Account Title	Classification	Financial Statement	Normal Balance
L			
Land	Plant Asset	Balance Sheet	Debit
Loss on Disposal of Plant Assets	Other Expense	Income Statement	Debit
M			
Maintenance and Repairs Expense	Operating Expense	Income Statement	Debit
Mortgage Payable	Long-Term Liability	Balance Sheet	Credit
N			
Notes Payable	Current Liability/ Long-Term Liability	Balance Sheet	Credit
O			
Owner's Capital	Owner's Equity	Owner's Equity and Balance Sheet	Credit
Owner's Drawings	Temporary account closed to Owner's Capital	Owner's Equity	Debit
P			
Patents	Intangible Asset	Balance Sheet	Debit
Paid-in Capital in Excess of Par— Common Stock	Stockholders' Equity	Balance Sheet	Credit
Paid-in Capital in Excess of Par— Preferred Stock	Stockholders' Equity	Balance Sheet	Credit
Preferred Stock	Stockholders' Equity	Balance Sheet	Credit
Premium on Bonds Payable	Long-Term Liability	Balance Sheet	Credit
Prepaid Insurance	Current Asset	Balance Sheet	Debit
Prepaid Rent	Current Asset	Balance Sheet	Debit
R			
Rent Expense	Operating Expense	Income Statement	Debit
Retained Earnings	Stockholders' Equity	Balance Sheet and Retained Earnings Statement	Credit
S			
Salaries and Wages Expense	Operating Expense	Income Statement	Debit
Salaries and Wages Payable	Current Liability	Balance Sheet	Credit
Sales Discounts	Revenue—Contra	Income Statement	Debit
Sales Returns and Allowances	Revenue—Contra	Income Statement	Debit
Sales Revenue	Revenue	Income Statement	Credit
Selling Expenses	Operating Expense	Income Statement	Debit
Service Revenue	Revenue	Income Statement	Credit
Stock Investments	Current Asset/Long-Term Investment	Balance Sheet	Debit
Supplies	Current Asset	Balance Sheet	Debit
Supplies Expense	Operating Expense	Income Statement	Debit
T			
Treasury Stock	Stockholders' Equity—Contra	Balance Sheet	Debit
U			
Unearned Service Revenue	Current Liability	Balance Sheet	Credit
Utilities Expense	Operating Expense	Income Statement	Debit

(1) The normal balance for Income Summary will be credit when there is a net income, debit when there is a net loss. The Income Summary account does not appear on any financial statement.

(2) If a periodic system is used, Inventory also appears on the income statement in the calculation of cost of goods sold.

The following is a sample chart of accounts. It does not represent a comprehensive chart of all the accounts used in this textbook but rather those accounts that are commonly used. This sample chart of accounts is for a company that generates both service revenue as well as sales revenue. It uses the perpetual approach to inventory. If a periodic system was used, the following temporary accounts would be needed to record inventory purchases: Purchases, Freight-In, Purchase Returns and Allowances, and Purchase Discounts.

CHART OF ACCOUNTS

Assets	Liabilities	Owner's and Stockholders' Equity	Revenues	Expenses
Cash	Notes Payable	Owner's Capital	Service Revenue	Advertising Expense
Accounts Receivable	Accounts Payable	Owner's Drawings	Sales Revenue	Amortization Expense
Allowance for Doubtful Accounts	Unearned Service Revenue	Common Stock	Sales Discounts	Bad Debt Expense
	Salaries and Wages Payable	Paid-in Capital in Excess of Par—Common Stock	Sales Returns and Allowances	Cost of Goods Sold
Interest Receivable	Unearned Rent Revenue	Preferred Stock	Interest Revenue	Depreciation Expense
Inventory	Interest Payable	Paid-in Capital in Excess of Par—Preferred Stock	Gain on Disposal of Plant Assets	Freight-Out
Supplies	Dividends Payable			Income Tax Expense
Prepaid Insurance	Income Taxes Payable	Treasury Stock		Insurance Expense
Prepaid Rent		Retained Earnings		Interest Expense
Land	Bonds Payable	Dividends		Loss on Disposal of Plant Assets
Equipment	Discount on Bonds Payable	Income Summary		Maintenance and Repairs Expense
Accumulated Depreciation—Equipment	Premium on Bonds Payable			Rent Expense
Buildings	Mortgage Payable			Salaries and Wages Expense
Accumulated Depreciation—Buildings				Supplies Expense
Copyrights				Utilities Expense
Goodwill				
Patents				

weygandt
kimmel
kieso
team for success

ACCOUNTING
PRINCIPLES 11e

Jerry J. Weygandt PhD, CPA
University of Wisconsin—Madison
Madison, Wisconsin

Paul D. Kimmel PhD, CPA
University of Wisconsin—Milwaukee
Milwaukee, Wisconsin

Donald E. Kieso PhD, CPA
Northern Illinois University
DeKalb, Illinois

WILEY

Dedicated to
*the **Wiley sales representatives***
who sell our books and service our
adopters in a professional and ethical
manner, and to
Enid, Merlynn, and Donna

Vice President & Executive Publisher	George Hoffman
Associate Publisher	Christopher DeJohn
Editorial Operations Manager	Yana Mermel
Content Editor	Ed Brislin
Senior Development Editor	Terry Ann Tatro
Development Editor	Margaret Thompson
Senior Content Manager	Dorothy Sinclair
Senior Production Editor	Valerie A. Vargas
Associate Director of Marketing	Amy Scholz
Marketing Manager	Karolina Zarychta Honsa
Senior Product Designer	Allison Morris
Product Designe	Greg Chaput
Media Specialist	Daniela DiMaggio
Design Director	Harry Nolan
Cover Design	Maureen Eide
Interior Design	Kristine Carney
Production Management Services	Ingrao Associates
Senior Photo Editor	Mary Ann Price
Editorial Assistant	Jaclyn MacKenzie
Marketing Assistant	Justine Kay
Cover and title page	© Moof/Cultura/Getty Images, Inc.
Brief Contents image	© Cherrus/Shutterstock
Continuing Cookie Chronicle icon	© Fekete Tibor/iStockphoto
Waterways Problem Set icon	© Perry Kroll/Photostock
Softbyte icon	© Cogal/iStockphoto
Pioneer Advertising Agency icon	© Mike Rodriguez/iStockphoto
Caterpillar icon	© Filonmar/iStockphoto
All other icons	Shutterstock

This book was set in New Aster by Aptara®, Inc. and printed and bound by Courier-Kendallville. The cover was printed by Courier-Kendallville.

Founded in 1807, John Wiley & Sons, Inc. has been a valued source of knowledge and understanding for more than 200 years, helping people around the world meet their needs and fulfill their aspirations. Our company is built on a foundation of principles that include responsibility to the communities we serve and where we live and work. In 2008, we launched a Corporate Citizenship Initiative, a global effort to address the environmental, social, economic, and ethical challenges we face in our business. Among the issues we are addressing are carbon impact, paper specifications and procurement, ethical conduct within our business and among our vendors, and community and charitable support. For more information, please visit our website: www.wiley.com/go/citizenship.

ISBN-13 978-1-118-13003-2

Binder-Ready Version ISBN 978-1-118-18089-1

Printed in the United States of America

10 9 8 7 6 5 4 3 2 1

Brief Contents

*Available at the book's companion website, **www.wiley.com/college/weygandt**.

read it!

REAL-WORLD CONTEXT
Real-world companies and business situations give you glimpses into how real companies use accounting.

Feature Stories introduce chapter topics in fun ways using real-world companies that are engaging.

Time Warner completed a spin-off of AOL after years of trying to integrate the two companies. One | analyst called the failed deal "a nine-year adventure akin to a marathon through mud."

Issues that affect today's business world are highlighted in the textbook.

Real-World Focus

BYP22-4 The Coca-Cola Company hardly needs an introduction. A line taken from the cover of a recent annual report says it all: If you measured time in servings of Coca-Cola, "a billion Coca-Cola's ago was yesterday morning." On average, every U.S. citizen drinks 363 8-ounce servings of Coca-Cola products each year. Coca-Cola's primary line of business is the making and selling of syrup to bottlers. These bottlers then sell the finished bottles and cans of Coca-Cola to the consumer.

In the annual report of Coca-Cola, the information shown below was provided.

THE COCA-COLA COMPANY
Management Discussion

Our gross margin declined to 61 percent this year from 62 percent in the prior year, primarily due to costs for materials such as sweeteners and packaging.

The increases [in selling expenses] in the last two years were primarily due to higher marketing expenditures in support of our Company's volume growth.

We measure ...
and (2) uni...

ANATOMY OF A FRAUD

Lawrence Fairbanks, the assistant vice-chancellor of communications at Aesop University, was allowed to make purchases of under $2,500 for his department without external approval. Unfortunately, he also sometimes bought items for himself, such as expensive antiques and other collectibles. How did he do it? He replaced the vendor invoices he received with fake vendor invoices that he created. The fake invoices had descriptions that were more consistent with the communications department's purchases. He submitted these fake invoices to the accounting department as the basis for their journal entries and to the accounts payable department as the basis for payment.

Total take: $475,000

THE MISSING CONTROL
Segregation of duties. The university had not properly segregated related purchasing activities. Lawrence was ordering items, receiving the items, and receiving the invoice. By receiving the invoice, he had control over the documents that were used to account for the purchase and thus was able to substitute a fake invoice.

Source: Adapted from Wells, Fraud Casebook (2007), pp. 3–15.

Insight Boxes frame real-world company issues through international, ethical, and other perspectives.

ACCOUNTING ACROSS THE ORGANIZATION
A Thousand Millionaires!

Traveling to space or embarking on an expedition to excavate lost Mayan ruins are normally the stuff of adventure novels. But for employees of Facebook, these and other lavish dreams moved closer to reality when the world's No. 1 online social network went public through an initial public offering (IPO) that may have created at least a thousand millionaires. The IPO was the largest in Internet history, valuing Facebook at over $104 billion.

With all these riches to be had, why did Mark Zuckerberg, the founder of Facebook, delay taking his company public? Consider that the main motivation for issuing shares to the public is to raise money so you can grow your business. However, unlike a manufacturer or even an online retailer, Facebook doesn't need major physical resources, it doesn't have inventory, and it doesn't really need much money for marketing. So in the past, the company hasn't had much need for additional cash beyond what it was already generating on its own. Finally, as head of a closely held, nonpublic company, Zuckerberg was subject to far fewer regulations than a public company.

Source: "Status Update: I'm Rich! Facebook Flotation to Create 1,000 Millionaires Among Company's Rank and File," Daily Mail Reporter (February 1, 2012).

? Why did Mark Zuckerberg, the CEO and founder of Facebook, delay taking his company's shares public through an initial public offering (IPO)? (See page 640.)

Financial Reporting and Analysis

Financial Reporting Problem: Apple Inc.

BYP1-1 The actual financial statements of Apple Inc. for 2011, are presented in Appendix A (at the bac...
incl...

A Look at IFRS

LEARNING OBJECTIVE 10
Describe the impact of international accounting standards on U.S. financial reporting.

Most agree that there is a need for one set of international accounting standards. Here is why:
Multinational corporations. Today's companies view the entire world as their market. For example, Coca-Cola, Intel, and McDonald's generate more than 50% of their sales outside the United States, and many foreign companies, such as Toyota, Nestlé, and Sony, find their largest market to be the United States.

Mergers and acquisitions. The mergers between Fiat/Chrysler and Vodafone/Mannesmann suggest that we will see even more such business combinations of companies from different countries in the future.

v

WILEY

see it!

CONTENT FOR ALL LEARNING STYLES

In addition to a textbook consistently reviewed as very readable, over 50% of the textbook provides visual presentations and interpretations of content.

Equation Analysis Illustrations visually walk you through the steps of journal transactions.

Basic Analysis	The expense Insurance Expense is increased $50, and the asset Prepaid Insurance is decreased $50.

Equation Analysis

$$(2) \quad \underset{-\$50}{\underset{\text{Prepaid Insurance}}{\text{Assets}}} = \text{Liabilities} + \underset{-\$50}{\underset{\text{Insurance Expense}}{\text{Owner's Equity}}}$$

Debit–Credit Analysis

Debits increase expenses: debit Insurance Expense $50.
Credits decrease assets: credit Prepaid Insurance $50.

Journal Entry

Oct. 31 | Insurance Expense | 50 |
Prepaid Insurance | | 50
(To record insurance expired)

Posting

Prepaid Insurance	130		Insurance Expense	722
Oct. 4	600	Oct. 31 Adj. 50	Oct. 31 Adj. 50	
Oct. 31 Bal. 550			Oct. 31 Bal. 50	

Cash Flow Analyses visually summarize the effects of transactions on cash flows.

A	=	L	+	SE
+2,000				
−2,000				

Cash Flows
+2,000

Retailer receives cash more quickly from credit card issuer

Infographics reinforce important textual concepts. All infographics were revised in the Eleventh Edition.

Illustrations are clearly identified and often present data in a real-world format.

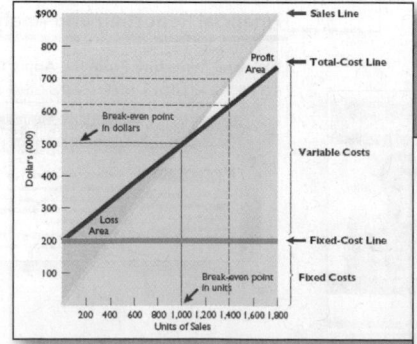

Hayes Company Direct Labor Budget.xls

HAYES COMPANY
Direct Labor Budget
For the Year Ending December 31, 2014

	Quarter				
	1	2	3	4	Year
Units to be produced (Illustration 23-5)	3,100	3,600	4,100	4,600	
Direct labor time (hours) per unit	× 2	× 2	× 2	× 2	
Total required direct labor hours	6,200	7,200	8,200	9,200	
Direct labor cost per hour	× $10	× $10	× $10	× $10	
Total direct labor cost	$62,000	$72,000	$82,000	$92,000	$308,000

kieso
weygandt
kimmel
warfield
team for success

do it!

KNOW THE FUNDAMENTALS

Knowing the fundamentals of accounting will help you understand what is happening in all areas of a business. **DO IT!** exercises throughout the textbook will help you practice your understanding of accounting.

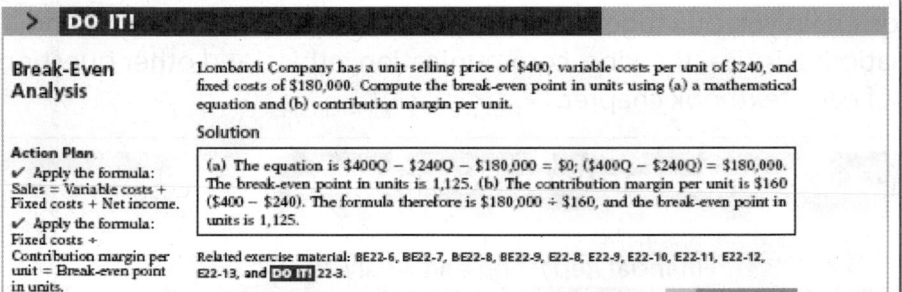

> **DO IT!**

Break-Even Analysis

Lombardi Company has a unit selling price of $400, variable costs per unit of $240, and fixed costs of $180,000. Compute the break-even point in units using (a) a mathematical equation and (b) contribution margin per unit.

Solution

Action Plan
✔ Apply the formula:
Sales = Variable costs + Fixed costs + Net income.
✔ Apply the formula:
Fixed costs + Contribution margin per unit = Break-even point in units.

(a) The equation is $400Q − $240Q − $180,000 = $0; ($400Q − $240Q) = $180,000. The break-even point in units is 1,125. (b) The contribution margin per unit is $160 ($400 − $240). The formula therefore is $180,000 ÷ $160, and the break-even point in units is 1,125.

Related exercise material: BE22-6, BE22-7, BE22-8, BE22-9, E22-8, E22-9, E22-10, E22-11, E22-12, E22-13, and **DO IT!** 22-3.

✔ The Navigator

Clear **DO IT!** exercises in the textbook narrative provide step-by-step applications of a concept at the precise moment you acquire the knowledge. Each **DO IT!** in the textbook narrative includes a solution, an Action Plan, and a path of related homework exercises.

Comprehensive DO IT!'s at the end of each chapter apply the **DO IT!** exercises and address **multiple** topics.

> **Comprehensive DO IT!**

B.T. Hernandez Company, maker of high-quality flashlights, has experienced steady growth over the last 6 years. However, increased competition has led Mr. Hernandez, the president, to believe that an aggressive campaign is needed next year to maintain the company's present growth. The company's accountant has presented Mr. Hernandez with the data on the next page for the current year, 2014, for use in preparing next year's advertising campaign.

> **DO IT! Review**

DO IT! 22-1 Heleña Company reports the following total costs at two levels of production.

Classify types of costs.
(LO 1, 3), C

	5,000 Units	10,000 Units
Indirect labor	$ 3,000	$ 6,000
Property taxes	7,000	7,000
Direct labor	28,000	56,000
Direct materials	22,000	44,000
Depreciation	4,000	4,000
Utilities	5,000	7,000
Maintenance	9,000	11,000

Classify each cost as variable, fixed, or mixed.

DO IT! 22-2 Westerville Company accumulates the following data concerning a mixed cost, using units produced as the activity level.

Compute costs using high-low method and estimate total cost.
(LO 3), AP

	Units Produced	Total Cost
March	10,000	$18,000
April	9,000	16,650
May	10,500	18,580
June	8,800	16,200
July	9,500	17,100

(a) Compute the variable- and fixed-cost elements using the high-low method.
(b) Estimate the total cost if the company produces 9,200 units.

End-of-Chapter DO IT! exercises provide further practice with alternate versions of the in-chapter **DO IT!** exercises.

WILEY

get it!

IMPROVE DECISION-MAKING SKILLS

As an employee, manager, or even a director of your own personal finances, you will make better decisions by learning how to analyze and solve business problems using materials provided at the end of each chapter.

Broadening Your Perspective questions help you pull together concepts from a particular chapter and apply them to real-world business situations. Critical thinking, communication, ethics, and other questions are included in this section at the end of each textbook chapter.

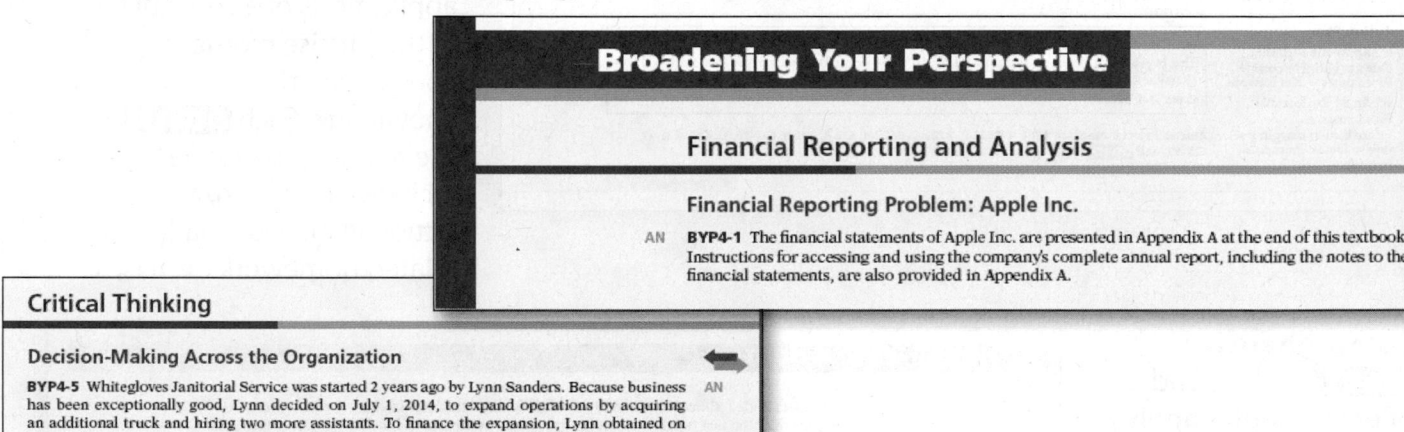

Broadening Your Perspective

Financial Reporting and Analysis

Financial Reporting Problem: Apple Inc.

AN **BYP4-1** The financial statements of Apple Inc. are presented in Appendix A at the end of this textbook. Instructions for accessing and using the company's complete annual report, including the notes to the financial statements, are also provided in Appendix A.

Critical Thinking

Decision-Making Across the Organization

BYP4-5 Whitegloves Janitorial Service was started 2 years ago by Lynn Sanders. Because business AN has been exceptionally good, Lynn decided on July 1, 2014, to expand operations by acquiring an additional truck and hiring two more assistants. To finance the expansion, Lynn obtained on

Continuing Cookie Chronicle, Waterways Continuing Problem, and Comprehensive Problems pull together concepts from multiple chapters and provide a macro perspective of accounting in action.

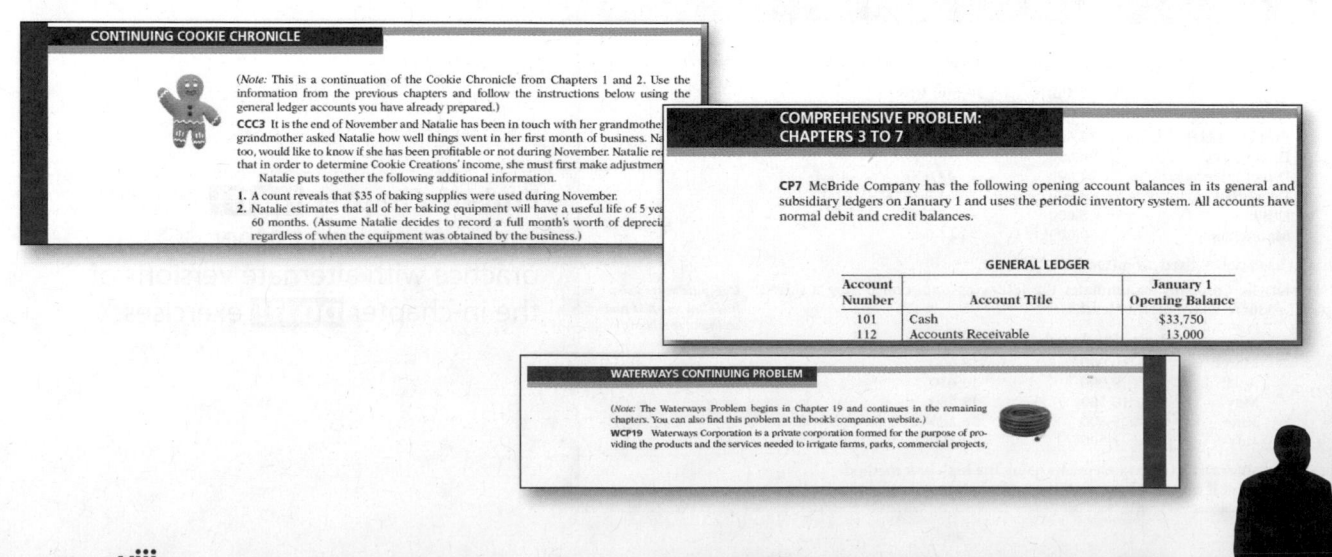

CONTINUING COOKIE CHRONICLE

(*Note:* This is a continuation of the Cookie Chronicle from Chapters 1 and 2. Use the information from the previous chapters and follow the instructions below using the general ledger accounts you have already prepared.)

CCC3 It is the end of November and Natalie has been in touch with her grandmother. Natalie's grandmother asked Natalie how well things went in her first month of business. Natalie, too, would like to know if she has been profitable or not during November. Natalie realizes that in order to determine Cookie Creations' income, she must first make adjustments.

Natalie puts together the following additional information.

1. A count reveals that $35 of baking supplies were used during November.
2. Natalie estimates that all of her baking equipment will have a useful life of 5 years or 60 months. (Assume Natalie decides to record a full month's worth of depreciation, regardless of when the equipment was obtained by the business.)

COMPREHENSIVE PROBLEM: CHAPTERS 3 TO 7

CP7 McBride Company has the following opening account balances in its general and subsidiary ledgers on January 1 and uses the periodic inventory system. All accounts have normal debit and credit balances.

GENERAL LEDGER

Account Number	Account Title	January 1 Opening Balance
101	Cash	$33,750
112	Accounts Receivable	13,000

WATERWAYS CONTINUING PROBLEM

(*Note:* The Waterways Problem begins in Chapter 19 and continues in the remaining chapters. You can also find this problem at the book's companion website.)

WCP19 Waterways Corporation is a private corporation formed for the purpose of providing the products and the services needed to irrigate farms, parks, commercial projects,

www.wileyteamforsuccess.com

Contents

1 | Accounting in Action

Feature Story

*The **Feature Story** helps you picture how the chapter topic relates to the real world of accounting and business. You will find references to the story throughout the chapter.*

Knowing the Numbers

Many students who take this course do not plan to be accountants. If you are in that group, you might be thinking, "If I'm not going to be an accountant, why do I need to know accounting?" Well, consider this quote from Harold Geneen, the former chairman of IT&T: "To be good at your business, you have to know the numbers—cold." In business, accounting and financial statements are the means for communicating the numbers. If you don't know how to read financial statements, you can't really know your business.

Many businesses agree with this view. They see the value of their employees being able to read financial statements and understand how their actions affect the company's financial results. For example, consider Clif Bar & Company. The original Clif Bar® energy bar was created in 1990 after six months of experimentation by Gary Erickson and his mother in her kitchen. Today, the company has almost 300 employees and is considered one of the leading Landor's Breakaway Brands®.

Clif Bar is guided by what it calls its Five Aspirations— Sustaining Our Business, Our Brands, Our People, Our

Community, and the Planet. Its website documents its ef and accomplishments in these five areas. Just a few exam include the company's use of organic products to protec water, and biodiversity; the "smart" solar array (the large North America), which provides nearly all the electrical n for its 115,000-square foot building; and the incentives (Bar provides to employees to reduce their personal envir mental impact, such as $6,500 toward the purchase of a efficient car or $1,000 per year for eco-friendly improven toward their homes.

One of the company's proudest moments was the creatic an employee stock ownership plan (ESOP) in 2010. This gives its employees 20% ownership of the company (Ga and his wife Kit own the other 80%). The ESOP also resu in Clif Bar enacting an open-book management program including the commitment to educate all employee-own about its finances. Armed with this basic financial knowl employees are more aware of the financial impact of the actions, which leads to better decisions.

Many other companies have adopted this open-book ma agement approach. Even in companies that do not pract

*The **Navigator** is a learning system designed to prompt you to use the learning aids in the chapter and set priorities as you study.*

 The Navigator

- ☐ Scan Learning Objectives
- ☐ Read Feature Story
- ☐ Read Preview
- ☐ Read text and answer **DO IT!** p. 11
    - ☐ p. 14   ☐ p. 21   ☐ p. 25
- ☐ Work Comprehensive **DO IT!** p. 26
- ☐ Review Summary of Learning Objectives
- ☐ Answer Self-Test Questions
- ☐ Complete Assignments
- ☐ Go to *WileyPLUS* for practice and tutorials
- **Read A Look at IFRS** p. 48

Learning Objectives give you a framework for learning the specific concepts covered in the chapter.

Learning Objectives   ✔ The Navigator

After studying this chapter, you should be able to:

[1] Explain what accounting is.

[2] Identify the users and uses of accounting.

[3] Understand why ethics is a fundamental business concept.

[4] Explain generally accepted accounting principles.

[5] Explain the monetary unit assumption and the economic entity assumption.

[6] State the accounting equation, and define its components.

[7] Analyze the effects of business transactions on the accounting equation.

[8] Understand the four financial statements and how they are prepared.

© Dan Moore/iStockphoto

open-book management, employers generally assume that managers in all areas of the company are "financially literate."

Taking this course will go a long way to making you financially literate. In this textbook, you will learn how to read and prepare financial statements, and

how to use basic tools to evaluate financial results. Throughout this textbook, we attempt to increase your familiarity with financial reporting by providing numerous references, questions, and exercises that encourage you to explore the financial statements of well-known companies.

Preview of Chapter 1

 ✔ The Navigator

The opening story about Clif Bar & Company highlights the importance of having good financial information and knowing how to use it to make effective business decisions. Whatever your pursuits or occupation, the need for financial information is inescapable. You cannot earn a living, spend money, buy on credit, make an investment, or pay taxes without receiving, using, or dispensing financial information. Good decision-making depends on good information.

The purpose of this chapter is to show you that accounting is the system used to provide useful financial information. The content and organization of Chapter 1 are as follows.

*The **Preview** describes and outlines the major topics and subtopics you will see in the chapter.*

ACCOUNTING IN ACTION

What Is Accounting?	The Building Blocks of Accounting	The Basic Accounting Equation	Using the Accounting Equation	Financial Statements
• Three activities • Who uses accounting data	• Ethics in financial reporting • Generally accepted accounting principles • Measurement principles • Assumptions	• Assets • Liabilities • Owner's equity	• Transaction analysis • Summary of transactions	• Income statement • Owner's equity statement • Balance sheet • Statement of cash flows

What Is Accounting?

What consistently ranks as one of the top career opportunities in business? What frequently rates among the most popular majors on campus? What was the undergraduate degree chosen by Nike founder Phil Knight, Home Depot co-founder Arthur Blank, former acting director of the Federal Bureau of Investigation (FBI) Thomas Pickard, and numerous members of Congress? Accounting.[1] Why did these people choose accounting? They wanted to understand what was happening financially to their organizations. Accounting is the financial information system that provides these insights. In short, to understand your organization, you have to know the numbers.

Accounting consists of three basic activities—it **identifies**, **records**, and **communicates** the economic events of an organization to interested users. Let's take a closer look at these three activities.

Three Activities

As a starting point to the accounting process, a company **identifies** the **economic events relevant to its business**. Examples of economic events are the sale of snack chips by PepsiCo, the provision of telephone services by AT&T, and the payment of wages by Ford Motor Company.

Once a company like PepsiCo identifies economic events, it **records** those events in order to provide a history of its financial activities. Recording consists of keeping a **systematic**, **chronological diary of events**, measured in dollars and cents. In recording, PepsiCo also classifies and summarizes economic events.

Finally, PepsiCo **communicates** the collected information to interested users by means of **accounting reports**. The most common of these reports are called **financial statements**. To make the reported financial information meaningful, PepsiCo reports the recorded data in a standardized way. It accumulates information resulting from similar transactions. For example, PepsiCo accumulates all sales transactions over a certain period of time and reports the data as one amount in the company's financial statements. Such data are said to be reported **in the aggregate**. By presenting the recorded data in the aggregate, the accounting process simplifies a multitude of transactions and makes a series of activities understandable and meaningful.

A vital element in communicating economic events is the accountant's ability to **analyze and interpret** the reported information. Analysis involves use of ratios, percentages, graphs, and charts to highlight significant financial trends and relationships. Interpretation involves **explaining the uses**, **meaning**, **and limitations of reported data**. Appendices A–E show the financial statements of Apple Inc., PepsiCo Inc., The Coca-Cola Company, Amazon.com, Inc., and Wal-Mart Stores, Inc., respectively. (In addition, in the *A Look at IFRS* section at the end of each chapter, the U.K. company Zetar plc is analyzed.) We refer to these statements at various places throughout the textbook. At this point, these financial statements probably strike you as complex and confusing. By the end of this course, you'll be surprised at your ability to understand, analyze, and interpret them.

Illustration 1-1 summarizes the activities of the accounting process.

---

[1]The appendix to this chapter describes job opportunities for accounting majors and explains why accounting is such a popular major.

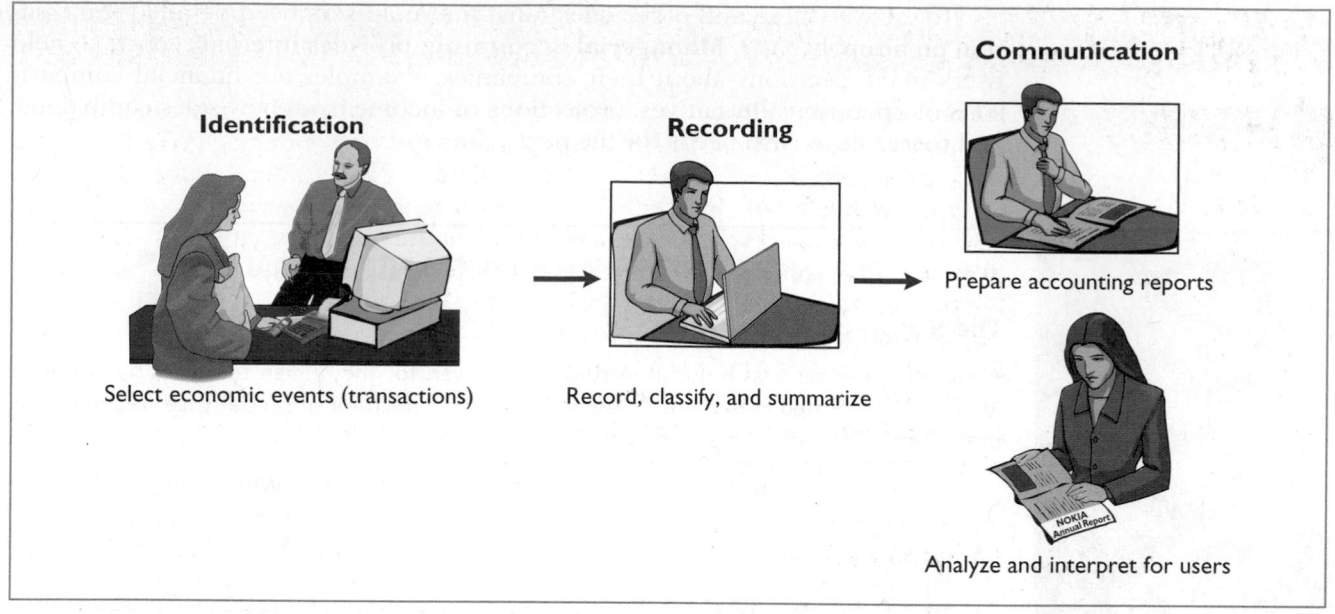

Identification

Select economic events (transactions)

Recording

Record, classify, and summarize

Communication

Prepare accounting reports

Analyze and interpret for users

Illustration 1-1
The activities of the accounting process

You should understand that the accounting process **includes** the bookkeeping function. **Bookkeeping** usually involves **only** the recording of economic events. It is therefore just one part of the accounting process. In total, accounting involves **the entire process of identifying, recording, and communicating economic events.**[2]

Essential terms are printed in blue when they first appear, and are defined in the end-of-chapter glossary.

Who Uses Accounting Data

The financial information that users need depends upon the kinds of decisions they make. There are two broad groups of users of financial information: internal users and external users.

LEARNING OBJECTIVE　2

Identify the users and uses of accounting.

INTERNAL USERS

Internal users of accounting information are managers who plan, organize, and run the business. These include marketing managers, production supervisors, finance directors, and company officers. In running a business, internal users must answer many important questions, as shown in Illustration 1-2.

Questions Asked by Internal Users

Snack chips　Beverages

Finance	**Marketing**	**Human Resources**	**Management**
Is cash sufficient to pay dividends to Microsoft stockholders?	What price should Apple charge for an iPod to maximize the company's net income?	Can General Motors afford to give its employees pay raises this year?	Which PepsiCo product line is the most profitable? Should any product lines be eliminated?

Illustration 1-2
Questions that internal users ask

---

[2]The origins of accounting are generally attributed to the work of Luca Pacioli, an Italian Renaissance mathematician. Pacioli was a close friend and tutor to Leonardo da Vinci and a contemporary of Christopher Columbus. In his 1494 text *Summa de Arithmetica, Geometria, Proportione et Proportionalite*, Pacioli described a system to ensure that financial information was recorded efficiently and accurately.

To answer these and other questions, internal users need detailed information on a timely basis. **Managerial accounting** provides internal reports to help users make decisions about their companies. Examples are financial comparisons of operating alternatives, projections of income from new sales campaigns, and forecasts of cash needs for the next year.

© Agnieszka Pastuszak-Maksim/
iStockphoto

Accounting Across the Organization boxes demonstrate applications of accounting information in various business functions.

ACCOUNTING ACROSS THE ORGANIZATION

The Scoop on Accounting

Accounting can serve as a useful recruiting tool even for the human resources department. Rhino Foods, located in Burlington, Vermont, is a manufacturer of specialty ice cream. Its corporate website includes the following:

> "Wouldn't it be great to work where you were part of a team? Where your input and hard work made a difference? Where you weren't kept in the dark about what management was thinking? . . . Well—it's not a dream! It's the way we do business . . . Rhino Foods believes in family, honesty and open communication—we really care about and appreciate our employees—and it shows. Operating results are posted and monthly group meetings inform all employees about what's happening in the Company. Employees also share in the Company's profits, in addition to having an excellent comprehensive benefits package."

Source: www.rhinofoods.com/workforus/workforus.html.

? What are the benefits to the company and to the employees of making the financial statements available to all employees? (See page 47.)

EXTERNAL USERS

External users are individuals and organizations outside a company who want financial information about the company. The two most common types of external users are investors and creditors. **Investors** (owners) use accounting information to decide whether to buy, hold, or sell ownership shares of a company. **Creditors** (such as suppliers and bankers) use accounting information to evaluate the risks of granting credit or lending money. Illustration 1-3 shows some questions that investors and creditors may ask.

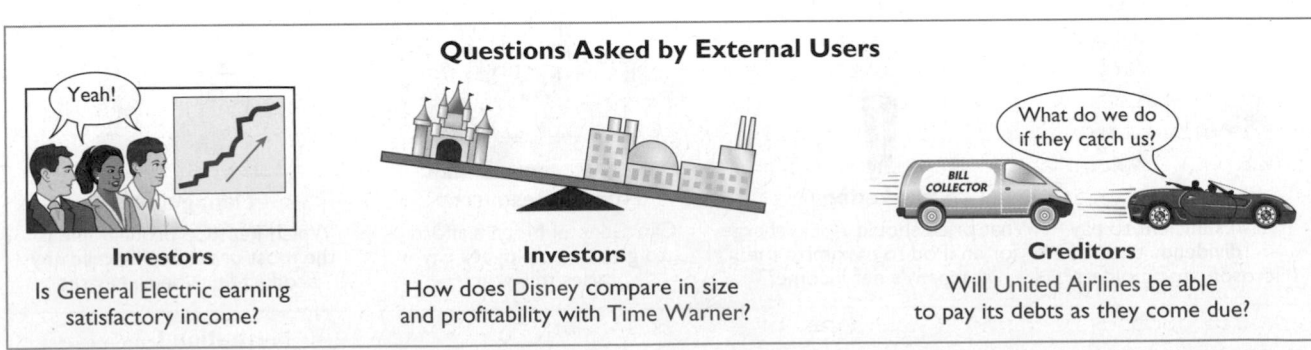

Illustration 1-3
Questions that external users ask

Financial accounting answers these questions. It provides economic and financial information for investors, creditors, and other external users. The information needs of external users vary considerably. **Taxing authorities**, such as the Internal Revenue Service, want to know whether the company complies with tax laws. **Regulatory agencies**, such as the Securities and Exchange Commission or the Federal Trade Commission, want to know whether the company is operating within prescribed rules. **Customers** are interested in whether a company like General Motors will continue to honor product warranties and support its product lines. **Labor unions** such as the Major League Baseball Players Association want to know whether the owners have the ability to pay increased wages and benefits.

The Building Blocks of Accounting

A doctor follows certain standards in treating a patient's illness. An architect follows certain standards in designing a building. An accountant follows certain standards in reporting financial information. For these standards to work, a fundamental business concept must be at work—ethical behavior.

> **LEARNING OBJECTIVE   3**
>
> Understand why ethics is a fundamental business concept.

Ethics in Financial Reporting

People won't gamble in a casino if they think it is "rigged." Similarly, people won't play the stock market if they think stock prices are rigged. In recent years, the financial press has been full of articles about financial scandals at Enron, WorldCom, HealthSouth, AIG, and other companies. As the scandals came to light, mistrust of financial reporting in general grew. One article in the *Wall Street Journal* noted that "repeated disclosures about questionable accounting practices have bruised investors' faith in the reliability of earnings reports, which in turn has sent stock prices tumbling." Imagine trying to carry on a business or invest money if you could not depend on the financial statements to be honestly prepared. Information would have no credibility. There is no doubt that a sound, well-functioning economy depends on accurate and dependable financial reporting.

United States regulators and lawmakers were very concerned that the economy would suffer if investors lost confidence in corporate accounting because of unethical financial reporting. In response, Congress passed the **Sarbanes-Oxley Act (SOX)**. Its intent is to reduce unethical corporate behavior and decrease the likelihood of future corporate scandals. As a result of SOX, top management must now certify the accuracy of financial information. In addition, penalties for fraudulent financial activity are much more severe. Also, SOX increased the independence requirements of the outside auditors who review the accuracy of corporate financial statements and increased the oversight role of boards of directors.

The standards of conduct by which actions are judged as right or wrong, honest or dishonest, fair or not fair, are **ethics**. Effective financial reporting depends on sound ethical behavior. To sensitize you to ethical situations in business and to give you practice at solving ethical dilemmas, we address ethics in a number of ways in this textbook:

> ## Ethics Note
>
> Circus-founder P.T. Barnum is alleged to have said, "Trust everyone, but cut the deck." What Sarbanes-Oxley does is to provide measures that (like cutting the deck of playing cards) help ensure that fraud will not occur.

Ethics Notes help sensitize you to some of the ethical issues in accounting.

1. A number of the *Feature Stories* and other parts of the textbook discuss the central importance of ethical behavior to financial reporting.

2. *Ethics Insight* boxes and marginal *Ethics Notes* highlight ethics situations and issues in actual business settings.

3. Many of the *People, Planet, and Profit Insight* boxes focus on ethical issues that companies face in measuring and reporting social and environmental issues.

4. At the end of the chapter, an *Ethics Case* simulates a business situation and asks you to put yourself in the position of a decision-maker in that case.

When analyzing these various ethics cases, as well as experiences in your own life, it is useful to apply the three steps outlined in Illustration 1-4.

1. Recognize an ethical situation and the ethical issues involved.	**2. Identify and analyze the principal elements in the situation.**	**3. Identify the alternatives, and weigh the impact of each alternative on various stakeholders.**
Use your personal ethics to identify ethical situations and issues. Some businesses and professional organizations provide written codes of ethics for guidance in some business situations.	Identify the **stakeholders**—persons or groups who may be harmed or benefited. Ask the question: What are the responsibilities and obligations of the parties involved?	Select the most ethical alternative, considering all the consequences. Sometimes there will be one right answer. Other situations involve more than one right solution; these situations require an evaluation of each and a selection of the best alternative.

Illustration 1-4
Steps in analyzing ethics cases and situations

Insight boxes provide examples of business situations from various perspectives—ethics, investor, international, and corporate social responsibility. Guideline answers are provided near the end of the chapter.

Gemunu Amarasinghe/AP Photo

ETHICS INSIGHT

The Numbers Behind Not-for-Profit Organizations

Accounting plays an important role for a wide range of business organizations worldwide. Just as the integrity of the numbers matters for business, it matters at least as much at not-for-profit organizations. Proper control and reporting help ensure that money is used the way donors intended. Donors are less inclined to give to an organization if they think the organization is subject to waste or theft. The accounting challenges of some large international not-for-profits rival those of the world's largest businesses. For example, after the Haitian earthquake, the Haitian-born musician Wyclef Jean was criticized for the poor accounting controls in a relief fund that he founded. In response, he hired a new accountant and improved the transparency regarding money raised and spent.

 What benefits does a sound accounting system provide to a not-for-profit organization? (See page 47.)

Generally Accepted Accounting Principles

LEARNING OBJECTIVE   4

Explain generally accepted accounting principles.

The accounting profession has developed standards that are generally accepted and universally practiced. This common set of standards is called **generally accepted accounting principles (GAAP)**. These standards indicate how to report economic events.

The primary accounting standard-setting body in the United States is the **Financial Accounting Standards Board (FASB)**. The **Securities and Exchange Commission (SEC)** is the agency of the U.S. government that oversees U.S. financial markets and accounting standard-setting bodies. The SEC relies on the FASB to develop accounting standards, which public companies must follow. Many countries outside of the United States have adopted the accounting standards issued by the **International Accounting Standards Board (IASB)**. These standards are called **International Financial Reporting Standards (IFRS)**.

As markets become more global, it is often desirable to compare the results of companies from different countries that report using different accounting standards. In order to increase comparability, in recent years the two standard-setting bodies have made efforts to reduce the differences between U.S. GAAP and IFRS. This process is referred to as **convergence**. As a result of these convergence efforts, it is likely that someday there will be a single set of high-quality accounting standards that are used by companies around the world. Because convergence is such an important issue, we highlight any major differences between GAAP and IFRS in *International Notes* (as shown in the margin here) and provide a more in-depth discussion in the *A Look at IRFS* section at the end of each chapter.

> ## International Note
>
> Over 100 countries use International Financial Reporting Standards (called IFRS). For example, all companies in the European Union follow international standards. The differences between U.S. and international standards are not generally significant.

International Notes highlight differences between U.S. and international accounting standards.

Measurement Principles

GAAP generally uses one of two measurement principles, the historical cost principle or the fair value principle. Selection of which principle to follow generally relates to trade-offs between relevance and faithful representation. **Relevance** means that financial information is capable of making a difference in a decision. **Faithful representation** means that the numbers and descriptions match what really existed or happened—they are factual.

Helpful Hint Relevance and faithful representation are two primary qualities that make accounting information useful for decision-making.

Helpful Hints further clarify concepts being discussed.

HISTORICAL COST PRINCIPLE

The **historical cost principle** (or cost principle) dictates that companies record assets at their cost. This is true not only at the time the asset is purchased, but also over the time the asset is held. For example, if Best Buy purchases land for $300,000, the company initially reports it in its accounting records at $300,000. But what does Best Buy do if, by the end of the next year, the fair value of the land has increased to $400,000? Under the historical cost principle, it continues to report the land at $300,000.

FAIR VALUE PRINCIPLE

The **fair value principle** states that assets and liabilities should be reported at fair value (the price received to sell an asset or settle a liability). Fair value information may be more useful than historical cost for certain types of assets and liabilities. For example, certain investment securities are reported at fair value because market price information is usually readily available for these types of assets. In determining which measurement principle to use, companies weigh the factual nature of cost figures versus the relevance of fair value. In general, most companies choose to use cost. Only in situations where assets are actively traded, such as investment securities, do companies apply the fair value principle extensively.

SeongJoonCho/Bloomberg/
Getty Images, Inc.

INTERNATIONAL INSIGHT
The Korean Discount

If you think that accounting standards don't matter, consider recent events in South Korea. For many years, international investors complained that the financial reports of South Korean companies were inadequate and inaccurate. Accounting practices there often resulted in huge differences between stated revenues and actual revenues. Because investors did not have faith in the accuracy of the numbers, they were unwilling to pay as much for the shares of these companies relative to shares of comparable companies in different countries. This difference in stock price was often referred to as the "Korean discount."

In response, Korean regulators decided that, beginning in 2011, companies would comply with international accounting standards. This change was motivated by a desire to "make the country's businesses more transparent" in order to build investor confidence and spur economic growth. Many other Asian countries, including China, India, Japan, and Hong Kong, have also decided either to adopt international standards or to create standards that are based on the international standards.

Source: Evan Ramstad, "End to 'Korea Discount'?" *Wall Street Journal* (March 16, 2007).

? What is meant by the phrase "make the country's businesses more transparent"? Why would increasing transparency spur economic growth? (See page 48.)

Assumptions

LEARNING OBJECTIVE   5

Explain the monetary unit assumption and the economic entity assumption.

Assumptions provide a foundation for the accounting process. Two main assumptions are the **monetary unit assumption** and the **economic entity assumption**.

MONETARY UNIT ASSUMPTION

The **monetary unit assumption** requires that companies include in the accounting records only transaction data that can be expressed in money terms. This assumption enables accounting to quantify (measure) economic events. The monetary unit assumption is vital to applying the historical cost principle.

This assumption prevents the inclusion of some relevant information in the accounting records. For example, the health of a company's owner, the quality of service, and the morale of employees are not included. The reason: Companies cannot quantify this information in money terms. Though this information is important, companies record only events that can be measured in money.

ECONOMIC ENTITY ASSUMPTION

An economic entity can be any organization or unit in society. It may be a company (such as Crocs, Inc.), a governmental unit (the state of Ohio), a municipality (Seattle), a school district (St. Louis District 48), or a church (Southern Baptist). The **economic entity assumption** requires that the activities of the entity be kept separate and distinct from the activities of its owner and all other economic entities. To illustrate, Sally Rider, owner of Sally's Boutique, must keep her personal living costs separate from the expenses of the business. Similarly, McDonald's, Coca-Cola, and Cadbury-Schweppes are segregated into separate economic entities for accounting purposes.

PROPRIETORSHIP A business owned by one person is generally a **proprietorship**. The owner is often the manager/operator of the business.

Ethics Note

The importance of the economic entity assumption is illustrated by scandals involving Adelphia. In this case, senior company employees entered into transactions that blurred the line between the employees' financial interests and those of the company. For example, Adelphia guaranteed over $2 billion of loans to the founding family.

Small service-type businesses (plumbing companies, beauty salons, and auto repair shops), farms, and small retail stores (antique shops, clothing stores, and used-book stores) are often proprietorships. **Usually only a relatively small amount of money (capital) is necessary to start in business as a proprietorship. The owner (proprietor) receives any profits, suffers any losses, and is personally liable for all debts of the business.** There is no legal distinction between the business as an economic unit and the owner, but the accounting records of the business activities are kept separate from the personal records and activities of the owner.

PARTNERSHIP A business owned by two or more persons associated as partners is a **partnership**. In most respects a partnership is like a proprietorship except that more than one owner is involved. Typically a partnership agreement (written or oral) sets forth such terms as initial investment, duties of each partner, division of net income (or net loss), and settlement to be made upon death or withdrawal of a partner. Each partner generally has unlimited personal liability for the debts of the partnership. **Like a proprietorship, for accounting purposes the partnership transactions must be kept separate from the personal activities of the partners.** Partnerships are often used to organize retail and service-type businesses, including professional practices (lawyers, doctors, architects, and certified public accountants).

CORPORATION A business organized as a separate legal entity under state corporation law and having ownership divided into transferable shares of stock is a **corporation**. The holders of the shares (stockholders) **enjoy limited liability**; that is, they are not personally liable for the debts of the corporate entity. Stockholders **may transfer all or part of their ownership shares to other investors at any time** (i.e., sell their shares). The ease with which ownership can change adds to the attractiveness of investing in a corporation. Because ownership can be transferred without dissolving the corporation, the corporation **enjoys an unlimited life**.

   Although the combined number of proprietorships and partnerships in the United States is more than five times the number of corporations, the revenue produced by corporations is eight times greater. Most of the largest companies in the United States—for example, ExxonMobil, Ford, Wal-Mart Stores, Inc., Citigroup, and Apple—are corporations.

*The **DO IT!** exercises ask you to put newly acquired knowledge to work. They outline the Action Plan necessary to complete the exercise, and they show a Solution.*

> **DO IT!**

Basic Concepts

Indicate whether each of the five statements presented below is true or false.

1. The three steps in the accounting process are identification, recording, and communication.
2. The two most common types of external users are investors and company officers.
3. Congress passed the Sarbanes-Oxley Act to reduce unethical behavior and decrease the likelihood of future corporate scandals.
4. The primary accounting standard-setting body in the United States is the Financial Accounting Standards Board (FASB).
5. The historical cost principle dictates that companies record assets at their cost. In later periods, however, the fair value of the asset must be used if fair value is higher than its cost.

Action Plan

✔ Review the basic concepts learned to date.

✔ Develop an understanding of the key terms used.

Solution

1. True   2. False. The two most common types of external users are investors and creditors.   3. True.   4. True.   5. False. The historical cost principle dictates that companies record assets at their cost. Under the historical cost principle, the company must also use cost in later periods.

Related exercise material: **E1-1, E1-2, E1-3, E1-4, and DO IT! 1-1.**

✔ **The Navigator**

ACCOUNTING ACROSS THE ORGANIZATION

Spinning the Career Wheel

How will the study of accounting help you? A working knowledge of accounting is desirable for virtually every field of business. Some examples of how accounting is used in business careers include:

General management: Managers of Ford Motors, Massachusetts General Hospital, California State University—Fullerton, a McDonald's franchise, and a Trek bike shop all need to understand accounting data in order to make wise business decisions.

Marketing: A marketing specialist at Procter & Gamble must be sensitive to costs and benefits, which accounting helps them quantify and understand. Making a sale is meaningless unless it is a profitable sale.

Finance: Do you want to be a banker for Citicorp, an investment analyst for Goldman Sachs, or a stock broker for Merrill Lynch? These fields rely heavily on accounting knowledge to analyze financial statements. In fact, it is difficult to get a good job in a finance function without two or three courses in accounting.

Real estate: Are you interested in being a real estate broker for Prudential Real Estate? Because a third party—the bank—is almost always involved in financing a real estate transaction, brokers must understand the numbers involved: Can the buyer afford to make the payments to the bank? Does the cash flow from an industrial property justify the purchase price? What are the tax benefits of the purchase?

? How might accounting help you? (See page 48.)

Josef Volavka/iStockphoto

The Basic Accounting Equation

LEARNING OBJECTIVE 6

State the accounting equation, and define its components.

The two basic elements of a business are what it owns and what it owes. **Assets** are the resources a business owns. For example, Google has total assets of approximately $40.5 billion. Liabilities and owner's equity are the rights or claims against these resources. Thus, Google has $40.5 billion of claims against its $40.5 billion of assets. Claims of those to whom the company owes money (creditors) are called **liabilities**. Claims of owners are called **owner's equity**. Google has liabilities of $4.5 billion and owners' equity of $36 billion.

We can express the relationship of assets, liabilities, and owner's equity as an equation, as shown in Illustration 1-5.

Illustration 1-5
The basic accounting equation

Assets	=	Liabilities	+	Owner's Equity

This relationship is the **basic accounting equation**. Assets must equal the sum of liabilities and owner's equity. Liabilities appear before owner's equity in the basic accounting equation because they are paid first if a business is liquidated.

The accounting equation applies to all **economic entities** regardless of size, nature of business, or form of business organization. It applies to a small proprietorship such as a corner grocery store as well as to a giant corporation such as PepsiCo. The equation provides the **underlying framework** for recording and summarizing economic events.

Let's look in more detail at the categories in the basic accounting equation.

Assets

As noted above, **assets** are resources a business owns. The business uses its assets in carrying out such activities as production and sales. The common characteristic possessed by all assets is **the capacity to provide future services or benefits**. In a business, that service potential or future economic benefit eventually results in cash inflows (receipts). For example, consider Campus Pizza, a local restaurant. It owns a delivery truck that provides economic benefits from delivering pizzas. Other assets of Campus Pizza are tables, chairs, jukebox, cash register, oven, tableware, and, of course, cash.

Liabilities

Liabilities are claims against assets—that is, existing debts and obligations. Businesses of all sizes usually borrow money and purchase merchandise on credit. These economic activities result in payables of various sorts:

- Campus Pizza, for instance, purchases cheese, sausage, flour, and beverages on credit from suppliers. These obligations are called **accounts payable**.
- Campus Pizza also has a **note payable** to First National Bank for the money borrowed to purchase the delivery truck.
- Campus Pizza may also have **salaries and wages payable** to employees and **sales and real estate taxes payable** to the local government.

All of these persons or entities to whom Campus Pizza owes money are its **creditors**.

Creditors may legally force the liquidation of a business that does not pay its debts. In that case, the law requires that creditor claims be paid **before** ownership claims.

Owner's Equity

The ownership claim on total assets is **owner's equity**. It is equal to total assets minus total liabilities. Here is why: The assets of a business are claimed by either creditors or owners. To find out what belongs to owners, we subtract the creditors' claims (the liabilities) from assets. The remainder is the owner's claim on the assets—the owner's equity. Since the claims of creditors must be paid **before** ownership claims, owner's equity is often referred to as **residual equity**.

INCREASES IN OWNER'S EQUITY

In a proprietorship, owner's investments and revenues increase owner's equity.

INVESTMENTS BY OWNER Investments by owner are the assets the owner puts into the business. These investments increase owner's equity. They are recorded in a category called **owner's capital**.

REVENUES Revenues are the **gross increase in owner's equity resulting from business activities entered into for the purpose of earning income**. Generally, revenues result from selling merchandise, performing services, renting property,

Helpful Hint In some places, we use the term "owner's equity" and in others we use "owners' equity." *Owner's* (singular, possessive) refers to one owner (the case with a sole proprietorship). *Owners'* (plural, possessive) refers to multiple owners (the case with partnerships or corporations).

and lending money. Common sources of revenue are sales, fees, services, commissions, interest, dividends, royalties, and rent.

Revenues usually result in an increase in an asset. They may arise from different sources and are called various names depending on the nature of the business. Campus Pizza, for instance, has two categories of sales revenues—pizza sales and beverage sales.

DECREASES IN OWNER'S EQUITY

In a proprietorship, owner's drawings and expenses decrease owner's equity.

DRAWINGS An owner may withdraw cash or other assets for personal use. We use a separate classification called **drawings** to determine the total withdrawals for each accounting period. **Drawings decrease owner's equity.** They are recorded in a category called owner's drawings.

EXPENSES **Expenses** are the cost of assets consumed or services used in the process of earning revenue. They are **decreases in owner's equity that result from operating the business**. For example, Campus Pizza recognizes the following expenses: cost of ingredients (meat, flour, cheese, tomato paste, mushrooms, etc.); cost of beverages; salaries and wages expense; utilities expense (electric, gas, and water expense); delivery expense (gasoline, repairs, licenses, etc.); supplies expense (napkins, detergents, aprons, etc.); rent expense; interest expense; and property tax expense.

In summary, owner's equity is increased by an owner's investments and by revenues from business operations. Owner's equity is decreased by an owner's withdrawals of assets and by expenses. Illustration 1-6 expands the basic accounting equation by showing the items that comprise owner's equity. This format is referred to as the **expanded accounting equation**.

Illustration 1-6
Expanded accounting equation

Basic Equation	Assets = Liabilities	+	Owner's Equity			
Expanded Equation	Assets = Liabilities	+	Owner's Capital	− Owner's Drawings	+ Revenues	− Expenses

---

> **DO IT!**

Owner's Equity Effects

Action Plan

✔ Understand the sources of revenue.

✔ Understand what causes expenses.

✔ Review the rules for changes in owner's equity: Investments and revenues increase owner's equity. Expenses and drawings decrease owner's equity.

✔ Recognize that drawings are withdrawals of cash or other assets from the business for personal use.

Classify the following items as investment by owner (I), owner's drawings (D), revenues (R), or expenses (E). Then indicate whether each item increases or decreases owner's equity.

1. Rent Expense
2. Service Revenue
3. Drawings
4. Salaries and Wages Expense

Solution

> 1. Rent Expense is an expense (E); it decreases owner's equity. 2. Service Revenue is revenue (R); it increases owner's equity. 3. Drawings is owner's drawings (D); it decreases owner's equity. 4. Salaries and Wages Expense is an expense (E); it decreases owner's equity.

Related exercise material: **BE1-1, BE1-2, BE1-3, BE1-4, BE1-5, E1-5, and DO IT! 1-2.**

✔ The Navigator

Using the Accounting Equation

Transactions (**business transactions**) are a business's economic events recorded by accountants. Transactions may be external or internal. **External transactions** involve economic events between the company and some outside enterprise. For example, Campus Pizza's purchase of cooking equipment from a supplier, payment of monthly rent to the landlord, and sale of pizzas to customers are external transactions. **Internal transactions** are economic events that occur entirely within one company. The use of cooking and cleaning supplies are internal transactions for Campus Pizza.

<table>
<tr><td>**LEARNING OBJECTIVE**</td><td>**7**</td></tr>
</table>

Analyze the effects of business transactions on the accounting equation.

Companies carry on many activities that do not represent business transactions. Examples are hiring employees, answering the telephone, talking with customers, and placing merchandise orders. Some of these activities may lead to business transactions: Employees will earn wages, and suppliers will deliver ordered merchandise. The company must analyze each event to find out if it affects the components of the accounting equation. If it does, the company will record the transaction. Illustration 1-7 demonstrates the transaction identification process.

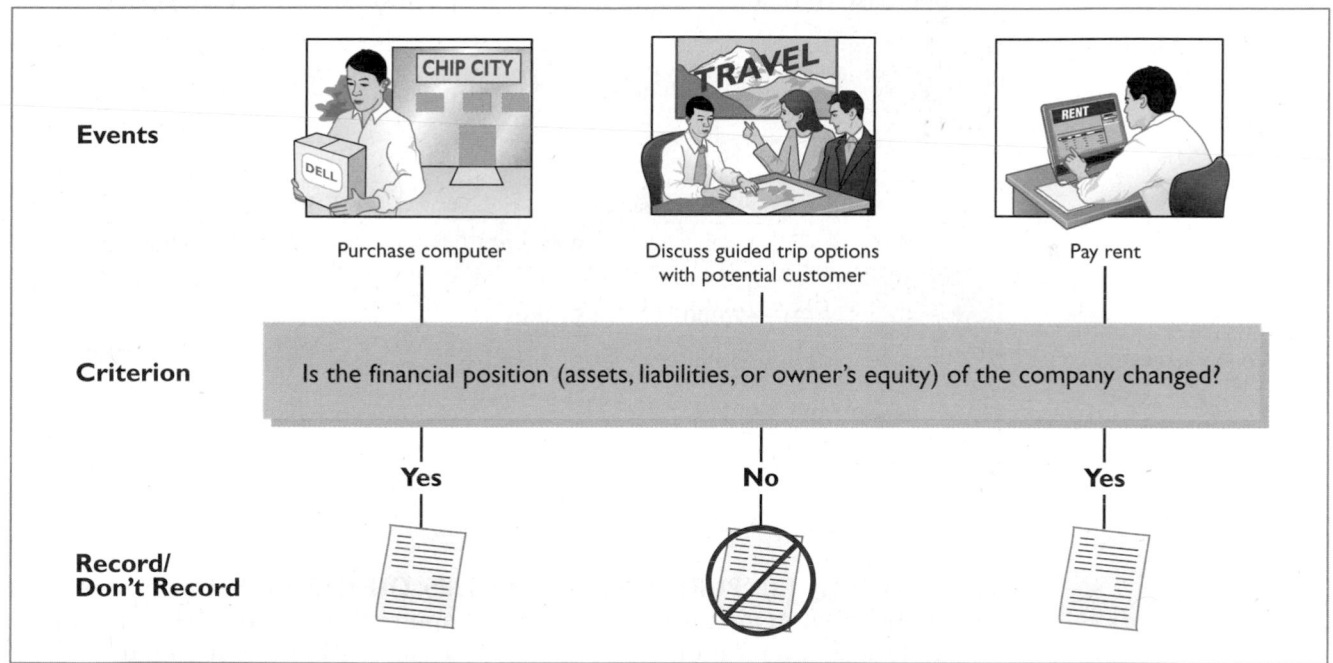

Events

Purchase computer | Discuss guided trip options with potential customer | Pay rent

Criterion — Is the financial position (assets, liabilities, or owner's equity) of the company changed?

Yes | No | Yes

Record/ Don't Record

Illustration 1-7
Transaction identification process

Each transaction must have a dual effect on the accounting equation. For example, if an asset is increased, there must be a corresponding (1) decrease in another asset, (2) increase in a specific liability, or (3) increase in owner's equity.

Two or more items could be affected. For example, as one asset is increased $10,000, another asset could decrease $6,000 and a liability could increase $4,000. Any change in a liability or ownership claim is subject to similar analysis.

Helpful Hint. You will want to study these transactions until you are sure you understand them. They are not difficult, but understanding them is important to your success in this course. The ability to analyze transactions in terms of the basic accounting equation is essential in accounting.

Transaction Analysis

To demonstrate how to analyze transactions in terms of the accounting equation, we will review the business activities of Softbyte, a computer programming business. The following business transactions occur during Softbyte's first month of operations.

TRANSACTION (1). INVESTMENT BY OWNER Ray Neal decides to open a computer programming service which he names Softbyte. On September 1, 2014, he invests $15,000 cash in the business. This transaction results in an equal increase in assets and owner's equity.

| Basic Analysis | The asset Cash increases $15,000, and owner's equity (identified as Owner's Capital) increases $15,000. |

Equation Analysis	Assets	=	Liabilities	+	Owner's Equity
	Cash	=			Owner's Capital
(1)	+$15,000	=			+$15,000 Initial investment

Observe that the equality of the accounting equation has been maintained. Note that the investments by the owner do not represent revenues, and they are excluded in determining net income. Therefore, it is necessary to make clear that the increase is an investment (increasing Owner's Capital) rather than revenue.

TRANSACTION (2). PURCHASE OF EQUIPMENT FOR CASH Softbyte purchases computer equipment for $7,000 cash. This transaction results in an equal increase and decrease in total assets, though the composition of assets changes.

| Basic Analysis | The asset Cash decreases $7,000, and the asset Equipment increases $7,000. |

Equation Analysis	Assets			=	Liabilities	+	Owner's Equity
	Cash	+	Equipment	=			Owner's Capital
	$15,000						$15,000
(2)	−7,000		+$7,000				
	$ 8,000	+	$7,000	=			$15,000
		$15,000					

Observe that total assets are still $15,000. Owner's equity also remains at $15,000, the amount of Ray Neal's original investment.

TRANSACTION (3). PURCHASE OF SUPPLIES ON CREDIT Softbyte purchases for $1,600 from Acme Supply Company computer paper and other supplies expected to last several months. Acme agrees to allow Softbyte to pay this bill in October. This transaction is a purchase on account (a credit purchase). Assets increase because of the expected future benefits of using the paper and supplies, and liabilities increase by the amount due to Acme Company.

| Basic Analysis | The asset Supplies increases $1,600, and the liability Accounts Payable increases by $1,600. |

Equation Analysis	Assets					=	Liabilities	+	Owner's Equity
	Cash	+	Supplies	+	Equipment	=	Accounts Payable	+	Owner's Capital
	$8,000				$7,000				$15,000
(3)			+$1,600				+$1,600		
	$8,000	+	$1,600	+	$7,000	=	$1,600	+	$15,000
			$16,600					$16,600	

Total assets are now $16,600. This total is matched by a $1,600 creditor's claim and a $15,000 ownership claim.

TRANSACTION (4). SERVICES PERFORMED FOR CASH Softbyte receives $1,200 cash from customers for programming services it has performed. This transaction represents Softbyte's principal revenue-producing activity. Recall that **revenue increases owner's equity**.

Basic Analysis	The asset Cash increases $1,200, and owner's equity increases $1,200 due to Service Revenue.

Equation Analysis		Assets			= Liabilities +	Owner's Equity		

		Cash	+ Supplies	+ Equipment	= Accounts Payable	+ Owner's Capital	+ Revenues	
		$8,000	$1,600	$7,000	$1,600	$15,000		
(4)		+1,200					+$1,200	Service Revenue
		$9,200 +	$1,600 +	$7,000	= $1,600	+ $15,000 +	$1,200	
			$17,800			$17,800		

The two sides of the equation balance at $17,800. Service Revenue is included in determining Softbyte's net income.

Note that we do not have room to give details for each individual revenue and expense account in this illustration. Thus, revenues (and expenses when we get to them) are summarized under one column heading for Revenues and one for Expenses. However, it is important to keep track of the category (account) titles affected (e.g., Service Revenue) as they will be needed when we prepare financial statements later in the chapter.

TRANSACTION (5). PURCHASE OF ADVERTISING ON CREDIT Softbyte receives a bill for $250 from the *Daily News* for advertising but postpones payment until a later date. This transaction results in an increase in liabilities and a decrease in owner's equity.

Basic Analysis	The liability Accounts Payable increases $250, and owner's equity decreases $250 due to Advertising Expense.

Equation Analysis									

	Assets			= Liabilities +	Owner's Equity			
Cash	+ Supplies	+ Equipment	= Accounts Payable	+ Owner's Capital	+ Revenues	− Expenses		
$9,200	$1,600	$7,000	$1,600	$15,000	$1,200			
(5)			+250			−$250		Advertising Expense
$9,200 +	$1,600 +	$7,000	= $1,850	+ $15,000 +	$1,200	− $250		
	$17,800			$17,800				

The two sides of the equation still balance at $17,800. Owner's equity decreases when Softbyte incurs the expense. Expenses are not always paid in cash at the time they are incurred. When Softbyte pays at a later date, the liability Accounts Payable will decrease, and the asset Cash will decrease [see Transaction (8)]. The cost of advertising is an expense (rather than an asset) because the company has **used** the benefits. Advertising Expense is included in determining net income.

TRANSACTION (6). SERVICES PERFORMED FOR CASH AND CREDIT Softbyte performs $3,500 of programming services for customers. The company receives cash of $1,500 from customers, and it bills the balance of $2,000 on account. This transaction results in an equal increase in assets and owner's equity.

Basic Analysis	Three specific items are affected: The asset Cash increases $1,500, the asset Accounts Receivable increases $2,000, and owner's equity increases $3,500 due to Service Revenue.

Equation Analysis

		Assets			= Liabilities +		Owner's Equity		
Cash	+ Accounts Receivable	+ Supplies	+ Equipment	=	Accounts Payable	+ Owner's Capital	+ Revenues	− Expenses	
$9,200		$1,600	$7,000		$1,850	$15,000	$1,200	$250	
(6) +1,500	+$2,000						+3,500		Service Revenue
$10,700 +	$2,000 +	$1,600 +	$7,000	=	$1,850 +	$15,000 +	$4,700	− $250	
		$21,300					$21,300		

Softbyte recognizes $3,500 in revenue when it performs the service. In exchange for this service, it received $1,500 in Cash and Accounts Receivable of $2,000. This Accounts Receivable represents customers' promises to pay $2,000 to Softbyte in the future. When it later receives collections on account, Softbyte will increase Cash and will decrease Accounts Receivable [see Transaction (9)].

TRANSACTION (7). PAYMENT OF EXPENSES Softbyte pays the following expenses in cash for September: store rent $600, salaries and wages of employees $900, and utilities $200. These payments result in an equal decrease in assets and owner's equity.

Basic Analysis	The asset Cash decreases $1,700, and owner's equity decreases $1,700 due to the specific expense categories (Rent Expense, Salaries and Wages Expense, and Utilities Expense).

Equation Analysis

		Assets			= Liabilities +		Owner's Equity		
Cash	+ Accounts Receivable	+ Supplies	+ Equipment	=	Accounts Payable	+ Owner's Capital	+ Revenues	− Expenses	
$10,700	$2,000	$1,600	$7,000		$1,850	$15,000	$4,700	$ 250	
(7) −1,700								−600	Rent Expense
								−900	Sal. and Wages Exp.
								−200	Utilities Exp.
$9,000 +	$2,000 +	$1,600 +	$7,000	=	$1,850 +	$15,000 +	$4,700	− $1,950	
		$19,600					$19,600		

The two sides of the equation now balance at $19,600. Three lines in the analysis indicate the different types of expenses that have been incurred.

TRANSACTION (8). PAYMENT OF ACCOUNTS PAYABLE Softbyte pays its $250 *Daily News* bill in cash. The company previously [in Transaction (5)] recorded the bill as an increase in Accounts Payable and a decrease in owner's equity.

Basic Analysis	This cash payment "on account" decreases the asset Cash by $250 and also decreases the liability Accounts Payable by $250.

Equation Analysis

	Cash	+	Accounts Receivable	+	Supplies	+	Equipment	=	Accounts Payable	+	Owner's Capital	+	Revenues	−	Expenses
	$9,000		$2,000		$1,600		$7,000		$1,850		$15,000		$4,700		$1,950
(8)	−250								−250						
	$8,750	+	$2,000	+	$1,600	+	$7,000	=	$1,600	+	$15,000	+	$4,700	−	$1,950

Assets = $19,350   Liabilities + Owner's Equity = $19,350

Observe that the payment of a liability related to an expense that has previously been recorded does not affect owner's equity. The company recorded this expense in Transaction (5) and should not record it again.

TRANSACTION (9). RECEIPT OF CASH ON ACCOUNT Softbyte receives $600 in cash from customers who had been billed for services [in Transaction (6)]. Transaction (9) does not change total assets, but it changes the composition of those assets.

Basic Analysis	The asset Cash increases $600, and the asset Accounts Receivable decreases $600.

Equation Analysis

	Cash	+	Accounts Receivable	+	Supplies	+	Equipment	=	Accounts Payable	+	Owner's Capital	+	Revenues	−	Expenses
	$8,750		$2,000		$1,600		$7,000		$1,600		$15,000		$4,700		$1,950
(9)	+600		−600												
	$9,350	+	$1,400	+	$1,600	+	$7,000	=	$1,600	+	$15,000	+	$4,700	−	$1,950

Assets = $19,350   Liabilities + Owner's Equity = $19,350

Note that the collection of an account receivable for services previously billed and recorded does not affect owner's equity. Softbyte already recorded this revenue in Transaction (6) and should not record it again.

TRANSACTION (10). WITHDRAWAL OF CASH BY OWNER Ray Neal withdraws $1,300 in cash from the business for his personal use. This transaction results in an equal decrease in assets and owner's equity.

Basic Analysis	The asset Cash decreases $1,300, and owner's equity decreases $1,300 due to owner's withdrawal (Owner's Drawings).

Equation Analysis

	Assets			= Liabilities +		Owner's Equity			
Cash +	Accounts Receivable +	Supplies +	Equipment =	Accounts Payable +	Owner's Capital −	Owner's Drawings +	Revenues −	Expenses	
$9,350	$1,400	$1,600	$7,000	$1,600	$15,000		$4,700	$1,950	
(10) −1,300						−$1,300			Drawings
$8,050 +	$1,400 +	$1,600 +	$7,000 =	$1,600 +	$15,000 −	$1,300 +	$4,700 −	$1,950	
	$18,050					$18,050			

Observe that the effect of a cash withdrawal by the owner is the opposite of the effect of an investment by the owner. **Owner's drawings are not expenses.** Expenses are incurred for the purpose of earning revenue. Drawings do not generate revenue. They are a **disinvestment**. Like owner's investment, the company excludes owner's drawings in determining net income.

Summary of Transactions

Illustration 1-8 summarizes the September transactions of Softbyte to show their cumulative effect on the basic accounting equation. It also indicates the transaction number and the specific effects of each transaction.

	Assets			= Liabilities +		Owner's Equity			
Cash +	Accounts Receivable +	Supplies +	Equipment =	Accounts Payable +	Owner's Capital −	Owner's Drawings +	Rev. −	Exp.	
(1) +$15,000					+ $15,000				Initial inv.
(2) −7,000			+$7,000						
(3)		+$1,600		+$1,600					
(4) +1,200							+$1,200		Ser. Rev.
(5)				+250				−$250	Adv. Exp.
(6) +1,500	+$2,000						+3,500		Ser. Rev.
(7) −600								−600	Rent Exp.
−900								−900	Sal./Wages Exp.
−200								−200	Utilities Exp.
(8) −250				−250					
(9) +600	−600								
(10) −1,300						−$1,300			Drawings
$ 8,050 +	$1,400 +	$1,600 +	$7,000 =	$1,600 +	$15,000 −	$1,300 +	$4,700 −	$1,950	
	$18,050					$18,050			

Illustration 1-8
Tabular summary of Softbyte transactions

Illustration 1-8 demonstrates some significant facts:

1. Each transaction is analyzed in terms of its effect on:
   (a) The three components of the basic accounting equation.
   (b) Specific items within each component.
2. The two sides of the equation must always be equal.

There! You made it through your first transaction analysis. If you feel a bit shaky on any of the transactions, it might be a good idea at this point to get up,

take a short break, and come back again for a 10- to 15-minute review of the transactions, to make sure you understand them before you go on to the next section.

> DO IT!

Tabular Analysis

Action Plan

✔ Analyze the effects of each transaction on the accounting equation.

✔ Use appropriate category names (not descriptions).

✔ Keep the accounting equation in balance.

Transactions made by Virmari & Co., a public accounting firm, for the month of August are shown below. Prepare a tabular analysis which shows the effects of these transactions on the expanded accounting equation, similar to that shown in Illustration 1-8.

1. The owner invested $25,000 cash in the business.
2. The company purchased $7,000 of office equipment on credit.
3. The company received $8,000 cash in exchange for services performed.
4. The company paid $850 for this month's rent.
5. The owner withdrew $1,000 cash for personal use.

Solution

	Assets			=	Liabilities	+			Owner's Equity				
	Cash	+	Equipment	=	Accounts Payable	+	Owner's Capital	−	Owner's Drawings	+	Revenues	−	Expenses
1.	+$25,000						+$25,000						
2.			+$7,000		+$7,000								
3.	+8,000										+$8,000		
4.	−850												−$850
5.	−1,000								−$1,000				
	$31,150	+	$7,000	=	$7,000	+	$25,000	−	$1,000	+	$8,000	=	$850

$38,150 $38,150

Related exercise material: **BE1-6, BE1-7, BE1-8, BE1-9, E1-6, E1-7, E1-8, E1-11, and DO IT! 1-3.**

 The Navigator

Financial Statements

Companies prepare four financial statements from the summarized accounting data:

1. An **income statement** presents the revenues and expenses and resulting net income or net loss for a specific period of time.

2. An **owner's equity statement** summarizes the changes in owner's equity for a specific period of time.

3. A **balance sheet** reports the assets, liabilities, and owner's equity at a specific date.

4. A **statement of cash flows** summarizes information about the cash inflows (receipts) and outflows (payments) for a specific period of time.

These statements provide relevant financial data for internal and external users. Illustration 1-9 (page 22) shows the financial statements of Softbyte.

> **LEARNING OBJECTIVE   8**
>
> Understand the four financial statements and how they are prepared.

> **International Note**
>
> The primary types of financial statements required by GAAP and IFRS are the same. In practice, some format differences do exist in presentations commonly employed by GAAP companies compared to IFRS companies.

Illustration 1-9
Financial statements and their interrelationships

Helpful Hint The heading of each statement identifies the company, the type of statement, and the specific date or time period covered by the statement.

SOFTBYTE
Income Statement
For the Month Ended September 30, 2014

Revenues		
Service revenue		$ 4,700
Expenses		
Salaries and wages expense	$900	
Rent expense	600	
Advertising expense	250	
Utilities expense	200	
Total expenses		1,950
Net income		**$ 2,750**

SOFTBYTE
Owner's Equity Statement
For the Month Ended September 30, 2014

Helpful Hint Note that final sums are double-underlined, and negative amounts (in the statement of cash flows) are presented in parentheses.

Owner's capital, September 1		$ –0–
Add: Investments	$15,000	
Net income	2,750	17,750
		17,750
Less: Drawings		1,300
Owner's capital, September 30		**$16,450**

SOFTBYTE
Balance Sheet
September 30, 2014

Assets

Cash	**$ 8,050**
Accounts receivable	1,400
Supplies	1,600
Equipment	7,000
Total assets	$ 18,050

Liabilities and Owner's Equity

Liabilities	
Accounts payable	$ 1,600
Owner's equity	
Owner's capital	**16,450**
Total liabilities and owner's equity	$ 18,050

SOFTBYTE
Statement of Cash Flows
For the Month Ended September 30, 2014

Helpful Hint The arrows in this illustration show the interrelationships of the four financial statements.

1. Net income is computed first and is needed to determine the ending balance in owner's equity.
2. The ending balance in owner's equity is needed in preparing the balance sheet.
3. The cash shown on the balance sheet is needed in preparing the statement of cash flows.

Cash flows from operating activities		
Cash receipts from revenues		$ 3,300
Cash payments for expenses		(1,950)
Net cash provided by operating activities		1,350
Cash flows from investing activities		
Purchase of equipment		(7,000)
Cash flows from financing activities		
Investments by owner	$15,000	
Drawings by owner	(1,300)	13,700
Net increase in cash		8,050
Cash at the beginning of the period		0
Cash at the end of the period		**$ 8,050**

Note that the statements shown in Illustration 1-9 are interrelated:

1. Net income of $2,750 on the **income statement** is added to the beginning balance of owner's capital in the **owner's equity statement**.
2. Owner's capital of $16,450 at the end of the reporting period shown in the **owner's equity statement** is reported on the **balance sheet**.
3. Cash of $8,050 on the **balance sheet** is reported on the **statement of cash flows**.

Also, explanatory notes and supporting schedules are an integral part of every set of financial statements. We illustrate these notes and schedules in later chapters of this textbook.

Be sure to carefully examine the format and content of each statement in Illustration 1-9. We describe the essential features of each in the following sections.

Helpful Hint The income statement, owner's equity statement, and statement of cash flows are all for a *period* of time, whereas the balance sheet is for a *point* in time.

Income Statement

The income statement reports the revenues and expenses for a specific period of time. (In Softbyte's case, this is "For the Month Ended September 30, 2014.") Softbyte's income statement is prepared from the data appearing in the owner's equity columns of Illustration 1-8 (page 20).

The income statement lists revenues first, followed by expenses. Finally the statement shows net income (or net loss). **Net income** results when revenues exceed expenses. **A net loss** occurs when expenses exceed revenues.

Although practice varies, we have chosen in our illustrations and homework solutions to list expenses in order of magnitude. (We will consider alternative formats for the income statement in later chapters.)

Note that the income statement does **not** include investment and withdrawal transactions between the owner and the business in measuring net income. For example, as explained earlier, Ray Neal's withdrawal of cash from Softbyte was not regarded as a business expense.

Alternative Terminology The income statement is sometimes referred to as the *statement of operations, earnings statement,* or *profit and loss statement.*

Alternative Terminology notes introduce other terms you might hear or read.

Owner's Equity Statement

The owner's equity statement reports the changes in owner's equity for a specific period of time. The time period is the same as that covered by the income statement. Data for the preparation of the owner's equity statement come from the owner's equity columns of the tabular summary (Illustration 1-8) and from the income statement. The first line of the statement shows the beginning owner's equity amount (which was zero at the start of the business). Then come the owner's investments, net income (or loss), and the owner's drawings. This statement indicates **why** owner's equity has increased or decreased during the period.

What if Softbyte had reported a net loss in its first month? Let's assume that during the month of September 2014, Softbyte lost $10,000. Illustration 1-10 shows the presentation of a net loss in the owner's equity statement.

SOFTBYTE
Owner's Equity Statement
For the Month Ended September 30, 2014

Owner's capital, September 1		$ –0–
Add: Investments		15,000
		15,000
Less: Drawings	$ 1,300	
Net loss	**10,000**	11,300
Owner's capital, September 30		$ 3,700

Illustration 1-10
Presentation of net loss

If the owner makes any additional investments, the company reports them in the owner's equity statement as investments.

Balance Sheet

Softbyte's balance sheet reports the assets, liabilities, and owner's equity at a specific date (in Softbyte's case, September 30, 2014). The company prepares the balance sheet from the column headings of the tabular summary (Illustration 1-8) and the month-end data shown in its last line.

Observe that the balance sheet lists assets at the top, followed by liabilities and owner's equity. Total assets must equal total liabilities and owner's equity. Softbyte reports only one liability—accounts payable—in its balance sheet. In most cases, there will be more than one liability. When two or more liabilities are involved, a customary way of listing is as follows.

Illustration 1-11
Presentation of liabilities

Liabilities	
Notes payable	$ 10,000
Accounts payable	63,000
Salaries and wages payable	18,000
Total liabilities	**$91,000**

The balance sheet is a snapshot of the company's financial condition at a specific moment in time (usually the month-end or year-end).

Statement of Cash Flows

The statement of cash flows provides information on the cash receipts and payments for a specific period of time. The statement of cash flows reports (1) the cash effects of a company's operations during a period, (2) its investing activities, (3) its financing activities, (4) the net increase or decrease in cash during the period, and (5) the cash amount at the end of the period.

Reporting the sources, uses, and change in cash is useful because investors, creditors, and others want to know what is happening to a company's most liquid resource. The statement of cash flows provides answers to the following simple but important questions.

1. Where did cash come from during the period?
2. What was cash used for during the period?
3. What was the change in the cash balance during the period?

As shown in Softbyte's statement of cash flows, cash increased $8,050 during the period. Net cash provided by operating activities increased cash $1,350. Cash flow from investing activities decreased cash $7,000. And cash flow from financing activities increased cash $13,700. At this time, you need not be concerned with how these amounts are determined. Chapter 17 will examine the statement of cash flows in detail.

PEOPLE, PLANET, AND PROFIT INSIGHT

Beyond Financial Statements

Should we expand our financial statements beyond the income statement, owner's equity statement, balance sheet, and statement of cash flows? Some believe we should take into account ecological and social performance, in addition to financial results, in evaluating a company. The argument is that a company's responsibility lies with anyone who is influenced by its actions. In other words, a company should be interested in benefiting many different parties, instead of only maximizing stockholders' interests.

A socially responsible business does not exploit or endanger any group of individuals. It follows fair trade practices, provides safe environments for workers, and bears responsibility for environmental damage. Granted, measurement of these factors is difficult. How to report this information is also controversial. But many interesting and useful efforts are underway. Throughout this textbook, we provide additional insights into how companies are attempting to meet the challenge of measuring and reporting their contributions to society, as well as their financial results, to stockholders.

? Why might a company's stockholders be interested in its environmental and social performance? (See page 48.)

> **DO IT!**

Financial Statement Items

Presented below is selected information related to Flanagan Company at December 31, 2014. Flanagan reports financial information monthly.

Equipment	$10,000	Utilities Expense	$ 4,000
Cash	8,000	Accounts Receivable	9,000
Service Revenue	36,000	Salaries and Wages Expense	7,000
Rent Expense	11,000	Notes Payable	16,500
Accounts Payable	2,000	Owner's Drawings	5,000

(a) Determine the total assets of Flanagan Company at December 31, 2014.
(b) Determine the net income that Flanagan Company reported for December 2014.
(c) Determine the owner's equity of Flanagan Company at December 31, 2014.

Solution

Action Plan

✔ Remember the basic accounting equation: assets must equal liabilities plus owner's equity.

✔ Review previous financial statements to determine how total assets, net income, and owner's equity are computed.

(a) The total assets are $27,000, comprised of Cash $8,000, Accounts Receivable $9,000, and Equipment $10,000.

(b) Net income is $14,000, computed as follows.

Revenues		
Service revenue		$36,000
Expenses		
Rent expense	$11,000	
Salaries and wages expense	7,000	
Utilities expense	4,000	
Total expenses		22,000
Net income		$14,000

(c) The ending owner's equity of Flanagan Company is $8,500. By rewriting the accounting equation, we can compute owner's equity as assets minus liabilities, as follows.

Total assets [as computed in (a)]		$27,000
Less: Liabilities		
Notes payable	$16,500	
Accounts payable	2,000	18,500
Owner's equity		$ 8,500

Note that it is not possible to determine the company's owner's equity in any other way because the beginning total for owner's equity is not provided.

Related exercise material: **BE1-10, BE1-11, E1-9, E1-12, E1-13, E1-14, E1-15, E1-16, and DO IT! 1-4.**

> Comprehensive DO IT!

*The **Comprehensive DO IT!** is a final review of the chapter. The **Action Plan** gives tips about how to approach the problem, and the **Solution** demonstrates both the form and content of complete answers.*

Joan Robinson opens her own law office on July 1, 2014. During the first month of operations, the following transactions occurred.

1. Joan invested $11,000 in cash in the law practice.
2. Paid $800 for July rent on office space.
3. Purchased office equipment on account $3,000.
4. Performed legal services to clients for cash $1,500.
5. Borrowed $700 cash from a bank on a note payable.
6. Performed legal services for client on account $2,000.
7. Paid monthly expenses: salaries and wages $500, utilities $300, and advertising $100.
8. Joan withdraws $1,000 cash for personal use.

Instructions
(a) Prepare a tabular summary of the transactions.
(b) Prepare the income statement, owner's equity statement, and balance sheet at July 31 for Joan Robinson, Attorney.

Solution to Comprehensive DO IT!

(a)

Trans-action	Cash	+	Accounts Receivable	+	Equipment	=	Notes Payable	+	Accounts Payable	+	Owner's Capital	−	Owner's Drawings	+	Revenues	−	Expenses
(1)	+$11,000					=					+$11,000						
(2)	−800																−$800
(3)					+$3,000	=			+$3,000								
(4)	+1,500														+$1,500		
(5)	+700						+$700										
(6)			+$2,000												+2,000		
(7)	−500																−500
	−300																−300
	−100																−100
(8)	−1,000												−$1,000				
	$10,500	+	$2,000	+	$3,000	=	$700	+	$3,000	+	$11,000	−	$1,000	+	$3,500	−	$1,700

Assets: $15,500

Liabilities + Owner's Equity: $15,500

Action Plan

✔ Make sure that assets equal liabilities plus owner's equity after each transaction.

✔ Investments and revenues increase owner's equity. Withdrawals and expenses decrease owner's equity.

✔ Prepare the financial statements in the order listed.

✔ The income statement shows revenues and expenses for a period of time.

✔ The owner's equity statement shows the changes in owner's equity for the same period of time as the income statement.

✔ The balance sheet reports assets, liabilities, and owner's equity at a specific date.

JOAN ROBINSON, ATTORNEY
Income Statement
Month Ended July 31, 2014

Revenues		
Service revenue		$3,500
Expenses		
Rent expense	$800	
Salaries and wages expense	500	
Utilities expense	300	
Advertising expense	100	
Total expenses		1,700
Net income		$1,800

JOAN ROBINSON, ATTORNEY
Owner's Equity Statement
Month Ended July 31, 2014

Owner's capital, July 1		$ 0
Add: Investments	$11,000	
Net income	1,800	12,800
		12,800
Less: Drawings		1,000
Owner's capital, July 31		$11,800

JOAN ROBINSON, ATTORNEY
Balance Sheet
July 31, 2014

Assets

Cash	$10,500
Accounts receivable	2,000
Equipment	3,000
Total assets	$15,500

Liabilities and Owner's Equity

Liabilities	
Notes payable	$ 700
Accounts payable	3,000
Total liabilities	3,700
Owner's equity	
Owner's capital	11,800
Total liabilities and owner's equity	$15,500

 The Navigator

 The Navigator

SUMMARY OF LEARNING OBJECTIVES

1 Explain what accounting is. Accounting is an information system that identifies, records, and communicates the economic events of an organization to interested users.

2 Identify the users and uses of accounting. The major users and uses of accounting are as follows. (a) Management uses accounting information to plan, organize, and run the business. (b) Investors (owners) decide whether to buy, hold, or sell their financial interests on the basis of accounting data. (c) Creditors (suppliers and bankers) evaluate the risks of granting credit or lending money on the basis of accounting information. Other groups that use accounting information are taxing authorities, regulatory agencies, customers, and labor unions.

3 Understand why ethics is a fundamental business concept. Ethics are the standards of conduct by which actions are judged as right or wrong. Effective financial reporting depends on sound ethical behavior.

4 Explain generally accepted accounting principles. Generally accepted accounting principles are a common set of standards used by accountants.

5 Explain the monetary unit assumption and the economic entity assumption. The monetary unit assumption requires that companies include in the accounting records only transaction data that can be expressed in terms of money. The economic entity assumption requires that the activities of each economic entity be kept separate from the activities of its owner(s) and other economic entities.

6 State the accounting equation, and define its components. The basic accounting equation is:

$$\text{Assets} = \text{Liabilities} + \text{Owner's Equity}$$

Assets are resources a business owns. Liabilities are creditorship claims on total assets. Owner's equity is the ownership claim on total assets.

The expanded accounting equation is:

$$\text{Assets} = \text{Liabilities} + \text{Owner's Capital} - \text{Owner's Drawings} + \text{Revenues} - \text{Expenses}$$

Owner's capital is assets the owner puts into the business. Owner's drawings are the assets the owner withdraws for personal use. Revenues are increases in assets resulting from income-earning activities. Expenses are the costs of assets consumed or services used in the process of earning revenue.

7 Analyze the effects of business transactions on the accounting equation. Each business transaction must have a dual effect on the accounting equation. For example, if an individual asset increases, there must be a corresponding (1) decrease in another asset, or (2) increase in a specific liability, or (3) increase in owner's equity.

8 Understand the four financial statements and how they are prepared. An income statement presents the revenues and expenses, and resulting net income or net loss, for a specific period of time. An owner's equity statement summarizes the changes in owner's equity for a specific period of time. A balance sheet reports the assets, liabilities, and owner's equity at a specific date. A statement of cash flows summarizes information about the cash inflows (receipts) and outflows (payments) for a specific period of time.

GLOSSARY

Accounting The information system that identifies, records, and communicates the economic events of an organization to interested users. (p. 4).

Assets Resources a business owns. (p. 13).

Balance sheet A financial statement that reports the assets, liabilities, and owner's equity at a specific date. (p. 21).

Basic accounting equation Assets = Liabilities + Owner's Equity. (p. 13).

Bookkeeping A part of accounting that involves only the recording of economic events. (p. 5).

Convergence The process of reducing the differences between U.S. GAAP and IFRS. (p. 9).

Corporation A business organized as a separate legal entity under state corporation law, having ownership divided into transferable shares of stock. (p. 11).

Drawings Withdrawal of cash or other assets from an unincorporated business for the personal use of the owner(s). (p. 14).

Economic entity assumption An assumption that requires that the activities of the entity be kept separate and distinct from the activities of its owner and all other economic entities. (p. 10).

Ethics The standards of conduct by which one's actions are judged as right or wrong, honest or dishonest, fair or not fair. (p. 7).

Expanded accounting equation Assets = Liabilities + Owner's Capital − Owner's Drawings + Revenues − Expenses. (p. 14).

Expenses The cost of assets consumed or services used in the process of earning revenue. (p. 14).

Fair value principle An accounting principle stating that assets and liabilities should be reported at fair value (the price received to sell an asset or settle a liability). (p. 9).

Faithful representation Numbers and descriptions match what really existed or happened—they are factual. (p. 9).

Financial accounting The field of accounting that provides economic and financial information for investors, creditors, and other external users. (p. 6).

Financial Accounting Standards Board (FASB) A private organization that establishes generally accepted accounting principles in the United States (GAAP). (p. 9).

Generally accepted accounting principles (GAAP) Common standards that indicate how to report economic events. (p. 8).

Historical cost principle An accounting principle that states that companies should record assets at their cost. (p. 9).

Income statement A financial statement that presents the revenues and expenses and resulting net income or net loss of a company for a specific period of time. (p. 21).

International Accounting Standards Board (IASB) An accounting standard-setting body that issues standards adopted by many countries outside of the United States. (p. 9).

International Financial Reporting Standards (IFRS) International accounting standards set by the International Accounting Standards Board (IASB). (p. 9).

Investments by owner The assets an owner puts into the business. (p. 13).

Liabilities Creditor claims against total assets. (p. 13).

Managerial accounting The field of accounting that provides internal reports to help users make decisions about their companies. (p. 6).

Monetary unit assumption An assumption stating that companies include in the accounting records only transaction data that can be expressed in terms of money. (p. 10).

Net income The amount by which revenues exceed expenses. (p. 23).

Net loss The amount by which expenses exceed revenues. (p. 23).

Owner's equity The ownership claim on total assets. (p. 13).

Owner's equity statement A financial statement that summarizes the changes in owner's equity for a specific period of time. (p. 21).

Partnership A business owned by two or more persons associated as partners. (p. 11).

Proprietorship A business owned by one person. (p. 10).

Relevance Financial information that is capable of making a difference in a decision. (p. 9).

Revenues The gross increase in owner's equity resulting from business activities entered into for the purpose of earning income. (p. 13).

Sarbanes-Oxley Act (SOX) Law passed by Congress intended to reduce unethical corporate behavior. (p. 7).

Securities and Exchange Commission (SEC) A governmental agency that oversees U.S. financial markets and accounting standard-setting bodies. (p. 9).

Statement of cash flows A financial statement that summarizes information about the cash inflows (receipts) and cash outflows (payments) for a specific period of time. (p. 21).

Transactions The economic events of a business that are recorded by accountants. (p. 15).

APPENDIX 1A   Accounting Career Opportunities

Why is accounting such a popular major and career choice? First, there are a lot of jobs. In many cities in recent years, the demand for accountants exceeded the supply. Not only are there a lot of jobs, but there are a wide array of opportunities. As one accounting organization observed, "accounting is one degree with 360 degrees of opportunity."

LEARNING OBJECTIVE	9
Explain the career opportunities in accounting.	

Accounting is also hot because it is obvious that accounting matters. Interest in accounting has increased, ironically, because of the attention caused by the accounting failures of companies such as Enron and WorldCom. These widely publicized scandals revealed the important role that accounting plays in society. Most people want to make a difference, and an accounting career provides many opportunities to contribute to society. Finally, the Sarbanes-Oxley Act (SOX) (see page 7) significantly increased the accounting and internal control requirements for corporations. This dramatically increased demand for professionals with accounting training.

Accountants are in such demand that it is not uncommon for accounting students to have accepted a job offer a year before graduation. As the following discussion reveals, the job options of people with accounting degrees are virtually unlimited.

Public Accounting

Individuals in **public accounting** offer expert service to the general public, in much the same way that doctors serve patients and lawyers serve clients. A major portion of public accounting involves **auditing**. In auditing, a certified public accountant (CPA) examines company financial statements and provides an opinion as to how accurately the financial statements present the company's results and financial position. Analysts, investors, and creditors rely heavily on these "audit opinions," which CPAs have the exclusive authority to issue.

Taxation is another major area of public accounting. The work that tax specialists perform includes tax advice and planning, preparing tax returns, and representing clients before governmental agencies such as the Internal Revenue Service.

A third area in public accounting is **management consulting**. It ranges from installing basic accounting software or highly complex enterprise resource planning systems, to performing support services for major marketing projects and merger and acquisition activities.

Many CPAs are entrepreneurs. They form small- or medium-sized practices that frequently specialize in tax or consulting services.

Private Accounting

Instead of working in public accounting, you might choose to be an employee of a for-profit company such as Starbucks, Google, or PepsiCo. In **private** (or **managerial**) **accounting**, you would be involved in activities such as cost accounting (finding the cost of producing specific products), budgeting, accounting information system design and support, and tax planning and preparation. You might also be a member of your company's internal audit team. In response to SOX, the internal auditors' job of reviewing the company's operations to ensure compliance with company policies and to increase efficiency has taken on increased importance.

Alternatively, many accountants work for not-for-profit organizations such as the Red Cross or the Bill and Melinda Gates Foundation, or for museums, libraries, or performing arts organizations.

Governmental Accounting

Another option is to pursue one of the many accounting opportunities in governmental agencies. For example, the Internal Revenue Service (IRS), Federal Bureau of Investigation (FBI), and the Securities and Exchange Commission (SEC) all employ accountants. The FBI has a stated goal that at least 15 percent of its new agents should be CPAs. There is also a very high demand for accounting educators at public colleges and universities and in state and local governments.

Forensic Accounting

Forensic accounting uses accounting, auditing, and investigative skills to conduct investigations into theft and fraud. It is listed among the top 20 career paths of the future. The job of forensic accountants is to catch the perpetrators of the estimated $600 billion per year of theft and fraud occurring at U.S. companies. This includes tracing money-laundering and identity-theft activities as well as tax evasion. Insurance companies hire forensic accountants to detect frauds such as arson, and law offices employ forensic accountants to identify marital assets in divorces. Forensic accountants often have FBI, IRS, or similar government experience.

"Show Me the Money"

How much can a new accountant make? Take a look at the average salaries for college graduates in public and private accounting. Keep in mind if you also have a CPA license, you'll make 10–15% more when you start out.

Illustration 1A-1

Salary estimates for jobs in public and corporate accounting

Employer	Jr. Level (0–3 yrs.)	Sr. Level (4–6 yrs.)
Public accounting (large firm)	$48,750–$69,250	$66,750–$86,000
Public accounting (small firm)	$41,000–$56,000	$54,000–$69,750
Corporate accounting (large company)	$38,000–$57,250	$55,750–$73,500
Corporate accounting (small company)	$33,500–$49,000	$46,500–$58,750

Serious earning potential over time gives CPAs great job security. Here are some examples of upper-level salaries for managers in corporate accounting. Note that geographic region, experience, education, CPA certification, and company size each play a role in determining salary.

Position	Large Company	Small to Medium Company
Chief financial officer	$183,250–$384,000	$94,250–$175,750
Corporate controller	$122,000–$180,000	$80,500–$134,750
Tax manager	$ 92,250–$130,250	$74,250–$100,250

Illustration 1A-2
Upper-level management salaries in corporate accounting

For up-to-date salary estimates, as well as a wealth of additional information regarding accounting as a career, check out **www.startheregoplaces.com.**

SUMMARY OF LEARNING OBJECTIVE FOR APPENDIX 1A

 The Navigator

9 Explain the career opportunities in accounting. Accounting offers many different jobs in fields such as public and private accounting, governmental, and forensic accounting. Accounting is a popular major because there are many different types of jobs, with unlimited potential for career advancement.

GLOSSARY FOR APPENDIX 1A

Auditing The examination of financial statements by a certified public accountant in order to express an opinion as to the fairness of presentation. (p. 29).

Forensic accounting An area of accounting that uses accounting, auditing, and investigative skills to conduct investigations into theft and fraud. (p. 30).

Management consulting An area of public accounting ranging from development of accounting and computer systems to support services for marketing projects and merger and acquisition activities. (p. 30).

Private (or managerial) accounting An area of accounting within a company that involves such activities

as cost accounting, budgeting, design and support of accounting information systems, and tax planning and preparation. (p. 30).

Public accounting An area of accounting in which the accountant offers expert service to the general public. (p. 29).

Taxation An area of public accounting involving tax advice, tax planning, preparing tax returns, and representing clients before governmental agencies. (p. 30).

 Self-Test, Brief Exercises, Exercises, Problem Set A, and many more components are available for practice in *WileyPLUS.*

*Note: All asterisked Questions, Exercises, and Problems relate to material in the appendix to the chapter.

SELF-TEST QUESTIONS

Answers are on page 48.

(LO 1) **1.** Which of the following is **not** a step in the accounting process?
  (a) Identification.   **(c)** Recording.
  (b) Verification.   **(d)** Communication.

(LO 2) **2.** Which of the following statements about users of accounting information is **incorrect**?
  (a) Management is an internal user.
  (b) Taxing authorities are external users.

  (c) Present creditors are external users.
  (d) Regulatory authorities are internal users.

3. The historical cost principle states that: (LO 4)
  (a) assets should be initially recorded at cost and adjusted when the fair value changes.
  (b) activities of an entity are to be kept separate and distinct from its owner.
  (c) assets should be recorded at their cost.

(d) only transaction data capable of being expressed in terms of money be included in the accounting records.

(LO 5) **4.** Which of the following statements about basic assumptions is **correct**?
    (a) Basic assumptions are the same as accounting principles.
    (b) The economic entity assumption states that there should be a particular unit of accountability.
    (c) The monetary unit assumption enables accounting to measure employee morale.
    (d) Partnerships are not economic entities.

(LO 5) **5.** The three types of business entities are:
    (a) proprietorships, small businesses, and partnerships.
    (b) proprietorships, partnerships, and corporations.
    (c) proprietorships, partnerships, and large businesses.
    (d) financial, manufacturing, and service companies.

(LO 6) **6.** Net income will result during a time period when:
    (a) assets exceed liabilities.
    (b) assets exceed revenues.
    (c) expenses exceed revenues.
    (d) revenues exceed expenses.

(LO 6) **7.** As of December 31, 2014, Kent Company has assets of $3,500 and owner's equity of $2,000. What are the liabilities for Kent Company as of December 31, 2014?
    (a) $1,500.
    (b) $1,000.
    (c) $2,500.
    (d) $2,000.

(LO 7) **8.** Performing services on account will have the following effects on the components of the basic accounting equation:
    (a) increase assets and decrease owner's equity.
    (b) increase assets and increase owner's equity.
    (c) increase assets and increase liabilities.
    (d) increase liabilities and increase owner's equity.

(LO 7) **9.** Which of the following events is **not** recorded in the accounting records?
    (a) Equipment is purchased on account.
    (b) An employee is terminated.
    (c) A cash investment is made into the business.
    (d) The owner withdraws cash for personal use.

(LO 7) **10.** During 2014, Bruske Company's assets decreased $50,000 and its liabilities decreased $90,000. Its owner's equity therefore:
    (a) increased $40,000.   **(c)** decreased $40,000.
    (b) decreased $140,000.   **(d)** increased $140,000.

(LO 7) **11.** Payment of an account payable affects the components of the accounting equation in the following way.
    (a) Decreases owner's equity and decreases liabilities.
    (b) Increases assets and decreases liabilities.
    (c) Decreases assets and increases owner's equity.
    (d) Decreases assets and decreases liabilities.

(LO 8) **12.** Which of the following statements is **false**?
    (a) A statement of cash flows summarizes information about the cash inflows (receipts) and outflows (payments) for a specific period of time.
    (b) A balance sheet reports the assets, liabilities, and owner's equity at a specific date.
    (c) An income statement presents the revenues, expenses, changes in owner's equity, and resulting net income or net loss for a specific period of time.
    (d) An owner's equity statement summarizes the changes in owner's equity for a specific period of time.

(LO 8) **13.** On the last day of the period, Alan Cesska Company buys a $900 machine on credit. This transaction will affect the:
    (a) income statement only.
    (b) balance sheet only.
    (c) income statement and owner's equity statement only.
    (d) income statement, owner's equity statement, and balance sheet.

(LO 8) **14.** The financial statement that reports assets, liabilities, and owner's equity is the:
    (a) income statement.
    (b) owner's equity statement.
    (c) balance sheet.
    (d) statement of cash flows.

(LO 9) ***15.** Services performed by a public accountant include:
    (a) auditing, taxation, and management consulting.
    (b) auditing, budgeting, and management consulting.
    (c) auditing, budgeting, and cost accounting.
    (d) internal auditing, budgeting, and management consulting.

Go to the book's companion website, www.wiley.com/college/weygandt, for additional Self-Test Questions.

 ✔ The Navigator

QUESTIONS

1. "Accounting is ingrained in our society and it is vital to our economic system." Do you agree? Explain.

2. Identify and describe the steps in the accounting process.

3. (a) Who are internal users of accounting data? (b) How does accounting provide relevant data to these users?

4. What uses of financial accounting information are made by (a) investors and (b) creditors?

5. "Bookkeeping and accounting are the same." Do you agree? Explain.

6. Trenton Travel Agency purchased land for $90,000 cash on December 10, 2014. At December 31, 2014, the land's value has increased to $93,000. What amount should be reported for land on Trenton's balance sheet at December 31, 2014? Explain.

7. What is the monetary unit assumption?

8. What is the economic entity assumption?

9. What are the three basic forms of business organizations for profit-oriented enterprises?

10. Rachel Hipp is the owner of a successful printing shop. Recently, her business has been increasing, and Rachel has been thinking about changing the organization of her business from a proprietorship to a corporation. Discuss some of the advantages Rachel would enjoy if she were to incorporate her business.

11. What is the basic accounting equation?

12. (a) Define the terms assets, liabilities, and owner's equity.
    (b) What items affect owner's equity?

13. Which of the following items are liabilities of Siebers Jewelry Stores?
    (a) Cash.
    (b) Accounts payable.
    (c) Owner's drawings.
    (d) Accounts receivable.
    (e) Supplies.
    (f) Equipment.
    (g) Salaries and wages payable.
    (h) Service revenue.
    (i) Rent expense.

14. Can a business enter into a transaction in which only the left side of the basic accounting equation is affected? If so, give an example.

15. Are the following events recorded in the accounting records? Explain your answer in each case.
    (a) The owner of the company dies.
    (b) Supplies are purchased on account.
    (c) An employee is fired.
    (d) The owner of the business withdraws cash from the business for personal use.

16. Indicate how the following business transactions affect the basic accounting equation.
    (a) Paid cash for janitorial services.
    (b) Purchased equipment for cash.
    (c) Invested cash in the business.
    (d) Paid accounts payable in full.

17. Listed below are some items found in the financial statements of Tony Gruber Co. Indicate in which financial statement(s) the following items would appear.
    (a) Service revenue.
    (b) Equipment.
    (c) Advertising expense.
    (d) Accounts receivable.
    (e) Owner's capital.
    (f) Salaries and wages payable.

18. In February 2014, Maria Osgood invested an additional $10,000 in her business, Osgood's Pharmacy, which is organized as a proprietorship. Osgood's accountant, Carl Sota, recorded this receipt as an increase in cash and revenues. Is this treatment appropriate? Why or why not?

19. "A company's net income appears directly on the income statement and the owner's equity statement, and it is included indirectly in the company's balance sheet." Do you agree? Explain.

20. Saylor Enterprises had a capital balance of $168,000 at the beginning of the period. At the end of the accounting period, the capital balance was $198,000.
    (a) Assuming no additional investment or withdrawals during the period, what is the net income for the period?
    (b) Assuming an additional investment of $13,000 but no withdrawals during the period, what is the net income for the period?

21. Summarized operations for Bayles Co. for the month of July are as follows.

    Revenues recognized: for cash $20,000; on account $70,000.

    Expenses incurred: for cash $26,000; on account $40,000.

    Indicate for Bayles Co. (a) the total revenues, (b) the total expenses, and (c) net income for the month of July.

22. The basic accounting equation is Assets = Liabilities + Owner's Equity. Replacing the words in that equation with dollar amounts, what is Apple's accounting equation at September 24, 2011? (*Hint:* Owner's equity is equivalent to shareholders' equity.)

BRIEF EXERCISES

BE1-1 Presented below is the basic accounting equation. Determine the missing amounts.

Use basic accounting equation.

(LO 6)

	Assets	=	Liabilities	+	Owner's Equity
(a)	$90,000		$50,000		?
(b)	?		$40,000		$70,000
(c)	$94,000		?		$53,000

BE1-2 Given the accounting equation, answer each of the following questions.

Use basic accounting equation.

(LO 6)

(a) The liabilities of Grieg Company are $120,000 and the owner's equity is $232,000. What is the amount of Grieg Company's total assets?

(b) The total assets of Grieg Company are $190,000 and its owner's equity is $91,000. What is the amount of its total liabilities?

(c) The total assets of Grieg Company are $800,000 and its liabilities are equal to one-half of its total assets. What is the amount of Grieg Company's owner's equity?

Use basic accounting equation.
(LO 6)

BE1-3 At the beginning of the year, Sielert Company had total assets of $800,000 and total liabilities of $300,000. Answer the following questions.

(a) If total assets increased $150,000 during the year and total liabilities decreased $80,000, what is the amount of owner's equity at the end of the year?

(b) During the year, total liabilities increased $100,000 and owner's equity decreased $70,000. What is the amount of total assets at the end of the year?

(c) If total assets decreased $80,000 and owner's equity increased $120,000 during the year, what is the amount of total liabilities at the end of the year?

Solve expanded accounting equation.
(LO 6)

BE1-4 Use the expanded accounting equation to answer each of the following questions.

(a) The liabilities of Roman Company are $90,000. Owner's capital account is $150,000; drawings are $40,000; revenues, $450,000; and expenses, $320,000. What is the amount of Roman Company's total assets?

(b) The total assets of Dylan Company are $57,000. Owner's capital account is $25,000; drawings are $7,000; revenues, $52,000; and expenses, $35,000. What is the amount of the company's total liabilities?

(c) The total assets of Capp Co. are $600,000 and its liabilities are equal to two-thirds of its total assets. What is the amount of Capp Co.'s owner's equity?

Identify assets, liabilities, and owner's equity.
(LO 6)

BE1-5 Indicate whether each of the following items is an asset (A), liability (L), or part of owner's equity (OE).

_____ **(a)** Accounts receivable   _____ **(d)** Supplies
_____ **(b)** Salaries and wages payable   _____ **(e)** Owner's capital
_____ **(c)** Equipment   _____ **(f)** Notes payable

Determine effect of transactions on basic accounting equation.
(LO 7)

BE1-6 Presented below are three business transactions. On a sheet of paper, list the letters (a), (b), and (c) with columns for assets, liabilities, and owner's equity. For each column, indicate whether the transactions increased (+), decreased (−), or had no effect (NE) on assets, liabilities, and owner's equity.

(a) Purchased supplies on account.
(b) Received cash for performing a service.
(c) Paid expenses in cash.

Determine effect of transactions on basic accounting equation.
(LO 7)

BE1-7 Follow the same format as in BE1-6. Determine the effect on assets, liabilities, and owner's equity of the following three transactions.

(a) Invested cash in the business.
(b) Withdrawal of cash by owner.
(c) Received cash from a customer who had previously been billed for services performed.

Classify items affecting owner's equity.
(LO 7)

BE1-8 Classify each of the following items as owner's drawings (D), revenue (R), or expense (E).

_____ **(a)** Advertising expense   _____ **(e)** Owner's drawings
_____ **(b)** Service revenue   _____ **(f)** Rent revenue
_____ **(c)** Insurance expense   _____ **(g)** Utilities expense
_____ **(d)** Salaries and wages expense

Determine effect of transactions on basic owner's equity.
(LO 7)

BE1-9 Presented below are three transactions. Mark each transaction as affecting owner's investment (I), owner's drawings (D), revenue (R), expense (E), or not affecting owner's equity (NOE).

_____ **(a)** Received cash for services performed
_____ **(b)** Paid cash to purchase equipment
_____ **(c)** Paid employee salaries

Prepare a balance sheet.
(LO 8)

BE1-10 In alphabetical order below are balance sheet items for Fritz Company at December 31, 2014. Molly Fritz is the owner of Fritz Company. Prepare a balance sheet, following the format of Illustration 1-9.

Accounts payable	$90,000
Accounts receivable	$72,500
Cash	$49,000
Owner's capital	$31,500

BE1-11 Indicate whether the following items would appear on the income statement (IS), balance sheet (BS), or owner's equity statement (OE).

_____ **(a)** Notes payable   _____ **(d)** Cash
_____ **(b)** Advertising expense   _____ **(e)** Service revenue
_____ **(c)** Owner's capital

Determine where items appear on financial statements.
(LO 8)

> DO IT! Review

DO IT! 1-1 Indicate whether each of the five statements presented below is true or false.

1. The three steps in the accounting process are identification, recording, and examination.
2. The two most common types of external users are investors and creditors.
3. Congress passed the Sarbanes-Oxley Act to ensure that investors invest only in companies that will be profitable.
4. The primary accounting standard-setting body in the United States is the Securities and Exchange Commission (SEC).
5. The historical cost principle dictates that companies record assets at their cost and continue to report them at their cost over the time the asset is held.

Review basic concepts.
(LO 1, 2, 3, 4)

DO IT! 1-2 Classify the following items as investment by owner (I), owner's drawings (D), revenues (R), or expenses (E). Then indicate whether each item increases or decreases owner's equity.

(1) Drawings.   **(3)** Advertising expense.
(2) Rent revenue.   **(4)** Owner puts personal assets into the business.

Evaluate effects of transactions on owner's equity.
(LO 6)

DO IT! 1-3 Transactions made by J. Depp and Co., a law firm, for the month of March are shown below. Prepare a tabular analysis which shows the effects of these transactions on the expanded accounting equation, similar to that shown in Illustration 1-8.

1. The company performed $20,000 of services for customers, on credit.
2. The company received $20,000 in cash from customers who had been billed for services (in transaction 1).
3. The company received a bill for $2,300 of advertising, but will not pay it until a later date.
4. J. Depp withdrew $3,600 cash from the business for personal use.

Prepare tabular analysis.
(LO 7)

DO IT! 1-4 Presented below is selected information related to Howard Company at December 31, 2014. Howard reports financial information monthly.

Calculate effects of transactions on financial statement items.
(LO 6, 8)

Accounts Payable	$ 3,000	Salaries and Wages Expense	$16,500
Cash	4,500	Notes Payable	25,000
Advertising Expense	6,000	Rent Expense	10,500
Service Revenue	51,500	Accounts Receivable	13,500
Equipment	29,000	Owner's Drawings	7,500

(a) Determine the total assets of Howard Company at December 31, 2014.
(b) Determine the net income that Howard Company reported for December 2014.
(c) Determine the owner's equity of Howard Company at December 31, 2014.

EXERCISES

E1-1 Zimmerman Company performs the following accounting tasks during the year.

_____Analyzing and interpreting information.
_____Classifying economic events.
_____Explaining uses, meaning, and limitations of data.
_____Keeping a systematic chronological diary of events.
_____Measuring events in dollars and cents.

Classify the three activities of accounting.
(LO 1)

_____Preparing accounting reports.

_____Reporting information in a standard format.

_____Selecting economic activities relevant to the company.

_____Summarizing economic events.

Accounting is "an information system that **identifies**, **records**, and **communicates** the economic events of an organization to interested users."

Instructions

Categorize the accounting tasks performed by Zimmerman as relating to either the identification (I), recording (R), or communication (C) aspects of accounting.

Identify users of accounting information.

(LO 2)

E1-2 (a) The following are users of financial statements.

_____Customers   _____Securities and Exchange Commission

_____Internal Revenue Service   _____Store manager

_____Labor unions   _____Suppliers

_____Marketing manager   _____Vice president of finance

_____Production supervisor

Instructions

Identify the users as being either **external users** or **internal users**.

(b) The following questions could be asked by an internal user or an external user.

_____Can we afford to give our employees a pay raise?

_____Did the company earn a satisfactory income?

_____Do we need to borrow in the near future?

_____How does the company's profitability compare to other companies?

_____What does it cost us to manufacture each unit produced?

_____Which product should we emphasize?

_____Will the company be able to pay its short-term debts?

Instructions

Identify each of the questions as being more likely asked by an **internal user** or an **external user**.

Discuss ethics and the historical cost principle.

(LO 3, 4)

E1-3 Jill Motta, president of Motta Company, has instructed Linda Berger, the head of the accounting department for Motta Company, to report the company's land in the company's accounting reports at its fair value of $170,000 instead of its cost of $100,000. Motta says, "Showing the land at $170,000 will make our company look like a better investment when we try to attract new investors next month."

Instructions

Explain the ethical situation involved for Linda Berger, identifying the stakeholders and the alternatives.

Use accounting concepts.

(LO 4, 5)

E1-4 The following situations involve accounting principles and assumptions.

1. Piang Company owns buildings that are worth substantially more than they originally cost. In an effort to provide more relevant information, Piang reports the buildings at fair value in its accounting reports.

2. Delta Company includes in its accounting records only transaction data that can be expressed in terms of money.

3. Luke Witte, owner of Luke's Photography, records his personal living costs as expenses of the business.

Instructions

For each of the three situations, say if the accounting method used is correct or incorrect. If correct, identify which principle or assumption supports the method used. If incorrect, identify which principle or assumption has been violated.

Classify accounts as assets, liabilities, and owner's equity.

(LO 6)

E1-5 Tomlin Cleaners has the following balance sheet items.

Accounts payable   Accounts receivable
Cash   Notes payable
Equipment   Salaries and wages payable
Supplies   Owner's capital

Instructions

Classify each item as an asset, liability, or owner's equity.

E1-6 Selected transactions for Tara Lawn Care Company are listed below.

1. Made cash investment to start business.
2. Paid monthly rent.
3. Purchased equipment on account.
4. Billed customers for services performed.
5. Withdrew cash for owner's personal use.
6. Received cash from customers billed in (4).
7. Incurred advertising expense on account.
8. Purchased additional equipment for cash.
9. Received cash from customers when service was performed.

Analyze the effect of transactions.
(LO 6, 7)

Instructions
List the numbers of the above transactions and describe the effect of each transaction on assets, liabilities, and owner's equity. For example, the first answer is: (1) Increase in assets and increase in owner's equity.

E1-7 Kam Computer Timeshare Company entered into the following transactions during May 2014.

1. Purchased computer terminals for $20,000 from Digital Equipment on account.
2. Paid $4,000 cash for May rent on storage space.
3. Received $17,000 cash from customers for contracts billed in April.
4. Performed computer services to Viking Construction Company for $3,000 cash.
5. Paid Tri-State Power Co. $11,000 cash for energy usage in May.
6. Kam invested an additional $29,000 in the business.
7. Paid Digital Equipment for the terminals purchased in (1) above.
8. Incurred advertising expense for May of $1,200 on account.

Analyze the effect of transactions on assets, liabilities, and owner's equity.
(LO 6, 7)

Instructions
Indicate with the appropriate letter whether each of the transactions above results in:

(a) An increase in assets and a decrease in assets.
(b) An increase in assets and an increase in owner's equity.
(c) An increase in assets and an increase in liabilities.
(d) A decrease in assets and a decrease in owner's equity.
(e) A decrease in assets and a decrease in liabilities.
(f) An increase in liabilities and a decrease in owner's equity.
(g) An increase in owner's equity and a decrease in liabilities.

E1-8 An analysis of the transactions made by Liam Agler & Co., a certified public accounting firm, for the month of August is shown below. The expenses were $650 for rent, $4,800 for salaries and wages, and $500 for utilities.

Analyze transactions and compute net income.
(LO 7)

	Cash	+	Accounts Receivable	+	Supplies	+	Equipment	=	Accounts Payable	+	Owner's Capital	−	Owner's Drawings	+	Revenues	−	Expenses
1.	+$15,000										+$15,000						
2.	−2,000						+$5,000		+$3,000								
3.	−750				+$750												
4.	+4,600		+$3,900												+$8,500		
5.	−1,500								−1,500								
6.	−2,000												−$2,000				
7.	−650																−$650
8.	+450		−450														
9.	−4,800																−4,800
10.									+500								−500

Instructions
(a) ▬▬ Describe each transaction that occurred for the month.
(b) Determine how much owner's equity increased for the month.
(c) Compute the amount of net income for the month.

E1-9 An analysis of transactions for Liam Agler & Co. was presented in E1-8.

Prepare financial statements.
(LO 8)

Instructions
Prepare an income statement and an owner's equity statement for August and a balance sheet at August 31, 2014. Assume that August is the company's first month of business.

Determine net income (or loss).
(LO 6, 8)

E1-10 Iverson Company had the following assets and liabilities on the dates indicated.

December 31	Total Assets	Total Liabilities
2013	$400,000	$250,000
2014	$460,000	$300,000
2015	$590,000	$400,000

Iverson began business on January 1, 2013, with an investment of $100,000.

Instructions

From an analysis of the change in owner's equity during the year, compute the net income (or loss) for:

(a) 2013, assuming Iverson's drawings were $15,000 for the year.

(b) 2014, assuming Iverson made an additional investment of $45,000 and had no drawings in 2014.

(c) 2015, assuming Iverson made an additional investment of $15,000 and had drawings of $25,000 in 2015.

Analyze financial statements items.
(LO 6, 8)

E1-11 Two items are omitted from each of the following summaries of balance sheet and income statement data for two proprietorships for the year 2014, Garba's Goods and Zahra Enterprises.

	Garba's Goods	Zahra Enterprises
Beginning of year:		
Total assets	$110,000	$129,000
Total liabilities	85,000	(c)
Total owner's equity	(a)	80,000
End of year:		
Total assets	160,000	180,000
Total liabilities	120,000	50,000
Total owner's equity	40,000	130,000
Changes during year in owner's equity:		
Additional investment	(b)	25,000
Drawings	29,000	(d)
Total revenues	215,000	100,000
Total expenses	175,000	60,000

Instructions

Determine the missing amounts.

Prepare income statement and owner's equity statement.
(LO 8)

E1-12 The following information relates to David Pande Co. for the year 2014.

Owner's capital, January 1, 2014	$48,000	Advertising expense	$ 1,800
Owner's drawings during 2014	6,000	Rent expense	10,400
Service revenue	63,600	Utilities expense	3,100
Salaries and wages expense	29,500		

Instructions

After analyzing the data, prepare an income statement and an owner's equity statement for the year ending December 31, 2014.

Correct an incorrectly prepared balance sheet.
(LO 8)

E1-13 Reza Lang is the bookkeeper for Taylor Company. Reza has been trying to get the balance sheet of Taylor Company to balance. Taylor's balance sheet is shown below.

TAYLOR COMPANY
Balance Sheet
December 31, 2014

Assets		Liabilities	
Cash	$15,000	Accounts payable	$21,000
Supplies	8,000	Accounts receivable	(9,500)
Equipment	46,000	Owner's capital	67,500
Owner's drawings	10,000	Total liabilities and	
Total assets	$79,000	owner's equity	$79,000

Instructions
Prepare a correct balance sheet.

E1-14 Andrew Tym is the sole owner of Deer Park, a public camping ground near the Lake Mead National Recreation Area. Andrew has compiled the following financial information as of December 31, 2014.

Compute net income and prepare a balance sheet.
(LO 8)

Revenues during 2014—camping fees	$140,000	Fair value of equipment	$140,000
Revenues during 2014—general store	65,000	Notes payable	60,000
Accounts payable	11,000	Expenses during 2014	150,000
Cash on hand	23,000	Accounts receivable	17,500
Original cost of equipment	105,500		

Instructions
(a) Determine Andrew Tym's net income from Deer Park for 2014.
(b) Prepare a balance sheet for Deer Park as of December 31, 2014.

E1-15 Presented below is financial information related to the 2014 operations of Gilligan Cruise Company.

Prepare an income statement.
(LO 8)

Maintenance and repairs expense	$ 95,000
Utilities expense	10,000
Salaries and wages expense	142,000
Advertising expense	24,500
Ticket revenue	410,000

Instructions
Prepare the 2014 income statement for Gilligan Cruise Company.

E1-16 Presented below is information related to the sole proprietorship of Huan Feng attorney.

Prepare an owner's equity statement.
(LO 6, 8)

Legal service revenue—2014	$335,000
Total expenses—2014	211,000
Assets, January 1, 2014	96,000
Liabilities, January 1, 2014	62,000
Assets, December 31, 2014	168,000
Liabilities, December 31, 2014	100,000
Drawings—2014	?

Instructions
Prepare the 2014 owner's equity statement for Huan Feng's legal practice.

EXERCISES: SET B AND CHALLENGE EXERCISES

Visit the book's companion website, at **www.wiley.com/college/weygandt**, and choose the Student Companion site to access Exercise Set B and Challenge Exercises.

PROBLEMS: SET A

P1-1A On April 1, Renato Uhrig established Renato's Travel Agency. The following transactions were completed during the month.

Analyze transactions and compute net income.
(LO 6, 7)

1. Invested $15,000 cash to start the agency.
2. Paid $600 cash for April office rent.
3. Purchased equipment for $3,000 cash.
4. Incurred $700 of advertising costs in the *Chicago Tribune*, on account.
5. Paid $800 cash for office supplies.
6. Performed services worth $10,000: $3,000 cash is received from customers, and the balance of $7,000 is billed to customers on account.
7. Withdrew $500 cash for personal use.

8. Paid *Chicago Tribune* $500 of the amount due in transaction (4).
9. Paid employees' salaries $2,500.
10. Received $4,000 in cash from customers who have previously been billed in transaction (6).

Instructions

(a) Total assets $20,900

(a) Prepare a tabular analysis of the transactions using the following column headings: Cash, Accounts Receivable, Supplies, Equipment, Accounts Payable, Owner's Capital, Owner's Drawings, Revenues, and Expenses.

(b) Net income $6,200

(b) From an analysis of the owner's equity columns, compute the net income or net loss for April.

Analyze transactions and prepare income statement, owner's equity statement, and balance sheet.

(LO 6, 7, 8)

P1-2A Sue Kojima opened a law office on July 1, 2014. On July 31, the balance sheet showed Cash $5,000, Accounts Receivable $1,500, Supplies $500, Equipment $6,000, Accounts Payable $4,200, and Owner's Capital $8,800. During August, the following transactions occurred.

1. Collected $1,200 of accounts receivable.
2. Paid $2,800 cash on accounts payable.
3. Recognized revenue of $7,500 of which $3,000 is collected in cash and the balance is due in September.
4. Purchased additional equipment for $2,000, paying $400 in cash and the balance on account.
5. Paid salaries $2,500, rent for August $900, and advertising expenses $400.
6. Withdrew $700 in cash for personal use.
7. Received $2,000 from Standard Federal Bank—money borrowed on a note payable.
8. Incurred utility expenses for month on account $270.

Instructions

(a) Total assets $16,800

(a) Prepare a tabular analysis of the August transactions beginning with July 31 balances. The column headings should be as follows: Cash + Accounts Receivable + Supplies + Equipment = Notes Payable + Accounts Payable + Owner's Capital − Owner's Drawings + Revenues − Expenses.

(b) Net income $3,430
    Ending capital $11,530

(b) Prepare an income statement for August, an owner's equity statement for August, and a balance sheet at August 31.

Prepare income statement, owner's equity statement, and balance sheet.

(LO 8)

P1-3A On June 1, Tamara Eder started Crazy Creations Co., a company that provides craft opportunities, by investing $12,000 cash in the business. Following are the assets and liabilities of the company at June 30 and the revenues and expenses for the month of June.

Cash	$10,150	Service Revenue	$6,700
Accounts Receivable	3,000	Advertising Expense	500
Supplies	2,000	Rent Expense	1,600
Equipment	10,000	Gasoline Expense	200
Notes Payable	9,000	Utilities Expense	150
Accounts Payable	1,200		

Tamara made no additional investment in June but withdrew $1,300 in cash for personal use during the month.

Instructions

(a) Net income $4,250
    Owner's equity $14,950
    Total assets $25,150
(b) Owner's equity $15,700

(a) Prepare an income statement and owner's equity statement for the month of June and a balance sheet at June 30, 2014.

(b) Prepare an income statement and owner's equity statement for June assuming the following data are not included above: (1) $900 of services were performed and billed but not collected at June 30, and (2) $150 of gasoline expense was incurred but not paid.

Analyze transactions and prepare financial statements.

(LO 6, 7, 8)

P1-4A Debra Menge started her own consulting firm, Menge Consulting, on May 1, 2014. The following transactions occurred during the month of May.

May 1	Debra invested $7,000 cash in the business.
2	Paid $900 for office rent for the month.
3	Purchased $600 of supplies on account.
5	Paid $125 to advertise in the *County News*.
9	Received $4,000 cash for services performed.
12	Withdrew $1,000 cash for personal use.
15	Performed $5,400 of services on account.

17 Paid $2,500 for employee salaries.
20 Paid for the supplies purchased on account on May 3.
23 Received a cash payment of $4,000 for services performed on account on May 15.
26 Borrowed $5,000 from the bank on a note payable.
29 Purchased equipment for $4,200 on account.
30 Paid $275 for utilities.

Instructions

(a) Show the effects of the previous transactions on the accounting equation using the following format.   (a) Total assets $20,800

	Assets			Liabilities		Owner's Equity			
		Accounts			Notes	Accounts	Owner's	Owner's		
Date	Cash +	Receivable +	Supplies +	Equipment =	Payable +	Payable +	Capital −	Drawings +	Revenues − Expenses

(b) Prepare an income statement for the month of May.   (b) Net income $5,600
(c) Prepare a balance sheet at May 31, 2014.   (c) Cash $14,600

P1-5A Financial statement information about four different companies is as follows.

Determine financial statement amounts and prepare owner's equity statement.

(LO 6, 8)

	Farrell Company	Prasad Company	Thao Company	Zinda Company
January 1, 2014				
Assets	$ 80,000	$ 90,000	(g)	$150,000
Liabilities	48,000	(d)	80,000	(j)
Owner's equity	(a)	40,000	49,000	90,000
December 31, 2014				
Assets	(b)	112,000	180,000	(k)
Liabilities	60,000	72,000	(h)	100,000
Owner's equity	50,000	(e)	82,000	151,000
Owner's equity changes in year				
Additional investment	(c)	8,000	10,000	15,000
Drawings	15,000	(f)	12,000	10,000
Total revenues	350,000	410,000	(i)	500,000
Total expenses	333,000	385,000	350,000	(l)

Instructions

(a) Determine the missing amounts. (*Hint:* For example, to solve for (a), Assets − Liabilities = Owner's equity = $32,000.)
(b) Prepare the owner's equity statement for Farrell Company.
(c) ━━━━ Write a memorandum explaining the sequence for preparing financial statements and the interrelationship of the owner's equity statement to the income statement and balance sheet.

PROBLEMS: SET B

P1-1B Solki's Repair Shop was started on May 1 by Solki Lee. A summary of May transactions is presented below.

Analyze transactions and compute net income.

(LO 6, 7)

1. Invested $10,000 cash to start the repair shop.
2. Purchased equipment for $5,000 cash.
3. Paid $400 cash for May office rent.
4. Paid $500 cash for supplies.
5. Incurred $250 of advertising costs in the *Beacon News* on account.
6. Received $6,100 in cash from customers for repair service.
7. Withdrew $1,000 cash for personal use.
8. Paid part-time employee salaries $2,000.
9. Paid utility bills $170.
10. Performed repair services worth $750 on account.
11. Collected cash of $120 for services billed in transaction (10).

(a) Total assets $13,280

(b) Net income $4,030

Instructions

(a) Prepare a tabular analysis of the transactions, using the following column headings: Cash, Accounts Receivable, Supplies, Equipment, Accounts Payable, Owner's Capital, Owner's Drawings, Revenues, and Expenses.

(b) From an analysis of the owner's equity columns, compute the net income or net loss for May.

Analyze transactions and prepare income statement, owner's equity statement, and balance sheet.

(LO 6, 7, 8)

P1-2B Peter Nimmer opened a veterinary business in Nashville, Tennessee, on August 1, 2014. On August 31, the balance sheet showed Cash $9,000, Accounts Receivable $1,700, Supplies $600, Equipment $6,000, Accounts Payable $3,600, and Owner's Capital $13,700. During September, the following transactions occurred.

1. Paid $2,900 cash on accounts payable.
2. Collected $1,300 of accounts receivable.
3. Purchased additional equipment for $2,100, paying $800 in cash and the balance on account.
4. Recognized revenue of $7,800, of which $2,500 is received in cash and the balance is due in October.
5. Withdrew $1,100 cash for personal use.
6. Paid salaries $1,700, rent for September $900, and advertising expense $450.
7. Incurred utilities expense for month on account $170.
8. Received $10,000 from Capital Bank (money borrowed on a note payable).

Instructions

(a) Total assets $29,350

(a) Prepare a tabular analysis of the September transactions beginning with August 31 balances. The column headings should be as follows: Cash + Accounts Receivable + Supplies + Equipment = Notes Payable + Accounts Payable + Owner's Capital − Owner's Drawings + Revenues − Expenses.

(b) Net income $4,580
    Ending capital $17,180

(b) Prepare an income statement for September, an owner's equity statement for September, and a balance sheet at September 30.

Prepare income statement, owner's equity statement, and balance sheet.

(LO 8)

P1-3B On May 1, R. C. Twining started RC Flying School, a company that provides flying lessons, by investing $40,000 cash in the business. Following are the assets and liabilities of the company on May 31, 2014, and the revenues and expenses for the month of May.

Cash	$ 3,400	Advertising Expense	$ 600
Accounts Receivable	4,900	Rent Expense	1,200
Equipment	64,000	Maintenance and Repairs Expense	400
Notes Payable	30,000	Gasoline Expense	2,500
Accounts Payable	800	Utilities Expense	400
Service Revenue	8,100		

R. C. Twining made no additional investment in May, but he withdrew $1,500 in cash for personal use.

Instructions

(a) Net income $3,000
    Owner's equity $41,500
    Total assets $72,300
(b) Owner's equity $40,900

(a) Prepare an income statement and owner's equity statement for the month of May and a balance sheet at May 31.

(b) Prepare an income statement and owner's equity statement for May assuming the following data are not included above: (1) $900 worth of services were performed and billed but not collected at May 31, and (2) $1,500 of gasoline expense was incurred but not paid.

Analyze transactions and prepare financial statements.

(LO 6, 7, 8)

P1-4B Dennis Luljak started his own delivery service, Luljak Deliveries, on June 1, 2014. The following transactions occurred during the month of June.

June 1	Dennis invested $10,000 cash in the business.
2	Purchased a used van for deliveries for $12,000. Dennis paid $2,000 cash and signed a note payable for the remaining balance.
3	Paid $500 for office rent for the month.
5	Performed $4,400 of services on account.
9	Withdrew $200 cash for personal use.
12	Purchased supplies for $150 on account.
15	Received a cash payment of $1,250 for services performed on June 5.
17	Purchased gasoline for $200 on account.
20	Received a cash payment of $1,300 for services performed.

23   Made a cash payment of $600 on the note payable.
26   Paid $250 for utilities.
29   Paid for the gasoline purchased on account on June 17.
30   Paid $1,000 for employee salaries.

Instructions
(a) Show the effects of the previous transactions on the accounting equation using the   (a) Total assets $23,100
following format.

	Assets				Liabilities		Owner's Equity			
		Accounts			Notes	Accounts	Owner's	Owner's		
Date	Cash +	Receivable +	Supplies +	Equipment =	Payable +	Payable +	Capital	− Drawings +	Revenues −	Expenses

(b) Prepare an income statement for the month of June.   (b) Net income $3,750
(c) Prepare a balance sheet at June 30, 2014.   (c) Cash $7,800

P1-5B Financial statement information about four different companies is as follows.   *Determine financial statement amounts and prepare owner's equity statement.*

(LO 6, 8)

	Luo Company	Foster Company	Usher Company	Merritt Company
January 1, 2014				
Assets	$ 95,000	$110,000	(g)	$170,000
Liabilities	50,000	(d)	75,000	(j)
Owner's equity	(a)	60,000	45,000	90,000
December 31, 2014				
Assets	(b)	141,000	200,000	(k)
Liabilities	55,000	75,000	(h)	80,000
Owner's equity	63,000	(e)	130,000	162,000
Owner's equity changes in year				
Additional investment	(c)	15,000	10,000	15,000
Drawings	25,000	(f)	14,000	20,000
Total revenues	350,000	420,000	(i)	520,000
Total expenses	320,000	385,000	342,000	(l)

Instructions
(a) Determine the missing amounts. (*Hint:* For example, to solve for (a), Assets − Liabilities = Owner's equity = $45,000.)
(b) Prepare the owner's equity statement for Foster Company.
(c) ━━━ Write a memorandum explaining the sequence for preparing financial statements and the interrelationship of the owner's equity statement to the income statement and balance sheet.

PROBLEMS: SET C

Visit the book's companion website, at **www.wiley.com/college/weygandt**, and choose the Student Companion site to access Problem Set C.

CONTINUING COOKIE CHRONICLE

CCC1 Natalie Koebel spent much of her childhood learning the art of cookie-making from her grandmother. They passed many happy hours mastering every type of cookie imaginable and later creating new recipes that were both healthy and delicious. Now at the start of her second year in college, Natalie is investigating various possibilities for starting her own business as part of the requirements of the entrepreneurship program in which she is enrolled.

*The **Continuing Cookie Chronicle** starts in this chapter and continues in every chapter. **You also can find this problem** at the book's Student Companion site.*

A long-time friend insists that Natalie has to somehow include cookies in her business plan. After a series of brainstorming sessions, Natalie settles on the idea of operating a cookie-making school. She will start on a part-time basis and offer her services in people's homes. Now that she has started thinking about it, the possibilities seem endless. During the fall, she will concentrate on holiday cookies. She will offer individual lessons and group sessions (which will probably be more entertainment than education for the participants). Natalie also decides to include children in her target market.

The first difficult decision is coming up with the perfect name for her business. In the end, she settles on "Cookie Creations" and then moves on to more important issues.

Instructions
(a) What form of business organization—proprietorship, partnership, or corporation—do you recommend that Natalie use for her business? Discuss the benefits and weaknesses of each form and give the reasons for your choice.
(b) Will Natalie need accounting information? If yes, what information will she need and why? How often will she need this information?
(c) Identify specific asset, liability, and owner's equity accounts that Cookie Creations will likely use to record its business transactions.
(d) Should Natalie open a separate bank account for the business? Why or why not?

Broadening Your Perspective

Financial Reporting and Analysis

Financial Reporting Problem: Apple Inc.

BYP1-1 The actual financial statements of Apple Inc. for 2011 are presented in Appendix A. Instructions for accessing and using the company's complete annual report, including the notes to the financial statements, are also provided in Appendix A.

Instructions
Refer to Apple's financial statements and answer the following questions.

(a) What were Apple's total assets at September 24, 2011? At September 25, 2010?
(b) How much cash (and cash equivalents) did Apple have on September 24, 2011?
(c) What amount of accounts payable did Apple report on September 24, 2011? On September 25, 2010?
(d) What were Apple's net sales in 2009? In 2010? In 2011?
(e) What is the amount of the change in Apple's net income from 2010 to 2011?

Comparative Analysis Problem: PepsiCo, Inc. vs. The Coca-Cola Company

BYP1-2 PepsiCo's financial statements are presented in Appendix B. Financial statements of The Coca-Cola Company are presented in Appendix C. Instructions for accessing and using the complete annual reports of PepsiCo and Coca-Cola, including the notes to the financial statements, are also provided in Appendices B and C, respectively.

Instructions
(a) Based on the information contained in these financial statements, determine the following for each company.
   (1) Total assets at December 31, 2011, for PepsiCo and for Coca-Cola at December 31, 2011.
   (2) Accounts (notes) receivable, net at December 31, 2011, for PepsiCo and at December 31, 2011, for Coca-Cola.
   (3) Net revenues for year ended in 2011.
   (4) Net income for year ended in 2011.
(b) What conclusions concerning the two companies can be drawn from these data?

Comparative Analysis Problem:
Amazon.com, Inc. vs. Wal-Mart Stores, Inc.

BYP1-3 Amazon.com, Inc.'s financial statements are presented in Appendix D. Financial statements for Wal-Mart Stores, Inc. are presented in Appendix E. Instructions for accessing and using the complete annual reports of Amazon and Wal-Mart, including the notes to the financial statements, are also provided in Appendices D and E, respectively.

Instructions

(a) Based on the information contained in these financial statements, determine the following for each company.
  (1) Total assets at December 31, 2011, for Amazon and for Wal-Mart at January 31, 2012.
  (2) Receivables (net) at December 31, 2011, for Amazon and for Wal-Mart at January 31, 2012.
  (3) Net sales (product only) for year ended in 2011 (2012 for Wal-Mart).
  (4) Net income for the year ended in 2011 (2012 for Wal-Mart).
(b) What conclusions concerning these two companies can be drawn from these data?

Real-World Focus

BYP1-4 This exercise will familiarize you with skill requirements, job descriptions, and salaries for accounting careers.

Address: **www.careers-in-accounting.com**, or go to **www.wiley.com/college/weygandt**

Instructions

Go to the site shown above. Answer the following questions.

(a) What are the three broad areas of accounting (from "Skills and Talents")?
(b) List eight skills required in accounting.
(c) How do the three accounting areas differ in terms of these eight required skills?
(d) Explain one of the key job options in accounting.
(e) What is the overall salary range for a junior staff accountant?

Critical Thinking

Decision-Making Across the Organization

BYP1-5 Kathy and James Mohr, local golf stars, opened the Chip-Shot Driving Range on March 1, 2014, by investing $25,000 of their cash savings in the business. A caddy shack was constructed for cash at a cost of $8,000, and $800 was spent on golf balls and golf clubs. The Mohrs leased five acres of land at a cost of $1,000 per month and paid the first month's rent. During the first month, advertising costs totaled $750, of which $150 was unpaid at March 31, and $400 was paid to members of the high-school golf team for retrieving golf balls. All revenues from customers were deposited in the company's bank account. On March 15, Kathy and James withdrew a total of $1,000 in cash for personal living expenses. A $100 utility bill was received on March 31 but was not paid. On March 31, the balance in the company's bank account was $18,900.

Kathy and James thought they had a pretty good first month of operations. But, their estimates of profitability ranged from a loss of $6,100 to net income of $2,450.

Instructions

With the class divided into groups, answer the following.

(a) How could the Mohrs have concluded that the business operated at a loss of $6,100? Was this a valid basis on which to determine net income?
(b) How could the Mohrs have concluded that the business operated at a net income of $2,450? (*Hint:* Prepare a balance sheet at March 31.) Was this a valid basis on which to determine net income?
(c) Without preparing an income statement, determine the actual net income for March.
(d) What was the revenue recognized in March?

Communication Activity

BYP1-6 Ashley Hirano, the bookkeeper for New York Company, has been trying to get the balance sheet to balance. The company's balance sheet is shown below.

NEW YORK COMPANY			
Balance Sheet			
For the Month Ended December 31, 2014			
Assets		**Liabilities**	
Equipment	$25,500	Owner's capital	$26,000
Cash	9,000	Accounts receivable	(6,000)
Supplies	2,000	Owner's drawings	(2,000)
Accounts payable	(8,000)	Notes payable	10,500
	$28,500		$28,500

Instructions

Explain to Ashley Hirano in a memo why the original balance sheet is incorrect, and what should be done to correct it.

Ethics Case

BYP1-7 After numerous campus interviews, Greg Thorpe, a senior at Great Northern College, received two office interview invitations from the Baltimore offices of two large firms. Both firms offered to cover his out-of-pocket expenses (travel, hotel, and meals). He scheduled the interviews for both firms on the same day, one in the morning and one in the afternoon. At the conclusion of each interview, he submitted to both firms his total out-of-pocket expenses for the trip to Baltimore: mileage $112 (280 miles at $0.40), hotel $130, meals $36, and parking and tolls $18, for a total of $296. He believes this approach is appropriate. If he had made two trips, his cost would have been two times $296. He is also certain that neither firm knew he had visited the other on that same trip. Within 10 days, Greg received two checks in the mail, each in the amount of $296.

Instructions

(a) Who are the stakeholders (affected parties) in this situation?
(b) What are the ethical issues in this case?
(c) What would you do in this situation?

All About You

BYP1-8 Some people are tempted to make their finances look worse to get financial aid. Companies sometimes also manage their financial numbers in order to accomplish certain goals. Earnings management is the planned timing of revenues, expenses, gains, and losses to smooth out bumps in net income. In managing earnings, companies' actions vary from being within the range of ethical activity, to being both unethical and illegal attempts to mislead investors and creditors.

Instructions

Provide responses for each of the following questions.

(a) Discuss whether you think each of the following actions (adapted from **www.finaid.org/fafsa/maximize.phtml**) to increase the chances of receiving financial aid is ethical.
  (1) Spend down the student's assets and income first, before spending parents' assets and income.
  (2) Accelerate necessary expenses to reduce available cash. For example, if you need a new car, buy it before applying for financial aid.
  (3) State that a truly financially dependent child is independent.
  (4) Have a parent take an unpaid leave of absence for long enough to get below the "threshold" level of income.

(b) What are some reasons why a **company** might want to overstate its earnings?

(c) What are some reasons why a **company** might want to understate its earnings?

(d) Under what circumstances might an otherwise ethical person decide to illegally overstate or understate earnings?

FASB Codification Activity

BYP1-9 The FASB has developed the Financial Accounting Standards Board Accounting Standards Codification (or more simply "the Codification"). The FASB's primary goal in developing the Codification is to provide in one place all the authoritative literature related to a particular topic. To provide easy access to the Codification, the FASB also developed the Financial Accounting Standards Board Codification Research System (CRS). CRS is an online, real-time database that provides easy access to the Codification. The Codification and the related CRS provide a topically organized structure, subdivided into topic, subtopics, sections, and paragraphs, using a numerical index system.

You may find this system useful in your present and future studies, and so we have provided an opportunity to use this online system as part of the *Broadening Your Perspective* section.

Instructions

Academic access to the FASB Codification is available through university subscriptions, obtained from the American Accounting Association (at **http://aaahq.org/FASB/Access.cfm**), for an annual fee of $150. This subscription covers an unlimited number of students within a single institution. Once this access has been obtained by your school, you should log in (at **http://aaahq.org/ascLogin. cfm**) and familiarize yourself with the resources that are accessible at the FASB Codification site.

Considering People, Planet, and Profit

BYP1-10 This chapter's Feature Story discusses the fact that although Clif Bar & Company is not a public company, it does share its financial information with its employees as part of its open-book management approach. Further, although it does not publicly share its financial information, it does provide a different form of an annual report to external users. In this report, the company provides information regarding its sustainability efforts.

Address: **www.clifbar.com/uploads/default/ClifBar_AA2010.pdf**

Instructions

Access the 2010 annual report of Clif Bar & Company at the site shown above and then answer the following questions.

(a) What are the Five Aspirations?

(b) What are the four key goals of the company's sustainability efforts related to the planet? Give one example of a recent initiative, and a measurable outcome for that initiative, that the company has taken related to each goal.

Answers to Chapter Questions

Answers to Insight and Accounting Across the Organization Questions

p. 6 The Scoop on Accounting Q: What are the benefits to the company and to the employees of making the financial statements available to all employees? **A:** If employees can read and use financial reports, a company will benefit in the following ways. The **marketing department** will make better decisions about products to offer and prices to charge. The **finance department** will make better decisions about debt and equity financing and how much to distribute in dividends. The **production department** will make better decisions about when to buy new equipment and how much inventory to produce. The **human resources department** will be better able to determine whether employees can be given raises. Finally, **all employees** will be better informed about the basis on which they are evaluated, which will increase employee morale.

p. 8 The Numbers Behind Not-for-Profit Organizations Q: What benefits does a sound accounting system provide to a not-for-profit organization? **A:** Accounting provides at least two benefits to not-for-profit organizations. First, it helps to ensure that money is used in the way that donors intended. Second, it assures donors that their money is not going to waste and thus increases the likelihood of future donations.

p. 10 The Korean Discount   Q: What is meant by the phrase "make the country's businesses more transparent"? Why would increasing transparency spur economic growth? **A:** Transparency refers to the extent to which outsiders have knowledge regarding a company's financial performance and financial position. If a company lacks transparency, its financial reports do not adequately inform investors of critical information that is needed to make investment decisions. If corporate transparency is increased, investors would be more willing to supply the financial capital that businesses need in order to grow, which would spur the country's economic growth.

p. 12 Spinning the Career Wheel   Q: How might accounting help you? **A:** You will need to understand financial reports in any enterprise with which you are associated. Whether you become a manager, a doctor, a lawyer, a social worker, a teacher, an engineer, an architect, or an entrepreneur, a working knowledge of accounting is relevant.

p. 25 Beyond Financial Statements   Q: Why might a company's stockholders be interested in its environmental and social performance? **A:** Many companies now recognize that being a socially responsible organization is not only the right thing to do, but it also is good for business. Many investment professionals understand, for example, that environmental, social, and proper corporate governance of companies affects the performance of their investment portfolios. For example, British Petroleum's oil spill disaster is a classic example of the problems that can occur for a company and its stockholders. BP's stock price was slashed, its dividend reduced, its executives replaced, and its reputation badly damaged. It is interesting that socially responsible investment funds are now gaining momentum in the marketplace such that companies now recognize this segment as an important investment group.

Answers to Self-Test Questions

1. b   **2.** d   **3.** c   **4.** b   **5.** b   **6.** d   **7.** a ($3,500 − $2,000)   **8.** b   **9.** b   **10.** a ($90,000 − $50,000)
11. d   **12.** c   **13.** b   **14.** c   *15. a

A Look at IFRS

LEARNING OBJECTIVE	**10**

Describe the impact of international accounting standards on U.S. financial reporting.

Most agree that there is a need for one set of international accounting standards. Here is why:

Multinational corporations. Today's companies view the entire world as their market. For example, Coca-Cola, Intel, and McDonald's generate more than 50% of their sales outside the United States, and many foreign companies, such as Toyota, Nestlé, and Sony, find their largest market to be the United States.

Mergers and acquisitions. The mergers between Fiat/Chrysler and Vodafone/Mannesmann suggest that we will see even more such business combinations of companies from different countries in the future.

Information technology. As communication barriers continue to topple through advances in technology, companies and individuals in different countries and markets are becoming more comfortable buying and selling goods and services from one another.

Financial markets. Financial markets are of international significance today. Whether it is currency, equity securities (stocks), bonds, or derivatives, there are active markets throughout the world trading these types of instruments.

Key Points

- International standards are referred to as **International Financial Reporting Standards (IFRS)**, developed by the International Accounting Standards Board (IASB).

- Recent events in the global capital markets have underscored the importance of financial disclosure and transparency not only in the United States but in markets around the world. As a result, many are examining which accounting and financial disclosure rules should be followed. As indicated in the graphic on the next page, much of the world has voted for the standards issued by the IASB. Over 115 countries require or permit use of IFRS.

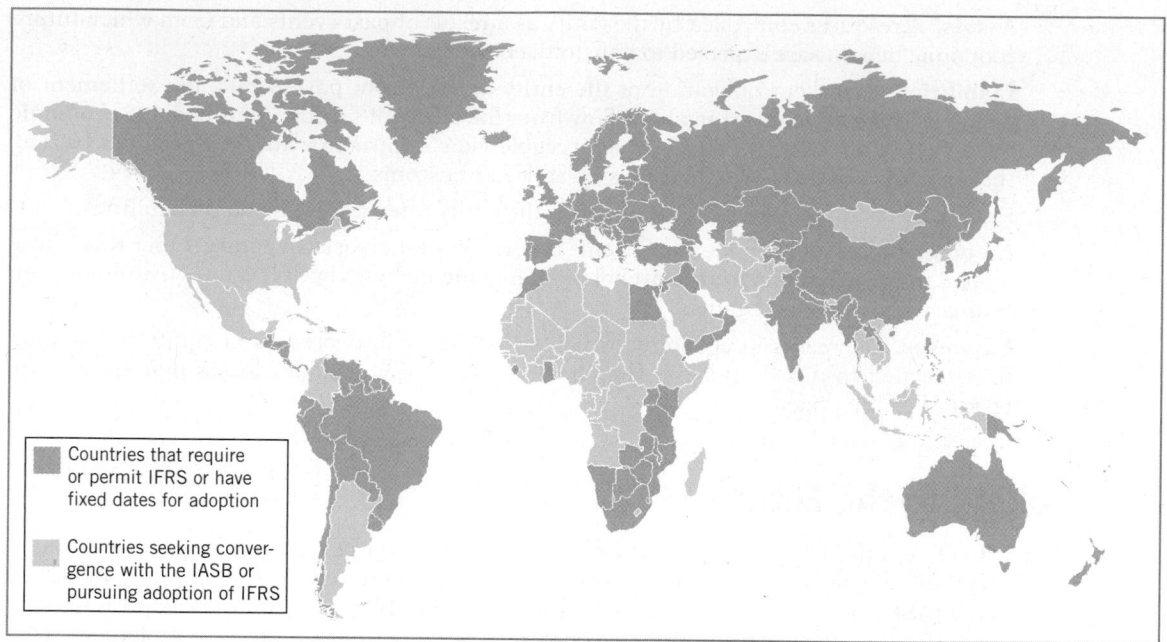

Countries that require or permit IFRS or have fixed dates for adoption

Countries seeking convergence with the IASB or pursuing adoption of IFRS

Source: http://www.pwc.com/us/en/issues/ifrs-reporting/country-adoption/index.jhtml.

- U.S standards, referred to as generally accepted accounting principles (GAAP), are developed by the Financial Accounting Standards Board (FASB). The fact that there are differences between what is in this textbook (which is based on U.S. standards) and IFRS should not be surprising because the FASB and IASB have responded to different user needs. In some countries, the primary users of financial statements are private investors; in others, the primary users are tax authorities or central government planners. It appears that the United States and the international standard-setting environment are primarily driven by meeting the needs of investors and creditors.

- The internal control standards applicable to Sarbanes-Oxley (SOX) apply only to large public companies listed on U.S. exchanges. There is a continuing debate as to whether non-U.S. companies should have to comply with this extra layer of regulation. Debate about international companies (non-U.S.) adopting SOX-type standards centers on whether the benefits exceed the costs. The concern is that the higher costs of SOX compliance are making the U.S. securities markets less competitive.

- The textbook mentions a number of ethics violations, such as Enron, WorldCom, and AIG. These problems have also occurred internationally, for example, at Satyam Computer Services (India), Parmalat (Italy), and Royal Ahold (the Netherlands).

- IFRS tends to be simpler in its accounting and disclosure requirements; some people say more "principles-based." GAAP is more detailed; some people say it is more "rules-based." This difference in approach has resulted in a debate about the merits of "principles-based" versus "rules-based" standards.

- U.S. regulators have recently eliminated the need for foreign companies that trade shares in U.S. markets to reconcile their accounting with GAAP.

- The three most common forms of business organization, proprietorships, partnerships, and corporations, are also found in countries that use IFRS. Because the choice of business organization is influenced by factors such as legal environment, tax rates and regulations, and degree of entrepreneurism, the relative use of each form will vary across countries.

- The conceptual framework that underlies IFRS is very similar to that used to develop GAAP. The basic definitions provided in this textbook for the key elements of financial statements, that is, assets, liabilities, equity, revenues (**referred to as income**), and expenses, are simplified versions of the official definitions provided by the FASB. The more substantive definitions, using the IASB definitional structure, are as follows.

Assets. A resource controlled by the entity as a result of past events and from which future economic benefits are expected to flow to the entity.

Liabilities. A present obligation of the entity arising from past events, the settlement of which is expected to result in an outflow from the entity of resources embodying economic benefits. Liabilities may be legally enforceable via a contract or law, but need not be, i.e., they can arise due to normal business practice or customs.

Equity. A residual interest in the assets of the entity after deducting all its liabilities.

Income. Increases in economic benefits that result in increases in equity (other than those related to contributions from shareholders). Income includes both revenues (resulting from ordinary activities) and gains.

Expenses. Decreases in economic benefits that result in decreases in equity (other than those related to distributions to shareholders). Expenses includes losses that are not the result of ordinary activities.

Looking to the Future

Both the IASB and the FASB are hard at work developing standards that will lead to the elimination of major differences in the way certain transactions are accounted for and reported. In fact, at one time the IASB stated that no new major standards would be issued for a period of time. The major reason for this policy was to provide companies the time to translate and implement IFRS into practice, as much has happened in a very short period of time. Consider, for example, that as a result of a joint project on the conceptual framework, the definitions of the most fundamental elements (assets, liabilities, equity, revenues, and expenses) may actually change. However, whether the IASB adopts internal control provisions similar to those in SOX remains to be seen.

IFRS Practice

IFRS Self-Test Questions

1. Which of the following is **not** a reason why a single set of high-quality international accounting standards would be beneficial?
   (a) Mergers and acquisition activity.
   (b) Financial markets.
   (c) Multinational corporations.
   (d) GAAP is widely considered to be a superior reporting system.

2. The Sarbanes-Oxley Act determines:
   (a) international tax regulations.
   (b) internal control standards as enforced by the IASB.
   (c) internal control standards of U.S. publicly traded companies.
   (d) U.S. tax regulations.

3. IFRS is considered to be more:
   (a) principles-based and less rules-based than GAAP.
   (b) rules-based and less principles-based than GAAP.
   (c) detailed than GAAP.
   (d) None of the above.

4. Which of the following statements is **false**?
   (a) IFRS is based on a conceptual framework that is similar to that used to develop GAAP.
   (b) Assets are defined by the IASB as resources controlled by the entity as a result of past events and from which future economic benefits are expected to flow to the entity.
   (c) Non-U.S. companies that trade shares in U.S. markets must reconcile their accounting with GAAP.
   (d) Proprietorships, partnerships, and corporations are also found in countries that use IFRS.

5. Which of the following statements is **true**?
  (a) Under IFRS, the term income refers to what would be called revenues and gains under GAAP.
  (b) The term income is not used under IFRS.
  (c) The term income refers only to gains on investments.
  (d) Under IFRS, expenses include distributions to owners.

IFRS Exercises

IFRS1-1 Who are the two key international players in the development of international accounting standards? Explain their role.

IFRS1-2 What might explain the fact that different accounting standard-setters have developed accounting standards that are sometimes quite different in nature?

IFRS1-3 What is the benefit of a single set of high-quality accounting standards?

IFRS1-4 Discuss the potential advantages and disadvantages that countries outside the United States should consider before adopting regulations, such as those in the Sarbanes-Oxley Act, that increase corporate internal control requirements.

International Financial Reporting Problem: Zetar plc

IFRS1-5 The financial statements of Zetar plc are presented in Appendix F. Instructions for accessing and using the company's complete annual report, including the notes to its financial statements, are also provided in Appendix F.

Instructions
Visit Zetar's corporate website and answer the following questions from Zetar's 2011 annual report.

  (a) What accounting firm performed the audit of Zetar's financial statements?
  (b) What is the address of the company's corporate headquarters?
  (c) What is the company's reporting currency?
  (d) What two segments does the company operate in, and what were the sales for each segment in the year ended April 30, 2011?

Answers to IFRS Self-Test Questions
1. d **2.** c **3.** a **4.** c **5.** a

 The Navigator

✔ Remember to go back to The Navigator box on the chapter opening page and check off your completed work.

2 | The Recording Process

Feature Story

Accidents Happen

How organized are you financially? Take a short quiz. Answer yes or no to each question:

- Does your wallet contain so many cash machine receipts that you've been declared a walking fire hazard?

- Do you wait until you debit card is denied before checking the status of your funds?

- Was Aaron Rodgers (the quarterback for the Green Bay Packers) playing high school football the last time you verified the accuracy of your bank account?

If you think it is hard to keep track of the many transactions that make up your life, imagine how difficult it is for a big corporation to do so. Not only that, but now consider how important it is for a large company to have good accounting records, especially if it has control of your life savings. MF Global Holdings Ltd is such a company. As a big investment broker, it held billions of dollars of investments for clients. If you had your life savings invested at MF Global, you might be slightly displeased if you heard this from one of its representatives: "You know, I kind of remember an account

for someone with a name like yours—now what did we with that?"

Unfortunately, that is almost exactly what happened to N Global's clients shortly before it recently filed for bankrup During the days immediately following the bankruptcy fi regulators and auditors struggled to piece things togethe the words of one regulator, "Their books are a disaster . we're trying to figure out what numbers are real number One company that considered buying an interest in MF Global walked away from the deal because it "couldn't c sense of what was on the balance sheet." That company the information that should have been instantly available instead took days to produce.

It now appears that MF Global did not properly segregate customer accounts from company accounts. And, becaus its sloppy recordkeeping, customers were not protected when the company had financial troubles. Total custome losses were approximately $1 billion. As you can see, accounting matters!

Source: S. Patterson and A. Lucchetti, "Inside the Hunt for MF Global C *Wall Street Journal Online* (November 11, 2011).

 The Navigator

- ■ Scan Learning Objectives
- ■ Read Feature Story
- ■ Read Preview
- ■ Read text and answer **DO IT!** p. 58
  - ■ p. 61 ■ p. 71 ■ p. 75
- ■ Work Comprehensive **DO IT!** p. 75
- ■ Review Summary of Learning Objectives
- ■ Answer Self-Test Questions
- ■ Complete Assignments
- ■ Go to *WileyPLUS* for practice and tutorials
- **Read A Look at IFRS** p. 96

Learning Objectives The Navigator

After studying this chapter, you should be able to:

[1] Explain what an account is and how it helps in the recording process.

[2] Define debits and credits and explain their use in recording business transactions.

[3] Identify the basic steps in the recording process.

[4] Explain what a journal is and how it helps in the recording process.

[5] Explain what a ledger is and how it helps in the recording process.

[6] Explain what posting is and how it helps in the recording process.

[7] Prepare a trial balance and explain its purposes.

Preview of Chapter 2

✔ The Navigator

In Chapter 1, we analyzed business transactions in terms of the accounting equation, and we presented the cumulative effects of these transactions in tabular form. Imagine a company like MF Global (as in the Feature Story) using the same tabular format as Softbyte to keep track of its transactions. In a single day, MF Global engaged in thousands of business transactions. To record each transaction this way would be impractical, expensive, and unnecessary. Instead, companies use a set of procedures and records to keep track of transaction data more easily. This chapter introduces and illustrates these basic procedures and records.

The content and organization of Chapter 2 are as follows.

THE RECORDING PROCESS		
The Account	**Steps in the Recording Process**	**The Trial Balance**
• Debits and credits • Owner's equity relationships • Summary of debit/credit rules	• Journal • Ledger • Posting • Chart of accounts • The recording process illustrated	• Limitations of a trial balance • Locating errors • Use of dollar signs

The Account

LEARNING OBJECTIVE   **1**

Explain what an account is and how it helps in the recording process.

An **account** is an individual accounting record of increases and decreases in a specific asset, liability, or owner's equity item. For example, Softbyte (the company discussed in Chapter 1) would have separate accounts for Cash, Accounts Receivable, Accounts Payable, Service Revenue, Salaries and Wages Expense, and so on. (Note that whenever we are referring to a specific account, we capitalize the name.)

In its simplest form, an account consists of three parts: (1) a title, (2) a left or debit side, and (3) a right or credit side. Because the format of an account resembles the letter T, we refer to it as a **T-account**. Illustration 2-1 shows the basic form of an account.

Illustration 2-1
Basic form of account

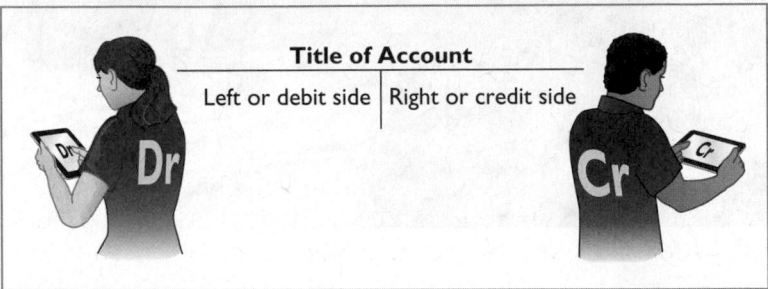

We use this form often throughout this book to explain basic accounting relationships.

Debits and Credits

LEARNING OBJECTIVE   **2**

Define debits and credits and explain their use in recording business transactions.

The term **debit** indicates the left side of an account, and **credit** indicates the right side. They are commonly abbreviated as **Dr.** for debit and **Cr.** for credit. They **do not** mean increase or decrease, as is commonly thought. We use the terms **debit** and **credit** repeatedly in the recording process to describe **where** entries are made in accounts. For example, the act of entering an amount on the left side of an account is called **debiting** the account. Making an entry on the right side is **crediting** the account.

When comparing the totals of the two sides, an account shows a **debit balance** if the total of the debit amounts exceeds the credits. An account shows a **credit balance** if the credit amounts exceed the debits. Note the position of the debit side and credit side in Illustration 2-1.

The procedure of recording debits and credits in an account is shown in Illustration 2-2 for the transactions affecting the Cash account of Softbyte. The data are taken from the Cash column of the tabular summary in Illustration 1-8 (page 20).

Illustration 2-2
Tabular summary and account form for Softbyte's Cash account

Tabular Summary	Account Form			
Cash	**Cash**			
$15,000	(Debits)	15,000	(Credits)	7,000
−7,000		1,200		1,700
1,200		1,500		250
1,500		600		1,300
−1,700	Balance	8,050		
−250	(Debit)			
600				
−1,300				
$ 8,050				

Every positive item in the tabular summary represents a receipt of cash. Every negative amount represents a payment of cash. **Notice that in the account form, we record the increases in cash as debits and the decreases in cash as credits.** For example, the $15,000 receipt of cash (in red) is debited to Cash, and the −$7,000 payment of cash (in blue) is credited to Cash.

Having increases on one side and decreases on the other reduces recording errors and helps in determining the totals of each side of the account as well as the account balance. The balance is determined by netting the two sides (subtracting one amount from the other). The account balance, a debit of $8,050, indicates that Softbyte had $8,050 more increases than decreases in cash. That is, since it started with a balance of zero, it has $8,050 in its Cash account.

DEBIT AND CREDIT PROCEDURE

In Chapter 1, you learned the effect of a transaction on the basic accounting equation. Remember that each transaction must affect two or more accounts to keep the basic accounting equation in balance. In other words, for each transaction, debits must equal credits. The equality of debits and credits provides the basis for the **double-entry system** of recording transactions.

Under the double-entry system, the dual (two-sided) effect of each transaction is recorded in appropriate accounts. This system provides a logical method for recording transactions. As discussed in the Feature Story about MF Global, the double-entry system also helps ensure the accuracy of the recorded amounts as well as the detection of errors. If every transaction is recorded with equal debits and credits, the sum of all the debits to the accounts must equal the sum of all the credits.

> ### International Note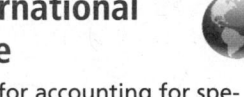
> Rules for accounting for specific events sometimes differ across countries. For example, European companies rely less on historical cost and more on fair value than U.S. companies. Despite the differences, the double-entry accounting system is the basis of accounting systems worldwide.

The double-entry system for determining the equality of the accounting equation is much more efficient than the plus/minus procedure used in Chapter 1. The following discussion illustrates debit and credit procedures in the double-entry system.

DR./CR. PROCEDURES FOR ASSETS AND LIABILITIES

In Illustration 2-2 for Softbyte, increases in Cash—an asset—were entered on the left side, and decreases in Cash were entered on the right side. We know that both sides of the basic equation (Assets = Liabilities + Owner's Equity) must be equal. It therefore follows that increases and decreases in liabilities will have to be recorded **opposite from** increases and decreases in assets. Thus, increases in liabilities must be entered on the right or credit side, and decreases in liabilities must be entered on the left or debit side. The effects that debits and credits have on assets and liabilities are summarized in Illustration 2-3.

Debits	Credits
Increase assets	Decrease assets
Decrease liabilities	Increase liabilities

Illustration 2-3
Debit and credit effects—assets and liabilities

Asset accounts normally show debit balances. That is, debits to a specific asset account should exceed credits to that account. Likewise, **liability accounts normally show credit balances**. That is, credits to a liability account should exceed debits to that account. The **normal balance** of an account is on the side where an increase in the account is recorded. Illustration 2-4 (page 56) shows the normal balances for assets and liabilities.

Knowing the normal balance in an account may help you trace errors. For example, a credit balance in an asset account such as Land or a debit balance in a liability account such as Salaries and Wages Payable usually indicates an error. Occasionally, though, an abnormal balance may be correct. The Cash account, for example, will have a credit balance when a company has overdrawn its bank balance (i.e., written a check that "bounced").

DR./CR. PROCEDURES FOR OWNER'S EQUITY

As Chapter 1 indicated, owner's investments and revenues increase owner's equity. Owner's drawings and expenses decrease owner's equity. Companies keep accounts for each of these types of transactions.

OWNER'S CAPITAL Investments by owners are credited to the Owner's Capital account. Credits increase this account, and debits decrease it. When an owner invests cash in the business, the company debits (increases) Cash and credits (increases) Owner's Capital. When the owner's investment in the business is reduced, Owner's Capital is debited (decreased).

Illustration 2-5 shows the rules of debit and credit for the Owner's Capital account.

Illustration 2-5
Debit and credit effects—Owner's Capital

Debits	Credits
Decrease Owner's Capital	Increase Owner's Capital

We can diagram the normal balance in Owner's Capital as follows.

Illustration 2-6
Normal balance—Owner's Capital

Owner's Capital

Debit for decrease	Credit for increase
	Normal balance

OWNER'S DRAWINGS An owner may withdraw cash or other assets for personal use. Withdrawals could be debited directly to Owner's Capital to indicate a decrease in owner's equity. However, it is preferable to use a separate account, called Owner's Drawings. This separate account makes it easier to determine total withdrawals for each accounting period. Owner's Drawings is increased by debits and decreased by credits. Normally, the drawings account will have a debit balance.

Illustration 2-7 shows the rules of debit and credit for the drawings account.

Illustration 2-7
Debit and credit effects—Owner's Drawings

Debits	Credits
Increase Owner's Drawings	Decrease Owner's Drawings

We can diagram the normal balance as shown in Illustration 2-8.

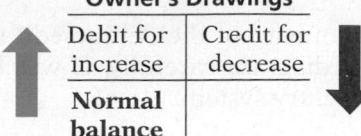

Owner's Drawings

Debit for increase	Credit for decrease
Normal balance	

Illustration 2-8
Normal balance—Owner's Drawings

The **Owner's Drawings** account decreases owner's equity. It is not an income statement account like revenues and expenses.

INVESTOR INSIGHT

Keeping Score

The Chicago Cubs baseball team probably has these major revenue and expense accounts:

Revenues	Expenses
Admissions (ticket sales)	Players' salaries
Concessions	Administrative salaries
Television and radio	Travel
Advertising	Ballpark maintenance

? Do you think that the Chicago Bears football team would be likely to have the same major revenue and expense accounts as the Cubs? (See page 95.)

Jonathan Daniel/Getty Images, Inc.

REVENUES AND EXPENSES The purpose of earning revenues is to benefit the owner(s) of the business. When a company earns revenues, owner's equity increases. Therefore, **the effect of debits and credits on revenue accounts is the same as their effect on Owner's Capital**. That is, revenue accounts are increased by credits and decreased by debits.

Expenses have the opposite effect. Expenses decrease owner's equity. Since expenses decrease net income and revenues increase it, it is logical that the increase and decrease sides of expense accounts should be the opposite of revenue accounts. Thus, expense accounts are increased by debits and decreased by credits. Illustration 2-9 shows the rules of debits and credits for revenues and expenses.

Helpful Hint Because revenues increase owner's equity, a revenue account has the same debit/credit rules as the Owner's Capital account. Expenses have the opposite effect.

Illustration 2-9
Debit and credit effects—revenues and expenses

Debits	Credits
Decrease revenues	Increase revenues
Increase expenses	Decrease expenses

Credits to revenue accounts should exceed debits. Debits to expense accounts should exceed credits. Thus, revenue accounts normally show credit balances, and expense accounts normally show debit balances. We can diagram the normal balances as follows.

Illustration 2-10
Normal balances—revenues and expenses

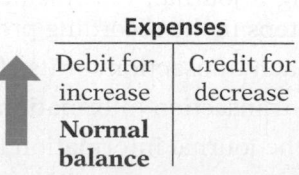

Revenues

Debit for decrease	Credit for increase
	Normal balance

Expenses

Debit for increase	Credit for decrease
Normal balance	

Helpful Hint You may want to bookmark Illustration 2-11. You probably will refer to it often.

Summary of Debit/Credit Rules

Illustration 2-11 shows a summary of the debit/credit rules and effects on each type of account. Study this diagram carefully. It will help you understand the fundamentals of the double-entry system.

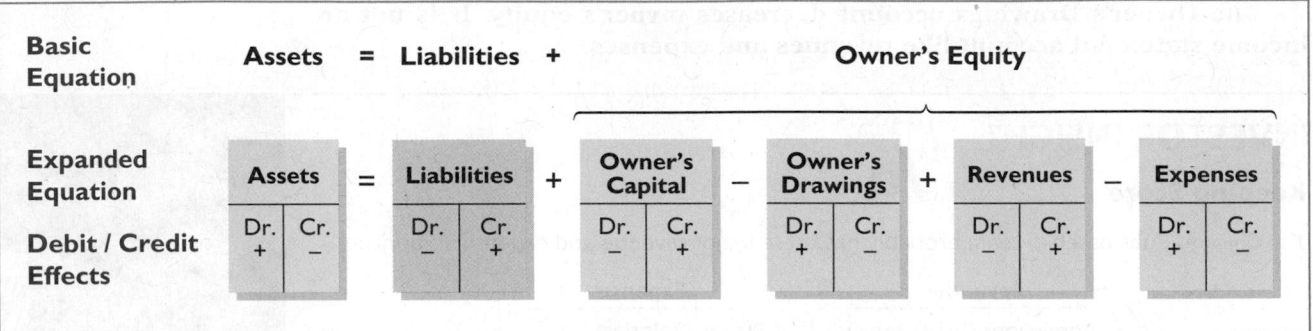

Illustration 2-11
Summary of debit/credit rules

> DO IT!

Normal Balances

Action Plan

✔ Determine the types of accounts needed. Kate will need asset accounts for each different type of asset she invests in the business and liability accounts for any debts she incurs.

✔ Understand the types of owner's equity accounts. Only Owner's Capital will be needed when Kate begins the business. Other owner's equity accounts will be needed later.

Kate Browne has just rented space in a shopping mall. In this space, she will open a hair salon to be called "Hair It Is." A friend has advised Kate to set up a double-entry set of accounting records in which to record all of her business transactions.

Identify the balance sheet accounts that Kate will likely need to record the transactions needed to open her business. Indicate whether the normal balance of each account is a debit or a credit.

Solution

Kate would likely need the following accounts in which to record the transactions necessary to ready her hair salon for opening day:

Cash (debit balance)

Equipment (debit balance)

Supplies (debit balance)

Accounts Payable (credit balance)

If she borrows money: Notes Payable (credit balance)

Owner's Capital (credit balance)

Related exercise material: **BE2-1, BE2-2, BE2-5, E2-1, E2-2, E2-4, and DO IT! 2-1.**

✔ The Navigator

Steps in the Recording Process

LEARNING OBJECTIVE **3**

Identify the basic steps in the recording process.

Although it is possible to enter transaction information directly into the accounts without using a journal, few businesses do so. Practically every business uses three basic steps in the recording process:

1. Analyze each transaction for its effects on the accounts.
2. Enter the transaction information in a **journal**.
3. Transfer the journal information to the appropriate accounts in the **ledger**.

The recording process begins with the transaction. **Business documents**, such as a sales slip, a check, a bill, or a cash register tape, provide evidence of the transaction. The company analyzes this evidence to determine the transaction's effects on specific accounts. The company then enters the transaction in the journal. Finally, it transfers the journal entry to the designated accounts in the ledger. Illustration 2-12 shows the recording process.

The steps in the recording process occur repeatedly. In Chapter 1, we illustrated the first step, the analysis of transactions, and will give further examples in this and later chapters. The other two steps in the recording process are explained in the next sections.

> ## Ethics Note
>
> Business documents provide evidence that transactions actually occurred. International Outsourcing Services, LLC was accused of submitting fraudulent documents (store coupons) to companies such as Kraft Foods and PepsiCo for reimbursement of as much as $250 million. Ensuring that all recorded transactions are backed up by proper business documents reduces the likelihood of fraudulent activity.

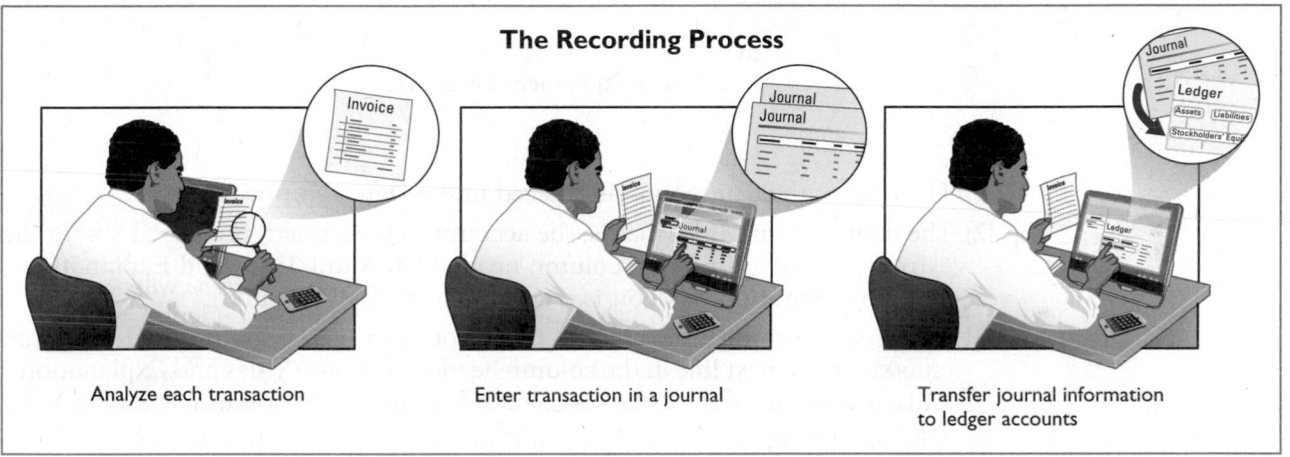

The Recording Process

Analyze each transaction | Enter transaction in a journal | Transfer journal information to ledger accounts

Illustration 2-12
The recording process

The Journal

Companies initially record transactions in chronological order (the order in which they occur). Thus, the **journal** is referred to as the book of original entry. For each transaction, the journal shows the debit and credit effects on specific accounts.

Companies may use various kinds of journals, but every company has the most basic form of journal, a **general journal**. Typically, a general journal has spaces for dates, account titles and explanations, references, and two amount columns. See the format of the journal in Illustration 2-13 (page 60). *Whenever we use the term "journal" in this textbook, we mean the general journal unless we specify otherwise.*

The journal makes several significant contributions to the recording process:

1. It discloses in one place the **complete effects of a transaction**.
2. It provides a **chronological record** of transactions.
3. It helps to **prevent or locate errors** because the debit and credit amounts for each entry can be easily compared.

LEARNING OBJECTIVE	4

Explain what a journal is and how it helps in the recording process.

JOURNALIZING

Entering transaction data in the journal is known as **journalizing**. Companies make separate journal entries for each transaction. A complete entry consists of (1) the date of the transaction, (2) the accounts and amounts to be debited and credited, and (3) a brief explanation of the transaction.

Illustration 2-13 shows the technique of journalizing, using the first two transactions of Softbyte. Recall that on September 1, Ray Neal invested $15,000 cash in the business, and Softbyte purchased computer equipment for $7,000 cash. The number J1 indicates that these two entries are recorded on the first page of the journal. Illustration 2-13 shows the standard form of journal entries for these two transactions. (The boxed numbers correspond to explanations in the list below the illustration.)

Illustration 2-13
Technique of journalizing

GENERAL JOURNAL				J1
Date	**Account Titles and Explanation**	**Ref.**	**Debit**	**Credit**
2014		⑤		
Sept. 1 ②	Cash		15,000	
① ③	Owner's Capital			15,000
④	(Owner's investment of cash in business)			
1	Equipment		7,000	
	Cash			7,000
	(Purchase of equipment for cash)			

① The date of the transaction is entered in the Date column.

② The debit account title (that is, the account to be debited) is entered first at the extreme left margin of the column headed "Account Titles and Explanation," and the amount of the debit is recorded in the Debit column.

③ The credit account title (that is, the account to be credited) is indented and entered on the next line in the column headed "Account Titles and Explanation," and the amount of the credit is recorded in the Credit column.

④ A brief explanation of the transaction appears on the line below the credit account title. A space is left between journal entries. The blank space separates individual journal entries and makes the entire journal easier to read.

⑤ The column titled Ref. (which stands for Reference) is left blank when the journal entry is made. This column is used later when the journal entries are transferred to the ledger accounts.

It is important to use correct and specific account titles in journalizing. Erroneous account titles lead to incorrect financial statements. However, some flexibility exists initially in selecting account titles. The main criterion is that each title must appropriately describe the content of the account. Once a company chooses the specific title to use, it should record under that account title all later transactions involving the account.[1]

SIMPLE AND COMPOUND ENTRIES

Some entries involve only two accounts, one debit and one credit. (See, for example, the entries in Illustration 2-13.) An entry like these is considered a **simple entry**. Some transactions, however, require more than two accounts in journalizing. An entry that requires three or more accounts is a **compound entry**. To illustrate, assume that on July 1, Butler Company purchases a delivery truck costing $14,000.

---

[1]*In homework problems, you should use specific account titles when they are given.* When account titles are not given, you may select account titles that identify the nature and content of each account. The account titles used in journalizing should not contain explanations such as Cash Paid or Cash Received.

It pays $8,000 cash now and agrees to pay the remaining $6,000 on account (to be paid later). The compound entry is as follows.

GENERAL JOURNAL				J1
Date	Account Titles and Explanation	Ref.	Debit	Credit
2014 July 1	Equipment		14,000	
	Cash			8,000
	Accounts Payable			6,000
	(Purchased truck for cash with balance on account)			

Illustration 2-14
Compound journal entry

In a compound entry, the standard format requires that all debits be listed before the credits.

ACCOUNTING ACROSS THE ORGANIZATION

Boosting Microsoft's Profits

At one time, Microsoft's Home and Entertainment Division lost over $4 billion, mostly due to losses on the original Xbox videogame console. With the Xbox 360 videogame console, the division's head of finance, Bryan Lee, hoped the division would become profitable. He set strict goals for sales, revenue, and profit. "A manager seeking to spend more on a feature such as a disk drive has to find allies in the group to cut spending elsewhere, or identify new revenue to offset the increase," he explained.

For example, Microsoft originally designed the Xbox 360 to have 256 megabytes of memory. But the design department said that amount of memory wouldn't support the best special effects. The purchasing department said that adding more memory would cost $30—which was 10% of the estimated selling price of $300. The marketing department, however, "determined that adding the memory would let Microsoft reduce marketing costs and attract more game developers, boosting royalty revenue. It would also extend the life of the console, generating more sales." As a result, Microsoft doubled the memory to 512 megabytes. Today, the division enjoys great success.

Source: Robert A. Guth, "New Xbox Aim for Microsoft: Profitability," *Wall Street Journal* (May 24, 2005), p. C1.

? In what ways is this Microsoft division using accounting to assist in its effort to become more profitable? (See page 95.)

> DO IT!

Recording Business Activities

Kate Browne engaged in the following activities in establishing her salon, Hair It Is:

1. Opened a bank account in the name of Hair It Is and deposited $20,000 of her own money in this account as her initial investment.
2. Purchased equipment on account (to be paid in 30 days) for a total cost of $4,800.
3. Interviewed three persons for the position of hair stylist.

In what form (type of record) should Kate record these three activities? Prepare the entries to record the transactions.

Action Plan

✔ Understand which activities need to be recorded and which do not. Any that affect assets, liabilities, or owner's capital should be recorded in a journal.

✔ Analyze the effects of transactions on asset, liability, and owner's equity accounts.

Solution

Each transaction that is recorded is entered in the general journal. The three activities would be recorded as follows.

1.	Cash	20,000	
	Owner's Capital		20,000
	(Owner's investment of cash in business)		
2.	Equipment	4,800	
	Accounts Payable		4,800
	(Purchase of equipment on account)		
3.	No entry because no transaction has occurred.		

Related exercise material: **BE2-3, BE2-6, E2-3, E2-5, E2-6, E2-7,** and **DO IT!** **2-2.**

✔ The Navigator

The Ledger

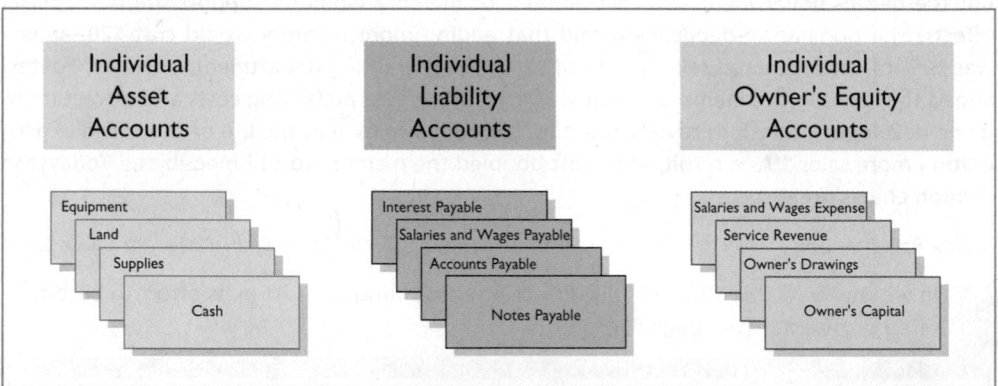

LEARNING OBJECTIVE   5

Explain what a ledger is and how it helps in the recording process.

The entire group of accounts maintained by a company is the **ledger**. The ledger provides the balance in each of the accounts as well as keeps track of changes in these balances.

Companies may use various kinds of ledgers, but every company has a general ledger. A **general ledger** contains all the asset, liability, and owner's equity accounts, as shown in Illustration 2-15 for J. Lind Company. *Whenever we use the term "ledger" in this textbook, we are referring to the general ledger unless we specify otherwise.*

Illustration 2-15
The general ledger, which contains all of a company's accounts

Companies arrange the ledger in the sequence in which they present the accounts in the financial statements, beginning with the balance sheet accounts. First in order are the asset accounts, followed by liability accounts, owner's capital, owner's drawings, revenues, and expenses. Each account is numbered for easier identification.

The ledger provides the balance in each of the accounts. For example, the Cash account shows the amount of cash available to meet current obligations. The Accounts Receivable account shows amounts due from customers. Accounts Payable shows amounts owed to creditors.

ETHICS INSIGHT

A Convenient Overstatement

Sometimes a company's investment securities suffer a permanent decline in value below their original cost. When this occurs, the company is supposed to reduce the recorded value of the securities on its balance sheet ("write-them down" in common financial lingo) and record a loss. It appears, however, that during the financial crisis, employees at some financial institutions chose to look the other way as the value of their investments skidded. A number of Wall Street traders that worked for the investment bank Credit Suisse Group were charged with intentionally overstating the value of securities that had suffered declines of approximately $2.85 billion. One reason that they may have been reluctant to record the losses is out of fear that the company's shareholders and clients would panic if they saw the magnitude of the losses. However, personal self-interest might have been equally to blame—the bonuses of the traders were tied to the value of the investment securities.

Source: S. Pulliam, J. Eaglesham, and M. Siconolfi, "U.S. Plans Changes on Bond Fraud," *Wall Street Journal Online* (February 1, 2012).

? What incentives might employees have had to overstate the value of these investment securities on the company's financial statements? (See page 95.)

STANDARD FORM OF ACCOUNT

The simple T-account form used in accounting textbooks is often very useful for illustration purposes. However, in practice, the account forms used in ledgers are much more structured. Illustration 2-16 shows a typical form, using assumed data from a cash account.

CASH					NO. 101
Date	Explanation	Ref.	Debit	Credit	Balance
2014					
June 1			25,000		25,000
2				8,000	17,000
3			4,200		21,200
9			7,500		28,700
17				11,700	17,000
20				250	16,750
30				7,300	9,450

Illustration 2-16
Three-column form of account

This format is called the **three-column form of account**. It has three money columns—debit, credit, and balance. The balance in the account is determined after each transaction. Companies use the explanation space and reference columns to provide special information about the transaction.

POSTING

Transferring journal entries to the ledger accounts is called **posting**. This phase of the recording process accumulates the effects of journalized transactions into the individual accounts. Posting involves the following steps.

1. In the **ledger**, in the appropriate columns of the account(s) debited, enter the date, journal page, and debit amount shown in the journal.

2. In the reference column of the **journal**, write the account number to which the debit amount was posted.

> **LEARNING OBJECTIVE   6**
>
> Explain what posting is and how it helps in the recording process.

3. In the **ledger**, in the appropriate columns of the account(s) credited, enter the date, journal page, and credit amount shown in the journal.

4. In the reference column of the **journal**, write the account number to which the credit amount was posted.

Illustration 2-17 shows these four steps using Softbyte's first journal entry. The boxed numbers indicate the sequence of the steps.

Illustration 2-17
Posting a journal entry

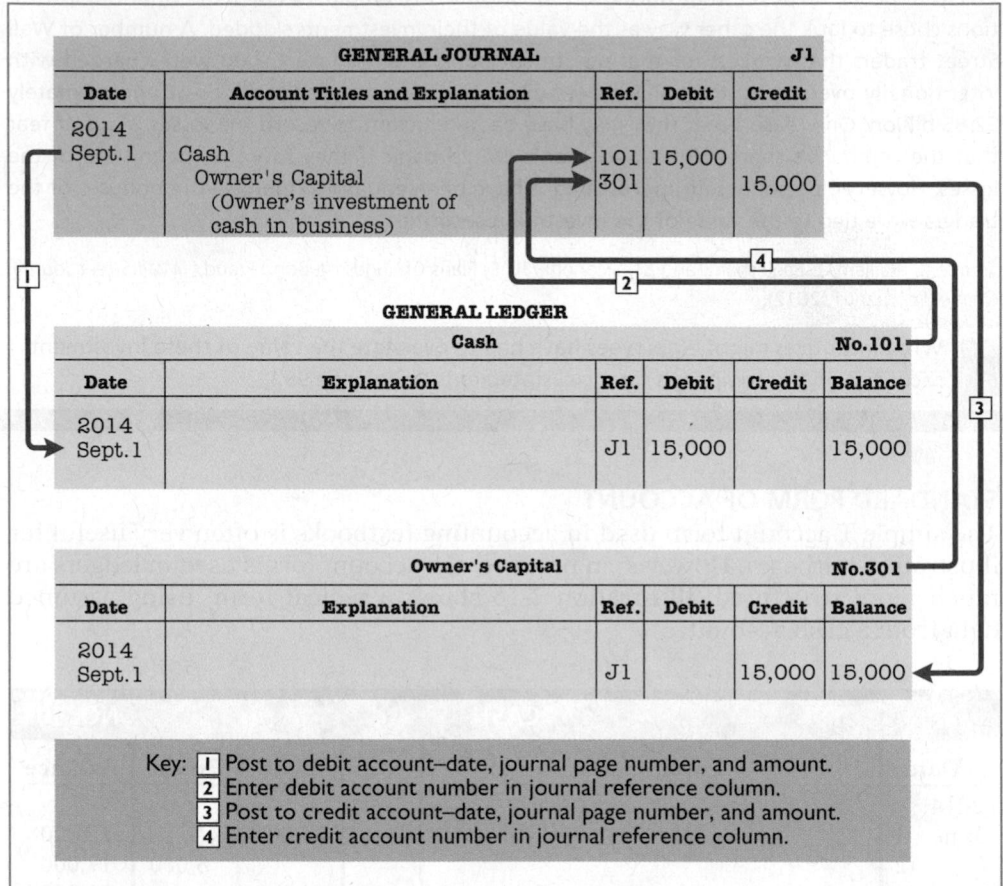

GENERAL JOURNAL — J1

Date	Account Titles and Explanation	Ref.	Debit	Credit
2014 Sept. 1	Cash	101	15,000	
	Owner's Capital	301		15,000
	(Owner's investment of cash in business)			

GENERAL LEDGER

Cash — No. 101

Date	Explanation	Ref.	Debit	Credit	Balance
2014 Sept. 1		J1	15,000		15,000

Owner's Capital — No. 301

Date	Explanation	Ref.	Debit	Credit	Balance
2014 Sept. 1		J1		15,000	15,000

Key: 1 Post to debit account—date, journal page number, and amount.
2 Enter debit account number in journal reference column.
3 Post to credit account—date, journal page number, and amount.
4 Enter credit account number in journal reference column.

Posting should be performed in chronological order. That is, the company should post all the debits and credits of one journal entry before proceeding to the next journal entry. Postings should be made on a timely basis to ensure that the ledger is up to date.[2]

The reference column of a ledger account indicates the journal page from which the transaction was posted.[3] The explanation space of the ledger account is used infrequently because an explanation already appears in the journal.

CHART OF ACCOUNTS

The number and type of accounts differ for each company. The number of accounts depends on the amount of detail management desires. For example, the management of one company may want a single account for all types of utility expense. Another may keep separate expense accounts for each type of utility, such as gas, electricity, and water. Similarly, a small company like Softbyte will

---

[2]*In homework problems, you can journalize all transactions before posting any of the journal entries.*
[3]After the last entry has been posted, the accountant should scan the reference column **in the journal**, to confirm that all postings have been made.

have fewer accounts than a corporate giant like Dell. Softbyte may be able to manage and report its activities in 20 to 30 accounts, while Dell may require thousands of accounts to keep track of its worldwide activities.

Most companies have a **chart of accounts**. This chart lists the accounts and the account numbers that identify their location in the ledger. The numbering system that identifies the accounts usually starts with the balance sheet accounts and follows with the income statement accounts.

In this and the next two chapters, we will be explaining the accounting for Pioneer Advertising Agency (a service company). Accounts 101–199 indicate asset accounts; 200–299 indicate liabilities; 301–350 indicate owner's equity accounts; 400–499, revenues; 601–799, expenses; 800–899, other revenues; and 900–999, other expenses. Illustration 2-18 shows Pioneer's chart of accounts. Accounts listed in red are used in this chapter; accounts shown in black are explained in later chapters.

Helpful Hint On the textbook's front endpapers, you also will find an expanded chart of accounts.

Illustration 2-18
Chart of accounts

PIONEER ADVERTISING AGENCY
Chart of Accounts

Assets	Owner's Equity
101 Cash	301 Owner's Capital
112 Accounts Receivable	306 Owner's Drawings
126 Supplies	350 Income Summary
130 Prepaid Insurance	
157 Equipment	**Revenues**
158 Accumulated Depreciation—Equipment	400 Service Revenue
Liabilities	**Expenses**
200 Notes Payable	631 Supplies Expense
201 Accounts Payable	711 Depreciation Expense
209 Unearned Service Revenue	722 Insurance Expense
212 Salaries and Wages Payable	726 Salaries and Wages Expense
230 Interest Payable	729 Rent Expense
	732 Utilities Expense
	905 Interest Expense

You will notice that there are gaps in the numbering system of the chart of accounts for Pioneer Advertising. Companies leave gaps to permit the insertion of new accounts as needed during the life of the business.

The Recording Process Illustrated

Illustrations 2-19 through 2-28 (pages 66–70) show the basic steps in the recording process, using the October transactions of Pioneer Advertising Agency. Pioneer's accounting period is a month. In these illustrations, a basic analysis, an equation analysis, and a debit-credit analysis precede the journal entry and posting of each transaction. For simplicity, we use the T-account form to show the posting instead of the standard account form.

Study these transaction analyses carefully. **The purpose of transaction analysis is first to identify the type of account involved, and then to determine whether to make a debit or a credit to the account.** You should always perform this type of analysis before preparing a journal entry. Doing so will help you understand the journal entries discussed in this chapter as well as more complex journal entries in later chapters.

Illustration 2-19
Investment of cash by owner

Cash Flows
+10,000

Helpful Hint Follow these steps:
1. Determine what type of account is involved.
2. Determine what items increased or decreased and by how much.
3. Translate the increases and decreases into debits and credits.

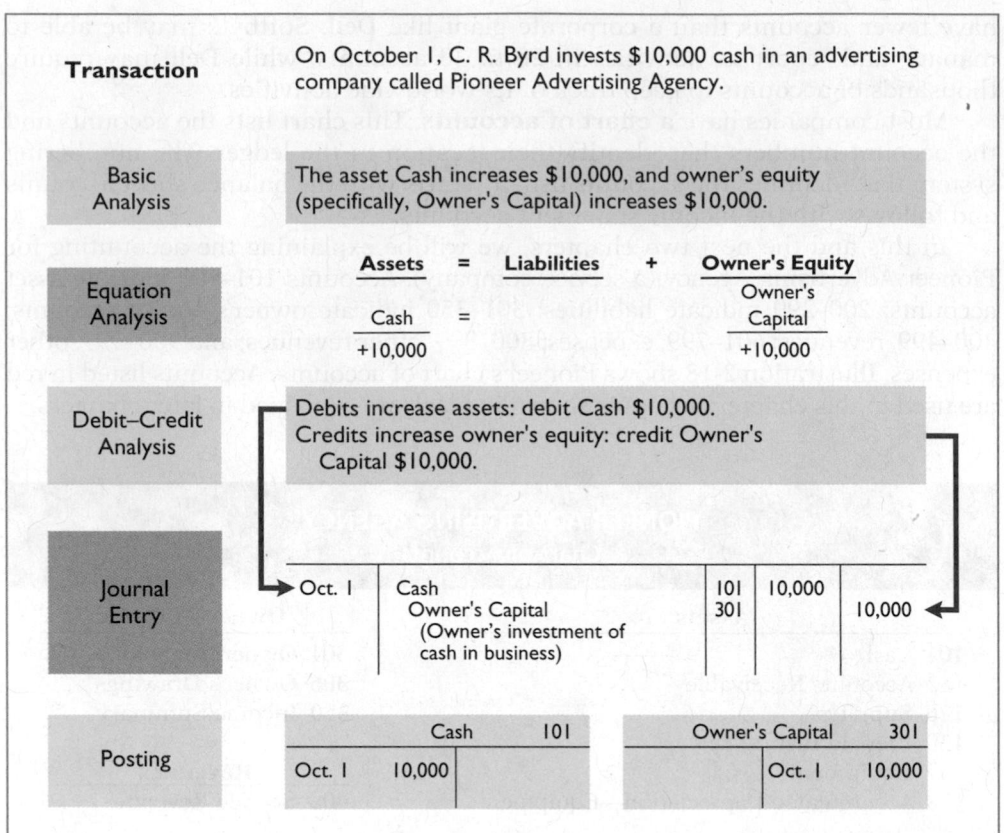

Transaction	On October 1, C. R. Byrd invests $10,000 cash in an advertising company called Pioneer Advertising Agency.
Basic Analysis	The asset Cash increases $10,000, and owner's equity (specifically, Owner's Capital) increases $10,000.

Equation Analysis

Assets	=	Liabilities	+	Owner's Equity
				Owner's Capital
Cash	=			Capital
+10,000				+10,000

Debit–Credit Analysis

Debits increase assets: debit Cash $10,000.
Credits increase owner's equity: credit Owner's Capital $10,000.

Journal Entry

Oct. 1	Cash	101	10,000	
	Owner's Capital	301		10,000
	(Owner's investment of cash in business)			

Posting

Cash	101		Owner's Capital	301
Oct. 1 10,000			Oct. 1	10,000

Illustration 2-20
Purchase of office equipment

Cash Flows
no effect

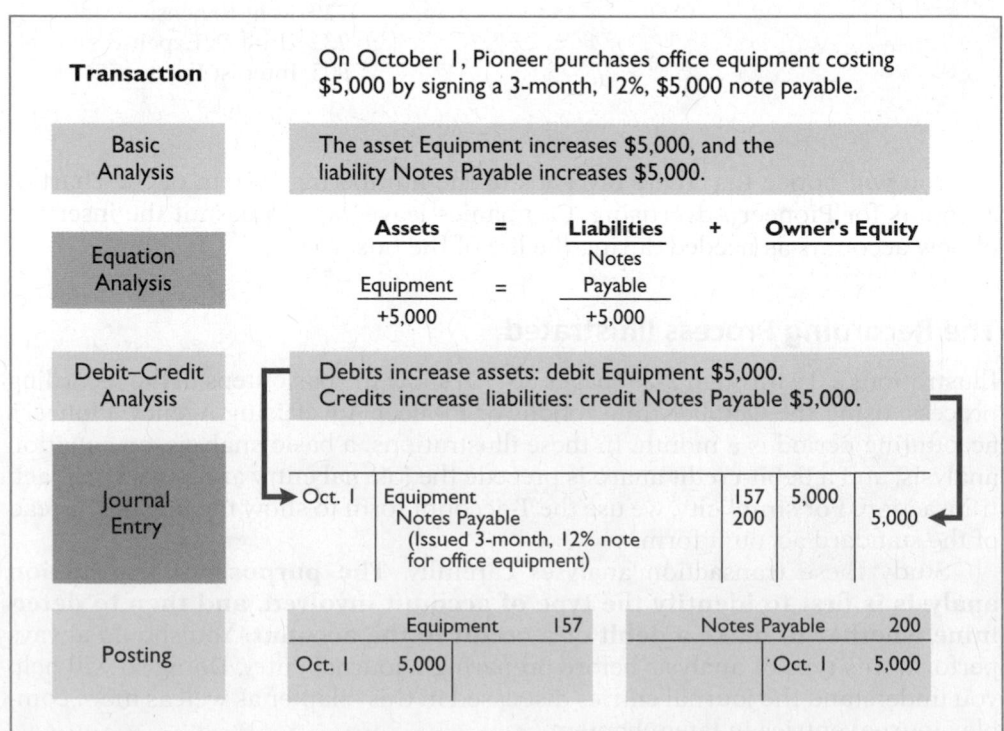

Transaction	On October 1, Pioneer purchases office equipment costing $5,000 by signing a 3-month, 12%, $5,000 note payable.
Basic Analysis	The asset Equipment increases $5,000, and the liability Notes Payable increases $5,000.

Equation Analysis

Assets	=	Liabilities	+	Owner's Equity
		Notes		
Equipment	=	Payable		
+5,000		+5,000		

Debit–Credit Analysis

Debits increase assets: debit Equipment $5,000.
Credits increase liabilities: credit Notes Payable $5,000.

Journal Entry

Oct. 1	Equipment	157	5,000	
	Notes Payable	200		5,000
	(Issued 3-month, 12% note for office equipment)			

Posting

Equipment	157		Notes Payable	200
Oct. 1 5,000			Oct. 1	5,000

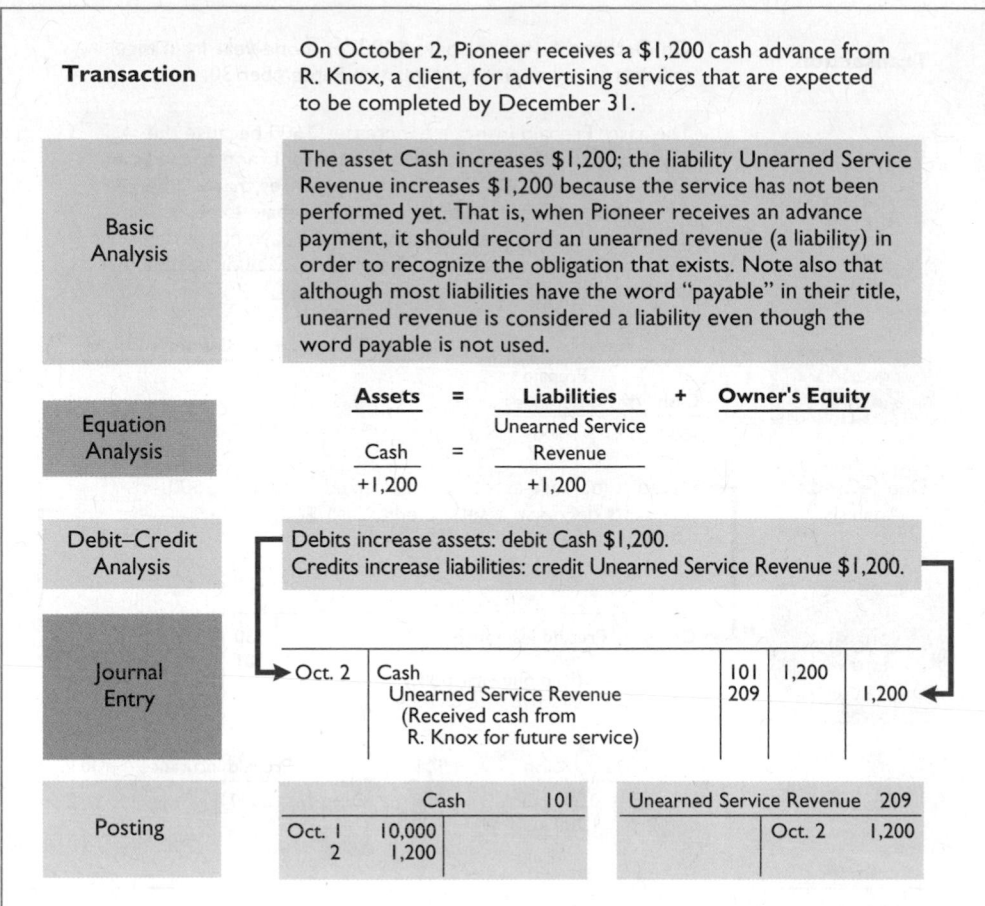

Illustration 2-21
Receipt of cash for future service

Cash Flows
+1,200

Illustration 2-22
Payment of monthly rent

Cash Flows
−900

Illustration 2-23
Payment for insurance

Cash Flows
−600

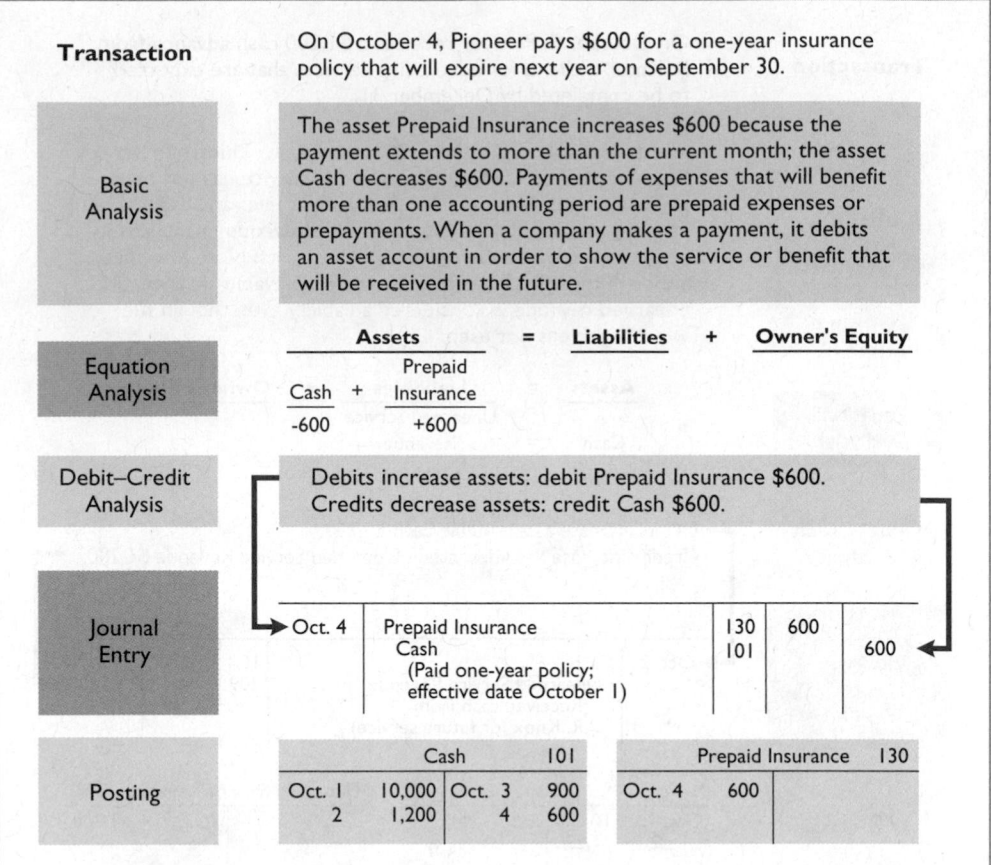

Transaction	On October 4, Pioneer pays $600 for a one-year insurance policy that will expire next year on September 30.
Basic Analysis	The asset Prepaid Insurance increases $600 because the payment extends to more than the current month; the asset Cash decreases $600. Payments of expenses that will benefit more than one accounting period are prepaid expenses or prepayments. When a company makes a payment, it debits an asset account in order to show the service or benefit that will be received in the future.

Equation Analysis

Assets		=	Liabilities	+	Owner's Equity
Cash	+	Prepaid Insurance			
−600		+600			

Debit–Credit Analysis

Debits increase assets: debit Prepaid Insurance $600.
Credits decrease assets: credit Cash $600.

Journal Entry

Oct. 4	Prepaid Insurance	130	600	
	Cash	101		600
	(Paid one-year policy; effective date October 1)			

Posting

Cash		101	Prepaid Insurance		130
Oct. 1	10,000	Oct. 3 900	Oct. 4	600	
2	1,200	4 600			

Illustration 2-24
Purchase of supplies on credit

Cash Flows
no effect

Transaction	On October 5, Pioneer purchases an estimated 3-month supply of advertising materials on account from Aero Supply for $2,500.
Basic Analysis	The asset Supplies increases $2,500; the liability Accounts Payable increases $2,500.

Equation Analysis

Assets	=	Liabilities	+	Owner's Equity
Supplies	=	Accounts Payable		
+2,500		+2,500		

Debit–Credit Analysis

Debits increase assets: debit Supplies $2,500.
Credits increase liabilities: credit Accounts Payable $2,500.

Journal Entry

Oct. 5	Supplies	126	2,500	
	Accounts Payable	201		2,500
	(Purchased supplies on account from Aero Supply)			

Posting

Supplies		126	Accounts Payable		201
Oct. 5	2,500			Oct. 5	2,500

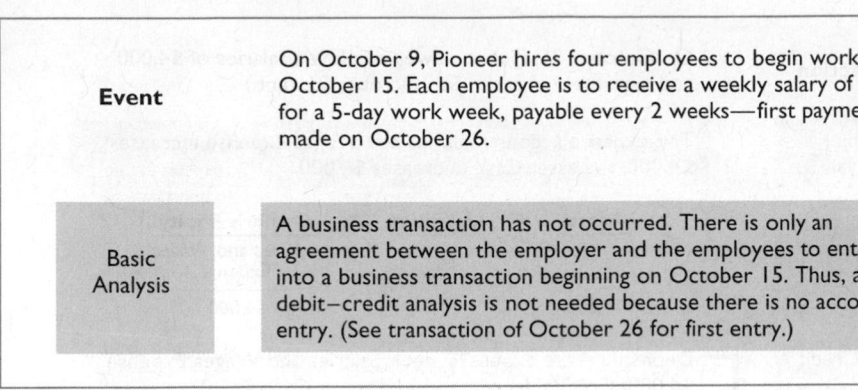

Illustration 2-25
Hiring of employees

Cash Flows
no effect

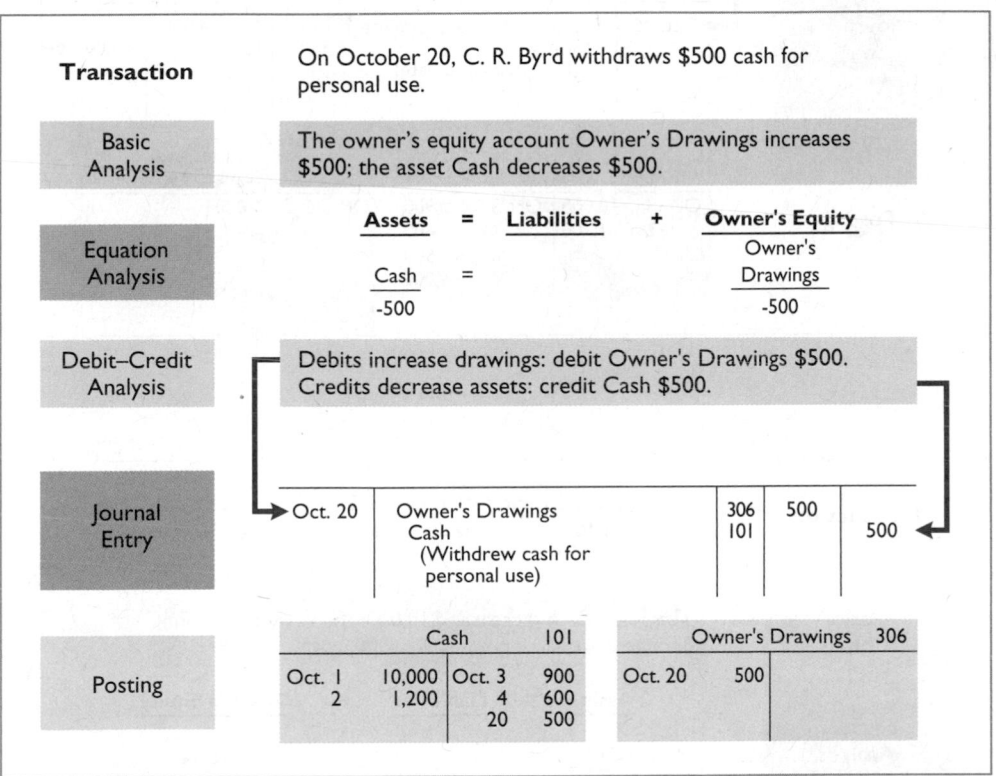

Illustration 2-26
Withdrawal of cash by owner

Cash Flows
−500

Illustration 2-27
Payment of salaries

Cash Flows
−4,000

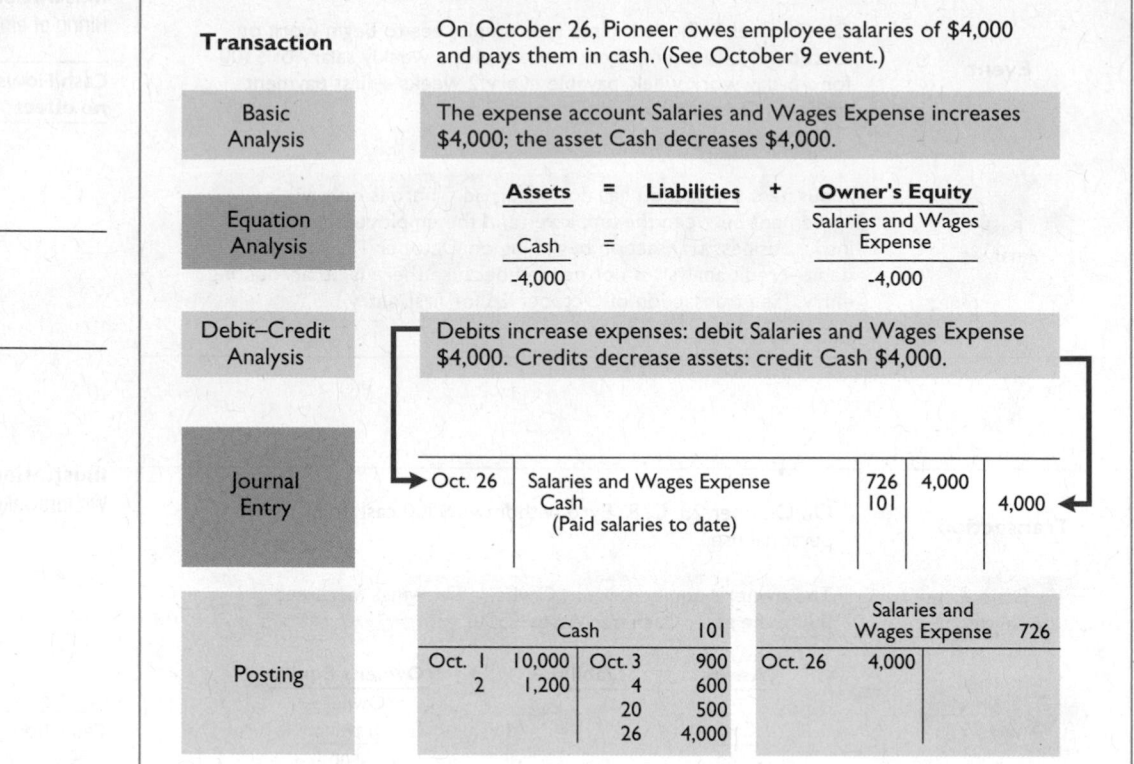

Transaction	On October 26, Pioneer owes employee salaries of $4,000 and pays them in cash. (See October 9 event.)
Basic Analysis	The expense account Salaries and Wages Expense increases $4,000; the asset Cash decreases $4,000.
Equation Analysis	**Assets** = **Liabilities** + **Owner's Equity** Salaries and Wages Expense
	Cash = −4,000 −4,000
Debit–Credit Analysis	Debits increase expenses: debit Salaries and Wages Expense $4,000. Credits decrease assets: credit Cash $4,000.

Journal Entry

Oct. 26	Salaries and Wages Expense	726	4,000	
	Cash	101		4,000
	(Paid salaries to date)			

Posting

		Cash		101			Salaries and Wages Expense	726
Oct. 1	10,000	Oct. 3		900		Oct. 26	4,000	
2	1,200	4		600				
		20		500				
		26		4,000				

Illustration 2-28
Receipt of cash for services performed

Cash Flows
+10,000

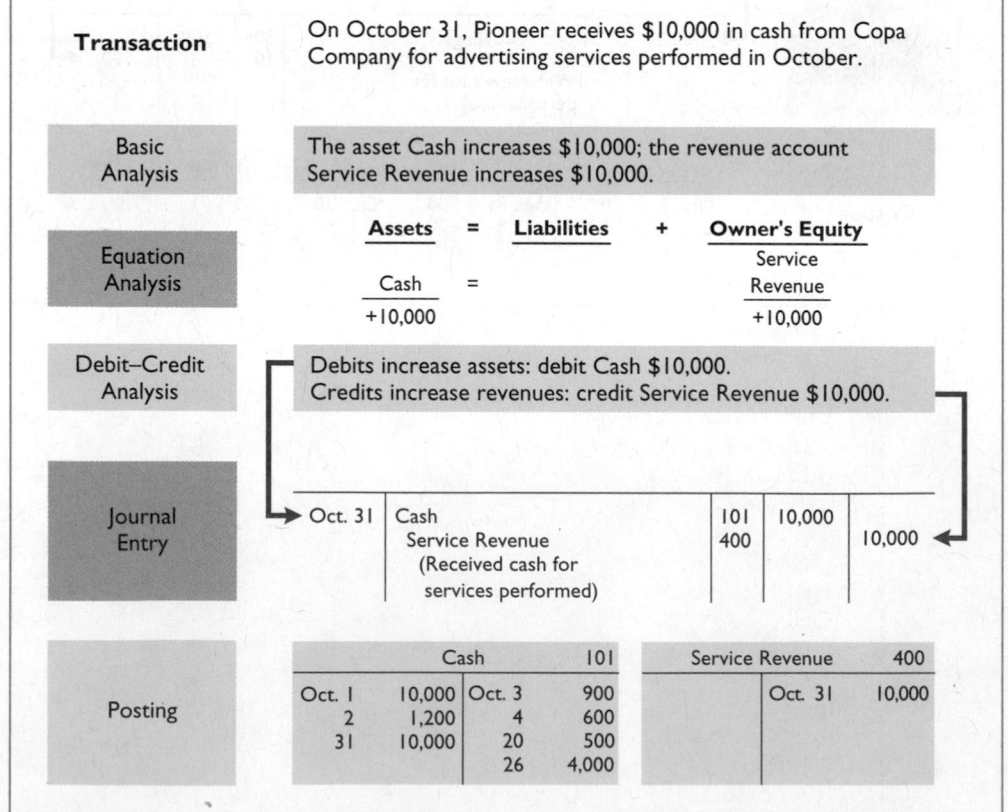

Transaction	On October 31, Pioneer receives $10,000 in cash from Copa Company for advertising services performed in October.
Basic Analysis	The asset Cash increases $10,000; the revenue account Service Revenue increases $10,000.
Equation Analysis	**Assets** = **Liabilities** + **Owner's Equity** Service Revenue
	Cash = +10,000 +10,000
Debit–Credit Analysis	Debits increase assets: debit Cash $10,000. Credits increase revenues: credit Service Revenue $10,000.

Journal Entry

Oct. 31	Cash	101	10,000	
	Service Revenue	400		10,000
	(Received cash for services performed)			

Posting

		Cash		101		Service Revenue		400
Oct. 1	10,000	Oct. 3		900			Oct. 31	10,000
2	1,200	4		600				
31	10,000	20		500				
		26		4,000				

> **DO IT!**

Posting

Kate Browne recorded the following transactions in a general journal during the month of March.

Mar. 4	Cash		2,280	
	Service Revenue			2,280
15	Salaries and Wages Expense		400	
	Cash			400
19	Utilities Expense		92	
	Cash			92

Post these entries to the Cash account of the general ledger to determine its ending balance. The beginning balance of Cash on March 1 was $600.

Action Plan

✔ Recall that posting involves transferring the journalized debits and credits to specific accounts in the ledger.

✔ Determine the ending balance by netting the total debits and credits.

Solution

Cash			
3/1	600	3/15	400
3/4	2,280	3/19	92
3/31 Bal.	2,388		

Related exercise material: **BE2-7, BE2-8, E2-8, E2-12, and DO IT! 2-3.**

✔ The Navigator

Summary Illustration of Journalizing and Posting

Illustration 2-29 shows the journal for Pioneer Advertising Agency for October.

GENERAL JOURNAL				PAGE J1
Date	**Account Titles and Explanation**	**Ref.**	**Debit**	**Credit**
2014				
Oct. 1	Cash	101	10,000	
	Owner's Capital	301		10,000
	(Owner's investment of cash in business)			
1	Equipment	157	5,000	
	Notes Payable	200		5,000
	(Issued 3-month, 12% note for office equipment)			
2	Cash	101	1,200	
	Unearned Service Revenue	209		1,200
	(Received cash from R. Knox for future service)			
3	Rent Expense	729	900	
	Cash	101		900
	(Paid October rent)			
4	Prepaid Insurance	130	600	
	Cash	101		600
	(Paid one-year policy; effective date October 1)			
5	Supplies	126	2,500	
	Accounts Payable	201		2,500
	(Purchased supplies on account from Aero Supply)			

Illustration 2-29
General journal entries

(continued)

Illustration 2-29
(*continued*)

Date	Account Titles and Explanation	Ref.	Debit	Credit
20	Owner's Drawings	306	500	
	Cash	101		500
	(Withdrew cash for personal use)			
26	Salaries and Wages Expense	726	4,000	
	Cash	101		4,000
	(Paid salaries to date)			
31	Cash	101	10,000	
	Service Revenue	400		10,000
	(Received cash for services performed)			

Illustration 2-30
General ledger

Illustration 2-30 shows the ledger, with all balances in red.

GENERAL LEDGER

Cash   No. 101

Date	Explanation	Ref.	Debit	Credit	Balance
2014					
Oct. 1		J1	10,000		10,000
2		J1	1,200		11,200
3		J1		900	10,300
4		J1		600	9,700
20		J1		500	9,200
26		J1		4,000	5,200
31		J1	10,000		**15,200**

Supplies   No. 126

Date	Explanation	Ref.	Debit	Credit	Balance
2014					
Oct. 5		J1	2,500		**2,500**

Prepaid Insurance   No. 130

Date	Explanation	Ref.	Debit	Credit	Balance
2014					
Oct. 4		J1	600		**600**

Equipment   No. 157

Date	Explanation	Ref.	Debit	Credit	Balance
2014					
Oct. 1		J1	5,000		**5,000**

Notes Payable   No. 200

Date	Explanation	Ref.	Debit	Credit	Balance
2014					
Oct. 1		J1		5,000	**5,000**

Accounts Payable   No. 201

Date	Explanation	Ref.	Debit	Credit	Balance
2014					
Oct. 5		J1		2,500	**2,500**

Unearned Service Revenue   No. 209

Date	Explanation	Ref.	Debit	Credit	Balance
2014					
Oct. 2		J1		1,200	**1,200**

Owner's Capital   No. 301

Date	Explanation	Ref.	Debit	Credit	Balance
2014					
Oct. 1		J1		10,000	**10,000**

Owner's Drawings   No. 306

Date	Explanation	Ref.	Debit	Credit	Balance
2014					
Oct. 20		J1	500		**500**

Service Revenue   No. 400

Date	Explanation	Ref.	Debit	Credit	Balance
2014					
Oct. 31		J1		10,000	**10,000**

Salaries and Wages Expense   No. 726

Date	Explanation	Ref.	Debit	Credit	Balance
2014					
Oct. 26		J1	4,000		**4,000**

Rent Expense   No. 729

Date	Explanation	Ref.	Debit	Credit	Balance
2014					
Oct. 3		J1	900		**900**

The Trial Balance

LEARNING OBJECTIVE 7

Prepare a trial balance and explain its purposes.

A **trial balance** is a list of accounts and their balances at a given time. Customarily, companies prepare a trial balance at the end of an accounting period. They list accounts in the order in which they appear in the ledger. Debit balances appear in the left column and credit balances in the right column.

The trial balance proves the mathematical equality of debits and credits after posting. Under the double-entry system, this equality occurs when the sum of the debit account balances equals the sum of the credit account balances. A trial balance may also uncover errors in journalizing and posting. For example, a trial balance may well have detected the error at MF Global discussed in the Feature Story. In addition, a trial balance is useful in the preparation of financial statements, as we will explain in the next two chapters.

The steps for preparing a trial balance are:

1. List the account titles and their balances in the appropriate debit or credit column.
2. Total the debit and credit columns.
3. Prove the equality of the two columns.

Illustration 2-31 shows the trial balance prepared from Pioneer Advertising's ledger. Note that the total debits equal the total credits.

Illustration 2-31
A trial balance

Helpful Hint Note that the order of presentation in the trial balance is:
Assets
Liabilities
Owner's equity
Revenues
Expenses

PIONEER ADVERTISING AGENCY Trial Balance October 31, 2014		
	Debit	**Credit**
Cash	$ 15,200	
Supplies	2,500	
Prepaid Insurance	600	
Equipment	5,000	
Notes Payable		$ 5,000
Accounts Payable		2,500
Unearned Service Revenue		1,200
Owner's Capital		10,000
Owner's Drawings	500	
Service Revenue		10,000
Salaries and Wages Expense	4,000	
Rent Expense	900	
	$28,700	**$28,700**

A trial balance is a necessary checkpoint for uncovering certain types of errors. For example, if only the debit portion of a journal entry has been posted, the trial balance would bring this error to light.

Limitations of a Trial Balance

A trial balance does not guarantee freedom from recording errors, however. Numerous errors may exist even though the totals of the trial balance columns agree. For example, the trial balance may balance even when:

1. A transaction is not journalized.
2. A correct journal entry is not posted.
3. A journal entry is posted twice.
4. Incorrect accounts are used in journalizing or posting.
5. Offsetting errors are made in recording the amount of a transaction.

As long as equal debits and credits are posted, even to the wrong account or in the wrong amount, the total debits will equal the total credits. **The trial balance does not prove that the company has recorded all transactions or that the ledger is correct.**

Ethics Note

An *error* is the result of an unintentional mistake; it is neither ethical nor unethical. An *irregularity* is an intentional misstatement, which *is* viewed as unethical.

Locating Errors

Errors in a trial balance generally result from mathematical mistakes, incorrect postings, or simply transcribing data incorrectly. What do you do if you are faced with a trial balance that does not balance? First, determine the amount of the difference between the two columns of the trial balance. After this amount is known, the following steps are often helpful:

1. If the error is $1, $10, $100, or $1,000, re-add the trial balance columns and recompute the account balances.
2. If the error is divisible by 2, scan the trial balance to see whether a balance equal to half the error has been entered in the wrong column.
3. If the error is divisible by 9, retrace the account balances on the trial balance to see whether they are incorrectly copied from the ledger. For example, if a balance was $12 and it was listed as $21, a $9 error has been made. Reversing the order of numbers is called a **transposition error**.
4. If the error is not divisible by 2 or 9, scan the ledger to see whether an account balance in the amount of the error has been omitted from the trial balance, and scan the journal to see whether a posting of that amount has been omitted.

Use of Dollar Signs

Note that dollar signs do not appear in journals or ledgers. Dollar signs are typically used only in the trial balance and the financial statements. Generally, a dollar sign is shown only for the first item in the column and for the total of that column. A single line (a totaling rule) is placed under the column of figures to be added or subtracted. Total amounts are double-underlined to indicate they are final sums.

Enviromatic/iStockphoto

INVESTOR INSIGHT

Why Accuracy Matters

While most companies record transactions very carefully, the reality is that mistakes still happen. For example, bank regulators fined Bank One Corporation (now Chase) $1.8 million because they felt that the unreliability of the bank's accounting system caused it to violate regulatory requirements.

Also, in recent years Fannie Mae, the government-chartered mortgage association, announced a series of large accounting errors. These announcements caused alarm among investors, regulators, and politicians because they fear that the errors may suggest larger, undetected problems. This is important because the home-mortgage market depends on Fannie Mae to buy hundreds of billions of dollars of mortgages each year from banks, thus enabling the banks to issue new mortgages.

Finally, before a major overhaul of its accounting system, the financial records of Waste Management Inc. were in such disarray that of the company's 57,000 employees, 10,000 were receiving pay slips that were in error.

The Sarbanes-Oxley Act was created to minimize the occurrence of errors like these by increasing every employee's responsibility for accurate financial reporting.

 In order for these companies to prepare and issue financial statements, their accounting equations (debits and credits) must have been in balance at year-end. How could these errors or misstatements have occurred? (See page 95.)

> DO IT!

Trial Balance

The following accounts come from the ledger of SnowGo Company at December 31, 2014.

157	Equipment	$88,000	301	Owner's Capital	$20,000
306	Owner's Drawings	8,000	212	Salaries and Wages	
201	Accounts Payable	22,000		Payable	2,000
726	Salaries and Wages		200	Notes Payable	19,000
	Expense	42,000	732	Utilities Expense	3,000
112	Accounts Receivable	4,000	130	Prepaid Insurance	6,000
400	Service Revenue	95,000	101	Cash	7,000

Prepare a trial balance in good form.

Solution

Action Plan

✔ Determine normal balances and list accounts in the order they appear in the ledger.

✔ Accounts with debit balances appear in the left column, and those with credit balances in the right column.

✔ Total the debit and credit columns to prove equality.

SNOWGO COMPANY
Trial Balance
December 31, 2014

	Debit	Credit
Cash	$ 7,000	
Accounts Receivable	4,000	
Prepaid Insurance	6,000	
Equipment	88,000	
Notes Payable		$ 19,000
Accounts Payable		22,000
Salaries and Wages Payable		2,000
Owner's Capital		20,000
Owner's Drawings	8,000	
Service Revenue		95,000
Utilities Expense	3,000	
Salaries and Wages Expense	42,000	
	$158,000	$158,000

Related exercise material: **BE2-9, BE2-10, E2-9, E2-10, E2-11, E2-13, E2-14, and DO IT! 2-4.**

✔ The Navigator

> Comprehensive DO IT!

Bob Sample opened the Campus Laundromat on September 1, 2014. During the first month of operations, the following transactions occurred.

Sept. 1. Bob invested $20,000 cash in the business.
2 The company paid $1,000 cash for store rent for September.
3 Purchased washers and dryers for $25,000, paying $10,000 in cash and signing a $15,000, 6-month, 12% note payable.
4 Paid $1,200 for a one-year accident insurance policy.
10 Received a bill from the *Daily News* for advertising the opening of the laundromat $200.
20 Bob withdrew $700 cash for personal use.
30 The company determined that cash receipts for laundry services for the month were $6,200.

The chart of accounts for the company is the same as that for Pioneer Advertising Agency plus No. 610 Advertising Expense.

Instructions

(a) Journalize the September transactions. (Use J1 for the journal page number.)

(b) Open ledger accounts and post the September transactions.

(c) Prepare a trial balance at September 30, 2014.

Solution to Comprehensive DO IT!

(a)

	GENERAL JOURNAL			J1
Date	**Account Titles and Explanation**	**Ref.**	**Debit**	**Credit**
2014				
Sept. 1	Cash	101	20,000	
	Owner's Capital	301		20,000
	(Owner's investment of cash in business)			
2	Rent Expense	729	1,000	
	Cash	101		1,000
	(Paid September rent)			
3	Equipment	157	25,000	
	Cash	101		10,000
	Notes Payable	200		15,000
	(Purchased laundry equipment for cash and 6-month, 12% note payable)			
4	Prepaid Insurance	130	1,200	
	Cash	101		1,200
	(Paid one-year insurance policy)			
10	Advertising Expense	610	200	
	Accounts Payable	201		200
	(Received bill from Daily News for advertising)			
20	Owner's Drawings	306	700	
	Cash	101		700
	(Withdrew cash for personal use)			
30	Cash	101	6,200	
	Service Revenue	400		6,200
	(Received cash for services performed)			

(b)   GENERAL LEDGER

Cash   **No. 101**

Date	Explanation	Ref.	Debit	Credit	Balance
2014					
Sept. 1		J1	20,000		20,000
2		J1		1,000	19,000
3		J1		10,000	9,000
4		J1		1,200	7,800
20		J1		700	7,100
30		J1	6,200		13,300

Prepaid Insurance   **No. 130**

Date	Explanation	Ref.	Debit	Credit	Balance
2014					
Sept. 4		J1	1,200		1,200

Equipment   **No. 157**

Date	Explanation	Ref.	Debit	Credit	Balance
2014					
Sept. 3		J1	25,000		25,000

Notes Payable   **No. 200**

Date	Explanation	Ref.	Debit	Credit	Balance
2014					
Sept. 3		J1		15,000	15,000

Accounts Payable   **No. 201**

Date	Explanation	Ref.	Debit	Credit	Balance
2014					
Sept. 10		J1		200	200

Owner's Capital   **No. 301**

Date	Explanation	Ref.	Debit	Credit	Balance
2014					
Sept. 1		J1		20,000	20,000

Owner's Drawings   **No. 306**

Date	Explanation	Ref.	Debit	Credit	Balance
2014					
Sept. 20		J1	700		700

(b)

GENERAL LEDGER (*continued*)

Service Revenue					No. 400
Date	Explanation	Ref.	Debit	Credit	Balance
2014					
Sept. 30		J1		6,200	6,200

Advertising Expense					No. 610
Date	Explanation	Ref.	Debit	Credit	Balance
2014					
Sept. 10		J1	200		200

Rent Expense					No. 729
Date	Explanation	Ref.	Debit	Credit	Balance
2014					
Sept. 2		J1	1,000		1,000

(c)

CAMPUS LAUNDROMAT
Trial Balance
September 30, 2014

	Debit	Credit
Cash	$13,300	
Prepaid Insurance	1,200	
Equipment	25,000	
Notes Payable		$15,000
Accounts Payable		200
Owner's Capital		20,000
Owner's Drawings	700	
Service Revenue		6,200
Advertising Expense	200	
Rent Expense	1,000	
	$41,400	$41,400

The Navigator

SUMMARY OF LEARNING OBJECTIVES

The Navigator

1 **Explain what an account is and how it helps in the recording process.** An account is a record of increases and decreases in specific asset, liability, and owner's equity items.

2 **Define debits and credits and explain their use in recording business transactions.** The terms debit and credit are synonymous with left and right. Assets, drawings, and expenses are increased by debits and decreased by credits. Liabilities, owner's capital, and revenues are increased by credits and decreased by debits.

3 **Identify the basic steps in the recording process.** The basic steps in the recording process are (a) analyze each transaction for its effects on the accounts, (b) enter the transaction information in a journal, (c) transfer the journal information to the appropriate accounts in the ledger.

4 **Explain what a journal is and how it helps in the recording process.** The initial accounting record of a transaction is entered in a journal before the data are entered in the accounts. A journal (a) discloses in one place the complete effects of a transaction, (b) provides a chronological record of transactions, and (c) prevents or locates errors because the debit and credit amounts for each entry can be easily compared.

5 **Explain what a ledger is and how it helps in the recording process.** The ledger is the entire group of accounts maintained by a company. The ledger provides the balance in each of the accounts as well as keeps track of changes in these balances.

6 **Explain what posting is and how it helps in the recording process.** Posting is the transfer of journal entries to the ledger accounts. This phase of the recording process accumulates the effects of journalized transactions in the individual accounts.

7 **Prepare a trial balance and explain its purposes.** A trial balance is a list of accounts and their balances at a given time. Its primary purpose is to prove the equality of debits and credits after posting. A trial balance also uncovers errors in journalizing and posting and is useful in preparing financial statements.

GLOSSARY

Account A record of increases and decreases in specific asset, liability, or owner's equity items. (p. 54).

Chart of accounts A list of accounts and the account numbers that identify their location in the ledger. (p. 65).

Compound entry A journal entry that involves three or more accounts. (p. 60).

Credit The right side of an account. (p. 54).

Debit The left side of an account. (p. 54).

Double-entry system A system that records in appropriate accounts the dual effect of each transaction. (p. 55).

General journal The most basic form of journal. (p. 59).

General ledger A ledger that contains all asset, liability, and owner's equity accounts. (p. 62).

Journal An accounting record in which transactions are initially recorded in chronological order. (p. 59).

Journalizing The entering of transaction data in the journal. (p. 59).

Ledger The entire group of accounts maintained by a company. (p. 62).

Normal balance An account balance on the side where an increase in the account is recorded. (p. 55).

Posting The procedure of transferring journal entries to the ledger accounts. (p. 63).

Simple entry A journal entry that involves only two accounts. (p. 60).

T-account The basic form of an account. (p. 54).

Three-column form of account A form with columns for debit, credit, and balance amounts in an account. (p. 63).

Trial balance A list of accounts and their balances at a given time. (p. 72).

 Self-Test, Brief Exercises, Exercises, Problem Set A, and many more components are available for practice in *WileyPLUS*.

SELF-TEST QUESTIONS

Answers are on page 96.

(LO 1) **1.** Which of the following statements about an account is **true**?
  (a) In its simplest form, an account consists of two parts.
  (b) An account is an individual accounting record of increases and decreases in specific asset, liability, and owner's equity items.
  (c) There are separate accounts for specific assets and liabilities but only one account for owner's equity items.
  (d) The left side of an account is the credit or decrease side.

(LO 2) **2.** Debits:
  (a) increase both assets and liabilities.
  (b) decrease both assets and liabilities.
  (c) increase assets and decrease liabilities.
  (d) decrease assets and increase liabilities.

(LO 2) **3.** A revenue account:
  (a) is increased by debits.
  (b) is decreased by credits.
  (c) has a normal balance of a debit.
  (d) is increased by credits.

(LO 2) **4.** Accounts that normally have debit balances are:
  (a) assets, expenses, and revenues.
  (b) assets, expenses, and owner's capital.
  (c) assets, liabilities, and owner's drawings.
  (d) assets, owner's drawings, and expenses.

(LO 2) **5.** The expanded accounting equation is:
  (a) Assets + Liabilities = Owner's Capital + Owner's Drawings + Revenues + Expenses
  (b) Assets = Liabilities + Owner's Capital + Owner's Drawings + Revenues − Expenses

  (c) Assets = Liabilities − Owner's Capital − Owner's Drawings − Revenues − Expenses
  (d) Assets = Liabilities + Owner's Capital − Owner's Drawings + Revenues − Expenses

6. Which of the following is **not** part of the recording process? (LO 3)
  (a) Analyzing transactions.
  (b) Preparing a trial balance.
  (c) Entering transactions in a journal.
  (d) Posting transactions.

7. Which of the following statements about a journal is (LO 4) **false**?
  (a) It is not a book of original entry.
  (b) It provides a chronological record of transactions.
  (c) It helps to locate errors because the debit and credit amounts for each entry can be readily compared.
  (d) It discloses in one place the complete effect of a transaction.

8. The purchase of supplies on account should result in: (LO 4)
  (a) a debit to Supplies Expense and a credit to Cash.
  (b) a debit to Supplies Expense and a credit to Accounts Payable.
  (c) a debit to Supplies and a credit to Accounts Payable.
  (d) a debit to Supplies and a credit to Accounts Receivable.

9. The order of the accounts in the ledger is: (LO 5)
  (a) assets, revenues, expenses, liabilities, owner's capital, owner's drawings.
  (b) assets, liabilities, owner's capital, owner's drawings, revenues, expenses.
  (c) owner's capital, assets, revenues, expenses, liabilities, owner's drawings.
  (d) revenues, assets, expenses, liabilities, owner's capital, owner's drawings.

(LO 5) 10. A ledger:
(a) contains only asset and liability accounts.
(b) should show accounts in alphabetical order.
(c) is a collection of the entire group of accounts maintained by a company.
(d) is a book of original entry.

(LO 6) 11. Posting:
(a) normally occurs before journalizing.
(b) transfers ledger transaction data to the journal.
(c) is an optional step in the recording process.
(d) transfers journal entries to ledger accounts.

(LO 6) 12. Before posting a payment of $5,000, the Accounts Payable of Senator Company had a normal balance of $16,000. The balance after posting this transaction was:
(a) $21,000.   (c) $11,000.
(b) $5,000.   (d) Cannot be determined.

(LO 7) 13. A trial balance:
(a) is a list of accounts with their balances at a given time.
(b) proves the mathematical accuracy of journalized transactions.

(c) will not balance if a correct journal entry is posted twice.
(d) proves that all transactions have been recorded.

14. A trial balance will not balance if: **(LO 7)**
(a) a correct journal entry is posted twice.
(b) the purchase of supplies on account is debited to Supplies and credited to Cash.
(c) a $100 cash drawing by the owner is debited to Owner's Drawings for $1,000 and credited to Cash for $100.
(d) a $450 payment on account is debited to Accounts Payable for $45 and credited to Cash for $45.

15. The trial balance of Jeong Company had accounts **(LO 7)** with the following normal balances: Cash $5,000, Service Revenue $85,000, Salaries and Wages Payable $4,000, Salaries and Wages Expense $40,000, Rent Expense $10,000, Owner's Capital $42,000; Owner's Drawings $15,000; Equipment $61,000. In preparing a trial balance, the total in the debit column is:
(a) $131,000.   (c) $91,000.
(b) $216,000.   (d) $116,000.

Go to the book's companion website, www.wiley.com/college/weygandt, for additional Self-Test Questions.

✔ **The Navigator**

QUESTIONS

1. Describe the parts of a T-account.
2. "The terms debit and credit mean increase and decrease, respectively." Do you agree? Explain.
3. Heath Precourt, a fellow student, contends that the double-entry system means each transaction must be recorded twice. Is Heath correct? Explain.
4. Erica Mendez, a beginning accounting student, believes debit balances are favorable and credit balances are unfavorable. Is Erica correct? Discuss.
5. State the rules of debit and credit as applied to (a) asset accounts, (b) liability accounts, and (c) the owner's equity accounts (revenue, expenses, owner's drawings, and owner's capital).
6. What is the normal balance for each of the following accounts? (a) Accounts Receivable. (b) Cash. (c) Owner's Drawings. (d) Accounts Payable. (e) Service Revenue. (f) Salaries and Wages Expense. (g) Owner's Capital.
7. Indicate whether each of the following accounts is an asset, a liability, or an owner's equity account and whether it has a normal debit or credit balance: (a) Accounts Receivable, (b) Accounts Payable, (c) Equipment, (d) Owner's Drawings, (e) Supplies.
8. For the following transactions, indicate the account debited and the account credited.
(a) Supplies are purchased on account.
(b) Cash is received on signing a note payable.
(c) Employees are paid salaries in cash.
9. Indicate whether the following accounts generally will have (a) debit entries only, (b) credit entries only, or (c) both debit and credit entries.

(1) Cash.
(2) Accounts Receivable.
(3) Owner's Drawings.
(4) Accounts Payable.
(5) Salaries and Wages Expense.
(6) Service Revenue.

10. What are the basic steps in the recording process?
11. What are the advantages of using a journal in the recording process?
12. (a) When entering a transaction in the journal, should the debit or credit be written first?
(b) Which should be indented, the debit or credit?
13. Describe a compound entry, and provide an example.
14. (a) Should business transaction debits and credits be recorded directly in the ledger accounts?
(b) What are the advantages of first recording transactions in the journal and then posting to the ledger?
15. The account number is entered as the last step in posting the amounts from the journal to the ledger. What is the advantage of this step?
16. Journalize the following business transactions.
(a) Qing Wei invests $9,000 cash in the business.
(b) Insurance of $800 is paid for the year.
(c) Supplies of $2,000 are purchased on account.
(d) Cash of $7,500 is received for services performed.
17. (a) What is a ledger?
(b) What is a chart of accounts and why is it important?
18. What is a trial balance and what are its purposes?
19. Victor Grimm is confused about how accounting information flows through the accounting system. He believes the flow of information is as follows.
(a) Debits and credits posted to the ledger.
(b) Business transaction occurs.

(c) Information entered in the journal.
(d) Financial statements are prepared.
(e) Trial balance is prepared.
Is Victor correct? If not, indicate to Victor the proper flow of the information.

20. Two students are discussing the use of a trial balance. They wonder whether the following errors, each considered separately, would prevent the trial balance from balancing.

(a) The bookkeeper debited Cash for $600 and credited Salaries and Wages Expense for $600 for payment of wages.
(b) Cash collected on account was debited to Cash for $900 and Service Revenue was credited for $90. What would you tell them?

21. What are the normal balances for Apple's Cash, Accounts Payable, and Interest Expense accounts?

BRIEF EXERCISES

Indicate debit and credit effects and normal balance.
(LO 2)

BE2-1 For each of the following accounts, indicate the effects of (a) a debit and (b) a credit on the accounts and (c) the normal balance of the account.

1. Accounts Payable.
2. Advertising Expense.
3. Service Revenue.
4. Accounts Receivable.
5. Owner's Capital.
6. Owner's Drawings.

Identify accounts to be debited and credited.
(LO 2)

BE2-2 Transactions for the George Lynch Company for the month of June are presented below. Identify the accounts to be debited and credited for each transaction.

June 1   George Lynch invests $5,000 cash in a small welding business of which he is the sole proprietor.
2   Purchases equipment on account for $2,100.
3    $800 cash is paid to landlord for June rent.
12   Sends a bill to M. Rodero for $300 for welding work performed on account.

Journalize transactions.
(LO 4)

BE2-3 Using the data in BE2-2, journalize the transactions. (You may omit explanations.)

Identify and explain steps in recording process.
(LO 3)

BE2-4 ———— Raymond Faust, a fellow student, is unclear about the basic steps in the recording process. Identify and briefly explain the steps in the order in which they occur.

Indicate basic and debit-credit analysis.
(LO 2)

BE2-5 H. Xiao has the following transactions during August of the current year. Indicate (a) the effect on the accounting equation and (b) the debit-credit analysis illustrated on pages 66–70 of the text.

Aug. 1   Opens an office as a financial advisor, investing $8,000 in cash.
4   Pays insurance in advance for 6 months, $1,800 cash.
16   Receives $3,400 from clients for services performed.
27   Pays secretary $1,000 salary.

Journalize transactions.
(LO 4)

BE2-6 Using the data in BE2-5, journalize the transactions. (You may omit explanations.)

Post journal entries to T-accounts.
(LO 6)

BE2-7 Selected transactions for the Joel Berges Company are presented in journal form below. Post the transactions to T-accounts. Make one T-account for each item and determine each account's ending balance.

J1

Date	Account Titles and Explanation	Ref.	Debit	Credit
May 5	Accounts Receivable		4,100	
	Service Revenue			4,100
	(Billed for services performed)			
12	Cash		2,400	
	Accounts Receivable			2,400
	(Received cash in payment of account)			
15	Cash		3,000	
	Service Revenue			3,000
	(Received cash for services performed)			

BE2-8 Selected journal entries for the Joel Berges Company are presented in BE2-7. Post the transactions using the standard form of account.

Post journal entries to standard form of account.
(LO 6)

BE2-9 From the ledger balances given below, prepare a trial balance for the Deroche Company at June 30, 2014. List the accounts in the order shown on page 73 of the text. All account balances are normal.

Prepare a trial balance.
(LO 7)

Accounts Payable $9,000, Cash $5,800, Owner's Capital $15,000, Owner's Drawings $1,200, Equipment $17,000, Service Revenue $10,000, Accounts Receivable $3,000, Salaries and Wages Expense $6,000, and Rent Expense $1,000.

BE2-10 An inexperienced bookkeeper prepared the following trial balance. Prepare a correct trial balance, assuming all account balances are normal.

Prepare a correct trial balance.
(LO 7)

HUEWITT COMPANY
Trial Balance
December 31, 2014

	Debit	Credit
Cash	$10,800	
Prepaid Insurance		$ 3,500
Accounts Payable		3,000
Unearned Service Revenue	2,200	
Owner's Capital		9,000
Owner's Drawings		4,500
Service Revenue		25,600
Salaries and Wages Expense	18,600	
Rent Expense		2,400
	$31,600	$48,000

> DO IT! Review

DO IT! 2-1 Ivan Klumb has just rented space in a strip mall. In this space, he will open a photography studio, to be called "Picture This!" A friend has advised Ivan to set up a double-entry set of accounting records in which to record all of his business transactions.

Identify the balance sheet accounts that Ivan will likely need to record the transactions needed to open his business. Indicate whether the normal balance of each account is a debit or credit.

Identify normal balances.
(LO 2)

DO IT! 2-2 Ivan Klumb engaged in the following activities in establishing his photography studio, Picture This!:

Record business activities.
(LO 4)

1. Opened a bank account in the name of Picture This! and deposited $6,300 of his own money into this account as his initial investment.

2. Purchased photography supplies at a total cost of $1,100. The business paid $400 in cash and the balance is on account.

3. Obtained estimates on the cost of photography equipment from three different manufacturers.

In what form (type of record) should Ivan record these three activities? Prepare the entries to record the transactions.

DO IT! 2-3 Ivan Klumb recorded the following transactions during the month of April.

Post transactions.
(LO 6)

April 3	Cash	3,400	
	Service Revenue		3,400
April 16	Rent Expense	700	
	Cash		700
April 20	Salaries and Wages Expense	300	
	Cash		300

Post these entries to the Cash T-account of the general ledger to determine the ending balance in cash. The beginning balance in cash on April 1 was $1,600.

Prepare a trial balance.
(LO 7)

DO IT! 2-4 The following accounts are taken from the ledger of Recha Company at December 31, 2014.

200	Notes Payable	$20,000	101	Cash		$ 6,000
301	Owner's Capital	28,000	126	Supplies		6,000
157	Equipment	80,000	729	Rent Expense		4,000
306	Owner's Drawings	8,000	212	Salaries and Wages Payable		3,000
726	Salaries and Wages Expense	38,000	201	Accounts Payable		11,000
400	Service Revenue	88,000	112	Accounts Receivable		8,000

Prepare a trial balance in good form.

EXERCISES

Analyze statements about accounting and the recording process.
(LO 1)

E2-1 Lixun Zhang has prepared the following list of statements about accounts.

1. An account is an accounting record of either a specific asset or a specific liability.
2. An account shows only increases, not decreases, in the item it relates to.
3. Some items, such as Cash and Accounts Receivable, are combined into one account.
4. An account has a left, or credit side, and a right, or debit side.
5. A simple form of an account consisting of just the account title, the left side, and the right side, is called a T-account.

Instructions
Identify each statement as true or false. If false, indicate how to correct the statement.

Identify debits, credits, and normal balances.
(LO 2)

E2-2 Selected transactions for R. Sparks, an interior decorator, in her first month of business, are as follows.

Jan.	2	Invested $10,000 cash in business.
	3	Purchased used car for $4,000 cash for use in business.
	9	Purchased supplies on account for $500.
	11	Billed customers $2,100 for services performed.
	16	Paid $350 cash for advertising.
	20	Received $700 cash from customers billed on January 11.
	23	Paid creditor $300 cash on balance owed.
	28	Withdrew $1,000 cash for personal use by owner.

Instructions
For each transaction, indicate the following.

(a) The basic type of account debited and credited (asset, liability, owner's equity).
(b) The specific account debited and credited (Cash, Rent Expense, Service Revenue, etc.).
(c) Whether the specific account is increased or decreased.
(d) The normal balance of the specific account.

Use the following format, in which the January 2 transaction is given as an example.

	Account Debited				Account Credited			
Date	(a) Basic Type	(b) Specific Account	(c) Effect	(d) Normal Balance	(a) Basic Type	(b) Specific Account	(c) Effect	(d) Normal Balance
Jan. 2	Asset	Cash	Increase	Debit	Owner's Equity	Owner's Capital	Increase	Credit

Journalize transactions.
(LO 4)

E2-3 Data for R. Sparks, interior decorator, are presented in E2-2.

Instructions
Journalize the transactions using journal page J1. (You may omit explanations.)

Analyze transactions and determine their effect on accounts.
(LO 2)

E2-4 Presented below is information related to Lachapelle Real Estate Agency.

Oct.	1	Arthur Lachapelle begins business as a real estate agent with a cash investment of $15,000.
	2	Hires an administrative assistant.
	3	Purchases office furniture for $1,900, on account.

6   Sells a house and lot for J. Baxter; bills J. Baxter $3,600 for realty services performed.
27 Pays $1,100 on the balance related to the transaction of October 3.
30 Pays the administrative assistant $2,500 in salary for October.

Instructions
Prepare the debit-credit analysis for each transaction as illustrated on pages 66–70.

E2-5 Transaction data for Lachapelle Real Estate Agency are presented in E2-4.

Journalize transactions.
(LO 4)

Instructions
Journalize the transactions. (You may omit explanations.)

E2-6 Federlin Industries had the following transactions.

Analyze transactions and journalize.
(LO 2, 3, 4)

1. Borrowed $5,000 from the bank by signing a note.
2. Paid $3,100 cash for a computer.
3. Purchased $850 of supplies on account.

Instructions
(a) Indicate what accounts are increased and decreased by each transaction.
(b) Journalize each transaction. (Omit explanations.)

E2-7 Kahl Enterprises had the following selected transactions.

Analyze transactions and journalize.
(LO 2, 3, 4)

1. Jo Kahl invested $4,000 cash in the business.
2. Paid office rent of $950.
3. Performed consulting services and billed a client $5,200.
4. Jo Kahl withdrew $750 cash for personal use.

Instructions
(a) Indicate the effect each transaction has on the accounting equation (Assets = Liabilities + Owner's Equity), using plus and minus signs.
(b) Journalize each transaction. (Omit explanations.)

E2-8 Janet Miyoshi has prepared the following list of statements about the general ledger.

Analyze statements about the ledger.
(LO 5)

1. The general ledger contains all the asset and liability accounts but no owner's equity accounts.
2. The general ledger is sometimes referred to as simply the ledger.
3. The accounts in the general ledger are arranged in alphabetical order.
4. Each account in the general ledger is numbered for easier identification.
5. The general ledger is a book of original entry.

Instructions
Identify each statement as true or false. If false, indicate how to correct the statement.

E2-9 Selected transactions from the journal of Trisha Spoor, investment broker, are presented below.

Post journal entries and prepare a trial balance.
(LO 6, 7)

Date	Account Titles and Explanation	Ref.	Debit	Credit
Aug. 1	Cash		5,000	
	Owner's Capital			5,000
	(Owner's investment of cash in business)			
10	Cash		2,400	
	Service Revenue			2,400
	(Received cash for services performed)			
12	Equipment		5,000	
	Cash			3,000
	Notes Payable			2,000
	(Purchased equipment for cash and notes payable)			
25	Accounts Receivable		1,700	
	Service Revenue			1,700
	(Billed clients for services performed)			
31	Cash		900	
	Accounts Receivable			900
	(Receipt of cash on account)			

Journalize transactions from account data and prepare a trial balance.

(LO 4, 7)

Instructions

(a) Post the transactions to T-accounts.

(b) Prepare a trial balance at August 31, 2014.

E2-10 The T-accounts below summarize the ledger of Zimmer Landscaping Company at the end of the first month of operations.

Cash			No. 101
4/1	12,000	4/15	1,300
4/12	900	4/25	1,500
4/29	400		
4/30	1,000		

Accounts Receivable			No. 112
4/7	3,200	4/29	400

Supplies			No. 126
4/4	1,800		

Accounts Payable			No. 201
4/25	1,500	4/4	1,800

Unearned Service Revenue			No. 209
		4/30	1,000

Owner's Capital			No. 301
		4/1	12,000

Service Revenue			No. 400
		4/7	3,200
		4/12	900

Salaries and Wages Expense			No. 726
4/15	1,300		

Instructions

(a) Prepare the complete general journal (including explanations) from which the postings to Cash were made.

(b) Prepare a trial balance at April 30, 2014.

Journalize transactions from account data and prepare a trial balance.

(LO 4, 7)

E2-11 Presented below is the ledger for Harbach Co.

Cash			No. 101
10/1	3,000	10/4	400
10/10	500	10/12	1,500
10/10	4,000	10/15	250
10/20	500	10/30	300
10/25	2,000	10/31	500

Accounts Receivable			No. 112
10/6	800	10/20	500
10/20	940		

Supplies			No. 126
10/4	400		

Equipment			No. 157
10/3	2,000		

Notes Payable			No. 200
		10/10	4,000

Accounts Payable			No. 201
10/12	1,500	10/3	2,000

Owner's Capital			No. 301
		10/1	3,000
		10/25	2,000

Owner's Drawings			No. 306
10/30	300		

Service Revenue			No. 400
		10/6	800
		10/10	500
		10/20	940

Salaries and Wages Expense			No. 726
10/31	500		

Rent Expense			No. 729
10/15	250		

Instructions

(a) Reproduce the journal entries for the transactions that occurred on October 1, 10, and 20, and provide explanations for each.

(b) Determine the October 31 balance for each of the accounts above, and prepare a trial balance at October 31, 2014.

E2-12 Selected transactions for Sandra Linke Company during its first month in business are presented below.

Prepare journal entries and post using standard account form.

(LO 4, 6)

Sept.	1	Invested $10,000 cash in the business.
	5	Purchased equipment for $12,000 paying $4,000 in cash and the balance on account.
	25	Paid $3,000 cash on balance owed for equipment.
	30	Withdrew $700 cash for personal use.

Linke's chart of accounts shows: No. 101 Cash, No. 157 Equipment, No. 201 Accounts Payable, No. 301 Owner's Capital, and No. 306 Owner's Drawings.

Instructions
(a) Journalize the transactions on page J1 of the journal. (Omit explanations.)
(b) Post the transactions using the standard account form.

E2-13 The bookkeeper for Jeff Sobol Equipment Repair made a number of errors in journalizing and posting, as described below.

Analyze errors and their effects on trial balance.

(LO 7)

1. A credit posting of $525 to Accounts Receivable was omitted.
2. A debit posting of $750 for Prepaid Insurance was debited to Insurance Expense.
3. A collection from a customer of $100 in payment of its account owed was journalized and posted as a debit to Cash $100 and a credit to Service Revenue $100.
4. A credit posting of $415 to Property Taxes Payable was made twice.
5. A cash purchase of supplies for $250 was journalized and posted as a debit to Supplies $25 and a credit to Cash $25.
6. A debit of $475 to Advertising Expense was posted as $457.

Instructions
For each error:

(a) Indicate whether the trial balance will balance.
(b) If the trial balance will not balance, indicate the amount of the difference.
(c) Indicate the trial balance column that will have the larger total.

Consider each error separately. Use the following form, in which error (1) is given as an example.

Error	(a) In Balance	(b) Difference	(c) Larger Column
(1)	No	$525	debit

E2-14 The accounts in the ledger of Longoria Delivery Service contain the following balances on July 31, 2014.

Prepare a trial balance.

(LO 2, 7)

Accounts Receivable	$ 7,642	Prepaid Insurance	$ 1,968
Accounts Payable	8,396	Maintenance and Repairs Expense	961
Cash	?	Service Revenue	10,610
Equipment	49,360	Owner's Drawings	700
Gasoline Expense	758	Owner's Capital	42,000
Utilities Expense	523	Salaries and Wages Expense	4,428
Notes Payable	17,000	Salaries and Wages Payable	815

Instructions
Prepare a trial balance with the accounts arranged as illustrated in the chapter and fill in the missing amount for Cash.

EXERCISES: SET B AND CHALLENGE EXERCISES

Visit the book's companion website, at **www.wiley.com/college/weygandt**, and choose the Student Companion site to access Exercise Set B and Challenge Exercises.

PROBLEMS: SET A

Journalize a series of transactions.

(LO 2, 4)

P2-1A McKay Disc Golf Course was opened on March 1 by Evan McKay. The following selected events and transactions occurred during March.

Mar. 1	Invested $20,000 cash in the business.
3	Purchased Sable's Golf Land for $15,000 cash. The price consists of land $12,000, shed $2,000, and equipment $1,000. (Make one compound entry.)
5	Paid advertising expenses of $700.
6	Paid cash $600 for a one-year insurance policy.
10	Purchased golf discs and other equipment for $1,050 from Taylor Company payable in 30 days.
18	Received $1,100 in cash for golf fees (McKay records golf fees as service revenue).
19	Sold 150 coupon books for $10 each. Each book contains 4 coupons that enable the holder to play one round of disc golf.
25	Withdrew $800 cash for personal use.
30	Paid salaries of $250.
30	Paid Taylor Company in full.
31	Received $2,100 cash for golf fees.

McKay Disc Golf uses the following accounts: Cash, Prepaid Insurance, Land, Buildings, Equipment, Accounts Payable, Unearned Service Revenue, Owner's Capital, Owner's Drawings, Service Revenue, Advertising Expense, and Salaries and Wages Expense.

Instructions
Journalize the March transactions.

Journalize transactions, post, and prepare a trial balance.

(LO 2, 4, 6, 7)

P2-2A Bridgette Keyes is a licensed dentist. During the first month of the operation of her business, the following events and transactions occurred.

April 1	Invested $20,000 cash in her business.
1	Hired a secretary-receptionist at a salary of $700 per week payable monthly.
2	Paid office rent for the month $1,100.
3	Purchased dental supplies on account from Smile Company $4,000.
10	Performed dental services and billed insurance companies $5,100.
11	Received $1,000 cash advance from Heather Greene for an implant.
20	Received $2,100 cash for services performed from James Chang.
30	Paid secretary-receptionist for the month $2,800.
30	Paid $2,400 to Smile Company for accounts payable due.

Bridgette uses the following chart of accounts: No. 101 Cash, No. 112 Accounts Receivable, No. 126 Supplies, No. 201 Accounts Payable, No. 209 Unearned Service Revenue, No. 301 Owner's Capital, No. 400 Service Revenue, No. 726 Salaries and Wages Expense, and No. 729 Rent Expense.

Instructions
(a) Journalize the transactions.
(b) Post to the ledger accounts.

(c) Trial balance totals $29,800   **(c)** Prepare a trial balance on April 30, 2014.

Journalize transactions, post, and prepare a trial balance.

(LO 2, 4, 6, 7)

P2-3A Santa Ana Services was formed on May 1, 2014. The following transactions took place during the first month.

Transactions on May 1:

1. Don Humes invested $40,000 cash in the company, as its sole owner.
2. Hired two employees to work in the warehouse. They will each be paid a salary of $3,050 per month.
3. Signed a 2-year rental agreement on a warehouse; paid $24,000 cash in advance for the first year.
4. Purchased furniture and equipment costing $30,000. A cash payment of $10,000 was made immediately; the remainder will be paid in 6 months.
5. Paid $1,800 cash for a one-year insurance policy on the furniture and equipment.

Transactions during the remainder of the month:

6. Purchased basic office supplies for $500 cash.
7. Purchased more office supplies for $1,500 on account.
8. Total revenues earned were $20,000—$8,000 cash and $12,000 on account.
9. Paid $400 to suppliers for accounts payable due.
10. Received $3,000 from customers in payment of accounts receivable.
11. Received utility bills in the amount of $350, to be paid next month.
12. Paid the monthly salaries of the two employees, totalling $6,100.

Instructions
(a) Prepare journal entries to record each of the events listed. (Omit explanations.)
(b) Post the journal entries to T-accounts.
(c) Prepare a trial balance as of May 31, 2014.

(c) Trial balance totals $81,450

P2-4A The trial balance of Marius Santiago Co. shown below does not balance.

Prepare a correct trial balance.

(LO 7)

MARIUS SANTIAGO CO.
Trial Balance
June 30, 2014

	Debit	Credit
Cash		$ 3,340
Accounts Receivable	$ 2,812	
Supplies	1,200	
Equipment	2,600	
Accounts Payable		3,666
Unearned Service Revenue	1,100	
Owner's Capital		8,000
Owner's Drawings	800	
Service Revenue		2,480
Salaries and Wages Expense	3,200	
Utilities Expense	810	
	$12,522	$17,486

Each of the listed accounts has a normal balance per the general ledger. An examination of the ledger and journal reveals the following errors.

1. Cash received from a customer in payment of its account was debited for $580, and Accounts Receivable was credited for the same amount. The actual collection was for $850.
2. The purchase of a computer on account for $710 was recorded as a debit to Supplies for $710 and a credit to Accounts Payable for $710.
3. Services were performed on account for a client for $980. Accounts Receivable was debited for $980, and Service Revenue was credited for $98.
4. A debit posting to Salaries and Wages Expense of $700 was omitted.
5. A payment of a balance due for $306 was credited to Cash for $306 and credited to Accounts Payable for $360.
6. The withdrawal of $600 cash for Santiago's personal use was debited to Salaries and Wages Expense for $600 and credited to Cash for $600.

Instructions
Prepare a correct trial balance. (*Hint:* It helps to prepare the correct journal entry for the transaction described and compare it to the mistake made.)

Trial balance totals $15,462

P2-5A The Lunt Theater, owned by Beth Saxena, will begin operations in March. The Lunt will be unique in that it will show only triple features of sequential theme movies. As of March 1, the ledger of Lunt showed: No. 101 Cash $3,000, No. 140 Land $24,000, No. 145 Buildings (concession stand, projection room, ticket booth, and screen) $10,000, No. 157 Equipment $10,000, No. 201 Accounts Payable $7,000, and No. 301 Owner's Capital $40,000. During the month of March, the following events and transactions occurred.

Journalize transactions, post, and prepare a trial balance.

(LO 2, 4, 6, 7)

Mar. 2   Rented the three *Indiana Jones* movies to be shown for the first 3 weeks of March. The film rental was $3,500; $1,500 was paid in cash and $2,000 will be paid on March 10.

3   Ordered the *Lord of the Rings* movies to be shown the last 10 days of March. It will cost $200 per night.

9	Received $4,000 cash from admissions.	

9   Received $4,000 cash from admissions.
10 Paid balance due on *Indiana Jones* movies rental and $2,100 on March 1 accounts payable.
11 Lunt Theater contracted with John Blume to operate the concession stand. Blume is to pay 15% of gross concession receipts, payable monthly, for the rental of the concession stand.
12 Paid advertising expenses $800.
20 Received $5,000 cash from customers for admissions.
20 Received the *Lord of the Rings* movies and paid the rental fee of $2,000.
31 Paid salaries of $3,100.
31 Received statement from John Blume showing gross receipts from concessions of $6,000 and the balance due to Lunt Theater of $900 ($6,000 × 15%) for March. Blume paid one-half the balance due and will remit the remainder on April 5.
31 Received $9,000 cash from customers for admissions.

In addition to the accounts identified above, the chart of accounts includes: No. 112 Accounts Receivable, No. 400 Service Revenue, No. 429 Rent Revenue, No. 610 Advertising Expense, No. 726 Salaries and Wages Expense, and No. 729 Rent Expense.

Instructions
(a) Enter the beginning balances in the ledger. Insert a check mark (✓) in the reference column of the ledger for the beginning balance.
(b) Journalize the March transactions. Lunt records admission revenue as service revenue, rental of the concession stand as rent revenue, and film rental expense as rent expense.
(c) Post the March journal entries to the ledger. Assume that all entries are posted from page 1 of the journal.
(d) Trial balance totals $63,800   **(d)** Prepare a trial balance on March 31, 2014.

PROBLEMS: SET B

Journalize a series of transactions.

(LO 2, 4)

P2-1B Frontier Park was started on April 1 by M. Preston. The following selected events and transactions occurred during April.

Apr. 1 Preston invested $35,000 cash in the business.
    4 Purchased land costing $27,000 for cash.
    8 Incurred advertising expense of $1,800 on account.
    11 Paid salaries to employees $1,500.
    12 Hired park manager at a salary of $4,000 per month, effective May 1.
    13 Paid $1,650 cash for a one-year insurance policy.
    17 Withdrew $1,000 cash for personal use.
    20 Received $6,800 in cash for admission fees.
    25 Sold 100 coupon books for $25 each. Each book contains 10 coupons that entitle the holder to one admission to the park.
    30 Received $8,900 in cash admission fees.
    30 Paid $900 on balance owed for advertising incurred on April 8.

Frontier Park uses the following accounts: Cash, Prepaid Insurance, Land, Accounts Payable, Unearned Service Revenue, Owner's Capital, Owner's Drawings, Service Revenue, Advertising Expense, and Salaries and Wages Expense.

Instructions
Journalize the April transactions.

Journalize transactions, post, and prepare a trial balance.

(LO 2, 4, 6, 7)

P2-2B Iris Beck is a licensed CPA. During the first month of operations of her business, the following events and transactions occurred.

May 1 Beck invested $20,000 cash in her business.
     2 Hired a secretary-receptionist at a salary of $2,000 per month.
     3 Purchased $2,500 of supplies on account from Tinio Supply Company.
     7 Paid office rent of $900 cash for the month.
    11 Completed a tax assignment and billed client $3,200 for services performed.
    12 Received $3,500 advance on a management consulting engagement.
    17 Received cash of $1,200 for services performed for Misra Co.
    31 Paid secretary-receptionist $2,000 salary for the month.
    31 Paid 60% of balance due Tinio Supply Company.

Iris uses the following chart of accounts: No. 101 Cash, No. 112 Accounts Receivable, No. 126 Supplies, No. 201 Accounts Payable, No. 209 Unearned Service Revenue, No. 301 Owner's Capital, No. 400 Service Revenue, No. 726 Salaries and Wages Expense, and No. 729 Rent Expense.

Instructions
(a) Journalize the transactions.
(b) Post to the ledger accounts.
(c) Prepare a trial balance on May 31, 2014.

(c) Trial balance totals $28,900

P2-3B Tony Vian owns and manages a computer repair service, which had the following trial balance on December 31, 2013 (the end of its fiscal year).

Journalize transactions, post, and prepare a trial balance.
(LO 2, 4, 6, 7)

VIAN REPAIR SERVICE
Trial Balance
December 31, 2013

	Debit	Credit
Cash	$ 8,000	
Accounts Receivable	15,000	
Supplies	13,000	
Prepaid Rent	3,000	
Equipment	20,000	
Accounts Payable		$19,000
Owner's Capital		40,000
	$59,000	$59,000

Summarized transactions for January 2014 were as follows.

1. Advertising costs, paid in cash, $1,000.
2. Additional supplies acquired on account $4,200.
3. Miscellaneous expenses, paid in cash, $2,000.
4. Cash collected from customers in payment of accounts receivable $14,000.
5. Cash paid to creditors for accounts payable due $15,000.
6. Repair services performed during January: for cash $6,000; on account $9,000.
7. Wages for January, paid in cash, $3,500.
8. Tony's drawings during January were $3,000.

Instructions
(a) Open T-accounts for each of the accounts listed in the trial balance, and enter the opening balances for 2014.
(b) Prepare journal entries to record each of the January transactions. (Omit explanations.)
(c) Post the journal entries to the accounts in the ledger. (Add accounts as needed.)
(d) Prepare a trial balance as of January 31, 2014.

(d) Trial balance totals $63,200

P2-4B The trial balance of the Sean Devine Company shown below does not balance.

Prepare a correct trial balance.
(LO 7)

SEAN DEVINE COMPANY
Trial Balance
May 31, 2014

	Debit	Credit
Cash	$ 5,850	
Accounts Receivable		$ 2,750
Prepaid Insurance	700	
Equipment	8,000	
Accounts Payable		4,500
Unearned Service Revenue	650	
Owner's Capital		11,700
Service Revenue	6,690	
Salaries and Wages Expense	4,200	
Advertising Expense		1,100
Utilities Expense	890	
	$26,980	$20,050

Your review of the ledger reveals that each account has a normal balance. You also discover the following errors.

1. The totals of the debit sides of Prepaid Insurance, Accounts Payable, and Utilities Expense were each understated $100.
2. Transposition errors were made in Accounts Receivable and Service Revenue. Based on postings made, the correct balances were $2,570 and $6,960, respectively.
3. A debit posting to Salaries and Wages Expense of $200 was omitted.
4. A $1,000 cash drawing by the owner was debited to Owner's Capital for $1,000 and credited to Cash for $1,000.
5. A $520 purchase of supplies on account was debited to Equipment for $520 and credited to Cash for $520.
6. A cash payment of $540 for advertising was debited to Advertising Expense for $54 and credited to Cash for $54.
7. A collection from a customer for $210 was debited to Cash for $210 and credited to Accounts Payable for $210.

Instructions

Trial balance totals $25,020

Prepare a correct trial balance. Note that the chart of accounts includes the following: Owner's Drawings and Supplies. (*Hint:* It helps to prepare the correct journal entry for the transaction described and compare it to the mistake made.)

Journalize transactions, post, and prepare a trial balance.

(LO 2, 4, 6, 7)

P2-5B The Classic Theater is owned by Kim Lockerby. All facilities were completed on March 31. At this time, the ledger showed: No. 101 Cash $4,000, No. 140 Land $10,000, No. 145 Buildings (concession stand, projection room, ticket booth, and screen) $8,000, No. 157 Equipment $6,000, No. 201 Accounts Payable $2,000, No. 275 Mortgage Payable $8,000, and No. 301 Owner's Capital $18,000. During April, the following events and transactions occurred.

Apr. 2 Paid film rental of $1,100 on first movie.
3 Ordered two additional films at $1,000 each.
9 Received $2,800 cash from admissions.
10 Made $2,000 payment on mortgage and $1,000 for accounts payable due.
11 Classic Theater contracted with Rhonda Humes to operate the concession stand. Humes is to pay Classic Theater 17% of gross concession receipts, payable monthly, for the rental of the concession stand.
12 Paid advertising expenses $500.
20 Received one of the films ordered on April 3 and was billed $1,000. The film will be shown in April.
25 Received $5,200 cash from admissions.
29 Paid salaries $2,000.
30 Received statement from Rhonda Humes showing gross concession receipts of $1,000 and the balance due to The Classic Theater of $170 ($1,000 × 17%) for April. Humes paid one-half of the balance due and will remit the remainder on May 5.
30 Prepaid $1,200 rental on special film to be run in May.

In addition to the accounts identified above, the chart of accounts shows: No. 112 Accounts Receivable, No. 136 Prepaid Rent, No. 400 Service Revenue, No. 429 Rent Revenue, No. 610 Advertising Expense, No. 726 Salaries and Wages Expense, and No. 729 Rent Expense.

Instructions
(a) Enter the beginning balances in the ledger as of April 1. Insert a check mark (✓) in the reference column of the ledger for the beginning balance.
(b) Journalize the April transactions. Classic records admission revenue as service revenue, rental of the concession stand as rent revenue, and film rental expense as rent expense.
(c) Post the April journal entries to the ledger. Assume that all entries are posted from page 1 of the journal.

(d) Trial balance totals $34,170

(d) Prepare a trial balance on April 30, 2014.

PROBLEMS: SET C

Visit the book's companion website, at **www.wiley.com/college/weygandt**, and choose the Student Companion site to access Problem Set C.

CONTINUING COOKIE CHRONICLE

(*Note:* This is a continuation of the Cookie Chronicle from Chapter 1.)

CCC2 After researching the different forms of business organization. Natalie Koebel decides to operate "Cookie Creations" as a proprietorship. She then starts the process of getting the business running. In November 2013, the following activities take place.

Nov. 8   Natalie cashes her U.S. Savings Bonds and receives $520, which she deposits in her personal bank account.

8   She opens a bank account under the name "Cookie Creations" and transfers $500 from her personal account to the new account.

11   Natalie pays $65 for advertising.

13   She buys baking supplies, such as flour, sugar, butter, and chocolate chips, for $125 cash. (*Hint:* Use Supplies account.)

14   Natalie starts to gather some baking equipment to take with her when teaching the cookie classes. She has an excellent top-of-the-line food processor and mixer that originally cost her $750. Natalie decides to start using it only in her new business. She estimates that the equipment is currently worth $300. She invests the equipment in the business.

16   Natalie realizes that her initial cash investment is not enough. Her grandmother lends her $2,000 cash, for which Natalie signs a note payable in the name of the business. Natalie deposits the money in the business bank account. (*Hint:* The note does not have to be repaid for 24 months. As a result, the note payable should be reported in the accounts as the last liability and also on the balance sheet as the last liability.)

17   She buys more baking equipment for $900 cash.

20   She teaches her first class and collects $125 cash.

25   Natalie books a second class for December 4 for $150. She receives $30 cash in advance as a down payment.

30   Natalie pays $1,320 for a one-year insurance policy that will expire on December 1, 2014.

Instructions

(a) Prepare journal entries to record the November transactions.
(b) Post the journal entries to general ledger accounts.
(c) Prepare a trial balance at November 30.

Broadening Your Perspective

Financial Reporting and Analysis

Financial Reporting Problem: Apple Inc.

BYP2-1 The financial statements of Apple Inc. are presented in Appendix A. Instructions for accessing and using the company's complete annual report, including the notes to the financial statements, are also provided in Appendix A.

Apple's financial statements contain the following selected accounts, stated in millions of dollars.

Accounts Payable	Cash and Cash Equivalents
Accounts Receivable	Research and Development Expense
Property, Plant, and Equipment	Inventories

Instructions

(a) Answer the following questions.
   (1) What is the increase and decrease side for each account?
   (2) What is the normal balance for each account?

(b) Identify the probable other account in the transaction and the effect on that account when:

(1) Accounts Receivable is decreased.

(2) Accounts Payable is decreased.

(3) Inventories are increased.

(c) Identify the other account(s) that ordinarily would be involved when:

(1) Research and Development Expense is increased.

(2) Property, Plant, and Equipment is increased.

Comparative Analysis Problem: Amazon.com, Inc. vs. Wal-Mart Stores, Inc.

BYP2-2 Amazon.com, Inc.'s financial statements are presented in Appendix D. Financial statements for Wal-Mart Stores, Inc. are presented in Appendix E. Instructions for accessing and using the complete annual reports of Amazon and Wal-Mart, including the notes to the financial statements, are also provided in Appendices D and E, respectively.

Instructions

(a) Based on the information contained in the financial statements, determine the normal balance of the listed accounts for each company.

Amazon	Wal-Mart
1. Interest Expense	**1.** Net Sales Revenues
2. Cash and Cash Equivalents	**2.** Inventories
3. Accounts Payable	**3.** Cost of Sales

(b) Identify the other account ordinarily involved when:

(1) Accounts Receivable is increased.

(2) Interest Expense is increased.

(3) Salaries and Wages Payable is decreased.

(4) Service Revenue is increased.

Real-World Focus

BYP2-3 Much information about specific companies is available on the Internet. Such information includes basic descriptions of the company's location, activities, industry, financial health, and financial performance.

Address: **biz.yahoo.com/i**, or go to **www.wiley.com/college/weygandt**

Steps

1. Type in a company name, or use index to find company name.

2. Choose **Profile**. Perform instructions (a)–(c) below.

3. Click on the company's specific industry to identify competitors. Perform instructions (d)–(g) below.

Instructions

Answer the following questions.

(a) What is the company's industry?

(b) What is the company's total sales?

(c) What is the company's net income?

(d) What are the names of four of the company's competitors?

(e) Choose one of these competitors.

(f) What is this competitor's name? What are its sales? What is its net income?

(g) Which of these two companies is larger by size of sales? Which one reported higher net income?

BYP2-4 The January 27, 2011, edition of the *New York Times* contains an article by Richard Sandomir entitled "N.F.L. Finances, as Seen Through Packers' Records." The article discusses the fact that the Green Bay Packers are the only NFL team that publicly publishes its annual report.

Instructions

Read the article and answer the following questions.

(a) Why are the Green Bay Packers the only professional football team to publish and distribute an annual report?

(b) Why is the football players' labor union particularly interested in the Packers' annual report?

(c) In addition to the players' labor union, what other outside party might be interested in the annual report?

(d) Even though the Packers' revenue increased in recent years, the company's operating profit fell significantly. How does the article explain this decline?

Critical Thinking

Decision-Making Across the Organization

BYP2-5 Dyanna Craig operates Craig Riding Academy. The academy's primary sources of revenue are riding fees and lesson fees, which are paid on a cash basis. Dyanna also boards horses for owners, who are billed monthly for boarding fees. In a few cases, boarders pay in advance of expected use. For its revenue transactions, the academy maintains the following accounts: Cash, Accounts Receivable, and Service Revenue.

The academy owns 10 horses, a stable, a riding corral, riding equipment, and office equipment. These assets are accounted for in these accounts: Horses, Buildings, and Equipment.

The academy also maintains the following accounts: Supplies, Prepaid Insurance, Accounts Payable, Salaries and Wages Expense, Advertising Expense, Utilities Expense, and Maintenance and Repairs Expense.

Dyanna makes periodic withdrawals of cash for personal living expenses. To record Dyanna's equity in the business and her drawings, two accounts are maintained: Owner's Capital and Owner's Drawings.

During the first month of operations, an inexperienced bookkeeper was employed. Dyanna Craig asks you to review the following eight entries of the 50 entries made during the month. In each case, the explanation for the entry is correct.

May 1	Cash	18,000	
	Owner's Capital		18,000
	(Invested $18,000 cash in business)		
5	Cash	250	
	Service Revenue		250
	(Received $250 cash for lessons provided)		
7	Cash	300	
	Service Revenue		300
	(Received $300 for boarding of horses		
	beginning June 1)		
14	Equipment	80	
	Cash		800
	(Purchased desk and other office		
	equipment for $800 cash)		
15	Salaries and Wages Expense	400	
	Cash		400
	(Issued check to Dyanna Craig for personal use)		
20	Cash	148	
	Service Revenue		184
	(Received $184 cash for riding fees)		
30	Maintenance and Repairs Expense	75	
	Accounts Payable		75
	(Received bill of $75 from carpenter for		
	repair services performed)		
31	Supplies	1,700	
	Cash		1,700
	(Purchased an estimated 2 months'		
	supply of feed and hay for $1,700 on account)		

Instructions

With the class divided into groups, answer the following.

(a) Identify each journal entry that is correct. For each journal entry that is incorrect, prepare the entry that should have been made by the bookkeeper.

(b) Which of the incorrect entries would prevent the trial balance from balancing?

(c) What was the correct net income for May, assuming the bookkeeper reported net income of $4,500 after posting all 50 entries?

(d) What was the correct cash balance at May 31, assuming the bookkeeper reported a balance of $12,475 after posting all 50 entries (and the only errors occurred in the items listed above)?

Communication Activity

BYP2-6 Keller's Maid Company offers home-cleaning service. Two recurring transactions for the company are billing customers for services performed and paying employee salaries. For example, on March 15, bills totaling $6,000 were sent to customers and $2,000 was paid in salaries to employees.

Instructions

Write a memo to your instructor that explains and illustrates the steps in the recording process for each of the March 15 transactions. Use the format illustrated in the text under the heading, "The Recording Process Illustrated" (p. 65).

Ethics Cases

BYP2-7 Meredith Ward is the assistant chief accountant at Frazier Company, a manufacturer of computer chips and cellular phones. The company presently has total sales of $20 million. It is the end of the first quarter. Meredith is hurriedly trying to prepare a trial balance so that quarterly financial statements can be prepared and released to management and the regulatory agencies. The total credits on the trial balance exceed the debits by $1,000. In order to meet the 4 p.m. deadline, Meredith decides to force the debits and credits into balance by adding the amount of the difference to the Equipment account. She chooses Equipment because it is one of the larger account balances; percentage-wise, it will be the least misstated. Meredith "plugs" the difference! She believes that the difference will not affect anyone's decisions. She wishes that she had another few days to find the error but realizes that the financial statements are already late.

Instructions

(a) Who are the stakeholders in this situation?

(b) What are the ethical issues involved in this case?

(c) What are Meredith's alternatives?

BYP2-8 If you haven't already done so, in the not-too-distant future you will prepare a résumé. In some ways, your résumé is like a company's annual report. Its purpose is to enable others to evaluate your past, in an effort to predict your future.

A résumé is your opportunity to create a positive first impression. It is important that it be impressive—but it should also be accurate. In order to increase their job prospects, some people are tempted to "inflate" their résumés by overstating the importance of some past accomplishments or positions. In fact, you might even think that "everybody does it" and that if you don't do it, you will be at a disadvantage.

David Edmondson, the president and CEO of well-known electronics retailer Radio Shack, overstated his accomplishments by claiming that he had earned a bachelor's of science degree, when in fact he had not. Apparently, his employer had not done a background check to ensure the accuracy of his résumé. Should Radio Shack have fired him?

YES: Radio Shack is a publicly traded company. Investors, creditors, employees, and others doing business with the company will not trust it if its leader is known to have poor integrity. The "tone at the top" is vital to creating an ethical organization.

NO: Mr. Edmondson had been a Radio Shack employee for 11 years. He had served the company in a wide variety of positions, and had earned the position of CEO through exceptional performance. While the fact that he lied 11 years earlier on his résumé was unfortunate, his service since then made this past transgression irrelevant. In addition, the company was in the midst of a massive restructuring, which included closing 700 of its 7,000 stores. It could not afford additional upheaval at this time.

Instructions

Write a response indicating your position regarding this situation. Provide support for your view.

All About You

BYP2-9 Every company needs to plan in order to move forward. Its top management must consider where it wants the company to be in three to five years. Like a company, you need to think about where you want to be three to five years from now, and you need to start taking steps now in order to get there.

Instructions
Provide responses to each of the following items.

(a) Where would you like to be working in three to five years? Describe your plan for getting there by identifying between five and 10 specific steps that you need to take.

(b) In order to get the job you want, you will need a résumé. Your résumé is the equivalent of a company's annual report. It needs to provide relevant and reliable information about your past accomplishments so that employers can decide whether to "invest" in you. Do a search on the Internet to find a good résumé format. What are the basic elements of a résumé?

(c) A company's annual report provides information about a company's accomplishments. In order for investors to use the annual report, the information must be reliable; that is, users must have faith that the information is accurate and believable. How can you provide assurance that the information on your résumé is reliable?

(d) Prepare a résumé assuming that you have accomplished the five to 10 specific steps you identified in part (a). Also, provide evidence that would give assurance that the information is reliable.

Considering People, Planet, and Profit

BYP2-10 Auditors provide a type of certification of corporate financial statements. Certification is used in many other aspects of business as well. For example, it plays a critical role in the sustainability movement. The February 7, 2012, issue of the *New York Times* contained an article by S. Amanda Caudill entitled "Better Lives in Better Coffee," which discusses the role of certification in the coffee business.

Address: **http://scientistatwork.blogs.nytimes.com/2012/02/07/better-lives-in-better-coffee**

Instructions
Read the article and answer the following questions.

(a) The article mentions three different certification types that coffee growers can obtain from three different certification bodies. Using financial reporting as an example, what potential problems might the existence of multiple certification types present to coffee purchasers?

(b) According to the author, which certification is most common among coffee growers? What are the possible reasons for this?

(c) What social and environmental benefits are coffee certifications trying to achieve? Are there also potential financial benefits to the parties involved?

Answers to Chapter Questions

Answers to Insight and Accounting Across the Organization Questions

p. 57 Keeping Score   Q: Do you think that the Chicago Bears football team would be likely to have the same major revenue and expense accounts as the Cubs? **A:** Because their businesses are similar—professional sports—many of the revenue and expense accounts for the baseball and football teams might be similar.

p. 61 Boosting Microsoft's Profits   Q: In what ways is this Microsoft division using accounting to assist in its effort to become more profitable? **A:** The division has used accounting to set very strict sales, revenue, and profit goals. In addition, the managers in this division use accounting to keep a tight rein on product costs. Also, accounting serves as the basis of communication so that the marketing managers and product designers can work with production managers, engineers, and accountants to create an exciting product within specified cost constraints.

p. 63 A Convenient Overstatement   Q: What incentives might employees have had to overstate the value of these investment securities on the company's financial statements? **A:** One reason that they may have been reluctant to record the losses is out of fear that the company's shareholders and clients would panic if they saw the magnitude of the losses. However, personal self-interest might have been equally to blame—the bonuses of the traders were tied to the value of the investment securities.

p. 74 Why Accuracy Matters   Q: In order for these companies to prepare and issue financial statements, their accounting equations (debits and credits) must have been in balance at year-end. How could these errors or misstatements have occurred? **A:** A company's accounting equation (its books) can be in balance yet its financial statements have errors or misstatements because of the following: entire transactions were not recorded; transactions were recorded at wrong amounts; transactions were recorded in the wrong accounts; transactions were recorded in the wrong accounting period. Audits of financial statements uncover some but obviously not all errors or misstatements.

Answers to Self-Test Questions

1. b **2.** c **3.** d **4.** d **5.** d **6.** b **7.** a **8.** c **9.** b **10.** c **11.** d **12.** c ($16,000 − $5,000) **13.** a **14.** c **15.** a ($5,000 + $40,000 + $10,000 + $15,000 + $61,000)

A Look at IFRS

LEARNING OBJECTIVE	**8**

Compare the procedures for the accounting process under GAAP and IFRS.

International companies use the same set of procedures and records to keep track of transaction data. Thus, the material in Chapter 2 dealing with the account, general rules of debit and credit, and steps in the recording process—the journal, ledger, and chart of accounts—is the same under both GAAP and IFRS.

Key Points

- Transaction analysis is the same under IFRS and GAAP but, as you will see in later chapters, different standards sometimes impact how transactions are recorded.

- Rules for accounting for specific events sometimes differ across countries. For example, European companies rely less on historical cost and more on fair value than U.S. companies. Despite the differences, the double-entry accounting system is the basis of accounting systems worldwide.

- Both the IASB and FASB go beyond the basic definitions provided in this textbook for the key elements of financial statements, that is, assets, liabilities, equity, revenues, and expenses. The more substantive definitions, using the IASB definitional structure, are provided in the Chapter 1 *A Look at IFRS* discussion.

- A trial balance under IFRS follows the same format as shown in the textbook.

- As shown in the textbook, dollars signs are typically used only in the trial balance and the financial statements. The same practice is followed under IFRS, using the currency of the country that the reporting company is headquartered.

- In February 2010, the SEC expressed a desire to continue working toward a single set of high-quality standards. In deciding whether the United States should adopt IFRS, some of the issues the SEC said should be considered are:

  ♦ Whether IFRS is sufficiently developed and consistent in application.

  ♦ Whether the IASB is sufficiently independent.

  ♦ Whether IFRS is established for the benefit of investors.

  ♦ The issues involved in educating investors about IFRS.

  ♦ The impact of a switch to IFRS on U.S. laws and regulations.

  ♦ The impact on companies including changes to their accounting systems, contractual arrangements, corporate governance, and litigation.

  ♦ The issues involved in educating accountants, so they can prepare financial statements under IFRS.

Looking to the Future

The basic recording process shown in this textbook is followed by companies across the globe. It is unlikely to change in the future. The definitional structure of assets, liabilities, equity, revenues, and expenses may change over time as the IASB and FASB evaluate their overall conceptual framework for establishing accounting standards.

IFRS Practice

IFRS Self-Test Questions

1. Which statement is **correct** regarding IFRS?
   (a) IFRS reverses the rules of debits and credits, that is, debits are on the right and credits are on the left.
   (b) IFRS uses the same process for recording transactions as GAAP.
   (c) The chart of accounts under IFRS is different because revenues follow assets.
   (d) None of the above statements are correct.

2. The expanded accounting equation under IFRS is as follows:
   (a) Assets = Liabilities + Owner's Capital + Owner's Drawings + Revenues − Expenses.
   (b) Assets + Liabilities = Owner's Capital + Owner's Drawings + Revenues − Expenses.
   (c) Assets = Liabilities + Owner's Capital − Owner's Drawings + Revenues − Expenses.
   (d) Assets = Liabilities + Owner's Capital + Owner's Drawings − Revenues − Expenses.

3. A trial balance:
   (a) is the same under IFRS and GAAP.
   (b) proves that transactions are recorded correctly.
   (c) proves that all transactions have been recorded.
   (d) will not balance if a correct journal entry is posted twice.

4. One difference between IFRS and GAAP is that:
   (a) GAAP uses accrual-accounting concepts and IFRS uses primarily the cash basis of accounting.
   (b) IFRS uses a different posting process than GAAP.
   (c) IFRS uses more fair value measurements than GAAP.
   (d) the limitations of a trial balance are different between IFRS and GAAP.

5. The general policy for using proper currency signs (dollar, yen, pound, etc.) is the same for both IFRS and this textbook. This policy is as follows:
   (a) Currency signs only appear in ledgers and journal entries.
   (b) Currency signs are only shown in the trial balance.
   (c) Currency signs are shown for all compound journal entries.
   (d) Currency signs are shown in trial balances and financial statements.

IFRS Exercises

IFRS2-1 Describe some of the issues the SEC must consider in deciding whether the United States should adopt IFRS.

International Financial Reporting Problem: Zetar plc

IFRS2-2 The financial statements of Zetar plc are presented in Appendix F. Instructions for accessing and using the company's complete annual report, including the notes to its financial statements, are also provided in Appendix F.

Instructions
Describe in which statement each of the following items is reported, and the position in the statement (e.g., current asset).

(a) Other administrative expenses.
(b) Cash at bank.
(c) Borrowings and overdrafts.
(d) Finance costs.

Answers to IFRS Self-Test Questions
1. b 2. c 3. a 4. c 5. d

✔ The Navigator

✔ Remember to go back to The Navigator box on the chapter opening page and check off your completed work.

3 | Adjusting the Accounts

Feature Story

Keeping Track of Groupons

Who doesn't like buying things at a discount? That's why it's not surprising that three years after it started as a company, Groupon was estimated to be worth $16 billion. This translates into an average increase in value of almost $15 million per day.

Now consider that Groupon had previously been estimated to be worth even more than that. What happened? Well, accounting regulators and investors began to question the way that Groupon had accounted for some of its transactions. But if Groupon sells only coupons ("groupons"), you're probably wondering how hard can it be to accurately account for that? It turns out that accounting for coupons is not as easy as you might think.

First, consider what happens when Groupon makes a sale. Suppose it sells a groupon for $30 for Highrise Hamburgers. When it receives the $30 from the customer, it must turn over half of that amount ($15) to Highrise Hamburgers. So should Groupon record revenue for the full $30 or just $15? Until recently, Groupon recorded the full $30. But, in response to an SEC ruling on the issue, Groupon now records revenue of $15 instead.

A second issue is a matter of timing. When should Group record this $15 revenue? Should it record the revenue w sells the groupon, or must it wait until the customer use groupon at Highrise Hamburgers? You can find the answ this question in the notes to Groupon's financial statem It recognizes the revenue once "the number of custome who purchase the daily deal exceeds the predetermined threshold, the Groupon has been electronically delivered the purchaser and a listing of Groupons sold has been r available to the merchant."

The accounting becomes even more complicated when consider the company's loyalty programs. Groupon offer or discounted groupons to its subscribers for doing thing such as referring new customers or participating in prom These groupons are to be used for future purchases, yet company must record the expense at the time the custo receives the groupon. The cost of these programs is hug Groupon, so the timing of this expense can definitely aff reported income.

The final kicker is that Groupon, like all other companie must rely on many estimates in its financial reporting. For example, Groupon reports that "estimates are utiliz

 The Navigator

- Scan Learning Objectives
- Read Feature Story
- Read Preview
- Read text and answer **DO IT!** p. 102
  - p. 110   p. 116   p. 121
- Work Comprehensive **DO IT!** p. 122
- Review Summary of Learning Objectives
- Answer Self-Test Questions
- Complete Assignments
- Go to *WileyPLUS* for practice and tutorials
- 🌐 **Read A Look at IFRS** p. 157

Learning Objectives   **The Navigator**

After studying this chapter, you should be able to:

[1] Explain the time period assumption.

[2] Explain the accrual basis of accounting.

[3] Explain the reasons for adjusting entries and identify the major types of adjusting entries.

[4] Prepare adjusting entries for deferrals.

[5] Prepare adjusting entries for accruals.

[6] Describe the nature and purpose of an adjusted trial balance.

Rudy Archuleta/Redux Pictures

for, but not limited to, stock-based compensation, income taxes, valuation of acquired goodwill and intangible assets, customer refunds, contingent liabilities and the depreciable lives of fixed assets."

It concludes by saying that "actual results could differ materially from those estimates." So, next time you use a coupon, think about what that means for the company's accountants!

Preview of Chapter 3

  The Navigator

In Chapter 1, you learned a neat little formula: Net income = Revenues − Expenses. In Chapter 2, you learned some rules for recording revenue and expense transactions. Guess what? Things are not really that nice and neat. In fact, it is often difficult for companies to determine in what time period they should report some revenues and expenses. In other words, in measuring net income, timing is everything.

The content and organization of Chapter 3 are as follows.

ADJUSTING THE ACCOUNTS

Timing Issues	The Basics of Adjusting Entries	The Adjusted Trial Balance and Financial Statements
• Fiscal and calendar years • Accrual- vs. cash-basis accounting • Recognizing revenues and expenses	• Types of adjusting entries • Adjusting entries for deferrals • Adjusting entries for accruals • Summary of basic relationships	• Preparing the adjusted trial balance • Preparing financial statements

Timing Issues

Time Period Assumption

If we could wait to prepare financial statements until a company ended its operations, no adjustments would be needed. At that point, we could easily determine its final balance sheet and the amount of lifetime income it earned.

However, most companies need immediate feedback about how well they are doing. For example, management usually wants monthly financial statements. The Internal Revenue Service requires all businesses to file annual tax returns. Therefore, **accountants divide the economic life of a business into artificial time periods**. This convenient assumption is referred to as the **time period assumption**.

Many business transactions affect more than one of these arbitrary time periods. For example, the airplanes purchased by Southwest Airlines five years ago are still in use today. We must determine the relevance of each business transaction to specific accounting periods. (How much of the cost of an airplane contributed to operations this year?)

Fiscal and Calendar Years

Both small and large companies prepare financial statements periodically in order to assess their financial condition and results of operations. **Accounting time periods are generally a month, a quarter, or a year.** Monthly and quarterly time periods are called **interim periods**. Most large companies must prepare both quarterly and annual financial statements.

An accounting time period that is one year in length is a **fiscal year**. A fiscal year usually begins with the first day of a month and ends 12 months later on the last day of a month. Most businesses use the **calendar year** (January 1 to December 31) as their accounting period. Some do not. Companies whose fiscal year differs from the calendar year include Delta Air Lines, June 30, and Walt Disney Productions, September 30. Sometimes a company's year-end will vary from year to year. For example, PepsiCo's fiscal year ends on the Friday closest to December 31, which was December 25 in 2010 and December 30 in 2011.

Accrual- versus Cash-Basis Accounting

What you will learn in this chapter is **accrual-basis accounting**. Under the accrual basis, companies record transactions that change a company's financial statements **in the periods in which the events occur**. For example, using the accrual basis to determine net income means companies recognize revenues when they perform services (rather than when they receive cash). It also means recognizing expenses when incurred (rather than when paid).

An alternative to the accrual basis is the cash basis. Under **cash-basis accounting**, companies record revenue when they receive cash. They record an expense when they pay out cash. The cash basis seems appealing due to its simplicity, but it often produces misleading financial statements. It fails to record revenue for a company that has performed services but for which it has not received the cash. As a result, it does not match expenses with revenues. **Cash-basis accounting is not in accordance with generally accepted accounting principles (GAAP)**.

Individuals and some small companies do use cash-basis accounting. The cash basis is justified for small businesses because they often have few receivables and payables. Medium and large companies use accrual-basis accounting.

Recognizing Revenues and Expenses

It can be difficult to determine when to report revenues and expenses. The revenue recognition principle and the expense recognition principle help in this task.

REVENUE RECOGNITION PRINCIPLE

When a company agrees to perform a service or sell a product to a customer, it has a **performance obligation**. When the company meets this performance obligation, it recognizes revenue. The **revenue recognition principle** therefore requires that companies recognize revenue in the accounting period in which the performance obligation is satisfied.[1] To illustrate, assume that Dave's Dry Cleaning cleans clothing on June 30 but customers do not claim and pay for their clothes until the first week of July. Dave's should record revenue in June when it performed the service (satisfied the performance obligation) rather than in July when it received the cash. At June 30, Dave's would report a receivable on its balance sheet and revenue in its income statement for the service performed.

EXPENSE RECOGNITION PRINCIPLE

Accountants follow a simple rule in recognizing expenses: "Let the expenses follow the revenues." Thus, expense recognition is tied to revenue recognition. In the dry cleaning example, this means that Dave's should report the salary expense incurred in performing the June 30 cleaning service in the same period in which it recognizes the service revenue. The critical issue in expense recognition is when the expense makes its contribution to revenue. This may or may not be the same period in which the expense is paid. If Dave's does not pay the salary incurred on June 30 until July, it would report salaries payable on its June 30 balance sheet.

This practice of expense recognition is referred to as the **expense recognition principle** (often referred to as the **matching principle**). It dictates that efforts (expenses) be matched with results (revenues). Illustration 3-1 summarizes the revenue and expense recognition principles.

Revenue Recognition
Satisfied performance obligation

Customer requests service → Cash received

Revenue is recognized when performance obligation is satisfied.

Expense Recognition
Matching Revenues

↑ Delivery

Advertising   Utilities

Expenses

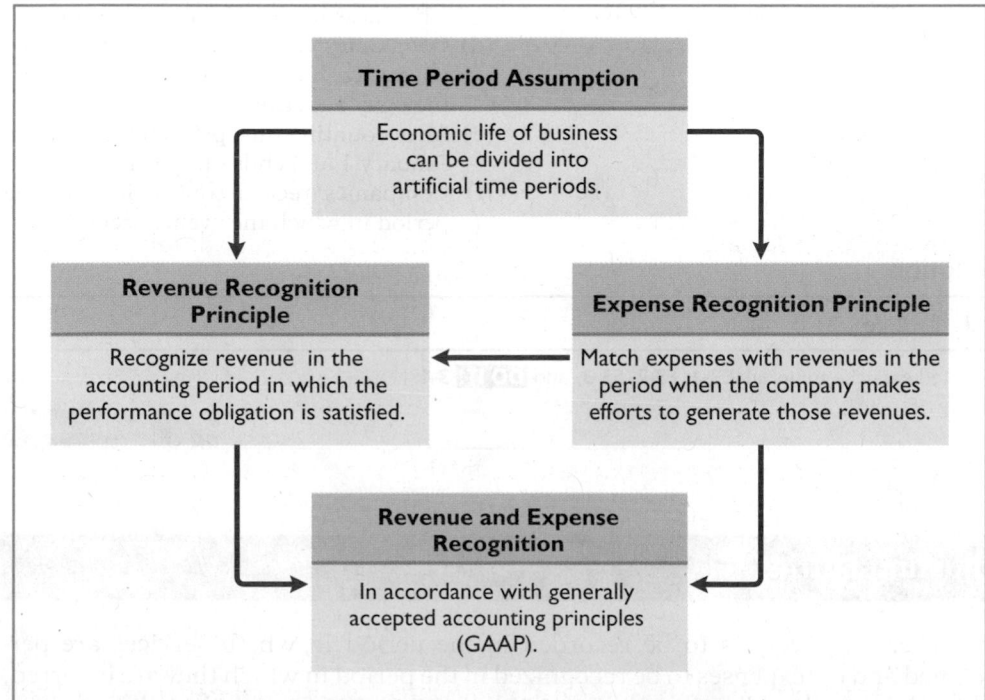

Illustration 3-1
GAAP relationships in revenue and expense recognition

[1]The definition for the revenue recognition principle is based on the revised exposure draft issued by the FASB.

ETHICS INSIGHT

Cooking the Books?

Allegations of abuse of the revenue recognition principle have become all too common in recent years. For example, it was alleged that Krispy Kreme sometimes doubled the number of doughnuts shipped to wholesale customers at the end of a quarter to boost quarterly results. The customers shipped the unsold doughnuts back after the beginning of the next quarter for a refund. Conversely, Computer Associates International was accused of backdating sales—that is, reporting a sale in one period that did not actually occur until the next period in order to achieve the earlier period's sales targets.

? What motivates sales executives and finance and accounting executives to participate in activities that result in inaccurate reporting of revenues? (See page 156.)

© Dean Turner/iStockphoto

> DO IT!

Timing Concepts

Several timing concepts are discussed on pages 100–101. A list of concepts is provided in the left column below, with a description of the concept in the right column below. There are more descriptions provided than concepts. Match the description of the concept to the concept.

1. ____Accrual-basis accounting.
2. ____Calendar year.
3. ____Time period assumption.
4. ____Expense recognition principle.

(a) Monthly and quarterly time periods.
(b) Efforts (expenses) should be matched with results (revenues).
(c) Accountants divide the economic life of a business into artificial time periods.
(d) Companies record revenues when they receive cash and record expenses when they pay out cash.
(e) An accounting time period that starts on January 1 and ends on December 31.
(f) Companies record transactions in the period in which the events occur.

Action Plan

✔ Review the glossary terms identified on page 124.

✔ Study carefully the revenue recognition principle, the expense recognition principle, and the time period assumption.

Solution

> **1.** f **2.** e **3.** c **4.** b

Related exercise material: **E3-1, E3-2, E3-3, and DO IT! 3-1.**

✔ **The Navigator**

The Basics of Adjusting Entries

| LEARNING OBJECTIVE | 3 |

Explain the reasons for adjusting entries and identify the major types of adjusting entries.

In order for revenues to be recorded in the period in which services are performed and for expenses to be recognized in the period in which they are incurred, companies make adjusting entries. **Adjusting entries ensure that the revenue recognition and expense recognition principles are followed**.

Adjusting entries are necessary because the **trial balance**—the first pulling together of the transaction data—may not contain up-to-date and complete data. This is true for several reasons:

1. Some events are not recorded daily because it is not efficient to do so. Examples are the use of supplies and the earning of wages by employees.

2. Some costs are not recorded during the accounting period because these costs expire with the passage of time rather than as a result of recurring daily transactions. Examples are charges related to the use of buildings and equipment, rent, and insurance.

3. Some items may be unrecorded. An example is a utility service bill that will not be received until the next accounting period.

Adjusting entries are required every time a company prepares financial statements. The company analyzes each account in the trial balance to determine whether it is complete and up to date for financial statement purposes. **Every adjusting entry will include one income statement account and one balance sheet account.**

International Note

Internal controls are a system of checks and balances designed to detect and prevent fraud and errors. The Sarbanes-Oxley Act requires U.S. companies to enhance their systems of internal control. However, many foreign companies do not have to meet strict internal control requirements. Some U.S. companies believe that this gives foreign firms an unfair advantage because developing and maintaining internal controls can be very expensive.

Types of Adjusting Entries

Adjusting entries are classified as either **deferrals** or **accruals**. As Illustration 3-2 shows, each of these classes has two subcategories.

Deferrals:

1. Prepaid expenses: Expenses paid in cash before they are used or consumed.

2. Unearned revenues: Cash received before services are performed.

Accruals:

1. Accrued revenues: Revenues for services performed but not yet received in cash or recorded.

2. Accrued expenses: Expenses incurred but not yet paid in cash or recorded.

Illustration 3-2
Categories of adjusting entries

Subsequent sections give examples of each type of adjustment. Each example is based on the October 31 trial balance of Pioneer Advertising Agency from Chapter 2, reproduced in Illustration 3-3.

Illustration 3-3
Trial balance

PIONEER ADVERTISING AGENCY		
Trial Balance		
October 31, 2014		
	Debit	**Credit**
Cash	$ 15,200	
Supplies	2,500	
Prepaid Insurance	600	
Equipment	5,000	
Notes Payable		$ 5,000
Accounts Payable		2,500
Unearned Service Revenue		1,200
Owner's Capital		10,000
Owner's Drawings	500	
Service Revenue		10,000
Salaries and Wages Expense	4,000	
Rent Expense	900	
	$28,700	$28,700

We assume that Pioneer Advertising uses an accounting period of one month. Thus, monthly adjusting entries are made. The entries are dated October 31.

Adjusting Entries for Deferrals

To defer means to postpone or delay. **Deferrals** are expenses or revenues that are recognized at a date later than the point when cash was originally exchanged. The two types of deferrals are prepaid expenses and unearned revenues.

PREPAID EXPENSES

When companies record payments of expenses that will benefit more than one accounting period, they record an asset called **prepaid expenses** or **prepayments**. When expenses are prepaid, an asset account is increased (debited) to show the service or benefit that the company will receive in the future. Examples of common prepayments are insurance, supplies, advertising, and rent. In addition, companies make prepayments when they purchase buildings and equipment.

Prepaid expenses are costs that expire either with the passage of time (e.g., rent and insurance) **or through use** (e.g., supplies). The expiration of these costs does not require daily entries, which would be impractical and unnecessary. Accordingly, companies postpone the recognition of such cost expirations until they prepare financial statements. At each statement date, they make adjusting entries to record the expenses applicable to the current accounting period and to show the remaining amounts in the asset accounts.

Prior to adjustment, assets are overstated and expenses are understated. Therefore, as shown in Illustration 3-4, **an adjusting entry for prepaid expenses results in an increase (a debit) to an expense account and a decrease (a credit) to an asset account**.

Illustration 3-4
Adjusting entries for prepaid expenses

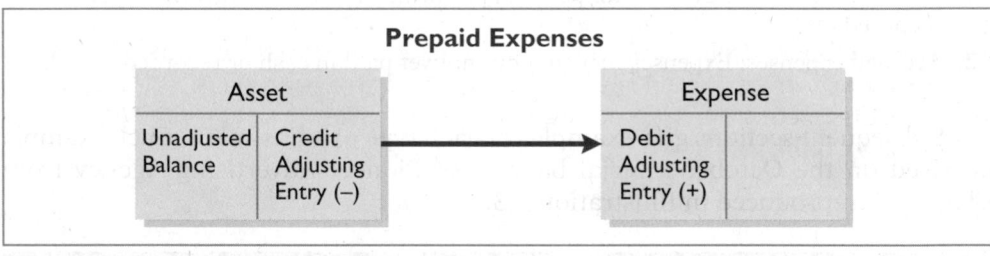

Let's look in more detail at some specific types of prepaid expenses, beginning with supplies.

Supplies

Oct. 5

Supplies purchased; record asset

Oct. 31
Supplies used; record supplies expense

SUPPLIES The purchase of supplies, such as paper and envelopes, results in an increase (a debit) to an asset account. During the accounting period, the company uses supplies. Rather than record supplies expense as the supplies are used, companies recognize supplies expense at the **end** of the accounting period. At the end of the accounting period, the company counts the remaining supplies. As shown in Illustration 3-5, the difference between the unadjusted balance in the Supplies (asset) account and the actual cost of supplies on hand represents the supplies used (an expense) for that period.

Recall from Chapter 2 that Pioneer Advertising Agency purchased supplies costing $2,500 on October 5. Pioneer recorded the purchase by increasing (debiting) the asset Supplies. This account shows a balance of $2,500 in the October 31 trial balance. An inventory count at the close of business on October 31 reveals that $1,000 of supplies are still on hand. Thus, the cost of supplies used is $1,500

($2,500 − $1,000). This use of supplies decreases an asset, Supplies. It also decreases owner's equity by increasing an expense account, Supplies Expense. This is shown in Illustration 3-5.

Illustration 3-5
Adjustment for supplies

After adjustment, the asset account Supplies shows a balance of $1,000, which is equal to the cost of supplies on hand at the statement date. In addition, Supplies Expense shows a balance of $1,500, which equals the cost of supplies used in October. **If Pioneer does not make the adjusting entry, October expenses are understated and net income is overstated by $1,500. Moreover, both assets and owner's equity will be overstated by $1,500 on the October 31 balance sheet**.

INSURANCE Companies purchase insurance to protect themselves from losses due to fire, theft, and unforeseen events. Insurance must be paid in advance, often for more than one year. The cost of insurance (premiums) paid in advance is recorded as an increase (debit) in the asset account Prepaid Insurance. At the financial statement date, companies increase (debit) Insurance Expense and decrease (credit) Prepaid Insurance for the cost of insurance that has expired during the period.

On October 4, Pioneer Advertising paid $600 for a one-year fire insurance policy. Coverage began on October 1. Pioneer recorded the payment by increasing (debiting) Prepaid Insurance. This account shows a balance of $600 in the October 31 trial balance. Insurance of $50 ($600 ÷ 12) expires each month. The expiration of prepaid insurance decreases an asset, Prepaid Insurance. It also decreases owner's equity by increasing an expense account, Insurance Expense.

As shown in Illustration 3-6 (page 106), the asset Prepaid Insurance shows a balance of $550, which represents the unexpired cost for the remaining 11 months of coverage. At the same time, the balance in Insurance Expense equals the insurance cost that expired in October. **If Pioneer does not make this adjustment, October expenses are understated by $50 and net income is overstated by $50. Moreover, both assets and owner's equity will be overstated by $50 on the October 31 balance sheet.**

Illustration 3-6
Adjustment for insurance

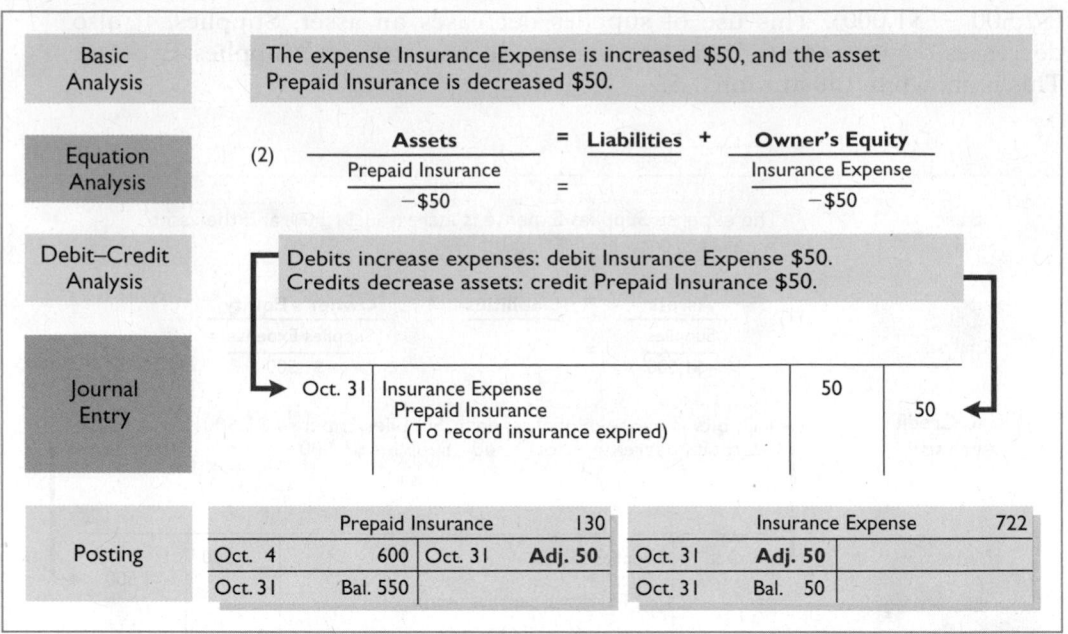

Basic Analysis	The expense Insurance Expense is increased $50, and the asset Prepaid Insurance is decreased $50.

Equation Analysis

(2)

Assets	=	Liabilities	+	Owner's Equity
Prepaid Insurance	=			Insurance Expense
−$50				−$50

Debit–Credit Analysis

Debits increase expenses: debit Insurance Expense $50.
Credits decrease assets: credit Prepaid Insurance $50.

Journal Entry

Oct. 31 | Insurance Expense .... | 50 |
| Prepaid Insurance .... | | 50 |
| (To record insurance expired) | | |

Posting

Prepaid Insurance	130
Oct. 4 600	Oct. 31 **Adj. 50**
Oct. 31 **Bal. 550**	

Insurance Expense	722
Oct. 31 **Adj. 50**	
Oct. 31 **Bal. 50**	

Depreciation

Oct. 2

Equipment purchased; record asset

Equipment			
Oct $40	Nov $40	Dec $40	Jan $40
Feb $40	March $40	April $40	May $40
June $40	July $40	Aug $40	Sept $40
Depreciation = $480/year			

Oct. 31
Depreciation recognized; record depreciation expense

Helpful Hint All contra accounts have increases, decreases, and normal balances opposite to the account to which they relate.

DEPRECIATION A company typically owns a variety of assets that have long lives, such as buildings, equipment, and motor vehicles. The period of service is referred to as the **useful life** of the asset. Because a building is expected to provide service for many years, it is recorded as an asset, rather than an expense, on the date it is acquired. As explained in Chapter 1, companies record such assets **at cost**, as required by the historical cost principle. To follow the expense recognition principle, companies allocate a portion of this cost as an expense during each period of the asset's useful life. **Depreciation** is the process of allocating the cost of an asset to expense over its useful life.

Need for Adjustment. The acquisition of long-lived assets is essentially a long-term prepayment for the use of an asset. An adjusting entry for depreciation is needed to recognize the cost that has been used (an expense) during the period and to report the unused cost (an asset) at the end of the period. One very important point to understand: **Depreciation is an allocation concept, not a valuation concept.** That is, depreciation **allocates an asset's cost to the periods in which it is used. Depreciation does not attempt to report the actual change in the value of the asset.**

For Pioneer Advertising, assume that depreciation on the equipment is $480 a year, or $40 per month. As shown in Illustration 3-7, rather than decrease (credit) the asset account directly, Pioneer instead credits Accumulated Depreciation—Equipment. Accumulated Depreciation is called a **contra asset account**. Such an account is offset against an asset account on the balance sheet. Thus, the Accumulated Depreciation—Equipment account offsets the asset Equipment. This account keeps track of the total amount of depreciation expense taken over the life of the asset. To keep the accounting equation in balance, Pioneer decreases owner's equity by increasing an expense account, Depreciation Expense.

The balance in the Accumulated Depreciation—Equipment account will increase $40 each month, and the balance in Equipment remains $5,000.

Statement Presentation. As indicated, Accumulated Depreciation—Equipment is a contra asset account. It is offset against Equipment on the balance sheet. The normal balance of a contra asset account is a credit. A theoretical alternative to using a contra asset account would be to decrease (credit) the asset account by the amount of depreciation each period. But using the contra account is preferable for a simple reason: It discloses **both** the original cost of the equipment **and**

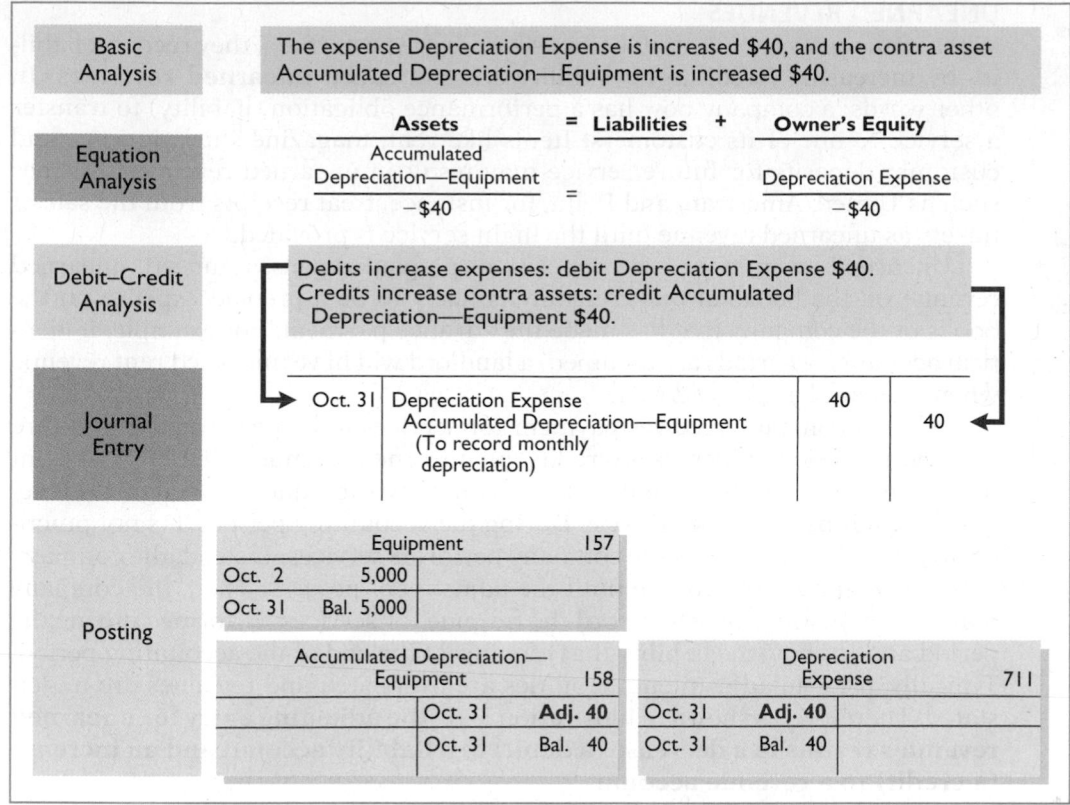

Basic Analysis	The expense Depreciation Expense is increased $40, and the contra asset Accumulated Depreciation—Equipment is increased $40.

Equation Analysis

Assets	=	Liabilities	+	Owner's Equity
Accumulated Depreciation—Equipment −$40	=			Depreciation Expense −$40

Debit–Credit Analysis

Debits increase expenses: debit Depreciation Expense $40.
Credits increase contra assets: credit Accumulated Depreciation—Equipment $40.

Journal Entry

Oct. 31	Depreciation Expense	40	
	Accumulated Depreciation—Equipment		40
	(To record monthly depreciation)		

Posting

Equipment		157
Oct. 2	5,000	
Oct. 31	Bal. 5,000	

Accumulated Depreciation—Equipment		158
	Oct. 31	Adj. 40
	Oct. 31	Bal. 40

Depreciation Expense		711
Oct. 31	Adj. 40	
Oct. 31	Bal. 40	

Illustration 3-7
Adjustment for depreciation

the total cost that has been expensed to date. Thus, in the balance sheet, Pioneer deducts Accumulated Depreciation—Equipment from the related asset account, as shown in Illustration 3-8.

Equipment	$ 5,000
Less: Accumulated depreciation—equipment	40
	$4,960

Illustration 3-8
Balance sheet presentation of accumulated depreciation

Book value is the difference between the cost of any depreciable asset and its related accumulated depreciation. In Illustration 3-8, the book value of the equipment at the balance sheet date is $4,960. The book value and the fair value of the asset are generally two different values. As noted earlier, **the purpose of depreciation is not valuation but a means of cost allocation**.

Depreciation expense identifies the portion of an asset's cost that expired during the period (in this case, in October). The accounting equation shows that without this adjusting entry, total assets, total owner's equity, and net income are overstated by $40 and depreciation expense is understated by $40.

Illustration 3-9 summarizes the accounting for prepaid expenses.

Alternative Terminology
Book value is also referred to as *carrying value*.

Illustration 3-9
Accounting for prepaid expenses

ACCOUNTING FOR PREPAID EXPENSES			
Examples	**Reason for Adjustment**	**Accounts Before Adjustment**	**Adjusting Entry**
Insurance, supplies, advertising, rent, depreciation	Prepaid expenses recorded in asset accounts have been used.	Assets overstated. Expenses understated.	Dr. Expenses Cr. Assets or Contra Assets

Unearned Revenues

Oct. 2

Thank you in advance for your work

I will finish by Dec. 31

$1,200

Cash is received in advance; liability is recorded

Oct. 31

Some service has been performed; some revenue is recorded

UNEARNED REVENUES

When companies receive cash before services are performed, they record a liability by increasing (crediting) a liability account called **unearned revenues**. In other words, a company now has a performance obligation (liability) to transfer a service to one of its customers. Items like rent, magazine subscriptions, and customer deposits for future service may result in unearned revenues. Airlines such as United, American, and Delta, for instance, treat receipts from the sale of tickets as unearned revenue until the flight service is provided.

Unearned revenues are the opposite of prepaid expenses. Indeed, unearned revenue on the books of one company is likely to be a prepaid expense on the books of the company that has made the advance payment. For example, if identical accounting periods are assumed, a landlord will have unearned rent revenue when a tenant has prepaid rent.

When a company receives payment for services to be performed in a future accounting period, it increases (credits) an unearned revenue (a liability) account to recognize the liability that exists. The company subsequently recognizes revenues when it performs the service. During the accounting period, it is not practical to make daily entries as the company performs services. Instead, the company delays recognition of revenue until the adjustment process. Then, the company makes an adjusting entry to record the revenue for services performed during the period and to show the liability that remains at the end of the accounting period. Typically, prior to adjustment, liabilities are overstated and revenues are understated. Therefore, as shown in Illustration 3-10, **the adjusting entry for unearned revenues results in a decrease (a debit) to a liability account and an increase (a credit) to a revenue account**.

Illustration 3-10
Adjusting entries for unearned revenues

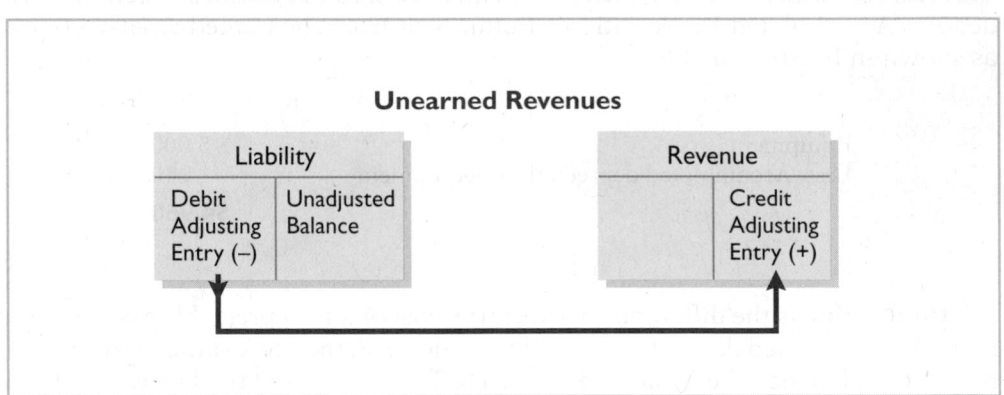

Unearned Revenues

Liability				Revenue	
Debit Adjusting Entry (−)	Unadjusted Balance				Credit Adjusting Entry (+)

Pioneer Advertising received $1,200 on October 2 from R. Knox for advertising services expected to be completed by December 31. Pioneer credited the payment to Unearned Service Revenue. This liability account shows a balance of $1,200 in the October 31 trial balance. From an evaluation of the service Pioneer performed for Knox during October, the company determines that it should recognize $400 of revenue in October. The liability (Unearned Service Revenue) is therefore decreased, and owner's equity (Service Revenue) is increased.

As shown in Illustration 3-11, the liability Unearned Service Revenue now shows a balance of $800. That amount represents the remaining advertising services expected to be performed in the future. At the same time, Service Revenue shows total revenue recognized in October of $10,400. **Without this adjustment, revenues and net income are understated by $400 in the income statement. Moreover, liabilities will be overstated and owner's equity will be understated by $400 on the October 31 balance sheet.**

| Basic Analysis | The liability Unearned Service Revenue is decreased $400, and the revenue Service Revenue is increased $400. |

Illustration 3-11
Service revenue accounts after adjustment

Illustration 3-12 summarizes the accounting for unearned revenues.

Illustration 3-12
Accounting for unearned revenues

ACCOUNTING FOR UNEARNED REVENUES

Examples	Reason for Adjustment	Accounts Before Adjustment	Adjusting Entry
Rent, magazine subscriptions, customer deposits for future service	Unearned revenues recorded in liability accounts are now recognized as revenue for services performed.	Liabilities overstated. Revenues understated.	Dr. Liabilities Cr. Revenues

ACCOUNTING ACROSS THE ORGANIZATION

Turning Gift Cards into Revenue

Those of you who are marketing majors (and even most of you who are not) know that gift cards are among the hottest marketing tools in merchandising today. Customers purchase gift cards and give them to someone for later use. In a recent year, gift-card sales topped $95 billion.

Although these programs are popular with marketing executives, they create accounting questions. Should revenue be recorded at the time the gift card is sold, or when it is exercised? How should expired gift cards be accounted for? In a recent balance sheet, Best Buy reported unearned revenue related to gift cards of $479 million.

Source: Robert Berner, "Gift Cards: No Gift to Investors," *BusinessWeek* (March 14, 2005), p. 86.

 Suppose that Robert Jones purchases a $100 gift card at Best Buy on December 24, 2013, and gives it to his wife, Mary Jones, on December 25, 2013. On January 3, 2014, Mary uses the card to purchase $100 worth of CDs. When do you think Best Buy should recognize revenue and why? (See page 156.)

© Skip ODonnell/iStockphoto

> **DO IT!**

Adjusting Entries for Deferrals

The ledger of Hammond Company, on March 31, 2014, includes these selected accounts before adjusting entries are prepared.

	Debit	Credit
Prepaid Insurance	$ 3,600	
Supplies	2,800	
Equipment	25,000	
Accumulated Depreciation—Equipment		$5,000
Unearned Service Revenue		9,200

An analysis of the accounts shows the following.

1. Insurance expires at the rate of $100 per month.
2. Supplies on hand total $800.
3. The equipment depreciates $200 a month.
4. During March, services were performed for one-half of the unearned service revenue.

Prepare the adjusting entries for the month of March.

Solution

Action Plan

✔ Make adjusting entries at the end of the period for revenues recognized and expenses incurred in the period.

✔ Don't forget to make adjusting entries for deferrals. Failure to adjust for deferrals leads to overstatement of the asset or liability and understatement of the related expense or revenue.

1. Insurance Expense	100	
Prepaid Insurance		100
(To record insurance expired)		
2. Supplies Expense	2,000	
Supplies		2,000
(To record supplies used)		
3. Depreciation Expense	200	
Accumulated Depreciation—Equipment		200
(To record monthly depreciation)		
4. Unearned Service Revenue	4,600	
Service Revenue		4,600
(To record revenue for services performed)		

Related exercise material: **BE3-3, BE3-4, BE3-5, BE3-6,** and **DO IT!** 3-2.

✔ **The Navigator**

Adjusting Entries for Accruals

LEARNING OBJECTIVE　**5**

Prepare adjusting entries for accruals.

The second category of adjusting entries is **accruals**. Prior to an accrual adjustment, the revenue account (and the related asset account) or the expense account (and the related liability account) are understated. Thus, the adjusting entry for accruals will **increase both a balance sheet and an income statement account**.

ACCRUED REVENUES

Revenues for services performed but not yet recorded at the statement date are **accrued revenues**. Accrued revenues may accumulate (accrue) with the passing of time, as in the case of interest revenue. These are unrecorded because the earning of interest does not involve daily transactions. Companies do not record interest revenue on a daily basis because it is often impractical to do so. Accrued revenues also may result from services that have been performed but not yet billed nor collected, as in the case of commissions and fees. These may be unrecorded because only a portion of the total service has been performed and the clients will not be billed until the service has been completed.

An adjusting entry records the receivable that exists at the balance sheet date and the revenue for the services performed during the period. Prior to adjustment, both assets and revenues are understated. As shown in Illustration 3-13, **an adjusting entry for accrued revenues results in an increase (a debit) to an asset account and an increase (a credit) to a revenue account**.

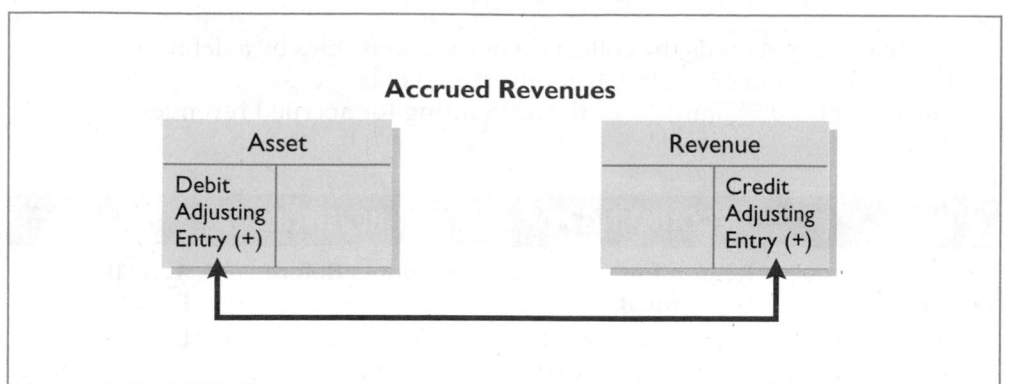

Illustration 3-13
Adjusting entries for accrued revenues

In October, Pioneer Advertising performed services worth $200 that were not billed to clients on or before October 31. Because these services are not billed, they are not recorded. The accrual of unrecorded service revenue increases an asset account, Accounts Receivable. It also increases owner's equity by increasing a revenue account, Service Revenue, as shown in Illustration 3-14.

Illustration 3-14
Adjustment for accrued revenue

The asset Accounts Receivable shows that clients owe Pioneer $200 at the balance sheet date. The balance of $10,600 in Service Revenue represents the total revenue for services performed by Pioneer during the month ($10,000 + $400 + $200). **Without the adjusting entry, assets and owner's equity on the balance sheet and revenues and net income on the income statement are understated.**

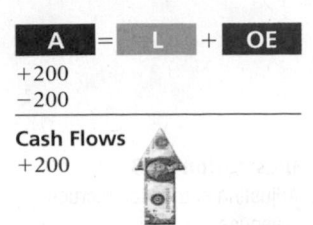

A = L + OE
+200
−200

Cash Flows
+200

Equation analyses summarize the effects of transactions on the three elements of the accounting equation, as well as the effect on cash flows.

Illustration 3-15
Accounting for accrued revenues

On November 10, Pioneer receives cash of $200 for the services performed in October and makes the following entry.

Nov. 10	Cash	200	
	Accounts Receivable		200
	(To record cash collected on account)		

The company records the collection of the receivables by a debit (increase) to Cash and a credit (decrease) to Accounts Receivable.

Illustration 3-15 summarizes the accounting for accrued revenues.

ACCOUNTING FOR ACCRUED REVENUES			
Examples	**Reason for Adjustment**	**Accounts Before Adjustment**	**Adjusting Entry**
Interest, rent, services	Services performed but not yet received in cash or recorded.	Assets understated. Revenues understated.	Dr. Assets Cr. Revenues

ACCRUED EXPENSES

Expenses incurred but not yet paid or recorded at the statement date are called **accrued expenses**. Interest, taxes, and salaries are common examples of accrued expenses.

Companies make adjustments for accrued expenses to record the obligations that exist at the balance sheet date and to recognize the expenses that apply to the current accounting period. Prior to adjustment, both liabilities and expenses are understated. Therefore, as Illustration 3-16 shows, **an adjusting entry for accrued expenses results in an increase (a debit) to an expense account and an increase (a credit) to a liability account.**

Illustration 3-16
Adjusting entries for accrued expenses

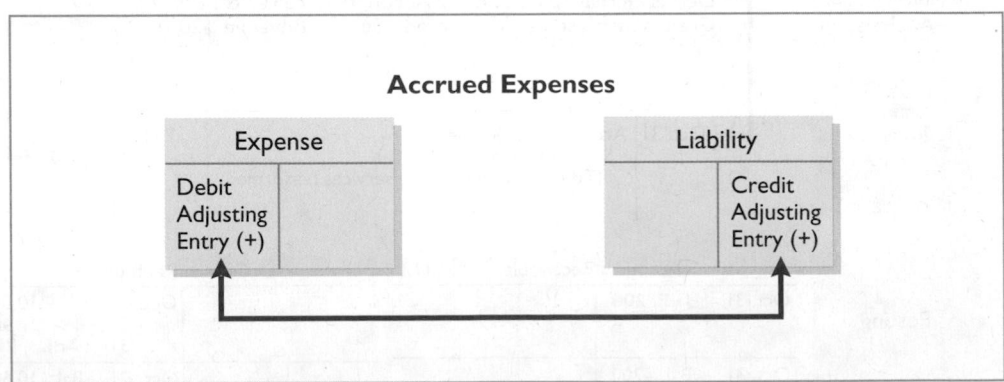

Let's look in more detail at some specific types of accrued expenses, beginning with accrued interest.

ACCRUED INTEREST Pioneer Advertising signed a three-month note payable in the amount of $5,000 on October 1. The note requires Pioneer to pay interest at an annual rate of 12%.

The amount of the interest recorded is determined by three factors: (1) the face value of the note; (2) the interest rate, which is always expressed as an annual rate; and (3) the length of time the note is outstanding. For Pioneer, the total interest due on the $5,000 note at its maturity date three months in the future is $150 ($5,000 × 12% × $\frac{3}{12}$), or $50 for one month. Illustration 3-17 shows the formula for computing interest and its application to Pioneer for the month of October.

Face Value of Note	×	Annual Interest Rate	×	Time in Terms of One Year	=	Interest
$5,000	×	12%	×	$\frac{1}{12}$	=	$50

Illustration 3-17
Formula for computing interest

Helpful Hint In computing interest, we express the time period as a fraction of a year.

As Illustration 3-18 shows, the accrual of interest at October 31 increases a liability account, Interest Payable. It also decreases owner's equity by increasing an expense account, Interest Expense.

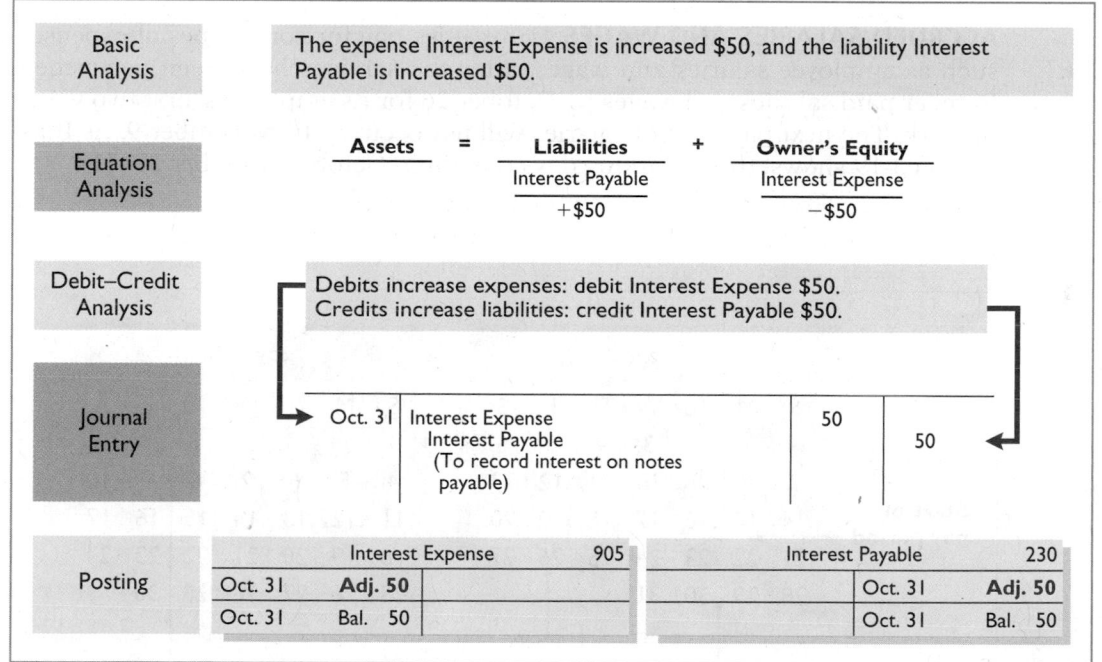

Illustration 3-18
Adjustment for accrued interest

Basic Analysis
The expense Interest Expense is increased $50, and the liability Interest Payable is increased $50.

Equation Analysis

Assets	=	Liabilities	+	Owner's Equity
		Interest Payable		Interest Expense
		+$50		−$50

Debit–Credit Analysis
Debits increase expenses: debit Interest Expense $50.
Credits increase liabilities: credit Interest Payable $50.

Journal Entry

Oct. 31	Interest Expense	50	
	Interest Payable		50
	(To record interest on notes payable)		

Posting

Interest Expense		905
Oct. 31	Adj. 50	
Oct. 31	Bal. 50	

Interest Payable		230
	Oct. 31	Adj. 50
	Oct. 31	Bal. 50

Interest Expense shows the interest charges for the month of October. Interest Payable shows the amount of interest the company owes at the statement date. Pioneer will not pay the interest until the note comes due at the end of three months. Companies use the Interest Payable account, instead of crediting Notes Payable, to disclose the two different types of obligations—interest and principal—in the accounts and statements. **Without this adjusting entry, liabilities and interest expense are understated, and net income and owner's equity are overstated.**

Günay Mutlu/iStockphoto

INTERNATIONAL INSIGHT

Cashing In on Accrual Accounting

The Chinese government, like most governments, uses cash accounting. A recent report, however, noted that it decided to use accrual accounting versus cash accounting for about $38 billion of expenditures in a recent budget projection. The Chinese government decided to expense the amount in the year in which it was originally allocated rather than when the payments would be made. Why did the Chinese government do this? It enabled the government to keep its projected budget deficit below a 3% threshold. While the Chinese government was able to keep its projected shortfall below 3%, it did suffer some criticism for its inconsistent accounting. Critics charge that this inconsistent treatment reduces the transparency of China's accounting information. That is, it is not easy for outsiders to accurately evaluate what is really going on.

Source: Andrew Batson, "China Altered Budget Accounting to Reduce Deficit Figure," *Wall Street Journal Online* (March 15, 2010).

? Accrual accounting is often considered superior to cash accounting. Why, then, were some people critical of China's use of accrual accounting in this instance? (See page 157.)

ACCRUED SALARIES AND WAGES Companies pay for some types of expenses, such as employee salaries and wages, after the services have been performed. Pioneer paid salaries and wages on October 26 for its employees' first two weeks of work. The next payment of salaries will not occur until November 9. As Illustration 3-19 shows, three working days remain in October (October 29–31).

Illustration 3-19
Calendar showing Pioneer's pay periods

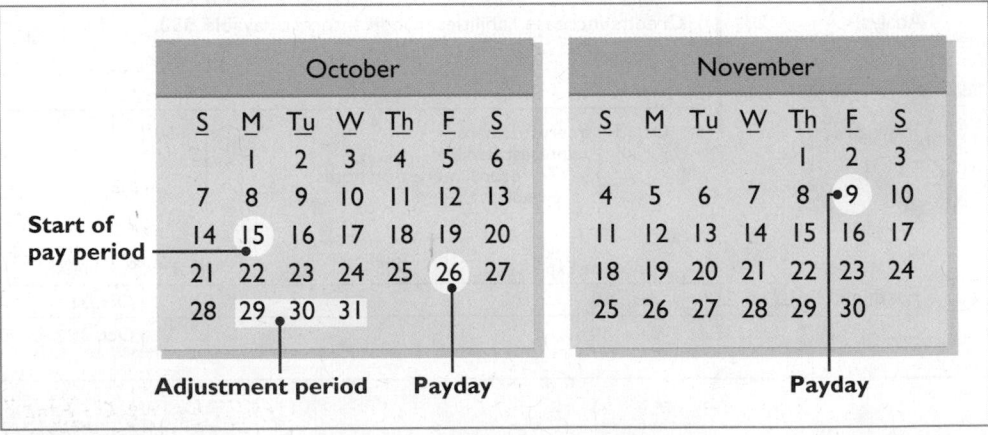

At October 31, the salaries and wages for these three days represent an accrued expense and a related liability to Pioneer. The employees receive total salaries and wages of $2,000 for a five-day work week, or $400 per day. Thus, accrued salaries and wages at October 31 are $1,200 ($400 × 3). This accrual increases a liability, Salaries and Wages Payable. It also decreases owner's equity by increasing an expense account, Salaries and Wages Expense, as shown in Illustration 3-20.

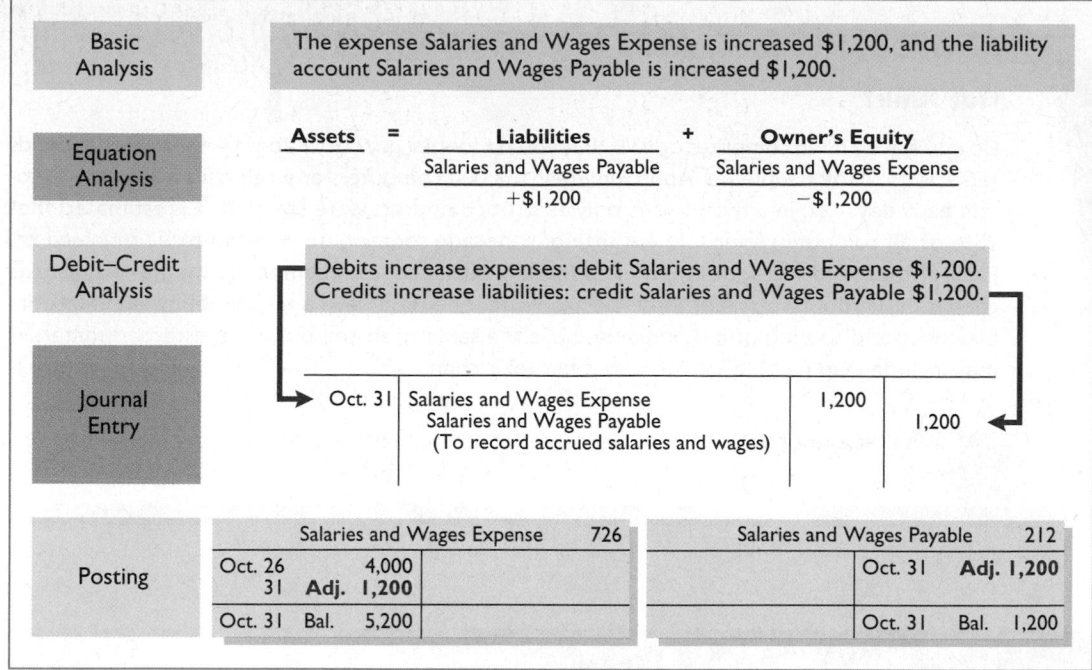

Illustration 3-20
Adjustment for accrued salaries and wages

After this adjustment, the balance in Salaries and Wages Expense of $5,200 (13 days × $400) is the actual salary and wages expense for October. The balance in Salaries and Wages Payable of $1,200 is the amount of the liability for salaries and wages Pioneer owes as of October 31. **Without the $1,200 adjustment for salaries and wages, Pioneer's expenses are understated $1,200 and its liabilities are understated $1,200.**

Pioneer Advertising pays salaries and wages every two weeks. Consequently, the next payday is November 9, when the company will again pay total salaries and wages of $4,000. The payment consists of $1,200 of salaries and wages payable at October 31 plus $2,800 of salaries and wages expense for November (7 working days, as shown in the November calendar × $400). Therefore, Pioneer makes the following entry on November 9.

Nov. 9	Salaries and Wages Payable	1,200	
	Salaries and Wages Expense	2,800	
	Cash		4,000
	(To record November 9 payroll)		

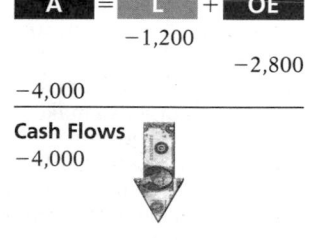

This entry eliminates the liability for Salaries and Wages Payable that Pioneer recorded in the October 31 adjusting entry, and it records the proper amount of Salaries and Wages Expense for the period between November 1 and November 9.

Illustration 3-21 summarizes the accounting for accrued expenses.

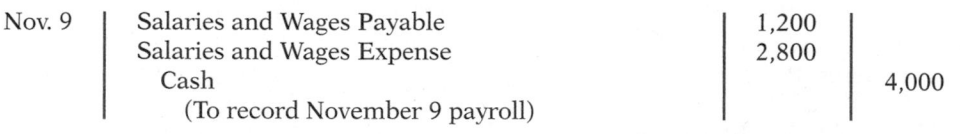

Illustration 3-21
Accounting for accrued expenses

ACCOUNTING FOR ACCRUED EXPENSES			
Examples	**Reason for Adjustment**	**Accounts Before Adjustment**	**Adjusting Entry**
Interest, rent, salaries	Expenses have been incurred but not yet paid in cash or recorded.	Expenses understated. Liabilities understated.	Dr. Expenses Cr. Liabilities

PEOPLE, PLANET, AND PROFIT INSIGHT

© Nathan Gleave/iStockphoto

Got Junk?

Do you have an old computer or two that you no longer use? How about an old TV that needs replacing? Many people do. Approximately 163,000 computers and televisions become obsolete **each day**. Yet, in a recent year, only 11% of computers were recycled. It is estimated that 75% of all computers ever sold are sitting in storage somewhere, waiting to be disposed of. Each of these old TVs and computers is loaded with lead, cadmium, mercury, and other toxic chemicals. If you have one of these electronic gadgets, you have a responsibility, and a probable cost, for disposing of it. Companies have the same problem, but their discarded materials may include lead paint, asbestos, and other toxic chemicals.

? What accounting issue might this cause for companies? (See page 157.)

> ### DO IT!

Adjusting Entries for Accruals

Micro Computer Services began operations on August 1, 2014. At the end of August 2014, management prepares monthly financial statements. The following information relates to August.

1. At August 31, the company owed its employees $800 in salaries and wages that will be paid on September 1.

2. On August 1, the company borrowed $30,000 from a local bank on a 15-year mortgage. The annual interest rate is 10%.

3. Revenue for services performed but unrecorded for August totaled $1,100.

Prepare the adjusting entries needed at August 31, 2014.

Solution

Action Plan

✔ Make adjusting entries at the end of the period to recognize revenues for services performed and for expenses incurred.

✔ Don't forget to make adjusting entries for accruals. Adjusting entries for accruals will increase both a balance sheet and an income statement account.

1. Salaries and Wages Expense	800	
Salaries and Wages Payable		800
(To record accrued salaries)		
2. Interest Expense	250	
Interest Payable		250
(To record accrued interest: $30,000 \times 10\% \times \frac{1}{12} = \$250$)		
3. Accounts Receivable	1,100	
Service Revenue		1,100
(To record revenue for services performed)		

Related exercise material: **BE3-2, BE3-7, E3-5, E3-6, E3-7, E3-8, E3-9, and DO IT! 3-3.**

✔ The Navigator

Summary of Basic Relationships

Illustration 3-22 summarizes the four basic types of adjusting entries. Take some time to study and analyze the adjusting entries. Be sure to note that **each adjusting entry affects one balance sheet account and one income statement account**.

Type of Adjustment	Accounts Before Adjustment	Adjusting Entry

Prepaid expenses	Assets overstated
	Expenses understated
		Dr. Expenses
		    Cr. Assets or
		    Contra Assets

Unearned revenues	Liabilities overstated Revenues understated	Dr. Liabilities Cr. Revenues
Accrued revenues	Assets understated Revenues understated	Dr. Assets Cr. Revenues
Accrued expenses	Expenses understated Liabilities understated	Dr. Expenses Cr. Liabilities

Illustration 3-22
Summary of adjusting entries

Illustrations 3-23 (below) and 3-24 (on page 118) show the journalizing and posting of adjusting entries for Pioneer Advertising Agency on October 31. The ledger identifies all adjustments by the reference J2 because they have been recorded on page 2 of the general journal. The company may insert a center caption "Adjusting Entries" between the last transaction entry and the first adjusting entry in the journal. When you review the general ledger in Illustration 3-24, note that the entries highlighted in color are the adjustments.

	GENERAL JOURNAL			J2
Date	Account Titles and Explanation	Ref.	Debit	Credit
2014 Oct. 31	Adjusting Entries Supplies Expense	631	1,500	
	Supplies	126		1,500
	(To record supplies used)			
31	Insurance Expense	722	50	
	Prepaid Insurance	130		50
	(To record insurance expired)			
31	Depreciation Expense	711	40	
	Accumulated Depreciation—Equipment	158		40
	(To record monthly depreciation)			
31	Unearned Service Revenue	209	400	
	Service Revenue	400		400
	(To record revenue for services performed)			
31	Accounts Receivable	112	200	
	Service Revenue	400		200
	(To record revenue for services performed)			
31	Interest Expense	905	50	
	Interest Payable	230		50
	(To record interest on notes payable)			
31	Salaries and Wages Expense	726	1,200	
	Salaries and Wages Payable	212		1,200
	(To record accrued salaries and wages)			

Illustration 3-23
General journal showing adjusting entries

Helpful Hint
(1) Adjusting entries should not involve debits or credits to Cash.
(2) Evaluate whether the adjustment makes sense. For example, an adjustment to recognize supplies used should increase Supplies Expense.
(3) Double-check all computations.
(4) Each adjusting entry affects one balance sheet account and one income statement account.

Illustration 3-24
General ledger after adjustment

Cash   No. 101

Date	Explanation	Ref.	Debit	Credit	Balance
2014					
Oct. 1		J1	10,000		10,000
2		J1	1,200		11,200
3		J1		900	10,300
4		J1		600	9,700
20		J1		500	9,200
26		J1		4,000	5,200
31		J1	10,000		15,200

Accounts Receivable   No. 112

Date	Explanation	Ref.	Debit	Credit	Balance
2014					
Oct. 31	Adj. entry	J2	200		200

Supplies   No. 126

Date	Explanation	Ref.	Debit	Credit	Balance
2014					
Oct. 5		J1	2,500		2,500
31	Adj. entry	J2		1,500	1,000

Prepaid Insurance   No. 130

Date	Explanation	Ref.	Debit	Credit	Balance
2014					
Oct. 4		J1	600		600
31	Adj. entry	J2		50	550

Equipment   No. 157

Date	Explanation	Ref.	Debit	Credit	Balance
2014					
Oct. 1		J1	5,000		5,000

Accumulated Depreciation—Equipment   No. 158

Date	Explanation	Ref.	Debit	Credit	Balance
2014					
Oct. 31	Adj. entry	J2		40	40

Notes Payable   No. 200

Date	Explanation	Ref.	Debit	Credit	Balance
2014					
Oct. 1		J1		5,000	5,000

Accounts Payable   No. 201

Date	Explanation	Ref.	Debit	Credit	Balance
2014					
Oct. 5		J1		2,500	2,500

Unearned Service Revenue   No. 209

Date	Explanation	Ref.	Debit	Credit	Balance
2014					
Oct. 2		J1		1,200	1,200
31	Adj. entry	J2	400		800

Salaries and Wages Payable   No. 212

Date	Explanation	Ref.	Debit	Credit	Balance
2014					
Oct. 31	Adj. entry	J2		1,200	1,200

Interest Payable   No. 230

Date	Explanation	Ref.	Debit	Credit	Balance
2014					
Oct. 31	Adj. entry	J2		50	50

Owner's Capital   No. 301

Date	Explanation	Ref.	Debit	Credit	Balance
2014					
Oct. 1		J1		10,000	10,000

Owner's Drawings   No. 306

Date	Explanation	Ref.	Debit	Credit	Balance
2014					
Oct. 20		J1	500		500

Service Revenue   No. 400

Date	Explanation	Ref.	Debit	Credit	Balance
2014					
Oct. 31		J1		10,000	10,000
31	Adj. entry	J2		400	10,400
31	Adj. entry	J2		200	10,600

Supplies Expense   No. 631

Date	Explanation	Ref.	Debit	Credit	Balance
2014					
Oct. 31	Adj. entry	J2	1,500		1,500

Depreciation Expense   No. 711

Date	Explanation	Ref.	Debit	Credit	Balance
2014					
Oct. 31	Adj. entry	J2	40		40

Insurance Expense   No. 722

Date	Explanation	Ref.	Debit	Credit	Balance
2014					
Oct. 31	Adj. entry	J2	50		50

Salaries and Wages Expense   No. 726

Date	Explanation	Ref.	Debit	Credit	Balance
2014					
Oct. 26		J1	4,000		4,000
31	Adj. entry	J2	1,200		5,200

Rent Expense   No. 729

Date	Explanation	Ref.	Debit	Credit	Balance
2014					
Oct. 3		J1	900		900

Interest Expense   No. 905

Date	Explanation	Ref.	Debit	Credit	Balance
2014					
Oct. 31	Adj. entry	J2	50		50

The Adjusted Trial Balance and Financial Statements

After a company has journalized and posted all adjusting entries, it prepares another trial balance from the ledger accounts. This trial balance is called an **adjusted trial balance**. It shows the balances of all accounts, including those adjusted, at the end of the accounting period. The purpose of an adjusted trial balance is to **prove the equality** of the total debit balances and the total credit balances in the ledger after all adjustments. Because the accounts contain all data needed for financial statements, the adjusted trial balance is the **primary basis for the preparation of financial statements**.

LEARNING OBJECTIVE   6

Describe the nature and purpose of an adjusted trial balance.

Preparing the Adjusted Trial Balance

Illustration 3-25 presents the adjusted trial balance for Pioneer Advertising Agency prepared from the ledger accounts in Illustration 3-24. The amounts affected by the adjusting entries are highlighted in color. Compare these amounts to those in the unadjusted trial balance in Illustration 3-3 on page 103. In this comparison, you will see that there are more accounts in the adjusted trial balance as a result of the adjusting entries made at the end of the month.

Illustration 3-25
Adjusted trial balance

PIONEER ADVERTISING AGENCY
Adjusted Trial Balance
October 31, 2014

	Dr.	Cr.
Cash	$ 15,200	
Accounts Receivable	200	
Supplies	1,000	
Prepaid Insurance	550	
Equipment	5,000	
Accumulated Depreciation—Equipment		$ 40
Notes Payable		5,000
Accounts Payable		2,500
Interest Payable		50
Unearned Service Revenue		800
Salaries and Wages Payable		1,200
Owner's Capital		10,000
Owner's Drawings	500	
Service Revenue		10,600
Salaries and Wages Expense	5,200	
Supplies Expense	1,500	
Rent Expense	900	
Insurance Expense	50	
Interest Expense	50	
Depreciation Expense	40	
	$30,190	$30,190

Preparing Financial Statements

Companies can prepare financial statements directly from the adjusted trial balance. Illustrations 3-26 (page 120) and 3-27 (page 121) present the inter-relationships of data in the adjusted trial balance and the financial statements.

As Illustration 3-26 shows, companies prepare the income statement from the revenue and expense accounts. Next, they use the owner's capital and drawings accounts and the net income (or net loss) from the income statement to prepare the owner's equity statement.

Illustration 3-26
Preparation of the income statement and owner's equity statement from the adjusted trial balance

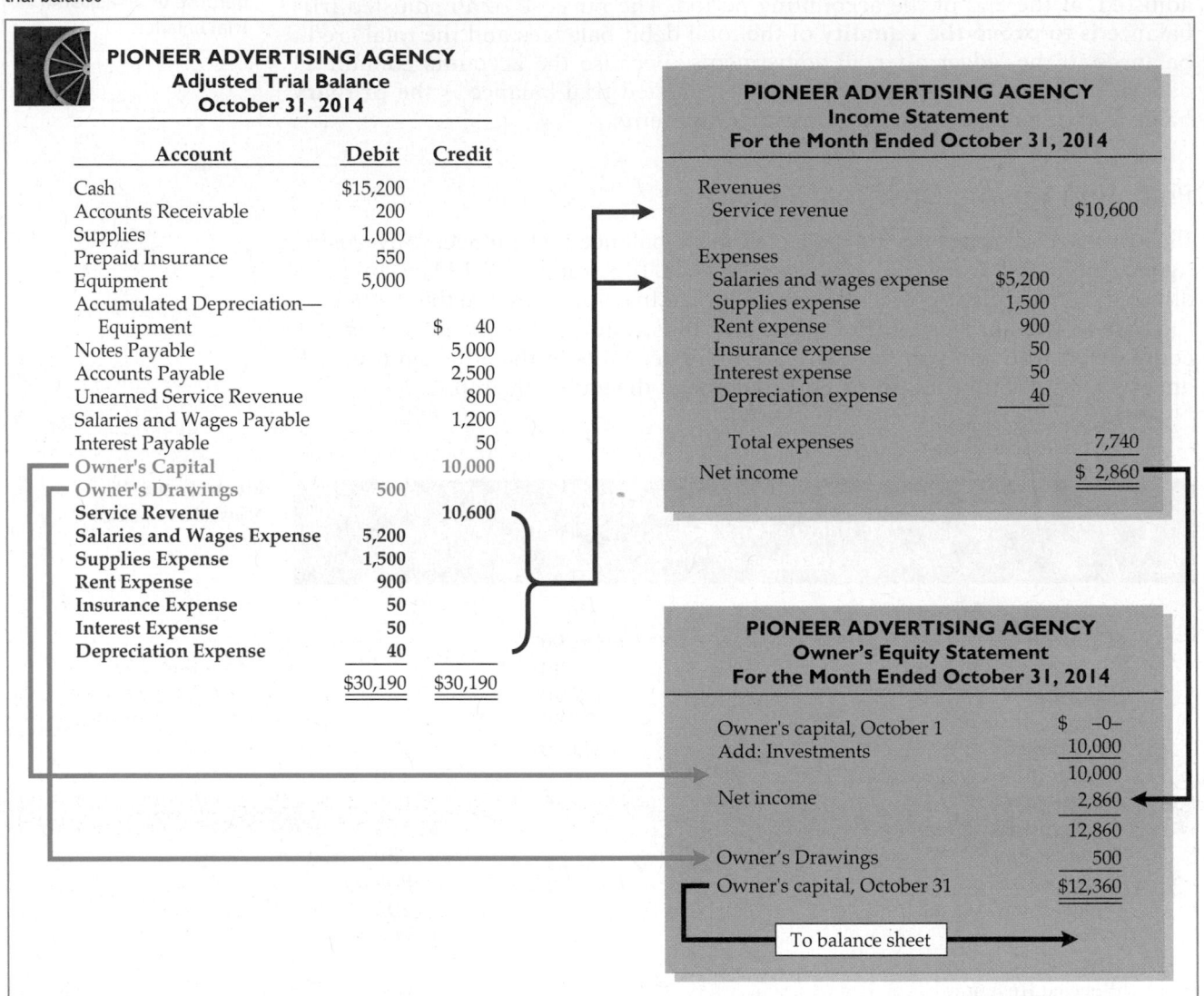

As Illustration 3-27 shows, companies then prepare the balance sheet from the asset and liability accounts and the ending owner's capital balance as reported in the owner's equity statement.

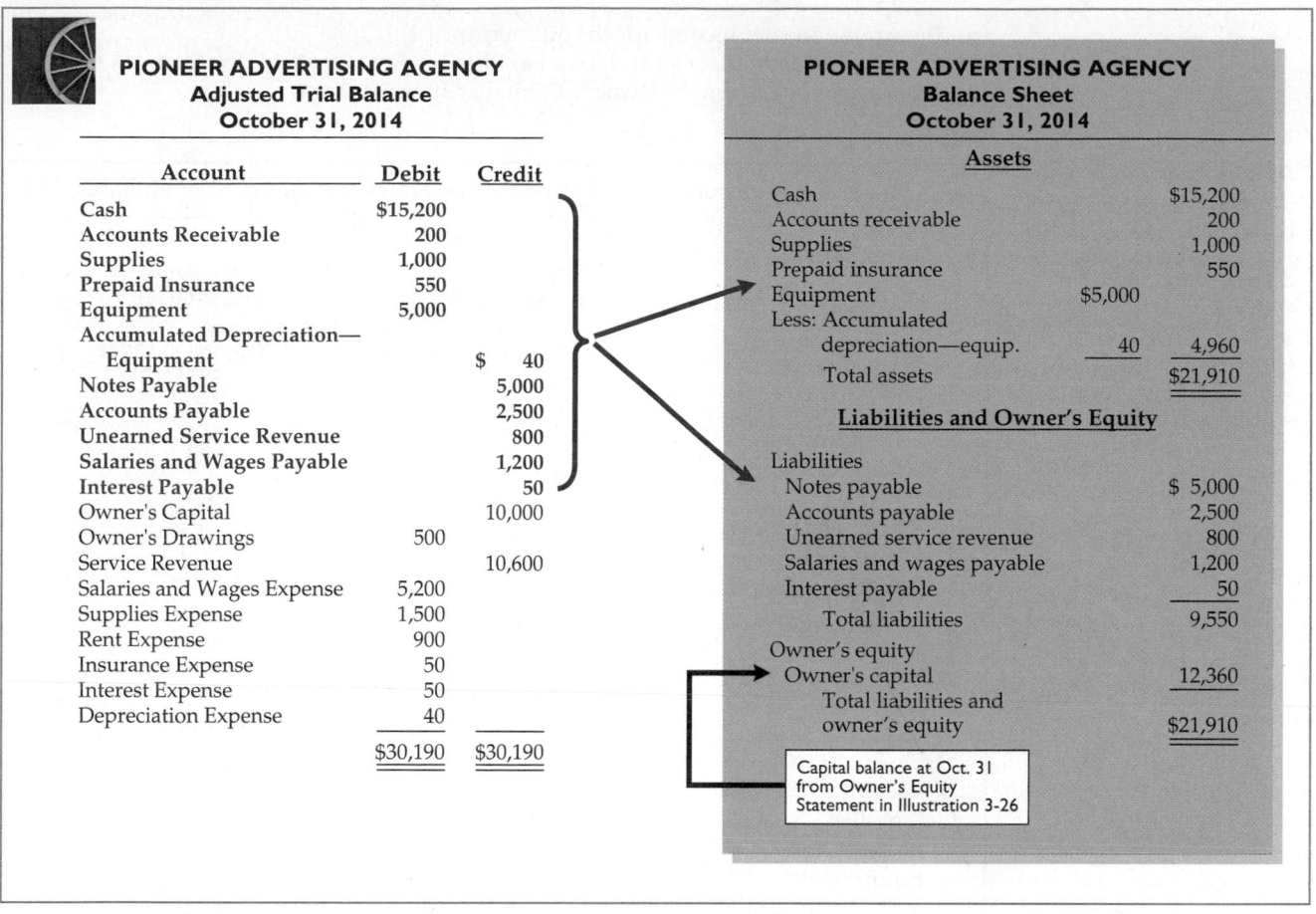

PIONEER ADVERTISING AGENCY
Adjusted Trial Balance
October 31, 2014

Account	Debit	Credit
Cash	$15,200	
Accounts Receivable	200	
Supplies	1,000	
Prepaid Insurance	550	
Equipment	5,000	
Accumulated Depreciation—		
Equipment		$ 40
Notes Payable		5,000
Accounts Payable		2,500
Unearned Service Revenue		800
Salaries and Wages Payable		1,200
Interest Payable		50
Owner's Capital		10,000
Owner's Drawings	500	
Service Revenue		10,600
Salaries and Wages Expense	5,200	
Supplies Expense	1,500	
Rent Expense	900	
Insurance Expense	50	
Interest Expense	50	
Depreciation Expense	40	
	$30,190	$30,190

PIONEER ADVERTISING AGENCY
Balance Sheet
October 31, 2014

Assets

Cash		$15,200
Accounts receivable		200
Supplies		1,000
Prepaid insurance		550
Equipment	$5,000	
Less: Accumulated		
depreciation—equip.	40	4,960
Total assets		$21,910

Liabilities and Owner's Equity

Liabilities		
Notes payable		$ 5,000
Accounts payable		2,500
Unearned service revenue		800
Salaries and wages payable		1,200
Interest payable		50
Total liabilities		9,550
Owner's equity		
Owner's capital		12,360
Total liabilities and		
owner's equity		$21,910

> Capital balance at Oct. 31 from Owner's Equity Statement in Illustration 3-26

Illustration 3-27
Preparation of the balance sheet from the adjusted trial balance

> DO IT!

Trial Balance

Skolnick Co. was organized on April 1, 2014. The company prepares quarterly financial statements. The adjusted trial balance amounts at June 30 are shown below.

	Debit		Credit
Cash	$ 6,700	Accumulated Depreciation—	
Accounts Receivable	600	Equipment	$ 850
Prepaid Rent	900	Notes Payable	5,000
Supplies	1,000	Accounts Payable	1,510
Equipment	15,000	Salaries and Wages Payable	400
Owner's Drawings	600	Interest Payable	50
Salaries and Wages Expense	9,400	Unearned Rent Revenue	500
Rent Expense	1,500	Owner's Capital	14,000
Depreciation Expense	850	Service Revenue	14,200
Supplies Expense	200	Rent Revenue	800
Utilities Expense	510		
Interest Expense	50		
	$37,310		$37,310

(a) Determine the net income for the quarter April 1 to June 30.
(b) Determine the total assets and total liabilities at June 30, 2014, for Skolnick Co.
(c) Determine the amount of Owner's Capital at June 30, 2014.

Solution

Action Plan

✔ In an adjusted trial balance, all asset, liability, revenue, and expense accounts are properly stated.

✔ To determine the ending balance in Owner's Capital, add net income and subtract dividends.

(a) The net income is determined by adding revenues and subtracting expenses. The net income is computed as follows.

Revenues		
Service revenue	$14,200	
Rent revenue	800	
Total revenues		$15,000
Expenses		
Salaries and wages expense	9,400	
Rent expense	1,500	
Depreciation expense	850	
Utilities expense	510	
Supplies expense	200	
Interest expense	50	
Total expenses		12,510
Net income		$ 2,490

(b) Total assets and liabilities are computed as follows.

Assets			Liabilities	
Cash		$ 6,700	Notes payable	$5,000
Accounts receivable		600	Accounts payable	1,510
Supplies		1,000	Unearned rent	
Prepaid rent		900	revenue	500
Equipment	$15,000		Salaries and wages	
Less: Accumulated			payable	400
depreciation—			Interest payable	50
equipment	850	14,150		
Total assets		$23,350	Total liabilities	$7,460

(c)

Owner's capital, April 1	$ 0
Add: Investments	14,000
Net income	2,490
Less: Owner's drawings	600
Owner's capital, June 30	$15,890

Related exercise material: **BE3-9, BE3-10, E3-11, E3-12, E3-13, and DO IT! 3-4.**

✔ **The Navigator**

> Comprehensive DO IT!

The Green Thumb Lawn Care Company began operations on April 1. At April 30, the trial balance shows the following balances for selected accounts.

Prepaid Insurance	$ 3,600
Equipment	28,000
Notes Payable	20,000
Unearned Service Revenue	4,200
Service Revenue	1,800

Analysis reveals the following additional data.

1. Prepaid insurance is the cost of a 2-year insurance policy, effective April 1.
2. Depreciation on the equipment is $500 per month.
3. The note payable is dated April 1. It is a 6-month, 12% note.
4. Seven customers paid for the company's 6-month lawn service package of $600 beginning in April. The company performed services for these customers in April.
5. Lawn services performed for other customers but not recorded at April 30 totaled $1,500.

Instructions
Prepare the adjusting entries for the month of April. Show computations.

Solution to Comprehensive **DO IT!**

Action Plan

✔ Note that adjustments are being made for one month.
✔ Make computations carefully.
✔ Select account titles carefully.
✔ Make sure debits are made first and credits are indented.
✔ Check that debits equal credits for each entry.

GENERAL JOURNAL					J1
Date	**Account Titles and Explanation**	**Ref.**	**Debit**		**Credit**
	Adjusting Entries				
Apr. 30	Insurance Expense		150		
	Prepaid Insurance				150
	(To record insurance expired: $3,600 ÷ 24 = $150 per month)				
30	Depreciation Expense		500		
	Accumulated Depreciation—Equipment				500
	(To record monthly depreciation)				
30	Interest Expense		200		
	Interest Payable				200
	(To record interest on notes payable: $20,000 × 12% × 1/12 = $200)				
30	Unearned Service Revenue		700		
	Service Revenue				700
	(To record revenue for services performed: $600 ÷ 6 = $100; $100 per month × 7 = $700)				
30	Accounts Receivable		1,500		
	Service Revenue				1,500
	(To record revenue for services performed)				

 ✔ The Navigator

SUMMARY OF LEARNING OBJECTIVES

✔ The Navigator

1 **Explain the time period assumption.** The time period assumption assumes that the economic life of a business is divided into artificial time periods.

2 **Explain the accrual basis of accounting.** Accrual-basis accounting means that companies record events that change a company's financial statements in the periods in which those events occur, rather than in the periods in which the company receives or pays cash.

3 **Explain the reasons for adjusting entries and identify the major types of adjusting entries.** Companies make adjusting entries at the end of an accounting period. Such entries ensure that companies recognize revenues in the period in which the performance obligation is satisfied and recognize expenses in the period in which they are incurred.

The major types of adjusting entries are deferrals (prepaid expenses and unearned revenues), and accruals (accrued revenues and accrued expenses).

4 Prepare adjusting entries for deferrals. Deferrals are either prepaid expenses or unearned revenues. Companies make adjusting entries for deferrals to record the portion of the prepayment that represents the expense incurred or the revenue for services performed in the current accounting period.

5 Prepare adjusting entries for accruals. Accruals are either accrued revenues or accrued expenses. Companies make adjusting entries for accruals to record revenues for services performed and expenses incurred in the current accounting period that have not been recognized through daily entries.

6 Describe the nature and purpose of an adjusted trial balance. An adjusted trial balance shows the balances of all accounts, including those that have been adjusted, at the end of an accounting period. Its purpose is to prove the equality of the total debit balances and total credit balances in the ledger after all adjustments.

GLOSSARY

Accrual-basis accounting Accounting basis in which companies record transactions that change a company's financial statements in the periods in which the events occur. (p. 100).

Accruals Adjusting entries for either accrued revenues or accrued expenses. (p. 103).

Accrued expenses Expenses incurred but not yet paid in cash or recorded. (p. 112).

Accrued revenues Revenues for services performed but not yet received in cash or recorded. (p. 110).

Adjusted trial balance A list of accounts and their balances after the company has made all adjustments. (p. 119).

Adjusting entries Entries made at the end of an accounting period to ensure that companies follow the revenue recognition and expense recognition principles. (p. 102).

Book value The difference between the cost of a depreciable asset and its related accumulated depreciation. (p. 107).

Calendar year An accounting period that extends from January 1 to December 31. (p. 100).

Cash-basis accounting Accounting basis in which companies record revenue when they receive cash and an expense when they pay cash. (p. 100).

Contra asset account An account offset against an asset account on the balance sheet. (p. 106).

Deferrals Adjusting entries for either prepaid expenses or unearned revenues. (p. 103).

Depreciation The process of allocating the cost of an asset to expense over its useful life. (p. 106).

Expense recognition principle (matching principle) The principle that companies match efforts (expenses) with accomplishments (revenues). (p. 101).

Fiscal year An accounting period that is one year in length. (p. 100).

Interim periods Monthly or quarterly accounting time periods. (p. 100).

Prepaid expenses (prepayments) Expenses paid in cash before they are used or consumed. (p. 104).

Revenue recognition principle The principle that companies recognize revenue in the accounting period in which the performance obligation is satisfied. (p. 101).

Time period assumption An assumption that accountants can divide the economic life of a business into artificial time periods. (p. 100).

Unearned revenues A liability recorded for cash received before services are performed. (p. 108).

Useful life The length of service of a long-lived asset. (p. 106).

APPENDIX 3A   Alternative Treatment of Prepaid Expenses and Unearned Revenues

<table>
<tr><td>LEARNING OBJECTIVE   **7**</td></tr>
<tr><td>Prepare adjusting entries for the alternative treatment of deferrals.</td></tr>
</table>

In discussing adjusting entries for prepaid expenses and unearned revenues, we illustrated transactions for which companies made the initial entries to balance sheet accounts. In the case of prepaid expenses, the company debited the prepayment to an asset account. In the case of unearned revenue, the company credited a liability account to record the cash received.

Some companies use an alternative treatment. (1) When a company prepays an expense, it debits that amount to an expense account. (2) When it receives payment for future services, it credits the amount to a revenue account. In this appendix, we describe the circumstances that justify such entries and the different adjusting entries that may be required. This alternative treatment of prepaid expenses and unearned revenues has the same effect on the financial statements as the procedures described in the chapter.

Prepaid Expenses

Prepaid expenses become expired costs either through the passage of time (e.g., insurance) or through consumption (e.g., advertising supplies). If at the time of purchase the company expects to consume the supplies before the next financial statement date, **it may choose to debit (increase) an expense account rather than an asset account. This alternative treatment is simply more convenient.**

Assume that Pioneer Advertising Agency expects that it will use before the end of the month all of the supplies purchased on October 5. A debit of $2,500 to Supplies Expense (rather than to the asset account Supplies) on October 5 will eliminate the need for an adjusting entry on October 31. At October 31, the Supplies Expense account will show a balance of $2,500, which is the cost of supplies used between October 5 and October 31.

But what if the company does not use all the supplies? For example, what if an inventory of $1,000 of advertising supplies remains on October 31? Obviously, the company would need to make an adjusting entry. Prior to adjustment, the expense account Supplies Expense is overstated $1,000, and the asset account Supplies is understated $1,000. Thus, Pioneer makes the following adjusting entry.

Oct. 31	Supplies	1,000	
	Supplies Expense		1,000
	(To record supplies inventory)		

A = L + OE
+1,000
+1,000 Exp

Cash Flows
no effect

After the company posts the adjusting entry, the accounts show:

Supplies			Supplies Expense			
10/31 Adj.	1,000		10/5	2,500	10/31 Adj.	1,000
			10/31 Bal.	1,500		

Illustration 3A-1
Prepaid expenses accounts after adjustment

After adjustment, the asset account Supplies shows a balance of $1,000, which is equal to the cost of supplies on hand at October 31. In addition, Supplies Expense shows a balance of $1,500. This is equal to the cost of supplies used between October 5 and October 31. Without the adjusting entry, expenses are overstated and net income is understated by $1,000 in the October income statement. Also, both assets and owner's equity are understated by $1,000 on the October 31 balance sheet.

Illustration 3A-2 compares the entries and accounts for advertising supplies in the two adjustment approaches.

Prepayment Initially Debited to Asset Account (per chapter)			Prepayment Initially Debited to Expense Account (per appendix)		
Oct. 5 Supplies	2,500		Oct. 5 Supplies Expense	2,500	
Accounts Payable		2,500	Accounts Payable		2,500
Oct. 31 Supplies Expense	1,500		Oct. 31 Supplies	1,000	
Supplies		1,500	Supplies Expense		1,000

Illustration 3A-2
Adjustment approaches—a comparison

After Pioneer posts the entries, the accounts appear as follows.

Illustration 3A-3
Comparison of accounts

	(per chapter) Supplies				(per appendix) Supplies	
10/5	2,500	10/31 Adj.	1,500	10/31 Adj.	1,000	
10/31 Bal.	1,000					

	Supplies Expense			Supplies Expense		
10/31 Adj.	1,500		10/5	2,500	10/31 Adj.	1,000
			10/31 Bal.	1,500		

Note that the account balances under each alternative are the same at October 31: Supplies $1,000 and Supplies Expense $1,500.

Unearned Revenues

Unearned revenues are recognized as revenue at the time services are performed. Similar to the case for prepaid expenses, companies may credit (increase) a revenue account when they receive cash for future services.

To illustrate, assume that Pioneer Advertising received $1,200 for future services on October 2. Pioneer expects to perform the services before October 31.[2] In such a case, the company credits Service Revenue. If Pioneer in fact performs the service before October 31, no adjustment is needed.

However, if at the statement date Pioneer has not performed $800 of the services, it would make an adjusting entry. Without the entry, the revenue account Service Revenue is overstated $800, and the liability account Unearned Service Revenue is understated $800. Thus, Pioneer makes the following adjusting entry.

Helpful Hint The required adjusted balances here are Service Revenue $400 and Unearned Service Revenue $800.

A = L + OE
−800 Rev
+800

Cash Flows
no effect

Oct. 31	Service Revenue	800	
	Unearned Service Revenue		800
	(To record unearned service revenue)		

After Pioneer posts the adjusting entry, the accounts show:

Illustration 3A-4
Unearned service revenue accounts after adjustment

Unearned Service Revenue			Service Revenue			
	10/31 Adj.	800	10/31 Adj.	800	10/2	1,200
					10/31 Bal.	400

The liability account Unearned Service Revenue shows a balance of $800. This equals the services that will be performed in the future. In addition, the balance in Service Revenue equals the services performed in October. Without the adjusting entry, both revenues and net income are overstated by $800 in the October income statement. Also, liabilities are understated by $800 and owner's equity is overstated by $800 on the October 31 balance sheet.

---

[2]This example focuses only on the alternative treatment of unearned revenues. For simplicity, we have ignored the entries to Service Revenue pertaining to the immediate recognition of revenue ($10,000) and the adjusting entry for accrued revenue ($200).

Illustration 3A-5 compares the entries and accounts for initially recording unearned service revenue in (1) a liability account or (2) a revenue account.

Unearned Service Revenue Initially Credited to Liability Account (per chapter)			Unearned Service Revenue Initially Credited to Revenue Account (per appendix)		
Oct. 2 Cash	1,200		Oct. 2 Cash	1,200	
Unearned Service Revenue		1,200	Service Revenue		1,200
Oct. 31 Unearned Service Revenue	400		Oct. 31 Service Revenue	800	
Service Revenue		400	Unearned Service Revenue		800

Illustration 3A-5
Adjustment approaches—a comparison

After Pioneer posts the entries, the accounts appear as follows.

Illustration 3A-6
Comparison of accounts

(per chapter) Unearned Service Revenue				(per appendix) Unearned Service Revenue			
10/31 Adj.	400	10/2	1,200			10/31 Adj.	800
		10/31 Bal.	800				

Service Revenue				Service Revenue			
		10/31 Adj.	400	10/31 Adj.	800	10/2	1,200
						10/31 Bal.	400

Note that the balances in the accounts are the same under the two alternatives: Unearned Service Revenue $800 and Service Revenue $400.

Summary of Additional Adjustment Relationships

Illustration 3A-7 provides a summary of basic relationships for deferrals.

Illustration 3A-7
Summary of basic relationships for deferrals

Type of Adjustment	Reason for Adjustment	Account Balances before Adjustment	Adjusting Entry
1. Prepaid expenses	(a) Prepaid expenses initially recorded in asset accounts have been used.	Assets overstated Expenses understated	Dr. Expenses Cr. Assets
	(b) **Prepaid expenses initially recorded in expense accounts have not been used.**	**Assets understated Expenses overstated**	**Dr. Assets Cr. Expenses**
2. Unearned revenues	(a) Unearned revenues initially recorded in liability accounts are now recognized as revenue.	Liabilities overstated Revenues understated	Dr. Liabilities Cr. Revenues
	(b) **Unearned revenues initially recorded in revenue accounts are still unearned.**	**Liabilities understated Revenues overstated**	**Dr. Revenues Cr. Liabilities**

Alternative adjusting entries **do not apply** to accrued revenues and accrued expenses because **no entries occur before companies make these types of adjusting entries**.

SUMMARY OF LEARNING OBJECTIVE FOR APPENDIX 3A

7 Prepare adjusting entries for the alternative treatment of deferrals. Companies may initially debit prepayments to an expense account. Likewise, they may credit unearned revenues to a revenue account. At the end of the period, these accounts may be overstated. The adjusting entries for prepaid expenses are a debit to an asset account and a credit to an expense account. Adjusting entries for unearned revenues are a debit to a revenue account and a credit to a liability account.

APPENDIX 3B　Concepts in Action

LEARNING OBJECTIVE　8

Discuss financial reporting concepts.

This appendix provides a summary of the concepts in action used in this textbook. In addition, it provides other useful concepts which accountants use as a basis for recording and reporting financial information.

Qualities of Useful Information

Recently, the FASB completed the first phase of a project in which it developed a conceptual framework to serve as the basis for future accounting standards. The framework begins by stating that the primary objective of financial reporting is to provide financial information that is **useful** to investors and creditors for making decisions about providing capital. Useful information should possess two fundamental qualities, relevance and faithful representation, as shown in Illustration 3B-1.

Illustration 3B-1
Fundamental qualities of useful information

"Tell me what I need to know."

BIG SHOT

Relevance Accounting information has **relevance** if it would make a difference in a business decision. Information is considered relevant if it provides information that has **predictive value**, that is, helps provide accurate expectations about the future, and has **confirmatory value**, that is, confirms or corrects prior expectations. **Materiality** is a company-specific aspect of relevance. An item is material when its **size** makes it likely to influence the decision of an investor or creditor.

Faithful Representation Faithful representation means that information accurately depicts what really happened. To provide a faithful representation, information must be **complete** (nothing important has been omitted), **neutral** (is not biased toward one position or another), and **free from error**.

ENHANCING QUALITIES

In addition to the two fundamental qualities, the FASB also describes a number of enhancing qualities of useful information. These include **comparability**, **consistency**, **verifiability**, **timeliness**, and **understandability**. In accounting, comparability results when different companies use the same accounting principles. Another characteristic that enhances comparability is consistency. **Consistency** means that a company uses the same accounting principles and methods from year to year. Information is **verifiable** if independent observers, using the same methods, obtain similar results. For accounting information to have relevance, it must be **timely**. That is, it must be available to decision-makers before it loses its capacity to influence decisions. For example, public companies like Google or Best Buy provide their annual reports to investors within 60 days of their year-end. Information has the quality of **understandability** if it is presented in a clear and concise fashion, so that reasonably informed users of that information can interpret it and comprehend its meaning.

Assumptions in Financial Reporting

To develop accounting standards, the FASB relies on some key assumptions, as shown in Illustration 3B-2. These include assumptions about the monetary unit, economic entity, time period, and going concern.

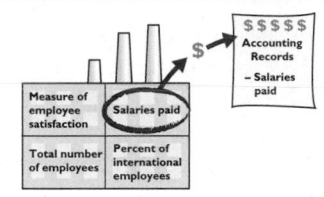

Monetary Unit Assumption The **monetary unit assumption** requires that only those things that can be expressed in money are included in the accounting records. This means that certain important information needed by investors, creditors, and managers, such as customer satisfaction, is not reported in the financial statements.

Economic Entity Assumption The **economic entity assumption** states that every economic entity can be separately identified and accounted for. In order to assess a company's performance and financial position accurately, it is important to not blur company transactions with personal transactions (especially those of its managers) or transactions of other companies.

Time Period Assumption Notice that the income statement, retained earnings statement, and statement of cash flows all cover periods of one year, and the balance sheet is prepared at the end of each year. The **time period assumption** states that the life of a business can be divided into artificial time periods and that useful reports covering those periods can be prepared for the business.

Going Concern Assumption The **going concern assumption** states that the business will remain in operation for the foreseeable future. Of course, many businesses do fail, but in general it is reasonable to assume that the business will continue operating.

Illustration 3B-2
Key assumptions in financial reporting

Principles in Financial Reporting

MEASUREMENT PRINCIPLES

GAAP generally uses one of two measurement principles, the historical cost principle or the fair value principle. Selection of which principle to follow generally relates to trade-offs between relevance and faithful representation.

HISTORICAL COST PRINCIPLE The **historical cost principle** (or cost principle, discussed in Chapter 1) dictates that companies record assets at their cost. This is true not only at the time the asset is purchased but also over the time the asset is held. For example, if land that was purchased for $30,000 increases in value to $40,000, it continues to be reported at $30,000.

FAIR VALUE PRINCIPLE The **fair value principle** (discussed in Chapter 1) indicates that assets and liabilities should be reported at fair value (the price received to sell an asset or settle a liability). Fair value information may be more useful than historical cost for certain types of assets and liabilities. For example, certain investment securities are reported at fair value because market price information is often readily available for these types of assets. In choosing between cost and fair value, two qualities that make accounting information useful for decision-making are used—relevance and faithful representation. In determining which measurement principle to use, the factual nature of cost figures are weighed versus the relevance of fair value. In general, most assets follow the historical cost principle because fair values may not be representationally faithful. Only in situations where assets are actively traded, such as investment securities, is the fair value principle applied.

REVENUE RECOGNITION PRINCIPLE

The **revenue recognition principle** requires that companies recognize revenue in the accounting period in which the performance obligation is satisfied. As discussed earlier in the chapter, in a service company, revenue is recognized at the time the service is performed. In a merchandising company, the performance obligation is generally satisfied when the goods transfer from the seller to the buyer (discussed in Chapter 5). At this point, the sales transaction is complete and the sales price established.

EXPENSE RECOGNITION PRINCIPLE

The **expense recognition principle** (often referred to as the matching principle, discussed earlier in the chapter) dictates that efforts (expenses) be matched with results (revenues). Thus, expenses follow revenues.

FULL DISCLOSURE PRINCIPLE

The **full disclosure principle** (discussed in Chapter 11) requires that companies disclose all circumstances and events that would make a difference to financial statement users. If an important item cannot reasonably be reported directly in one of the four types of financial statements, then it should be discussed in notes that accompany the statements.

Cost Constraint

Providing information is costly. In deciding whether companies should be required to provide a certain type of information, accounting standard-setters consider the **cost constraint**. It weighs the cost that companies will incur to provide the information against the benefit that financial statement users will gain from having the information available.

SUMMARY OF LEARNING OBJECTIVE FOR APPENDIX 3B

 ✔ **The Navigator**

8 Discuss financial reporting concepts To be judged useful, information should have the primary characteristics of relevance and faithful representation. In addition, it should be comparable, consistent, verifiable, timely, and understandable.

The **monetary unit assumption** requires that companies include in the accounting records only transaction data that can be expressed in terms of money. The **economic entity assumption** states that economic events can be identified with a particular unit of accountability. The **time period assumption** states that the economic life of a business can be divided into artificial time periods and that meaningful accounting reports can be prepared for each period. The **going concern assumption** states that the company will continue in operation long enough to carry out its existing objectives and commitments.

The **historical cost principle** states that companies should record assets at their cost. The **fair value principle** indicates that assets and liabilities should be reported at fair value. The **revenue recognition principle** requires that companies recognize revenue in the accounting period in which the performance obligation is satisfied. The **expense recognition principle** dictates that efforts (expenses) be matched with results (revenues). The **full disclosure principle** requires that companies disclose circumstances and events that matter to financial statement users.

The **cost constraint** weighs the cost that companies incur to provide a type of information against its benefits to financial statement users.

GLOSSARY FOR APPENDIX 3B

Comparability Ability to compare the accounting information of different companies because they use the same accounting principles. (p. 129).

Consistency Use of the same accounting principles and methods from year to year within a company. (p. 129).

Cost constraint Constraint that weighs the cost that companies will incur to provide the information against the benefit that financial statement users will gain from having the information available. (p. 130).

Economic entity assumption An assumption that every economic entity can be separately identified and accounted for. (p. 129).

Expense recognition principle Efforts (expenses) should be matched with results (revenues). (p. 130).

Fair value principle Assets and liabilities should be reported at fair value (the price received to sell an asset or settle a liability). (p. 130).

Faithful representation Information that accurately depicts what really happened. (p. 128).

Full disclosure principle Accounting principle that dictates that companies disclose circumstances and events that make a difference to financial statement users. (p. 130).

Going concern assumption The assumption that the company will continue in operation for the foreseeable future. (p. 129).

Historical cost principle An accounting principle that states that companies should record assets at their cost. (p. 130).

Materiality A company-specific aspect of relevance. An item is material when its size makes it likely to influence the decision of an investor or creditor. (p. 128).

Monetary unit assumption An assumption that requires that only those things that can be expressed in money are included in the accounting records. (p. 129).

Relevance The quality of information that indicates the information makes a difference in a decision. (p. 128).

Revenue recognition principle Companies recognize revenue in the accounting period in which the performance obligation is satisfied. (p. 130).

Timely Information that is available to decision-makers before it loses its capacity to influence decisions. (p. 129).

Time period assumption An assumption that the life of a business can be divided into artificial time periods and that useful reports covering those periods can be prepared for the business. (p. 129).

Understandability Information presented in a clear and concise fashion so that users can interpret it and comprehend its meaning. (p. 129).

Verifiable The quality of information that occurs when independent observers, using the same methods, obtain similar results. (p. 129).

Self-Test, Brief Exercises, Exercises, Problem Set A, and many more components are available for practice in *WileyPLUS*.

*****Note:** All asterisked Questions, Exercises, and Problems relate to material in the appendices to the chapter.

SELF-TEST QUESTIONS

Answers are on page 157.

(LO 1) **1.** The revenue recognition principle states that:
  (a) revenue should be recognized in the accounting period in which a performance obligation is satisfied.
  (b) expenses should be matched with revenues.
  (c) the economic life of a business can be divided into artificial time periods.
  (d) the fiscal year should correspond with the calendar year.

(LO 2) **2.** The time period assumption states that:
  (a) companies must wait until the calendar year is completed to prepare financial statements.
  (b) companies use the fiscal year to report financial information.
  (c) the economic life of a business can be divided into artificial time periods.
  (d) companies record information in the time period in which the events occur.

(LO 2) **3.** Which of the following statements about the accrual basis of accounting is **false**?
  (a) Events that change a company's financial statements are recorded in the periods in which the events occur.
  (b) Revenue is recognized in the period in which services are performed.
  (c) This basis is in accord with generally accepted accounting principles.
  (d) Revenue is recorded only when cash is received, and expense is recorded only when cash is paid.

(LO 2) **4.** The principle or assumption dictating that efforts (expenses) be matched with accomplishments (revenues) is the:
  (a) expense recognition principle.
  (b) cost assumption.
  (c) time period assumption.
  (d) revenue recognition principle.

(LO 3) **5.** Adjusting entries are made to ensure that:
  (a) expenses are recognized in the period in which they are incurred.
  (b) revenues are recorded in the period in which services are performed.
  (c) balance sheet and income statement accounts have correct balances at the end of an accounting period.
  (d) All the responses above are correct.

(LO 3) **6.** Each of the following is a major type (or category) of adjusting entries **except**:
  (a) prepaid expenses.
  (b) accrued revenues.
  (c) accrued expenses.
  (d) recognized revenues.

7. The trial balance shows Supplies $1,350 and Supplies (LO 4) Expense $0. If $600 of supplies are on hand at the end of the period, the adjusting entry is:

  (a) Supplies | 600 |
    Supplies Expense | | 600
  (b) Supplies | 750 |
    Supplies Expense | | 750
  (c) Supplies Expense | 750 |
    Supplies | | 750
  (d) Supplies Expense | 600 |
    Supplies | | 600

8. Adjustments for prepaid expenses: (LO 4)
  (a) decrease assets and increase revenues.
  (b) decrease expenses and increase assets.
  (c) decrease assets and increase expenses.
  (d) decrease revenues and increase assets.

9. Accumulated Depreciation is: (LO 4)
  (a) a contra asset account.
  (b) an expense account.
  (c) an owner's equity account.
  (d) a liability account.

10. Rivera Company computes depreciation on delivery (LO 4) equipment at $1,000 for the month of June. The adjusting entry to record this depreciation is as follows.

  (a) Depreciation Expense | 1,000 |
    Accumulated Depreciation— Rivera Company | | 1,000
  (b) Depreciation Expense | 1,000 |
    Equipment | | 1,000
  (c) Depreciation Expense | 1,000 |
    Accumulated Depreciation— Equipment | | 1,000
  (d) Equipment Expense | 1,000 |
    Accumulated Depreciation— Equipment | | 1,000

11. Adjustments for unearned revenues: (LO 4)
  (a) decrease liabilities and increase revenues.
  (b) have an assets and revenues account relationship.
  (c) increase assets and increase revenues.
  (d) decrease revenues and decrease assets.

12. Adjustments for accrued revenues: (LO 5)
  (a) have a liabilities and revenues account relationship.
  (b) have an assets and revenues account relationship.
  (c) decrease assets and revenues.
  (d) decrease liabilities and increase revenues.

13. Anika Wilson earned a salary of $400 for the last week (LO 5) of September. She will be paid on October 1. The adjusting entry for Anika's employer at September 30 is:
  (a) No entry is required.
  (b) Salaries and Wages Expense | 400 |
    Salaries and Wages Payable | | 400

(c)	Salaries and Wages Expense	400	
	Cash		400
(d)	Salaries and Wages Payable	400	
	Cash		400

(LO 6) **14.** Which of the following statements is **incorrect** concerning the adjusted trial balance?
   (a) An adjusted trial balance proves the equality of the total debit balances and the total credit balances in the ledger after all adjustments are made.
   (b) The adjusted trial balance provides the primary basis for the preparation of financial statements.
   (c) The adjusted trial balance lists the account balances segregated by assets and liabilities.
   (d) The adjusted trial balance is prepared after the adjusting entries have been journalized and posted.

(LO 7)***15.** The trial balance shows Supplies $0 and Supplies Expense $1,500. If $800 of supplies are on hand at the end of the period, the adjusting entry is:

   (a) Debit Supplies $800 and credit Supplies Expense $800.
   (b) Debit Supplies Expense $800 and credit Supplies $800.
   (c) Debit Supplies $700 and credit Supplies Expense $700.
   (d) Debit Supplies Expense $700 and credit Supplies $700.

*16. Neutrality is an ingredient of: (LO 8)

	Faithful Representation	**Relevance**
(a)	Yes	Yes
(b)	No	No
(c)	Yes	No
(d)	No	Yes

*17. Which item is a constraint in financial accounting?   (LO 8)
   (a) Comparability.   **(c)** Cost.
   (b) Materiality.   **(d)** Consistency.

Go to the book's companion website, www.wiley.com/college/weygandt, for additional Self-Test Questions.

QUESTIONS

1. (a) How does the time period assumption affect an accountant's analysis of business transactions?
   (b) Explain the terms fiscal year, calendar year, and interim periods.

2. Define two generally accepted accounting principles that relate to adjusting the accounts.

3. Susan Zupan, a lawyer, accepts a legal engagement in March, performs the work in April, and is paid in May. If Zupan's law firm prepares monthly financial statements, when should it recognize revenue from this engagement? Why?

4. Why do accrual-basis financial statements provide more useful information than cash-basis statements?

5. In completing the engagement in Question 3, Zupan pays no costs in March, $2,000 in April, and $2,500 in May (incurred in April). How much expense should the firm deduct from revenues in the month when it recognizes the revenue? Why?

6. "Adjusting entries are required by the historical cost principle of accounting." Do you agree? Explain.

7. Why may a trial balance not contain up-to-date and complete financial information?

8. Distinguish between the two categories of adjusting entries, and identify the types of adjustments applicable to each category.

9. What is the debit/credit effect of a prepaid expense adjusting entry?

10. "Depreciation is a valuation process that results in the reporting of the fair value of the asset." Do you agree? Explain.

11. Explain the differences between depreciation expense and accumulated depreciation.

12. J. Brownlee Company purchased equipment for $18,000. By the current balance sheet date, $6,000 had been depreciated. Indicate the balance sheet presentation of the data.

13. What is the debit/credit effect of an unearned revenue adjusting entry?

14. A company fails to recognize revenue for services performed but not yet received in cash or recorded. Which of the following accounts are involved in the adjusting entry: (a) asset, (b) liability, (c) revenue, or (d) expense? For the accounts selected, indicate whether they would be debited or credited in the entry.

15. A company fails to recognize an expense incurred but not paid. Indicate which of the following accounts is debited and which is credited in the adjusting entry: (a) asset, (b) liability, (c) revenue, or (d) expense.

16. A company makes an accrued revenue adjusting entry for $900 and an accrued expense adjusting entry for $700. How much was net income understated prior to these entries? Explain.

17. On January 9, a company pays $5,000 for salaries and wages of which $2,000 was reported as Salaries and Wages Payable on December 31. Give the entry to record the payment.

18. For each of the following items before adjustment, indicate the type of adjusting entry (prepaid expense, unearned revenue, accrued revenue, or accrued expense) that is needed to correct the misstatement. If an item could result in more than one type of adjusting entry, indicate each of the types.
   (a) Assets are understated.
   (b) Liabilities are overstated.
   (c) Liabilities are understated.
   (d) Expenses are understated.
   (e) Assets are overstated.
   (f) Revenue is understated.

19. One-half of the adjusting entry is given below. Indicate the account title for the other half of the entry.
    (a) Salaries and Wages Expense is debited.
    (b) Depreciation Expense is debited.
    (c) Interest Payable is credited.
    (d) Supplies is credited.
    (e) Accounts Receivable is debited.
    (f) Unearned Service Revenue is debited.
20. "An adjusting entry may affect more than one balance sheet or income statement account." Do you agree? Why or why not?
21. Why is it possible to prepare financial statements directly from an adjusted trial balance?
*22. Dashan Company debits Supplies Expense for all purchases of supplies and credits Rent Revenue for all advanced rentals. For each type of adjustment, give the adjusting entry.
*23. (a) What is the primary objective of financial reporting?
    (b) Identify the characteristics of useful accounting information.

*24. Dan Fineman, the president of King Company, is pleased. King substantially increased its net income in 2014 while keeping its unit inventory relatively the same. Howard Gross, chief accountant, cautions Dan, however. Gross says that since King changed its method of inventory valuation, there is a consistency problem and it is difficult to determine whether King is better off. Is Gross correct? Why or why not?
*25. What is the distinction between comparability and consistency?
*26. Describe the constraint inherent in the presentation of accounting information.
*27. Laurie Belk is president of Better Books. She has no accounting background. Belk cannot understand why fair value is not used as the basis for all accounting measurement and reporting. Discuss.
*28. What is the economic entity assumption? Give an example of its violation.

BRIEF EXERCISES

Indicate why adjusting entries are needed.
(LO 3)

BE3-1 The ledger of Jung Company includes the following accounts. Explain why each account may require adjustment.
(a) Prepaid Insurance.
(b) Depreciation Expense.
(c) Unearned Service Revenue.
(d) Interest Payable.

Identify the major types of adjusting entries.
(LO 3, 4, 5)

BE3-2 Moteki Company accumulates the following adjustment data at December 31. Indicate (a) the type of adjustment (prepaid expense, accrued revenues and so on), and (b) the status of accounts before adjustment (overstated or understated).
1. Supplies of $100 are on hand.
2. Services provided but not recorded total $900.
3. Interest of $200 has accumulated on a note payable.
4. Rent collected in advance totaling $650 has been earned.

Prepare adjusting entry for supplies.
(LO 4)

BE3-3 Ritter Advertising Company's trial balance at December 31 shows Supplies $6,700 and Supplies Expense $0. On December 31, there are $2,500 of supplies on hand. Prepare the adjusting entry at December 31, and using T-accounts, enter the balances in the accounts, post the adjusting entry, and indicate the adjusted balance in each account.

Prepare adjusting entry for depreciation.
(LO 4)

BE3-4 At the end of its first year, the trial balance of Nygaard Company shows Equipment $30,000 and zero balances in Accumulated Depreciation—Equipment and Depreciation Expense. Depreciation for the year is estimated to be $4,000. Prepare the adjusting entry for depreciation at December 31, post the adjustments to T-accounts, and indicate the balance sheet presentation of the equipment at December 31.

Prepare adjusting entry for prepaid expense.
(LO 4)

BE3-5 On July 1, 2014, Dobbs Co. pays $14,400 to Kalter Insurance Co. for a 3-year insurance contract. Both companies have fiscal years ending December 31. For Dobbs Co., journalize and post the entry on July 1 and the adjusting entry on December 31.

Prepare adjusting entry for unearned revenue.
(LO 4)

BE3-6 Using the data in BE3-5, journalize and post the entry on July 1 and the adjusting entry on December 31 for Kalter Insurance Co. Kalter uses the accounts Unearned Service Revenue and Service Revenue.

Prepare adjusting entries for accruals.
(LO 5)

BE3-7 The bookkeeper for Bradbury Company asks you to prepare the following accrued adjusting entries at December 31.
1. Interest on notes payable of $400 is accrued.
2. Services performed but not recorded total $1,900.
3. Salaries earned by employees of $900 have not been recorded.

Use the following account titles: Service Revenue, Accounts Receivable, Interest Expense, Interest Payable, Salaries and Wages Expense, and Salaries and Wages Payable.

BE3-8 The trial balance of Yewlett Company includes the following balance sheet accounts, which may require adjustment. For each account that requires adjustment, indicate (a) the type of adjusting entry (prepaid expenses, unearned revenues, accrued revenues, and accrued expenses) and (b) the related account in the adjusting entry.

Analyze accounts in an unadjusted trial balance.
(LO 3, 4, 5)

Accounts Receivable   Interest Payable
Prepaid Insurance   Unearned Service Revenue
Accumulated Depreciation—Equipment

BE3-9 The adjusted trial balance of Parsons Company at December 31, 2014, includes the following accounts: Owner's Capital $15,600, Owner's Drawings $7,000, Service Revenue $37,000, Salaries and Wages Expense $16,000, Insurance Expense $2,000, Rent Expense $4,000, Supplies Expense $1,500, and Depreciation Expense $1,300. Prepare an income statement for the year.

Prepare an income statement from an adjusted trial balance.
(LO 6)

BE3-10 Partial adjusted trial balance data for Parsons Company is presented in BE3-9. The balance in Owner's Capital is the balance as of January 1. Prepare an owner's equity statement for the year assuming net income is $12,200 for the year.

Prepare an owner's equity statement from an adjusted trial balance.
(LO 6)

*BE3-11 Mayes Company records all prepayments in income statement accounts. At April 30, the trial balance shows Supplies Expense $2,800, Service Revenue $9,200, and zero balances in related balance sheet accounts. Prepare the adjusting entries at April 30 assuming (a) $700 of supplies on hand and (b) $3,000 of service revenue should be reported as unearned.

Prepare adjusting entries under alternative treatment of deferrals.
(LO 7)

*BE3-12 The accompanying chart shows the qualitative characteristics of useful accounting information. Fill in the blanks.

Identify characteristics of useful information.
(LO 8)

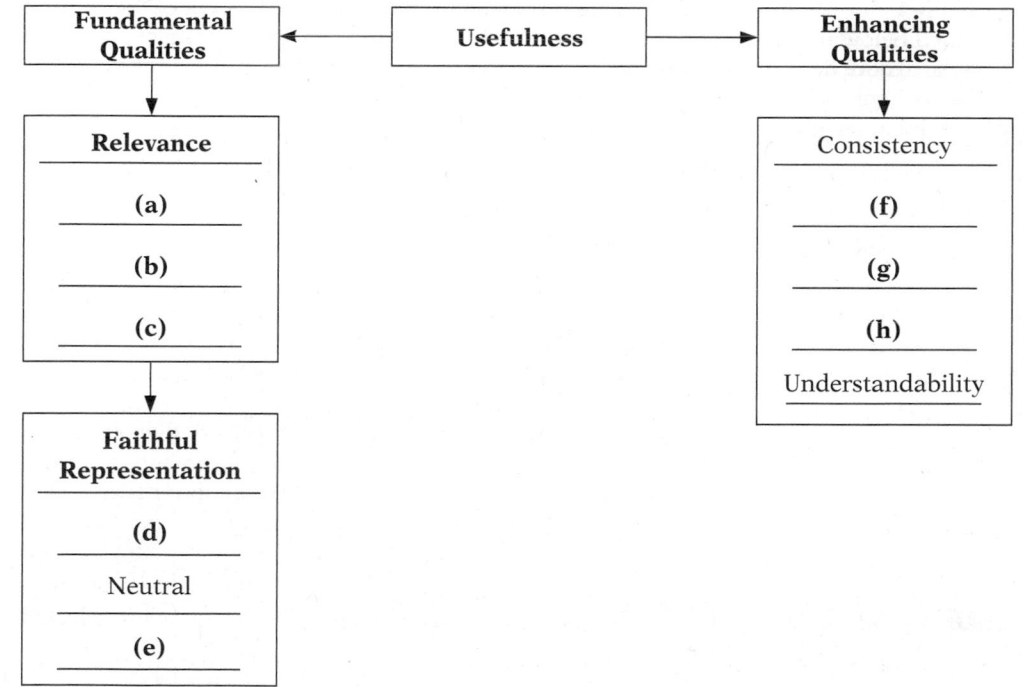

*BE3-13 Given the characteristics of useful accounting information, complete each of the following statements.

Identify characteristics of useful information.
(LO 8)

(a) For information to be _____, it should have predictive value, confirmatory value, and be material.

(b) _____ is the quality of information that gives assurance that the information accurately depicts what really happened.

(c) _____ means using the same accounting principles and methods from year to year within a company.

Identify characteristics of useful information.

(LO 8)

***BE3-14** Here are some qualitative characteristics of useful accounting information:

1. Predictive value   **3.** Verifiable

2. Neutral   **4.** Timely

Match each qualitative characteristic to one of the following statements.

_____ **(a)** Accounting information should help provide accurate expectations about future events.

_____ **(b)** Accounting information cannot be selected, prepared, or presented to favor one set of interested users over another.

_____ **(c)** The quality of information that occurs when independent observers, using the same methods, obtain similar results.

_____ **(d)** Accounting information must be available to decision-makers before it loses its capacity to influence their decisions.

Define full disclosure principle.

(LO 8)

***BE3-15** The full disclosure principle dictates that:

(a) financial statements should disclose all assets at their cost.

(b) financial statements should disclose only those events that can be measured in currency.

(c) financial statements should disclose all events and circumstances that would matter to users of financial statements.

(d) financial statements should not be relied on unless an auditor has expressed an unqualified opinion on them.

> DO IT! Review

Identify timing concepts.

(LO 1, 2)

DO IT! 3-1 Several timing concepts are discussed on pages 100–101. A list of concepts is provided below in the left column, with a description of the concept in the right column. There are more descriptions provided than concepts. Match the description of the concept to the concept.

1. ____ Cash-basis accounting.

2. ____ Fiscal year.

3. ____ Revenue recognition principle.

4. ____ Expense recognition principle.

(a) Monthly and quarterly time periods.

(b) Accountants divide the economic life of a business into artificial time periods.

(c) Efforts (expenses) should be matched with accomplishments (revenues).

(d) Companies record revenues when they receive cash and record expenses when they pay out cash.

(e) An accounting time period that is one year in length.

(f) An accounting time period that starts on January 1 and ends on December 31.

(g) Companies record transactions in the period in which the events occur.

(h) Recognize revenue in the accounting period in which a performance obligation is satisfied.

Prepare adjusting entries for deferrals.

(LO 4)

DO IT! 3-2 The ledger of Herrera, Inc. on March 31, 2014, includes the following selected accounts before adjusting entries.

	Debit	Credit
Prepaid Insurance	2,400	
Supplies	2,500	
Equipment	30,000	
Unearned Service Revenue		9,000

An analysis of the accounts shows the following.

1. Insurance expires at the rate of $300 per month.

2. Supplies on hand total $1,100.

3. The equipment depreciates $500 per month.

4. During March, services were performed for two-fifths of the unearned service revenue.

Prepare the adjusting entries for the month of March.

DO IT! 3-3 Javier Computer Services began operations in July 2014. At the end of the month, the company prepares monthly financial statements. It has the following information for the month.

Prepare adjusting entries for accruals.

(LO 5)

1. At July 31, the company owed employees $1,300 in salaries that the company will pay in August.

2. On July 1, the company borrowed $20,000 from a local bank on a 10-year note. The annual interest rate is 12%.

3. Service revenue unrecorded in July totaled $2,400.

Prepare the adjusting entries needed at July 31, 2014.

DO IT! 3-4 Lumina Co. was organized on April 1, 2014. The company prepares quarterly financial statements. The adjusted trial balance amounts at June 30 are shown below.

Calculate amounts from trial balance.

(LO 6)

	Debit		Credit
Cash	$ 5,360	Accumulated Depreciation—	
Accounts Receivable	480	Equipment	$ 700
Prepaid Rent	720	Notes Payable	4,000
Supplies	920	Accounts Payable	790
Equipment	12,000	Salaries and Wages Payable	300
Owner's Drawings	500	Interest Payable	40
Salaries and Wages Expense	7,400	Unearned Rent Revenue	400
Rent Expense	1,200	Owner's Capital	11,200
Depreciation Expense	700	Service Revenue	11,360
Supplies Expense	160	Rent Revenue	1,100
Utilities Expense	410		$29,890
Interest Expense	40		
	$29,890		

(a) Determine the net income for the quarter April 1 to June 30.
(b) Determine the total assets and total liabilities at June 30, 2014 for Lumina Company.
(c) Determine the amount that appears for Owner's Capital at June 30, 2014.

EXERCISES

E3-1 Ian Muse has prepared the following list of statements about the time period assumption.

Explain the time period assumption.

(LO 1)

1. Adjusting entries would not be necessary if a company's life were not divided into artificial time periods.
2. The IRS requires companies to file annual tax returns.
3. Accountants divide the economic life of a business into artificial time periods, but each transaction affects only one of these periods.
4. Accounting time periods are generally a month, a quarter, or a year.
5. A time period lasting one year is called an interim period.
6. All fiscal years are calendar years, but not all calendar years are fiscal years.

Instructions
Identify each statement as true or false. If false, indicate how to correct the statement.

E3-2 On numerous occasions, proposals have surfaced to put the federal government on the accrual basis of accounting. This is no small issue. If this basis were used, it would mean that billions in unrecorded liabilities would have to be booked, and the federal deficit would increase substantially.

Distinguish between cash and accrual basis of accounting.

(LO 2)

Instructions
(a) What is the difference between accrual-basis accounting and cash-basis accounting?
(b) Why would politicians prefer the cash basis over the accrual basis?
(c) Write a letter to your senator explaining why the federal government should adopt the accrual basis of accounting.

Compute cash and accrual accounting income.
(LO 2)

E3-3 Primo Industries collected $105,000 from customers in 2014. Of the amount collected, $25,000 was for services performed in 2013. In addition, Primo performed services worth $40,000 in 2014, which will not be collected until 2015.

Primo Industries also paid $72,000 for expenses in 2014. Of the amount paid, $30,000 was for expenses incurred on account in 2013. In addition, Primo incurred $42,000 of expenses in 2014, which will not be paid until 2015.

Instructions
(a) Compute 2014 cash-basis net income.
(b) Compute 2014 accrual-basis net income.

Identify the type of adjusting entry needed.
(LO 3, 4, 5)

E3-4 Hart Corporation encounters the following situations:

1. Hart collects $1,300 from a customer in 2014 for services to be performed in 2015.
2. Hart incurs utility expense which is not yet paid in cash or recorded.
3. Hart's employees worked 3 days in 2014 but will not be paid until 2015.
4. Hart performs services for customers but has not yet received cash or recorded the transaction.
5. Hart paid $2,400 rent on December 1 for the 4 months starting December 1.
6. Hart received cash for future services and recorded a liability until the service was performed.
7. Hart performed consulting services for a client in December 2014. On December 31, it had not billed the client for services provided of $1,200.
8. Hart paid cash for an expense and recorded an asset until the item was used up.
9. Hart purchased $900 of supplies in 2014; at year-end, $400 of supplies remain unused.
10. Hart purchased equipment on January 1, 2014; the equipment will be used for 5 years.
11. Hart borrowed $10,000 on October 1, 2014, signing an 8% one-year note payable.

Instructions
Identify what type of adjusting entry (prepaid expense, unearned revenue, accrued expense, or accrued revenue) is needed in each situation at December 31, 2014.

Prepare adjusting entries from selected data.
(LO 4, 5)

E3-5 Verne Cova Company has the following balances in selected accounts on December 31, 2014.

Accounts Receivable	$ –0–
Accumulated Depreciation—Equipment	–0–
Equipment	7,000
Interest Payable	–0–
Notes Payable	10,000
Prepaid Insurance	2,100
Salaries and Wages Payable	–0–
Supplies	2,450
Unearned Service Revenue	30,000

All the accounts have normal balances. The information below has been gathered at December 31, 2014.

1. Verne Cova Company borrowed $10,000 by signing a 12%, one-year note on September 1, 2014.
2. A count of supplies on December 31, 2014, indicates that supplies of $900 are on hand.
3. Depreciation on the equipment for 2014 is $1,000.
4. Verne Cova Company paid $2,100 for 12 months of insurance coverage on June 1, 2014.
5. On December 1, 2014, Verne Cova collected $30,000 for consulting services to be performed from December 1, 2014, through March 31, 2015.
6. Verne Cova performed consulting services for a client in December 2014. The client will be billed $4,200.
7. Verne Cova Company pays its employees total salaries of $9,000 every Monday for the preceding 5-day week (Monday through Friday). On Monday, December 29, employees were paid for the week ending December 26. All employees worked the last 3 days of 2014.

Instructions
Prepare adjusting entries for the seven items described above.

E3-6 Lei Company accumulates the following adjustment data at December 31.

1. Services performed but not recorded total $1,000.
2. Supplies of $300 have been used.
3. Utility expenses of $225 are unpaid.
4. Services related to unearned service revenue of $260 were performed.
5. Salaries of $800 are unpaid.
6. Prepaid insurance totaling $350 has expired.

Identify types of adjustments and account relationships.
(LO 3, 4, 5)

Instructions
For each of the above items indicate the following.

(a) The type of adjustment (prepaid expense, unearned revenue, accrued revenue, or accrued expense).
(b) The status of accounts before adjustment (overstatement or understatement).

E3-7 The ledger of Perez Rental Agency on March 31 of the current year includes the selected accounts, shown below, before adjusting entries have been prepared.

Prepare adjusting entries from selected account data.
(LO 4, 5)

	Debit	Credit
Prepaid Insurance	$ 3,600	
Supplies	2,800	
Equipment	25,000	
Accumulated Depreciation—Equipment		$ 8,400
Notes Payable		20,000
Unearned Rent Revenue		10,200
Rent Revenue		60,000
Interest Expense	–0–	
Salaries and Wages Expense	14,000	

An analysis of the accounts shows the following.

1. The equipment depreciates $400 per month.
2. One-third of the unearned rent revenue was earned during the quarter.
3. Interest of $500 is accrued on the notes payable.
4. Supplies on hand total $900.
5. Insurance expires at the rate of $200 per month.

Instructions
Prepare the adjusting entries at March 31, assuming that adjusting entries are made **quarterly**. Additional accounts are Depreciation Expense, Insurance Expense, Interest Payable, and Supplies Expense.

E3-8 Robin Shalit, D.D.S., opened a dental practice on January 1, 2014. During the first month of operations, the following transactions occurred.

Prepare adjusting entries.
(LO 4, 5)

1. Performed services for patients who had dental plan insurance. At January 31, $875 of such services were performed but not yet recorded.
2. Utility expenses incurred but not paid prior to January 31 totaled $650.
3. Purchased dental equipment on January 1 for $80,000, paying $20,000 in cash and signing a $60,000, 3-year note payable. The equipment depreciates $400 per month. Interest is $500 per month.
4. Purchased a one-year malpractice insurance policy on January 1 for $24,000.
5. Purchased $1,600 of dental supplies. On January 31, determined that $400 of supplies were on hand.

Instructions
Prepare the adjusting entries on January 31. Account titles are Accumulated Depreciation—Equipment, Depreciation Expense, Service Revenue, Accounts Receivable, Insurance Expense, Interest Expense, Interest Payable, Prepaid Insurance, Supplies, Supplies Expense, Utilities Expense, and Utilities Payable.

E3-9 The trial balance for Pioneer Advertising Agency is shown in Illustration 3-3 (page 103). Instead of the adjusting entries shown in the text at October 31, assume the following adjustment data.

Prepare adjusting entries.
(LO 4, 5)

1. Supplies on hand at October 31 total $500.
2. Expired insurance for the month is $100.
3. Depreciation for the month is $50.
4. Services related to unearned service revenue in October worth $600 were performed.
5. Services performed but not recorded at October 31 are $300.
6. Interest accrued at October 31 is $95.
7. Accrued salaries at October 31 are $1,625.

Instructions
Prepare the adjusting entries for the items above.

Prepare correct income statement.
(LO 2, 4, 5, 6)

E3-10 The income statement of Gopitkumar Co. for the month of July shows net income of $1,400 based on Service Revenue $5,500, Salaries and Wages Expense $2,300, Supplies Expense $1,200, and Utilities Expense $600. In reviewing the statement, you discover the following.

1. Insurance expired during July of $400 was omitted.
2. Supplies expense includes $250 of supplies that are still on hand at July 31.
3. Depreciation on equipment of $150 was omitted.
4. Accrued but unpaid salaries and wages at July 31 of $300 were not included.
5. Services performed but unrecorded totaled $650.

Instructions
Prepare a correct income statement for July 2014.

Analyze adjusted data.
(LO 3, 4, 5, 6)

E3-11 A partial adjusted trial balance of Gehring Company at January 31, 2014, shows the following.

GEHRING COMPANY
Adjusted Trial Balance
January 31, 2014

	Debit	Credit
Supplies	$ 850	
Prepaid Insurance	2,400	
Salaries and Wages Payable		$ 800
Unearned Service Revenue		750
Supplies Expense	950	
Insurance Expense	400	
Salaries and Wages Expense	2,900	
Service Revenue		2,000

Instructions
Answer the following questions, assuming the year begins January 1.

(a) If the amount in Supplies Expense is the January 31 adjusting entry, and $1,000 of supplies was purchased in January, what was the balance in Supplies on January 1?
(b) If the amount in Insurance Expense is the January 31 adjusting entry, and the original insurance premium was for one year, what was the total premium and when was the policy purchased?
(c) If $3,500 of salaries was paid in January, what was the balance in Salaries and Wages Payable at December 31, 2013?

Journalize basic transactions and adjusting entries.
(LO 4, 5, 6)

E3-12 Selected accounts of Koffman Company are shown below and on the next page.

Supplies Expense	
7/31	800

Supplies			
7/1 Bal.	1,100	7/31	800
7/10	650		

Salaries and Wages Payable			
		7/31	1,200

Accounts Receivable			Unearned Service Revenue			
7/31	500		7/31	1,150	7/1 Bal.	1,500
					7/20	1,000

Salaries and Wages Expense			Service Revenue		
7/15	1,200			7/14	2,000
7/31	1,200			7/31	1,150
				7/31	500

Instructions

After analyzing the accounts, journalize **(a)** the July transactions and **(b)** the adjusting entries that were made on July 31. (*Hint:* July transactions were for cash.)

E3-13 The trial balances before and after adjustment for Frinzi Company at the end of its fiscal year are presented below.

Prepare adjusting entries from analysis of trial balances.

(LO 4, 5, 6)

FRINZI COMPANY
Trial Balance
August 31, 2014

	Before Adjustment		After Adjustment	
	Dr.	Cr.	Dr.	Cr.
Cash	$10,400		$10,400	
Accounts Receivable	8,800		10,800	
Supplies	2,300		900	
Prepaid Insurance	4,000		2,500	
Equipment	14,000		14,000	
Accumulated Depreciation—Equipment		$ 3,600		$ 4,500
Accounts Payable		5,800		5,800
Salaries and Wages Payable		–0–		1,100
Unearned Rent Revenue		1,500		600
Owner's Capital		15,600		15,600
Service Revenue		34,000		36,000
Rent Revenue		11,000		11,900
Salaries and Wages Expense	17,000		18,100	
Supplies Expense	–0–		1,400	
Rent Expense	15,000		15,000	
Insurance Expense	–0–		1,500	
Depreciation Expense	–0–		900	
	$71,500	$71,500	$75,500	$75,500

Instructions

Prepare the adjusting entries that were made.

E3-14 The adjusted trial balance for Frinzi Company is given in E3-13.

Prepare financial statements from adjusted trial balance.

(LO 6)

Instructions

Prepare the income and owner's equity statements for the year and the balance sheet at August 31.

E3-15 The following data are taken from the comparative balance sheets of Cascade Billiards Club, which prepares its financial statements using the accrual basis of accounting.

Record transactions on accrual basis; convert revenue to cash receipts.

(LO 4, 5)

December 31	2014	2013
Accounts receivable from members	$14,000	$ 9,000
Unearned service revenue	17,000	25,000

Members are billed based upon their use of the club's facilities. Unearned service revenues arise from the sale of gift certificates, which members can apply to their future use of club facilities. The 2014 income statement for the club showed that service revenue of $161,000 was earned during the year.

Instructions

(*Hint:* You will probably find it helpful to use T-accounts to analyze these data.)

(a) Prepare journal entries for each of the following events that took place during 2014.
   (1) Accounts receivable from 2013 were all collected.
   (2) Gift certificates outstanding at the end of 2013 were all redeemed.
   (3) An additional $38,000 worth of gift certificates were sold during 2014. A portion of these was used by the recipients during the year; the remainder was still outstanding at the end of 2014.
   (4) Services performed for members for 2014 were billed to members.
   (5) Accounts receivable for 2014 (i.e., those billed in item [4] above) were partially collected.

(b) Determine the amount of cash received by the club, with respect to member services, during 2014.

Journalize adjusting entries.
(LO 7)

*E3-16 Aaron Lynch Company has the following balances in selected accounts on December 31, 2014.

Service Revenue	$40,000
Insurance Expense	2,700
Supplies Expense	2,450

All the accounts have normal balances. Aaron Lynch Company debits prepayments to expense accounts when paid, and credits unearned revenues to revenue accounts when received. The following information below has been gathered at December 31, 2014.

1. Aaron Lynch Company paid $2,700 for 12 months of insurance coverage on June 1, 2014.
2. On December 1, 2014, Aaron Lynch Company collected $40,000 for consulting services to be performed from December 1, 2014, through March 31, 2015.
3. A count of supplies on December 31, 2014, indicates that supplies of $900 are on hand.

Instructions

Prepare the adjusting entries needed at December 31, 2014.

Journalize transactions and adjusting entries.
(LO 7)

*E3-17 At Cambridge Company, prepayments are debited to expense when paid, and unearned revenues are credited to revenue when cash is received. During January of the current year, the following transactions occurred.

Jan. 2 Paid $1,920 for fire insurance protection for the year.
    10 Paid $1,700 for supplies.
    15 Received $6,100 for services to be performed in the future.

On January 31, it is determined that $2,500 of the services were performed and that there are $650 of supplies on hand.

Instructions

(a) Journalize and post the January transactions. (Use T-accounts.)
(b) Journalize and post the adjusting entries at January 31.
(c) Determine the ending balance in each of the accounts.

Identify accounting assumptions and principles.
(LO 8)

*E3-18 Presented below are the assumptions and principles discussed in this chapter.

1. Full disclosure principle.   4. Time period assumption.
2. Going concern assumption.   5. Historical cost principle.
3. Monetary unit assumption.   6. Economic entity assumption.

Instructions

Identify by number the accounting assumption or principle that is described below. Do not use a number more than once.

_____ **(a)** Is the rationale for why plant assets are not reported at liquidation value. (*Note:* Do not use the historical cost principle.)
_____ **(b)** Indicates that personal and business record-keeping should be separately maintained.
_____ **(c)** Assumes that the monetary unit is the "measuring stick" used to report on financial performance.
_____ **(d)** Separates financial information into time periods for reporting purposes.

_____ **(e)** Measurement basis used when a reliable estimate of fair value is not available.

_____ **(f)** Dictates that companies should disclose all circumstances and events that make a difference to financial statement users.

*__**E3-19**__ Rosman Co. had three major business transactions during 2014.

(a) Reported at its fair value of $260,000 merchandise inventory with a cost of $208,000.

(b) The president of Rosman Co., Jay Rosman, purchased a truck for personal use and charged it to his expense account.

(c) Rosman Co. wanted to make its 2014 income look better, so it added 2 more weeks to the year (a 54-week year). Previous years were 52 weeks.

Identify the assumption or principle that has been violated.

(LO 8)

Instructions

In each situation, identify the assumption or principle that has been violated, if any, and discuss what the company should have done.

*__**E3-20**__ The following characteristics, assumptions, principles, or constraint guide the FASB when it creates accounting standards.

Identify financial accounting concepts and principles.

(LO 8)

Relevance
Faithful representation
Comparability
Consistency
Monetary unit assumption
Economic entity assumption

Expense recognition principle
Time period assumption
Going concern assumption
Historical cost principle
Full disclosure principle
Materiality

Match each item above with a description below.

1. _____ Ability to easily evaluate one company's results relative to another's.
2. _____ Belief that a company will continue to operate for the foreseeable future.
3. _____ The judgment concerning whether an item's size is large enough to matter to decision-makers.
4. _____ The reporting of all information that would make a difference to financial statement users.
5. _____ The practice of preparing financial statements at regular intervals.
6. _____ The quality of information that indicates the information makes a difference in a decision.
7. _____ A belief that items should be reported on the balance sheet at the price that was paid to acquire them.
8. _____ A company's use of the same accounting principles and methods from year to year.
9. _____ Tracing accounting events to particular companies.
10. _____ The desire to minimize bias in financial statements.
11. _____ Reporting only those things that can be measured in monetary units.
12. _____ Dictates that efforts (expenses) be matched with results (revenues).

*__**E3-21**__ Net Nanny Software International Inc., headquartered in Vancouver, Canada, specializes in Internet safety and computer security products for both the home and commercial markets. In a recent balance sheet, it reported a deficit of US$5,678,288. It has reported only net losses since its inception. In spite of these losses, Net Nanny's shares of stock have traded anywhere from a high of $3.70 to a low of $0.32 on the Canadian Venture Exchange.

Comment on the objective and qualitative characteristics of accounting information.

(LO 8)

Net Nanny's financial statements have historically been prepared in Canadian dollars. Recently, the company adopted the U.S. dollar as its reporting currency.

Instructions

(a) What is the objective of financial reporting? How does this objective meet or not meet Net Nanny's investors' needs?

(b) Why would investors want to buy Net Nanny's shares if the company has consistently reported losses over the last few years? Include in your answer an assessment of the relevance of the information reported on Net Nanny's financial statements.

(c) Comment on how the change in reporting information from Canadian dollars to U.S. dollars likely affected the readers of Net Nanny's financial statements. Include in your answer an assessment of the comparability of the information.

Comment on the objective and qualitative characteristics of financial reporting.

(LO 8)

*E3-22 A friend of yours, Ana Gehrig, recently completed an undergraduate degree in science and has just started working with a biotechnology company. Ana tells you that the owners of the business are trying to secure new sources of financing which are needed in order for the company to proceed with development of a new health-care product. Ana said that her boss told her that the company must put together a report to present to potential investors.

Ana thought that the company should include in this package the detailed scientific findings related to the Phase I clinical trials for this product. She said, "I know that the biotech industry sometimes has only a 10% success rate with new products, but if we report all the scientific findings, everyone will see what a sure success this is going to be! The president was talking about the importance of following some set of accounting principles. Why do we need to look at some accounting rules? What they need to realize is that we have scientific results that are quite encouraging, some of the most talented employees around, and the start of some really great customer relationships. We haven't made any sales yet, but we will. We just need the funds to get through all the clinical testing and get government approval for our product. Then these investors will be quite happy that they bought in to our company early!"

Instructions
(a) What is accounting information?
(b) Comment on how Ana's suggestions for what should be reported to prospective investors conforms to the qualitative characteristics of accounting information. Do you think that the things that Ana wants to include in the information for investors will conform to financial reporting guidelines?

EXERCISES: SET B AND CHALLENGE EXERCISES

Visit the book's companion website, at **www.wiley.com/college/weygandt**, and choose the Student Companion site to access Exercise Set B and Challenge Exercises.

PROBLEMS: SET A

Prepare adjusting entries, post to ledger accounts, and prepare an adjusted trial balance.

(LO 4, 5, 6)

P3-1A Deanna Nardelli started her own consulting firm, Nardelli Consulting, on May 1, 2014. The trial balance at May 31 is as follows.

NARDELLI CONSULTING
Trial Balance
May 31, 2014

Account Number		Debit	Credit
101	Cash	$ 4,500	
112	Accounts Receivable	6,000	
126	Supplies	1,900	
130	Prepaid Insurance	3,600	
149	Equipment	11,400	
201	Accounts Payable		$ 4,500
209	Unearned Service Revenue		2,000
301	Owner's Capital		17,700
400	Service Revenue		7,500
726	Salaries and Wages Expense	3,400	
729	Rent Expense	900	
		$31,700	$31,700

In addition to those accounts listed on the trial balance, the chart of accounts for Nardelli Consulting also contains the following accounts and account numbers: No. 150 Accumulated Depreciation—Equipment, No. 212 Salaries and Wages Payable, No. 631 Supplies Expense, No. 717 Depreciation Expense, No. 722 Insurance Expense, and No. 732 Utilities Expense.

Other data:

1. $900 of supplies have been used during the month.
2. Utilities expense incurred but not paid on May 31, 2014, $250.
3. The insurance policy is for 2 years.
4. $400 of the balance in the unearned service revenue account remains unearned at the end of the month.
5. May 31 is a Wednesday, and employees are paid on Fridays. Nardelli Consulting has two employees, who are paid $900 each for a 5-day work week.
6. The office furniture has a 5-year life with no salvage value. It is being depreciated at $190 per month for 60 months.
7. Invoices representing $1,700 of services performed during the month have not been recorded as of May 31.

Instructions

(a) Prepare the adjusting entries for the month of May. Use J4 as the page number for your journal.
(b) Post the adjusting entries to the ledger accounts. Enter the totals from the trial balance as beginning account balances and place a check mark in the posting reference column.
(c) Prepare an adjusted trial balance at May 31, 2014.

(c) Adj. trial balance $34,920

P3-2A The Skyline Motel opened for business on May 1, 2014. Its trial balance before adjustment on May 31 is as follows.

Prepare adjusting entries, post, and prepare adjusted trial balance and financial statements.

(LO 4, 5, 6)

SKYLINE MOTEL
Trial Balance
May 31, 2014

Account Number		Debit	Credit
101	Cash	$ 3,500	
126	Supplies	2,080	
130	Prepaid Insurance	2,400	
140	Land	12,000	
141	Buildings	60,000	
149	Equipment	15,000	
201	Accounts Payable		$ 4,800
208	Unearned Rent Revenue		3,300
275	Mortgage Payable		40,000
301	Owner's Capital		41,380
429	Rent Revenue		10,300
610	Advertising Expense	600	
726	Salaries and Wages Expense	3,300	
732	Utilities Expense	900	
		$99,780	$99,780

In addition to those accounts listed on the trial balance, the chart of accounts for Skyline Motel also contains the following accounts and account numbers: No. 142 Accumulated Depreciation—Buildings, No. 150 Accumulated Depreciation—Equipment, No. 212 Salaries and Wages Payable, No. 230 Interest Payable, No. 619 Depreciation Expense, No. 631 Supplies Expense, No. 718 Interest Expense, and No. 722 Insurance Expense.

Other data:

1. Prepaid insurance is a 1-year policy starting May 1, 2014.
2. A count of supplies shows $750 of unused supplies on May 31.
3. Annual depreciation is $3,000 on the buildings and $1,500 on equipment.

4. The mortgage interest rate is 12%. (The mortgage was taken out on May 1.)
5. Two-thirds of the unearned rent revenue has been earned.
6. Salaries of $750 are accrued and unpaid at May 31.

Instructions
(a) Journalize the adjusting entries on May 31.
(b) Prepare a ledger using the three-column form of account. Enter the trial balance amounts and post the adjusting entries. (Use J1 as the posting reference.)
(c) Prepare an adjusted trial balance on May 31.
(d) Prepare an income statement and an owner's equity statement for the month of May and a balance sheet at May 31.

(c) Adj. trial balance $101,305
(d) Net income $4,645
Ending capital balance $46,025
Total assets $93,075

Prepare adjusting entries and financial statements.
(LO 4, 5, 6)

P3-3A Everett Co. was organized on July 1, 2014. Quarterly financial statements are prepared. The unadjusted and adjusted trial balances as of September 30 are shown below.

EVERETT CO.
Trial Balance
September 30, 2014

	Unadjusted		Adjusted	
	Dr.	**Cr.**	**Dr.**	**Cr.**
Cash	$ 8,700		$ 8,700	
Accounts Receivable	10,400		11,500	
Supplies	1,500		650	
Prepaid Rent	2,200		1,200	
Equipment	18,000		18,000	
Accumulated Depreciation—Equipment		$ –0–		$ 700
Notes Payable		10,000		10,000
Accounts Payable		2,500		2,500
Salaries and Wages Payable		–0–		725
Interest Payable		–0–		100
Unearned Rent Revenue		1,900		1,050
Owner's Capital		22,000		22,000
Owner's Drawings	1,600		1,600	
Service Revenue		16,000		17,100
Rent Revenue		1,410		2,260
Salaries and Wages Expense	8,000		8,725	
Rent Expense	1,900		2,900	
Depreciation Expense			700	
Supplies Expense			850	
Utilities Expense	1,510		1,510	
Interest Expense			100	
	$53,810	$53,810	$56,435	$56,435

Instructions
(a) Journalize the adjusting entries that were made.
(b) Prepare an income statement and an owner's equity statement for the 3 months ending September 30 and a balance sheet at September 30.
(c) If the note bears interest at 12%, how many months has it been outstanding?

(b) Net income $4,575
Ending capital $24,975
Total assets $39,350

Prepare adjusting entries.
(LO 4, 5)

P3-4A A review of the ledger of Carmel Company at December 31, 2014, produces the following data pertaining to the preparation of annual adjusting entries.

1. Prepaid Insurance $10,440. The company has separate insurance policies on its buildings and its motor vehicles. Policy B4564 on the building was purchased on April 1, 2013, for $7,920. The policy has a term of 3 years. Policy A2958 on the vehicles was purchased on January 1, 2014, for $4,500. This policy has a term of 2 years.

2. Unearned Rent Revenue $429,000. The company began subleasing office space in its new building on November 1. At December 31, the company had the following rental contracts that are paid in full for the entire term of the lease.

1. Insurance expense $4,890

2. Rent revenue $84,000

Date	Term (in months)	Monthly Rent	Number of Leases
Nov. 1	9	$5,000	5
Dec. 1	6	$8,500	4

3. Notes Payable $120,000. This balance consists of a note for 9 months at an annual interest rate of 9%, dated November 1.

3. Interest expense $1,800

4. Salaries and Wages Payable $0. There are eight salaried employees. Salaries are paid every Friday for the current week. Five employees receive a salary of $700 each per week, and three employees earn $500 each per week. Assume December 31 is a Tuesday. Employees do not work weekends. All employees worked the last 2 days of December.

4. Salaries and wages expense $2,000

Instructions
Prepare the adjusting entries at December 31, 2014.

P3-5A On November 1, 2014, the account balances of Schilling Equipment Repair were as follows.

Journalize transactions and follow through accounting cycle to preparation of financial statements.

(LO 4, 5, 6)

GLS

No.		Debit	No.		Credit
101	Cash	$ 2,400	154	Accumulated Depreciation—Equipment	$ 2,000
112	Accounts Receivable	4,250	201	Accounts Payable	2,600
126	Supplies	1,800	209	Unearned Service Revenue	1,200
153	Equipment	12,000	212	Salaries and Wages Payable	700
			301	Owner's Capital	13,950
		$20,450			$20,450

During November, the following summary transactions were completed.

Nov. 8   Paid $1,700 for salaries due employees, of which $700 is for October salaries.
   10   Received $3,420 cash from customers on account.
   12   Received $3,100 cash for services performed in November.
   15   Purchased equipment on account $2,000.
   17   Purchased supplies on account $700.
   20   Paid creditors on account $2,700.
   22   Paid November rent $400.
   25   Paid salaries $1,700.
   27   Performed services on account and billed customers for services provided $1,900.
   29   Received $600 from customers for future service.

Adjustment data consist of:

1. Supplies on hand $1,400.
2. Accrued salaries payable $350.
3. Depreciation for the month is $200.
4. Services related to unearned service revenue of $1,250 were performed.

Instructions
(a) Enter the November 1 balances in the ledger accounts.
(b) Journalize the November transactions.
(c) Post to the ledger accounts. Use J1 for the posting reference. Use the following additional accounts: No. 407 Service Revenue, No. 615 Depreciation Expense, No. 631 Supplies Expense, No. 726 Salaries and Wages Expense, and No. 729 Rent Expense.
(d) Prepare a trial balance at November 30.
(e) Journalize and post adjusting entries.
(f) Prepare an adjusted trial balance.
(g) Prepare an income statement and an owner's equity statement for November and a balance sheet at November 30.

(d) Trial balance $25,350

(f) Adj. trial balance $25,900

(g) Net income $1,500;
    Ending capital $15,450
    Total assets $18,950

*Prepare adjusting entries,
adjusted trial balance, and
financial statements using
appendix.*

(LO 4, 5, 6, 7)

*P3-6A Sommer Graphics Company was organized on January 1, 2014, by Krystal Sommer. At the end of the first 6 months of operations, the trial balance contained the accounts shown below.

	Debit		Credit
Cash	$ 8,600	Notes Payable	$ 20,000
Accounts Receivable	14,000	Accounts Payable	9,000
Equipment	45,000	Owner's Capital	22,000
Insurance Expense	2,700	Sales Revenue	52,100
Salaries and Wages Expense	30,000	Service Revenue	6,000
Supplies Expense	3,700		
Advertising Expense	1,900		
Rent Expense	1,500		
Utilities Expense	1,700		
	$109,100		$109,100

Analysis reveals the following additional data.

1. The $3,700 balance in Supplies Expense represents supplies purchased in January. At June 30, $1,500 of supplies are on hand.
2. The note payable was issued on February 1. It is a 9%, 6-month note.
3. The balance in Insurance Expense is the premium on a one-year policy, dated March 1, 2014.
4. Service revenues are credited to revenue when received. At June 30, services revenue of $1,300 are unearned.
5. Revenue for services performed but unrecorded at June 30 totals $2,000.
6. Depreciation is $2,250 per year.

Instructions

(b) Adj. trial balance
    $112,975
(c) Net income $18,725
    Ending capital $40,725
    Total assets $71,775

(a) Journalize the adjusting entries at June 30. (Assume adjustments are recorded every 6 months.)
(b) Prepare an adjusted trial balance.
(c) Prepare an income statement and owner's equity statement for the 6 months ended June 30 and a balance sheet at June 30.

PROBLEMS: SET B

*Prepare adjusting entries,
post to ledger accounts, and
prepare adjusted trial balance.*

(LO 4, 5, 6)

P3-1B Jason Elsner started his own consulting firm, Elsner Company, on June 1, 2014. The trial balance at June 30 is shown below.

ELSNER COMPANY
Trial Balance
June 30, 2014

Account Number		Debit	Credit
101	Cash	$ 7,150	
112	Accounts Receivable	6,000	
126	Supplies	2,000	
130	Prepaid Insurance	3,000	
157	Equipment	15,000	
201	Accounts Payable		$ 4,500
209	Unearned Service Revenue		4,000
301	Owner's Capital		21,750
400	Service Revenue		7,900
726	Salaries and Wages Expense	4,000	
729	Rent Expense	1,000	
		$38,150	$38,150

In addition to those accounts listed on the trial balance, the chart of accounts for Elsner Company also contains the following accounts and account numbers: No. 158 Accumulated Depreciation—Equipment, No. 212 Salaries and Wages Payable, No. 631 Supplies Expense, No. 711 Depreciation Expense, No. 722 Insurance Expense, and No. 732 Utilities Expense.

Other data:

1. Supplies on hand at June 30 are $750.
2. A utility bill for $150 has not been recorded and will not be paid until next month.
3. The insurance policy is for a year.
4. $2,800 of unearned service revenue is recognized for services performed during the month.
5. Salaries of $1,900 are accrued at June 30.
6. The equipment has a 5-year life with no salvage value. It is being depreciated at $250 per month for 60 months.
7. Invoices representing $1,200 of services performed during the month have not been recorded as of June 30.

Instructions
(a) Prepare the adjusting entries for the month of June. Use J3 as the page number for your journal.
(b) Post the adjusting entries to the ledger accounts. Enter the totals from the trial balance as beginning account balances and place a check mark in the posting reference column.
(c) Prepare an adjusted trial balance at June 30, 2014.

(c) Adj. trial balance $41,650

P3-2B Maquoketa River Resort opened for business on June 1 with eight air-conditioned units. Its trial balance before adjustment on August 31 is as follows.

Prepare adjusting entries, post, and prepare adjusted trial balance and financial statements.

(LO 4, 5, 6)

MAQUOKETA RIVER RESORT
Trial Balance
August 31, 2014

Account Number		Debit	Credit
101	Cash	$ 19,600	
126	Supplies	3,300	
130	Prepaid Insurance	6,000	
140	Land	25,000	
143	Buildings	125,000	
149	Equipment	26,000	
201	Accounts Payable		$ 6,500
208	Unearned Rent Revenue		7,400
275	Mortgage Payable		80,000
301	Owner's Capital		100,000
306	Owner's Drawings	5,000	
429	Rent Revenue		80,000
622	Maintenance and Repairs Expense	3,600	
726	Salaries and Wages Expense	51,000	
732	Utilities Expense	9,400	
		$273,900	$273,900

In addition to those accounts listed on the trial balance, the chart of accounts for Maquoketa River Resort also contains the following accounts and account numbers: No. 112 Accounts Receivable, No. 144 Accumulated Depreciation—Buildings, No. 150 Accumulated Depreciation—Equipment, No. 212 Salaries and Wages Payable, No. 230 Interest Payable, No. 620 Depreciation Expense, No. 631 Supplies Expense, No. 718 Interest Expense, and No. 722 Insurance Expense.

Other data:

1. Insurance expires at the rate of $300 per month.
2. A count on August 31 shows $800 of supplies on hand.

3. Annual depreciation is $6,000 on buildings and $2,400 on equipment.
4. Unearned rent revenue of $4,800 was earned prior to August 31.
5. Salaries of $400 were unpaid at August 31.
6. Rentals of $4,000 were due from tenants at August 31. (Use Accounts Receivable.)
7. The mortgage interest rate is 9% per year. (The mortgage was taken out on August 1.)

Instructions

(c) Adj. trial balance
$281,000

(d) Net income $18,300
Ending capital balance
$113,300
Total assets $203,400

(a) Journalize the adjusting entries on August 31 for the 3-month period June 1–August 31.
(b) Prepare a ledger using the three-column form of account. Enter the trial balance amounts and post the adjusting entries. (Use J1 as the posting reference.)
(c) Prepare an adjusted trial balance on August 31.
(d) Prepare an income statement and an owner's equity statement for the 3 months ending August 31 and a balance sheet as of August 31.

Prepare adjusting entries and financial statements.

(LO 4, 5, 6)

P3-3B Delgado Advertising Agency was founded by Maria Delgado in January of 2013. Presented below are both the adjusted and unadjusted trial balances as of December 31, 2014.

DELGADO ADVERTISING AGENCY
Trial Balance
December 31, 2014

	Unadjusted		Adjusted	
	Dr.	Cr.	Dr.	Cr.
Cash	$ 11,000		$ 11,000	
Accounts Receivable	20,000		21,500	
Supplies	8,600		4,800	
Prepaid Insurance	3,350		2,500	
Equipment	60,000		60,000	
Accumulated Depreciation—Equipment		$ 28,000		$ 34,000
Accounts Payable		5,000		5,000
Interest Payable		–0–		150
Notes Payable		5,000		5,000
Unearned Service Revenue		7,200		5,900
Salaries and Wages Payable		–0–		2,100
Owner's Capital		25,500		25,500
Owner's Drawings	12,000		12,000	
Service Revenue		58,600		61,400
Salaries and Wages Expense	10,000		12,100	
Insurance Expense			850	
Interest Expense	350		500	
Depreciation Expense			6,000	
Supplies Expense			3,800	
Rent Expense	4,000		4,000	
	$129,300	$129,300	$139,050	$139,050

Instructions

(b) Net income $34,150
Ending capital $47,650
Total assets $65,800

(c) (1) 6%
(2) $2,500

(a) Journalize the annual adjusting entries that were made.
(b) Prepare an income statement and an owner's equity statement for the year ending December 31, 2014, and a balance sheet at December 31.
(c) Answer the following questions.
   (1) If the note has been outstanding 6 months, what is the annual interest rate on that note?
   (2) If the company paid $12,500 in salaries in 2014, what was the balance in Salaries and Wages Payable on December 31, 2013?

Preparing adjusting entries.

(LO 4, 5)

1. Salaries and wages
expense $2,640

P3-4B A review of the ledger of Almquist Company at December 31, 2014, produces the following data pertaining to the preparation of annual adjusting entries.

1. Salaries and Wages Payable $0. There are eight salaried employees. Salaries are paid every Friday for the current week. Five employees receive a salary of $900 each

per week, and three employees earn $700 each per week. Assume December 31 is a Tuesday. Employees do not work weekends. All employees worked the last 2 days of December.

2. Unearned Rent Revenue $354,000. The company began subleasing office space in its new building on November 1. At December 31, the company had the following rental contracts that are paid in full for the entire term of the lease.

2. Rent revenue $84,000

Date	Term (in months)	Monthly Rent	Number of Leases
Nov. 1	6	$5,000	5
Dec. 1	6	$8,500	4

3. Prepaid Advertising $15,600. This balance consists of payments on two advertising contracts. The contracts provide for monthly advertising in two trade magazines. The terms of the contracts are as follows.

3. Advertising expense $5,200

Contract	Date	Amount	Number of Magazine Issues
A650	May 1	$6,000	12
B974	Oct. 1	9,600	24

The first advertisement runs in the month in which the contract is signed.

4. Notes Payable $120,000. This balance consists of a note for one year at an annual interest rate of 9%, dated June 1.

4. Interest expense $6,300

Instructions
Prepare the adjusting entries at December 31, 2014. (Show all computations.)

P3-5B On September 1, 2014, the account balances of Percy Equipment Repair were as follows.

Journalize transactions and follow through accounting cycle to preparation of financial statements.
(LO 4, 5, 6)

No.		Debit	No.		Credit
101	Cash	$ 4,880	154	Accumulated Depreciation—Equipment	$ 1,500
112	Accounts Receivable	3,520	201	Accounts Payable	3,400
126	Supplies	2,000	209	Unearned Service Revenue	1,400
153	Equipment	15,000	212	Salaries and Wages Payable	500
			301	Owner's Capital	18,600
		$25,400			$25,400

During September, the following summary transactions were completed.

Sept. 8 Paid $1,400 for salaries due employees, of which $900 is for September.
10 Received $1,200 cash from customers on account.
12 Received $3,400 cash for services performed in September.
15 Purchased store equipment on account $3,000.
17 Purchased supplies on account $1,200.
20 Paid creditors $4,500 on account.
22 Paid September rent $500.
25 Paid salaries $1,250.
27 Performed services on account and billed customers $2,100 for these services.
29 Received $650 from customers for future service.

Adjustment data consist of:

1. Supplies on hand $1,300.
2. Accrued salaries payable $300.
3. Depreciation is $100 per month.
4. Services related to unearned service revenue of $1,450 were performed.

Instructions
(a) Enter the September 1 balances in the ledger accounts.
(b) Journalize the September transactions.
(c) Post to the ledger accounts. Use J1 for the posting reference. Use the following additional accounts: No. 407 Service Revenue, No. 615 Depreciation Expense, No. 631 Supplies Expense, No. 726 Salaries and Wages Expense, and No. 729 Rent Expense.
(d) Prepare a trial balance at September 30.
(e) Journalize and post adjusting entries.
(f) Prepare an adjusted trial balance.
(g) Prepare an income statement and an owner's equity statement for September and a balance sheet at September 30.

(d) Trial balance $30,750
(f) Adj. trial balance $31,150
(g) Net income $2,000
　 Ending capital $20,600
　 Total assets $24,600

PROBLEMS: SET C

Visit the book's companion website, at **www.wiley.com/college/weygandt**, and choose the Student Companion site to access Problem Set C.

CONTINUING COOKIE CHRONICLE

(*Note:* This is a continuation of the Cookie Chronicle from Chapters 1 and 2. Use the information from the previous chapters and follow the instructions below using the general ledger accounts you have already prepared.)

CCC3 It is the end of November and Natalie has been in touch with her grandmother. Her grandmother asked Natalie how well things went in her first month of business. Natalie, too, would like to know if she has been profitable or not during November. Natalie realizes that in order to determine Cookie Creations' income, she must first make adjustments.

Natalie puts together the following additional information.

1. A count reveals that $35 of baking supplies were used during November.
2. Natalie estimates that all of her baking equipment will have a useful life of 5 years or 60 months. (Assume Natalie decides to record a full month's worth of depreciation, regardless of when the equipment was obtained by the business.)
3. Natalie's grandmother has decided to charge interest of 6% on the note payable extended on November 16. The loan plus interest is to be repaid in 24 months. (Assume that half a month of interest accrued during November.)
4. On November 30, a friend of Natalie's asks her to teach a class at the neighborhood school. Natalie agrees and teaches a group of 35 first-grade students how to make gingerbread cookies. The next day, Natalie prepares an invoice for $300 and leaves it with the school principal. The principal says that he will pass the invoice along to the head office, and it will be paid sometime in December.
5. Natalie receives a utilities bill for $45. The bill is for utilities consumed by Natalie's business during November and is due December 15.

Instructions
Using the information that you have gathered through Chapter 2, and based on the new information above, do the following.

(a) Prepare and post the adjusting journal entries.
(b) Prepare an adjusted trial balance.
(c) Using the adjusted trial balance, calculate Cookie Creations' net income or net loss for the month of November. Do not prepare an income statement.

Broadening Your Perspective

Financial Reporting and Analysis

Financial Reporting Problem: Apple Inc.

BYP3-1 The financial statements of Apple Inc. are presented in Appendix A at the end of this textbook. Instructions for accessing and using the company's complete annual report, including the notes to the financial statements, are also provided in Appendix A.

Instructions
(a) Using the consolidated financial statements and related information, identify items that may result in adjusting entries for prepayments.
(b) Using the consolidated financial statements and related information, identify items that may result in adjusting entries for accruals.
(c) What has been the trend since 2009 for net income?

Comparative Analysis Problem:
PepsiCo, Inc. vs. The Coca-Cola Company

BYP3-2 PepsiCo's financial statements are presented in Appendix B. Financial statements for The Coca-Cola Company are presented in Appendix C. Instructions for accessing and using the complete annual reports of PepsiCo and Coca-Cola, including the notes to the financial statements, are also provided in Appendices B and C, respectively.

Instructions
Based on information contained in these financial statements, determine the following for each company.

(a) Net increase (decrease) in property, plant, and equipment (net) from 2010 to 2011.
(b) Increase (decrease) in selling, general, and administrative expenses from 2010 to 2011.
(c) Increase (decrease) in long-term debt (obligations) from 2010 to 2011.
(d) Increase (decrease) in net income from 2010 to 2011.
(e) Increase (decrease) in cash and cash equivalents from 2010 to 2011.

Comparative Analysis Problem:
Amazon.com, Inc. vs. Wal-Mart Stores, Inc.

BYP3-3 Amazon.com, Inc.'s financial statements are presented in Appendix D. Financial statements for Wal-Mart Stores, Inc. are presented in Appendix E. Instructions for accessing and using the complete annual reports of Amazon and Wal-Mart, including the notes to the financial statements, are also provided in Appendices D and E, respectively.

Instructions
Based on information contained in these financial statements, determine the following for each company.

1. (a) Increase (decrease) in interest expense from 2010 to 2011.
   (b) Increase (decrease) in net income from 2010 to 2011.
   (c) Increase (decrease) in cash flow from operations from 2010 to 2011.
2. Cash flow from operations and net income for each company is different. What are some possible reasons for these differences?

Real-World Focus

BYP3-4 No financial decision-maker should ever rely solely on the financial information reported in the annual report to make decisions. It is important to keep abreast of financial news. This activity demonstrates how to search for financial news on the Internet.

Address: **http://biz.yahoo.com/i**, or go to **www.wiley.com/college/weygandt**

Steps:
1. Type in either Wal-Mart, Target Corp., or Kmart.
2. Choose **News**.
3. Select an article that sounds interesting to you and that would be relevant to an investor in these companies.

Instructions
(a) What was the source of the article (e.g., Reuters, Businesswire, Prnewswire)?
(b) Assume that you are a personal financial planner and that one of your clients owns stock in the company. Write a brief memo to your client summarizing the article and explaining the implications of the article for their investment.

BYP3-5 The July 6, 2011, edition of the *Wall Street Journal Online* includes an article by Michael Rapoport entitled "U.S. Firms Clash Over Accounting Rules." The article discusses why some U.S. companies favored adoption of International Financial Reporting Standards (IFRS) while other companies opposed it.

Instructions
Read the article and answer the following questions.

(a) The articles says that the switch to IFRS tends to be favored by "larger companies, big accounting firms, and rule makers." What reasons are given for favoring the switch?
(b) What two reasons are given by many smaller companies that oppose the switch?
(c) What criticism of IFRS is raised with regard to regulated companies?
(d) Explain what is meant by "condorsement."

Critical Thinking

 ## Decision-Making Across the Organization

BYP3-6 Happy Camper Park was organized on April 1, 2013, by Barbara Evans. Barbara is a good manager but a poor accountant. From the trial balance prepared by a part-time bookkeeper, Barbara prepared the following income statement for the quarter that ended March 31, 2014.

HAPPY CAMPER PARK
Income Statement
For the Quarter Ended March 31, 2014

Revenues		
Rent revenue		$90,000
Operating expenses		
Advertising	$ 5,200	
Salaries and wages	29,800	
Utilities	900	
Depreciation	800	
Maintenance and repairs	4,000	
Total operating expenses		40,700
Net income		$49,300

Barbara thought that something was wrong with the statement because net income had never exceeded $20,000 in any one quarter. Knowing that you are an experienced accountant, she asks you to review the income statement and other data.

You first look at the trial balance. In addition to the account balances reported above in the income statement, the ledger contains the following additional selected balances at March 31, 2014.

Supplies	$ 6,200
Prepaid Insurance	7,200
Notes Payable	12,000

You then make inquiries and discover the following.

1. Rent revenues include advanced rentals for summer occupancy $15,000.
2. There were $1,700 of supplies on hand at March 31.
3. Prepaid insurance resulted from the payment of a one-year policy on January 1, 2014.
4. The mail on April 1, 2014, brought the following bills: advertising for week of March 24, $110; repairs made March 10, $260; and utilities, $180.
5. There are four employees, who receive wages totaling $300 per day. At March 31, 2 days' salaries and wages have been incurred but not paid.
6. The note payable is a 3-month, 10% note dated January 1, 2014.

Instructions
With the class divided into groups, answer the following.

(a) Prepare a correct income statement for the quarter ended March 31, 2014.
(b) Explain to Barbara the generally accepted accounting principles that she did not recognize in preparing her income statement and their effect on her results.

Communication Activity

BYP3-7 In reviewing the accounts of Gloria Jean Co. at the end of the year, you discover that adjusting entries have not been made.

Instructions
Write a memo to Gloria Jean Hall, the owner of Gloria Jean Co., that explains the following: the nature and purpose of adjusting entries, why adjusting entries are needed, and the types of adjusting entries that may be made.

Ethics Case

BYP3-8 Kellner Company is a pesticide manufacturer. Its sales declined greatly this year due to the passage of legislation outlawing the sale of several of Kellner's chemical pesticides. In the coming year, Kellner will have environmentally safe and competitive chemicals to replace these discontinued products. Sales in the next year are expected to greatly exceed any prior year's. The decline in sales and profits appears to be a one-year aberration. But even so, the company president fears a large dip in the current year's profits. He believes that such a dip could cause a significant drop in the market price of Kellner's stock and make the company a takeover target.

To avoid this possibility, the company president calls in Melissa Ray, controller, to discuss this period's year-end adjusting entries. He urges her to accrue every possible revenue and to defer as many expenses as possible. He says to Melissa, "We need the revenues this year, and next year can easily absorb expenses deferred from this year. We can't let our stock price be hammered down!" Melissa didn't get around to recording the adjusting entries until January 17, but she dated the entries December 31 as if they were recorded then. Melissa also made every effort to comply with the president's request.

Instructions
(a) Who are the stakeholders in this situation?
(b) What are the ethical considerations of (1) the president's request and (2) Melissa dating the adjusting entries December 31?
(c) Can Melissa accrue revenues and defer expenses and still be ethical?

All About You

BYP3-9 Companies must report or disclose in their financial statement information about all liabilities, including potential liabilities related to environmental cleanup. There are many situations in which you will be asked to provide personal financial information about your assets, liabilities, revenue, and expenses. Sometimes you will face difficult decisions regarding what to disclose and how to disclose it.

Instructions
Suppose that you are putting together a loan application to purchase a home. Based on your income and assets, you qualify for the mortgage loan, but just barely. How would you address each

of the following situations in reporting your financial position for the loan application? Provide responses for each of the following situations.

(a) You signed a guarantee for a bank loan that a friend took out for $20,000. If your friend doesn't pay, you will have to pay. Your friend has made all of the payments so far, and it appears he will be able to pay in the future.

(b) You were involved in an auto accident in which you were at fault. There is the possibility that you may have to pay as much as $50,000 as part of a settlement. The issue will not be resolved before the bank processes your mortgage request.

(c) The company for which you work isn't doing very well, and it has recently laid off employees. You are still employed, but it is quite possible that you will lose your job in the next few months.

Considering People, Planet, and Profit

BYP3-10 Many companies have potential pollution or environmental-disposal problems—not only for electronic gadgets, but also for the lead paint or asbestos they sold. How do we fit these issues into the accounting equation? Are these costs and related liabilities that companies should report?

YES: As more states impose laws holding companies responsible, and as more courts levy pollution-related fines, it becomes increasingly likely that companies will have to pay large amounts in the future.

NO: The amounts still are too difficult to estimate. Putting inaccurate estimates on the financial statements reduces their usefulness. Instead, why not charge the costs later, when the actual environmental cleanup or disposal occurs, at which time the company knows the actual cost?

Instructions
Write a response indicating your position regarding this situation. Provide support for your view.

FASB Codification Activity

BYP3-11 If your school has a subscription to the FASB Codification, go to **http://aaahq.org/ asclogin.cfm** to log in and prepare responses to the following.

Instructions
Access the glossary ("Master Glossary") to answer the following.

(a) What is the definition of revenue?
(b) What is the definition of compensation?

Answers to Chapter Questions

Answers to Insight and Accounting Across the Organization Questions

p. 102 Cooking the Books? Q: What motivates sales executives and finance and accounting executives to participate in activities that result in inaccurate reporting of revenues? **A:** Sales executives typically receive bonuses based on their ability to meet quarterly sales targets. In addition, they often face the possibility of losing their jobs if they miss those targets. Executives in accounting and finance are very aware of the earnings targets of Wall Street analysts and investors. If they fail to meet these targets, the company's stock price will fall. As a result of these pressures, executives sometimes knowingly engage in unethical efforts to misstate revenues. As a result of the Sarbanes-Oxley Act, the penalties for such behavior are now much more severe.

p. 109 Turning Gift Cards into Revenue Q: Suppose that Robert Jones purchases a $100 gift card at Best Buy on December 24, 2013, and gives it to his wife, Mary Jones, on December 25, 2013. On January 3, 2014, Mary uses the card to purchase $100 worth of CDs. When do you think Best Buy should recognize revenue and why? **A:** According to the revenue recognition principle, companies should recognize revenue when the performance obligation is satisfied. In this case, revenue results when Best Buy provides the goods. Thus, when Best Buy receives cash in exchange for the gift card on December 24, 2013, it should recognize a liability, Unearned Sales Revenue, for $100. On January 3, 2014, when Mary Jones exchanges the card for merchandise, Best Buy should recognize revenue and eliminate $100 from the balance in the Unearned Sales Revenue account.

p. 114 Cashing In on Accrual Accounting **Q:** Accrual accounting is often considered superior to cash accounting. Why, then, were some people critical of China's use of accrual accounting in this instance? **A:** In this case, some people were critical because, in general, China uses cash accounting. By switching to accrual accounting for this transaction, China was not being consistent in its accounting practices. Lack of consistency reduces the transparency and usefulness of accounting information.

p. 116 Got Junk? **Q:** What accounting issue might this cause for companies? **A:** The balance sheet should provide a fair representation of what a company owns and what it owes. If significant obligations of the company are not reported on the balance sheet, the company's net worth (its equity) will be overstated. While it is true that it is not possible to estimate the **exact** amount of future environmental cleanup costs, it is becoming clear that companies will be held accountable. Therefore, it seems reasonable to accrue for environmental costs. Recognition of these liabilities provides a more accurate picture of the company's financial position. It also has the potential to improve the environment. As companies are forced to report these amounts on their financial statements, they will start to look for more effective and efficient means to reduce toxic waste and therefore reduce their costs.

Answers to Self-Test Questions

1. a **2.** c **3.** d **4.** a **5.** d **6.** d **7.** c ($1,350 − $600) **8.** c **9.** a **10.** c **11.** a **12.** b
13. b **14.** c ***15.** a ***16.** c ***17.** c

A Look at IFRS

It is often difficult for companies to determine in what time period they should report particular revenues and expenses. Both the IASB and FASB are working on a joint project to develop a common conceptual framework that will enable companies to better use the same principles to record transactions consistently over time.

> **LEARNING OBJECTIVE**   **9**
>
> Compare the procedures for adjusting entries under GAAP and IFRS.

Key Points

- In this chapter, you learned accrual-basis accounting applied under GAAP. Companies applying IFRS also use accrual-basis accounting to ensure that they record transactions that change a company's financial statements in the period in which events occur.

- Similar to GAAP, cash-basis accounting is not in accordance with IFRS.

- IFRS also divides the economic life of companies into artificial time periods. Under both GAAP and IFRS, this is referred to as the **time period assumption**.

- IFRS requires that companies present a complete set of financial statements, including comparative information, annually.

- The **general** revenue recognition principle required by GAAP that is used in this textbook is similar to that used under IFRS.

- Revenue recognition fraud is a major issue in U.S. financial reporting. The same situation occurs in other countries, as evidenced by revenue recognition breakdowns at Dutch software company Baan NV, Japanese electronics giant NEC, and Dutch grocer Ahold NV.

- Under IFRS, revaluation (using fair value) of items such as land and buildings is permitted. IFRS allows depreciation based on revaluation of assets, which is not permitted under GAAP.

- The terminology used for revenues and gains, and expenses and losses, differs somewhat between IFRS and GAAP. For example, income under IFRS is defined as:

  > Increases in economic benefits during the accounting period in the form of inflows or enhancements of assets or decreases of liabilities that result in increases in equity, other than those relating to contributions from shareholders.

  Income includes both revenues, which arise during the normal course of operating activities, and gains, which arise from activities outside of the normal sales of goods and services. The term income is not used this way under GAAP. Instead, under GAAP income refers to the net difference between revenues and expenses. Expenses under IFRS are defined as:

> Decreases in economic benefits during the accounting period in the form of outflows or depletions of assets or incurrences of liabilities that result in decreases in equity other than those relating to distributions to shareholders.

Note that under IFRS, expenses include both those costs incurred in the normal course of operations as well as losses that are not part of normal operations. This is in contrast to GAAP, which defines each separately.

Looking to the Future

The IASB and FASB are completing a joint project on revenue recognition. The purpose of this project is to develop comprehensive guidance on when to recognize revenue. It is hoped that this approach will lead to more consistent accounting in this area. For more on this topic, see **www.fasb.org/project/revenue_recognition.shtml**.

IFRS Practice

IFRS Self-Test Questions

1. IFRS:
   (a) uses accrual accounting.
   (b) uses cash-basis accounting.
   (c) allows revenue to be recognized when a customer makes an order.
   (d) requires that revenue not be recognized until cash is received.

2. Which of the following statements is **false**?
   (a) IFRS employs the time period assumption.
   (b) IFRS employs accrual accounting.
   (c) IFRS requires that revenues and costs must be capable of being measured reliably.
   (d) IFRS uses the cash basis of accounting.

3. As a result of the revenue recognition project by the FASB and IASB:
   (a) revenue recognition places more emphasis on when the performance obligation is satisfied.
   (b) revenue recognition places more emphasis on when revenue is realized.
   (c) revenue recognition places more emphasis on when expenses are incurred.
   (d) revenue is no longer recorded unless cash has been received.

4. Which of the following is **false**?
   (a) Under IFRS, the term income describes both revenues and gains.
   (b) Under IFRS, the term expenses includes losses.
   (c) Under IFRS, companies do not engage in the adjusting process.
   (d) Under IFRS, revenue recognition fraud is a major issue.

5. Accrual-basis accounting:
   (a) is optional under IFRS.
   (b) results in companies recording transactions that change a company's financial statements in the period in which events occur.
   (c) has been eliminated as a result of the IASB/FASB joint project on revenue recognition.
   (d) is not consistent with the IASB conceptual framework.

IFRS Exercises

IFRS3-1 Compare and contrast the rules regarding revenue recognition under IFRS versus GAAP.

IFRS3-2 Under IFRS, do the definitions of revenues and expenses include gains and losses? Explain.

International Financial Reporting Problem: Zetar plc

IFRS3-3 The financial statements of Zetar plc are presented in Appendix F. Instructions for accessing and using the company's complete annual report, including the notes to its financial statements, are also provided in Appendix F.

Instructions

Visit Zetar's corporate website and answer the following questions from Zetar's 2011 annual report.

(a) From the notes to the financial statements, how does the company determine the amount of revenue to record at the time of a sale?

(b) From the notes to the financial statements, how does the company determine whether a sale has occurred?

(c) Using the consolidated income statement and consolidated statement of financial position, identify items that may result in adjusting entries for deferrals.

(d) Using the consolidated income statement, identify two items that may result in adjusting entries for accruals.

Answers to IFRS Self-Test Questions

1. a **2.** d **3.** a **4.** c **5.** b

✔ **The Navigator**

4 | Completing the Accounting Cycle

Feature Story

Everyone Likes to Win

When Ted Castle was a hockey coach at the University of Vermont, his players were self-motivated by their desire to win. Hockey was a game you usually either won or lost. But at Rhino Foods, Inc., a bakery-foods company he founded in Burlington, Vermont, he discovered that manufacturing-line workers were not so self-motivated. Ted thought, what if he turned the food-making business into a game, with rules, strategies, and trophies?

In a game, knowing the score is all-important. Ted felt that only if the employees know the score—know exactly how the business is doing daily, weekly, monthly—could he turn food-making into a game. But Rhino is a closely held, family-owned business, and its financial statements and profits were confidential. Ted wondered, should he open Rhino's books to the employees?

A consultant put Ted's concerns in perspective when he said, "Imagine you're playing touch football. You play for an hour or two, and the whole time I'm sitting there with a book,

keeping score. All of a sudden I blow the whistle, and I 'OK, that's it. Everybody go home.' I close my book and away. How would you feel?" Ted opened his books anc revealed the financial statements to his employees.

The next step was to teach employees the rules and str of how to "win" at making food. The first lesson: "You opponent at Rhino is expenses. You must cut and contr expenses." Ted and his staff distilled those lessons into scorecards—production reports and income statements keep Rhino's employees up-to-date on the game. At no each day, Ted posts the previous day's results at the entr to the production room. Everyone checks whether they or lost money on what they produced the day before. A not just an academic exercise: There's a bonus check fo employee at the end of every four-week "game" that n profitability guidelines.

Rhino has flourished since the first game. Employment increased from 20 to 130 people, while both revenues profits have grown dramatically.

Learning Objectives   ✔ The Navigator

After studying this chapter, you should be able to:

[1] Prepare a worksheet.

[2] Explain the process of closing the books.

[3] Describe the content and purpose of a post-closing trial balance.

[4] State the required steps in the accounting cycle.

[5] Explain the approaches to preparing correcting entries.

[6] Identify the sections of a classified balance sheet.

Preview of Chapter 4

✔ The Navigator

At Rhino Foods, Inc., financial statements help employees understand what is happening in the business. In Chapter 3, we prepared financial statements directly from the adjusted trial balance. However, with so many details involved in the end-of-period accounting procedures, it is easy to make errors. One way to minimize errors in the records and to simplify the end-of-period procedures is to use a worksheet.

In this chapter, we will explain the role of the worksheet in accounting. We also will study the remaining steps in the accounting cycle, especially the closing process, again using Pioneer Advertising Agency as an example. Then we will consider correcting entries and classified balance sheets. The content and organization of Chapter 4 are as follows.

COMPLETING THE ACCOUNTING CYCLE

Using a Worksheet	Closing the Books	Summary of the Accounting Cycle	Classified Balance Sheet
• Steps in preparation • Preparing financial statements • Preparing adjusting entries	• Preparing closing entries • Posting closing entries • Preparing a post-closing trial balance	• Reversing entries—An optional step • Correcting entries—An avoidable step	• Current assets • Long-term investments • Property, plant, and equipment • Intangible assets • Current liabilities • Long-term liabilities • Owner's equity

Using a Worksheet

LEARNING OBJECTIVE   **1**

Prepare a worksheet.

A **worksheet** is a multiple-column form used in the adjustment process and in preparing financial statements. As its name suggests, the worksheet is a working tool. **It is not a permanent accounting record.** It is neither a journal nor a part of the general ledger. The worksheet is merely a device used in preparing adjusting entries and the financial statements. Companies generally computerize worksheets using an electronic spreadsheet program such as Excel.

Illustration 4-1 shows the basic form of a worksheet and the five steps for preparing it. Each step is performed in sequence. **The use of a worksheet is optional.** When a company chooses to use one, it prepares financial statements directly from the worksheet. It enters the adjustments in the worksheet columns and then journalizes and posts the adjustments after it has prepared the financial statements. Thus, worksheets make it possible to provide the financial statements to management and other interested parties at an earlier date.

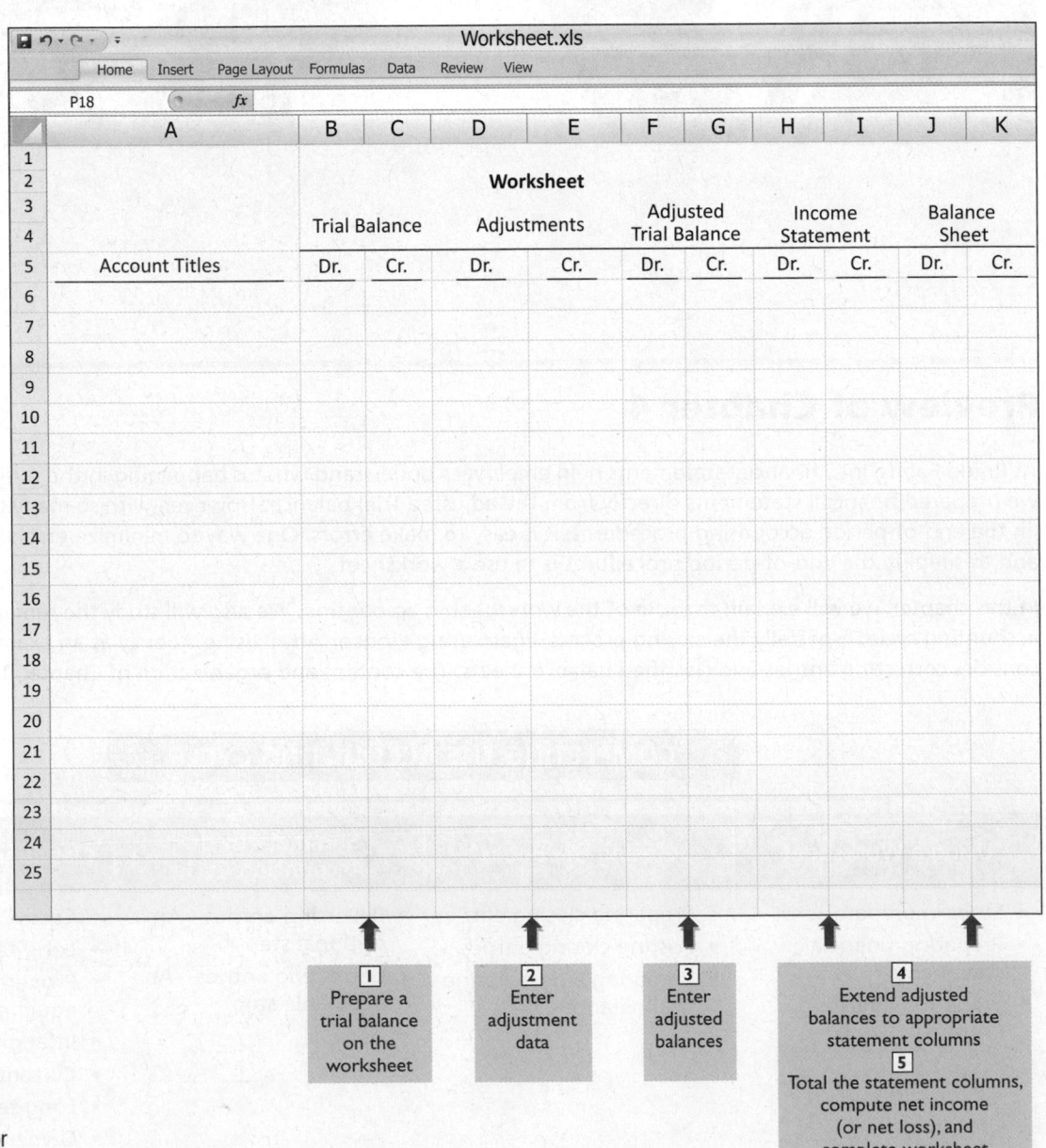

Illustration 4-1
Form and procedure for a worksheet

Steps in Preparing a Worksheet

We will use the October 31 trial balance and adjustment data of Pioneer Advertising Agency from Chapter 3 to illustrate how to prepare a worksheet. We describe each step of the process and demonstrate these steps in Illustration 4-2 (page 164) and transparencies 4-3A, B, C, and D.

STEP 1. PREPARE A TRIAL BALANCE ON THE WORKSHEET

Enter all ledger accounts with balances in the account titles column. Enter debit and credit amounts from the ledger in the trial balance columns. Illustration 4-2 shows the worksheet trial balance for Pioneer Advertising Agency. This trial balance is the same one that appears in Illustration 2-31 (page 73) and Illustration 3-3 (page 103).

STEP 2. ENTER THE ADJUSTMENTS IN THE ADJUSTMENTS COLUMNS

Turn over the first transparency, Illustration 4-3A. When using a worksheet, enter all adjustments in the adjustments columns. In entering the adjustments, use applicable trial balance accounts. If additional accounts are needed, insert them on the lines immediately below the trial balance totals. A different letter identifies the debit and credit for each adjusting entry. The term used to describe this process is **keying. Companies do not journalize the adjustments until after they complete the worksheet and prepare the financial statements.**

The adjustments for Pioneer Advertising Agency are the same as the adjustments in Illustration 3-23 (page 117). They are keyed in the adjustments columns of the worksheet as follows.

(a) Pioneer debits an additional account, Supplies Expense, $1,500 for the cost of supplies used, and credits Supplies $1,500.

(b) Pioneer debits an additional account, Insurance Expense, $50 for the insurance that has expired, and credits Prepaid Insurance $50.

(c) The company needs two additional depreciation accounts. It debits Depreciation Expense $40 for the month's depreciation, and credits Accumulated Depreciation—Equipment $40.

(d) Pioneer debits Unearned Service Revenue $400 for services performed, and credits Service Revenue $400.

(e) Pioneer debits an additional account, Accounts Receivable, $200 for services performed but not billed, and credits Service Revenue $200.

(f) The company needs two additional accounts relating to interest. It debits Interest Expense $50 for accrued interest, and credits Interest Payable $50.

(g) Pioneer debits Salaries and Wages Expense $1,200 for accrued salaries, and credits an additional account, Salaries and Wages Payable, $1,200.

After Pioneer has entered all the adjustments, the adjustments columns are totaled to prove their equality.

STEP 3. ENTER ADJUSTED BALANCES IN THE ADJUSTED TRIAL BALANCE COLUMNS

Turn over the second transparency, Illustration 4-3B. Pioneer determines the adjusted balance of an account by combining the amounts entered in the first four columns of the worksheet for each account. For example, the Prepaid Insurance account in the trial balance columns has a $600 debit balance and a $50 credit in the adjustments columns. The result is a $550 debit balance recorded in the adjusted trial balance columns. **For each account, the amount in the adjusted**

(**Note:** Text continues on page 165, following acetate overlays.)

Illustration 4-2
Preparing a trial balance

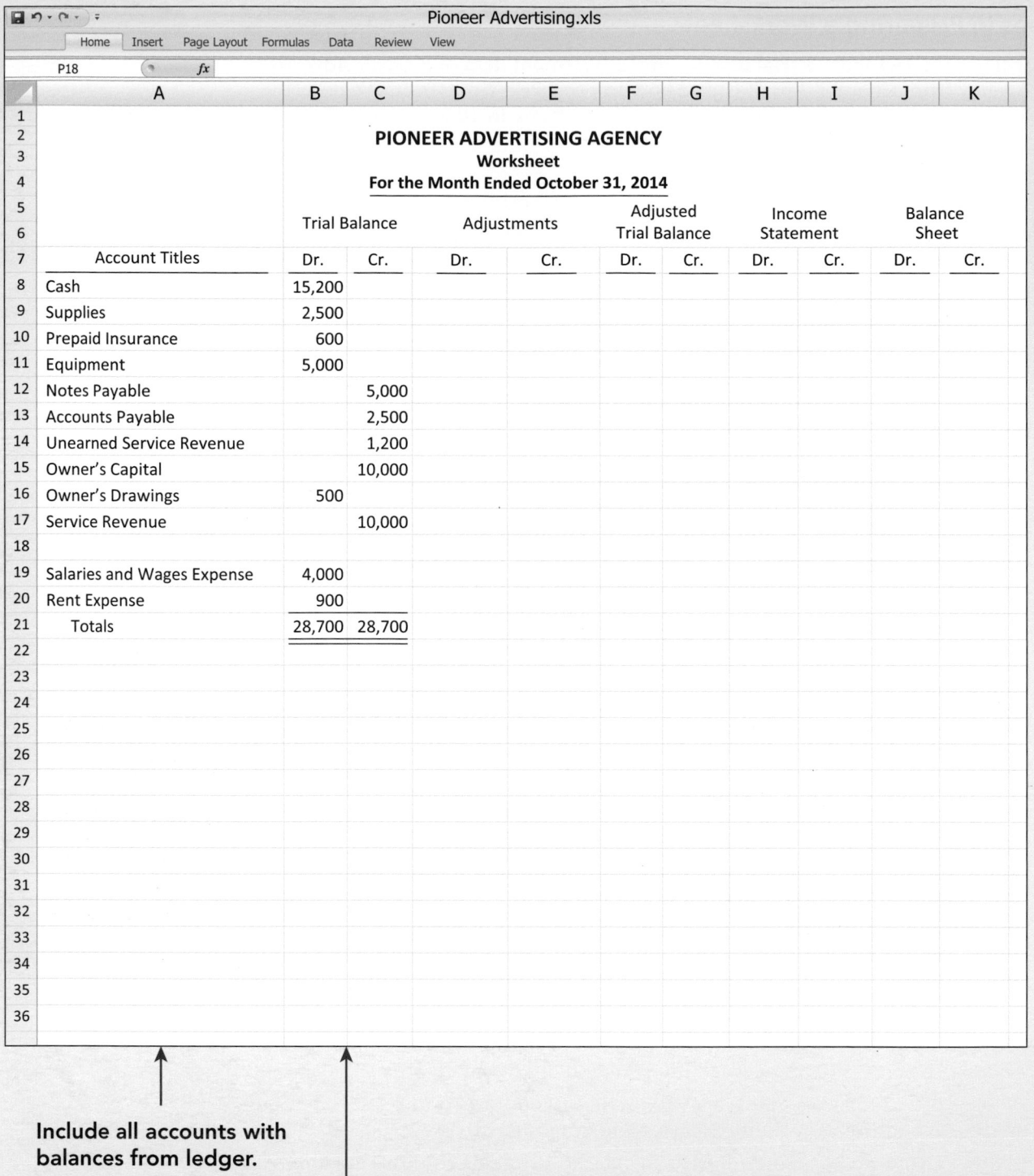

PIONEER ADVERTISING.xls

Home | Insert | Page Layout | Formulas | Data | Review | View

P18

	A	B	C	D	E	F	G	H	I	J	K
1											
2		**PIONEER ADVERTISING AGENCY**									
3		Worksheet									
4		For the Month Ended October 31, 2014									
5		Trial Balance		Adjustments		Adjusted Trial Balance		Income Statement		Balance Sheet	
6											
7	Account Titles	Dr.	Cr.	Dr.	Cr.	Dr.	Cr.	Dr.	Cr.	Dr.	Cr.
8	Cash	15,200									
9	Supplies	2,500									
10	Prepaid Insurance	600									
11	Equipment	5,000									
12	Notes Payable		5,000								
13	Accounts Payable		2,500								
14	Unearned Service Revenue		1,200								
15	Owner's Capital		10,000								
16	Owner's Drawings	500									
17	Service Revenue		10,000								
18											
19	Salaries and Wages Expense	4,000									
20	Rent Expense	900									
21	Totals	28,700	28,700								
22											
23											
24											
25											
26											
27											
28											
29											
30											
31											
32											
33											
34											
35											
36											

Include all accounts with balances from ledger.

Trial balance amounts come directly from ledger accounts.

Illustrati...

Entering th...

Add additio...
as needed t...
the adjustm...

(a) Supplies U
(b) Insurance
(c) Depreciat...
(d) Service R...
(e) Service R...
(f) Interest A...
(g) Salaries A...

Steps in Preparing a Worksheet

We will use the October 31 trial balance and adjustment data of Pioneer Advertising Agency from Chapter 3 to illustrate how to prepare a worksheet. We describe each step of the process and demonstrate these steps in Illustration 4-2 (page 164) and transparencies 4-3A, B, C, and D.

STEP 1. PREPARE A TRIAL BALANCE ON THE WORKSHEET

Enter all ledger accounts with balances in the account titles column. Enter debit and credit amounts from the ledger in the trial balance columns. Illustration 4-2 shows the worksheet trial balance for Pioneer Advertising Agency. This trial balance is the same one that appears in Illustration 2-31 (page 73) and Illustration 3-3 (page 103).

STEP 2. ENTER THE ADJUSTMENTS IN THE ADJUSTMENTS COLUMNS

Turn over the first transparency, Illustration 4-3A. When using a worksheet, enter all adjustments in the adjustments columns. In entering the adjustments, use applicable trial balance accounts. If additional accounts are needed, insert them on the lines immediately below the trial balance totals. A different letter identifies the debit and credit for each adjusting entry. The term used to describe this process is **keying. Companies do not journalize the adjustments until after they complete the worksheet and prepare the financial statements.**

The adjustments for Pioneer Advertising Agency are the same as the adjustments in Illustration 3-23 (page 117). They are keyed in the adjustments columns of the worksheet as follows.

(a) Pioneer debits an additional account, Supplies Expense, $1,500 for the cost of supplies used, and credits Supplies $1,500.

(b) Pioneer debits an additional account, Insurance Expense, $50 for the insurance that has expired, and credits Prepaid Insurance $50.

(c) The company needs two additional depreciation accounts. It debits Depreciation Expense $40 for the month's depreciation, and credits Accumulated Depreciation—Equipment $40.

(d) Pioneer debits Unearned Service Revenue $400 for services performed, and credits Service Revenue $400.

(e) Pioneer debits an additional account, Accounts Receivable, $200 for services performed but not billed, and credits Service Revenue $200.

(f) The company needs two additional accounts relating to interest. It debits Interest Expense $50 for accrued interest, and credits Interest Payable $50.

(g) Pioneer debits Salaries and Wages Expense $1,200 for accrued salaries, and credits an additional account, Salaries and Wages Payable, $1,200.

After Pioneer has entered all the adjustments, the adjustments columns are totaled to prove their equality.

STEP 3. ENTER ADJUSTED BALANCES IN THE ADJUSTED TRIAL BALANCE COLUMNS

Turn over the second transparency, Illustration 4-3B. Pioneer determines the adjusted balance of an account by combining the amounts entered in the first four columns of the worksheet for each account. For example, the Prepaid Insurance account in the trial balance columns has a $600 debit balance and a $50 credit in the adjustments columns. The result is a $550 debit balance recorded in the adjusted trial balance columns. **For each account, the amount in the adjusted**

(**Note:** Text continues on page 165, following acetate overlays.)

Illustration 4-2
Preparing a trial balance

	Pioneer Advertising.xls									

Home Insert Page Layout Formulas Data Review View

P18

	A	B	C	D	E	F	G	H	I	J	K
1											
2			**PIONEER ADVERTISING AGENCY**								
3			Worksheet								
4			**For the Month Ended October 31, 2014**								
5		Trial Balance		Adjustments		Adjusted Trial Balance		Income Statement		Balance Sheet	
6											
7	Account Titles	Dr.	Cr.	Dr.	Cr.	Dr.	Cr.	Dr.	Cr.	Dr.	Cr.
8	Cash	15,200									
9	Supplies	2,500									
10	Prepaid Insurance	600									
11	Equipment	5,000									
12	Notes Payable		5,000								
13	Accounts Payable		2,500								
14	Unearned Service Revenue		1,200								
15	Owner's Capital		10,000								
16	Owner's Drawings	500									
17	Service Revenue		10,000								
18											
19	Salaries and Wages Expense	4,000									
20	Rent Expense	900									
21	Totals	28,700	28,700								
22											
23											
24											
25											
26											
27											
28											
29											
30											
31											
32											
33											
34											
35											
36											

Include all accounts with balances from ledger.

Trial balance amounts come directly from ledger accounts.

trial balance columns is the balance that will appear in the ledger after journalizing and posting the adjusting entries. The balances in these columns are the same as those in the adjusted trial balance in Illustration 3-25 (page 119).

After Pioneer has entered all account balances in the adjusted trial balance columns, the columns are totaled to prove their equality. If the column totals do not agree, the financial statement columns will not balance and the financial statements will be incorrect.

STEP 4. EXTEND ADJUSTED TRIAL BALANCE AMOUNTS TO APPROPRIATE FINANCIAL STATEMENT COLUMNS

Turn over the third transparency, Illustration 4-3C. The fourth step is to extend adjusted trial balance amounts to the income statement and balance sheet columns of the worksheet. Pioneer enters balance sheet accounts in the appropriate balance sheet debit and credit columns. For instance, it enters Cash in the balance sheet debit column, and Notes Payable in the balance sheet credit column. Pioneer extends Accumulated Depreciation—Equipment to the balance sheet credit column. The reason is that accumulated depreciation is a contra asset account with a credit balance.

Because the worksheet does not have columns for the owner's equity statement, Pioneer extends the balance in owner's capital to the balance sheet credit column. In addition, it extends the balance in owner's drawings to the balance sheet debit column because it is an owner's equity account with a debit balance.

The company enters the expense and revenue accounts such as Salaries and Wages Expense and Service Revenue in the appropriate income statement columns. Illustration 4-3C shows all of these extensions.

STEP 5. TOTAL THE STATEMENT COLUMNS, COMPUTE THE NET INCOME (OR NET LOSS), AND COMPLETE THE WORKSHEET

Turn over the fourth transparency, Illustration 4-3D. The company now must total each of the financial statement columns. The net income or loss for the period is the difference between the totals of the two income statement columns. If total credits exceed total debits, the result is net income. In such a case, as shown in Illustration 4-3D, the company inserts the words "Net Income" in the account titles space. It then enters the amount in the income statement debit column and the balance sheet credit column. **The debit amount balances the income statement columns; the credit amount balances the balance sheet columns.** In addition, the credit in the balance sheet column indicates the increase in owner's equity resulting from net income.

What if total debits in the income statement columns exceed total credits? In that case, the company has a net loss. It enters the amount of the net loss in the income statement credit column and the balance sheet debit column.

After entering the net income or net loss, the company determines new column totals. The totals shown in the debit and credit income statement columns will match. So will the totals shown in the debit and credit balance sheet columns. If either the income statement columns or the balance sheet columns are not equal after the net income or net loss has been entered, there is an error in the worksheet. Illustration 4-3D shows the completed worksheet for Pioneer Advertising Agency.

Preparing Financial Statements from a Worksheet

After a company has completed a worksheet, it has at hand all the data required for preparation of financial statements. The income statement is prepared from the income statement columns. The balance sheet and owner's equity statement are prepared from the balance sheet columns. Illustration 4-4 (page 166) shows the financial statements prepared from Pioneer's worksheet. At this point, the company

Helpful Hint Every adjusted trial balance amount must be extended to one of the four statement columns.

Illustration 4-4
Financial statements from a
worksheet

PIONEER ADVERTISING AGENCY
Income Statement
For the Month Ended October 31, 2014

Revenues		
Service revenue		$10,600
Expenses		
Salaries and wages expense	$5,200	
Supplies expense	1,500	
Rent expense	900	
Insurance expense	50	
Interest expense	50	
Depreciation expense	40	
Total expenses		7,740
Net income		$ 2,860

PIONEER ADVERTISING AGENCY
Owner's Equity Statement
For the Month Ended October 31, 2014

Owner's capital, October 1		$ –0–
Add: Investments	$10,000	
Net income	2,860	12,860
		12,860
Less: Drawings		500
Owner's capital, October 31		$12,360

PIONEER ADVERTISING AGENCY
Balance Sheet
October 31, 2014

Assets

Cash		$15,200
Accounts receivable		200
Supplies		1,000
Prepaid insurance		550
Equipment	$5,000	
Less: Accumulated depreciation—equipment	40	4,960
Total assets		$21,910

Liabilities and Owner's Equity

Liabilities		
Notes payable	$5,000	
Accounts payable	2,500	
Interest payable	50	
Unearned service revenue	800	
Salaries and wages payable	1,200	
Total liabilities		$ 9,550
Owner's equity		
Owner's capital		12,360
Total liabilities and owner's equity		$21,910

has not journalized or posted adjusting entries. Therefore, ledger balances for some accounts are not the same as the financial statement amounts.

The amount shown for owner's capital on the worksheet is the account balance **before considering drawings and net income (or loss)**. When the owner has made no additional investments of capital during the period, this worksheet amount for owner's capital is the balance at the beginning of the period.

Using a worksheet, companies can prepare financial statements before they journalize and post adjusting entries. **However, the completed worksheet is not a substitute for formal financial statements.** The format of the data in the financial statement columns of the worksheet is not the same as the format of the financial statements. **A worksheet is essentially a working tool of the accountant**; companies do not distribute it to management and other parties.

Preparing Adjusting Entries from a Worksheet

A worksheet is not a journal, and it cannot be used as a basis for posting to ledger accounts. To adjust the accounts, the company must journalize the adjustments and post them to the ledger. **The adjusting entries are prepared from the adjustments columns of the worksheet.** The reference letters in the adjustments columns and the explanations of the adjustments at the bottom of the worksheet help identify the adjusting entries. The journalizing and posting of adjusting entries **follows** the preparation of financial statements when a worksheet is used. The adjusting entries on October 31 for Pioneer Advertising Agency are the same as those shown in Illustration 3-23 (page 117).

Helpful Hint Note that writing the explanation to the adjustment at the bottom of the worksheet is not required.

> ## DO IT!

Worksheet

Action Plan

✔ Balance sheet: Extend assets to debit column. Extend liabilities to credit column. Extend contra assets to credit column. Extend drawings account to debit column.

✔ Income statement: Extend expenses to debit column. Extend revenues to credit column.

Susan Elbe is preparing a worksheet. Explain to Susan how she should extend the following adjusted trial balance accounts to the financial statement columns of the worksheet.

Cash	Owner's Drawings
Accumulated Depreciation—Equipment	Service Revenue
Accounts Payable	Salaries and Wages Expense

Solution

Income statement debit column—Salaries and Wages Expense
Income statement credit column—Service Revenue
Balance sheet debit column—Cash; Owner's Drawings
Balance sheet credit column—Accumulated Depreciation—Equipment; Accounts Payable

Related exercise material: **BE4-1, BE4-2, BE4-3, E4-1, E4-2, E4-5, E4-6, and DO IT! 4-1.**

✔ **The Navigator**

Closing the Books

At the end of the accounting period, the company makes the accounts ready for the next period. This is called **closing the books**. In closing the books, the company distinguishes between temporary and permanent accounts.

Temporary accounts relate only to a given accounting period. They include all income statement accounts and the owner's drawings account. **The company closes all temporary accounts at the end of the period.**

LEARNING OBJECTIVE   2

Explain the process of closing the books.

Alternative Terminology
Temporary accounts are sometimes called *nominal accounts*, and permanent accounts are sometimes called *real accounts*.

Illustration 4-5
Temporary versus permanent accounts

In contrast, **permanent accounts** relate to one or more future accounting periods. They consist of all balance sheet accounts, including the owner's capital account. **Permanent accounts are not closed from period to period.** Instead, the company carries forward the balances of permanent accounts into the next accounting period. Illustration 4-5 identifies the accounts in each category.

TEMPORARY These accounts are closed	PERMANENT These accounts are not closed
All revenue accounts	All asset accounts
All expense accounts	All liability accounts
Owner's drawings account	Owner's capital account

Preparing Closing Entries

At the end of the accounting period, the company transfers temporary account balances to the permanent owner's equity account, Owner's Capital, by means of closing entries.[1]

Closing entries formally recognize in the ledger the transfer of net income (or net loss) and owner's drawings to owner's capital. The owner's equity statement shows the results of these entries. **Closing entries also produce a zero balance in each temporary account.** The temporary accounts are then ready to accumulate data in the next accounting period separate from the data of prior periods. Permanent accounts are not closed.

Journalizing and posting closing entries is a required step in the accounting cycle. (See Illustration 4-12 on page 175.) The company performs this step after it has prepared financial statements. In contrast to the steps in the cycle that you have already studied, companies generally journalize and post closing entries **only at the end of the annual accounting period**. Thus, all temporary accounts will contain data for the entire year.

In preparing closing entries, companies could close each income statement account directly to owner's capital. However, to do so would result in excessive detail in the permanent Owner's Capital account. Instead, companies close the revenue and expense accounts to another temporary account, **Income Summary**, and they transfer the resulting net income or net loss from this account to owner's capital.

Companies **record closing entries in the general journal**. A center caption, Closing Entries, inserted in the journal between the last adjusting entry and the first closing entry, identifies these entries. Then the company posts the closing entries to the ledger accounts.

Companies generally prepare closing entries directly from the adjusted balances in the ledger. They could prepare separate closing entries for each nominal account, but the following four entries accomplish the desired result more efficiently:

1. Debit each revenue account for its balance, and credit Income Summary for total revenues.

2. Debit Income Summary for total expenses, and credit each expense account for its balance.

---

[1]We explain closing entries for a partnership and for a corporation in Chapters 12 and 13, respectively.

3. Debit Income Summary and credit Owner's Capital for the amount of net income.
4. Debit Owner's Capital for the balance in the Owner's Drawings account, and credit Owner's Drawings for the same amount.

Illustration 4-6 presents a diagram of the closing process. In it, the boxed numbers refer to the four entries required in the closing process.

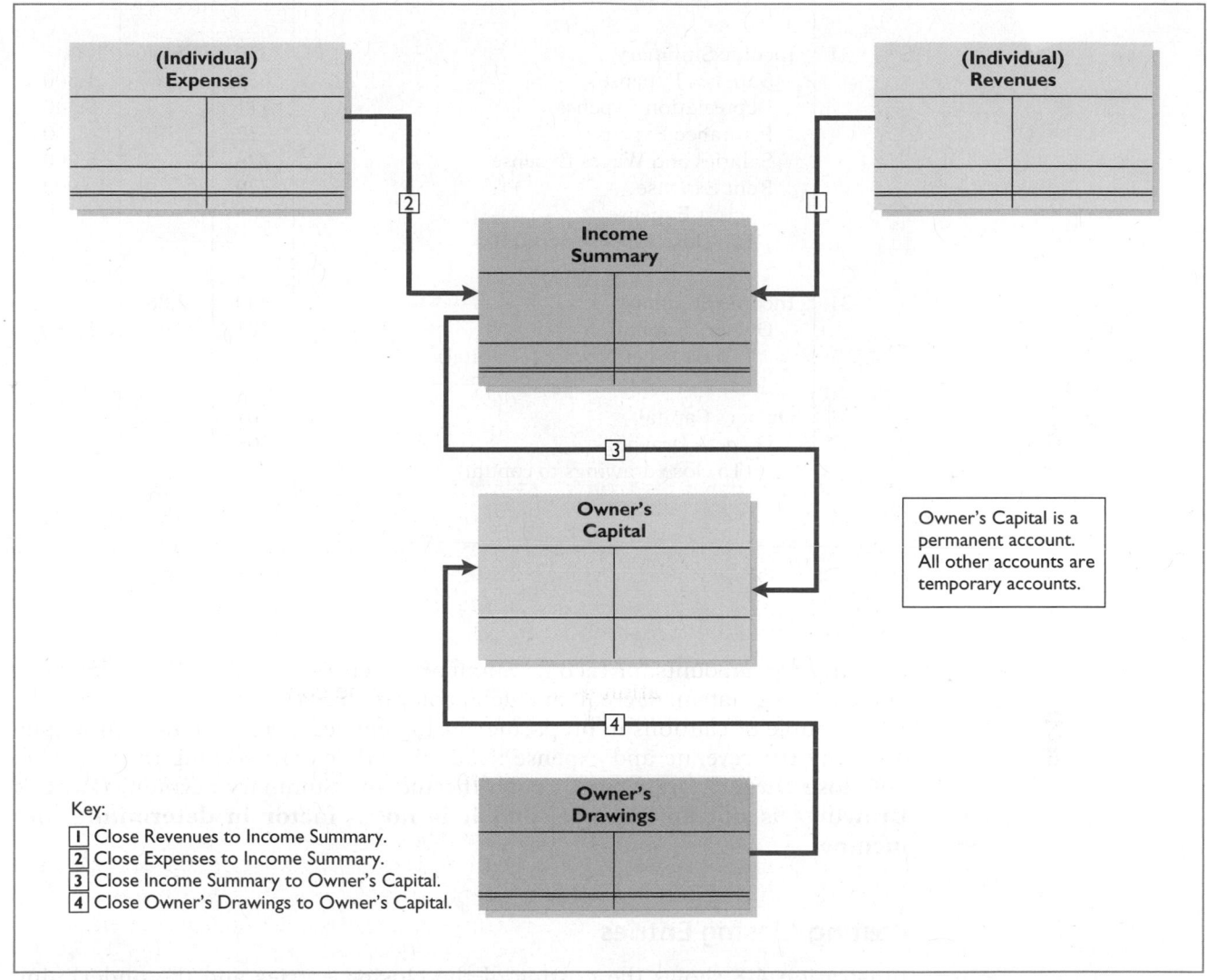

Key:
1. Close Revenues to Income Summary.
2. Close Expenses to Income Summary.
3. Close Income Summary to Owner's Capital.
4. Close Owner's Drawings to Owner's Capital.

Owner's Capital is a permanent account. All other accounts are temporary accounts.

Illustration 4-6
Diagram of closing process—proprietorship

If there were a net loss (because expenses exceeded revenues), entry 3 in Illustration 4-6 would be reversed: there would be a credit to Income Summary and a debit to Owner's Capital.

CLOSING ENTRIES ILLUSTRATED

In practice, companies generally prepare closing entries only at the end of the annual accounting period. However, to illustrate the journalizing and posting of closing entries, we will assume that Pioneer Advertising Agency closes its books monthly. Illustration 4-7 (page 170) shows the closing entries at October 31. (The numbers in parentheses before each entry correspond to the four entries diagrammed in Illustration 4-6.)

	GENERAL JOURNAL			J3
Date	Account Titles and Explanation	Ref.	Debit	Credit
	Closing Entries			
2014	(1)			
Oct. 31	Service Revenue	400	10,600	
	Income Summary	350		10,600
	(To close revenue account)			
	(2)			
31	Income Summary	350	7,740	
	Supplies Expense	631		1,500
	Depreciation Expense	711		40
	Insurance Expense	722		50
	Salaries and Wages Expense	726		5,200
	Rent Expense	729		900
	Interest Expense	905		50
	(To close expense accounts)			
	(3)			
31	Income Summary	350	2,860	
	Owner's Capital	301		2,860
	(To close net income to capital)			
	(4)			
31	Owner's Capital	301	500	
	Owner's Drawings	306		500
	(To close drawings to capital)			

Note that the amounts for Income Summary in entries (1) and (2) are the totals of the income statement credit and debit columns, respectively, in the worksheet.

A couple of cautions in preparing closing entries: (1) Avoid unintentionally doubling the revenue and expense balances rather than zeroing them. (2) Do not close Owner's Drawings through the Income Summary account. **Owner's Drawings is not an expense, and it is not a factor in determining net income.**

Posting Closing Entries

Illustration 4-8 shows the posting of the closing entries and the underlining (ruling) of the accounts. Note that all temporary accounts have zero balances after posting the closing entries. In addition, notice that the balance in owner's capital (Owner's Capital) represents the total equity of the owner at the end of the accounting period. This balance is shown on the balance sheet and is the ending capital reported on the owner's equity statement, as shown in Illustration 4-4 on page 166. Pioneer uses the Income Summary account only in closing. It does not journalize and post entries to this account during the year.

As part of the closing process, Pioneer totals, balances, and double-underlines its temporary accounts—revenues, expenses, and Owner's Drawings, as shown in T-account form in Illustration 4-8. It does not close its permanent accounts—assets, liabilities, and Owner's Capital. Instead, Pioneer draws a single underline beneath the current-period entries for the permanent accounts. The account balance is then entered below the single underline and is carried forward to the next period. (For example, see Owner's Capital.)

Helpful Hint The balance in Income Summary before it is closed must equal the net income or net loss for the period.

Supplies Expense   631

1,500	(2)	1,500

Service Revenue   400

(1)	10,600	10,000
		400
		200
	10,600	10,600

Depreciation Expense   711

40	(2)	40

Insurance Expense   722

50	(2)	50

Income Summary   350

(2)	7,740	(1)	10,600
(3)	2,860		
	10,600		10,600

Salaries and Wages Expense   726

4,000	(2)	5,200
1,200		
5,200		5,200

Owner's Capital   301

(4)	500	10,000
		(3) 2,860
		Bal. 12,360

Rent Expense   729

900	(2)	900

Key:
1 Close Revenues to Income Summary.
2 Close Expenses to Income Summary.
3 Close Income Summary to Owner's Capital.
4 Close Owner's Drawings to Owner's Capital.

Interest Expense   905

50	(2)	50

Owner's Drawings   306

500	(4)	500

Illustration 4-8
Posting of closing entries

ACCOUNTING ACROSS THE ORGANIZATION

Cisco Performs the Virtual Close

Technology has dramatically shortened the closing process. Recent surveys have reported that the average company now takes only six to seven days to close, rather than 20 days. But a few companies do much better. Cisco Systems can perform a "virtual close"—closing within 24 hours on any day in the quarter. The same is true at Lockheed Martin Corp., which improved its closing time by 85% in just the last few years. Not very long ago, it took 14 to 16 days. Managers at these companies emphasize that this increased speed has not reduced the accuracy and completeness of the data.

This is not just showing off. Knowing exactly where you are financially all of the time allows the company to respond faster than competitors. It also means that the hundreds of people who used to spend 10 to 20 days a quarter tracking transactions can now be more usefully employed on things such as mining data for business intelligence to find new business opportunities.

Source: "Reporting Practices: Few Do It All," *Financial Executive* (November 2003), p. 11.

? Who else benefits from a shorter closing process? (See page 211.)

> **DO IT!**

Closing Entries

The worksheet for Hancock Company shows the following in the financial statement columns:

Owner's drawings $15,000
Owner's capital $42,000
Net income $18,000

Prepare the closing entries at December 31 that affect owner's capital.

Action Plan

✔ Close Income Summary to Owner's Capital.

✔ Close Owner's Drawings to Owner's Capital.

Solution

Dec. 31	Income Summary	18,000	
	Owner's Capital		18,000
	(To close net income to capital)		
31	Owner's Capital	15,000	
	Owner's Drawings		15,000
	(To close drawings to capital)		

Related exercise material: **BE4-4, BE4-5, BE4-6, E4-4, E4-7, E4-8, E4-11,** and **DO IT!** **4-2.**

✔ The Navigator

Preparing a Post-Closing Trial Balance

LEARNING OBJECTIVE　3

Describe the content and purpose of a post-closing trial balance.

After Pioneer has journalized and posted all closing entries, it prepares another trial balance, called a **post-closing trial balance**, from the ledger. The post-closing trial balance lists permanent accounts and their balances after the journalizing and posting of closing entries. The purpose of the post-closing trial balance is **to prove the equality of the permanent account balances carried forward into the next accounting period.** Since all temporary accounts will have zero balances, **the post-closing trial balance will contain only permanent—balance sheet—accounts**.

Illustration 4-9 shows the post-closing trial balance for Pioneer Advertising Agency.

Illustration 4-9
Post-closing trial balance

PIONEER ADVERTISING AGENCY
Post-Closing Trial Balance
October 31, 2014

	Debit	Credit
Cash	$ 15,200	
Accounts Receivable	200	
Supplies	1,000	
Prepaid Insurance	550	
Equipment	5,000	
Accumulated Depreciation—Equipment		$　40
Notes Payable		5,000
Accounts Payable		2,500
Unearned Service Revenue		800
Salaries and Wages Payable		1,200
Interest Payable		50
Owner's Capital		12,360
	$21,950	**$21,950**

Pioneer prepares the post-closing trial balance from the permanent accounts in the ledger. Illustration 4-10 shows the permanent accounts in Pioneer's general ledger.

Illustration 4-10
General ledger, permanent accounts

(Permanent Accounts Only)

GENERAL LEDGER

Cash   No. 101

Date	Explanation	Ref.	Debit	Credit	Balance
2014					
Oct. 1		J1	10,000		10,000
2		J1	1,200		11,200
3		J1		900	10,300
4		J1		600	9,700
20		J1		500	9,200
26		J1		4,000	5,200
31		J1	10,000		15,200

Accounts Receivable   No. 112

Date	Explanation	Ref.	Debit	Credit	Balance
2014					
Oct. 31	Adj. entry	J2	200		200

Supplies   No. 126

Date	Explanation	Ref.	Debit	Credit	Balance
2014					
Oct. 5		J1	2,500		2,500
31	Adj. entry	J2		1,500	1,000

Prepaid Insurance   No. 130

Date	Explanation	Ref.	Debit	Credit	Balance
2014					
Oct. 4		J1	600		600
31	Adj. entry	J2		50	550

Equipment   No. 157

Date	Explanation	Ref.	Debit	Credit	Balance
2014					
Oct. 1		J1	5,000		5,000

Accumulated Depreciation—Equipment   No. 158

Date	Explanation	Ref.	Debit	Credit	Balance
2014					
Oct. 31	Adj. entry	J2		40	40

Notes Payable   No. 200

Date	Explanation	Ref.	Debit	Credit	Balance
2014					
Oct. 1		J1		5,000	5,000

Accounts Payable   No. 201

Date	Explanation	Ref.	Debit	Credit	Balance
2014					
Oct. 5		J1		2,500	2,500

Unearned Service Revenue   No. 209

Date	Explanation	Ref.	Debit	Credit	Balance
2014					
Oct. 2		J1		1,200	1,200
31	Adj. entry	J2	400		800

Salaries and Wages Payable   No. 212

Date	Explanation	Ref.	Debit	Credit	Balance
2014					
Oct. 31	Adj. entry	J2		1,200	1,200

Interest Payable   No. 230

Date	Explanation	Ref.	Debit	Credit	Balance
2014					
Oct. 31	Adj. entry	J2		50	50

Owner's Capital   No. 301

Date	Explanation	Ref.	Debit	Credit	Balance
2014					
Oct. 1		J1		10,000	10,000
31	Closing entry	J3		2,860	12,860
31	Closing entry	J3	500		12,360

Note: The permanent accounts for Pioneer Advertising Agency are shown here. Illustration 4-11 (page 174) shows the temporary accounts. Both permanent and temporary accounts are part of the general ledger. They are segregated here to aid in learning.

A post-closing trial balance provides evidence that the company has properly journalized and posted the closing entries. It also shows that the accounting equation is in balance at the end of the accounting period. However, like the trial balance, it does not prove that Pioneer has recorded all transactions or that the ledger is correct. For example, the post-closing trial balance still will balance even if a transaction is not journalized and posted or if a transaction is journalized and posted twice.

The remaining accounts in the general ledger are temporary accounts, shown in Illustration 4-11. After Pioneer correctly posts the closing entries, each temporary account has a zero balance. These accounts are double-underlined to finalize the closing process.

Illustration 4-11
General ledger, temporary accounts

(Temporary Accounts Only)

GENERAL LEDGER

Owner's Drawings　No. 306

Date	Explanation	Ref.	Debit	Credit	Balance
2014					
Oct. 20		J1	500		500
31	Closing entry	J3		500	–0–

Income Summary　No. 350

Date	Explanation	Ref.	Debit	Credit	Balance
2014					
Oct.31	Closing entry	J3		10,600	10,600
31	Closing entry	J3	7,740		2,860
31	Closing entry	J3	2,860		–0–

Service Revenue　No. 400

Date	Explanation	Ref.	Debit	Credit	Balance
2014					
Oct. 31		J1		10,000	10,000
31	Adj. entry	J2		400	10,400
31	Adj. entry	J2		200	10,600
31	Closing entry	J3	10,600		–0–

Supplies Expense　No. 631

Date	Explanation	Ref.	Debit	Credit	Balance
2014					
Oct. 31	Adj. entry	J2	1,500		1,500
31	Closing entry	J3		1,500	–0–

Depreciation Expense　No. 711

Date	Explanation	Ref.	Debit	Credit	Balance
2014					
Oct. 31	Adj. entry	J2	40		40
31	Closing entry	J3		40	–0–

Insurance Expense　No. 722

Date	Explanation	Ref.	Debit	Credit	Balance
2014					
Oct. 31	Adj. entry	J2	50		50
31	Closing entry	J3		50	–0–

Salaries and Wages Expense　No. 726

Date	Explanation	Ref.	Debit	Credit	Balance
2014					
Oct. 26		J1	4,000		4,000
31	Adj. entry	J2	1,200		5,200
31	Closing entry	J3		5,200	–0–

Rent Expense　No. 729

Date	Explanation	Ref.	Debit	Credit	Balance
2014					
Oct. 3		J1	900		900
31	Closing entry	J3		900	–0–

Interest Expense　No. 905

Date	Explanation	Ref.	Debit	Credit	Balance
2014					
Oct. 31	Adj. entry	J2	50		50
31	Closing entry	J3		50	–0–

Note: The temporary accounts for Pioneer Advertising Agency are shown here. Illustration 4-10 (page 173) shows the permanent accounts. Both permanent and temporary accounts are part of the general ledger. They are segregated here to aid in learning.

Summary of the Accounting Cycle

LEARNING OBJECTIVE　4

State the required steps in the accounting cycle.

Illustration 4-12 summarizes the steps in the accounting cycle. You can see that the cycle begins with the analysis of business transactions and ends with the preparation of a post-closing trial balance.

Illustration 4-12
Steps in the accounting cycle

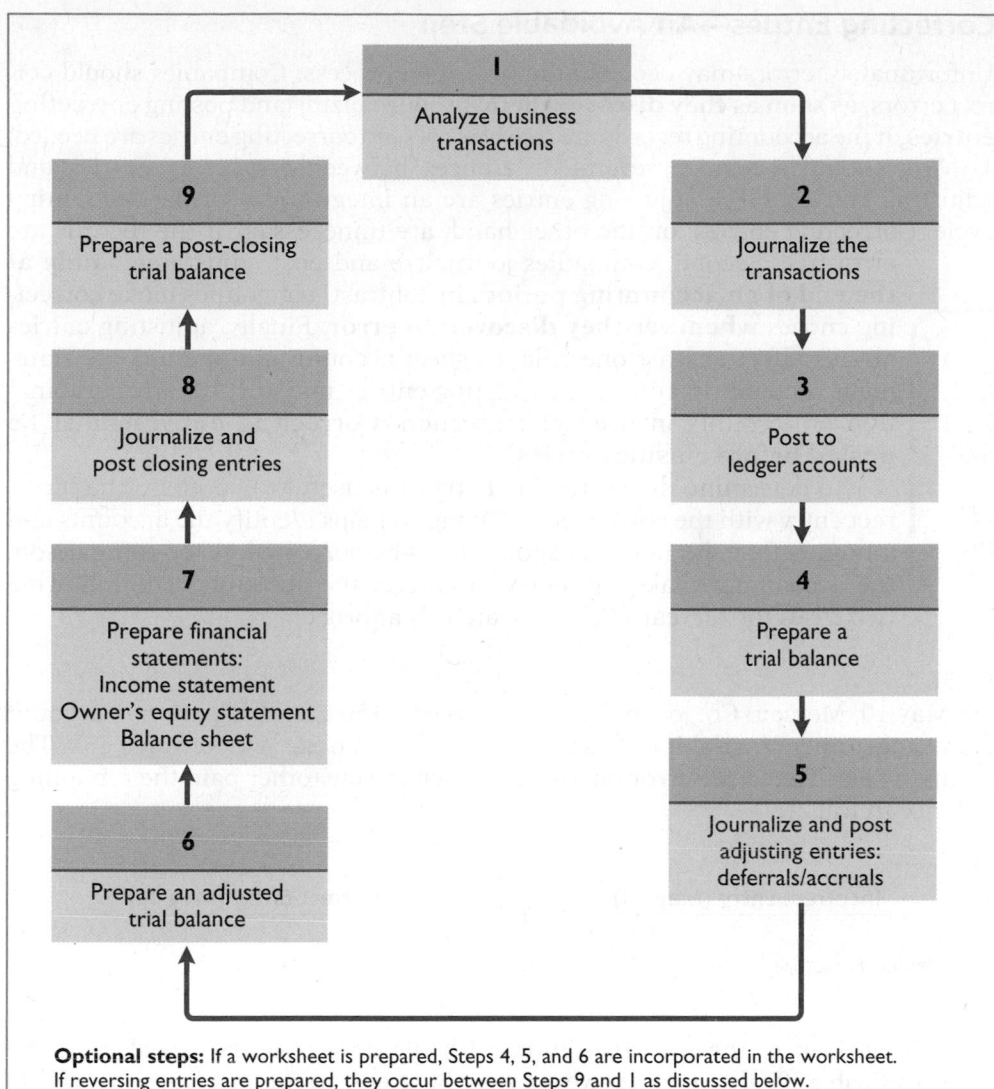

Optional steps: If a worksheet is prepared, Steps 4, 5, and 6 are incorporated in the worksheet. If reversing entries are prepared, they occur between Steps 9 and 1 as discussed below.

Steps 1–3 may occur daily during the accounting period. Companies perform Steps 4–7 on a periodic basis, such as monthly, quarterly, or annually. Steps 8 and 9—closing entries and a post-closing trial balance—usually take place only at the end of a company's **annual** accounting period.

There are also two **optional steps** in the accounting cycle. As you have seen, companies may use a worksheet in preparing adjusting entries and financial statements. In addition, they may use reversing entries, as explained below.

Reversing Entries—An Optional Step

Some accountants prefer to reverse certain adjusting entries by making a **reversing entry** at the beginning of the next accounting period. A reversing entry is the exact opposite of the adjusting entry made in the previous period. **Use of reversing entries is an optional bookkeeping procedure; it is not a required step in the accounting cycle.** Accordingly, we have chosen to cover this topic in an appendix at the end of the chapter.

Correcting Entries—An Avoidable Step

LEARNING OBJECTIVE   **5**

Explain the approaches to preparing correcting entries.

Ethics Note

When companies find errors in previously released income statements, they restate those numbers. Perhaps because of the increased scrutiny caused by Sarbanes-Oxley, in a recent year companies filed a record 1,195 restatements.

Unfortunately, errors may occur in the recording process. Companies should correct errors, **as soon as they discover them**, by journalizing and posting **correcting entries**. If the accounting records are free of errors, no correcting entries are needed.

You should recognize several differences between correcting entries and adjusting entries. First, adjusting entries are an integral part of the accounting cycle. Correcting entries, on the other hand, are unnecessary if the records are error-free. Second, companies journalize and post adjustments **only at the end of an accounting period**. In contrast, companies make correcting entries **whenever they discover an error**. Finally, adjusting entries always affect at least one balance sheet account and one income statement account. In contrast, correcting entries may involve any combination of accounts in need of correction. **Correcting entries must be posted before closing entries.**

To determine the correcting entry, it is useful to compare the incorrect entry with the correct entry. Doing so helps identify the accounts and amounts that should—and should not—be corrected. After comparison, the accountant makes an entry to correct the accounts. The following two cases for Mercato Co. illustrate this approach.

CASE 1

On May 10, Mercato Co. journalized and posted a $50 cash collection on account from a customer as a debit to Cash $50 and a credit to Service Revenue $50. The company discovered the error on May 20, when the customer paid the remaining balance in full.

Illustration 4-13
Comparison of entries

Incorrect Entry (May 10)			Correct Entry (May 10)		
Cash	50		Cash	50	
Service Revenue		50	Accounts Receivable		50

Comparison of the incorrect entry with the correct entry reveals that the debit to Cash $50 is correct. However, the $50 credit to Service Revenue should have been credited to Accounts Receivable. As a result, both Service Revenue and Accounts Receivable are overstated in the ledger. Mercato makes the following correcting entry.

Illustration 4-14
Correcting entry

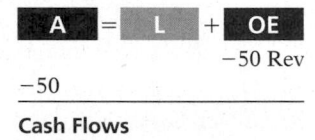

−50

Cash Flows
no effect

Correcting Entry

May 20	Service Revenue	50	
	Accounts Receivable		50
	(To correct entry of May 10)		

CASE 2

On May 18, Mercato purchased on account equipment costing $450. The transaction was journalized and posted as a debit to Equipment $45 and a credit to Accounts Payable $45. The error was discovered on June 3, when Mercato received the monthly statement for May from the creditor.

Illustration 4-15
Comparison of entries

Incorrect Entry (May 18)			Correct Entry (May 18)		
Equipment	45		Equipment	450	
Accounts Payable		45	Accounts Payable		450

Comparison of the two entries shows that two accounts are incorrect. Equipment is understated $405, and Accounts Payable is understated $405. Mercato makes the following correcting entry.

	Correcting Entry		
June 3	Equipment	405	
	Accounts Payable		405
	(To correct entry of May 18)		

A = L + OE
+405
+405

Cash Flows
no effect

Illustration 4-16
Correcting entry

Instead of preparing a correcting entry, **it is possible to reverse the incorrect entry and then prepare the correct entry**. This approach will result in more entries and postings than a correcting entry, but it will accomplish the desired result.

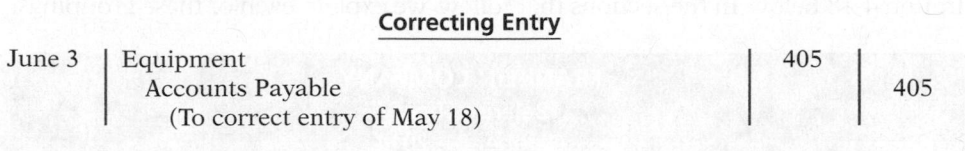

ACCOUNTING ACROSS THE ORGANIZATION

Yale Express Loses Some Transportation Bills

Yale Express, a short-haul trucking firm, turned over much of its cargo to local truckers to complete deliveries. Yale collected the entire delivery charge. When billed by the local trucker, Yale sent payment for the final phase to the local trucker. Yale used a cutoff period of 20 days into the next accounting period in making its adjusting entries for accrued liabilities. That is, it waited 20 days to receive the local truckers' bills to determine the amount of the unpaid but incurred delivery charges as of the balance sheet date.

On the other hand, Republic Carloading, a nationwide, long-distance freight forwarder, frequently did not receive transportation bills from truckers to whom it passed on cargo until months after the year-end. In making its year-end adjusting entries, Republic waited for months in order to include all of these outstanding transportation bills.

When Yale Express merged with Republic Carloading, Yale's vice president employed the 20-day cutoff procedure for both firms. As a result, millions of dollars of Republic's accrued transportation bills went unrecorded. When the company detected the error and made correcting entries, these and other errors changed a reported profit of $1.14 million into a loss of $1.88 million!

© Christian Lagereek/iStockphoto

 What might Yale Express's vice president have done to produce more accurate financial statements without waiting months for Republic's outstanding transportation bills? (See page 211.)

The Classified Balance Sheet

The balance sheet presents a snapshot of a company's financial position at a point in time. To improve users' understanding of a company's financial position, companies often use a classified balance sheet. A **classified balance sheet** groups together similar assets and similar liabilities, using a number of standard classifications and sections. This is useful because items within a group have similar economic characteristics. A classified balance sheet generally contains the standard classifications listed in Illustration 4-17.

LEARNING OBJECTIVE 6

Identify the sections of a classified balance sheet.

Assets	Liabilities and Owner's Equity
Current assets	Current liabilities
Long-term investments	Long-term liabilities
Property, plant, and equipment	Owner's (Stockholders') equity
Intangible assets	

Illustration 4-17
Standard balance sheet classifications

These groupings help financial statement readers determine such things as (1) whether the company has enough assets to pay its debts as they come due, and (2) the claims of short- and long-term creditors on the company's total assets. Many of these groupings can be seen in the balance sheet of Franklin Company shown in Illustration 4-18 below. In the sections that follow, we explain each of these groupings.

Illustration 4-18
Classified balance sheet

FRANKLIN COMPANY
Balance Sheet
October 31, 2014

Assets

Current assets			
Cash		$ 6,600	
Debt investments		2,000	
Accounts receivable		7,000	
Notes receivable		1,000	
Inventory		3,000	
Supplies		2,100	
Prepaid insurance		400	
Total current assets			$22,100
Long-term investments			
Stock investments		5,200	
Investment in real estate		2,000	7,200
Property, plant, and equipment			
Land		10,000	
Equipment	$24,000		
Less: Accumulated depreciation—			
equipment	5,000	19,000	29,000
Intangible assets			
Patents			3,100
Total assets			$61,400

Helpful Hint Recall that the basic accounting equation is Assets = Liabilities + Owner's Equity.

Liabilities and Owner's Equity

Current liabilities			
Notes payable		$11,000	
Accounts payable		2,100	
Unearned service revenue		900	
Salaries and wages payable		1,600	
Interest payable		450	
Total current liabilities			$16,050
Long-term liabilities			
Mortgage payable		10,000	
Notes payable		1,300	
Total long-term liabilities			11,300
Total liabilities			27,350
Owner's equity			
Owner's capital			34,050
Total liabilities and owner's equity			$61,400

Current Assets

Current assets are assets that a company expects to convert to cash or use up within one year or its operating cycle, whichever is longer. In Illustration 4-18, Franklin Company had current assets of $22,100. For most businesses the cutoff for classification as current assets is one year from the balance sheet date. For example, accounts receivable are current assets because the company will collect them and convert them to cash within one year. Supplies is a current asset because the company expects to use them up in operations within one year.

Some companies use a period longer than one year to classify assets and liabilities as current because they have an operating cycle longer than one year. The **operating cycle** of a company is the average time that it takes to purchase inventory, sell it on account, and then collect cash from customers. For most businesses this cycle takes less than a year, so they use a one-year cutoff. But, for some businesses, such as vineyards or airplane manufacturers, this period may be longer than a year. **Except where noted, we will assume that companies use one year to determine whether an asset or liability is current or long-term.**

Common types of current assets are (1) cash, (2) investments (such as short-term U.S. government securities), (3) receivables (notes receivable, accounts receivable, and interest receivable), (4) inventories, and (5) prepaid expenses (supplies and insurance). **On the balance sheet, companies usually list these items in the order in which they expect to convert them into cash.**

Illustration 4-19 presents the current assets of Southwest Airlines Co.

Illustration 4-19
Current assets section

Real World	**SOUTHWEST AIRLINES CO.** Balance Sheet (partial) (in millions)	
Current assets		
Cash and cash equivalents		$1,390
Short-term investments		369
Accounts receivable		241
Inventories		181
Prepaid expenses and other current assets		420
Total current assets		$2,601

As explained later in the chapter, a company's current assets are important in assessing its short-term debt-paying ability.

Long-Term Investments

Long-term investments are generally (1) investments in stocks and bonds of other companies that are normally held for many years, (2) long-term assets such as land or buildings that a company is not currently using in its operating activities, and (3) long-term notes receivable. In Illustration 4-18, Franklin Company reported total long-term investments of $7,200 on its balance sheet.

Yahoo! Inc. reported long-term investments in its balance sheet as shown in Illustration 4-20.

Alternative Terminology
Long-term investments are often referred to simply as *investments*.

Illustration 4-20
Long-term investments section

Real World	**YAHOO! INC.** Balance Sheet (partial) (in thousands)	
Long-term investments		
Investments in securities		$90,266

International Note

Property, Plant, and Equipment

Property, plant, and equipment are assets with relatively long useful lives that a company is currently using in operating the business. This category includes land, buildings, machinery and equipment, delivery equipment, and furniture. In Illustration 4-18, Franklin Company reported property, plant, and equipment of $29,000.

Depreciation is the practice of allocating the cost of assets to a number of years. Companies do this by systematically assigning a portion of an asset's cost as an expense each year (rather than expensing the full purchase price in the year of purchase). The assets that the company depreciates are reported on the balance sheet at cost less accumulated depreciation. The **accumulated depreciation** account shows the total amount of depreciation that the company has expensed thus far in the asset's life. In Illustration 4-18, Franklin Company reported accumulated depreciation of $5,000.

Illustration 4-21 presents the property, plant, and equipment of Cooper Tire & Rubber Company.

Illustration 4-21
Property, plant, and equipment section

Real World	COOPER TIRE & RUBBER COMPANY Balance Sheet (partial) (in thousands)		
Property, plant, and equipment			
Land and land improvements		$ 41,553	
Buildings		298,706	
Machinery and equipment		1,636,091	
Molds, cores, and rings		268,158	$2,244,508
Less: Accumulated depreciation			1,252,692
			$ 991,816

Intangible Assets

Many companies have long-lived assets that do not have physical substance yet often are very valuable. We call these assets **intangible assets**. One significant intangible asset is goodwill. Others include patents, copyrights, and trademarks or trade names that give the company **exclusive right** of use for a specified period of time. In Illustration 4-18, Franklin Company reported intangible assets of $3,100.

Illustration 4-22 shows the intangible assets of media giant Time Warner, Inc.

Illustration 4-22
Intangible assets section

Real World	TIME WARNER, INC. Balance Sheet (partial) (in millions)	
Intangible assets		
Goodwill		$40,953
Film library		2,690
Customer lists		2,540
Cable television franchises		38,048
Sports franchises		262
Brands, trademarks, and other intangible assets		8,313
		$92,806

PEOPLE, PLANET, AND PROFIT INSIGHT

Regaining Goodwill

After falling to unforeseen lows amidst scandals, recalls, and economic crises, the American public's positive perception of the reputation of corporate America is on the rise. Overall corporate reputation is experiencing rehabilitation as the American public gives high marks overall to corporate America, specific industries, and the largest number of individual companies in a dozen years. This is according to the findings of the *2011 Harris Interactive RQ Study*, which measures the reputations of the 60 most visible companies in the United States.

The survey focuses on six reputational dimensions that influence reputation and consumer behavior. Four of these dimensions, along with the five corporations that ranked highest within each, are as follows.

- **Social Responsibility**: (1) Whole Foods Market, (2) Johnson & Johnson, (3) Google, (4) The Walt Disney Company, (5) Procter & Gamble Co.

- **Emotional Appeal**: (1) Johnson & Johnson, (2) Amazon.com, (3) UPS, (4) General Mills, (5) Kraft Foods

- **Financial Performance**: (1) Google, (2) Berkshire Hathaway, (3) Apple, (4) Intel, (5) The Walt Disney Company

- **Products and Services**: (1) Intel Corporation, (2) 3M Company, (3) Johnson & Johnson, (4) Google, (5) Procter & Gamble Co.

© Gehringj/iStockphoto

Source: www.harrisinteractive.com.

? Name two industries today which are probably rated low on the reputational characteristics of "being trusted" and "having high ethical standards." (See page 212.)

> DO IT!

Assets Section of Classified Balance Sheet

Baxter Hoffman recently received the following information related to Hoffman Company's December 31, 2014, balance sheet.

Prepaid insurance	$ 2,300	Inventory	$3,400
Cash	800	Accumulated depreciation—	
Equipment	10,700	equipment	2,700
		Accounts receivable	1,100

Prepare the assets section of Hoffman Company's classified balance sheet.

Solution

Action Plan

✔ Present current assets first. Current assets are cash and other resources that the company expects to convert to cash or use up within one year.

✔ Present current assets in the order in which the company expects to convert them into cash.

✔ Subtract accumulated depreciation—equipment from equipment to determine the book value of equipment.

Assets		
Current assets		
Cash	$ 800	
Accounts receivable	1,100	
Inventory	3,400	
Prepaid insurance	2,300	
Total current assets		$ 7,600
Property, plant, and equipment		
Equipment	10,700	
Less: Accumulated depreciation—equipment	2,700	8,000
Total assets		$15,600

Related exercise material: **BE4-10 and DO IT! 4-3.**

 The Navigator

Current Liabilities

In the liabilities and owner's equity section of the balance sheet, the first grouping is current liabilities. **Current liabilities** are obligations that the company is to pay within the coming year or its operating cycle, whichever is longer. Common examples are accounts payable, salaries and wages payable, notes payable, interest payable, and income taxes payable. Also included as current liabilities are current maturities of long-term obligations—payments to be made within the next year on long-term obligations. In Illustration 4-18, Franklin Company reported five different types of current liabilities, for a total of $16,050.

Illustration 4-23 shows the current liabilities section adapted from the balance sheet of Marcus Corporation.

Illustration 4-23
Current liabilities section

| MARCUS CORPORATION |
| Balance Sheet (partial) |
| (in thousands) |

Real World

Current liabilities	
Notes payable	$ 239
Accounts payable	24,242
Current maturities of long-term debt	57,250
Other current liabilities	27,477
Income taxes payable	11,215
Salaries and wages payable	6,720
Total current liabilities	$127,143

Users of financial statements look closely at the relationship between current assets and current liabilities. This relationship is important in evaluating a company's **liquidity**—its ability to pay obligations expected to be due within the next year. When current assets exceed current liabilities, the likelihood for paying the liabilities is favorable. When the reverse is true, short-term creditors may not be paid, and the company may ultimately be forced into bankruptcy.

ACCOUNTING ACROSS THE ORGANIZATION

Can a Company Be Too Liquid?

There actually is a point where a company can be too liquid—that is, it can have too much working capital (current assets less current liabilities). While it is important to be liquid enough to be able to pay short-term bills as they come due, a company does not want to tie up its cash in extra inventory or receivables that are not earning the company money.

By one estimate from the REL Consultancy Group, the thousand largest U.S. companies have on their books cumulative excess working capital of $764 billion. Based on this figure, companies could have reduced debt by 36% or increased net income by 9%. Given that managers throughout a company are interested in improving profitability, it is clear that they should have an eye toward managing working capital. They need to aim for a "Goldilocks solution"—not too much, not too little, but just right.

Source: K. Richardson, "Companies Fall Behind in Cash Management," *Wall Street Journal* (June 19, 2007).

 What can various company managers do to ensure that working capital is managed efficiently to maximize net income? (See page 212.)

Long-Term Liabilities

Long-term liabilities are obligations that a company expects to pay **after** one year. Liabilities in this category include bonds payable, mortgages payable, long-term notes payable, lease liabilities, and pension liabilities. Many companies report long-term debt maturing after one year as a single amount in the balance sheet and show the details of the debt in notes that accompany the financial statements. Others list the various types of long-term liabilities. In Illustration 4-18, Franklin Company reported long-term liabilities of $11,300.

Illustration 4-24 shows the long-term liabilities that The Procter & Gamble Company reported in its balance sheet.

Illustration 4-24
Long-term liabilities section

THE PROCTER & GAMBLE COMPANY Balance Sheet (partial) (in millions)	
Long-term liabilities	
Long-term debt	$23,375
Deferred income taxes	12,015
Other noncurrent liabilities	5,147
Total long-term liabilities	$40,537

Real World

Owner's Equity

The content of the owner's equity section varies with the form of business organization. In a proprietorship, there is one capital account. In a partnership, there is a capital account for each partner. Corporations divide owners' equity into two accounts—Common Stock (sometimes referred to as Capital Stock) and Retained Earnings. Corporations record stockholders' investments in the company by debiting an asset account and crediting the Common Stock account. They record in the Retained Earnings account income retained for use in the business. Corporations combine the Common Stock and Retained Earnings accounts and report them on the balance sheet as **stockholders' equity**. (We'll learn more about these corporation accounts in later chapters.) Nordstrom, Inc. recently reported its stockholders' equity section as follows.

Alternative Terminology
Common stock is sometimes called *capital stock*.

Illustration 4-25
Stockholders' equity section

NORDSTROM, INC. Balance Sheet (partial) ($ in thousands)	
Stockholders' equity	
Common stock, 271,331 shares	$ 685,934
Retained earnings	1,406,747
Total stockholders' equity	$2,092,681

Real World

> DO IT!

Balance Sheet Classifications

The following accounts were taken from the financial statements of Callahan Company.

_____ Salaries and wages payable
_____ Service revenue
_____ Interest payable
_____ Goodwill
_____ Debt investments (short-term)
_____ Mortgage payable (due in 3 years)

_____ Stock investments (long-term)
_____ Equipment
_____ Accumulated depreciation—equipment
_____ Depreciation expense
_____ Owner's capital
_____ Unearned service revenue

Match each of the following to its proper balance sheet classification, shown below. If the item would not appear on a balance sheet, use "NA."

Current assets (CA)   Current liabilities (CL)
Long-term investments (LTI)   Long-term liabilities (LTL)
Property, plant, and equipment (PPE)   Owner's equity (OE)
Intangible assets (IA)

Solution

__CL__	Salaries and wages payable	__LTI__	Stock investments (long-term)
__NA__	Service revenue	__PPE__	Equipment
__CL__	Interest payable	__PPE__	Accumulated depreciation—
__IA__	Goodwill		equipment
__CA__	Debt investments (short-term)	__NA__	Depreciation expense
__LTL__	Mortgage payable (due	__OE__	Owner's capital
	in 3 years)	__CL__	Unearned service revenue

Related exercise material: **BE4-11, E4-14, E4-15, E4-16, E4-17, and DO IT! 4-4.**

✔ The Navigator

> Comprehensive DO IT!

At the end of its first month of operations, Watson Answering Service has the following unadjusted trial balance.

WATSON ANSWERING SERVICE
August 31, 2014
Trial Balance

	Debit	Credit
Cash	$ 5,400	
Accounts Receivable	2,800	
Supplies	1,300	
Prepaid Insurance	2,400	
Equipment	60,000	
Notes Payable		$40,000
Accounts Payable		2,400
Owner's Capital		30,000
Owner's Drawings	1,000	
Service Revenue		4,900
Salaries and Wages Expense	3,200	
Utilities Expense	800	
Advertising Expense	400	
	$77,300	$77,300

Other data:

1. Insurance expires at the rate of $200 per month.
2. $1,000 of supplies are on hand at August 31.
3. Monthly depreciation on the equipment is $900.
4. Interest of $500 on the notes payable has accrued during August.

Instructions
(a) Prepare a worksheet.
(b) Prepare a classified balance sheet assuming $35,000 of the notes payable are long-term.
(c) Journalize the closing entries.

Solution to Comprehensive DO IT!

(a)

WATSON ANSWERING SERVICE
Worksheet for the Month Ended August 31, 2014

Account Titles	Trial Balance Dr.	Trial Balance Cr.	Adjustments Dr.	Adjustments Cr.	Adjusted Trial Balance Dr.	Adjusted Trial Balance Cr.	Income Statement Dr.	Income Statement Cr.	Balance Sheet Dr.	Balance Sheet Cr.
Cash	5,400				5,400				5,400	
Accounts Receivable	2,800				2,800				2,800	
Supplies	1,300			(b) 300	1,000				1,000	
Prepaid Insurance	2,400			(a) 200	2,200				2,200	
Equipment	60,000				60,000				60,000	
Notes Payable		40,000				40,000				40,000
Accounts Payable		2,400				2,400				2,400
Owner's Capital		30,000				30,000				30,000
Owner's Drawings	1,000				1,000				1,000	
Service Revenue		4,900				4,900		4,900		
Salaries and										
Wages Expense	3,200				3,200		3,200			
Utilities Expense	800				800		800			
Advertising Expense	400				400		400			
Totals	77,300	77,300								
Insurance Expense			(a) 200		200		200			
Supplies Expense			(b) 300		300		300			
Depreciation Expense			(c) 900		900		900			
Accumulated Depreciation—										
Equipment				(c) 900		900				900
Interest Expense			(d) 500		500		500			
Interest Payable				(d) 500		500				500
Totals			1,900	1,900	78,700	78,700	6,300	4,900	72,400	73,800
Net Loss								1,400	1,400	
Totals							6,300	6,300	73,800	73,800

Explanation: (a) insurance expired, (b) supplies used, (c) depreciation expensed, (d) interest accrued.

(b)

WATSON ANSWERING SERVICE
Balance Sheet
August 31, 2014

Assets

Current assets		
Cash	$ 5,400	
Accounts receivable	2,800	
Supplies	1,000	
Prepaid insurance	2,200	
Total current assets		$11,400
Property, plant, and equipment		
Equipment	60,000	
Less: Accumulated depreciation—equipment	900	59,100
Total assets		$70,500

Liabilities and Owner's Equity

Current liabilities		
Notes payable	$ 5,000	
Accounts payable	2,400	
Interest payable	500	
Total current liabilities		$ 7,900
Long-term liabilities		
Notes payable		35,000
Total liabilities		42,900
Owner's equity		
Owner's capital		27,600*
Total liabilities and owner's equity		$70,500

*Owner's capital, $30,000 less drawings $1,000 and net loss $1,400.

(c)

Date	Account Titles	Debit	Credit
Aug. 31	Service Revenue	4,900	
	Income Summary		4,900
	(To close revenue account)		
31	Income Summary	6,300	
	Salaries and Wages Expense		3,200
	Depreciation Expense		900
	Utilities Expense		800
	Interest Expense		500
	Advertising Expense		400
	Supplies Expense		300
	Insurance Expense		200
	(To close expense accounts)		
31	Owner's Capital	1,400	
	Income Summary		1,400
	(To close net loss to capital)		
31	Owner's Capital	1,000	
	Owner's Drawings		1,000
	(To close drawings to capital)		

✔ The Navigator

SUMMARY OF LEARNING OBJECTIVES

1 Prepare a worksheet. The steps in preparing a worksheet are as follows. (a) Prepare a trial balance on the worksheet. (b) Enter the adjustments in the adjustments columns. (c) Enter adjusted balances in the adjusted trial balance columns. (d) Extend adjusted trial balance amounts to appropriate financial statement columns. (e) Total the statement columns, compute net income (or net loss), and complete the worksheet.

2 Explain the process of closing the books. Closing the books occurs at the end of an accounting period. The process is to journalize and post closing entries and then underline and balance all accounts. In closing the books, companies make separate entries to close revenues and expenses to Income Summary, Income Summary to Owner's Capital, and Owner's Drawings to Owner's Capital. Only temporary accounts are closed.

3 Describe the content and purpose of a post-closing trial balance. A post-closing trial balance contains the balances in permanent accounts that are carried forward to the next accounting period. The purpose of this trial balance is to prove the equality of these balances.

4 State the required steps in the accounting cycle. The required steps in the accounting cycle are (1) analyze business transactions, (2) journalize the transactions, (3) post to ledger accounts, (4) prepare a trial balance, (5) journalize and post adjusting entries, (6) prepare an adjusted trial balance, (7) prepare financial statements, (8) journalize and post closing entries, and (9) prepare a post-closing trial balance.

5 Explain the approaches to preparing correcting entries. One way to determine the correcting entry is to compare the incorrect entry with the correct entry. After comparison, the company makes a correcting entry to correct the accounts. An alternative to a correcting entry is to reverse the incorrect entry and then prepare the correct entry.

6 Identify the sections of a classified balance sheet. A classified balance sheet categorizes assets as current assets; long-term investments; property, plant, and equipment; and intangibles. Liabilities are classified as either current or long-term. There is also an owner's (owners') equity section, which varies with the form of business organization.

GLOSSARY

Classified balance sheet A balance sheet that contains standard classifications or sections. (p. 177).

Closing entries Entries made at the end of an accounting period to transfer the balances of temporary accounts to a permanent owner's equity account, Owner's Capital. (p. 168).

Correcting entries Entries to correct errors made in recording transactions. (p. 176).

Current assets Assets that a company expects to convert to cash or use up within one year. (p. 178).

Current liabilities Obligations that a company expects to pay within the coming year or its operating cycle, whichever is longer. (p. 182).

Income Summary A temporary account used in closing revenue and expense accounts. (p. 168).

Intangible assets Noncurrent assets that do not have physical substance. (p. 180).

Liquidity The ability of a company to pay obligations expected to be due within the next year. (p. 182).

Long-term investments Generally, (1) investments in stocks and bonds of other companies that companies normally hold for many years, and (2) long-term assets, such as land and buildings, not currently being used in operations. (p. 179).

Long-term liabilities Obligations that a company expects to pay after one year. (p. 183).

Operating cycle The average time that it takes to purchase inventory, sell it on account, and then collect cash from customers. (p. 179).

Permanent (real) accounts Accounts that relate to one or more future accounting periods. Consist of all balance sheet accounts. Balances are carried forward to next accounting period. (p. 168).

Post-closing trial balance A list of permanent accounts and their balances after a company has journalized and posted closing entries. (p. 172).

Property, plant, and equipment Assets with relatively long useful lives and currently being used in operations. (p. 180).

Reversing entry An entry, made at the beginning of the next accounting period, that is the exact opposite of the adjusting entry made in the previous period. (p. 175).

Stockholders' equity The ownership claim of shareholders on total assets. It is to a corporation what owner's equity is to a proprietorship. (p. 183).

Temporary (nominal) accounts Accounts that relate only to a given accounting period. Consist of all income statement accounts and owner's drawings account. All temporary accounts are closed at end of the accounting period. (p. 167).

Worksheet A multiple-column form that may be used in making adjusting entries and in preparing financial statements. (p. 162).

APPENDIX 4A   Reversing Entries

After preparing the financial statements and closing the books, it is often helpful to reverse some of the adjusting entries before recording the regular transactions of the next period. Such entries are **reversing entries**. Companies make **a reversing entry at the beginning of the next accounting period**. Each reversing entry **is the exact opposite of the adjusting entry made in the previous period**. The recording of reversing entries is an **optional step** in the accounting cycle.

The purpose of reversing entries is to simplify the recording of a subsequent transaction related to an adjusting entry. For example, in Chapter 3 (page 115), the payment of salaries after an adjusting entry resulted in two debits: one to Salaries and Wages Payable and the other to Salaries and Wages Expense. With reversing entries, the company can debit the entire subsequent payment to Salaries and Wages Expense. **The use of reversing entries does not change the amounts reported in the financial statements.** What it does is simplify the recording of subsequent transactions.

Reversing Entries Example

Companies most often use reversing entries to reverse two types of adjusting entries: accrued revenues and accrued expenses. To illustrate the optional use of reversing entries for accrued expenses, we will use the salaries expense transactions for Pioneer Advertising Agency as illustrated in Chapters 2, 3, and 4. The transaction and adjustment data are as follows.

1. October 26 (initial salary entry): Pioneer pays $4,000 of salaries and wages earned between October 15 and October 26.

2. October 31 (adjusting entry): Salaries and wages earned between October 29 and October 31 are $1,200. The company will pay these in the November 9 payroll.

3. November 9 (subsequent salary entry): Salaries and wages paid are $4,000. Of this amount, $1,200 applied to accrued salaries and wages payable and $2,800 was earned between November 1 and November 9.

Illustration 4A-1 shows the entries with and without reversing entries.

The first three entries are the same whether or not Pioneer uses reversing entries. The last two entries are different. The November 1 **reversing entry** eliminates the $1,200 balance in Salaries and Wages Payable created by the October 31 adjusting entry. The reversing entry also creates a $1,200 credit balance in the Salaries and Wages Expense account. As you know, it is unusual for an expense account to have a credit balance. The balance is correct in this instance, though, because it anticipates that the entire amount of the first salaries and wages payment in the new accounting period will be debited to Salaries and Wages Expense. This debit will eliminate the credit balance. The resulting debit balance in the expense account will equal the salaries and wages expense incurred in the new accounting period ($2,800 in this example).

If Pioneer makes reversing entries, it can debit all cash payments of expenses to the expense account. This means that on November 9 (and every payday) Pioneer can debit Salaries and Wages Expense for the amount paid, without regard to any accrued salaries and wages payable. Being able to make the **same entry each time** simplifies the recording process. The company can record subsequent transactions as if the related adjusting entry had never been made.

Without Reversing Entries (per chapter)			With Reversing Entries (per appendix)		
Initial Salary Entry			**Initial Salary Entry**		
Oct. 26 Salaries and Wages Expense	4,000		Oct. 26 (Same entry)		
Cash		4,000			
Adjusting Entry			**Adjusting Entry**		
Oct. 31 Salaries and Wages Expense	1,200		Oct. 31 (Same entry)		
Salaries and Wages Payable		1,200			
Closing Entry			**Closing Entry**		
Oct. 31 Income Summary	5,200		Oct. 31 (Same entry)		
Salaries and Wages Expense		5,200			
Reversing Entry			**Reversing Entry**		
Nov. 1 No reversing entry is made.			Nov. 1 **Salaries and Wages Payable**	**1,200**	
			Salaries and Wages Expense		**1,200**
Subsequent Salary Entry			**Subsequent Salary Entry**		
Nov. 9 Salaries and Wages Payable	1,200		Nov. 9 **Salaries and Wages Expense**	**4,000**	
Salaries and Wages Expense	2,800		**Cash**		**4,000**
Cash		4,000			

Illustration 4A-1
Comparative entries—not reversing vs. reversing

Illustration 4A-2 shows the posting of the entries with reversing entries.

Salaries and Wages Expense

10/26 Paid	4,000	10/31 Closing	5,200
31 Adjusting	1,200		
	5,200		5,200
11/9 Paid	4,000	**11/1 Reversing**	**1,200**

Salaries and Wages Payable

11/1 Reversing	**1,200**	10/31 Adjusting	1,200

Illustration 4A-2
Postings with reversing entries

A company can also use reversing entries for accrued revenue adjusting entries. For Pioneer Advertising Agency, the adjusting entry was Accounts Receivable (Dr.) $200 and Service Revenue (Cr.) $200. Thus, the reversing entry on November 1 is:

Nov. 1	Service Revenue	200	
	Accounts Receivable		200
	(To reverse October 31 adjusting entry)		

A = L + OE
−200 Rev
−200
Cash Flows
no effect

When Pioneer collects the accrued service revenue, it debits Cash and credits Service Revenue.

SUMMARY OF LEARNING OBJECTIVE FOR APPENDIX 4A

7 Prepare reversing entries. Reversing entries are the opposite of the adjusting entries made in the preceding period. Some companies choose to make reversing entries at the beginning of a new accounting period to simplify the recording of later transactions related to the adjusting entries. In most cases, only accrued adjusting entries are reversed.

*Note: All asterisked Questions, Exercises, and Problems relate to material in the appendix to the chapter.

SELF-TEST QUESTIONS

Answers are on page 212.

(LO 1) 1. Which of the following statements is **incorrect** concerning the worksheet?
  (a) The worksheet is essentially a working tool of the accountant.
  (b) The worksheet is distributed to management and other interested parties.
  (c) The worksheet cannot be used as a basis for posting to ledger accounts.
  (d) Financial statements can be prepared directly from the worksheet before journalizing and posting the adjusting entries.

(LO 1) 2. In a worksheet, net income is entered in the following columns:
  (a) income statement (Dr) and balance sheet (Dr).
  (b) income statement (Cr) and balance sheet (Dr).
  (c) income statement (Dr) and balance sheet (Cr).
  (d) income statement (Cr) and balance sheet (Cr).

(LO 1) 3. In the unadjusted trial balance of its worksheet for the year ended December 31, 2014, Knox Company reported Equipment of $120,000. The year-end adjusting entries require an adjustment of $15,000 for depreciation expense for the equipment. After adjustment, the following adjusted amount should be reported:
  (a) a debit of $105,000 for Equipment in the balance sheet column.
  (b) a credit of $15,000 for Depreciation Expense—Equipment in the income statement column.
  (c) a debit of $120,000 for Equipment in the balance sheet column.
  (d) a debit of $15,000 for Accumulated Depreciation—Equipment in the balance sheet column.

(LO 2) 4. An account that will have a zero balance after closing entries have been journalized and posted is:
  (a) Service Revenue.
  (b) Supplies.
  (c) Prepaid Insurance.
  (d) Accumulated Depreciation—Equipment.

(LO 2) 5. When a net loss has occurred, Income Summary is:
  (a) debited and Owner's Capital is credited.
  (b) credited and Owner's Capital is debited.
  (c) debited and Owner's Drawings is credited.
  (d) credited and Owner's Drawings is debited.

(LO 2) 6. The closing process involves separate entries to close (1) expenses, (2) drawings, (3) revenues, and (4) income summary. The correct sequencing of the entries is:
  (a) (4), (3), (2), (1)   (c) (3), (1), (4), (2)
  (b) (1), (2), (3), (4)   (d) (3), (2), (1), (4)

(LO 3) 7. Which types of accounts will appear in the post-closing trial balance?

  (a) Permanent (real) accounts.
  (b) Temporary (nominal) accounts.
  (c) Accounts shown in the income statement columns of a worksheet.
  (d) None of the above.

(LO 4) 8. All of the following are required steps in the accounting cycle **except**:
  (a) journalizing and posting closing entries.
  (b) preparing financial statements.
  (c) journalizing the transactions.
  (d) preparing a worksheet.

(LO 4) 9. The proper order of the following steps in the accounting cycle is:
  (a) prepare unadjusted trial balance, journalize transactions, post to ledger accounts, journalize and post adjusting entries.
  (b) journalize transactions, prepare unadjusted trial balance, post to ledger accounts, journalize and post adjusting entries.
  (c) journalize transactions, post to ledger accounts, prepare unadjusted trial balance, journalize and post adjusting entries.
  (d) prepare unadjusted trial balance, journalize and post adjusting entries, journalize transactions, post to ledger accounts.

(LO 5) 10. When Ramirez Company purchased supplies worth $500, it incorrectly recorded a credit to Supplies for $5,000 and a debit to Cash for $5,000. Before correcting this error:
  (a) Cash is overstated and Supplies is overstated.
  (b) Cash is understated and Supplies is understated.
  (c) Cash is understated and Supplies is overstated.
  (d) Cash is overstated and Supplies is understated.

(LO 5) 11. Cash of $100 received at the time the service was performed was journalized and posted as a debit to Cash $100 and a credit to Accounts Receivable $100. Assuming the incorrect entry is not reversed, the correcting entry is:
  (a) debit Service Revenue $100 and credit Accounts Receivable $100.
  (b) debit Accounts Receivable $100 and credit Service Revenue $100.
  (c) debit Cash $100 and credit Service Revenue $100.
  (d) debit Accounts Receivable $100 and credit Cash $100.

(LO 6) 12. The correct order of presentation in a classified balance sheet for the following current assets is:
  (a) accounts receivable, cash, prepaid insurance, inventory.
  (b) cash, inventory, accounts receivable, prepaid insurance.

(c) cash, accounts receivable, inventory, prepaid insurance.

(d) inventory, cash, accounts receivable, prepaid insurance.

(LO 6) **13.** A company has purchased a tract of land. It expects to build a production plant on the land in approximately 5 years. During the 5 years before construction, the land will be idle. The land should be reported as:
(a) property, plant, and equipment.
(b) land expense.
(c) a long-term investment.
(d) an intangible asset.

(LO 6) **14.** In a classified balance sheet, assets are usually classified using the following categories:
(a) current assets; long-term assets; property, plant, and equipment; and intangible assets.
(b) current assets; long-term investments; property, plant, and equipment; and tangible assets.
(c) current assets; long-term investments; tangible assets; and intangible assets.

(d) current assets; long-term investments; property, plant, and equipment; and intangible assets.

15. Current assets are listed: (LO 6)
(a) by expected conversion to cash.
(b) by importance.
(c) by longevity.
(d) alphabetically.

*16. On December 31, Kevin Hartman Company correctly (LO 7) made an adjusting entry to recognize $2,000 of accrued salaries payable. On January 8 of the next year, total salaries of $3,400 were paid. Assuming the correct reversing entry was made on January 1, the entry on January 8 will result in a credit to Cash $3,400 and the following debit(s):
(a) Salaries and Wages Payable $1,400 and Salaries and Wages Expense $2,000.
(b) Salaries and Wages Payable $2,000 and Salaries and Wages Expense $1,400.
(c) Salaries and Wages Expense $3,400.
(d) Salaries and Wages Payable $3,400.

Go to the book's companion website, www.wiley.com/college/weygandt, for additional Self-Test Questions.

✔ **The Navigator**

QUESTIONS

1. "A worksheet is a permanent accounting record and its use is required in the accounting cycle." Do you agree? Explain.

2. Explain the purpose of the worksheet.

3. What is the relationship, if any, between the amount shown in the adjusted trial balance column for an account and that account's ledger balance?

4. If a company's revenues are $125,000 and its expenses are $113,000, in which financial statement columns of the worksheet will the net income of $12,000 appear? When expenses exceed revenues, in which columns will the difference appear?

5. Why is it necessary to prepare formal financial statements if all of the data are in the statement columns of the worksheet?

6. Identify the account(s) debited and credited in each of the four closing entries, assuming the company has net income for the year.

7. Describe the nature of the Income Summary account and identify the types of summary data that may be posted to this account.

8. What are the content and purpose of a post-closing trial balance?

9. Which of the following accounts would not appear in the post-closing trial balance? Interest Payable; Equipment; Depreciation Expense; Owner's Drawings; Unearned Service Revenue; Accumulated Depreciation—Equipment; and Service Revenue.

10. Distinguish between a reversing entry and an adjusting entry. Are reversing entries required?

11. Indicate, in the sequence in which they are made, the three required steps in the accounting cycle that involve journalizing.

12. Identify, in the sequence in which they are prepared, the three trial balances that are often used to report financial information about a company.

13. How do correcting entries differ from adjusting entries?

14. What standard classifications are used in preparing a classified balance sheet?

15. What is meant by the term "operating cycle?"

16. Define current assets. What basis is used for arranging individual items within the current assets section?

17. Distinguish between long-term investments and property, plant, and equipment.

18. (a) What is the term used to describe the owner's equity section of a corporation? (b) Identify the two owners' equity accounts in a corporation and indicate the purpose of each.

19. Using Apple's annual report, determine its current liabilities at September 25, 2010, and September 24, 2011. Were current liabilities higher or lower than current assets in these two years?

*20. Cigale Company prepares reversing entries. If the adjusting entry for interest payable is reversed, what type of an account balance, if any, will there be in Interest Payable and Interest Expense after the reversing entry is posted?

*21. At December 31, accrued salaries payable totaled $3,500. On January 10, total salaries of $8,000 are paid. (a) Assume that reversing entries are made at January 1. Give the January 10 entry, and indicate the Salaries and Wages Expense account balance after the entry is posted. (b) Repeat part (a) assuming reversing entries are not made.

BRIEF EXERCISES

List the steps in preparing a worksheet.

(LO 1)

BE4-1 The steps in using a worksheet are presented in random order below. List the steps in the proper order by placing numbers 1–5 in the blank spaces.

(a) _____ Prepare a trial balance on the worksheet.
(b) _____ Enter adjusted balances.
(c) _____ Extend adjusted balances to appropriate statement columns.
(d) _____ Total the statement columns, compute net income (loss), and complete the worksheet.
(e) _____ Enter adjustment data.

Prepare partial worksheet.

(LO 1)

BE4-2 The ledger of Clayton Company includes the following unadjusted balances: Prepaid Insurance $3,000, Service Revenue $58,000, and Salaries and Wages Expense $25,000. Adjusting entries are required for (a) expired insurance $1,800; (b) services performed $1,100, but unbilled and uncollected; and (c) accrued salaries payable $800. Enter the unadjusted balances and adjustments into a worksheet and complete the worksheet for all accounts. (*Note:* You will need to add the following accounts: Accounts Receivable, Salaries and Wages Payable, and Insurance Expense.)

Identify worksheet columns for selected accounts.

(LO 1)

BE4-3 The following selected accounts appear in the adjusted trial balance columns of the worksheet for Goulet Company: Accumulated Depreciation; Depreciation Expense; Owner's Capital; Owner's Drawings; Service Revenue; Supplies; and Accounts Payable. Indicate the financial statement column (income statement Dr., balance sheet Cr., etc.) to which each balance should be extended.

Prepare closing entries from ledger balances.

(LO 2)

BE4-4 The ledger of Rios Company contains the following balances: Owner's Capital $30,000; Owner's Drawings $2,000; Service Revenue $50,000; Salaries and Wages Expense $27,000; and Supplies Expense $7,000. Prepare the closing entries at December 31.

Post closing entries; underline and balance T-accounts.

(LO 2)

BE4-5 Using the data in BE4-4, enter the balances in T-accounts, post the closing entries, and underline and balance the accounts.

Journalize and post closing entries using the three-column form of account.

(LO 2)

BE4-6 The income statement for Weeping Willow Golf Club for the month ending July 31 shows Service Revenue $16,400, Salaries and Wages Expense $8,200, Maintenance and Repairs Expense $2,500, and Net Income $5,700. Prepare the entries to close the revenue and expense accounts. Post the entries to the revenue and expense accounts, and complete the closing process for these accounts using the three-column form of account.

Identify post-closing trial balance accounts.

(LO 3)

BE4-7 Using the data in BE4-3, identify the accounts that would be included in a post-closing trial balance.

List the required steps in the accounting cycle in sequence.

(LO 4)

BE4-8 The steps in the accounting cycle are listed in random order below. List the steps in proper sequence, assuming no worksheet is prepared, by placing numbers 1–9 in the blank spaces.

(a) _____ Prepare a trial balance.
(b) _____ Journalize the transactions.
(c) _____ Journalize and post closing entries.
(d) _____ Prepare financial statements.
(e) _____ Journalize and post adjusting entries.
(f) _____ Post to ledger accounts.
(g) _____ Prepare a post-closing trial balance.
(h) _____ Prepare an adjusted trial balance.
(i) _____ Analyze business transactions.

Prepare correcting entries.

(LO 5)

BE4-9 At Creighton Company, the following errors were discovered after the transactions had been journalized and posted. Prepare the correcting entries.

1. A collection on account from a customer for $870 was recorded as a debit to Cash $870 and a credit to Service Revenue $870.
2. The purchase of store supplies on account for $1,570 was recorded as a debit to Supplies $1,750 and a credit to Accounts Payable $1,750.

Prepare the current assets section of a balance sheet.

(LO 6)

BE4-10 The balance sheet debit column of the worksheet for Hamidi Company includes the following accounts: Accounts Receivable $12,500; Prepaid Insurance $3,600; Cash $4,100; Supplies $5,200; and Debt Investments (short-term) $6,700. Prepare the current assets section of the balance sheet, listing the accounts in proper sequence.

BE4-11 The following are the major balance sheet classifications:

Current assets (CA)
Long-term investments (LTI)
Property, plant, and equipment (PPE)
Intangible assets (IA)

Current liabilities (CL)
Long-term liabilities (LTL)
Owner's equity (OE)

Classify accounts on balance sheet.
(LO 6)

Match each of the following accounts to its proper balance sheet classification.

_____ Accounts payable
_____ Accounts receivable
_____ Accumulated depreciation—buildings
_____ Buildings
_____ Cash
_____ Copyrights

_____ Income taxes payable
_____ Debt investments (long-term)
_____ Land
_____ Inventory
_____ Patents
_____ Supplies

*BE4-12 At October 31, Burgess Company made an accrued expense adjusting entry of $2,100 for salaries. Prepare the reversing entry on November 1, and indicate the balances in Salaries and Wages Payable and Salaries and Wages Expense after posting the reversing entry.

Prepare reversing entries.
(LO 7)

> DO IT! Review

DO IT! 4-1 Bradley Decker is preparing a worksheet. Explain to Bradley how he should extend the following adjusted trial balance accounts to the financial statement columns of the worksheet.

Prepare a worksheet.
(LO 1)

Service Revenue
Notes Payable
Owner's Capital

Accounts Receivable
Accumulated Depreciation
Utilities Expense

DO IT! 4-2 The worksheet for Tsai Company shows the following in the financial statement columns.

Prepare closing entries.
(LO 2)

Owner's drawings $22,000
Owner's capital   70,000
Net income   41,000

Prepare the closing entries at December 31 that affect owner's capital.

DO IT! 4-3 Ryan Newton recently received the following information related to Ryan Company's December 31, 2014, balance sheet.

Prepare assets section of the balance sheet.
(LO 6)

Inventory	$ 2,900	Debt investments (short-term)	$1,200
Cash	4,300	Accumulated depreciation	5,700
Equipment	21,700	Accounts receivable	4,300
Stock investments (long-term)	6,500		

Prepare the assets section of Ryan Company's classified balance sheet.

DO IT! 4-4 The following accounts were taken from the financial statements of Lee Company.

Match accounts to balance sheet classifications.
(LO 6)

_____ Interest revenue
_____ Utilities payable
_____ Accounts payable
_____ Supplies
_____ Bonds payable
_____ Goodwill

_____ Owner's capital
_____ Accumulated depreciation—equipment
_____ Equipment
_____ Salaries and wages expense
_____ Debt investments (long-term)
_____ Unearned rent revenue

Match each of the accounts to its proper balance sheet classification, as shown below. If the item would not appear on a balance sheet, use "NA."

Current assets (CA)
Long-term investments (LTI)
Property, plant, and equipment (PPE)
Intangible assets (IA)

Current liabilities (CL)
Long-term liabilities (LTL)
Owner's equity (OE)

Complete the worksheet.
(LO 1)

E4-1 The trial balance columns of the worksheet for Nanduri Company at June 30, 2014, are as follows.

NANDURI COMPANY
Worksheet
For the Month Ended June 30, 2014

	Trial Balance	
Account Titles	Dr.	Cr.
Cash	2,320	
Accounts Receivable	2,440	
Supplies	1,880	
Accounts Payable		1,120
Unearned Service Revenue		240
Owner's Capital		3,600
Service Revenue		2,400
Salaries and Wages Expense	560	
Miscellaneous Expense	160	
	7,360	7,360

Other data:

1. A physical count reveals $500 of supplies on hand.
2. $100 of the unearned revenue is still unearned at month-end.
3. Accrued salaries are $210.

Instructions
Enter the trial balance on a worksheet and complete the worksheet.

Complete the worksheet.
(LO 1)

E4-2 The adjusted trial balance columns of the worksheet for DeSousa Company are as follows.

DESOUSA COMPANY
Worksheet (partial)
For the Month Ended April 30, 2014

	Adjusted Trial Balance		Income Statement		Balance Sheet	
Account Titles	Dr.	Cr.	Dr.	Cr.	Dr.	Cr.
Cash	10,000					
Accounts Receivable	7,840					
Prepaid Rent	2,280					
Equipment	23,050					
Accumulated Depreciation—Equip.		4,921				
Notes Payable		5,700				
Accounts Payable		4,920				
Owner's Capital		27,960				
Owner's Drawings	3,650					
Service Revenue		15,590				
Salaries and Wages Expense	10,840					
Rent Expense	760					
Depreciation Expense	671					
Interest Expense	57					
Interest Payable		57				
Totals	59,148	59,148				

Instructions
Complete the worksheet.

E4-3 Worksheet data for DeSousa Company are presented in E4-2. The owner did not make any additional investments in the business in April.

Prepare financial statements from worksheet.
(LO 1, 6)

Instructions
Prepare an income statement, an owner's equity statement, and a classified balance sheet.

E4-4 Worksheet data for DeSousa Company are presented in E4-2.

Journalize and post closing entries and prepare a post-closing trial balance.
(LO 2, 3)

Instructions
(a) Journalize the closing entries at April 30.
(b) Post the closing entries to Income Summary and Owner's Capital. Use T-accounts.
(c) Prepare a post-closing trial balance at April 30.

E4-5 The adjustments columns of the worksheet for Misra Company are shown below.

Prepare adjusting entries from a worksheet, and extend balances to worksheet columns.
(LO 1)

Account Titles	Adjustments Debit	Adjustments Credit
Accounts Receivable	1,100	
Prepaid Insurance		300
Accumulated Depreciation—Equipment		900
Salaries and Wages Payable		500
Service Revenue		1,100
Salaries and Wages Expense	500	
Insurance Expense	300	
Depreciation Expense	900	
	2,800	2,800

Instructions
(a) Prepare the adjusting entries.
(b) Assuming the adjusted trial balance amount for each account is normal, indicate the financial statement column to which each balance should be extended.

E4-6 Selected worksheet data for Elsayed Company are presented below.

Derive adjusting entries from worksheet data.
(LO 1)

Account Titles	Trial Balance Dr.	Trial Balance Cr.	Adjusted Trial Balance Dr.	Adjusted Trial Balance Cr.
Accounts Receivable	?		34,000	
Prepaid Insurance	26,000		20,000	
Supplies	7,000		?	
Accumulated Depreciation—Equipment		12,000		?
Salaries and Wages Payable		?		5,600
Service Revenue		88,000		97,000
Insurance Expense			?	
Depreciation Expense			10,000	
Supplies Expense			4,500	
Salaries and Wages Expense	?		49,000	

Instructions
(a) Fill in the missing amounts.
(b) Prepare the adjusting entries that were made.

Prepare closing entries, and prepare a post-closing trial balance.
(LO 2, 3)

E4-7 Kay Magill Company had the following adjusted trial balance.

KAY MAGILL COMPANY
Adjusted Trial Balance
For the Month Ended June 30, 2014

	Adjusted Trial Balance	
Account Titles	**Debit**	**Credit**
Cash	$ 3,712	
Accounts Receivable	3,904	
Supplies	480	
Accounts Payable		$ 1,556
Unearned Service Revenue		160
Owner's Capital		5,760
Owner's Drawings	628	
Service Revenue		4,300
Salaries and Wages Expense	1,344	
Miscellaneous Expense	256	
Supplies Expense	1,900	
Salaries and Wages Payable		448
	$12,224	$12,224

Instructions
(a) Prepare closing entries at June 30, 2014.
(b) Prepare a post-closing trial balance.

Journalize and post closing entries, and prepare a post-closing trial balance.
(LO 2, 3)

E4-8 Plevin Company ended its fiscal year on July 31, 2014. The company's adjusted trial balance as of the end of its fiscal year is shown below.

PLEVIN COMPANY
Adjusted Trial Balance
July 31, 2014

No.	**Account Titles**	**Debit**	**Credit**
101	Cash	$ 9,840	
112	Accounts Receivable	8,780	
157	Equipment	15,900	
158	Accumulated Depreciation—Equip.		$ 7,400
201	Accounts Payable		4,220
208	Unearned Rent Revenue		1,800
301	Owner's Capital		45,200
306	Owner's Drawings	16,000	
400	Service Revenue		64,000
429	Rent Revenue		6,500
711	Depreciation Expense	8,000	
726	Salaries and Wages Expense	55,700	
732	Utilities Expense	14,900	
		$129,120	$129,120

Instructions
(a) Prepare the closing entries using page J15.
(b) Post to Owner's Capital and No. 350 Income Summary accounts. (Use the three-column form.)
(c) Prepare a post-closing trial balance at July 31.

Prepare financial statements.
(LO 6)

E4-9 The adjusted trial balance for Plevin Company is presented in E4-8.

Instructions
(a) Prepare an income statement and an owner's equity statement for the year. Plevin did not make any capital investments during the year.
(b) Prepare a classified balance sheet at July 31.

E4-10 Janis Engle has prepared the following list of statements about the accounting cycle.

Answer questions related to the accounting cycle.
(LO 4)

1. "Journalize the transactions" is the first step in the accounting cycle.
2. Reversing entries are a required step in the accounting cycle.
3. Correcting entries do not have to be part of the accounting cycle.
4. If a worksheet is prepared, some steps of the accounting cycle are incorporated into the worksheet.
5. The accounting cycle begins with the analysis of business transactions and ends with the preparation of a post-closing trial balance.
6. All steps of the accounting cycle occur daily during the accounting period.
7. The step of "post to the ledger accounts" occurs before the step of "journalize the transactions."
8. Closing entries must be prepared before financial statements can be prepared.

Instructions
Identify each statement as true or false. If false, indicate how to correct the statement.

E4-11 Selected accounts for Heather's Salon are presented below. All June 30 postings are from closing entries.

Prepare closing entries.
(LO 2)

Salaries and Wages Expense				Service Revenue				Owner's Capital			
6/10	3,200	6/30	8,800	6/30	18,100	6/15	9,700	6/30	2,500	6/1	12,000
6/28	5,600					6/24	8,400			6/30	5,000
										Bal.	14,500

Supplies Expense				Rent Expense				Owner's Drawings			
6/12	600	6/30	1,300	6/1	3,000	6/30	3,000	6/13	1,000	6/30	2,500
6/24	700							6/25	1,500		

Instructions
(a) Prepare the closing entries that were made.
(b) Post the closing entries to Income Summary.

E4-12 Andrew Clark Company discovered the following errors made in January 2014.

Prepare correcting entries.
(LO 5)

1. A payment of Salaries and Wages Expense of $700 was debited to Equipment and credited to Cash, both for $700.
2. A collection of $1,000 from a client on account was debited to Cash $100 and credited to Service Revenue $100.
3. The purchase of equipment on account for $760 was debited to Equipment $670 and credited to Accounts Payable $670.

Instructions
(a) Correct the errors by reversing the incorrect entry and preparing the correct entry.
(b) Correct the errors without reversing the incorrect entry.

E4-13 Keenan Company has an inexperienced accountant. During the first 2 weeks on the job, the accountant made the following errors in journalizing transactions. All entries were posted as made.

Prepare correcting entries.
(LO 5)

1. A payment on account of $840 to a creditor was debited to Accounts Payable $480 and credited to Cash $480.
2. The purchase of supplies on account for $560 was debited to Equipment $56 and credited to Accounts Payable $56.
3. A $500 withdrawal of cash for P. Keenan's personal use was debited to Salaries and Wages Expense $500 and credited to Cash $500.

Instructions
Prepare the correcting entries.

E4-14 The adjusted trial balance for Martell Bowling Alley at December 31, 2014, contains the accounts shown on page 198.

Prepare a classified balance sheet.
(LO 6)

	Debit		Credit
Buildings	$128,800	Owner's Capital	$115,000
Accounts Receivable	14,520	Accumulated Depreciation—Buildings	42,600
Prepaid Insurance	4,680	Accounts Payable	12,300
Cash	18,040	Notes Payable	97,780
Equipment	62,400	Accumulated Depreciation—Equipment	18,720
Land	67,000	Interest Payable	2,600
Insurance Expense	780	Service Revenue	17,180
Depreciation Expense	7,360		$306,180
Interest Expense	2,600		
	$306,180		

Instructions

(a) Prepare a classified balance sheet; assume that $22,000 of the note payable will be paid in 2015.

(b) ━━━━ Comment on the liquidity of the company.

Classify accounts on balance sheet.

(LO 6)

E4-15 The following are the major balance sheet classifications.

Current assets (CA)
Long-term investments (LTI)
Property, plant, and equipment (PPE)
Intangible assets (IA)

Current liabilities (CL)
Long-term liabilities (LTL)
Owner's equity (OE)

Instructions

Classify each of the following accounts taken from Raman Company's balance sheet.

_____ Accounts payable	_____ Accumulated depreciation—equipment
_____ Accounts receivable	_____ Buildings
_____ Cash	_____ Land (in use)
_____ Owner's capital	_____ Notes payable (due in 2 years)
_____ Patents	_____ Supplies
_____ Salaries and wages payable	_____ Equipment
_____ Inventory	_____ Prepaid expenses
_____ Stock investments (to be sold in 7 months)	

Prepare a classified balance sheet.

(LO 6)

E4-16 The following items were taken from the financial statements of D. Gygi Company. (All amounts are in thousands.)

Long-term debt	$ 1,000	Accumulated depreciation—equipment	$ 5,655
Prepaid insurance	880	Accounts payable	1,444
Equipment	11,500	Notes payable (due after 2015)	400
Stock investments (long-term)	264	Owner's capital	12,955
Debt investments (short-term)	3,690	Accounts receivable	1,696
Notes payable (due in 2015)	500	Inventory	1,256
Cash	2,668		

Instructions

Prepare a classified balance sheet in good form as of December 31, 2014.

Prepare financial statements.

(LO 6)

E4-17 These financial statement items are for Norsted Company at year-end, July 31, 2014.

Salaries and wages payable	$ 2,080	Notes payable (long-term)	$ 1,800
Salaries and wages expense	51,700	Cash	14,200
Utilities expense	22,600	Accounts receivable	9,780
Equipment	30,400	Accumulated depreciation—equipment	6,000
Accounts payable	4,100	Owner's drawings	3,000
Service revenue	62,000	Depreciation expense	4,000
Rent revenue	8,500	Owner's capital (beginning of the year)	51,200

Instructions

(a) Prepare an income statement and an owner's equity statement for the year. The owner did not make any new investments during the year.

(b) Prepare a classified balance sheet at July 31.

*E4-18 Reblin Company pays salaries of $12,000 every Monday for the preceding 5-day week (Monday through Friday). Assume December 31 falls on a Tuesday, so Reblin's employees have worked 2 days without being paid.

Use reversing entries.

(LO 7)

Instructions

(a) Assume the company does not use reversing entries. Prepare the December 31 adjusting entry and the entry on Monday, January 6, when Reblin pays the payroll.

(b) Assume the company does use reversing entries. Prepare the December 31 adjusting entry, the January 1 reversing entry, and the entry on Monday, January 6, when Reblin pays the payroll.

*E4-19 On December 31, the adjusted trial balance of Cisneros Employment Agency shows the following selected data.

Prepare closing and reversing entries.

(LO 2, 4, 7)

Accounts Receivable	$24,500	Service Revenue	$92,500
Interest Expense	8,300	Interest Payable	2,000

Analysis shows that adjusting entries were made to (1) accrue $5,000 of service revenue and (2) accrue $2,000 interest expense.

Instructions

(a) Prepare the closing entries for the temporary accounts shown above at December 31.

(b) Prepare the reversing entries on January 1.

(c) Post the entries in (a) and (b). Underline and balance the accounts. (Use T-accounts.)

(d) Prepare the entries to record (1) the collection of the accrued revenue on January 10 and (2) the payment of all interest due ($3,000) on January 15.

(e) Post the entries in (d) to the temporary accounts.

EXERCISES: SET B AND CHALLENGE EXERCISES

Visit the book's companion website, at **www.wiley.com/college/weygandt**, and choose the Student Companion site to access Exercise Set B and Challenge Exercises.

PROBLEMS: SET A

P4-1A The trial balance columns of the worksheet for Lampert Roofing at March 31, 2014, are as follows.

Prepare a worksheet, financial statements, and adjusting and closing entries.

(LO 1, 2, 3, 6)

LAMPERT ROOFING
Worksheet
For the Month Ended March 31, 2014

Account Titles	Trial Balance	
	Dr.	**Cr.**
Cash	4,500	
Accounts Receivable	3,200	
Supplies	2,000	
Equipment	11,000	
Accumulated Depreciation—Equipment		1,250
Accounts Payable		2,500
Unearned Service Revenue		550
Owner's Capital		12,900
Owner's Drawings	1,100	
Service Revenue		6,300
Salaries and Wages Expense	1,300	
Miscellaneous Expense	400	
	23,500	23,500

Other data:

1. A physical count reveals only $550 of roofing supplies on hand.
2. Depreciation for March is $250.
3. Unearned revenue amounted to $210 at March 31.
4. Accrued salaries are $700.

Instructions

(a) Adjusted trial balance
  $24,450
(b) Net income $2,540
  Total assets $17,750

(a) Enter the trial balance on a worksheet and complete the worksheet.
(b) Prepare an income statement and owner's equity statement for the month of March and a classified balance sheet at March 31. C. Lampert made an additional investment in the business of $10,000 in March.
(c) Journalize the adjusting entries from the adjustments columns of the worksheet.
(d) Journalize the closing entries from the financial statement columns of the worksheet.

Complete worksheet; prepare financial statements, closing entries, and post-closing trial balance.

(LO 1, 2, 3, 6)

GLS

P4-2A The adjusted trial balance columns of the worksheet for Alshwer Company, owned by M. Alshwer, are as follows.

ALSHWER COMPANY
Worksheet
For the Year Ended December 31, 2014

Account No.	Account Titles	Adjusted Trial Balance Dr.	Cr.
101	Cash	5,300	
112	Accounts Receivable	10,800	
126	Supplies	1,500	
130	Prepaid Insurance	2,000	
157	Equipment	27,000	
158	Accumulated Depreciation—Equipment		5,600
200	Notes Payable		15,000
201	Accounts Payable		6,100
212	Salaries and Wages Payable		2,400
230	Interest Payable		600
301	Owner's Capital		13,000
306	Owner's Drawings	7,000	
400	Service Revenue		61,000
610	Advertising Expense	8,400	
631	Supplies Expense	4,000	
711	Depreciation Expense	5,600	
722	Insurance Expense	3,500	
726	Salaries and Wages Expense	28,000	
905	Interest Expense	600	
	Totals	103,700	103,700

Instructions

(a) Net income $10,900

(b) Current assets $19,600
  Current liabilities $14,100

(e) Post-closing trial balance
  $46,600

Prepare financial statements, closing entries, and post-closing trial balance.

(LO 1, 2, 3, 6)

(a) Complete the worksheet by extending the balances to the financial statement columns.
(b) Prepare an income statement, owner's equity statement, and a classified balance sheet. (*Note:* $5,000 of the notes payable become due in 2015.) M. Alshwer did not make any additional investments in the business during the year.
(c) Prepare the closing entries. Use J14 for the journal page.
(d) Post the closing entries. Use the three-column form of account. Income Summary is No. 350.
(e) Prepare a post-closing trial balance.

P4-3A The completed financial statement columns of the worksheet for Fleming Company are shown on the next page.

FLEMING COMPANY
Worksheet
For the Year Ended December 31, 2014

Account No.	Account Titles	Income Statement Dr.	Income Statement Cr.	Balance Sheet Dr.	Balance Sheet Cr.
101	Cash			8,900	
112	Accounts Receivable			10,800	
130	Prepaid Insurance			2,800	
157	Equipment			24,000	
158	Accumulated Depreciation—Equip.				4,500
201	Accounts Payable				9,000
212	Salaries and Wages Payable				2,400
301	Owner's Capital				19,500
306	Owner's Drawings			11,000	
400	Service Revenue		60,000		
622	Maintenance and Repairs Expense	1,600			
711	Depreciation Expense	3,100			
722	Insurance Expense	1,800			
726	Salaries and Wages Expense	30,000			
732	Utilities Expense	1,400			
	Totals	37,900	60,000	57,500	35,400
	Net Income	22,100			22,100
		60,000	60,000	57,500	57,500

Instructions

(a) Prepare an income statement, an owner's equity statement, and a classified balance sheet.

(b) Prepare the closing entries. J. Fleming did not make any additional investments during the year.

(c) Post the closing entries and underline and balance the accounts. (Use T-accounts.) Income Summary is account No. 350.

(d) Prepare a post-closing trial balance.

(a) Ending capital $30,600
Total current assets
$22,500

(d) Post-closing trial balance
$46,500

P4-4A Jarmuz Management Services began business on January 1, 2014, with a capital investment of $120,000. The company manages condominiums for owners (Service Revenue) and rents space in its own office building (Rent Revenue). The trial balance and adjusted trial balance columns of the worksheet at the end of the first year are as follows.

Complete worksheet; prepare classified balance sheet, entries, and post-closing trial balance.

(LO 1, 2, 3, 6)

JARMUZ MANAGEMENT SERVICES
Worksheet
For the Year Ended December 31, 2014

Account Titles	Trial Balance Dr.	Trial Balance Cr.	Adjusted Trial Balance Dr.	Adjusted Trial Balance Cr.
Cash	13,800		13,800	
Accounts Receivable	28,300		28,300	
Prepaid Insurance	3,600		2,400	
Land	67,000		67,000	
Buildings	127,000		127,000	
Equipment	59,000		59,000	
Accounts Payable		12,500		12,500
Unearned Rent Revenue		6,000		1,500
Mortgage Payable		120,000		120,000
Owner's Capital		144,000		144,000
Owner's Drawings	22,000		22,000	
Service Revenue		90,700		90,700
Rent Revenue		29,000		33,500
Salaries and Wages Expense	42,000		42,000	
Advertising Expense	20,500		20,500	
Utilities Expense	19,000		19,000	
Totals	402,200	402,200		

Account Titles	Trial Balance		Adjusted Trial Balance	
	Dr.	Cr.	Dr.	Cr.
Insurance Expense			1,200	
Depreciation Expense			6,600	
Accumulated Depreciation—Buildings				3,000
Accumulated Depreciation—Equipment				3,600
Interest Expense			10,000	
Interest Payable				10,000
Totals			418,800	418,800

Instructions

(a) Net income $24,900

(b) Total current assets $44,500

(e) Post-closing trial balance $297,500

(a) Prepare a complete worksheet.

(b) Prepare a classified balance sheet. (*Note*: $30,000 of the mortgage note payable is due for payment next year.)

(c) Journalize the adjusting entries.

(d) Journalize the closing entries.

(e) Prepare a post-closing trial balance.

Complete all steps in accounting cycle.

(LO 1, 2, 3, 4, 6)

P4-5A Heidi Jara opened Jara's Cleaning Service on July 1, 2014. During July, the following transactions were completed.

July	1	Jara invested $20,000 cash in the business.
	1	Purchased used truck for $9,000, paying $4,000 cash and the balance on account.
	3	Purchased cleaning supplies for $2,100 on account.
	5	Paid $1,800 cash on a 1-year insurance policy effective July 1.
	12	Billed customers $4,500 for cleaning services.
	18	Paid $1,500 cash on amount owed on truck and $1,400 on amount owed on cleaning supplies.
	20	Paid $2,500 cash for employee salaries.
	21	Collected $3,400 cash from customers billed on July 12.
	25	Billed customers $6,000 for cleaning services.
	31	Paid $350 for the monthly gasoline bill for the truck.
	31	Withdraw $5,600 cash for personal use.

The chart of accounts for Jara's Cleaning Service contains the following accounts: No. 101 Cash, No. 112 Accounts Receivable, No. 126 Supplies, No. 130 Prepaid Insurance, No. 157 Equipment, No. 158 Accumulated Depreciation—Equipment, No. 201 Accounts Payable, No. 212 Salaries and Wages Payable, No. 301 Owner's Capital, No. 306 Owner's Drawings, No. 350 Income Summary, No. 400 Service Revenue, No. 631 Supplies Expense, No. 633 Gasoline Expense, No. 711 Depreciation Expense, No. 722 Insurance Expense, and No. 726 Salaries and Wages Expense.

Instructions

(a) Journalize and post the July transactions. Use page J1 for the journal and the three-column form of account.

(b) Trial balance $34,700

(c) Adjusted trial balance $38,900

(b) Prepare a trial balance at July 31 on a worksheet.

(c) Enter the following adjustments on the worksheet and complete the worksheet.

   (1) Unbilled and uncollected revenue for services performed at July 31 were $2,700.

   (2) Depreciation on equipment for the month was $500.

   (3) One-twelfth of the insurance expired.

   (4) An inventory count shows $600 of cleaning supplies on hand at July 31.

   (5) Accrued but unpaid employee salaries were $1,000.

(d) Net income $7,200 Total assets $26,800

(d) Prepare the income statement and owner's equity statement for July and a classified balance sheet at July 31.

(e) Journalize and post adjusting entries. Use page J2 for the journal.

(f) Journalize and post closing entries and complete the closing process. Use page J3 for the journal.

(g) Post-closing trial balance $27,300

(g) Prepare a post-closing trial balance at July 31.

P4-6A Dao Vang, CPA, was retained by Universal Cable to prepare financial statements for April 2014. Vang accumulated all the ledger balances per Universal's records and found the following.

Analyze errors and prepare correcting entries and trial balance.

(LO 5)

UNIVERSAL CABLE
Trial Balance
April 30, 2014

	Debit	Credit
Cash	$ 4,100	
Accounts Receivable	3,200	
Supplies	800	
Equipment	10,600	
Accumulated Depreciation—Equip.		$ 1,350
Accounts Payable		2,100
Salaries and Wages Payable		700
Unearned Service Revenue		890
Owner's Capital		12,900
Service Revenue		5,450
Salaries and Wages Expense	3,300	
Advertising Expense	600	
Miscellaneous Expense	290	
Depreciation Expense	500	
	$23,390	$23,390

Dao Vang reviewed the records and found the following errors.

1. Cash received from a customer on account was recorded as $950 instead of $590.
2. A payment of $75 for advertising expense was entered as a debit to Miscellaneous Expense $75 and a credit to Cash $75.
3. The first salary payment this month was for $1,900, which included $700 of salaries payable on March 31. The payment was recorded as a debit to Salaries and Wages Expense $1,900 and a credit to Cash $1,900. (No reversing entries were made on April 1.)
4. The purchase on account of a printer costing $310 was recorded as a debit to Supplies and a credit to Accounts Payable for $310.
5. A cash payment of repair expense on equipment for $96 was recorded as a debit to Equipment $69 and a credit to Cash $69.

Instructions
(a) Prepare an analysis of each error showing (1) the incorrect entry, (2) the correct entry, and (3) the correcting entry. Items 4 and 5 occurred on April 30, 2014.
(b) Prepare a correct trial balance.

(b) Trial balance $22,690

PROBLEMS: SET B

P4-1B Michael Pevnick began operations as a private investigator on January 1, 2014. The trial balance columns of the worksheet for Michael Pevnick, P.I., at March 31 are as follows.

Prepare worksheet, financial statements, and adjusting and closing entries.

(LO 1, 2, 3, 6)

MICHAEL PEVNICK, P.I.
Worksheet
For the Quarter Ended March 31, 2014

	Trial Balance	
Account Titles	Dr.	Cr.
Cash	11,400	
Accounts Receivable	5,620	
Supplies	1,050	
Prepaid Insurance	2,400	
Equipment	30,000	

Account Titles	Trial Balance Dr.	Trial Balance Cr.
Notes Payable		10,000
Accounts Payable		12,350
Owner's Capital		20,000
Owner's Drawings	600	
Service Revenue		13,620
Salaries and Wages Expense	2,200	
Travel Expense	1,300	
Rent Expense	1,200	
Miscellaneous Expense	200	
	55,970	55,970

Other data:

1. Supplies on hand total $480.
2. Depreciation is $800 per quarter.
3. Interest accrued on 6-month note payable, issued January 1, $300.
4. Insurance expires at the rate of $200 per month.
5. Services performed but unbilled at March 31 total $1,030.

Instructions

(a) Adjusted trial balance
$58,100

(b) Net income $7,480
Total assets $49,530

(a) Enter the trial balance on a worksheet and complete the worksheet.
(b) Prepare an income statement and owner's equity statement for the quarter and a classified balance sheet at March 31. M. Pevnick did not make any additional investments in the business during the quarter ended March 31, 2014.
(c) Journalize the adjusting entries from the adjustments columns of the worksheet.
(d) Journalize the closing entries from the financial statement columns of the worksheet.

Complete worksheet; prepare financial statements, closing entries, and post-closing trial balance.

(LO 1, 2, 3, 6)

P4-2B The adjusted trial balance columns of the worksheet for Greenwood Company are as follows.

GREENWOOD COMPANY
Worksheet
For the Year Ended December 31, 2014

Account No.	Account Titles	Adjusted Trial Balance Dr.	Adjusted Trial Balance Cr.
101	Cash	18,800	
112	Accounts Receivable	16,200	
126	Supplies	2,300	
130	Prepaid Insurance	4,400	
157	Equipment	46,000	
158	Accumulated Depreciation—Equipment		20,000
200	Notes Payable		20,000
201	Accounts Payable		8,000
212	Salaries and Wages Payable		2,600
230	Interest Payable		1,000
301	Owner's Capital		26,000
306	Owner's Drawings	12,000	
400	Service Revenue		87,800
610	Advertising Expense	10,000	
631	Supplies Expense	3,700	
711	Depreciation Expense	8,000	
722	Insurance Expense	4,000	
726	Salaries and Wages Expense	39,000	
905	Interest Expense	1,000	
	Totals	165,400	165,400

Instructions

(a) Complete the worksheet by extending the balances to the financial statement columns.

(b) Prepare an income statement, owner's equity statement, and a classified balance sheet. (*Note:* $5,000 of the notes payable become due in 2015.) T. Greenwood did not make any additional investments in the business during 2014.

(c) Prepare the closing entries. Use J14 for the journal page.

(d) Post the closing entries. Use the three-column form of account. Income Summary is account No. 350.

(e) Prepare a post-closing trial balance.

(a) Net income $22,100

(b) Current assets $41,700
Current liabilities $16,600

(e) Post-closing trial balance $87,700

P4-3B The completed financial statement columns of the worksheet for Niho Company are shown below.

Prepare financial statements, closing entries, and post-closing trial balance.

(LO 1, 2, 3, 6)

NIHO COMPANY
Worksheet
For the Year Ended December 31, 2014

Account No.	Account Titles	Income Statement Dr.	Income Statement Cr.	Balance Sheet Dr.	Balance Sheet Cr.
101	Cash			6,200	
112	Accounts Receivable			7,500	
130	Prepaid Insurance			1,800	
157	Equipment			33,000	
158	Accumulated Depreciation—Equip.				8,600
201	Accounts Payable				11,700
212	Salaries and Wages Payable				3,000
301	Owner's Capital				34,000
306	Owner's Drawings			7,200	
400	Service Revenue		46,000		
622	Maintenance and Repairs Expense	4,400			
711	Depreciation Expense	2,800			
722	Insurance Expense	1,200			
726	Salaries and Wages Expense	35,200			
732	Utilities Expense	4,000			
	Totals	47,600	46,000	55,700	57,300
	Net Loss		1,600	1,600	
		47,600	47,600	57,300	57,300

Instructions

(a) Prepare an income statement, owner's equity statement, and a classified balance sheet. S. Niho made an additional investment in the business of $4,000 during 2014.

(b) Prepare the closing entries.

(c) Post the closing entries and underline and balance the accounts. (Use T-accounts.) Income Summary is account No. 350.

(d) Prepare a post-closing trial balance.

(a) Net loss $1,600
Ending capital $25,200
Total assets $39,900

(d) Post-closing trial balance $48,500

P4-4B Avalon Amusement Park has a fiscal year ending on September 30. Selected data from the September 30 worksheet are presented below.

Complete worksheet; prepare classified balance sheet, entries, and post-closing trial balance.

(LO 1, 2, 3, 6)

AVALON AMUSEMENT PARK
Worksheet
For the Year Ended September 30, 2014

	Trial Balance Dr.	Trial Balance Cr.	Adjusted Trial Balance Dr.	Adjusted Trial Balance Cr.
Cash	41,400		41,400	
Supplies	18,600		2,200	
Prepaid Insurance	31,900		10,900	
Land	80,000		80,000	
Equipment	120,000		120,000	

	Trial Balance		Adjusted Trial Balance	
	Dr.	Cr.	Dr.	Cr.
Accumulated Depreciation—Equip.		36,200		42,200
Accounts Payable		14,600		14,600
Unearned Ticket Revenue		3,700		1,000
Mortgage Payable		50,000		50,000
Owner's Capital		109,700		109,700
Owner's Drawings	14,000		14,000	
Ticket Revenue		277,500		280,200
Salaries and Wages Expense	105,000		105,000	
Maintenance and Repairs Expense	30,500		30,500	
Advertising Expense	9,400		9,400	
Utilities Expense	16,900		16,900	
Property Tax Expense	18,000		21,000	
Interest Expense	6,000		10,000	
Totals	491,700	491,700		
Insurance Expense			21,000	
Supplies Expense			16,400	
Interest Payable				4,000
Depreciation Expense			6,000	
Property Taxes Payable				3,000
Totals			504,700	504,700

Instructions

(a) Net income $44,000

(b) Total current assets $54,500

(e) Post-closing trial balance $254,500

(a) Prepare a complete worksheet.

(b) Prepare a classified balance sheet. (*Note:* $15,000 of the mortgage note payable is due for payment in the next fiscal year.)

(c) Journalize the adjusting entries using the worksheet as a basis.

(d) Journalize the closing entries using the worksheet as a basis.

(e) Prepare a post-closing trial balance.

Complete all steps in accounting cycle.

(LO 1, 2, 3, 4, 6)

P4-5B Gillian Shaw opened Shaw's Carpet Cleaners on March 1. During March, the following transactions were completed.

Mar. 1   Invested $10,000 cash in the business.
  1   Purchased used truck for $6,000, paying $3,000 cash and the balance on account.
  3   Purchased cleaning supplies for $1,200 on account.
  5   Paid $1,200 cash on a 1-year insurance policy effective March 1.
  14   Billed customers $4,800 for cleaning services.
  18   Paid $1,500 cash on amount owed on truck and $500 on amount owed on cleaning supplies.
  20   Paid $1,800 cash for employee salaries.
  21   Collected $1,400 cash from customers billed on March 14.
  28   Billed customers $2,500 for cleaning services.
  31   Paid $200 for the monthly gasoline bill for the truck.
  31   Withdrew $700 cash for personal use.

The chart of accounts for Shaw's Carpet Cleaners contains the following accounts: No. 101 Cash, No. 112 Accounts Receivable, No. 126 Supplies, No. 130 Prepaid Insurance, No. 157 Equipment, No. 158 Accumulated Depreciation—Equipment, No. 201 Accounts Payable, No. 212 Salaries and Wages Payable, No. 301 Owner's Capital, No. 306 Owner's Drawings, No. 350 Income Summary, No. 400 Service Revenue, No. 631 Supplies Expense, No. 633 Gasoline Expense, No. 711 Depreciation Expense, No. 722 Insurance Expense, and No. 726 Salaries and Wages Expense.

Instructions

(a) Journalize and post the March transactions. Use page J1 for the journal and the three-column form of account.

(b) Trial balance $19,500

(c) Adjusted trial balance $20,850

(b) Prepare a trial balance at March 31 on a worksheet.

(c) Enter the following adjustments on the worksheet and complete the worksheet.
  (1) Unbilled revenue for services performed at March 31 was $500.
  (2) Depreciation on equipment for the month was $300.

(3) One-twelfth of the insurance expired.
(4) An inventory count shows $250 of cleaning supplies on hand at March 31.
(5) Accrued but unpaid employee salaries were $550.

(d) Prepare the income statement and owner's equity statement for March and a classified balance sheet at March 31.

(d) Net income $3,900
   Total assets $15,950

(e) Journalize and post adjusting entries. Use page J2 for the journal.
(f) Journalize and post closing entries and complete the closing process. Use page J3 for the journal.
(g) Prepare a post-closing trial balance at March 31.

(g) Post-closing trial balance
   $16,250

PROBLEMS: SET C

Visit the book's companion website, at **www.wiley.com/college/weygandt**, and choose the Student Companion site to access Problem Set C.

COMPREHENSIVE PROBLEM:
CHAPTERS 2 TO 4

CP4 Kristin Malone opened Kristin's Maids Cleaning Service on July 1, 2014. During July, the company completed the following transactions.

July 1   Invested $14,000 cash in the business.
     1   Purchased a used truck for $10,000, paying $3,000 cash and the balance on account.
     3   Purchased cleaning supplies for $800 on account.
     5   Paid $1,800 on a 1-year insurance policy, effective July 1.
    12   Billed customers $3,800 for cleaning services.
    18   Paid $1,000 of amount owed on truck, and $400 of amount owed on cleaning supplies.
    20   Paid $1,600 for employee salaries.
    21   Collected $1,400 from customers billed on July 12.
    25   Billed customers $1,500 for cleaning services.
    31   Paid gasoline for the month on the truck, $400.
    31   Withdrew $600 cash for personal use.

The chart of accounts for Kristin's Maids Cleaning Service contains the following accounts: No. 101 Cash, No. 112 Accounts Receivable, No. 126 Supplies, No. 130 Prepaid Insurance, No. 157 Equipment, No. 158 Accumulated Depreciation—Equipment, No. 201 Accounts Payable, No. 212 Salaries and Wages Payable, No. 301 Owner's Capital, No. 306 Owner's Drawings, No. 350 Income Summary, No. 400 Service Revenue, No. 631 Supplies Expense, No. 633 Gasoline Expense, No. 711 Depreciation Expense, No. 722 Insurance Expense, and No. 726 Salaries and Wages Expense.

Instructions
(a) Journalize and post the July transactions. Use page J1 for the journal.
(b) Prepare a trial balance at July 31 on a worksheet.
(c) Enter the following adjustments on the worksheet, and complete the worksheet.

(b) Trial balance totals
   $25,700

   (1) Unbilled fees for services performed at July 31 were $1,300.
   (2) Depreciation on equipment for the month was $200.
   (3) One-twelfth of the insurance expired.
   (4) An inventory count shows $100 of cleaning supplies on hand at July 31.
   (5) Accrued but unpaid employee salaries were $500.

(d) Prepare the income statement and owner's equity statement for July, and a classified balance sheet at July 31, 2014.

(d) Net income $3,050
   Total assets $23,350

(e) Journalize and post the adjusting entries. Use page J2 for the journal.
(f) Journalize and post the closing entries, and complete the closing process. Use page J3 for the journal.
(g) Prepare a post-closing trial balance at July 31.

(g) Trial balance totals
   $23,550

CONTINUING COOKIE CHRONICLE

(*Note:* This is a continuation of the Cookie Chronicle from Chapters 1 through 3.)

CCC4 Natalie had a very busy December. At the end of the month, after journalizing and posting the December transactions and adjusting entries, Natalie prepared the following adjusted trial balance.

COOKIE CREATIONS
Adjusted Trial Balance
December 31, 2013

	Debit	Credit
Cash	$1,180	
Accounts Receivable	875	
Supplies	350	
Prepaid Insurance	1,210	
Equipment	1,200	
Accumulated Depreciation—Equipment		$ 40
Accounts Payable		75
Salaries and Wages Payable		56
Interest Payable		15
Unearned Service Revenue		300
Notes Payable		2,000
Owner's Capital		800
Owner's Drawings	500	
Service Revenue		4,515
Salaries and Wages Expense	1,006	
Utilities Expense	125	
Advertising Expense	165	
Supplies Expense	1,025	
Depreciation Expense	40	
Insurance Expense	110	
Interest Expense	15	
	$7,801	$7,801

Instructions

Using the information in the adjusted trial balance, do the following.

(a) Prepare an income statement and an owner's equity statement for the 2 months ended December 31, 2013, and a classified balance sheet at December 31, 2013. The note payable has a stated interest rate of 6%, and the principal and interest are due on November 16, 2015.

(b) Natalie has decided that her year-end will be December 31, 2013. Prepare and post closing entries as of December 31, 2013.

(c) Prepare a post-closing trial balance.

Broadening Your Perspective

Financial Reporting and Analysis

Financial Reporting Problem: Apple Inc.

BYP4-1 The financial statements of Apple Inc. are presented in Appendix A at the end of this textbook. Instructions for accessing and using the company's complete annual report, including the notes to the financial statements, are also provided in Appendix A.

Instructions

Answer the questions below using Apple's Consolidated Balance Sheets.

(a) What were Apple's total current assets at September 24, 2011, and September 25, 2010?

(b) Are assets that Apple included under current assets listed in proper order? Explain.

(c) How are Apple's assets classified?

(d) What was Apple's "Cash and cash equivalents" at September 24, 2011?

(e) What were Apple's total current liabilities at September 24, 2011, and September 25, 2010?

Comparative Analysis Problem:
PepsiCo, Inc. vs. The Coca-Cola Company

BYP4-2 PepsiCo's financial statements are presented in Appendix B. Financial statements for The Coca-Cola Company are presented in Appendix C. Instructions for accessing and using the complete annual reports of PepsiCo and Coca-Cola, including the notes to the financial statements, are also provided in Appendices B and C, respectively.

Instructions

(a) Based on the information contained in these financial statements, determine each of the following for PepsiCo at December 31, 2011, and for Coca-Cola at December 31, 2011.

    (1) Total current assets.

    (2) Net amount of property, plant, and equipment (land, buildings, and equipment).

    (3) Total current liabilities.

    (4) Total equity.

(b) What conclusions concerning the companies' respective financial positions can be drawn?

Comparative Analysis Problem:
Amazon.com, Inc. vs. Wal-Mart Stores, Inc.

BYP4-3 Amazon.com, Inc.'s financial statements are presented in Appendix D. Financial statements for Wal-Mart Stores, Inc. are presented in Appendix E. Instructions for accessing and using the complete annual reports of Amazon and Wal-Mart, including the notes to the financial statements, are also provided in Appendices D and E, respectively.

Instructions

(a) Based on the information contained in these financial statements, determine the following for Amazon at December 31, 2011, and Wal-Mart at January 31, 2012.

    (1) Total current assets.

    (2) Net amount of property and equipment (fixed assets), net.

    (3) Total current liabilities.

    (4) Total equity.

(b) What conclusions concerning these two companies can be drawn from these data?

Real-World Focus

BYP4-4 Numerous companies have established home pages on the Internet, e.g., Capt'n Eli Root Beer Company (**www.captneli.com/rootbeer.php**) and Kodak (**www.kodak.com**).

Instructions

Examine the home pages of any two companies and answer the following questions.

(a) What type of information is available?

(b) Is any accounting-related information presented?

(c) Would you describe the home page as informative, promotional, or both? Why?

Critical Thinking

Decision-Making Across the Organization

BYP4-5 Whitegloves Janitorial Service was started 2 years ago by Lynn Sanders. Because business has been exceptionally good, Lynn decided on July 1, 2014, to expand operations by acquiring an additional truck and hiring two more assistants. To finance the expansion, Lynn obtained on

July 1, 2014, a $25,000, 10% bank loan, payable $10,000 on July 1, 2015, and the balance on July 1, 2016. The terms of the loan require the borrower to have $10,000 more current assets than current liabilities at December 31, 2014. If these terms are not met, the bank loan will be refinanced at 15% interest. At December 31, 2014, the accountant for Whitegloves Janitorial Service Inc. prepared the balance sheet shown below.

   Lynn presented the balance sheet to the bank's loan officer on January 2, 2015, confident that the company had met the terms of the loan. The loan officer was not impressed. She said, "We need financial statements audited by a CPA." A CPA was hired and immediately realized that the balance sheet had been prepared from a trial balance and not from an adjusted trial balance. The adjustment data at the balance sheet date consisted of the following.

1. Unbilled janitorial services performed were $3,700.
2. Janitorial supplies on hand were $2,500.
3. Prepaid insurance was a 3-year policy dated January 1, 2014.
4. December expenses incurred but unpaid at December 31, $500.
5. Interest on the bank loan was not recorded.
6. The amounts for property, plant, and equipment presented in the balance sheet were reported net of accumulated depreciation (cost less accumulated depreciation). These amounts were $4,000 for cleaning equipment and $5,000 for delivery trucks as of January 1, 2014. Depreciation for 2014 was $2,000 for cleaning equipment and $5,000 for delivery trucks.

WHITEGLOVES JANITORIAL SERVICE
Balance Sheet
December 31, 2014

Assets		Liabilities and Owner's Equity	
Current assets		Current liabilities	
Cash	$ 6,500	Notes payable	$10,000
Accounts receivable	9,000	Accounts payable	2,500
Supplies	5,200	Total current liabilities	12,500
Prepaid insurance	4,800	Long-term liability	
Total current assets	25,500	Notes payable	15,000
Property, plant, and equipment		Total liabilities	27,500
Equipment (net)	22,000	Owner's equity	
Delivery trucks (net)	34,000	Owner's capital	54,000
Total property, plant, and equipment	56,000		
Total assets	$81,500	Total liabilities and owner's equity	$81,500

Instructions
With the class divided into groups, answer the following.

(a) Prepare a correct balance sheet.
(b) Were the terms of the bank loan met? Explain.

Communication Activity

BYP4-6 The accounting cycle is important in understanding the accounting process.

Instructions
Write a memo to your instructor that lists the steps of the accounting cycle in the order they should be completed. End with a paragraph that explains the optional steps in the cycle.

Ethics Case

BYP4-7 As the controller of Take No Prisoners Perfume Company, you discover a misstatement that overstated net income in the prior year's financial statements. The misleading financial statements appear in the company's annual report which was issued to banks and other creditors less than a month ago. After much thought about the consequences of telling the president, Jeb Wilde, about this misstatement, you gather your courage to inform him. Jeb says, "Hey! What they don't know won't hurt them. But, just so we set the record straight, we'll adjust this year's financial

statements for last year's misstatement. We can absorb that misstatement better in this year than in last year anyway! Just don't make such a mistake again."

Instructions
(a) Who are the stakeholders in this situation?
(b) What are the ethical issues in this situation?
(c) What would you do as a controller in this situation?

All About You

BYP4-8 Companies prepare balance sheets in order to know their financial position at a specific point in time. This enables them to make a comparison to their position at previous points in time, and gives them a basis for planning for the future. In order to evaluate your financial position, you need to prepare a personal balance sheet. Assume that you have compiled the following information regarding your finances. (*Hint:* Some of the items might not be used in your personal balance sheet.)

Amount owed on student loan balance (long-term)	$ 5,000
Balance in checking account	1,200
Certificate of deposit (6-month)	3,000
Annual earnings from part-time job	11,300
Automobile	7,000
Balance on automobile loan (current portion)	1,500
Balance on automobile loan (long-term portion)	4,000
Home computer	800
Amount owed to you by younger brother	300
Balance in money market account	1,800
Annual tuition	6,400
Video and stereo equipment	1,250
Balance owed on credit card (current portion)	150
Balance owed on credit card (long-term portion)	1,650

Instructions
Prepare a personal balance sheet using the format you have learned for a classified balance sheet for a company. For the capital account, use Owner's Capital.

FASB Codification Activity

BYP4-9 If your school has a subscription to the FASB Codification, go to **http://aaahq.org/ascLogin.cfm** to log in and prepare responses to the following.

Instructions
(a) Access the glossary ("Master Glossary") at the FASB Codification website to answer the following.
    (1) What is the definition of current assets?
    (2) What is the definition of current liabilities?
(b) A company wants to offset its accounts payable against its cash account and show a cash amount net of accounts payable on its balance sheet. Identify the criteria (found in the FASB Codification) under which a company has the right of set off. Does the company have the right to offset accounts payable against the cash account?

Answers to Chapter Questions

Answers to Insight and Accounting Across the Organization Questions

p. 171 Cisco Performs the Virtual Close   Q: Who else benefits from a shorter closing process? **A:** Investors benefit from a shorter closing process. The shorter the closing, the sooner the company can report its financial results. This means that the financial information is more timely and therefore more relevant to investors.

p. 177 Yale Express Loses Some Transportation Bills   Q: What might Yale Express's vice president have done to produce more accurate financial statements without waiting months for

Republic's outstanding transportation bills? **A:** Yale's vice president could have engaged his accountants and auditors to prepare an adjusting entry based on an estimate of the outstanding transportation bills. (The estimate could have been made using past experience and the current volume of business.)

p. 181 Regaining Goodwill **Q:** Name two industries today which are probably rated low on the reputational characteristics of "being trusted" and "having high ethical standards." **A:** Two possible industries are financial companies (Goldman Sachs or AIG) or oil companies (BP).

p. 182 Can a Company Be Too Liquid? **Q:** What can various company managers do to ensure that working capital is managed efficiently to maximize net income? **A:** Marketing and sales managers must understand that by extending generous repayment terms, they are expanding the company's receivables balance and slowing the company's cash flow. Production managers must strive to minimize the amount of excess inventory on hand. Managers must coordinate efforts to speed up the collection of receivables, while also ensuring that the company pays its payables on time but never too early.

Answers to Self-Test Questions

1. b **2.** c **3.** c **4.** a **5.** b **6.** c **7.** a **8.** d **9.** c **10.** d **11.** b **12.** c **13.** c **14.** d **15.** a ***16.** c

A Look at IFRS

LEARNING OBJECTIVE	8

Compare the procedures for the closing process under GAAP and IFRS.

The classified balance sheet, although generally required internationally, contains certain variations in format when reporting under IFRS.

Key Points

- The procedures of the closing process are applicable to all companies, whether they are using IFRS or GAAP.

- IFRS recommends but does not require the use of the title "statement of financial position" rather than balance sheet.

- The format of statement of financial position information is often presented differently under IFRS. Although no specific format is required, most companies that follow IFRS present statement of financial position information in this order:
  - ◆ Noncurrent assets
  - ◆ Current assets
  - ◆ Equity
  - ◆ Noncurrent liabilities
  - ◆ Current liabilities

- IFRS requires a classified statement of financial position except in very limited situations. IFRS follows the same guidelines as this textbook for distinguishing between current and noncurrent assets and liabilities.

- Under IFRS, current assets are usually listed in the reverse order of liquidity. For example, under GAAP cash is listed first, but under IFRS it is listed last.

- Some companies report the subtotal **net assets**, which equals total assets minus total liabilities. See, for example, the statement of financial position of Zetar plc in Appendix F.

- IFRS has many differences in terminology from what are shown in your textbook. For example, in the sample statement of financial position illustrated on the next page, notice in the investment category that stock is called shares.

FRANKLIN COMPANY
Statement of Financial Position
October 31, 2014

Assets

Intangible assets			
Patents			$ 3,100
Property, plant, and equipment			
Land		$10,000	
Equipment	$24,000		
Less: Accumulated depreciation	5,000	19,000	29,000
Long-term investments			
Share investments		5,200	
Investment in real estate		2,000	7,200
Current assets			
Prepaid insurance		400	
Supplies		2,100	
Inventory		3,000	
Notes receivable		1,000	
Accounts receivable		7,000	
Debt investments		2,000	
Cash		6,600	22,100
Total assets			$61,400

Equity and Liabilities

Equity			
Owner's capital			$34,050
Non-current liabilities			
Mortgage payable		$10,000	
Notes payable		1,300	11,300
Current liabilities			
Notes payable		11,000	
Accounts payable		2,100	
Salaries and wages payable		1,600	
Unearned service revenue		900	
Interest payable		450	16,050
Total equity and liabilities			$61,400

- Both IFRS and GAAP require disclosures about (1) accounting policies followed, (2) judgments that management has made in the process of applying the entity's accounting policies, and (3) the key assumptions and estimation uncertainty that could result in a material adjustment to the carrying amounts of assets and liabilities within the next financial year.

- Comparative prior-period information must be presented and financial statements must be prepared annually.

- Both GAAP and IFRS are increasing the use of fair value to report assets. However, at this point IFRS has adopted it more broadly. As examples, under IFRS companies can apply fair value to property, plant, and equipment; natural resources; and in some cases intangible assets.

Looking to the Future

The IASB and the FASB are working on a project to converge their standards related to financial statement presentation. A key feature of the proposed framework is that each of the statements will be organized in the same format, to separate an entity's financing activities from its operating and investing activities and, further, to separate financing activities into transactions with owners and creditors. Thus, the same classifications used in the statement of financial position would also be used in the income statement and the statement of cash flows. The project has three phases. You can follow the joint financial presentation project at the following link: **http://www.fasb.org/project/ financial_statement_presentation.shtml**.

The IASB and the FASB face a difficult task in attempting to update, modify, and complete a converged conceptual framework. For example, how do companies choose between information that is highly relevant but difficult to verify versus information that is less relevant but easy to verify? How do companies define control when developing a definition of an asset? Is a liability the future sacrifice itself or the obligation to make the sacrifice? Should a single measurement method, such as historical cost or fair value, be used, or does it depend on whether it is an asset or liability that is being measured? It appears that the new document will be a significant improvement over its predecessors and will lead to principles-based standards, which will help financial statement users make better decisions.

IFRS Practice

IFRS Self-Test Questions

1. Which of the following statements is **false**?
   (a) Assets equals liabilities plus equity.
   (b) Under IFRS, companies sometimes net liabilities against assets to report "net assets."
   (c) The FASB and IASB are working on a joint conceptual framework project.
   (d) Under IFRS, the statement of financial position is usually referred to as the statement of assets and equity.

2. A company has purchased a tract of land and expects to build a production plant on the land in approximately 5 years. During the 5 years before construction, the land will be idle. Under IFRS, the land should be reported as:
   (a) land expense.
   (b) property, plant, and equipment.
   (c) an intangible asset.
   (d) a long-term investment.

3. Current assets under IFRS are listed generally:
   (a) by importance.
   (b) in the reverse order of their expected conversion to cash.
   (c) by longevity.
   (d) alphabetically.

4. Companies that use IFRS:
   (a) may report all their assets on the statement of financial position at fair value.
   (b) may offset assets against liabilities and show net assets and net liabilities on their statement of financial positions, rather than the underlying detailed line items.
   (c) may report noncurrent assets before current assets on the statement of financial position.
   (d) do not have any guidelines as to what should be reported on the statement of financial position.

5. Companies that follow IFRS to prepare a statement of financial position generally use the following order of classification:
   (a) current assets, current liabilities, noncurrent assets, noncurrent liabilities, equity.
   (b) noncurrent assets, noncurrent liabilities, current assets, current liabilities, equity.
   (c) noncurrent assets, current assets, equity, noncurrent liabilities, current liabilities.
   (d) equity, noncurrent assets, current assets, noncurrent liabilities, current liabilities.

IFRS Exercises

IFRS4-1 In what ways does the format of a statement of financial of position under IFRS often differ from a balance sheet presented under GAAP?

IFRS4-2 What term is commonly used under IFRS in reference to the balance sheet?

IFRS4-3 The statement of financial position for Sundell Company includes the following accounts (in British pounds): Accounts Receivable £12,500; Prepaid Insurance £3,600; Cash £15,400; Supplies £5,200; and Debt Investments (short-term) £6,700. Prepare the current assets section of the statement of financial position, listing the accounts in proper sequence.

IFRS4-4 Glarus Company recently received the following information related to the company's December 31, 2014, statement of financial position (in Swiss francs).

Inventory	CHF 2,900	Debt investments (short-term)	CHF 120
Cash	13,400	Accumulated depreciation—	
Equipment	21,700	equipment	5,700
Share investments		Accounts receivable	4,300
(long-term)	6,500		

Prepare the assets section of the company's classified statement of financial position.

IFRS4-5 The following information is available for Lessila Bowling Alley at December 31, 2014.

Buildings	$128,800	Owner's Capital	$115,000
Accounts Receivable	14,520	Accumulated Depreciation—Buildings	42,600
Prepaid Insurance	4,680	Accounts Payable	12,300
Cash	18,040	Notes Payable	97,780
Equipment	62,400	Accumulated Depreciation—Equipment	18,720
Land	64,000	Interest Payable	2,600
Insurance Expense	780	Bowling Revenues	14,180
Depreciation Expense	7,360		
Interest Expense	2,600		

Prepare a classified statement of financial position. Assume that $13,900 of the notes payable will be paid in 2015.

IFRS4-6 Nate Roche is interested in comparing the liquidity and solvency of a U.S. software company with a Chinese competitor. Is this possible if the two companies report using different currencies?

International Comparative Analysis Problem:
Apple vs. Zetar plc

IFRS4-7 The financial statements of Zetar plc are presented in Appendix F. Instructions for accessing and using the company's complete annual report, including the notes to its financial statements, are also provided in Appendix F.

Instructions
Identify five differences in the format of the statement of financial position used by Zetar plc compared to a company, such as Apple, that follows GAAP. (Apple's financial statements are available in Appendix A.)

Answers to IFRS Self-Test Questions
1. d **2.** d **3.** b **4.** c **5.** c

The Navigator

✔ Remember to go back to The Navigator box on the chapter opening page and check off your completed work.

5 | Accounting for Merchandising Operations

Buy Now, Vote Later

Have you ever shopped for outdoor gear at an REI (Recreational Equipment Incorporated) store? If so, you might have been surprised if a salesclerk asked if you were a member. A member? What do you mean a member? You soon realize that REI might not be your typical store. In fact, there's a lot about REI that makes it different.

REI is a consumer cooperative, or "co-op" for short. To figure out what that means, consider this quote from the company's annual report:

> As a cooperative, the Company is owned by its members. Each member is entitled to one vote in the election of the Company's Board of Directors. Since January 1, 2008, the nonrefundable, nontransferable, one-time membership fee has been $20 dollars. As of December 31, 2010, there were approximately 10.8 million members.

Voting rights? Now that's something you don't get from shopping at Wal-Mart. REI members get other benefits as well, including sharing in the company's profits through a dividend at the end of the year, which can be used for purchases at REI stores during the next two years. The m you spend, the bigger your dividend.

Since REI is a co-op, you might wonder whether manage- ment's incentives might be a little different. For example, management still concerned about making a profit? The answer is yes, as it ensures the long-term viability of the company. At the same time, REI's members want the com pany to be run efficiently, so that prices remain low. In or for its members to evaluate just how well management is doing, REI publishes an audited annual report, just like publicly traded companies do. So, while profit maximizati might not be the ultimate goal for REI, the accounting an reporting issues are similar to those of a typical corporatio

How well is this business model working for REI? Well, it consistently been rated as one of the best places to work the United States. It was ranked 8th on *Fortune*'s 2012 lis Also, REI had sustainable business practices long before s responsibility became popular at other companies. The C Stewardship Report states "we reduced the absolute amo of energy we use despite opening four new stores and growing our business; we grew the amount of FSC-certif

✔ **The Navigator**

- Scan Learning Objectives
- Read Feature Story
- Read Preview
- Read text and answer **DO IT!** p. 225
  - p. 229   ■ p. 232   ■ p. 237
- Work Comprehensive **DO IT!** p. 238
- Review Summary of Learning Objectives
- Answer Self-Test Questions
- Complete Assignments
- Go to *WileyPLUS* for practice and tutorials
- **Read A Look at IFRS** p. 271

Learning Objectives ✔ The Navigator

After studying this chapter, you should be able to:

[1] Identify the differences between service and merchandising companies.

[2] Explain the recording of purchases under a perpetual inventory system.

[3] Explain the recording of sales revenues under a perpetual inventory system.

[4] Explain the steps in the accounting cycle for a merchandising company.

[5] Distinguish between a multiple-step and a single-step income statement.

paper we use to 58.4 percent of our total paper footprint—including our cash register receipt paper; we facilitated 2.2 million volunteer hours and we provided $3.7 million to more than 330 conservation and recreation nonprofits."

So, while REI, like other retailers, closely monitors its financial results, it also strives to succeed in other areas. And, with over 10 million votes at stake, REI's management knows that it has to deliver.

Preview of Chapter 5

 The Navigator

Merchandising is one of the largest and most influential industries in the United States. It is likely that a number of you will work for a merchandiser. Therefore, understanding the financial statements of merchandising companies is important. In this chapter, you will learn the basics about reporting merchandising transactions. In addition, you will learn how to prepare and analyze a commonly used form of the income statement—the multiple-step income statement. The content and organization of the chapter are as follows.

ACCOUNTING FOR MERCHANDISING OPERATIONS

Merchandising Operations	Recording Purchases of Merchandise	Recording Sales of Merchandise	Completing the Accounting Cycle	Forms of Financial Statements
• Operating cycles • Flow of costs—perpetual and periodic inventory systems • Advantages of the perpetual system	• Freight costs • Purchase returns and allowances • Purchase discounts • Summary of purchasing transactions	• Sales returns and allowances • Sales discounts	• Adjusting entries • Closing entries • Summary of merchandising entries	• Multiple-step income statement • Single-step income statement • Classified balance sheet

Merchandising Operations

REI, Wal-Mart, and Amazon.com are called merchandising companies because they buy and sell merchandise rather than perform services as their primary source of revenue. Merchandising companies that purchase and sell directly to consumers are called **retailers**. Merchandising companies that sell to retailers are known as **wholesalers**. For example, retailer Walgreens might buy goods from wholesaler McKesson. Retailer Office Depot might buy office supplies from wholesaler United Stationers. The primary source of revenues for merchandising companies is the sale of merchandise, often referred to simply as **sales revenue** or **sales**. A merchandising company has two categories of expenses: cost of goods sold and operating expenses.

Cost of goods sold is the total cost of merchandise sold during the period. This expense is directly related to the revenue recognized from the sale of goods. Illustration 5-1 shows the income measurement process for a merchandising company. The items in the two blue boxes are unique to a merchandising company; they are not used by a service company.

Illustration 5-1

Income measurement process for a merchandising company

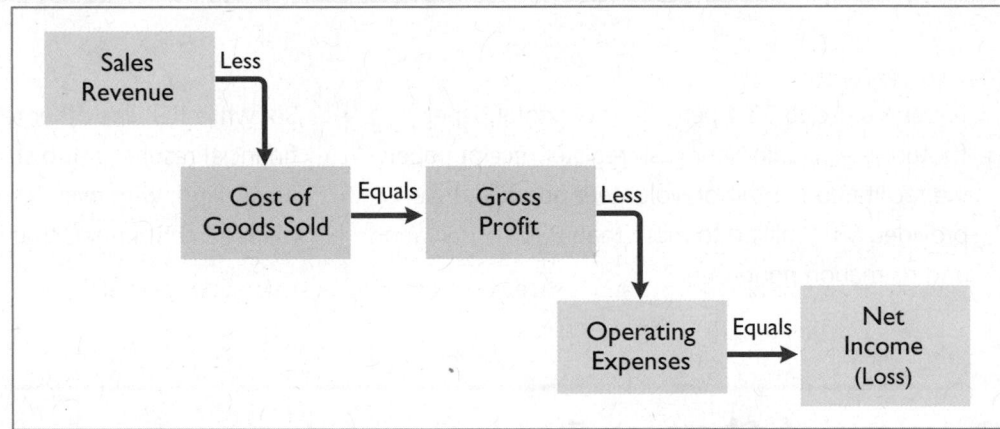

Operating Cycles

The operating cycle of a merchandising company ordinarily is longer than that of a service company. The purchase of merchandise inventory and its eventual sale lengthen the cycle. Illustration 5-2 shows the operating cycle of a service company.

Illustration 5-2

Operating cycle for a service company

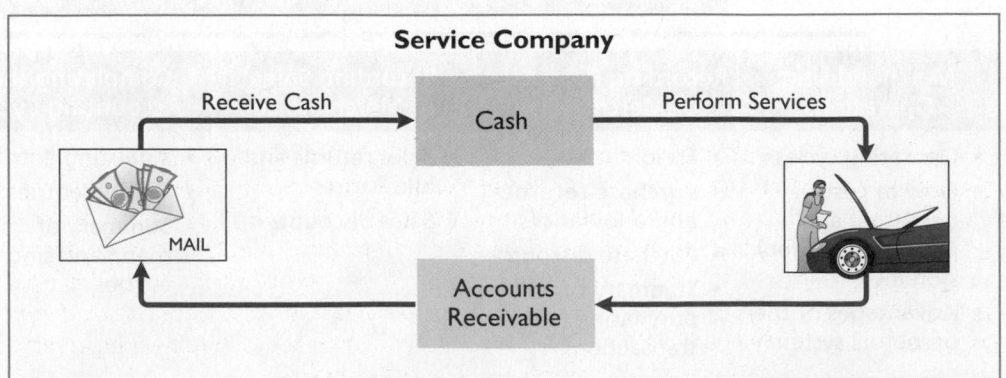

Illustration 5-3 shows the operating cycle of a merchandising company.

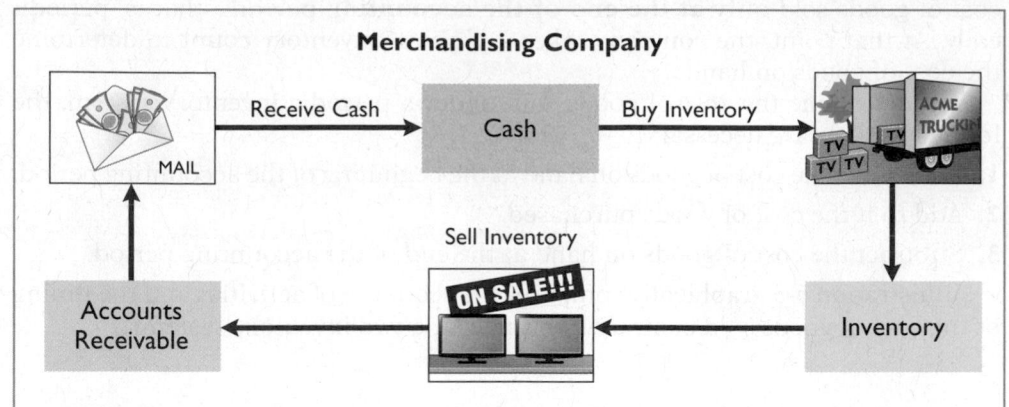

Illustration 5-3
Operating cycle for a
merchandising company

Note that the added asset account for a merchandising company is the Inventory account. Companies report inventory as a current asset on the balance sheet.

Flow of Costs

The flow of costs for a merchandising company is as follows. Beginning inventory plus the cost of goods purchased is the cost of goods available for sale. As goods are sold, they are assigned to cost of goods sold. Those goods that are not sold by the end of the accounting period represent ending inventory. Illustration 5-4 describes these relationships. Companies use one of two systems to account for inventory: a **perpetual inventory system** or a **periodic inventory system**.

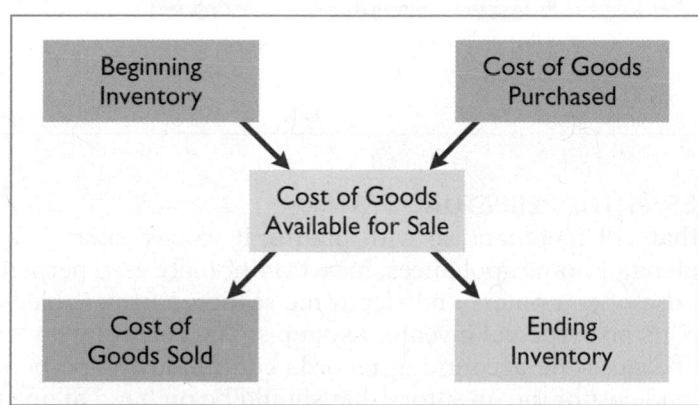

Illustration 5-4
Flow of costs

PERPETUAL SYSTEM

In a **perpetual inventory system**, companies keep detailed records of the cost of each inventory purchase and sale. These records continuously—perpetually— show the inventory that should be on hand for every item. For example, a Ford dealership has separate inventory records for each automobile, truck, and van on its lot and showroom floor. Similarly, a Kroger grocery store uses bar codes and optical scanners to keep a daily running record of every box of cereal and every jar of jelly that it buys and sells. Under a perpetual inventory system, a company determines the cost of goods sold **each time a sale occurs**.

Helpful Hint For control purposes, companies take a physical inventory count under the perpetual system, even though it is not needed to determine cost of goods sold.

PERIODIC SYSTEM

In a **periodic inventory system**, companies do not keep detailed inventory records of the goods on hand throughout the period. Instead, they determine the cost of goods sold **only at the end of the accounting period**—that is, periodically. At that point, the company takes a physical inventory count to determine the cost of goods on hand.

To determine the cost of goods sold under a periodic inventory system, the following steps are necessary:

1. Determine the cost of goods on hand at the beginning of the accounting period.
2. Add to it the cost of goods purchased.
3. Subtract the cost of goods on hand at the end of the accounting period.

Illustration 5-5 graphically compares the sequence of activities and the timing of the cost of goods sold computation under the two inventory systems.

Illustration 5-5
Comparing perpetual and periodic inventory systems

ADVANTAGES OF THE PERPETUAL SYSTEM

Companies that sell merchandise with high unit values, such as automobiles, furniture, and major home appliances, have traditionally used perpetual systems. The growing use of computers and electronic scanners has enabled many more companies to install perpetual inventory systems. The perpetual inventory system is so named because the accounting records continuously—perpetually—show the quantity and cost of the inventory that should be on hand at any time.

A perpetual inventory system provides better control over inventories than a periodic system. Since the inventory records show the quantities that should be on hand, the company can count the goods at any time to see whether the amount of goods actually on hand agrees with the inventory records. If shortages are uncovered, the company can investigate immediately. Although a perpetual inventory system requires additional clerical work and additional cost to maintain the subsidiary records, a computerized system can minimize this cost. Much of Amazon.com's success is attributed to its sophisticated inventory system.

Some businesses find it either unnecessary or uneconomical to invest in a sophisticated, computerized perpetual inventory system such as Amazon's. Many small merchandising businesses find that basic computerized accounting packages provide some of the essential benefits of a perpetual inventory system. Also, managers of some small businesses still find that they can control their merchandise and manage day-to-day operations using a periodic inventory system.

Because of the widespread use of the perpetual inventory system, we illustrate it in this chapter. Appendix 5B describes the journal entries for the periodic system.

INVESTOR INSIGHT

Morrow Snowboards Improves Its Stock Appeal

Investors are often eager to invest in a company that has a hot new product. However, when snowboard-maker Morrow Snowboards, Inc. issued shares of stock to the public for the first time, some investors expressed reluctance to invest in Morrow because of a number of accounting control problems. To reduce investor concerns, Morrow implemented a perpetual inventory system to improve its control over inventory. In addition, it stated that it would perform a physical inventory count every quarter until it felt that the perpetual inventory system was reliable.

? If a perpetual system keeps track of inventory on a daily basis, why do companies ever need to do a physical count? (See page 270.)

Recording Purchases of Merchandise

Companies purchase inventory using cash or credit (on account). They normally record purchases when they receive the goods from the seller. Every purchase should be supported by business documents that provide written evidence of the transaction. Each cash purchase should be supported by a canceled check or a cash register receipt indicating the items purchased and amounts paid. Companies record cash purchases by an increase in Inventory and a decrease in Cash.

> **LEARNING OBJECTIVE 2**
>
> Explain the recording of purchases under a perpetual inventory system.

A **purchase invoice** should support each credit purchase. This invoice indicates the total purchase price and other relevant information. However, the purchaser does not prepare a separate purchase invoice. Instead, the purchaser uses as a purchase invoice a copy of the sales invoice sent by the seller. In Illustration 5-6 (page 222), for example, Sauk Stereo (the buyer) uses as a purchase invoice the sales invoice prepared by PW Audio Supply (the seller).

Sauk Stereo makes the following journal entry to record its purchase from PW Audio Supply. The entry increases (debits) Inventory and increases (credits) Accounts Payable.

May 4	Inventory		3,800	
	Accounts Payable			3,800
	(To record goods purchased on account from PW Audio Supply)			

A = L + OE
+3,800
　　　+3,800

Cash Flows
no effect

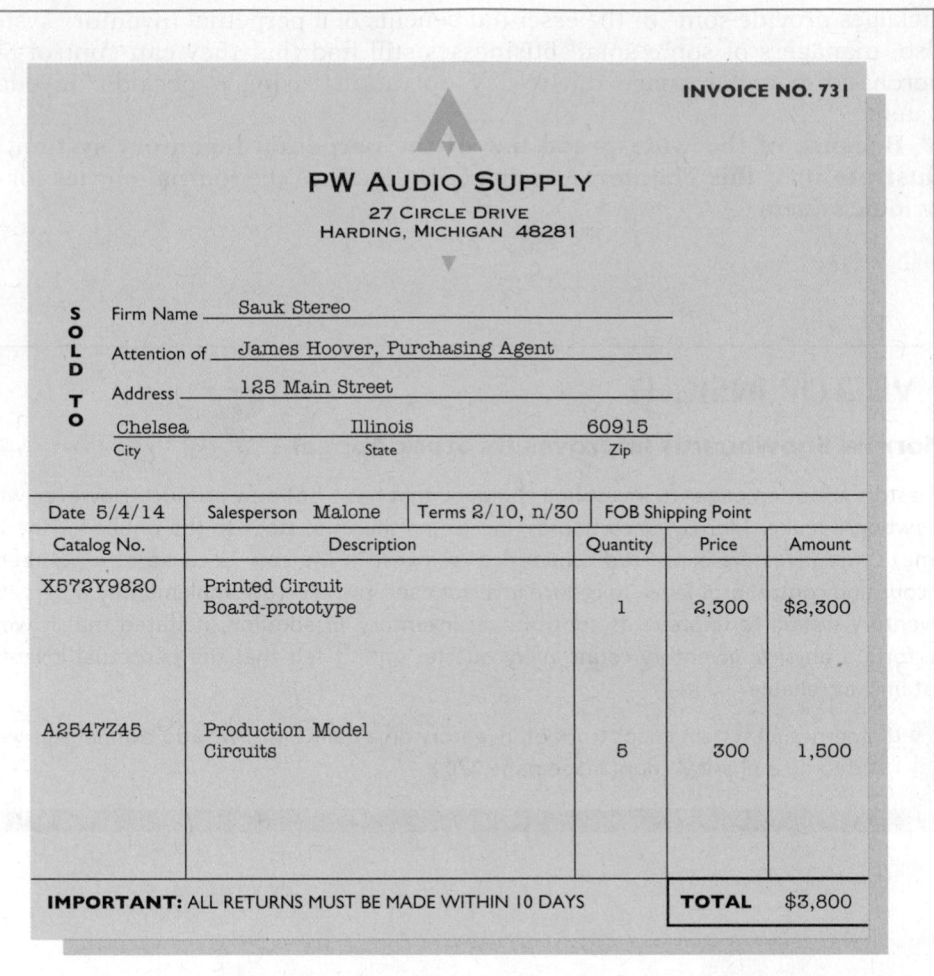

Helpful Hint To better understand the contents of this invoice, identify these items:
1. Seller
2. Invoice date
3. Purchaser
4. Salesperson
5. Credit terms
6. Freight terms
7. Goods sold: catalog number, description, quantity, price per unit
8. Total invoice amount

Under the perpetual inventory system, companies record purchases of merchandise for sale in the Inventory account. Thus, REI would increase (debit) Inventory for clothing, sporting goods, and anything else purchased for resale to customers.

Not all purchases are debited to Inventory, however. Companies record purchases of assets acquired for use and not for resale, such as supplies, equipment, and similar items, as increases to specific asset accounts rather than to Inventory. For example, to record the purchase of materials used to make shelf signs or for cash register receipt paper, REI would increase (debit) Supplies.

Freight Costs

The sales agreement should indicate who—the seller or the buyer—is to pay for transporting the goods to the buyer's place of business. When a common carrier such as a railroad, trucking company, or airline transports the goods, the carrier prepares a freight bill in accord with the sales agreement.

Freight terms are expressed as either FOB shipping point or FOB destination. The letters FOB mean **free on board**. Thus, **FOB shipping point** means that the seller places the goods free on board the carrier, and the buyer pays the freight costs. Conversely, **FOB destination** means that the seller places the goods free on board to the buyer's place of business, and the seller pays the freight. For example, the sales invoice in Illustration 5-6 indicates FOB shipping point. Thus, the buyer (Sauk Stereo) pays the freight charges. Illustration 5-7 (on the next page) illustrates these shipping terms.

Illustration 5-7
Shipping terms

FREIGHT COSTS INCURRED BY THE BUYER

When the buyer incurs the transportation costs, these costs are considered part of the cost of purchasing inventory. Therefore, the buyer debits (increases) the Inventory account. For example, if Sauk Stereo (the buyer) pays Public Carrier Co. $150 for freight charges on May 6, the entry on Sauk Stereo's books is:

May 6	Inventory	150	
	Cash		150
	(To record payment of freight on goods purchased)		

Thus, any freight costs incurred by the buyer are part of the cost of merchandise purchased. The reason: Inventory cost should include all costs to acquire the inventory, including freight necessary to deliver the goods to the buyer. Companies recognize these costs as cost of goods sold when inventory is sold.

FREIGHT COSTS INCURRED BY THE SELLER

In contrast, **freight costs incurred by the seller on outgoing merchandise are an operating expense to the seller**. These costs increase an expense account titled Freight-Out (sometimes called Delivery Expense). For example, if the freight terms on the invoice in Illustration 5-6 had required PW Audio Supply (the seller) to pay the freight charges, the entry by PW Audio Supply would be:

May 4	Freight-Out (or Delivery Expense)	150	
	Cash		150
	(To record payment of freight on goods sold)		

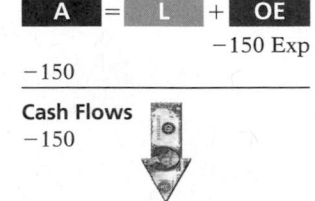

When the seller pays the freight charges, the seller will usually establish a higher invoice price for the goods to cover the shipping expense.

Purchase Returns and Allowances

A purchaser may be dissatisfied with the merchandise received because the goods are damaged or defective, of inferior quality, or do not meet the purchaser's specifications. In such cases, the purchaser may return the goods to the seller for credit if the sale was made on credit, or for a cash refund if the purchase was for cash. This transaction is known as a **purchase return**. Alternatively, the purchaser may choose to keep the merchandise if the seller is willing to grant an allowance (deduction) from the purchase price. This transaction is known as a **purchase allowance**.

Assume that Sauk Stereo returned goods costing $300 to PW Audio Supply on May 8. The following entry by Sauk Stereo for the returned merchandise decreases (debits) Accounts Payable and decreases (credits) Inventory.

A = L + OE
−300
−300

Cash Flows
no effect

May 8	Accounts Payable	300	
	Inventory		300
	(To record return of goods purchased		
	from PW Audio Supply)		

Because Sauk Stereo increased Inventory when the goods were received, Inventory is decreased when Sauk Stereo returns the goods.

Suppose instead that Sauk Stereo chose to keep the goods after being granted a $50 allowance (reduction in price). It would reduce (debit) Accounts Payable and reduce (credit) Inventory for $50.

Purchase Discounts

The credit terms of a purchase on account may permit the buyer to claim a cash discount for prompt payment. The buyer calls this cash discount a **purchase discount**. This incentive offers advantages to both parties. The purchaser saves money, and the seller is able to shorten the operating cycle by converting the accounts receivable into cash.

Credit terms specify the amount of the cash discount and time period in which it is offered. They also indicate the time period in which the purchaser is expected to pay the full invoice price. In the sales invoice in Illustration 5-6 (page 222), credit terms are 2/10, n/30, which is read "two-ten, net thirty." This means that the buyer may take a 2% cash discount on the invoice price, less ("net of") any returns or allowances, if payment is made within 10 days of the invoice date (the **discount period**). Otherwise, the invoice price, less any returns or allowances, is due 30 days from the invoice date.

Alternatively, the discount period may extend to a specified number of days following the month in which the sale occurs. For example, 1/10 EOM (end of month) means that a 1% discount is available if the invoice is paid within the first 10 days of the next month.

When the seller elects not to offer a cash discount for prompt payment, credit terms will specify only the maximum time period for paying the balance due. For example, the invoice may state the time period as n/30, n/60, or n/10 EOM. This means, respectively, that the buyer must pay the net amount in 30 days, 60 days, or within the first 10 days of the next month.

When the buyer pays an invoice within the discount period, the amount of the discount decreases Inventory. Why? Because companies record inventory at cost and, by paying within the discount period, the buyer has reduced its cost. To illustrate, assume Sauk Stereo pays the balance due of $3,500 (gross invoice price of $3,800 less purchase returns and allowances of $300) on May 14, the last day of the discount period. The cash discount is $70 ($3,500 × 2%), and Sauk Stereo pays $3,430 ($3,500 − $70). The entry Sauk Stereo makes to record its May 14 payment decreases (debits) Accounts Payable by the amount of the gross invoice price, reduces (credits) Inventory by the $70 discount, and reduces (credits) Cash by the net amount owed.

Helpful Hint The term *net* in "net 30" means the remaining amount due after subtracting any sales returns and allowances and partial payments.

A = L + OE
−3,500
−3,430
−70

Cash Flows
−3,430

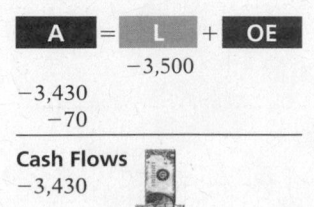

May 14	Accounts Payable	3,500	
	Cash		3,430
	Inventory		70
	(To record payment within discount		
	period)		

If Sauk Stereo failed to take the discount, and instead made full payment of $3,500 on June 3, it would debit Accounts Payable and credit Cash for $3,500 each.

June 3	Accounts Payable	3,500	
	Cash		3,500
	(To record payment with no discount taken)		

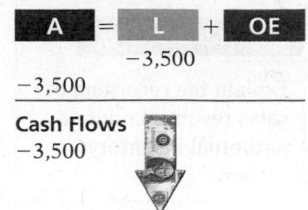

A = L + OE

−3,500

−3,500

Cash Flows
−3,500

A merchandising company usually should take all available discounts. Passing up the discount may be viewed as **paying interest** for use of the money. For example, passing up the discount offered by PW Audio Supply would be comparable to Sauk Stereo paying an interest rate of 2% for the use of $3,500 for 20 days. This is the equivalent of an annual interest rate of approximately 36.5% (2% $\times$ 365/20). Obviously, it would be better for Sauk Stereo to borrow at prevailing bank interest rates of 6% to 10% than to lose the discount.

Summary of Purchasing Transactions

The following T-account (with transaction descriptions in red) provides a summary of the effect of the previous transactions on Inventory. Sauk Stereo originally purchased $3,800 worth of inventory for resale. It then returned $300 of goods. It paid $150 in freight charges, and finally, it received a $70 discount off the balance owed because it paid within the discount period. This results in a balance in Inventory of $3,580.

Inventory

Purchase	May 4	3,800	May 8	300	Purchase return
Freight-in	6	150	14	70	Purchase discount
Balance		3,580			

> ## DO IT!

Purchase Transactions

On September 5, De La Hoya Company buys merchandise on account from Junot Diaz Company. The selling price of the goods is $1,500, and the cost to Diaz Company was $800. On September 8, De La Hoya returns defective goods with a selling price of $200. Record the transactions on the books of De La Hoya Company.

Solution

Sept. 5	Inventory	1,500	
	Accounts Payable		1,500
	(To record goods purchased on account)		
8	Accounts Payable	200	
	Inventory		200
	(To record return of defective goods)		

Action Plan

✔ Purchaser records goods at cost.

✔ When goods are returned, purchaser reduces Inventory.

Related exercise material: **BE5-2, BE5-4, E5-2, E5-3, E5-4,** and **DO IT!** 5-1.

✔ **The Navigator**

Recording Sales of Merchandise

In accordance with the revenue recognition principle, companies record sales revenue when the performance obligation is satisfied. Typically, the performance obligation is satisfied when the goods transfer from the seller to the buyer. At this point, the sales transaction is complete and the sales price established.

Sales may be made on credit or for cash. A **business document** should support every sales transaction, to provide written evidence of the sale. **Cash register documents** provide evidence of cash sales. A **sales invoice**, like the one shown in Illustration 5-6 (page 222), provides support for a credit sale. The original copy of the invoice goes to the customer, and the seller keeps a copy for use in recording the sale. The invoice shows the date of sale, customer name, total sales price, and other relevant information.

The seller makes two entries for each sale. **The first entry records the sale**: The seller increases (debits) Cash (or Accounts Receivable, if a credit sale) and also increases (credits) Sales Revenue. **The second entry records the cost of the merchandise sold**: The seller increases (debits) Cost of Goods Sold and also decreases (credits) Inventory for the cost of those goods. As a result, the Inventory account will show at all times the amount of inventory that should be on hand.

To illustrate a credit sales transaction, PW Audio Supply records its May 4 sale of $3,800 to Sauk Stereo (see Illustration 5-6) as follows (assume the merchandise cost PW Audio Supply $2,400).

A	=	L	+	OE
+3,800				
				+3,800 Rev

Cash Flows
no effect

A	=	L	+	OE
				−2,400 Exp
−2,400				

Cash Flows
no effect

May 4	Accounts Receivable	3,800	
	Sales Revenue		3,800
	(To record credit sale to Sauk Stereo per invoice #731)		
4	Cost of Goods Sold	2,400	
	Inventory		2,400
	(To record cost of merchandise sold on invoice #731 to Sauk Stereo)		

For internal decision-making purposes, merchandising companies may use more than one sales account. For example, PW Audio Supply may decide to keep separate sales accounts for its sales of TV sets, DVD recorders, and microwave ovens. REI might use separate accounts for camping gear, children's clothing, and ski equipment—or it might have even more narrowly defined accounts. By using separate sales accounts for major product lines, rather than a single combined sales account, company management can more closely monitor sales trends and respond more strategically to changes in sales patterns. For example, if TV sales are increasing while microwave oven sales are decreasing, PW Audio Supply might reevaluate both its advertising and pricing policies on these items to ensure they are optimal.

On its income statement presented to outside investors, a merchandising company normally would provide only a single sales figure—the sum of all of its individual sales accounts. This is done for two reasons. First, providing detail on all of its individual sales accounts would add considerable length to its income statement. Second, companies do not want their competitors to know the details of their operating results. However, Microsoft recently expanded its disclosure of revenue from three to five types. The reason: The additional categories enabled financial statement users to better evaluate the growth of the company's consumer and Internet businesses.

Ethics Note

Many companies are trying to improve the quality of their financial reporting. For example, General Electric now provides more detail on its revenues and operating profits.

ANATOMY OF A FRAUD[1]

Holly Harmon was a cashier at a national superstore for only a short while when she began stealing merchandise using three methods. Under the first method, her husband or friends took UPC labels from cheaper items and put them on more expensive items. Holly then scanned the goods at the register. Using the second method Holly scanned an item at the register but then voided the sale and left the merchandise in the shopping cart. A third approach was to put goods into large plastic containers. She scanned the plastic containers but not the goods within them. One day, Holly did not call in sick or show up for work. In such instances, the company reviews past surveillance tapes to look for suspicious activity by employees. This enabled the store to observe the thefts and to identify the participants.

Total take: $12,000

THE MISSING CONTROLS

Human resource controls. A background check would have revealed Holly's previous criminal record. She would not have been hired as a cashier.

Physical controls. Software can flag high numbers of voided transactions or a high number of sales of low-priced goods. Random comparisons of video records with cash register records can ensure that the goods reported as sold on the register are the same goods that are shown being purchased on the video recording. Finally, employees should be aware that they are being monitored.

Source: Adapted from Wells, *Fraud Casebook* (2007), pp. 251–259.

At the end of "Anatomy of a Fraud" stories, which describe some recent real-world frauds, we discuss the missing control activity that would likely have prevented or uncovered the fraud.

Sales Returns and Allowances

We now look at the "flip side" of purchase returns and allowances, which the seller records as **sales returns and allowances**. These are transactions where the seller either accepts goods back from the buyer (a return) or grants a reduction in the purchase price (an allowance) so the buyer will keep the goods. PW Audio Supply's entries to record credit for returned goods involve (1) an increase (debit) in Sales Returns and Allowances (a contra account to Sales Revenue) and a decrease (credit) in Accounts Receivable at the $300 selling price, and (2) an increase (debit) in Inventory (assume a $140 cost) and a decrease (credit) in Cost of Goods Sold, as shown below (assuming that the goods were not defective).

May 8	Sales Returns and Allowances	300	
	Accounts Receivable		300
	(To record credit granted to Sauk Stereo for returned goods)		
8	Inventory	140	
	Cost of Goods Sold		140
	(To record cost of goods returned)		

A = L + OE
−300   −300 Rev

Cash Flows
no effect

A = L + OE
+140   +140 Exp

Cash Flows
no effect

If Sauk Stereo returns goods because they are damaged or defective, then PW Audio Supply's entry to Inventory and Cost of Goods Sold should be for the fair value of the returned goods, rather than their cost. For example, if the returned

---

[1]The "Anatomy of a Fraud" stories in this textbook are adapted from *Fraud Casebook: Lessons from the Bad Side of Business,* edited by Joseph T. Wells (Hoboken, NJ: John Wiley & Sons, Inc., 2007). Used by permission. The names of some of the people and organizations in the stories are fictitious, but the facts in the stories are true.

goods were defective and had a fair value of $50, PW Audio Supply would debit Inventory for $50 and credit Cost of Goods Sold for $50.

What happens if the goods are not returned but the seller grants the buyer an allowance by reducing the purchase price? In this case, the seller debits Sales Returns and Allowances and credits Accounts Receivable for the amount of the allowance. An allowance has no impact on Inventory or Cost of Goods Sold.

As mentioned above, Sales Returns and Allowances is a **contra revenue account** to Sales Revenue. This means that it is offset against a revenue account on the income statement. The normal balance of Sales Returns and Allowances is a debit. Companies use a contra account, instead of debiting Sales Revenue, to disclose in the accounts and in the income statement the amount of sales returns and allowances. Disclosure of this information is important to management. Excessive returns and allowances may suggest problems—inferior merchandise, inefficiencies in filling orders, errors in billing customers, or delivery or shipment mistakes. Moreover, a decrease (debit) recorded directly to Sales Revenue would obscure the relative importance of sales returns and allowances as a percentage of sales. It also could distort comparisons between total sales in different accounting periods.

ACCOUNTING ACROSS THE ORGANIZATION

Should Costco Change Its Return Policy?

In most industries, sales returns are relatively minor. But returns of consumer electronics can really take a bite out of profits. Recently, the marketing executives at Costco Wholesale Corp. faced a difficult decision. Costco has always prided itself on its generous return policy. Most goods have had an unlimited grace period for returns. A new policy will require that certain electronics must be returned within 90 days of their purchase. The reason? The cost of returned products such as high-definition TVs, computers, and iPods cut an estimated 8¢ per share off Costco's earnings per share, which was $2.30.

Source: Kris Hudson, "Costco Tightens Policy on Returning Electronics," *Wall Street Journal* (February 27, 2007), p. B4.

© Jacob Wackerhausen/iStockphoto

 If a company expects significant returns, what are the implications for revenue recognition? (See page 270.)

Sales Discounts

As mentioned in our discussion of purchase transactions, the seller may offer the customer a cash discount—called by the seller a **sales discount**—for the prompt payment of the balance due. Like a purchase discount, a sales discount is based on the invoice price less returns and allowances, if any. The seller increases (debits) the Sales Discounts account for discounts that are taken. For example, PW Audio Supply makes the following entry to record the cash receipt on May 14 from Sauk Stereo within the discount period.

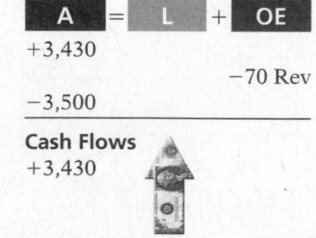

A = L + OE
+3,430
        −70 Rev
−3,500

Cash Flows
+3,430

May 14	Cash	3,430	
	Sales Discounts	70	
	Accounts Receivable		3,500
	(To record collection within 2/10, n/30 discount period from Sauk Stereo)		

Like Sales Returns and Allowances, Sales Discounts is a **contra revenue account** to Sales Revenue. Its normal balance is a debit. PW Audio Supply uses this account, instead of debiting Sales Revenue, to disclose the amount of cash discounts taken by customers. If Sauk Stereo does not take the discount, PW

Audio Supply increases (debits) Cash for $3,500 and decreases (credits) Accounts Receivable for the same amount at the date of collection.

The following T-accounts summarize the three sales-related transactions and show their combined effect on net sales.

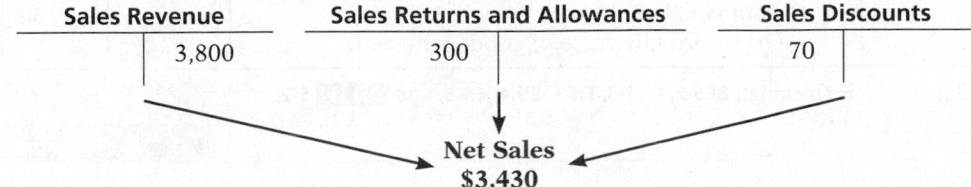

Sales Revenue	Sales Returns and Allowances	Sales Discounts
3,800	300	70

Net Sales
$3,430

PEOPLE, PLANET, AND PROFIT INSIGHT

Selling Green

Helen Sessions/Alamy

Here is a question an executive of PepsiCo was asked: Should PepsiCo market green? The executive indicated that the company should, as he believes it's the No. 1 thing consumers all over the world care about. Here are some of his thoughts on this issue:

"Sun Chips are part of the food business I run. It's a 'healthy snack.' We decided that Sun Chips, if it's a healthy snack, should be made in facilities that have a net-zero footprint. In other words, I want off the electric grid everywhere we make Sun Chips. We did that. Sun Chips should be made in a facility that puts back more water than it uses. It does that. And we partnered with our suppliers and came out with the world's first compostable chip package.

Now, there was an issue with this package: It was louder than the New York subway, louder than jet engines taking off. What would a company that's committed to green do: walk away or stay committed? If your people are passionate, they're going to fix it for you as long as you stay committed. Six months later, the compostable bag has half the noise of our current package.

So the view today is: we should market green, we should be proud to do it . . . it has to be a 360-degree process, both internal and external. And if you do that, you can monetize environmental sustainability for the shareholders."

Source: "Four Problems—and Solutions," *Wall Street Journal* (March 7, 2011), p. R2.

What is meant by "monetize environmental sustainability" for shareholders? (See page 270.)

> DO IT!

Sales Transactions

Action Plan

✔ Seller records both the sale and the cost of goods sold at the time of the sale.

✔ When goods are returned, the seller records the return in a contra account, Sales Returns and Allowances, and reduces Accounts Receivable.

On September 5, De La Hoya Company buys merchandise on account from Junot Diaz Company. The selling price of the goods is $1,500, and the cost to Diaz Company was $800. On September 8, De La Hoya returns defective goods with a selling price of $200 and a fair value of $30. Record the transactions on the books of Junot Diaz Company.

Solution

Sept. 5	Accounts Receivable	1,500	
	Sales Revenue		1,500
	(To record credit sale)		
5	Cost of Goods Sold	800	
	Inventory		800
	(To record cost of goods sold on account)		

Action Plan (cont'd)

✔ Any goods returned increase Inventory and reduce Cost of Goods Sold. Defective or damaged inventory is recorded at fair value (scrap value).

8	Sales Returns and Allowances		200	
	Accounts Receivable			200
	(To record credit granted for receipt of returned goods)			
8	Inventory		30	
	Cost of Goods Sold			30
	(To record fair value of goods returned)			

Related exercise material: **BE5-2, BE5-3, E5-3, E5-4, E5-5, and DO IT! 5-2.**

✔ **The Navigator**

Completing the Accounting Cycle

LEARNING OBJECTIVE **4**

Explain the steps in the accounting cycle for a merchandising company.

Up to this point, we have illustrated the basic entries for transactions relating to purchases and sales in a perpetual inventory system. Now we consider the remaining steps in the accounting cycle for a merchandising company. Each of the required steps described in Chapter 4 for service companies apply to merchandising companies. Appendix 5A to this chapter shows use of a worksheet by a merchandiser (an optional step).

Adjusting Entries

A merchandising company generally has the same types of adjusting entries as a service company. However, a merchandiser using a perpetual system will require one additional adjustment to make the records agree with the actual inventory on hand. Here's why: At the end of each period, for control purposes, a merchandising company that uses a perpetual system will take a physical count of its goods on hand. The company's unadjusted balance in Inventory usually does not agree with the actual amount of inventory on hand. The perpetual inventory records may be incorrect due to recording errors, theft, or waste. Thus, the company needs to adjust the perpetual records to make the recorded inventory amount agree with the inventory on hand. **This involves adjusting Inventory and Cost of Goods Sold.**

For example, suppose that PW Audio Supply has an unadjusted balance of $40,500 in Inventory. Through a physical count, PW Audio Supply determines that its actual merchandise inventory at year-end is $40,000. The company would make an adjusting entry as follows.

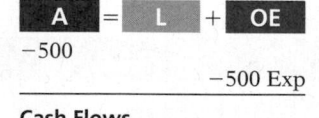
−500
    −500 Exp

Cash Flows
no effect

Cost of Goods Sold		500	
Inventory			500
(To adjust inventory to physical count)			

Closing Entries

A merchandising company, like a service company, closes to Income Summary all accounts that affect net income. In journalizing, the company credits all temporary accounts with debit balances, and debits all temporary accounts with credit balances, as shown below for PW Audio Supply. Note that PW Audio Supply closes Cost of Goods Sold to Income Summary.

Helpful Hint The easiest way to prepare the first two closing entries is to identify the temporary accounts by their balances and then prepare one entry for the credits and one for the debits.

Dec. 31	Sales Revenue		480,000	
	Income Summary			480,000
	(To close income statement accounts with credit balances)			

31	Income Summary	450,000	
	Sales Returns and Allowances		12,000
	Sales Discounts		8,000
	Cost of Goods Sold		316,000
	Salaries and Wages Expense		64,000
	Freight-Out		7,000
	Advertising Expense		16,000
	Utilities Expense		17,000
	Depreciation Expense		8,000
	Insurance Expense		2,000
	(To close income statement accounts with debit balances)		
31	Income Summary	30,000	
	Owner's Capital		30,000
	(To close net income to capital)		
31	Owner's Capital	15,000	
	Owner's Drawings		15,000
	(To close drawings to capital)		

After PW Audio Supply has posted the closing entries, all temporary accounts have zero balances. Also, Owner's Capital has a balance that is carried over to the next period.

Summary of Merchandising Entries

Illustration 5-8 summarizes the entries for the merchandising accounts using a perpetual inventory system.

Illustration 5-8
Daily recurring and adjusting and closing entries

	Transactions	Daily Recurring Entries	Dr.	Cr.
Sales Transactions	Selling merchandise to customers.	Cash or Accounts Receivable	XX	
		Sales Revenue		XX
		Cost of Goods Sold	XX	
		Inventory		XX
	Granting sales returns or allowances to customers.	Sales Returns and Allowances	XX	
		Cash or Accounts Receivable		XX
		Inventory	XX	
		Cost of Goods Sold		XX
	Paying freight costs on sales; FOB destination.	Freight-Out	XX	
		Cash		XX
	Receiving payment from customers within discount period.	Cash	XX	
		Sales Discounts	XX	
		Accounts Receivable		XX
Purchase Transactions	Purchasing merchandise for resale.	Inventory	XX	
		Cash or Accounts Payable		XX
	Paying freight costs on merchandise purchased; FOB shipping point.	Inventory	XX	
		Cash		XX
	Receiving purchase returns or allowances from suppliers.	Cash or Accounts Payable	XX	
		Inventory		XX
	Paying suppliers within discount period.	Accounts Payable	XX	
		Inventory		XX
		Cash		XX

Events	Adjusting and Closing Entries		
Adjust because book amount is higher than the inventory amount determined to be on hand.	Cost of Goods Sold Inventory	XX	 XX
Closing temporary accounts with credit balances.	Sales Revenue Income Summary	XX	 XX

Closing temporary accounts with debit balances.	Income Summary
	    Sales Returns and Allowances
	    Sales Discounts
	    Cost of Goods Sold
	    Freight-Out
	    Expenses
		XX	
			XX
			XX
			XX
			XX
			XX

Illustration 5-8
(*continued*)

> **DO IT!**

Closing Entries

The trial balance of Celine's Sports Wear Shop at December 31 shows Inventory $25,000, Sales Revenue $162,400, Sales Returns and Allowances $4,800, Sales Discounts $3,600, Cost of Goods Sold $110,000, Rent Revenue $6,000, Freight-Out $1,800, Rent Expense $8,800, and Salaries and Wages Expense $22,000. Prepare the closing entries for the above accounts.

Solution

Action Plan

✔ Close all temporary accounts with credit balances to Income Summary by debiting these accounts.

✔ Close all temporary accounts with debit balances, except drawings, to Income Summary by crediting these accounts.

The two closing entries are:

Dec. 31	Sales Revenue	162,400	
	Rent Revenue	6,000	
	Income Summary		168,400
	(To close accounts with credit balances)		
31	Income Summary	151,000	
	Cost of Goods Sold		110,000
	Sales Returns and Allowances		4,800
	Sales Discounts		3,600
	Freight-Out		1,800
	Rent Expense		8,800
	Salaries and Wages Expense		22,000
	(To close accounts with debit balances)		

Related exercise material: **BE5-5, BE5-6, E5-6, E5-7, E5-8, and DO IT! 5-3.**

✔ **The Navigator**

Forms of Financial Statements

LEARNING OBJECTIVE 5

Distinguish between a multiple-step and a single-step income statement.

Merchandising companies widely use the classified balance sheet introduced in Chapter 4 and one of two forms for the income statement. This section explains the use of these financial statements by merchandisers.   .

Multiple-Step Income Statement

The **multiple-step income statement** is so named because it shows several steps in determining net income. Two of these steps relate to the company's principal operating activities. A multiple-step statement also distinguishes between operating and **nonoperating activities**. Finally, the statement also highlights intermediate components of income and shows subgroupings of expenses.

INCOME STATEMENT PRESENTATION OF SALES

The multiple-step income statement begins by presenting **sales revenue**. It then deducts contra revenue accounts—sales returns and allowances, and sales discounts—from sales revenue to arrive at **net sales**. Illustration 5-9 presents the sales revenues section for PW Audio Supply, using assumed data.

Illustration 5-9
Computation of net sales

PW AUDIO SUPPLY		
Income Statement (partial)		
Sales revenues		
Sales revenue		$ 480,000
Less: Sales returns and allowances	$12,000	
Sales discounts	8,000	20,000
Net sales		**$460,000**

GROSS PROFIT

From Illustration 5-1, you learned that companies deduct cost of goods sold from sales revenue to determine **gross profit**. For this computation, companies use **net sales** (which takes into consideration Sales Returns and Allowances and Sales Discounts) as the amount of sales revenue. On the basis of the sales data in Illustration 5-9 (net sales of $460,000) and cost of goods sold under the perpetual inventory system (assume $316,000), PW Audio Supply's gross profit is $144,000, computed as follows.

Alternative Terminology
Gross profit is sometimes referred to as *gross margin*.

Net sales	$ 460,000
Cost of goods sold	316,000
Gross profit	**$144,000**

Illustration 5-10
Computation of gross profit

We also can express a company's gross profit as a percentage, called the **gross profit rate**. To do so, we divide the amount of gross profit by net sales. For PW Audio Supply, the **gross profit rate** is 31.3%, computed as follows.

Gross Profit	÷	Net Sales	=	Gross Profit Rate
$144,000	÷	$460,000	=	31.3%

Illustration 5-11
Gross profit rate formula and computation

Analysts generally consider the gross profit **rate** to be more useful than the gross profit **amount**. The rate expresses a more meaningful (qualitative) relationship between net sales and gross profit. For example, a gross profit of $1,000,000 may sound impressive. But if it is the result of a gross profit rate of only 7%, it is not so impressive. The gross profit rate tells how many cents of each sales dollar go to gross profit.

Gross profit represents the **merchandising profit** of a company. It is not a measure of the overall profitability because operating expenses are not yet deducted. But managers and other interested parties closely watch the amount and trend of gross profit. They compare current gross profit with amounts reported in past periods. They also compare the company's gross profit rate with rates of competitors and with industry averages. Such comparisons provide information about the effectiveness of a company's purchasing function and the soundness of its pricing policies.

OPERATING EXPENSES AND NET INCOME

Operating expenses are the next component in measuring net income for a merchandising company. They are the expenses incurred in the process of earning sales revenue. These expenses are similar in merchandising and service companies. At PW Audio Supply, operating expenses were $114,000. The company determines its net income by subtracting operating expenses from gross profit. Thus, net income is $30,000, as shown below.

Illustration 5-12
Operating expenses in computing net income

Gross profit	$144,000
Operating expenses	**114,000**
Net income	$ 30,000

The net income amount is the so-called "bottom line" of a company's income statement.

NONOPERATING ACTIVITIES

Nonoperating activities consist of various revenues and expenses and gains and losses that are unrelated to the company's main line of operations. When nonoperating items are included, the label "**Income from operations**" (or "Operating income") precedes them. This label clearly identifies the results of the company's normal operations, an amount determined by subtracting cost of goods sold and operating expenses from net sales. The results of nonoperating activities are shown in the categories "**Other revenues and gains**" and "**Other expenses and losses.**" Illustration 5-13 lists examples of each.

Illustration 5-13
Other items of nonoperating activities

Other Revenues and Gains

Interest revenue from notes receivable and marketable securities.

Dividend revenue from investments in common stock.

Rent revenue from subleasing a portion of the store.

Gain from the sale of property, plant, and equipment.

Other Expenses and Losses

Interest expense on notes and loans payable.

Casualty losses from recurring causes, such as vandalism and accidents.

Loss from the sale or abandonment of property, plant, and equipment.

Loss from strikes by employees and suppliers.

Ethics Note

Companies manage earnings in various ways. ConAgra Foods recorded a non-recurring gain for $186 million from the sale of Pilgrim's Pride stock to help meet an earnings projection for the quarter.

Merchandising companies report the nonoperating activities in the income statement immediately after the company's operating activities. Illustration 5-14 shows these sections for PW Audio Supply, using assumed data.

The distinction between operating and nonoperating activities is crucial to many external users of financial data. These users view operating income as sustainable and many nonoperating activities as nonrecurring. Therefore, when forecasting next year's income, analysts put the most weight on this year's operating income, and less weight on this year's nonoperating activities.

PW AUDIO SUPPLY
Income Statement
For the Year Ended December 31, 2014

Calculation of gross profit

Sales		
Sales revenue		$480,000
Less: Sales returns and allowances	$12,000	
Sales discounts	8,000	20,000
Net sales		460,000
Cost of goods sold		316,000
Gross profit		144,000

Calculation of income from operations

Operating expenses		
Salaries and wages expense	64,000	
Utilities expense	17,000	
Advertising expense	16,000	
Depreciation expense	8,000	
Freight-out	7,000	
Insurance expense	2,000	
Total operating expenses		114,000
Income from operations		30,000

Results of nonoperating activities

Other revenues and gains		
Interest revenue	3,000	
Gain on disposal of plant assets	600	3,600
Other expenses and losses		
Interest expense	1,800	
Casualty loss from vandalism	200	2,000
Net income		$ 31,600

ETHICS INSIGHT

Disclosing More Details

After Enron, increased investor criticism and regulator scrutiny forced many companies to improve the clarity of their financial disclosures. For example, IBM began providing more detail regarding its "Other gains and losses." It had previously included these items in its selling, general, and administrative expenses, with little disclosure.

Disclosing other gains and losses in a separate line item on the income statement will not have any effect on bottom-line income. However, analysts complained that burying these details in the selling, general, and administrative expense line reduced their ability to fully understand how well IBM was performing. For example, previously if IBM sold off one of its buildings at a gain, it would include this gain in the selling, general and administrative expense line item, thus reducing that expense. This made it appear that the company had done a better job of controlling operating expenses than it actually had.

As another example, when eBay recently sold the remainder of its investment in Skype to Microsoft, it reported a gain in "Other revenues and gains" of $1.7 billion. Since eBay's total income from operations was $2.4 billion, it was very important that the gain from the Skype sale not be buried in operating income.

ImageRite/Getty Images, Inc.

 Why have investors and analysts demanded more accuracy in isolating "Other gains and losses" from operating items? (See page 270.)

Single-Step Income Statement

Another income statement format is the **single-step income statement**. The statement is so named because only one step—subtracting total expenses from total revenues—is required in determining net income.

In a single-step statement, all data are classified into two categories: (1) **revenues**, which include both operating revenues and other revenues and gains; and (2) **expenses**, which include cost of goods sold, operating expenses, and other expenses and losses. Illustration 5-15 shows a single-step statement for PW Audio Supply.

Illustration 5-15
Single-step income statement

PW AUDIO SUPPLY		
Income Statement		
For the Year Ended December 31, 2014		
Revenues		
Net sales		$460,000
Interest revenue		3,000
Gain on disposal of plant assets		600
Total revenues		463,600
Expenses		
Cost of goods sold	$316,000	
Operating expenses	114,000	
Interest expense	1,800	
Casualty loss from vandalism	200	
Total expenses		432,000
Net income		$ 31,600

There are two primary reasons for using the single-step format. (1) A company does not realize any type of profit or income until total revenues exceed total expenses, so it makes sense to divide the statement into these two categories. (2) The format is simpler and easier to read. *For homework problems, however, you should use the single-step format only when specifically instructed to do so.*

Classified Balance Sheet

In the balance sheet, merchandising companies report inventory as a current asset immediately below accounts receivable. Recall from Chapter 4 that companies generally list current asset items in the order of their closeness to cash (liquidity). Inventory is less close to cash than accounts receivable because the goods must first be sold and then collection made from the customer. Illustration 5-16 presents the assets section of a classified balance sheet for PW Audio Supply.

Illustration 5-16
Assets section of a classified balance sheet

Helpful Hint The $40,000 is the cost of the inventory on hand, not its expected selling price.

PW AUDIO SUPPLY		
Balance Sheet (Partial)		
December 31, 2014		
Assets		
Current assets		
Cash		$ 9,500
Accounts receivable		16,100
Inventory		40,000
Prepaid insurance		1,800
Total current assets		67,400
Property, plant, and equipment		
Equipment	$80,000	
Less: Accumulated depreciation—equipment	24,000	56,000
Total assets		$123,400

> DO IT!

Financial Statement Classifications

You are presented with the following list of accounts from the adjusted trial balance for merchandiser Gorman Company. Indicate in which financial statement and under what classification each of the following would be reported.

Accounts Payable	Interest Payable
Accounts Receivable	Inventory
Accumulated Depreciation—Buildings	Land
Accumulated Depreciation—Equipment	Notes Payable (due in 3 years)
Advertising Expense	Owner's Capital (beginning balance)
Buildings	Owner's Drawings
Cash	Property Taxes Payable
Depreciation Expense	Salaries and Wages Expense
Equipment	Salaries and Wages Payable
Freight-Out	Sales Returns and Allowances
Gain on Disposal of Plant Assets	Sales Revenue
Insurance Expense	Utilities Expense
Interest Expense	

Solution

Action Plan

✔ Review the major sections of the income statement: sales revenues, cost of goods sold, operating expenses, other revenues and gains, and other expenses and losses.

✔ Add net income and investments to beginning capital and deduct drawings to arrive at ending capital in the owner's equity statement.

✔ Review the major sections of the balance sheet, income statement, and owner's equity statement.

Account	Financial Statement	Classification
Accounts Payable	Balance sheet	Current liabilities
Accounts Receivable	Balance sheet	Current assets
Accumulated Depreciation—Buildings	Balance sheet	Property, plant, and equipment
Accumulated Depreciation—Equipment	Balance sheet	Property, plant, and equipment
Advertising Expense	Income statement	Operating expenses
Buildings	Balance sheet	Property, plant, and equipment
Cash	Balance sheet	Current assets
Depreciation Expense	Income statement	Operating expenses
Equipment	Balance sheet	Property, plant, and equipment
Freight-Out	Income statement	Operating expenses
Gain on Disposal of Plant Assets	Income statement	Other revenues and gains
Insurance Expense	Income statement	Operating expenses
Interest Expense	Income statement	Other expenses and losses
Interest Payable	Balance sheet	Current liabilities
Inventory	Balance sheet	Current assets
Land	Balance sheet	Property, plant, and equipment
Notes Payable (due in 3 years)	Balance sheet	Long-term liabilities
Owner's Capital	Owner's equity statement	Beginning balance
Owner's Drawings	Owner's equity statement	Deduction section
Property Taxes Payable	Balance sheet	Current liabilities
Salaries and Wages Expense	Income statement	Operating expenses
Salaries and Wages Payable	Balance sheet	Current liabilities
Sales Returns and Allowances	Income statement	Sales revenues
Sales Revenue	Income statement	Sales revenues
Utilities Expense	Income statement	Operating expenses

Related exercise material: **BE5-7, BE5-8, BE5-9, E5-9, E5-10, E5-12, E5-13, E5-14, and DO IT!** 5-4.

 ✔ The Navigator

> Comprehensive DO IT!

The adjusted trial balance columns of Falcetto Company's worksheet for the year ended December 31, 2014, are as follows.

	Debit		Credit
Cash	14,500	Accumulated Depreciation—	
Accounts Receivable	11,100	Equipment	18,000
Inventory	29,000	Notes Payable	25,000
Prepaid Insurance	2,500	Accounts Payable	10,600
Equipment	95,000	Owner's Capital	81,000
Owner's Drawings	12,000	Sales Revenue	536,800
Sales Returns and Allowances	6,700	Interest Revenue	2,500
Sales Discounts	5,000		673,900
Cost of Goods Sold	363,400		
Freight-Out	7,600		
Advertising Expense	12,000		
Salaries and Wages Expense	56,000		
Utilities Expense	18,000		
Rent Expense	24,000		
Depreciation Expense	9,000		
Insurance Expense	4,500		
Interest Expense	3,600		
	673,900		

Instructions

Prepare a multiple-step income statement for Falcetto Company.

Solution to Comprehensive DO IT!

Action Plan

✔ Remember that the key components of the income statement are net sales, cost of goods sold, gross profit, total operating expenses, and net income (loss). Report these components in the right-hand column of the income statement.

✔ Put nonoperating items after income from operations.

FALCETTO COMPANY
Income Statement
For the Year Ended December 31, 2014

Sales revenues		
Sales revenue		$536,800
Less: Sales returns and allowances	$ 6,700	
Sales discounts	5,000	11,700
Net sales		525,100
Cost of goods sold		363,400
Gross profit		161,700
Operating expenses		
Salaries and wages expense	56,000	
Rent expense	24,000	
Utilities expense	18,000	
Advertising expense	12,000	
Depreciation expense	9,000	
Freight-out	7,600	
Insurance expense	4,500	
Total operating expenses		131,100
Income from operations		30,600
Other revenues and gains		
Interest revenue	2,500	
Other expenses and losses		
Interest expense	3,600	1,100
Net income		$ 29,500

SUMMARY OF LEARNING OBJECTIVES

✔ The Navigator

1 **Identify the differences between service and merchandising companies.** Because of inventory, a merchandising company has sales revenue, cost of goods sold, and gross profit. To account for inventory, a merchandising company must choose between a perpetual and a periodic inventory system.

2 **Explain the recording of purchases under a perpetual inventory system.** The company debits the Inventory account for all purchases of merchandise and freight-in, and credits it for purchase discounts and purchase returns and allowances.

3 **Explain the recording of sales revenues under a perpetual inventory system.** When a merchandising company sells inventory, it debits Accounts Receivable (or Cash) and credits Sales Revenue for the **selling price** of the merchandise. At the same time, it debits Cost of Goods Sold and credits Inventory for the **cost** of the inventory items sold. Sales Returns and Allowances and Sales Discounts are debited and are contra revenue accounts.

4 **Explain the steps in the accounting cycle for a merchandising company.** Each of the required steps in the accounting cycle for a service company applies to a merchandising company. A worksheet is again an optional step. Under a perpetual inventory system, the company must adjust the Inventory account to agree with the physical count.

5 **Distinguish between a multiple-step and a single-step income statement.** A multiple-step income statement shows numerous steps in determining net income, including nonoperating activities sections. A single-step income statement classifies all data under two categories, revenues or expenses, and determines net income in one step.

GLOSSARY

Contra revenue account An account that is offset against a revenue account on the income statement. (p. 228).

Cost of goods sold The total cost of merchandise sold during the period. (p. 218).

FOB destination Freight terms indicating that the seller places the goods free on board to the buyer's place of business, and the seller pays the freight. (p. 222).

FOB shipping point Freight terms indicating that the seller places goods free on board the carrier, and the buyer pays the freight costs. (p. 222).

Gross profit The excess of net sales over the cost of goods sold. (p. 233).

Gross profit rate Gross profit expressed as a percentage, by dividing the amount of gross profit by net sales. (p. 233).

Income from operations Income from a company's principal operating activity; determined by subtracting cost of goods sold and operating expenses from net sales. (p. 234).

Multiple-step income statement An income statement that shows several steps in determining net income. (p. 232).

Net sales Sales revenue less sales returns and allowances and less sales discounts. (p. 233).

Nonoperating activities Various revenues, expenses, gains, and losses that are unrelated to a company's main line of operations. (p. 234).

Operating expenses Expenses incurred in the process of earning sales revenue. (p. 234).

Other expenses and losses A nonoperating-activities section of the income statement that shows expenses and losses unrelated to the company's main line of operations. (p. 234).

Other revenues and gains A nonoperating-activities section of the income statement that shows revenues and gains unrelated to the company's main line of operations. (p. 234).

Periodic inventory system An inventory system under which the company does not keep detailed inventory records throughout the accounting period but determines the cost of goods sold only at the end of an accounting period. (p. 220).

Perpetual inventory system An inventory system under which the company keeps detailed records of the cost of each inventory purchase and sale, and the records continuously show the inventory that should be on hand. (p. 219).

Purchase allowance A deduction made to the selling price of merchandise, granted by the seller so that the buyer will keep the merchandise. (p. 223).

Purchase discount A cash discount claimed by a buyer for prompt payment of a balance due. (p. 224).

Purchase invoice A document that supports each credit purchase. (p. 221).

Purchase return A return of goods from the buyer to the seller for a cash or credit refund. (p. 223).

Sales discount A reduction given by a seller for prompt payment of a credit sale. (p. 228).

Sales invoice A document that supports each credit sale. (p. 226).

Sales returns and allowances Purchase returns and allowances from the seller's perspective. See *Purchase return* and *Purchase allowance*, above. (p. 227).

Sales revenue (Sales) The primary source of revenue in a merchandising company. (p. 218).

Single-step income statement An income statement that shows only one step in determining net income. (p. 236).

APPENDIX 5A   Worksheet for a Merchandising Company—Perpetual Inventory

Using a Worksheet

LEARNING OBJECTIVE 6

Prepare a worksheet for a merchandising company.

As indicated in Chapter 4, a worksheet enables companies to prepare financial statements before they journalize and post adjusting entries. The steps in preparing a worksheet for a merchandising company are the same as for a service company (see pages 163–165). Illustration 5A-1 shows the worksheet for PW Audio Supply (excluding nonoperating items). The unique accounts for a merchandiser using a **perpetual inventory system** are in red.

PW Audio Supply.xls

Home   Insert   Page Layout   Formulas   Data   Review   View

P18   fx

PW AUDIO SUPPLY
Worksheet
For the Year Ended December 31, 2014

Accounts	Trial Balance Dr.	Trial Balance Cr.	Adjustments Dr.	Adjustments Cr.	Adjusted Trial Balance Dr.	Adjusted Trial Balance Cr.	Income Statement Dr.	Income Statement Cr.	Balance Sheet Dr.	Balance Sheet Cr.
Cash	9,500				9,500				9,500	
Accounts Receivable	16,100				16,100				16,100	
Inventory	40,500			(a) 500	40,000				40,000	
Prepaid Insurance	3,800			(b) 2,000	1,800				1,800	
Equipment	80,000				80,000				80,000	
Accumulated Depreciation— Equipment		16,000		(c) 8,000		24,000				24,000
Accounts Payable		20,400				20,400				20,400
Owner's Capital		83,000				83,000				83,000
Owner's Drawings	15,000				15,000				15,000	
Sales Revenue		480,000				480,000		480,000		
Sales Returns and Allowances	12,000				12,000		12,000			
Sales Discounts	8,000				8,000		8,000			
Cost of Goods Sold	315,500		(a) 500		316,000		316,000			
Freight-Out	7,000				7,000		7,000			
Advertising Expense	16,000				16,000		16,000			
Salaries and Wages Expense	59,000		(d) 5,000		64,000		64,000			
Utilities Expense	17,000				17,000		17,000			
Totals	599,400	599,400								
Insurance Expense			(b) 2,000		2,000		2,000			
Depreciation Expense			(c) 8,000		8,000		8,000			
Salaries and Wages Payable				(d) 5,000		5,000				5,000
Totals			15,500	15,500	612,400	612,400	450,000	480,000	162,400	132,400
Net Income							30,000			30,000
Totals							480,000	480,000	162,400	162,400

Key: (a) Adjustment to inventory on hand. (b) Insurance expired. (c) Depreciation expense. (d) Salaries accrued.

Illustration 5A-1
Worksheet for merchandising company—perpetual inventory system

TRIAL BALANCE COLUMNS

Data for the trial balance come from the ledger balances of PW Audio Supply at December 31. The amount shown for Inventory, $40,500, is the year-end inventory amount from the perpetual inventory system.

ADJUSTMENTS COLUMNS

A merchandising company generally has the same types of adjustments as a service company. As you see in the worksheet, adjustments (b), (c), and (d) are for insurance, depreciation, and salaries. Pioneer Advertising Agency, as illustrated in Chapters 3 and 4, also had these adjustments. Adjustment (a) was required to adjust the perpetual inventory carrying amount to the actual count.

After PW Audio Supply enters all adjustments data on the worksheet, it establishes the equality of the adjustments column totals. It then extends the balances in all accounts to the adjusted trial balance columns.

ADJUSTED TRIAL BALANCE

The adjusted trial balance shows the balance of all accounts after adjustment at the end of the accounting period.

INCOME STATEMENT COLUMNS

Next, the merchandising company transfers the accounts and balances that affect the income statement from the adjusted trial balance columns to the income statement columns. PW Audio Supply shows Sales Revenue of $480,000 in the credit column. It shows the contra revenue accounts Sales Returns and Allowances $12,000 and Sales Discounts $8,000 in the debit column. The difference of $460,000 is the net sales shown on the income statement (Illustration 5-14, page 235).

Finally, the company totals all the credits in the income statement column and compares those totals to the total of the debits in the income statement column. If the credits exceed the debits, the company has net income. PW Audio Supply has net income of $30,000. If the debits exceed the credits, the company would report a net loss.

BALANCE SHEET COLUMNS

The major difference between the balance sheets of a service company and a merchandiser is inventory. PW Audio Supply shows the ending inventory amount of $40,000 in the balance sheet debit column. The information to prepare the owner's equity statement is also found in these columns. That is, the Owner's Capital account is $83,000. Owner's Drawings are $15,000. Net income results when the total of the debit column exceeds the total of the credit column in the balance sheet columns. A net loss results when the total of the credits exceeds the total of the debit balances.

SUMMARY OF LEARNING OBJECTIVE FOR APPENDIX 5A

The Navigator

6 Prepare a worksheet for a merchandising company. The steps in preparing a worksheet for a merchandising company are the same as for a service company. The unique accounts for a merchandiser are Inventory, Sales Revenue, Sales Returns and Allowances, Sales Discounts, and Cost of Goods Sold.

APPENDIX 5B   Periodic Inventory System

As described in this chapter, companies may use one of two basic systems of accounting for inventories: (1) the perpetual inventory system or (2) the periodic inventory system. In the chapter, we focused on the characteristics of the perpetual inventory system. In this appendix, we discuss and illustrate the **periodic**

LEARNING OBJECTIVE   7

Explain the recording of purchases and sales of inventory under a periodic inventory system.

inventory system. One key difference between the two systems is the point at which the company computes cost of goods sold. For a visual reminder of this difference, refer back to Illustration 5-5 (on page 220).

Determining Cost of Goods Sold Under a Periodic System

Determining cost of goods sold is different when a periodic inventory system is used rather than a perpetual system. As you have seen, a company using a **perpetual system** makes an entry to record cost of goods sold and to reduce inventory each time a sale is made. A company using a **periodic system** does not determine cost of goods sold until the end of the period. At the end of the period, the company performs a count to determine the ending balance of inventory. It then **calculates cost of goods sold by subtracting ending inventory from the goods available for sale**. Goods available for sale is the sum of beginning inventory plus purchases, as shown in Illustration 5B-1.

Illustration 5B-1
Basic formula for cost of goods sold using the periodic system

	Beginning Inventory
+	Cost of Goods Purchased
	Cost of Goods Available for Sale
−	Ending Inventory
	Cost of Goods Sold

Another difference between the two approaches is that the perpetual system directly adjusts the Inventory account for any transaction that affects inventory (such as freight costs, returns, and discounts). The periodic system does not do this. Instead, it creates different accounts for purchases, freight costs, returns, and discounts. These various accounts are shown in Illustration 5B-2, which presents the calculation of cost of goods sold for PW Audio Supply using the periodic approach.

Illustration 5B-2
Cost of goods sold for a merchandiser using a periodic inventory system

PW AUDIO SUPPLY
Cost of Goods Sold
For the Year Ended December 31, 2014

Cost of goods sold			
Inventory, January 1			$ 36,000
Purchases		$325,000	
Less: Purchase returns and allowances	$10,400		
Purchase discounts	6,800	17,200	
Net purchases		307,800	
Add: Freight-in		12,200	
Cost of goods purchased			320,000
Cost of goods available for sale			356,000
Inventory, December 31			40,000
Cost of goods sold			$316,000

Helpful Hint The far right column identifies the primary items that make up cost of goods sold of $316,000. The middle column explains cost of goods purchased of $320,000. The left column reports contra purchase items of $17,200.

Note that the basic elements from Illustration 5B-1 are highlighted in Illustration 5B-2. You will learn more in Chapter 6 about how to determine cost of goods sold using the periodic system.

The use of the periodic inventory system does not affect the form of presentation in the balance sheet. As under the perpetual system, a company reports inventory in the current assets section.

Recording Merchandise Transactions

In a **periodic inventory system**, companies record revenues from the sale of merchandise when sales are made, just as in a perpetual system. Unlike the perpetual system, however, companies **do not attempt on the date of sale to record the cost of the merchandise sold**. Instead, they take a physical inventory count at the **end of the period** to determine (1) the cost of the merchandise then on hand and (2) the cost of the goods sold during the period. And, **under a periodic system, companies record purchases of merchandise in the Purchases account rather than the Inventory account**. Also, in a periodic system, purchase returns and allowances, purchase discounts, and freight costs on purchases are recorded in separate accounts.

To illustrate the recording of merchandise transactions under a periodic inventory system, we will use purchase/sale transactions between PW Audio Supply and Sauk Stereo, as illustrated for the perpetual inventory system in this chapter.

Recording Purchases of Merchandise

On the basis of the sales invoice (Illustration 5-6, shown on page 222) and receipt of the merchandise ordered from PW Audio Supply, Sauk Stereo records the $3,800 purchase as follows.

Helpful Hint Be careful not to debit purchases of equipment or supplies to a Purchases account.

May 4	Purchases	3,800	
	Accounts Payable		3,800
	(To record goods purchased on account from PW Audio Supply)		

Purchases is a temporary account whose normal balance is a debit.

FREIGHT COSTS

When the purchaser directly incurs the freight costs, it debits the account Freight-In (or Transportation-In). For example, if Sauk Stereo pays Public Carrier Co. $150 for freight charges on its purchase from PW Audio Supply on May 6, the entry on Sauk Stereo's books is:

Alternative Terminology Freight-In is also called *Transportation-In.*

May 6	Freight-In (Transportation-In)	150	
	Cash		150
	(To record payment of freight on goods purchased)		

Like Purchases, Freight-In is a temporary account whose normal balance is a debit. **Freight-In is part of cost of goods purchased.** The reason is that cost of goods purchased should include any freight charges necessary to bring the goods to the purchaser. Freight costs are not subject to a purchase discount. Purchase discounts apply only to the invoice cost of the merchandise.

PURCHASE RETURNS AND ALLOWANCES

Sauk Stereo returns $300 of goods to PW Audio Supply and prepares the following entry to recognize the return.

May 8	Accounts Payable	300	
	Purchase Returns and Allowances		300
	(To record return of goods purchased		
	from PW Audio Supply)		

Purchase Returns and Allowances is a temporary account whose normal balance is a credit.

PURCHASE DISCOUNTS

On May 14, Sauk Stereo pays the balance due on account to PW Audio Supply, taking the 2% cash discount allowed by PW Audio Supply for payment within 10 days. Sauk Stereo records the payment and discount as follows.

May 14	Accounts Payable ($3,800 − $300)	3,500	
	Purchase Discounts ($3,500 × .02)		70
	Cash		3,430
	(To record payment within the		
	discount period)		

Purchase Discounts is a temporary account whose normal balance is a credit.

Recording Sales of Merchandise

The seller, PW Audio Supply, records the sale of $3,800 of merchandise to Sauk Stereo on May 4 (sales invoice No. 731, Illustration 5-6, page 222) as follows.

May 4	Accounts Receivable	3,800	
	Sales Revenue		3,800
	(To record credit sales per invoice #731		
	to Sauk Stereo)		

SALES RETURNS AND ALLOWANCES

To record the returned goods received from Sauk Stereo on May 8, PW Audio Supply records the $300 sales return as follows.

May 8	Sales Returns and Allowances	300	
	Accounts Receivable		300
	(To record credit granted to Sauk Stereo		
	for returned goods)		

SALES DISCOUNTS

On May 14, PW Audio Supply receives payment of $3,430 on account from Sauk Stereo. PW Audio Supply honors the 2% cash discount and records the payment of Sauk Stereo's account receivable in full as follows.

May 14	Cash	3,430	
	Sales Discounts ($3,500 × .02)	70	
	Accounts Receivable ($3,800 − $300)		3,500
	(To record collection within 2/10, n/30		
	discount period from Sauk Stereo)		

COMPARISON OF ENTRIES—PERPETUAL VS. PERIODIC

Illustration 5B-3 summarizes the periodic inventory entries shown in this appendix and compares them to the perpetual-system entries from the chapter. Entries that differ in the two systems are shown in color.

ENTRIES ON SAUK STEREO'S BOOKS					
Transaction	**Perpetual Inventory System**		**Periodic Inventory System**		
May 4 Purchase of merchandise on credit.	Inventory Accounts Payable	3,800 3,800	Purchases Accounts Payable	3,800 3,800	
6 Freight costs on purchases.	Inventory Cash	150 150	Freight-In Cash	150 150	
8 Purchase returns and allowances.	Accounts Payable Inventory	300 300	Accounts Payable Purchase Returns and Allowances	300 300	
14 Payment on account with a discount.	Accounts Payable Cash Inventory	3,500 3,430 70	Accounts Payable Cash Purchase Discounts	3,500 3,430 70	

ENTRIES ON PW AUDIO SUPPLY'S BOOKS					
Transaction	**Perpetual Inventory System**		**Periodic Inventory System**		
May 4 Sale of merchandise on credit.	Accounts Receivable Sales Revenue	3,800 3,800	Accounts Receivable Sales Revenue	3,800 3,800	
	Cost of Goods Sold Inventory	2,400 2,400	No entry for cost of goods sold		
8 Return of merchandise sold.	Sales Returns and Allowances Accounts Receivable	300 300	Sales Returns and Allowances Accounts Receivable	300 300	
	Inventory Cost of Goods Sold	140 140	No entry		
14 Cash received on account with a discount.	Cash Sales Discounts Accounts Receivable	3,430 70 3,500	Cash Sales Discounts Accounts Receivable	3,430 70 3,500	

Illustration 5B-3
Comparison of entries for perpetual and periodic inventory systems

Journalizing and Posting Closing Entries

For a merchandising company, like a service company, all accounts that affect the determination of net income are closed to Income Summary. Data for the preparation of closing entries may be obtained from the income statement columns of the worksheet. In journalizing, all debit column amounts are credited, and all credit columns amounts are debited. To close the merchandise inventory in a periodic inventory system:

1. The beginning inventory balance is debited to Income Summary and credited to Inventory.

2. The ending inventory balance is debited to Inventory and credited to Income Summary.

The two entries for PW Audio Supply are:

(1)

Dec. 31	Income Summary	36,000	
	Inventory		36,000
	(To close beginning inventory)		

(2)

31	Inventory	40,000	
	Income Summary		40,000
	(To record ending inventory)		

After posting, the Inventory and Income Summary accounts will show the following.

Illustration 5B-4
Posting closing entries for merchandise inventory

Inventory		Income Summary	
1/1 Bal. 36,000	12/31 Close **36,000**	12/31 Close **36,000**	12/31 Close **40,000**
12/31 Close **40,000**			
12/31 Bal. 40,000			

Often, the closing of inventory is included with other closing entries, as shown below for PW Audio Supply.

Helpful Hint Except for merchandise inventory, the easiest way to prepare the first two closing entries is to identify the temporary accounts by their balances and then prepare one entry for the credits and one for the debits.

Helpful Hint Close inventory with other accounts in homework problems unless stated otherwise.

			Debit	Credit
Dec. 31	**Inventory (Dec. 31)**		**40,000**	
	Sales Revenue		480,000	
	Purchase Returns and Allowances		10,400	
	Purchase Discounts		6,800	
	Income Summary			537,200
	(To record ending inventory and close accounts with credit balances)			
31	Income Summary		507,200	
	Inventory (Jan. 1)			**36,000**
	Sales Returns and Allowances			12,000
	Sales Discounts			8,000
	Purchases			325,000
	Freight-In			12,200
	Salaries and Wages Expense			64,000
	Freight-Out			7,000
	Advertising Expense			16,000
	Utilities Expense			17,000
	Depreciation Expense			8,000
	Insurance Expense			2,000
	(To close beginning inventory and other income statement accounts with debit balances)			
31	Income Summary		30,000	
	Owner's Capital			30,000
	(To transfer net income to capital)			
31	Owner's Capital		15,000	
	Owner's Drawings			15,000
	(To close drawings to capital)			

After the closing entries are posted, all temporary accounts have zero balances. In addition, Owner's Capital has a credit balance of $98,000: beginning balance + net income − drawings ($83,000 + $30,000 − $15,000).

Using a Worksheet

As indicated in Chapter 4, a worksheet enables companies to prepare financial statements before journalizing and posting adjusting entries. The steps in preparing a worksheet for a merchandising company are the same as they are for a service company (see pages 163–165).

TRIAL BALANCE COLUMNS
Data for the trial balance come from the ledger balances of PW Audio Supply at December 31. The amount shown for Inventory, $36,000, is the beginning inventory amount from the periodic inventory system.

ADJUSTMENTS COLUMNS

A merchandising company generally has the same types of adjustments as a service company. As you see in the worksheet in Illustration 5B-5, adjustments (a), (b), and (c) are for insurance, depreciation, and salaries and wages. These adjustments were also required for Pioneer Advertising Agency, as illustrated in Chapters 3 and 4. The unique accounts for a merchandiser using a **periodic inventory system** are shown in capital red letters. Note, however, that the worksheet excludes nonoperating items.

After all adjustment data are entered on the worksheet, the equality of the adjustment column totals is established. The balances in all accounts are then extended to the adjusted trial balance columns.

Illustration 5B-5
Worksheet for merchandising company—periodic inventory system

PW Audio Supply.xls

P18

PW AUDIO SUPPLY
Worksheet
For the Year Ended December 31, 2014

Accounts	Trial Balance Dr.	Trial Balance Cr.	Adjustments Dr.	Adjustments Cr.	Adjusted Trial Balance Dr.	Adjusted Trial Balance Cr.	Income Statement Dr.	Income Statement Cr.	Balance Sheet Dr.	Balance Sheet Cr.
Cash	9,500				9,500				9,500	
Accounts Receivable	16,100				16,100				16,100	
INVENTORY	36,000				36,000		36,000	40,000	40,000	
Prepaid Insurance	3,800			(a) 2,000	1,800				1,800	
Equipment	80,000				80,000				80,000	
Accumulated Depreciation—Equipment		16,000		(b) 8,000		24,000				24,000
Accounts Payable		20,400				20,400				20,400
Owner's Capital		83,000				83,000				83,000
Owner's Drawings	15,000				15,000				15,000	
SALES REVENUE		480,000				480,000		480,000		
SALES RETURNS AND ALLOWANCES	12,000				12,000		12,000			
SALES DISCOUNTS	8,000				8,000		8,000			
PURCHASES	325,000				325,000		325,000			
PURCHASE RETURNS AND ALLOWANCES		10,400				10,400		10,400		
PURCHASE DISCOUNTS		6,800				6,800		6,800		
FREIGHT-IN	12,200				12,200		12,200			
Freight-Out	7,000				7,000		7,000			
Advertising Expense	16,000				16,000		16,000			
Salaries and Wages Expense	59,000		(c) 5,000		64,000		64,000			
Utilities Expense	17,000				17,000		17,000			
Totals	616,600	616,600								
Insurance Expense			(a) 2,000		2,000		2,000			
Depreciation Expense			(b) 8,000		8,000		8,000			
Salaries and Wages Payable				(c) 5,000		5,000				5,000
Totals			15,000	15,000	629,600	629,600	507,200	537,200	162,400	132,400
Net Income							30,000			30,000
Totals							537,200	537,200	162,400	162,400

Key: (a) Insurance expired. (b) Depreciation expense. (c) Salaries and wages accrued.

INCOME STATEMENT COLUMNS

Next, PW Audio Supply transfers the accounts and balances that affect the income statement from the adjusted trial balance columns to the income statements columns. The company shows Sales Revenue of $480,000 in the credit column. It shows the contra revenue accounts, Sales Returns and Allowances of $12,000 and Sales Discounts of $8,000 in the debit column. The difference of $460,000 is the net sales shown on the income statement (Illustration 5-9, page 233). Similarly, Purchases of $325,000 and Freight-In of $12,200 are extended to the debit column. The contra purchase accounts, Purchase Returns and Allowances of $10,400 and Purchase Discounts of $6,800, are extended to the credit columns.

The worksheet procedures for the Inventory account merit specific comment. The procedures are:

1. The beginning balance, $36,000, is extended from the adjusted trial balance column to the **income statement debit column**. From there it can be added in reporting cost of goods available for sale in the income statement.

2. The ending inventory, $40,000, is added to the worksheet by an **income statement credit and a balance sheet debit**. The credit makes it possible to deduct ending inventory from the cost of goods available for sale in the income statement to determine cost of goods sold. The debit means the ending inventory can be reported as an asset on the balance sheet.

These two procedures are specifically illustrated below:

Illustration 5B-6
Worksheet procedures for inventories

	Income Statement		Balance Sheet	
	Dr.	Cr.	Dr.	Cr.
Inventory	(1) 36,000	40,000 ◄─── (2) ───► 40,000		

The computation for cost of goods sold, taken from the income statement column in Illustration 5B-5, is as follows.

Illustration 5B-7
Computation of cost of goods sold from worksheet columns

Debit Column		Credit Column	
Beginning inventory	$ 36,000	Ending inventory	$40,000
Purchases	325,000	Purchase returns and allowances	10,400
Freight-in	12,200	Purchase discounts	6,800
Total debits	373,200	Total credits	$57,200
Less: Total credits	57,200		
Cost of goods sold	**$316,000**		

Helpful Hint In a periodic system, cost of goods sold is a computation—it is not a separate account with a balance.

Finally, PW Audio Supply totals all the credits in the income statement column and compares these totals to the total of the debits in the income statement column. If the credits exceed the debits, the company has net income. PW Audio Supply has net income of $30,000. If the debits exceed the credits, the company would report a net loss.

BALANCE SHEET COLUMNS

The major difference between the balance sheets of a service company and a merchandising company is inventory. PW Audio Supply shows ending inventory of $40,000 in the balance sheet debit column. The information to prepare the owner's equity statement is also found in these columns. That is, the Owner's Capital account is $83,000. Owner's Drawings are $15,000. Net income results when the total of the debit column exceeds the total of the credit column in the balance sheet columns. A net loss results when the total of the credits exceeds the total of the debit balances.

SUMMARY OF LEARNING OBJECTIVE FOR APPENDIX 5B

7 Explain the recording of purchases and sales of inventory under a periodic inventory system. In recording purchases under a periodic system, companies must make entries for (a) cash and credit purchases, (b) purchase returns and allowances, (c) purchase discounts, and (d) freight costs. In recording sales, companies must make entries for (a) cash and credit sales, (b) sales returns and allowances, and (c) sales discounts.

 **Self-Test, Brief Exercises, Exercises, Problem Set A, and many more components are available for practice in *WileyPLUS*.**

*Note: All asterisked Questions, Exercises, and Problems relate to material in the appendices to the chapter.

SELF-TEST QUESTIONS

Answers are on page 271.

(LO 1) **1.** Gross profit will result if:
- **(a)** operating expenses are less than net income.
- **(b)** sales revenues are greater than operating expenses.
- **(c)** sales revenues are greater than cost of goods sold.
- **(d)** operating expenses are greater than cost of goods sold.

(LO 2) **2.** Under a perpetual inventory system, when goods are purchased for resale by a company:
- **(a)** purchases on account are debited to Inventory.
- **(b)** purchases on account are debited to Purchases.
- **(c)** purchase returns are debited to Purchase Returns and Allowances.
- **(d)** freight costs are debited to Freight-Out.

(LO 3) **3.** The sales accounts that normally have a debit balance are:
- **(a)** Sales Discounts.
- **(b)** Sales Returns and Allowances.
- **(c)** Both (a) and (b).
- **(d)** Neither (a) nor (b).

(LO 3) **4.** A credit sale of $750 is made on June 13, terms 2/10, net/30. A return of $50 is granted on June 16. The amount received as payment in full on June 23 is:
- **(a)** $700.
- **(c)** $685.
- **(b)** $686.
- **(d)** $650.

(LO 2) **5.** Which of the following accounts will normally appear in the ledger of a merchandising company that uses a perpetual inventory system?
- **(a)** Purchases.
- **(c)** Cost of Goods Sold.
- **(b)** Freight-In.
- **(d)** Purchase Discounts.

(LO 3) **6.** To record the sale of goods for cash in a perpetual inventory system:
- **(a)** only one journal entry is necessary to record cost of goods sold and reduction of inventory.
- **(b)** only one journal entry is necessary to record the receipt of cash and the sales revenue.
- **(c)** two journal entries are necessary: one to record the receipt of cash and sales revenue, and one to record the cost of goods sold and reduction of inventory.
- **(d)** two journal entries are necessary: one to record the receipt of cash and reduction of inventory, and one to record the cost of goods sold and sales revenue.

7. The steps in the accounting cycle for a merchandising (LO 4) company are the same as those in a service company **except:**
- **(a)** an additional adjusting journal entry for inventory may be needed in a merchandising company.
- **(b)** closing journal entries are not required for a merchandising company.
- **(c)** a post-closing trial balance is not required for a merchandising company.
- **(d)** a multiple-step income statement is required for a merchandising company.

8. The multiple-step income statement for a merchan- (LO 5) dising company shows each of the following features **except:**
- **(a)** gross profit.
- **(b)** cost of goods sold.
- **(c)** a sales revenue section.
- **(d)** an investing activities section.

9. If sales revenues are $400,000, cost of goods sold is (LO 5) $310,000, and operating expenses are $60,000, the gross profit is:
- **(a)** $30,000.
- **(c)** $340,000.
- **(b)** $90,000.
- **(d)** $400,000.

10. A single-step income statement: (LO 5)
- **(a)** reports gross profit.
- **(b)** does not report cost of goods sold.
- **(c)** reports sales revenues and "Other revenues and gains" in the revenues section of the income statement.
- **(d)** reports operating income separately.

11. Which of the following appears on both a single-step (LO 5) and a multiple-step income statement?
- **(a)** Inventory.
- **(b)** Gross profit.
- **(c)** Income from operations.
- **(d)** Cost of goods sold.

(LO 6) *12. In a worksheet using a perpetual inventory system, Inventory is shown in the following columns:
  (a) adjusted trial balance debit and balance sheet debit.
  (b) income statement debit and balance sheet debit.
  (c) income statement credit and balance sheet debit.
  (d) income statement credit and adjusted trial balance debit.

(LO 7) *13. In determining cost of goods sold in a periodic system:
  (a) purchase discounts are deducted from net purchases.
  (b) freight-out is added to net purchases.
  (c) purchase returns and allowances are deducted from net purchases.
  (d) freight-in is added to net purchases.

*14. If beginning inventory is $60,000, cost of goods pur- (LO 7) chased is $380,000, and ending inventory is $50,000, cost of goods sold is:
  (a) $390,000.   (c) $330,000.
  (b) $370,000.   (d) $420,000.

*15. When goods are purchased for resale by a company (LO 7) using a periodic inventory system:
  (a) purchases on account are debited to Inventory.
  (b) purchases on account are debited to Purchases.
  (c) purchase returns are debited to Purchase Returns and Allowances.
  (d) freight costs are debited to Purchases.

Go to the book's companion website, www.wiley.com/college/weygandt, for additional Self-Test Questions.

 The Navigator

QUESTIONS

1. (a) "The steps in the accounting cycle for a merchandising company are different from the accounting cycle for a service company." Do you agree or disagree? (b) Is the measurement of net income for a merchandising company conceptually the same as for a service company? Explain.

2. Why is the normal operating cycle for a merchandising company likely to be longer than for a service company?

3. (a) How do the components of revenues and expenses differ between merchandising and service companies? (b) Explain the income measurement process in a merchandising company.

4. How does income measurement differ between a merchandising and a service company?

5. When is cost of goods sold determined in a perpetual inventory system?

6. Distinguish between FOB shipping point and FOB destination. Identify the freight terms that will result in a debit to Inventory by the buyer and a debit to Freight-Out by the seller.

7. Explain the meaning of the credit terms 2/10, n/30.

8. Goods costing $2,000 are purchased on account on July 15 with credit terms of 2/10, n/30. On July 18, a $200 credit memo is received from the supplier for damaged goods. Give the journal entry on July 24 to record payment of the balance due within the discount period using a perpetual inventory system.

9. Ming Xu believes revenues from credit sales may be recorded before they are collected in cash. Do you agree? Explain.

10. (a) What is the primary source document for recording (1) cash sales, (2) credit sales. (b) Using XXs for amounts, give the journal entry for each of the transactions in part (a).

11. A credit sale is made on July 10 for $900, terms 2/10, n/30. On July 12, $100 of goods are returned for credit. Give the journal entry on July 19 to record the receipt of the balance due within the discount period.

12. Explain why the Inventory account will usually require adjustment at year-end.

13. Prepare the closing entries for the Sales Revenue account, assuming a balance of $200,000 and the Cost of Goods Sold account with a $145,000 balance.

14. What merchandising account(s) will appear in the post-closing trial balance?

15. Minnick Co. has sales revenue of $105,000, cost of goods sold of $70,000, and operating expenses of $20,000. What is its gross profit and its gross profit rate?

16. Paul Scott Company reports net sales of $800,000, gross profit of $370,000, and net income of $240,000. What are its operating expenses?

17. Identify the distinguishing features of an income statement for a merchandising company.

18. Identify the sections of a multiple-step income statement that relate to (a) operating activities, and (b) nonoperating activities.

19. How does the single-step form of income statement differ from the multiple-step form?

20. Determine Apple's gross profit rate for 2011 and 2010. Indicate whether it increased or decreased from 2010 to 2011.

*21. Indicate the columns of the worksheet in a perpetual system in which (a) inventory and (b) cost of goods sold will be shown.

*22. Identify the accounts that are added to or deducted from Purchases in a periodic system to determine the cost of goods purchased. For each account, indicate whether it is added or deducted.

*23. Goods costing $3,000 are purchased on account on July 15 with credit terms of 2/10, n/30. On July 18, a $200 credit was received from the supplier for damaged goods. Give the journal entry on July 24 to record payment of the balance due within the discount period, assuming a periodic inventory system.

BRIEF EXERCISES

BE5-1 Presented below are the components in Gates Company's income statement. Determine the missing amounts.

	Sales Revenue	Cost of Goods Sold	Gross Profit	Operating Expenses	Net Income
(a)	$75,000	?	$30,000	?	$10,800
(b)	$108,000	$70,000	?	?	$29,500
(c)	?	$83,900	$79,600	$39,500	?

Compute missing amounts in determining net income.
(LO 1)

BE5-2 Radomir Company buys merchandise on account from Lemke Company. The selling price of the goods is $780, and the cost of the goods is $470. Both companies use perpetual inventory systems. Journalize the transaction on the books of both companies.

Journalize perpetual inventory entries.
(LO 2, 3)

BE5-3 Prepare the journal entries to record the following transactions on Kwang Company's books using a perpetual inventory system.

Journalize sales transactions.
(LO 3)

(a) On March 2, Kwang Company sold $900,000 of merchandise to Sensat Company, terms 2/10, n/30. The cost of the merchandise sold was $620,000.

(b) On March 6, Sensat Company returned $90,000 of the merchandise purchased on March 2. The cost of the returned merchandise was $62,000.

(c) On March 12, Kwang Company received the balance due from Sensat Company.

BE5-4 From the information in BE5-3, prepare the journal entries to record these transactions on Sensat Company's books under a perpetual inventory system.

Journalize purchase transactions.
(LO 2)

BE5-5 At year-end, the perpetual inventory records of Litwin Company showed merchandise inventory of $98,000. The company determined, however, that its actual inventory on hand was $95,700. Record the necessary adjusting entry.

Prepare adjusting entry for inventory.
(LO 4)

BE5-6 Hudson Company has the following account balances: Sales Revenue $195,000, Sales Discounts $2,000, Cost of Goods Sold $117,000, and Inventory $40,000. Prepare the entries to record the closing of these items to Income Summary.

Prepare closing entries for accounts.
(LO 4)

BE5-7 Arndt Company provides the following information for the month ended October 31, 2014: sales on credit $280,000, cash sales $100,000, sales discounts $5,000, and sales returns and allowances $11,000. Prepare the sales revenues section of the income statement based on this information.

Prepare sales revenues section of income statement.
(LO 5)

BE5-8 ———— Explain where each of the following items would appear on (1) a multiple-step income statement, and on (2) a single-step income statement: (a) gain on sale of equipment, (b) interest expense, (c) casualty loss from vandalism, and (d) cost of goods sold.

Contrast presentation in multiple-step and single-step income statements.
(LO 5)

BE5-9 Assume Kader Company has the following reported amounts: Sales revenue $510,000, Sales returns and allowances $15,000, Cost of goods sold $330,000, and Operating expenses $110,000. Compute the following: (a) net sales, (b) gross profit, (c) income from operations, and (d) gross profit rate. (Round to one decimal place.)

Compute net sales, gross profit, income from operations, and gross profit rate.
(LO 5)

*BE5-10 Presented below is the format of the worksheet using the perpetual inventory system presented in Appendix 5A.

Identify worksheet columns for selected accounts.
(LO 6)

Trial Balance		Adjustments		Adjusted Trial Balance		Income Statement		Balance Sheet	
Dr.	Cr.	Dr.	Cr.	Dr.	Cr.	Dr.	Cr.	Dr.	Cr.

Indicate where the following items will appear on the worksheet: (a) Cash, (b) Inventory, (c) Sales revenue, and (d) Cost of goods sold.

Example:
Cash: Trial balance debit column; Adjusted trial balance debit column; and Balance sheet debit column.

Compute net purchases and cost of goods purchased.
(LO 7)

*BE5-11 Assume that Gallant Company uses a periodic inventory system and has these account balances: Purchases $450,000; Purchase Returns and Allowances $13,000; Purchase Discounts $8,000; and Freight-In $16,000. Determine net purchases and cost of goods purchased.

Compute cost of goods sold and gross profit.
(LO 7)

*BE5-12 Assume the same information as in BE5-11 and also that Gallant Company has beginning inventory of $60,000, ending inventory of $90,000, and net sales of $730,000. Determine the amounts to be reported for cost of goods sold and gross profit.

Journalize purchase transactions.
(LO 7)

*BE5-13 Prepare the journal entries to record these transactions on Nimmer Company's books using a periodic inventory system.

(a) On March 2, Nimmer Company purchased $900,000 of merchandise from Sen Company, terms 2/10, n/30.

(b) On March 6, Nimmer Company returned $130,000 of the merchandise purchased on March 2.

(c) On March 12, Nimmer Company paid the balance due to Sen Company.

Prepare closing entries for merchandise accounts.
(LO 7)

*BE5-14 A. Hall Company has the following merchandise account balances: Sales Revenue $180,000, Sales Discounts $2,000, Purchases $120,000, and Purchases Returns and Allowances $30,000. In addition, it has a beginning inventory of $40,000 and an ending inventory of $30,000. Prepare the entries to record the closing of these items to Income Summary using the periodic inventory system.

Identify worksheet columns for selected accounts
(LO 7)

*BE5-15 Presented below is the format of the worksheet using the periodic inventory system presented in Appendix 5B.

Trial Balance		Adjustments		Adjusted Trial Balance		Income Statement		Balance Sheet	
Dr.	Cr.	Dr.	Cr.	Dr.	Cr.	Dr.	Cr.	Dr.	Cr.

Indicate where the following items will appear on the worksheet: (a) cash, (b) beginning inventory, (c) accounts payable, (d) ending inventory.

Example
Cash: Trial balance debit column; Adjustment trial balance debit column; and Balance sheet debit column.

> DO IT! Review

Record transactions of purchasing company.
(LO 2)

DO IT! 5-1 On October 5, Loomis Company buys merchandise on account from Brooke Company. The selling price of the goods is $5,000, and the cost to Brooke Company is $3,100. On October 8, Loomis returns defective goods with a selling price of $650 and a fair value of $100. Record the transactions on the books of Loomis Company.

Record transactions of selling company.
(LO 3)

DO IT! 5-2 Assume information similar to that in **DO IT!** 5-1: On October 5, Loomis Company buys merchandise on account from Brooke Company. The selling price of the goods is $5,000, and the cost to Brooke Company is $3,100. On October 8, Loomis returns defective goods with a selling price of $650 and a fair value of $100. Record the transactions on the books of Brooke Company.

Prepare closing entries for a merchandising company.
(LO 4)

DO IT! 5-3 The trial balance of Optique Boutique at December 31 shows Inventory $21,000, Sales Revenue $156,000, Sales Returns and Allowances $4,000, Sales Discounts $3,000, Cost of Goods Sold $92,400, Interest Revenue $5,000, Freight-Out $1,500, Utilities Expense $7,400, and Salaries and Wages Expense $19,500. Prepare the closing entries for Optique.

Classify financial statement accounts.
(LO 5)

DO IT! 5-4 Estes Company is preparing its multiple-step income statement, owner's equity statement, and classified balance sheet. Using the column heads **Account, Financial Statement, and Classification**, indicate in which financial statement and under what classification each of the following would be reported.

Account	Financial Statement	Classification
Accounts Payable		
Accounts Receivable		
Accumulated Depreciation—Buildings		
Cash		
Casualty Loss from Vandalism		
Cost of Goods Sold		
Depreciation Expense		
Equipment		
Freight-Out		
Insurance Expense		
Interest Payable		
Inventory		
Land		
Notes Payable (due in 5 years)		
Owner's Capital (beginning balance)		
Owner's Drawings		
Property Taxes Payable		
Salaries and Wages Expense		
Salaries and Wages Payable		
Sales Returns and Allowances		
Sales Revenue		
Unearned Rent Revenue		
Utilities Expense		

EXERCISES

E5-1 Mr. Etemadi has prepared the following list of statements about service companies and merchandisers.

Answer general questions about merchandisers.
(LO 1)

1. Measuring net income for a merchandiser is conceptually the same as for a service company.
2. For a merchandiser, sales less operating expenses is called gross profit.
3. For a merchandiser, the primary source of revenues is the sale of inventory.
4. Sales salaries and wages is an example of an operating expense.
5. The operating cycle of a merchandiser is the same as that of a service company.
6. In a perpetual inventory system, no detailed inventory records of goods on hand are maintained.
7. In a periodic inventory system, the cost of goods sold is determined only at the end of the accounting period.
8. A periodic inventory system provides better control over inventories than a perpetual system.

Instructions
Identify each statement as true or false. If false, indicate how to correct the statement.

E5-2 Information related to Harwick Co. is presented below.

Journalize purchase transactions.
(LO 2)

1. On April 5, purchased merchandise from Botham Company for $23,000, terms 2/10, net/30, FOB shipping point.
2. On April 6, paid freight costs of $900 on merchandise purchased from Botham.
3. On April 7, purchased equipment on account for $26,000.
4. On April 8, returned damaged merchandise to Botham Company and was granted a $3,000 credit for returned merchandise.
5. On April 15, paid the amount due to Botham Company in full.

Instructions
(a) Prepare the journal entries to record these transactions on the books of Harwick Co. under a perpetual inventory system.
(b) Assume that Harwick Co. paid the balance due to Botham Company on May 4 instead of April 15. Prepare the journal entry to record this payment.

Journalize perpetual inventory entries.
(LO 2, 3)

E5-3 On September 1, Boylan Office Supply had an inventory of 30 calculators at a cost of $18 each. The company uses a perpetual inventory system. During September, the following transactions occurred.

Sept. 6   Purchased with cash 80 calculators at $20 each from Guthrie.
      9   Paid freight of $80 on calculators purchased from Guthrie Co.
    10   Returned 3 calculators to Guthrie Co. for $63 credit (including freight) because they did not meet specifications.
    12   Sold 26 calculators costing $21 (including freight) for $31 each to Lee Book Store, terms n/30.
    14   Granted credit of $31 to Lee Book Store for the return of one calculator that was not ordered.
    20   Sold 30 calculators costing $21 for $32 each to Orr's Card Shop, terms n/30.

Instructions
Journalize the September transactions.

Prepare purchase and sale entries.
(LO 2, 3)

E5-4 On June 10, Tuzun Company purchased $8,000 of merchandise from Epps Company, FOB shipping point, terms 2/10, n/30. Tuzun pays the freight costs of $400 on June 11. Damaged goods totaling $300 are returned to Epps for credit on June 12. The fair value of these goods is $70. On June 19, Tuzun pays Epps Company in full, less the purchase discount. Both companies use a perpetual inventory system.

Instructions
(a) Prepare separate entries for each transaction on the books of Tuzun Company.
(b) Prepare separate entries for each transaction for Epps Company. The merchandise purchased by Tuzun on June 10 had cost Epps $4,800.

Journalize sales transactions.
(LO 3)

E5-5 Presented below are transactions related to Bogner Company.

1. On December 3, Bogner Company sold $570,000 of merchandise to Maris Co., terms 2/10, n/30, FOB shipping point. The cost of the merchandise sold was $350,000.
2. On December 8, Maris Co. was granted an allowance of $20,000 for merchandise purchased on December 3.
3. On December 13, Bogner Company received the balance due from Maris Co.

Instructions
(a) Prepare the journal entries to record these transactions on the books of Bogner Company using a perpetual inventory system.
(b) Assume that Bogner Company received the balance due from Maris Co. on January 2 of the following year instead of December 13. Prepare the journal entry to record the receipt of payment on January 2.

Prepare sales revenues section and closing entries.
(LO 4, 5)

E5-6 The adjusted trial balance of Tsai Company shows the following data pertaining to sales at the end of its fiscal year October 31, 2014: Sales Revenue $820,000, Freight-Out $16,000, Sales Returns and Allowances $25,000, and Sales Discounts $13,000.

Instructions
(a) Prepare the sales revenues section of the income statement.
(b) Prepare separate closing entries for (1) sales revenue, and (2) the contra accounts to sales revenue.

Prepare adjusting and closing entries.
(LO 4)

E5-7 Juan Morales Company had the following account balances at year-end: Cost of Goods Sold $60,000; Inventory $15,000; Operating Expenses $29,000; Sales Revenue $115,000; Sales Discounts $1,200; and Sales Returns and Allowances $1,700. A physical count of inventory determines that merchandise inventory on hand is $13,900.

Instructions
(a) Prepare the adjusting entry necessary as a result of the physical count.
(b) Prepare closing entries.

Prepare adjusting and closing entries.
(LO 4)

E5-8 Presented below is information related to Garland Co. for the month of January 2014.

Ending inventory per perpetual records	$ 21,600	Insurance expense	$ 12,000
		Rent expense	20,000
Ending inventory actually on hand	21,000	Salaries and wages expense	55,000
		Sales discounts	10,000
Cost of goods sold	218,000	Sales returns and allowances	13,000
Freight-out	7,000	Sales revenue	380,000

Instructions
(a) Prepare the necessary adjusting entry for inventory.
(b) Prepare the necessary closing entries.

E5-9 Presented below is information for Furlow Company for the month of March 2014.

Cost of goods sold	$212,000	Rent expense	$ 32,000
Freight-out	7,000	Sales discounts	8,000
Insurance expense	6,000	Sales returns and allowances	13,000
Salaries and wages expense	58,000	Sales revenue	380,000

Prepare multiple-step income statement.
(LO 5)

Instructions
(a) Prepare a multiple-step income statement.
(b) Compute the gross profit rate.

E5-10 In its income statement for the year ended December 31, 2014, Lemere Company reported the following condensed data.

Operating expenses	$ 725,000	Interest revenue	$ 28,000
Cost of goods sold	1,289,000	Loss on disposal of plant assets	17,000
Interest expense	70,000	Net sales	2,200,000

Prepare multiple-step and single-step income statements.
(LO 5)

Instructions
(a) Prepare a multiple-step income statement.
(b) Prepare a single-step income statement.

E5-11 An inexperienced accountant for Huang Company made the following errors in recording merchandising transactions.

1. A $195 refund to a customer for faulty merchandise was debited to Sales Revenue $195 and credited to Cash $195.
2. A $180 credit purchase of supplies was debited to Inventory $180 and credited to Cash $180.
3. A $215 sales discount was debited to Sales Revenue.
4. A cash payment of $20 for freight on merchandise purchases was debited to Freight-Out $200 and credited to Cash $200.

Prepare correcting entries for sales and purchases.
(LO 2, 3)

Instructions
Prepare separate correcting entries for each error, assuming that the incorrect entry is not reversed. (Omit explanations.)

E5-12 In 2014, Matt Cruz Company had net sales of $900,000 and cost of goods sold of $522,000. Operating expenses were $225,000, and interest expense was $11,000. Cruz prepares a multiple-step income statement.

Compute various income measures.
(LO 5)

Instructions
(a) Compute Cruz's gross profit.
(b) Compute the gross profit rate. Why is this rate computed by financial statement users?
(c) What is Cruz's income from operations and net income?
(d) If Cruz prepared a single-step income statement, what amount would it report for net income?
(e) In what section of its classified balance sheet should Cruz report merchandise inventory?

E5-13 Presented below is financial information for two different companies.

Compute missing amounts and compute gross profit rate.
(LO 5)

	May Company	Reed Company
Sales revenue	$90,000	(d)
Sales returns	(a)	$ 5,000
Net sales	87,000	102,000
Cost of goods sold	56,000	(e)
Gross profit	(b)	41,500
Operating expenses	15,000	(f)
Net income	(c)	15,000

Instructions
(a) Determine the missing amounts.
(b) Determine the gross profit rates. (Round to one decimal place.)

Compute missing amounts.
(LO 5)

E5-14 Financial information is presented below for three different companies.

	Allen Cosmetics	Bast Grocery	Corr Wholesalers
Sales revenue	$90,000	$ (e)	$122,000
Sales returns and allowances	(a)	5,000	12,000
Net sales	86,000	95,000	(i)
Cost of goods sold	56,000	(f)	(j)
Gross profit	(b)	38,000	24,000
Operating expenses	15,000	(g)	18,000
Income from operations	(c)	(h)	(k)
Other expenses and losses	4,000	7,000	(l)
Net income	(d)	11,000	5,000

Instructions
Determine the missing amounts.

Complete worksheet using a perpetual inventory system.
(LO 6)

*E5-15 Presented below are selected accounts for Salazar Company as reported in the worksheet using a perpetual inventory system at the end of May 2014.

Accounts	Adjusted Trial Balance		Income Statement		Balance Sheet	
	Dr.	Cr.	Dr.	Cr.	Dr.	Cr.
Cash	11,000					
Inventory	76,000					
Sales Revenue		480,000				
Sales Returns and Allowances	10,000					
Sales Discounts	9,000					
Cost of Goods Sold	300,000					

Instructions
Complete the worksheet by extending amounts reported in the adjusted trial balance to the appropriate columns in the worksheet. Do not total individual columns.

Prepare a worksheet using a perpetual inventory system.
(LO 6)

*E5-16 The trial balance columns of the worksheet using a perpetual inventory system for Marquez Company at June 30, 2014, are as follows.

MARQUEZ COMPANY
Worksheet
For the Month Ended June 30, 2014

Account Titles	Trial Balance	
	Debit	Credit
Cash	1,920	
Accounts Receivable	2,440	
Inventory	11,640	
Accounts Payable		1,120
Owner's Capital		3,500
Sales Revenue		42,500
Cost of Goods Sold	20,560	
Operating Expenses	10,560	
	47,120	47,120

Other data:
Operating expenses incurred on account, but not yet recorded, total $1,500.

Instructions
Enter the trial balance on a worksheet and complete the worksheet.

*E5-17 The trial balance of D. Savage Company at the end of its fiscal year, August 31, 2014, includes these accounts: Inventory $17,200; Purchases $149,000; Sales Revenue $190,000; Freight-In $5,000; Sales Returns and Allowances $3,000; Freight-Out $1,000; and Purchase Returns and Allowances $2,000. The ending merchandise inventory is $23,000.

Prepare cost of goods sold section.
(LO 7)

Instructions
Prepare a cost of goods sold section for the year ending August 31 (periodic inventory).

*E5-18 On January 1, 2014, Christel Madan Corporation had inventory of $50,000. At December 31, 2014, Christel Madan had the following account balances.

Compute various income statement items.
(LO 7)

Freight-in	$ 4,000
Purchases	509,000
Purchase discounts	6,000
Purchase returns and allowances	2,000
Sales revenue	840,000
Sales discounts	5,000
Sales returns and allowances	10,000

At December 31, 2014, Christel Madan determines that its ending inventory is $60,000.

Instructions
(a) Compute Christel Madan's 2014 gross profit.
(b) Compute Christel Madan's 2014 operating expenses if net income is $130,000 and there are no nonoperating activities.

*E5-19 Below is a series of cost of goods sold sections for companies B, F, L, and R.

Prepare cost of goods sold section.
(LO 7)

	B	F	L	R
Beginning inventory	$ 150	$ 70	$1,000	$ (j)
Purchases	1,620	1,060	(g)	43,590
Purchase returns and allowances	40	(d)	290	(k)
Net purchases	(a)	1,030	6,210	41,090
Freight-in	110	(e)	(h)	2,240
Cost of goods purchased	(b)	1,280	7,940	(l)
Cost of goods available for sale	1,840	1,350	(i)	49,530
Ending inventory	310	(f)	1,450	6,230
Cost of goods sold	(c)	1,230	7,490	43,300

Instruction
Fill in the lettered blanks to complete the cost of goods sold sections.

*E5-20 This information relates to Rana Co.

Journalize purchase transactions.
(LO 7)

1. On April 5, purchased merchandise from Craig Company for $25,000, terms 2/10, net/30, FOB shipping point.
2. On April 6, paid freight costs of $900 on merchandise purchased from Craig Company.
3. On April 7, purchased equipment on account for $30,000.
4. On April 8, returned some of April 5 merchandise, which cost $2,800, to Craig Company.
5. On April 15, paid the amount due to Craig Company in full.

Instructions
(a) Prepare the journal entries to record these transactions on the books of Rana Co. using a periodic inventory system.
(b) Assume that Rana Co. paid the balance due to Craig Company on May 4 instead of April 15. Prepare the journal entry to record this payment.

*E5-21 Presented below is information related to Lor Co.

Journalize purchase transactions.
(LO 7)

1. On April 5, purchased merchandise from Garcia Company for $19,000, terms 2/10, net/30, FOB shipping point.
2. On April 6, paid freight costs of $800 on merchandise purchased from Garcia.
3. On April 7, purchased equipment on account from Holifield Mfg. Co. for $23,000.
4. On April 8, returned merchandise, which cost $4,000, to Garcia Company.
5. On April 15, paid the amount due to Garcia Company in full.

Instructions

(a) Prepare the journal entries to record these transactions on the books of Lor Co. using a periodic inventory system.

(b) Assume that Lor Co. paid the balance due to Garcia Company on May 4 instead of April 15. Prepare the journal entry to record this payment.

Complete worksheet.
(LO 7)

*E5-22 Presented below are selected accounts for B. Midler Company as reported in the worksheet at the end of May 2014. Ending inventory is $75,000.

Accounts	Adjusted Trial Balance		Income Statement		Balance Sheet	
	Dr.	Cr.	Dr.	Cr.	Dr.	Cr.
Cash	9,000					
Inventory	80,000					
Purchases	240,000					
Purchase Returns and Allowances		30,000				
Sales Revenue		450,000				
Sales Returns and Allowances	10,000					
Sales Discounts	5,000					
Rent Expense	42,000					

Instructions

Complete the worksheet by extending amounts reported in the adjustment trial balance to the appropriate columns in the worksheet. The company uses the periodic inventory system.

EXERCISES: SET B AND CHALLENGE EXERCISES

Visit the book's companion website, at **www.wiley.com/college/weygandt**, and choose the Student Companion site to access Exercise Set B and Challenge Exercises.

PROBLEMS: SET A

Journalize purchase and sales transactions under a perpetual inventory system.
(LO 2, 3)

P5-1A Powell's Book Warehouse distributes hardcover books to retail stores and extends credit terms of 2/10, n/30 to all of its customers. At the end of May, Powell's inventory consisted of books purchased for $1,800. During June, the following merchandising transactions occurred.

June 1   Purchased books on account for $1,600 from Kline Publishers, FOB destination, terms 2/10, n/30. The appropriate party also made a cash payment of $50 for the freight on this date.

3   Sold books on account to Reading Rainbow for $2,500. The cost of the books sold was $1,440.

6   Received $100 credit for books returned to Kline Publishers.

9   Paid Kline Publishers in full, less discount.

15   Received payment in full from Reading Rainbow.

17   Sold books on account to Blanco Books for $1,800. The cost of the books sold was $1,080.

20   Purchased books on account for $1,500 from Dietz Publishers, FOB destination, terms 2/15, n/30. The appropriate party also made a cash payment of $50 for the freight on this date.

24   Received payment in full from Blanco Books.

26   Paid Dietz Publishers in full, less discount.

28   Sold books on account to Reddy Bookstore for $1,400. The cost of the books sold was $850.

30   Granted Reddy Bookstore $120 credit for books returned costing $72.

Powell's Book Warehouse's chart of accounts includes the following: No. 101 Cash, No. 112 Accounts Receivable, No. 120 Inventory, No. 201 Accounts Payable, No. 401 Sales Revenue, No. 412 Sales Returns and Allowances, No. 414 Sales Discounts, and No. 505 Cost of Goods Sold.

Instructions

Journalize the transactions for the month of June for Powell's Book Warehouse using a perpetual inventory system.

P5-2A Latona Hardware Store completed the following merchandising transactions in the month of May. At the beginning of May, the ledger of Latona showed Cash of $5,000 and Owner's Capital of $5,000.

Journalize, post, and prepare a partial income statement.

(LO 2, 3, 5)

May 1   Purchased merchandise on account from Gray's Wholesale Supply $4,200, terms 2/10, n/30.

2   Sold merchandise on account $2,100, terms 1/10, n/30. The cost of the merchandise sold was $1,300.

5   Received credit from Gray's Wholesale Supply for merchandise returned $300.

9   Received collections in full, less discounts, from customers billed on sales of $2,100 on May 2.

10   Paid Gray's Wholesale Supply in full, less discount.

11   Purchased supplies for cash $400.

12   Purchased merchandise for cash $1,400.

15   Received refund for poor quality merchandise from supplier on cash purchase $150.

17   Purchased merchandise from Amland Distributors $1,300, FOB shipping point, terms 2/10, n/30.

19   Paid freight on May 17 purchase $130.

24   Sold merchandise for cash $3,200. The merchandise sold had a cost of $2,000.

25   Purchased merchandise from Horvath, Inc. $620, FOB destination, terms 2/10, n/30.

27   Paid Amland Distributors in full, less discount.

29   Made refunds to cash customers for defective merchandise $70. The returned merchandise had a fair value of $30.

31   Sold merchandise on account $1,000 terms n/30. The cost of the merchandise sold was $560.

Latona Hardware's chart of accounts includes the following: No. 101 Cash, No. 112 Accounts Receivable, No. 120 Inventory, No. 126 Supplies, No. 201 Accounts Payable, No. 301 Owner's Capital, No. 401 Sales Revenue, No. 412 Sales Returns and Allowances, No. 414 Sales Discounts, and No. 505 Cost of Goods Sold.

Instructions

(a) Journalize the transactions using a perpetual inventory system.

(b) Enter the beginning cash and capital balances and post the transactions. (Use J1 for the journal reference.)

(c) Prepare an income statement through gross profit for the month of May 2014.

(c) Gross profit $2,379

P5-3A The Deluxe Store is located in midtown Madison. During the past several years, net income has been declining because of suburban shopping centers. At the end of the company's fiscal year on November 30, 2014, the following accounts appeared in two of its trial balances.

Prepare financial statements and adjusting and closing entries.

(LO 4, 5)

	Unadjusted	Adjusted		Unadjusted	Adjusted
Accounts Payable	$ 25,200	$ 25,200	Notes Payable	$ 37,000	$ 37,000
Accounts Receivable	30,500	30,500	Owner's Capital	101,700	101,700
Accumulated Depr.—Equip.	34,000	45,000	Owner's Drawings	10,000	10,000
Cash	26,000	26,000	Prepaid Insurance	10,500	3,500
Cost of Goods Sold	507,000	507,000	Property Tax Expense		2,500
Freight-Out	6,500	6,500	Property Taxes Payable		2,500
Equipment	146,000	146,000	Rent Expense	15,000	15,000
Depreciation Expense		11,000	Salaries and Wages Expense	96,000	96,000
Insurance Expense		7,000	Sales Revenue	700,000	700,000
Interest Expense	6,400	6,400	Sales Commissions Expense	6,500	11,000
Interest Revenue	8,000	8,000	Sales Commissions Payable		4,500
Inventory	29,000	29,000	Sales Returns and Allowances	8,000	8,000
			Utilities Expense	8,500	8,500

(a) Net income $29,100
     Owner's capital $120,800
     Total assets $190,000

Instructions

(a) Prepare a multiple-step income statement, an owner's equity statement, and a classified balance sheet. Notes payable are due in 2017.

(b) Journalize the adjusting entries that were made.

(c) Journalize the closing entries that are necessary.

Journalize, post, and prepare a trial balance.

(LO 2, 3, 4)

P5-4A Adam Nichols, a former disc golf star, operates Adam's Discorama. At the beginning of the current season on April 1, the ledger of Adam's Discorama showed Cash $1,800, Inventory $2,500, and Owner's Capital $4,300. The following transactions were completed during April.

Apr. 5   Purchased golf discs, bags, and other inventory on account from Rayford Co. $1,200, FOB shipping point, terms 2/10, n/60.

      7   Paid freight on the Rayford purchase $50.

      9   Received credit from Rayford Co. for merchandise returned $100.

     10   Sold merchandise on account for $900, terms n/30. The merchandise sold had a cost of $540.

     12   Purchased disc golf shirts and other accessories on account from Galaxy Sportswear $670, terms 1/10, n/30.

     14   Paid Rayford Co. in full, less discount.

     17   Received credit from Galaxy Sportswear for merchandise returned $70.

     20   Made sales on account for $610, terms n/30. The cost of the merchandise sold was $370.

     21   Paid Galaxy Sportswear in full, less discount.

     27   Granted an allowance to customers for clothing that was flawed $20.

     30   Received payments on account from customers $900.

The chart of accounts for the store includes the following: No. 101 Cash, No. 112 Accounts Receivable, No. 120 Inventory, No. 201 Accounts Payable, No. 301 Owner's Capital, No. 401 Sales Revenue, No. 412 Sales Returns and Allowances, and No. 505 Cost of Goods Sold.

Instructions

(a) Journalize the April transactions using a perpetual inventory system.

(b) Enter the beginning balances in the ledger accounts and post the April transactions. (Use J1 for the journal reference.)

(c) Total debits $5,810

(c) Prepare a trial balance on April 30, 2014.

Complete accounting cycle beginning with a worksheet.

(LO 4, 5, 6)

*P5-5A The trial balance of Valdez Fashion Center contained the following accounts at November 30, the end of the company's fiscal year.

VALDEZ FASHION CENTER
Trial Balance
November 30, 2014

	Debit	Credit
Cash	$ 8,700	
Accounts Receivable	30,700	
Inventory	44,700	
Supplies	6,200	
Equipment	133,000	
Accumulated Depreciation—Equipment		$ 28,000
Notes Payable		51,000
Accounts Payable		48,500
Owner's Capital		90,000
Owner's Drawings	12,000	
Sales Revenue		755,200
Sales Returns and Allowances	8,800	
Cost of Goods Sold	497,400	
Salaries and Wages Expense	140,000	
Advertising Expense	24,400	
Utilities Expense	14,000	
Maintenance and Repairs Expense	12,100	
Freight-Out	16,700	
Rent Expense	24,000	
Totals	$972,700	$972,700

Adjustment data:

1. Supplies on hand totaled $2,000.
2. Depreciation is $11,500 on the equipment.
3. Interest of $4,000 is accrued on notes payable at November 30.
4. Inventory actually on hand is $44,400.

Instructions
(a) Enter the trial balance on a worksheet, and complete the worksheet.
(b) Prepare a multiple-step income statement and an owner's equity statement for the year, and a classified balance sheet as of November 30, 2014. Notes payable of $20,000 are due in January 2015.
(c) Journalize the adjusting entries.
(d) Journalize the closing entries.
(e) Prepare a post-closing trial balance.

(a) Adj. trial balance
$988,200
Net loss $2,200
(b) Gross profit $248,700
Total assets $179,300

*P5-6A At the end of Dayton Department Store's fiscal year on November 30, 2014, these accounts appeared in its adjusted trial balance.

Determine cost of goods sold and gross profit under periodic approach.

(LO 5, 7)

Freight-In	$ 7,500
Inventory	40,000
Purchases	585,000
Purchase Discounts	6,300
Purchase Returns and Allowances	2,700
Sales Revenue	1,000,000
Sales Returns and Allowances	20,000

Additional facts:

1. Merchandise inventory on November 30, 2014, is $52,600.
2. Dayton Department Store uses a periodic system.

Instructions
Prepare an income statement through gross profit for the year ended November 30, 2014.

Gross profit $409,100

Calculate missing amounts and assess profitability.

(LO 5, 7)

*P5-7A Alana Inc. operates a retail operation that purchases and sells home entertainment products. The company purchases all merchandise inventory on credit and uses a periodic inventory system. The Accounts Payable account is used for recording inventory purchases only; all other current liabilities are accrued in separate accounts. You are provided with the following selected information for the fiscal years 2011 through 2014, inclusive.

	2011	2012	2013	2014
Income Statement Data				
Sales revenue		$55,000	$ (e)	$47,000
Cost of goods sold		(a)	13,800	14,300
Gross profit		38,300	35,200	(i)
Operating expenses		34,900	(f)	28,600
Net income		$ (b)	$ 2,500	$ (j)
Balance Sheet Data				
Inventory	$7,200	$ (c)	$ 8,100	$ (k)
Accounts payable	3,200	3,600	2,500	(l)
Additional Information				
Purchases of merchandise inventory on account		$14,200	$ (g)	$13,200
Cash payments to suppliers		(d)	(h)	13,600

(c) $4,700

(g) $17,200

(i) $32,700

Instructions

(a) Calculate the missing amounts.

(b) Sales declined over the 3-year fiscal period, 2012–2014. Does that mean that profitability necessarily also declined? Explain, computing the gross profit rate and the profit margin for each fiscal year to help support your answer. (Round to one decimal place.)

Journalize, post, and prepare trial balance and partial income statement using periodic approach.

(LO 7)

*P5-8A At the beginning of the current season on April 1, the ledger of Kokott Pro Shop showed Cash $3,000; Inventory $4,000; and Owner's Capital $7,000. These transactions occurred during April 2014.

Apr. 5   Purchased golf bags, clubs, and balls on account from Hogan Co. $1,200, FOB shipping point, terms 2/10, n/60.
     7   Paid freight on Hogan Co. purchases $50.
     9   Received credit from Hogan Co. for merchandise returned $100.
    10   Sold merchandise on account to customers $600, terms n/30.
    12   Purchased golf shoes, sweaters, and other accessories on account from Duffer Sportswear $450, terms 1/10, n/30.
    14   Paid Hogan Co. in full.
    17   Received credit from Duffer Sportswear for merchandise returned $50.
    20   Made sales on account to customers $600, terms n/30.
    21   Paid Duffer Sportswear in full.
    27   Granted credit to customers for clothing that had flaws $35.
    30   Received payments on account from customers $600.

The chart of accounts for the pro shop includes Cash, Accounts Receivable, Inventory, Accounts Payable, Owner's Capital, Sales Revenue, Sales Returns and Allowances, Purchases, Purchase Returns and Allowances, Purchase Discounts, and Freight-In.

Instructions

(a) Journalize the April transactions using a periodic inventory system.

(b) Using T-accounts, enter the beginning balances in the ledger accounts and post the April transactions.

(c) Tot. trial balance $8,376

Gross profit $465

(c) Prepare a trial balance on April 30, 2014.

(d) Prepare an income statement through gross profit, assuming merchandise inventory on hand at April 30 is $4,824.

PROBLEMS: SET B

P5-1B Urdan Co. distributes suitcases to retail stores and extends credit terms of 1/10, n/30 to all of its customers. At the end of June, Urdan's inventory consisted of suitcases costing $1,200. During the month of July, the following merchandising transactions occurred.

Journalize purchase and sales transactions under a perpetual inventory system.
(LO 2, 3)

July 1 Purchased suitcases on account for $1,800 from Hostad Manufacturers, FOB destination, terms 2/10, n/30. The appropriate party also made a cash payment of $100 for freight on this date.
 3 Sold suitcases on account to Kaye Satchels for $2,000. The cost of suitcases sold is $1,200.
 9 Paid Hostad Manufacturers in full.
 12 Received payment in full from Kaye Satchels.
 17 Sold suitcases on account to The Going Concern for $1,800. The cost of the suitcases sold was $1,080.
 18 Purchased suitcases on account for $1,900 from Nelson Manufacturers, FOB shipping point, terms 1/10, n/30. The appropriate party also made a cash payment of $125 for freight on this date.
 20 Received $300 credit (including freight) for suitcases returned to Nelson Manufacturers.
 21 Received payment in full from The Going Concern.
 22 Sold suitcases on account to Wopat's for $2,250. The cost of suitcases sold was $1,350.
 30 Paid Nelson Manufacturers in full.
 31 Granted Wopat's $200 credit for suitcases returned costing $120.

Urdan's chart of accounts includes the following: No. 101 Cash, No. 112 Accounts Receivable, No. 120 Inventory, No. 201 Accounts Payable, No. 401 Sales Revenue, No. 412 Sales Returns and Allowances, No. 414 Sales Discounts, and No. 505 Cost of Goods Sold.

Instructions

Journalize the transactions for the month of July for Urdan using a perpetual inventory system.

P5-2B Rose Distributing Company completed the following merchandising transactions in the month of April. At the beginning of April, the ledger of Rose showed Cash of $9,000 and Owner's Capital of $9,000.

Journalize, post, and prepare a partial income statement.
(LO 2, 3, 5)

Apr. 2 Purchased merchandise on account from Kwon Supply Co. $6,900, terms 1/10, n/30.
 4 Sold merchandise on account $6,500, FOB destination, terms 1/10, n/30. The cost of the merchandise sold was $3,900.
 5 Paid $240 freight on April 4 sale.
 6 Received credit from Kwon Supply Co. for merchandise returned $500.
 11 Paid Kwon Supply Co. in full, less discount.
 13 Received collections in full, less discounts, from customers billed on April 4.
 14 Purchased merchandise for cash $3,800.
 16 Received refund from supplier for returned goods on cash purchase of April 14, $500.
 18 Purchased merchandise from Davis Distributors $4,500, FOB shipping point, terms 2/10, n/30.
 20 Paid freight on April 18 purchase $100.
 23 Sold merchandise for cash $7,400. The merchandise sold had a cost of $4,120.
 26 Purchased merchandise for cash $2,300.
 27 Paid Davis Distributors in full, less discount.
 29 Made refunds to cash customers for defective merchandise $90. The returned merchandise had a fair value of $30.
 30 Sold merchandise on account $3,700, terms n/30. The cost of the merchandise sold was $2,800.

Rose Distributing Company's chart of accounts includes the following: No. 101 Cash, No. 112 Accounts Receivable, No. 120 Inventory, No. 201 Accounts Payable, No. 301 Owner's Capital, No. 401 Sales Revenue, No. 412 Sales Returns and Allowances, No. 414 Sales Discounts, No. 505 Cost of Goods Sold, and No. 644 Freight-Out.

Instructions
(a) Journalize the transactions using a perpetual inventory system.
(b) Enter the beginning cash and capital balances, and post the transactions. (Use J1 for the journal reference.)

(c) Gross profit $6,655

(c) Prepare the income statement through gross profit for the month of April 2014.

Prepare financial statements and adjusting and closing entries.

(LO 4, 5)

P5-3B Mackey Department Store is located near the Village Shopping Mall. At the end of the company's calendar year on December 31, 2014, the following accounts appeared in two of its trial balances.

	Unadjusted	Adjusted		Unadjusted	Adjusted
Accounts Payable	$ 79,300	$ 80,300	Inventory	$ 75,000	$ 75,000
Accounts Receivable	50,300	50,300	Mortgage Payable	80,000	80,000
Accumulated Depr.—Buildings	42,100	52,500	Owner's Capital	176,600	176,600
Accumulated Depr.—Equipment	29,600	42,900	Owner's Drawings	28,000	28,000
Buildings	290,000	290,000	Prepaid Insurance	9,600	2,400
Cash	23,800	23,800	Property Tax Expense		4,800
Cost of Goods Sold	412,700	412,700	Property Taxes Payable		4,800
Depreciation Expense		23,700	Salaries and Wages Expense	108,000	108,000
Equipment	110,000	110,000	Sales Commissions Expense	10,200	14,500
Insurance Expense		7,200	Sales Commissions Payable		4,300
Interest Expense	3,000	12,000	Sales Returns and Allowances	8,000	8,000
Interest Payable		9,000	Sales Revenue	728,000	728,000
Interest Revenue	4,000	4,000	Utilities Expense	11,000	12,000

Instructions

(a) Net income $129,100
Owner's capital $277,700
Total assets $456,100

(a) Prepare a multiple-step income statement, an owner's equity statement, and a classi-fied balance sheet. $25,000 of the mortgage payable is due for payment next year.
(b) Journalize the adjusting entries that were made.
(c) Journalize the closing entries that are necessary.

Journalize, post, and prepare a trial balance.

(LO 2, 3, 4)

P5-4B Alex Diaz, a former professional tennis star, operates Diaz Tennis Shop at the Cedar Lake Resort. At the beginning of the current season, the ledger of Diaz Tennis Shop showed Cash $2,500, Inventory $1,700, and Owner's Capital $4,200. The following transactions were completed during April.

Apr.	4	Purchased racquets and balls from Marx Co. $840, FOB shipping point, terms 2/10, n/30.
	6	Paid freight on purchase from Marx Co. $40.
	8	Sold merchandise to members $1,150, terms n/30. The merchandise sold had a cost of $790.
	10	Received credit of $40 from Marx Co. for a racquet that was returned.
	11	Purchased tennis shoes from Rupp Sports for cash, $420.
	13	Paid Marx Co. in full.
	14	Purchased tennis shirts and shorts from Hayley's Sportswear $900, FOB shipping point, terms 3/10, n/60.
	15	Received cash refund of $50 from Rupp Sports for damaged merchandise that was returned.
	17	Paid freight on Hayley's Sportswear purchase $30.
	18	Sold merchandise to members $900, terms n/30. The cost of the merchandise sold was $540.
	20	Received $600 in cash from customers in settlement of their accounts.
	21	Paid Hayley's Sportswear in full.
	27	Granted an allowance of $40 to members for tennis clothing that did not fit properly.
	30	Received cash payments on account from customers, $710.

The chart of accounts for the tennis shop includes the following: No. 101 Cash, No. 112 Accounts Receivable, No. 120 Inventory, No. 201 Accounts Payable, No. 301 Owner's Capital, No. 401 Sales Revenue, No. 412 Sales Returns and Allowances, and No. 505 Cost of Goods Sold.

Instructions
(a) Journalize the April transactions using a perpetual inventory system.
(b) Enter the beginning balances in the ledger accounts and post the April transactions. (Use J1 for the journal reference.)
(c) Prepare a trial balance on April 30, 2014.

(c) Total debits $6,250

*P5-5B At the end of Roshek Department Store's fiscal year on December 31, 2014, these accounts appeared in its adjusted trial balance.

Determine cost of goods sold and gross profit under periodic approach.

(LO 5, 7)

Freight-In	$ 5,600
Inventory	40,500
Purchases	447,000
Purchase Discounts	12,000
Purchase Returns and Allowances	6,400
Sales Revenue	725,000
Sales Returns and Allowances	11,000

Additional facts:

1. Merchandise inventory on December 31, 2014, is $65,000.
2. Roshek Department Store uses a periodic system.

Instructions
Prepare an income statement through gross profit for the year ended December 31, 2014.

Gross profit $304,300

*P5-6B Val Knight operates a retail clothing operation. She purchases all merchandise inventory on credit and uses a periodic inventory system. The Accounts Payable account is used for recording inventory purchases only; all other current liabilities are accrued in separate accounts. You are provided with the following selected information for the fiscal years 2011–2014.

Calculate missing amounts and assess profitability.

(LO 5, 7)

	2011	2012	2013	2014
Inventory (ending)	$13,000	$ 11,300	$ 14,700	$ 12,200
Accounts payable (ending)	20,000			
Sales revenue		239,000	237,000	235,000
Purchases of merchandise inventory on account		146,000	145,000	129,000
Cash payments to suppliers		135,000	161,000	127,000

Instructions
(a) Calculate cost of goods sold for each of the 2012, 2013, and 2014 fiscal years.
(b) Calculate the gross profit for each of the 2012, 2013, and 2014 fiscal years.
(c) Calculate the ending balance of accounts payable for each of the 2012, 2013, and 2014 fiscal years.
(d) Sales declined in fiscal 2014. Does that mean that profitability, as measured by the gross profit rate, necessarily also declined? Explain, calculating the gross profit rate for each fiscal year to help support your answer. (Round to one decimal place.)

(a) 2013 $141,600

(c) 2013 Ending accts payable $15,000

*P5-7B At the beginning of the current season, the ledger of Everett Tennis Shop showed Cash $2,500; Inventory $1,700; and Owner's Capital $4,200. The following transactions were completed during April.

Journalize, post, and prepare trial balance and partial income statement using periodic approach.

(LO 7)

Apr.	4	Purchased racquets and balls from Riggs Co. $740, terms 3/10, n/30.
	6	Paid freight on Riggs Co. purchase $60.
	8	Sold merchandise to customers $900, terms n/30.
	10	Received credit of $40 from Riggs Co. for a racquet that was returned.
	11	Purchased tennis shoes from King Sports for cash $300.
	13	Paid Riggs Co. in full.
	14	Purchased tennis shirts and shorts from BJ Sportswear $700, terms 2/10, n/60.
	15	Received cash refund of $50 from King Sports for damaged merchandise that was returned.

17   Paid freight on BJ Sportswear purchase $30.
18   Sold merchandise to customers $1,000, terms n/30.
20   Received $500 in cash from customers in settlement of their accounts.
21   Paid BJ Sportswear in full.
27   Granted an allowance of $25 to customers for tennis clothing that did not fit properly.
30   Received cash payments on account from customers $550.

The chart of accounts for the tennis shop includes Cash, Accounts Receivable, Inventory, Accounts Payable, Owner's Capital, Sales Revenue, Sales Returns and Allowances, Purchases, Purchase Returns and Allowances, Purchase Discounts, and Freight-In.

Instructions

(a) Journalize the April transactions using a periodic inventory system.
(b) Using T-accounts, enter the beginning balances in the ledger accounts and post the April transactions.
(c) Tot. trial balance $6,225   **(c)** Prepare a trial balance on April 30, 2014.
(d) Gross profit $766   **(d)** Prepare an income statement through gross profit, assuming inventory on hand at April 30 is $2,296.

PROBLEMS: SET C

Visit the book's companion website, at **www.wiley.com/college/weygandt**, and choose the Student Companion site to access Problem Set C.

COMPREHENSIVE PROBLEM

CP5 On December 1, 2014, Prosen Distributing Company had the following account balances.

	Debit		Credit
Cash	$ 7,200	Accumulated Depreciation—	
Accounts Receivable	4,600	Equipment	$ 2,200
Inventory	12,000	Accounts Payable	4,500
Supplies	1,200	Salaries and Wages Payable	1,000
Equipment	22,000	Owner's Capital	39,300
	$47,000		$47,000

During December, the company completed the following summary transactions.

Dec.   6   Paid $1,600 for salaries and wages due employees, of which $600 is for December and $1,000 is for November salaries and wages payable.
8   Received $1,900 cash from customers in payment of account (no discount allowed).
10   Sold merchandise for cash $6,300. The cost of the merchandise sold was $4,100.
13   Purchased merchandise on account from Maglio Co. $9,000, terms 2/10, n/30.
15   Purchased supplies for cash $2,000.
18   Sold merchandise on account $12,000, terms 3/10, n/30. The cost of the merchandise sold was $8,000.
20   Paid salaries and wages $1,800.
23   Paid Maglio Co. in full, less discount.
27   Received collections in full, less discounts, from customers billed on December 18.

Adjustment data:

1. Accrued salaries and wages payable $800.
2. Depreciation $200 per month.
3. Supplies on hand $1,500.

Instructions

(a) Journalize the December transactions using a perpetual inventory system.

(b) Enter the December 1 balances in the ledger T-accounts and post the December transactions. Use Cost of Goods Sold, Depreciation Expense, Salaries and Wages Expense, Sales Revenue, Sales Discounts, and Supplies Expense.

(c) Journalize and post adjusting entries.

(d) Prepare an adjusted trial balance.   (d) Totals $65,300

(e) Prepare an income statement and an owner's equity statement for December and a   (e) Net income $740
classified balance sheet at December 31.

CONTINUING COOKIE CHRONICLE

(*Note:* This is a continuation of the Cookie Chronicle from Chapters 1 through 4.)

CCC5 Because Natalie has had such a successful first few months, she is considering other opportunities to develop her business. One opportunity is the sale of fine European mixers. The owner of Kzinski Supply Company has approached Natalie to become the exclusive U.S. distributor of these fine mixers in her state. The current cost of a mixer is approximately $525 (U.S.), and Natalie would sell each one for $1,050. Natalie comes to you for advice on how to account for these mixers.

*Go to the book's companion website, **www.wiley.com/college/weygandt**, to see the completion of this problem.*

Broadening Your Perspective

Financial Reporting and Analysis

Financial Reporting Problem: Apple Inc.

BYP5-1 The financial statements of Apple Inc. are presented in Appendix A at the end of this textbook. Instructions for accessing and using the company's complete annual report, including the notes to the financial statements, are also provided in Appendix A.

Instructions

Answer the following questions using Apple's Consolidated Statement of Income.

(a) What was the percentage change in (1) sales and in (2) net income from 2009 to 2010 and from 2010 to 2011?

(b) What was the company's gross profit rate in 2009, 2010, and 2011?

(c) What was the company's percentage of net income to net sales in 2009, 2010, and 2011? Comment on any trend in this percentage.

Comparative Analysis Problem:
PepsiCo, Inc. vs. The Coca-Cola Company

BYP5-2 PepsiCo's financial statements are presented in Appendix B. Financial statements of The Coca-Cola Company are presented in Appendix C. Instructions for accessing and using the complete annual reports of PepsiCo and Coca-Cola, including the notes to the financial statements, are also provided in Appendices B and C, respectively.

Instructions

(a) Based on the information contained in these financial statements, determine each of the following for each company.

(1) Gross profit for 2011.

(2) Gross profit rate for 2011.

(3) Operating income for 2011.

(4) Percentage change in operating income from 2010 to 2011.

(b) What conclusions concerning the relative profitability of the two companies can you draw from these data?

Comparative Analysis Problem: Amazon.com, Inc. vs. Wal-Mart Stores, Inc.

BYP5-3 Amazon.com, Inc.'s financial statements are presented in Appendix D. Financial statements of Wal-Mart Stores, Inc. are presented in Appendix E. (Use Wal-Mart's January 31, 2012, financial statements for comparative purposes.) Instructions for accessing and using the complete annual reports of Amazon and Wal-Mart, including the notes to the financial statements, are also provided in Appendices D and E, respectively.

Instructions

(a) Based on the information contained in these financial statements, determine each of the following for each company. Use Amazon's net product sales to compute gross profit information.

(1) Gross profit for 2011.

(2) Gross profit rate for 2011.

(3) Operating income for 2011.

(4) Percentage change in operating income from 2010 to 2011.

(b) What conclusions concerning the relative profitability of the two companies can you draw from these data?

Real-World Focus

BYP5-4 No financial decision-maker should ever rely solely on the financial information reported in the annual report to make decisions. It is important to keep abreast of financial news. This activity demonstrates how to search for financial news on the Web.

Address: **biz.yahoo.com/i**, or go to **www.wiley.com/college/weygandt**

Steps:

1. Type in either PepsiCo or Coca-Cola.

2. Choose **News**.

3. Select an article that sounds interesting to you.

Instructions

(a) What was the source of the article (e.g., Reuters, Businesswire, PR Newswire)?

(b) Assume that you are a personal financial planner and that one of your clients owns stock in the company. Write a brief memo to your client, summarizing the article and explaining the implications of the article for his or her investment.

Critical Thinking

 ## Decision-Making Across the Organization

BYP5-5 Three years ago, Dana Mann and her brother-in-law Eric Boldt opened Family Department Store. For the first two years, business was good, but the following condensed income results for 2013 were disappointing.

FAMILY DEPARTMENT STORE
Income Statement
For the Year Ended December 31, 2013

Net sales		$700,000
Cost of goods sold		553,000
Gross profit		147,000
Operating expenses		
Selling expenses	$100,000	
Administrative expenses	20,000	120,000
Net income		$ 27,000

Dana believes the problem lies in the relatively low gross profit rate (gross profit divided by net sales) of 21%. Eric believes the problem is that operating expenses are too high.

Dana thinks the gross profit rate can be improved by making both of the following changes. She does not anticipate that these changes will have any effect on operating expenses.

1. Increase average selling prices by 17%. This increase is expected to lower sales volume so that total sales will increase only 6%.
2. Buy merchandise in larger quantities and take all purchase discounts. These changes are expected to increase the gross profit rate by 3 percentage points.

Eric thinks expenses can be cut by making both of the following changes. He feels that these changes will not have any effect on net sales.

1. Cut 2013 sales salaries of $60,000 in half and give sales personnel a commission of 2% of net sales.
2. Reduce store deliveries to one day per week rather than twice a week. This change will reduce 2013 delivery expenses of $30,000 by 40%.

Dana and Eric come to you for help in deciding the best way to improve net income.

Instructions
With the class divided into groups, answer the following.

(a) Prepare a condensed income statement for 2014, assuming (1) Dana's changes are implemented and (2) Eric's ideas are adopted.
(b) What is your recommendation to Dana and Eric?
(c) Prepare a condensed income statement for 2014, assuming both sets of proposed changes are made.

Communication Activity

BYP5-6 The following situation is in chronological order.

1. Connor decides to buy a surfboard.
2. He calls Surfing USA Co. to inquire about its surfboards.
3. Two days later, he requests Surfing USA Co. to make a surfboard.
4. Three days later, Surfing USA Co. sends him a purchase order to fill out.
5. He sends back the purchase order.
6. Surfing USA Co. receives the completed purchase order.
7. Surfing USA Co. completes the surfboard.
8. Connor picks up the surfboard.
9. Surfing USA Co. bills Connor.
10. Surfing USA Co. receives payment from Connor.

Instructions
In a memo to the president of Surfing USA Co., answer the following.

(a) When should Surfing USA Co. record the sale?
(b) Suppose that with his purchase order, Connor is required to make a down payment. Would that change your answer?

Ethics Case

BYP5-7 Jacquie Boynton was just hired as the assistant treasurer of Key West Stores. The company is a specialty chain store with nine retail stores concentrated in one metropolitan area. Among other things, the payment of all invoices is centralized in one of the departments Jacquie will manage. Her primary responsibility is to maintain the company's high credit rating by paying all bills when due and to take advantage of all cash discounts.

Phelan Carter, the former assistant treasurer who has been promoted to treasurer, is training Jacquie in her new duties. He instructs Jacquie that she is to continue the practice of preparing all checks "net of discount" and dating the checks the last day of the discount period. "But," Phelan continues, "we always hold the checks at least 4 days beyond the discount period before mailing them. That way, we get another 4 days of interest on our money. Most of our creditors need our business and don't complain. And, if they scream about our missing the discount period, we blame it on the mail room or the post office. We've only lost one discount out of every hundred we take that way. I think everybody does it. By the way, welcome to our team!"

Instructions
(a) What are the ethical considerations in this case?
(b) Who are the stakeholders that are harmed or benefitted in this situation?
(c) Should Jacquie continue the practice started by Phelan? Does she have any choice?

All About You

BYP5-8 There are many situations in business where it is difficult to determine the proper period in which to record revenue. Suppose that after graduation with a degree in finance, you take a job as a manager at a consumer electronics store called Impact Electronics. The company has expanded rapidly in order to compete with Best Buy. Impact has also begun selling gift cards for its electronic products. The cards are available in any dollar amount and allow the holder of the card to purchase an item for up to 2 years from the time the card is purchased. If the card is not used during that 2 years, it expires.

Instructions
Answer the following questions.

At what point should the revenue from the gift cards be recognized? Should the revenue be recognized at the time the card is sold, or should it be recorded when the card is redeemed? Explain the reasoning to support your answers.

FASB Codification Activity

BYP5-9 If your school has a subscription to the FASB Codification, go to **http://aaahq.org/ascLogin.cfm** to log in and prepare responses to the following.

Instructions
(a) Access the glossary ("Master Glossary") to answer the following:
   (1) What is the definition provided for inventory?
   (2) What is a customer?
(b) What guidance does the Codification provide concerning reporting inventories above cost?

Answers to Chapter Questions

Answers to Insight and Accounting Across the Organization Questions

p. 221 Morrow Snowboards Improves Its Stock Appeal   Q: If a perpetual system keeps track of inventory on a daily basis, why do companies ever need to do a physical count? **A:** A perpetual system keeps track of all sales and purchases on a continuous basis. This provides a constant record of the number of units in the inventory. However, if employees make errors in recording sales or purchases, or if there is theft, the inventory value will not be correct. As a consequence, all companies do a physical count of inventory at least once a year.

p. 228 Should Costco Change Its Return Policy?   Q: If a company expects significant returns, what are the implications for revenue recognition? **A:** If a company expects significant returns, it should make an adjusting entry at the end of the year, reducing sales by the estimated amount of sales returns. This is necessary so as not to overstate the amount of revenue recognized in the period.

p. 229 Selling Green   Q: What is meant by "monetize environmental sustainability" for shareholders? **A:** By marketing green, not only does PepsiCo help the environment in the long run, but it also leads to long-term profitability as well. In other words, sound sustainability practices are good business and lead to sound financial results.

p. 235 Disclosing More Details   Q: Why have investors and analysts demanded more accuracy in isolating "Other gains and losses" from operating items? **A:** Greater accuracy in the classification of operating versus nonoperating ("Other gains and losses") items permits investors and analysts to judge the real operating margin, the results of continuing operations, and management's ability to control operating expenses.

A Look at IFRS

The basic accounting entries for merchandising are the same under both GAAP and IFRS. The income statement is a required statement under both sets of standards. The basic format is similar although some differences do exist.

LEARNING OBJECTIVE 8

Compare the accounting procedures for merchandising under GAAP and IFRS.

Key Points

- Under both GAAP and IFRS, a company can choose to use either a perpetual or a periodic system.

- Inventories are defined by IFRS as held-for-sale in the ordinary course of business, in the process of production for such sale, or in the form of materials or supplies to be consumed in the production process or in the providing of services.

- Under GAAP, companies generally classify income statement items by function. Classification by function leads to descriptions like administration, distribution, and manufacturing. Under IFRS, companies must classify expenses either by nature or by function. Classification by nature leads to descriptions such as the following: salaries, depreciation expense, and utilities expense. If a company uses the functional-expense method on the income statement, disclosure by nature is required in the notes to the financial statements.

- Presentation of the income statement under GAAP follows either a single-step or multiple-step format. IFRS does not mention a single-step or multiple-step approach.

- Under IFRS, revaluation of land, buildings, and intangible assets is permitted. The initial gains and losses resulting from this revaluation are reported as adjustments to equity, often referred to as **other comprehensive income**. The effect of this difference is that the use of IFRS results in more transactions affecting equity (other comprehensive income) but not net income.

- *IAS 1*, "Presentation of Financial Statements," provides general guidelines for the reporting of income statement information. Subsequently, a number of international standards have been issued that provide additional guidance to issues related to income statement presentation.

- Similar to GAAP, comprehensive income under IFRS includes unrealized gains and losses (such as those on so-called "non-trading securities") that are not included in the calculation of net income.

- IFRS requires that two years of income statement information be presented, whereas GAAP requires three years.

Looking to the Future

The IASB and FASB are working on a project that would rework the structure of financial statements. Specifically, this project will address the issue of how to classify various items in the income statement. A main goal of this new approach is to provide information that better represents how businesses are run. In addition, this approach draws attention away from just one number—net income. It will adopt major groupings similar to those currently used by the statement of cash flows (operating, investing, and financing), so that numbers can be more readily traced across statements. For example, the amount of income that is generated by operations would be traceable to the assets and liabilities used to generate the income. Finally, this approach would also provide detail, beyond that currently seen in most statements (either GAAP or IFRS), by requiring that line items be presented both by function and by nature. The new financial statement format was heavily influenced by suggestions from financial statement analysts.

IFRS Practice

IFRS Self-Test Questions

1. Which of the following would **not** be included in the definition of inventory under IFRS?
   (a) Photocopy paper held for sale by an office-supply store.
   (b) Stereo equipment held for sale by an electronics store.
   (c) Used office equipment held for sale by the human relations department of a plastics company.
   (d) All of the above would meet the definition.

2. Which of the following would **not** be a line item of a company reporting costs by nature?
   (a) Depreciation expense.
   (b) Salaries expense.
   (c) Interest expense.
   (d) Manufacturing expense.

3. Which of the following would **not** be a line item of a company reporting costs by function?
   (a) Administration.
   (b) Manufacturing.
   (c) Utilities expense.
   (d) Distribution.

4. Which of the following statements is **false**?
   (a) IFRS specifically requires use of a multiple-step income statement.
   (b) Under IFRS, companies can use either a perpetual or periodic system.
   (c) The proposed new format for financial statements was heavily influenced by the suggestions of financial statement analysts.
   (d) The new income statement format will try to de-emphasize the focus on the "net income" line item.

5. Under the new format for financial statements being proposed under a joint IASB/FASB project:
   (a) all financial statements would adopt headings similar to the current format of the balance sheet.
   (b) financial statements would be presented consistent with the way management usually run companies.
   (c) companies would be required to report income statement line items by function only.
   (d) the amount of detail shown in the income statement would decrease compared to current presentations.

IFRS Exercises

IFRS5-1 Explain the difference between the "nature-of-expense" and "function-of-expense" classifications.

IFRS5-2 For each of the following income statement line items, state whether the item is a "by nature" expense item or a "by function" expense item.

_____ Cost of goods sold
_____ Depreciation expense
_____ Salaries and wages expense
_____ Selling expenses
_____ Utilities expense
_____ Delivery expense
_____ General and administrative expenses

IFRS5-3 Matilda Company reported the following amounts (in euros) in 2014: Net income, €150,000; Unrealized gain related to revaluation of buildings, €10,000; and Unrealized loss on non-trading securities, €(35,000). Determine Matilda's total comprehensive income for 2014.

International Financial Reporting Problem: Zetar plc

IFRS5-4 The financial statements of Zetar plc are presented in Appendix F. Instructions for accessing and using the company's complete annual report, including the notes to its financial statements, are also provided in Appendix F.

Instructions

Use Zetar's annual report to answer the following questions.

(a) Does Zetar use a multiple-step or a single-step income statement format? Explain how you made your determination.
(b) Instead of "interest expense," what label does Zetar use for interest costs that it incurs?
(c) Using the notes to the company's financial statements, explain what each of the following are:
   (1) Adjusted results.
   (2) One-off items.

Answers to IFRS Self-Test Questions
1. c   2. d   3. c   4. a   5. b

✔ **The Navigator**

6 | Inventories

Feature Story

"Where Is That Spare Bulldozer Blade?"

Let's talk inventory—big, bulldozer-size inventory. Caterpillar Inc. is the world's largest manufacturer of construction and mining equipment, diesel and natural gas engines, and industrial gas turbines. It sells its products in over 200 countries, making it one of the most successful U.S. exporters. More than 70% of its productive assets are located domestically, and nearly 50% of its sales are foreign.

In the past, Caterpillar's profitability suffered, but today it is very successful. A big part of this turnaround can be attributed to effective management of its inventory. Imagine what it costs Caterpillar to have too many bulldozers sitting around in inventory—a situation the company definitely wants to avoid. Conversely, Caterpillar must make sure it has enough inventory to meet demand.

At one time during a 7-year period, Caterpillar's sales increased by 100%, while its inventory increased by only 50%. To

achieve this dramatic reduction in the amount of resource tied up in inventory, while continuing to meet customers' needs, Caterpillar used a two-pronged approach. First, it completed a factory modernization program, which great increased its production efficiency. The program reduced 60% the amount of inventory the company processed at one time. It also reduced by an incredible 75% the time it takes to manufacture a part.

Second, Caterpillar dramatically improved its parts distribu system. It ships more than 100,000 items daily from its 2? distribution centers strategically located around the worlc (10 million square feet of warehouse space—remember, v talking bulldozers). The company can virtually guarantee it can get any part to anywhere in the world within 24 ho

After these changes, Caterpillar had record exports, profi and revenues. It would seem that things couldn't be bett But industry analysts, as well as the company's managers, thought otherwise. In order to maintain Caterpillar's posi as the industry leader, management began another majo

✔ The Navigator

- Scan Learning Objectives
- Read Feature Story
- Read Preview
- Read text and answer **DO IT!** p. 280
    - p. 286   - p. 291   - p. 294
- Work Comprehensive **DO IT! 1** p. 294
    - **2** p. 299
- Review Summary of Learning Objectives
- Answer Self-Test Questions
- Complete Assignments
- Go to *WileyPLUS* for practice and tutorials
- 🌐 **Read A Look at IFRS** p. 324

Learning Objectives

✔ The Navigator

After studying this chapter, you should be able to:

[1] Determine how to classify inventory and inventory quantities.

[2] Explain the accounting for inventories and apply the inventory cost flow methods.

[3] Explain the financial effects of the inventory cost flow assumptions.

[4] Explain the lower-of-cost-or-market basis of accounting for inventories.

[5] Indicate the effects of inventory errors on the financial statements.

[6] Compute and interpret the inventory turnover.

overhaul of inventory production and inventory management processes. The goal: to cut the number of repairs in half, increase productivity by 20%, and increase inventory turnover by 40%.

In short, Caterpillar's ability to manage its inventory has been a key reason for its past success, and inventory management will very likely play a huge part in its ability to succeed in the future.

Preview of Chapter 6

In the previous chapter, we discussed the accounting for merchandise inventory using a perpetual inventory system. In this chapter, we explain the methods used to calculate the cost of inventory on hand at the balance sheet date and the cost of goods sold.

The content and organization of this chapter are as follows.

INVENTORIES			
Classifying and Determining Inventory	Inventory Costing	Inventory Errors	Statement Presentation and Analysis
• Classifying inventory • Determining inventory quantities	• Specific identification • Cost flow assumptions • Financial statement and tax effects • Consistent use • Lower-of-cost-or-market	• Income statement effects • Balance sheet effects	• Presentation • Analysis

Classifying and Determining Inventory

LEARNING OBJECTIVE   **1**

Determine how to classify inventory and inventory quantities.

Two important steps in the reporting of inventory at the end of the accounting period are the classification of inventory based on its degree of completeness and the determination of inventory amounts.

Classifying Inventory

How a company classifies its inventory depends on whether the firm is a merchandiser or a manufacturer. In a **merchandising** company, such as those described in Chapter 5, inventory consists of many different items. For example, in a grocery store, canned goods, dairy products, meats, and produce are just a few of the inventory items on hand. These items have two common characteristics: (1) They are owned by the company, and (2) they are in a form ready for sale to customers in the ordinary course of business. Thus, merchandisers need only one inventory classification, **merchandise inventory**, to describe the many different items that make up the total inventory.

In a **manufacturing** company, some inventory may not yet be ready for sale. As a result, manufacturers usually classify inventory into three categories: finished goods, work in process, and raw materials. **Finished goods inventory** is manufactured items that are completed and ready for sale. **Work in process** is that portion of manufactured inventory that has been placed into the production process but is not yet complete. **Raw materials** are the basic goods that will be used in production but have not yet been placed into production.

For example, Caterpillar classifies earth-moving tractors completed and ready for sale as **finished goods**. It classifies the tractors on the assembly line in various stages of production as **work in process**. The steel, glass, tires, and other components that are on hand waiting to be used in the production of tractors are identified as **raw materials**. Illustration 6-1 shows an excerpt from Note 7 of Caterpillar's annual report, which shows the significant increases in each type of Caterpillar's inventory levels as the economy began to recover during this period.

Helpful Hint Regardless of the classification, companies report all inventories under Current Assets on the balance sheet.

Illustration 6-1
Composition of Caterpillar's inventory

(millions of dollars)	December 31		
	2011	**2010**	**2009**
Raw materials	$ 3,872	$2,766	$1,979
Work-in-process	2,845	1,483	656
Finished goods	7,570	5,098	3,465
Other	257	240	260
Total inventories	**$14,544**	**$9,587**	**$6,360**

By observing the levels and changes in the levels of these three inventory types, financial statement users can gain insight into management's production plans. For example, low levels of raw materials and high levels of finished goods suggest that management believes it has enough inventory on hand, and production will be slowing down—perhaps in anticipation of a recession. On the other hand, high levels of raw materials and low levels of finished goods probably signal that management is planning to step up production.

Many companies have significantly lowered inventory levels and costs using **just-in-time (JIT) inventory** methods. Under a just-in-time method, companies manufacture or purchase goods just in time for use. Dell is famous for having developed a system for making computers in response to individual customer requests. Even though it makes each computer to meet each customer's particular specifications, Dell is able to assemble the computer and put it on a truck in less than 48 hours. The success of the JIT system depends on reliable suppliers. By integrating its information systems with those of its suppliers, Dell reduced its inventories to nearly zero. This is a huge advantage in an industry where products become obsolete nearly overnight.

The accounting concepts discussed in this chapter apply to the inventory classifications of both merchandising and manufacturing companies. Our focus here is on merchandise inventory. Additional issues specific to manufacturing companies are discussed later in the managerial section of this textbook (Chapters 19–26).

ACCOUNTING ACROSS THE ORGANIZATION

A Big Hiccup

JIT can save a company a lot of money, but it isn't without risk. An unexpected disruption in the supply chain can cost a company a lot of money. Japanese automakers experienced just such a disruption when a 6.8-magnitude earthquake caused major damage to the company that produces 50% of their piston rings. The rings themselves cost only $1.50, but without them you cannot make a car. No other supplier could quickly begin producing sufficient quantities of the rings to match the desired specifications. As a result, the automakers were forced to shut down production for a few days—a loss of tens of thousands of cars.

Similarly, a major snowstorm halted production at Canadian plants of General Motors and Ford. A Ford spokesperson said, "Because the plants run with just-in-time inventory, we don't have large stockpiles of parts sitting around. When you have a somewhat significant disruption, you can pretty quickly run out of parts."

Source: Amy Chozick, "A Key Strategy of Japan's Car Makers Backfires," *Wall Street Journal* (July 20, 2007); Kate Linebaugh, "Canada Military Evacuates Motorists Stranded by Snow," *Wall Street Journal* (December 15, 2010).

?   What steps might the companies take to avoid such a serious disruption in the future? (See page 324.)

© PeskyMonkey/iStockphoto

Determining Inventory Quantities

No matter whether they are using a periodic or perpetual inventory system, all companies need to determine inventory quantities at the end of the accounting period. If using a perpetual system, companies take a physical inventory for the following reasons:

1. To check the accuracy of their perpetual inventory records.
2. To determine the amount of inventory lost due to wasted raw materials, shoplifting, or employee theft.

Companies using a periodic inventory system take a physical inventory for **two different purposes**: to determine the inventory on hand at the balance sheet date, and to determine the cost of goods sold for the period.

Determining inventory quantities involves two steps: (1) taking a physical inventory of goods on hand and (2) determining the ownership of goods.

TAKING A PHYSICAL INVENTORY

Companies take a physical inventory at the end of the accounting period. Taking a physical inventory involves actually counting, weighing, or measuring each kind of inventory on hand. In many companies, taking an

Ethics Note

In a famous fraud, a salad oil company filled its storage tanks mostly with water. The oil rose to the top, so auditors thought the tanks were full of oil. The company also said it had more tanks than it really did: It repainted numbers on the tanks to confuse auditors.

inventory is a formidable task. Retailers such as Target, True Value Hardware, or Home Depot have thousands of different inventory items. An inventory count is generally more accurate when goods are not being sold or received during the counting. Consequently, companies often "take inventory" when the business is closed or when business is slow. Many retailers close early on a chosen day in January—after the holiday sales and returns, when inventories are at their lowest level—to count inventory. Wal-Mart Stores, Inc., for example, has a year-end of January 31.

© Greg Brookes/iStockphoto

ETHICS INSIGHT

Falsifying Inventory to Boost Income

Managers at women's apparel maker Leslie Fay were convicted of falsifying inventory records to boost net income—and consequently to boost management bonuses. In another case, executives at Craig Consumer Electronics were accused of defrauding lenders by manipulating inventory records. The indictment said the company classified "defective goods as new or refurbished" and claimed that it owned certain shipments "from overseas suppliers" when, in fact, Craig either did not own the shipments or the shipments did not exist.

? What effect does an overstatement of inventory have on a company's financial statements? (See page 324.)

DETERMINING OWNERSHIP OF GOODS

One challenge in computing inventory quantities is determining what inventory a company owns. To determine ownership of goods, two questions must be answered: Do all of the goods included in the count belong to the company? Does the company own any goods that were not included in the count?

GOODS IN TRANSIT A complication in determining ownership is **goods in transit** (on board a truck, train, ship, or plane) at the end of the period. The company may have purchased goods that have not yet been received, or it may have sold goods that have not yet been delivered. To arrive at an accurate count, the company must determine ownership of these goods.

Goods in transit should be included in the inventory of the company that has legal title to the goods. Legal title is determined by the terms of the sale, as shown in Illustration 6-2 and described below.

Illustration 6-2
Terms of sale

1. When the terms are **FOB (free on board) shipping point**, ownership of the goods passes to the buyer when the public carrier accepts the goods from the seller.
2. When the terms are **FOB destination**, ownership of the goods remains with the seller until the goods reach the buyer.

If goods in transit at the statement date are ignored, inventory quantities may be seriously miscounted. Assume, for example, that Hargrove Company has 20,000 units of inventory on hand on December 31. It also has the following goods in transit:

1. Sales of 1,500 units shipped December 31 FOB destination.

2. Purchases of 2,500 units shipped FOB shipping point by the seller on December 31.

Hargrove has legal title to both the 1,500 units sold and the 2,500 units purchased. If the company ignores the units in transit, it would understate inventory quantities by 4,000 units (1,500 + 2,500).

As we will see later in the chapter, inaccurate inventory counts affect not only the inventory amount shown on the balance sheet but also the cost of goods sold calculation on the income statement.

CONSIGNED GOODS In some lines of business, it is common to hold the goods of other parties and try to sell the goods for them for a fee, but without taking ownership of the goods. These are called **consigned goods**.

For example, you might have a used car that you would like to sell. If you take the item to a dealer, the dealer might be willing to put the car on its lot and charge you a commission if it is sold. Under this agreement, the dealer **would not take ownership** of the car, which would still belong to you. Therefore, if an inventory count were taken, the car would not be included in the dealer's inventory because the dealer does not own it.

Many car, boat, and antique dealers sell goods on consignment to keep their inventory costs down and to avoid the risk of purchasing an item that they will not be able to sell. Today, even some manufacturers are making consignment agreements with their suppliers in order to keep their inventory levels low.

ANATOMY OF A FRAUD

Ted Nickerson, CEO of clock manufacturer Dally Industries, was feared by all of his employees. Ted also had expensive tastes. To support his expensive tastes, Ted took out large loans, which he collateralized with his shares of Dally Industries stock. If the price of Dally's stock fell, he was required to provide the bank with more shares of stock. To achieve target net income figures and thus maintain the stock price, Ted coerced employees in the company to alter inventory figures. Inventory quantities were manipulated by changing the amounts on inventory control tags after the year-end physical inventory count. For example, if a tag said there were 20 units of a particular item, the tag was changed to 220. Similarly, the unit costs that were used to determine the value of ending inventory were increased from, for example, $125 per unit to $1,250. Both of these fraudulent changes had the effect of increasing the amount of reported ending inventory. This reduced cost of goods sold and increased net income.

Total take: $245,000

THE MISSING CONTROL

Independent internal verification. The company should have spot-checked its inventory records periodically, verifying that the number of units in the records agreed with the amount on hand and that the unit costs agreed with vendor price sheets.

Source: Adapted from Wells, *Fraud Casebook* (2007), pp. 502–509.

> **DO IT!**

Rules of Ownership

Hasbeen Company completed its inventory count. It arrived at a total inventory value of $200,000. As a new member of Hasbeen's accounting department, you have been given the information listed below. Discuss how this information affects the reported cost of inventory.

1. Hasbeen included in the inventory goods held on consignment for Falls Co., costing $15,000.
2. The company did not include in the count purchased goods of $10,000 which were in transit (terms: FOB shipping point).
3. The company did not include in the count sold inventory with a cost of $12,000 which was in transit (terms: FOB shipping point).

Solution

Action Plan

✔ Apply the rules of ownership to goods held on consignment.

✔ Apply the rules of ownership to goods in transit.

The goods of $15,000 held on consignment should be deducted from the inventory count. The goods of $10,000 purchased FOB shipping point should be added to the inventory count. Sold goods of $12,000 which were in transit FOB shipping point should not be included in the ending inventory. Thus, inventory should be carried at $195,000 ($200,000 − $15,000 + $10,000).

Related exercise material: **BE6-1, E6-1, E6-2, and DO IT! 6-1.**

 The Navigator

Inventory Costing

LEARNING OBJECTIVE 2

Explain the accounting for inventories and apply the inventory cost flow methods.

Inventory is accounted for at cost. Cost includes all expenditures necessary to acquire goods and place them in a condition ready for sale. For example, freight costs incurred to acquire inventory are added to the cost of inventory, but the cost of shipping goods to a customer are a selling expense.

After a company has determined the quantity of units of inventory, it applies unit costs to the quantities to compute the total cost of the inventory and the cost of goods sold. This process can be complicated if a company has purchased inventory items at different times and at different prices.

For example, assume that Crivitz TV Company purchases three identical 50-inch TVs on different dates at costs of $700, $750, and $800. During the year, Crivitz sold two sets at $1,200 each. These facts are summarized in Illustration 6-3.

Illustration 6-3
Data for inventory costing example

Purchases

February 3	1 TV	at	$700
March 5	1 TV	at	$750
May 22	1 TV	at	$800

Sales

June 1	2 TVs	for	$2,400 ($1,200 × 2)

Cost of goods sold will differ depending on which two TVs the company sold. For example, it might be $1,450 ($700 + $750), or $1,500 ($700 + $800), or $1,550 ($750 + $800). In this section, we discuss alternative costing methods available to Crivitz.

Specific Identification

If Crivitz can positively identify which particular units it sold and which are still in ending inventory, it can use the **specific identification method** of inventory costing. For example, if Crivitz sold the TVs it purchased on February 3 and May 22, then its cost of goods sold is $1,500 ($700 + $800), and its ending inventory is $750 (see Illustration 6-4). Using this method, companies can accurately determine ending inventory and cost of goods sold.

Illustration 6-4
Specific identification method

Specific identification requires that companies keep records of the original cost of each individual inventory item. Historically, specific identification was possible only when a company sold a limited variety of high-unit-cost items that could be identified clearly from the time of purchase through the time of sale. Examples of such products are cars, pianos, or expensive antiques.

Today, bar coding, electronic product codes, and radio frequency identification make it theoretically possible to do specific identification with nearly any type of product. The reality is, however, that this practice is still relatively rare. Instead, rather than keep track of the cost of each particular item sold, most companies make assumptions, called **cost flow assumptions**, about which units were sold.

Cost Flow Assumptions

Because specific identification is often impractical, other cost flow methods are permitted. These differ from specific identification in that they **assume** flows of costs that may be unrelated to the physical flow of goods. There are three assumed cost flow methods:

1. First-in, first-out (FIFO)
2. Last-in, first-out (LIFO)
3. Average-cost

There is no accounting requirement that the cost flow assumption be consistent with the physical movement of the goods. Company management selects the appropriate cost flow method.

To demonstrate the three cost flow methods, we will use a **periodic** inventory system. We assume a periodic system because **very few companies use** *perpetual* **LIFO, FIFO, or average-cost** to cost their inventory and related cost of goods sold. Instead, companies that use perpetual systems often use an assumed cost (called a standard cost) to record cost of goods sold at the time of sale. Then, at the end of the period when they count their inventory, they **recalculate cost of**

Ethics Note

A major disadvantage of the specific identification method is that management may be able to manipulate net income. For example, it can boost net income by selling units purchased at a low cost, or reduce net income by selling units purchased at a high cost.

goods sold using *periodic* **FIFO, LIFO, or average-cost** as shown in this chapter and adjust cost of goods sold to this recalculated number.[1]

To illustrate the three inventory cost flow methods, we will use the data for Houston Electronics' Astro condensers, shown in Illustration 6-5.

Illustration 6-5
Data for Houston Electronics

HOUSTON ELECTRONICS Astro Condensers				
Date	**Explanation**	**Units**	**Unit Cost**	**Total Cost**
Jan. 1	Beginning inventory	100	$10	$ 1,000
Apr. 15	Purchase	200	11	2,200
Aug. 24	Purchase	300	12	3,600
Nov. 27	Purchase	400	13	5,200
	Total units available for sale	1,000		$12,000
	Units in ending inventory	450		
	Units sold	550		

The cost of goods sold formula in a periodic system is:

> **(Beginning Inventory + Purchases) − Ending Inventory = Cost of Goods Sold**

Houston Electronics had a total of 1,000 units available to sell during the period (beginning inventory plus purchases). The total cost of these 1,000 units is $12,000, referred to as **cost of goods available for sale**. A physical inventory taken at December 31 determined that there were 450 units in ending inventory. Therefore, Houston sold 550 units (1,000 − 450) during the period. To determine the cost of the 550 units that were sold (the cost of goods sold), we assign a cost to the ending inventory and subtract that value from the cost of goods available for sale. The value assigned to the ending inventory **will depend on which cost flow method we use**. No matter which cost flow assumption we use, though, the sum of cost of goods sold plus the cost of the ending inventory must equal the cost of goods available for sale—in this case, $12,000.

FIRST-IN, FIRST-OUT (FIFO)

The **first-in, first-out (FIFO) method** assumes that the **earliest goods** purchased are the first to be sold. FIFO often parallels the actual physical flow of merchandise. That is, it generally is good business practice to sell the oldest units first. Under the FIFO method, therefore, the **costs** of the earliest goods purchased are the first to be recognized in determining cost of goods sold. (This does not necessarily mean that the oldest units **are** sold first, but that the costs of the oldest units are **recognized** first. In a bin of picture hangers at the hardware store, for example, no one really knows, nor would it matter, which hangers are sold first.) Illustration 6-6 shows the allocation of the cost of goods available for sale at Houston Electronics under FIFO.

---

[1]Also, some companies use a perpetual system to keep track of units, but they do not make an entry for perpetual cost of goods sold. In addition, firms that employ LIFO tend to use **dollar-value LIFO**, a method discussed in upper-level courses. FIFO periodic and FIFO perpetual give the same result. Therefore, companies should not incur the additional cost to use FIFO perpetual. Few companies use perpetual average-cost because of the added cost of recordkeeping. Finally, for instructional purposes, we believe it is easier to demonstrate the cost flow assumptions under the periodic system, which makes it more pedagogically appropriate.

Illustration 6-6
Allocation of costs—FIFO method

COST OF GOODS AVAILABLE FOR SALE				
Date	Explanation	Units	Unit Cost	Total Cost
Jan. 1	Beginning inventory	100	$10	$ 1,000
Apr. 15	Purchase	200	11	2,200
Aug. 24	Purchase	300	12	3,600
Nov. 27	Purchase	400	13	5,200
	Total	1,000		$12,000

Helpful Hint Note the sequencing of the allocation: (1) Compute ending inventory, and (2) determine cost of goods sold.

STEP 1: ENDING INVENTORY   **STEP 2: COST OF GOODS SOLD**

Date	Units	Unit Cost	Total Cost			
Nov. 27	400	$13	$ 5,200	Cost of goods available for sale	$12,000
Aug. 24	50	12	600	Less: Ending inventory	5,800
Total	450		$5,800	Cost of goods sold	$ 6,200

Helpful Hint Another way of thinking about the calculation of FIFO ending inventory is the *LISH assumption*—last in still here.

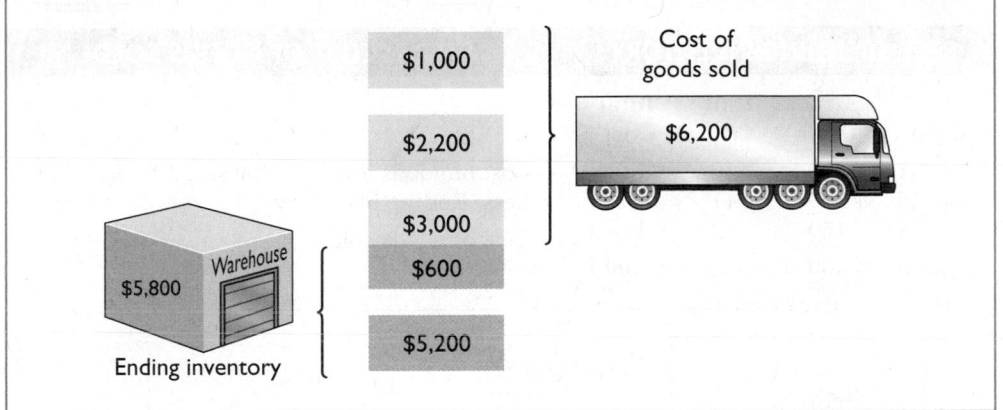

Under FIFO, since it is assumed that the first goods purchased were the first goods sold, ending inventory is based on the prices of the most recent units purchased. That is, **under FIFO, companies obtain the cost of the ending inventory by taking the unit cost of the most recent purchase and working backward until all units of inventory have been costed**. In this example, Houston Electronics prices the 450 units of ending inventory using the **most recent** prices. The last purchase was 400 units at $13 on November 27. The remaining 50 units are priced using the unit cost of the second most recent purchase, $12, on August 24. Next, Houston Electronics calculates cost of goods sold by subtracting the cost of the units **not sold** (ending inventory) from the cost of all goods available for sale.

Illustration 6-7 demonstrates that companies also can calculate cost of goods sold by pricing the 550 units sold using the prices of the first 550 units acquired. Note that of the 300 units purchased on August 24, only 250 units are assumed sold. This agrees with our calculation of the cost of ending inventory, where 50 of these units were assumed unsold and thus included in ending inventory.

Date	Units	Unit Cost	Total Cost
Jan. 1	100	$10	$ 1,000
Apr. 15	200	11	2,200
Aug. 24	250	12	3,000
Total	550		$6,200

Illustration 6-7
Proof of cost of goods sold

LAST-IN, FIRST-OUT (LIFO)

The **last-in, first-out (LIFO) method** assumes that the **latest goods** purchased are the first to be sold. LIFO seldom coincides with the actual physical flow of inventory. (Exceptions include goods stored in piles, such as coal or hay, where goods are removed from the top of the pile as they are sold.) Under the LIFO method, the **costs** of the latest goods purchased are the first to be recognized in determining cost of goods sold. Illustration 6-8 shows the allocation of the cost of goods available for sale at Houston Electronics under LIFO.

Illustration 6-8
Allocation of costs—LIFO method

COST OF GOODS AVAILABLE FOR SALE				
Date	Explanation	Units	Unit Cost	Total Cost
Jan. 1	Beginning inventory	100	$10	$ 1,000
Apr. 15	Purchase	200	11	2,200
Aug. 24	Purchase	300	12	3,600
Nov. 27	Purchase	400	13	5,200
	Total	1,000		$12,000

STEP 1: ENDING INVENTORY				STEP 2: COST OF GOODS SOLD	
Date	Units	Unit Cost	Total Cost		
Jan. 1	100	$10	$ 1,000	Cost of goods available for sale	$12,000
Apr. 15	200	11	2,200	Less: Ending inventory	5,000
Aug. 24	150	12	1,800	Cost of goods sold	$ 7,000
Total	450		$5,000		

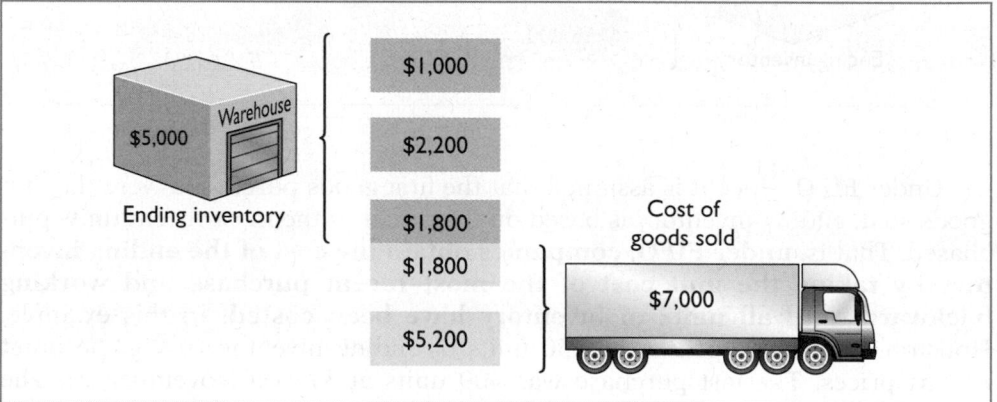

Helpful Hint Another way of thinking about the calculation of LIFO **ending inventory** is the *FISH assumption*—first in still here.

Under LIFO, since it is assumed that the first goods sold were those that were most recently purchased, ending inventory is based on the prices of the oldest units purchased. That is, **under LIFO, companies obtain the cost of the ending inventory by taking the unit cost of the earliest goods available for sale and working forward until all units of inventory have been costed**. In this example, Houston Electronics prices the 450 units of ending inventory using the **earliest** prices. The first purchase was 100 units at $10 in the January 1 beginning inventory. Then, 200 units were purchased at $11. The remaining 150 units needed are priced at $12 per unit (August 24 purchase). Next, Houston Electronics calculates cost of goods sold by subtracting the cost of the units **not sold** (ending inventory) from the cost of all goods available for sale.

Illustration 6-9 demonstrates that companies also can calculate cost of goods sold by pricing the 550 units sold using the prices of the last 550 units acquired. Note that of the 300 units purchased on August 24, only 150 units are assumed sold. This agrees with our calculation of the cost of ending inventory, where 150 of these units were assumed unsold and thus included in ending inventory.

Illustration 6-9
Proof of cost of goods sold

Date	Units	Unit Cost	Total Cost
Nov. 27	400	$13	$5,200
Aug. 24	150	12	1,800
Total	550		$7,000

Under a periodic inventory system, which we are using here, **all goods purchased during the period are assumed to be available for the first sale, regardless of the date of purchase**.

AVERAGE-COST

The **average-cost method** allocates the cost of goods available for sale on the basis of the **weighted-average unit cost** incurred. The average-cost method assumes that goods are similar in nature. Illustration 6-10 presents the formula and a sample computation of the weighted-average unit cost.

Illustration 6-10
Formula for weighted-average unit cost

Cost of Goods Available for Sale	÷	Total Units Available for Sale	=	Weighted- Average Unit Cost
$12,000	÷	1,000	=	$12

The company then applies the weighted-average unit cost to the units on hand to determine the cost of the ending inventory. Illustration 6-11 shows the allocation of the cost of goods available for sale at Houston Electronics using average-cost.

Illustration 6-11
Allocation of costs—average-cost method

COST OF GOODS AVAILABLE FOR SALE

Date	Explanation	Units	Unit Cost	Total Cost
Jan. 1	Beginning inventory	100	$10	$ 1,000
Apr. 15	Purchase	200	11	2,200
Aug. 24	Purchase	300	12	3,600
Nov. 27	Purchase	400	13	5,200
	Total	1,000		$12,000

STEP 1: ENDING INVENTORY   STEP 2: COST OF GOODS SOLD

$12,000	÷	1,000	=	$12	Cost of goods available for sale	$12,000
		Unit		Total	Less: Ending inventory	5,400
Units		Cost		Cost	Cost of goods sold	$ 6,600
450		$12		$5,400		

$$\frac{\$12,000}{1,000 \text{ units}} = \$12 \text{ per unit}$$

Cost per unit

450 units × $12 = $5,400   Warehouse

Ending inventory

$12,000 − $5,400 = $6,600

Cost of goods sold

We can verify the cost of goods sold under this method by multiplying the units sold times the weighted-average unit cost (550 × $12 = $6,600). Note that this method does not use the average of the unit costs. That average is $11.50 ($10 + $11 + $12 + $13 = $46; $46 ÷ 4). The average-cost method instead uses the average **weighted by** the quantities purchased at each unit cost.

> **DO IT!**

Cost Flow Methods

The accounting records of Shumway Ag Implements show the following data.

Beginning inventory	4,000 units at $ 3
Purchases	6,000 units at $ 4
Sales	7,000 units at $12

Determine the cost of goods sold during the period under a periodic inventory system using (a) the FIFO method, (b) the LIFO method, and (c) the average-cost method.

Solution

Action Plan

✔ Understand the periodic inventory system.

✔ Allocate costs between goods sold and goods on hand (ending inventory) for each cost flow method.

✔ Compute cost of goods sold for each method.

Cost of goods available for sale = (4,000 × $3) + (6,000 × $4) = $36,000

Ending inventory = 10,000 − 7,000 = 3,000 units

(a) FIFO: $36,000 − (3,000 × $4) = $24,000

(b) LIFO: $36,000 − (3,000 × $3) = $27,000

(c) Average cost per unit: [(4,000 @ $3) + (6,000 @ $4)] ÷ 10,000 = $3.60
Average-cost: $36,000 − (3,000 × $3.60) = $25,200

Related exercise material: **BE6-3, BE6-4, BE6-5, E6-3, E6-4, E6-5, E6-6, E6-7, E6-8, and DO IT! 6-2.**

✔ The Navigator

Financial Statement and Tax Effects of Cost Flow Methods

LEARNING OBJECTIVE   3

Explain the financial effects of the inventory cost flow assumptions.

Each of the three assumed cost flow methods is acceptable for use. For example, Reebok International Ltd. and Wendy's International currently use the FIFO method of inventory costing. Campbell Soup Company, Krogers, and Walgreen Drugs use LIFO for part or all of their inventory. Bristol-Myers Squibb, Starbucks, and Motorola use the average-cost method. In fact, a company may also use more than one cost flow method at the same time. Stanley Black & Decker Manufacturing Company, for example, uses LIFO for domestic inventories and FIFO for foreign inventories. Illustration 6-12 (in the margin) shows the use of the three cost flow methods in 500 large U.S. companies.

The reasons companies adopt different inventory cost flow methods are varied, but they usually involve one of three factors: (1) income statement effects, (2) balance sheet effects, or (3) tax effects.

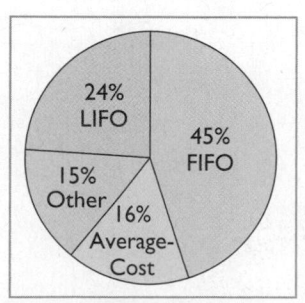

Illustration 6-12
Use of cost flow methods in major U.S. companies

INCOME STATEMENT EFFECTS

To understand why companies might choose a particular cost flow method, let's examine the effects of the different cost flow assumptions on the financial statements of Houston Electronics. The condensed income statements in Illustration 6-13 assume that Houston sold its 550 units for $18,500, had operating expenses of $9,000, and is subject to an income tax rate of 30%.

Illustration 6-13
Comparative effects of cost flow methods

HOUSTON ELECTRONICS Condensed Income Statements	FIFO	LIFO	Average-Cost
Sales revenue	$18,500	$18,500	$18,500
Beginning inventory	1,000	1,000	1,000
Purchases	11,000	11,000	11,000
Cost of goods available for sale	12,000	12,000	12,000
Ending inventory	**5,800**	**5,000**	**5,400**
Cost of goods sold	6,200	7,000	6,600
Gross profit	12,300	11,500	11,900
Operating expenses	9,000	9,000	9,000
Income before income taxes*	3,300	2,500	2,900
Income tax expense (30%)	990	750	870
Net income	**$ 2,310**	**$ 1,750**	**$ 2,030**

*We are assuming that Houston Electronics is a corporation, and corporations are required to pay income taxes.

Note the cost of goods available for sale ($12,000) is the same under each of the three inventory cost flow methods. However, the ending inventories and the costs of goods sold are different. This difference is due to the unit costs that the company allocated to cost of goods sold and to ending inventory. Each dollar of difference in ending inventory results in a corresponding dollar difference in income before income taxes. For Houston, an $800 difference exists between FIFO and LIFO cost of goods sold.

In periods of changing prices, the cost flow assumption can have a significant impact on income and on evaluations based on income. In most instances, prices are rising (inflation). In a period of inflation, FIFO produces a higher net income because the lower unit costs of the first units purchased are matched against revenues. In a period of rising prices (as is the case in the Houston example), FIFO reports the highest net income ($2,310) and LIFO the lowest ($1,750); average-cost falls in the middle ($2,030). If prices are falling, the results from the use of FIFO and LIFO are reversed. FIFO will report the lowest net income and LIFO the highest.

To management, higher net income is an advantage. It causes external users to view the company more favorably. In addition, management bonuses, if based on net income, will be higher. Therefore, when prices are rising (which is usually the case), companies tend to prefer FIFO because it results in higher net income.

Some argue that the use of LIFO in a period of inflation enables the company to avoid reporting **paper** (or **phantom**) **profit** as economic gain. To illustrate, assume that Kralik Company buys 200 units of a product at $20 per unit on January 10 and 200 more on December 31 at $24 each. During the year, Kralik sells 200 units at $30 each. Illustration 6-14 shows the results under FIFO and LIFO.

Illustration 6-14
Income statement effects compared

	FIFO	LIFO
Sales revenue (200 × $30)	$6,000	$6,000
Cost of goods sold	4,000 (200 × $20)	4,800 (200 × $24)
Gross profit	$2,000	$1,200

Under LIFO, Kralik Company has recovered the current replacement cost ($4,800) of the units sold. Thus, the gross profit in economic terms is real. However, under FIFO, the company has recovered only the January 10 cost ($4,000). To replace the units sold, it must reinvest $800 (200 × $4) of the gross profit. Thus, $800 of the gross profit is said to be phantom or illusory. As a result, reported net income is also overstated in real terms.

BALANCE SHEET EFFECTS

A major advantage of the FIFO method is that in a period of inflation, the costs allocated to ending inventory will approximate their current cost. For example, for Houston Electronics, 400 of the 450 units in the ending inventory are costed under FIFO at the higher November 27 unit cost of $13.

Conversely, a major shortcoming of the LIFO method is that in a period of inflation, the costs allocated to ending inventory may be significantly understated in terms of current cost. The understatement becomes greater over prolonged periods of inflation if the inventory includes goods purchased in one or more prior accounting periods. For example, Caterpillar has used LIFO for more than 50 years. Its balance sheet shows ending inventory of $14,544 million. But the inventory's actual current cost if FIFO had been used is $16,966 million.

TAX EFFECTS

Helpful Hint A tax rule, often referred to as the *LIFO conformity rule*, requires that if companies use LIFO for tax purposes they must also use it for financial reporting purposes. This means that if a company chooses the LIFO method to reduce its tax bills, it will also have to report lower net income in its financial statements.

We have seen that both inventory on the balance sheet and net income on the income statement are higher when companies use FIFO in a period of inflation. Yet, many companies have selected LIFO. Why? The reason is that LIFO results in the lowest income taxes (because of lower net income) during times of rising prices. For example, at Houston Electronics, income taxes are $750 under LIFO, compared to $990 under FIFO. The tax savings of $240 makes more cash available for use in the business.

Using Inventory Cost Flow Methods Consistently

Whatever cost flow method a company chooses, it should use that method consistently from one accounting period to another. This approach is often referred to as the **consistency concept**, which means that a company uses the same accounting principles and methods from year to year. Consistent application enhances the comparability of financial statements over successive time periods. In contrast, using the FIFO method one year and the LIFO method the next year would make it difficult to compare the net incomes of the two years.

Although consistent application is preferred, it does not mean that a company may never change its inventory costing method. When a company adopts a different method, it should disclose in the financial statements the change and its effects on net income. Illustration 6-15 shows a typical disclosure, using information from recent financial statements of Quaker Oats (now a unit of PepsiCo).

Illustration 6-15
Disclosure of change in cost flow method

> | Real World | **QUAKER OATS** |
> | --- | --- |
> | | Notes to the Financial Statements |

> **Note 1:** Effective July 1, the Company adopted the LIFO cost flow assumption for valuing the majority of U.S. Grocery Products inventories. The Company believes that the use of the LIFO method better matches current costs with current revenues. The effect of this change on the current year was to decrease net income by $16.0 million.

INTERNATIONAL INSIGHT

Is LIFO Fair?

ExxonMobil Corporation, like many U.S. companies, uses LIFO to value its inventory for financial reporting and tax purposes. In one recent year, this resulted in a cost of goods sold figure that was $5.6 billion higher than under FIFO. By increasing cost of goods sold, ExxonMobil reduces net income, which reduces taxes. Critics say that LIFO provides an unfair "tax dodge." As Congress looks for more sources of tax revenue, some lawmakers favor the elimination of LIFO. Supporters of LIFO argue that the method is conceptually sound because it matches current costs with current revenues. In addition, they point out that this matching provides protection against inflation.

International accounting standards do not allow the use of LIFO. Because of this, the net income of foreign oil companies such as BP and Royal Dutch Shell are not directly comparable to U.S. companies, which makes analysis difficult.

Source: David Reilly, "Big Oil's Accounting Methods Fuel Criticism," *Wall Street Journal* (August 8, 2006), p. C1.

? What are the arguments for and against the use of LIFO? (See page 324.)

Lower-of-Cost-or-Market

The value of inventory for companies selling high-technology or fashion goods can drop very quickly due to changes in technology or fashions. These circumstances sometimes call for inventory valuation methods other than those presented so far. For example, at one time purchasing managers at Ford decided to make a large purchase of palladium, a precious metal used in vehicle emission devices. They made this purchase because they feared a future shortage. The shortage did not materialize, and by the end of the year the price of palladium had plummeted. Ford's inventory was then worth $1 billion less than its original cost. Do you think Ford's inventory should have been stated at cost, in accordance with the historical cost principle, or at its lower replacement cost?

As you probably reasoned, this situation requires a departure from the cost basis of accounting. This is done by valuing the inventory at the **lower-of-cost-or-market (LCM)** in the period in which the price decline occurs. LCM is a basis whereby inventory is stated at the lower of either its cost or market value as determined by current replacement cost. LCM is an example of the accounting convention of **conservatism**. Conservatism means that the approach adopted among accounting alternatives is the method that is least likely to overstate assets and net income.

Companies apply LCM to the items in inventory after they have used one of the cost flow methods (specific identification, FIFO, LIFO, or average-cost) to determine cost. Under the LCM basis, market is defined as **current replacement cost**, not selling price. For a merchandising company, current replacement cost is the cost of purchasing the same goods at the present time from the usual suppliers in the usual quantities. Current replacement cost is used because a decline in the replacement cost of an item usually leads to a decline in the selling price of the item.

To illustrate the application of LCM, assume that Ken Tuckie TV has the following lines of merchandise with costs and market values as indicated. LCM produces the results shown in Illustration 6-16 (page 290). Note that the amounts shown in the final column are the lower-of-cost-or-market amounts for each item.

> **LEARNING OBJECTIVE 4**
>
> Explain the lower-of-cost-or-market basis of accounting for inventories.

> **International Note**
>
> Under U.S. GAAP, companies cannot reverse inventory write-downs if inventory increases in value in subsequent periods. IFRS permits companies to reverse write-downs in some circumstances.

Illustration 6-16
Computation of lower-of-cost-or-market

	Cost	Market	Lower-of-Cost-or-Market
Flat-screen TVs	$60,000	$55,000	$ 55,000
Satellite radios	45,000	52,000	45,000
DVD recorders	48,000	45,000	45,000
DVDs	15,000	14,000	14,000
Total inventory			$159,000

Inventory Errors

LEARNING OBJECTIVE 5

Indicate the effects of inventory errors on the financial statements.

Unfortunately, errors occasionally occur in accounting for inventory. In some cases, errors are caused by failure to count or price the inventory correctly. In other cases, errors occur because companies do not properly recognize the transfer of legal title to goods that are in transit. When errors occur, they affect both the income statement and the balance sheet.

Income Statement Effects

Under a periodic inventory system, both the beginning and ending inventories appear in the income statement. The ending inventory of one period automatically becomes the beginning inventory of the next period. Thus, inventory errors affect the computation of cost of goods sold and net income in two periods.

The effects on cost of goods sold can be computed by entering incorrect data in the formula in Illustration 6-17 and then substituting the correct data.

Illustration 6-17
Formula for cost of goods sold

$$\text{Beginning Inventory} + \text{Cost of Goods Purchased} - \text{Ending Inventory} = \text{Cost of Goods Sold}$$

If the error understates **beginning** inventory, cost of goods sold will be understated. If the error understates **ending** inventory, cost of goods sold will be overstated. Illustration 6-18 shows the effects of inventory errors on the current year's income statement.

Illustration 6-18
Effects of inventory errors on current year's income statement

When Inventory Error:	Cost of Goods Sold Is:	Net Income Is:
Understates beginning inventory	Understated	Overstated
Overstates beginning inventory	Overstated	Understated
Understates ending inventory	Overstated	Understated
Overstates ending inventory	Understated	Overstated

Ethics Note

Inventory fraud increases during recessions. Such fraud includes pricing inventory at amounts in excess of its actual value, or claiming to have inventory when no inventory exists. Inventory fraud usually overstates ending inventory, thereby understating cost of goods sold and creating higher income.

So far, the effects of inventory errors are fairly straightforward. Now, though, comes the (at first) surprising part: An error in the ending inventory of the current period will have a **reverse effect on net income of the next accounting period**. Illustration 6-19 shows this effect. As you study the illustration, you will see that the reverse effect comes from the fact that understating ending inventory in 2013 results in understating beginning inventory in 2014 and overstating net income in 2014.

Over the two years, though, total net income is correct because the errors **offset each other**. Notice that total income using incorrect data is $35,000 ($22,000 + $13,000), which is the same as the total income of

	2013			2014		
	Incorrect		**Correct**	**Incorrect**		**Correct**
Sales revenue		$80,000	$80,000		$90,000	$90,000
Beginning inventory	$20,000		$20,000	**$12,000**	**$15,000**	
Cost of goods purchased	40,000		40,000	68,000	68,000	
Cost of goods available for sale	60,000		60,000	80,000	83,000	
Ending inventory	**12,000**		**15,000**	23,000	23,000	
Cost of goods sold		48,000	45,000	57,000		60,000
Gross profit		32,000	35,000	33,000		30,000
Operating expenses		10,000	10,000	20,000		20,000
Net income		$22,000	$25,000	$13,000		$10,000

SAMPLE COMPANY — Condensed Income Statements

$(3,000) Net income understated

$3,000 Net income overstated

The errors cancel. Thus the combined total income for the 2-year period is correct.

Illustration 6-19 Effects of inventory errors on two years' income statements

$35,000 ($25,000 + $10,000) using correct data. Also note in this example that an error in the beginning inventory does not result in a corresponding error in the ending inventory for that period. The correctness of the ending inventory depends entirely on the accuracy of taking and costing the inventory at the balance sheet date under the periodic inventory system.

Balance Sheet Effects

Companies can determine the effect of ending inventory errors on the balance sheet by using the basic accounting equation: Assets = Liabilities + Owner's Equity. Errors in the ending inventory have the effects shown in Illustration 6-20.

Illustration 6-20 Effects of ending inventory errors on balance sheet

Ending Inventory Error	Assets	Liabilities	Owner's Equity
Overstated	Overstated	No effect	Overstated
Understated	Understated	No effect	Understated

The effect of an error in ending inventory on the subsequent period was shown in Illustration 6-19. Recall that if the error is not corrected, the combined total net income for the two periods would be correct. Thus, total owner's equity reported on the balance sheet at the end of 2014 will also be correct.

> DO IT!

LCM Basis; Inventory Errors

(a) Tracy Company sells three different types of home heating stoves (gas, wood, and pellet). The cost and market value of its inventory of stoves are as follows.

	Cost	Market
Gas	$ 84,000	$ 79,000
Wood	250,000	280,000
Pellet	112,000	101,000

Determine the value of the company's inventory under the lower-of-cost-or-market approach.

Solution

> The lowest value for each inventory type is gas $79,000, wood $250,000, and pellet $101,000. The total inventory value is the sum of these amounts, $430,000.

(b) Visual Company overstated its 2013 ending inventory by $22,000. Determine the impact this error has on ending inventory, cost of goods sold, and owner's equity in 2013 and 2014.

Solution

	2013	2014
Ending inventory	$22,000 overstated	No effect
Cost of goods sold	$22,000 understated	$22,000 overstated
Owner's equity	$22,000 overstated	No effect

Related exercise material: **BE6-7, BE6-8, E6-9, E6-10, E6-11, E6-12, and** **6-3.**

Statement Presentation and Analysis

Presentation

As indicated in Chapter 5, inventory is classified in the balance sheet as a current asset immediately below receivables. In a multiple-step income statement, cost of goods sold is subtracted from sales. There also should be disclosure of (1) the major inventory classifications, (2) the basis of accounting (cost, or lower-of-cost-or-market), and (3) the cost method (FIFO, LIFO, or average-cost).

Wal-Mart Stores, Inc., for example, in its January 31, 2011, balance sheet reported inventories of $36,318 million under current assets. The accompanying notes to the financial statements, as shown in Illustration 6-21, disclosed the following information.

Illustration 6-21
Inventory disclosures by Wal-Mart

Real World   **WAL-MART STORES, INC.**
Notes to the Financial Statements

Note 1. Summary of Significant Accounting Policies

Inventories

The Company values inventories at the lower of cost or market as determined primarily by the retail method of accounting, using the last-in, first-out ("LIFO") method for substantially all of the WalMart U.S. segment's merchandise inventories. The retail method of accounting results in inventory being valued at the lower of cost or market since permanent markdowns are currently taken as a reduction of the retail value of inventory. The Sam's Club segment's merchandise is valued based on the weighted-average cost using the LIFO method. Inventories for the Walmart International operations are primarily valued by the retail method of accounting and are stated using the first-in, first-out ("FIFO") method. At January 31, 2011 and 2010, our inventories valued at LIFO approximate those inventories as if they were valued at FIFO.

As indicated in this note, Wal-Mart values its inventories at the lower-of-cost-or-market using LIFO and FIFO.

Analysis

The amount of inventory carried by a company has significant economic consequences. And inventory management is a double-edged sword that requires constant attention. On the one hand, management wants to have a great variety and quantity on hand so that customers have a wide selection and items are always in stock. But, such a policy may incur high carrying costs (e.g., investment, storage, insurance, obsolescence, and damage). On the other hand, low inventory levels lead to stock-outs and lost sales. Common ratios used to manage and evaluate inventory levels are inventory turnover and a related measure, days in inventory.

Inventory turnover measures the number of times on average the inventory is sold during the period. Its purpose is to measure the liquidity of the inventory. The inventory turnover is computed by dividing cost of goods sold by the average inventory during the period. Unless seasonal factors are significant, average inventory can be computed from the beginning and ending inventory balances. For example, Wal-Mart reported in its 2011 annual report a beginning inventory of $32,713 million, an ending inventory of $36,318 million, and cost of goods sold for the year ended January 31, 2011, of $315,287 million. The inventory turnover formula and computation for Wal-Mart are shown below.

Cost of Goods Sold	÷	Average Inventory	=	Inventory Turnover
$315,287	÷	$\dfrac{\$36,318 + \$32,713}{2}$	=	**9.1 times**

Illustration 6-22
Inventory turnover formula and computation for Wal-Mart

A variant of the inventory turnover is **days in inventory**. This measures the average number of days inventory is held. It is calculated as 365 divided by the inventory turnover. For example, Wal-Mart's inventory turnover of 9.1 times divided into 365 is approximately 40.1 days. This is the approximate time that it takes a company to sell the inventory once it arrives at the store.

There are typical levels of inventory in every industry. Companies that are able to keep their inventory at lower levels and higher turnovers and still satisfy customer needs are the most successful.

ACCOUNTING ACROSS THE ORGANIZATION

Too Many TVs or Too Few?

Financial analysts closely monitored the inventory management practices of companies during the recent recession. For example, some analysts following Sony expressed concern because the company built up its inventory of televisions in an attempt to sell 25 million liquid crystal display (LCD) TVs—a 60% increase over the prior year. A year earlier, Sony had cut its inventory levels so that its quarterly days in inventory was down to 38 days, compared to 61 days for the same quarter a year before that. But now, as a result of its inventory build-up, days in inventory rose to 59 days. While management was saying that it didn't think that Sony's inventory levels were now too high, analysts were concerned that the company would have to engage in very heavy discounting in order to sell off its inventory. Analysts noted that the losses from discounting can be "punishing."

Source: Daisuke Wakabayashi, "Sony Pledges to Corral Inventory," *Wall Street Journal* Online (November 2, 2010).

 For Sony, what are the advantages and disadvantages of having a low days in inventory measure? (See page 324.)

DO IT!

Inventory Turnover

Early in 2014, Westmoreland Company switched to a just-in-time inventory system. Its sales revenue, cost of goods sold, and inventory amounts for 2013 and 2014 are shown below.

	2013	2014
Sales revenue	$2,000,000	$1,800,000
Cost of goods sold	1,000,000	910,000
Beginning inventory	290,000	210,000
Ending inventory	210,000	50,000

Determine the inventory turnover and days in inventory for 2013 and 2014. Discuss the changes in the amount of inventory, the inventory turnover and days in inventory, and the amount of sales across the two years.

Solution

Action Plan

✔ To find the inventory turnover, divide cost of goods sold by average inventory.

✔ To determine days in inventory, divide 365 days by the inventory turnover.

✔ Just-in-time inventory reduces the amount of inventory on hand, which reduces carrying costs. Reducing inventory levels by too much has potential negative implications for sales.

	2013	2014
Inventory turnover	$\dfrac{\$1,000,000}{(\$290,000 + \$210,000)/2} = 4$	$\dfrac{\$910,000}{(\$210,000 + \$50,000)/2} = 7$
Days in inventory	$365 \div 4 = 91.3$ days	$365 \div 7 = 52.1$ days

The company experienced a very significant decline in its ending inventory as a result of the just-in-time inventory. This decline improved its inventory turnover and its days in inventory. However, its sales declined by 10%. It is possible that this decline was caused by the dramatic reduction in the amount of inventory that was on hand, which increased the likelihood of "stock-outs." To determine the optimal inventory level, management must weigh the benefits of reduced inventory against the potential lost sales caused by stock-outs.

Related exercise material: **BE6-9, E6-13, E6-14, and DO IT! 6-4.**

 The Navigator

Comprehensive DO IT! 1

Gerald D. Englehart Company has the following inventory, purchases, and sales data for the month of March.

Inventory:	March 1	200 units @ $4.00	$ 800
Purchases:			
	March 10	500 units @ $4.50	2,250
	March 20	400 units @ $4.75	1,900
	March 30	300 units @ $5.00	1,500
Sales:			
	March 15	500 units	
	March 25	400 units	

The physical inventory count on March 31 shows 500 units on hand.

Instructions

Under a **periodic inventory system**, determine the cost of inventory on hand at March 31 and the cost of goods sold for March under (a) FIFO, (b) LIFO, and (c) average-cost.

Solution to Comprehensive DO IT! 1

The cost of goods available for sale is $6,450, as follows.

Inventory:		200 units @ $4.00	$ 800
Purchases:			
	March 10	500 units @ $4.50	2,250
	March 20	400 units @ $4.75	1,900
	March 30	300 units @ $5.00	1,500
Total:		1,400	$6,450

Under a **periodic inventory system**, the cost of goods sold under each cost flow method is as follows.

FIFO Method

Ending inventory:

Date	Units	Unit Cost	Total Cost	
March 30	300	$5.00	$1,500	
March 20	200	4.75	950	$2,450

Cost of goods sold: $6,450 − $2,450 = $4,000

LIFO Method

Ending inventory:

Date	Units	Unit Cost	Total Cost	
March 1	200	$4.00	$ 800	
March 10	300	4.50	1,350	$2,150

Cost of goods sold: $6,450 − $2,150 = $4,300

Average-Cost Method

Average unit cost: $6,450 ÷ 1,400 = $4.607
Ending inventory: 500 × $4.607 = $2,303.50

Cost of goods sold: $6,450 − $2,303.50 = $4,146.50

✔ The Navigator

SUMMARY OF LEARNING OBJECTIVES

✔ The Navigator

1 Determine how to classify inventory and inventory quantities. Merchandisers need only one inventory classification, merchandise inventory, to describe the different items that make up total inventory. Manufacturers, on the other hand, usually classify inventory into three categories: finished goods, work in process, and raw materials. To determine inventory quantities, manufacturers (1) take a physical inventory of goods on hand and (2) determine the ownership of goods in transit or on consignment.

2 **Explain the accounting for inventories and apply the inventory cost flow methods.** The primary basis of accounting for inventories is cost. Cost of goods available for sale includes (a) cost of beginning inventory and (b) cost of goods purchased. The inventory cost flow methods are specific identification and three assumed cost flow methods—FIFO, LIFO, and average-cost.

3 **Explain the financial effects of the inventory cost flow assumptions.** Companies may allocate the cost of goods available for sale to cost of goods sold and ending inventory by specific identification or by a method based on an assumed cost flow. When prices are rising, the first-in, first-out (FIFO) method results in lower cost of goods sold and higher net income than the other methods. The reverse is true when prices are falling. In the balance sheet, FIFO results in an ending inventory that is closest to current value. Inventory under LIFO is the farthest from current value. LIFO results in the lowest income taxes.

4 **Explain the lower-of-cost-or-market basis of accounting for inventories.** Companies use the lower-of-cost-or-market (LCM) basis when the current replacement cost (market) is less than cost. Under LCM, companies recognize the loss in the period in which the price decline occurs.

5 **Indicate the effects of inventory errors on the financial statements.** In the income statement of the current year: (a) An error in beginning inventory will have a reverse effect on net income. (b) An error in ending inventory will have a similar effect on net income. In the following period, its effect on net income for that period is reversed, and total net income for the two years will be correct.

In the balance sheet: Ending inventory errors will have the same effect on total assets and total owner's equity and no effect on liabilities.

6 **Compute and interpret the inventory turnover.** The inventory turnover is cost of goods sold divided by average inventory. To convert it to average days in inventory, divide 365 days by the inventory turnover.

GLOSSARY

Average-cost method Inventory costing method that uses the weighted-average unit cost to allocate to ending inventory and cost of goods sold the cost of goods available for sale. (p. 285).

Consigned goods Goods held for sale by one party although ownership of the goods is retained by another party. (p. 279).

Consistency concept Dictates that a company use the same accounting principles and methods from year to year. (p. 288).

Current replacement cost The current cost to replace an inventory item. (p. 289).

Days in inventory Measure of the average number of days inventory is held; calculated as 365 divided by inventory turnover. (p. 293).

Finished goods inventory Manufactured items that are completed and ready for sale. (p. 276).

First-in, first-out (FIFO) method Inventory costing method that assumes that the costs of the earliest goods purchased are the first to be recognized as cost of goods sold. (p. 282).

FOB (free on board) destination Freight terms indicating that ownership of the goods remains with the seller until the goods reach the buyer. (p. 278).

FOB (free on board) shipping point Freight terms indicating that ownership of the goods passes to the buyer when the public carrier accepts the goods from the seller. (p. 278).

Inventory turnover A ratio that measures the number of times on average the inventory sold during the period; computed by dividing cost of goods sold by the average inventory during the period. (p. 293).

Just-in-time (JIT) inventory Inventory system in which companies manufacture or purchase goods just in time for use. (p. 276).

Last-in, first-out (LIFO) method Inventory costing method that assumes the costs of the latest units purchased are the first to be allocated to cost of goods sold. (p. 284).

Lower-of-cost-or-market (LCM) A basis whereby inventory is stated at the lower of either its cost or its market value as determined by current replacement cost. (p. 289).

Raw materials Basic goods that will be used in production but have not yet been placed into production. (p. 276).

Specific identification method An actual physical flow costing method in which items still in inventory are specifically costed to arrive at the total cost of the ending inventory. (p. 281).

Weighted-average unit cost Average cost that is weighted by the number of units purchased at each unit cost. (p. 285).

Work in process That portion of manufactured inventory that has been placed into the production process but is not yet complete. (p. 276).

APPENDIX 6A   Inventory Cost Flow Methods in Perpetual Inventory Systems

What inventory cost flow methods do companies employ if they use a perpetual inventory system? Simple—they can use any of the inventory cost flow methods described in the chapter. To illustrate the application of the three assumed cost flow methods (FIFO, LIFO, and average-cost), we will use the data shown in Illustration 6A-1 and in this chapter for Houston Electronics' Astro condensers.

LEARNING OBJECTIVE 7

Apply the inventory cost flow methods to perpetual inventory records.

Illustration 6A-1
Inventoriable units and costs

HOUSTON ELECTRONICS
Astro Condensers

Date	Explanation	Units	Units Cost	Total Cost	Balance in Units
1/1	Beginning inventory	100	$10	$ 1,000	100
4/15	Purchases	200	11	2,200	300
8/24	Purchases	300	12	3,600	600
9/10	Sale	550			50
11/27	Purchases	400	13	5,200	450
				$12,000	

First-In, First-Out (FIFO)

Under perpetual FIFO, the company charges to cost of goods sold the cost of the earliest goods on hand **prior to each sale**. Therefore, the cost of goods sold on September 10 consists of the units on hand January 1 and the units purchased April 15 and August 24. Illustration 6A-2 shows the inventory under a FIFO method perpetual system.

Illustration 6A-2
Perpetual system—FIFO

Date	Purchases	Cost of Goods Sold	Balance (in units and cost)
January 1			(100 @ $10) $ 1,000
April 15	(200 @ $11) $2,200		(100 @ $10) } (200 @ $11) } $ 3,200
August 24	(300 @ $12) $3,600		(100 @ $10) } (200 @ $11) } (300 @ $12) } $ 6,800
September 10		(100 @ $10) (200 @ $11) (250 @ $12)	(50 @ $12) $ 600
		$6,200	*Cost of goods sold*
November 27	(400 @ $13) $5,200		(50 @ $12) } (400 @ $13) } **$5,800** *Ending inventory*

The ending inventory in this situation is $5,800, and the cost of goods sold is $6,200 [(100 @ $10) + (200 @ $11) + (250 @ $12)].

Compare Illustrations 6-6 (page 283) and 6A-2. You can see that the results under FIFO in a perpetual system are the **same as in a periodic system**. In both cases, the ending inventory is $5,800 and cost of goods sold is $6,200. Regardless of the system, the first costs in are the costs assigned to cost of goods sold.

Last-In, First-Out (LIFO)

Under the LIFO method using a perpetual system, the company charges to cost of goods sold the cost of the most recent purchase prior to sale. Therefore, the cost of the goods sold on September 10 consists of all the units from the August 24 and April 15 purchases plus 50 of the units in beginning inventory. Illustration 6A-3 shows the computation of the ending inventory under the LIFO method.

Illustration 6A-3
Perpetual system—LIFO

Date	Purchases	Cost of Goods Sold	Balance (in units and cost)
January 1			(100 @ $10) $ 1,000
April 15	(200 @ $11) $2,200		(100 @ $10) (200 @ $11) } $ 3,200
August 24	(300 @ $12) $3,600		(100 @ $10) (200 @ $11) } $ 6,800 (300 @ $12)
September 10		(300 @ $12) (200 @ $11) (50 @ $10)	(50 @ $10) $ 500
Cost of goods sold		**$6,300**	
November 27	(400 @ $13) $5,200		(50 @ $10) (400 @ $13) } **$5,700**
Ending inventory			

The use of LIFO in a perpetual system will usually produce cost allocations that differ from those using LIFO in a periodic system. In a perpetual system, the company allocates the latest units purchased **prior to each sale** to cost of goods sold. In contrast, in a periodic system, the latest units purchased **during the period** are allocated to cost of goods sold. Thus, when a purchase is made after the last sale, the LIFO periodic system will apply this purchase to the previous sale. Compare Illustrations 6-8 (page 284) and 6A-3. Illustration 6-8 shows that the 400 units at $13 purchased on November 27 applied to the sale of 550 units on September 10. Under the LIFO perpetual system in Illustration 6A-3, the 400 units at $13 purchased on November 27 are all applied to the ending inventory.

The ending inventory in this LIFO perpetual illustration is $5,700, and cost of goods sold is $6,300, as compared to the LIFO periodic Illustration 6-8 (on page 284) where the ending inventory is $5,000 and cost of goods sold is $7,000.

Average-Cost

The average-cost method in a perpetual inventory system is called the **moving-average method**. Under this method, the company computes a new average **after each purchase**, by dividing the cost of goods available for sale by the units on hand. The average cost is then applied to (1) the units sold, to determine the cost of goods sold, and (2) the remaining units on hand, to determine the ending inventory amount. Illustration 6A-4 shows the application of the moving-average cost method by Houston Electronics.

Illustration 6A-4
Perpetual system—average-cost method

Date	Purchases	Cost of Goods Sold	Balance (in units and cost)
January 1			(100 @ $10) $ 1,000
April 15	(200 @ $11) $2,200		(300 @ $10.667) $ 3,200
August 24	(300 @ $12) $3,600		(600 @ $11.333) $ 6,800
September 10		(550 @ $11.333)	(50 @ $11.333) $ 567
Cost of goods sold		**$6,233**	
November 27	(400 @ $13) $5,200		(450 @ $12.816) **$5,767**
Ending inventory			

As indicated, Houston Electronics computes **a new average each time it makes a purchase**. On April 15, after it buys 200 units for $2,200, a total of 300 units costing $3,200 ($1,000 + $2,200) are on hand. The average unit cost is $10.667 ($3,200 ÷ 300). On August 24, after Houston Electronics buys 300 units for $3,600, a total of 600 units costing $6,800 ($1,000 + $2,200 + $3,600) are on hand, at an average cost per unit of $11.333 ($6,800 ÷ 600). Houston Electronics uses this unit cost of $11.333 in costing sales until it makes another purchase, when the company computes a new unit cost. Accordingly, the unit cost of the 550 units sold on September 10 is $11.333, and the total cost of goods sold is $6,233. On November 27, following the purchase of 400 units for $5,200, there are 450 units on hand costing $5,767 ($567 + $5,200) with a new average cost of $12.816 ($5,767 ÷ 450).

Compare this moving-average cost under the perpetual inventory system to Illustration 6-11 (on page 285) showing the average-cost method under a periodic inventory system.

> Comprehensive DO IT! 2

Comprehensive **DO IT!** 1 on page 294 showed cost of goods sold computations under a periodic inventory system. Now let's assume that Gerald D. Englehart Company uses a perpetual inventory system. The company has the same inventory, purchases, and sales data for the month of March as shown earlier:

Inventory:	March 1	200 units @ $4.00	$ 800
Purchases:	March 10	500 units @ $4.50	2,250
	March 20	400 units @ $4.75	1,900
	March 30	300 units @ $5.00	1,500
Sales:	March 15	500 units	
	March 25	400 units	

The physical inventory count on March 31 shows 500 units on hand.

Instructions
Under a **perpetual inventory system**, determine the cost of inventory on hand at March 31 and the cost of goods sold for March under (a) FIFO, (b) LIFO, and (c) moving-average cost.

Action Plan

✔ Compute the cost of goods sold under the perpetual FIFO method by allocating to the goods sold the **earliest** cost of goods purchased.

✔ Compute the cost of goods sold under the perpetual LIFO method by allocating to the goods sold the **latest** cost of goods purchased.

✔ Compute the cost of goods sold under the perpetual average-cost method by allocating to the goods sold a **moving-average** cost.

Solution to Comprehensive DO IT! 2

The cost of goods available for sale is $6,450, as follows.

Inventory:		200 units @ $4.00	$ 800
Purchases:	March 10	500 units @ $4.50	2,250
	March 20	400 units @ $4.75	1,900
	March 30	300 units @ $5.00	1,500
Total:		1,400	$6,450

Under a **perpetual inventory system**, the cost of goods sold under each cost flow method is as follows.

FIFO Method

Date	Purchases	Cost of Goods Sold	Balance
March 1			(200 @ $4.00) $ 800
March 10	(500 @ $4.50) $2,250		(200 @ $4.00) } $3,050 (500 @ $4.50)

Date	Purchases	Cost of Goods Sold	Balance
March 15		(200 @ $4.00)	
		(300 @ $4.50)	(200 @ $4.50) $ 900
		$2,150	
March 20	(400 @ $4.75) $1,900		(200 @ $4.50) $2,800
			(400 @ $4.75)
March 25		(200 @ $4.50)	
		(200 @ $4.75)	(200 @ $4.75) $ 950
		$1,850	
March 30	(300 @ $5.00) $1,500		(200 @ $4.75) $2,450
			(300 @ $5.00)
	Ending inventory $2,450	Cost of goods sold: $2,150 + $1,850 = $4,000	

LIFO Method

Date	Purchases	Cost of Goods Sold	Balance
March 1			(200 @ $4.00) $ 800
March 10	(500 @ $4.50) $2,250		(200 @ $4.00) $3,050
			(500 @ $4.50)
March 15		(500 @ $4.50) $2,250	(200 @ $4.00) $ 800
March 20	(400 @ $4.75) $1,900		(200 @ $4.00) $2,700
			(400 @ $4.75)
March 25		(400 @ $4.75) $1,900	(200 @ $4.00) $ 800
March 30	(300 @ $5.00) $1,500		(200 @ $4.00) $2,300
			(300 @ $5.00)
	Ending inventory $2,300	Cost of goods sold: $2,250 + $1,900 = $4,150	

Moving-Average Cost Method

Date	Purchases	Cost of Goods Sold	Balance
March 1			(200 @ $ 4.00) $ 800
March 10	(500 @ $4.50) $2,250		(700 @ $4.357) $3,050
March 15		(500 @ $4.357) $2,179	(200 @ $4.357) $ 871
March 20	(400 @ $4.75) $1,900		(600 @ $4.618) $2,771
March 25		(400 @ $4.618) $1,847	(200 @ $4.618) $ 924
March 30	(300 @ $5.00) $1,500		(500 @ $4.848) $2,424
	Ending inventory $2,424	Cost of goods sold: $2,179 + $1,847 = $4,026	

✔ The Navigator

SUMMARY OF LEARNING OBJECTIVE FOR APPENDIX 6A

✔ The Navigator

7 Apply the inventory cost flow methods to perpetual inventory records. Under FIFO and a perpetual inventory system, companies charge to cost of goods sold the cost of the earliest goods on hand prior to each sale. Under LIFO and a perpetual system, companies charge to cost of goods sold the cost of the most recent purchase prior to sale. Under the moving-average (average cost) method and a perpetual system, companies compute a new average cost after each purchase.

APPENDIX 6B Estimating Inventories

LEARNING OBJECTIVE | **8**

Describe the two methods of estimating inventories.

In the chapter, we assumed that a company would be able to physically count its inventory. What if it cannot? What if the inventory were destroyed by fire or flood, for example? In that case, the company would use an estimate.

Two circumstances explain why companies sometimes estimate inventories. First, a casualty such as fire, flood, or earthquake may make it impossible to take a physical inventory. Second, managers may want monthly or quarterly financial statements, but a physical inventory is taken only annually. The need for estimating inventories occurs primarily with a periodic inventory system because of the absence of perpetual inventory records.

There are two widely used methods of estimating inventories: (1) the gross profit method, and (2) the retail inventory method.

Gross Profit Method

The **gross profit method** estimates the cost of ending inventory by applying a gross profit rate to net sales. This method is relatively simple but effective. Accountants, auditors, and managers frequently use the gross profit method to test the reasonableness of the ending inventory amount. It will detect large errors.

To use this method, a company needs to know its net sales, cost of goods available for sale, and gross profit rate. The company then can estimate its gross profit for the period. Illustration 6B-1 shows the formulas for using the gross profit method.

Step 1:	Net Sales	−	Estimated Gross Profit	=	Estimated Cost of Goods Sold
Step 2:	Cost of Goods Available for Sale	−	Estimated Cost of Goods Sold	=	Estimated Cost of Ending Inventory

Illustration 6B-1
Gross profit method formulas

To illustrate, assume that Kishwaukee Company wishes to prepare an income statement for the month of January. Its records show net sales of $200,000, beginning inventory $40,000, and cost of goods purchased $120,000. In the preceding year, the company realized a 30% gross profit rate. It expects to earn the same rate this year. Given these facts and assumptions, Kishwaukee can compute the estimated cost of the ending inventory at January 31 under the gross profit method as follows.

Illustration 6B-2
Example of gross profit method

Step 1:

Net sales	$ 200,000
Less: Estimated gross profit (30% × $200,000)	60,000
Estimated cost of goods sold	**$140,000**

Step 2:

Beginning inventory	$ 40,000
Cost of goods purchased	120,000
Cost of goods available for sale	160,000
Less: Estimated cost of goods sold	140,000
Estimated cost of ending inventory	**$ 20,000**

The gross profit method is based on the assumption that the gross profit rate will remain constant. But, it may not remain constant, due to a change in merchandising policies or in market conditions. In such cases, the company should adjust the rate to reflect current operating conditions. In some cases, companies can obtain a more accurate estimate by applying this method on a department or product-line basis.

Note that companies should not use the gross profit method to prepare financial statements at the end of the year. These statements should be based on a physical inventory count.

Retail Inventory Method

A retail store such as Home Depot, Ace Hardware, or Wal-Mart has thousands of different types of merchandise at low unit costs. In such cases, it is difficult and time-consuming to apply unit costs to inventory quantities. An alternative is to use the **retail inventory method** to estimate the cost of inventory. Most retail companies can establish a relationship between cost and sales price. The company then applies the cost-to-retail percentage to the ending inventory at retail prices to determine inventory at cost.

Under the retail inventory method, a company's records must show both the cost and retail value of the goods available for sale. Illustration 6B-3 presents the formulas for using the retail inventory method.

Illustration 6B-3
Retail inventory method formulas

Step 1:	Goods Available for Sale at Retail	−	Net Sales	=	Ending Inventory at Retail
Step 2:	Goods Available for Sale at Cost	÷	Goods Available for Sale at Retail	=	Cost-to-Retail Ratio
Step 3:	Ending Inventory at Retail	×	Cost-to-Retail Ratio	=	Estimated Cost of Ending Inventory

We can demonstrate the logic of the retail method by using unit-cost data. Assume that Ortiz Inc. has marked 10 units purchased at $7 to sell for $10 per unit. Thus, the cost-to-retail ratio is 70% ($70 ÷ $100). If four units remain unsold, their retail value is $40 (4 × $10), and their cost is $28 ($40 × 70%). This amount agrees with the total cost of goods on hand on a per unit basis (4 × $7).

Illustration 6B-4 shows application of the retail method for Valley West. Note that it is not necessary to take a physical inventory to determine the estimated cost of goods on hand at any given time.

Illustration 6B-4
Application of retail inventory method

	At Cost	At Retail
Beginning inventory	$14,000	$ 21,500
Goods purchased	61,000	78,500
Goods available for sale	$75,000	100,000
Less: Net sales		70,000
Step (1) Ending inventory at retail =		**$ 30,000**

Step (2) Cost-to-retail ratio = $75,000 ÷ $100,000 = 75%
Step (3) Estimated cost of ending inventory = $30,000 × 75% = $22,500

The retail inventory method also facilitates taking a physical inventory at the end of the year. Valley West can value the goods on hand at the prices marked on the merchandise, and then apply the cost-to-retail ratio to the goods on hand at retail to determine the ending inventory at cost.

The major disadvantage of the retail method is that it is an averaging technique. Thus, it may produce an incorrect inventory valuation if the mix of the ending inventory is not representative of the mix in the goods available for sale. Assume, for example, that the cost-to-retail ratio of 75% for Valley West consists of equal proportions of inventory items that have cost-to-retail ratios of 70%, 75%, and 80%. If the ending inventory contains only items with a 70% ratio, an incorrect inventory cost will result. Companies can minimize this problem by applying the retail method on a department or product-line basis.

SUMMARY OF LEARNING OBJECTIVE FOR APPENDIX 6B

8 Describe the two methods of estimating inventories. The two methods of estimating inventories are the gross profit method and the retail inventory method. Under the gross profit method, companies apply a gross profit rate to net sales to determine estimated cost of goods sold. They then subtract estimated cost of goods sold from cost of goods available for sale to determine the estimated cost of the ending inventory.

Under the retail inventory method, companies compute a cost-to-retail ratio by dividing the cost of goods available for sale by the retail value of the goods available for sale. They then apply this ratio to the ending inventory at retail to determine the estimated cost of the ending inventory.

GLOSSARY FOR APPENDIX 6B

Gross profit method A method for estimating the cost of the ending inventory by applying a gross profit rate to net sales and subtracting estimated cost of goods sold from cost of goods available for sale. (p. 301).

Retail inventory method A method for estimating the cost of the ending inventory by applying a cost-to-retail ratio to the ending inventory at retail. (p. 302).

 Self-Test, Brief Exercises, Exercises, Problem Set A, and many more components are available for practice in *WileyPLUS*.

***Note:** All asterisked Questions, Exercises, and Problems relate to material in the appendices to the chapter.

SELF-TEST QUESTIONS

Answers are on page 324.

(LO 1) **1.** Which of the following should **not** be included in the physical inventory of a company?
 (a) Goods held on consignment from another company.
 (b) Goods shipped on consignment to another company.
 (c) Goods in transit from another company shipped FOB shipping point.
 (d) None of the above.

(LO 1) **2.** As a result of a thorough physical inventory, Railway Company determined that it had inventory worth $180,000 at December 31, 2014. This count did not take into consideration the following facts: Rogers Consignment store currently has goods worth $35,000 on its sales floor that belong to Railway but are being sold on consignment by Rogers. The selling price of these goods is $50,000. Railway purchased $13,000 of goods that were shipped on December 27, FOB destination, that will be received by Railway on January 3. Determine the correct amount of inventory that Railway should report.
 (a) $230,000.   **(c)** $228,000.
 (b) $215,000.   **(d)** $193,000.

3. Cost of goods available for sale consists of two elements: beginning inventory and (LO 2)
 (a) ending inventory.
 (b) cost of goods purchased.
 (c) cost of goods sold.
 (d) All of the above.

(LO 2) **4.** Poppins Company has the following:

	Units	Unit Cost
Inventory, Jan. 1	8,000	$11
Purchase, June 19	13,000	12
Purchase, Nov. 8	5,000	13

If Poppins has 9,000 units on hand at December 31, the cost of the ending inventory under FIFO is:
- **(a)** $99,000.
- **(b)** $108,000.
- **(c)** $113,000.
- **(d)** $117,000.

(LO 2) **5.** Using the data in Question 4 above, the cost of the ending inventory under LIFO is:
- **(a)** $113,000.
- **(b)** $108,000.
- **(c)** $99,000.
- **(d)** $100,000.

(LO 2) **6.** Hansel Electronics has the following:

	Units	Unit Cost
Inventory, Jan. 1	5,000	$ 8
Purchase, April 2	15,000	$10
Purchase, Aug. 28	20,000	$12

If Hansel has 7,000 units on hand at December 31, the cost of ending inventory under the average-cost method is:
- **(a)** $84,000.
- **(b)** $70,000.
- **(c)** $56,000.
- **(d)** $75,250.

(LO 3) **7.** In periods of rising prices, LIFO will produce:
- **(a)** higher net income than FIFO.
- **(b)** the same net income as FIFO.
- **(c)** lower net income than FIFO.
- **(d)** higher net income than average-cost.

(LO 3) **8.** Factors that affect the selection of an inventory costing method do **not** include:
- **(a)** tax effects.
- **(b)** balance sheet effects.
- **(c)** income statement effects.
- **(d)** perpetual vs. periodic inventory system.

(LO 4) **9.** Norton Company purchased 1,000 widgets and has 200 widgets in its ending inventory at a cost of $91 each and a current replacement cost of $80 each. The ending inventory under lower-of-cost-or-market is:
- **(a)** $91,000.
- **(b)** $80,000.
- **(c)** $18,200.
- **(d)** $16,000.

(LO 5) **10.** Falk Company's ending inventory is understated $4,000. The effects of this error on the current year's cost of goods sold and net income, respectively, are:

- **(a)** understated, overstated.
- **(b)** overstated, understated.
- **(c)** overstated, overstated.
- **(d)** understated, understated.

(LO 4) **11.** Pauline Company overstated its inventory by $15,000 at December 31, 2013. It did not correct the error in 2013 or 2014. As a result, Pauline's owner's equity was:
- **(a)** overstated at December 31, 2013, and understated at December 31, 2014.
- **(b)** overstated at December 31, 2013, and properly stated at December 31, 2014.
- **(c)** understated at December 31, 2013, and understated at December 31, 2014.
- **(d)** overstated at December 31, 2013, and overstated at December 31, 2014.

(LO 5) **12.** Santana Company had beginning inventory of $80,000, ending inventory of $110,000, cost of goods sold of $285,000, and sales of $475,000. Santana's days in inventory is:
- **(a)** 73 days.
- **(b)** 121.7 days.
- **(c)** 102.5 days.
- **(d)** 84.5 days.

(LO 6) **13.** Which of these would cause the inventory turnover to increase the most?
- **(a)** Increasing the amount of inventory on hand.
- **(b)** Keeping the amount of inventory on hand constant but increasing sales.
- **(c)** Keeping the amount of inventory on hand constant but decreasing sales.
- **(d)** Decreasing the amount of inventory on hand and increasing sales.

(LO 7) ***14.** In a perpetual inventory system:
- **(a)** LIFO cost of goods sold will be the same as in a periodic inventory system.
- **(b)** average costs are a simple average of unit costs incurred.
- **(c)** a new average is computed under the average-cost method after each sale.
- **(d)** FIFO cost of goods sold will be the same as in a periodic inventory system.

(LO 8) ***15.** King Company has sales of $150,000 and cost of goods available for sale of $135,000. If the gross profit rate is 30%, the estimated cost of the ending inventory under the gross profit method is:
- **(a)** $15,000.
- **(b)** $30,000.
- **(c)** $45,000.
- **(d)** $75,000.

Go to the book's companion website, www.wiley.com/college/weygandt, for additional Self-Test Questions.

✔ **The Navigator**

QUESTIONS

1. "The key to successful business operations is effective inventory management." Do you agree? Explain.

2. An item must possess two characteristics to be classified as inventory by a merchandiser. What are these two characteristics?

3. Your friend Theo Dolan has been hired to help take the physical inventory in Silker Hardware Store. Explain to Theo Dolan what this job will entail.

4. (a) Rochelle Company ships merchandise to Jay Company on December 30. The merchandise reaches the buyer on January 6. Indicate the terms of sale that will result in the goods being included in (1) Rochelle's December 31 inventory, and (2) Jay's December 31 inventory.

(b) Under what circumstances should Rochelle Company include consigned goods in its inventory?

5. Katz Hat Shop received a shipment of hats for which it paid the wholesaler $2,970. The price of the hats was $3,000 but Katz was given a $30 cash discount and required to pay freight charges of $50. In addition, Katz paid $130 to cover the travel expenses of an employee who negotiated the purchase of the hats. What amount will Katz record for inventory? Why?

6. Explain the difference between the terms FOB shipping point and FOB destination.

7. Kyle Ebert believes that the allocation of inventoriable costs should be based on the actual physical flow of the goods. Explain to Kyle why this may be both impractical and inappropriate.

8. What is a major advantage and a major disadvantage of the specific identification method of inventory costing?

9. "The selection of an inventory cost flow method is a decision made by accountants." Do you agree? Explain. Once a method has been selected, what accounting requirement applies?

10. Which assumed inventory cost flow method:
   (a) usually parallels the actual physical flow of merchandise?
   (b) assumes that goods available for sale during an accounting period are identical?
   (c) assumes that the latest units purchased are the first to be sold?

11. In a period of rising prices, the inventory reported in Gumby Company's balance sheet is close to the current cost of the inventory. Pokey Company's inventory is considerably below its current cost. Identify the inventory cost flow method being used by each company. Which company has probably been reporting the higher gross profit?

12. Davey Company has been using the FIFO cost flow method during a prolonged period of rising prices. During the same time period, Davey has been paying out all of its net income as dividends. What adverse effects may result from this policy?

13. Josh Kuchin is studying for the next accounting midterm examination. What should Josh know about (a) departing from the cost basis of accounting for inventories and (b) the meaning of "market" in the lower-of-cost-or-market method?

14. Taylor Music Center has 5 CD players on hand at the balance sheet date. Each cost $400. The current replacement cost is $380 per unit. Under the lower-of-cost-or-market basis of accounting for inventories, what value should be reported for the CD players on the balance sheet? Why?

15. Bonnie Stores has 20 toasters on hand at the balance sheet date. Each costs $27. The current replacement cost is $30 per unit. Under the lower-of-cost-or-market basis of accounting for inventories, what value should Bonnie report for the toasters on the balance sheet? Why?

16. Kuzu Company discovers in 2014 that its ending inventory at December 31, 2013, was $7,000 understated. What effect will this error have on (a) 2013 net income, (b) 2014 net income, and (c) the combined net income for the 2 years?

17. Ryder Company's balance sheet shows Inventory $162,800. What additional disclosures should be made?

18. Under what circumstances might inventory turnover be too high? That is, what possible negative consequences might occur?

19. What inventory cost flow does Apple use for its inventories? (*Hint:* You will need to examine the notes for Apple's financial statements.)

*20. "When perpetual inventory records are kept, the results under the FIFO and LIFO methods are the same as they would be in a periodic inventory system." Do you agree? Explain.

*21. How does the average-cost method of inventory costing differ between a perpetual inventory system and a periodic inventory system?

*22. When is it necessary to estimate inventories?

*23. Both the gross profit method and the retail inventory method are based on averages. For each method, indicate the average used, how it is determined, and how it is applied.

*24. Wiggins Company has net sales of $400,000 and cost of goods available for sale of $300,000. If the gross profit rate is 35%, what is the estimated cost of the ending inventory? Show computations.

*25. Emporia Shoe Shop had goods available for sale in 2014 with a retail price of $120,000. The cost of these goods was $84,000. If sales during the period were $80,000, what is the ending inventory at cost using the retail inventory method?

BRIEF EXERCISES

BE6-1 Farley Company identifies the following items for possible inclusion in the taking of a physical inventory. Indicate whether each item should be included or excluded from the inventory taking.

Identify items to be included in taking a physical inventory.
(LO 1)

(a) Goods shipped on consignment by Farley to another company.
(b) Goods in transit from a supplier shipped FOB destination.

(c) Goods sold but being held for customer pickup.
(d) Goods held on consignment from another company.

Identify the components of goods available for sale.
(LO 2)

BE6-2 Wilbur Company has the following items: (a) Freight-In, (b) Purchase Returns and Allowances, (c) Purchases, (d) Sales Discounts, and (e) Purchase Discounts. Identify which items are included in goods available for sale.

Compute ending inventory using FIFO and LIFO.
(LO 2)

BE6-3 In its first month of operations, Bethke Company made three purchases of merchandise in the following sequence: (1) 300 units at $6, (2) 400 units at $7, and (3) 200 units at $8. Assuming there are 360 units on hand, compute the cost of the ending inventory under the (a) FIFO method and (b) LIFO method. Bethke uses a periodic inventory system.

Compute the ending inventory using average-cost.
(LO 2)

BE6-4 Data for Bethke Company are presented in BE6-3. Compute the cost of the ending inventory under the average-cost method, assuming there are 360 units on hand.

Explain the financial statement effect of inventory cost flow assumptions.
(LO 3)

BE6-5 The management of Svetlana Corp. is considering the effects of inventory-costing methods on its financial statements and its income tax expense. Assuming that the price the company pays for inventory is increasing, which method will:

(a) Provide the highest net income?
(b) Provide the highest ending inventory?
(c) Result in the lowest income tax expense?
(d) Result in the most stable earnings over a number of years?

Explain the financial statement effect of inventory cost flow assumptions.
(LO 3)

BE6-6 In its first month of operation, Franklin Company purchased 120 units of inventory for $6, then 200 units for $7, and finally 140 units for $8. At the end of the month, 180 units remained. Compute the amount of phantom profit that would result if the company used FIFO rather than LIFO. Explain why this amount is referred to as **phantom profit**. The company uses the periodic method.

Determine the LCM valuation using inventory categories.
(LO 4)

BE6-7 Central Appliance Center accumulates the following cost and market data at December 31.

Inventory Categories	Cost Data	Market Data
Cameras	$12,000	$12,100
Camcorders	9,500	9,700
DVD players	14,000	12,800

Compute the lower-of-cost-or-market valuation for the company's total inventory.

Determine correct income statement amounts.
(LO 5)

BE6-8 Pettit Company reports net income of $90,000 in 2014. However, ending inventory was understated $7,000. What is the correct net income for 2014? What effect, if any, will this error have on total assets as reported in the balance sheet at December 31, 2014?

Compute inventory turnover and days in inventory.
(LO 6)

BE6-9 At December 31, 2014, the following information was available for A. Kamble Company: ending inventory $40,000, beginning inventory $60,000, cost of goods sold $270,000, and sales revenue $380,000. Calculate inventory turnover and days in inventory for A. Kamble Company.

Apply cost flow methods to perpetual inventory records.
(LO 7)

*BE6-10 Gregory Department Store uses a perpetual inventory system. Data for product E2-D2 include the following purchases.

Date	Number of Units	Unit Price
May 7	50	$10
July 28	30	13

On June 1, Gregory sold 26 units, and on August 27, 40 more units. Prepare the perpetual inventory schedule for the above transactions using (a) FIFO, (b) LIFO, and (c) moving-average cost.

Apply the gross profit method.
(LO 8)

*BE6-11 At May 31, Suarez Company has net sales of $330,000 and cost of goods available for sale of $230,000. Compute the estimated cost of the ending inventory, assuming the gross profit rate is 35%.

Apply the retail inventory method.
(LO 8)

*BE6-12 On June 30, Calico Fabrics has the following data pertaining to the retail inventory method. Goods available for sale: at cost $38,000; at retail $50,000; net sales $40,000; and ending inventory at retail $10,000. Compute the estimated cost of the ending inventory using the retail inventory method.

> DO IT! Review

DO IT! 6-1 Gomez Company just took its physical inventory. The count of inventory items on hand at the company's business locations resulted in a total inventory cost of $300,000. In reviewing the details of the count and related inventory transactions, you have discovered the following.

Apply rules of ownership to determine inventory cost.

(LO 1)

1. Gomez has sent inventory costing $26,000 on consignment to Kako Company. All of this inventory was at Kako's showrooms on December 31.

2. The company did not include in the count inventory (cost, $20,000) that was sold on December 28, terms FOB shipping point. The goods were in transit on December 31.

3. The company did not include in the count inventory (cost, $17,000) that was purchased with terms of FOB shipping point. The goods were in transit on December 31.

Compute the correct December 31 inventory.

DO IT! 6-2 The accounting records of Old Towne Electronics show the following data.

Compute cost of goods sold under different cost flow methods.

(LO 2)

Beginning inventory	3,000 units at $5
Purchases	8,000 units at $7
Sales	9,400 units at $10

Determine cost of goods sold during the period under a periodic inventory system using (a) the FIFO method, (b) the LIFO method, and (c) the average-cost method. (Round unit cost to nearest tenth of a cent.)

DO IT! 6-3 (a) Moberg Company sells three different categories of tools (small, medium, and large). The cost and market value of its inventory of tools are as follows.

Compute inventory value under LCM.

(LO 4)

	Cost	Market Value
Small	$ 64,000	$ 73,000
Medium	290,000	260,000
Large	152,000	171,000

Determine the value of the company's inventory under the lower-of-cost-or-market approach.

(b) Janus Company understated its 2013 ending inventory by $31,000. Determine the impact this error has on ending inventory, cost of goods sold, and owner's equity in 2013 and 2014.

DO IT! 6-4 Early in 2014, Chien Company switched to a just-in-time inventory system. Its sales, cost of goods sold, and inventory amounts for 2013 and 2014 are shown below.

Compute inventory turnover and assess inventory level.

(LO 6)

	2013	2014
Sales	$3,120,000	$3,713,000
Cost of goods sold	1,200,000	1,425,000
Beginning inventory	180,000	220,000
Ending inventory	220,000	100,000

Determine the inventory turnover and days in inventory for 2013 and 2014. Discuss the changes in the amount of inventory, the inventory turnover and days in inventory, and the amount of sales across the two years.

EXERCISES

E6-1 Tri-State Bank and Trust is considering giving Josef Company a loan. Before doing so, management decides that further discussions with Josef's accountant may be desirable. One area of particular concern is the inventory account, which has a year-end balance of $297,000. Discussions with the accountant reveal the following.

Determine the correct inventory amount.

(LO 1)

1. Josef sold goods costing $38,000 to Sorci Company, FOB shipping point, on December 28. The goods are not expected to arrive at Sorci until January 12. The goods were not included in the physical inventory because they were not in the warehouse.

2. The physical count of the inventory did not include goods costing $95,000 that were shipped to Josef FOB destination on December 27 and were still in transit at year-end.
3. Josef received goods costing $22,000 on January 2. The goods were shipped FOB shipping point on December 26 by Solita Co. The goods were not included in the physical count.
4. Josef sold goods costing $35,000 to Natali Co., FOB destination, on December 30. The goods were received at Natali on January 8. They were not included in Josef's physical inventory.
5. Josef received goods costing $44,000 on January 2 that were shipped FOB destination on December 29. The shipment was a rush order that was supposed to arrive December 31. This purchase was included in the ending inventory of $297,000.

Instructions
Determine the correct inventory amount on December 31.

Determine the correct inventory amount.

(LO 1)

E6-2 Rachel Warren, an auditor with Laplante CPAs, is performing a review of Schuda Company's inventory account. Schuda did not have a good year, and top management is under pressure to boost reported income. According to its records, the inventory balance at year-end was $740,000. However, the following information was not considered when determining that amount.

1. Included in the company's count were goods with a cost of $250,000 that the company is holding on consignment. The goods belong to Harmon Corporation.
2. The physical count did not include goods purchased by Schuda with a cost of $40,000 that were shipped FOB destination on December 28 and did not arrive at Schuda warehouse until January 3.
3. Included in the inventory account was $14,000 of office supplies that were stored in the warehouse and were to be used by the company's supervisors and managers during the coming year.
4. The company received an order on December 29 that was boxed and sitting on the loading dock awaiting pick-up on December 31. The shipper picked up the goods on January 1 and delivered them on January 6. The shipping terms were FOB shipping point. The goods had a selling price of $40,000 and a cost of $28,000. The goods were not included in the count because they were sitting on the dock.
5. On December 29, Schuda shipped goods with a selling price of $80,000 and a cost of $60,000 to Reza Sales Corporation FOB shipping point. The goods arrived on January 3. Reza Sales had only ordered goods with a selling price of $10,000 and a cost of $8,000. However, a sales manager at Schuda had authorized the shipment and said that if Reza wanted to ship the goods back next week, it could.
6. Included in the count was $40,000 of goods that were parts for a machine that the company no longer made. Given the high-tech nature of Schuda's products, it was unlikely that these obsolete parts had any other use. However, management would prefer to keep them on the books at cost, "since that is what we paid for them, after all."

Instructions
Prepare a schedule to determine the correct inventory amount. Provide explanations for each item above, saying why you did or did not make an adjustment for each item.

Calculate cost of goods sold using specific identification and FIFO.

(LO 2, 3)

E6-3 On December 1, Marzion Electronics Ltd. has three DVD players left in stock. All are identical, all are priced to sell at $150. One of the three DVD players left in stock, with serial #1012, was purchased on June 1 at a cost of $100. Another, with serial #1045, was purchased on November 1 for $90. The last player, serial #1056, was purchased on November 30 for $80.

Instructions
(a) Calculate the cost of goods sold using the FIFO periodic inventory method assuming that two of the three players were sold by the end of December, Marzion Electronics' year-end.
(b) If Marzion Electronics used the specific identification method instead of the FIFO method, how might it alter its earnings by "selectively choosing" which particular players to sell to the two customers? What would Marzion's cost of goods sold be if the company wished to minimize earnings? Maximize earnings?
(c) Which of the two inventory methods do you recommend that Marzion use? Explain why.

E6-4 Linda's Boards sells a snowboard, Xpert, that is popular with snowboard enthusiasts. Information relating to Linda's purchases of Xpert snowboards during September is shown below. During the same month, 121 Xpert snowboards were sold. Linda's uses a periodic inventory system.

Compute inventory and cost of goods sold using FIFO and LIFO.

(LO 2)

Date	Explanation	Units	Unit Cost	Total Cost
Sept. 1	Inventory	26	$ 97	$ 2,522
Sept. 12	Purchases	45	102	4,590
Sept. 19	Purchases	20	104	2,080
Sept. 26	Purchases	50	105	5,250
	Totals	141		$14,442

Instructions
(a) Compute the ending inventory at September 30 and cost of goods sold using the FIFO and LIFO methods. Prove the amount allocated to cost of goods sold under each method.
(b) For both FIFO and LIFO, calculate the sum of ending inventory and cost of goods sold. What do you notice about the answers you found for each method?

E6-5 Xiong Co. uses a periodic inventory system. Its records show the following for the month of May, in which 65 units were sold.

Compute inventory and cost of goods sold using FIFO and LIFO.

(LO 2)

		Units	Unit Cost	Total Cost
May 1	Inventory	30	$ 8	$240
15	Purchases	25	11	275
24	Purchases	35	12	420
	Totals	90		$935

Instructions
Compute the ending inventory at May 31 and cost of goods sold using the FIFO and LIFO methods. Prove the amount allocated to cost of goods sold under each method.

E6-6 Kaleta Company reports the following for the month of June.

Compute inventory and cost of goods sold using FIFO and LIFO.

(LO 2, 3)

		Units	Unit Cost	Total Cost
June 1	Inventory	200	$5	$1,000
12	Purchase	400	6	2,400
23	Purchase	300	7	2,100
30	Inventory	100		

Instructions
(a) Compute the cost of the ending inventory and the cost of goods sold under (1) FIFO and (2) LIFO.
(b) Which costing method gives the higher ending inventory? Why?
(c) Which method results in the higher cost of goods sold? Why?

E6-7 Lisa Company had 100 units in beginning inventory at a total cost of $10,000. The company purchased 200 units at a total cost of $26,000. At the end of the year, Lisa had 80 units in ending inventory.

Compute inventory under FIFO, LIFO, and average-cost.

(LO 2, 3)

Instructions
(a) Compute the cost of the ending inventory and the cost of goods sold under (1) FIFO, (2) LIFO, and (3) average-cost.
(b) Which cost flow method would result in the highest net income?
(c) Which cost flow method would result in inventories approximating current cost in the balance sheet?
(d) Which cost flow method would result in Lisa paying the least taxes in the first year?

E6-8 Inventory data for Kaleta Company are presented in E6-6.

Compute inventory and cost of goods sold using average-cost.

(LO 2, 3)

Instructions
(a) Compute the cost of the ending inventory and the cost of goods sold using the average-cost method.
(b) Will the results in (a) be higher or lower than the results under (1) FIFO and (2) LIFO?
(c) Why is the average unit cost not $6?

Determine ending inventory under LCM.

(LO 4)

E6-9 Optix Camera Shop uses the lower-of-cost-or-market basis for its inventory. The following data are available at December 31.

Item	Units	Unit Cost	Market
Cameras:			
Minolta	5	$170	$156
Canon	6	150	152
Light meters:			
Vivitar	12	125	115
Kodak	14	120	135

Instructions

Determine the amount of the ending inventory by applying the lower-of-cost-or-market basis.

Compute lower-of-cost-or-market.

(LO 4)

E6-10 Serebin Company applied FIFO to its inventory and got the following results for its ending inventory.

Cameras	100 units at a cost per unit of $65
DVD players	150 units at a cost per unit of $75
iPods	125 units at a cost per unit of $80

The cost of purchasing units at year-end was cameras $71, DVD players $67, and iPods $78.

Instructions

Determine the amount of ending inventory at lower-of-cost-or-market.

Determine effects of inventory errors.

(LO 5)

E6-11 Hamid's Hardware reported cost of goods sold as follows.

	2013	2014
Beginning inventory	$ 20,000	$ 30,000
Cost of goods purchased	150,000	175,000
Cost of goods available for sale	170,000	205,000
Ending inventory	30,000	35,000
Cost of goods sold	$140,000	$170,000

Hamid's made two errors: (1) 2013 ending inventory was overstated $3,000, and (2) 2014 ending inventory was understated $6,000.

Instructions

Compute the correct cost of goods sold for each year.

Prepare correct income statements.

(LO 5)

E6-12 Rulix Watch Company reported the following income statement data for a 2-year period.

	2013	2014
Sales revenue	$220,000	$250,000
Cost of goods sold		
Beginning inventory	32,000	44,000
Cost of goods purchased	173,000	202,000
Cost of goods available for sale	205,000	246,000
Ending inventory	44,000	52,000
Cost of goods sold	161,000	194,000
Gross profit	$ 59,000	$ 56,000

Rulix uses a periodic inventory system. The inventories at January 1, 2013, and December 31, 2014, are correct. However, the ending inventory at December 31, 2013, was overstated $6,000.

Instructions

(a) Prepare correct income statement data for the 2 years.
(b) What is the cumulative effect of the inventory error on total gross profit for the 2 years?
(c) ━━━━━ Explain in a letter to the president of Rulix Watch Company what has happened, i.e., the nature of the error and its effect on the financial statements.

E6-13 This information is available for Quick's Photo Corporation for 2012, 2013, and 2014.

Compute inventory turnover, days in inventory, and gross profit rate.
(LO 6)

	2012	2013	2014
Beginning inventory	$ 100,000	$ 300,000	$ 400,000
Ending inventory	300,000	400,000	480,000
Cost of goods sold	900,000	1,120,000	1,300,000
Sales revenue	1,200,000	1,600,000	1,900,000

Instructions
Calculate inventory turnover, days in inventory, and gross profit rate (from Chapter 5) for Quick's Photo Corporation for 2012, 2013, and 2014. Comment on any trends.

E6-14 The cost of goods sold computations for Alpha Company and Omega Company are shown below.

Compute inventory turnover and days in inventory.
(LO 6)

	Alpha Company	Omega Company
Beginning inventory	$ 45,000	$ 71,000
Cost of goods purchased	200,000	290,000
Cost of goods available for sale	245,000	361,000
Ending inventory	55,000	69,000
Cost of goods sold	$190,000	$292,000

Instructions
(a) Compute inventory turnover and days in inventory for each company.
(b) Which company moves its inventory more quickly?

*E6-15 Bufford Appliance uses a perpetual inventory system. For its flat-screen television sets, the January 1 inventory was 3 sets at $600 each. On January 10, Bufford purchased 6 units at $660 each. The company sold 2 units on January 8 and 4 units on January 15.

Apply cost flow methods to perpetual records.
(LO 7)

Instructions
Compute the ending inventory under (1) FIFO, (2) LIFO, and (3) moving-average cost.

*E6-16 Kaleta Company reports the following for the month of June.

Calculate inventory and cost of goods sold using three cost flow methods in a perpetual inventory system.
(LO 7)

Date	Explanation	Units	Unit Cost	Total Cost
June 1	Inventory	200	$5	$1,000
12	Purchase	400	6	2,400
23	Purchase	300	7	2,100
30	Inventory	100		

Instructions
(a) Calculate the cost of the ending inventory and the cost of goods sold for each cost flow assumption, using a perpetual inventory system. Assume a sale of 440 units occurred on June 15 for a selling price of $8 and a sale of 360 units on June 27 for $9.
(b) How do the results differ from E6-6 and E6-8?
(c) Why is the average unit cost not $6 [($5 + $6 + $7) ÷ 3 = $6]?

*E6-17 Information about Linda's Boards is presented in E6-4. Additional data regarding Linda's sales of Xpert snowboards are provided below. Assume that Linda's uses a perpetual inventory system.

Apply cost flow methods to perpetual records.
(LO 7)

Date		Units	Unit Price	Total Revenue
Sept. 5	Sale	12	$199	$ 2,388
Sept. 16	Sale	50	199	9,950
Sept. 29	Sale	59	209	12,331
	Totals	121		$24,669

Instructions
(a) Compute ending inventory at September 30 using FIFO, LIFO, and moving-average cost.
(b) Compare ending inventory using a perpetual inventory system to ending inventory using a periodic inventory system (from E6-4).
(c) Which inventory cost flow method (FIFO, LIFO) gives the same ending inventory value under both periodic and perpetual? Which method gives different ending inventory values?

Use the gross profit method to estimate inventory.

(LO 8)

*E6-18 Brenda Company reported the following information for November and December 2014.

	November	December
Cost of goods purchased	$536,000	$ 610,000
Inventory, beginning-of-month	130,000	120,000
Inventory, end-of-month	120,000	?
Sales revenue	840,000	1,000,000

Brenda's ending inventory at December 31 was destroyed in a fire.

Instructions

(a) Compute the gross profit rate for November.

(b) Using the gross profit rate for November, determine the estimated cost of inventory lost in the fire.

Determine merchandise lost using the gross profit method of estimating inventory.

(LO 8)

*E6-19 The inventory of Hauser Company was destroyed by fire on March 1. From an examination of the accounting records, the following data for the first 2 months of the year are obtained: Sales Revenue $51,000, Sales Returns and Allowances $1,000, Purchases $31,200, Freight-In $1,200, and Purchase Returns and Allowances $1,400.

Instructions

Determine the merchandise lost by fire, assuming:

(a) A beginning inventory of $20,000 and a gross profit rate of 40% on net sales.

(b) A beginning inventory of $30,000 and a gross profit rate of 30% on net sales.

Determine ending inventory at cost using retail method.

(LO 8)

*E6-20 Gepetto Shoe Store uses the retail inventory method for its two departments, Women's Shoes and Men's Shoes. The following information for each department is obtained.

XLS

Item	Women's Shoes	Men's Shoes
Beginning inventory at cost	$ 25,000	$ 45,000
Cost of goods purchased at cost	110,000	136,300
Net sales	178,000	185,000
Beginning inventory at retail	46,000	60,000
Cost of goods purchased at retail	179,000	185,000

Instructions

Compute the estimated cost of the ending inventory for each department under the retail inventory method.

EXERCISES: SET B AND CHALLENGE EXERCISES

Visit the book's companion website, at **www.wiley.com/college/weygandt**, and choose the Student Companion site to access Exercise Set B and Challenge Exercises.

PROBLEMS: SET A

Determine items and amounts to be recorded in inventory.

(LO 1)

P6-1A Austin Limited is trying to determine the value of its ending inventory as of February 28, 2014, the company's year-end. The following transactions occurred, and the accountant asked your help in determining whether they should be recorded or not.

(a) On February 26, Austin shipped goods costing $800 to a customer and charged the customer $1,000. The goods were shipped with terms FOB shipping point and the receiving report indicates that the customer received the goods on March 2.

(b) On February 26, Louis Inc. shipped goods to Austin under terms FOB shipping point. The invoice price was $450 plus $30 for freight. The receiving report indicates that the goods were received by Austin on March 2.

(c) Austin had $650 of inventory isolated in the warehouse. The inventory is designated for a customer who has requested that the goods be shipped on March 10.

(d) Also included in Austin's warehouse is $700 of inventory that Ryhn Producers shipped to Austin on consignment.

(e) On February 26, Austin issued a purchase order to acquire goods costing $900. The goods were shipped with terms FOB destination on February 27. Austin received the goods on March 2.

(f) On February 26, Austin shipped goods to a customer under terms FOB destination. The invoice price was $350; the cost of the items was $200. The receiving report indicates that the goods were received by the customer on March 2.

Instructions

For each of the above transactions, specify whether the item in question should be included in ending inventory, and if so, at what amount.

P6-2A Express Distribution markets CDs of the performing artist Fishe. At the beginning of October, Express had in beginning inventory 2,000 of Fishe's CDs with a unit cost of $7. During October, Express made the following purchases of Fishe's CDs.

Oct. 3 2,500 @ $8	Oct. 19 3,000 @ $10
Oct. 9 3,500 @ $9	Oct. 25 4,000 @ $11

During October, 10,900 units were sold. Express uses a periodic inventory system.

Instructions

(a) Determine the cost of goods available for sale.

(b) Determine (1) the ending inventory and (2) the cost of goods sold under each of the assumed cost flow methods (FIFO, LIFO, and average-cost). Prove the accuracy of the cost of goods sold under the FIFO and LIFO methods.

(c) Which cost flow method results in (1) the highest inventory amount for the balance sheet and (2) the highest cost of goods sold for the income statement?

Determine cost of goods sold and ending inventory using FIFO, LIFO, and average-cost with analysis.

(LO 2, 3)

(b)(2) Cost of goods sold:
FIFO $ 94,500
LIFO $108,700
Average $101,370

P6-3A Ziad Company had a beginning inventory on January 1 of 150 units of Product 4-18-15 at a cost of $20 per unit. During the year, the following purchases were made.

Mar. 15 400 units at $23	Sept. 4 350 units at $26
July 20 250 units at $24	Dec. 2 100 units at $29

1,000 units were sold. Ziad Company uses a periodic inventory system.

Instructions

(a) Determine the cost of goods available for sale.

(b) Determine (1) the ending inventory, and (2) the cost of goods sold under each of the assumed cost flow methods (FIFO, LIFO, and average-cost). Prove the accuracy of the cost of goods sold under the FIFO and LIFO methods.

(c) Which cost flow method results in (1) the highest inventory amount for the balance sheet, and (2) the highest cost of goods sold for the income statement?

Determine cost of goods sold and ending inventory, using FIFO, LIFO, and average-cost with analysis.

(LO 2, 3)

(b)(2) Cost of goods sold:
FIFO $23,400
LIFO $24,900
Average $24,160

P6-4A The management of Felipe Inc. is reevaluating the appropriateness of using its present inventory cost flow method, which is average-cost. The company requests your help in determining the results of operations for 2014 if either the FIFO or the LIFO method had been used. For 2014, the accounting records show these data:

Compute ending inventory, prepare income statements, and answer questions using FIFO and LIFO.

(LO 2, 3)

Inventories		Purchases and Sales	
Beginning (7,000 units) $14,000		Total net sales (180,000 units) $747,000	
Ending (17,000 units)		Total cost of goods purchased	
		(190,000 units) 466,000	

Purchases were made quarterly as follows.

Quarter	Units	Unit Cost	Total Cost
1	50,000	$2.20	$110,000
2	40,000	2.35	94,000
3	40,000	2.50	100,000
4	60,000	2.70	162,000
	190,000		$466,000

Operating expenses were $130,000, and the company's income tax rate is 40%.

Instructions

(a) Prepare comparative condensed income statements for 2014 under FIFO and LIFO. (Show computations of ending inventory.)

(a) Gross profit:
FIFO $312,900
LIFO $303,000

(b) ━━━ Answer the following questions for management.
(1) Which cost flow method (FIFO or LIFO) produces the more meaningful inventory amount for the balance sheet? Why?
(2) Which cost flow method (FIFO or LIFO) produces the more meaningful net income? Why?
(3) Which cost flow method (FIFO or LIFO) is more likely to approximate the actual physical flow of goods? Why?
(4) How much more cash will be available for management under LIFO than under FIFO? Why?
(5) Will gross profit under the average-cost method be higher or lower than FIFO? Than LIFO? (*Note:* It is not necessary to quantify your answer.)

Calculate ending inventory, cost of goods sold, gross profit, and gross profit rate under periodic method; compare results.

(LO 2, 3)

P6-5A You are provided with the following information for Najera Inc. for the month ended June 30, 2014. Najera uses the periodic method for inventory.

Date	Description	Quantity	Unit Cost or Selling Price
June 1	Beginning inventory	40	$40
June 4	Purchase	135	44
June 10	Sale	110	70
June 11	Sale return	15	70
June 18	Purchase	55	46
June 18	Purchase return	10	46
June 25	Sale	65	75
June 28	Purchase	30	50

Instructions
(a) Calculate (i) ending inventory, (ii) cost of goods sold, (iii) gross profit, and (iv) gross profit rate under each of the following methods.
(1) LIFO.   (2) FIFO.   (3) Average-cost.
(b) Compare results for the three cost flow assumptions.

(a) (iii) Gross profit:
LIFO $4,215
FIFO $4,645
Average $4,414.60

Compare specific identification, FIFO, and LIFO under periodic method; use cost flow assumption to justify price increase.

(LO 2, 3)

P6-6A You are provided with the following information for Barton Inc. Barton Inc. uses the periodic method of accounting for its inventory transactions.

March 1 Beginning inventory 2,000 liters at a cost of 60¢ per liter.
March 3 Purchased 2,500 liters at a cost of 65¢ per liter.
March 5 Sold 2,300 liters for $1.05 per liter.
March 10 Purchased 4,000 liters at a cost of 72¢ per liter.
March 20 Purchased 2,500 liters at a cost of 80¢ per liter.
March 30 Sold 5,200 liters for $1.25 per liter.

Instructions
(a) Prepare partial income statements through gross profit, and calculate the value of ending inventory that would be reported on the balance sheet, under each of the following cost flow assumptions. (Round ending inventory and cost of goods sold to the nearest dollar.)
(1) Specific identification method assuming:
  (i) The March 5 sale consisted of 1,000 liters from the March 1 beginning inventory and 1,300 liters from the March 3 purchase; and
  (ii) The March 30 sale consisted of the following number of units sold from beginning inventory and each purchase: 450 liters from March 1; 550 liters from March 3; 2,900 liters from March 10; 1,300 liters from March 20.
(2) FIFO.
(3) LIFO.
(b) How can companies use a cost flow method to justify price increases? Which cost flow method would best support an argument to increase prices?

(a) Gross profit:
(1) Specific identification
$3,715

(2) FIFO $3,930
(3) LIFO $3,385

Compute ending inventory, prepare income statements, and answer questions using FIFO and LIFO.

(LO 2, 3)

P6-7A The management of Sherlynn Co. asks your help in determining the comparative effects of the FIFO and LIFO inventory cost flow methods. For 2014, the accounting records provide the following data.

Inventory, January 1 (10,000 units)		$ 45,000
Cost of 100,000 units purchased		532,000
Selling price of 80,000 units sold		700,000
Operating expenses		140,000

Units purchased consisted of 35,000 units at $5.10 on May 10; 35,000 units at $5.30 on August 15; and 30,000 units at $5.60 on November 20. Income taxes are 30%.

Instructions

(a) Prepare comparative condensed income statements for 2014 under FIFO and LIFO. (Show computations of ending inventory.)

(b) ◂━━━━ Answer the following questions for management.

(1) Which inventory cost flow method produces the most meaningful inventory amount for the balance sheet? Why?

(2) Which inventory cost flow method produces the most meaningful net income? Why?

(3) Which inventory cost flow method is most likely to approximate actual physical flow of the goods? Why?

(4) How much additional cash will be available for management under LIFO than under FIFO? Why?

(5) How much of the gross profit under FIFO is illusory in comparison with the gross profit under LIFO?

(a) Net income
FIFO $105,700
LIFO $91,000

*P6-8A Mercer Inc. is a retailer operating in British Columbia. Mercer uses the perpetual inventory method. All sales returns from customers result in the goods being returned to inventory; the inventory is not damaged. Assume that there are no credit transactions; all amounts are settled in cash. You are provided with the following information for Mercer Inc. for the month of January 2014.

Calculate cost of goods sold and ending inventory under LIFO, FIFO, and moving-average cost under the perpetual system; compare gross profit under each assumption.

(LO 7)

Date	Description	Quantity	Unit Cost or Selling Price
January 1	Beginning inventory	100	$15
January 5	Purchase	140	18
January 8	Sale	110	28
January 10	Sale return	10	28
January 15	Purchase	55	20
January 16	Purchase return	5	20
January 20	Sale	90	32
January 25	Purchase	20	22

Instructions

(a) For each of the following cost flow assumptions, calculate (i) cost of goods sold, (ii) ending inventory, and (iii) gross profit.

(1) LIFO.   (2) FIFO.   (3) Moving-average cost.

(b) Compare results for the three cost flow assumptions.

(a)(iii) Gross profit:
LIFO $2,160
FIFO $2,560
Average $2,421

*P6-9A Terando Co. began operations on July 1. It uses a perpetual inventory system. During July, the company had the following purchases and sales.

Determine ending inventory under a perpetual inventory system.

(LO 7)

	Purchases		
Date	Units	Unit Cost	Sales Units
July 1	5	$120	
July 6			4
July 11	7	$136	
July 14			3
July 21	8	$147	
July 27			6

Instructions

(a) Determine the ending inventory under a perpetual inventory system using (1) FIFO, (2) moving-average cost, and (3) LIFO.

(b) Which costing method produces the highest ending inventory valuation?

(a) Ending inventory
FIFO $1,029
Avg. $994
LIFO $958

*P6-10A Suzuki Company lost all of its inventory in a fire on December 26, 2014. The accounting records showed the following gross profit data for November and December.

	November	December (to 12/26)
Net sales	$600,000	$700,000
Beginning inventory	32,000	36,000
Purchases	389,000	420,000
Purchase returns and allowances	13,300	14,900
Purchase discounts	8,500	9,500
Freight-in	8,800	9,900
Ending inventory	36,000	?

Suzuki is fully insured for fire losses but must prepare a report for the insurance company.

Instructions

(a) Gross profit rate 38%

(a) Compute the gross profit rate for November.

(b) Using the gross profit rate for November, determine the estimated cost of the inventory lost in the fire.

*P6-11A Dixon Books uses the retail inventory method to estimate its monthly ending inventories. The following information is available for two of its departments at October 31, 2014.

	Hardcovers		Paperbacks	
	Cost	Retail	Cost	Retail
Beginning inventory	$ 420,000	$ 700,000	$ 280,000	$ 360,000
Purchases	2,135,000	3,200,000	1,155,000	1,540,000
Freight-in	24,000		12,000	
Purchase discounts	44,000		22,000	
Net sales		3,100,000		1,570,000

At December 31, Dixon Books takes a physical inventory at retail. The actual retail values of the inventories in each department are Hardcovers $790,000 and Paperbacks $335,000.

Instructions

(a) Hardcovers: End. Inv.
$520,000

(a) Determine the estimated cost of the ending inventory for each department at **October 31**, 2014, using the retail inventory method.

(b) Compute the ending inventory at cost for each department at **December 31**, assuming the cost-to-retail ratios for the year are 65% for Hardcovers and 75% for Paperbacks.

PROBLEMS: SET B

P6-1B Weber Limited is trying to determine the value of its ending inventory at February 28, 2014, the company's year-end. The accountant counted everything that was in the warehouse as of February 28, which resulted in an ending inventory valuation of $48,000. However, she didn't know how to treat the following transactions so she didn't record them.

(a) On February 26, Weber shipped to a customer goods costing $800. The goods were shipped FOB shipping point, and the receiving report indicates that the customer received the goods on March 2.

(b) On February 26, Gretel Inc. shipped goods to Weber FOB destination. The invoice price was $350. The receiving report indicates that the goods were received by Weber on March 2.

(c) Weber had $500 of inventory at a customer's warehouse "on approval." The customer was going to let Weber know whether it wanted the merchandise by the end of the week, March 4.

(d) Weber also had $400 of inventory on consignment at a Roslyn craft shop.

(e) On February 26, Weber ordered goods costing $750. The goods were shipped FOB shipping point on February 27. Weber received the goods on March 1.

(f) On February 28, Weber packaged goods and had them ready for shipping to a customer FOB destination. The invoice price was $350; the cost of the items was $250. The receiving report indicates that the goods were received by the customer on March 2.

(g) Weber had damaged goods set aside in the warehouse because they are no longer saleable. These goods cost $400 and Weber originally expected to sell these items for $600.

Instructions

For each of the above transactions, specify whether the item in question should be included in ending inventory and, if so, at what amount. For each item that is not included in ending inventory, indicate who owns it and in what account, if any, it should have been recorded.

P6-2B Xinxin Distribution markets CDs of the performing artist Carly. At the beginning of March, Xinxin had in beginning inventory 1,500 Carly CDs with a unit cost of $7. During March Xinxin made the following purchases of Carly CDs.

Determine cost of goods sold and ending inventory using FIFO, LIFO, and average-cost with analysis.

(LO 2, 3)

| March 5 | 3,000 @ $8 | March 21 | 4,000 @ $10 |
| March 13 | 4,500 @ $9 | March 26 | 2,500 @ $11 |

During March, 12,000 units were sold. Xinxin uses a periodic inventory system.

Instructions

(a) Determine the cost of goods available for sale.

(b) Determine (1) the ending inventory and (2) the cost of goods sold under each of the assumed cost flow methods (FIFO, LIFO, and average-cost). Prove the accuracy of the cost of goods sold under the FIFO and LIFO methods.

(c) Which cost flow method results in (1) the highest inventory amount for the balance sheet and (2) the highest cost of goods sold for the income statement?

(b)(2) Cost of goods sold:
FIFO $105,000
LIFO $116,000
Average $110,321

P6-3B Walz Company had a beginning inventory of 400 units of Product Ribo at a cost of $8 per unit. During the year, purchases were:

Determine cost of goods sold and ending inventory using FIFO, LIFO, and average-cost with analysis.

(LO 2, 3)

| Feb. 20 | 600 units at $9 | Aug. 12 | 300 units at $11 |
| May 5 | 500 units at $10 | Dec. 8 | 200 units at $12 |

Walz Company uses a periodic inventory system. Sales totaled 1,500 units.

Instructions

(a) Determine the cost of goods available for sale.

(b) Determine (1) the ending inventory and (2) the cost of goods sold under each of the assumed cost flow methods (FIFO, LIFO, and average-cost). Prove the accuracy of the cost of goods sold under the FIFO and LIFO methods.

(c) Which cost flow method results in (1) the lowest inventory amount for the balance sheet, and (2) the lowest cost of goods sold for the income statement?

(b) Cost of goods sold:
FIFO $13,600
LIFO $15,200
Average $14,475

P6-4B The management of Patel Co. is reevaluating the appropriateness of using its present inventory cost flow method, which is average-cost. They request your help in determining the results of operations for 2014 if either the FIFO method or the LIFO method had been used. For 2014, the accounting records show the following data.

Compute ending inventory, prepare income statements, and answer questions using FIFO and LIFO.

(LO 2, 3)

Inventories		Purchases and Sales	
Beginning (15,000 units)	$32,000	Total net sales (217,000 units)	$865,000
Ending (28,000 units)		Total cost of goods purchased (230,000 units)	600,000

Purchases were made quarterly as follows.

Quarter	Units	Unit Cost	Total Cost
1	60,000	$2.40	$144,000
2	50,000	2.50	125,000
3	50,000	2.70	135,000
4	70,000	2.80	196,000
	230,000		$600,000

Operating expenses were $147,000, and the company's income tax rate is 34%.

Instructions

(a) Prepare comparative condensed income statements for 2014 under FIFO and LIFO. (Show computations of ending inventory.)

(a) Net income
FIFO $108,504
LIFO $98,472

(b) ━━━ Answer the following questions for management.

  (1) Which cost flow method (FIFO or LIFO) produces the more meaningful inventory amount for the balance sheet? Why?

  (2) Which cost flow method (FIFO or LIFO) produces the more meaningful net income? Why?

  (3) Which cost flow method (FIFO or LIFO) is more likely to approximate actual physical flow of the goods? Why?

(b)(4) $5,168

  (4) How much additional cash will be available for management under LIFO than under FIFO? Why?

  (5) Will gross profit under the average-cost method be higher or lower than (i) FIFO and (ii) LIFO? (*Note:* It is not necessary to quantify your answer.)

Calculate ending inventory, cost of goods sold, gross profit, and gross profit rate under periodic method; compare results.

(LO 2, 3)

P6-5B You are provided with the following information for Perkins Inc. for the month ended October 31, 2014. Perkins uses a periodic method for inventory.

Date	Description	Units	Unit Cost or Selling Price
October 1	Beginning inventory	60	$25
October 9	Purchase	120	26
October 11	Sale	100	35
October 17	Purchase	70	27
October 22	Sale	60	40
October 25	Purchase	80	28
October 29	Sale	110	40

Instructions

(a)(iii) Gross profit:
LIFO $3,050
FIFO $3,230
Average $3,141

(a) Calculate (i) ending inventory, (ii) cost of goods sold, (iii) gross profit, and (iv) gross profit rate under each of the following methods.

  (1) LIFO.
  (2) FIFO.
  (3) Average-cost.

(b) Compare results for the three cost flow assumptions.

Compare specific identification, FIFO and LIFO under periodic method; use cost flow assumption to influence earnings.

(LO 2, 3)

P6-6B You have the following information for Princess Diamonds. Princess Diamonds uses the periodic method of accounting for its inventory transactions. Princess only carries one brand and size of diamonds—all are identical. Each batch of diamonds purchased is carefully coded and marked with its purchase cost.

March 1 Beginning inventory 150 diamonds at a cost of $300 per diamond.
March 3 Purchased 200 diamonds at a cost of $360 each.
March 5 Sold 180 diamonds for $600 each.
March 10 Purchased 350 diamonds at a cost of $380 each.
March 25 Sold 400 diamonds for $650 each.

Instructions

(a) Gross profit:
(1) Maximum $163,600

(2) Minimum $154,000

(a) Assume that Princess Diamonds uses the specific identification cost flow method.

  (1) Demonstrate how Princess Diamonds could maximize its gross profit for the month by specifically selecting which diamonds to sell on March 5 and March 25.

  (2) Demonstrate how Princess Diamonds could minimize its gross profit for the month by selecting which diamonds to sell on March 5 and March 25.

(b) Assume that Princess Diamonds uses the FIFO cost flow assumption. Calculate cost of goods sold. How much gross profit would Princess Diamonds report under this cost flow assumption?

(c) Assume that Princess Diamonds uses the LIFO cost flow assumption. Calculate cost of goods sold. How much gross profit would the company report under this cost flow assumption?

Compute ending inventory, prepare income statements, and answer questions using FIFO and LIFO.

(LO 2, 3)

(d) Which cost flow method should Princess Diamonds select? Explain.

P6-7B The management of Chelsea Inc. asks your help in determining the comparative effects of the FIFO and LIFO inventory cost flow methods. For 2014, the accounting records provide the following data.

Inventory, January 1 (10,000 units)	$ 35,000
Cost of 120,000 units purchased	504,500
Selling price of 100,000 units sold	665,000
Operating expenses	130,000

Units purchased consisted of 35,000 units at $4.00 on May 10; 60,000 units at $4.20 on August 15; and 25,000 units at $4.50 on November 20. Income taxes are 28%.

Instructions

(a) Prepare comparative condensed income statements for 2014 under FIFO and LIFO. (Show computations of ending inventory.)

(b) ◄─────── Answer the following questions for management in the form of a business letter.

    (1) Which inventory cost flow method produces the most meaningful inventory amount for the balance sheet? Why?

    (2) Which inventory cost flow method produces the most meaningful net income? Why?

    (3) Which inventory cost flow method is most likely to approximate the actual physical flow of the goods? Why?

    (4) How much more cash will be available for management under LIFO than under FIFO? Why?

    (5) How much of the gross profit under FIFO is illusionary in comparison with the gross profit under LIFO?

(a) Gross profit:
FIFO $259,000
LIFO $240,500

*P6-8B Minsoo Ltd. is a retailer operating in Edmonton, Alberta. Minsoo uses the perpetual inventory method. All sales returns from customers result in the goods being returned to inventory; the inventory is not damaged. Assume that there are no credit transactions; all amounts are settled in cash. You are provided with the following information for Minsoo Ltd. for the month of January 2014.

Calculate cost of goods sold and ending inventory for FIFO, moving-average cost, and LIFO under the perpetual system; compare gross profit under each assumption.

(LO 7)

Date	Description	Quantity	Unit Cost or Selling Price
December 31	Ending inventory	160	$17
January 2	Purchase	100	21
January 6	Sale	150	40
January 9	Sale return	10	40
January 9	Purchase	80	24
January 10	Purchase return	10	24
January 10	Sale	60	45
January 23	Purchase	100	28
January 30	Sale	110	50

Instructions

(a) For each of the following cost flow assumptions, calculate (i) cost of goods sold, (ii) ending inventory, and (iii) gross profit.

    (1) LIFO.   (2) FIFO.   (3) Moving-average cost.

(b) Compare results for the three cost flow assumptions.

(a)(iii) Gross profit:
LIFO $6,540
FIFO $7,780
Average $7,354

*P6-9B Buffet Appliance Mart began operations on May 1. It uses a perpetual inventory system. During May, the company had the following purchases and sales for its Model 25 Sureshot camera.

Determine ending inventory under a perpetual inventory system.

(LO 7)

Date	Purchases Units	Purchases Unit Cost	Sales Units
May 1	7	$150	
4			4
8	8	$170	
12			5
15	6	$185	
20			3
25			4

Instructions

(a) Determine the ending inventory under a perpetual inventory system using (1) FIFO, (2) moving-average cost, and (3) LIFO.

(b) Which costing method produces (1) the highest ending inventory valuation and (2) the lowest ending inventory valuation?

(a) FIFO $925
Average $874
LIFO $790

Estimate inventory loss using gross profit method.
(LO 8)

*P6-10B Liis Company lost 70% of its inventory in a fire on March 25, 2014. The accounting records showed the following gross profit data for February and March.

	February	March (to 3/25)
Net sales	$300,000	$250,000
Net purchases	176,800	139,000
Freight-in	3,900	3,000
Beginning inventory	4,500	20,200
Ending inventory	20,200	?

Liis Company is fully insured for fire losses but must prepare a report for the insurance company.

Instructions

(a) Gross profit rate 45%

(a) Compute the gross profit rate for the month of February.

(b) Using the gross profit rate for February, determine both the estimated total inventory and inventory lost in the fire in March.

Compute ending inventory using retail method.
(LO 8)

*P6-11B Belden Department Store uses the retail inventory method to estimate its monthly ending inventories. The following information is available for two of its departments at August 31, 2014.

	Sporting Goods		Jewelry and Cosmetics	
	Cost	Retail	Cost	Retail
Net sales		$1,000,000		$1,160,000
Purchases	$675,000	1,066,000	$741,000	1,158,000
Purchase returns	(26,000)	(40,000)	(12,000)	(20,000)
Purchase discounts	(12,360)	—	(2,440)	—
Freight-in	9,000	—	14,000	—
Beginning inventory	47,360	74,000	39,440	62,000

At December 31, Belden Department Store takes a physical inventory at retail. The actual retail values of the inventories in each department are Sporting Goods $95,000 and Jewelry and Cosmetics $44,000.

Instructions

(b) Sporting Goods: End. Inv. $63,000

(a) Determine the estimated cost of the ending inventory for each department on **August 31**, 2014, using the retail inventory method.

(b) Compute the ending inventory at cost for each department at **December 31**, assuming the cost-to-retail ratios are 60% for Sporting Goods and 64% for Jewelry and Cosmetics.

PROBLEMS: SET C

Visit the book's companion website, at **www.wiley.com/college/weygandt**, and choose the Student Companion site to access Problem Set C.

COMPREHENSIVE PROBLEM

CP6 On December 1, 2014, Matthias Company had the account balances shown below.

Debit			Credit
Cash	$ 4,800	Accumulated Depreciation—Equipment	$ 1,500
Accounts Receivable	3,900	Accounts Payable	3,000
Inventory	1,800*	Owner's Capital	27,000
Equipment	21,000		$31,500
	$31,500		

*(3,000 × $0.60)

The following transactions occurred during December.

Dec. 3   Purchased 4,000 units of inventory on account at a cost of $0.72 per unit.
     5   Sold 4,400 units of inventory on account for $0.90 per unit. (It sold 3,000 of
          the $0.60 units and 1,400 of the $0.72.)
     7   Granted the December 5 customer $180 credit for 200 units of inventory
          returned costing $120. These units were returned to inventory.
     17   Purchased 2,200 units of inventory for cash at $0.80 each.
     22   Sold 2,000 units of inventory on account for $0.95 per unit. (It sold 2,000 of
          the $0.72 units.)

Adjustment data:

1. Accrued salaries payable $400.
2. Depreciation $200 per month.

Instructions

(a) Journalize the December transactions and adjusting entries, assuming Matthias uses
the perpetual inventory method.

(b) Enter the December 1 balances in the ledger T-accounts and post the December transactions. In addition to the accounts mentioned above, use the following additional
accounts: Cost of Goods Sold, Depreciation Expense, Salaries and Wages Expense,
Salaries and Wages Payable, Sales Revenue, and Sales Returns and Allowances.

(c) Prepare an adjusted trial balance as of December 31, 2014.

(d) Prepare an income statement for December 2014 and a classified balance sheet at
December 31, 2014.

(e) Compute ending inventory and cost of goods sold under FIFO, assuming Matthias
Company uses the periodic inventory system.

(f) Compute ending inventory and cost of goods sold under LIFO, assuming Matthias
Company uses the periodic inventory system.

CONTINUING COOKIE CHRONICLE

(*Note:* This is a continuation of the Cookie Chronicle from Chapters 1 through 5.)

CCC6 Natalie is busy establishing both divisions of her business (cookie classes and mixer
sales) and completing her business degree. Her goals for the next 11 months are to sell one
mixer per month and to give two to three classes per week.

The cost of the fine European mixers is expected to increase. Natalie has just negotiated new terms with Kzinski that include shipping costs in the negotiated purchase price
(mixers will be shipped FOB destination). Natalie must choose a cost flow assumption for
her mixer inventory.

Go to the book's companion website, **www.wiley.com/college/weygandt,** *to see the completion
of this problem.*

Broadening Your Perspective

Financial Reporting and Analysis

Financial Reporting Problem: Apple Inc.

BYP6-1 The notes that accompany a company's financial statements provide informative details that
would clutter the amounts and descriptions presented in the statements. Refer to the financial statements
of Apple Inc. in Appendix A as well as its annual report. Instructions for accessing and using the company's
complete annual report, including the notes to the financial statements, are also provided in Appendix A.

Instructions

Answer the following questions. Complete the requirements in millions of dollars, as shown in
Apple's annual report.

(a) What did Apple report for the amount of inventories in its consolidated balance sheet at
September 25, 2010? At September 24, 2011?

(b) Compute the dollar amount of change and the percentage change in inventories between 2010 and 2011. Compute inventory as a percentage of current assets at September 24, 2011.

(c) How does Apple value its inventories? Which inventory cost flow method does Apple use? (See Notes to the Financial Statements.)

(d) What is the cost of sales (cost of goods sold) reported by Apple for 2011, 2010, and 2009? Compute the percentage of cost of sales to net sales in 2011.

Comparative Analysis Problem: PepsiCo, Inc. vs. The Coca-Cola Company

BYP6-2 PepsiCo's financial statements are presented in Appendix B. Financial statements of The Coca-Cola Company are presented in Appendix C. Instructions for accessing and using the complete annual reports of PepsiCo and Coca-Cola, including the notes to the financial statements, are also provided in Appendices B and C, respectively.

Instructions

(a) Based on the information contained in these financial statements, compute the following 2011 ratios for each company.
  (1) Inventory turnover.
  (2) Days in inventory.

(b) What conclusions concerning the management of the inventory can you draw from these data?

Comparative Analysis Problem: Amazon.com, Inc. vs. Wal-Mart Stores, Inc.

BYP6-3 Amazon.com, Inc.'s financial statements are presented in Appendix D. Financial statements of Wal-Mart Stores, Inc. are presented in Appendix E. Instructions for accessing and using the complete annual reports of Amazon and Wal-Mart, including the notes to the financial statements, are also provided in Appendices D and E, respectively.

Instructions

(a) Based on the information contained in these financial statements, compute the following 2011 ratios for each company.
  (1) Inventory turnover.
  (2) Days in inventory.

(b) What conclusions concerning the management of the inventory can you draw from these data?

Real-World Focus

BYP6-4 A company's annual report usually will identify the inventory method used. Knowing that, you can analyze the effects of the inventory method on the income statement and balance sheet.

Address: **www.cisco.com**, or go to **www.wiley.com/college/weygandt**

Instructions

Answer the following questions based on the current year's annual report on Cisco's website.

(a) At Cisco's fiscal year-end, what was the inventory on the balance sheet?

(b) How has this changed from the previous fiscal year-end?

(c) How much of the inventory was finished goods?

(d) What inventory method does Cisco use?

Critical Thinking

 ## Decision-Making Across the Organization

BYP6-5 On April 10, 2014, fire damaged the office and warehouse of Corvet Company. Most of the accounting records were destroyed, but the following account balances were determined as of March 31, 2014: Inventory (January 1, 2014), $80,000; Sales Revenue (January 1–March 31, 2014), $180,000; Purchases (January 1–March 31, 2014), $94,000.

The company's fiscal year ends on December 31. It uses a periodic inventory system.

From an analysis of the April bank statement, you discover cancelled checks of $4,200 for cash purchases during the period April 1–10. Deposits during the same period totaled $18,500. Of that amount, 60% were collections on accounts receivable, and the balance was cash sales.

Correspondence with the company's principal suppliers revealed $12,400 of purchases on account from April 1 to April 10. Of that amount, $1,600 was for merchandise in transit on April 10 that was shipped FOB destination.

Correspondence with the company's principal customers produced acknowledgments of credit sales totaling $37,000 from April 1 to April 10. It was estimated that $5,600 of credit sales will never be acknowledged or recovered from customers.

Corvet Company reached an agreement with the insurance company that its fire-loss claim should be based on the average of the gross profit rates for the preceding 2 years. The financial statements for 2012 and 2013 showed the following data.

	2013	2012
Net sales	$600,000	$480,000
Cost of goods purchased	404,000	356,000
Beginning inventory	60,000	40,000
Ending inventory	80,000	60,000

Inventory with a cost of $17,000 was salvaged from the fire.

Instructions
With the class divided into groups, answer the following.

(a) Determine the balances in (1) Sales Revenue and (2) Purchases at April 10.
*(b) Determine the average gross profit rate for the years 2012 and 2013. (*Hint:* Find the gross profit rate for each year and divide the sum by 2.)
*(c) Determine the inventory loss as a result of the fire, using the gross profit method.

Communication Activity

BYP6-6 You are the controller of Small Toys Inc. Marta Johns, the president, recently mentioned to you that she found an error in the 2013 financial statements which she believes has corrected itself. She determined, in discussions with the Purchasing Department, that 2013 ending inventory was overstated by $1 million. Marta says that the 2014 ending inventory is correct. Thus, she assumes that 2014 income is correct. Marta says to you, "What happened has happened—there's no point in worrying about it anymore."

Instructions
You conclude that Marta is incorrect. Write a brief, tactful memo to Marta, clarifying the situation.

Ethics Case

BYP6-7 R. J. Graziano Wholesale Corp. uses the LIFO method of inventory costing. In the current year, profit at R. J. Graziano is running unusually high. The corporate tax rate is also high this year, but it is scheduled to decline significantly next year. In an effort to lower the current year's net income and to take advantage of the changing income tax rate, the president of R. J. Graziano Wholesale instructs the plant accountant to recommend to the purchasing department a large purchase of inventory for delivery 3 days before the end of the year. The price of the inventory to be purchased has doubled during the year, and the purchase will represent a major portion of the ending inventory value.

Instructions
(a) What is the effect of this transaction on this year's and next year's income statement and income tax expense? Why?
(b) If R. J. Graziano Wholesale had been using the FIFO method of inventory costing, would the president give the same directive?
(c) Should the plant accountant order the inventory purchase to lower income? What are the ethical implications of this order?

All About You

BYP6-8 Some of the largest business frauds ever perpetrated have involved the misstatement of inventory. Two classics were at Leslie Fay and McKesson Corporation.

Instructions
There is considerable information regarding inventory frauds available on the Internet. Search for information about one of the two cases mentioned above, or inventory fraud at any other company, and prepare a short explanation of the nature of the inventory fraud.

FASB Codification Activity

BYP6-9 If your school has a subscription to the FASB Codification, go to **http://aaahq.org/ascLogin.cfm** to log in and prepare responses to the following.

Instructions
(a) The primary basis for accounting for inventories is cost. How is cost defined in the Codification?
(b) What does the Codification state regarding the use of consistency in the selection or employment of a basis for inventory?
(c) What does the Codification indicate is a justification for the use of the lower-of-cost-or-market for inventory valuation?

Answers to Chapter Questions

Answers to Insight and Accounting Across the Organization Questions

p. 277 A Big Hiccup   Q: What steps might the companies take to avoid such a serious disruption in the future? **A:** The manufacturer of the piston rings should spread its manufacturing facilities across a few locations that are far enough apart that they would not all be at risk at once. In addition, the automakers might consider becoming less dependent on a single supplier as well as having weather contingency plans.

p. 278 Falsifying Inventory to Boost Income   Q: What effect does an overstatement of inventory have on a company's financial statements? **A:** The balance sheet looks stronger because inventory and retained earnings are overstated. The income statement looks better because cost of goods sold is understated and income is overstated.

p. 289 Is LIFO Fair?   Q: What are the arguments for and against the use of LIFO? **A:** Proponents of LIFO argue that it is conceptually superior because it matches the most recent cost with the most recent selling price. Critics contend that it artificially understates the company's net income and consequently reduces tax payments. Also, because most foreign companies are not allowed to use LIFO, its use by U.S. companies reduces the ability of investors to compare U.S. companies with foreign companies.

p. 293 Too Many TVs or Too Few?   Q: For Sony, what are the advantages and disadvantages of having a low days in inventory measure? **A:** If Sony has a low days in inventory, it reduces the amount of cash it has tied up in inventory. It also minimizes the risk it will be stuck with excess inventory that could force it to provide big discounts, resulting in punishing losses. Sony also faces the risk that the TVs will become obsolete before they are sold. However, Sony increases the risk that it will encounter "stock-outs," that is, it will not have adequate inventory to meet customer demand.

Answers to Self-Test Questions

1. a   **2.** b ($180,000 + $35,000)   **3.** b   **4.** c [(5,000 × $13) + (4,000 × $12)]   **5.** d [(8,000 × $11) + (1,000 × $12)]   **6.** d ((5,000 × $8) + (15,000 × $10) + (20,000 × $12)) ÷ 40,000 = $10.75; $10.75 × 7,000   **7.** c   **8.** d   **9.** d (200 × $80)   **10.** b   **11.** b   **12.** b $285,000 ÷ [($80,000 + $110,000) ÷ 2] = 3; 365 ÷ 3   **13.** d   *14. d   *15. b [$150,000 − (30% × $150,000)] = $105,000; $135,000 − $105,000

A Look at IFRS

LEARNING OBJECTIVE   9
Compare the accounting procedures for inventories under GAAP and IFRS.

The major IFRS requirements related to accounting and reporting for inventories are the same as GAAP. The major differences are that IFRS prohibits the use of the LIFO cost flow assumption and determines market in the lower-of-cost-or-market inventory valuation differently.

Key Points

- The requirements for accounting for and reporting inventories are more principles-based under IFRS. That is, GAAP provides more detailed guidelines in inventory accounting.

- The definitions for inventory are essentially similar under IFRS and GAAP. Both define inventory as assets held-for-sale in the ordinary course of business, in the process of production for sale (work in process), or to be consumed in the production of goods or services (e.g., raw materials).

- Who owns the goods—goods in transit or consigned goods—as well as the costs to include in inventory, are accounted for the same under IFRS and GAAP.

- Both GAAP and IFRS permit specific identification where appropriate. IFRS actually requires that the specific identification method be used where the inventory items are not interchangeable (i.e., can be specifically identified). If the inventory items are not specifically identifiable, a cost flow assumption is used. GAAP does not specify situations in which specific identification must be used.

- A major difference between IFRS and GAAP relates to the LIFO cost flow assumption. GAAP permits the use of LIFO for inventory valuation. IFRS prohibits its use. FIFO and average-cost are the only two acceptable cost flow assumptions permitted under IFRS.

- IFRS requires companies to use the same cost flow assumption for all goods of a similar nature. GAAP has no specific requirement in this area.

- In the lower-of-cost-or-market test for inventory valuation, IFRS defines market as net realizable value. Net realizable value is the estimated selling price in the ordinary course of business, less the estimated costs of completion and estimated selling expenses. In other words, net realizable value is the best estimate of the net amounts that inventories are expected to realize. GAAP, on the other hand, defines market as essentially replacement cost.

- Under GAAP, if inventory is written down under the lower-of-cost-or-market valuation, the new basis is now considered its cost. As a result, the inventory may not be written back up to its original cost in a subsequent period. Under IFRS, the write-down may be reversed in a subsequent period up to the amount of the previous write-down. Both the write-down and any subsequent reversal should be reported on the income statement as an expense. An item-by-item approach is generally followed under IFRS.

- An example of the use of lower-of-cost-or-net realizable value (LCNRV) under IFRS follows.

Mendel Company has the following four items in its ending inventory as of December 31, 2014. The company uses the lower-of-cost-or-net realizable value approach for inventory valuation following IFRS.

Item No.	Cost	Net Realizable Value
1320	$3,600	$3,400
1333	4,000	4,100
1428	2,800	2,100
1510	5,000	4,700

The computation of the ending inventory value to be reported in the financial statements at December 31, 2014, is as follows.

Item No.	Cost	Net Realizable Value	LCNRV
1320	$ 3,600	$ 3,400	$ 3,400
1333	4,000	4,100	4,000
1428	2,800	2,100	2,100
1510	5,000	4,700	4,700
Total	$15,400	$14,300	$14,200

- Unlike property, plant, and equipment, IFRS does not permit the option of valuing inventories at fair value. As indicated above, IFRS requires inventory to be written down, but inventory cannot be written up above its original cost.

- Similar to GAAP, certain agricultural products and mineral products can be reported at net realizable value using IFRS.

- IFRS allows companies to report inventory at standard cost if it does not differ significantly from actual cost. Standard cost is addressed in managerial accounting courses.

Looking to the Future

One convergence issue that will be difficult to resolve relates to the use of the LIFO cost flow assumption. As indicated, IFRS specifically prohibits its use. Conversely, the LIFO cost flow assumption is widely used in the United States because of its favorable tax advantages. In addition, many argue that LIFO from a financial reporting point of view provides a better matching of current costs against revenue and, therefore, enables companies to compute a more realistic income.

IFRS Practice

IFRS Self-Test Questions

1. Which of the following should **not** be included in the inventory of a company using IFRS?
   (a) Goods held on consignment from another company.
   (b) Goods shipped on consignment to another company.
   (c) Goods in transit from another company shipped FOB shipping point.
   (d) None of the above.

2. Which method of inventory costing is prohibited under IFRS?
   (a) Specific identification.   (c) FIFO.
   (b) LIFO.   (d) Average-cost.

3. Yang Company purchased 2,000 widgets and has 400 widgets in its ending inventory at a cost of $90 each and a current replacement cost of $80 each. The net realizable value of each unit in the ending inventory is $70. The ending inventory under lower-of-cost-or-net realizable value is:
   (a) $36,000.   (c) $28,000.
   (b) $32,000.   (d) None of the above.

4. Specific identification:
   (a) must be used under IFRS if the inventory items are not interchangeable.
   (b) cannot be used under IFRS.
   (c) cannot be used under GAAP.
   (d) must be used under IFRS if it would result in the most conservative net income.

5. IFRS requires the following:
   (a) Ending inventory is written up and down to net realizable value each reporting period.
   (b) Ending inventory is written down to net realizable value but cannot be written up.
   (c) Ending inventory is written down to net realizable value and may be written up in future periods to its net realizable value but not above its original cost.
   (d) Ending inventory is written down to net realizable value and may be written up in future periods to its net realizable value.

IFRS Exercises

IFRS6-1 Briefly describe some of the similarities and differences between GAAP and IFRS with respect to the accounting for inventories.

IFRS6-2 LaTour Inc. is based in France and prepares its financial statements (in euros) in accordance with IFRS. In 2014, it reported cost of goods sold of €578 million and average inventory of €154 million. Briefly discuss how analysis of LaTour's inventory turnover (and comparisons to a company using GAAP) might be affected by differences in inventory accounting between IFRS and GAAP.

IFRS6-3 Franklin Company has the following four items in its ending inventory as of December 31, 2014. The company uses the lower-of-cost-or-net realizable value approach for inventory valuation following IFRS.

Item No.	Cost	Net Realizable Value
AB	$1,700	$1,400
TRX	2,200	2,300
NWA	7,800	7,100
SGH	3,000	3,700

Compute the lower-of-cost-or-net realizable value.

International Financial Reporting Problem: Zetar plc

IFRS6-4 The financial statements of Zetar plc are presented in Appendix F. Instructions for accessing and using the company's complete annual report, including the notes to its financial statements, are also provided in Appendix F.

Instructions

Using the notes to the company's financial statements, answer the following questions.

(a) What cost flow assumption does the company use to value inventory?

(b) What was the amount of expense that the company reported for inventory write-downs during 2011?

(c) What amount of raw materials, work in process, and finished goods inventory did the company report at April 30, 2011?

Answers to IFRS Self-Test Questions
1. a   2. b   3. c   4. a   5. c

 ✔ The Navigator

✔ Remember to go back to The Navigator box on the chapter opening page and check off your completed work.

Feature Story

QuickBooks® Helps This Retailer Sell Guitars

Starting a small business requires many decisions. For example, you have to decide where to locate, how much space you need, how much inventory to have, how many employees to hire, and where to advertise. Small business owners are typically so concerned about the product and sales side of their business that they often do not give enough thought to something that is critical to their success—how to keep track of financial results.

Small business owners today can choose either manual or computerized accounting systems. For example, Paul and Laura West are the owners of the first independent dealership of Carvin guitars and professional audio equipment. When they founded their company, in Sacramento, California, they decided to purchase a computerized accounting system that would integrate many aspects of their retail operations. They wanted to use their accounting software to manage their inventory of guitars and amplifiers, enter sales, record and report financial data, and process credit card and debit card

transactions. They evaluated a number of options and cho QuickBooks® by Intuit Inc.

QuickBooks®, like most other popular software packages, programs designed for the needs of a specific business, w in this case is retailing. This QuickBooks® retailing package automatically collects sales information from its point-of-s scanning devices. It also keeps track of inventory levels ar automatically generates purchase orders for popular item when re-order points are reached. It even supports sales efforts by compiling a customer database from which the Wests send out targeted direct mailings to potential custor The computerized system enables data files to be emailed the company's accountant. This keeps costs down and makes it easier and more efficient to generate financial reports as needed. The Wests believe that the investment the computerized system has saved them time and mone and allowed them to spend more time on other aspects c their business.

Source: Intuit Inc., "QuickBooks® and ProAdvisor® Help Make Guitar Store Hit," *Journal of Accountancy* (May 2006), p. 101.

 The Navigator

- Scan Learning Objectives
- Read Feature Story
- Read Preview
- Read text and answer **DO IT!** p. 335
  - p. 348
- Work Comprehensive **DO IT!** p. 349
- Review Summary of Learning Objectives
- Answer Self-Test Questions
- Complete Assignments
- Go to *WileyPLUS* for practice and tutorials
- **Read A Look at IFRS** p. 371

Learning Objectives   **The Navigator**

After studying this chapter, you should be able to:

[1] Identify the basic concepts of an accounting information system.

[2] Describe the nature and purpose of a subsidiary ledger.

[3] Explain how companies use special journals in journalizing.

Terra Images/Age Fotostock America, Inc.

Preview of Chapter 7

✔ The Navigator

As you see from the Feature Story, a reliable information system is a necessity for any company. Whether companies use pen, pencil, or computers in maintaining accounting records, certain principles and procedures apply. The purpose of this chapter is to explain and illustrate these features.

The content and organization of Chapter 7 are as follows.

ACCOUNTING INFORMATION SYSTEMS		
Basic Concepts of Accounting Information Systems	**Subsidiary Ledgers**	**Special Journals**
• Computerized accounting systems • Manual accounting systems	• Example • Advantages	• Sales journal • Cash receipts journal • Purchases journal • Cash payments journal • Effects of special journals on general journal

Basic Concepts of Accounting Information Systems

The **accounting information system** collects and processes transaction data and communicates financial information to decision-makers. It includes each of the steps in the accounting cycle that you studied in earlier chapters. It also includes the documents that provide evidence of the transactions, and the records, trial balances, worksheets, and financial statements that result. An **accounting system** may be either manual or computerized. Most businesses these days use some sort of computerized accounting system, whether it is an off-the-shelf system for small businesses, like QuickBooks or Peachtree, or a more complex custom-made system.

Efficient and effective accounting information systems are based on certain basic principles. These principles, as described in Illustration 7-1, are (1) cost-effectiveness, (2) usefulness, and (3) flexibility. If the accounting system is cost-effective, provides useful output, and has the flexibility to meet future needs, it can contribute to both individual and organizational goals.

Illustration 7-1

Principles of an efficient and effective accounting information system

Cost-Effectiveness

The accounting system must be cost-effective. Benefits of information must outweigh the cost of providing it.

Useful Output

To be useful, information must be understandable, relevant, reliable, timely, and accurate. Designers of accounting systems must consider the needs and knowledge of various users.

Flexibility

The accounting system should accommodate a variety of users and changing information needs. The system should be sufficiently flexible to meet the resulting changes in the demands made upon it.

Computerized Accounting Systems

Many small businesses eventually replace their manual accounting system with a computerized general ledger accounting system. **General ledger accounting systems** are software programs that integrate the various accounting functions related to sales, purchases, receivables, payables, cash receipts and disbursements, and payroll. They also generate financial statements. Computerized systems have a number of advantages over manual systems. First, the company typically enters data only once in a computerized system. Second, because the computer does most steps automatically, it eliminates many errors resulting from human intervention in a manual system, such as errors in posting or preparation of financial statements. Computerized systems also provide information up-to-the-minute. More timely information results in better business decisions. Many different general ledger software packages are available.

CHOOSING A SOFTWARE PACKAGE

To identify the right software for your business, you must understand your company's operations. For example, consider its needs with regard to inventory, billing, payroll, and cash management. In addition, the company might have specific needs that are not supported by all software systems. For example, you might want to track employees' hours on individual jobs or to extract information for determining sales commissions. Choosing the right system is critical because installation of even a basic system is time-consuming, and learning a new system will require many hours of employee time.

ENTRY-LEVEL SOFTWARE

Software publishers tend to classify businesses into groups based on revenue and the number of employees. Companies with revenues of less than $5 million and up to 20 employees generally use **entry-level programs**. The two leading entry-level programs are Intuit's QuickBooks and The Sage Group's Sage 50. These programs control more than 90% of the market. Each of these entry-level programs comes in many different industry-specific versions. For example, some are designed for very specific industry applications such as restaurants, retailing, construction, manufacturing, or nonprofit.

Quality entry-level packages typically involve more than recording transactions and preparing financial statements. Here are some common features and benefits:

- **Easy data access and report preparation.** Users can easily access information related to specific customers or suppliers. For example, you can view all transactions, invoices, payments, as well as contact information for a specific client.

- **Audit trail.** As a result of the Sarbanes-Oxley Act, companies are now far more concerned that their accounting system minimizes opportunities for fraud. Many programs provide an "audit trail" that enables the tracking of all transactions.

- **Internal controls.** Some systems have an internal accounting review that identifies suspicious transactions or likely mistakes such as wrong account numbers or duplicate transactions.

- **Customization.** This feature enables the company to create data fields specific to the needs of its business.

- **Network-compatibility.** Multiple users in the company can access the system at the same time.

Ethics Note

Entire books and movies have used computer-system tampering as a major theme. Most programmers would agree that tamper-proofing and debugging programs are the most difficult and time-consuming phases of their jobs.

ENTERPRISE RESOURCE PLANNING SYSTEMS

Enterprise resource planning (ERP) systems are typically used by manufacturing companies with more than 500 employees and $500 million in sales. The best-known of these systems are SAP AG's SAP ERP (the most widely used) and Oracle's ERP. ERP systems go far beyond the functions of an entry-level general ledger package. They integrate all aspects of the organization, including accounting, sales, human resource management, and manufacturing. Because of the complexity of an ERP system, implementation can take three years and cost five times as much as the purchase price of the system. Purchase and implementation of ERP systems can cost from $250,000 to as much as $50 million for the largest multi-national corporations.

ETHICS INSIGHT

Curbing Fraudulent Activity with Software

The Sarbanes-Oxley Act (SOX) requires that companies demonstrate that they have adequate controls in place to detect significant fraudulent behavior by employees. Recently, about 15% of publicly traded companies reported at least one material weakness in their controls that needed to be remedied.

The SOX requirements have created a huge market for software that can monitor and trace every recorded transaction and adjusting entry. This enables companies to pinpoint who used the accounting system and when they used it. These systems also require "electronic signatures" by employees for all significant transactions. Such signatures verify that employees have followed all required procedures, and that all actions are properly authorized. SOX-related technology spending was estimated to be approximately $2 billion at one time. One firm that specializes in compliance software had 10 clients prior to SOX and 250 after SOX.

Source: W. M. Bulkeley and C. Forelle, "Anti-Crime Program: How Corporate Scandals Gave Tech Firms a New Business Line," *Wall Street Journal* (December 9, 2005), p. A1.

 Why might this software help reduce fraudulent activity by employees? (See page 371.)

Manual Accounting Systems

Manual accounting systems perform each of the steps in the accounting cycle by hand. For example, someone manually enters each accounting transaction in the journal and manually posts each to the ledger. Other manual computations must be made to obtain ledger account balances and to prepare a trial balance and financial statements. In the remainder of this chapter, we illustrate the use of a manual system.

You might be wondering, "Why cover manual accounting systems if the real world uses computerized systems?" First, small businesses still abound. Most of them begin operations with manual accounting systems and convert to computerized systems as the business grows. You may work in a small business or start your own someday, so it is useful to know how a manual system works. Second, to understand what computerized accounting systems do, you also need to understand manual accounting systems.

The manual accounting system represented in the first six chapters of this textbook is satisfactory in a company with a low volume of transactions. However, in most companies, it is necessary to add additional ledgers and journals to the accounting system to record transaction data efficiently.

Subsidiary Ledgers

LEARNING OBJECTIVE 2

Describe the nature and purpose of a subsidiary ledger.

Imagine a business that has several thousand charge (credit) customers and shows the transactions with these customers in only one general ledger account—Accounts Receivable. It would be nearly impossible to determine the balance owed by an individual customer at any specific time. Similarly, the amount payable to one creditor would be difficult to locate quickly from a single Accounts Payable account in the general ledger.

Instead, companies use subsidiary ledgers to keep track of individual balances. A **subsidiary ledger** is a group of accounts with a common characteristic (for example, all accounts receivable). It is an addition to and an expansion of the general ledger. The subsidiary ledger frees the general ledger from the details of individual balances.

Two common subsidiary ledgers are:

1. The **accounts receivable** (or **customers'**) **subsidiary ledger**, which collects transaction data of individual customers.

2. The **accounts payable** (or **creditors'**) **subsidiary ledger**, which collects transaction data of individual creditors.

In each of these subsidiary ledgers, companies usually arrange individual accounts in alphabetical order.

A general ledger account summarizes the detailed data from a subsidiary ledger. For example, the detailed data from the accounts receivable subsidiary ledger are summarized in Accounts Receivable in the general ledger. The general ledger account that summarizes subsidiary ledger data is called a **control account**. Illustration 7-2 presents an overview of the relationship of subsidiary ledgers to the general ledger. There, the general ledger control accounts and subsidiary ledger accounts are in green. Note that Cash and Owner's Capital in this illustration are not control accounts because there are no subsidiary ledger accounts related to these accounts.

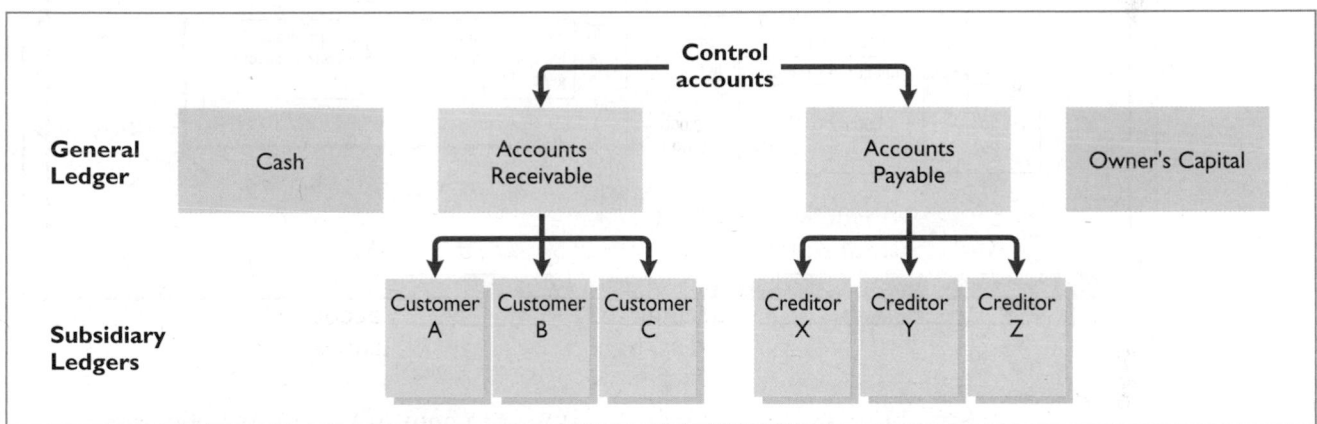

Illustration 7-2
Relationship of general ledger and subsidiary ledgers

At the end of an accounting period, each general ledger control account balance must equal the composite balance of the individual accounts in the related subsidiary ledger. For example, the balance in Accounts Payable in Illustration 7-2 must equal the total of the subsidiary balances of Creditors X + Y + Z.

Subsidiary Ledger Example

Illustration 7-3 lists credit sales and collections on account for Pujols Company.

Illustration 7-3
Sales and collection transactions

Credit Sales			Collections on Account		
Jan. 10	Aaron Co.	$ 6,000	Jan. 19	Aaron Co.	$4,000
12	Branden Inc.	3,000	21	Branden Inc.	3,000
20	Caron Co.	3,000	29	Caron Co.	1,000
		$12,000			$8,000

Illustration 7-4
Relationship between general
and subsidiary ledgers

Illustration 7-4 provides an example of a control account and subsidiary ledger for Pujols Company. (Due to space considerations, the explanation column in these accounts is not shown in this and subsequent illustrations.) Illustration 7-4 is based on the transactions listed in Illustration 7-3.

Pujols can reconcile the total debits ($12,000) and credits ($8,000) in Accounts Receivable in the general ledger to the detailed debits and credits in the subsidiary accounts. Also, the balance of $4,000 in the control account agrees with the total of the balances in the individual accounts (Aaron Co. $2,000 + Branden Inc. $0 + Caron Co. $2,000) in the subsidiary ledger.

As Illustration 7-4 shows, companies make monthly postings to the control accounts in the general ledger. This practice allows them to prepare monthly financial statements. Companies post to the individual accounts in the subsidiary ledger daily. Daily posting ensures that account information is current. This enables the company to monitor credit limits, bill customers, and answer inquiries from customers about their account balances.

Advantages of Subsidiary Ledgers

Subsidiary ledgers have several advantages:

1. **They show in a single account transactions affecting one customer or one creditor**, thus providing up-to-date information on specific account balances.
2. **They free the general ledger of excessive details.** As a result, a trial balance of the general ledger does not contain vast numbers of individual account balances.

3. **They help locate errors in individual accounts** by reducing the number of accounts in one ledger and by using control accounts.
4. **They make possible a division of labor** in posting. One employee can post to the general ledger while someone else posts to the subsidiary ledgers.

ACCOUNTING ACROSS THE ORGANIZATION

"I'm John Smith, a.k.a. 13695071642"

Rather than relying on customer or creditor names in a subsidiary ledger, a computerized system expands the account number of the control account in a pre-specified manner. For example, if Accounts Receivable was numbered 10010, the first account in the accounts receivable subsidiary ledger might be numbered 10010–0001. Most systems allow inquiries about specific accounts in the subsidiary ledger (by account number) or about the control account. With the latter, the system would automatically total all the subsidiary accounts whenever an inquiry to the control account was made.

© Niels Laan/iStockphoto

? Why use numbers to identify names in a computerized system? (See page 371.)

> DO IT!

Subsidiary Ledgers

Presented below is information related to Sims Company for its first month of operations. Determine the balances that appear in the accounts payable subsidiary ledger. What Accounts Payable balance appears in the general ledger at the end of January?

	Credit Purchases			Cash Paid	
Jan. 5	Devon Co.	$11,000	Jan. 9	Devon Co.	$7,000
11	Shelby Co.	7,000	14	Shelby Co.	2,000
22	Taylor Co.	14,000	27	Taylor Co.	9,000

Action Plan

✔ Subtract cash paid from credit purchases to determine the balances in the accounts payable subsidiary ledger.

✔ Sum the individual balances to determine the Accounts Payable balance.

Solution

Subsidiary ledger balances:

Devon Co. $4,000 ($11,000 − $7,000)

Shelby Co. $5,000 ($7,000 − $2,000)

Taylor Co. $5,000 ($14,000 − $9,000)

General ledger Accounts Payable balance: $14,000 ($4,000 + $5,000 + $5,000)

Related exercise material: **BE7-4, BE7-5, E7-1, E7-2, E7-4, E7-5, and DO IT! 7-1.**

✔ **The Navigator**

Special Journals

So far you have learned to journalize transactions in a two-column general journal and post each entry to the general ledger. This procedure is satisfactory in only very small companies. To expedite journalizing and posting, most companies use special journals **in addition to the general journal**.

LEARNING OBJECTIVE 3

Explain how companies use special journals in journalizing.

Companies use **special journals** to record similar types of transactions. Examples are all sales of merchandise on account or all cash receipts. The types of transactions that occur frequently in a company determine what special journals the company uses. Most merchandising companies record daily transactions using the journals shown in Illustration 7-5.

Illustration 7-5
Use of special journals and the general journal

Sales Journal	**Cash Receipts Journal**	**Purchases Journal**	**Cash Payments Journal**	**General Journal**
Used for: All sales of merchandise on account	Used for: All cash received (including cash sales)	Used for: All purchases of merchandise on account	Used for: All cash paid (including cash purchases)	Used for: Transactions that cannot be entered in a special journal, including correcting, adjusting, and closing entries

If a transaction cannot be recorded in a special journal, the company records it in the general journal. For example, if a company had special journals for only the four types of transactions listed above, it would record purchase returns and allowances in the general journal. Similarly, **correcting**, **adjusting, and closing entries are recorded in the general journal.** In some situations, companies might use special journals other than those listed above. For example, when sales returns and allowances are frequent, a company might use a special journal to record these transactions.

Special journals **permit greater division of labor** because several people can record entries in different journals at the same time. For example, one employee may journalize all cash receipts, and another may journalize all credit sales. Also, the use of special journals **reduces the time needed to complete the posting process**. With special journals, companies may post some accounts monthly, instead of daily, as we will illustrate later in the chapter. On the following pages, we discuss the four special journals shown in Illustration 7-5.

Sales Journal

In the **sales journal**, companies record **sales of merchandise on account**. Cash sales of merchandise go in the cash receipts journal. Credit sales of assets other than merchandise go in the general journal.

JOURNALIZING CREDIT SALES

Helpful Hint Postings are also made daily to individual ledger accounts in the inventory subsidiary ledger to maintain a perpetual inventory.

To demonstrate use of a sales journal, we will use data for Karns Wholesale Supply, which uses a **perpetual inventory system**. Under this system, each entry in the sales journal results in one entry **at selling price** and another entry **at cost**. The entry at selling price is a debit to Accounts Receivable (a control account) and a credit of equal amount to Sales Revenue. The entry at cost is a debit to Cost of Goods Sold and a credit of equal amount to Inventory (a control account). Using a sales journal with two amount columns, the company can show on only one line a sales transaction at both selling price and cost. Illustration 7-6 shows this two-column sales journal of Karns Wholesale Supply, using assumed credit sales transactions (for sales invoices 101–107).

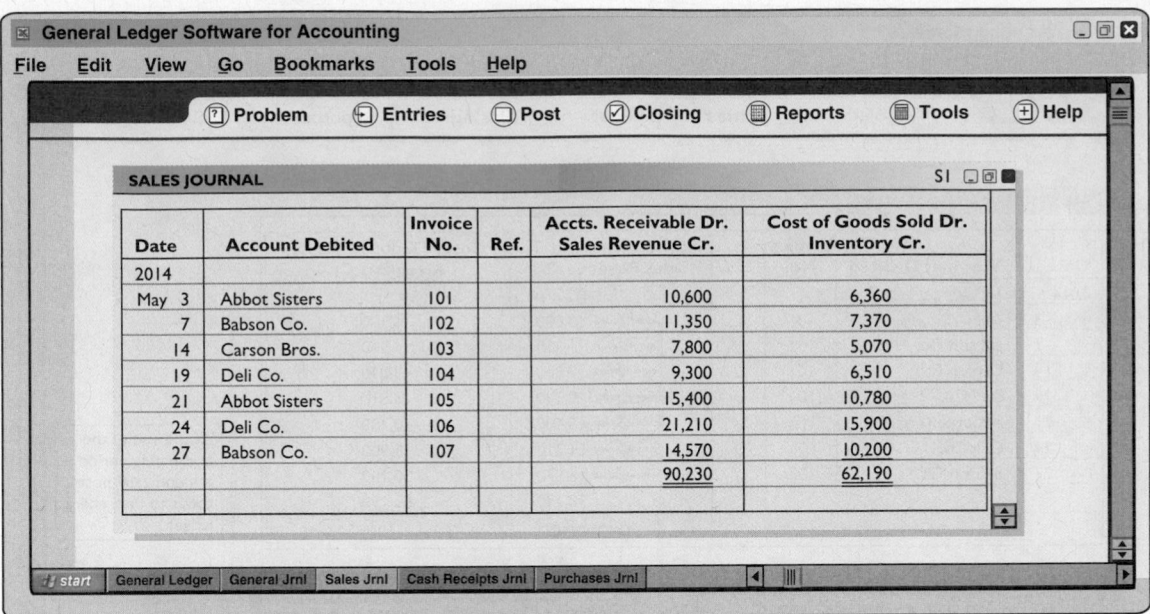

Illustration 7-6
Journalizing the sales journal—perpetual inventory system

Note that, unlike the general journal, an explanation is not required for each entry in a special journal. Also, note that use of prenumbered invoices ensures that all invoices are journalized and no invoices are duplicated. Finally, note that the reference (Ref.) column is not used in journalizing. It is used in posting the sales journal, as explained in the next section.

POSTING THE SALES JOURNAL

Companies make daily postings from the sales journal **to the individual accounts receivable** in the subsidiary ledger. Posting **to the general ledger** is done **monthly**. Illustration 7-7 (page 338) shows both the daily and monthly postings.

A check mark (✓) is inserted in the reference column to indicate that the daily posting to the customer's account has been made. If the subsidiary ledger accounts were numbered, the account number would be entered in place of the check mark. At the end of the month, Karns posts the column totals of the sales journal to the general ledger. Here, the column totals are as follows. From the selling-price column, a debit of $90,230 to Accounts Receivable (account No. 112), and a credit of $90,230 to Sales Revenue (account No. 401). From the cost column, a debit of $62,190 to Cost of Goods Sold (account No. 505), and a credit of $62,190 to Inventory (account No. 120). Karns inserts the account numbers below the column totals to indicate that the postings have been made. In both the general ledger and subsidiary ledger accounts, the reference **S1** indicates that the posting came from page 1 of the sales journal.

PROVING THE LEDGERS

The next step is to "prove" the ledgers. To do so, Karns must determine two things: (1) The total of the general ledger debit balances must equal the total of the general ledger credit balances. (2) The sum of the subsidiary ledger balances must equal the balance in the control account. Illustration 7-8 (page 339) shows the proof of the postings from the sales journal to the general and subsidiary ledgers.

ADVANTAGES OF THE SALES JOURNAL

The use of a special journal to record sales on account has a number of advantages. First, the one-line entry for each sales transaction saves time. In the sales journal, it is not necessary to write out the four account titles for each transaction.

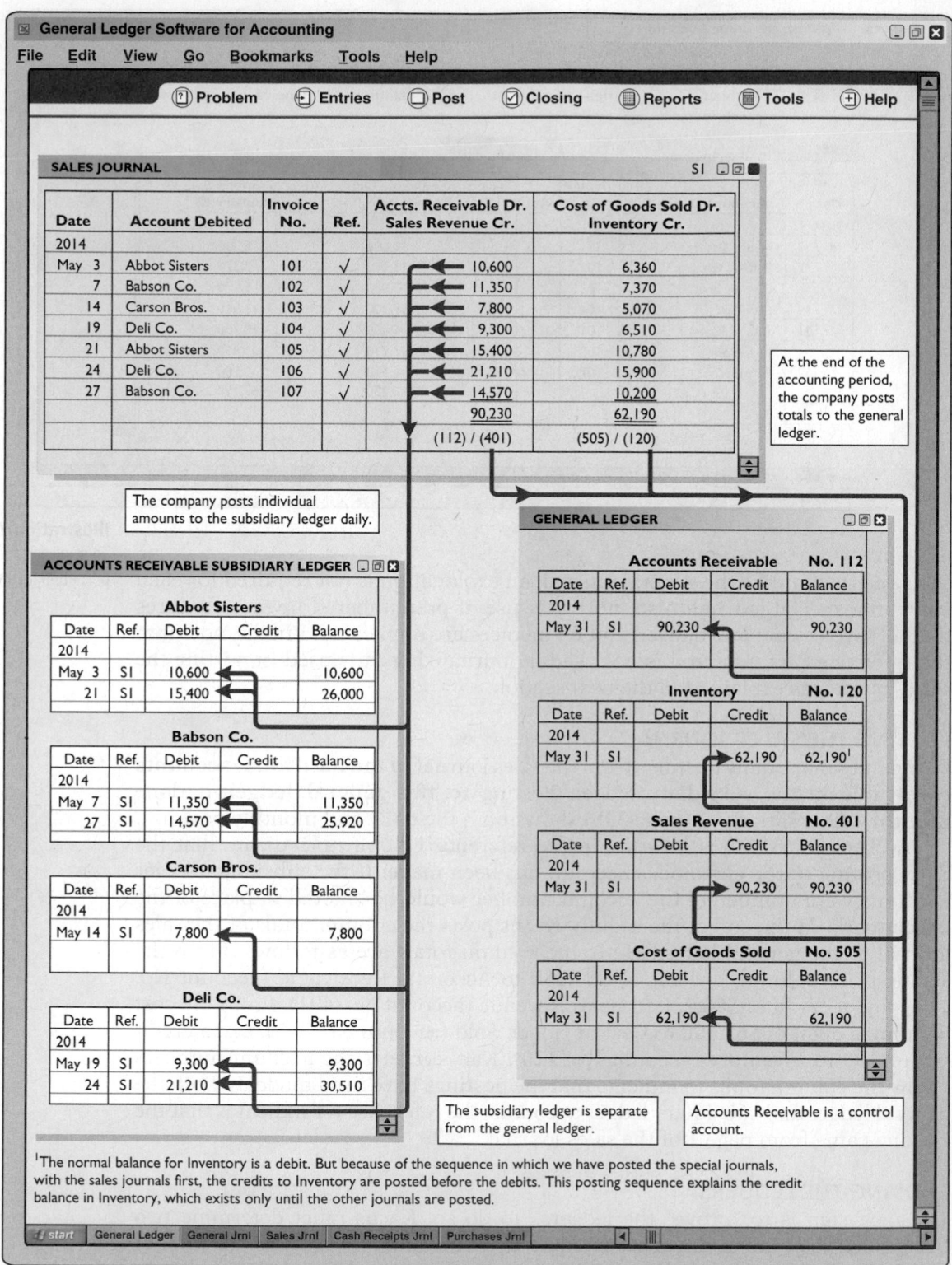

Illustration 7-7
Posting the sales journal

Second, only totals, rather than individual entries, are posted to the general ledger. This saves posting time and reduces the possibilities of errors in posting. Finally, a division of labor results because one individual can take responsibility for the sales journal.

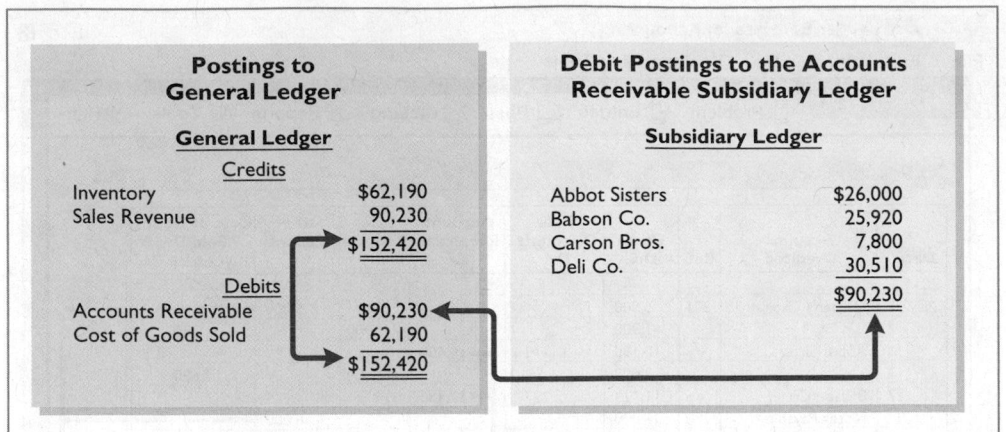

Illustration 7-8
Proving the equality of the
postings from the sales journal

Cash Receipts Journal

In the **cash receipts journal**, companies record all receipts of cash. The most common types of cash receipts are cash sales of merchandise and collections of accounts receivable. Many other possibilities exist, such as receipt of money from bank loans and cash proceeds from disposal of equipment. A one- or two-column cash receipts journal would not have space enough for all possible cash receipt transactions. Therefore, companies use a multiple-column cash receipts journal.

Generally, a cash receipts journal includes the following columns: debit columns for Cash and Sales Discounts, and credit columns for Accounts Receivable, Sales Revenue, and "Other Accounts." Companies use the "Other Accounts" category when the cash receipt does not involve a cash sale or a collection of accounts receivable. Under a perpetual inventory system, each sales entry also is accompanied by an entry that debits Cost of Goods Sold and credits Inventory for the cost of the merchandise sold. Illustration 7-9 (page 340) shows a six-column cash receipts journal.

Companies may use additional credit columns if these columns significantly reduce postings to a specific account. For example, a loan company such as Household International receives thousands of cash collections from customers. Using separate credit columns for Loans Receivable and Interest Revenue, rather than the Other Accounts credit column, would reduce postings.

JOURNALIZING CASH RECEIPTS TRANSACTIONS

To illustrate the journalizing of cash receipts transactions, we will continue with the May transactions of Karns Wholesale Supply. Collections from customers relate to the entries recorded in the sales journal in Illustration 7-6. The entries in the cash receipts journal are based on the following cash receipts.

May 1   D. A. Karns makes an investment of $5,000 in the business.
    7   Cash sales of merchandise total $1,900 (cost, $1,240).
  10   Received a check for $10,388 from Abbot Sisters in payment of invoice No. 101 for $10,600 less a 2% discount.
  12   Cash sales of merchandise total $2,600 (cost, $1,690).
  17   Received a check for $11,123 from Babson Co. in payment of invoice No. 102 for $11,350 less a 2% discount.
  22   Received cash by signing a note for $6,000.
  23   Received a check for $7,644 from Carson Bros. in full for invoice No. 103 for $7,800 less a 2% discount.
  28   Received a check for $9,114 from Deli Co. in full for invoice No. 104 for $9,300 less a 2% discount.

Further information about the columns in the cash receipts journal is listed on page 341.

Illustration 7-9
Journalizing and posting the cash receipts journal

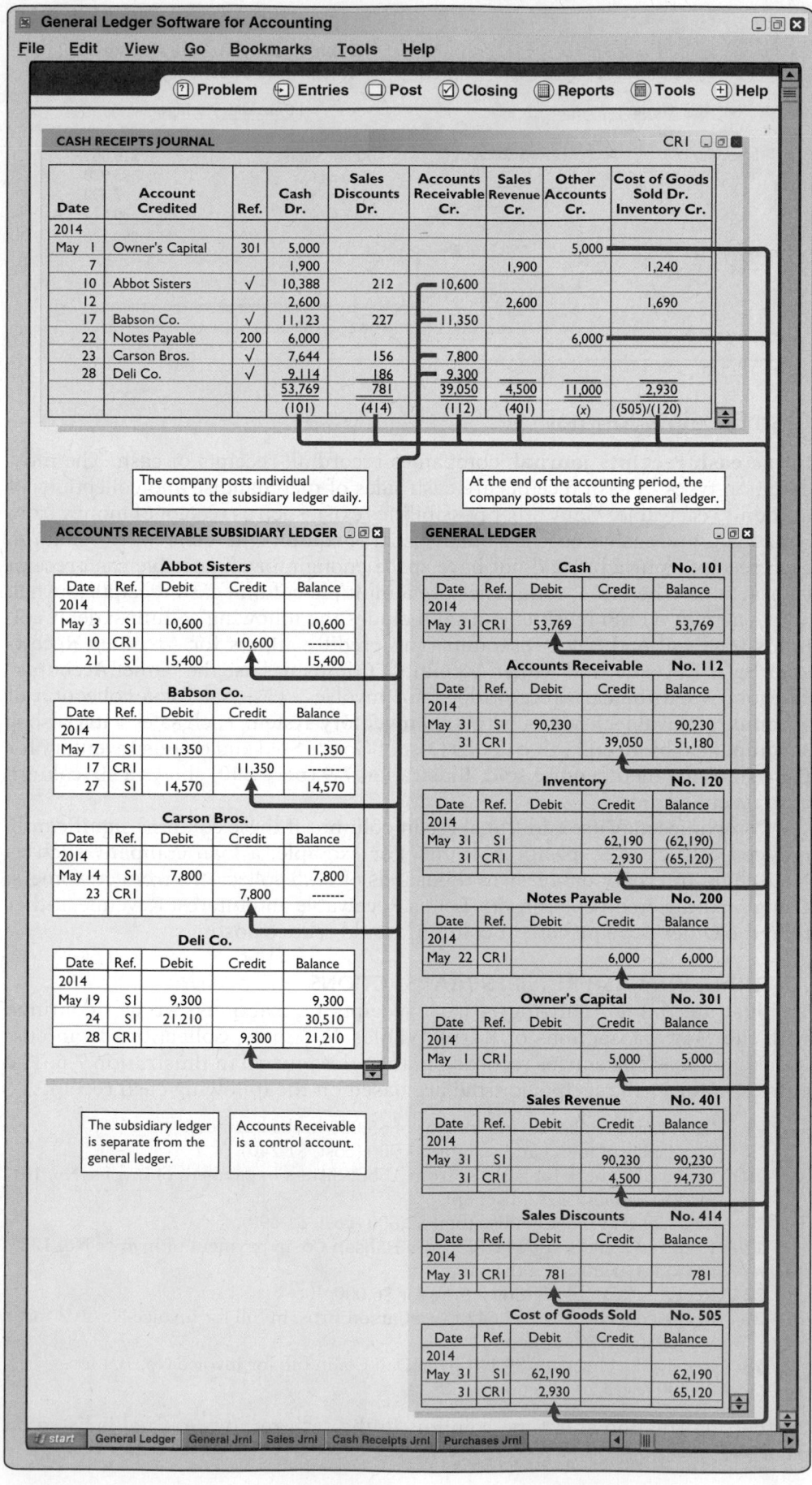

Debit Columns:

1. **Cash.** Karns enters in this column the amount of cash actually received in each transaction. The column total indicates the total cash receipts for the month.

2. **Sales Discounts.** Karns includes a Sales Discounts column in its cash receipts journal. By doing so, it does not need to enter sales discount items in the general journal. As a result, the cash receipts journal shows on one line the collection of an account receivable within the discount period.

Credit Columns:

3. **Accounts Receivable.** Karns uses the Accounts Receivable column to record cash collections on account. The amount entered here is the amount to be credited to the individual customer's account.

4. **Sales Revenue.** The Sales Revenue column records all cash sales of merchandise. Cash sales of other assets (plant assets, for example) are not reported in this column.

5. **Other Accounts.** Karns uses the Other Accounts column whenever the credit is other than to Accounts Receivable or Sales Revenue. For example, in the first entry, Karns enters $5,000 as a credit to Owner's Capital. This column is often referred to as the sundry accounts column.

Debit and Credit Column:

6. **Cost of Goods Sold and Inventory.** This column records debits to Cost of Goods Sold and credits to Inventory.

In a multi-column journal, generally only one line is needed for each entry. Debit and credit amounts for each line must be equal. When Karns journalizes the collection from Abbot Sisters on May 10, for example, three amounts are indicated. Note also that the Account Credited column identifies both general ledger and subsidiary ledger account titles. General ledger accounts are illustrated in the May 1 and May 22 entries. A subsidiary account is illustrated in the May 10 entry for the collection from Abbot Sisters.

When Karns has finished journalizing a multi-column journal, it totals the amount columns and compares the totals to prove the equality of debits and credits. Illustration 7-10 shows the proof of the equality of Karns's cash receipts journal.

Helpful Hint When is an account title entered in the "Account Credited" column of the cash receipts journal? Answer: A *subsidiary ledger* account is entered when the entry involves a collection of accounts receivable. A *general ledger* account is entered when the account is not shown in a special column (and an amount must be entered in the Other Accounts column). Otherwise, no account is shown in the "Account Credited" column.

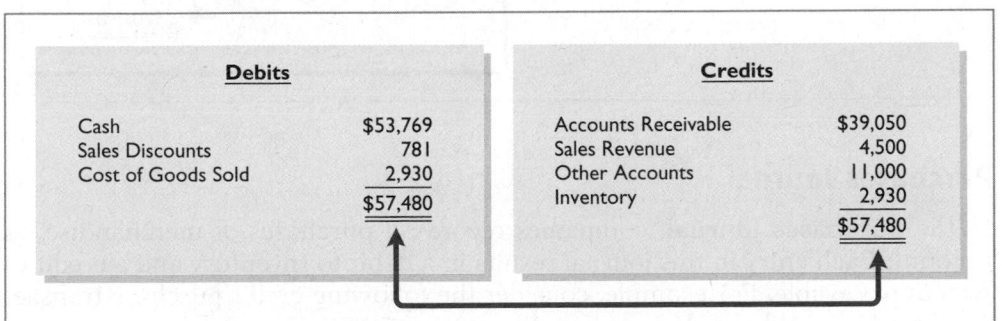

Illustration 7-10
Proving the equality of the cash receipts journal

Debits		Credits	
Cash	$53,769	Accounts Receivable	$39,050
Sales Discounts	781	Sales Revenue	4,500
Cost of Goods Sold	2,930	Other Accounts	11,000
	$57,480	Inventory	2,930
			$57,480

Totaling the columns of a journal and proving the equality of the totals is called **footing** and **cross-footing** a journal.

POSTING THE CASH RECEIPTS JOURNAL

Posting a multi-column journal (Illustration 7-9, page 340) involves the following steps.

1. **At the end of the month**, the company posts all column totals, except for the Other Accounts total, to the account title(s) specified in the column heading

(such as Cash or Accounts Receivable). The company then enters account numbers below the column totals to show that they have been posted. For example, Karns has posted Cash to account No. 101, Accounts Receivable to account No. 112, Inventory to account No. 120, Sales Revenue to account No. 401, Sales Discounts to account No. 414, and Cost of Goods Sold to account No. 505.

2. The company **separately posts the individual amounts comprising the Other Accounts total** to the general ledger accounts specified in the Account Credited column. See, for example, the credit posting to Owner's Capital. The total amount of this column has not been posted. The symbol (X) is inserted below the total to this column to indicate that the amount has not been posted.

3. The individual amounts in a column, posted in total to a control account (Accounts Receivable, in this case), are posted **daily to the subsidiary ledger** account specified in the Account Credited column. See, for example, the credit posting of $10,600 to Abbot Sisters.

The symbol **CR**, used in both the subsidiary and general ledgers, identifies postings from the cash receipts journal.

PROVING THE LEDGERS

After posting of the cash receipts journal is completed, Karns proves the ledgers. As shown in Illustration 7-11, the general ledger totals agree. Also, the sum of the subsidiary ledger balances equals the control account balance.

Illustration 7-11

Proving the ledgers after posting the sales and the cash receipts journals

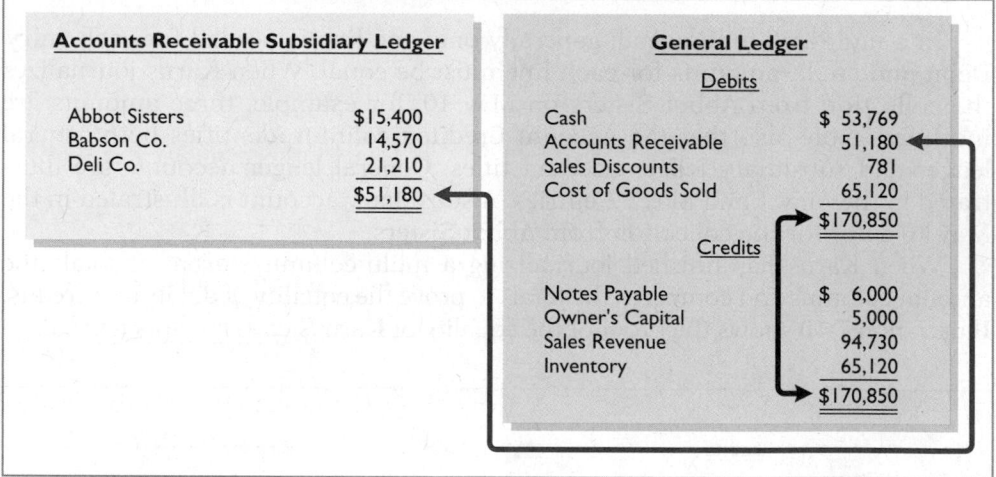

Accounts Receivable Subsidiary Ledger		General Ledger	
		Debits	
Abbot Sisters	$15,400	Cash	$ 53,769
Babson Co.	14,570	Accounts Receivable	51,180
Deli Co.	21,210	Sales Discounts	781
	$51,180	Cost of Goods Sold	65,120
			$170,850
		Credits	
		Notes Payable	$ 6,000
		Owner's Capital	5,000
		Sales Revenue	94,730
		Inventory	65,120
			$170,850

Purchases Journal

In the **purchases journal**, companies record all purchases of merchandise on account. Each entry in this journal results in a debit to Inventory and a credit to Accounts Payable. For example, consider the following credit purchase transactions for Karns Wholesale Supply in Illustration 7-12.

Illustration 7-12

Credit purchase transactions

Date	Supplier	Amount
5/6	Jasper Manufacturing Inc.	$11,000
5/10	Eaton and Howe Inc.	7,200
5/14	Fabor and Son	6,900
5/19	Jasper Manufacturing Inc.	17,500
5/26	Fabor and Son	8,700
5/29	Eaton and Howe Inc.	12,600

Illustration 7-13 shows the purchases journal for Karns Wholesale Supply. When using a one-column purchases journal (as in Illustration 7-13), a company cannot journalize other types of purchases on account or cash purchases in it. For example, in the purchases journal in Illustration 7-13, Karns would have to record credit purchases of equipment or supplies in the general journal. Likewise, all cash purchases would be entered in the cash payments journal. As illustrated later, companies that make numerous credit purchases for items other than merchandise often expand the purchases journal to a multi-column format. (See Illustration 7-15 on page 345.)

Illustration 7-13
Journalizing and posting the purchases journal

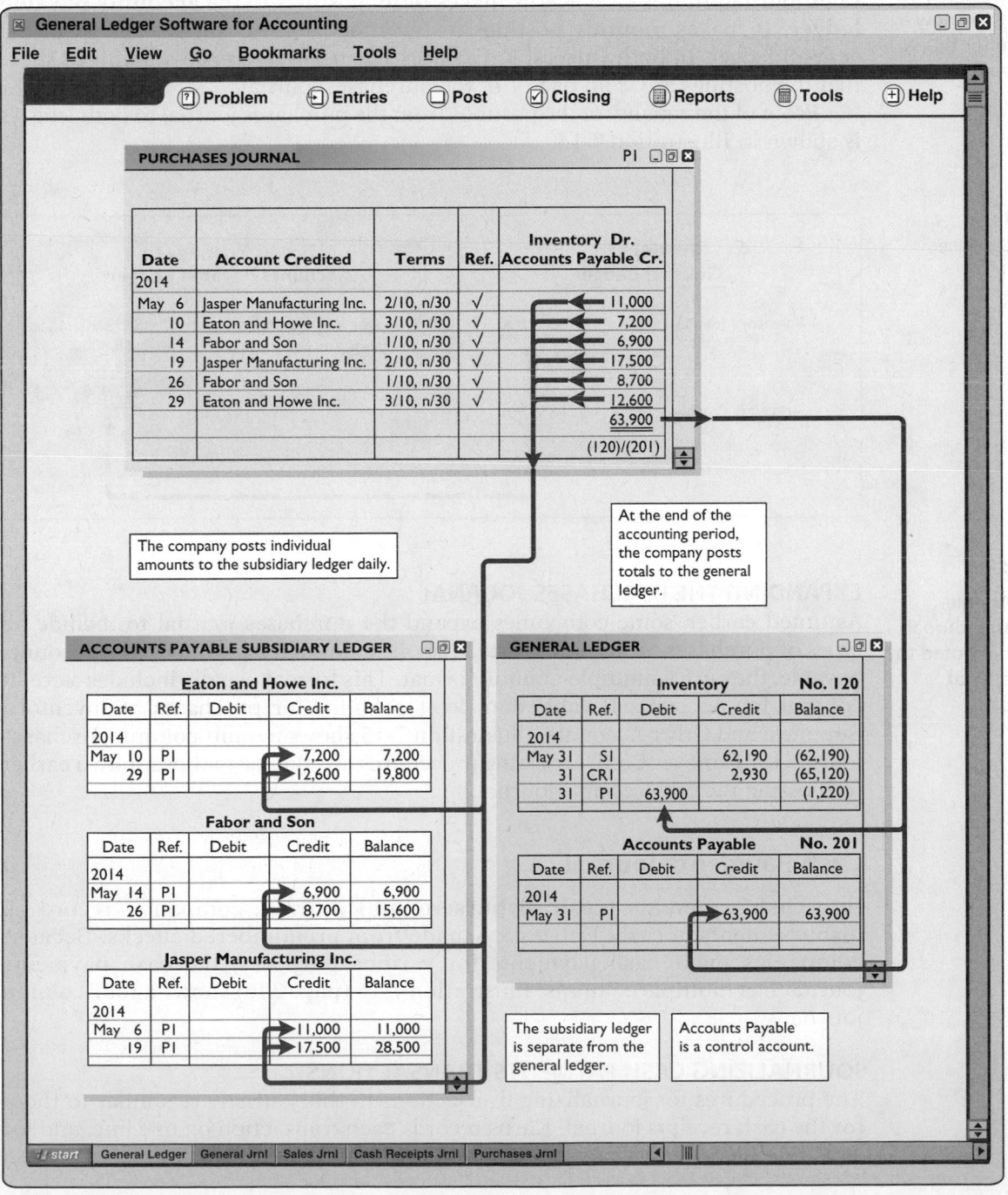

JOURNALIZING CREDIT PURCHASES OF MERCHANDISE

The journalizing procedure is similar to that for a sales journal. Companies make entries in the purchases journal from purchase invoices. In contrast to the sales journal, the purchases journal may not have an invoice number column because invoices received from different suppliers will not be in numerical sequence. To ensure that they record all purchase invoices, some companies consecutively number each invoice upon receipt and then use an internal document number column in the purchases journal. The entries for Karns Wholesale Supply are based on the assumed credit purchases listed in Illustration 7-12.

POSTING THE PURCHASES JOURNAL

The procedures for posting the purchases journal are similar to those for the sales journal. In this case, Karns makes **daily** postings to the **accounts payable ledger**. It makes **monthly** postings to Inventory and Accounts Payable in the general ledger. In both ledgers, Karns uses **P1** in the reference column to show that the postings are from page 1 of the purchases journal.

Proof of the equality of the postings from the purchases journal to both ledgers is shown in Illustration 7-14.

Illustration 7-14
Proving the equality of the purchases journal

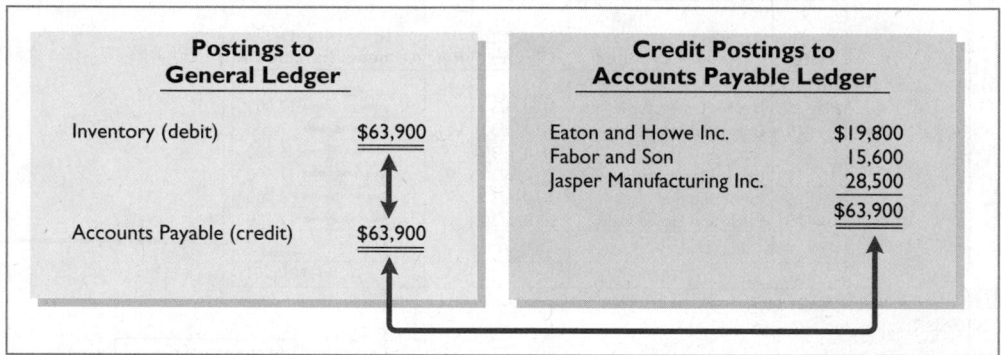

EXPANDING THE PURCHASES JOURNAL

As noted earlier, some companies expand the purchases journal to include all types of purchases on account. Instead of one column for inventory and accounts payable, they use a multiple-column format. This format usually includes a credit column for Accounts Payable and debit columns for purchases of Inventory, Supplies, and Other Accounts. Illustration 7-15 shows a multi-column purchases journal for Hanover Co. The posting procedures are similar to those shown earlier for posting the cash receipts journal.

Cash Payments Journal

In a **cash payments (cash disbursements) journal**, companies record all disbursements of cash. Entries are made from prenumbered checks. Because companies make cash payments for various purposes, the cash payments journal has multiple columns. Illustration 7-16 (page 346) shows a four-column journal.

JOURNALIZING CASH PAYMENTS TRANSACTIONS

The procedures for journalizing transactions in this journal are similar to those for the cash receipts journal. Karns records each transaction on one line, and for each line there must be equal debit and credit amounts. The entries in the cash

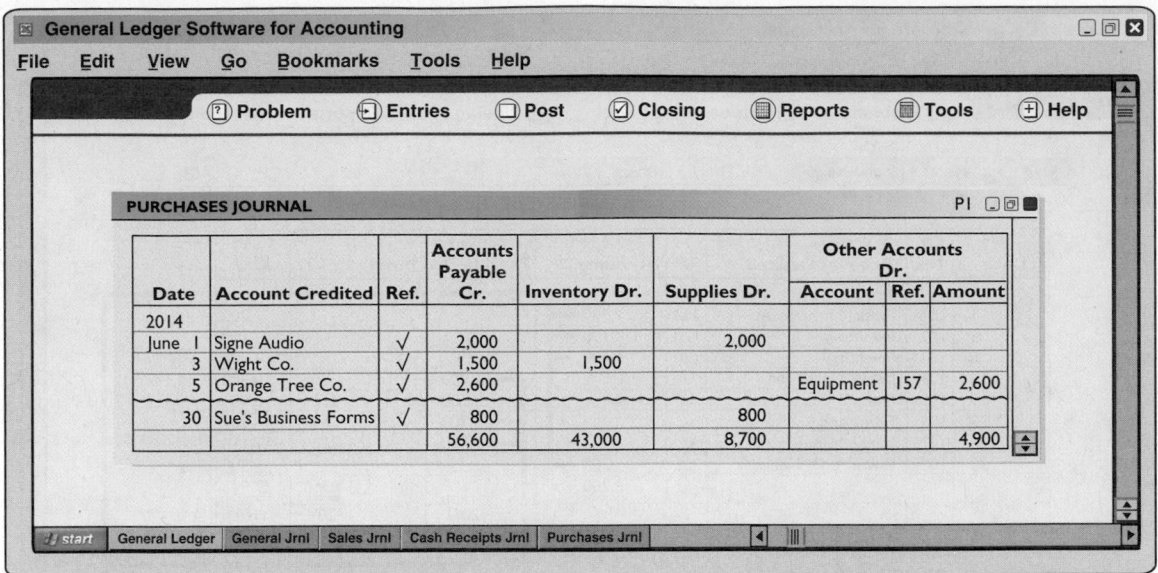

Illustration 7-15
Multi-column purchases journal

payments journal in Illustration 7-16 are based on the following transactions for Karns Wholesale Supply.

May 1   Issued check No. 101 for $1,200 for the annual premium on a fire insurance policy.

3   Issued check No. 102 for $100 in payment of freight when terms were FOB shipping point.

8   Issued check No. 103 for $4,400 for the purchase of merchandise.

10   Sent check No. 104 for $10,780 to Jasper Manufacturing Inc. in payment of May 6 invoice for $11,000 less a 2% discount.

19   Mailed check No. 105 for $6,984 to Eaton and Howe Inc. in payment of May 10 invoice for $7,200 less a 3% discount.

23   Sent check No. 106 for $6,831 to Fabor and Son in payment of May 14 invoice for $6,900 less a 1% discount.

28   Sent check No. 107 for $17,150 to Jasper Manufacturing Inc. in payment of May 19 invoice for $17,500 less a 2% discount.

30   Issued check No. 108 for $500 to D. A. Karns as a cash withdrawal for personal use.

Note that whenever Karns enters an amount in the Other Accounts column, it must identify a specific general ledger account in the Account Debited column. The entries for checks No. 101, 102, 103, and 108 illustrate this situation. Similarly, Karns must identify a subsidiary account in the Account Debited column whenever it enters an amount in the Accounts Payable column. See, for example, the entry for check No. 104.

After Karns journalizes the cash payments journal, it totals the columns. The totals are then balanced to prove the equality of debits and credits.

POSTING THE CASH PAYMENTS JOURNAL

The procedures for posting the cash payments journal are similar to those for the cash receipts journal. Karns posts the amounts recorded in the Accounts Payable column individually to the subsidiary ledger and in total to the control account. It posts Inventory and Cash only in total at the end of the month. Transactions in the Other Accounts column are posted individually to the appropriate account(s) affected. The company does not post totals for the Other Accounts column.

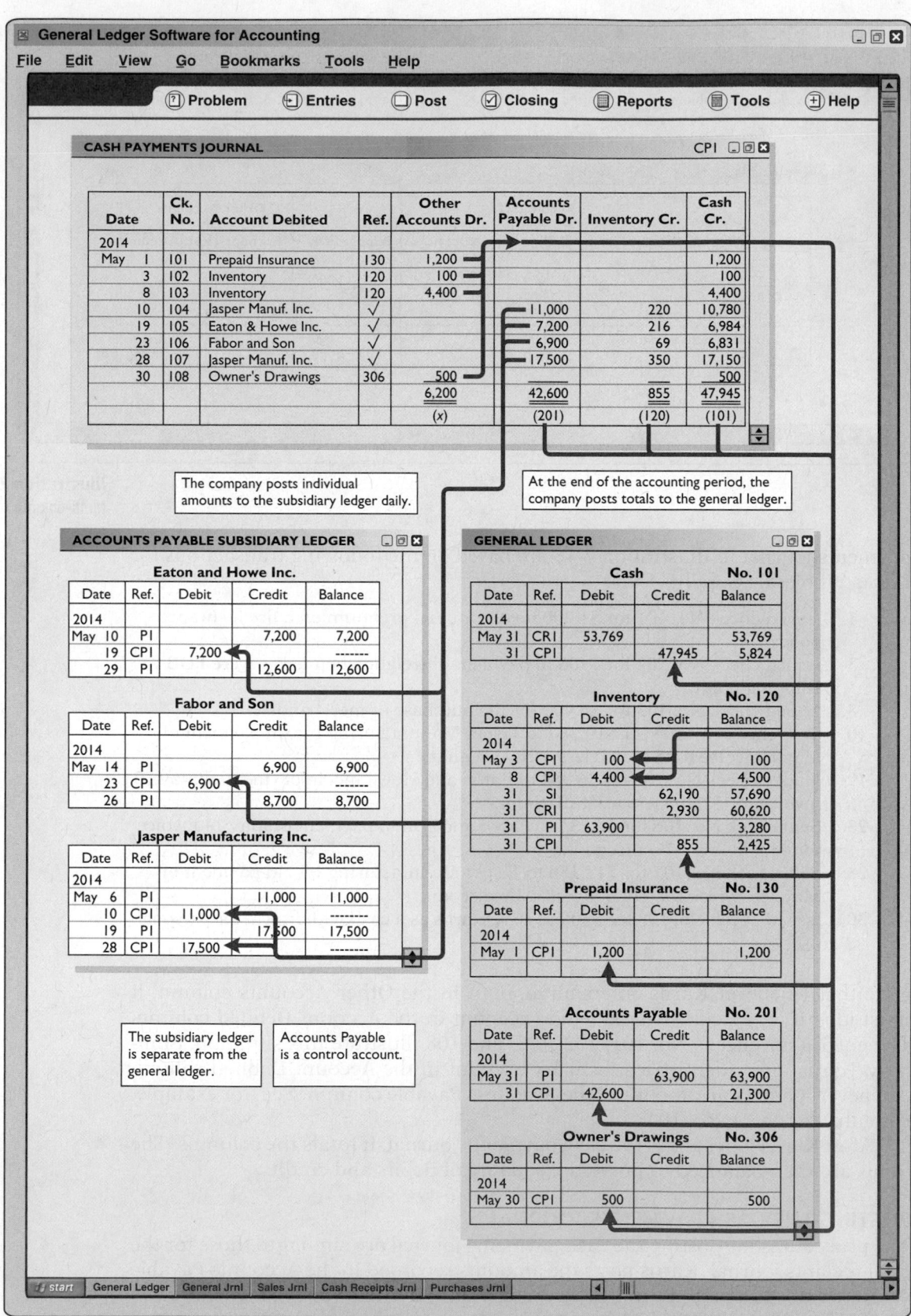

Illustration 7-16
Journalizing and posting the cash payments journal

Illustration 7-16 shows the posting of the cash payments journal. Note that Karns uses the symbol **CP** as the posting reference. After postings are completed, the company proves the equality of the debit and credit balances in the general ledger. In addition, the control account balances should agree with the subsidiary ledger total balance. Illustration 7-17 shows the agreement of these balances.

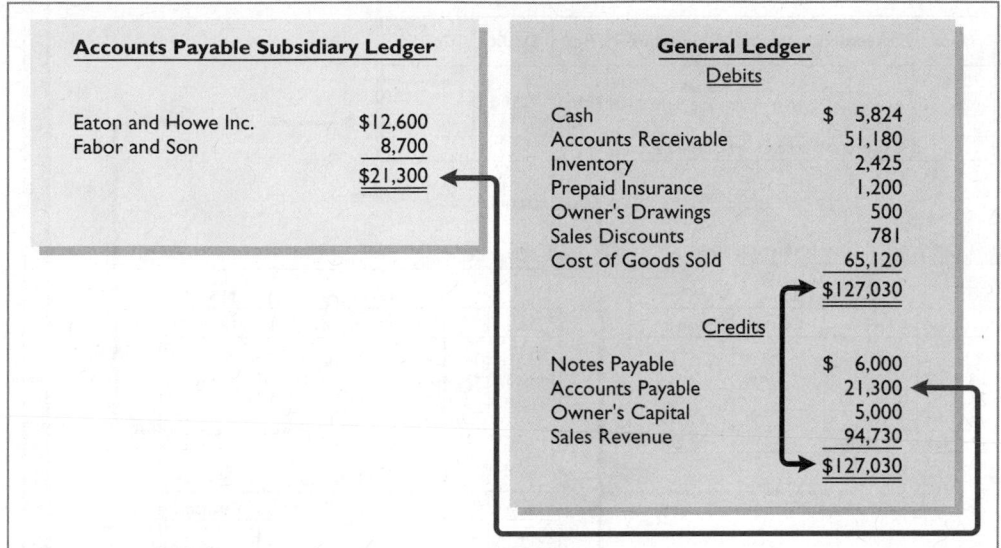

Illustration 7-17
Proving the ledgers after postings from the sales, cash receipts, purchases, and cash payments journals

Effects of Special Journals on the General Journal

Special journals for sales, purchases, and cash substantially reduce the number of entries that companies make in the general journal. **Only transactions that cannot be entered in a special journal are recorded in the general journal.** For example, a company may use the general journal to record such transactions as granting of credit to a customer for a sales return or allowance, granting of credit from a supplier for purchases returned, acceptance of a note receivable from a customer, and purchase of equipment by issuing a note payable. Also, **correcting, adjusting, and closing entries are made in the general journal.**

The general journal has columns for date, account title and explanation, reference, and debit and credit amounts. When control and subsidiary accounts are not involved, the procedures for journalizing and posting of transactions are the same as those described in earlier chapters. When control and subsidiary accounts are involved, companies make two changes from the earlier procedures:

1. In **journalizing**, they identify both the control and the subsidiary accounts.
2. In **posting**, there must be a **dual posting**: once to the control account and once to the subsidiary account.

To illustrate, assume that on May 31, Karns Wholesale Supply returns $500 of merchandise for credit to Fabor and Son. Illustration 7-18 (page 348) shows the entry in the general journal and the posting of the entry. Note that if Karns receives cash instead of credit on this return, then it would record the transaction in the cash receipts journal.

Note that the general journal indicates two accounts (Accounts Payable, and Fabor and Son) for the debit, and two postings ("201/✓") in the reference column. One debit is posted to the control account and another debit to the creditor's account in the subsidiary ledger.

Illustration 7-18
Journalizing and posting the
general journal

> DO IT!

Special Journals

Action Plan

✔ Determine if the
transaction involves the
receipt of cash (cash
receipts journal) or the
payment of cash (cash
payments journal).

✔ Determine if the
transaction is a sale of
merchandise on account
(sales journal) or a
purchase of merchandise
on account (purchases
journal).

✔ All other transactions
are recorded in the
general journal.

Swisher Company had the following transactions during March.
1. Collected cash on account from Oakland Company.
2. Purchased equipment by signing a note payable.
3. Sold merchandise on account.
4. Purchased merchandise on account.
5. Paid $2,400 for a 2-year insurance policy.

Identify the journal in which each of the transactions above is recorded.

Solution

1. Collected cash on account from Oakland Company.	Cash receipts journal
2. Purchased equipment by signing a note payable.	General journal
3. Sold merchandise on account.	Sales journal
4. Purchased merchandise on account.	Purchases journal
5. Paid $2,400 for a 2-year insurance policy.	Cash payments journal

Related exercise material: **BE7-6, BE7-7, BE7-8, BE7-9, BE7-10, E7-6, E7-7, E7-8, E7-10, and DO IT! 7-2.**

✔ The Navigator

Comprehensive DO IT!

Cassandra Wilson Company uses a six-column cash receipts journal with the following columns.

Cash (Dr.)   Other Accounts (Cr.)
Sales Discounts (Dr.)   Cost of Goods Sold (Dr.) and
Accounts Receivable (Cr.)   Inventory (Cr.)
Sales Revenue (Cr.)

Cash receipts transactions for the month of July 2014 are as follows.

July 3 Cash sales total $5,800 (cost, $3,480).
    5   Received a check for $6,370 from Jeltz Company in payment of an invoice dated June 26 for $6,500, terms 2/10, n/30.
    9   Cassandra Wilson, the proprietor, made an additional investment of $5,000 in cash in the business.
    10 Cash sales total $12,519 (cost, $7,511).
    12 Received a check for $7,275 from R. Eliot & Co. in payment of a $7,500 invoice dated July 3, terms 3/10, n/30.
    15 Received an advance of $700 cash for future services.
    20 Cash sales total $15,472 (cost, $9,283).
    22 Received a check for $5,880 from Beck Company in payment of $6,000 invoice dated July 13, terms 2/10, n/30.
    29 Cash sales total $17,660 (cost, $10,596).
    31 Received cash of $200 on interest earned for July.

Action Plan

✔ Record all cash receipts in the cash receipts journal.

✔ The "account credited" indicates items posted individually to the subsidiary ledger or to the general ledger.

✔ Record cash sales in the cash receipts journal—not in the sales journal.

✔ The total debits must equal the total credits.

Instructions

(a) Journalize the transactions in the cash receipts journal.
(b) Contrast the posting of the Accounts Receivable and Other Accounts columns.

Solution to Comprehensive DO IT!

(a)

CASSANDRA WILSON COMPANY
Cash Receipts Journal   CR1

Date	Account Credited	Ref.	Cash Dr.	Sales Discounts Dr.	Accounts Receivable Cr.	Sales Revenue Cr.	Other Accounts Cr.	Cost of Goods Sold Dr. Inventory Cr.
2014								
7/3			5,800			5,800		3,480
5	Jeltz Company		6,370	130	6,500			
9	Owner's Capital		5,000				5,000	
10			12,519			12,519		7,511
12	R. Eliot & Co.		7,275	225	7,500			
15	Unearned Service Revenue		700				700	
20			15,472			15,472		9,283
22	Beck Company		5,880	120	6,000			
29			17,660			17,660		10,596
31	Interest Revenue		200				200	
			76,876	475	20,000	51,451	5,900	30,870

(b) The Accounts Receivable column total is posted as a credit to Accounts Receivable. The individual amounts are credited to the customers' accounts identified in the Account Credited column, which are maintained in the accounts receivable subsidiary ledger.

The amounts in the Other Accounts column are posted individually. They are credited to the account titles identified in the Account Credited column.

The Navigator

SUMMARY OF LEARNING OBJECTIVES

1 Identify the basic concepts of an accounting information system. The basic principles in developing an accounting information system are cost-effectiveness, useful output, and flexibility. Most companies use a computerized accounting system. Smaller companies use entry-level software such as QuickBooks or Sage 50. Larger companies use custom-made software packages, which often integrate all aspects of the organization.

2 Describe the nature and purpose of a subsidiary ledger. A subsidiary ledger is a group of accounts with a common

characteristic. It facilitates the recording process by freeing the general ledger from details of individual balances.

3 Explain how companies use special journals in journalizing. Companies use special journals to group similar types of transactions. In a special journal, generally only one line is used to record a complete transaction.

GLOSSARY

Accounting information system A system that collects and processes transaction data and communicates financial information to decision-makers. (p. 330).

Accounts payable (creditors') subsidiary ledger A subsidiary ledger that collects transaction data of individual creditors. (p. 333).

Accounts receivable (customers') subsidiary ledger A subsidiary ledger that collects transaction data of individual customers. (p. 333).

Cash payments (cash disbursements) journal A special journal that records all disbursements of cash. (p. 344).

Cash receipts journal A special journal that records all cash received. (p. 339).

Control account An account in the general ledger that summarizes subsidiary ledger data. (p. 333).

Manual accounting system A system in which someone performs each of the steps in the accounting cycle by hand. (p. 332).

Purchases journal A special journal that records all purchases of merchandise on account. (p. 342).

Sales journal A special journal that records all sales of merchandise on account. (p. 336).

Special journal A journal that records similar types of transactions, such as all credit sales. (p. 336).

Subsidiary ledger A group of accounts with a common characteristic. (p. 332).

 **Self-Test, Brief Exercises, Exercises, Problem Set A, and many more components are available for practice in *WileyPLUS*.**

SELF-TEST QUESTIONS

Answers are on page 371.

(LO 1) **1.** The basic principles of an accounting information system include all of the following **except**:
  (a) cost-effectiveness.   **(c)** useful output.
  (b) flexibility.   **(d)** periodicity.

(LO 1) **2.** Which of the following is **not** an advantage of computerized accounting systems?
  (a) Data is entered only once in computerized accounting systems.
  (b) Computerized accounting systems provide up-to-date information.
  (c) Computerized accounting systems eliminate entering of transaction information.

  (d) Computerized accounting systems eliminate many errors resulting from human intervention.

3. Which of the following is **incorrect** concerning sub- (LO 2) sidiary ledgers?
  (a) The purchases ledger is a common subsidiary ledger for creditor accounts.
  (b) The accounts receivable ledger is a subsidiary ledger.
  (c) A subsidiary ledger is a group of accounts with a common characteristic.
  (d) An advantage of the subsidiary ledger is that it permits a division of labor in posting.

(LO 2) **4.** Two common subsidiary ledgers are:
  (a) accounts receivable and cash receipts.
  (b) accounts payable and cash payments.
  (c) accounts receivable and accounts payable.
  (d) sales and cost of goods sold.

(LO 2) **5.** At the beginning of the month, the accounts receivable subsidiary ledger showed balances for Apple Company $5,000 and Berry Company $7,000. During the month, credit sales were made to Apple $6,000, Berry $4,500, and Cantaloupe $8,500. Cash was collected on account from Berry $11,500 and Cantaloupe $3,000. At the end of the month, the control account Accounts Receivable in the general ledger should have a balance of:
  (a) $11,000.   **(c)** $16,500.
  (b) $12,000.   **(d)** $31,000.

(LO 3) **6.** A sales journal will be used for:

	Credit Sales	Cash Sales	Sales Discounts
(a)	no	yes	yes
(b)	yes	no	yes
(c)	yes	no	no
(d)	yes	yes	no

(LO 3) **7.** A purchase of equipment on account is recorded in the:
  (a) cash receipts journal.   **(c)** cash payments journal.
  (b) purchases journal.   **(d)** general journal.

(LO 3) **8.** A purchase of equipment using cash is recorded in the:
  (a) cash receipts journal.   **(c)** cash payments journal.
  (b) purchases journal.   **(d)** general journal.

(LO 3) **9.** Which of the following statements is **correct**?
  (a) The sales discount column is included in the cash receipts journal.
  (b) The purchases journal records all purchases of merchandise whether for cash or on account.
  (c) The cash receipts journal records sales on account.
  (d) Merchandise returned by the buyer is recorded by the seller in the purchases journal.

(LO 3) **10.** Dotel Company's cash receipts journal includes an Accounts Receivable column and an Other Accounts column. At the end of the month, these columns are posted to the general ledger as:

	Accounts Receivable	Other Accounts
(a)	a column total	a column total
(b)	individual amounts	a column total
(c)	individual amounts	individual amounts
(d)	a column total	individual amounts

(LO 3) **11.** Which of the following is **incorrect** concerning the posting of the cash receipts journal?
  (a) The total of the Other Accounts column is not posted.
  (b) All column totals except the total for the Other Accounts column are posted once at the end of the month to the account title(s) specified in the column heading.
  (c) The totals of all columns are posted daily to the accounts specified in the column heading.
  (d) The individual amounts in a column posted in total to a control account are posted daily to the subsidiary ledger account specified in the Account Credited column.

(LO 3) **12.** Postings from the purchases journal to the subsidiary ledger are generally made:
  (a) yearly.
  (b) monthly.
  (c) weekly.
  (d) daily.

(LO 3) **13.** Which statement is **incorrect** regarding the general journal?
  (a) Only transactions that cannot be entered in a special journal are recorded in the general journal.
  (b) Dual postings are always required in the general journal.
  (c) The general journal may be used to record acceptance of a note receivable in payment of an account receivable.
  (d) Correcting, adjusting, and closing entries are made in the general journal.

(LO 3) **14.** When companies use special journals:
  (a) they record all purchase transactions in the purchases journal.
  (b) they record all cash received, except from cash sales, in the cash receipts journal.
  (c) they record all cash disbursements in the cash payments journal.
  (d) a general journal is not necessary.

(LO 3) **15.** If a customer returns goods for credit, the selling company normally makes an entry in the:
  (a) cash payments journal.
  (b) sales journal.
  (c) general journal.
  (d) cash receipts journal.

Go to the book's companion website, www.wiley.com/college/weygandt, for additional Self-Test Questions.

✔ **The Navigator**

QUESTIONS

1. (a) What is an accounting information system? (b) "An accounting information system applies only to a manual system." Do you agree? Explain.

2. Certain principles should be followed in the development of an accounting information system. Identify and explain each of the principles.

3. What are common features of computerized accounting packages beyond recording transactions and preparing financial statements?
4. How does an enterprise resource planning (ERP) system differ from an entry-level computerized accounting system?
5. What are the advantages of using subsidiary ledgers?
6. (a) When do companies normally post to (1) the subsidiary accounts and (2) the general ledger control accounts? (b) Describe the relationship between a control account and a subsidiary ledger.
7. Identify and explain the four special journals discussed in the chapter. List an advantage of using each of these journals rather than using only a general journal.
8. Kensington Company uses special journals. It recorded in a sales journal a sale made on account to R. Stiner for $435. A few days later, R. Stiner returns $70 worth of merchandise for credit. Where should Kensington Company record the sales return? Why?
9. A $500 purchase of merchandise on account from Lore Company was properly recorded in the purchases journal. When posted, however, the amount recorded in the subsidiary ledger was $50. How might this error be discovered?
10. Why would special journals used in different businesses not be identical in format? What type of business would maintain a cash receipts journal but not include a column for accounts receivable?
11. The cash and the accounts receivable columns in the cash receipts journal were mistakenly over-added by $4,000 at the end of the month. (a) Will the customers' ledger agree with the Accounts Receivable control account? (b) Assuming no other errors, will the trial balance totals be equal?
12. One column total of a special journal is posted at month-end to only two general ledger accounts. One of

these two accounts is Accounts Receivable. What is the name of this special journal? What is the other general ledger account to which that same month-end total is posted?
13. In what journal would the following transactions be recorded? (Assume that a two-column sales journal and a single-column purchases journal are used.)
    (a) Recording of depreciation expense for the year.
    (b) Credit given to a customer for merchandise purchased on credit and returned.
    (c) Sales of merchandise for cash.
    (d) Sales of merchandise on account.
    (e) Collection of cash on account from a customer.
    (f) Purchase of office supplies on account.
14. In what journal would the following transactions be recorded? (Assume that a two-column sales journal and a single-column purchases journal are used.)
    (a) Cash received from signing a note payable.
    (b) Investment of cash by the owner of the business.
    (c) Closing of the expense accounts at the end of the year.
    (d) Purchase of merchandise on account.
    (e) Credit received for merchandise purchased and returned to supplier.
    (f) Payment of cash on account due a supplier.
15. What transactions might be included in a multiple-column purchases journal that would not be included in a single-column purchases journal?
16. Give an example of a transaction in the general journal that causes an entry to be posted twice (i.e., to two accounts), one in the general ledger, the other in the subsidiary ledger. Does this affect the debit/credit equality of the general ledger?
17. Give some examples of appropriate general journal transactions for an organization using special journals.

BRIEF EXERCISES

Identify basic concepts of an accounting information system.

(LO 1)

BE7-1 Indicate whether each of the following statements is true or false.

1. When designing an accounting system, we need to think about the needs and knowledge of both the top managers and various other users.
2. When the environment changes as a result of technological advances, increased competition, or government regulation, an accounting system does not have to be sufficiently flexible to meet the changes in order to save money.
3. In developing an accounting system, cost is relevant. The benefits obtained from the information disseminated must outweigh the cost of providing it.

Identify basic concepts of an accounting information system.

(LO 1)

BE7-2 Here is a list of words or phrases related to computerized accounting systems.

1. Entry-level software.
2. Enterprise resource planning systems.
3. Network-compatible.
4. Audit trail.
5. Internal control.

Instructions

Match each word or phrase with the best description of it.

_____ (a) Allows multiple users to access the system at the same time.
_____ (b) Enables the tracking of all transactions.

_____ **(c)** Identifies suspicious transactions or likely mistakes such as wrong account numbers or duplicate transactions.

_____ **(d)** Large-scale computer systems that integrate all aspects of the organization including accounting, sales, human resource management, and manufacturing.

_____ **(e)** System for companies with revenues of less than $5 million and up to 20 employees.

BE7-3 Benji Borke has prepared the following list of statements about accounting information systems.

1. The accounting information system includes each of the steps of the accounting cycle, the documents that provide evidence of transactions that have occurred, and the accounting records.
2. The benefits obtained from information provided by the accounting information system need not outweigh the cost of providing that information.
3. Designers of accounting systems must consider the needs and knowledge of various users.
4. If an accounting information system is cost-effective and provides useful output, it does not need to be flexible.

Identify basic concepts of an accounting information system.
(LO 1)

Instructions
Identify each statement as true or false. If false, indicate how to correct the statement.

BE7-4 Presented below is information related to Gantner Company for its first month of operations. Identify the balances that appear in the accounts receivable subsidiary ledger and the accounts receivable balance that appears in the general ledger at the end of January.

Identify subsidiary ledger balances.
(LO 2)

Credit Sales			Cash Collections		
Jan. 7	Austin Co.	$10,000	Jan. 17	Austin Co.	$7,000
15	Diaz Co.	8,000	24	Diaz Co.	4,000
23	Noble Co.	9,000	29	Noble Co.	9,000

BE7-5 Identify in what ledger (general or subsidiary) each of the following accounts is shown.

(a) Rent Expense.
(b) Accounts Receivable—Cabrera.
(c) Notes Payable.
(d) Accounts Payable—Pacheco.

Identify subsidiary ledger accounts.
(LO 2)

BE7-6 Identify the journal in which each of the following transactions is recorded.

(a) Cash sales.
(b) Owner withdrawal of cash.
(c) Cash purchase of land.
(d) Credit sales.
(e) Purchase of merchandise on account.
(f) Receipt of cash for services performed.

Identify special journals.
(LO 3)

BE7-7 Indicate whether each of the following debits and credits is included in the cash receipts journal. (Use "Yes" or "No" to answer this question.)

(a) Debit to Sales Revenue.
(b) Credit to Inventory.
(c) Credit to Accounts Receivable.
(d) Debit to Accounts Payable.

Identify entries to cash receipts journal.
(LO 3)

BE7-8 Villar Co. uses special journals and a general journal. Identify the journal in which each of the following transactions is recorded.

(a) Purchased equipment on account.
(b) Purchased merchandise on account.
(c) Paid utility expense in cash.
(d) Sold merchandise on account.

Identify transactions for special journals.
(LO 3)

BE7-9 Identify the special journal(s) in which the following column headings appear.

(a) Sales Discounts Dr.
(b) Accounts Receivable Cr.
(c) Cash Dr.
(d) Sales Revenue Cr.
(e) Inventory Dr.

Identify transactions for special journals.
(LO 3)

BE7-10 Rauch Computer Components Inc. uses a multi-column cash receipts journal. Indicate which column(s) is/are posted only in total, only daily, or both in total and daily.

(a) Accounts Receivable.
(b) Sales Discounts.
(c) Cash.
(d) Other Accounts.

Indicate postings for cash receipts journal.
(LO 3)

> DO IT! Review

DO IT! 7-1 Presented below is information related to Rizzo Company for its first month of operations. Determine the balances that appear in the accounts payable subsidiary ledger. What Accounts Payable balance appears in the general ledger at the end of January?

Credit Purchases			Cash Paid		
Jan. 6	Gorst Company	$11,000	Jan. 11	Gorst Company	$ 6,500
Jan. 10	Tian Company	12,000	Jan. 16	Tian Company	12,000
Jan. 23	Maddox Company	10,000	Jan. 29	Maddox Company	7,700

DO IT! 7-2 Hinske Company had the following transactions during April.

1. Sold merchandise on account.
2. Purchased merchandise on account.
3. Collected cash from a sale to Renfro Company.
4. Recorded accrued interest on a note payable.
5. Paid $2,000 for supplies.

Identify the journal in which each of the transactions above is recorded.

EXERCISES

E7-1 Nex Company uses both special journals and a general journal as described in this chapter. On June 30, after all monthly postings had been completed, the Accounts Receivable control account in the general ledger had a debit balance of $340,000; the Accounts Payable control account had a credit balance of $77,000.

The July transactions recorded in the special journals are summarized below. No entries affecting accounts receivable and accounts payable were recorded in the general journal for July.

Sales journal	Total sales $161,400
Purchases journal	Total purchases $66,400
Cash receipts journal	Accounts receivable column total $131,000
Cash payments journal	Accounts payable column total $47,500

Instructions
(a) What is the balance of the Accounts Receivable control account after the monthly postings on July 31?
(b) What is the balance of the Accounts Payable control account after the monthly postings on July 31?
(c) To what account(s) is the column total of $161,400 in the sales journal posted?
(d) To what account(s) is the accounts receivable column total of $131,000 in the cash receipts journal posted?

E7-2 Presented below is the subsidiary accounts receivable account of Jill Longley.

Date	Ref.	Debit	Credit	Balance
2014				
Sept. 2	S31	61,000		61,000
9	G4		14,000	47,000
27	CR8		47,000	—

Instructions
Write a memo to Sara Fogelman, chief financial officer, that explains each transaction.

E7-3 On September 1, the balance of the Accounts Receivable control account in the general ledger of Montgomery Company was $10,960. The customers' subsidiary ledger contained account balances as follows: Hurley $1,440, Andino $2,640, Fowler $2,060, Sogard $4,820. At the end of September, the various journals contained the following information.

Post various journals to control and subsidiary accounts.

(LO 2, 3)

Sales journal: Sales to Sogard $800; to Hurley $1,260; to Giambi $1,330; to Fowler $1,600.

Cash receipts journal: Cash received from Fowler $1,310; from Sogard $3,300; from Giambi $380; from Andino $1,800; from Hurley $1,240.

General journal: An allowance is granted to Sogard $220.

Instructions

(a) Set up control and subsidiary accounts and enter the beginning balances. Do not construct the journals.

(b) Post the various journals. Post the items as individual items or as totals, whichever would be the appropriate procedure. (No sales discounts given.)

(c) Prepare a list of customers and prove the agreement of the controlling account with the subsidiary ledger at September 30, 2014.

E7-4 Kieschnick Company has a balance in its Accounts Receivable control account of $10,000 on January 1, 2014. The subsidiary ledger contains three accounts: Bixler Company, balance $4,000; Cuddyer Company, balance $2,500; and Freeze Company. During January, the following receivable-related transactions occurred.

Determine control and subsidiary ledger balances for accounts receivable.

(LO 2)

	Credit Sales	Collections	Returns
Bixler Company	$9,000	$8,000	$ -0-
Cuddyer Company	7,000	2,500	3,000
Freeze Company	8,500	9,000	-0-

Instructions

(a) What is the January 1 balance in the Freeze Company subsidiary account?

(b) What is the January 31 balance in the control account?

(c) Compute the balances in the subsidiary accounts at the end of the month.

(d) Which January transaction would not be recorded in a special journal?

E7-5 Pennington Company has a balance in its Accounts Payable control account of $9,250 on January 1, 2014. The subsidiary ledger contains three accounts: Hale Company, balance $3,000; Janish Company, balance $1,875; and Valdez Company. During January, the following payable-related transactions occurred.

Determine control and subsidiary ledger balances for accounts payable.

(LO 2)

	Purchases	Payments	Returns
Hale Company	$6,750	$6,000	$ -0-
Janish Company	5,250	1,875	2,250
Valdez Company	6,375	6,750	-0-

Instructions

(a) What is the January 1 balance in the Valdez Company subsidiary account?

(b) What is the January 31 balance in the control account?

(c) Compute the balances in the subsidiary accounts at the end of the month.

(d) Which January transaction would not be recorded in a special journal?

E7-6 Gomes Company uses special journals and a general journal. The following transactions occurred during September 2014.

Record transactions in sales and purchases journal.

(LO 3)

Sept. 2 Sold merchandise on account to H. Drew, invoice no. 101, $620, terms n/30. The cost of the merchandise sold was $420.

10 Purchased merchandise on account from A. Pagan $650, terms 2/10, n/30.

12 Purchased office equipment on account from R. Cairo $6,500.

21 Sold merchandise on account to G. Holliday, invoice no. 102 for $800, terms 2/10, n/30. The cost of the merchandise sold was $480.

25 Purchased merchandise on account from D. Downs $860, terms n/30.

27 Sold merchandise to S. Miller for $700 cash. The cost of the merchandise sold was $400.

Instructions

(a) Prepare a sales journal (see Illustration 7-7) and a single-column purchases journal (see Illustration 7-13). (Use page 1 for each journal.)

(b) Record the transaction(s) for September that should be journalized in the sales journal and the purchases journal.

Record transactions in cash receipts and cash payments journal.

(LO 3)

E7-7 R. Santiago Co. uses special journals and a general journal. The following transactions occurred during May 2014.

May	1	R. Santiago invested $40,000 cash in the business.
	2	Sold merchandise to Lawrie Co. for $6,300 cash. The cost of the merchandise sold was $4,200.
	3	Purchased merchandise for $7,700 from J. Moskos using check no. 101.
	14	Paid salary to H. Rivera $700 by issuing check no. 102.
	16	Sold merchandise on account to K. Stanton for $900, terms n/30. The cost of the merchandise sold was $630.
	22	A check of $9,000 is received from M. Mangini in full for invoice 101; no discount given.

Instructions

(a) Prepare a multiple-column cash receipts journal (see Illustration 7-9) and a multiple-column cash payments journal (see Illustration 7-16). (Use page 1 for each journal.)

(b) Record the transaction(s) for May that should be journalized in the cash receipts journal and cash payments journal.

Explain journalizing in cash journals.

(LO 3)

E7-8 Francisco Company uses the columnar cash journals illustrated in the textbook. In April, the following selected cash transactions occurred.

1. Made a refund to a customer as an allowance for damaged goods.
2. Received collection from customer within the 3% discount period.
3. Purchased merchandise for cash.
4. Paid a creditor within the 3% discount period.
5. Received collection from customer after the 3% discount period had expired.
6. Paid freight on merchandise purchased.
7. Paid cash for office equipment.
8. Received cash refund from supplier for merchandise returned.
9. Withdrew cash for personal use of owner.
10. Made cash sales.

Instructions

Indicate (a) the journal, and (b) the columns in the journal that should be used in recording each transaction.

Journalize transactions in general journal and explain postings.

(LO 3)

E7-9 Hasselback Company has the following selected transactions during March.

Mar.	2	Purchased equipment costing $7,400 from Bole Company on account.
	5	Received credit of $410 from Carwell Company for merchandise damaged in shipment to Hasselback.
	7	Issued credit of $400 to Dempsey Company for merchandise the customer returned. The returned merchandise had a cost of $260.

Hasselback Company uses a one-column purchases journal, a sales journal, the columnar cash journals used in the text, and a general journal.

Instructions

(a) Journalize the transactions in the general journal.

(b) ⸺ In a brief memo to the president of Hasselback Company, explain the postings to the control and subsidiary accounts from each type of journal.

Indicate journalizing in special journals.

(LO 3)

E7-10 Below are some typical transactions incurred by Ricketts Company.

1. Payment of creditors on account.
2. Return of merchandise sold for credit.
3. Collection on account from customers.
4. Sale of land for cash.
5. Sale of merchandise on account.
6. Sale of merchandise for cash.

7. Received credit for merchandise purchased on credit.
8. Sales discount taken on goods sold.
9. Payment of employee wages.
10. Income summary closed to owner's capital.
11. Depreciation on building.
12. Purchase of office supplies for cash.
13. Purchase of merchandise on account.

Instructions

For each transaction, indicate whether it would normally be recorded in a cash receipts journal, cash payments journal, sales journal, single-column purchases journal, or general journal.

E7-11 The general ledger of Hensley Company contained the following Accounts Payable control account (in T-account form). Also shown is the related subsidiary ledger.

Explain posting to control account and subsidiary ledger.

(LO 2, 3)

GENERAL LEDGER

Accounts Payable

Feb. 15	General journal	1,400	Feb. 1	Balance	26,025
28	?	?	5	General journal	265
			11	General journal	550
			28	Purchases	13,400
			Feb. 28	Balance	10,500

ACCOUNTS PAYABLE LEDGER

Benton

Feb. 28	Bal. 4,600

Parks

Feb. 28	Bal.	?

Dooley

Feb. 28	Bal. 2,300

Instructions

(a) Indicate the missing posting reference and amount in the control account, and the missing ending balance in the subsidiary ledger.
(b) Indicate the amounts in the control account that were dual-posted (i.e., posted to the control account and the subsidiary accounts).

E7-12 Selected accounts from the ledgers of Youngblood Company at July 31 showed the following.

Prepare purchases and general journals.

(LO 2, 3)

GENERAL LEDGER

Equipment   No. 157

Date	Explanation	Ref.	Debit	Credit	Balance
July 1		G1	3,900		3,900

Accounts Payable   No. 201

Date	Explanation	Ref.	Debit	Credit	Balance
July 1		G1		3,900	3,900
15		G1		400	4,300
18		G1	100		4,200
25		G1	200		4,000
31		P1		9,300	13,300

Inventory   No. 120

Date	Explanation	Ref.	Debit	Credit	Balance
July 15		G1	400		400
18		G1		100	300
25		G1		200	100
31		P1	9,300		9,400

ACCOUNTS PAYABLE LEDGER

Flaherty Equipment Co.

Date	Explanation	Ref.	Debit	Credit	Balance
July 1		G1		3,900	3,900

Weller Co.

Date	Explanation	Ref.	Debit	Credit	Balance
July 14		P1		1,100	1,100
25		G1	200		900

Marsh Co.

Date	Explanation	Ref.	Debit	Credit	Balance
July 3		P1		2,400	2,400
20		P1		1,700	4,100

Yates Co.

Date	Explanation	Ref.	Debit	Credit	Balance
July 12		P1		500	500
21		P1		600	1,100

Lange Corp

Date	Explanation	Ref.	Debit	Credit	Balance
July 17		P1		1,400	1,400
18		G1	100		1,300
29		P1		1,600	2,900

Bernardo Inc.

Date	Explanation	Ref.	Debit	Credit	Balance
July 15		G1		400	400

Instructions

From the data prepare:

(a) The single-column purchases journal for July.
(b) The general journal entries for July.

Determine correct posting amount to control account.
(LO 2, 3)

E7-13 Tresh Products uses both special journals and a general journal as described in this chapter. Tresh also posts customers' accounts in the accounts receivable subsidiary ledger. The postings for the most recent month are included in the subsidiary T-accounts below.

	Estes				**Gehrke**	
Bal.	340	250		Bal.	150	150
	200				290	

	Truong				**Weiser**	
Bal.	–0–	145		Bal.	120	120
	145				190	
					150	

Instructions

Determine the correct amount of the end-of-month posting from the sales journal to the Accounts Receivable control account.

Compute balances in various accounts.
(LO 3)

E7-14 Selected account balances for Hulse Company at January 1, 2014, are presented below.

Accounts Payable	$14,000
Accounts Receivable	22,000
Cash	17,000
Inventory	13,500

Hulse's sales journal for January shows a total of $110,000 in the selling price column, and its one-column purchases journal for January shows a total of $77,000.

The column totals in Hulse's cash receipts journal are: Cash Dr. $61,000; Sales Discounts Dr. $1,100; Accounts Receivable Cr. $45,000; Sales Revenue Cr. $6,000; and Other Accounts Cr. $11,100.

The column totals in Hulse's cash payments journal for January are: Cash Cr. $55,000; Inventory Cr. $1,000; Accounts Payable Dr. $46,000; and Other Accounts Dr. $10,000. Hulse's total cost of goods sold for January is $63,600.

Accounts Payable, Accounts Receivable, Cash, Inventory, and Sales Revenue are not involved in the "Other Accounts" column in either the cash receipts or cash payments journal, and are not involved in any general journal entries.

Instructions

Compute the January 31 balance for Hulse in the following accounts.

(a) Accounts Payable.
(b) Accounts Receivable.

(c) Cash.
(d) Inventory.
(e) Sales Revenue.

EXERCISES: SET B AND CHALLENGE EXERCISES

Visit the book's companion website, at **www.wiley.com/college/weygandt**, and choose the Student Companion site to access Exercise Set B and Challenge Exercises.

PROBLEMS: SET A

P7-1A Kozma Company's chart of accounts includes the following selected accounts.

101	Cash	401	Sales Revenue
112	Accounts Receivable	414	Sales Discounts
120	Inventory	505	Cost of Goods Sold
301	Owner's Capital		

Journalize transactions in cash receipts journal; post to control account and subsidiary ledger.

(LO 2, 3)

On April 1, the accounts receivable ledger of Kozma Company showed the following balances: Morrow $1,550, Rose $1,200, Jennings Co. $2,900, and Dent $2,200. The April transactions involving the receipt of cash were as follows.

Apr. 1   The owner, T. Kozma, invested additional cash in the business $7,200.
    4   Received check for payment of account from Dent less 2% cash discount.
    5   Received check for $920 in payment of invoice no. 307 from Jennings Co.
    8   Made cash sales of merchandise totaling $7,245. The cost of the merchandise sold was $4,347.
  10   Received check for $600 in payment of invoice no. 309 from Morrow.
  11   Received cash refund from a supplier for damaged merchandise $740.
  23   Received check for $1,000 in payment of invoice no. 310 from Jennings Co.
  29   Received check for payment of account from Rose.

Instructions
(a) Journalize the transactions above in a six-column cash receipts journal with columns for Cash Dr., Sales Discounts Dr., Accounts Receivable Cr., Sales Revenue Cr., Other Accounts Cr., and Cost of Goods Sold Dr./Inventory Cr. Foot and cross-foot the journal.
(b) Insert the beginning balances in the Accounts Receivable control and subsidiary accounts, and post the April transactions to these accounts.
(c) Prove the agreement of the control account and subsidiary account balances.

(a) Balancing totals $21,105

(c) Accounts Receivable $1,930

P7-2A Reineke Company's chart of accounts includes the following selected accounts.

101	Cash	201	Accounts Payable
120	Inventory	306	Owner's Drawings
130	Prepaid Insurance	505	Cost of Goods Sold
157	Equipment		

Journalize transactions in cash payments journal; post to control account and subsidiary ledgers.

(LO 2, 3)

On October 1, the accounts payable ledger of Reineke Company showed the following balances: Uggla Company $2,700, Orr Co. $2,500, Rosenthal Co. $1,800, and Clevenger Company $3,700. The October transactions involving the payment of cash were as follows.

Oct. 1   Purchased merchandise, check no. 63, $300.
    3   Purchased equipment, check no. 64, $800.
    5   Paid Uggla Company balance due of $2,700, less 2% discount, check no. 65, $2,646.
  10   Purchased merchandise, check no. 66, $2,550.
  15   Paid Rosenthal Co. balance due of $1,800, check no. 67.
  16   C. Reineke, the owner, pays his personal insurance premium of $400, check no. 68.
  19   Paid Orr Co. in full for invoice no. 610, $2,000 less 2% cash discount, check no. 69, $1,960.
  29   Paid Clevenger Company in full for invoice no. 264, $2,500, check no. 70.

(a) Balancing totals $13,050

Instructions

(a) Journalize the transactions above in a four-column cash payments journal with columns for Other Accounts Dr., Accounts Payable Dr., Inventory Cr., and Cash Cr. Foot and cross-foot the journal.

(c) Accounts Payable $1,700

(b) Insert the beginning balances in the Accounts Payable control and subsidiary accounts, and post the October transactions to these accounts.

(c) Prove the agreement of the control account and the subsidiary account balances.

Journalize transactions in multi-column purchases journal and sales journal; post to the general and subsidiary ledgers.

(LO 2, 3)

P7-3A The chart of accounts of LR Company includes the following selected accounts.

112	Accounts Receivable	401	Sales Revenue
120	Inventory	412	Sales Returns and Allowances
126	Supplies	505	Cost of Goods Sold
157	Equipment	610	Advertising Expense
201	Accounts Payable		

In July, the following selected transactions were completed. All purchases and sales were on account. The cost of all merchandise sold was 70% of the sales price.

July 1 Purchased merchandise from Eby Company $8,000.
   2 Received freight bill from Shaw Shipping on Eby purchase $400.
   3 Made sales to Fort Company $1,300 and to Hefner Bros. $1,500.
   5 Purchased merchandise from Getz Company $3,200.
   8 Received credit on merchandise returned to Getz Company $300.
   13 Purchased store supplies from Dayne Supply $720.
   15 Purchased merchandise from Eby Company $3,600 and from Bosco Company $4,300.
   16 Made sales to Aybar Company $3,450 and to Hefner Bros. $1,870.
   18 Received bill for advertising from Welton Advertisements $600.
   21 Sales were made to Fort Company $310 and to Duncan Company $2,800.
   22 Granted allowance to Fort Company for merchandise damaged in shipment $40.
   24 Purchased merchandise from Getz Company $3,000.
   26 Purchased equipment from Dayne Supply $900.
   28 Received freight bill from Shaw Shipping on Getz purchase of July 24, $380.
   30 Sales were made to Aybar Company $5,600.

Instructions

(a) Purchases journal—
Accounts Payable $25,100
Sales journal—Sales
Revenue total $16,830

(c) Accounts Receivable
$16,790
Accounts Payable $24,800

(a) Journalize the transactions above in a purchases journal, a sales journal, and a general journal. The purchases journal should have the following column headings: Date, Account Credited (Debited), Ref., Accounts Payable Cr., Inventory Dr., and Other Accounts Dr.

(b) Post to both the general and subsidiary ledger accounts. (Assume that all accounts have zero beginning balances.)

(c) Prove the agreement of the control and subsidiary accounts.

Journalize transactions in special journals.

(LO 2, 3)

P7-4A Selected accounts from the chart of accounts of Mercer Company are shown below.

101	Cash	401	Sales Revenue
112	Accounts Receivable	412	Sales Returns and Allowances
120	Inventory	414	Sales Discounts
126	Supplies	505	Cost of Goods Sold
157	Equipment	726	Salaries and Wages Expense
201	Accounts Payable		

The cost of all merchandise sold was 60% of the sales price. During January, Mercer completed the following transactions.

Jan. 3 Purchased merchandise on account from Gallagher Co. $9,000.
   4 Purchased supplies for cash $80.
   4 Sold merchandise on account to Wheeler $5,250, invoice no. 371, terms 1/10, n/30.
   5 Returned $300 worth of damaged goods purchased on account from Gallagher Co. on January 3.
   6 Made cash sales for the week totaling $3,150.
   8 Purchased merchandise on account from Phegley Co. $4,500.
   9 Sold merchandise on account to Linton Corp. $5,400, invoice no. 372, terms 1/10, n/30.

11	Purchased merchandise on account from Cora Co. $3,700.
13	Paid in full Gallagher Co. on account less a 2% discount.
13	Made cash sales for the week totaling $6,260.
15	Received payment from Linton Corp. for invoice no. 372.
15	Paid semi-monthly salaries of $14,300 to employees.
17	Received payment from Wheeler for invoice no. 371.
17	Sold merchandise on account to Delaney Co. $1,200, invoice no. 373, terms 1/10, n/30.
19	Purchased equipment on account from Dozier Corp. $5,500.
20	Cash sales for the week totaled $3,200.
20	Paid in full Phegley Co. on account less a 2% discount.
23	Purchased merchandise on account from Gallagher Co. $7,800.
24	Purchased merchandise on account from Atchison Corp. $5,100.
27	Made cash sales for the week totaling $4,230.
30	Received payment from Delaney Co. for invoice no. 373.
31	Paid semi-monthly salaries of $13,200 to employees.
31	Sold merchandise on account to Wheeler $9,330, invoice no. 374, terms 1/10, n/30.

Mercer Company uses the following journals.

1. Sales journal.
2. Single-column purchases journal.
3. Cash receipts journal with columns for Cash Dr., Sales Discounts Dr., Accounts Receivable Cr., Sales Revenue Cr., Other Accounts Cr., and Cost of Goods Sold Dr./Inventory Cr.
4. Cash payments journal with columns for Other Accounts Dr., Accounts Payable Dr., Inventory Cr., and Cash Cr.
5. General journal.

Instructions
Using the selected accounts provided:

(a) Record the January transactions in the appropriate journal noted.
(b) Foot and cross-foot all special journals.
(c) Show how postings would be made by placing ledger account numbers and checkmarks as needed in the journals. (Actual posting to ledger accounts is not required.)

(a) Sales journal $21,180
    Purchases journal $30,100
    Cash receipts journal
      balancing total $28,690
    Cash payments journal
      balancing total $40,780

P7-5A Presented below are the purchases and cash payments journals for Fornelli Co. for its first month of operations.

Journalize in sales and cash receipts journals; post; prepare a trial balance; prove control to subsidiary; prepare adjusting entries; prepare an adjusted trial balance.

(LO 2, 3)

GLS

PURCHASES JOURNAL   P1

Date	Account Credited	Ref.	Inventory Dr. Accounts Payable Cr.
July 4	N. Alvarado		6,800
5	F. Rees		8,100
11	J. Gallup		5,920
13	C. Werly		15,300
20	M. Mangus		7,900
			44,020

CASH PAYMENTS JOURNAL   CP1

Date	Account Debited	Ref.	Other Accounts Dr.	Accounts Payable Dr.	Inventory Cr.	Cash Cr.
July 4	Supplies		600			600
10	F. Rees			8,100	81	8,019
11	Prepaid Rent		6,000			6,000
15	N. Alvarado			6,800		6,800
19	Owner's Drawings		2,500			2,500
21	C. Werly			15,300	153	15,147
			9,100	30,200	234	39,066

In addition, the following transactions have not been journalized for July. The cost of all merchandise sold was 65% of the sales price.

July 1 The founder, N. Fornelli, invests $80,000 in cash.
      6 Sell merchandise on account to Dow Co. $6,200 terms 1/10, n/30.
      7 Make cash sales totaling $8,000.
      8 Sell merchandise on account to S. Goebel $4,600, terms 1/10, n/30.
     10 Sell merchandise on account to W. Leiss $4,900, terms 1/10, n/30.
     13 Receive payment in full from S. Goebel.
     16 Receive payment in full from W. Leiss.
     20 Receive payment in full from Dow Co.
     21 Sell merchandise on account to H. Kenney $5,000, terms 1/10, n/30.
     29 Returned damaged goods to N. Alvarado and received cash refund of $420.

Instructions
(a) Open the following accounts in the general ledger.

101 Cash	306 Owner's Drawings
112 Accounts Receivable	401 Sales Revenue
120 Inventory	414 Sales Discounts
126 Supplies	505 Cost of Goods Sold
131 Prepaid Rent	631 Supplies Expense
201 Accounts Payable	729 Rent Expense
301 Owner's Capital	

(b) Journalize the transactions that have not been journalized in the sales journal and the cash receipts journal (see Illustration 7-9).
(c) Post to the accounts receivable and accounts payable subsidiary ledgers. Follow the sequence of transactions as shown in the problem.
(d) Post the individual entries and totals to the general ledger.
(e) Prepare a trial balance at July 31, 2014.
(f) Determine whether the subsidiary ledgers agree with the control accounts in the general ledger.
(g) The following adjustments at the end of July are necessary.
    (1) A count of supplies indicates that $140 is still on hand.
    (2) Recognize rent expense for July, $500.
    Prepare the necessary entries in the general journal. Post the entries to the general ledger.
(h) Prepare an adjusted trial balance at July 31, 2014.

P7-6A The post-closing trial balance for Horner Co. is shown below.

HORNER CO.
Post-Closing Trial Balance
December 31, 2014

	Debit	Credit
Cash	$ 41,500	
Accounts Receivable	15,000	
Notes Receivable	45,000	
Inventory	23,000	
Equipment	6,450	
Accumulated Depreciation—Equipment		$ 1,500
Accounts Payable		43,000
Owner's Capital		86,450
	$130,950	$130,950

The subsidiary ledgers contain the following information: (1) accounts receivable—B. Hannigan $2,500, I. Kirk $7,500, and T. Hodges $5,000; (2) accounts payable—T. Igawa $12,000, D. Danford $18,000, and K. Thayer $13,000. The cost of all merchandise sold was 60% of the sales price.

(b) Sales journal total
$20,700
Cash receipts journal
balancing totals $104,120

(e) Totals $122,520
(f) Accounts Receivable
$5,000
Accounts Payable $13,820

(h) Totals $122,520

Journalize in special journals; post; prepare a trial balance.
(LO 2, 3)

GLS

The transactions for January 2015 are as follows.

Jan. 3   Sell merchandise to M. Ziesmer $8,000, terms 2/10, n/30.
      5   Purchase merchandise from E. Pheatt $2,000, terms 2/10, n/30.
      7   Receive a check from T. Hodges $3,500.
     11   Pay freight on merchandise purchased $300.
     12   Pay rent of $1,000 for January.
     13   Receive payment in full from M. Ziesmer.
     14   Post all entries to the subsidiary ledgers. Issued credit of $300 to B. Hannigan for
          returned merchandise.
     15   Send K. Thayer a check for $12,870 in full payment of account, discount $130.
     17   Purchase merchandise from G. Roland $1,600, terms 2/10, n/30.
     18   Pay sales salaries of $2,800 and office salaries $2,000.
     20   Give D. Danford a 60-day note for $18,000 in full payment of account payable.
     23   Total cash sales amount to $9,100.
     24   Post all entries to the subsidiary ledgers. Sell merchandise on account to I. Kirk
          $7,400, terms 1/10, n/30.
     27   Send E. Pheatt a check for $950.
     29   Receive payment on a note of $40,000 from B. Stout.
     30   Post all entries to the subsidiary ledgers. Return merchandise of $300 to G.
          Roland for credit.

Instructions
(a) Open general and subsidiary ledger accounts for the following.

101 Cash   301 Owner's Capital
112 Accounts Receivable   401 Sales Revenue
115 Notes Receivable   412 Sales Returns and Allowances
120 Inventory   414 Sales Discounts
157 Equipment   505 Cost of Goods Sold
158 Accumulated Depreciation—Equipment   726 Salaries and Wages Expense
200 Notes Payable   729 Rent Expense
201 Accounts Payable

(b) Record the January transactions in a sales journal, a single-column purchases journal, a
cash receipts journal (see Illustration 7-9), a cash payments journal (see Illustration 7-16),
and a general journal.
(c) Post the appropriate amounts to the general ledger.
(d) Prepare a trial balance at January 31, 2015.
(e) Determine whether the subsidiary ledgers agree with controlling accounts in the
general ledger.

(b) Sales journal $15,400
    Purchases journal $3,600
    Cash receipts journal
    (balancing) $60,600
    Cash payments journal
    (balancing) $20,050
(d) Totals $144,800
(e) Accounts Receivable
    $18,600
    Accounts Payable $14,350

PROBLEMS: SET B

P7-1B Belt Company's chart of accounts includes the following selected accounts.

101 Cash   401 Sales Revenue
112 Accounts Receivable   414 Sales Discounts
120 Inventory   505 Cost of Goods Sold
301 Owner's Capital

On June 1, the accounts receivable ledger of Belt Company showed the following balances:
Suppan & Son $3,000, Guthrie Co. $2,800, Quentin Bros. $2,400, and Hinshaw Co. $2,000.
The June transactions involving the receipt of cash were as follows.

June 1   The owner, Jim Belt, invested additional cash in the business $15,000.
      3   Received check in full from Hinshaw Co. less 2% cash discount.
      6   Received check in full from Guthrie Co. less 2% cash discount.
      7   Made cash sales of merchandise totaling $8,700. The cost of the merchandise
          sold was $5,000.
      9   Received check in full from Suppan & Son less 2% cash discount.
     11   Received cash refund from a supplier for damaged merchandise $450.

*Journalize transactions in
cash receipts journal; post to
control account and
subsidiary ledger.*

(LO 2, 3)

15 Made cash sales of merchandise totaling $6,500. The cost of the merchandise sold was $4,000.

20 Received check in full from Quentin Bros. $2,400.

Instructions

(a) Balancing totals $40,850
(a) Journalize the transactions above in a six-column cash receipts journal with columns for Cash Dr., Sales Discounts Dr., Accounts Receivable Cr., Sales Revenue Cr., Other Accounts Cr., and Cost of Goods Sold Dr./Inventory Cr. Foot and cross-foot the journal.

(b) Insert the beginning balances in the Accounts Receivable control and subsidiary accounts, and post the June transactions to these accounts.

(c) Accounts Receivable $0
(c) Prove the agreement of the control account and subsidiary account balances.

Journalize transactions in cash payments journal; post to the general and subsidiary ledgers.

(LO 2, 3)

P7-2B Schellhammer Company's chart of accounts includes the following selected accounts.

101 Cash	157 Equipment
120 Inventory	201 Accounts Payable
130 Prepaid Insurance	306 Owner's Drawings

On November 1, the accounts payable ledger of Schellhammer Company showed the following balances: S. Gentry $4,000, D. Montero $2,100, R. Trumbo $800, and W. Olivo $1,800. The November transactions involving the payment of cash were as follows.

Nov. 1 Purchased merchandise, check no. 11, $950.
3 Purchased store equipment, check no. 12, $1,400.
5 Paid W. Olivo balance due of $1,800, less 1% discount, check no. 13, $1,782.
11 Purchased merchandise, check no. 14, $1,700.
15 Paid R. Trumbo balance due of $800, less 3% discount, check no. 15, $776.
16 M. Richey, the owner, withdrew $400 cash for own use, check no. 16.
19 Paid D. Montero in full for invoice no. 1245, $2,100 less 2% discount, check no. 17, $2,058.
25 Paid premium due on one-year insurance policy, check no. 18, $2,400.
30 Paid S. Gentry in full for invoice no. 832, $2,700, check no. 19.

Instructions

(a) Balancing totals $14,250
(a) Journalize the transactions above in a four-column cash payments journal with columns for Other Accounts Dr., Accounts Payable Dr., Inventory Cr., and Cash Cr. Foot and cross-foot the journal.

(b) Insert the beginning balances in the Accounts Payable control and subsidiary accounts, and post the November transactions to these accounts.

(c) Accounts Payable $1,300
(c) Prove the agreement of the control account and the subsidiary account balances.

Journalize transactions in multi-column purchases journal; post to the general and subsidiary ledgers.

(LO 2, 3)

P7-3B The chart of accounts of Henry Company includes the following selected accounts.

112 Accounts Receivable	401 Sales Revenue
120 Inventory	412 Sales Returns and Allowances
126 Supplies	505 Cost of Goods Sold
157 Equipment	610 Advertising Expense
201 Accounts Payable	

In May, the following selected transactions were completed. All purchases and sales were on account except as indicated. The cost of all merchandise sold was 60% of the sales price.

May 2 Purchased merchandise from Berkman Company $5,000.
3 Received freight bill from Fast Freight on Berkman purchase $250.
5 Sales were made to Persinger Company $1,300, Fehr Bros. $2,300, and Mount Company $1,000.
8 Purchased merchandise from Kayser Company $5,400 and Neufeld Company $3,000.
10 Received credit on merchandise returned to Neufeld Company $350.
15 Purchased supplies from Rabel's Supplies $600.
16 Purchased merchandise from Berkman Company $3,100, and Kayser Company $4,200.
17 Returned supplies to Rabel's Supplies, receiving credit $70. (*Hint:* Credit Supplies.)
18 Received freight bills on May 16 purchases from Fast Freight $325.
20 Returned merchandise to Berkman Company receiving credit $200.
23 Made sales to Fehr Bros. $1,600 and to Mount Company $2,500.
25 Received bill for advertising from Mock Advertising $620.
26 Granted allowance to Mount Company for merchandise damaged in shipment $140.
28 Purchased equipment from Rabel's Supplies $400.

Instructions

(a) Journalize the transactions above in a purchases journal, a sales journal, and a general journal. The purchases journal should have the following column headings: Date, Account Credited (Debited), Ref., Accounts Payable Cr., Inventory Dr., and Other Accounts Dr.

(b) Post to both the general and subsidiary ledger accounts. (Assume that all accounts have zero beginning balances.)

(c) Prove the agreement of the control and subsidiary accounts.

P7-4B Selected accounts from the chart of accounts of Conley Company are shown below.

101 Cash	201 Accounts Payable
112 Accounts Receivable	401 Sales Revenue
120 Inventory	414 Sales Discounts
126 Supplies	505 Cost of Goods Sold
140 Land	610 Advertising Expense
145 Building	

The cost of all merchandise sold was 65% of the sales price. During October, Conley Company completed the following transactions.

Oct. 2 Purchased merchandise on account from Kent Company $15,000.
4 Sold merchandise on account to Doumit Co. $5,600. Invoice no. 204, terms 2/10, n/30.
5 Purchased supplies for cash $60.
7 Made cash sales for the week totaling $6,700.
9 Paid in full the amount owed Kent Company less a 2% discount.
10 Purchased merchandise on account from Wrigley Corp. $2,600.
12 Received payment from Doumit Co. for invoice no. 204.
13 Returned $150 worth of damaged goods purchased on account from Wrigley Corp. on October 10.
14 Made cash sales for the week totaling $6,000.
16 Sold a parcel of land for $20,000 cash, the land's original cost.
17 Sold merchandise on account to JR's Warehouse $4,900, invoice no. 205, terms 2/10, n/30.
18 Purchased merchandise for cash $1,600.
21 Made cash sales for the week totaling $6,000.
23 Paid in full the amount owed Wrigley Corp. for the goods kept (no discount).
25 Purchased supplies on account from Francisco Co. $190.
25 Sold merchandise on account to Fryer Corp. $3,800, invoice no. 206, terms 2/10, n/30.
25 Received payment from JR's Warehouse for invoice no. 205.
26 Purchased for cash a small parcel of land and a building on the land to use as a storage facility. The total cost of $26,000 was allocated $16,000 to the land and $10,000 to the building.
27 Purchased merchandise on account from Marte Co. $6,200.
28 Made cash sales for the week totaling $5,500.
30 Purchased merchandise on account from Kent Company $10,000.
30 Paid advertising bill for the month from the *Gazette*, $290.
30 Sold merchandise on account to JR's Warehouse $3,400, invoice no. 207, terms 2/10, n/30.

Conley Company uses the following journals.

1. Sales journal.
2. Single-column purchases journal.
3. Cash receipts journal with columns for Cash Dr., Sales Discounts Dr., Accounts Receivable Cr., Sales Revenue Cr., Other Accounts Cr., and Cost of Goods Sold Dr./Inventory Cr.
4. Cash payments journal with columns for Other Accounts Dr., Accounts Payable Dr., Inventory Cr., and Cash Cr.
5. General journal.

Instructions

Using the selected accounts provided:

(a) Record the October transactions in the appropriate journals.
(b) Foot and cross-foot all special journals.

Margin notes

(a) Purchases journal—
Accounts Payable, Cr.
$22,895
Sales journal—Sales
Revenue total $8,700

(c) Accounts Receivable
$8,560
Accounts Payable $22,275
Journalize transactions in special journals.

(LO 2, 3)

(b) Sales journal $17,700
Purchases journal
$33,800
Cash receipts journal—
Cash, Dr. $54,490
Cash payments journal,
Cash, Cr. $45,100

Journalize in purchases and cash payments journals; post; prepare a trial balance; prove control to subsidiary; prepare adjusting entries; prepare an adjusted trial balance.

(LO 2, 3)

GLS

(c) Show how postings would be made by placing ledger account numbers and check marks as needed in the journals. (Actual posting to ledger accounts is not required.)

P7-5B Presented below are the sales and cash receipts journals for Lowery Co. for its first month of operations.

SALES JOURNAL				**S1**

Date	Account Debited	Ref.	Accounts Receivable Dr. Sales Revenue Cr.	Cost of Goods Sold Dr. Inventory Cr.
Feb. 3	C. Ogleby		4,000	2,400
9	S. Hauke		5,000	3,000
12	T. Ghosh		6,500	3,900
26	W. Hoy		5,500	3,300
			21,000	12,600

CASH RECEIPTS JOURNAL							**CR1**

Date	Owner's Account Credited	Ref.	Cash Dr.	Sales Discounts Dr.	Accounts Receivable Cr.	Sales Revenue Cr.	Other Accounts Cr.	Cost of Goods Sold Dr. Inventory Cr.
Feb. 1	Owner's Capital		23,000				23,000	
2			4,500			4,500		2,700
13	C. Ogleby		3,960	40	4,000			
18	Inventory		120				120	
26	S. Hauke		5,000		5,000			
			36,580	40	9,000	4,500	23,120	2,700

In addition, the following transactions have not been journalized for February 2014.

Feb. 2 Purchased merchandise on account from B. Setterstrom for $5,600, terms 2/10, n/30.

7 Purchased merchandise on account from A. Dambro for $23,000, terms 1/10, n/30.

9 Paid cash of $980 for purchase of supplies.

12 Paid $5,488 to B. Setterstrom in payment for $5,600 invoice, less 2% discount.

15 Purchased equipment for $4,500 cash.

16 Purchased merchandise on account from D. Budke $1,900, terms 2/10, n/30.

17 Paid $22,770 to A. Dambro in payment of $23,000 invoice, less 1% discount.

20 S. Lowery withdrew cash of $800 from the business for personal use.

21 Purchased merchandise on account from Eberle Company for $8,000, terms 1/10, n/30.

28 Paid $1,900 to D. Budke in payment of $1,900 invoice.

Instructions

(a) Open the following accounts in the general ledger.

101 Cash	301 Owner's Capital
112 Accounts Receivable	306 Owner's Drawings
120 Inventory	401 Sales Revenue
126 Supplies	414 Sales Discounts
157 Equipment	505 Cost of Goods Sold
158 Accumulated Depreciation—Equipment	631 Supplies Expense
201 Accounts Payable	711 Depreciation Expense

(b) Purchases journal total $38,500
Cash payments journal—Cash, Cr. $36,438

(b) Journalize the transactions that have not been journalized in a one-column purchases journal and the cash payments journal (see Illustration 7-16).

(c) Post to the accounts receivable and accounts payable subsidiary ledgers. Follow the sequence of transactions as shown in the problem.

(d) Post the individual entries and totals to the general ledger.
(e) Prepare a trial balance at February 28, 2014.
(f) Determine that the subsidiary ledgers agree with the control accounts in the general ledger.
(g) The following adjustments at the end of February are necessary.
   (1) A count of supplies indicates that $200 is still on hand.
   (2) Depreciation on equipment for February is $150.
   Prepare the adjusting entries and then post the adjusting entries to the general ledger.
(h) Prepare an adjusted trial balance at February 28, 2014.

(e) Totals $56,500

(f) Accounts Receivable
    $12,000
    Accounts Payable $8,000

(h) Totals $56,650

PROBLEMS: SET C

Visit the book's companion website, at **www.wiley.com/college/weygandt**, and choose the Student Companion site to access Problem Set C.

COMPREHENSIVE PROBLEM: CHAPTERS 3 TO 7

CP7 McBride Company has the following opening account balances in its general and subsidiary ledgers on January 1 and uses the periodic inventory system. All accounts have normal debit and credit balances.

GENERAL LEDGER

Account Number	Account Title	January 1 Opening Balance
101	Cash	$33,750
112	Accounts Receivable	13,000
115	Notes Receivable	39,000
120	Inventory	20,000
126	Supplies	1,000
130	Prepaid Insurance	2,000
157	Equipment	6,450
158	Accumulated Depreciation—Equip.	1,500
201	Accounts Payable	35,000
301	Owner's Capital	78,700

Accounts Receivable Subsidiary Ledger

Customer	January 1 Opening Balance
R. Kotsay	$1,500
B. Boxberger	7,500
S. Andrus	4,000

Accounts Payable Subsidiary Ledger

Creditor	January 1 Opening Balance
S. Otero	$ 9,000
R. Rasmus	15,000
D. Baroni	11,000

In addition, the following transactions have not been journalized for January 2014.

Jan. 3   Sell merchandise on account to B. Berg $3,600, invoice no. 510, and J. Lutz $1,800, invoice no. 511.

     5   Purchase merchandise on account from S. Colt $5,000 and D. Kahn $2,700.

     7   Receive checks for $4,000 from S. Andrus and $2,000 from B. Boxberger.

     8   Pay freight on merchandise purchased $180.

     9   Send checks to S. Otero for $9,000 and D. Baroni for $11,000.

 9   Issue credit of $300 to J. Lutz for merchandise returned.
10   Summary cash sales total $15,500.
11   Sell merchandise on account to R. Kotsay for $2,900, invoice no. 512, and to
       S. Andrus $900, invoice no. 513.
       Post all entries to the subsidiary ledgers.
12   Pay rent of $1,000 for January.
13   Receive payment in full from B. Berg and J. Lutz.
15   Withdraw $800 cash by I. McBride for personal use.
16   Purchase merchandise on account from D. Baroni for $12,000, from S. Otero
       for $13,900, and from S. Colt for $1,500.
17   Pay $400 cash for supplies.
18   Return $200 of merchandise to S. Otero and receive credit.
20   Summary cash sales total $17,500.
21   Issue $15,000 note to R. Rasmus in payment of balance due.
21   Receive payment in full from S. Andrus.
       Post all entries to the subsidiary ledgers.
22   Sell merchandise on account to B. Berg for $3,700, invoice no. 514, and to
       R. Kotsay for $800, invoice no. 515.
23   Send checks to D. Baroni and S. Otero in full payment.
25   Sell merchandise on account to B. Boxberger for $3,500, invoice no. 516, and
       to J. Lutz for $6,100, invoice no. 517.
27   Purchase merchandise on account from D. Baroni for $12,500, from D. Kahn
       for $1,200, and from S. Colt for $2,800.
28   Pay $200 cash for office supplies.
31   Summary cash sales total $22,920.
31   Pay sales salaries of $4,300 and office salaries of $3,600.

Instructions

(a) Record the January transactions in the appropriate journal—sales, purchases, cash
receipts, cash payments, and general.

(b) Post the journals to the general and subsidiary ledgers. Add and number new accounts
in an orderly fashion as needed.

(c) Trial balance totals
     $200,320;
     Adj. T/B totals $200,475

(c) Prepare a trial balance at January 31, 2014, using a worksheet. Complete the worksheet using the following additional information.
  (1) Supplies at January 31 total $700.
  (2) Insurance coverage expires on October 31, 2014.
  (3) Annual depreciation on the equipment is $1,500.
  (4) Interest of $30 has accrued on the note payable.
  (5) Inventory at January 31 is $15,000.

(d) Net income $12,185
     Total assets $130,815

(d) Prepare a multiple-step income statement and an owner's equity statement for January
and a classified balance sheet at the end of January.

(e) Prepare and post the adjusting and closing entries.

(f) Post-closing T/B totals
     $132,440

(f) Prepare a post-closing trial balance, and determine whether the subsidiary ledgers
agree with the control accounts in the general ledger.

Broadening Your Perspective

Financial Reporting and Analysis

Financial Reporting Problem—Mini Practice Set

BYP7-1 Jeter Co. uses a perpetual inventory system and both an accounts receivable and an
accounts payable subsidiary ledger. Balances related to both the general ledger and the subsidiary
ledger for Jeter are indicated in the working papers. Presented on the next page are a series of
transactions for Jeter Co. for the month of January. Credit sales terms are 2/10, n/30. The cost of all
merchandise sold was 60% of the sales price.

Jan. 3 Sell merchandise on account to B. Corpas $3,600, invoice no. 510, and to J. Revere $1,800, invoice no. 511.

5 Purchase merchandise from S. Gamel $5,000 and D. Posey $2,200, terms n/30.

7 Receive checks from S. Mahay $4,000 and B. Santos $2,000 after discount period has lapsed.

8 Pay freight on merchandise purchased $235.

9 Send checks to S. Meek for $9,000 less 2% cash discount, and to D. Saito for $11,000 less 1% cash discount.

9 Issue credit of $300 to J. Revere for merchandise returned.

10 Summary daily cash sales total $15,500.

11 Sell merchandise on account to R. Beltre $1,600, invoice no. 512, and to S. Mahay $900, invoice no. 513.

12 Pay rent of $1,000 for January.

13 Receive payment in full from B. Corpas and J. Revere less cash discounts.

15 Withdraw $800 cash by M. Jeter for personal use.

15 Post all entries to the subsidiary ledgers.

16 Purchase merchandise from D. Saito $15,000, terms 1/10, n/30; S. Meek $14,200, terms 2/10, n/30; and S. Gamel $1,500, terms n/30.

17 Pay $400 cash for office supplies.

18 Return $200 of merchandise to S. Meek and receive credit.

20 Summary daily cash sales total $20,100.

21 Issue $15,000 note, maturing in 90 days, to R. Moses in payment of balance due.

21 Receive payment in full from S. Mahay less cash discount.

22 Sell merchandise on account to B. Corpas $2,700, invoice no. 514, and to R. Beltre $2,300, invoice no. 515.

22 Post all entries to the subsidiary ledgers.

23 Send checks to D. Saito and S. Meek in full payment less cash discounts.

25 Sell merchandise on account to B. Santos $3,500, invoice no. 516, and to J. Revere $6,100, invoice no. 517.

27 Purchase merchandise from D. Saito $14,500, terms 1/10, n/30; D. Posey $3,200, terms n/30; and S. Gamel $5,400, terms n/30.

27 Post all entries to the subsidiary ledgers.

28 Pay $200 cash for office supplies.

31 Summary daily cash sales total $21,300.

31 Pay sales salaries $4,300 and office salaries $3,800.

Instructions

(a) Record the January transactions in a sales journal, a single-column purchases journal, a cash receipts journal as shown on page 340, a cash payments journal as shown on page 346, and a two-column general journal.

(b) Post the journals to the general ledger.

(c) Prepare a trial balance at January 31, 2014, in the trial balance columns of the worksheet. Complete the worksheet using the following additional information.

  (1) Office supplies at January 31 total $900.

  (2) Insurance coverage expires on October 31, 2014.

  (3) Annual depreciation on the equipment is $1,500.

  (4) Interest of $50 has accrued on the note payable.

(d) Prepare a multiple-step income statement and an owner's equity statement for January and a classified balance sheet at the end of January.

(e) Prepare and post adjusting and closing entries.

(f) Prepare a post-closing trial balance, and determine whether the subsidiary ledgers agree with the control accounts in the general ledger.

Real-World Focus

BYP7-2 Intuit provides some of the leading accounting software packages. Information related to its products is found at its website.

Address: **http://quickbooks.intuit.com** or go to **www.wiley.com/college/weygandt**

Instructions

Look under product and services for the product QuickBooks Premier for Accountants. Be ready to discuss its new features with the class.

Critical Thinking

Decision-Making Across the Organization

BYP7-3 Ermler & Trump is a wholesaler of small appliances and parts. Ermler & Trump is operated by two owners, Jack Ermler and Andrea Trump. In addition, the company has one employee, a repair specialist, who is on a fixed salary. Revenues are earned through the sale of appliances to retailers (approximately 75% of total revenues), appliance parts to do-it-yourselfers (10%), and the repair of appliances brought to the store (15%). Appliance sales are made on both a credit and cash basis. Customers are billed on prenumbered sales invoices. Credit terms are always net/30 days. All parts sales and repair work are cash only.

Merchandise is purchased on account from the manufacturers of both the appliances and the parts. Practically all suppliers offer cash discounts for prompt payments, and it is company policy to take all discounts. Most cash payments are made by check. Checks are most frequently issued to suppliers, to trucking companies for freight on merchandise purchases, and to newspapers, radio, and TV stations for advertising. All advertising bills are paid as received. Jack and Andrea each make a monthly drawing in cash for personal living expenses. The salaried repairman is paid twice monthly. Ermler & Trump currently has a manual accounting system.

Instructions

With the class divided into groups, answer the following.

(a) Identify the special journals that Ermler & Trump should have in its manual accounting system. List the column headings appropriate for each of the special journals.

(b) What control and subsidiary accounts should be included in Ermler & Trump's manual accounting system? Why?

Communication Activity

BYP7-4 Jill Locey, a classmate, has a part-time bookkeeping job. She is concerned about the inefficiencies in journalizing and posting transactions. Ben Newell is the owner of the company where Jill works. In response to numerous complaints from Jill and others, Ben hired two additional bookkeepers a month ago. However, the inefficiencies have continued at an even higher rate. The accounting information system for the company has only a general journal and a general ledger. Ben refuses to install a computerized accounting system.

Instructions

Now that Jill is an expert in manual accounting information systems, she decides to send a letter to Ben Newell explaining (1) why the additional personnel did not help and (2) what changes should be made to improve the efficiency of the accounting department. Write the letter that you think Jill should send.

Ethics Case

BYP7-5 Wiemers Products Company operates three divisions, each with its own manufacturing plant and marketing/sales force. The corporate headquarters and central accounting office are in Wiemers, and the plants are in Freeport, Rockport, and Bayport, all within 50 miles of Wiemers. Corporate management treats each division as an independent profit center and encourages competition among them. They each have similar but different product lines. As a competitive incentive, bonuses are awarded each year to the employees of the fastest-growing and most-profitable division.

Indy Grover is the manager of Wiemers's centralized computerized accounting operation that enters the sales transactions and maintains the accounts receivable for all three divisions. Indy came up in the accounting ranks from the Bayport division where his wife, several relatives, and many friends still work.

As sales documents are entered into the computer, the originating division is identified by code. Most sales documents (95%) are coded, but some (5%) are not coded or are coded incorrectly. As the manager, Indy has instructed the data-entry personnel to assign the Bayport code to all uncoded and incorrectly coded sales documents. This is done, he says, "in order to expedite processing and to keep the computer files current since they are updated daily." All receivables and cash collections for all three divisions are handled by Wiemers as one subsidiary accounts receivable ledger.

Instructions
(a) Who are the stakeholders in this situation?
(b) What are the ethical issues in this case?
(c) How might the system be improved to prevent this situation?

All About You

BYP7-6 In this chapter, you learned about a basic manual accounting information system. Computerized accounting systems range from the very basic and inexpensive to the very elaborate and expensive. However, even the most sophisticated systems are based on the fundamental structures and relationships that you learned in this chapter.

Instructions
Go to the book's companion site for this textbook, **www.wiley.com/college/weygandt**, and review the demonstration that is provided for the general ledger software package that is used with this textbook. Prepare a brief explanation of how the general ledger system works—that is, how it is used, and what information it provides.

Answers to Chapter Questions

Answers to Insight and Accounting Across the Organization Questions

p. 332 Curbing Fraudulent Activity with Software   Q: Why might this software help reduce fraudulent activity by employees? **A:** By pinpointing who used the accounting system and when they used it, the software can hold employees more accountable for their actions. Companies hope that this will reduce efforts by employees to enter false accounting entries, change the dates of transactions, or create unauthorized expenditures. If employees do engage in these activities, there will be significant evidence of their activities.

p. 335 "I'm John Smith, a.k.a. 13695071642"   Q: Why use numbers to identify names in a computerized system? **A:** Computerized systems process numbers faster than letters. Also, letters sometimes cause problems because you may have two people with the same name. Computerized systems avoid this problem by giving different customers, including those with the same names, different account numbers.

Answers to Self-Test Questions

1. d **2.** c **3.** a **4.** c **5.** c ($5,000 + $7,000 + $6,000 + $4,500 + $8,500 − $11,500 − $3,000)
6. c **7.** d **8.** c **9.** a **10.** d **11.** c **12.** d **13.** b **14.** c **15.** c

A Look at IFRS

As discussed in Chapter 1, IFRS is growing in acceptance around the world. For example, recent statistics indicate a substantial number of the Global Fortune 500 companies use IFRS. And the chair of the IASB predicts that IFRS adoption will grow from its current level of 115 countries to nearly 150 countries in the near future.

> **LEARNING OBJECTIVE   4**
> Compare the procedures for accounting information systems under GAAP and IFRS.

When countries accept IFRS for use as accepted accounting policies, companies need guidance to ensure that their first IFRS financial statements contain high-quality information. Specifically, *IFRS 1* requires that information in a company's first IFRS statements (1) be transparent, (2) provide a suitable starting point, and (3) have a cost that does not exceed the benefits.

Key Points

- The basic concepts related to an accounting information system are the same under GAAP and IFRS.
- The use of subsidiary ledgers and control accounts, as well as the system used for recording transactions, are the same under GAAP and IFRS.
- Many companies will be going through a substantial conversion process to switch from their current reporting standards to IFRS.

- The overriding principle in converting to IFRS is full retrospective application of IFRS. Retrospective application—recasting prior financial statements on the basis of IFRS—provides financial statement users with comparable information.
- As indicated, the objective of the conversion process is to present a set of IFRS statements as if the company always reported under IFRS. To achieve this objective, a company follows these steps.
  1. Identify the timing of its first IFRS statements.
  2. Prepare an opening balance sheet at the date of transition to IFRS.
  3. Select accounting principles that comply with IFRS, and apply these principles retrospectively.
  4. Make extensive disclosures to explain the transition to IFRS.
- Once a company decides to convert to IFRS, it must decide on the transition date and the reporting date. The transition date is the beginning of the earliest period for which full comparative IFRS information is presented. The reporting date is the closing balance sheet date for the first IFRS financial statements.
- To illustrate, assume that FirstChoice Company plans to provide its first IFRS statements for the year ended December 31, 2014. FirstChoice decides to present comparative information for one year only. Therefore, its date of transition to IFRS is January 1, 2013, and its reporting date is December 31, 2014.
- The timeline for first-time adoption is presented in the following graphic.

The graphic shows the following.

1. The opening IFRS statement of financial position for FirstChoice on January 1, 2013, serves as the starting point (date of transition) for the company's accounting under IFRS.
2. The first full IFRS statements are shown for FirstChoice for December 31, 2014. In other words, a minimum of two years of IFRS statements must be presented before a conversion to IFRS occurs. As a result, FirstChoice must prepare at least one year of comparative financial statements for 2013 using IFRS.
3. FirstChoice presents financial statements in accordance with U.S. GAAP annually to December 31, 2013.

Following this conversion process, FirstChoice provides users of the financial statements with comparable IFRS statements for 2013 and 2014.

- Upon first-time adoption of IFRS, a company must present at least one year of comparative information under IFRS.

Looking to the Future

The basic recording process shown in this textbook is followed by companies around the globe. It is unlikely to change in the future. The definitional structure of assets, liabilities, equity, revenues, and expenses may change over time as the IASB and FASB evaluate their overall conceptual framework for establishing accounting standards. In addition, high-quality international accounting requires both high-quality accounting standards and high-quality auditing. Similar to the convergence of U.S. GAAP and IFRS, there is a movement to improve international auditing standards. The International Auditing and Assurance Standards Board (IAASB) functions as an independent standard-setting body. It works to establish high-quality auditing and assurance and quality-control standards throughout the world. Whether the IAASB adopts internal control provisions similar to those in SOX remains to be seen. You can follow developments in the international audit arena at **http://www.ifac.org/laasb/**.

IFRS Practice

IFRS Self-Test Questions

1. Information in a company's first IFRS statements must:
  (a) have a cost that does not exceed the benefits.
  (b) be transparent.
  (c) provide a suitable starting point.
  (d) All the above.

2. Indicate which of these statements is **false**.
  (a) The use of subsidiary ledgers is the same under IFRS and GAAP.
  (b) GAAP and IFRS use the same accounting principles.
  (c) The use of special journals is the same under IFRS and GAAP.
  (d) At conversion, companies should retrospectively adjust the financial statements presented following IFRS.

3. The transition date is the date:
  (a) when a company no longer reports under its national standards.
  (b) when the company issues its most recent financial statement under IFRS.
  (c) three years prior to the reporting date.
  (d) None of the above.

4. When converting to IFRS, a company must:
  (a) recast previously issued financial statements in accordance with IFRS.
  (b) use U.S. GAAP in the reporting period but subsequently use IFRS.
  (c) prepare at least three years of comparative statements.
  (d) use U.S. GAAP in the transition year but IFRS in the reporting year.

5. The purpose of presenting comparative information in the transition to IFRS is:
  (a) to ensure that the information is reliable.
  (b) in accordance with the Sarbanes-Oxley Act.
  (c) to provide users of the financial statements with information on U.S. GAAP in one period and IFRS in the other period.
  (d) to provide users of the financial statements with information on IFRS for at least two periods.

IFRS Exercises

IFRS7-1 How is the date of transition and the date of reporting determined in first-time adoption of IFRS?

IFRS7-2 What are the characteristics of high-quality information in a company's first IFRS financial statements?

IFRS7-3 What are the steps to be completed in preparing the opening IFRS statement of financial position?

IFRS7-4 Becker Ltd. is planning to adopt IFRS and prepare its first IFRS financial statements at December 31, 2014. What is the date of Becker's opening balance sheet assuming one year of comparative information? What periods will be covered in Becker's first IFRS financial statements?

IFRS7-5 Stengel plc is preparing its opening IFRS balance sheet on January 1, 2014. Under its previous GAAP, Stengel used the LIFO inventory method. Under LIFO, its inventory is reported at £250,000 (in British pounds). Under FIFO, which Stengel will use upon adoption of IFRS, the inventory is valued at £265,000. Explain what Stengel must do.

Answers to IFRS Self-Test Questions
1. d **2.** b **3.** d **4.** a **5.** d

✔ The Navigator

✔ Remember to go back to The Navigator box on the chapter opening page and check off your completed work.

Feature Story

✔ The Naviga

Minding the Money in Moose Jaw

If you're ever looking for a cappuccino in Moose Jaw, Saskatchewan, stop by Stephanie's Gourmet Coffee and More, located on Main Street. Staff there serve, on average, 650 cups of coffee a day, including both regular and specialty coffees, not to mention soups, Italian sandwiches, and a wide assortment of gourmet cheesecakes.

"We've got high school students who come here, and students from the community college," says owner/manager Stephanie Mintenko, who has run the place since opening it in 1995. "We have customers who are retired, and others who are working people and have only 30 minutes for lunch. We have to be pretty quick."

That means that the cashiers have to be efficient. Like most businesses where purchases are low-cost and high-volume, cash control has to be simple.

"We have an electronic cash register, but it's not the fancy new kind where you just punch in the item," explains Ms. Mintenko. "You have to punch in the prices." The machine does keep track of sales in several categories,

however. Cashiers punch a button to indicate whether ea item is a beverage, a meal, or other type of item. An inter tape in the machine keeps a record of all transactions. Th customer receives a receipt only upon request.

There is only one cash register. "Up to three of us might operate it on any given shift, including myself," says Ms. Mintenko.

She and her staff do two "cashouts" each day—one wit the shift change at 5:00 p.m. and one when the shop clo at 10:00 p.m. At each cashout, they count the cash in the register drawer. That amount, minus the cash change car forward (the float), should match the shift total on the register tape. If there's a discrepancy, they do another count. Then, if necessary, "we go through the whole tap to find the mistake," she explains. "It usually turns out to be someone who punched in $18 instead of $1.80, or something like that."

Ms. Mintenko sends all the cash tapes and float totals to bookkeeper, who double-checks everything and provides regular reports. "We try to keep the accounting simple, so we can concentrate on making great coffee and food.

✔ **The Navigator**

- Scan Learning Objectives
- Read Feature Story
- Read Preview
- Read text and answer **DO IT!** p. 385
    - p. 388 ■ p. 393 ■ p. 401
- Work Comprehensive **DO IT!** p. 403
- Review Summary of Learning Objectives
- Answer Self-Test Questions
- Complete Assignments
- Go to *WileyPLUS* for practice and tutorials
 Read A Look at IFRS p. 425

Learning Objectives   ✔ The Navigator

After studying this chapter, you should be able to:

[1] Define fraud and internal control.

[2] Identify the principles of internal control activities.

[3] Explain the applications of internal control principles to cash receipts.

[4] Explain the applications of internal control principles to cash disbursements.

[5] Describe the operation of a petty cash fund.

[6] Indicate the control features of a bank account.

[7] Prepare a bank reconciliation.

[8] Explain the reporting of cash.

© James Pauls/iStockphoto

Preview of Chapter 8

 The Navigator

As the story about recording cash sales at Stephanie's Gourmet Coffee and More indicates, control of cash is important to ensure that fraud does not occur. Companies also need controls to safeguard other types of assets. For example, Stephanie's undoubtedly has controls to prevent the theft of food and supplies, and controls to prevent the theft of tableware and dishes from its kitchen.

In this chapter, we explain the essential features of an internal control system and how it prevents fraud. We also describe how those controls apply to a specific asset—cash. The applications include some controls with which you may be already familiar, such as the use of a bank.

The content and organization of Chapter 8 are as follows.

FRAUD, INTERNAL CONTROL, AND CASH

Fraud and Internal Control	Cash Controls	Control Features: Use of a Bank	Reporting Cash
• Fraud • The Sarbanes-Oxley Act • Internal control • Principles of internal control activities • Limitations	• Cash receipts controls • Cash disbursements controls • Petty cash fund	• Making deposits • Writing checks • Bank statements • Reconciling the bank account • Electronic funds transfer (EFT) system	• Cash equivalents • Restricted cash

Fraud and Internal Control

The Feature Story describes many of the internal control procedures used by Stephanie's Gourmet Coffee and More. These procedures are necessary to discourage employees from fraudulent activities.

Fraud

A **fraud** is a dishonest act by an employee that results in personal benefit to the employee at a cost to the employer. Examples of fraud reported in the financial press include:

- A bookkeeper in a small company diverted $750,000 of bill payments to a personal bank account over a three-year period.
- A shipping clerk with 28 years of service shipped $125,000 of merchandise to himself.
- A computer operator embezzled $21 million from Wells Fargo Bank over a two-year period.
- A church treasurer "borrowed" $150,000 of church funds to finance a friend's business dealings.

Why does fraud occur? The three main factors that contribute to fraudulent activity are depicted by the **fraud triangle** in Illustration 8-1 (in the margin).

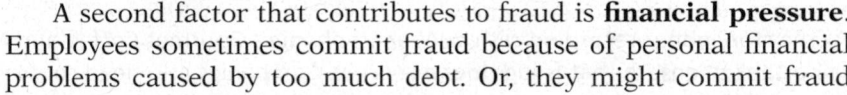

Illustration 8-1
Fraud triangle

The most important element of the fraud triangle is **opportunity**. For an employee to commit fraud, the workplace environment must provide opportunities that an employee can take advantage of. Opportunities occur when the workplace lacks sufficient controls to deter and detect fraud. For example, inadequate monitoring of employee actions can create opportunities for theft and can embolden employees because they believe they will not be caught.

A second factor that contributes to fraud is **financial pressure**. Employees sometimes commit fraud because of personal financial problems caused by too much debt. Or, they might commit fraud because they want to lead a lifestyle that they cannot afford on their current salary.

The third factor that contributes to fraud is **rationalization**. In order to justify their fraud, employees rationalize their dishonest actions. For example, employees sometimes justify fraud because they believe they are underpaid while the employer is making lots of money. Employees feel justified in stealing because they believe they deserve to be paid more.

The Sarbanes-Oxley Act

What can be done to prevent or to detect fraud? After numerous corporate scandals came to light in the early 2000s, Congress addressed this issue by passing the **Sarbanes-Oxley Act (SOX)**. Under SOX, all publicly traded U.S. corporations are required to maintain an adequate system of internal control. Corporate executives and boards of directors must ensure that these controls are reliable and effective. In addition, independent outside auditors must attest to the adequacy of the internal control system. Companies that fail to comply are subject to fines, and company officers can be imprisoned. SOX also created the Public Company Accounting Oversight Board (PCAOB) to establish auditing standards and regulate auditor activity.

One poll found that 60% of investors believe that SOX helps safeguard their stock investments. Many say they would be unlikely to invest in a company that fails to follow SOX requirements. Although some corporate executives have criticized the time and expense involved in following the SOX requirements, SOX appears to be working well. For example, the chief accounting officer of Eli Lily noted that SOX triggered a comprehensive review of how the company documents controls. This review uncovered redundancies and pointed out controls that needed to be added. In short, it added up to time and money well spent. And the finance chief at General Electric noted, "We have seen value in SOX. It helps build investors' trust and gives them more confidence."[1]

Internal Control

Internal control consists of all the related methods and measures adopted within an organization to safeguard assets, enhance the reliability of accounting records, increase efficiency of operations, and ensure compliance with laws and regulations. Internal control systems have five primary components as listed below.[2]

- **A control environment.** It is the responsibility of top management to make it clear that the organization values integrity and that unethical activity will not be tolerated. This component is often referred to as the "tone at the top."

- **Risk assessment.** Companies must identify and analyze the various factors that create risk for the business and must determine how to manage these risks.

- **Control activities.** To reduce the occurrence of fraud, management must design policies and procedures to address the specific risks faced by the company.

- **Information and communication.** The internal control system must capture and communicate all pertinent information both down and up the organization, as well as communicate information to appropriate external parties.

- **Monitoring.** Internal control systems must be monitored periodically for their adequacy. Significant deficiencies need to be reported to top management and/or the board of directors.

PEOPLE, PLANET, AND PROFIT INSIGHT

And the Controls Are . . .

Internal controls are important for an effective financial reporting system. The same is true for sustainability reporting. An effective system of internal controls for sustainability reporting will help in the following ways: (1) prevent the unauthorized use of data; (2) provide reasonable assurance that the information is accurate, valid, and complete; and (3) report information that is consistent with overall sustainability accounting policies. With these types of controls, users will have the confidence that they can use the sustainability information effectively.

Some regulators are calling for even more assurance through audits of this information. Companies that potentially can cause environmental damage through greenhouse gases are subject to reporting requirements as well as companies in the mining and extractive industries. And, as demand for more information in the sustainability area expands, the need for audits of this information will grow.

© Karl Dolenc/iStockphoto

 Why is sustainability information important to investors? (See page 424.)

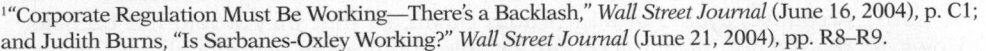

[1]"Corporate Regulation Must Be Working—There's a Backlash," *Wall Street Journal* (June 16, 2004), p. C1; and Judith Burns, "Is Sarbanes-Oxley Working?" *Wall Street Journal* (June 21, 2004), pp. R8–R9.

[2]The Committee of Sponsoring Organizations of the Treadway Commission, "Internal Control—Integrated Framework," *www.coso.org/publications/executive_summary_integrated_framework.htm* (accessed March 2008).

Principles of Internal Control Activities

Each of the five components of an internal control system is important. Here, we will focus on one component, the control activities. The reason? These activities are the backbone of the company's efforts to address the risks it faces, such as fraud. The specific control activities used by a company will vary, depending on management's assessment of the risks faced. This assessment is heavily influenced by the size and nature of the company.

The six principles of control activities are as follows.

- Establishment of responsibility
- Segregation of duties
- Documentation procedures
- Physical controls
- Independent internal verification
- Human resource controls

We explain these principles in the following sections. You should recognize that they apply to most companies and are relevant to both manual and computerized accounting systems.

ESTABLISHMENT OF RESPONSIBILITY

An essential principle of internal control is to assign responsibility to specific employees. **Control is most effective when only one person is responsible for a given task.**

It's your shift now. I'm turning in my cash drawer and heading home.

Transfer of cash drawers

To illustrate, assume that the cash on hand at the end of the day in a Safeway supermarket is $10 short of the cash entered in the cash register. If only one person has operated the register, the shift manager can quickly determine responsibility for the shortage. If two or more individuals have worked the register, it may be impossible to determine who is responsible for the error. In the Feature Story, the principle of establishing responsibility does not appear to be strictly applied by Stephanie's Gourmet Coffee and More, since three people operate the cash register on any given shift.

Many retailers solve this problem by having registers with multiple drawers. This makes it possible for more than one person to operate a register but still allows identification of a particular employee with a specific drawer. Only the signed-in cashier has access to his or her drawer.

Establishing responsibility often requires limiting access only to authorized personnel, and then identifying those personnel. For example, the automated systems used by many companies have mechanisms such as identifying passcodes that keep track of who made a journal entry, who entered a sale, or who went into an inventory storeroom at a particular time. Use of identifying passcodes enables the company to establish responsibility by identifying the particular employee who carried out the activity.

ANATOMY OF A FRAUD

Maureen Frugali was a training supervisor for claims processing at Colossal Healthcare. As a standard part of the claims-processing training program, Maureen created fictitious claims for use by trainees. These fictitious claims were then sent to the accounts payable department. After the training claims had been processed, she was to notify Accounts Payable of all fictitious claims, so that they would not be paid. However, she did not inform Accounts Payable about every fictitious claim. She created some fictitious claims for entities that she controlled (that is, she would receive the payment), and she let Accounts Payable pay her.

THE MISSING CONTROL
Establishment of responsibility. The health-care company did not adequately restrict the responsibility for authorizing and approving claims transactions. The training supervisor should not have been authorized to create claims in the company's "live" system.

Source: Adapted from Wells, *Fraud Casebook* (2007), pp. 61–70.

SEGREGATION OF DUTIES

Segregation of duties is indispensable in an internal control system. There are two common applications of this principle:

1. Different individuals should be responsible for related activities.
2. The responsibility for record-keeping for an asset should be separate from the physical custody of that asset.

The rationale for segregation of duties is this: **The work of one employee should, without a duplication of effort, provide a reliable basis for evaluating the work of another employee.** For example, the personnel that design and program computerized systems should not be assigned duties related to day-to-day use of the system. Otherwise, they could design the system to benefit them personally and conceal the fraud through day-to-day use.

SEGREGATION OF RELATED ACTIVITIES. Making one individual responsible for related activities increases the potential for errors and irregularities. Instead, companies should, for example, assign related **purchasing activities** to different individuals. Related purchasing activities include ordering merchandise, order approval, receiving goods, authorizing payment, and paying for goods or services. Various frauds are possible when one person handles related purchasing activities:

- If a purchasing agent is allowed to order goods without obtaining supervisory approval, the likelihood of the purchasing agent receiving kickbacks from suppliers increases.
- If an employee who orders goods also handles receipt of the goods and invoice, as well as payment authorization, he or she might authorize payment for a fictitious invoice.

These abuses are less likely to occur when companies divide the purchasing tasks.

Similarly, companies should assign related **sales activities** to different individuals. Related selling activities include making a sale, shipping (or delivering) the goods to the customer, billing the customer, and receiving payment. Various frauds are possible when one person handles related sales activities:

- If a salesperson can make a sale without obtaining supervisory approval, he or she might make sales at unauthorized prices to increase sales commissions.
- A shipping clerk who also has access to accounting records could ship goods to himself.
- A billing clerk who handles billing and receipt could understate the amount billed for sales made to friends and relatives.

These abuses are less likely to occur when companies divide the sales tasks: The salespeople make the sale; the shipping department ships the goods on the basis of the sales order; and the billing department prepares the sales invoice after comparing the sales order with the report of goods shipped.

ANATOMY OF A FRAUD

Lawrence Fairbanks, the assistant vice-chancellor of communications at Aesop University, was allowed to make purchases of under $2,500 for his department without external approval. Unfortunately, he also sometimes bought items for himself, such as expensive antiques and other collectibles. How did he do it? He replaced the vendor invoices he received with fake vendor invoices that he created. The fake invoices had descriptions that were more consistent with the communications department's purchases. He submitted these fake invoices to the accounting department as the basis for their journal entries and to the accounts payable department as the basis for payment.

Total take: $475,000

THE MISSING CONTROL

Segregation of duties. The university had not properly segregated related purchasing activities. Lawrence was ordering items, receiving the items, and receiving the invoice. By receiving the invoice, he had control over the documents that were used to account for the purchase and thus was able to substitute a fake invoice.

Source: Adapted from Wells, *Fraud Casebook* (2007), pp. 3–15.

Accounting employee A
Maintains cash
balances per books

Segregation of duties
(Accountability for assets)

Assistant cashier B
Maintains custody
of cash on hand

SEGREGATION OF RECORD-KEEPING FROM PHYSICAL CUSTODY. The accountant should have neither physical custody of the asset nor access to it. Likewise, the custodian of the asset should not maintain or have access to the accounting records. **The custodian of the asset is not likely to convert the asset to personal use when one employee maintains the record of the asset, and a different employee has physical custody of the asset.** The separation of accounting responsibility from the custody of assets is especially important for cash and inventories because these assets are very vulnerable to fraud.

ANATOMY OF A FRAUD

Angela Bauer was an accounts payable clerk for Aggasiz Construction Company. Angela prepared and issued checks to vendors and reconciled bank statements. She perpetrated a fraud in this way: She wrote checks for costs that the company had not actually incurred (e.g., fake taxes). A supervisor then approved and signed the checks. Before issuing the check, though, Angela would "white-out" the payee line on the check and change it to personal accounts that she controlled. She was able to conceal the theft because she also reconciled the bank account. That is, nobody else ever saw that the checks had been altered.

Total take: $570,000

THE MISSING CONTROL

Segregation of duties. Aggasiz Construction Company did not properly segregate record-keeping from physical custody. Angela had physical custody of the checks, which essentially was control of the cash. She also had record-keeping responsibility because she prepared the bank reconciliation.

Source: Adapted from Wells, *Fraud Casebook* (2007), pp. 100–107.

DOCUMENTATION PROCEDURES

Documents provide evidence that transactions and events have occurred. At Stephanie's Gourmet Coffee and More, the cash register tape is the restaurant's documentation for the sale and the amount of cash received. More sophisticated registers, called point-of-sale terminals, do not rely on tapes. Rather, they are networked with the company's computing and accounting records, which results in direct documentation.

Similarly, a shipping document indicates that the goods have been shipped, and a sales invoice indicates that the company has billed the customer for the goods. By requiring signatures (or initials) on the documents, the company can identify the individual(s) responsible for the transaction or event. Companies should document transactions when the transaction occurs.

Companies should establish procedures for documents. First, whenever possible, companies should use **prenumbered documents, and all documents should be accounted for**. Prenumbering helps to prevent a transaction from being recorded more than once, or conversely, from not being recorded at all. Second, the control system should require that employees **promptly forward source documents for accounting entries to the accounting department. This control measure helps to ensure timely recording of the transaction** and contributes directly to the accuracy and reliability of the accounting records.

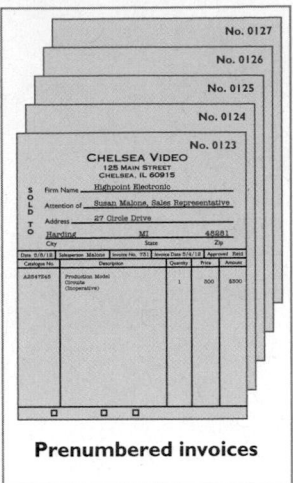

Prenumbered invoices

ANATOMY OF A FRAUD

To support their reimbursement requests for travel costs incurred, employees at Mod Fashions Corporation's design center were required to submit receipts. The receipts could include the detailed bill provided for a meal, the credit card receipt provided when the credit card payment is made, or a copy of the employee's monthly credit card bill that listed the item. A number of the designers who frequently traveled together came up with a fraud scheme: They submitted claims for the same expenses. For example, if they had a meal together that cost $200, one person submitted the detailed meal bill, another submitted the credit card receipt, and a third submitted a monthly credit card bill showing the meal as a line item. Thus, all three received a $200 reimbursement.

Total take: $75,000

THE MISSING CONTROL

Documentation procedures. Mod Fashions should require the original, detailed receipt. It should not accept photocopies, and it should not accept credit card statements. In addition, documentation procedures could be further improved by requiring the use of a corporate credit card (rather than a personal credit card) for all business expenses.

Source: Adapted from Wells, *Fraud Casebook* (2007), pp. 79–90.

PHYSICAL CONTROLS

Use of physical controls is essential. **Physical controls** relate to the safeguarding of assets and enhance the accuracy and reliability of the accounting records. Illustration 8-2 shows examples of these controls.

Illustration 8-2
Physical controls

Physical Controls

Safes, vaults, and safety deposit boxes for cash and business papers	Locked warehouses and storage cabinets for inventories and records	Computer facilities with pass key access or fingerprint or eyeball scans	Alarms to prevent break-ins	Television monitors and garment sensors to deter theft	Time clocks for recording time worked

ANATOMY OF A FRAUD

At Centerstone Health, a large insurance company, the mailroom each day received insurance applications from prospective customers. Mailroom employees scanned the applications into electronic documents before the applications were processed. Once the applications were scanned, they could be accessed online by authorized employees.

Insurance agents at Centerstone Health earn commissions based upon successful applications. The sales agent's name is listed on the application. However, roughly 15% of the applications are from customers who did not work with a sales agent. Two friends—Alex, an employee in record-keeping, and Parviz, a sales agent—thought up a way to perpetrate a fraud. Alex identified scanned applications that did not list a sales agent. After business hours, he entered the mailroom and found the hard-copy applications that did not show a sales agent. He wrote in Parviz's name as the sales agent and then rescanned the application for processing. Parviz received the commission, which the friends then split.

Total take: $240,000

THE MISSING CONTROL
Physical controls. Centerstone Health lacked two basic physical controls that could have prevented this fraud. First, the mailroom should have been locked during non-business hours, and access during business hours should have been tightly controlled. Second, the scanned applications supposedly could be accessed only by authorized employees using their passwords. However, the password for each employee was the same as the employee's user ID. Since employee user-ID numbers were available to all other employees, all employees knew all other employees' passwords. Unauthorized employees could access the scanned applications. Thus, Alex could enter the system using another employee's password and access the scanned applications.

Source: Adapted from Wells, *Fraud Casebook* (2007), pp. 316–326.

INDEPENDENT INTERNAL VERIFICATION

Most internal control systems provide for **independent internal verification**. This principle involves the review of data prepared by employees. To obtain maximum benefit from independent internal verification:

1. Companies should verify records periodically or on a surprise basis.

2. An employee who is independent of the personnel responsible for the information should make the verification.

3. Discrepancies and exceptions should be reported to a management level that can take appropriate corrective action.

Independent internal verification is especially useful in comparing recorded accountability with existing assets. The reconciliation of the cash register tape with the cash in the register at Stephanie's Gourmet Coffee and More is an example of this internal control principle. Another common example is the reconciliation of a company's cash balance per books with the cash balance per bank and the verification of the perpetual inventory records through a count of physical inventory. Illustration 8-3 shows the relationship between this principle and the segregation of duties principle.

ANATOMY OF A FRAUD

Bobbi Jean Donnelly, the office manager for Mod Fashions Corporations design center, was responsible for preparing the design center budget and reviewing expense reports submitted by design center employees. Her desire to upgrade her wardrobe got the better of her, and she enacted a fraud that involved filing expense-reimbursement requests for her own personal clothing purchases. Bobbi Jean was able to conceal the fraud because she was responsible for reviewing all expense reports, including her

Illustration 8-3
Comparison of segregation of duties principle with independent internal verification principle

own. In addition, she sometimes was given ultimate responsibility for signing off on the expense reports when her boss was "too busy." Also, because she controlled the budget, when she submitted her expenses, she coded them to budget items that she knew were running under budget, so that they would not catch anyone's attention.

Total take: $275,000

THE MISSING CONTROL
Independent internal verification. Bobbi Jean's boss should have verified her expense reports. When asked what he thought her expenses for a year were, the boss said about $10,000. At $115,000 per year, her actual expenses were more than 10 times what would have been expected. However, because he was "too busy" to verify her expense reports or to review the budget, he never noticed.

Source: Adapted from Wells, *Fraud Casebook* (2007), pp. 79–90.

Large companies often assign independent internal verification to internal auditors. **Internal auditors** are company employees who continuously evaluate the effectiveness of the company's internal control systems. They review the activities of departments and individuals to determine whether prescribed internal controls are being followed. They also recommend improvements when needed. For example, WorldCom was at one time the second largest U.S. telecommunications company. The fraud that caused its bankruptcy (the largest ever when it occurred) involved billions of dollars. It was uncovered by an internal auditor.

HUMAN RESOURCE CONTROLS
Human resource control activities include the following.

1. **Bond employees who handle cash. Bonding** involves obtaining insurance protection against theft by employees. It contributes to the safeguarding of cash in two ways. First, the insurance company carefully screens all individuals before adding them to the policy and may reject risky applicants. Second, bonded employees know that the insurance company will vigorously prosecute all offenders.

2. **Rotate employees' duties and require employees to take vacations.** These measures deter employees from attempting thefts since they will not be able to permanently conceal their improper actions. Many banks, for example,

If I take a vacation they will know that I've been stealing.

have discovered employee thefts when the employee was on vacation or assigned to a new position.

3. **Conduct thorough background checks.** Many believe that the most important and inexpensive measure any business can take to reduce employee theft and fraud is for the human resources department to conduct thorough background checks. Two tips: (1) Check to see whether job applicants actually graduated from the schools they list. (2) Never use telephone numbers for previous employers provided by the applicant. Always look them up yourself.

ANATOMY OF A FRAUD

Ellen Lowry was the desk manager and Josephine Rodriguez was the head of housekeeping at the Excelsior Inn, a luxury hotel. The two best friends were so dedicated to their jobs that they never took vacations, and they frequently filled in for other employees. In fact, Ms. Rodriguez, whose job as head of housekeeping did not include cleaning rooms, often cleaned rooms herself, "just to help the staff keep up." These two "dedicated" employees, working as a team, found a way to earn a little more cash. Ellen, the desk manager, provided significant discounts to guests who paid with cash. She kept the cash and did not register the guest in the hotel's computerized system. Instead, she took the room out of circulation "due to routine maintenance." Because the room did not show up as being used, it did not receive a normal housekeeping assignment. Instead, Josephine, the head of housekeeping, cleaned the rooms during the guests' stay.

Total take: $95,000

THE MISSING CONTROL

Human resource controls. Ellen, the desk manager, had been fired by a previous employer after being accused of fraud. If the Excelsior Inn had conducted a thorough background check, it would not have hired her. The hotel fraud was detected when Ellen missed work for a few days due to illness. A system of mandatory vacations and rotating days off would have increased the chances of detecting the fraud before it became so large.

Source: Adapted from Wells, *Fraud Casebook* (2007), pp. 145–155.

Stockbyte/Getty Images, Inc.

ACCOUNTING ACROSS THE ORGANIZATION

SOX Boosts the Role of Human Resources

Under SOX, a company needs to keep track of employees' degrees and certifications to ensure that employees continue to meet the specified requirements of a job. Also, to ensure proper employee supervision and proper separation of duties, companies must develop and monitor an organizational chart. When one corporation went through this exercise, it found that out of 17,000 employees, there were 400 people who did not report to anyone. The corporation also had 35 people who reported to each other. In addition, if an employee complains of an unfair firing and mentions financial issues at the company, HR should refer the case to the company audit committee and possibly to its legal counsel.

 Why would unsupervised employees or employees who report to each other represent potential internal control threats? (See page 424.)

Limitations of Internal Control

Companies generally design their systems of internal control to provide **reasonable assurance** of proper safeguarding of assets and reliability of the accounting records. The concept of reasonable assurance rests on the premise that the costs of establishing control procedures should not exceed their expected benefit.

To illustrate, consider shoplifting losses in retail stores. Stores could eliminate such losses by having a security guard stop and search customers as they leave the store. But store managers have concluded that the negative effects of such a procedure cannot be justified. Instead, they have attempted to control shoplifting losses by less costly procedures. They post signs saying, "We reserve the right to inspect all packages" and "All shoplifters will be prosecuted." They use hidden TV cameras and store detectives to monitor customer activity, and they install sensor equipment at exits.

The **human element** is an important factor in every system of internal control. A good system can become ineffective as a result of employee fatigue, carelessness, or indifference. For example, a receiving clerk may not bother to count goods received and may just "fudge" the counts. Occasionally, two or more individuals may work together to get around prescribed controls. Such **collusion** can significantly reduce the effectiveness of a system, eliminating the protection offered by segregation of duties. No system of internal control is perfect.

The **size of the business** also may impose limitations on internal control. Small companies often find it difficult to segregate duties or to provide for independent internal verification. A study by the Association of Certified Fraud Examiners (*2012 Report to the Nation on Occupational Fraud and Abuse*) indicates that businesses with fewer than 100 employees are most at risk for employee theft. In fact, 31% of frauds occurred at companies with fewer than 100 employees. The median loss at small companies was $147,000, which was higher than the median fraud at companies with more than 10,000 employees ($140,000). A $147,000 loss can threaten the very existence of a small company.

Helpful Hint Controls may vary with the risk level of the activity. For example, management may consider cash to be high risk and maintaining inventories in the stockroom as low risk. Thus, management would have stricter controls for cash.

> ## DO IT!

Control Activities

Identify which control activity is violated in each of the following situations, and explain how the situation creates an opportunity for a fraud.

1. The person with primary responsibility for reconciling the bank account and making all bank deposits is also the company's accountant.

2. Wellstone Company's treasurer received an award for distinguished service because he had not taken a vacation in 30 years.

3. In order to save money spent on order slips and to reduce time spent keeping track of order slips, a local bar/restaurant does not buy prenumbered order slips.

Solution

Action Plan

✔ Familiarize yourself with each of the control activities summarized on page 378.

✔ Understand the nature of the frauds that each control activity is intended to address.

1. Violates the control activity of segregation of duties. Record-keeping should be separate from physical custody. As a consequence, the employee could embezzle cash and make journal entries to hide the theft.

2. Violates the control activity of human resource controls. Key employees must take vacations. Otherwise, the treasurer, who manages the company's cash, might embezzle cash and use his position to conceal the theft.

3. Violates the control activity of documentation procedures. If prenumbered documents are not used, then it is virtually impossible to account for the documents. As a consequence, an employee could write up a dinner sale, receive the cash from the customer, and then throw away the order slip and keep the cash.

Related exercise material: **BE8-1, BE8-2, BE8-3, BE8-4, E8-1, and** **DO IT!** **8-1.**

 The Navigator

Cash Controls

LEARNING OBJECTIVE 3

Explain the applications
of internal control
principles to cash receipts.

Cash is the one asset that is readily convertible into any other type of asset. It also is easily concealed and transported, and is highly desired. Because of these characteristics, **cash is the asset most susceptible to fraudulent activities**. In addition, because of the large volume of cash transactions, numerous errors may occur in executing and recording them. To safeguard cash and to ensure the accuracy of the accounting records for cash, effective internal control over cash is critical.

Cash Receipts Controls

Illustration 8-4 shows how the internal control principles explained earlier apply to cash receipts transactions. As you might expect, companies vary considerably in how they apply these principles. To illustrate internal control over cash receipts, we will examine control activities for a retail store with both over-the-counter and mail receipts.

Illustration 8-4
Application of internal control principles to cash receipts

Cash Receipts Controls

Establishment of Responsibility
Only designated personnel are authorized to handle cash receipts (cashiers)

Segregation of Duties
Different individuals receive cash, record cash receipts, and hold the cash

Documentation Procedures
Use remittance advice (mail receipts), cash register tapes or computer records, and deposit slips

Physical Controls
Store cash in safes and bank vaults; limit access to storage areas; use cash registers

Independent Internal Verification
Supervisors count cash receipts daily; assistant treasurer compares total receipts to bank deposits daily

Human Resource Controls
Bond personnel who handle cash; require employees to take vacations; conduct background checks

OVER-THE-COUNTER RECEIPTS

In retail businesses, control of over-the-counter receipts centers on cash registers that are visible to customers. A cash sale is entered in a cash register, with the amount clearly visible to the customer. This activity prevents the cashier from entering a lower amount and pocketing the difference. The customer receives an itemized cash register receipt slip and is expected to count the change received.

(One weakness at Stephanie's Gourmet Coffee and More in the Feature Story is that customers were only given a receipt if they requested it.) The cash register's tape is locked in the register until a supervisor removes it. This tape accumulates the daily transactions and totals.

At the end of the clerk's shift, the clerk counts the cash and sends the cash and the count to the cashier. The cashier counts the cash, prepares a deposit slip, and deposits the cash at the bank. The cashier also sends a duplicate of the deposit slip to the accounting department to indicate cash received. The supervisor removes the cash register tape and sends it to the accounting department as the basis for a journal entry to record the cash received. Illustration 8-5 summarizes this process.

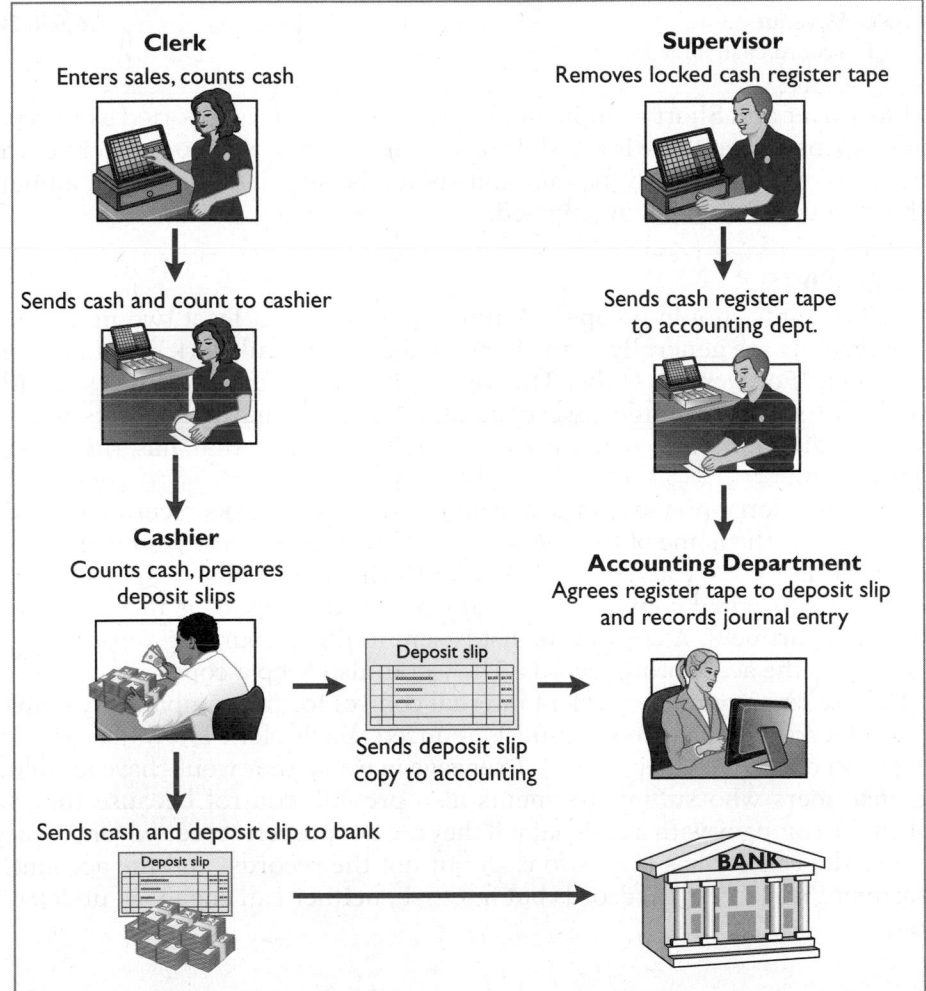

Illustration 8-5
Control of over-the-counter receipts

Helpful Hint Flowcharts such as this one enhance the understanding of the flow of documents, the processing steps, and the internal control procedures.

This system for handling cash receipts uses an important internal control principle—segregation of record-keeping from physical custody. The supervisor has access to the cash register tape but **not** to the cash. The clerk and the cashier have access to the cash but **not** to the register tape. In addition, the cash register tape provides documentation and enables independent internal verification. Use of these three principles of internal control (segregation of record-keeping from physical custody, documentation, and independent internal verification) provides an effective system of internal control. Any attempt at fraudulent activity should be detected unless there is collusion among the employees.

In some instances, the amount deposited at the bank will not agree with the cash recorded in the accounting records based on the cash register tape. These differences often result because the clerk hands incorrect change back to the retail customer. In this case, the difference between the actual cash and the amount reported on the cash register tape is reported in a Cash Over and Short account. For example, suppose that the cash register tape indicated sales of $6,956.20 but the amount of cash was only $6,946.10. A cash shortfall of $10.10 exists. To account for this cash shortfall and related cash, the company makes the following entry.

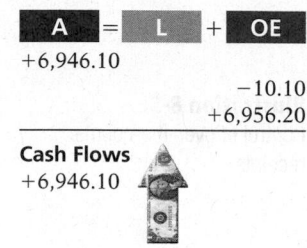

Cash	6,946.10	
Cash Over and Short	10.10	
Sales Revenue		6,956.20
(To record cash shortfall)		

Cash Over and Short is an income statement item. It is reported as miscellaneous expense when there is a cash shortfall, and as miscellaneous revenue when there is an overage. Clearly, the amount should be small. Any material amounts in this account should be investigated.

MAIL RECEIPTS

All mail receipts should be opened in the presence of at least two mail clerks. These receipts are generally in the form of checks. A mail clerk should endorse each check "For Deposit Only." This restrictive endorsement reduces the likelihood that someone could divert the check to personal use. Banks will not give an individual cash when presented with a check that has this type of endorsement.

The mail clerks prepare, in triplicate, a list of the checks received each day. This list shows the name of the check issuer, the purpose of the payment, and the amount of the check. Each mail clerk signs the list to establish responsibility for the data. The original copy of the list, along with the checks, is then sent to the cashier's department. A copy of the list is sent to the accounting department for recording in the accounting records. The clerks also keep a copy.

This process provides excellent internal control for the company. By employing two clerks, the chance of fraud is reduced. Each clerk knows he or she is being observed by the other clerk(s). To engage in fraud, they would have to collude. The customers who submit payments also provide control because they will contact the company with a complaint if they are not properly credited for payment. Because the cashier has access to cash but not the records, and the accounting department has access to records but not cash, neither can engage in undetected fraud.

> **DO IT!**

Control over Cash Receipts

L. R. Cortez is concerned about the control over cash receipts in his fast-food restaurant, Big Cheese. The restaurant has two cash registers. At no time do more than two employees take customer orders and enter sales. Work shifts for employees range from 4 to 8 hours. Cortez asks your help in installing a good system of internal control over cash receipts.

Action Plan

✔ Differentiate among the internal control principles of (1) establishing responsibility, (2) using physical controls, and (3) independent internal verification.

✔ Design an effective system of internal control over cash receipts.

Solution

Cortez should assign a separate cash register drawer to each employee at the start of each work shift, with register totals set at zero. Each employee should have access to only the assigned register drawer to enter all sales. Each customer should be given a receipt. At the end of the shift, the employee should do a cash count. A separate employee should compare the cash count with the register tape to be sure they agree. In addition, Cortez should install an automated system that would enable the company to compare orders entered in the register to orders processed by the kitchen.

Related exercise material: **BE8-5, BE8-6, BE8-7, E8-2,** and **DO IT!** 8-2.

✔ The Navigator

Cash Disbursements Controls

Companies disburse cash for a variety of reasons, such as to pay expenses and liabilities or to purchase assets. **Generally, internal control over cash disbursements is more effective when companies pay by check or electronic funds transfer (EFT) rather than by cash.** One exception is **payments for incidental amounts that are paid out of petty cash.**[3]

Companies generally issue checks only after following specified control procedures. Illustration 8-6 (page 390) shows how principles of internal control apply to cash disbursements.

LEARNING OBJECTIVE 4

Explain the applications of internal control principles to cash disbursements.

VOUCHER SYSTEM CONTROLS

Most medium and large companies use vouchers as part of their internal control over cash disbursements. A **voucher system** is a network of approvals by authorized individuals, acting independently, to ensure that all disbursements by check are proper.

The system begins with the authorization to incur a cost or expense. It ends with the issuance of a check for the liability incurred. A **voucher** is an authorization form prepared for each expenditure. Companies require vouchers for all types of cash disbursements except those from petty cash.

The starting point in preparing a voucher is to fill in the appropriate information about the liability on the face of the voucher. The vendor's invoice provides most of the needed information. Then, an employee in accounts payable records the voucher (in a journal called a **voucher register**) and files it according to the date on which it is to be paid. The company issues and sends a check on that date, and stamps the voucher "paid." The paid voucher is sent to the accounting department for recording (in a journal called the **check register**). A voucher system involves two journal entries, one to record the liability when the voucher is issued and a second to pay the liability that relates to the voucher.

The use of a voucher system, whether done manually or electronically, improves internal control over cash disbursements. First, the authorization process inherent in a voucher system establishes responsibility. Each individual has responsibility to review the underlying documentation to ensure that it is correct. In addition, the voucher system keeps track of the documents that back up each transaction. By keeping these documents in one place, a supervisor can independently verify the authenticity of each transaction. Consider, for example, the case of Aesop University presented on page 380. Aesop did not use a voucher system for

---

[3]We explain the operation of a petty cash fund on pages 390–392.

Cash Disbursements Controls

  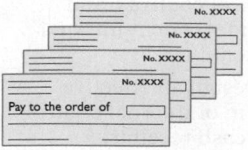

Establishment of Responsibility
Only designated personnel are authorized to sign checks (treasurer) and approve vendors

Segregation of Duties
Different individuals approve and make payments; check-signers do not record disbursements

Documentation Procedures
Use prenumbered checks and account for them in sequence; each check must have an approved invoice; require employees to use corporate credit cards for reimbursable expenses; stamp invoices "paid"

Physical Controls
Store blank checks in safes, with limited access; print check amounts by machine in indelible ink

Independent Internal Verification
Compare checks to invoices; reconcile bank statement monthly

Human Resource Controls
Bond personnel who handle cash; require employees to take vacations; conduct background checks

Illustration 8-6
Application of internal control principles to cash disbursements

transactions under $2,500. As a consequence, there was no independent verification of the documents, which enabled the employee to submit fake invoices to hide his unauthorized purchases.

Petty Cash Fund

LEARNING OBJECTIVE 5

Describe the operation of a petty cash fund.

As you just learned, better internal control over cash disbursements is possible when companies make payments by check. However, using checks to pay small amounts is both impractical and a nuisance. For instance, a company would not want to write checks to pay for postage due, working lunches, or taxi fares. A common way of handling such payments, while maintaining satisfactory control, is to use a **petty cash fund** to pay relatively small amounts. The operation of a petty cash fund, often called an **imprest system**, involves (1) establishing the fund, (2) making payments from the fund, and (3) replenishing the fund.[4]

---

[4]The term "imprest" means an advance of money for a designated purpose.

ESTABLISHING THE PETTY CASH FUND

Two essential steps in establishing a petty cash fund are (1) appointing a petty cash custodian who will be responsible for the fund, and (2) determining the size of the fund. Ordinarily, a company expects the amount in the fund to cover anticipated disbursements for a three- to four-week period.

To establish the fund, a company issues a check payable to the petty cash custodian for the stipulated amount. For example, if Laird Company decides to establish a $100 fund on March 1, the general journal entry is:

Mar. 1	Petty Cash	100	
	Cash		100
	(To establish a petty cash fund)		

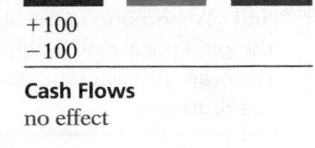

A = L + OE
+100
−100

Cash Flows
no effect

The fund custodian cashes the check and places the proceeds in a locked petty cash box or drawer. Most petty cash funds are established on a fixed-amount basis. The company will make no additional entries to the Petty Cash account unless management changes the stipulated amount of the fund. For example, if Laird Company decides on July 1 to increase the size of the fund to $250, it would debit Petty Cash $150 and credit Cash $150.

Ethics Note

Petty cash funds are authorized and legitimate. In contrast, "slush" funds are unauthorized and hidden (under the table).

MAKING PAYMENTS FROM THE PETTY CASH FUND

The petty cash custodian has the authority to make payments from the fund that conform to prescribed management policies. Usually, management limits the size of expenditures that come from petty cash. Likewise, it may not permit use of the fund for certain types of transactions (such as making short-term loans to employees).

Each payment from the fund must be documented on a prenumbered petty cash receipt (or petty cash voucher), as shown in Illustration 8-7. The signatures of both the fund custodian and the person receiving payment are required on the receipt. If other supporting documents such as a freight bill or invoice are available, they should be attached to the petty cash receipt.

Helpful Hint The petty cash receipt satisfies two internal control procedures: (1) establishing responsibility (signature of custodian), and (2) documentation procedures.

Illustration 8-7
Petty cash receipt

No. 7	LAIRD COMPANY
	Petty Cash Receipt

Date 3/6/14

Paid to   Acme Express Agency   Amount $18.00

For   Collect Express Charges

CHARGE TO   Freight-in

Approved   Received Payment

L. A. Bird Custodian   *R.E. Meins*

The petty cash custodian keeps the receipts in the petty cash box until the fund is replenished. The sum of the petty cash receipts and the money in the fund should equal the established total at all times. Management can (and should) make surprise counts at any time to determine whether the fund is being maintained correctly.

The company does not make an accounting entry to record a payment when it is made from petty cash. It is considered both inexpedient and unnecessary to do so. Instead, the company recognizes the accounting effects of each payment when it replenishes the fund.

REPLENISHING THE PETTY CASH FUND

When the money in the petty cash fund reaches a minimum level, the company replenishes the fund. The petty cash custodian initiates a request for reimbursement. The individual prepares a schedule (or summary) of the payments that have been made and sends the schedule, supported by petty cash receipts and other documentation, to the treasurer's office. The treasurer's office examines the receipts and supporting documents to verify that proper payments from the fund were made. The treasurer then approves the request and issues a check to restore the fund to its established amount. At the same time, all supporting documentation is stamped "paid" so that it cannot be submitted again for payment.

To illustrate, assume that on March 15 Laird's petty cash custodian requests a check for $87. The fund contains $13 cash and petty cash receipts for postage $44, freight-out $38, and miscellaneous expenses $5. The general journal entry to record the check is:

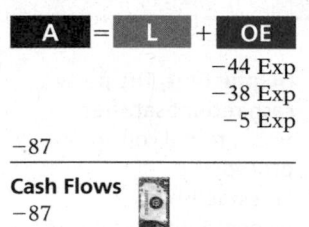

Mar. 15	Postage Expense	44	
	Freight-Out	38	
	Miscellaneous Expense	5	
	Cash		87
	(To replenish petty cash fund)		

Note that the reimbursement entry does not affect the Petty Cash account. Replenishment changes the composition of the fund by replacing the petty cash receipts with cash. It does not change the balance in the fund.

Occasionally, in replenishing a petty cash fund, the company may need to recognize a cash shortage or overage. This results when the total of the cash plus receipts in the petty cash box does not equal the established amount of the petty cash fund. To illustrate, assume that Laird's petty cash custodian has only $12 in cash in the fund plus the receipts as listed. The request for reimbursement would therefore be for $88, and Laird would make the following entry.

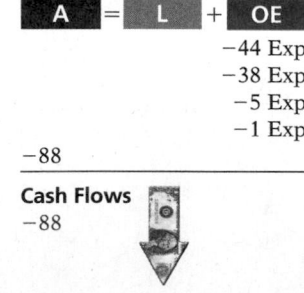

Mar. 15	Postage Expense	44	
	Freight-Out	38	
	Miscellaneous Expense	5	
	Cash Over and Short	1	
	Cash		88
	(To replenish petty cash fund)		

Conversely, if the custodian has $14 in cash, the reimbursement request would be for $86. The company would credit Cash Over and Short for $1 (overage). A company reports a debit balance in Cash Over and Short in the income statement as miscellaneous expense. It reports a credit balance in the account as miscellaneous revenue. The company closes Cash Over and Short to Income Summary at the end of the year.

Companies should replenish a petty cash fund at the end of the accounting period, regardless of the cash in the fund. Replenishment at this time is necessary in order to recognize the effects of the petty cash payments on the financial statements.

Helpful Hint Cash over and short situations result from mathematical errors or from failure to keep accurate records.

ETHICS INSIGHT

How Employees Steal

A recent study by the Association of Certified Fraud Examiners found that two-thirds of all employee thefts involved a fraudulent disbursement by an employee. The most common form (24.9% of cases) was fraudulent billing schemes. In these, the employee causes the company to issue a payment to the employee by submitting a bill for nonexistent goods or services, purchases of personal goods by the employee, or inflated invoices. The graph below shows various types of fraudulent disbursements and the median loss from each.

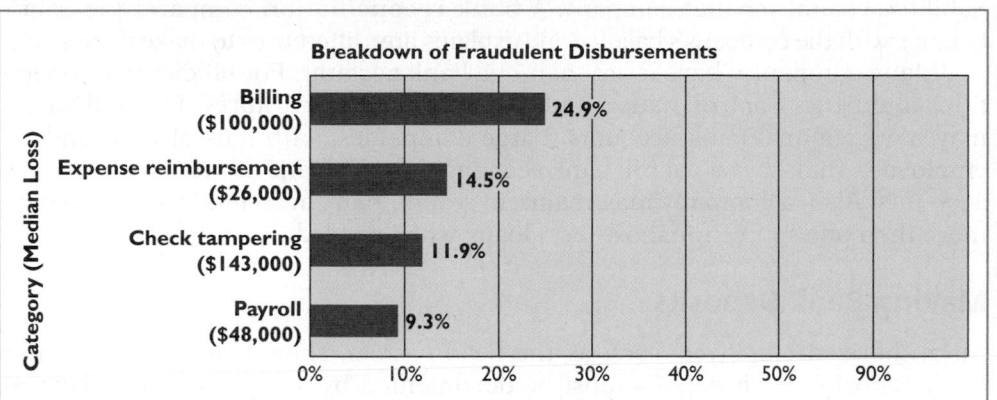

Breakdown of Fraudulent Disbursements

Category (Median Loss)

- Billing ($100,000) — 24.9%
- Expense reimbursement ($26,000) — 14.5%
- Check tampering ($143,000) — 11.9%
- Payroll ($48,000) — 9.3%

(0% 10% 20% 30% 40% 50% 90%)

© Chris Fernig/iStockphoto

Source: 2012 Report to the Nation on Occupational Fraud and Abuse, Association of Certified Fraud Examiners, *www.acfe.com/uploadedfiles/ACFE_website/content/rttn/2012-report-to-nations.pdf*, p. 12.

? How can companies reduce the likelihood of fraudulent disbursements? (See page 424.)

> DO IT!

Petty Cash Fund

Action Plan

✔ To establish the fund, set up a separate general ledger account.

✔ Determine how much cash is needed to replenish the fund: subtract the cash remaining from the petty cash fund balance.

✔ Total the petty cash receipts. Determine any cash over or short—the difference between the cash needed to replenish the fund and the total of the petty cash receipts.

✔ Record the expenses incurred according to the petty cash receipts when replenishing the fund.

Bateer Company established a $50 petty cash fund on July 1. On July 30, the fund had $12 cash remaining and petty cash receipts for postage $14, office supplies $10, and delivery expense $15. Prepare journal entries to establish the fund on July 1 and to replenish the fund on July 30.

Solution

July 1	Petty Cash	50	
	Cash		50
	(To establish petty cash fund)		
30	Postage Expense	14	
	Supplies	10	
	Delivery Expense	15	
	Cash Over and Short		1
	Cash ($50 − $12)		38
	(To replenish petty cash)		

Related exercise material: BE8-9, E8-7, E8-8, and **DO IT!** 8-3.

 ✔ The Navigator

Control Features: Use of a Bank

The use of a bank contributes significantly to good internal control over cash. A company can safeguard its cash by using a bank as a depository and as a clearinghouse for checks received and written. Use of a bank minimizes the amount of currency that a company must keep on hand. Also, use of a bank facilitates the control of cash because it creates a double record of all bank transactions—one by the company and the other by the bank. The asset account Cash maintained by the company should have the same balance as the bank's liability account for that company. A **bank reconciliation** compares the bank's balance with the company's balance and explains any differences to make them agree.

Many companies have more than one bank account. For efficiency of operations and better control, national retailers like Wal-Mart Stores, Inc. and Target may have regional bank accounts. Large companies, with tens of thousands of employees, may have a payroll bank account, as well as one or more general bank accounts. Also, a company may maintain several bank accounts in order to have more than one source for short-term loans when needed.

Making Bank Deposits

An authorized employee, such as the head cashier, should make a company's bank deposits. Each deposit must be documented by a deposit slip (ticket), as shown in Illustration 8-8.

Illustration 8-8
Deposit slip

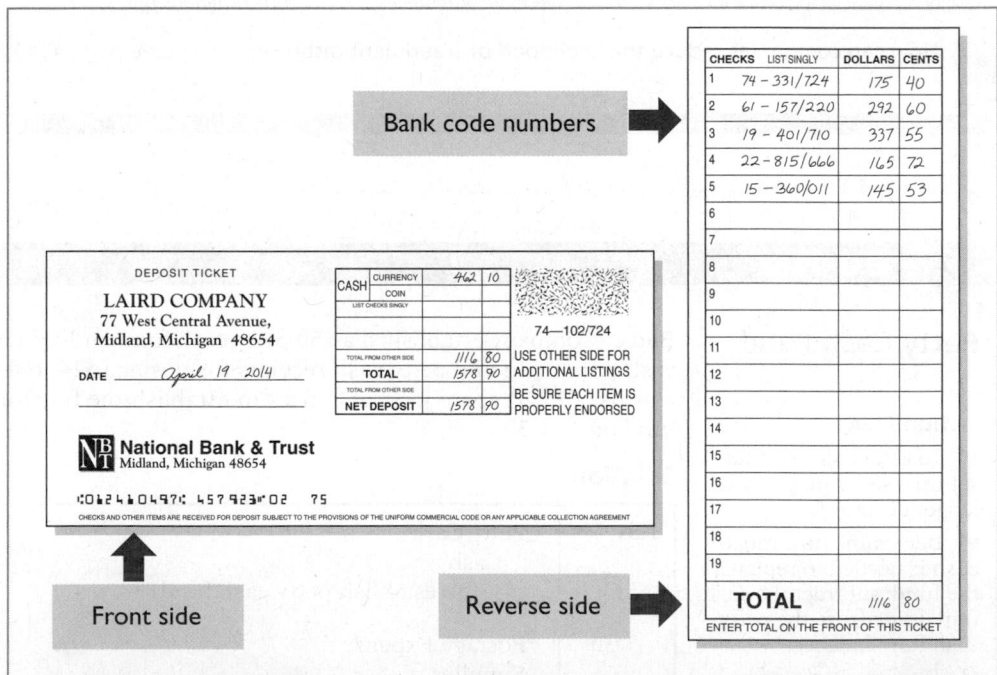

Deposit slips are prepared in duplicate. The bank retains the original; the depositor keeps the duplicate, machine-stamped by the bank to establish its authenticity.

Writing Checks

Most of us write checks without thinking very much about them. A **check** is a written order signed by the depositor directing the bank to pay a specified sum of money to a designated recipient. There are three parties to a check: (1) the **maker** (or drawer) who issues the check, (2) the **bank** (or payer) on which the check is drawn, and (3) the **payee** to whom the check is payable. A check is a **negotiable instrument** that one party can transfer to another party by endorsement. Each check should be accompanied by an explanation of its purpose. In many companies, a remittance advice attached to the check, as shown in Illustration 8-9, explains the check's purpose.

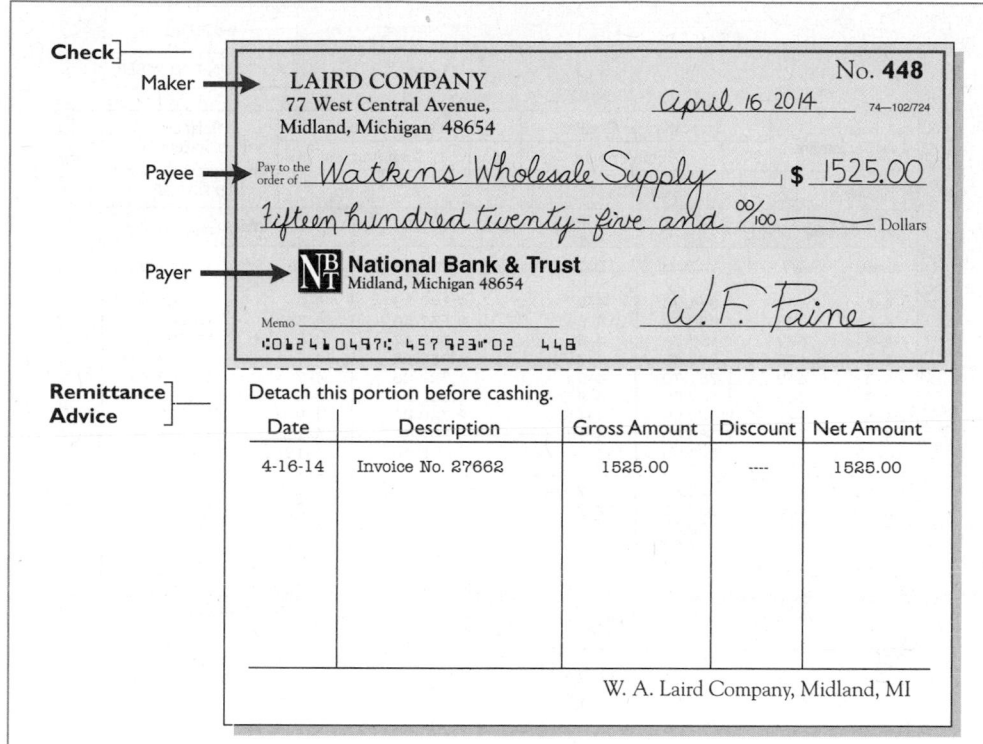

Illustration 8-9
Check with remittance advice

It is important to know the balance in the checking account at all times. To keep the balance current, the depositor should enter each deposit and check on running-balance memo forms (or online statements) provided by the bank or on the check stubs in the checkbook.

Bank Statements

If you have a personal checking account, you are probably familiar with bank statements. A **bank statement** shows the depositor's bank transactions and balances.[5] Each month, a depositor receives a statement from the bank. Illustration 8-10 (page 396) presents a typical bank statement for Laird Company. It shows (1) checks paid and other debits (such as debit card transactions or direct withdrawals for bill payments) that reduce the balance in the depositor's account, (2) deposits and other credits that increase the balance in the depositor's account, and (3) the account balance after each day's transactions.

Helpful Hint Essentially, the bank statement is a copy of the bank's records sent to the customer (or available online) for review.

[5]Our presentation assumes that the depositor makes all adjustments at the end of the month. In practice, a company may also make journal entries during the month as it reviews information from the bank regarding its account.

Illustration 8-10
Bank statement

Helpful Hint The bank *credits* to the customer's account every deposit it receives. The reverse occurs when the bank "pays" a check issued by a company on its checking account balance. Payment reduces the bank's liability. Thus, the bank *debits* check payments to the customer's account with the bank.

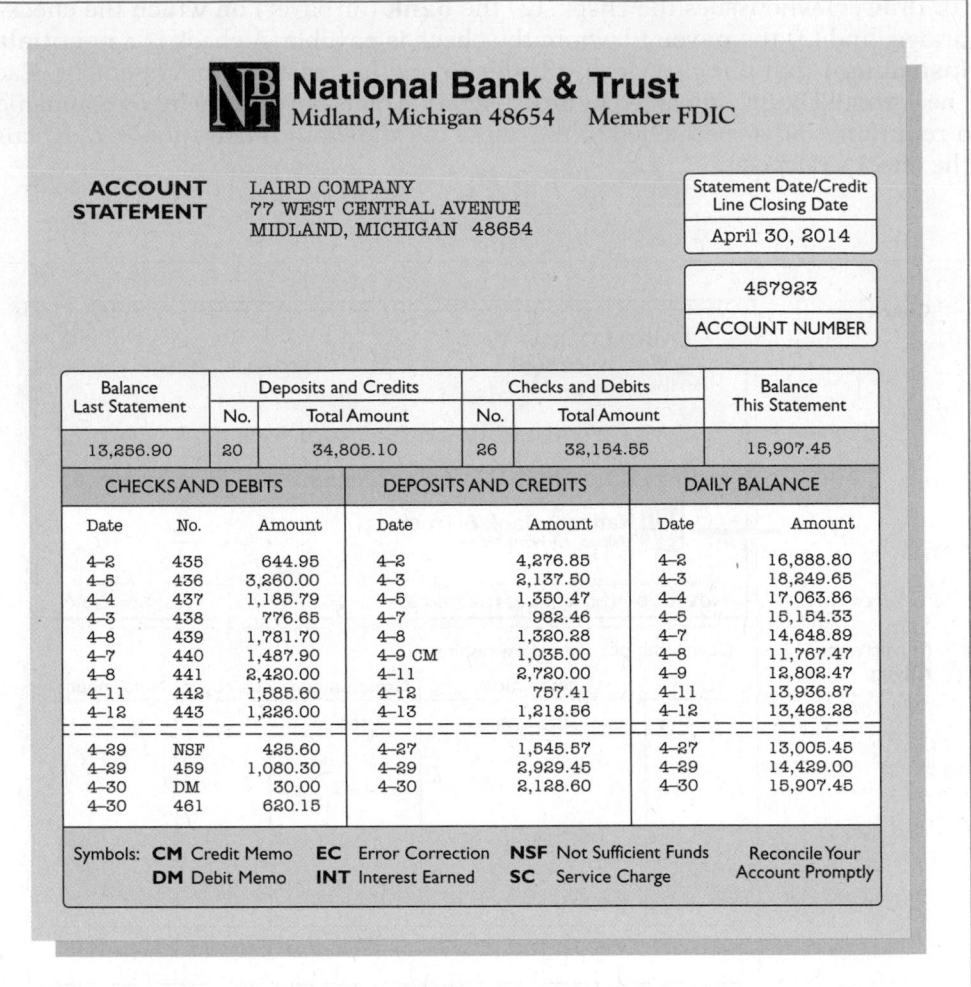

The bank statement lists in numerical sequence all "paid" checks, along with the date the check was paid and its amount. Upon paying a check, the bank stamps the check "paid"; a paid check is sometimes referred to as a **canceled** check. On the statement, the bank also includes memoranda explaining other debits and credits it made to the depositor's account.

DEBIT MEMORANDUM

Some banks charge a monthly fee for their services. Often, they charge this fee only when the average monthly balance in a checking account falls below a specified amount. They identify the fee, called a **bank service charge**, on the bank statement by a symbol such as **SC**. The bank also sends with the statement a debit memorandum explaining the charge noted on the statement. Other debit memoranda may also be issued for other bank services such as the cost of printing checks, issuing traveler's checks, and wiring funds to other locations. The symbol **DM** is often used for such charges.

Banks also use a debit memorandum when a deposited check from a customer "bounces" because of insufficient funds. For example, assume that Scott Company, a customer of Laird Company, sends a check for $800 to Laird Company for services performed. Unfortunately, Scott does not have sufficient funds at its bank to pay for these services. In such a case, Scott's bank marks the check **NSF** (not sufficient funds) and returns it to Laird's (the depositor's) bank. Laird's bank then debits Laird's account, as shown by the symbol NSF on the bank statement in Illustration 8-10. The bank sends the NSF check and debit memorandum to Laird as notification of the charge. Laird then records an Account Receivable from Scott Company (the writer of the bad check) and reduces cash for the NSF check.

CREDIT MEMORANDUM

Sometimes a depositor asks the bank to collect its notes receivable. In such a case, the bank will credit the depositor's account for the cash proceeds of the note. This is illustrated by the symbol **CM** on the Laird Company bank statement. The bank issues and sends with the statement a credit memorandum to explain the entry. Many banks also offer interest on checking accounts. The interest earned may be indicated on the bank statement by the symbol **CM** or **INT**.

Reconciling the Bank Account

The bank and the depositor maintain independent records of the depositor's checking account. People tend to assume that the respective balances will always agree. In fact, the two balances are seldom the same at any given time, and both balances differ from the "correct" or "true" balance. Therefore, it is necessary to make the balance per books and the balance per bank agree with the correct or true amount—a process called **reconciling the bank account**. The need for agreement has two causes:

LEARNING OBJECTIVE **7**

Prepare a bank reconciliation.

1. **Time lags** that prevent one of the parties from recording the transaction in the same period as the other party.
2. **Errors** by either party in recording transactions.

Time lags occur frequently. For example, several days may elapse between the time a company mails a check to a payee and the date the bank pays the check. Similarly, when the depositor uses the bank's night depository to make its deposits, there will be a difference of at least one day between the time the depositor records the deposit and the time the bank does so. A time lag also occurs whenever the bank mails a debit or credit memorandum to the depositor.

The incidence of errors depends on the effectiveness of the internal controls maintained by the company and the bank. Bank errors are infrequent. However, either party could accidentally record a $450 check as $45 or $540. In addition, the bank might mistakenly charge a check drawn by C. D. Berg to the account of C. D. Burg.

RECONCILIATION PROCEDURE
The bank reconciliation should be prepared by an employee who has no other responsibilities pertaining to cash. If a company fails to follow this internal control principle of independent internal verification, cash embezzlements may go unnoticed. For example, a cashier who prepares the reconciliation can embezzle cash and conceal the embezzlement by misstating the reconciliation. Thus, the bank accounts would reconcile, and the embezzlement would not be detected.

In reconciling the bank account, it is customary to reconcile the balance per books and balance per bank to their adjusted (correct or true) cash balances. The starting point in preparing the reconciliation is to enter the balance per bank statement and balance per books on the reconciliation schedule. The company then makes various adjustments, as shown in Illustration 8-11 (page 398).

Illustration 8-11
Bank reconciliation adjustments

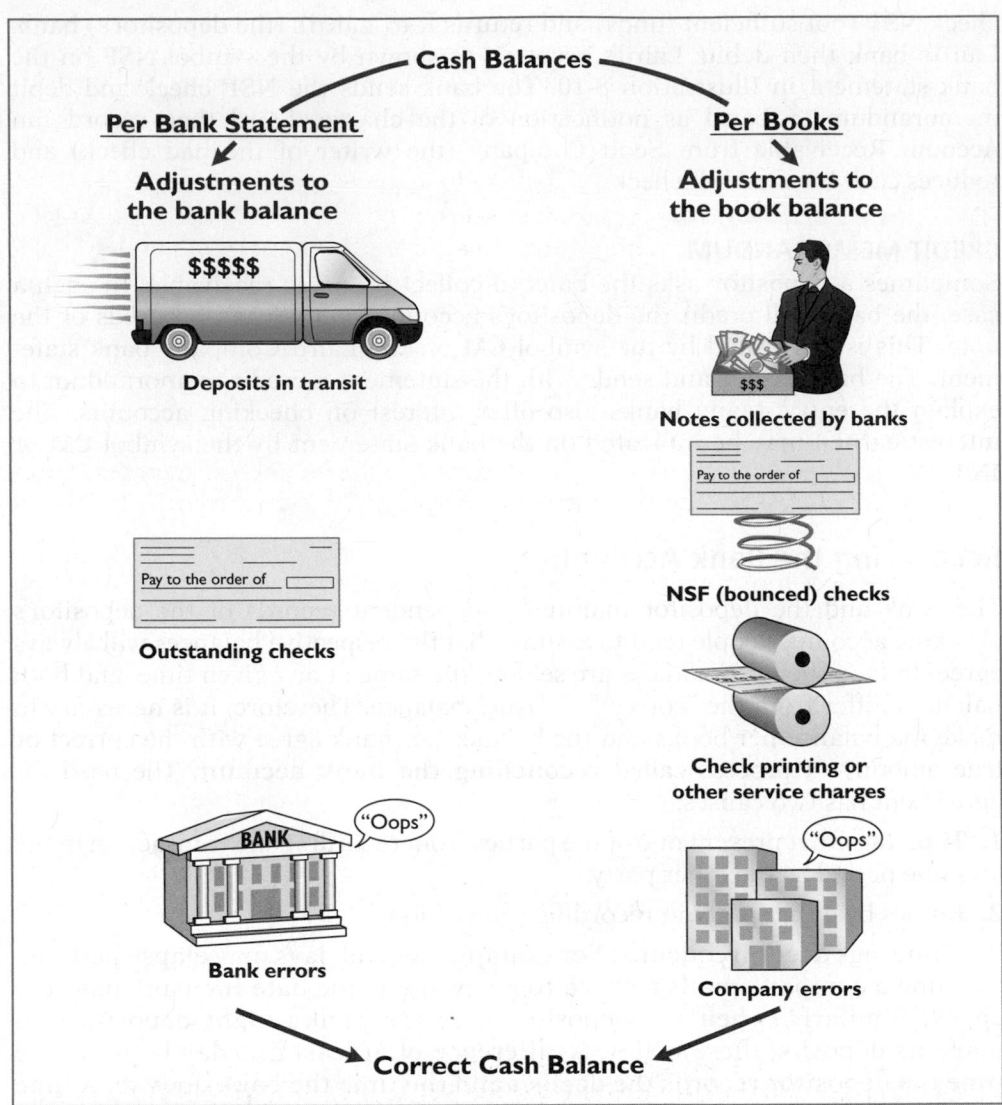

The following steps should reveal all the reconciling items that cause the difference between the two balances.

Step 1. Deposits in transit. Compare the individual deposits listed on the bank statement with deposits in transit from the preceding bank reconciliation and with the deposits per company records or duplicate deposit slips. Deposits recorded by the depositor that have not been recorded by the bank are the **deposits in transit**. Add these deposits to the balance per bank.

Step 2. Outstanding checks. Compare the paid checks shown on the bank statement with (a) checks outstanding from the previous bank reconciliation, and (b) checks issued by the company as recorded in the cash payments journal (or in the check register in your personal checkbook). Issued checks recorded by the company but that have not yet been paid by the bank are **outstanding checks**. Deduct outstanding checks from the balance per the bank.

Step 3. Errors. Note any errors discovered in the foregoing steps and list them in the appropriate section of the reconciliation schedule. For example, if the company mistakenly recorded as $169 a paid check correctly written

Helpful Hint Deposits in transit and outstanding checks are reconciling items because of time lags.

for $196, it would deduct the error of $27 from the balance per books. All errors made by the depositor are reconciling items in determining the adjusted cash balance per books. In contrast, all errors made by the bank are reconciling items in determining the adjusted cash balance per the bank.

Step 4. Bank memoranda. Trace bank memoranda to the depositor's records. List in the appropriate section of the reconciliation schedule any unrecorded memoranda. For example, the company would deduct from the balance per books a $5 debit memorandum for bank service charges. Similarly, it would add to the balance per books $32 of interest earned.

BANK RECONCILIATION ILLUSTRATED

The bank statement for Laird Company, in Illustration 8-10, shows a balance per bank of $15,907.45 on April 30, 2014. On this date the balance of cash per books is $11,589.45. Using the four reconciliation steps, Laird determines the following reconciling items.

Step 1. Deposits in transit: April 30 deposit (received by bank on May 1).	$2,201.40
Step 2. Outstanding checks: No. 453, $3,000.00; no. 457, $1,401.30; no. 460, $1,502.70.	5,904.00
Step 3. Errors: Laird wrote check no. 443 for $1,226.00 and the bank correctly paid that amount. However, Laird recorded the check as $1,262.00.	36.00
Step 4. Bank memoranda:	
a. Debit—NSF check from J. R. Baron for $425.60.	425.60
b. Debit—Charge for printing company checks $30.00.	30.00
c. Credit—Collection of note receivable for $1,000 plus interest earned $50, less bank collection fee $15.00.	1,035.00

Illustration 8-12 shows Laird's bank reconciliation.

Helpful Hint Note in the bank statement on page 396 that checks no. 459 and 461 have been paid but check no. 460 is not listed. Thus, this check is outstanding. If a complete bank statement were provided, checks no. 453 and 457 would also not be listed. The amounts for these three checks are obtained from the company's cash payments records.

LAIRD COMPANY
Bank Reconciliation
April 30, 2014

Cash balance per bank statement		$ 15,907.45
Add: Deposits in transit		2,201.40
		18,108.85
Less: Outstanding checks		
No. 453	$3,000.00	
No. 457	1,401.30	
No. 460	1,502.70	5,904.00
Adjusted cash balance per bank		**$12,204.85** ←
Cash balance per books		$ 11,589.45
Add: Collection of note receivable $1,000, plus		
interest earned $50, less collection fee $15	$1,035.00	
Error in recording check no. 443	36.00	1,071.00
		12,660.45
Less: NSF check	425.60	
Bank service charge	30.00	455.60
Adjusted cash balance per books		**$12,204.85** ←

Illustration 8-12
Bank reconciliation

Alternative Terminology
The terms *adjusted cash balance, true cash balance,* and *correct cash balance* are used interchangeably.

Helpful Hint The entries that follow are adjusting entries. In prior chapters, Cash was an account that did not require adjustment. That was a simplifying assumption for learning purposes because we had not yet explained a bank reconciliation.

ENTRIES FROM BANK RECONCILIATION

The company records each reconciling item used to determine the **adjusted cash balance per books**. **If the company does not journalize and post these items, the Cash account will not show the correct balance.** Laird Company would make the following entries on April 30.

COLLECTION OF NOTE RECEIVABLE. This entry involves four accounts. Assuming that the interest of $50 has not been accrued and the collection fee is charged to Miscellaneous Expense, the entry is:

Apr. 30	Cash	1,035.00	
	Miscellaneous Expense	15.00	
	Notes Receivable		1,000.00
	Interest Revenue		50.00
	(To record collection of note		
	receivable by bank)		

BOOK ERROR. The cash disbursements journal shows that check no. 443 was a payment on account to Andrea Company, a supplier. The correcting entry is:

Apr. 30	Cash	36.00	
	Accounts Payable—Andrea Company		36.00
	(To correct error in recording check		
	no. 443)		

NSF CHECK. As indicated earlier, an NSF check becomes an account receivable to the depositor. The entry is:

Apr. 30	Accounts Receivable—J. R. Baron	425.60	
	Cash		425.60
	(To record NSF check)		

BANK SERVICE CHARGES. Depositors debit check printing charges (DM) and other bank service charges (SC) to Miscellaneous Expense because they are usually nominal in amount. The entry is:

Apr. 30	Miscellaneous Expense	30.00	
	Cash		30.00
	(To record charge for printing company		
	checks)		

Instead of making four separate entries, Laird could combine them into one compound entry.

After Laird has posted the entries, the Cash account will show the following.

Illustration 8-13
Adjusted balance in Cash account

Cash					
Apr. 30 Bal.	11,589.45		Apr. 30		425.60
30	1,035.00		30		30.00
30	36.00				
Apr. 30 Bal.	**12,204.85**				

The adjusted cash balance in the ledger should agree with the adjusted cash balance per books in the bank reconciliation in Illustration 8-12 (page 399).

What entries does the bank make? If the company discovers any bank errors in preparing the reconciliation, it should notify the bank. The bank then can make the necessary corrections in its records. The bank does not make any entries for deposits in transit or outstanding checks. Only when these items reach the bank will the bank record these items.

Electronic Funds Transfer (EFT) System

It is not surprising that companies and banks have developed approaches to transfer funds among parties without the use of paper (deposit tickets, checks, etc.). Such procedures, called **electronic funds transfers (EFT)**, are disbursement systems that use wire, telephone, or computers to transfer cash balances from one location to another. Use of EFT is quite common. For example, many employees receive no formal payroll checks from their employers. Instead, employers send electronic payroll data to the appropriate banks. Also, individuals and companies now frequently make regular payments such as those for house, car, and utilities by EFT.

EFT transactions normally result in better internal control since no cash or checks are handled by company employees. This does not mean that opportunities for fraud are eliminated. In fact, the same basic principles related to internal control apply to EFT transfers. For example, without proper segregation of duties and authorizations, an employee might be able to redirect electronic payments into a personal bank account and conceal the theft with fraudulent accounting entries.

INVESTOR INSIGHT

Madoff's Ponzi Scheme

No recent fraud has generated more interest and rage than the one perpetrated by Bernard Madoff. Madoff was an elite New York investment fund manager who was highly regarded by securities regulators. Investors flocked to him because he delivered very steady returns of between 10% and 15%, no matter whether the market was going up or going down. However, for many years, Madoff did not actually invest the cash that people gave to him. Instead, he was running a Ponzi scheme: He paid returns to existing investors using cash received from new investors. As long as the size of his investment fund continued to grow from new investments at a rate that exceeded the amounts that he needed to pay out in returns, Madoff was able to operate his fraud smoothly. To conceal his misdeeds, he fabricated false investment statements that were provided to investors. In addition, Madoff hired an auditor that never verified the accuracy of the investment records but automatically issued unqualified opinions each year. Although a competing fund manager warned the SEC a number of times over a nearly 10-year period that he thought Madoff was engaged in fraud, the SEC never aggressively investigated the allegations. Investors, many of which were charitable organizations, lost more than $18 billion. Madoff was sentenced to a jail term of 150 years.

Mary Altaffer/©AP/Wide World Photos

? How was Madoff able to conceal such a giant fraud? (See page 424.)

> DO IT!

Bank Reconciliation

Sally Kist owns Linen Kist Fabrics. Sally asks you to explain how she should treat the following reconciling items when reconciling the company's bank account: (1) a debit memorandum for an NSF check, (2) a credit memorandum for a note collected by the bank, (3) outstanding checks, and (4) a deposit in transit.

Action Plan

✔ Understand the purpose of a bank reconciliation.

✔ Identify time lags and explain how they cause reconciling items.

Solution

Sally should treat the reconciling items as follows.

(1) NSF check: Deduct from balance per books.

(2) Collection of note: Add to balance per books.

(3) Outstanding checks: Deduct from balance per bank.

(4) Deposit in transit: Add to balance per bank.

Related exercise material: **BE8-11, BE8-12, BE8-13, BE8-14, E8-9, E8-10, E8-11, E8-12, E8-13, and** **DO IT! 8-4.**

✔ The Navigator

Reporting Cash

LEARNING OBJECTIVE 8

Explain the reporting of cash.

Cash consists of coins, currency (paper money), checks, money orders, and money on hand or on deposit in a bank or similar depository. Companies report cash in two different statements: the balance sheet and the statement of cash flows. The balance sheet reports the amount of cash available at a given point in time. The statement of cash flows shows the sources and uses of cash during a period of time. The statement of cash flows was introduced in Chapter 1 and will be discussed in much detail in Chapter 17. In this section, we discuss some important points regarding the presentation of cash in the balance sheet.

When presented in a balance sheet, cash on hand, cash in banks, and petty cash are often combined and reported simply as **Cash**. Because it is the most liquid asset owned by the company, cash is listed first in the current assets section of the balance sheet.

Cash Equivalents

Many companies use the designation "Cash and cash equivalents" in reporting cash. (See Illustration 8-14 for an example.) **Cash equivalents** are short-term, highly liquid investments that are both:

1. Readily convertible to known amounts of cash, and

2. So near their maturity that their market value is relatively insensitive to changes in interest rates.

Illustration 8-14
Balance sheet presentation of cash

Real World	**DELTA AIR LINES, INC.** Balance Sheet (partial) December 31, 2011 (in millions)	
Assets		
Current assets		
Cash and cash equivalents		**$2,657**
Short-term investments		958
Restricted cash		**305**
Accounts receivable and other net		1,563
Parts inventories		367
Prepaid expenses and other		1,879
Total current assets		$ 7,729

Examples of cash equivalents are Treasury bills, commercial paper (short-term corporate notes), and money market funds. All typically are purchased with cash that is in excess of immediate needs.

Occasionally, a company will have a net negative balance in its bank account. In this case, the company should report the negative balance among current liabilities. For example, farm equipment manufacturer Ag-Chem recently reported "Checks outstanding in excess of cash balances" of $2,145,000 among its current liabilities.

Restricted Cash

A company may have **restricted cash**, cash that is not available for general use but rather is restricted for a special purpose. For example, landfill companies are often required to maintain a fund of restricted cash to ensure they will have adequate resources to cover closing and clean-up costs at the end of a landfill site's useful life. McKesson Corp. recently reported restricted cash of $962 million to be paid out as the result of investor lawsuits.

Cash restricted in use should be reported separately on the balance sheet as restricted cash. If the company expects to use the restricted cash within the next year, it reports the amount as a current asset. When this is not the case, it reports the restricted funds as a noncurrent asset.

Illustration 8-14 shows restricted cash reported in the financial statements of Delta Air Lines. The company is required to maintain restricted cash as collateral to support insurance obligations related to workers' compensation claims. Delta does not have access to these funds for general use, and so it must report them separately, rather than as part of cash and cash equivalents.

> **Ethics Note**
>
> Recently, some companies were forced to restate their financial statements because they had too broadly interpreted which types of investments could be treated as cash equivalents. By reporting these items as cash equivalents, the companies made themselves look more liquid.

> ## > Comprehensive DO IT!

Poorten Company's bank statement for May 2014 shows the following data.

Balance 5/1	$12,650	Balance 5/31	$14,280
Debit memorandum:		Credit memorandum:	
NSF check	$175	Collection of note receivable	$505

The cash balance per books at May 31 is $13,319. Your review of the data reveals the following.

1. The NSF check was from Copple Co., a customer.

2. The note collected by the bank was a $500, 3-month, 12% note. The bank charged a $10 collection fee. No interest has been accrued.

3. Outstanding checks at May 31 total $2,410.

4. Deposits in transit at May 31 total $1,752.

5. A Poorten Company check for $352, dated May 10, cleared the bank on May 25. The company recorded this check, which was a payment on account, for $325.

Instructions
(a) Prepare a bank reconciliation at May 31.
(b) Journalize the entries required by the reconciliation.

Solution to Comprehensive DO IT!

Action Plan

✔ Follow the four steps in the reconciliation procedure (pp. 398–399).

✔ Work carefully to minimize mathematical errors in the reconciliation.

✔ Prepare entries from reconciling items per books.

✔ Make sure the cash ledger balance after posting the reconciling entries agrees with the adjusted cash balance per books.

(a)

POORTEN COMPANY
Bank Reconciliation
May 31, 2014

Cash balance per bank statement		$14,280
Add: Deposits in transit		1,752
		16,032
Less: Outstanding checks		2,410
Adjusted cash balance per bank		$13,622
Cash balance per books		$13,319
Add: Collection of note receivable $500, plus $15		
interest, less collection fee $10		505
		13,824
Less: NSF check	$175	
Error in recording check	27	202
Adjusted cash balance per books		$13,622

(b)

May 31	Cash	505	
	Miscellaneous Expense	10	
	Notes Receivable		500
	Interest Revenue		15
	(To record collection of note by bank)		
31	Accounts Receivable—Copple Co.	175	
	Cash		175
	(To record NSF check from Copple Co.)		
31	Accounts Payable	27	
	Cash		27
	(To correct error in recording check)		

✔ The Navigator

SUMMARY OF LEARNING OBJECTIVES
✔ The Navigator

1 Define fraud and internal control. A fraud is a dishonest act by an employee that results in personal benefit to the employee at a cost to the employer. The fraud triangle refers to the three factors that contribute to fraudulent activity by employees: opportunity, financial pressure, and rationalization. Internal control consists of all the related methods and measures adopted within an organization to safeguard its assets, enhance the reliability of its accounting records, increase efficiency of operations, and ensure compliance with laws and regulations.

2 Identify the principles of internal control activities. The principles of internal control are establishment of responsibility; segregation of duties; documentation procedures; physical controls; independent internal verification; and human resource controls such as bonding and requiring employees to take vacations.

3 Explain the applications of internal control principles to cash receipts. Internal controls over cash receipts include (a) designating specific personnel to handle

cash; (b) assigning different individuals to receive cash, record cash, and maintain custody of cash; (c) using remittance advices for mail receipts, cash register tapes for over-the-counter receipts, and deposit slips for bank deposits; (d) using company safes and bank vaults to store cash with access limited to authorized personnel, and using cash registers in executing over-the-counter receipts; (e) making independent daily counts of register receipts and daily comparison of total receipts with total deposits; and (f) bonding personnel that handle cash and requiring them to take vacations.

4 Explain the applications of internal control principles to cash disbursements. Internal controls over cash disbursements include (a) having specific individuals such as the treasurer authorized to sign checks and approve invoices; (b) assigning different individuals to approve items for payment, pay the items, and record the payment; (c) using prenumbered checks and accounting for all checks, with each check supported by an approved invoice; (d) storing blank checks in a safe or vault with access restricted to authorized personnel, and using a check-writing machine to imprint amounts on checks; (e) comparing each check with the approved invoice before issuing the check, and making monthly reconciliations of bank and book balances; and (f) bonding personnel who handle cash, requiring employees to take vacations, and conducting background checks.

5 Describe the operation of a petty cash fund. Companies operate a petty cash fund to pay relatively small amounts of cash. They must establish the fund, make payments from the fund, and replenish the fund when the cash in the fund reaches a minimum level.

6 Indicate the control features of a bank account. A bank account contributes to good internal control by providing physical controls for the storage of cash. It minimizes the amount of currency that a company must keep on hand, and it creates a double record of a depositor's bank transactions.

7 Prepare a bank reconciliation. It is customary to reconcile the balance per books and balance per bank to their adjusted balances. The steps in the reconciling process are to determine deposits in transit, outstanding checks, errors by the depositor or the bank, and unrecorded bank memoranda.

8 Explain the reporting of cash. Companies list cash first in the current assets section of the balance sheet. In some cases, they report cash together with cash equivalents. Cash restricted for a special purpose is reported separately as a current asset or as a noncurrent asset, depending on when the cash is expected to be used.

GLOSSARY

Bank reconciliation The process of comparing the bank's balance of an account with the company's balance and explaining any differences to make them agree. (p. 394).

Bank service charge A fee charged by a bank for the use of its services. (p. 396).

Bank statement A monthly statement from the bank that shows the depositor's bank transactions and balances. (p. 395).

Bonding Obtaining insurance protection against misappropriation of assets by employees. (p. 383).

Cash Resources that consist of coins, currency, checks, money orders, and money on hand or on deposit in a bank or similar depository. (p. 402).

Cash equivalents Short-term, highly liquid investments that can be converted to a specific amount of cash. (p. 402).

Check A written order signed by a bank depositor, directing the bank to pay a specified sum of money to a designated recipient. (p. 394).

Deposits in transit Deposits recorded by the depositor but not yet recorded by the bank. (p. 398).

Electronic funds transfer (EFT) A disbursement system that uses wire, telephone, or computers to transfer funds from one location to another. (p. 401).

Fraud A dishonest act by an employee that results in personal benefit to the employee at a cost to the employer. (p. 376).

Fraud triangle The three factors that contribute to fraudulent activity by employees: opportunity, financial pressure, and rationalization. (p. 376).

Internal auditors Company employees who continuously evaluate the effectiveness of the company's internal control system. (p. 383).

Internal control All of the related methods and activities adopted within an organization to safeguard assets and enhance the accuracy and reliability of accounting records. (p. 377).

NSF check A check that is not paid by a bank because of insufficient funds in a customer's bank account. (p. 397).

Outstanding checks Checks issued and recorded by a company but not yet paid by the bank. (p. 398).

Petty cash fund A cash fund used to pay relatively small amounts. (p. 390).

Restricted cash Cash that must be used for a special purpose. (p. 403).

Sarbanes-Oxley Act (SOX) Regulations passed by Congress to try to reduce unethical corporate behavior. (p. 376).

Voucher An authorization form prepared for each payment in a voucher system. (p. 389).

Voucher system A network of approvals by authorized individuals acting independently to ensure that all disbursements by check are proper. (p. 389).

Self-Test, Brief Exercises, Exercises, Problem Set A, and many more components are available for practice in *WileyPLUS*.

SELF-TEST QUESTIONS

Answers are on page 425.

(LO 1) **1.** Which of the following is **not** an element of the fraud triangle?
   (a) Rationalization.   **(c)** Segregation of duties.
   (b) Financial pressure.   **(d)** Opportunity.

2. An organization uses internal control to enhance (LO 1) the accuracy and reliability of accounting records and to:
   (a) safeguard assets.
   (b) eliminate fraud.

(c) produce correct financial statements.

(d) deter employee dishonesty.

(LO 1) 3. Which of the following was **not** a result of the Sarbanes-Oxley Act?

(a) Companies must file financial statements with the Internal Revenue Service.

(b) All publicly traded companies must maintain adequate internal controls.

(c) The Public Company Accounting Oversight Board was created to establish auditing standards and regulate auditor activity.

(d) Corporate executives and board of directors must ensure that controls are reliable and effective, and they can be fined or imprisoned for failure to do so.

(LO 2) 4. The principles of internal control do **not** include:

(a) establishment of responsibility.

(b) documentation procedures.

(c) management responsibility.

(d) independent internal verification.

(LO 2) 5. Physical controls do **not** include:

(a) safes and vaults to store cash.

(b) independent bank reconciliations.

(c) locked warehouses for inventories.

(d) bank safety deposit boxes for important papers.

(LO 2) 6. Which of the following control activities is **not** relevant when a company uses a computerized (rather than manual) accounting system?

(a) Establishment of responsibility.

(b) Segregation of duties.

(c) Independent internal verification.

(d) All of these control activities are relevant to a computerized system.

(LO 3) 7. Permitting only designated personnel to handle cash receipts is an application of the principle of:

(a) segregation of duties.

(b) establishment of responsibility.

(c) independent internal verification.

(d) human resource controls.

(LO 4) 8. The use of prenumbered checks in disbursing cash is an application of the principle of:

(a) establishment of responsibility.

(b) segregation of duties.

(c) physical controls.

(d) documentation procedures.

(LO 5) 9. A company writes a check to replenish a $100 petty cash fund when the fund contains receipts of $94 and $4 in cash. In recording the check, the company should:

(a) debit Cash Over and Short for $2.

(b) debit Petty Cash for $94.

(c) credit Cash for $94.

(d) credit Petty Cash for $2.

(LO 6) 10. The control features of a bank account do **not** include:

(a) having bank auditors verify the correctness of the bank balance per books.

(b) minimizing the amount of cash that must be kept on hand.

(c) providing a double record of all bank transactions.

(d) safeguarding cash by using a bank as a depository.

(LO 7) 11. In a bank reconciliation, deposits in transit are:

(a) deducted from the book balance.

(b) added to the book balance.

(c) added to the bank balance.

(d) deducted from the bank balance.

(LO 7) 12. The reconciling item in a bank reconciliation that will result in an adjusting entry by the depositor is:

(a) outstanding checks.   (c) a bank error.

(b) deposit in transit.   (d) bank service charges.

(LO 8) 13. Which of the following items in a cash drawer at November 30 is **not** cash?

(a) Money orders.

(b) Coins and currency.

(c) An NSF check.

(d) A customer check dated November 28.

(LO 8) 14. Which of the following statements correctly describes the reporting of cash?

(a) Cash cannot be combined with cash equivalents.

(b) Restricted cash funds may be combined with cash.

(c) Cash is listed first in the current assets section.

(d) Restricted cash funds cannot be reported as a current asset.

Go to the book's companion website, www.wiley.com/college/weygandt, for additional Self-Test Questions.

✔ **The Navigator**

QUESTIONS

1. A local bank reported that it lost $150,000 as the result of an employee fraud. Edward Jasso is not clear on what is meant by an "employee fraud." Explain the meaning of fraud to Edward and give an example of frauds that might occur at a bank.

2. Fraud experts often say that there are three primary factors that contribute to employee fraud. Identify the three factors and explain what is meant by each.

3. Identify and describe the five components of a good internal control system.

4. "Internal control is concerned only with enhancing the accuracy of the accounting records." Do you agree? Explain.

5. What principles of internal control apply to most organizations?

6. At the corner grocery store, all sales clerks make change out of one cash register drawer. Is this a violation of internal control? Why?

7. Liz Kelso is reviewing the principle of segregation of duties. What are the two common applications of this principle?

8. How do documentation procedures contribute to good internal control?

9. What internal control objectives are met by physical controls?

10. (a) Explain the control principle of independent internal verification. (b) What practices are important in applying this principle?

11. The management of Nickle Company asks you, as the company accountant, to explain (a) the concept of reasonable assurance in internal control and (b) the importance of the human factor in internal control.

12. Riverside Fertilizer Co. owns the following assets at the balance sheet date.

Cash in bank savings account	$ 8,000
Cash on hand	850
Cash refund due from the IRS	1,000
Checking account balance	14,000
Postdated checks	500

What amount should Riverside report as cash in the balance sheet?

13. What principle(s) of internal control is (are) involved in making daily cash counts of over-the-counter receipts?

14. Seaton Department Stores has just installed new electronic cash registers in its stores. How do cash registers improve internal control over cash receipts?

15. At Kellum Wholesale Company, two mail clerks open all mail receipts. How does this strengthen internal control?

16. "To have maximum effective internal control over cash disbursements, all payments should be made by check." Is this true? Explain.

17. Ken Deangelo Company's internal controls over cash disbursements provide for the treasurer to sign checks imprinted by a check-writing machine in indelible ink after comparing the check with the approved invoice. Identify the internal control principles that are present in these controls.

18. How do the principles of (a) physical controls and (b) documentation controls apply to cash disbursements?

19. (a) What is a voucher system? (b) What principles of internal control apply to a voucher system?

20. What is the essential feature of an electronic funds transfer (EFT) procedure?

21. (a) Identify the three activities that pertain to a petty cash fund, and indicate an internal control principle that is applicable to each activity. (b) When are journal entries required in the operation of a petty cash fund?

22. "The use of a bank contributes significantly to good internal control over cash." Is this true? Why or why not?

23. Anna Korte is confused about the lack of agreement between the cash balance per books and the balance per bank. Explain the causes for the lack of agreement to Anna, and give an example of each cause.

24. What are the four steps involved in finding differences between the balance per books and balance per bank?

25. Heather Kemp asks your help concerning an NSF check. Explain to Heather (a) what an NSF check is, (b) how it is treated in a bank reconciliation, and (c) whether it will require an adjusting entry.

26. (a) "Cash equivalents are the same as cash." Do you agree? Explain. (b) How should restricted cash funds be reported on the balance sheet?

27. At what amount does Apple report cash and cash equivalents in its 2011 consolidated balance sheet?

BRIEF EXERCISES

BE8-1 Match each situation with the fraud triangle factor—opportunity, financial pressure, or rationalization—that best describes it.

Identify fraud triangle concepts.

(LO 1)

1. An employee's monthly credit card payments are nearly 75% of his or her monthly earnings.
2. An employee earns minimum wage at a firm that has reported record earnings for each of the last five years.
3. An employee has an expensive gambling habit.
4. An employee has check-writing and -signing responsibilities for a small company, as well as reconciling the bank account.

BE8-2 Shelly Eckert has prepared the following list of statements about internal control.

Indicate internal control concepts.

(LO 1)

1. One of the objectives of internal control is to safeguard assets from employee theft, robbery, and unauthorized use.
2. One of the objectives of internal control is to enhance the accuracy and reliability of the accounting records.
3. No laws require U.S. corporations to maintain an adequate system of internal control.

Identify each statement as true or false. If false, indicate how to correct the statement.

BE8-3 Jessica Mahan is the new owner of Penny Parking. She has heard about internal control but is not clear about its importance for her business. Explain to Jessica the four purposes of internal control and give her one application of each purpose for Penny Parking.

Explain the importance of internal control.

(LO 1)

Identify internal control principles.
(LO 2)

BE8-4 The internal control procedures in Valentine Company provide that:

1. Employees who have physical custody of assets do not have access to the accounting records.
2. Each month, the assets on hand are compared to the accounting records by an internal auditor.
3. A prenumbered shipping document is prepared for each shipment of goods to customers.

Identify the principles of internal control that are being followed.

Identify the internal control principles applicable to cash receipts.
(LO 3)

BE8-5 Rosenquist Company has the following internal control procedures over cash receipts. Identify the internal control principle that is applicable to each procedure.

1. All over-the-counter receipts are entered in cash registers.
2. All cashiers are bonded.
3. Daily cash counts are made by cashier department supervisors.
4. The duties of receiving cash, recording cash, and custody of cash are assigned to different individuals.
5. Only cashiers may operate cash registers.

Make journal entries for cash overage and shortfall.
(LO 3)

BE8-6 The cash register tape for Bluestem Industries reported sales of $6,871.50. Record the journal entry that would be necessary for each of the following situations. (a) Cash to be accounted for exceeds cash on hand by $50.75. (b) Cash on hand exceeds cash to be accounted for by $28.32.

Make journal entry using cash count sheet.
(LO 3)

BE8-7 While examining cash receipts information, the accounting department determined the following information: opening cash balance $160, cash on hand $1,125.74, and cash sales per register tape $980.83. Prepare the required journal entry based upon the cash count sheet.

Identify the internal control principles applicable to cash disbursements.
(LO 4)

BE8-8 Pennington Company has the following internal control procedures over cash disbursements. Identify the internal control principle that is applicable to each procedure.

1. Company checks are prenumbered.
2. The bank statement is reconciled monthly by an internal auditor.
3. Blank checks are stored in a safe in the treasurer's office.
4. Only the treasurer or assistant treasurer may sign checks.
5. Check-signers are not allowed to record cash disbursement transactions.

Prepare entry to replenish a petty cash fund.
(LO 5)

BE8-9 On March 20, Dody's petty cash fund of $100 is replenished when the fund contains $9 in cash and receipts for postage $52, freight-out $26, and travel expense $10. Prepare the journal entry to record the replenishment of the petty cash fund.

Identify the control features of a bank account.
(LO 6)

BE8-10 Lance Bachman is uncertain about the control features of a bank account. Explain the control benefits of (a) a check and (b) a bank statement.

Indicate location of reconciling items in a bank reconciliation.
(LO 7)

BE8-11 The following reconciling items are applicable to the bank reconciliation for Ellington Company: (1) outstanding checks, (2) bank debit memorandum for service charge, (3) bank credit memorandum for collecting a note for the depositor, and (4) deposits in transit. Indicate how each item should be shown on a bank reconciliation.

Identify reconciling items that require adjusting entries.
(LO 7)

BE8-12 Using the data in BE8-11, indicate (a) the items that will result in an adjustment to the depositor's records and (b) why the other items do not require adjustment.

Prepare partial bank reconciliation.
(LO 7)

BE8-13 At July 31, Ramirez Company has the following bank information: cash balance per bank $7,420, outstanding checks $762, deposits in transit $1,620, and a bank service charge $20. Determine the adjusted cash balance per bank at July 31.

Prepare partial bank reconciliation.
(LO 7)

BE8-14 At August 31, Pratt Company has a cash balance per books of $9,500 and the following additional data from the bank statement: charge for printing Pratt Company checks $35, interest earned on checking account balance $40, and outstanding checks $800. Determine the adjusted cash balance per books at August 31.

Explain the statement presentation of cash balances.
(LO 8)

BE8-15 Zhang Company has the following cash balances: Cash in Bank $15,742, Payroll Bank Account $6,000, and Plant Expansion Fund Cash $25,000 to be used two years from now. Explain how each balance should be reported on the balance sheet.

> DO IT! Review

DO IT! 8-1 Identify which control activity is violated in each of the following situations, and explain how the situation creates an opportunity for fraud or inappropriate accounting practices.

1. Once a month, the sales department sends sales invoices to the accounting department to be recorded.
2. Leah Hutcherson orders merchandise for Rice Lake Company; he also receives merchandise and authorizes payment for merchandise.
3. Several clerks at Great Foods use the same cash register drawer.

Identify violations of control activities.
(LO 2)

DO IT! 8-2 Gary Stanten is concerned with control over mail receipts at Gary's Sporting Goods. All mail receipts are opened by Al Krane. Al sends the checks to the accounting department, where they are stamped "For Deposit Only." The accounting department records and deposits the mail receipts weekly. Gary asks for your help in installing a good system of internal control over mail receipts.

Design system of internal control over cash receipts.
(LO 3)

DO IT! 8-3 Wilkinson Company established a $100 petty cash fund on August 1. On August 31, the fund had $7 cash remaining and petty cash receipts for postage $31, office supplies $42, and miscellaneous expense $16. Prepare journal entries to establish the fund on August 1 and replenish the fund on August 31.

Make journal entries for petty cash fund.
(LO 5)

DO IT! 8-4 Roger Richman owns Richman Blankets. Richman asks you to explain how he should treat the following reconciling items when reconciling the company's bank account.

1. Outstanding checks.
2. A deposit in transit.
3. The bank charged to our account a check written by another company.
4. A debit memorandum for a bank service charge.

Explain treatment of items in bank reconciliation.
(LO 7)

EXERCISES

E8-1 Eve Herschel is the owner of Herschel's Pizza. Herschel's is operated strictly on a carryout basis. Customers pick up their orders at a counter where a clerk exchanges the pizza for cash. While at the counter, the customer can see other employees making the pizzas and the large ovens in which the pizzas are baked.

Identify the principles of internal control.
(LO 2)

Instructions
Identify the six principles of internal control and give an example of each principle that you might observe when picking up your pizza. (*Note:* It may not be possible to observe all the principles.)

E8-2 The following control procedures are used at Torres Company for over-the-counter cash receipts.

1. To minimize the risk of robbery, cash in excess of $100 is stored in an unlocked attaché case in the stock room until it is deposited in the bank.
2. All over-the-counter receipts are registered by three clerks who use a cash register with a single cash drawer.
3. The company accountant makes the bank deposit and then records the day's receipts.
4. At the end of each day, the total receipts are counted by the cashier on duty and reconciled to the cash register total.
5. Cashiers are experienced; they are not bonded.

Identify internal control weaknesses over cash receipts and suggest improvements.
(LO 2, 3)

Instructions
(a) For each procedure, explain the weakness in internal control, and identify the control principle that is violated.
(b) For each weakness, suggest a change in procedure that will result in good internal control.

Identify internal control weaknesses over cash disbursements and suggest improvements.

(LO 2, 4)

E8-3 The following control procedures are used in Mendy Lang's Boutique Shoppe for cash disbursements.

1. The company accountant prepares the bank reconciliation and reports any discrepancies to the owner.
2. The store manager personally approves all payments before signing and issuing checks.
3. Each week, 100 company checks are left in an unmarked envelope on a shelf behind the cash register.
4. After payment, bills are filed in a paid invoice folder.
5. The company checks are unnumbered.

Instructions
(a) For each procedure, explain the weakness in internal control, and identify the internal control principle that is violated.
(b) For each weakness, suggest a change in the procedure that will result in good internal control.

Identify internal control weaknesses for cash disbursements and suggest improvements.

(LO 4)

E8-4 At Danner Company, checks are not prenumbered because both the purchasing agent and the treasurer are authorized to issue checks. Each signer has access to unissued checks kept in an unlocked file cabinet. The purchasing agent pays all bills pertaining to goods purchased for resale. Prior to payment, the purchasing agent determines that the goods have been received and verifies the mathematical accuracy of the vendor's invoice. After payment, the invoice is filed by the vendor name, and the purchasing agent records the payment in the cash disbursements journal. The treasurer pays all other bills following approval by authorized employees. After payment, the treasurer stamps all bills PAID, files them by payment date, and records the checks in the cash disbursements journal. Danner Company maintains one checking account that is reconciled by the treasurer.

Instructions
(a) List the weaknesses in internal control over cash disbursements.
(b) ━━━━ Write a memo to the company treasurer indicating your recommendations for improvement.

Indicate whether procedure is good or weak internal control.

(LO 2, 3, 4)

E8-5 Listed below are five procedures followed by Eikenberry Company.

1. Several individuals operate the cash register using the same register drawer.
2. A monthly bank reconciliation is prepared by someone who has no other cash responsibilities.
3. Joe Cockrell writes checks and also records cash payment journal entries.
4. One individual orders inventory, while a different individual authorizes payments.
5. Unnumbered sales invoices from credit sales are forwarded to the accounting department every four weeks for recording.

Instructions
Indicate whether each procedure is an example of good internal control or of weak internal control. If it is an example of good internal control, indicate which internal control principle is being followed. If it is an example of weak internal control, indicate which internal control principle is violated. Use the table below.

Procedure	IC Good or Weak?	Related Internal Control Principle
1.		
2.		
3.		
4.		
5.		

Indicate whether procedure is good or weak internal control.

(LO 2, 3, 4)

E8-6 Listed below are five procedures followed by Gilmore Company.

1. Employees are required to take vacations.
2. Any member of the sales department can approve credit sales.
3. Paul Jaggard ships goods to customers, bills customers, and receives payment from customers.
4. Total cash receipts are compared to bank deposits daily by someone who has no other cash responsibilities.
5. Time clocks are used for recording time worked by employees.

Instructions

Indicate whether each procedure is an example of good internal control or of weak internal control. If it is an example of good internal control, indicate which internal control principle is being followed. If it is an example of weak internal control, indicate which internal control principle is violated. Use the table below.

Procedure	IC Good or Weak?	Related Internal Control Principle
1.		
2.		
3.		
4.		
5.		

E8-7 Setterstrom Company established a petty cash fund on May 1, cashing a check for $100. The company reimbursed the fund on June 1 and July 1 with the following results.

Prepare journal entries for a petty cash fund.

(LO 5)

June 1: Cash in fund $1.75. Receipts: delivery expense $31.25; postage expense $39.00; and miscellaneous expense $25.00.

July 1: Cash in fund $3.25. Receipts: delivery expense $21.00; entertainment expense $51.00; and miscellaneous expense $24.75.

On July 10, Setterstrom increased the fund from $100 to $130.

Instructions

Prepare journal entries for Setterstrom Company for May 1, June 1, July 1, and July 10.

E8-8 Horvath Company uses an imprest petty cash system. The fund was established on March 1 with a balance of $100. During March, the following petty cash receipts were found in the petty cash box.

Prepare journal entries for a petty cash fund.

(LO 5)

Date	Receipt No.	For	Amount
3/5	1	Stamp Inventory	$39
7	2	Freight-Out	21
9	3	Miscellaneous Expense	6
11	4	Travel Expense	24
14	5	Miscellaneous Expense	5

The fund was replenished on March 15 when the fund contained $2 in cash. On March 20, the amount in the fund was increased to $175.

Instructions

Journalize the entries in March that pertain to the operation of the petty cash fund.

E8-9 Don Wyatt is unable to reconcile the bank balance at January 31. Don's reconciliation is as follows.

Prepare bank reconciliation and adjusting entries.

(LO 7)

Cash balance per bank	$3,560.20
Add: NSF check	490.00
Less: Bank service charge	25.00
Adjusted balance per bank	$4,025.20
Cash balance per books	$3,875.20
Less: Deposits in transit	530.00
Add: Outstanding checks	730.00
Adjusted balance per books	$4,075.20

Instructions

(a) Prepare a correct bank reconciliation.

(b) Journalize the entries required by the reconciliation.

E8-10 On April 30, the bank reconciliation of Westbrook Company shows three outstanding checks: no. 254, $650; no. 255, $620; and no. 257, $410. The May bank statement and the May cash payments journal show the following.

Determine outstanding checks.

(LO 7)

Bank Statement		
Checks Paid		
Date	Check No.	Amount
5/4	254	$650
5/2	257	410
5/17	258	159
5/12	259	275
5/20	261	500
5/29	263	480
5/30	262	750

Cash Payments Journal		
Checks Issued		
Date	Check No.	Amount
5/2	258	$159
5/5	259	275
5/10	260	890
5/15	261	500
5/22	262	750
5/24	263	480
5/29	264	560

Instructions

Using Step 2 in the reconciliation procedure, list the outstanding checks at May 31.

Prepare bank reconciliation and adjusting entries.

(LO 7)

E8-11 The following information pertains to Crane Video Company.

1. Cash balance per bank, July 31, $7,263.
2. July bank service charge not recorded by the depositor $28.
3. Cash balance per books, July 31, $7,284.
4. Deposits in transit, July 31, $1,300.
5. Bank collected $700 note for Crane in July, plus interest $36, less fee $20. The collection has not been recorded by Crane, and no interest has been accrued.
6. Outstanding checks, July 31, $591.

Instructions

(a) Prepare a bank reconciliation at July 31.
(b) Journalize the adjusting entries at July 31 on the books of Crane Video Company.

Prepare bank reconciliation and adjusting entries.

(LO 7)

E8-12 The information below relates to the Cash account in the ledger of Minton Company.

Balance September 1—$17,150; Cash deposited—$64,000.
Balance September 30—$17,404; Checks written—$63,746.

The September bank statement shows a balance of $16,422 on September 30 and the following memoranda.

Credits		Debits	
Collection of $2,500 note plus interest $30	$2,530	NSF check: Richard Nance	$425
Interest earned on checking account	$45	Safety deposit box rent	$65

At September 30, deposits in transit were $5,450, and outstanding checks totaled $2,383.

Instructions

(a) Prepare the bank reconciliation at September 30.
(b) Prepare the adjusting entries at September 30, assuming (1) the NSF check was from a customer on account, and (2) no interest had been accrued on the note.

Compute deposits in transit and outstanding checks for two bank reconciliations.

(LO 7)

E8-13 The cash records of Dawes Company show the following four situations.

1. The June 30 bank reconciliation indicated that deposits in transit total $920. During July, the general ledger account Cash shows deposits of $15,750, but the bank statement indicates that only $15,600 in deposits were received during the month.
2. The June 30 bank reconciliation also reported outstanding checks of $680. During the month of July, Dawes Company's books show that $17,200 of checks were issued. The bank statement showed that $16,400 of checks cleared the bank in July.
3. In September, deposits per the bank statement totaled $26,700, deposits per books were $26,400, and deposits in transit at September 30 were $2,100.
4. In September, cash disbursements per books were $23,700, checks clearing the bank were $25,000, and outstanding checks at September 30 were $2,100.

There were no bank debit or credit memoranda. No errors were made by either the bank or Dawes Company.

Instructions

Answer the following questions.

(a) In situation (1), what were the deposits in transit at July 31?
(b) In situation (2), what were the outstanding checks at July 31?

(c) In situation (3), what were the deposits in transit at August 31?

(d) In situation (4), what were the outstanding checks at August 31?

E8-14 Wynn Company has recorded the following items in its financial records.

Show presentation of cash in financial statements.

(LO 8)

Cash in bank	$ 42,000
Cash in plant expansion fund	100,000
Cash on hand	12,000
Highly liquid investments	34,000
Petty cash	500
Receivables from customers	89,000
Stock investments	61,000

The highly liquid investments had maturities of 3 months or less when they were purchased. The stock investments will be sold in the next 6 to 12 months. The plant expansion project will begin in 3 years.

Instructions

(a) What amount should Wynn report as "Cash and cash equivalents" on its balance sheet?

(b) Where should the items not included in part (a) be reported on the balance sheet?

(c) What disclosures should Wynn make in its financial statements concerning "cash and cash equivalents"?

EXERCISES: SET B AND CHALLENGE EXERCISES

Visit the book's companion website, at **www.wiley.com/college/weygandt**, and choose the Student Companion site to access Exercise Set B and Challenge Exercises.

PROBLEMS: SET A

P8-1A Bolz Office Supply Company recently changed its system of internal control over cash disbursements. The system includes the following features.

Identify internal control principles over cash disbursements.

(LO 2, 4)

Instead of being unnumbered and manually prepared, all checks must now be pre-numbered and written by using the new check-writing machine purchased by the company. Before a check can be issued, each invoice must have the approval of Kathy Moon, the purchasing agent, and Robin Self, the receiving department supervisor. Checks must be signed by either Jennifer Edwards, the treasurer, or Rich Woodruff, the assistant treasurer. Before signing a check, the signer is expected to compare the amount of the check with the amount on the invoice.

After signing a check, the signer stamps the invoice PAID and inserts within the stamp, the date, check number, and amount of the check. The "paid" invoice is then sent to the accounting department for recording.

Blank checks are stored in a safe in the treasurer's office. The combination to the safe is known only by the treasurer and assistant treasurer. Each month, the bank statement is reconciled with the bank balance per books by the assistant chief accountant. All employees who handle or account for cash are bonded.

Instructions

Identify the internal control principles and their application to cash disbursements of Bolz Office Supply Company.

P8-2A Forney Company maintains a petty cash fund for small expenditures. The following transactions occurred over a 2-month period.

Journalize and post petty cash fund transactions.

(LO 5)

July	1	Established petty cash fund by writing a check on Scranton Bank for $200.
	15	Replenished the petty cash fund by writing a check for $196.00. On this date the fund consisted of $4.00 in cash and the following petty cash receipts: freight-out $92.00, postage expense $42.40, entertainment expense $46.60, and miscellaneous expense $11.20.

31   Replenished the petty cash fund by writing a check for $192.00. At this date, the fund consisted of $8.00 in cash and the following petty cash receipts: freight-out $82.10, charitable contributions expense $45.00, postage expense $25.50, and miscellaneous expense $39.40.

Aug. 15   Replenished the petty cash fund by writing a check for $187.00. On this date, the fund consisted of $13.00 in cash and the following petty cash receipts: freight-out $77.60, entertainment expense $43.00, postage expense $33.00, and miscellaneous expense $37.00.

16   Increased the amount of the petty cash fund to $300 by writing a check for $100.

31   Replenished the petty cash fund by writing a check for $284.00. On this date, the fund consisted of $16 in cash and the following petty cash receipts: postage expense $140.00, travel expense $95.60, and freight-out $47.10.

Instructions

(a) Journalize the petty cash transactions.

(b) Post to the Petty Cash account.

(c) What internal control features exist in a petty cash fund?

(a) July 15, Cash short $3.80

(b) Aug. 31 balance $300

Prepare a bank reconciliation and adjusting entries.

(LO 7)

P8-3A On May 31, 2014, Reber Company had a cash balance per books of $6,781.50. The bank statement from New York State Bank on that date showed a balance of $6,404.60. A comparison of the statement with the Cash account revealed the following facts.

1. The statement included a debit memo of $40 for the printing of additional company checks.

2. Cash sales of $836.15 on May 12 were deposited in the bank. The cash receipts journal entry and the deposit slip were incorrectly made for $886.15. The bank credited Reber Company for the correct amount.

3. Outstanding checks at May 31 totaled $576.25. Deposits in transit were $2,416.15.

4. On May 18, the company issued check No. 1181 for $685 to Lynda Carsen on account. The check, which cleared the bank in May, was incorrectly journalized and posted by Reber Company for $658.

5. A $3,000 note receivable was collected by the bank for Reber Company on May 31 plus $80 interest. The bank charged a collection fee of $20. No interest has been accrued on the note.

6. Included with the cancelled checks was a check issued by Stiner Company to Ted Cress for $800 that was incorrectly charged to Reber Company by the bank.

7. On May 31, the bank statement showed an NSF charge of $680 for a check issued by Sue Allison, a customer, to Reber Company on account.

Instructions

(a) Prepare the bank reconciliation at May 31, 2014.

(b) Prepare the necessary adjusting entries for Reber Company at May 31, 2014.

(a) Adjusted cash balance per bank $9,044.50

Prepare a bank reconciliation and adjusting entries from detailed data.

(LO 7)

P8-4A The bank portion of the bank reconciliation for Langer Company at November 30, 2014, was as follows.

LANGER COMPANY
Bank Reconciliation
November 30, 2014

Cash balance per bank		$14,367.90
Add: Deposits in transit		2,530.20
		16,898.10

Less: Outstanding checks		
Check Number	Check Amount	
3451	$2,260.40	
3470	720.10	
3471	844.50	
3472	1,426.80	
3474	1,050.00	6,301.80
Adjusted cash balance per bank		$10,596.30

The adjusted cash balance per bank agreed with the cash balance per books at November 30.

The December bank statement showed the following checks and deposits.

Bank Statement				
Checks			**Deposits**	
Date	Number	Amount	Date	Amount
12-1	3451	$ 2,260.40	12-1	$ 2,530.20
12-2	3471	844.50	12-4	1,211.60
12-7	3472	1,426.80	12-8	2,365.10
12-4	3475	1,640.70	12-16	2,672.70
12-8	3476	1,300.00	12-21	2,945.00
12-10	3477	2,130.00	12-26	2,567.30
12-15	3479	3,080.00	12-29	2,836.00
12-27	3480	600.00	12-30	1,025.00
12-30	3482	475.50	Total	$18,152.90
12-29	3483	1,140.00		
12-31	3485	540.80		
	Total	$15,438.70		

The cash records per books for December showed the following.

Cash Payments Journal						Cash Receipts Journal	
Date	Number	Amount	Date	Number	Amount	Date	Amount
12-1	3475	$1,640.70	12-20	3482	$ 475.50	12-3	$ 1,211.60
12-2	3476	1,300.00	12-22	3483	1,140.00	12-7	2,365.10
12-2	3477	2,130.00	12-23	3484	798.00	12-15	2,672.70
12-4	3478	621.30	12-24	3485	450.80	12-20	2,954.00
12-8	3479	3,080.00	12-30	3486	889.50	12-25	2,567.30
12-10	3480	600.00	Total		$13,933.20	12-28	2,836.00
12-17	3481	807.40				12-30	1,025.00
						12-31	1,690.40
						Total	$17,322.10

The bank statement contained two memoranda:

1. A credit of $5,145 for the collection of a $5,000 note for Langer Company plus interest of $160 and less a collection fee of $15. Langer Company has not accrued any interest on the note.
2. A debit of $572.80 for an NSF check written by L. Rees, a customer. At December 31, the check had not been redeposited in the bank.

At December 31, the cash balance per books was $12,485.20, and the cash balance per the bank statement was $20,154.30. The bank did not make any errors, but two errors were made by Langer Company.

Instructions
(a) Using the four steps in the reconciliation procedure, prepare a bank reconciliation at December 31.
(b) Prepare the adjusting entries based on the reconciliation. (*Hint:* The correction of any errors pertaining to recording checks should be made to Accounts Payable. The correction of any errors relating to recording cash receipts should be made to Accounts Receivable.)

(a) Adjusted balance per books $16,958.40

Prepare a bank reconciliation and adjusting entries.
(LO 7)

P8-5A Rodriguez Company maintains a checking account at the Imura Bank. At July 31, selected data from the ledger balance and the bank statement are shown below.

	Cash in Bank	
	Per Books	**Per Bank**
Balance, July 1	$17,600	$16,800
July receipts	81,400	
July credits		82,470
July disbursements	77,150	
July debits		74,756
Balance, July 31	$21,850	$24,514

Analysis of the bank data reveals that the credits consist of $79,000 of July deposits and a credit memorandum of $4,470 for the collection of a $4,400 note plus interest revenue of $70. The July debits per bank consist of checks cleared $74,700 and a debit memorandum of $56 for printing additional company checks.

You also discover the following errors involving July checks: (1) A check for $230 to a creditor on account that cleared the bank in July was journalized and posted as $320. (2) A salary check to an employee for $255 was recorded by the bank for $155.

The June 30 bank reconciliation contained only two reconciling items: deposits in transit $8,000 and outstanding checks of $6,200.

Instructions

(a) Adjusted balance per books $26,354

(a) Prepare a bank reconciliation at July 31, 2014.
(b) Journalize the adjusting entries to be made by Rodriguez Company. Assume that interest on the note has not been accrued.

Identify internal control weaknesses in cash receipts and cash disbursements.
(LO 2, 3, 4)

P8-6A Rondelli Middle School wants to raise money for a new sound system for its auditorium. The primary fund-raising event is a dance at which the famous disc jockey D.J. Sound will play classic and not-so-classic dance tunes. Matt Ballester, the music and theater instructor, has been given the responsibility for coordinating the fund-raising efforts. This is Matt's first experience with fund-raising. He decides to put the eighth-grade choir in charge of the event; he will be a relatively passive observer.

Matt had 500 unnumbered tickets printed for the dance. He left the tickets in a box on his desk and told the choir students to take as many tickets as they thought they could sell for $5 each. In order to ensure that no extra tickets would be floating around, he told them to dispose of any unsold tickets. When the students received payment for the tickets, they were to bring the cash back to Matt and he would put it in a locked box in his desk drawer.

Some of the students were responsible for decorating the gymnasium for the dance. Matt gave each of them a key to the money box and told them that if they took money out to purchase materials, they should put a note in the box saying how much they took and what it was used for. After 2 weeks the money box appeared to be getting full, so Matt asked Jeff Kenney to count the money, prepare a deposit slip, and deposit the money in a bank account Matt had opened.

The day of the dance, Matt wrote a check from the account to pay the DJ. D.J. Sound, however, said that he accepted only cash and did not give receipts. So Matt took $200 out of the cash box and gave it to D.J. At the dance, Matt had Sam Copper working at the entrance to the gymnasium, collecting tickets from students, and selling tickets to those who had not prepurchased them. Matt estimated that 400 students attended the dance.

The following day, Matt closed out the bank account, which had $250 in it, and gave that amount plus the $180 in the cash box to Principal Finke. Principal Finke seemed surprised that, after generating roughly $2,000 in sales, the dance netted only $430 in cash. Matt did not know how to respond.

Instructions

Identify as many internal control weaknesses as you can in this scenario, and suggest how each could be addressed.

PROBLEMS: SET B

P8-1B Granada Theater is located in the Brooklyn Mall. A cashier's booth is located near the entrance to the theater. Three cashiers are employed. One works from 1–5 P.M., another from 5–9 P.M. The shifts are rotated among the three cashiers. The cashiers receive cash from customers and operate a machine that ejects serially numbered tickets. The rolls of tickets are inserted and locked into the machine by the theater manager at the beginning of each cashier's shift.

Identify internal control weaknesses over cash receipts.

(LO 2, 3)

After purchasing a ticket, the customer takes the ticket to an usher stationed at the entrance of the theater lobby some 60 feet from the cashier's booth. The usher tears the ticket in half, admits the customer, and returns the ticket stub to the customer. The other half of the ticket is dropped into a locked box by the usher.

At the end of each cashier's shift, the theater manager removes the ticket rolls from the machine and makes a cash count. The cash count sheet is initialed by the cashier. At the end of the day, the manager deposits the receipts in total in a bank night deposit vault located in the mall. The manager also sends copies of the deposit slip and the initialed cash count sheets to the theater company treasurer for verification and to the company's accounting department. Receipts from the first shift are stored in a safe located in the manager's office.

Instructions

(a) Identify the internal control principles and their application to the cash receipts transactions of the Granada Theater.

(b) If the usher and cashier decide to collaborate to misappropriate cash, what actions might they take?

P8-2B Haig Company maintains a petty cash fund for small expenditures. The following transactions occurred over a 2-month period.

Journalize and post petty cash fund transactions.

(LO 5)

July 1   Established petty cash fund by writing a check on China Bank for $100.
15   Replenished the petty cash fund by writing a check for $96.90. On this date the fund consisted of $3.10 in cash and the following petty cash receipts: freight-out $51.00, postage expense $20.50, entertainment expense $23.10, and miscellaneous expense $6.10.
31   Replenished the petty cash fund by writing a check for $95.90. At this date, the fund consisted of $4.10 in cash and the following petty cash receipts: freight-out $43.50, charitable contributions expense $20.00, postage expense $20.10, and miscellaneous expense $12.30.
Aug. 15   Replenished the petty cash fund by writing a check for $98.00. On this date, the fund consisted of $2.00 in cash and the following petty cash receipts: freight-out $40.20, entertainment expense $21.00, postage expense $16.00, and miscellaneous expense $19.80.
16   Increased the amount of the petty cash fund to $150 by writing a check for $50.
31   Replenished petty cash fund by writing a check for $137.00. On this date, the fund consisted of $13 in cash and the following petty cash receipts: freight-out $74.00, entertainment expense $43.20, and postage expense $17.70.

Instructions

(a) Journalize the petty cash transactions.
(b) Post to the Petty Cash account.
(c) What internal control features exist in a petty cash fund?

(a) July 15 Cash over $3.80
(b) Aug. 31 balance $150

P8-3B Davaney Genetics Company of Milwaukee, Wisconsin, spreads herbicides and applies liquid fertilizer for local farmers. On May 31, 2014, the company's Cash account per its general ledger showed the following balance.

Prepare a bank reconciliation and adjusting entries.

(LO 7)

CASH					NO. 101
Date	Explanation	Ref.	Debit	Credit	Balance
May 31	Balance				13,287

The bank statement from Milwaukee State Bank on that date showed the following balance.

MILWAUKEE STATE BANK

Checks and Debits	Deposits and Credits	Daily Balance
XXX	XXX	5/31 13,332

A comparison of the details on the bank statement with the details in the Cash account revealed the following facts.

1. The statement included a debit memo of $35 for the printing of additional company checks.
2. Cash sales of $1,720 on May 12 were deposited in the bank. The cash receipts journal entry and the deposit slip were incorrectly made for $1,820. The bank credited Davaney Genetics Company for the correct amount.
3. Outstanding checks at May 31 totaled $1,225, and deposits in transit were $2,600.
4. On May 18, the company issued check no. 1181 for $911 to J. Tallgrass on account. The check, which cleared the bank in May, was incorrectly journalized and posted by Davaney Genetics Company for $119.
5. A $4,500 note receivable was collected by the bank for Davaney Genetics Company on May 31 plus $80 interest. The bank charged a collection fee of $25. No interest has been accrued on the note.
6. Included with the cancelled checks was a check issued by Morray Company to Terry Irvin for $900 that was incorrectly charged to Davaney Genetics Company by the bank.
7. On May 31, the bank statement showed an NSF charge of $1,308 for a check issued by Peter Reser, a customer, to Davaney Genetics Company on account.

Instructions

(a) Adj. cash bal. $15,607

(a) Prepare the bank reconciliation at May 31, 2014.
(b) Prepare the necessary adjusting entries for Davaney Genetics Company at May 31, 2014.

Prepare a bank reconciliation and adjusting entries from detailed data.

(LO 7)

P8-4B The bank portion of the bank reconciliation for Phillips Company at October 31, 2014, was as follows.

PHILLIPS COMPANY
Bank Reconciliation
October 31, 2014

Cash balance per bank		$6,000
Add: Deposits in transit		842
		6,842

Less: Outstanding checks

Check Number	Check Amount	
2451	$700	
2470	396	
2471	464	
2472	270	
2474	578	2,408
Adjusted cash balance per bank		$4,434

The adjusted cash balance per bank agreed with the cash balance per books at October 31. The November bank statement showed the following checks and deposits:

Bank Statement

	Checks			Deposits	
Date	Number	Amount	Date		Amount
11-1	2470	$ 396	11-1		$ 842
11-2	2471	464	11-4		666
11-5	2474	578	11-8		545
11-4	2475	903	11-13		1,416
11-8	2476	1,556	11-18		810
11-10	2477	330	11-21		1,624
11-15	2479	980	11-25		1,412
11-18	2480	714	11-28		908
11-27	2481	382	11-30		652
11-30	2483	317	Total		$8,875
11-29	2486	495			
	Total	$7,115			

The cash records per books for November showed the following.

Cash Payments Journal

Date	Number	Amount	Date	Number	Amount
11-1	2475	$ 903	11-20	2483	$ 317
11-2	2476	1,556	11-22	2484	460
11-2	2477	330	11-23	2485	525
11-4	2478	300	11-24	2486	495
11-8	2479	890	11-29	2487	210
11-10	2480	714	11-30	2488	635
11-15	2481	382	Total		$8,067
11-18	2482	350			

Cash Receipts Journal

Date	Amount
11-3	$ 666
11-7	545
11-12	1,416
11-17	810
11-20	1,642
11-24	1,412
11-27	908
11-29	652
11-30	2,541
Total	$10,592

The bank statement contained two bank memoranda:

1. A credit of $2,375 for the collection of a $2,300 note for Phillips Company plus interest of $91 and less a collection fee of $16. Phillips Company has not accrued any interest on the note.
2. A debit for the printing of additional company checks $34.

At November 30, the cash balance per books was $5,958, and the cash balance per the bank statement was $9,100. The bank did not make any errors, but two errors were made by Phillips Company.

Instructions
(a) Using the four steps in the reconciliation procedure described on pages 398–399, prepare a bank reconciliation at November 30.
(b) Prepare the adjusting entries based on the reconciliation. (*Hint:* The correction of any errors pertaining to recording checks should be made to Accounts Payable. The correction of any errors relating to recording cash receipts should be made to Accounts Receivable.)

(a) Adjusted cash balance per bank $8,191

P8-5B Zhang Company's bank statement from Nguyen National Bank at August 31, 2014, shows the information below.

Prepare a bank reconciliation and adjusting entries.

(LO 7)

Balance, August 1	$11,284	Bank credit memoranda:	
August deposits	47,521	Collection of note	
Checks cleared in August	46,475	receivable plus $105	
Balance, August 31	16,856	interest	$5,105
		Interest earned	41
		Bank debit memorandum:	
		Safety deposit box rent	20

A summary of the Cash account in the ledger for August shows: balance, August 1, $10,959; receipts $50,050; disbursements $47,794; and balance, August 31, $13,215. Analysis reveals that the only reconciling items on the July 31 bank reconciliation were a deposit in transit for $3,200 and outstanding checks of $2,925. The deposit in transit was the first deposit recorded by the bank in August. In addition, you determine that there were two errors involving company checks drawn in August: (1) A check for $340 to a creditor on account that cleared the bank in August was journalized and posted for $430. (2) A salary check to an employee for $275 was recorded by the bank for $277.

Instructions

(a) Prepare a bank reconciliation at August 31.

(b) Journalize the adjusting entries to be made by Zhang Company at August 31. Assume that interest on the note has not been accrued by the company.

(a) Adjusted balance per books $18,431

Prepare a comprehensive bank reconciliation with theft and internal control deficiencies.

(LO 2, 3, 4, 7)

P8-6B Gamel Company is a very profitable small business. It has not, however, given much consideration to internal control. For example, in an attempt to keep clerical and office expenses to a minimum, the company has combined the jobs of cashier and book-keeper. As a result, Jan Worthy handles all cash receipts, keeps the accounting records, and prepares the monthly bank reconciliations.

The balance per the bank statement on October 31, 2014, was $15,313. Outstanding checks were: no. 62 for $107.74, no. 183 for $127.50, no. 284 for $215.26, no. 862 for $132.10, no. 863 for $192.78, and no. 864 for $140.49. Included with the statement was a credit memorandum of $460 indicating the collection of a note receivable for Gamel Company by the bank on October 25. This memorandum has not been recorded by Gamel Company.

The company's ledger showed one cash account with a balance of $18,608.81. The balance included undeposited cash on hand. Because of the lack of internal controls, Jan took for personal use all of the undeposited receipts in excess of $3,226.18. She then prepared the following bank reconciliation in an effort to conceal her theft of cash.

BANK RECONCILIATION

Cash balance per books, October 31		$18,608.81
Add: Outstanding checks		
No. 862	$132.10	
No. 863	192.78	
No. 864	140.49	390.37
		18,999.18
Less: Undeposited receipts		3,226.18
Unadjusted balance per bank, October 31		15,773.00
Less: Bank credit memorandum		460.00
Cash balance per bank statement, October 31		$15,313.00

Instructions

(a) Adjusted balance per books $17,623.31

(a) Prepare a correct bank reconciliation. (*Hint:* Deduct the amount of the theft from the adjusted balance per books.)

(b) Indicate the three ways that Jan attempted to conceal the theft and the dollar amount pertaining to each method.

(c) What principles of internal control were violated in this case?

PROBLEMS: SET C

Visit the book's companion website, at **www.wiley.com/college/weygandt**, and choose the Student Companion site to access Problem Set C.

COMPREHENSIVE PROBLEM

CP8 On December 1, 2014, Fullerton Company had the following account balances.

	Debit		Credit
Cash	$18,200	Accumulated Depreciation—	
Notes Receivable	2,200	Equipment	$ 3,000
Accounts Receivable	7,500	Accounts Payable	6,100
Inventory	16,000	Owner's Capital	64,400
Prepaid Insurance	1,600		$73,500
Equipment	28,000		
	$73,500		

During December, the company completed the following transactions.

Dec. 7   Received $3,600 cash from customers in payment of account (no discount allowed).
12   Purchased merchandise on account from Vance Co. $12,000, terms 1/10, n/30.
17   Sold merchandise on account $16,000, terms 2/10, n/30. The cost of the merchandise sold was $10,000.
19   Paid salaries $2,200.
22   Paid Vance Co. in full, less discount.
26   Received collections in full, less discounts, from customers billed on December 17.
31   Received $2,700 cash from customers in payment of account (no discount allowed).

Adjustment data:

1. Depreciation $200 per month.
2. Insurance expired $400.

Instructions
(a) Journalize the December transactions. (Assume a perpetual inventory system.)
(b) Enter the December 1 balances in the ledger T-accounts and post the December transactions. Use Cost of Goods Sold, Depreciation Expense, Insurance Expense, Salaries and Wages Expense, Sales Revenue, and Sales Discounts.
(c) The statement from Jackson County Bank on December 31 showed a balance of $26,130. A comparison of the bank statement with the Cash account revealed the following facts.
   1. The bank collected a note receivable of $2,200 for Fullerton Company on December 15.
   2. The December 31 receipts were deposited in a night deposit vault on December 31. These deposits were recorded by the bank in January.
   3. Checks outstanding on December 31 totaled $1,210.
   4. On December 31, the bank statement showed an NSF charge of $680 for a check received by the company from L. Bryan, a customer, on account.

   Prepare a bank reconciliation as of December 31 based on the available information. (*Hint:* The cash balance per books is $26,100. This can be proven by finding the balance in the Cash account from parts (a) and (b).)
(d) Journalize the adjusting entries resulting from the bank reconciliation and adjustment data.
(e) Post the adjusting entries to the ledger T-accounts.
(f) Prepare an adjusted trial balance.
(g) Prepare an income statement for December and a classified balance sheet at December 31.

CONTINUING COOKIE CHRONICLE

(*Note:* This is a continuation of the Cookie Chronicle from Chapters 1 through 7.)

CCC8 Part 1   Natalie is struggling to keep up with the recording of her accounting transactions. She is spending a lot of time marketing and selling mixers and giving her cookie classes. Her friend John is an accounting student who runs his own accounting service. He has asked Natalie if she would like to have him do her accounting. John and Natalie meet and discuss her business.

Part 2   Natalie decides that she cannot afford to hire John to do her accounting. One way that she can ensure that her cash account does not have any errors and is accurate and up-to-date is to prepare a bank reconciliation at the end of each month. Natalie would like you to help her.

Go to the book's companion website, **www.wiley.com/college/weygandt**, *to see the completion of this problem.*

Broadening Your Perspective

Financial Reporting and Analysis

Financial Reporting Problem: Apple Inc.

BYP8-1 The financial statements of Apple Inc. are presented in Appendix A at the end of this textbook. Instructions for accessing and using the company's complete annual report, including the notes to the financial statements, are also provided in Appendix A.

Instructions
(a) What comments, if any, are made about cash in the report of the independent registered public accounting firm?
(b) What data about cash and cash equivalents are shown in the consolidated balance sheet?
(c) In its notes to Consolidated Financial Statements, how does Apple define cash equivalents?
(d) In management's Annual Report on Internal Control over Financial Reporting (Item 9), what does Apple's management say about internal control?

Comparative Analysis Problem: PepsiCo, Inc. vs. The Coca-Cola Company

BYP8-2 PepsiCo's financial statements are presented in Appendix B. Financial statements of The Coca-Cola Company are presented in Appendix C. Instructions for accessing and using the complete annual reports of PepsiCo and Coca-Cola, including the notes to the financial statements, are also provided in Appendices B and C, respectively.

Instructions
(a) Based on the information contained in these financial statements, determine each of the following for each company:
(1) Cash and cash equivalents balance at December 31, 2011, for PepsiCo and at December 31, 2011, for Coca-Cola.
(2) Increase (decrease) in cash and cash equivalents from 2010 to 2011.
(3) Cash provided by operating activities during the year ended December 2011 (from statement of cash flows).
(b) What conclusions concerning the management of cash can be drawn from these data?

Comparative Analysis Problem: Amazon.com, Inc. vs. Wal-Mart Stores, Inc.

BYP8-3 Amazon.com, Inc.'s financial statements are presented in Appendix D. Financial statements of Wal-Mart Stores, Inc. are presented in Appendix E. Instructions for accessing and using the complete annual reports of Amazon and Wal-Mart, including the notes to the financial statements, are also provided in Appendices D and E, respectively.

Instructions
(a) Based on the information contained in these financial statements, determine each of the following for each company:
(1) Cash and cash equivalents balance at December 31, 2011, for Amazon and at January 31, 2012, for Wal-Mart.
(2) Increase (decrease) in cash and cash equivalents from 2011 to 2010.
(3) Net cash provided by operating activities during the year ended December 31, 2011, for Amazon and January 31, 2012, for Wal-Mart from statement of cash flows.
(b) What conclusions concerning the management of cash can be drawn from these data?

Real-World Focus

BYP8-4 All organizations should have systems of internal control. Universities are no exception. This site discusses the basics of internal control in a university setting.

Address: **www.bc.edu/offices/audit/controls**, or go to **www.wiley.com/college/weygandt**

Steps: Go to the site shown above.

Instructions
The home page of this site provides links to pages that answer six critical questions. Use these links to answer the following questions.

(a) In a university setting, who has responsibility for evaluating the adequacy of the system of internal control?

(b) What do reconciliations ensure in the university setting? Who should review the reconciliation?

(c) What are some examples of physical controls?

(d) What are two ways to accomplish inventory counts?

Critical Thinking

Decision-Making Across the Organization

BYP8-5 The board of trustees of a local church is concerned about the internal accounting controls for the offering collections made at weekly services. The trustees ask you to serve on a three-person audit team with the internal auditor of a local college and a CPA who has just joined the church.

At a meeting of the audit team and the board of trustees you learn the following.

1. The church's board of trustees has delegated responsibility for the financial management and audit of the financial records to the finance committee. This group prepares the annual budget and approves major disbursements. It is not involved in collections or record keeping. No audit has been made in recent years because the same trusted employee has kept church records and served as financial secretary for 15 years. The church does not carry any fidelity insurance.

2. The collection at the weekly service is taken by a team of ushers who volunteer to serve one month. The ushers take the collection plates to a basement office at the rear of the church. They hand their plates to the head usher and return to the church service. After all plates have been turned in, the head usher counts the cash received. The head usher then places the cash in the church safe along with a notation of the amount counted. The head usher volunteers to serve for 3 months.

3. The next morning the financial secretary opens the safe and recounts the collection. The secretary withholds $150–$200 in cash, depending on the cash expenditures expected for the week, and deposits the remainder of the collections in the bank. To facilitate the deposit, church members who contribute by check are asked to make their checks payable to "Cash."

4. Each month, the financial secretary reconciles the bank statement and submits a copy of the reconciliation to the board of trustees. The reconciliations have rarely contained any bank errors and have never shown any errors per books.

Instructions
With the class divided into groups, answer the following.

(a) Indicate the weaknesses in internal accounting control over the handling of collections.

(b) List the improvements in internal control procedures that you plan to make at the next meeting of the audit team for (1) the ushers, (2) the head usher, (3) the financial secretary, and (4) the finance committee.

(c) What church policies should be changed to improve internal control?

Communication Activity

BYP8-6 As a new auditor for the CPA firm of Eaton, Quayle, and Hale, you have been assigned to review the internal controls over mail cash receipts of Pritchard Company. Your review reveals the following. Checks are promptly endorsed "For Deposit Only," but no list of the checks is prepared by the person opening the mail. The mail is opened either by the cashier or by the employee who maintains the accounts receivable records. Mail receipts are deposited in the bank weekly by the cashier.

Instructions
Write a letter to Danny Peak, owner of Pritchard Company, explaining the weaknesses in internal control and your recommendations for improving the system.

Ethics Case

BYP8-7 You are the assistant controller in charge of general ledger accounting at Linbarger Bottling Company. Your company has a large loan from an insurance company. The loan agreement requires that the company's cash account balance be maintained at $200,000 or more, as reported monthly.

At June 30, the cash balance is $80,000, which you report to Lisa Infante, the financial vice president. Lisa excitedly instructs you to keep the cash receipts book open for one additional day for purposes of the June 30 report to the insurance company. Lisa says, "If we don't get that cash balance over $200,000, we'll default on our loan agreement. They could close us down, put us all out of our jobs!" Lisa continues, "I talked to Oconto Distributors (one of Linbarger's largest customers) this morning. They said they sent us a check for $150,000 yesterday. We should receive it tomorrow. If we include just that one check in our cash balance, we'll be in the clear. It's in the mail!"

Instructions
(a) Who will suffer negative effects if you do not comply with Lisa Infante's instructions? Who will suffer if you do comply?
(b) What are the ethical considerations in this case?
(c) What alternatives do you have?

All About You

BYP8-8 The print and electronic media are full of stories about potential security risks that may arise from your personal computer. It is important to keep in mind, however, that there are also many other ways that your identity can be stolen other than from your computer. The federal government provides many resources to help protect you from identity thieves.

Instructions
Go to **http://onguardonline.gov/idtheft.html**, click **Video and Media,** and then click on **ID Theft Faceoff**. Complete the quiz provided there.

FASB Codification Activity

BYP8-9 If your school has a subscription to the FASB Codification, go to **http://aaahq.org/ ascLogin.cfm** to log in and prepare responses to the following.

(a) How is cash defined in the Codification?
(b) How are cash equivalents defined in the Codification?
(c) What are the disclosure requirements related to cash and cash equivalents?

Answers to Chapter Questions

Answers to Insight and Accounting Across the Organization Questions

p. 377 And the Controls Are. . .   **Q:** Why is sustainability information important to investors? **A:** Investors, customers, suppliers, and employees want more information about companies' long-term impact on society. There is a growing awareness that sustainability issues can affect a company's financial performance. Proper reporting on sustainability issues develops a solid reputation for transparency and provides confidence to shareholders.

p. 384 SOX Boosts the Role of Human Resources   **Q:** Why would unsupervised employees or employees who report to each other represent potential internal control threats? **A:** An unsupervised employee may have a fraudulent job (or may even be a fictitious person), e.g., a person drawing a paycheck without working. Or, if two employees supervise each other, there is no real separation of duties, and they can conspire to defraud the company.

p. 393 How Employees Steal   **Q:** How can companies reduce the likelihood of fraudulent disbursements? **A:** To reduce the occurrence of fraudulent disbursements, a company should follow the procedures discussed in this chapter. These include having only designated personnel sign checks; having different personnel approve payments and make payments; ensuring that check-signers do not record disbursements; using prenumbered checks and matching each check to an approved invoice; storing blank checks securely; reconciling the bank statement; and stamping invoices PAID.

p. 401 Madoff's Ponzi Scheme   **Q:** How was Madoff able to conceal such a giant fraud? **A:** Madoff fabricated false investment statements that were provided to investors. In addition, his auditor never verified these investment statements even though the auditor issued an unqualified opinion each year.

Answers to Self-Test Questions
1. c   **2.** a   **3.** a   **4.** c   **5.** b   **6.** d   **7.** b   **8.** d   **9.** a ($100 − ($94 + $4))   **10.** a   **11.** c   **12.** d   **13.** c
14. c

A Look at IFRS

Fraud can occur anywhere. Because the three main factors that contribute to fraud are universal in nature, the principles of internal control activities are used globally by companies. While Sarbanes-Oxley (SOX) does not apply to international companies, most large international companies have internal controls similar to those indicated in the chapter. IFRS and GAAP are also very similar in accounting for cash. *IAS No. 1 (revised)*, "Presentation of Financial Statements," is the only standard that discusses issues specifically related to cash.

> **LEARNING OBJECTIVE   9**
>
> **Compare the accounting procedures for fraud, internal control, and cash under GAAP and IFRS.**

Key Points

- The fraud triangle discussed in this chapter is applicable to all international companies. Some of the major frauds on an international basis are Parmalat (Italy), Royal Ahold (the Netherlands), and Satyam Computer Services (India).

- Rising economic crime poses a growing threat to companies, with nearly one-third of all organizations worldwide being victims of fraud in a recent 12-month period. The survey data shows that the incidence of economic crime varies by territory; some countries, mainly those in emerging markets, experienced much higher levels of fraud than the average, as much as 71% in one country; by industry sector, some (notably insurance, financial services, and communications) reporting higher levels of fraud than others; and by size and type of organization. However, no organization is immune (*PricewaterhouseCoopers' Global Economic Crime Survey*, 2009).

- Economic crime takes on many different forms, some more common than others. The chart below shows the types of economic crime suffered by those companies who reported experiencing economic crime in the last 12 months.

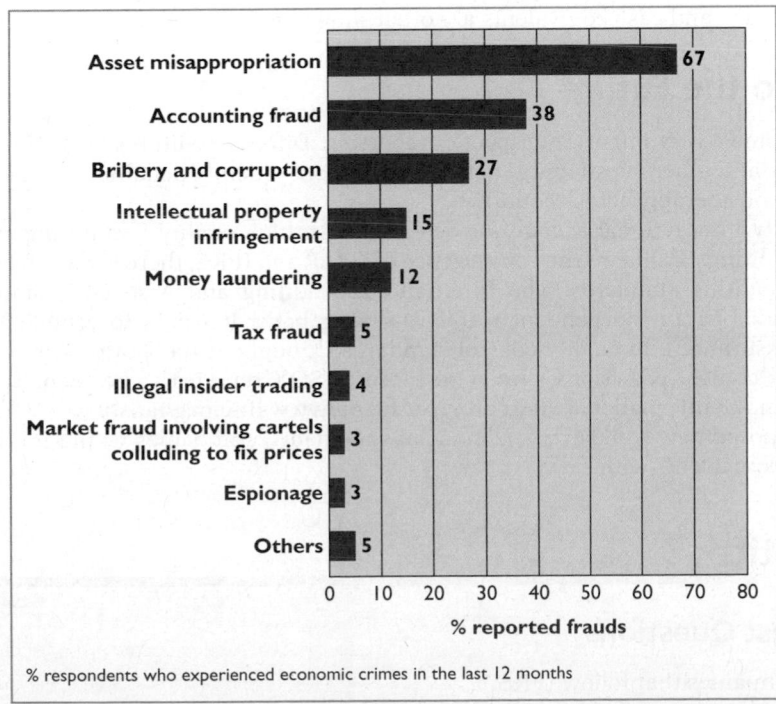

This chart shows that the three most common types of economic crimes experienced in the last 12 months were asset misappropriation, accounting fraud, and bribery and corruption (*PricewaterhouseCoopers' Global Economic Crime Survey*, 2009).

- Accounting scandals both in the United States and internationally have re-ignited the debate over the relative merits of GAAP, which takes a "rules-based" approach to accounting, versus IFRS, which takes a "principles-based" approach. The FASB announced that it intends to introduce more principles-based standards.

- On a lighter note, at one time the Ig Nobel Prize in Economics went to the CEOs of those companies involved in the corporate accounting scandals of that year for "adapting the mathematical concept of imaginary numbers for use in the business world." A parody of the Nobel Prizes, the Ig Nobel Prizes (read Ignoble, as not noble) are given each year in early October for 10 achievements that "first make people laugh, and then make them think." Organized by the scientific humor magazine *Annals of Improbable Research* (*AIR*), they are presented by a group that includes genuine Nobel laureates at a ceremony at Harvard University's Sanders Theater. (See **en.wikipedia.org/wiki/Ig_Nobel_Prize.**)

- Internal controls are a system of checks and balances designed to prevent and detect fraud and errors. While most companies have these systems in place, many have never completely documented them, nor had an independent auditor attest to their effectiveness. Both of these actions are required under SOX.

- Companies find that internal control review is a costly process but badly needed. One study estimates the cost of SOX compliance for U.S. companies at over $35 billion, with audit fees doubling in the first year of compliance. At the same time, examination of internal controls indicates lingering problems in the way companies operate. One study of first compliance with the internal-control testing provisions documented material weaknesses for about 13% of companies reporting in a two-year period (*PricewaterhouseCoopers' Global Economic Crime Survey*, 2005).

- The SOX internal control standards apply only to companies listed on U.S. exchanges. There is continuing debate over whether foreign issuers should have to comply with this extra layer of regulation.

- The accounting and internal control procedures related to cash are essentially the same under both IFRS and this textbook. In addition, the definition used for cash equivalents is the same.

- Most companies report cash and cash equivalents together under IFRS, as shown in this textbook. In addition, IFRS follows the same accounting policies related to the reporting of restricted cash.

- IFRS defines cash and cash equivalents as follows.
  - ♦ **Cash** is comprised of cash on hand and demand deposits.
  - ♦ **Cash equivalents** are short-term, highly liquid investments that are readily convertible to known amounts of cash and which are subject to an insignificant risk of changes in value.

- Under IFRS, cash and cash equivalents are often shown in the statement of financial position.

Looking to the Future

Ethics has become a very important aspect of reporting. Different cultures have different perspectives on bribery and other questionable activities, and consequently penalties for engaging in such activities vary considerably across countries.

High-quality international accounting requires both high-quality accounting standards and high-quality auditing. Similar to the convergence of GAAP and IFRS, there is movement to improve international auditing standards. The International Auditing and Assurance Standards Board (IAASB) functions as an independent standard-setting body. It works to establish high-quality auditing and assurance and quality-control standards throughout the world. Whether the IAASB adopts internal control provisions similar to those in SOX remains to be seen. You can follow developments in the international audit arena at **http://www.ifac.org/iaasb/**.

Under proposed new standards for financial statements, companies would not be allowed to combine cash equivalents with cash.

IFRS Practice

IFRS Self-Test Questions

1. Non-U.S companies that follow IFRS:
   (a) do not normally use the principles of internal control activities described in this textbook.
   (b) often offset cash with accounts payable on the balance sheet.
   (c) are not required to follow SOX.
   (d) None of the above.

2. Which of the following is the correct accounting under IFRS for cash?
   (a) Cash cannot be combined with cash equivalents.
   (b) Restricted cash funds may be reported as a current or non-current asset depending on the circumstances.
   (c) Restricted cash funds cannot be reported as a current asset.
   (d) Cash on hand is not reported on the balance sheet as Cash.

3. The Sarbanes-Oxley Act applies to:
   (a) all U.S. companies listed on U.S. exchanges.
   (b) all companies that list stock on any stock exchange in any country.
   (c) all European companies listed on European exchanges.
   (d) Both (a) and (c).

4. High-quality international accounting requires both high-quality accounting standards and:
   (a) a reconsideration of SOX to make it less onerous.
   (b) high-quality auditing standards.
   (c) government intervention to ensure that the public interest is protected.
   (d) the development of new principles of internal control activities.

5. Cash equivalents under IFRS:
   (a) are significantly different than the cash equivalents discussed in the textbook.
   (b) are generally disclosed separately from cash.
   (c) may be required to be reported separately from cash in the future.
   (d) None of the above.

IFRS Exercises

IFRS8-1 Some people argue that the internal control requirements of the Sarbanes-Oxley Act (SOX) put U.S. companies at a competitive disadvantage to companies outside the United States. Discuss the competitive implications (both pros and cons) of SOX.

IFRS8-2 State whether each of the following is true or false. For those that are false, explain why.

(a) A proposed new financial accounting standard would not allow cash equivalents to be reported in combination with cash.
(b) Perspectives on bribery and penalties for engaging in bribery are the same across all countries.
(c) Cash equivalents are comprised of cash on hand and demand deposits.
(d) SOX was created by the International Accounting Standards Board.

International Financial Reporting Problem: Zetar plc

IFRS8–3 The financial statements of Zetar plc are presented in Appendix F. Instructions for accessing and using the company's complete annual report, including the notes to its financial statements, are also provided in Appendix F.

Instructions
Using the notes to the company's financial statements, answer the following questions.

(a) Which committee of the board of directors is responsible for considering management's reports on internal control?
(b) What are the company's key control procedures?
(c) Does the company have an internal audit department?
(d) In what section or sections does Zetar report its bank overdrafts?

Answers to IFRS Self-Test Questions
1. c   2. b   3. a   4. b   5. c

✔ The Navigator

9 | Accounting for Receivables

✔ The Naviga

Feature Story

A Dose of Careful Management Keeps Receivables Healthy

"Sometimes you have to know when to be very tough, and sometimes you can give them a bit of a break," says Vivi Su. She's not talking about her children but about the customers of a subsidiary of pharmaceutical company Whitehall-Robins, where she works as supervisor of credit and collections.

For example, while the company's regular terms are 1/15, n/30 (1% discount if paid within 15 days), a customer might ask for and receive a few days of grace and still get the discount. Or a customer might place orders above its credit limit, in which case, depending on its payment history and the circumstances, Ms. Su might authorize shipment of the goods anyway.

"It's not about drawing a line in the sand, and that's all," she explains. "You want a good relationship with your customers—but you also need to bring in the money."

"The money," in Whitehall-Robins' case, amounts to some $170 million in sales a year. Nearly all of it comes in through the credit accounts Ms. Su manages. The process starts with the decision to grant a customer an account in the first place, Ms. Su explains. The sales rep gives the customer a credit application. "My department reviews this application very carefully; a customer needs to supply three good referenc and we also run a check with a credit firm like Equifax. If accept them, then based on their size and history, we ass a credit limit."

Once accounts are established, "I get an aging report eve single day," says Ms. Su. "The rule of thumb is that we sh always have at least 85% of receivables current—meaning they were billed less than 30 days ago," she continues. "B we try to do even better than that—I like to see 90%."

At 15 days overdue, Whitehall-Robins phones the client. A 45 days, Ms. Su notes, "I send a letter. Then a second not sent in writing. After the third and final notice, the client I 10 days to pay, and then I hand it over to a collection age and it's out of my hands."

Ms. Su's boss, Terry Norton, records an estimate for ba debts every year, based on a percentage of receivables percentage depends on the current aging history. He a calculates and monitors the company's accounts receiv turnover, which the company reports in its financial statements.

✔ The Navigator

- ■ Scan Learning Objectives
- ■ Read Feature Story
- ■ Read Preview
- ■ Read text and answer **DO IT!** p. 438
  - ■ p. 440   ■ p. 446   ■ p. 448
- ■ Work Comprehensive **DO IT!** p. 448
- ■ Review Summary of Learning Objectives
- ■ Answer Self-Test Questions
- ■ Complete Assignments
- ■ Go to *WileyPLUS* for practice and tutorials
- **Read A Look at IFRS** p. 468

Learning Objectives

✔ The Navigator

After studying this chapter, you should be able to:

[1] Identify the different types of receivables.

[2] Explain how companies recognize accounts receivable.

[3] Distinguish between the methods and bases companies use to value accounts receivable.

[4] Describe the entries to record the disposition of accounts receivable.

[5] Compute the maturity date of and interest on notes receivable.

[6] Explain how companies recognize notes receivable.

[7] Describe how companies value notes receivable.

[8] Describe the entries to record the disposition of notes receivable.

[9] Explain the statement presentation and analysis of receivables.

Ms. Su knows that she and Mr. Norton are crucial to the profitability of Whitehall-Robins. "Receivables are generally the second-largest asset of any company (after its capital assets)," she points out. "So it's no wonder we keep a very close eye on them."

Preview of Chapter 9

 The Navigator

As indicated in the Feature Story, receivables are a significant asset for many pharmaceutical companies. Because a large portion of sales in the United States are done on credit, receivables are important to companies in other industries as well. As a consequence, companies must pay close attention to their receivables and manage them carefully. In this chapter you will learn what journal entries companies make when they sell products, when they collect cash from those sales, and when they write off accounts they cannot collect.

The content and organization of the chapter are as follows.

ACCOUNTING FOR RECEIVABLES

Types of Receivables	Accounts Receivable	Notes Receivable	Statement Presentation and Analysis
• Accounts receivable • Notes receivable • Other receivables	• Recognizing accounts receivable • Valuing accounts receivable • Disposing of accounts receivable	• Determining maturity date • Computing interest • Recognizing notes receivable • Valuing notes receivable • Disposing of notes receivable	• Presentation • Analysis

Types of Receivables

LEARNING OBJECTIVE 1

Identify the different types of receivables.

The term **receivables** refers to amounts due from individuals and companies. Receivables are claims that are expected to be collected in cash. The management of receivables is a very important activity for any company that sells goods or services on credit.

Receivables are important because they represent one of a company's most liquid assets. For many companies, receivables are also one of the largest assets. For example, receivables represented 21.9% of the current assets of pharmaceutical giant Rite Aid in 2011. Illustration 9-1 lists receivables as a percentage of total assets for five other well-known companies in a recent year.

Illustration 9-1
Receivables as a percentage of assets

Company	Receivables as a Percentage of Total Assets
General Electric	52%
Ford Motor Company	42%
Minnesota Mining and Manufacturing Company (3M)	14%
DuPont Co.	17%
Intel Corporation	5%

The relative significance of a company's receivables as a percentage of its assets depends on various factors: its industry, the time of year, whether it extends long-term financing, and its credit policies. To reflect important differences among receivables, they are frequently classified as (1) accounts receivable, (2) notes receivable, and (3) other receivables.

Accounts receivable are amounts customers owe on account. They result from the sale of goods and services. Companies generally expect to collect accounts receivable within 30 to 60 days. They are usually the most significant type of claim held by a company.

Notes receivable are a written promise (as evidenced by a formal instrument) for amounts to be received. The note normally requires the collection of interest and extends for time periods of 60–90 days or longer. Notes and accounts receivable that result from sales transactions are often called **trade receivables**.

Other receivables include nontrade receivables such as interest receivable, loans to company officers, advances to employees, and income taxes refundable. These do not generally result from the operations of the business. Therefore, they are generally classified and reported as separate items in the balance sheet.

Ethics Note

Companies report receivables from employees separately in the financial statements. The reason: Sometimes those assets are not the result of an "arm's-length" transaction.

Accounts Receivable

LEARNING OBJECTIVE 2

Explain how companies recognize accounts receivable.

Three accounting issues associated with accounts receivable are:

1. **Recognizing** accounts receivable.
2. **Valuing** accounts receivable.
3. **Disposing** of accounts receivable.

Recognizing Accounts Receivable

Recognizing accounts receivable is relatively straightforward. A service organization records a receivable when it performs service on account. A merchandiser records accounts receivable at the point of sale of merchandise on account. When a merchandiser sells goods, it increases (debits) Accounts Receivable and increases (credits) Sales Revenue.

The seller may offer terms that encourage early payment by providing a discount. Sales returns also reduce receivables. The buyer might find some of the goods unacceptable and choose to return the unwanted goods.

To review, assume that Jordache Co. on July 1, 2014, sells merchandise on account to Polo Company for $1,000, terms 2/10, n/30. On July 5, Polo returns merchandise worth $100 to Jordache Co. On July 11, Jordache receives payment from Polo Company for the balance due. The journal entries to record these transactions on the books of Jordache Co. are as follows. **(Cost of goods sold entries are omitted.)**

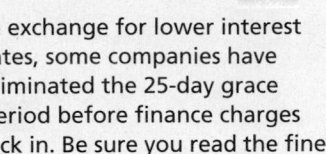

Ethics Note

In exchange for lower interest rates, some companies have eliminated the 25-day grace period before finance charges kick in. Be sure you read the fine print in any credit agreement you sign.

July	1	Accounts Receivable—Polo Company	1,000	
		Sales Revenue		1,000
		(To record sales on account)		

July	5	Sales Returns and Allowances	100	
		Accounts Receivable—Polo Company		100
		(To record merchandise returned)		

July	11	Cash ($900 − $18)	882	
		Sales Discounts ($900 × .02)	18	
		Accounts Receivable—Polo Company		900
		(To record collection of accounts receivable)		

Helpful Hint These entries are the same as those described in Chapter 5. For simplicity, we have omitted inventory and cost of goods sold from this set of journal entries and from end-of-chapter material.

Some retailers issue their own credit cards. When you use a retailer's credit card (JCPenney, for example), the retailer charges interest on the balance due if not paid within a specified period (usually 25–30 days).

To illustrate, assume that you use your JCPenney Company credit card to purchase clothing with a sales price of $300 on June 1, 2014. JCPenney will increase (debit) Accounts Receivable for $300 and increase (credit) Sales Revenue for $300 (cost of goods sold entry omitted) as follows.

June	1	Accounts Receivable	300	
		Sales Revenue		300
		(To record sale of merchandise)		

A	=	L	+	OE
+300				
				+300 Rev

Cash Flows
no effect

Assuming that you owe $300 at the end of the month and JCPenney charges 1.5% per month on the balance due, the adjusting entry that JCPenney makes to record interest revenue of $4.50 ($300 × 1.5%) on June 30 is as follows.

June	30	Accounts Receivable	4.50	
		Interest Revenue		4.50
		(To record interest on amount due)		

A	=	L	+	OE
+4.50				
				+4.50 Rev

Cash Flows
no effect

Interest revenue is often substantial for many retailers.

ANATOMY OF A FRAUD

Tasanee was the accounts receivable clerk for a large non-profit foundation that provided performance and exhibition space for the performing and visual arts. Her responsibilities included activities normally assigned to an accounts receivable clerk, such as recording revenues from various sources that included donations, facility rental fees, ticket revenue, and bar receipts. However, she was also responsible for handling all cash and checks from the time they were received until the time she deposited them, as well as preparing the bank reconciliation. Tasanee took advantage of her situation by falsifying bank deposits and bank reconciliations so that she could steal cash from the bar receipts. Since nobody else logged the donations or matched the donation receipts to pledges prior to Tasanee receiving them, she was able to offset the cash that was stolen against donations that she received but didn't record. Her crime was made easier by the fact that her boss, the company's controller, only did a very superficial review of the bank reconciliation and thus didn't notice that some numbers had been cut out from other documents and taped onto the bank reconciliation.

Total take: $1.5 million

THE MISSING CONTROL

Segregation of duties. The foundation should not have allowed an accounts receivable clerk, whose job was to record receivables, to also handle cash, record cash, make deposits, and especially prepare the bank reconciliation.

Independent internal verification. The controller was supposed to perform a thorough review of the bank reconciliation. Because he did not, he was terminated from his position.

Source: Adapted from Wells, *Fraud Casebook* (2007), pp. 183–194.

Valuing Accounts Receivable

Once companies record receivables in the accounts, the next question is: How should they report receivables in the financial statements? Companies report accounts receivable on the balance sheet as an asset. But determining the **amount** to report is sometimes difficult because some receivables will become uncollectible.

Each customer must satisfy the credit requirements of the seller before the credit sale is approved. Inevitably, though, some accounts receivable become uncollectible. For example, a customer may not be able to pay because of a decline in its sales revenue due to a downturn in the economy. Similarly, individuals may be laid off from their jobs or faced with unexpected hospital bills. Companies record credit losses as debits to **Bad Debt Expense** (or Uncollectible Accounts Expense). Such losses are a normal and necessary risk of doing business on a credit basis.

Recently, when U.S. home prices fell, home foreclosures rose and the economy in general slowed, lenders experienced huge increases in their bad debt expense. For example, during one quarter Wachovia (a large U.S. bank now owned by Wells Fargo) increased bad debt expense from $108 million to $408 million. Similarly, American Express increased its bad debt expense by 70%.

Two methods are used in accounting for uncollectible accounts: (1) the direct write-off method and (2) the allowance method. The following sections explain these methods.

DIRECT WRITE-OFF METHOD FOR UNCOLLECTIBLE ACCOUNTS

Under the **direct write-off method**, when a company determines a particular account to be uncollectible, it charges the loss to Bad Debt Expense. Assume, for example, that Warden Co. writes off as uncollectible M. E. Doran's $200 balance on December 12. Warden's entry is:

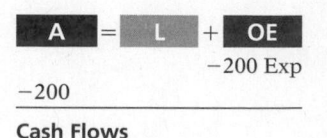

A = L + OE

−200 −200 Exp

Cash Flows
no effect

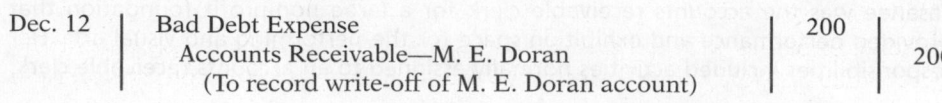

Dec. 12	Bad Debt Expense	200	
	Accounts Receivable—M. E. Doran		200
	(To record write-off of M. E. Doran account)		

Under this method, Bad Debt Expense will show only **actual losses** from uncollectibles. The company will report accounts receivable at its gross amount.

Although this method is simple, its use can reduce the usefulness of both the income statement and balance sheet. Consider the following example. Assume that in 2014, Quick Buck Computer Company decided it could increase its revenues by offering computers to college students without requiring any money down and with no credit-approval process. On campuses across the country, it distributed one million computers with a selling price of $800 each. This increased Quick Buck's revenues and receivables by $800 million. The promotion was a huge success! The 2014 balance sheet and income statement looked great. Unfortunately, during 2015, nearly 40% of the customers defaulted on their loans. This made the 2015 income statement and balance sheet look terrible. Illustration 9-2 shows the effect of these events on the financial statements if the direct write-off method is used.

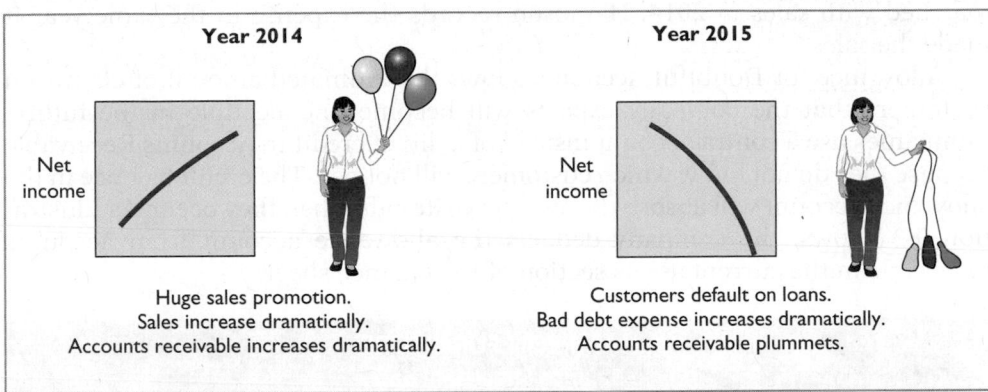

Illustration 9-2
Effects of direct write-off method

Under the direct write-off method, companies often record bad debt expense in a period different from the period in which they record the revenue. The method does not attempt to match bad debt expense to sales revenues in the income statement. Nor does the direct write-off method show accounts receivable in the balance sheet at the amount the company actually expects to receive. **Consequently, unless bad debt losses are insignificant, the direct write-off method is not acceptable for financial reporting purposes.**

ALLOWANCE METHOD FOR UNCOLLECTIBLE ACCOUNTS

The **allowance method** of accounting for bad debts involves estimating uncollectible accounts at the end of each period. This provides better matching on the income statement. It also ensures that companies state receivables on the balance sheet at their cash (net) realizable value. **Cash (net) realizable value** is the net amount the company expects to receive in cash. It excludes amounts that the company estimates it will not collect. Thus, this method reduces receivables in the balance sheet by the amount of estimated uncollectible receivables.

GAAP requires the allowance method for financial reporting purposes when bad debts are material in amount. This method has three essential features:

1. Companies **estimate** uncollectible accounts receivable. They match this estimated expense **against revenues** in the same accounting period in which they record the revenues.

2. Companies debit estimated uncollectibles to Bad Debt Expense and credit them to Allowance for Doubtful Accounts through an adjusting entry at the end of each period. Allowance for Doubtful Accounts is a contra account to Accounts Receivable.

3. When companies write off a specific account, they debit actual uncollectibles to Allowance for Doubtful Accounts and credit that amount to Accounts Receivable.

Helpful Hint In this context, *material* means significant or important to financial statement users.

RECORDING ESTIMATED UNCOLLECTIBLES To illustrate the allowance method, assume that Hampson Furniture has credit sales of $1,200,000 in 2014. Of this amount, $200,000 remains uncollected at December 31. The credit manager estimates that $12,000 of these sales will be uncollectible. The adjusting entry to record the estimated uncollectibles increases (debits) Bad Debt Expense and increases (credits) Allowance for Doubtful Accounts, as follows.

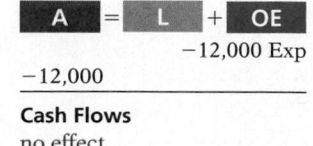

−12,000   −12,000 Exp

Cash Flows
no effect

Dec. 31	Bad Debt Expense	12,000	
	Allowance for Doubtful Accounts		12,000
	(To record estimate of uncollectible		
	accounts)		

Hampson reports Bad Debt Expense in the income statement as an operating expense (usually as a selling expense). Thus, the estimated uncollectibles are matched with sales in 2014. Hampson records the expense in the same year it made the sales.

Allowance for Doubtful Accounts shows the estimated amount of claims on customers that the company expects will become uncollectible in the future. Companies use a contra account instead of a direct credit to Accounts Receivable because they do not know which customers will not pay. The credit balance in the allowance account will absorb the specific write-offs when they occur. As Illustration 9-3 shows, the company deducts the allowance account from accounts receivable in the current assets section of the balance sheet.

Illustration 9-3
Presentation of allowance for doubtful accounts

HAMPSON FURNITURE		
Balance Sheet (partial)		
Current assets		
Cash		$ 14,800
Accounts receivable	$200,000	
Less: Allowance for doubtful accounts	12,000	188,000
Inventory		310,000
Supplies		25,000
Total current assets		$537,800

Helpful Hint Cash realizable value is sometimes referred to as *accounts receivable (net)*.

The amount of $188,000 in Illustration 9-3 represents the expected **cash realizable value** of the accounts receivable at the statement date. **Companies do not close Allowance for Doubtful Accounts at the end of the fiscal year.**

RECORDING THE WRITE-OFF OF AN UNCOLLECTIBLE ACCOUNT As described in the Feature Story, companies use various methods of collecting past-due accounts, such as letters, calls, and legal action. When they have exhausted all means of collecting a past-due account and collection appears impossible, the company writes off the account. In the credit card industry, for example, it is standard practice to write off accounts that are 210 days past due. To prevent premature or unauthorized write-offs, authorized management personnel should formally approve each write-off. To maintain segregation of duties, the employee authorized to write off accounts should not have daily responsibilities related to cash or receivables.

To illustrate a receivables write-off, assume that the financial vice president of Hampson Furniture authorizes a write-off of the $500 balance owed by R. A. Ware on March 1, 2015. The entry to record the write-off is:

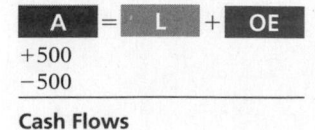

+500
−500

Cash Flows
no effect

Mar. 1	Allowance for Doubtful Accounts	500	
	Accounts Receivable—R. A. Ware		500
	(Write-off of R. A. Ware account)		

Bad Debt Expense does not increase when the write-off occurs. **Under the allowance method, companies debit every bad debt write-off to the allowance account rather than to Bad Debt Expense.** A debit to Bad Debt Expense would be incorrect because the company has already recognized the expense when it made the adjusting entry for estimated bad debts. Instead, the entry to record the write-off of an uncollectible account reduces both Accounts Receivable and Allowance for Doubtful Accounts. After posting, the general ledger accounts appear as shown in Illustration 9-4.

Accounts Receivable				Allowance for Doubtful Accounts			
Jan. 1 Bal. 200,000		Mar. 1	500	Mar. 1	500	Jan. 1 Bal.	12,000
Mar. 1 Bal. 199,500						Mar. 1 Bal.	11,500

Illustration 9-4
General ledger balances after write-off

A write-off affects **only balance sheet accounts**—not income statement accounts. The write-off of the account reduces both Accounts Receivable and Allowance for Doubtful Accounts. Cash realizable value in the balance sheet, therefore, remains the same, as Illustration 9-5 shows.

	Before Write-Off	After Write-Off
Accounts receivable	$ 200,000	$ 199,500
Allowance for doubtful accounts	12,000	11,500
Cash realizable value	**$188,000**	**$188,000**

Illustration 9-5
Cash realizable value comparison

RECOVERY OF AN UNCOLLECTIBLE ACCOUNT Occasionally, a company collects from a customer after it has written off the account as uncollectible. The company makes two entries to record the recovery of a bad debt: (1) It reverses the entry made in writing off the account. This reinstates the customer's account. (2) It journalizes the collection in the usual manner.

To illustrate, assume that on July 1, R. A. Ware pays the $500 amount that Hampson had written off on March 1. Hampson makes these entries:

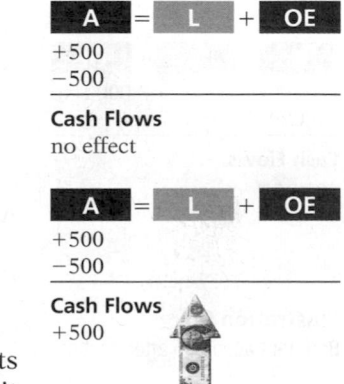

(1)

July 1	Accounts Receivable—R. A. Ware	500	
	Allowance for Doubtful Accounts		500
	(To reverse write-off of R. A. Ware account)		

A = L + OE
+500
−500

Cash Flows
no effect

(2)

July 1	Cash	500	
	Accounts Receivable—R. A. Ware		500
	(To record collection from R. A. Ware)		

A = L + OE
+500
−500

Cash Flows
+500

Note that the recovery of a bad debt, like the write-off of a bad debt, affects **only balance sheet accounts**. The net effect of the two entries above is a debit to Cash and a credit to Allowance for Doubtful Accounts for $500. Accounts Receivable and Allowance for Doubtful Accounts both increase in entry (1) for two reasons. First, the company made an error in judgment when it wrote off the account receivable. Second, after R. A. Ware did pay, Accounts Receivable in the general ledger and Ware's account in the subsidiary ledger should show the collection for possible future credit purposes.

ESTIMATING THE ALLOWANCE For Hampson Furniture in Illustration 9-3, the amount of the expected uncollectibles was given. However, in "real life," companies must estimate that amount when they use the allowance method. Two bases are used to determine this amount: **(1) percentage of sales** and **(2) percentage of receivables**. Both bases are generally accepted. The choice is a management decision. It depends on the relative emphasis that management wishes to give to expenses and revenues on the one hand or to cash realizable value of the accounts receivable on the other. The choice is whether to emphasize income statement or balance sheet relationships. Illustration 9-6 compares the two bases.

Illustration 9-6
Comparison of bases for estimating uncollectibles

The percentage-of-sales basis results in a better matching of expenses with revenues—an income statement viewpoint. The percentage-of-receivables basis produces the better estimate of cash realizable value—a balance sheet viewpoint. Under both bases, the company must determine its past experience with bad debt losses.

Percentage-of-Sales. In the **percentage-of-sales basis**, management estimates what percentage of credit sales will be uncollectible. This percentage is based on past experience and anticipated credit policy.

The company applies this percentage to either total credit sales or net credit sales of the current year. To illustrate, assume that Gonzalez Company elects to use the percentage-of-sales basis. It concludes that 1% of net credit sales will become uncollectible. If net credit sales for 2014 are $800,000, the estimated bad debt expense is $8,000 (1% × $800,000). The adjusting entry is:

A	=	L	+	OE
				−8,000 Exp
−8,000				

Cash Flows
no effect

Dec. 31	Bad Debt Expense	8,000	
	Allowance for Doubtful Accounts		8,000
	(To record estimated bad debts for year)		

After the adjusting entry is posted, assuming the allowance account already has a credit balance of $1,723, the accounts of Gonzalez Company will show the following.

Illustration 9-7
Bad debt accounts after posting

Bad Debt Expense		Allowance for Doubtful Accounts	
Dec. 31 Adj. **8,000**			Jan. 1 Bal. 1,723
			Dec. 31 Adj. **8,000**
			Dec. 31 Bal. 9,723

This basis of estimating uncollectibles emphasizes the matching of expenses with revenues. As a result, Bad Debt Expense will show a direct percentage relationship to the sales base on which it is computed. **When the**

company makes the adjusting entry, it disregards the existing balance in Allowance for Doubtful Accounts. The adjusted balance in this account should be a reasonable approximation of the realizable value of the receivables. If actual write-offs differ significantly from the amount estimated, the company should modify the percentage for future years.

Percentage-of-Receivables. Under the **percentage-of-receivables basis**, management estimates what percentage of receivables will result in losses from uncollectible accounts. The company prepares an **aging schedule**, in which it classifies customer balances by the length of time they have been unpaid. Because of its emphasis on time, the analysis is often called **aging the accounts receivable**. In the Feature Story, Whitehall-Robins prepared an aging report daily.

After the company arranges the accounts by age, it determines the expected bad debt losses. It applies percentages based on past experience to the totals in each category. The longer a receivable is past due, the less likely it is to be collected. Thus, the estimated percentage of uncollectible debts increases as the number of days past due increases. Illustration 9-8 shows an aging schedule for Dart Company. Note that the estimated percentage uncollectible increases from 2% to 40% as the number of days past due increases.

Helpful Hint Where appropriate, companies may use only a single percentage rate.

Illustration 9-8
Aging schedule

Worksheet.xls

Home | Insert | Page Layout | Formulas | Data | Review | View

P18   fx

	A	B	C	D	E	F	G
1				Number of Days Past Due			
2			Not				
3	Customer	Total	Yet Due	1–30	31–60	61–90	Over 90
4	T. E. Adert	$ 600		$ 300		$ 200	$ 100
5	R. C. Bortz	300	$ 300				
6	B. A. Carl	450		200	$ 250		
7	O. L. Diker	700	500			200	
8	T. O. Ebbet	600			300		300
9	Others	36,950	26,200	5,200	2,450	1,600	1,500
10		$39,600	$27,000	$5,700	$3,000	$2,000	$1,900
11	Estimated Percentage Uncollectible		2%	4%	10%	20%	40%
12	Total Estimated Bad Debts	$ 2,228	$ 540	$ 228	$ 300	$ 400	$ 760
13							

Helpful Hint The older categories have higher percentages because the longer an account is past due, the less likely it is to be collected.

Total estimated bad debts for Dart Company ($2,228) represent the amount of existing customer claims the company expects will become uncollectible in the future. This amount represents the **required balance** in Allowance for Doubtful Accounts at the balance sheet date. **The amount of the bad debt adjusting entry is the difference between the required balance and the existing balance in the allowance account.** If the trial balance shows Allowance for Doubtful Accounts with a credit balance of $528, the company will make an adjusting entry for $1,700 ($2,228 − $528), as shown here.

Dec. 31	Bad Debt Expense	1,700	
	Allowance for Doubtful Accounts		1,700
	(To adjust allowance account to total estimated uncollectibles)		

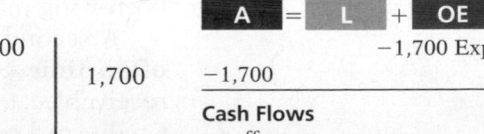

A = L + OE
−1,700 Exp
−1,700

Cash Flows
no effect

After Dart posts its adjusting entry, its accounts will appear as follows.

Illustration 9-9
Bad debt accounts after posting

Bad Debt Expense			Allowance for Doubtful Accounts	
Dec. 31 Adj. **1,700**			Bal.	528
			Dec. 31 Adj. **1,700**	
			Bal.	2,228

Allowance for Doubtful Accounts			
Dec. 31 Unadj. Bal. 500		Dec. 31 Adj. 2,728	
		Dec. 31 Bal. 2,228	

Occasionally, the allowance account will have a **debit balance** prior to adjustment. This occurs when write-offs during the year have exceeded previous provisions for bad debts. In such a case, the company **adds the debit balance to the required balance** when it makes the adjusting entry. Thus, if there had been a $500 debit balance in the allowance account before adjustment, the adjusting entry would have been for $2,728 ($2,228 + $500) to arrive at a credit balance of $2,228 (see T-account in margin). The percentage-of-receivables basis will normally result in the better approximation of cash realizable value.

> **DO IT!**

Uncollectible Accounts Receivable

Action Plan

✔ Report receivables at their cash (net) realizable value.

✔ Estimate the amount the company does not expect to collect.

✔ Consider the existing balance in the allowance account when using the percentage-of-receivables basis.

Brule Co. has been in business five years. The unadjusted trial balance at the end of the current year shows:

Accounts Receivable	$30,000 Dr.
Sales Revenue	$180,000 Cr.
Allowance for Doubtful Accounts	$2,000 Dr.

Brule estimates bad debts to be 10% of receivables. Prepare the entry necessary to adjust Allowance for Doubtful Accounts.

Solution

The following entry should be made to bring the balance in Allowance for Doubtful Accounts up to a normal credit balance of $3,000 (10% × $30,000):

Bad Debt Expense [(10% × $30,000) + $2,000]	5,000	
Allowance for Doubtful Accounts		5,000
(To record estimate of uncollectible accounts)		

Related exercise material: **BE9-3, BE9-4, BE9-5, BE9-6, BE9-7, E9-3, E9-4, E9-5, E9-6, and DO IT! 9-1.**

 ✔ **The Navigator**

Disposing of Accounts Receivable

LEARNING OBJECTIVE   4

Describe the entries to record the disposition of accounts receivable.

In the normal course of events, companies collect accounts receivable in cash and remove the receivables from the books. However, as credit sales and receivables have grown in significance, the "normal course of events" has changed. Companies now frequently sell their receivables to another company for cash, thereby shortening the cash-to-cash operating cycle.

Companies sell receivables for two major reasons. First, **they may be the only reasonable source of cash**. When money is tight, companies may not be able to borrow money in the usual credit markets. Or if money is available, the cost of borrowing may be prohibitive.

A second reason for selling receivables is that **billing and collection are often time-consuming and costly**. It is often easier for a retailer to sell the receivables to another party with expertise in billing and collection matters. Credit card companies such as MasterCard, Visa, and Discover specialize in billing and collecting accounts receivable.

SALE OF RECEIVABLES

A common sale of receivables is a sale to a factor. A **factor** is a finance company or bank that buys receivables from businesses and then collects the payments directly from the customers. Factoring is a multibillion dollar business.

Factoring arrangements vary widely. Typically, the factor charges a commission to the company that is selling the receivables. This fee ranges from 1–3% of the amount of receivables purchased. To illustrate, assume that Hendredon Furniture factors $600,000 of receivables to Federal Factors. Federal Factors assesses a service charge of 2% of the amount of receivables sold. The journal entry to record the sale by Hendredon Furniture on April 2, 2014, is as follows.

Apr. 2	Cash	588,000	
	Service Charge Expense (2% × $600,000)	12,000	
	Accounts Receivable		600,000
	(To record the sale of accounts receivable)		

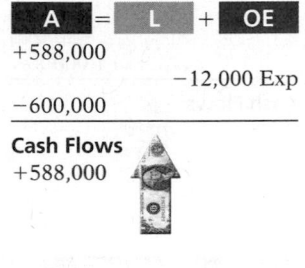

A = L + OE
+588,000
−12,000 Exp
−600,000

Cash Flows
+588,000

If the company often sells its receivables, it records the service charge expense (such as that incurred by Hendredon) as a selling expense. If the company infrequently sells receivables, it may report this amount in the "Other expenses and losses" section of the income statement.

CREDIT CARD SALES

Over one billion credit cards are in use in the United States—more than three credit cards for every man, woman, and child in this country. Visa, MasterCard, and American Express are the national credit cards that most individuals use. Three parties are involved when national credit cards are used in retail sales: (1) the credit card issuer, who is independent of the retailer; (2) the retailer; and (3) the customer. A retailer's acceptance of a national credit card is another form of selling (factoring) the receivable.

Illustration 9-10 shows the major advantages of national credit cards to the retailer. In exchange for these advantages, the retailer pays the credit card issuer a fee of 2–6% of the invoice price for its services.

Illustration 9-10
Advantages of credit cards to the retailer

ACCOUNTING FOR CREDIT CARD SALES The retailer generally considers sales from the use of national credit card sales as **cash sales**. The retailer must pay to the bank that issues the card a fee for processing the transactions. The retailer records the credit card slips in a similar manner as checks deposited from a cash sale.

To illustrate, Anita Ferreri purchases $1,000 of compact discs for her restaurant from Karen Kerr Music Co., using her Visa First Bank Card. First Bank charges a service fee of 3%. The entry to record this transaction by Karen Kerr Music on March 22, 2014, is as follows.

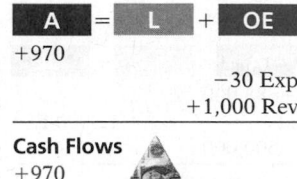

A = L + OE
+970
　　　　　　−30 Exp
　　　　　　+1,000 Rev

Cash Flows
+970

Mar. 22	Cash	970	
	Service Charge Expense	30	
	Sales Revenue		1,000
	(To record Visa credit card sales)		

© Michael Braun/iStockphoto

ACCOUNTING ACROSS THE ORGANIZATION

How Does a Credit Card Work?

Most of you know how to use a credit card, but do you know what happens in the transaction and how the transaction is processed? Suppose that you use a Visa card to purchase some new ties at Nordstrom. The salesperson swipes your card, which allows the information on the magnetic strip on the back of the card to be read. The salesperson then enters in the amount of the purchase. The machine contacts the Visa computer, which routes the call back to the bank that issued your Visa card. The issuing bank verifies that the account exists, that the card is not stolen, and that you have not exceeded your credit limit. At this point, the slip is printed, which you sign.

Visa acts as the clearing agent for the transaction. It transfers funds from the issuing bank to Nordstrom's bank account. Generally this transfer of funds, from sale to the receipt of funds in the merchant's account, takes two to three days.

In the meantime, Visa puts a pending charge on your account for the amount of the tie purchase; that amount counts immediately against your available credit limit. At the end of the billing period, Visa sends you an invoice (your credit card bill) which shows the various charges you made, and the amounts that Visa expended on your behalf, for the month. You then must "pay the piper" for your stylish new ties.

? Assume that Nordstrom prepares a bank reconciliation at the end of each month. If some credit card sales have not been processed by the bank, how should Nordstrom treat these transactions on its bank reconciliation? (See page 467.)

> DO IT!

Disposition of Accounts Receivable

Mehl Wholesalers Co. has been expanding faster than it can raise capital. According to its local banker, the company has reached its debt ceiling. Mehl's suppliers (creditors) are demanding payment within 30 days of the invoice date for goods acquired, but Mehl's customers are slow in paying (60–90 days). As a result, Mehl has a cash flow problem.

Mehl needs $120,000 in cash to safely cover next Friday's payroll. Its balance of outstanding accounts receivable totals $750,000. To alleviate this cash crunch, Mehl sells $125,000 of its receivables on September 7, 2014. Record the entry that Mehl would make when it raises the needed cash. (Assume a 1% service charge.)

Action Plan

✔ To speed up the collection of cash, sell receivables to a factor.

✔ Calculate service charge expense as a percentage of the factored receivables.

Solution

If Mehl Wholesalers factors $125,000 of its accounts receivable at a 1% service charge, it would make the following entry.

Sept. 7	Cash	123,750	
	Service Charge Expense (1% × $125,000)	1,250	
	Accounts Receivable		125,000
	(To record sale of receivables to factor)		

Related exercise material: **BE9-8, E9-7, E9-8, E9-9, and** **DO IT!** **9-2.**

 ✔ **The Navigator**

Notes Receivable

Companies may also grant credit in exchange for a formal credit instrument known as a promissory note. A **promissory note** is a written promise to pay a specified amount of money on demand or at a definite time. Promissory notes may be used (1) when individuals and companies lend or borrow money, (2) when the amount of the transaction and the credit period exceed normal limits, or (3) in settlement of accounts receivable.

In a promissory note, the party making the promise to pay is called the **maker**. The party to whom payment is to be made is called the **payee**. The note may specifically identify the payee by name or may designate the payee simply as the bearer of the note.

In the note shown in Illustration 9-11, Calhoun Company is the maker and Wilma Company is the payee. To Wilma Company, the promissory note is a note receivable. To Calhoun Company, it is a note payable.

> **LEARNING OBJECTIVE   5**
>
> **Compute the maturity date of and interest on notes receivable.**

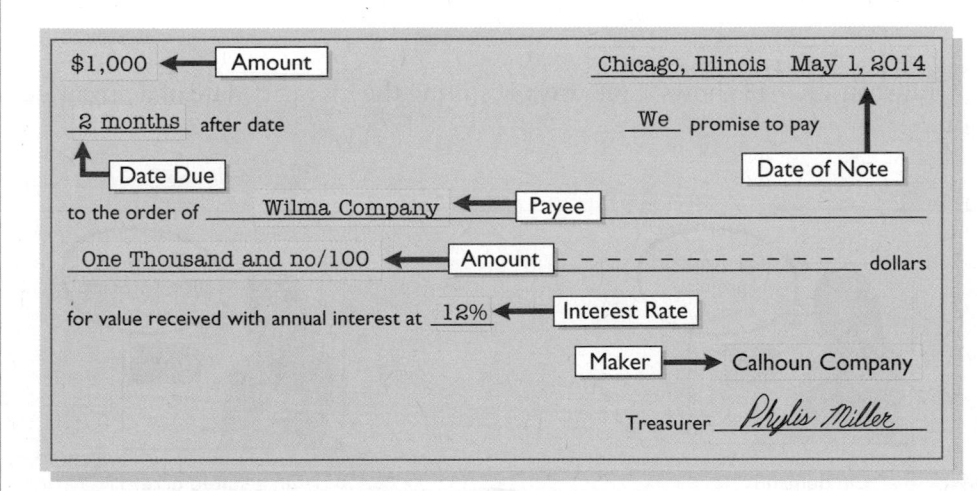

Illustration 9-11
Promissory note

Helpful Hint Who are the two key parties to a note, and what entry does each party make when the note is issued?

Answer:
1. The maker, Calhoun Company, debits Cash and credits Notes Payable.
2. The payee, Wilma Company, debits Notes Receivable and credits Cash.

Notes receivable give the holder a stronger legal claim to assets than do accounts receivable. Like accounts receivable, notes receivable can be readily sold to another party. Promissory notes are negotiable instruments (as are checks), which means that they can be transferred to another party by endorsement.

Companies frequently accept notes receivable from customers who need to extend the payment of an outstanding account receivable. They often require such notes from high-risk customers. In some industries (such as the pleasure and sport boat industry), all credit sales are supported by notes. The majority of notes, however, originate from loans.

The basic issues in accounting for notes receivable are the same as those for accounts receivable:

1. **Recognizing** notes receivable.
2. **Valuing** notes receivable.
3. **Disposing** of notes receivable.

On the following pages, we will look at these issues. Before we do, we need to consider two issues that do not apply to accounts receivable: maturity date and computing interest.

Determining the Maturity Date

When the life of a note is expressed in terms of months, you find the date when it matures by counting the months from the date of issue. For example, the maturity date of a three-month note dated May 1 is August 1. A note drawn on the last day of a month matures on the last day of a subsequent month. That is, a July 31 note due in two months matures on September 30.

When the due date is stated in terms of days, you need to count the exact number of days to determine the maturity date. In counting, **omit the date the note is issued but include the due date**. For example, the maturity date of a 60-day note dated July 17 is September 15, computed as follows.

Illustration 9-12
Computation of maturity date

Term of note		60 days
July (31 − 17)	14	
August	31	45
Maturity date: September		**15**

Illustration 9-13 shows three ways of stating the maturity date of a promissory note.

Illustration 9-13
Maturity date of different notes

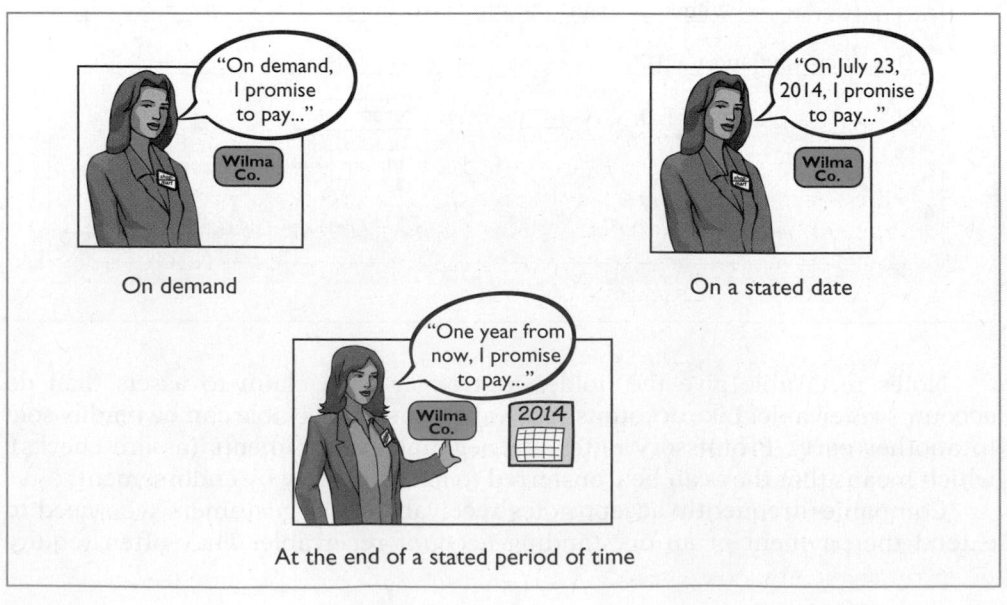

On demand

On a stated date

At the end of a stated period of time

Computing Interest

Illustration 9-14 gives the basic formula for computing interest on an interest-bearing note.

Face Value of Note	×	Annual Interest Rate	×	Time in Terms of One Year	=	Interest

Illustration 9-14
Formula for computing interest

The interest rate specified in a note is an **annual** rate of interest. The time factor in the computation in Illustration 9-14 expresses the fraction of a year that the note is outstanding. When the maturity date is stated in days, the time factor is often the number of days divided by 360. When counting days, omit the date that the note is issued but include the due date. When the due date is stated in months, the time factor is the number of months divided by 12. Illustration 9-15 shows computation of interest for various time periods.

Helpful Hint The interest rate specified is the *annual* rate.

Terms of Note	Interest Computation
	Face × Rate × Time = Interest
$ 730, 12%, 120 days	$ 730 × 12% × **120/360** = $ 29.20
$1,000, 9%, 6 months	$1,000 × 9% × **6/12** = $ 45.00
$2,000, 6%, 1 year	$2,000 × 6% × **1/1** = $120.00

Illustration 9-15
Computation of interest

There are different ways to calculate interest. For example, the computation in Illustration 9-15 assumes 360 days for the length of the year. Most financial instruments use 365 days to compute interest. *For homework problems, assume 360 days to simplify computations.*

Recognizing Notes Receivable

To illustrate the basic entry for notes receivable, we will use Calhoun Company's $1,000, two-month, 12% promissory note dated May 1. Assuming that Calhoun Company wrote the note to settle an open account, Wilma Company makes the following entry for the receipt of the note.

LEARNING OBJECTIVE 6
Explain how companies recognize notes receivable.

May 1	Notes Receivable	1,000	
	Accounts Receivable—Calhoun Company		1,000
	(To record acceptance of Calhoun Company note)		

A = L + OE
+1,000
−1,000

Cash Flows
no effect

The company records the note receivable at its **face value**, the amount shown on the face of the note. No interest revenue is reported when the note is accepted, because the revenue recognition principle does not recognize revenue until the performance obligation is satisfied. Interest is earned (accrued) as time passes.

If a company lends money using a note, the entry is a debit to Notes Receivable and a credit to Cash in the amount of the loan.

Valuing Notes Receivable

Valuing short-term notes receivable is the same as valuing accounts receivable. Like accounts receivable, companies report short-term notes receivable at their **cash (net) realizable value**. The notes receivable allowance account is Allowance for Doubtful Accounts. The estimations involved in determining cash realizable value and in recording bad debt expense and the related allowance are done similarly to accounts receivable.

LEARNING OBJECTIVE 7
Describe how companies value notes receivable.

INTERNATIONAL INSIGHT

Can Fair Value Be Unfair?

The FASB and the International Accounting Standards Board (IASB) are considering proposals for how to account for financial instruments. The FASB has proposed that loans and receivables be accounted for at their fair value (the amount they could currently be sold for), as are most investments. The FASB believes that this would provide a more accurate view of a company's financial position. It might be especially useful as an early warning when a bank is in trouble because of poor-quality loans. But, banks argue that fair values are difficult to estimate accurately. They are also concerned that volatile fair values could cause large swings in a bank's reported net income.

Source: David Reilly, "Banks Face a Mark-to-Market Challenge," *Wall Street Journal Online* (March 15, 2010).

 What are the arguments in favor of and against fair value accounting for loans and receivables? (See page 467.)

Disposing of Notes Receivable

Notes may be held to their maturity date, at which time the face value plus accrued interest is due. In some situations, the maker of the note defaults, and the payee must make an appropriate adjustment. In other situations, similar to accounts receivable, the holder of the note speeds up the conversion to cash by selling the receivables (as described later in this chapter).

HONOR OF NOTES RECEIVABLE

A note is **honored** when its maker pays in full at its maturity date. For each interest-bearing note, the **amount due at maturity** is the face value of the note plus interest for the length of time specified on the note.

To illustrate, assume that Wolder Co. lends Higley Co. $10,000 on June 1, accepting a five-month, 9% interest note. In this situation, interest is $375 ($10,000 × 9% × $\frac{5}{12}$). The amount due, **the maturity value**, is $10,375 ($10,000 + $375). To obtain payment, Wolder (the payee) must present the note either to Higley Co. (the maker) or to the maker's agent, such as a bank. If Wolder presents the note to Higley Co. on November 1, the maturity date, Wolder's entry to record the collection is:

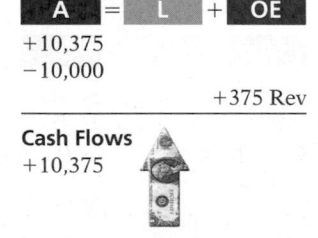

A = L + OE
+10,375
−10,000
          +375 Rev

Cash Flows
+10,375

Nov. 1	Cash	10,375	
	Notes Receivable		10,000
	Interest Revenue ($10,000 × 9% × $\frac{5}{12}$)		375
	(To record collection of Higley note and interest)		

ACCRUAL OF INTEREST RECEIVABLE

Suppose instead that Wolder Co. prepares financial statements as of September 30. The timeline in Illustration 9-16 presents this situation.

Illustration 9-16
Timeline of interest earned

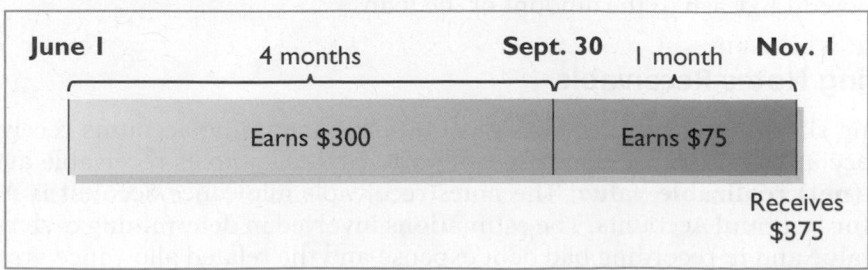

| June 1 | 4 months | Sept. 30 | 1 month | Nov. 1 |

Earns $300   Earns $75

Receives $375

To reflect interest earned but not yet received, Wolder must accrue interest on September 30. In this case, the adjusting entry by Wolder is for four months of interest, or $300, as shown below.

Sept. 30	Interest Receivable ($10,000 × 9% × $\frac{4}{12}$)	300	
	Interest Revenue		300
	(To accrue 4 months' interest on Higley note)		

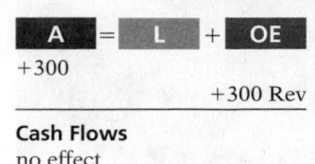

A = L + OE
+300
+300 Rev

Cash Flows
no effect

At the note's maturity on November 1, Wolder receives $10,375. This amount represents repayment of the $10,000 note as well as five months of interest, or $375, as shown below. The $375 is comprised of the $300 Interest Receivable accrued on September 30 plus $75 earned during October. Wolder's entry to record the honoring of the Higley note on November 1 is:

Nov. 1	Cash [$10,000 + (10,000 × 9% × $\frac{5}{12}$)]	10,375	
	Notes Receivable		10,000
	Interest Receivable		300
	Interest Revenue (10,000 × 9% × $\frac{1}{12}$)]		75
	(To record collection of Higley note and interest)		

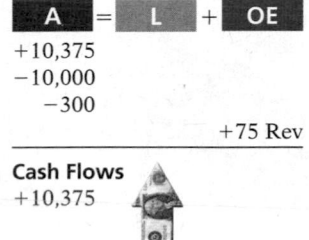

A = L + OE
+10,375
−10,000
−300
+75 Rev

Cash Flows
+10,375

In this case, Wolder credits Interest Receivable because the receivable was established in the adjusting entry on September 30.

DISHONOR OF NOTES RECEIVABLE

A **dishonored (defaulted) note** is a note that is not paid in full at maturity. A dishonored note receivable is no longer negotiable. However, the payee still has a claim against the maker of the note for both the note and the interest. Therefore the note holder usually transfers the Notes Receivable account to an Account Receivable.

To illustrate, assume that Higley Co. on November 1 indicates that it cannot pay at the present time. The entry to record the dishonor of the note depends on whether Wolder Co. expects eventual collection. If it does expect eventual collection, Wolder Co. debits the amount due (face value and interest) on the note to Accounts Receivable. It would make the following entry at the time the note is dishonored (assuming no previous accrual of interest).

Nov. 1	Accounts Receivable—Higley	10,375	
	Notes Receivable		10,000
	Interest Revenue		375
	(To record the dishonor of Higley note)		

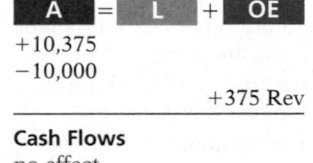

A = L + OE
+10,375
−10,000
+375 Rev

Cash Flows
no effect

If instead, on November 1, there is no hope of collection, the note holder would write off the face value of the note by debiting Allowance for Doubtful Accounts. No interest revenue would be recorded because collection will not occur.

SALE OF NOTES RECEIVABLE

The accounting for the sale of notes receivable is recorded similarly to the sale of accounts receivable. The accounting entries for the sale of notes receivable are left for a more advanced course.

ACCOUNTING ACROSS THE ORGANIZATION

Bad Information Can Lead to Bad Loans

Many factors have contributed to the recent credit crisis. One significant factor that resulted in many bad loans was a failure by lenders to investigate loan customers sufficiently. For example, Countrywide Financial Corporation wrote many loans under its "Fast and Easy" loan program. That program allowed borrowers to provide little or no documentation for their income or their assets. Other lenders had similar programs, which earned the nickname "liars' loans." One study found that in these situations, 60% of applicants overstated their incomes by more than 50% in order to qualify for a loan. Critics of the banking industry say that because loan officers were compensated for loan volume and because banks were selling the loans to investors rather than holding them, the lenders had little incentive to investigate the borrowers' creditworthiness.

Source: Glenn R. Simpson and James R. Hagerty, "Countrywide Loss Focuses Attention on Underwriting," *Wall Street Journal* (April 30, 2008), p. B1; and Michael Corkery, "Fraud Seen as Driver in Wave of Foreclosures," *Wall Street Journal* (December 21, 2007), p. A1.

 What steps should the banks have taken to ensure the accuracy of financial information provided on loan applications? (See page 467.)

> DO IT!

Notes Receivable

Gambit Stores accepts from Leonard Co. a $3,400, 90-day, 6% note dated May 10 in settlement of Leonard's overdue account. (a) What is the maturity date of the note? (b) What entry does Gambit make at the maturity date, assuming Leonard pays the note and interest in full at that time?

Solution

(a) The maturity date is August 8, computed as follows.

Term of note:		90 days
May (31−10)	21	
June	30	
July	31	82
Maturity date: August		8

(b) The interest payable at the maturity date is $51, computed as follows.

Face × Rate × Time = Interest
$3,400 × 6% × 90/360 = $51

The entry recorded by Gambit Stores at the maturity date is:

Cash	3,451	
Notes Receivable		3,400
Interest Revenue		51
(To record collection of Leonard note)		

Related exercise material: **BE9-9, BE9-10, BE9-11, E9-10, E9-11, E9-12, E9-13, and DO IT! 9-3.**

Action Plan

✔ Count the exact number of days to determine the maturity date. Omit the date the note is issued, but include the due date.

✔ Determine whether interest was accrued.

✔ Compute the accrued interest.

✔ Prepare the entry for payment of the note and interest.

✔ The entry to record interest at maturity in this solution assumes no interest has been previously accrued on this note.

✔ The Navigator

Presentation

Companies should identify in the balance sheet or in the notes to the financial statements each of the major types of receivables. Short-term receivables appear in the current assets section of the balance sheet. Short-term investments appear before short-term receivables because these investments are more liquid (nearer to cash). Companies report both the gross amount of receivables and the allowance for doubtful accounts.

In a multiple-step income statement, companies report bad debt expense and service charge expense as selling expenses in the operating expenses section. Interest revenue appears under "Other revenues and gains" in the nonoperating activities section of the income statement.

LEARNING OBJECTIVE 9

Explain the statement presentation and analysis of receivables.

Analysis

Investors and corporate managers compute financial ratios to evaluate the liquidity of a company's accounts receivable. They use the **accounts receivable turnover** to assess the liquidity of the receivables. This ratio measures the number of times, on average, the company collects accounts receivable during the period. It is computed by dividing net credit sales (net sales less cash sales) by the average net accounts receivable during the year. Unless seasonal factors are significant, average net accounts receivable outstanding can be computed from the beginning and ending balances of net accounts receivable.

For example, in 2011 Cisco Systems had net sales of $34,526 million for the year. It had a beginning accounts receivable (net) balance of $4,929 million and an ending accounts receivable (net) balance of $4,698 million. Assuming that Cisco's sales were all on credit, its accounts receivable turnover is computed as follows.

Net Credit Sales	÷	Average Net Accounts Receivable	=	Accounts Receivable Turnover
$34,526	÷	$\frac{\$4,929 + \$4,698}{2}$	=	7.2 times

Illustration 9-17
Accounts receivable turnover and computation

The result indicates an accounts receivable turnover of 7.2 times per year. The higher the turnover, the more liquid the company's receivables.

A variant of the accounts receivable turnover that makes the liquidity even more evident is its conversion into an **average collection period** in terms of days. This is done by dividing the accounts receivable turnover into 365 days. For example, Cisco's turnover of 7.2 times is divided into 365 days, as shown in Illustration 9-18, to obtain approximately 51 days. This means that it takes Cisco 51 days to collect its accounts receivable.

Days in Year	÷	Accounts Receivable Turnover	=	Average Collection Period in Days
365 days	÷	7.2 times	=	51 days

Illustration 9-18
Average collection period for receivables formula and computation

Companies frequently use the average collection period to assess the effectiveness of a company's credit and collection policies. The general rule is that the collection period should not greatly exceed the credit term period (that is, the time allowed for payment).

> **DO IT!**

Analysis of Receivables

In 2014, Phil Mickelson Company has net credit sales of $923,795 for the year. It had a beginning accounts receivable (net) balance of $38,275 and an ending accounts receivable (net) balance of $35,988. Compute Phil Mickelson Company's (a) accounts receivable turnover and (b) average collection period in days.

Solution

Action Plan

✔ Review the formula to compute the accounts receivable turnover.

✔ Make sure that both the beginning and ending accounts receivable balances are considered in the computation.

✔ Review the formula to compute the average collection period in days.

(a)

$$\text{Net credit sales} \div \frac{\text{Average net}}{\text{accounts receivable}} = \frac{\text{Accounts receivable}}{\text{turnover}}$$

$$\$923,795 \div \frac{\$38,275 + \$35,988}{2} = 24.9 \text{ times}$$

(b)

$$\text{Days in year} \div \frac{\text{Accounts receivable}}{\text{turnover}} = \frac{\text{Average collection}}{\text{period in days}}$$

$$365 \div 24.9 \text{ times} = 14.7 \text{ days}$$

Related exercise material: **BE9-12, E9-14, and DO IT! 9-4.**

✔ **The Navigator**

> **Comprehensive DO IT!**

The following selected transactions relate to Dylan Company.

Mar.	1	Sold $20,000 of merchandise to Potter Company, terms 2/10, n/30.
	11	Received payment in full from Potter Company for balance due on existing accounts receivable.
	12	Accepted Juno Company's $20,000, 6-month, 12% note for balance due.
	13	Made Dylan Company credit card sales for $13,200.
	15	Made Visa credit card sales totaling $6,700. A 3% service fee is charged by Visa.
Apr.	11	Sold accounts receivable of $8,000 to Harcot Factor. Harcot Factor assesses a service charge of 2% of the amount of receivables sold.
	13	Received collections of $8,200 on Dylan Company credit card sales and added finance charges of 1.5% to the remaining balances.
May	10	Wrote off as uncollectible $16,000 of accounts receivable. Dylan uses the percentage-of-sales basis to estimate bad debts.
June	30	Credit sales recorded during the first 6 months total $2,000,000. The bad debt percentage is 1% of credit sales. At June 30, the balance in the allowance account is $3,500 before adjustment.
July	16	One of the accounts receivable written off in May was from J. Simon, who pays the amount due, $4,000, in full.

Instructions

Prepare the journal entries for the transactions.

Solution to Comprehensive DO IT!

Action Plan

✔ Generally, record accounts receivable at invoice price.

✔ Recognize that sales returns and allowances and cash discounts reduce the amount received on accounts receivable.

Date	Account	Debit	Credit
Mar. 1	Accounts Receivable—Potter	20,000	
	Sales Revenue		20,000
	(To record sales on account)		
11	Cash	19,600	
	Sales Discounts (2% × $20,000)	400	
	Accounts Receivable—Potter		20,000
	(To record collection of accounts receivable)		

Action Plan (Contd.)

✔ Record service charge expense on the seller's books when accounts receivable are sold.

✔ Prepare an adjusting entry for bad debt expense.

✔ Ignore any balance in the allowance account under the percentage-of-sales basis. Recognize the balance in the allowance account under the percentage-of-receivables basis.

✔ Record write-offs of accounts receivable only in balance sheet accounts.

Date	Account	Debit	Credit
12	Notes Receivable	20,000	
	Accounts Receivable—Juno		20,000
	(To record acceptance of Juno Company note)		
13	Accounts Receivable	13,200	
	Sales Revenue		13,200
	(To record company credit card sales)		
15	Cash	6,499	
	Service Charge Expense (3% × $6,700)	201	
	Sales Revenue		6,700
	(To record credit card sales)		
Apr. 11	Cash	7,840	
	Service Charge Expense (2% × $8,000)	160	
	Accounts Receivable		8,000
	(To record sale of receivables to factor)		
13	Cash	8,200	
	Accounts Receivable		8,200
	(To record collection of accounts receivable)		
	Accounts Receivable [($13,200 − $8,200) × 1.5%]	75	
	Interest Revenue		75
	(To record interest on amount due)		
May 10	Allowance for Doubtful Accounts	16,000	
	Accounts Receivable		16,000
	(To record write-off of accounts receivable)		
June 30	Bad Debt Expense ($2,000,000 × 1%)	20,000	
	Allowance for Doubtful Accounts		20,000
	(To record estimate of uncollectible accounts)		
July 16	Accounts Receivable—J. Simon	4,000	
	Allowance for Doubtful Accounts		4,000
	(To reverse write-off of accounts receivable)		
	Cash	4,000	
	Accounts Receivable—J. Simon		4,000
	(To record collection of accounts receivable)		

✔ The Navigator

SUMMARY OF LEARNING OBJECTIVES

 ✔ The Navigator

1 Identify the different types of receivables. Receivables are frequently classified as (1) accounts, (2) notes, and (3) other. Accounts receivable are amounts customers owe on account. Notes receivable are claims for which lenders issue formal instruments of credit as proof of the debt. Other receivables include nontrade receivables such as interest receivable, loans to company officers, advances to employees, and income taxes refundable.

2 Explain how companies recognize accounts receivable. Companies record accounts receivable when they provide a service on account or at the point of sale of merchandise on account. Accounts receivable are reduced by sales returns and allowances. Cash discounts reduce the amount received on accounts receivable. When

interest is charged on a past due receivable, the company adds this interest to the accounts receivable balance and recognizes it as interest revenue.

3 Distinguish between the methods and bases companies use to value accounts receivable. There are two methods of accounting for uncollectible accounts: the allowance method and the direct write-off method. Companies may use either the percentage-of-sales or the percentage-of-receivables basis to estimate uncollectible accounts using the allowance method. The percentage-of-sales basis emphasizes the expense recognition (matching) principle. The percentage-of-receivables basis emphasizes the cash realizable value of the accounts receivable. An aging schedule is often used with this basis.

4 **Describe the entries to record the disposition of accounts receivable.** When a company collects an account receivable, it credits Accounts Receivable. When a company sells (factors) an account receivable, a service charge expense reduces the amount received.

5 **Compute the maturity date of and interest on notes receivable.** For a note stated in months, the maturity date is found by counting the months from the date of issue. For a note stated in days, the number of days is counted, omitting the issue date and counting the due date. The formula for computing interest is Face value × Interest rate × Time.

6 **Explain how companies recognize notes receivable.** Companies record notes receivable at face value. In some cases, it is necessary to accrue interest prior to maturity. In this case, companies debit Interest Receivable and credit Interest Revenue.

7 **Describe how companies value notes receivable.** As with accounts receivable, companies report notes receivable at their cash (net) realizable value. The notes receivable allowance account is Allowance for Doubtful Accounts. The computation and estimations involved in valuing notes receivable at cash realizable value, and in recording the proper amount of bad debt expense and the related allowance, are similar to those for accounts receivable.

8 **Describe the entries to record the disposition of notes receivable.** Notes can be held to maturity. At that time the face value plus accrued interest is due, and the note is removed from the accounts. In many cases, the holder of the note speeds up the conversion by selling the receivable to another party (a factor). In some situations, the maker of the note dishonors the note (defaults), in which case the company transfers the note and accrued interest to an account receivable or writes off the note.

9 **Explain the statement presentation and analysis of receivables.** Companies should identify in the balance sheet or in the notes to the financial statements each major type of receivable. Short-term receivables are considered current assets. Companies report the gross amount of receivables and the allowance for doubtful accounts. They report bad debt and service charge expenses in the multiple-step income statement as operating (selling) expenses. Interest revenue appears under other revenues and gains in the nonoperating activities section of the statement. Managers and investors evaluate accounts receivable for liquidity by computing a turnover ratio and an average collection period.

GLOSSARY

Accounts receivable Amounts owed by customers on account. (p. 430).

Accounts receivable turnover A measure of the liquidity of accounts receivable; computed by dividing net credit sales by average net accounts receivable. (p. 447).

Aging the accounts receivable The analysis of customer balances by the length of time they have been unpaid. (p. 437).

Allowance method A method of accounting for bad debts that involves estimating uncollectible accounts at the end of each period. (p. 433).

Average collection period The average amount of time that a receivable is outstanding; calculated by dividing 365 days by the accounts receivable turnover. (p. 447).

Bad Debt Expense An expense account to record uncollectible receivables. (p. 432).

Cash (net) realizable value The net amount a company expects to receive in cash. (p. 433).

Direct write-off method A method of accounting for bad debts that involves expensing accounts at the time they are determined to be uncollectible. (p. 432).

Dishonored (defaulted) note A note that is not paid in full at maturity. (p. 445).

Factor A finance company or bank that buys receivables from businesses and then collects the payments directly from the customers. (p. 439).

Maker The party in a promissory note who is making the promise to pay. (p. 441).

Notes receivable Written promise (as evidenced by a formal instrument) for amounts to be received. (p. 430).

Other receivables Various forms of nontrade receivables, such as interest receivable and income taxes refundable. (p. 430).

Payee The party to whom payment of a promissory note is to be made. (p. 441).

Percentage-of-receivables basis Management estimates what percentage of receivables will result in losses from uncollectible accounts. (p. 437).

Percentage-of-sales basis Management estimates what percentage of credit sales will be uncollectible. (p. 436).

Promissory note A written promise to pay a specified amount of money on demand or at a definite time. (p. 441).

Receivables Amounts due from individuals and other companies. (p. 430).

Trade receivables Notes and accounts receivable that result from sales transactions. (p. 430).

 Self-Test, Brief Exercises, Exercises, Problem Set A, and many more components are available for practice in *WileyPLUS*.

SELF-TEST QUESTIONS

Answers are on page 467.

(LO 1) **1.** Receivables are frequently classified as:
   (a) accounts receivable, company receivables, and other receivables.
   (b) accounts receivable, notes receivable, and employee receivables.
   (c) accounts receivable and general receivables.
   (d) accounts receivable, notes receivable, and other receivables.

(LO 2) **2.** Buehler Company on June 15 sells merchandise on account to Chaz Co. for $1,000, terms 2/10, n/30. On June 20, Chaz Co. returns merchandise worth $300 to Buehler Company. On June 24, payment is received from Chaz Co. for the balance due. What is the amount of cash received?
   (a) $700.   **(c)** $686.
   (b) $680.   **(d)** None of the above.

(LO 3) **3.** Which of the following approaches for bad debts is best described as a balance sheet method?
   (a) Percentage-of-receivables basis.
   (b) Direct write-off method.
   (c) Percentage-of-sales basis.
   (d) Both percentage-of-receivables basis and direct write-off method.

(LO 3) **4.** Hughes Company has a credit balance of $5,000 in its Allowance for Doubtful Accounts before any adjustments are made at the end of the year. Based on review and aging of its accounts receivable at the end of the year, Hughes estimates that $60,000 of its receivables are uncollectible. The amount of bad debt expense which should be reported for the year is:
   (a) $5,000.   **(c)** $60,000.
   (b) $55,000.   **(d)** $65,000.

(LO 3) **5.** Use the same information as in Question 4, except that Hughes has a debit balance of $5,000 in its Allowance for Doubtful Accounts before any adjustments are made at the end of the year. In this situation, the amount of bad debt expense that should be reported for the year is:
   (a) $5,000.   **(c)** $60,000.
   (b) $55,000.   **(d)** $65,000.

(LO 3) **6.** Net sales for the month are $800,000, and bad debts are expected to be 1.5% of net sales. The company uses the percentage-of-sales basis. If Allowance for Doubtful Accounts has a credit balance of $15,000 before adjustment, what is the balance after adjustment?
   (a) $15,000.   **(c)** $23,000.
   (b) $27,000.   **(d)** $31,000.

(LO 3) **7.** In 2014, Roso Carlson Company had net credit sales of $750,000. On January 1, 2014, Allowance for Doubtful Accounts had a credit balance of $18,000. During 2014, $30,000 of uncollectible accounts receivable were written off. Past experience indicates that 3% of net credit sales become uncollectible. What should be the adjusted balance of Allowance for Doubtful Accounts at December 31, 2014?
   (a) $10,050.   **(c)** $22,500.
   (b) $10,500.   **(d)** $40,500.

(LO 3) **8.** An analysis and aging of the accounts receivable of Prince Company at December 31 reveals the following data.

Accounts receivable	$800,000
Allowance for doubtful accounts per books before adjustment	50,000
Amounts expected to become uncollectible	65,000

The cash realizable value of the accounts receivable at December 31, after adjustment, is:
   (a) $685,000.   **(c)** $800,000.
   (b) $750,000.   **(d)** $735,000.

(LO 4) **9.** Which of the following statements about Visa credit card sales is **incorrect**?
   (a) The credit card issuer makes the credit investigation of the customer.
   (b) The retailer is not involved in the collection process.
   (c) Two parties are involved.
   (d) The retailer receives cash more quickly than it would from individual customers on account.

(LO 4) **10.** Blinka Retailers accepted $50,000 of Citibank Visa credit card charges for merchandise sold on July 1. Citibank charges 4% for its credit card use. The entry to record this transaction by Blinka Retailers will include a credit to Sales Revenue of $50,000 and a debit(s) to:
   (a) Cash $48,000
            and Service Charge Expense $2,000
   (b) Accounts Receivable $48,000
            and Service Charge Expense $2,000
   (c) Cash $50,000
   (d) Accounts Receivable $50,000

(LO 6) **11.** One of the following statements about promissory notes is incorrect. The **incorrect** statement is:
   (a) The party making the promise to pay is called the maker.

(b) The party to whom payment is to be made is called the payee.

(c) A promissory note is not a negotiable instrument.

(d) A promissory note is often required from high-risk customers.

(LO 6) **12.** Foti Co. accepts a $1,000, 3-month, 6% promissory note in settlement of an account with Bartelt Co. The entry to record this transaction is as follows.

(a)	Notes Receivable	1,015	
	Accounts Receivable		1,015
(b)	Notes Receivable	1,000	
	Accounts Receivable		1,000
(c)	Notes Receivable	1,000	
	Sales Revenue		1,000
(d)	Notes Receivable	1,030	
	Accounts Receivable		1,030

(LO 8) **13.** Ginter Co. holds Kolar Inc.'s $10,000, 120-day, 9% note. The entry made by Ginter Co. when the note is collected, assuming no interest has been previously accrued, is:

(a)	Cash	10,300	
	Notes Receivable		10,300
(b)	Cash	10,000	
	Notes Receivable		10,000
(c)	Accounts Receivable	10,300	
	Notes Receivable		10,000
	Interest Revenue		300
(d)	Cash	10,300	
	Notes Receivable		10,000
	Interest Revenue		300

14. Accounts and notes receivable are reported in the current assets section of the balance sheet at: (LO 9)

(a) cash (net) realizable value.

(b) net book value.

(c) lower-of-cost-or-market value.

(d) invoice cost.

15. Oliveras Company had net credit sales during the year   (LO 9) of $800,000 and cost of goods sold of $500,000. The balance in accounts receivable at the beginning of the year was $100,000, and the end of the year it was $150,000. What were the accounts receivable turnover and the average collection period in days?

(a) 4.0 and 91.3 days.

(b) 5.3 and 68.9 days.

(c) 6.4 and 57 days.

(d) 8.0 and 45.6 days.

Go to the book's companion website, www.wiley.com/college/weygandt, for additional Self-Test Questions.

 The Navigator

QUESTIONS

1. What is the difference between an account receivable and a note receivable?

2. What are some common types of receivables other than accounts receivable and notes receivable?

3. Texaco Oil Company issues its own credit cards. Assume that Texaco charges you $40 interest on an unpaid balance. Prepare the journal entry that Texaco makes to record this revenue.

4. What are the essential features of the allowance method of accounting for bad debts?

5. Roger Holloway cannot understand why cash realizable value does not decrease when an uncollectible account is written off under the allowance method. Clarify this point for Roger.

6. Distinguish between the two bases that may be used in estimating uncollectible accounts.

7. Borke Company has a credit balance of $3,000 in Allowance for Doubtful Accounts. The estimated bad debt expense under the percentage-of-sales basis is $4,100. The total estimated uncollectibles under the percentage-of-receivables basis is $5,800. Prepare the adjusting entry under each basis.

8. How are bad debts accounted for under the direct write-off method? What are the disadvantages of this method?

9. Freida Company accepts both its own credit cards and national credit cards. What are the advantages of accepting both types of cards?

10. An article recently appeared in the *Wall Street Journal* indicating that companies are selling their receivables at a record rate. Why are companies selling their receivables?

11. Westside Textiles decides to sell $800,000 of its accounts receivable to First Factors Inc. First Factors assesses a service charge of 3% of the amount of receivables sold. Prepare the journal entry that Westside Textiles makes to record this sale.

12. Your roommate is uncertain about the advantages of a promissory note. Compare the advantages of a note receivable with those of an account receivable.

13. How may the maturity date of a promissory note be stated?

14. Indicate the maturity date of each of the following promissory notes:

Date of Note	Terms
(a) March 13	one year after date of note
(b) May 4	3 months after date
(c) June 20	30 days after date
(d) July 1	60 days after date

15. Compute the missing amounts for each of the following notes.

	Principal	Annual Interest Rate	Time	Total Interest
(a)	?	9%	120 days	$ 450
(b)	$30,000	10%	3 years	?
(c)	$60,000	?	5 months	$1,500
(d)	$45,000	8%	?	$1,200

16. In determining interest revenue, some financial institutions use 365 days per year and others use 360 days. Why might a financial institution use 360 days?

17. Jana Company dishonors a note at maturity. What are the options available to the lender?

18. General Motors Corporation has accounts receivable and notes receivable. How should the receivables be reported on the balance sheet?

19. The accounts receivable turnover is 8.14, and average net receivables during the period are $400,000. What is the amount of net credit sales for the period?

20. What percentage does Apple's allowance for doubtful accounts represent as a percentage of its gross receivables?

BRIEF EXERCISES

BE9-1 Presented below are three receivables transactions. Indicate whether these receivables are reported as accounts receivable, notes receivable, or other receivables on a balance sheet.

Identify different types of receivables.

(LO 1)

(a) Sold merchandise on account for $64,000 to a customer.
(b) Received a promissory note of $57,000 for services performed.
(c) Advanced $10,000 to an employee.

BE9-2 Record the following transactions on the books of RAS Co.

Record basic accounts receivable transactions.

(LO 2)

(a) On July 1, RAS Co. sold merchandise on account to Waegelein Inc. for $17,200, terms 2/10, n/30.
(b) On July 8, Waegelein Inc. returned merchandise worth $3,800 to RAS Co.
(c) On July 11, Waegelein Inc. paid for the merchandise.

BE9-3 During its first year of operations, Gavin Company had credit sales of $3,000,000; $600,000 remained uncollected at year-end. The credit manager estimates that $31,000 of these receivables will become uncollectible.

Prepare entry for allowance method and partial balance sheet.

(LO 3, 9)

(a) Prepare the journal entry to record the estimated uncollectibles.
(b) Prepare the current assets section of the balance sheet for Gavin Company. Assume that in addition to the receivables it has cash of $90,000, inventory of $130,000, and prepaid insurance of $7,500.

BE9-4 At the end of 2014, Carpenter Co. has accounts receivable of $700,000 and an allowance for doubtful accounts of $54,000. On January 24, 2015, the company learns that its receivable from Megan Gray is not collectible, and management authorizes a write-off of $6,200.

Prepare entry for write-off; determine cash realizable value.

(LO 3)

(a) Prepare the journal entry to record the write-off.
(b) What is the cash realizable value of the accounts receivable (1) before the write-off and (2) after the write-off?

BE9-5 Assume the same information as BE9-4. On March 4, 2015, Carpenter Co. receives payment of $6,200 in full from Megan Gray. Prepare the journal entries to record this transaction.

Prepare entries for collection of bad debt write-off.

(LO 3)

BE9-6 Farr Co. elects to use the percentage-of-sales basis in 2014 to record bad debt expense. It estimates that 2% of net credit sales will become uncollectible. Sales revenues are $800,000 for 2014, sales returns and allowances are $40,000, and the allowance for doubtful accounts has a credit balance of $9,000. Prepare the adjusting entry to record bad debt expense in 2014.

Prepare entry using percentage-of-sales method.

(LO 3)

BE9-7 Kingston Co. uses the percentage-of-receivables basis to record bad debt expense. It estimates that 1% of accounts receivable will become uncollectible. Accounts receivable are $420,000 at the end of the year, and the allowance for doubtful accounts has a credit balance of $1,500.

Prepare entry using percentage-of-receivables method.

(LO 3)

(a) Prepare the adjusting journal entry to record bad debt expense for the year.
(b) If the allowance for doubtful accounts had a debit balance of $800 instead of a credit balance of $1,500, determine the amount to be reported for bad debt expense.

BE9-8 Presented below are two independent transactions.

Prepare entries to dispose of accounts receivable.

(LO 4)

(a) Tony's Restaurant accepted a Visa card in payment of a $175 lunch bill. The bank charges a 4% fee. What entry should Tony's make?

(b) Larkin Company sold its accounts receivable of $60,000. What entry should Larkin make, given a service charge of 3% on the amount of receivables sold?

Compute interest and determine maturity dates on notes.

(LO 5)

BE9-9 Compute interest and find the maturity date for the following notes.

	Date of Note	Principal	Interest Rate (%)	Terms
(a)	June 10	$80,000	6%	60 days
(b)	July 14	$64,000	7%	90 days
(c)	April 27	$12,000	8%	75 days

Determine maturity dates and compute interest and rates on notes.

(LO 5)

BE9-10 Presented below are data on three promissory notes. Determine the missing amounts.

Date of Note	Terms	Maturity Date	Principal	Annual Interest Rate	Total Interest
(a) April 1	60 days	?	$600,000	6%	?
(b) July 2	30 days	?	90,000	?	$600
(c) March 7	6 months	?	120,000	10%	?

Prepare entry for notes receivable exchanged for account receivable.

(LO 6)

BE9-11 On January 10, 2014, Perez Co. sold merchandise on account to Robertsen Co. for $15,600, n/30. On February 9, Robertsen Co. gave Perez Co. a 10% promissory note in settlement of this account. Prepare the journal entry to record the sale and the settlement of the account receivable.

Compute ratios to analyze receivables.

(LO 9)

BE9-12 The financial statements of Minnesota Mining and Manufacturing Company (3M) report net sales of $20.0 billion. Accounts receivable (net) are $2.7 billion at the beginning of the year and $2.8 billion at the end of the year. Compute 3M's accounts receivable turnover. Compute 3M's average collection period for accounts receivable in days.

> DO IT! Review

Prepare entry for uncollectible accounts.

(LO 3)

DO IT! 9-1 Gonzalez Company has been in business several years. At the end of the current year, the ledger shows:

Accounts Receivable	$ 310,000 Dr.
Sales Revenue	2,200,000 Cr.
Allowance for Doubtful Accounts	6,100 Cr.

Bad debts are estimated to be 5% of receivables. Prepare the entry to adjust Allowance for Doubtful Accounts.

Prepare entry for factored accounts.

(LO 4)

DO IT! 9-2 Wynn Distributors is a growing company whose ability to raise capital has not been growing as quickly as its expanding assets and sales. Wynn's local banker has indicated that the company cannot increase its borrowing for the foreseeable future. Wynn's suppliers are demanding payment for goods acquired within 30 days of the invoice date, but Wynn's customers are slow in paying for their purchases (60–90 days). As a result, Wynn has a cash flow problem.

Wynn needs $160,000 to cover next Friday's payroll. Its balance of outstanding accounts receivable totals $1,000,000. To alleviate this cash crunch, Wynn sells $200,000 of its receivables. Record the entry that Wynn would make when it raises the needed cash. (Assume a 3% service charge.)

Prepare entries for notes receivable.

(LO 5, 8)

DO IT! 9-3 Gentry Wholesalers accepts from Benton Stores a $6,200, 4-month, 9% note dated May 31 in settlement of Benton's overdue account. (a) What is the maturity date of the note? (b) What is the entry made by Gentry at the maturity date, assuming Benton pays the note and interest in full at that time?

Compute ratios for receivables.

(LO 9)

DO IT! 9-4 In 2014, Wainwright Company has net credit sales of $1,300,000 for the year. It had a beginning accounts receivable (net) balance of $101,000 and an ending accounts receivable (net) balance of $107,000. Compute Wainwright Company's (a) accounts receivable turnover and (b) average collection period in days.

EXERCISES

E9-1 Presented below are selected transactions of Molina Company. Molina sells in large quantities to other companies and also sells its product in a small retail outlet.

Journalize entries related to accounts receivable.

(LO 2)

March 1   Sold merchandise on account to Dodson Company for $5,000, terms 2/10, n/30.

       3   Dodson Company returned merchandise worth $500 to Molina.

       9   Molina collected the amount due from Dodson Company from the March 1 sale.

     15   Molina sold merchandise for $400 in its retail outlet. The customer used his Molina credit card.

     31   Molina added 1.5% monthly interest to the customer's credit card balance.

Instructions

Prepare journal entries for the transactions above.

E9-2 Presented below are two independent situations.

Journalize entries for recognizing accounts receivable.

(LO 2)

(a) On January 6, Brumbaugh Co. sells merchandise on account to Pryor Inc. for $7,000, terms 2/10, n/30. On January 16, Pryor Inc. pays the amount due. Prepare the entries on Brumbaugh's books to record the sale and related collection.

(b) On January 10, Andrew Farley uses his Paltrow Co. credit card to purchase merchandise from Paltrow Co. for $9,000. On February 10, Farley is billed for the amount due of $9,000. On February 12, Farley pays $5,000 on the balance due. On March 10, Farley is billed for the amount due, including interest at 1% per month on the unpaid balance as of February 12. Prepare the entries on Paltrow Co.'s books related to the transactions that occurred on January 10, February 12, and March 10.

E9-3 The ledger of Costello Company at the end of the current year shows Accounts Receivable $110,000, Sales Revenue $840,000, and Sales Returns and Allowances $20,000.

Journalize entries to record allowance for doubtful accounts using two different bases.

(LO 3)

Instructions

(a) If Costello uses the direct write-off method to account for uncollectible accounts, journalize the adjusting entry at December 31, assuming Costello determines that L. Dole's $1,400 balance is uncollectible.

(b) If Allowance for Doubtful Accounts has a credit balance of $2,100 in the trial balance, journalize the adjusting entry at December 31, assuming bad debts are expected to be (1) 1% of net sales, and (2) 10% of accounts receivable.

(c) If Allowance for Doubtful Accounts has a debit balance of $200 in the trial balance, journalize the adjusting entry at December 31, assuming bad debts are expected to be (1) 0.75% of net sales and (2) 6% of accounts receivable.

E9-4 Menge Company has accounts receivable of $93,100 at March 31. An analysis of the accounts shows the following information.

Determine bad debt expense; prepare the adjusting entry for bad debt expense.

(LO 3)

Month of Sale	Balance, March 31
March	$60,000
February	17,600
January	8,500
Prior to January	7,000
	$93,100

Credit terms are 2/10, n/30. At March 31, Allowance for Doubtful Accounts has a credit balance of $1,200 prior to adjustment. The company uses the percentage-of-receivables basis for estimating uncollectible accounts. The company's estimate of bad debts is shown below.

Age of Accounts	Estimated Percentage Uncollectible
1–30 days	2.0%
31–60 days	5.0%
61–90 days	20.0%
Over 90 days	50.0%

Journalize write-off and recovery.

(LO 3)

Instructions
(a) Determine the total estimated uncollectibles.
(b) Prepare the adjusting entry at March 31 to record bad debt expense.

E9-5 At December 31, 2013, Finzelberg Company had a credit balance of $15,000 in Allowance for Doubtful Accounts. During 2014, Finzelberg wrote off accounts totaling $11,000. One of those accounts ($1,800) was later collected. At December 31, 2014, an aging schedule indicated that the balance in Allowance for Doubtful Accounts should be $19,000.

Instructions
Prepare journal entries to record the 2014 transactions of Finzelberg Company.

Journalize percentage of sales basis, write-off, recovery.

(LO 3)

E9-6 On December 31, 2014, Ling Co. estimated that 2% of its net sales of $450,000 will become uncollectible. The company recorded this amount as an addition to Allowance for Doubtful Accounts. On May 11, 2015, Ling Co. determined that the Jeff Shoemaker account was uncollectible and wrote off $1,100. On June 12, 2015, Shoemaker paid the amount previously written off.

Instructions
Prepare the journal entries on December 31, 2014, May 11, 2015, and June 12, 2015.

Journalize entries for the sale of accounts receivable.

(LO 4)

E9-7 Presented below are two independent situations.

(a) On March 3, Kitselman Appliances sells $650,000 of its receivables to Ervay Factors Inc. Ervay Factors assesses a finance charge of 3% of the amount of receivables sold. Prepare the entry on Kitselman Appliances' books to record the sale of the receivables.
(b) On May 10, Fillmore Company sold merchandise for $3,000 and accepted the customer's America Bank MasterCard. America Bank charges a 4% service charge for credit card sales. Prepare the entry on Fillmore Company's books to record the sale of merchandise.

Journalize entries for credit card sales.

(LO 4)

E9-8 Presented below are two independent situations.

(a) On April 2, Jennifer Elston uses her JCPenney Company credit card to purchase merchandise from a JCPenney store for $1,500. On May 1, Elston is billed for the $1,500 amount due. Elston pays $500 on the balance due on May 3. On June 1, Elston receives a bill for the amount due, including interest at 1.0% per month on the unpaid balance as of May 3. Prepare the entries on JCPenney Co.'s books related to the transactions that occurred on April 2, May 3, and June 1.
(b) On July 4, Spangler's Restaurant accepts a Visa card for a $200 dinner bill. Visa charges a 2% service fee. Prepare the entry on Spangler's books related to this transaction.

Journalize credit card sales, and indicate the statement presentation of financing charges and service charge expense.

(LO 4)

E9-9 Colaw Stores accepts both its own and national credit cards. During the year, the following selected summary transactions occurred.

Jan. 15	Made Colaw credit card sales totaling $18,000. (There were no balances prior to January 15.)
20	Made Visa credit card sales (service charge fee 2%) totaling $4,500.
Feb. 10	Collected $10,000 on Colaw credit card sales.
15	Added finance charges of 1.5% to Colaw credit card account balances.

Instructions
(a) Journalize the transactions for Colaw Stores.
(b) Indicate the statement presentation of the financing charges and the credit card service charge expense for Colaw Stores.

Journalize entries for notes receivable transactions.

(LO 5, 6)

E9-10 Elburn Supply Co. has the following transactions related to notes receivable during the last 2 months of 2014. The company does not make entries to accrue interest except at December 31.

Nov. 1	Loaned $30,000 cash to Manny Lopez on a 12 month, 10% note.
Dec. 11	Sold goods to Ralph Kremer, Inc., receiving a $6,750, 90-day, 8% note.
16	Received a $4,000, 180 day, 9% note in exchange for Joe Fernetti's outstanding accounts receivable.
31	Accrued interest revenue on all notes receivable.

Instructions
(a) Journalize the transactions for Elburn Supply Co.
(b) Record the collection of the Lopez note at its maturity in 2015.

E9-11 Record the following transactions for Redeker Co. in the general journal.

2014

May 1   Received a $9,000, 12-month, 10% note in exchange for Mark Chamber's
          outstanding accounts receivable.
Dec. 31   Accrued interest on the Chamber note.
Dec. 31   Closed the interest revenue account.

2015

May 1   Received principal plus interest on the Chamber note. (No interest has been
          accrued in 2015.)

Journalize entries for notes receivable.
(LO 5, 6)

E9-12 Vandiver Company had the following select transactions.

Apr. 1, 2014	Accepted Goodwin Company's 12-month, 12% note in settlement of a $30,000 account receivable.
July 1, 2014	Loaned $25,000 cash to Thomas Slocombe on a 9-month, 10% note.
Dec. 31, 2014	Accrued interest on all notes receivable.
Apr. 1, 2015	Received principal plus interest on the Goodwin note.
Apr. 1, 2015	Thomas Slocombe dishonored its note; Vandiver expects it will eventually collect.

Prepare entries for note receivable transactions.
(LO 5, 6, 8)

Instructions

Prepare journal entries to record the transactions. Vandiver prepares adjusting entries once a year on December 31.

E9-13 On May 2, McLain Company lends $9,000 to Chang, Inc., issuing a 6-month, 9% note. At the maturity date, November 2, Chang indicates that it cannot pay.

Journalize entries for dishonor of notes receivable.
(LO 5, 8)

Instructions

(a) Prepare the entry to record the issuance of the note.

(b) Prepare the entry to record the dishonor of the note, assuming that McLain Company expects collection will occur.

(c) Prepare the entry to record the dishonor of the note, assuming that McLain Company does not expect collection in the future.

E9-14 Kerwick Company had accounts receivable of $100,000 on January 1, 2014. The only transactions that affected accounts receivable during 2014 were net credit sales of $1,000,000, cash collections of $920,000, and accounts written off of $30,000.

Compute accounts receivable turnover and average collection period.
(LO 9)

Instructions

(a) Compute the ending balance of accounts receivable.

(b) Compute the accounts receivable turnover for 2014.

(c) Compute the average collection period in days.

EXERCISES: SET B AND CHALLENGE EXERCISES

Visit the book's companion website, at **www.wiley.com/college/weygandt**, and choose the Student Companion site to access Exercise Set B and Challenge Exercises.

PROBLEMS: SET A

P9-1A At December 31, 2013, House Co. reported the following information on its balance sheet.

Prepare journal entries related to bad debt expense.
(LO 2, 3, 9)

Accounts receivable	$960,000
Less: Allowance for doubtful accounts	80,000

During 2014, the company had the following transactions related to receivables.

1.	Sales on account	$3,700,000
2.	Sales returns and allowances	50,000
3.	Collections of accounts receivable	2,810,000
4.	Write-offs of accounts receivable deemed uncollectible	90,000
5.	Recovery of bad debts previously written off as uncollectible	29,000

Instructions

(a) Prepare the journal entries to record each of these five transactions. Assume that no cash discounts were taken on the collections of accounts receivable.

(b) Accounts receivable
$1,710,000
ADA $19,000

(b) Enter the January 1, 2014, balances in Accounts Receivable and Allowance for Doubtful Accounts, post the entries to the two accounts (use T-accounts), and determine the balances.

(c) Bad debt expense $96,000

(c) Prepare the journal entry to record bad debt expense for 2014, assuming that an aging of accounts receivable indicates that expected bad debts are $115,000.

(d) Compute the accounts receivable turnover for 2014 assuming the expected bad debt information provided in (c).

Compute bad debt amounts.

(LO 3)

P9-2A Information related to Mingenback Company for 2014 is summarized below.

Total credit sales	$2,500,000
Accounts receivable at December 31	875,000
Bad debts written off	33,000

Instructions

(a) What amount of bad debt expense will Mingenback Company report if it uses the direct write-off method of accounting for bad debts?

(b) Assume that Mingenback Company estimates its bad debt expense to be 2% of credit sales. What amount of bad debt expense will Mingenback record if it has an Allowance for Doubtful Accounts credit balance of $4,000?

(c) Assume that Mingenback Company estimates its bad debt expense based on 6% of accounts receivable. What amount of bad debt expense will Mingenback record if it has an Allowance for Doubtful Accounts credit balance of $3,000?

(d) Assume the same facts as in (c), except that there is a $3,000 debit balance in Allowance for Doubtful Accounts. What amount of bad debt expense will Mingenback record?

(e) ————— What is the weakness of the direct write-off method of reporting bad debt expense?

Journalize entries to record transactions related to bad debts.

(LO 2, 3)

P9-3A Presented below is an aging schedule for Halleran Company.

	Worksheet.xls						

Home   Insert   Page Layout   Formulas   Data   Review   View

P18   fx

	A	B	C	D	E	F	G·
1				Number of Days Past Due			
2			Not				
3	**Customer**	**Total**	**Yet Due**	**1–30**	**31–60**	**61–90**	**Over 90**
4	Anders	$ 22,000		$10,000	$12,000		
5	Blake	40,000	$ 40,000				
6	Coulson	57,000	16,000	6,000		$35,000	
7	Deleon	34,000					$34,000
8	Others	132,000	96,000	16,000	14,000		6,000
9		$285,000	$152,000	$32,000	$26,000	$35,000	$40,000
10	Estimated Percentage Uncollectible		3%	6%	13%	25%	50%
11	Total Estimated Bad Debts	$ 38,610	$ 4,560	$ 1,920	$ 3,380	$ 8,750	$20,000
12							

At December 31, 2014, the unadjusted balance in Allowance for Doubtful Accounts is a credit of $12,000.

Instructions

(a) Bad debt expense
$26,610

(a) Journalize and post the adjusting entry for bad debts at December 31, 2014.

(b) Journalize and post to the allowance account the following events and transactions in the year 2015.

(1) On March 31, a $1,000 customer balance originating in 2014 is judged uncollectible.

(2) On May 31, a check for $1,000 is received from the customer whose account was written off as uncollectible on March 31.

(c) Journalize the adjusting entry for bad debts on December 31, 2015, assuming that the unadjusted balance in Allowance for Doubtful Accounts is a debit of $800 and the aging schedule indicates that total estimated bad debts will be $31,600.

(c) Bad debt expense
$32,400

P9-4A Rigney Inc. uses the allowance method to estimate uncollectible accounts receivable. The company produced the following aging of the accounts receivable at year-end.

Journalize transactions related to bad debts.

(SO 2, 3)

				Worksheet.xls				
Home	Insert	Page Layout	Formulas	Data	Review	View		
P18		*fx*						
	A	B	C	D	E	F	G
1				**Number of Days Outstanding**				
2								
3		**Total**	**0–30**	**31–60**	**61–90**	**91–120**	**Over 120**
4	Accounts receivable	200,000	77,000	46,000	39,000	23,000	$15,000
5	% uncollectible		1%	4%	5%	8%	20%
6	Estimated bad debts						
7							

Instructions

(a) Calculate the total estimated bad debts based on the above information.

(b) Prepare the year-end adjusting journal entry to record the bad debts using the aged uncollectible accounts receivable determined in (a). Assume the current balance in Allowance for Doubtful Accounts is a $8,000 debit.

(c) Of the above accounts, $5,000 is determined to be specifically uncollectible. Prepare the journal entry to write off the uncollectible account.

(d) The company collects $5,000 subsequently on a specific account that had previously been determined to be uncollectible in (c). Prepare the journal entry(ies) necessary to restore the account and record the cash collection.

(e) Comment on how your answers to (a)–(d) would change if Rigney Inc. used 4% of **total** accounts receivable rather than aging the accounts receivable. What are the advantages to the company of aging the accounts receivable rather than applying a percentage to total accounts receivable?

(a) Tot. est. bad debts $9,400

P9-5A At December 31, 2014, the trial balance of Darby Company contained the following amounts before adjustment.

Journalize entries to record transactions related to bad debts.

(LO 3)

	Debit	Credit
Accounts Receivable	$385,000	
Allowance for Doubtful Accounts		$ 1,000
Sales Revenue		970,000

Instructions

(a) Based on the information given, which method of accounting for bad debts is Darby Company using—the direct write-off method or the allowance method? How can you tell?

(b) Prepare the adjusting entry at December 31, 2014, for bad debt expense under each of the following independent assumptions.

(1) An aging schedule indicates that $11,750 of accounts receivable will be uncollectible.

(2) The company estimates that 1% of sales will be uncollectible.

(c) Repeat part (b) assuming that instead of a credit balance there is an $1,000 debit balance in Allowance for Doubtful Accounts.

(d) During the next month, January 2015, a $3,000 account receivable is written off as uncollectible. Prepare the journal entry to record the write-off.

(e) Repeat part (d) assuming that Darby uses the direct write-off method instead of the allowance method in accounting for uncollectible accounts receivable.

(f) ——— What type of account is Allowance for Doubtful Accounts? How does it affect how accounts receivable is reported on the balance sheet at the end of the accounting period?

(b)(2) $9,700

Prepare entries for various notes receivable transactions.

(LO 2, 4, 5, 8, 9)

P9-6A Farwell Company closes its books monthly. On September 30, selected ledger account balances are:

Notes Receivable	$37,000
Interest Receivable	183

Notes Receivable include the following.

Date	Maker	Face	Term	Interest
Aug. 16	K. Goza Inc.	$12,000	60 days	8%
Aug. 25	Holt Co.	9,000	60 days	7%
Sept. 30	Noblitt Corp.	16,000	6 months	9%

Interest is computed using a 360-day year. During October, the following transactions were completed.

Oct.	7	Made sales of $6,900 on Farwell credit cards.
	12	Made sales of $900 on MasterCard credit cards. The credit card service charge is 3%.
	15	Added $460 to Farwell customer balances for finance charges on unpaid balances.
	15	Received payment in full from K. Goza Inc. on the amount due.
	24	Received notice that the Holt note has been dishonored. (Assume that Holt is expected to pay in the future.)

Instructions

(a) Journalize the October transactions and the October 31 adjusting entry for accrued interest receivable.

(b) Accounts receivable $16,465

(b) Enter the balances at October 1 in the receivable accounts. Post the entries to all of the receivable accounts.

(c) Total receivables $32,585

(c) Show the balance sheet presentation of the receivable accounts at October 31.

Prepare entries for various receivable transactions.

(LO 2, 4, 5, 6, 8)

P9-7A On January 1, 2014, Harter Company had Accounts Receivable $139,000, Notes Receivable $25,000, and Allowance for Doubtful Accounts $13,200. The note receivable is from Willingham Company. It is a 4-month, 9% note dated December 31, 2013. Harter Company prepares financial statements annually at December 31. During the year, the following selected transactions occurred.

Jan.	5	Sold $20,000 of merchandise to Sheldon Company, terms n/15.
	20	Accepted Sheldon Company's $20,000, 3-month, 8% note for balance due.
Feb.	18	Sold $8,000 of merchandise to Patwary Company and accepted Patwary's $8,000, 6-month, 9% note for the amount due.
Apr.	20	Collected Sheldon Company note in full.
	30	Received payment in full from Willingham Company on the amount due.
May	25	Accepted Potter Inc.'s $6,000, 3-month, 7% note in settlement of a past-due balance on account.
Aug.	18	Received payment in full from Patwary Company on note due.
	25	The Potter Inc. note was dishonored. Potter Inc. is not bankrupt; future payment is anticipated.
Sept.	1	Sold $12,000 of merchandise to Stanbrough Company and accepted a $12,000, 6-month, 10% note for the amount due.

Instructions

Journalize the transactions.

PROBLEMS: SET B

Prepare journal entries related to bad debt expense.

(LO 2, 3, 9)

P9-1B At December 31, 2013, Obermeyer Imports reported the following information on its balance sheet.

Accounts receivable	$250,000
Less: Allowance for doubtful accounts	15,000

During 2014, the company had the following transactions related to receivables.

1.	Sales on account	$2,600,000
2.	Sales returns and allowances	45,000

3. Collections of accounts receivable 2,250,000
4. Write-offs of accounts receivable deemed uncollectible 10,000
5. Recovery of bad debts previously written off as uncollectible 3,000

Instructions

(a) Prepare the journal entries to record each of these five transactions. Assume that no cash discounts were taken on the collections of accounts receivable.

(b) Enter the January 1, 2014, balances in Accounts Receivable and Allowance for Doubtful Accounts. Post the entries to the two accounts (use T-accounts), and determine the balances.

(c) Prepare the journal entry to record bad debt expense for 2014, assuming that an aging of accounts receivable indicates that estimated bad debts are $22,000.

(d) Compute the accounts receivable turnover for the year 2014.

(b) Accounts receivable
$545,000
ADA $8,000

(c) Bad debt expense
$14,000

P9-2B Information related to Miracle Company for 2014 is summarized below.

Total credit sales	$1,000,000
Accounts receivable at December 31	369,000
Bad debts written off	22,150

Compute bad debt amounts.
(LO 3)

XLS

Instructions

(a) What amount of bad debt expense will Miracle Company report if it uses the direct write-off method of accounting for bad debts?

(b) Assume that Miracle Company decides to estimate its bad debt expense to be 2% of credit sales. What amount of bad debt expense will Miracle record if Allowance for Doubtful Accounts has a credit balance of $3,000?

(c) Assume that Miracle Company decides to estimate its bad debt expense based on 5% of accounts receivable. What amount of bad debt expense will Miracle Company record if Allowance for Doubtful Accounts has a credit balance of $4,000?

(d) Assume the same facts as in (c), except that there is a $2,000 debit balance in Allowance for Doubtful Accounts. What amount of bad debt expense will Miracle record?

(e) ——— What is the weakness of the direct write-off method of reporting bad debt expense?

P9-3B Presented below is an aging schedule for Loucks Company.

Journalize entries to record transactions related to bad debts.
(LO 2, 3)

XLS

Worksheet.xls

Home Insert Page Layout Formulas Data Review View

P18   fx

	A	B	C	D	E	F	G
1					Number of Days Past Due		
2			Not				
3	**Customer**	**Total**	**Yet Due**	**1–30**	**31–60**	**61–90**	**Over 90**
4	Alma	$ 30,000		$ 13,500	$16,500		
5	Browne	45,000	$ 45,000				
6	Conlon	75,000	22,500	7,500		$45,000	
7	Dalton	57,000					$57,000
8	Others	189,000	138,000	22,500	19,500		9,000
9		$396,000	$205,500	$43,500	$36,000	$45,000	$66,000
10	Estimated Percentage Uncollectible		2%	6%	10%	25%	40%
11	Total Estimated Bad Debts	$ 47,970	$ 4,110	$ 2,610	$ 3,600	$ 11,250	$26,400
12							

At December 31, 2014, the unadjusted balance in Allowance for Doubtful Accounts is a credit of $16,000.

Instructions

(a) Journalize and post the adjusting entry for bad debts at December 31, 2014.

(b) Journalize and post to the allowance account the following events and transactions in the year 2015.

(1) March 1, a $1,900 customer balance originating in 2014 is judged uncollectible.

(2) May 1, a check for $1,900 is received from the customer whose account was written off as uncollectible on March 1.

(a) Bad debt expense
$31,970

(c) Bad debt expense
$40,300

(c) Journalize the adjusting entry for bad debts on December 31, 2015. Assume that the unadjusted balance in Allowance for Doubtful Accounts is a debit of $2,000, and the aging schedule indicates that total estimated bad debts will be $38,300.

Journalize transactions related to bad debts.

(LO 2, 3)

P9-4B The following represents selected information taken from a company's aging schedule to estimate uncollectible accounts receivable at year-end.

	Worksheet.xls						
Home	Insert	Page Layout	Formulas	Data	Review	View	
P18	*fx*						
	A	B	C	D	E	F	G
1				**Number of Days Outstanding**			
2							
3		**Total**	**0–30**	**31–60**	**61–90**	**91–120**	**Over 120**
4	Accounts receivable	$375,000	$220,000	$90,000	$40,000	$10,000	$15,000
5	% uncollectible		1%	4%	5%	8%	20%
6	Estimated bad debts						
7							

Instructions

(a) Tot. est.
    bad debts $11,600

(a) Calculate the total estimated bad debts based on the above information.

(b) Prepare the year-end adjusting journal entry to record the bad debts using the allowance method and the aged uncollectible accounts receivable determined in (a). Assume the current balance in Allowance for Doubtful Accounts is a $3,000 credit.

(c) Of the above accounts, $1,600 is determined to be specifically uncollectible. Prepare the journal entry to write off the uncollectible accounts.

(d) The company subsequently collects $700 on a specific account that had previously been determined to be uncollectible in (c). Prepare the journal entry(ies) necessary to restore the account and record the cash collection.

(e) Explain how establishing an allowance account satisfies the expense recognition principle.

Journalize entries to record transactions related to bad debts.

(LO 3)

P9-5B At December 31, 2014, the trial balance of Markowitz Company contained the following amounts before adjustment.

	Debit	Credit
Accounts Receivable	$250,000	
Allowance for Doubtful Accounts		$ 1,100
Sales Revenue		650,000

Instructions

(a)(2) $13,000

(a) Prepare the adjusting entry at December 31, 2014, to record bad debt expense under each of the following independent assumptions.

  (1) An aging schedule indicates that $13,500 of accounts receivable will be uncollectible.

  (2) The company estimates that 2% of sales will be uncollectible.

(b) Repeat part (a) assuming that instead of a credit balance, there is a $1,100 debit balance in Allowance for Doubtful Accounts.

(c) During the next month, January 2015, a $3,200 account receivable is written off as uncollectible. Prepare the journal entry to record the write-off.

(d) Repeat part (c) assuming that Markowitz Company uses the direct write-off method instead of the allowance method in accounting for uncollectible accounts receivable.

(e) ⬤━━━ What are the advantages of using the allowance method in accounting for uncollectible accounts as compared to the direct write-off method?

Prepare entries for various notes receivable transactions.

(LO 2, 4, 5, 8, 9)

P9-6B Sauer Co. closes its books monthly. On June 30, selected ledger account balances are:

Notes Receivable	$47,000
Interest Receivable	285

Notes Receivable include the following.

Date	Maker	Face	Term	Interest
May 16	Eddy Inc.	$12,000	60 days	7%
May 25	Masasi Co.	20,000	60 days	9%
June 30	Pelsma Corp.	15,000	6 months	8%

During July, the following transactions were completed.

July 5 Made sales of $7,200 on Sauer Co. credit cards.
  14 Made sales of $1,000 on Visa credit cards. The credit card service charge is 3%.
  14 Added $510 to Sauer Co. credit card customer balances for finance charges on unpaid balances.
  15 Received payment in full from Eddy Inc. on the amount due.
  24 Received notice that the Masasi Co. note has been dishonored. (Assume that Masasi Co. is expected to pay in the future.)

Instructions
(a) Journalize the July transactions and the July 31 adjusting entry for accrued interest receivable. (Interest is computed using 360 days.)
(b) Enter the balances at July 1 in the receivable accounts. Post the entries to all of the receivable accounts.
(c) Show the balance sheet presentation of the receivable accounts at July 31.

(b) Accounts receivable $28,010

(c) Total receivables $43,110

P9-7B On January 1, 2014, Morfitt Company had Accounts Receivable $98,000 and Allowance for Doubtful Accounts $8,100. Morfitt Company prepares financial statements annually. During the year, the following selected transactions occurred.

Prepare entries for various receivable transactions.
(LO 2, 4, 5, 6, 8)

Jan. 5 Sold $10,800 of merchandise to Motte Company, terms n/30.
Feb. 2 Accepted a $10,800, 4-month, 9% promissory note from Motte Company for the balance due.
  12 Sold $13,500 of merchandise to Gitchel Company and accepted Gitchel's $13,500, 2-month, 8% note for the balance due.
  26 Sold $9,000 of merchandise to Benedict Co., terms n/10.
Apr. 5 Accepted a $9,000, 3-month, 8% note from Benedict Co. for the balance due.
  12 Collected Gitchel Company note in full.
June 2 Collected Motte Company note in full.
July 5 Benedict Co. dishonors its note of April 5. It is expected that Benedict will eventually pay the amount owed.
  15 Sold $12,000 of merchandise to Kriley Co. and accepted Kriley's $12,000, 3-month, 12% note for the amount due.
Oct. 15 Kriley Co.'s note was dishonored. Kriley Co. is bankrupt, and there is no hope of future settlement.

Instructions
Journalize the transactions.

PROBLEMS: SET C

Visit the book's companion website, at **www.wiley.com/college/weygandt**, and choose the Student Companion site to access Problem Set C.

COMPREHENSIVE PROBLEM

CP9 Winter Company's balance sheet at December 31, 2013, is presented below.

WINTER COMPANY
Balance Sheet
December 31, 2013

Cash	$13,100	Accounts payable	$ 8,750
Accounts receivable	19,780	Owner's capital	32,730
Allowance for doubtful accounts	(800)		$41,480
Inventory	9,400		
	$41,480		

During January 2014, the following transactions occurred. Winter uses the perpetual inventory method.

Jan. 1   Winter accepted a 4-month, 8% note from Merando Company in payment of Merando's $1,200 account.

3   Winter wrote off as uncollectible the accounts of Inwood Corporation ($450) and Goza Company ($280).

8   Winter purchased $17,200 of inventory on account.

11   Winter sold for $28,000 on account inventory that cost $19,600.

15   Winter sold inventory that cost $700 to Mark Lauber for $1,000. Lauber charged this amount on his Visa First Bank card. The service fee charged Winter by First Bank is 3%.

17   Winter collected $22,900 from customers on account.

21   Winter paid $14,300 on accounts payable.

24   Winter received payment in full ($280) from Goza Company on the account written off on January 3.

27   Winter purchased supplies for $1,400 cash.

31   Winter paid other operating expenses, $3,718.

Adjustment data:

1. Interest is recorded for the month on the note from January 1.

2. Bad debts are expected to be 6% of the January 31, 2014, accounts receivable.

3. A count of supplies on January 31, 2014, reveals that $560 remains unused.

Instructions

(You may want to set up T-accounts to determine ending balances.)

(a) Prepare journal entries for the transactions listed above and adjusting entries. (Include entries for cost of goods sold using the perpetual system.)

(b) Totals $74,585

(c) Tot. assets $47,473

(b) Prepare an adjusted trial balance at January 31, 2014.

(c) Prepare an income statement and an owner's equity statement for the month ending January 31, 2014, and a classified balance sheet as of January 31, 2014.

CONTINUING COOKIE CHRONICLE

(*Note:* This is a continuation of the Cookie Chronicle from Chapters 1 through 8.)

CCC9 One of Natalie's friends, Curtis Lesperance, runs a coffee shop where he sells specialty coffees and prepares and sells muffins and cookies. He is eager to buy one of Natalie's fine European mixers, which would enable him to make larger batches of muffins and cookies. However, Curtis cannot afford to pay for the mixer for at least 30 days. He asks Natalie if she would be willing to sell him the mixer on credit. Natalie comes to you for advice.

Go to the book's companion website, **www.wiley.com/college/weygandt,** *to see the completion of this problem.*

Broadening Your Perspective

Financial Reporting and Analysis

Financial Reporting Problem: RLF Company

BYP9-1 RLF Company sells office equipment and supplies to many organizations in the city and surrounding area on contract terms of 2/10, n/30. In the past, over 75% of the credit customers have taken advantage of the discount by paying within 10 days of the invoice date.

The number of customers taking the full 30 days to pay has increased within the last year. Current indications are that less than 60% of the customers are now taking the discount. Bad debts as a percentage of gross credit sales have risen from the 2.5% provided in past years to about 4.5% in the current year.

The company's Finance Committee has requested more information on the collections of accounts receivable. The controller responded to this request with the report reproduced below.

RLF COMPANY
Accounts Receivable Collections
May 31, 2014

The fact that some credit accounts will prove uncollectible is normal. Annual bad debt write-offs have been 2.5% of gross credit sales over the past 5 years. During the last fiscal year, this percentage increased to slightly less than 4.5%. The current Accounts Receivable balance is $1,400,000. The condition of this balance in terms of age and probability of collection is as follows.

Proportion of Total	Age Categories	Probability of Collection
60%	not yet due	98%
22%	less than 30 days past due	96%
9%	30 to 60 days past due	94%
5%	61 to 120 days past due	91%
$2\frac{1}{2}$%	121 to 180 days past due	75%
$1\frac{1}{2}$%	over 180 days past due	30%

Allowance for Doubtful Accounts had a credit balance of $29,500 on June 1, 2013. RLF has provided for a monthly bad debt expense accrual during the current fiscal year based on the assumption that 4.5% of gross credit sales will be uncollectible. Total gross credit sales for the 2013–2014 fiscal year amounted to $2,900,000. Write-offs of bad accounts during the year totaled $102,000.

Instructions
(a) Prepare an accounts receivable aging schedule for RLF Company using the age categories identified in the controller's report to the Finance Committee showing the following.
    (1) The amount of accounts receivable outstanding for each age category and in total.
    (2) The estimated amount that is uncollectible for each category and in total.
(b) Compute the amount of the year-end adjustment necessary to bring Allowance for Doubtful Accounts to the balance indicated by the age analysis. Then prepare the necessary journal entry to adjust the accounting records.
(c) In a recessionary environment with tight credit and high interest rates:
    (1) Identify steps RLF Company might consider to improve the accounts receivable situation.
    (2) Then evaluate each step identified in terms of the risks and costs involved.

Comparative Analysis Problem: PepsiCo, Inc. vs. The Coca-Cola Company

BYP9-2 PepsiCo, Inc.'s financial statements are presented in Appendix B. Financial statements of The Coca-Cola Company are presented in Appendix C. Instructions for accessing and using the complete annual reports of PepsiCo and Coca-Cola, including the notes to the financial statements, are also provided in Appendices B and C, respectively.

Instructions
(a) Based on the information in these financial statements, compute the following 2011 ratios for each company. (Assume all sales are credit sales and that PepsiCo's receivables on its balance sheet are all trade receivables.)
    (1) Accounts receivable turnover.
    (2) Average collection period for receivables.
(b) What conclusions about managing accounts receivable can you draw from these data?

Comparative Analysis Problem: Amazon.com, Inc. vs. Wal-Mart Stores, Inc.

BYP9-3 Amazon.com, Inc.'s financial statements are presented in Appendix D. Financial statements of Wal-Mart Stores, Inc. are presented in Appendix E. Instructions for accessing and using the complete annual reports of Amazon and Wal-Mart, including the notes to the finanial statements, are also provided in Appendices D and E, respectively.

Instructions
(a) Based on the information in these financial statements, compute the following ratios for each company (for the most recent year shown). (Assume all sales are credit sales.)
    (1) Accounts receivable turnover.
    (2) Average collection period for receivables.

(b) What conclusions about managing accounts receivable can you draw from these data?

Real-World Focus

BYP9-4 Purpose: To learn more about factoring.

Address: **www.ccapital.net**, or go to **www.wiley.com/college/weygandt**

Steps: Go to the website, click on **Invoice Factoring**, and answer the following questions.
(a) What are some of the benefits of factoring?
(b) What is the range of the percentages of the typical discount rate?
(c) If a company factors its receivables, what percentage of the value of the receivables can it expect to receive from the factor in the form of cash, and how quickly will it receive the cash?

Critical Thinking

Decision-Making Across the Organization

BYP9-5 Carol and Sam Foyle own Campus Fashions. From its inception Campus Fashions has sold merchandise on either a cash or credit basis, but no credit cards have been accepted. During the past several months, the Foyles have begun to question their sales policies. First, they have lost some sales because of refusing to accept credit cards. Second, representatives of two metropolitan banks have been persuasive in almost convincing them to accept their national credit cards. One bank, City National Bank, has stated that its credit card fee is 4%.

The Foyles decide that they should determine the cost of carrying their own credit sales. From the accounting records of the past 3 years, they accumulate the following data.

	2015	2014	2013
Net credit sales	$500,000	$550,000	$400,000
Collection agency fees for slow-paying customers	2,450	2,500	2,300
Salary of part-time accounts receivable clerk	4,100	4,100	4,100

Credit and collection expenses as a percentage of net credit sales are uncollectible accounts 1.6%, billing and mailing costs 0.5%, and credit investigation fee on new customers 0.15%.

Carol and Sam also determine that the average accounts receivable balance outstanding during the year is 5% of net credit sales. The Foyles estimate that they could earn an average of 8% annually on cash invested in other business opportunities.

Instructions
With the class divided into groups, answer the following.

(a) Prepare a table showing, for each year, total credit and collection expenses in dollars and as a percentage of net credit sales.
(b) Determine the net credit and collection expense in dollars and as a percentage of sales after considering the revenue not earned from other investment opportunities.
(c) Discuss both the financial and nonfinancial factors that are relevant to the decision.

Communication Activity

BYP9-6 Jill Epp, a friend of yours, overheard a discussion at work about changes her employer wants to make in accounting for uncollectible accounts. Jill knows little about accounting, and she asks you to help make sense of what she heard. Specifically, she asks you to explain the differences between the percentage-of-sales, percentage-of-receivables, and the direct write-off methods for uncollectible accounts.

Instructions
In a letter of one page (or less), explain to Jill the three methods of accounting for uncollectibles. Be sure to discuss differences among these methods.

Ethics Case

BYP9-7 The controller of Diaz Co. believes that the yearly allowance for doubtful accounts for Diaz Co. should be 2% of net credit sales. The president of Diaz Co., nervous that the stockholders might expect the company to sustain its 10% growth rate, suggests that the controller increase the

allowance for doubtful accounts to 4%. The president thinks that the lower net income, which reflects a 6% growth rate, will be a more sustainable rate for Diaz Co.

Instructions
(a) Who are the stakeholders in this case?
(b) Does the president's request pose an ethical dilemma for the controller?
(c) Should the controller be concerned with Diaz Co.'s growth rate? Explain your answer.

All About You

BYP9-8 Credit card usage in the United States is substantial. Many startup companies use credit cards as a way to help meet short-term financial needs. The most common forms of debt for startups are use of credit cards and loans from relatives.

Suppose that you start up Brothers Sandwich Shop. You invested your savings of $20,000 and borrowed $70,000 from your relatives. Although sales in the first few months are good, you see that you may not have sufficient cash to pay expenses and maintain your inventory at acceptable levels, at least in the short term. You decide you may need to use one or more credit cards to fund the possible cash shortfall.

Instructions
(a) Go to the Internet and find two sources that provide insight into how to compare credit card terms.
(b) Develop a list, in descending order of importance, as to what features are most important to you in selecting a credit card for your business.
(c) Examine the features of your present credit card. (If you do not have a credit card, select a likely one online for this exercise.) Given your analysis above, what are the three major disadvantages of your present credit card?

FASB Codification Activity

BYP9-9 If your school has a subscription to the FASB Codification, go to **http://aaahq.org/ascLogin.cfm** to log in and prepare responses to the following.

(a) How are receivables defined in the Codification?
(b) What are the conditions under which losses from uncollectible receivables (Bad Debt Expense) should be reported?

Answers to Chapter Questions

Answers to Insight and Accounting Across the Organization Questions

p. 440 How Does a Credit Card Work? **Q:** Assume that Nordstrom prepares a bank reconciliation at the end of each month. If some credit card sales have not been processed by the bank, how should Nordstrom treat these transactions on its bank reconciliation? **A:** Nordstrom would treat the credit card receipts as deposits in transit. It has already recorded the receipts as cash. Its bank will increase Nordstrom's cash account when it receives the receipts.

p. 444 Can Fair Value Be Unfair? **Q:** What are the arguments in favor of and against fair value accounting for loans and receivables? **A:** Arguments in favor of fair value accounting for loans and receivables are that fair value would provide a more accurate view of a company's financial position. This might provide a useful early warning of when a bank or other financial institution was in trouble because its loans were of poor quality. But, banks argue that estimating fair values is very difficult to do accurately. They are also concerned that volatile fair values could cause large swings in a bank's reported net income.

p. 446 Bad Information Can Lead to Bad Loans **Q:** What steps should the banks have taken to ensure the accuracy of financial information provided on loan applications? **A:** At a minimum, the bank should have requested copies of recent income tax forms and contacted the supposed employer to verify income. To verify ownership and value of assets, it should have examined bank statements, investment statements, and title documents and should have employed appraisers.

Answers to Self-Test Questions

1. d   **2.** c ($1,000 − $300) × (100% − 2%)   **3.** a   **4.** b ($60,000 − $5,000)   **5.** d ($60,000 + $5,000)   **6.** b ($800,000 × 1.5%) + $15,000   **7.** b ($750,000 × 3%) + ($18,000 − $30,000)   **8.** d ($800,000 − $65,000)   **9.** c   **10.** a   **11.** c   **12.** b   **13.** d $10,000 + ($10,000 × 120/360 × 9%)   **14.** a
15. c $800,000 ÷ [($100,000 + $150,000) ÷ 2] and 365 ÷ 4

A Look at IFRS

LEARNING OBJECTIVE   10

Compare the accounting procedures for receivables under GAAP and IFRS.

The basic accounting and reporting issues related to recognition and measurement of receivables, such as the use of allowance accounts, how to record discounts, use of the allowance method to account for bad debts, and factoring, are essentially the same between IFRS and GAAP.

Key Points

- IFRS requires that loans and receivables be accounted for at amortized cost, adjusted for allowances for doubtful accounts. IFRS sometimes refers to these allowances as **provisions**. The entry to record the allowance would be:

Bad Debt Expense	xxxxxx	
Allowance for Doubtful Accounts		xxxxxx

- Although IFRS implies that receivables with different characteristics should be reported separately, there is no standard that mandates this segregation.

- The FASB and IASB have worked to implement fair value measurement (the amount they currently could be sold for) for financial instruments. Both Boards have faced bitter opposition from various factions. As a consequence, the Boards have adopted a piecemeal approach. The first step is disclosure of fair value information in the notes. The second step is the fair value option, which permits but does not require companies to record some types of financial instruments at fair values in the financial statements.

- IFRS requires a two-tiered approach to test whether the value of loans and receivables are impaired. First, a company should look at specific loans and receivables to determine whether they are impaired. Then, the loans and receivables as a group should be evaluated for impairment. GAAP does not prescribe a similar two-tiered approach.

- IFRS and GAAP differ in the criteria used to determine how to record a factoring transaction. IFRS uses a combination approach focused on risks and rewards and loss of control. GAAP uses loss of control as the primary criterion. In addition, IFRS permits partial derecognition of receivables; GAAP does not.

Looking to the Future

It appears likely that the question of recording fair values for financial instruments will continue to be an important issue to resolve as the Boards work toward convergence. Both the IASB and the FASB have indicated that they believe that financial statements would be more transparent and understandable if companies recorded and reported all financial instruments at fair value. That said, in *IFRS 9*, which was issued in 2009, the IASB created a split model, where some financial instruments are recorded at fair value, but other financial assets, such as loans and receivables, can be accounted for at amortized cost if certain criteria are met. Critics say that this can result in two companies with identical securities accounting for those securities in different ways. A proposal by the FASB would require that nearly all financial instruments, including loans and receivables, be accounted for at fair value. It has been suggested that *IFRS 9* will likely be changed or replaced as the FASB and IASB continue to deliberate the best treatment for financial instruments. In fact, one past member of the IASB said that companies should ignore *IFRS 9* and continue to report under the old standard. In his opinion, it was extremely likely that it would be changed before 2013, the mandatory adoption date of the standard.

IFRS Practice

IFRS Self-Test Questions

1. Under IFRS, loans and receivables are to be reported on the balance sheet at:
   (a) amortized cost.
   (b) amortized cost adjusted for estimated loss provisions.

(c) historical cost.

(d) replacement cost.

2. Which of the following statements is **false**?

   (a) Loans and receivables include equity securities purchased by the company.

   (b) Loans and receivables include credit card receivables.

   (c) Loans and receivables include amounts owed by employees as a result of company loans to employees.

   (d) Loans and receivables include amounts resulting from transactions with customers.

3. In recording a factoring transaction:

   (a) IFRS focuses on loss of control.

   (b) GAAP focuses on loss of control and risks and rewards.

   (c) IFRS and GAAP allow partial derecognition.

   (d) IFRS allows partial derecognition

4. Under IFRS:

   (a) the entry to record estimated uncollected accounts is the same as GAAP.

   (b) loans and receivables should only be tested for impairment as a group.

   (c) it is always acceptable to use the direct write-off method.

   (d) all financial instruments are recorded at fair value.

5. Which of the following statements is **true**?

   (a) The fair value option requires that some types of financial instruments be recorded at fair value.

   (b) The fair value option allows, but does not require, that some types of financial instruments be recorded at amortized cost.

   (c) The fair value option allows, but does not require, that some types of financial instruments be recorded at fair value.

   (d) The FASB and IASB would like to reduce the reliance on fair value accounting for financial instruments in the future.

IFRS Exercises

IFRS9-1 What are some steps taken by both the FASB and IASB to move to fair value measurement for financial instruments? In what ways have some of the approaches differed?

International Financial Reporting Problem: Zetar plc

IFRS9-2 The financial statements of Zetar plc are presented in Appendix F. Instructions for accessing and using the company's complete annual report, including the notes to its financial statements, are also provided in Appendix F.

Instructions

Use the company's annual report to answer the following questions.

(a) According to the Operational Review of Financial Performance, what was one reason why the balance in receivables increased relative to the previous year?

(b) According to the notes to the financial statements, how are loans and receivables defined?

(c) Using the notes to the financial statements, what amount of trade receivables were written off (utilised) during 2011?

(d) Using information in the notes to the financial statements, determine what percentage the provision for impairment of receivables was as a percentage of total trade receivables for 2011 and 2010. How did the ratio change from 2010 to 2011, and what does this suggest about the company's receivables?

Answers to IFRS Self-Test Questions

1. b   2. a   3. d   4. a   5. c

 Remember to go back to The Navigator box on the chapter opening page and check off your completed work.

10 Plant Assets, Natural Resources, and Intangible Assets

How Much for a Ride to the Beach?

It's spring break. Your plane has landed, you've finally found your bags, and you're dying to hit the beach—but first you need a "vehicular unit" to get you there. As you turn away from baggage claim, you see a long row of rental agency booths. Many are names you are familiar with—Hertz, Avis, and Budget. But a booth at the far end catches your eye— Rent-A-Wreck. Now there's a company making a clear statement!

Any company that relies on equipment to generate revenues must make decisions about what kind of equipment to buy, how long to keep it, and how vigorously to maintain it. Rent-A-Wreck has decided to rent used rather than new cars and trucks. It rents these vehicles across the United States, Europe, and Asia. While the big-name agencies push vehicles with that "new car smell," Rent-A-Wreck competes on price.

Rent-A-Wreck's message is simple: Rent a used car and sa some cash. It's not a message that appeals to everyone. If you're a marketing executive wanting to impress a big clie you probably don't want to pull up in a Rent-A-Wreck car But if you want to get from point A to point B for the minimum cash per mile, then Rent-A-Wreck is playing you tune. The company's message seems to be getting across the right clientele. Revenues have increased significantly.

When you rent a car from Rent-A-Wreck, you are renting from an independent business person. This owner has pa "franchise fee" for the right to use the Rent-A-Wreck nan In order to gain a franchise, he or she must meet financia and other criteria, and must agree to run the rental agenc according to rules prescribed by Rent-A-Wreck. Some of these rules require that each franchise maintain its cars in a reasonable fashion. This ensures that, though you won' be cruising down Daytona Beach's Atlantic Avenue in a Mercedes convertible, you can be reasonably assured tha you won't be calling a towtruck.

✔ **The Navigator**

- Scan Learning Objectives
- Read Feature Story
- Read Preview
- Read text and answer **DO IT!** p. 475
  - p. 481 ■ p. 482 ■ p. 486 ■ p. 491
- Work Comprehensive **DO IT! 1** p. 494
  - **2** p. 495
- Review Summary of Learning Objectives
- Answer Self-Test Questions
- Complete Assignments
- Go to *WileyPLUS* for practice and tutorials
- 🌐 **Read A Look at IFRS** p. 517

Learning Objectives

✔ **The Navigator**

After studying this chapter, you should be able to:

[1] Describe how the historical cost principle applies to plant assets.

[2] Explain the concept of depreciation and how to compute it.

[3] Distinguish between revenue and capital expenditures, and explain the entries for each.

[4] Explain how to account for the disposal of a plant asset.

[5] Compute periodic depletion of natural resources.

[6] Explain the basic issues related to accounting for intangible assets.

[7] Indicate how plant assets, natural resources, and intangible assets are reported.

Preview of Chapter 10

✔ The Navigator

The accounting for long-term assets has important implications for a company's reported results. In this chapter, we explain the application of the historical cost principle of accounting to property, plant, and equipment, such as Rent-A-Wreck vehicles, as well as to natural resources and intangible assets such as the "Rent-A-Wreck" trademark. We also describe the methods that companies may use to allocate an asset's cost over its useful life. In addition, we discuss the accounting for expenditures incurred during the useful life of assets, such as the cost of replacing tires and brake pads on rental cars.

The content and organization of Chapter 10 are as follows.

PLANT ASSETS, NATURAL RESOURCES, AND INTANGIBLE ASSETS

Plant Assets	Natural Resources	Intangible Assets	Statement Presentation and Analysis
• Determining the cost of plant assets • Depreciation • Expenditures during useful life • Plant asset disposals	• Depletion • Presentation	• Accounting for intangibles • Research and development costs	• Presentation • Analysis

Plant Assets

LEARNING OBJECTIVE 1

Describe how the historical cost principle applies to plant assets.

Plant assets are resources that have three characteristics. They have a physical substance (a definite size and shape), are used in the operations of a business, and are not intended for sale to customers. They are also called **property, plant, and equipment; plant and equipment;** and **fixed assets**. These assets are expected to be of use to the company for a number of years. Except for land, plant assets decline in service potential over their useful lives.

Because plant assets play a key role in ongoing operations, companies keep plant assets in good operating condition. They also replace worn-out or outdated plant assets, and expand productive resources as needed. Many companies have substantial investments in plant assets. Illustration 10-1 shows the percentages of plant assets in relation to total assets of companies in a number of industries.

Illustration 10-1
Percentages of plant assets in relation to total assets

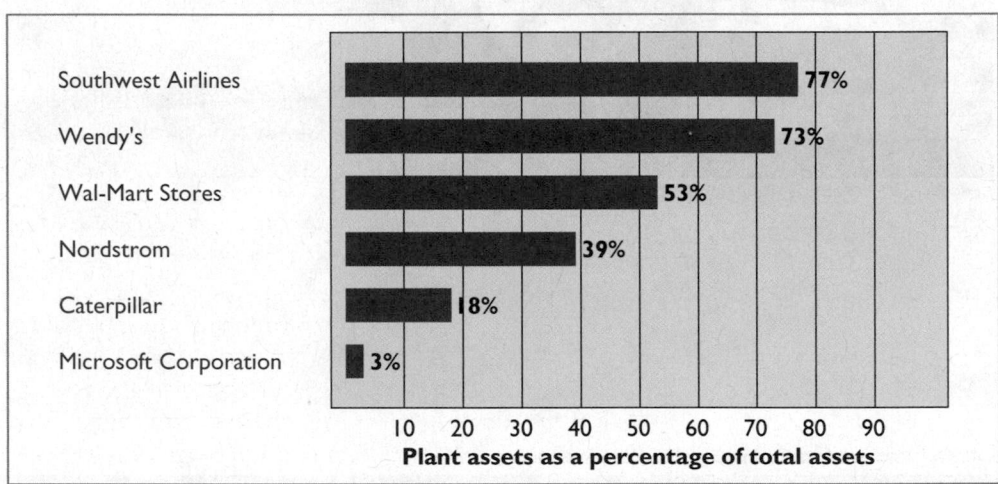

Plant assets as a percentage of total assets

Determining the Cost of Plant Assets

The historical cost principle requires that companies record plant assets at cost. Thus, Rent-A-Wreck records its vehicles at cost. **Cost consists of all expenditures necessary to acquire the asset and make it ready for its intended use.** For example, the cost of factory machinery includes the purchase price, freight costs paid by the purchaser, and installation costs. Once cost is established, the company uses that amount as the basis of accounting for the plant asset over its useful life.

In the following sections, we explain the application of the historical cost principle to each of the major classes of plant assets.

LAND

Companies often use **land** as a building site for a manufacturing plant or office building. The cost of land includes (1) the cash purchase price, (2) closing costs such as title and attorney's fees, (3) real estate brokers' commissions, and (4) accrued property taxes and other liens assumed by the purchaser. For example, if the cash price is $50,000 and the purchaser agrees to pay accrued taxes of $5,000, the cost of the land is $55,000.

Helpful Hint Management's intended use is important in applying the historical cost principle.

Companies record as debits (increases) to the Land account all necessary costs incurred to make land **ready for its intended use**. When a company acquires vacant land, these costs include expenditures for clearing, draining, filling, and grading. Sometimes the land has a building on it that must be removed before construction of a new building. In this case, the company debits to the Land account all demolition and removal costs, less any proceeds from salvaged materials.

To illustrate, assume that Hayes Company acquires real estate at a cash cost of $100,000. The property contains an old warehouse that is razed at a net cost of $6,000 ($7,500 in costs less $1,500 proceeds from salvaged materials). Additional expenditures are the attorney's fee, $1,000, and the real estate broker's commission, $8,000. The cost of the land is $115,000, computed as shown in Illustration 10-2.

Illustration 10-2
Computation of cost of land

Land	
Cash price of property	$ 100,000
Net removal cost of warehouse ($7,500 − $1,500)	6,000
Attorney's fee	1,000
Real estate broker's commission	8,000
Cost of land	**$115,000**

When Hayes records the acquisition, it debits Land for $115,000 and credits Cash for $115,000.

LAND IMPROVEMENTS

Land improvements are structural additions made to land. Examples are driveways, parking lots, fences, landscaping, and underground sprinklers. The cost of land improvements includes all expenditures necessary to make the improvements ready for their intended use. For example, the cost of a new parking lot for Home Depot includes the amount paid for paving, fencing, and lighting. Thus, Home Depot debits to Land Improvements the total of all of these costs.

Land improvements have limited useful lives, and their maintenance and replacement are the responsibility of the company. As a result, companies expense (depreciate) the cost of land improvements over their useful lives.

BUILDINGS

Buildings are facilities used in operations, such as stores, offices, factories, warehouses, and airplane hangars. Companies debit to the Buildings account all necessary expenditures related to the purchase or construction of a building. When a building is **purchased**, such costs include the purchase price, closing costs (attorney's fees, title insurance, etc.), and real estate broker's commission. Costs to make the building ready for its intended use include expenditures for remodeling and replacing or repairing the roof, floors, electrical wiring, and plumbing. When a new building is **constructed**, cost consists of the contract price plus payments for architects' fees, building permits, and excavation costs.

In addition, companies charge certain interest costs to the Buildings account. Interest costs incurred to finance the project are included in the cost of the building when a significant period of time is required to get the building ready for use. In these circumstances, interest costs are considered as necessary as materials and labor. However, the inclusion of interest costs in the cost of a constructed building is **limited to the construction period**. When construction has been completed, the company records subsequent interest payments on funds borrowed to finance the construction as debits (increases) to Interest Expense.

EQUIPMENT

Equipment includes assets used in operations, such as store check-out counters, office furniture, factory machinery, delivery trucks, and airplanes. The cost of equipment, such as Rent-A-Wreck vehicles, consists of the cash purchase price, sales taxes, freight charges, and insurance during transit paid by the purchaser. It also includes expenditures required in assembling, installing, and testing the unit. However, Rent-A-Wreck does not include motor vehicle licenses and accident insurance on company vehicles in the cost of equipment. These costs represent annual recurring expenditures and do not benefit future periods. Thus, they are treated as **expenses** as they are incurred.

To illustrate, assume Merten Company purchases factory machinery at a cash price of $50,000. Related expenditures are for sales taxes $3,000, insurance during shipping $500, and installation and testing $1,000. The cost of the factory machinery is $54,500, computed in Illustration 10-3.

Illustration 10-3

Computation of cost of factory machinery

Factory Machinery

Cash price	$ 50,000
Sales taxes	3,000
Insurance during shipping	500
Installation and testing	1,000
Cost of factory machinery	**$54,500**

Merten makes the following summary entry to record the purchase and related expenditures.

A = L + OE
+54,500
−54,500

Cash Flows
−54,500

Equipment	54,500	
Cash		54,500
(To record purchase of factory machine)		

For another example, assume that Lenard Company purchases a delivery truck at a cash price of $22,000. Related expenditures consist of sales taxes $1,320, painting and lettering $500, motor vehicle license $80, and a three-year accident insurance policy $1,600. The cost of the delivery truck is $23,820, computed as follows.

Illustration 10-4

Computation of cost of delivery truck

Delivery Truck

Cash price	$ 22,000
Sales taxes	1,320
Painting and lettering	500
Cost of delivery truck	**$23,820**

Lenard treats the cost of the motor vehicle license as an expense, and the cost of the insurance policy as a prepaid asset. Thus, Lenard makes the following entry to record the purchase of the truck and related expenditures:

A = L + OE
+23,820
　　　　−80 Exp
+ 1,600
−25,500

Cash Flows
−25,500

Equipment	23,820	
License Expense	80	
Prepaid Insurance	1,600	
Cash		25,500
(To record purchase of delivery truck and related		
expenditures)		

ACCOUNTING ACROSS THE ORGANIZATION

Many U.S. Firms Use Leases

Leasing is big business for U.S. companies. For example, business investment in equipment in a recent year totaled $709 billion. Leasing accounted for about 31% of all business investment ($218 billion).

Who does the most leasing? Interestingly, major banks such as Continental Bank, J.P. Morgan Leasing, and US Bancorp Equipment Finance are the major lessors. Also, many companies have established separate leasing companies, such as Boeing Capital Corporation, Dell Financial Services, and John Deere Capital Corporation. And, as an excellent example of the magnitude of leasing, leased planes account for nearly 40% of the U.S. fleet of commercial airlines. In addition, leasing is becoming increasingly common in the hotel industry. Marriott, Hilton, and InterContinental are increasingly choosing to lease hotels that are owned by someone else.

? Why might airline managers choose to lease rather than purchase their planes? (See page 517.)

> ## DO IT!

Cost of Plant Assets

Assume that Drummond Heating and Cooling Co. purchases a delivery truck for $15,000 cash, plus sales taxes of $900 and delivery costs of $500. The buyer also pays $200 for painting and lettering, $600 for an annual insurance policy, and $80 for a motor vehicle license. Explain how each of these costs would be accounted for.

Solution

Action Plan

✔ Identify expenditures made in order to get delivery equipment ready for its intended use.

✔ Treat operating costs as expenses.

The first four payments ($15,000, $900, $500, and $200) are expenditures necessary to make the truck ready for its intended use. Thus, the cost of the truck is $16,600. The payments for insurance and the license are operating costs and therefore are expensed.

Related exercise material: BE10-1, BE10-2, E10-1, E10-2, E10-3, and **DO IT!** 10-1.

✔ **The Navigator**

Depreciation

As explained in Chapter 3, **depreciation is the process of allocating to expense the cost of a plant asset over its useful (service) life in a rational and systematic manner**. Cost allocation enables companies to properly match expenses with revenues in accordance with the expense recognition principle, as shown in Illustration 10-5.

LEARNING OBJECTIVE 2

Explain the concept of depreciation and how to compute it.

Illustration 10-5
Depreciation as a cost allocation concept

Ethics Note

When a business is acquired, proper allocation of the purchase price to various asset classes is important since different depreciation treatments can materially affect income. For example, buildings are depreciated, but land is not.

It is important to understand that **depreciation is a process of cost allocation. It is not a process of asset valuation.** No attempt is made to measure the change in an asset's fair value during ownership. So, the **book value** (cost less accumulated depreciation) of a plant asset may be quite different from its fair value. In fact, if an asset is fully depreciated, it can have a zero book value but still have a significant fair value.

Depreciation applies to three classes of plant assets: land improvements, buildings, and equipment. Each asset in these classes is considered to be a **depreciable asset**. Why? Because the usefulness to the company and revenue-producing ability of each asset will decline over the asset's useful life. Depreciation **does not apply to land** because its usefulness and revenue-producing ability generally remain intact over time. In fact, in many cases, the usefulness of land is greater over time because of the scarcity of good land sites. Thus, **land is not a depreciable asset**.

During a depreciable asset's useful life, its revenue-producing ability declines because of **wear and tear**. A delivery truck that has been driven 100,000 miles will be less useful to a company than one driven only 800 miles.

Revenue-producing ability may also decline because of obsolescence. **Obsolescence** is the process of becoming out of date before the asset physically wears out. For example, major airlines moved from Chicago's Midway Airport to Chicago-O'Hare International Airport because Midway's runways were too short for jumbo jets. Similarly, many companies replace their computers long before they originally planned to do so because improvements in new computing technology make the old computers obsolete.

Recognizing depreciation on an asset does not result in an accumulation of cash for replacement of the asset. The balance in Accumulated Depreciation represents the total amount of the asset's cost that the company has charged to expense. It is not a cash fund.

Note that the concept of depreciation is consistent with the going-concern assumption. The **going-concern assumption** states that the company will continue in operation for the foreseeable future. If a company does not use a going-concern assumption, then plant assets should be stated at their fair value. In that case, depreciation of these assets is not needed.

FACTORS IN COMPUTING DEPRECIATION

Three factors affect the computation of depreciation, as shown in Illustration 10-6.

Illustration 10-6
Three factors in computing depreciation

Helpful Hint Depreciation expense is reported on the income statement. Accumulated depreciation is reported on the balance sheet as a deduction from plant assets.

Cost: all expenditures necessary to acquire the asset and make it ready for intended use

Useful life: estimate of the expected life based on need for repair, service life, and vulnerability to obsolescence

Salvage value: estimate of the asset's value at the end of its useful life

1. **Cost.** Earlier, we explained the issues affecting the cost of a depreciable asset. Recall that companies record plant assets at cost, in accordance with the historical cost principle.

2. **Useful life. Useful life** is an estimate of the expected productive life, also called service life, of the asset for its owner. Useful life may be expressed in terms of time, units of activity (such as machine hours), or units of output. Useful life is an estimate. In making the estimate, management considers such factors as the intended use of the asset, its expected repair and maintenance, and its vulnerability to obsolescence. Past experience with similar assets is often helpful in deciding on expected useful life. We might reasonably expect Rent-A-Wreck and Avis to use different estimated useful lives for their vehicles.

3. **Salvage value. Salvage value** is an estimate of the asset's value at the end of its useful life. This value may be based on the asset's worth as scrap or on its expected trade-in value. Like useful life, salvage value is an estimate. In making the estimate, management considers how it plans to dispose of the asset and its experience with similar assets.

Alternative Terminology
Another term sometimes used for salvage value is *residual value*.

DEPRECIATION METHODS

Depreciation is generally computed using one of the following methods:

1. Straight-line
2. Units-of-activity
3. Declining-balance

Each method is acceptable under generally accepted accounting principles. Management selects the method(s) it believes to be appropriate. The objective is to select the method that best measures an asset's contribution to revenue over its useful life. Once a company chooses a method, it should apply it consistently over the useful life of the asset. Consistency enhances the comparability of financial statements. Depreciation affects the balance sheet through accumulated depreciation and the income statement through depreciation expense.

We will compare the three depreciation methods using the following data for a small delivery truck purchased by Barb's Florists on January 1, 2014.

Cost	$13,000
Expected salvage value	$ 1,000
Estimated useful life in years	5
Estimated useful life in miles	100,000

Illustration 10-7
Delivery truck data

Illustration 10-8 (in the margin) shows the use of the primary depreciation methods in a sample of the largest companies in the United States.

STRAIGHT-LINE Under the **straight-line method**, companies expense the same amount of depreciation for each year of the asset's useful life. It is measured solely by the passage of time.

To compute depreciation expense under the straight-line method, companies need to determine depreciable cost. **Depreciable cost** is the cost of the asset less its salvage value. It represents the total amount subject to depreciation. Under the straight-line method, to determine annual depreciation expense, we divide depreciable cost by the asset's useful life. Illustration 10-9 (page 478) shows the computation of the first year's depreciation expense for Barb's Florists.

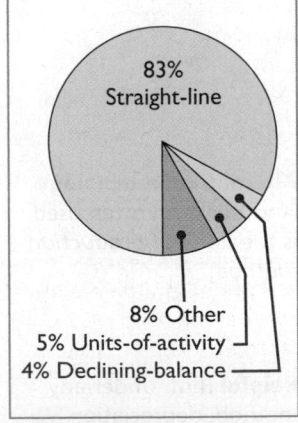

Illustration 10-8
Use of depreciation methods in large U.S. companies

Illustration 10-9
Formula for straight-line method

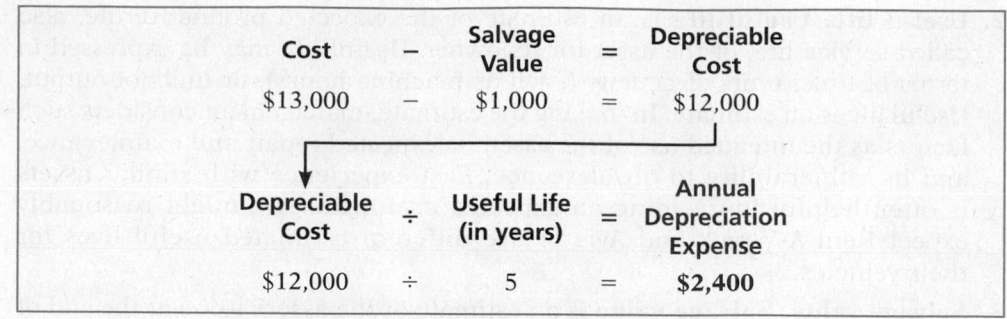

Cost	−	Salvage Value	=	Depreciable Cost
$13,000	−	$1,000	=	$12,000

Depreciable Cost	÷	Useful Life (in years)	=	Annual Depreciation Expense
$12,000	÷	5	=	$2,400

Alternatively, we also can compute an annual **rate** of depreciation. In this case, the rate is 20% (100% ÷ 5 years). When a company uses an annual straight-line rate, it applies the percentage rate to the depreciable cost of the asset. Illustration 10-10 shows a **depreciation schedule** using an annual rate.

Illustration 10-10
Straight-line depreciation schedule

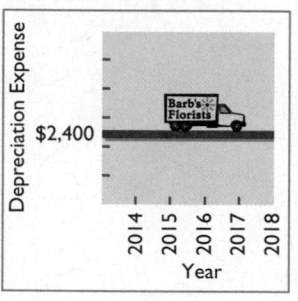

	BARB'S FLORISTS					
	Computation			Annual	End of Year	
Year	Depreciable Cost	×	Depreciation Rate	= Depreciation Expense	Accumulated Depreciation	Book Value
2014	$12,000		20%	$2,400	$ 2,400	$10,600*
2015	12,000		20	2,400	4,800	8,200
2016	12,000		20	2,400	7,200	5,800
2017	12,000		20	2,400	9,600	3,400
2018	12,000		20	2,400	12,000	1,000

*Book value = Cost − Accumulated depreciation = ($13,000 − $2,400).

Note that the depreciation expense of $2,400 is the same each year. The book value (computed as cost minus accumulated depreciation) at the end of the useful life is equal to the expected $1,000 salvage value.

What happens to these computations for an asset purchased **during** the year, rather than on January 1? In that case, it is necessary to **prorate the annual depreciation** on a time basis. If Barb's Florists had purchased the delivery truck on April 1, 2014, the company would own the truck for nine months of the first year (April–December). Thus, depreciation for 2014 would be $1,800 ($12,000 × 20% × 9/12 of a year).

The straight-line method predominates in practice. Such large companies as Campbell Soup, Marriott, and General Mills use the straight-line method. It is simple to apply, and it matches expenses with revenues when the use of the asset is reasonably uniform throughout the service life.

Alternative Terminology
Another term often used is the *units-of-production method.*

Helpful Hint Under any method, depreciation stops when the asset's book value equals expected salvage value.

UNITS-OF-ACTIVITY Under the **units-of-activity method**, useful life is expressed in terms of the total units of production or use expected from the asset, rather than as a time period. The units-of-activity method is ideally suited to factory machinery. Manufacturing companies can measure production in units of output or in machine hours. This method can also be used for such assets as delivery equipment (miles driven) and airplanes (hours in use). The units-of-activity method is generally not suitable for buildings or furniture because depreciation for these assets is more a function of time than of use.

To use this method, companies estimate the total units of activity for the entire useful life, and then divide these units into depreciable cost. The resulting number represents the depreciable cost per unit. The depreciable cost per unit is then applied to the units of activity during the year to determine the annual depreciation expense.

To illustrate, assume that Barb's Florists drives its delivery truck 15,000 miles in the first year. Illustration 10-11 shows the units-of-activity formula and the computation of the first year's depreciation expense.

Illustration 10-11
Formula for units-of-activity method

The units-of-activity depreciation schedule, using assumed mileage, is as follows.

BARB'S FLORISTS					
	Computation		**Annual**	**End of Year**	
Year	**Units of Activity** ×	**Depreciable Cost/Unit** =	**Depreciation Expense**	**Accumulated Depreciation**	**Book Value**
2014	15,000	$0.12	**$1,800**	$ 1,800	$11,200*
2015	30,000	0.12	**3,600**	5,400	7,600
2016	20,000	0.12	**2,400**	7,800	5,200
2017	25,000	0.12	**3,000**	10,800	2,200
2018	10,000	0.12	**1,200**	12,000	**1,000**

*($13,000 − $1,800).

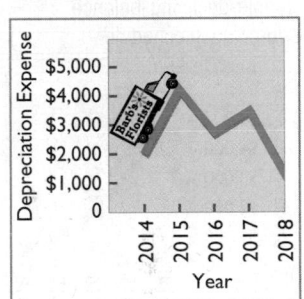

Illustration 10-12
Units-of-activity depreciation schedule

This method is easy to apply for assets purchased mid-year. In such a case, the company computes the depreciation using the productivity of the asset for the partial year.

The units-of-activity method is not nearly as popular as the straight-line method (see Illustration 10-8, page 477) primarily because it is often difficult for companies to reasonably estimate total activity. However, some very large companies, such as Chevron and Boise Cascade (a forestry company), do use this method. When the productivity of an asset varies significantly from one period to another, the units-of-activity method results in the best matching of expenses with revenues.

DECLINING-BALANCE The **declining-balance method** produces a decreasing annual depreciation expense over the asset's useful life. The method is so named because the periodic depreciation is based on a **declining book value** (cost less accumulated depreciation) of the asset. With this method, companies compute annual depreciation expense by multiplying the book value at the beginning of the year by the declining-balance depreciation rate. **The depreciation rate remains constant from year to year, but the book value to which the rate is applied declines each year.**

At the beginning of the first year, book value is the cost of the asset. This is because the balance in accumulated depreciation at the beginning of the asset's useful life is zero. In subsequent years, book value is the difference between cost and accumulated depreciation to date. Unlike the other depreciation methods, the declining-balance method does not use depreciable cost in computing annual depreciation expense. That is, **it ignores salvage value in determining the amount to which the declining-balance rate is applied**. Salvage value, however, does limit the total depreciation that can be taken. Depreciation stops when the asset's book value equals expected salvage value.

A common declining-balance rate is double the straight-line rate. The method is often called the **double-declining-balance method**. If Barb's Florists uses the double-declining-balance method, it uses a depreciation rate of 40% (2 × the straight-line rate of 20%). Illustration 10-13 shows the declining-balance formula and the computation of the first year's depreciation on the delivery truck.

Illustration 10-13
Formula for declining-balance method

Book Value at Beginning of Year	×	Declining-Balance Rate	=	Annual Depreciation Expense
$13,000	×	40%	=	$5,200

The depreciation schedule under this method is as follows.

Illustration 10-14
Double-declining-balance depreciation schedule

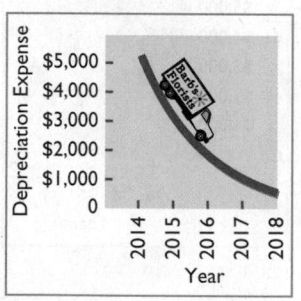

	BARB'S FLORISTS					
	Computation			**Annual**	**End of Year**	
Year	**Book Value Beginning of Year**	**× Depreciation Rate =**		**Depreciation Expense**	**Accumulated Depreciation**	**Book Value**
2014	$13,000	40%		**$5,200**	$ 5,200	$7,800
2015	7,800	40		**3,120**	8,320	4,680
2016	4,680	40		**1,872**	10,192	2,808
2017	2,808	40		**1,123**	11,315	1,685
2018	1,685	40		**685***	12,000	**1,000**

*Computation of $674 ($1,685 × 40%) is adjusted to $685 in order for book value to equal salvage value.

Helpful Hint The method recommended for an asset that is expected to be significantly more productive in the first half of its useful life is the declining-balance method.

The delivery equipment is 69% depreciated ($8,320 ÷ $12,000) at the end of the second year. Under the straight-line method, the truck would be depreciated 40% ($4,800 ÷ $12,000) at that time. Because the declining-balance method produces higher depreciation expense in the early years than in the later years, it is considered an **accelerated-depreciation method**. The declining-balance method is compatible with the expense recognition principle. It matches the higher depreciation expense in early years with the higher benefits received in these years. It also recognizes lower depreciation expense in later years, when the asset's contribution to revenue is less. Some assets lose usefulness rapidly because of obsolescence. In these cases, the declining-balance method provides the most appropriate depreciation amount.

When a company purchases an asset during the year, it must prorate the first year's declining-balance depreciation on a time basis. For example, if Barb's Florists had purchased the truck on April 1, 2014, depreciation for 2014 would become $3,900 ($13,000 × 40% × 9/12). The book value at the beginning of 2015 is then $9,100 ($13,000 − $3,900), and the 2015 depreciation is $3,640 ($9,100 × 40%). Subsequent computations would follow from those amounts.

> DO IT!

Straight-Line Depreciation

On January 1, 2014, Iron Mountain Ski Corporation purchased a new snow-grooming machine for $50,000. The machine is estimated to have a 10-year life with a $2,000 salvage value. What journal entry would Iron Mountain Ski Corporation make at December 31, 2014, if it uses the straight-line method of depreciation?

Solution

Action Plan

✔ Calculate depreciable cost (Cost − Salvage value).

✔ Divide the depreciable cost by the asset's estimated useful life.

$$\text{Depreciation expense} = \frac{\text{Cost} - \text{Salvage value}}{\text{Useful life}} = \frac{\$50,000 - \$2,000}{10} = \$4,800$$

The entry to record the first year's depreciation would be:

Dec. 31	Depreciation Expense	4,800	
	Accumulated Depreciation—Equipment		4,800
	(To record annual depreciation on		
	snow-grooming machine)		

Related exercise material: **BE10-3, BE10-4, E10-4, and DO IT! 10-2.**

 ✔ The Navigator

COMPARISON OF METHODS Illustration 10-15 compares annual and total depreciation expense under each of the three methods for Barb's Florists.

Year	Straight-Line	Units-of-Activity	Declining-Balance
2014	$ 2,400	$ 1,800	$ 5,200
2015	2,400	3,600	3,120
2016	2,400	2,400	1,872
2017	2,400	3,000	1,123
2018	2,400	1,200	685
	$12,000	**$12,000**	**$12,000**

Illustration 10-15
Comparison of depreciation methods

Annual depreciation varies considerably among the methods, but **total depreciation expense is the same ($12,000) for the five-year period** under all three methods. Each method is acceptable in accounting because each recognizes in a rational and systematic manner the decline in service potential of the asset. Illustration 10-16 graphs the depreciation expense pattern under each method.

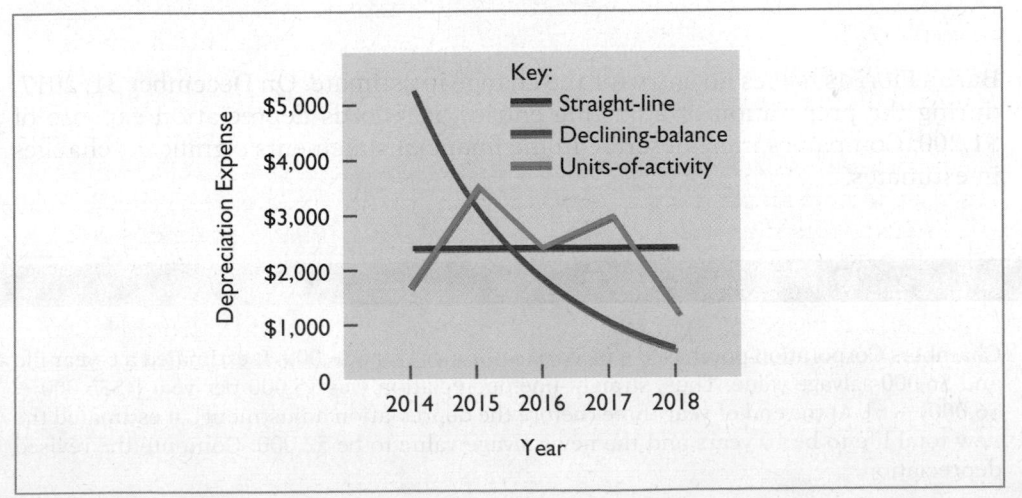

Illustration 10-16
Patterns of depreciation

DEPRECIATION AND INCOME TAXES

The Internal Revenue Service (IRS) allows taxpayers to deduct depreciation expense when they compute taxable income. However, the IRS does not require taxpayers to use the same depreciation method on the tax return that is used in preparing financial statements.

Many corporations use straight-line in their financial statements to maximize net income. At the same time, they use a special accelerated-depreciation method on their tax returns to minimize their income taxes. Taxpayers must use on their tax returns either the straight-line method or a special accelerated-depreciation method called the **Modified Accelerated Cost Recovery System** (MACRS).

REVISING PERIODIC DEPRECIATION

Depreciation is one example of the use of estimation in the accounting process. Management should periodically review annual depreciation expense. If wear and tear or obsolescence indicate that annual depreciation estimates are inadequate or excessive, the company should change the amount of depreciation expense.

When a change in an estimate is required, the company makes the change in **current and future years**. **It does not change depreciation in prior periods.** The rationale is that continual restatement of prior periods would adversely affect confidence in financial statements.

Helpful Hint Use a step-by-step approach: (1) determine new depreciable cost; (2) divide by remaining useful life.

To determine the new annual depreciation expense, the company first computes the asset's depreciable cost at the time of the revision. It then allocates the revised depreciable cost to the remaining useful life.

To illustrate, assume that Barb's Florists decides on January 1, 2017, to extend the useful life of the truck one year (a total life of six years) and increase its salvage value to $2,200. The company has used the straight-line method to depreciate the asset to date. Depreciation per year was $2,400 [($13,000 − $1,000) ÷ 5]. Accumulated depreciation after three years (2014–2016) is $7,200 ($2,400 × 3), and book value is $5,800 ($13,000 − $7,200). The new annual depreciation is $1,200, computed as shown in Illustration 10-17.

Illustration 10-17
Revised depreciation computation

Book value, 1/1/17	$ 5,800
Less: Salvage value	2,200
Depreciable cost	$ 3,600
Remaining useful life	3 years (2017–2019)
Revised annual depreciation ($3,600 ÷ 3)	**$ 1,200**

Barb's Florists makes no entry for the change in estimate. On December 31, 2017, during the preparation of adjusting entries, it records depreciation expense of $1,200. Companies must describe in the financial statements significant changes in estimates.

> **DO IT!**

Revised Depreciation

Chambers Corporation purchased a piece of equipment for $36,000. It estimated a 6-year life and $6,000 salvage value. Thus, straight-line depreciation was $5,000 per year [($36,000 − $6,000) ÷ 6]. At the end of year three (before the depreciation adjustment), it estimated the new total life to be 10 years and the new salvage value to be $2,000. Compute the revised depreciation.

Action Plan

✔ Calculate remaining depreciable cost.

✔ Divide remaining depreciable cost by new remaining life.

Solution

Original depreciation expense = [($36,000 − $6,000) ÷ 6] = $5,000
Accumulated depreciation after 2 years = 2 × $5,000 = $10,000
Book value = $36,000 − $10,000 = $26,000

Book value after 2 years of depreciation	$26,000
Less: New salvage value	2,000
Depreciable cost	$24,000
Remaining useful life	8 years
Revised annual depreciation ($24,000 ÷ 8)	$ 3,000

Related exercise material: **BE10-7, E10-8,** and **DO IT!** 10-3.

✔ The Navigator

Expenditures During Useful Life

During the useful life of a plant asset, a company may incur costs for ordinary repairs, additions, or improvements. **Ordinary repairs** are expenditures to **maintain** the operating efficiency and productive life of the unit. They usually are fairly small amounts that occur frequently. Examples are motor tune-ups and oil changes, the painting of buildings, and the replacing of worn-out gears on machinery. Companies record such repairs as debits to Maintenance and Repairs Expense as they are incurred. Because they are immediately charged as an expense against revenues, these costs are often referred to as **revenue expenditures**.

In contrast, **additions and improvements** are costs incurred to **increase** the operating efficiency, productive capacity, or useful life of a plant asset. They are usually material in amount and occur infrequently. Additions and improvements increase the company's investment in productive facilities. Companies generally debit these amounts to the plant asset affected. They are often referred to as **capital expenditures**.

Companies must use good judgment in deciding between a revenue expenditure and capital expenditure. For example, assume that Rodriguez Co. purchases a number of wastepaper baskets. Although the proper accounting would appear to be to capitalize and then depreciate these wastepaper baskets over their useful life, it would be more usual for Rodriguez to expense them immediately. This practice is justified on the basis of **materiality**. Materiality refers to the impact of an item's size on a company's financial operations. The **materiality concept** states that if an item would not make a difference in decision-making, the company does not have to follow GAAP in reporting that item.

LEARNING OBJECTIVE 3

Distinguish between revenue and capital expenditures, and explain the entries for each.

ANATOMY OF A FRAUD

Bernie Ebbers was the founder and CEO of the phone company WorldCom. The company engaged in a series of increasingly large, debt-financed acquisitions of other companies. These acquisitions made the company grow quickly, which made the stock price increase dramatically. However, because the acquired companies all had different accounting systems, WorldCom's financial records were a mess. When WorldCom's performance started to flatten out, Bernie coerced WorldCom's accountants to engage in a number of fraudulent activities to make net income look better than it really was and thus prop up the stock price. One of these frauds involved treating $7 billion of line costs as capital expenditures. The line costs, which were rental fees paid to other phone companies to use their phone lines, had always been properly expensed in previous years. Capitalization delayed expense recognition to future periods and thus boosted current-period profits.

> **Total take: $7 billion**

THE MISSING CONTROLS

Documentation procedures. The company's accounting system was a disorganized collection of non-integrated systems, which resulted from a series of corporate acquisitions. Top management took advantage of this disorganization to conceal its fraudulent activities.

Independent internal verification. A fraud of this size should have been detected by a routine comparison of the actual physical assets with the list of physical assets shown in the accounting records.

Plant Asset Disposals

LEARNING OBJECTIVE 4

Explain how to account for the disposal of a plant asset.

Companies dispose of plant assets that are no longer useful to them. Illustration 10-18 shows the three ways in which companies make plant asset disposals.

Whatever the disposal method, the company must determine the book value of the plant asset at the disposal date to determine the gain or loss. Recall that the book value is the difference between the cost of the plant asset and the accumulated depreciation to date. If the disposal occurs at any time during the year, the company must record depreciation for the fraction of the year to the date of disposal. The company then eliminates the book value by reducing (debiting) Accumulated Depreciation for the total depreciation associated with that asset to the date of disposal and reducing (crediting) the asset account for the cost of the asset.

Illustration 10-18
Methods of plant asset disposal

In this chapter, we examine the accounting for the retirement and sale of plant assets. In the appendix to the chapter, we discuss and illustrate the accounting for exchanges of plant assets.

RETIREMENT OF PLANT ASSETS

To illustrate the retirement of plant assets, assume that Hobart Company retires its computer printers, which cost $32,000. The accumulated depreciation on these printers is $32,000. The equipment, therefore, is fully depreciated (zero book value). The entry to record this retirement is as follows.

A = L + OE
+32,000
−32,000

Cash Flows
no effect

Accumulated Depreciation—Equipment	32,000	
Equipment		32,000
(To record retirement of fully depreciated equipment)		

Helpful Hint When a company disposes of a plant asset, the company must remove from the accounts all amounts related to the asset. This includes the original cost in the asset account and the total depreciation to date in the accumulated depreciation account.

What happens if a fully depreciated plant asset is still useful to the company? In this case, the asset and its accumulated depreciation continue to be reported on the balance sheet, without further depreciation adjustment, until the company retires the asset. Reporting the asset and related accumulated depreciation on the balance sheet informs the financial statement reader that the asset is still in use. Once fully depreciated, no additional depreciation should be taken, even if an asset is still being used. In no situation can the accumulated depreciation on a plant asset exceed its cost.

If a company retires a plant asset before it is fully depreciated and no cash is received for scrap or salvage value, a loss on disposal occurs. For example, assume that Sunset Company discards delivery equipment that cost $18,000 and has accumulated depreciation of $14,000. The entry is as follows.

Accumulated Depreciation—Equipment	14,000	
Loss on Disposal of Plant Assets	4,000	
Equipment		18,000
(To record retirement of delivery equipment at a loss)		

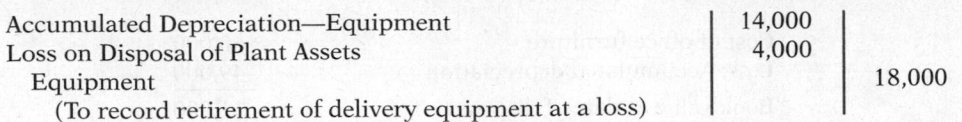

A = L + OE
+14,000
−18,000   −4,000 Exp

Cash Flows
no effect

Companies report a loss on disposal of plant assets in the "Other expenses and losses" section of the income statement.

SALE OF PLANT ASSETS

In a disposal by sale, the company compares the book value of the asset with the proceeds received from the sale. If the proceeds of the sale **exceed** the book value of the plant asset, **a gain on disposal occurs**. If the proceeds of the sale **are less than** the book value of the plant asset sold, **a loss on disposal occurs**.

Only by coincidence will the book value and the fair value of the asset be the same when the asset is sold. Gains and losses on sales of plant assets are therefore quite common. For example, Delta Airlines reported a $94,343,000 gain on the sale of five Boeing B727-200 aircraft and five Lockheed L-1011-1 aircraft.

GAIN ON SALE To illustrate a gain on sale of plant assets, assume that on July 1, 2014, Wright Company sells office furniture for $16,000 cash. The office furniture originally cost $60,000. As of January 1, 2014, it had accumulated depreciation of $41,000. Depreciation for the first six months of 2014 is $8,000. Wright records depreciation expense and updates accumulated depreciation to July 1 with the following entry.

July 1	Depreciation Expense	8,000	
	Accumulated Depreciation—Equipment		8,000
	(To record depreciation expense for the first		
	6 months of 2014)		

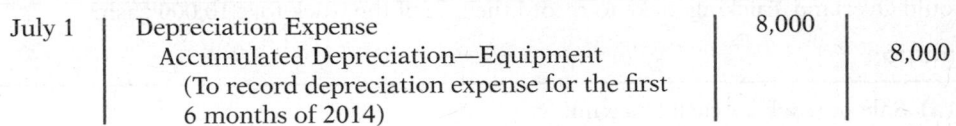

A = L + OE
              −8,000 Exp
−8,000

Cash Flows
no effect

After the accumulated depreciation balance is updated, the company computes the gain or loss. The gain or loss is the difference between the proceeds from the sale and the book value at the date of disposal. Illustration 10-19 shows this computation for Wright Company, which has a gain on disposal of $5,000.

Cost of office furniture	$60,000
Less: Accumulated depreciation ($41,000 + $8,000)	49,000
Book value at date of disposal	11,000
Proceeds from sale	16,000
Gain on disposal of plant asset	**$ 5,000**

Illustration 10-19
Computation of gain on disposal

Wright records the sale and the gain on disposal of the plant asset as follows.

July 1	Cash	16,000	
	Accumulated Depreciation—Equipment	49,000	
	Equipment		60,000
	Gain on Disposal of Plant Assets		5,000
	(To record sale of office furniture		
	at a gain)		

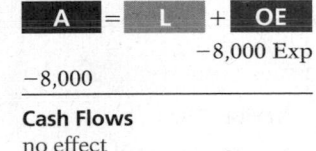

A = L + OE
+16,000
+49,000
−60,000
             +5,000 Rev

Cash Flows
+16,000

Companies report a gain on disposal of plant assets in the "Other revenues and gains" section of the income statement.

LOSS ON SALE Assume that instead of selling the office furniture for $16,000, Wright sells it for $9,000. In this case, Wright computes a loss of $2,000 as follows.

Illustration 10-20
Computation of loss on disposal

Cost of office furniture	$60,000
Less: Accumulated depreciation	49,000
Book value at date of disposal	11,000
Proceeds from sale	9,000
Loss on disposal of plant asset	**$ 2,000**

Wright records the sale and the loss on disposal of the plant asset as follows.

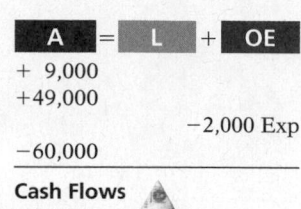

A = L + OE
+ 9,000
+49,000
          −2,000 Exp
−60,000

Cash Flows
+9,000

July 1	Cash	9,000	
	Accumulated Depreciation—Equipment	49,000	
	Loss on Disposal of Plant Assets	2,000	
	Equipment		60,000
	(To record sale of office furniture at a loss)		

Companies report a loss on disposal of plant assets in the "Other expenses and losses" section of the income statement.

> **DO IT!**

Plant Asset Disposal

Action Plan

✔ At the time of disposal, determine the book value of the asset.

✔ Compare the asset's book value with the proceeds received to determine whether a gain or loss has occurred.

Overland Trucking has an old truck that cost $30,000, and it has accumulated depreciation of $16,000 on this truck. Overland has decided to sell the truck. (a) What entry would Overland Trucking make to record the sale of the truck for $17,000 cash? (b) What entry would Overland Trucking make to record the sale of the truck for $10,000 cash?

Solution

(a) Sale of truck for cash at a gain:

Cash	17,000	
Accumulated Depreciation—Equipment	16,000	
Equipment		30,000
Gain on Disposal of Plant Assets		
[$17,000 − ($30,000 − $16,000)]		3,000
(To record sale of truck at a gain)		

(b) Sale of truck for cash at a loss:

Cash	10,000	
Accumulated Depreciation—Equipment	16,000	
Loss on Disposal of Plant Assets		
[$10,000 − ($30,000 − $16,000)]	4,000	
Equipment		30,000
(To record sale of truck at a loss)		

Related exercise material: **BE10-9, BE10-10, E10-9, E10-10, and DO IT! 10-4.**

✔ The Navigator

Natural Resources

LEARNING OBJECTIVE   5

Compute periodic depletion of natural resources.

Natural resources consist of standing timber and underground deposits of oil, gas, and minerals. These long-lived productive assets have two distinguishing characteristics: (1) They are physically extracted in operations (such as mining, cutting, or pumping). (2) They are replaceable only by an act of nature.

The acquisition cost of a natural resource is the price needed to acquire the resource **and** prepare it for its intended use. For an already-discovered resource, such as an existing coal mine, cost is the price paid for the property.

Helpful Hint On a balance sheet, natural resources may be described more specifically as *timberlands, mineral deposits, oil reserves*, and so on.

Depletion

The allocation of the cost of natural resources to expense in a rational and systematic manner over the resource's useful life is called **depletion**. (That is, depletion is to natural resources as depreciation is to plant assets.) **Companies generally use the units-of-activity method** (learned earlier in the chapter) **to compute depletion**. The reason is that **depletion generally is a function of the units extracted during the year**.

Under the units-of-activity method, companies divide the total cost of the natural resource minus salvage value by the number of units estimated to be in the resource. The result is a **depletion cost per unit of product**. They then multiply the depletion cost per unit by the number of units extracted and sold. The result is the **annual depletion expense**. Illustration 10-21 shows the formula to compute depletion expense.

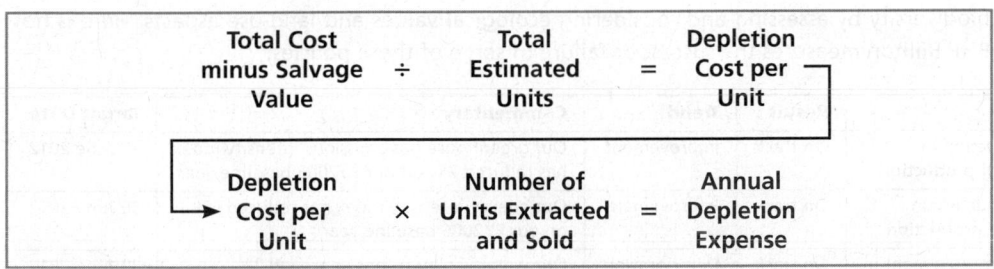

Illustration 10-21
Formula to compute depletion expense

To illustrate, assume that Lane Coal Company invests $5 million in a mine estimated to have 10 million tons of coal and no salvage value. In the first year, Lane extracts and sells 800,000 tons of coal. Using the formulas above, Lane computes the depletion expense as follows.

$$\$5{,}000{,}000 \div 10{,}000{,}000 = \$0.50 \text{ depletion cost per ton}$$

$$\$0.50 \times 800{,}000 = \$400{,}000 \text{ annual depletion expense}$$

Lane records depletion expense for the first year of operation as follows.

Ethics Note

Investors were stunned at news that Royal Dutch/Shell Group had significantly overstated its reported oil reserves—and perhaps had done so intentionally.

Dec. 31	Depletion Expense	400,000	
	Accumulated Depletion		400,000
	(To record depletion expense on coal deposits)		

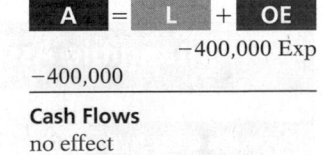

A = L + OE
−400,000 Exp
−400,000

Cash Flows
no effect

Presentation

The company reports the account Depletion Expense as a part of the cost of producing the product. Accumulated Depletion is a contra asset account, similar to accumulated depreciation. It is deducted from the cost of the natural resource in the balance sheet, as Illustration 10-22 shows.

LANE COAL COMPANY
Balance Sheet (partial)

| Coal mine | $5,000,000 | |
| **Less: Accumulated depletion** | **400,000** | $4,600,000 |

Illustration 10-22
Statement presentation of accumulated depletion

Many companies do not use an Accumulated Depletion account. In such cases, the company credits the amount of depletion directly to the natural resources account.

Sometimes, a company will extract natural resources in one accounting period but not sell them until a later period. In this case, the company does not expense the depletion until it sells the resource. It reports the amount not sold as inventory in the current assets section.

PEOPLE, PLANET, AND PROFIT INSIGHT

Sustainability Report Please

© Christian Uhrig/iStockphoto

Sustainability reports identify how the company is meeting its corporate social responsibilities. Many companies, both large and small, are now issuing these reports. For example, companies such as Disney, Best Buy, Microsoft, Ford, and ConocoPhilips issue these reports. Presented below is an adapted section of BHP Billiton's (a global mining, oil, and gas company) sustainability report on its environmental policies. These policies are to (1) take action to address the challenges of climate change, (2) set and achieve targets that reduce pollution, and (3) enhance biodiversity by assessing and considering ecological values and land-use aspects. Here is how BHP Billiton measures the success or failure of some of these policies:

Environment	Result	Trend	Commentary	Target Date
Aggregate Group target of 6% reduction in greenhouse gas emissions per unit of production	On track	Improvement	Our greenhouse gas emissions intensity index has reduced 7% on our FY2006 baseline year	30 June 2012
Aggregate Group target of 13% reduction in carbon-based energy use per unit of production	On track	Improvement	Our energy intensity index has reduced 6% on our FY2006 baseline year	30 June 2012
Aggregate Group target of a 10% improvement in the ratio of water recycled/reused to high-quality water consumed	On track	Deterioration	Our water use index has improved 7% on our FY2007 baseline year	30 June 2012

In addition to the environment, BHP Billiton has sections in its sustainability report which discuss people, safety, health, and community.

Source: BHP Billiton, *2010 Sustainability Report.*

? Why do you believe companies issue sustainability reports? (See page 517.)

Intangible Assets

LEARNING OBJECTIVE **6**

Explain the basic issues related to accounting for intangible assets.

Intangible assets are rights, privileges, and competitive advantages that result from the ownership of long-lived assets that do not possess physical substance. Evidence of intangibles may exist in the form of contracts or licenses. Intangibles may arise from the following sources:

1. Government grants, such as patents, copyrights, licenses, trademarks, and trade names.

2. Acquisition of another business, in which the purchase price includes a payment for **goodwill**.

3. Private monopolistic arrangements arising from contractual agreements, such as franchises and leases.

Some widely known intangibles are Microsoft's patents, McDonald's franchises, Apple's trade name iPod, J.K. Rowling's copyrights on the *Harry Potter* books, and the trademark Rent-A-Wreck in the Feature Story.

Accounting for Intangible Assets

Companies record intangible assets at cost. Intangibles are categorized as having either a limited life or an indefinite life. If an intangible has a **limited life**, the company allocates its cost over the asset's useful life using a process similar to depreciation. The process of allocating the cost of intangibles is referred to as **amortization**. The cost of intangible assets with **indefinite lives should not be amortized**.

To record amortization of an intangible asset, a company increases (debits) Amortization Expense, and decreases (credits) the specific intangible asset. (Unlike depreciation, no contra account, such as Accumulated Amortization, is usually used.)

Intangible assets are typically amortized on a straight-line basis. For example, the legal life of a patent is 20 years. Companies **amortize the cost of a patent over its 20-year life or its useful life, whichever is shorter**. To illustrate the computation of patent amortization, assume that National Labs purchases a patent at a cost of $60,000. If National estimates the useful life of the patent to be eight years, the annual amortization expense is $7,500 ($60,000 ÷ 8). National records the annual amortization as follows.

> **Helpful Hint** *Amortization* is to intangibles what *depreciation* is to plant assets and *depletion* is to natural resources.

Dec. 31	Amortization Expense	7,500	
	Patents		7,500
	(To record patent amortization)		

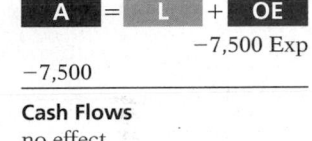

A = L + OE

−7,500 Exp

−7,500

Cash Flows
no effect

Companies classify Amortization Expense as an operating expense in the income statement.

There is a difference between intangible assets and plant assets in determining cost. For plant assets, cost includes both the purchase price of the asset and the costs incurred in designing and constructing the asset. In contrast, the initial cost for an intangible asset includes **only the purchase price**. Companies expense any costs incurred in developing an intangible asset.

PATENTS

A **patent** is an exclusive right issued by the U.S. Patent Office that enables the recipient to manufacture, sell, or otherwise control an invention for a period of 20 years from the date of the grant. A patent is nonrenewable. But, companies can extend the legal life of a patent by obtaining new patents for improvements or other changes in the basic design. **The initial cost of a patent is the cash or cash equivalent price paid to acquire the patent.**

The saying, "A patent is only as good as the money you're prepared to spend defending it," is very true. Many patents are subject to litigation by competitors. Any legal costs an owner incurs in successfully defending a patent in an infringement suit are considered necessary to establish the patent's validity. **The owner adds those costs to the Patents account and amortizes them over the remaining life of the patent.**

The patent holder amortizes the cost of a patent over its 20-year legal life or its useful life, whichever is shorter. Companies consider obsolescence and inadequacy in determining useful life. These factors may cause a patent to become economically ineffective before the end of its legal life.

COPYRIGHTS

The federal government grants **copyrights**, which give the owner the exclusive right to reproduce and sell an artistic or published work. Copyrights extend for the life of the creator plus 70 years. The cost of a copyright is the **cost of acquiring and defending it**. The cost may be only the small fee paid to the U.S. Copyright Office. Or, it may amount to much more if an infringement suit is involved.

The useful life of a copyright generally is significantly shorter than its legal life. Therefore, copyrights usually are amortized over a relatively short period of time.

TRADEMARKS AND TRADE NAMES

A **trademark** or **trade name** is a word, phrase, jingle, or symbol that identifies a particular enterprise or product. Trade names like Wheaties, Monopoly, Big Mac, Kleenex, Coca-Cola, and Jeep create immediate product identification. They also generally enhance the sale of the product. The creator or original user may obtain exclusive legal right to the trademark or trade name by registering it with the U.S. Patent Office. Such registration provides 20 years of protection. The registration may be renewed indefinitely as long as the trademark or trade name is in use.

If a company purchases the trademark or trade name, its cost is the purchase price. If a company develops and maintains the trademark or trade name, any costs related to these activities are expensed as incurred. Because trademarks and trade names have indefinite lives, they are not amortized.

FRANCHISES

When you fill up your tank at the corner Shell station, eat lunch at Subway, or rent a car from Rent-A-Wreck, you are dealing with franchises. A **franchise** is a contractual arrangement between a franchisor and a franchisee. The franchisor grants the franchisee the right to sell certain products, perform specific services, or use certain trademarks or trade names, usually within a designated geographic area.

Another type of franchise is a **license**. A license granted by a governmental body permits a company to use public property in performing its services. Examples are the use of city streets for a bus line or taxi service, the use of public land for telephone and electric lines, and the use of airwaves for radio or TV broadcasting. In a recent license agreement, FOX, CBS, and NBC agreed to pay $27.9 billion for the right to broadcast NFL football games over an eight-year period. Franchises and licenses may by granted for a definite period of time, an indefinite period, or perpetually.

When a company can identify costs with the purchase of a franchise or license, it should recognize an intangible asset. Companies should amortize the cost of a limited-life franchise (or license) over its useful life. If the life is indefinite, the cost is not amortized. Annual payments made under a franchise agreement are recorded as **operating expenses** in the period in which they are incurred.

GOODWILL

Usually, the largest intangible asset that appears on a company's balance sheet is goodwill. **Goodwill** represents the value of all favorable attributes that relate to a company that are not attributable to any other specific asset. These include exceptional management, desirable location, good customer relations, skilled employees, high-quality products, and harmonious relations with labor unions. Goodwill is unique. Unlike assets such as investments and plant assets, which can be sold **individually** in the marketplace, goodwill can be identified only with the business **as a whole**.

If goodwill can be identified only with the business as a whole, how can its amount be determined? One could try to put a dollar value on the factors listed above (exceptional management, desirable location, and so on). But, the results would be very subjective, and such subjective valuations would not contribute to the reliability of financial statements. **Therefore, companies record goodwill only when an entire business is purchased. In that case, goodwill is the excess of cost over the fair value of the net assets (assets less liabilities) acquired.**

In recording the purchase of a business, the company debits (increases) the identifiable acquired assets, credits liabilities at their fair values, credits cash for the purchase price, and records the difference as goodwill. **Goodwill is not**

amortized because it is considered to have an indefinite life. Companies report goodwill in the balance sheet under intangible assets.

INTERNATIONAL INSIGHT

Should Companies Write Up Goodwill?

Softbank Corp. was Japan's biggest Internet company. At one time, it boosted the profit margin of its mobile-phone unit from 3.2% to 11.2% through what appeared to some as accounting tricks. What did it do? It wrote down the value of its mobile-phone-unit assets by half. This would normally result in a huge loss. But rather than take a loss, the company wrote up goodwill by the same amount. How did this move increase earnings? The assets were being depreciated over 10 years, but the company amortizes goodwill over 20 years. (Amortization of goodwill was allowed under the accounting standards it followed at that time.) While the new treatment did not break any rules, the company was criticized by investors for not providing sufficient justification or a detailed explanation for the sudden shift in policy.

Source: Andrew Morse and Yukari Iwatani Kane, "Softbank's Accounting Shift Raises Eyebrows," *Wall Street Journal* (August 28, 2007), p. C1.

?   Do you think that this treatment would be allowed under U.S. GAAP? (See page 517.)

© Pixtal/SuperStock

Research and Development Costs

Research and development costs are expenditures that may lead to patents, copyrights, new processes, and new products. Many companies spend considerable sums of money on research and development (R&D). For example, in a recent year, IBM spent over $5.1 billion on R&D.

Research and development costs present accounting problems. For one thing, it is sometimes difficult to assign the costs to specific projects. Also, there are uncertainties in identifying the extent and timing of future benefits. As a result, companies usually record R&D costs **as an expense when incurred**, whether the research and development is successful or not.

To illustrate, assume that Laser Scanner Company spent $3 million on R&D that resulted in two highly successful patents. It spent $20,000 on legal fees for the patents. The company would add the lawyers' fees to the patent account. The R&D costs, however, cannot be included in the cost of the patent. Instead, the company would record the R&D costs as an expense when incurred.

Many disagree with this accounting approach. They argue that expensing R&D costs leads to understated assets and net income. Others, however, argue that capitalizing these costs will lead to highly speculative assets on the balance sheet. Who is right is difficult to determine.

Helpful Hint Research and development (R&D) costs are not intangible assets. But because they may lead to patents and copyrights, we discuss them in this section.

> **DO IT!**

Classification Concepts

Match the statement with the term most directly associated with it.

Copyrights   Depletion
Intangible assets   Franchises
Research and development costs

1. _____ The allocation of the cost of a natural resource to expense in a rational and systematic manner.

2. _____ Rights, privileges, and competitive advantages that result from the ownership of long-lived assets that do not possess physical substance.

3. _____ An exclusive right granted by the federal government to reproduce and sell an artistic or published work.

4. _____ A right to sell certain products or services or to use certain trademarks or trade names within a designated geographic area.

5. _____ Costs incurred by a company that often lead to patents or new products. These costs must be expensed as incurred.

Action Plan

✔ Know that the accounting for intangibles often depends on whether the item has a finite or indefinite life.

✔ Recognize the many similarities and differences between the accounting for natural resources, plant assets, and intangible assets.

Solution

1. Depletion	4. Franchises
2. Intangible assets	5. Research and development costs
3. Copyrights	

Related exercise material: **BE10-11, BE10-12, E10-11, E10-12, E10-13, and DO IT! 10-5.**

✔ **The Navigator**

Statement Presentation and Analysis

Presentation

Usually, companies combine plant assets and natural resources under "Property, plant, and equipment" in the balance sheet. They show intangibles separately. Companies disclose either in the balance sheet or the notes the balances of the major classes of assets, such as land, buildings, and equipment, and accumulated depreciation by major classes or in total. In addition, they should describe the depreciation and amortization methods that were used, as well as disclose the amount of depreciation and amortization expense for the period.

Illustration 10-23 shows a typical financial statement presentation of property, plant, and equipment and intangibles for The Procter & Gamble Company

Illustration 10-23
P&G's presentation of property, plant, and equipment, and intangible assets

	THE PROCTER & GAMBLE COMPANY Balance Sheet (partial) (in millions)		
Real World			
		June 30	
		2011	**2010**
Property, plant, and equipment			
Buildings		$ 7,753	$ 6,868
Machinery and equipment		32,820	29,294
Land		934	850
		41,507	37,012
Accumulated depreciation		(20,214)	(17,768)
Net property, plant, and equipment		21,293	19,244
Goodwill and other intangible assets			
Goodwill		57,562	54,012
Trademarks and other intangible assets, net		32,620	31,636
Net goodwill and other intangible assets		$90,182	$85,648

(P&G) in its 2011 balance sheet. The notes to P&G's financial statements present greater details about the accounting for its long-term tangible and intangible assets.

Illustration 10-24 shows another comprehensive presentation of property, plant, and equipment from the balance sheet of Owens-Illinois. The notes to the financial statements of Owens-Illinois identify the major classes of property, plant, and equipment. They also indicate that depreciation and amortization are by the straight-line method, and depletion is by the units-of-activity method.

Illustration 10-24
Owens-Illinois' presentation of property, plant, and equipment, and intangible assets

Real World	**OWENS-ILLINOIS, INC.** Balance Sheet (partial) (in millions)		
Property, plant, and equipment			
Timberlands, at cost, less accumulated depletion		$ 95.4	
Buildings and equipment, at cost	$2,207.1		
Less: Accumulated depreciation	1,229.0	978.1	
Total property, plant, and equipment			$1,073.5
Intangibles			
Patents			410.0
Total			$1,483.5

Analysis

Using ratios, we can analyze how efficiently a company uses its assets to generate sales. The **asset turnover** analyzes the productivity of a company's assets. It tells us how many dollars of sales a company generates for each dollar invested in assets. This ratio is computed by dividing net sales by average total assets for the period. Illustration 10-25 shows the computation of the asset turnover for The Procter & Gamble Company. P&G's net sales for 2011 were $82,559 million. Its total ending assets were $138,354 million, and beginning assets were $128,172 million.

Illustration 10-25
Asset turnover formula and computation

Net Sales	÷	Average Total Assets	=	Asset Turnover
$82,559	÷	$\dfrac{\$128{,}172 + \$138{,}354}{2}$	=	.62 times

Thus, each dollar invested in assets produced $0.62 in sales for P&G. If a company is using its assets efficiently, each dollar of assets will create a high amount of sales. This ratio varies greatly among different industries—from those that are asset-intensive (utilities) to those that are not (services).

> Comprehensive DO IT! 1

DuPage Company purchases a factory machine at a cost of $18,000 on January 1, 2014. DuPage expects the machine to have a salvage value of $2,000 at the end of its 4-year useful life.

During its useful life, the machine is expected to be used 160,000 hours. Actual annual hourly use was 2014, 40,000; 2015, 60,000; 2016, 35,000; and 2017, 25,000.

Instructions

Prepare depreciation schedules for the following methods: (a) straight-line, (b) units-of-activity, and (c) declining-balance using double the straight-line rate.

Solution to Comprehensive DO IT! 1

Action Plan

✔ Under the straight-line method, apply the depreciation rate to depreciable cost.

✔ Under the units-of-activity method, compute the depreciable cost per unit by dividing depreciable cost by total units of activity.

✔ Under the declining-balance method, apply the depreciation rate to **book value** at the beginning of the year.

(a)

Straight-Line Method

	Computation			Annual	End of Year	
Year	Depreciable Cost*	×	Depreciation Rate =	Depreciation Expense	Accumulated Depreciation	Book Value
2014	$16,000		25%	$4,000	$ 4,000	$14,000**
2015	16,000		25%	4,000	8,000	10,000
2016	16,000		25%	4,000	12,000	6,000
2017	16,000		25%	4,000	16,000	2,000

*$18,000 − $2,000.
**$18,000 − $4,000.

(b)

Units-of-Activity Method

	Computation			Annual	End of Year	
Year	Units of Activity	×	Depreciable Cost/Unit =	Depreciation Expense	Accumulated Depreciation	Book Value
2014	40,000		$0.10*	$4,000	$ 4,000	$14,000
2015	60,000		0.10	6,000	10,000	8,000
2016	35,000		0.10	3,500	13,500	4,500
2017	25,000		0.10	2,500	16,000	2,000

*($18,000 − $2,000) ÷ 160,000.

(c)

Declining-Balance Method

	Computation			Annual	End of Year	
Year	Book Value Beginning of Year	×	Depreciation Rate* =	Depreciation Expense	Accumulated Depreciation	Book Value
2014	$18,000		50%	$9,000	$ 9,000	$9,000
2015	9,000		50%	4,500	13,500	4,500
2016	4,500		50%	2,250	15,750	2,250
2017	2,250		50%	250**	16,000	2,000

*¼ × 2.
**Adjusted to $250 because ending book value should not be less than expected salvage value.

✔ **The Navigator**

> Comprehensive DO IT! 2

On January 1, 2014, Skyline Limousine Co. purchased a limo at an acquisition cost of $28,000. The vehicle has been depreciated by the straight-line method using a 4-year service life and a $4,000 salvage value. The company's fiscal year ends on December 31.

Instructions

Prepare the journal entry or entries to record the disposal of the limousine assuming that it was:

(a) Retired and scrapped with no salvage value on January 1, 2018.

(b) Sold for $5,000 on July 1, 2017.

Solution to Comprehensive DO IT! 2

Action Plan

✔ At the time of disposal, determine the book value of the asset.

✔ Recognize any gain or loss from disposal of the asset.

✔ Remove the book value of the asset from the records by debiting Accumulated Depreciation for the total depreciation to date of disposal and crediting the asset account for the cost of the asset.

(a) 1/1/18	Accumulated Depreciation—Equipment	24,000	
	Loss on Disposal of Plant Assets	4,000	
	Equipment		28,000
	(To record retirement of limousine)		
(b) 7/1/17	Depreciation Expense	3,000	
	Accumulated Depreciation—Equipment		3,000
	(To record depreciation to date		
	of disposal)		
	Cash	5,000	
	Accumulated Depreciation—Equipment	21,000	
	Loss on Disposal of Plant Assets	2,000	
	Equipment		28,000
	(To record sale of limousine)		

 The Navigator

SUMMARY OF LEARNING OBJECTIVES

 The Navigator

1 Describe how the historical cost principle applies to plant assets. The cost of plant assets includes all expenditures necessary to acquire the asset and make it ready for its intended use. Once cost is established, the company uses that amount as the basis of accounting for the plant assets over its useful life.

2 Explain the concept of depreciation and how to compute it. Depreciation is the allocation of the cost of a plant asset to expense over its useful (service) life in a rational and systematic manner. Depreciation is not a process of valuation, nor is it a process that results in an accumulation of cash.

Three depreciation methods are:

Method	Effect on Annual Depreciation	Formula
Straight-line	Constant amount	Depreciable cost ÷ Useful life (in years)
Units-of-activity	Varying amount	Depreciable cost per unit × Units of activity during the year
Declining-balance	Decreasing amount	Book value at beginning of year × Declining-balance rate

Companies make revisions of periodic depreciation in present and future periods, not retroactively. They determine the new annual depreciation by dividing the depreciable cost at the time of the revision by the remaining useful life.

3 Distinguish between revenue and capital expenditures, and explain the entries for each. Companies incur revenue expenditures to maintain the operating efficiency and productive life of an asset. They debit these expenditures to Maintenance and Repairs Expense as incurred. Capital expenditures increase the operating efficiency, productive capacity, or expected useful life of the asset. Companies generally debit these expenditures to the plant asset affected.

4 Explain how to account for the disposal of a plant asset. The accounting for disposal of a plant asset through retirement or sale is as follows. (a) Eliminate the book value of the plant asset at the date of disposal. (b) Record cash proceeds, if any. (c) Account for the difference between the book value and the cash proceeds as a gain or loss on disposal.

5 Compute periodic depletion of natural resources. Companies compute depletion cost per unit by dividing the total cost of the natural resource minus salvage value by the number of units estimated to be in the resource. They then multiply the depletion cost per unit by the number of units extracted and sold.

6 Explain the basic issues related to accounting for intangible assets. The process of allocating the cost of an intangible asset is referred to as amortization. The cost of intangible assets with indefinite lives is not amortized. Companies normally use the straight-line method for amortizing intangible assets.

7 Indicate how plant assets, natural resources, and intangible assets are reported. Companies usually combine plant assets and natural resources under

property, plant, and equipment. They show intangibles separately under intangible assets. Either within the balance sheet or in the notes, companies should disclose the balances of the major classes of assets, such as land, buildings, and equipment, and accumulated depreciation by major classes or in total. They also should describe the depreciation and amortization methods used, and should disclose the amount of depreciation and amortization expense for the period. The asset turnover measures the productivity of a company's assets in generating sales.

GLOSSARY

Accelerated-depreciation method Depreciation method that produces higher depreciation expense in the early years than in the later years. (p. 480).

Additions and improvements Costs incurred to increase the operating efficiency, productive capacity, or useful life of a plant asset. (p. 483).

Amortization The allocation of the cost of an intangible asset to expense over its useful life in a systematic and rational manner. (p. 489).

Asset turnover A measure of how efficiently a company uses its assets to generate sales; calculated as net sales divided by average total assets. (p. 493).

Capital expenditures Expenditures that increase the company's investment in productive facilities. (p. 483).

Copyrights Exclusive grant from the federal government that allows the owner to reproduce and sell an artistic or published work. (p. 489).

Declining-balance method Depreciation method that applies a constant rate to the declining book value of the asset and produces a decreasing annual depreciation expense over the useful life of the asset. (p. 479).

Depletion The allocation of the cost of a natural resource to expense in a rational and systematic manner over the resource's useful life. (p. 487).

Depreciable cost The cost of a plant asset less its salvage value. (p. 477).

Depreciation The process of allocating to expense the cost of a plant asset over its useful (service) life in a rational and systematic manner. (p. 475).

Franchise (license) A contractual arrangement under which the franchisor grants the franchisee the right to sell certain products, perform specific services, or use certain trademarks or trade names, usually within a designated geographic area. (p. 490).

Going-concern assumption States that the company will continue in operation for the foreseeable future. (p. 476).

Goodwill The value of all favorable attributes that relate to a company that is not attributable to any other specific asset. (p. 490).

Intangible assets Rights, privileges, and competitive advantages that result from the ownership of long-lived assets that do not possess physical substance. (p. 488).

Materiality concept If an item would not make a difference in decision-making, a company does not have to follow GAAP in reporting it. (p. 483).

Natural resources Assets that consist of standing timber and underground deposits of oil, gas, and minerals. (p. 486).

Ordinary repairs Expenditures to maintain the operating efficiency and productive life of the unit. (p. 483).

Patent An exclusive right issued by the U.S. Patent Office that enables the recipient to manufacture, sell, or otherwise control an invention for a period of 20 years from the date of the grant. (p. 489).

Plant assets Tangible resources that are used in the operations of the business and are not intended for sale to customers. (p. 472).

Research and development (R&D) costs Expenditures that may lead to patents, copyrights, new processes, or new products. (p. 491).

Revenue expenditures Expenditures that are immediately charged against revenues as an expense. (p. 483).

Salvage value An estimate of an asset's value at the end of its useful life. (p. 477).

Straight-line method Depreciation method in which periodic depreciation is the same for each year of the asset's useful life. (p. 477).

Trademark (trade name) A word, phrase, jingle, or symbol that identifies a particular enterprise or product. (p. 490).

Units-of-activity method Depreciation method in which useful life is expressed in terms of the total units of production or use expected from an asset. (p. 478).

Useful life An estimate of the expected productive life, also called service life, of an asset. (p. 477).

APPENDIX 10A   Exchange of Plant Assets

Ordinarily, companies record a gain or loss on the exchange of plant assets. The rationale for recognizing a gain or loss is that most exchanges have **commercial substance**. An exchange has commercial substance if the future cash flows change as a result of the exchange.

To illustrate, Ramos Co. exchanges some of its equipment for land held by Brodhead Inc. It is likely that the timing and amount of the cash flows arising from the land will differ significantly from the cash flows arising from the equipment. As a result, both Ramos and Brodhead are in different economic positions. Therefore, **the exchange has commercial substance**, and the companies recognize a gain or loss in the exchange. Because most exchanges have commercial substance (even when similar assets are exchanged), we illustrate only this type of situation, for both a loss and a gain.

> **LEARNING OBJECTIVE   8**
>
> Explain how to account for the exchange of plant assets.

Loss Treatment

To illustrate an exchange that results in a loss, assume that Roland Company exchanged a set of used trucks plus cash for a new semi-truck. The used trucks have a combined book value of $42,000 (cost $64,000 less $22,000 accumulated depreciation). Roland's purchasing agent, experienced in the second-hand market, indicates that the used trucks have a fair value of $26,000. In addition to the trucks, Roland must pay $17,000 for the semi-truck. Roland computes the cost of the semi-truck as follows.

Fair value of used trucks	$26,000
Cash paid	17,000
Cost of semi-truck	$43,000

Illustration 10A-1
Cost of semi-truck

Roland incurs a loss on disposal of plant assets of $16,000 on this exchange. The reason is that the book value of the used trucks is greater than the fair value of these trucks. The computation is as follows.

Book value of used trucks ($64,000 − $22,000)	$ 42,000
Fair value of used trucks	26,000
Loss on disposal of plant assets	**$16,000**

Illustration 10A-2
Computation of loss on disposal

In recording an exchange at a loss, three steps are required: (1) eliminate the book value of the asset given up, (2) record the cost of the asset acquired, and (3) recognize the loss on disposal of plant assets. Roland Company thus records the exchange on the loss as follows.

Equipment (new)	43,000	
Accumulated Depreciation—Equipment	22,000	
Loss on Disposal of Plant Assets	16,000	
Equipment (old)		64,000
Cash		17,000
(To record exchange of used trucks for semi-truck)		

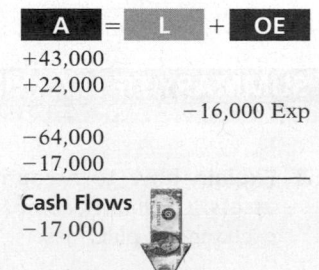

A	=	L	+	OE

+43,000
+22,000
           −16,000 Exp
−64,000
−17,000

Cash Flows
−17,000

Gain Treatment

To illustrate a gain situation, assume that Mark Express Delivery decides to exchange its old delivery equipment plus cash of $3,000 for new delivery equipment. The book value of the old delivery equipment is $12,000 (cost $40,000 less accumulated depreciation $28,000). The fair value of the old delivery equipment is $19,000.

The cost of the new asset is the fair value of the old asset exchanged plus any cash paid (or other consideration given up). The cost of the new delivery equipment is $22,000, computed as follows.

Illustration 10A-3
Cost of new delivery equipment

Fair value of old delivery equipment	$ 19,000
Cash paid	3,000
Cost of new delivery equipment	**$22,000**

A gain results when the fair value of the old delivery equipment is greater than its book value. For Mark Express, there is a gain of $7,000 on disposal of plant assets, computed as follows.

Illustration 10A-4
Computation of gain on disposal

Fair value of old delivery equipment	$19,000
Book value of old delivery equipment ($40,000 − $28,000)	12,000
Gain on disposal of plant assets	**$ 7,000**

Mark Express Delivery records the exchange as follows.

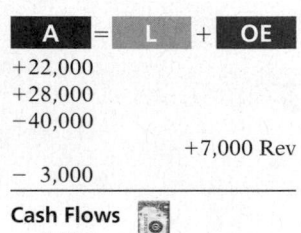

A	=	L	+	OE
+22,000				
+28,000				
−40,000				
				+7,000 Rev
− 3,000				

Cash Flows
− 3,000

Equipment (new)	22,000	
Accumulated Depreciation—Equipment (old)	28,000	
Equipment (old)		40,000
Gain on Disposal of Plant Assets		7,000
Cash		3,000
(To record exchange of old delivery equipment for		
new delivery equipment)		

In recording an exchange at a gain, the following three steps are involved: (1) eliminate the book value of the asset given up, (2) record the cost of the asset acquired, and (3) recognize the gain on disposal of plant assets. Accounting for exchanges of plant assets becomes more complex if the transaction does not have commercial substance. This issue is discussed in more advanced accounting classes.

SUMMARY OF LEARNING OBJECTIVE FOR APPENDIX 10A

    The Navigator

8 Explain how to account for the exchange of plant assets. Ordinarily, companies record a gain or loss on the exchange of plant assets. The rationale for recognizing a gain or loss is that most exchanges have commercial substance. An exchange has commercial substance if the future cash flows change as a result of the exchange.

Self-Test, Brief Exercises, Exercises, Problem Set A, and many more components are available for practice in *WileyPLUS*.

Note: All asterisked Questions, Exercises, and Problems relate to material in the appendix to the chapter.

SELF-TEST QUESTIONS

Answers are on page 517.

(LO 1) **1.** Erin Danielle Company purchased equipment and incurred the following costs.

Cash price	$24,000
Sales taxes	1,200
Insurance during transit	200
Installation and testing	400
Total costs	$25,800

What amount should be recorded as the cost of the equipment?
   (a) $24,000.   (c) $25,400.
   (b) $25,200.   (d) $25,800.

(LO 2) **2.** Depreciation is a process of:
   (a) valuation.   (c) cash accumulation.
   (b) cost allocation.   (d) appraisal.

(LO 2) **3.** Micah Bartlett Company purchased equipment on January 1, 2013, at a total invoice cost of $400,000. The equipment has an estimated salvage value of $10,000 and an estimated useful life of 5 years. The amount of accumulated depreciation at December 31, 2014, if the straight-line method of depreciation is used, is:
   (a) $80,000.   (c) $78,000.
   (b) $160,000.   (d) $156,000.

(LO 2) **4.** Ann Torbert purchased a truck for $11,000 on January 1, 2013. The truck will have an estimated salvage value of $1,000 at the end of 5 years. Using the units-of-activity method, the balance in accumulated depreciation at December 31, 2014, can be computed by the following formula:
   (a) ($11,000 ÷ Total estimated activity) × Units of activity for 2014.
   (b) ($10,000 ÷ Total estimated activity) × Units of activity for 2014.
   (c) ($11,000 ÷ Total estimated activity) × Units of activity for 2013 and 2014.
   (d) ($10,000 ÷ Total estimated activity) × Units of activity for 2013 and 2014.

(LO 2) **5.** Jefferson Company purchased a piece of equipment on January 1, 2014. The equipment cost $60,000 and has an estimated life of 8 years and a salvage value of $8,000. What was the depreciation expense for the asset for 2015 under the double-declining-balance method?
   (a) $6,500.   (c) $15,000.
   (b) $11,250.   (d) $6,562.

(LO 2) **6.** When there is a change in estimated depreciation:
   (a) previous depreciation should be corrected.
   (b) current and future years' depreciation should be revised.

   (c) only future years' depreciation should be revised.
   (d) None of the above.

(LO 2) **7.** Able Towing Company purchased a tow truck for $60,000 on January 1, 2012. It was originally depreciated on a straight-line basis over 10 years with an assumed salvage value of $12,000. On December 31, 2014, before adjusting entries had been made, the company decided to change the remaining estimated life to 4 years (including 2014) and the salvage value to $2,000. What was the depreciation expense for 2014?
   (a) $6,000.   (c) $15,000.
   (b) $4,800.   (d) $12,100.

(LO 3) **8.** Additions to plant assets are:
   (a) revenue expenditures.
   (b) debited to the Maintenance and Repairs Expense account.
   (c) debited to the Purchases account.
   (d) capital expenditures.

(LO 4) **9.** Bennie Razor Company has decided to sell one of its old manufacturing machines on June 30, 2014. The machine was purchased for $80,000 on January 1, 2010, and was depreciated on a straight-line basis for 10 years assuming no salvage value. If the machine was sold for $26,000, what was the amount of the gain or loss recorded at the time of the sale?
   (a) $18,000.   (c) $22,000.
   (b) $54,000.   (d) $46,000.

(LO 5) **10.** Maggie Sharrer Company expects to extract 20 million tons of coal from a mine that cost $12 million. If no salvage value is expected and 2 million tons are mined and sold in the first year, the entry to record depletion will include a:
   (a) debit to Accumulated Depletion of $2,000,000.
   (b) credit to Depletion Expense of $1,200,000.
   (c) debit to Depletion Expense of $1,200,000.
   (d) credit to Accumulated Depletion of $2,000,000.

(LO 6) **11.** Which of the following statements is **false**?
   (a) If an intangible asset has a finite life, it should be amortized.
   (b) The amortization period of an intangible asset can exceed 20 years.
   (c) Goodwill is recorded only when a business is purchased.
   (d) Research and development costs are expensed when incurred, except when the research and development expenditures result in a successful patent.

(LO 6) **12.** Martha Beyerlein Company incurred $150,000 of research and development costs in its laboratory to develop a patent granted on January 2, 2014. On July 31, 2014, Beyerlein paid $35,000 for legal fees in a successful defense of the patent. The total amount debited to Patents through July 31, 2014, should be:

(a) $150,000.　　　　(c) $185,000.
(b) $35,000.　　　　(d) $170,000.

(LO 7) **13.** Indicate which of the following statements is **true**.

(a) Since intangible assets lack physical substance, they need be disclosed only in the notes to the financial statements.

(b) Goodwill should be reported as a contra account in the owner's equity section.

(c) Totals of major classes of assets can be shown in the balance sheet, with asset details disclosed in the notes to the financial statements.

(d) Intangible assets are typically combined with plant assets and natural resources and shown in the property, plant, and equipment section.

(LO 7) **14.** Lake Coffee Company reported net sales of $180,000, net income of $54,000, beginning total assets of $200,000, and ending total assets of $300,000. What was the company's asset turnover?

(a) 0.90.　　　　(c) 0.72.
(b) 0.20.　　　　(d) 1.39.

*15. Schopenhauer Company exchanged an old machine, (LO 8) with a book value of $39,000 and a fair value of $35,000, and paid $10,000 cash for a similar new machine. The transaction has commercial substance. At what amount should the machine acquired in the exchange be recorded on Schopenhauer's books?

(a) $45,000.
(b) $46,000.
(c) $49,000.
(d) $50,000.

*16. In exchanges of assets in which the exchange has (LO 8) commercial substance:

(a) neither gains nor losses are recognized immediately.
(b) gains, but not losses, are recognized immediately.
(c) losses, but not gains, are recognized immediately.
(d) both gains and losses are recognized immediately.

Go to the book's companion website, www.wiley.com/college/weygandt, for additional Self-Test Questions.

 The Navigator

QUESTIONS

1. Sid Watney is uncertain about the applicability of the historical cost principle to plant assets. Explain the principle to Sid.

2. What are some examples of land improvements?

3. Lynn Company acquires the land and building owned by Noble Company. What types of costs may be incurred to make the asset ready for its intended use if Lynn Company wants to use (a) only the land, and (b) both the land and the building?

4. In a recent newspaper release, the president of Downs Company asserted that something has to be done about depreciation. The president said, "Depreciation does not come close to accumulating the cash needed to replace the asset at the end of its useful life." What is your response to the president?

5. Andrew is studying for the next accounting examination. He asks your help on two questions: (a) What is salvage value? (b) Is salvage value used in determining periodic depreciation under each depreciation method? Answer Andrew's questions.

6. Contrast the straight-line method and the units-of-activity method as to (a) useful life, and (b) the pattern of periodic depreciation over useful life.

7. Contrast the effects of the three depreciation methods on annual depreciation expense.

8. In the fourth year of an asset's 5-year useful life, the company decides that the asset will have a 6-year service life. How should the revision of depreciation be recorded? Why?

9. Distinguish between revenue expenditures and capital expenditures during useful life.

10. How is a gain or loss on the sale of a plant asset computed?

11. Romero Corporation owns a machine that is fully depreciated but is still being used. How should Romero account for this asset and report it in the financial statements?

12. What are natural resources, and what are their distinguishing characteristics?

13. Explain what depletion is and how it is computed.

14. What are the similarities and differences between the terms depreciation, depletion, and amortization?

15. Rowand Company hires an accounting intern who says that intangible assets should always be amortized over their legal lives. Is the intern correct? Explain.

16. Goodwill has been defined as the value of all favorable attributes that relate to a business. What types of attributes could result in goodwill?

17. Jimmy West, a business major, is working on a case problem for one of his classes. In the case problem, the company needs to raise cash to market a new product it developed. Ron Thayer, an engineering major, takes one look at the company's balance sheet and says, "This company has an awful lot of goodwill. Why don't you recommend that they sell some of it to raise cash?" How should Jimmy respond to Ron?

18. Under what conditions is goodwill recorded?

19. Often, research and development costs provide companies with benefits that last a number of years. (For example, these costs can lead to the development of a patent that will increase the company's income for many years.) However, generally accepted accounting principles require that such costs be recorded as an expense when incurred. Why?

20. McDonald's Corporation reports total average assets of $28.9 billion and net sales of $20.5 billion. What is the company's asset turnover?

21. Stark Corporation and Zuber Corporation operate in the same industry. Stark uses the straight-line method to account for depreciation; Zuber uses an accelerated method. Explain what complications might arise in trying to compare the results of these two companies.

22. Gomez Corporation uses straight-line depreciation for financial reporting purposes but an accelerated method for tax purposes. Is it acceptable to use different methods for the two purposes? What is Gomez's motivation for doing this?

23. You are comparing two companies in the same industry. You have determined that Ace Corp. depreciates its plant assets over a 40-year life, whereas Liu Corp. depreciates its plant assets over a 20-year life. Discuss the implications this has for comparing the results of the two companies.

24. Sosa Company is doing significant work to revitalize its warehouses. It is not sure whether it should capitalize these costs or expense them. What are the implications for current-year net income and future net income of expensing versus capitalizing these costs?

*25. When assets are exchanged in a transaction involving commercial substance, how is the gain or loss on disposal of plant assets computed?

*26. Unruh Refrigeration Company trades in an old machine on a new model when the fair value of the old machine is greater than its book value. The transaction has commercial substance. Should Unruh recognize a gain on disposal of plant assets? If the fair value of the old machine is less than its book value, should Unruh recognize a loss on disposal of plant assets?

BRIEF EXERCISES

BE10-1 The following expenditures were incurred by McCoy Company in purchasing land: cash price $50,000, accrued taxes $3,000, attorneys' fees $2,500, real estate broker's commission $2,000, and clearing and grading $3,500. What is the cost of the land?

Determine the cost of land.
(LO 1)

BE10-2 Rich Castillo Company incurs the following expenditures in purchasing a truck: cash price $30,000, accident insurance $2,000, sales taxes $2,100, motor vehicle license $100, and painting and lettering $400. What is the cost of the truck?

Determine the cost of a truck.
(LO 1)

BE10-3 Corales Company acquires a delivery truck at a cost of $38,000. The truck is expected to have a salvage value of $6,000 at the end of its 4-year useful life. Compute annual depreciation expense for the first and second years using the straight-line method.

Compute straight-line depreciation.
(LO 2)

BE10-4 Chisenhall Company purchased land and a building on January 1, 2014. Management's best estimate of the value of the land was $100,000 and of the building $200,000. However, management told the accounting department to record the land at $220,000 and the building at $80,000. The building is being depreciated on a straight-line basis over 15 years with no salvage value. Why do you suppose management requested this accounting treatment? Is it ethical?

Compute depreciation and evaluate treatment.
(LO 2)

BE10-5 Depreciation information for Corales Company is given in BE10-3. Assuming the declining-balance depreciation rate is double the straight-line rate, compute annual depreciation for the first and second years under the declining-balance method.

Compute declining-balance depreciation.
(LO 2)

BE10-6 Rosco Taxi Service uses the units-of-activity method in computing depreciation on its taxicabs. Each cab is expected to be driven 150,000 miles. Taxi no. 10 cost $39,500 and is expected to have a salvage value of $500. Taxi no. 10 is driven 30,000 miles in year 1 and 20,000 miles in year 2. Compute the depreciation for each year.

Compute depreciation using the units-of-activity method.
(LO 2)

BE10-7 On January 1, 2014, the Morgantown Company ledger shows Equipment $32,000 and Accumulated Depreciation—Equipment $9,000. The depreciation resulted from using the straight-line method with a useful life of 10 years and salvage value of $2,000. On this date, the company concludes that the equipment has a remaining useful life of only 4 years with the same salvage value. Compute the revised annual depreciation.

Compute revised depreciation.
(LO 2)

BE10-8 Flaherty Company had the following two transactions related to its delivery truck.

1. Paid $45 for an oil change.
2. Paid $400 to install special gear unit, which increases the operating efficiency of the truck.

Prepare Flaherty's journal entries to record these two transactions.

Prepare entries for delivery truck costs.
(LO 3)

BE10-9 Prepare journal entries to record the following.

(a) Sound Tracker Company retires its delivery equipment, which cost $41,000. Accumulated depreciation is also $41,000 on this delivery equipment. No salvage value is received.

(b) Assume the same information as (a), except that accumulated depreciation is $37,000, instead of $41,000, on the delivery equipment.

Prepare entries for disposal by retirement.
(LO 4)

Prepare entries for disposal by sale.
(LO 4)

BE10-10 Gunkelson Company sells equipment on September 30, 2014, for $18,000 cash. The equipment originally cost $72,000 and as of January 1, 2014, had accumulated depreciation of $42,000. Depreciation for the first 9 months of 2014 is $5,250. Prepare the journal entries to (a) update depreciation to September 30, 2014, and (b) record the sale of the equipment.

Prepare depletion expense entry and balance sheet presentation for natural resources.
(LO 5)

BE10-11 Franceour Mining Co. purchased for $7 million a mine that is estimated to have 35 million tons of ore and no salvage value. In the first year, 5 million tons of ore are extracted and sold.

(a) Prepare the journal entry to record depletion expense for the first year.
(b) Show how this mine is reported on the balance sheet at the end of the first year.

Prepare amortization expense entry and balance sheet presentation for intangibles.
(LO 6)

BE10-12 Campanez Company purchases a patent for $140,000 on January 2, 2014. Its estimated useful life is 10 years.

(a) Prepare the journal entry to record amortization expense for the first year.
(b) Show how this patent is reported on the balance sheet at the end of the first year.

Classify long-lived assets on balance sheet.
(LO 7)

BE10-13 Information related to plant assets, natural resources, and intangibles at the end of 2014 for Dent Company is as follows: buildings $1,100,000; accumulated depreciation—buildings $600,000; goodwill $410,000; coal mine $500,000; accumulated depletion—coal mine $108,000. Prepare a partial balance sheet of Dent Company for these items.

Analyze long-lived assets.
(LO 7)

BE10-14 In a recent annual report, Target reported beginning total assets of $44.1 billion; ending total assets of $44.5 billion; and net sales of $63.4 billion. Compute Target's asset turnover.

Prepare entry for disposal by exchange.
(LO 8)

*BE10-15 Olathe Company exchanges old delivery equipment for new delivery equipment. The book value of the old delivery equipment is $31,000 (cost $61,000 less accumulated depreciation $30,000). Its fair value is $24,000, and cash of $5,000 is paid. Prepare the entry to record the exchange, assuming the transaction has commercial substance.

Prepare entry for disposal by exchange.
(LO 8)

*BE10-16 Assume the same information as BE10-15, except that the fair value of the old delivery equipment is $33,000. Prepare the entry to record the exchange.

> DO IT! Review

Explain accounting for cost of plant assets.
(LO 1)

DO IT! 10-1 Lofton Company purchased a delivery truck. The total cash payment was $27,900, including the following items.

Negotiated purchase price	$24,000
Installation of special shelving	1,100
Painting and lettering	900
Motor vehicle license	100
Annual insurance policy	500
Sales tax	1,300
Total paid	$27,900

Explain how each of these costs would be accounted for.

Calculate depreciation expense and make journal entry.
(LO 2)

DO IT! 10-2 On January 1, 2014, Emporia Country Club purchased a new riding mower for $15,000. The mower is expected to have an 8-year life with a $3,000 salvage value. What journal entry would Emporia make at December 31, 2014, if it uses straight-line depreciation?

Calculate revised depreciation
(LO 2)

DO IT! 10-3 Pinewood Corporation purchased a piece of equipment for $70,000. It estimated an 8-year life and $2,000 salvage value. At the end of year four (before the depreciation adjustment), it estimated the new total life to be 10 years and the new salvage value to be $6,000. Compute the revised depreciation.

Make journal entries to record plant asset disposal.
(LO 4)

DO IT! 10-4 Napoli Manufacturing has old equipment that cost $52,000. The equipment has accumulated depreciation of $28,000. Napoli has decided to sell the equipment.

(a) What entry would Napoli make to record the sale of the equipment for $26,000 cash?
(b) What entry would Napoli make to record the sale of the equipment for $15,000 cash?

DO IT! 10-5 Match the statement with the term most directly associated with it.

Match intangibles classifications concepts.

(LO 5, 6)

Goodwill   Amortization
Intangible assets   Franchises
Research and development costs

1. _____ Rights, privileges, and competitive advantages that result from the ownership of long-lived assets that do not possess physical substance.

2. _____ The allocation of the cost of an intangible asset to expense in a rational and systematic manner.

3. _____ A right to sell certain products or services, or use certain trademarks or trade names within a designated geographic area.

4. _____ Costs incurred by a company that often lead to patents or new products. These costs must be expensed as incurred.

5. _____ The excess of the cost of a company over the fair value of the net assets acquired.

EXERCISES

E10-1 The following expenditures relating to plant assets were made by Prather Company during the first 2 months of 2014.

Determine cost of plant acquisitions.

(LO 1)

1. Paid $5,000 of accrued taxes at time plant site was acquired.
2. Paid $200 insurance to cover possible accident loss on new factory machinery while the machinery was in transit.
3. Paid $850 sales taxes on new delivery truck.
4. Paid $17,500 for parking lots and driveways on new plant site.
5. Paid $250 to have company name and advertising slogan painted on new delivery truck.
6. Paid $8,000 for installation of new factory machinery.
7. Paid $900 for one-year accident insurance policy on new delivery truck.
8. Paid $75 motor vehicle license fee on the new truck.

Instructions
(a) Explain the application of the historical cost principle in determining the acquisition cost of plant assets.
(b) List the numbers of the foregoing transactions, and opposite each indicate the account title to which each expenditure should be debited.

E10-2 Benedict Company incurred the following costs.

Determine property, plant, and equipment costs.

(LO 1)

1. Sales tax on factory machinery purchased	$ 5,000
2. Painting of and lettering on truck immediately upon purchase	700
3. Installation and testing of factory machinery	2,000
4. Real estate broker's commission on land purchased	3,500
5. Insurance premium paid for first year's insurance on new truck	880
6. Cost of landscaping on property purchased	7,200
7. Cost of paving parking lot for new building constructed	17,900
8. Cost of clearing, draining, and filling land	13,300
9. Architect's fees on self-constructed building	10,000

Instructions
Indicate to which account Benedict would debit each of the costs.

E10-3 On March 1, 2014, Westmorlan Company acquired real estate on which it planned to construct a small office building. The company paid $75,000 in cash. An old warehouse on the property was razed at a cost of $8,600; the salvaged materials were sold for $1,700. Additional expenditures before construction began included $1,100 attorney's fee for work concerning the land purchase, $5,000 real estate broker's fee, $7,800 architect's fee, and $14,000 to put in driveways and a parking lot.

Determine acquisition costs of land.

(LO 1)

Instructions
(a) Determine the amount to be reported as the cost of the land.
(b) For each cost not used in part (a), indicate the account to be debited.

Understand depreciation concepts.

(LO 2)

E10-4 Tom Parkey has prepared the following list of statements about depreciation.

1. Depreciation is a process of asset valuation, not cost allocation.
2. Depreciation provides for the proper matching of expenses with revenues.
3. The book value of a plant asset should approximate its fair value.
4. Depreciation applies to three classes of plant assets: land, buildings, and equipment.
5. Depreciation does not apply to a building because its usefulness and revenue-producing ability generally remain intact over time.
6. The revenue-producing ability of a depreciable asset will decline due to wear and tear and to obsolescence.
7. Recognizing depreciation on an asset results in an accumulation of cash for replacement of the asset.
8. The balance in accumulated depreciation represents the total cost that has been charged to expense.
9. Depreciation expense and accumulated depreciation are reported on the income statement.
10. Four factors affect the computation of depreciation: cost, useful life, salvage value, and residual value.

Instructions

Identify each statement as true or false. If false, indicate how to correct the statement.

Compute depreciation under units-of-activity method.

(LO 2)

E10-5 Yello Bus Lines uses the units-of-activity method in depreciating its buses. One bus was purchased on January 1, 2014, at a cost of $148,000. Over its 4-year useful life, the bus is expected to be driven 100,000 miles. Salvage value is expected to be $8,000.

Instructions

(a) Compute the depreciable cost per unit.

(b) Prepare a depreciation schedule assuming actual mileage was: 2014, 26,000; 2015, 32,000; 2016, 25,000; and 2017, 17,000.

Determine depreciation for partial periods.

(LO 2)

E10-6 Rottino Company purchased a new machine on October 1, 2014, at a cost of $150,000. The company estimated that the machine will have a salvage value of $12,000. The machine is expected to be used for 10,000 working hours during its 5-year life.

Instructions

Compute the depreciation expense under the following methods for the year indicated.

(a) Straight-line for 2014.

(b) Units-of-activity for 2014, assuming machine usage was 1,700 hours.

(c) Declining-balance using double the straight-line rate for 2014 and 2015.

Compute depreciation using different methods.

(LO 2)

E10-7 Linton Company purchased a delivery truck for $34,000 on January 1, 2014. The truck has an expected salvage value of $2,000, and is expected to be driven 100,000 miles over its estimated useful life of 8 years. Actual miles driven were 15,000 in 2014 and 12,000 in 2015.

Instructions

(a) Compute depreciation expense for 2014 and 2015 using (1) the straight-line method, (2) the units-of-activity method, and (3) the double-declining-balance method.

(b) Assume that Linton uses the straight-line method.

   (1) Prepare the journal entry to record 2014 depreciation.

   (2) Show how the truck would be reported in the December 31, 2014, balance sheet.

Compute revised annual depreciation.

(LO 2)

E10-8 Terry Wade, the new controller of Hellickson Company, has reviewed the expected useful lives and salvage values of selected depreciable assets at the beginning of 2014. His findings are as follows.

Type of Asset	Date Acquired	Cost	Accumulated Depreciation 1/1/14	Useful Life in Years		Salvage Value	
				Old	Proposed	Old	Proposed
Building	1/1/08	$800,000	$114,000	40	50	$40,000	$26,000
Warehouse	1/1/09	100,000	19,000	25	20	5,000	6,000

All assets are depreciated by the straight-line method. Hellickson Company uses a calendar year in preparing annual financial statements. After discussion, management has agreed to accept Terry's proposed changes.

Instructions
(a) Compute the revised annual depreciation on each asset in 2014. (Show computations.)
(b) Prepare the entry (or entries) to record depreciation on the building in 2014.

E10-9 Presented below are selected transactions at Ridge Company for 2014.

Jan. 1   Retired a piece of machinery that was purchased on January 1, 2004. The machine cost $62,000 on that date. It had a useful life of 10 years with no salvage value.

June 30   Sold a computer that was purchased on January 1, 2011. The computer cost $45,000. It had a useful life of 5 years with no salvage value. The computer was sold for $14,000.

Dec. 31   Discarded a delivery truck that was purchased on January 1, 2010. The truck cost $33,000. It was depreciated based on a 6-year useful life with a $3,000 salvage value.

Instructions
Journalize all entries required on the above dates, including entries to update depreciation, where applicable, on assets disposed of. Ridge Company uses straight-line depreciation. (Assume depreciation is up to date as of December 31, 2013.)

E10-10 Pryce Company owns equipment that cost $65,000 when purchased on January 1, 2011. It has been depreciated using the straight-line method based on estimated salvage value of $5,000 and an estimated useful life of 5 years.

Instructions
Prepare Pryce Company's journal entries to record the sale of the equipment in these four independent situations.

(a) Sold for $31,000 on January 1, 2014.
(b) Sold for $31,000 on May 1, 2014.
(c) Sold for $11,000 on January 1, 2014.
(d) Sold for $11,000 on October 1, 2014.

E10-11 On July 1, 2014, Friedman Inc. invested $720,000 in a mine estimated to have 900,000 tons of ore of uniform grade. During the last 6 months of 2014, 100,000 tons of ore were mined and sold.

Instructions
(a) Prepare the journal entry to record depletion expense.
(b) Assume that the 100,000 tons of ore were mined, but only 80,000 units were sold. How are the costs applicable to the 20,000 unsold units reported?

E10-12 The following are selected 2014 transactions of Pedigo Corporation.

Jan. 1   Purchased a small company and recorded goodwill of $150,000. Its useful life is indefinite.

May 1   Purchased for $75,000 a patent with an estimated useful life of 5 years and a legal life of 20 years.

Instructions
Prepare necessary adjusting entries at December 31 to record amortization required by the events above.

E10-13 Gill Company, organized in 2014, has the following transactions related to intangible assets.

1/2/14	Purchased patent (7-year life)	$595,000
4/1/14	Goodwill purchased (indefinite life)	360,000
7/1/14	10-year franchise; expiration date 7/1/2024	480,000
9/1/14	Research and development costs	185,000

Instructions
Prepare the necessary entries to record these intangibles. All costs incurred were for cash. Make the adjusting entries as of December 31, 2014, recording any necessary amortization and reflecting all balances accurately as of that date.

E10-14 During 2014 Paola Corporation reported net sales of $3,500,000 and net income of $1,500,000. Its balance sheet reported average total assets of $1,400,000.

Instructions
Calculate the asset turnover.

Journalize entries for exchanges.

(LO 8)

*E10-15 Presented below are two independent transactions. Both transactions have commercial substance.

1. Mercy Co. exchanged old trucks (cost $64,000 less $22,000 accumulated depreciation) plus cash of $17,000 for new trucks. The old trucks had a fair value of $38,000.
2. Pence Inc. trades its used machine (cost $12,000 less $4,000 accumulated depreciation) for a new machine. In addition to exchanging the old machine (which had a fair value of $11,000), Pence also paid cash of $3,000.

Instructions
(a) Prepare the entry to record the exchange of assets by Mercy Co.
(b) Prepare the entry to record the exchange of assets by Pence Inc.

Journalize entries for the exchange of plant assets.

(LO 8)

*E10-16 Rizzo's Delivery Company and Overland's Express Delivery exchanged delivery trucks on January 1, 2014. Rizzo's truck cost $22,000. It has accumulated depreciation of $15,000 and a fair value of $3,000. Overland's truck cost $10,000. It has accumulated depreciation of $8,000 and a fair value of $3,000. The transaction has commercial substance.

Instructions
(a) Journalize the exchange for Rizzo's Delivery Company.
(b) Journalize the exchange for Overland's Express Delivery.

EXERCISES: SET B AND CHALLENGE EXERCISES

Visit the book's companion website, at **www.wiley.com/college/weygandt**, and choose the Student Companion site to access Exercise Set B and Challenge Exercises.

PROBLEMS: SET A

Determine acquisition costs of land and building.

(LO 1)

P10-1A Venable Company was organized on January 1. During the first year of operations, the following plant asset expenditures and receipts were recorded in random order.

	Debit
1. Cost of filling and grading the land	$ 4,000
2. Full payment to building contractor	690,000
3. Real estate taxes on land paid for the current year	5,000
4. Cost of real estate purchased as a plant site (land $100,000 and building $45,000)	145,000
5. Excavation costs for new building	35,000
6. Architect's fees on building plans	10,000
7. Accrued real estate taxes paid at time of purchase of real estate	2,000
8. Cost of parking lots and driveways	14,000
9. Cost of demolishing building to make land suitable for construction of new building	25,000
	$930,000

	Credit
10. Proceeds from salvage of demolished building	$ 3,500

Totals

Land $172,500
Buildings $735,000

Instructions
Analyze the foregoing transactions using the following column headings. Insert the number of each transaction in the Item space, and insert the amounts in the appropriate columns. For amounts entered in the Other Accounts column, also indicate the account titles.

Item	**Land**	**Buildings**	**Other Accounts**

Compute depreciation under different methods.

(LO 2)

P10-2A In recent years, Avery Transportation purchased three used buses. Because of frequent turnover in the accounting department, a different accountant selected the depreciation method for each bus, and various methods were selected. Information concerning the buses is summarized as follows.

Bus	Acquired	Cost	Salvage Value	Useful Life in Years	Depreciation Method
1	1/1/12	$ 96,000	$ 6,000	5	Straight-line
2	1/1/12	110,000	10,000	4	Declining-balance
3	1/1/13	92,000	8,000	5	Units-of-activity

For the declining-balance method, the company uses the double-declining rate. For the units-of-activity method, total miles are expected to be 120,000. Actual miles of use in the first 3 years were 2013, 24,000; 2014, 34,000; and 2015, 30,000.

Instructions
(a) Compute the amount of accumulated depreciation on each bus at December 31, 2014.
(b) If Bus 2 was purchased on April 1 instead of January 1, what is the depreciation expense for this bus in (1) 2012 and (2) 2013?

(a) Bus 2, 2013, $82,500

P10-3A On January 1, 2014, Evers Company purchased the following two machines for use in its production process.

Compute depreciation under different methods.
(LO 2)

Machine A: The cash price of this machine was $48,000. Related expenditures included: sales tax $1,700, shipping costs $150, insurance during shipping $80, installation and testing costs $70, and $100 of oil and lubricants to be used with the machinery during its first year of operations. Evers estimates that the useful life of the machine is 5 years with a $5,000 salvage value remaining at the end of that time period. Assume that the straight-line method of depreciation is used.

Machine B: The recorded cost of this machine was $180,000. Evers estimates that the useful life of the machine is 4 years with a $10,000 salvage value remaining at the end of that time period.

Instructions
(a) Prepare the following for Machine A.
  (1) The journal entry to record its purchase on January 1, 2014.
  (2) The journal entry to record annual depreciation at December 31, 2014.
(b) Calculate the amount of depreciation expense that Evers should record for Machine B each year of its useful life under the following assumptions.
  (1) Evers uses the straight-line method of depreciation.
  (2) Evers uses the declining-balance method. The rate used is twice the straight-line rate.
  (3) Evers uses the units-of-activity method and estimates that the useful life of the machine is 125,000 units. Actual usage is as follows: 2014, 45,000 units; 2015, 35,000 units; 2016, 25,000 units; 2017, 20,000 units.
(c) Which method used to calculate depreciation on Machine B reports the highest amount of depreciation expense in year 1 (2014)? The highest amount in year 4 (2017)? The highest total amount over the 4-year period?

(b) (2) 2014 DDB depreciation $90,000

P10-4A At the beginning of 2012, Mazzaro Company acquired equipment costing $120,000. It was estimated that this equipment would have a useful life of 6 years and a salvage value of $12,000 at that time. The straight-line method of depreciation was considered the most appropriate to use with this type of equipment. Depreciation is to be recorded at the end of each year.

Calculate revisions to depreciation expense.
(LO 2)

During 2014 (the third year of the equipment's life), the company's engineers reconsidered their expectations, and estimated that the equipment's useful life would probably be 7 years (in total) instead of 6 years. The estimated salvage value was not changed at that time. However, during 2017 the estimated salvage value was reduced to $5,000.

Instructions
Indicate how much depreciation expense should be recorded each year for this equipment, by completing the following table.

Year	Depreciation Expense	Accumulated Depreciation
2012		
2013		
2014		
2015		
2016		
2017		
2018		

2018 depreciation expense, $17,900

P10-5A At December 31, 2014, Grand Company reported the following as plant assets.

Land		$ 4,000,000
Buildings	$28,500,000	
Less: Accumulated depreciation—buildings	12,100,000	16,400,000
Equipment	48,000,000	
Less: Accumulated depreciation—equipment	5,000,000	43,000,000
Total plant assets		$63,400,000

During 2015, the following selected cash transactions occurred.

April 1   Purchased land for $2,130,000.
May 1   Sold equipment that cost $750,000 when purchased on January 1, 2011. The equipment was sold for $450,000.
June 1   Sold land purchased on June 1, 2005 for $1,500,000. The land cost $400,000.
July 1   Purchased equipment for $2,500,000.
Dec.31   Retired equipment that cost $500,000 when purchased on December 31, 2005. No salvage value was received.

Instructions

(a) Journalize the above transactions. The company uses straight-line depreciation for buildings and equipment. The buildings are estimated to have a 50-year life and no salvage value. The equipment is estimated to have a 10-year useful life and no salvage value. Update depreciation on assets disposed of at the time of sale or retirement.
(b) Record adjusting entries for depreciation for 2015.
(c) Prepare the plant assets section of Grand's balance sheet at December 31, 2015.

P10-6A Ceda Co. has equipment that cost $80,000 and that has been depreciated $50,000.

Instructions

Record the disposal under the following assumptions.

(a) It was scrapped as having no value.
(b) It was sold for $21,000.
(c) It was sold for $31,000.

P10-7A The intangible assets section of Sappelt Company at December 31, 2014, is presented below.

Patents ($70,000 cost less $7,000 amortization)	$63,000
Franchises ($48,000 cost less $19,200 amortization)	28,800
Total	$91,800

The patent was acquired in January 2014 and has a useful life of 10 years. The franchise was acquired in January 2011 and also has a useful life of 10 years. The following cash transactions may have affected intangible assets during 2015.

Jan. 2   Paid $27,000 legal costs to successfully defend the patent against infringement by another company.
Jan.–June   Developed a new product, incurring $140,000 in research and development costs. A patent was granted for the product on July 1. Its useful life is equal to its legal life.
Sept. 1   Paid $50,000 to an extremely large defensive lineman to appear in commercials advertising the company's products. The commercials will air in September and October.
Oct. 1   Acquired a franchise for $140,000. The franchise has a useful life of 50 years.

Instructions

(a) Prepare journal entries to record the transactions above.
(b) Prepare journal entries to record the 2015 amortization expense.
(c) Prepare the intangible assets section of the balance sheet at December 31, 2015.

P10-8A Due to rapid turnover in the accounting department, a number of transactions involving intangible assets were improperly recorded by the Goins Company in 2014.

1. Goins developed a new manufacturing process, incurring research and development costs of $136,000. The company also purchased a patent for $60,000. In early January, Goins capitalized $196,000 as the cost of the patents. Patent amortization expense of $19,600 was recorded based on a 10-year useful life.

2. On July 1, 2014, Goins purchased a small company and as a result acquired goodwill of $92,000. Goins recorded a half-year's amortization in 2014, based on a 50-year life ($920 amortization). The goodwill has an indefinite life.

Instructions

Prepare all journal entries necessary to correct any errors made during 2014. Assume the books have not yet been closed for 2014.

1. R&D Exp. $136,000

P10-9A LaPorta Company and Lott Corporation, two corporations of roughly the same size, are both involved in the manufacture of in-line skates. Each company depreciates its plant assets using the straight-line approach. An investigation of their financial statements reveals the following information.

Calculate and comment on asset turnover.
(LO 7)

	LaPorta Co.	Lott Corp.
Net income	$ 800,000	$1,000,000
Sales revenue	1,300,000	1,180,000
Average total assets	2,500,000	2,000,000
Average plant assets	1,800,000	1,000,000

Instructions

(a) For each company, calculate the asset turnover.

(b) ▬▬ Based on your calculations in part (a), comment on the relative effectiveness of the two companies in using their assets to generate sales and produce net income.

PROBLEMS: SET B

P10-1B Russo Company was organized on January 1. During the first year of operations, the following plant asset expenditures and receipts were recorded in random order.

Determine acquisition costs of land and building.
(LO 1)

Debit

1. Accrued real estate taxes paid at time of purchase of real estate	$ 5,000
2. Real estate taxes on land paid for the current year	7,500
3. Full payment to building contractor	490,000
4. Excavation costs for new building	19,000
5. Cost of real estate purchased as a plant site (land $75,000 and building $25,000)	100,000
6. Cost of parking lots and driveways	18,000
7. Architect's fees on building plans	9,000
8. Installation cost of fences around property	6,000
9. Cost of demolishing building to make land suitable for construction of new building	27,000
	$681,500

Credit

10. Proceeds from salvage of demolished building	$ 3,500

Instructions

Analyze the foregoing transactions using the following column headings. Insert the number of each transaction in the Item space, and insert the amounts in the appropriate columns. For amounts entered in the Other Accounts column, also indicate the account title.

Totals
Land $128,500
Buildings $518,000

Item	Land	Buildings	Other Accounts

P10-2B In recent years, Darnell Company purchased three machines. Because of heavy turnover in the accounting department, a different accountant was in charge of selecting the depreciation method for each machine, and each selected a different method. Information concerning the machines is summarized below.

Compute depreciation under different methods.
(LO 2)

Machine	Acquired	Cost	Salvage Value	Useful Life in Years	Depreciation Method
1	1/1/11	$105,000	$ 5,000	10	Straight-line
2	1/1/12	180,000	10,000	8	Declining-balance
3	11/1/14	125,000	15,000	6	Units-of-activity

For the declining-balance method, the company uses the double-declining rate. For the units-of-activity method, total machine hours are expected to be 25,000. Actual hours of use in the first 3 years were 2014, 2,000; 2015, 4,500; and 2016, 5,500.

Instructions

(a) Machine 2, 2013, $78,750

(a) Compute the amount of accumulated depreciation on each machine at December 31, 2014.

(b) If Machine 2 had been purchased on May 1 instead of January 1, what would be the depreciation expense for this machine in (1) 2012 and (2) 2013?

Compute depreciation under different methods.

(LO 2)

P10-3B On January 1, 2014, Bourgeois Company purchased the following two machines for use in its production process.

Machine A: The cash price of this machine was $58,000. Related expenditures included: sales tax $2,750, shipping costs $100, insurance during shipping $75, installation and testing costs $75, and $90 of oil and lubricants to be used with the machinery during its first year of operation. Bourgeois estimates that the useful life of the machine is 4 years with a $5,000 salvage value remaining at the end of that time period.

Machine B: The recorded cost of this machine was $120,000. Bourgeois estimates that the useful life of the machine is 4 years with a $10,000 salvage value remaining at the end of that time period.

Instructions

(a) Prepare the following for Machine A.

(a) (2) $14,000

(1) The journal entry to record its purchase on January 1, 2014.

(2) The journal entry to record annual depreciation at December 31, 2014, assuming the straight-line method of depreciation is used.

(b) Calculate the amount of depreciation expense that Bourgeois should record for Machine B each year of its useful life under the following assumption.

(1) Bourgeois uses the straight-line method of depreciation.

(2) Bourgeois uses the declining-balance method. The rate used is twice the straight-line rate.

(3) Bourgeois uses the units-of-activity method and estimates the useful life of the machine is 25,000 units. Actual usage is as follows: 2014, 5,500 units; 2015, 7,000 units; 2016, 8,000 units; 2017, 4,500 units.

(c) Which method used to calculate depreciation on Machine B reports the lowest amount of depreciation expense in year 1 (2014)? The lowest amount in year 4 (2017)? The lowest total amount over the 4-year period?

Calculate revisions to depreciation expense.

(LO 2)

P10-4B At the beginning of 2012, Sullivan Company acquired equipment costing $300,000. It was estimated that this equipment would have a useful life of 6 years and a salvage value of $30,000 at that time. The straight-line method of depreciation was considered the most appropriate to use with this type of equipment. Depreciation is to be recorded at the end of each year.

During 2014 (the third year of the equipment's life), the company's engineers reconsidered their expectations, and estimated that the equipment's useful life would probably be 7 years (in total) instead of 6 years. The estimated salvage value was not changed at that time. However, during 2017 the estimated salvage value was reduced to $5,000.

Instructions

Indicate how much depreciation expense should be recorded for this equipment each year by completing the following table.

Year	Depreciation Expense	Accumulated Depreciation
2012		
2013		
2014		
2015		
2016		
2017		
2018		

2018 depreciation expense, $48,500

P10-5B At December 31, 2014, Torrealba Company reported the following as plant assets.

Land		$ 2,000,000
Buildings	$20,000,000	
Less: Accumulated depreciation—buildings	8,000,000	12,000,000
Equipment	30,000,000	
Less: Accumulated depreciation—equipment	4,000,000	26,000,000
Total plant assets		$40,000,000

Journalize a series of equipment transactions related to purchase, sale, retirement, and depreciation.

(LO 2, 4, 7)

During 2015, the following selected cash transactions occurred.

April 1	Purchased land for $1,200,000.
May 1	Sold equipment that cost $450,000 when purchased on January 1, 2011. The equipment was sold for $260,000.
June 1	Sold land purchased on June 1, 2005, for $1,000,000. The land cost $340,000.
July 1	Purchased equipment for $1,500,000.
Dec. 31	Retired equipment that cost $300,000 when purchased on December 31, 2005. No salvage value was received.

Instructions
(a) Journalize the above transactions. Torrealba uses straight-line depreciation for buildings and equipment. The buildings are estimated to have a 50-year useful life and no salvage value. The equipment is estimated to have a 10-year useful life and no salvage value. Update depreciation on assets disposed of at the time of sale or retirement.
(b) Record adjusting entries for depreciation for 2015.
(c) Prepare the plant assets section of Torrealba's balance sheet at December 31, 2015.

(b) Depreciation Expense—
Buildings $400,000;
Equipment $3,000,000
(c) Total plant assets
$38,660,000

P10-6B Dickey's has equipment that cost $45,000 and that has been depreciated $26,000.

Record disposals.
(LO 4)

Instructions
Record the disposal under the following assumptions.

(a) It was scrapped as having no value.
(b) It was sold for $29,000.
(c) It was sold for $10,000.

(b) 10,000 gain

P10-7B The intangible assets section of Willingham Company at December 31, 2014, is presented below.

Prepare entries to record transactions related to acquisition and amortization of intangibles; prepare the intangible assets section.

(LO 6, 7)

Patents ($100,000 cost less $10,000 amortization)	$ 90,000
Copyrights ($60,000 cost less $24,000 amortization)	36,000
Total	$126,000

The patent was acquired in January 2014 and has a useful life of 10 years. The copyright was acquired in January 2011 and also has a useful life of 10 years. The following cash transactions may have affected intangible assets during 2015.

Jan. 2	Paid $36,000 legal costs to successfully defend the patent against infringement by another company.
Jan.–June	Developed a new product, incurring $230,000 in research and development costs. A patent was granted for the product on July 1. Its useful life is equal to its legal life.
Sept. 1	Paid $125,000 to an Xgames star to appear in commercials advertising the company's products. The commercials will air in September and October.
Oct. 1	Acquired a copyright for $300,000. The copyright has a useful life of 50 years.

Instructions
(a) Prepare journal entries to record the transactions above.
(b) Prepare journal entries to record the 2015 amortization expense for intangible assets.
(c) Prepare the intangible assets section of the balance sheet at December 31, 2015.
(d) ━━━ Prepare the note to the financials on Willingham's intangibles as of December 31, 2015.

(b) Amortization Expense
(patents) $14,000;
Amortization Expense
(copyrights) $7,500
(c) Total intangible assets,
$440,500

P10-8B Due to rapid turnover in the accounting department, a number of transactions involving intangible assets were improperly recorded by Farnsworth Company in 2014.

Prepare entries to correct errors made in recording and amortizing intangible assets.

(LO 6)

1. Farnsworth developed a new manufacturing process, incurring research and development costs of $110,000. The company also purchased a patent for $50,000. In early January,

Farnsworth capitalized $160,000 as the cost of the patents. Patent amortization expense of $16,000 was recorded based on a 10-year useful life.

2. On July 1, 2014, Farnsworth purchased a small company and as a result acquired goodwill of $200,000. Farnsworth recorded a half-year's amortization in 2014, based on a 50-year life ($2,000 amortization). The goodwill has an indefinite life.

R&D Exp. $110,000

Instructions
Prepare all journal entries necessary to correct any errors made during 2014. Assume the books have not yet been closed for 2014.

Calculate and comment on asset turnover.

(LO 7)

P10-9B Auer Corporation and Marte Corporation, two corporations of roughly the same size, are both involved in the manufacture of canoes and sea kayaks. Each company depreciates its plant assets using the straight-line approach. An investigation of their financial statements reveals the following information.

	Auer Corp.	**Marte Corp.**
Net income	$ 300,000	$ 325,000
Sales revenue	1,050,000	945,000
Average total assets	1,000,000	1,050,000
Average plant assets	750,000	770,000

Instructions
(a) For each company, calculate the asset turnover.
(b) ———— Based on your calculations in part (a), comment on the relative effectiveness of the two companies in using their assets to generate sales and produce net income.

PROBLEMS: SET C

Visit the book's companion website, at **www.wiley.com/college/weygandt**, and choose the Student Companion site to access Problem Set C.

COMPREHENSIVE PROBLEM: CHAPTERS 3 TO 10

CP10 Hassellhouf Company's trial balance at December 31, 2014, is presented below. All 2014 transactions have been recorded except for the items described on page 513.

	Debit	Credit
Cash	$ 28,000	
Accounts Receivable	36,800	
Notes Receivable	10,000	
Interest Receivable	–0–	
Inventory	36,200	
Prepaid Insurance	3,600	
Land	20,000	
Buildings	150,000	
Equipment	60,000	
Patents	9,000	
Allowance for Doubtful Accounts		$ 500
Accumulated Depreciation—Buildings		50,000
Accumulated Depreciation—Equipment		24,000
Accounts Payable		27,300
Salaries and Wages Payable		–0–
Unearned Rent Revenue		6,000
Notes Payable (due in 2015)		11,000
Interest Payable		–0–
Notes Payable (due after 2015)		30,000
Owner's Capital		113,600
Owner's Drawings	12,000	

	Debit	Credit
Sales Revenue		905,000
Interest Revenue		–0–
Rent Revenue		–0–
Gain on Disposal of Plant Assets		–0–
Bad Debt Expense	–0–	
Cost of Goods Sold	630,000	
Depreciation Expense	–0–	
Insurance Expense	–0–	
Interest Expense	–0–	
Other Operating Expenses	61,800	
Amortization Expense	–0–	
Salaries and Wages Expense	110,000	
Total	$1,167,400	$1,167,400

Unrecorded transactions:

1. On May 1, 2014, Hassellhouf purchased equipment for $21,200 plus sales taxes of $1,600 (all paid in cash).
2. On July 1, 2014, Hassellhouf sold for $3,500 equipment which originally cost $5,000. Accumulated depreciation on this equipment at January 1, 2014, was $1,800; 2014 depreciation prior to the sale of the equipment was $450.
3. On December 31, 2014, Hassellhouf sold for $9,000 on account inventory that cost $6,300.
4. Hassellhouf estimates that uncollectible accounts receivable at year-end is $4,000.
5. The note receivable is a one-year, 8% note dated April 1, 2014. No interest has been recorded.
6. The balance in prepaid insurance represents payment of a $3,600 6-month premium on September 1, 2014.
7. The building is being depreciated using the straight-line method over 30 years. The salvage value is $30,000.
8. The equipment owned prior to this year is being depreciated using the straight-line method over 5 years. The salvage value is 10% of cost.
9. The equipment purchased on May 1, 2014, is being depreciated using the straight-line method over 5 years, with a salvage value of $1,800.
10. The patent was acquired on January 1, 2014, and has a useful life of 10 years from that date.
11. Unpaid salaries and wages at December 31, 2014, total $5,200.
12. The unearned rent revenue of $6,000 was received on December 1, 2014, for 3 months rent.
13. Both the short-term and long-term notes payable are dated January 1, 2014, and carry a 9% interest rate. All interest is payable in the next 12 months.

Instructions
(a) Prepare journal entries for the transactions listed above.
(b) Prepare an updated December 31, 2014, trial balance.
(c) Prepare a 2014 income statement and an owner's equity statement.
(d) Prepare a December 31, 2014, classified balance sheet.

(b) Totals $1,205,040

(d) Total assets $259,200

CONTINUING COOKIE CHRONICLE

(*Note:* This is a continuation of the Cookie Chronicle from Chapters 1 through 9.)

CCC10 Natalie is also thinking of buying a van that will be used only for business. Natalie is concerned about the impact of the van's cost on her income statement and balance sheet. She has come to you for advice on calculating the van's depreciation.

Go to the book's companion website, **www.wiley.com/college/weygandt***, to see the completion of this problem.*

Broadening Your Perspective

Financial Reporting and Analysis

Financial Reporting Problem: Apple Inc.

BYP10-1 The financial statements of Apple Inc. are presented in Appendix A. Instructions for accessing and using the company's complete annual report, including the notes to the financial statements, are also provided in Appendix A.

Instructions
Refer to Apple's financial statements and answer the following questions.

(a) What was the total cost and book value of property, plant, and equipment at September 24, 2011?
(b) What was the amount of depreciation and amortization expense for each of the three years 2009–2011?
(c) Using the statement of cash flows, what is the amount of capital spending in 2011 and 2010?
(d) Where does the company disclose its intangible assets, and what types of intangibles did it have at September 24, 2011?

Comparative Analysis Problem: PepsiCo, Inc. vs. The Coca-Cola Company

BYP10-2 PepsiCo, Inc.'s financial statements are presented in Appendix B. Financial statements of The Coca-Cola Company are presented in Appendix C. Instructions for accessing and using the complete annual reports of PepsiCo and Coca-Cola, including the notes to the financial statements, are also provided in Appendices B and C, respectively.

Instructions
(a) Compute the asset turnover for each company for 2011.
(b) What conclusions concerning the efficiency of assets can be drawn from these data?

Comparative Analysis Problem: Amazon.com, Inc. vs. Wal-Mart Stores, Inc.

BYP10-3 Amazon.com, Inc.'s financial statements are presented in Appendix D. Financial statements of Wal-Mart Stores, Inc. are presented in Appendix E. Instructions for accessing and using the complete annual reports of Amazon and Wal-Mart, including the notes to the financial statements, are also provided in Appendices D and E, respectively.

Instructions
(a) Compute the asset turnover for each company for 2011.
(b) What conclusions concerning the efficiency of assets can be drawn from these data?

Real-World Focus

BYP10-4 A company's annual report identifies the amount of its plant assets and the depreciation method used.

Address: **www.annualreports.com**, or go to **www.wiley.com/college/weygandt**

Steps
1. Select a particular company.
2. Search by company name.
3. Follow instructions below.

Instructions
Answer the following questions.

(a) What is the name of the company?
(b) What is the Internet address of the annual report?
(c) At fiscal year-end, what is the net amount of its plant assets?
(d) What is the accumulated depreciation?
(e) Which method of depreciation does the company use?

Critical Thinking

Decision-Making Across the Organization

BYP10-5 Pinson Company and Estes Company are two proprietorships that are similar in many respects. One difference is that Pinson Company uses the straight-line method and Estes Company uses the declining-balance method at double the straight-line rate. On January 2, 2012, both companies acquired the depreciable assets shown below.

Asset	Cost	Salvage Value	Useful Life
Buildings	$360,000	$20,000	40 years
Equipment	130,000	10,000	10 years

Including the appropriate depreciation charges, annual net income for the companies in the years 2012, 2013, and 2014 and total income for the 3 years were as follows.

	2012	2013	2014	Total
Pinson Company	$84,000	$88,400	$90,000	$262,400
Estes Company	68,000	76,000	85,000	229,000

At December 31, 2014, the balance sheets of the two companies are similar except that Estes Company has more cash than Pinson Company.
  Lynda Peace is interested in buying one of the companies. She comes to you for advice.

Instructions
With the class divided into groups, answer the following.

(a) Determine the annual and total depreciation recorded by each company during the 3 years.
(b) Assuming that Estes Company also uses the straight-line method of depreciation instead of the declining-balance method as in (a), prepare comparative income data for the 3 years.
(c) Which company should Lynda Peace buy? Why?

Communication Activity

BYP10-6 The following was published with the financial statements to American Exploration Company.

AMERICAN EXPLORATION COMPANY
Notes to the Financial Statements

Property, Plant, and Equipment—The Company accounts for its oil and gas exploration and production activities using the successful efforts method of accounting. Under this method, acquisition costs for proved and unproved properties are capitalized when incurred.... The costs of drilling exploratory wells are capitalized pending determination of whether each well has discovered proved reserves. If proved reserves are not discovered, such drilling costs are charged to expense.... Depletion of the cost of producing oil and gas properties is computed on the units-of-activity method.

Instructions
Write a brief memo to your instructor discussing American Exploration Company's note regarding property, plant, and equipment. Your memo should address what is meant by the "successful efforts method" and "units-of-activity method."

Ethics Case

BYP10-7 Turner Container Company is suffering declining sales of its principal product, nonbio-degradeable plastic cartons. The president, Robert Griffin, instructs his controller, Alexis Landrum, to lengthen asset lives to reduce depreciation expense. A processing line of automated plastic extruding equipment, purchased for $3.5 million in January 2014, was originally estimated to have a useful life of 8 years and a salvage value of $300,000. Depreciation has been recorded for 2 years on that basis. Robert wants the estimated life changed to 12 years total, and the straight-line method continued. Alexis is hesitant to make the change, believing it is unethical to increase net income in this manner. Robert says, "Hey, the life is only an estimate, and I've heard that our competition uses a 12-year life on their production equipment."

Instructions
(a) Who are the stakeholders in this situation?
(b) Is the change in asset life unethical, or is it simply a good business practice by an astute president?
(c) What is the effect of Robert Griffin's proposed change on income before taxes in the year of change?

All About You

BYP10-8 The Feature Story at the beginning of the chapter discussed the company Rent-A-Wreck. Note that the trade name Rent-A-Wreck is a very important asset to the company, as it creates immediate product identification. As indicated in the chapter, companies invest substantial sums to ensure that their product is well-known to the consumer. Test your knowledge of who owns some famous brands and their impact on the financial statements.

Instructions
(a) Provide an answer to the five multiple-choice questions below.
  (1) Which company owns both Taco Bell and Pizza Hut?
      (a) McDonald's.   (c) Yum Brands.
      (b) CKE.   (d) Wendy's.
  (2) Dairy Queen belongs to:
      (a) Breyer.   (c) GE.
      (b) Berkshire Hathaway.   (d) The Coca-Cola Company.
  (3) Philip Morris, the cigarette maker, is owned by:
      (a) Altria.   (c) Boeing.
      (b) GE.   (d) ExxonMobil.
  (4) AOL, a major Internet provider, belongs to:
      (a) Microsoft.   (c) NBC.
      (b) Cisco.   (d) Time Warner.
  (5) ESPN, the sports broadcasting network, is owned by:
      (a) Procter & Gamble.   (c) Walt Disney.
      (b) Altria.   (d) The Coca-Cola Company.
(b) How do you think the value of these brands is reported on the appropriate company's balance sheet?

FASB Codification Activity

BYP10-9 If your school has a subscription to the FASB Codification, go to **http://aaahq.org/ ascLogin.cfm** to log in and prepare responses to the following.

(a) What does it mean to capitalize an item?
(b) What is the definition provided for an intangible asset?
(c) Your great-uncle, who is a CPA, is impressed that you are taking an accounting class. Based on his experience, he believes that depreciation is something that companies do based on past practice, not on the basis of authoritative guidance. Provide the authoritative literature to support the practice of fixed-asset depreciation.

Answers to Chapter Questions

Answers to Insight and Accounting Across the Organization Questions

p. 475 Many U.S. Firms Use Leases   Q: Why might airline managers choose to lease rather than purchase their planes? **A:** The reasons for leasing include favorable tax treatment, better financing options, increased flexibility, reduced risk of obsolescence, and often less debt shown on the balance sheet.

p. 488 Sustainability Report Please   Q: Why do you believe companies issue sustainability reports?   **A:** It is important that companies clearly describe the things they value in addition to overall profitability. Most companies recognize that the health, safety, and environmental protections of their workforce and community are important components in developing strategies for continued growth and longevity. Without a strong commitment to the principles of corporate social responsibility, it is unlikely that a company will be able to maintain long-term stability and profitability. The development of a sustainability report helps companies to consider these issues and develop measures to assess whether they are meeting their goals in this area.

p. 491 Should Companies Write Up Goodwill?   Q: Do you think that this treatment would be allowed under U.S. GAAP?   **A:** The write-down of assets would have been allowed if it could be shown that the assets had declined in value (an impairment). However, the creation of goodwill to offset the write-down would not have been allowed. Goodwill can be recorded only when it results from the acquisition of a business. It cannot be recorded as the result of being created internally.

Answers to Self-Test Questions

1. d ($24,000 + $1,200 + $200 + $400)   **2.** b   **3.** d [($400,000 − $10,000) ÷ 5] × 2   **4.** d   **5.** b $60,000 × 25% = $15,000; ($60,000 − $15,000) × 25% = $11,250   **6.** b   **7.** d [($60,000 − $12,000) ÷ 10] × 2 = $9,600; ($60,000 − $9,600 − $2,000) ÷ 4   **8.** d   **9.** a [($80,000 ÷ 10) × 4.5] = $36,000; ($80,000 − $36,000) − $26,000   **10.** c ($12 million ÷ 20 million) × 2 million   **11.** d   **12.** b   **13.** c **14.** c $180,000 ÷ [($200,000 + $300,000) ÷ 2]   *15. a ($35,000 + $10,000)   *16. d

A Look at IFRS

IFRS follows most of the same principles as GAAP in the accounting for property, plant, and equipment. There are, however, some significant differences in the implementation. IFRS allows the use of revaluation of property, plant, and equipment, and it also requires the use of component depreciation. In addition, there are some significant differences in the accounting for both intangible assets and impairments.

LEARNING OBJECTIVE	9

Compare the accounting procedure for long-lived assets under GAAP and IFRS.

Key Points

- The definition for plant assets for both IFRS and GAAP is essentially the same.

- Both IFRS and GAAP follow the historical cost principle when accounting for property, plant, and equipment at date of acquisition. Cost consists of all expenditures necessary to acquire the asset and make it ready for its intended use.

- Under both IFRS and GAAP, interest costs incurred during construction are capitalized. Recently, IFRS converged to GAAP requirements in this area.

- IFRS, like GAAP, capitalizes all direct costs in self-constructed assets such as raw materials and labor. IFRS does not address the capitalization of fixed overhead although in practice these costs are generally capitalized.

- IFRS also views depreciation as an allocation of cost over an asset's useful life. IFRS permits the same depreciation methods (e.g., straight-line, accelerated, and units-of-activity) as GAAP. However, a major difference is that IFRS requires component depreciation. **Component depreciation** specifies that any significant parts of a depreciable asset that have different estimated useful lives should be separately depreciated. Component depreciation is allowed under GAAP but is seldom used.

To illustrate, assume that Lexure Construction builds an office building for $4,000,000, not including the cost of the land. If the $4,000,000 is allocated over the 40-year useful life of the building, Lexure reports $100,000 of depreciation per year, assuming straight-line depreciation and no disposal value. However, assume that $320,000 of the cost of the building relates to personal property and $600,000 relates to land improvements. The personal property has a depreciable life of 5 years, and the land improvements have a depreciable life of 10 years. In accordance with IFRS, Lexure must use component depreciation. It must reclassify $320,000 of the cost of the building to personal property and $600,000 to the cost of land improvements. Assuming that Lexure uses straight-line depreciation, component depreciation for the first year of the office building is computed as follows.

Building cost adjusted ($4,000,000 − $320,000 − $600,000)	$3,080,000
Building cost depreciation per year ($3,080,000/40)	$ 77,000
Personal property depreciation ($320,000/5)	64,000
Land improvements depreciation ($600,000/10)	60,000
Total component depreciation in first year	$ 201,000

- IFRS uses the term **residual value** rather than salvage value to refer to an owner's estimate of an asset's value at the end of its useful life for that owner.
- IFRS allows companies to revalue plant assets to fair value at the reporting date. Companies that choose to use the revaluation framework must follow revaluation procedures. If revaluation is used, it must be applied to all assets in a class of assets. Assets that are experiencing rapid price changes must be revalued on an annual basis, otherwise less frequent revaluation is acceptable.

To illustrate asset revaluation accounting, assume that Pernice Company applies revaluation to plant assets with a carrying value of $1,000,000, a useful life of 5 years, and no residual value. Pernice makes the following journal entries in year 1, assuming straight-line depreciation.

Depreciation Expense	200,000	
Accumulated Depreciation—Plant Assets		200,000
(To record depreciation expense in year 1)		

After this entry, Pernice's plant assets have a carrying amount of $800,000 ($1,000,000 − $200,000). At the end of year 1, independent appraisers determine that the asset has a fair value of $850,000. To report the plant assets at fair value, or $850,000, Pernice eliminates the Accumulated Depreciation—Plant Assets account, reduces Plant Assets to its fair value of $850,000, and records Revaluation Surplus of $50,000. The entry to record the revaluation is as follows.

Accumulated Depreciation—Plant Assets	200,000	
Plant Assets		150,000
Revaluation Surplus		50,000
(To record adjusting the plant assets to fair value)		

Thus, Pernice follows a two-step process. First, Pernice records depreciation based on the cost basis of $1,000,000. As a result, it reports depreciation expense of $200,000 on the income statement. Second, it records the revaluation. It does this by eliminating any accumulated depreciation, adjusting the recorded value of the plant assets to fair value, and debiting or crediting the Revaluation Surplus account. In this example, the revaluation surplus is $50,000, which is the difference between the fair value of $850,000 and the book value of $800,000. Revaluation surplus is an example of an item reported as other comprehensive income, as discussed in the *A Look at IFRS* section of Chapter 5. Pernice now reports the following information in its statement of financial position at the end of year 1.

Plant assets ($1,000,000 − $150,000)	$850,000
Accumulated depreciation—plant assets	0
	$850,000
Revaluation surplus (equity)	$ 50,000

As indicated, $850,000 is the new basis of the asset. Pernice reports depreciation expense of $200,000 in the income statement and $50,000 in other comprehensive income. Assuming no change in the total useful life, depreciation in year 2 will be $212,500 ($850,000 ÷ 4).

- Under both GAAP and IFRS, changes in the depreciation method used and changes in useful life are handled in current and future periods. Prior periods are not affected. GAAP recently conformed to international standards in the accounting for changes in depreciation methods.
- The accounting for subsequent expenditures, such as ordinary repairs and additions, are essentially the same under IFRS and GAAP.
- The accounting for plant asset disposals is essentially the same under IFRS and GAAP.
- Initial costs to acquire natural resources are essentially the same under IFRS and GAAP.
- The definition of intangible assets is essentially the same under IFRS and GAAP.
- As in GAAP, under IFRS the costs associated with research and development are segregated into the two components. Costs in the research phase are always expensed under both IFRS and GAAP. Under IFRS, however, costs in the development phase are capitalized as Development Costs once technological feasibility is achieved.

  To illustrate, assume that Laser Scanner Company spent $1 million on research and $2 million on development of new products. Of the $2 million in development costs, $500,000 was incurred prior to technological feasibility and $1,500,000 was incurred after technological feasibility had been demonstrated. The company would record these costs as follows.

Research Expense	1,000,000	
Development Expense	500,000	
Development Costs	1,500,000	
Cash		3,000,000
(To record research and development costs)		

- IFRS permits revaluation of intangible assets (except for goodwill). GAAP prohibits revaluation of intangible assets.
- IFRS requires an impairment test at each reporting date for plant assets and intangibles and records an impairment if the asset's carrying amount exceeds its recoverable amount. The recoverable amount is the higher of the asset's fair value less costs to sell or its value-in-use. Value-in-use is the future cash flows to be derived from the particular asset, discounted to present value. Under GAAP, impairment loss is measured as the excess of the carrying amount over the asset's fair value.
- IFRS allows reversal of impairment losses when there has been a change in economic conditions or in the expected use of the asset. Under GAAP, impairment losses cannot be reversed for assets to be held and used; the impairment loss results in a new cost basis for the asset. IFRS and GAAP are similar in the accounting for impairments of assets held for disposal.
- The accounting for exchanges of nonmonetary assets has recently converged between IFRS and GAAP. GAAP now requires that gains on exchanges of nonmonetary assets be recognized if the exchange has commercial substance. This is the same framework used in IFRS.

Looking to the Future

With respect to revaluations, as part of the conceptual framework project, the Boards will examine the measurement bases used in accounting. It is too early to say whether a converged conceptual framework will recommend fair value measurement (and revaluation accounting) for plant assets and intangibles. However, this is likely to be one of the more contentious issues, given the long-standing use of historical cost as a measurement basis in GAAP.

The IASB and FASB have identified a project that would consider expanded recognition of internally generated intangible assets. IFRS permits more recognition of intangibles compared to GAAP. Thus, it will be challenging to develop converged standards for intangible assets, given the long-standing prohibition on capitalizing internally generated intangible assets and research and development costs in GAAP.

IFRS Practice

IFRS Self-Test Questions

1. Which of the following statements is **correct**?
   (a) Both IFRS and GAAP permit revaluation of property, plant, and equipment and intangible assets (except for goodwill).
   (b) IFRS permits revaluation of property, plant, and equipment and intangible assets (except for goodwill).
   (c) Both IFRS and GAAP permit revaluation of property, plant, and equipment but not intangible assets.
   (d) GAAP permits revaluation of property, plant, and equipment but not intangible assets.

2. International Company has land that cost $450,000 but now has a fair value of $600,000. International Company decides to use the revaluation method specified in IFRS to account for the land. Which of the following statements is **correct**?
   (a) International Company must continue to report the land at $450,000.
   (b) International Company would report a net income increase of $150,000 due to an increase in the value of the land.
   (c) International Company would debit Revaluation Surplus for $150,000.
   (d) International Company would credit Revaluation Surplus by $150,000.

3. Francisco Corporation is constructing a new building at a total initial cost of $10,000,000. The building is expected to have a useful life of 50 years with no residual value. The building's finished surfaces (e.g., roof cover and floor cover) are 5% of this cost and have a useful life of 20 years. Building services systems (e.g., electric, heating, and plumbing) are 20% of the cost and have a useful life of 25 years. The depreciation in the first year using component depreciation, assuming straight-line depreciation with no residual value, is:
   (a) $200,000.
   (b) $215,000.
   (c) $255,000.
   (d) None of the above.

4. Research and development costs are:
   (a) expensed under GAAP.
   (b) expensed under IFRS.
   (c) expensed under both GAAP and IFRS.
   (d) None of the above.

5. Under IFRS, value-in-use is defined as:
   (a) net realizable value.
   (b) fair value.
   (c) future cash flows discounted to present value.
   (d) total future undiscounted cash flows.

IFRS Exercises

IFRS10-1 What is component depreciation, and when must it be used?

IFRS10-2 What is revaluation of plant assets? When should revaluation be applied?

IFRS10-3 Some product development expenditures are recorded as development expenses and others as development costs. Explain the difference between these accounts and how a company decides which classification is appropriate.

IFRS10-4 Beckham Company constructed a warehouse for $280,000. Beckham estimates that the warehouse has a useful life of 20 years and no residual value. Construction records indicate that $50,000 of the cost of the warehouse relates to its heating, ventilation, and air conditioning (HVAC) system, which has an estimated useful life of only 10 years. Compute the first year of depreciation expense using straight-line component depreciation.

IFRS10-5 At the end of its first year of operations, Escobar Company chose to use the revaluation framework allowed under IFRS. Escobar's ledger shows Plant Assets $475,000 and Accumulated Depreciation—Plant Assets $60,000. Prepare journal entries to record the following.

(a) Independent appraisers determine that the plant assets have a fair value of $460,000.
(b) Independent appraisers determine that the plant assets have a fair value of $400,000.

IFRS10-6 Odessa Industries spent $350,000 on research and $600,000 on development of a new product. Of the $600,000 in development costs, $400,000 was incurred prior to technological feasibility and $200,000 after technological feasibility had been demonstrated. Prepare the journal entry to record research and development costs.

International Financial Statement Analysis: Zetar plc

IFRS10-7 The financial statements of Zetar plc are presented in Appendix F. Instructions for accessing and using the company's complete annual report, including the notes to its financial statements, are also provided in Appendix F.

Instructions
Use the company's annual report to answer the following questions.

(a) According to the notes to the financial statements, what method or methods does the company use to depreciate "plant and equipment?" What rate does it use to depreciate plant and equipment?
(b) According to the notes to the financial statements, how often is goodwill tested for impairment?
(c) Using the notes to the financial statements, as well as information from the statement of cash flows, prepare the journal entry to record the disposal of property, plant, and equipment during 2011. (Round your amounts to the nearest thousand.)

Answers to IFRS Self-Test Questions
1. b   **2.** d   **3.** c ($10,000,000 × .05/20) + ($10,000,000 × .20/25) + ($10,000,000 × .75/50)   **4.** a
5. c

 The Navigator

11 | Current Liabilities and Payroll Accounting

Feature Story

Financing His Dreams

What would you do if you had a great idea for a new product but couldn't come up with the cash to get the business off the ground? Small businesses often cannot attract investors. Nor can they obtain traditional debt financing through bank loans or bond issuances. Instead, they often resort to unusual, and costly, forms of nontraditional financing.

Such was the case for Wilbert Murdock. Murdock grew up in a New York housing project and always had great ambitions. This ambitious spirit led him into some business ventures that failed: a medical diagnostic tool, a device to eliminate carpal tunnel syndrome, custom-designed sneakers, and a device to keep people from falling asleep while driving.

Another idea was computerized golf clubs that analyze a golfer's swing and provide immediate feedback. Murdock saw great potential in the idea. Many golfers are willing to shell out considerable sums of money for devices that might improve their game. But Murdock had no cash to develop his product, and banks and other lenders had shied away. Rather than give up, Murdock resorted to credit cards—in a big He quickly owed $25,000 to credit card companies.

While funding a business with credit cards might sound unusual, it isn't. A recent study found that one-third of businesses with fewer than 20 employees financed at lea part of their operations with credit cards. As Murdock explained, credit cards are an appealing way to finance a start-up because "credit-card companies don't care how money is spent." However, they do care how they are pa And so Murdock faced high interest charges and a barra credit card collection letters.

Murdock's debt forced him to sacrifice nearly everything order to keep his business afloat. His car stopped running barely had enough money to buy food, and he lived and worked out of a dimly lit apartment in his mother's basen Through it all he tried to maintain a positive spirit, joking that, if he becomes successful, he might some day get to appear in an American Express commercial.

Source: Rodney Ho, "Banking on Plastic: To Finance a Dream, Many Entrepreneurs Binge on Credit Cards," *Wall Street Journal* (March 9, 19 p. A1.

 The Navigator

- ■ Scan Learning Objectives
- ■ Read Feature Story
- ■ Read Preview
- ■ Read text and answer **DO IT!** p. 527
  - ■ p. 531　■ p. 538　■ p. 541
- ■ Work Comprehensive **DO IT!** p. 543
- ■ Review Summary of Learning Objectives
- ■ Answer Self-Test Questions
- ■ Complete Assignments
- ■ Go to *WileyPLUS* for practice and tutorials
- **Read A Look at IFRS** p. 564

Learning Objectives　 The Navigator

After studying this chapter, you should be able to:

[1] Explain a current liability, and identify the major types of current liabilities.

[2] Describe the accounting for notes payable.

[3] Explain the accounting for other current liabilities.

[4] Explain the financial statement presentation and analysis of current liabilities.

[5] Describe the accounting and disclosure requirements for contingent liabilities.

[6] Compute and record the payroll for a pay period.

[7] Describe and record employer payroll taxes.

[8] Discuss the objectives of internal control for payroll.

Cary Westfall/iStockphoto

Preview of Chapter 11

 The Navigator

Inventor-entrepreneur Wilbert Murdock, as you can tell from the Feature Story, had to use multiple credit cards to finance his business ventures. Murdock's credit card debts would be classified as **current liabilities** because they are due every month. Yet, by making minimal payments and paying high interest each month, Murdock used this credit source long-term. Some credit card balances remain outstanding for years as they accumulate interest.

Earlier, we defined liabilities as creditors' claims on total assets and as existing debts and obligations. These claims, debts, and obligations must be settled or paid at some time **in the future** by the transfer of assets or services. The future date on which they are due or payable (maturity date) is a significant feature of liabilities. This "future date" feature gives rise to two basic classifications of liabilities: (1) current liabilities and (2) long-term liabilities. We will explain current liabilities, along with payroll accounting, in this chapter. We will explain long-term liabilities in Chapter 15.

The content and organization of Chapter 11 are as follows.

CURRENT LIABILITIES AND PAYROLL ACCOUNTING

Current Liabilities	Contingent Liabilities	Payroll Accounting
• Notes payable • Sales taxes payable • Unearned revenues • Current maturities of long-term debt • Statement presentation and analysis	• Recording • Disclosure	• Determining the payroll • Recording the payroll • Employer payroll taxes • Filing and remitting payroll taxes • Internal control for payroll

Current Liabilities

LEARNING OBJECTIVE **1**

Explain a current liability, and identify the major types of current liabilities.

As explained in Chapter 4, a **current liability** is a debt that a company expects to pay within one year or the operating cycle, whichever is longer. Debts that do not meet this criterion are classified as long-term liabilities.

Companies must carefully monitor the relationship of current liabilities to current assets. This relationship is critical in evaluating a company's short-term debt-paying ability. A company that has more current liabilities than current assets may not be able to meet its current obligations when they become due.

Current liabilities include notes payable, accounts payable, and unearned revenues. They also include accrued liabilities such as taxes, salaries and wages, and interest payable. In the sections that follow, we discuss a few of the common types of current liabilities.

Notes Payable

LEARNING OBJECTIVE **2**

Describe the accounting for notes payable.

Companies record obligations in the form of written notes as **notes payable**. Notes payable are often used instead of accounts payable because they give the lender formal proof of the obligation in case legal remedies are needed to collect the debt. Companies frequently issue notes payable to meet short-term financing needs. Notes payable usually require the borrower to pay interest.

Notes are issued for varying periods of time. **Those due for payment within one year of the balance sheet date are usually classified as current liabilities.**

To illustrate the accounting for notes payable, assume that First National Bank agrees to lend $100,000 on September 1, 2014, if Cole Williams Co. signs a $100,000, 12%, four-month note maturing on January 1. When a company issues an interest-bearing note, the amount of assets it receives upon issuance of the note generally equals the note's face value. Cole Williams Co. therefore will receive $100,000 cash and will make the following journal entry.

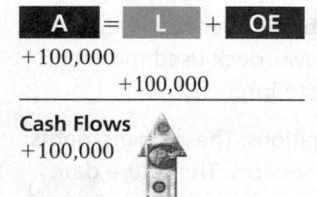

A = L + OE
+100,000
         +100,000

Cash Flows
+100,000

Sept. 1	Cash	100,000	
	Notes Payable		100,000
	(To record issuance of 12%, 4-month note		
	to First National Bank)		

Interest accrues over the life of the note, and the company must periodically record that accrual. If Cole Williams Co. prepares financial statements annually, it makes an adjusting entry at December 31 to recognize interest expense and interest payable of $4,000 ($100,000 × 12% × 4/12). Illustration 11-1 shows the formula for computing interest and its application to Cole Williams Co.'s note.

Illustration 11-1
Formula for computing interest

Face Value of Note	×	Annual Interest Rate	×	Time in Terms of One Year	=	Interest
$100,000	×	12%	×	4/12	=	**$4,000**

Cole Williams makes an adjusting entry as follows.

A = L + OE
        −4,000 Exp
        +4,000

Cash Flows
no effect

Dec. 31	Interest Expense	4,000	
	Interest Payable		4,000
	(To accrue interest for 4 months on		
	First National Bank note)		

In the December 31 financial statements, the current liabilities section of the balance sheet will show notes payable $100,000 and interest payable $4,000. In addition, the company will report interest expense of $4,000 under "Other expenses and losses" in the income statement. If Cole Williams Co. prepared financial statements monthly, the adjusting entry at the end of each month would be $1,000 ($100,000 × 12% × 1/12).

At maturity (January 1, 2015), Cole Williams Co. must pay the face value of the note ($100,000) plus $4,000 interest ($100,000 × 12% × 4/12). It records payment of the note and accrued interest as follows.

Jan. 1	Notes Payable	100,000	
	Interest Payable	4,000	
	Cash		104,000
	(To record payment of First National Bank interest-bearing note and accrued interest at maturity)		

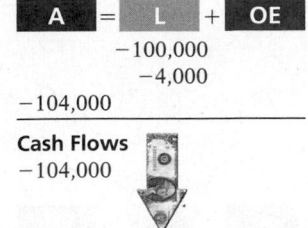

Sales Taxes Payable

As a consumer, you know that many of the products you purchase at retail stores are subject to sales taxes. Many states also are now collecting sales taxes on purchases made on the Internet as well. Sales taxes are expressed as a percentage of the sales price. The selling company collects the tax from the customer when the sale occurs. Periodically (usually monthly), the retailer remits the collections to the state's department of revenue. Collecting sales taxes is important. For example, the state of New York recently sued Sprint Corporation for $300 million for its alleged failure to collect sales taxes on phone calls.

Under most state sales tax laws, the selling company must enter separately in the cash register the amount of the sale and the amount of the sales tax collected. (Gasoline sales are a major exception.) The company then uses the cash register readings to credit Sales Revenue and Sales Taxes Payable. For example, if the March 25 cash register reading for Cooley Grocery shows sales of $10,000 and sales taxes of $600 (sales tax rate of 6%), the journal entry is:

LEARNING OBJECTIVE 3

Explain the accounting for other current liabilities.

Mar. 25	Cash	10,600	
	Sales Revenue		10,000
	Sales Taxes Payable		600
	(To record daily sales and sales taxes)		

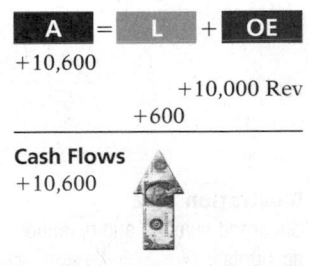

When the company remits the taxes to the taxing agency, it debits Sales Taxes Payable and credits Cash. The company does not report sales taxes as an expense. It simply forwards to the government the amount paid by the customers. Thus, Cooley Grocery serves only as a **collection agent** for the taxing authority.

Sometimes companies do not enter sales taxes separately in the cash register. To determine the amount of sales in such cases, divide total receipts by 100% plus the sales tax percentage. To illustrate, assume that in the above example Cooley Grocery enters total receipts of $10,600. The receipts from the sales are equal to the sales price (100%) plus the tax percentage (6% of sales), or 1.06 times the sales total. We can compute the sales amount as follows.

$$\$10,600 \div 1.06 = \$10,000$$

Thus, Cooley Grocery could find the sales tax amount it must remit to the state ($600) by subtracting sales from total receipts ($10,600 − $10,000).

Helpful Hint Alternatively, Cooley could find the tax by multiplying sales by the sales tax rate ($10,000 × .06).

Unearned Revenues

A magazine publisher, such as Sports Illustrated, receives customers' checks when they order magazines. An airline company, such as American Airlines, often receives cash when it sells tickets for future flights. Season tickets for concerts, sporting events, and theater programs are also paid for in advance. How do companies account for unearned revenues that are received before goods are delivered or services are performed?

1. When a company receives the advance payment, it debits Cash, and credits a current liability account identifying the source of the unearned revenue.

2. When the company recognizes revenue, it debits an unearned revenue account, and credits a revenue account.

To illustrate, assume that Superior University sells 10,000 season football tickets at $50 each for its five-game home schedule. The university makes the following entry for the sale of season tickets.

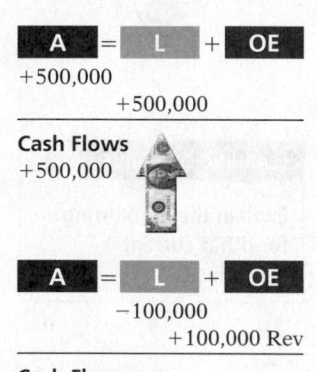

Aug. 6	Cash	500,000	
	Unearned Ticket Revenue		500,000
	(To record sale of 10,000 season tickets)		

As each game is completed, Superior records the recognition of revenue with the following entry.

Sept. 7	Unearned Ticket Revenue	100,000	
	Ticket Revenue		100,000
	(To record football ticket revenue)		

The account Unearned Ticket Revenue represents unearned revenue, and Superior reports it as a current liability. As the school recognizes revenue, it reclassifies the amount from unearned revenue to Ticket Revenue. Unearned revenue is material for some companies. In the airline industry, for example, tickets sold for future flights represent almost 50% of total current liabilities. At United Air Lines, unearned ticket revenue is its largest current liability, recently amounting to over $1 billion.

Illustration 11-2 shows specific unearned revenue and revenue accounts used in selected types of businesses.

Illustration 11-2
Unearned revenue and revenue accounts

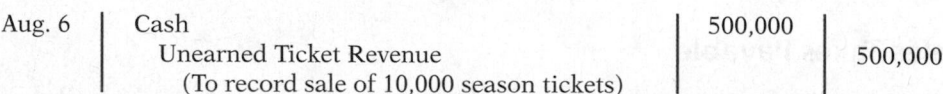

| | Account Title | |
Type of Business	Unearned Revenue	Revenue
Airline	Unearned Ticket Revenue	Ticket Revenue
Magazine publisher	Unearned Subscription Revenue	Subscription Revenue
Hotel	Unearned Rent Revenue	Rent Revenue

Current Maturities of Long-Term Debt

Companies often have a portion of long-term debt that comes due in the current year. That amount is considered a current liability. As an example, assume that Wendy Construction issues a five-year, interest-bearing $25,000 note on January 1, 2013. This note specifies that each January 1, starting January 1, 2014, Wendy should pay $5,000 of the note. When the company prepares financial statements on December 31, 2013, it should report $5,000 as a current liability and $20,000 as a long-term liability. (The $5,000 amount is the portion of the note that is due to be paid within the next 12 months.) Companies often identify current maturities of long-term debt on the balance sheet as **long-term debt due within one year**.

It is not necessary to prepare an adjusting entry to recognize the current maturity of long-term debt. At the balance sheet date, all obligations due within one year are classified as current, and all other obligations as long-term.

> **DO IT!**

Current Liabilities

Action Plan

✔ Use the interest formula: Face value of note × Annual interest rate × Time in terms of one year.

✔ Divide total receipts by 100% plus the tax rate to determine sales revenue; then subtract sales revenue from the total receipts.

✔ Determine what fraction of the total unearned rent should be recognized this year.

You and several classmates are studying for the next accounting examination. They ask you to answer the following questions.

1. If cash is borrowed on a $50,000, 6-month, 12% note on September 1, how much interest expense would be incurred by December 31?

2. How is the sales tax amount determined when the cash register total includes sales taxes?

3. If $15,000 is collected in advance on November 1 for 3 months' rent, what amount of rent revenue should be recognized by December 31?

Solution

1. $50,000 × 12% × 4/12 = $2,000
2. First, divide the total cash register receipts by 100% plus the sales tax percentage to find the sales revenue amount. Second, subtract the sales revenue amount from the total cash register receipts to determine the sales taxes.
3. $15,000 × 2/3 = $10,000

Related exercise material: **BE11-2, BE11-3, BE11-4, E11-1, E11-2, E11-3, E11-4, and DO IT! 11-1.**

 ✔ The Navigator

Statement Presentation and Analysis

PRESENTATION

As indicated in Chapter 4, current liabilities are the first category under liabilities on the balance sheet. Each of the principal types of current liabilities is listed separately. In addition, companies disclose the terms of notes payable and other key information about the individual items in the notes to the financial statements.

> LEARNING OBJECTIVE 4
>
> Explain the financial statement presentation and analysis of current liabilities.

Companies seldom list current liabilities in the order of liquidity. The reason is that varying maturity dates may exist for specific obligations such as notes payable. A more common method of presenting current liabilities is to list them by **order of magnitude**, with the largest ones first. Or, as a matter of custom, many companies show notes payable first, and then accounts payable, regardless of amount. Then the remaining current liabilities are listed by magnitude. (*Use this approach in your homework*.) Illustration 11-3 (page 528) provides an adapted excerpt from Caterpillar Inc.'s balance sheet, which illustrates its order of presentation.

ANALYSIS

Use of current and noncurrent classifications makes it possible to analyze a company's liquidity. **Liquidity** refers to the ability to pay maturing obligations and meet unexpected needs for cash. The relationship of current assets to current liabilities is critical in analyzing liquidity. We can express this relationship as a dollar amount (working capital) and as a ratio (the current ratio).

Illustration 11-3
Balance sheet presentation of current liabilities

Real World	**CATERPILLAR INC.** Balance Sheet December 31, 2011 (in millions)

Assets

Current assets	$38,128
Property, plant and equipment (net)	14,395
Other long-term assets	28,923
Total assets	$81,446

Liabilities and Stockholders' Equity

Current liabilities	
Short-term borrowings (notes payable)	$ 3,988
Accounts payable	8,161
Accrued expenses	3,386
Accrued wages, salaries, and employee benefits	2,410
Customer advances	2,691
Dividends payable	298
Other current liabilities	1,967
Long-term debt due within one year	5,660
Total current liabilities	28,561
Noncurrent liabilities	39,483
Total liabilities	68,044
Stockholders' equity	13,402
Total liabilities and stockholders' equity	$81,446

Helpful Hint For other examples of current liabilities sections, refer to the PepsiCo and Coca-Cola balance sheets in Appendices B and C.

The excess of current assets over current liabilities is **working capital**. Illustration 11-4 shows the formula for the computation of Caterpillar's working capital (dollar amounts in millions).

Illustration 11-4
Working capital formula and computation

Current Assets	−	Current Liabilities	=	Working Capital
$38,128	−	$28,561	=	$9,567

As an absolute dollar amount, working capital offers limited informational value. For example, $1 million of working capital may be more than needed for a small company but inadequate for a large corporation. Also, $1 million of working capital may be adequate for a company at one time but inadequate at another time.

The **current ratio** permits us to compare the liquidity of different-sized companies and of a single company at different times. The current ratio is calculated as current assets divided by current liabilities. Illustration 11-5 shows the formula for this ratio, along with its computation using Caterpillar's current asset and current liability data (dollar amounts in millions).

Illustration 11-5
Current ratio formula and computation

Current Assets	÷	Current Liabilities	=	Current Ratio
$38,128	÷	$28,561	=	1.33:1

Historically, companies and analysts considered a current ratio of 2:1 to be the standard for a good credit rating. In recent years, however, many healthy companies have maintained ratios well below 2:1 by improving management of their current assets and liabilities. Caterpillar's ratio of 1.33:1 is adequate but certainly below the standard of 2:1.

Contingent Liabilities

LEARNING OBJECTIVE   5

Describe the accounting and disclosure requirements for contingent liabilities.

With notes payable, interest payable, accounts payable, and sales taxes payable, we know that an obligation to make a payment exists. But, suppose that your company is involved in a dispute with the Internal Revenue Service (IRS) over the amount of its income tax liability. Should you report the disputed amount as a liability on the balance sheet? Or, suppose your company is involved in a lawsuit which, if you lose, might result in bankruptcy. How should you report this major contingency? The answers to these questions are difficult because these liabilities are dependent—contingent—upon some future event. In other words, a **contingent liability** is a potential liability that may become an actual liability in the future.

How should companies report contingent liabilities? They use the following guidelines:

1. If the contingency is **probable** (if it is likely to occur) **and** the amount can be **reasonably estimated**, the liability should be recorded in the accounts.

2. If the contingency is only **reasonably possible** (if it could happen), then it needs to be disclosed only in the notes that accompany the financial statements.

3. If the contingency is **remote** (if it is unlikely to occur), it need not be recorded or disclosed.

ACCOUNTING ACROSS THE ORGANIZATION

Contingencies: How Big Are They?

Contingent liabilities abound in the real world. Consider the following. Manville Corp. filed for bankruptcy when it was hit by billions of dollars in asbestos product-liability claims. Companies having multiple toxic waste sites are faced with cleanup costs that average $10 to $30 million and can reach as high as $500 million depending on the type of waste. For life and health insurance companies and their stockholders, the cost of diseases such as diabetes, Alzheimer's, and AIDS is like an iceberg: Everyone wonders how big such costs really are and what damage they might do in the future. And frequent-flyer programs are so popular that airlines at one time owed participants more than 3 million round-trip domestic tickets. That's enough to fly at least 5.4 billion miles—free for the passengers, but at what future cost to the airlines?

 Why do you think most companies disclose, but do not record, contingent liabilities? (See page 563.)

Recording a Contingent Liability

Product warranties are an example of a contingent liability that companies should record in the accounts. Warranty contracts result in future costs that companies may incur in replacing defective units or repairing malfunctioning units. Generally, a manufacturer, such as Stanley Black & Decker, knows that it will incur some warranty costs. From prior experience with the product, the company usually can reasonably estimate the anticipated cost of servicing (honoring) the warranty.

The accounting for warranty costs is based on the expense recognition principle. **The estimated cost of honoring product warranty contracts should be recognized as an expense in the period in which the sale occurs.** To illustrate, assume that in 2014 Denson Manufacturing Company sells 10,000 washers and dryers at an average price of $600 each. The selling price includes a one-year warranty on parts. Denson expects that 500 units (5%) will be defective and that warranty repair costs will average $80 per unit. In 2014, the company honors warranty contracts on 300 units, at a total cost of $24,000.

At December 31, it is necessary to accrue the estimated warranty costs on the 2014 sales. Denson computes the estimated warranty liability as follows.

Illustration 11-6
Computation of estimated warranty liability

Number of units sold	10,000
Estimated rate of defective units	× 5%
Total estimated defective units	500
Average warranty repair cost	× $80
Estimated warranty liability	**$40,000**

The company makes the following adjusting entry.

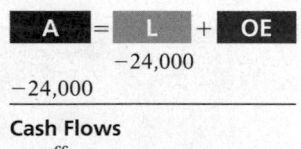

Cash Flows
no effect

Dec. 31	Warranty Expense	40,000	
	Warranty Liability		40,000
	(To accrue estimated warranty costs)		

Denson records those repair costs incurred in 2014 to honor warranty contracts on 2014 sales as shown below.

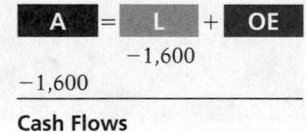

Cash Flows
no effect

Jan. 1–	Warranty Liability	24,000	
Dec. 31	Repair Parts		24,000
	(To record honoring of 300 warranty contracts on 2014 sales)		

The company reports warranty expense of $40,000 under selling expenses in the income statement. It classifies warranty liability of $16,000 ($40,000 − $24,000) as a current liability on the balance sheet.

In the following year, Denson should debit to Warranty Liability all expenses incurred in honoring warranty contracts on 2014 sales. To illustrate, assume that the company replaces 20 defective units in January 2015, at an average cost of $80 in parts and labor. The summary entry for the month of January 2015 is:

A = L + OE
−1,600
−1,600

Cash Flows
no effect

Jan. 31	Warranty Liability	1,600	
	Repair Parts		1,600
	(To record honoring of 20 warranty contracts on 2014 sales)		

Disclosure of Contingent Liabilities

When it is probable that a company will incur a contingent liability but it cannot reasonably estimate the amount, or when the contingent liability is only reasonably possible, only disclosure of the contingency is required. Examples of contingencies that may require disclosure are pending or threatened lawsuits and assessment of additional income taxes pending an IRS audit of the tax return.

The disclosure should identify the nature of the item and, if known, the amount of the contingency and the expected outcome of the future event. Disclosure is usually accomplished through a note to the financial statements, as shown in Illustration 11-7.

Illustration 11-7
Disclosure of contingent liability

Real World	**YAHOO! INC.** Notes to the Financial Statements

Contingencies. From time to time, third parties assert patent infringement claims against the company. Currently the company is engaged in several lawsuits regarding patent issues and has been notified of a number of other potential patent disputes. In addition, from time to time the company is subject to other legal proceedings and claims in the ordinary course of business, including claims for infringement of trademarks, copyrights and other intellectual property rights.... The company does not believe, based on current knowledge, that any of the foregoing legal proceedings or claims are likely to have a material adverse effect on the financial position, results of operations or cash flows.

The required disclosure for contingencies is a good example of the use of the full-disclosure principle. The **full-disclosure principle** requires that companies disclose all circumstances and events that would make a difference to financial statement users. Some important financial information, such as contingencies, is not easily reported in the financial statements. Reporting information on contingencies in the notes to the financial statements will help investors be aware of events that can affect the financial health of a company.

> **DO IT!**

Current Liabilities

Lepid Company has the following account balances at December 31, 2014.

Notes payable ($80,000 due after 12/31/15)	$200,000
Unearned service revenue	75,000
Other long-term debt ($30,000 due in 2015)	150,000
Salaries and wages payable	22,000
Other accrued expenses	15,000
Accounts payable	100,000

In addition, Lepid is involved in a lawsuit. Legal counsel feels it is probable Lepid will pay damages of $38,000 in 2015.

(a) Prepare the current liability section of Lepid's December 31, 2014, balance sheet.
(b) Lepid's current assets are $504,000. Compute Lepid's working capital and current ratio.

Solution

Action Plan

✔ Determine which liabilities will be paid within one year or the operating cycle and include those as current liabilities.

✔ If the contingent liability is probable and reasonably estimable, include it as a current liability.

✔ Use the formula for working capital: Current assets − Current liabilities.

✔ Use the formula for the current ratio: Current assets ÷ Current liabilities.

(a) Current liabilities

Notes payable	$120,000
Accounts payable	100,000
Unearned service revenue	75,000
Lawsuit liability	38,000
Salaries and wages payable	22,000
Other accrued expenses	15,000
Long-term debt due within one year	30,000
Total current liabilities	$400,000

(b) Working capital = Current assets − Current liabilities = $504,000 − $400,000 = $104,000
Current ratio = Current assets ÷ Current liabilities = $504,000 ÷ $400,000 = 1.26:1

Related exercise material: **BE11-5, E11-7, E11-8, E11-9, and DO IT! 11-2.**

 The Navigator

Payroll Accounting

Payroll and related fringe benefits often make up a large percentage of current liabilities. Employee compensation is often the most significant expense that a company incurs. For example, Costco recently reported total employees of 103,000 and labor and fringe benefits costs which approximated 70% of the company's total cost of operations.

Payroll accounting involves more than paying employees' wages. Companies are required by law to maintain payroll records for each employee, to file and pay payroll taxes, and to comply with state and federal tax laws related to employee compensation.

The term "payroll" **pertains to both salaries and wages of employees**. Managerial, administrative, and sales personnel are generally paid **salaries**. Salaries are often expressed in terms of a specified amount per month or per year rather than an hourly rate. Store clerks, factory employees, and manual laborers are normally paid **wages**. Wages are based on a rate per hour or on a piecework basis (such as per unit of product). Frequently, people use the terms "salaries" and "wages" interchangeably.

The term "payroll" **does not apply to payments made for services of professionals** such as certified public accountants, attorneys, and architects. Such professionals are independent contractors rather than salaried employees. Payments to them are called **fees**. This distinction is important because government regulations relating to the payment and reporting of payroll taxes apply only to employees.

Determining the Payroll

Determining the payroll involves computing three amounts: (1) gross earnings, (2) payroll deductions, and (3) net pay.

GROSS EARNINGS

Gross earnings is the total compensation earned by an employee. It consists of wages or salaries, plus any bonuses and commissions.

Companies determine total **wages** for an employee by multiplying the hours worked by the hourly rate of pay. In addition to the hourly pay rate, most companies are required by law to pay hourly workers a minimum of 1½ times the regular hourly rate for overtime work in excess of eight hours per day or 40 hours per week. In addition, many employers pay overtime rates for work done at night, on weekends, and on holidays.

For example, assume that Michael Jordan, an employee of Academy Company, worked 44 hours for the weekly pay period ending January 14. His regular wage is $12 per hour. For any hours in excess of 40, the company pays at one-and-a-half times the regular rate. Academy computes Jordan's gross earnings (total wages) as follows.

Illustration 11-8
Computation of total wages

Type of Pay	Hours	×	Rate	=	Gross Earnings
Regular	40	×	$12	=	$ 480
Overtime	4	×	18	=	72
Total wages					**$552**

This computation assumes that Jordan receives 1½ times his regular hourly rate ($12 × 1.5) for his overtime hours. Union contracts often require that overtime rates be as much as twice the regular rates.

An employee's **salary** is generally based on a monthly or yearly rate. The company then prorates these rates to its payroll periods (e.g., biweekly or monthly). Most executive and administrative positions are salaried. Federal law does not require overtime pay for employees in such positions.

Many companies have **bonus** agreements for employees. One survey found that over 94% of the largest U.S. manufacturing companies offer annual bonuses to key executives. Bonus arrangements may be based on such factors as increased sales or net income. Companies may pay bonuses in cash and/or by granting employees the opportunity to acquire shares of company stock at favorable prices (called stock option plans).

Ethics Note

Bonuses often reward outstanding individual performance, but successful corporations also need considerable teamwork. A challenge is to motivate individuals while preventing an unethical employee from taking another's idea for his or her own advantage.

PAYROLL DEDUCTIONS

As anyone who has received a paycheck knows, gross earnings are usually very different from the amount actually received. The difference is due to **payroll deductions**.

Payroll deductions may be mandatory or voluntary. **Mandatory deductions are required by law and consist of FICA taxes and income taxes.** Voluntary deductions are at the option of the employee. Illustration 11-9 summarizes common types of payroll deductions. Such deductions do not result in payroll tax expense to the employer. The employer is merely a collection agent, and subsequently transfers the deducted amounts to the government and designated recipients.

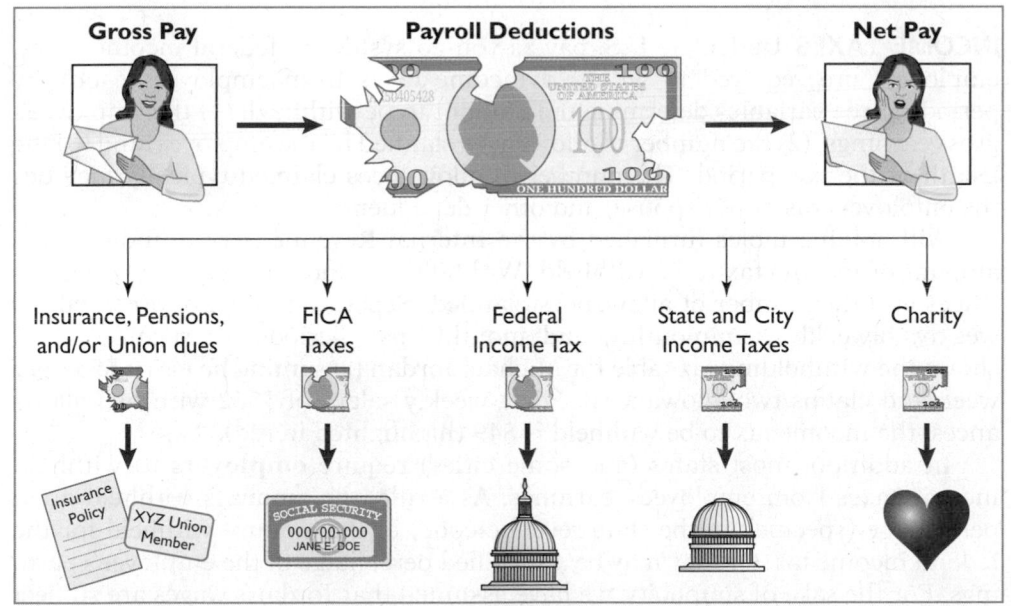

Illustration 11-9
Payroll deductions

FICA TAXES In 1937, Congress enacted the Federal Insurance Contribution Act (FICA). **FICA taxes are designed to provide workers with supplemental retirement, employment disability, and medical benefits.** In 1965, Congress extended benefits to include Medicare for individuals over 65 years of age. The benefits are financed by a tax levied on employees' earnings.

FICA taxes consist of a Social Security tax and a Medicare tax. They are paid by both employee and employer.[1] The FICA tax rate is 7.65% (6.2% Social Security

---

[1]Congress sets the tax rate and the tax base for FICA taxes. For example, in 2011 the tax rate on gross earnings subject to Social Security taxes for employees was lowered to 4.2% to provide more spendable income to stimulate the economy.

tax plus 1.45%) on the first $110,100 of salary and wages for each employee. In addition, the Medicare tax of 1.45% continues for an employee's salary and wages in excess of $110,100. These tax rate and tax base requirements are shown in Illustration 11-10.

Illustration 11-10
FICA tax rate and tax base

Social Security taxes

| Employee and employer | 6.2% on salary and wages up to $110,100 |

Medicare taxes

| Employee and employer | 1.45% on all salary and wages without limitation |

To illustrate the computation of FICA taxes, assume that Mario Ruez has total wages for the year of $100,000. In this case, Mario pays FICA taxes of $7,650 ($100,000 × 7.65%). If Mario has total wages of $114,000, Mario pays FICA taxes of $8,479.20, as shown in Illustration 11-11.

Illustration 11-11
FICA tax computation

Social Security tax	($110,100 × 6.2%)	$6,826.20
Medicare tax	($114,000 × 1.45%)	1,653.00
Total FICA taxes		$8,479.20

Mario's employer is also required to pay $8,479.20.

INCOME TAXES Under the U.S. pay-as-you-go system of federal income taxes, employers are required to withhold income taxes from employees each pay period. Three variables determine the amount to be withheld: (1) the employee's gross earnings, (2) the number of allowances claimed by the employee, and (3) the length of the pay period. The number of allowances claimed typically includes the employee, his or her spouse, and other dependents.

Withholding tables furnished by the Internal Revenue Service indicate the amount of income tax to be withheld. Withholding amounts are based on gross wages and the number of allowances claimed. Separate tables are provided for weekly, biweekly, semimonthly, and monthly pay periods. Illustration 11-12 shows the withholding tax table for Michael Jordan (assuming he earns $552 per week and claims two allowances). For a weekly salary of $552 with two allowances, the income tax to be withheld is $49 (highlighted in red).

In addition, most states (and some cities) require **employers** to withhold income taxes from employees' earnings. As a rule, the amounts withheld are a percentage (specified in the state revenue code) of the amount withheld for the federal income tax. Or they may be a specified percentage of the employee's earnings. For the sake of simplicity, we have assumed that Jordan's wages are subject to state income taxes of 2%, or $11.04 (2% × $552) per week.

There is no limit on the amount of gross earnings subject to income tax withholdings. In fact, under our progressive system of taxation, the higher the earnings, the higher the percentage of income withheld for taxes.

OTHER DEDUCTIONS Employees may voluntarily authorize withholdings for charitable organizations, retirement, and other purposes. All voluntary deductions from gross earnings should be authorized in writing by the employee. The authorization(s) may be made individually or as part of a group plan. Deductions for charitable organizations, such as the United Fund, or for financial arrangements, such as U.S. savings bonds and repayment of loans from company credit unions, are made individually. Deductions for union dues, health and life insurance, and pension plans are often made on a group basis. We will assume that

Illustration 11-12
Withholding tax table

MARRIED Persons — WEEKLY Payroll Period
(For Wages Paid in 2014)

If the wages are —		And the number of withholding allowances claimed is —										
At least	But less than	0	1	2	3	4	5	6	7	8	9	10
		The amount of income tax to be withheld is —										
490	500	56	48	40	32	24	17	9	1	0	0	0
500	510	57	49	42	34	26	18	10	3	0	0	0
510	520	59	51	43	35	27	20	12	4	0	0	0
520	530	60	52	45	37	29	21	13	6	0	0	0
530	540	62	54	46	38	30	23	15	7	0	0	0
540	550	63	55	48	40	32	24	16	9	1	0	0
550	560	65	57	49	41	33	26	18	10	2	0	0
560	570	66	58	51	43	35	27	19	12	4	0	0
570	580	68	60	52	44	36	29	21	13	5	0	0
580	590	69	61	54	46	38	30	22	15	7	0	0
590	600	71	63	55	47	39	32	24	16	8	1	0
600	610	72	64	57	49	41	33	25	18	10	2	0
610	620	74	66	58	50	42	35	27	19	11	4	0
620	630	75	67	60	52	44	36	28	21	13	5	0
630	640	77	69	61	53	45	38	30	22	14	7	0
640	650	78	70	63	55	47	39	31	24	16	8	0
650	660	80	72	64	56	48	41	33	25	17	10	2
660	670	81	73	66	58	50	42	34	27	19	11	3
670	680	83	75	67	59	51	44	36	28	20	13	5
680	690	84	76	69	61	53	45	37	30	22	14	6

Jordan has weekly voluntary deductions of $10 for the United Fund and $5 for union dues.

NET PAY

Academy Company determines **net pay** by subtracting payroll deductions from gross earnings. Illustration 11-13 shows the computation of Jordan's net pay for the pay period.

Alternative Terminology
Net pay is also called *take-home pay.*

Illustration 11-13
Computation of net pay

Gross earnings		$ 552.00
Payroll deductions:		
FICA taxes	$42.23	
Federal income taxes	49.00	
State income taxes	11.04	
United Fund	10.00	
Union dues	5.00	117.27
Net pay		**$434.73**

Assuming that Michael Jordan's wages for each week during the year are $552, total wages for the year are $28,704 (52 × $552). Thus, all of Jordan's wages are subject to FICA tax during the year. In comparison, let's assume that Jordan's department head earns $2,200 per week, or $114,400 for the year. Since only the first $110,100 is subject to FICA taxes, the maximum FICA withholdings on the department head's earnings would be $8,485 [($110,100 × 6.20%) + ($114,400 × 1.45%)].

Recording the Payroll

Recording the payroll involves maintaining payroll department records, recognizing payroll expenses and liabilities, and recording payment of the payroll.

MAINTAINING PAYROLL DEPARTMENT RECORDS

To comply with state and federal laws, an employer must keep a cumulative record of each employee's gross earnings, deductions, and net pay during the year. The record that provides this information is the **employee earnings record**. Illustration 11-14 shows Michael Jordan's employee earnings record.

| | | Academy Company.xls | | | | | | | | | | | |

Home   Insert   Page Layout   Formulas   Data   Review   View

P18   fx

	A	B	C	D	E	F	G	H	I	J	K	L	M	N

ACADEMY COMPANY
Employee Earnings Record
For the Year 2014

Name	Michael Jordan		Address	2345 Mifflin Ave.
Social Security Number	329-35-9547			Hampton, Michigan 48292
Date of Birth	December 24, 1964		Telephone	555-238-9051
Date Employed	September 1, 2005		Date Employment Ended	
Sex	Male		Exemptions	2
Single _____	Married ___x___			

2014 Period Ending	Total Hours	Gross Earnings				Deductions						Payment	
		Regular	Overtime	Total	Cumulative	FICA	Fed. Inc. Tax	State Inc. Tax	United Fund	Union Dues	Total	Net Amount	Check No.
1/7	42	480.00	36.00	516.00	516.00	39.47	43.00	10.32	10.00	5.00	107.79	408.21	974
1/14	44	480.00	72.00	552.00	1,068.00	42.23	49.00	11.04	10.00	5.00	117.27	434.73	1028
1/21	43	480.00	54.00	534.00	1,602.00	40.85	46.00	10.68	10.00	5.00	112.53	421.47	1077
1/28	42	480.00	36.00	516.00	2,118.00	39.47	43.00	10.32	10.00	5.00	107.79	408.21	1133
Jan. Total		1,920.00	198.00	2,118.00		162.02	181.00	42.36	40.00	20.00	445.38	1,672.62	

Illustration 11-14
Employee earnings record

Companies keep a separate earnings record for each employee and update these records after each pay period. The employer uses the cumulative payroll data on the earnings record to: (1) determine when an employee has earned the maximum earnings subject to FICA taxes, (2) file state and federal payroll tax returns (as explained later), and (3) provide each employee with a statement of gross earnings and tax withholdings for the year. Illustration 11-18 on page 542 shows this statement.

In addition to employee earnings records, many companies find it useful to prepare a **payroll register**. This record accumulates the gross earnings, deductions, and net pay by employee for each pay period. Illustration 11-15 presents Academy Company's payroll register. It provides the documentation for preparing a paycheck for each employee. For example, it shows the data for Michael Jordan in the wages section. In this example, Academy Company's total weekly payroll is $17,210, as shown in the gross earnings column (column E, row 24).

Note that this record is a listing of each employee's payroll data for the pay period. In some companies, a payroll register is a journal or book of original entry. Postings are made from it directly to ledger accounts. In other companies, the payroll register is a memorandum record that provides the data for a general journal entry and subsequent posting to the ledger accounts. At Academy Company, the latter procedure is followed.

	A	B	C	D	E	F	G	H	I	J	K	L	M	N
							ACADEMY COMPANY							
							Payroll Register							
							For the Week Ending January 14, 2014							
5			Earnings				Deductions					Paid		Account Debited
6							Federal	State						Salaries and
7		Total		Over-			Income	Income	United	Union			Check	Wages
8	Employee	Hours	Regular	time	Gross	FICA	Tax	Tax	Fund	Dues	Total	Net Pay	No.	Expense
10	Arnold, Patricia	40	580.00		580.00	44.37	61.00	11.60	15.00		131.97	448.03	998	580.00
11	Canton, Matthew	40	590.00		590.00	45.14	63.00	11.80	20.00		139.94	450.06	999	590.00
21	Mueller, William	40	530.00		530.00	40.55	54.00	10.60	11.00		116.15	413.85	1000	530.00
22	Bennett, Robin	42	480.00	36.00	516.00	39.47	43.00	10.32	18.00	5.00	115.79	400.21	1025	516.00
23	Jordan, Michael	44	480.00	72.00	552.00	42.23	49.00	11.04	10.00	5.00	117.27	434.73	1028	552.00
29	Milroy, Lee	43	480.00	54.00	534.00	40.85	46.00	10.68	10.00	5.00	112.53	421.47	1029	534.00
31	Total		16,200.00	1,010.00	17,210.00	1,316.57	3,490.00	344.20	421.50	115.00	5,687.27	11,522.73		17,210.00

Illustration 11-15
Payroll register

RECOGNIZING PAYROLL EXPENSES AND LIABILITIES

From the payroll register in Illustration 11-15, Academy Company makes a journal entry to record the payroll. For the week ending January 14, the entry is:

Jan. 14	Salaries and Wages Expense	17,210.00	
	FICA Taxes Payable		1,316.57
	Federal Income Taxes Payable		3,490.00
	State Income Taxes Payable		344.20
	United Fund Payable		421.50
	Union Dues Payable		115.00
	Salaries and Wages Payable		11,522.73
	(To record payroll for the week ending January 14)		

A = L + OE
−17,210.00 Exp
+1,316.57
+3,490.00
+344.20
+421.50
+115.00
+11,522.73

Cash Flows
no effect

The company credits specific liability accounts for the mandatory and voluntary deductions made during the pay period. In the example, Academy debits Salaries and Wages Expense for the gross earnings of its employees. The amount credited to Salaries and Wages Payable is the sum of the individual checks the employees will receive.

RECORDING PAYMENT OF THE PAYROLL

A company makes payments by check (or electronic funds transfer) either from its regular bank account or a payroll bank account. Each paycheck is usually accompanied by a detachable **statement of earnings** document. This shows the employee's gross earnings, payroll deductions, and net pay, both for the period and for the year-to-date. Academy Company uses its regular bank account for payroll checks. Illustration 11-16 (page 538) shows the paycheck and statement of earnings for Michael Jordan.

Illustration 11-16
Paycheck and statement of earnings

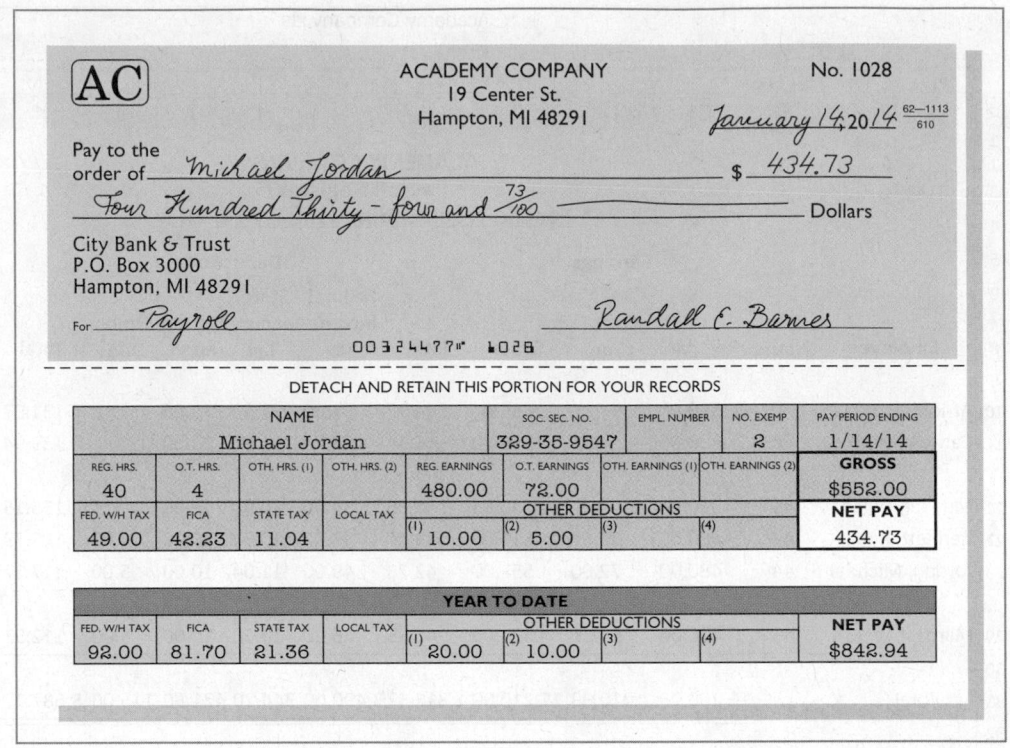

Helpful Hint Do any of the income tax liabilities result in payroll tax expense for the employer?
Answer: No. The employer is acting only as a collection agent for the government.

Following payment of the payroll, the company enters the check numbers in the payroll register. Academy Company records payment of the payroll as follows.

| A | = | L | + | OE |

−11,522.73
−11,522.73

Cash Flows
−11,522.73

Jan. 14	Salaries and Wages Payable	11,522.73	
	Cash		11,522.73
	(To record payment of payroll)		

Many medium- and large-size companies use a payroll processing center that performs payroll recordkeeping services. Companies send the center payroll information about employee pay rates and hours worked. The center maintains the payroll records and prepares the payroll checks. In most cases, it costs less to process the payroll through the center (outsource) than if the company did so internally.

> **DO IT!**

Payroll

Action Plan

✔ Determine net pay by subtracting payroll deductions from gross earnings.

✔ Record gross earnings as Salaries and Wages Expense, record payroll deductions as liabilities, and record net pay as Salaries and Wages Payable.

In January, gross earnings in Ramirez Company were $40,000. All earnings are subject to 7.65% FICA taxes. Federal income tax withheld was $9,000, and state income tax withheld was $1,000. (a) Calculate net pay for January, and (b) record the payroll.

Solution

(a) Net pay: $40,000 − (7.65% × $40,000) − $9,000 − $1,000 = $26,940

(b) Salaries and Wages Expense	40,000	
FICA Taxes Payable		3,060
Federal Income Taxes Payable		9,000
State Income Taxes Payable		1,000
Salaries and Wages Payable		26,940
(To record payroll)		

Related exercise material: **BE11-7, BE11-8, E11-10, E11-11, E11-12, E11-13, and DO IT! 11-3.**

✔ The Navigator

Employer Payroll Taxes

Payroll tax expense for businesses results from three taxes that governmental agencies levy **on employers**. These taxes are (1) FICA, (2) federal unemployment tax, and (3) state unemployment tax. These taxes plus such items as paid vacations and pensions (discussed in the appendix to this chapter) are collectively referred to as **fringe benefits**. As indicated earlier, the cost of fringe benefits in many companies is substantial.

> **LEARNING OBJECTIVE   7**
>
> Describe and record employer payroll taxes.

FICA TAXES

Each employee must pay FICA taxes. In addition, employers must match each employee's FICA contribution. This means the employer must remit to the federal government 12.4% of each employee's first $110,100 of taxable earnings, plus 2.9% of each employee's earnings, regardless of amount. The matching contribution results in **payroll tax expense** to the employer. The employer's tax is subject to the same rate and maximum earnings as the employee's. The company uses the same account, FICA Taxes Payable, to record both the employee's and the employer's FICA contributions. For the January 14 payroll, Academy Company's FICA tax contribution is $1,316.57 ($17,210.00 × 7.65%).

FEDERAL UNEMPLOYMENT TAXES

The Federal Unemployment Tax Act (FUTA) is another feature of the federal Social Security program. **Federal unemployment taxes** provide benefits for a limited period of time to employees who lose their jobs through no fault of their own. The FUTA tax rate is 6.2% of taxable wages. The taxable wage base is the first $7,000 of wages paid to each employee in a calendar year. Employers who pay the state unemployment tax on a timely basis will receive an offset credit of up to 5.4%. Therefore, the net federal tax rate is generally 0.8% (6.2% − 5.4%). This rate would equate to a maximum of $56 of federal tax per employee per year (0.8% × $7,000). State tax rates are based on state law.

The **employer** bears the entire federal unemployment tax. There is no deduction or withholding from employees. Companies use the account Federal Unemployment Taxes Payable to recognize this liability. The federal unemployment tax for Academy Company for the January 14 payroll is $137.68 ($17,210.00 × 0.8%).

Helpful Hint Both the employer and employee pay FICA taxes. Federal unemployment taxes and (in most states) the state unemployment taxes are borne entirely by the employer.

STATE UNEMPLOYMENT TAXES

All states have unemployment compensation programs under state unemployment tax acts (SUTA). Like federal unemployment taxes, **state unemployment taxes** provide benefits to employees who lose their jobs. These taxes are levied on employers.[2] The basic rate is usually 5.4% on the first $7,000 of wages paid to an employee during the year. The state adjusts the basic rate according to the employer's experience rating: Companies with a history of stable employment may pay less than 5.4%. Companies with a history of unstable employment may pay more than the basic rate. Regardless of the rate paid, the company's credit on the federal unemployment tax is still 5.4%.

Companies use the account State Unemployment Taxes Payable for this liability. The state unemployment tax for Academy Company for the January 14 payroll is $929.34 ($17,210.00 × 5.4%). Illustration 11-17 (page 540) summarizes the types of employer payroll taxes.

RECORDING EMPLOYER PAYROLL TAXES

Companies usually record employer payroll taxes at the same time they record the payroll. The entire amount of gross pay ($17,210.00) shown in the payroll register in Illustration 11-15 is subject to each of the three taxes mentioned above.

---

[2]In a few states, the employee is also required to make a contribution. *In this textbook, including the homework, we will assume that the tax is only on the employer.*

Illustration 11-17
Employer payroll
taxes

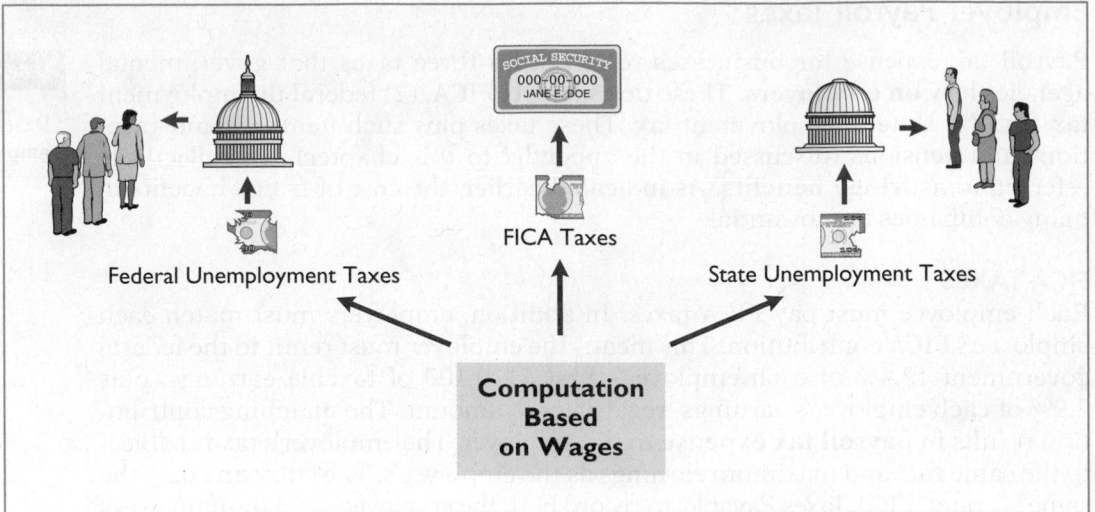

Federal Unemployment Taxes   FICA Taxes   State Unemployment Taxes

Computation
Based
on Wages

Accordingly, Academy records the payroll tax expense associated with the January 14 payroll with the following entry.

A	=	L	+	OE
		−2,383.59 Exp		
+1,316.57				
+137.68				
+929.34				

Cash Flows
no effect

Jan. 14	Payroll Tax Expense	2,383.59	
	FICA Taxes Payable		1,316.57
	Federal Unemployment Taxes Payable		137.68
	State Unemployment Taxes Payable		929.34
	(To record employer's payroll taxes on January 14 payroll)		

Note that Academy uses separate liability accounts instead of a single credit to Payroll Taxes Payable. Why? Because these liabilities are payable to different taxing authorities at different dates. Companies classify the liability accounts in the balance sheet as current liabilities since they will be paid within the next year. They classify Payroll Tax Expense on the income statement as an operating expense.

ACCOUNTING ACROSS THE ORGANIZATION

It Costs $74,000 to Put $44,000 in Sally's Pocket

© svetikd/iStockphoto

Sally works for Bogan Communications, a small company in New Jersey that provides audio systems. She makes $59,000 a year but only nets $44,000. What happened to the other $15,000? Well, $2,376 goes for Sally's share of the medical and dental insurance that Bogan provides, $126 for state unemployment insurance, $149 for disability insurance, and $856 for Medicare. New Jersey takes $1,893 in income taxes, and the federal government gets $3,658 for Social Security and another $6,250 for income tax withholding. All of this adds up to some 22% of Sally's gross pay going to Washington or Trenton.

Employing Sally costs Bogan plenty too. Bogan has to write checks for $74,000 so Sally can receive her $59,000 in base pay. Health insurance is the biggest cost: While Sally pays nearly $2,400 for coverage, Bogan pays the rest—$9,561. Then, the federal and state governments take $56 for federal unemployment coverage, $149 for disability insurance, $300 for workers' comp, and $505 for state unemployment insurance. Finally, the government requires Bogan to pay $856 for Sally's Medicare and $3,658 for her Social Security.

When you add it all up, it costs $74,000 to put $44,000 in Sally's pocket and to give her $12,000 in benefits.

Source: Michael P. Fleischer, "Why I'm Not Hiring," *Wall Street Journal* (August 9, 2010), p. A17.

? How are the Social Security and Medicare taxes computed for Sally's salary? (See page 563.)

> **DO IT!**

Employer's Payroll Taxes

In January, the payroll supervisor determines that gross earnings for Halo Company are $70,000. All earnings are subject to 7.65% FICA taxes, 5.4% state unemployment taxes, and 0.8% federal unemployment taxes. Halo asks you to record the employer's payroll taxes.

Action Plan

✔ Compute the employer's payroll taxes on the period's gross earnings.

✔ Identify the expense account(s) to be debited.

✔ Identify the liability account(s) to be credited.

Solution

The entry to record the employer's payroll taxes is:

Payroll Tax Expense	9,695	
FICA Taxes Payable ($70,000 × 7.65%)		5,355
Federal Unemployment Taxes Payable ($70,000 × 0.8%)		560
State Unemployment Taxes Payable ($70,000 × 5.4%)		3,780
(To record employer's payroll taxes on January payroll)		

Related exercise material: **BE11-9, E11-12, E11-14, and DO IT! 11-4.**

✔ **The Navigator**

Filing and Remitting Payroll Taxes

Preparation of payroll tax returns is the responsibility of the payroll department. The treasurer's department makes the tax payment. Much of the information for the returns is obtained from employee earnings records.

For purposes of reporting and remitting to the IRS, the company combines the FICA taxes and federal income taxes that it withheld. **Companies must report the taxes quarterly**, no later than one month following the close of each quarter. The remitting requirements depend on the amount of taxes withheld and the length of the pay period. Companies remit funds through deposits in either a Federal Reserve bank or an authorized commercial bank.

Companies generally file and remit federal unemployment taxes **annually** on or before January 31 of the subsequent year. Earlier payments are required when the tax exceeds a specified amount. Companies usually must file and pay state unemployment taxes by the **end of the month following each quarter**. When payroll taxes are paid, companies debit payroll liability accounts, and credit Cash.

ANATOMY OF A FRAUD

Art was a custodial supervisor for a large school district. The district was supposed to employ between 35 and 40 regular custodians, as well as 3 or 4 substitute custodians to fill in when regular custodians were missing. Instead, in addition to the regular custodians, Art "hired" 77 substitutes. In fact, almost none of these people worked for the district. Instead, Art submitted time cards for these people, collected their checks at the district office, and personally distributed the checks to the "employees." If a substitute's check was for $1,200, that person would cash the check, keep $200, and pay Art $1,000.

Total take: $150,000

The Missing Controls

Human Resource Controls. Thorough background checks should be performed. No employees should begin work until they have been approved by the Board of Education and entered into the payroll system. No employees should be entered into the payroll system until they have been approved by a supervisor. All paychecks should be distributed directly to employees at the official school locations by designated employees.

Independent internal verification. Budgets should be reviewed monthly to identify situations where actual costs significantly exceed budgeted amounts.

Source: Adapted from Wells, *Fraud Casebook* (2007), pp. 164–171.

Employers also must provide each employee with a **Wage and Tax Statement (Form W-2)** by January 31 following the end of a calendar year. This statement shows gross earnings, FICA taxes withheld, and income taxes withheld for the year. The required W-2 form for Michael Jordan, using assumed annual data, is shown in Illustration 11-18. The employer must send a copy of each employee's Wage and Tax Statement (Form W-2) to the Social Security Administration. This agency subsequently furnishes the Internal Revenue Service with the income data required.

Illustration 11-18
W-2 form

22222	Void ☐	a Employee's social security number 329-35-9547	For Official Use Only ► OMB No. 1545-0008	

b Employer identification number (EIN) 36-2167852

c Employer's name, address, and ZIP code
Academy Company
19 Center St.
Hampton, MI 48291

d Control number

e Employee's first name and initial: Michael   Last name: Jordan   Suff.
2345 Mifflin Ave.
Hampton, MI 48292

f Employee's address and ZIP code

Box	Description	Amount
1	Wages, tips, other compensation	26,300.00
2	Federal income tax withheld	2,248.00
3	Social security wages	26,300.00
4	Social security tax withheld	2,011.95
5	Medicare wages and tips	26,300.00
6	Medicare tax withheld	
7	Social security tips	
8	Allocated tips	
9	Advance EIC payment	
10	Dependent care benefits	
11	Nonqualified plans	
12a	See instructions for box 12	
13	Statutory employee ☐ Retirement plan ☐ Third-party sick pay ☐	
12b		
14	Other	
12c		
12d		

15 State	Employer's state ID number	16 State wages, tips, etc.	17 State income tax	18 Local wages, tips, etc.	19 Local income tax	20 Locality name
MI	423-1466-3	26,300.00	526.00			

Form **W-2** Wage and Tax Statement   **2014**   Department of the Treasury—Internal Revenue Service

Copy A For Social Security Administration — Send this entire page with Form W-3 to the Social Security Administration; photocopies are **not** acceptable.

For Privacy Act and Paperwork Reduction Act Notice, see back of Copy D.

Cat. No. 10134D

Internal Control for Payroll

Chapter 8 introduced internal control. As applied to payrolls, the objectives of internal control are (1) to safeguard company assets against unauthorized payments of payrolls, and (2) to ensure the accuracy and reliability of the accounting records pertaining to payrolls.

Irregularities often result if internal control is lax. Frauds involving payroll include overstating hours, using unauthorized pay rates, adding fictitious employees to the payroll, continuing terminated employees on the payroll, and distributing duplicate payroll checks. Moreover, inaccurate records will result in incorrect paychecks, financial statements, and payroll tax returns.

Payroll activities involve four functions: hiring employees, timekeeping, preparing the payroll, and paying the payroll. For effective internal control, companies should assign these four functions to different departments or individuals. Illustration 11-19 highlights these functions and illustrates their internal control features.

Payroll Function		Payroll Function	
Hiring Employees	**Internal control feature:** Human Resources department documents and authorizes employment. **Fraud prevented:** Fictitious employees are not added to payroll.	**Preparing the Payroll**	**Internal control feature:** Two (or more) employees verify payroll amounts; supervisor approves. **Fraud prevented:** Payroll calculations are accurate and relevant.
Timekeeping	**Internal control feature:** Supervisors monitor hours worked through time cards and time reports. **Fraud prevented:** Employee not paid for hours not worked.	**Paying the Payroll**	**Internal control feature:** Treasurer signs and distributes prenumbered checks. **Fraud prevented:** Checks are not lost, misappropriated, or unavailable for proof of payment; endorsed check provides proof of payment.

Illustration 11-19
Internal control for payroll

> Comprehensive DO IT!

Indiana Jones Company had the following selected transactions.

Feb. 1 Signs a $50,000, 6-month, 9%-interest-bearing note payable to CitiBank and receives $50,000 in cash.

10 Cash register sales total $43,200, which includes an 8% sales tax.

28 The payroll for the month consists of salaries and wages of $50,000. All wages are subject to 7.65% FICA taxes. A total of $8,900 federal income taxes are withheld. The salaries are paid on March 1.

28 The company develops the following adjustment data.
1. Interest expense of $375 has been incurred on the note.
2. Employer payroll taxes include 7.65% FICA taxes, a 5.4% state unemployment tax, and a 0.8% federal unemployment tax.
3. Some sales were made under warranty. Of the units sold under warranty, 350 are expected to become defective. Repair costs are estimated to be $40 per unit.

Instructions
(a) Journalize the February transactions.
(b) Journalize the adjusting entries at February 28.

Solution to Comprehensive DO IT!

Action Plan

✔ To determine sales revenue, divide the cash register total by 100% plus the sales tax percentage.

✔ Base payroll taxes on gross earnings.

✔ Expense warranty costs in the period in which the sale occurs.

(a) Feb. 1	Cash	50,000	
	Notes Payable		50,000
	(Issued 6-month, 9%-interest-bearing note to CitiBank)		
10	Cash	43,200	
	Sales Revenue ($43,200 ÷ 1.08)		40,000
	Sales Taxes Payable ($40,000 × 8%)		3,200
	(To record sales revenue and sales taxes payable)		

28	Salaries and Wages Expense		50,000	
		FICA Taxes Payable (7.65% × $50,000)		3,825
		Federal Income Taxes Payable		8,900
		Salaries and Wages Payable		37,275
		(To record February salaries)		
(b) Feb. 28	Interest Expense		375	
		Interest Payable		375
		(To record accrued interest for February)		
28	Payroll Tax Expense		6,925	
		FICA Taxes Payable		3,825
		Federal Unemployment Taxes Payable (0.8% × $50,000)		400
		State Unemployment Taxes Payable (5.4% × $50,000)		2,700
		(To record employer's payroll taxes on February payroll)		
28	Warranty Expense (350 × $40)		14,000	
		Warranty Liability		14,000
		(To record estimated warranty liability)		

 The Navigator

SUMMARY OF LEARNING OBJECTIVES

The Navigator

1 Explain a current liability, and identify the major types of current liabilities. A current liability is a debt that a company expects to pay within one year or the operating cycle, whichever is longer. The major types of current liabilities are notes payable, accounts payable, sales taxes payable, unearned revenues, and accrued liabilities such as taxes, salaries and wages, and interest payable.

2 Describe the accounting for notes payable. When a promissory note is interest-bearing, the amount of assets received upon the issuance of the note is generally equal to the face value of the note. Interest expense accrues over the life of the note. At maturity, the amount paid equals the face value of the note plus accrued interest.

3 Explain the accounting for other current liabilities. Companies record sales taxes payable at the time the related sales occur. The company serves as a collection agent for the taxing authority. Sales taxes are not an expense to the company. Companies initially record unearned revenues in an Unearned Revenue account. As a company recognizes revenue, a transfer from unearned revenue to revenue occurs. Companies report the current maturities of long-term debt as a current liability in the balance sheet.

4 Explain the financial statement presentation and analysis of current liabilities. Companies should report the nature and amount of each current liability in the balance sheet or in schedules in the notes accompanying the statements. The liquidity of a company may be analyzed by computing working capital and the current ratio.

5 Describe the accounting and disclosure requirements for contingent liabilities. If the contingency is **probable** (likely to occur) and the amount is reasonably estimable, the company should record the liability in the accounts. If the contingency is only **reasonably possible** (it could happen), then it should be disclosed only in the notes to the financial statements. If the possibility that the contingency will happen is **remote** (unlikely to occur), it need not be recorded or disclosed.

6 Compute and record the payroll for a pay period. The computation of the payroll involves gross earnings, payroll deductions, and net pay. In recording the payroll, companies debit Salaries and Wages Expense for gross earnings, credit individual tax and other liability accounts for payroll deductions, and credit Salaries and Wages Payable for net pay. When the payroll is paid, companies debit Salaries and Wages Payable and credit Cash.

7 Describe and record employer payroll taxes. Employer payroll taxes consist of FICA, federal unemployment taxes, and state unemployment taxes. The taxes are usually accrued at the time the company records the payroll, by debiting Payroll Tax Expense and crediting separate liability accounts for each type of tax.

8 Discuss the objectives of internal control for payroll. The objectives of internal control for payroll are (1) to safeguard company assets against unauthorized payments of payrolls, and (2) to ensure the accuracy of the accounting records pertaining to payrolls.

GLOSSARY

Bonus Compensation to management and other personnel, based on factors such as increased sales or the amount of net income. (p. 533).

Contingent liability A potential liability that may become an actual liability in the future. (p. 529).

Current ratio A measure of a company's liquidity; computed as current assets divided by current liabilities. (p. 528).

Employee earnings record A cumulative record of each employee's gross earnings, deductions, and net pay during the year. (p. 536).

Federal unemployment taxes Taxes imposed on the employer by the federal government that provide benefits for a limited time period to employees who lose their jobs through no fault of their own. (p. 539).

Fees Payments made for the services of professionals. (p. 532).

FICA taxes Taxes designed to provide workers with supplemental retirement, employment disability, and medical benefits. (p. 533).

Full-disclosure principle Requires that companies disclose all circumstances and events that would make a difference to financial statement users. (p. 531).

Gross earnings Total compensation earned by an employee. (p. 532).

Net pay Gross earnings less payroll deductions. (p. 535).

Notes payable Obligations in the form of written notes. (p. 524).

Payroll deductions Deductions from gross earnings to determine the amount of a paycheck. (p. 533).

Payroll register A payroll record that accumulates the gross earnings, deductions, and net pay by employee for each pay period. (p. 536).

Salaries Employee pay based on a specified amount rather than an hourly rate. (p. 532).

Statement of earnings A document attached to a paycheck that indicates the employee's gross earnings, payroll deductions, and net pay. (p. 537).

State unemployment taxes Taxes imposed on the employer by states that provide benefits to employees who lose their jobs. (p. 539).

Wage and Tax Statement (Form W-2) A form showing gross earnings, FICA taxes withheld, and income taxes withheld, prepared annually by an employer for each employee. (p. 542).

Wages Amounts paid to employees based on a rate per hour or on a piecework basis. (p. 532).

Working capital A measure of a company's liquidity; computed as current assets minus current liabilities. (p. 528).

APPENDIX 11A   Additional Fringe Benefits

In addition to the traditional payroll-tax fringe benefits (Social Security taxes, Medicare taxes, and state and federal unemployment taxes), employers incur other substantial fringe benefit costs. Two of the most important are paid absences and postretirement benefits.

> **LEARNING OBJECTIVE   9**
>
> Identify additional fringe benefits associated with employee compensation.

Paid Absences

Employees often are given rights to receive compensation for absences when they meet certain conditions of employment. The compensation may be for paid vacations, sick pay benefits, and paid holidays. When the payment for such absences is **probable** and the amount can be **reasonably estimated**, the company should accrue a liability for paid future absences. When the amount cannot be reasonably estimated, the company should instead disclose the potential liability. Ordinarily, vacation pay is the only paid absence that is accrued. The other types of paid absences are only disclosed.

To illustrate, assume that Academy Company employees are entitled to one day's vacation for each month worked. If 30 employees earn an average of $110 per day in a given month, the accrual for vacation benefits in one month is $3,300. Academy records the liability at the end of the month by the following adjusting entry.

Jan. 31	Vacation Benefits Expense	3,300	
	Vacation Benefits Payable		3,300
	(To accrue vacation benefits expense)		

A = L + OE
−3,300 Exp
+3,300

Cash Flows
no effect

This accrual is required by the expense recognition principle. Academy would report Vacation Benefits Expense as an operating expense in the income statement, and Vacation Benefits Payable as a current liability in the balance sheet.

Later, when Academy pays vacation benefits, it debits Vacation Benefits Payable and credits Cash. For example, if employees take 10 days of vacation in July, the entry is:

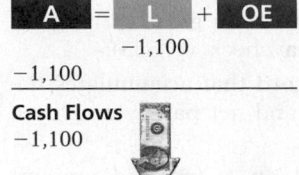

July 31	Vacation Benefits Payable	1,100	
	Cash		1,100
	(To record payment of vacation benefits)		

The magnitude of unpaid absences has gained employers' attention. Consider the case of an assistant superintendent of schools who worked for 20 years and rarely took a vacation or sick day. A month or so before she retired, the school district discovered that she was due nearly $30,000 in accrued benefits. Yet the school district had never accrued the liability.

Postretirement Benefits

Postretirement benefits are benefits that employers provide to retired employees for (1) pensions and (2) health care and life insurance. Companies account for both types of postretirement benefits on the accrual basis. The cost of postretirement benefits is getting steep. For example, states and localities must deal with a $1 trillion deficit in public employees' retirement benefit funds. This shortfall amounts to more than $8,800 for every household in the nation.

The average American has debt of approximately $10,000 (not counting the mortgage on their home) and has little in the way of savings. What will happen at retirement for these people? The picture is not pretty—people are living longer, the future of Social Security is unclear, and companies are cutting back on postretirement benefits. This situation may lead to one of the great social and moral dilemmas this country faces in the next 40 years. The more you know about postretirement benefits, the better you will understand the issues involved in this dilemma.

POSTRETIREMENT HEALTH-CARE AND LIFE INSURANCE BENEFITS

Providing medical and related health-care benefits for retirees was at one time an inexpensive and highly effective way of generating employee goodwill. This practice has now turned into one of corporate America's most worrisome financial problems. Runaway medical costs, early retirement, and increased longevity are sending the liability for retiree health plans through the roof.

Companies estimate and expense postretirement costs during the working years of the employee because the company benefits from the employee's services during this period. However, the company rarely sets up funds to meet the cost of the future benefits. It follows a pay-as-you-go basis for these costs. The major reason is that the company does not receive a tax deduction until it actually pays the medical bill.

PENSION PLANS

A **pension plan** is an agreement whereby an employer provides benefits (payments) to employees after they retire. The need for good accounting for pension plans becomes apparent when we consider the size of existing pension funds. Over 50 million workers currently participate in pension plans in the United States. Most pension plans are subject to the provisions of ERISA (Employee Retirement Income Security Act), a law enacted to curb abuses in the administration and funding of such plans.

Three parties are generally involved in a pension plan. The **employer** (company) sponsors the pension plan. The **plan administrator** receives the contributions from the employer, invests the pension assets, and makes the benefit payments to the **pension recipients** (retired employees). Illustration 11A-1 indicates the flow of cash among the three parties involved in a pension plan.

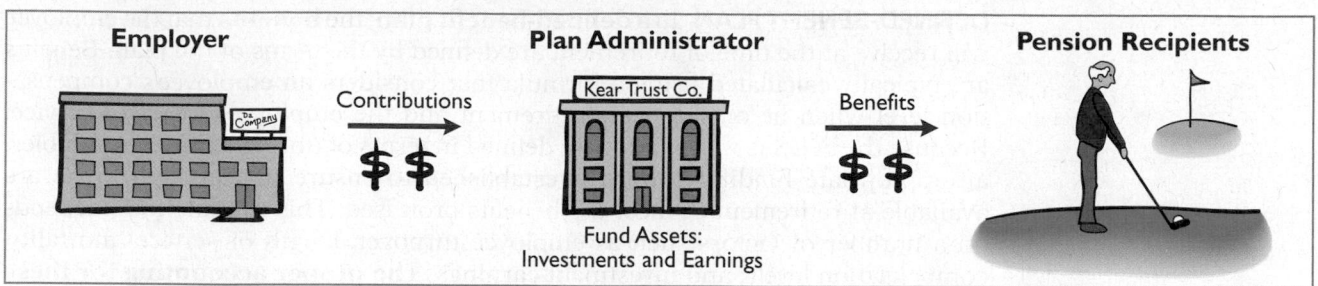

Illustration 11A-1
Parties in a pension plan

An employer-financed pension is part of the employees' compensation. ERISA establishes the minimum contribution that a company must make each year toward employee pensions. The most popular type of pension plan used is the 401(k) plan. A 401(k) plan works as follows. As an employee, you can contribute up to a certain percentage of your pay into a 401(k) plan, and your employer will match a percentage of your contribution. These contributions are then generally invested in stocks and bonds through mutual funds. These funds will grow without being taxed and can be withdrawn beginning at age 59-1/2. If you must access the funds earlier, you may be able to do so, but a penalty usually occurs along with a payment of tax on the proceeds. Any time you have the opportunity to be involved in a 401(k) plan, you should avail yourself of this benefit!

Companies record pension costs as an expense while the employees are working because that is when the company receives benefits from the employees' services. Generally, the pension expense is reported as an operating expense in the company's income statement. Frequently, the amount contributed by the company to the pension plan is different from the amount of the pension expense. A **liability** is recognized when the pension expense to date is **more than** the company's contributions to date. An **asset** is recognized when the pension expense to date is **less than** the company's contributions to date. Further consideration of the accounting for pension plans is left for more advanced courses.

The two most common types of pension arrangements for providing benefits to employees after they retire are defined-contribution plans and defined-benefit plans.

DEFINED-CONTRIBUTION PLAN In a **defined-contribution plan**, the plan defines the employer's contribution but not the benefit that the employee will receive at retirement. That is, the employer agrees to contribute a certain sum each period based on a formula. A 401(k) plan is typically a defined-contribution plan.

The accounting for a defined-contribution plan is straightforward. The employer simply makes a contribution each year based on the formula established in the plan. As a result, the employer's obligation is easily determined. It follows that the company reports **the amount of the contribution required each period as pension expense. The employer reports a liability only if it has not made the contribution in full.**

To illustrate, assume that Alba Office Interiors has a defined-contribution plan in which it contributes $200,000 each year to the pension fund for its employees. The entry to record this transaction is:

Pension Expense	200,000	
Cash		200,000
(To record pension expense and contribution		
to pension fund)		

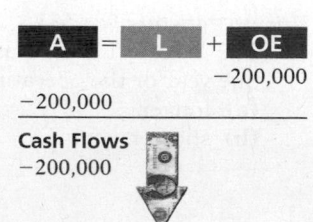

A	=	L	+	OE
				−200,000
−200,000				

Cash Flows
−200,000

To the extent that Alba did not contribute the $200,000 defined contribution, it would record a liability. Pension payments to retired employees are made from the pension fund by the plan administrator.

DEFINED-BENEFIT PLAN In a **defined-benefit plan**, the **benefits** that the employee will receive at the time of retirement are defined by the terms of the plan. Benefits are typically calculated using a formula that considers an employee's compensation level when he or she nears retirement and the employee's years of service. Because the benefits in this plan are defined in terms of uncertain future variables, an appropriate funding pattern is established to ensure that enough funds are available at retirement to meet the benefits promised. This funding level depends on a number of factors such as employee turnover, length of service, mortality, compensation levels, and investment earnings. **The proper accounting for these plans is complex and is considered in more advanced accounting courses.**

POSTRETIREMENT BENEFITS AS LONG-TERM LIABILITIES
While part of the liability associated with (1) postretirement health-care and life insurance benefits and (2) pension plans is generally a current liability, the greater portion of these liabilities extends many years into the future. Therefore, many companies are required to report significant amounts as long-term liabilities for postretirement benefits.

SUMMARY OF LEARNING OBJECTIVE FOR APPENDIX 11A

 The Navigator

9 **Identify additional fringe benefits associated with employee compensation.** Additional fringe benefits associated with wages are paid absences (paid vacations, sick pay benefits, and paid holidays), and postretirement benefits (pensions, health care, and life insurance).

GLOSSARY FOR APPENDIX 11A

Defined-benefit plan A pension plan in which the benefits that the employee will receive at retirement are defined by the terms of the plan. (p. 548).

Defined-contribution plan A pension plan in which the employer's contribution to the plan is defined by the terms of the plan. (p. 547).

Pension plan An agreement whereby an employer provides benefits to employees after they retire. (p. 546).

Postretirement benefits Payments by employers to retired employees for health care, life insurance, and pensions. (p. 546).

 Self-Test, Brief Exercises, Exercises, Problem Set A, and many more components are available for practice in *WileyPLUS*.

*Note: All asterisked Questions, Exercises, and Problems relate to material in the appendix to the chapter.

SELF-TEST QUESTIONS

Answers are on page 563.

(LO 1) **1.** The time period for classifying a liability as current is one year or the operating cycle, whichever is:
(a) longer.
(b) shorter.
(c) probable.
(d) possible.

2. To be classified as a current liability, a debt must be (LO 1) expected to be paid within:
(a) one year.
(b) the operating cycle.
(c) 2 years.
(d) (a) or (b), whichever is longer.

(LO 2) **3.** Maggie Sharrer Company borrows $88,500 on September 1, 2014, from Sandwich State Bank by signing an $88,500, 12%, one-year note. What is the accrued interest at December 31, 2014?
    (a) $2,655.   **(c)** $4,425.
    (b) $3,540.   **(d)** $10,620.

(LO 2) **4.** RS Company borrowed $70,000 on December 1 on a 6-month, 6% note. At December 31:
    (a) neither the note payable nor the interest payable is a current liability.
    (b) the note payable is a current liability, but the interest payable is not.
    (c) the interest payable is a current liability but the note payable is not.
    (d) both the note payable and the interest payable are current liabilities.

(LO 3) **5.** Becky Sherrick Company has total proceeds from sales of $4,515. If the proceeds include sales taxes of 5%, the amount to be credited to Sales Revenue is:
    (a) $4,000.   **(c)** $4,289.25.
    (b) $4,300.   **(d)** No correct answer given.

(LO 3) **6.** Sensible Insurance Company collected a premium of $18,000 for a 1-year insurance policy on April 1. What amount should Sensible report as a current liability for Unearned Service Revenue at December 31?
    (a) $0.   **(c)** $13,500.
    (b) $4,500.   **(d)** $18,000.

(LO 4) **7.** Working capital is calculated as:
    (a) current assets minus current liabilities.
    (b) total assets minus total liabilities.
    (c) long-term liabilities minus current liabilities.
    (d) Both (b) and (c).

(LO 4) **8.** The current ratio is computed as:
    (a) total assets divided by total liabilities.
    (b) total assets divided by current liabilities.
    (c) current assets divided by total liabilities.
    (d) current assets divided by current liabilities.

(LO 5) **9.** A contingent liability should be recorded in the accounts when:
    (a) it is probable the contingency will happen, but the amount cannot be reasonably estimated.
    (b) it is reasonably possible the contingency will happen, and the amount can be reasonably estimated.

    (c) it is probable the contingency will happen, and the amount can be reasonably estimated.
    (d) it is reasonably possible the contingency will happen, but the amount cannot be reasonably estimated.

10. At December 31, Hanes Company prepares an adjust- (LO 5)
ing entry for a product warranty contract. Which of the following accounts is/are included in the entry?
    (a) Miscellaneous Expense.
    (b) Warranty Liability.
    (c) Repair Parts.
    (d) Both (a) and (b).

11. Andy Manion earns $14 per hour for a 40-hour week (LO 6)
and $21 per hour for any overtime work. If Manion works 45 hours in a week, gross earnings are:
    (a) $560.   **(c)** $650.
    (b) $630.   **(d)** $665.

12. When recording payroll: (LO 6)
    (a) gross earnings are recorded as salaries and wages payable.
    (b) net pay is recorded as salaries and wages expense.
    (c) payroll deductions are recorded as liabilities.
    (d) More than one of the above.

13. Employer payroll taxes do **not** include: (LO 7)
    (a) federal unemployment taxes.
    (b) state unemployment taxes.
    (c) federal income taxes.
    (d) FICA taxes.

14. FICA Taxes Payable was credited for $7,500 in the (LO 7)
entry when Antonio Company recorded payroll. When Antonio Company records employer's payroll taxes, FICA Taxes Payable should be credited for:
    (a) $0.   **(c)** $15,000.
    (b) $7,500.   **(d)** Some other amount.

15. The department that should pay the payroll is the: (LO 8)
    (a) timekeeping department.
    (b) human resources department.
    (c) payroll department.
    (d) treasurer's department.

*16. Which of the following is **not** an additional fringe (LO 9)
benefit?
    (a) Postretirement pensions.   **(c)** Paid vacations.
    (b) Paid absences.   **(d)** Salaries.

Go to the book's companion website, www.wiley.com/college/weygandt, for additional Self-Test Questions.

QUESTIONS

1. Lori Randle believes a current liability is a debt that can be expected to be paid in one year. Is Lori correct? Explain.

2. Petrocelli Company obtains $40,000 in cash by signing a 7%, 6-month, $40,000 note payable to First Bank on July 1. Petrocelli's fiscal year ends on September 30. What information should be reported for the note payable in the annual financial statements?

3. (a) Your roommate says, "Sales taxes are reported as an expense in the income statement." Do you agree? Explain.

    (b) Jensen Company has cash proceeds from sales of $8,400. This amount includes $400 of sales taxes. Give the entry to record the proceeds.

4. Ottawa University sold 15,000 season football tickets at $80 each for its six-game home schedule. What entries should be made (a) when the tickets were sold, and (b) after each game?

5. What is liquidity? What are two measures of liquidity?
6. What is a contingent liability? Give an example of a contingent liability that is usually recorded in the accounts.
7. Under what circumstances is a contingent liability disclosed only in the notes to the financial statements? Under what circumstances is a contingent liability not recorded in the accounts nor disclosed in the notes to the financial statements?
8. What is the difference between gross pay and net pay? Which amount should a company record as wages and salaries expense?
9. Which payroll tax is levied on both employers and employees?
10. Are the federal and state income taxes withheld from employee paychecks a payroll tax expense for the employer? Explain your answer.
11. What do the following acronyms stand for: FICA, FUTA, and SUTA?
12. What information is shown in a W-2 statement?
13. Distinguish between the two types of payroll deductions and give examples of each.

14. What are the primary uses of the employee earnings record?
15. (a) Identify the three types of employer payroll taxes.
    (b) How are tax liability accounts and payroll tax expense accounts classified in the financial statements?
16. You are a newly hired accountant with Nolasco Company. On your first day, the controller asks you to identify the main internal control objectives related to payroll accounting. How would you respond?
17. What are the four functions associated with payroll activities?
*18. Identify two additional types of fringe benefits associated with employees' compensation.
*19. Often during job interviews, the candidate asks the potential employer about the firm's paid absences policy. What are paid absences? How are they accounted for?
*20. What are two types of postretirement benefits?
*21. Explain how a 401(k) plan works.
*22. What is the principal difference between a defined-contribution pension plan and a defined-benefit pension plan?

BRIEF EXERCISES

Identify whether obligations are current liabilities.

(LO 1)

BE11-1 Jamison Company has the following obligations at December 31: (a) a note payable for $100,000 due in 2 years, (b) a 10-year mortgage payable of $300,000 payable in ten $30,000 annual payments, (c) interest payable of $15,000 on the mortgage, and (d) accounts payable of $60,000. For each obligation, indicate whether it should be classified as a current liability. (Assume an operating cycle of less than one year.)

Prepare entries for an interest-bearing note payable.

(LO 2)

BE11-2 Peralta Company borrows $60,000 on July 1 from the bank by signing a $60,000, 10%, one-year note payable.

(a) Prepare the journal entry to record the proceeds of the note.
(b) Prepare the journal entry to record accrued interest at December 31, assuming adjusting entries are made only at the end of the year.

Compute and record sales taxes payable.

(LO 3)

BE11-3 Coghlan Auto Supply does not segregate sales and sales taxes at the time of sale. The register total for March 16 is $16,380. All sales are subject to a 5% sales tax. Compute sales taxes payable, and make the entry to record sales taxes payable and sales revenue.

Prepare entries for unearned revenues.

(LO 3)

BE11-4 Derby University sells 4,000 season basketball tickets at $210 each for its 12-game home schedule. Give the entry to record (a) the sale of the season tickets and (b) the revenue recognized by playing the first home game.

Analyze liquidity.

(LO 4)

BE11-5 Yahoo! Inc.'s recent financial statements contain the following selected data (in thousands).

Current assets	$ 4,594,772	Current liabilities	$1,717,728
Total assets	14,936,030	Total liabilities	2,417,394

Compute (a) working capital and (b) current ratio.

Prepare adjusting entry for warranty costs.

(LO 5)

BE11-6 On December 1, Bruney Company introduces a new product that includes a one-year warranty on parts. In December, 1,000 units are sold. Management believes that 5% of the units will be defective and that the average warranty costs will be $90 per unit. Prepare the adjusting entry at December 31 to accrue the estimated warranty cost.

Compute gross earnings and net pay.

(LO 6)

BE11-7 Beth Corbin's regular hourly wage rate is $16, and she receives an hourly rate of $24 for work in excess of 40 hours. During a January pay period, Beth works 45 hours. Beth's federal income tax withholding is $95, and she has no voluntary deductions. Compute Beth Corbin's gross earnings and net pay for the pay period.

BE11-8 Data for Beth Corbin are presented in BE11-7. Prepare the journal entries to record (a) Beth's pay for the period and (b) the payment of Beth's wages. Use January 15 for the end of the pay period and the payment date.

Record a payroll and the payment of wages.

(LO 6)

BE11-9 In January, gross earnings in Lugo Company totaled $80,000. All earnings are subject to 7.65% FICA taxes, 5.4% state unemployment taxes, and 0.8% federal unemployment taxes. Prepare the entry to record January payroll tax expense.

Record employer payroll taxes.

(LO 7)

BE11-10 Swenson Company has the following payroll procedures.

(a) Supervisor approves overtime work.
(b) The human resources department prepares hiring authorization forms for new hires.
(c) A second payroll department employee verifies payroll calculations.
(d) The treasurer's department pays employees.

Identify the payroll function to which each procedure pertains.

Identify payroll functions.

(LO 8)

*BE11-11 At Ward Company, employees are entitled to one day's vacation for each month worked. In January, 70 employees worked the full month. Record the vacation pay liability for January, assuming the average daily pay for each employee is $120.

Record estimated vacation benefits.

(LO 9)

> DO IT! Review

DO IT! 11-1 You and several classmates are studying for the next accounting examination. They ask you to answer the following questions:

Answer questions about current liabilities.

(LO 2, 3)

1. If cash is borrowed on a $70,000, 9-month, 6% note on August 1, how much interest expense would be incurred by December 31?

2. The cash register total including sales taxes is $42,000, and the sales tax rate is 5%. What is the sales taxes payable?

3. If $45,000 is collected in advance on November 1 for 6-month magazine subscriptions, what amount of subscription revenue should be recognized by December 31?

DO IT! 11-2 Medlen Company, has the following account balances at December 31, 2014.

Prepare current liabilities section and compute liquidity measures.

(LO 4, 5)

Notes payable ($60,000 due after 12/31/15)	$100,000
Unearned service revenue	70,000
Other long-term debt ($90,000 due in 2015)	250,000
Salaries and wages payable	32,000
Accounts payable	63,000

In addition, Medlen is involved in a lawsuit. Legal counsel feels it is probable Medlen will pay damages of $25,000 in 2015.

(a) Prepare the current liability section of Medlen's December 31, 2014, balance sheet.
(b) Medlen's current assets are $570,000. Compute Medlen's working capital and current ratio.

DO IT! 11-3 In January, gross earnings in Burrell Company were $80,000. All earnings are subject to 7.65% FICA taxes. Federal income tax withheld was $14,000, and state income tax withheld was $1,600. (a) Calculate net pay for January, and (b) record the payroll.

Calculate net pay and record payroll.

(LO 6)

DO IT! 11-4 In January, the payroll supervisor determines that gross earnings for Carlyle Company are $120,000. All earnings are subject to 7.65% FICA taxes, 5.4% state unemployment taxes, and 0.8% federal unemployment taxes. Record the employer's payroll taxes.

Record employer's payroll taxes.

(LO 7)

EXERCISES

E11-1 C.S. Lewis Company had the following transactions involving notes payable.

Prepare entries for interest-bearing notes.

(LO 2)

July 1, 2014	Borrows $50,000 from First National Bank by signing a 9-month, 8% note.
Nov. 1, 2014	Borrows $60,000 from Lyon County State Bank by signing a 3-month, 6% note.

Dec. 31, 2014   Prepares adjusting entries.
Feb. 1, 2015   Pays principal and interest to Lyon County State Bank.
Apr. 1, 2015   Pays principal and interest to First National Bank.

Instructions
Prepare journal entries for each of the transactions.

Prepare entries for interest-bearing notes.
(LO 2)

E11-2 On June 1, Merando Company borrows $90,000 from First Bank on a 6-month, $90,000, 8% note.

Instructions
(a) Prepare the entry on June 1.
(b) Prepare the adjusting entry on June 30.
(c) Prepare the entry at maturity (December 1), assuming monthly adjusting entries have been made through November 30.
(d) What was the total financing cost (interest expense)?

Journalize sales and related taxes.
(LO 3)

E11-3 In performing accounting services for small businesses, you encounter the following situations pertaining to cash sales.

1. Poole Company enters sales and sales taxes separately on its cash register. On April 10, the register totals are sales $30,000 and sales taxes $1,500.
2. Waterman Company does not segregate sales and sales taxes. Its register total for April 15 is $25,680, which includes a 7% sales tax.

Instructions
Prepare the entry to record the sales transactions and related taxes for each client.

Journalize unearned subscription revenue.
(LO 3)

E11-4 Moreno Company publishes a monthly sports magazine, *Fishing Preview*. Subscriptions to the magazine cost $20 per year. During November 2014, Moreno sells 15,000 subscriptions beginning with the December issue. Moreno prepares financial statements quarterly and recognizes subscription revenue at the end of the quarter. The company uses the accounts Unearned Subscription Revenue and Subscription Revenue.

Instructions
(a) Prepare the entry in November for the receipt of the subscriptions.
(b) Prepare the adjusting entry at December 31, 2014, to record sales revenue recognized in December 2014.
(c) Prepare the adjusting entry at March 31, 2015, to record sales revenue recognized in the first quarter of 2015.

Record estimated liability and expense for warranties.
(LO 5)

E11-5 Betancourt Company sells automatic can openers under a 75-day warranty for defective merchandise. Based on past experience, Betancourt estimates that 3% of the units sold will become defective during the warranty period. Management estimates that the average cost of replacing or repairing a defective unit is $15. The units sold and units defective that occurred during the last 2 months of 2014 are as follows.

Month	Units Sold	Units Defective Prior to December 31
November	30,000	600
December	32,000	400

Instructions
(a) Determine the estimated warranty liability at December 31 for the units sold in November and December.
(b) Prepare the journal entries to record the estimated liability for warranties and the costs incurred in honoring 1,000 warranty claims. (Assume actual costs of $15,000.)
(c) Give the entry to record the honoring of 500 warranty contracts in January at an average cost of $15.

Record and disclose contingent liabilities.
(LO 5)

E11-6 Gallardo Co. is involved in a lawsuit as a result of an accident that took place September 5, 2014. The lawsuit was filed on November 1, 2014, and claims damages of $1,000,000.

Instructions
(a) At December 31, 2014, Gallardo's attorneys feel it is remote that Gallardo will lose the lawsuit. How should the company account for the effects of the lawsuit?

(b) Assume instead that at December 31, 2014, Gallardo's attorneys feel it is probable that Gallardo will lose the lawsuit and be required to pay $1,000,000. How should the company account for this lawsuit?

(c) Assume instead that at December 31, 2014, Gallardo's attorneys feel it is reasonably possible that Gallardo could lose the lawsuit and be required to pay $1,000,000. How should the company account for this lawsuit?

E11-7 Younger Online Company has the following liability accounts after posting adjusting entries: Accounts Payable $73,000, Unearned Ticket Revenue $24,000, Warranty Liability $18,000, Interest Payable $8,000, Mortgage Payable $120,000, Notes Payable $80,000, and Sales Taxes Payable $10,000. Assume the company's operating cycle is less than 1 year, ticket revenue will be recognized within 1 year, warranty costs are expected to be incurred within 1 year, and the notes mature in 3 years.

Prepare the current liability section of the balance sheet.

(LO 1, 2, 3, 4, 5)

Instructions

(a) Prepare the current liabilities section of the balance sheet, assuming $30,000 of the mortgage is payable next year.

(b) Comment on Younger Online Company's liquidity, assuming total current assets are $300,000.

E11-8 Suppose Kroger Co.'s 2014 financial statements contained the following data (in millions).

Calculate liquidity ratios.

(LO 4)

Current assets	$ 7,450	Accounts receivable	$909
Total assets	23,093	Interest expense	502
Current liabilities	7,714	Income tax expense	532
Total liabilities	18,187	Net income	70
Cash	424		

Instructions

Compute these values:

(a) Working capital.   **(b)** Current ratio.

E11-9 Suppose the following financial data were reported by 3M Company for 2013 and 2014 (dollars in millions).

Calculate current ratio and working capital before and after paying accounts payable.

(LO 4)

3M COMPANY
Balance Sheets (partial)

	2014	2013
Current assets		
Cash and cash equivalents	$ 3,040	$1,849
Accounts receivable, net	3,250	3,195
Inventories	2,639	3,013
Other current assets	1,866	1,541
Total current assets	$10,795	$9,598
Current liabilities	$ 4,897	$5,839

Instructions

(a) Calculate the current ratio and working capital for 3M for 2013 and 2014.

(b) Suppose that at the end of 2014, 3M management used $200 million cash to pay off $200 million of accounts payable. How would its current ratio and working capital have changed?

E11-10 Maria Garza's regular hourly wage rate is $16, and she receives a wage of 1½ times the regular hourly rate for work in excess of 40 hours. During a March weekly pay period, Maria worked 42 hours. Her gross earnings prior to the current week were $6,000. Maria is married and claims three withholding allowances. Her only voluntary deduction is for group hospitalization insurance at $25 per week.

Compute net pay and record pay for one employee.

(LO 6)

Instructions

(a) Compute the following amounts for Maria's wages for the current week.
   (1) Gross earnings.
   (2) FICA taxes. (Assume a 7.65% rate on maximum of $110,100.)

(3) Federal income taxes withheld. (Use the withholding table in the text, page 535.)
(4) State income taxes withheld. (Assume a 2.0% rate.)
(5) Net pay.
(b) Record Maria's pay.

Compute maximum FICA deductions.

(LO 6)

E11-11 Employee earnings records for Slaymaker Company reveal the following gross earnings for four employees through the pay period of December 15.

J. Seligman	$93,500	L. Marshall	$108,100
R. Eby	$106,600	T. Olson	$112,500

For the pay period ending December 31, each employee's gross earnings is $4,500. The FICA tax rate is 7.65% on gross earnings of $110,100.

Instructions
Compute the FICA withholdings that should be made for each employee for the December 31 pay period. (Show computations.)

Prepare payroll register and record payroll and payroll tax expense.

(LO 6, 7)

E11-12 Ramirez Company has the following data for the weekly payroll ending January 31.

	Hours						Hourly Rate	Federal Income Tax Withholding	Health Insurance
Employee	M	T	W	T	F	S			
L. Helton	8	8	9	8	10	3	$12	$34	$10
R. Kenseth	8	8	8	8	8	2	14	37	25
D. Tavaras	9	10	8	8	9	0	15	58	25

Employees are paid 1½ times the regular hourly rate for all hours worked in excess of 40 hours per week. FICA taxes are 7.65% on the first $110,100 of gross earnings. Ramirez Company is subject to 5.4% state unemployment taxes and 0.8% federal unemployment taxes on the first $7,000 of gross earnings.

Instructions
(a) Prepare the payroll register for the weekly payroll.
(b) Prepare the journal entries to record the payroll and Ramirez's payroll tax expense.

Compute missing payroll amounts and record payroll.

(LO 6)

E11-13 Selected data from a February payroll register for Sutton Company are presented below. Some amounts are intentionally omitted.

Gross earnings:		State income taxes	$ (3)
Regular	$9,100	Union dues	100
Overtime	(1)	Total deductions	(4)
Total	(2)	Net pay	$7,595
Deductions:		Account debited:	
FICA taxes	$ 765	Salaries and wages expense	(5)
Federal income taxes	1,140		

FICA taxes are 7.65%. State income taxes are 4% of gross earnings.

Instructions
(a) Fill in the missing amounts.
(b) Journalize the February payroll and the payment of the payroll.

Determine employer's payroll taxes; record payroll tax expense.

(LO 7)

E11-14 According to a payroll register summary of Frederickson Company, the amount of employees' gross pay in December was $850,000, of which $80,000 was not subject to FICA tax and $750,000 was not subject to state and federal unemployment taxes.

Instructions
(a) Determine the employer's payroll tax expense for the month, using the following rates: FICA 7.65%, state unemployment 5.4%, and federal unemployment 0.8%.
(b) Prepare the journal entry to record December payroll tax expense.

Prepare adjusting entries for fringe benefits.

(LO 9)

*E11-15 Mayberry Company has two fringe benefit plans for its employees:

1. It grants employees 2 days' vacation for each month worked. Ten employees worked the entire month of March at an average daily wage of $140 per employee.
2. In its pension plan, the company recognizes 10% of gross earnings as a pension expense. Gross earnings in March were $40,000. No contribution has been made to the pension fund.

Instructions
Prepare the adjusting entries at March 31.

*E11-16 Podsednik Corporation has 20 employees who each earn $140 a day. The follow-ing information is available.

1. At December 31, Podsednik recorded vacation benefits. Each employee earned 5 vaca-tion days during the year.
2. At December 31, Podsednik recorded pension expense of $100,000, and made a contri-bution of $70,000 to the pension plan.
3. In January, 18 employees used one vacation day each.

Prepare journal entries for fringe benefits.
(LO 9)

Instructions
Prepare Podsednik's journal entries to record these transactions.

Visit the book's companion website, at **www.wiley.com/college/weygandt**, and choose the Student Companion site to access Exercise Set B and Challenge Exercises.

P11-1A On January 1, 2014, the ledger of Accardo Company contains the following liability accounts.

Prepare current liability entries, adjusting entries, and current liabilities section.
(LO 1, 2, 3, 4, 5)

Accounts Payable	$52,000
Sales Taxes Payable	7,700
Unearned Service Revenue	16,000

During January, the following selected transactions occurred.

Jan. 5 Sold merchandise for cash totaling $20,520, which includes 8% sales taxes.
   12 Performed services for customers who had made advance payments of $10,000. (Credit Service Revenue.)
   14 Paid state revenue department for sales taxes collected in December 2013 ($7,700).
   20 Sold 900 units of a new product on credit at $50 per unit, plus 8% sales tax. This new product is subject to a 1-year warranty.
   21 Borrowed $27,000 from Girard Bank on a 3-month, 8%, $27,000 note.
   25 Sold merchandise for cash totaling $12,420, which includes 8% sales taxes.

Instructions
(a) Journalize the January transactions.
(b) Journalize the adjusting entries at January 31 for (1) the outstanding notes payable, and (2) estimated warranty liability, assuming warranty costs are expected to equal 7% of sales of the new product. (*Hint:* Use one-third of a month for the Girard Bank note.)
(c) Prepare the current liabilities section of the balance sheet at January 31, 2014. Assume no change in accounts payable.

*(c) Current liability total
$94,250*

P11-2A The following are selected transactions of Blanco Company. Blanco prepares financial statements **quarterly**.

Journalize and post note transactions; show balance sheet presentation.
(LO 2)

Jan. 2 Purchased merchandise on account from Nunez Company, $30,000, terms 2/10, n/30. (Blanco uses the perpetual inventory system.)
Feb. 1 Issued a 9%, 2-month, $30,000 note to Nunez in payment of account.
Mar. 31 Accrued interest for 2 months on Nunez note.
Apr. 1 Paid face value and interest on Nunez note.
July 1 Purchased equipment from Marson Equipment paying $11,000 in cash and signing a 10%, 3-month, $60,000 note.
Sept. 30 Accrued interest for 3 months on Marson note.
Oct. 1 Paid face value and interest on Marson note.
Dec. 1 Borrowed $24,000 from the Paola Bank by issuing a 3-month, 8% note with a face value of $24,000.
Dec. 31 Recognized interest expense for 1 month on Paola Bank note.

Instructions

(a) Prepare journal entries for the listed transactions and events.
(b) Post to the accounts Notes Payable, Interest Payable, and Interest Expense.
(c) Show the balance sheet presentation of notes and interest payable at December 31.
(d) What is total interest expense for the year?

(d) $2,110

Prepare payroll register and payroll entries.

(LO 6, 7)

P11-3A Mann Hardware has four employees who are paid on an hourly basis plus time-and-a-half for all hours worked in excess of 40 a week. Payroll data for the week ended March 15, 2014, are presented below.

Employee	Hours Worked	Hourly Rate	Federal Income Tax Withholdings	United Fund
Ben Abel	40	$15.00	$?	$5.00
Rita Hager	42	16.00	?	5.00
Jack Never	44	13.00	60	8.00
Sue Perez	46	13.00	61	5.00

Abel and Hager are married. They claim 0 and 4 withholding allowances, respectively. The following tax rates are applicable: FICA 7.65%, state income taxes 3%, state unemployment taxes 5.4%, and federal unemployment 0.8%.

Instructions

(a) Net pay $1,985.30

(a) Prepare a payroll register for the weekly payroll. (Use the wage-bracket withholding table in the text for federal income tax withholdings.)

(b) Payroll tax expense $349.43

(b) Journalize the payroll on March 15, 2014, and the accrual of employer payroll taxes.
(c) Journalize the payment of the payroll on March 16, 2014.

(d) Cash paid $632.02

(d) Journalize the deposit in a Federal Reserve bank on March 31, 2014, of the FICA and federal income taxes payable to the government.

Journalize payroll transactions and adjusting entries.

(LO 6, 7, 9)

P11-4A The following payroll liability accounts are included in the ledger of Harmon Company on January 1, 2014.

FICA Taxes Payable	$ 760.00
Federal Income Taxes Payable	1,204.60
State Income Taxes Payable	108.95
Federal Unemployment Taxes Payable	288.95
State Unemployment Taxes Payable	1,954.40
Union Dues Payable	870.00
U.S. Savings Bonds Payable	360.00

In January, the following transactions occurred.

Jan. 10   Sent check for $870.00 to union treasurer for union dues.
    12   Remitted check for $1,964.60 to the Federal Reserve bank for FICA taxes and federal income taxes withheld.
    15   Purchased U.S. Savings Bonds for employees by writing check for $360.00.
    17   Paid state income taxes withheld from employees.
    20   Paid federal and state unemployment taxes.
    31   Completed monthly payroll register, which shows salaries and wages $58,000, FICA taxes withheld $4,437, federal income taxes payable $2,158, state income taxes payable $454, union dues payable $400, United Fund contributions payable $1,888, and net pay $48,663.
    31   Prepared payroll checks for the net pay and distributed checks to employees.

At January 31, the company also makes the following accrued adjustments pertaining to employee compensation.

1. Employer payroll taxes: FICA taxes 7.65%, federal unemployment taxes 0.8%, and state unemployment taxes 5.4%.
***2.** Vacation pay: 6% of gross earnings.

Instructions

(b) Payroll tax expense $8,033; Vacation benefits expense $3,480

(a) Journalize the January transactions.
(b) Journalize the adjustments pertaining to employee compensation at January 31.

P11-5A For the year ended December 31, 2014, Denkinger Electrical Repair Company reports the following summary payroll data.

Prepare entries for payroll and payroll taxes; prepare W-2 data.

(LO 6, 7)

Gross earnings:	
Administrative salaries	$200,000
Electricians' wages	370,000
Total	$570,000

Deductions:	
FICA taxes	$ 38,645
Federal income taxes withheld	174,400
State income taxes withheld (3%)	17,100
United Fund contributions payable	27,500
Health insurance premiums	17,200
Total	$274,845

Denkinger Company's payroll taxes are Social Security tax 6.2%, Medicare tax 1.45%, state unemployment 2.5% (due to a stable employment record), and 0.8% federal unemployment. Gross earnings subject to Social Security taxes of 6.2% total $490,000, and gross earnings subject to unemployment taxes total $135,000.

Instructions

(a) Prepare a summary journal entry at December 31 for the full year's payroll.

(b) Journalize the adjusting entry at December 31 to record the employer's payroll taxes.

(c) The W-2 Wage and Tax Statement requires the following dollar data.

(a) Salaries and wages payable $295,155
(b) Payroll tax expense $43,100

Wages, Tips, Other Compensation	Federal Income Tax Withheld	State Income Tax Withheld	FICA Wages	FICA Tax Withheld

Complete the required data for the following employees.

Employee	Gross Earnings	Federal Income Tax Withheld
Maria Sandoval	$59,000	$28,500
Jennifer Mingenback	26,000	10,200

PROBLEMS: SET B

P11-1B On January 1, 2014, the ledger of Werth Company contains the following liability accounts.

Prepare current liability entries, adjusting entries, and current liabilities section.

(LO 1, 2, 3, 4, 5)

Accounts Payable	$35,000
Sales Taxes Payable	5,000
Unearned Service Revenue	12,000

During January, the following selected transactions occurred.

Jan. 1 Borrowed $30,000 in cash from Platteville Bank on a 4-month, 6%, $30,000 note.

5 Sold merchandise for cash totaling $11,130, which includes 6% sales taxes.

12 Performed services for customers who had made advance payments of $8,000. (Credit Service Revenue.)

14 Paid state treasurer's department for sales taxes collected in December 2013, $5,000.

20 Sold 750 units of a new product on credit at $44 per unit, plus 6% sales tax. This new product is subject to a 1-year warranty.

25 Sold merchandise for cash totaling $16,536, which includes 6% sales taxes.

Instructions

(a) Journalize the January transactions.

(b) Journalize the adjusting entries at January 31 for (1) the outstanding notes payable, and (2) estimated warranty liability, assuming warranty costs are expected to equal 5% of sales of the new product.

(c) Prepare the current liabilities section of the balance sheet at January 31, 2014. Assume no change in accounts payable.

(c) Current liability total $74,346

Journalize and post note transactions and show balance sheet presentation.

(LO 2)

P11-2B The following are selected transactions of Lindblom Company. Lindblom prepares financial statements **quarterly**.

Jan. 2 Purchased merchandise on account from Evers Company, $20,000, terms 2/10, n/30. (Lindblom uses the perpetual inventory system.)

Feb. 1 Issued a 12%, 2-month, $20,000 note to Evers in payment of account.

Mar. 31 Accrued interest for 2 months on Evers note.

Apr. 1 Paid face value and interest on Evers note.

July 1 Purchased equipment from Francisco Equipment paying $12,000 in cash and signing a 10%, 3-month, $40,000 note.

Sept. 30 Accrued interest for 3 months on Francisco note.

Oct. 1 Paid face value and interest on Francisco note.

Dec. 1 Borrowed $25,000 from the National Bank by issuing a 3-month, 12% note with a face value of $25,000.

Dec. 31 Recognized interest expense for 1 month on National Bank note.

Instructions

(a) Prepare journal entries for the above transactions and events.

(b) Post to the accounts, Notes Payable, Interest Payable, and Interest Expense.

(c) Show the balance sheet presentation of notes and interest payable at December 31.

(d) $1,650

(d) What is total interest expense for the year?

Prepare payroll register and payroll entries.

(LO 6, 7)

P11-3B Otto Drug Store has four employees who are paid on an hourly basis plus time-and-a-half for all hours worked in excess of 40 a week. Payroll data for the week ended February 15, 2014, are shown below.

Employee	Hours Worked	Hourly Rate	Federal Income Tax Withholdings	United Fund Contributions
M. Dingler	39	$12.00	$34	$ –0–
D. Patel	42	12.00	20	10.00
L. Grimmett	44	10.00	51	5.00
A. Bly	46	10.00	36	5.00

The following tax rates are applicable: FICA 7.65%, state income taxes 3%, state unemployment taxes 5.4%, and federal unemployment 0.8%. The first three employees are sales clerks (store wages expense). The fourth employee performs administrative duties (office wages expense).

Instructions

(a) Net pay $1,567.03

(a) Prepare a payroll register for the weekly payroll.

(b) Payroll tax expense $267.86

(b) Journalize the payroll on February 15, 2014, and the accrual of employer payroll taxes.

(c) Journalize the payment of the payroll on February 16, 2014.

(d) Cash paid $436.90

(d) Journalize the remittance to the Federal Reserve bank on February 28, 2014, of the FICA and federal income taxes payable to the government.

Journalize payroll transactions and adjusting entries.

(LO 6, 7, 9)

P11-4B The following payroll liability accounts are included in the ledger of Grandon Company on January 1, 2014.

FICA Taxes Payable	$ 540
Federal Income Taxes Payable	1,100
State Income Taxes Payable	210
Federal Unemployment Taxes Payable	54
State Unemployment Taxes Payable	365
Union Dues Payable	200
U.S. Savings Bonds Payable	300

In January, the following transactions occurred.

Jan. 10 Sent check for $200 to union treasurer for union dues.

12 Remitted check for $1,640 to the Federal Reserve bank for FICA taxes and federal income taxes withheld.

15 Purchased U.S. Savings Bonds for employees by writing check for $300.

17 Paid state income taxes withheld from employees.

20 Paid federal and state unemployment taxes.

31 Completed monthly payroll register, which shows salaries and wages $42,000, FICA taxes withheld $3,213, federal income taxes payable $2,540, state income

taxes payable $500, union dues payable $300, United Fund contributions payable $1,300, and net pay $34,147.

31 Prepared payroll checks for the net pay and distributed checks to employees.

At January 31, the company also makes the following accruals pertaining to employee compensation.

1. Employer payroll taxes: FICA taxes 7.65%, state unemployment taxes 5.4%, and federal unemployment taxes 0.8%.

*2. Vacation pay: 5% of gross earnings.

Instructions

(a) Journalize the January transactions.

(b) Journalize the adjustments pertaining to employee compensation at January 31.

(b) Payroll tax expense $5,817; Vacation benefits expense $2,100

P11-5B For the year ended December 31, 2014, Stone Company reports the following summary payroll data.

Prepare entries for payroll and payroll taxes; prepare W-2 data.

(LO 6, 7)

Gross earnings:		Deductions:	
Administrative salaries	$150,000	FICA taxes	$ 26,735
Electricians' wages	240,000	Federal income taxes withheld	78,000
Total	$390,000	State income taxes withheld (3%)	11,700
		United Fund contributions payable	17,000
		Health insurance premiums	12,000
		Total	$145,435

Stone Company's payroll taxes are Social Security tax 6.2%, Medicare tax 1.45%, state unemployment 2.5% (due to a stable employment record), and 0.8% federal unemployment. Gross earnings subject to Social Security taxes of 6.2% total $340,000, and gross earnings subject to unemployment taxes total $90,000.

Instructions

(a) Prepare a summary journal entry at December 31 for the full year's payroll.

(b) Journalize the adjusting entry at December 31 to record the employer's payroll taxes.

(c) The W-2 Wage and Tax Statement requires the dollar data shown below.

(a) Salaries and wages payable $244,565

(b) Payroll tax expense $29,705

Wages, Tips, Other Compensation	Federal Income Tax Withheld	State Income Tax Withheld	FICA Wages	FICA Tax Withheld

Complete the required data for the following employees.

Employee	Gross Earnings	Federal Income Tax Withheld
A. Chavez	$50,000	$18,300
E. Kremer	24,000	4,800

PROBLEMS: SET C

Visit the book's companion website, at **www.wiley.com/college/weygandt**, and choose the Student Companion site to access Problem Set C.

COMPREHENSIVE PROBLEM

CP11 Morgan Company's balance sheet at December 31, 2013, is presented below.

MORGAN COMPANY
Balance Sheet
December 31, 2013

Cash	$ 30,000	Accounts Payable	$ 13,750
Inventory	30,750	Interest Payable	250
Prepaid Insurance	6,000	Notes Payable	50,000
Equipment	38,000	Owner's Capital	40,750
	$104,750		$104,750

During January 2014, the following transactions occurred. (Morgan Company uses the perpetual inventory system.)

1. Morgan paid $250 interest on the note payable on January 1, 2014. The note is due December 31, 2015.
2. Morgan purchased $261,100 of inventory on account.
3. Morgan sold for $440,000 cash, inventory which cost $265,000. Morgan also collected $28,600 in sales taxes.
4. Morgan paid $230,000 in accounts payable.
5. Morgan paid $17,000 in sales taxes to the state.
6. Paid other operating expenses of $30,000.
7. On January 31, 2014, the payroll for the month consists of salaries and wages of $60,000. All salaries and wages are subject to 7.65% FICA taxes. A total of $8,900 federal income taxes are withheld. The salaries and wages are paid on February 1.

Adjustment data:

8. Interest expense of $250 has been incurred on the notes payable.
9. The insurance for the year 2014 was prepaid on December 31, 2013.
10. The equipment was acquired on December 31, 2013, and will be depreciated on a straight-line basis over 5 years with a $2,000 salvage value.
11. Employer's payroll taxes include 7.65% FICA taxes, a 5.4% state unemployment tax, and an 0.8% federal unemployment tax.

Instructions
(You may need to set up T-accounts to determine ending balances.)

(a) Prepare journal entries for the transactions listed above and the adjusting entries.
(b) Prepare an adjusted trial balance at January 31, 2014.
(c) Prepare an income statement, an owner's equity statement for the month ending January 31, 2014, and a classified balance sheet as of January 31, 2014.

CONTINUING COOKIE CHRONICLE

(*Note:* This is a continuation of the Cookie Chronicle from Chapters 1 through 10.)

CCC11 Recall that Cookie Creations sells fine European mixers that it purchases from Kzinski Supply Co. Kzinski warrants the mixers to be free of defects in material and workmanship for a period of one year from the date of original purchase. If the mixer has such a defect, Kzinski will repair or replace the mixer free of charge for parts and labor.

*Go to the book's companion website, **www.wiley.com/college/weygandt**, to see the completion of this problem.*

Broadening Your Perspective

Financial Reporting and Analysis

Financial Reporting Problem: Apple Inc.

BYP11-1 The financial statements of Apple Inc. and the notes to consolidated financial statements appear in Appendix A. Instructions for accessing and using the company's complete annual report, including the notes to the financial statements, are also provided in Appendix A.

Instructions
Refer to Apple's financial statements and answer the following questions about current and contingent liabilities and payroll costs.

(a) What were Apple's total current liabilities at September 24, 2011? What was the increase/decrease in Apple's total current liabilities from the prior year?

(b) In Apple's Note 1 ("Summary of Significant Accounting Policies"), the company explains the nature of its contingencies. Under what conditions does Apple recognize (record and report) liabilities for contingencies?

(c) What were the components of total current liabilities on September 24, 2011?

Comparative Analysis Problem:
PepsiCo, Inc. vs. The Coca-Cola Company

BYP11-2 PepsiCo, Inc.'s financial statements are presented in Appendix B. Financial statements of The Coca-Cola Company are presented in Appendix C. Instructions for accessing and using the complete annual reports of PepsiCo and Coca-Cola, including the notes to the financial statements, are also provided in Appendices B and C, respectively.

Instructions
(a) At December 31, 2011, what was PepsiCo's largest current liability account? What were its total current liabilities? At December 31, 2011, what was Coca-Cola's largest current liability account? What were its total current liabilities?

(b) Based on information contained in those financial statements, compute the following 2011 values for each company:
 (1) Working capital.
 (2) Current ratio.

(c) What conclusions concerning the relative liquidity of these companies can be drawn from these data?

Comparative Analysis Problem:
Amazon.com, Inc. vs. Wal-Mart Stores, Inc.

BYP11-3 Amazon.com Inc.'s financial statements are presented in Appendix D. Financial statements for Wal-Mart Stores, Inc. are presented in Appendix E. Instructions for accessing and using the complete annual reports of Amazon and Wal-Mart, including the notes to the financial statements, are also provided in Appendices D and E, respectively.

Instructions
(a) At December 31, 2011, what was Amazon's largest current liability account? What were its total current liabilities? At January 31, 2012, what was Wal-Mart's largest current liability account? What were its total current liabilities?

(b) Based on information in these financial statements, compute the following 2011 values for Amazon and 2012 values for Wal-Mart:
 (1) Working capital.
 (2) Current ratio.

(c) What conclusions concerning the relative liquidity of these companies can be drawn from these data?

Real-World Focus

BYP11-4 The Internal Revenue Service provides considerable information over the Internet. The following site answers payroll tax questions faced by employers.

Address: **www.irs.ustreas.gov/formspubs/index.html**, or go to **www.wiley.com/college/weygandt**

Steps
1. Go to the site shown above.
2. Choose **View Online, Tax Publications**.
3. Choose **Publication 15, Circular E, Employer's Tax Guide**.

Instructions
Answer each of the following questions.

(a) How does the government define "employees"?
(b) What are the special rules for Social Security and Medicare regarding children who are employed by their parents?
(c) How can an employee obtain a Social Security card if he or she doesn't have one?
(d) Must employees report to their employer tips received from customers? If so, how?
(e) Where should the employer deposit Social Security taxes withheld or contributed?

Critical Thinking

Decision-Making Across the Organization

BYP11-5 Cunningham Processing Company performs word-processing services for business clients and students in a university community. The work for business clients is fairly steady throughout the year. The work for students peaks significantly in December and May as a result of term papers, research project reports, and dissertations.

Two years ago, the company attempted to meet the peak demand by hiring part-time help. This led to numerous errors and much customer dissatisfaction. A year ago, the company hired four experienced employees on a permanent basis in place of part-time help. This proved to be much better in terms of productivity and customer satisfaction. But, it has caused an increase in annual payroll costs and a significant decline in annual net income.

Recently, Melissa Braun, a sales representative of Banister Services Inc., has made a proposal to the company. Under her plan, Banister will provide up to four experienced workers at a daily rate of $80 per person for an 8-hour workday. Banister workers are not available on an hourly basis. Cunningham would have to pay only the daily rate for the workers used.

The owner of Cunningham Processing, Carol Holt, asks you, as the company's accountant, to prepare a report on the expenses that are pertinent to the decision. If the Banister plan is adopted, Carol will terminate the employment of two permanent employees and will keep two permanent employees. At the moment, each employee earns an annual income of $22,000. Cunningham pays 7.65% FICA taxes, 0.8% federal unemployment taxes, and 5.4% state unemployment taxes. The unemployment taxes apply to only the first $7,000 of gross earnings. In addition, Cunningham pays $40 per month for each employee for medical and dental insurance. Carol indicates that if the Banister Services plan is accepted, her needs for temporary workers will be as follows.

Months	Number of Employees	Working Days per Month
January–March	2	20
April–May	3	25
June–October	2	18
November–December	3	23

Instructions

With the class divided into groups, answer the following.

(a) Prepare a report showing the comparative payroll expense of continuing to employ permanent workers compared to adopting the Banister Services Inc. plan.

(b) What other factors should Carol consider before finalizing her decision?

Communication Activity

BYP11-6 Mike Falcon, president of the Brownlee Company, has recently hired a number of additional employees. He recognizes that additional payroll taxes will be due as a result of this hiring, and that the company will serve as the collection agent for other taxes.

Instructions

In a memorandum to Mike Falcon, explain each of the taxes, and identify the taxes that result in payroll tax expense to Brownlee Company.

Ethics Case

BYP11-7 Robert Eberle owns and manages Robert's Restaurant, a 24-hour restaurant near the city's medical complex. Robert employs 9 full-time employees and 16 part-time employees. He pays all of the full-time employees by check, the amounts of which are determined by Robert's public accountant, Anne Farr. Robert pays all of his part-time employees in currency. He computes their wages and withdraws the cash directly from his cash register.

Anne has repeatedly urged Robert to pay all employees by check. But as Robert has told his competitor and friend, Danny Gall, who owns the Greasy Diner, "My part-time employees prefer the currency over a check. Also, I don't withhold or pay any taxes or worker's compensation insurance on those cash wages because they go totally unrecorded and unnoticed."

Instructions
(a) Who are the stakeholders in this situation?
(b) What are the legal and ethical considerations regarding Robert's handling of his payroll?
(c) Anne Farr is aware of Robert's payment of the part-time payroll in currency. What are her ethical responsibilities in this case?
(d) What internal control principle is violated in this payroll process?

All About You

BYP11-8 Medical costs are substantial and rising. But will they be the most substantial expense over your lifetime? Not likely. Will it be housing or food? Again, not likely. The answer is taxes. On average, Americans work 107 days to afford their taxes. Companies, too, have large tax burdens. They look very hard at tax issues in deciding where to build their plants and where to locate their administrative headquarters.

Instructions
(a) Determine what your state income taxes are if your taxable income is $60,000 and you file as a single taxpayer in the state in which you live.
(b) Assume that you own a home worth $200,000 in your community and the tax rate is 2.1%. Compute the property taxes you would pay.
(c) Assume that the total gasoline bill for your automobile is $1,200 a year (300 gallons at $4 per gallon). What are the amounts of state and federal taxes that you pay on the $1,200?
(d) Assume that your purchases for the year total $9,000. Of this amount, $5,000 was for food and prescription drugs. What is the amount of sales tax you would pay on these purchases? (Many states do not levy a sales tax on food or prescription drugs. Does yours?)
(e) Determine what your Social Security taxes are if your income is $60,000.
(f) Determine what your federal income taxes are if your taxable income is $60,000 and you file as a single taxpayer.
(g) Determine your total taxes paid based on the above calculations, and determine the percentage of income that you would pay in taxes based on the following formula: Total taxes paid ÷ Total income.

FASB Codification Activity

BYP11-9 If your school has a subscription to the FASB Codification, go to **http://aaahq.org/ascLogin.cfm** to log in and prepare responses to the following.
(a) What is the definition of current liabilities?
(b) What is the definition of a contingent liability?
(c) What guidance does the Codification provide for the disclosure of contingent liabilities?

Answers to Chapter Questions

Answers to Accounting Across the Organization Questions

p. 529 Contingencies: How Big Are They?   Q: Why do you think most companies disclose, but do not record, contingent liabilities? **A:** A contingent liability may be probable, but often its amount is difficult to determine. If it cannot be determined, the company is not required to accrue it as a liability.

p. 540 It Costs $74,000 to Put $44,000 in Sally's Pocket   Q: How are the Social Security and Medicare taxes computed for Sally's salary? **A:** As indicated in the story, Sally's gross earnings were $59,000. The Social Security tax is 6.2% for both employee and employer up to gross earnings of $110,100 (2012 guidelines). As shown, both Sally and Bogan pay $3,658, which is 6.2% × $59,000. In addition, the Medicare tax is 1.45% on all gross earnings for both employee and employer. As shown, both Sally and Bogan pay $856, which is 1.45% × $59,000.

Answers to Self-Test Questions

1. a **2.** d **3.** b ($88,500 × 12% × 4/12) **4.** d **5.** b ($4,515 ÷ 1.05) **6.** b ($18,000 × 3/12) **7.** a
8. d **9.** c **10.** b **11.** d ($14 × 40) + ($21 × 5) **12.** c **13.** c **14.** b **15.** d *****16.** d

A Look at IFRS

LEARNING OBJECTIVE 10

Compare the accounting for payroll under GAAP and IFRS.

IFRS and GAAP have similar definitions of liabilities. IFRS related to reporting and recognition of liabilities are found in *IAS 1 (revised)* ("Presentation of Financial Statements") and *IAS 37* ("Provisions, Contingent Liabilities, and Contingent Assets"). The general recording procedures for payroll are similar, although differences occur depending on the types of benefits that are provided in different countries. For example, companies in other countries often have different forms of pensions, unemployment benefits, welfare payments, and so on. The accounting for various forms of compensation plans under IFRS is found in *IAS 19* ("Employee Benefits") and *IFRS 2* ("Share-based Payments"). *IAS 19* addresses the accounting for a wide range of compensation elements, including wages, bonuses, post-employment benefits, and compensated absences. Both of these standards were recently amended, resulting in significant convergence between IFRS and GAAP.

Key Points

- The basic definition of a liability under GAAP and IFRS is very similar. In a more technical way, liabilities are defined by the IASB as a present obligation of the entity arising from past events, the settlement of which is expected to result in an outflow from the entity of resources embodying economic benefits. Liabilities may be legally enforceable via a contract or law but need not be; that is, they can arise due to normal business practice or customs.

- IFRS requires that companies classify liabilities as current or noncurrent on the face of the statement of financial position (balance sheet), except in industries where a **presentation** based on liquidity would be considered to provide more useful information (such as financial institutions). When current liabilities (also called short-term liabilities) are presented, they are generally presented in order of liquidity.

- Under IFRS, liabilities are classified as current if they are expected to be paid within 12 months.

- Similar to GAAP, items are normally reported in order of liquidity. Companies sometimes show liabilities before assets. Also, they will sometimes show long-term liabilities before current liabilities.

- Under IFRS, companies sometimes will net current liabilities against current assets to show working capital on the face of the statement of financial position. (This is evident in the Zetar financial statements in Appendix F.)

- Under GAAP, some contingent liabilities are recorded in the financial statements, others are disclosed, and in some cases no disclosure is required. Unlike GAAP, IFRS reserves the use of the term **contingent liability** to refer only to possible obligations that are **not** recognized in the financial statements but may be disclosed if certain criteria are met. Contingent liabilities are defined in *IAS 37* as being:

  ♦ A possible obligation that arises from past events and whose existence will be confirmed only by the occurrence or nonoccurrence of one or more uncertain future events not wholly within the control of the entity; or

  ♦ A present obligation that arises from past events but is not recognized because:
    - It is not probable that an outflow of resources embodying economic benefits will be required to settle the obligation; or
    - The amount of the obligation cannot be measured with sufficient reliability.

- For those items that GAAP would treat as recordable contingent liabilities, IFRS instead uses the term provisions. **Provisions** are defined as liabilities of uncertain timing or amount. Examples of provisions would be provisions for warranties, employee vacation pay, or anticipated losses. Under IFRS, the measurement of a provision related to an uncertain obligation is based on the best estimate of the expenditure required to settle the obligation.

- IFRS and GAAP separate plans into defined benefit and defined contribution. The accounting for defined contribution plans is similar. For defined benefit plans, there are still some significant technical differences in the reporting between GAAP and IFRS. However, the IASB and FASB are working on a joint project on pensions that will most likely eliminate the differences between the two, while dramatically changing the approach used by both.

Looking to the Future

The FASB and IASB are currently involved in two projects, each of which has implications for the accounting for liabilities. One project is investigating approaches to differentiate between debt and equity instruments. The other project, the elements phase of the conceptual framework project, will evaluate the definitions of the fundamental building blocks of accounting. The results of these projects could change the classification of many debt and equity securities.

IFRS Practice

IFRS Self-Test Questions

1. Which of the following is **false**?
   (a) Under IFRS, current liabilities must always be presented before noncurrent liabilities.
   (b) Under IFRS, an item is a current liability if it will be paid within the next 12 months.
   (c) Under IFRS, current liabilities are shown in order of liquidity.
   (d) Under IFRS, a liability is only recognized if it is a present obligation.

2. Under IFRS, a contingent liability is:
   (a) disclosed in the notes if certain criteria are met.
   (b) reported on the face of the financial statements if certain criteria are met.
   (c) the same as a provision.
   (d) not covered by IFRS.

3. Under IFRS, obligations related to warranties are considered:
   (a) contingent liabilities.
   (b) provisions.
   (c) possible obligations.
   (d) None of these.

4. Which of the following statements is **true**?
   (a) The accounting for issues related to payroll are not covered in any IFRS.
   (b) The accounting for payrolls is similar under IFRS and U.S. GAAP.
   (c) Salary and wages payable is considered a contingent liability under IFRS.
   (d) IFRS does not normally report liabilities in order of liquidity.

5. The joint projects of the FASB and IASB could potentially:
   (a) change the definition of liabilities.
   (b) change the definition of equity.
   (c) change the definition of assets.
   (d) All of the above.

IFRS Exercises

IFRS11-1 Define a provision and give an example.

IFRS11-2 Define a contingent liability and give an example.

IFRS11-3 Briefly describe some of the similarities and differences between GAAP and IFRS with respect to the accounting for liabilities.

International Financial Statement Analysis: Zetar plc

IFRS11-4 The financial statements of Zetar plc are presented in Appendix F. Instructions for accessing and using Zetar's annual report are also provided in Appendix F.

Instructions
Use the company's complete annual report to answer the following questions.

(a) According to the notes to the financial statements, what types of transactions do trade payables relate to? What was the average amount of time it took the company to pay its payables?
(b) Note 3.4 discusses provisions that the company records for certain types of activities. What do the provisions relate to, what are the estimates based on, and what could cause those estimates to change in subsequent periods?
(c) What was the average interest rate paid on bank loans and overdrafts?

Answers to IFRS Self-Test Questions
1. a   2. a   3. b   4. b   5. d

✔ **The Navigator**

✔ Remember to go back to The Navigator box on the chapter opening page and check off your completed work.

12 | Accounting for Partnerships

Feature Story

From Trials to the Top Ten

In 1990, Cliff Chenfield and Craig Balsam gave up the razors, ties, and six-figure salaries they had become accustomed to as New York lawyers. Instead, they set up a partnership, Razor & Tie Music, in Cliff's living room. Ten years later, it became the only record company in the country that had achieved success in selling music both on television and in stores. Razor & Tie's entertaining and effective TV commercials have yielded unprecedented sales for multi-artist music compilations. At the same time, its hot retail label has been behind some of the most recent original, progressive releases from artists such as Kelly Sweet, All That Remains, EndeverafteR, Angelique Kidjo, Ryan Shaw, Dave Barnes, Twisted Sister, Dar Williams, Danko Jones, and Yerba Buena.

Razor & Tie may be best known for its wildly popular *Kidz Bop* CD series, the top-selling children's audio product in the United States. Advertised on Nickelodeon, the Cartoon Network, and elsewhere, *Kidz Bop* titles have sold millions of copies. Many of its releases in the series have "gone Gold."

Razor & Tie got its start with its first TV release, *Those Fabulous '70s* (100,000 copies sold), followed by *Disco Fever* (over 300,000 sold).

After restoring the respectability of the oft-maligned mu the 1970s, the partners forged into the musical '80s with same zeal that elicited success with their first releases. In 1993, Razor & Tie released *Totally '80s*, a collection of To singles from the 1980s that has sold over 450,000 units. Featuring the tag line, "The greatest hits from the decad when communism died and music videos were born," *To '80s* was the best-selling direct-response album in the co in 1993.

In 1995, Razor & Tie broke into the contemporary music world with *Living in the '90s*, the most successful record the history of the company. Featuring a number of song were still hits on the radio at the time the package initial aired, *Living in the '90s* was a blockbuster. It received Gc certification in less than nine months and rewrote the ru on direct-response albums. For the first time, contempor music was available through an album offered only throu direct-response spots. Razor & Tie pursued that same str with its 2002 introduction of the *Kidz Bop* titles.

In fact, Razor & Tie is now a vertically integrated busines includes a music company with major label distribution, music publishing business, a media buying company, a h

 The Navigator

- Scan Learning Objectives
- Read Feature Story
- Read Preview
- Read text and answer **DO IT!** p. 571
  - p. 577   p. 580   p. 583
- Work Comprehensive **DO IT!** p. 584
- Review Summary of Learning Objectives
- Answer Self-Test Questions
- Complete Assignments
- Go to *WileyPLUS* for practice and tutorials

As partnership accounting is essentially the same under GAAP and IFRS, there is

Learning Objectives   ✔ The Navigator

After studying this chapter, you should be able to:

[1] Identify the characteristics of the partnership form of business organization.

[2] Explain the accounting entries for the formation of a partnership.

[3] Identify the bases for dividing net income or net loss.

[4] Describe the form and content of partnership financial statements.

[5] Explain the effects of the entries to record the liquidation of a partnership.

video company, a direct marketing operation, and a growing database of entertainment consumers.

Razor & Tie has carved out a sizable piece of the market through the complementary talents of the two partners. Their imagination and savvy, along with exciting new releases planned for the coming years, ensure Razor & Tie's continued growth.

Preview of Chapter 12

✔ **The Navigator**

It is not surprising that when Cliff Chenfield and Craig Balsam began Razor & Tie, they decided to use the partnership form of organization. Both saw the need for hands-on control of their product and its promotion. In this chapter, we discuss reasons why businesses select the partnership form of organization. We also explain the major issues in accounting for partnerships.

The content and organization of Chapter 12 are as follows.

ACCOUNTING FOR PARTNERSHIPS

Partnership Form of Organization	Basic Partnership Accounting	Liquidation of a Partnership
• Characteristics • Organizations with partnership characteristics • Advantages/disadvantages • Partnership agreement	• Forming a partnership • Dividing net income/net loss • Partnership financial statements	• No capital deficiency • Capital deficiency

Partnership Form of Organization

LEARNING OBJECTIVE   1

Identify the characteristics of the partnership form of business organization.

A **partnership** is an association of two or more persons to carry on as co-owners of a business for profit. Partnerships are sometimes used in small retail, service, or manufacturing companies. Also accountants, lawyers, and doctors find it desirable to form partnerships with other professionals in the field.

Characteristics of Partnerships

Partnerships are fairly easy to form. People form partnerships simply by a verbal agreement or more formally by written agreement. We explain the principal characteristics of partnerships in the following sections.

ASSOCIATION OF INDIVIDUALS

Association of Individuals

A partnership is a legal entity. A partnership can own property (land, buildings, equipment) and can sue or be sued. **A partnership also is an accounting entity.** Thus, the personal assets, liabilities, and transactions of the partners are excluded from the accounting records of the partnership, just as they are in a proprietorship.

The net income of a partnership is not taxed as a separate entity. But, a partnership must file an information tax return showing partnership net income and each partner's share of that net income. Each partner's share is taxable at **personal tax rates**, regardless of the amount of net income each withdraws from the business during the year.

MUTUAL AGENCY

Mutual Agency

Mutual agency means that each partner acts on behalf of the partnership when engaging in partnership business. The act of any partner is binding on all other partners. This is true even when partners act beyond the scope of their authority, so long as the act appears to be appropriate for the partnership. For example, a partner of a grocery store who purchases a delivery truck creates a binding contract in the name of the partnership, even if the partnership agreement denies this authority. On the other hand, if a partner in a law firm purchased a snowmobile for the partnership, such an act would not be binding on the partnership. The purchase is clearly outside the scope of partnership business.

LIMITED LIFE

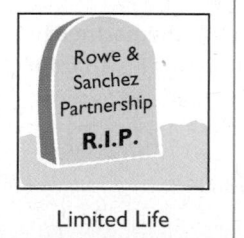

Limited Life

Corporations have unlimited life. Partnerships do not. A partnership may be ended voluntarily at any time through the acceptance of a new partner or the withdrawal of a partner. It may be ended involuntarily by the death or incapacity of a partner. **Partnership dissolution** occurs whenever a partner withdraws or a new partner is admitted. Dissolution does not necessarily mean that the business ends. If the continuing partners agree, operations can continue without interruption by forming a new partnership.

UNLIMITED LIABILITY

Each partner is **personally and individually liable** for all partnership liabilities. Creditors' claims attach first to partnership assets. If these are insufficient, the claims then attach to the personal resources of any partner, irrespective of that partner's equity in the partnership. Because each partner is responsible for all the debts of the partnership, each partner is said to have **unlimited liability**.

CO-OWNERSHIP OF PROPERTY

Unlimited Liability

Partners jointly own partnership assets. If the partnership is dissolved, each partner has a claim on total assets equal to the balance in his or her respective capital account. This claim does not attach to **specific assets** that an individual partner contributed to the firm. Similarly, if a partner invests a building in the partnership valued at $100,000 and the building is later sold at a gain of $20,000, the partners all share in the gain.

Partnership net income (or net loss) is also co-owned. **If the partnership contract does not specify to the contrary, all net income or net loss is shared equally by the partners.** As you will see later, though, partners may agree to unequal sharing of net income or net loss.

Co-ownership of Property

Organizations with Partnership Characteristics

If you are starting a business with a friend and each of you has little capital and your business is not risky, you probably want to use a partnership. As indicated above, the partnership is easy to establish and its cost is minimal. These types of partnerships are often called **regular partnerships**. However if your business is risky—say, roof repair or performing some type of professional service—you will want to limit your liability and not use a regular partnership. As a result, special forms of business organizations with partnership characteristics are now often used to provide protection from unlimited liability for people who wish to work together in some activity.

The special partnership forms are limited partnerships, limited liability partnerships, and limited liability companies. These special forms use the same accounting procedures as those described for a regular partnership. In addition, for taxation purposes, all the profits and losses pass through these organizations (similar to the regular partnership) to the owners, who report their share of partnership net income or losses on their personal tax returns.

LIMITED PARTNERSHIPS

In a **limited partnership**, one or more partners have **unlimited liability** and one or more partners have **limited liability** for the debts of the firm. Those with unlimited liability are **general partners**. Those with limited liability are **limited partners**. Limited partners are responsible for the debts of the partnership up to the limit of their investment in the firm.

The words "Limited Partnership," "Ltd.," or "LP" identify this type of organization. For the privilege of limited liability, the limited partner usually accepts less compensation than a general partner and exercises less influence in the affairs of the firm. If the limited partners get involved in management, they risk their liability protection.

LIMITED LIABILITY PARTNERSHIP

Most states allow professionals such as lawyers, doctors, and accountants to form a **limited liability partnership** or "LLP." The LLP is designed to protect innocent partners from malpractice or negligence claims resulting from the acts of another partner. LLPs generally carry large insurance policies as protection against malpractice suits. These professional partnerships vary in size from a medical partnership of three to five doctors, to 150 to 200 partners in a large law firm, to more than 2,000 partners in an international accounting firm.

LIMITED LIABILITY COMPANIES

A hybrid form of business organization with certain features like a corporation and others like a limited partnership is the **limited liability company** or "LLC." An LLC usually has a limited life. The owners, called **members**, have limited liability like owners of a corporation. Whereas limited partners do not actively participate in the management of a limited partnership (LP), the members of a limited liability company (LLC) can assume an active management role. For income tax purposes, the IRS usually classifies an LLC as a partnership.

International Note

Much of the funding for successful new U.S. businesses comes from "venture capital" firms, which are organized as limited partnerships. To develop its own venture capital industry, China believes that it needs the limited liability form. Therefore, China has taken steps to model its partnership laws to allow for limited partnerships like those in the United States.

Helpful Hint In an LLP, *all* partners have limited liability. There are no general partners.

ACCOUNTING ACROSS THE ORGANIZATION

Limited Liability Companies Gain in Popularity

The proprietorship form of business organization is still the most popular, followed by the corporate form. But whenever a group of individuals wants to form a partnership, the limited liability company is usually the popular choice.

One other form of business organization is a **subchapter S corporation**. A subchapter S corporation has many of the characteristics of a partnership—especially, taxation as a partnership—but it is losing its popularity. The reason: It involves more paperwork and expense than a limited liability company, which in most cases offers similar advantages.

 Why do you think that the use of the limited liability company is gaining in popularity? (See page 605.)

© Daniel Laflor/iStockphoto

Illustration 12-1 summarizes different forms of organizations that have partnership characteristics.

Illustration 12-1
Different forms of organizations with partnership characteristics

	Major Advantages	Major Disadvantages
Regular Partnership General Partners	Simple and inexpensive to create and operate.	Owners (partners) personally liable for business debts.
Limited Partnership General Partner Limited Partners	Limited partners have limited personal liability for business debts as long as they do not participate in management. General partners can raise cash without involving outside investors in management of business.	General partners personally liable for business debts. More expensive to create than regular partnership. Suitable mainly for companies that invest in real estate.
Limited Liability Partnership	Mostly of interest to partners in old-line professions such as law, medicine, and accounting. Owners (partners) are not personally liable for the malpractice of other partners.	Unlike a limited liability company, owners (partners) remain personally liable for many types of obligations owed to business creditors, lenders, and landlords. Often limited to a short list of professions.
Limited Liability Company	Owners have limited personal liability for business debts even if they participate in management.	More expensive to create than regular partnership.

Source: www.nolo.com (accessed June 2010).

Advantages and Disadvantages of Partnerships

Why do people choose partnerships? One major advantage of a partnership is to combine the skills and resources of two or more individuals. In addition, partnerships are easily formed and are relatively free from government regulations and restrictions. A partnership does not have to contend with the "red tape" that a corporation must face. Also, partners generally can make decisions quickly on substantive business matters without having to consult a board of directors.

On the other hand, partnerships also have some major disadvantages. **Unlimited liability** is particularly troublesome. Many individuals fear they may lose not only their initial investment but also their personal assets, if those assets are needed to pay partnership creditors.

Illustration 12-2 summarizes the advantages and disadvantages of the regular partnership form of business organization. As indicated in the previous section, different types of partnership forms have evolved to reduce some of the disadvantages.

Advantages	Disadvantages
Combining skills and resources of two or more individuals	Mutual agency
Ease of formation	Limited life
Freedom from governmental regulations and restrictions	Unlimited liability
Ease of decision-making	

Illustration 12-2
Advantages and disadvantages of a partnership

> **DO IT!**

Partnership Organization

Indicate whether each of the following statements is true or false.

_____ 1. Partnerships have unlimited life. Corporations do not.

_____ 2. Partners jointly own partnership assets. A partner's claim on partnership assets does not attach to specific assets.

_____ 3. In a limited partnership, the general partners have unlimited liability.

_____ 4. The members of a limited liability company have limited liability, like shareholders of a corporation, and they are taxed like corporate shareholders.

_____ 5. Because of mutual agency, the act of any partner is binding on all other partners.

Action Plan

✔ When forming a business, carefully consider what type of organization would best suit the needs of the business.

✔ Keep in mind the new, "hybrid" organizational forms that have many of the best characteristics of partnerships and corporations.

Solution

1. False. Corporations have unlimited life. Partnerships do not.
2. True.
3. True.
4. False. The members of a limited liability company are taxed like partners in a partnership.
5. True.

Related exercise material: **E12-1** and **DO IT!** 12-1.

 The Navigator

The Partnership Agreement

Ideally, the agreement of two or more individuals to form a partnership should be expressed in a written contract, called the **partnership agreement** or **articles of co-partnership**. The partnership agreement contains such basic information as

Ethics Note

A well-developed partnership agreement reduces ethical conflict among partners. It specifies in clear and concise language the process by which the partners will resolve ethical and legal problems. This issue is especially significant when the partnership experiences financial distress.

the name and principal location of the firm, the purpose of the business, and date of inception. In addition, it should specify relationships among the partners, such as:

1. Names and capital contributions of partners.
2. Rights and duties of partners.
3. Basis for sharing net income or net loss.
4. Provision for withdrawals of assets.
5. Procedures for submitting disputes to arbitration.
6. Procedures for the withdrawal or addition of a partner.
7. Rights and duties of surviving partners in the event of a partner's death.

We cannot overemphasize the importance of a written contract. The agreement should attempt to anticipate all possible situations, contingencies, and disagreements. The help of a lawyer is highly desirable in preparing the agreement.

PhotoDisc/Getty Images, Inc.

ACCOUNTING ACROSS THE ORGANIZATION

How to Part Ways Nicely

What should you do when you and your business partner do not agree on things, to the point where you are no longer on speaking terms? Given how heated business situations can get, this is not an unusual occurrence. Unfortunately, in many instances the partners do everything they can to undermine the other partner, eventually destroying the business. In some instances people even steal from the partnership because they either feel that they "deserve it" or they assume that the other partners are stealing from them.

It would be much better to follow the example of Jennifer Appel and her partner. They found that after opening a successful bakery and writing a cookbook, they couldn't agree on how the business should be run. The other partner bought out Ms. Appel's share of the business. Ms. Appel went on to start her own style of bakery, which she ultimately franchised.

Source: Paulette Thomas, "As Partnership Sours, Parting Is Sweet," *Wall Street Journal*, (July 6, 2004), p. A20.

How can partnership conflicts be minimized and more easily resolved? (See page 605.)

Basic Partnership Accounting

LEARNING OBJECTIVE   2

Explain the accounting entries for the formation of a partnership.

We now turn to the basic accounting for partnerships. The major accounting issues relate to forming the partnership, dividing income or loss, and preparing financial statements.

Forming a Partnership

Each partner's initial investment in a partnership is entered in the partnership records. The partnership should record these investments at the **fair value of the assets at the date of their transfer to the partnership**. All partners must agree to the values assigned.

To illustrate, assume that A. Rolfe and T. Shea combine their proprietorships to start a partnership named U.S. Software. The firm will specialize in developing financial modeling software packages. Rolfe and Shea have the following assets prior to the formation of the partnership.

	Book Value		Fair Value	
	A. Rolfe	T. Shea	A. Rolfe	T. Shea
Cash	$ 8,000	$ 9,000	$ 8,000	$ 9,000
Equipment	5,000		4,000	
Accumulated depreciation—equipment	(2,000)			
Accounts receivable		4,000		4,000
Allowance for doubtful accounts		(700)		(1,000)
	$11,000	$12,300	$12,000	$12,000

Illustration 12-3
Book and fair values of assets invested

*Items under **owners' equity (OE)** in the accounting equation analyses (in margins) are not labeled in this partnership chapter. Nearly all affect partners' **capital** accounts.*

The partnership records the investments as follows.

Investment of A. Rolfe

Cash	8,000	
Equipment	4,000	
A. Rolfe, Capital		12,000
(To record investment of Rolfe)		

Investment of T. Shea

Cash	9,000	
Accounts Receivable	4,000	
Allowance for Doubtful Accounts		1,000
T. Shea, Capital		12,000
(To record investment of Shea)		

A = L + OE
+8,000
+4,000
+12,000

Cash Flows
+8,000

A = L + OE
+9,000
+4,000
−1,000
+12,000

Cash Flows
+9,000

Note that the partnership records neither the original cost of the office equipment ($5,000) nor its book value ($5,000 − $2,000). It records the equipment at its fair value, $4,000. The partnership does not carry forward any accumulated depreciation from the books of previous entities (in this case, the two proprietorships).

In contrast, the gross claims on customers ($4,000) are carried forward to the partnership. The partnership adjusts the allowance for doubtful accounts to $1,000, to arrive at a cash (net) realizable value of $3,000. A partnership may start with an allowance for doubtful accounts because it will continue to collect existing accounts receivable, some of which are expected to be uncollectible. In addition, this procedure maintains the control and subsidiary relationship between Accounts Receivable and the accounts receivable subsidiary ledger.

After formation of the partnership, the accounting for transactions is similar to any other type of business organization. For example, the partners record all transactions with outside parties, such as the purchase or sale of inventory and the payment or receipt of cash, the same as would a sole proprietor.

The steps in the accounting cycle described in Chapter 4 for a proprietorship also apply to a partnership. For example, the partnership prepares a trial balance and journalizes and posts adjusting entries. A worksheet may be used. There are minor differences in journalizing and posting closing entries and in preparing financial statements, as we explain in the following sections. The differences occur because there is more than one owner.

Dividing Net Income or Net Loss

<table><tr><td>LEARNING OBJECTIVE</td><td>3</td></tr></table>

Identify the bases for dividing net income or net loss.

Partners equally share partnership net income or net loss unless the partnership contract indicates otherwise. The same basis of division usually applies to both net income and net loss. It is customary to refer to this basis as the **income ratio**, the **income and loss ratio**, or the **profit and loss (P&L) ratio**. Because of its wide acceptance, we will use the term **income ratio** to identify the basis for dividing net income and net loss. The partnership recognizes a partner's share of net income or net loss in the accounts through closing entries.

CLOSING ENTRIES

As in the case of a proprietorship, a partnership must make four entries in preparing closing entries. The entries are:

1. Debit each revenue account for its balance, and credit Income Summary for total revenues.
2. Debit Income Summary for total expenses, and credit each expense account for its balance.
3. Debit Income Summary for its balance, and credit each partner's capital account for his or her share of net income. Or, credit Income Summary, and debit each partner's capital account for his or her share of net loss.
4. Debit each partner's capital account for the balance in that partner's drawing account, and credit each partner's drawing account for the same amount.

The first two entries are the same as in a proprietorship. The last two entries are different because (1) there are two or more owners' capital and drawing accounts, and (2) it is necessary to divide net income (or net loss) among the partners.

To illustrate the last two closing entries, assume that AB Company has net income of $32,000 for 2014. The partners, L. Arbor and D. Barnett, share net income and net loss equally. Drawings for the year were Arbor $8,000 and Barnett $6,000. The last two closing entries are:

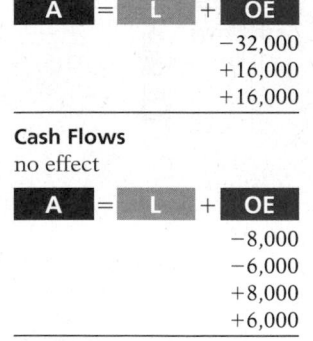

A = L + OE			
−32,000			
+16,000			
+16,000			

Cash Flows
no effect

Dec. 31	Income Summary	32,000	
	L. Arbor, Capital ($32,000 × 50%)		16,000
	D. Barnett, Capital ($32,000 × 50%)		16,000
	(To transfer net income to partners' capital accounts)		

A = L + OE			
−8,000			
−6,000			
+8,000			
+6,000			

Cash Flows
no effect

Dec. 31	L. Arbor, Capital	8,000	
	D. Barnett, Capital	6,000	
	L. Arbor, Drawings		8,000
	D. Barnett, Drawings		6,000
	(To close drawing accounts to capital accounts)		

Assume that the beginning capital balance is $47,000 for Arbor and $36,000 for Barnett. After posting the closing entries, the capital and drawing accounts will appear as shown in Illustration 12-4.

Illustration 12-4
Partners' capital and drawing accounts after closing

L. Arbor, Capital					D. Barnett, Capital			
12/31 **Clos.**	**8,000**	1/1 Bal.	47,000		12/31 **Clos.**	**6,000**	1/1 Bal.	36,000
		12/31 **Clos.**	**16,000**				12/31 **Clos.**	**16,000**
		12/31 Bal.	55,000				12/31 Bal.	46,000

L. Arbor, Drawings					D. Barnett, Drawings			
12/31 Bal.	8,000	12/31 **Clos.**	**8,000**		12/31 Bal.	6,000	12/31 **Clos.**	**6,000**

As in a proprietorship, the partners' capital accounts are permanent accounts. Their drawing accounts are temporary accounts. Normally, the capital accounts will have credit balances, and the drawing accounts will have debit balances. Drawing accounts are debited when partners withdraw cash or other assets from the partnership for personal use.

INCOME RATIOS

As noted earlier, the partnership agreement should specify the basis for sharing net income or net loss. The following are typical income ratios.

1. A fixed ratio, expressed as a proportion (6:4), a percentage (70% and 30%), or a fraction (2/3 and 1/3).

2. A ratio based either on capital balances at the beginning of the year or on average capital balances during the year.

3. Salaries to partners and the remainder on a fixed ratio.

4. Interest on partners' capital balances and the remainder on a fixed ratio.

5. Salaries to partners, interest on partners' capital, and the remainder on a fixed ratio.

The objective is to settle on a basis that will equitably reflect the partners' capital investment and service to the partnership.

A **fixed ratio** is easy to apply, and it may be an equitable basis in some circumstances. Assume, for example, that Hughes and Lane are partners. Each contributes the same amount of capital, but Hughes expects to work full-time in the partnership and Lane expects to work only half-time. Accordingly, the partners agree to a fixed ratio of 2/3 to Hughes and 1/3 to Lane.

A **ratio based on capital balances** may be appropriate when the funds invested in the partnership are considered the critical factor. Capital ratios may also be equitable when the partners hire a manager to run the business and do not plan to take an active role in daily operations.

The three remaining ratios (items 3, 4, and 5) give specific recognition to differences among partners. These ratios provide salary allowances for time worked and interest allowances for capital invested. Then, the partnership allocates any remaining net income or net loss on a fixed ratio.

Salaries to partners and interest on partners' capital are not expenses of the partnership. Therefore, these items do not enter into the matching of expenses with revenues and the determination of net income or net loss. For a partnership, as for other entities, salaries and wages expense pertains to the cost of services performed by employees. Likewise, interest expense relates to the cost of borrowing from creditors. But partners, as owners, are not considered either **employees** or **creditors**. When the partnership agreement permits the partners to make monthly withdrawals of cash based on their "salary," the partnership debits these withdrawals to the partner's drawing account.

SALARIES, INTEREST, AND REMAINDER ON A FIXED RATIO

Under income ratio (5) in the list above, the partnership must apply salaries and interest **before** it allocates the remainder on the specified fixed ratio. **This is true even if the provisions exceed net income. It is also true even if the partnership has suffered a net loss for the year.** The partnership's income statement should show, below net income, detailed information concerning the division of net income or net loss.

To illustrate, assume that Sara King and Ray Lee are co-partners in the Kingslee Company. The partnership agreement provides for (1) salary allowances of $8,400 to King and $6,000 to Lee, (2) interest allowances of 10% on capital balances at the beginning of the year, and (3) the remaining income to be divided equally. Capital balances on January 1 were King $28,000, and Lee $24,000. In 2014, partnership net income is $22,000. The division of net income is as shown on page 576.

Illustration 12-5
Division of net income schedule

KINGSLEE COMPANY			
Division of Net Income			
For the Year Ended December 31, 2014			

	Net income			$ 22,000	

Division of Net Income

	Sara King	Ray Lee	Total
Salary allowance	$ 8,400	$6,000	$14,400
Interest allowance on partners' capital			
Sara King ($28,000 × 10%)	2,800		
Ray Lee ($24,000 × 10%)		2,400	
Total interest allowance			5,200
Total salaries and interest	11,200	8,400	19,600
Remaining income, $2,400			
($22,000 − $19,600)			
Sara King ($2,400 × 50%)	1,200		
Ray Lee ($2,400 × 50%)		1,200	
Total remainder			2,400
Total division of net income	**$12,400**	**$9,600**	**$22,000**

Kingslee records the division of net income as follows.

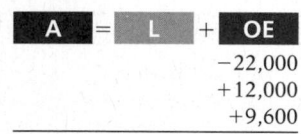

Cash Flows
no effect

Dec. 31	Income Summary	22,000	
	Sara King, Capital		12,400
	Ray Lee, Capital		9,600
	(To close net income to partners' capital)		

Now let's look at a situation in which the salary and interest allowances **exceed** net income. Assume that Kingslee Company's net income is only $18,000. In this case, the salary and interest allowances will create a deficiency of $1,600 ($18,000 − $19,600). The computations of the allowances are the same as those in the preceding example. Beginning with total salaries and interest, we complete the division of net income as shown in Illustration 12-6.

Illustration 12-6
Division of net income—income deficiency

	Sara King	Ray Lee	Total
Total salaries and interest	$11,200	$8,400	$19,600
Remaining deficiency ($1,600)			
($18,000 − $19,600)			
Sara King ($1,600 × 50%)	(800)		
Ray Lee ($1,600 × 50%)		(800)	
Total remainder			(1,600)
Total division	**$10,400**	**$7,600**	**$18,000**

Partnership Financial Statements

LEARNING OBJECTIVE 4

Describe the form and content of partnership financial statements.

The financial statements of a partnership are similar to those of a proprietorship. The differences are due to the number of owners involved. The income statement for a partnership is identical to the income statement for a proprietorship except for the division of net income, as shown earlier.

The owners' equity statement for a partnership is called the **partners' capital statement**. It explains the changes in each partner's capital account and in total partnership capital during the year. Illustration 12-7 shows the partners' capital statement for Kingslee Company. It is based on the division of $22,000 of net income in Illustration 12-5. The statement includes assumed data for the additional investment and drawings. The partnership prepares the partners' capital statement from the income statement and the partners' capital and drawing accounts.

Illustration 12-7
Partners' capital statement

KINGSLEE COMPANY Partners' Capital Statement For the Year Ended December 31, 2014			
	Sara King	Ray Lee	Total
Capital, January 1	$28,000	$24,000	$52,000
Add: Additional investment	2,000		2,000
Net income	12,400	9,600	22,000
	42,400	33,600	76,000
Less: Drawings	7,000	5,000	12,000
Capital, December 31	$35,400	$28,600	$64,000

Helpful Hint As in a proprietorship, partners' capital may change due to (1) additional investment, (2) drawings, and (3) net income or net loss.

The balance sheet for a partnership is the same as for a proprietorship except for the owners' equity section. For a partnership, the balance sheet shows the capital balances of each partner. The owners' equity section for Kingslee Company would show the following.

Illustration 12-8
Owners' equity section of a partnership balance sheet

KINGSLEE COMPANY Balance Sheet (partial) December 31, 2014		
Total liabilities (assumed amount)		$115,000
Owners' equity		
Sara King, capital	$35,400	
Ray Lee, capital	28,600	
Total owners' equity		64,000
Total liabilities and owners' equity		$179,000

> **DO IT!**

Division of Net Income

LeeMay Company reports net income of $57,000. The partnership agreement provides for salaries of $15,000 to L. Lee and $12,000 to R. May. They will share the remainder on a 60:40 basis (60% to Lee). L. Lee asks your help to divide the net income between the partners and to prepare the closing entry.

Solution

Action Plan

✔ Compute net income exclusive of any salaries to partners and interest on partners' capital.

✔ Deduct salaries to partners from net income.

✔ Apply the partners' income ratios to the remaining net income.

The division of net income is as follows.

	L. Lee	R. May	Total
Salary allowance	$15,000	$12,000	$27,000
Remaining income $30,000 ($57,000 − $27,000)			
L. Lee (60% × $30,000)	18,000		
R. May (40% × $30,000)		12,000	
Total remaining income			30,000
Total division of net income	$33,000	$24,000	$57,000

Action Plan (cont'd.)

✔ Prepare the closing entry distributing net income or net loss among the partners' capital accounts.

The closing entry for net income therefore is:

Income Summary	57,000	
L. Lee, Capital		33,000
R. May, Capital		24,000
(To close net income to partners' capital accounts)		

Related exercise material: **BE12-3, BE12-4, BE12-5, E12-4, E12-5, and** **DO IT!** **12-2.**

✔ **The Navigator**

Liquidation of a Partnership

LEARNING OBJECTIVE   **5**

Explain the effects of the entries to record the liquidation of a partnership.

Liquidation of a business involves selling the assets of the firm, paying liabilities, and distributing any remaining assets. Liquidation may result from the sale of the business by mutual agreement of the partners, from the death of a partner, or from bankruptcy. **Partnership liquidation** ends both the legal and economic life of the entity.

From an accounting standpoint, the partnership should complete the accounting cycle for the final operating period prior to liquidation. This includes preparing adjusting entries and financial statements. It also involves preparing closing entries and a post-closing trial balance. Thus, only balance sheet accounts should be open as the liquidation process begins.

In liquidation, the sale of noncash assets for cash is called **realization**. Any difference between book value and the cash proceeds is called the **gain or loss on realization**. To liquidate a partnership, it is necessary to:

> ## Ethics Note
>
> The process of selling noncash assets and then distributing the cash reduces the likelihood of partner disputes. If, instead, the partnership distributes noncash assets to partners to liquidate the firm, the partners would need to agree on the value of the noncash assets, which can be very difficult to determine.

1. Sell noncash assets for cash and recognize a gain or loss on realization.
2. Allocate gain/loss on realization to the partners based on their income ratios.
3. Pay partnership liabilities in cash.
4. Distribute remaining cash to partners on the basis of their **capital balances**.

Each of the steps must be performed in sequence. The partnership must pay creditors **before** partners receive any cash distributions. Also, an accounting entry must record each step.

When a partnership is liquidated, all partners may have credit balances in their capital accounts. This situation is called **no capital deficiency**. Or, one or more partners may have a debit balance in the capital account. This situation is termed a **capital deficiency**. To illustrate each of these conditions, assume that Ace Company is liquidated when its ledger shows the following assets, liabilities, and owners' equity accounts.

Illustration 12-9
Account balances prior to liquidation

Assets		Liabilities and Owners' Equity	
Cash	$ 5,000	Notes Payable	$15,000
Accounts Receivable	15,000	Accounts Payable	16,000
Inventory	18,000	R. Arnet, Capital	15,000
Equipment	35,000	P. Carey, Capital	17,800
Accum. Depr.—Equipment	(8,000)	W. Eaton, Capital	1,200
	$65,000		$65,000

No Capital Deficiency

The partners of Ace Company agree to liquidate the partnership on the following terms. (1) The partnership will sell its noncash assets to Jackson Enterprises for $75,000 cash. (2) The partnership will pay its partnership liabilities. The income ratios of the partners are 3:2:1, respectively. The steps in the liquidation process are as follows.

1. Ace sells the noncash assets (accounts receivable, inventory, and equipment) for $75,000. The book value of these assets is $60,000 ($15,000 + $18,000 + $35,000 − $8,000). Thus, Ace realizes a gain of $15,000 on the sale. The entry is:

(1)

Cash	75,000	
Accumulated Depreciation–Equipment	8,000	
Accounts Receivable		15,000
Inventory		18,000
Equipment		35,000
Gain on Realization		15,000
(To record realization of noncash assets)		

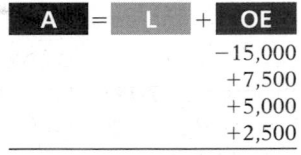

A	=	L	+	OE
+75,000				
+8,000				
−15,000				
−18,000				
−35,000				
				+15,000

Cash Flows
+75,000

2. Ace allocates the $15,000 gain on realization to the partners based on their income ratios, which are 3:2:1. The entry is:

(2)

Gain on Realization	15,000	
R. Arnet, Capital ($15,000 × 3/6)		7,500
P. Carey, Capital ($15,000 × 2/6)		5,000
W. Eaton, Capital ($15,000 × 1/6)		2,500
(To allocate gain to partners' capital accounts)		

A	=	L	+	OE
				−15,000
				+7,500
				+5,000
				+2,500

Cash Flows
no effect

3. Partnership liabilities consist of Notes Payable $15,000 and Accounts Payable $16,000. Ace pays creditors in full by a cash payment of $31,000. The entry is:

(3)

Notes Payable	15,000	
Accounts Payable	16,000	
Cash		31,000
(To record payment of partnership liabilities)		

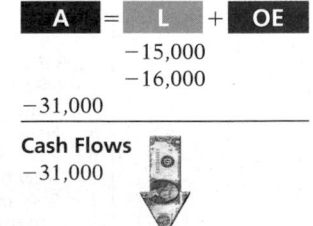

A	=	L	+	OE
		−15,000		
		−16,000		
−31,000				

Cash Flows
−31,000

4. Ace distributes the remaining cash to the partners on the basis of **their capital balances**. After posting the entries in the first three steps, all partnership accounts, including Gain on Realization, will have zero balances except for four accounts: Cash $49,000; R. Arnet, Capital $22,500; P. Carey, Capital $22,800; and W. Eaton, Capital $3,700, as shown below.

Illustration 12-10
Ledger balances before distribution of cash

Cash		R. Arnet, Capital	P. Carey, Capital	W. Eaton, Capital
Bal. 5,000	(3) 31,000	Bal. 15,000	Bal. 17,800	Bal. 1,200
(1) 75,000		(2) 7,500	(2) 5,000	(2) 2,500
Bal. 49,000		**Bal. 22,500**	**Bal. 22,800**	**Bal. 3,700**

Ace records the distribution of cash as follows.

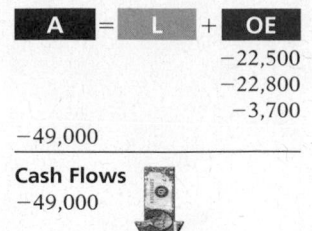

−22,500
−22,800
−3,700
−49,000

Cash Flows
−49,000

(4)

R. Arnet, Capital	22,500	
P. Carey, Capital	22,800	
W. Eaton, Capital	3,700	
Cash		49,000
(To record distribution of cash to partners)		

After posting this entry, all partnership accounts will have zero balances.

A word of caution: **Partnerships should not distribute remaining cash to partners on the basis of their income-sharing ratios.** On this basis, Arnet would receive three-sixths, or $24,500, which would produce an erroneous debit balance of $2,000. The income ratio is the proper basis for allocating net income or loss. **It is not a proper basis for making the final distribution of cash to the partners.**

SCHEDULE OF CASH PAYMENTS

Alternative Terminology
The schedule of cash payments is sometimes called a *safe cash payments schedule.*

The **schedule of cash payments** shows the distribution of cash to the partners in a partnership liquidation. A cash payments schedule is sometimes prepared to determine the distribution of cash to the partners in the liquidation of a partnership. The schedule of cash payments is organized around the basic accounting equation. Illustration 12-11 shows the schedule for Ace Company. The numbers in parentheses refer to the four required steps in the liquidation of a partnership. They also identify the accounting entries that Ace must make. The cash payments schedule is especially useful when the liquidation process extends over a period of time.

Illustration 12-11
Schedule of cash payments, no capital deficiency

ACE Company.xls

Home   Insert   Page Layout   Formulas   Data   Review   View

P18   *fx*

ACE COMPANY
Schedule of Cash Payments

Item		Cash	+	Noncash Assets	=	Liabilities	+	R. Arnet, Capital	+	P. Carey, Capital	+	W. Eaton, Capital
Balances before liquidation		5,000	+	60,000	=	31,000	+	15,000	+	17,800	+	1,200
Sale of noncash assets and allocation of gain	(1)&(2)	75,000	+	(60,000)	=			7,500	+	5,000	+	2,500
New balances		80,000	+	−0−	=	31,000	+	22,500	+	22,800	+	3,700
Pay liabilities	(3)	(31,000)			=	(31,000)						
New balances		49,000	+	−0−	=	−0−	+	22,500	+	22,800	+	3,700
Cash distribution to partners	(4)	(49,000)			=			(22,500)	+	(22,800)	+	(3,700)
Final balances		−0−		−0−		−0−		−0−		−0−		−0−

> DO IT!

Partnership Liquidation—No Capital Deficiency

The partners of Grafton Company have decided to liquidate their business. Noncash assets were sold for $115,000. The income ratios of the partners Kale D., Croix D., and Marais K. are 2:3:3, respectively. Complete the following schedule of cash payments for Grafton Company.

Action Plan

✔ First, sell the noncash assets and determine the gain.

✔ Allocate the gain to the partners based on their income ratios.

✔ Use cash to pay off liabilities.

✔ Distribute remaining cash on the basis of their capital balances.

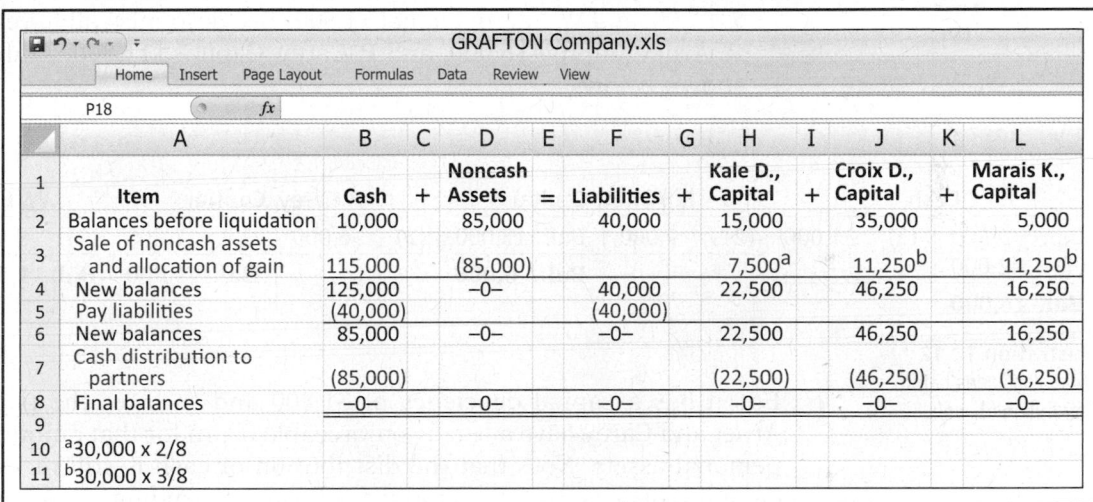

GRAFTON Company.xls

Item	Cash +	Noncash Assets =	Liabilities +	Kale D., Capital +	Croix D., Capital +	Marais K., Capital
1						
2 Balances before liquidation	10,000	85,000	40,000	15,000	35,000	5,000
3 Sale of noncash assets and allocation of gain						
4 New balances						
5 Pay liabilities						
6 New balances						
7 Cash distribution to partners						
8 Final balances						
9						
10						

Solution

GRAFTON Company.xls

Item	Cash +	Noncash Assets =	Liabilities +	Kale D., Capital +	Croix D., Capital +	Marais K., Capital
1						
2 Balances before liquidation	10,000	85,000	40,000	15,000	35,000	5,000
3 Sale of noncash assets and allocation of gain	115,000	(85,000)		7,500[a]	11,250[b]	11,250[b]
4 New balances	125,000	–0–	40,000	22,500	46,250	16,250
5 Pay liabilities	(40,000)		(40,000)			
6 New balances	85,000	–0–	–0–	22,500	46,250	16,250
7 Cash distribution to partners	(85,000)			(22,500)	(46,250)	(16,250)
8 Final balances	–0–	–0–	–0–	–0–	–0–	–0–
9						
10 [a]30,000 x 2/8						
11 [b]30,000 x 3/8						

Related exercise material: **BE12-6, E12-8, E12-9, and DO IT! 12-3.**

✔ The Navigator

Capital Deficiency

A capital deficiency may result from recurring net losses, excessive drawings, or losses from realization suffered during liquidation. To illustrate, assume that Ace Company is on the brink of bankruptcy. The partners decide to liquidate by having a "going-out-of-business" sale. They sell merchandise at substantial discounts, and sell the equipment at auction. Cash proceeds from these sales and collections from customers total only $42,000. Thus, the loss from liquidation is $18,000 ($60,000 − $42,000). The steps in the liquidation process are as follows.

1. The entry for the realization of noncash assets is:

(1)

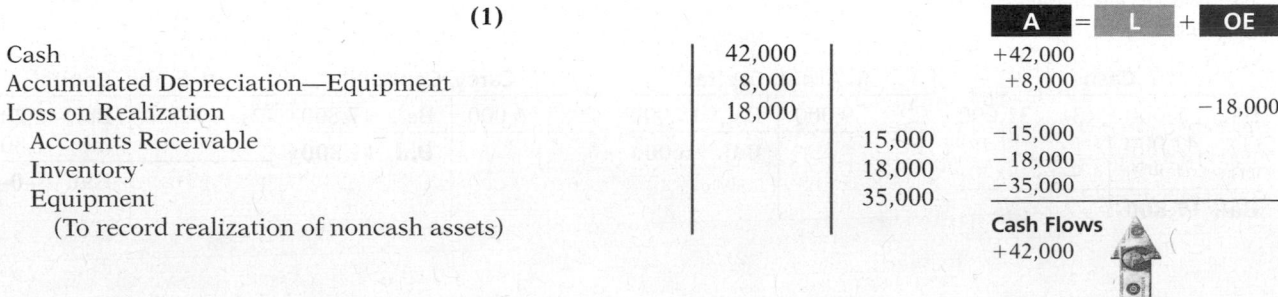

			A = L + OE
Cash	42,000		+42,000
Accumulated Depreciation—Equipment	8,000		+8,000
Loss on Realization	18,000		−18,000
Accounts Receivable		15,000	−15,000
Inventory		18,000	−18,000
Equipment		35,000	−35,000
(To record realization of noncash assets)			**Cash Flows** +42,000

2. Ace allocates the loss on realization to the partners on the basis of their income ratios. The entry is:

(2)

R. Arnet, Capital ($18,000 × 3/6)	9,000	
P. Carey, Capital ($18,000 × 2/6)	6,000	
W. Eaton, Capital ($18,000 × 1/6)	3,000	
Loss on Realization		18,000
(To allocate loss on realization to partners)		

A = L + OE
−9,000
−6,000
−3,000
+18,000

Cash Flows
no effect

3. Ace pays the partnership liabilities. This entry is the same as the previous one.

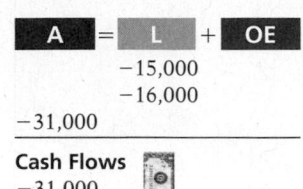

A = L + OE
−15,000
−16,000
−31,000

Cash Flows
−31,000

(3)

Notes Payable	15,000	
Accounts Payable	16,000	
Cash		31,000
(To record payment of partnership liabilities)		

4. After posting the three entries, two accounts will have debit balances—Cash $16,000, and W. Eaton, Capital $1,800. Two accounts will have credit balances—R. Arnet, Capital $6,000, and P. Carey, Capital $11,800. All four accounts are shown below.

Cash				R. Arnet, Capital				P. Carey, Capital				W. Eaton, Capital			
Bal.	5,000	(3)	31,000	(2)	9,000	Bal.	15,000	(2)	6,000	Bal.	17,800	(2)	3,000	Bal.	1,200
(1)	42,000					**Bal.**	**6,000**			**Bal.**	**11,800**	**Bal.**	**1,800**		
Bal.	**16,000**														

Illustration 12-12
Ledger balances before distribution of cash

Eaton has a capital deficiency of $1,800 and so owes the partnership $1,800. Arnet and Carey have a legally enforceable claim for that amount against Eaton's personal assets. Note that the distribution of cash is still made on the basis of capital balances. But, the amount will vary depending on how Eaton settles the deficiency. Two alternatives are presented in the following sections.

PAYMENT OF DEFICIENCY

If the partner with the capital deficiency pays the amount owed the partnership, the deficiency is eliminated. To illustrate, assume that Eaton pays $1,800 to the partnership. The entry is:

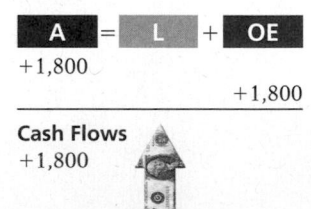

A = L + OE
+1,800
+1,800

Cash Flows
+1,800

(a)

Cash	1,800	
W. Eaton, Capital		1,800
(To record payment of capital deficiency by Eaton)		

After posting this entry, account balances are as follows.

Illustration 12-13
Ledger balances after paying capital deficiency

Cash				R. Arnet, Capital				P. Carey, Capital				W. Eaton, Capital			
Bal.	5,000	(3)	31,000	(2)	9,000	Bal.	15,000	(2)	6,000	Bal.	17,800	(2)	3,000	Bal.	1,200
(1)	42,000					**Bal.**	**6,000**			**Bal.**	**11,800**			(a)	1,800
(a)	1,800													**Bal.**	**–0–**
Bal.	**17,800**														

The cash balance of $17,800 is now equal to the credit balances in the capital accounts (Arnet $6,000 + Carey $11,800). Ace now distributes cash on the basis of these balances. The entry is:

R. Arnet, Capital	6,000	
P. Carey, Capital	11,800	
Cash		17,800
(To record distribution of cash to the partners)		

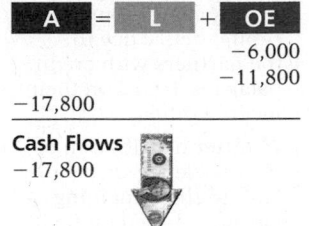

After posting this entry, all accounts will have zero balances.

NONPAYMENT OF DEFICIENCY

If a partner with a capital deficiency is unable to pay the amount owed to the partnership, the partners with credit balances must absorb the loss. The partnership allocates the loss on the basis of the income ratios that exist between the partners with credit balances.

The income ratios of Arnet and Carey are 3:2, or 3/5 and 2/5, respectively. Thus, Ace would make the following entry to remove Eaton's capital deficiency.

(a)

R. Arnet, Capital ($1,800 × 3/5)	1,080	
P. Carey, Capital ($1,800 × 2/5)	720	
W. Eaton, Capital		1,800
(To record write-off of capital deficiency)		

After posting this entry, the cash and capital accounts will have the following balances.

Cash			R. Arnet, Capital			P. Carey, Capital			W. Eaton, Capital		
Bal. 5,000	(3) 31,000		(2) 9,000	Bal. 15,000		(2) 6,000	Bal. 17,800		(2) 3,000	Bal. 1,200	
(1) 42,000			(a) 1,080			(a) 720				(a) 1,800	
Bal. 16,000				Bal. 4,920			Bal. 11,080			Bal. –0–	

Illustration 12-14
Ledger balances after nonpayment of capital deficiency

The cash balance ($16,000) now equals the sum of the credit balances in the capital accounts (Arnet $4,920 + Carey $11,080). Ace records the distribution of cash as:

R. Arnet, Capital	4,920	
P. Carey, Capital	11,080	
Cash		16,000
(To record distribution of cash to the partners)		

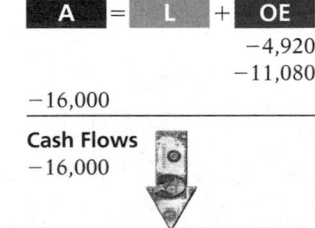

After posting this entry, all accounts will have zero balances.

> **DO IT!**

Partnership Liquidation— Capital Deficiency

Kessington Company wishes to liquidate the firm by distributing the company's cash to the three partners. Prior to the distribution of cash, the company's balances are Cash $45,000; Rollings, Capital (Cr.) $28,000; Havens, Capital (Dr.) $12,000; and Ostergard, Capital (Cr.) $29,000. The income ratios of the three partners are 4:4:2, respectively. Prepare the entry to record the absorption of Havens' capital deficiency by the other partners and the distribution of cash to the partners with credit balances.

Action Plan

✔ Allocate any unpaid capital deficiency to the partners with credit balances, based on their income ratios.

✔ After distribution of the deficiency, distribute cash to the remaining partners, based on their capital balances.

Solution

Rollings, Capital ($12,000 × 4/6)	8,000	
Ostergard, Capital ($12,000 × 2/6)	4,000	
Havens, Capital		12,000
(To record write-off of capital deficiency)		
Rollings, Capital ($28,000 − $8,000)	20,000	
Ostergard, Capital ($29,000 − $4,000)	25,000	
Cash		45,000
(To record distribution of cash to partners)		

Related exercise material: **E12-10 and DO IT! 12-4.**

✔ **The Navigator**

> Comprehensive DO IT!

On January 1, 2014, the capital balances in Hollingsworth Company are Lois Holly $26,000, and Jim Worth $24,000. In 2014 the partnership reports net income of $30,000. The income ratio provides for salary allowances of $12,000 for Holly and $10,000 to Worth and the remainder equally. Neither partner had any drawings in 2014.

Instructions

(a) Prepare a schedule showing the distribution of net income in 2014.
(b) Journalize the division of 2014 net income to the partners.

Solution to Comprehensive DO IT!

Action Plan

✔ Compute the net income of the partnership.

✔ Allocate the partners' salaries.

✔ Divide the remaining net income among the partners, applying the income/loss ratio.

✔ Journalize the division of net income in a closing entry.

(a)   Net income $30,000

Division of Net Income

	Lois Holly	Jim Worth	Total
Salary allowance	$12,000	$10,000	$22,000
Remaining income $8,000 ($30,000 − $22,000)			
Lois Holly ($8,000 × 50%)	4,000		
Jim Worth ($8,000 × 50%)		4,000	
Total remainder			8,000
Total division of net income	$16,000	$14,000	$30,000

(b) 12/31/14

Income Summary	30,000	
Lois Holly, Capital		16,000
Jim Worth, Capital		14,000
(To close net income to partners' capital)		

✔ **The Navigator**

SUMMARY OF LEARNING OBJECTIVES

✔ **The Navigator**

1 **Identify the characteristics of the partnership form of business organization.** The principal characteristics of a partnership are (a) association of individuals, (b) mutual agency, (c) limited life, (d) unlimited liability, and (e) co-ownership of property.

2 **Explain the accounting entries for the formation of a partnership.** When formed, a partnership records each partner's initial investment at the fair value of the assets at the date of their transfer to the partnership.

3 **Identify the bases for dividing net income or net loss.** Partnerships divide net income or net loss on the basis of the income ratio, which may be (a) a fixed ratio, (b) a ratio based on beginning or average capital balances, (c) salaries to partners and the remainder on a fixed ratio, (d) interest on partners' capital and the remainder on a fixed ratio, and (e) salaries to partners, interest on partners' capital, and the remainder on a fixed ratio.

4 **Describe the form and content of partnership financial statements.** The financial statements of a partnership are similar to those of a proprietorship. The principal differences are as follows. (a) The partnership shows the division of net income on the income statement. (b) The owners' equity statement is called a partners' capital statement. (c) The partnership reports each partner's capital on the balance sheet.

5 **Explain the effects of the entries to record the liquidation of a partnership.** When a partnership is liquidated, it is necessary to record the (a) sale of noncash assets, (b) allocation of the gain or loss on realization, (c) payment of partnership liabilities, and (d) distribution of cash to the partners on the basis of their capital balances.

GLOSSARY

Capital deficiency A debit balance in a partner's capital account after allocation of gain or loss. (p. 578).

General partners Partners who have unlimited liability for the debts of the firm. (p. 569).

Income ratio The basis for dividing net income and net loss in a partnership. (p. 574).

Limited liability company A form of business organization, usually classified as a partnership for tax purposes and usually with limited life, in which partners, who are called members, have limited liability. (p. 569).

Limited liability partnership A partnership of professionals in which partners are given limited liability and the public is protected from malpractice by insurance carried by the partnership. (p. 569).

Limited partners Partners whose liability for the debts of the firm is limited to their investment in the firm. (p. 569).

Limited partnership A partnership in which one or more general partners have unlimited liability and one or more partners have limited liability for the obligations of the firm. (p. 569).

No capital deficiency All partners have credit balances after allocation of gain or loss. (p. 578).

Partners' capital statement The owners' equity statement for a partnership which shows the changes in each partner's capital account and in total partnership capital during the year. (p. 576).

Partnership An association of two or more persons to carry on as co-owners of a business for profit. (p. 568).

Partnership agreement A written contract expressing the voluntary agreement of two or more individuals in a partnership. (p. 571).

Partnership dissolution A change in partners due to withdrawal or admission, which does not necessarily terminate the business. (p. 568).

Partnership liquidation An event that ends both the legal and economic life of a partnership. (p. 578).

Schedule of cash payments A schedule showing the distribution of cash to the partners in a partnership liquidation. (p. 580).

APPENDIX 12A   Admission and Withdrawal of Partners

The chapter explained how the basic accounting for a partnership works. We now look at how to account for a common occurrence in partnerships—the addition or withdrawal of a partner.

Admission of a Partner

The admission of a new partner results in the **legal dissolution** of the existing partnership and the beginning of a new one. From an economic standpoint, however, the admission of a new partner (or partners) may be of minor significance in the continuity of the business. For example, in large public accounting or law firms, partners are admitted annually without any change in operating policies. **To recognize the economic effects, it is necessary only to open a capital account for each new partner.** In the entries illustrated in this appendix, we assume that the accounting records of the predecessor firm will continue to be used by the new partnership.

> **LEARNING OBJECTIVE   6**
>
> Explain the effects of the entries when a new partner is admitted.

Helpful Hint In a purchase of an interest, the partnership is not a participant in the transaction. In this transaction, the new partner contributes *no* cash to the partnership.

A new partner may be admitted either by (1) purchasing the interest of one or more existing partners or (2) investing assets in the partnership. The former affects only the capital accounts of the partners who are parties to the transaction. The latter increases both net assets and total capital of the partnership.

PURCHASE OF A PARTNER'S INTEREST

The **admission** of a partner **by purchase of an interest** is a personal transaction between one or more existing partners and the new partner. Each party acts as an individual separate from the partnership entity. The individuals involved negotiate the price paid. It may be equal to or different from the capital equity acquired. The purchase price passes directly from the new partner to the partners who are giving up part or all of their ownership claims.

Any money or other consideration exchanged is the personal property of the participants and **not** the property of the partnership. Upon purchase of an interest, the new partner acquires each selling partner's capital interest and income ratio.

Accounting for the purchase of an interest is straightforward. The partnership records only the changes in partners' capital. **Partners' capital accounts are debited for any ownership claims sold.** At the same time, the new partner's capital account is credited for the capital equity purchased. Total assets, total liabilities, and total capital remain unchanged, as do all individual asset and liability accounts.

To illustrate, assume that L. Carson agrees to pay $10,000 each to C. Ames and D. Barker for 33⅓% (one-third) of their interest in the Ames–Barker partnership. At the time of the admission of Carson, each partner has a $30,000 capital balance. Both partners, therefore, give up $10,000 of their capital equity. The entry to record the admission of Carson is:

C. Ames, Capital	10,000	
D. Barker, Capital	10,000	
L. Carson, Capital		20,000
(To record admission of Carson by purchase)		

The effect of this transaction on net assets and partners' capital is shown below.

Net Assets	C. Ames, Capital		D. Barker, Capital		L. Carson, Capital
60,000	**10,000**	30,000	**10,000**	30,000	**20,000**
		Bal. 20,000		Bal. 20,000	

Illustration 12A-1
Ledger balances after purchase of a partner's interest

Note that net assets remain unchanged at $60,000, and each partner has a $20,000 capital balance. Ames and Barker continue as partners in the firm, but the capital interest of each has changed. The cash paid by Carson goes directly to the individual partners and not to the partnership.

Regardless of the amount paid by Carson for the one-third interest, the entry is exactly the same. If Carson pays $12,000 each to Ames and Barker for one-third of the partnership, the partnership still makes the entry shown above.

INVESTMENT OF ASSETS IN A PARTNERSHIP

The admission of a partner by an investment of assets is a transaction between the new partner and the partnership. Often referred to simply as **admission by investment**, the transaction **increases both the net assets and total capital of the partnership.**

Assume, for example, that instead of purchasing an interest, Carson invests $30,000 in cash in the Ames-Barker partnership for a 33$\frac{1}{3}$% capital interest. In such a case, the entry is:

Cash	30,000	
L. Carson, Capital		30,000
(To record admission of Carson by investment)		

The effects of this transaction on the partnership accounts would be:

Net Assets	C. Ames, Capital	D. Barker, Capital	L. Carson, Capital
60,000	30,000	30,000	**30,000**
30,000			
Bal. 90,000			

Illustration 12A-2
Ledger balances after investment of assets

Note that both net assets and total capital have increased by $30,000.

Remember that Carson's one-third capital interest might not result in a one-third income ratio. The new partnership agreement should specify Carson's income ratio, and it may or may not be equal to the one-third capital interest.

The comparison of the net assets and capital balances in Illustration 12A-3 shows the different effects of the purchase of an interest and admission by investment.

Illustration 12A-3
Comparison of purchase of an interest and admission by investment

Purchase of an Interest		Admission by Investment	
Net assets	$60,000	Net assets	$90,000
Capital		Capital	
C. Ames	$20,000	C. Ames	$30,000
D. Barker	20,000	D. Barker	30,000
L. Carson	20,000	L. Carson	30,000
Total capital	$60,000	Total capital	$90,000

When a new partner purchases an interest, the total net assets and total capital of the partnership **do not change**. When a partner is admitted by investment, both the total net assets and the total capital **change**.

In the case of admission by investment, further complications occur when the new partner's investment differs from the capital equity acquired. When those amounts are not the same, the difference is considered a **bonus** either to (1) the existing (old) partners or (2) the new partner.

BONUS TO OLD PARTNERS For both personal and business reasons, the existing partners may be unwilling to admit a new partner without receiving a bonus. In an established firm, existing partners may insist on a bonus as compensation for the work they have put into the company over the years. Two accounting factors underlie the business reason. First, total partners' capital equals the **book value** of the recorded net assets of the partnership. When the new partner is admitted, the fair values of assets such as land and buildings may be higher than their book values. The bonus will help make up the difference between fair value and book value. Second, when the partnership has been profitable, goodwill may exist. But, the partnership balance sheet does not report goodwill. The new partner is usually willing to pay the bonus to become a partner.

A bonus to old partners results when the new partner's investment in the firm is greater than the capital credit on the date of admittance. The bonus results in **an increase in the capital balances of the old partners. The partnership allocates the bonus to them on the basis of their income ratios before the**

admission of the new partner. To illustrate, assume that the Bart-Cohen partnership, owned by Sam Bart and Tom Cohen, has total capital of $120,000. Lea Eden acquires a 25% ownership (capital) interest in the partnership by making a cash investment of $80,000. The procedure for determining Eden's capital credit and the bonus to the old partners is as follows.

1. **Determine the total capital of the new partnership.** Add the new partner's investment to the total capital of the old partnership. In this case, the total capital of the new firm is $200,000, computed as follows.

Total capital of existing partnership	$120,000
Investment by new partner, Eden	80,000
Total capital of new partnership	$200,000

2. **Determine the new partner's capital credit.** Multiply the total capital of the new partnership by the new partner's ownership interest. Eden's capital credit is $50,000 ($200,000 × 25%).

3. **Determine the amount of bonus.** Subtract the new partner's capital credit from the new partner's investment. The bonus in this case is $30,000 ($80,000 − $50,000).

4. **Allocate the bonus to the old partners on the basis of their income ratios.** Assuming the ratios are Bart 60%, and Cohen 40%, the allocation is Bart $18,000 ($30,000 × 60%) and Cohen $12,000 ($30,000 × 40%).

The entry to record the admission of Eden is:

Cash	80,000	
Sam Bart, Capital		18,000
Tom Cohen, Capital		12,000
Lea Eden, Capital		50,000
(To record admission of Eden and bonus to old partners)		

A = L + OE
+80,000
+18,000
+12,000
+50,000

Cash Flows
+80,000

BONUS TO NEW PARTNER A bonus to a new partner results when the new partner's investment in the firm is less than his or her capital credit. This may occur when the new partner possesses special attributes that the partnership wants. For example, the new partner may be able to supply cash that the firm needs for expansion or to meet maturing debts. Or the new partner may be a recognized expert in a relevant field. Thus, an engineering firm may be willing to give a renowned engineer a bonus to join the firm. The partners of a restaurant may offer a bonus to a sports celebrity in order to add the athlete's name to the partnership. A bonus to a new partner may also result when recorded book values on the partnership books are higher than their fair values.

A bonus to a new partner results in a **decrease in the capital balances of the old partners. The amount of the decrease for each partner is based on the income ratios before the admission of the new partner.** To illustrate, assume that Lea Eden invests $20,000 in cash for a 25% ownership interest in the Bart–Cohen partnership. The computations for Eden's capital credit and the bonus are as follows, using the four procedures described in the preceding section.

Illustration 12A-4
Computation of capital credit and bonus to new partner

1. Total capital of Bart–Cohen partnership		$120,000
Investment by new partner, Eden		20,000
Total capital of new partnership		$140,000
2. **Eden's capital credit** (25% × $140,000)		**$ 35,000**
3. **Bonus to Eden** ($35,000 − $20,000)		**$ 15,000**
4. Allocation of bonus to old partners:		
Bart ($15,000 × 60%)	$9,000	
Cohen ($15,000 × 40%)	6,000	$ 15,000

The partnership records the admission of Eden as follows.

Cash	20,000	
Sam Bart, Capital	9,000	
Tom Cohen, Capital	6,000	
Lea Eden, Capital		35,000
(To record Eden's admission and bonus)		

A = L + OE
+20,000
−9,000
−6,000
+35,000

Cash Flows
+20,000

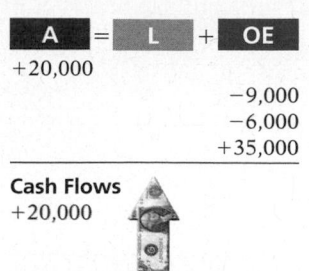

Withdrawal of a Partner

LEARNING OBJECTIVE 7

Describe the effects of the entries when a partner withdraws from the firm.

Now let's look at the opposite situation–the withdrawal of a partner. A partner may withdraw from a partnership **voluntarily**, by selling his or her equity in the firm. Or, he or she may withdraw **involuntarily**, by reaching mandatory retirement age or by dying. The withdrawal of a partner, like the admission of a partner, legally dissolves the partnership. The legal effects may be recognized by dissolving the firm. However, it is customary to record only the economic effects of the partner's withdrawal, while the firm continues to operate and reorganizes itself legally.

As indicated earlier, the partnership agreement should specify the terms of withdrawal. The withdrawal of a partner may be accomplished by (1) payment from partners' personal assets or (2) payment from partnership assets. The former affects only the partners' capital accounts. The latter decreases total net assets and total capital of the partnership.

PAYMENT FROM PARTNERS' PERSONAL ASSETS

Withdrawal by payment from partners' personal assets is a personal transaction between the partners. **It is the direct opposite of admitting a new partner who purchases a partner's interest.** The remaining partners pay the retiring partner directly from their personal assets. **Partnership assets are not involved in any way, and total capital does not change.** The effect on the partnership is limited to changes in the partners' capital balances.

To illustrate, assume that partners Morz, Nead, and Odom have capital balances of $25,000, $15,000, and $10,000, respectively. Morz and Nead agree to buy out Odom's interest. Each of them agrees to pay Odom $8,000 in exchange for one-half of Odom's total interest of $10,000. The entry to record the withdrawal is:

J. Odom, Capital	10,000	
A. Morz, Capital		5,000
M. Nead, Capital		5,000
(To record purchase of Odom's interest)		

A = L + OE
−10,000
+5,000
+5,000

Cash Flows
no effect

The effect of this entry on the partnership accounts is shown below.

Net Assets		A. Morz, Capital		M. Nead, Capital		J. Odom, Capital	
50,000			25,000		15,000	**10,000**	10,000
			5,000		**5,000**		
			Bal. 30,000		Bal. 20,000		Bal. –0–

Illustration 12A-5
Ledger balances after payment from partners' personal assets

Note that net assets and total capital remain the same at $50,000.

What about the $16,000 paid to Odom? You've probably noted that it is not recorded. The entry debited Odom's capital only for $10,000, not for the $16,000 that she received. Similarly, both Morz and Nead credit their capital accounts for only $5,000, not for the $8,000 they each paid.

After Odom's withdrawal, Morz and Nead will share net income or net loss equally unless they indicate another income ratio in the partnership agreement.

PAYMENT FROM PARTNERSHIP ASSETS

Withdrawal by payment from partnership assets is a transaction that involves the partnership. **Both partnership net assets and total capital decrease as a result.** Using partnership assets to pay for a withdrawing partner's interest is the **reverse** of admitting a partner through the investment of assets in the partnership.

Many partnership agreements provide that the amount paid should be based on the fair value of the assets at the time of the partner's withdrawal. When this basis is required, some maintain that any differences between recorded asset balances and their fair values should be (1) recorded by an adjusting entry, and (2) allocated to all partners on the basis of their income ratios. This position has serious flaws. Recording the revaluations violates the historical cost principle, which requires that assets be stated at original cost. It also violates the going-concern assumption, which assumes the entity will continue indefinitely. The terms of the partnership contract should not dictate the accounting for this event.

In accounting for a withdrawal by payment from partnership assets, the partnership should not record asset revaluations. Instead, it should consider any difference between the amount paid and the withdrawing partner's capital balance as **a bonus** to the retiring partner or to the remaining partners.

BONUS TO RETIRING PARTNER A partnership may pay a bonus to a retiring partner when:

1. The fair value of partnership assets is more than their book value,
2. There is unrecorded goodwill resulting from the partnership's superior earnings record, or
3. The remaining partners are eager to remove the partner from the firm.

The partnership deducts the bonus from the remaining partners' capital balances on the basis of their income ratios at the time of the withdrawal.

To illustrate, assume that the following capital balances exist in the RST partnership: Roman $50,000, Sand $30,000, and Terk $20,000. The partners share income in the ratio of 3:2:1, respectively. Terk retires from the partnership and receives a cash payment of $25,000 from the firm. The procedure for determining the bonus to the retiring partner and the allocation of the bonus to the remaining partners is as follows.

1. **Determine the amount of the bonus.** Subtract the retiring partner's capital balance from the cash paid by the partnership. The bonus in this case is $5,000 ($25,000 − $20,000).
2. **Allocate the bonus to the remaining partners on the basis of their income ratios.** The ratios of Roman and Sand are 3:2. Thus, the allocation of the $5,000 bonus is: Roman $3,000 ($5,000 × 3/5) and Sand $2,000 ($5,000 × 2/5).

The partnership records the withdrawal of Terk as follows.

Helpful Hint Compare this entry to the one on page 591.

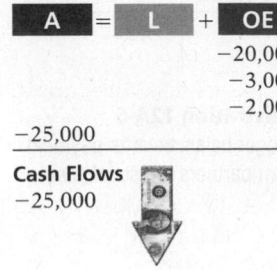

B. Terk, Capital	20,000	
F. Roman, Capital	3,000	
D. Sand, Capital	2,000	
Cash		25,000
(To record withdrawal of and bonus to Terk)		

The remaining partners, Roman and Sand, will recover the bonus given to Terk as the partnership sells or uses the undervalued assets.

BONUS TO REMAINING PARTNERS The retiring partner may give a bonus to the remaining partners when:

1. Recorded assets are overvalued,
2. The partnership has a poor earnings record, or
3. The partner is eager to leave the partnership.

In such cases, the cash paid to the retiring partner will be less than the retiring partner's capital balance. **The partnership allocates (credits) the bonus to the capital accounts of the remaining partners on the basis of their income ratios.**

To illustrate, assume instead that the partnership pays Terk only $16,000 for her $20,000 equity when she withdraws from the partnership. In that case:

1. The bonus to remaining partners is $4,000 ($20,000 − $16,000).
2. The allocation of the $4,000 bonus is: Roman $2,400 ($4,000 × 3/5) and Sand $1,600 ($4,000 × 2/5).

Under these circumstances, the entry to record the withdrawal is:

B. Terk, Capital	20,000	
F. Roman, Capital		2,400
D. Sand, Capital		1,600
Cash		16,000
(To record withdrawal of Terk and bonus to		
remaining partners)		

Helpful Hint Compare this entry to the one on page 590.

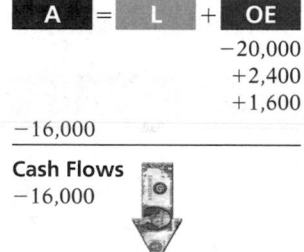

A = L + OE
−20,000
+2,400
+1,600
−16,000

Cash Flows
−16,000

Note that if Sand had withdrawn from the partnership, Roman and Terk would divide any bonus on the basis of their income ratio, which is 3:1 or 75% and 25%.

DEATH OF A PARTNER

The death of a partner dissolves the partnership. However, partnership agreements usually contain a provision for the surviving partners to continue operations. When a partner dies, it usually is necessary to determine the partner's equity at the date of death. This is done by (1) determining the net income or loss for the year to date, (2) closing the books, and (3) preparing financial statements. The partnership agreement may also require an independent audit and a revaluation of assets.

The surviving partners may agree to purchase the deceased partner's equity from their personal assets. Or they may use partnership assets to settle with the deceased partner's estate. In both instances, the entries to record the withdrawal of the partner are similar to those presented earlier.

To facilitate payment from partnership assets, some partnerships obtain life insurance policies on each partner, with the partnership named as the beneficiary. The partnership then uses the proceeds from the insurance policy on the deceased partner to settle with the estate.

SUMMARY OF LEARNING OBJECTIVES FOR APPENDIX 12A

✔ The Navigator

6 Explain the effects of the entries when a new partner is admitted. The entry to record the admittance of a new partner by purchase of a partner's interest affects only partners' capital accounts. The entries to record the admittance by investment of assets in the partnership (a) increase both net assets and total capital and (b) may result in recognition of a bonus to either the old partners or the new partner.

7 Describe the effects of the entries when a partner withdraws from the firm. The entry to record a withdrawal from the firm when the partners pay from their personal assets affects only partners' capital accounts. The entry to record a withdrawal when payment is made from partnership assets (a) decreases net assets and total capital and (b) may result in recognizing a bonus either to the retiring partner or the remaining partners.

GLOSSARY FOR APPENDIX 12A

Admission by investment Admission of a partner by investing assets in the partnership, causing both partnership net assets and total capital to increase. (p. 586).

Admission by purchase of an interest Admission of a partner in a personal transaction between one or more existing partners and the new partner; does not change total partnership assets or total capital. (p. 586).

Withdrawal by payment from partners' personal assets Withdrawal of a partner in a personal transaction between partners; does not change total partnership assets or total capital. (p. 589).

Withdrawal by payment from partnership assets Withdrawal of a partner in a transaction involving the partnership, causing both partnership net assets and total capital to decrease. (p. 590).

 **Self-Test, Brief Exercises, Exercises, Problem Set A, and many more components are available for practice in *WileyPLUS*.**

*Note: All asterisked Questions, Exercises, and Problems relate to material in the appendix to the chapter.

SELF-TEST QUESTIONS

Answers are on page 605.

(LO 1) **1.** Which of the following is **not** a characteristic of a partnership?
  (a) Taxable entity.
  (b) Co-ownership of property.
  (c) Mutual agency.
  (d) Limited life.

(LO 1) **2.** A partnership agreement should include each of the following except:
  (a) names and capital contributions of partners.
  (b) rights and duties of partners as well as basis for sharing net income or loss.
  (c) basis for splitting partnership income taxes.
  (d) provision for withdrawal of assets.

(LO 1) **3.** The advantages of a partnership do **not** include:
  (a) ease of formation.
  (b) unlimited liability.
  (c) freedom from government regulation.
  (d) ease of decision-making.

(LO 2) **4.** Upon formation of a partnership, each partner's initial investment of assets should be recorded at their:
  (a) book values.   (c) fair values.
  (b) cost.   (d) appraised values.

(LO 2) **5.** Ben and Sam Jenkins formed a partnership. Ben contributed $8,000 cash and a used truck that originally cost $35,000 and had accumulated depreciation of $15,000. The truck's fair value was $16,000. Sam, a builder, contributed a new storage garage. His cost of construction was $40,000. The garage has a fair value of $55,000. What is the combined total capital that would be recorded on the partnership books for the two partners?
  (a) $79,000.   (c) $75,000.
  (b) $60,000.   (d) $90,000.

(LO 3) **6.** The NBC Company reports net income of $60,000. If partners N, B, and C have an income ratio of 50%, 30%, and 20%, respectively, C's share of the net income is:

  (a) $30,000.   (c) $18,000.
  (b) $12,000.   (d) No correct answer is given.

7. Using the data in Self-Test Question 6, what is B's (LO 3) share of net income if the percentages are applicable after each partner receives a $10,000 salary allowance?
  (a) $12,000.   (c) $19,000.
  (b) $20,000.   (d) $21,000.

8. To close a partner's drawing account, an entry must be (LO 3) made that:
  (a) debits that partner's drawing account and credits Income Summary.
  (b) debits that partner's drawing account and credits that partner's capital account.
  (c) credits that partner's drawing account and debits that partner's capital account.
  (d) credits that partner's drawing account and debits the firm's dividend account.

9. Which of the following statements about partnership (LO 4) financial statements is **true**?
  (a) Details of the distribution of net income are shown in the owners' equity statement.
  (b) The distribution of net income is shown on the balance sheet.
  (c) Only the total of all partner capital balances is shown in the balance sheet.
  (d) The owners' equity statement is called the partners' capital statement.

10. In the liquidation of a partnership, it is necessary to (LO 5) (1) distribute cash to the partners, (2) sell noncash assets, (3) allocate any gain or loss on realization to the partners, and (4) pay liabilities. These steps should be performed in the following order:
  (a) (2), (3), (4), (1).
  (b) (2), (3), (1), (4).
  (c) (3), (2), (1), (4).
  (d) (3), (2), (4), (1).

Use the following account balance information for Creekville Partnership to answer Self-Test Questions 11 and 12. Income ratios are 2:4:4 for Harriet, Mike, and Elly, respectively.

Assets		Liabilities and Owners' Equity	
Cash	$ 9,000	Accounts payable	$ 21,000
Accounts		Harriet, capital	23,000
receivable	22,000	Mike, capital	8,000
Inventory	73,000	Elly, capital	52,000
	$104,000		$104,000

(LO 5) **11.** Assume that as part of liquidation proceedings, Creekville sells its noncash assets for $85,000. The amount of cash that would ultimately be distributed to Elly would be:
(a) $52,000.   (c) $34,000.
(b) $48,000.   (d) $86,000.

(LO 5) **12.** Assume that as part of liquidation proceedings, Creekville sells its noncash assets for $60,000. As a result, one of the partners has a capital deficiency which that partner decides not to repay. The amount of cash that would ultimately be distributed to Elly would be:
(a) $52,000.   (c) $24,000.
(b) $38,000.   (d) $34,000.

***13.** Louisa Santiago purchases 50% of Leo Lemon's capital interest in the K & L partnership for $22,000. If the capital balance of Kate Kildare and Leo Lemon are $40,000 and $30,000, respectively, Santiago's capital balance following the purchase is:
(a) $22,000.   (c) $20,000.
(b) $35,000.   (d) $15,000.

(LO 6)

***14.** Capital balances in the MEM partnership are Mary, Capital $60,000; Ellen, Capital $50,000; and Mills, Capital $40,000, and income ratios are 5:3:2, respectively. The MEMO partnership is formed by admitting Oleg to the firm with a cash investment of $60,000 for a 25% capital interest. The bonus to be credited to Mills, Capital in admitting Oleg is:
(a) $10,000.   (c) $3,750.
(b) $7,500.   (d) $1,500.

(LO 6)

***15.** Capital balances in the MURF partnership are Molly, Capital $50,000; Ursula, Capital $40,000; Ray, Capital $30,000; and Fred, Capital $20,000, and income ratios are 4:3:2:1, respectively. Fred withdraws from the firm following payment of $29,000 in cash from the partnership. Ursula's capital balance after recording the withdrawal of Fred is:
(a) $36,000.   (c) $38,000.
(b) $37,000.   (d) $40,000.

(LO 7)

Go to the book's companion website, www.wiley.com/college/weygandt, for additional Self-Test Questions.

✔ The Navigator

QUESTIONS

1. The characteristics of a partnership include the following: (a) association of individuals, (b) limited life, and (c) co-ownership of property. Explain each of these terms.

2. Kevin Mathis is confused about the partnership characteristics of (a) mutual agency and (b) unlimited liability. Explain these two characteristics for Kevin.

3. Lance Kosinski and Matt Morrisen are considering a business venture. They ask you to explain the advantages and disadvantages of the partnership form of organization.

4. Why might a company choose to use a limited partnership?

5. Newland and Palermo form a partnership. Newland contributes land with a book value of $50,000 and a fair value of $60,000. Newland also contributes equipment with a book value of $52,000 and a fair value of $57,000. The partnership assumes a $20,000 mortgage on the land. What should be the balance in Newland's capital account upon formation of the partnership?

6. W. Jenson, N. Emch, and W. Gilligan have a partnership called Outlaws. A dispute has arisen among the partners. Jenson has invested twice as much in assets as the other two partners, and he believes net income and net losses should be shared in accordance with

the capital ratios. The partnership agreement does not specify the division of profits and losses. How will net income and net loss be divided?

7. Mutt and Jeff are discussing how income and losses should be divided in a partnership they plan to form. What factors should be considered in determining the division of net income or net loss?

8. M. Elston and R. Ogle have partnership capital balances of $40,000 and $80,000, respectively. The partnership agreement indicates that net income or net loss should be shared equally. If net income for the partnership is $42,000, how should the net income be divided?

9. S. Pletcher and F. Holt share net income and net loss equally. (a) Which account(s) is (are) debited and credited to record the division of net income between the partners? (b) If S. Pletcher withdraws $30,000 in cash for personal use in lieu of salary, which account is debited and which is credited?

10. Partners T. Greer and R. Parks are provided salary allowances of $30,000 and $25,000, respectively. They divide the remainder of the partnership income in a ratio of 3:2. If partnership net income is $40,000, how much is allocated to Greer and Parks?

11. Are the financial statements of a partnership similar to those of a proprietorship? Discuss.

12. How does the liquidation of a partnership differ from the dissolution of a partnership?

13. Roger Fuller and Mike Rangel are discussing the liquidation of a partnership. Roger maintains that all cash should be distributed to partners on the basis of their income ratios. Is he correct? Explain.

14. In continuing their discussion from Question 13, Mike says that even in the case of a capital deficiency, all cash should still be distributed on the basis of capital balances. Is Mike correct? Explain.

15. Norris, Madson, and Howell have income ratios of 5:3:2 and capital balances of $34,000, $31,000, and $28,000, respectively. Noncash assets are sold at a gain. After creditors are paid, $103,000 of cash is available for distribution to the partners. How much cash should be paid to Madson?

16. Before the final distribution of cash, account balances are: Cash $27,000; S. Shea, Capital $19,000 (Cr.); L. Seastrom, Capital $12,000 (Cr.); and M. Luthi, Capital $4,000 (Dr.). Luthi is unable to pay any of the capital deficiency. If the income-sharing ratios are 5:3:2, respectively, how much cash should be paid to L. Seastrom?

17. Why is Apple not a partnership?

*18. Susan Turnbull decides to purchase from an existing partner for $50,000 a one-third interest in a partnership. What effect does this transaction have on partnership net assets?

*19. Jerry Park decides to invest $25,000 in a partnership for a one-sixth capital interest. How much do the partnership's net assets increase? Does Park also acquire a one-sixth income ratio through this investment?

*20. Jill Parsons purchases for $72,000 Jamar's interest in the Tholen-Jamar partnership. Assuming that Jamar has a $68,000 capital balance in the partnership, what journal entry is made by the partnership to record this transaction?

*21. Jaime Keller has a $41,000 capital balance in a partnership. She sells her interest to Sam Parmenter for $45,000 cash. What entry is made by the partnership for this transaction?

*22. Andrea Riley retires from the partnership of Jaggard, Pester, and Riley. She receives $85,000 of partnership assets in settlement of her capital balance of $81,000. Assuming that the income-sharing ratios are 5:3:2, respectively, how much of Riley's bonus is debited to Pester's capital account?

*23. Your roommate argues that partnership assets should be revalued in situations like those in Question 21. Why is this generally not done?

*24. How is a deceased partner's equity determined?

BRIEF EXERCISES

Journalize entries in forming a partnership.
(LO 2)

BE12-1 Barbara Ripley and Fred Nichols decide to organize the ALL-Star partnership. Ripley invests $15,000 cash, and Nichols contributes $10,000 cash and equipment having a book value of $3,500. Prepare the entry to record Nichols's investment in the partnership, assuming the equipment has a fair value of $4,000.

Prepare portion of opening balance sheet for partnership.
(LO 2)

BE12-2 Penner and Torres decide to merge their proprietorships into a partnership called Pentor Company. The balance sheet of Torres Co. shows:

Accounts receivable	$16,000	
Less: Allowance for doubtful accounts	1,200	$14,800
Equipment	20,000	
Less: Accumulated depreciation—equip.	7,000	13,000

The partners agree that the net realizable value of the receivables is $14,500 and that the fair value of the equipment is $11,000. Indicate how the accounts should appear in the opening balance sheet of the partnership.

Journalize the division of net income using fixed income ratios.
(LO 3)

BE12-3 Rod Dall Co. reports net income of $75,000. The income ratios are Rod 60% and Dall 40%. Indicate the division of net income to each partner, and prepare the entry to distribute the net income.

Compute division of net income with a salary allowance and fixed ratios.
(LO 3)

BE12-4 PFW Co. reports net income of $45,000. Partner salary allowances are Pitts $15,000, Filbert $5,000, and Witten $5,000. Indicate the division of net income to each partner, assuming the income ratio is 50:30:20, respectively.

Show division of net income when allowances exceed net income.
(LO 3)

BE12-5 Nabb & Fry Co. reports net income of $31,000. Interest allowances are Nabb $7,000 and Fry $5,000; salary allowances are Nabb $15,000 and Fry $10,000; the remainder is shared equally. Show the distribution of income on the income statement.

Journalize final cash distribution in liquidation.
(LO 5)

BE12-6 After liquidating noncash assets and paying creditors, account balances in the Mann Co. are Cash $21,000, A Capital (Cr.) $8,000, B Capital (Cr.) $9,000, and C Capital (Cr.) $4,000. The partners share income equally. Journalize the final distribution of cash to the partners.

*BE12-7 Gamma Co. capital balances are: Barr $30,000, Croy $25,000, and Eubank $22,000. The partners share income equally. Tovar is admitted to the firm by purchasing one-half of Eubank's interest for $13,000. Journalize the admission of Tovar to the partnership.

Journalize admission by purchase of an interest.
(LO 6)

*BE12-8 In Eastwood Co., capital balances are Irey $40,000 and Pedigo $50,000. The partners share income equally. Vernon is admitted to the firm with a 45% interest by an investment of cash of $58,000. Journalize the admission of Vernon.

Journalize admission by investment.
(LO 6)

*BE12-9 Capital balances in Pelmar Co. are Lango $40,000, Oslo $30,000, and Fernetti $20,000. Lango and Oslo each agree to pay Fernetti $12,000 from their personal assets. Lango and Oslo each receive 50% of Fernetti's equity. The partners share income equally. Journalize the withdrawal of Fernetti.

Journalize withdrawal paid by personal assets.
(LO 7)

*BE12-10 Data pertaining to Pelmar Co. are presented in BE12-9. Instead of payment from personal assets, assume that Fernetti receives $24,000 from partnership assets in withdrawing from the firm. Journalize the withdrawal of Fernetti.

Journalize withdrawal paid by partnership assets.
(LO 7)

> ## DO IT! Review

DO IT! 12-1 Indicate whether each of the following statements is true or false.

Analyze statements about partnership organization.
(LO 1)

_____ **1.** Each partner is personally and individually liable for all partnership liabilities.

_____ **2.** If a partnership dissolves, each partner has a claim to the specific assets he/she contributed to the firm.

_____ **3.** In a limited partnership, all partners have limited liability.

_____ **4.** A major advantage of regular partnership is that it is simple and inexpensive to create and operate.

_____ **5.** Members of a limited liability company can take an active management role.

DO IT! 12-2 Frontenac Company reported net income of $75,000. The partnership agreement provides for salaries of $25,000 to Miley and $18,000 to Guthrie. They divide the remainder 40% to Miley and 60% to Guthrie. Miley asks your help to divide the net income between the partners and to prepare the closing entry.

Divide net income and prepare closing entry.
(LO 3)

DO IT! 12-3 The partners of LR Company have decided to liquidate their business. Noncash assets were sold for $125,000. The income ratios of the partners Cisneros, Gunselman, and Forren are 3:2:3, respectively. Complete the following schedule of cash payments for LR Company

Complete schedule of partnership liquidation payments.
(LO 5)

LR Company.xls

Home   Insert   Page Layout   Formulas   Data   Review   View

P18   fx

	A	B	C	D	E	F	G	H	I	J	K	L
1	Item	Cash	+	Noncash Assets	=	Liabilities	+	Cisneros, Capital	+	Gunselman, Capital	+	Forren, Capital
2	Balances before liquidation	15,000		90,000		40,000		20,000		32,000		13,000
3	Sale of noncash assets and allocation of gain											
4	New balances											
5	Pay liabilities											
6	New balances											
7	Cash distribution to partners											
8	Final balances											
9												
10												

DO IT! 12-4 Parsons Company wishes to liquidate the firm by distributing the company's cash to the three partners. Prior to the distribution of cash, the company's balances are: Cash $73,000; Oakley, Capital (Cr.) $47,000; Quaney, Capital (Dr.) $14,000; and Ellis, Capital (Cr.) $40,000. The income ratios of the three partners are 3:3:4, respectively. Prepare the entry to record the absorption of Quaney's capital deficiency by the other partners and the distribution of cash to the partners with credit balances.

Prepare entries to record absorption of capital deficiency and distribution of cash.
(LO 5)

EXERCISES

Identify characteristics of partnership.
(LO 1)

E12-1 Mark Rensing has prepared the following list of statements about partnerships.

1. A partnership is an association of three or more persons to carry on as co-owners of a business for profit.
2. The legal requirements for forming a partnership can be quite burdensome.
3. A partnership is not an entity for financial reporting purposes.
4. The net income of a partnership is taxed as a separate entity.
5. The act of any partner is binding on all other partners, even when partners perform business acts beyond the scope of their authority.
6. Each partner is personally and individually liable for all partnership liabilities.
7. When a partnership is dissolved, the assets legally revert to the original contributor.
8. In a limited partnership, one or more partners have unlimited liability and one or more partners have limited liability for the debts of the firm.
9. Mutual agency is a major advantage of the partnership form of business.

Instructions

Identify each statement as true or false. If false, indicate how to correct the statement.

Journalize entry for formation of a partnership.
(LO 2)

E12-2 K. Decker, S. Rosen, and E. Toso are forming a partnership. Decker is transferring $50,000 of personal cash to the partnership. Rosen owns land worth $15,000 and a small building worth $80,000, which she transfers to the partnership. Toso transfers to the partnership cash of $9,000, accounts receivable of $32,000 and equipment worth $39,000. The partnership expects to collect $29,000 of the accounts receivable.

Instructions

(a) Prepare the journal entries to record each of the partners' investments.
(b) What amount would be reported as total owners' equity immediately after the investments?

Journalize entry for formation of a partnership.
(LO 2)

E12-3 Suzy Vopat has owned and operated a proprietorship for several years. On January 1, she decides to terminate this business and become a partner in the firm of Vopat and Sigma. Vopat's investment in the partnership consists of $12,000 in cash, and the following assets of the proprietorship: accounts receivable $14,000 less allowance for doubtful accounts of $2,000, and equipment $30,000 less accumulated depreciation of $4,000. It is agreed that the allowance for doubtful accounts should be $3,000 for the partnership. The fair value of the equipment is $23,500.

Instructions

Journalize Vopat's admission to the firm of Vopat and Sigma.

Prepare schedule showing distribution of net income and closing entry.
(LO 3)

E12-4 McGill and Smyth have capital balances on January 1 of $50,000 and $40,000, respectively. The partnership income-sharing agreement provides for (1) annual salaries of $22,000 for McGill and $13,000 for Smyth, (2) interest at 10% on beginning capital balances, and (3) remaining income or loss to be shared 60% by McGill and 40% by Smyth.

Instructions

(a) Prepare a schedule showing the distribution of net income, assuming net income is (1) $50,000 and (2) $36,000.
(b) Journalize the allocation of net income in each of the situations above.

Prepare journal entries to record allocation of net income.
(LO 3)

E12-5 Coburn (beginning capital, $60,000) and Webb (beginning capital $90,000) are partners. During 2014, the partnership earned net income of $80,000, and Coburn made drawings of $18,000 while Webb made drawings of $24,000.

Instructions

(a) Assume the partnership income-sharing agreement calls for income to be divided 45% to Coburn and 55% to Webb. Prepare the journal entry to record the allocation of net income.
(b) Assume the partnership income-sharing agreement calls for income to be divided with a salary of $30,000 to Coburn and $25,000 to Webb, with the remainder divided 45%

to Coburn and 55% to Webb. Prepare the journal entry to record the allocation of net income.

(c) Assume the partnership income-sharing agreement calls for income to be divided with a salary of $40,000 to Coburn and $35,000 to Webb, interest of 10% on beginning capital, and the remainder divided 50%–50%. Prepare the journal entry to record the allocation of net income.

(d) Compute the partners' ending capital balances under the assumption in part (c).

E12-6 For National Co., beginning capital balances on January 1, 2014, are Nancy Payne $20,000 and Ann Dody $18,000. During the year, drawings were Payne $8,000 and Dody $5,000. Net income was $40,000, and the partners share income equally.

Prepare partners' capital statement and partial balance sheet.
(LO 4)

Instructions

(a) Prepare the partners' capital statement for the year.

(b) Prepare the owners' equity section of the balance sheet at December 31, 2014.

E12-7 Terry, Nick, and Frank are forming The Doctor Partnership. Terry is transferring $30,000 of personal cash and equipment worth $25,000 to the partnership. Nick owns land worth $28,000 and a small building worth $75,000, which he transfers to the partnership. There is a long-term mortgage of $20,000 on the land and building, which the partnership assumes. Frank transfers cash of $7,000, accounts receivable of $36,000, supplies worth $3,000, and equipment worth $27,000 to the partnership. The partnership expects to collect $32,000 of the accounts receivable.

Prepare a classified balance sheet of a partnership.
(LO 4)

Instructions

Prepare a classified balance sheet for the partnership after the partners' investments on December 31, 2014.

E12-8 Sedgwick Company at December 31 has cash $20,000, noncash assets $100,000, liabilities $55,000, and the following capital balances: Floyd $45,000 and DeWitt $20,000. The firm is liquidated, and $105,000 in cash is received for the noncash assets. Floyd and DeWitt income ratios are 60% and 40%, respectively.

Prepare cash payments schedule.
(LO 5)

Instructions

Prepare a schedule of cash payments.

E12-9 Data for Sedgwick Company are presented in E12-8.

Journalize transactions in a liquidation.
(LO 5)

Instructions

Prepare the entries to record:

(a) The sale of noncash assets.

(b) The allocation of the gain or loss on realization to the partners.

(c) Payment of creditors.

(d) Distribution of cash to the partners.

E12-10 Prior to the distribution of cash to the partners, the accounts in the VUP Company are: Cash $24,000; Vogel, Capital (Cr.) $17,000; Utech, Capital (Cr.) $15,000; and Pena, Capital (Dr.) $8,000. The income ratios are 5:3:2, respectively.

Journalize transactions with a capital deficiency.
(LO 5)

Instructions

(a) Prepare the entry to record (1) Pena's payment of $8,000 in cash to the partnership and (2) the distribution of cash to the partners with credit balances.

(b) Prepare the entry to record (1) the absorption of Pena's capital deficiency by the other partners and (2) the distribution of cash to the partners with credit balances.

*E12-11 K. Kolmer, C. Eidman, and C. Ryno share income on a 5:3:2 basis. They have capital balances of $34,000, $26,000, and $21,000, respectively, when Don Jernigan is admitted to the partnership.

Journalize admission of a new partner by purchase of an interest.
(LO 6)

Instructions

Prepare the journal entry to record the admission of Don Jernigan under each of the following assumptions.

(a) Purchase of 50% of Kolmer's equity for $19,000.

(b) Purchase of 50% of Eidman's equity for $12,000.

(c) Purchase of 33$\frac{1}{3}$% of Ryno's equity for $9,000.

Journalize admission of a new partner by investment.
(LO 6)

*E12-12 S. Pagan and T. Tabor share income on a 6:4 basis. They have capital balances of $100,000 and $60,000, respectively, when W. Wolford is admitted to the partnership.

Instructions
Prepare the journal entry to record the admission of W. Wolford under each of the following assumptions.

(a) Investment of $90,000 cash for a 30% ownership interest with bonuses to the existing partners.

(b) Investment of $50,000 cash for a 30% ownership interest with a bonus to the new partner.

Journalize withdrawal of a partner with payment from partners' personal assets.
(LO 7)

*E12-13 N. Essex, C. Gilmore, and C. Heganbart have capital balances of $50,000, $40,000, and $30,000, respectively. Their income ratios are 5:3:2. Heganbart withdraws from the partnership under each of the following independent conditions.

1. Essex and Gilmore agree to purchase Heganbart's equity by paying $17,000 each from their personal assets. Each purchaser receives 50% of Heganbart's equity.
2. Gilmore agrees to purchase all of Heganbart's equity by paying $22,000 cash from her personal assets.
3. Essex agrees to purchase all of Heganbart's equity by paying $26,000 cash from his personal assets.

Instructions
Journalize the withdrawal of Heganbart under each of the assumptions above.

Journalize withdrawal of a partner with payment from partnership assets.
(LO 7)

*E12-14 B. Higgins, J. Mayo, and N. Rice have capital balances of $95,000, $75,000, and $60,000, respectively. They share income or loss on a 5:3:2 basis. Rice withdraws from the partnership under each of the following conditions.

1. Rice is paid $64,000 in cash from partnership assets, and a bonus is granted to the retiring partner.
2. Rice is paid $52,000 in cash from partnership assets, and bonuses are granted to the remaining partners.

Instructions
Journalize the withdrawal of Rice under each of the assumptions above.

Journalize entry for admission and withdrawal of partners.
(LO 6, 7)

*E12-15 Foss, Albertson, and Espinosa are partners who share profits and losses 50%, 30%, and 20%, respectively. Their capital balances are $100,000, $60,000, and $40,000, respectively.

Instructions
(a) Assume Garrett joins the partnership by investing $88,000 for a 25% interest with bonuses to the existing partners. Prepare the journal entry to record his investment.
(b) Assume instead that Foss leaves the partnership. Foss is paid $110,000 with a bonus to the retiring partner. Prepare the journal entry to record Foss's withdrawal.

EXERCISES: SET B AND CHALLENGE EXERCISES

Visit the book's companion website, at **www.wiley.com/college/weygandt**, and choose the Student Companion site to access Exercise Set B and Challenge Exercises.

PROBLEMS: SET A

P12-1A The post-closing trial balances of two proprietorships on January 1, 2014, are presented below.

Prepare entries for formation of a partnership and a balance sheet.
(LO 2, 4)

GLS

	Sorensen Company		Lucas Company	
	Dr.	Cr.	Dr.	Cr.
Cash	$ 14,000		$12,000	
Accounts receivable	17,500		26,000	
Allowance for doubtful accounts		$ 3,000		$ 4,400
Inventory	26,500		18,400	
Equipment	45,000		29,000	
Accumulated depreciation—equipment		24,000		11,000
Notes payable		18,000		15,000
Accounts payable		22,000		31,000
Sorensen, capital		36,000		
Lucas, capital				24,000
	$103,000	$103,000	$85,400	$85,400

Sorensen and Lucas decide to form a partnership, Solu Company, with the following agreed upon valuations for noncash assets.

	Sorensen Company	Lucas Company
Accounts receivable	$17,500	$26,000
Allowance for doubtful accounts	4,500	4,000
Inventory	28,000	20,000
Equipment	25,000	15,000

All cash will be transferred to the partnership, and the partnership will assume all the liabilities of the two proprietorships. Further, it is agreed that Sorensen will invest an additional $5,000 in cash, and Lucas will invest an additional $19,000 in cash.

Instructions
(a) Prepare separate journal entries to record the transfer of each proprietorship's assets and liabilities to the partnership.
(b) Journalize the additional cash investment by each partner.
(c) Prepare a classified balance sheet for the partnership on January 1, 2014.

(a) Sorensen, Capital $40,000
Lucas, Capital $23,000

(c) Total assets $173,000

P12-2A At the end of its first year of operations on December 31, 2014, NBS Company's accounts show the following.

Journalize divisions of net income and prepare a partners' capital statement.
(LO 3, 4)

Partner	Drawings	Capital
Art Niensted	$23,000	$48,000
Greg Bolen	14,000	30,000
Krista Sayler	10,000	25,000

The capital balance represents each partner's initial capital investment. Therefore, net income or net loss for 2014 has not been closed to the partners' capital accounts.

Instructions
(a) Journalize the entry to record the division of net income for the year 2014 under each of the following independent assumptions.
  (1) Net income is $30,000. Income is shared 6:3:1.
  (2) Net income is $40,000. Niensted and Bolen are given salary allowances of $15,000 and $10,000, respectively. The remainder is shared equally.
  (3) Net income is $19,000. Each partner is allowed interest of 10% on beginning capital balances. Niensted is given a $15,000 salary allowance. The remainder is shared equally.

(a) (1) Niensted $18,000
(2) Niensted $20,000
(3) Niensted $17,700

(b) Prepare a schedule showing the division of net income under assumption (3) above.

(c) Niensted $42,700

(c) Prepare a partners' capital statement for the year under assumption (3) above.

Prepare entries with a capital deficiency in liquidation of a partnership.

(LO 5)

P12-3A The partners in Crawford Company decide to liquidate the firm when the balance sheet shows the following.

CRAWFORD COMPANY
Balance Sheet
May 31, 2014

Assets		Liabilities and Owners' Equity	
Cash	$ 27,500	Notes payable	$ 13,500
Accounts receivable	25,000	Accounts payable	27,000
Allowance for doubtful accounts	(1,000)	Salaries and wages payable	4,000
Inventory	34,500	A. Jamison, capital	33,000
Equipment	21,000	S. Moyer, capital	21,000
Accumulated depreciation—equipment	(5,500)	P. Roper, capital	3,000
	$101,500		$101,500

The partners share income and loss 5:3:2. During the process of liquidation, the following transactions were completed in the following sequence.

1. A total of $51,000 was received from converting noncash assets into cash.
2. Gain or loss on realization was allocated to partners.
3. Liabilities were paid in full.
4. P. Roper paid his capital deficiency.
5. Cash was paid to the partners with credit balances.

Instructions

(a) Loss on realization
   $23,000
   Cash paid: to Jamison
   $21,500; to Moyer
   $14,100

(a) Prepare the entries to record the transactions.
(b) Post to the cash and capital accounts.
(c) Assume that Roper is unable to pay the capital deficiency.
  (1) Prepare the entry to allocate Roper's debit balance to Jamison and Moyer.
  (2) Prepare the entry to record the final distribution of cash.

Journalize admission of a partner under different assumptions.

(LO 6)

*P12-4A At April 30, partners' capital balances in PDL Company are: G. Donley $52,000, C. Lamar $48,000, and J. Pinkston $18,000. The income sharing ratios are 5:4:1, respectively. On May 1, the PDLT Company is formed by admitting J. Terrell to the firm as a partner.

Instructions

(a) Journalize the admission of Terrell under each of the following independent assumptions.

(a) (1) Terrell $9,000
   (2) Terrell $16,000
   (3) Terrell $54,000
   (4) Terrell $48,000

  (1) Terrell purchases 50% of Pinkston's ownership interest by paying Pinkston $16,000 in cash.
  (2) Terrell purchases 33$\frac{1}{3}$% of Lamar's ownership interest by paying Lamar $15,000 in cash.
  (3) Terrell invests $62,000 for a 30% ownership interest, and bonuses are given to the old partners.
  (4) Terrell invests $42,000 for a 30% ownership interest, which includes a bonus to the new partner.
(b) Lamar's capital balance is $32,000 after admitting Terrell to the partnership by investment. If Lamar's ownership interest is 20% of total partnership capital, what were (1) Terrell's cash investment and (2) the bonus to the new partner?

Journalize withdrawal of a partner under different assumptions.

(LO 7)

*P12-5A On December 31, the capital balances and income ratios in TEP Company are as follows.

Partner	Capital Balance	Income Ratio
Trayer	$60,000	50%
Emig	40,000	30%
Posada	30,000	20%

Instructions

(a) Journalize the withdrawal of Posada under each of the following assumptions.

    (1) Each of the continuing partners agrees to pay $18,000 in cash from personal funds to purchase Posada's ownership equity. Each receives 50% of Posada's equity.

    (2) Emig agrees to purchase Posada's ownership interest for $25,000 cash.

    (3) Posada is paid $34,000 from partnership assets, which includes a bonus to the retiring partner.

    (4) Posada is paid $22,000 from partnership assets, and bonuses to the remaining partners are recognized.

(b) If Emig's capital balance after Posada's withdrawal is $43,600, what were (1) the total bonus to the remaining partners and (2) the cash paid by the partnership to Posada?

(a) (1) Emig, Capital $15,000
(2) Emig, Capital $30,000
(3) Bonus $4,000
(4) Bonus $8,000

PROBLEMS: SET B

P12-1B The post-closing trial balances of two proprietorships on January 1, 2014, are presented below.

Prepare entries for formation of a partnership and a balance sheet.

(LO 2, 4)

	Utech Company		Flott Company	
	Dr.	**Cr.**	**Dr.**	**Cr.**
Cash	$ 10,000		$ 8,000	
Accounts receivable	18,000		30,000	
Allowance for doubtful accounts		$ 2,000		$ 3,000
Inventory	35,000		20,000	
Equipment	60,000		35,000	
Accumulated depreciation—equipment		28,000		15,000
Notes payable		20,000		
Accounts payable		30,000		40,000
Utech, capital		43,000		
Flott, capital				35,000
	$123,000	$123,000	$93,000	$93,000

Utech and Flott decide to form a partnership, Commander Company, with the following agreed upon valuations for noncash assets.

	Utech Company	Flott Company
Accounts receivable	$18,000	$30,000
Allowance for doubtful accounts	2,500	4,000
Inventory	38,000	25,000
Equipment	35,000	18,000

All cash will be transferred to the partnership, and the partnership will assume all the liabilities of the two proprietorships. Further, it is agreed that Utech will invest an additional $3,500 in cash, and Flott will invest an additional $16,000 in cash.

Instructions

(a) Prepare separate journal entries to record the transfer of each proprietorship's assets and liabilities to the partnership.

(b) Journalize the additional cash investment by each partner.

(c) Prepare a classified balance sheet for the partnership on January 1, 2014.

(a) Utech, Capital $48,500
Flott, Capital $37,000

(c) Total assets $195,000

P12-2B At the end of its first year of operations on December 31, 2014, RKC Company's accounts show the following.

Journalize divisions of net income and prepare a partners' capital statement.

(LO 3, 4)

Partner	Drawings	Capital
Riles	$15,000	$40,000
Kinder	10,000	25,000
Crifui	5,000	15,000

The capital balance represents each partner's initial capital investment. Therefore, net income or net loss for 2014 has not been closed to the partners' capital accounts.

Instructions

(a) Journalize the entry to record the division of net income for 2014 under each of the independent assumptions shown below.

(a) (1) Riles $25,000
　　(2) Riles $21,000
　　(3) Riles $26,000

    (1) Net income is $50,000. Income is shared 5:3:2.

    (2) Net income is $43,000. Riles and Kinder are given salary allowances of $15,000 and $10,000, respectively. The remainder is shared equally.

    (3) Net income is $34,000. Each partner is allowed interest of 10% on beginning capital balances. Riles is given a $20,000 salary allowance. The remainder is shared equally.

(b) Prepare a schedule showing the division of net income under assumption (3) above.

(c) Riles $51,000

(c) Prepare a partners' capital statement for the year under assumption (3) above.

Prepare entries and schedule of cash payments in liquidation of a partnership

(LO 5)

P12-3B The partners in Newman Company decide to liquidate the firm when the balance sheet shows the following.

NEWMAN COMPANY
Balance Sheet
April 30, 2014

Assets		Liabilities and Owners' Equity	
Cash	$ 30,000	Notes payable	$ 20,000
Accounts receivable	25,000	Accounts payable	30,000
Allowance for doubtful accounts	(2,000)	Salaries and wages payable	2,500
Inventory	35,000	Mallory, capital	28,000
Equipment	20,000	Bosco, capital	13,650
Accumulated depreciation—equipment	(8,000)	Renteria, capital	5,850
	$100,000		$100,000

The partners share income and loss 5:3:2. During the process of liquidation, the transactions below were completed in the following sequence.

1. A total of $55,000 was received from converting noncash assets into cash.

2. Gain or loss on realization was allocated to partners.

3. Liabilities were paid in full.

4. Cash was paid to the partners with credit balances.

Instructions

(a) Loss on realization $15,000
  Cash paid: to Mallory
  $20,500; to Renteria $2,850

(a) Prepare a schedule of cash payments.

(b) Prepare the entries to record the transactions.

(c) Post to the cash and capital accounts.

Journalize admission of a partner under different assumptions.

(LO 6)

*P12-4B At April 30, partners' capital balances in YBG Company are: Younger $30,000, Beyer $16,000, and Giger $10,000. The income-sharing ratios are 5:3:2, respectively. On May 1, the YBGE Company is formed by admitting Edelman to the firm as a partner.

Instructions

(a) Journalize the admission of Edelman under each of the following independent assumptions.

(a) (1) Edelman, Capital $5,000
　　(2) Edelman $8,000
　　(3) Edelman $34,000
　　(4) Edelman $16,000

    (1) Edelman purchases 50% of Giger's ownership interest by paying Giger $4,000 in cash.

    (2) Edelman purchases 50% of Beyer's ownership interest by paying Beyer $10,000 in cash.

    (3) Edelman invests $29,000 cash in the partnership for a 40% ownership interest that includes a bonus to the new partner.

    (4) Edelman invests $24,000 in the partnership for a 20% ownership interest, and bonuses are given to the old partners.

(b) Beyer's capital balance is $25,000 after admitting Edelman to the partnership by investment. If Beyer's ownership interest is 25% of total partnership capital, what were (1) Edelman's cash investment and (2) the total bonus to the old partners?

*P12-5B On December 31, the capital balances and income ratios in DUYP Company are as follows.

Journalize withdrawal of a partner under different assumptions.

(LO 7)

GLS

Partner	Capital Balance	Income Ratio
Dunlap	$100,000	60%
Yevak	51,000	30
Piper	28,000	10

Instructions

(a) Journalize the withdrawal of Piper under each of the following independent assumptions.

(1) Each of the remaining partners agrees to pay $15,000 in cash from personal funds to purchase Piper's ownership equity. Each receives 50% of Piper's equity.

(2) Yevak agrees to purchase Piper's ownership interest for $22,000 in cash.

(3) From partnership assets, Piper is paid $34,000, which includes a bonus to the retiring partner.

(4) Piper is paid $19,000 from partnership assets. Bonuses to the remaining partners are recognized.

(b) If Yevak's capital balance after Piper's withdrawal is $57,000, what were (1) the total bonus to the remaining partners and (2) the cash paid by the partnership to Piper?

(a) (1) Yevak, Capital $14,000
(2) Yevak, Capital $28,000
(3) Bonus $6,000
(4) Bonus $9,000

PROBLEMS: SET C

Visit the book's companion website, at **www.wiley.com/college/weygandt**, and choose the Student Companion site to access Problem Set C.

CONTINUING COOKIE CHRONICLE

(*Note:* This is a continuation of the Cookie Chronicle from Chapters 1 through 11.)

CCC12 Natalie's high school friend, Katy Peterson, has been operating a bakery for approximately 18 months. Because Natalie has been so successful operating Cookie Creations, Katy would like to have Natalie become her partner. Katy believes that together they will create a thriving cookie-making business. Natalie is quite happy with her current business set-up. Up until now, she had not considered joining forces with anyone. However, Natalie thinks that it may be a good idea to establish a partnership with Katy, and decides to look into it.

Go to the book's companion website, **www.wiley.com/college/weygandt,** *to see the completion of this problem.*

Broadening Your Perspective

Financial Reporting and Analysis

Real-World Focus

BYP12-1 This exercise is an introduction to the Big Four accounting firms, all of which are partnerships.

Addresses

Deloitte & Touche	**www.deloitte.com/**
Ernst & Young	**www.ey.com/**
KPMG	**www.us.kpmg.com/**
PricewaterhouseCoopers	**www.pwc.com/**

or go to **www.wiley.com/college/weygandt**

Steps
1. Select a firm that is of interest to you.
2. Go to the firm's homepage.

Instructions
(a) Name two services performed by the firm.
(b) What is the firm's total annual revenue?
(c) How many clients does it service?
(d) How many people are employed by the firm?
(e) How many partners are there in the firm?

Critical Thinking

 ## Decision-Making Across the Organization

BYP12-2 Stephen Wadson and Mary Shively, two professionals in the finance area, have worked for Morrisen Leasing for a number of years. Morrisen Leasing is a company that leases high-tech medical equipment to hospitals. Stephen and Mary have decided that, with their financial expertise, they might start their own company to perform consulting services for individuals interested in leasing equipment. One form of organization they are considering is a partnership.

   If they start a partnership, each individual plans to contribute $50,000 in cash. In addition, Stephen has a used IBM computer that originally cost $3,700, which he intends to invest in the partnership. The computer has a present fair value of $1,500.

   Although both Stephen and Mary are financial wizards, they do not know a great deal about how a partnership operates. As a result, they have come to you for advice.

Instructions
With the class divided into groups, answer the following.

(a) What are the major disadvantages of starting a partnership?
(b) What type of document is needed for a partnership, and what should this document contain?
(c) Both Stephen and Mary plan to work full-time in the new partnership. They believe that net income or net loss should be shared equally. However, they are wondering how they can provide compensation to Stephen Wadson for his additional investment of the computer. What would you tell them?
(d) Stephen is not sure how the computer equipment should be reported on his tax return. What would you tell him?
(e) As indicated above, Stephen and Mary have worked together for a number of years. Stephen's skills complement Mary's and vice versa. If one of them dies, it will be very difficult for the other to maintain the business, not to mention the difficulty of paying the deceased partner's estate for his or her partnership interest. What would you advise them to do?

Communication Activity

BYP12-3 You are an expert in the field of forming partnerships. Ronald Hrabik and Meg Percival want to establish a partnership to start "Pasta Shop," and they are going to meet with you to discuss their plans. Prior to the meeting, you will send them a memo discussing the issues they need to consider before their visit.

Instructions
Write a memo in good form to be sent to Hrabik and Percival.

Ethics Case

 BYP12-4 Alexandra and Kellie operate a beauty salon as partners who share profits and losses equally. The success of their business has exceeded their expectations; the salon is operating quite profitably. Kellie is anxious to maximize profits and schedules appointments from 8 a.m. to 6 p.m. daily, even sacrificing some lunch hours to accommodate regular customers. Alexandra schedules her appointments from 9 a.m. to 5 p.m. and takes long lunch hours. Alexandra regularly makes

significantly larger withdrawals of cash than Kellie does, but, she says, "Kellie, you needn't worry, I never make a withdrawal without you knowing about it, so it is properly recorded in my drawing account and charged against my capital at the end of the year." Alexandra's withdrawals to date are double Kellie's.

Instructions

(a) Who are the stakeholders in this situation?

(b) Identify the problems with Alexandra's actions and discuss the ethical considerations of her actions.

(c) How might the partnership agreement be revised to accommodate the differences in Alexandra's and Kellie's work and withdrawal habits?

All About You

BYP12-5 As this chapter indicates, the partnership form of organization has advantages and disadvantages. The chapter noted that different types of partnerships have been developed to minimize some of these disadvantages. Alternatively, an individual or company can choose the proprietorship or corporate form of organization.

Instructions

Go to two local businesses that are different, such as a restaurant, a retailer, a construction company, or a professional office (dentist, doctor, etc.), and find the answers to the following questions.

(a) What form of organization do you use in your business?

(b) What do you believe are the two major advantages of this form of organization for your business?

(c) What do you believe are the two major disadvantages of this form of organization for your business?

(d) Do you believe that eventually you may choose another form of organization?

(e) Did you have someone help you form this organization (attorney, accountant, relative, etc.)?

Answers to Chapter Questions

Answers to Insight and Accounting Across the Organization Questions

p. 570 Limited Liability Companies Gain in Popularity   Q: Why do you think that the use of the limited liability company is gaining in popularity? **A:** The LLC is gaining in popularity because owners in such companies have limited liability for business debts even if they participate in management. As a result, the LLC form has a distinct advantage over regular partnerships. In addition, the other limited-type partnerships discussed in Illustration 12-1 are restrictive as to their use. As a result, it is not surprising that limited liability companies are now often used as the form of organization when individuals want to set up a partnership.

p. 572 How to Part Ways Nicely   Q: How can partnership conflicts be minimized and more easily resolved? **A:** First, it is important to develop a business plan that all parties agree to. Second, it is vital to have a well-thought-out partnership agreement. Third, it can be useful to set up a board of mutually agreed upon and respected advisors to consult when making critical decisions.

Answers to Self-Test Questions

1. a **2.** c **3.** b **4.** c **5.** a ($8,000 + $16,000 + $55,000) **6.** b ($60,000 × 20%) **7.** c [$60,000 − ($10,000 × 3)] × 30% = $9,000; $10,000 + $9,000 **8.** c **9.** d **10.** a **11.** b ($22,000 + $73,000) − $85,000 = $10,000 loss; Ely $52,000 − (40% × 10,000) **12.** d ($22,000 + $73,000) − $60,000 = $35,000 loss; loss allocation Harriett $23,000 − (20% × 35,000); Mike $8,000 − (40% × 35,000); Elly $52,000 − (40% × 35,000); Mike deficiency is $6,000; allocated to Elly $38,000 − ($6,000 × 4/6) ***13.** d ($30,000 × 50%) ***14.** d ($60,000 + $50,000 + $40,000 + $60,000) = $210,000; $210,000 × 25% = $52,500; ($60,000 − $52,500) × 20% ***15.** b ($29,000 − $20,000) = $9,000 loss; $40,000 − ($9,000 × 3/9)

 The Navigator

✔ Remember to go back to The Navigator box on the chapter opening page and check off your completed work.

13 | Corporations: Organization and Capital Stock Transactions

✔ The Naviga

Feature Story

What's Cooking?

What major U.S. corporation got its start 41 years ago with a waffle iron? *Hint:* It doesn't sell food. *Another hint:* Swoosh. *Another hint:* "Just do it." That's right, Nike. In 1971, Nike co-founder Bill Bowerman put a piece of rubber into a kitchen waffle iron, and the trademark waffle sole was born. It seems fair to say that at Nike, "They don't make 'em like they used to."

Nike was co-founded by Bowerman and Phil Knight, a member of Bowerman's University of Oregon track team. Each began in the shoe business independently during the early 1960s. Bowerman got his start by making hand-crafted running shoes for his University of Oregon track team. Knight, after completing graduate school, started a small business importing low-cost, high-quality shoes from Japan. In 1964, the two joined forces, each contributing $500, and formed Blue Ribbon Sports, a partnership that marketed Japanese shoes.

It wasn't until 1971 that the company began manufacturing its own line of shoes. With the new shoes came a new corporate name–Nike–the Greek goddess of victory. It is hard to imagine that the company that now boasts a stable ful world-class athletes as promoters at one time had part-tir employees selling shoes out of car trunks at track meets. Nike has achieved its success through relentless innovatio combined with unbridled promotion.

By 1980, Nike was sufficiently established and issued its f stock to the public. That same year, it created a stock ow ship program for its employees, allowing them to share ir company's success. Since then, Nike has enjoyed phenom growth, with 2011 sales reaching $20.7 billion and total dividends paid of $569 million.

Nike is not alone in its quest for the top of the sport shoe world. Reebok used to be Nike's arch rival (get it? "arch" but then Reebok was acquired by the German company adidas. Now adidas pushes Nike every step of the way.

The shoe market is fickle, with new styles becoming pop almost daily and vast international markets still lying untar Whether one of these two giants does eventually take co of the pedi-planet remains to be seen. Meanwhile, the shareholders sit anxiously in the stands as this Olympic-si drama unfolds.

✔ The Navigator

- ☐ Scan Learning Objectives
- ☐ Read Feature Story
- ☐ Read Preview
- ☐ Read text and answer **DO IT!** p. 615
  - ☐ p. 617 ☐ p. 620 ☐ p. 624 ☐ p. 626
- ☐ Work Comprehensive **DO IT!** p. 627
- ☐ Review Summary of Learning Objectives
- ☐ Answer Self-Test Questions
- ☐ Complete Assignments
- ☐ Go to *WileyPLUS* for practice and tutorials

 Read A Look at IFRS p. 644

Learning Objectives
 ✔ The Navigator

After studying this chapter, you should be able to:

[1] Identify the major characteristics of a corporation.

[2] Differentiate between paid-in capital and retained earnings.

[3] Record the issuance of common stock.

[4] Explain the accounting for treasury stock.

[5] Differentiate preferred stock from common stock.

[6] Prepare a stockholders' equity section.

Preview of Chapter 13

✔ The Navigator

Corporations like Nike and adidas have substantial resources at their disposal. In fact, the corporation is the dominant form of business organization in the United States in terms of sales, earnings, and number of employees. All of the 500 largest companies in the United States are corporations. In this chapter, we will explain the essential features of a corporation and the accounting for a corporation's capital stock transactions. In Chapter 14, we will look at other issues related to accounting for corporations.

The content and organization of Chapter 13 are as follows.

CORPORATIONS: ORGANIZATION AND CAPITAL STOCK TRANSACTIONS

The Corporate Form of Organization	Accounting for Issues of Common Stock	Accounting for Treasury Stock	Accounting for Preferred Stock	Statement Presentation
• Characteristics • Formation • Stockholder rights • Stock issue considerations • Corporate capital	• Issuing par value stock • Issuing no-par stock • Issuing stock for services or noncash assets	• Purchase of treasury stock • Disposal of treasury stock	• Dividend preferences • Liquidation preference	• Paid-in capital • Retained earnings

The Corporate Form of Organization

LEARNING OBJECTIVE   1

Identify the major characteristics of a corporation.

In 1819, Chief Justice John Marshall defined a corporation as "an artificial being, invisible, intangible, and existing only in contemplation of law." This definition is the foundation for the prevailing legal interpretation that a **corporation** is an **entity separate and distinct from its owners**.

A corporation is created by law, and its continued existence depends upon the statutes of the state in which it is incorporated. As a legal entity, a corporation has most of the rights and privileges of a person. The major exceptions relate to privileges that only a living person can exercise, such as the right to vote or to hold public office. A corporation is subject to the same duties and responsibilities as a person. For example, it must abide by the laws, and it must pay taxes.

Two common ways to classify corporations are by **purpose** and by **ownership**. A corporation may be organized for the purpose of making a profit, or it may be not-for-profit. For-profit corporations include such well-known companies as McDonald's, Nike, PepsiCo, and Google. Not-for-profit corporations are organized for charitable, medical, or educational purposes. Examples are the Salvation Army and the American Cancer Society.

Classification by ownership differentiates publicly held and privately held corporations. A **publicly held corporation** may have thousands of stockholders. Its stock is regularly traded on a national securities exchange such as the New York Stock Exchange. Examples are IBM, Caterpillar, and General Electric.

In contrast, a **privately held corporation** usually has only a few stockholders, and does not offer its stock for sale to the general public. Privately held companies are generally much smaller than publicly held companies, although some notable exceptions exist. Cargill Inc., a private corporation that trades in grain and other commodities, is one of the largest companies in the United States.

Alternative Terminology
Privately held corporations are also referred to as *closely held corporations.*

Stockholders
Legal existence separate from owners

Characteristics of a Corporation

In 1964, when Nike's founders Phil Knight and Bill Bowerman were just getting started in the running shoe business, they formed their original organization as a partnership. In 1968, they reorganized the company as a corporation. A number of characteristics distinguish corporations from proprietorships and partnerships. We explain the most important of these characteristics below.

SEPARATE LEGAL EXISTENCE

As an entity separate and distinct from its owners, the corporation acts under its own name rather than in the name of its stockholders. Nike may buy, own, and sell property. It may borrow money, and may enter into legally binding contracts in its own name. It may also sue or be sued, and it pays its own taxes.

In a partnership, the acts of the owners (partners) bind the partnership. In contrast, the acts of its owners (stockholders) do not bind the corporation unless such owners are **agents** of the corporation. For example, if you owned shares of Nike stock, you would not have the right to purchase inventory for the company unless you were designated as an agent of the corporation.

Stockholders
Limited liability of stockholders

LIMITED LIABILITY OF STOCKHOLDERS

Since a corporation is a separate legal entity, creditors have recourse only to corporate assets to satisfy their claims. The liability of stockholders is normally limited to their investment in the corporation. Creditors have no legal claim on the personal assets of the owners unless fraud has occurred. Even in the event of bankruptcy, stockholders' losses are generally limited to their capital investment in the corporation.

TRANSFERABLE OWNERSHIP RIGHTS

Transferable ownership rights

Shares of capital stock give ownership in a corporation. These shares are transferable units. Stockholders may dispose of part or all of their interest in a corporation simply by selling their stock. The transfer of an ownership interest in a partnership requires the consent of each owner. In contrast, the transfer of stock is entirely at the discretion of the stockholder. It does not require the approval of either the corporation or other stockholders.

The transfer of ownership rights between stockholders normally has no effect on the daily operating activities of the corporation. Nor does it affect the corporation's assets, liabilities, and total ownership equity. The transfer of these ownership rights is a transaction between individual owners. The company does not participate in the transfer of these ownership rights after the original sale of the capital stock.

ABILITY TO ACQUIRE CAPITAL

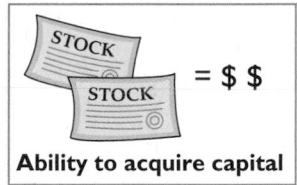

Ability to acquire capital

It is relatively easy for a corporation to obtain capital through the issuance of stock. Buying stock in a corporation is often attractive to an investor because a stockholder has limited liability and shares of stock are readily transferable. Also, numerous individuals can become stockholders by investing relatively small amounts of money.

CONTINUOUS LIFE

Continuous life

The life of a corporation is stated in its charter. The life may be perpetual, or it may be limited to a specific number of years. If it is limited, the company can extend the life through renewal of the charter. Since a corporation is a separate legal entity, its continuance as a going concern is not affected by the withdrawal, death, or incapacity of a stockholder, employee, or officer. As a result, a successful company can have a continuous and perpetual life.

CORPORATION MANAGEMENT

Stockholders legally own the corporation. However, they manage the corporation indirectly through a board of directors they elect. Philip Knight is the chairman of Nike. The board, in turn, formulates the operating policies for the company. The board also selects officers, such as a president and one or more vice presidents, to execute policy and to perform daily management functions. As a result of the Sarbanes-Oxley Act, the board is now required to monitor management's actions more closely. Many feel that the failures of Enron, WorldCom, and more recently MF Global could have been avoided by more diligent boards.

Illustration 13-1 (page 610) presents a typical organization chart showing the delegation of responsibility.

The chief executive officer (CEO) has overall responsibility for managing the business. As the organization chart shows, the CEO delegates responsibility to other officers. The chief accounting officer is the **controller**. The controller's responsibilities include (1) maintaining the accounting records, (2) maintaining an adequate system of internal control, and (3) preparing financial statements, tax returns, and internal reports. The **treasurer** has custody of the corporation's funds and is responsible for maintaining the company's cash position.

The organizational structure of a corporation enables a company to hire professional managers to run the business. On the other hand, the separation of ownership and management often reduces an owner's ability to actively manage the company.

Ethics Note

Managers who are not owners are often compensated based on the performance of the firm. They thus may be tempted to exaggerate firm performance by inflating income figures.

Illustration 13-1
Corporation organization chart

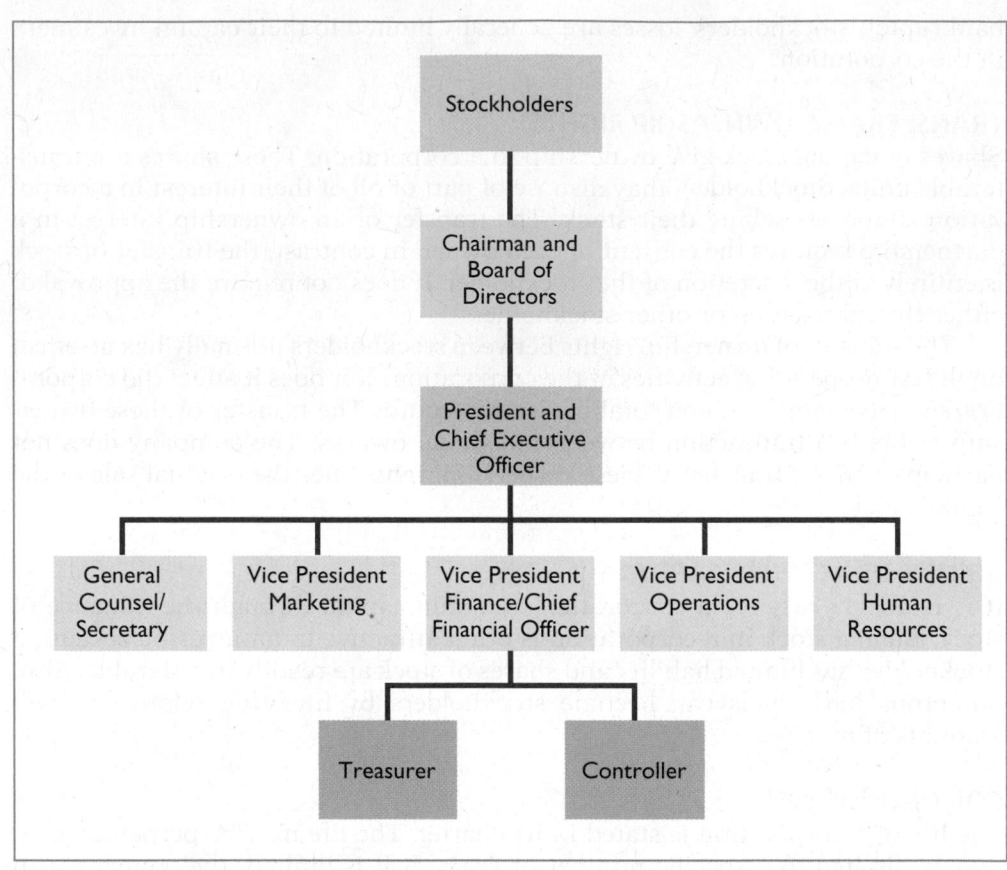

GOVERNMENT REGULATIONS

A corporation is subject to numerous state and federal regulations. For example, state laws usually prescribe the requirements for issuing stock, the distributions of earnings permitted to stockholders, and the acceptable methods for buying back and retiring stock. Federal securities laws govern the sale of capital stock to the general public. Also, most publicly held corporations are required to make extensive disclosure of their financial affairs to the Securities and Exchange Commission (SEC) through quarterly and annual reports. In addition, when a corporation lists its stock on organized securities exchanges, it must comply with the reporting requirements of these exchanges. Government regulations are designed to protect the owners of the corporation.

Government regulations

ADDITIONAL TAXES

Owners of proprietorships and partnerships report their share of earnings on their personal income tax returns. The individual owner then pays taxes on this amount. Corporations, on the other hand, must pay federal and state income taxes **as a separate legal entity**. These taxes can be substantial. They can amount to as much as 40% of taxable income.

In addition, stockholders must pay taxes on cash dividends (pro rata distributions of net income). Thus, many argue that the government taxes corporate income **twice (double taxation)**—once at the corporate level and again at the individual level.

In summary, Illustration 13-2 shows the advantages and disadvantages of a corporation compared to a proprietorship and a partnership.

Additional taxes

Forming a Corporation

A corporation is formed by grant of a state **charter**. The charter is a document that describes the name and purpose of the corporation, the types and number of shares of stock that are authorized to be issued, the names of the individuals that

Advantages	Disadvantages
Separate legal existence	Corporation management—separation of
Limited liability of stockholders	ownership and management
Transferable ownership rights	Government regulations
Ability to acquire capital	Additional taxes
Continuous life	
Corporation management—professional	
managers	

Illustration 13-2
Advantages and disadvantages of a corporation

formed the company, and the number of shares that these individuals agreed to purchase. Regardless of the number of states in which a corporation has operating divisions, it is incorporated in only one state.

It is to the company's advantage to incorporate in a state whose laws are favorable to the corporate form of business organization. For example, although General Motors has its headquarters in Michigan, it is incorporated in New Jersey. In fact, more and more corporations have been incorporating in states with rules that favor existing management. For example, Gulf Oil changed its state of incorporation to Delaware to thwart possible unfriendly takeovers. There, certain defensive tactics against takeovers can be approved by the board of directors alone, without a vote by shareholders.

Upon receipt of its charter from the state of incorporation, the corporation establishes **by-laws**. The by-laws establish the internal rules and procedures for conducting the affairs of the corporation. Corporations engaged in interstate commerce must also obtain a **license** from each state in which they do business. The license subjects the corporation's operating activities to the general corporation laws of the state.

Costs incurred in the formation of a corporation are called **organization costs**. These costs include legal and state fees, and promotional expenditures involved in the organization of the business. **Corporations expense organization costs as incurred.** Determining the amount and timing of future benefits is so difficult that it is standard procedure to take a conservative approach of expensing these costs immediately.

Alternative Terminology
The charter is often referred to as the *articles of incorporation.*

ACCOUNTING ACROSS THE ORGANIZATION

A Thousand Millionaires!

Traveling to space or embarking on an expedition to excavate lost Mayan ruins are normally the stuff of adventure novels. But for employees of Facebook, these and other lavish dreams moved closer to reality when the world's No. 1 online social network went public through an initial public offering (IPO) that may have created at least a thousand millionaires. The IPO was the largest in Internet history, valuing Facebook at over $104 billion.

With all these riches to be had, why did Mark Zuckerberg, the founder of Facebook, delay taking his company public? Consider that the main motivation for issuing shares to the public is to raise money so you can grow your business. However, unlike a manufacturer or even an online retailer, Facebook doesn't need major physical resources, it doesn't have inventory, and it doesn't really need much money for marketing. So in the past, the company hasn't had much need for additional cash beyond what it was already generating on its own. Finally, as head of a closely held, nonpublic company, Zuckerberg was subject to far fewer regulations than a public company.

Source: "Status Update: I'm Rich! Facebook Flotation to Create 1,000 Millionaires Among Company's Rank and File," *Daily Mail Reporter* (February 1, 2012).

Jeff Chiu/AP/Wide World Photos

 Why did Mark Zuckerberg, the CEO and founder of Facebook, delay taking his company's shares public through an initial public offering (IPO)? (See page 643.)

Stockholder Rights

When chartered, the corporation may begin selling shares of stock. When a corporation has only one class of stock, it is **common stock**. Each share of common stock gives the stockholder the ownership rights pictured in Illustration 13-3. The articles of incorporation or the by-laws state the ownership rights of a share of stock.

Illustration 13-3
Ownership rights of stockholders

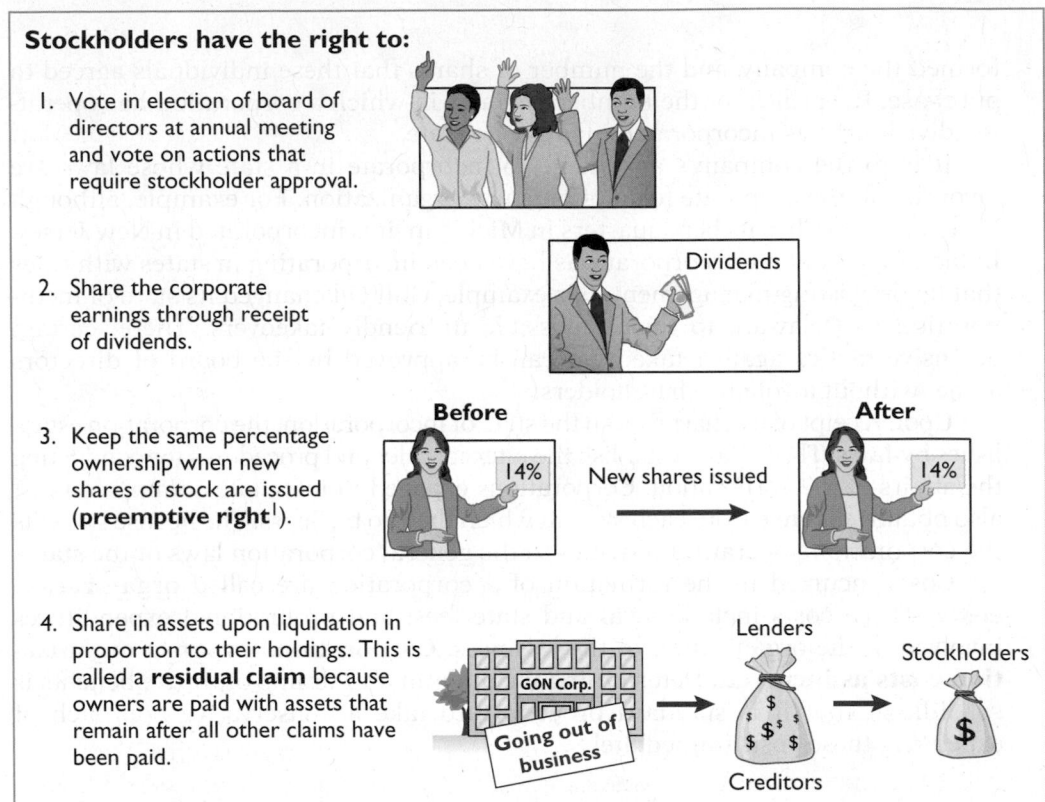

Stockholders have the right to:

1. Vote in election of board of directors at annual meeting and vote on actions that require stockholder approval.

2. Share the corporate earnings through receipt of dividends.

3. Keep the same percentage ownership when new shares of stock are issued (**preemptive right**[1]).

4. Share in assets upon liquidation in proportion to their holdings. This is called a **residual claim** because owners are paid with assets that remain after all other claims have been paid.

Proof of stock ownership is evidenced by a form known as a **stock certificate**. As Illustration 13-4 shows, the face of the certificate shows the name of the corporation, the stockholder's name, the class and special features of the stock, the number of shares owned, and the signatures of authorized corporate officials. Prenumbered certificates facilitate accountability. They may be issued for any quantity of shares.

Stock Issue Considerations

Although Nike incorporated in 1968, it did not sell stock to the public until 1980. At that time, Nike evidently decided it would benefit from the infusion of cash that a public sale would bring. When a corporation decides to issue stock, it must resolve a number of basic questions: How many shares should it authorize for sale? How should it issue the stock? What value should the corporation assign to the stock? We address these questions in the following sections.

---

[1]A number of companies have eliminated the preemptive right because they believe it makes an unnecessary and cumbersome demand on management. For example, by stockholder approval, IBM has dropped its preemptive right for stockholders.

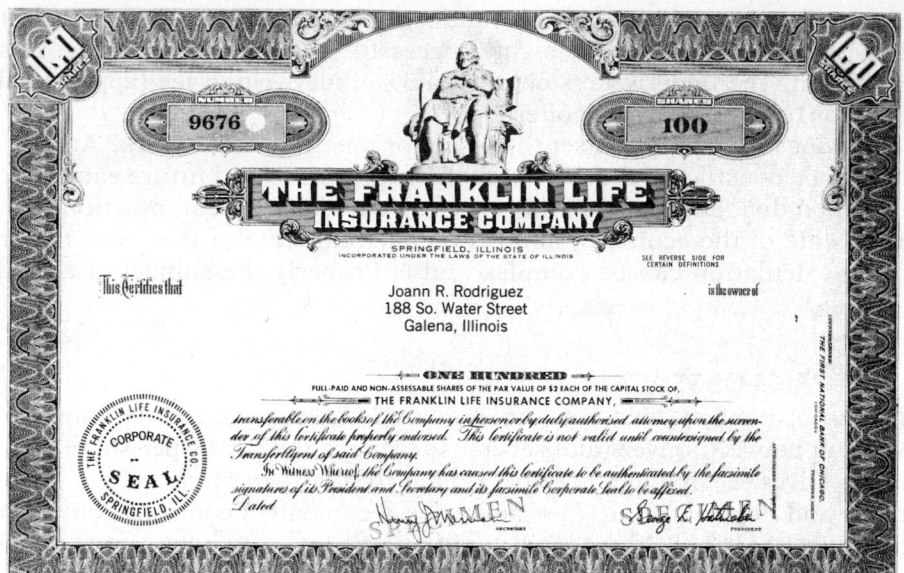

Illustration 13-4
A stock certificate

AUTHORIZED STOCK

The charter indicates the amount of stock that a corporation is **authorized** to sell. The total amount of **authorized stock** at the time of incorporation normally anticipates both initial and subsequent capital needs. As a result, the number of shares authorized generally exceeds the number initially sold. If it sells all authorized stock, a corporation must obtain consent of the state to amend its charter before it can issue additional shares.

The authorization of capital stock does not result in a formal accounting entry. The reason is that the event has no immediate effect on either corporate assets or stockholders' equity. However, the number of authorized shares is often reported in the stockholders' equity section. It is then simple to determine the number of unissued shares that the corporation can issue without amending the charter: subtract the total shares issued from the total authorized. For example, if Advanced Micro was authorized to sell 100,000 shares of common stock and issued 80,000 shares, 20,000 shares would remain unissued.

ISSUANCE OF STOCK

A corporation can issue common stock **directly** to investors. Alternatively, it can issue the stock **indirectly** through an investment banking firm that specializes in bringing securities to the attention of prospective investors. Direct issue is typical in closely held companies. Indirect issue is customary for a publicly held corporation.

In an indirect issue, the investment banking firm may agree to **underwrite** the entire stock issue. In this arrangement, the investment banker buys the stock from the corporation at a stipulated price and resells the shares to investors. The corporation thus avoids any risk of being unable to sell the shares. Also, it obtains immediate use of the cash received from the underwriter. The investment banking firm, in turn, assumes the risk of reselling the shares, in return for an underwriting fee.[2]

Indirect issuance

---

[2] Alternatively, the investment banking firm may agree only to enter into a **best-efforts** contract with the corporation. In such cases, the banker agrees to sell as many shares as possible at a specified price. The corporation bears the risk of unsold stock. Under a best-efforts arrangement, the banking firm is paid a fee or commission for its services.

For example, Google (the world's number-one Internet search engine) used underwriters when it issued a highly successful initial public offering, raising $1.67 billion. The underwriters charged a 3% underwriting fee (approximately $50 million) on Google's stock offering.

How does a corporation set the price for a new issue of stock? Among the factors to be considered are (1) the company's anticipated future earnings, (2) its expected dividend rate per share, (3) its current financial position, (4) the current state of the economy, and (5) the current state of the securities market. The calculation can be complex and is properly the subject of a finance course.

MARKET PRICE OF STOCK

The stock of publicly held companies is traded on organized exchanges. The interaction between buyers and sellers determines the prices per share. In general, the prices set by the marketplace tend to follow the trend of a company's earnings and dividends. But, factors beyond a company's control, such as an oil embargo, changes in interest rates, and the outcome of a presidential election, may cause day-to-day fluctuations in market prices.

The trading of capital stock on securities exchanges involves the transfer of **already issued shares** from an existing stockholder to another investor. These transactions have **no impact** on a corporation's stockholders' equity.

Joe Robbins/Getty Images, Inc.

INVESTOR INSIGHT

How to Read Stock Quotes

Organized exchanges trade the stock of publicly held companies at dollar prices per share established by the interaction between buyers and sellers. For each listed security, the financial press reports the high and low prices of the stock during the year, the total volume of stock traded on a given day, the high and low prices for the day, and the closing market price, with the net change for the day. Nike is listed on the New York Stock Exchange. Here is a listing for Nike:

	52 Weeks						
Stock	High	Low	Volume	High	Low	Close	Net Change
Nike	78.55	48.76	5,375,651	72.44	69.78	70.61	−1.69

These numbers indicate the following. The high and low market prices for the last 52 weeks have been $78.55 and $48.76. The trading volume for the day was 5,375,651 shares. The high, low, and closing prices for that date were $72.44, $69.78, and $70.61, respectively. The net change for the day was a decrease of $1.69 per share.

 For stocks traded on organized exchanges, how are the dollar prices per share established? What factors might influence the price of shares in the marketplace? (See page 643.)

PAR AND NO-PAR VALUE STOCKS

Par value stock is capital stock to which the charter has assigned a value per share. Years ago, par value determined the **legal capital** per share that a company must retain in the business for the protection of corporate creditors. That amount was not available for withdrawal by stockholders. Thus, in the past, most states required the corporation to sell its shares at par or above.

However, par value was often immaterial relative to the value of the company's stock—even at the time of issue. Thus, its usefulness as a protective device to creditors was questionable. For example, Loews Corporation's par value is $0.01 per share, yet a new issue in 2012 would have sold at a **market price** in the $32 per share range. Thus, par has no relationship with market price. In the vast majority of cases, it is an immaterial amount. As a consequence, today many states do not require a par value. Instead, they use other means to protect creditors.

No-par value stock is capital stock to which the charter has not assigned a value. No-par value stock is fairly common today. For example, Nike and Procter & Gamble both have no-par stock. In many states, the board of directors assigns a **stated value** to no-par shares.

> ## DO IT!

Corporate Organization

Indicate whether each of the following statements is true or false.

_____ **1.** Similar to partners in a partnership, stockholders of a corporation have unlimited liability.

_____ **2.** It is relatively easy for a corporation to obtain capital through the issuance of stock.

_____ **3.** The separation of ownership and management is an advantage of the corporate form of business.

_____ **4.** The journal entry to record the authorization of capital stock includes a credit to the appropriate capital stock account.

_____ **5.** All states require a par value per share for capital stock.

Solution

1. False. The liability of stockholders is normally limited to their investment in the corporation.

2. True.

3. False. The separation of ownership and management is a disadvantage of the corporate form of business.

4. False. The authorization of capital stock does not result in a formal accounting entry.

5. False. Many states do not require a par value.

Related exercise material: **BE13-1, E13-1, E13-2, and DO IT! 13-1.**

Action Plan

✔ Review the characteristics of a corporation and understand which are advantages and which are disadvantages.

✔ Understand that corporations raise capital through the issuance of stock, which can be par or no-par.

✔ The Navigator

Corporate Capital

Owners' equity is identified by various names: **stockholders' equity, shareholders' equity,** or **corporate capital**. The stockholders' equity section of a corporation's balance sheet consists of two parts: (1) paid-in (contributed) capital and (2) retained earnings (earned capital).

The distinction between **paid-in capital** and **retained earnings** is important from both a legal and a financial point of view. Legally, corporations can make distributions of earnings (declare dividends) out of retained earnings in all states. However, in many states they cannot declare dividends out of paid-in capital. Management, stockholders, and others often look to retained earnings for the continued existence and growth of the corporation.

LEARNING OBJECTIVE   2

Differentiate between paid-in capital and retained earnings.

PAID-IN CAPITAL

Paid-in capital is the total amount of cash and other assets paid in to the corporation by stockholders in exchange for capital stock. As noted earlier, when a corporation has only one class of stock, it is **common stock**.

RETAINED EARNINGS

Retained earnings is net income that a corporation retains for future use. Net income is recorded in Retained Earnings by a closing entry that debits Income Summary and credits Retained Earnings. For example, assuming that net income for Delta Robotics in its first year of operations is $130,000, the closing entry is:

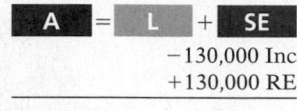

−130,000 Inc
+130,000 RE

Cash Flows
no effect

Income Summary	130,000	
Retained Earnings		130,000
(To close Income Summary and transfer net income to retained earnings)		

If Delta Robotics has a balance of $800,000 in common stock at the end of its first year, its stockholders' equity section is as follows.

Illustration 13-5
Stockholders' equity section

DELTA ROBOTICS
Balance Sheet (partial)

Stockholders' equity		
Paid-in capital		
Common stock	$800,000	
Retained earnings	130,000	
Total stockholders' equity		**$930,000**

Illustration 13-6 compares the owners' equity (stockholders' equity) accounts reported on a balance sheet for a proprietorship, a partnership, and a corporation.

Illustration 13-6
Comparison of owners' equity accounts

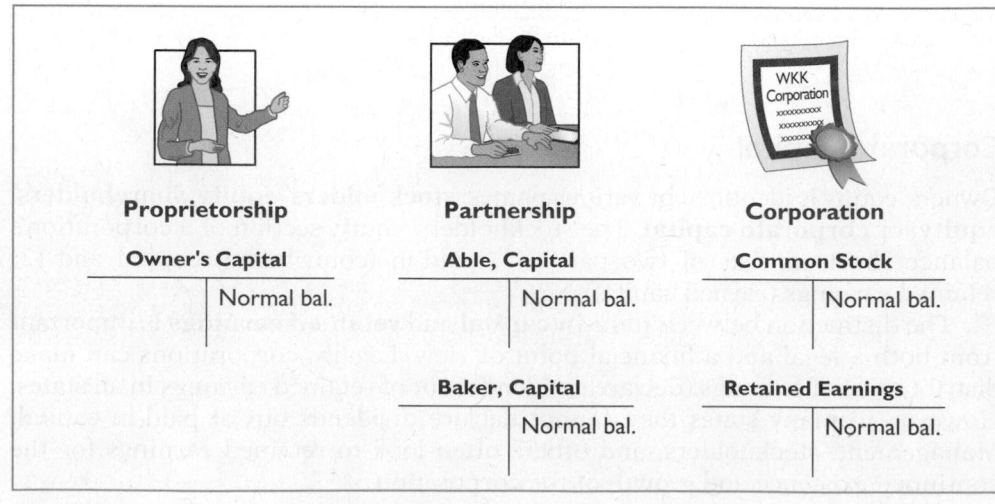

PEOPLE, PLANET, AND PROFIT INSIGHT

The Impact of Corporate Social Responsibility

A recent survey conducted by Institutional Shareholder Services, a proxy advisory firm, shows that 83% of investors now believe environmental and social factors can significantly impact shareholder value over the long term. This belief is clearly visible in the rising level of support for shareholder proposals requesting action related to social and environmental issues.

The following table shows that the number of corporate social responsibility (CSR)-related shareholder proposals rose from 150 in 2000 to 191 in 2010. Moreover, those proposals received average voting support of 18.4% of votes cast versus just 7.5% a decade earlier.

Trends in Shareholder Proposals on Corporate Responsibility

	2000	2005	2010
Number of proposals voted	150	155	191
Average voting support	7.5%	9.9%	18.4%
Percent proposals receiving >10% support	16.7%	31.2%	52.1%

Source: Investor Responsibility Research Center, Ernst & Young, *Seven Questions CEOs and Boards Should Ask About: "Triple Bottom Line" Reporting.*

? Why are CSR-related shareholder proposals increasing? (See page 643.)

> ## DO IT!

Corporate Capital

At the end of its first year of operation, Doral Corporation has $750,000 of common stock and net income of $122,000. Prepare (a) the closing entry for net income and (b) the stockholders' equity section at year-end.

Solution

Action Plan

✔ Record net income in Retained Earnings by a closing entry in which Income Summary is debited and Retained Earnings is credited.

✔ In the stockholders' equity section, show (1) paid-in capital and (2) retained earnings.

(a) Income Summary		122,000	
Retained Earnings			122,000
(To close Income Summary and transfer net income to retained earnings)			
(b) Stockholders' equity			
Paid-in capital			
Common stock		$750,000	
Retained earnings		122,000	
Total stockholders' equity			$872,000

Related exercise material: **BE13-2 and DO IT! 13-2.**

✔ **The Navigator**

Accounting for Issues of Common Stock

Let's now look at how to account for issues of common stock. The primary objectives in accounting for the issuance of common stock are (1) to identify the specific sources of paid-in capital, and (2) to maintain the distinction between paid-in capital and retained earnings. **The issuance of common stock affects only paid-in capital accounts.**

LEARNING OBJECTIVE   3

Record the issuance of common stock.

Issuing Par Value Common Stock for Cash

As discussed earlier, par value does not indicate a stock's market price. Therefore, the cash proceeds from issuing par value stock may be equal to, greater than, or less than par value. When the company records issuance of common stock for cash, it credits the par value of the shares to Common Stock. It also records in a separate paid-in capital account the portion of the proceeds that is above or below par value.

To illustrate, assume that Hydro-Slide, Inc. issues 1,000 shares of $1 par value common stock at par for cash. The entry to record this transaction is:

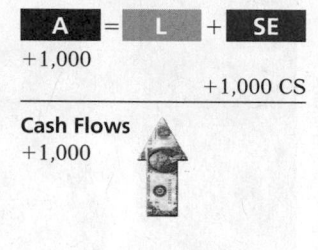

Cash	1,000	
Common Stock		1,000
(To record issuance of 1,000 shares of $1 par common stock at par)		

Now assume that Hydro-Slide issues an additional 1,000 shares of the $1 par value common stock for cash at $5 per share. The amount received above the par value, in this case $4 ($5 − $1), is credited to Paid-in Capital in Excess of Par—Common Stock. The entry is:

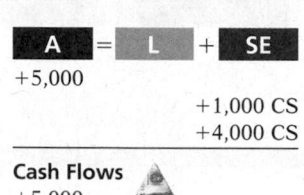

Cash	5,000	
Common Stock		1,000
Paid-in Capital in Excess of Par—Common Stock		4,000
(To record issuance of 1,000 shares of $1 par common stock)		

The total paid-in capital from these two transactions is $6,000, and the legal capital is $2,000. Assuming Hydro-Slide, Inc. has retained earnings of $27,000, Illustration 13-7 shows the company's stockholders' equity section.

Illustration 13-7
Stockholders' equity—paid-in capital in excess of par

HYDRO-SLIDE, INC.		
Balance Sheet (partial)		
Stockholders' equity		
Paid-in capital		
Common stock	$ 2,000	
Paid-in capital in excess of par— common stock	**4,000**	
Total paid-in capital	6,000	
Retained earnings	27,000	
Total stockholders' equity	$33,000	

Alternative Terminology
Paid-in Capital in Excess of Par is also called *Premium on Stock*.

When a corporation issues stock for less than par value, it debits the account Paid-in Capital in Excess of Par—Common Stock if a credit balance exists in this account. If a credit balance does not exist, then the corporation debits to Retained Earnings the amount less than par. This situation occurs only rarely. Most states do not permit the sale of common stock below par value because stockholders may be held personally liable for the difference between the price paid upon original sale and par value.

Issuing No-Par Common Stock for Cash

When no-par common stock has a stated value, the entries are similar to those illustrated for par value stock. The corporation credits the stated value to Common Stock. Also, when the selling price of no-par stock exceeds stated value, the corporation credits the excess to Paid-in Capital in Excess of Stated Value—Common Stock.

For example, assume that instead of $1 par value stock, Hydro-Slide, Inc. has $5 stated value no-par stock and the company issues 5,000 shares at $8 per share for cash. The entry is:

Cash	40,000	
Common Stock		25,000
Paid-in Capital in Excess of Stated Value—Common Stock		15,000
(To record issue of 5,000 shares of $5 stated		
value no-par stock)		

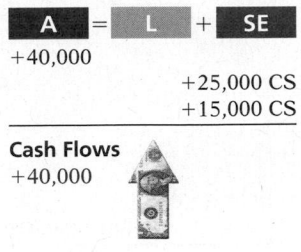

Hydro-Slide, Inc. reports Paid-in Capital in Excess of Stated Value—Common Stock as part of paid-in capital in the stockholders' equity section.

What happens when no-par stock does not have a stated value? In that case, the corporation credits the entire proceeds to Common Stock. Thus, if Hydro-Slide does not assign a stated value to its no-par stock, it records the issuance of the 5,000 shares at $8 per share for cash as follows.

Cash	40,000	
Common Stock		40,000
(To record issue of 5,000 shares of no-par stock)		

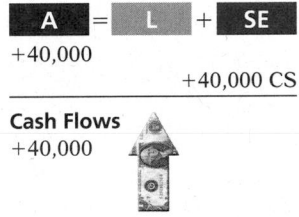

Issuing Common Stock for Services or Noncash Assets

Corporations also may issue stock for services (compensation to attorneys or consultants) or for noncash assets (land, buildings, and equipment). In such cases, what cost should be recognized in the exchange transaction? To comply with the **historical cost principle**, in a noncash transaction **cost is the cash equivalent price**. Thus, **cost is either the fair value of the consideration given up or the fair value of the consideration received**, whichever is more clearly determinable.

To illustrate, assume that attorneys have helped Jordan Company incorporate. They have billed the company $5,000 for their services. They agree to accept 4,000 shares of $1 par value common stock in payment of their bill. At the time of the exchange, there is no established market price for the stock. In this case, the fair value of the consideration received, $5,000, is more clearly evident. Accordingly, Jordan Company makes the following entry.

Organization Expense	5,000	
Common Stock		4,000
Paid-in Capital in Excess of Par—Common Stock		1,000
(To record issuance of 4,000 shares of $1 par value		
stock to attorneys)		

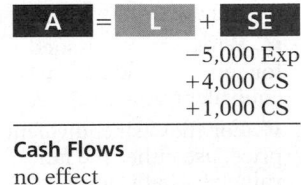

As explained on page 611, organization costs are expensed as incurred.

In contrast, assume that Athletic Research Inc. is an existing publicly held corporation. Its $5 par value stock is actively traded at $8 per share. The company issues 10,000 shares of stock to acquire land recently advertised for sale at $90,000. The most clearly evident value in this noncash transaction is the market price of the consideration given, $80,000. The company records the transaction as follows.

Land	80,000	
Common Stock		50,000
Paid-in Capital in Excess of Par—Common Stock		30,000
(To record issuance of 10,000 shares of $5 par value		
stock for land)		

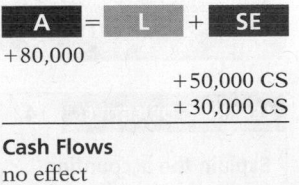

As illustrated in these examples, **the par value of the stock is never a factor in determining the cost of the assets received**. This is also true of the stated value of no-par stock.

ANATOMY OF A FRAUD

The president, chief operating officer, and chief financial officer of SafeNet, a software encryption company, were each awarded employee stock options by the company's board of directors as part of their compensation package. Stock options enable an employee to buy a company's stock sometime in the future at the price that existed when the stock option was awarded. For example, suppose that you received stock options today, when the stock price of your company was $30. Three years later, if the stock price rose to $100, you could "exercise" your options and buy the stock for $30 per share, thereby making $70 per share. After being awarded their stock options, the three employees changed the award dates in the company's records to dates in the past, when the company's stock was trading at historical lows. For example, using the previous example, they would choose a past date when the stock was selling for $10 per share, rather than the $30 price on the actual award date. In our example, this would increase the profit from exercising the options to $90 per share.

Total take: $1.7 million

THE MISSING CONTROL

Independent internal verification. The company's board of directors should have ensured that the awards were properly administered. For example, the date on the minutes from the board meeting could be compared to the dates that were recorded for the awards. In addition, the dates should again be confirmed upon exercise.

> DO IT!

Issuance of Stock

Action Plan

✔ In issuing shares for cash, credit Common Stock for par value per share.

✔ Credit any additional proceeds in excess of par to a separate paid-in capital account.

✔ When stock is issued for services, use the cash equivalent price.

✔ For the cash equivalent price, use either the fair value of what is given up or the fair value of what is received, whichever is more clearly determinable.

Cayman Corporation begins operations on March 1 by issuing 100,000 shares of $10 par value common stock for cash at $12 per share. On March 15, it issues 5,000 shares of common stock to attorneys in settlement of their bill of $50,000 for organization costs. Journalize the issuance of the shares, assuming the stock is not publicly traded.

Solution

Mar. 1	Cash		1,200,000	
		Common Stock		1,000,000
		Paid-in Capital in Excess of Par—		
		Common Stock		200,000
		(To record issuance of 100,000 shares		
		at $12 per share)		
Mar. 15	Organization Expense		50,000	
		Common Stock		50,000
		(To record issuance of 5,000 shares		
		for attorneys' fees)		

Related exercise material: **BE13-3, BE13-4, BE13-5, E13-3, E13-4, E13-6,** and **DO IT!** **13-3.**

✔ The Navigator

Accounting for Treasury Stock

LEARNING OBJECTIVE   4

Explain the accounting for treasury stock.

Treasury stock is a corporation's own stock that it has issued and subsequently reacquired from shareholders but not retired. A corporation may acquire treasury stock for various reasons:

1. To reissue the shares to officers and employees under bonus and stock compensation plans.

2. To increase trading of the company's stock in the securities market. Companies expect that buying their own stock will signal that management believes the stock is underpriced, which they hope will enhance its market price.

3. To have additional shares available for use in the acquisition of other companies.

4. To reduce the number of shares outstanding and thereby increase earnings per share.

Another infrequent reason for purchasing shares is that management may want to eliminate hostile shareholders by buying them out.

Many corporations have treasury stock. For example, approximately 65% of U.S. companies have treasury stock.[3] In a recent year, Nike purchased more than 6 million treasury shares.

Purchase of Treasury Stock

Companies generally account for treasury stock by **the cost method**. This method uses the cost of the shares purchased to value the treasury stock. Under the cost method, the company debits **Treasury Stock** for the **price paid to reacquire the shares**. When the company disposes of the shares, it credits to Treasury Stock **the same amount** it paid to reacquire the shares.

To illustrate, assume that on January 1, 2014, the stockholders' equity section of Mead, Inc. has 400,000 shares authorized and 100,000 shares of $5 par value common stock outstanding (all issued at par value) and Retained Earnings of $200,000. The stockholders' equity section before purchase of treasury stock is as follows.

MEAD, INC.	
Balance Sheet (partial)	
Stockholders' equity	
Paid-in capital	
Common stock, $5 par value, 400,000 shares authorized, 100,000 shares issued and outstanding	$500,000
Retained earnings	200,000
Total stockholders' equity	$700,000

Illustration 13-8
Stockholders' equity with no treasury stock

On February 1, 2014, Mead acquires 4,000 shares of its stock at $8 per share. The entry is:

Feb. 1	Treasury Stock	32,000	
	Cash		32,000
	(To record purchase of 4,000 shares of treasury stock at $8 per share)		

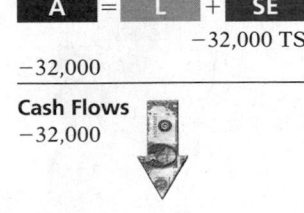

A = L + SE
                    −32,000 TS
−32,000

Cash Flows
−32,000

Mead debits Treasury Stock for the cost of the shares purchased ($32,000). Is the original paid-in capital account, Common Stock, affected? No, because the number of issued shares does not change.

In the stockholders' equity section of the balance sheet, Mead deducts treasury stock from total paid-in capital and retained earnings. Treasury Stock is a **contra stockholders' equity account**. Thus, the acquisition of treasury stock

---

[3]*Accounting Trends & Techniques 2011* (New York: American Institute of Certified Public Accountants).

reduces stockholders' equity. The stockholders' equity section of Mead, Inc. after purchase of treasury stock is as follows.

Illustration 13-9
Stockholders' equity with treasury stock

MEAD, INC.	
Balance Sheet (partial)	
Stockholders' equity	
Paid-in capital	
Common stock, $5 par value, 400,000 shares authorized,	
100,000 shares issued, and 96,000 shares outstanding	$500,000
Retained earnings	200,000
Total paid-in capital and retained earnings	700,000
Less: Treasury stock (4,000 shares)	**32,000**
Total stockholders' equity	$668,000

Ethics Note

The purchase of treasury stock reduces the cushion (cash available) for creditors and preferred stockholders. A restriction for the cost of treasury stock purchased is often required. The restriction is usually applied to retained earnings.

Mead discloses in the balance sheet both the number of shares issued (100,000) and the number in the treasury (4,000). The difference is the number of shares of stock outstanding (96,000). The term **outstanding stock** means the number of shares of issued stock that are being held by stockholders.

Some maintain that companies should report treasury stock as an asset because it can be sold for cash. But under this reasoning, companies would also show unissued stock as an asset, which is clearly incorrect. Rather than being an asset, treasury stock reduces stockholder claims on corporate assets. This effect is correctly shown by reporting treasury stock as a deduction from total paid-in capital and retained earnings.

Han Myung-Gu/WireImage/Getty Images, Inc.

ACCOUNTING ACROSS THE ORGANIZATION

Why Did Reebok Buy Its Own Stock?

In a bold (and some would say risky) move, Reebok at one time bought back nearly a third of its shares. This repurchase of shares dramatically reduced Reebok's available cash. In fact, the company borrowed significant funds to accomplish the repurchase. In a press release, management stated that it was repurchasing the shares because it believed its stock was severely underpriced. The repurchase of so many shares was meant to signal management's belief in good future earnings.

Skeptics, however, suggested that Reebok's management was repurchasing shares to make it less likely that another company would acquire Reebok (in which case Reebok's top managers would likely lose their jobs). By depleting its cash, Reebok became a less attractive acquisition target. Acquiring companies like to purchase companies with large cash balances so they can pay off debt used in the acquisition.

? What signal might a large stock repurchase send to investors regarding management's belief about the company's growth opportunities? (See page 644.)

Disposal of Treasury Stock

Treasury stock is usually sold or retired. The accounting for its sale differs when treasury stock is sold above cost than when it is sold below cost.

SALE OF TREASURY STOCK ABOVE COST

If the selling price of the treasury shares is equal to their cost, the company records the sale of the shares by a debit to Cash and a credit to Treasury Stock. When the selling price of the shares is greater than their cost, the company credits the difference to Paid-in Capital from Treasury Stock.

To illustrate, assume that on July 1, Mead, Inc. sells for $10 per share the 1,000 shares of its treasury stock previously acquired at $8 per share. The entry is as follows.

July 1	Cash	10,000	
	Treasury Stock		8,000
	Paid-in Capital from Treasury Stock		2,000
	(To record sale of 1,000 shares of treasury stock above cost)		

Helpful Hint Treasury stock transactions are classified as capital stock transactions. As in the case when stock is issued, the income statement is not involved.

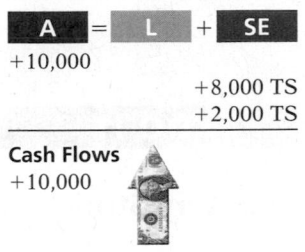

Mead does not record a $2,000 gain on sale of treasury stock for two reasons. (1) Gains on sales occur when **assets** are sold, and treasury stock is not an asset. (2) A corporation does not realize a gain or suffer a loss from stock transactions with its own stockholders. Thus, companies should not include in net income any paid-in capital arising from the sale of treasury stock. Instead, they report Paid-in Capital from Treasury Stock separately on the balance sheet, as a part of paid-in capital.

SALE OF TREASURY STOCK BELOW COST

When a company sells treasury stock below its cost, it usually debits to Paid-in Capital from Treasury Stock the excess of cost over selling price. Thus, if Mead, Inc. sells an additional 800 shares of treasury stock on October 1 at $7 per share, it makes the following entry.

Oct. 1	Cash	5,600	
	Paid-in Capital from Treasury Stock	800	
	Treasury Stock		6,400
	(To record sale of 800 shares of treasury stock below cost)		

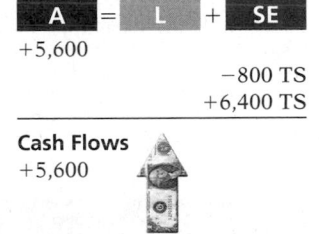

Observe the following from the two sales entries. (1) Mead credits Treasury Stock at cost in each entry. (2) Mead uses Paid-in Capital from Treasury Stock for the difference between cost and the resale price of the shares. (3) The original paid-in capital account, Common Stock, is not affected. **The sale of treasury stock increases both total assets and total stockholders' equity.**

After posting the foregoing entries, the treasury stock accounts will show the following balances on October 1.

Treasury Stock				Paid-in Capital from Treasury Stock			
Feb. 1	32,000	July 1	8,000	Oct. 1	800	July 1	2,000
		Oct. 1	6,400			Oct. 1 Bal.	1,200
Oct. 1 Bal.	17,600						

Illustration 13-10
Treasury stock accounts

When a company fully depletes the credit balance in Paid-in Capital from Treasury Stock, it debits to Retained Earnings any additional excess of cost over selling price. To illustrate, assume that Mead, Inc. sells its remaining 2,200 shares at $7 per share on December 1. The excess of cost over selling price is $2,200 [2,200 × ($8 − $7)]. In this case, Mead debits $1,200 of the excess to Paid-in

Capital from Treasury Stock. It debits the remainder to Retained Earnings. The entry is:

A	=	L	+	SE
+15,400				
				−1,200 TS
				−1,000 RE
				+17,600 TS

Cash Flows
+15,400

Dec. 1	Cash	15,400	
	Paid-in Capital from Treasury Stock	1,200	
	Retained Earnings	1,000	
	Treasury Stock		17,600
	(To record sale of 2,200 shares of treasury		
	stock at $7 per share)		

> DO IT!

Treasury Stock

Action Plan

✔ Record the purchase of treasury stock at cost.

✔ When treasury stock is sold above its cost, credit the excess of the selling price over cost to Paid-in Capital from Treasury Stock.

✔ When treasury stock is sold below its cost, debit the excess of cost over selling price to Paid-in Capital from Treasury Stock.

Santa Anita Inc. purchases 3,000 shares of its $50 par value common stock for $180,000 cash on July 1. It will hold the shares in the treasury until resold. On November 1, the corporation sells 1,000 shares of treasury stock for cash at $70 per share. Journalize the treasury stock transactions.

Solution

July 1	Treasury Stock	180,000	
	Cash		180,000
	(To record the purchase of 3,000 shares		
	at $60 per share)		
Nov. 1	Cash	70,000	
	Treasury Stock		60,000
	Paid-in Capital from Treasury Stock		10,000
	(To record the sale of 1,000 shares		
	at $70 per share)		

Related exercise material: **BE13-6, E13-5, E13-7, E13-8, and DO IT! 13-4.**

✔ **The Navigator**

Accounting for Preferred Stock

LEARNING OBJECTIVE   **5**

Differentiate preferred stock from common stock.

To appeal to a larger segment of potential investors, a corporation may issue an additional class of stock, called preferred stock. **Preferred stock** has contractual provisions that give it some preference or priority over common stock. Typically, preferred stockholders have a priority as to (1) distributions of earnings (dividends) and (2) assets in the event of liquidation. However, they generally do not have voting rights.

Like common stock, corporations may issue preferred stock for cash or for noncash assets. The entries for these transactions are similar to the entries for common stock. When a corporation has more than one class of stock, each paid-in capital account title should identify the stock to which it relates. A company might have the following accounts: Preferred Stock, Common Stock, Paid-in Capital in Excess of Par—Preferred Stock, and Paid-in Capital in Excess of Par—Common Stock.

For example, if Stine Corporation issues 10,000 shares of $10 par value preferred stock for $12 cash per share, the entry to record the issuance is:

A	=	L	+	SE
+120,000				
				+100,000 PS
				+20,000 PS

Cash Flows
+120,000

Cash	120,000	
Preferred Stock		100,000
Paid-in Capital in Excess of Par—Preferred Stock		20,000
(To record the issuance of 10,000 shares of $10 par		
value preferred stock)		

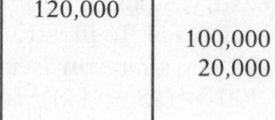

Preferred stock may have either a par value or no-par value. In the stockholders' equity section of the balance sheet, companies list preferred stock first because of its dividend and liquidation preferences over common stock.

Dividend Preferences

As indicated above, **preferred stockholders have the right to receive dividends before common stockholders**. For example, if the dividend rate on preferred stock is $5 per share, common shareholders will not receive any dividends in the current year until preferred stockholders have received $5 per share. The first claim to dividends does not, however, guarantee the payment of dividends. Dividends depend on many factors, such as adequate retained earnings and availability of cash. If a company does not pay dividends to preferred stockholders, it cannot of course pay dividends to common stockholders.

For preferred stock, companies state the per share dividend amount as a percentage of the par value or as a specified amount. For example, Earthlink specifies a 3% dividend on its $100 par value preferred. PepsiCo pays $4.56 per share on its no-par value stock.

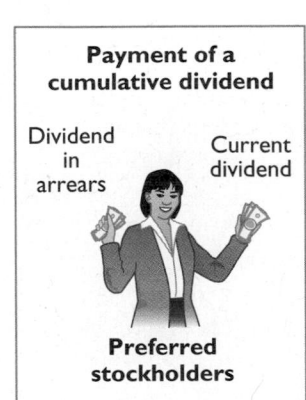

Preferred   Common
stockholders   stockholders

Dividend preferences

CUMULATIVE DIVIDEND

Preferred stock often contains a **cumulative dividend** feature. This right means that preferred stockholders must be paid both current-year dividends and any unpaid prior-year dividends before common stockholders receive dividends. When preferred stock is cumulative, preferred dividends not declared in a given period are called **dividends in arrears**.

To illustrate, assume that Scientific Leasing has 5,000 shares of 7%, $100 par value, cumulative preferred stock outstanding. Each $100 share pays a $7 dividend (.07 × $100). The annual dividend is $35,000 (5,000 × $7 per share). If dividends are two years in arrears, preferred stockholders are entitled to receive the following dividends in the current year.

Dividends in arrears ($35,000 × 2)	$ 70,000
Current-year dividends	35,000
Total preferred dividends	**$105,000**

Illustration 13-11
Computation of total dividends to preferred stock

The company cannot pay dividends to common stockholders until it pays the entire preferred dividend. In other words, companies cannot pay dividends to common stockholders while any preferred dividends are in arrears.

Are dividends in arrears considered a liability? **No—no payment obligation exists until the board of directors declares a dividend.** However, companies should disclose in the notes to the financial statements the amount of dividends in arrears. Doing so enables investors to assess the potential impact of this commitment on the corporation's financial position.

The investment community does not look favorably on companies that are unable to meet their dividend obligations. As a financial officer noted in discussing one company's failure to pay its cumulative preferred dividend for a period of time, "Not meeting your obligations on something like that is a major black mark on your record." The accounting entries for preferred stock dividends are explained in Chapter 14.

Liquidation Preference

Most preferred stocks also have a preference on corporate assets if the corporation fails. This feature provides security for the preferred stockholder. The preference to assets may be for the par value of the shares or for a specified liquidating value.

For example, Commonwealth Edison's preferred stock entitles its holders to receive $31.80 per share, plus accrued and unpaid dividends, in the event of liquidation. The liquidation preference establishes the respective claims of creditors and preferred stockholders in litigation involving bankruptcy lawsuits.

Statement Presentation

LEARNING OBJECTIVE 6

Prepare a stockholders' equity section.

Alternative Terminology
Paid-in capital is sometimes called *contributed capital*.

Companies report paid-in capital and retained earnings in the stockholders' equity section of the balance sheet. They identify the specific sources of paid-in capital, using the following classifications.

1. **Capital stock.** This category consists of preferred and common stock. Preferred stock appears before common stock because of its preferential rights. Companies report par value, shares authorized, shares issued, and shares outstanding for each class of stock.

2. **Additional paid-in capital.** This category includes the excess of amounts paid in over par or stated value and paid-in capital from treasury stock.

The stockholders' equity section of Connally Inc. in Illustration 13-12 includes most of the accounts discussed in this chapter. The disclosures pertaining to Connally's common stock indicate that the company issued 400,000 shares; 100,000 shares are unissued (500,000 authorized less 400,000 issued); and 390,000 shares are outstanding (400,000 issued less 10,000 shares in treasury).

Illustration 13-12
Stockholders' equity section

CONNALLY INC.
Balance Sheet (partial)

Stockholders' equity		
Paid-in capital		
Capital stock		
9% preferred stock, $100 par value cumulative,		
10,000 shares authorized, 6,000		
shares issued and outstanding		$ 600,000
Common stock, no par, $5 stated value, 500,000		
shares authorized, 400,000 shares issued, and		
390,000 shares outstanding		2,000,000
Total capital stock		2,600,000
Additional paid-in capital		
In excess of par—preferred stock	$ 30,000	
In excess of stated value—common stock	860,000	
From treasury stock	140,000	
Total additional paid-in capital		1,030,000
Total paid-in capital		3,630,000
Retained earnings		1,058,000
Total paid-in capital and retained earnings		4,688,000
Less: Treasury stock (10,000 common shares) (at cost)		80,000
Total stockholders' equity		$4,608,000

> DO IT!

Stockholders' Equity Section

Jennifer Corporation has issued 300,000 shares of $3 par value common stock. It authorized 600,000 shares. The paid-in capital in excess of par on the common stock is $380,000. The corporation has reacquired 15,000 shares at a cost of $50,000 and is currently holding those shares. Treasury stock was reissued in prior years for $72,000 more than its cost.

The corporation also has 4,000 shares issued and outstanding of 8%, $100 par value preferred stock. It authorized 10,000 shares. The paid-in capital in excess of par on the preferred stock is $25,000. Retained earnings is $610,000.

Prepare the stockholders' equity section of the balance sheet.

Solution

Action Plan

✔ Present capital stock first; list preferred stock before common stock.

✔ Present additional paid-in capital after capital stock.

✔ Report retained earnings after capital stock and additional paid-in capital.

✔ Deduct treasury stock from total paid-in capital and retained earnings.

JENNIFER CORPORATION Balance Sheet (partial)		
Stockholders' equity		
Paid-in capital		
Capital stock		
8% preferred stock, $100 par value, 10,000 shares authorized, 4,000 shares issued and outstanding		$ 400,000
Common stock, $3 par value, 600,000 shares authorized, 300,000 shares issued, and 285,000 shares outstanding		900,000
Total capital stock		1,300,000
Additional paid-in capital		
In excess of par—preferred stock	$ 25,000	
In excess of par—common stock	380,000	
From treasury stock	72,000	
Total additional paid-in capital		477,000
Total paid-in capital		1,777,000
Retained earnings		610,000
Total paid-in capital and retained earnings		2,387,000
Less: Treasury stock (15,000 common shares) (at cost)		50,000
Total stockholders' equity		$2,337,000

Related exercise material: **BE13-8, E13-9, E13-12, E13-13, E13-14, E13-15, and DO IT! 13-5.**

✔ **The Navigator**

> Comprehensive DO IT!

Rolman Corporation is authorized to issue 1,000,000 shares of $5 par value common stock. In its first year, the company has the following stock transactions.

Jan. 10   Issued 400,000 shares of stock at $8 per share.

July 1   Issued 100,000 shares of stock for land. The land had an asking price of $900,000. The stock is currently selling on a national exchange at $8.25 per share.

Sept. 1   Purchased 10,000 shares of common stock for the treasury at $9 per share.

Dec. 1   Sold 4,000 shares of the treasury stock at $10 per share.

Instructions

(a) Journalize the transactions.

(b) Prepare the stockholders' equity section assuming the company had retained earnings of $200,000 at December 31.

Solution to Comprehensive DO IT!

Action Plan

✔ When common stock has a par value, credit Common Stock for par value.

(a) Jan. 10	Cash	3,200,000	
	Common Stock		2,000,000
	Paid-in Capital in Excess of Par—Common Stock		1,200,000
	(To record issuance of 400,000 shares of $5 par value stock)		

Action Plan (cont'd)

✔ Use fair value in a noncash transaction.

✔ Debit and credit the Treasury Stock account at cost.

✔ Record differences between the cost and selling price of treasury stock in stockholders' equity accounts, not as gains or losses.

July 1	Land	825,000	
	Common Stock		500,000
	Paid-in Capital in Excess		
	of Par—Common Stock		325,000
	(To record issuance of		
	100,000 shares of $5 par		
	value stock for land)		
Sept. 1	Treasury Stock	90,000	
	Cash		90,000
	(To record purchase of		
	10,000 shares of treasury		
	stock at cost)		
Dec. 1	Cash	40,000	
	Treasury Stock		36,000
	Paid-in Capital from Treasury		
	Stock		4,000
	(To record sale of 4,000 shares		
	of treasury stock above cost)		

(b)

ROLMAN CORPORATION
Balance Sheet (partial)

Stockholders' equity		
Paid-in capital		
Capital stock		
Common stock, $5 par value, 1,000,000 shares		
authorized, 500,000 shares issued, 494,000		
shares outstanding		$2,500,000
Additional paid-in capital		
In excess of par—common stock	$1,525,000	
From treasury stock	4,000	
Total additional paid-in capital		1,529,000
Total paid-in capital		4,029,000
Retained earnings		200,000
Total paid-in capital and retained earnings		4,229,000
Less: Treasury stock (6,000 shares)		54,000
Total stockholders' equity		$4,175,000

 The Navigator

SUMMARY OF LEARNING OBJECTIVES

 The Navigator

1 Identify the major characteristics of a corporation. The major characteristics of a corporation are separate legal existence, limited liability of stockholders, transferable ownership rights, ability to acquire capital, continuous life, corporation management, government regulations, and additional taxes.

2 Differentiate between paid-in capital and retained earnings. Paid-in capital is the total amount paid in on capital stock. It is often called contributed capital. Retained earnings is net income retained in a corporation. It is often called earned capital.

3 Record the issuance of common stock. When companies record the issuance of common stock for cash, they credit the par value of the shares to Common Stock. They record in a separate paid-in capital account the portion of the proceeds that is above or below par value. When no-par common stock has a stated value, the entries are similar to those for par value stock. When no-par stock does not have a stated value, companies credit the entire proceeds to Common Stock.

4 Explain the accounting for treasury stock. The cost method is generally used in accounting for treasury stock. Under this approach, companies debit Treasury Stock at the price paid to reacquire the shares. They credit the same amount to Treasury Stock when they sell the shares. The difference between the sales price and cost is recorded in stockholders' equity accounts, not in income statement accounts.

5 **Differentiate preferred stock from common stock.** Preferred stock has contractual provisions that give it priority over common stock in certain areas. Typically, preferred stockholders have preferences (1) to dividends and (2) to assets in liquidation. They usually do not have voting rights.

6 **Prepare a stockholders' equity section.** In the stockholders' equity section, companies report paid-in capital and retained earnings and identify specific sources of paid-in capital. Within paid-in capital, two classifications are shown: capital stock and additional paid-in capital. If a corporation has treasury stock, it deducts the cost of treasury stock from total paid-in capital and retained earnings to obtain total stockholders' equity.

GLOSSARY

Authorized stock The amount of stock that a corporation is authorized to sell as indicated in its charter. (p. 613).

Charter A document that is issued by the state to set forth important terms and features regarding the creation of a corporation. (p. 610).

Corporation A business organized as a legal entity separate and distinct from its owners under state corporation law. (p. 608).

Cumulative dividend A feature of preferred stock entitling the stockholder to receive current and unpaid prior-year dividends before common stockholders receive dividends. (p. 625).

No-par value stock Capital stock that has not been assigned a value in the corporate charter. (p. 615).

Organization costs Costs incurred in the formation of a corporation. (p. 611).

Outstanding stock Capital stock that has been issued and is being held by stockholders. (p. 622).

Paid-in capital Total amount of cash and other assets paid in to the corporation by stockholders in exchange for capital stock. (p. 616).

Par value stock Capital stock that has been assigned a value per share in the corporate charter. (p. 614).

Preferred stock Capital stock that has some preferences over common stock. (p. 624).

Privately held corporation A corporation that has only a few stockholders and whose stock is not available for sale to the general public. (p. 608).

Publicly held corporation A corporation that may have thousands of stockholders and whose stock is regularly traded on a national securities exchange. (p. 608).

Retained earnings Net income that the corporation retains for future use. (p. 616).

Stated value The amount per share assigned by the board of directors to no-par value stock. (p. 615).

Treasury stock A corporation's own stock that has been issued and subsequently reacquired from shareholders by the corporation but not retired. (p. 620).

 **Self-Test, Brief Exercises, Exercises, Problem Set A, and many more components are available for practice in *WileyPLUS*.**

SELF-TEST QUESTIONS

Answers are on page 644.

(LO 1) 1. Which of the following is **not** a major advantage of a corporate form of organization?
   (a) Separate legal existence.
   (b) Continuous life.
   (c) Government regulations.
   (d) Transferable ownership rights.

(LO 1) 2. A major disadvantage of a corporation is:
   (a) limited liability of stockholders.
   (b) additional taxes.
   (c) transferable ownership rights.
   (d) separate legal existence.

(LO 1) 3. Costs incurred in the formation of a corporation:
   (a) do not include legal fees.
   (b) are expensed as incurred.
   (c) are recorded as an asset.

   (d) provide future benefits whose amounts and timing are easily determined.

4. Which of the following statements is **false**? (LO 1)
   (a) Ownership of common stock gives the owner a voting right.
   (b) The stockholders' equity section begins with paid-in capital.
   (c) The authorization of capital stock does not result in a formal accounting entry.
   (d) Legal capital per share applies to par value stock but not to no-par value stock.

5. Total stockholders' equity (in the absence of treasury stock) equals: (LO 2)
   (a) Total paid-in capital + Retained earnings.
   (b) Paid-in capital + Capital stock + Retained earnings.

(c) Capital stock + Additional paid-in capital − Retained earnings.

(d) Common stock + Retained earnings.

(LO 2) 6. The account Retained Earnings is:
  (a) a subdivision of paid-in capital.
  (b) net income retained in the corporation.
  (c) reported as an expense in the income statement.
  (d) closed to capital stock.

(LO 3) 7. A-Team Corporation issued 1,000 shares of $5 par value stock for land. The stock is actively traded at $9 per share. The land was advertised for sale at $10,500. The land should be recorded at:
  (a) $4,000.   **(c)** $9,000.
  (b) $5,000.   **(d)** $10,500.

(LO 3) 8. ABC Corporation issues 1,000 shares of $10 par value common stock at $12 per share. In recording the transaction, credits are made to:
  (a) Common Stock $10,000 and Paid-in Capital in Excess of Stated Value $2,000.
  (b) Common Stock $12,000.
  (c) Common Stock $10,000 and Paid-in Capital in Excess of Par $2,000.
  (d) Common Stock $10,000 and Retained Earnings $2,000.

(LO 4) 9. Treasury stock may be repurchased:
  (a) to reissue the shares to officers and employees under bonus and stock compensation plans.
  (b) to signal to the stock market that management believes the stock is underpriced.
  (c) to have additional shares available for use in the acquisition of other companies.
  (d) More than one of the above.

(LO 4) 10. XYZ, Inc. sells 100 shares of $5 par value treasury stock at $13 per share. If the cost of acquiring the shares was $10 per share, the entry for the sale should include credits to:
  (a) Treasury Stock $1,000 and Paid-in Capital from Treasury Stock $300.

(b) Treasury Stock $500 and Paid-in Capital from Treasury Stock $800.

(c) Treasury Stock $1,000 and Retained Earnings $300.

(d) Treasury Stock $500 and Paid-in Capital in Excess of Par $800.

11. In the stockholders' equity section, the cost of trea- (LO 4) sury stock is deducted from:
  (a) total paid-in capital and retained earnings.
  (b) retained earnings.
  (c) total stockholders' equity.
  (d) common stock in paid-in capital.

12. Preferred stock may have priority over common stock (LO 5) **except** in:
  (a) dividends.
  (b) assets in the event of liquidation.
  (c) cumulative dividend features.
  (d) voting.

13. M-Bot Corporation has 10,000 shares of 8%, $100 par (LO 5) value, cumulative preferred stock outstanding at December 31, 2014. No dividends were declared in 2012 or 2013. If M-Bot wants to pay $375,000 of dividends in 2014, common stockholders will receive:
  (a) $0.   **(c)** $215,000.
  (b) $295,000.   **(d)** $135,000.

14. Which of the following is **not** reported under addi- (LO 6) tional paid-in capital?
  (a) Paid-in capital in excess of par.
  (b) Common stock.
  (c) Paid-in capital in excess of stated value.
  (d) Paid-in capital from treasury stock.

15. In the stockholders' equity section of the balance (LO 6) sheet, common stock:
  (a) is listed before preferred stock.
  (b) is added to total capital stock.
  (c) is part of paid-in capital.
  (d) is part of additional paid-in capital.

Go to the book's companion website, www.wiley.com/college/weygandt, for additional Self-Test Questions.

 The Navigator

QUESTIONS

1. Mark Kemp, a student, asks your help in understanding the following characteristics of a corporation: (a) separate legal existence, (b) limited liability of stockholders, and (c) transferable ownership rights. Explain these characteristics to Mark.

2. **(a)** Your friend Katie Fehr cannot understand how the characteristic of corporation management is both an advantage and a disadvantage. Clarify this problem for Katie.
   (b) Identify and explain two other disadvantages of a corporation.

3. **(a)** The following terms pertain to the forming of a corporation: (1) charter, (2) by-laws, and (3) organization costs. Explain the terms.

(b) Donna Fleming believes a corporation must be incorporated in the state in which its headquarters' office is located. Is Donna correct? Explain.

4. What are the basic ownership rights of common stockholders in the absence of restrictive provisions?

5. **(a)** What are the two principal components of stockholders' equity?
   (b) What is paid-in capital? Give three examples.

6. How do the financial statements for a corporation differ from the statements for a proprietorship?

7. The corporate charter of Luney Corporation allows the issuance of a maximum of 100,000 shares of common stock. During its first two years of operations,

Luney sold 70,000 shares to shareholders and reac-quired 7,000 of these shares. After these transactions, how many shares are authorized, issued, and out-standing?

8. Which is the better investment—common stock with a par value of $5 per share, or common stock with a par value of $20 per share? Why?

9. What factors help determine the market price of stock?

10. What effect does the issuance of stock at a price above par value have on the issuer's net income? Explain.

11. Why is common stock usually not issued at a price that is less than par value?

12. Land appraised at $80,000 is purchased by issuing 1,000 shares of $20 par value common stock. The market price of the shares at the time of the exchange, based on active trading in the securities market, is $95 per share. Should the land be recorded at $20,000, $80,000, or $95,000? Explain.

13. For what reasons might a company like IBM repur-chase some of its stock (treasury stock)?

14. Meng, Inc. purchases 1,000 shares of its own previ-ously issued $5 par common stock for $12,000. Assuming the shares are held in the treasury, what effect does this transaction have on (a) net income, (b) total assets, (c) total paid-in capital, and (d) total stockholders' equity?

15. The treasury stock purchased in Question 14 is resold by Meng, Inc. for $16,000. What effect does this transaction have on (a) net income, (b) total assets, (c) total paid-in capital, and (d) total stockholders' equity?

16. (a) What are the principal differences between com-mon stock and preferred stock?
    (b) Preferred stock may be cumulative. Discuss this feature.
    (c) How are dividends in arrears presented in the financial statements?

17. Diaz Inc.'s common stock has a par value of $1 and a current market price of $15. Explain why these amounts are different.

18. Indicate how each of the following accounts should be classified in the stockholders' equity section.
    (a) Common stock.
    (b) Paid-in capital in excess of par—common stock.
    (c) Retained earnings.
    (d) Treasury stock.
    (e) Paid-in capital from treasury stock.
    (f) Paid-in capital in excess of stated value—common stock.
    (g) Preferred stock.

19. How many shares of common stock did Apple have at September 24, 2011, and at September 25, 2010?

BRIEF EXERCISES

BE13-1 Angie Baden is studying for her accounting midterm examination. Identify for Angie the advantages and disadvantages of the corporate form of business organization.

List the advantages and disadvantages of a corporation.
(LO 1)

BE13-2 At December 31, Ortiz Corporation reports net income of $480,000. Prepare the entry to close net income.

Prepare closing entries.
(LO 2)

BE13-3 On May 10, Jack Corporation issues 2,000 shares of $10 par value common stock for cash at $18 per share. Journalize the issuance of the stock.

Prepare entries for issuance of par value common stock.
(LO 3)

BE13-4 On June 1, Noonan Inc. issues 4,000 shares of no-par common stock at a cash price of $6 per share. Journalize the issuance of the shares assuming the stock has a stated value of $1 per share.

Prepare entries for issuance of no-par value common stock.
(LO 3)

BE13-5 Lei Inc.'s $10 par value common stock is actively traded at a market price of $15 per share. Lei issues 5,000 shares to purchase land advertised for sale at $85,000. Journalize the issuance of the stock in acquiring the land.

Prepare entries for issuance of stock in a noncash transaction.
(LO 3)

BE13-6 On July 1, Raney Corporation purchases 500 shares of its $5 par value common stock for the treasury at a cash price of $9 per share. On September 1, it sells 300 shares of the treasury stock for cash at $11 per share. Journalize the two treasury stock transactions.

Prepare entries for treasury stock transactions.
(LO 4)

BE13-7 Garb Inc. issues 5,000 shares of $100 par value preferred stock for cash at $130 per share. Journalize the issuance of the preferred stock.

Prepare entries for issuance of preferred stock.
(LO 5)

BE13-8 Pine Corporation has the following accounts at December 31: Common Stock, $10 par, 5,000 shares issued, $50,000; Paid-in Capital in Excess of Par—Common Stock $30,000; Retained Earnings $45,000; and Treasury Stock, 500 shares, $11,000. Prepare the stockholders' equity section of the balance sheet.

Prepare stockholders' equity section.
(LO 6)

> DO IT! Review

Analyze statements about corporate organization.
(LO 1)

DO IT! 13-1 Indicate whether each of the following statements is true or false.

_____ **1.** The corporation is an entity separate and distinct from its owners.

_____ **2.** The liability of stockholders is normally limited to their investment in the corporation.

_____ **3.** The relative lack of government regulation is an advantage of the corporate form of business.

_____ **4.** There is no journal entry to record the authorization of capital stock.

_____ **5.** No-par value stock is quite rare today.

Close net income and prepare stockholders' equity section.
(LO 2)

DO IT! 13-2 At the end of its first year of operation, Goss Corporation has $1,000,000 of common stock and net income of $236,000. Prepare (a) the closing entry for net income and (b) the stockholders' equity section at year-end.

Journalize issuance of stock.
(LO 3)

DO IT! 13-3 Beauty Island Corporation began operations on April 1 by issuing 60,000 shares of $5 par value common stock for cash at $13 per share. On April 19, it issued 2,000 shares of common stock to attorneys in settlement of their bill of $27,500 for organization costs. Journalize both issuances, assuming the stock is not publicly traded.

Journalize treasury stock transactions.
(LO 4)

DO IT! 13-4 Fouts Corporation purchased 2,000 shares of its $10 par value common stock for $130,000 on August 1. It will hold these shares in the treasury until resold. On December 1, the corporation sold 1,200 shares of treasury stock for cash at $72 per share. Journalize the treasury stock transactions.

Prepare stockholders' equity section.
(LO 6)

DO IT! 13-5 Anders Corporation has issued 100,000 shares of $5 par value common stock. It authorized 500,000 shares. The paid-in capital in excess of par on the common stock is $240,000. The corporation has reacquired 7,000 shares at a cost of $46,000 and is currently holding those shares. Treasury stock was reissued in prior years for $47,000 more than its cost.

The corporation also has 2,000 shares issued and outstanding of 7%, $100 par value preferred stock. It authorized 10,000 shares. The paid-in capital in excess of par on the preferred stock is $23,000. Retained earnings is $372,000.

Prepare the stockholders' equity section of the balance sheet.

EXERCISES

Identify characteristics of a corporation.
(LO 1)

E13-1 Andrea has prepared the following list of statements about corporations.

1. A corporation is an entity separate and distinct from its owners.
2. As a legal entity, a corporation has most of the rights and privileges of a person.
3. Most of the largest U.S. corporations are privately held corporations.
4. Corporations may buy, own, and sell property; borrow money; enter into legally binding contracts; and sue and be sued.
5. The net income of a corporation is not taxed as a separate entity.
6. Creditors have a legal claim on the personal assets of the owners of a corporation if the corporation does not pay its debts.
7. The transfer of stock from one owner to another requires the approval of either the corporation or other stockholders.
8. The board of directors of a corporation legally owns the corporation.
9. The chief accounting officer of a corporation is the controller.
10. Corporations are subject to fewer state and federal regulations than partnerships or proprietorships.

Instructions
Identify each statement as true or false. If false, indicate how to correct the statement.

Identify characteristics of a corporation.
(LO 1, 2)

E13-2 Andrea (see E13-1) has studied the information you gave her in that exercise and has come to you with more statements about corporations.

1. Corporation management is both an advantage and a disadvantage of a corporation compared to a proprietorship or a partnership.
2. Limited liability of stockholders, government regulations, and additional taxes are the major disadvantages of a corporation.
3. When a corporation is formed, organization costs are recorded as an asset.
4. Each share of common stock gives the stockholder the ownership rights to vote at stockholder meetings, share in corporate earnings, keep the same percentage ownership when new shares of stock are issued, and share in assets upon liquidation.
5. The number of issued shares is always greater than or equal to the number of authorized shares.
6. A journal entry is required for the authorization of capital stock.
7. Publicly held corporations usually issue stock directly to investors.
8. The trading of capital stock on a securities exchange involves the transfer of already issued shares from an existing stockholder to another investor.
9. The market price of common stock is usually the same as its par value.
10. Retained earnings is the total amount of cash and other assets paid in to the corporation by stockholders in exchange for capital stock.

Instructions
Identify each statement as true or false. If false, indicate how to correct the statement.

E13-3 During its first year of operations, Foyle Corporation had the following transactions pertaining to its common stock.

Journalize issuance of common stock.

(LO 3)

Jan. 10   Issued 70,000 shares for cash at $5 per share.
July 1   Issued 40,000 shares for cash at $7 per share.

Instructions
(a) Journalize the transactions, assuming that the common stock has a par value of $5 per share.
(b) Journalize the transactions, assuming that the common stock is no-par with a stated value of $1 per share.

E13-4 Osage Corporation issued 2,000 shares of stock.

Journalize issuance of common stock.

(LO 3)

Instructions
Prepare the entry for the issuance under the following assumptions.

(a) The stock had a par value of $5 per share and was issued for a total of $52,000.
(b) The stock had a stated value of $5 per share and was issued for a total of $52,000.
(c) The stock had no par or stated value and was issued for a total of $52,000.
(d) The stock had a par value of $5 per share and was issued to attorneys for services during incorporation valued at $52,000.
(e) The stock had a par value of $5 per share and was issued for land worth $52,000.

E13-5 Quay Co. had the following transactions during the current period.

Journalize issuance of common and preferred stock and purchase of treasury stock.

(LO 3, 4, 5)

Mar.   2   Issued 5,000 shares of $5 par value common stock to attorneys in payment of a bill for $30,000 for services performed in helping the company to incorporate.
June 12   Issued 60,000 shares of $5 par value common stock for cash of $375,000.
July 11   Issued 1,000 shares of $100 par value preferred stock for cash at $110 per share.
Nov. 28   Purchased 2,000 shares of treasury stock for $80,000.

Instructions
Journalize the transactions.

E13-6 As an auditor for the CPA firm of Hinkson and Calvert, you encounter the following situations in auditing different clients.

Journalize noncash common stock transactions.

(LO 3)

1. LR Corporation is a closely held corporation whose stock is not publicly traded. On December 5, the corporation acquired land by issuing 5,000 shares of its $20 par value common stock. The owners' asking price for the land was $120,000, and the fair value of the land was $110,000.
2. Vera Corporation is a publicly held corporation whose common stock is traded on the securities markets. On June 1, it acquired land by issuing 20,000 shares of its $10 par value stock. At the time of the exchange, the land was advertised for sale at $250,000. The stock was selling at $11 per share.

Instructions
Prepare the journal entries for each of the situations above.

Journalize treasury stock transactions.

(LO 4)

E13-7 On January 1, 2014, the stockholders' equity section of Newlin Corporation shows common stock ($5 par value) $1,500,000; paid-in capital in excess of par $1,000,000; and retained earnings $1,200,000. During the year, the following treasury stock transactions occurred.

Mar. 1   Purchased 50,000 shares for cash at $15 per share.
July 1   Sold 10,000 treasury shares for cash at $17 per share.
Sept. 1   Sold 8,000 treasury shares for cash at $14 per share.

Instructions
(a) Journalize the treasury stock transactions.
(b) Restate the entry for September 1, assuming the treasury shares were sold at $12 per share.

Journalize treasury stock transactions.

(LO 4)

E13-8 Rinehart Corporation purchased from its stockholders 5,000 shares of its own previously issued stock for $255,000. It later resold 2,000 shares for $54 per share, then 2,000 more shares for $49 per share, and finally 1,000 shares for $43 per share.

Instructions
Prepare journal entries for the purchase of the treasury stock and the three sales of treasury stock.

Journalize preferred stock transactions and indicate statement presentation.

(LO 5, 6)

E13-9 Tran Corporation is authorized to issue both preferred and common stock. The par value of the preferred is $50. During the first year of operations, the company had the following events and transactions pertaining to its preferred stock.

Feb. 1   Issued 20,000 shares for cash at $53 per share.
July 1   Issued 12,000 shares for cash at $57 per share.

Instructions
(a) Journalize the transactions.
(b) Post to the stockholders' equity accounts.
(c) Indicate the financial statement presentation of the related accounts.

Differentiate between preferred and common stock.

(LO 5)

E13-10 Hodge Corporation issued 100,000 shares of $20 par value, cumulative, 6% preferred stock on January 1, 2013, for $2,300,000. In December 2015, Hodge declared its first dividend of $500,000.

Instructions
(a) Prepare Hodge's journal entry to record the issuance of the preferred stock.
(b) If the preferred stock is **not** cumulative, how much of the $500,000 would be paid to **common** stockholders?
(c) If the preferred stock is cumulative, how much of the $500,000 would be paid to **common** stockholders?

Prepare correct entries for capital stock transactions.

(LO 3, 4, 5)

E13-11 Gilliam Corporation recently hired a new accountant with extensive experience in accounting for partnerships. Because of the pressure of the new job, the accountant was unable to review his textbooks on the topic of corporation accounting. During the first month, the accountant made the following entries for the corporation's capital stock.

May 2	Cash		130,000	
	Capital Stock			130,000
	(Issued 10,000 shares of $10 par value common stock at $13 per share)			
10	Cash		600,000	
	Capital Stock			600,000
	(Issued 10,000 shares of $50 par value preferred stock at $60 per share)			
15	Capital Stock		15,000	
	Cash			15,000
	(Purchased 1,000 shares of common stock for the treasury at $15 per share)			

31	Cash	8,000	
	Capital Stock		5,000
	Gain on Sale of Stock		3,000
	(Sold 500 shares of treasury stock at $16 per share)		

Instructions
On the basis of the explanation for each entry, prepare the entry that should have been made for the capital stock transactions.

E13-12 The following stockholders' equity accounts, arranged alphabetically, are in the ledger of Eudaley Corporation at December 31, 2014.

Prepare a stockholders' equity section.
(LO 6)

Common Stock ($5 stated value)	$1,500,000
Paid-in Capital in Excess of Par—Preferred Stock	280,000
Paid-in Capital in Excess of Stated Value—Common Stock	900,000
Preferred Stock (8%, $100 par, noncumulative)	500,000
Retained Earnings	1,234,000
Treasury Stock (10,000 common shares)	120,000

Instructions
Prepare the stockholders' equity section of the balance sheet at December 31, 2014.

E13-13 The stockholders' equity section of Haley Corporation at December 31 is as follows.

Answer questions about stockholders' equity section.
(LO 3, 4, 5, 6)

HALEY CORPORATION
Balance Sheet (partial)

Paid-in capital	
Preferred stock, cumulative, 10,000 shares authorized, 6,000 shares issued and outstanding	$ 300,000
Common stock, no par, 750,000 shares authorized, 600,000 shares issued	1,200,000
Total paid-in capital	1,500,000
Retained earnings	1,858,000
Total paid-in capital and retained earnings	3,358,000
Less: Treasury stock (10,000 common shares)	64,000
Total stockholders' equity	$3,294,000

Instructions
From a review of the stockholders' equity section, as chief accountant, write a memo to the president of the company answering the following questions.

(a) How many shares of common stock are outstanding?
(b) Assuming there is a stated value, what is the stated value of the common stock?
(c) What is the par value of the preferred stock?
(d) If the annual dividend on preferred stock is $30,000, what is the dividend rate on preferred stock?
(e) If dividends of $60,000 were in arrears on preferred stock, what would be the balance in Retained Earnings?

E13-14 The stockholders' equity section of Aluminum Company of America (Alcoa) showed the following (in alphabetical order): additional paid-in capital $6,101, common stock $925, preferred stock $55, retained earnings $7,428, and treasury stock 2,828. All dollar data are in millions.
    The preferred stock has 557,740 shares authorized, with a par value of $100 and an annual $3.75 per share cumulative dividend preference. At December 31 of the current year, 557,649 shares of preferred are issued and 546,024 shares are outstanding. There are 1.8 billion shares of $1 par value common stock authorized, of which 924.6 million are issued and 844.8 million are outstanding at December 31.

Prepare a stockholders' equity section.
(LO 6)

Instructions
Prepare the stockholders' equity section of the current year, including disclosure of all relevant data.

Classify stockholders' equity accounts.

(LO 6)

E13-15 The ledger of Rolling Hills Corporation contains the following accounts: Common Stock, Preferred Stock, Treasury Stock, Paid-in Capital in Excess of Par—Preferred Stock, Paid-in Capital in Excess of Stated Value—Common Stock, Paid-in Capital from Treasury Stock, and Retained Earnings.

Instructions

Classify each account using the following table headings.

	Paid-in Capital			
Account	Capital Stock	Additional	Retained Earnings	Other

EXERCISES: SET B AND CHALLENGE EXERCISES

Visit the book's companion website, at **www.wiley.com/college/weygandt**, and choose the Student Companion site to access Exercise Set B and Challenge Exercises.

PROBLEMS: SET A

Journalize stock transactions, post, and prepare paid-in capital section.

(LO 3, 5, 6)

P13-1A DeLong Corporation was organized on January 1, 2014. It is authorized to issue 10,000 shares of 8%, $100 par value preferred stock, and 500,000 shares of no-par common stock with a stated value of $2 per share. The following stock transactions were completed during the first year.

Jan. 10	Issued 80,000 shares of common stock for cash at $4 per share.
Mar. 1	Issued 5,000 shares of preferred stock for cash at $105 per share.
Apr. 1	Issued 24,000 shares of common stock for land. The asking price of the land was $90,000. The fair value of the land was $85,000.
May 1	Issued 80,000 shares of common stock for cash at $4.50 per share.
Aug. 1	Issued 10,000 shares of common stock to attorneys in payment of their bill of $30,000 for services performed in helping the company organize.
Sept. 1	Issued 10,000 shares of common stock for cash at $5 per share.
Nov. 1	Issued 1,000 shares of preferred stock for cash at $109 per share.

Instructions

(a) Journalize the transactions.

(c) Total paid-in capital $1,479,000

(b) Post to the stockholders' equity accounts. (Use J5 as the posting reference.)

(c) Prepare the paid-in capital section of stockholders' equity at December 31, 2014.

Journalize and post treasury stock transactions, and prepare stockholders' equity section.

(LO 4, 6)

P13-2A Fechter Corporation had the following stockholders' equity accounts on January 1, 2014: Common Stock ($5 par) $500,000, Paid-in Capital in Excess of Par—Common Stock $200,000, and Retained Earnings $100,000. In 2014, the company had the following treasury stock transactions.

Mar. 1	Purchased 5,000 shares at $8 per share.
June 1	Sold 1,000 shares at $12 per share.
Sept. 1	Sold 2,000 shares at $10 per share.
Dec. 1	Sold 1,000 shares at $7 per share.

Fechter Corporation uses the cost method of accounting for treasury stock. In 2014, the company reported net income of $30,000.

Instructions

(a) Journalize the treasury stock transactions, and prepare the closing entry at December 31, 2014, for net income.

(b) Treasury Stock $8,000

(c) Total stockholders' equity $829,000

(b) Open accounts for (1) Paid-in Capital from Treasury Stock, (2) Treasury Stock, and (3) Retained Earnings. Post to these accounts using J10 as the posting reference.

(c) Prepare the stockholders' equity section for Fechter Corporation at December 31, 2014.

P13-3A The stockholders' equity accounts of Castle Corporation on January 1, 2014, were as follows.

Journalize and post transactions, and prepare stockholders' equity section.

(LO 2, 3, 4, 6)

Preferred Stock (8%, $50 par, cumulative, 10,000 shares authorized)	$ 400,000
Common Stock ($1 stated value, 2,000,000 shares authorized)	1,000,000
Paid-in Capital in Excess of Par—Preferred Stock	100,000
Paid-in Capital in Excess of Stated Value—Common Stock	1,450,000
Retained Earnings	1,816,000
Treasury Stock (10,000 common shares)	50,000

During 2014, the corporation had the following transactions and events pertaining to its stockholders' equity.

Feb.	1	Issued 25,000 shares of common stock for $120,000.
Apr.	14	Sold 6,000 shares of treasury stock—common for $33,000.
Sept.	3	Issued 5,000 shares of common stock for a patent valued at $35,000.
Nov.	10	Purchased 1,000 shares of common stock for the treasury at a cost of $6,000.
Dec.	31	Determined that net income for the year was $452,000.

No dividends were declared during the year.

Instructions
(a) Journalize the transactions and the closing entry for net income.
(b) Enter the beginning balances in the accounts, and post the journal entries to the stockholders' equity accounts. (Use J5 for the posting reference.)
(c) Prepare a stockholders' equity section at December 31, 2014, including the disclosure of the preferred dividends in arrears.

(c) Total stockholders' equity
$5,350,000

P13-4A Peck Corporation is authorized to issue 20,000 shares of $50 par value, 10% preferred stock and 125,000 shares of $5 par value common stock. On January 1, 2014, the ledger contained the following stockholders' equity balances.

Journalize and post stock transactions, and prepare stockholders' equity section.

(LO 2, 3, 5, 6)

Preferred Stock (10,000 shares)	$500,000
Paid-in Capital in Excess of Par—Preferred Stock	75,000
Common Stock (70,000 shares)	350,000
Paid-in Capital in Excess of Par—Common Stock	700,000
Retained Earnings	300,000

During 2014, the following transactions occurred.

Feb.	1	Issued 2,000 shares of preferred stock for land having a fair value of $120,000.
Mar.	1	Issued 1,000 shares of preferred stock for cash at $65 per share.
July	1	Issued 16,000 shares of common stock for cash at $7 per share.
Sept.	1	Issued 400 shares of preferred stock for a patent. The asking price of the patent was $30,000. Market price for the preferred stock was $70 and the fair value for the patent was indeterminable.
Dec.	1	Issued 8,000 shares of common stock for cash at $7.50 per share.
Dec.	31	Net income for the year was $260,000. No dividends were declared.

Instructions
(a) Journalize the transactions and the closing entry for net income.
(b) Enter the beginning balances in the accounts, and post the journal entries to the stockholders' equity accounts. (Use J2 for the posting reference.)
(c) Prepare a stockholders' equity section at December 31, 2014.

(c) Total stockholders' equity
$2,570,000

P13-5A The following stockholders' equity accounts arranged alphabetically are in the ledger of Galindo Corporation at December 31, 2014.

Prepare stockholders' equity section.

(LO 6)

Common Stock ($5 stated value)	$2,000,000
Paid-in Capital from Treasury Stock	10,000
Paid-in Capital in Excess of Par—Preferred Stock	679,000
Paid-in Capital in Excess of Stated Value—Common Stock	1,600,000
Preferred Stock (8%, $50 par, noncumulative)	800,000
Retained Earnings	1,748,000
Treasury Stock (10,000 common shares)	130,000

Total stockholders' equity
$6,707,000

Prepare entries for stock transactions and prepare stockholders' equity section.

(LO 3, 4, 5, 6)

Instructions

Prepare a stockholders' equity section at December 31, 2014.

P13-6A Irwin Corporation has been authorized to issue 20,000 shares of $100 par value, 10%, noncumulative preferred stock and 1,000,000 shares of no-par common stock. The corporation assigned a $2.50 stated value to the common stock. At December 31, 2014, the ledger contained the following balances pertaining to stockholders' equity.

Preferred Stock	$ 120,000
Paid-in Capital in Excess of Par—Preferred Stock	20,000
Common Stock	1,000,000
Paid-in Capital in Excess of Stated Value—Common Stock	1,800,000
Treasury Stock (1,000 common shares)	11,000
Paid-in Capital from Treasury Stock	1,500
Retained Earnings	82,000

The preferred stock was issued for land having a fair value of $140,000. All common stock issued was for cash. In November, 1,500 shares of common stock were purchased for the treasury at a per share cost of $11. In December, 500 shares of treasury stock were sold for $14 per share. No dividends were declared in 2014.

Instructions

(a) Prepare the journal entries for the:
   (1) Issuance of preferred stock for land.
   (2) Issuance of common stock for cash.
   (3) Purchase of common treasury stock for cash.
   (4) Sale of treasury stock for cash.

(b) Total stockholders' equity
$3,012,500

(b) Prepare the stockholders' equity section at December 31, 2014.

PROBLEMS: SET B

Journalize stock transactions, post, and prepare paid-in capital section.

(LO 3, 5, 6)

P13-1B Mendoza Corporation was organized on January 1, 2014. It is authorized to issue 20,000 shares of 6%, $40 par value preferred stock, and 500,000 shares of no-par common stock with a stated value of $2 per share. The following stock transactions were completed during the first year.

Jan. 10	Issued 100,000 shares of common stock for cash at $3 per share.
Mar. 1	Issued 10,000 shares of preferred stock for cash at $55 per share.
Apr. 1	Issued 25,000 shares of common stock for land. The asking price of the land was $90,000. The company's estimate of fair value of the land was $75,000.
May 1	Issued 75,000 shares of common stock for cash at $4 per share.
Aug. 1	Issued 10,000 shares of common stock to attorneys in payment of their bill for $50,000 for services performed in helping the company organize.
Sept. 1	Issued 5,000 shares of common stock for cash at $6 per share.
Nov. 1	Issued 2,000 shares of preferred stock for cash at $60 per share.

Instructions

(a) Journalize the transactions.

(c) Total paid-in capital
$1,425,000

(b) Post to the stockholders' equity accounts. (Use J1 as the posting reference.)

(c) Prepare the paid-in capital section of stockholders' equity at December 31, 2014.

Journalize and post treasury stock transactions, and prepare stockholders' equity section.

(LO 4, 6)

P13-2B Hawthorne Corporation had the following stockholders' equity accounts on January 1, 2014: Common Stock ($1 par) $400,000, Paid-in Capital in Excess of Par—Common Stock $500,000, and Retained Earnings $100,000. In 2014, the company had the following treasury stock transactions.

Mar. 1	Purchased 5,000 shares at $7 per share.
June 1	Sold 1,000 shares at $10 per share.
Sept. 1	Sold 2,000 shares at $9 per share.
Dec. 1	Sold 1,000 shares at $5 per share.

Hawthorne Corporation uses the cost method of accounting for treasury stock. In 2014, the company reported net income of $80,000.

Instructions
(a) Journalize the treasury stock transactions, and prepare the closing entry at December 31, 2014, for net income.
(b) Open accounts for (1) Paid-in Capital from Treasury Stock, (2) Treasury Stock, and (3) Retained Earnings. Post to these accounts using J12 as the posting reference.
(c) Prepare the stockholders' equity section for Hawthorne Corporation at December 31, 2014.

(b) Treasury Stock $7,000

(c) Total stockholders' equity
    $1,078,000

P13-3B The stockholders' equity accounts of Lore Corporation on January 1, 2014, were as follows.

Journalize and post transactions, and prepare stockholders' equity section.

(LO 2, 3, 4, 6)

Preferred Stock (10%, $100 par, noncumulative, 5,000 shares authorized)	$ 300,000
Common Stock ($5 stated value, 300,000 shares authorized)	1,000,000
Paid-in Capital in Excess of Par—Preferred Stock	20,000
Paid-in Capital in Excess of Stated Value—Common Stock	425,000
Retained Earnings	488,000
Treasury Stock (5,000 common shares)	40,000

During 2014, the corporation had the following transactions and events pertaining to its stockholders' equity.

Feb. 1	Issued 3,000 shares of common stock for $25,500.
Mar. 20	Purchased 1,500 additional shares of common treasury stock at $8 per share.
June 14	Sold 4,000 shares of treasury stock—common for $36,000.
Sept. 3	Issued 2,000 shares of common stock for a patent valued at $19,000.
Dec. 31	Determined that net income for the year was $350,000.

Instructions
(a) Journalize the transactions and the closing entry for net income.
(b) Enter the beginning balances in the accounts and post the journal entries to the stockholders' equity accounts. (Use J1 as the posting reference.)
(c) Prepare a stockholders' equity section at December 31, 2014.

(c) Total stockholders' equity
    $2,611,500

P13-4B Gerstner Corporation is authorized to issue 10,000 shares of $40 par value, 10% preferred stock and 200,000 shares of $5 par value common stock. On January 1, 2014, the ledger contained the following stockholders' equity balances.

Journalize and post stock transactions, and prepare stockholders' equity section.

(LO 2, 3, 5, 6)

Preferred Stock (5,000 shares)	$200,000
Paid-in Capital in Excess of Par—Preferred Stock	60,000
Common Stock (70,000 shares)	350,000
Paid-in Capital in Excess of Par—Common Stock	700,000
Retained Earnings	300,000

During 2014, the following transactions occurred.

Feb. 1	Issued 1,000 shares of preferred stock for land having a fair value of $65,000.
Mar. 1	Issued 2,000 shares of preferred stock for cash at $60 per share.
July 1	Issued 20,000 shares of common stock for cash at $5.80 per share.
Sept. 1	Issued 800 shares of preferred stock for a patent. The asking price of the patent was $60,000. Market price for the preferred stock was $65 and the fair value for the patent was indeterminable.
Dec. 1	Issued 10,000 shares of common stock for cash at $6 per share.
Dec. 31	Net income for the year was $210,000. No dividends were declared.

Instructions
(a) Journalize the transactions and the closing entry for net income.
(b) Enter the beginning balances in the accounts, and post the journal entries to the stockholders' equity accounts. (Use J2 as the posting reference.)
(c) Prepare a stockholders' equity section at December 31, 2014.

(c) Total stockholders' equity
    $2,233,000

P13-5B The following stockholders' equity accounts arranged alphabetically are in the ledger of Alpers Corporation at December 31, 2014.

Prepare stockholders' equity section.

(LO 6)

Common Stock ($10 stated value)	$1,200,000
Paid-in Capital from Treasury Stock	6,000
Paid-in Capital in Excess of Par—Preferred Stock	288,400
Paid-in Capital in Excess of Stated Value—Common Stock	690,000
Preferred Stock (8%, $100 par, noncumulative)	300,000
Retained Earnings	826,000
Treasury Stock (8,000 common shares)	88,000

Total stockholders' equity
$3,222,400

Prepare entries for stock transactions and prepare stockholders' equity section.

(LO 3, 4, 5, 6)

Instructions

Prepare a stockholders' equity section at December 31, 2014.

P13-6B Kingsley Corporation has been authorized to issue 40,000 shares of $100 par value, 8%, noncumulative preferred stock and 2,000,000 shares of no-par common stock. The corporation assigned a $5 stated value to the common stock. At December 31, 2014, the ledger contained the following balances pertaining to stockholders' equity.

Preferred Stock	$ 240,000
Paid-in Capital in Excess of Par—Preferred Stock	56,000
Common Stock	2,000,000
Paid-in Capital in Excess of Stated Value—Common Stock	4,400,000
Treasury Stock (1,000 common shares)	22,000
Paid-in Capital from Treasury Stock	3,000
Retained Earnings	560,000

The preferred stock was issued for land having a fair value of $296,000. All common stock issued was for cash. In November, 1,500 shares of common stock were purchased for the treasury at a per share cost of $22. In December, 500 shares of treasury stock were sold for $28 per share. No dividends were declared in 2014.

Instructions

(a) Prepare the journal entries for the:
   (1) Issuance of preferred stock for land.
   (2) Issuance of common stock for cash.
   (3) Purchase of common treasury stock for cash.
   (4) Sale of treasury stock for cash.

(b) Total stockholders' equity
$7,237,000

(b) Prepare the stockholders' equity section at December 31, 2014.

PROBLEMS: SET C

Visit the book's companion website, at **www.wiley.com/college/weygandt**, and choose the Student Companion site to access Problem Set C.

CONTINUING COOKIE CHRONICLE

(*Note:* This is a continuation of the Cookie Chronicle from Chapters 1 through 12.)

CCC13 Natalie's friend, Curtis Lesperance, decides to meet with Natalie after hearing that her discussions about a possible business partnership with her friend Katy Peterson have failed. Because Natalie has been so successful with Cookie Creations and Curtis has been just as successful with his coffee shop, they both conclude that they could benefit from each other's business expertise. Curtis and Natalie next evaluate the different types of business organization. Because of the advantage of limited personal liability, they decide to form a corporation. Natalie and Curtis are very excited about this new business venture. They come to you with information about their businesses and with a number of questions.

Go to the book's companion website, **www.wiley.com/college/weygandt***, to see the completion of this problem.*

Broadening Your Perspective

Financial Reporting and Analysis

Financial Reporting Problem: Apple Inc.

BYP13-1 The stockholders' equity section for Apple Inc. is shown in Appendix A. Instructions for accessing and using the company's complete annual report, including the notes to the financial statements, are also provided in Appendix A.

Instructions
(a) What is the par or stated value per share of Apple's common stock?
(b) What percentage of Apple's authorized common stock was issued at September 24, 2011?

Comparative Analysis Problem:
PepsiCo vs. Coca-Cola

BYP13-2 PepsiCo, Inc.'s financial statements are presented in Appendix B. Financial statements of The Coca-Cola Company are presented in Appendix C. Instructions for accessing and using the complete annual reports of PepsiCo and Coca-Cola, including the notes to the financial statements, are also provided in Appendices B and C, respectively.

Instructions
(a) What is the par or stated value of Coca-Cola's and PepsiCo's common stock?
(b) What percentage of authorized shares was issued by Coca-Cola at December 31, 2011, and by PepsiCo at December 31, 2011?
(c) How many shares are held as treasury stock by Coca-Cola at December 31, 2011, and by PepsiCo at December 31, 2011?
(d) How many Coca-Cola common shares are outstanding at December 31, 2011? How many PepsiCo shares of common stock are outstanding at December 31, 2011?

Comparative Analysis Problem:
Amazon.com, Inc. vs. Wal-Mart Stores, Inc.

BYP13-3 Amazon.com, Inc.'s financial statements are presented in Appendix D. Financial statements of Wal-Mart Stores, Inc. are presented in Appendix E. Instructions for accessing and using the complete annual reports of Amazon and Wal-Mart, including the notes to the financial statements, are also provided in Appendices D and E, respectively.

Instructions
(a) What is the par or stated value of Amazon's and Wal-Mart's common stock?
(b) What percentage of authorized shares was issued by Amazon at December 31, 2011, and by Wal-Mart at January 31, 2012?
(c) How many shares are held as treasury stock by Amazon at December 31, 2011, and by Wal-Mart at January 31, 2012?
(d) How many Amazon common shares are outstanding at December 31, 2011? How many Wal-Mart shares of common stock are outstanding at January 31, 2012?

Real-World Focus

BYP13-4 SEC filings of publicly traded companies are available to view online.

Address: **http://biz.yahoo.com/i**, or go to **www.wiley.com/college/weygandt**

Steps
1. Pick a company and type in the company's name.
2. Choose **Quote**.

Instructions
Answer the following questions.

(a) What company did you select?
(b) What is its stock symbol?
(c) What was the stock's trading range today?
(d) What was the stock's trading range for the year?

Critical Thinking

Decision-Making Across the Organization

BYP13-5 The stockholders' meeting for Percival Corporation has been in progress for some time. The chief financial officer for Percival is presently reviewing the company's financial statements and is explaining the items that comprise the stockholders' equity section of the balance sheet for

the current year. The stockholders' equity section of Percival Corporation at December 31, 2014, is as follows.

PERCIVAL CORPORATION
Balance Sheet (partial)
December 31, 2014

Paid-in capital		
Capital stock		
Preferred stock, authorized 1,000,000 shares cumulative, $100 par value, $8 per share, 6,000 shares issued and outstanding		$ 600,000
Common stock, authorized 5,000,000 shares, $1 par value, 3,000,000 shares issued, and 2,700,000 outstanding		3,000,000
Total capital stock		3,600,000
Additional paid-in capital		
In excess of par—preferred stock	$ 50,000	
In excess of par—common stock	25,000,000	
Total additional paid-in capital		25,050,000
Total paid-in capital		28,650,000
Retained earnings		900,000
Total paid-in capital and retained earnings		29,550,000
Less: Treasury stock (300,000 common shares)		9,300,000
Total stockholders' equity		$20,250,000

At the meeting, stockholders have raised a number of questions regarding the stockholders' equity section.

Instructions
With the class divided into groups, answer the following questions as if you were the chief financial officer for Percival Corporation.

(a) "What does the cumulative provision related to the preferred stock mean?"
(b) "I thought the common stock was presently selling at $29.75, but the company has the stock stated at $1 per share. How can that be?"
(c) "Why is the company buying back its common stock? Furthermore, the treasury stock has a debit balance because it is subtracted from stockholders' equity. Why is treasury stock not reported as an asset if it has a debit balance?"

Communication Activity

BYP13-6 Joe Moyer, your uncle, is an inventor who has decided to incorporate. Uncle Joe knows that you are an accounting major at U.N.O. In a recent letter to you, he ends with the question, "I'm filling out a state incorporation application. Can you tell me the difference in the following terms: (1) authorized stock, (2) issued stock, (3) outstanding stock, (4) preferred stock?"

Instructions
In a brief note, differentiate for Uncle Joe among the four different stock terms. Write the letter to be friendly, yet professional.

Ethics Case

BYP13-7 The R&D division of Piqua Chemical Corp. has just developed a chemical for sterilizing the vicious Brazilian "killer bees" which are invading Mexico and the southern states of the United States. The president of the company is anxious to get the chemical on the market to boost the company's profits. He believes his job is in jeopardy because of decreasing sales and profits. The company has an opportunity to sell this chemical in Central American countries, where the laws are much more relaxed than in the United States.

The director of Piqua's R&D division strongly recommends further testing in the laboratory for side-effects of this chemical on other insects, birds, animals, plants, and even humans. He cautions the president, "We could be sued from all sides if the chemical has tragic side-effects that we didn't even test for in the labs." The president answers, "We can't wait an additional year for your lab tests. We can avoid losses from such lawsuits by establishing a separate wholly owned corporation to shield Piqua Corp. from such lawsuits. We can't lose any more than our investment in the new corporation, and we'll invest in just the patent covering this chemical. We'll reap the benefits if the chemical works and is safe, and avoid the losses from lawsuits if it's a disaster." The following week, Piqua creates a new wholly owned corporation called Finlay Inc., sells the chemical patent to it for $10, and watches the spraying begin.

Instructions
(a) Who are the stakeholders in this situation?
(b) Are the president's motives and actions ethical?
(c) Can Piqua shield itself against losses of Finlay Inc.?

All About You

BYP13-8 A high percentage of Americans own stock in corporations. As a shareholder in a corporation, you will receive an annual report. One of the goals of this course is for you to learn how to navigate your way around an annual report.

Instructions
Use the annual report provided in Appendix A to answer the following questions.

(a) What CPA firm performed the audit of Apple's financial statements?
(b) What was the amount of Apple's earnings per share in 2011?
(c) What were net sales in 2011?
(d) How much cash did Apple spend on capital expenditures in 2011?
(e) Over what life does the company depreciate its buildings?
(f) What were the proceeds from issuance of common stock in 2011?

FASB Codification Activity

BYP13-9 If your school has a subscription to the FASB Codification, go to **http://aaahq.org/ascLogin.cfm** to log in and prepare responses to the following.

(a) How is common stock defined?
(b) How is preferred stock defined?
(c) What is the meaning of the term shares?

Answers to Chapter Questions

Answers to Insight and Accounting Across the Organization Questions

p. 611 A Thousand Millonaires!   Q: Why did Mark Zuckerberg, the CEO and founder of Facebook, delay taking his company's shares public through an initial public offering (IPO)? **A:** Facebook did not need to invest in factories, distribution systems, or even marketing, so it did not need to raise a lot of cash. Also, by delaying the decision to go public, Zuckerberg had more control over the direction of the company. In addition, publicly traded companies face many more financial reporting disclosure requirements.

p. 614 How to Read Stock Quotes   Q: For stocks traded on organized stock exchanges, how are the dollar prices per share established? **A:** The dollar prices per share are established by the interaction between buyers and sellers of the shares.   **Q:** What factors might influence the price of shares in the marketplace? **A:** The price of shares is influenced by a company's earnings and dividends as well as by factors beyond a company's control, such as changes in interest rates, labor strikes, scarcity of supplies or resources, and politics. The number of willing buyers and sellers (demand and supply) also plays a part in the price of shares.

p. 617 The Impact of Corporate Social Responsibility   Q: Why are CSR-related shareholder proposals increasing? **A:** The increase in shareholder proposals reflects a growing belief that a company's social and environmental policies correlate strongly with its risk-management strategy and ultimately its financial performance.

p. 622 Why Did Reebok Buy Its Own Stock?   Q: What signal might a large stock repurchase send to investors regarding management's belief about the company's growth opportunities? **A:** When a company has many growth opportunities, it will normally conserve its cash in order to be better able to fund expansion. A large use of cash to buy back stock (and essentially shrink the company) would suggest that management was not optimistic about its growth opportunities.

Answers to Self-Test Questions

1. c **2.** b **3.** b **4.** d **5.** a **6.** b **7.** c (1,000 × $9) **8.** c **9.** d **10.** a **11.** a **12.** d **13.** d **14.** b **15.** c

A Look at IFRS

<table>
<tr><td>**LEARNING OBJECTIVE**   **7**

Compare the accounting procedures for stockholders' equity under GAAP and IFRS.</td><td>The accounting for transactions related to stockholders' equity, such as issuance of shares and purchase of treasury stock, are similar under both IFRS and GAAP. Major differences relate to terminology used, introduction of items such as revaluation surplus, and presentation of stockholders' equity information.</td></tr>
</table>

Key Points

- Under IFRS, the term **reserves** is used to describe all equity accounts other than those arising from contributed (paid-in) capital. This would include, for example, reserves related to retained earnings, asset revaluations, and fair value differences.

- Many countries have a different mix of investor groups than in the United States. For example, in Germany, financial institutions like banks are not only major creditors of corporations but often are the largest corporate stockholders as well. In the United States, Asia, and the United Kingdom, many companies rely on substantial investment from private investors.

- There are often terminology differences for equity accounts. The following summarizes some of the common differences in terminology.

GAAP	IFRS
Common stock	Share capital—ordinary
Stockholders	Shareholders
Par value	Nominal or face value
Authorized stock	Authorized share capital
Preferred stock	Share capital—preference
Paid-in capital	Issued/allocated share capital
Paid-in capital in excess of par—common stock	Share premium—ordinary
Paid-in capital in excess of par—preferred stock	Share premium—preference
Retained earnings	Retained earnings or Retained profits
Retained earnings deficit	Accumulated losses
Accumulated other comprehensive income	General reserve and other reserve accounts

As an example of how similar transactions use different terminology under IFRS, consider the accounting for the issuance of 1,000 shares of $1 par value common stock for $5 per share. Under IFRS, the entry is as follows.

Cash	5,000	
Share Capital—Ordinary		1,000
Share Premium—Ordinary		4,000

- The accounting for treasury stock differs somewhat between IFRS and GAAP. (However, many of the differences are beyond the scope of this course.) Like GAAP, IFRS does not allow a company to record gains or losses on purchases of its own shares. One difference worth noting is that, when a company purchases its own shares, IFRS treats it as a reduction of stockholders' equity, but it does not specify which particular stockholders' equity accounts are to be affected. Therefore, it could be shown as an increase to a contra equity account (Treasury Stock) or a decrease to retained earnings or share capital.

- A major difference between IFRS and GAAP relates to the account Revaluation Surplus. Revaluation surplus arises under IFRS because companies are permitted to revalue their property, plant, and equipment to fair value under certain circumstances. This account is part of general reserves under IFRS and is not considered contributed capital.

- IFRS often uses terms such as **retained profits** or **accumulated profit or loss** to describe retained earnings. The term **retained earnings** is also often used.

- Equity is given various descriptions under IFRS, such as shareholders' equity, owners' equity, capital and reserves, and shareholders' funds.

Looking to the Future

As indicated in earlier discussions, the IASB and the FASB are currently working on a project related to financial statement presentation. An important part of this study is to determine whether certain line items, subtotals, and totals should be clearly defined and required to be displayed in the financial statements.

IFRS Practice

IFRS Self-Test Questions

1. Under IFRS, a purchase by a company of its own shares is recorded by:
   (a) an increase in Treasury Stock.
   (b) a decrease in contributed capital.
   (c) a decrease in share capital.
   (d) All of these are acceptable treatments.

2. Which of the following is **true**?
   (a) In the United States, the primary corporate stockholders are financial institutions.
   (b) Share capital means total assets under IFRS.
   (c) The IASB and FASB are presently studying how financial statement information should be presented.
   (d) The accounting for treasury stock differs extensively between GAAP and IFRS.

3. Under IFRS, the amount of capital received in excess of par value would be credited to:
   (a) Retained Earnings.
   (b) Contributed Capital.
   (c) Share Premium.
   (d) Par value is not used under IFRS.

4. Which of the following is **false**?
   (a) Under GAAP, companies cannot record gains on transactions involving their own shares.
   (b) Under IFRS, companies cannot record gains on transactions involving their own shares.
   (c) Under IFRS, the statement of stockholders' equity is a required statement.
   (d) Under IFRS, a company records a revaluation surplus when it experiences an increase in the price of its common stock.

5. Which of the following does **not** represent a pair of GAAP/IFRS-comparable terms?
   (a) Additional paid-in capital/Share premium.
   (b) Treasury stock/Repurchase reserve.
   (c) Common stock/Share capital.
   (d) Preferred stock/Preference shares.

IFRS Exercises

IFRS13-1 On May 10, Jaurez Corporation issues 1,000 shares of $10 par value ordinary shares for cash at $18 per share. Journalize the issuance of the shares.

IFRS13-2 Meenen Corporation has the following accounts at December 31 (in euros): Share Capital—Ordinary, €10 par, 5,000 shares issued, €50,000; Share Premium—Ordinary €10,000; Retained Earnings €45,000; and Treasury Shares—Ordinary, 500 shares, €11,000. Prepare the equity section of the statement of financial position.

IFRS13-3 Overton Co. had the following transactions during the current period.

Mar. 2   Issued 5,000 shares of $1 par value ordinary shares to attorneys in payment of a bill for $30,000 for services provided in helping the company to incorporate.
June 12   Issued 60,000 shares of $1 par value ordinary shares for cash of $375,000.
July 11   Issued 1,000 shares of $100 par value preference shares for cash at $110 per share.
Nov. 28   Purchased 2,000 treasury shares for $80,000.

Instructions
Journalize the above transactions.

International Financial Reporting Problem: Zetar plc

IFRS13-4 The financial statements of Zetar plc are presented in Appendix F. Instructions for accessing and using the company's complete annual report, including the notes to its financial statements, are also provided in Appendix F.

Instructions
Use the company's annual report to answer the following questions.

(a) Using the information in the statement of changes in equity, prepare the journal entry to record the issuance of ordinary shares during the year ended April 30, 2010.
(b) Examine the equity section of the company's balance sheet. For each item in the equity section, provide the comparable label that would be used under GAAP.

Answers to IFRS Self-Test Questions
1. d   2. c   3. c   4. d   5. b

✔ **The Navigator**

14 | Corporations: Dividends, Retained Earnings, and Income Reporting

 Feature Story

Owning a Piece of the Action

Van Meter Industrial, Inc., an electrical-parts distributor in Cedar Rapids, Iowa, is 100% employee-owned. For many years, the company has issued bonuses in the form of shares of company stock to all of its employees. These bonus distributions typically have a value equal to several weeks of pay. Top management always thought that this was a great program. Therefore, it came as quite a surprise a few years ago when an employee stood up at a company-wide meeting and said that he did not see any real value in receiving the company's shares. Instead, he wanted "a few hundred extra bucks for beer and cigarettes."

As it turned out, many of the company's 340 employees felt this way. Rather than end the stock bonus program, however, the company decided to educate its employees on the value of share ownership. The employees are now taught how to determine the worth of their shares, the rights that come

with share ownership, and what they can do to help incr the value of those shares.

As part of the education program, management develope a slogan, "Work ten, get five free." The idea is that after working 10 years, an employee's shares would be worth equivalent of about five years' worth of salary. For examp a person earning a $30,000 salary would earn $300,000 wages over a 10-year period. During that same 10-year period, it was likely that the value of the employee's shar would accumulate to about $150,000 (five years' worth salary). This demonstrates in more concrete terms why employees should be excited about share ownership.

A 12-member employee committee has the responsibility educating new employees about the program. The commi also runs training programs so that employees understand their cost-saving actions improve the company's results—a stock price. It appears that the company's education progr

✔ **The Navigator**

- ■ Scan Learning Objectives
- ■ Read Feature Story
- ■ Read Preview
- ■ Read text and answer **DO IT!** p. 653
  - ■ p. 657 ■ p. 661 ■ p. 664
- ■ Work Comprehensive **DO IT!** p. 665
- ■ Review Summary of Learning Objectives
- ■ Answer Self-Test Questions
- ■ Complete Assignments
- ■ Go to *WileyPLUS* for practice and tutorials
- 🌐 **Read A Look at IFRS** p. 682

Learning Objectives

After studying this chapter, you should be able to:

[1] Prepare the entries for cash dividends and stock dividends.

[2] Identify the items reported in a retained earnings statement.

[3] Prepare and analyze a comprehensive stockholders' equity section.

[4] Describe the form and content of corporation income statements.

[5] Compute earnings per share.

encourage employees to act like owners is working. Profitability has increased rapidly, and employee turnover has fallen from 18% to 8%. Given Van Meter's success, many of the 10,000 other employee-owned companies in the United States might want to investigate whether their employees understand the benefits of share ownership.

Source: Adapted from Simona Covel, "How to Get Workers to Think and Act Like Owners," *Wall Street Journal Online* (February 15, 2008).

Preview of Chapter 14

 The Navigator

As indicated in the Feature Story, a profitable corporation like Van Meter Industrial, Inc. can provide real benefits to employees through its stock bonus plan. And as employees learn more about the role of dividends, retained earnings, and earnings per share, they develop an understanding and appreciation for what the company is providing to them.

The content and organization of Chapter 14 are as follows.

CORPORATIONS: DIVIDENDS, RETAINED EARNINGS, AND INCOME REPORTING

Dividends	Retained Earnings	Statement Presentation and Analysis
• Cash dividends • Stock dividends • Stock splits	• Retained earnings restrictions • Prior period adjustments • Retained earnings statement	• Presentation • Analysis • Income statement presentation • Income statement analysis

Dividends

LEARNING OBJECTIVE 1

Prepare the entries for cash dividends and stock dividends.

A dividend is a corporation's distribution of cash or stock to its stockholders on a pro rata (proportional to ownership) basis. Pro rata means that if you own 10% of the common shares, you will receive 10% of the dividend. Dividends can take four forms: cash, property, scrip (a promissory note to pay cash), or stock. Cash dividends predominate in practice. Also, companies declare stock dividends with some frequency. These two forms of dividends are the focus of discussion in this chapter.

Investors are very interested in a company's dividend practices. In the financial press, **dividends are generally reported quarterly as a dollar amount per share**. (Sometimes they are reported on an annual basis.) For example, Nike's **quarterly** dividend rate in the fourth quarter of 2011 was 36 cents per share. The dividend rate for the fourth quarter of 2011 for GE was 15 cents, and for ConAgra Foods it was 24 cents.

Cash Dividends

A **cash dividend** is a pro rata distribution of cash to stockholders. Cash dividends are not paid on treasury shares. For a corporation to pay a cash dividend, it must have the following.

1. **Retained earnings.** The legality of a cash dividend depends on the laws of the state in which the company is incorporated. Payment of cash dividends from retained earnings is legal in all states. In general, cash dividend distributions from only the balance in common stock (legal capital) are illegal.

   A dividend declared out of paid-in capital is termed a **liquidating dividend**. Such a dividend reduces or "liquidates" the amount originally paid in by stockholders. Statutes vary considerably with respect to cash dividends based on paid-in capital in excess of par or stated value. Many states permit such dividends.

2. **Adequate cash.** The legality of a dividend and the ability to pay a dividend are two different things. For example, Nike, with retained earnings of over $5.8 billion, could legally declare a dividend of at least $5.8 billion. But Nike's cash balance is only $1.9 billion.

   Before declaring a cash dividend, a company's board of directors must carefully consider both current and future demands on the company's cash resources. In some cases, current liabilities may make a cash dividend inappropriate. In other cases, a major plant expansion program may warrant only a relatively small dividend.

3. **Declared dividends.** A company does not pay dividends unless its board of directors decides to do so, at which point the board "declares" the dividend. The board of directors has full authority to determine the amount of income to distribute in the form of a dividend and the amount to retain in the business. Dividends do not accrue like interest on a note payable, and they are not a liability until declared.

The amount and timing of a dividend are important issues for management to consider. The payment of a large cash dividend could lead to liquidity problems for the company. On the other hand, a small dividend or a missed dividend may cause unhappiness among stockholders. Many stockholders expect to receive a reasonable cash payment from the company on a periodic basis. Many companies declare and pay cash dividends quarterly. On the other hand, a number of high-growth companies pay no dividends, preferring to conserve cash to finance future capital expenditures.

ENTRIES FOR CASH DIVIDENDS

Three dates are important in connection with dividends: (1) the declaration date, (2) the record date, and (3) the payment date. Normally, there are two to four weeks between each date. Companies make accounting entries on the declaration date and the payment date.

On the **declaration date**, the board of directors formally declares (authorizes) the cash dividend and announces it to stockholders. The declaration of a cash dividend **commits the corporation to a legal obligation**. The company must make an entry to recognize the increase in Cash Dividends and the increase in the liability Dividends Payable.

To illustrate, assume that on December 1, 2014, the directors of Media General declare a 50 cents per share cash dividend on 100,000 shares of $10 par value common stock. The dividend is $50,000 (100,000 × $0.50). The entry to record the declaration is:

Declaration Date

Dec. 1	Cash Dividends	50,000	
	Dividends Payable		50,000
	(To record declaration of cash dividend)		

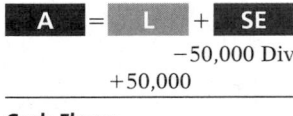

−50,000 Div
+50,000

Cash Flows
no effect

Media General debits the account Cash Dividends. Cash dividends decrease retained earnings. We use the specific title Cash Dividends to differentiate it from other types of dividends, such as stock dividends. Dividends Payable is a current liability. It will normally be paid within the next several months. When using a Cash Dividends account, the company transfers the balance of that account to Retained Earnings at the end of the year by a closing entry. *For homework problems, you should use the Cash Dividends account for recording dividend declarations.*

At the **record date**, the company determines ownership of the outstanding shares for dividend purposes. The stockholders' records maintained by the corporation supply this information. In the interval between the declaration date and the record date, the corporation updates its stock ownership records. For Media General, the record date is December 22. No entry is required on this date because the corporation's liability recognized on the declaration date is unchanged.

Helpful Hint The purpose of the record date is to identify the persons or entities that will receive the dividend, not to determine the amount of the dividend liability.

Record Date

Dec. 22	No entry		

On the **payment date**, the company makes cash dividend payments to the stockholders of record (as of December 22) and records the payment of the dividend. If January 20 is the payment date for Media General, the entry on that date is:

Payment Date

Jan. 20	Dividends Payable	50,000	
	Cash		50,000
	(To record payment of cash dividend)		

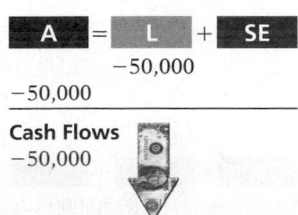

−50,000
−50,000

Cash Flows
−50,000

Note that payment of the dividend reduces both current assets and current liabilities. It has no effect on stockholders' equity. The cumulative effect of the declaration and payment of a cash dividend is to **decrease both stockholders' equity and total assets**. Illustration 14-1 (page 652) summarizes the three important dates associated with dividends for Media General.

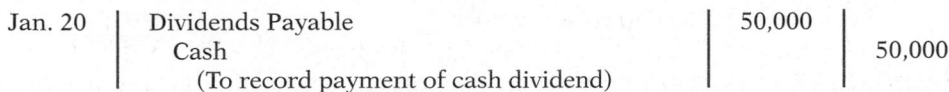

Illustration 14-1
Key dividend dates

ALLOCATING CASH DIVIDENDS BETWEEN PREFERRED AND COMMON STOCK

As explained in Chapter 13, preferred stock has priority over common stock in regard to dividends. Holders of cumulative preferred stock must be paid any unpaid prior-year dividends and their current year's dividend before common stockholders receive dividends.

To illustrate, assume that at December 31, 2014, IBR Inc. has 1,000 shares of 8%, $100 par value cumulative preferred stock. It also has 50,000 shares of $10 par value common stock outstanding. The dividend per share for preferred stock is $8 ($100 par value × 8%). The required annual dividend for preferred stock is therefore $8,000 (1,000 shares × $8). At December 31, 2014, the directors declare a $6,000 cash dividend. In this case, the entire dividend amount goes to preferred stockholders because of their dividend preference. The entry to record the declaration of the dividend is:

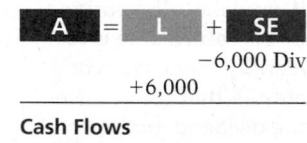
−6,000 Div
+6,000

Cash Flows
no effect

Dec. 31	Cash Dividends	6,000	
	Dividends Payable		6,000
	(To record $6 per share cash dividend to preferred stockholders)		

Because of the cumulative feature, dividends of $2 ($8 − $6) per share are in arrears on preferred stock for 2014. IBR must pay these dividends to preferred stockholders before it can pay any future dividends to common stockholders. IBR should disclose dividends in arrears in the financial statements.

At December 31, 2015, IBR declares a $50,000 cash dividend. The allocation of the dividend to the two classes of stock is as follows.

Illustration 14-2
Allocating dividends to preferred and common stock

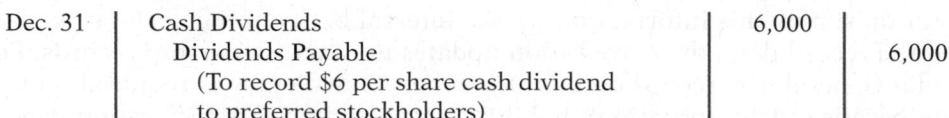

Total dividend		$50,000
Allocated to preferred stock		
Dividends in arrears, 2014 (1,000 × $2)	**$2,000**	
2015 dividend (1,000 × $8)	**8,000**	**10,000**
Remainder allocated to common stock		$40,000

The entry to record the declaration of the dividend is:

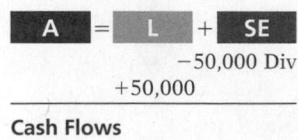
−50,000 Div
+50,000

Cash Flows
no effect

Dec. 31	Cash Dividends	50,000	
	Dividends Payable		50,000
	(To record declaration of cash dividends of $10,000 to preferred stock and $40,000 to common stock)		

If IBR's preferred stock is not cumulative, preferred stockholders receive only $8,000 in dividends in 2015. Common stockholders receive $42,000.

ACCOUNTING ACROSS THE ORGANIZATION

Up, Down, and ??

The decision whether to pay a dividend, and how much to pay, is a very important management decision. As the chart below shows, from 2002 to 2007, many companies substantially increased their dividends. Total dividends paid by U.S. companies hit record levels. One reason for the increase is that Congress lowered, from 39% to 15%, the tax rate paid by investors on dividends received, making dividends more attractive to investors.

Then the financial crisis of 2008 occurred. As result, in 2009, 804 companies cut their dividends (see chart) at the highest rate since the S&P started collecting data in 1995. In 2010, more companies started increasing their dividends. However, potential higher taxes on dividends in the future and the possibility of a low-growth economy may stall any significant increase.

Source: Matt Phillips and Jay Miller, "Last Year's Dividend Slash Was $58 Billion," *Wall Street Journal* (January 8, 2010), p. C5.

 What factors must management consider in deciding how large a dividend to pay?
(See page 681.)

> DO IT!

Dividends on Preferred and Common Stock

MasterMind Corporation has 2,000 shares of 6%, $100 par value preferred stock outstanding at December 31, 2014. At December 31, 2014, the company declared a $60,000 cash dividend. Determine the dividend paid to preferred stockholders and common stockholders under each of the following scenarios.

1. The preferred stock is noncumulative, and the company has not missed any dividends in previous years.
2. The preferred stock is noncumulative, and the company did not pay a dividend in each of the two previous years.
3. The preferred stock is cumulative, and the company did not pay a dividend in each of the two previous years.

Solution

1. The company has not missed past dividends and the preferred stock is noncumulative. Thus, the preferred stockholders are paid only this year's dividend. The dividend paid to preferred stockholders would be $12,000 (2,000 × .06 × $100). The dividend paid to common stockholders would be $48,000 ($60,000 − $12,000).

2. The preferred stock is noncumulative. Thus, past unpaid dividends do not have to be paid. The dividend paid to preferred stockholders would be $12,000 (2,000 × .06 × $100). The dividend paid to common stockholders would be $48,000 ($60,000 − $12,000).

3. The preferred stock is cumulative. Thus, dividends that have been missed (dividends in arrears) must be paid. The dividend paid to preferred stockholders would be $36,000 (3 × 2,000 × .06 × $100). The dividend paid to common stockholders would be $24,000 ($60,000 − $36,000).

Related exercise material: **E14-2 and 14-1.**

✔ **The Navigator**

Stock Dividends

A **stock dividend** is a pro rata (proportional to ownership) distribution of the corporation's own stock to stockholders. Whereas a company pays cash in a cash dividend, a company issues shares of stock in a stock dividend. **A stock dividend results in a decrease in retained earnings and an increase in paid-in capital.** Unlike a cash dividend, a stock dividend does not decrease total stockholders' equity or total assets.

To illustrate, assume that you have a 2% ownership interest in Cetus Inc. That is, you own 20 of its 1,000 shares of common stock. If Cetus declares a 10% stock dividend, it would issue 100 shares (1,000 × 10%) of stock. You would receive two shares (2% × 100). Would your ownership interest change? No, it would remain at 2% (22 ÷ 1,100). **You now own more shares of stock, but your ownership interest has not changed.**

Cetus has disbursed no cash and has assumed no liabilities. What, then, are the purposes and benefits of a stock dividend? Corporations issue stock dividends generally for one or more of the following reasons.

1. To satisfy stockholders' dividend expectations without spending cash.

2. To increase the marketability of the corporation's stock. When the number of shares outstanding increases, the market price per share decreases. Decreasing the market price of the stock makes it easier for smaller investors to purchase the shares.

3. To emphasize that a company has permanently reinvested in the business a portion of stockholders' equity, which therefore is unavailable for cash dividends.

When the dividend is declared, the board of directors determines the size of the stock dividend and the value assigned to each dividend.

Generally, if the company issues a **small stock dividend** (less than 20–25% of the corporation's issued stock), the value assigned to the dividend is the fair value per share. This treatment is based on the assumption that a small stock dividend will have little effect on the market price of the shares previously outstanding. Thus, many stockholders consider small stock dividends to be distributions of earnings equal to the market price of the shares distributed. If a company issues a **large stock dividend** (greater than 20–25%), the price assigned to the dividend is the par or stated value. Small stock dividends predominate in practice. Thus, we will illustrate only entries for small stock dividends.

ENTRIES FOR STOCK DIVIDENDS

To illustrate the accounting for small stock dividends, assume that Medland Corporation has a balance of $300,000 in retained earnings. It declares a 10% stock dividend on its 50,000 shares of $10 par value common stock. The current market price of its stock is $15 per share. The number of shares to be issued is 5,000 (10% × 50,000). Therefore, the total amount to be debited to Stock Dividends is $75,000 (5,000 × $15). The entry to record the declaration of the stock dividend is as follows.

Stock Dividends	75,000	
Common Stock Dividends Distributable		50,000
Paid-in Capital in Excess of Par—Common Stock		25,000
(To record declaration of 10% stock dividend)		

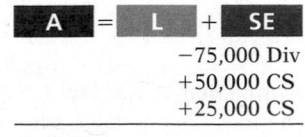

A = L + SE
−75,000 Div
+50,000 CS
+25,000 CS

Cash Flows
no effect

Medland debits Stock Dividends for the market price of the stock issued ($15 × 5,000). (Similar to Cash Dividends, Stock Dividends decrease retained earnings.) Medland also credits Common Stock Dividends Distributable for the par value of the dividend shares ($10 × 5,000) and credits Paid-in Capital in Excess of Par—Common Stock for the excess of the market price over par ($5 × 5,000).

Common Stock Dividends Distributable is a **stockholders' equity account**. It is not a liability because assets will not be used to pay the dividend. If the company prepares a balance sheet before it issues the dividend shares, it reports the distributable account under paid-in capital as shown in Illustration 14-3.

Paid-in capital	
Common stock	$500,000
Common stock dividends distributable	**50,000**
Paid-in capital in excess of par—common stock	25,000
Total paid-in capital	$575,000

Illustration 14-3
Statement presentation of common stock dividends distributable

When Medland issues the dividend shares, it debits Common Stock Dividends Distributable and credits Common Stock, as follows.

Common Stock Dividends Distributable	50,000	
Common Stock		50,000
(To record issuance of 5,000 shares in a stock dividend)		

A = L + SE
−50,000 CS
+50,000 CS

Cash Flows
no effect

EFFECTS OF STOCK DIVIDENDS

How do stock dividends affect stockholders' equity? They **change the composition of stockholders' equity** because they transfer to paid-in capital a portion of retained earnings. However, **total stockholders' equity remains the same**. Stock dividends also have no effect on the par or stated value per share. But the number of shares outstanding increases. Illustration 14-4 shows these effects for Medland Corporation.

	Before Dividend	After Dividend
Stockholders' equity		
Paid-in capital		
Common stock, $10 par	$ 500,000	$ 550,000
Paid-in capital in excess of par—common stock	—	25,000
Total paid-in capital	500,000	575,000
Retained earnings	300,000	225,000
Total stockholders' equity	**$800,000**	**$800,000**
Outstanding shares	**50,000**	**55,000**
Par value per share	**$10.00**	**$10.00**

Illustration 14-4
Stock dividend effects

In this example, total paid-in capital increases by $75,000 (50,000 shares × 10% × $15) and retained earnings decreases by the same amount. Note also that total stockholders' equity remains unchanged at $800,000. The number of shares increases by 5,000 (50,000 × 10%).

Stock Splits

A **stock split**, like a stock dividend, involves issuance of additional shares to stockholders according to their percentage ownership. **However, a stock split results in a reduction in the par or stated value per share.** The purpose of a stock split is to increase the marketability of the stock by lowering its market price per share. This, in turn, makes it easier for the corporation to issue additional stock.

The effect of a split on market price is generally **inversely proportional** to the size of the split. For example, after a 2-for-1 stock split, the market price of Nike's stock fell from $111 to approximately $55. The lower market price stimulated market activity. Within one year, the stock was trading above $100 again. Illustration 14-5 shows the effect of a 4-for-1 stock split for stockholders.

Illustration 14-5
Effect of stock split for stockholders

In a stock split, the number of shares increases in the same proportion that par or stated value per share decreases. For example, in a 2-for-1 split, one share of $10 par value stock is exchanged for two shares of $5 par value stock. **A stock split does not have any effect on total paid-in capital, retained earnings, or total stockholders' equity.** But, the number of shares outstanding increases, and par value per share decreases. Illustration 14-6 shows these effects for Medland Corporation, assuming that it splits its 50,000 shares of common stock on a 2-for-1 basis.

Illustration 14-6
Stock split effects

	Before Stock Split	After Stock Split
Stockholders' equity		
Paid-in capital		
Common stock	$ 500,000	$ 500,000
Paid-in capital in excess of par—common stock	–0–	–0–
Total paid-in capital	500,000	500,000
Retained earnings	300,000	300,000
Total stockholders' equity	**$800,000**	**$800,000**
Outstanding shares	**50,000**	**100,000**
Par value per share	**$10.00**	**$5.00**

A stock split does not affect the balances in any stockholders' equity accounts. Therefore, **it is not necessary to journalize a stock split**.

Illustration 14-7 summarizes the differences between stock splits and stock dividends.

Item	Stock Split	Stock Dividend
Total paid-in capital	No change	Increase
Total retained earnings	No change	Decrease
Total par value (common stock)	No change	Increase
Par value per share	Decrease	No change
Total stockholders' equity	No change	No change

Illustration 14-7
Differences between the effects of stock splits and stock dividends

INVESTOR INSIGHT

A No-Split Philosophy

Warren Buffett's company, Berkshire Hathaway, has two classes of shares. Until recently, the company had never split either class of stock. As a result, the class A stock had a market price of $97,000 and the class B sold for about $3,200 per share. Because the price per share is so high, the stock does not trade as frequently as the stock of other companies. Buffett has always opposed stock splits because he feels that a lower stock price attracts short-term investors. He appears to be correct. For example, while more than 6 million shares of IBM are exchanged on the average day, only about 1,000 class A shares of Berkshire are traded. Despite Buffett's aversion to splits, in order to accomplish a recent acquisition, Berkshire decided to split its class B shares 50 to 1.

Dietmar Klement/iStockphoto

Source: Scott Patterson, "Berkshire Nears Smaller Baby B's," *Wall Street Journal Online* (January 19, 2010).

? Why does Warren Buffett usually oppose stock splits? (See page 681.)

> DO IT!

Stock Dividends and Stock Splits

Action Plan

✔ Calculate the stock dividend's effect on retained earnings by multiplying the number of new shares times the market price of the stock (or par value for a large stock dividend).

✔ Recall that a stock dividend increases the number of shares without affecting total stockholders' equity.

✔ Recall that a stock split only increases the number of shares outstanding and decreases the par value per share.

Sing CD Company has had five years of record earnings. Due to this success, the market price of its 500,000 shares of $2 par value common stock has tripled from $15 per share to $45. During this period, paid-in capital remained the same at $2,000,000. Retained earnings increased from $1,500,000 to $10,000,000. President Joan Elbert is considering either a 10% stock dividend or a 2-for-1 stock split. She asks you to show the before-and-after effects of each option on retained earnings and total stockholders' equity.

Solution

The stock dividend amount is $2,250,000 [(500,000 × 10%) × $45]. The new balance in retained earnings is $7,750,000 ($10,000,000 − $2,250,000). The retained earnings balance after the stock split is the same as it was before the split: $10,000,000. Total stockholders' equity does not change. The effects on the stockholders' equity accounts are as follows.

	Original Balances	After Dividend	After Split
Paid-in capital	$ 2,000,000	$ 4,250,000	$ 2,000,000
Retained earnings	10,000,000	7,750,000	10,000,000
Total stockholders' equity	$12,000,000	$12,000,000	$12,000,000
Shares outstanding	500,000	550,000	1,000,000

Related exercise material: **BE14-3, E14-3, E14-4, E14-5, E14-6, E14-7, and DO IT! 14-2.**

✔ The Navigator

Retained Earnings

As you learned in Chapter 13, **retained earnings** is net income that a company retains in the business. The balance in retained earnings is part of the stockholders' claim on the total assets of the corporation. It does not, though, represent a claim on any specific asset. Nor can the amount of retained earnings be associated with the balance of any asset account. For example, a $100,000 balance in retained earnings does not mean that there should be $100,000 in cash. The reason is that the company may have used the cash resulting from the excess of revenues over expenses to purchase buildings, equipment, and other assets.

To demonstrate that retained earnings and cash may be quite different, Illustration 14-8 shows recent amounts of retained earnings and cash in selected companies.

Illustration 14-8
Retained earnings and cash balances

	(in millions)	
Company	Retained Earnings	Cash
Facebook	$ 1,606	$ 1,512
Google	20,082	10,198
Nike, Inc.	4,885	1,855
Starbucks Coffee Company	2,189	281
Amazon.com	(1,375)	2,539

Remember from Chapter 13 that when a company has net income, it closes net income to retained earnings. The closing entry is a debit to Income Summary and a credit to Retained Earnings.

Helpful Hint Remember that Retained Earnings is a stockholders' equity account, whose normal balance is a credit.

When a company has a **net loss** (expenses exceed revenues), it also closes this amount to retained earnings. The closing entry in this case is a debit to Retained Earnings and a credit to Income Summary. This is done even if it results in a debit balance in Retained Earnings. **Companies do not debit net losses to paid-in capital accounts.** To do so would destroy the distinction between paid-in and earned capital. If cumulative losses exceed cumulative income over a company's life, a debit balance in Retained Earnings results. A debit balance in Retained Earnings is identified as a **deficit**. A company reports a deficit as a deduction in the stockholders' equity section, as shown in Illustration 14-9.

Illustration 14-9
Stockholders' equity with deficit

Balance Sheet (partial)

Stockholders' equity	
Paid-in capital	
Common stock	$800,000
Retained earnings (deficit)	**(50,000)**
Total stockholders' equity	$750,000

Retained Earnings Restrictions

The balance in retained earnings is generally available for dividend declarations. Some companies state this fact. For example, Lockheed Martin Corporation states the following in the notes to its financial statements.

Illustration 14-10
Disclosure of unrestricted
retained earnings

LOCKHEED MARTIN CORPORATION
Notes to the Financial Statements

At December 31, retained earnings were unrestricted and available for dividend payments.

In some cases, there may be **retained earnings restrictions**. These make a portion of the retained earnings balance currently unavailable for dividends. Restrictions result from one or more of the following causes.

1. **Legal restrictions.** Many states require a corporation to restrict retained earnings for the cost of treasury stock purchased. The restriction keeps intact the corporation's legal capital that is being temporarily held as treasury stock. When the company sells the treasury stock, the restriction is lifted.
2. **Contractual restrictions.** Long-term debt contracts may restrict retained earnings as a condition for the loan. The restriction limits the use of corporate assets for payment of dividends. Thus, it increases the likelihood that the corporation will be able to meet required loan payments.
3. **Voluntary restrictions.** The board of directors may voluntarily create retained earnings restrictions for specific purposes. For example, the board may authorize a restriction for future plant expansion. By reducing the amount of retained earnings available for dividends, the company makes more cash available for the planned expansion.

Companies generally disclose **retained earnings restrictions** in the notes to the financial statements. For example, as shown in Illustration 14-11, Tektronix Inc., a manufacturer of electronic measurement devices, had total retained earnings of $774 million, but the unrestricted portion was only $223.8 million.

Illustration 14-11
Disclosure of restriction

TEKTRONIX INC.
Notes to the Financial Statements

Certain of the Company's debt agreements require compliance with debt covenants. Management believes that the Company is in compliance with such requirements. The Company had unrestricted retained earnings of $223.8 million after meeting those requirements.

Prior Period Adjustments

Suppose that a corporation has closed its books and issued financial statements. The corporation then discovers that it made a material error in reporting net income of a prior year. How should the company record this situation in the accounts and report it in the financial statements?

The correction of an error in previously issued financial statements is known as a **prior period adjustment**. The company makes the correction directly to Retained Earnings because the effect of the error is now in this account. The net income for the prior period has been recorded in retained earnings through the journalizing and posting of closing entries.

To illustrate, assume that General Microwave discovers in 2014 that it understated depreciation expense on equipment in 2013 by $300,000 due to computational errors. These errors overstated both net income for 2013 and the current balance in retained earnings. The entry for the prior period adjustment, ignoring all tax effects, is as follows.

Cash Flows
no effect

Retained Earnings	300,000	
Accumulated Depreciation—Equipment		300,000
(To adjust for understatement of depreciation in a		
prior period)		

A debit to an income statement account in 2014 is incorrect because the error pertains to a prior year.

Companies report prior period adjustments in the retained earnings statement.[1] They add (or deduct, as the case may be) these adjustments from the beginning retained earnings balance. This results in an adjusted beginning balance. For example, assuming a beginning balance of $800,000 in retained earnings, General Microwave reports the prior period adjustment as follows.

Illustration 14-12
Statement presentation of prior period adjustments

GENERAL MICROWAVE	
Retained Earnings Statement (partial)	
Balance, January 1, as reported	$ 800,000
Correction for overstatement of net income	
in prior period (depreciation error)	**(300,000)**
Balance, January 1, as adjusted	$ 500,000

Again, reporting the correction in the current year's income statement would be incorrect because it applies to a prior year's income statement.

Retained Earnings Statement

The **retained earnings statement** shows the changes in retained earnings during the year. The company prepares the statement from the Retained Earnings account. Illustration 14-13 shows (in T-account form) transactions that affect retained earnings.

Illustration 14-13
Debits and credits to retained earnings

Retained Earnings	
1. Net loss	1. Net income
2. Prior period adjustments for overstatement of net income	2. Prior period adjustments for understatement of net income
3. Cash dividends and stock dividends	
4. Some disposals of treasury stock	

As indicated, net income increases retained earnings, and a net loss decreases retained earnings. Prior period adjustments may either increase or decrease retained earnings. Both cash dividends and stock dividends decrease retained earnings. The circumstances under which treasury stock transactions decrease retained earnings are explained in Chapter 13, page 623.

A complete retained earnings statement for Graber Inc., based on assumed data, is as follows.

---

[1]A complete retained earnings statement is shown in Illustration 14-14 on the next page.

GRABER INC.
Retained Earnings Statement
For the Year Ended December 31, 2014

Illustration 14-14
Retained earnings
statement

Balance, January 1, as reported		$1,050,000
Correction for understatement of net income		
in prior period (inventory error)		50,000
Balance, January 1, as adjusted		1,100,000
Add: Net income		360,000
		1,460,000
Less: Cash dividends	$100,000	
Stock dividends	200,000	300,000
Balance, December 31		$1,160,000

> DO IT!

Retained Earnings Statement

Vega Corporation has retained earnings of $5,130,000 on January 1, 2014. During the year, Vega earned $2,000,000 of net income. It declared and paid a $250,000 cash dividend. In 2014, Vega recorded an adjustment of $180,000 due to the understatement (from a mathematical error) of 2013 depreciation expense. Prepare a retained earnings statement for 2014.

Solution

Action Plan

✔ Recall that a retained earnings statement begins with retained earnings, as reported at the end of the previous year.

✔ Add or subtract any prior period adjustments to arrive at the adjusted beginning figure.

✔ Add net income and subtract dividends declared to arrive at the ending balance in retained earnings.

VEGA CORPORATION
Retained Earnings Statement
For the Year Ended December 31, 2014

Balance, January 1, as reported	$5,130,000
Correction for overstatement of net income	
in prior period (depreciation error)	(180,000)
Balance, January 1, as adjusted	4,950,000
Add: Net income	2,000,000
	6,950,000
Less: Cash dividends	250,000
Balance, December 31	$6,700,000

Related exercise material: **BE14-4, BE14-5, E14-8, E14-9, and DO IT! 14-3.**

 ✔ The Navigator

Statement Presentation and Analysis

Presentation

Illustration 14-15 (page 662) presents the stockholders' equity section of Graber Inc.'s balance sheet. Note the following. (1) "Common stock dividends distributable" is shown under "Capital stock," in "Paid-in capital." (2) A note (Note R) discloses a retained earnings restriction.

LEARNING OBJECTIVE **3**

Prepare and analyze a comprehensive stockholders' equity section.

Illustration 14-15
Comprehensive stockholders'
equity section

GRABER INC. Balance Sheet (partial)		
Stockholders' equity		
Paid-in capital		
Capital stock		
9% Preferred stock, $100 par value, cumulative, callable at $120, 10,000 shares authorized, 6,000 shares issued and outstanding		$ 600,000
Common stock, no par, $5 stated value, 500,000 shares authorized, 400,000 shares issued and 390,000 shares outstanding	$2,000,000	
Common stock dividends distributable	**50,000**	2,050,000
Total capital stock		2,650,000
Additional paid-in capital		
In excess of par—preferred stock	30,000	
In excess of stated value—common stock	1,050,000	
Total additional paid-in capital		1,080,000
Total paid-in capital		3,730,000
Retained earnings **(see Note R)**		1,160,000
Total paid-in capital and retained earnings		4,890,000
Less: Treasury stock (10,000 common shares)		80,000
Total stockholders' equity		$4,810,000

Note R: Retained earnings is restricted for the cost of treasury stock, $80,000.

Instead of presenting a detailed stockholders' equity section in the balance sheet and a retained earnings statement, many companies prepare a **stockholders' equity statement**. This statement shows the changes (1) in each stockholders' equity account and (2) in total that occurred during the year. An example of a stockholders' equity statement appears in Apple's financial statements in Appendix A.

Analysis

Investors and analysts can measure profitability from the viewpoint of the common stockholder by the **return on common stockholders' equity**. This ratio, as shown in Illustration 14-16, indicates how many dollars of net income the company earned for each dollar invested by the common stockholders. It is computed by dividing **net income available to common stockholders** (which is net income minus preferred stock dividends) by average common stockholders' equity.

To illustrate, Walt Disney Company's beginning-of-the-year and end-of-the-year common stockholders' equity were $31,820 and $30,753 million, respectively. Its net income was $4,687 million, and no preferred stock was outstanding. The return on common stockholders' equity is computed as follows.

Illustration 14-16
Return on common
stockholders' equity
and computation

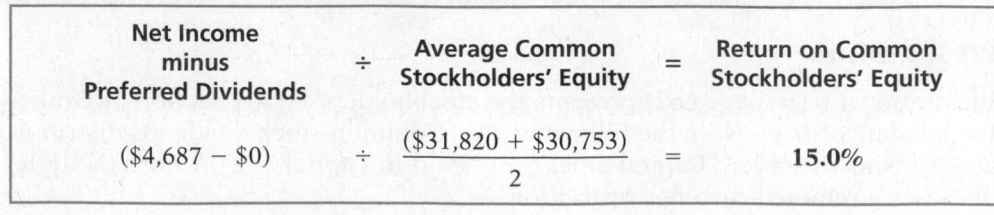

Net Income minus Preferred Dividends	÷	Average Common Stockholders' Equity	=	Return on Common Stockholders' Equity
($4,687 − $0)	÷	$\dfrac{(\$31,820 + \$30,753)}{2}$	=	15.0%

As shown on page 662, if a company has preferred stock, we would deduct the amount of **preferred dividends** from the company's net income to compute income available to common stockholders. Also, the par value of preferred stock is deducted from total stockholders' equity when computing the average common stockholders' equity.

Income Statement Presentation

Income statements for **corporations are the same as the statements for proprietorships or partnerships except for one thing: the reporting of income taxes**. For income tax purposes, corporations are a separate legal entity. As a result, corporations report **income tax expense** in a separate section of the corporation income statement, before net income. The condensed income statement for Leads Inc. in Illustration 14-17 shows a typical presentation. Note that the corporation reports income before income taxes as one line item and income tax expense as another.

LEARNING OBJECTIVE 4

Describe the form and content of corporation income statements.

LEADS INC.
Income Statement
For the Year Ended December 31, 2014

Sales revenue	$800,000
Cost of goods sold	600,000
Gross profit	200,000
Operating expenses	50,000
Income from operations	150,000
Other revenues and gains	10,000
Other expenses and losses	(4,000)
Income before income taxes	**156,000**
Income tax expense	**46,800**
Net income	$109,200

Illustration 14-17
Income statement with income taxes

Companies record income tax expense and the related liability for income taxes payable as part of the adjusting process. Using the data for Leads Inc., in Illustration 14-17, the adjusting entry for income tax expense at December 31, 2014, is:

Income Tax Expense	46,800	
Income Taxes Payable		46,800
(To record income taxes for 2014)		

A = L + SE
−46,800 Exp
+46,800

Cash Flows
no effect

The income statement of Apple (in Appendix A) presents another illustration of income taxes.

Income Statement Analysis

The financial press frequently reports earnings data. Stockholders and potential investors widely use these data in evaluating the profitability of a company. A convenient measure of earnings is **earnings per share (EPS)**, which indicates the net income earned by each share of outstanding **common stock**.

LEARNING OBJECTIVE 5

Compute earnings per share.

EPS AND PREFERRED DIVIDENDS

The existence of preferred dividends slightly complicates the calculation of EPS. When a corporation has both preferred and common stock, we must subtract the current year's preferred dividend from net income, to arrive at **income available to common stockholders**. Illustration 14-18 shows the formula for computing EPS.

Illustration 14-18
Formula for earnings per share

Net Income minus Preferred Dividends	÷	Weighted-Average Common Shares Outstanding	=	Earnings per Share

Ethics Note

In order to meet market expectations for EPS, some managers engage in elaborate treasury stock transactions. These transactions can be very costly for the remaining shareholders.

To illustrate, assume that Rally Inc. reports net income of $211,000 on its 102,500 weighted-average common shares.[2] During the year, it also declares a $6,000 dividend on its preferred stock. Therefore, the amount Rally has available for common stock dividends is $205,000 ($211,000 − $6,000). Earnings per share is $2 ($205,000 ÷ 102,500). If the preferred stock is cumulative, Rally deducts the dividend for the current year, whether or not it is declared. Remember that companies report **earnings per share only for common stock**.

Investors often attempt to link earnings per share to the market price per share of a company's stock.[3] Because of the importance of earnings per share, most companies must report it on the face of the income statement. Generally, companies simply report this amount below net income on the statement. For Rally Inc., the presentation is as follows.

Illustration 14-19
Basic earnings per share disclosure

RALLY INC.
Income Statement (partial)

Net income	$211,000
Earnings per share	**$2.00**

> DO IT!

Stockholders' Equity and EPS

On January 1, 2014, Siena Corporation purchased 2,000 shares of treasury stock. Other information regarding Siena Corporation is provided below.

	2013	2014
Net income	$110,000	$110,000
Dividends on preferred stock	$10,000	$10,000
Dividends on common stock	$2,000	$1,600
Weighted-average number of shares outstanding	10,000	8,000*
Common stockholders' equity, beginning of year	$500,000	$400,000*
Common stockholders' equity, end of year	$500,000	$400,000

*Adjusted for purchase of treasury stock.

Compute (a) return on common stockholders' equity for each year and (b) earnings per share for each year, and (c) discuss the changes in each.

---

[2]The calculation of the weighted average of common shares outstanding is discussed in advanced accounting courses.

[3]The ratio of the market price per share to the earnings per share is called the **price/earnings (P/E) ratio**. The financial media report this ratio for common stocks listed on major stock exchanges.

Solution

(a)

	2013	2014
Return on common stockholders' equity	$\dfrac{(\$110{,}000 - \$10{,}000)}{(\$500{,}000 + \$500{,}000)/2} = 20\%$	$\dfrac{(\$110{,}000 - \$10{,}000)}{(\$400{,}000 + \$400{,}000)/2} = 25\%$

(b)

	2013	2014
Earnings per share	$\dfrac{(\$110{,}000 - \$10{,}000)}{10{,}000} = \$10$	$\dfrac{(\$110{,}000 - \$10{,}000)}{8{,}000} = \$12.50$

(c) Between 2013 and 2014, return on common stockholders' equity improved from 20% to 25%. Earnings per share increased from $10 to $12.50. While this would appear to be good news for the company's common stockholders, these increases should be carefully evaluated. It is important to note that net income did not change during this period. The increase in both ratios was due to the purchase of treasury shares, which reduced the denominator of each ratio. As the company repurchases its own shares, it becomes more reliant on debt and thus increases its risk.

Related exercise material: **BE14-6, BE14-7, BE14-9, BE14-10, E14-12, E14-13, E14-14, E14-15, E14-16, E14-17, and DO IT! 14-4.**

 The Navigator

> Comprehensive DO IT!

On January 1, 2014, Hayslett Corporation had the following stockholders' equity accounts.

Common Stock ($10 par value, 260,000 shares issued and outstanding)	$2,600,000
Paid-in Capital in Excess of Par—Common Stock	1,500,000
Retained Earnings	3,200,000

During the year, the following transactions occurred.

April	1	Declared a $1.50 cash dividend per share to stockholders of record on April 15, payable May 1.
May	1	Paid the dividend declared in April.
June	1	Announced a 2-for-1 stock split. Prior to the split, the market price per share was $24.
Aug.	1	Declared a 10% stock dividend to stockholders of record on August 15, distributable August 31. On August 1, the market price of the stock was $10 per share.
	31	Issued the shares for the stock dividend.
Dec.	1	Declared a $1.50 per share dividend to stockholders of record on December 15, payable January 5, 2015.
	31	Determined that net income for the year was $600,000.

Instructions
(a) Journalize the transactions and the closing entry for net income.
(b) Prepare a stockholders' equity section at December 31.

Solution to Comprehensive DO IT!

(a) Apr.	1	Cash Dividends (260,000 × $1.50)	390,000	
		Dividends Payable		390,000
May	1	Dividends Payable	390,000	
		Cash		390,000

Action Plan (cont'd)

✔ Use market price of stock to determine the value of a small stock dividend.

✔ Close Income Summary to Retained Earnings.

June 1	Memo—two-for-one stock split increases number of shares to 520,000 (260,000 × 2) and reduces par value to $5 per share.		
Aug. 1	Stock Dividends (52,000* × $10)	520,000	
	Common Stock Dividends Distributable (52,000 × $5)		260,000
	Paid-in Capital in Excess of Par—Common Stock (52,000 × $5)		260,000
	*520,000 × .10		
31	Common Stock Dividends Distributable	260,000	
	Common Stock		260,000
Dec. 1	Cash Dividends (572,000** × $1.50)	858,000	
	Dividends Payable		858,000
	**(260,000 × 2) + 52,000		
31	Income Summary	600,000	
	Retained Earnings		600,000

(b)

HAYSLETT CORPORATION
Balance Sheet (Partial)

Stockholders' equity	
Paid-in capital	
Capital stock	
Common stock, $5 par value, 572,000 shares issued and outstanding	$2,860,000
Paid-in capital in excess of par—common stock	1,760,000
Total paid-in capital	4,620,000
Retained earnings	2,032,000*
Total stockholders' equity	$6,652,000

*$3,200,000 + $600,000 − $390,000 − $520,000 − $858,000

✔ **The Navigator**

SUMMARY OF LEARNING OBJECTIVES

✔ **The Navigator**

1 Prepare the entries for cash dividends and stock dividends. Companies make entries for both cash and stock dividends at the declaration date and at the payment date. At the **declaration date**, the entries are: cash dividend—debit Cash Dividends and credit Dividends Payable; small stock dividend—debit Stock Dividends, credit Paid-in Capital in Excess of Par (or Stated Value)—Common Stock, and credit Common Stock Dividends Distributable. At the **payment date**, the entries for cash and stock dividends are: cash dividend—debit Dividends Payable and credit Cash; small stock dividend—debit Common Stock Dividends Distributable and credit Common Stock.

2 Identify the items reported in a retained earnings statement. Companies report each of the individual debits and credits to retained earnings in the retained earnings statement. Additions consist of net income and prior period adjustments to correct understatements of prior years' net income. Deductions consist of net loss, adjustments to correct overstatements of prior years' net income, cash and stock dividends, and some disposals of treasury stock.

3 Prepare and analyze a comprehensive stockholders' equity section. A comprehensive stockholders' equity section includes all stockholders' equity accounts. It consists of two sections: paid-in capital and retained earnings. It should also include notes to the financial statements that explain any restrictions on retained earnings and any dividends in arrears. One measure of profitability is the return on common stockholders' equity. It is calculated by dividing net income minus preferred stock dividends by average common stockholders' equity.

4 Describe the form and content of corporation income statements. The form and content of corporation income statements are similar to the statements of proprietorships and partnerships with one exception: Corporations must report income taxes or income tax expense in a separate section before net income in the income statement.

5 Compute earnings per share. Companies compute earnings per share by dividing net income by the weighted-average number of common shares outstanding during the period. When preferred stock dividends exist, they must be deducted from net income in order to calculate EPS.

GLOSSARY

Cash dividend A pro rata distribution of cash to stockholders. (p. 650).

Declaration date The date the board of directors formally declares (authorizes) a dividend and announces it to stockholders. (p. 651).

Deficit A debit balance in retained earnings. (p. 658).

Dividend A corporation's distribution of cash or stock to its stockholders on a pro rata (proportional) basis. (p. 650).

Earnings per share The net income earned by each share of outstanding common stock. (p. 663).

Liquidating dividend A dividend declared out of paid-in capital. (p. 650).

Payment date The date dividend checks are mailed to stockholders. (p. 651).

Prior period adjustment The correction of an error in previously issued financial statements. (p. 659).

Record date The date when ownership of outstanding shares is determined for dividend purposes. (p. 651).

Retained earnings Net income that a company retains in the business. (p. 658).

Retained earnings restrictions Circumstances that make a portion of retained earnings currently unavailable for dividends. (p. 659).

Retained earnings statement A financial statement that shows the changes in retained earnings during the year. (p. 660).

Return on common stockholders' equity A measure of profitability that shows how many dollars of net income were earned for each dollar invested by the owners; computed as net income minus preferred dividends divided by average common stockholders' equity. (p. 662).

Stock dividend A pro rata distribution to stockholders of the corporation's own stock. (p. 654).

Stockholders' equity statement A statement that shows the changes in each stockholders' equity account and in total stockholders' equity during the year. (p. 662).

Stock split The issuance of additional shares of stock to stockholders according to their percentage ownership. It is accompanied by a reduction in the par or stated value per share. (p. 656).

Self-Test, Brief Exercises, Exercises, Problem Set A, and many more components are available for practice in *WileyPLUS*.

SELF-TEST QUESTIONS

Answers are on page 681.

(LO 1) **1.** Entries for cash dividends are required on the:
  (a) declaration date and the payment date.
  (b) record date and the payment date.
  (c) declaration date, record date, and payment date.
  (d) declaration date and the record date.

(LO 1) **2.** Which of the following statements about small stock dividends is **true**?

  (a) A debit to Retained Earnings for the par value of the shares issued should be made.
  (b) A small stock dividend decreases total stockholders' equity.
  (c) Market price per share should be assigned to the dividend shares.
  (d) A small stock dividend ordinarily will have an effect on par value per share of stock.

(LO 1) **3.** Which of the following statements about a 3-for-1 stock split is **true**?
(a) It will triple the market price of the stock.
(b) It will triple the amount of total stockholders' equity.
(c) It will have no effect on total stockholders' equity.
(d) It requires the company to distribute cash.

(LO 1) **4.** Encore Inc. declared an $80,000 cash dividend. It currently has 3,000 shares of 7%, $100 par value cumulative preferred stock outstanding. It is one year in arrears on its preferred stock. How much cash will Encore distribute to the common stockholders?
(a) $38,000.   (c) $59,000.
(b) $42,000.   (d) None.

(LO 1) **5.** Raptor Inc. has retained earnings of $500,000 and total stockholders' equity of $2,000,000. It has 100,000 shares of $8 par value common stock outstanding, which is currently selling for $30 per share. If Raptor declares a 10% stock dividend on its common stock:
(a) net income will decrease by $80,000.
(b) retained earnings will decrease by $80,000 and total stockholders' equity will increase by $80,000.
(c) retained earnings will decrease by $300,000 and total stockholders' equity will increase by $300,000.
(d) retained earnings will decrease by $300,000 and total paid-in capital will increase by $300,000.

(LO 2) **6.** Which of the following can cause a restriction in retained earnings?
(a) State laws regarding treasury stock.
(b) Long-term debt contract terms.
(c) Authorizations by the board of directors in light of planned expansion of corporate facilities.
(d) All of the above.

(LO 2) **7.** All **but one** of the following is reported in a retained earnings statement. The exception is:
(a) cash and stock dividends.
(b) net income and net loss.
(c) sales revenue.
(d) prior period adjustments.

(LO 2) **8.** A prior period adjustment is:
(a) reported in the income statement as a nontypical item.
(b) a correction of an error that is recorded directly to retained earnings.
(c) reported directly in the stockholders' equity section.
(d) reported in the retained earnings statement as an adjustment of the ending balance of retained earnings.

(LO 3) **9.** In the stockholders' equity section, Common Stock Dividends Distributable is reported as a(n):
(a) deduction from total paid-in capital and retained earnings.

(b) addition to additional paid-in capital.
(c) deduction from retained earnings.
(d) addition to capital stock.

(LO 3) **10.** Katie Inc. reported net income of $186,000 during 2014 and paid dividends of $26,000 on common stock. It also has 10,000 shares of 6%, $100 par value, non-cumulative preferred stock outstanding and paid dividends of $60,000 on preferred stock. Common stockholders' equity was $1,200,000 on January 1, 2014, and $1,600,000 on December 31, 2014. The company's return on common stockholders' equity for 2014 is:
(a) 10.0%.   (c) 7.1%.
(b) 9.0%.   (d) 13.3%.

(LO 3) **11.** The return on common stockholders' equity is defined as:
(a) net income divided by total assets.
(b) cash dividends divided by average common stockholders' equity.
(c) income available to common stockholders divided by average common stockholders' equity.
(d) None of these is correct.

(LO 4) **12.** During 2014, Talon Inc. had sales revenue $376,000, gross profit $176,000, operating expenses $66,000, cash dividends $30,000, other expenses and losses $20,000. Its corporate tax rate is 30%. What was Talon's income tax expense for the year?
(a) $18,000.   (c) $112,800.
(b) $52,800.   (d) $27,000.

(LO 4) **13.** Corporation income statements may be the same as the income statements for unincorporated companies **except** for:
(a) gross profit.
(b) income tax expense.
(c) operating income.
(d) net sales.

(LO 5) **14.** If everything else is held constant, earnings per share is increased by:
(a) the payment of a cash dividend to common shareholders.
(b) the payment of a cash dividend to preferred shareholders.
(c) the issuance of new shares of common stock.
(d) the purchase of treasury stock.

(LO 5) **15.** The income statement for Nadeen, Inc. shows income before income taxes $700,000, income tax expense $210,000, and net income $490,000. If Nadeen has 100,000 shares of common stock outstanding throughout the year, earnings per share is:
(a) $7.00.
(b) $4.90.
(c) $2.10.
(d) No correct answer is given.

Go to the book's companion website, www.wiley.com/college/weygandt, for additional Self-Test Questions.

✔ The Navigator

QUESTIONS

1. **(a)** What is a dividend? **(b)** "Dividends must be paid in cash." Do you agree? Explain.

2. Jan Kimler maintains that adequate cash is the only requirement for the declaration of a cash dividend. Is Jan correct? Explain.

3. **(a)** Three dates are important in connection with cash dividends. Identify these dates, and explain their significance to the corporation and its stockholders.

   (b) Identify the accounting entries that are made for a cash dividend and the date of each entry.

4. Farley Inc. declares a $55,000 cash dividend on December 31, 2014. The required annual dividend on preferred stock is $10,000. Determine the allocation of the dividend to preferred and common stockholders assuming the preferred stock is cumulative and dividends are 1 year in arrears.

5. Contrast the effects of a cash dividend and a stock dividend on a corporation's balance sheet.

6. Rich Mordica asks, "Since stock dividends don't change anything, why declare them?" What is your answer to Rich?

7. Gorton Corporation has 30,000 shares of $10 par value common stock outstanding when it announces a 2-for-1 stock split. Before the split, the stock had a market price of $120 per share. After the split, how many shares of stock will be outstanding? What will be the approximate market price per share?

8. The board of directors is considering either a stock split or a stock dividend. They understand that total stockholders' equity will remain the same under either action. However, they are not sure of the different effects of the two types of actions on other aspects of stockholders' equity. Explain the differences to the directors.

9. What is a prior period adjustment, and how is it reported in the financial statements?

10. NAJ Corporation has a retained earnings balance of $230,000 on January 1. During the year, a prior period adjustment of $50,000 is recorded because of the understatement of depreciation in the prior period. Show the retained earnings statement presentation of these data.

11. What is the purpose of a retained earnings restriction? Identify the possible causes of retained earnings restrictions.

12. How are retained earnings restrictions generally reported in the financial statements?

13. Identify the events that result in debits and credits to retained earnings.

14. Rafy Furcal believes that both the beginning and ending balances in retained earnings are shown in the stockholders' equity section. Is Rafy correct? Discuss.

15. Dean Percival, who owns many investments in common stock, says, "I don't care what a company's net income is. The stock price tells me everything I need to know!" How do you respond to Dean?

16. What is the unique feature of a corporation income statement? Illustrate this feature, using assumed data.

17. Why must preferred stock dividends be subtracted from net income in computing earnings per share?

18. What were the amounts of basic earnings per share of common stock that Apple reported in the years 2007 to 2011?

BRIEF EXERCISES

BE14-1 Greenwood Corporation has 80,000 shares of common stock outstanding. It declares a $1 per share cash dividend on November 1 to stockholders of record on December 1. The dividend is paid on December 31. Prepare the entries on the appropriate dates to record the declaration and payment of the cash dividend.

Prepare entries for a cash dividend.

(LO 1)

BE14-2 Langley Corporation has 50,000 shares of $10 par value common stock outstanding. It declares a 15% stock dividend on December 1 when the market price per share is $16. The dividend shares are issued on December 31. Prepare the entries for the declaration and payment of the stock dividend.

Prepare entries for a stock dividend.

(LO 1)

BE14-3 The stockholders' equity section of Pretzer Corporation consists of common stock ($10 par) $2,000,000 and retained earnings $500,000. A 10% stock dividend (20,000 shares) is declared when the market price per share is $14. Show the before-and-after effects of the dividend on the following.

(a) The components of stockholders' equity.
(b) Shares outstanding.
(c) Par value per share.

Show before-and-after effects of a stock dividend.

(LO 1)

Prepare a retained earnings statement.

(LO 2)

BE14-4 For the year ending December 31, 2014, Soto Inc. reports net income $170,000 and dividends $85,000. Prepare the retained earnings statement for the year assuming the balance in retained earnings on January 1, 2014, was $220,000.

Prepare a retained earnings statement.

(LO 2)

BE14-5 The balance in retained earnings on January 1, 2014, for Palmer Inc. was $800,000. During the year, the corporation paid cash dividends of $90,000 and distributed a stock dividend of $8,000. In addition, the company determined that it had understated its depreciation expense in prior years by $50,000. Net income for 2014 was $120,000. Prepare the retained earnings statement for 2014.

Calculate the return on common stockholders' equity.

(LO 3)

BE14-6 SUPERVALU, one of the largest grocery retailers in the United States, is headquartered in Minneapolis. Suppose the following financial information (in millions) was taken from the company's 2014 annual report: net sales $40,597, net income $393, beginning common stockholders' equity $2,581, and ending common stockholders' equity $2,887. Compute the return on common stockholders' equity.

Compute the return on common stockholders' equity.

(LO 3)

BE14-7 Whetzel Corporation reported net income of $152,000, declared dividends on common stock of $50,000, and had an ending balance in retained earnings of $360,000. Common stockholders' equity was $700,000 at the beginning of the year and $820,000 at the end of the year. Compute the return on common stockholders' equity.

Prepare a corporate income statement.

(LO 4)

BE14-8 The following information is available for Reinsch Corporation for the year ended December 31, 2014: cost of goods sold $205,000, sales revenue $350,000, other revenues and gains $50,000, and operating expenses $75,000. Assuming a corporate tax rate of 30%, prepare an income statement for the company.

Compute earnings per share.

(LO 5)

BE14-9 Ziegler Corporation reports net income of $380,000 and a weighted-average of 200,000 shares of common stock outstanding for the year. Compute the earnings per share of common stock.

Compute earnings per share with cumulative preferred stock.

(LO 5)

BE14-10 Income and common stock data for Ziegler Corporation are presented in BE14-9. Assume also that Ziegler has cumulative preferred stock dividends for the current year of $30,000 that were declared and paid. Compute the earnings per share of common stock.

> ### DO IT! Review

Determine dividends paid to preferred and common stockholders.

(LO 1)

DO IT! 14-1 Herr Corporation has 3,000 shares of 7%, $100 par value preferred stock outstanding at December 31, 2014. At December 31, 2014, the company declared a $105,000 cash dividend. Determine the dividend paid to preferred stockholders and common stockholders under each of the following scenarios.

1. The preferred stock is noncumulative, and the company has not missed any dividends in previous years.

2. The preferred stock is noncumulative, and the company did not pay a dividend in each of the two previous years.

3. The preferred stock is cumulative, and the company did not pay a dividend in each of the two previous years.

Determine effects of stock dividend and stock split.

(LO 1)

DO IT! 14-2 Jurgens Company has had 4 years of net income. Due to this success, the market price of its 400,000 shares of $3 par value common stock has increased from $12 per share to $46. During this period, paid-in capital remained the same at $2,800,000. Retained earnings increased from $1,800,000 to $12,000,000. President E. Rife is considering either a 15% stock dividend or a 2-for-1 stock split. He asks you to show the before-and-after effects of each option on (a) retained earnings and (b) total stockholders' equity.

Prepare a retained earnings statement.

(LO 2)

DO IT! 14-3 Foley Corporation has retained earnings of $3,100,000 on January 1, 2014. During the year, Foley earned $1,200,000 of net income. It declared and paid a $150,000 cash dividend. In 2014, Foley recorded an adjustment of $110,000 due to the overstatement (from mathematical error) of 2013 depreciation expense. Prepare a retained earnings statement for 2014.

Compute return on stockholders' equity and EPS and discuss changes in each.

(LO 3, 5)

DO IT! 14-4 On January 1, 2014, Vahsholtz Corporation purchased 5,000 shares of treasury stock. Other information regarding Vahsholtz Corporation is provided on page 671.

	2013	2014
Net income	$100,000	$110,000
Dividends on preferred stock	$30,000	$30,000
Dividends on common stock	$20,000	$25,000
Weighted-average number of common shares outstanding	50,000	45,000
Common stockholders' equity beginning of year	$600,000	$750,000
Common stockholders' equity end of year	$750,000	$830,000

Compute (a) return on common stockholders' equity for each year and (b) earnings per share for each year, and (c) discuss the changes in each.

EXERCISES

E14-1 On January 1, Guillen Corporation had 95,000 shares of no-par common stock issued and outstanding. The stock has a stated value of $5 per share. During the year, the following occurred.

Journalize cash dividends; indicate statement presentation.

(LO 1)

Apr.	1	Issued 25,000 additional shares of common stock for $17 per share.
June	15	Declared a cash dividend of $1 per share to stockholders of record on June 30.
July	10	Paid the $1 cash dividend.
Dec.	1	Issued 2,000 additional shares of common stock for $19 per share.
	15	Declared a cash dividend on outstanding shares of $1.20 per share to stockholders of record on December 31.

Instructions

(a) Prepare the entries, if any, on each of the three dividend dates.

(b) How are dividends and dividends payable reported in the financial statements prepared at December 31?

E14-2 Knudsen Corporation was organized on January 1, 2013. During its first year, the corporation issued 2,000 shares of $50 par value preferred stock and 100,000 shares of $10 par value common stock. At December 31, the company declared the following cash dividends: 2013, $5,000; 2014, $12,000; and 2015, $28,000.

Allocate cash dividends to preferred and common stock.

(LO 1)

Instructions

(a) Show the allocation of dividends to each class of stock, assuming the preferred stock dividend is 6% and noncumulative.

(b) Show the allocation of dividends to each class of stock, assuming the preferred stock dividend is 7% and cumulative.

(c) Journalize the declaration of the cash dividend at December 31, 2015, under part (b).

E14-3 On January 1, 2014, Frontier Corporation had $1,000,000 of common stock outstanding that was issued at par. It also had retained earnings of $750,000. The company issued 40,000 shares of common stock at par on July 1 and earned net income of $400,000 for the year.

Journalize stock dividends.

(LO 1)

Instructions

Journalize the declaration of a 15% stock dividend on December 10, 2014, for the following independent assumptions.

(a) Par value is $10, and market price is $18.

(b) Par value is $5, and market price is $20.

E14-4 On October 31, the stockholders' equity section of Heins Company consists of common stock $500,000 and retained earnings $900,000. Heins is considering the following two courses of action: (1) declaring a 5% stock dividend on the 50,000, $10 par value shares outstanding, or (2) effecting a 2-for-1 stock split that will reduce par value to $5 per share. The current market price is $14 per share.

Compare effects of a stock dividend and a stock split.

(LO 1)

Instructions

Prepare a tabular summary of the effects of the alternative actions on the components of stockholders' equity, outstanding shares, and par value per share. Use the following column headings: Before Action, After Stock Dividend, and After Stock Split.

Indicate account balances after a stock dividend.

(LO 1, 3)

E14-5 On October 1, Little Bobby Corporation's stockholders' equity is as follows.

Common stock, $5 par value	$400,000
Paid-in capital in excess of par—common stock	25,000
Retained earnings	155,000
Total stockholders' equity	$580,000

On October 1, Little Bobby declares and distributes a 10% stock dividend when the market price of the stock is $15 per share.

Instructions

(a) Compute the par value per share (1) before the stock dividend and (2) after the stock dividend.

(b) Indicate the balances in the three stockholders' equity accounts after the stock dividend shares have been distributed.

Indicate the effects on stockholders' equity components.

(LO 1, 2, 3)

E14-6 During 2014, Roblez Corporation had the following transactions and events.

1. Declared a cash dividend.
2. Issued par value common stock for cash at par value.
3. Completed a 2-for-1 stock split in which $10 par value stock was changed to $5 par value stock.
4. Declared a small stock dividend when the market price was higher than par value.
5. Made a prior period adjustment for overstatement of net income.
6. Issued the shares of common stock required by the stock dividend declaration in item no. 4 above.
7. Paid the cash dividend in item no. 1 above.
8. Issued par value common stock for cash above par value.

Instructions

Indicate the effect(s) of each of the foregoing items on the subdivisions of stockholders' equity. Present your answer in tabular form with the following columns. Use (I) for increase, (D) for decrease, and (NE) for no effect. Item no. 1 is given as an example.

	Paid-in Capital		
Item	**Capital Stock**	**Additional**	**Retained Earnings**
1	NE	NE	D

Prepare correcting entries for dividends and a stock split.

(LO 1)

E14-7 Before preparing financial statements for the current year, the chief accountant for Toso Company discovered the following errors in the accounts.

1. The declaration and payment of $50,000 cash dividend was recorded as a debit to Interest Expense $50,000 and a credit to Cash $50,000.
2. A 10% stock dividend (1,000 shares) was declared on the $10 par value stock when the market price per share was $18. The only entry made was Stock Dividends (Dr.) $10,000 and Dividend Payable (Cr.) $10,000. The shares have not been issued.
3. A 4-for-1 stock split involving the issue of 400,000 shares of $5 par value common stock for 100,000 shares of $20 par value common stock was recorded as a debit to Retained Earnings $2,000,000 and a credit to Common Stock $2,000,000.

Instructions

Prepare the correcting entries at December 31.

Prepare a retained earnings statement.

(LO 2)

E14-8 On January 1, 2014, Eddy Corporation had retained earnings of $650,000. During the year, Eddy had the following selected transactions.

1. Declared cash dividends $120,000.
2. Corrected overstatement of 2013 net income because of depreciation error $40,000.
3. Earned net income $350,000.
4. Declared stock dividends $90,000.

Instructions

Prepare a retained earnings statement for the year.

E14-9 Newland Company reported retained earnings at December 31, 2013, of $310,000. Newland had 200,000 shares of common stock outstanding at the beginning of 2014.

The following transactions occurred during 2014.

1. An error was discovered. In 2012, depreciation expense was recorded at $70,000, but the correct amount was $50,000.
2. A cash dividend of $0.50 per share was declared and paid.
3. A 5% stock dividend was declared and distributed when the market price per share was $15 per share.
4. Net income was $285,000.

Prepare a retained earnings statement.
(LO 2)

Instructions
Prepare a retained earnings statement for 2014.

E14-10 Dirk Company reported the following balances at December 31, 2013: common stock $500,000, paid-in capital in excess of par value—common stock $100,000, and retained earnings $250,000. During 2014, the following transactions affected stockholder's equity.

1. Issued preferred stock with a par value of $125,000 for $200,000.
2. Purchased treasury stock (common) for $40,000.
3. Earned net income of $180,000.
4. Declared and paid cash dividends of $56,000.

Prepare a stockholders' equity section.
(LO 3)

Instructions
Prepare the stockholders' equity section of Dirk Company's December 31, 2014, balance sheet.

E14-11 The following accounts appear in the ledger of Horner Inc. after the books are closed at December 31.

Prepare a stockholders' equity section.
(LO 3)

Common Stock, no par, $1 stated value, 400,000 shares authorized;	
300,000 shares issued	$ 300,000
Common Stock Dividends Distributable	30,000
Paid-in Capital in Excess of Stated Value—Common Stock	1,200,000
Preferred Stock, $5 par value, 8%, 40,000 shares authorized;	
30,000 shares issued	150,000
Retained Earnings	800,000
Treasury Stock (10,000 common shares)	74,000
Paid-in Capital in Excess of Par—Preferred Stock	344,000

Instructions
Prepare the stockholders' equity section at December 31, assuming retained earnings is restricted for plant expansion in the amount of $100,000.

E14-12 The following information is available for Norman Corporation for the year ended December 31, 2014: sales revenue $700,000, other revenues and gains $92,000, operating expenses $110,000, cost of goods sold $465,000, other expenses and losses $32,000, and preferred stock dividends $30,000. The company's tax rate was 30%, and it had 50,000 shares outstanding during the entire year.

Prepare an income statement and compute earnings per share.
(LO 4, 5)

Instructions
(a) Prepare a corporate income statement.
(b) Calculate earnings per share.

E14-13 In 2014, Pennington Corporation had net sales of $600,000 and cost of goods sold of $360,000. Operating expenses were $153,000, and interest expense was $7,500. The corporation's tax rate is 30%. The corporation declared preferred dividends of $15,000 in 2014, and its average common stockholders' equity during the year was $200,000.

Prepare an income statement and compute return on equity.
(LO 3, 4)

Instructions
(a) Prepare an income statement for Pennington Corporation.
(b) Compute Pennington Corporation's return on common stockholders' equity for 2014.

E14-14 Ringgold Corporation has outstanding at December 31, 2014, 50,000 shares of $20 par value, cumulative, 6% preferred stock and 200,000 shares of $5 par value common stock. All shares were outstanding the entire year. During 2014, Ringgold earned total revenues of $2,000,000 and incurred total expenses (except income taxes) of $1,300,000. Ringgold's income tax rate is 30%.

Compute EPS.
(LO 4, 5)

Calculate ratios to evaluate earnings performance.

(LO 3, 5)

Instructions

Compute Ringgold's 2014 earnings per share.

E14-15 The following financial information is available for Plummer Corporation.

	2014	2013
Average common stockholders' equity	$1,200,000	$900,000
Dividends paid to common stockholders	50,000	30,000
Dividends paid to preferred stockholders	20,000	20,000
Net income	290,000	200,000
Market price of common stock	20	15

The weighted-average number of shares of common stock outstanding was 80,000 for 2013 and 100,000 for 2014.

Instructions

Calculate earnings per share and return on common stockholders' equity for 2014 and 2013.

Calculate ratios to evaluate earnings performance.

(LO 3, 5)

E14-16 This financial information is available for Klinger Corporation.

	2014	2013
Average common stockholders' equity	$1,800,000	$1,900,000
Dividends paid to common stockholders	90,000	70,000
Dividends paid to preferred stockholders	20,000	20,000
Net income	200,000	191,000
Market price of common stock	20	25

The weighted-average number of shares of common stock outstanding was 180,000 for 2013 and 150,000 for 2014.

Instructions

Calculate earnings per share and return on common stockholders' equity for 2014 and 2013.

Compute earnings per share under different assumptions.

(LO 5)

E14-17 At December 31, 2014, Millwood Corporation has 2,000 shares of $100 par value, 8%, preferred stock outstanding and 100,000 shares of $10 par value common stock issued. Millwood's net income for the year is $241,000.

Instructions

Compute the earnings per share of common stock under the following independent situations. (Round to two decimals.)

(a) The dividend to preferred stockholders was declared. There has been no change in the number of shares of common stock outstanding during the year.

(b) The dividend to preferred stockholders was not declared. The preferred stock is cumulative. Millwood held 10,000 shares of common treasury stock throughout the year.

EXERCISES: SET B AND CHALLENGE EXERCISES

Visit the book's companion website, at **www.wiley.com/college/weygandt**, and choose the Student Companion site to access Exercise Set B and Challenge Exercises.

PROBLEMS: SET A

Prepare dividend entries and stockholders' equity section.

(LO 1, 3)

P14-1A On January 1, 2014, Geffrey Corporation had the following stockholders' equity accounts.

Common Stock ($20 par value, 60,000 shares issued and outstanding)	$1,200,000
Paid-in Capital in Excess of Par—Common Stock	200,000
Retained Earnings	600,000

During the year, the following transactions occurred.

Feb. 1   Declared a $1 cash dividend per share to stockholders of record on February 15, payable March 1.

Mar. 1   Paid the dividend declared in February.

Apr. 1   Announced a 2-for-1 stock split. Prior to the split, the market price per share was $36.

July 1   Declared a 10% stock dividend to stockholders of record on July 15, distributable July 31. On July 1, the market price of the stock was $13 per share.

   31   Issued the shares for the stock dividend.

Dec. 1   Declared a $0.50 per share dividend to stockholders of record on December 15, payable January 5, 2015.

   31   Determined that net income for the year was $350,000.

Instructions

(a) Journalize the transactions and the closing entries for net income and dividends.

(b) Enter the beginning balances, and post the entries to the stockholders' equity accounts. (*Note:* Open additional stockholders' equity accounts as needed.)

(c) Prepare a stockholders' equity section at December 31.

(c) Total stockholders' equity $2,224,000

P14-2A The stockholders' equity accounts of Karp Company at January 1, 2014, are as follows.

Preferred Stock, 6%, $50 par	$600,000
Common Stock, $5 par	800,000
Paid-in Capital in Excess of Par—Preferred Stock	200,000
Paid-in Capital in Excess of Par—Common Stock	300,000
Retained Earnings	800,000

Journalize and post transactions; prepare retained earnings statement and stockholders' equity section.

(LO 1, 2, 3)

There were no dividends in arrears on preferred stock. During 2014, the company had the following transactions and events.

July 1   Declared a $0.60 cash dividend per share on common stock.

Aug. 1   Discovered $25,000 understatement of 2013 depreciation on equipment. (Ignore income taxes.)

Sept. 1   Paid the cash dividend declared on July 1.

Dec. 1   Declared a 15% stock dividend on common stock when the market price of the stock was $18 per share.

   15   Declared a 6% cash dividend on preferred stock payable January 15, 2015.

   31   Determined that net income for the year was $355,000.

   31   Recognized a $200,000 restriction of retained earnings for plant expansion.

Instructions

(a) Journalize the transactions, events, and closing entries for net income and dividends.

(b) Enter the beginning balances in the accounts, and post to the stockholders' equity accounts. (*Note:* Open additional stockholders' equity accounts as needed.)

(c) Prepare a retained earnings statement for the year.

(d) Prepare a stockholders' equity section at December 31, 2014.

(c) Ending balance $566,000
(d) Total stockholders' equity $2,898,000

P14-3A The post-closing trial balance of Storey Corporation at December 31, 2014, contains the following stockholders' equity accounts.

Preferred Stock (15,000 shares issued)	$ 750,000
Common Stock (250,000 shares issued)	2,500,000
Paid-in Capital in Excess of Par—Preferred Stock	250,000
Paid-in Capital in Excess of Par—Common Stock	400,000
Common Stock Dividends Distributable	250,000
Retained Earnings	1,042,000

Prepare retained earnings statement and stockholders' equity section, and compute allocation of dividends and earnings per share.

(LO 1, 2, 3, 5)

A review of the accounting records reveals the following.

1. No errors have been made in recording 2014 transactions or in preparing the closing entry for net income.

2. Preferred stock is $50 par, 6%, and cumulative; 15,000 shares have been outstanding since January 1, 2013.

3. Authorized stock is 20,000 shares of preferred, 500,000 shares of common with a $10 par value.
4. The January 1 balance in Retained Earnings was $1,170,000.
5. On July 1, 20,000 shares of common stock were issued for cash at $16 per share.
6. On September 1, the company discovered an understatement error of $90,000 in computing depreciation in 2013. The net of tax effect of $63,000 was properly debited directly to Retained Earnings.
7. A cash dividend of $250,000 was declared and properly allocated to preferred and common stock on October 1. No dividends were paid to preferred stockholders in 2013.
8. On December 31, a 10% common stock dividend was declared out of retained earnings on common stock when the market price per share was $16.
9. Net income for the year was $585,000.
10. On December 31, 2014, the directors authorized disclosure of a $200,000 restriction of retained earnings for plant expansion. (Use Note X.)

Instructions
(a) Reproduce the Retained Earnings account (T-account) for 2014.
(b) Prepare a retained earnings statement for 2014.
(c) Prepare a stockholders' equity section at December 31, 2014.
(d) Compute the allocation of the cash dividend to preferred and common stock.

(c) Total stockholders' equity $5,192,000

Prepare the stockholders' equity section, reflecting dividends and stock split.

(LO 1, 2, 3)

P14-4A On January 1, 2014, Ven Corporation had the following stockholders' equity accounts.

Common Stock (no par value, 90,000 shares issued and outstanding)	$1,600,000
Retained Earnings	500,000

During the year, the following transactions occurred.

Feb. 1	Declared a $1 cash dividend per share to stockholders of record on February 15, payable March 1.
Mar. 1	Paid the dividend declared in February.
Apr. 1	Announced a 3-for-1 stock split. Prior to the split, the market price per share was $36.
July 1	Declared a 5% stock dividend to stockholders of record on July 15, distributable July 31. On July 1, the market price of the stock was $16 per share.
31	Issued the shares for the stock dividend.
Dec. 1	Declared a $0.50 per share dividend to stockholders of record on December 15, payable January 5, 2015.
31	Determined that net income for the year was $350,000.

Instructions
Prepare the stockholders' equity section of the balance sheet at (a) March 31, (b) June 30, (c) September 30, and (d) December 31, 2014.

(d) Total stockholders' equity $2,218,250

Prepare the stockholders' equity section, reflecting various events.

(LO 1, 2, 3)

P14-5A On January 1, 2014, Shellenburger Inc. had the following stockholders' equity account balances.

Common Stock, no-par value (500,000 shares issued)	$1,500,000
Common Stock Dividends Distributable	200,000
Retained Earnings	600,000

During 2014, the following transactions and events occurred.

1. Issued 50,000 shares of common stock as a result of a 10% stock dividend declared on December 15, 2013.
2. Issued 30,000 shares of common stock for cash at $6 per share.
3. Corrected an error that had understated the net income for 2012 by $70,000.
4. Declared and paid a cash dividend of $80,000.
5. Earned net income of $300,000.

Instructions
Prepare the stockholders' equity section of the balance sheet at December 31, 2014.

Total stockholders' equity $2,770,000

PROBLEMS: SET B

P14-1B On January 1, 2014, Chen Corporation had the following stockholders' equity accounts.

Common Stock ($5 par value, 200,000 shares issued and outstanding)	$1,000,000
Paid-in Capital in Excess of Par—Common Stock	200,000
Retained Earnings	840,000

Prepare dividend entries and stockholders' equity section.

(LO 1, 3)

During the year, the following transactions occurred.

Jan. 15 Declared a $1 cash dividend per share to stockholders of record on January 31, payable February 15.
Feb. 15 Paid the dividend declared in January.
Apr. 15 Declared a 10% stock dividend to stockholders of record on April 30, distributable May 15. On April 15, the market price of the stock was $15 per share.
May 15 Issued the shares for the stock dividend.
July 1 Announced a 2-for-1 stock split. The market price per share prior to the announcement was $17. (The new par value is $2.50.)
Dec. 1 Declared a $0.50 per share cash dividend to stockholders of record on December 15, payable January 10, 2015.
     31 Determined that net income for the year was $250,000.

Instructions
(a) Journalize the transactions and the closing entries for net income and dividends.
(b) Enter the beginning balances, and post the entries to the stockholders' equity accounts. (*Note:* Open additional stockholders' equity accounts as needed.)
(c) Prepare a stockholders' equity section at December 31.

(c) Total stockholders' equity $1,870,000

P14-2B The stockholders' equity accounts of Holt Inc., at January 1, 2014, are as follows.

Preferred Stock, $100 par, 7%	$600,000
Common Stock, $10 par	900,000
Paid-in Capital in Excess of Par—Preferred Stock	100,000
Paid-in Capital in Excess of Par—Common Stock	200,000
Retained Earnings	500,000

Journalize and post transactions; prepare retained earnings statement and stockholders' equity section.

(LO 1, 2, 3)

There were no dividends in arrears on preferred stock. During 2014, the company had the following transactions and events.

July 1 Declared a $0.50 cash dividend per share on common stock.
Aug. 1 Discovered a $72,000 overstatement of 2013 depreciation on equipment. (Ignore income taxes.)
Sept. 1 Paid the cash dividend declared on July 1.
Dec. 1 Declared a 10% stock dividend on common stock when the market price of the stock was $16 per share.
     15 Declared a 7% cash dividend on preferred stock payable January 31, 2015.
     31 Determined that net income for the year was $350,000.

Instructions
(a) Journalize the transactions and the closing entries for net income and dividends.
(b) Enter the beginning balances in the accounts and post to the stockholders' equity accounts. (*Note:* Open additional stockholders' equity accounts as needed.)
(c) Prepare a retained earnings statement for the year.
(d) Prepare a stockholders' equity section at December 31, 2014.

(c) Ending balance $691,000
(d) Total stockholders' equity $2,635,000

P14-3B The ledger of Giffin Corporation at December 31, 2014, after the books have been closed, contains the following stockholders' equity accounts.

Preferred Stock (10,000 shares issued)	$1,000,000
Common Stock (400,000 shares issued)	2,000,000
Paid-in Capital in Excess of Par—Preferred Stock	200,000
Paid-in Capital in Excess of Stated Value—Common Stock	1,180,000
Common Stock Dividends Distributable	200,000
Retained Earnings	2,560,000

Prepare retained earnings statement and stockholders' equity section, and compute allocation of dividends and earnings per share.

(LO 1, 2, 3, 5)

A review of the accounting records reveals the following.

1. No errors have been made in recording 2014 transactions or in preparing the closing entry for net income.
2. Preferred stock is 6%, $100 par value, noncumulative, and callable at $125. Since January 1, 2013, 10,000 shares have been outstanding; 20,000 shares are authorized.
3. Common stock is no-par with a stated value of $5 per share; 600,000 shares are authorized.
4. The January 1 balance in Retained Earnings was $2,450,000.
5. On October 1, 100,000 shares of common stock were sold for cash at $8 per share.
6. A cash dividend of $500,000 was declared and properly allocated to preferred and common stock on November 1. No dividends were paid to preferred stockholders in 2013.
7. On December 31, a 10% common stock dividend was declared out of retained earnings on common stock when the market price per share was $9.
8. Net income for the year was $970,000.
9. On December 31, 2014, the directors authorized disclosure of a $100,000 restriction of retained earnings for plant expansion. (Use Note A.)

Instructions
(a) Reproduce the Retained Earnings account (T-account) for 2014.
(b) Prepare a retained earnings statement for 2014.
(c) Prepare a stockholders' equity section at December 31, 2014.
(d) Compute the allocation of the cash dividend to preferred and common stock.

(c) Total stockholders' equity
$7,140,000

Prepare the stockholders'
equity section, reflecting
dividends and stock split.
(LO 1, 2, 3)

P14-4B On January 1, 2014, Dingler Corporation had the following stockholders' equity accounts.

Common Stock (no-par value, 100,000 shares issued and outstanding)	$2,800,000
Retained Earnings	1,000,000

During the year, the following transactions occurred.

Feb.	1	Declared a $1 cash dividend per share to stockholders of record on February 15, payable March 1.
Mar.	1	Paid the dividend declared in February.
Apr.	1	Announced a 4-for-1 stock split. Prior to the split, the market price per share was $36.
July	1	Declared a 5% stock dividend to stockholders of record on July 15, distributable July 31. On July 1, the market price of the stock was $13 per share.
	31	Issued the shares for the stock dividend.
Dec.	1	Declared a $0.50 per share dividend to stockholders of record on December 15, payable January 5, 2015.
	31	Determined that net income for the year was $700,000.

Instructions

(d) Total, stockholders'
equity $4,190,000

Prepare the stockholders' equity section of the balance sheet at (a) March 31, (b) June 30, (c) September 30, and (d) December 31, 2014.

Prepare the stockholders'
equity section, reflecting
various events.
(LO 1, 2, 3)

P14-5B On January 1, 2014, Hammond Inc. had the following shareholders' equity balances.

Common Stock, no-par value (1,000,000 shares issued)	$3,000,000
Common Stock Dividends Distributable	400,000
Retained Earnings	1,200,000

During 2014, the following transactions and events occurred.

1. Issued 100,000 shares of common stock as a result of a 10% stock dividend declared on December 15, 2013.
2. Issued 60,000 shares of common stock for cash at $5 per share.
3. Corrected an error that had understated the net income for 2012 by $140,000.
4. Declared and paid a cash dividend of $300,000.
5. Earned net income of $600,000.

Total stockholders' equity
$5,340,000

Instructions
Prepare the stockholders' equity section of the balance sheet at December 31, 2014.

PROBLEMS: SET C

Visit the book's companion website, at **www.wiley.com/college/weygandt**, and choose the Student Companion site to access Problem Set C.

CONTINUING COOKIE CHRONICLE

(*Note:* This is a continuation of the Cookie Chronicle from Chapters 1 through 13.)

CCC14 After establishing their company's fiscal year-end to be October 31, Natalie and Curtis began operating Cookie & Coffee Creations Inc. on November 1, 2014. On that date, they issued both preferred and common stock. After the first year of operations, Natalie and Curtis want to prepare financial information for the year.

Go to the book's companion website, **www.wiley.com/college/weygandt**, *to see the completion of this problem.*

Broadening Your Perspective

Financial Reporting and Analysis

Financial Reporting Problem: Apple Inc.

BYP14-1 The financial statements of Apple Inc. are presented in Appendix A. Instructions for accessing and using the company's complete annual report, including the notes to the financial statements, are also provided in Appendix A.

Instructions
Refer to Apple's financial statements and answer the following question.
What amount, if any, did Apple declare in dividends on common stock in the year ended September 24, 2011?

Comparative Analysis Problem:
PepsiCo, Inc. vs. The Coca-Cola Company

BYP14-2 PepsiCo's financial statements are presented in Appendix B. Financial statements of The Coca-Cola Company are presented in Appendix C. Instructions for accessing and using the complete annual reports of PepsiCo and Coca-Cola, including the notes to the financial statements, are also provided in Appendices B and C, respectively.

Instructions
(a) Compute earnings per share and return on common stockholders' equity for both companies for 2011. Assume PepsiCo's weighted-average shares were 1,580 million and Coca-Cola's weighted-average shares were 2,284 million. Can these measures be used to compare the profitability of the two companies? Why or why not?
(b) What was the total amount of dividends paid by each company in 2011?

Comparative Analysis Problem:
Amazon.com, Inc. vs. Wal-Mart Stores, Inc.

BYP14-3 Amazon.com, Inc.'s financial statements are presented in Appendix D. Financial statements of Wal-Mart Stores, Inc. are presented in Appendix E. Instructions for accessing and using the complete annual reports of Amazon and Wal-Mart, including the notes to the financial statements, are also provided in Appendices D and E, respectively.

Instructions

(a) What are the basic earnings per share for both Amazon and Wal-Mart as of December 31, 2011, and January 31, 2012, respectively?

(b) What was the total amount of dividends, if any, paid by Amazon for the year ending December 31, 2011? What was the total dividends paid by Wal-Mart for the year ending January 31, 2012?

Real-World Focus

BYP14-4 Use the stockholders' equity section of an annual report and identify the major components.

Address: **www.annualreports.com,** or go to **www.wiley.com/college/weygandt**

Steps

1. From the Annual Reports Homepage, choose **Search by Alphabet**, and choose a letter.
2. Select a particular company.
3. Choose Annual Report.
4. Follow instructions below.

Instructions

Answer the following questions.

(a) What is the company's name?

(b) What classes of capital stock has the company issued?

(c) For each class of stock:
   (1) How many shares are authorized, issued, and/or outstanding?
   (2) What is the par value?

(d) What are the company's retained earnings?

(e) Has the company acquired treasury stock? How many shares?

Critical Thinking

Decision-Making Across the Organization

BYP14-5 The stockholders' equity accounts of Gonzalez, Inc., at January 1, 2014, are as follows.

Preferred Stock, no par, 4,000 shares issued	$400,000
Common Stock, no par, 140,000 shares issued	700,000
Retained Earnings	550,000

During 2014, the company had the following transactions and events.

July	1	Declared a $0.50 cash dividend per share on common stock.
Aug.	1	Discovered a $72,000 overstatement of 2013 depreciation expense. (Ignore income taxes.)
Sept.	1	Paid the cash dividend declared on July 1.
Dec.	1	Declared a 10% stock dividend on common stock when the market price of the stock was $12 per share.
	15	Declared a $6 per share cash dividend on preferred stock, payable January 31, 2015.
	31	Determined that net income for the year was $320,000.

Instructions

With the class divided into groups, answer the following questions.

(a) Prepare a retained earnings statement for the year. There are no preferred dividends in arrears.

(b) Discuss why the overstatement of 2013 depreciation expense is not treated as an adjustment of the current year's income.

(c) Discuss the reasons why a company might decide to issue a stock dividend rather than a cash dividend.

Communication Activity

BYP14-6 In the past year, Gosser Corporation declared a 10% stock dividend, and Jenks, Inc. announced a 2-for-1 stock split. Your parents own 100 shares of each company's $50 par value common stock. During a recent phone call, your parents ask you, as an accounting student, to explain the differences between the two events.

Instructions

Write a letter to your parents that explains the effects of the two events on them as stockholders and the effects of each event on the financial statements of each corporation.

Ethics Case

BYP14-7 Molina Corporation has paid 60 consecutive quarterly cash dividends (15 years). The last 6 months, however, have been a cash drain on the company, as profit margins have been greatly narrowed by increasing competition. With a cash balance sufficient to meet only day-to-day operating needs, the president, Rob Lowery, has decided that a stock dividend instead of a cash dividend should be declared. He tells Molina's financial vice president, Debbie Oler, to issue a press release stating that the company is extending its consecutive dividend record with the issuance of a 5% stock dividend. "Write the press release convincing the stockholders that the stock dividend is just as good as a cash dividend," he orders. "Just watch our stock rise when we announce the stock dividend. It must be a good thing if that happens."

Instructions

(a) Who are the stakeholders in this situation?

(b) Is there anything unethical about Lowery's intentions or actions?

(c) What is the effect of a stock dividend on a corporation's stockholders' equity accounts? Which would you rather receive as a stockholder—a cash dividend or a stock dividend? Why?

All About You

BYP14-8 In this textbook, you learned that in response to the Sarbanes-Oxley Act, many companies have implemented formal ethics codes. Many other organizations also have ethics codes.

Instructions

Obtain the ethics code from an organization that you belong to (e.g., student organization, business school, employer, or a volunteer organization). Evaluate the ethics code based on how clearly it identifies proper and improper behavior. Discuss its strengths, and how it might be improved.

FASB Codification Activity

BYP14-9 If your school has a subscription to the FASB Codification, go to **http://aaahq.org/ascLogin.cfm** to log in and prepare responses to the following.

(a) What is the stock dividend?

(b) What is a stock split?

(c) At what percentage point does the issuance of additional shares qualify as a stock dividend, as opposed to a stock split?

Answers to Chapter Questions

Answers to Insight and Accounting Across the Organization Questions

p. 653 Up, Down, and ??   Q: What factors must management consider in deciding how large a dividend to pay? **A:** Management must consider the size of the company's retained earnings balance, the amount of available cash, the company's expected near-term cash needs, the company's growth opportunities, and what level of dividend the company will be able to sustain based upon its expected future earnings.

p. 657 A No-Split Philosophy   Q: Why does Warren Buffett usually oppose stock splits? **A:** Buffett prefers to attract shareholders who will make a long-term commitment to his company, as opposed to traders who will only hold their investment for a short period of time. He believes that a high stock price discourages short-term investment.

Answers to Self-Test Questions

1. a **2.** c **3.** c **4.** a $80,000 − [(3,000 × 7% × $100) × 2] **5.** d (100,000 × 10% × $30) **6.** d **7.** c
8. b **9.** d **10.** b $186,000 − (6% × $100 × 10,000) = $126,000; ($1,200,000 + $1,600,000) ÷ 2 = $1,400,000; ($126,000 ÷ $1,400,000) **11.** c **12.** d ($176,000 − $66,000 − $20,000) × 30%
13. b **14.** d **15.** b ($490,000 ÷ 100,000)

A Look at IFRS

LEARNING OBJECTIVE   **6**

Compare the accounting for dividends, retained earnings, and income reporting under GAAP and IFRS.

The basic accounting for cash and stock dividends is essentially the same under both GAAP and IFRS although IFRS terminology may differ.

Key Points

- The term **reserves** is used in IFRS to indicate all non–contributed (non–paid-in) capital. Reserves include retained earnings and other comprehensive income items, such as revaluation surplus and unrealized gains or losses on available-for sale securities.

- IFRS often uses terms such as **retained profits** or **accumulated profit or loss** to describe retained earnings. The term retained earnings is also often used.

- The accounting related to prior period adjustment is essentially the same under IFRS and GAAP. IFRS addresses the accounting for errors in *IAS 8* ("Accounting Policies, Changes in Accounting Estimates, and Errors"). One area where IFRS and GAAP differ in reporting relates to error corrections in previously issued financial statements. While IFRS requires restatement with some exceptions, GAAP does not permit any exceptions.

- The stockholders' equity section is essentially the same under IFRS and GAAP. However, terminology used to describe certain components is often different. These differences are discussed in Chapter 13.

- Equity is given various descriptions under IFRS, such as shareholders' equity, owners' equity, capital and reserves, and shareholders' funds.

- The income statement using IFRS is called the **statement of comprehensive income**. A statement of comprehensive income is presented in a one- or two-statement format. The single-statement approach includes all items of income and expense, as well as each component of other comprehensive income or loss by its individual characteristic. In the two-statement approach, a traditional income statement is prepared. It is then followed by a statement of comprehensive income, which starts with net income or loss and then adds other comprehensive income or loss items. Regardless of which approach is reported, income tax expense is required to be reported.

- The computations related to earnings per share are essentially the same under IFRS and GAAP.

Looking to the Future

The IASB and the FASB are currently working on a project related to financial statement presentation. An important part of this study is to determine whether certain line items, subtotals, and totals should be clearly defined and required to be displayed in the financial statements. For example, it is likely that the statement of stockholders' equity and its presentation will be examined closely.

Both the IASB and FASB are working toward convergence of any remaining differences related to earnings per share computations. This convergence will deal with highly technical changes beyond the scope of this textbook.

IFRS Practice

IFRS Self-Test Questions

1. The basic accounting for cash dividends and stock dividends:
    (a) is different under IFRS versus GAAP.
    (b) is the same under IFRS and GAAP.
    (c) differs only for the accounting for cash dividends between GAAP and IFRS.
    (d) differs only for the accounting for stock dividends between GAAP and IFRS.

2. Which item in **not** considered part of reserves?
   (a) Unrealized loss on available-for-sale investments.
   (b) Revaluation surplus.
   (c) Retained earnings.
   (d) Issued shares.

3. Under IFRS, a statement of comprehensive income must include:
   (a) accounts payable.
   (b) retained earnings.
   (c) income tax expense.
   (d) preference stock.

4. Which set of terms can be used to describe total stockholders' equity under IFRS?
   (a) Shareholders' equity, capital and reserves, other comprehensive income.
   (b) Capital and reserves, shareholders' equity, shareholders' funds.
   (c) Capital and reserves, retained earnings, shareholders' equity.
   (d) All of the above.

5. Earnings per share computations related to IFRS and GAAP:
   (a) are essentially similar.
   (b) result in an amount referred to as earnings per share.
   (c) must deduct preferred (preference) dividends when computing earnings per share.
   (d) All of the above.

IFRS Exercise

International Financial Reporting Problem: Zetar plc

IFRS14-1 The financial statements of Zetar plc are presented in Appendix F. Instructions for accessing and using the company's complete annual report, including the notes to its financial statements, are also provided in Appendix F.

Instructions
Use the company's annual report to answer the following questions.

(a) Did the company declare and pay any dividends for the year ended April 30, 2011?
(b) Compute the company's return on ordinary shareholders' equity for the year ended April 30, 2011.
(c) What was Zetar's earnings per share for the year ended April 30, 2011?

Answers to IFRS Self-Test Questions
1. b **2.** d **3.** c **4.** b **5.** d

✔ **The Navigator**

15 | Long-Term Liabilities

Feature Story

And Then There Were Two

Debt can help a company acquire the things it needs to grow, but it is often the very thing that kills a company. A brief history of Maxwell Car Company illustrates the role of debt in the U.S. auto industry. In 1920, Maxwell Car Company was on the brink of financial ruin. Because it was unable to pay its bills, its creditors stepped in and took over. They hired a former General Motors (GM) executive named Walter Chrysler to reorganize the company. By 1925, he had taken over the company and renamed it Chrysler. By 1933, Chrysler was booming, with sales surpassing even those of Ford.

But the next few decades saw Chrysler make a series of blunders. By 1980, with its creditors pounding at the gates, Chrysler was again on the brink of financial ruin.

At that point, Chrysler brought in a former Ford executive named Lee Iacocca to save the company. Iacocca argued that the United States could not afford to let Chrysler fail because of the loss of jobs. He convinced the federal government to grant loan guarantees—promises that if Chrysler failed to pay its creditors, the government would pay them. Iacocca then

streamlined operations and brought out some profitable products. Chrysler repaid all of its government-guarantee loans by 1983, seven years ahead of the scheduled final payment.

To compete in today's global vehicle market, you must be big—really big. So in 1998, Chrysler merged with German automaker Daimler-Benz to form DaimlerChrysler. For a t this left just two U.S.-based auto manufacturers—GM ar Ford. But in 2007, DaimlerChrysler sold 81% of Chrysler Cerberus, an investment group, to provide much-needed infusions to the automaker. In 2009, Daimler turned ove remaining stake to Cerberus. Three days later, Chrysler fi for bankruptcy. But by 2010, it was beginning to show s of a turnaround.

The car companies are giants. GM and Ford typically ran among the top five U.S. firms in total assets. But GM an Ford accumulated truckloads of debt on their way to get big. Although debt made it possible to get so big, the Chrysler story, and GM's recent bankruptcy, make it clea debt can also threaten a company's survival.

✔ **The Navigator**

- ☐ Scan Learning Objectives
- ☐ Read Feature Story
- ☐ Read Preview
- ☐ Read text and answer **DO IT!** p. 690
  - ☐ p. 694 ☐ p. 696 ☐ p. 698
  - ☐ p. 702
- ☐ Work Comprehensive **DO IT!** p. 702
- ☐ Review Summary of Learning Objectives
- ☐ Answer Self-Test Questions
- ☐ Complete Assignments
- ☐ Go to *WileyPLUS* for practice and tutorials
- 🌐 **Read A Look at IFRS** p. 735

Learning Objectives ✔ The Navigator

After studying this chapter, you should be able to:

[1] Explain why bonds are issued.

[2] Prepare the entries for the issuance of bonds and interest expense.

[3] Describe the entries when bonds are redeemed or converted.

[4] Describe the accounting for long-term notes payable.

[5] Contrast the accounting for operating and capital leases.

[6] Identify the methods for the presentation and analysis of long-term liabilities.

Preview of Chapter 15

✔ The Navigator

As you can see from the Feature Story, having liabilities can be dangerous in difficult economic times. In this chapter, we will explain the accounting for the major types of long-term liabilities reported on the balance sheet. **Long-term liabilities** are obligations that are expected to be paid more than one year in the future. These liabilities may be bonds, long-term notes, or lease obligations.

The content and organization of Chapter 15 are as follows.

LONG-TERM LIABILITIES				
Bond Basics	**Bond Issuances**	**Bond Redemptions**	**Other Long-Term Liabilities**	**Statement Presentation and Analysis**
• Types of bonds • Issuing procedures • Market price	• Issuing bonds at face value • Discount or premium • Issuing bonds at a discount • Issuing bonds at a premium	• Redeeming bonds at maturity • Redeeming bonds before maturity • Converting bonds into common stock	• Long-term notes payable • Lease liabilities	• Presentation • Analysis

© Henrik Jonsson/iStockphoto

Bond Basics

LEARNING OBJECTIVE   **1**

Explain why bonds are issued.

Bonds are a form of interest-bearing notes payable. To obtain **large amounts of long-term capital**, corporate management usually must decide whether to issue common stock (equity financing) or bonds (debt financing). Bonds offer three advantages over common stock, as shown in Illustration 15-1.

Illustration 15-1
Advantages of bond financing over common stock

Bond Financing	Advantages
Ballot	1. **Stockholder control is not affected.** Bondholders do not have voting rights, so current owners (stockholders) retain full control of the company.
Tax Bill	2. **Tax savings result.** Bond interest is deductible for tax purposes; dividends on stock are not.
$ / STOCK	3. **Return on common stockholders' equity may be higher.** Although bond interest expense reduces net income, return on common stockholders' equity often is higher under bond financing because no additional shares of common stock are issued.

As Illustration 15-1 shows, one reason to issue bonds is that they do not affect stockholder control. Because bondholders do not have voting rights, owners can raise capital with bonds and still maintain corporate control. In addition, bonds are attractive to corporations because the cost of bond interest is tax-deductible. As a result of this tax treatment, which stock dividends do not offer, bonds may result in lower cost of capital than equity financing.

To illustrate another advantage of bond financing, assume that Microsystems, Inc. is considering two plans for financing the construction of a new $5 million plant. Plan A involves issuance of 200,000 shares of common stock at the current market price of $25 per share. Plan B involves issuance of $5 million, 8% bonds at face value. Income before interest and taxes on the new plant will be $1.5 million. Income taxes are expected to be 30%. Microsystems currently has 100,000 shares of common stock outstanding. Illustration 15-2 shows the alternative effects on earnings per share.

Illustration 15-2
Effects on earnings per share—stocks vs. bonds

	Plan A Issue Stock	Plan B Issue Bonds
Income before interest and taxes	$1,500,000	$1,500,000
Interest (8% × $5,000,000)	—	400,000
Income before income taxes	1,500,000	1,100,000
Income tax expense (30%)	450,000	330,000
Net income	$1,050,000	$ 770,000
Outstanding shares	300,000	100,000
Earnings per share	**$3.50**	**$7.70**

Note that net income is $280,000 less ($1,050,000 − $770,000) with long-term debt financing (bonds). However, earnings per share is higher because there are 200,000 fewer shares of common stock outstanding.

One disadvantage in using bonds is that the company must **pay interest** on a periodic basis. In addition, the company must also **repay the principal** at the due date. A company with fluctuating earnings and a relatively weak cash position may have great difficulty making interest payments when earnings are low.

A corporation may also obtain long-term financing from notes payable and leasing. However, notes payable and leasing are seldom sufficient to furnish the amount of funds needed for plant expansion and major projects like new buildings.

Bonds are sold in relatively small denominations (usually $1,000 multiples). As a result of their size and the variety of their features, bonds attract many investors.

Helpful Hint Besides corporations, governmental agencies and universities also issue bonds to raise capital.

Types of Bonds

Bonds may have many different features. In the following sections, we describe the types of bonds commonly issued.

SECURED AND UNSECURED BONDS

Secured bonds have specific assets of the issuer pledged as collateral for the bonds. A bond secured by real estate, for example, is called a **mortgage bond**. A bond secured by specific assets set aside to redeem (retire) the bonds is called a **sinking fund bond**.

Unsecured bonds, also called **debenture bonds**, are issued against the general credit of the borrower. Companies with good credit ratings use these bonds extensively. For example, at one time, DuPont reported over $2 billion of debenture bonds outstanding.

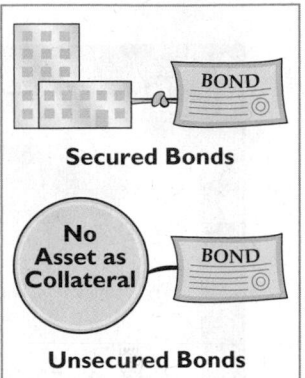
Secured Bonds

Unsecured Bonds

TERM AND SERIAL BONDS

Bonds that mature–are due for payment–at a single specified future date are **term bonds**. In contrast, bonds that mature in installments are **serial bonds**.

REGISTERED AND BEARER BONDS

Bonds issued in the name of the owner are **registered bonds**. Interest payments on registered bonds are made by check to bondholders of record. Bonds not registered are **bearer** (or **coupon**) **bonds**. Holders of bearer bonds must send in coupons to receive interest payments. Most bonds issued today are registered bonds.

CONVERTIBLE AND CALLABLE BONDS

Bonds that can be converted into common stock at the bondholder's option are **convertible bonds**. The conversion feature generally is attractive to bond buyers. Bonds that the issuing company can redeem (buy back) at a stated dollar amount prior to maturity are **callable bonds**. A call feature is included in nearly all corporate bond issues.

Convertible Bonds

Callable Bonds

Issuing Procedures

State laws grant corporations the power to issue bonds. Both the board of directors and stockholders usually must approve bond issues. **In authorizing the bond issue, the board of directors must stipulate the number of bonds to be authorized, total face value, and contractual interest rate.** The total bond authorization often exceeds the number of bonds the company originally issues. This gives the corporation the flexibility to issue more bonds, if needed, to meet future cash requirements.

The **face value** is the amount of principal due at the maturity date. The **maturity date** is the date that the final payment is due to the investor from the issuing company. The **contractual interest rate**, often referred to as the **stated rate**, is the rate used to determine the amount of cash interest the borrower pays and the investor receives. Usually the contractual rate is stated as an annual rate. Interest is generally paid semiannually.

The terms of the bond issue are set forth in a legal document called a **bond indenture**. The indenture shows the terms and summarizes the rights of the bondholders and their trustees, and the obligations of the issuing company. The **trustee** (usually a financial institution) keeps records of each bondholder, maintains custody of unissued bonds, and holds conditional title to pledged property.

Ethics Note

Some companies try to minimize the amount of debt reported on their balance sheet by not reporting certain types of commitments as liabilities. This subject is of intense interest in the financial community.

In addition, the issuing company arranges for the printing of **bond certificates**. The indenture and the certificate are separate documents. As shown in Illustration 15-3, a bond certificate provides the following information: name of the issuer, face value, contractual interest rate, and maturity date. An investment company that specializes in selling securities generally sells the bonds for the issuing company.

Issuer of bonds

Maturity date

No. $5000

INTERNATIONAL MINERALS & CHEMICAL CORPORATION
11.875% SINKING FUND DEBENTURE DUE MAY 1, 2018
INTERNATIONAL MINERALS & CHEMICAL CORPORATION, a New York corporation (herein referred to as the "Company"), for value received, hereby promises to pay to

CUSIP 459884 AC 6
SEE REVERSE FOR CERTAIN DEFINITIONS

11.875%
DUE 2018

SPECIMEN

11.875%
DUE 2018

or registered assigns,
the principal sum of

FIVE THOUSAND DOLLARS

CERTIFICATE OF AUTHENTICATION
This is one of the Debentures described in the within-mentioned Indenture.
THE FIRST NATIONAL BANK OF CHICAGO,
Trustee,
By

INTERNATIONAL MINERALS & CHEMICAL CORPORATION

Authorized Officer

Attest:

Secretary

By

Chairman of the Board

Face or par value

Contractual interest rate

Illustration 15-3
Bond certificate

2014
$1 million

≠

2034
$1 million

Same dollars at different times are not equal.

Determining the Market Price of a Bond

If you were an investor wanting to purchase a bond, how would you determine how much to pay? To be more specific, assume that Coronet, Inc. issues a **zero-interest bond** (pays no interest) with a face value of $1,000,000 due in 20 years. For this bond, the only cash you receive is a million dollars at the end of 20 years. Would you pay a million dollars for this bond? We hope not! A million dollars received 20 years from now is not the same as a million dollars received today.

The term **time value of money** is used to indicate the relationship between time and money—that a dollar received today is worth more than a dollar promised at some time in the future. If you had $1 million today, you would invest it. From that investment, you would earn interest such that at the end of 20 years, you would have much more than $1 million. Thus, if someone is going to pay you $1 million 20 years from now, you would want to find its equivalent today, or its present value. In other words, you would want to determine the value today of the amount to be received in the future after taking into account current interest rates.

The current market price (present value) of a bond is the value at which it should sell in the marketplace. Market price therefore is a function of the three factors that determine present value: (1) the dollar amounts to be received, (2) the length of time until the amounts are received, and (3) the market rate of interest. The **market interest rate** is the rate investors demand for loaning funds. Appendix 15A discusses the process of finding the present value for bonds. Appendix G near the end of the textbook also provides additional material for time value of money computations.

ACCOUNTING ACROSS THE ORGANIZATION

How About Those 30-Year Bonds?

Companies like Philip Morris International, Medtronic Inc., Plains All American Pipeline LP, and Simon Properties Group all sold 30-year bonds in 2012. The chart below indicates that companies are on pace to issue a record number of investment-grade bonds of 30-year maturities in 2012.

These companies are looking to extend their debt to lock in low interest rates and take advantage of investor demand.

The issuers of these bonds are benefitting from "a massive sentiment shift" says one bond expert. The belief that the economy will recover is making investors more comfortable holding longer-term bonds, as they search for investments that offer better returns than U.S. Treasury bonds.

Source: Vipal Monga, "The Big Number," *Wall Street Journal* (March 20, 2012), p. B5.

 What are the advantages for companies of issuing 30-year bonds instead of 5-year bonds? (See page 735.)

> **DO IT!**

Bond Terminology

State whether each of the following statements is true or false.

_____ **1.** Mortgage bonds and sinking fund bonds are both examples of secured bonds.

_____ **2.** Unsecured bonds are also known as debenture bonds.

_____ **3.** The stated rate is the rate investors demand for loaning funds.

_____ **4.** The face value is the amount of principal the issuing company must pay at the maturity date.

_____ **5.** The market price of a bond is equal to its maturity value.

Action Plan

✔ Review the types of bonds and the basic terms associated with bonds.

Solution

1. True.

2. True.

3. False.   The stated rate is the contractual interest rate used to determine the amount of cash interest the borrower pays.

4. True.

5. False.   The market price of a bond is the value at which it should sell in the marketplace. As a result, the present value of the bond and its maturity value are often different.

Related exercise material: **BE15-1, E15-1, E15-2, and DO IT! 15-1.**

✔ **The Navigator**

Accounting for Bond Issues

LEARNING OBJECTIVE   2

Prepare the entries for the issuance of bonds and interest expense.

A corporation records bond transactions when it issues (sells) or redeems (buys back) bonds and when bondholders convert bonds into common stock. If bondholders sell their bond investments to other investors, the issuing firm receives no further money on the transaction, **nor does the issuing corporation journalize the transaction** (although it does keep records of the names of bondholders in some cases).

Bonds may be issued at face value, below face value (discount), or above face value (premium). Bond prices for both new issues and existing bonds are quoted as **a percentage of the face value of the bond. Face value is usually $1,000.** Thus, a $1,000 bond with a quoted price of 97 means that the selling price of the bond is 97% of face value, or $970.

Issuing Bonds at Face Value

To illustrate the accounting for bonds issued at face value, assume that on January 1, 2014, Candlestick, Inc. issues $100,000, five-year, 10% bonds at 100 (100% of face value). The entry to record the sale is:

A = L + SE
+100,000
        +100,000

Cash Flows
+100,000

Jan. 1	Cash	100,000	
	Bonds Payable		100,000
	(To record sale of bonds at face value)		

Candlestick reports bonds payable in the long-term liabilities section of the balance sheet because the maturity date is January 1, 2019 (more than one year away).

Over the term (life) of the bonds, companies make entries to record bond interest. Interest on bonds payable is computed in the same manner as interest on notes payable, as explained in Chapter 11 (page 524). Assume that interest is payable semiannually on January 1 and July 1 on the Candlestick bonds. In that case, Candlestick must pay interest of $5,000 ($100,000 × 10% × 6/12) on July 1, 2014. The entry for the payment, assuming no previous accrual of interest, is:

July 1	Interest Expense	5,000	
	Cash		5,000
	(To record payment of bond interest)		

At December 31, Candlestick recognizes the $5,000 of interest expense incurred since July 1 with the following adjusting entry:

Dec. 31	Interest Expense	5,000	
	Interest Payable		5,000
	(To accrue bond interest)		

Companies classify interest payable as a current liability because it is scheduled for payment within the next year. When Candlestick pays the interest on January 1, 2015, it debits (decreases) Interest Payable and credits (decreases) Cash for $5,000.

Candlestick records the payment on January 1 as follows.

Jan. 1	Interest Payable	5,000	
	Cash		5,000
	(To record payment of bond interest)		

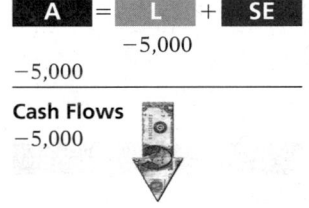

Discount or Premium on Bonds

The previous illustrations assumed that the contractual (stated) interest rate and the market (effective) interest rate paid on the bonds were the same. Recall that the **contractual interest rate** is the rate applied to the face (par) value to arrive at the interest paid in a year. The **market interest rate** is the rate investors demand for loaning funds to the corporation. When the contractual interest rate and the market interest rate are the same, bonds sell **at face value (par value)**.

However, market interest rates change daily. The type of bond issued, the state of the economy, current industry conditions, and the company's performance all affect market interest rates. As a result, contractual and market interest rates often differ. To make bonds salable when the two rates differ, bonds sell below or above face value.

To illustrate, suppose that a company issues 10% bonds at a time when other bonds of similar risk are paying 12%. Investors will not be interested in buying the 10% bonds, so their value will fall below their face value. When a bond is sold for less than its face value, the difference between the face value of a bond and its selling price is called a **discount**. As a result of the decline in the bonds' selling price, the actual interest rate incurred by the company increases to the level of the current market interest rate.

Conversely, if the market rate of interest is **lower than** the contractual interest rate, investors will have to pay more than face value for the bonds. That is, if the market rate of interest is 8% but the contractual interest rate on the bonds is 10%, the price of the bonds will be bid up. When a bond is sold for more than its face value, the difference between the face value and its selling price is called a **premium**. Illustration 15-4 (page 692) shows these relationships graphically.

Illustration 15-4
Interest rates and bond prices

Issuance of bonds at an amount different from face value is quite common. By the time a company prints the bond certificates and markets the bonds, it will be a coincidence if the market rate and the contractual rate are the same. Thus, the issuance of bonds at a discount does not mean that the issuer's financial strength is suspect. Conversely, the sale of bonds at a premium does not indicate that the financial strength of the issuer is exceptional.

Issuing Bonds at a Discount

To illustrate issuance of bonds at a discount, assume that on January 1, 2014, Candlestick, Inc. sells $100,000, five-year, 10% bonds for $92,639 (92.639% of face value). Interest is payable on July 1 and January 1. The entry to record the issuance is:

+92,639
   −7,361
   +100,000

Cash Flows
+92,639

Jan. 1	Cash	92,639	
	Discount on Bonds Payable	7,361	
	Bonds Payable		100,000
	(To record sale of bonds at a discount)		

Although Discount on Bonds Payable has a debit balance, **it is not an asset**. Rather, it is a **contra account**. This account is **deducted from bonds payable** on the balance sheet, as shown in Illustration 15-5.

Illustration 15-5
Statement presentation of
discount on bonds payable

CANDLESTICK, INC.
Balance Sheet (partial)

Long-term liabilities		
Bonds payable	$100,000	
Less: Discount on bonds payable	**7,361**	$92,639

Helpful Hint Carrying value (book value) of bonds issued at a discount is determined by subtracting the balance of the discount account from the balance of the Bonds Payable account.

The $92,639 represents the **carrying (or book) value** of the bonds. On the date of issue, this amount equals the market price of the bonds.

The issuance of bonds below face value—at a discount—causes the total cost of borrowing to differ from the bond interest paid. That is, the issuing corporation must pay not only the contractual interest rate over the term of the bonds but also the face value (rather than the issuance price) at maturity. Therefore, the difference between the issuance price and face value of the bonds—the discount—is an

additional cost of borrowing. The company records this additional cost as **interest expense** over the life of the bonds. Appendices 15B and 15C show the procedures for recording this additional cost.

The total cost of borrowing $92,639 for Candlestick, Inc. is $57,361, computed as follows.

Illustration 15-6
Total cost of borrowing—bonds issued at a discount

Bonds Issued at a Discount	
Semiannual interest payments ($100,000 × 10% × ½ = $5,000; $5,000 × 10)	$50,000
Add: Bond discount ($100,000 − $92,639)	7,361
Total cost of borrowing	**$57,361**

Alternatively, we can compute the total cost of borrowing as follows.

Illustration 15-7
Alternative computation of total cost of borrowing—bonds issued at a discount

Bonds Issued at a Discount	
Principal at maturity	$100,000
Semiannual interest payments ($5,000 × 10)	50,000
Cash to be paid to bondholders	150,000
Cash received from bondholders	92,639
Total cost of borrowing	**$ 57,361**

Issuing Bonds at a Premium

To illustrate the issuance of bonds at a premium, we now assume the Candlestick, Inc. bonds described above sell for $108,111 (108.111% of face value) rather than for $92,639. The entry to record the sale is:

Jan. 1	Cash	108,111	
	Bonds Payable		100,000
	Premium on Bonds Payable		8,111
	(To record sale of bonds at a premium)		

A = L + SE
+108,111
+100,000
+8,111

Cash Flows
+108,111

Candlestick adds the premium on bonds payable **to the bonds payable amount** on the balance sheet, as shown in Illustration 15-8.

Illustration 15-8
Statement presentation of bond premium

CANDLESTICK, INC.
Balance Sheet (partial)

Long-term liabilities		
Bonds payable	$100,000	
Add: Premium on bonds payable	**8,111**	**$108,111**

Helpful Hint
Premium on Bonds Payable

Decrease Debit	Increase Credit
	↓
	Normal Balance

The sale of bonds above face value causes the total cost of borrowing to be **less than the bond interest paid**. The reason: The borrower is not required to pay the bond premium at the maturity date of the bonds. Thus, the bond premium is considered to be **a reduction in the cost of borrowing**. The company credits the bond premium to Interest Expense over the life of the bonds. Appendices 15B and 15C show the procedures for recording this reduction in the cost of borrowing. The total cost of borrowing $108,111 for Candlestick, Inc. is computed as follows.

Illustration 15-9
Total cost of borrowing—bonds issued at a premium

Bonds Issued at a Premium	
Semiannual interest payments	
($100,000 × 10% × ½ = $5,000; $5,000 × 10)	$ 50,000
Less: Bond premium ($108,111 − $100,000)	8,111
Total cost of borrowing	**$41,889**

Alternatively, we can compute the cost of borrowing as follows.

Illustration 15-10
Alternative computation of total cost of borrowing—bonds issued at a premium

Bonds Issued at a Premium	
Principal at maturity	$100,000
Semiannual interest payments ($5,000 × 10)	50,000
Cash to be paid to bondholders	150,000
Cash received from bondholders	108,111
Total cost of borrowing	**$ 41,889**

> DO IT!

Bond Issuance

Giant Corporation issues $200,000 of bonds for $189,000. (a) Prepare the journal entry to record the issuance of the bonds, and (b) show how the bonds would be reported on the balance sheet at the date of issuance.

Solution

Action Plan

✔ Record cash received, bonds payable at face value, and the difference as a discount or premium.

✔ Report discount as a deduction from bonds payable and premium as an addition to bonds payable.

(a)

Cash	189,000	
Discount on Bonds Payable	11,000	
Bonds Payable		200,000
(To record sale of bonds at a discount)		

(b)

Long-term liabilities		
Bonds payable	$200,000	
Less: Discount on bonds payable	11,000	$189,000

Related exercise material: **BE15-2, BE15-3, BE15-4, E15-3, E15-4, E15-7,** and **DO IT!** 15-2.

✔ **The Navigator**

Accounting for Bond Redemptions

LEARNING OBJECTIVE	3

Describe the entries when bonds are redeemed or converted.

An issuing corporation retires bonds either when it buys back (redeems) the bonds or when bondholders convert them into common stock. We explain the entries for these transactions in the following sections.

Redeeming Bonds at Maturity

Regardless of the issue price of bonds, the book value of the bonds at maturity will equal their face value. Assuming that the company pays and records separately the interest for the last interest period, Candlestick records the redemption of its bonds at maturity as follows.

Jan. 1	Bonds Payable	100,000	
	Cash		100,000
	(To record redemption of bonds at maturity)		

A = L + SE
−100,000
−100,000

Cash Flows
−100,000

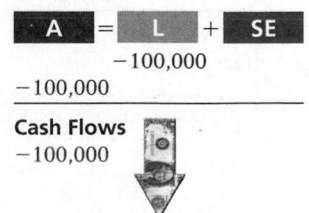

Redeeming Bonds before Maturity

Bonds also may be redeemed before maturity. A company may decide to redeem bonds before maturity to reduce interest cost and to remove debt from its balance sheet. A company should redeem debt early only if it has sufficient cash resources.

When a company redeems bonds before maturity, it is necessary to (1) eliminate the carrying value of the bonds at the redemption date, (2) record the cash paid, and (3) recognize the gain or loss on redemption. The **carrying value** of the bonds is the face value of the bonds less any remaining bond discount or plus any remaining bond premium at the redemption date.

To illustrate, assume that Candlestick, Inc. has sold its bonds at a premium. At the end of the eighth period, Candlestick redeems these bonds at 103 after paying the semiannual interest. Assume also that the carrying value of the bonds at the redemption date is $101,623. Candlestick makes the following entry to record the redemption at the end of the eighth interest period (January 1, 2018).

Helpful Hint Question: A bond is redeemed prior to its maturity date. Its carrying value exceeds its redemption price. Will this result in a gain or a loss on redemption? Answer: Gain.

Jan. 1	Bonds Payable	100,000	
	Premium on Bonds Payable	1,623	
	Loss on Bond Redemption	1,377	
	Cash		103,000
	(To record redemption of bonds at 103)		

A = L + SE
−100,000
−1,623
−1,377 Exp
−103,000

Cash Flows
−103,000

Note that the loss of $1,377 is the difference between the cash paid of $103,000 and the carrying value of the bonds of $101,623.

Converting Bonds into Common Stock

Convertible bonds have features that are attractive both to bondholders and to the issuer. The conversion often gives bondholders an opportunity to benefit if the market price of the common stock increases substantially. Until conversion, though, the bondholder receives interest on the bond. For the issuer of convertible bonds, the bonds sell at a higher price and pay a lower rate of interest than comparable debt securities without the conversion option. Many corporations, such as Intel, Ford, and Wells Fargo, have convertible bonds outstanding.

When the issuing company records a conversion, the company ignores the current market prices of the bonds and stock. Instead, the company transfers the **carrying value** of the bonds to paid-in capital accounts. **No gain or loss is recognized.**

To illustrate, assume that on July 1, Saunders Associates converts $100,000 bonds sold at face value into 2,000 shares of $10 par value common stock. Both the bonds and the common stock have a market value of $130,000. Saunders makes the following entry to record the conversion.

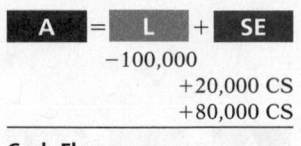

Cash Flows
no effect

July 1	Bonds Payable	100,000	
	Common Stock		20,000
	Paid-in Capital in Excess of Par—		
	Common Stock		80,000
	(To record bond conversion)		

Note that the company does not consider the current market value of the bonds and stock ($130,000) in making the entry. This method of recording the bond conversion is often referred to as the **carrying (or book) value method**.

> ## DO IT!

Bond Redemption

R & B Inc. issued $500,000, 10-year bonds at a premium. Prior to maturity, when the carrying value of the bonds is $508,000, the company redeems the bonds at 102. Prepare the entry to record the redemption of the bonds.

Solution

Action Plan

✔ Determine and eliminate the carrying value of the bonds.

✔ Record the cash paid.

✔ Compute and record the gain or loss (the difference between the first two items).

There is a loss on redemption. The cash paid, $510,000 ($500,000 × 102%), is greater than the carrying value of $508,000. The entry is:

Bonds Payable	500,000	
Premium on Bonds Payable	8,000	
Loss on Bond Redemption	2,000	
Cash		510,000
(To record redemption of bonds at 102)		

Related exercise material: **BE15-5, E15-5, E15-6, E15-8, E15-9, and DO IT! 15-3.**

✔ The Navigator

Accounting for Other Long-Term Liabilities

LEARNING OBJECTIVE 4

Describe the accounting for long-term notes payable.

Other common types of long-term obligations are notes payable and lease liabilities. The accounting for these liabilities is explained in the following sections.

Long-Term Notes Payable

The use of notes payable in long-term debt financing is quite common. **Long-term notes payable** are similar to short-term interest-bearing notes payable except that the term of the notes exceeds one year. In periods of unstable interest rates, lenders may tie the interest rate on long-term notes to changes in the market rate for comparable loans. Examples are the 8.03% adjustable rate notes issued by General Motors and the floating-rate notes issued by American Express Company.

A long-term note may be secured by a **mortgage** that pledges title to specific assets as security for a loan. Individuals widely use **mortgage notes payable** to purchase homes, and many small and some large companies use them to acquire plant assets. At one time, approximately 18% of McDonald's long-term debt related to mortgage notes on land, buildings, and improvements.

Like other long-term notes payable, the mortgage loan terms may stipulate either a **fixed** or an **adjustable** interest rate. The interest rate on a fixed-rate mortgage remains the same over the life of the mortgage. The interest rate on an adjustable-rate mortgage is adjusted periodically to reflect changes in the market rate of interest. Typically, the terms require the borrower to make equal installment payments over the term of the loan. Each payment consists of (1) interest on the unpaid balance of the loan and (2) a reduction of loan principal. While the total amount of the payment remains constant, the interest decreases each period, while the portion applied to the loan principal increases.

Companies initially record mortgage notes payable at face value. They subsequently make entries for each installment payment. To illustrate, assume that Porter Technology Inc. issues a $500,000, 12%, 20-year mortgage note on December 31, 2014, to obtain needed financing for a new research laboratory. The terms provide for semiannual installment payments of $33,231 (not including real estate taxes and insurance). The installment payment schedule for the first two years is as follows.

Semiannual Interest Period	(A) Cash Payment	(B) Interest Expense (D) × 6%	(C) Reduction of Principal (A) − (B)	(D) Principal Balance (D) − (C)
12/31/14				$500,000
06/30/15	$33,231	$30,000	$3,231	496,769
12/31/15	33,231	29,806	3,425	493,344
06/30/16	33,231	29,601	3,630	489,714
12/31/16	33,231	29,383	3,848	485,866

Illustration 15-11
Mortgage installment payment schedule

Porter records the mortgage loan on December 31, 2014, as follows.

Dec. 31	Cash	500,000	
	Mortgage Payable		500,000
	(To record mortgage loan)		

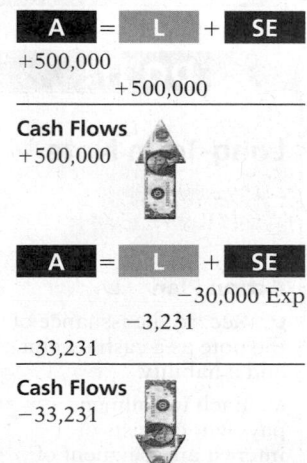

A = L + SE
+500,000
+500,000

Cash Flows
+500,000

On June 30, 2015, Porter records the first installment payment as follows.

June 30	Interest Expense	30,000	
	Mortgage Payable	3,231	
	Cash		33,231
	(To record semiannual payment on mortgage)		

A = L + SE
−30,000 Exp
−3,231
−33,231

Cash Flows
−33,231

In the balance sheet, the company reports the reduction in principal for the next year as a current liability, and it classifies the remaining unpaid principal balance as a long-term liability. At December 31, 2015, the total liability is $493,344. Of that amount, $7,478 ($3,630 + $3,848) is current, and $485,866 ($493,344 − $7,478) is long-term.

ACCOUNTING ACROSS THE ORGANIZATION

Bonds versus Notes?

Companies have a choice in the form of long-term borrowing they undertake—issue bonds or issue notes. Notes are generally issued to a single lender (usually through a loan from a bank). Bonds, on the other hand, allow the company to divide the borrowing into many small investing units, thereby enabling more than one investor to participate in the borrowing. As indicated in the graph below, companies are recently borrowing more from bond investors than from banks and other loan providers in a bid to lock in cheap, long-term funding.

Corporate Bonds/Corporate Loans

Why this trend? For one thing, low interest rates and rising inflows into fixed-income funds have triggered record bond issuances as banks cut back lending. In addition, for some high-rated companies, it can be riskier to borrow from a bank than the bond markets. The reason: High-rated companies tended to rely on short-term financing to fund working capital but were left stranded when these markets froze up. Some are now financing themselves with longer-term bonds instead.

Source: A. Sakoui and N. Bullock, "Companies Choose Bonds for Cheap Funds," *Financial Times* (October 12, 2009).

? Why might companies prefer bond financing instead of short-term financing? (See page 735.)

> DO IT!

Long-Term Note

Cole Research issues a $250,000, 8%, 20-year mortgage note to obtain needed financing for a new lab. The terms call for semiannual payments of $12,631 each. Prepare the entries to record the mortgage loan and the first installment payment.

Action Plan

✔ Record the issuance of the note as a cash receipt and a liability.

✔ Each installment payment consists of interest and payment of principal.

Solution

Cash	250,000	
Mortgage Payable		250,000
(To record mortgage loan)		
Interest Expense	10,000*	
Mortgage Payable	2,361	
Cash		12,361
(To record semiannual payment on mortgage)		

*Interest expense = $250,000 × 8% × 6/12.

Related exercise material: **BE15-6, E15-10, E15-11,** and **DO IT!** 15-4.

 ✔ The Navigator

Lease Liabilities

A lease is a contractual arrangement between a lessor (owner of the property) and a lessee (renter of the property). It grants the right to use specific property for a period of time in return for cash payments. Leasing is big business. The global leasing market has recently been between $600 to $700 billion for capital equipment. This represents approximately one-third of equipment financed in a year. The two most common types of leases are operating leases and capital leases.

LEARNING OBJECTIVE	5

Contrast the accounting for operating and capital leases.

OPERATING LEASES

The renting of an apartment and the rental of a car at an airport are examples of **operating leases**. **In an operating lease, the intent is temporary use of the property by the lessee, while the lessor continues to own the property.**

In an operating lease, the lessee records the lease (or rental) payments as an expense. The lessor records the payments as revenue. For example, assume that a sales representative for Western Inc. leases a car from Hertz Car Rental at the Los Angeles airport and that Hertz charges a total of $275. Western, the lessee, records the rental as follows.

Rent Expense	275	
Cash		275
(To record payment of lease rental charge)		

A	=	L	+	SE
				−275 Exp
−275				

Cash Flows
−275

The lessee may incur other costs during the lease period. For example, in the case above, Western will generally incur costs for gas. Western would report these costs as an expense.

CAPITAL LEASES

In most lease contracts, the lessee makes a periodic payment and records that payment in the income statement as rent expense. In some cases, however, the lease contract transfers to the lessee substantially all the benefits and risks of ownership. Such a lease is in effect a purchase of the property. This type of lease is a **capital lease**. Its name comes from the fact that the company capitalizes the present value of the cash payments for the lease and records that amount as an asset. Illustration 15-12 indicates the major difference between operating and capital leases.

Illustration 15-12
Types of leases

Operating lease	Capital lease
Lessor has substantially all of the benefits and risks of ownership	**Lessee** has substantially all of the benefits and risks of ownership

Helpful Hint A capital lease situation is one that, although legally a rental case, is *in substance* an installment purchase by the lessee. Accounting standards require that substance over form be used in such a situation.

If **any one** of the following conditions exists, the lessee must record a lease **as an asset**—that is, as a capital lease:

1. **The lease transfers ownership of the property to the lessee.** *Rationale:* If during the lease term the lessee receives ownership of the asset, the lessee should report the leased item as an asset on its books.

2. **The lease contains a bargain purchase option.** *Rationale:* If during the term of the lease the lessee can purchase the asset at a price substantially below its fair value, the lessee will exercise this option. Thus, the lessee should report the leased item as an asset on its books.

3. **The lease term is equal to 75% or more of the economic life of the leased property.** *Rationale:* If the lease term is for much of the asset's useful life, the lessee should report the leased item as an asset on its books.

4. **The present value of the lease payments equals or exceeds 90% of the fair value of the leased property.** *Rationale:* If the present value of the lease payments is equal to or almost equal to the fair value of the asset, the lessee has essentially purchased the asset. As a result, the lessee should report the leased item as an asset on its books.

To illustrate, assume that Gonzalez Company decides to lease new equipment. The lease period is four years. The economic life of the leased equipment is estimated to be five years. The present value of the lease payments is $190,000, which is equal to the fair value of the equipment. There is no transfer of ownership during the lease term, nor is there any bargain purchase option.

In this example, Gonzalez has essentially purchased the equipment. Conditions 3 and 4 have been met. First, the lease term is 75% or more of the economic life of the asset. Second, the present value of cash payments is equal to the equipment's fair value. Gonzalez records the transaction as follows.

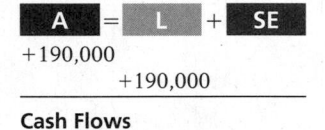

+190,000

   +190,000

Cash Flows
no effect

Leased Asset—Equipment	190,000	
Lease Liability		190,000
(To record leased asset and lease liability)		

The lessee reports a leased asset on the balance sheet under plant assets. It reports the lease liability on the balance sheet as a liability. **The portion of the lease liability expected to be paid in the next year is a current liability. The remainder is classified as a long-term liability.**

Most lessees do not like to report leases on their balance sheets. Why? Because the lease liability increases the company's total liabilities. This, in turn, may make it more difficult for the company to obtain needed funds from lenders. As a result, companies attempt to keep leased assets and lease liabilities off the balance sheet by structuring leases so as not to meet any of the four conditions discussed earlier. The practice of keeping liabilities off the balance sheet is referred to as **off–balance-sheet financing**.

Ethics Note

Accounting standard-setters are attempting to rewrite rules on lease accounting because of concerns that abuse of the current standards is reducing the usefulness of financial statements.

Statement Presentation and Analysis

LEARNING OBJECTIVE   6

Identify the methods for the presentation and analysis of long-term liabilities.

Presentation

Companies report long-term liabilities in a separate section of the balance sheet immediately following current liabilities, as shown in Illustration 15-13. Alternatively, companies may present summary data in the balance sheet, with detailed data (interest rates, maturity dates, conversion privileges, and assets pledged as collateral) shown in a supporting schedule.

LAX CORPORATION
Balance Sheet (partial)

Long-term liabilities		
Bonds payable 10% due in 2019	$1,000,000	
Less: Discount on bonds payable	80,000	$ 920,000
Mortgage payable, 11%, due in 2025 and secured by plant assets		500,000
Lease liability		440,000
Total long-term liabilities		$1,860,000

Illustration 15-13
Balance sheet presentation of long-term liabilities

Companies report the current maturities of long-term debt under current liabilities if they are to be paid within one year or the operating cycle, whichever is longer.

Analysis

Long-term creditors and stockholders are interested in a company's long-run solvency. Of particular interest is the company's ability to pay interest as it comes due and to repay the face value of the debt at maturity. Here we look at two ratios that provide information about debt-paying ability and long-run solvency.

The **debt to assets ratio** measures the percentage of the total assets provided by creditors. It is computed by dividing debt (both current and long-term liabilities) by assets. To illustrate, we use data from a recent Kellogg Company annual report. The company reported total liabilities of $8,925 million, total assets of $11,200 million, interest expense of $295 million, income taxes of $476 million, and net income of $1,208 million. As shown in Illustration 15-14, Kellogg's debt to assets ratio is 79.7%. The higher the percentage of debt to assets, the greater the risk that the company may be unable to meet its maturing obligation.

Debt	÷	Assets	=	Debt to Assets Ratio
$8,925	÷	$11,200	=	79.7%

Illustration 15-14
Debt to assets ratio

Times interest earned indicates the company's ability to meet interest payments as they come due. It is computed by dividing income before income taxes and interest expense by interest expense. As shown in Illustration 15-15, Kellogg's times interest earned is 6.71 times. This interest coverage is considered safe.

Income before Income Taxes and Interest Expense	÷	Interest Expense	=	Times Interest Earned
$1,208 + $476 + $295	÷	$295	=	6.71 times

Illustration 15-15
Times interest earned

Paul Fleet/Alamy

INVESTOR INSIGHT

"Covenant-Lite" Debt

In many corporate loans and bond issuances, the lending agreement specifies debt covenants. These covenants typically are specific financial measures, such as minimum levels of retained earnings, cash flows, times interest earned, or other measures that a company must maintain during the life of the loan. If the company violates a covenant, it is considered to have violated the loan agreement. The creditors can then demand immediate repayment, or they can renegotiate the loan's terms. Covenants protect lenders because they enable lenders to step in and try to get their money back before the borrower gets too deep into trouble.

During the 1990s, most traditional loans specified between three to six covenants or "triggers." In more recent years, when lots of cash was available, lenders began reducing or completely eliminating covenants from loan agreements in order to be more competitive with other lenders. When the economy declined, lenders lost big money when companies defaulted.

Source: Cynthia Koons, "Risky Business: Growth of 'Covenant-Lite' Debt," *Wall Street Journal* (June 18, 2007), p. C2.

 How can financial ratios such as those covered in this chapter provide protection for creditors? (See page 735.)

> DO IT!

Lease Liability; Analysis of Long-Term Liabilities

Action Plan

✔ Record the present value of the lease payments as an asset and a liability.

✔ Use the formula for the debt to assets ratio (debt divided by assets).

FX Corporation leases new equipment on December 31, 2014. The lease transfers ownership to FX at the end of the lease. The present value of the lease payments is $240,000. After recording this lease, FX has assets of $2,000,000, liabilities of $1,200,000, and stockholders' equity of $800,000. (a) Prepare the entry to record the lease, and (b) compute and discuss the debt to assets ratio at year-end.

Solution

(a)

Leased Asset—Equipment	240,000	
Lease Liability		240,000
(To record leased asset and lease liability)		

(b) The debt to assets ratio = $1,200,000 ÷ $2,000,000 = 60%. This means that 60% of its assets were provided by creditors. The higher the percentage of debt to assets, the greater the risk that the company may be unable to meet its maturing obligations.

Related exercise material: **BE15-7, E15-12, E15-14, and DO IT! 15-5.**

 The Navigator

> Comprehensive DO IT!

Snyder Software Inc. has successfully developed a new spreadsheet program. To produce and market the program, the company needed $2 million of additional financing. On January 1, 2014, Snyder borrowed money as follows.

1. Snyder issued $500,000, 11%, 10-year convertible bonds. The bonds sold at face value and pay semiannual interest on January 1 and July 1. Each $1,000 bond is convertible into 30 shares of Snyder's $20 par value common stock.

2. Snyder issued $1 million, 10%, 10-year bonds at face value. Interest is payable semiannually on January 1 and July 1.

3. Snyder also issued a $500,000, 12%, 15-year mortgage payable. The terms provide for semiannual installment payments of $36,324 on June 30 and December 31.

Instructions

1. For the convertible bonds, prepare journal entries for:
   (a) The issuance of the bonds on January 1, 2014.
   (b) Interest expense on July 1 and December 31, 2014.
   (c) The payment of interest on January 1, 2015.
   (d) The conversion of all bonds into common stock on January 1, 2015, when the market price of the common stock was $67 per share.

2. For the 10-year, 10% bonds:
   (a) Journalize the issuance of the bonds on January 1, 2014.
   (b) Prepare the journal entries for interest expense in 2014. Assume no accrual of interest on June 30.
   (c) Prepare the entry for the redemption of the bonds at 101 on January 1, 2017, after paying the interest due on this date.

3. For the mortgage payable:
   (a) Prepare the entry for the issuance of the note on January 1, 2014.
   (b) Prepare a payment schedule for the first four installment payments.
   (c) Indicate the current and noncurrent amounts for the mortgage payable at December 31, 2014.

Solution to Comprehensive DO IT!

Action Plan

✔ Compute interest semiannually (six months).

✔ Record the accrual and payment of interest on appropriate dates.

✔ Record the conversion of the bonds into common stock by removing the book (carrying) value of the bonds from the liability account.

1. (a) 2014

Jan. 1	Cash		500,000	
	Bonds Payable			500,000
	(To record issue of 11%, 10-year convertible bonds at face value)			

(b) 2014

July 1	Interest Expense		27,500	
	Cash ($500,000 × 0.055)			27,500
	(To record payment of semiannual interest)			
Dec. 31	Interest Expense		27,500	
	Interest Payable			27,500
	(To record accrual of semiannual bond interest)			

(c) 2015

Jan. 1	Interest Payable		27,500	
	Cash			27,500
	(To record payment of accrued interest)			

(d) Jan. 1

	Bonds Payable		500,000	
	Common Stock			300,000*
	Paid-in Capital in Excess of Par—Common Stock			200,000
	(To record conversion of bonds into common stock)			

*($500,000 ÷ $1,000 = 500 bonds; 500 × 30 = 15,000 shares; 15,000 × $20 = $300,000)

Action Plan

✔ Record the issuance of the bonds.

✔ Compute interest expense for each period.

✔ Compute the loss on bond redemption as the excess of the cash paid over the carrying value of the redeemed bonds.

2. (a) 2014

Jan. 1	Cash		1,000,000	
	Bonds Payable			1,000,000
	(To record issuance of bonds)			

(b) 2014

July 1	Interest Expense	50,000	
	Cash		50,000
	(To record payment of semiannual interest)		
Dec. 31	Interest Expense	50,000	
	Interest Payable		50,000
	(To record accrual of semiannual interest)		

(c) 2017

Jan. 1	Bonds Payable	1,000,000	
	Loss on Bond Redemption	10,000*	
	Cash		1,010,000
	(To record redemption of bonds at 101)		

*($1,010,000 − $1,000,000)

Action Plan

✔ Compute periodic interest expense on a mortgage payable, recognizing that as the principal amount decreases, so does the interest expense.

✔ Record mortgage payments, recognizing that each payment consists of (1) interest on the unpaid loan balance and (2) a reduction of the loan principal.

3. (a) 2014

Jan. 1	Cash	500,000	
	Mortgage Payable		500,000
	(To record issuance of mortgage payable)		

(b)

Semiannual Interest Period	Cash Payment	Interest Expense	Reduction of Principal	Principal Balance
Issue date				$500,000
1	$36,324	$30,000	$6,324	493,676
2	36,324	29,621	6,703	486,973
3	36,324	29,218	7,106	479,867
4	36,324	28,792	7,532	472,335

(c) Current liability: $14,638 ($7,106 + $7,532)
Long-term liability: $472,335

✔ The Navigator

SUMMARY OF LEARNING OBJECTIVES

 The Navigator

1 Explain why bonds are issued. Companies may sell bonds to investors to raise long-term capital. Bonds offer the following advantages over common stock: (a) stockholder control is not affected, (b) tax savings result, and (c) earnings per share of common stock may be higher.

2 Prepare the entries for the issuance of bonds and interest expense. When companies issue bonds, they debit Cash for the cash proceeds and credit Bonds Payable for the face value of the bonds. The account Premium on Bonds Payable shows a bond premium. Discount on Bonds Payable shows a bond discount.

3 Describe the entries when bonds are redeemed or converted. When bondholders redeem bonds at maturity, the issuing company credits Cash and debits Bonds Payable for the face value of the bonds. When bonds are redeemed before maturity, the issuing company

(a) eliminates the carrying value of the bonds at the redemption date, (b) records the cash paid, and (c) recognizes the gain or loss on redemption. When bonds are converted to common stock, the issuing company transfers the carrying (or book) value of the bonds to appropriate paid-in capital accounts. No gain or loss is recognized.

4 Describe the accounting for long-term notes payable. Each payment consists of (1) interest on the unpaid balance of the loan and (2) a reduction of loan principal. The interest decreases each period, while the portion applied to the loan principal increases.

5 Contrast the accounting for operating and capital leases. For an operating lease, the lessee (renter) records lease (rental) payments as an expense. For a capital lease, the lessee records the asset and related obligation at the present value of the future lease payments.

6 Identify the methods for the presentation and analysis of long-term liabilities. Companies should report the nature and amount of each long-term debt in the balance sheet or in the notes accompanying the financial statements. Stockholders and long-term creditors are interested in a company's long-run solvency. Debt to assets and times interest earned are two ratios that provide information about debt-paying ability and long-run solvency.

GLOSSARY

Bearer (coupon) bonds Bonds not registered in the name of the owner. (p. 687).

Bond certificate A legal document that indicates the name of the issuer, the face value of the bonds, the contractual interest rate, and maturity date of the bonds. (p. 688).

Bond indenture A legal document that sets forth the terms of the bond issue. (p. 687).

Bonds A form of interest-bearing notes payable issued by corporations, universities, and governmental entities. (p. 686).

Callable bonds Bonds that are subject to redemption (buy back) at a stated dollar amount prior to maturity at the option of the issuer. (p. 687).

Capital lease A contractual arrangement that transfers substantially all the benefits and risks of ownership to the lessee so that the lease is in effect a purchase of the property. (p. 699).

Contractual interest rate Rate used to determine the amount of cash interest the borrower pays and the investor receives. (p. 687).

Convertible bonds Bonds that permit bondholders to convert them into common stock at the bondholders' option. (p. 687).

Debenture bonds Bonds issued against the general credit of the borrower. Also called unsecured bonds. (p. 687).

Debt to assets ratio A solvency measure that indicates the percentage of total assets provided by creditors; computed as debt divided by assets. (p. 701).

Discount (on a bond) The difference between the face value of a bond and its selling price, when the bond is sold for less than its face value. (p. 691).

Face value Amount of principal due at the maturity date of the bond. (p. 687).

Long-term liabilities Obligations expected to be paid more than one year in the future. (p. 685).

Market interest rate The rate investors demand for loaning funds to the corporation. (p. 689).

Maturity date The date on which the final payment on the bond is due from the bond issuer to the investor. (p. 687).

Mortgage bond A bond secured by real estate. (p. 687).

Mortgage notes payable A long-term note secured by a mortgage that pledges title to specific assets as security for a loan. (p. 696).

Operating lease A contractual arrangement giving the lessee temporary use of the property, with continued ownership of the property by the lessor. (p. 699).

Premium (on a bond) The difference between the selling price and the face value of a bond, when the bond is sold for more than its face value. (p. 691).

Registered bonds Bonds issued in the name of the owner. (p. 687).

Secured bonds Bonds that have specific assets of the issuer pledged as collateral. (p. 687).

Serial bonds Bonds that mature in installments. (p. 687).

Sinking fund bonds Bonds secured by specific assets set aside to redeem them. (p. 687).

Term bonds Bonds that mature at a single specified future date. (p. 687).

Times interest earned A solvency measure that indicates a company's ability to meet interest payments; computed by dividing income before income taxes and interest expense by interest expense. (p. 701).

Time value of money The relationship between time and money. A dollar received today is worth more than a dollar promised at some time in the future. (p. 688).

Unsecured bonds Bonds issued against the general credit of the borrower. Also called debenture bonds. (p. 687).

APPENDIX 15A   Present Value Concepts Related to Bond Pricing

Congratulations! You have a winning lottery ticket and the state has provided you with three possible options for payment. They are:

1. Receive $10,000,000 in three years.
2. Receive $7,000,000 immediately.
3. Receive $3,500,000 at the end of each year for three years.

LEARNING OBJECTIVE	7
Compute the market price of a bond.	

Which of these options would you select? The answer is not easy to determine at a glance. To make a dollar-maximizing choice, you must perform present value computations. A present value computation is based on the concept of time value of money. Time value of money concepts are useful for the lottery situation and for pricing other amounts to be received in the future. This appendix discusses how to use present value concepts to price bonds. It also will tell you how to determine what option you should take as a lottery winner.

Present Value of a Single Amount

To illustrate present value concepts, assume that you are willing to invest a sum of money that will yield $1,000 at the end of one year. In other words, what amount would you need to invest today to have $1,000 one year from now? If you want to earn 10%, the investment (or present value) is $909.09 ($1,000 ÷ 1.10). Illustration 15A-1 shows the computation.

Illustration 15A-1
Present value computation—
$1,000 discounted at 10%
for one year

Present Value	×	(1 + Interest Rate)	=	Future Amount
Present value	×	(1 + 10%)	=	$1,000
Present value			=	$1,000 ÷ 1.10
Present value			=	$909.09

The future amount ($1,000), the interest rate (10%), and the number of periods (1) are known. We can depict the variables in this situation as shown in the time diagram in Illustration 15A-2.

Illustration 15A-2
Finding present value if
discounted for one period

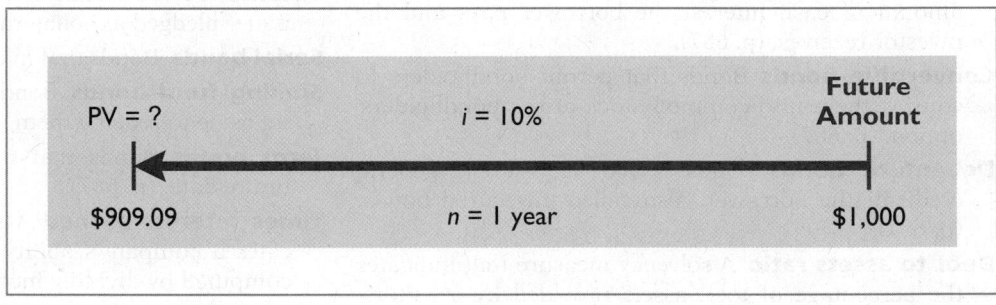

If you are to receive the single future amount of $1,000 **in two years**, discounted at 10%, its present value is $826.45 [($1,000 ÷ 1.10) ÷ 1.10], depicted as follows.

Illustration 15A-3
Finding present value if
discounted for two periods

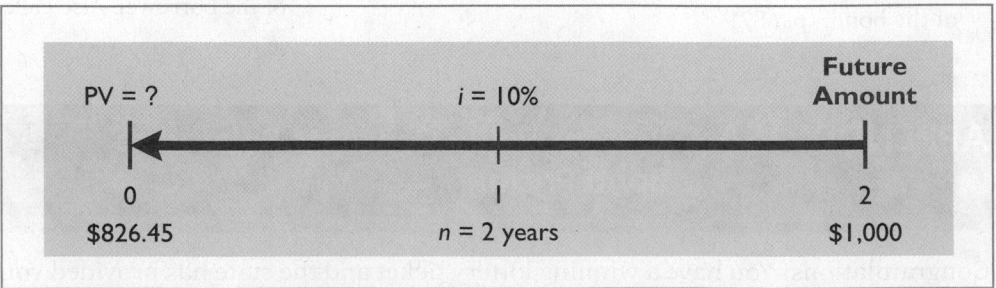

We also can determine the present value of 1 through tables that show the present value of 1 for n periods. In Table 15A-1, n is the number of discounting periods involved. The percentages are the periodic interest rates or discount rates, and the 5-digit decimal numbers in the respective columns are the present value of 1 factors.

When using Table 15A-1, we multiply the future amount by the present value factor specified at the intersection of the number of periods and the interest rate. For example, the present value factor for 1 period at an interest rate of 10% is .90909, which equals the $909.09 ($1,000 × .90909) computed in Illustration 15A-1.

TABLE 15A-1
Present Value of 1

(n) Periods	4%	5%	6%	7%	8%	9%	10%	11%	12%	15%
1	.96154	.95238	.94340	.93458	.92593	.91743	.90909	.90090	.89286	.86957
2	.92456	.90703	.89000	.87344	.85734	.84168	.82645	.81162	.79719	.75614
3	.88900	.86384	.83962	.81630	.79383	.77218	.75132	.73119	.71178	.65752
4	.85480	.82270	.79209	.76290	.73503	.70843	.68301	.65873	.63552	.57175
5	.82193	.78353	.74726	.71299	.68058	.64993	.62092	.59345	.56743	.49718
6	.79031	.74622	.70496	.66634	.63017	.59627	.56447	.53464	.50663	.43233
7	.75992	.71068	.66506	.62275	.58349	.54703	.51316	.48166	.45235	.37594
8	.73069	.67684	.62741	.58201	.54027	.50187	.46651	.43393	.40388	.32690
9	.70259	.64461	.59190	.54393	.50025	.46043	.42410	.39092	.36061	.28426
10	.67556	.61391	.55839	.50835	.46319	.42241	.38554	.35218	.32197	.24719

For two periods at an interest rate of 10%, the present value factor is .82645, which equals the $826.45 ($1,000 × .82645) computed previously.

Let's now go back to our lottery example. Given the present value concepts just learned, we can determine whether receiving $10,000,000 in three years is better than receiving $7,000,000 today, assuming the appropriate discount rate is 9%. The computation is as follows.

Illustration 15A-4
Present value of $10,000,000 to be received in three years

$10,000,000 × PV of 1 due in 3 years at 9% =	
$10,000,000 × .77218 (Table 15A-1)	$7,721,800
Amount to be received from state immediately	7,000,000
Difference	$ 721,800

What this computation shows you is that you would be $721,800 better off receiving the $10,000,000 at the end of three years rather than taking $7,000,000 immediately.

Present Value of Interest Payments (Annuities)

In addition to receiving the face value of a bond at maturity, an investor also receives periodic interest payments over the life of the bonds. These periodic payments are called **annuities**.

In order to compute the present value of an annuity, we need to know: (1) the interest rate, (2) the number of interest periods, and (3) the amount of the periodic receipts or payments. To illustrate the computation of the present value of an annuity, assume that you will receive $1,000 cash annually for three years and the interest rate is 10%. The time diagram in Illustration 15A-5 (page 708) depicts this situation.

Illustration 15A-5
Time diagram for a three-year annuity

The present value in this situation may be computed as follows.

Illustration 15A-6
Present value of a series of future amounts computation

Future Amount	×	Present Value of 1 Factor at 10%	=	Present Value
$1,000 (1 year away)		.90909		$ 909.09
1,000 (2 years away)		.82645		826.45
1,000 (3 years away)		.75132		751.32
		2.48686		**$2,486.86**

We also can use annuity tables to value annuities. As illustrated in Table 15A-2 below, these tables show the present value of 1 to be received periodically for a given number of periods.

TABLE 15A-2
Present Value of an Annuity of 1

(n) Periods	4%	5%	6%	7%	8%	9%	10%	11%	12%	15%
1	.96154	.95238	.94340	.93458	.92593	.91743	.90909	.90090	.89286	.86957
2	1.88609	1.85941	1.83339	1.80802	1.78326	1.75911	1.73554	1.71252	1.69005	1.62571
3	2.77509	2.72325	2.67301	2.62432	2.57710	2.53130	2.48685	2.44371	2.40183	2.28323
4	3.62990	3.54595	3.46511	3.38721	3.31213	3.23972	3.16986	3.10245	3.03735	2.85498
5	4.45182	4.32948	4.21236	4.10020	3.99271	3.88965	3.79079	3.69590	3.60478	3.35216
6	5.24214	5.07569	4.91732	4.76654	4.62288	4.48592	4.35526	4.23054	4.11141	3.78448
7	6.00205	5.78637	5.58238	5.38929	5.20637	5.03295	4.86842	4.71220	4.56376	4.16042
8	6.73274	6.46321	6.20979	5.97130	5.74664	5.53482	5.33493	5.14612	4.96764	4.48732
9	7.43533	7.10782	6.80169	6.51523	6.24689	5.99525	5.75902	5.53705	5.32825	4.77158
10	8.11090	7.72173	7.36009	7.02358	6.71008	6.41766	6.14457	5.88923	5.65022	5.01877

From Table 15A-2 you can see that the present value factor of an annuity of 1 for three periods at 10% is 2.48685.[1] This present value factor is the total of the three individual present value factors as shown in Illustration 15A-6. Applying this amount to the annual cash flow of $1,000 produces a present value of $2,486.85.

Let's now go back to our lottery example. We determined that you would get more money if you wait and take the $10,000,000 in three years rather than take

---

[1]The difference of .00001 between 2.48686 and 2.48685 is due to rounding.

$7,000,000 immediately. But there is still another option—to receive $3,500,000 at the end of **each year** for three years (an annuity). The computation to evaluate this option (again assuming a 9% discount rate) is as follows.

$3,500,000 × PV of 1 due yearly for 3 years at 9% =	
$3,500,000 × 2.53130 (Table 15A-2)	$8,859,550
Present value of $10,000,000 to be received in 3 years	7,721,800
Difference	$1,137,750

Illustration 15A-7
Present value of lottery payments to be received over three years

If you take the annuity of $3,500,000 for each of 3 years, you will be $1,137,750 richer as a result.

Time Periods and Discounting

We have used an **annual** interest rate to determine present value. Present value computations may also be done over shorter periods of time, such as monthly, quarterly, or semiannually. When the time frame is less than one year, it is necessary to convert the annual interest rate to the shorter time frame.

Assume, for example, that the investor in Illustration 15A-6 received $500 **semiannually** for three years instead of $1,000 annually. In this case, the number of periods becomes 6 (3 × 2), the interest rate is 5% (10% ÷ 2), the present value factor from Table 15A-2 is 5.07569, and the present value of the future cash flows is $2,537.85 (5.07569 × $500). This amount is slightly higher than the $2,486.86 computed in Illustration 15A-6 because interest is computed twice during the same year. That is, interest is earned on the first half year's interest.

Computing the Present Value of a Bond

The present value (or market price) of a bond is a function of three variables: (1) the payment amounts, (2) the length of time until the amounts are paid, and (3) the interest (discount) rate.

The first variable (dollars to be paid) is made up of two elements: (1) a series of interest payments (an annuity), and (2) the principal amount (a single sum). To compute the present value of the bond, we must discount both the interest payments and the principal amount.

When the investor's interest (discount) rate is equal to the bond's contractual interest rate, the present value of the bonds will equal the face value of the bonds. To illustrate, assume a bond issue of 10%, five-year bonds with a face value of $100,000 with interest payable **semiannually** on January 1 and July 1. If the discount rate is the same as the contractual rate, the bonds will sell **at face value**. In this case, the investor will receive: (1) $100,000 at maturity and (2) a series of ten $5,000 interest payments [$100,000 × (10% ÷ 2)] over the term of the bonds. The length of time is expressed in terms of interest periods (in this case, 10) and the discount rate per interest period (5%). The time diagram in Illustration 15A-8 (page 710) depicts the variables involved in this discounting situation.

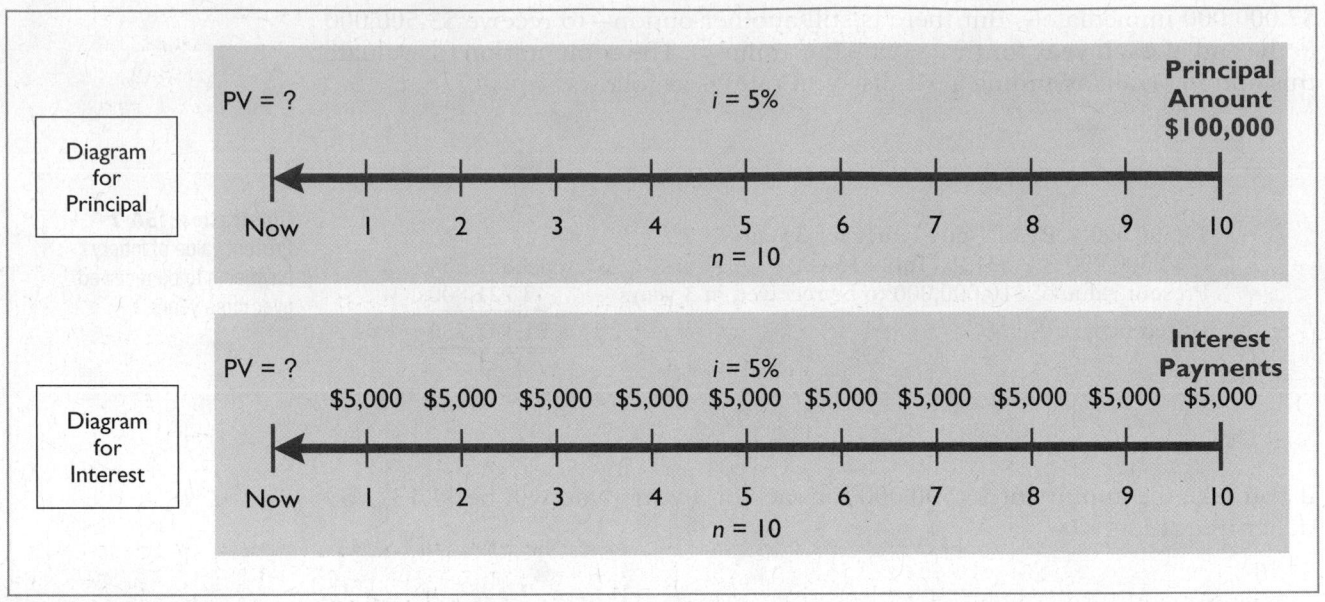

Illustration 15A-8
Time diagram for the present value of a 10%, five-year bond paying interest semiannually

Illustration 15A-9
Present value of principal and interest (face value)

The computation of the present value of Candlestick's bonds, assuming they were issued at face value (page 690), is shown below.

10% Contractual Rate—10% Discount Rate

Present value of principal to be received at maturity	
$100,000 × PV of 1 due in 10 periods at 5%	
$100,000 × .61391 (Table 15A-1)	$ 61,391
Present value of interest to be received periodically over the term of the bonds	
$5,000 × PV of 1 due periodically for 10 periods at 5%	
$5,000 × 7.72173 (Table 15A-2)	38,609*
Present value of bonds	**$100,000**

*(Rounded).

Now assume that the investor's required rate of return is 12%, not 10%. The future amounts are again $100,000 and $5,000, respectively. But now we must use a discount rate of 6% (12% ÷ 2). The present value of Candlestick's bonds issued at a discount (page 692) is $92,639 as computed below.

Illustration 15A-10
Present value of principal and interest (discount)

10% Contractual Rate—12% Discount Rate

Present value of principal to be received at maturity	
$100,000 × .55839 (Table 15A-1)	$ 55,839
Present value of interest to be received periodically over the term of the bonds	
$5,000 × 7.36009 (Table 15A-2)	36,800
Present value of bonds	**$92,639**

If the discount rate is 8% and the contractual rate is 10%, the present value of Candlestick's bonds issued at a premium (page 693) is $108,111, computed as shown in Illustration 15A-11.

10% Contractual Rate—8% Discount Rate	
Present value of principal to be received at maturity	
$100,000 × .67556 (Table 15A-1)	$ 67,556
Present value of interest to be received periodically over the term of the bonds	
$5,000 × 8.11090 (Table 15A-2)	40,555
Present value of bonds	**$108,111**

Illustration 15A-11
Present value of principal and interest (premium)

SUMMARY OF LEARNING OBJECTIVE FOR APPENDIX 15A

7 Compute the market price of a bond. Time value of money concepts are useful for pricing bonds. The present value (or market price) of a bond is a function of three variables: (1) the payment amounts, (2) the length of time until the amounts are paid, and (3) the interest rate.

APPENDIX 15B   Effective-Interest Method of Bond Amortization

Under the **effective-interest method**, the amortization of bond discount or bond premium results in periodic interest expense equal to a **constant percentage** of the carrying value of the bonds. The effective-interest method results in varying amounts of amortization and interest expense per period but **a constant percentage rate**.

The following steps are required under the effective-interest method.

LEARNING OBJECTIVE 8

Apply the effective-interest method of amortizing bond discount and bond premium.

1. Compute the **bond interest expense**. To do so, multiply the carrying value of the bonds at the beginning of the interest period by the effective-interest rate.
2. Compute the **bond interest paid** (or accrued). To do so, multiply the face value of the bonds by the contractual interest rate.
3. Compute the **amortization amount**. To do so, determine the difference between the amounts computed in steps (1) and (2).

Illustration 15B-1 depicts these steps.

```
        (1)                              (2)                    (3)
 Bond Interest Expense            Bond Interest Paid

( Carrying Value        Effective-    ( Face        Contractual
  of Bonds at      ×    Interest   -    Amount of × Interest   ) =  Amortization
  Beginning of         Rate      )     Bonds        Rate            Amount
  Period )
```

Illustration 15B-1
Computation of amortization—effective-interest method

When the difference between the straight-line method of amortization (Appendix 15C) and the effective-interest method is material, GAAP requires the use of the effective-interest method.

Amortizing Bond Discount

To illustrate the effective-interest method of bond discount amortization, assume that Candlestick, Inc. issues $100,000 of 10%, five-year bonds on January 1, 2014, with interest payable each July 1 and January 1 (pages 692–693). The bonds sell for $92,639 (92.639% of face value). This sales price results in a bond discount of $7,361 ($100,000 − $92,639) and an effective-interest rate of 12%. A bond discount amortization schedule, as shown in Illustration 15B-2 (page 712), facilitates the recording of interest expense and the discount amortization. Note that interest expense as a percentage of carrying value remains constant at 6%.

			Candlestick Inc.xls			

Home   Insert   Page Layout   Formulas   Data   Review   View

P18   fx

	A	B	C	D	E	F
1			**CANDLESTICK, INC.**			
2			**Bond Discount Amortization**			
3			**Effective-Interest Method—Semiannual Interest Payments**			
4			**10% Bonds Issued at 12%**			
5						
6			**(B)** **Interest Expense**	**(C)**	**(D)**	**(E)**
7	**Semiannual**	**(A)**	**to Be Recorded**	**Discount**	**Unamortized**	**Bond**
8	**Interest**	**Interest to Be Paid**	**(6% × Preceding Bond**	**Amortization**	**Discount**	**Carrying Value**
	Periods	**(5% × $100,000)**	**Carrying Value)**	**(B) – (A)**	**(D) – (C)**	**($100,000 – D)**
9	Issue date				$7,361	$92,639
10	1	$ 5,000	$ 5,558 (6% × $92,639)	$ 558	6,803	93,197
11	2	5,000	5,592 (6% × $93,197)	592	6,211	93,789
12	3	5,000	5,627 (6% × $93,789)	627	5,584	94,416
13	4	5,000	5,665 (6% × $94,416)	665	4,919	95,081
14	5	5,000	5,705 (6% × $95,081)	705	4,214	95,786
15	6	5,000	5,747 (6% × $95,786)	747	3,467	96,533
16	7	5,000	5,792 (6% × $96,533)	792	2,675	97,325
17	8	5,000	5,840 (6% × $97,325)	840	1,835	98,165
18	9	5,000	5,890 (6% × $98,165)	890	945	99,055
19	10	5,000	5,945* (6% × $99,055)	945	–0–	100,000
20		$50,000	$57,361	$7,361		
21						
22	Column **(A)** remains constant because the face value of the bonds ($100,000) is multiplied by the semiannual contractual interest rate (5%) each period.					
23	Column **(B)** is computed as the preceding bond carrying value times the semiannual effective-interest rate (6%).					
24	Column **(C)** indicates the discount amortization each period.					
25	Column **(D)** decreases each period until it reaches zero at maturity.					
26	Column **(E)** increases each period until it equals face value at maturity.					
27						
28	*$2 difference due to rounding.					

Illustration 15B-2
Bond discount amortization schedule

We have highlighted columns (A), (B), and (C) in the amortization schedule to emphasize their importance. These three columns provide the numbers for each period's journal entries. They are the primary reason for preparing the schedule.

For the first interest period, the computations of interest expense and the bond discount amortization are:

Illustration 15B-3
Computation of bond discount amortization

Interest expense ($92,639 × 6%)	$5,558
Contractual interest ($100,000 × 5%)	5,000
Bond discount amortization	**$ 558**

Candlestick records the payment of interest and amortization of bond discount on July 1, 2014, as follows.

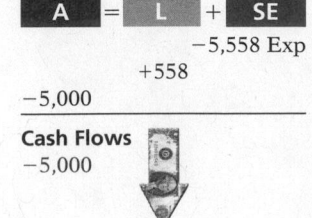

$A = L + SE$
            −5,558 Exp
    +558
−5,000

Cash Flows
−5,000

July 1	Interest Expense	5,558	
	Discount on Bonds Payable		558
	Cash		5,000
	(To record payment of bond interest and amortization of bond discount)		

For the second interest period, bond interest expense will be $5,592 ($93,197 × 6%), and the discount amortization will be $592. At December 31, Candlestick makes the following adjusting entry.

Dec. 31	Interest Expense	5,592	
	Discount on Bonds Payable		592
	Interest Payable		5,000
	(To record accrued interest and amortization of bond discount)		

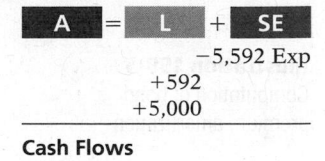

−5,592 Exp
+592
+5,000

Cash Flows
no effect

Total interest expense for 2014 is $11,150 ($5,558 + $5,592). On January 1, Candlestick records payment of the interest by a debit to Interest Payable and a credit to Cash.

Helpful Hint When a bond sells for $108,111, it is quoted as 108.111% of face value. Note that $108,111 can be proven as shown in Appendix 15A.

Amortizing Bond Premium

The amortization of bond premium by the effective-interest method is similar to the procedures described for bond discount. For example, assume that Candlestick, Inc. issues $100,000, 10%, five-year bonds on January 1, 2014, with interest payable on July 1 and January 1 (pages 693–694). In this case, the bonds sell for $108,111. This sales price results in bond premium of $8,111 and an effective-interest rate of 8%. Illustration 15B-4 shows the bond premium amortization schedule.

Illustration 15B-4
Bond premium amortization schedule

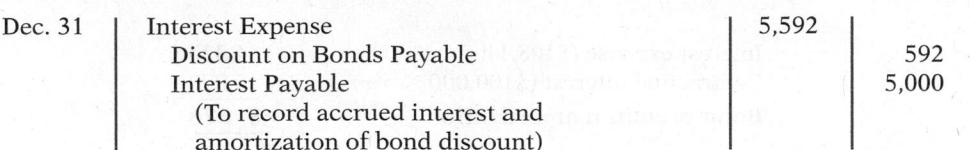

Candlestick Inc.xls

Home Insert Page Layout Formulas Data Review View

P18

	A	B	C		D	E	F
1			**CANDLESTICK, INC.**				
2			**Bond Premium Amortization**				
3			**Effective-Interest Method—Semiannual Interest Payments**				
4			**10% Bonds Issued at 8%**				
5							
6			**(B)**				
7	**Semiannual**	**(A)**	**Interest Expense to Be Recorded**		**(C)**	**(D)**	**(E)**
8	**Interest**	**Interest to Be Paid**	**(4% × Preceding Bond**		**Premium**	**Unamortized**	**Bond**
9	**Periods**	**(5% × $100,000)**	**Carrying Value)**		**Amortization (A) – (B)**	**Premium (D) – (C)**	**Carrying Value ($100,000 + D)**
10	Issue date					$8,111	$108,111
11	1	$ 5,000	$ 4,324	(4% × $108,111)	$ 676	7,435	107,435
12	2	5,000	4,297	(4% × $107,435)	703	6,732	106,732
13	3	5,000	4,269	(4% × $106,732)	731	6,001	106,001
14	4	5,000	4,240	(4% × $106,001)	760	5,241	105,241
15	5	5,000	4,210	(4% × $105,241)	790	4,451	104,451
16	6	5,000	4,178	(4% × $104,451)	822	3,629	103,629
17	7	5,000	4,145	(4% × $103,629)	855	2,774	102,774
18	8	5,000	4,111	(4% × $102,774)	889	1,885	101,885
19	9	5,000	4,075	(4% × $101,885)	925	960	100,960
20	10	5,000	4,040*	(4% × $100,960)	960	–0–	100,000
21		$50,000	$41,889		$8,111		
22							
23	Column **(A)** remains constant because the face value of the bonds ($100,000) is multiplied by the semiannual contractual interest rate (5%) each period.						
24	Column **(B)** is computed as the carrying value of the bonds times the semiannual effective-interest rate (4%).						
25	Column **(C)** indicates the premium amortization each period.						
26	Column **(D)** decreases each period until it reaches zero at maturity.						
27	Column **(E)** decreases each period until it equals face value at maturity.						
28							
29	*$2 difference due to rounding.						

8 Apply the effective-interest method of amortizing bond discount and bond premium. The effective-interest method results in varying amounts of amortization and interest expense per period but a constant percentage rate of interest. When the difference between the straight-line and effective-interest method is material, GAAP requires the use of the effective-interest method.

Effective-interest method of amortization A method of amortizing bond discount or bond premium that results in periodic interest expense equal to a constant percentage of the carrying value of the bonds. (p. 711).

APPENDIX 15C   Straight-Line Amortization

Amortizing Bond Discount

Under the **straight-line method of amortization**, the amortization of bond discount or bond premium results in periodic interest expense of the same amount in each interest period. In other words, the straight-line method results in a constant amount of amortization and interest expense per period. The amount is determined using the formula in Illustration 15C-1.

Bond Discount	÷	Number of Interest Periods	=	Bond Discount Amortization

> **LEARNING OBJECTIVE   9**
>
> Apply the straight-line method of amortizing bond discount and bond premium.

Illustration 15C-1
Formula for straight-line method of bond discount amortization

In the Candlestick, Inc. example (pages 692–693), the company sold $100,000, five-year, 10% bonds on January 1, 2014, for $92,639. This price resulted in a $7,361 bond discount ($100,000 − $92,639). Interest is payable on July 1 and January 1. The bond discount amortization for each interest period is $736 ($7,361 ÷ 10). Candlestick records the payment of bond interest and the amortization of bond discount on the first interest date (July 1, 2014) as follows.

July 1	Interest Expense	5,736	
	Discount on Bonds Payable		736
	Cash		5,000
	(To record payment of bond interest and amortization of bond discount)		

At December 31, Candlestick makes the following adjusting entry.

Dec. 31	Interest Expense	5,736	
	Discount on Bonds Payable		736
	Interest Payable		5,000
	(To record accrued bond interest and amortization of bond discount)		

A = L + SE
−5,736 Exp
+736
−5,000

Cash Flows
−5,000

A = L + SE
−5,736 Exp
+736
+5,000

Cash Flows
no effect

Over the term of the bonds, the balance in Discount on Bonds Payable will decrease annually by the **same amount** until it has a zero balance at the maturity date of the bonds. Thus, the carrying value of the bonds at maturity will be equal to the face value.

It is useful to prepare a bond discount amortization schedule as shown in Illustration 15C-2. The schedule shows interest expense, discount amortization, and the carrying value of the bond for each interest period. As indicated, the interest expense recorded **each period** for the Candlestick bond is $5,736. Also note that the carrying value of the bond increases $736 each period until it reaches its face value $100,000 at the end of period 10.

Illustration 15C-2
Bond discount amortization schedule

	Candlestick Inc.xls					
Home Insert Page Layout Formulas Data Review View						
P18	fx					
	A	B	C	D	E	F
1		**CANDLESTICK, INC.**				
2		**Bond Discount Amortization**				
3		**Straight-Line Method—Semiannual Interest Payments**				
4						
5	**Semiannual**	**(A)** **Interest to**	**(B)** **Interest Expense**	**(C)** **Discount**	**(D)** **Unamortized**	**(E)** **Bond**
6	**Interest**	**Be Paid**	**to Be Recorded**	**Amortization**	**Discount**	**Carrying Value**
7	**Periods**	**(5% × $100,000)**	**(A) + (C)**	**($7,361 ÷ 10)**	**(D) – (C)**	**($100,000 – D)**
8	Issue date				$7,361	$92,639
9	1	$ 5,000	$ 5,736	$ 736	6,625	93,375
10	2	5,000	5,736	736	5,889	94,111
11	3	5,000	5,736	736	5,153	94,847
12	4	5,000	5,736	736	4,417	95,583
13	5	5,000	5,736	736	3,681	96,319
14	6	5,000	5,736	736	2,945	97,055
15	7	5,000	5,736	736	2,209	97,791
16	8	5,000	5,736	736	1,473	98,527
17	9	5,000	5,736	736	737	99,263
18	10	5,000	5,737*	737*	–0–	100,000
19		$50,000	$57,361	$7,361		
20						
21	Column **(A)** remains constant because the face value of the bonds ($100,000) is multiplied by the semiannual contractual interest rate (5%) each period.					
22	Column **(B)** is computed as the interest paid (Column A) plus the discount amortization (Column C).					
23	Column **(C)** indicates the discount amortization each period.					
24	Column **(D)** decreases each period by the same amount until it reaches zero at maturity.					
25	Column **(E)** increases each period by the same amount of discount amortization until it equals the face value at maturity.					
26						
27	*One dollar difference due to rounding.					

We have highlighted columns (A), (B), and (C) in the amortization schedule to emphasize their importance. These three columns provide the numbers for each period's journal entries. They are the primary reason for preparing the schedule.

Amortizing Bond Premium

The amortization of bond premium parallels that of bond discount. Illustration 15C-3 presents the formula for determining bond premium amortization under the straight-line method.

Illustration 15C-3
Formula for straight-line method of bond premium amortization

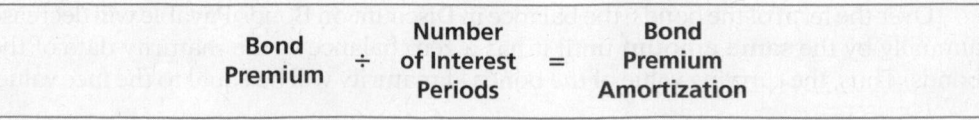

Continuing our example, assume that Candlestick sells the bonds for $108,111, rather than $92,639 (pages 693–694). This sale price results in a bond premium of $8,111 ($108,111 − $100,000). The bond premium amortization for each interest period is $811 ($8,111 ÷ 10). Candlestick records the first payment of interest on July 1 as follows.

July 1	Interest Expense	4,189	
	Premium on Bonds Payable	811	
	Cash		5,000
	(To record payment of bond interest and amortization of bond premium)		

At December 31, the company makes the following adjusting entry.

Dec. 31	Interest Expense	4,189	
	Premium on Bonds Payable	811	
	Interest Payable		5,000
	(To record accrued bond interest and amortization of bond premium)		

A = L + SE
−4,189 Exp
−811
−5,000

Cash Flows
−5,000

A = L + SE
−4,189 Exp
−811
+5,000

Cash Flows
no effect

Over the term of the bonds, the balance in Premium on Bonds Payable will decrease annually **by the same amount** until it has a zero balance at maturity.

It is useful to prepare a bond premium amortization schedule as shown in Illustration 15C-4. It shows interest expense, premium amortization, and the carrying

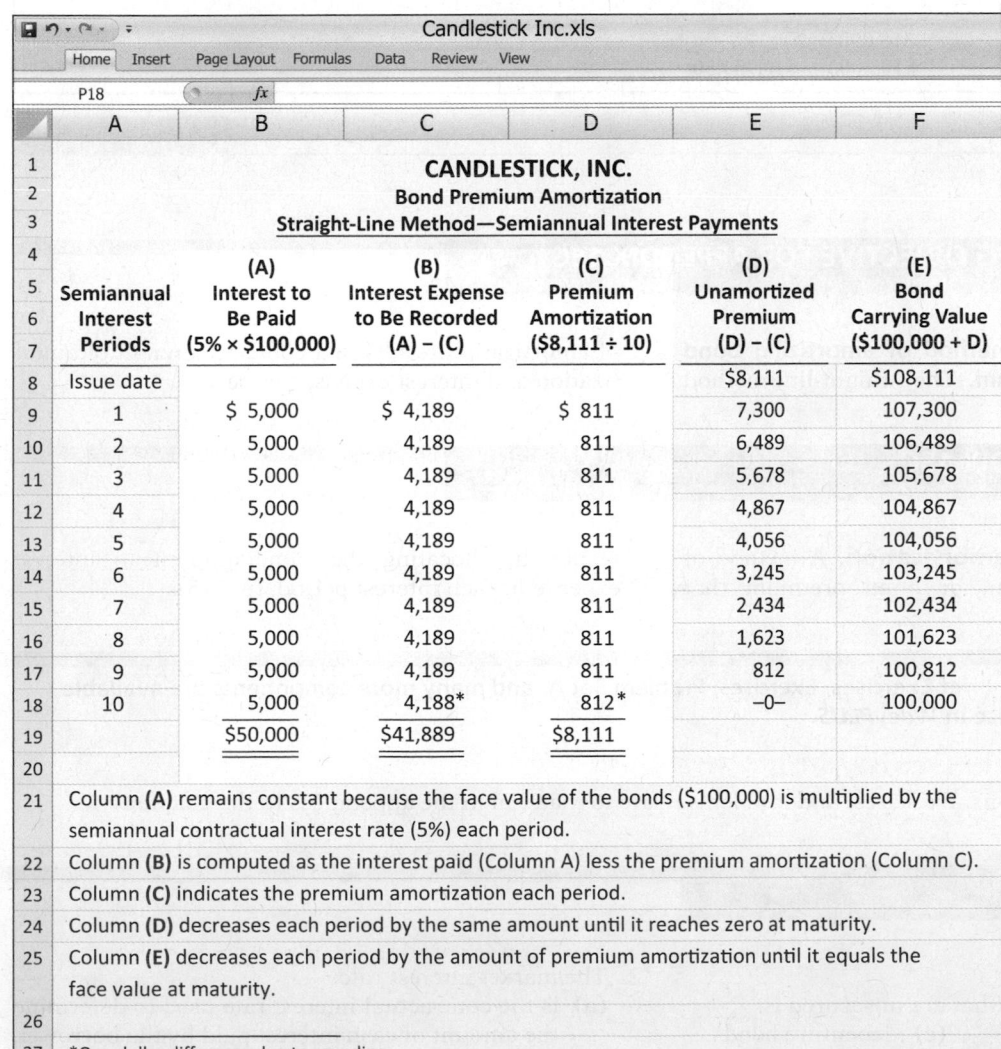

Semiannual Interest Periods	(A) Interest to Be Paid (5% × $100,000)	(B) Interest Expense to Be Recorded (A) − (C)	(C) Premium Amortization ($8,111 ÷ 10)	(D) Unamortized Premium (D) − (C)	(E) Bond Carrying Value ($100,000 + D)
Issue date				$8,111	$108,111
1	$ 5,000	$ 4,189	$ 811	7,300	107,300
2	5,000	4,189	811	6,489	106,489
3	5,000	4,189	811	5,678	105,678
4	5,000	4,189	811	4,867	104,867
5	5,000	4,189	811	4,056	104,056
6	5,000	4,189	811	3,245	103,245
7	5,000	4,189	811	2,434	102,434
8	5,000	4,189	811	1,623	101,623
9	5,000	4,189	811	812	100,812
10	5,000	4,188*	812*	–0–	100,000
	$50,000	$41,889	$8,111		

CANDLESTICK, INC.
Bond Premium Amortization
Straight-Line Method—Semiannual Interest Payments

Column **(A)** remains constant because the face value of the bonds ($100,000) is multiplied by the semiannual contractual interest rate (5%) each period.

Column **(B)** is computed as the interest paid (Column A) less the premium amortization (Column C).

Column **(C)** indicates the premium amortization each period.

Column **(D)** decreases each period by the same amount until it reaches zero at maturity.

Column **(E)** decreases each period by the amount of premium amortization until it equals the face value at maturity.

*One dollar difference due to rounding.

Illustration 15C-4
Bond premium amortization schedule

value of the bond. The interest expense recorded each period for the Candlestick bond is $4,189. Also note that the carrying value of the bond decreases $811 each period until it reaches its face value ($100,000) at the end of period 10.

> DO IT!

Glenda Corporation issues $1,750,000, 10-year, 12% bonds on January 1, 2014, for $1,968,090 to yield 10%. The bonds pay semiannual interest July 1 and January 1. Glenda uses the straight-line method of amortization.

Action Plan

✔ Compute credit to cash (or interest payable) by multiplying the face value of the bonds by the contractual interest rate.

✔ Compute bond premium or discount amortization by dividing bond premium or discount by the total number of periods.

✔ Understand that interest expense decreases when bonds are issued at a premium. The reason is that the amortization of premium reduces the total cost of borrowing.

Instructions
(a) Prepare the journal entry to record the issuance of the bonds.
(b) Prepare the journal entry to record the payment of interest on July 1, 2014.

Solution

(a)	2014			
	Jan. 1	Cash	1,968,090	
		Bonds Payable		1,750,000
		Premium on Bonds Payable		218,090
(b)	2014			
	July 1	Interest Expense	94,095.50**	
		Premium on Bonds Payable	10,904.50*	
		Cash		105,000

*$218,090 ÷ 20
**$105,000 − $10,904.50

 The Navigator

SUMMARY OF LEARNING OBJECTIVE FOR APPENDIX 15C

9 Apply the straight-line method of amortizing bond discount and bond premium. The straight-line method of amortization results in a constant amount of amortization and interest expense per period.

GLOSSARY FOR APPENDIX 15C

Straight-line method of amortization. A method of amortizing bond discount or bond premium that results in allocating the same amount to interest expense in each interest period. (p. 715).

 Self-Test, Brief Exercises, Exercises, Problem Set A, and many more components are available for practice in *WileyPLUS*.

***Note:** All asterisked Questions, Exercises, and Problems relate to material in the appendices to the chapter.

SELF-TEST QUESTIONS

Answers are on page 735.

(LO 1) **1.** The term used for bonds that are unsecured is:
  (a) callable bonds.
  (b) indenture bonds.
  (c) debenture bonds.
  (d) bearer bonds.

2. The market interest rate: (LO 1)
  (a) is the contractual interest rate used to determine the amount of cash interest paid by the borrower.
  (b) is listed in the bond indenture.

(c) is the rate investors demand for loaning funds.
(d) More than one of the above is true.

(LO 2) **3.** Karson Inc. issues 10-year bonds with a maturity value of $200,000. If the bonds are issued at a premium, this indicates that:
(a) the contractual interest rate exceeds the market interest rate.
(b) the market interest rate exceeds the contractual interest rate.
(c) the contractual interest rate and the market interest rate are the same.
(d) no relationship exists between the two rates.

(LO 2) **4.** Four-Nine Corporation issued bonds that pay interest every July 1 and January 1. The entry to accrue bond interest at December 31 includes a:
(a) debit to Interest Payable.
(b) credit to Cash.
(c) credit to Interest Expense.
(d) credit to Interest Payable.

(LO 3) **5.** Gester Corporation redeems its $100,000 face value bonds at 105 on January 1, following the payment of semiannual interest. The carrying value of the bonds at the redemption date is $103,745. The entry to record the redemption will include a:
(a) credit of $3,745 to Loss on Bond Redemption.
(b) debit of $3,745 to Premium on Bonds Payable.
(c) credit of $1,255 to Gain on Bond Redemption.
(d) debit of $5,000 to Premium on Bonds Payable.

(LO 3) **6.** Colson Inc. converts $600,000 of bonds sold at face value into 10,000 shares of common stock, par value $1. Both the bonds and the stock have a market value of $760,000. What amount should be credited to Paid-in Capital in Excess of Par—Common Stock as a result of the conversion?
(a) $10,000.   **(c)** $600,000.
(b) $160,000.   **(d)** $590,000.

(LO 4) **7.** Howard Corporation issued a 20-year mortgage note payable on January 1, 2014. At December 31, 2014, the unpaid principal balance will be reported as:
(a) a current liability.
(b) a long-term liability.
(c) part current and part long-term liability.
(d) interest payable.

(LO 4) **8.** Andrews Inc. issues a $497,000, 10% 3-year mortgage note on January 1. The note will be paid in three annual installments of $200,000, each payable at the end of the year. What is the amount of interest expense that should be recognized by Andrews Inc. in the second year?
(a) $16,567.   **(c)** $34,670.
(b) $49,700.   **(d)** $346,700.

(LO 5) **9.** Lease A does not contain a bargain purchase option, but the lease term is equal to 90% of the estimated economic life of the leased property. Lease B does not transfer ownership of the property to the lessee by the end of the lease term, but the lease term is equal to 75% of the estimated economic life of the leased property. How should the lessee classify these leases?

	Lease A	Lease B
(a)	Operating lease	Capital lease
(b)	Operating lease	Operating lease
(c)	Capital lease	Operating lease
(d)	Capital lease	Capital lease

(LO 6) **10.** For 2014, Corn Flake Corporation reported net income of $300,000. Interest expense was $40,000 and income taxes were $100,000. The times interest earned was:
(a) 3 times.   **(c)** 7.5 times.
(b) 4.4 times.   **(d)** 11 times.

(LO 7) *11. The market price of a bond is dependent on:
(a) the payment amounts.
(b) the length of time until the amounts are paid.
(c) the interest rate.
(d) All of the above.

(LO 8) *12. On January 1, Besalius Inc. issued $1,000,000, 9% bonds for $938,554. The market rate of interest for these bonds is 10%. Interest is payable annually on December 31. Besalius uses the effective-interest method of amortizing bond discount. At the end of the first year, Besalius should report unamortized bond discount of:
(a) $54,900.   **(c)** $51,610.
(b) $57,591.   **(d)** $51,000.

(LO 8) *13. On January 1, Dias Corporation issued $1,000,000, 10%, 5-year bonds with interest payable on July 1 and January 1. The bonds sold for $1,081,105. The market rate of interest for these bonds was 8%. On the first interest date, using the effective-interest method, the debit entry to Interest Expense is for:
(a) $50,000.   **(c)** $43,244.
(b) $54,055.   **(d)** $100,811.

(LO 9) *14. On January 1, Hurley Corporation issues $500,000, 5-year, 12% bonds at 96 with interest payable on July 1 and January 1. The entry on July 1 to record payment of bond interest and the amortization of bond discount using the straight-line method will include a:
(a) debit to Interest Expense $30,000.
(b) debit to Interest Expense $60,000.
(c) credit to Discount on Bonds Payable $4,000.
(d) credit to Discount on Bonds Payable $2,000.

(LO 9) *15. For the bonds issued in Question 14 above, what is the carrying value of the bonds at the end of the third interest period?
(a) $486,000.   **(c)** $472,000.
(b) $488,000.   **(d)** $464,000.

Go to the book's companion website, www.wiley.com/college/weygandt, for additional Self-Test Questions.

✔ **The Navigator**

QUESTIONS

1. (a) What are long-term liabilities? Give three examples. (b) What is a bond?

2. (a) As a source of long-term financing, what are the major advantages of bonds over common stock?

(b) What are the major disadvantages in using bonds for long-term financing?

3. Contrast the following types of bonds: (a) secured and unsecured, (b) term and serial, (c) registered and bearer, and (d) convertible and callable.

4. The following terms are important in issuing bonds: (a) face value, (b) contractual interest rate, (c) bond indenture, and (d) bond certificate. Explain each of these terms.

5. Describe the two major obligations incurred by a company when bonds are issued.

6. Assume that Remington Inc. sold bonds with a face value of $100,000 for $104,000. Was the market interest rate equal to, less than, or greater than the bonds' contractual interest rate? Explain.

7. If a 7%, 10-year, $800,000 bond is issued at face value and interest is paid semiannually, what is the amount of the interest payment at the end of the first semiannual period?

8. If the Bonds Payable account has a balance of $900,000 and the Discount on Bonds Payable account has a balance of $120,000, what is the carrying value of the bonds?

9. Which accounts are debited and which are credited if a bond issue originally sold at a premium is redeemed before maturity at 97 immediately following the payment of interest?

10. Rattigan Corporation is considering issuing a convertible bond. What is a convertible bond? Discuss the advantages of a convertible bond from the standpoint of (a) the bondholders and (b) the issuing corporation.

11. Rob Grier, a friend of yours, has recently purchased a home for $125,000, paying $25,000 down and the remainder financed by a 10.5%, 20-year mortgage, payable at $998.38 per month. At the end of the first month, Rob receives a statement from the bank indicating that only $123.38 of principal was paid during the month. At this rate, he calculates that it will take over 67 years to pay off the mortgage. Is he right? Discuss.

12. (a) What is a lease agreement? (b) What are the two most common types of leases? (c) Distinguish between the two types of leases.

13. Jhutti Company rents a warehouse on a month-to-month basis for the storage of its excess inventory. The company periodically must rent space when its production greatly exceeds actual sales. What is the nature of this type of lease agreement and what accounting treatment should be used?

14. Benedict Company entered into an agreement to lease 12 computers from Haley Electronics, Inc. The present value of the lease payments is $186,300. Assuming that this is a capital lease, what entry would Benedict Company make on the date of the lease agreement?

15. In general, what are the requirements for the financial statement presentation of long-term liabilities?

16. Did Apple redeem any of its debt during the fiscal year ended September 24, 2011? (*Hint:* Examine Apple's statement of cash flows.)

*17. Kelli Deane is discussing the advantages of the effective-interest method of bond amortization with her accounting staff. What do you think Kelli is saying?

*18. Windsor Corporation issues $500,000 of 9%, 5-year bonds on January 1, 2014, at 104. If Windsor uses the effective-interest method in amortizing the premium, will the annual interest expense increase or decrease over the life of the bonds? Explain.

*19. Jill Grey and Mike Goreman are discussing how the market price of a bond is determined. Jill believes that the market price of a bond is solely a function of the amount of the principal payment at the end of the term of a bond. Is she right? Discuss.

*20. Explain the straight-line method of amortizing discount and premium on bonds payable.

*21. DeWeese Corporation issues $400,000 of 8%, 5-year bonds on January 1, 2014, at 105. Assuming that the straight-line method is used to amortize the premium, what is the total amount of interest expense for 2014?

BRIEF EXERCISES

Compare bond versus stock financing.

(LO 1)

BE15-1 Moby Inc. is considering two alternatives to finance its construction of a new $2 million plant.

(a) Issuance of 200,000 shares of common stock at the market price of $10 per share.
(b) Issuance of $2 million, 8% bonds at face value.

Complete the following table, and indicate which alternative is preferable.

	Issue Stock	Issue Bond
Income before interest and taxes	$700,000	$700,000
Interest expense from bonds	_____	_____
Income before income taxes		
Income tax expense (30%)	_____	_____
Net income	$ _____	$ _____
Outstanding shares		500,000
Earnings per share	_____	_____

BE15-2 Meera Corporation issued 4,000, 8%, 5-year, $1,000 bonds dated January 1, 2014, at 100.

(a) Prepare the journal entry to record the sale of these bonds on January 1, 2014.
(b) Prepare the journal entry to record the first interest payment on July 1, 2014 (interest payable semiannually), assuming no previous accrual of interest.
(c) Prepare the adjusting journal entry on December 31, 2014, to record interest expense.

Prepare entries for bonds issued at face value.

(LO 2)

BE15-3 Nasreen Company issues $2 million, 10-year, 8% bonds at 97, with interest payable on July 1 and January 1.

(a) Prepare the journal entry to record the sale of these bonds on January 1, 2014.
(b) Assuming instead that the above bonds sold for 104, prepare the journal entry to record the sale of these bonds on January 1, 2014.

Prepare entries for bonds sold at a discount and a premium.

(LO 2)

BE15-4 Frankum Company has issued three different bonds during 2014. Interest is payable semiannually on each of these bonds.

1. On January 1, 2014, 1,000, 8%, 5-year, $1,000 bonds dated January 1, 2014, were issued at face value.
2. On July 1, $900,000, 9%, 5-year bonds dated July 1, 2014, were issued at 102.
3. On September 1, $400,000, 7%, 5-year bonds dated September 1, 2014, were issued at 98.

Prepare the journal entry to record each bond transaction at the date of issuance.

Prepare entries for bonds issued.

(LO 2)

BE15-5 The balance sheet for Miley Consulting reports the following information on July 1, 2014.

Long-term liabilities	
Bonds payable	$1,000,000
Less: Discount on bonds payable	60,000 $940,000

Miley decides to redeem these bonds at 101 after paying semiannual interest. Prepare the journal entry to record the redemption on July 1, 2014.

Prepare entry for redemption of bonds.

(LO 3)

BE15-6 Hanschu Inc. issues an $800,000, 10%, 10-year mortgage note on December 31, 2014, to obtain financing for a new building. The terms provide for semiannual installment payments of $64,195. Prepare the entry to record the mortgage loan on December 31, 2014, and the first installment payment.

Prepare entries for long-term notes payable.

(LO 4)

BE15-7 Prepare the journal entries that the lessee should make to record the following transactions.

1. The lessee makes a lease payment of $80,000 to the lessor in an operating lease transaction.
2. Imhoff Company leases a new building from Noble Construction, Inc. The present value of the lease payments is $700,000. The lease qualifies as a capital lease.

Contrast accounting for operating and capital leases.

(LO 5)

BE15-8 Presented below are long-term liability items for Lind Company at December 31, 2014. Prepare the long-term liabilities section of the balance sheet for Lind Company.

Bonds payable, due 2016	$600,000
Lease liability	70,000
Notes payable, due 2019	80,000
Discount on bonds payable	45,000

Prepare statement presentation of long-term liabilities.

(LO 6)

*BE15-9 (a) What is the present value of $10,000 due 8 periods from now, discounted at 10%?

(b) What is the present value of $20,000 to be received at the end of each of 6 periods, discounted at 8%?

Determine present value.

(LO 7)

*BE15-10 Presented below is the partial bond discount amortization schedule for Ferree Corp. Ferree uses the effective-interest method of amortization.

Use effective-interest method of bond amortization.

(LO 2, 8)

Semiannual Interest Periods	Interest to Be Paid	Interest Expense to Be Recorded	Discount Amortization	Unamortized Discount	Bond Carrying Value
Issue date				$62,311	$937,689
1	$45,000	$46,884	$1,884	60,427	939,573
2	45,000	46,979	1,979	58,448	941,552

(a) Prepare the journal entry to record the payment of interest and the discount amortization at the end of period 1.

(b) ⟶ Explain why interest expense is greater than interest paid.

(c) Explain why interest expense will increase each period.

Prepare entries for bonds issued at a discount.

(LO 2,9)

*BE15-11 Sweetwood Company issues $5 million, 10-year, 9% bonds at 96, with interest payable on July 1 and January 1. The straight-line method is used to amortize bond discount.

(a) Prepare the journal entry to record the sale of these bonds on January 1, 2014.

(b) Prepare the journal entry to record interest expense and bond discount amortization on July 1, 2014, assuming no previous accrual of interest.

Prepare entries for bonds issued at a premium.

(LO 2,9)

*BE15-12 Golden Inc. issues $4 million, 5-year, 10% bonds at 102, with interest payable on July 1 and January 1. The straight-line method is used to amortize bond premium.

(a) Prepare the journal entry to record the sale of these bonds on January 1, 2014.

(b) Prepare the journal entry to record interest expense and bond premium amortization on July 1, 2014, assuming no previous accrual of interest.

> DO IT! Review

Evaluate statements about bonds.

(LO 1)

DO IT! 15-1 State whether each of the following statements is true or false.

_____ **1.** Mortgage bonds and sinking fund bonds are both examples of debenture bonds.

_____ **2.** Convertible bonds are also known as callable bonds.

_____ **3.** The market rate is the rate investors demand for loaning funds.

_____ **4.** Semiannual interest on bonds is equal to the face value times the stated rate times 6/12.

_____ **5.** The present value of a bond is the value at which it should sell in the market.

Prepare journal entry for bond issuance and show balance sheet presentation.

(LO 2)

DO IT! 15-2 Eubank Corporation issues $500,000 of bonds for $520,000. (a) Prepare the journal entry to record the issuance of the bonds, and (b) show how the bonds would be reported on the balance sheet at the date of issuance.

Prepare entry for bond redemption.

(LO 3)

DO IT! 15-3 Prater Corporation issued $400,000 of 10-year bonds at a discount. Prior to maturity, when the carrying value of the bonds was $390,000, the company redeemed the bonds at 99. Prepare the entry to record the redemption of the bonds.

Prepare entries for mortgage note and installment payment on note.

(LO 4)

DO IT! 15-4 Detwiler Orchard issues a $700,000, 6%, 15-year mortgage note to obtain needed financing for a new lab. The terms call for semiannual payments of $35,714 each. Prepare the entries to record the mortgage loan and the first installment payment.

Prepare entry for lease, and compute debt to assets ratio.

(LO 5, 6)

DO IT! 15-5 Huebner Corporation leases new equipment on December 31, 2014. The lease transfers ownership of the equipment to Huebner at the end of the lease. The present value of the lease payments is $192,000. After recording this lease, Huebner has assets of $1,800,000, liabilities of $1,100,000, and stockholders' equity of $700,000. (a) Prepare the entry to record the lease, and (b) compute and discuss the debt to assets ratio at year-end.

EXERCISES

Evaluate statements about bonds.

(LO 1)

E15-1 Nick Bosch has prepared the following list of statements about bonds.

1. Bonds are a form of interest-bearing notes payable.

2. When seeking long-term financing, an advantage of issuing bonds over issuing common stock is that stockholder control is not affected.

3. When seeking long-term financing, an advantage of issuing common stock over issuing bonds is that tax savings result.

4. Secured bonds have specific assets of the issuer pledged as collateral for the bonds.

5. Secured bonds are also known as debenture bonds.

6. Bonds that mature in installments are called term bonds.

7. A conversion feature may be added to bonds to make them more attractive to bond buyers.

8. The rate used to determine the amount of cash interest the borrower pays is called the stated rate.
9. Bond prices are usually quoted as a percentage of the face value of the bond.
10. The present value of a bond is the value at which it should sell in the marketplace.

Instructions

Identify each statement as true or false. If false, indicate how to correct the statement.

E15-2 Gilliland Airlines is considering two alternatives for the financing of a purchase of a fleet of airplanes. These two alternatives are:

Compare two alternatives of financing—issuance of common stock vs. issuance of bonds.
(LO 1)

1. Issue 90,000 shares of common stock at $30 per share. (Cash dividends have not been paid nor is the payment of any contemplated.)
2. Issue 10%, 10-year bonds at face value for $2,700,000.

It is estimated that the company will earn $800,000 before interest and taxes as a result of this purchase. The company has an estimated tax rate of 30% and has 120,000 shares of common stock outstanding prior to the new financing.

Instructions

Determine the effect on net income and earnings per share for these two methods of financing.

E15-3 On January 1, Klosterman Company issued $500,000, 10%, 10-year bonds at face value. Interest is payable semiannually on July 1 and January 1.

Prepare entries for issuance of bonds, and payment and accrual of bond interest.
(LO 2)

Instructions

Prepare journal entries to record the following.

(a) The issuance of the bonds.
(b) The payment of interest on July 1, assuming that interest was not accrued on June 30.
(c) The accrual of interest on December 31.

E15-4 On January 1, Forrester Company issued $400,000, 8%, 5-year bonds at face value. Interest is payable semiannually on July 1 and January 1.

Prepare entries for bonds issued at face value.
(LO 2)

Instructions

Prepare journal entries to record the following events.

(a) The issuance of the bonds.
(b) The payment of interest on July 1, assuming no previous accrual of interest.
(c) The accrual of interest on December 31.

E15-5 Laudie Company issued $400,000 of 9%, 10-year bonds on January 1, 2014, at face value. Interest is payable semiannually on July 1 and January 1.

Prepare entries for bonds issued at face value.
(LO 2, 3)

Instructions

Prepare the journal entries to record the following events.

(a) The issuance of the bonds.
(b) The payment of interest on July 1, assuming no previous accrual of interest.
(c) The accrual of interest on December 31.
(d) The redemption of bonds at maturity, assuming interest for the last interest period has been paid and recorded.

E15-6 Swisher Company issued $2,000,000 of bonds on January 1, 2014.

Prepare entries for issuance, redemption, and conversion of bonds.
(LO 2, 3)

Instructions

(a) Prepare the journal entry to record the issuance of the bonds if they are issued at (1) 100, (2) 98, and (3) 103.
(b) Prepare the journal entry to record the redemption of the bonds at maturity, assuming the bonds were issued at 100.
(c) Prepare the journal entry to record the redemption of the bonds before maturity at 98. Assume the balance in Premium on Bonds Payable is $9,000.
(d) Prepare the journal entry to record the conversion of the bonds into 60,000 shares of $10 par value common stock. Assume the bonds were issued at par.

E15-7 Whitmore Company issued $500,000 of 5-year, 8% bonds at 97 on January 1, 2014. The bonds pay interest twice a year.

Prepare entries to record issuance of bonds at discount and premium.
(LO 2)

Instructions

(a) (1) Prepare the journal entry to record the issuance of the bonds.
    (2) Compute the total cost of borrowing for these bonds.
(b) Repeat the requirements from part (a), assuming the bonds were issued at 105.

Prepare entries for bond interest and redemption.
(LO 2, 3)

E15-8 The following section is taken from Ohlman Corp.'s balance sheet at December 31, 2013.

Current liabilities	
Interest payable	$ 56,000
Long-term liabilities	
Bonds payable, 7%, due January 1, 2018	1,600,000

Bond interest is payable semiannually on January 1 and July 1. The bonds are callable on any interest date.

Instructions

(a) Journalize the payment of the bond interest on January 1, 2014.

(b) Assume that on January 1, 2014, after paying interest, Ohlman calls bonds having a face value of $600,000. The call price is 103. Record the redemption of the bonds.

(c) Prepare the entry to record the payment of interest on July 1, 2014, assuming no previous accrual of interest on the remaining bonds.

Prepare entries for redemption of bonds and conversion of bonds into common stock.
(LO 3)

E15-9 Presented below are three independent situations.

1. Longbine Corporation redeemed $130,000 face value, 12% bonds on June 30, 2014, at 102. The carrying value of the bonds at the redemption date was $117,500. The bonds pay semiannual interest, and the interest payment due on June 30, 2014, has been made and recorded.

2. Tastove Inc. redeemed $150,000 face value, 12.5% bonds on June 30, 2014, at 98. The carrying value of the bonds at the redemption date was $151,000. The bonds pay semiannual interest, and the interest payment due on June 30, 2014, has been made and recorded.

3. Precision Company has $80,000, 8%, 12-year convertible bonds outstanding. These bonds were sold at face value and pay semiannual interest on June 30 and December 31 of each year. The bonds are convertible into 30 shares of Precision $5 par value common stock for each $1,000 worth of bonds. On December 31, 2014, after the bond interest has been paid, $20,000 face value bonds were converted. The market price of Precision common stock was $44 per share on December 31, 2014.

Instructions

For each independent situation above, prepare the appropriate journal entry for the redemption or conversion of the bonds.

Prepare entries to record mortgage note and installment payments.
(LO 4)

E15-10 Jernigan Co. receives $300,000 when it issues a $300,000, 10%, mortgage note payable to finance the construction of a building at December 31, 2014. The terms provide for semiannual installment payments of $25,000 on June 30 and December 31.

Instructions

Prepare the journal entries to record the mortgage loan and the first two installment payments.

Prepare entries to record mortgage note and installment payments.
(LO 4)

E15-11 Dreiling Company borrowed $300,000 on January 1, 2014, by issuing a $300,000, 8% mortgage note payable. The terms call for semiannual installment payments of $20,000 on June 30 and December 31.

Instructions

(a) Prepare the journal entries to record the mortgage loan and the first two installment payments.

(b) Indicate the amount of mortgage note payable to be reported as a current liability and as a long-term liability at December 31, 2014.

Prepare entries for operating lease and capital lease.
(LO 5)

E15-12 Presented below are two independent situations.

1. Flinthills Car Rental leased a car to Jayhawk Company for one year. Terms of the operating lease agreement call for monthly payments of $500.

2. On January 1, 2014, Throm Inc. entered into an agreement to lease 20 computers from Drummond Electronics. The terms of the lease agreement require three annual rental payments of $20,000 (including 10% interest) beginning December 31, 2014. The present value of the three rental payments is $49,735. Throm considers this a capital lease.

Instructions

(a) Prepare the appropriate journal entry to be made by Jayhawk Company for the first lease payment.

(b) Prepare the journal entry to record the lease agreement on the books of Throm Inc. on January 1, 2014.

E15-13 The adjusted trial balance for Karr Farm Corporation at the end of the current year contained the following accounts.

Prepare long-term liabilities section.

(LO 6)

Interest Payable	$ 9,000
Lease Liability	89,500
Bonds Payable, due 2019	180,000
Premium on Bonds Payable	32,000

Instructions
Prepare the long-term liabilities section of the balance sheet.

E15-14 Hatfield Corporation reports the following amounts in its 2014 financial statements:

Compute debt to assets ratio and times interest earned.

(LO 6)

	At December 31, 2014	For the Year 2014
Total assets	$1,000,000	
Total liabilities	580,000	
Total stockholders' equity	?	
Interest expense		$ 20,000
Income tax expense		100,000
Net income		150,000

Instructions
(a) Compute the December 31, 2014, balance in stockholders' equity.
(b) Compute the debt to assets ratio at December 31, 2014.
(c) Compute times interest earned for 2014.

*E15-15 England Corporation is issuing $200,000 of 8%, 5-year bonds when potential bond investors want a return of 10%. Interest is payable semiannually.

Compute market price of bonds.

(LO 7)

Instructions
Compute the market price (present value) of the bonds.

*E15-16 Lorance Corporation issued $800,000, 9%, 10-year bonds on January 1, 2014, for $750,150. This price resulted in an effective-interest rate of 10% on the bonds. Interest is payable semiannually on July 1 and January 1. Lorance uses the effective-interest method to amortize bond premium or discount.

Prepare entries for issuance of bonds, payment of interest, and amortization of discount using effective-interest method.

(LO 2, 8)

Instructions
Prepare the journal entries to record the following. (Round to the nearest dollar.)

(a) The issuance of the bonds.
(b) The payment of interest and the discount amortization on July 1, 2014, assuming that interest was not accrued on June 30.
(c) The accrual of interest and the discount amortization on December 31, 2014.

*E15-17 LRNA Company issued $300,000, 11%, 10-year bonds on January 1, 2014, for $318,694. This price resulted in an effective-interest rate of 10% on the bonds. Interest is payable semiannually on July 1 and January 1. LRNA uses the effective-interest method to amortize bond premium or discount.

Prepare entries for issuance of bonds, payment of interest, and amortization of premium using effective-interest method.

(LO 2, 8)

Instructions
Prepare the journal entries to record the following. (Round to the nearest dollar.)

(a) The issuance of the bonds.
(b) The payment of interest and the premium amortization on July 1, 2014, assuming that interest was not accrued on June 30.
(c) The accrual of interest and the premium amortization on December 31, 2014.

*E15-18 Adcock Company issued $600,000, 9%, 20-year bonds on January 1, 2014, at 103. Interest is payable semiannually on July 1 and January 1. Adcock uses straight-line amortization for bond premium or discount.

Prepare entries to record issuance of bonds, payment of interest, amortization of premium, and redemption at maturity.

(LO 2, 3, 9)

Instructions
Prepare the journal entries to record the following.

(a) The issuance of the bonds.
(b) The payment of interest and the premium amortization on July 1, 2014, assuming that interest was not accrued on June 30.
(c) The accrual of interest and the premium amortization on December 31, 2014.
(d) The redemption of the bonds at maturity, assuming interest for the last interest period has been paid and recorded.

Prepare entries to record issuance of bonds, payment of interest, amortization of discount, and redemption at maturity.

(LO 2, 3, 9)

*E15-19 Gridley Company issued $800,000, 11%, 10-year bonds on December 31, 2013, for $730,000. Interest is payable semiannually on June 30 and December 31. Gridley Company uses the straight-line method to amortize bond premium or discount.

Instructions
Prepare the journal entries to record the following.
(a) The issuance of the bonds.
(b) The payment of interest and the discount amortization on June 30, 2014.
(c) The payment of interest and the discount amortization on December 31, 2014.
(d) The redemption of the bonds at maturity, assuming interest for the last interest period has been paid and recorded.

EXERCISES: SET B AND CHALLENGE EXERCISES

Visit the book's companion website, at **www.wiley.com/college/weygandt**, and choose the Student Companion site to access Exercise Set B and Challenge Exercises.

PROBLEMS: SET A

Prepare entries to record issuance of bonds, interest accrual, and bond redemption.

(LO 2, 3, 6)

P15-1A On May 1, 2014, Herron Corp. issued $600,000, 9%, 5-year bonds at face value. The bonds were dated May 1, 2014, and pay interest semiannually on May 1 and November 1. Financial statements are prepared annually on December 31.

Instructions
(a) Prepare the journal entry to record the issuance of the bonds.
(b) Prepare the adjusting entry to record the accrual of interest on December 31, 2014.
(c) Show the balance sheet presentation on December 31, 2014.

(d) Int. exp. $18,000

(d) Prepare the journal entry to record payment of interest on May 1, 2015, assuming no accrual of interest from January 1, 2015, to May 1, 2015.
(e) Prepare the journal entry to record payment of interest on November 1, 2015.

(f) Loss $12,000

(f) Assume that on November 1, 2015, Herron calls the bonds at 102. Record the redemption of the bonds.

Prepare entries to record issuance of bonds, interest accrual, and bond redemption.

(LO 2, 3, 6)

P15-2A Asquith Electric sold $750,000, 10%, 10-year bonds on January 1, 2014. The bonds were dated January 1 and paid interest on January 1 and July 1. The bonds were sold at 104.

Instructions
(a) Prepare the journal entry to record the issuance of the bonds on January 1, 2014.
(b) At December 31, 2014, the balance in the Premium on Bonds Payable account is $27,000. Show the balance sheet presentation of accrued interest and the bond liability at December 31, 2014.

(c) Loss $13,500

(c) On January 1, 2016, when the carrying value of the bonds was $774,000, the company redeemed the bonds at 105. Record the redemption of the bonds assuming that interest for the period has already been paid.

Prepare installment payments schedule and journal entries for a mortgage note payable.

(LO 4)

P15-3A Talkington Electronics issues a $400,000, 8%, 10-year mortgage note on December 31, 2013. The proceeds from the note are to be used in financing a new research laboratory. The terms of the note provide for semiannual installment payments, exclusive of real estate taxes and insurance, of $29,433. Payments are due June 30 and December 31.

Instructions

(b) June 30 debit Mortgage Payable $13,433

(a) Prepare an installment payments schedule for the first 2 years.
(b) Prepare the entries for (1) the loan and (2) the first two installment payments.

(c) Current liability—2014 $29,639

(c) Show how the total mortgage liability should be reported on the balance sheet at December 31, 2014.

P15-4A Presented below are three different lease transactions that occurred for Ruggiero Inc. in 2014. Assume that all lease contracts start on January 1, 2014. In no case does Ruggiero receive title to the properties leased during or at the end of the lease term.

Analyze three different lease situations and prepare journal entries.

(LO 5)

	Lessor		
	Judson Delivery	**Hester Co.**	**Gunselman Auto**
Type of property	Computer	Delivery equipment	Automobile
Yearly rental	$ 5,000	$ 4,200	$ 3,700
Lease term	6 years	4 years	2 years
Estimated economic life	7 years	7 years	5 years
Fair value of lease asset	$27,500	$19,000	$11,000
Present value of the lease rental payments	$26,000	$13,000	$ 6,400
Bargain purchase option	None	None	None

Instructions

(a) Which of the leases are operating leases and which are capital leases? Explain.

(b) How should the lease transaction for Hester Co. be recorded in 2014?

(c) How should the lease transaction for Judson Delivery be recorded on January 1, 2014?

*P15-5A On July 1, 2014, Flanagin Corporation issued $2,000,000, 10%, 10-year bonds at $2,271,813. This price resulted in an effective-interest rate of 8% on the bonds. Flanagin uses the effective-interest method to amortize bond premium or discount. The bonds pay semiannual interest July 1 and January 1.

Prepare entries to record issuance of bonds, payment of interest, and amortization of bond premium using effective-interest method.

(LO 2, 8)

Instructions

(Round all computations to the nearest dollar.)

(a) Prepare the journal entry to record the issuance of the bonds on July 1, 2014.

(b) Prepare an amortization table through December 31, 2015 (3 interest periods), for this bond issue.

(c) Prepare the journal entry to record the accrual of interest and the amortization of the premium on December 31, 2014.

(c) Amortization $9,127

(d) Prepare the journal entry to record the payment of interest and the amortization of the premium on July 1, 2015, assuming no accrual of interest on June 30.

(d) Amortization $9,493

(e) Prepare the journal entry to record the accrual of interest and the amortization of the premium on December 31, 2015.

(e) Amortization $9,872

*P15-6A On July 1, 2014, Kellerman Company issued $5,000,000, 8%, 10-year bonds at $4,376,892. This price resulted in an effective-interest rate of 10% on the bonds. Kellerman uses the effective-interest method to amortize bond premium or discount. The bonds pay semiannual interest July 1 and January 1.

Prepare entries to record issuance of bonds, payment of interest, and amortization of discount using effective-interest method. In addition, answer questions.

(LO 2, 6, 8)

Instructions

(Round all computations to the nearest dollar.)

(a) Prepare the journal entries to record the following transactions.

(1) The issuance of the bonds on July 1, 2014.

(2) The accrual of interest and the amortization of the discount on December 31, 2014.

(3) The payment of interest and the amortization of the discount on July 1, 2015, assuming no accrual of interest on June 30.

(a) (3) Amortization $19,787

(4) The accrual of interest and the amortization of the discount on December 31, 2015.

(a) (4) Amortization $20,776

(b) Show the proper balance sheet presentation for the liability for bonds payable on the December 31, 2015, balance sheet.

(b) Bond carrying value $4,436,300

(c) ———— Provide the answers to the following questions in letter form.

(1) What amount of interest expense is reported for 2015?

(2) Would the bond interest expense reported in 2015 be the same as, greater than, or less than the amount that would be reported if the straight-line method of amortization were used?

(3) Determine the total cost of borrowing over the life of the bond.

(4) Would the total bond interest expense be greater than, the same as, or less than the total interest expense that would be reported if the straight-line method of amortization were used?

Prepare entries to record issuance of bonds, interest accrual, and straight-line amortization for 2 years.

(LO 2, 6, 9)

(b) Amortization $6,000

(d) Premium on bonds payable $96,000

*P15-7A Wainwright Electric sold $3,000,000, 10%, 10-year bonds on January 1, 2014. The bonds were dated January 1 and pay interest July 1 and January 1. Wainwright Electric uses the straight-line method to amortize bond premium or discount. The bonds were sold at 104. Assume no interest is accrued on June 30.

Instructions
(a) Prepare the journal entry to record the issuance of the bonds on January 1, 2014.
(b) Prepare a bond premium amortization schedule for the first 4 interest periods.
(c) Prepare the journal entries for interest and the amortization of the premium in 2014 and 2015.
(d) Show the balance sheet presentation of the bond liability at December 31, 2015.

Prepare entries to record issuance of bonds, interest, and straight-line amortization of bond premium and discount.

(LO 2, 6, 9)

(a) Amortization $7,000
(b) Amortization $3,500
(c) Premium on bonds payable $133,000
Discount on bonds payable $66,500

*P15-8A Saberhagen Company sold $3,500,000, 8%, 10-year bonds on July 1, 2014. The bonds were dated July 1, 2014, and pay interest July 1 and January 1. Saberhagen Company uses the straight-line method to amortize bond premium or discount. Assume no interest is accrued on June 30.

Instructions
(a) Prepare all the necessary journal entries to record the issuance of the bonds and bond interest expense for 2014, assuming that the bonds sold at 104.
(b) Prepare journal entries as in part (a) assuming that the bonds sold at 98.
(c) Show balance sheet presentation for the bonds at December 31, 2014.

Prepare entries to record interest payments, straight-line premium amortization, and redemption of bonds.

(LO 2, 3, 9)

*P15-9A The following is taken from the Colaw Company balance sheet.

COLAW COMPANY
Balance Sheet (partial)
December 31, 2014

Current liabilities		
Interest payable (for 6 months		
from July 1 to December 31)		$ 105,000
Long-term liabilities		
Bonds payable, 7% due January 1, 2025	$3,000,000	
Add: Premium on bonds payable	200,000	3,200,000

Interest is payable semiannually on January 1 and July 1. The bonds are callable on any semiannual interest date. Colaw uses straight-line amortization for any bond premium or discount. From December 31, 2014, the bonds will be outstanding for an additional 10 years (120 months).

Instructions
(a) Journalize the payment of bond interest on January 1, 2015.

(b) Amortization $10,000

(b) Prepare the entry to amortize bond premium and to pay the interest due on July 1, 2015, assuming no accrual of interest on June 30.

(c) Gain $64,000

(c) Assume that on July 1, 2015, after paying interest, Colaw Company calls bonds having a face value of $1,200,000. The call price is 101. Record the redemption of the bonds.

(d) Amortization $6,000

(d) Prepare the adjusting entry at December 31, 2015, to amortize bond premium and to accrue interest on the remaining bonds.

PROBLEMS: SET B

Prepare entries to record issuance of bonds, interest accrual, and bond redemption.

(LO 2, 3, 6)

(d) Int. exp. $75,000

P15-1B On June 1, 2014, Weller Corp. issued $2,000,000, 9%, 5-year bonds at face value. The bonds were dated June 1, 2014, and pay interest semiannually on June 1 and December 1. Financial statements are prepared annually on December 31.

Instructions
(a) Prepare the journal entry to record the issuance of the bonds.
(b) Prepare the adjusting entry to record the accrual of interest on December 31, 2014.
(c) Show the balance sheet presentation on December 31, 2014.
(d) Prepare the journal entry to record payment of interest on June 1, 2015, assuming no accrual of interest from January 1, 2015, to June 1, 2015.

(e) Prepare the journal entry to record payment of interest on December 1, 2015.

(f) Assume that on December 1, 2015, Weller calls the bonds at 102. Record the redemption of the bonds.

(f) Loss $40,000

P15-2B Shonrock Co. sold $800,000, 9%, 10-year bonds on January 1, 2014. The bonds were dated January 1, and interest is paid on January 1 and July 1. The bonds were sold at 105.

Prepare entries to record issuance of bonds, interest accrual, and bond redemption.

(LO 2, 3, 6)

Instructions

(a) Prepare the journal entry to record the issuance of the bonds on January 1, 2014.

(b) At December 31, 2014, the balance in the Premium on Bonds Payable account is $36,000. Show the balance sheet presentation of accrued interest and the bond liability at December 31, 2014.

(c) On January 1, 2016, when the carrying value of the bonds was $832,000, the company redeemed the bonds at 105. Record the redemption of the bonds assuming that interest for the period has already been paid.

(c) Loss $8,000

P15-3B Crosetti's Electronics issues a $600,000, 8%, 10-year mortgage note on December 31, 2014, to help finance a plant expansion program. The terms provide for semiannual installment payments, not including real estate taxes and insurance, of $44,149. Payments are due June 30 and December 31.

Prepare installment payments schedule and journal entries for a mortgage note payable.

(LO 4)

Instructions

(a) Prepare an installment payments schedule for the first 2 years.

(b) Prepare the entries for (1) the mortgage loan and (2) the first two installment payments.

(b) June 30 debit Mortgage Payable $20,149

(c) Show how the total mortgage liability should be reported on the balance sheet at December 31, 2015.

(c) Current liability—2015: $44,458

P15-4B Presented below are three different lease transactions in which Naylor Enterprises engaged in 2014. Assume that all lease transactions start on January 1, 2014. In no case does Naylor receive title to the properties leased during or at the end of the lease term.

Analyze three different lease situations and prepare journal entries.

(LO 5)

	Lessor		
	Baxter Springs Co.	**Mendenhall Co.**	**Midas Inc.**
Type of property	Bulldozer	Truck	Furniture
Bargain purchase option	None	None	None
Lease term	4 years	6 years	3 years
Estimated economic life	8 years	7 years	5 years
Yearly rental	$13,000	$20,000	$ 3,000
Fair value of leased asset	$80,000	$96,000	$20,500
Present value of the lease rental payments	$48,000	$82,000	$ 9,000

Instructions

(a) Identify the leases above as operating or capital leases. Explain.

(b) How should the lease transaction for Mendenhall Co. be recorded on January 1, 2014?

(c) How should the lease transaction for Midas Inc. be recorded in 2014?

*P15-5B On July 1, 2014, Witherspoon Satellites issued $4,500,000, 9%, 10-year bonds at $4,219,600. This price resulted in an effective-interest rate of 10% on the bonds. Witherspoon uses the effective-interest method to amortize bond premium or discount. The bonds pay semiannual interest July 1 and January 1.

Prepare entries to record issuance of bonds, payment of interest, and amortization of bond discount using effective-interest method.

(LO 2, 8)

Instructions

(Round all computations to the nearest dollar.)

(a) Prepare the journal entry to record the issuance of the bonds on July 1, 2014.

(b) Prepare an amortization table through December 31, 2015 (3 interest periods), for this bond issue.

(c) Prepare the journal entry to record the accrual of interest and the amortization of the discount on December 31, 2014.

(c) Amortization $8,480

(d) Prepare the journal entry to record the payment of interest and the amortization of the discount on July 1, 2015, assuming that interest was not accrued on June 30.

(d) Amortization $8,904

(e) Prepare the journal entry to record the accrual of interest and the amortization of the discount on December 31, 2015.

(e) Amortization $9,349

Prepare entries to record issuance of bonds, payment of interest, and amortization of premium using effective-interest method. In addition, answer questions.

(LO 2, 6, 8)

(a) (2) Amortization $18,255
(a) (3) Amortization $18,985

(a) (4) Amortization $19,745
(b) Bond carrying value $4,486,642

*P15-6B On July 1, 2014, Ashlock Chemical Company issued $4,000,000, 10%, 10 year bonds at $4,543,627. This price resulted in an 8% effective-interest rate on the bonds. Ashlock uses the effective-interest method to amortize bond premium or discount. The bonds pay semiannual interest on each July 1 and January 1.

Instructions
(Round all computations to the nearest dollar.)

(a) Prepare the journal entries to record the following transactions.
   (1) The issuance of the bonds on July 1, 2014.
   (2) The accrual of interest and the amortization of the premium on December 31, 2014.
   (3) The payment of interest and the amortization of the premium on July 1, 2015, assuming no accrual of interest on June 30.
   (4) The accrual of interest and the amortization of the premium on December 31, 2015.
(b) Show the proper balance sheet presentation for the liability for bonds payable on the December 31, 2015, balance sheet.
(c) ●——— Provide the answers to the following questions in letter form.
   (1) What amount of interest expense is reported for 2015?
   (2) Would the bond interest expense reported in 2015 be the same as, greater than, or less than the amount that would be reported if the straight-line method of amortization were used?
   (3) Determine the total cost of borrowing over the life of the bond.
   (4) Would the total bond interest expense be greater than, the same as, or less than the total interest expense if the straight-line method of amortization were used?

Prepare entries to record issuance of bonds, interest accrual, and straight-line amortization for 2 years.

(LO 2, 6, 9)

(b) Amortization $6,000

(d) Discount on bonds payable $216,000

*P15-7B Fernetti Company sold $6,000,000, 9%, 20-year bonds on January 1, 2014. The bonds were dated January 1, 2014, and pay interest on January 1 and July 1. Fernetti Company uses the straight-line method to amortize bond premium or discount. The bonds were sold at 96. Assume no interest is accrued on June 30.

Instructions
(a) Prepare the journal entry to record the issuance of the bonds on January 1, 2014.
(b) Prepare a bond discount amortization schedule for the first 4 interest periods.
(c) Prepare the journal entries for interest and the amortization of the discount in 2014 and 2015.
(d) Show the balance sheet presentation of the bond liability at December 31, 2015.

Prepare entries to record issuance of bonds, interest, and straight-line amortization of bond premium and discount.

(LO 2, 6, 9)

(a) Amortization $6,000
(b) Amortization $8,000
(c) Premium on bonds payable $108,000
   Discount on bonds payable $144,000

*P15-8B Roswell Corporation sold $4,000,000, 8%, 10-year bonds on January 1, 2014. The bonds were dated January 1, 2014, and pay interest on July 1 and January 1. Roswell Corporation uses the straight-line method to amortize bond premium or discount. Assume no interest is accrued on June 30.

Instructions
(a) Prepare all the necessary journal entries to record the issuance of the bonds and bond interest expense for 2014, assuming that the bonds sold at 103.
(b) Prepare journal entries as in part (a) assuming that the bonds sold at 96.
(c) Show balance sheet presentation for the bonds at December 31, 2014.

Prepare entries to record interest payments, straight-line discount amortization, and redemption of bonds.

(LO 2, 3, 9)

*P15-9B The following is taken from the Sinjh Corporation balance sheet.

SINJH CORPORATION
Balance Sheet (partial)
December 31, 2014

Current liabilities		
Interest payable (for 6 months from July 1 to December 31)		$ 108,000
Long-term liabilities		
Bonds payable, 9%, due January 1, 2025	$2,400,000	
Less: Discount on bonds payable	90,000	2,310,000

Interest is payable semiannually on January 1 and July 1. The bonds are callable on any semiannual interest date. Sinjh uses straight-line amortization for any bond premium or discount. From December 31, 2014, the bonds will be outstanding for an additional 10 years (120 months).

Instructions

(Round all computations to the nearest dollar).

(a) Journalize the payment of bond interest on January 1, 2015.

(b) Prepare the entry to amortize bond discount and to pay the interest due on July 1, 2015, assuming that interest was not accrued on June 30.

(b) Amortization $4,500

(c) Assume that on July 1, 2015, after paying interest, Sinjh Corp. calls bonds having a face value of $800,000. The call price is 102. Record the redemption of the bonds.

(c) Loss $44,500

(d) Prepare the adjusting entry at December 31, 2015, to amortize bond discount and to accrue interest on the remaining bonds.

(d) Amortization $3,000

PROBLEMS: SET C

Visit the book's companion website, at **www.wiley.com/college/weygandt**, and choose the Student Companion site to access Problem Set C.

COMPREHENSIVE PROBLEM: CHAPTERS 13 TO 15

CP15 Quigley Corporation's trial balance at December 31, 2014, is presented below. All 2014 transactions have been recorded except for the items described below.

	Debit	Credit
Cash	$ 23,000	
Accounts Receivable	51,000	
Inventory	22,700	
Land	65,000	
Buildings	95,000	
Equipment	40,000	
Allowance for Doubtful Accounts		$ 450
Accumulated Depreciation—Buildings		30,000
Accumulated Depreciation—Equipment		14,400
Accounts Payable		19,300
Interest Payable		–0–
Dividends Payable		–0–
Unearned Rent Revenue		8,000
Bonds Payable (10%)		50,000
Common Stock ($10 par)		30,000
Paid-in Capital in Excess of Par—Common Stock		6,000
Preferred Stock ($20 par)		–0–
Paid-in Capital in Excess of Par—Preferred Stock		–0–
Retained Earnings		75,050
Treasury Stock	–0–	
Cash Dividends	–0–	
Sales Revenue		570,000
Rent Revenue		–0–
Bad Debt Expense	–0–	
Interest Expense	2,500	
Cost of Goods Sold	400,000	
Depreciation Expense	–0–	
Other Operating Expenses	39,000	
Salaries and Wages Expense	65,000	
Total	$803,200	$803,200

Unrecorded transactions

1. On January 1, 2014, Quigley issued 1,000 shares of $20 par, 6% preferred stock for $22,000.
2. On January 1, 2014, Quigley also issued 1,000 shares of common stock for $23,000.
3. Quigley reacquired 300 shares of its common stock on July 1, 2014, for $49 per share.
4. On December 31, 2014, Quigley declared the annual preferred stock dividend and a $1.50 per share dividend on the outstanding common stock, all payable on January 15, 2015.
5. Quigley estimates that uncollectible accounts receivable at year-end is $5,100.
6. The building is being depreciated using the straight-line method over 30 years. The salvage value is $5,000.
7. The equipment is being depreciated using the straight-line method over 10 years. The salvage value is $4,000.
8. The unearned rent was collected on October 1, 2014. It was receipt of 4 months' rent in advance (October 1, 2014 through January 31, 2015).
9. The 10% bonds payable pay interest every January 1 and July 1. The interest for the 6 months ended December 31, 2014, has not been paid or recorded.

Instructions
(Ignore income taxes.)

(b) Total $868,700

(a) Prepare journal entries for the transactions listed above.
(b) Prepare an updated December 31, 2014, trial balance, reflecting the unrecorded transactions.
(c) Prepare a multiple-step income statement for the year ending December 31, 2014.
(d) Prepare a retained earnings statement for the year ending December 31, 2014.

(e) Total assets $270,900

(e) Prepare a classified balance sheet as of December 31, 2014.

CONTINUING COOKIE CHRONICLE

(*Note:* This is a continuation of the Cookie Chronicle from Chapters 1 through 14.)

CCC15 Natalie and Curtis have been experiencing great demand for their cookies and muffins. As a result, they are now thinking about buying a commercial oven. They know which oven they want and how much it will cost. They have some cash set aside for the purchase and will need to borrow the rest. They met with a bank manager to discuss their options.

Go to the book's companion website, **www.wiley.com/college/weygandt**, *to see the completion of this problem.*

Broadening Your Perspective

Financial Reporting and Analysis

Financial Reporting Problem: Apple Inc.

BYP15-1 Refer to the financial statements of Apple Inc. in Appendix A. Instructions for accessing and using the company's complete annual report, including the notes to the financial statements, are also provided in Appendix A.

Instructions
(a) What were Apple's total long-term liabilities at September 24, 2011? What was the increase/decrease in total long-term liabilities from the prior year?
(b) Determine whether Apple redeemed (bought back) any long-term liabilities during the fiscal year ended September 24, 2011.

Comparative Analysis Problem:
PepsiCo, Inc. vs. The Coca-Cola Company

BYP15-2 PepsiCo's financial statements are presented in Appendix B. Financial statements of The Coca-Cola Company are presented in Appendix C. Instructions for accessing and using the complete annual reports of PepsiCo and Coca-Cola, including the notes to the financial statements, are also provided in Appendices B and C, respectively.

Instructions

(a) Based on the information contained in these financial statements, compute the following 2011 ratios for each company.
  (1) Debt to assets.
  (2) Times interest earned.
(b) What conclusions concerning the companies' long-run solvency can be drawn from these ratios?

Comparative Analysis Problem:
Amazon.com, Inc. vs. Wal-Mart Stores, Inc.

BYP15-3 Amazon.com, Inc.'s financial statements are presented in Appendix D. Financial statements of Wal-Mart Stores, Inc. are presented in Appendix E. Instructions for accessing and using the complete annual reports of Amazon and Wal-Mart, including the notes to the financial statements, are also provided in Appendices D and E, respectively.

Instructions

(a) Based on the information contained in these financial statements, compute the following 2011 ratios for each company.
  (1) Debt to assets.
  (2) Times interest earned.
(b) What conclusions concerning the companies' long-run solvency can be drawn from these ratios?

REAL-WORLD FOCUS

BYP15-4 Bond or debt securities pay a stated rate of interest. This rate of interest is dependent on the risk associated with the investment. Also, bond prices change when the risks associated with those bonds change. Standard & Poor's provides ratings for companies that issue debt securities.

Address: **www.standardandpoors.com/ratings/definitions-and-faqs/en/us**, or go to
www.wiley.com/college/weygandt

Instructions
Go to the website shown and answer the following questions.

(a) Explain the meaning of an "A" rating. Explain the meaning of a "C" rating.
(b) What types of things can cause a change in a company's credit rating?
(c) Explain the relationship between a company's credit rating and the merit of an investment in that company's bonds.

Critical Thinking

Decision-Making Across the Organization

*BYP15-5 On January 1, 2012, Glover Corporation issued $2,400,000 of 5-year, 8% bonds at 95. The bonds pay interest semiannually on July 1 and January 1. By January 1, 2014, the market rate of interest for bonds of risk similar to those of Glover Corporation had risen. As a result, the market value of these bonds was $2,000,000 on January 1, 2014—below their carrying value. Joanna Glover, president of the company, suggests repurchasing all of these bonds in the open market at the $2,000,000 price. To do so, the company will have to issue $2,000,000 (face value) of new 10-year, 11% bonds at par. The president asks you, as controller, "What is the feasibility of my proposed repurchase plan?"

Instructions

With the class divided into groups, answer the following.

(a) What is the carrying value of the outstanding Glover Corporation 5-year bonds on January 1, 2014? (Assume straight-line amortization.)

(b) Prepare the journal entry to redeem the 5-year bonds on January 1, 2014. Prepare the journal entry to issue the new 10-year bonds.

(c) Prepare a short memo to the president in response to her request for advice. List the economic factors that you believe should be considered for her repurchase proposal.

Communication Activity

BYP15-6 Sam Masasi, president of Masasi Corporation, is considering the issuance of bonds to finance an expansion of his business. He has asked you to (1) discuss the advantages of bonds over common stock financing, (2) indicate the types of bonds he might issue, and (3) explain the issuing procedures used in bond transactions.

Instructions

Write a memo to the president, answering his request.

Ethics Case

BYP15-7 Ken Iwig is the president, founder, and majority owner of Olathe Medical Corporation, an emerging medical technology products company. Olathe is in dire need of additional capital to keep operating and to bring several promising products to final development, testing, and production. Ken, as owner of 51% of the outstanding stock, manages the company's operations. He places heavy emphasis on research and development and on long-term growth. The other principal stockholder is Barb Lowery who, as a nonemployee investor, owns 40% of the stock. Barb would like to deemphasize the R&D functions and emphasize the marketing function, to maximize short-run sales and profits from existing products. She believes this strategy would raise the market price of Olathe's stock.

All of Ken's personal capital and borrowing power is tied up in his 51% stock ownership. He knows that any offering of additional shares of stock will dilute his controlling interest because he won't be able to participate in such an issuance. But, Barb has money and would likely buy enough shares to gain control of Olathe. She then would dictate the company's future direction, even if it meant replacing Ken as president and CEO.

The company already has considerable debt. Raising additional debt will be costly, will adversely affect Olathe's credit rating, and will increase the company's reported losses due to the growth in interest expense. Barb and the other minority stockholders express opposition to the assumption of additional debt, fearing the company will be pushed to the brink of bankruptcy. Wanting to maintain his control and to preserve the direction of "his" company, Ken is doing everything to avoid a stock issuance. He is contemplating a large issuance of bonds, even if it means the bonds are issued with a high effective-interest rate.

Instructions

(a) Who are the stakeholders in this situation?

(b) What are the ethical issues in this case?

(c) What would you do if you were Ken?

All About You

BYP15-8 Numerous articles have been written that identify early warning signs that you might be getting into trouble with your personal debt load. You can find many good articles on this topic on the Internet.

Instructions

Find an article that identifies early warning signs of personal debt trouble. Write a summary of the article and bring your summary and the article to class to share.

FASB Codification Activity

BYP15-9 If your school has a subscription to the FASB Codification, go to **http://aaahq.org/ ascLogin.cfm** to log in and prepare responses to the following:

(a) What is the long-term obligation?

(b) What guidance does the Codification provide for the disclosure of long-term obligations?

Answers to Chapter Questions

Answers to Insight and Accounting Across the Organization Questions

p. 689 How About Those 30-Year Bonds? **Q:** What are the advantages for companies of issuing 30-year bonds instead of 5-year bonds? **A:** The major advantages for companies are to extend their debt and to pay low interest rates. This locks in these low rates for a considerable period of time.

p. 698 Bonds versus Notes? **Q:** Why might companies prefer bond financing instead of short-term financing? **A:** In some cases, it is difficult to get loans from banks. In addition, low interest rates have encouraged companies to go more long-term and fix their rate. Recently, short-term loans suddenly froze, leading to liquidity problems for certain companies.

p. 702 "Covenant-Lite" Debt **Q:** How can financial ratios such as those covered in this chapter provide protection for creditors? **A:** Financial ratios such as the current ratio, debt to assets ratio, and times interest earned provide indications of a company's liquidity and solvency. By specifying minimum levels of liquidity and solvency, as measured by these ratios, a creditor creates triggers that enable it to step in before a company's financial situation becomes too dire.

Answers to Self-Test Questions

1. c **2.** c **3.** a **4.** d **5.** b **6.** d $600,000 - (10,000 \times \$1)$ **7.** c **8.** c $\$200,000 - (10\% \times \$497,000) = \$150,300$; $(\$497,000 - \$150,300) \times 10\%$ **9.** d **10.** d $(\$300,000 + \$40,000 + \$100,000) \div \$40,000$ ***11.** d ***12.** b $[(\$938,554 \times 10\%) - (\$1,000,000 \times 9\%)] = \$3,855$; $(\$1,000,000 - \$938,554) - \$3,855$ ***13.** c $(\$1,081,105 \times 8\%) \div 2$ ***14.** d $[\$500,000 - (96\% \times \$500,000)] = \$20,000$; $(\$20,000 \div 10)$ ***15.** a $500,000 \times .96) = 480,000$; $(\$480,000 + \$2,000 + \$2,000 + \$2,000)$

A Look at IFRS

IFRS and GAAP have similar definitions of liabilities. IFRSs related to reporting and recognition of liabilities are found in *IAS I (revised)* ("Presentation of Financial Statements") and *IAS 37* ("Provisions, Contingent Liabilities, and Contingent Assets").

LEARNING OBJECTIVE **10**

Compare the accounting for long-term liabilities under GAAP and IFRS.

Key Points

- As indicated in Chapter 11, in general GAAP and IFRS define liabilities similarly.

- IFRS requires that companies classify liabilities as current or noncurrent on the face of the statement of financial position (balance sheet), except in industries where a **presentation** based on liquidity would be considered to provide more useful information (such as financial institutions). When current liabilities (also called short-term liabilities) are presented, they are generally presented in order of liquidity.

- Under IFRS, liabilities are classified as current if they are expected to be paid within 12 months.

- Similar to GAAP, items are normally reported in order of liquidity. Companies sometimes show liabilities before assets. Also, they will sometimes show noncurrent (long-term) liabilities before current liabilities.

- Under both GAAP and IFRS, preferred stock that is required to be redeemed at a specific point in time in the future must be reported as debt, rather than being presented as either equity or in a "mezzanine" area between debt and equity.

- The basic calculation for bond valuation is the same under GAAP and IFRS. In addition, the accounting for bond liability transactions is essentially the same between GAAP and IFRS.

- IFRS requires use of the effective-interest method for amortization of bond discounts and premiums. GAAP also requires the effective-interest method, except that it allows use of the straight-line method where the difference is not material. Under IFRS, companies do not use a premium or discount account but instead show the bond at its net amount. For example, if a $100,000 bond was issued at 97, under IFRS a company would record:

| Cash | 97,000 | |
| Bonds Payable | | 97,000 |

- The accounting for convertible bonds differs between IFRS and GAAP. Unlike GAAP, IFRS splits the proceeds from the convertible bond between an equity component and a debt component. The equity conversion rights are reported in equity.

    To illustrate, assume that Harris Corp. issues convertible 7% bonds with a face value of $1,000,000 and receives $1,000,000. Comparable bonds without a conversion feature would have required a 9% rate of interest. To determine how much of the proceeds would be allocated to debt and how much to equity, the promised payments of the bond obligation would be discounted at the market rate of 9%. Suppose that this results in a present value of $850,000. The entry to record the issuance would be:

Cash	1,000,000	
Bonds Payable		850,000
Share Premium—Conversion Equity		150,000

- The IFRS leasing standard is *IAS 17*. Both Boards share the same objective of recording leases by lessees and lessors according to their economic substance—that is, according to the definitions of assets and liabilities. However, GAAP for leases is much more "rules-based" with specific bright-line criteria (such as the "90% of fair value" test) to determine if a lease arrangement transfers the risks and rewards of ownership; IFRS is more conceptual in its provisions. Rather than a 90% cut-off, it asks whether the agreement transfers substantially all of the risks and rewards associated with ownership.

Looking to the Future

The FASB and IASB are currently involved in two projects, each of which has implications for the accounting for liabilities. One project is investigating approaches to differentiate between debt and equity instruments. The other project, the elements phase of the conceptual framework project, will evaluate the definitions of the fundamental building blocks of accounting. The results of these projects could change the classification of many debt and equity securities.

    In addition to these projects, the FASB and IASB have also identified leasing as one of the most problematic areas of accounting. A joint project is now focused on lessee accounting. One of the first areas studied is, "What are the assets and liabilities to be recognized related to a lease contract?" Should the focus remain on the leased item or the right to use the leased item? This question is tied to the Boards' joint project on the conceptual framework—defining an "asset" and a "liability."

IFRS Practice

IFRS Self-Test Questions

1. The accounting for bonds payable is:
    (a) essentially the same under IFRS and GAAP.
    (b) differs in that GAAP requires use of the straight-line method for amortization of bond premium and discount.
    (c) the same except that market prices may be different because the present value calculations are different between IFRS and GAAP.
    (d) not covered by IFRS.
2. Stevens Corporation issued 5% convertible bonds with a total face value of $3,000,000 for $3,000,000. If the bonds had not had a conversion feature, they would have sold for $2,600,000. Under IFRS, the entry to record the transaction would require a credit to:
    (a) Bonds Payable for $3,000,000.
    (b) Bonds Payable for $400,000.
    (c) Share Premium—Conversion Equity for $400,000.
    (d) Discount on Bonds Payable for $400,000.

3. Under IFRS, if preference shares (preferred stock) have a requirement to be redeemed at a specific point in time in the future, they are treated:
  (a) as a type of asset account.
  (b) as ordinary shares (common stock).
  (c) in the same fashion as other types of preference shares.
  (d) as a liability.
4. The leasing standards employed by IFRS:
  (a) rely more heavily on interpretation of the conceptual meaning of assets and liabilities than GAAP.
  (b) are more "rules based" than those of GAAP.
  (c) employ the same "bright-line test" as GAAP.
  (d) are identical to those of GAAP.
5. The joint projects of the FASB and IASB could potentially:
  (a) change the definition of liabilities.
  (b) change the definition of equity.
  (c) change the definition of assets.
  (d) All of the above.

IFRS Exercises

IFRS15-1 Briefly describe some of the similarities and differences between GAAP and IFRS with respect to the accounting for liabilities.

IFRS15-2 Ratzlaff Company issues (in euros) €2 million, 10-year, 8% bonds at 97, with interest payable on July 1 and January 1.

Instructions
(a) Prepare the journal entry to record the sale of these bonds on January 1, 2014.
(b) Assuming instead that the above bonds sold for 104, prepare the journal entry to record the sale of these bonds on January 1, 2014.

IFRS15-3 Archer Company issued (in pounds) £4,000,000 par value, 7% convertible bonds at 99 for cash. The net present value of the debt without the conversion feature is £3,800,000. Prepare the journal entry to record the issuance of the convertible bonds.

International Financial Statement Analysis: Zetar plc

IFRS15-4 The financial statements of Zetar plc are presented in Appendix F. Instructions for accessing and using the company's complete annual report, including the notes to its financial statements, are also provided in Appendix F.

Instructions
Use the company's annual report to answer the following questions.
(a) According to the notes to the financial statements, what types of transactions do trade payables relate to? What was the average amount of time it took the company to pay its payables?
(b) Note 4.2 discusses provisions that the company records for certain types of activities. What do the provisions relate to, what are the estimates based on, and what could cause those estimates to change in subsequent periods?
(c) What was the average interest rate paid on bank loans and overdrafts?

Answers to IFRS Self-Test Questions
1. a **2.** c **3.** d **4.** a **5.** d

✔ **The Navigator**

16 | Investments

Feature Story

"Is There Anything Else We Can Buy?"

In a rapidly changing world, you must change rapidly or suffer the consequences. In business, change requires investment.

A case in point is found in the entertainment industry. Technology is bringing about innovations so quickly that it is nearly impossible to guess which technologies will last and which will soon fade away. For example, will both satellite TV and cable TV survive? Or, will both be replaced by something else?

Consider the publishing industry as well. Will paper newspapers and magazines be replaced completely by online news? If you are a publisher, you have to make your best guess about what the future holds and invest accordingly.

Time Warner, Inc. lives at the center of this arena. It is not an environment for the timid, and Time Warner's philosophy is anything but that. Instead, it might be characterized as, "If we can't beat you, we will buy you." Its mantra is "invest, invest, invest." A list of Time Warner's holdings gives an idea of its reach:

Magazines: *People, Time, Life, Sports Illustrated, Fortune.*

Book publishers: Time-Life Books, Book-of-the-Month Cl∪, Little, Brown & Co, Sunset Books.

Television and movies: Warner Bros. ("ER," "Without a Trace," the WB Network), HBO, and movies like *Harry Potte* *and the Deathly Hollows: Part 2* and *the Dark Knight Rises.*

Broadcasting: TNT, CNN news, and Turner's library of thousands of classic movies.

Internet: America Online and AOL Anywhere.

Time Warner owns more information and entertainment copyrights and brands than any other company in the world.

The merger of America Online (AOL) with Time Warner, one of the biggest mergers ever, was originally perceived many as the gateway to the future. In actuality, it was a financial disaster. It is largely responsible for much of the decline in Time Warner's stock price, from a high of $95 to a recent level of $32. Ted Turner, who was at one tim Time Warner's largest shareholder, lost billions of dollars the deal and eventually sold most of his shares. In 2009,

✔ The Navigator

- ☐ Scan Learning Objectives
- ☐ Read Feature Story
- ☐ Read Preview
- ☐ Read text and answer **DO IT!** p. 742
  - ☐ p. 747   ☐ p. 751   ☐ p. 754
- ☐ Work Comprehensive **DO IT!** p. 756
- ☐ Review Summary of Learning Objectives
- ☐ Answer Self-Test Questions
- ☐ Complete Assignments
- ☐ Go to *WileyPLUS* for practice and tutorials

Learning Objectives

After studying this chapter, you should be able to:

[1] Discuss why corporations invest in debt and stock securities.

[2] Explain the accounting for debt investments.

[3] Explain the accounting for stock investments.

[4] Describe the use of consolidated financial statements.

[5] Indicate how debt and stock investments are reported in financial statements.

[6] Distinguish between short-term and long-term investments.

Warner Bros/Photofest

Time Warner completed a spin-off of AOL after years of trying to integrate the two companies. One analyst called the failed deal "a nine-year adventure akin to a marathon through mud."

Preview of Chapter 16

 The Navigator

Time Warner's management believes in aggressive growth through investing in the stock of existing companies. Besides purchasing stock, companies also purchase other securities such as bonds issued by corporations or by governments. Companies can make investments for a short or long period of time, as a passive investment, or with the intent to control another company. As you will see in this chapter, the way in which a company accounts for its investments is determined by a number of factors.

The content and organization of Chapter 16 are as follows.

INVESTMENTS

Why Corporations Invest	Accounting for Debt Investments	Accounting for Stock Investments	Valuing and Reporting Investments
• Cash management • Investment income • Strategic reasons	• Recording acquisition of bonds • Recording bond interest • Recording sale of bonds	• Holdings of less than 20% • Holdings between 20% and 50% • Holdings of more than 50%	• Categories of securities • Balance sheet presentation • Realized and unrealized gain or loss • Classified balance sheet

Why Corporations Invest

<table><tr><td>LEARNING OBJECTIVE</td><td>1</td></tr></table>

Discuss why corporations invest in debt and stock securities.

Corporations purchase investments in debt or stock securities generally for one of three reasons. First, a corporation may **have excess cash** that it does not need for the immediate purchase of operating assets. For example, many companies experience seasonal fluctuations in sales. A Cape Cod marina has more sales in the spring and summer than in the fall and winter. The reverse is true for an Aspen ski shop. Thus, at the end of an operating cycle, many companies may have cash on hand that is temporarily idle until the start of another operating cycle. These companies may invest the excess funds to earn—through interest and dividends—a greater return than they would get by just holding the funds in the bank. The role that such temporary investments play in the operating cycle is shown in Illustration 16-1.

Illustration 16-1
Temporary investments and the operating cycle

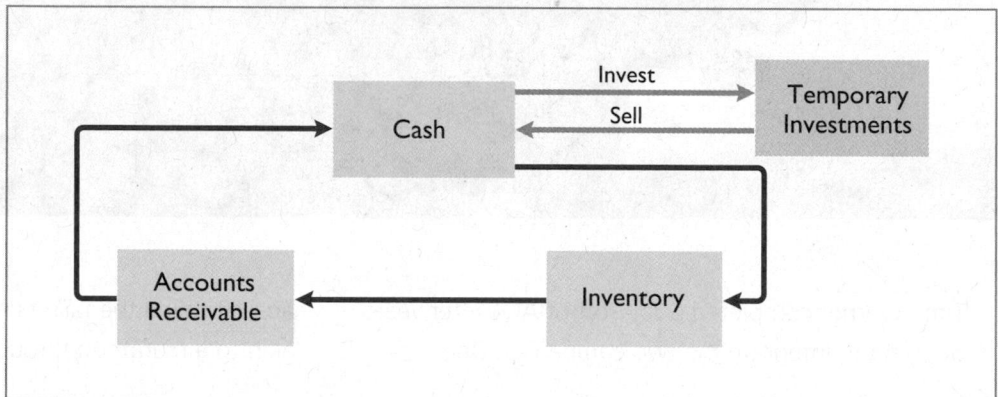

Excess cash may also result from economic cycles. For example, when the economy is booming, General Electric generates considerable excess cash. It uses some of this cash to purchase new plant and equipment, and pays out some of the cash in dividends. But, it may also invest excess cash in liquid assets in anticipation of a future downturn in the economy. It can then liquidate these investments during a recession, when sales slow and cash is scarce.

When investing excess cash for short periods of time, corporations invest in low-risk, highly liquid securities—most often short-term government securities. It is generally not wise to invest short-term excess cash in shares of common stock because stock investments can experience rapid price changes. If you did invest your short-term excess cash in stock and the price of the stock declined significantly just before you needed cash again, you would be forced to sell your stock investment at a loss.

A second reason some companies purchase investments is to generate **earnings from investment income**. For example, banks make most of their earnings by lending money, but they also generate earnings by investing in debt. Conversely, mutual stock funds invest primarily in equity securities in order to benefit from stock-price appreciation and dividend revenue.

Third, companies also invest for **strategic reasons**. A company can exercise some influence over a customer or supplier by purchasing a significant, but not controlling, interest in that company. Or, a company may purchase a noncontrolling interest in another company in a related industry in which it wishes to establish a presence. For example, Time Warner initially purchased an interest of less than 20% in Turner Broadcasting to have a stake in Turner's expanding business opportunities. At a later date, Time Warner acquired the remaining 80%. Subsequently, Time Warner merged with AOL and became AOL Time Warner, Inc. Now, it is again just Time Warner, Inc., as indicated in the Feature Story.

A corporation may also choose to purchase a controlling interest in another company. For example, as the *Accounting Across the Organization* box on page 746 shows, Procter & Gamble purchased Gillette. Such purchases might be done to enter a new industry without incurring the tremendous costs and risks associated with starting from scratch. Or, a company might purchase another company in its same industry.

In summary, businesses invest in other companies for the reasons shown in Illustration 16-2.

Reason	Typical Investment
To house excess cash until needed	Low-risk, highly liquid, short-term securities such as government-issued securities
To generate earnings *I need 1,000 Treasury bills by tonight.*	Debt securities (banks and other financial institutions) and stock securities (mutual funds and pension funds)
To meet strategic goals	Stocks of companies in a related industry or in an unrelated industry that the company wishes to enter

Illustration 16-2
Why corporations invest

Accounting for Debt Investments

Debt investments are investments in government and corporation bonds. In accounting for debt investments, companies make entries to record (1) the acquisition, (2) the interest revenue, and (3) the sale.

LEARNING OBJECTIVE   2

Explain the accounting for debt investments.

Recording Acquisition of Bonds

At acquisition, debt investments are recorded at cost. Cost includes all expenditures necessary to acquire these investments, such as the price paid plus brokerage fees (commissions), if any.

For example, assume that Kuhl Corporation acquires 50 Doan Inc. 8%, 10-year, $1,000 bonds on January 1, 2014, for $50,000. Kuhl records the investment as:

Jan. 1	Debt Investments	50,000	
	Cash		50,000
	(To record purchase of 50 Doan Inc. bonds)		

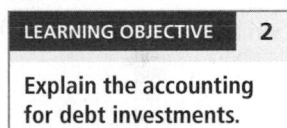

A = L + SE
+50,000
−50,000

Cash Flows
−50,000

Recording Bond Interest

The Doan Inc. bonds pay interest of $2,000 semiannually on July 1 and January 1 ($50,000 × 8% × ½). The entry for the receipt of interest on July 1 is:

July 1	Cash	2,000	
	Interest Revenue		2,000
	(To record receipt of interest on		
	Doan Inc. bonds)		

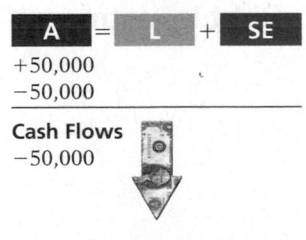

A = L + SE
+2,000
+2,000 Rev

Cash Flows
+2,000

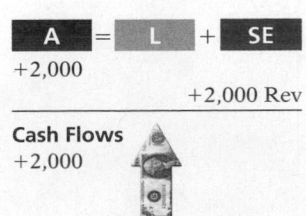

If Kuhl Corporation's fiscal year ends on December 31, it accrues the interest of $2,000 earned since July 1. The adjusting entry is:

A = L + SE
+2,000
          +2,000 Rev

Cash Flows
no effect

Dec. 31	Interest Receivable	2,000	
	Interest Revenue		2,000
	(To accrue interest on Doan Inc. bonds)		

Kuhl reports Interest Receivable as a current asset in the balance sheet. It reports Interest Revenue under "Other revenues and gains" in the income statement.
Kuhl reports receipt of the interest on January 1 as follows.

A = L + SE
+2,000
−2,000

Cash Flows
+2,000

Jan. 1	Cash	2,000	
	Interest Receivable		2,000
	(To record receipt of accrued interest)		

A credit to Interest Revenue at this time is incorrect because the company earned and accrued interest revenue in the **preceding** accounting period.

Recording Sale of Bonds

When Kuhl sells the bonds, it credits the investment account for the cost of the bonds. Kuhl records as a gain or loss any difference between the net proceeds from the sale (sales price less brokerage fees) and the cost of the bonds.

Assume, for example, that Kuhl Corporation receives net proceeds of $54,000 on the sale of the Doan Inc. bonds on January 1, 2015, after receiving the interest due. Since the securities cost $50,000, the company realizes a gain of $4,000. It records the sale as:

A = L + SE
+54,000
−50,000
          +4,000 Rev

Cash Flows
+54,000

Jan. 1	Cash	54,000	
	Debt Investments		50,000
	Gain on Sale of Debt Investments		4,000
	(To record sale of Doan Inc. bonds)		

Kuhl reports the gain on sale of debt investments under "Other revenues and gains" in the income statement and reports losses under "Other expenses and losses."

> **DO IT!**

Debt Investments

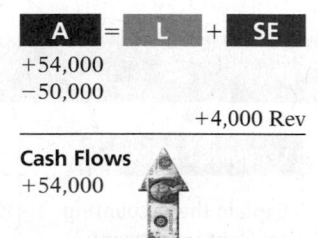

Waldo Corporation had the following transactions pertaining to debt investments.

Jan. 1 Purchased 30, $1,000 Hillary Co. 10% bonds for $30,000. Interest is payable semiannually on July 1 and January 1.
July 1 Received semiannual interest on Hillary Co. bonds.
July 1 Sold 15 Hillary Co. bonds for $14,600.

(a) Journalize the transactions, and (b) prepare the adjusting entry for the accrual of interest on December 31.

Solution

(a) Jan. 1	Debt Investments	30,000	
	Cash		30,000
	(To record purchase of 30 Hillary Co. bonds)		

Action Plan

✔ Record bond investments at cost.

✔ Record interest when received and/or accrued.

✔ When bonds are sold, credit the investment account for the cost of the bonds.

✔ Record any difference between the cost and the net proceeds as a gain or loss.

July 1	Cash		1,500	
	Interest Revenue ($30,000 × .10 × 6/12)			1,500
	(To record receipt of interest on Hillary Co. bonds)			
July 1	Cash		14,600	
	Loss on Sale of Debt Investments		400	
	Debt Investments ($30,000 × 15/30)			15,000
	(To record sale of 15 Hillary Co. bonds)			
(b) Dec. 31	Interest Receivable		750	
	Interest Revenue ($15,000 × .10 × 6/12)			750
	(To accrue interest on Hillary Co. bonds)			

Related exercise material: **BE16-1, E16-2, E16-3, and DO IT! 16-1.**

✔ **The Navigator**

Accounting for Stock Investments

Stock investments are investments in the capital stock of other corporations. When a company holds stock (and/or debt) of several different corporations, the group of securities is identified as an **investment portfolio**.

The accounting for investments in common stock depends on the extent of the investor's influence over the operating and financial affairs of the issuing corporation (the **investee**). Illustration 16-3 shows the general guidelines.

LEARNING OBJECTIVE 3

Explain the accounting for stock investments.

Investor's Ownership Interest in Investee's Common Stock	Presumed Influence on Investee	Accounting Guidelines
Less than 20%	Insignificant	Cost method
Between 20% and 50%	Significant	Equity method
More than 50%	Controlling	Consolidated financial statements

Illustration 16-3
Accounting guidelines for stock investments

Companies are required to use judgment instead of blindly following the guidelines.[1] We explain the application of each guideline next.

Holdings of Less than 20%

In accounting for stock investments of less than 20%, companies use the cost method. Under the **cost method**, companies record the investment at cost, and recognize revenue only when cash dividends are received.

Helpful Hint The entries for investments in common stock also apply to investments in preferred stock.

[1]Among the questions that are considered in determining an investor's influence are these:
(1) Does the investor have representation on the investee's board? (2) Does the investor participate in the investee's policy-making process? (3) Are there material transactions between the investor and investee? (4) Is the common stock held by other stockholders concentrated or dispersed?

RECORDING ACQUISITION OF STOCK INVESTMENTS

At acquisition, stock investments are recorded at cost. Cost includes all expenditures necessary to acquire these investments, such as the price paid plus any brokerage fees (commissions), if any.

For example, assume that on July 1, 2014, Sanchez Corporation acquires 1,000 shares (10% ownership) of Beal Corporation common stock. Sanchez pays $40 per share. The entry for the purchase is:

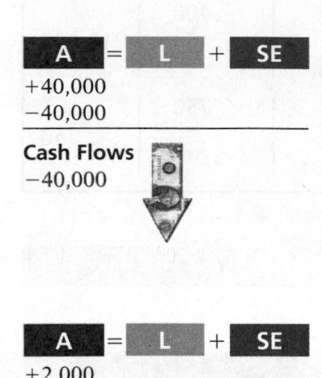

July 1	Stock Investments	40,000	
	Cash		40,000
	(To record purchase of 1,000 shares of Beal Corporation common stock)		

RECORDING DIVIDENDS

During the time Sanchez owns the stock, it makes entries for any cash dividends received. If Sanchez receives a $2 per share dividend on December 31, the entry is:

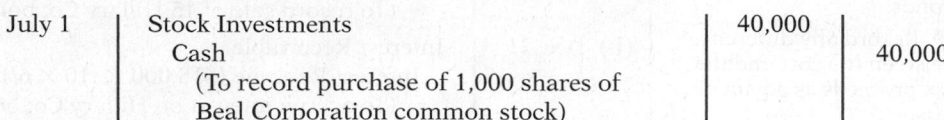

Dec. 31	Cash (1,000 × $2)	2,000	
	Dividend Revenue		2,000
	(To record receipt of a cash dividend)		

Sanchez reports Dividend Revenue under "Other revenues and gains" in the income statement. Unlike interest on notes and bonds, dividends do not accrue. Therefore, companies do not make adjusting entries to accrue dividends.

RECORDING SALE OF STOCK

When a company sells a stock investment, it recognizes as a gain or a loss the difference between the net proceeds from the sale (sales price less brokerage fees) and the cost of the stock.

Assume that Sanchez Corporation receives net proceeds of $39,000 on the sale of its Beal stock on February 10, 2015. Because the stock cost $40,000, Sanchez incurred a loss of $1,000. The entry to record the sale is:

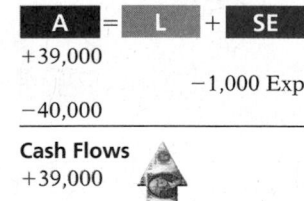

Feb. 10	Cash	39,000	
	Loss on Sale of Stock Investments	1,000	
	Stock Investments		40,000
	(To record sale of Beal common stock)		

Sanchez reports the loss under "Other expenses and losses" in the income statement. It would show a gain on sale under "Other revenues and gains."

Holdings Between 20% and 50%

When an investor company owns only a small portion of the shares of stock of another company, the investor cannot exercise control over the investee. But, when an investor owns between 20% and 50% of the common stock of a corporation, it is presumed that the investor has significant influence over the financial and operating activities of the investee. The investor probably has a representative on the investee's board of directors. Through that representative, the investor may exercise some control over the investee. The investee company in some sense becomes part of the investor company.

For example, even prior to purchasing all of Turner Broadcasting, Time Warner owned 20% of Turner. Because it exercised significant control over major decisions made by Turner, Time Warner used an approach called the equity method.

Under the **equity method, the investor records its share of the net income of the investee in the year when it is earned**. An alternative might be to delay recognizing the investor's share of net income until the investee declares a cash dividend. But, that approach would ignore the fact that the investor and investee are, in some sense, one company, making the investor better off by the investee's earned income.

Under the equity method, the investor company initially records the investment in common stock at cost. After that, it **adjusts** the investment account annually to show the investor's equity in the investee. Each year, the investor does the following. (1) It increases (debits) the investment account and increases (credits) revenue for its share of the investee's net income.[2] (2) The investor also decreases (credits) the investment account for the amount of dividends received. The investment account is reduced for dividends received because payment of a dividend decreases the net assets of the investee.

Helpful Hint Under the equity method, the investor recognizes revenue on the accrual basis—i.e., when it is earned by the investee.

RECORDING ACQUISITION OF STOCK INVESTMENTS

Assume that Milar Corporation acquires 30% of the common stock of Beck Company for $120,000 on January 1, 2014. The entry to record this transaction is:

Jan. 1	Stock Investments	120,000	
	Cash		120,000
	(To record purchase of Beck common stock)		

A	=	L	+	SE
+120,000				
−120,000				

Cash Flows
−120,000

RECORDING REVENUE AND DIVIDENDS

For 2014, Beck reports net income of $100,000. It declares and pays a $40,000 cash dividend. Milar records (1) its share of Beck's income, $30,000 (30% × $100,000) and (2) the reduction in the investment account for the dividends received, $12,000 ($40,000 × 30%). The entries are:

(1)

Dec. 31	Stock Investments	30,000	
	Revenue from Stock Investments		30,000
	(To record 30% equity in Beck's 2014 net income)		

A	=	L	+	SE
+30,000				
				+30,000 Rev

Cash Flows
no effect

(2)

Dec. 31	Cash	12,000	
	Stock Investments		12,000
	(To record dividends received)		

A	=	L	+	SE
+12,000				
−12,000				

Cash Flows
+12,000

After Milar posts the transactions for the year, its investment and revenue accounts will show the following.

Stock Investments			
Jan. 1	120,000	Dec. 31	**12,000**
Dec. 31	**30,000**		
Dec. 31 Bal.	138,000		

Revenue from Stock Investments		
	Dec. 31	**30,000**

Illustration 16-4
Investment and revenue accounts after posting

During the year, the net increase in the investment account was $18,000. As indicated above, the investment account increased by $30,000 due to Milar's share of Beck's income, and it decreased by $12,000 due to dividends received from Beck.

---

[2]Or, the investor increases (debits) a loss account and decreases (credits) the investment account for its share of the investee's net loss.

In addition, Milar reports $30,000 of revenue from its investment, which is 30% of Beck's net income of $100,000.

Note that the difference between reported revenue under the cost method and reported revenue under the equity method can be significant. For example, Milar would report only $12,000 of dividend revenue (30% × $40,000) if it used the cost method.

Holdings of More than 50%

LEARNING OBJECTIVE 4

Describe the use of consolidated financial statements.

Helpful Hint If parent (A) has three wholly owned subsidiaries (B, C, & D), there are four separate legal entities. From the viewpoint of the shareholders of the parent company, there is only one economic entity.

A company that owns more than 50% of the common stock of another entity is known as the **parent company**. The entity whose stock the parent company owns is called the **subsidiary (affiliated) company**. Because of its stock ownership, the parent company has a **controlling interest** in the subsidiary.

When a company owns more than 50% of the common stock of another company, it usually prepares **consolidated financial statements**. These statements present the total assets and liabilities controlled by the parent company. They also present the total revenues and expenses of the subsidiary companies. Companies prepare consolidated statements **in addition to** the financial statements for the parent and individual subsidiary companies.

As noted earlier, when Time Warner had a 20% investment in Turner, it reported this investment in a single line item—Other Investments. After the merger, Time Warner instead consolidated Turner's results with its own. Under this approach, Time Warner included Turner's individual assets and liabilities with its own. Its plant and equipment were added to Time Warner's plant and equipment, its receivables were added to Time Warner's receivables, and so on.

ACCOUNTING ACROSS THE ORGANIZATION

How Procter & Gamble Accounts for Gillette

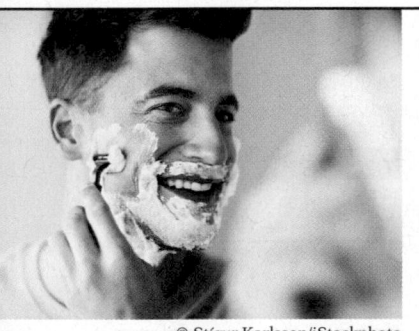

© Stígur Karlsson/iStockphoto

Several years ago, Procter & Gamble Company acquired Gillette Company for $53.4 billion. The common stockholders of Procter & Gamble elect the board of directors of the company, who, in turn, select the officers and managers of the company. Procter & Gamble's board of directors controls the property owned by the corporation, which includes the common stock of Gillette. Thus, they are in a position to elect the board of directors of Gillette and, in effect, control its operations. These relationships are graphically illustrated here.

 Where on Procter & Gamble's balance sheet will you find its investment in Gillette Company? (See page 773.)

Consolidated statements are useful to the stockholders, board of directors, and management of the parent company. These statements indicate the magnitude and scope of operations of the companies under common control. For example, regulators and the courts undoubtedly used the consolidated statements of AT&T to determine whether a breakup of the company was in the public interest. Illustration 16-5 lists three companies that prepare consolidated statements and some of the companies they have owned.

PepsiCo	Cendant	The Disney Company
Frito-Lay	Howard Johnson	Capital Cities/ABC, Inc.
Tropicana	Ramada Inn	Disneyland, Disney World
Quaker Oats	Century 21	Mighty Ducks
Pepsi-Cola	Coldwell Banker	Anaheim Angels
Gatorade	Avis	ESPN

Illustration 16-5
Examples of consolidated companies and their subsidiaries

> ## DO IT!

Stock Investments

Presented below are two independent situations.

1. Rho Jean Inc. acquired 5% of the 400,000 shares of common stock of Stillwater Corp. at a total cost of $6 per share on May 18, 2014. On August 30, Stillwater declared and paid a $75,000 dividend. On December 31, Stillwater reported net income of $244,000 for the year.

2. Debbie, Inc. obtained significant influence over North Sails by buying 40% of North Sails' 60,000 outstanding shares of common stock at a cost of $12 per share on January 1, 2014. On April 15, North Sails declared and paid a cash dividend of $45,000. On December 31, North Sails reported net income of $120,000 for the year.

Prepare all necessary journal entries for 2014 for (1) Rho Jean Inc. and (2) Debbie, Inc.

Solution

Action Plan

✔ Presume that the investor has relatively little influence over the investee when an investor owns less than 20% of the common stock of another corporation. In this case, net income earned by the investee is not considered a proper basis for recognizing income from the investment by the investor.

✔ Presume significant influence for investments of 20%–50%. Therefore, record the investor's share of the net income of the investee.

(1) May 18	Stock Investments (20,000 × $6)		120,000	
	Cash			120,000
	(To record purchase of 20,000 shares of Stillwater Co. stock)			
Aug. 30	Cash		3,750	
	Dividend Revenue ($75,000 × 5%)			3,750
	(To record receipt of cash dividend)			
(2) Jan. 1	Stock Investments (60,000 × 40% × $12)		288,000	
	Cash			288,000
	(To record purchase of 24,000 shares of North Sails' stock)			
Apr. 15	Cash		18,000	
	Stock Investments ($45,000 × 40%)			18,000
	(To record receipt of cash dividend)			
Dec. 31	Stock Investments ($120,000 × 40%)		48,000	
	Revenue from Stock Investments			48,000
	(To record 40% equity in North Sails' net income)			

Related exercise material: **BE16-2, BE16-3, E16-4, E16-5, E16-6, E16-7, E16-8, and DO IT! 16-2.**

 The Navigator

Valuing and Reporting Investments

LEARNING OBJECTIVE　**5**

Indicate how debt and stock investments are reported in financial statements.

The value of debt and stock investments may fluctuate greatly during the time they are held. For example, in one 12-month period, the stock price of Time Warner hit a high of $58.50 and a low of $9. In light of such price fluctuations, how should companies value investments at the balance sheet date? Valuation could be at cost, at fair value, or at the lower-of-cost-or-market value.

Many people argue that fair value offers the best approach because it represents the expected cash realizable value of securities. **Fair value** is the amount for which a security could be sold in a normal market. Others counter that unless a security is going to be sold soon, the fair value is not relevant because the price of the security will likely change again.

Categories of Securities

For purposes of valuation and reporting at a financial statement date, companies classify debt investments into three categories:

1. **Trading securities** are bought and held primarily for sale in the near term to generate income on short-term price differences.
2. **Available-for-sale securities** are held with the intent of selling them sometime in the future.
3. **Held-to-maturity securities** are debt securities that the investor has the intent and ability to hold to maturity.[3]

Stock investments are classified into two categories:

1. **Trading securities** (as defined above).
2. **Available-for-sale securities** (as defined above).

Stock investments have no maturity date. Therefore, they are never classified as held-to-maturity securities.

Illustration 16-6 shows the valuation guidelines for these securities. **These guidelines apply to all debt securities and all stock investments in which the holdings are less than 20%.**

Illustration 16-6
Valuation guidelines

---

[3]This category is provided for completeness. The accounting and valuation issues related to held-to-maturity securities are discussed in more advanced accounting courses.

TRADING SECURITIES

Companies hold trading securities with the intention of selling them in a short period (generally less than a month). **Trading** means frequent buying and selling. As indicated in Illustration 16-7, companies adjust trading securities to fair value at the end of each period. They report changes from cost as part of net income. The changes are reported as **unrealized gains or losses** because the securities have not been sold. The unrealized gain or loss is the difference between the **total cost** of trading securities and their **total fair value**. Companies classify trading securities as current assets.

Illustration 16-7 shows the cost and fair values for investments Pace Corporation classified as trading securities on December 31, 2014. Pace has an unrealized gain of $7,000 because total fair value of $147,000 is $7,000 greater than total cost of $140,000.

Illustration 16-7
Valuation of trading securities

Trading Securities, December 31, 2014			
Investments	**Cost**	**Fair Value**	**Unrealized Gain (Loss)**
Yorkville Company bonds	$ 50,000	$ 48,000	$(2,000)
Kodak Company stock	90,000	99,000	9,000
Total	$140,000	$147,000	$ 7,000

Pace records fair value and unrealized gain or loss through an adjusting entry at the time it prepares financial statements. In this entry, the company uses a valuation allowance account, Fair Value Adjustment—Trading, to record the difference between the total cost and the total fair value of the securities. The adjusting entry for Pace Corporation is:

 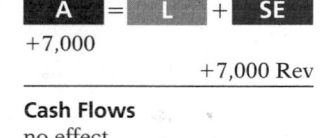

Dec. 31	Fair Value Adjustment—Trading	7,000	
	Unrealized Gain—Income		7,000
	(To record unrealized gain on trading securities)		

A = L + SE
+7,000
+7,000 Rev

Cash Flows
no effect

The use of a Fair Value Adjustment—Trading account enables Pace to maintain a record of the investment cost. It needs actual cost to determine the gain or loss realized when it sells the securities. Pace adds the debit balance (or subtracts a credit balance) of the Fair Value Adjustment—Trading balance to the cost of the investments to arrive at a fair value for the trading securities.

The fair value of the securities is the amount Pace reports on its balance sheet. It reports the unrealized gain in the income statement in the "Other revenues and gains" section. The term "Income" in the account title indicates that the gain affects net income.

If the total cost of the trading securities is greater than total fair value, an unrealized loss has occurred. In such a case, the adjusting entry is a debit to Unrealized Loss—Income and a credit to Fair Value Adjustment—Trading. Companies report the unrealized loss under "Other expenses and losses" in the income statement.

The Fair Value Adjustment—Trading account is carried forward into future accounting periods. The company does not make any entry to the account until the end of each reporting period. At that time, the company adjusts the balance in the account to the difference between cost and fair value. For trading securities, it closes the Unrealized Gain (Loss)—Income account at the end of the reporting period.

ACCOUNTING ACROSS THE ORGANIZATION

And the Correct Way to Report Investments Is...?

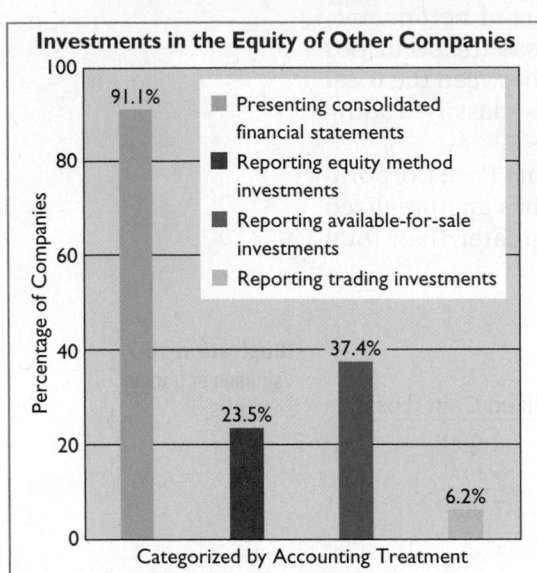

The accompanying graph presents an estimate of the percentage of companies on the major exchanges that have investments in the equity of other entities.

As the graph indicates, many companies have equity investments of some type. These investments can be substantial. For example, the total amount of equity-method investments appearing on company balance sheets is approximately $403 billion, and the amount shown in the income statements in any one year for all companies is approximately $38 billion.

Source: "Report and Recommendations Pursuant to Section 401(c) of the Sarbanes-Oxley Act of 2002 on Arrangements with Off-Balance Sheet Implications, Special Purpose Entities, and Transparency of Filings by Issuers," United States Securities and Exchange Commission—Office of Chief Accountant, Office of Economic Analyses, Division of Corporation Finance (June 2005), pp. 36–39.

 Why might the use of the equity method not lead to full disclosure in the financial statements? (See page 773.)

AVAILABLE-FOR-SALE SECURITIES

As indicated earlier, companies hold available-for-sale securities with the intent of selling these investments sometime in the future. If the intent is to sell the securities within the next year or operating cycle, the investor classifies the securities as current assets in the balance sheet. Otherwise, it classifies them as long-term assets in the investments section of the balance sheet.

Companies report available-for-sale securities at fair value. The procedure for determining fair value and the unrealized gain or loss for these securities is the same as for trading securities. To illustrate, assume that Ingrao Corporation has two securities that it classifies as available-for-sale. Illustration 16-8 provides information on the cost, fair value, and amount of the unrealized gain or loss on December 31, 2014. There is an unrealized loss of $9,537 because total cost of $293,537 is $9,537 more than total fair value of $284,000.

Ethics Note

Some managers seem to hold their available-for-sale securities that have experienced losses, while selling those that have gains, thus increasing income. Do you think this is ethical?

Illustration 16-8
Valuation of available-for-sale securities

Available-for-Sale Securities, December 31, 2014

Investments	Cost	Fair Value	Unrealized Gain (Loss)
Campbell Soup Corporation 8% bonds	$ 93,537	$103,600	$10,063
Hershey Company stock	200,000	180,400	(19,600)
Total	$293,537	$284,000	$(9,537)

Both the adjusting entry and the reporting of the unrealized gain or loss for Ingrao's available-for-sale securities differ from those illustrated for trading securities. The differences result because Ingrao does not expect to sell these securities in the near term. Thus, prior to actual sale it is more likely that changes in fair value may change either unrealized gains or losses. Therefore, Ingrao does not report an unrealized gain or loss in the income statement. Instead, it reports it as a **separate component of stockholders' equity**.

In the adjusting entry, Ingrao identifies the fair value adjustment account with available-for-sale securities, and it identifies the unrealized gain or loss account with stockholders' equity. Ingrao records the unrealized loss of $9,537 as follows.

Dec. 31	Unrealized Gain or Loss—Equity	9,537	
	Fair Value Adjustment—Available-for-Sale		9,537
	(To record unrealized loss on available-for-sale securities)		

A	=	L	+	SE

−9,537 Exp

−9,537

Cash Flows
no effect

If total fair value exceeds total cost, Ingrao debits Fair Value Adjustment—Available-for-Sale and credits Unrealized Gain or Loss—Equity.

For available-for-sale securities, the company carries forward the Unrealized Gain or Loss—Equity account to future periods. At each future balance sheet date, Ingrao adjusts the Fair Value Adjustment—Available-for-Sale account and the Unrealized Gain or Loss—Equity account to show the difference between cost and fair value at that time.

> **Ethics Note**
>
> At one time, the SEC accused investment bank Morgan Stanley of overstating the value of certain bond investments by $75 million. The SEC stated that, in applying market value accounting, Morgan Stanley used its own more-optimistic assumptions rather than relying on external pricing sources.

> DO IT!

Trading and Available-for-Sale Securities

Some of Powderhorn Corporation's investment securities are classified as trading securities and some are classified as available-for-sale. The cost and fair value of each category at December 31, 2014, are shown below.

	Cost	Fair Value	Unrealized Gain (Loss)
Trading securities	$93,600	$94,900	$1,300
Available-for-sale securities	$48,800	$51,400	$2,600

At December 31, 2013, the Fair Value Adjustment—Trading account had a debit balance of $9,200, and the Fair Value Adjustment—Available-for-Sale account had a credit balance of $5,750. Prepare the required journal entries for each group of securities for December 31, 2014.

Solution

Action Plan

✔ Mark trading securities to fair value and report the adjustment in current-period income.

✔ Mark available-for-sale securities to fair value and report the adjustment as a separate component of stockholders' equity.

Trading securities:

Unrealized Loss—Income	7,900*	
Fair Value Adjustment—Trading		7,900
(To record unrealized loss on trading securities)		

  *$9,200 − $1,300

Available-for-sale securities:

Fair Value Adjustment—Available-for-Sale	8,350**	
Unrealized Gain or Loss—Equity		8,350
(To record unrealized gain on available-for-sale securities)		

  **$5,750 + $2,600

Related exercise material: **BE16-4, BE16-5, BE16-6, BE16-7, E16-10, E16-11, E16-12, and DO IT! 16-3.**

 The Navigator

Balance Sheet Presentation

In the balance sheet, companies classify investments as either short-term or long-term.

SHORT-TERM INVESTMENTS

Short-term investments (also called **marketable securities**) are securities held by a company that are (1) **readily marketable** and (2) **intended to be converted into cash** within the next year or operating cycle, whichever is longer. Investments that do not meet **both criteria** are classified as **long-term investments.**

Helpful Hint Trading securities are always classified as short-term. Available-for-sale securities can be either short-term or long-term.

READILY MARKETABLE An investment is readily marketable when it can be sold easily whenever the need for cash arises. Short-term paper[4] meets this criterion. It can be readily sold to other investors. Stocks and bonds traded on organized securities exchanges, such as the New York Stock Exchange, are readily marketable. They can be bought and sold daily. In contrast, there may be only a limited market for the securities issued by small corporations, and no market for the securities of a privately held company.

INTENT TO CONVERT Intent to convert means that management intends to sell the investment within the next year or operating cycle, whichever is longer. Generally, this criterion is satisfied when the investment is considered a resource that the investor will use whenever the need for cash arises. For example, a ski resort may invest idle cash during the summer months with the intent to sell the securities to buy supplies and equipment shortly before the winter season. This investment is considered short-term even if lack of snow cancels the next ski season and eliminates the need to convert the securities into cash as intended.

Because of their high liquidity, short-term investments appear immediately below Cash in the "Current assets" section of the balance sheet. They are reported at fair value. For example, Pace Corporation would report its trading securities as shown in Illustration 16-9.

Illustration 16-9
Presentation of short-term investments

PACE CORPORATION	
Balance Sheet (partial)	
Current assets	
Cash	$ 21,000
Short-term investments, at fair value	147,000

LONG-TERM INVESTMENTS

Companies generally report long-term investments in a separate section of the balance sheet immediately below "Current assets," as shown later in Illustration 16-12 (page 755). Long-term investments in available-for-sale securities are reported at

---

[4]**Short-term paper** includes (1) certificates of deposit (CDs) issued by banks, (2) money market certificates issued by banks and savings and loan associations, (3) Treasury bills issued by the U.S. government, and (4) commercial paper (notes) issued by corporations with good credit ratings.

fair value. Investments in common stock accounted for under the equity method are reported at equity.

Presentation of Realized and Unrealized Gain or Loss

Companies must present in the financial statements gains and losses on investments, whether realized or unrealized. In the income statement, companies report gains and losses in the nonoperating activities section under the categories listed in Illustration 16-10. Interest and dividend revenue are also reported in that section.

Other Revenue and Gains	Other Expenses and Losses
Interest Revenue	Loss on Sale of Investments
Dividend Revenue	Unrealized Loss—Income
Gain on Sale of Investments	
Unrealized Gain—Income	

Illustration 16-10
Nonoperating items related to investments

As indicated earlier, companies report an unrealized gain or loss on available-for-sale securities as a separate component of stockholders' equity. To illustrate, assume that Dawson Inc. has common stock of $3,000,000, retained earnings of $1,500,000, and an unrealized loss on available-for-sale securities of $100,000. Illustration 16-11 shows the balance sheet presentation of the unrealized loss.

Illustration 16-11
Unrealized loss in stockholders' equity section

DAWSON INC.	
Balance Sheet (partial)	
Stockholders' equity	
Common stock	$3,000,000
Retained earnings	1,500,000
Total paid-in capital and retained earnings	4,500,000
Less: Unrealized loss on available-for-sale securities	**100,000**
Total stockholders' equity	$4,400,000

Note that the loss decreases stockholders' equity. An unrealized gain is added to stockholders' equity. Reporting the unrealized gain or loss in the stockholders' equity section serves two purposes. (1) It reduces the volatility of net income due to fluctuations in fair value. (2) It informs the financial statement user of the gain or loss that would occur if the securities were sold at fair value.

Companies must report items such as this, which affect stockholders' equity but are not included in the calculation of net income, as part of a more inclusive measure called **comprehensive income**. We discuss comprehensive income more fully in Chapter 18.

Classified Balance Sheet

We have presented many sections of classified balance sheets in this and preceding chapters. The classified balance sheet in Illustration 16-12 includes, in one place, key topics from previous chapters: the issuance of par value common stock, restrictions of retained earnings, and issuance of long-term bonds. From this chapter, the statement includes (highlighted in red) short-term and long-term investments. The investments in short-term securities are considered trading securities. The long-term investments in stock of less than 20% owned companies are considered available-for-sale securities. Illustration 16-12 also includes a long-term investment reported at equity and descriptive notations within the statement, such as the basis for valuing inventory and one note to the statement.

> **DO IT!**

Financial Statement Presentation of Investments

Identify where each of the following items would be reported in the financial statements.

1. Interest earned on investments in bonds.
2. Fair value adjustment—available-for-sale.
3. Unrealized loss on available-for-sale securities.
4. Gain on sale of investments in stock.
5. Unrealized gain on trading securities.

Use the following possible categories:

Balance sheet:

Current assets	Current liabilities
Investments	Long-term liabilities
Property, plant, and equipment	Stockholders' equity
Intangible assets	

Income statement:

Other revenues and gains	Other expenses and losses

Solution

Item	Financial Statement	Category
1. Interest earned on investments in bonds.	Income statement	Other revenues and gains
2. Fair value adjustment—available-for-sale	Balance sheet	Investments
3. Unrealized loss on available-for-sale securities	Balance sheet	Stockholders' equity
4. Gain on sale of investments in stock	Income statement	Other revenues and gains
5. Unrealized gain on trading securities	Income statement	Other revenues and gains

Related exercise material: **BE16-5, BE16-7, BE16-8, E16-10, E16-11, E16-12, and DO IT! 16-4.**

Action Plan

✔ Classify investments as current assets if they will be held for less than one year.

✔ Report unrealized gains or losses on trading securities in income.

✔ Report unrealized gains or losses on available-for-sale securities in equity.

✔ Report realized earnings on investments in the income statement as "Other revenues and gains" or as "Other expenses and losses."

✔ **The Navigator**

Illustration 16-12
Classified balance sheet

PACE CORPORATION
Balance Sheet
December 31, 2014

Assets

Current assets			
Cash			$ 21,000
Short-term investments, at fair value			**147,000**
Accounts receivable		$ 84,000	
Less: Allowance for doubtful accounts		4,000	80,000
Inventory, at FIFO cost			43,000
Prepaid insurance			23,000
Total current assets			314,000
Investments			
Investments in stock of less than 20%			
owned companies, at fair value		50,000	
Investment in stock of 20–50% owned			
company, at equity		150,000	
Total investments			200,000
Property, plant, and equipment			
Land		200,000	
Buildings	$800,000		
Less: Accumulated depreciation—buildings	200,000	600,000	
Equipment	180,000		
Less: Accumulated depreciation—equipment	54,000	126,000	
Total property, plant, and equipment			926,000
Intangible assets			
Goodwill			270,000
Total assets			$1,710,000

Liabilities and Stockholders' Equity

Current liabilities		
Accounts payable		$ 185,000
Federal income taxes payable		60,000
Interest payable		10,000
Total current liabilities		255,000
Long-term liabilities		
Bonds payable, 10%, due 2021	$ 300,000	
Less: Discount on bonds	10,000	
Total long-term liabilities		290,000
Total liabilities		545,000
Stockholders' equity		
Paid-in capital		
Common stock, $10 par value,		
200,000 shares authorized, 80,000 shares		
issued and outstanding	800,000	
Paid-in capital in excess of par—		
common stock	100,000	
Total paid-in capital	900,000	
Retained earnings (Note 1)	255,000	
Total paid-in capital and retained earnings	1,155,000	
Add: Unrealized gain on available-for-sale		
securities	10,000	
Total stockholders' equity		1,165,000
Total liabilities and stockholders' equity		$1,710,000

Note 1. Retained earnings of $100,000 is restricted for plant expansion.

> Comprehensive DO IT!

In its first year of operations, DeMarco Company had the following selected transactions in stock investments that are considered trading securities.

June 1   Purchased for cash 600 shares of Sanburg common stock at $24 per share.
July 1   Purchased for cash 800 shares of Cey Corporation common stock at $33 per share.
Sept. 1 Received a $1 per share cash dividend from Cey Corporation.
Nov. 1   Sold 200 shares of Sanburg common stock for cash at $27 per share.
Dec. 15 Received a $0.50 per share cash dividend on Sanburg common stock.

At December 31, the fair values per share were Sanburg $25 and Cey $30.

Instructions
(a) Journalize the transactions.
(b) Prepare the adjusting entry at December 31 to report the securities at fair value.

Solution to Comprehensive DO IT!

Action Plan

✔ Record the price paid as the cost of the investment.

✔ Compute the gain or loss on sales as the difference between selling price and the cost of the securities.

✔ Base the adjustment to fair value on the total difference between the cost and the fair value of the securities.

(a) June 1	Stock Investments		14,400	
	Cash (600 × $24)			14,400
	(To record purchase of 600 shares of Sanburg common stock)			
July 1	Stock Investments		26,400	
	Cash (800 × $33)			26,400
	(To record purchase of 800 shares of Cey common stock)			
Sept. 1	Cash (800 × $1.00)		800	
	Dividend Revenue			800
	(To record receipt of $1 per share cash dividend from Cey Corporation)			
Nov. 1	Cash (200 × $27)		5,400	
	Stock Investments ($14,400 × 200/600)			4,800
	Gain on Sale of Stock Investments			600
	(To record sale of 200 shares of Sanburg common stock)			
Dec. 15	Cash [(600 − 200) × $0.50]		200	
	Dividend Revenue			200
	(To record receipt of $0.50 per share dividend from Sanburg)			
(b) Dec. 31	Unrealized Loss—Income		2,000	
	Fair Value Adjustment—Trading			2,000
	(To record unrealized loss on trading securities)			

Investment	Cost	Fair Value	Unrealized Gain (Loss)
Sanburg common stock	$ 9,600	$10,000	$ 400
Cey common stock	26,400	24,000	(2,400)
Totals	$36,000	$34,000	$(2,000)

 The Navigator

SUMMARY OF LEARNING OBJECTIVES

 The Navigator

1 Discuss why corporations invest in debt and stock securities. Corporations invest for three primary reasons. (a) They have excess cash. (b) They view investments as a significant revenue source. (c) They have strategic goals such as gaining control of a competitor or moving into a new line of business.

2 Explain the accounting for debt investments. Companies record investments in debt securities when they purchase bonds, receive or accrue interest, and sell the bonds. They report gains or losses on the sale of bonds in the "Other revenues and gains" or "Other expenses and losses" sections of the income statement.

3 Explain the accounting for stock investments. Companies record investments in common stock when they purchase the stock, receive dividends, and sell the stock. When ownership is less than 20%, the cost method is used. When ownership is between 20% and 50%, the equity method should be used. When ownership is more than 50%, companies prepare consolidated financial statements.

4 Describe the use of consolidated financial statements. When a company owns more than 50% of the common stock of another company, it usually prepares consolidated financial statements. These statements indicate the magnitude and scope of operations of the companies under common control.

5 Indicate how debt and stock investments are reported in financial statements. Investments in debt securities are classified as trading, available-for-sale, or held-to-maturity securities for valuation and reporting purposes. Stock investments are classified either as trading or available-for-sale securities. Stock investments have no maturity date and therefore are never classified as held-to-maturity securities. Trading securities are reported as current assets at fair value, with changes from cost reported in net income. Available-for-sale securities are also reported at fair value, with the changes from cost reported in stockholders' equity. Available-for-sale securities are classified as short-term or long-term, depending on their expected future sale date.

6 Distinguish between short-term and long-term investments. Short-term investments are securities that are (a) readily marketable and (b) intended to be converted to cash within the next year or operating cycle, whichever is longer. Investments that do not meet both criteria are classified as long-term investments.

GLOSSARY

Available-for-sale securities Securities that are held with the intent of selling them sometime in the future. (p. 748).

Consolidated financial statements Financial statements that present the assets and liabilities controlled by the parent company and the total revenues and expenses of the subsidiary companies. (p. 746).

Controlling interest Ownership of more than 50% of the common stock of another entity. (p. 746).

Cost method An accounting method in which the investment in common stock is recorded at cost, and revenue is recognized only when cash dividends are received. (p. 743).

Debt investments Investments in government and corporation bonds. (p. 741).

Equity method An accounting method in which the investment in common stock is initially recorded at cost, and the investment account is then adjusted annually to show the investor's equity in the investee. (p. 745).

Fair value Amount for which a security could be sold in a normal market. (p. 748).

Held-to-maturity securities Debt securities that the investor has the intent and ability to hold to their maturity date. (p. 748).

Investment portfolio A group of stocks and/or debt securities in different corporations held for investment purposes. (p. 743).

Long-term investments Investments that are not readily marketable or that management does not intend to convert into cash within the next year or operating cycle, whichever is longer. (p. 752).

Parent company A company that owns more than 50% of the common stock of another entity. (p. 746).

Short-term investments Investments that are readily marketable and intended to be converted into cash within the next year or operating cycle, whichever is longer. (p. 752).

Stock investments Investments in the capital stock of other corporations. (p. 743).

Subsidiary (affiliated) company A company in which more than 50% of its stock is owned by another company. (p. 746).

Trading securities Securities bought and held primarily for sale in the near term to generate income on short-term price differences. (p. 748).

Self-Test, Brief Exercises, Exercises, Problem Set A, and many more components are available for practice in *WileyPLUS*.

SELF-TEST QUESTIONS

Answers are on page 773.

(LO 1) **1.** Which of the following is **not** a primary reason why corporations invest in debt and equity securities?
(a) They wish to gain control of a competitor.
(b) They have excess cash.

(c) They wish to move into a new line of business.
(d) They are required to by law.

2. Debt investments are initially recorded at: (LO 2)
(a) cost.
(b) cost plus accrued interest.

(c) fair value.

(d) face value.

(LO 2) **3.** Hanes Company sells debt investments costing $26,000 for $28,000. In journalizing the sale, credits are to:

(a) Debt Investments and Loss on Sale of Debt Investments.

(b) Debt Investments and Gain on Sale of Debt Investments.

(c) Stock Investments and Gain on Sale of Stock Investments.

(d) No correct answer is given.

(LO 3) **4.** Pryor Company receives net proceeds of $42,000 on the sale of stock investments that cost $39,500. This transaction will result in reporting in the income statement a:

(a) loss of $2,500 under "Other expenses and losses."

(b) loss of $2,500 under "Operating expenses."

(c) gain of $2,500 under "Other revenues and gains."

(d) gain of $2,500 under "Operating revenues."

(LO 3) **5.** The equity method of accounting for long-term investments in stock should be used when the investor has significant influence over an investee and owns:

(a) between 20% and 50% of the investee's common stock.

(b) 20% or more of the investee's common stock.

(c) more than 50% of the investee's common stock.

(d) less than 20% of the investee's common stock.

(LO 3) **6.** Assume that Horicon Corp acquired 25% of the common stock of Sheboygan Corp. on January 1, 2014, for $300,000. During 2014, Sheboygan Corp. reported net income of $160,000 and paid total dividends of $60,000. If Horicon uses the equity method to account for its investment, the balance in the investment account on December 31, 2014, will be:

(a) $300,000.   (c) $400,000.

(b) $325,000.   (d) $340,000.

(LO 3) **7.** Using the information in Self-Test Question 6, what entry would Horicon make to record the receipt of the dividend from Sheboygan?

(a) Debit Cash and credit Revenue from Stock Investments.

(b) Debit Cash Dividends and credit Revenue from Stock Investments.

(c) Debit Cash and credit Stock Investments.

(d) Debit Cash and credit Dividend Revenue.

(LO 3) **8.** You have a controlling interest if:

(a) you own more than 20% of a company's stock.

(b) you are the president of the company.

(c) you use the equity method.

(d) you own more than 50% of a company's stock.

(LO 4) **9.** Which of the following statements is **false**? Consolidated financial statements are useful to:

(a) determine the profitability of specific subsidiaries.

(b) determine the total profitability of companies under common control.

(c) determine the breadth of a parent company's operations.

(d) determine the full extent of total obligations of companies under common control.

10. At the end of the first year of operations, the total cost (LO 5) of the trading securities portfolio is $120,000. Total fair value is $115,000. The financial statements should show:

(a) a reduction of an asset of $5,000 and a realized loss of $5,000.

(b) a reduction of an asset of $5,000 and an unrealized loss of $5,000 in the stockholders' equity section.

(c) a reduction of an asset of $5,000 in the current assets section and an unrealized loss of $5,000 in "Other expenses and losses."

(d) a reduction of an asset of $5,000 in the current assets section and a realized loss of $5,000 in "Other expenses and losses."

11. At December 31, 2014, the fair value of available- (LO 5) for-sale securities is $41,300 and the cost is $39,800. At January 1, 2014, there was a credit balance of $900 in the Fair Value Adjustment—Available-for-Sale account. The required adjusting entry would be:

(a) Debit Fair Value Adjustment—Available-for-Sale for $1,500 and credit Unrealized Gain or Loss—Equity for $1,500.

(b) Debit Fair Value Adjustment—Available-for-Sale for $600 and credit Unrealized Gain or Loss—Equity for $600.

(c) Debit Fair Value Adjustment—Available-for-Sale for $2,400 and credit Unrealized Gain or Loss—Equity for $2,400.

(d) Debit Unrealized Gain or Loss—Equity for $2,400 and credit Fair Value Adjustment—Available-for-Sale for $2,400.

12. In the balance sheet, a debit balance in Unrealized (LO 5) Gain or Loss—Equity is reported as a(n):

(a) increase to stockholders' equity.

(b) decrease to stockholders' equity.

(c) loss in the income statement.

(d) loss in the retained earnings statement.

13. Short-term debt investments must be readily market- (LO 6) able and expected to be sold within:

(a) 3 months from the date of purchase.

(b) the next year or operating cycle, whichever is shorter.

(c) the next year or operating cycle, whichever is longer.

(d) the operating cycle.

Go to the book's companion website, www.wiley.com/college/weygandt, for additional Self-Test Questions.

✔ **The Navigator**

QUESTIONS

1. What are the reasons that corporations invest in securities?
2. **(a)** What is the cost of an investment in bonds?
   (b) When is interest on bonds recorded?
3. Alex Ramirez is confused about losses and gains on the sale of debt investments. Explain to Alex (a) how the gain or loss is computed, and (b) the statement presentation of the gains and losses.
4. Seibel Company sells Mayo's bonds costing $40,000 for $45,000, including $500 of accrued interest. Seibel records a $5,000 gain on this sale. Is this correct? Explain.
5. What is the cost of an investment in stock?
6. To acquire Peoples Corporation stock, J. Rich pays $62,000 in cash. What entry should be made for this investment?
7. (a) When should a long-term investment in common stock be accounted for by the equity method? (b) When is revenue recognized under this method?
8. Ling Corporation uses the equity method to account for its ownership of 35% of the common stock of Gorman Packing. During 2014, Gorman reported a net income of $80,000 and declares and pays cash dividends of $10,000. What recognition should Ling Corporation give to these events?
9. What constitutes "significant influence" when an investor's financial interest is below the 50% level?
10. Distinguish between the cost and equity methods of accounting for investments in stocks.
11. What are consolidated financial statements?
12. What are the classification guidelines for investments at a balance sheet date?
13. Jill Hollern is the controller of Chavez Inc. At December 31, the company's investments in trading securities cost $74,000. They have a fair value of $72,000. Indicate how Jill would report these data in the financial statements prepared on December 31.
14. Using the data in Question 13, how would Jill report the data if the investment were long-term and the securities were classified as available-for-sale?
15. Culver Company's investments in available-for-sale securities at December 31 show total cost of $195,000 and total fair value of $205,000. Prepare the adjusting entry.
16. Using the data in Question 15, prepare the adjusting entry assuming the securities are classified as trading securities.
17. What is the proper statement presentation of the account Unrealized Loss—Equity?
18. What purposes are served by reporting Unrealized Gain or Loss—Equity in the stockholders' equity section?
19. Deering Wholesale Supply owns stock in Orr Corporation. Deering intends to hold the stock indefinitely because of some negative tax consequences if sold. Should the investment in Orr be classified as a short-term investment? Why or why not?
20. What does Apple state regarding its accounting policy involving consolidated financial statements?

BRIEF EXERCISES

BE16-1 Ownbey Corporation purchased debt investments for $52,000 on January 1, 2014. On July 1, 2014, Ownbey received cash interest of $2,340. Journalize the purchase and the receipt of interest. Assume that no interest has been accrued.

Journalize entries for debt investments.
(LO 2)

BE16-2 On August 1, Shaw Company buys 1,000 shares of Estrada common stock for $37,000 cash. On December 1, Shaw sells the stock investments for $40,000 in cash. Journalize the purchase and sale of the common stock.

Journalize entries for stock investments.
(LO 3)

BE16-3 Noler Company owns 25% of Lauer Company. For the current year, Lauer reports net income of $180,000 and declares and pays a $50,000 cash dividend. Record Noler's equity in Lauer's net income and the receipt of dividends from Lauer.

Record transactions under the equity method of accounting.
(LO 3)

BE16-4 The cost of the trading securities of Munoz Company at December 31, 2014, is $64,000. At December 31, 2014, the fair value of the securities is $59,000. Prepare the adjusting entry to record the securities at fair value.

Prepare adjusting entry using fair value.
(LO 5)

BE16-5 For the data presented in BE16-4, show the financial statement presentation of the trading securities and related accounts.

Indicate statement presentation using fair value.
(LO 5, 6)

BE16-6 Godfrey Corporation holds, as a long-term investment, available-for-sale securities costing $72,000. At December 31, 2014, the fair value of the securities is $68,000. Prepare the adjusting entry to record the securities at fair value.

Prepare adjusting entry using fair value.
(LO 5)

BE16-7 For the data presented in BE16-6, show the financial statement presentation of the available-for-sale securities and related accounts. Assume the available-for-sale securities are noncurrent.

Indicate statements presentation using fair value.
(LO 5, 6)

Prepare investments section of balance sheet.

(LO 5, 6)

BE16-8 Kruger Corporation has the following long-term investments. (1) Common stock of Eidman Co. (10% ownership) held as available-for-sale securities, cost $108,000, fair value $115,000. (2) Common stock of Pickerill Inc. (30% ownership), cost $210,000, equity $260,000. Prepare the investments section of the balance sheet.

> DO IT! Review

Make journal entry for bond purchase and adjusting entry for interest accrual.

(LO 2)

DO IT! 16-1 Kurtyka Corporation had the following transactions relating to debt investments:

Jan. 1   Purchased 50, $1,000, 10% Spiller Company bonds for $50,000. Interest is payable semiannually on January 1 and July 1.
July 1   Received semiannual interest from Spiller Company bonds.
July 1   Sold 30 Spiller Company bonds for $29,000.

(a) Journalize the transactions, and **(b)** prepare the adjusting entry for the accrual of interest on December 31.

Make journal entries for stock investments.

(LO 3)

DO IT! 16-2 Presented below are two independent situations:

1. Edelman Inc. acquired 10% of the 500,000 shares of common stock of Schuberger Corporation at a total cost of $11 per share on June 17, 2014. On September 3, Schuberger declared and paid a $160,000 dividend. On December 31, Schuberger reported net income of $550,000 for the year.
2. Wen Corporation obtained significant influence over Hunsaker Company by buying 30% of Hunsaker's 100,000 outstanding shares of common stock at a cost of $18 per share on January 1, 2014. On May 15, Hunsaker declared and paid a cash dividend of $150,000. On December 31, Hunsaker reported net income of $270,000 for the year.

Prepare all necessary journal entries for 2014 for (a) Edelman and (b) Wen.

Make journal entries for trading and available-for-sale securities.

(LO 5)

DO IT! 16-3 Some of Tollakson Corporation's investment securities are classified as trading securities and some are classified as available-for-sale. The cost and fair value of each category at December 31, 2014, were as follows.

	Cost	Fair Value	Unrealized Gain (Loss)
Trading securities	$96,300	$84,900	$(11,400)
Available-for-sale securities	$59,000	$63,200	$ 4,200

At December 31, 2013, the Fair Value Adjustment—Trading account had a debit balance of $3,200, and the Fair Value Adjustment—Available-for-Sale account had a credit balance of $5,750. Prepare the required journal entries for each group of securities for December 31, 2014.

Indicate financial statement presentation of investments.

(LO 6)

DO IT! 16-4 Identify where each of the following items would be reported in the financial statements.

1. Loss on sale of investments in stock.
2. Unrealized gain on available-for-sale securities.
3. Fair value adjustment—trading.
4. Interest earned on investments in bonds.
5. Unrealized loss on trading securities.

Use the following possible categories:

Balance sheet:

Current assets	Current liabilities
Investments	Long-term liabilities
Property, plant, and equipment	Stockholders' equity
Intangible assets	

Income statement:

Other revenues and gains	Other expenses and losses

EXERCISES

E16-1 Mr. Taliaferro is studying for an accounting test and has developed the following questions about investments.

1. What are three reasons why companies purchase investments in debt or stock securities?
2. Why would a corporation have excess cash that it does not need for operations?
3. What is the typical investment when investing cash for short periods of time?
4. What are the typical investments when investing cash to generate earnings?
5. Why would a company invest in securities that provide no current cash flows?
6. What is the typical stock investment when investing cash for strategic reasons?

Understand debt and stock investments.
(LO 1)

Instructions
Provide answers for Mr. Taliaferro.

E16-2 Jenek Corporation had the following transactions pertaining to debt investments.

Journalize debt investment transactions and accrue interest.
(LO 2)

Jan. 1	Purchased 50 9%, $1,000 Leeds Co. bonds for $50,000 cash. Interest is payable semiannually on July 1 and January 1.
July 1	Received semiannual interest on Leeds Co. bonds.
July 1	Sold 30 Leeds Co. bonds for $33,000.

Instructions
(a) Journalize the transactions.
(b) Prepare the adjusting entry for the accrual of interest at December 31.

E16-3 Flynn Company purchased 70 Rinehart Company 12%, 10-year, $1,000 bonds on January 1, 2014, for $70,000. The bonds pay interest semiannually on July 1 and January 1. On January 1, 2015, after receipt of interest, Flynn Company sold 40 of the bonds for $38,500.

Journalize debt investment transactions, accrue interest, and record sale.
(LO 2)

Instructions
Prepare the journal entries to record the transactions described above.

E16-4 Hulse Company had the following transactions pertaining to stock investments.

Journalize stock investment transactions.
(LO 3)

Feb. 1	Purchased 600 shares of Wade common stock (2%) for $7,200 cash.
July 1	Received cash dividends of $1 per share on Wade common stock.
Sept. 1	Sold 300 shares of Wade common stock for $4,300.
Dec. 1	Received cash dividends of $1 per share on Wade common stock.

Instructions
(a) Journalize the transactions.
(b) Explain how dividend revenue and the gain (loss) on sale should be reported in the income statement.

E16-5 Nosker Inc. had the following transactions pertaining to investments in common stock.

Journalize transactions for investments in stocks.
(LO 3)

Jan. 1	Purchased 2,500 shares of Escalante Corporation common stock (5%) for $152,000 cash.
July 1	Received a cash dividend of $3 per share.
Dec. 1	Sold 500 shares of Escalante Corporation common stock for $32,000 cash.
Dec. 31	Received a cash dividend of $3 per share.

Instructions
Journalize the transactions.

E16-6 On February 1, Rinehart Company purchased 500 shares (2% ownership) of Givens Company common stock for $32 per share. On March 20, Rinehart Company sold 100 shares of Givens stock for $2,900. Rinehart received a dividend of $1.00 per share on April 25. On June 15, Rinehart sold 200 shares of Givens stock for $7,600. On July 28, Rinehart received a dividend of $1.25 per share.

Journalize transactions for investments in stocks.
(LO 3)

Instructions
Prepare the journal entries to record the transactions described above.

*Journalize and post transac-
tions, under the equity
method.*
(LO 3)

E16-7 On January 1, Zabel Corporation purchased a 25% equity in Helbert Corporation for $180,000. At December 31, Helbert declared and paid a $60,000 cash dividend and reported net income of $200,000.

Instructions

(a) Journalize the transactions.

(b) Determine the amount to be reported as an investment in Helbert stock at December 31.

*Journalize entries under cost
and equity methods.*
(LO 3, 5)

E16-8 Presented below are two independent situations.

1. Gambino Cosmetics acquired 10% of the 200,000 shares of common stock of Nevins Fashion at a total cost of $13 per share on March 18, 2014. On June 30, Nevins declared and paid a $60,000 dividend. On December 31, Nevins reported net income of $122,000 for the year. At December 31, the market price of Nevins Fashion was $15 per share. The stock is classified as available-for-sale.

2. Kanza, Inc., obtained significant influence over Rogan Corporation by buying 40% of Rogan's 30,000 outstanding shares of common stock at a total cost of $9 per share on January 1, 2014. On June 15, Rogan declared and paid a cash dividend of $30,000. On December 31, Rogan reported a net income of $80,000 for the year.

Instructions

Prepare all the necessary journal entries for 2014 for (a) Gambino Cosmetics and (b) Kanza, Inc.

*Understand the usefulness of
consolidated statements.*
(LO 4)

E16-9 Agee Company purchased 70% of the outstanding common stock of Himes Corporation.

Instructions

(a) Explain the relationship between Agee Company and Himes Corporation.

(b) How should Agee account for its investment in Himes?

(c) Why is the accounting treatment described in (b) useful?

*Prepare adjusting entry to
record fair value, and indicate
statement presentation.*
(LO 5, 6)

E16-10 At December 31, 2014, the trading securities for Storrer, Inc. are as follows.

Security	Cost	Fair Value
A	$17,500	$16,000
B	12,500	14,000
C	23,000	21,000
	$53,000	$51,000

Instructions

(a) Prepare the adjusting entry at December 31, 2014, to report the securities at fair value.

(b) Show the balance sheet and income statement presentation at December 31, 2014, after adjustment to fair value.

*Prepare adjusting entry to
record fair value, and indicate
statement presentation.*
(LO 5, 6)

E16-11 Data for investments in stock classified as trading securities are presented in E16-10. Assume instead that the investments are classified as available-for-sale securities. They have the same cost and fair value. The securities are considered to be a long-term investment.

Instructions

(a) Prepare the adjusting entry at December 31, 2014, to report the securities at fair value.

(b) Show the statement presentation at December 31, 2014, after adjustment to fair value.

(c) ———— E. Kretsinger, a member of the board of directors, does not understand the reporting of the unrealized gains or losses. Write a letter to Ms. Kretsinger explaining the reporting and the purposes that it serves.

*Prepare adjusting entries for
fair value, and indicate
statement presentation for
two classes of securities.*
(LO 5, 6)

E16-12 Uttinger Company has the following data at December 31, 2014.

Securities	Cost	Fair Value
Trading	$120,000	$126,000
Available-for-sale	100,000	96,000

The available-for-sale securities are held as a long-term investment.

Instructions

(a) Prepare the adjusting entries to report each class of securities at fair value.

(b) Indicate the statement presentation of each class of securities and the related unrealized gain (loss) accounts.

EXERCISES: SET B AND CHALLENGE EXERCISES

Visit the book's companion website, at **www.wiley.com/college/weygandt**, and choose the Student Companion site to access Exercise Set B and Challenge Exercises.

PROBLEMS: SET A

P16-1A Vilander Carecenters Inc. provides financing and capital to the health-care industry, with a particular focus on nursing homes for the elderly. The following selected transactions relate to bonds acquired as an investment by Vilander, whose fiscal year ends on December 31.

Journalize debt investment transactions and show financial statement presentation.

(LO 2, 5, 6)

2014

Jan. 1   Purchased at face value $2,000,000 of Javier Nursing Centers, Inc., 10-year, 8% bonds dated January 1, 2014, directly from Javier.
July 1   Received the semiannual interest on the Javier bonds.
Dec. 31   Accrual of interest at year-end on the Javier bonds.

(Assume that all intervening transactions and adjustments have been properly recorded and that the number of bonds owned has not changed from December 31, 2014, to December 31, 2016.)

2017

Jan. 1   Received the semiannual interest on the Javier bonds.
Jan. 1   Sold $1,000,000 Javier bonds at 106.
July 1   Received the semiannual interest on the Javier bonds.
Dec. 31   Accrual of interest at year-end on the Javier bonds.

Instructions

(a) Journalize the listed transactions for the years 2014 and 2017.

(b) Assume that the fair value of the bonds at December 31, 2014, was $2,200,000. These bonds are classified as available-for-sale securities. Prepare the adjusting entry to record these bonds at fair value.

(c) Based on your analysis in part (b), show the balance sheet presentation of the bonds and interest receivable at December 31, 2014. Assume the investments are considered long-term. Indicate where any unrealized gain or loss is reported in the financial statements.

(a) Gain on sale of debt investment $60,000

P16-2A In January 2014, the management of Kinzie Company concludes that it has sufficient cash to permit some short-term investments in debt and stock securities. During the year, the following transactions occurred.

Journalize investment transactions, prepare adjusting entry, and show statement presentation.

(LO 2, 3, 5, 6)

Feb. 1   Purchased 600 shares of Muninger common stock for $32,400.
Mar. 1   Purchased 800 shares of Tatman common stock for $20,000.
Apr. 1   Purchased 50 $1,000, 7% Yoakem bonds for $50,000. Interest is payable semiannually on April 1 and October 1.
July 1   Received a cash dividend of $0.60 per share on the Muninger common stock.
Aug. 1   Sold 200 shares of Muninger common stock at $58 per share.
Sept. 1   Received a $1 per share cash dividend on the Tatman common stock.
Oct. 1   Received the semiannual interest on the Yoakem bonds.
Oct. 1   Sold the Yoakem bonds for $49,000.

At December 31, the fair value of the Muninger common stock was $55 per share. The fair value of the Tatman common stock was $24 per share.

Instructions

(a) Journalize the transactions and post to the accounts Debt Investments and Stock Investments. (Use the T-account form.)

(b) Prepare the adjusting entry at December 31, 2014, to report the investment securities at fair value. All securities are considered to be trading securities.

(a) Gain on sale of stock investment $800

(c) Show the balance sheet presentation of investment securities at December 31, 2014.

(d) Identify the income statement accounts and give the statement classification of each account.

Journalize transactions and adjusting entry for stock investments.

(LO 3, 5, 6)

P16-3A On December 31, 2014, Turnball Associates owned the following securities, held as a long-term investment. The securities are not held for influence or control of the investee.

Common Stock	Shares	Cost
Gehring Co.	2,000	$60,000
Wooderson Co.	5,000	45,000
Kitselton Co.	1,500	30,000

On December 31, 2014, the total fair value of the securities was equal to its cost. In 2015, the following transactions occurred.

July 1 Received $1 per share semiannual cash dividend on Wooderson Co. common stock.

Aug. 1 Received $0.50 per share cash dividend on Gehring Co. common stock.

Sept. 1 Sold 1,500 shares of Wooderson Co. common stock for cash at $8 per share.

Oct. 1 Sold 800 shares of Gehring Co. common stock for cash at $33 per share.

Nov. 1 Received $1 per share cash dividend on Kitselton Co. common stock.

Dec. 15 Received $0.50 per share cash dividend on Gehring Co. common stock.

31 Received $1 per share semiannual cash dividend on Wooderson Co. common stock.

At December 31, the fair values per share of the common stocks were: Gehring Co. $32, Wooderson Co. $8, and Kitselton Co. $18.

Instructions

(a) Journalize the 2015 transactions and post to the account Stock Investments. (Use the T-account form.)

(b) Prepare the adjusting entry at December 31, 2015, to show the securities at fair value. The stock should be classified as available-for-sale securities.

(c) Show the balance sheet presentation of the investments at December 31, 2015. At this date, Turnball Associates has common stock $1,500,000 and retained earnings $1,000,000.

(b) Unrealized loss $4,100

Prepare entries under the cost and equity methods, and tabulate differences.

(LO 3)

P16-4A Heidebrecht Design acquired 20% of the outstanding common stock of Quayle Company on January 1, 2014, by paying $800,000 for the 30,000 shares. Quayle declared and paid $0.30 per share cash dividends on March 15, June 15, September 15, and December 15, 2014. Quayle reported net income of $320,000 for the year. At December 31, 2014, the market price of Quayle common stock was $34 per share.

Instructions

(a) Prepare the journal entries for Heidebrecht Design for 2014 assuming Heidebrecht Design cannot exercise significant influence over Quayle. (Use the cost method and assume that Quayle common stock should be classified as a trading security.)

(b) Prepare the journal entries for Heidebrecht Design for 2014, assuming Heidebrecht Design can exercise significant influence over Quayle. Use the equity method.

(c) Indicate the balance sheet and income statement account balances at December 31, 2014, under each method of accounting.

(a) Total dividend revenue $36,000

(b) Revenue from stock investments $64,000

Journalize stock investment transactions and show statement presentation.

(LO 3, 5, 6)

P16-5A The following securities are in Frederick Company's portfolio of long-term available-for-sale securities at December 31, 2014.

	Cost
1,000 shares of Willhite Corporation common stock	$52,000
1,400 shares of Hutcherson Corporation common stock	84,000
1,200 shares of Downing Corporation preferred stock	33,600

On December 31, 2014, the total cost of the portfolio equaled total fair value. Frederick had the following transactions related to the securities during 2015.

Jan. 20 Sold all 1,000 shares of Willhite Corporation common stock at $55 per share.

28 Purchased 400 shares of $70 par value common stock of Liggett Corporation at $78 per share.

30 Received a cash dividend of $1.15 per share on Hutcherson Corp. common stock.

Feb. 8   Received cash dividends of $0.40 per share on Downing Corp. preferred stock.
     18   Sold all 1,200 shares of Downing Corp. preferred stock at $27 per share.
July 30   Received a cash dividend of $1.00 per share on Hutcherson Corp. common stock.
Sept. 6   Purchased an additional 900 shares of $10 par value common stock of Liggett
          Corporation at $82 per share.
Dec. 1   Received a cash dividend of $1.50 per share on Liggett Corporation common stock.

At December 31, 2015, the fair values of the securities were:

Hutcherson Corporation common stock	$64 per share
Liggett Corporation common stock	$72 per share

Instructions
(a) Prepare journal entries to record the transactions.
(b) Post to the investment accounts. (Use T-accounts.)
(c) Prepare the adjusting entry at December 31, 2015 to report the portfolio at fair value.
(d) Show the balance sheet presentation at December 31, 2015, for the investment-related accounts.

(a) Loss on sale of stock investment $1,200

(c) Unrealized loss $5,800

P16-6A The following data, presented in alphabetical order, are taken from the records of Nieto Corporation.

Prepare a balance sheet.
(LO 5, 6)

Accounts payable	$ 260,000
Accounts receivable	140,000
Accumulated depreciation—buildings	180,000
Accumulated depreciation—equipment	52,000
Allowance for doubtful accounts	6,000
Bonds payable (10%, due 2022)	500,000
Buildings	950,000
Cash	62,000
Common stock ($10 par value; 500,000 shares authorized, 150,000 shares issued)	1,500,000
Dividends payable	80,000
Equipment	275,000
Fair value adjustment—available-for-sale securities (Dr)	8,000
Goodwill	200,000
Income taxes payable	120,000
Inventory	170,000
Investment in Mara common stock (30% ownership), at equity	380,000
Investment in Sasse common stock (10% ownership), at cost	278,000
Land	390,000
Notes payable (due 2015)	70,000
Paid-in capital in excess of par—common stock	130,000
Premium on bonds payable	40,000
Prepaid insurance	16,000
Retained earnings	103,000
Short-term investments, at fair value (and cost)	180,000
Unrealized gain—available-for-sale securities	8,000

The investment in Sasse common stock is considered to be a long-term available-for-sale security.

Instructions
Prepare a classified balance sheet at December 31, 2014.

Total assets $2,811,000

P16-1B Cheese Farms is a grower of hybrid seed corn for Mukenthaler Genetics Corporation. It has had two exceptionally good years and has elected to invest its excess funds in bonds. The selected transactions, shown on the next page, relate to bonds acquired as an investment by Cheese Farms, whose fiscal year ends on December 31.

Journalize debt investment transactions and show financial statement presentation.
(LO 2, 5, 6)

2014

Jan.   1   Purchased at face value $400,000 of Wilkerson Corporation 10-year, 9% bonds dated January 1, 2014, directly from the issuing corporation.

July   1   Received the semiannual interest on the Wilkerson bonds.

Dec. 31   Accrual of interest at year-end on the Wilkerson bonds.

(Assume that all intervening transactions and adjustments have been properly recorded and the number of bonds owned has not changed from December 31, 2014, to December 31, 2016.)

2017

Jan.   1   Received the semiannual interest on the Wilkerson bonds.

Jan.   1   Sold $200,000 of Wilkerson bonds at 114.

July   1   Received the semiannual interest on the Wilkerson bonds.

Dec. 31   Accrual of interest at year-end on the Wilkerson bonds.

Instructions

(a) Gain on sale of debt investments $28,000

(a) Journalize the listed transactions for the years 2014 and 2017.

(b) Assume that the fair value of the bonds at December 31, 2014, was $385,000. These bonds are classified as available-for-sale securities. Prepare the adjusting entry to record these bonds at fair value.

(c) Based on your analysis in part (b), show the balance sheet presentation of the bonds and interest receivable at December 31, 2014. Assume the investments are considered long-term. Indicate where any unrealized gain or loss is reported in the financial statements.

Journalize investment transactions, prepare adjusting entry, and show statement presentation.

(LO 2, 3, 5, 6)

P16-2B In January 2014, the management of Kord Company concludes that it has sufficient cash to purchase some short-term investments in debt and stock securities. During the year, the following transactions occurred.

Feb.   1   Purchased 500 shares of Day common stock for $30,800.

Mar.   1   Purchased 600 shares of Eldridge common stock for $20,300.

Apr.   1   Purchased 40 $1,000, 9% Lorenz bonds for $40,000. Interest is payable semiannually on April 1 and October 1.

July   1   Received a cash dividend of $0.60 per share on the Day common stock.

Aug.   1   Sold 300 shares of Day common stock at $69 per share.

Sept. 1   Received a $1 per share cash dividend on the Eldridge common stock.

Oct.   1   Received the semiannual interest on the Lorenz bonds.

Oct.   1   Sold the Lorenz bonds for $44,000.

At December 31, the fair value of the Day common stock was $66 per share. The fair value of the Eldridge common stock was $29 per share.

Instructions

(b) Unrealized loss $2,020

(a) Journalize the transactions and post to the accounts Debt Investments and Stock Investments. (Use the T-account form.)

(b) Prepare the adjusting entry at December 31, 2014, to report the investments at fair value. All securities are considered to be trading securities.

(c) Show the balance sheet presentation of investment securities at December 31, 2014.

(d) Identify the income statement accounts and give the statement classification of each account.

Journalize transactions and adjusting entry for stock investments.

(LO 3, 5, 6)

P16-3B On December 31, 2014, Bly Associates owned the following securities, held as long-term investments.

Common Stock	Shares	Cost
Woolridge Co.	4,000	$100,000
Coria Co.	5,000	30,000
Sterling Motors Co.	3,000	60,000

On this date, the total fair value of the securities was equal to its cost. The securities are not held for influence or control over the investees. In 2015, the following transactions occurred.

July   1   Received $1 per share semiannual cash dividend on Coria Co. common stock.

Aug.   1   Received $0.50 per share cash dividend on Woolridge Co. common stock.

Sept. 1 Sold 1,500 shares of Coria Co. common stock for cash at $7 per share.
Oct. 1   Sold 600 shares of Woolridge Co. common stock for cash at $30 per share.
Nov. 1   Received $1 per share cash dividend on Sterling Motor Co. common stock.
Dec. 15 Received $0.50 per share cash dividend on Woolridge Co. common stock.
    31   Received $1 per share semiannual cash dividend on Coria Co. common stock.

At December 31, the fair values per share of the common stocks were Woolridge Co. $23, Coria Co. $7, and Sterling Motors Co. $19.

Instructions

(a) Journalize the 2015 transactions and post to the account Stock Investments. (Use the T-account form.)

(b) Prepare the adjusting entry at December 31, 2015, to show the securities at fair value. The stock should be classified as available-for-sale securities.

(c) Show the balance sheet presentation of the investment-related accounts at December 31, 2015. At this date, Bly Associates has common stock $2,000,000 and retained earnings $1,200,000.

(a) Gain on sale, $1,500 and $3,000

P16-4B Wooden's Concrete acquired 20% of the outstanding common stock of Hoag, Inc. on January 1, 2014, by paying $1,100,000 for 40,000 shares. Hoag declared and paid a $0.50 per share cash dividend on June 30 and again on December 31, 2014. Hoag reported net income of $600,000 for the year. At December 31, 2014, the market price of Hoag's common stock was $30 per share.

Prepare entries under the cost and equity methods, and tabulate differences.

(LO 3)

Instructions

(a) Prepare the journal entries for Wooden's Concrete for 2014, assuming Wooden's cannot exercise significant influence over Hoag. Use the cost method and assume Hoag common stock should be classified as available-for-sale.

(b) Prepare the journal entries for Wooden's Concrete for 2014, assuming Wooden's can exercise significant influence over Hoag. Use the equity method.

(c) Indicate the balance sheet and income statement account balances at December 31, 2014, under each method of accounting.

(a) Total dividend revenue $40,000

(b) Revenue from investment $120,000

P16-5B The following are in Rodriguez's Company's portfolio of long-term available-for-sale securities at December 31, 2014.

Journalize stock investment transactions and show statement presentation.

(LO 3, 5, 6)

	Cost
700 shares of Parra Corporation common stock	$35,000
900 shares of Robison Corporation common stock	42,000
800 shares of Vega Corporation preferred stock	22,400

On December 31, the total cost of the portfolio equaled total fair value. Rodriguez's Company had the following transactions related to the securities during 2015.

Jan. 7   Sold 700 shares of Parra Corporation common stock at $55 per share.
    10   Purchased 300 shares, $70 par value common stock of Younker Corporation at $78 per share.
    26   Received a cash dividend of $1.15 per share on Robison Corporation common stock.
Feb. 2   Received cash dividends of $0.40 per share on Vega Corporation preferred stock.
    10   Sold all 800 shares of Vega Corporation preferred stock at $26 per share.
July 1   Received a cash dividend of $1.00 per share on Robison Corporation common stock.
Sept. 1 Purchased an additional 800 shares of the $70 par value common stock of Younker Corporation at $75 per share.
Dec. 15 Received a cash dividend of $1.50 per share on Younker Corporation common stock.

At December 31, 2015, the fair values of the securities were:

Robison Corporation common stock	$48 per share
Younker Corporation common stock	$72 per share

Instructions

(a) Prepare journal entries to record the transactions.

(b) Post to the investment accounts. (Use T-accounts.)

(a) Loss on sale $1,600

(c) Unrealized loss $3,000

(c) Prepare the adjusting entry at December 31, 2015, to report the portfolio at fair value.
(d) Show the balance sheet presentation at December 31, 2015, for the investment-related accounts.

Prepare a balance sheet.
(LO 5, 6)

P16-6B The following data, presented in alphabetical order, are taken from the records of Mussatto Corporation.

Accounts payable	$ 375,000
Accounts receivable	135,000
Accumulated depreciation—buildings	270,000
Accumulated depreciation—equipment	80,000
Allowance for doubtful accounts	10,000
Bonds payable (10%, due 2024)	600,000
Buildings	1,350,000
Cash	210,000
Common stock ($5 par value; 500,000 shares authorized, 440,000 shares issued)	2,200,000
Discount on bonds payable	30,000
Dividends payable	75,000
Equipment	415,000
Goodwill	300,000
Income taxes payable	180,000
Inventory	255,000
Investment in Sanchez Inc. stock (30% ownership), at equity	900,000
Land	780,000
Notes payable (due 2015)	110,000
Paid-in capital in excess of par—common stock	300,000
Prepaid insurance	25,000
Retained earnings	480,000
Short-term investments, at fair value (and cost)	280,000

Instructions

Total assets $4,290,000

Prepare a classified balance sheet at December 31, 2014.

PROBLEMS: SET C

Visit the book's companion website, at **www.wiley.com/college/weygandt**, and choose the Student Companion site to access Problem Set C.

COMPREHENSIVE PROBLEM: CHAPTERS 12 TO 16

CP16 Part I Debby Kauffman and her two colleagues, Jamie Hiatt and Ella Rincon, are personal trainers at an upscale health spa/resort in Tampa, Florida. They want to start a health club that specializes in health plans for people in the 50+ age range. The growing population in this age range and strong consumer interest in the health benefits of physical activity have convinced them they can profitably operate their own club. In addition to many other decisions, they need to determine what type of business organization they want. Jamie believes there are more advantages to the corporate form than a partnership, but he hasn't yet convinced Debby and Ella. They have come to you, a small-business consulting specialist, seeking information and advice regarding the choice of starting a partnership versus a corporation.

Instructions
(a) ——— Prepare a memo (dated May 26, 2013) that describes the advantages and disadvantages of both partnerships and corporations. Advise Debby, Jamie, and Ella regarding which organizational form you believe would better serve their purposes. Make sure to include reasons supporting your advice.

Part II After deciding to incorporate, each of the three investors receives 20,000 shares of $2 par common stock on June 12, 2013, in exchange for their co-owned building ($200,000 fair value) and $100,000 total cash they contributed to the business. The next decision that Debby, Jamie, and Ella need to make is how to obtain financing for renovation and equipment. They understand the difference between equity securities and debt securities, but do not understand the tax, net income, and earnings per share consequences of equity versus debt financing on the future of their business.

Instructions

(b) Prepare notes for a discussion with the three entrepreneurs in which you will compare the consequences of using equity versus debt financing. As part of your notes, show the differences in interest and tax expense assuming $1,400,000 is financed with common stock, and then alternatively with debt. Assume that when common stock is used, 140,000 shares will be issued. When debt is used, assume the interest rate on debt is 9%, the tax rate is 32%, and income before interest and taxes is $300,000. (You may want to use an electronic spreadsheet.)

Part III During the discussion about financing, Ella mentions that one of her clients, Timothy Hansen, has approached her about buying a significant interest in the new club. Having an interested investor sways the three to issue equity securities to provide the financing they need. On July 21, 2013, Mr. Hansen buys 90,000 shares at a price of $10 per share.

The club, LifePath Fitness, opens on January 12, 2014, and after a slow start begins to produce the revenue desired by the owners. The owners decide to pay themselves a stock dividend since cash has been less than abundant since they opened their doors. The 10% stock dividend is declared by the owners on July 27, 2014. The market price of the stock is $3 on the declaration date. The date of record is July 31, 2014 (there have been no changes in stock ownership since the initial issuance), and the issue date is August 15, 2014. By the middle of the fourth quarter of 2014, the cash flow of LifePath Fitness has improved to the point that the owners feel ready to pay themselves a cash dividend. They declare a $0.05 cash dividend on December 4, 2014. The record date is December 14, 2014, and the payment date is December 24, 2014.

Instructions

(c) (1) Record all of the transactions related to the common stock of LifePath Fitness during the years 2013 and 2014. (2) Indicate how many shares are issued and outstanding after the stock dividend is issued.

Part IV Since the club opened, a major concern has been the pool facilities. Although the existing pool is adequate, Debby, Jamie, and Ella all desire to make LifePath a cutting-edge facility. Until the end of 2014, financing concerns prevented this improvement. However, because there has been steady growth in clientele, revenue, and income since the fourth quarter of 2014, the owners have explored possible financing options. They are hesitant to issue stock and change the ownership mix because they have been able to work together as a team with great effectiveness. They have formulated a plan to issue secured term bonds to raise the needed $600,000 for the pool facilities. By the end of April 2015, everything was in place for the bond issue to go ahead. On June 1, 2015, the bonds were issued for $548,000. The bonds pay semiannual interest of 3% (6% annual) on December 1 and June 1 of each year. The bonds mature in 10 years, and amortization is computed using the straight-line method.

Instructions

(d) Record (1) the issuance of the secured bonds, (2) the interest payment made on December 1, 2015, (3) the adjusting entry required at December 31, 2015, and (4) the interest payment made on June 1, 2016.

Part V Mr. Hansen's purchase of the stock of LifePath Fitness was done through his business. The stock investment has always been accounted for using the cost method on his firm's books. However, early in 2016 he decided to take his company public. He is preparing an IPO (initial public offering), and he needs to have the firm's financial statements audited. One of the issues to be resolved is to restate the stock investment in LifePath Fitness using the equity method since Mr. Hansen's ownership percentage is greater than 20%.

Instructions

(e) **(1)** Give the entries that would have been made on Hansen's books if the equity method of accounting for investments had been used from the initial investment through 2015. Assume the following data for LifePath.

	2013	2014	2015
Net income	$30,000	$70,000	$105,000
Total cash dividends	$ 2,100	$20,000	$ 50,000

(2) Compute the balance in the Stock Investment account (as it relates to LifePath Fitness) at the end of 2015.

CONTINUING COOKIE CHRONICLE

(*Note:* This is a continuation of the Cookie Chronicle from Chapters 1 through 15.)

CCC16 Natalie has been approached by Ken Thornton, a shareholder of The Beanery Coffee Inc. Ken wants to retire and would like to sell his 1,000 shares in The Beanery Coffee, which represents 30% of all shares issued. The Beanery is currently operated by Ken's twin daughters, who each own 35% of the common shares. The Beanery not only operates a coffee shop but also roasts and sells beans to retailers, under the name "Rocky Mountain Beanery."

Ken has met with Curtis and Natalie to discuss the business operation. All have concluded that there would be many advantages for Cookie & Coffee Creations Inc. to acquire an interest in The Beanery Coffee. Despite the apparent advantages, however, Natalie and Curtis are still not convinced that they should participate in this business venture.

*Go to the book's companion website, **www.wiley.com/college/weygandt**, to see the completion of this problem.*

Broadening Your Perspective

Financial Reporting and Analysis

Financial Reporting Problem: Apple Inc.

BYP16-1 The annual report of Apple Inc. is presented in Appendix A. Instructions for accessing and using the company's complete annual report, including the notes to the financial statements, are also provided in Appendix A.

Instructions

(a) Determine the percentage increase for (1) short-term marketable securities from 2010 to 2011, and (2) long-term marketable securities from 2010 to 2011.
(b) Using Apple's consolidated statement of cash flows, determine:
  (1) Purchases of marketable securities during the current year.
  (2) How much was spent for business acquisitions, net of cash acquired during the current year.

Comparative Analysis Problem:
PepsiCo, Inc. vs. The Coca-Cola Company

BYP16-2 PepsiCo's financial statements are presented in Appendix B. Financial statements of The Coca-Cola Company are presented in Appendix C. Instructions for accessing and using the complete annual reports of PepsiCo and Coca-Cola, including the notes to the financial statements, are also provided in Appendices B and C, respectively.

Instructions

(a) Based on the information contained in these financial statements, determine the following for each company.
  (1) Net cash used in investing (investment) activities for the current year (from the statement of cash flows).
  (2) Cash used for capital expenditures during the current year.
(b) Each of PepsiCo's financial statements is labeled "consolidated." What has been consolidated? That is, from the contents of PepsiCo's annual report, identify by name the corporations that have been consolidated (parent and subsidiaries).

Comparative Analysis Problem:
Amazon.com, Inc. vs. Wal-Mart Stores, Inc.

BYP16-3 Amazon.com, Inc.'s financial statements are presented in Appendix D. Financial statements of Wal-Mart Stores, Inc. are presented in Appendix E. Instructions for accessing and using the complete annual reports of Amazon and Wal-Mart, including the notes to the financial statements, are also provided in Appendices D and E, respectively.

Instructions

(a) Based on the information contained in these financial statements, determine the following for each company.
  (1) Net cash used for investing (investment) activities for the current year (from the statement of cash flows).
  (2) Cash used for business acquisitions, net of cash acquired during the current year.
(b) Each of Amazon's financial statements is labeled "consolidated." What has been consolidated? That is, from the contents of Amazon's annual report, identify by name the corporations that have been consolidated (parent and subsidiaries).

Real-World Focus

BYP16-4 Most publicly traded companies are examined by numerous analysts. These analysts often don't agree about a company's future prospects. In this exercise, you will find analysts' ratings about companies and make comparisons over time and across companies in the same industry. You will also see to what extent the analysts experienced "earnings surprises." Earnings surprises can cause changes in stock prices.

Address: **biz.yahoo.com/i**, or go to **www.wiley.com/college/weygandt**

Steps
1. Choose a company.
2. Use the index to find the company's name.
3. Choose **Research**.

Instructions
(a) How many analysts rated the company?
(b) What percentage rated it a strong buy?
(c) What was the average rating for the week?
(d) Did the average rating improve or decline relative to the previous week?
(e) What was the amount of the earnings surprise percentage during the last quarter?

Critical Thinking

Decision-Making Across the Organization

BYP16-5 At the beginning of the question-and-answer portion of the annual stockholders' meeting of Neosho Corporation, stockholder John Linton asks, "Why did management sell the holdings in JMB Company at a loss when this company has been very profitable during the period Neosho held its stock?"

Since president Tony Cedeno has just concluded his speech on the recent success and bright future of Neosho, he is taken aback by this question and responds, "I remember we paid $1,300,000 for that stock some years ago. I am sure we sold that stock at a much higher price. You must be mistaken."

Linton retorts, "Well, right here in footnote number 7 to the annual report it shows that 240,000 shares, a 30% interest in JMB, were sold on the last day of the year. Also, it states that JMB earned $520,000 this year and paid out $160,000 in cash dividends. Further, a summary statement indicates that in past years, while Neosho held JMB stock, JMB earned $1,240,000 and paid out $440,000 in dividends. Finally, the income statement for this year shows a loss on the sale of JMB stock of $180,000. So, I doubt that I am mistaken."

Red-faced, president Cedeno turns to you.

Instructions

With the class divided into groups, answer the following.

(a) What dollar amount did Neosho receive upon the sale of the JMB stock?

(b) Explain why both stockholder Linton and president Cedeno are correct.

Communication Activity

BYP16-6 Fegan Corporation has purchased two securities for its portfolio. The first is a stock investment in Plummer Corporation, one of its suppliers. Fegan purchased 10% of Plummer with the intention of holding it for a number of years, but has no intention of purchasing more shares. The second investment was a purchase of debt securities. Fegan purchased the debt securities because its analysts believe that changes in market interest rates will cause these securities to increase in value in a short period of time. Fegan intends to sell the securities as soon as they have increased in value.

Instructions

Write a memo to Sam Nichols, the chief financial officer, explaining how to account for each of these investments. Explain what the implications for reported income are from this accounting treatment.

Ethics Case

BYP16-7 Harding Financial Services Company holds a large portfolio of debt and stock securities as an investment. The total fair value of the portfolio at December 31, 2014, is greater than total cost. Some securities have increased in value and others have decreased. Ann Bales, the financial vice president, and Kim Reeble, the controller, are in the process of classifying for the first time the securities in the portfolio.

Bales suggests classifying the securities that have increased in value as trading securities in order to increase net income for the year. She wants to classify the securities that have decreased in value as long-term available-for-sale securities, so that the decreases in value will not affect 2014 net income.

Reeble disagrees. She recommends classifying the securities that have decreased in value as trading securities and those that have increased in value as long-term available-for-sale securities. Reeble argues that the company is having a good earnings year and that recognizing the losses now will help to smooth income for this year. Moreover, for future years, when the company may not be as profitable, the company will have built-in gains.

Instructions

(a) Will classifying the securities as Bales and Reeble suggest actually affect earnings as each says it will?

(b) Is there anything unethical in what Bales and Reeble propose? Who are the stakeholders affected by their proposals?

(c) Assume that Bales and Reeble properly classify the portfolio. At year-end, Bales proposes to sell the securities that will increase 2014 net income, and that Reeble proposes to sell the securities that will decrease 2014 net income. Is this unethical?

All About You

BYP16-8 The Securities and Exchange Commission (SEC) is the primary regulatory agency of U.S. financial markets. Its job is to ensure that the markets remain fair for all investors. The following SEC sites provide useful information for investors.

Address: **www.sec.gov/answers.shtml** and **http://www.sec.gov/investor/tools/quiz.htm**, or go to **www.wiley.com/college/weygandt**.

Instructions

(a) Go to the first SEC site and find the definition of the following terms.

   (i) Ask price.

   (ii) Margin.

   (iii) Prospectus.

   (iv) Index fund.

(b) Go to the second SEC site and take the short quiz.

FASB Codification Activity

BYP16-9 If your school has a subscription to the FASB Codification, go to **http://aaahq.org/ascLogin.cfm** to log in and prepare responses to the following.

(a) What is the definition of a trading security?

(b) What is the definition of an available-for-sale security?

(c) What is definition of a holding gain or loss?

Answers to Chapter Questions

Answers to Insight and Accounting Across the Organization Questions

p. 746 How Procter & Gamble Accounts for Gillette   **Q:** Where on Procter & Gamble's balance sheet will you find its investment in Gillette Company? **A:** Because Procter & Gamble owns 90% of Gillette, Procter & Gamble does not report Gillette in the investment section of its balance sheet. Instead, Gillette's assets and liabilities are included and commingled with the assets and liabilities of Procter & Gamble.

p. 750 And the Correct Way to Report Investments Is... ?   **Q:** Why might the use of the equity method not lead to full disclosure in the financial statements? **A:** Under the equity method, the investment in common stock of another company is initially recorded at cost. After that, the investment account is adjusted at each reporting date to show the investor's equity in the investee. However, on the investor's balance sheet, only the investment account is shown. The pro rata share of the investee's assets and liabilities are not reported. Because the pro rata share of the investee's assets and liabilities are not shown, some argue that the full disclosure principle is violated.

Answers to Self-Test Questions

1. d **2.** a **3.** b **4.** c **5.** a **6.** b $300,000 + [25\% \times (\$160,000 - \$60,000)]$ **7.** c **8.** d **9.** a **10.** c
11. c $(\$41,300 - \$39,800) + \$900$ **12.** b **13.** c

A Look at IFRS

Until recently, when the IASB issued *IFRS 9*, the accounting and reporting for investments under IFRS and GAAP were for the most part very similar. However, *IFRS 9* introduces new investment classifications and increases the situations when investments are accounted for at fair value, with gains and losses recorded in income.

> **LEARNING OBJECTIVE   7**
>
> **Compare the accounting for investments under GAAP and IFRS.**

Key Points

• The basic accounting entries to record the acquisition of debt securities, the receipt of interest, and the sale of debt securities are the same under IFRS and GAAP.

• The basic accounting entries to record the acquisition of stock investments, the receipt of dividends, and the sale of stock securities are the same under IFRS and GAAP.

- Both IFRS and GAAP use the same criteria to determine whether the equity method of accounting should be used—that is, significant influence with a general guide of over 20% ownership, IFRS uses the term **associate investment** rather than equity investment to describe its investment under the equity method.

- Under IFRS, both the investor and an associate company should follow the same accounting policies. As a result, in order to prepare financial information, adjustments are made to the associate's policies to conform to the investor's books. GAAP does not have that requirement.

- The basis for consolidation under IFRS is control. Under GAAP, a bipolar approach is used, which is a risk-and-reward model (often referred to as a variable-entity approach) and a voting-interest approach. However, under both systems, for consolidation to occur, the investor company must generally own 50% of another company.

- In general, IFRS requires that companies determine how to measure their financial assets based on two criteria:
  - ♦ The company's business model for managing their financial assets; and
  - ♦ The contractual cash flow characteristics of the financial asset.

  If a company has (1) a business model whose objective is to hold assets in order to collect contractual cash flows and (2) the contractual terms of the financial asset gives specified dates to cash flows that are solely payments of principal and interest on the principal amount outstanding, then the company should use cost (often referred to as amortized cost).

  For example, assume that Mitsubishi purchases a bond investment that it intends to hold to maturity (held-for-collection). Its business model for this type of investment is to collect interest and then principal at maturity. The payment dates for the interest rate and principal are stated on the bond. In this case, Mitsubishi accounts for the investment at cost. If, on the other hand, Mitsubishi purchased the bonds as part of a trading strategy to speculate on interest rate changes (a trading investment), then the debt investment is reported at fair value. As a result, only debt investments such as receivables, loans, and bond investments that meet the two criteria above are recorded at amortized cost. All other debt investments are recorded and reported at fair value.

- Equity investments are generally recorded and reported at fair value under IFRS. Equity investments do not have a fixed interest or principal payment schedule and therefore cannot be accounted for at amortized cost. In general, equity investments are valued at fair value, with all gains and losses reported in income.

- GAAP classifies investments as trading, available-for-sale (both debt and equity investments), and held-to-maturity (only for debt investments). IFRS uses held-for-collection (debt investments), trading (both debt and equity investments), and non-trading equity investment classifications. GAAP classifications are based on management's intent with respect to the investment. IFRS classifications are based on the business model used to manage the investments and the type of security.

- The accounting for trading investments is the same between GAAP and IFRS. Held-to-maturity (GAAP) and held-for-collection (IFRS) investments are accounted for at amortized cost. Gains and losses related to available-for-sale securities (GAAP) and non-trading equity investments (IFRS) are reported in other comprehensive income.

- Unrealized gains and losses related to available-for-sale securities are reported in other comprehensive income under GAAP and IFRS. These gains and losses that accumulate are then reported in the balance sheet.

- IFRS does not use "Other revenues and gains" or "Other expenses and losses" in its income statement presentation. It will generally classify these items as unusual items or financial items.

Looking to the Future

As indicated earlier, both the FASB and IASB have indicated that they believe that all financial instruments should be reported at fair value and that changes in fair value should be reported as part of net income. It seems likely, as more companies choose the fair value option for financial instruments, that we will eventually arrive at fair value measurement for all financial instruments.

IFRS Practice

IFRS Self-Test Questions

1. The following asset is **not** considered a financial asset under IFRS:
  (a) trading securities.   **(c)** held-for-collection securities.
  (b) equity securities.   **(d)** inventories.

2. Under IFRS, the equity method of accounting for long-term investments in common stock should be used when the investor has significant influence over an investee and owns:
  (a) between 20% and 50% of the investee's common stock.
  (b) 30% or more of the investee's common stock.
  (c) more than 50% of the investee's common stock.
  (d) less than 20% of the investee's common stock.

3. Under IFRS, at the end of the first year of operations, the total cost of the trading investments portfolio is $120,000. Total fair value is $115,000. The financial statement should show:
  (a) a reduction in the carrying value of the asset of $5,000 and an unrealized loss of $5,000 in other expenses and losses.
  (b) a reduction in the carrying value of the asset of $5,000 and an unrealized loss of $5,000 in the stockholders' equity section.
  (c) a reduction in the carrying value of the asset of $5,000 in current assets and an unrealized loss of $5,000 in other comprehensive income.
  (d) a reduction in the carrying value of the asset of $5,000 in current assets and a realized loss of $5,000 in other expenses and losses.

4. Under IFRS, unrealized gains on non-trading stock investments should:
  (a) be reported in the income statement as part of net income.
  (b) be reported as other gains on the income statement as part of net income.
  (c) not be reported on the income statement or balance sheet.
  (d) be reported as other comprehensive income.

5. Under IFRS, the unrealized loss on trading investments should be reported:
  (a) as part of other comprehensive loss reducing net income.
  (b) on the income statement reducing net income.
  (c) as part of other comprehensive loss not affecting net income.
  (d) directly to stockholders' equity bypassing the income statement.

Answers to IFRS Self-Test Questions
1. d   **2.** a   **3.** a   **4.** d   **5.** b

✔ **The Navigator**

✔ Remember to go back to The Navigator box on the chapter opening page and check off your completed work.

17 | Statement of Cash Flows

Feature Story

Got Cash?

Companies must be ready to respond to changes quickly in order to survive and thrive. This requires careful management of cash. One company that managed cash successfully in its early years was Microsoft. During those years, the company paid much of its payroll with stock options (rights to purchase company stock in the future at a given price) instead of cash. This conserved cash and turned more than a thousand of its employees into millionaires.

In recent years, Microsoft has had a different kind of cash problem. Now that it has reached a more "mature" stage in life, it generates so much cash—roughly $1 billion per month—that it cannot always figure out what to do with it. At one time, Microsoft had accumulated $60 billion.

The company said it was accumulating cash to invest in new opportunities, buy other companies, and pay off pending lawsuits. Microsoft's stockholders complained that holding all this cash was putting a drag on the company's profitability. Why? Because Microsoft had the cash invested in very low-yielding government securities. Stockholders felt that the company either should find new investment projects that would bring higher returns, or return some of the cash to stockholders.

Finally, Microsoft announced a plan to return cash to stockholders by paying a special one-time $32 billion dividend. This special dividend was so large that, according to the U.S. Commerce Department, it caused total personal income in the United States to rise by 3.7% in one month—the largest increase ever recorded by the agency. (It also made the holiday season brighter, especially for retailers in the Seattle area.) Microsoft also doubled its regular annual dividend to $3.50 per share. Further, it announced that it would spend another $30 billion buying treasury stock.

In recent years, Apple also encountered this cash "problem." At the end of 2011, Apple had nearly $100 billion in liquid assets (cash, cash equivalents, and investment securities). At that time it was generating $37 billion of cash per year from its operating activities but spending only about $7 billion on plant assets and purchases of patents. Shareholders pressured Apple to unload some of this cash. In response, Apple announced that it would begin to pay a quarterly dividend of $2.65 per share and it would buy back up to $10 billion of its stock. Analysts noted that the dividend consumes only $10 billion of cash per year. This leaves Apple wallowing in cash. The rest of us should have such problems!

Source: "Business: An End to Growth? Microsoft's Cash Bonanza," *The Economist* (July 23, 2005), p. 61.

✔ The Navigator

- ■ Scan Learning Objectives
- ■ Read Feature Story
- ■ Read Preview
- ■ Read text and answer **DO IT!** p. 781
    - ■ p. 788   ■ p. 791   ■ p. 795
- ■ Work Comprehensive **DO IT! 1** p. 796
- ■ Review Summary of Learning Objectives
- ■ Work Comprehensive **DO IT! 2** p. 805
- ■ Answer Self-Test Questions
- ■ Complete Assignments
- ■ Go to *WileyPLUS* for practice and tutorials
- 🌐 **Read A Look at IFRS** p. 837

Learning Objectives   ✔ The Navigator

After studying this chapter, you should be able to:

[1] Indicate the usefulness of the statement of cash flows.

[2] Distinguish among operating, investing, and financing activities.

[3] Prepare a statement of cash flows using the indirect method.

[4] Analyze the statement of cash flows.

Preview of Chapter 17

✔ The Navigator

The balance sheet, income statement, and retained earnings statement do not always show the whole picture of the financial condition of a company or institution. In fact, looking at the financial statements of some well-known companies, a thoughtful investor might ask questions like these: How did Eastman Kodak finance cash dividends of $649 million in a year in which it earned only $17 million? How could United Air Lines purchase new planes that cost $1.9 billion in a year in which it reported a net loss of over $2 billion? How did the companies that spent a combined fantastic $3.4 trillion on mergers and acquisitions in a recent year finance those deals? Answers to these and similar questions can be found in this chapter, which presents the statement of cash flows.

The content and organization of this chapter are as follows.

STATEMENT OF CASH FLOWS

The Statement of Cash Flows: Usefulness and Format	Preparing the Statement of Cash Flows—Indirect Method	Using Cash Flows to Evaluate a Company
• Usefulness • Classification • Significant noncash activities • Format • Preparation • Indirect and direct methods	• Step 1: Operating activities • Step 2: Investing and financing activities • Step 3: Net change in cash	• Free cash flow

The Statement of Cash Flows: Usefulness and Format

The balance sheet, income statement, and retained earnings statement provide only limited information about a company's cash flows (cash receipts and cash payments). For example, comparative balance sheets show the increase in property, plant, and equipment during the year. But, they do not show how the additions were financed or paid for. The income statement shows net income. But, it does not indicate the amount of cash generated by operating activities. The retained earnings statement shows cash dividends declared but not the cash dividends paid during the year. None of these statements presents a detailed summary of where cash came from and how it was used.

Usefulness of the Statement of Cash Flows

The **statement of cash flows** reports the cash receipts, cash payments, and net change in cash resulting from operating, investing, and financing activities during a period. The information in a statement of cash flows should help investors, creditors, and others assess:

1. **The entity's ability to generate future cash flows.** By examining relationships between items in the statement of cash flows, investors can make predictions of the amounts, timing, and uncertainty of future cash flows better than they can from accrual-basis data.

2. **The entity's ability to pay dividends and meet obligations.** If a company does not have adequate cash, it cannot pay employees, settle debts, or pay dividends. Employees, creditors, and stockholders should be particularly interested in this statement, because it alone shows the flows of cash in a business.

> **Ethics Note**
>
> Though we would discourage reliance on cash flows to the exclusion of accrual accounting, comparing net cash provided by operating activities to net income can reveal important information about the "quality" of reported net income. Such a comparison can reveal the extent to which net income provides a good measure of actual performance.

3. **The reasons for the difference between net income and net cash provided (used) by operating activities.** Net income provides information on the success or failure of a business. However, some financial statement users are critical of accrual-basis net income because it requires many estimates. As a result, users often challenge the reliability of the number. Such is not the case with cash. Many readers of the statement of cash flows want to know the reasons for the difference between net income and net cash provided by operating activities. Then they can assess for themselves the reliability of the income number.

4. **The cash investing and financing transactions during the period.** By examining a company's investing and financing transactions, a financial statement reader can better understand why assets and liabilities changed during the period.

Classification of Cash Flows

The statement of cash flows classifies cash receipts and cash payments as operating, investing, and financing activities. Transactions and other events characteristic of each kind of activity are as follows.

1. **Operating activities** include the cash effects of transactions that create revenues and expenses. They thus enter into the determination of net income.

2. **Investing activities** include (a) acquiring and disposing of investments and property, plant, and equipment, and (b) lending money and collecting the loans.

3. **Financing activities** include (a) obtaining cash from issuing debt and repaying the amounts borrowed, and (b) obtaining cash from stockholders, repurchasing shares, and paying dividends.

The operating activities category is the most important. It shows the cash provided by company operations. This source of cash is generally considered to be the best measure of a company's ability to generate sufficient cash to continue as a going concern.

Illustration 17-1 lists typical cash receipts and cash payments within each of the three classifications. **Study the list carefully.** It will prove very useful in solving homework exercises and problems.

TYPES OF CASH INFLOWS AND OUTFLOWS

Illustration 17-1
Typical receipt and payment classifications

Operating activities—Income statement items
Cash inflows:
    From sale of goods or services.
    From interest received and dividends received.
Cash outflows:
    To suppliers for inventory.
    To employees for wages.
    To government for taxes.
    To lenders for interest.
    To others for expenses.

Operating activities

Investing activities—Changes in investments and long-term assets
Cash inflows:
    From sale of property, plant, and equipment.
    From sale of investments in debt or equity securities of other entities.
    From collection of principal on loans to other entities.
Cash outflows:
    To purchase property, plant, and equipment.
    To purchase investments in debt or equity securities of other entities.
    To make loans to other entities.

Investing activities

Financing activities—Changes in long-term liabilities and stockholders' equity
Cash inflows:
    From sale of common stock.
    From issuance of debt (bonds and notes).
Cash outflows:
    To stockholders as dividends.
    To redeem long-term debt or reacquire capital stock (treasury stock).

Financing activities

Note the following general guidelines:

1. Operating activities involve income statement items.

2. Investing activities involve cash flows resulting from changes in investments and long-term asset items.

3. Financing activities involve cash flows resulting from changes in long-term liability and stockholders' equity items.

Companies classify as operating activities some cash flows related to investing or financing activities. For example, receipts of investment revenue (interest and dividends) are classified as operating activities. So are payments of interest to lenders. Why are these considered operating activities? **Because companies report these items in the income statement, where results of operations are shown.**

Significant Noncash Activities

Not all of a company's significant activities involve cash. Examples of significant noncash activities are:

1. Direct issuance of common stock to purchase assets.

2. Conversion of bonds into common stock.

3. Direct issuance of debt to purchase assets.

4. Exchanges of plant assets.

Helpful Hint Do not include noncash investing and financing activities in the body of the statement of cash flows. Report this information in a separate schedule.

Companies do not report in the body of the statement of cash flows significant financing and investing activities that do not affect cash. Instead, they report these activities in either a **separate schedule** at the bottom of the statement of cash flows or in a **separate note or supplementary schedule** to the financial statements. The reporting of these noncash activities in a separate schedule satisfies the **full disclosure principle**.

In solving homework assignments, you should present significant noncash investing and financing activities in a separate schedule at the bottom of the statement of cash flows. (See the last entry in Illustration 17-2 on the next page for an example.)

ACCOUNTING ACROSS THE ORGANIZATION

Net *What*?

Net income is not the same as net cash provided by operating activities. Below are some results from recent annual reports (dollars in millions). Note the wide disparity among these companies, all of which engaged in retail merchandising.

Darren McCollester/Getty Images, Inc.

Company	Net Income	Net Cash Provided by Operating Activities
Kohl's Corporation	$ 1,083	$ 1,234
Wal-Mart Stores, Inc.	11,284	20,169
J. C. Penney Company, Inc.	1,153	1,255
Costco Wholesale Corp.	1,082	2,076
Target Corporation	2,849	4,125

? In general, why do differences exist between net income and net cash provided by operating activities? (See page 837.)

Format of the Statement of Cash Flows

The general format of the statement of cash flows presents the results of the three activities discussed previously—operating, investing, and financing—plus the significant noncash investing and financing activities. Illustration 17-2 shows a widely used form of the statement of cash flows.

Illustration 17-2
Format of statement of cash flows

COMPANY NAME Statement of Cash Flows Period Covered		
Cash flows from operating activities		
(List of individual items)	XX	
Net cash provided (used) by operating activities		XXX
Cash flows from investing activities		
(List of individual inflows and outflows)	XX	
Net cash provided (used) by investing activities		XXX
Cash flows from financing activities		
(List of individual inflows and outflows)	XX	
Net cash provided (used) by financing activities		XXX
Net increase (decrease) in cash		XXX
Cash at beginning of period		XXX
Cash at end of period		XXX
Noncash investing and financing activities		
(List of individual noncash transactions)		XXX

The cash flows from operating activities section always appears first, followed by the investing activities section and then the financing activities section. The sum of the operating, investing, and financing sections equals the net increase or decrease in cash for the period. This amount is added to the beginning cash balance to arrive at the ending cash balance—the same amount reported on the balance sheet.

> **DO IT!**

Classification of Cash Flows

Action Plan

✔ Identify the three types of activities used to report all cash inflows and outflows.

✔ Report as operating activities the cash effects of transactions that create revenues and expenses and enter into the determination of net income.

✔ Report as investing activities transactions that (a) acquire and dispose of investments and long-term assets and (b) lend money and collect loans.

✔ Report as financing activities transactions that (a) obtain cash from issuing debt and repay the amounts borrowed and (b) obtain cash from stockholders and pay them dividends.

During its first week, Duffy & Stevenson Company had these transactions.

1. Issued 100,000 shares of $5 par value common stock for $800,000 cash.
2. Borrowed $200,000 from Castle Bank, signing a 5-year note bearing 8% interest.
3. Purchased two semi-trailer trucks for $170,000 cash.
4. Paid employees $12,000 for salaries and wages.
5. Collected $20,000 cash for services performed.

Classify each of these transactions by type of cash flow activity.

Solution

1. Financing activity	4. Operating activity
2. Financing activity	5. Operating activity
3. Investing activity	

Related exercise material: **BE17-1, BE17-2, BE17-3, E17-1, E17-2, E17-3, and DO IT! 17-1.**

✔ The Navigator

Preparing the Statement of Cash Flows

Companies prepare the statement of cash flows differently from the three other basic financial statements. First, it is not prepared from an adjusted trial balance. It requires detailed information concerning the changes in account balances that occurred between two points in time. An adjusted trial balance will not provide the necessary data. Second, the statement of cash flows deals with cash receipts and payments. As a result, the company **adjusts** the effects of the use of accrual accounting **to determine cash flows**.

The information to prepare this statement usually comes from three sources:

- **Comparative balance sheets.** Information in the comparative balance sheets indicates the amount of the changes in assets, liabilities, and stockholders' equities from the beginning to the end of the period.

- **Current income statement.** Information in this statement helps determine the amount of net cash provided or used by operating activities during the period.

- **Additional information.** Such information includes transaction data that are needed to determine how cash was provided or used during the period.

Preparing the statement of cash flows from these data sources involves three major steps, explained in Illustration 17-3.

Illustration 17-3
Three major steps in preparing the statement of cash flows

STEP 1: Determine net cash provided/used by operating activities by converting net income from an accrual basis to a cash basis.

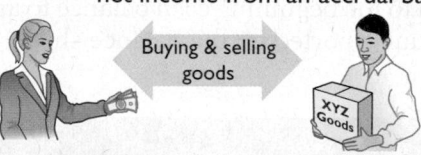

Buying & selling goods

XYZ Goods

This step involves analyzing not only the current year's income statement but also comparative balance sheets and selected additional data.

STEP 2: Analyze changes in noncurrent asset and liability accounts and record as investing and financing activities, or disclose as noncash transactions.

FOR SALE

BANK

Investing

Financing

This step involves analyzing comparative balance sheet data and selected additional information for their effects on cash.

STEP 3: Compare the net change in cash on the statement of cash flows with the change in the Cash account reported on the balance sheet to make sure the amounts agree.

Year 1   Year 2   Difference

The difference between the beginning and ending cash balances can be easily computed from comparative balance sheets.

Indirect and Direct Methods

In order to perform Step 1, a company **must convert net income from an accrual basis to a cash basis**. This conversion may be done by either of two methods: (1) the indirect method or (2) the direct method. **Both methods arrive at the same total amount** for "Net cash provided by operating activities." They differ in **how** they arrive at the amount.

The **indirect method** adjusts net income for items that do not affect cash. A great majority of companies (98%) use this method, as shown in the nearby chart.[1] Companies favor the indirect method for two reasons. (1) It is easier and less costly to prepare, and (2) it focuses on the differences between net income and net cash flow from operating activities.

The **direct method** shows operating cash receipts and payments. It is prepared by adjusting each item in the income statement from the accrual basis to the cash basis. The FASB has expressed a preference for the direct method, but allows the use of either method.

The next section illustrates the more popular indirect method. Appendix 17A illustrates the direct method.

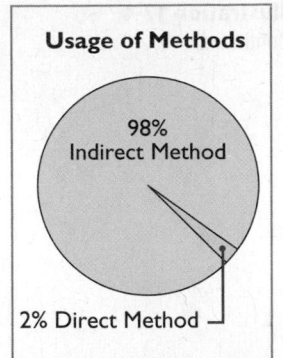

Usage of Methods

98% Indirect Method

2% Direct Method

Preparing the Statement of Cash Flows—Indirect Method

To explain how to prepare a statement of cash flows using the indirect method, we use financial information from Computer Services Company. Illustration 17-4 presents Computer Services' current and previous-year balance sheets, its current-year income statement, and related financial information for the current year.

LEARNING OBJECTIVE   3

Prepare a statement of cash flows using the indirect method.

Illustration 17-4
Comparative balance sheets, income statement, and additional information for Computer Services Company

COMPUTER SERVICES COMPANY
Comparative Balance Sheets
December 31

Assets	2014	2013	Change in Account Balance Increase/Decrease
Current assets			
Cash	$ 55,000	$ 33,000	$ 22,000 Increase
Accounts receivable	20,000	30,000	10,000 Decrease
Inventory	15,000	10,000	5,000 Increase
Prepaid expenses	5,000	1,000	4,000 Increase
Property, plant, and equipment			
Land	130,000	20,000	110,000 Increase
Buildings	160,000	40,000	120,000 Increase
Accumulated depreciation—buildings	(11,000)	(5,000)	6,000 Increase
Equipment	27,000	10,000	17,000 Increase
Accumulated depreciation—equipment	(3,000)	(1,000)	2,000 Increase
Total assets	$398,000	$138,000	
Liabilities and Stockholders' Equity			
Current liabilities			
Accounts payable	$ 28,000	$ 12,000	$ 16,000 Increase
Income taxes payable	6,000	8,000	2,000 Decrease
Long-term liabilities			
Bonds payable	130,000	20,000	110,000 Increase
Stockholders' equity			
Common stock	70,000	50,000	20,000 Increase
Retained earnings	164,000	48,000	116,000 Increase
Total liabilities and stockholders' equity	$398,000	$138,000	

---

[1]*Accounting Trends and Techniques—2011* (New York: American Institute of Certified Public Accountants, 2011).

Illustration 17-4
(continued)

COMPUTER SERVICES COMPANY		
Income Statement		
For the Year Ended December 31, 2014		
Sales revenue		$507,000
Cost of goods sold	$150,000	
Operating expenses (excluding depreciation)	111,000	
Depreciation expense	9,000	
Loss on disposal of equipment	3,000	
Interest expense	42,000	315,000
Income before income tax		192,000
Income tax expense		47,000
Net income		$145,000

Additional information for 2014:
1. Depreciation expense was comprised of $6,000 for building and $3,000 for equipment.
2. The company sold equipment with a book value of $7,000 (cost $8,000, less accumulated depreciation $1,000) for $4,000 cash.
3. Issued $110,000 of long-term bonds in direct exchange for land.
4. A building costing $120,000 was purchased for cash. Equipment costing $25,000 was also purchased for cash.
5. Issued common stock for $20,000 cash.
6. The company declared and paid a $29,000 cash dividend.

We will now apply the three steps to the information provided for Computer Services Company.

Step 1: Operating Activities

DETERMINE NET CASH PROVIDED/USED BY OPERATING ACTIVITIES BY CONVERTING NET INCOME FROM AN ACCRUAL BASIS TO A CASH BASIS

To determine net cash provided by operating activities under the indirect method, companies **adjust net income in numerous ways**. A useful starting point is to understand **why** net income must be converted to net cash provided by operating activities.

Under generally accepted accounting principles, most companies use the accrual basis of accounting. This basis requires that companies record revenue when their performance obligation is satisfied and record expenses when incurred. Revenues include credit sales for which the company has not yet collected cash. Expenses incurred include some items that it has not yet paid in cash. Thus, under the accrual basis, net income is not the same as net cash provided by operating activities.

Therefore, under the **indirect method**, companies must adjust net income to convert certain items to the cash basis. The indirect method (or reconciliation method) starts with net income and converts it to net cash provided by operating activities. Illustration 17-5 lists the three types of adjustments.

Illustration 17-5
Three types of adjustments to convert net income to net cash provided by operating activities

Net Income	+/−	Adjustments	=	Net Cash Provided/ Used by Operating Activities
		• **Add back noncash expenses**, such as depreciation expense, amortization, or depletion.		
		• **Deduct gains and add losses** that resulted from investing and financing activities.		
		• **Analyze changes** to noncash current asset and current liability accounts.		

We explain the three types of adjustments in the next three sections.

DEPRECIATION EXPENSE

Computer Services' income statement reports depreciation expense of $9,000. Although depreciation expense reduces net income, it does not reduce cash. In other words, depreciation expense is a noncash charge. The company must add it back to net income to arrive at net cash provided by operating activities. Computer Services reports depreciation expense in the statement of cash flows as shown below.

Helpful Hint Depreciation is similar to any other expense in that it reduces net income. It differs in that it does not involve a current cash outflow. That is why it must be *added back* to net income to arrive at net cash provided by operating activities.

Illustration 17-6
Adjustment for depreciation

Cash flows from operating activities	
Net income	$145,000
Adjustments to reconcile net income to net cash provided by operating activities:	
Depreciation expense	**9,000**
Net cash provided by operating activities	$154,000

As the first adjustment to net income in the statement of cash flows, companies frequently list depreciation and similar noncash charges such as amortization of intangible assets, depletion expense, and bad debt expense.

LOSS ON DISPOSAL OF EQUIPMENT

Illustration 17-1 states that cash received from the sale (disposal) of plant assets is reported in the investing activities section. Because of this, **companies eliminate from net income all gains and losses related to the disposal of plant assets, to arrive at net cash provided by operating activities**.

In our example, Computer Services' income statement reports a $3,000 loss on the disposal of equipment (book value $7,000, less $4,000 cash received from disposal of equipment). The company's loss of $3,000 should not be included in the operating activities section of the statement of cash flows. Illustration 17-7 shows that the $3,000 loss is eliminated by adding $3,000 back to net income to arrive at net cash provided by operating activities.

Illustration 17-7
Adjustment for loss on disposal of equipment

Cash flows from operating activities		
Net income		$145,000
Adjustments to reconcile net income to net cash provided by operating activities:		
Depreciation expense	$9,000	
Loss on disposal of equipment	**3,000**	12,000
Net cash provided by operating activities		$157,000

If a gain on disposal occurs, the company deducts the gain from net income in order to determine net cash provided by operating activities. **In the case of either a gain or a loss, companies report as a source of cash in the investing activities section of the statement of cash flows the actual amount of cash received from the sale.**

CHANGES TO NONCASH CURRENT ASSET AND CURRENT LIABILITY ACCOUNTS

A final adjustment in reconciling net income to net cash provided by operating activities involves examining all changes in current asset and current liability accounts. The accrual-accounting process records revenues in the period in which the performance obligation is satisfied and expenses in the period incurred. For example, Accounts Receivable reflects amounts owed to the company for sales that have been made but for which cash collections have not yet been received. Prepaid Insurance reflects insurance that has been paid for but which has not yet expired (therefore has not been expensed). Similarly, Salaries and Wages Payable reflects salaries and wages expense that has been incurred but has not been paid.

As a result, we need to adjust net income for these accruals and prepayments to determine net cash provided by operating activities. Thus, we must analyze the change in each current asset and current liability account to determine its impact on net income and cash.

CHANGES IN NONCASH CURRENT ASSETS.   The adjustments required for changes in noncash current asset accounts are as follows. **Deduct from net income increases in current asset accounts, and add to net income decreases in current asset accounts, to arrive at net cash provided by operating activities.** We observe these relationships by analyzing the accounts of Computer Services Company.

DECREASE IN ACCOUNTS RECEIVABLE Computer Services Company's accounts receivable decreased by $10,000 (from $30,000 to $20,000) during the period. For Computer Services, this means that cash receipts were $10,000 higher than sales revenue. The Accounts Receivable account in Illustration 17-8 shows that Computer Services Company had $507,000 in sales revenue (as reported on the income statement), but it collected $517,000 in cash.

Illustration 17-8
Analysis of accounts receivable

		Accounts Receivable		
1/1/14	Balance	30,000	**Receipts from customers**	**517,000**
	Sales revenue	**507,000**		
12/31/14	Balance	20,000		

As shown in Illustration 17-9 (page 787), to adjust net income to net cash provided by operating activities, the company adds to net income the decrease of $10,000 in accounts receivable. When the Accounts Receivable balance increases, cash receipts are lower than sales revenue earned under the accrual basis. Therefore, the company deducts from net income the amount of the increase in accounts receivable, to arrive at net cash provided by operating activities.

INCREASE IN INVENTORY Computer Services Company's inventory increased $5,000 (from $10,000 to $15,000) during the period. The change in the Inventory account reflects the difference between the amount of inventory purchased and the amount sold. For Computer Services, this means that the cost of merchandise purchased exceeded the cost of goods sold by $5,000. As a result, cost of goods sold does not reflect $5,000 of cash payments made for merchandise. The company deducts from net income this inventory increase of $5,000 during the period, to arrive at net cash provided by operating activities (see Illustration 17-9). If inventory decreases, the company adds to net income the amount of the change, to arrive at net cash provided by operating activities.

INCREASE IN PREPAID EXPENSES Computer Services' prepaid expenses increased during the period by $4,000. This means that cash paid for expenses is higher than expenses reported on an accrual basis. In other words, the company has made cash payments in the current period but will not charge expenses to income until future periods (as charges to the income statement). To adjust net income to net cash provided by operating activities, the company deducts from net income the $4,000 increase in prepaid expenses (see Illustration 17-9).

Cash flows from operating activities
  Net income $145,000
  Adjustments to reconcile net income to net cash
    provided by operating activities:
    Depreciation expense $ 9,000
    Loss on disposal of equipment   3,000
    Decrease in accounts receivable   10,000
    Increase in inventory   (5,000)
    Increase in prepaid expenses   (4,000)   13,000
      Net cash provided by operating activities $158,000

Illustration 17-9
Adjustments for changes in current asset accounts

If prepaid expenses decrease, reported expenses are higher than the expenses paid. Therefore, the company adds to net income the decrease in prepaid expenses, to arrive at net cash provided by operating activities.

CHANGES IN CURRENT LIABILITIES.   The adjustments required for changes in current liability accounts are as follows. **Add to net income increases in current liability accounts and deduct from net income decreases in current liability accounts, to arrive at net cash provided by operating activities.**

INCREASE IN ACCOUNTS PAYABLE For Computer Services Company, Accounts Payable increased by $16,000 (from $12,000 to $28,000) during the period. That means the company received $16,000 more in goods than it actually paid for. As shown in Illustration 17-10 (below), to adjust net income to determine net cash provided by operating activities, the company adds to net income the $16,000 increase in Accounts Payable.

DECREASE IN INCOME TAXES PAYABLE When a company incurs income tax expense but has not yet paid its taxes, it records income tax payable. A change in the Income Taxes Payable account reflects the difference between income tax expense incurred and income tax actually paid. Computer Services' Income Taxes Payable account decreased by $2,000. That means the $47,000 of income tax expense reported on the income statement was $2,000 less than the amount of taxes paid during the period of $49,000. As shown in Illustration 17-10, to adjust net income to a cash basis, the company must reduce net income by $2,000.

Illustration 17-10
Adjustments for changes in current liability accounts

Cash flows from operating activities
  Net income $145,000
  Adjustments to reconcile net income to net cash
    provided by operating activities:
    Depreciation expense $ 9,000
    Loss on disposal of equipment   3,000
    Decrease in accounts receivable   10,000
    Increase in inventory   (5,000)
    Increase in prepaid expenses   (4,000)
    Increase in accounts payable   16,000
    Decrease in income taxes payable   (2,000)   27,000
      Net cash provided by operating activities $172,000

Illustration 17-10 shows that after starting with net income of $145,000 the sum of all of the adjustments to net income was $27,000. This resulted in net cash provided by operating activities of $172,000.

Summary of Conversion to Net Cash Provided by Operating Activities—Indirect Method

As shown in the previous illustrations, the statement of cash flows prepared by the indirect method starts with net income. It then adds or deducts items to arrive at net cash provided by operating activities. The required adjustments are of three types:

1. Noncash charges such as depreciation, amortization, and depletion.
2. Gains and losses on the disposal of plant assets.
3. Changes in noncash current asset and current liability accounts.

Illustration 17-11 provides a summary of these changes.

Illustration 17-11
Adjustments required to convert net income to net cash provided by operating activities

		Adjustments Required to Convert Net Income to Net Cash Provided by Operating Activities
Noncash Charges	Depreciation expense	Add
	Amortization expense	Add
	Depletion expense	Add
Gains and Losses	Loss on disposal of plant assets	Add
	Gain on disposal of plant assets	Deduct
Changes in Current Assets and Current Liabilities	Increase in current asset account	Deduct
	Decrease in current asset account	Add
	Increase in current liability account	Add
	Decrease in current liability account	Deduct

ANATOMY OF A FRAUD

For more than a decade, the top executives at the Italian dairy products company Parmalat engaged in multiple frauds that overstated cash and other assets by more than $1 billion while understating liabilities by between $8 and $12 billion. Much of the fraud involved creating fictitious sources and uses of cash. Some of these activities incorporated sophisticated financial transactions with subsidiaries created with the help of large international financial institutions. However, much of the fraud employed very basic, even sloppy, forgery of documents. For example, when outside auditors requested confirmation of bank accounts (such as a fake $4.8 billion account in the Cayman Islands), documents were created on scanners, with signatures that were cut and pasted from other documents. These were then passed through a fax machine numerous times to make them look real (if difficult to read). Similarly, fictitious bills were created in order to divert funds to other businesses owned by the Tanzi family (who controlled Parmalat).

Total take: Billions of dollars

THE MISSING CONTROL
Independent internal verification. Internal auditors at the company should have independently verified bank accounts and major transfers of cash to outside companies that were controlled by the Tanzi family.

> DO IT!

Cash from Operating Activities

Josh's PhotoPlus reported net income of $73,000 for 2014. Included in the income statement were depreciation expense of $7,000 and a gain on disposal of equipment of $2,500. Josh's comparative balance sheets show the following balances.

	12/31/13	12/31/14
Accounts receivable	$17,000	$21,000
Accounts payable	6,000	2,200

Action Plan

✔ Add noncash charges such as depreciation back to net income to compute net cash provided by operating activities.

✔ Deduct from net income gains on the disposal of plant assets, or add losses back to net income, to compute net cash provided by operating activities.

✔ Use changes in noncash current asset and current liability accounts to compute net cash provided by operating activities.

Calculate net cash provided by operating activities for Josh's PhotoPlus.

Solution

Cash flows from operating activities			
Net income			$73,000
Adjustments to reconcile net income to net cash provided by operating activities:			
Depreciation expense		$ 7,000	
Gain on disposal of equipment		(2,500)	
Increase in accounts receivable		(4,000)	
Decrease in accounts payable		(3,800)	(3,300)
Net cash provided by operating activities			$69,700

Related exercise material: **BE17-4, BE17-5, BE17-6, E17-4, E17-5, E17-6, and DO IT!** 17-2.

✔ **The Navigator**

Step 2: Investing and Financing Activities

ANALYZE CHANGES IN NONCURRENT ASSET AND LIABILITY ACCOUNTS AND RECORD AS INVESTING AND FINANCING ACTIVITIES, OR AS NONCASH INVESTING AND FINANCING ACTIVITIES

INCREASE IN LAND As indicated from the change in the Land account and the additional information, Computer Services Company purchased land of $110,000 by directly exchanging bonds for land. The issuance of bonds payable for land has no effect on cash. But, it is a significant noncash investing and financing activity that merits disclosure in a separate schedule. (See Illustration 17-13 on page 790.)

INCREASE IN BUILDINGS As the additional data indicate, Computer Services Company acquired an office building for $120,000 cash. This is a cash outflow reported in the investing activities section. (See Illustration 17-13 on page 790.)

INCREASE IN EQUIPMENT The Equipment account increased $17,000. The additional information explains that this net increase resulted from two transactions: (1) a purchase of equipment of $25,000, and (2) the sale for $4,000 of equipment costing $8,000. These transactions are investing activities. The company should report each transaction separately. Thus, it reports the purchase of equipment as an outflow of cash for $25,000. It reports the sale as an inflow of cash for $4,000. The T-account below shows the reasons for the change in this account during the year.

Illustration 17-12
Analysis of equipment

	Equipment		
1/1/14 Balance	10,000	Cost of equipment sold	8,000
Purchase of equipment	25,000		
12/31/14 Balance	27,000		

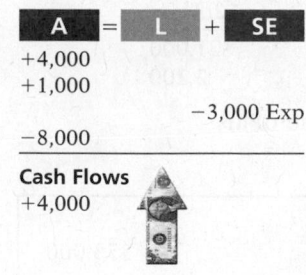

A	=	L	+	SE
+4,000				
+1,000				
				−3,000 Exp
−8,000				

Cash Flows
+4,000

Helpful Hint When companies issue stocks or bonds for cash, the actual proceeds will appear in the statement of cash flows as a financing inflow (rather than the par value of the stocks or face value of bonds).

The following entry shows the details of the equipment sale transaction.

Cash	4,000	
Accumulated Depreciation—Equipment	1,000	
Loss on Disposal of Equipment	3,000	
Equipment		8,000

INCREASE IN BONDS PAYABLE The Bonds Payable account increased $110,000. As indicated in the additional information, the company acquired land from the issuance of these bonds. It reports this noncash transaction in a separate schedule at the bottom of the statement.

INCREASE IN COMMON STOCK The balance sheet reports an increase in Common Stock of $20,000. The additional information section notes that this increase resulted from the issuance of new shares of stock. This is a cash inflow reported in the financing activities section.

INCREASE IN RETAINED EARNINGS Retained earnings increased $116,000 during the year. This increase can be explained by two factors. (1) Net income of $145,000 increased retained earnings. (2) Dividends of $29,000 decreased retained earnings. The company adjusts net income to net cash provided by operating activities in the operating activities section. Payment of the dividends (not the declaration) is a **cash outflow that the company reports as a financing activity**.

STATEMENT OF CASH FLOWS—2014
Using the previous information, we can now prepare a statement of cash flows for 2014 for Computer Services Company as shown in Illustration 17-13.

Step 3: Net Change in Cash

COMPARE THE NET CHANGE IN CASH ON THE STATEMENT OF CASH FLOWS WITH THE CHANGE IN THE CASH ACCOUNT REPORTED ON THE BALANCE SHEET TO MAKE SURE THE AMOUNTS AGREE
Illustration 17-13 indicates that the net change in cash during the period was an increase of $22,000. This agrees with the change in Cash account reported on the balance sheet in Illustration 17-4 (page 784).

Illustration 17-13
Statement of cash flows, 2014—indirect method

Helpful Hint Note that in the investing and financing activities sections, positive numbers indicate cash inflows (receipts), and negative numbers indicate cash outflows (payments).

COMPUTER SERVICES COMPANY		
Statement of Cash Flows—Indirect Method		
For the Year Ended December 31, 2014		
Cash flows from operating activities		
Net income		$145,000
Adjustments to reconcile net income to net cash provided by operating activities:		
Depreciation expense	$ 9,000	
Loss on disposal of equipment	3,000	
Decrease in accounts receivable	10,000	
Increase in inventory	(5,000)	
Increase in prepaid expenses	(4,000)	
Increase in accounts payable	16,000	
Decrease in income taxes payable	(2,000)	27,000
Net cash provided by operating activities		172,000

Illustration 17-13
(continued)

Cash flows from investing activities		
Purchase of building	(120,000)	
Purchase of equipment	(25,000)	
Sale of equipment	4,000	
Net cash used by investing activities		(141,000)
Cash flows from financing activities		
Issuance of common stock	20,000	
Payment of cash dividends	(29,000)	
Net cash used by financing activities		(9,000)
Net increase in cash		22,000
Cash at beginning of period		33,000
Cash at end of period		$ 55,000
Noncash investing and financing activities		
Issuance of bonds payable to purchase land		$110,000

> **DO IT!**

Indirect Method

Use the information below and on page 792 to prepare a statement of cash flows using the indirect method.

REYNOLDS COMPANY
Comparative Balance Sheets
December 31

Assets	2014	2013	Change Increase/Decrease
Cash	$ 54,000	$ 37,000	$ 17,000 Increase
Accounts receivable	68,000	26,000	42,000 Increase
Inventory	54,000	–0–	54,000 Increase
Prepaid expenses	4,000	6,000	2,000 Decrease
Land	45,000	70,000	25,000 Decrease
Buildings	200,000	200,000	–0–
Accumulated depreciation—buildings	(21,000)	(11,000)	10,000 Increase
Equipment	193,000	68,000	125,000 Increase
Accumulated depreciation—equipment	(28,000)	(10,000)	18,000 Increase
Totals	$569,000	$386,000	
Liabilities and Stockholders' Equity			
Accounts payable	$ 23,000	$ 40,000	$ 17,000 Decrease
Accrued expenses payable	10,000	–0–	10,000 Increase
Bonds payable	110,000	150,000	40,000 Decrease
Common stock ($1 par)	220,000	60,000	160,000 Increase
Retained earnings	206,000	136,000	70,000 Increase
Totals	$569,000	$386,000	

REYNOLDS COMPANY
Income Statement
For the Year Ended December 31, 2014

Sales revenue		$890,000
Cost of goods sold	$465,000	
Operating expenses	221,000	
Interest expense	12,000	
Loss on disposal of equipment	2,000	700,000
Income before income taxes		190,000
Income tax expense		65,000
Net income		$125,000

Additional information:
1. Operating expenses include depreciation expense of $33,000 and charges from prepaid expenses of $2,000.
2. Land was sold at its book value for cash.
3. Cash dividends of $55,000 were declared and paid in 2014.
4. Interest expense of $12,000 was paid in cash.
5. Equipment with a cost of $166,000 was purchased for cash. Equipment with a cost of $41,000 and a book value of $36,000 was sold for $34,000 cash.
6. Bonds of $10,000 were redeemed at their face value for cash. Bonds of $30,000 were converted into common stock.
7. Common stock ($1 par) of $130,000 was issued for cash.
8. Accounts payable pertain to merchandise suppliers.

Solution

Action Plan

✔ Determine net cash provided/used by operating activities by adjusting net income for items that did not affect cash.

✔ Determine net cash provided/used by investing activities and financing activities.

✔ Determine the net increase/decrease in cash.

Helpful Hint

1. Determine net cash provided/used by operating activities, recognizing that operating activities generally relate to changes in current assets and current liabilities.

2. Determine net cash provided/used by investing activities, recognizing that investing activities generally relate to changes in noncurrent assets.

3. Determine net cash provided/used by financing

REYNOLDS COMPANY
Statement of Cash Flows—Indirect Method
For the Year Ended December 31, 2014

Cash flows from operating activities		
Net income		$ 125,000
Adjustments to reconcile net income to net		
cash provided by operating activities:		
Depreciation expense	$ 33,000	
Loss on disposal of equipment	2,000	
Increase in accounts receivable	(42,000)	
Increase in inventory	(54,000)	
Decrease in prepaid expenses	2,000	
Decrease in accounts payable	(17,000)	
Increase in accrued expenses payable	10,000	(66,000)
Net cash provided by operating activities		59,000
Cash flows from investing activities		
Sale of land	25,000	
Sale of equipment	34,000	
Purchase of equipment	(166,000)	
Net cash used by investing activities		(107,000)
Cash flows from financing activities		
Redemption of bonds	(10,000)	
Sale of common stock	130,000	
Payment of dividends	(55,000)	
Net cash provided by financing activities		65,000

activities, recognizing that financing activities generally relate to changes in long-term liabilities and stockholders' equity accounts.

Net increase in cash	17,000
Cash at beginning of period	37,000
Cash at end of period	$54,000
Noncash investing and financing activities	
Conversion of bonds into common stock	$30,000

Related exercise material: **BE17-4, BE17-5, BE17-6, BE17-7, E17-4, E17-5, and E17-6.**

 The Navigator

ACCOUNTING ACROSS THE ORGANIZATION

Burning Through Our Cash

Kodak used to dominate the market for photographic film—back when most cameras used film. But when digital cameras arrived, the company's cash flows steadily declined. Investors began to wonder whether Kodak's cash would run out before the company came up with an alternative source of income. Eventually, the company was forced to sell plant assets and intangibles such as patents in order to supplement its cash from operating activities. Finally, Kodak decided to borrow money against its line of credit. Investors in Kodak's stocks and bonds interpreted this as a desperate move (because it further increased the company's debt). The price of its stock and its bonds plummeted. Within months, Kodak had filed for bankruptcy.

Source: Dana Mattioli and Matt Marzemsky, "Clock Ticks as Kodak Burns Cash," *Wall Street Journal* (September 27, 2011).

© Soubrette/iStockphoto

? What impact did Kodak's sale of plant assets have on its net cash provided by investing activities? (See page 837.)

Using Cash Flows to Evaluate a Company

Traditionally, investors and creditors used ratios based on accrual accounting. These days, cash-based ratios are gaining increased acceptance among analysts.

LEARNING OBJECTIVE 4

Analyze the statement of cash flows.

Free Cash Flow

In the statement of cash flows, net cash provided by operating activities is intended to indicate the cash-generating capability of the company. Analysts have noted, however, that **net cash provided by operating activities fails to take into account that a company must invest in new fixed assets** just to maintain its current level of operations. Companies also must at least **maintain dividends at current levels** to satisfy investors. The measurement of free cash flow provides additional insight regarding a company's cash-generating ability. **Free cash flow** describes the net cash provided by operating activities after adjustment for capital expenditures and dividends.

Consider the following example. Suppose that MPC produced and sold 10,000 personal computers this year. It reported $100,000 net cash provided by operating activities. In order to maintain production at 10,000 computers, MPC invested $15,000 in equipment. It chose to pay $5,000 in dividends. Its free cash flow was $80,000 ($100,000 − $15,000 − $5,000). The company could use this $80,000 either to purchase new assets to expand the business or to pay an $80,000 dividend and continue to produce 10,000 computers. In practice, free cash flow is often calculated with the formula in Illustration 17-14. (Alternative definitions also exist.)

Illustration 17-14
Free cash flow

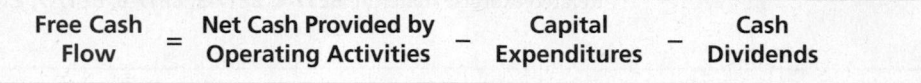

Free Cash Flow	=	Net Cash Provided by Operating Activities	−	Capital Expenditures	−	Cash Dividends

Illustration 17-15 provides basic information (in billions) excerpted from the 2011 statement of cash flows of Microsoft Corporation.

Illustration 17-15
Microsoft's cash flow information's ($ in millions)

MICROSOFT CORPORATION
Real World
Statement of Cash Flows (partial)
2011

Cash provided by operating activities		$26,994
Cash flows from investing activities		
Additions to property and equipment	$ (2,355)	
Purchases of investments	(35,993)	
Sales of investments	15,880	
Acquisitions of companies	(71)	
Maturities of investments	6,897	
Other	1,026	
Cash used by investing activities		(14,616)
Cash paid for dividends		(5,180)

Microsoft's free cash flow is calculated as shown in Illustration 17-16.

Illustration 17-16
Calculation of Microsoft's free cash flow ($ in millions)

Cash provided by operating activities	$26,994
Less: Expenditures on property, plant, and equipment	2,355
Dividends paid	5,180
Free cash flow	**$19,459**

Microsoft generated approximately $19.5 billion of free cash flow. This is a tremendous amount of cash generated in a single year. It is available for the acquisition of new assets, the retirement of stock or debt, or the payment of dividends.

Also note that Microsoft's cash from operations of $27 billion exceeds its 2011 net income of $23.2 billion. This lends additional credibility to Microsoft's income number as an indicator of potential future performance. If anything, Microsoft's net income might understate its actual performance.

Oracle Corporation is one of the world's largest sellers of database software and information management services. Like Microsoft, its success depends on continuing to improve its existing products while developing new products to keep pace with rapid changes in technology. Oracle's free cash flow for 2011 was $9.7 billion. This is impressive but significantly less than Microsoft's amazing ability to generate cash.

> DO IT!

Free Cash Flow

Chicago Corporation issued the following statement of cash flows for 2014.

CHICAGO CORPORATION
Statement of Cash Flows—Indirect Method
For the Year Ended December 31, 2014

Cash flows from operating activities		
Net income		$ 19,000
Adjustments to reconcile net income to net cash		
provided by operating activities:		
Depreciation expense	$ 8,100	
Loss on disposal of plant assets	1,300	
Decrease in accounts receivable	6,900	
Increase in inventory	(4,000)	
Decrease in accounts payable	(2,000)	10,300
Net cash provided by operating activities		29,300
Cash flows from investing activities		
Sale of investments	1,100	
Purchase of equipment	(19,000)	
Net cash used by investing activities		(17,900)
Cash flows from financing activities		
Issuance of stock	10,000	
Payment on long-term note payable	(5,000)	
Payment for dividends	(9,000)	
Net cash used by financing activities		(4,000)
Net increase in cash		7,400
Cash at beginning of year		10,000
Cash at end of year		$ 17,400

(a) Compute free cash flow for Chicago Corporation. (b) Explain why free cash flow often provides better information than "Net cash provided by operating activities."

Solution

Action Plan

✔ Compute free cash flow as: Net cash provided by operating activities – Capital expenditures – Cash dividends.

(a) Free cash flow = $29,300 – $19,000 – $9,000 = $1,300

(b) Net cash provided by operating activities fails to take into account that a company must invest in new plant assets just to maintain the current level of operations. Companies must also maintain dividends at current levels to satisfy investors. The measurement of free cash flow provides additional insight regarding a company's cash-generating ability.

Related exercise material: **BE17-8, BE17-9, BE17-10, BE17-11, E17-7, E17-9, and DO IT! 17-3.**

 The Navigator

> **Comprehensive DO IT! 1**

The income statement for the year ended December 31, 2014, for Kosinski Manufacturing Company contains the following condensed information.

KOSINSKI MANUFACTURING COMPANY
Income Statement
For the Year Ended December 31, 2014

Sales revenue		$6,583,000
Operating expenses (excluding depreciation)	$4,920,000	
Depreciation expense	880,000	5,800,000
Income before income taxes		783,000
Income tax expense		353,000
Net income		$ 430,000

Included in operating expenses is a $24,000 loss resulting from the sale of equipment for $270,000 cash. Equipment was purchased at a cost of $750,000.

The following balances are reported on Kosinski's comparative balance sheets at December 31.

KOSINSKI MANUFACTURING COMPANY
Comparative Balance Sheets (partial)

	2014	**2013**
Cash	$672,000	$130,000
Accounts receivable	775,000	610,000
Inventory	834,000	867,000
Accounts payable	521,000	501,000

Income tax expense of $353,000 represents the amount paid in 2014. Dividends declared and paid in 2014 totaled $200,000.

Instructions
Prepare the statement of cash flows using the indirect method.

Action Plan

✔ Determine net cash from operating activities. Operating activities generally relate to changes in current assets and current liabilities.

✔ Determine net cash from investing activities. Investing activities generally relate to changes in noncurrent assets.

✔ Determine net cash from financing activities. Financing activities generally relate to changes in long-term liabilities and stockholders' equity accounts.

Solution to Comprehensive DO IT! 1

KOSINSKI MANUFACTURING COMPANY
Statement of Cash Flows—Indirect Method
For the Year Ended December 31, 2014

Cash flows from operating activities		
Net income		$ 430,000
Adjustments to reconcile net income to net cash provided by operating activities:		
Depreciation expense	$ 880,000	
Loss on disposal of equipment	24,000	
Increase in accounts receivable	(165,000)	
Decrease in inventory	33,000	
Increase in accounts payable	20,000	792,000
Net cash provided by operating activities		1,222,000

Cash flows from investing activities		
Sale of equipment	270,000	
Purchase of equipment	(750,000)	
Net cash used by investing activities		(480,000)
Cash flows from financing activities		
Payment of cash dividends		(200,000)
Net increase in cash		542,000
Cash at beginning of period		130,000
Cash at end of period		$ 672,000

 The Navigator

SUMMARY OF LEARNING OBJECTIVES

 The Navigator

1 Indicate the usefulness of the statement of cash flows. The statement of cash flows provides information about the cash receipts, cash payments, and net change in cash resulting from the operating, investing, and financing activities of a company during the period.

2 Distinguish among operating, investing, and financing activities. Operating activities include the cash effects of transactions that enter into the determination of net income. Investing activities involve cash flows resulting from changes in investments and long-term asset items. Financing activities involve cash flows resulting from changes in long-term liability and stockholders' equity items.

3 Prepare a statement of cash flows using the indirect method. The preparation of a statement of cash flows

involves three major steps: (1) Determine net cash provided/used by operating activities by converting net income from an accrual basis to a cash basis. (2) Analyze changes in noncurrent asset and liability accounts and record as investing and financing activities, or disclose as noncash transactions. (3) Compare the net change in cash on the statement of cash flows with the change in the Cash account reported on the balance sheet to make sure the amounts agree.

4 Analyze the statement of cash flows. Free cash flow indicates the amount of cash a company generated during the current year that is available for the payment of additional dividends or for expansion.

GLOSSARY

Direct method A method that shows operating cash receipts and payments, making it more consistent with the objective of the statement of cash flows. (p. 783).

Financing activities Cash flow activities that include (a) obtaining cash from issuing debt and repaying the amounts borrowed and (b) obtaining cash from stockholders, repurchasing shares, and paying dividends. (p. 779).

Free cash flow Net cash provided by operating activities adjusted for capital expenditures and dividends paid. (p. 793).

Indirect method A method of preparing a statement of cash flows in which net income is adjusted for items that do not affect cash, to determine net cash provided by operating activities. (pp. 783, 784).

Investing activities Cash flow activities that include (a) purchasing and disposing of investments and property, plant, and equipment using cash and (b) lending money and collecting the loans. (p. 778).

Operating activities Cash flow activities that include the cash effects of transactions that create revenues and expenses and thus enter into the determination of net income. (p. 778).

Statement of cash flows A basic financial statement that provides information about the cash receipts, cash payments, and net change in cash during a period, resulting from operating, investing, and financing activities. (p. 778).

APPENDIX 17A   Statement of Cash Flows—Direct Method

LEARNING OBJECTIVE   **5**

Prepare a statement of cash flows using the direct method.

To explain and illustrate the direct method, we will use the transactions of Computer Services Company for 2014, to prepare a statement of cash flows. Illustration 17A-1 presents information related to 2014 for Computer Services Company.

Illustration 17A-1
Comparative balance sheets, income statement, and additional information for Computer Services Company

COMPUTER SERVICES COMPANY
Comparative Balance Sheets
December 31

Assets	2014	2013	Change in Account Balance Increase/Decrease
Current assets			
Cash	$ 55,000	$ 33,000	$ 22,000 Increase
Accounts receivable	20,000	30,000	10,000 Decrease
Inventory	15,000	10,000	5,000 Increase
Prepaid expenses	5,000	1,000	4,000 Increase
Property, plant, and equipment			
Land	130,000	20,000	110,000 Increase
Buildings	160,000	40,000	120,000 Increase
Accumulated depreciation—buildings	(11,000)	(5,000)	6,000 Increase
Equipment	27,000	10,000	17,000 Increase
Accumulated depreciation—equipment	(3,000)	(1,000)	2,000 Increase
Total assets	$398,000	$138,000	
Liabilities and Stockholders' Equity			
Current liabilities			
Accounts payable	$ 28,000	$ 12,000	$ 16,000 Increase
Income taxes payable	6,000	8,000	2,000 Decrease
Long-term liabilities			
Bonds payable	130,000	20,000	110,000 Increase
Stockholders' equity			
Common stock	70,000	50,000	20,000 Increase
Retained earnings	164,000	48,000	116,000 Increase
Total liabilities and stockholders' equity	$398,000	$138,000	

COMPUTER SERVICES COMPANY
Income Statement
For the Year Ended December 31, 2014

Sales revenue		$507,000
Cost of goods sold	$150,000	
Operating expenses (excluding depreciation)	111,000	
Depreciation expense	9,000	
Loss on disposal of equipment	3,000	
Interest expense	42,000	315,000
Income before income tax		192,000
Income tax expense		47,000
Net income		$145,000

Additional information for 2014:

1. Depreciation expense was comprised of $6,000 for building and $3,000 for equipment.
2. The company sold equipment with a book value of $7,000 (cost $8,000, less accumulated depreciation $1,000) for $4,000 cash.
3. Issued $110,000 of long-term bonds in direct exchange for land.
4. A building costing $120,000 was purchased for cash. Equipment costing $25,000 was also purchased for cash.
5. Issued common stock for $20,000 cash.
6. The company declared and paid a $29,000 cash dividend.

To prepare a statement of cash flows under the direct approach, we will apply the three steps outlined in Illustration 17-3 (page 782).

Step 1: Operating Activities

DETERMINE NET CASH PROVIDED/USED BY OPERATING ACTIVITIES BY CONVERTING NET INCOME FROM AN ACCRUAL BASIS TO A CASH BASIS

Under the **direct method**, companies compute net cash provided by operating activities by **adjusting each item in the income statement** from the accrual basis to the cash basis. To simplify and condense the operating activities section, companies **report only major classes of operating cash receipts and cash payments**. For these major classes, the difference between cash receipts and cash payments is the net cash provided by operating activities. These relationships are as shown in Illustration 17A-2.

Illustration 17A-2
Major classes of cash receipts and payments

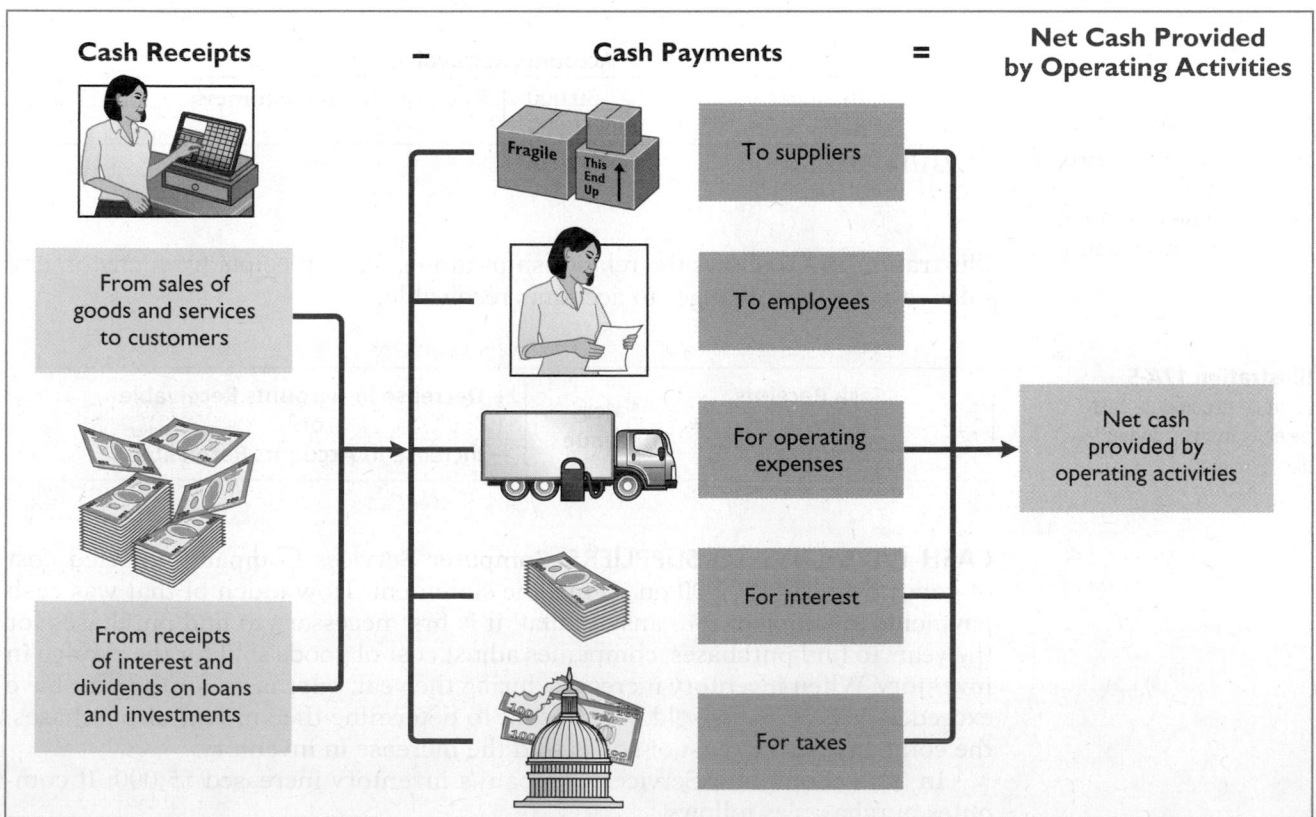

An efficient way to apply the direct method is to analyze the items reported in the income statement in the order in which they are listed. We then determine cash receipts and cash payments related to these revenues and expenses. The following pages present the adjustments required to prepare a statement of cash flows for Computer Services Company using the direct approach.

CASH RECEIPTS FROM CUSTOMERS The income statement for Computer Services Company reported sales revenue from customers of $507,000. How much of that was cash receipts? To answer that, companies need to consider the change in accounts receivable during the year. When accounts receivable increase during the year, revenues on an accrual basis are higher than cash receipts from customers. Operations led to revenues, but not all of those revenues resulted in cash receipts.

To determine the amount of cash receipts, the company deducts from sales revenue the increase in accounts receivable. On the other hand, there may be a decrease in accounts receivable. That would occur if cash receipts from customers exceeded sales revenue. In that case, the company adds to sales revenue the decrease in accounts receivable. For Computer Services Company, accounts receivable decreased $10,000. Thus, cash receipts from customers were $517,000, computed as shown in Illustration 17A-3.

Illustration 17A-3
Computation of cash receipts from customers

Sales revenue	$ 507,000
Add: Decrease in accounts receivable	10,000
Cash receipts from customers	**$517,000**

Computer Services can also determine cash receipts from customers from an analysis of the Accounts Receivable account, as shown in Illustration 17A-4.

Illustration 17A-4
Analysis of accounts receivable

	Accounts Receivable			
1/1/14	Balance	30,000	**Receipts from customers**	**517,000**
	Sales revenue	507,000		
12/31/14	Balance	20,000		

Helpful Hint The T-account shows that sales revenue plus decrease in accounts receivable equals cash receipts.

Illustration 17A-5 shows the relationships among cash receipts from customers, sales revenue, and changes in accounts receivable.

Illustration 17A-5
Formula to compute cash receipts from customers— direct method

Cash Receipts from Customers	=	Sales Revenue	+ Decrease in Accounts Receivable
			or
			− Increase in Accounts Receivable

CASH PAYMENTS TO SUPPLIERS Computer Services Company reported cost of goods sold of $150,000 on its income statement. How much of that was cash payments to suppliers? To answer that, it is first necessary to find purchases for the year. To find purchases, companies adjust cost of goods sold for the change in inventory. When inventory increases during the year, purchases for the year have exceeded cost of goods sold. As a result, to determine the amount of purchases, the company adds to cost of goods sold the increase in inventory.

In 2014, Computer Services Company's inventory increased $5,000. It computes purchases as follows.

Cost of goods sold	$ 150,000
Add: Increase in inventory	5,000
Purchases	**$155,000**

Illustration 17A-6
Computation of purchases

After computing purchases, a company can determine cash payments to suppliers. This is done by adjusting purchases for the change in accounts payable. When accounts payable increase during the year, purchases on an accrual basis are higher than they are on a cash basis. As a result, to determine cash payments to suppliers, a company deducts from purchases the increase in accounts payable. On the other hand, if cash payments to suppliers exceed purchases, there may be a decrease in accounts payable. In that case, a company adds to purchases the decrease in accounts payable. For Computer Services Company, cash payments to suppliers were $139,000, computed as follows.

Purchases	$ 155,000
Deduct: Increase in accounts payable	16,000
Cash payments to suppliers	**$139,000**

Illustration 17A-7
Computation of cash payments to suppliers

Computer Services also can determine cash payments to suppliers from an analysis of the Accounts Payable account, as shown in Illustration 17A-8

Accounts Payable

Payments to suppliers	139,000	1/1/14	Balance	12,000
			Purchases	155,000
		12/31/14	Balance	28,000

Illustration 17A-8
Analysis of accounts payable

Helpful Hint The T-account shows that purchases less increase in accounts payable equals payments to suppliers.

Illustration 17A-9 shows the relationships among cash payments to suppliers, cost of goods sold, changes in inventory, and changes in accounts payable.

| Cash Payments to Suppliers | = | Cost of Goods Sold | + Increase in Inventory or − Decrease in Inventory | + Decrease in Accounts Payable or − Increase in Accounts Payable |

Illustration 17A-9
Formula to compute cash payments to suppliers—direct method

CASH PAYMENTS FOR OPERATING EXPENSES Computer Services reported on its income statement operating expenses of $111,000. How much of that amount was cash paid for operating expenses? To answer that, we need to adjust this amount for any changes in prepaid expenses and accrued expenses payable. For example, if prepaid expenses increased during the year, cash paid for operating expenses is higher than operating expenses reported on the income statement. To convert operating expenses to cash payments for operating expenses, a company adds the increase in prepaid expenses to operating expenses. On the other hand, if prepaid expenses decrease during the year, it deducts the decrease from operating expenses.

Companies must also adjust operating expenses for changes in accrued expenses payable. When accrued expenses payable increase during the year, operating expenses on an accrual basis are higher than they are in a cash basis. As a result, to determine cash payments for operating expenses, a company deducts from operating expenses an increase in accrued expenses payable. On the other hand, a company adds to operating expenses a decrease in accrued expenses payable because cash payments exceed operating expenses.

Computer Services Company's cash payments for operating expenses were $115,000, computed as follows.

Illustration 17A-10
Computation of cash payments for operating expenses

Operating expenses	$ 111,000
Add: Increase in prepaid expenses	4,000
Cash payments for operating expenses	**$115,000**

Illustration 17A-11 shows the relationships among cash payments for operating expenses, changes in prepaid expenses, and changes in accrued expenses payable.

Illustration 17A-11
Formula to compute cash payments for operating expenses—direct method

Cash Payments for Operating Expenses	=	Operating Expenses	+ Increase in Prepaid Expenses or − Decrease in Prepaid Expenses	+ Decrease in Accrued Expenses Payable or − Increase in Accrued Expenses Payable

DEPRECIATION EXPENSE AND LOSS ON DISPOSAL OF EQUIPMENT Computer Services' depreciation expense in 2014 was $9,000. Depreciation expense is not shown on a statement of cash flows under the direct method because it is a noncash charge. If the amount for operating expenses includes depreciation expense, operating expenses must be reduced by the amount of depreciation to determine cash payments for operating expenses.

The loss on disposal of equipment of $3,000 is also a noncash charge. The loss on disposal of equipment reduces net income, but it does not reduce cash. Thus, the loss on disposal of equipment is not shown on the statement of cash flows under the direct method.

Other charges to expense that do not require the use of cash, such as the amortization of intangible assets, depletion expense, and bad debt expense, are treated in the same manner as depreciation.

CASH PAYMENTS FOR INTEREST Computer Services reported on the income statement interest expense of $42,000. Since the balance sheet did not include an accrual for interest payable for 2013 or 2014, the amount reported as expense is the same as the amount of interest paid.

CASH PAYMENTS FOR INCOME TAXES Computer Services reported income tax expense of $47,000 on the income statement. Income taxes payable, however, decreased $2,000. This decrease means that income taxes paid were more than income taxes reported in the income statement. Cash payments for income taxes were, therefore, $49,000 as shown below.

Illustration 17A-12
Computation of cash payments for income taxes

Income tax expense	$ 47,000
Add: Decrease in income taxes payable	2,000
Cash payments for income taxes	**$49,000**

Illustration 17A-13 shows the relationships among cash payments for income taxes, income tax expense, and changes in income taxes payable.

Cash Payments for Income Taxes	=	Income Tax Expense	$\Bigg\{$	+ Decrease in Income Taxes Payable or − Increase in Income Taxes Payable

Illustration 17A-13
Formula to compute cash payments for income taxes— direct method

The operating activities section of the statement of cash flows of Computer Services Company is shown in Illustration 17A-14.

Illustration 17A-14
Operating activities section of the statement of cash flows

Cash flows from operating activities
    Cash receipts from customers $517,000
    Less: Cash payments:
        To suppliers $139,000
        For operating expenses   115,000
        For interest expense   42,000
        For income taxes   49,000   345,000
        Net cash provided by operating activities $172,000

When a company uses the direct method, it must also provide in a **separate schedule** (not shown here) the net cash flows from operating activities as computed under the indirect method.

Step 2: Investing and Financing Activities

ANALYZE CHANGES IN NONCURRENT ASSET AND LIABILITY ACCOUNTS AND RECORD AS INVESTING AND FINANCING ACTIVITIES, OR DISCLOSE AS NON-CASH TRANSACTIONS

INCREASE IN LAND As indicated from the change in the Land account and the additional information, Computer Services Company purchased land of $110,000 by directly exchanging bonds for land. The exchange of bonds payable for land has no effect on cash. But, it is a significant noncash investing and financing activity that merits disclosure in a separate schedule. (See Illustration 17A-16.)

Helpful Hint The investing and financing activities are measured and reported the same under both the direct and indirect methods.

INCREASE IN BUILDINGS As the additional data indicate, Computer Services Company acquired an office building for $120,000 cash. This is a cash outflow reported in the investing activities section. (See Illustration 17A-16.)

INCREASE IN EQUIPMENT The Equipment account increased $17,000. The additional information explains that this was a net increase that resulted from two transactions: (1) a purchase of equipment of $25,000, and (2) the sale for $4,000 of equipment costing $8,000. These transactions are investing activities. The company should report each transaction separately. The statement in Illustration 17A-16 reports the purchase of equipment as an outflow of cash for $25,000. It reports the sale as an inflow of cash for $4,000. The T-account below shows the reasons for the change in this account during the year.

Illustration 17A-15
Analysis of equipment

Equipment

1/1/14 Balance	10,000	Cost of equipment sold	8,000
Purchase of equipment	**25,000**		
12/31/14 Balance	27,000		

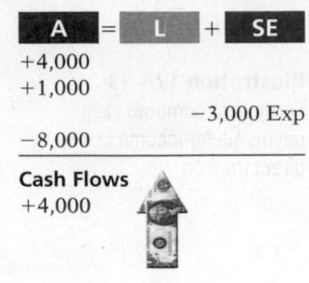

A = L + SE
+4,000
+1,000
      −3,000 Exp
−8,000

Cash Flows
+4,000

The following entry shows the details of the equipment sale transaction.

Cash	4,000	
Accumulated Depreciation	1,000	
Loss on Disposal of Equipment	3,000	
Equipment		8,000

INCREASE IN BONDS PAYABLE The Bonds Payable account increased $110,000. As indicated in the additional information, the company acquired land by directly exchanging bonds for land. Illustration 17A-16 reports this noncash transaction in a separate schedule at the bottom of the statement.

INCREASE IN COMMON STOCK The balance sheet reports an increase in Common Stock of $20,000. The additional information section notes that this increase resulted from the issuance of new shares of stock. This is a cash inflow reported in the financing activities section in Illustration 17A-16.

INCREASE IN RETAINED EARNINGS Retained earnings increased $116,000 during the year. This increase can be explained by two factors. (1) Net income of $145,000 increased retained earnings and (2) dividends of $29,000 decreased retained earnings. The company adjusts net income to net cash provided by operating activities in the operating activities section. **Payment** of the dividends (not the declaration) is a **cash outflow that the company reports as a financing activity in Illustration 17A-16**.

STATEMENT OF CASH FLOWS—2014
Illustration 17A-16 shows the statement of cash flows for Computer Services Company.

Helpful Hint When companies issue stocks or bonds for cash, the actual proceeds will appear in the statement of cash flows as a financing inflow (rather than the par value of the stocks or face value of bonds).

Illustration 17A-16
Statement of cash flows, 2014—direct method

COMPUTER SERVICES COMPANY
Statement of Cash Flows—Direct Method
For the Year Ended December 31, 2014

Cash flows from operating activities		
Cash receipts from customers		$ 517,000
Less: Cash payments:		
To suppliers	$ 139,000	
For operating expenses	115,000	
For income taxes	49,000	
For interest expense	42,000	345,000
Net cash provided by operating activities		172,000
Cash flows from investing activities		
Sale of equipment	4,000	
Purchase of building	(120,000)	
Purchase of equipment	(25,000)	
Net cash used by investing activities		(141,000)
Cash flows from financing activities		
Issuance of common stock	20,000	
Payment of cash dividends	(29,000)	
Net cash used by financing activities		(9,000)
Net increase in cash		22,000
Cash at beginning of period		33,000
Cash at end of period		$ 55,000
Noncash investing and financing activities		
Issuance of bonds payable to purchase land		$ 110,000

Step 3: Net Change in Cash

COMPARE THE NET CHANGE IN CASH ON THE STATEMENT OF CASH FLOWS WITH THE CHANGE IN THE CASH ACCOUNT REPORTED ON THE BALANCE SHEET TO MAKE SURE THE AMOUNTS AGREE

Illustration 17A-16 indicates that the net change in cash during the period was an increase of $22,000. This agrees with the change in balances in the Cash account reported on the balance sheets in Illustration 17A-1 (page 798).

SUMMARY OF LEARNING OBJECTIVE FOR APPENDIX 17A

5 Prepare a statement of cash flows using the direct method. The preparation of the statement of cash flows involves three major steps. (1) Determine net cash provided/used by operating activities by converting net income from an accrual basis to a cash basis. (2) Analyze changes in noncurrent asset and liability accounts and record as investing and financing activities, or disclose as noncash transactions. (3) Compare the net change in cash on the statement of cash flows with the change in the Cash account reported on the balance sheet to make sure the amounts agree. The direct method reports cash receipts less cash payments to arrive at net cash provided by operating activities.

> Comprehensive DO IT! 2

The income statement for Kosinski Manufacturing Company contains the following condensed information.

KOSINSKI MANUFACTURING COMPANY
Income Statement
For the Year Ended December 31, 2014

Sales revenue		$6,583,000
Operating expenses, excluding depreciation	$4,920,000	
Depreciation expense	880,000	5,800,000
Income before income taxes		783,000
Income tax expense		353,000
Net income		$ 430,000

Included in operating expenses is a $24,000 loss resulting from the sale of equipment for $270,000 cash. Equipment was purchased at a cost of $750,000. The following balances are reported on Kosinski's comparative balance sheet at December 31.

KOSINSKI MANUFACTURING COMPANY
Comparative Balance Sheets (partial)

	2014	2013
Cash	$672,000	$130,000
Accounts receivable	775,000	610,000
Inventory	834,000	867,000
Accounts payable	521,000	501,000

Income tax expense of $353,000 represents the amount paid in 2014. Dividends declared and paid in 2014 totaled $200,000.

Instructions

Prepare the statement of cash flows using the direct method.

Solution to Comprehensive DO IT! 2

Action Plan

✔ Determine net cash from operating activities. Each item in the income statement must be adjusted to the cash basis.

✔ Determine net cash from investing activities. Investing activities generally relate to changes in noncurrent assets.

✔ Determine net cash from financing activities. Financing activities generally relate to changes in long-term liabilities and stockholders' equity accounts.

KOSINSKI MANUFACTURING COMPANY
Statement of Cash Flows—Direct Method
For the Year Ended December 31, 2014

Cash flows from operating activities		
Cash collections from customers		$6,418,000*
Cash payments:		
For operating expenses	$4,843,000**	
For income taxes	353,000	5,196,000
Net cash provided by operating activities		1,222,000
Cash flows from investing activities		
Sale of equipment	270,000	
Purchase of equipment	(750,000)	
Net cash used by investing activities		(480,000)
Cash flows from financing activities		
Payment of cash dividends	(200,000)	
Net cash used by financing activities		(200,000)
Net increase in cash		542,000
Cash at beginning of period		130,000
Cash at end of period		$ 672,000

Direct-Method Computations:

*Computation of cash collections from customers:

Sales revenue	$6,583,000
Deduct: Increase in accounts receivable	(165,000)
Cash collections from customers	$6,418,000

**Computation of cash payments for operating expenses:

Operating expenses	$4,920,000
Deduct: Loss on disposal of equipment	(24,000)
Deduct: Decrease in inventories	(33,000)
Deduct: Increase in accounts payable	(20,000)
Cash payments for operating expenses	$4,843,000

✔ **The Navigator**

APPENDIX17B   Using a Worksheet to Prepare the Statement of Cash Flows—Indirect Method

LEARNING OBJECTIVE 6

Explain how to use a worksheet to prepare the statement of cash flows using the indirect method.

When preparing a statement of cash flows, companies may need to make numerous adjustments of net income. In such cases, they often use **a worksheet to assemble and classify the data that will appear on the statement**. The worksheet is merely an aid in preparing the statement. Its use is optional. Illustration 17B-1 shows the skeleton format of the worksheet for preparation of the statement of cash flows. The following guidelines are important in preparing a worksheet.

1. In the balance sheet accounts section, **list accounts with debit balances separately from those with credit balances**. This means, for example, that Accumulated Depreciation appears under credit balances and not as a contra account under debit balances. Enter the beginning and ending balances of each account in the appropriate columns. Enter as reconciling items in the two middle columns the transactions that caused the change in the account balance during the year.

Illustration 17B-1
Format of worksheet

	A	B	C	D	E
			XYZ Company.xls		
	Home Insert Page Layout Formulas Data Review View				
	P18		fx		
1					
2			**XYZ COMPANY**		
3			**Worksheet**		
4		**Statement of Cash Flows For the Year Ended . . .**			
5					
6		End of			End of
7		Last Year	Reconciling Items		Current Year
8	**Balance Sheet Accounts**	Balances	Debit	Credit	Balances
9	Debit balance accounts	XX	XX	XX	XX
10		XX	XX	XX	XX
11	Totals	XXX			XXX
12	Credit balance accounts	XX	XX	XX	XX
13		XX	XX	XX	XX
14	Totals	XXX			XXX
15					
16	**Statement of Cash**				
17	**Flows Effects**				
18	Operating activities				
19	Net income		XX		
20	Adjustments to net income		XX	XX	
21	Investing activities				
22	Receipts and payments		XX	XX	
23	Financing activities				
24	Receipts and payments		XX	XX	
25	Totals		XXX	XXX	
26	Increase (decrease) in cash		(XX)	XX	
27	Totals		XXX	XXX	
28					

After all reconciling items have been entered, each line pertaining to a balance sheet account should "foot across." That is, the beginning balance plus or minus the reconciling item(s) must equal the ending balance. When this agreement exists for all balance sheet accounts, all changes in account balances have been reconciled.

2. The bottom portion of the worksheet consists of the operating, investing, and financing activities sections. It provides the information necessary to prepare the formal statement of cash flows. **Enter inflows of cash as debits in the reconciling columns. Enter outflows of cash as credits in the reconciling columns.** Thus, in this section, the sale of equipment for cash at book value appears as a debit under investing activities. Similarly, the purchase of land for cash appears as a credit under investing activities.

3. **The reconciling items shown in the worksheet are not entered in any journal or posted to any account.** They do not represent either adjustments or corrections of the balance sheet accounts. They are used only to facilitate the preparation of the statement of cash flows.

Preparing the Worksheet

As in the case of worksheets illustrated in earlier chapters, preparing a worksheet involves a series of prescribed steps. The steps in this case are:

1. Enter in the balance sheet accounts section the balance sheet accounts and their beginning and ending balances.

2. Enter in the reconciling columns of the worksheet the data that explain the changes in the balance sheet accounts other than cash and their effects on the statement of cash flows.

3. Enter on the cash line and at the bottom of the worksheet the increase or decrease in cash. This entry should enable the totals of the reconciling columns to be in agreement.

To illustrate the preparation of a worksheet, we will use the 2014 data for Computer Services Company. Your familiarity with these data (from the chapter) should help you understand the use of a worksheet. For ease of reference, the comparative balance sheets, income statement, and selected data for 2014 are presented in Illustration 17B-2.

Illustration 17B-2
Comparative balance sheets, income statement, and additional information for Computer Services Company

COMPUTER SERVICES COMPANY
Comparative Balance Sheets
December 31

Assets	2014	2013	Change in Account Balance Increase/Decrease
Current assets			
Cash	$ 55,000	$ 33,000	$ 22,000 Increase
Accounts receivable	20,000	30,000	10,000 Decrease
Inventory	15,000	10,000	5,000 Increase
Prepaid expenses	5,000	1,000	4,000 Increase
Property, plant, and equipment			
Land	130,000	20,000	110,000 Increase
Buildings	160,000	40,000	120,000 Increase
Accumulated depreciation—buildings	(11,000)	(5,000)	6,000 Increase
Equipment	27,000	10,000	17,000 Increase
Accumulated depreciation—equipment	(3,000)	(1,000)	2,000 Increase
Total assets	$398,000	$138,000	
Liabilities and Stockholders' Equity			
Current liabilities			
Accounts payable	$ 28,000	$ 12,000	$ 16,000 Increase
Income taxes payable	6,000	8,000	2,000 Decrease
Long-term liabilities			
Bonds payable	130,000	20,000	110,000 Increase
Stockholders' equity			
Common stock	70,000	50,000	20,000 Increase
Retained earnings	164,000	48,000	116,000 Increase
Total liabilities and stockholders' equity	$398,000	$138,000	

COMPUTER SERVICES COMPANY
Income Statement
For the Year Ended December 31, 2014

Sales revenue		$507,000
Cost of goods sold	$150,000	
Operating expenses (excluding depreciation)	111,000	
Depreciation expense	9,000	
Loss on disposal of equipment	3,000	
Interest expense	42,000	315,000
Income before income tax		192,000
Income tax expense		47,000
Net income		$145,000

Additional information for 2014:
1. Depreciation expense was comprised of $6,000 for building and $3,000 for equipment.
2. The company sold equipment with a book value of $7,000 (cost $8,000, less accumulated depreciation $1,000) for $4,000 cash.
3. Issued $110,000 of long-term bonds in direct exchange for land.
4. A building costing $120,000 was purchased for cash. Equipment costing $25,000 was also purchased for cash.
5. Issued common stock for $20,000 cash.
6. The company declared and paid a $29,000 cash dividend.

DETERMINING THE RECONCILING ITEMS

Companies can use one of several approaches to determine the reconciling items. For example, they can first complete the changes affecting net cash provided by operating activities, and then can determine the effects of financing and investing transactions. Or, they can analyze the balance sheet accounts in the order in which they are listed on the worksheet. We will follow this latter approach for Computer Services, except for cash. As indicated in step 3, **cash is handled last**.

ACCOUNTS RECEIVABLE The decrease of $10,000 in accounts receivable means that cash collections from sales revenue are higher than the sales revenue reported in the income statement. To convert net income to net cash provided by operating activities, we add the decrease of $10,000 to net income. The entry in the reconciling columns of the worksheet is:

| (a) | Operating—Decrease in Accounts Receivable | 10,000 | |
| | Accounts Receivable | | 10,000 |

INVENTORY Computer Services Company's inventory balance increases $5,000 during the period. The Inventory account reflects the difference between the amount of inventory that the company purchased and the amount that it sold. For Computer Services, this means that the cost of merchandise purchased exceeds the cost of goods sold by $5,000. As a result, cost of goods sold does not reflect $5,000 of cash payments made for merchandise. We deduct this inventory increase of $5,000 during the period from net income to arrive at net cash provided by operating activities. The worksheet entry is:

| (b) | Inventory | 5,000 | |
| | Operating—Increase in Inventory | | 5,000 |

PREPAID EXPENSES An increase of $4,000 in prepaid expenses means that expenses deducted in determining net income are less than expenses that were paid in cash. We deduct the increase of $4,000 from net income in determining net cash provided by operating activities. The worksheet entry is:

| (c) | Prepaid Expenses | 4,000 | |
| | Operating—Increase in Prepaid Expenses | | 4,000 |

LAND The increase in land of $110,000 resulted from a purchase through the issuance of long-term bonds. The company should report this transaction as a significant noncash investing and financing activity. The worksheet entry is:

| (d) | Land | 110,000 | |
| | Bonds Payable | | 110,000 |

Helpful Hint These amounts are asterisked in the worksheet to indicate that they result from a significant noncash transaction.

BUILDINGS The cash purchase of a building for $120,000 is an investing activity cash outflow. The entry in the reconciling columns of the worksheet is:

| (e) | Buildings | 120,000 | |
| | Investing—Purchase of Building | | 120,000 |

EQUIPMENT The increase in equipment of $17,000 resulted from a cash purchase of $25,000 and the disposal of equipment costing $8,000. The book value of the equipment was $7,000, the cash proceeds were $4,000, and a loss of $3,000 was recorded. The worksheet entries are:

| (f) | Equipment | 25,000 | |
| | Investing—Purchase of Equipment | | 25,000 |

(g)	Investing—Sale of Equipment	4,000	
	Operating—Loss on Disposal of Equipment	3,000	
	Accumulated Depreciation—Equipment	1,000	
	Equipment		8,000

ACCOUNTS PAYABLE We must add the increase of $16,000 in accounts payable to net income to determine net cash provided by operating activities. The worksheet entry is:

| **(h)** | Operating—Increase in Accounts Payable | 16,000 | |
| | Accounts Payable | | 16,000 |

INCOME TAXES PAYABLE When a company incurs income tax expense but has not yet paid its taxes, it records income taxes payable. A change in the Income Taxes Payable account reflects the difference between income tax expense incurred and income tax actually paid. Computer Services' Income Taxes Payable account decreases by $2,000. That means the $47,000 of income tax expense reported on the income statement was $2,000 less than the amount of taxes paid during the period of $49,000. To adjust net income to a cash basis, we must reduce net income by $2,000. The worksheet entry is:

(i)	Income Taxes Payable	2,000	
	Operating—Decrease in Income Taxes		
	Payable		2,000

BONDS PAYABLE The increase of $110,000 in this account resulted from the issuance of bonds for land. This is a significant noncash investing and financing activity. Worksheet entry (d) above is the only entry necessary.

COMMON STOCK The balance sheet reports an increase in Common Stock of $20,000. The additional information section notes that this increase resulted from the issuance of new shares of stock. This is a cash inflow reported in the financing section. The worksheet entry is:

| **(j)** | Financing—Issuance of Common Stock | 20,000 | |
| | Common Stock | | 20,000 |

ACCUMULATED DEPRECIATION—BUILDINGS, AND ACCUMULATED DEPRECIATION—EQUIPMENT Increases in these accounts of $6,000 and $3,000, respectively, resulted from depreciation expense. Depreciation expense is a **noncash charge that we must add to net income** to determine net cash provided by operating activities. The worksheet entries are:

| **(k)** | Operating—Depreciation Expense | 6,000 | |
| | Accumulated Depreciation—Buildings | | 6,000 |

| **(l)** | Operating—Depreciation Expense | 3,000 | |
| | Accumulated Depreciation—Equipment | | 3,000 |

RETAINED EARNINGS The $116,000 increase in retained earnings resulted from net income of $145,000 and the declaration and payment of a $29,000 cash dividend. Net income is included in net cash provided by operating activities, and the dividends are a financing activity cash outflow. The entries in the reconciling columns of the worksheet are:

| **(m)** | Operating—Net Income | 145,000 | |
| | Retained Earnings | | 145,000 |

| **(n)** | Retained Earnings | 29,000 | |
| | Financing—Payment of Dividends | | 29,000 |

DISPOSITION OF CHANGE IN CASH The firm's cash increased $22,000 in 2014. The final entry on the worksheet, therefore, is:

(o)	Cash	22,000	
	Increase in Cash		22,000

As shown in the worksheet, we enter the increase in cash in the reconciling credit column as a **balancing** amount. This entry should complete the reconciliation of the changes in the balance sheet accounts. Also, it should permit the totals of the reconciling columns to be in agreement. When all changes have been explained and the reconciling columns are in agreement, the reconciling columns are ruled to complete the worksheet. The completed worksheet for Computer Services Company is shown in Illustration 17B-3.

Illustration 17B-3
Completed worksheet—indirect method

	Computer Services Company.xls			
Home Insert Page Layout Formulas Data Review View				
P18 *fx*				

	A	B	C	D	E
1	**COMPUTER SERVICES COMPANY**				
2	**Worksheet**				
3	**Statement of Cash Flows For the Year Ended December 31, 2014**				
4					
5		**Balance**	**Reconciling Items**		**Balance**
6	**Balance Sheet Accounts**	**12/31/13**	**Debit**	**Credit**	**12/31/14**
7	Debits				
8	Cash	33,000	(o) 22,000		55,000
9	Accounts Receivable	30,000		(a) 10,000	20,000
10	Inventory	10,000	(b) 5,000		15,000
11	Prepaid Expenses	1,000	(c) 4,000		5,000
12	Land	20,000	(d) 110,000*		130,000
13	Buildings	40,000	(e) 120,000		160,000
14	Equipment	10,000	(f) 25,000	(g) 8,000	27,000
15	Total	144,000			412,000
16	Credits				
17	Accounts Payable	12,000		(h) 16,000	28,000
18	Income Taxes Payable	8,000	(i) 2,000		6,000
19	Bonds Payable	20,000		(d) 110,000*	130,000
20	Accumulated Depreciation—Buildings	5,000		(k) 6,000	11,000
21	Accumulated Depreciation—Equipment	1,000	(g) 1,000	(l) 3,000	3,000
22	Common Stock	50,000		(j) 20,000	70,000
23	Retained Earnings	48,000	(n) 29,000	(m) 145,000	164,000
24	Total	144,000			412,000
25					
26	**Statement of Cash Flows Effects**				
27	Operating activities				
28	Net income		(m) 145,000		
29	Decrease in accounts receivable		(a) 10,000		
30	Increase in inventory			(b) 5,000	
31	Increase in prepaid expenses			(c) 4,000	
32	Increase in accounts payable		(h) 16,000		
33	Decrease in income taxes payable			(i) 2,000	
34	Depreciation expense		{(k) 6,000		
35			{(l) 3,000		
36	Loss on disposal of equipment		(g) 3,000		
37	Investing activities				
38	Purchase of building			(e) 120,000	
39	Purchase of equipment			(f) 25,000	
40	Sale of equipment		(g) 4,000		
41	Financing activities				
42	Issuance of common stock		(j) 20,000		
43	Payment of dividends			(n) 29,000	
44	Totals		525,000	503,000	
45	Increase in cash			(o) 22,000	
46	Totals		525,000	525,000	
47					

* Significant noncash investing and financing activity.

6 Explain how to use a worksheet to prepare the statement of cash flows using the indirect method. When there are numerous adjustments, a worksheet can be a helpful tool in preparing the statement of cash flows. Key guidelines for using a worksheet are as follows. (1) List accounts with debit balances separately from those with credit balances. (2) In the reconciling columns in the bottom portion of the worksheet, show cash inflows as debits and cash outflows as credits. (3) Do not enter reconciling items in any journal or account, but use them only to help prepare the statement of cash flows.

The steps in preparing the worksheet are as follows. (1) Enter beginning and ending balances of balance sheet accounts. (2) Enter debits and credits in reconciling columns. (3) Enter the increase or decrease in cash in two places as a balancing amount.

APPENDIX 17C Statement of Cash Flows—T-Account Approach

LEARNING OBJECTIVE **7**
Use the T-account approach to prepare a statement of cash flows.

Many people like to use T-accounts to provide structure to the preparation of a statement of cash flows. The use of T-accounts is based on the accounting equation that you learned in Chapter 1. The basic equation is:

$$\text{Assets = Liabilities + Equity}$$

Now, let's rewrite the left-hand side as:

$$\text{Cash + Noncash Assets = Liabilities + Equity}$$

Next, rewrite the equation by subtracting Noncash Assets from each side to isolate Cash on the left-hand side:

$$\text{Cash = Liabilities + Equity − Noncash Assets}$$

Finally, if we insert the Δ symbol (which means "change in"), we have:

$$\Delta \text{ Cash} = \Delta \text{ Liabilities} + \Delta \text{ Equity} - \Delta \text{ Noncash Assets}$$

What this means is that the change in cash is equal to the change in all of the other balance sheet accounts. Another way to think about this is that if we analyze the changes in all of the noncash balance sheet accounts, we will explain the change in the Cash account. This, of course, is exactly what we are trying to do with the statement of cash flows.

To implement this approach, first prepare a large Cash T-account with sections for operating, investing, and financing activities. Then, prepare smaller T-accounts for all of the other noncash balance sheet accounts. Insert the beginning and ending balances for each of these accounts. Once you have done this, then walk through the steps outlined in Illustration 17-3 (page 782). As you walk through the steps, enter debit and credit amounts into the affected accounts. When all of the changes in the T-accounts have been explained, you are done. To demonstrate, we will apply this approach to the example of Computer Services Company that is presented in the chapter. Each of the adjustments in Illustration 17C-1 is numbered so you can follow them through the T-accounts.

1. Post net income as a debit to the operating section of the Cash T-account and a credit to Retained Earnings. Make sure to label all adjustments to the Cash T-account. It also helps to number each adjustment so you can trace all of them if you make an error.

2. Post depreciation expense as a debit to the operating section of Cash and a credit to each of the appropriate accumulated depreciation accounts.

3. Post any gains or losses on the sale of property, plant, and equipment. To do this, it is best to first prepare the journal entry that was recorded at the time

Cash

Operating			
(1) Net income	145,000	5,000	Inventory (5)
(2) Depreciation expense	9,000	4,000	Prepaid expenses (6)
(3) Loss on equipment	3,000	2,000	Income taxes payable (8)
(4) Accounts receivable	10,000		
(7) Accounts payable	16,000		
Net cash provided by operating activities	172,000		
Investing			
(3) Sold equipment	4,000	120,000	Purchased building (10)
		25,000	Purchased equipment (11)
		141,000	Net cash used by investing activities
Financing			
(12) Issued common stock	20,000	29,000	Dividend paid (13)
		9,000	Net cash used by financing activities
	22,000		

Accounts Receivable		**Inventory**		**Prepaid Expenses**		**Land**	
30,000		10,000		1,000		20,000	
	10,000 (4)	(5) 5,000		(6) 4,000		(9) 110,000	
20,000		15,000		5,000		130,000	

Buildings		**Accumulated Depreciation—Buildings**		**Equipment**		**Accumulated Depreciation—Equipment**	
40,000			5,000	10,000			1,000
(10) 120,000			6,000 (2)	(11) 25,000	8,000 (3)	(3) 1,000	3,000 (2)
160,000			11,000	27,000			3,000

Accounts Payable		**Income Taxes Payable**		**Bonds Payable**		**Common Stock**		**Retained Earnings**	
	12,000		8,000		20,000		50,000		48,000
	16,000 (7)	(8) 2,000			110,000 (9)		20,000 (12)		145,000 (1)
	28,000		6,000		130,000		70,000	(13) 29,000	
									164,000

Illustration 17C-1
T-account approach

of the sale and then post each element of the journal entry. For example, for Computer Services the entry was:

Cash	4,000	
Accumulated Depreciation—Equipment	1,000	
Loss on Disposal of Equipment	3,000	
Equipment		8,000

The $4,000 cash entry is a source of cash in the investing section of the Cash account. Accumulated Depreciation—Equipment is debited for $1,000. The Loss on Disposal of Equipment is a debit to the operating section of the Cash T-account. Finally, Equipment is credited for $8,000.

4–8. Next, post each of the changes to the noncash current asset and current liability accounts. For example, to explain the $10,000 decline in Computer Services' accounts receivable, credit Accounts Receivable for $10,000 and debit the operating section of the Cash T-account for $10,000.

9. Analyze the changes in the noncurrent accounts. Land was purchased by issuing bonds payable. This requires a debit to Land for $110,000 and a credit to Bonds Payable for $110,000. Note that this is a significant noncash event that requires disclosure at the bottom of the statement of cash flows.

10. Buildings is debited for $120,000, and the investing section of the Cash T-account is credited for $120,000 as a use of cash from investing.

11. Equipment is debited for $25,000 and the investing section of the Cash T-account is credited for $25,000 as a use of cash from investing.

12. Common Stock is credited for $20,000 for the issuance of shares of stock, and the financing section of the Cash T-account is debited for $20,000.

13. Retained Earnings is debited to reflect the payment of the $29,000 dividend, and the financing section of the Cash T-account is credited to reflect the use of Cash.

At this point, all of the changes in the noncash accounts have been explained. All that remains is to subtotal each section of the Cash T-account and compare the total change in cash with the change shown on the balance sheet. Once this is done, the information in the Cash T-account can be used to prepare a statement of cash flows.

SUMMARY OF LEARNING OBJECTIVE FOR APPENDIX 17C

7 Use the T-account approach to prepare a statement of cash flows. To use T-accounts to prepare the statement of cash flows: (1) prepare a large Cash T-account with sections for operating, investing, and financing activities; (2) prepare smaller T-accounts for all other noncash accounts; (3) insert beginning and ending balances for all accounts; and (4) follows the steps in Illustration 17-3 (page 782), entering debit and credit amounts as needed.

 **Self-Test, Brief Exercises, Exercises, Problem Set A, and many more components are available for practice in *WileyPLUS*.**

*****Note:** All asterisked Questions, Exercises, and Problems relate to material in the appendices to the chapter.

SELF-TEST QUESTIONS

Answers are on page 837.

(LO 1) **1.** Which of the following is **incorrect** about the statement of cash flows?
  (a) It is a fourth basic financial statement.
  (b) It provides information about cash receipts and cash payments of an entity during a period.
  (c) It reconciles the ending cash account balance to the balance per the bank statement.
  (d) It provides information about the operating, investing, and financing activities of the business.

(LO 1) **2.** Which of the following will **not** be reported in the statement of cash flows?
  (a) The net change in stockholders' equity during the year.
  (b) Cash payments for plant assets during the year.
  (c) Cash receipts from sales of plant assets during the year.
  (d) How acquisitions of plant assets during the year were financed.

(LO 2) **3.** The statement of cash flows classifies cash receipts and cash payments by these activities:

  (a) operating and nonoperating.
  (b) investing, financing, and operating.
  (c) financing, operating, and nonoperating.
  (d) investing, financing, and nonoperating.

(LO 2) **4.** Which is an example of a cash flow from an operating activity?
  (a) Payment of cash to lenders for interest.
  (b) Receipt of cash from the sale of capital stock.
  (c) Payment of cash dividends to the company's stockholders.
  (d) None of the above.

(LO 2) **5.** Which is an example of a cash flow from an investing activity?
  (a) Receipt of cash from the issuance of bonds payable.
  (b) Payment of cash to repurchase outstanding capital stock.
  (c) Receipt of cash from the sale of equipment.
  (d) Payment of cash to suppliers for inventory.

(LO 2) **6.** Cash dividends paid to stockholders are classified on the statement of cash flows as:
  (a) operating activities.
  (b) investing activities.
  (c) a combination of (a) and (b).
  (d) financing activities.

(LO 2) **7.** Which is an example of a cash flow from a financing activity?
  (a) Receipt of cash from sale of land.
  (b) Issuance of debt for cash.
  (c) Purchase of equipment for cash.
  (d) None of the above

(LO 2) **8.** Which of the following is **incorrect** about the statement of cash flows?
  (a) The direct method may be used to report cash provided by operations.
  (b) The statement shows the net cash provided (used) for three categories of activity.
  (c) The operating section is the last section of the statement.
  (d) The indirect method may be used to report net cash provided by operating activities.

Questions 9 through 11 apply only to the indirect method.

(LO 3) **9.** Net income is $132,000, accounts payable increased $10,000 during the year, inventory decreased $6,000 during the year, and accounts receivable increased $12,000 during the year. Under the indirect method, what is net cash provided by operating activities?
  (a) $102,000. **(c)** $124,000.
  (b) $112,000. **(d)** $136,000.

(LO 3) **10.** Items that are added back to net income in determining net cash provided by operating activities under the indirect method do **not** include:
  (a) depreciation expense.
  (b) an increase in inventory.
  (c) amortization expense.
  (d) loss on disposal of equipment.

(LO 3) **11.** The following data are available for Allen Clapp Corporation.

Net income	$200,000
Depreciation expense	40,000
Dividends paid	60,000
Gain on disposal of land	10,000
Decrease in accounts receivable	20,000
Decrease in accounts payable	30,000

Net cash provided by operating activities is:
  (a) $160,000. **(c)** $240,000.
  (b) $220,000. **(d)** $280,000.

(LO 3) **12.** The following data are available for Orange Peels Corporation.

Sale of land	$100,000
Sale of equipment	50,000
Issuance of common stock	70,000
Purchase of equipment	30,000
Payment of cash dividends	60,000

Net cash provided by investing activities is:
  (a) $120,000. **(c)** $150,000.
  (b) $130,000. **(d)** $190,000.

(LO 3) **13.** The following data are available for Something Strange!

Increase in accounts payable	$ 40,000
Increase in bonds payable	100,000
Sale of investment	50,000
Issuance of common stock	60,000
Payment of cash dividends	30,000

Net cash provided by financing activities is:
  (a) $90,000. **(c)** $160,000.
  (b) $130,000. **(d)** $170,000.

(LO 4) **14.** The statement of cash flows should **not** be used to evaluate an entity's ability to:
  (a) earn net income.
  (b) generate future cash flows.
  (c) pay dividends.
  (d) meet obligations.

(LO 4) **15.** Free cash flow provides an indication of a company's ability to:
  (a) generate net income.
  (b) generate cash to pay dividends.
  (c) generate cash to invest in new capital expenditures.
  (d) Both (b) and (c).

Questions 16 and 17 apply only to the direct method.

(LO 5) ***16.** The beginning balance in accounts receivable is $44,000, the ending balance is $42,000, and sales during the period are $129,000. What are cash receipts from customers?
  (a) $127,000. **(c)** $131,000.
  (b) $129,000. **(d)** $141,000.

(LO 5) ***17.** Which of the following items is reported on a statement of cash flows prepared by the direct method?
  (a) Loss on disposal of building.
  (b) Increase in accounts receivable.
  (c) Depreciation expense.
  (d) Cash payments to suppliers.

(LO 6) ***18.** In a worksheet for the statement of cash flows, a decrease in accounts receivable is entered in the reconciling columns as a credit to Accounts Receivable and a debit in the:
  (a) investing activities section.
  (b) operating activities section.
  (c) financing activities section.
  (d) None of the above.

(LO 6) ***19.** In a worksheet for the statement of cash flows, a worksheet entry that includes a credit to accumulated depreciation will also include a:
  (a) credit in the operating activities section and a debit in another section.
  (b) debit in the operating activities section.
  (c) debit in the investing activities section.
  (d) debit in the financing activities section.

Go to the book's companion website, www.wiley.com/college/weygandt, for additional Self-Test Questions.

✔ The Navigator

QUESTIONS

1. **(a)** What is a statement of cash flows?
   (b) Mark Paxson maintains that the statement of cash flows is an optional financial statement. Do you agree? Explain.

2. What questions about cash are answered by the statement of cash flows?

3. Distinguish among the three types of activities reported in the statement of cash flows.

4. **(a)** What are the major sources (inflows) of cash in a statement of cash flows?
   (b) What are the major uses (outflows) of cash?

5. Why is it important to disclose certain noncash transactions? How should they be disclosed?

6. Diane Hollowell and Terry Parmenter were discussing the format of the statement of cash flows of Snow Candy Co. At the bottom of Snow Candy's statement of cash flows was a separate section entitled "Noncash investing and financing activities." Give three examples of significant noncash transactions that would be reported in this section.

7. Why is it necessary to use comparative balance sheets, a current income statement, and certain transaction data in preparing a statement of cash flows?

8. Contrast the advantages and disadvantages of the direct and indirect methods of preparing the statement of cash flows. Are both methods acceptable? Which method is preferred by the FASB? Which method is more popular?

9. When the total cash inflows exceed the total cash outflows in the statement of cash flows, how and where is this excess identified?

10. Describe the indirect method for determining net cash provided (used) by operating activities.

11. Why is it necessary to convert accrual-basis net income to cash-basis income when preparing a statement of cash flows?

12. The president of Merando Company is puzzled. During the last year, the company experienced a net loss of $800,000, yet its cash increased $300,000 during the same period of time. Explain to the president how this could occur.

13. Identify five items that are adjustments to convert net income to net cash provided by operating activities under the indirect method.

14. Why and how is depreciation expense reported in a statement prepared using the indirect method?

15. Why is the statement of cash flows useful?

16. During 2014, Doubleday Company converted $1,700,000 of its total $2,000,000 of bonds payable into common stock. Indicate how the transaction would be reported on a statement of cash flows, if at all.

17. In its 2011 statement of cash flows, what amount did Apple report for net cash (a) provided by operating activities, (b) used for investing activities, and (c) used for financing activities?

*18. Describe the direct method for determining net cash provided by operating activities.

*19. Give the formulas under the direct method for computing (a) cash receipts from customers and (b) cash payments to suppliers.

*20. Molino Inc. reported sales revenue of $2 million for 2014. Accounts receivable decreased $200,000 and accounts payable increased $300,000. Compute cash receipts from customers, assuming that the receivable and payable transactions related to operations.

*21. In the direct method, why is depreciation expense not reported in the cash flows from operating activities section?

*22. Why is it advantageous to use a worksheet when preparing a statement of cash flows? Is a worksheet required to prepare a statement of cash flows?

BRIEF EXERCISES

Indicate statement presentation of selected transactions.
(LO 2)

BE17-1 Each of the items below must be considered in preparing a statement of cash flows for Baskerville Co. for the year ended December 31, 2014. For each item, state how it should be shown in the statement of cash flows for 2014.

(a) Issued bonds for $200,000 cash.
(b) Purchased equipment for $150,000 cash.
(c) Sold land costing $20,000 for $20,000 cash.
(d) Declared and paid a $50,000 cash dividend.

Classify items by activities.
(LO 2)

BE17-2 Classify each item as an operating, investing, or financing activity. Assume all items involve cash unless there is information to the contrary.

(a) Purchase of equipment.
(b) Sale of building.
(c) Redemption of bonds.
(d) Depreciation.
(e) Payment of dividends.
(f) Issuance of capital stock.

BE17-3 The following T-account is a summary of the Cash account of Cuellar Company.

Identify financing activity transactions.

(LO 2)

Cash (Summary Form)

Balance, Jan. 1	8,000		
Receipts from customers	364,000	Payments for goods	200,000
Dividends on stock investments	6,000	Payments for operating expenses	140,000
Proceeds from sale of equipment	36,000	Interest paid	10,000
Proceeds from issuance of		Taxes paid	8,000
bonds payable	300,000	Dividends paid	50,000
Balance, Dec. 31	306,000		

What amount of net cash provided (used) by financing activities should be reported in the statement of cash flows?

BE17-4 Telfer, Inc. reported net income of $2.8 million in 2014. Depreciation for the year was $160,000, accounts receivable decreased $350,000, and accounts payable decreased $280,000. Compute net cash provided by operating activities using the indirect method.

Compute net cash provided by operating activities— indirect method.

(LO 3)

BE17-5 The net income for Metz Co. for 2014 was $280,000. For 2014, depreciation on plant assets was $70,000, and the company incurred a loss on disposal of plant assets of $12,000. Compute net cash provided by operating activities under the indirect method.

Compute net cash provided by operating activities— indirect method.

(LO 3)

BE17-6 The comparative balance sheets for Montalvo Company show these changes in noncash current asset accounts: accounts receivable decrease $80,000, prepaid expenses increase $28,000, and inventories increase $30,000. Compute net cash provided by operating activities using the indirect method assuming that net income is $300,000.

Compute net cash provided by operating activities— indirect method.

(LO 3)

BE17-7 The T-accounts for Equipment and the related Accumulated Depreciation— Equipment for Luo Company at the end of 2014 are shown here.

Determine cash received from sale of equipment.

(LO 3)

Equipment

Beg. bal.	80,000	Disposals	22,000
Acquisitions	41,600		
End. bal.	99,600		

Accumulated Depreciation——Equipment

Disposals	5,500	Beg. bal.	44,500
		Depr. exp.	12,000
		End. bal.	51,000

In addition, Luo Company's income statement reported a loss on the disposal of equipment of $5,500. What amount was reported on the statement of cash flows as "cash flow from sale of equipment"?

BE17-8 Assume that during 2014, Cypress Semiconductor Corporation reported net cash provided by operating activities of $155,793,000, net cash used in investing of $207,826,000, and net cash used in financing of $33,372,000. In addition, cash spent for fixed assets during the period was $132,280,000. No dividends were paid. Calculate free cash flow.

Calculate free cash flow.

(LO 4)

BE17-9 Hinck Corporation reported net cash provided by operating activities of $360,000, net cash used by investing activities of $250,000, and net cash provided by financing activities of $70,000. In addition, cash spent for capital assets during the period was $200,000. No dividends were paid. Calculate free cash flow.

Calculate free cash flow.

(LO 4)

BE17-10 Suppose in a recent quarter, Alliance Atlantis Communications Inc. reported net cash provided by operating activities of $45,600,000 and revenues of $264,800,000. Cash spent on plant asset additions during the quarter was $1,600,000. No dividends were paid. Calculate free cash flow.

Calculate free cash flow.

(LO 4)

BE17-11 The management of Morrow Inc. is trying to decide whether it can increase its dividend. During the current year, it reported net income of $875,000. It had net cash provided by operating activities of $734,000, paid cash dividends of $70,000, and had capital expenditures of $280,000. Compute the company's free cash flow, and discuss whether an increase in the dividend appears warranted. What other factors should be considered?

Calculate and analyze free cash flow.

(LO 4)

*BE17-12 Suppose Columbia Sportswear Company had accounts receivable of $206,024,000 at the beginning of a recent year, and $267,653,000 at year-end. Sales revenue was $1,095,307,000 for the year. What is the amount of cash receipts from customers?

Compute receipts from customers—direct method.

(LO 5)

Compute cash payments for income taxes—direct method.
(LO 5)

*BE17-13 Howell Corporation reported income taxes of $340,000,000 on its 2014 income statement and income taxes payable of $297,000,000 at December 31, 2013, and $522,000,000 at December 31, 2014. What amount of cash payments were made for income taxes during 2014?

Compute cash payments for operating expenses—direct method.
(LO 5)

*BE17-14 Sisson Corporation reports operating expenses of $80,000 excluding depreciation expense of $15,000 for 2014. During the year, prepaid expenses decreased $6,600 and accrued expenses payable increased $4,400. Compute the cash payments for operating expenses in 2014.

Indicate entries in worksheet.
(LO 6)

*BE17-15 During the year, prepaid expenses decreased $5,600, and accrued expenses increased $2,400. Indicate how the changes in prepaid expenses and accrued expenses payable should be entered in the reconciling columns of a worksheet. Assume that beginning balances were prepaid expenses $18,600 and accrued expenses payable $8,200.

> DO IT! Review

Classify transactions by type of cash flow activity.
(LO 2)

DO IT! 17-1 Ragsdell Corporation had the following transactions.

1. Issued $200,000 of bonds payable.
2. Paid utilities expense.
3. Issued 500 shares of preferred stock for $45,000.
4. Sold land and a building for $250,000.
5. Lent $30,000 to Tegtmeier Corporation, receiving Tegtmeier's 1-year, 12% note.

Classify each of these transactions by type of cash flow activity (operating, investing, or financing).

Calculate net cash from operating activities.
(LO 3)

DO IT! 17-2 Wise Photography reported net income of $130,000 for 2014. Included in the income statement were depreciation expense of $6,000, amortization expense of $2,000, and a gain on disposal of equipment of $3,600. Wise's comparative balance sheets show the following balances.

	12/31/13	12/31/14
Accounts receivable	$27,000	$21,000
Accounts payable	6,000	9,200

Calculate net cash provided by operating activities for Wise Photography.

Compute and discuss free cash flow.
(LO 4)

DO IT! 17-3 Obermeyer Corporation issued the following statement of cash flows for 2014.

OBERMEYER CORPORATION
Statement of Cash Flows—Indirect Method
For the Year Ended December 31, 2014

Cash flows from operating activities		
Net income		$59,000
Adjustments to reconcile net income to net cash		
provided by operating activities:		
Depreciation expense	$ 9,100	
Loss on disposal of equipment	9,500	
Increase in inventory	(5,000)	
Decrease in accounts receivable	3,300	
Decrease in accounts payable	(2,200)	14,700
Net cash provided by operating activities		73,700
Cash flows from investing activities		
Sale of investments	3,100	
Purchase of equipment	(27,000)	
Net cash used by investing activities		(23,900)

Cash flows from financing activities		
Issuance of stock	20,000	
Payment on long-term note payable	(10,000)	
Payment for dividends	(15,000)	
Net cash used by financing activities		(5,000)
Net increase in cash		44,800
Cash at beginning of year		13,000
Cash at end of year		$57,800

(a) Compute free cash flow for Obermeyer Corporation. (b) Explain why free cash flow often provides better information than "Net cash provided by operating activities."

EXERCISES

E17-1 Tabares Corporation had these transactions during 2014.

(a) Issued $50,000 par value common stock for cash.
(b) Purchased a machine for $30,000, giving a long-term note in exchange.
(c) Issued $200,000 par value common stock upon conversion of bonds having a face value of $200,000.
(d) Declared and paid a cash dividend of $18,000.
(e) Sold a long-term investment with a cost of $15,000 for $15,000 cash.
(f) Collected $16,000 of accounts receivable.
(g) Paid $18,000 on accounts payable.

Classify transactions by type of activity.

(LO 2)

Instructions
Analyze the transactions and indicate whether each transaction resulted in a cash flow from operating activities, investing activities, financing activities, or noncash investing and financing activities.

E17-2 An analysis of comparative balance sheets, the current year's income statement, and the general ledger accounts of Wellman Corp. uncovered the following items. Assume all items involve cash unless there is information to the contrary.

Classify transactions by type of activity.

(LO 2)

(a) Payment of interest on notes payable.
(b) Exchange of land for patent.
(c) Sale of building at book value.
(d) Payment of dividends.
(e) Depreciation.
(f) Receipt of dividends on investment in stock.
(g) Receipt of interest on notes receivable.
(h) Issuance of capital stock.
(i) Amortization of patent.
(j) Issuance of bonds for land.
(k) Purchase of land.
(l) Conversion of bonds into common stock.
(m) Loss on sale of land.
(n) Retirement of bonds.

Instructions
Indicate how each item should be classified in the statement of cash flows using these four major classifications: operating activity (indirect method), investing activity, financing activity, and significant noncash investing and financing activity.

E17-3 Cushenberry Corporation had the following transactions.

1. Sold land (cost $12,000) for $15,000.
2. Issued common stock at par for $20,000.
3. Recorded depreciation on buildings for $17,000.
4. Paid salaries of $9,000.
5. Issued 1,000 shares of $1 par value common stock for equipment worth $8,000.
6. Sold equipment (cost $10,000, accumulated depreciation $7,000) for $1,200.

Prepare journal entry and determine effect on cash flows.

(LO 2)

Instructions
For each transaction above, (a) prepare the journal entry, and (b) indicate how it would affect the statement of cash flows using the indirect method.

Prepare the operating activities section—indirect method.
(LO 3)

E17-4 Gutierrez Company reported net income of $225,000 for 2014. Gutierrez also reported depreciation expense of $45,000 and a loss of $5,000 on the disposal of equipment. The comparative balance sheet shows a decrease in accounts receivable of $15,000 for the year, a $17,000 increase in accounts payable, and a $4,000 decrease in prepaid expenses.

Instructions
Prepare the operating activities section of the statement of cash flows for 2014. Use the indirect method.

Prepare the operating activities section—indirect method.
(LO 3)

E17-5 The current sections of Scoggin Inc.'s balance sheets at December 31, 2013 and 2014, are presented here. Scoggin's net income for 2014 was $153,000. Depreciation expense was $24,000.

	2014	2013
Current assets		
Cash	$105,000	$ 99,000
Accounts receivable	110,000	89,000
Inventory	158,000	172,000
Prepaid expenses	27,000	22,000
Total current assets	$400,000	$382,000
Current liabilities		
Accrued expenses payable	$ 15,000	$ 5,000
Accounts payable	85,000	92,000
Total current liabilities	$100,000	$ 97,000

Instructions
Prepare the net cash provided by operating activities section of the company's statement of cash flows for the year ended December 31, 2014, using the indirect method.

Prepare partial statement of cash flows—indirect method.
(LO 3)

E17-6 The three accounts shown below appear in the general ledger of Herrick Corp. during 2014.

Equipment

Date		Debit	Credit	Balance
Jan. 1	Balance			160,000
July 31	Purchase of equipment	70,000		230,000
Sept. 2	Cost of equipment constructed	53,000		283,000
Nov. 10	Cost of equipment sold		49,000	234,000

Accumulated Depreciation—Equipment

Date		Debit	Credit	Balance
Jan. 1	Balance			71,000
Nov. 10	Accumulated depreciation on equipment sold	30,000		41,000
Dec. 31	Depreciation for year		28,000	69,000

Retained Earnings

Date		Debit	Credit	Balance
Jan. 1	Balance			105,000
Aug. 23	Dividends (cash)	14,000		91,000
Dec. 31	Net income		77,000	168,000

Instructions
From the postings in the accounts, indicate how the information is reported on a statement of cash flows using the indirect method. The loss on disposal of equipment was $7,000. (*Hint:* Cost of equipment constructed is reported in the investing activities section as a decrease in cash of $53,000.)

E17-7 Rojas Corporation's comparative balance sheets are presented below.

Prepare statement of cash flows and compute free cash flow.

(LO 3, 4)

ROJAS CORPORATION
Comparative Balance Sheets
December 31

	2014	2013
Cash	$ 14,300	$ 10,700
Accounts receivable	21,200	23,400
Land	20,000	26,000
Buildings	70,000	70,000
Accumulated depreciation—buildings	(15,000)	(10,000)
Total	$110,500	$120,100
Accounts payable	$ 12,370	$ 31,100
Common stock	75,000	69,000
Retained earnings	23,130	20,000
Total	$110,500	$120,100

Additional information:

1. Net income was $22,630. Dividends declared and paid were $19,500.
2. All other changes in noncurrent account balances had a direct effect on cash flows, except the change in accumulated depreciation. The land was sold for $4,900.

Instructions
(a) Prepare a statement of cash flows for 2014 using the indirect method.
(b) Compute free cash flow.

E17-8 Here are comparative balance sheets for Velo Company.

Prepare a statement of cash flows—indirect method.

(LO 3)

VELO COMPANY
Comparative Balance Sheets
December 31

Assets	2014	2013
Cash	$ 63,000	$ 22,000
Accounts receivable	85,000	76,000
Inventory	170,000	189,000
Land	75,000	100,000
Equipment	270,000	200,000
Accumulated depreciation—equipment	(66,000)	(32,000)
Total	$597,000	$555,000
Liabilities and Stockholders' Equity		
Accounts payable	$ 39,000	$ 47,000
Bonds payable	150,000	200,000
Common stock ($1 par)	216,000	174,000
Retained earnings	192,000	134,000
Total	$597,000	$555,000

Additional information:

1. Net income for 2014 was $93,000.
2. Cash dividends of $35,000 were declared and paid.
3. Bonds payable amounting to $50,000 were redeemed for cash $50,000.
4. Common stock was issued for $42,000 cash.
5. No equipment was sold during 2014, but land was sold at cost.

Instructions
Prepare a statement of cash flows for 2014 using the indirect method.

*Prepare statement of cash
flows and compute free cash
flow.*
(LO 3, 4)

E17-9 Rodriquez Corporation's comparative balance sheets are presented below.

RODRIQUEZ CORPORATION
Comparative Balance Sheets
December 31

	2014	2013
Cash	$ 15,200	$ 17,700
Accounts receivable	25,200	22,300
Investments	20,000	16,000
Equipment	60,000	70,000
Accumulated depreciation—equipment	(14,000)	(10,000)
Total	$106,400	$116,000
Accounts payable	$ 14,600	$ 11,100
Bonds payable	10,000	30,000
Common stock	50,000	45,000
Retained earnings	31,800	29,900
Total	$106,400	$116,000

Additional information:

1. Net income was $18,300. Dividends declared and paid were $16,400.
2. Equipment which cost $10,000 and had accumulated depreciation of $1,200 was sold for $3,300.
3. All other changes in noncurrent account balances had a direct effect on cash flows, except the change in accumulated depreciation.

Instructions
(a) Prepare a statement of cash flows for 2014 using the indirect method.
(b) Compute free cash flow.

*Compute net cash provided
by operating activities—direct
method.*
(LO 5)

*E17-10 Macgregor Company completed its first year of operations on December 31, 2014. Its initial income statement showed that Macgregor had revenues of $192,000 and operating expenses of $78,000. Accounts receivable and accounts payable at year-end were $60,000 and $23,000, respectively. Assume that accounts payable related to operating expenses. Ignore income taxes.

Instructions
Compute net cash provided by operating activities using the direct method.

*Compute cash payments—
direct method.*
(LO 5)

*E17-11 Suppose a recent income statement for McDonald's Corporation shows cost of goods sold $4,852.7 million and operating expenses (including depreciation expense of $1,201 million) $10,671.5 million. The comparative balance sheet for the year shows that inventory increased $18.1 million, prepaid expenses increased $56.3 million, accounts payable (merchandise suppliers) increased $136.9 million, and accrued expenses payable increased $160.9 million.

Instructions
Using the direct method, compute (a) cash payments to suppliers and (b) cash payments for operating expenses.

*Compute cash flow from
operating activities—direct
method.*
(LO 5)

*E17-12 The 2014 accounting records of Blocker Transport reveal these transactions and events.

Payment of interest	$ 10,000	Collection of accounts receivable	$182,000
Cash sales	48,000	Payment of salaries and wages	53,000
Receipt of dividend revenue	18,000	Depreciation expense	16,000
Payment of income taxes	12,000	Proceeds from sale of vehicles	12,000
Net income	38,000	Purchase of equipment for cash	22,000
Payment of accounts payable		Loss on disposal of vehicles	3,000
for merchandise	115,000	Payment of dividends	14,000
Payment for land	74,000	Payment of operating expenses	28,000

Instructions
Prepare the cash flows from operating activities section using the direct method. (Not all of the items will be used.)

*E17-13 The following information is taken from the 2014 general ledger of Swisher Company.

Calculate cash flows—direct method.

(LO 5)

Rent	Rent expense	$ 48,000
	Prepaid rent, January 1	5,900
	Prepaid rent, December 31	9,000
Salaries	Salaries and wages expense	$ 54,000
	Salaries and wages payable, January 1	10,000
	Salaries and wages payable, December 31	8,000
Sales	Sales revenue	$175,000
	Accounts receivable, January 1	16,000
	Accounts receivable, December 31	7,000

Instructions

In each case, compute the amount that should be reported in the operating activities section of the statement of cash flows under the direct method.

*E17-14 Comparative balance sheets for International Company are presented below.

Prepare a worksheet.

(LO 6)

INTERNATIONAL COMPANY
Comparative Balance Sheets
December 31

Assets	2014	2013
Cash	$ 73,000	$ 22,000
Accounts receivable	85,000	76,000
Inventory	180,000	189,000
Land	75,000	100,000
Equipment	250,000	200,000
Accumulated depreciation—equipment	(66,000)	(42,000)
Total	$597,000	$545,000

Liabilities and Stockholders' Equity	2014	2013
Accounts payable	$ 34,000	$ 47,000
Bonds payable	150,000	200,000
Common stock ($1 par)	214,000	164,000
Retained earnings	199,000	134,000
Total	$597,000	$545,000

Additional information:

1. Net income for 2014 was $135,000.
2. Cash dividends of $70,000 were declared and paid.
3. Bonds payable amounting to $50,000 were redeemed for cash $50,000.
4. Common stock was issued for $50,000 cash.
5. Depreciation expense was $24,000.
6. Sales for the year were $978,000.

Instructions

Prepare a worksheet for a statement of cash flows for 2014 using the indirect method. Enter the reconciling items directly on the worksheet, using letters to cross-reference each entry.

EXERCISES: SET B AND CHALLENGE EXERCISES

Visit the book's companion website, at **www.wiley.com/college/weygandt**, and choose the Student Companion site to access Exercise Set B and Challenge Exercises.

PROBLEMS: SET A

P17-1A You are provided with the following transactions that took place during a recent fiscal year.

Distinguish among operating, investing, and financing activities.   (LO 2)

Transaction	Statement of Cash Flow Activity Affected	Cash Inflow, Outflow, or No Effect?
(a) Recorded depreciation expense on the plant assets.		
(b) Recorded and paid interest expense.		
(c) Recorded cash proceeds from a disposal of plant assets.		
(d) Acquired land by issuing common stock.		
(e) Paid a cash dividend to preferred stockholders.		
(f) Paid a cash dividend to common stockholders.		
(g) Recorded cash sales.		
(h) Recorded sales on account.		
(i) Purchased inventory for cash.		
(j) Purchased inventory on account.		

Instructions

Complete the table indicating whether each item (1) affects operating (O) activities, investing (I) activities, financing (F) activities, or is a noncash (NC) transaction reported in a separate schedule, and (2) represents a cash inflow or cash outflow or has no cash flow effect. Assume use of the indirect approach.

Determine cash flow effects of changes in equity accounts.

(LO 3)

P17-2A The following account balances relate to the stockholders' equity accounts of Kerbs Corp. at year-end.

	2014	2013
Common stock, 10,500 and 10,000 shares, respectively, for 2014 and 2013	$170,000	$140,000
Preferred stock, 5,000 shares	125,000	125,000
Retained earnings	300,000	250,000

A small stock dividend was declared and issued in 2014. The market value of the shares was $10,500. Cash dividends were $15,000 in both 2014 and 2013. The common stock has no par or stated value.

Instructions

(a) Net income $75,500

(a) What was the amount of net income reported by Kerbs Corp. in 2014?

(b) Determine the amounts of any cash inflows or outflows related to the common stock and dividend accounts in 2014.

(c) Indicate where each of the cash inflows or outflows identified in (b) would be classified on the statement of cash flows.

Prepare the operating activities section—indirect method.

(LO 3)

P17-3A The income statement of Whitlock Company is presented here.

WHITLOCK COMPANY
Income Statement
For the Year Ended November 30, 2014

Sales revenue		$7,700,000
Cost of goods sold		
Beginning inventory	$1,900,000	
Purchases	4,400,000	
Goods available for sale	6,300,000	
Ending inventory	1,400,000	
Total cost of goods sold		4,900,000
Gross profit		2,800,000
Operating expenses		1,150,000
Net income		$1,650,000

Additional information:

1. Accounts receivable increased $200,000 during the year, and inventory decreased $500,000.
2. Prepaid expenses increased $150,000 during the year.

3. Accounts payable to suppliers of merchandise decreased $340,000 during the year.
4. Accrued expenses payable decreased $100,000 during the year.
5. Operating expenses include depreciation expense of $70,000.

Instructions

Prepare the operating activities section of the statement of cash flows for the year ended November 30, 2014, for Whitlock Company, using the indirect method.

*P17-4A Data for Whitlock Company are presented in P17-3A.

Instructions

Prepare the operating activities section of the statement of cash flows using the direct method.

P17-5A Zumbrunn Company's income statement contained the condensed information below.

ZUMBRUNN COMPANY
Income Statement
For the Year Ended December 31, 2014

Service revenue		$970,000
Operating expenses, excluding depreciation	$624,000	
Depreciation expense	60,000	
Loss on disposal of equipment	16,000	700,000
Income before income taxes		270,000
Income tax expense		40,000
Net income		$230,000

Zumbrunn's balance sheet contained the comparative data at December 31, shown below.

	2014	2013
Accounts receivable	$75,000	$65,000
Accounts payable	46,000	28,000
Income taxes payable	11,000	7,000

Accounts payable pertain to operating expenses.

Instructions

Prepare the operating activities section of the statement of cash flows using the indirect method.

*P17-6A Data for Zumbrunn Company are presented in P17-5A.

Instructions

Prepare the operating activities section of the statement of cash flows using the direct method.

P17-7A Presented below are the financial statements of Nosker Company.

NOSKER COMPANY
Comparative Balance Sheets
December 31

Assets	2014	2013
Cash	$ 38,000	$ 20,000
Accounts receivable	30,000	14,000
Inventory	27,000	20,000
Equipment	60,000	78,000
Accumulated depreciation—equipment	(29,000)	(24,000)
Total	$126,000	$108,000

Liabilities and Stockholders' Equity	2014	2013
Accounts payable	$ 24,000	$ 15,000
Income taxes payable	7,000	8,000
Bonds payable	27,000	33,000
Common stock	18,000	14,000
Retained earnings	50,000	38,000
Total	$126,000	$108,000

Cash from operations
$1,430,000

Prepare the operating activities section—direct method.

(LO 5)

Cash from operations
$1,430,000

Prepare the operating activities section—indirect method.

(LO 3)

Cash from operations
$318,000

Prepare the operating activities section—direct method.

(LO 5)

Cash from operations
$318,000

Prepare a statement of cash flows—indirect method, and compute free cash flow.

(LO 3, 4)

NOSKER COMPANY
Income Statement
For the Year Ended December 31, 2014

Sales revenue	$242,000
Cost of goods sold	175,000
Gross profit	67,000
Operating expenses	24,000
Income from operations	43,000
Interest expense	3,000
Income before income taxes	40,000
Income tax expense	8,000
Net income	$ 32,000

Additional data:

1. Dividends declared and paid were $20,000.
2. During the year equipment was sold for $8,500 cash. This equipment cost $18,000 originally and had a book value of $8,500 at the time of sale.
3. All depreciation expense, $14,500, is in the operating expenses.
4. All sales and purchases are on account.

(a) Cash from operations
    $31,500

Instructions

(a) Prepare a statement of cash flows using the indirect method.
(b) Compute free cash flow.

Prepare a statement of cash flows—direct method, and compute free cash flow.

(LO 4, 5)

XLS

*P17-8A Data for Nosker Company are presented in P17-7A. Further analysis reveals the following.

1. Accounts payable pertain to merchandise suppliers.
2. All operating expenses except for depreciation were paid in cash.

Instructions

(a) Cash from operations
    $31,500

(a) Prepare a statement of cash flows for Nosker Company using the direct method.
(b) Compute free cash flow.

Prepare a statement of cash flows—indirect method.

(LO 3)

P17-9A Condensed financial data of Cheng Inc. follow.

CHENG INC.
Comparative Balance Sheets
December 31

Assets	2014	2013
Cash	$ 80,800	$ 48,400
Accounts receivable	92,800	33,000
Inventory	117,500	102,850
Prepaid expenses	28,400	26,000
Investments	143,000	114,000
Equipment	270,000	242,500
Accumulated depreciation—equipment	(50,000)	(52,000)
Total	$682,500	$514,750

Liabilities and Stockholders' Equity	2014	2013
Accounts payable	$112,000	$ 67,300
Accrued expenses payable	16,500	17,000
Bonds payable	110,000	150,000
Common stock	220,000	175,000
Retained earnings	224,000	105,450
Total	$682,500	$514,750

CHENG INC.
Income Statement
For the Year Ended December 31, 2014

Sales revenue		$392,780
Less:		
Cost of goods sold	$135,460	
Operating expenses, excluding depreciation	12,410	
Depreciation expense	46,500	
Income tax expense	27,280	
Interest expense	4,730	
Loss on disposal of plant assets	7,500	233,880
Net income		$158,900

Additional information:

1. New equipment costing $85,000 was purchased for cash during the year.
2. Old equipment having an original cost of $57,500 was sold for $1,500 cash.
3. Bonds matured and were paid off at face value for cash.
4. A cash dividend of $40,350 was declared and paid during the year.

Instructions
Prepare a statement of cash flows using the indirect method.

Cash from operations $180,250

P17-10A Data for Cheng Inc. are presented in P17-9A. Further analysis reveals that accounts payable pertain to merchandise creditors.

Prepare a statement of cash flows—direct method.

(LO 5)

Instructions
Prepare a statement of cash flows for Cheng Inc. using the direct method.

Cash from operations $180,250

P17-11A The comparative balance sheets for Rothlisberger Company as of December 31 are presented below.

Prepare a statement of cash flows—indirect method.

(LO 3)

ROTHLISBERGER COMPANY
Comparative Balance Sheets
December 31

Assets	2014	2013
Cash	$ 81,000	$ 45,000
Accounts receivable	41,000	62,000
Inventory	151,450	142,000
Prepaid expenses	15,280	21,000
Land	105,000	130,000
Buildings	200,000	200,000
Accumulated depreciation—buildings	(60,000)	(40,000)
Equipment	221,000	155,000
Accumulated depreciation—equipment	(45,000)	(35,000)
Total	$709,730	$680,000

Liabilities and Stockholders' Equity	2014	2013
Accounts payable	$ 47,730	$ 40,000
Bonds payable	260,000	300,000
Common stock, $1 par	200,000	160,000
Retained earnings	202,000	180,000
Total	$709,730	$680,000

Additional information:

1. Operating expenses include depreciation expense of $42,000 and charges from prepaid expenses of $5,720.
2. Land was sold for cash at book value.

Cash from operations
$113,000

3. Cash dividends of $20,000 were paid.
4. Net income for 2014 was $42,000.
5. Equipment was purchased for $88,000 cash. In addition, equipment costing $22,000 with a book value of $10,000 was sold for $6,000 cash.
6. Bonds were converted at face value by issuing 40,000 shares of $1 par value common stock.

Instructions

Prepare a statement of cash flows for the year ended December 31, 2014, using the indirect method.

Prepare a worksheet—indirect method.

(LO 6)

*P17-12A Condensed financial data of Oakley Company appear below.

OAKLEY COMPANY
Comparative Balance Sheets
December 31

Assets	2014	2013
Cash	$ 82,700	$ 47,250
Accounts receivable	90,800	57,000
Inventory	126,900	102,650
Investments	84,500	87,000
Equipment	255,000	205,000
Accumulated depreciation—buildings	(49,500)	(40,000)
	$590,400	$458,900

Liabilities and Stockholders' Equity		
Accounts payable	$ 57,700	$ 48,280
Accrued expenses payable	12,100	18,830
Bonds payable	100,000	70,000
Common stock	250,000	200,000
Retained earnings	170,600	121,790
	$590,400	$458,900

OAKLEY COMPANY
Income Statement
For the Year Ended December 31, 2014

Sales revenue		$297,500
Gain on disposal of equipment		8,750
		306,250
Less:		
Cost of goods sold	$99,460	
Operating expenses (excluding depreciation expense)	14,670	
Depreciation expense	49,700	
Income tax expense	7,270	
Interest expense	2,940	174,040
Net income		$132,210

Additional information:

1. Equipment costing $97,000 was purchased for cash during the year.
2. Investments were sold at cost.
3. Equipment costing $47,000 was sold for $15,550, resulting in gain of $8,750.
4. A cash dividend of $83,400 was declared and paid during the year.

Instructions

Reconciling items total
$610,210

Prepare a worksheet for the statement of cash flows using the indirect method. Enter the reconciling items directly in the worksheet columns, using letters to cross-reference each entry.

PROBLEMS: SET B

P17-1B You are provided with the following transactions that took place during a recent fiscal year.

Distinguish among operating, investing, and financing activities.

(LO 2)

Transaction	Statement of Cash Flow Activity Affected	Cash Inflow, Outflow, or No Effect?
(a) Recorded depreciation expense on the plant assets.		
(b) Incurred a loss on disposal of plant assets.		
(c) Acquired a building by paying cash.		
(d) Made principal repayments on a mortgage.		
(e) Issued common stock.		
(f) Purchased shares of another company to be held as a long-term equity investment.		
(g) Paid cash dividends to common stockholders.		
(h) Sold inventory on credit. The company uses a perpetual inventory system.		
(i) Purchased inventory on credit.		
(j) Paid wages to employees.		

Instructions

Complete the table indicating whether each item (1) affects operating (O) activities, investing (I) activities, financing (F) activities, or is a noncash (NC) transaction reported in a separate schedule, and (2) represents a cash inflow or cash outflow or has no cash flow effect. Assume use of the indirect approach.

P17-2B The following selected account balances relate to the plant asset accounts of Diaz Inc. at year-end.

Determine cash flow effects of changes in plant asset accounts.

(LO 3)

	2014	2013
Accumulated depreciation—buildings	$337,500	$300,000
Accumulated depreciation—equipment	144,000	96,000
Buildings	750,000	750,000
Depreciation expense	101,500	85,500
Equipment	300,000	240,000
Land	100,000	70,000
Loss on disposal of equipment	8,000	0

Additional information:

1. Diaz purchased $95,000 of equipment and $30,000 of land for cash in 2014.
2. Diaz also sold equipment in 2014.
3. Depreciation expense in 2014 was $37,500 on building and $64,000 on equipment.

Instructions

(a) Determine the amounts of any cash inflows or outflows related to the plant asset accounts in 2014.

(a) Cash proceeds $11,000

(b) Indicate where each of the cash inflows or outflows identified in (a) would be classified on the statement of cash flows.

P17-3B The income statement of Eichorn Company is presented on the next page.

Additional information:

1. Accounts receivable decreased $320,000 during the year, and inventory increased $120,000.
2. Prepaid expenses increased $175,000 during the year.

Prepare the operating activities section—indirect method.

(LO 3)

3. Accounts payable to merchandise suppliers increased $50,000 during the year.
4. Accrued expenses payable increased $155,000 during the year.

EICHORN COMPANY
Income Statement
For the Year Ended December 31, 2014

Sales revenue		$5,400,000
Cost of goods sold		
Beginning inventory	$1,780,000	
Purchases	3,430,000	
Goods available for sale	5,210,000	
Ending inventory	1,900,000	
Total cost of goods sold		3,310,000
Gross profit		2,090,000
Operating expenses		
Depreciation expense	105,000	
Amortization expense	20,000	
Other expenses	945,000	1,070,000
Net income		$1,020,000

Instructions
Prepare the operating activities section of the statement of cash flows for the year ended December 31, 2014, for Eichorn Company, using the indirect method.

Cash from operations $1,375,000

Prepare the operating activities section—direct method.

(LO 5)

Cash from operations $1,375,000

***P17-4B** Data for Eichorn Company are presented in P17-3B.

Instructions
Prepare the operating activities section of the statement of cash flows using the direct method.

Prepare the operating activities section—indirect method.

(LO 3)

P17-5B The income statement of Darbyshire Inc. reported the following condensed information.

DARBYSHIRE INC.
Income Statement
For the Year Ended December 31, 2014

Service revenue	$545,000
Operating expenses	400,000
Income from operations	145,000
Income tax expense	36,000
Net income	$109,000

Darbyshire's balance sheet contained these comparative data at December 31.

	2014	2013
Accounts receivable	$50,000	$70,000
Accounts payable	30,000	51,000
Income taxes payable	10,000	4,000

Darbyshire has no depreciable assets. Accounts payable pertain to operating expenses.

Cash from operations $114,000

Instructions
Prepare the operating activities section of the statement of cash flows using the indirect method.

Prepare the operating activities section—direct method.

(LO 5)

Cash from operations $114,000

***P17-6B** Data for Darbyshire Inc. are presented in P17-5B.

Instructions
Prepare the operating activities section of the statement of cash flows using the direct method.

P17-7B Presented below are the financial statements of Johnston Company.

Prepare a statement of cash flows–indirect method, and compute free cash flow.

(LO 3, 4)

JOHNSTON COMPANY
Comparative Balance Sheets
December 31

Assets		2014		2013
Cash		$ 24,000		$ 33,000
Accounts receivable		25,000		14,000
Inventory		41,000		25,000
Equipment	$ 70,000		$ 78,000	
Less: Accumulated depreciation—				
equipment	(27,000)	43,000	(24,000)	54,000
Total		$133,000		$126,000

Liabilities and Stockholders' Equity		2014		2013
Accounts payable		$ 31,000		$ 43,000
Income taxes payable		24,000		20,000
Bonds payable		20,000		10,000
Common stock		25,000		25,000
Retained earnings		33,000		28,000
Total		$133,000		$126,000

JOHNSTON COMPANY
Income Statement
For the Year Ended December 31, 2014

Sales revenue	$286,000
Cost of goods sold	204,000
Gross profit	82,000
Operating expenses	37,000
Income from operations	45,000
Interest expense	7,000
Income before income taxes	38,000
Income tax expense	10,000
Net income	$ 28,000

Additional data:

1. Dividends of $23,000 were declared and paid.
2. During the year equipment was sold for $10,000 cash. This equipment cost $15,000 originally and had a book value of $10,000 at the time of sale.
3. All depreciation expense, $8,000, is in the operating expenses.
4. All sales and purchases are on account.
5. Additional equipment was purchased for $7,000 cash.

Instructions
(a) Prepare a statement of cash flows using the indirect method.
(b) Compute free cash flow.

(a) Cash from operations $1,000

Prepare a statement of cash flows—direct method, and compute free cash flow.

(LO 4, 5)

*P17-8B Data for Johnston Company are presented in P17-7B. Further analysis reveals the following.

1. Accounts payable pertains to merchandise creditors.
2. All operating expenses except for depreciation are paid in cash.

Instructions
(a) Prepare a statement of cash flows using the direct method.
(b) Compute free cash flow.

(a) Cash from operations $1,000

Prepare a statement of cash flows—indirect method.

(LO 3)

P17-9B Condensed financial data of Saffordville Company are shown below.

SAFFORDVILLE COMPANY
Comparative Balance Sheets
December 31

Assets	2014	2013
Cash	$102,700	$ 33,400
Accounts receivable	60,800	37,000
Inventory	126,900	102,650
Investments	79,500	107,000
Equipment	315,000	205,000
Accumulated depreciation—equipment	(44,500)	(40,000)
Total	$640,400	$445,050

Liabilities and Stockholders' Equity		
Accounts payable	$ 57,700	$ 48,280
Accrued expenses payable	15,100	18,830
Bonds payable	145,000	70,000
Common stock	250,000	200,000
Retained earnings	172,600	107,940
Total	$640,400	$445,050

SAFFORDVILLE COMPANY
Income Statement
For the Year Ended December 31, 2014

Sales revenue		$297,500
Gain on disposal of plant assets		5,000
		302,500
Less:		
Cost of goods sold	$99,460	
Operating expenses, excluding depreciation expense	19,670	
Depreciation expense	30,500	
Income tax expense	37,270	
Interest expense	2,940	189,840
Net income		$112,660

Additional information:

1. New equipment costing $146,000 was purchased for cash during the year.
2. Investments were sold at cost.

Cash from operations
$95,800

3. Equipment costing $36,000 was sold for $15,000, resulting in a gain of $5,000.
4. A cash dividend of $48,000 was declared and paid during the year.

Instructions
Prepare a statement of cash flows using the indirect method.

Prepare a statement of cash flows—direct method.

(LO 5)

*P17-10B Data for Saffordville Company are presented in P17-9B. Further analysis reveals that accounts payable pertain to merchandise creditors.

Cash from operations
$95,800

Instructions
Prepare a statement of cash flows for Saffordville Company using the direct method.

Prepare a statement of cash flows—indirect method.

(LO 3)

P17-11B Presented on the next page are the comparative balance sheets for Pester Company at December 31.

PESTER COMPANY
Comparative Balance Sheets
December 31

Assets	2014	2013
Cash	$ 41,000	$ 57,000
Accounts receivable	77,000	64,000
Inventory	172,000	140,000
Prepaid expenses	12,140	16,540
Land	110,000	150,000
Buildings	250,000	250,000
Accumulated depreciation—buildings	(70,000)	(50,000)
Equipment	215,000	175,000
Accumulated depreciation—equipment	(70,000)	(42,000)
Total	$737,140	$760,540
Liabilities and Stockholders' Equity		
Accounts payable	$ 58,000	$ 45,000
Bonds payable	235,000	265,000
Common stock, $1 par	280,000	250,000
Retained earnings	164,140	200,540
Total	$737,140	$760,540

Additional information:

1. Operating expenses include depreciation expense $55,000 and charges from prepaid expenses of $4,400.
2. Land was sold for cash at cost.
3. Cash dividends of $84,290 were paid.
4. Net income for 2014 was $47,890.
5. Equipment was purchased for $80,000 cash. In addition, equipment costing $40,000 with a book value of $33,000 was sold for $37,000 cash.
6. Bonds were converted at face value by issuing 30,000 shares of $1 par value common stock.

Instructions
Prepare a statement of cash flows for 2014 using the indirect method.

Cash from operations
$71,290

PROBLEMS: SET C

Visit the book's companion website, at **www.wiley.com/college/weygandt**, and choose the Student Companion site to access Problem Set C.

CONTINUING COOKIE CHRONICLE

(*Note:* This is a continuation of the Cookie Chronicle from Chapters 1 through 16.)

CCC17 Natalie has prepared the balance sheet and income statement of Cookie & Coffee Creations Inc. and would like you to prepare the statement of cash flows.

Go to the book's companion website, **www.wiley.com/college/weygandt**, *to see the completion of this problem.*

Broadening Your Perspective

Financial Reporting and Analysis

Financial Reporting Problem: Apple Inc.

BYP17-1 The financial statements of Apple Inc. are presented in Appendix A. Instructions for accessing and using the company's complete annual report, including the notes to the financial statements, are also provided in Appendix A.

Instructions
Answer the following questions.

(a) What was the amount of net cash provided by operating activities for the year ended September 24, 2011? For the year ended September 25, 2010?

(b) What was the amount of increase or decrease in cash and cash equivalents for the year ended September 24, 2011? For the year ended September 25, 2010?

(c) Which method of computing net cash provided by operating activities does Apple use?

(d) From your analysis of the 2011 statement of cash flows, did the change in accounts and notes receivable require or provide cash? Did the change in inventories require or provide cash? Did the change in accounts payable and other current liabilities require or provide cash?

(e) What was the net outflow or inflow of cash from investing activities for the year ended September 24, 2011?

(f) What was the amount of income taxes paid in the year ended September 24, 2011?

Comparative Analysis Problem:
PepsiCo, Inc. vs. The Coca-Cola Company

BYP17-2 PepsiCo's financial statements are presented in Appendix B. Financial statements of The Coca-Cola Company are presented in Appendix C. Instructions for accessing and using the complete annual reports of PepsiCo and Coca-Cola, including the notes to the financial statements, are also provided in Appendices B and C, respectively.

Instructions
(a) Based on the information contained in these financial statements, compute free cash flow for each company.

(b) What conclusions concerning the management of cash can be drawn from these data?

Comparative Analysis Problem:
Amazon.com, Inc. vs. Wal-Mart Stores, Inc.

BYP17-3 Amazon.com, Inc.'s financial statements are presented in Appendix D. Financial statements of Wal-Mart Stores, Inc. are presented in Appendix E. Instructions for accessing and using the complete annual reports of Amazon and Wal-Mart, including the notes to the financial statements, are also provided in Appendices D and E, respectively.

Instructions
(a) Based on the information contained in these financial statements, compute free cash flow for each company.

(b) What conclusions concerning the management of cash can be drawn from these data?

Real-World Focus

BYP17-4 Purpose: Learn about the SEC.

Address: **www.sec.gov/index.html**, or go to **www.wiley.com/college/weygandt**

From the SEC homepage, choose **About the SEC**.

Instructions

Answer the following questions.

(a) How many enforcement actions does the SEC take each year against securities law violators? What are typical infractions?

(b) After the Depression, Congress passed the Securities Acts of 1933 and 1934 to improve investor confidence in the markets. What two "common sense" notions are these laws based on?

(c) Who was the President of the United States at the time of the creation of the SEC? Who was the first SEC Chairperson?

BYP17-5 Purpose: Use the Internet to view SEC filings.

Address: **biz.yahoo.com/i**, or go to **www.wiley.com/college/weygandt**

Steps:
1. Type in a company name.
2. Choose **Profile**.
3. Choose **SEC Filings**. (This will take you to Yahoo-Edgar Online.)

Instructions

Answer the following questions.

(a) What company did you select?
(b) Which filing is the most recent? What is the date?
(c) What other recent SEC filings are available for your viewing?

Critical Thinking

Decision-Making Across the Organization

BYP17-6 Tom Epps and Mary Jones are examining the following statement of cash flows for Guthrie Company for the year ended January 31, 2014.

GUTHRIE COMPANY
Statement of Cash Flows
For the Year Ended January 31, 2014

Sources of cash	
From sales of merchandise	$380,000
From sale of capital stock	420,000
From sale of investment (purchased below)	80,000
From depreciation	55,000
From issuance of note for truck	20,000
From interest on investments	6,000
Total sources of cash	961,000
Uses of cash	
For purchase of fixtures and equipment	330,000
For merchandise purchased for resale	258,000
For operating expenses (including depreciation)	160,000
For purchase of investment	75,000
For purchase of truck by issuance of note	20,000
For purchase of treasury stock	10,000
For interest on note payable	3,000
Total uses of cash	856,000
Net increase in cash	$105,000

Tom claims that Guthrie's statement of cash flows is an excellent portrayal of a superb first year with cash increasing $105,000. Mary replies that it was not a superb first year. Rather, she says, the year was an operating failure, that the statement is presented incorrectly, and that $105,000 is not the actual increase in cash. The cash balance at the beginning of the year was $140,000.

Instructions

With the class divided into groups, answer the following.

(a) Using the data provided, prepare a statement of cash flows in proper form using the indirect method. The only noncash items in the income statement are depreciation and the gain from the sale of the investment.

(b) With whom do you agree, Tom or Mary? Explain your position.

Communication Activity

BYP17-7 Will Hardin, the owner-president of Computer Services Company, is unfamiliar with the statement of cash flows that you, as his accountant, prepared. He asks for further explanation.

Instructions

Write him a brief memo explaining the form and content of the statement of cash flows as shown in Illustration 17-13 (pages 790–791).

Ethics Case

BYP17-8 Wesley Corp. is a medium-sized wholesaler of automotive parts. It has 10 stockholders who have been paid a total of $1 million in cash dividends for 8 consecutive years. The board's policy requires that, for this dividend to be declared, net cash provided by operating activities as reported in Wesley's current year's statement of cash flows must exceed $1 million. President and CEO Samuel Gunkle's job is secure so long as he produces annual operating cash flows to support the usual dividend.

At the end of the current year, controller Gerald Rondelli presents president Samuel Gunkle with some disappointing news: The net cash provided by operating activities is calculated by the indirect method to be only $970,000. The president says to Gerald, "We must get that amount above $1 million. Isn't there some way to increase operating cash flow by another $30,000?" Gerald answers, "These figures were prepared by my assistant. I'll go back to my office and see what I can do." The president replies, "I know you won't let me down, Gerald."

Upon close scrutiny of the statement of cash flows, Gerald concludes that he can get the operating cash flows above $1 million by reclassifying a $60,000, 2-year note payable listed in the financing activities section as "Proceeds from bank loan—$60,000." He will report the note instead as "Increase in payables—$60,000" and treat it as an adjustment of net income in the operating activities section. He returns to the president, saying, "You can tell the board to declare their usual dividend. Our net cash flow provided by operating activities is $1,030,000." "Good man, Gerald! I knew I could count on you," exults the president.

Instructions

(a) Who are the stakeholders in this situation?

(b) Was there anything unethical about the president's actions? Was there anything unethical about the controller's actions?

(c) Are the board members or anyone else likely to discover the misclassification?

All About You

BYP17-9 In this chapter, you learned that companies prepare a statement of cash flows in order to keep track of their sources and uses of cash and to help them plan for their future cash needs. Planning for your own short- and long-term cash needs is every bit as important as it is for a company.

Instructions

Read the article ("Financial Uh-Oh? No Problem") provided at **www.fool.com/personal-finance/ saving/index.aspx**, and answer the following questions.

(a) Describe the three factors that determine how much money you should set aside for short-term needs.

(b) How many months of living expenses does the article suggest to set aside?

(c) Estimate how much you should set aside based upon your current situation. Are you closer to Cliff's scenario or to Prudence's?

FASB Codification Activity

BYP17-10 If your school has a subscription to the FASB Codification, go to **http://aaahq.org/ ascLogin.cfm** to log in and prepare responses to the following. Use the Master Glossary to determine the proper definitions.

(a) What are cash equivalents?
(b) What are financing activities?
(c) What are investing activities?
(d) What are operating activities?
(e) What is the primary objective for the statement of cash flow? Is working capital the basis for meeting this objective?
(f) Do companies need to disclose information about investing and financing activities that do not affect cash receipts or cash payments? If so, how should such information be disclosed?

Answers to Chapter Questions

Answers to Insight and Accounting Across the Organization Questions

p. 780 Net *What*?   Q: In general, why do differences exist between net income and net cash provided by operating activities?   **A:** The differences are explained by differences in the timing of the reporting of revenues and expenses under accrual accounting versus cash accounting. Under accrual accounting, companies report revenues when their performance obligation is satisfied, even if cash hasn't been received, and they report expenses when incurred, even if cash hasn't been paid.

p. 793 Burning Through Our Cash   Q: What impact did Kodak's sale of plant assets have on its net cash provided by investing activities? **A:** Kodak sold its plant assets to increase its net cash provided by investing activities. This net cash increase allowed Kodak to then invest in new product ideas.

Answers to Self-Test Questions

1. c **2.** a **3.** b **4.** a **5.** c **6.** d **7.** b **8.** c **9.** d ($132,000 + $10,000 + $6,000 − $12,000) **10.** b
11. b ($200,000 + $40,000 − $10,000 + $20,000 − $30,000) **12.** a ($100,000 + $50,000 − $30,000) **13.** b ($100,000 + $60,000 − $30,000) **14.** a **15.** d ***16.** c [$129,000 + ($44,000 − $42,000)] ***17.** d ***18.** b ***19.** b

 # A Look at IFRS

As in GAAP, the statement of cash flows is a required statement for IFRS. In addition, the content and presentation of an IFRS statement of cash flows is similar to the one used for GAAP. However, the disclosure requirements related to the statement of cash flows are more extensive under GAAP. *IAS 7* ("Cash Flow Statements") provides the overall IFRS requirements for cash flow information.

LEARNING OBJECTIVE   8

Discuss the accounting procedures for the statement of cash flows under GAAP and IFRS.

Key Points

- Companies preparing financial statements under IFRS must prepare a statement of cash flows as an integral part of the financial statements.

- Both IFRS and GAAP require that the statement of cash flows should have three major sections—operating, investing, and financing activities—along with changes in cash and cash equivalents.

- Similar to GAAP, the statement of cash flows can be prepared using either the indirect or direct method under IFRS. In both U.S. and international settings, companies choose for the most part to use the indirect method for reporting net cash flows from operating activities.

- The definition of cash equivalents used in IFRS is similar to that used in GAAP. A major difference is that in certain situations, bank overdrafts are considered part of cash and cash equivalents under IFRS (which is not the case in GAAP). Under GAAP, bank overdrafts are classified as financing activities in the statement of cash flows and are reported as liabilities on the balance sheet.

- IFRS requires that noncash investing and financing activities be excluded from the statement of cash flows. Instead, these noncash activities should be reported elsewhere. This requirement is interpreted to mean that noncash investing and financing activities should be disclosed in the notes to the financial statements instead of in the financial statements. Under GAAP, companies may present this information on the face of the statement of cash flows.

- One area where there can be substantial differences between IFRS and GAAP relates to the classification of interest, dividends, and taxes. The following table indicates the differences between the two approaches.

Item	IFRS	GAAP
Interest paid	Operating or financing	Operating
Interest received	Operating or investing	Operating
Dividends paid	Operating or financing	Financing
Dividends received	Operating or investing	Operating
Taxes paid	Operating—unless specific identification with financing or investing activity	Operating

- Under IFRS, some companies present the operating section in a single line item, with a full reconciliation provided in the notes to the financial statements. This presentation is not seen under GAAP.

- Similar to GAAP, under IFRS companies must disclose the amount of taxes and interest paid. Under GAAP, companies disclose this in the notes to the financial statements. Under IFRS, some companies disclose this information in the notes, but others provide individual line items on the face of the statement. In order to provide this information on the face of the statement, companies first add back the amount of interest expense and tax expense (similar to adding back depreciation expense) and then further down the statement they subtract the cash amount paid for interest and taxes. This treatment can be seen in the statement of cash flows provided for Zetar in Appendix F.

Looking to the Future

Presently, the FASB and the IASB are involved in a joint project on the presentation and organization of information in the financial statements. One interesting approach, revealed in a published proposal from that project, is that in the future the income statement and balance sheet would adopt headings similar to those of the statement of cash flows. That is, the income statement and balance sheet would be broken into operating, investing, and financing sections.

With respect to the statement of cash flows specifically, the notion of **cash equivalents** will probably not be retained. That is, cash equivalents will not be combined with cash but instead will be reported as a form of highly liquid, low-risk investment. The definition of cash in the existing literature would be retained, and the statement of cash flows would present information on changes in cash only. In addition, the FASB favors presentation of operating cash flows using the direct method only. However, the majority of IASB members express a preference for not requiring use of the direct method of reporting operating cash flows. The two Boards will have to resolve their differences in this area in order to issue a converged standard for the statement of cash flows.

IFRS Practice

IFRS Self-Test Questions

1. Under IFRS, interest paid can be reported as:
   (a) only a financing activity.
   (b) a financing activity or an investing activity.
   (c) a financing activity or an operating activity.
   (d) only an operating activity.

2. IFRS requires that noncash items:
   (a) be reported in the section to which they relate, that is, a noncash investing activity would be reported in the investing section.
   (b) be disclosed in the notes to the financial statements.

(c) do not need to be reported.

(d) be treated in a fashion similar to cash equivalents.

3. In the future, it appears likely that:

(a) the income statement and balance sheet will have headings of operating, investing, and financing, much like the statement of cash flows.

(b) cash and cash equivalents will be combined in a single line item.

(c) the IASB will not allow companies to use the direct approach to the statement of cash flows.

(d) None of the above.

4. Under IFRS:

(a) taxes are always treated as an operating activity.

(b) the income statement uses the headings operating, investing, and financing.

(c) dividends received can be either an operating or investing activity.

(d) dividends paid can be either an operating or investing activity.

5. Which of the following is **correct**?

(a) Under IFRS, the statement of cash flows is optional.

(b) IFRS requires use of the direct approach in preparing the statement of cash flows.

(c) The majority of companies following GAAP and the majority following IFRS employ the indirect approach to the statement of cash flows.

(d) Cash and cash equivalents are reported as separate line items under IFRS.

IFRS Exercises

IFRS17-1 Discuss the differences that exist in the treatment of bank overdrafts under GAAP and IFRS.

IFRS17-2 Describe the treatment of each of the following items under IFRS versus GAAP.

(a) Interest paid.

(b) Interest received.

(c) Dividends paid.

(d) Dividends received.

IFRS17-3 Explain how the treatment of cash equivalents will probably change in the future.

International Financial Reporting Problem: Zetar plc

IFRS17-4 The financial statements of Zetar plc are presented in Appendix F. Instructions for accessing and using the company's complete annual report, including the notes to its financial statements, are also provided in Appendix F.

Instructions

Use the company's annual report to answer the following questions.

(a) In which section (operating, investing, or financing) does Zetar report interest paid (finance costs)?

(b) Explain why the amount that Zetar reports for cash and cash equivalents in its statement of cash flows is negative.

(c) If Zetar reported under GAAP rather than IFRS, how would its treatment of bank overdrafts differ?

(d) Zetar's statement of cash flows reports negative "net movement in working capital" in 2011 of £(6,040) (in thousands). According to the statement of cash flows, what were the components of this "net movement"?

Answers to IFRS Self-Test Questions

1. c   2. b   3. a   4. c   5. c

✔ **The Navigator**

✔ Remember to go back to The Navigator box on the chapter opening page and check off your completed work.

Feature Story

It Pays to Be Patient

A recent issue of *Forbes* magazine listed Warren Buffett as the richest person in the world. His estimated wealth was $62 billion, give or take a few million. How much is $62 billion? If you invested $62 billion in an investment earning just 4%, you could spend $6.8 million per day—every day—forever.

So, how does Buffett spend his money? Basically, he doesn't! He still lives in the same house that he purchased in Omaha, Nebraska, in 1958 for $31,500. He still drives his own car (a Cadillac DTS). And, in case you were thinking that his kids are riding the road to Easy Street, think again. Buffett has committed to donate virtually all of his money to charity before he dies.

How did Buffett amass this wealth? Through careful investing. Buffett epitomizes a "value investor." He applies the basic techniques he learned in the 1950s from the great value investor Benjamin Graham. He looks for companies that have good long-term potential but are currently underpriced. He invests in companies that have low exposure to debt and that reinvest their earnings for future growth. He does not get caught up in fads or the latest trends.

Buffett sat out on the dot-com mania in the 1990s. Whe other investors put lots of money into fledgling high-tech firms, Buffett didn't bite because he did not find dot-com companies that met his criteria. He didn't get to enjoy th stock price boom on the way up, but on the other hand, didn't have to ride the price back down to Earth. When t dot-com bubble burst, everyone else was suffering from investment shock. Buffett swooped in and scooped up de on companies that he had been following for years.

In 2012, the stock market had again reached near record highs. Buffett's returns had been significantly lagging the market. Only 26% of his investments at that time were in stock, and he was sitting on $38 billion in cash. One com tator noted that "if the past is any guide, just when Buffe seems to look most like a loser, the party is about to end.

If you think you want to follow Buffett's example and tra form your humble nest egg into a mountain of cash, be warned. His techniques have been widely circulated and emulated, but never practiced with the same degree of success. You should probably start by honing your finan analysis skills. A good way for you to begin your career a

 The Navigator

- Scan Learning Objectives
- Read Feature Story
- Read Preview
- Read text and answer **DO IT!** p. 846
    - p. 859 ■ p. 864 ■ p. 866
- Work Comprehensive **DO IT!** p. 867
- Review Summary of Learning Objectives
- Answer Self-Test Questions
- Complete Assignments
- Go to *WileyPLUS* for practice and tutorials

 Read A Look at IFRS p. 889

Learning Objectives

 The Navigator

After studying this chapter, you should be able to:

[1] Discuss the need for comparative analysis.

[2] Identify the tools of financial statement analysis.

[3] Explain and apply horizontal analysis.

[4] Describe and apply vertical analysis.

[5] Identify and compute ratios used in analyzing a firm's liquidity, profitability, and solvency.

[6] Understand the concept of earning power, and how irregular items are presented.

[7] Understand the concept of quality of earnings.

successful investor is to master the fundamentals of financial analysis discussed in this chapter.

Source: Jason Zweig, "Buffett Is Out of Step," *Wall Street Journal* (May 7, 2012).

Preview of Chapter 18

✔ The Navigator

We can all learn an important lesson from Warren Buffett. Study companies carefully if you wish to invest. Do not get caught up in fads but instead find companies that are financially healthy. Using some of the basic decision tools presented in this textbook, you can perform a rudimentary analysis on any U.S. company and draw basic conclusions about its financial health. Although it would not be wise for you to bet your life savings on a company's stock relying solely on your current level of knowledge, we strongly encourage you to practice your new skills wherever possible. Only with practice will you improve your ability to interpret financial numbers.

Before unleashing you on the world of high finance, we will present a few more important concepts and techniques, as well as provide you with one more comprehensive review of corporate financial statements. We use all of the decision tools presented in this text to analyze a single company—Macy's, Inc.—one of the country's oldest and largest retail store chains.

The content and organization of Chapter 18 are as follows.

FINANCIAL STATEMENT ANALYSIS

Basics of Financial Statement Analysis	Horizontal and Vertical Analysis	Ratio Analysis	Earning Power and Irregular Items	Quality of Earnings
• Need for comparative analysis • Tools of analysis	• Balance sheet • Income statement • Retained earnings statement	• Liquidity • Profitability • Solvency • Summary	• Discontinued operations • Extraordinary items • Changes in accounting principle • Comprehensive income	• Alternative accounting methods • Pro forma income • Improper recognition

Basics of Financial Statement Analysis

Analyzing financial statements involves evaluating three characteristics: a company's liquidity, profitability, and solvency. A **short-term creditor**, such as a bank, is primarily interested in liquidity—the ability of the borrower to pay obligations when they come due. The liquidity of the borrower is extremely important in evaluating the safety of a loan. A **long-term creditor**, such as a bondholder, looks to profitability and solvency measures that indicate the company's ability to survive over a long period of time. Long-term creditors consider such measures as the amount of debt in the company's capital structure and its ability to meet interest payments. Similarly, **stockholders** look at the profitability and solvency of the company. They want to assess the likelihood of dividends and the growth potential of the stock.

Need for Comparative Analysis

Every item reported in a financial statement has significance. When Macy's, Inc. reports cash and cash equivalents of $3 billion on its balance sheet, we know the company had that amount of cash on the balance sheet date. But, we do not know whether the amount represents an increase over prior years, or whether it is adequate in relation to the company's need for cash. To obtain such information, we need to compare the amount of cash with other financial statement data.

Comparisons can be made on a number of different bases. Three are illustrated in this chapter.

Intracompany

1. **Intracompany basis.** Comparisons within a company are often useful to detect changes in financial relationships and significant trends. For example, a comparison of Macy's current year's cash amount with the prior year's cash amount shows either an increase or a decrease. Likewise, a comparison of Macy's year-end cash amount with the amount of its total assets at year-end shows the proportion of total assets in the form of cash.

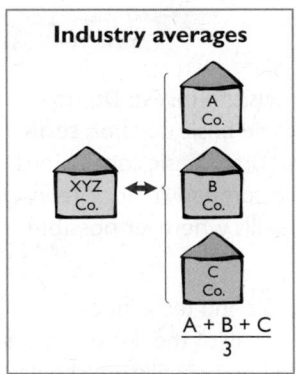

Industry averages

2. **Industry averages.** Comparisons with industry averages provide information about a company's relative position within the industry. For example, financial statement readers can compare Macy's financial data with the averages for its industry compiled by financial rating organizations such as Dun & Bradstreet, Moody's, and Standard & Poor's, or with information provided on the Internet by organizations such as Yahoo! on its financial site.

Intercompany

3. **Intercompany basis.** Comparisons with other companies provide insight into a company's competitive position. For example, investors can compare Macy's total sales for the year with the total sales of its competitors in retail, such as J.C. Penney.

Tools of Analysis

We use various tools to evaluate the significance of financial statement data. Three commonly used tools are as follows:

- **Horizontal analysis** evaluates a series of financial statement data over a period of time.
- **Vertical analysis** evaluates financial statement data by expressing each item in a financial statement as a percentage of a base amount.
- **Ratio analysis** expresses the relationship among selected items of financial statement data.

Horizontal analysis is used primarily in intracompany comparisons. Two features in published financial statements and annual report information facilitate this type of comparison. First, each of the basic financial statements presents comparative financial data for a minimum of two years. Second, a summary of selected financial data is presented for a series of five to 10 years or more. Vertical analysis is used in both intra- and intercompany comparisons. Ratio analysis is used in all three types of comparisons. In the following sections, we explain and illustrate each of the three types of analysis.

Horizontal Analysis

Horizontal analysis, also called **trend analysis**, is a technique for evaluating a series of financial statement data over a period of time. Its purpose is to determine the increase or decrease that has taken place. This change may be expressed as either an amount or a percentage. For example, Illustration 18-1 shows recent net sales figures of Macy's, Inc.

> **LEARNING OBJECTIVE**   **3**
>
> **Explain and apply horizontal analysis.**

Real World	MACY'S, INC. Net Sales (in millions)		
	2011	**2010**	**2009**
	$26,405	$25,003	$23,489

Illustration 18-1
Macy's, Inc.'s net sales

If we assume that 2009 is the base year, we can measure all percentage increases or decreases from this base period amount as follows.

$$\text{Change Since Base Period} = \frac{\text{Current Year Amount} - \text{Base Year Amount}}{\text{Base Year Amount}}$$

Illustration 18-2
Formula for horizontal analysis of changes since base period

For example, we can determine that net sales for Macy's increased from 2009 to 2010 approximately 6.4% [($25,003 − $23,489) ÷ $23,489]. Similarly, we can determine that net sales increased from 2009 to 2011 approximately 12.4% [($26,405 − $23,489) ÷ $23,489].

Alternatively, we can express current year sales as a percentage of the base period. We do this by dividing the current year amount by the base year amount, as shown below.

$$\text{Current Results in Relation to Base Period} = \frac{\text{Current Year Amount}}{\text{Base Year Amount}}$$

Illustration 18-3
Formula for horizontal analysis of current year in relation to base year

Illustration 18-4 presents this analysis for Macy's for a three-year period using 2009 as the base period.

Real World	MACY'S, INC. Net Sales (in millions) in relation to base period 2009		
	2011	**2010**	**2009**
	$26,405	$25,003	$23,489
	112.4%	106.4%	100%

Illustration 18-4
Horizontal analysis of Macy's, Inc.'s net sales in relation to base period

Balance Sheet

To further illustrate horizontal analysis, we will use the financial statements of Quality Department Store Inc., a fictional retailer. Illustration 18-5 presents a horizontal analysis of its two-year condensed balance sheets, showing dollar and percentage changes.

Illustration 18-5
Horizontal analysis of balance sheets

QUALITY DEPARTMENT STORE INC.
Condensed Balance Sheets
December 31

	2011	2010	Increase or (Decrease) during 2011 Amount	Percent
Assets				
Current assets	$1,020,000	$ 945,000	$ 75,000	7.9%
Plant assets (net)	800,000	632,500	167,500	26.5%
Intangible assets	15,000	17,500	(2,500)	(14.3%)
Total assets	$1,835,000	$1,595,000	$240,000	15.0%
Liabilities				
Current liabilities	$ 344,500	$ 303,000	$ 41,500	13.7%
Long-term liabilities	487,500	497,000	(9,500)	(1.9%)
Total liabilities	832,000	800,000	32,000	4.0%
Stockholders' Equity				
Common stock, $1 par	275,400	270,000	5,400	2.0%
Retained earnings	727,600	525,000	202,600	38.6%
Total stockholders' equity	1,003,000	795,000	208,000	26.2%
Total liabilities and stockholders' equity	$1,835,000	$1,595,000	$240,000	15.0%

The comparative balance sheets in Illustration 18-5 show that a number of significant changes have occurred in Quality Department Store's financial structure from 2010 to 2011:

- In the assets section, plant assets (net) increased $167,500, or 26.5%.
- In the liabilities section, current liabilities increased $41,500, or 13.7%.
- In the stockholders' equity section, retained earnings increased $202,600, or 38.6%.

These changes suggest that the company expanded its asset base during 2011 and **financed this expansion primarily by retaining income** rather than assuming additional long-term debt.

Income Statement

Illustration 18-6 presents a horizontal analysis of the two-year condensed income statements of Quality Department Store Inc. for the years 2011 and 2010. Horizontal analysis of the income statements shows the following changes:

- Net sales increased $260,000, or 14.2% ($260,000 ÷ $1,837,000).
- Cost of goods sold increased $141,000, or 12.4% ($141,000 ÷ $1,140,000).
- Total operating expenses increased $37,000, or 11.6% ($37,000 ÷ $320,000).

Overall, gross profit and net income were up substantially. Gross profit increased 17.1%, and net income, 26.5%. Quality's profit trend appears favorable.

Illustration 18-6
Horizontal analysis of income statements

QUALITY DEPARTMENT STORE INC. Condensed Income Statements For the Years Ended December 31				
			Increase or (Decrease) during 2011	
	2011	2010	Amount	Percent
Sales revenue	$2,195,000	$1,960,000	$235,000	12.0%
Sales returns and allowances	98,000	123,000	(25,000)	(20.3%)
Net sales	2,097,000	1,837,000	260,000	14.2%
Cost of goods sold	1,281,000	1,140,000	141,000	12.4%
Gross profit	816,000	697,000	119,000	17.1%
Selling expenses	253,000	211,500	41,500	19.6%
Administrative expenses	104,000	108,500	(4,500)	(4.1%)
Total operating expenses	357,000	320,000	37,000	11.6%
Income from operations	459,000	377,000	82,000	21.8%
Other revenues and gains				
Interest and dividends	9,000	11,000	(2,000)	(18.2%)
Other expenses and losses				
Interest expense	36,000	40,500	(4,500)	(11.1%)
Income before income taxes	432,000	347,500	84,500	24.3%
Income tax expense	168,200	139,000	29,200	21.0%
Net income	$ 263,800	$ 208,500	$ 55,300	26.5%

Helpful Hint Note that though the amount column is additive (the total is $55,300), the percentage column is not additive (26.5% is not the column total). A separate percentage has been calculated for each item.

Retained Earnings Statement

Illustration 18-7 presents a horizontal analysis of Quality Department Store's comparative retained earnings statements. Analyzed horizontally, net income increased $55,300, or 26.5%, whereas dividends on the common stock increased only $1,200, or 2%. We saw in the horizontal analysis of the balance sheet that ending retained earnings increased 38.6%. As indicated earlier, the company retained a significant portion of net income to finance additional plant facilities.

Illustration 18-7
Horizontal analysis of retained earnings statements

QUALITY DEPARTMENT STORE INC. Retained Earnings Statements For the Years Ended December 31				
			Increase or (Decrease) during 2011	
	2011	2010	Amount	Percent
Retained earnings, Jan. 1	$525,000	$376,500	$148,500	39.4%
Add: Net income	263,800	208,500	55,300	26.5%
	788,800	585,000	203,800	
Deduct: Dividends	61,200	60,000	1,200	2.0%
Retained earnings, Dec. 31	$727,600	$525,000	$202,600	38.6%

Horizontal analysis of changes from period to period is relatively straightforward and is quite useful. But, complications can occur in making the computations. If an item has no value in a base year or preceding year but does have a value in the next year, we cannot compute a percentage change. Similarly, if a negative amount appears in the base or preceding period and a positive amount exists the following year (or vice versa), no percentage change can be computed.

> **DO IT!**

Horizontal Analysis

Summary financial information for Rosepatch Company is as follows.

	December 31, 2014	December 31, 2013
Current assets	$234,000	$180,000
Plant assets (net)	756,000	420,000
Total assets	$990,000	$600,000

Compute the amount and percentage changes in 2014 using horizontal analysis, assuming 2013 is the base year.

Solution

Action Plan

✔ Find the percentage change by dividing the amount of the increase by the 2013 amount (base year).

	Increase in 2014	
	Amount	**Percent**
Current assets	$ 54,000	30% [($234,000 − $180,000) ÷ $180,000]
Plant assets (net)	336,000	80% [($756,000 − $420,000) ÷ $420,000]
Total assets	$390,000	65% [($990,000 − $600,000) ÷ $600,000]

Related exercise material: **BE18-2, BE18-3, BE18-6, BE18-7, E18-1, E18-3, E18-4, and DO IT! 18-1.**

✔ **The Navigator**

Vertical Analysis

LEARNING OBJECTIVE   4

Describe and apply vertical analysis.

Vertical analysis, also called **common-size analysis**, is a technique that expresses each financial statement item as a percentage of a base amount. On a balance sheet, we might say that current assets are 22% of total assets—total assets being the base amount. Or on an income statement, we might say that selling expenses are 16% of net sales—net sales being the base amount.

Balance Sheet

Illustration 18-8 presents the vertical analysis of Quality Department Store Inc.'s comparative balance sheets. The base for the asset items is **total assets**. The base for the liability and stockholders' equity items is **total liabilities and stockholders' equity**.

Vertical analysis shows the relative size of each category in the balance sheet. It also can show the **percentage change** in the individual asset, liability, and stockholders' equity items. For example, we can see that current assets decreased from 59.2% of total assets in 2010 to 55.6% in 2011 (even though the absolute dollar amount increased $75,000 in that time). Plant assets (net) have increased from 39.7% to 43.6% of total assets. Retained earnings have increased from 32.9% to 39.7% of total liabilities and stockholders' equity. These results reinforce the earlier observations that **Quality Department Store is choosing to finance its growth through retention of earnings rather than through issuing additional debt**.

QUALITY DEPARTMENT STORE INC.
Condensed Balance Sheets
December 31

Assets	2011 Amount	2011 Percent	2010 Amount	2010 Percent
Current assets	$1,020,000	55.6%	$ 945,000	59.2%
Plant assets (net)	800,000	43.6%	632,500	39.7%
Intangible assets	15,000	0.8%	17,500	1.1%
Total assets	$1,835,000	100.0%	$1,595,000	100.0%
Liabilities				
Current liabilities	$ 344,500	18.8%	$ 303,000	19.0%
Long-term liabilities	487,500	26.5%	497,000	31.2%
Total liabilities	832,000	45.3%	800,000	50.2%
Stockholders' Equity				
Common stock, $1 par	275,400	15.0%	270,000	16.9%
Retained earnings	727,600	39.7%	525,000	32.9%
Total stockholders' equity	1,003,000	54.7%	795,000	49.8%
Total liabilities and stockholders' equity	$1,835,000	100.0%	$1,595,000	100.0%

Illustration 18-8
Vertical analysis of balance sheets

Helpful Hint The formula for calculating these balance sheet percentages is:
$$\frac{\text{Each item on B/S}}{\text{Total assets}} = \%$$

Income Statement

Illustration 18-9 shows vertical analysis of Quality Department Store's income statements. Cost of goods sold as a percentage of net sales declined 1% (62.1% vs. 61.1%), and total operating expenses declined 0.4% (17.4% vs. 17.0%). As a result,

QUALITY DEPARTMENT STORE INC.
Condensed Income Statements
For the Years Ended December 31

	2011 Amount	2011 Percent	2010 Amount	2010 Percent
Sales revenue	$2,195,000	104.7%	$1,960,000	106.7%
Sales returns and allowances	98,000	4.7%	123,000	6.7%
Net sales	2,097,000	100.0%	1,837,000	100.0%
Cost of goods sold	1,281,000	61.1%	1,140,000	62.1%
Gross profit	816,000	38.9%	697,000	37.9%
Selling expenses	253,000	12.0%	211,500	11.5%
Administrative expenses	104,000	5.0%	108,500	5.9%
Total operating expenses	357,000	17.0%	320,000	17.4%
Income from operations	459,000	21.9%	377,000	20.5%
Other revenues and gains				
Interest and dividends	9,000	0.4%	11,000	0.6%
Other expenses and losses				
Interest expense	36,000	1.7%	40,500	2.2%
Income before income taxes	432,000	20.6%	347,500	18.9%
Income tax expense	168,200	8.0%	139,000	7.5%
Net income	$ 263,800	12.6%	$ 208,500	11.4%

Illustration 18-9
Vertical analysis of income statements

Helpful Hint The formula for calculating these income statement percentages is:
$$\frac{\text{Each item on I/S}}{\text{Net sales}} = \%$$

it is not surprising to see net income as a percentage of net sales increase from 11.4% to 12.6%. Quality Department Store appears to be a profitable business that is becoming even more successful.

An associated benefit of vertical analysis is that it enables you to compare companies of different sizes. For example, Quality Department Store's main competitor is a Macy's store in a nearby town. Using vertical analysis, we can compare the condensed income statements of Quality Department Store Inc. (a small retail company) with Macy's, Inc.[1] (a giant international retailer), as shown in Illustration 18-10.

Illustration 18-10
Intercompany income statement comparison

Condensed Income Statements (in thousands)				
	Quality Department Store Inc.		**Macy's, Inc.**	
	Dollars	**Percent**	**Dollars**	**Percent**
Net sales	$2,097	100.0%	$26,405,000	100.0%
Cost of goods sold	1,281	61.1%	15,738,000	59.6%
Gross profit	816	38.9%	10,667,000	40.4%
Selling and administrative expenses	357	17.0%	8,256,000	31.3%
Income from operations	459	21.9%	2,411,000	9.1%
Other expenses and revenues (including income taxes)	195	9.3%	1,155,000	4.4%
Net income	$ 264	12.6%	$ 1,256,000	4.7%

Macy's net sales are 12,592 times greater than the net sales of relatively tiny Quality Department Store. But vertical analysis eliminates this difference in size. The percentages show that Quality's and Macy's gross profit rates were comparable at 38.9% and 40.4%, respectively. However, the percentages related to income from operations were significantly different at 21.9% and 9.1%, respectively. This disparity can be attributed to Quality's selling and administrative expense percentage (17%) which is much lower than Macy's (31.3%). Although Macy's earned net income more than 4,757 times larger than Quality's, Macy's net income as a **percentage of each sales dollar** (4.7%) is only 37% of Quality's (12.6%).

Ratio Analysis

LEARNING OBJECTIVE 5

Identify and compute ratios used in analyzing a firm's liquidity, profitability, and solvency.

Ratio analysis expresses the relationship among selected items of financial statement data. A **ratio** expresses the mathematical relationship between one quantity and another. The relationship is expressed in terms of either a percentage, a rate, or a simple proportion. To illustrate, in 2011 Nike, Inc. had current assets of $11,297 million and current liabilities of $3,958 million. We can find the relationship between these two measures by dividing current assets by current liabilities. The alternative means of expression are:

Percentage: Current assets are 285% of current liabilities.
Rate: Current assets are 2.85 times current liabilities.
Proportion: The relationship of current assets to liabilities is 2.85:1.

To analyze the primary financial statements, we can use ratios to evaluate liquidity, profitability, and solvency. Illustration 18-11 describes these classifications.

---

[1] *2011 Annual Report*, Macy's, Inc. (Cincinnati, Ohio).

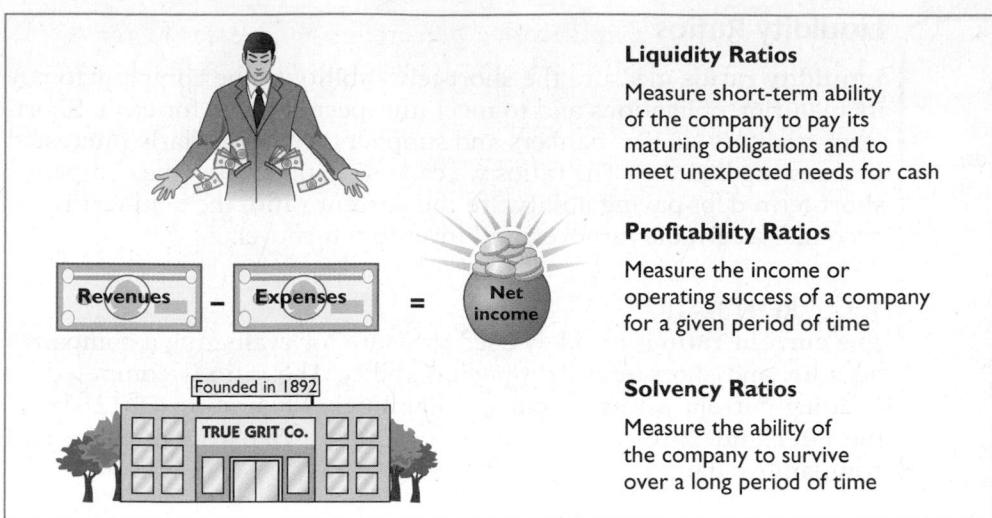

Illustration 18-11
Financial ratio classifications

Liquidity Ratios

Measure short-term ability of the company to pay its maturing obligations and to meet unexpected needs for cash

Profitability Ratios

Measure the income or operating success of a company for a given period of time

Solvency Ratios

Measure the ability of the company to survive over a long period of time

Ratios can provide clues to underlying conditions that may not be apparent from individual financial statement components. However, a single ratio by itself is not very meaningful. Thus, in the discussion of ratios we will use the following types of comparisons.

1. **Intracompany comparisons** for two years for Quality Department Store.
2. **Industry average comparisons** based on median ratios for department stores.
3. **Intercompany comparisons** based on Macy's, Inc. as Quality Department Store's principal competitor.

ANATOMY OF A FRAUD

This final *Anatomy of a Fraud* box demonstrates that sometimes relationships between numbers can be used by companies to detect fraud. The numeric relationships that can reveal fraud can be such things as financial ratios that appear abnormal, or statistical abnormalities in the numbers themselves. For example, the fact that WorldCom's line costs, as a percentage of either total expenses or revenues, differed very significantly from its competitors should have alerted people to the possibility of fraud. Or, consider the case of a bank manager, who cooperated with a group of his friends to defraud the bank's credit card department. The manager's friends would apply for credit cards and then run up balances of slightly less than $5,000. The bank had a policy of allowing bank personnel to write-off balances of less than $5,000 without seeking supervisor approval. The fraud was detected by applying statistical analysis based on Benford's Law. Benford's Law states that in a random collection of numbers, the frequency of lower digits (e.g., 1, 2, or 3) should be much higher than higher digits (e.g., 7, 8, or 9). In this case, bank auditors analyzed the first two digits of amounts written off. There was a spike at 48 and 49, which was not consistent with what would be expected if the numbers were random.

Total take: Thousands of dollars

THE MISSING CONTROLS
Independent internal verification. While it might be efficient to allow employees to write off accounts below a certain level, it is important that these write-offs be reviewed and verified periodically. Such a review would likely call attention to an employee with large amounts of write-offs, or in this case, write-offs that were frequently very close to the approval threshold.

Source: Mark J. Nigrini, "I've Got Your Number," *Journal of Accountancy Online* (May 1999).

Liquidity Ratios

Liquidity ratios measure the short-term ability of the company to pay its maturing obligations and to meet unexpected needs for cash. Short-term creditors such as bankers and suppliers are particularly interested in assessing liquidity. The ratios we can use to determine the company's short-term debt-paying ability are the current ratio, the acid-test ratio, accounts receivable turnover, and inventory turnover.

1. CURRENT RATIO

The **current ratio** is a widely used measure for evaluating a company's liquidity and short-term debt-paying ability. The ratio is computed by dividing current assets by current liabilities. Illustration 18-12 shows the 2011 and 2010 current ratios for Quality Department Store and comparative data.

Illustration 18-12
Current ratio

$$\text{Current Ratio} = \frac{\text{Current Assets}}{\text{Current Liabilities}}$$

Quality Department Store

2011	2010
$\dfrac{\$1,020,000}{\$344,500} = 2.96:1$	$\dfrac{\$945,000}{\$303,000} = 3.12:1$
Industry average	Macy's, Inc.
1.70:1	**1.40:1**

Helpful Hint Can any company operate successfully without working capital? Yes, if it has very predictable cash flows and solid earnings. A number of companies (e.g., Whirlpool, American Standard, and Campbell's Soup) are pursuing this goal. The rationale: Less money tied up in working capital means more money to invest in the business.

What does the ratio actually mean? The 2011 ratio of 2.96:1 means that for every dollar of current liabilities, Quality has $2.96 of current assets. Quality's current ratio has decreased in the current year. But, compared to the industry average of 1.70:1, Quality appears to be reasonably liquid. Macy's has a current ratio of 1.40:1, which indicates it has adequate current assets relative to its current liabilities.

The current ratio is sometimes referred to as the **working capital ratio**. **Working capital** is current assets minus current liabilities. The current ratio is a more dependable indicator of liquidity than working capital. Two companies with the same amount of working capital may have significantly different current ratios.

The current ratio is only one measure of liquidity. It does not take into account the **composition** of the current assets. For example, a satisfactory current ratio does not disclose the fact that a portion of the current assets may be tied up in slow-moving inventory. A dollar of cash would be more readily available to pay the bills than a dollar of slow-moving inventory.

2. ACID-TEST RATIO

The **acid-test (quick) ratio** is a measure of a company's immediate short-term liquidity. We compute this ratio by dividing the sum of cash, short-term investments, and net accounts receivable by current liabilities. Thus, it is an important complement to the current ratio. For example, assume that the current assets of Quality Department Store for 2011 and 2010 consist of the items shown in Illustration 18-13.

Illustration 18-13
Current assets of Quality
Department Store

QUALITY DEPARTMENT STORE INC. Balance Sheet (partial)		
	2011	**2010**
Current assets		
Cash	**$ 100,000**	**$155,000**
Short-term investments	**20,000**	**70,000**
Accounts receivable (net*)	**230,000**	**180,000**
Inventory	620,000	500,000
Prepaid expenses	50,000	40,000
Total current assets	$1,020,000	$ 945,000

*Allowance for doubtful accounts is $10,000 at the end of each year.

Cash, short-term investments, and accounts receivable (net) are highly liquid compared to inventory and prepaid expenses. The inventory may not be readily saleable, and the prepaid expenses may not be transferable to others. Thus, the acid-test ratio measures **immediate** liquidity. The 2011 and 2010 acid-test ratios for Quality Department Store and comparative data are as follows.

Illustration 18-14
Acid-test ratio

$$\text{Acid-Test Ratio} = \frac{\text{Cash} + \text{Short-Term Investments} + \text{Accounts Receivable (Net)}}{\text{Current Liabilities}}$$

Quality Department Store

2011

$$\frac{\$100,000 + \$20,000 + \$230,000}{\$344,500} = 1.02:1$$

Industry average

0.70:1

2010

$$\frac{\$155,000 + \$70,000 + \$180,000}{\$303,000} = 1.34:1$$

Macy's, Inc.

0.51:1

The ratio has declined in 2011. Is an acid-test ratio of 1.02:1 adequate? This depends on the industry and the economy. When compared with the industry average of 0.70:1 and Macy's of 0.51:1, Quality's acid-test ratio seems adequate.

INVESTOR INSIGHT

How to Manage the Current Ratio

The apparent simplicity of the current ratio can have real-world limitations because adding equal amounts to both the numerator and the denominator causes the ratio to decrease.

Assume, for example, that a company has $2,000,000 of current assets and $1,000,000 of current liabilities. Thus, its current ratio is 2:1. If the company purchases $1,000,000 of inventory on account, it will have $3,000,000 of current assets and $2,000,000 of current liabilities. Its current ratio therefore decreases to 1.5:1. If, instead, the company pays off $500,000 of its current liabilities, it will have $1,500,000 of current assets and $500,000 of current liabilities. Its current ratio then increases to 3:1. Thus, any trend analysis should be done with care because the ratio is susceptible to quick changes and is easily influenced by management.

SuperStock

? How might management influence a company's current ratio? (See page 889.)

3. ACCOUNTS RECEIVABLE TURNOVER

We can measure liquidity by how quickly a company can convert certain assets to cash. How liquid, for example, are the accounts receivable? The ratio used to assess the liquidity of the receivables is **accounts receivable turnover**. It measures the number of times, on average, the company collects receivables during the period. We compute accounts receivable turnover by dividing net credit sales (net sales less cash sales) by the average net accounts receivable. Unless seasonal factors are significant, average net accounts receivable can be computed from the beginning and ending balances of the net accounts receivable.[2]

Assume that all sales are credit sales. The balance of net accounts receivable at the beginning of 2010 is $200,000. Illustration 18-15 shows the accounts receivable turnover for Quality Department Store and comparative data. Quality's accounts receivable turnover improved in 2011. The turnover of 10.2 times is substantially lower than Macy's 74.8 times, and is also lower than the department store industry's average of 46.4 times.

Illustration 18-15
Accounts receivable turnover

AVERAGE COLLECTION PERIOD A popular variant of the accounts receivable turnover is to convert it to an **average collection period** in terms of days. To do so, we divide the accounts receivable turnover into 365 days. For example, the accounts receivable turnover of 10.2 times divided into 365 days gives an average collection period of approximately 36 days. This means that accounts receivable are collected on average every 36 days, or about every 5 weeks. Analysts frequently use the average collection period to assess the effectiveness of a company's credit and collection policies. The general rule is that the collection period should not greatly exceed the credit term period (the time allowed for payment).

4. INVENTORY TURNOVER

Inventory turnover measures the number of times, on average, the inventory is sold during the period. Its purpose is to measure the liquidity of the inventory. We compute the inventory turnover by dividing cost of goods sold by the average inventory. Unless seasonal factors are significant, we can use the beginning and ending inventory balances to compute average inventory.

Assuming that the inventory balance for Quality Department Store at the beginning of 2010 was $450,000, its inventory turnover and comparative data are as shown in Illustration 18-16. Quality's inventory turnover declined slightly in 2011. The turnover of 2.3 times is low compared with the industry average of 4.3

---

[2]If seasonal factors are significant, the average accounts receivable balance might be determined by using monthly amounts.

and Macy's 3.2. Generally, the faster the inventory turnover, the less cash a company has tied up in inventory and the less the chance of inventory obsolescence.

Illustration 18-16
Inventory turnover

DAYS IN INVENTORY A variant of inventory turnover is the **days in inventory**. We calculate it by dividing the inventory turnover into 365. For example, Quality's 2011 inventory turnover of 2.3 times divided into 365 is approximately 159 days. An average selling time of 159 days is also high compared with the industry average of 84.9 days (365 ÷ 4.3) and Macy's 114.1 days (365 ÷ 3.2).

Inventory turnovers vary considerably among industries. For example, grocery store chains have a turnover of 17.1 times and an average selling period of 21 days. In contrast, jewelry stores have an average turnover of 0.80 times and an average selling period of 456 days.

Profitability Ratios

Profitability ratios measure the income or operating success of a company for a given period of time. Income, or the lack of it, affects the company's ability to obtain debt and equity financing. It also affects the company's liquidity position and the company's ability to grow. As a consequence, both creditors and investors are interested in evaluating earning power—profitability. Analysts frequently use profitability as the ultimate test of management's operating effectiveness.

5. PROFIT MARGIN

Profit margin is a measure of the percentage of each dollar of sales that results in net income. We can compute it by dividing net income by net sales. Illustration 18-17 shows Quality Department Store's profit margin and comparative data.

Illustration 18-17
Profit margin

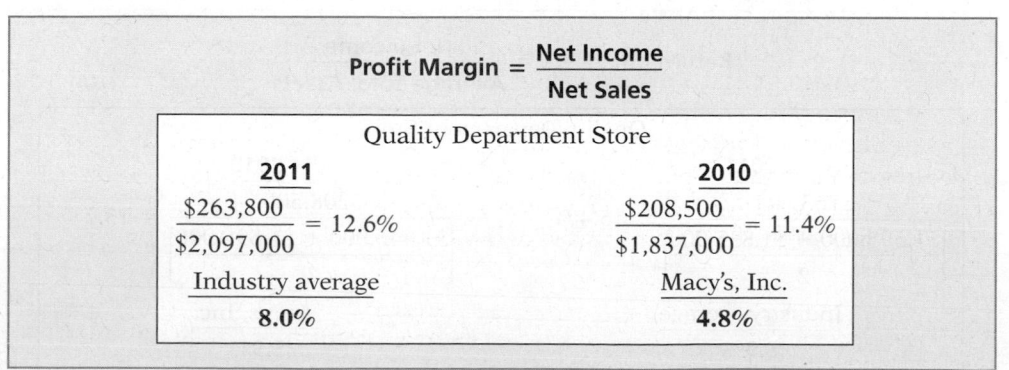

Quality experienced an increase in its profit margin from 2010 to 2011. Its profit margin is unusually high in comparison with the industry average of 8% and Macy's 4.8%.

High-volume (high inventory turnover) businesses, such as grocery stores (Safeway or Kroger) and discount stores (Kmart or Wal-Mart), generally experience low profit margins. In contrast, low-volume businesses, such as jewelry stores (Tiffany & Co.) or airplane manufacturers (Boeing Co.), have high profit margins.

6. ASSET TURNOVER

Asset turnover measures how efficiently a company uses its assets to generate sales. It is determined by dividing net sales by average total assets. The resulting number shows the dollars of sales produced by each dollar invested in assets. Unless seasonal factors are significant, we can use the beginning and ending balance of total assets to determine average total assets. Assuming that total assets at the beginning of 2010 were $1,446,000, the 2011 and 2010 asset turnover for Quality Department Store and comparative data are shown in Illustration 18-18.

Illustration 18-18
Asset turnover

$$\text{Asset Turnover} = \frac{\text{Net Sales}}{\text{Average Total Assets}}$$

Quality Department Store

2011		**2010**	
$\dfrac{\$2,097,000}{\left[\dfrac{\$1,595,000 + \$1,835,000}{2}\right]}$	= 1.2 times	$\dfrac{\$1,837,000}{\left[\dfrac{\$1,446,000 + \$1,595,000}{2}\right]}$	= 1.2 times
Industry average		Macy's, Inc.	
1.4 times		**1.2 times**	

Asset turnover shows that in 2011 Quality generated sales of $1.20 for each dollar it had invested in assets. The ratio changed very little from 2010 to 2011. Quality's asset turnover is below the industry average of 1.4 times and equal to Macy's ratio of 1.2 times.

Asset turnovers vary considerably among industries. For example, a large utility company like Consolidated Edison (New York) has a ratio of 0.4 times, and the large grocery chain Kroger Stores has a ratio of 3.4 times.

7. RETURN ON ASSETS

An overall measure of profitability is **return on assets**. We compute this ratio by dividing net income by average total assets. The 2011 and 2010 return on assets for Quality Department Store and comparative data are shown below.

Illustration 18-19
Return on assets

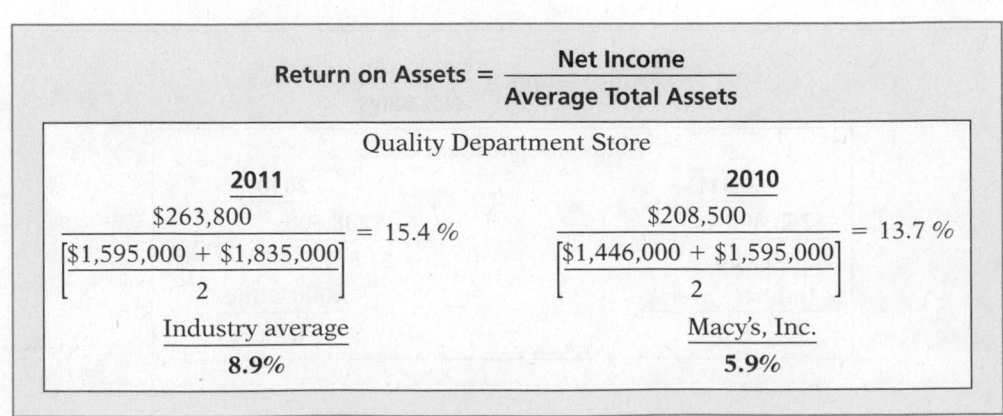

$$\text{Return on Assets} = \frac{\text{Net Income}}{\text{Average Total Assets}}$$

Quality Department Store

2011		**2010**	
$\dfrac{\$263,800}{\left[\dfrac{\$1,595,000 + \$1,835,000}{2}\right]}$	= 15.4 %	$\dfrac{\$208,500}{\left[\dfrac{\$1,446,000 + \$1,595,000}{2}\right]}$	= 13.7 %
Industry average		Macy's, Inc.	
8.9%		**5.9%**	

Quality's return on assets improved from 2010 to 2011. Its return of 15.4% is very high compared with the department store industry average of 8.9% and Macy's 5.9%.

8. RETURN ON COMMON STOCKHOLDERS' EQUITY

Another widely used profitability ratio is **return on common stockholders' equity**. It measures profitability from the common stockholders' viewpoint. This ratio shows how many dollars of net income the company earned for each dollar invested by the owners. We compute it by dividing net income by average common stockholders' equity. Assuming that common stockholders' equity at the beginning of 2010 was $667,000, Illustration 18-20 shows the 2011 and 2010 ratios for Quality Department Store and comparative data.

Illustration 18-20
Return on common stockholders' equity

Quality's rate of return on common stockholders' equity is high at 29.3%, considering an industry average of 18.3% and a rate of 21.9% for Macy's.

WITH PREFERRED STOCK When a company has preferred stock, we must deduct **preferred dividend** requirements from net income to compute income available to common stockholders. Similarly, we deduct the par value of preferred stock (or call price, if applicable) from total stockholders' equity to determine the amount of common stockholders' equity used in this ratio. The ratio then appears as follows.

$$\text{Return on Common Stockholders' Equity} = \frac{\text{Net Income} - \text{Preferred Dividends}}{\text{Average Common Stockholders' Equity}}$$

Illustration 18-21
Return on common stockholders' equity with preferred stock

Note that Quality's rate of return on stockholders' equity (29.3%) is substantially higher than its rate of return on assets (15.4%). The reason is that Quality has made effective use of **leverage**. **Leveraging** or **trading on the equity** at a gain means that the company has borrowed money at a lower rate of interest than it is able to earn by using the borrowed money. Leverage enables Quality Department Store to use money supplied by nonowners to increase the return to the owners. A comparison of the rate of return on total assets with the rate of interest paid for borrowed money indicates the profitability of trading on the equity. Quality Department Store earns more on its borrowed funds than it has to pay in the form of interest. Thus, the return to stockholders exceeds the return on the assets, due to benefits from the positive leveraging.

9. EARNINGS PER SHARE (EPS)

Earnings per share (EPS) is a measure of the net income earned on each share of common stock. It is computed by dividing net income by the number of weighted-average common shares outstanding during the year. A measure of net income earned on a per share basis provides a useful perspective for determining profitability. Assuming that there is no change in the number of outstanding shares during 2010 and that the 2011 increase occurred midyear, Illustration 18-22 shows the net income per share for Quality Department Store for 2011 and 2010.

Illustration 18-22
Earnings per share

$$\text{Earnings per Share} = \frac{\text{Net Income}}{\text{Weighted-Average Common Shares Outstanding}}$$

Quality Department Store

2011

$$\frac{\$263,800}{\left[\dfrac{270{,}000 + 275{,}400}{2}\right]} = \$0.97$$

2010

$$\frac{\$208,500}{\$270,000} = \$0.77$$

Note that no industry or Macy's data are presented. Such comparisons are not meaningful because of the wide variations in the number of shares of outstanding stock among companies. The only meaningful EPS comparison is an intracompany trend comparison: Quality's earnings per share increased 20 cents per share in 2011. This represents a 26% increase over the 2010 earnings per share of 77 cents.

The terms "earnings per share" and "net income per share" refer to the amount of net income applicable to each share of **common stock**. Therefore, in computing EPS, if there are preferred dividends declared for the period, we must deduct them from net income to determine income available to the common stockholders.

10. PRICE-EARNINGS RATIO

The **price-earnings (P-E) ratio** is an oft-quoted measure of the ratio of the market price of each share of common stock to the earnings per share. The price-earnings (P-E) ratio reflects investors' assessments of a company's future earnings. We compute it by dividing the market price per share of the stock by earnings per share. Assuming that the market price of Quality Department Store Inc. stock is $8 in 2010 and $12 in 2011, the price-earnings ratio computation is as follows.

Illustration 18-23
Price-earnings ratio

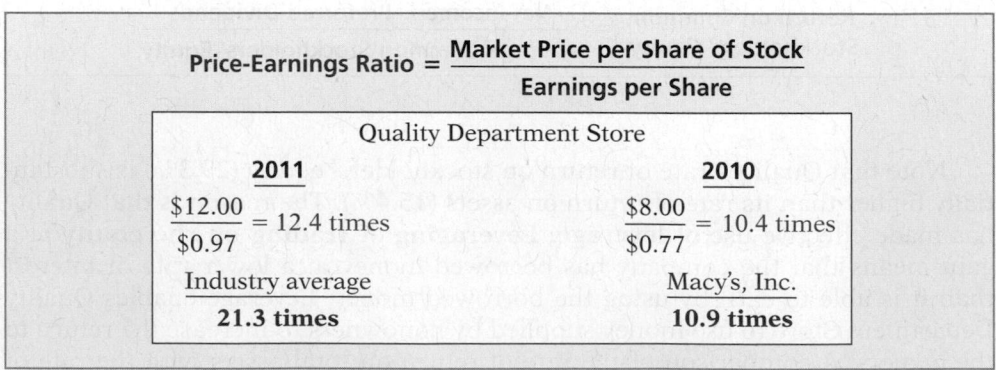

$$\text{Price-Earnings Ratio} = \frac{\text{Market Price per Share of Stock}}{\text{Earnings per Share}}$$

Quality Department Store

2011

$$\frac{\$12.00}{\$0.97} = 12.4 \text{ times}$$

Industry average
21.3 times

2010

$$\frac{\$8.00}{\$0.77} = 10.4 \text{ times}$$

Macy's, Inc.
10.9 times

In 2011, each share of Quality's stock sold for 12.4 times the amount that the company earned on each share. Quality's price-earnings ratio is lower than the industry average of 21.3 times but higher than the ratio of 10.9 times for Macy's.

The average price-earnings ratio for the stocks that constitute the Standard and Poor's 500 Index (500 largest U.S. firms) in late 2012 was approximately 15.9 times.

11. PAYOUT RATIO

The **payout ratio** measures the percentage of earnings distributed in the form of cash dividends. We compute it by dividing cash dividends by net income. Companies that have high growth rates generally have low payout ratios because they reinvest most of their net income into the business. The 2011 and 2010 payout ratios for Quality Department Store are computed as shown in Illustration 18-24.

Illustration 18-24
Payout ratio

$$\text{Payout Ratio} = \frac{\text{Cash Dividends}}{\text{Net Income}}$$

Quality Department Store

2011	2010
$\dfrac{\$61,200}{\$263,800} = 23.2\%$	$\dfrac{\$60,000}{\$208,500} = 28.8\%$
Industry average	Macy's, Inc.
16.1%	**11.8%**

Quality's payout ratio is higher than the industry average payout ratio of 16.1%.

Solvency Ratios

Solvency ratios measure the ability of a company to survive over a long period of time. Long-term creditors and stockholders are particularly interested in a company's ability to pay interest as it comes due and to repay the face value of debt at maturity. Debt to assets and times interest earned are two ratios that provide information about debt-paying ability.

12. DEBT TO ASSETS RATIO

The **debt to assets ratio** measures the percentage of the total assets that creditors provide. We compute it by dividing debt (both current and long-term liabilities) by assets. This ratio indicates the company's degree of leverage. It also provides some indication of the company's ability to withstand losses without impairing the interests of creditors. The higher the percentage of debt to assets, the greater the risk that the company may be unable to meet its maturing obligations. The 2011 and 2010 ratios for Quality Department Store and comparative data are as follows.

Illustration 18-25
Debt to assets ratio

$$\text{Debt to Assets Ratio} = \frac{\text{Debt}}{\text{Assets}}$$

Quality Department Store

2011	2010
$\dfrac{\$832,000}{\$1,835,000} = 45.3\%$	$\dfrac{\$800,000}{\$1,595,000} = 50.2\%$
Industry average	Macy's, Inc.
34.2%	**73.1%**

A ratio of 45.3% means that creditors have provided 45.3% of Quality Department Store's total assets. Quality's 45.3% is above the industry average of 34.2%.

It is considerably below the high 73.1% ratio of Macy's. The lower the ratio, the more equity "buffer" there is available to the creditors. Thus, from the creditors' point of view, a low ratio of debt to assets is usually desirable.

The adequacy of this ratio is often judged in the light of the company's earnings. Generally, companies with relatively stable earnings (such as public utilities) have higher debt to assets ratios than cyclical companies with widely fluctuating earnings (such as many high-tech companies).

13. TIMES INTEREST EARNED

Alternative Terminology
Times interest earned is also called *interest coverage.*

Times interest earned provides an indication of the company's ability to meet interest payments as they come due. We compute it by dividing income before interest expense and income taxes by interest expense. Illustration 18-26 shows the 2011 and 2010 ratios for Quality Department Store and comparative data. Note that times interest earned uses income before income taxes and interest expense. This represents the amount available to cover interest. For Quality Department Store, the 2011 amount of $468,000 is computed by taking the income before income taxes of $432,000 and adding back the $36,000 of interest expense.

Illustration 18-26
Times interest earned

$$\text{Times Interest Earned} = \frac{\text{Income before Income Taxes and Interest Expense}}{\text{Interest Expense}}$$

Quality Department Store

2011
$$\frac{\$468,000}{\$36,000} = 13 \text{ times}$$

Industry average
16.1 times

2010
$$\frac{\$388,000}{\$40,500} = 9.6 \text{ times}$$

Macy's, Inc.
5.4 times

Quality's interest expense is well covered at 13 times, compared with the industry average of 16.1 times and Macy's 5.4 times.

Summary of Ratios

Illustration 18-27
Summary of liquidity, profitability, and solvency ratios

Illustration 18-27 summarizes the ratios discussed in this chapter. The summary includes the formula and purpose or use of each ratio.

Ratio	Formula	Purpose or Use
Liquidity Ratios		
1. Current ratio	$\dfrac{\text{Current assets}}{\text{Current liabilities}}$	Measures short-term debt-paying ability.
2. Acid-test (quick) ratio	$\dfrac{\text{Cash + Short-term investments + Accounts receivable (net)}}{\text{Current liabilities}}$	Measures immediate short-term liquidity.
3. Accounts receivable turnover	$\dfrac{\text{Net credit sales}}{\text{Average net accounts receivable}}$	Measures liquidity of accounts receivable.
4. Inventory turnover	$\dfrac{\text{Cost of goods sold}}{\text{Average inventory}}$	Measures liquidity of inventory.
Profitability Ratios		
5. Profit margin	$\dfrac{\text{Net income}}{\text{Net sales}}$	Measures net income generated by each dollar of sales.
6. Asset turnover	$\dfrac{\text{Net sales}}{\text{Average total assets}}$	Measures how efficiently assets are used to generate sales.

Ratio	Formula	Purpose or Use
7. Return on assets	$\dfrac{\text{Net income}}{\text{Average total assets}}$	Measures overall profitability of assets.
8. Return on common stockholders' equity	$\dfrac{\text{Net income} - \text{Preferred dividends}}{\text{Average common stockholders' equity}}$	Measures profitability of owners' investment.
9. Earnings per share (EPS)	$\dfrac{\text{Net income} - \text{Preferred dividends}}{\text{Weighted-average common shares outstanding}}$	Measures net income earned on each share of common stock.
10. Price-earnings (P-E) ratio	$\dfrac{\text{Market price per share of stock}}{\text{Earnings per share}}$	Measures the ratio of the market price per share to earnings per share.
11. Payout ratio	$\dfrac{\text{Cash dividends}}{\text{Net income}}$	Measures percentage of earnings distributed in the form of cash dividends.
Solvency Ratios		
12. Debt to assets ratio	$\dfrac{\text{Debt}}{\text{Assets}}$	Measures the percentage of total assets provided by creditors.
13. Times interest earned	$\dfrac{\text{Income before income taxes and interest expense}}{\text{Interest expense}}$	Measures ability to meet interest payments as they come due.

> **DO IT!**

Ratio Analysis

The condensed financial statements of John Cully Company, for the years ended June 30, 2014 and 2013, are presented below.

JOHN CULLY COMPANY
Balance Sheets
June 30

	(in thousands)	
Assets	**2014**	**2013**
Current assets		
Cash and cash equivalents	$ 553.3	$ 611.6
Accounts receivable (net)	776.6	664.9
Inventory	768.3	653.5
Prepaid expenses and other current assets	204.4	269.2
Total current assets	2,302.6	2,199.2
Property, plant, and equipment (net)	694.2	647.0
Investments	12.3	12.6
Intangibles and other assets	876.7	849.3
Total assets	$3,885.8	$3,708.1
Liabilities and Stockholders' Equity		
Current liabilities	$1,497.7	$1,322.0
Long-term liabilities	679.5	637.1
Stockholders' equity—common	1,708.6	1,749.0
Total liabilities and stockholders' equity	$3,885.8	$3,708.1

	JOHN CULLY COMPANY	
	Income Statements	
	For the Year Ended June 30	

	(in thousands)	
	2014	**2013**
Sales revenue	$6,336.3	$5,790.4
Costs and expenses		
Cost of goods sold	1,617.4	1,476.3
Selling and administrative expenses	4,007.6	3,679.0
Interest expense	13.9	27.1
Total costs and expenses	5,638.9	5,182.4
Income before income taxes	697.4	608.0
Income tax expense	291.3	232.6
Net income	$ 406.1	$ 375.4

Compute the following ratios for 2014 and 2013.

(a) Current ratio.
(b) Inventory turnover. (Inventory on 6/30/12 was $599.0.)
(c) Profit margin ratio.
(d) Return on assets. (Assets on 6/30/12 were $3,349.9.)
(e) Return on common stockholders' equity. (Stockholders' equity on 6/30/12 was $1,795.9.)
(f) Debt to assets ratio.
(g) Times interest earned.

Solution

Action Plan

✔ Remember that the current ratio includes all current assets. The acid-test ratio uses only cash, short-term investments, and net accounts receivable.

✔ Use average balances for turnover ratios like inventory, accounts receivable, and asset.

	2014	**2013**
(a) Current ratio:		
$2,302.6 ÷ $1,497.7 =	1.5:1	
$2,199.2 ÷ $1,322.0 =		1.7:1
(b) Inventory turnover:		
$1,617.4 ÷ [($768.3 + $653.5) ÷ 2] =	2.3 times	
$1,476.3 ÷ [($653.5 + $599.0) ÷ 2] =		2.4 times
(c) Profit margin:		
$406.1 ÷ $6,336.3 =	6.4%	
$375.4 ÷ $5,790.4 =		6.5%
(d) Return on assets:		
$406.1 ÷ [($3,885.8 + $3,708.1) ÷ 2] =	10.7%	
$375.4 ÷ [($3,708.1 + $3,349.9) ÷ 2] =		10.6%
(e) Return on common stockholders' equity:		
($406.1 − $0) ÷ [($1,708.6 + $1,749.0) ÷ 2] =	23.5%	
($375.4 − $0) ÷ [($1,749.0 + $1,795.9) ÷ 2] =		21.2%
(f) Debt to assets ratio:		
($1,497.7 + $679.5) ÷ $3,885.8 =	56.0%	
($1,322.0 + $637.1) ÷ $3,708.1 =		52.8%
(g) Times interest earned:		
($406.1 + $291.3 + $13.9) ÷ $13.9 =	51.2 times	
($375.4 + $232.6 + $27.1) ÷ $27.1 =		23.4 times

Related exercise material: **BE18-9, BE18-10, BE18-12, BE18-13, E18-5, E18-7, E18-8, E18-9, E18-10, E18-11, and DO IT! 18-2.**

✔ **The Navigator**

Earning Power and Irregular Items

Users of financial statements are interested in the concept of earning power. **Earning power** means the normal level of income to be obtained in the future. Earning power differs from actual net income by the amount of irregular revenues, expenses, gains, and losses. Users are interested in earning power because it helps them derive an estimate of future earnings without the "noise" of irregular items.

For users of financial statements to determine earning power or regular income, the "irregular" items are separately identified on the income statement. Companies report two types of "irregular" items.

1. Discontinued operations.

2. Extraordinary items.

These "irregular" items are reported net of income taxes. That is, the income statement first reports income tax on the income before "irregular" items. Then the amount of tax for each of the listed "irregular" items is computed. The general concept is "let the tax follow income or loss."

Discontinued Operations

Discontinued operations refers to the disposal of a **significant component** of a business, such as the elimination of a major class of customers, or an entire activity. For example, to downsize its operations, General Dynamics Corp. sold its missile business to Hughes Aircraft Co. for $450 million. In its income statement, General Dynamics reported the sale in a separate section entitled "Discontinued operations."

Following the disposal of a significant component, the company should report on its income statement both income from continuing operations and income (or loss) from discontinued operations. **The income (loss) from discontinued operations consists of two parts: the income (loss) from operations and the gain (loss) on disposal of the component**.

To illustrate, assume that during 2014 Acro Energy Inc. has income before income taxes of $800,000. During 2014, Acro discontinued and sold its unprofitable chemical division. The loss in 2014 from chemical operations (net of $60,000 taxes) was $140,000. The loss on disposal of the chemical division (net of $30,000 taxes) was $70,000. Assuming a 30% tax rate on income, Illustration 18-28 shows Acro's income statement presentation.

Illustration 18-28
Statement presentation of discontinued operations

ACRO ENERGY INC. Income Statement (partial) For the Year Ended December 31, 2014		
Income before income taxes		$800,000
Income tax expense		240,000
Income from continuing operations		560,000
Discontinued operations		
Loss from operations of chemical division, net of $60,000 income tax saving	$140,000	
Loss from disposal of chemical division, net of $30,000 income tax saving	70,000	210,000
Net income		$350,000

Helpful Hint Observe the dual disclosures. (1) The results of operations of the discontinued division must be eliminated from the results of continuing operations. (2) The company must also report the disposal of the operation.

Note that the statement uses the caption "Income from continuing operations" and adds a new section "Discontinued operations." **The new section reports both the operating loss and the loss on disposal net of applicable income taxes.** This presentation clearly indicates the separate effects of continuing operations and discontinued operations on net income.

Extraordinary Items

Extraordinary items are events and transactions that meet two conditions. They are (1) **unusual in nature,** and (2) **infrequent in occurrence**. To be unusual, the item should be abnormal and only incidentally related to the company's customary activities. To be infrequent, the item should not be reasonably expected to recur in the foreseeable future.

A company must evaluate both criteria in terms of its operating environment. Thus, Weyerhaeuser Co. reported the $36 million in damages to its timberland caused by the volcanic eruption of Mount St. Helens as an extraordinary item. The eruption was both unusual and infrequent. In contrast, Florida Citrus Company does not report frost damage to its citrus crop as an extraordinary item, because frost damage is not infrequent. Illustration 18-29 shows the classification of extraordinary and ordinary items.

Extraordinary items

1. Effects of major natural casualties, if rare in the area.

2. Expropriation (takeover) of property by a foreign government.

3. Effects of a newly enacted law or regulation, such as a condemnation action.

Ordinary items

1. Effects of major natural casualties, not uncommon in the area.

2. Write-down of inventories or write-off of receivables.

3. Losses attributable to labor strikes.

4. Gains or losses from sales of property, plant, or equipment.

Illustration 18-29
Examples of extraordinary and ordinary items

Companies report extraordinary items net of taxes in a separate section of the income statement, immediately below discontinued operations. To illustrate, assume that in 2014 a foreign government expropriated property held as an investment by Acro Energy Inc. If the loss is $70,000 before applicable income taxes of $21,000, the income statement will report a deduction of $49,000, as shown in Illustration 18-30. When there is an extraordinary item to report, the company adds the caption "Income before extraordinary item" immediately before the section for the extraordinary item. This presentation clearly indicates the effect of the extraordinary item on net income.

Illustration 18-30
Statement presentation of
extraordinary items

ACRO ENERGY INC.		
Income Statement (partial)		
For the Year Ended December 31, 2014		
Income before income taxes		$800,000
Income tax expense		240,000
Income from continuing operations		560,000
Discontinued operations		
Loss from operations of chemical division,		
net of $60,000 income tax saving	$140,000	
Loss from disposal of chemical division,		
net of $30,000 income tax saving	70,000	210,000
Income before extraordinary item		350,000
Extraordinary item		
Expropriation of investment, net of		
$21,000 income tax saving		**49,000**
Net income		$301,000

Helpful Hint If there are no discontinued operations, the third line of the income statement would be labeled "Income before extraordinary item."

What if a transaction or event meets one (but not both) of the criteria for an extraordinary item? In that case, the company reports it under either "Other revenues and gains" or "Other expenses and losses" at its gross amount (not net of tax). This is true, for example, of gains (losses) resulting from the sale of property, plant, and equipment, as explained in Chapter 10. It is quite common for companies to use the label "Non-recurring charges" for losses that do not meet the extraordinary item criteria.

INVESTOR INSIGHT

What Does "Non-Recurring" Really Mean?

Many companies incur restructuring charges as they attempt to reduce costs. They often label these items in the income statement as "non-recurring" charges to suggest that they are isolated events which are unlikely to occur in future periods. The question for analysts is, are these costs really one-time, "non-recurring" events, or do they reflect problems that the company will be facing for many periods in the future? If they are one-time events, they can be largely ignored when trying to predict future earnings.

But some companies report "one-time" restructuring charges over and over again. For example, toothpaste and other consumer-goods giant Procter & Gamble Co. reported a restructuring charge in 12 consecutive quarters. Motorola had "special" charges in 14 consecutive quarters. On the other hand, other companies have a restructuring charge only once in a 5- or 10-year period. There appears to be no substitute for careful analysis of the numbers that comprise net income.

 If a company takes a large restructuring charge, what is the effect on the company's current income statement versus future ones? (See page 889.)

Changes in Accounting Principle

For ease of comparison, users of financial statements expect companies to prepare such statements on a basis **consistent** with the preceding period. A **change in accounting principle** occurs when the principle used in the current year is different from the one used in the preceding year. Accounting rules permit a change when management can show that the new principle is preferable to the old principle. An example is a change in inventory costing methods (such as FIFO to average cost).

Ethics Note

Changes in accounting principle should result in financial statements that are more informative for statement users. They should *not* be used to artificially improve the reported performance or financial position of the corporation.

Companies report most changes in accounting principle retroactively. That is, they report both the current period and previous periods using the new principle. As a result, the same principle applies in all periods. This treatment improves the ability to compare results across years.

Comprehensive Income

The income statement reports most revenues, expenses, gains, and losses recognized during the period. However, over time, specific exceptions to this general practice have developed. Certain items now bypass income and are reported directly in stockholders' equity.

For example, in Chapter 16 you learned that companies do not include in income any unrealized gains and losses on available-for-sale securities. Instead, they report such gains and losses in the balance sheet as adjustments to stockholders' equity. Why are these gains and losses on available-for-sale securities excluded from net income? Because disclosing them separately (1) reduces the volatility of net income due to fluctuations in fair value, yet (2) informs the financial statement user of the gain or loss that would be incurred if the securities were sold at fair value.

Many analysts have expressed concern over the significant increase in the number of items that bypass the income statement. They feel that such reporting has reduced the usefulness of the income statement. To address this concern, in addition to reporting net income, a company must also report comprehensive income. **Comprehensive income** includes all changes in stockholders' equity during a period except those resulting from investments by stockholders and distributions to stockholders. A number of alternative formats for reporting comprehensive income are allowed. These formats are discussed in advanced accounting courses.

> DO IT!

Irregular Items

In its proposed 2014 income statement, AIR Corporation reports income before income taxes $400,000, extraordinary loss due to earthquake $100,000, income taxes $120,000 (not including irregular items), loss on operation of discontinued flower division $50,000, and loss on disposal of discontinued flower division $90,000. The income tax rate is 30%. Prepare a correct income statement, beginning with "Income before income taxes."

Action Plan

✔ Recall that a loss is extraordinary if it is both unusual and infrequent.

✔ Disclose the income tax effect of each component of income, beginning with income before any irregular items.

✔ Show discontinued operations before extraordinary items.

Solution

AIR CORPORATION Income Statement (partial) For the Year Ended December 31, 2014		
Income before income taxes		$400,000
Income tax expense		120,000
Income from continuing operations		280,000
Discontinued operations		
Loss from operation of flower division, net of $15,000 tax saving	$35,000	
Loss on disposal of flower division, net of $27,000 tax saving	63,000	98,000
Income before extraordinary item		182,000
Extraordinary earthquake loss, net of $30,000 tax saving		70,000
Net income		$112,000

Related exercise material: **BE18-14, BE18-15, E18-12, E18-13,** and **DO IT!** 18-3.

 The Navigator

Quality of Earnings

In evaluating the financial performance of a company, the quality of a company's earnings is of extreme importance to analysts. A company that has a high **quality of earnings** provides full and transparent information that will not confuse or mislead users of the financial statements.

LEARNING OBJECTIVE   7

Understand the concept of quality of earnings.

The issue of quality of earnings has taken on increasing importance because recent accounting scandals suggest that some companies are spending too much time managing their income and not enough time managing their business. Here are some of the factors affecting quality of earnings.

Alternative Accounting Methods

Variations among companies in the application of generally accepted accounting principles may hamper comparability and reduce quality of earnings. For example, one company may use the FIFO method of inventory costing, while another company in the same industry may use LIFO. If inventory is a significant asset to both companies, it is unlikely that their current ratios are comparable. For example, if General Motors Corporation had used FIFO instead of LIFO for inventory valuation, its inventories in a recent year would have been 26% higher, which significantly affects the current ratio (and other ratios as well).

In addition to differences in inventory costing methods, differences also exist in reporting such items as depreciation, depletion, and amortization. Although these differences in accounting methods might be detectable from reading the notes to the financial statements, adjusting the financial data to compensate for the different methods is often difficult, if not impossible.

Pro Forma Income

Companies whose stock is publicly traded are required to present their income statement following generally accepted accounting principles (GAAP). In recent years, many companies have also reported a second measure of income, called pro forma income. **Pro forma income** usually excludes items that the company thinks are unusual or non-recurring. For example, at one time, Cisco Systems (a high-tech company) reported a quarterly net loss under GAAP of $2.7 billion. Cisco reported pro forma income for the same quarter as a profit of $230 million. This large difference in profits between GAAP income numbers and pro forma income is not unusual these days. For example, during one 9-month period the 100 largest firms on the Nasdaq stock exchange reported a total pro forma income of $19.1 billion but a total loss as measured by GAAP of $82.3 billion—a difference of about $100 billion!

To compute pro forma income, companies generally can exclude any items they deem inappropriate for measuring their performance. Many analysts and investors are critical of the practice of using pro forma income because these numbers often make companies look better than they really are. As the financial press noted, pro forma numbers might be called EBS, which stands for "earnings before bad stuff." Companies, on the other hand, argue that pro forma numbers more clearly indicate sustainable income because they exclude unusual and non-recurring expenses. "Cisco's technique gives readers of financial statements a clear picture of Cisco's normal business activities," the company said in a statement issued in response to questions about its pro forma income accounting.

The SEC has provided guidance on how companies should present pro forma information. Stay tuned: Everyone seems to agree that pro forma numbers can be useful if they provide insights into determining a company's sustainable income. However, many companies have abused the flexibility that pro forma numbers allow and have used the measure as a way to put their companies in a good light.

Improper Recognition

Due to pressure from Wall Street to continually increase earnings, some managers have manipulated the earnings numbers to meet these expectations. The most common abuse is the improper recognition of revenue. One practice that companies are using is **channel stuffing**. Offering deep discounts on their products to customers, companies encourage their customers to buy early (stuff the channel) rather than later. This lets the company report good earnings in the current period, but it often leads to a disaster in subsequent periods because customers have no need for additional goods. To illustrate, Bristol-Myers Squibb at one time indicated that it used sales incentives to encourage wholesalers to buy more drugs than needed to meet patients' demands. As a result, the company had to issue revised financial statements showing corrected revenues and income.

Another practice is the improper capitalization of operating expenses. The classic case is WorldCom. It capitalized over $7 billion of operating expenses so that it would report positive net income. In other situations, companies fail to report all their liabilities. Enron had promised to make payments on certain contracts if financial difficulty developed, but these guarantees were not reported as liabilities. In addition, disclosure was so lacking in transparency that it was impossible to understand what was happening at the company.

> **DO IT!**

Quality of Earnings, Financial Statement Analysis

Match each of the following terms with the phrase that best describes it.

Comprehensive income	Vertical analysis
Quality of earnings	Pro forma income
Solvency ratio	Extraordinary item

1. _____ Measures the ability of the company to survive over a long period of time.

2. _____ Usually excludes items that a company thinks are unusual or non-recurring.

3. _____ Includes all changes in stockholders' equity during a period except those resulting from investments by stockholders and distributions to stockholders.

4. _____ Indicates the level of full and transparent information provided to users of the financial statements.

5. _____ Describes events and transactions that are unusual in nature and infrequent in occurrence.

6. _____ Expresses each item within a financial statement as a percentage of a base amount.

Solution

1. Solvency ratio: Measures the ability of the company to survive over a long period of time.

2. Pro forma income: Usually excludes items that a company thinks are unusual or non-recurring.

3. Comprehensive income: Includes all changes in stockholders' equity during a period except those resulting from investments by stockholders and distributions to stockholders.

4. Quality of earnings: Indicates the level of full and transparent information provided to users of the financial statements.

5. Extraordinary item: Describes events and transactions that are unusual in nature and infrequent in occurrence.

6. Vertical analysis: Expresses each item within a financial statement as a percentage of a base amount.

Action Plan

✔ Develop a sound understanding of basic methods used for financial reporting.

✔ Understand the use of fundamental analysis techniques.

Related exercise material: **DO IT!** 18-4.

✔ The Navigator

> Comprehensive DO IT!

The events and transactions of Dever Corporation for the year ending December 31, 2014, resulted in the following data.

Cost of goods sold	$2,600,000
Net sales	4,400,000
Other expenses and losses	9,600
Other revenues and gains	5,600
Selling and administrative expenses	1,100,000
Income from operations of plastics division	70,000
Gain from disposal of plastics division	500,000
Loss from tornado disaster (extraordinary loss)	600,000

Analysis reveals that:

1. All items are before the applicable income tax rate of 30%.

2. The plastics division was sold on July 1.

3. All operating data for the plastics division have been segregated.

Instructions

Prepare an income statement for the year.

Solution to Comprehensive DO IT!

Action Plan

✔ Report material items not typical of continuing operations in separate sections, net of taxes.

✔ Associate income taxes with the item that affects the taxes.

✔ Apply the corporate tax rate to income before income taxes to determine tax expense.

✔ Recall that all data presented in determining income before income taxes are the same as for unincorporated companies.

DEVER CORPORATION
Income Statement
For the Year Ended December 31, 2014

Net sales		$4,400,000
Cost of goods sold		2,600,000
Gross profit		1,800,000
Selling and administrative expenses		1,100,000
Income from operations		700,000
Other revenues and gains	$ 5,600	
Other expenses and losses	9,600	4,000
Income before income taxes		696,000
Income tax expense ($696,000 × 30%)		208,800
Income from continuing operations		487,200
Discontinued operations		
Income from operations of plastics division, net of		
$21,000 income taxes ($70,000 × 30%)	49,000	
Gain from disposal of plastics division, net of $150,000		
income taxes ($500,000 × 30%)	350,000	399,000
Income before extraordinary item		886,200
Extraordinary item		
Tornado loss, net of $180,000 income tax saving		
($600,000 × 30%)		420,000
Net income		$ 466,200

 The Navigator

SUMMARY OF LEARNING OBJECTIVES

✔ The Navigator

1 Discuss the need for comparative analysis. There are three bases of comparison: (1) intracompany, which compares an item or financial relationship with other data within a company; (2) industry, which compares company data with industry averages; and (3) intercompany, which compares an item or financial relationship of a company with data of one or more competing companies.

2 Identify the tools of financial statement analysis. Financial statements can be analyzed horizontally, vertically, and with ratios.

3 Explain and apply horizontal analysis. Horizontal analysis is a technique for evaluating a series of data over a period of time to determine the increase or decrease that has taken place, expressed as either an amount or a percentage.

4 Describe and apply vertical analysis. Vertical analysis is a technique that expresses each item within a financial statement in terms of a percentage of a relevant total or a base amount.

5 Identify and compute ratios used in analyzing a firm's liquidity, profitability, and solvency. The formula and purpose of each ratio is presented in Illustration 18-27 (pages 858–859).

6 Understand the concept of earning power, and how irregular items are presented. Earning power refers to a company's ability to sustain its profits from operations. "Irregular items"—discontinued operations and extraordinary items—are presented net of tax below income from continuing operations to highlight their unusual nature.

7 Understand the concept of quality of earnings. A high quality of earnings provides full and transparent information that will not confuse or mislead users of the financial statements. Issues related to quality of earnings are (1) alternative accounting methods, (2) pro forma income, and (3) improper recognition.

GLOSSARY

Accounts receivable turnover A measure of the liquidity of accounts receivable; computed by dividing net credit sales by average net accounts receivable. (p. 852).

Acid-test (quick) ratio A measure of a company's immediate short-term liquidity; computed by dividing the sum of cash, short-term investments, and net accounts receivable by current liabilities. (p. 850).

Asset turnover A measure of how efficiently a company uses its assets to generate sales; computed by dividing net sales by average total assets. (p. 854).

Change in accounting principle The use of a principle in the current year that is different from the one used in the preceding year. (p. 863).

Comprehensive income Includes all changes in stockholders' equity during a period except those resulting from investments by stockholders and distributions to stockholders. (p. 864).

Current ratio A measure used to evaluate a company's liquidity and short-term debt-paying ability; computed by dividing current assets by current liabilities. (p. 850).

Debt to assets ratio Measures the percentage of assets provided by creditors; computed by dividing debt by assets. (p. 857).

Discontinued operations The disposal of a significant component of a business. (p. 861).

Earnings per share (EPS) The net income earned on each share of common stock; computed by dividing net income minus preferred dividends (if any) by the number of weighted-average common shares outstanding. (p. 856).

Extraordinary items Events and transactions that are unusual in nature and infrequent in occurrence. (p. 862).

Horizontal analysis A technique for evaluating a series of financial statement data over a period of time, to determine the increase (decrease) that has taken place, expressed as either an amount or a percentage. (p. 843).

Inventory turnover A measure of the liquidity of inventory; computed by dividing cost of goods sold by average inventory. (p. 852).

Leveraging See *Trading on the equity*. (p. 855).

Liquidity ratios Measures of the short-term ability of the company to pay its maturing obligations and to meet unexpected needs for cash. (p. 850).

Payout ratio Measures the percentage of earnings distributed in the form of cash dividends; computed by dividing cash dividends by net income. (p. 857).

Price-earnings (P-E) ratio Measures the ratio of the market price of each share of common stock to the earnings per share; computed by dividing the market price of the stock by earnings per share. (p. 856).

Profit margin Measures the percentage of each dollar of sales that results in net income; computed by dividing net income by net sales. (p. 853).

Profitability ratios Measures of the income or operating success of a company for a given period of time. (p. 853).

Pro forma income A measure of income that usually excludes items that a company thinks are unusual or non-recurring. (p. 865).

Quality of earnings Indicates the level of full and transparent information provided to users of the financial statements. (p. 865).

Ratio An expression of the mathematical relationship between one quantity and another. The relationship may be expressed either as a percentage, a rate, or a simple proportion. (p. 848).

Ratio analysis A technique for evaluating financial statements that expresses the relationship between selected financial statement data. (p. 848).

Return on assets An overall measure of profitability; computed by dividing net income by average total assets. (p. 854).

Return on common stockholders' equity Measures the dollars of net income earned for each dollar invested by the owners; computed by dividing net income minus preferred dividends (if any) by average common stockholders' equity. (p. 855).

Solvency ratios Measures of the ability of the company to survive over a long period of time. (p. 857).

Times interest earned Measures a company's ability to meet interest payments as they come due; computed by dividing income before interest expense and income taxes by interest expense. (p. 858).

Trading on the equity Borrowing money at a lower rate of interest than can be earned by using the borrowed money. (p. 855).

Vertical analysis A technique for evaluating financial statement data that expresses each item within a financial statement as a percentage of a base amount. (p. 846).

Self-Test, Brief Exercises, Exercises, Problem Set A, and many more components are available for practice in *WileyPLUS*.

SELF-TEST QUESTIONS

Answers are on page 889.

(LO 1) **1.** Comparisons of data within a company are an example of the following comparative basis:
  (a) Industry averages.   **(c)** Intercompany.
  (b) Intracompany.   **(d)** Both (b) and (c).

(LO 3) **2.** In horizontal analysis, each item is expressed as a percentage of the:
  (a) net income amount.
  (b) stockholders' equity amount.
  (c) total assets amount.
  (d) base year amount.

(LO 3) **3.** Sammy Corporation reported net sales of $300,000, $330,000, and $360,000 in the years, 2012, 2013, and 2014, respectively. If 2012 is the base year, what is the trend percentage for 2014?
  (a) 77%.   **(c)** 120%.
  (b) 108%.   **(d)** 130%.

(LO 4) **4.** The following schedule is a display of what type of analysis?

	Amount	Percent
Current assets	$200,000	25%
Property, plant, and equipment	600,000	75%
Total assets	$800,000	

  (a) Horizontal analysis.   **(c)** Vertical analysis.
  (b) Differential analysis.   **(d)** Ratio analysis.

(LO 4) **5.** In vertical analysis, the base amount for depreciation expense is generally:
  (a) net sales.
  (b) depreciation expense in a previous year.
  (c) gross profit.
  (d) fixed assets.

(LO 5) **6.** Which of the following measures is an evaluation of a firm's ability to pay current liabilities?
  (a) Acid-test ratio.
  (b) Current ratio.
  (c) Both (a) and (b).
  (d) None of the above.

(LO 5) **7.** A measure useful in evaluating the efficiency in managing inventories is:
  (a) inventory turnover.
  (b) days in inventory.
  (c) Both (a) and (b).
  (d) None of the above.

Use the following financial statement information as of the end of each year to answer Self-Test Questions 8-12.

	2014	2013
Inventory	$ 54,000	$ 48,000
Current assets	81,000	106,000
Total assets	382,000	326,000
Current liabilities	27,000	36,000
Total liabilities	102,000	88,000
Preferred stock	40,000	40,000
Common stockholders' equity	240,000	198,000
Net sales	784,000	697,000
Cost of goods sold	306,000	277,000
Net income	134,000	90,000
Tax expense	22,000	18,000
Interest expense	12,000	12,000
Dividends paid to preferred stockholders	4,000	4,000
Dividends paid to common stockholders	15,000	10,000

(LO 5) **8.** Compute the days in inventory for 2014.
  (a) 64.4 days.   (c) 6 days.
  (b) 60.8 days.   (d) 24 days.
(LO 5) **9.** Compute the current ratio for 2014.
  (a) 1.26:1.   (c) .80:1.
  (b) 3.0:1.   (d) 3.75:1.
(LO 5) **10.** Compute the profit margin for 2014.
  (a) 17.1%.   (c) 37.9%.
  (b) 18.1%.   (d) 5.9%.
(LO 5) **11.** Compute the return on common stockholders' equity for 2014.
  (a) 47.9%.   (c) 61.2%.
  (b) 51.7%.   (d) 59.4%.
(LO 5) **12.** Compute the times interest earned for 2014.
  (a) 11.2 times.   (c) 14.0 times.
  (b) 65.3 times.   (d) 13.0 times.
(LO 6) **13.** In reporting discontinued operations, the income statement should show in a special section:
  (a) gains and losses on the disposal of the discontinued component.

  (b) gains and losses from operations of the discontinued component.
  (c) Both (a) and (b).
  (d) None of these answer choices are correct.
14. Scout Corporation has income before taxes of $400,000 (LO 6) and an extraordinary loss of $100,000. If the income tax rate is 25% on all items, the income statement should show income before extraordinary items and extraordinary items, respectively, of:
  (a) $325,000 and $100,000.
  (b) $325,000 and $75,000.
  (c) $300,000 and $100,000
  (d) $300,000 and $75,000.
15. Which situation below might indicate a company has (LO 7) a low quality of earnings?
  (a) The same accounting principles are used each year.
  (b) Revenue is recognized when earned.
  (c) Maintenance costs are expensed as incurred.
  (d) The company is continually reporting pro forma income numbers.

Go to the book's companion website, www.wiley.com/college/weygandt, for additional Self-Test Questions.

 ✔ The Navigator

QUESTIONS

1. (a) Jose Ramirez believes that the analysis of financial statements is directed at two characteristics of a company: liquidity and profitability. Is Jose correct? Explain.
  (b) Are short-term creditors, long-term creditors, and stockholders interested primarily in the same characteristics of a company? Explain.
2. (a) Distinguish among the following bases of comparison: (1) intracompany, (2) industry averages, and (3) intercompany.
  (b) Give the principal value of using each of the three bases of comparison.
3. Two popular methods of financial statement analysis are horizontal analysis and vertical analysis. Explain the difference between these two methods.
4. (a) If Peoples Company had net income of $390,000 in 2014 and it experienced a 24.5% increase in net income for 2015, what is its net income for 2015?
  (b) If six cents of every dollar of Peoples revenue is net income in 2014, what is the dollar amount of 2014 revenue?
5. What is a ratio? What are the different ways of expressing the relationship of two amounts? What information does a ratio provide?
6. Name the major ratios useful in assessing (a) liquidity and (b) solvency.
7. Roberto Perez is puzzled. His company had a profit margin of 10% in 2014. He feels that this is an indication that the company is doing well. Julie Beck, his accountant, says that more information is needed to determine the firm's financial well-being. Who is correct? Why?

8. What do the following classes of ratios measure? (a) Liquidity ratios. (b) Profitability ratios. (c) Solvency ratios.
9. What is the difference between the current ratio and the acid-test ratio?
10. Hizar Company, a retail store, has an accounts receivable turnover of 4.5 times. The industry average is 12.5 times. Does Hizar have a collection problem with its accounts receivable?
11. Which ratios should be used to help answer the following questions?
  (a) How efficient is a company in using its assets to produce sales?
  (b) How near to sale is the inventory on hand?
  (c) How many dollars of net income were earned for each dollar invested by the owners?
  (d) How able is a company to meet interest charges as they fall due?
12. The price-earnings ratio of General Motors (automobile builder) was 8, and the price-earnings ratio of Microsoft (computer software) was 38. Which company did the stock market favor? Explain.
13. What is the formula for computing the payout ratio? Would you expect this ratio to be high or low for a growth company?
14. Holding all other factors constant, indicate whether each of the following changes generally signals good or bad news about a company.
  (a) Increase in profit margin.
  (b) Decrease in inventory turnover.
  (c) Increase in the current ratio.

(d) Decrease in earnings per share.

(e) Increase in price-earnings ratio.

(f) Increase in debt to assets ratio.

(g) Decrease in times interest earned.

15. The return on assets for Zhang Corporation is 7.6%. During the same year, Zhang's return on common stockholders' equity is 12.8%. What is the explanation for the difference in the two rates?

16. Which two ratios do you think should be of greatest interest to:

(a) A pension fund considering the purchase of 20-year bonds?

(b) A bank contemplating a short-term loan?

(c) A common stockholder?

17. Why must preferred dividends be subtracted from net income in computing earnings per share?

18. (a) What is meant by trading on the equity?

(b) How would you determine the profitability of trading on the equity?

19. Lippert Inc. has net income of $160,000, weighted-average shares of common stock outstanding of 50,000, and preferred dividends for the period of $40,000. What is Lippert's earnings per share of common stock? Kate Lippert, the president of Lippert Inc., believes the computed EPS of the company is high. Comment.

20. Why is it important to report discontinued operations separately from income from continuing operations?

21. You are considering investing in Wingert Transportation. The company reports 2014 earnings per share of $6.50 on income before extraordinary items and $4.75 on net income. Which EPS figure would you consider more relevant to your investment decision? Why?

22. RAF Inc. reported 2013 earnings per share of $3.20 and had no extraordinary items. In 2014, EPS on income before extraordinary items was $2.99, and EPS on net income was $3.49. Is this a favorable trend?

23. Indicate which of the following items would be reported as an extraordinary item in Stumfol Corporation's income statement.

(a) Loss from damages caused by volcano eruption.

(b) Loss from sale of temporary investments.

(c) Loss attributable to a labor strike.

(d) Loss caused when manufacture of a product was prohibited by the Food and Drug Administration.

(e) Loss from flood damage. (The nearby Black River floods every 2 to 3 years.)

(f) Write-down of obsolete inventory.

(g) Expropriation of a factory by a foreign government.

24. Identify and explain factors that affect quality of earnings.

25. Identify the specific sections in Apple's 2011 annual report where horizontal and vertical analyses of financial data are presented.

BRIEF EXERCISES

Follow the rounding procedures used in the chapter.

BE18-1 You recently received a letter from your Uncle Sammy. A portion of the letter is presented below.

Discuss need for comparative analysis.

(LO 1)

You know that I have a significant amount of money I saved over the years. I am thinking about starting an investment program. I want to do the investing myself, based on my own research and analysis of financial statements. I know that you are studying accounting, so I have a couple of questions for you. I have heard that different users of financial statements are interested in different characteristics of companies. Is this true and, if so, why? Also, some of my friends who are already investing have told me that comparisons involving a company's financial data can be made on a number of different bases. Can you explain these bases to me?

Instructions

Write a letter to your Uncle Sammy which answers his questions.

BE18-2 Schellhammer Corporation reported the following amounts in 2013, 2014, and 2015.

Identify and use tools of financial statement analysis.

(LO 2, 3, 4, 5)

	2013	2014	2015
Current assets	$200,000	$210,000	$240,000
Current liabilities	$150,000	$168,000	$184,000
Total assets	$500,000	$600,000	$620,000

Instructions

(a) Identify and describe the three tools of financial statement analysis. (b) Perform each of the three types of analysis on Schellhammer's current assets.

Prepare horizontal analysis.
(LO 3)
BE18-3 Using the following data from the comparative balance sheet of Goody Company, illustrate horizontal analysis.

	December 31, 2015	December 31, 2014
Accounts receivable	$ 520,000	$ 400,000
Inventory	$ 840,000	$ 600,000
Total assets	$3,000,000	$2,500,000

Prepare vertical analysis.
(LO 4)
BE18-4 Using the same data presented above in BE18-3 for Goody Company, illustrate vertical analysis.

Calculate percentage of change.
(LO 3)
BE18-5 Net income was $500,000 in 2013, $450,000 in 2014, and $522,000 in 2015. What is the percentage of change from (a) 2013 to 2014 and (b) 2014 to 2015? Is the change an increase or a decrease?

Calculate net income.
(LO 3)
BE18-6 If Sappington Company had net income of $585,000 in 2015 and it experienced a 20% increase in net income over 2014, what was its 2014 net income?

Calculate change in net income.
(LO 3)
BE18-7 Horizontal analysis (trend analysis) percentages for Dody Company's sales revenue, cost of goods sold, and expenses are shown below.

Horizontal Analysis	2015	2014	2013
Sales revenue	96.2	106.8	100.0
Cost of goods sold	102.0	97.0	100.0
Expenses	109.6	98.4	100.0

Did Dody's net income increase, decrease, or remain unchanged over the 3-year period?

Calculate change in net income.
(LO 4)
BE18-8 Vertical analysis (common size) percentages for Kochheim Company's sales revenue, cost of goods sold, and expenses are shown below.

Vertical Analysis	2015	2014	2013
Sales revenue	100.0	100.0	100.0
Cost of goods sold	60.2	62.4	63.5
Expenses	25.0	25.6	27.5

Did Kochheim's net income as a percentage of sales increase, decrease, or remain unchanged over the 3-year period? Provide numerical support for your answer.

Calculate liquidity ratios.
(LO 5)
BE18-9 Selected condensed data taken from a recent balance sheet of Heidebrecht Inc. are as follows.

HEIDEBRECHT INC.
Balance Sheet (partial)

Cash	$ 8,041,000
Short-term investments	4,947,000
Accounts receivable	12,545,000
Inventory	14,814,000
Other current assets	5,571,000
Total current assets	$45,918,000
Total current liabilities	$40,644,000

What are the (a) working capital, (b) current ratio, and (c) acid-test ratio?

Calculate profitability ratios.
(LO 5)
BE18-10 Linebarger Corporation has net income of $11.44 million and net revenue of $95 million in 2014. Its assets are $14 million at the beginning of the year and $18 million at the end of the year. What are Linebarger's (a) asset turnover and (b) profit margin?

Evaluate collection of accounts receivable.
(LO 5)
BE18-11 The following data are taken from the financial statements of Rainsberger Company.

	2015	2014
Accounts receivable (net), end of year	$ 550,000	$ 520,000
Net sales on account	3,960,000	3,100,000
Terms for all sales are 1/10, n/60.		

(a) Compute for each year (1) the accounts receivable turnover and (2) the average collection period. At the end of 2013, accounts receivable (net) was $480,000.

(b) ————— What conclusions about the management of accounts receivable can be drawn from these data?

BE18-12 The following data are from the income statements of Haskin Company.

	2015	2014
Sales revenue	$6,420,000	$6,240,000
Beginning inventory	940,000	860,000
Purchases	4,340,000	4,661,000
Ending inventory	1,020,000	940,000

(a) Compute for each year (1) the inventory turnover and (2) the days in inventory.
(b) ⸻ What conclusions concerning the management of the inventory can be drawn from these data?

Evaluate management of inventory.
(LO 5)

BE18-13 Guo Company has owners' equity of $400,000 and net income of $66,000. It has a payout ratio of 20% and a return on assets of 15%. How much did Guo pay in cash dividends, and what were its average assets?

Calculate amounts from profitability ratios.
(LO 5)

BE18-14 An inexperienced accountant for Silva Corporation showed the following in the income statement: income before income taxes and extraordinary item $450,000, and extraordinary loss from flood (before taxes) $70,000. The extraordinary loss and taxable income are both subject to a 30% tax rate. Prepare a correct income statement.

Prepare income statement including extraordinary items.
(LO 6)

BE18-15 On June 30, Holloway Corporation discontinued its operations in Europe. During the year, the operating loss was $300,000 before taxes. On September 1, Holloway disposed of its European facilities at a pretax loss of $120,000. The applicable tax rate is 30%. Show the discontinued operations section of the income statement.

Prepare discontinued operations section of income statement.
(LO 6)

> DO IT! Review

DO IT! 18-1 Summary financial information for Wolford Company is as follows.

Prepare horizontal analysis.
(LO 3)

	December 31, 2015	December 31, 2014
Current assets	$ 199,000	$ 220,000
Plant assets	821,000	780,000
Total assets	$1,020,000	$1,000,000

Compute the amount and percentage changes in 2015 using horizontal analysis, assuming 2014 is the base year.

DO IT! 18-2 The condensed financial statements of Murawski Company for the years 2013 and 2014 are presented below and on page 874.

Compute ratios.
(LO 5)

MURAWSKI COMPANY
Balance Sheets
December 31

	2014	2013
Current assets		
Cash and cash equivalents	$ 330	$ 360
Accounts receivable (net)	470	400
Inventory	460	390
Prepaid expenses	120	160
Total current assets	1,380	1,310
Property, plant, and equipment	420	380
Investments	10	10
Intangibles and other assets	530	510
Total assets	$2,340	$2,210
Current liabilities	$ 900	$ 790
Long-term liabilities	410	380
Stockholders' equity—common	1,030	1,040
Total liabilities and stockholders' equity	$2,340	$2,210

MURAWSKI COMPANY
Income Statements
For the Years Ended December 31

	2014	2013
Sales revenue	$3,800	$3,460
Costs and expenses		
Cost of goods sold	955	890
Selling & administrative expenses	2,400	2,330
Interest expense	25	20
Total costs and expenses	3,380	3,240
Income before income taxes	420	220
Income tax expense	126	66
Net income	$ 294	$ 154

Compute the following ratios for 2014 and 2013.

(a) Current ratio.
(b) Inventory turnover. (Inventory on 12/31/12 was $340.)
(c) Profit margin.
(d) Return on assets. (Assets on 12/31/12 were $1,900.)
(e) Return on common stockholders' equity. (Stockholders' equity on 12/31/12 was $900.)
(f) Debt to assets ratio.
(g) Times interest earned.

Prepare income statement, including irregular items.
(LO 6)

DO IT! 18-3 In its proposed 2014 income statement, Hrabik Corporation reports income before income taxes $500,000, extraordinary loss due to earthquake $150,000, income taxes $200,000 (not including irregular items), loss on operation of discontinued music division $60,000, and gain on disposal of discontinued music division $40,000. The income tax rate is 30%. Prepare a correct income statement, beginning with income before income taxes.

Match terms relating to quality of earnings and financial statement analysis.
(LO 3, 4, 5, 6, 7)

DO IT! 18-4 Match each of the following terms with the phrase that best describes it.

Quality of earnings	Pro forma income
Current ratio	Discontinued operations
Horizontal analysis	Comprehensive income

1. _____ A measure used to evaluate a company's liquidity.

2. _____ Usually excludes items that a company thinks are unusual or non-recurring.

3. _____ Indicates the level of full and transparent information provided to users of the financial statements.

4. _____ The disposal of a significant component of a business.

5. _____ Determines increases or decreases in a series of financial statement data.

6. _____ Includes all changes in stockholders' equity during a period except those resulting from investments by stockholders and distributions to stockholders.

EXERCISES

Prepare horizontal analysis.
(LO 3)

XLS

Follow the rounding procedures used in the chapter.

E18-1 Financial information for Kurzen Inc. is presented below.

	December 31, 2015	December 31, 2014
Current assets	$125,000	$100,000
Plant assets (net)	396,000	330,000
Current liabilities	91,000	70,000
Long-term liabilities	133,000	95,000
Common stock, $1 par	161,000	115,000
Retained earnings	136,000	150,000

Instructions
Prepare a schedule showing a horizontal analysis for 2015 using 2014 as the base year.

E18-2 Operating data for Navarro Corporation are presented below.

Prepare vertical analysis.
(LO 4)

	2015	2014
Net sales	$750,000	$600,000
Cost of goods sold	465,000	390,000
Selling expenses	105,000	66,000
Administrative expenses	60,000	54,000
Income tax expense	36,000	27,000
Net income	84,000	63,000

Instructions
Prepare a schedule showing a vertical analysis for 2015 and 2014.

E18-3 The comparative condensed balance sheets of Gurley Corporation are presented below.

Prepare horizontal and vertical analyses.
(LO 3, 4)

GURLEY CORPORATION
Comparative Condensed Balance Sheets
December 31

	2015	2014
Assets		
Current assets	$ 74,000	$ 80,000
Property, plant, and equipment (net)	99,000	90,000
Intangibles	27,000	40,000
Total assets	$200,000	$210,000
Liabilities and stockholders' equity		
Current liabilities	$ 42,000	$ 48,000
Long-term liabilities	143,000	150,000
Stockholders' equity	15,000	12,000
Total liabilities and stockholders' equity	$200,000	$210,000

Instructions
(a) Prepare a horizontal analysis of the balance sheet data for Gurley Corporation using 2014 as a base.
(b) Prepare a vertical analysis of the balance sheet data for Gurley Corporation in columnar form for 2015.

E18-4 The comparative condensed income statements of Emley Corporation are shown below.

Prepare horizontal and vertical analyses.
(LO 3, 4)

EMLEY CORPORATION
Comparative Condensed Income Statements
For the Years Ended December 31

	2015	2014
Net sales	$660,000	$600,000
Cost of goods sold	483,000	420,000
Gross profit	177,000	180,000
Operating expenses	125,000	120,000
Net income	$ 52,000	$ 60,000

Instructions
(a) Prepare a horizontal analysis of the income statement data for Emley Corporation using 2014 as a base. (Show the amounts of increase or decrease.)
(b) Prepare a vertical analysis of the income statement data for Emley Corporation in columnar form for both years.

Compute liquidity ratios and compare results.

(LO 5)

E18-5 Suppose Nordstrom, Inc., which operates department stores in numerous states, has the following selected financial statement data for the year ending January 30, 2014.

NORDSTROM, INC.
Balance Sheet (partial)

(in millions)	End-of-Year	Beginning-of-Year
Cash and cash equivalents	$ 795	$ 72
Accounts receivable (net)	2,035	1,942
Inventory	898	900
Prepaid expenses	88	93
Other current assets	238	210
Total current assets	$4,054	$3,217
Total current liabilities	$2,014	$1,601

For the year, net sales were $8,258 and cost of goods sold was $5,328 (in millions).

Instructions
(a) Compute the four liquidity ratios at the end of the year.
(b) Using the data in the chapter, compare Nordstrom's liquidity with (1) that of Macy's Inc., and (2) the industry averages for department stores.

Perform current and acid-test ratio analysis.

(LO 5)

E18-6 Keener Incorporated had the following transactions occur involving current assets and current liabilities during February 2014.

Feb. 3   Accounts receivable of $15,000 are collected.
      7   Equipment is purchased for $28,000 cash.
      11 Paid $3,000 for a 3-year insurance policy.
      14 Accounts payable of $12,000 are paid.
      18 Cash dividends of $5,000 are declared.

Additional information:

1. As of February 1, 2014, current assets were $110,000, and current liabilities were $50,000.
2. As of February 1, 2014, current assets included $15,000 of inventory and $2,000 of prepaid expenses.

Instructions
(a) Compute the current ratio as of the beginning of the month and after each transaction.
(b) Compute the acid-test ratio as of the beginning of the month and after each transaction.

Compute selected ratios.

(LO 5)

E18-7 Frizell Company has the following comparative balance sheet data.

FRIZELL COMPANY
Balance Sheets
December 31

	2015	2014
Cash	$ 15,000	$ 30,000
Accounts receivable (net)	70,000	60,000
Inventory	60,000	50,000
Plant assets (net)	200,000	180,000
	$345,000	$320,000
Accounts payable	$ 50,000	$ 60,000
Mortgage payable (6%)	100,000	100,000
Common stock, $10 par	140,000	120,000
Retained earnings	55,000	40,000
	$345,000	$320,000

Additional information for 2015:

1. Net income was $25,000.
2. Sales on account were $410,000. Sales returns and allowances were $20,000.
3. Cost of goods sold was $198,000.

Instructions
Compute the following ratios at December 31, 2015.

(a) Current ratio.
(b) Acid-test ratio.
(c) Accounts receivable turnover.
(d) Inventory turnover.

E18-8 Selected comparative statement data for Queen Products Company are presented below. All balance sheet data are as of December 31.

Compute selected ratios.
(LO 5)

	2015	2014
Net sales	$750,000	$720,000
Cost of goods sold	480,000	440,000
Interest expense	7,000	5,000
Net income	45,000	42,000
Accounts receivable	120,000	100,000
Inventory	85,000	75,000
Total assets	580,000	500,000
Total common stockholders' equity	430,000	325,000

Instructions
Compute the following ratios for 2015.

(a) Profit margin.
(b) Asset turnover.
(c) Return on assets.
(d) Return on common stockholders' equity.

E18-9 The income statement for Sutherland, Inc., appears below.

Compute selected ratios.
(LO 5)

SUTHERLAND, INC.
Income Statement
For the Year Ended December 31, 2014

Net sales	$400,000
Cost of goods sold	230,000
Gross profit	170,000
Expenses (including $16,000 interest and $24,000 income taxes)	105,000
Net income	$ 65,000

Additional information:

1. The weighted-average common shares outstanding in 2014 were 30,000 shares.
2. The market price of Sutherland, Inc. stock was $13 in 2014.
3. Cash dividends of $26,000 were paid, $5,000 of which were to preferred stockholders.

Instructions
Compute the following ratios for 2014.

(a) Earnings per share.
(b) Price-earnings ratio.
(c) Payout ratio.
(d) Times interest earned.

E18-10 Lingenfelter Corporation experienced a fire on December 31, 2015, in which its financial records were partially destroyed. It has been able to salvage some of the records and has ascertained the following balances.

Compute amounts from ratios.
(LO 5)

	December 31, 2015	December 31, 2014
Cash	$ 30,000	$ 10,000
Accounts receivable (net)	72,500	126,000
Inventory	200,000	180,000
Accounts payable	50,000	90,000
Notes payable	30,000	60,000
Common stock, $100 par	400,000	400,000
Retained earnings	113,500	101,000

Additional information:

1. The inventory turnover is 4.5 times.
2. The return on common stockholders' equity is 16%. The company had no additional paid-in capital.
3. The accounts receivable turnover is 8.8 times.
4. The return on assets is 12.5%.
5. Total assets at December 31, 2014, were $655,000.

Instructions
Compute the following for Lingenfelter Corporation.

(a) Cost of goods sold for 2015.
(b) Net sales (credit) for 2015.
(c) Net income for 2015.
(d) Total assets at December 31, 2015.

Compute ratios.
(LO 5)

E18-11 Wiemers Corporation's comparative balance sheets are presented below.

WIEMERS CORPORATION
Balance Sheets
December 31

	2014	2013
Cash	$ 4,300	$ 3,700
Accounts receivable (net)	21,200	23,400
Inventory	10,000	7,000
Land	20,000	26,000
Buildings	70,000	70,000
Accumulated depreciation—buildings	(15,000)	(10,000)
Total	$110,500	$120,100
Accounts payable	$ 12,370	$ 31,100
Common stock	75,000	69,000
Retained earnings	23,130	20,000
Total	$110,500	$120,100

Wiemers's 2014 income statement included net sales of $100,000, cost of goods sold of $60,000, and net income of $15,000.

Instructions
Compute the following ratios for 2014.

(a) Current ratio.
(b) Acid-test ratio.
(c) Accounts receivable turnover.
(d) Inventory turnover.
(e) Profit margin.
(f) Asset turnover.
(g) Return on assets.
(h) Return on common stockholders' equity.
(i) Debt to assets ratio.

Prepare a correct income statement.
(LO 6)

E18-12 For its fiscal year ending October 31, 2014, Haas Corporation reports the following partial data shown below.

Income before income taxes	$540,000
Income tax expense (30% × $420,000)	126,000
Income before extraordinary items	414,000
Extraordinary loss from flood	120,000
Net income	$294,000

The flood loss is considered an extraordinary item. The income tax rate is 30% on all items.

Instructions
(a) Prepare a correct income statement, beginning with income before income taxes.
(b) ———— Explain in memo form why the income statement data are misleading.

Prepare income statement.
(LO 6)

E18-13 Trayer Corporation has income from continuing operations of $290,000 for the year ended December 31, 2014. It also has the following items (before considering income taxes).

1. An extraordinary loss of $80,000.
2. A gain of $30,000 on the discontinuance of a division.
3. A correction of an error in last year's financial statements that resulted in a $20,000 understatement of 2013 net income.

Assume all items are subject to income taxes at a 30% tax rate.

Instructions
(a) Prepare an income statement, beginning with income from continuing operations.
(b) Indicate the statement presentation of any item not included in (a) above.

EXERCISES: SET B AND CHALLENGE EXERCISES

Visit the book's companion website, at **www.wiley.com/college/weygandt**, and choose the Student Companion site to access Exercise Set B and Challenge Exercises.

PROBLEMS

Follow the rounding procedures used in the chapter.

P18-1 Comparative statement data for Farris Company and Ratzlaff Company, two competitors, appear below. All balance sheet data are as of December 31, 2015, and December 31, 2014.

Prepare vertical analysis and comment on profitability.
(LO 4, 5)

	Farris Company		Ratzlaff Company	
	2015	**2014**	**2015**	**2014**
Net sales	$1,549,035		$339,038	
Cost of goods sold	1,080,490		241,000	
Operating expenses	302,275		79,000	
Interest expense	8,980		2,252	
Income tax expense	54,500		6,650	
Current assets	325,975	$312,410	83,336	$ 79,467
Plant assets (net)	521,310	500,000	139,728	125,812
Current liabilities	65,325	75,815	35,348	30,281
Long-term liabilities	108,500	90,000	29,620	25,000
Common stock, $10 par	500,000	500,000	120,000	120,000
Retained earnings	173,460	146,595	38,096	29,998

Instructions
(a) Prepare a vertical analysis of the 2015 income statement data for Farris Company and Ratzlaff Company in columnar form.
(b) ⸺ Comment on the relative profitability of the companies by computing the return on assets and the return on common stockholders' equity for both companies.

P18-2 The comparative statements of Painter Tool Company are presented below and on page 880.

Compute ratios from balance sheet and income statement.
(LO 5)

PAINTER TOOL COMPANY
Income Statement
For the Years Ended December 31

	2015	**2014**
Net sales	$1,818,500	$1,750,500
Cost of goods sold	1,011,500	996,000
Gross profit	807,000	754,500
Selling and administrative expenses	499,000	479,000
Income from operations	308,000	275,500
Other expenses and losses		
Interest expense	18,000	14,000
Income before income taxes	290,000	261,500
Income tax expense	87,000	77,000
Net income	$ 203,000	$ 184,500

LANDWEHR CORPORATION
Income Statement
For the Years Ended December 31

	2015	2014
Sales revenue	$740,000	$700,000
Less: Sales returns and allowances	40,000	50,000
Net sales	700,000	650,000
Cost of goods sold	420,000	400,000
Gross profit	280,000	250,000
Operating expenses (including income taxes)	235,000	220,000
Net income	$ 45,000	$ 30,000

Additional information:

1. The market price of Landwehr's common stock was $4.00, $5.00, and $8.00 for 2013, 2014, and 2015, respectively.
2. All dividends were paid in cash.

Instructions

(a) Compute the following ratios for 2014 and 2015.
   (1) Profit margin.
   (2) Asset turnover.
   (3) Earnings per share. (Weighted-average common shares in 2015 were 32,000 and in 2014 were 31,000.)
   (4) Price-earnings ratio.
   (5) Payout ratio.
   (6) Debt to assets ratio.
(b) ━━━━━ Based on the ratios calculated, discuss briefly the improvement or lack thereof in financial position and operating results from 2014 to 2015 of Landwehr Corporation.

P18-4 Financial information for Messersmith Company is presented below and on page 882.

Compute ratios, and comment on overall liquidity and profitability.

(LO 5)

MESSERSMITH COMPANY
Balance Sheets
December 31

Assets	2015	2014
Cash	$ 70,000	$ 65,000
Short-term investments	52,000	40,000
Accounts receivable (net)	98,000	80,000
Inventory	125,000	135,000
Prepaid expenses	29,000	23,000
Land	130,000	130,000
Building and equipment (net)	180,000	175,000
	$684,000	$648,000

Liabilities and Stockholders' Equity		
Notes payable	$100,000	$100,000
Accounts payable	48,000	42,000
Accrued liabilities	50,000	40,000
Bonds payable, due 2016	150,000	150,000
Common stock, $10 par	200,000	200,000
Retained earnings	136,000	116,000
	$684,000	$648,000

MESSERSMITH COMPANY
Income Statement
For the Years Ended December 31

	2015	2014
Net sales	$850,000	$790,000
Cost of goods sold	620,000	575,000
Gross profit	230,000	215,000
Operating expenses	187,000	173,000
Net income	$ 43,000	$ 42,000

Additional information:

1. Inventory at the beginning of 2014 was $118,000.
2. Total assets at the beginning of 2014 were $630,000.
3. No common stock transactions occurred during 2014 or 2015.
4. All sales were on account. Accounts receivable, net at the beginning of 2014, were $88,000.
5. Notes payable are classified as current liabilities.

Instructions

(a) Indicate, by using ratios, the change in liquidity and profitability of Messersmith Company from 2014 to 2015. (*Note:* Not all profitability ratios can be computed.)
(b) Given below are three independent situations and a ratio that may be affected. For each situation, compute the affected ratio (1) as of December 31, 2015, and (2) as of December 31, 2016, after giving effect to the situation. Net income for 2016 was $50,000. Total assets on December 31, 2016, were $700,000.

Situation	Ratio
(1) 18,000 shares of common stock were sold at par on July 1, 2016.	Return on common stockholders' equity
(2) All of the notes payable were paid in 2016. The only change in liabilities was that the notes payable were paid.	Debt to assets ratio
(3) Market price of common stock was $9 on December 31, 2015, and $12.80 on December 31, 2016.	Price-earnings ratio

Compute selected ratios, and compare liquidity, profitability, and solvency for two companies.

(LO 5)

P18-5 Selected financial data of Target and Wal-Mart for a recent year are presented here (in millions).

	Target Corporation	Wal-Mart Stores, Inc.
	Income Statement Data for Year	
Net sales	$61,471	$374,526
Cost of goods sold	41,895	286,515
Selling and administrative expenses	16,200	70,847
Interest expense	647	1,798
Other income (expense)	1,896	4,273
Income tax expense	1,776	6,908
Net income	$ 2,849	$ 12,731
	Balance Sheet Data (End of Year)	
Current assets	$18,906	$ 47,585
Noncurrent assets	25,654	115,929
Total assets	$44,560	$163,514
Current liabilities	$11,782	$ 58,454
Long-term debt	17,471	40,452
Total stockholders' equity	15,307	64,608
Total liabilities and stockholders' equity	$44,560	$163,514

	Target Corporation	Wal-Mart Stores, Inc.
	Beginning-of-Year Balances	
Total assets	$37,349	$151,587
Total stockholders' equity	15,633	61,573
Current liabilities	11,117	52,148
Total liabilities	21,716	90,014
	Other Data	
Average net accounts receivable	$ 7,124	$ 3,247
Average inventory	6,517	34,433
Net cash provided by operating activities	4,125	20,354

Instructions

(a) For each company, compute the following ratios.

(1) Current ratio.		(7) Asset turnover.	
(2) Accounts receivable turnover.		(8) Return on assets.	
(3) Average collection period.		(9) Return on common stockholders' equity.	
(4) Inventory turnover.		(10) Debt to assets ratio.	
(5) Days in inventory.		(11) Times interest earned.	
(6) Profit margin.			

(b) Compare the liquidity, profitability, and solvency of the two companies.

P18-6 The comparative statements of Corbin Company are presented below and on page 884.   *Compute numerous ratios.*
(LO 5)

CORBIN COMPANY
Income Statement
For the Years Ended December 31

	2015	2014
Net sales (all on account)	$595,000	$520,000
Expenses		
Cost of goods sold	415,000	354,000
Selling and administrative	120,800	114,800
Interest expense	7,800	6,000
Income tax expense	15,000	14,000
Total expenses	558,600	488,800
Net income	$ 36,400	$ 31,200

CORBIN COMPANY
Balance Sheets
December 31

Assets	2015	2014
Current assets		
Cash	$ 21,000	$ 18,000
Short-term investments	18,000	15,000
Accounts receivable (net)	91,000	74,000
Inventory	85,000	70,000
Total current assets	215,000	177,000
Plant assets (net)	423,000	383,000
Total assets	$638,000	$560,000

Liabilities and Stockholders' Equity	2015	2014
Current liabilities		
Accounts payable	$122,000	$110,000
Income taxes payable	23,000	20,000
Total current liabilities	145,000	130,000
Long-term liabilities		
Bonds payable	120,000	80,000
Total liabilities	265,000	210,000
Stockholders' equity		
Common stock ($5 par)	150,000	150,000
Retained earnings	223,000	200,000
Total stockholders' equity	373,000	350,000
Total liabilities and stockholders' equity	$638,000	$560,000

Additional data:

The common stock recently sold at $19.50 per share.

Instructions

Compute the following ratios for 2015.

(a) Current ratio.
(b) Acid-test ratio.
(c) Accounts receivable turnover.
(d) Inventory turnover.
(e) Profit margin.
(f) Asset turnover.
(g) Return on assets.

(h) Return on common stockholders' equity.
(i) Earnings per share.
(j) Price-earnings ratio.
(k) Payout ratio.
(l) Debt to assets ratio.
(m) Times interest earned.

Compute missing information given a set of ratios.

(LO 5)

P18-7 An incomplete income statement and an incomplete comparative balance sheet of Deines Corporation are presented below and on page 885.

DEINES CORPORATION
Income Statement
For the Year Ended December 31, 2015

Net sales	$11,000,000
Cost of goods sold	?
Gross profit	?
Operating expenses	1,665,000
Income from operations	?
Other expenses and losses	
Interest expense	?
Income before income taxes	?
Income tax expense	560,000
Net income	$?

DEINES CORPORATION
Balance Sheets
December 31

Assets	2015	2014
Current assets		
Cash	$ 450,000	$ 375,000
Accounts receivable (net)	?	950,000
Inventory	?	1,720,000
Total current assets	?	3,045,000
Plant assets (net)	4,620,000	3,955,000
Total assets	$?	$7,000,000

Liabilities and Stockholders' Equity	2015	2014
Current liabilities	$?	$ 825,000
Long-term notes payable	?	2,800,000
Total liabilities	?	3,625,000
Common stock, $1 par	3,000,000	3,000,000
Retained earnings	400,000	375,000
Total stockholders' equity	3,400,000	3,375,000
Total liabilities and stockholders' equity	$?	$7,000,000

Additional information:

1. The accounts receivable turnover for 2015 is 10 times.
2. All sales are on account.
3. The profit margin for 2015 is 14.5%.
4. Return on assets is 22% for 2015.
5. The current ratio on December 31, 2015, is 3.0.
6. The inventory turnover for 2015 is 4.8 times.

Instructions

Compute the missing information given the ratios above. Show computations. (*Note:* Start with one ratio and derive as much information as possible from it before trying another ratio. List all missing amounts under the ratio used to find the information.)

P18-8 Terwilliger Corporation owns a number of cruise ships and a chain of hotels. The hotels, which have not been profitable, were discontinued on September 1, 2014. The 2014 operating results for the company were as follows.

Prepare income statement with discontinued operations and extraordinary loss.

(LO 6)

Operating revenues	$12,850,000
Operating expenses	8,700,000
Operating income	$ 4,150,000

Analysis discloses that these data include the operating results of the hotel chain, which were operating revenues $1,500,000 and operating expenses $2,400,000. The hotels were sold at a gain of $200,000 before taxes. This gain is not included in the operating results. During the year, Terwilliger suffered an extraordinary loss of $600,000 before taxes, which is not included in the operating results. In 2014, the company had other revenues and gains of $100,000, which are not included in the operating results. The corporation is in the 30% income tax bracket.

Instructions

Prepare a condensed income statement.

P18-9 The ledger of Jaime Corporation at December 31, 2014, contains the following summary data.

Prepare income statement with nontypical items.

(LO 6)

Net sales	$1,700,000	Cost of goods sold	$1,100,000
Selling expenses	120,000	Administrative expenses	150,000
Other revenues and gains	20,000	Other expenses and losses	28,000

Your analysis reveals the following additional information that is not included in the above data.

1. The entire Puzzles Division was discontinued on August 31. The income from operations for this division before income taxes was $20,000. The Puzzles Division was sold at a loss of $90,000 before income taxes.
2. On May 15, company property was expropriated for an interstate highway. The settlement resulted in an extraordinary gain of $120,000 before income taxes.
3. The income tax rate on all items is 30%.

Instructions

Prepare an income statement for the year ended December 31, 2014. Use the format illustrated in the Comprehensive DO IT! (page 867).

PROBLEMS: SET B

Visit the book's companion website, at **www.wiley.com/college/weygandt**, and choose the Student Companion site to access Problem Set B.

CONTINUING COOKIE CHRONICLE

(*Note:* This is a continuation of the Cookie Chronicle from Chapters 1 through 17.)

CCC18 Natalie and Curtis have the balance sheet and income statement for the first year of operations for Cookie & Coffee Creations Inc. They have been told that they can use these financial statements to prepare horizontal and vertical analyses, and to calculate financial ratios, to determine how their business is doing and to make some decisions they have been considering.

Go to the book's companion website, **www.wiley.com/college/weygandt,** *to see the completion of this problem.*

Broadening Your Perspective

Financial Reporting and Analysis

Financial Reporting Problem: Apple Inc.

BYP18-1 Your parents are considering investing in Apple Inc. common stock. They ask you, as an accounting expert, to make an analysis of the company for them. Apple's financial statements are presented in Appendix A. Instructions for accessing and using Apple's complete annual report, including the notes to the financial statements, are also provided in Appendix A.

Instructions
(Follow the approach in the chapter for rounding numbers.)

(a) Make a 3-year trend analysis, using 2009 as the base year, of (1) net sales and (2) net income. Comment on the significance of the trend results.

(b) Compute for 2011 and 2010 the (1) profit margin, (2) asset turnover, (3) return on assets, and (4) return on common stockholders' equity. How would you evaluate Apple's profitability? Total assets at September 26, 2009, were $47,501 and total stockholders' equity at September 26, 2009, was $31,640.

(c) Compute for 2011 and 2010 the (1) debt to assets ratio and (2) times interest earned. How would you evaluate Apple's long-term solvency?

(d) What information outside the annual report may also be useful to your parents in making a decision about Apple?

Comparative Analysis Problem: PepsiCo, Inc. vs. The Coca-Cola Company

BYP18-2 PepsiCo's financial statements are presented in Appendix B. Financial statements of The Coca-Cola Company are presented in Appendix C. Instructions for accessing and using the complete annual reports of PepsiCo and Coca-Cola, including the notes to the financial statements, are also provided in Appendices B and C, respectively.

Instructions

(a) Based on the information contained in these financial statements, determine each of the following for each company.

   (1) The percentage increase (decrease) in (i) net sales and (ii) net income from 2010 to 2011.
   (2) The percentage increase in (i) total assets and (ii) total common stockholders' (shareholders') equity from 2010 to 2011.
   (3) The basic earnings per share and price-earnings ratio for 2011. (For both PepsiCo and Coca-Cola, use the basic earnings per share.) Coca-Cola's common stock had a market price of $75.05 at the end of fiscal-year 2011, and PepsiCo's common stock had a market price of $66.35.

(b) What conclusions concerning the two companies can be drawn from these data?

Comparative Analysis Problem:
Amazon.com, Inc. vs. Wal-Mart Stores, Inc.

BYP18-3 Amazon.com, Inc.'s financial statements are presented in Appendix D. Financial statements of Wal-Mart Stores, Inc. are presented in Appendix E. Instructions for accessing and using the complete annual reports of Amazon and Wal-Mart, including the notes to the financial statements, are also provided in Appendices D and E, respectively.

Instructions

(a) Based on the information contained in these financial statements, determine each of the following for each company.

   (1) The percentage increase (decrease) in (i) net sales and (ii) net income from 2010 to 2011.
   (2) The percentage increase in (i) total assets and (ii) total common stockholders' (shareholders') equity from 2010 to 2011.
   (3) The basic earnings per share and price-earnings ratio for 2011. (For both Amazon and Wal-Mart, use the basic earnings per share.) Amazon's common stock had a market price of $214.75 at the end of fiscal-year 2011, and Wal-Mart's common stock had a market price of $57.90.

(b) What conclusions concerning the two companies can be drawn from these data?

Real-World Focus

BYP18-4 The Management Discussion and Analysis section of an annual report addresses corporate performance for the year and sometimes uses financial ratios to support its claims.

Address: **www.ibm.com/investor/tools/index.phtml** or go to **www.wiley.com/college/weygandt**

Steps
1. Choose **How to read annual reports** (in the Guides section).
2. Choose **Anatomy**.

Instructions
Using the information from the above site, answer the following questions.

(a) What are the optional elements that are often included in an annual report?
(b) What are the elements of an annual report that are required by the SEC?
(c) Describe the contents of the Management Discussion.
(d) Describe the contents of the Auditors' Report.
(e) Describe the contents of the Selected Financial Data.

Critical Thinking

Decision-Making Across the Organization

BYP18-5 As the CPA for Gandara Manufacturing Inc., you have been asked to develop some key ratios from the comparative financial statements. This information is to be used to convince creditors that the company is solvent and will continue as a going concern. The data requested and the computations developed from the financial statements follow.

	2014	**2013**
Current ratio	3.1 times	2.1 times
Acid-test ratio	.8 times	1.4 times
Asset turnover	2.8 times	2.2 times
Net income	Up 32%	Down 8%
Earnings per share	$3.30	$2.50

Instructions

With the class divided into groups, complete the following.

Gandara Manufacturing Inc. asks you to prepare a list of brief comments stating how each of these items supports the solvency and going-concern potential of the business. The company wishes to use these comments to support its presentation of data to its creditors. You are to prepare the comments as requested, giving the implications and the limitations of each item separately. Then prepare a collective inference that may be drawn from the individual items about Gandara's solvency and going-concern potential.

Communication Activity

BYP18-6 Abby Landis is the CEO of Pletcher's Electronics. Landis is an expert engineer but a novice in accounting. She asks you to explain (1) the bases for comparison in analyzing Pletcher's financial statements, and (2) the factors affecting quality of earnings.

Instructions

Write a letter to Abby Landis that explains the bases for comparison and factors affecting quality of earnings.

Ethics Case

BYP18-7 Dave Schonhardt, president of Schonhardt Industries, wishes to issue a press release to bolster his company's image and maybe even its stock price, which has been gradually falling. As controller, you have been asked to provide a list of 20 financial ratios along with some other operating statistics relative to Schonhardt Industries' first quarter financials and operations.

Two days after you provide the ratios and data requested, Steven Verlin, the public relations director of Schonhardt, asks you to prove the accuracy of the financial and operating data contained in the press release written by the president and edited by Steven. In the press release, the president highlights the sales increase of 25% over last year's first quarter and the positive change in the current ratio from 1.5:1 last year to 3:1 this year. He also emphasizes that production was up 50% over the prior year's first quarter.

You note that the press release contains only positive or improved ratios and none of the negative or deteriorated ratios. For instance, no mention is made that the debt to assets ratio has increased from 35% to 55%, that inventories are up 89%, and that while the current ratio improved, the acid-test ratio fell from 1:1 to. 5:1. Nor is there any mention that the reported profit for the quarter would have been a loss had not the estimated lives of Schonhardt's plant and machinery been increased by 30%. Steven emphasizes, "The prez wants this release by early this afternoon."

Instructions

(a) Who are the stakeholders in this situation?

(b) Is there anything unethical in president Schonhardt's actions?

(c) Should you as controller remain silent? Does Steven have any responsibility?

All About You

BYP18-8 In this chapter, you learned how to use many tools for performing a financial analysis of a company. When making personal investments, however, it is most likely that you won't be buying stocks and bonds in individual companies. Instead, when most people want to invest in stock, they buy mutual funds. By investing in a mutual fund, you reduce your risk because the fund diversifies by buying the stock of a variety of different companies, bonds, and other investments, depending on the stated goals of the fund.

Before you invest in a fund, you will need to decide what type of fund you want. For example, do you want a fund that has the potential of high growth (but also high risk), or are you looking for lower risk and a steady stream of income? Do you want a fund that invests only in U.S. companies, or do you want one that invests globally? Many resources are available to help you with these types of decisions.

Instructions

Go to **http://web.archive.org/web/20050210200843/http://www.cnb1.com/invallocmdl.htm** and complete the investment allocation questionnaire. Add up your total points to determine the type of investment fund that would be appropriate for you.

FASB Codification Activity

BYP18-9 If your school has a subscription to the FASB Codification, go to **http://aaahq.org/ascLogin.cfm** to log in and prepare responses to the following. Use the Master Glossary for determining the proper definitions.

(a) Discontinued operations.
(b) Extraordinary items.
(c) Comprehensive income.

Answers to Chapter Questions

Answers to Insight and Accounting Across the Organization Questions

p. 851 How to Manage the Current Ratio   Q: How might management influence a company's current ratio? **A:** Management can affect the current ratio by speeding up or withholding payments on accounts payable just before the balance sheet date. Management can alter the cash balance by increasing or decreasing long-term assets or long-term debt, or by issuing or purchasing common stock.

p. 863 What Does "Non-Recurring" Really Mean?   Q: If a company takes a large restructuring charge, what is the effect on the company's current income statement versus future ones? **A:** The current period's net income can be greatly diminished by a large restructuring charge. The net incomes in future periods can be enhanced because they are relieved of costs (i.e., depreciation and labor expenses) that would have been charged to them.

Answers to Self-Test Questions

1. b   **2.** d   **3.** c ($360,000 ÷ 300,000)   **4.** c   **5.** a   **6.** c   **7.** c   **8.** b $306,000 ÷ [($54,000 + $48,000) ÷ 2] = 6; 365 ÷ 6   **9.** b ($81,000 ÷ $27,000)   **10.** a $134,000 ÷ $784,000   **11.** d ($134,000 − $4,000) ÷ [($240,000 + $198,000) ÷ 2]   **12.** c ($134,000 + $22,000 + $12,000) ÷ $12,000   **13.** c   **14.** d ($400,000 − (25% × $400,000); $300,000 − [$100,000 − (25% × $100,000)]   **15.** d

A Look at IFRS

The tools of financial statement analysis, covered in the first section of this chapter, are the same throughout the world. Techniques such as vertical and horizontal analysis, for example, are tools used by analysts regardless of whether GAAP- or IFRS-related financial statements are being evaluated. In addition, the ratios provided in the textbook are the same ones that are used internationally.

The latter part of this chapter relates to the income statement and irregular items. As in GAAP, the income statement is a required statement under IFRS. In addition, the content and presentation of an IFRS income statement is similar to the one used for GAAP. *IAS 1* (revised), "Presentation of Financial Statements," provides general guidelines for the reporting of income statement information. In general, the differences in the presentation of financial statement information are relatively minor.

> **LEARNING OBJECTIVE   8**
>
> Compare financial statement analysis and income statement presentation under GAAP and IFRS.

IFRS Additions to the Textbook

- The tools of financial statement analysis covered in this chapter are universal and therefore no significant differences exist in the analysis methods used.
- The basic objectives of the income statement are the same under both GAAP and IFRS. As indicated in the textbook, a very important objective is to ensure that users of the income statement can evaluate the earning power of the company. Earning power is the normal level of income to be obtained in the future. Thus, both the IASB and the FASB are interested in distinguishing normal levels of income from irregular items in order to better predict a company's future profitability.
- The basic accounting for discontinued operations is the same under IFRS and GAAP.
- Under IFRS, there is no classification for extraordinary items. In other words, extraordinary item treatment is prohibited under IFRS. All revenue and expense items are considered ordinary in nature. Disclosure, however, is extensive for items that are considered material to the financial results. Examples are write-downs of inventory or plant assets, or gains and losses on the sale of plant assets.
- The accounting for changes in accounting principles and changes in accounting estimates are the same for both GAAP and IFRS.
- Both GAAP and IFRS follow the same approach in reporting comprehensive income. The statement of comprehensive income can be prepared under the one-statement approach or the two-statement approach.
- The issues related to quality of earnings are the same under both GAAP and IFRS. It is hoped that by adopting a more principles-based approach, as found in IFRS, that many of the earning quality issues will disappear.

Looking to the Future

The FASB and the IASB are working on a project that would rework the structure of financial statements. Recently, the IASB decided to require a statement of comprehensive income, similar to what was required under GAAP. In addition, another part of this project addresses the issue of how to classify various items in the income statement. A main goal of this new approach is to provide information that better represents how businesses are run. In addition, the approach draws attention away from one number—net income.

IFRS Practice

IFRS Self-Test Questions

1. The basic tools of financial analysis are the same under both GAAP and IFRS **except** that:
   (a) horizontal analysis cannot be done because the format of the statements is sometimes different.
   (b) analysis is different because vertical analysis cannot be done under IFRS.
   (c) the current ratio cannot be computed because current liabilities are often reported before current assets in IFRS statements of position.
   (d) None of the above.

2. Under IFRS:
   (a) the reporting of discontinued items is different than under GAAP.
   (b) the reporting of extraordinary items is prohibited.
   (c) the reporting of changes in accounting principles is different than under GAAP.
   (d) None of the above.

3. Presentation of comprehensive income must be reported under IFRS in:
   (a) the statement of stockholders' equity.
   (b) the income statement ending with net income.
   (c) the notes to the financial statements.
   (d) a statement of comprehensive income.

4. In preparing its income statement for 2014, Parmalane assembles the following information.

Sales revenue	$500,000
Cost of goods sold	300,000
Operating expenses	40,000
Loss on discontinued operations	20,000
Loss from flood disaster (an extraordinary item under GAAP)	10,000

Ignoring income taxes, what is Parmalane's income from continuing operations for 2014 under IFRS?
(a) $260,000. **(c)** $240,000.
(b) $250,000 **(d)** $150,000.

5. Using the same information as Question 4, which statement is **incorrect**?
(a) Net income under GAAP and IFRS are the same.
(b) Under GAAP, special reporting is provided for extraordinary items.
(c) Both GAAP and IFRS report the same amount for income from continuing operations.
(d) IFRS would not provide separate disclosure for discontinued operations.

International Financial Reporting Problem: Zetar plc

IFRS18-1 The financial statements of Zetar plc are presented in Appendix F. Instructions for accessing and using the company's complete annual report, including the notes to its financial statements, are also provided in Appendix F.

Instructions
Use the company's **2009 annual report** to answer the following questions.

(a) The company's income statement reports a loss on discontinued operations. What business did the company discontinue, and why did it choose to discontinue the business?
(b) For the year ended April 30, 2009, what amount did the company lose on the operation of the discontinued business, and what amount did it lose on disposal?
(c) What was the total recorded value of the net assets at the date of disposal, and what was the amount of costs incurred to dispose of the business?

Answers to IFRS Self-Test Questions
1. d 2. b 3. d 4. d 5. d

The Navigator

19 | Managerial Accounting

Feature Story

Just Add Water ... and Paddle

Mike Cichanowski grew up on the Mississippi River in Winona, Minnesota. At a young age, he learned to paddle a canoe so he could explore the river. Before long, Mike began crafting his own canoes from bent wood and fiberglass in his dad's garage. Then, when his canoe-making shop outgrew the garage, he moved it into an old warehouse. When that was going to be torn down, Mike came to a critical juncture in his life. He took out a bank loan and built his own small shop, giving birth to the company Wenonah Canoe.

Wenonah Canoe soon became known as a pioneer in developing techniques to get the most out of new materials such as plastics, composites, and carbon fibers—maximizing strength while minimizing weight.

In the 1990s, as kayaking became popular, Mike made another critical decision when he acquired Current Designs, a premier Canadian kayak manufacturer. This venture allowed Wenonah to branch out with new product lines while providing Current Designs with much-needed capacity expansion as well as manufacturing expertise. Mike moved Current Designs' headquarters to Minnesota and made a big (and potentially risky) investment in a new production facility. Today, the company's 90 employees produce and sell about 12,000 canoes and kayaks per year, across the country and around the world.

Mike will tell you that business success is "a three-legged stool." The first leg is the knowledge and commitment to make a great product. Wenonah's canoes and Current Designs' kayaks are widely regarded as among the very best. The second leg is the ability to sell your product. Mike's company started off making great canoes, but it took a little longer to figure out how to sell them. The third leg is not something that most of you would immediately associate with entrepreneurial success. It is what goes on behind the scenes—accounting. Good accounting information is absolutely critical to the countless decisions, big and small, that ensure the survival and growth of the company.

Bottom line: No matter how good your product is and no matter how many units you sell, if you don't have a firm on your numbers, you are up a creek without a paddle.

Watch the **What Is Managerial Accounting?** video in WileyPLUS for an introduction to managerial accounting.

Source: www.wenonah.com.

✔ The Navigator

- ☐ Scan Learning Objectives
- ☐ Read Feature Story
- ☐ Read Preview
- ☐ Read text and answer **DO IT!** p. 898
  - ☐ p. 902   ☐ p. 904   ☐ p. 911
- ☐ Work Comprehensive **DO IT! 1** p. 912
  - ☐ **2** p. 913
- ☐ Review Summary of Learning Objectives
- ☐ Answer Self-Test Questions
- ☐ Complete Assignments
- ☐ Go to *WileyPLUS* for practice and tutorials

Learning Objectives   ✔ The Navigator

After studying this chapter, you should be able to:

[1] Explain the distinguishing features of managerial accounting.

[2] Identify the three broad functions of management.

[3] Define the three classes of manufacturing costs.

[4] Distinguish between product and period costs.

[5] Explain the difference between a merchandising and a manufacturing income statement.

[6] Indicate how cost of goods manufactured is determined.

[7] Explain the difference between a merchandising and a manufacturing balance sheet.

[8] Identify trends in managerial accounting.

courtesy Current Designs

Preview of Chapter 19

✔ The Navigator

This chapter focuses on issues illustrated in the Feature Story about Current Designs and its parent company Wenonah Canoe. To succeed, the company needs to determine and control the costs of material, labor, and overhead, and understand the relationship between costs and profits. Managers often make decisions that determine their company's fate—and their own. Managers are evaluated on the results of their decisions. Managerial accounting provides tools for assisting management in making decisions and for evaluating the effectiveness of those decisions.

The content and organization of this chapter are as follows.

MANAGERIAL ACCOUNTING			
Managerial Accounting Basics	**Managerial Cost Concepts**	**Manufacturing Costs in Financial Statements**	**Managerial Accounting Today**
• Comparing managerial and financial accounting • Management functions • Organizational structure • Business ethics	• Manufacturing costs • Product vs. period costs	• Income statement • Cost of goods manufactured • Balance sheet • Cost concepts—A review • Product costing for service industries	• Focus on the value chain • Balanced scorecard • Corporate social responsibility

Managerial Accounting Basics

Managerial accounting provides economic and financial information for managers and other internal users. Understanding managerial accounting will be vital to your future success in business. You don't believe us? Let's look at some examples of some of the crucial activities of employees at Current Designs, and where those activities are addressed in this textbook.

In order to know whether it is making a profit, Current Designs needs accurate information about the cost of each kayak (Chapters 20 and 21). And to stay profitable, Current Designs must adjust the number of kayaks it produces in light of changes in economic conditions and consumer tastes. It then needs to understand how changes in the number of kayaks it produces impact its production costs and profitability (Chapter 22). Further, Current Designs' managers must often consider alternative courses of action. For example, should the company accept a special order from a customer, produce a particular kayak component internally or outsource it, or continue or discontinue a particular product line (Chapter 26)?

In order to plan for the future, Current Designs prepares budgets (Chapter 23), and it then compares its budgeted numbers with its actual results to evaluate performance and identify areas that need to change (Chapters 24 and 25). Finally, it sometimes needs to make substantial investment decisions, such as the building of a new plant or the purchase of new equipment (Chapter 26).

Someday, you are going to face decisions just like these. You may end up in sales, marketing, management, production, or finance. You may work for a company that provides medical care, produces software, or serves up mouth-watering meals. No matter what your position is and no matter what your product, knowledge of managerial accounting will increase your chances of business success. Put another way, in business you can either guess, or you can make an informed decision. As the CEO of Microsoft once noted: "If you're supposed to be making money in business and supposed to be satisfying customers and building market share, there are numbers that characterize those things. And if somebody can't speak to me quantitatively about it, then I'm nervous."

Comparing Managerial and Financial Accounting

There are both similarities and differences between managerial and financial accounting. First, each field of accounting deals with the economic events of a business. For example, **determining** the unit cost of manufacturing a product is part of managerial accounting. **Reporting** the total cost of goods manufactured and sold is part of financial accounting. In addition, both managerial and financial accounting require that a company's economic events be quantified and communicated to interested parties. Illustration 19-1 summarizes the principal differences between financial accounting and managerial accounting.

Management Functions

Managers' activities and responsibilities can be classified into three broad functions:

1. Planning.
2. Directing.
3. Controlling.

Feature	Financial Accounting	Managerial Accounting
Primary Users of Reports	External users: stockholders, creditors, and regulators.	Internal users: officers and managers.
Types and Frequency of Reports	Financial statements. Quarterly and annually.	Internal reports. As frequently as needed.
Purpose of Reports	General-purpose.	Special-purpose for specific decisions.
Content of Reports	Pertains to business as a whole. Highly aggregated (condensed). Limited to double-entry accounting and cost data. Generally accepted accounting principles.	Pertains to subunits of the business. Very detailed. Extends beyond double-entry accounting to any relevant data. Standard is relevance to decisions.
Verification Process	Audited by CPA.	No independent audits.

Illustration 19-1
Differences between financial and managerial accounting

In performing these functions, managers make decisions that have a significant impact on the organization.

Planning requires managers to look ahead and to establish objectives. These objectives are often diverse: maximizing short-term profits and market share, maintaining a commitment to environmental protection, and contributing to social programs. For example, Hewlett-Packard, in an attempt to gain a stronger foothold in the computer industry, has greatly reduced its prices to compete with Dell. A key objective of management is to **add value** to the business under its control. Value is usually measured by the trading price of the company's stock and by the potential selling price of the company.

Directing involves coordinating a company's diverse activities and human resources to produce a smooth-running operation. This function relates to implementing planned objectives and providing necessary incentives to motivate employees. For example, manufacturers such as Campbell Soup Company, General Motors, and Dell must coordinate purchasing, manufacturing, warehousing, and selling. Service corporations such as American Airlines, Federal Express, and AT&T must coordinate scheduling, sales, service, and acquisitions of equipment and supplies. Directing also involves selecting executives, appointing managers and supervisors, and hiring and training employees.

The third management function, **controlling**, is the process of keeping the company's activities on track. In controlling operations, managers determine whether planned goals are being met. When there are deviations from targeted objectives, managers must decide what changes are needed to get back on track. Scandals at companies like Enron, Lucent, and Xerox attest to the fact that companies must have adequate controls to ensure that the company develops and distributes accurate information.

How do managers achieve control? A smart manager in a very small operation can make personal observations, ask good questions, and know how to evaluate the answers. But using this approach in a larger organization would result in chaos. Imagine the president of Current Designs attempting to determine whether the company is meeting its planned objectives, without some record of what has happened and what is expected to occur. Thus, large businesses typically use a formal system of evaluation. These systems include such features as budgets, responsibility centers, and performance evaluation reports—all of which are features of managerial accounting.

Decision-making is not a separate management function. Rather, it is the outcome of the exercise of good judgment in planning, directing, and controlling.

MANAGEMENT INSIGHT

Even the Best Have to Get Better

© camilla wisbauer/iStockphoto

Louis Vuitton is a French manufacturer of high-end handbags, wallets, and suitcases. Its reputation for quality and style allows it to charge extremely high prices–for example, $700 for a tote bag. But often in the past, when demand was hot, supply was nonexistent–shelves were empty, and would-be buyers left empty-handed.

Luxury-goods manufacturers used to consider stockouts to be a good thing, but recently Louis Vuitton changed its attitude. The company adopted "lean" processes used by car manufacturers and electronics companies to speed up production of "hot" products. Work is done by flexible teams, with jobs organized based on how long a task takes. By reducing wasted time and eliminating bottlenecks, what used to take 20 to 30 workers eight days to do now takes 6 to 12 workers one day. Also, production employees who used to specialize on a single task on a single product are now multiskilled. This allows them to quickly switch products to meet demand.

To make sure that the factory is making the right products, within a week of a product launch, Louis Vuitton stores around the world feed sales information to the headquarters in France, and production is adjusted accordingly. Finally, the new production processes have also improved quality. Returns of some products are down by two-thirds, which makes quite a difference to the bottom line when the products are pricey.

Source: Christina Passariello, "Louis Vuitton Tries Modern Methods on Factory Lines," *Wall Street Journal* (October 9, 2006).

 What are some of the steps that this company has taken in order to ensure that production meets demand? (See page 937.)

Organizational Structure

Most companies prepare **organization charts** to show the interrelationships of activities and the delegation of authority and responsibility within the company. Illustration 19-2 shows a typical organization chart.

Stockholders own the corporation, but they manage it indirectly through a **board of directors** they elect. The board formulates the operating policies for the company or organization. The board also selects officers, such as a president and one or more vice presidents, to execute policy and to perform daily management functions.

The **chief executive officer (CEO)** has overall responsibility for managing the business. As the organization chart on the next page shows, the CEO delegates responsibilities to other officers.

Responsibilities within the company are frequently classified as either line or staff positions. Employees with **line positions** are directly involved in the company's primary revenue-generating operating activities. Examples of line positions include the vice president of operations, vice president of marketing, plant managers, supervisors, and production personnel. Employees with **staff positions** are involved in activities that support the efforts of the line employees. In a company like General Electric or Facebook, employees in finance, legal, and human resources have staff positions. While activities of staff employees are vital

Illustration 19-2
Corporation's organization chart

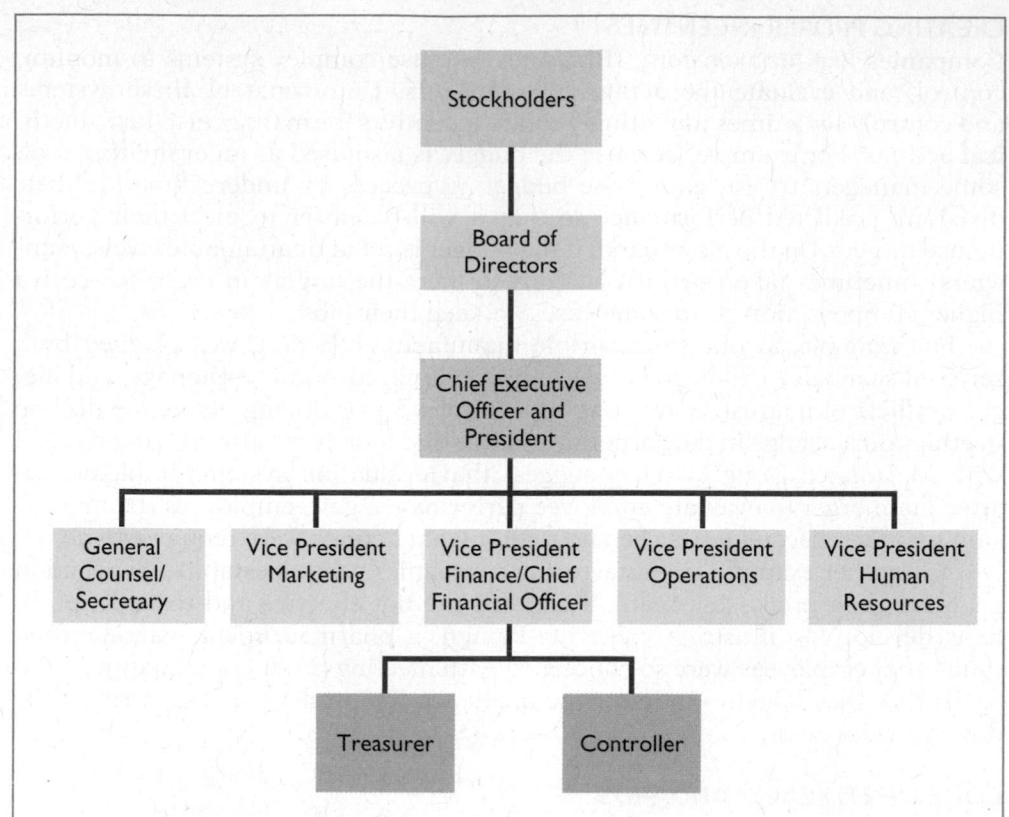

to the company, these employees are nonetheless there to serve the line employees who engage in the company's primary operations.

The **chief financial officer (CFO)** is responsible for all of the accounting and finance issues the company faces. The CFO is supported by the **controller** and the **treasurer**. The controller's responsibilities include (1) maintaining the accounting records, (2) maintaining an adequate system of internal control, and (3) preparing financial statements, tax returns, and internal reports. The treasurer has custody of the corporation's funds and is responsible for maintaining the company's cash position.

Also serving the CFO is the internal audit staff. The staff's responsibilities include reviewing the reliability and integrity of financial information provided by the controller and treasurer. Staff members also ensure that internal control systems are functioning properly to safeguard corporate assets. In addition, they investigate compliance with policies and regulations, and in many companies they determine whether resources are being used in the most economical and efficient fashion.

The vice president of operations oversees employees with line positions. For example, the company might have multiple plant managers, each of whom would report to the vice president of operations. Each plant would also have department managers, such as fabricating, painting, and shipping, each of whom would report to the plant manager.

Business Ethics

All employees within an organization are expected to act ethically in their business activities. Given the importance of ethical behavior to corporations and their owners (stockholders), an increasing number of organizations provide codes of business ethics for their employees.

CREATING PROPER INCENTIVES

Companies like Amazon.com, IBM, and Nike use complex systems to monitor, control, and evaluate the actions of managers. Unfortunately, these systems and controls sometimes unwittingly create incentives for managers to take unethical actions. For example, because the budget is also used as an evaluation tool, some managers try to "game" the budgeting process by underestimating their division's predicted performance so that it will be easier to meet their performance targets. On the other hand, if the budget is set at unattainable levels, managers sometimes take unethical actions to meet the targets in order to receive higher compensation or, in some cases, to keep their jobs.

For example, at one time, airline manufacturer Boeing was plagued by a series of scandals including charges of over-billing, corporate espionage, and illegal conflicts of interest. Some long-time employees of Boeing blame the decline in ethics on a change in the corporate culture that took place after Boeing merged with McDonnell Douglas. They suggest that evaluation systems implemented after the merger to evaluate employee performance gave employees the impression that they needed to succeed no matter what actions were required to do so.

As another example, manufacturing companies need to establish production goals for their processes. Again, if controls are not effective and realistic, problems develop. To illustrate, Schering-Plough, a pharmaceutical manufacturer, found that employees were so concerned with meeting production quantity standards that they failed to monitor the quality of the product, and as a result the dosages were often wrong.

CODE OF ETHICAL STANDARDS

In response to corporate scandals, the U.S. Congress enacted the **Sarbanes-Oxley Act (SOX)** to help prevent lapses in internal control. One result of SOX was to clarify top management's responsibility for the company's financial statements. CEOs and CFOs must now certify that financial statements give a fair presentation of the company's operating results and its financial condition. In addition, top managers must certify that the company maintains an adequate system of internal controls to safeguard the company's assets and ensure accurate financial reports.

Another result of SOX is that companies now pay more attention to the composition of the board of directors. In particular, the audit committee of the board of directors must be comprised entirely of independent members (that is, non-employees) and must contain at least one financial expert. Finally, the law substantially increases the penalties for misconduct.

To provide guidance for managerial accountants, the Institute of Management Accountants (IMA) has developed a code of ethical standards, entitled *IMA Statement of Ethical Professional Practice.* Management accountants should not commit acts in violation of these standards. Nor should they condone such acts by others within their organizations. We include the IMA code of ethical standards in Appendix I. Throughout the remaining chapters, we will address various ethical issues managers face.

> **DO IT!**

Managerial Accounting Concepts

Indicate whether the following statements are true or false.

1. Managerial accountants have a single role within an organization, collecting and reporting costs to management.
2. Financial accounting reports are general-purpose and intended for external users.

3. Managerial accounting reports are special-purpose and issued as frequently as needed.

4. Managers' activities and responsibilities can be classified into three broad functions: cost accounting, budgeting, and internal control.

5. As a result of the Sarbanes-Oxley Act, managerial accounting reports must now comply with generally accepted accounting principles (GAAP).

6. Top managers must certify that a company maintains an adequate system of internal controls.

Action Plan

✔ Understand that managerial accounting is a field of accounting that provides economic and financial information for managers and other internal users.

✔ Understand that financial accounting provides information for external users.

✔ Analyze which users require which different types of information.

Solution

1. False. Managerial accountants determine product costs. In addition, managerial accountants are now held responsible for evaluating how well the company is employing its resources. As a result, when the company makes critical strategic decisions, managerial accountants serve as team members alongside personnel from production, marketing, and engineering.

2. True.

3. True.

4. False. Managers' activities are classified into three broad functions: planning, directing, and controlling. Planning requires managers to look ahead to establish objectives. Directing involves coordinating a company's diverse activities and human resources to produce a smooth-running operation. Controlling keeps the company's activities on track.

5. False. SOX clarifies top management's responsibility for the company's financial statements. In addition, top managers must certify that the company maintains an adequate system of internal control to safeguard the company's assets and ensure accurate financial reports.

6. True.

Related exercise material: **BE19-1, BE19-2, BE19-3, E19-1, and DO IT! 19-1.**

✔ The Navigator

Managerial Cost Concepts

In order for managers at a company like Current Designs to plan, direct, and control operations effectively, they need good information. One very important type of information is related to costs. Managers should ask questions such as the following.

LEARNING OBJECTIVE 3

Define the three classes of manufacturing costs.

1. What costs are involved in making a product or performing a service?

2. If we decrease production volume, will costs decrease?

3. What impact will automation have on total costs?

4. How can we best control costs?

To answer these questions, managers need reliable and relevant cost information. We now explain and illustrate the various cost categories that companies use.

Manufacturing Costs

Manufacturing consists of activities and processes that convert raw materials into finished goods. Contrast this type of operation with merchandising, which sells merchandise in the form in which it is purchased. Manufacturing costs are classified as direct materials, direct labor, and manufacturing overhead.

DIRECT MATERIALS

Direct Materials

To obtain the materials that will be converted into the finished product, the manufacturer purchases raw materials. **Raw materials** are the basic materials and parts used in the manufacturing process.

Raw materials that can be physically and directly associated with the finished product during the manufacturing process are **direct materials**. Examples include flour in the baking of bread, syrup in the bottling of soft drinks, and steel in the making of automobiles. A primary direct material of many Current Designs' kayaks is polyethylene powder. Some of its high-performance kayaks use Kevlar®.

Some raw materials cannot be easily associated with the finished product. These are called indirect materials. **Indirect materials** have one of two characteristics: (1) They do not physically become part of the finished product (such as lubricants used by Current Designs in its equipment and polishing compounds used for the finishing touches on kayaks). Or, (2) they are impractical to trace to the finished product because their physical association with the finished product is too small in terms of cost (such as cotter pins and lock washers). Companies account for indirect materials as part of **manufacturing overhead**.

DIRECT LABOR

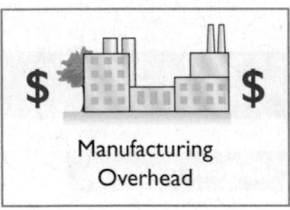

Direct Labor

The work of factory employees that can be physically and directly associated with converting raw materials into finished goods is **direct labor**. Bottlers at Coca-Cola, bakers at Sara Lee, and equipment operators at Current Designs are employees whose activities are usually classified as direct labor. **Indirect labor** refers to the work of factory employees that has no physical association with the finished product, or for which it is impractical to trace costs to the goods produced. Examples include wages of factory maintenance people, factory time-keepers, and factory supervisors. Like indirect materials, companies classify indirect labor as **manufacturing overhead**.

MANUFACTURING OVERHEAD

Manufacturing overhead consists of costs that are indirectly associated with the manufacture of the finished product. Overhead costs include manufacturing costs that cannot be classified as direct materials or direct labor. Manufacturing overhead includes indirect materials, indirect labor, depreciation on factory buildings and machines, and insurance, taxes, and maintenance on factory facilities.

Alternative Terminology
Some companies use terms such as *factory overhead, indirect manufacturing costs,* and *burden* instead of manufacturing overhead.

One study of manufactured goods found the following magnitudes of the three different product costs as a percentage of the total product cost: direct materials 54%, direct labor 13%, and manufacturing overhead 33%. Note that the direct labor component is the smallest. This component of product cost is dropping substantially because of automation. Companies are working hard to increase productivity by decreasing labor. In some companies, direct labor has become as little as 5% of the total cost.

Allocating direct materials and direct labor costs to specific products is fairly straightforward. Good recordkeeping can tell a company how much plastic it used in making each type of gear, or how many hours of factory labor it took to assemble a part. But allocating overhead costs to specific products presents problems. How much of the purchasing agent's salary is attributable to the hundreds of different products made in the same plant? What about the grease that keeps the machines humming, or the computers that make sure paychecks come out on time? Boiled down to its simplest form, the question becomes: Which products cause the incurrence of which costs? In subsequent chapters, we show various methods of allocating overhead to products.

MANAGEMENT INSIGHT

Why Manufacturing Matters for U.S. Workers

Prior to 2010, U.S. manufacturing employment fell at an average rate of 0.1% per year for 60 years. At the same time, U.S. factory output increased by an average rate of 3.4%. As manufacturers relied more heavily on automation, the number of people they needed declined. However, factory jobs are important because the average wage of a factory worker is $22, twice the average wage of employees in the service sector. Fortunately, manufacturing jobs in the United States increased by 1.2% in 2010, and they are forecast to continue to increase through at least 2015. Why? Because companies like Whirlpool, Caterpillar, and Dow are building huge new plants in the United States to replace old, inefficient U.S. facilities. For many products that are ultimately sold in the United States, it makes more sense to produce them domestically and save on the shipping costs. In addition, these efficient new plants, combined with an experienced workforce, will make it possible to compete with manufacturers in other countries, thereby increasing export potential.

Source: Bob Tita, "Whirlpool to Invest in Tennessee Plant," *Wall Street Journal Online* (September 1, 2010); and James R. Hagerty, "U.S. Factories Buck Decline," *Wall Street Journal Online* (January 19, 2011).

? In what ways does the shift to automated factories change the amount and composition of product costs? (See page 937.)

Product versus Period Costs

Each of the manufacturing cost components—direct materials, direct labor, and manufacturing overhead—are product costs. As the term suggests, **product costs** are costs that are a necessary and integral part of producing the finished product. Companies record product costs, when incurred, as inventory. These costs do not become expenses until the company sells the finished goods inventory. At that point, the company records the expense as cost of goods sold.

Period costs are costs that are matched with the revenue of a specific time period rather than included as part of the cost of a salable product. These are non-manufacturing costs. Period costs include selling and administrative expenses. In order to determine net income, companies deduct these costs from revenues in the period in which they are incurred.

Illustration 19-3 summarizes these relationships and cost terms. Our main concern in this chapter is with product costs.

LEARNING OBJECTIVE   4

Distinguish between product and period costs.

Alternative Terminology
Product costs are also called *inventoriable costs.*

Illustration 19-3
Product versus period costs

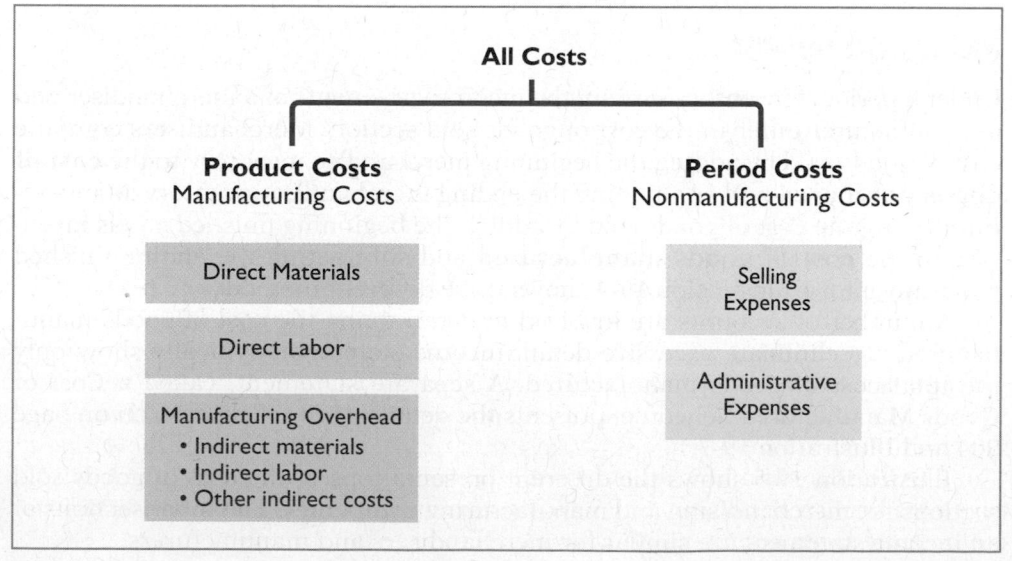

> DO IT!

Managerial Cost Concepts

Action Plan

✔ Classify as direct materials any raw materials that can be physically and directly associated with the finished product.

✔ Classify as direct labor the work of factory employees that can be physically and directly associated with the finished product.

✔ Classify as manufacturing overhead any costs that are indirectly associated with the finished product.

A bicycle company has these costs: tires, salaries of employees who put tires on the wheels, factory building depreciation, lubricants, spokes, salary of factory manager, handlebars, and salaries of factory maintenance employees. Classify each cost as direct materials, direct labor, or manufacturing overhead.

Solution

> Tires, spokes, and handlebars are direct materials. Salaries of employees who put tires on the wheels are direct labor. All of the other costs are manufacturing overhead.

Related exercise material: **BE19-4, BE19-5, BE19-6, BE19-7, E19-2, E19-3, E19-4, E19-5, E19-6, E19-7,** and **DO IT!** **19-2.**

✔ The Navigator

Manufacturing Costs in Financial Statements

LEARNING OBJECTIVE **5**

Explain the difference between a merchandising and a manufacturing income statement.

The financial statements of a manufacturer are similar to those of a merchandiser. For example, you will find many of the same sections and same accounts in the financial statements of Procter & Gamble that you find in the financial statements of Dick's Sporting Goods. The main differences between their financial statements occur in two places: the cost of goods sold section in the income statement and the current assets section in the balance sheet.

Income Statement

Under a periodic inventory system, the income statements of a merchandiser and a manufacturer differ in the cost of goods sold section. Merchandisers compute cost of goods sold by adding the beginning merchandise inventory to the **cost of goods purchased** and subtracting the ending merchandise inventory. Manufacturers compute cost of goods sold by adding the beginning finished goods inventory to the **cost of goods manufactured** and subtracting the ending finished goods inventory. Illustration 19-4 shows these different methods.

A number of accounts are involved in determining the cost of goods manufactured. To eliminate excessive detail, income statements typically show only the total cost of goods manufactured. A separate statement, called a Cost of Goods Manufactured Schedule, presents the details. (See the discussion on page 904 and Illustration 19-7.)

Illustration 19-5 shows the different presentations of the cost of goods sold sections for merchandising and manufacturing companies. The other sections of an income statement are similar for merchandisers and manufacturers.

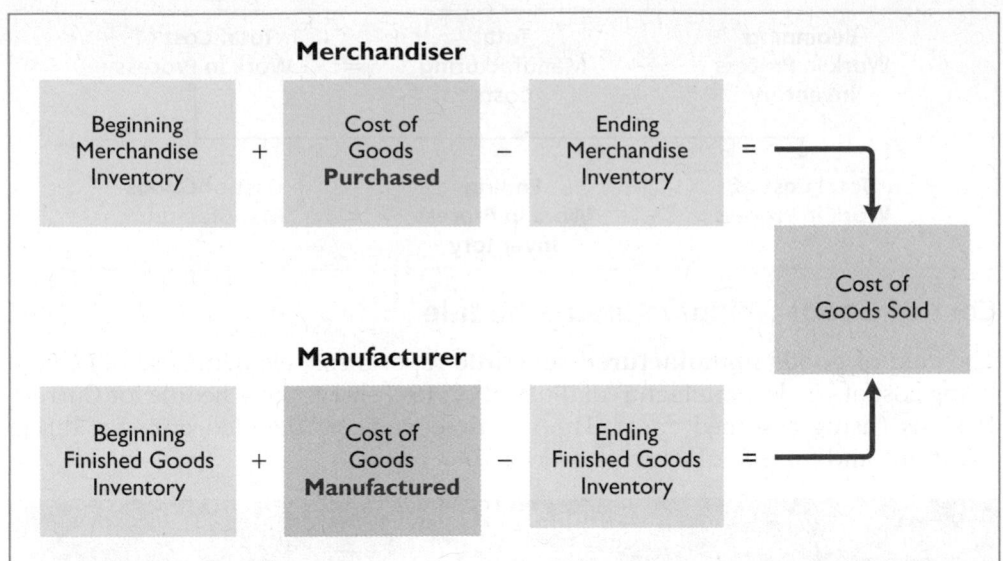

Illustration 19-4
Cost of goods sold components

Helpful Hint We assume a periodic inventory system in this illustration.

Illustration 19-5
Cost of goods sold sections of merchandising and manufacturing income statements

MERCHANDISING COMPANY Income Statement (partial) For the Year Ended December 31, 2014		MANUFACTURING COMPANY Income Statement (partial) For the Year Ended December 31, 2014	
Cost of goods sold		Cost of goods sold	
Merchandise inventory, Jan. 1	$ 70,000	Finished goods inventory, Jan. 1	$ 90,000
Cost of goods purchased	650,000	Cost of goods manufactured (see Illustration 19-7)	370,000
Cost of goods available for sale	720,000	Cost of goods available for sale	460,000
Less: Merchandise inventory, Dec. 31	400,000	Less: Finished goods inventory, Dec. 31	80,000
Cost of goods sold	$ 320,000	Cost of goods sold	$ 380,000

Cost of Goods Manufactured

An example may help show how companies determine the cost of goods manufactured. Assume that on January 1, Current Designs has a number of kayaks in various stages of production. In total, these partially completed units are called **beginning work in process inventory**. The costs the company assigns to beginning work in process inventory are based on the **manufacturing costs incurred in the prior period**.

Current Designs first incurs manufacturing costs in the current year to complete the work that was in process on January 1. It then incurs manufacturing costs for production of new orders. The sum of the direct materials costs, direct labor costs, and manufacturing overhead incurred in the current year is the **total manufacturing costs** for the current period.

We now have two cost amounts: (1) the cost of the beginning work in process and (2) the total manufacturing costs for the current period. The sum of these costs is the **total cost of work in process** for the year.

At the end of the year, Current Designs may have some kayaks that are only partially completed. The costs of these units become the cost of the **ending work in process inventory**. To find the **cost of goods manufactured**, we subtract this cost from the total cost of work in process. Illustration 19-6 (page 904) shows the formula for determining the cost of goods manufactured.

LEARNING OBJECTIVE	6

Indicate how cost of goods manufactured is determined.

Illustration 19-6
Cost of goods manufactured formula

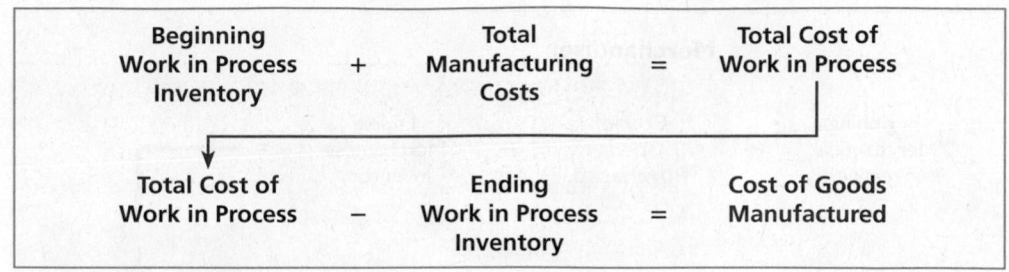

Cost of Goods Manufactured Schedule

The **cost of goods manufactured schedule** reports cost elements used in calculating cost of goods manufactured. Illustration 19-7 shows the schedule for Current Designs (using assumed data). The schedule presents detailed data for direct materials and for manufacturing overhead.

Illustration 19-7
Cost of goods manufactured schedule

CURRENT DESIGNS			
Cost of Goods Manufactured Schedule			
For the Year Ended December 31, 2014			
Work in process, January 1			$ 18,400
Direct materials			
Raw materials inventory, January 1	$ 16,700		
Raw materials purchases	152,500		
Total raw materials available for use	169,200		
Less: Raw materials inventory, December 31	22,800		
Direct materials used		$146,400	
Direct labor		175,600	
Manufacturing overhead			
Indirect labor	14,300		
Factory repairs	12,600		
Factory utilities	10,100		
Factory depreciation	9,440		
Factory insurance	8,360		
Total manufacturing overhead		54,800	
Total manufacturing costs			376,800
Total cost of work in process			395,200
Less: Work in process, December 31			25,200
Cost of goods manufactured			$370,000

Review Illustration 19-6 and then examine the cost of goods manufactured schedule in Illustration 19-7. You should be able to distinguish between "Total manufacturing costs" and "Cost of goods manufactured." The difference is the effect of the change in work in process during the period.

> **DO IT!**

Cost of Goods Manufactured

The following information is available for Keystone Company.

		March 1	March 31
Raw materials inventory		$12,000	$10,000
Work in process inventory		2,500	4,000
Materials purchased in March	$ 90,000		
Direct labor in March	75,000		
Manufacturing overhead in March	220,000		

Prepare the cost of goods manufactured schedule for the month of March.

Action Plan

✔ Start with beginning work in process as the first item in the cost of goods manufactured schedule.

✔ Sum direct materials used, direct labor, and manufacturing overhead to determine total manufacturing costs.

✔ Sum beginning work in process and total manufacturing costs to determine total cost of work in process.

✔ Cost of goods manufactured is the total cost of work in process less ending work in process.

Solution

KEYSTONE COMPANY Cost of Goods Manufactured Schedule For the Month Ended March 31			
Work in process, March 1			$ 2,500
Direct materials			
Raw materials, March 1	$ 12,000		
Raw material purchases	90,000		
Total raw materials available for use	102,000		
Less: Raw materials, March 31	10,000		
Direct materials used		$ 92,000	
Direct labor		75,000	
Manufacturing overhead		220,000	
Total manufacturing costs			387,000
Total cost of work in process			389,500
Less: Work in process, March 31			4,000
Cost of goods manufactured			$385,500

Related exercise material: **BE19-8, BE19-10, BE19-11, E19-8, E19-9, E19-10, E19-11, E19-12, E19-13, E19-14, E19-15, E19-16, E19-17,** and **DO IT!** **19-3.**

✔ **The Navigator**

Balance Sheet

The balance sheet for a merchandising company shows just one category of inventory. In contrast, the balance sheet for a manufacturer may have three inventory accounts, as shown in Illustration 19-8.

LEARNING OBJECTIVE   7

Explain the difference between a merchandising and a manufacturing balance sheet.

Raw Materials Inventory	Work in Process Inventory	Finished Goods Inventory
Shows the cost of raw materials on hand.	Shows the cost applicable to units that have been started into production but are only partially completed.	Shows the cost of completed goods on hand.

Illustration 19-8
Inventory accounts for a manufacturer

Finished Goods Inventory is to a manufacturer what Inventory is to a merchandiser. Each of these classifications represents the goods that the company has available for sale.

The current assets sections presented in Illustration 19-9 (page 906) contrast the presentations of inventories for merchandising and manufacturing companies. Manufacturing companies generally list their inventories in the order of their liquidity—the order in which they are expected to be realized in cash. Thus, finished goods inventory comes first. The remainder of the balance sheet is similar for the two types of companies.

MERCHANDISING COMPANY Balance Sheet December 31, 2014			MANUFACTURING COMPANY Balance Sheet December 31, 2014		
Current assets			Current assets		
Cash		$100,000	Cash		$180,000
Receivables (net)		210,000	Receivables (net)		210,000
Merchandise inventory		**400,000**	**Inventories**		
Prepaid expenses		22,000	**Finished goods**	**$80,000**	
Total current assets		$732,000	**Work in process**	**25,200**	
			Raw materials	**22,800**	128,000
			Prepaid expenses		18,000
			Total current assets		$536,000

Illustration 19-9
Current assets sections of merchandising and manufacturing balance sheets

Each step in the accounting cycle for a merchandiser applies to a manufacturer. For example, prior to preparing financial statements, manufacturers make adjusting entries. The adjusting entries are essentially the same as those of a merchandiser. The closing entries are also similar for manufacturers and merchandisers.

Cost Concepts—A Review

You have learned a number of cost concepts in this chapter. Because many of these concepts are new, we provide here an extended example for review. Suppose you started your own snowboard factory, Terrain Park Boards. Think that's impossible? Burton Snowboards was started by Jake Burton Carpenter, when he was only 23 years old. Jake initially experimented with 100 different prototype designs before settling on a final design. Then Jake, along with two relatives and a friend, started making 50 boards per day in Londonderry, Vermont. Unfortunately, while they made a lot of boards in their first year, they were only able to sell 300 of them. To get by during those early years, Jake taught tennis and tended bar to pay the bills.

Here are some of the costs that your snowboard factory would incur.

1. The materials cost of each snowboard (wood cores, fiberglass, resins, metal screw holes, metal edges, and ink) is $30.
2. The labor costs (for example, to trim and shape each board using jig saws and band saws) are $40.
3. Depreciation on the factory building and equipment (for example, presses, grinding machines, and lacquer machines) used to make the snowboards is $25,000 per year.
4. Property taxes on the factory building (where the snowboards are made) are $6,000 per year.
5. Advertising costs (mostly online and catalogue) are $60,000 per year.
6. Sales commissions related to snowboard sales are $20 per snowboard.
7. Salaries for factory maintenance employees are $45,000 per year.
8. The salary of the plant manager is $70,000.
9. The cost of shipping is $8 per snowboard.

Illustration 19-10 shows how Terrain Park Boards would assign these manufacturing and selling costs to the various categories.

Illustration 19-10
Assignment of costs to cost categories

Terrain Park Boards

	Product Costs			
Cost Item	Direct Materials	Direct Labor	Manufacturing Overhead	Period Costs
1. Material cost ($30 per board)	X			
2. Labor costs ($40 per board)		X		
3. Depreciation on factory equipment ($25,000 per year)			X	
4. Property taxes on factory building ($6,000 per year)			X	
5. Advertising costs ($60,000 per year)				X
6. Sales commissions ($20 per board)				X
7. Maintenance salaries (factory facilities) ($45,000 per year)			X	
8. Salary of plant manager ($70,000 per year)			X	
9. Cost of shipping boards ($8 per board)				X

Remember that total manufacturing costs are the sum of the **product costs—** direct materials, direct labor, and manufacturing overhead. If Terrain Park Boards produces 10,000 snowboards the first year, the total manufacturing costs would be $846,000 as shown in Illustration 19-11.

Illustration 19-11
Computation of total manufacturing costs

Cost Number and Item	Manufacturing Cost
1. Material cost ($30 × 10,000)	$ 300,000
2. Labor cost ($40 × 10,000)	400,000
3. Depreciation on factory equipment	25,000
4. Property taxes on factory building	6,000
7. Maintenance salaries (factory facilities)	45,000
8. Salary of plant manager	70,000
Total manufacturing costs	**$846,000**

Knowing the total manufacturing costs, Terrain Park Boards can compute the manufacturing cost per unit. Assuming 10,000 units, the cost to produce one snowboard is $84.60 ($846,000 ÷ 10,000 units).

In subsequent chapters, we will use extensively the cost concepts discussed in this chapter. So study Illustration 19-10 carefully. If you do not understand any of these classifications, go back and reread the appropriate section in this chapter.

Product Costing for Service Industries

Much of the U.S. economy has shifted toward an emphasis on services. Today, more than 50% of U.S. workers are employed by service companies. Airlines, marketing agencies, cable companies, and governmental agencies are just a few examples of service companies. How do service companies differ from manufacturing companies? One difference is that services are consumed immediately. For example, when a restaurant produces a meal, that meal is not put in inventory, but it is instead consumed immediately. An airline uses special equipment to provide its product, but again, the output of that equipment is consumed immediately by the customer in the form of a flight. And a marketing agency performs services for its clients that are immediately consumed by the customer in the form of a marketing plan. For a manufacturing company, like Boeing, it often has a long lead time before its airplane is used or consumed by the customer.

Ethics Note

Do telecommunications companies have an obligation to provide service to remote or low-user areas for a fee that may be less than the cost of the service?

This chapter's examples used manufacturing companies because accounting for the manufacturing environment requires the use of the broadest range of accounts. That is, the accounts used by service companies represent a subset of those used by manufacturers because service companies are not producing inventory. Neither the restaurant, the airline, or the marketing agency discussed above produces an inventoriable product. However, just like a manufacturer, each needs to keep track of the costs of its services in order to know whether it is generating a profit. A successful restaurateur needs to know the cost of each offering on the menu, an airline needs to know the cost of flight service to each destination, and a marketing agency needs to know the cost to develop a marketing plan. Thus, the techniques shown in this chapter, to accumulate manufacturing costs to determine manufacturing inventory, are equally useful for determining the costs of performing services.

For example, let's consider the costs that Hewlett-Packard (HP) might incur on a consulting engagement. A significant portion of its costs would be salaries of consulting personnel. It might also incur travel costs, materials, software costs, and depreciation charges on equipment used by the employees to provide the consulting service. In the same way that it needs to keep track of the cost of manufacturing its computers and printers, HP needs to know what its costs are on each consulting job. It could prepare a cost of services performed schedule similar to the cost of goods manufactured schedule in Illustration 19-7 (page 904). The structure would be essentially the same as the cost of goods manufactured schedule, but section headings would be reflective of the costs of the particular service organization.

Many of the examples we present in subsequent chapters will be based on service companies. To highlight the relevance of the techniques used in this course for service companies, we have placed a service company icon 👤 next to those items in the text and end-of-chapter materials that relate to nonmanufacturing companies.

SERVICE COMPANY INSIGHT

Low Fares but Decent Profits

During 2008, when other airlines were cutting flight service due to the recession, Allegiant Airlines increased capacity by 21%. Sounds crazy, doesn't it? But it must know something, because while the other airlines were losing money, it was generating profits. Consider also that its average one-way fare is only $83. So how does it make money? As a low-budget airline, it focuses on controlling costs. It purchases used planes for $4 million each rather than new planes for $40 million. It flies out of small towns, so wages are low and competition is nonexistent. It only flies a route if its 150-passenger planes are nearly full (it averages about 90% of capacity). If a route isn't filling up, it quits flying it as often or cancels it altogether. It adjusts its prices weekly. The bottom line is that it knows its costs to the penny. Knowing what your costs are might not be glamorous, but it sure beats losing money.

Source: Susan Carey, "For Allegiant, Getaways Mean Profits," *Wall Street Journal Online* (February 18, 2009).

? What are some of the line items that would appear in the cost of services performed schedule of an airline? (See page 937.)

Managerial Accounting Today

The business environment never stands still. Regulations are always changing, global competition continues to intensify, and technology is a source of constant upheaval. In this rapidly changing world, managerial accounting must continue to innovate in order to provide managers with the information they need.

LEARNING OBJECTIVE 8

Identify trends in managerial accounting.

Focus on the Value Chain

The **value chain** refers to all business processes associated with providing a product or performing a service. Illustration 19-12 depicts the value chain for a manufacturer. Many of the most significant business innovations in recent years have resulted either directly, or indirectly, from a focus on the value chain. For example, so-called **lean manufacturing**, originally pioneered by Japanese automobile manufacturer Toyota but now widely practiced, reviews all business processes in an effort to increase productivity and eliminate waste, all while continually trying to improve quality.

Illustration 19-12
A manufacturer's value chain

| Research & development and product design | Acquisition of raw materials | Production | Sales and marketing | Delivery | Customer relations and subsequent services |

Ethics Note

Does just-in-time inventory justify "just-in-time" employees obtained through the temporary employment services?

Just-in-time (JIT) inventory methods, which have significantly lowered inventory levels and costs for many companies, are one innovation that resulted from the focus on the value chain. Under the JIT inventory method, goods are manufactured or purchased just in time for sale. For example, Dell can deliver a computer within 48 hours of a customer's custom order. However, JIT also necessitates increased emphasis on product quality. Because JIT companies do not have excess inventory on hand, they cannot afford to stop production because of defects or machine breakdowns. If they have to stop production, deliveries will be delayed and customers will be unhappy. For example, a recent design flaw in an Intel computer chip was estimated to cost the company $1 billion in repairs and reduced revenue. As a consequence, many companies now focus on **total quality management (TQM)** to reduce defects in finished products, with the goal of zero defects. The TQM philosophy has been employed by some of the most successful businesses to improve all aspects of the value chain.

Another innovation, the **theory of constraints**, involves identification of "bottlenecks"—constraints within the value chain that limit a company's profitability. Once a major constraint has been identified and eliminated, the company moves on to fix the next most significant constraint. General Motors found that by eliminating bottlenecks, it improved its use of overtime labor while meeting customer demand. An application of the theory of constraints is presented in Chapter 26.

Technology has played a big role in the focus on the value chain and the implementation of lean manufacturing. For example, **enterprise resource planning (ERP) systems**, such as those provided by SAP, provide a comprehensive, centralized, integrated source of information to manage all major business processes—from purchasing, to manufacturing, to sales, to human resources. ERP systems have, in some large companies, replaced as many as 200 individual software packages. In addition, the focus on improving efficiency in the value chain has also resulted in adoption of automated manufacturing processes. Many companies now use computer-integrated manufacturing. These systems often reduce the reliance on manual labor by using robotic equipment. This increases overhead costs as a percentage of total product costs.

As overhead costs increased because of factory automation, the accuracy of overhead cost allocation to specific products became more important. Managerial accounting devised an approach, called **activity-based costing (ABC)**, which allocates overhead based on each product's use of particular activities in making the product. In addition to providing more accurate product costing, ABC also can contribute to increased efficiency in the value chain. For example, suppose one of a company's overhead pools is allocated based on the number of setups that each product requires. If a particular product's cost is high because it is allocated a lot of overhead due to a high number of setups, management will be motivated to try to reduce the number of setups and thus reduce its overhead allocation. ABC is discussed further in Chapter 21.

Balanced Scorecard

As companies implement various business practice innovations, managers sometimes focus too enthusiastically on the latest innovation, to the detriment of other areas of the business. For example, by focusing on total quality management, companies sometimes lose sight of cost/benefit considerations. Similarly, in focusing on reducing inventory levels through just-in-time inventory methods, companies sometimes lose sales due to inventory shortages. The **balanced scorecard** corrects for this limited perspective: This approach uses both financial and nonfinancial measures to evaluate all aspects of a company's operations in an integrated fashion. The performance measures are linked in a cause-and-effect fashion to ensure that they all tie to the company's overall objectives. For example, to increase return on assets, the company could try to increase sales. To increase sales, the company could try to increase customer satisfaction. To increase customer satisfaction, the company could try to reduce product defects. Finally, to reduce product defects, the company could increase employee training. The balanced scorecard, which is discussed further in Chapter 25, is now used by many companies, including Hilton Hotels, Wal-Mart Stores, Inc., and HP.

Corporate Social Responsibility

The balanced scorecard attempts to take a broader, more inclusive view of corporate profitability measures. Many companies, however, have begun to evaluate not just corporate profitability but also **corporate social responsibility**. In addition to profitability, corporate social responsibility considers a company's efforts to employ sustainable business practices with regard to its employees and the environment. This is sometimes referred to as the **triple bottom line** because it evaluates a company's performance with regard to **people, planet, and profit**. Make no mistake, these companies are still striving to maximize profits—in a competitive world, they won't survive long if they don't. In fact, you might recognize a few of the names on the Forbes.com list of the 100 most sustainable companies in the world. Ever hear of General Electric, adidas, Toyota, Coca-Cola, or Starbucks? These companies have learned that with a long-term, sustainable approach, they can maximize profits while also acting in the best interest of their employees, their communities, and the environment.

> DO IT!

Trends in Managerial Accounting

Match the descriptions that follow with the corresponding terms.

Descriptions:

1. _____ All activities associated with providing a product or performing a service.
2. _____ A method of allocating overhead based on each product's use of activities in making the product.
3. _____ Systems implemented to reduce defects in finished products with the goal of achieving zero defects.
4. _____ A performance-measurement approach that uses both financial and nonfinancial measures, tied to company objectives, to evaluate a company's operations in an integrated fashion.
5. _____ Inventory system in which goods are manufactured or purchased just as they are needed for use.

Terms:

a. Activity-based costing
b. Balanced scorecard
c. Just-in-time (JIT) inventory
d. Total quality management (TQM)
e. Value chain

Action Plan

✔ Develop a forward-looking view, in order to advise and provide information to various members of the organization.

✔ Understand current business trends and issues.

Solution

1. e   2. a   3. d   4. b   5. c

Related exercise material: **E19-18 and DO IT! 19-4.**

 The Navigator

> ## Comprehensive DO IT! 1

Giant Bike Co. Ltd. produces many different models of bicycles. Assume that the market has responded enthusiastically to a new model, the Jaguar. As a result, the company has established a separate manufacturing facility to produce these bicycles. The company produces 1,000 bicycles per month. Giant's monthly manufacturing costs and other data are as follows.

1. Rent on manufacturing equipment (lease cost)	$2,000/month
2. Insurance on manufacturing building	$750/month
3. Raw materials (frames, tires, etc.)	$80/bicycle
4. Utility costs for manufacturing facility	$1,000/month
5. Supplies for administrative office	$800/month
6. Wages for assembly line workers in manufacturing facility	$30/bicycle
7. Depreciation on office equipment	$650/month
8. Miscellaneous manufacturing materials (lubricants, solders, etc.)	$1.20/bicycle
9. Property taxes on manufacturing building	$2,400/year
10. Manufacturing supervisor's salary	$3,000/month
11. Advertising for bicycles	$30,000/year
12. Sales commissions	$10/bicycle
13. Depreciation on manufacturing building	$1,500/month

Instructions

(a) Prepare an answer sheet with the following column headings.

	Product Costs			
Cost Item	Direct Materials	Direct Labor	Manufacturing Overhead	Period Costs

Enter each cost item on your answer sheet, placing an "X" mark under the appropriate headings.

(b) Compute total manufacturing costs for the month.

Solution to Comprehensive DO IT! 1

Action Plan

✔ Classify as direct materials any raw materials that can be physically and directly associated with the finished product.

✔ Classify as direct labor the work of factory employees that can be physically and directly associated with the finished product.

✔ Classify as manufacturing overhead any costs that are indirectly associated with the finished product.

✔ Classify as period costs those costs that are matched with revenue of a specific time period rather than as part of the cost of a salable product.

(a)

	Product Costs			
Cost Item	Direct Materials	Direct Labor	Manufacturing Overhead	Period Costs
1. Rent on manufacturing equipment ($2,000/month)			X	
2. Insurance on manufacturing building ($750/month)			X	
3. Raw materials ($80/bicycle)	X			
4. Manufacturing utilities ($1,000/month)			X	
5. Office supplies ($800/month)				X
6. Wages for assembly workers ($30/bicycle)		X		
7. Depreciation on office equipment ($650/month)				X
8. Miscellaneous manufacturing materials ($1.20/bicycle)			X	
9. Property taxes on manufacturing building ($2,400/year)			X	

Cost Item	Product Costs			Period Costs
	Direct Materials	Direct Labor	Manufacturing Overhead	
10. Manufacturing supervisor's salary ($3,000/month)			X	
11. Advertising cost ($30,000/year)				X
12. Sales commissions ($10/bicycle)				X
13. Depreciation on manufacturing building ($1,500/month)			X	

(b) Cost Item	Manufacturing Cost
Rent on manufacturing equipment	$ 2,000
Insurance on manufacturing building	750
Raw materials ($80 × 1,000)	80,000
Manufacturing utilities	1,000
Labor ($30 × 1,000)	30,000
Miscellaneous materials ($1.20 × 1,000)	1,200
Property taxes on manufacturing building ($2,400 ÷ 12)	200
Manufacturing supervisor's salary	3,000
Depreciation on manufacturing building	1,500
Total manufacturing costs	$119,650

✔ **The Navigator**

> ## Comprehensive DO IT! 2

Superior Company has the following cost and expense data for the year ending December 31, 2014.

Raw materials, 1/1/14	$ 30,000	Insurance, factory	$ 14,000
Raw materials, 12/31/14	20,000	Property taxes, factory building	6,000
Raw materials purchases	205,000	Sales revenue	1,500,000
Indirect materials	15,000	Delivery expenses	100,000
Work in process, 1/1/14	80,000	Sales commissions	150,000
Work in process, 12/31/14	50,000	Indirect labor	90,000
Finished goods, 1/1/14	110,000	Factory machinery rent	40,000
Finished goods, 12/31/14	120,000	Factory utilities	65,000
Direct labor	350,000	Depreciation, factory building	24,000
Factory manager's salary	35,000	Administrative expenses	300,000

Instructions
(a) Prepare a cost of goods manufactured schedule for Superior Company for 2014.
(b) Prepare an income statement for Superior Company for 2014.
(c) Assume that Superior Company's accounting records show the balances of the following current asset accounts: Cash $17,000, Accounts Receivable (net) $120,000, Prepaid Expenses $13,000, and Debt Investments (short-term) $26,000. Prepare the current assets section of the balance sheet for Superior Company as of December 31, 2014.

Solution to Comprehensive DO IT! **2**

(a)

SUPERIOR COMPANY
Cost of Goods Manufactured Schedule
For the Year Ended December 31, 2014

Work in process, 1/1			$ 80,000
Direct materials			
Raw materials inventory, 1/1	$ 30,000		
Raw materials purchases	205,000		
Total raw materials available for use	235,000		
Less: Raw materials inventory, 12/31	20,000		
Direct materials used		$215,000	
Direct labor		350,000	
Manufacturing overhead			
Indirect labor	90,000		
Factory utilities	65,000		
Factory machinery rent	40,000		
Factory manager's salary	35,000		
Depreciation, factory building	24,000		
Indirect materials	15,000		
Insurance, factory	14,000		
Property taxes, factory building	6,000		
Total manufacturing overhead		289,000	
Total manufacturing costs			854,000
Total cost of work in process			934,000
Less: Work in process, 12/31			50,000
Cost of goods manufactured			$ 884,000

(b)

SUPERIOR COMPANY
Income Statement
For the Year Ended December 31, 2014

Sales revenue		$1,500,000
Cost of goods sold		
Finished goods inventory, January 1	$110,000	
Cost of goods manufactured	884,000	
Cost of goods available for sale	994,000	
Less: Finished goods inventory,		
December 31	120,000	
Cost of goods sold		874,000
Gross profit		626,000
Operating expenses		
Administrative expenses	300,000	
Sales commissions	150,000	
Delivery expenses	100,000	
Total operating expenses		550,000
Net income		$ 76,000

(c)

SUPERIOR COMPANY Balance Sheet (partial) December 31, 2014		
Current assets		
Cash		$ 17,000
Debt investments (short-term)		26,000
Accounts receivable (net)		120,000
Inventories		
Finished goods	$120,000	
Work in process	50,000	
Raw materials	20,000	190,000
Prepaid expenses		13,000
Total current assets		$366,000

✔ The Navigator

SUMMARY OF LEARNING OBJECTIVES

✔ The Navigator

1 Explain the distinguishing features of managerial accounting. The primary users of managerial accounting reports are internal users, who are officers, department heads, managers, and supervisors in the company. Managerial accounting issues internal reports as frequently as the need arises. The purpose of these reports is to provide special-purpose information for a particular user for a specific decision. The content of managerial accounting reports pertains to subunits of the business, may be very detailed, and may extend beyond the double-entry accounting system. The reporting standard is relevance to the decision being made. No independent audits are required in managerial accounting.

2 Identify the three broad functions of management. The three functions are planning, directing, and controlling. Planning requires management to look ahead and to establish objectives. Directing involves coordinating the diverse activities and human resources of a company to produce a smooth-running operation. Controlling is the process of keeping the activities on track.

3 Define the three classes of manufacturing costs. Manufacturing costs are typically classified as either (1) direct materials, (2) direct labor, or (3) manufacturing overhead. Raw materials that can be physically and directly associated with the finished product during the manufacturing process are called direct materials. The work of factory employees that can be physically and directly associated with converting raw materials into finished goods is considered direct labor. Manufacturing overhead consists of costs that are indirectly associated with the manufacture of the finished product.

4 Distinguish between product and period costs. Product costs are costs that are a necessary and integral part of producing the finished product. Product costs are also called inventoriable costs. Under the expense recognition principle, these costs do not become expenses until the company sells the finished goods inventory. Period costs are costs that are identified with a specific time period rather than with a salable product. These costs relate to nonmanufacturing costs and therefore are not inventoriable costs.

5 Explain the difference between a merchandising and a manufacturing income statement. The difference between a merchandising and a manufacturing income statement is in the cost of goods sold section. A manufacturing cost of goods sold section shows beginning and ending finished goods inventories and the cost of goods manufactured.

6 Indicate how cost of goods manufactured is determined. Companies add the cost of the beginning work in process to the total manufacturing costs for the current year to arrive at the total cost of work in process for the year. They then subtract the ending work in process from the total cost of work in process to arrive at the cost of goods manufactured.

7 Explain the difference between a merchandising and a manufacturing balance sheet. The difference between a merchandising and a manufacturing balance sheet is in the current assets section. The current assets section of a manufacturing company's balance sheet presents three inventory accounts: finished goods inventory, work in process inventory, and raw materials inventory.

8 Identify trends in managerial accounting. Managerial accounting has experienced many changes in recent years. Improved practices include a focus on managing the value chain through techniques such as just-in-time inventory, total quality management, activity-based costing, and theory of constraints. The balanced scorecard is now used by many companies in order to attain a more comprehensive view of the company's operations. Finally, companies are now evaluating their performance with regard to their corporate social responsibility.

GLOSSARY

Activity-based costing (ABC) A method of allocating overhead based on each product's use of activities in making the product. (p. 910).

Balanced scorecard A performance-measurement approach that uses both financial and nonfinancial measures, tied to company objectives, to evaluate a company's operations in an integrated fashion. (p. 910).

Board of directors The group of officials elected by the stockholders of a corporation to formulate operating policies and select the officers who manage the company. (p. 896).

Chief executive officer (CEO) Corporate officer who has overall responsibility for managing the business and delegates responsibilities to other corporate officers. (p. 896).

Chief financial officer (CFO) Corporate officer who is responsible for all of the accounting and finance issues of the company. (p. 897).

Controller Financial officer responsible for a company's accounting records, system of internal control, and preparation of financial statements, tax returns, and internal reports. (p. 897).

Corporate social responsibility The efforts of a company to employ sustainable business practices with regard to its employees and the environment. (p. 911).

Cost of goods manufactured Total cost of work in process less the cost of the ending work in process inventory. (p. 903).

Direct labor The work of factory employees that can be physically and directly associated with converting raw materials into finished goods. (p. 900).

Direct materials Raw materials that can be physically and directly associated with manufacturing the finished product. (p. 900).

Enterprise resource planning (ERP) system Software that provides a comprehensive, centralized, integrated source of information used to manage all major business processes. (p. 910).

Indirect labor Work of factory employees that has no physical association with the finished product, or for which it is impractical to trace the costs to the goods produced. (p. 900).

Indirect materials Raw materials that do not physically become part of the finished product or for which it is

impractical to trace to the finished product because their physical association with the finished product is too small. (p. 900).

Just-in-time (JIT) inventory Inventory system in which goods are manufactured or purchased just in time for sale. (p. 910).

Line positions Jobs that are directly involved in a company's primary revenue-generating operating activities. (p. 896).

Managerial accounting A field of accounting that provides economic and financial information for managers and other internal users. (p. 894).

Manufacturing overhead Manufacturing costs that are indirectly associated with the manufacture of the finished product. (p. 900).

Period costs Costs that are matched with the revenue of a specific time period and charged to expense as incurred. (p. 901).

Product costs Costs that are a necessary and integral part of producing the finished product. (p. 901).

Sarbanes-Oxley Act (SOX) Law passed by Congress intended to reduce unethical corporate behavior. (p. 898).

Staff positions Jobs that support the efforts of line employees. (p. 896).

Theory of constraints A specific approach used to identify and manage constraints in order to achieve the company's goals. (p. 910).

Total cost of work in process Cost of the beginning work in process plus total manufacturing costs for the current period. (p. 903).

Total manufacturing costs The sum of direct materials, direct labor, and manufacturing overhead incurred in the current period. (p. 903).

Total quality management (TQM) Systems implemented to reduce defects in finished products with the goal of achieving zero defects. (p. 910).

Treasurer Financial officer responsible for custody of a company's funds and for maintaining its cash position. (p. 897).

Triple bottom line The evaluation of a company's social responsibility performance with regard to people, planet, and profit. (p. 911).

Value chain All business processes associated with providing a product or performing a service. (p. 909).

 Self-Test, Brief Exercises, Exercises, Problem Set A, and many more resources are available for practice in *WileyPLUS*.

SELF-TEST QUESTIONS

Answers are on page 937.

(LO 1) **1.** Managerial accounting:
(a) is governed by generally accepted accounting principles.
(b) places emphasis on special-purpose information.
(c) pertains to the entity as a whole and is highly aggregated.
(d) is limited to cost data.

(LO 2) **2.** The management of an organization performs several broad functions. They are:
(a) planning, directing, and selling.
(b) planning, directing, and controlling.
(c) planning, manufacturing, and controlling.
(d) directing, manufacturing, and controlling.

(LO 2) **3.** After passage of the Sarbanes-Oxley Act:
(a) reports prepared by managerial accountants must by audited by CPAs.
(b) CEOs and CFOs must certify that financial statements give a fair presentation of the company's operating results.
(c) the audit committee, rather than top management, is responsible for the company's financial statements.
(d) reports prepared by managerial accountants must comply with generally accepted accounting principles (GAAP).

(LO 3) **4.** Direct materials are a:

	Product Cost	Manufacturing Overhead	Period Cost
(a)	Yes	Yes	No
(b)	Yes	No	No
(c)	Yes	Yes	Yes
(d)	No	No	No

(LO 3) **5.** Which of the following costs would a computer manufacturer include in manufacturing overhead?
(a) The cost of the disk drives.
(b) The wages earned by computer assemblers.
(c) The cost of the memory chips.
(d) Depreciation on testing equipment.

(LO 3) **6.** Which of the following is **not** an element of manufacturing overhead?
(a) Sales manager's salary.
(b) Plant manager's salary.
(c) Factory repairman's wages.
(d) Product inspector's salary.

(LO 4) **7.** Indirect labor is a:
(a) nonmanufacturing cost.
(b) raw material cost.
(c) product cost.
(d) period cost.

(LO 4) **8.** Which of the following costs are classified as a period cost?
(a) Wages paid to a factory custodian.
(b) Wages paid to a production department supervisor.
(c) Wages paid to a cost accounting department supervisor.
(d) Wages paid to an assembly worker.

(LO 5) **9.** For the year, Redder Company has cost of goods manufactured of $600,000, beginning finished goods inventory of $200,000, and ending finished goods inventory of $250,000. The cost of goods sold is:
(a) $450,000.   (c) $550,000.
(b) $500,000.   (d) $600,000.

(LO 5) **10.** Cost of goods available for sale is a step in the calculation of cost of goods sold of:
(a) a merchandising company but not a manufacturing company.
(b) a manufacturing company but not a merchandising company.
(c) a merchandising company and a manufacturing company.
(d) neither a manufacturing company nor a merchandising company.

(LO 6) **11.** A cost of goods manufactured schedule shows beginning and ending inventories for:
(a) raw materials and work in process only.
(b) work in process only.
(c) raw materials only.
(d) raw materials, work in process, and finished goods.

(LO 6) **12.** The formula to determine the cost of goods manufactured is:
(a) Beginning raw materials inventory + Total manufacturing costs − Ending work in process inventory.
(b) Beginning work in process inventory + Total manufacturing costs − Ending finished goods inventory.
(c) Beginning finished good inventory + Total manufacturing costs − Ending finished goods inventory.
(d) Beginning work in process inventory + Total manufacturing costs − Ending work in process inventory.

(LO 7) **13.** A manufacturer may report three inventories on its balance sheet: (1) raw materials, (2) work in process, and (3) finished goods. Indicate in what sequence these inventories generally appear on a balance sheet.
(a) (1), (2), (3)
(b) (2), (3), (1)
(c) (3), (1), (2)
(d) (3), (2), (1)

(LO 8) **14.** Which of the following managerial accounting techniques attempts to allocate manufacturing overhead in a more meaningful fashion?
  (a) Just-in-time inventory.
  (b) Total quality management.
  (c) Balanced scorecard.
  (d) Activity-based costing.

(LO 8) **15.** Corporate social responsibility refers to:
  (a) the practice by management of reviewing all business processes in an effort to increase productivity and eliminate waste.

  (b) an approach used to allocate overhead based on each product's use of activities.
  (c) the attempt by management to identify and eliminate constraints within the value chain.
  (d) efforts by companies to employ sustainable business practices with regard to employees and the environment.

Go to the book's companion website, www.wiley.com/college/weygandt, for additional Self-Test Questions.

 ✔ The Navigator

QUESTIONS

1. (a) "Managerial accounting is a field of accounting that provides economic information for all interested parties." Do you agree? Explain.
   (b) Joe Delong believes that managerial accounting serves only manufacturing firms. Is Joe correct? Explain.
2. Distinguish between managerial and financial accounting as to (a) primary users of reports, (b) types and frequency of reports, and (c) purpose of reports.
3. How do the content of reports and the verification of reports differ between managerial and financial accounting?
4. In what ways can the budgeting process create incentives for unethical behavior?
5. Linda Olsen is studying for the next accounting midterm examination. Summarize for Linda what she should know about management functions.
6. "Decision-making is management's most important function." Do you agree? Why or why not?
7. Explain the primary difference between line positions and staff positions, and give examples of each.
8. What new rules were enacted under the Sarbanes-Oxley Act to address unethical accounting practices?
9. Tony Andres is studying for his next accounting examination. Explain to Tony what he should know about the differences between the income statements for a manufacturing and for a merchandising company.
10. Jerry Lang is unclear as to the difference between the balance sheets of a merchandising company and a manufacturing company. Explain the difference to Jerry.
11. How are manufacturing costs classified?
12. Mel Finney claims that the distinction between direct and indirect materials is based entirely on physical association with the product. Is Mel correct? Why?
13. Tina Burke is confused about the differences between a product cost and a period cost. Explain the differences to Tina.

14. Identify the differences in the cost of goods sold section of an income statement between a merchandising company and a manufacturing company.
15. The determination of the cost of goods manufactured involves the following factors: (A) beginning work in process inventory, (B) total manufacturing costs, and (C) ending work in process inventory. Identify the meaning of x in the following formulas:
   (a) $A + B = x$ (b) $A + B - C = x$
16. Sealy Company has beginning raw materials inventory $12,000, ending raw materials inventory $15,000, and raw materials purchases $170,000. What is the cost of direct materials used?
17. Tate Inc. has beginning work in process $26,000, direct materials used $240,000, direct labor $220,000, total manufacturing overhead $180,000, and ending work in process $32,000. What are the total manufacturing costs?
18. Using the data in Question 17, what are (a) the total cost of work in process and (b) the cost of goods manufactured?
19. In what order should manufacturing inventories be listed in a balance sheet?
20. How does the output of manufacturing operations differ from that of service operations?
21. Discuss whether the product costing techniques discussed in this chapter apply equally well to manufacturers and service companies.
22. What is the value chain? Describe, in sequence, the main components of a manufacturer's value chain.
23. What is an enterprise resource planning (ERP) system? What are its primary benefits?
24. Why is product quality important for companies that implement a just-in-time inventory system?
25. Explain what is meant by "balanced" in the balanced scorecard approach.
26. What is activity-based costing, and what are its potential benefits?

BRIEF EXERCISES

BE19-1 Complete the following comparison table between managerial and financial accounting.

Distinguish between managerial and financial accounting.
(LO 1)

	Financial Accounting	Managerial Accounting
Primary users of reports		
Types of reports		
Frequency of reports		
Purpose of reports		
Content of reports		
Verification process		

BE19-2 The Sarbanes-Oxley Act (SOX) has important implications for the financial community. Explain two implications of SOX.

Identify important regulatory changes.
(LO 2)

BE19-3 Listed below are the three functions of the management of an organization.

Identify the three management functions.
(LO 2)

1. Planning   2. Directing   3. Controlling

Identify which of the following statements best describes each of the above functions.

(a) _____ requires management to look ahead and to establish objectives. A key objective of management is to add value to the business.

(b) _____ involves coordinating the diverse activities and human resources of a company to produce a smooth-running operation. This function relates to the implementation of planned objectives.

(c) _____ is the process of keeping the activities on track. Management must determine whether goals are being met and what changes are necessary when there are deviations.

BE19-4 Determine whether each of the following costs should be classified as direct materials (DM), direct labor (DL), or manufacturing overhead (MO).

Classify manufacturing costs.
(LO 3)

(a) _____ Frames and tires used in manufacturing bicycles.
(b) _____ Wages paid to production workers.
(c) _____ Insurance on factory equipment and machinery.
(d) _____ Depreciation on factory equipment.

BE19-5 Indicate whether each of the following costs of an automobile manufacturer would be classified as direct materials, direct labor, or manufacturing overhead.

Classify manufacturing costs.
(LO 3)

(a) _____ Windshield.
(b) _____ Engine.
(c) _____ Wages of assembly line worker.
(d) _____ Depreciation of factory machinery.
(e) _____ Factory machinery lubricants.
(f) _____ Tires.
(g) _____ Steering wheel.
(h) _____ Salary of painting supervisor.

BE19-6 Identify whether each of the following costs should be classified as product costs or period costs.

Identify product and period costs.
(LO 4)

(a) _____ Manufacturing overhead.
(b) _____ Selling expenses.
(c) _____ Administrative expenses.
(d) _____ Advertising expenses.
(e) _____ Direct labor.
(f) _____ Direct material.

BE19-7 Presented below are Dieker Company's monthly manufacturing cost data related to its personal computer products.

Classify manufacturing costs.
(LO 3)

(a) Utilities for manufacturing equipment $116,000
(b) Raw material (CPU, chips, etc.) $ 85,000
(c) Depreciation on manufacturing building $880,000
(d) Wages for production workers $191,000

Enter each cost item in the following table, placing an "X" under the appropriate headings.

	Product Costs		
	Direct Materials	Direct Labor	Factory Overhead
(a)			
(b)			
(c)			
(d)			

Compute total manufacturing costs and total cost of work in process.
(LO 6)

BE19-8 Francum Company has the following data: direct labor $209,000, direct materials used $180,000, total manufacturing overhead $208,000, and beginning work in process $25,000. Compute (a) total manufacturing costs and (b) total cost of work in process.

Prepare current assets section
(LO 7)

BE19-9 In alphabetical order below are current asset items for Ruiz Company's balance sheet at December 31, 2014. Prepare the current assets section (including a complete heading).

Accounts receivable	$200,000
Cash	62,000
Finished goods	91,000
Prepaid expenses	38,000
Raw materials	73,000
Work in process	87,000

Determine missing amounts in computing total manufacturing costs.
(LO 6)

BE19-10 Presented below are incomplete manufacturing cost data. Determine the missing amounts for three different situations.

	Direct Materials Used	Direct Labor Used	Factory Overhead	Total Manufacturing Costs
(a)	$40,000	$61,000	$ 50,000	?
(b)	?	$75,000	$140,000	$296,000
(c)	$55,000	?	$111,000	$310,000

Determine missing amounts in computing cost of goods manufactured.
(LO 6)

BE19-11 Use the same data from BE19–10 above and the data below. Determine the missing amounts.

	Total Manufacturing Costs	Work in Process (1/1)	Work in Process (12/31)	Cost of Goods Manufactured
(a)	?	$120,000	$82,000	?
(b)	$296,000	?	$98,000	$321,000
(c)	$310,000	$463,000	?	$715,000

> DO IT! Review

Identify managerial accounting concepts.
(LO 1, 2)

DO IT! 19-1 Indicate whether the following statements are true or false.

1. Managerial accountants explain and report manufacturing and nonmanufacturing costs, determine cost behaviors, and perform cost-volume-profit analysis, but are not involved in the budget process.

2. Financial accounting reports pertain to subunits of the business and are very detailed.

3. Managerial accounting reports must follow GAAP and are audited by CPAs.

4. Managers' activities and responsibilities can be classified into three broad functions: planning, directing, and controlling.

5. As a result of the Sarbanes-Oxley Act (SOX), top managers must certify that the company maintains an adequate system of internal control.

6. Management accountants follow a code of ethics developed by the Institute of Management Accountants.

Identify managerial cost concepts.
(LO 3, 4)

DO IT! 19-2 A music company has these costs:

Advertising	Paper inserts for CD cases
Blank CDs	CD plastic cases
Depreciation of CD image burner	Salaries of sales representatives
	Salaries of factory maintenance employees
Salary of factory manager	Salaries of employees who burn music onto CDs
Factory supplies used	

Classify each cost as a period or a product cost. Within the product cost category, indicate if the cost is part of direct materials (DM), direct labor (DL), or manufacturing overhead (MO).

DO IT! 19-3 The following information is available for Fishel Company.

Prepare cost of goods manufactured schedule.

(LO 6)

	April 1	April 30
Raw materials inventory	$10,000	$14,000
Work in process inventory	5,000	3,500

Materials purchased in April	$ 98,000
Direct labor in April	80,000
Manufacturing overhead in April	180,000

Prepare the cost of goods manufactured schedule for the month of April.

DO IT! 19-4 Match the descriptions that follow with the corresponding terms.

Identify trends in managerial accounting.

(LO 8)

Descriptions:

1. _____ Inventory system in which goods are manufactured or purchased just as they are needed for sale.

2. _____ A method of allocating overhead based on each product's use of activities in making the product.

3. _____ Systems that are especially important to firms adopting just-in-time inventory methods.

4. _____ One part of the value chain for a manufacturing company.

5. _____ The U.S. economy is trending toward this.

6. _____ A performance-measurement approach that uses both financial and nonfinancial measures, tied to company objectives, to evaluate a company's operations in an integrated fashion.

Terms:

(a) Activity-based costing
(b) Balanced scorecard
(c) Total quality management (TQM)
(d) Research and development, and product design
(e) Service industries
(f) Just-in-time (JIT) inventory

EXERCISES

E19-1 Richard Larkin has prepared the following list of statements about managerial accounting and financial accounting.

Identify distinguishing features of managerial accounting.

(LO 1)

1. Financial accounting focuses on providing information to internal users.
2. Analyzing cost-volume-profit relationships is part of managerial accounting.
3. Preparation of budgets is part of financial accounting.
4. Managerial accounting applies only to merchandising and manufacturing companies.
5. Both managerial accounting and financial accounting deal with many of the same economic events.
6. Managerial accounting reports are prepared only quarterly and annually.
7. Financial accounting reports are general-purpose reports.
8. Managerial accounting reports pertain to subunits of the business.
9. Managerial accounting reports must comply with generally accepted accounting principles.
10. Although managerial accountants are expected to behave ethically, there is no code of ethical standards for managerial accountants.

Instructions
Identify each statement as true or false. If false, indicate how to correct the statement.

E19-2 Presented below and on the next page is a list of costs and expenses usually incurred by Barnum Corporation, a manufacturer of furniture, in its factory.

Classify costs into three classes of manufacturing costs.

(LO 3)

1. Salaries for assembly line inspectors.
2. Insurance on factory machines.

3. Property taxes on the factory building.
4. Factory repairs.
5. Upholstery used in manufacturing furniture.
6. Wages paid to assembly line workers.
7. Factory machinery depreciation.
8. Glue, nails, paint, and other small parts used in production.
9. Factory supervisors' salaries.
10. Wood used in manufacturing furniture.

Instructions

Classify the above items into the following categories: (a) direct materials, (b) direct labor, and (c) manufacturing overhead.

Identify types of cost and explain their accounting.
(LO 3, 4)

E19-3 Ryan Corporation incurred the following costs while manufacturing its product.

Materials used in product	$100,000	Advertising expense	$45,000
Depreciation on plant	60,000	Property taxes on plant	14,000
Property taxes on store	7,500	Delivery expense	21,000
Labor costs of assembly-line workers	110,000	Sales commissions	35,000
Factory supplies used	13,000	Salaries paid to sales clerks	50,000

Instructions

(a) Identify each of the above costs as direct materials, direct labor, manufacturing overhead, or period costs.
(b) Explain the basic difference in accounting for product costs and period costs.

Determine the total amount of various types of costs.
(LO 3, 4)

E19-4 Knight Company reports the following costs and expenses in May.

Factory utilities	$ 15,500	Direct labor	$69,100
Depreciation on factory equipment	12,650	Sales salaries	46,400
Depreciation on delivery trucks	3,800	Property taxes on factory building	2,500
Indirect factory labor	48,900	Repairs to office equipment	1,300
Indirect materials	80,800	Factory repairs	2,000
Direct materials used	137,600	Advertising	15,000
Factory manager's salary	8,000	Office supplies used	2,640

Instructions

From the information, determine the total amount of:

(a) Manufacturing overhead.
(b) Product costs.
(c) Period costs.

Classify various costs into different cost categories.
(LO 3, 4)

E19-5 Ikerd Company is a manufacturer of personal computers. Various costs and expenses associated with its operations are as follows.

1. Property taxes on the factory building.
2. Production superintendents' salaries.
3. Memory boards and chips used in assembling computers.
4. Depreciation on the factory equipment.
5. Salaries for assembly-line quality control inspectors.
6. Sales commissions paid to sell personal computers.
7. Electrical components used in assembling computers.
8. Wages of workers assembling personal computers.
9. Soldering materials used on factory assembly lines.
10. Salaries for the night security guards for the factory building.

The company intends to classify these costs and expenses into the following categories: (a) direct materials, (b) direct labor, (c) manufacturing overhead, and (d) period costs.

Instructions

List the items (1) through (10). For each item, indicate the cost category to which it belongs.

Classify various costs into different cost categories.
(LO 3)

E19-6 The administrators of Crawford County's Memorial Hospital are interested in identifying the various costs and expenses that are incurred in producing a patient's X-ray. A list of such costs and expenses is as follows.

1. Salaries for the X-ray machine technicians.
2. Wages for the hospital janitorial personnel.
3. Film costs for the X-ray machines.

4. Property taxes on the hospital building.
5. Salary of the X-ray technicians' supervisor.
6. Electricity costs for the X-ray department.
7. Maintenance and repairs on the X-ray machines.
8. X-ray department supplies.
9. Depreciation on the X-ray department equipment.
10. Depreciation on the hospital building.

The administrators want these costs and expenses classified as: (a) direct materials, (b) direct labor, or (c) service overhead.

Instructions
List the items (1) through (10). For each item, indicate the cost category to which the item belongs.

E19-7 Kwik Delivery Service reports the following costs and expenses in June 2014.

Classify various costs into different cost categories.

(LO 4)

Indirect materials	$ 5,400	Drivers' salaries	$16,000
Depreciation on delivery equipment	11,200	Advertising	3,600
Dispatcher's salary	5,000	Delivery equipment repairs	300
Property taxes on office building	870	Office supplies	650
CEO's salary	12,000	Office utilities	990
Gas and oil for delivery trucks	2,200	Repairs on office equipment	180

Instructions
Determine the total amount of (a) delivery service (product) costs and (b) period costs.

E19-8 Lopez Corporation incurred the following costs while manufacturing its product.

Compute cost of goods manufactured and sold.

(LO 5, 6)

Materials used in product	$120,000	Advertising expense	$45,000
Depreciation on plant	60,000	Property taxes on plant	14,000
Property taxes on store	7,500	Delivery expense	21,000
Labor costs of assembly-line		Sales commissions	35,000
workers	110,000	Salaries paid to sales	
Factory supplies used	23,000	clerks	50,000

Work in process inventory was $12,000 at January 1 and $15,500 at December 31. Finished goods inventory was $60,000 at January 1 and $45,600 at December 31.

Instructions
(a) Compute cost of goods manufactured.
(b) Compute cost of goods sold.

E19-9 An incomplete cost of goods manufactured schedule is presented below.

Determine missing amounts in cost of goods manufactured schedule.

(LO 6)

MOLINA COMPANY
Cost of Goods Manufactured Schedule
For the Year Ended December 31, 2014

Work in process (1/1)		$210,000
Direct materials		
Raw materials inventory (1/1)	$?	
Add: Raw materials purchases	158,000	
Total raw materials available for use	?	
Less: Raw materials inventory (12/31)	22,500	
Direct materials used		$190,000
Direct labor		?
Manufacturing overhead		
Indirect labor	18,000	
Factory depreciation	36,000	
Factory utilities	68,000	
Total overhead		122,000
Total manufacturing costs		?
Total cost of work in process		?
Less: Work in process (12/31)		81,000
Cost of goods manufactured		$530,000

Instructions
Complete the cost of goods manufactured schedule for Molina Company.

Determine the missing amount of different cost items.
(LO 6)

E19-10 Manufacturing cost data for Copa Company are presented below.

	Case A	Case B	Case C
Direct materials used	$ (a)	$68,400	$130,000
Direct labor	57,000	86,000	(g)
Manufacturing overhead	46,500	81,600	102,000
Total manufacturing costs	195,650	(d)	253,700
Work in process 1/1/14	(b)	16,500	(h)
Total cost of work in process	221,500	(e)	337,000
Work in process 12/31/14	(c)	11,000	70,000
Cost of goods manufactured	185,275	(f)	(i)

Instructions
Indicate the missing amount for each letter (a) through (i).

Determine the missing amount of different cost items, and prepare a condensed cost of goods manufactured schedule.
(LO 6)

E19-11 Incomplete manufacturing cost data for Colaw Company for 2014 are presented as follows for four different situations.

	Direct Materials Used	Direct Labor Used	Manufac-turing Overhead	Total Manufac-turing Costs	Work in Process 1/1	Work in Process 12/31	Cost of Goods Manufac-tured
(1)	$127,000	$140,000	$ 87,000	$ (a)	$33,000	$ (b)	$360,000
(2)	(c)	200,000	132,000	450,000	(d)	40,000	470,000
(3)	80,000	100,000	(e)	255,000	60,000	80,000	(f)
(4)	70,000	(g)	75,000	288,000	45,000	(h)	270,000

Instructions
(a) Indicate the missing amount for each letter.
(b) Prepare a condensed cost of goods manufactured schedule for situation (1) for the year ended December 31, 2014.

Prepare a cost of goods manufactured schedule and a partial income statement.
(LO 5, 6)

E19-12 Cepeda Corporation has the following cost records for June 2014.

Indirect factory labor	$ 4,500	Factory utilities	$ 400
Direct materials used	20,000	Depreciation, factory equipment	1,400
Work in process, 6/1/14	3,000	Direct labor	40,000
Work in process, 6/30/14	3,800	Maintenance, factory equipment	1,800
Finished goods, 6/1/14	5,000	Indirect materials	2,200
Finished goods, 6/30/14	7,500	Factory manager's salary	3,000

Instructions
(a) Prepare a cost of goods manufactured schedule for June 2014.
(b) Prepare an income statement through gross profit for June 2014 assuming sales revenue is $92,100.

Classify various costs into different categories and prepare cost of services performed schedule.
(LO 4, 5, 6)

E19-13 Joyce Tombert, the bookkeeper for Marks Consulting, a political consulting firm, has recently completed a managerial accounting course at her local college. One of the topics covered in the course was the cost of goods manufactured schedule. Joyce wondered if such a schedule could be prepared for her firm. She realized that, as a service-oriented company, it would have no work in process inventory to consider.

Listed below are the costs her firm incurred for the month ended August 31, 2014.

Supplies used on consulting contracts	$ 1,200
Supplies used in the administrative offices	1,500
Depreciation on equipment used for contract work	900
Depreciation used on administrative office equipment	1,050
Salaries of professionals working on contracts	15,600
Salaries of administrative office personnel	7,700
Janitorial services for professional offices	400
Janitorial services for administrative offices	500
Insurance on contract operations	800
Insurance on administrative operations	900
Utilities for contract operations	1,400
Utilities for administrative offices	1,300

Instructions
(a) Prepare a schedule of cost of contract services performed (similar to a cost of goods manufactured schedule) for the month.
(b) For those costs not included in (a), explain how they would be classified and reported in the financial statements.

E19-14 The following information is available for Aikman Company.

Prepare a cost of goods manufactured schedule and a partial income statement.
(LO 5, 6, 7)

	January 1, 2014	2014	December 31, 2014
Raw materials inventory	$21,000		$30,000
Work in process inventory	13,500		17,200
Finished goods inventory	27,000		21,000
Materials purchased		$150,000	
Direct labor		220,000	
Manufacturing overhead		180,000	
Sales revenue		910,000	

Instructions
(a) Compute cost of goods manufactured.
(b) Prepare an income statement through gross profit.
(c) Show the presentation of the ending inventories on the December 31, 2014, balance sheet.
(d) How would the income statement and balance sheet of a merchandising company be different from Aikman's financial statements?

E19-15 Chambers Company produces blankets. From its accounting records, it prepares the following schedule and financial statements on a yearly basis.

Indicate in which schedule or financial statement(s) different cost items will appear.
(LO 5, 6, 7)

(a) Cost of goods manufactured schedule.
(b) Income statement.
(c) Balance sheet.

The following items are found in its ledger and accompanying data.

1. Direct labor
2. Raw materials inventory, 1/1
3. Work in process inventory, 12/31
4. Finished goods inventory, 1/1
5. Indirect labor
6. Depreciation on factory machinery
7. Work in process, 1/1
8. Finished goods inventory, 12/31
9. Factory maintenance salaries
10. Cost of goods manufactured
11. Depreciation on delivery equipment
12. Cost of goods available for sale
13. Direct materials used
14. Heat and electricity for factory
15. Repairs to roof of factory building
16. Cost of raw materials purchases

Instructions
List the items (1)–(16). For each item, indicate by using the appropriate letter or letters, the schedule and/or financial statement(s) in which the item will appear.

E19-16 An analysis of the accounts of Roberts Company reveals the following manufacturing cost data for the month ended June 30, 2014.

Prepare a cost of goods manufactured schedule, and present the ending inventories on the balance sheet.
(LO 6, 7)

Inventories	Beginning	Ending
Raw materials	$9,000	$13,100
Work in process	5,000	7,000
Finished goods	9,000	8,000

Costs incurred: raw materials purchases $54,000, direct labor $47,000, manufacturing overhead $19,900. The specific overhead costs were: indirect labor $5,500, factory insurance $4,000, machinery depreciation $4,000, machinery repairs $1,800, factory utilities $3,100, miscellaneous factory costs $1,500. Assume that all raw materials used were direct materials.

Determine the amount of cost to appear in various accounts, and indicate in which financial statements these accounts would appear.

(LO 5, 6, 7)

Instructions

(a) Prepare the cost of goods manufactured schedule for the month ended June 30, 2014.

(b) Show the presentation of the ending inventories on the June 30, 2014, balance sheet.

E19-17 Buhler Motor Company manufactures automobiles. During September 2014, the company purchased 5,000 head lamps at a cost of $10 per lamp. Buhler withdrew 4,650 lamps from the warehouse during the month. Fifty of these lamps were used to replace the head lamps in autos used by traveling sales staff. The remaining 4,600 lamps were put in autos manufactured during the month.

Of the autos put into production during September 2014, 90% were completed and transferred to the company's storage lot. Of the cars completed during the month, 70% were sold by September 30.

Instructions

(a) Determine the cost of head lamps that would appear in each of the following accounts at September 30, 2014: Raw Materials, Work in Process, Finished Goods, Cost of Goods Sold, and Selling Expenses.

(b) ▬▬▬ Write a short memo to the chief accountant, indicating whether and where each of the accounts in (a) would appear on the income statement or on the balance sheet at September 30, 2014.

Identify various managerial accounting practices.

(LO 8)

E19-18 The following is a list of terms related to managerial accounting practices.

1. Activity-based costing.

2. Just-in-time inventory.

3. Balanced scorecard.

4. Value chain.

Instructions

Match each of the terms with the statement below that best describes the term.

(a) _____ A performance-measurement technique that attempts to consider and evaluate all aspects of performance using financial and nonfinancial measures in an integrated fashion.

(b) _____ The group of activities associated with providing a product or performing a service.

(c) _____ An approach used to reduce the cost associated with handling and holding inventory by reducing the amount of inventory on hand.

(d) _____ A method used to allocate overhead to products based on each product's use of the activities that cause the incurrence of the overhead cost.

EXERCISES: SET B AND CHALLENGE EXERCISES

Visit the book's companion website, at **www.wiley.com/college/weygandt**, and choose the Student Companion site to access Exercise Set B and Challenge Exercises.

PROBLEMS: SET A

Classify manufacturing costs into different categories and compute the unit cost.

(LO 3, 4)

P19-1A Lott Company specializes in manufacturing a unique model of bicycle helmet. The model is well accepted by consumers, and the company has enough orders to keep the factory production at 10,000 helmets per month (80% of its full capacity). Lott's monthly manufacturing cost and other expense data are as follows.

Rent on factory equipment	$ 9,000
Insurance on factory building	1,500
Raw materials (plastics, polystyrene, etc.)	75,000
Utility costs for factory	900
Supplies for general office	300
Wages for assembly line workers	53,000

Depreciation on office equipment	$ 800
Miscellaneous materials (glue, thread, etc.)	1,100
Factory manager's salary	5,700
Property taxes on factory building	400
Advertising for helmets	14,000
Sales commissions	10,000
Depreciation on factory building	1,500

Instructions

(a) Prepare an answer sheet with the following column headings.

Cost Item	Direct Materials	Direct Labor	Manufacturing Overhead	Period Costs

Enter each cost item on your answer sheet, placing the dollar amount under the appropriate headings. Total the dollar amounts in each of the columns.

(b) Compute the cost to produce one helmet.

P19-2A Bell Company, a manufacturer of audio systems, started its production in October 2014. For the preceding 3 years, Bell had been a retailer of audio systems. After a thorough survey of audio system markets, Bell decided to turn its retail store into an audio equipment factory.

Raw materials cost for an audio system will total $74 per unit. Workers on the production lines are on average paid $12 per hour. An audio system usually takes 5 hours to complete. In addition, the rent on the equipment used to assemble audio systems amounts to $4,900 per month. Indirect materials cost $5 per system. A supervisor was hired to oversee production; her monthly salary is $3,000.

Factory janitorial costs are $1,300 monthly. Advertising costs for the audio system will be $9,500 per month. The factory building depreciation expense is $7,800 per year. Property taxes on the factory building will be $9,000 per year.

Classify manufacturing costs into different categories and compute the unit cost.

(LO 3, 4)

Instructions

(a) Prepare an answer sheet with the following column headings.

Cost Item	Direct Materials	Direct Labor	Manufacturing Overhead	Period Costs

(a) DM $111,000
DL $ 90,000
MO $ 18,100
PC $ 9,500

Assuming that Bell manufactures, on average, 1,500 audio systems per month, enter each cost item on your answer sheet, placing the dollar amount per month under the appropriate headings. Total the dollar amounts in each of the columns.

(b) Compute the cost to produce one audio system.

P19-3A Incomplete manufacturing costs, expenses, and selling data for two different cases are as follows.

Indicate the missing amount of different cost items, and prepare a condensed cost of goods manufactured schedule, an income statement, and a partial balance sheet.

(LO 5, 6, 7)

(a) DM $75,000
DL $53,000
MO $20,100
PC $25,100

	Case 1	Case 2
Direct materials used	$ 9,600	$ (g)
Direct labor	5,000	8,000
Manufacturing overhead	8,000	4,000
Total manufacturing costs	(a)	16,000
Beginning work in process inventory	1,000	(h)
Ending work in process inventory	(b)	3,000
Sales revenue	24,500	(i)
Sales discounts	2,500	1,400
Cost of goods manufactured	17,000	22,000
Beginning finished goods inventory	(c)	3,300
Goods available for sale	20,000	(j)
Cost of goods sold	(d)	(k)
Ending finished goods inventory	3,400	2,500
Gross profit	(e)	7,000
Operating expenses	2,500	(l)
Net income	(f)	5,000

Instructions

(a) Indicate the missing amount for each letter.

(b) Prepare a condensed cost of goods manufactured schedule for Case 1.

(c) Prepare an income statement and the current assets section of the balance sheet for Case 1. Assume that in Case 1 the other items in the current assets section are as follows: Cash $4,000, Receivables (net) $15,000, Raw Materials $600, and Prepaid Expenses $400.

(b) Ending WIP $ 6,600
(c) Current assets $30,000

Prepare a cost of goods manufactured schedule, a partial income statement, and a partial balance sheet.

(LO 5, 6, 7)

P19-4A The following data were taken from the records of Clarkson Company for the fiscal year ended June 30, 2014.

Raw Materials		Factory Insurance	$ 4,600
Inventory 7/1/13	$ 48,000	Factory Machinery	
Raw Materials		Depreciation	16,000
Inventory 6/30/14	39,600	Factory Utilities	27,600
Finished Goods		Office Utilities Expense	8,650
Inventory 7/1/13	96,000	Sales Revenue	534,000
Finished Goods		Sales Discounts	4,200
Inventory 6/30/14	75,900	Plant Manager's Salary	58,000
Work in Process		Factory Property Taxes	9,600
Inventory 7/1/13	19,800	Factory Repairs	1,400
Work in Process		Raw Materials Purchases	96,400
Inventory 6/30/14	18,600	Cash	32,000
Direct Labor	139,250		
Indirect Labor	24,460		
Accounts Receivable	27,000		

Instructions

(a) Prepare a cost of goods manufactured schedule. (Assume all raw materials used were direct materials.)

(b) Prepare an income statement through gross profit.

(c) Prepare the current assets section of the balance sheet at June 30, 2014.

(a) CGM $386,910

(b) Gross profit $122,790
(c) Current assets $193,100

Prepare a cost of goods manufactured schedule and a correct income statement.

(LO 5, 6)

P19-5A Phillips Company is a manufacturer of computers. Its controller resigned in October 2014. An inexperienced assistant accountant has prepared the following income statement for the month of October 2014.

PHILLIPS COMPANY
Income Statement
For the Month Ended October 31, 2014

Sales revenue		$780,000
Less: Operating expenses		
Raw materials purchases	$264,000	
Direct labor cost	190,000	
Advertising expense	90,000	
Selling and administrative salaries	75,000	
Rent on factory facilities	60,000	
Depreciation on sales equipment	45,000	
Depreciation on factory equipment	31,000	
Indirect labor cost	28,000	
Utilities expense	12,000	
Insurance expense	8,000	803,000
Net loss		$ (23,000)

Prior to October 2014, the company had been profitable every month. The company's president is concerned about the accuracy of the income statement. As her friend, you have been asked to review the income statement and make necessary corrections. After examining other manufacturing cost data, you have acquired additional information as follows.

1. Inventory balances at the beginning and end of October were:

	October 1	October 31
Raw materials	$18,000	$29,000
Work in process	16,000	14,000
Finished goods	30,000	45,000

2. Only 75% of the utilities expense and 60% of the insurance expense apply to factory operations. The remaining amounts should be charged to selling and administrative activities.

Instructions
(a) Prepare a schedule of cost of goods manufactured for October 2014.
(b) Prepare a correct income statement for October 2014.

(a) CGM $577,800
(b) NI $ 1,000

PROBLEMS: SET B

P19-1B Agler Company specializes in manufacturing motorcycle helmets. The company has enough orders to keep the factory production at 1,000 motorcycle helmets per month. Agler's monthly manufacturing cost and other expense data are shown below.

Classify manufacturing costs into different categories and compute the unit cost.

(LO 3, 4)

Maintenance costs on factory building	$ 1,500
Factory manager's salary	5,500
Advertising for helmets	8,000
Sales commissions	4,000
Depreciation on factory building	700
Rent on factory equipment	6,000
Insurance on factory building	3,000
Raw materials (plastic, polystyrene, etc.)	25,000
Utility costs for factory	800
Supplies for general office	200
Wages for assembly line workers	54,000
Depreciation on office equipment	500
Miscellaneous materials (glue, thread, etc.)	2,000

Instructions
(a) Prepare an answer sheet with the following column headings.

(a) DM $25,000
DL $54,000
MO $19,500
PC $12,700

	Product Costs			
Cost Item	Direct Materials	Direct Labor	Manufacturing Overhead	Period Costs

Enter each cost item on your answer sheet, placing the dollar amount under the appropriate headings. Total the dollar amounts in each of the columns.
(b) Compute the cost to produce one motorcycle helmet.

P19-2B Elliott Company, a manufacturer of tennis rackets, started production in November 2013. For the preceding 5 years, Elliott had been a retailer of sports equipment. After a thorough survey of tennis racket markets, Elliott decided to turn its retail store into a tennis racket factory.

Raw materials cost for a tennis racket will total $23 per racket. Workers on the production lines are paid on average $15 per hour. A racket usually takes 2 hours to complete. In addition, the rent on the equipment used to produce rackets amounts to $1,300 per month. Indirect materials cost $3 per racket. A supervisor was hired to oversee production; her monthly salary is $3,500.

Classify manufacturing costs into different categories and compute the unit cost.

(LO 3, 4)

Janitorial costs are $1,400 monthly. Advertising costs for the rackets will be $8,000 per month. The factory building depreciation expense is $8,400 per year. Property taxes on the factory building will be $9,600 per year.

Instructions

(a) DM $57,500
DL $75,000
MO $15,200
PC $ 8,000

(a) Prepare an answer sheet with the following column headings.

	Product Costs			
Cost Item	**Direct Materials**	**Direct Labor**	**Manufacturing Overhead**	**Period Costs**

Assuming that Elliott manufactures, on average, 2,500 tennis rackets per month, enter each cost item on your answer sheet, placing the dollar amount per month under the appropriate headings. Total the dollar amounts in each of the columns.

(b) Compute the cost to produce one racket.

Indicate the missing amount of different cost items, and prepare a condensed cost of goods manufactured schedule, an income statement, and a partial balance sheet.

(LO 5, 6, 7)

P19-3B Incomplete manufacturing costs, expenses, and selling data for two different cases are as follows.

	Case	
	A	**B**
Direct materials used	$ 6,300	$ (g)
Direct labor	3,000	4,000
Manufacturing overhead	6,000	5,000
Total manufacturing costs	(a)	16,000
Beginning work in process inventory	1,000	(h)
Ending work in process inventory	(b)	2,000
Sales revenue	22,500	(i)
Sales discounts	1,500	1,200
Cost of goods manufactured	15,800	20,000
Beginning finished goods inventory	(c)	5,000
Goods available for sale	18,300	(j)
Cost of goods sold	(d)	(k)
Ending finished goods inventory	1,200	2,500
Gross profit	(e)	6,000
Operating expenses	2,700	(l)
Net income	(f)	2,200

Instructions

(a) Indicate the missing amount for each letter.

(b) Prepare a condensed cost of goods manufactured schedule for Case A.

(b) End. WIP $500
(c) Current assets $15,600

(c) Prepare an income statement and the current assets section of the balance sheet for Case A. Assume that in Case A the other items in the current assets section are as follows: Cash $3,000, Receivables (net) $10,000, Raw Materials $700, and Prepaid Expenses $200.

Prepare a cost of goods manufactured schedule, a partial income statement, and a partial balance sheet.

(LO 5, 6, 7)

P19-4B The following data were taken from the records of Moxie Company for the year ended December 31, 2014.

Raw Materials		Factory Insurance	$ 7,400
Inventory 1/1/14	$ 47,000	Factory Machinery	
Raw Materials		Depreciation	7,700
Inventory 12/31/14	44,200	Factory Utilities	12,900
Finished Goods		Office Utilities Expense	8,600
Inventory 1/1/14	85,000	Sales Revenue	465,000
Finished Goods		Sales Discounts	2,500
Inventory 12/31/14	57,800	Plant Manager's Salary	60,000
Work in Process		Factory Property Taxes	6,100
Inventory 1/1/14	9,500	Factory Repairs	800
Work in Process		Raw Materials Purchases	62,500
Inventory 12/31/14	8,000	Cash	18,000
Direct Labor	145,100		
Indirect Labor	18,100		
Accounts Receivable	27,000		

Instructions
(a) Prepare a cost of goods manufactured schedule. (Assume all raw materials used were direct materials.)
(b) Prepare an income statement through gross profit.
(c) Prepare the current assets section of the balance sheet at December 31.

(a) CGM $324,900

(b) Gross profit $110,400
(c) Current assets $155,000

P19-5B Ortiz Company is a manufacturer of toys. Its controller resigned in August 2014. An inexperienced assistant accountant has prepared the following income statement for the month of August 2014.

Prepare a cost of goods manufactured schedule and a correct income statement.
(LO 5, 6)

ORTIZ COMPANY
Income Statement
For the Month Ended August 31, 2014

Sales revenue		$675,000
Less: Operating expenses		
Raw materials purchases	$220,000	
Direct labor cost	160,000	
Advertising expense	75,000	
Selling and administrative salaries	70,000	
Rent on factory facilities	60,000	
Depreciation on sales equipment	50,000	
Depreciation on factory equipment	35,000	
Indirect labor cost	20,000	
Utilities expense	10,000	
Insurance expense	5,000	705,000
Net loss		$(30,000)

Prior to August 2014, the company had been profitable every month. The company's president is concerned about the accuracy of the income statement. As her friend, you have been asked to review the income statement and make necessary corrections. After examining other manufacturing cost data, you have acquired additional information as follows.

1. Inventory balances at the beginning and end of August were:

	August 1	August 31
Raw materials	$19,500	$35,000
Work in process	25,000	21,000
Finished goods	40,000	52,000

2. Only 60% of the utilities expense and 70% of the insurance expense apply to factory operations; the remaining amounts should be charged to selling and administrative activities.

Instructions
(a) Prepare a cost of goods manufactured schedule for August 2014.
(b) Prepare a correct income statement for August 2014.

(a) CGM $493,000
(b) NL $ (6,500)

PROBLEMS: SET C

Visit the book's companion website, at **www.wiley.com/college/weygandt**, and choose the Student Companion site to access Problem Set C.

WATERWAYS CONTINUING PROBLEM

(*Note:* The Waterways Problem begins in Chapter 19 and continues in the remaining chapters. You can also find this problem at the book's companion website.)
WCP19   Waterways Corporation is a private corporation formed for the purpose of providing the products and the services needed to irrigate farms, parks, commercial projects,

and private lawns. It has a centrally located factory in a U.S. city that manufactures the products it markets to retail outlets across the nation. It also maintains a division that provides installation and warranty servicing in six metropolitan areas.

The mission of Waterways is to manufacture quality parts that can be used for effective irrigation projects that also conserve water. By that effort, the company hopes to satisfy its customers, provide rapid and responsible service, and serve the community and the employees who represent them in each community.

The company has been growing rapidly, so management is considering new ideas to help the company continue its growth and maintain the high quality of its products.

Waterways was founded by Will Winkman, who is the company president and chief executive officer (CEO). Working with him from the company's inception is Will's brother, Ben, whose sprinkler designs and ideas about the installation of proper systems have been a major basis of the company's success. Ben is the vice president who oversees all aspects of design and production in the company.

The factory itself is managed by Todd Senter who hires his line managers to supervise the factory employees. The factory makes all of the parts for the irrigation systems. The purchasing department is managed by Hector Hines.

The installation and training division is overseen by vice president Henry Writer, who supervises the managers of the six local installation operations. Each of these local managers hires his or her own local service people. These service employees are trained by the home office under Henry Writer's direction because of the uniqueness of the company's products.

There is a small human resources department under the direction of Sally Fenton, a vice president who handles the employee paperwork, though hiring is actually performed by the separate departments. Sam Totter is the vice president who heads the sales and marketing area; he oversees 10 well-trained salespeople.

The accounting and finance division of the company is run by Abe Headman, who is the chief financial officer (CFO) and a company vice president. He is a member of the Institute of Management Accountants and holds a certificate in management accounting. He has a small staff of certified public accountants, including a controller and a treasurer, and a staff of accounting input operators who maintain the financial records.

A partial list of Waterways' accounts and their balances for the month of November follows.

Accounts Receivable	$ 290,000
Advertising Expenses	54,000
Cash	260,000
Depreciation—Factory Equipment	16,800
Depreciation—Office Equipment	2,400
Direct Labor	22,000
Factory Supplies Used	16,000
Factory Utilities	10,200
Finished Goods Inventory, November 30	68,800
Finished Goods Inventory, October 31	72,550
Indirect Labor	48,000
Office Supplies Expense	1,600
Other Administrative Expenses	72,000
Prepaid Expenses	42,150
Raw Materials Inventory, November 30	52,700
Raw Materials Inventory, October 31	38,000
Raw Materials Purchases	184,500
Rent—Factory Equipment	47,000
Repairs—Factory Equipment	4,500
Salaries	325,000
Sales Revenue	1,350,000
Sales Commissions	40,500
Work in Process Inventory, October 31	52,900
Work in Process Inventory, November 30	42,000

Instructions

(a) Based on the information given, construct an organizational chart of Waterways Corporation.

(b) A list of accounts and their values are given above. From this information, prepare a cost of goods manufactured schedule, an income statement, and a partial balance sheet for Waterways Corporation for the month of November.

Broadening Your Perspective

Management Decision-Making

Beginning with Chapter 19 and continuing in the remaining chapters, we offer an exercise based on Current Designs, the company that was featured at the beginning of this chapter. We are excited to present managerial accounting situations that are based on the operations of a real company. However, to protect the proprietary nature of this information, the amounts in these exercises are realistic but not necessarily the actual data that would be found in Current Designs' accounting records. We sincerely appreciate the cooperation of the people at Current Designs, particularly Mike Cichanowski, Jim Brown, Diane Buswell, and Jake Greseth, who made these exercises possible.

Decision-Making Problem: Current Designs

BYP19-1 Mike Cichanowski founded Wenonah Canoe and later purchased Current Designs, a company that designs and manufactures kayaks. The kayak-manufacturing facility is located just a few minutes from the canoe company's headquarters in Winona, Minnesota.

Current Designs makes kayaks using two different processes. (See **www.cdkayak.com/ craftsmanship/index.php** for the details of each method.) The rotational molding process uses high temperature to melt polyethylene powder in a closed rotating metal mold to produce a complete kayak hull and deck in a single piece. These kayaks are less labor-intensive and less expensive for the company to produce and sell.

Its other kayaks use the vacuum-bagged composite lamination process (which we will refer to as the composite process). Layers of fiberglass or Kevlar® are carefully placed by hand in a mold and are bonded with resin. Then, a high-pressure vacuum is used to eliminate any excess resin that would otherwise add weight and reduce strength of the finished kayak. These kayaks require a great deal of skilled labor as each boat is individually finished. The exquisite finish of the vacuum-bagged composite kayaks gave rise to Current Designs' tag line, "A work of art, made for life."

Current Designs has the following managers:

Mike Cichanowski, CEO
Diane Buswell, Controller
Deb Welch, Purchasing Manager
Bill Johnson, Sales Manager
Dave Thill, Kayak Plant Manager
Rick Thrune, Production Manager for Composite Kayaks

Instructions

(a) What are the primary information needs of each manager?

(b) Name one special-purpose management accounting report that could be designed for each manager. Include the name of the report, the information it would contain, and how frequently it should be issued.

(c) When Diane Buswell, controller for Current Designs, reviewed the accounting records for a recent period, she noted the following items. Classify each item as a product cost or a period cost. If an item is a product cost, note if it is a direct materials, direct labor, or manufacturing overhead item.

| Payee | Purpose | Product Costs | | | Period Costs |
		Direct Materials	Direct Labor	Manufacturing Overhead	
Winona Agency	Property insurance for the manufacturing plant				
Bill Johnson (sales manager)	Payroll check—payment to sales manager				
Xcel Energy	Electricity for manufacturing plant				
Winona Printing	Price lists for salespeople				
Jim Kaiser (sales representative)	Sales commissions				
Dave Thill (plant manager)	Payroll check—payment to plant manager				
Dana Schultz (kayak assembler)	Payroll check—payment to kayak assembler				
Composite One	Bagging film used when kayaks are assembled; it is discarded after use				
Fastenal	Shop supplies—brooms, paper towels, etc.				
Ravago	Polyethylene powder which is the main ingredient for the rotational molded kayaks				
Winona County	Property taxes on manufacturing plant				
North American Composites	Kevlar® fabric for composite kayaks				
Waste Management	Trash disposal for the company office building				
None	Journal entry to record depreciation of manufacturing equipment				

 ## Decision-Making Across the Organization

BYP19-2 Wendall Company specializes in producing fashion outfits. On July 31, 2014, a tornado touched down at its factory and general office. The inventories in the warehouse and the factory were completely destroyed as was the general office nearby. Next morning, through a careful search of the disaster site, however, Bill Francis, the company's controller, and Elizabeth Walton, the cost accountant, were able to recover a small part of manufacturing cost data for the current month.

"What a horrible experience," sighed Bill "And the worst part is that we may not have enough records to use in filing an insurance claim."

"It was terrible," replied Elizabeth. "However, I managed to recover some of the manufacturing cost data that I was working on yesterday afternoon. The data indicate that our direct labor cost in July totaled $250,000 and that we had purchased $365,000 of raw materials. Also, I recall that the amount of raw materials used for July was $350,000. But I'm not sure this information will help. The rest of our records are blown away."

"Well, not exactly," said Bill. "I was working on the year-to-date income statement when the tornado warning was announced. My recollection is that our sales in July were $1,240,000 and our gross profit ratio has been 40% of sales. Also, I can remember that our cost of goods available for sale was $770,000 for July."

"Maybe we can work something out from this information!" exclaimed Elizabeth. "My experience tells me that our manufacturing overhead is usually 60% of direct labor."

"Hey, look what I just found," cried Elizabeth. "It's a copy of this June's balance sheet, and it shows that our inventories as of June 30 are Finished goods $38,000, Work in process $25,000, and Raw materials $19,000."

"Super," yelled Bill. "Let's go work something out."

In order to file an insurance claim, Wendall Company must determine the amount of its inventories as of July 31, 2014, the date of the tornado touchdown.

Instructions
With the class divided into groups, determine the amount of cost in the Raw Materials, Work in Process, and Finished Goods inventory accounts as of the date of the tornado touchdown.

Managerial Analysis

BYP19-3 Tenrack is a fairly large manufacturing company located in the southern United States. The company manufactures tennis rackets, tennis balls, tennis clothing, and tennis shoes, all bearing the company's distinctive logo, a large green question mark on a white flocked tennis ball. The company's sales have been increasing over the past 10 years.

The tennis racket division has recently implemented several advanced manufacturing techniques. Robot arms hold the tennis rackets in place while glue dries, and machine vision systems check for defects. The engineering and design team uses computerized drafting and testing of new products. The following managers work in the tennis racket division:

Jason Dennis, Sales Manager (supervises all sales representatives)
Peggy Groneman, Technical Specialist (supervises computer programmers)
Dave Marley, Cost Accounting Manager (supervises cost accountants)
Kevin Carson, Production Supervisor (supervises all manufacturing employees)
Sally Renner, Engineer (supervises all new-product design teams)

Instructions
(a) What are the primary information needs of each manager?
(b) Which, if any, financial accounting report(s) is each likely to use?
(c) Name one special-purpose management accounting report that could be designed for each manager. Include the name of the report, the information it would contain, and how frequently it should be issued.

Real-World Focus

BYP19-4 Anchor Glass Container Corporation, the third largest manufacturer of glass containers in the United States, supplies beverage and food producers and consumer products manufacturers nationwide. Parent company Consumers Packaging Inc. (*Toronto Stock Exchange:* CGC) is a leading international designer and manufacturer of glass containers.

The management discussion below appeared in a recent annual report of Anchor Glass.

ANCHOR GLASS CONTAINER CORPORATION
Management Discussion

Cost of Products Sold Cost of products sold as a percentage of net sales was 89.3% in the current year compared to 87.6% in the prior year. The increase in cost of products sold as a percentage of net sales principally reflected the impact of operational problems during the second quarter of the current year at a major furnace at one of the Company's plants, higher downtime, and costs and expenses associated with an increased number of scheduled capital improvement projects, increases in labor, and certain other manufacturing costs (with no corresponding selling price increases in the current year). Reduced fixed costs from the closing of the Streator, Illinois, plant in June of the current year and productivity and efficiency gains partially offset these cost increases.

Instructions
What factors affect the costs of products sold at Anchor Glass Container Corporation?

BYP19-5 The Institute of Management Accountants (IMA) is an organization dedicated to excellence in the practice of management accounting and financial management.

Address: **www.imanet.org**, or go to **www.wiley.com/college/weygandt**

Instructions
At the IMA's home page, locate the answers to the following questions.

(a) How many members does the IMA have, and what are their job titles?
(b) What are some of the benefits of joining the IMA as a student?
(c) Use the chapter locator function to locate the IMA chapter nearest you, and find the name of the chapter president.

Critical Thinking

Communication Activity

BYP19-6 Refer to P19–5A and add the following requirement.

Prepare a letter to the president of the company, Shelly Phillips, describing the changes you made. Explain clearly why net income is different after the changes. Keep the following points in mind as you compose your letter.

1. This is a letter to the president of a company, who is your friend. The style should be generally formal, but you may relax some requirements. For example, you may call the president by her first name.
2. Executives are very busy. Your letter should tell the president your main results first (for example, the amount of net income).
3. You should include brief explanations so that the president can understand the changes you made in the calculations.

Ethics Case

BYP19-7 Steve Morgan, controller for Newton Industries, was reviewing production cost reports for the year. One amount in these reports continued to bother him—advertising. During the year, the company had instituted an expensive advertising campaign to sell some of its slower-moving products. It was still too early to tell whether the advertising campaign was successful.

There had been much internal debate as how to report advertising cost. The vice president of finance argued that advertising costs should be reported as a cost of production, just like direct materials and direct labor. He therefore recommended that this cost be identified as manufacturing overhead and reported as part of inventory costs until sold. Others disagreed. Morgan believed that this cost should be reported as an expense of the current period, so as not to overstate net income. Others argued that it should be reported as prepaid advertising and reported as a current asset.

The president finally had to decide the issue. He argued that these costs should be reported as inventory. His arguments were practical ones. He noted that the company was experiencing financial difficulty and expensing this amount in the current period might jeopardize a planned bond offering. Also, by reporting the advertising costs as inventory rather than as prepaid advertising, less attention would be directed to it by the financial community.

Instructions
(a) Who are the stakeholders in this situation?
(b) What are the ethical issues involved in this situation?
(c) What would you do if you were Steve Morgan?

All About You

BYP19-8 The primary purpose of managerial accounting is to provide information useful for management decisions. Many of the managerial accounting techniques that you learn in this course will be useful for decisions you make in your everyday life.

Instructions
For each of the following managerial accounting techniques, read the definition provided and then provide an example of a personal situation that would benefit from use of this technique.

(a) Break-even point (page 1041).
(b) Budget (page 1076).
(c) Balanced scorecard (page 910).
(d) Capital budgeting (page 1240).

Considering Your Costs and Benefits

BYP19-9 As noted in this chapter, because of global competition, companies have become increasingly focused on reducing costs. To reduce costs and remain competitive, many companies are turning to outsourcing. Outsourcing means hiring an outside supplier to provide elements of a product or service rather than producing them internally.

Suppose you are the managing partner in a CPA firm with 30 full-time staff. Larger firms in your community have begun to outsource basic tax-return preparation work to India. Should you outsource your basic tax-return work to India as well? You estimate that you would have to lay off six staff members if you outsource the work. The basic arguments for and against are as follows.

YES: The wages paid to Indian accountants are very low relative to U.S. wages. You will not be able to compete unless you outsource.

NO: Tax-return data is highly sensitive. Many customers will be upset to learn that their data is being emailed around the world.

Instructions

Write a response indicating your position regarding this situation. Provide support for your view.

Answers to Chapter Questions

Answers to Insight and Accounting Across the Organization Questions

p. 896 Even the Best Have to Get Better Q: What are some of the steps that this company has taken in order to ensure that production meets demand? **A:** The company has organized flexible teams, with jobs arranged by the amount of time a task takes. Employees now are multiskilled, so they can switch between tasks and products. Also, the stores now provide sales data more quickly to the manufacturing facility, so that production levels can be changed more quickly in response to demand.

p. 901 Why Manufacturing Matters for U.S. Workers Q: In what ways does the shift to automated factories change the amount and composition of product costs? **A:** As factories become more automated, they become more efficient, increasing output and decreasing cost per unit. The composition of those costs also switches: Factory labor costs decline, and factory overhead costs (e.g., depreciation and maintenance on equipment) increase.

p. 909 Low Fares but Decent Profits Q: What are some of the line items that would appear in the cost of services performed schedule of an airline? **A:** Some of the line items that would appear in the cost of services performed schedule of an airline would be fuel, flight crew salaries, maintenance wages, depreciation on equipment, airport gate fees, and food-service costs.

Answers to Self-Test Questions

1. b **2.** b **3.** b **4.** b **5.** d **6.** a **7.** c **8.** c **9.** c ($200,000 + $600,000 − $250,000) **10.** c **11.** a **12.** d **13.** d **14.** d **15.** d

✔ **The Navigator**

20 | Job Order Costing

Feature Story

She Succeeds Where Others Have Failed

The financial press is fond of highlighting the fact that, sporting stilettos and leather skirts, Lynn Tilton does not dress like your typical manufacturing executive. Much more important, however, is the fact that her business success is also far from typical. In fact, as the full or partial owner of 74 companies with revenues of more than $8 billion, Tilton is one of the wealthiest female entrepreneurs in the United States. Her company, Patriarch Partners, is sometimes referred to as the largest woman-owned business in America.

Her path to success is an inspiring tale of determination. Tilton started on Wall Street as a single mother, working 15-hour days as she put herself through business school. During years of employment at numerous financial institutions, she developed a knack for analyzing balance sheets and interpreting complex financial information. Eventually, Tilton started her own company, Patriarch Partners, and invested in the debt of a number of distressed companies. She quickly figured out that the only way she was going to make money on those investments was to take control of the companies and try to make them profitable. Thus, seemingly almost by accident, she became the CEO of dozens of failing manufacturing

companies. Amazingly, she was able to make these com profitable when others had given up on them.

As a result of this initial success, Tilton made corporate tu arounds the focus of her company. Once a business is acq she installs a new management team, improves productiv and identifies new products for the company to produce. example, she turned a failed paper mill into a producer of alternative fuels, and saved a helicopter company by iden new customers. When others were fleeing the auto indus she dove in and bought a number of auto-parts companie

While she is a tough negotiator, Tilton also has the resp of her workers. Duane Ludgon, a union negotiator says, "Workers really take to Lynn. She's just human and hon with people. I don't say that about many CEOs." In fact Tilton is a crusader for U.S. manufacturing. She says, "T key to America's future is manufacturing. We simply hav to become a country that can make things again."

Not all of her investments are immediate successes. Her investment in a fire-truck manufacturer, American LaFra was slow to turn a profit. But everyone involved figured was only a matter of time before her persistent approac made this fire-truck maker another business that she sa before it went up in smoke.

 The Navigator

- Scan Learning Objectives
- Read Feature Story
- Read Preview
- Read Text and answer **DO IT!** p. 944
    - p. 952
    - p. 955
    - p. 959
- Work Comprehensive **DO IT!** p. 960
- Review Summary of Learning Objectives
- Answer Self-Test Questions
- Complete Assignments
- Go to *WileyPLUS* for practice and tutorials

Learning Objectives 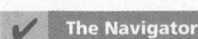 **The Navigator**

After studying this chapter, you should be able to:

[1] Explain the characteristics and purposes of cost accounting.

[2] Describe the flow of costs in a job order cost system.

[3] Explain the nature and importance of a job cost sheet.

[4] Indicate how the predetermined overhead rate is determined and used.

[5] Prepare entries for jobs completed and sold.

[6] Distinguish between under- and overapplied manufacturing overhead.

Watch the **Making a Hollywood Movie** video in WileyPLUS to learn more about job order costing in the real world.

Source: Robert Frank, "Tilton Flaunts Her Style at Patriarch," *Wall Street Journal Online* (January 8, 2011).

Mark Peterson/Redux Pictures

Preview of Chapter 20

 The Navigator

The Feature Story about Patriarch Partners describes the approach Lynn Tilton uses to turn around a failing company. Accurate costing is critical to this process. For example, in order to submit accurate bids on new jobs and to know whether it profited from past jobs, the company needs a good costing system. This chapter illustrates how these costs are assigned to specific jobs, such as the manufacture of individual fire trucks at one of Tilton's companies, American LaFrance. We begin the discussion in this chapter with an overview of the flow of costs in a job order cost accounting system. We then use a case study to explain and illustrate the documents, entries, and accounts in this type of cost accounting system.

The content and organization of Chapter 20 are as follows.

JOB ORDER COSTING

Cost Accounting Systems	Job Order Cost Flow	Reporting Job Cost Data
• Job order cost system • Process cost system	• Accumulating costs • Assigning costs to work in process • Assigning costs to finished goods • Assigning costs to cost of goods sold • Summary of job order cost flows • Job order costing for service companies • Advantages and disadvantages	• Cost of goods manufactured schedule • Income statement presentation • Under- or overapplied manufacturing overhead

Cost Accounting Systems

Cost accounting involves measuring, recording, and reporting product costs. Companies determine both the total cost and the unit cost of each product. The accuracy of the product cost information is critical to the success of the company. Companies use this information to determine which products to produce, what price to charge, and the amounts to produce. Accurate product cost information is also vital for effective evaluation of employee performance.

A **cost accounting system** consists of accounts for the various manufacturing costs. These accounts are fully integrated into the general ledger of a company. An important feature of a cost accounting system is the use of **a perpetual inventory system**. Such a system **provides immediate, up-to-date information on the cost of a product**.

There are two basic types of cost accounting systems: (1) a job order cost system and (2) a process cost system. Although cost accounting systems differ widely from company to company, most involve one of these two traditional product costing systems.

Job Order Cost System

Under a **job order cost system**, the company assigns costs to each **job** or to each **batch** of goods. An example of a job is the manufacture of a mainframe computer by IBM, the production of a movie by Disney, or the making of a fire truck by American LaFrance. An example of a batch is the printing of 225 wedding invitations by a local print shop, or the printing of a weekly issue of *Fortune* magazine by a high-tech printer such as Quad Graphics.

An important feature of job order costing is that each job or batch has its own distinguishing characteristics. For example, each house is custom built, each consulting engagement by a CPA firm is unique, and each printing job is different. **The objective is to compute the cost per job.** At each point in manufacturing a product or performing a service, the company can identify the job and its associated costs. A job order cost system measures costs for each completed job, rather than for set time periods. Illustration 20-1 shows the recording of costs in a job order cost system.

Illustration 20-1
Job order cost system

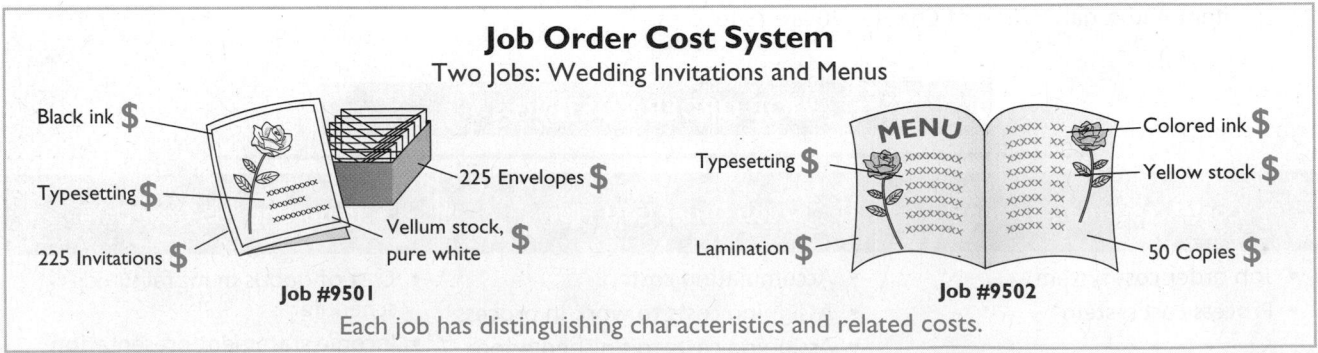

Process Cost System

A company uses a **process cost system** when it manufactures a large volume of similar products. Production is continuous. Examples of a process cost system are the manufacture of cereal by Kellogg, the refining of petroleum by ExxonMobil, and the production of ice cream by Ben & Jerry's. Process costing accumulates product-related costs **for a period of time** (such as a week or a month) instead of assigning costs to specific products or job orders. In process costing, companies assign the costs to departments or processes for the specified period of time. Illustration 20-2 shows examples of the use of a process cost system. We will discuss the process cost system further in Chapter 21.

Illustration 20-2
Process cost system

Process Cost System
Potato Chips Production

| I. Harvest | 2. Clean | 3. Slice | 4. Fry | 5. Bag |

Similar products are produced over a specified time period.

Can a company use both types of cost systems? Yes. For example, General Motors uses process cost accounting for its standard model cars, such as Malibus and Corvettes, and job order cost accounting for a custom-made limousine for the President of the United States.

The objective of both cost accounting systems is to provide unit cost information for product pricing, cost control, inventory valuation, and financial statement presentation.

MANAGEMENT INSIGHT

Jobs Won, Money Lost

Many companies suffer from poor cost accounting. As a result, they sometimes make products they should not be selling at all, or they buy product components that they could more profitably make themselves. Also, inaccurate cost data leads companies to misallocate capital and frustrates efforts by plant managers to improve efficiency.

For example, consider the case of a diversified company in the business of rebuilding diesel locomotives. The managers thought they were making money, but a consulting firm found that the company had seriously underestimated costs. The company bailed out of the business, and not a moment too soon. Says the consultant who advised the company, "The more contracts it won, the more money it lost." Given that situation, a company cannot stay in business very long!

 What type of costs do you think the company had been underestimating? (See page 980.)

© Tony Tremblay/iStockphoto

Job Order Cost Flow

The flow of costs (direct materials, direct labor, and manufacturing overhead) in job order cost accounting parallels the physical flow of the materials as they are converted into finished goods. As shown in Illustration 20-3 (page 942), companies first **accumulate** manufacturing costs in the form of raw materials, factory labor,

LEARNING OBJECTIVE	2
Describe the flow of costs in a job order cost system.	

or manufacturing overhead. They then **assign** manufacturing costs to the Work in Process Inventory account. When a job is completed, the company transfers the cost of the job to Finished Goods Inventory. Later when the goods are sold, the company transfers their cost to Cost of Goods Sold.

Illustration 20-3
Flow of costs in job order costing

Illustration 20-3 provides a basic overview of the flow of costs in a manufacturing setting. A more detailed presentation of the flow of costs is summarized near the end of this chapter in Illustration 20-15. There are two major steps in the flow of costs: (1) **accumulating** the manufacturing costs incurred, and (2) **assigning** the accumulated costs to the work done. The following discussion shows that the company accumulates manufacturing costs incurred by debits to Raw Materials Inventory, Factory Labor, and Manufacturing Overhead. When the company incurs these costs, it does not attempt to associate the costs with specific jobs. The company makes additional entries to assign manufacturing costs incurred. In the remainder of this chapter, we will use a case study to explain how a job order cost system operates.

Accumulating Manufacturing Costs

To illustrate a job order cost system, we will use the January transactions of Wallace Company, which makes custom electronic sensors for corporate safety applications (such as fire and carbon monoxide) and security applications (such as theft and corporate espionage).

RAW MATERIALS COSTS

When Wallace receives the raw materials it has purchased, **it debits the cost of the materials to Raw Materials Inventory**. The company would debit this account for the invoice cost of the raw materials and freight costs chargeable to the purchaser. It would credit the account for purchase discounts taken and purchase returns and allowances. Wallace makes **no effort at this point to associate the cost of materials with specific jobs or orders**.

To illustrate, assume that Wallace purchases 2,000 lithium batteries (Stock No. AA2746) at $5 per unit ($10,000) and 800 electronic modules (Stock No. AA2850) at $40 per unit ($32,000) for a total cost of $42,000 ($10,000 + $32,000). The entry to record this purchase on January 4 is:

	(1)[1]			Raw Materials Inventory
Jan. 4	Raw Materials Inventory	42,000		42,000
	Accounts Payable		42,000	
	(Purchase of raw materials			
	on account)			

At this point, Raw Materials Inventory has a balance of $42,000, as shown in the T-account in the margin. As we will explain later in the chapter, the company subsequently assigns direct raw materials inventory to work in process and indirect raw materials inventory to manufacturing overhead.

FACTORY LABOR COSTS

Some of a company's employees are involved in the manufacturing process, while others are not. As discussed in Chapter 19, wages and salaries of nonmanufacturing employees are expensed as period costs (e.g., Salaries and Wages Expense). Costs related to manufacturing employees are accumulated in Factory Labor to ensure their treatment as product costs. Factory labor consists of three costs: (1) gross earnings of factory workers, (2) employer payroll taxes on these earnings, and (3) fringe benefits (such as sick pay, pensions, and vacation pay) incurred by the employer. **Companies debit labor costs to Factory Labor as they incur those costs.**

To illustrate, assume that Wallace incurs $32,000 of factory labor costs. Of that amount, $27,000 relates to wages payable and $5,000 relates to payroll taxes payable in February. The entry to record factory labor for the month is:

	(2)			Factory Labor
Jan. 31	Factory Labor	32,000		32,000
	Factory Wages Payable		27,000	
	Employer Payroll Taxes Payable		5,000	
	(To record factory labor costs)			

At this point, Factory Labor has a balance of $32,000, as shown in the T-account in the margin. The company subsequently assigns direct factory labor to work in process and indirect factory labor to manufacturing overhead.

MANUFACTURING OVERHEAD COSTS

A company has many types of overhead costs. If these overhead costs, such as property taxes, depreciation, insurance, and repairs, relate to overhead costs of a nonmanufacturing facility, such as an office building, then these costs are expensed as period costs (e.g., Property Tax Expense, Depreciation Expense, Insurance Expense, and Repairs Expense). If the costs relate to the manufacturing process, then they are accumulated in Manufacturing Overhead, to ensure their treatment as product costs.

Using assumed data, the summary entry for manufacturing overhead in Wallace Company is:

	(3)			Manufacturing Overhead
Jan. 31	Manufacturing Overhead	13,800		13,800
	Utilities Payable		4,800	
	Prepaid Insurance		2,000	
	Accounts Payable (for repairs)		2,600	
	Accumulated Depreciation		3,000	
	Property Taxes Payable		1,400	
	(To record overhead costs)			

---

[1]The numbers placed above the entries for Wallace Company are used for reference purposes in the summary provided in Illustration 20-15.

At this point, Manufacturing Overhead has a balance of $13,800, as shown in the T-account in the margin. The company subsequently assigns manufacturing overhead to work in process.

> **DO IT!**

Manufacturing Costs

During the current month, Ringling Company incurs the following manufacturing costs:

(a) Raw material purchases of $4,200 on account.

(b) Incurs factory labor of $18,000. Of that amount, $15,000 relates to wages payable and $3,000 relates to payroll taxes payable.

(c) Factory utilities of $2,200 are payable, prepaid factory insurance of $1,800 has expired, and depreciation on the factory building is $3,500.

Prepare journal entries for each type of manufacturing cost.

Solution

Action Plan

✔ In accumulating manufacturing costs, debit at least one of three accounts: Raw Materials Inventory, Factory Labor, and Manufacturing Overhead.

✔ Manufacturing overhead costs may be recognized daily. Or manufacturing overhead may be recorded periodically through a summary entry.

(a) Raw Materials Inventory	4,200	
Accounts Payable		4,200
(Purchases of raw materials on account)		
(b) Factory Labor	18,000	
Factory Wages Payable		15,000
Employer Payroll Taxes Payable		3,000
(To record factory labor costs)		
(c) Manufacturing Overhead	7,500	
Utilities Payable		2,200
Prepaid Insurance		1,800
Accumulated Depreciation		3,500
(To record overhead costs)		

Related exercise material: **BE20-1, BE20-2, E20-1, E20-7, E20-8, E20-11, and DO IT! 20-1.**

✔ **The Navigator**

Assigning Manufacturing Costs to Work in Process

LEARNING OBJECTIVE 3

Explain the nature and importance of a job cost sheet.

Assigning manufacturing costs to work in process results in the following entries.

1. **Debits** made to Work in Process Inventory.

2. **Credits** made to Raw Materials Inventory, Factory Labor, and Manufacturing Overhead.

An essential accounting record in assigning costs to jobs is a **job cost sheet**, as shown in Illustration 20-4. A **job cost sheet** is a form used to record the costs chargeable to a specific job and to determine the total and unit costs of the completed job.

Companies keep a separate job cost sheet for each job. The job cost sheets constitute the subsidiary ledger for the Work in Process Inventory account. A **subsidiary ledger** consists of individual records for each individual item—in this case, each job. The Work in Process account is referred to as a **control account** because it summarizes the detailed data regarding specific jobs contained in the job cost sheets. **Each entry to Work in Process Inventory must be accompanied by a corresponding posting to one or more job cost sheets.**

Illustration 20-4
Job cost sheet

Job Cost Sheet

Job No. _____   Quantity _____
Item _____   Date Requested _____
For _____   Date Completed _____

Date	Direct Materials	Direct Labor	Manufacturing Overhead

Cost of completed job
   Direct materials $ _____
   Direct labor   _____
   Manufacturing overhead   _____
Total cost $ _____
Unit cost (total dollars ÷ quantity) $ _____

Helpful Hint In today's electronic environment, companies typically maintain job cost sheets as computer files.

RAW MATERIALS COSTS

Companies assign raw materials costs to jobs when their materials store-room issues the materials in response to requests. Requests for issuing raw materials are made on a prenumbered **materials requisition slip**. The materials issued may be used directly on a job, or they may be considered indirect materials. As Illustration 20-5 shows, the requisition should indicate the quantity and type of materials withdrawn and the account to be charged. The company will charge direct materials to Work in Process Inventory, and indirect materials to Manufacturing Overhead.

Helpful Hint Approvals are an important part of a materials requisition slip because they help to establish individual accountability over inventory.

Illustration 20-5
Materials requisition slip

Wallace Company
Materials Requisition Slip

Deliver to: Assembly Department   Req. No.   R247
Charge to: Work in Process–Job No. 101   Date: 1/6/14

Quantity	Description	Stock No.	Cost per Unit	Total
200	Lithium batteries	AA2746	$5.00	$1,000

Requested by _Bruce Howart_   Received by _Herb Crowley_
Approved by _Kap Shin_   Costed by _Heather Remmers_

Helpful Hint Note the specific job to be charged.

Ethics Note
The internal control principle of documentation includes prenumbering to enhance accountability.

The company may use any of the inventory costing methods (FIFO, LIFO, or average-cost) in costing the requisitions **to the individual job cost sheets**.

Periodically, the company journalizes the requisitions. For example, if Wallace uses $24,000 of direct materials and $6,000 of indirect materials in January, the entry is:

(4)

Jan. 31	Work in Process Inventory	24,000	
	Manufacturing Overhead	6,000	
	Raw Materials Inventory		30,000
	(To assign materials to jobs and overhead)		

This entry reduces Raw Materials Inventory by $30,000, increases Work in Process Inventory by $24,000, and increases Manufacturing Overhead by $6,000, as shown below.

Illustration 20-6 shows the posting of requisition slip R247 to Job No. 101 and other assumed postings to the job cost sheets for materials. The requisition slips provide

Illustration 20-6
Job cost sheets–direct materials

Helpful Hint Companies post to control accounts monthly, and post to job cost sheets daily.

Helpful Hint Prove the $24,000 direct materials charge to Work in Process Inventory by totaling the charges by jobs:

101	$12,000
102	7,000
103	5,000
	$24,000

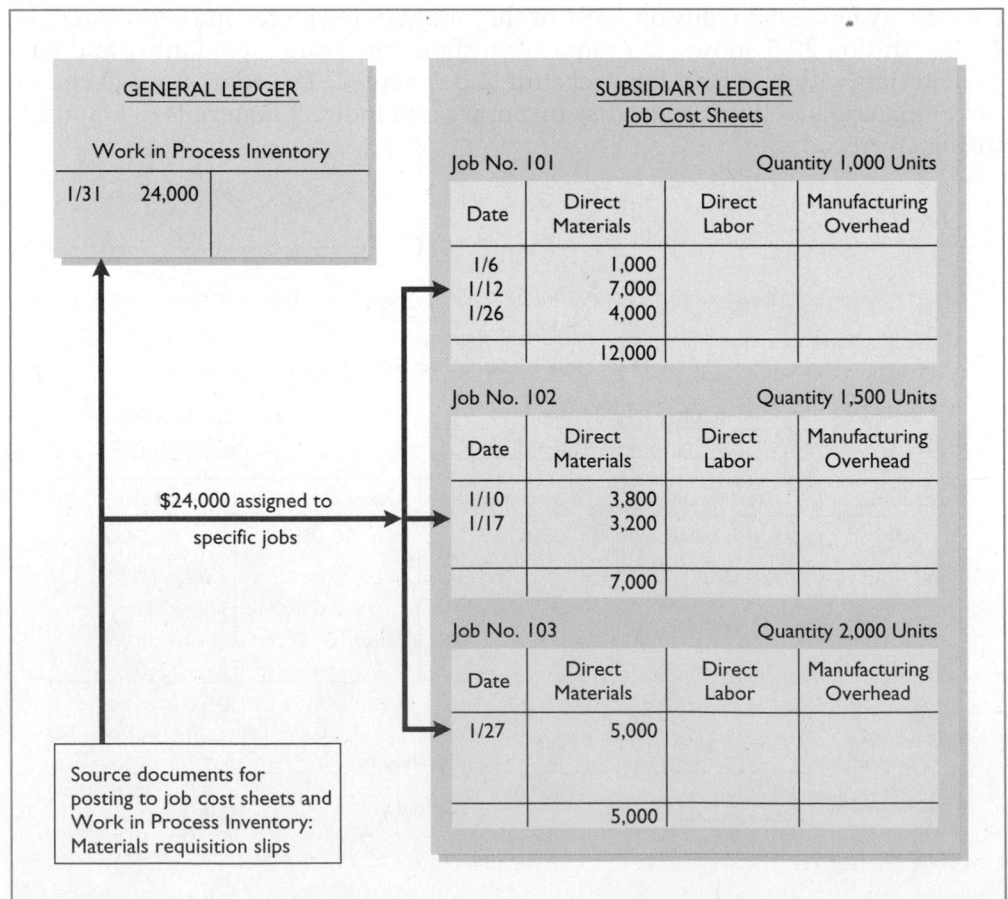

the basis for total direct materials costs of $12,000 for Job No. 101, $7,000 for Job No. 102, and $5,000 for Job No. 103. After the company has completed all postings, the sum of the direct materials columns of the job cost sheets (the subsidiary account amounts of $12,000, $7,000, and $5,000) should equal the direct materials debited to Work in Process Inventory (the control account amount of $24,000).

MANAGEMENT INSIGHT

The Cost of an iPhone? Just Tear One Apart

All companies need to know what it costs to make their own products—but a lot of companies would also like to know the cost of their competitors' products as well. That's where iSuppli steps in. For a price, iSuppli will tear apart sophisticated electronic devices to tell you what it would cost to replicate. In the case of smart-phones, which often have more than 1,000 tiny components, that is no small feat. As shown in the chart below, components of many smart-phones cost about $170. Assembly is only about another $6.50. The difference between what you pay and the "cost" is not all profit. Consider the additional nonproduction costs of research, design, marketing, patent fees, and selling costs.

Sum of the Parts
Cost of components[a], 2009

	Palm Pre	Apple iPhone[b]	Toshiba TG01	Motorola Droid
Integrated circuits	$ 83.96	$ 91.38	$ 68.39	$ 60.83
Display/ touchscreen	38.80	34.65	35.30	35.25
Mechanical[c]	19.63	17.80	21.88	20.23
Camera	7.50	9.35	12.80	14.25
Battery	4.25	5.07	4.71	4.25
Other	16.51	11.82	30.60	44.30
Total	**$170.65**	**$170.07**	**$173.68**	**$179.11**

[a] Latest data available
[b] 3GS 16GB
[c] Includes electromechanical
Source: iSuppli.

Source: "The Business of Dissecting Electronics: The Lowdown on Teardowns," *The Economist.com* (January 21, 2010).

 What type of costs are marketing and selling costs, and how are they treated for accounting purposes? (See page 980.)

FACTORY LABOR COSTS

Companies assign factory labor costs to jobs on the basis of time tickets prepared when the work is performed. The **time ticket** indicates the employee, the hours worked, the account and job to be charged, and the total labor cost. Many companies accumulate these data through the use of bar coding and scanning devices. When they start and end work, employees scan bar codes on their identification badges and bar codes associated with each job they work on. When direct labor is involved, the time ticket must indicate the job number, as shown in Illustration 20-7 (page 948). The employee's supervisor should approve all time tickets.

The time tickets are later sent to the payroll department, which applies the employee's hourly wage rate and computes the total labor cost. Finally, the company journalizes the time tickets. It debits the account Work in Process Inventory

Illustration 20-7
Time ticket

Wallace Company
Time Ticket

Date: _1/6/14_

Employee _____John Nash_____   Employee No. ___124___

Charge to: _____Work in Process_____   Job No. ___101___

Time			Hourly Rate	Total Cost
Start	Stop	Total Hours		
0800	1200	4	10.00	40.00

Approved by _Bob Kadler_   Costed by _M Cher_

for direct labor and debits Manufacturing Overhead for indirect labor. For example, if the $32,000 total factory labor cost consists of $28,000 of direct labor and $4,000 of indirect labor, the entry is:

(5)

Jan. 31	Work in Process Inventory	28,000	
	Manufacturing Overhead	4,000	
	Factory Labor		32,000
	(To assign labor to jobs and overhead)		

As a result of this entry, Factory Labor is reduced by $32,000 so it has a zero balance, and labor costs are assigned to the appropriate manufacturing accounts. The entry increases Work in Process Inventory by $28,000 and increases Manufacturing Overhead by $4,000, as shown below.

Let's assume that the labor costs chargeable to Wallace's three jobs are $15,000, $9,000, and $4,000. Illustration 20-8 shows the Work in Process Inventory and job cost sheets after posting. As in the case of direct materials, the postings to the direct labor columns of the job cost sheets should equal the posting of direct labor to Work in Process Inventory.

LEARNING OBJECTIVE   4

Indicate how the predetermined overhead rate is determined and used.

Manufacturing Overhead Costs

Companies charge the actual costs of direct materials and direct labor to specific jobs. In contrast, manufacturing **overhead** relates to production operations **as a whole**. As a result, overhead costs cannot be assigned to specific jobs on the basis

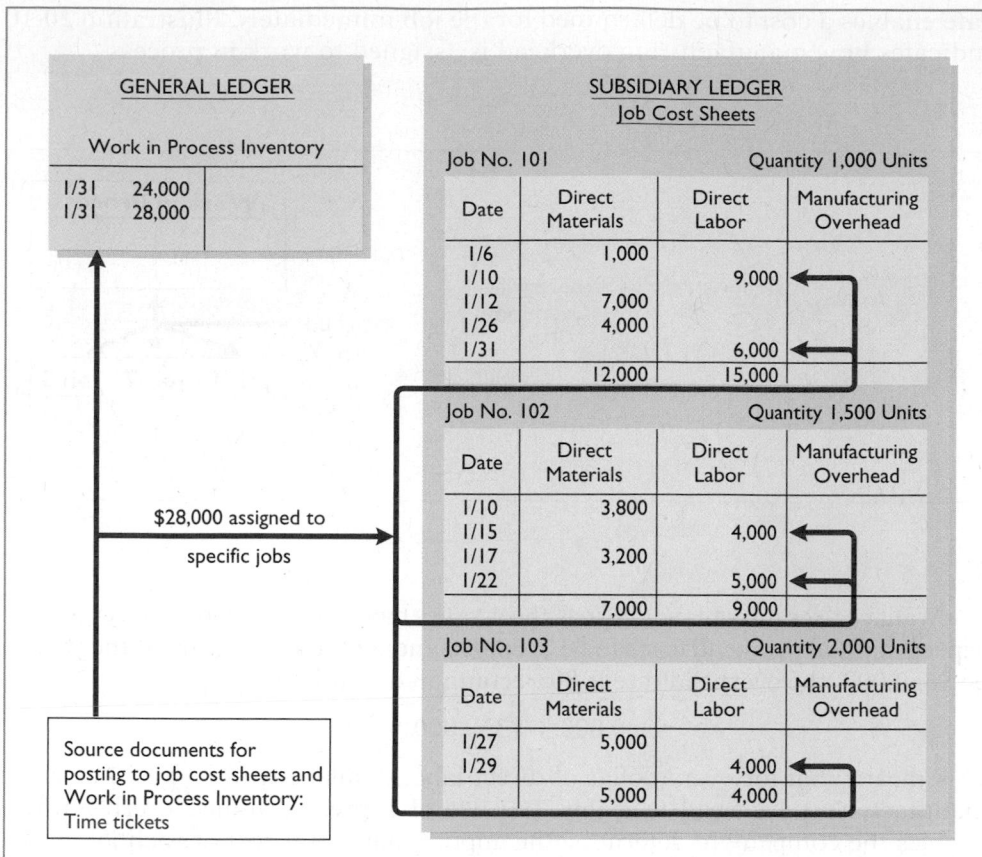

Illustration 20-8
Job cost sheets—direct labor

Helpful Hint Prove the $28,000 direct labor charge to Work in Process Inventory by totaling the charges by jobs:

101	$15,000
102	9,000
103	4,000
	$28,000

of actual costs incurred. Instead, companies assign manufacturing overhead to work in process and to specific jobs **on an estimated basis through the use of a predetermined overhead rate**.

The **predetermined overhead rate** is based on the relationship between estimated annual overhead costs and expected annual operating activity, expressed in terms of a common **activity base**. The company may state the activity in terms of direct labor costs, direct labor hours, machine hours, or any other measure that will provide an equitable basis for applying overhead costs to jobs. Companies establish the predetermined overhead rate at the beginning of the year. Small companies often use a single, company-wide pre-determined overhead rate. Large companies often use rates that vary from department to department. The formula for a predetermined overhead rate is as follows.

Estimated Annual Overhead Costs	÷	**Expected Annual Operating Activity**	=	**Predetermined Overhead Rate**

Illustration 20-9
Formula for predetermined overhead rate

Overhead relates to production operations as a whole. To know what "the whole" is, the logical thing is to wait until the end of the year's operations. At that time, the company knows all of its costs for the period. As a practical matter, though, managers cannot wait until the end of the year. To price products effectively as they are completed, managers need information about product costs of specific jobs completed during the year. Using a predetermined overhead rate enables a cost to be determined for the job immediately. Illustration 20-10 indicates how manufacturing overhead is assigned to work in process.

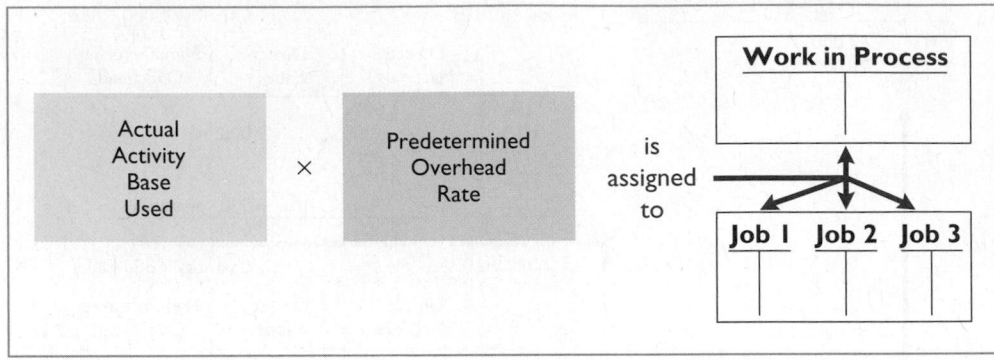

Wallace uses direct labor cost as the activity base. Assuming that the company expects annual overhead costs to be $280,000 and direct labor costs for the year to be $350,000, the overhead rate is 80%, computed as follows.

$$\$280,000 \div \$350,000 = 80\%$$

This means that for every dollar of direct labor, Wallace will assign 80 cents of manufacturing overhead to a job. The use of a predetermined overhead rate enables the company to determine the approximate total cost of each job **when it completes the job**.

Historically, companies used direct labor costs or direct labor hours as the activity base. The reason was the relatively high correlation between direct labor and manufacturing overhead. Today more companies are using **machine hours as the activity base, due to increased reliance on automation in manufacturing operations**. Or, as mentioned in Chapter 19 (and discussed more fully in Chapter 21), many companies now use activity-based costing to more accurately allocate overhead costs based on the activities that give rise to the costs.

A company may use more than one activity base. For example, if a job is manufactured in more than one factory department, each department may have its own overhead rate. In the Feature Story, American LaFrance might use two bases in assigning overhead to fire-truck jobs: direct materials dollars for indirect materials, and direct labor hours for such costs as insurance and supervisors' salaries.

Wallace Company applies manufacturing overhead to work in process when it assigns direct labor costs. It also applies manufacturing overhead to specific jobs at the same time. For January, Wallace applied overhead of $22,400 in response to its assignment of $28,000 of direct labor costs (direct labor cost of $28,000 × 80%). The following entry records this application.

(6)

Jan. 31	Work in Process Inventory	22,400	
	Manufacturing Overhead		22,400
	(To assign overhead to jobs)		

This entry reduces the balance in Manufacturing Overhead and increases Work in Process Inventory by $22,400, as follows.

The overhead that Wallace applies to each job will be 80% of the direct labor cost of the job for the month. Illustration 20-11 shows the Work in Process Inventory account and the job cost sheets after posting. Note that the debit of $22,400 to Work in Process Inventory equals the sum of the overhead applied to jobs: Job 101 $12,000 + Job 102 $7,200 + Job 103 $3,200.

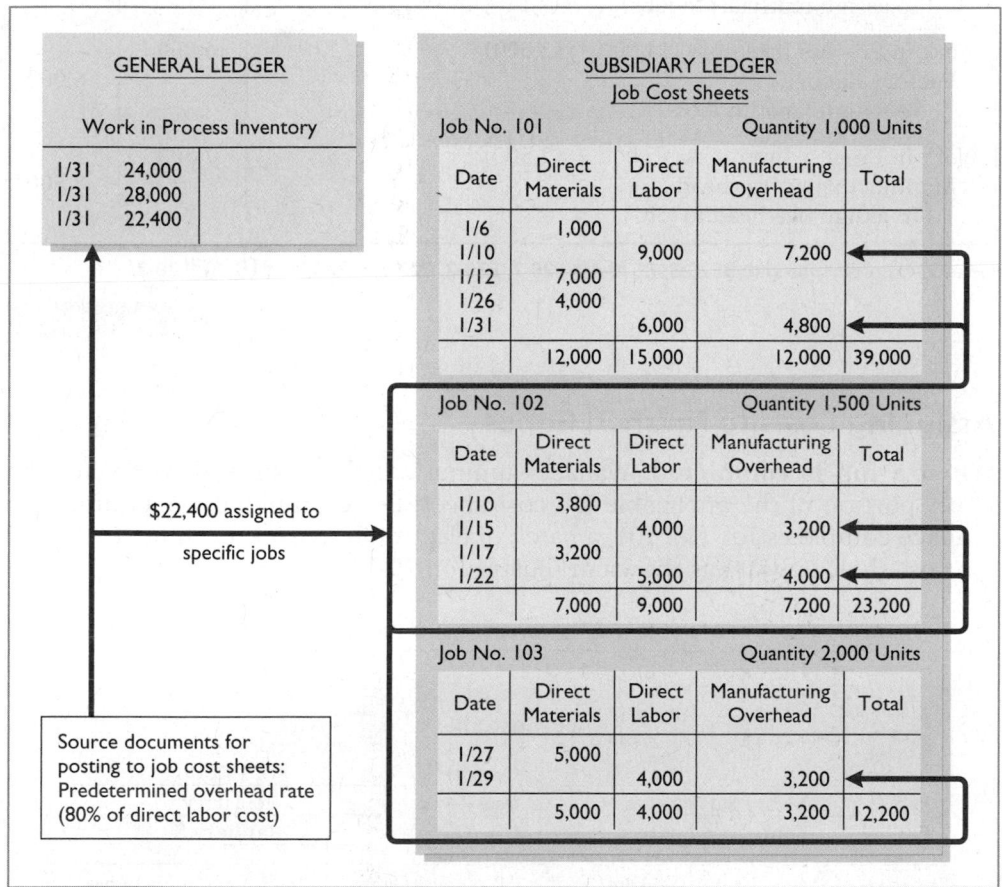

Illustration 20-11
Job cost sheets–manufacturing overhead applied

At the end of each month, the **balance in Work in Process Inventory should equal the sum of the costs shown on the job cost sheets of unfinished jobs**. Illustration 20-12 presents proof of the agreement of the control and subsidiary accounts in Wallace. (It assumes that all jobs are still in process.)

Work in Process Inventory		Job Cost Sheets	
Jan. 31	24,000	No. 101	$ 39,000
31	28,000	102	23,200
31	22,400	103	12,200
	74,400		**$74,400**

Illustration 20-12
Proof of job cost sheets to work in process inventory

> ### DO IT!

Work in Process

Danielle Company is working on two job orders. The job cost sheets show the following:

> Direct materials—Job 120 $6,000; Job 121 $3,600
> Direct labor—Job 120 $4,000; Job 121 $2,000
> Manufacturing overhead—Job 120 $5,000; Job 121 $2,500

Prepare the three summary entries to record the assignment of costs to Work in Process from the data on the job cost sheets.

Solution

Work in Process Inventory ($6,000 + $3,600)	9,600	
Raw Materials Inventory		9,600
(To assign materials to jobs)		
Work in Process Inventory ($4,000 + $2,000)	6,000	
Factory Labor		6,000
(To assign labor to jobs)		
Work in Process Inventory ($5,000 + $2,500)	7,500	
Manufacturing Overhead		7,500
(To assign overhead to jobs)		

Related exercise material: **BE20-3, BE20-4, BE20-7, E20-2, E20-7, E20-8,** and **DO IT!** **20-2.**

✔ **The Navigator**

Action Plan

✔ Recognize that Work in Process Inventory is the control account for all unfinished job cost sheets.

✔ Debit Work in Process Inventory for the materials, labor, and overhead charged to the job cost sheets.

✔ Credit the accounts that were debited when the manufacturing costs were accumulated.

Assigning Costs to Finished Goods

LEARNING OBJECTIVE 5

Prepare entries for jobs completed and sold.

When a job is completed, Wallace summarizes the costs and completes the lower portion of the applicable job cost sheet. For example, if we assume that Wallace completes Job No. 101, a batch of electronic sensors, on January 31, the job cost sheet appears as shown in Illustration 20-13.

Illustration 20-13
Completed job cost sheet

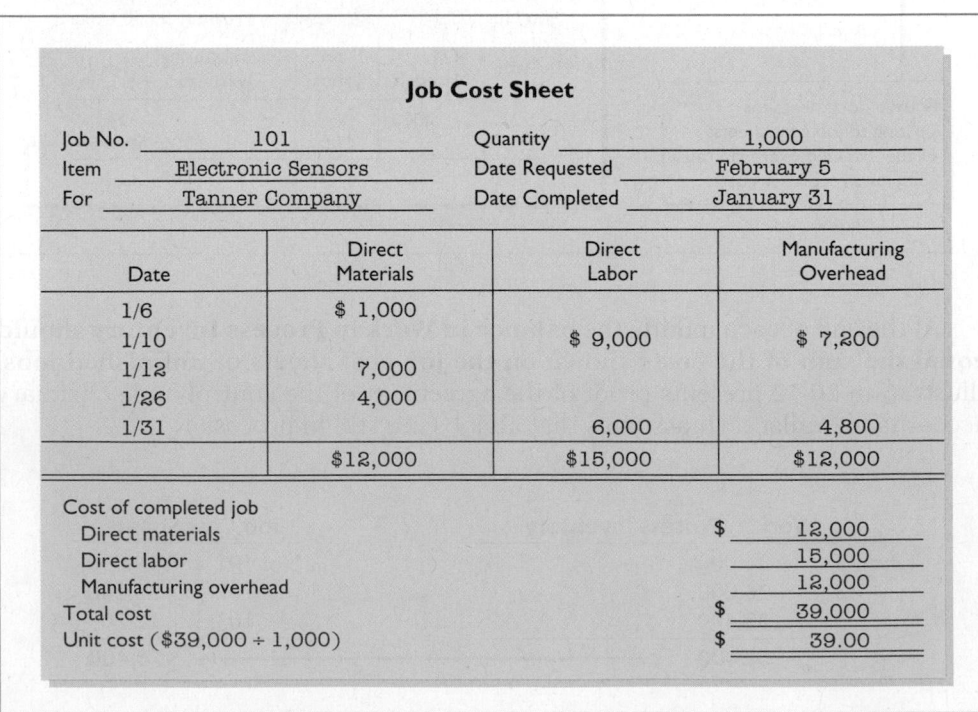

Job Cost Sheet

Job No.	101	Quantity	1,000
Item	Electronic Sensors	Date Requested	February 5
For	Tanner Company	Date Completed	January 31

Date	Direct Materials	Direct Labor	Manufacturing Overhead
1/6	$ 1,000		
1/10		$ 9,000	$ 7,200
1/12	7,000		
1/26	4,000		
1/31		6,000	4,800
	$12,000	$15,000	$12,000

Cost of completed job		
Direct materials	$	12,000
Direct labor		15,000
Manufacturing overhead		12,000
Total cost	$	39,000
Unit cost ($39,000 ÷ 1,000)	$	39.00

When a job is finished, Wallace makes an entry to transfer its total cost to finished goods inventory. The entry is as follows.

(7)

Jan. 31	Finished Goods Inventory	39,000	
	Work in Process Inventory		39,000
	(To record completion of		
	Job No. 101)		

This entry increases Finished Goods Inventory and reduces Work in Process Inventory by $39,000, as shown in the T-accounts below.

Work in Process Inventory		Finished Goods Inventory	
24,000	39,000 →	39,000	
28,000			
22,400			

Finished Goods Inventory is a control account. It controls individual finished goods records in a finished goods subsidiary ledger. The company posts directly from completed job cost sheets to the receipts columns. Illustration 20-14 shows the finished goods inventory record for Job No. 101.

Assigning Costs to Cost of Goods Sold

Companies recognize cost of goods sold when each sale occurs. To illustrate the entries a company makes when it sells a completed job, assume that on January 31 Wallace sells on account Job 101. The job cost $39,000, and it sold for $50,000. The entries to record the sale and recognize cost of goods sold are:

(8)

Jan. 31	Accounts Receivable	50,000	
	Sales Revenue		50,000
	(To record sale of Job No. 101)		
31	Cost of Goods Sold	39,000	
	Finished Goods Inventory		39,000
	(To record cost of Job No. 101)		

As Illustration 20-14 shows, Wallace records, in the issues section of the finished goods record, the units sold, the cost per unit, and the total cost of goods sold for each job sold.

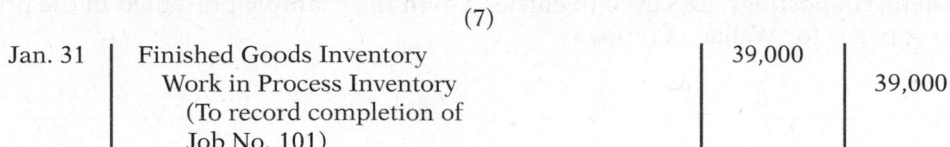

A	B	C	D	E	F	G	H	I	J
Item: Electronic Sensors								**Job No: 101**	
		Receipts			Issues			Balance	
Date	Units	Cost	Total	Units	Cost	Total	Units	Cost	Total
1/31	1,000	$39	$39,000				1,000	$39	$39,000
1/31				1,000	$39	$39,000			– 0 –

Illustration 20-14
Finished goods record

Summary of Job Order Cost Flows

Illustration 20-15 shows a completed flowchart for a job order cost accounting system. All postings are keyed to entries 1–8 in the example presented in the previous pages for Wallace Company.

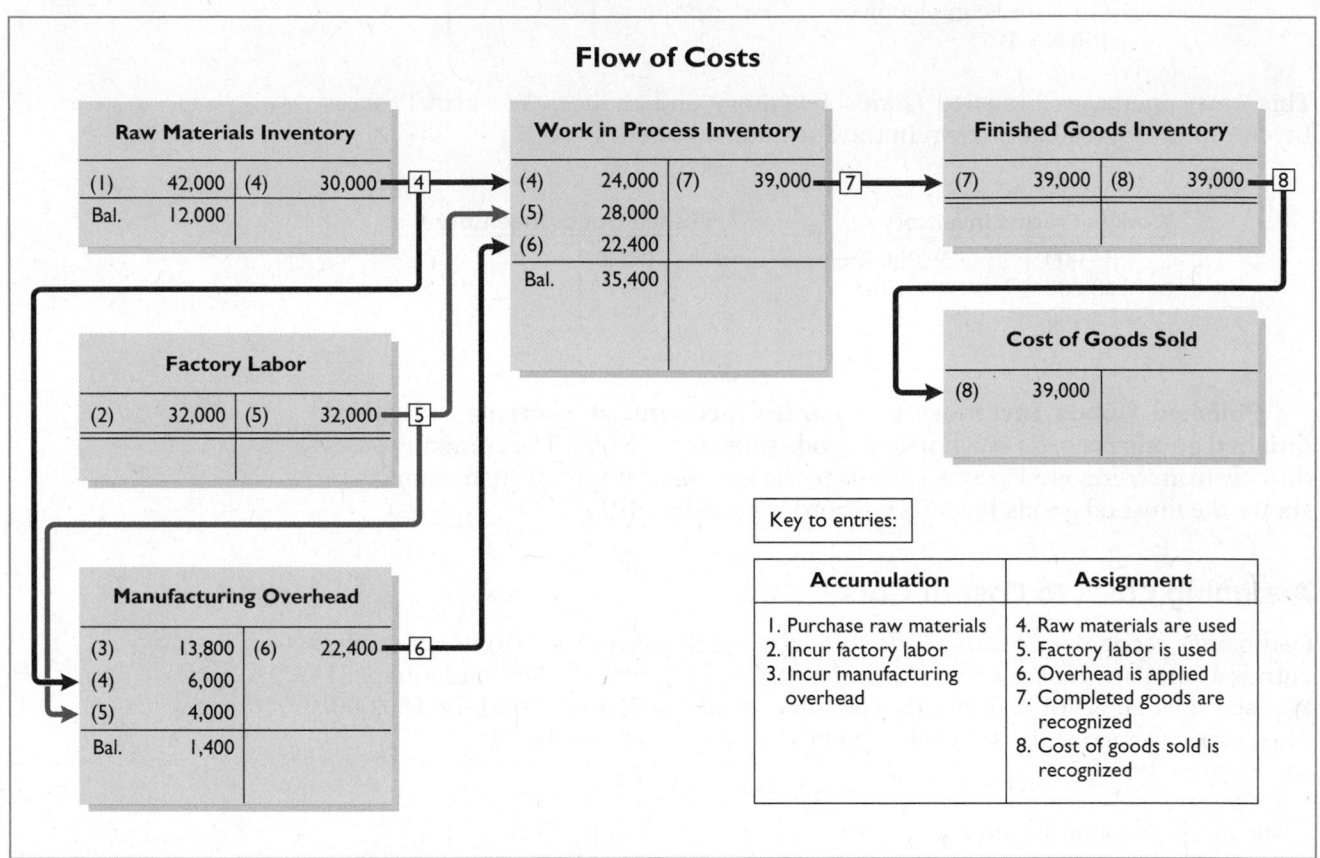

Illustration 20-15
Flow of costs in a job order cost system

The cost flows in the diagram can be categorized as one of four types:

- **Accumulation.** The company first accumulates costs by (1) purchasing raw materials, (2) incurring labor costs, and (3) incurring manufacturing overhead costs.

- **Assignment to jobs.** Once the company has incurred manufacturing costs, it must assign them to specific jobs. For example, as it uses raw materials on specific jobs (4), it assigns them to work in process, or treats them as manufacturing overhead if the raw materials cannot be associated with a specific job. Similarly, it either assigns factory labor (5) to work in process, or treats it as manufacturing overhead if the factory labor cannot be associated with a specific job. Finally it assigns manufacturing overhead (6) to work in process using a predetermined overhead rate. This deserves emphasis: **Do not assign overhead using actual overhead costs, but instead use a predetermined rate.**

- **Completed jobs.** As jobs are completed (7), the company transfers the cost of the completed job out of work in process inventory into finished goods inventory.

- **When goods are sold.** As specific items are sold (8), the company transfers their cost out of finished goods inventory into cost of goods sold.

Illustration 20-16 summarizes the flow of documents in a job order cost system.

Illustration 20-16
Flow of documents in a job
order cost system

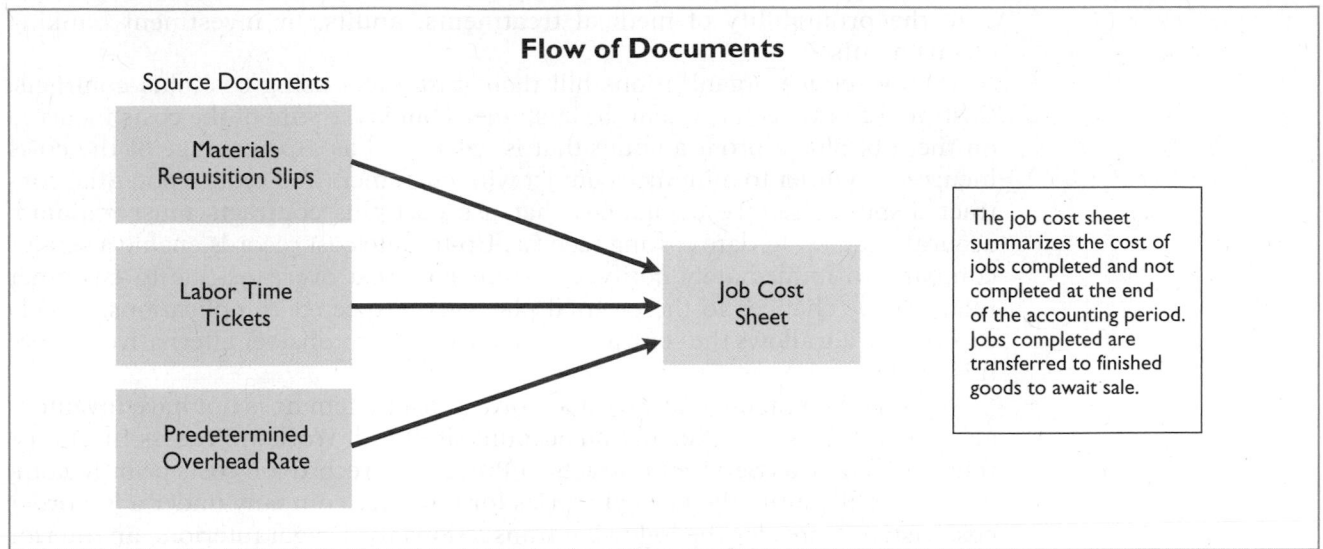

Flow of Documents

Source Documents

Materials Requisition Slips

Labor Time Tickets

Predetermined Overhead Rate

Job Cost Sheet

The job cost sheet summarizes the cost of jobs completed and not completed at the end of the accounting period. Jobs completed are transferred to finished goods to await sale.

> **DO IT!**

Completion and Sale of Jobs

Action Plan

✔ Debit Finished Goods Inventory for the cost of completed jobs.

✔ Debit Cost of Goods Sold for the cost of jobs sold.

During the current month, Onyx Corporation completed Job 109 and Job 112. Job 109 cost $19,000 and Job 112 cost $27,000. Job 112 was sold on account for $42,000. Journalize the entries for the completion of the two jobs and the sale of Job 112.

Solution

Finished Goods Inventory	46,000	
Work in Process Inventory		46,000
(To record completion of Job 109, costing $19,000 and Job 112, costing $27,000)		
Accounts Receivable	42,000	
Sales Revenue		42,000
(To record sale of Job 112)		
Cost of Goods Sold	27,000	
Finished Goods Inventory		27,000
(To record cost of goods sold for Job 112)		

Related exercise material: **BE20-8, E20-2, E20-3, E20-4, E20-6, E20-7, E20-10, and DO IT! 20-3.**

✔ The Navigator

Job Order Costing for Service Companies

Our extended job order costing example focuses on a manufacturer so that you see the flow of costs through the inventory accounts. It is important to understand, however, that job order costing is also commonly used by service companies. While service companies do not have inventory, the techniques of job order costing are still quite useful in many service-industry environments. Consider, for example, the Mayo Clinic (health care), PriceWaterhouseCoopers (accounting), and Goldman Sachs (investment banking). These companies need to keep track of the cost of jobs performed for specific customers to evaluate the profitability of medical treatments, audits, or investment banking engagements.

Many service organizations bill their customers using cost-plus contracts. Cost-plus contracts mean that the customer's bill is the sum of the costs incurred on the job, plus a profit amount that is calculated as a percentage of the costs incurred. In order to minimize conflict with customers and reduce potential contract disputes, service companies that use cost-plus contracts must maintain accurate and up-to-date costing records. Up-to-date cost records enable a service company to immediately notify a customer of cost overruns due to customer requests for changes to the original plan or unexpected complications. Timely recordkeeping allows the contractor and customer to consider alternatives before it is too late.

A service company that uses a job order cost system does not have inventory accounts. It does, however, use an account similar to Work in Process Inventory, referred to here as Service Contracts in Process, to record job costs prior to completion. To illustrate the journal entries for a service company under a job order cost system, consider the following transactions for Frugal Interiors, an interior design company. The entry to record the assignment of $9,000 of supplies to projects ($7,000 direct and $2,000 indirect) is:

Service Contracts in Process	7,000	
Operating Overhead	2,000	
Supplies		9,000
(To assign supplies to projects)		

The entry to record the assignment of service salaries and wages of $100,000 ($84,000 direct and $16,000 indirect) is:

Service Contracts in Process	84,000	
Operating Overhead	16,000	
Service Salaries and Wages		100,000
(To assign personnel costs to projects)		

Frugal Interiors applies operating overhead at a rate of 50% of direct labor costs. The entry to record the application of overhead ($84,000 × 50%) based on the direct labor costs is:

Service Contracts in Process	42,000	
Operating Overhead		42,000
(To assign operating overhead to projects)		

Finally, upon completion, the job cost sheet of a design project for Sampson Corporation shows a total cost of $34,000. The entry to record completion of this project is:

Cost of Completed Service Contracts	34,000	
Service Contracts in Process		34,000
(To record completion of Sampson project)		

Job cost sheets for a service company keep track of materials, labor, and overhead used on a particular job similar to a manufacturer. A number of exercises at the end of this chapter apply job order costing to service companies.

SERVICE COMPANY INSIGHT

Sales Are Nice, but Service Revenue Pays the Bills

Jet engines are one of the many products made by the industrial operations division of General Electric (GE). At prices as high as $30 million per engine, you can bet that GE does its best to keep track of costs. It might surprise you that GE doesn't make much profit on the sale of each engine. So why does it bother making them? Service revenue—during one recent year, about 75% of the division's revenues came from servicing its own products. One estimate is that the $13 billion in aircraft engines sold during a recent three-year period will generate about $90 billion in service revenue over the 30-year life of the engines. Because of the high product costs, both the engines themselves and the subsequent service are most likely accounted for using job order costing. Accurate service cost records are important because GE needs to generate high profit margins on its service jobs to make up for the low margins on the original sale. It also needs good cost records for its service jobs in order to control its costs. Otherwise, a competitor, such as Pratt and Whitney, might submit lower bids for service contracts and take lucrative service jobs away from GE.

Source: Paul Glader, "GE's Focus on Services Faces Test," *Wall Street Journal Online* (March 3, 2009).

? Explain why GE would use job order costing to keep track of the cost of repairing a malfunctioning engine for a major airline. (See page 980.)

© Christian Lagereek/iStockphoto

Advantages and Disadvantages of Job Order Costing

An advantage of job order costing is it is more precise in assignment of costs to projects than process costing. For example, assume that a construction company, Juan Company, builds 10 custom homes a year at a total cost of $2,000,000. One way to determine the cost of the homes is to divide the total construction cost incurred during the year by the number of homes produced during the year. For Juan Company, an average cost of $200,000 ($2,000,000 ÷ 10) is computed. If the homes are nearly identical, then this approach is adequate for purposes of determining profit per home. But if the homes vary in terms of size, style, and material types, using the average cost of $200,000 to determine profit per home is inappropriate. Instead, Juan Company should use a job order cost system to determine the specific cost incurred to build each home and the amount of profit made on each. Thus, job order costing provides more useful information for determining the profitability of particular projects and for estimating costs when preparing bids on future jobs.

One disadvantage of job order costing is that it requires a significant amount of data entry. For Juan Company, it is much easier to simply keep track of total costs incurred during the year than it is to keep track of the costs incurred on each job (home built). Recording this information is time-consuming, and if the data is not entered accurately, then the product costs are not accurate. In recent years, technological advances, such as bar-coding devices for both labor costs and materials, have increased the accuracy and reduced the effort needed to record costs on specific jobs. These innovations expand the opportunities to apply job order costing in a wider variety of business settings, thus improving management's ability to control costs and make better informed decisions.

A common problem of all costing systems is how to allocate overhead to the finished product. Overhead often represents more than 50% of a product's cost, and this cost is often difficult to allocate meaningfully to the product. How, for example, is the salary of a project manager allocated to the various homes, which may differ in size, style, and materials used, that she oversees? The accuracy of the job order cost system is largely dependent on the accuracy of the overhead allocation process. Even if the company does a good job of keeping track of the specific amounts of materials and labor used on each job, if the overhead costs are not allocated to individual jobs in a meaningful way, the product costing information is not useful. This issue will be addressed in more detail in Chapter 21.

Reporting Job Cost Data

LEARNING OBJECTIVE   6

Distinguish between under- and overapplied manufacturing overhead.

At the end of a period, companies prepare financial statements that present aggregate data on all jobs manufactured and sold. The cost of goods manufactured schedule in job order costing is the same as in Chapter 19 with one exception: **The schedule shows manufacturing overhead applied, rather than actual overhead costs. The company adds this amount to direct materials and direct labor to determine total manufacturing costs.**

Companies prepare the cost of goods manufactured schedule directly from the Work in Process Inventory account. Illustration 20-17 shows a condensed schedule for Wallace Company for January.

Illustration 20-17
Cost of goods manufactured schedule

WALLACE COMPANY		
Cost of Goods Manufactured Schedule		
For the Month Ending January 31, 2014		
Work in process, January 1		$ −0−
Direct materials used	$ 24,000	
Direct labor	28,000	
Manufacturing overhead applied	**22,400**	
Total manufacturing costs		74,400
Total cost of work in process		74,400
Less: Work in process, January 31		35,400
Cost of goods manufactured		$39,000

Note that the cost of goods manufactured ($39,000) agrees with the amount transferred from Work in Process Inventory to Finished Goods Inventory in journal entry No. 7 in Illustration 20-15 (page 954).

The income statement and balance sheet are the same as those illustrated in Chapter 19. For example, Illustration 20-18 shows the partial income statement for Wallace for the month of January.

Illustration 20-18
Partial income statement

WALLACE COMPANY		
Income Statement (partial)		
For the Month Ending January 31, 2014		
Sales revenue		$50,000
Cost of goods sold		
Finished goods inventory, January 1	$ −0−	
Cost of goods manufactured (see Illustration 20-17)	**39,000**	
Cost of goods available for sale	39,000	
Less: Finished goods inventory, January 31	−0−	
Cost of goods sold		39,000
Gross profit		$11,000

Under- or Overapplied Manufacturing Overhead

When Manufacturing Overhead has a **debit balance**, overhead is said to be underapplied. **Underapplied overhead** means that the overhead assigned to work in process is less than the overhead incurred. Conversely, when manufacturing overhead has a **credit balance**, overhead is overapplied. **Overapplied overhead** means that the overhead assigned to work in process is greater than the overhead incurred. Illustration 20-19 shows these concepts.

Illustration 20-19
Under- and overapplied overhead

Manufacturing Overhead	
Actual (Costs incurred)	Applied (Costs assigned)

Manufacturing Overhead

If actual is **greater** than applied, manufacturing overhead is underapplied.

If actual is **less** than applied, manufacturing overhead is overapplied.

YEAR-END BALANCE

At the end of the year, all manufacturing overhead transactions are complete. There is no further opportunity for offsetting events to occur. At this point, Wallace eliminates any balance in Manufacturing Overhead by an adjusting entry. It considers under- or overapplied overhead to be an **adjustment to cost of goods sold**. Thus, Wallace **debits underapplied overhead to Cost of Goods Sold**. It **credits overapplied overhead to Cost of Goods Sold**.

To illustrate, assume that Wallace has a $2,500 credit balance in Manufacturing Overhead at December 31. The adjusting entry for the overapplied overhead is:

Dec. 31	Manufacturing Overhead	2,500	
	Cost of Goods Sold		2,500
	(To transfer overapplied overhead to cost of goods sold)		

After Wallace posts this entry, Manufacturing Overhead has a zero balance. In preparing an income statement for the year, Wallace reports cost of goods sold **after adjusting it** for either under- or overapplied overhead.

Conceptually, some argue, under- or overapplied overhead at the end of the year should be allocated among ending work in process, finished goods, and cost of goods sold. The discussion of this possible allocation approach is left to more advanced courses.

> **DO IT!**

Applied Manufacturing Overhead

Action Plan

✔ Calculate the amount of overhead applied by multiplying the pre-determined overhead rate by actual activity.

✔ If actual manufacturing overhead is greater than applied, manufacturing overhead is underapplied.

✔ If actual manufacturing overhead is less than applied, manufacturing overhead is overapplied.

For Karr Company, the predetermined overhead rate is 140% of direct labor cost. During the month, Karr incurred $90,000 of factory labor costs, of which $80,000 is direct labor and $10,000 is indirect labor. Actual overhead incurred was $119,000.

Compute the amount of manufacturing overhead applied during the month. Determine the amount of under- or overapplied manufacturing overhead.

Solution

Manufacturing overhead applied = (140% × $80,000) = $112,000
Underapplied manufacturing overhead = ($119,000 − $112,000) = $7,000

Related exercise material: **BE20-10, E20-5, E20-12, E20-13, and DO IT! 20-4.**

 The Navigator

> Comprehensive DO IT!

Cardella Company applies overhead on the basis of direct labor costs. The company estimates annual overhead costs will be $760,000, and annual direct labor costs will be $950,000. During February, Cardella works on two jobs: A16 and B17. Summary data concerning these jobs are as follows.

Manufacturing Costs Incurred

Purchased $54,000 of raw materials on account.
Factory labor $76,000, plus $4,000 employer payroll taxes.
Manufacturing overhead exclusive of indirect materials and indirect labor $59,800.

Assignment of Costs

Direct materials: Job A16 $27,000, Job B17 $21,000
Indirect materials: $3,000
Direct labor: Job A16 $52,000, Job B17 $26,000
Indirect labor: $2,000

The company completed Job A16 and sold it on account for $150,000. Job B17 was only partially completed.

Instructions

(a) Compute the predetermined overhead rate.
(b) Journalize the February transactions in the sequence followed in the chapter.
(c) What was the amount of under- or overapplied manufacturing overhead?

Solution to Comprehensive DO IT!

Action Plan

✔ Predetermined overhead rate = Estimated annual overhead cost ÷ Expected annual operating activity.

✔ In accumulating costs, debit three accounts: Raw Materials Inventory, Factory Labor, and Manufacturing Overhead.

✔ When Work in Process Inventory is debited, credit one of the three accounts listed above.

✔ Debit Finished Goods Inventory for the cost of completed jobs. Debit Cost of Goods Sold for the cost of jobs sold.

✔ Overhead is underapplied when Manufacturing Overhead has a debit balance.

(a)

Estimated annual overhead costs	÷	Expected annual operating activity	=	Predetermined overhead rate
$760,000	÷	$950,000	=	80%

(b)

(1)

Feb. 28	Raw Materials Inventory	54,000	
	Accounts Payable		54,000
	(Purchase of raw materials on account)		

(2)

28	Factory Labor	80,000	
	Factory Wages Payable		76,000
	Employer Payroll Taxes Payable		4,000
	(To record factory labor costs)		

(3)

28	Manufacturing Overhead	59,800	
	Accounts Payable, Accumulated		
	Depreciation, and Prepaid Insurance		59,800
	(To record overhead costs)		

(4)

28	Work in Process Inventory	48,000	
	Manufacturing Overhead	3,000	
	Raw Materials Inventory		51,000
	(To assign raw materials to production)		

(5)

28	Work in Process Inventory	78,000	
	Manufacturing Overhead	2,000	
	Factory Labor		80,000
	(To assign factory labor to production)		

	(6)		
28	Work in Process Inventory	62,400	
	Manufacturing Overhead		62,400
	(To assign overhead to jobs—		
	80% × $78,000)		

	(7)		
28	Finished Goods Inventory	120,600	
	Work in Process Inventory		120,600
	(To record completion of Job A16: direct		
	materials $27,000, direct labor $52,000,		
	and manufacturing overhead $41,600)		

	(8)		
28	Accounts Receivable	150,000	
	Sales Revenue		150,000
	(To record sale of Job A16)		

28	Cost of Goods Sold	120,600	
	Finished Goods Inventory		120,600
	(To record cost of sale for Job A16)		

(c) Manufacturing Overhead has a debit balance of $2,400 as shown below.

Manufacturing Overhead

(3)	59,800	(6)	62,400
(4)	3,000		
(5)	2,000		
Bal.	2,400		

Thus, manufacturing overhead is underapplied for the month.

 The Navigator

SUMMARY OF LEARNING OBJECTIVES

✔ The Navigator

1 Explain the characteristics and purposes of cost accounting. Cost accounting involves the procedures for measuring, recording, and reporting product costs. From the data accumulated, companies determine the total cost and the unit cost of each product. The two basic types of cost accounting systems are job order cost and process cost.

2 Describe the flow of costs in a job order cost system. In job order costing, companies first accumulate manufacturing costs in three accounts: Raw Materials Inventory, Factory Labor, and Manufacturing Overhead. They then assign the accumulated costs to Work in Process Inventory and eventually to Finished Goods Inventory and Cost of Goods Sold.

3 Explain the nature and importance of a job cost sheet. A job cost sheet is a form used to record the costs chargeable to a specific job and to determine the total and unit costs of the completed job. Job cost sheets constitute the subsidiary ledger for the Work in Process Inventory control account.

4 Indicate how the predetermined overhead rate is determined and used. The predetermined overhead rate is based on the relationship between estimated annual overhead costs and expected annual operating activity. This is expressed in terms of a common activity base, such as direct labor cost. Companies use this rate to assign overhead costs to work in process and to specific jobs.

5 Prepare entries for jobs completed and sold. When jobs are completed, companies debit the cost to Finished Goods Inventory and credit it to Work in Process Inventory. When a job is sold, the entries are (a) debit Cash or Accounts Receivable and credit Sales Revenue for the selling price; and (b) debit Cost of Goods Sold and credit Finished Goods Inventory for the cost of the goods.

6 Distinguish between under- and overapplied manufacturing overhead. Underapplied manufacturing overhead indicates that the overhead assigned to work in process is less than the overhead incurred. Overapplied overhead indicates that the overhead assigned to work in process is greater than the overhead incurred.

Cost accounting An area of accounting that involves measuring, recording, and reporting product costs. (p. 940).

Cost accounting system Manufacturing cost accounts that are fully integrated into the general ledger of a company. (p. 940).

Job cost sheet A form used to record the costs chargeable to a specific job and to determine the total and unit costs of the completed job. (p. 944).

Job order cost system A cost accounting system in which costs are assigned to each job or batch. (p. 940).

Materials requisition slip A document authorizing the issuance of raw materials from the storeroom to production. (p. 945).

Overapplied overhead A situation in which overhead assigned to work in process is greater than the overhead incurred. (p. 959).

Predetermined overhead rate A rate based on the relationship between estimated annual overhead costs and expected annual operating activity, expressed in terms of a common activity base. (p. 949).

Process cost system A cost accounting system used when a company manufactures a large volume of similar products. (p. 940).

Time ticket A document that indicates the employee, the hours worked, the account and job to be charged, and the total labor cost. (p. 947).

Underapplied overhead A situation in which overhead assigned to work in process is less than the overhead incurred. (p. 958).

Self-Test, Brief Exercises, Exercises, Problem Set A, and many more resources are available for practice in *WileyPLUS.*

SELF-TEST QUESTIONS

Answers are on page 980.

(LO 1) **1.** Cost accounting involves the measuring, recording, and reporting of:
  (a) product costs.
  (b) future costs.
  (c) manufacturing processes.
  (d) managerial accounting decisions.

(LO 1) **2.** A company is more likely to use a job order cost system if:
  (a) it manufactures a large volume of similar products.
  (b) its production is continuous.
  (c) it manufactures products with unique characteristics.
  (d) it uses a periodic inventory system.

(LO 2) **3.** In accumulating raw materials costs, companies debit the cost of raw materials purchased in a perpetual system to:
  (a) Raw Materials Purchases.
  (b) Raw Materials Inventory.
  (c) Purchases.
  (d) Work in Process.

(LO 2) **4.** When incurred, factory labor costs are debited to:
  (a) Work in Process.
  (b) Factory Wages Expense.
  (c) Factory Labor.
  (d) Factory Wages Payable.

(LO 2) **5.** The flow of costs in job order costing:
  (a) begins with work in process inventory and ends with finished goods inventory.
  (b) begins as soon as a sale occurs.

  (c) parallels the physical flow of materials as they are converted into finished goods.
  (d) is necessary to prepare the cost of goods manufactured schedule.

6. Raw materials are assigned to a job when: (LO 3)
  (a) the job is sold.
  (b) the materials are purchased.
  (c) the materials are received from the vendor.
  (d) the materials are issued by the materials storeroom.

7. The source documents for assigning costs to job cost   (LO 3) sheets are:
  (a) invoices, time tickets, and the predetermined overhead rate.
  (b) materials requisition slips, time tickets, and the actual overhead costs.
  (c) materials requisition slips, payroll register, and the predetermined overhead rate.
  (d) materials requisition slips, time tickets, and the predetermined overhead rate.

8. In recording the issuance of raw materials in a job   (LO 3) order cost system, it would be **incorrect** to:
  (a) debit Work in Process Inventory.
  (b) debit Finished Goods Inventory.
  (c) debit Manufacturing Overhead.
  (d) credit Raw Materials Inventory.

9. The entry when direct factory labor is assigned to jobs   (LO 3) is a debit to:
  (a) Work in Process Inventory and a credit to Factory Labor.
  (b) Manufacturing Overhead and a credit to Factory Labor.

(c) Factory Labor and a credit to Manufacturing Overhead.

(d) Factory Labor and a credit to Work in Process Inventory.

(LO 4) **10.** The formula for computing the predetermined manufacturing overhead rate is estimated annual overhead costs divided by an expected annual operating activity, expressed as:

(a) direct labor cost.　　**(c)** machine hours.

(b) direct labor hours.　　**(d)** Any of the above.

(LO 4) **11.** In Crawford Company, the predetermined overhead rate is 80% of direct labor cost. During the month, Crawford incurs $210,000 of factory labor costs, of which $180,000 is direct labor and $30,000 is indirect labor. Actual overhead incurred was $200,000. The amount of overhead debited to Work in Process Inventory should be:

(a) $200,000.　　　**(c)** $168,000.

(b) $144,000.　　　**(d)** $160,000.

(LO 5) **12.** Mynex Company completes Job No. 26 at a cost of $4,500 and later sells it for $7,000 cash. A **correct** entry is:

(a) debit Finished Goods Inventory $7,000 and credit Work in Process Inventory $7,000.

(b) debit Cost of Goods Sold $7,000 and credit Finished Goods Inventory $7,000.

(c) debit Finished Goods Inventory $4,500 and credit Work in Process Inventory $4,500.

(d) debit Accounts Receivable $7,000 and credit Sales Revenue $7,000.

(LO 5) **13.** At the end of an accounting period, a company using a job order cost system calculates the cost of goods manufactured:

(a) from the job cost sheet.

(b) from the Work in Process Inventory account.

(c) by adding direct materials used, direct labor incurred, and manufacturing overhead incurred.

(d) from the Cost of Goods Sold account.

14. Which of the following statements is **true**?　(LO 5)

(a) Job order costing requires less data entry than process costing.

(b) Allocation of overhead is easier under job order costing than process costing.

(c) Job order costing provides more precise costing for custom jobs than process costing.

(d) The use of job order costing has declined because more companies have adopted automated accounting systems.

15. At end of the year, a company has a $1,200 debit balance in Manufacturing Overhead. The company:　(LO 6)

(a) makes an adjusting entry by debiting Manufacturing Overhead Applied for $1,200 and crediting Manufacturing Overhead for $1,200.

(b) makes an adjusting entry by debiting Manufacturing Overhead Expense for $1,200 and crediting Manufacturing Overhead for $1,200.

(c) makes an adjusting entry by debiting Cost of Goods Sold for $1,200 and crediting Manufacturing Overhead for $1,200.

(d) makes no adjusting entry because differences between actual overhead and the amount applied are a normal part of job order costing and will average out over the next year.

16. Manufacturing overhead is underapplied if:　(LO 6)

(a) actual overhead is less than applied.

(b) actual overhead is greater than applied.

(c) the predetermined rate equals the actual rate.

(d) actual overhead equals applied overhead.

Go to the book's companion website, **www.wiley.com/college/weygandt,** for additional Self-Test Questions.

 The Navigator

QUESTIONS

1. (a) Mary Barett is not sure about the difference between cost accounting and a cost accounting system. Explain the difference to Mary.

(b) What is an important feature of a cost accounting system?

2. (a) Distinguish between the two types of cost accounting systems.

(b) Can a company use both types of cost accounting systems?

3. What type of industry is likely to use a job order cost system? Give some examples.

4. What type of industry is likely to use a process cost system? Give some examples.

5. Your roommate asks your help in understanding the major steps in the flow of costs in a job order cost system. Identify the steps for your roommate.

6. There are three inventory control accounts in a job order system. Identify the control accounts and their subsidiary ledgers.

7. What source documents are used in accumulating direct labor costs?

8. "Entries to Manufacturing Overhead normally are only made daily." Do you agree? Explain.

9. Stan Kaiser is confused about the source documents used in assigning materials and labor costs. Identify the documents and give the entry for each document.

10. What is the purpose of a job cost sheet?

11. Indicate the source documents that are used in charging costs to specific jobs.

12. Explain the purpose and use of a "materials requisition slip" as used in a job order cost system.

13. Sam Bowden believes actual manufacturing overhead should be charged to jobs. Do you agree? Why or why not?

14. What elements are involved in computing a predetermined overhead rate?

15. How can the agreement of Work in Process Inventory and job cost sheets be verified?

16. Jane Neff believes that the cost of goods manufactured schedule in job order cost accounting is the same as shown in Chapter 19. Is Jane correct? Explain.

17. Matt Litkee is confused about under- and overapplied manufacturing overhead. Define the terms for Matt, and indicate the balance in the manufacturing overhead account applicable to each term.

18. "At the end of the year, under- or overapplied overhead is closed to Income Summary." Is this correct? If not, indicate the customary treatment of this amount.

BRIEF EXERCISES

Prepare a flowchart of a job order cost accounting system, and identify transactions.
(LO 2)

BE20-1 Knox Company begins operations on January 1. Because all work is done to customer specifications, the company decides to use a job order cost system. Prepare a flowchart of a typical job order system with arrows showing the flow of costs. Identify the eight transactions.

Prepare entries in accumulating manufacturing costs.
(LO 2)

BE20-2 During January, its first month of operations, Knox Company accumulated the following manufacturing costs: raw materials $4,000 on account, factory labor $6,000 of which $5,200 relates to factory wages payable and $800 relates to payroll taxes payable, and utilities payable $2,000. Prepare separate journal entries for each type of manufacturing cost.

Prepare entry for the assignment of raw materials costs.
(LO 3)

BE20-3 In January, Knox Company requisitions raw materials for production as follows: Job 1 $900, Job 2 $1,400, Job 3 $700, and general factory use $600. Prepare a summary journal entry to record raw materials used.

Prepare entry for the assignment of factory labor costs.
(LO 3)

BE20-4 Factory labor data for Knox Company is given in BE20-2. During January, time tickets show that the factory labor of $6,000 was used as follows: Job 1 $2,200, Job 2 $1,600, Job 3 $1,400, and general factory use $800. Prepare a summary journal entry to record factory labor used.

Prepare job cost sheets.
(LO 3)

BE20-5 Data pertaining to job cost sheets for Knox Company are given in BE20-3 and BE20-4. Prepare the job cost sheets for each of the three jobs. (*Note:* You may omit the column for Manufacturing Overhead.)

Compute predetermined overhead rates.
(LO 4)

BE20-6 Marquis Company estimates that annual manufacturing overhead costs will be $900,000. Estimated annual operating activity bases are direct labor cost $500,000, direct labor hours 50,000, and machine hours 100,000. Compute the predetermined overhead rate for each activity base.

Assign manufacturing overhead to production.
(LO 4)

BE20-7 During the first quarter, Roland Company incurs the following direct labor costs: January $40,000, February $30,000, and March $50,000. For each month, prepare the entry to assign overhead to production using a predetermined rate of 80% of direct labor cost.

Prepare entries for completion and sale of completed jobs.
(LO 5)

BE20-8 In March, Stinson Company completes Jobs 10 and 11. Job 10 cost $20,000 and Job 11 $30,000. On March 31, Job 10 is sold to the customer for $35,000 in cash. Journalize the entries for the completion of the two jobs and the sale of Job 10.

Prepare entries for service salaries and wages and operating overhead.
(LO 5)

BE20-9 Preprah Engineering Contractors incurred service salaries and wages of $32,000 ($24,000 direct and $8,000 indirect) on an engineering project. The company applies overhead at a rate of 25% of direct labor. Record the entries to assign service salaries and wages and to apply overhead.

Prepare adjusting entries for under- and overapplied overhead.
(LO 6)

BE20-10 At December 31, balances in Manufacturing Overhead are Shimeca Company—debit $1,200, Garcia Company—credit $900. Prepare the adjusting entry for each company at December 31, assuming the adjustment is made to cost of goods sold.

> ## DO IT! Review

DO IT! 20-1 During the current month, Tomlin Company incurs the following manufacturing costs.

(a) Purchased raw materials of $16,000 on account.
(b) Incurred factory labor of $40,000. Of that amount, $31,000 relates to wages payable and $9,000 relates to payroll taxes payable.
(c) Factory utilities of $3,100 are payable, prepaid factory property taxes of $2,400 have expired, and depreciation on the factory building is $9,500.

Prepare journal entries for each type of manufacturing cost. (Use a summary entry to record manufacturing overhead.)

Prepare journal entries for manufacturing costs.
(LO 2)

DO IT! 20-2 Milner Company is working on two job orders. The job cost sheets show the following.

Assign costs to work in process.
(LO 3, 4)

	Job 201	Job 202
Direct materials	$7,200	$9,000
Direct labor	4,000	8,000
Manufacturing overhead	5,200	9,800

Prepare the three summary entries to record the assignment of costs to Work in Process from the data on the job cost sheets.

DO IT! 20-3 During the current month, Reyes Corporation completed Job 310 and Job 312. Job 310 cost $60,000 and Job 312 cost $50,000. Job 312 was sold on account for $90,000. Journalize the entries for the completion of the two jobs and the sale of Job 312.

Prepare entries for completion and sale of jobs.
(LO 5)

DO IT! 20-4 For Eckstein Company, the predetermined overhead rate is 130% of direct labor cost. During the month, Eckstein incurred $100,000 of factory labor costs, of which $85,000 is direct labor and $15,000 is indirect labor. Actual overhead incurred was $115,000. Compute the amount of manufacturing overhead applied during the month. Determine the amount of under- or overapplied manufacturing overhead.

Apply manufacturing overhead and determine under- or overapplication.
(LO 6)

EXERCISES

E20-1 The gross earnings of the factory workers for Vargas Company during the month of January are $66,000. The employer's payroll taxes for the factory payroll are $8,000. The fringe benefits to be paid by the employer on this payroll are $6,000. Of the total accumulated cost of factory labor, 85% is related to direct labor and 15% is attributable to indirect labor.

Prepare entries for factory labor.
(LO 2, 3)

Instructions
(a) Prepare the entry to record the factory labor costs for the month of January.
(b) Prepare the entry to assign factory labor to production.

E20-2 Stine Company uses a job order cost system. On May 1, the company has a balance in Work in Process Inventory of $3,500 and two jobs in process: Job No. 429 $2,000, and Job No. 430 $1,500. During May, a summary of source documents reveals the following.

Prepare journal entries for manufacturing costs.
(LO 2, 3, 4, 5)

Job Number	Materials Requisition Slips		Labor Time Tickets	
429	$2,500		$1,900	
430	3,500		3,000	
431	4,400	$10,400	7,600	$12,500
General use		800		1,200
		$11,200		$13,700

Stine Company applies manufacturing overhead to jobs at an overhead rate of 60% of direct labor cost. Job No. 429 is completed during the month.

Instructions

(a) Prepare summary journal entries to record (i) the requisition slips, (ii) the time tickets, (iii) the assignment of manufacturing overhead to jobs, and (iv) the completion of Job No. 429.

(b) Post the entries to Work in Process Inventory, and prove the agreement of the control account with the job cost sheets. (Use a T-account.)

Analyze a job cost sheet and prepare entries for manufacturing costs.

(LO 2, 3, 4, 5)

E20-3 A job order cost sheet for Lowry Company is shown below.

Job No. 92			For 2,000 Units
Date	Direct Materials	Direct Labor	Manufacturing Overhead
Beg. bal. Jan. 1	5,000	6,000	5,100
8	6,000		
12		8,000	6,400
25	2,000		
27		4,000	3,200
	13,000	18,000	14,700

Cost of completed job:	
Direct materials	$13,000
Direct labor	18,000
Manufacturing overhead	14,700
Total cost	$45,700
Unit cost ($45,700 ÷ 2,000)	$22.85

Instructions

(a) ▸————— On the basis of the foregoing data, answer the following questions.

  (1) What was the balance in Work in Process Inventory on January 1 if this was the only unfinished job?

  (2) If manufacturing overhead is applied on the basis of direct labor cost, what overhead rate was used in each year?

(b) Prepare summary entries at January 31 to record the current year's transactions pertaining to Job No. 92.

Analyze costs of manufacturing and determine missing amounts.

(LO 2, 6)

E20-4 Manufacturing cost data for Orlando Company, which uses a job order cost system, are presented below.

	Case A	Case B	Case C
Direct materials used	$ (a)	$ 83,000	$ 63,150
Direct labor	50,000	140,000	(h)
Manufacturing overhead applied	42,500	(d)	(i)
Total manufacturing costs	145,650	(e)	213,000
Work in process 1/1/14	(b)	15,500	18,000
Total cost of work in process	201,500	(f)	(j)
Work in process 12/31/14	(c)	11,800	(k)
Cost of goods manufactured	192,300	(g)	222,000

Instructions

Indicate the missing amount for each letter. Assume that in all cases manufacturing overhead is applied on the basis of direct labor cost and the rate is the same.

Compute the manufacturing overhead rate and under- or overapplied overhead.

(LO 4, 6)

E20-5 Duggan Company applies manufacturing overhead to jobs on the basis of machine hours used. Overhead costs are expected to total $325,000 for the year, and machine usage is estimated at 125,000 hours.

For the year, $342,000 of overhead costs are incurred and 130,000 hours are used.

Instructions
(a) Compute the manufacturing overhead rate for the year.
(b) What is the amount of under- or overapplied overhead at December 31?
(c) Prepare the adjusting entry to assign the under- or overapplied overhead for the year
to cost of goods sold.

E20-6 A job cost sheet of Sandoval Company is given below.

Analyze job cost sheet and prepare entry for completed job.
(LO 2, 3, 4, 5)

Job Cost Sheet

JOB NO.   469   Quantity   2,500
ITEM   White Lion Cages   Date Requested   7/2
FOR   Todd Company   Date Completed   7/31

Date	Direct Materials	Direct Labor	Manufacturing Overhead
7/10	700		
12	900		
15		440	550
22		380	475
24	1,600		
27	1,500		
31		540	675

Cost of completed job:
  Direct materials   ——
  Direct labor   ——
  Manufacturing overhead   ——
Total cost   ——
Unit cost   ——

Instructions
(a) ———— Answer the following questions.
  (1) What are the source documents for direct materials, direct labor, and manufacturing overhead costs assigned to this job?
  (2) What is the predetermined manufacturing overhead rate?
  (3) What are the total cost and the unit cost of the completed job? (Round unit cost to nearest cent.)
(b) Prepare the entry to record the completion of the job.

E20-7 Torre Corporation incurred the following transactions.

1. Purchased raw materials on account $46,300.
2. Raw materials of $36,000 were requisitioned to the factory. An analysis of the materials requisition slips indicated that $6,800 was classified as indirect materials.
3. Factory labor costs incurred were $55,900, of which $51,000 pertained to factory wages payable and $4,900 pertained to employer payroll taxes payable.
4. Time tickets indicated that $50,000 was direct labor and $5,900 was indirect labor.
5. Manufacturing overhead costs incurred on account were $80,500.
6. Depreciation on the company's office building was $8,100.
7. Manufacturing overhead was applied at the rate of 150% of direct labor cost.
8. Goods costing $88,000 were completed and transferred to finished goods.
9. Finished goods costing $75,000 to manufacture were sold on account for $103,000.

Instructions
Journalize the transactions. (Omit explanations.)

Prepare entries for manufacturing and nonmanufacturing costs.
(LO 2, 3, 4, 5)

E20-8 Enos Printing Corp. uses a job order cost system. The following data summarize the operations related to the first quarter's production.

1. Materials purchased on account $192,000, and factory wages incurred $87,300.
2. Materials requisitioned and factory labor used by job:

Prepare entries for manufacturing and nonmanufacturing costs.
(LO 2, 3, 4, 5)

Job Number	Materials	Factory Labor
A20	$ 35,240	$18,000
A21	42,920	22,000
A22	36,100	15,000
A23	39,270	25,000
General factory use	4,470	7,300
	$158,000	$87,300

3. Manufacturing overhead costs incurred on account $49,500.
4. Depreciation on factory equipment $14,550.
5. Depreciation on the company's office building was $14,300.
6. Manufacturing overhead rate is 90% of direct labor cost.
7. Jobs completed during the quarter: A20, A21, and A23.

Instructions
Prepare entries to record the operations summarized above. (Prepare a schedule showing the individual cost elements and total cost for each job in item 7.)

Prepare a cost of goods manufactured schedule and partial financial statements.
(LO 2, 5)

XLS

E20-9 At May 31, 2014, the accounts of Mantle Company show the following.

1. May 1 inventories—finished goods $12,600, work in process $14,700, and raw materials $8,200.
2. May 31 inventories—finished goods $9,500, work in process $17,900, and raw materials $7,100.
3. Debit postings to work in process were direct materials $62,400, direct labor $50,000, and manufacturing overhead applied $40,000.
4. Sales revenue totaled $210,000.

Instructions
(a) Prepare a condensed cost of goods manufactured schedule.
(b) Prepare an income statement for May through gross profit.
(c) Indicate the balance sheet presentation of the manufacturing inventories at May 31, 2014.

Compute work in process and finished goods from job cost sheets.
(LO 3, 5)

E20-10 Tierney Company begins operations on April 1. Information from job cost sheets shows the following.

	Manufacturing Costs Assigned			
Job Number	April	May	June	Month Completed
10	$5,200	$4,400		May
11	4,100	3,900	$2,000	June
12	1,200			April
13		4,700	4,500	June
14		5,900	3,600	Not complete

Job 12 was completed in April. Job 10 was completed in May. Jobs 11 and 13 were completed in June. Each job was sold for 25% above its cost in the month following completion.

Instructions
(a) What is the balance in Work in Process Inventory at the end of each month?
(b) What is the balance in Finished Goods Inventory at the end of each month?
(c) What is the gross profit for May, June, and July?

Prepare entries for costs of services performed.
(LO 2, 4, 5)

E20-11 Shown below are the job cost related accounts for the law firm of Jack, Bob, and Will and their manufacturing equivalents:

Law Firm Accounts	Manufacturing Firm Accounts
Supplies	Raw Materials
Salaries and Wages Payable	Factory Wages Payable
Operating Overhead	Manufacturing Overhead
Service Contracts in Process	Work in Process
Cost of Completed Service Contracts	Cost of Goods Sold

Cost data for the month of March follow.

1. Purchased supplies on account $1,500.
2. Issued supplies $1,200 (60% direct and 40% indirect).
3. Assigned labor costs based on time cards for the month which indicated labor costs of $60,000 (80% direct and 20% indirect).
4. Operating overhead costs incurred for cash totaled $40,000.
5. Operating overhead is applied at a rate of 90% of direct attorney cost.
6. Work completed totaled $75,000.

Instructions
(a) Journalize the transactions for March. (Omit explanations.)
(b) Determine the balance of the Service Contracts in Process account. (Use a T-account.)

E20-12 Don Lieberman and Associates, a CPA firm, uses job order costing to capture the costs of its audit jobs. There were no audit jobs in process at the beginning of November. Listed below are data concerning the three audit jobs conducted during November.

Determine cost of jobs and ending balance in work in process and overhead accounts.

(LO 3, 4, 6)

	Lynn	**Brian**	**Mike**
Direct materials	$600	$400	$200
Auditor labor costs	$5,400	$6,600	$3,375
Auditor hours	72	88	45

Overhead costs are applied to jobs on the basis of auditor hours, and the predetermined overhead rate is $50 per auditor hour. The Lynn job is the only incomplete job at the end of November. Actual overhead for the month was $11,000.

Instructions
(a) Determine the cost of each job.
(b) Indicate the balance of the Service Contracts in Process account at the end of November.
(c) Calculate the ending balance of the Operating Overhead account for November.

E20-13 Pure Decorating uses a job order cost system to collect the costs of its interior decorating business. Each client's consultation is treated as a separate job. Overhead is applied to each job based on the number of decorator hours incurred. Listed below are data for the current year.

Determine predetermined overhead rate, apply overhead and determine whether balance under- or overapplied.

(LO 4, 6)

Estimated overhead	$920,000
Actual overhead	$942,800
Estimated decorator hours	40,000
Actual decorator hours	40,500

The company uses Operating Overhead in place of Manufacturing Overhead.

Instructions
(a) Compute the predetermined overhead rate.
(b) Prepare the entry to apply the overhead for the year.
(c) Determine whether the overhead was under- or overapplied and by how much.

EXERCISES: SET B AND CHALLENGE EXERCISES

Visit the book's companion website, at **www.wiley.com/college/weygandt**, and choose the Student Companion site to access Exercise Set B and Challenge Exercises.

PROBLEMS: SET A

P20-1A Degelman Company uses a job order cost system and applies overhead to production on the basis of direct labor costs. On January 1, 2014, Job No. 50 was the only job in process. The costs incurred prior to January 1 on this job were as follows: direct materials

Prepare entries in a job order cost system and job cost sheets.

(LO 2, 3, 4, 5, 6)

$20,000, direct labor $12,000, and manufacturing overhead $16,000. As of January 1, Job No. 49 had been completed at a cost of $90,000 and was part of finished goods inventory. There was a $15,000 balance in the Raw Materials Inventory account.

During the month of January, Degelman Company began production on Jobs 51 and 52, and completed Jobs 50 and 51. Jobs 49 and 50 were also sold on account during the month for $122,000 and $158,000, respectively. The following additional events occurred during the month.

1. Purchased additional raw materials of $90,000 on account.
2. Incurred factory labor costs of $70,000. Of this amount $16,000 related to employer payroll taxes.
3. Incurred manufacturing overhead costs as follows: indirect materials $17,000; indirect labor $20,000; depreciation expense on equipment $19,000; and various other manufacturing overhead costs on account $16,000.
4. Assigned direct materials and direct labor to jobs as follows.

Job No.	Direct Materials	Direct Labor
50	$10,000	$ 5,000
51	39,000	25,000
52	30,000	20,000

Instructions
(a) Calculate the predetermined overhead rate for 2014, assuming Degelman Company estimates total manufacturing overhead costs of $980,000, direct labor costs of $700,000, and direct labor hours of 20,000 for the year.
(b) Open job cost sheets for Jobs 50, 51, and 52. Enter the January 1 balances on the job cost sheet for Job No. 50.
(c) Prepare the journal entries to record the purchase of raw materials, the factory labor costs incurred, and the manufacturing overhead costs incurred during the month of January.
(d) Prepare the journal entries to record the assignment of direct materials, direct labor, and manufacturing overhead costs to production. In assigning manufacturing overhead costs, use the overhead rate calculated in (a). Post all costs to the job cost sheets as necessary.

(e) Job 50, $70,000
Job 51, $99,000

(e) Total the job cost sheets for any job(s) completed during the month. Prepare the journal entry (or entries) to record the completion of any job(s) during the month.
(f) Prepare the journal entry (or entries) to record the sale of any job(s) during the month.
(g) What is the balance in the Finished Goods Inventory account at the end of the month? What does this balance consist of?
(h) What is the amount of over- or underapplied overhead?

Prepare entries in a job order cost system and partial income statement.
(LO 2, 3, 4, 5, 6)

P20-2A For the year ended December 31, 2014, the job cost sheets of Cinta Company contained the following data.

Job Number	Explanation	Direct Materials	Direct Labor	Manufacturing Overhead	Total Costs
7640	Balance 1/1	$25,000	$24,000	$28,800	$ 77,800
	Current year's costs	30,000	36,000	43,200	109,200
7641	Balance 1/1	11,000	18,000	21,600	50,600
	Current year's costs	43,000	48,000	57,600	148,600
7642	Current year's costs	58,000	55,000	66,000	179,000

Other data:

1. Raw materials inventory totaled $15,000 on January 1. During the year, $140,000 of raw materials were purchased on account.
2. Finished goods on January 1 consisted of Job No. 7638 for $87,000 and Job No. 7639 for $92,000.
3. Job No. 7640 and Job No. 7641 were completed during the year.
4. Job Nos. 7638, 7639, and 7641 were sold on account for $530,000.

5. Manufacturing overhead incurred on account totaled $120,000.
6. Other manufacturing overhead consisted of indirect materials $14,000, indirect labor $18,000, and depreciation on factory machinery $8,000.

Instructions
(a) Prove the agreement of Work in Process Inventory with job cost sheets pertaining to unfinished work. (*Hint:* Use a single T-account for Work in Process Inventory.) Calculate each of the following, then post each to the T-account: (1) beginning balance, (2) direct materials, (3) direct labor, (4) manufacturing overhead, and (5) completed jobs.
(b) Prepare the adjusting entry for manufacturing overhead, assuming the balance is allocated entirely to Cost of Goods Sold.
(c) Determine the gross profit to be reported for 2014.

(a) $179,000; Job 7642: $179,000

(b) Amount = $6,800

(c) $158,600

P20-3A Stellar Inc. is a construction company specializing in custom patios. The patios are constructed of concrete, brick, fiberglass, and lumber, depending upon customer preference. On June 1, 2014, the general ledger for Stellar Inc. contains the following data.

Prepare entries in a job order cost system and cost of goods manufactured schedule.
(LO 2, 3, 4, 5)

Raw Materials Inventory	$4,200	Manufacturing Overhead Applied	$32,640
Work in Process Inventory	$5,540	Manufacturing Overhead Incurred	$31,650

Subsidiary data for Work in Process Inventory on June 1 are as follows.

Job Cost Sheets

	Customer Job		
Cost Element	Gannon	Rosenthal	Linton
Direct materials	$ 600	$ 800	$ 900
Direct labor	320	540	580
Manufacturing overhead	400	675	725
	$1,320	$2,015	$2,205

During June, raw materials purchased on account were $4,900, and all wages were paid. Additional overhead costs consisted of depreciation on equipment $700 and miscellaneous costs of $400 incurred on account.
A summary of materials requisition slips and time tickets for June shows the following.

Customer Job	Materials Requisition Slips	Time Tickets
Gannon	$ 800	$ 450
Koss	2,000	800
Rosenthal	500	360
Linton	1,300	1,200
Gannon	300	390
	4,900	3,200
General use	1,500	1,200
	$6,400	$4,400

Overhead was charged to jobs at the same rate of $1.25 per dollar of direct labor cost. The patios for customers Gannon, Rosenthal, and Linton were completed during June and sold for a total of $18,900. Each customer paid in full.

Instructions
(a) Journalize the June transactions: (i) for purchase of raw materials, factory labor costs incurred, and manufacturing overhead costs incurred; (ii) assignment of direct materials, labor, and overhead to production; and (iii) completion of jobs and sale of goods.
(b) Post the entries to Work in Process Inventory.
(c) Reconcile the balance in Work in Process Inventory with the costs of unfinished jobs.
(d) Prepare a cost of goods manufactured schedule for June.

(d) Cost of goods manufactured $13,840

Compute predetermined overhead rates, apply overhead, and calculate under- or overapplied overhead.

(LO 4, 6)

P20-4A Agassi Company uses a job order cost system in each of its three manufacturing departments. Manufacturing overhead is applied to jobs on the basis of direct labor cost in Department D, direct labor hours in Department E, and machine hours in Department K.

In establishing the predetermined overhead rates for 2014, the following estimates were made for the year.

	Department		
	D	**E**	**K**
Manufacturing overhead	$1,200,000	$1,500,000	$900,000
Direct labor costs	$1,500,000	$1,250,000	$450,000
Direct labor hours	100,000	125,000	40,000
Machine hours	400,000	500,000	120,000

During January, the job cost sheets showed the following costs and production data.

	Department		
	D	**E**	**K**
Direct materials used	$140,000	$126,000	$78,000
Direct labor costs	$120,000	$110,000	$37,500
Manufacturing overhead incurred	$ 99,000	$124,000	$79,000
Direct labor hours	8,000	11,000	3,500
Machine hours	34,000	45,000	10,400

(a) 80%, $12, $7.50
(b) $356,000, $368,000, $193,500
(c) $3,000, $(8,000), $1,000

Instructions
(a) Compute the predetermined overhead rate for each department.
(b) Compute the total manufacturing costs assigned to jobs in January in each department.
(c) Compute the under- or overapplied overhead for each department at January 31.

Analyze manufacturing accounts and determine missing amounts.

(LO 2, 3, 4, 5, 6)

P20-5A Rodman Corporation's fiscal year ends on November 30. The following accounts are found in its job order cost accounting system for the first month of the new fiscal year.

Raw Materials Inventory

Dec. 1	Beginning balance	(a)	Dec. 31	Requisitions	16,850
31	Purchases	19,225			
Dec. 31	Ending balance	7,975			

Work in Process Inventory

Dec. 1	Beginning balance	(b)	Dec. 31	Jobs completed	(f)
31	Direct materials	(c)			
31	Direct labor	8,800			
31	Overhead	(d)			
Dec. 31	Ending balance	(e)			

Finished Goods Inventory

Dec. 1	Beginning balance	(g)	Dec. 31	Cost of goods sold	(i)
31	Completed jobs	(h)			
Dec. 31	Ending balance	(j)			

Factory Labor

Dec. 31	Factory wages	12,025	Dec. 31	Wages assigned	(k)

Manufacturing Overhead

Dec. 31	Indirect materials	1,900	Dec. 31	Overhead applied	(m)
31	Indirect labor	(l)			
31	Other overhead	1,245			

Other data:

1. On December 1, two jobs were in process: Job No. 154 and Job No. 155. These jobs had combined direct materials costs of $9,750 and direct labor costs of $15,000. Overhead was applied at a rate that was 75% of direct labor cost.

2. During December, Job Nos. 156, 157, and 158 were started. On December 31, Job No. 158 was unfinished. This job had charges for direct materials $3,800 and direct labor $4,800, plus manufacturing overhead. All jobs, except for Job No. 158, were completed in December.

3. On December 1, Job No. 153 was in the finished goods warehouse. It had a total cost of $5,000. On December 31, Job No. 157 was the only job finished that was not sold. It had a cost of $4,000.

4. Manufacturing overhead was $230 overapplied in December.

Instructions

List the letters (a) through (m) and indicate the amount pertaining to each letter.

(c) $14,950
(f) $54,150
(i) $55,150

PROBLEMS: SET B

P20-1B Pedriani Company uses a job order cost system and applies overhead to production on the basis of direct labor hours. On January 1, 2014, Job No. 25 was the only job in process. The costs incurred prior to January 1 on this job were as follows: direct materials $10,000; direct labor $6,000; and manufacturing overhead $9,000. Job No. 23 had been completed at a cost of $42,000 and was part of finished goods inventory. There was a $5,000 balance in the Raw Materials Inventory account.

Prepare entries in a job order cost system and job cost sheets.

(LO 2, 3, 4, 5, 6)

During the month of January, the company began production on Jobs 26 and 27, and completed Jobs 25 and 26. Jobs 23 and 25 were sold on account during the month for $63,000 and $74,000, respectively. The following additional events occurred during the month.

1. Purchased additional raw materials of $45,000 on account.

2. Incurred factory labor costs of $33,500. Of this amount, $7,500 related to employer payroll taxes.

3. Incurred manufacturing overhead costs as follows: indirect materials $10,000; indirect labor $9,500; depreciation expense on equipment $12,000; and various other manufacturing overhead costs on account $11,000.

4. Assigned direct materials and direct labor to jobs as follows.

Job No.	Direct Materials	Direct Labor
25	$ 5,000	$ 3,000
26	17,000	12,000
27	13,000	9,000

5. The company uses direct labor hours as the activity base to assign overhead. Direct labor hours incurred on each job were as follows: Job No. 25, 200; Job No. 26, 800; and Job No. 27, 600.

Instructions

(a) Calculate the predetermined overhead rate for the year 2014, assuming Pedriani Company estimates total manufacturing overhead costs of $440,000, direct labor costs of $300,000, and direct labor hours of 20,000 for the year.

(b) Open job cost sheets for Jobs 25, 26, and 27. Enter the January 1 balances on the job cost sheet for Job No. 25.

(c) Prepare the journal entries to record the purchase of raw materials, the factory labor costs incurred, and the manufacturing overhead costs incurred during the month of January.

(d) Prepare the journal entries to record the assignment of direct materials, direct labor, and manufacturing overhead costs to production. In assigning manufacturing overhead costs, use the overhead rate calculated in (a). Post all costs to the job cost sheets as necessary.

(e) Total the job cost sheets for any job(s) completed during the month. Prepare the journal entry (or entries) to record the completion of any job(s) during the month.

(e) Job 25, $37,400
    Job 26, $46,600

(f) Prepare the journal entry (or entries) to record the sale of any job(s) during the month.

(g) What is the balance in the Work in Process Inventory account at the end of the month? What does this balance consist of?

(h) What is the amount of over- or underapplied overhead?

Prepare entries in a job order cost system and partial income statement.

(LO 2, 3, 4, 5, 6)

P20-2B For the year ended December 31, 2014, the job cost sheets of Dosey Company contained the following data.

Job Number	Explanation	Direct Materials	Direct Labor	Manufacturing Overhead	Total Costs
7650	Balance 1/1	$18,000	$20,000	$25,000	$ 63,000
	Current year's costs	32,000	36,000	45,000	113,000
7651	Balance 1/1	12,000	16,000	20,000	48,000
	Current year's costs	30,000	40,000	50,000	120,000
7652	Current year's costs	35,000	68,000	85,000	188,000

Other data:

1. Raw materials inventory totaled $20,000 on January 1. During the year, $100,000 of raw materials were purchased on account.
2. Finished goods on January 1 consisted of Job No. 7648 for $93,000 and Job No. 7649 for $62,000.
3. Job No. 7650 and Job No. 7651 were completed during the year.
4. Job Nos. 7648, 7649, and 7650 were sold on account for $490,000.
5. Manufacturing overhead incurred on account totaled $135,000.
6. Other manufacturing overhead consisted of indirect materials $12,000, indirect labor $16,000, and depreciation on factory machinery $19,500.

Instructions

(a) (1) $111,000
    (4) $180,000
Unfinished job 7652,
$188,000

(b) Amount = $2,500

(c) $156,500

(a) Prove the agreement of Work in Process Inventory with job cost sheets pertaining to unfinished work. (*Hint:* Use a single T-account for Work in Process Inventory.) Calculate each of the following, then post each to the T-account: (1) beginning balance, (2) direct materials, (3) direct labor, (4) manufacturing overhead, and (5) completed jobs.
(b) Prepare the adjusting entry for manufacturing overhead, assuming the balance is allocated entirely to cost of goods sold.
(c) Determine the gross profit to be reported for 2014.

Prepare entries in a job order cost system and cost of goods manufactured schedule.

(LO 2, 3, 4, 5)

P20-3B Robert Perez is a contractor specializing in custom-built jacuzzis. On May 1, 2014, his ledger contains the following data.

Raw Materials Inventory	$30,000
Work in Process Inventory	12,200
Manufacturing Overhead	2,500 (dr.)

The Manufacturing Overhead account has debit totals of $12,500 and credit totals of $10,000. Subsidiary data for Work in Process Inventory on May 1 include:

Job Cost Sheets

Job by Customer	Direct Materials	Direct Labor	Manufacturing Overhead
Stiner	$2,500	$2,000	$1,400
Alton	2,000	1,200	840
Herman	900	800	560
	$5,400	$4,000	$2,800

During May, the following costs were incurred: raw materials purchased on account $4,000, labor paid $7,000, and manufacturing overhead paid $1,400.

A summary of materials requisition slips and time tickets for the month of May reveals the following.

Job by Customer	Materials Requisition Slips	Time Tickets
Stiner	$ 500	$ 400
Alton	600	1,000
Herman	2,300	1,300
Smith	1,900	2,300
	5,300	5,000
General use	1,500	2,000
	$6,800	$7,000

Overhead was charged to jobs on the basis of $0.70 per dollar of direct labor cost. The jacuzzis for customers Stiner, Alton, and Herman were completed during May. The three jacuzzis were sold for a total of $36,000.

Instructions
(a) Prepare journal entries for the May transactions: (i) for purchase of raw materials, factory labor costs incurred, and manufacturing overhead costs incurred; (ii) assignment of raw materials, labor, and overhead to production; and (iii) completion of jobs and sale of goods.
(b) Post the entries to Work in Process Inventory.
(c) Reconcile the balance in Work in Process Inventory with the costs of unfinished jobs.
(d) Prepare a cost of goods manufactured schedule for May.

(d) Cost of goods manufactured $20,190

P20-4B Net Play Company uses a job order cost system in each of its three manufacturing departments. Manufacturing overhead is applied to jobs on the basis of direct labor cost in Department A, direct labor hours in Department B, and machine hours in Department C.

In establishing the predetermined overhead rates for 2014, the following estimates were made for the year.

Compute predetermined overhead rates, apply overhead, and calculate under- or overapplied overhead.

(LO 4, 6)

	Department		
	A	B	C
Manufacturing overhead	$720,000	$640,000	$900,000
Direct labor cost	$600,000	$100,000	$600,000
Direct labor hours	50,000	40,000	40,000
Machine hours	100,000	120,000	150,000

During January, the job cost sheets showed the following costs and production data.

	Department		
	A	B	C
Direct materials used	$92,000	$86,000	$64,000
Direct labor cost	$48,000	$35,000	$50,400
Manufacturing overhead incurred	$60,000	$60,000	$72,100
Direct labor hours	4,000	3,500	4,200
Machine hours	8,000	10,500	12,600

Instructions
(a) Compute the predetermined overhead rate for each department.
(b) Compute the total manufacturing costs assigned to jobs in January in each department.
(c) Compute the under- or overapplied overhead for each department at January 31.

(a) 120%, $16, $6
(b) $197,600, $177,000, $190,000
(c) $2,400 $4,000, $(3,500)

P20-5B Bell Company's fiscal year ends on June 30. The following accounts are found in its job order cost accounting system for the first month of the new fiscal year.

Analyze manufacturing accounts and determine missing amounts.

(LO 2, 3, 4, 5, 6)

Raw Materials Inventory

July 1	Beginning balance	19,000	July 31	Requisitions	(a)
31	Purchases	90,400			
July 31	Ending balance	(b)			

Work in Process Inventory

July 1	Beginning balance	(c)	July 31	Jobs completed	(f)
31	Direct materials	80,000			
31	Direct labor	(d)			
31	Overhead	(e)			
July 31	Ending balance	(g)			

Finished Goods Inventory

July 1	Beginning balance	(h)	July 31	Cost of goods sold	(j)
31	Completed jobs	(i)			
July 31	Ending balance	(k)			

Factory Labor

July 31	Factory wages	(l)	July 31	Wages assigned	(m)

Manufacturing Overhead

July 31	Indirect materials	8,900	July 31	Overhead applied	117,000
31	Indirect labor	16,000			
31	Other overhead	(n)			

Other data:

1. On July 1, two jobs were in process: Job No. 4085 and Job No. 4086, with costs of $19,000 and $8,200, respectively.
2. During July, Job Nos. 4087, 4088, and 4089 were started. On July 31, only Job No. 4089 was unfinished. This job had charges for direct materials $2,000 and direct labor $1,500, plus manufacturing overhead. Manufacturing overhead was applied at the rate of 130% of direct labor cost.
3. On July 1, Job No. 4084, costing $145,000, was in the finished goods warehouse. On July 31, Job No. 4088, costing $138,000, was in finished goods.
4. Overhead was $3,000 underapplied in July.

Instructions

(d) $ 90,000
(f) $308,750
(l) $106,000

List the letters (a) through (n) and indicate the amount pertaining to each letter. Show computations.

PROBLEMS: SET C

Visit the book's companion website, at **www.wiley.com/college/weygandt**, and choose the Student Companion site to access Problem Set C.

WATERWAYS CONTINUING PROBLEM

(*Note:* This is a continuation of the Waterways Problem from Chapter 19.)

WCP20 Waterways has two major public-park projects to provide with comprehensive irrigation in one of its service locations this month. Job J57 and Job K52 involve 15 acres of landscaped terrain which will require special-order sprinkler heads to meet the specifications of the project. This problem asks you to help Waterways use a job order cost system to account for production of these parts.

Go to the book's companion website, at **www.wiley.com/college/weygandt**, *to find the completion of this problem.*

Broadening Your Perspective

Management Decision-Making

Decision-Making Problem: Current Designs

BYP20-1 Huegel Hollow Resort has ordered 20 rotomolded kayaks from Current Designs. Each kayak will be formed in the rotomolded oven, cooled, and then the excess plastic trimmed away. Then, the hatches, seat, ropes, and bungees will be attached to the kayak.

Dave Thill, the kayak plant manager, knows that manufacturing each kayak requires 54 pounds of polyethylene powder and a finishing kit (rope, seat, hardware, etc.). The polyethylene powder used in these kayaks costs $1.50 per pound, and the finishing kits cost $170 each. Each kayak will use two kinds of labor: 2 hours of more-skilled type I labor from people who run the oven and trim the plastic, and 3 hours of less-skilled type II labor from people who attach the hatches and seat and other hardware. The type I employees are paid $15 per hour, and the type II employees are paid $12 per hour. For purposes of this problem, assume that overhead is allocated to all jobs at a rate of 150% of direct labor costs.

Instructions
Determine the total cost of the Huegel Hollow order and the cost of each individual kayak in the order. Identify costs as direct materials, direct labor, or manufacturing overhead.

Decision-Making Across the Organization

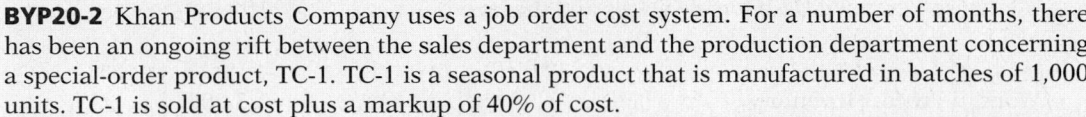

BYP20-2 Khan Products Company uses a job order cost system. For a number of months, there has been an ongoing rift between the sales department and the production department concerning a special-order product, TC-1. TC-1 is a seasonal product that is manufactured in batches of 1,000 units. TC-1 is sold at cost plus a markup of 40% of cost.

The sales department is unhappy because fluctuating unit production costs significantly affect selling prices. Sales personnel complain that this has caused excessive customer complaints and the loss of considerable orders for TC-1.

The production department maintains that each job order must be fully costed on the basis of the costs incurred during the period in which the goods are produced. Production personnel maintain that the only real solution to the problem is for the sales department to increase sales in the slack periods.

Andrea Parley, president of the company, asks you as the company accountant to collect quarterly data for the past year on TC-1. From the cost accounting system, you accumulate the following production quantity and cost data.

Costs	Quarter			
	1	2	3	4
Direct materials	$100,000	$220,000	$ 80,000	$200,000
Direct labor	60,000	132,000	48,000	120,000
Manufacturing overhead	105,000	153,000	97,000	125,000
Total	$265,000	$505,000	$225,000	$445,000
Production in batches	5	11	4	10
Unit cost (per batch)	$ 53,000	$ 45,909	$ 56,250	$ 44,500

Instructions
With the class divided into groups, answer the following questions.

(a) What manufacturing cost element is responsible for the fluctuating unit costs? Why?
(b) What is your recommended solution to the problem of fluctuating unit cost?
(c) Restate the quarterly data on the basis of your recommended solution.

Managerial Analysis

BYP20-3 In the course of routine checking of all journal entries prior to preparing year-end reports, Betty Eller discovered several strange entries. She recalled that the president's son Joe had come in to help out during an especially busy time and that he had recorded some journal entries. She was relieved that there were only a few of his entries, and even more relieved that he had included rather lengthy explanations. The entries Joe made were:

(1)

Work in Process Inventory	25,000	
Cash		25,000

(This is for materials put into process. I don't find the record that we paid for these, so I'm crediting Cash because I know we'll have to pay for them sooner or later.)

(2)

| Manufacturing Overhead | 12,000 | |
| Cash | | 12,000 |

(This is for bonuses paid to salespeople. I know they're part of overhead, and I can't find an account called "Non-Factory Overhead" or "Other Overhead" so I'm putting it in Manufacturing Overhead. I have the check stubs, so I know we paid these.)

(3)

| Wages Expense | 120,000 | |
| Cash | | 120,000 |

(This is for the factory workers' wages. I have a note that payroll taxes are $18,000. I still think that's part of wages expense and that we'll have to pay it all in cash sooner or later, so I credited Cash for the wages and the taxes.)

(4)

| Work in Process Inventory | 3,000 | |
| Raw Materials Inventory | | 3,000 |

(This is for the glue used in the factory. I know we used this to make the products, even though we didn't use very much on any one of the products. I got it out of inventory, so I credited an inventory account.)

Instructions
(a) How should Joe have recorded each of the four events?
(b) If the entry was not corrected, which financial statements (income statement or balance sheet) would be affected? What balances would be overstated or understated?

Real-World Focus

BYP 20-4 Founded in 1970, Parlex Corporation is a world leader in the design and manufacture of flexible interconnect products. Utilizing proprietary and patented technologies, Parlex produces custom flexible interconnects including flexible circuits, polymer thick film, laminated cables, and value-added assemblies for sophisticated electronics used in automotive, telecommunications, computer, diversified electronics, and aerospace applications. In addition to manufacturing sites in Methuen, Massachusetts; Salem, New Hampshire; Cranston, Rhode Island; San Jose, California; Shanghai, China; Isle of Wight, UK; and Empalme, Mexico, Parlex has logistic support centers and strategic alliances throughout North America, Asia, and Europe.

The following information was provided in the company's annual report.

PARLEX COMPANY
Notes to the Financial Statements

The Company's products are manufactured on a job order basis to customers' specifications. Customers submit requests for quotations on each job, and the Company prepares bids based on its own cost estimates. The Company attempts to reflect the impact of changing costs when establishing prices. However, during the past several years, the market conditions for flexible circuits and the resulting price sensitivity haven't always allowed this to transpire. Although still not satisfactory, the Company was able to reduce the cost of products sold as a percentage of sales to 85% this year versus 87% that was experienced in the two immediately preceding years. Management continues to focus on improving operational efficiency and further reducing costs.

Instructions
(a) Parlex management discusses the job order cost system employed by their company. What are several advantages of using the job order approach to costing?
(b) Contrast the products produced in a job order environment, like Parlex, to those produced when process cost systems are used.

BYP20-5 The Institute of Management Accountants sponsors a certification for management accountants, allowing them to obtain the title of Certified Management Accountant.

Address: **www.imanet.org,** or go to **www.wiley.com/college/weygandt**

Steps
1. Go to the site shown above.
2. Choose **CMA Certification**, and then, **Earning & Maintaining Your Credential**.

Instructions
(a) What is the experience qualification requirement?
(b) How many hours of continuing education are required, and what types of courses qualify?

Critical Thinking

Communication Activity

BYP20-6 You are the management accountant for Williams Company. Your company does custom carpentry work and uses a job order cost system. Williams sends detailed job cost sheets to its customers, along with an invoice. The job cost sheets show the date materials were used, the dollar cost of materials, and the hours and cost of labor. A predetermined overhead application rate is used, and the total overhead applied is also listed.

Nancy Kopay is a customer who recently had custom cabinets installed. Along with her check in payment for the work done, she included a letter. She thanked the company for including the detailed cost information but questioned why overhead was estimated. She stated that she would be interested in knowing exactly what costs were included in overhead, and she thought that other customers would, too.

Instructions
Prepare a letter to Ms. Kopay (address: 123 Cedar Lane, Altoona, KS 66651) and tell her why you did not send her information on exact costs of overhead included in her job. Respond to her suggestion that you provide this information.

Ethics Case

BYP20-7 LRF Printing performs printing services for many different corporate clients. Although LRF bids most jobs, some jobs, particularly new ones, are negotiated on a "cost-plus" basis. Cost-plus means that the buyer is willing to pay the actual cost plus a return (profit) on these costs to LRF.

Alice Reiley, controller for LRF, has recently returned from a meeting where LRF's president stated that he wanted her to find a way to charge more costs to any project that was on a cost-plus basis. The president noted that the company needed more profits to meet its stated goals this period. By charging more costs to the cost-plus projects and therefore fewer costs to the jobs that were bid, the company should be able to increase its profit for the current year.

Alice knew why the president wanted to take this action. Rumors were that he was looking for a new position and if the company reported strong profits, the president's opportunities would be enhanced. Alice also recognized that she could probably increase the cost of certain jobs by changing the basis used to allocate manufacturing overhead.

Instructions
(a) Who are the stakeholders in this situation?
(b) What are the ethical issues in this situation?
(c) What would you do if you were Alice Reiley?

All About You

BYP20-8 Many of you will work for a small business. Some of you will even own your own business. In order to operate a small business, you will need a good understanding of managerial accounting, as well as many other skills. Much information is available to assist people who are interested in starting a new business. A great place to start is the website provided by the Small Business Administration, which is an agency of the federal government whose purpose is to support small business.

Instructions

Go to **www.sba.gov** and in the Small Business Planner, Plan Your Business link, review the material under "Get Ready." Answer the following questions.

(a) What are some of the characteristics required of a small business owner?

(b) What are the top 10 reasons given for business failure?

Considering Your Costs and Benefits

BYP20-9 After graduating, you might decide to start a small business. As discussed in this chapter, owners of any business need to know how to calculate the cost of their products. In fact, many small businesses fail because they don't accurately calculate their product costs, so they don't know if they are making a profit or losing money—until it's too late.

Suppose that you decide to start a landscape business. You use an old pickup truck that you've fully paid for. You store the truck and other equipment in your parents' barn, and you store trees and shrubs on their land. Your parents will not charge you for the use of these facilities for the first two years, but beginning in the third year they will charge a reasonable rent. Your mother helps you by answering phone calls and providing customers with information. She doesn't charge you for this service, but she plans on doing it for only your first two years in business. In pricing your services, should you include charges for the truck, the barn, the land, and your mother's services when calculating your product cost? The basic arguments for and against are as follows.

YES: If you don't include charges for these costs, your costs are understated and your profitability is overstated.

NO: At this point, you are not actually incurring costs related to these activities; therefore, you shouldn't record charges.

Instructions

Write a response indicating your position regarding this situation. Provide support for your view.

Answers to Chapter Questions

Answers to Insight and Accounting Across the Organization Questions

p. 941 Jobs Won, Money Lost   Q: What type of costs do you think the company had been underestimating? **A:** It is most likely that the company failed to estimate and track overhead. In a highly diversified company, overhead associated with the diesel locomotive jobs may have been "lost" in the total overhead pool for the entire company.

p. 947 The Cost of an iPhone? Just Tear One Apart   Q: What type of costs are marketing and selling costs, and how are they treated for accounting purposes? **A:** Product costs include materials, labor, and overhead. Costs not related to production, such as marketing and selling costs, are period costs which are expensed in the period that they are incurred.

p. 957 Sales Are Nice, but Service Revenue Pays the Bills   Q: Explain why GE would use job order costing to keep track of the cost of repairing a malfunctioning engine for a major airline. **A:** GE operates in a competitive environment. Other companies offer competing bids to win service contracts on GE's airplane engines. GE needs to know what it costs to repair engines, so that it can present competitive bids while still generating a reasonable profit.

Answers to Self-Test Questions

1. a   **2.** c   **3.** b   **4.** c   **5.** c   **6.** d   **7.** d   **8.** b   **9.** a   **10.** d   **11.** b ($180,000 × 80%)   **12.** c   **13.** b   **14.** c   **15.** c   **16.** b

✔   **The Navigator**

21 | Process Costing

Ben & Jerry's Tracks Its Mix-Ups

Ben & Jerry's Homemade, Inc., based in Waterbury, Vermont, started its first ice cream shop in a former gas station in 1978.

Making ice cream is a process—a movement of product from a mixing department to a prepping department to a pint department. The mixing department is where the ice cream is created. In the prep area, the production process adds extras such as cherries and dark chocolate to make plain ice cream into "Cherry Garcia," Ben & Jerry's most popular flavor, or fudge-covered waffle cone pieces and a swirl of caramel for "Stephen Colbert's Americone Dream." The pint department is where the ice cream is actually put into containers. As the product is processed from one department to the next, the appropriate materials, labor, and overhead are added to determine its cost.

"The incoming ingredients from the shipping and receiving departments are stored in certain locations, either in a freezer or dry warehouse," says Beecher Eurich, staff accountant.

"As ingredients get added, so do the costs associated with them." How much ice cream is produced? Running plan around the clock, the company produces 18 million gallo a year.

With the company's process cost system, Eurich can tell how much a certain batch of ice cream costs to make—materials, labor, and overhead in each of the production departments. She generates reports for the production department heads but makes sure not to overdo it. "You can get bogged down in numbers," says Eurich. "If you generating a report that no one can use, then that's a w of time."

It's more likely, though, that Ben & Jerry's production pe want to know how efficient they are. Why? Many own in the company.

Watch the Jones Soda video in WileyPLUS to learn more about process costing in the real world.

The Navigator

- Scan Learning Objectives
- Read Feature Story
- Read Preview
- Read Text and answer **DO IT!** p. 986
  - p. 989 ■ p. 992 ■ p. 996
  - p. 1002
- Work Comprehensive **DO IT!** p. 1002
- Review Summary of Learning Objectives
- Answer Self-Test Questions
- Complete Assignments
- Go to *WileyPLUS* for practice and tutorials

Learning Objectives

After studying this chapter, you should be able to:

[1] Understand who uses process cost systems.

[2] Explain the similarities and differences between job order cost and process cost systems.

[3] Explain the flow of costs in a process cost system.

[4] Make the journal entries to assign manufacturing costs in a process cost system.

[5] Compute equivalent units.

[6] Explain the four steps necessary to prepare a production cost report.

[7] Prepare a production cost report.

[8] Explain just-in-time (JIT) processing.

[9] Explain activity-based costing (ABC).

Richard B. Levine/Alamy

Preview of Chapter 21

✔ The Navigator

The cost accounting system used by companies such as Ben & Jerry's is **process cost accounting**. In contrast to job order cost accounting, which focuses on the individual job, process cost accounting focuses on the **processes** involved in mass-producing products that are identical or very similar in nature. The primary objective of this chapter is to explain and illustrate process costing.

The content and organization of this chapter are as follows.

PROCESS COSTING

Nature of Process Cost Systems	Equivalent Units	Production Cost Report	Contemporary Developments
• Uses • Service companies • Similarities and differences • Process cost flow • Assigning manufacturing costs	• Weighted-average method • Refinements	• Physical units • Equivalent units of production • Unit production costs • Cost reconciliation schedule • Production cost report • Costing systems—Final comments	• Just-in-time processing • Activity-based costing

The Nature of Process Cost Systems

Uses of Process Cost Systems

Companies use **process cost systems** to apply costs to similar products that are mass-produced in a continuous fashion. Ben & Jerry's uses a process cost system. Production of the ice cream, once it begins, continues until the ice cream emerges, and the processing is the same for the entire run—with precisely the same amount of materials, labor, and overhead. Each finished pint of ice cream is indistinguishable from another.

A company such as USX uses process costing in the manufacturing of steel. Kellogg and General Mills use process costing for cereal production; ExxonMobil uses process costing for its oil refining. Sherwin Williams uses process costing for its paint products. At a bottling company like Coca-Cola, the manufacturing process begins with the blending of ingredients. Next, automated machinery moves the bottles into position and fills them. The production process then caps, packages, and forwards the bottles to the finished goods warehouse. Illustration 21-1 shows this process.

Illustration 21-1
Manufacturing processes

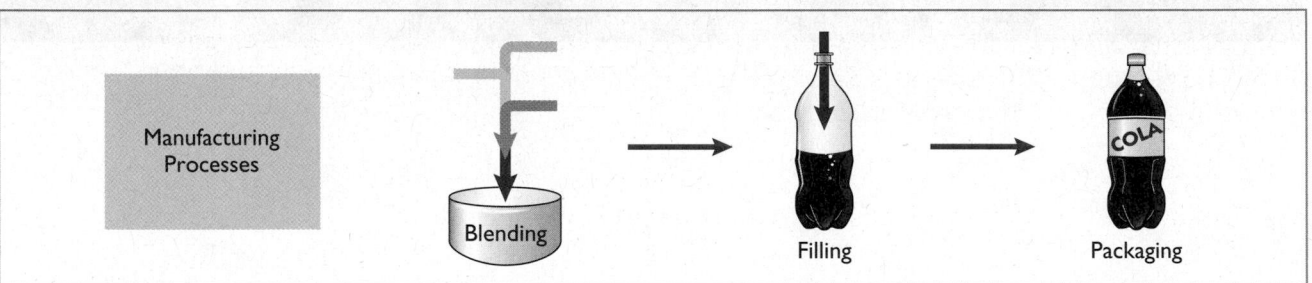

For Coca-Cola, as well as the other companies just mentioned, once production begins, it continues until the finished product emerges, and each unit of finished product is like every other unit.

In comparison, a job order cost system assigns costs to a **specific job**. Examples are the construction of a customized home, the making of a motion picture, or the manufacturing of a specialized machine. Illustration 21-2 provides examples of companies that primarily use either a process cost system or a job order cost system.

Illustration 21-2
Process cost and job order cost companies and products

Process Cost System			Job Order Cost System		
Company	**Product**		**Company**	**Product**	
Coca-Cola, PepsiCo	Soft drinks		Young & Rubicam, J. Walter Thompson	Advertising	
ExxonMobil, Royal Dutch Shell	Oil		Walt Disney, Warner Brothers	Motion pictures	
Intel, Advanced Micro Devices	Computer chips		Center Ice Consultants, Ice Pro	Ice rinks	
Dow Chemical, DuPont	Chemicals		Kaiser, Mayo Clinic	Patient health care	

Process Costing for Service Companies

Frequently, when we think of service companies, we think of specific, nonroutine tasks, such as rebuilding an automobile engine, performing consulting services on a business acquisition, or working on a major lawsuit. However, many service companies specialize in performing repetitive, routine aspects of a particular business. For example, auto-care vendors such as Jiffy Lube focus on the routine aspects of car care. H&R Block focuses on the routine aspects of basic tax practice, and many large law firms focus on routine legal services, such as uncomplicated divorces. Service companies that perform specific, nonroutine services will probably benefit from using a job order cost system. Those that perform routine, repetitive services will probably be better off with a process cost system.

Similarities and Differences Between Job Order Cost and Process Cost Systems

In a job order cost system, companies assign costs to each job. In a process cost system, companies track costs through a series of connected manufacturing processes or departments, rather than by individual jobs. Thus, companies use process cost systems when they produce a large volume of uniform or relatively homogeneous products. Illustration 21-3 shows the basic flow of costs in these two systems, and the following analysis highlights the basic similarities and differences between these two systems.

LEARNING OBJECTIVE   2

Explain the similarities and differences between job order cost and process cost systems.

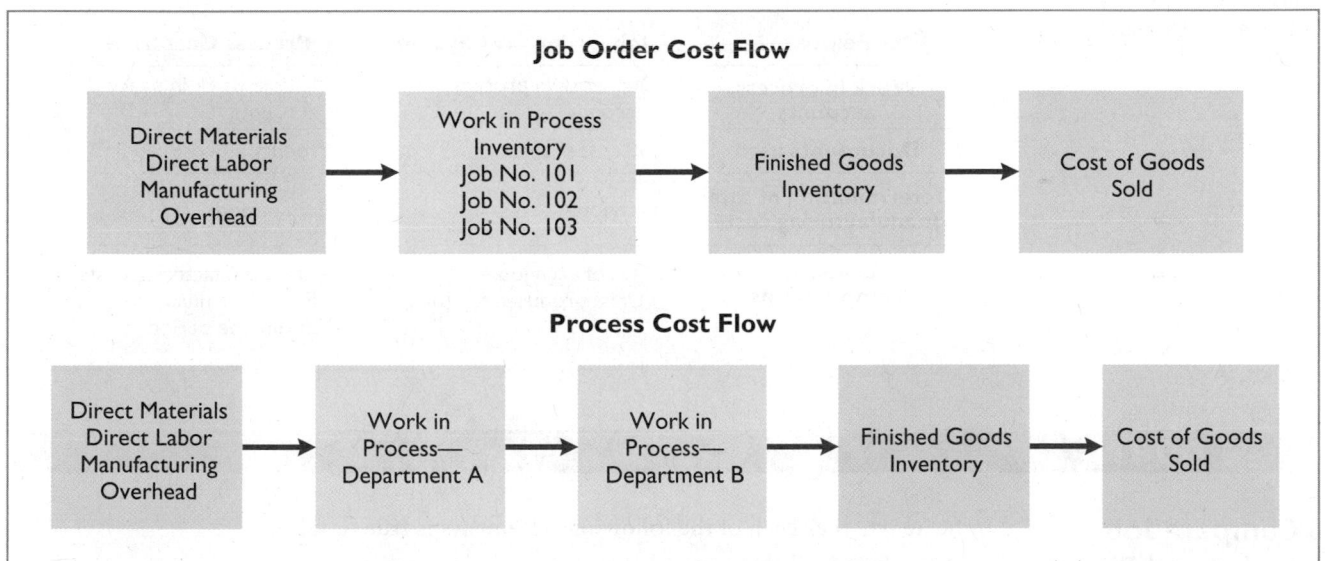

Illustration 21-3
Job order cost and process cost flow

SIMILARITIES

Job order cost and process cost systems are similar in three ways:

1. **The manufacturing cost elements.** Both costing systems track three manufacturing cost elements—direct materials, direct labor, and manufacturing overhead.
2. **The accumulation of the costs of materials, labor, and overhead.** Both costing systems debit raw materials to Raw Materials Inventory, factory labor to Factory Labor, and manufacturing overhead costs to Manufacturing Overhead.
3. **The flow of costs.** As noted above, both systems accumulate all manufacturing costs by debits to Raw Materials Inventory, Factory Labor, and Manufacturing

Overhead. Both systems then assign these costs to the same accounts—Work in Process, Finished Goods Inventory, and Cost of Goods Sold. **The methods of assigning costs, however, differ significantly.** These differences are explained and illustrated later in the chapter.

DIFFERENCES

The differences between a job order cost and a process cost system are as follows.

1. **The number of work in process accounts used.** A job order cost system uses only one work in process account. A process cost system uses multiple work in process accounts.

2. **Documents used to track costs.** A job order cost system charges costs to individual jobs and summarizes them in a job cost sheet. A process cost system summarizes costs in a production cost report for each department.

3. **The point at which costs are totaled.** A job order cost system totals costs when the job is completed. A process cost system totals costs at the end of a period of time.

4. **Unit cost computations.** In a job order cost system, the unit cost is the total cost per job divided by the units produced. In a process cost system, the unit cost is total manufacturing costs for the period divided by the equivalent units produced during the period.

Illustration 21-4 summarizes the major differences between a job order cost and a process cost system.

Illustration 21-4
Job order versus process cost systems

Feature	Job Order Cost System	Process Cost System
Work in process accounts	One work in process account	Multiple work in process accounts
Documents used	Job cost sheets	Production cost reports
Determination of total manufacturing costs	Each job	Each period
Unit-cost computations	Cost of each job ÷ Units produced for the job	Total manufacturing costs ÷ Equivalent units produced during the period

---

> **DO IT!**

Compare Job Order and Process Cost Systems

Action Plan

✔ Use job order costing in situations where unit costs are high, unit volume is low, and products are unique.

✔ Use process costing when there is a large volume of relatively homogeneous products.

Indicate whether each of the following statements is true or false.

1. A law firm is likely to use process costing for major lawsuits.
2. A manufacturer of paintballs is likely to use process costing.
3. Both job order and process costing determine product costs at the end of a period of time, rather than when a product is completed.
4. Process costing does not keep track of manufacturing overhead.

Solution

1. False.	2. True.	3. False.	4. False.

Related exercise material: **E21-1** and **DO IT!** **21-1.**

 The Navigator

Process Cost Flow

Illustration 21-5 shows the flow of costs in the process cost system for Tyler Company. Tyler Company manufactures roller blade and skateboard wheels that it sells to manufacturers and retail outlets. Manufacturing consists of two processes: machining and assembly. The Machining Department shapes, hones, and drills the raw materials. The Assembly Department assembles and packages the parts.

LEARNING OBJECTIVE 3

Explain the flow of costs in a process cost system.

Illustration 21-5
Flow of costs in process cost system

As the flow of costs indicates, the company can add materials, labor, and manufacturing overhead in both the Machining and Assembly departments. When it finishes its work, the Machining Department transfers the partially completed units to the Assembly Department. The Assembly Department finishes the goods and then transfers them to the finished goods inventory. Upon sale, Tyler removes the goods from the finished goods inventory. Within each department, a similar set of activities is performed on each unit processed.

Assigning Manufacturing Costs—Journal Entries

As indicated, the accumulation of the costs of materials, labor, and manufacturing overhead is the same in a process cost system as in a job order cost system. That is, both systems follow these procedures:

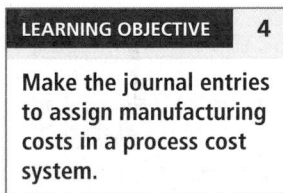

LEARNING OBJECTIVE 4

Make the journal entries to assign manufacturing costs in a process cost system.

- Companies debit all raw materials to Raw Materials Inventory at the time of purchase.
- They debit all factory labor to Factory Labor as the labor costs are incurred.
- They debit overhead costs to Manufacturing Overhead as these costs are incurred.

However, the assignment of the three manufacturing cost elements to Work in Process in a process cost system is different from a job order cost system. Here we'll look at how companies assign these manufacturing cost elements in a process cost system.

MATERIALS COSTS

All raw materials issued for production are a materials cost to the producing department. A process cost system may use materials requisition slips, but **it generally requires fewer requisitions than in a job order cost system, because the materials are used for processes rather than for specific jobs** and therefore typically are for larger quantities.

At the beginning of the first process, a company usually adds most of the materials needed for production. However, other materials may be added at various points. For example, in the manufacture of Hershey candy bars, the chocolate and other ingredients are added at the beginning of the first process, and the wrappers and cartons are added at the end of the packaging process. Tyler Company

Materials

adds materials at the beginning of each process. Tyler makes the following entry to record the materials used.

Work in Process—Machining	XXXX	
Work in Process—Assembly	XXXX	
Raw Materials Inventory		XXXX
(To record materials used)		

Ice cream maker Ben & Jerry's adds materials in three departments: milk and flavoring in the mixing department, extras such as cherries and dark chocolate in the prepping department, and cardboard containers in the pinting (packaging) department.

FACTORY LABOR COSTS

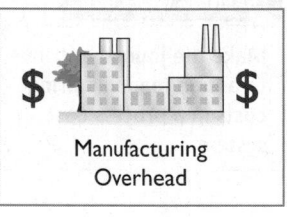

Factory Labor

In a process cost system, as in a job order cost system, companies may use time tickets to determine the cost of labor assignable to production departments. Since they assign labor costs to a process rather than a job, they can obtain, from the payroll register or departmental payroll summaries, the labor cost chargeable to a process.

Labor costs for the Machining and Assembly Departments will include the wages of employees who shape, hone, drill, and assemble the materials. The entry to assign these costs for Tyler Company is:

Work in Process—Machining	XXXX	
Work in Process—Assembly	XXXX	
Factory Labor		XXXX
(To assign factory labor to production)		

MANUFACTURING OVERHEAD COSTS

The objective in assigning overhead in a process cost system is to allocate the overhead costs to the production departments on an objective and equitable basis. That basis is the activity that "drives" or causes the costs. A primary driver of overhead costs in continuous manufacturing operations is **machine time used**, not direct labor. Thus, companies **widely use machine hours** in allocating manufacturing overhead costs using predetermined overhead rates. Tyler's entry to allocate overhead to the two processes is:

Work in Process—Machining	XXXX	
Work in Process—Assembly	XXXX	
Manufacturing Overhead		XXXX
(To assign overhead to production)		

TRANSFER TO NEXT DEPARTMENT

At the end of the month, Tyler needs an entry to record the cost of the goods transferred out of the Machining Department. In this case, the transfer is to the Assembly Department, and Tyler makes the following entry.

Work in Process—Assembly	XXXXX	
Work in Process—Machining		XXXXX
(To record transfer of units to the Assembly		
Department)		

TRANSFER TO FINISHED GOODS

When the Assembly Department completes the units, it transfers them to the finished goods warehouse. The entry for this transfer is as follows.

Finished Goods Inventory	XXXXX	
Work in Process—Assembly		XXXXX
(To record transfer of units to finished goods)		

TRANSFER TO COST OF GOODS SOLD

When Tyler sells the finished goods, it records the cost of goods sold as follows.

Cost of Goods Sold	XXXXX	
Finished Goods Inventory		XXXXX
(To record cost of units sold)		

> ## DO IT!

Manufacturing Costs in Process Costing

Ruth Company manufactures ZEBO through two processes: blending and bottling. In June, raw materials used were Blending $18,000 and Bottling $4,000. Factory labor costs were Blending $12,000 and Bottling $5,000. Manufacturing overhead costs were Blending $6,000 and Bottling $2,500. The company transfers units completed at a cost of $19,000 in the Blending Department to the Bottling Department. The Bottling Department transfers units completed at a cost of $11,000 to Finished Goods. Journalize the assignment of these costs to the two processes and the transfer of units as appropriate.

Solution

Action Plan

✔ In process cost accounting, keep separate work in process accounts for each process.

✔ When the costs are assigned to production, debit the separate work in process accounts.

✔ Transfer cost of completed units to the next process or to Finished Goods.

The entries are:

Work in Process—Blending	18,000	
Work in Process—Bottling	4,000	
Raw Materials Inventory		22,000
(To record materials used)		
Work in Process—Blending	12,000	
Work in Process—Bottling	5,000	
Factory Labor		17,000
(To assign factory labor to production)		
Work in Process—Blending	6,000	
Work in Process—Bottling	2,500	
Manufacturing Overhead		8,500
(To assign overhead to production)		
Work in Process—Bottling	19,000	
Work in Process—Blending		19,000
(To record transfer of units to the Bottling Department)		
Finished Goods Inventory	11,000	
Work in Process—Bottling		11,000
(To record transfer of units to finished goods)		

Related exercise material: **BE21-1, BE21-2, BE21-3, E21-2, E21-4, and DO IT! 21-2.**

✔ The Navigator

Equivalent Units

LEARNING OBJECTIVE **5**

Compute equivalent units.

Illustration 21-6
Information for full-time student example

Suppose you have a work-study job in the office of your college's president, and she asks you to compute the cost of instruction per full-time equivalent student at your college. The college's vice president for finance provides the following information.

Costs:
Total cost of instruction	$9,000,000

Student population:
Full-time students	900
Part-time students	1,000

Part-time students take 60% of the classes of a full-time student during the year. To compute the number of full-time equivalent students per year, you would make the following computation.

Illustration 21-7
Full-time equivalent unit computation

Full-Time Students	+	Equivalent Units of Part-Time Students	=	Full-Time Equivalent Students
900	+	(60% × 1,000)	=	1,500

The cost of instruction per full-time equivalent student is therefore the total cost of instruction ($9,000,000) divided by the number of full-time equivalent students (1,500), which is $6,000 ($9,000,000 ÷ 1,500).

A process cost system uses the same idea, called equivalent units of production. **Equivalent units of production** measure the work done during the period, expressed in fully completed units. Companies use this measure to determine the cost per unit of completed product.

Weighted-Average Method

The formula to compute equivalent units of production is as follows.

Illustration 21-8
Equivalent units of production formula

Units Completed and Transferred Out	+	Equivalent Units of Ending Work in Process	=	Equivalent Units of Production

To better understand this concept of equivalent units, consider the following two separate examples.

Example 1. In a specific period, the entire output of Sullivan Company's Blending Department consists of ending work in process of 4,000 units which are 60% complete as to materials, labor, and overhead. The equivalent units of production for the Blending Department are therefore 2,400 units (4,000 × 60%).

Example 2. The output of Kori Company's Packaging Department during the period consists of 10,000 units completed and transferred out, and 5,000 units in ending work in process which are 70% completed. The equivalent units of production are therefore 13,500 [10,000 + (5,000 × 70%)].

This method of computing equivalent units is referred to as the **weighted-average method**. It considers the degree of completion (weighting) of the units completed and transferred out and the ending work in process.

Refinements on the Weighted-Average Method

Kellogg Company has produced Eggo® Waffles since 1970. Three departments produce these waffles: Mixing, Baking, and Freezing/Packaging. The Mixing Department combines dry ingredients, including flour, salt, and baking powder, with liquid ingredients, including eggs and vegetable oil, to make waffle batter. Illustration 21-9 provides information related to the Mixing Department at the end of June.

MIXING DEPARTMENT			
		Percentage Complete	
	Physical Units	**Materials**	**Conversion Costs**
Work in process, June 1	100,000	100%	70%
Started into production	800,000		
Total units	900,000		
Units transferred out	700,000		
Work in process, June 30	200,000	100%	60%
Total units	900,000		

Illustration 21-9
Information for Mixing Department

Illustration 21-9 indicates that the beginning work in process is 100% complete as to materials cost and 70% complete as to conversion costs. **Conversion costs are the sum of labor costs and overhead costs.** In other words, Kellogg adds both the dry and liquid ingredients (materials) at the beginning of the waffle-making process, and the conversion costs (labor and overhead) related to the mixing of these ingredients are incurred uniformly and are 70% complete. The ending work in process is 100% complete as to materials cost and 60% complete as to conversion costs.

We then use the Mixing Department information to determine equivalent units. **In computing equivalent units, the beginning work in process is not part of the equivalent-units-of-production formula.** The units transferred out to the Baking Department are fully complete as to both materials and conversion costs. The ending work in process is fully complete as to materials, but only 60% complete as to conversion costs. We therefore need to make **two equivalent unit computations**: one for materials, and the other for conversion costs. Illustration 21-10 shows these computations.

Ethics Note

An unethical manager might use incorrect completion percentages when determining equivalent units. This results in either raising or lowering costs. Since completion percentages are somewhat subjective, this form of income manipulation can be difficult to detect.

MIXING DEPARTMENT		
	Equivalent Units	
	Materials	**Conversion Costs**
Units transferred out	700,000	700,000
Work in process, June 30		
200,000 × 100%	200,000	
200,000 × 60%		120,000
Total equivalent units	900,000	820,000

Illustration 21-10
Computation of equivalent units—Mixing Department

We can refine the earlier formula used to compute equivalent units of production (Illustration 21-8, page 990). Illustration 21-11 (page 992) shows the computations for materials and for conversion costs.

Illustration 21-11
Refined equivalent units of production formula

Units Completed and Transferred Out—Materials	+	Equivalent Units of Ending Work in Process—Materials	=	Equivalent Units of Production—Materials
Units Completed and Transferred Out—Conversion Costs	+	Equivalent Units of Ending Work in Process—Conversion Costs	=	Equivalent Units of Production—Conversion Costs

PEOPLE, PLANET, AND PROFIT INSIGHT

Haven't I Seen That Before?

© Nicole Hofmann/iStockphoto

For a variety of reasons, many companies, including Caterpillar, General Electric, and Eastman Kodak, are making a big push to remanufacture goods that have been thrown away. Items getting a second chance include cell phones, computers, home appliances, car parts, vacuum cleaners, and medical equipment. Businesses have figured out that profit margins on remanufactured goods are significantly higher than on new goods. As commodity prices such as copper and steel increase, reusing parts makes more sense. Also, as more local governments initiate laws requiring that electronics and appliances be recycled rather than thrown away, the cost of remanufacturing declines because the gathering of used goods becomes far more efficient. Besides benefitting the manufacturer, remanufacturing provides goods at a much lower price to consumers, reduces waste going to landfills, saves energy, reuses scarce resources, and reduces emissions. For example, it was estimated that a remanufactured car starter results in about 50% less carbon dioxide emissions than making a new one.

Source: James R. Hagerty and Paul Glader, "From Trash Heap to Store Shelf," *Wall Street Journal Online* (January 24, 2011).

? In what ways might the relative composition (materials, labor, and overhead) of a remanufactured product's cost differ from that of a newly made product? (See page 1028.)

> DO IT!

Equivalent Units

The fabricating department has the following production and cost data for the current month.

Beginning Work in Process	Units Transferred Out	Ending Work in Process
–0–	15,000	10,000

Materials are entered at the beginning of the process. The ending work in process units are 30% complete as to conversion costs. Compute the equivalent units of production for (a) materials and (b) conversion costs.

Action Plan

✔ To measure the work done during the period, expressed in fully completed units, compute equivalent units of production.

✔ Use the appropriate formula: Units completed and transferred out + Equivalent units of ending work in process = Equivalent units of production.

Solution

(a) Since materials are entered at the beginning of the process, the equivalent units of ending work in process are 10,000. Thus, 15,000 units + 10,000 units = 25,000 equivalent units of production for materials.

(b) Since ending work in process is only 30% complete as to conversion costs, the equivalent units of ending work in process are 3,000 (30% × 10,000 units). Thus, 15,000 units + 3,000 units = 18,000 equivalent units of production for conversion costs.

Related exercise material: **BE21-4, BE21-9, E21-5, E21-6, E21-8, E21-9, E21-10, E21-11, E21-13, E21-14, E21-15, and DO IT! 21-3.**

 The Navigator

Production Cost Report

As mentioned earlier, companies prepare a production cost report for each department. A **production cost report** is the key document that management uses to understand the activities in a department; it shows the production quantity and cost data related to that department. For example, in producing Eggo® Waffles, Kellogg Company uses three production cost reports: Mixing, Baking, and Freezing/Packaging. Illustration 21-12 shows the flow of costs to make an Eggo® Waffle and the related production cost reports for each department.

<table>
<tr><td>LEARNING OBJECTIVE</td><td>6</td></tr>
</table>

Explain the four steps necessary to prepare a production cost report.

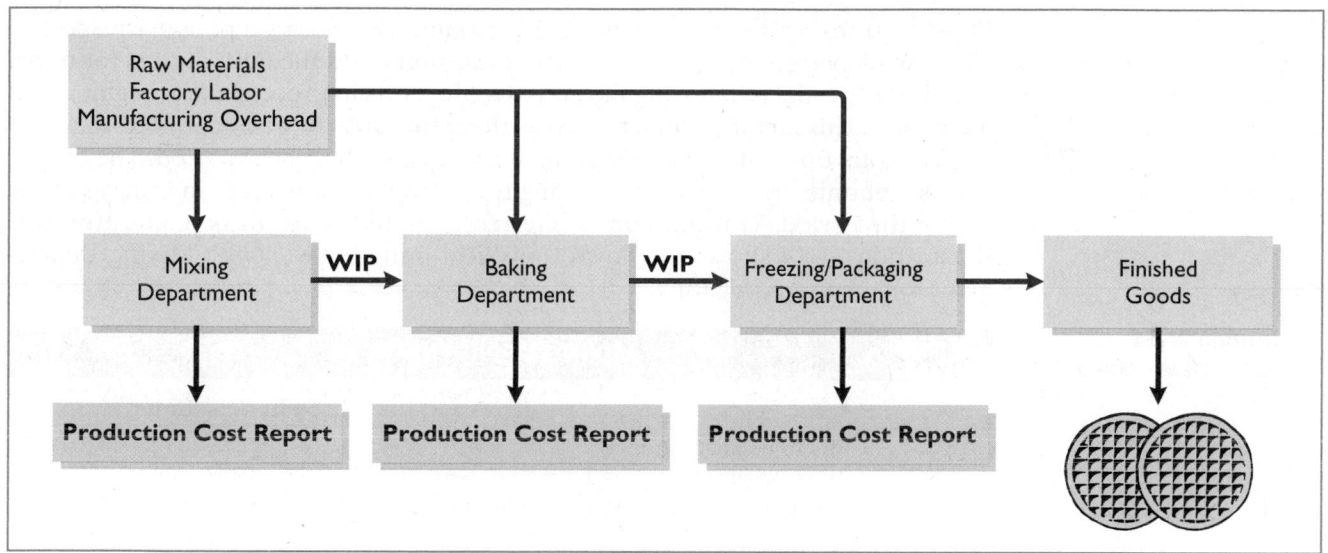

Illustration 21-12
Flow of costs in making Eggo® Waffles

In order to complete a production cost report, the company must perform four steps, which, as a whole, make up the process cost system.

1. Compute the physical unit flow.
2. Compute the equivalent units of production.
3. Compute unit production costs.
4. Prepare a cost reconciliation schedule.

Illustration 21-13 shows assumed data for the Mixing Department at Kellogg Company for the month of June. We will use this information to complete a production cost report for the Mixing Department.

Illustration 21-13
Unit and cost data—Mixing Department

MIXING DEPARTMENT	
Units	
Work in process, June 1	100,000
Direct materials: 100% complete	
Conversion costs: 70% complete	
Units started into production during June	800,000
Units completed and transferred out to Baking Department	700,000
Work in process, June 30	200,000
Direct materials: 100% complete	
Conversion costs: 60% complete	

Illustration 21-13
(*continued*)

Costs	
Work in process, June 1	
Direct materials: 100% complete	$ 50,000
Conversion costs: 70% complete	35,000
Cost of work in process, June 1	$ 85,000
Costs incurred during production in June	
Direct materials	$400,000
Conversion costs	170,000
Costs incurred in June	$570,000

Compute the Physical Unit Flow (Step 1)

Physical units are the actual units to be accounted for during a period, irrespective of any work performed. To keep track of these units, add the units started (or transferred) into production during the period to the units in process at the beginning of the period. This amount is referred to as the **total units to be accounted for**.

The total units then are accounted for by the output of the period. The output consists of units transferred out during the period and any units in process at the end of the period. This amount is referred to as the **total units accounted for**. Illustration 21-14 shows the flow of physical units for Kellogg's Mixing Department for the month of June.

Illustration 21-14
Physical unit flow—Mixing Department

MIXING DEPARTMENT	
	Physical Units
Units to be accounted for	
Work in process, June 1	100,000
Started (transferred) into production	800,000
Total units	**900,000**
Units accounted for	
Completed and transferred out	700,000
Work in process, June 30	200,000
Total units	**900,000**

The records indicate that the Mixing Department must account for 900,000 units. Of this sum, 700,000 units were transferred to the Baking Department and 200,000 units were still in process.

Compute the Equivalent Units of Production (Step 2)

Helpful Hint Materials are not always added at the beginning of the process. For example, materials are sometimes added uniformly during the process.

Once the physical flow of the units is established, Kellogg must measure the Mixing Department's productivity in terms of equivalent units of production. The Mixing Department adds materials at the beginning of the process, and it incurs conversion costs uniformly during the process. Thus, we need two computations of equivalent units: one for materials and one for conversion costs. The equivalent unit computation is as follows.

Illustration 21-15
Computation of equivalent units—Mixing Department

Helpful Hint Remember that we ignore the beginning work in process in this computation.

	Equivalent Units	
	Materials	**Conversion Costs**
Units transferred out	700,000	700,000
Work in process, June 30		
200,000 × 100%	200,000	
200,000 × 60%		120,000
Total equivalent units	900,000	820,000

Compute Unit Production Costs (Step 3)

Armed with the knowledge of the equivalent units of production, we can now compute the unit production costs. **Unit production costs** are costs expressed in terms of equivalent units of production. When equivalent units of production are different for materials and conversion costs, we compute three unit costs: (1) materials, (2) conversion, and (3) total manufacturing.

The computation of total materials cost related to Eggo® Waffles is as follows.

Work in process, June 1	
Direct materials cost	$ 50,000
Costs added to production during June	
Direct materials cost	400,000
Total materials cost	$450,000

Illustration 21-16
Total materials cost computation

The computation of unit materials cost is as follows.

Total Materials Cost	÷	Equivalent Units of Materials	=	Unit Materials Cost
$450,000	÷	900,000	=	$0.50

Illustration 21-17
Unit materials cost computation

Illustration 21-18 shows the computation of total conversion costs.

Work in process, June 1	
Conversion costs	$ 35,000
Costs added to production during June	
Conversion costs	170,000
Total conversion costs	$205,000

Illustration 21-18
Total conversion costs computation

The computation of unit conversion cost is as follows.

Total Conversion Costs	÷	Equivalent Units of Conversion Costs	=	Unit Conversion Cost
$205,000	÷	820,000	=	$0.25

Illustration 21-19
Unit conversion cost computation

Total manufacturing cost per unit is therefore computed as shown in Illustration 21-20.

Unit Materials Cost	÷	Unit Conversion Cost	=	Total Manufacturing Cost per Unit
$0.50	+	$0.25	=	$0.75

Illustration 21-20
Total manufacturing cost per unit

Prepare a Cost Reconciliation Schedule (Step 4)

We are now ready to determine the cost of goods transferred out of the Mixing Department to the Baking Department and the costs in ending work in process. Kellogg charged total costs of $655,000 to the Mixing Department in June, calculated as shown in Illustration 21-21 (page 996).

Illustration 21-21
Costs charged to Mixing
Department

Costs to be accounted for	
Work in process, June 1	$ 85,000
Started into production	570,000
Total costs	**$655,000**

The company then prepares a cost reconciliation schedule to assign these costs to (a) units transferred out to the Baking Department and (b) ending work in process.

Illustration 21-22
Cost reconciliation schedule—
Mixing Department

MIXING DEPARTMENT		
Cost Reconciliation Schedule		
Costs accounted for		
Transferred out (700,000 × $0.75)		$ 525,000
Work in process, June 30		
Materials (200,000 × $0.50)	$100,000	
Conversion costs (120,000 × $0.25)	30,000	130,000
Total costs		**$655,000**

Kellogg uses the total manufacturing cost per unit, $0.75, in costing the **units completed** and transferred to the Baking Department. In contrast, the unit cost of materials and the unit cost of conversion are needed in costing **units in process**. The **cost reconciliation schedule** shows that the **total costs accounted for** (Illustration 21-22) equal the **total costs to be accounted for** (Illustration 21-21).

Preparing the Production Cost Report

At this point, Kellogg is ready to prepare the production cost report for the Mixing Department. As indicated earlier, this report is an internal document for management that shows production quantity and cost data for a production department.

There are four steps in preparing a production cost report:

1. Compute the physical unit flow.
2. Compute the equivalent units of production.
3. Compute unit production costs.
4. Prepare a cost reconciliation schedule.

Illustration 21-23 shows the production cost report for the Mixing Department. The report identifies the four steps.

Production cost reports provide a basis for evaluating the productivity of a department. In addition, managers can use the cost data to assess whether unit costs and total costs are reasonable. By comparing the quantity and cost data with predetermined goals, top management can also judge whether current performance is meeting planned objectives.

> **DO IT!**

Cost Reconciliation Schedule

In March, Rodayo Manufacturing had the following unit production costs: materials $6 and conversion costs $9. On March 1, it had zero work in process. During March, Rodayo transferred out 12,000 units. As of March 31, 800 units that were 25% complete as to conversion costs and 100% complete as to materials were in ending work in process. Assign the costs to the units transferred out and in process.

Action Plan

✔ Assign the total manufacturing cost of $15 per unit to the 12,000 units transferred out.

✔ Assign the materials cost and conversion costs based on equivalent units of production to units in ending work in process.

Solution

The assignment of costs is as follows.

Costs accounted for		
Transferred out (12,000 × $15)		$180,000
Work in process, March 31		
Materials (800 × $6)	$4,800	
Conversion costs (200ᵃ × $9)	1,800	6,600
Total costs		$186,600

ᵃ800 × 25%

Related exercise material: **BE21-5, BE21-6, BE21-7, BE21-8, E21-5, E21-6, E21-7, E21-8, E21-9, E21-10, E21-11, E21-12, E21-13, E21-14, E21-15, and DO IT! 21-4.**

Illustration 21-23
Production cost report

Mixing Department.xls

Home   Insert   Page Layout   Formulas   Data   Review   View

P18   fx

	A	B	C	D	E
1		**Mixing Department**			
2		**Production Cost Report**			
3		**For the Month Ended June 30, 2014**			
4			**Equivalent Units**		
5		Physical Units	Materials	Conversion Costs	
6	QUANTITIES	Step 1	Step 2		
7	Units to be accounted for				
8	Work in process, June 1	100,000			
9	Started into production	800,000			
10	Total units	900,000			
11	Units accounted for				
12	Transferred out	700,000	700,000	700,000	
13	Work in process, June 30	200,000	200,000	120,000	(200,000 × 60%)
14	Total units	900,000	900,000	820,000	
15	COSTS				
16	Unit costs Step 3		Materials	Conversion Costs	Total
17	Total cost	(a)	$450,000	$205,000	$655,000
18	Equivalent units	(b)	900,000	820,000	
19	Unit costs [(a) ÷ (b)]		$0.50	$0.25	$0.75
20	Costs to be accounted for				
21	Work in process, June 1				$85,000
22	Started into production				570,000
23	Total costs				$655,000
24	Cost Reconciliation Schedule Step 4				
25	Costs accounted for				
26	Transferred out (700,000 × $0.75)				$525,000
27	Work in process, June 30				
28	Materials (200,000 × $0.50)			$100,000	
29	Conversion costs (120,000 × $0.25)			30,000	130,000
30	Total costs				$655,000
31					

Costing Systems—Final Comments

Companies often use a combination of a process cost and a job order cost system. Called **operations costing**, this hybrid system is similar to process costing in its assumption that standardized methods are used to manufacture the product. At the same time, the product may have some customized, individual features that require the use of a job order cost system.

Consider, for example, the automobile manufacturer Ford Motor Company. Each vehicle at a given plant goes through the same assembly line, but Ford uses different materials (such as seat coverings, paint, and tinted glass) for different vehicles. Similarly, Kellogg's Pop-Tarts® toaster pastries go through numerous standardized processes—mixing, filling, baking, frosting, and packaging. The pastry dough, though, comes in different flavors—plain, chocolate, and graham—and fillings include Smucker's® real fruit, chocolate fudge, vanilla creme, brown sugar cinnamon, and s'mores.

A cost-benefit trade-off occurs as a company decides which costing system to use. A job order cost system, for example, provides detailed information related to the cost of the product. Because each job has its own distinguishing characteristics, the system can provide an accurate cost per job. This information is useful in controlling costs and pricing products. However, the cost of implementing a job order cost system is often expensive because of the accounting costs involved.

On the other hand, for a company like Intel, which makes computer chips, is there a benefit in knowing whether the cost of the one-hundredth chip produced is different from the one-thousandth chip produced? Probably not. An average cost of the product will suffice for control and pricing purposes.

In summary, when deciding to use one of these systems, or a combination system, a company must weigh the costs of implementing the system against the benefits from the additional information provided.

Contemporary Developments

LEARNING OBJECTIVE   8

Explain just-in-time (JIT) processing.

As indicated in Chapter 19, two contemporary developments in managerial accounting are just-in-time processing and activity-based costing. We explain these innovations in the following sections.

Just-in-Time Processing

Traditionally, continuous process manufacturing has been based on a **just-in-case** philosophy. Companies hold inventories of raw materials **just in case** some items are of poor quality or a key supplier is shut down by a strike. They manufacture and store subassembly parts **just in case** these parts are needed later in the manufacturing process. Companies complete and store finished goods **just in case** they receive unexpected and rush customer orders. This philosophy often results in a "**push approach**." Raw materials and subassembly parts are pushed through each process. Traditional processing often results in the buildup of extensive manufacturing inventories.

Primarily in response to foreign competition, many U.S. firms have switched to **just-in-time (JIT) processing**. JIT manufacturing is dedicated to having the right amount of materials, parts, or products just as they are needed. JIT first hit the United States in the early 1980s when automobile companies adopted it to compete with foreign automakers. Many companies, including Dell, Caterpillar, and Harley-Davidson now successfully use JIT. Under JIT processing, companies receive raw materials **just in time** for use in production, they complete subassembly parts **just in time** for use in finished goods, and they complete finished goods **just in time** to be sold. Illustration 21-24 shows the sequence of activities in just-in-time processing.

Illustration 21-24
Just-in-time processing

OBJECTIVE OF JIT PROCESSING

A primary objective of JIT is to eliminate all manufacturing inventories. Inventories have an adverse effect on net income because they tie up funds and storage space that could be put to more productive uses. JIT strives to eliminate inventories by using a **"pull approach"** in manufacturing. This approach begins with the customer placing an order with the company, which starts the process of pulling the product through the manufacturing process. A computer at the final workstation sends a signal to the preceding workstation. This signal indicates the exact materials (parts and subassemblies) needed to complete the production of a specified product for a specified time period, such as an eight-hour shift. The next preceding process, in turn, sends its signal to other processes back up the line. The goal is a smooth continuous flow in the manufacturing process and no buildup of inventories at any point.

ELEMENTS OF JIT PROCESSING

There are three important elements in JIT processing:

1. **Dependable suppliers.** Suppliers must be willing to deliver on short notice exact quantities of raw materials according to precise quality specifications (even including multiple deliveries within the same day). Suppliers must also be willing to deliver the raw materials at specified work stations rather than at

a central receiving department. This type of purchasing requires constant and direct communication. Such communication is facilitated by an online computer linkage between the company and its suppliers.

2. **A multiskilled workforce.** Under JIT, machines are often strategically grouped around work cells or workstations. Much of the work is automated. As a result, one worker may operate and maintain several different types of machines.

3. **A total quality control system.** The company must establish total quality control throughout the manufacturing operations. Total quality control means **no defects**. Since the pull approach signals only required quantities, any defects at any workstation will shut down operations at subsequent workstations. Total quality control requires continuous monitoring by both employees and supervisors at each workstation.

BENEFITS OF JIT PROCESSING
The major benefits of implementing JIT processing are:

1. Significant reduction or elimination of manufacturing inventories.
2. Enhanced product quality.
3. Reduction or elimination of rework costs and inventory storage costs.
4. Production cost savings from the improved flow of goods through the processes.

The effects in many cases have been dramatic. For example, after using JIT for two years, a major division of Hewlett-Packard found that work in process inventories (in dollars) were down 82%, scrap/rework costs were down 30%, space utilization improved by 40%, and labor efficiency improved 50%. As indicated, JIT not only reduces inventory but also enables a manufacturer to produce a better product faster and with less waste.

One of the major accounting benefits of JIT is the elimination of separate raw materials and work in process inventory accounts. These accounts are replaced by **one account**, Raw and In-Process Inventory. All materials and conversion costs are charged to this account. The reduction (or elimination) of in-process inventories results in a simpler computation of equivalent units of production.

Activity-Based Costing

LEARNING OBJECTIVE 9

Explain activity-based costing (ABC).

Activity-based costing (ABC) focuses on the activities performed in producing a product. An ABC system is similar to conventional costing systems in accounting for direct materials and direct labor, but it differs in regard to manufacturing overhead.

A conventional cost system uses a **single unit-level** basis to allocate overhead costs to products. The basis may be direct labor or machine hours used to manufacture the product. The assumption in this approach is that as volume of units produced increases, so does the cost of overhead. However, in recent years the amount of direct labor used in many industries has greatly **decreased**, and total overhead costs resulting from depreciation on expensive equipment and machinery, utilities, repairs, and maintenance have significantly **increased**.

In ABC costing, the cost of a product is equal to the sum of the costs of all activities performed to manufacture it. ABC recognizes that to have accurate and meaningful cost data, **more than one basis** of allocating activity costs to products is needed.

In selecting the allocation basis, ABC seeks to identify the **cost drivers** that measure the activities performed on the product. **A cost driver** may be any factor or activity that has a direct cause–effect relationship with the resources consumed. Examples of activities and possible cost drivers are as follows.

Activity	Cost Driver
Ordering raw materials	Ordering hours; number of orders
Receiving raw materials	Receiving hours; number of shipments
Materials handling	Number of requisitions; weight of materials; handling hours
Production scheduling	Number of orders
Machine setups	Setup hours; number of setups
Machining (fabricating, assembling, etc.)	Machine hours
Quality control inspections	Number of inspections
Factory supervision	Number of employees

Illustration 21-25
Activities and cost drivers in ABC

Two important assumptions must be met in order to obtain accurate product costs under ABC:

1. All overhead costs related to the activity must be driven by the cost driver used to assign costs to products.

2. All overhead costs related to the activity should respond proportionally to changes in the activity level of the cost driver.

For example, if there is little or no correlation between changes in the cost driver and consumption of the overhead cost, inaccurate product costs are inevitable. An example of the use of ABC is illustrated in the appendix at the end of this chapter.

Activity-based costing may be used with either a job order or a process cost accounting system. The primary benefit of ABC is more accurate and meaningful product costing. Also, improved cost data about an activity can lead to reduced costs for the activity. In sum, ABC makes managers realize that it is **activities**, and not products, that determine the profitability of a company—a realization that should lead to better management decisions.

SERVICE COMPANY INSIGHT

Using ABC to Aid in Employee Evaluation

Although most publicized ABC applications are in manufacturing companies or large service firms, very small service businesses can apply it also. Mahany Welding Supply, a small family-run welding service business in Rochester, New York, used ABC to determine the cost of servicing customers and to identify feasible cost-reduction opportunities.

Application of ABC at Mahany Welding's operations provided information about the five employees who were involved in different activities of revenue generation—i.e., delivery of supplies (rural versus city), welding services, repairs, telephone sales, field or door-to-door sales, repeat business sales, and cold-call sales. Managers applied activity cost pools to the five revenue-producing employees using relevant cost drivers. ABC revealed annual net income (loss) by employee as follows.

Employee #1	$65,431	Employee #4	$(10,957)
Employee #2	$35,154	Employee #5	$(46,180)
Employee #3	$13,731		

This comparative information was an eye-opener to the owner of Mahany Welding—who was Employee #5!

Source: Michael Krupnicki and Thomas Tyson, "Using ABC to Determine the Cost of Servicing Customers," *Management Accounting* (December 31, 1997), pp. 40–46.

? What positive implications does application of ABC have for the employees of this company? (See page 1028.)

© kryczka/iStockphoto

> DO IT!

JIT and ABC

Action Plan

✔ JIT manufacturing is dedicated to having the right amounts of materials, parts, or products just as they are needed.

✔ ABC focuses on the activities performed in producing a product. It recognizes that to have accurate and meaningful cost data, more than one basis of allocating costs to products is needed.

Indicate whether each of the following statements is true or false.

1. Continuous process manufacturing often results in a reduction of inventory.
2. Companies that use just-in-time processing complete and store finished goods all the time to meet rush orders from customers.
3. A major benefit of just-in-time processing is production cost savings from the improved flow of goods through the processes.
4. An ABC system is similar to traditional costing systems in accounting for manufacturing costs but differs in regard to period costs.
5. The primary benefit of ABC is more accurate and meaningful costs.
6. In recent years, the amount of direct labor used in many industries has greatly increased and total overhead costs have significantly decreased.

Solution

1. False.	2. False.	3. True.	4. False.	5. True.	6. False.

Related exercise material: **BE21-11** and **DO IT!** 21-5.

✔ **The Navigator**

> Comprehensive DO IT!

Essence Company manufactures a high-end after-shave lotion, called Eternity, in 10-ounce plastic bottles. Because the market for after-shave lotion is highly competitive, the company is very concerned about keeping its costs under control. Eternity is manufactured through three processes: mixing, filling, and corking. Materials are added at the beginning of each of the processes, and labor and overhead are incurred uniformly throughout each process. The company uses a weighted-average method to cost its product. A partially completed production cost report for the month of May for the Mixing Department is shown below.

ESSENCE COMPANY
Mixing Department
Production Cost Report
For the Month Ended May 31, 2014

QUANTITIES	Physical Units	Equivalent Units Materials	Conversion Costs
Units to be accounted for	Step 1		Step 2
Work in process, May 1	1,000		
Started into production	2,000		
Total units	3,000		
Units accounted for			
Transferred out	2,200	?	?
Work in process, May 31	800	?	?
Total units	3,000	?	?

COSTS		Materials	Conversion Costs	Total
Unit costs Step 3				
Costs in May	(a)	?	?	?
Equivalent units	(b)	?	?	
Unit costs [(a) ÷ (b)]		?	?	?
Costs to be accounted for				
Work in process, May 1				$ 56,300
Started into production				119,320
Total costs				$175,620

COST RECONCILIATION SCHEDULE Step 4

Costs accounted for			
Transferred out			?
Work in process, May 31			
Materials		?	
Conversion costs		?	?
Total costs			?

Additional information:
Work in process, May 1, 1,000 units

Materials cost, 1,000 units (100% complete)	$49,100	
Conversion costs, 1,000 units (70% complete)	7,200	$56,300
Materials cost for May, 2,000 units		$100,000
Conversion costs for May		$19,320

Work in process, May 31, 800 units, 100% complete as to materials and 50% complete as to conversion costs.

Instructions

(a) Prepare a production cost report for the Mixing Department for the month of May.
(b) Prepare the journal entry to record the transfer of goods from the Mixing Department to the Filling Department.
(c) Explain why Essence Company is using a process cost system to account for its costs.

Solution to Comprehensive DO IT!

Action Plan

✔ Compute the physical unit flow—that is, the units to be accounted for and the units accounted for.

✔ Compute the equivalent units of production.

✔ Compute the unit production costs, expressed in terms of equivalent units of production.

✔ Prepare a cost reconciliation schedule, which shows that the total costs accounted for equal the total costs to be accounted for.

(a) A completed production cost report for the Mixing Department is shown below. Computations to support the amounts reported follow the report.

ESSENCE COMPANY
Mixing Department
Production Cost Report
For the Month Ended May 31, 2014

	Physical	Equivalent Units	
QUANTITIES	Units	Materials	Conversion Costs
Units to be accounted for	Step 1	Step 2	
Work in process, May 1	1,000		
Started into production	2,000		
Total units	3,000		

QUANTITIES	Physical Units	Equivalent Units	
		Materials	Conversion Costs
Units accounted for			
Transferred out	2,200	2,200	2,200
Work in process, May 31	800	800	400 (800 × 50%)
Total units	3,000	3,000	2,600

COSTS		Materials	Conversion Costs	Total
Unit costs Step 3				
Costs in May	(a)	$149,100	$26,520	$175,620
Equivalent units	(b)	3,000	2,600	
Unit costs [(a) ÷ (b)]		$49.70	$10.20	$59.90
Costs to be accounted for				
Work in process, May 1				$ 56,300
Started into production				119,320
Total costs				$175,620

COST RECONCILIATION SCHEDULE Step 4

Costs accounted for		
Transferred out (2,200 × $59.90)		$131,780
Work in process, May 31		
Materials (800 × $49.70)	$39,760	
Conversion costs (400 × $10.20)	4,080	43,840
Total costs		$175,620

Additional computations to support production cost report data:
Materials cost—$49,100 + $100,000
Conversion costs—$7,200 + $19,320 ($119,320 − $100,000)

(b) Work in Process—Filling   131,780
      Work in Process—Mixing   131,780

(c) Companies use process cost systems to apply costs to similar products that are mass-produced in a continuous fashion. Essence Company uses a process cost system because production of the after-shave lotion, once it begins, continues until the after-shave lotion emerges. The processing is the same for the entire run—with precisely the same amount of materials, labor, and overhead. Each bottle of Eternity after-shave lotion is indistinguishable from another.

 The Navigator

SUMMARY OF LEARNING OBJECTIVES

✔ The Navigator

1 Understand who uses process cost systems. Companies that mass-produce similar products in a continuous fashion use process cost systems. Once production begins, it continues until the finished product emerges. Each unit of finished product is indistinguishable from every other unit.

2 Explain the similarities and differences between job order cost and process cost systems. Job order cost systems are similar to process cost systems in three ways: (1) Both systems track the same cost elements—direct materials, direct labor, and manufacturing overhead. (2) Both accumulate costs in the same accounts—Raw

Materials Inventory, Factory Labor, and Manufacturing Overhead. (3) Both assign accumulated costs to the same accounts—Work in Process, Finished Goods Inventory, and Cost of Goods Sold. However, the method of assigning costs differs significantly.

There are four main differences between the two cost systems: (1) A process cost system uses separate accounts for each department or manufacturing process, rather than only one work in process account used in a job order cost system. (2) A process cost system summarizes costs in a production cost report for each department. A job cost system charges costs to individual jobs and summarizes them in a job cost sheet. (3) Costs are totaled at the end of a time period in a process cost system, but at the completion of a job in a job cost system. (4) A process cost system calculates unit cost as Total manufacturing costs for the period ÷ Units produced during the period. A job cost system calculates unit cost as Total cost per job ÷ Units produced.

3 Explain the flow of costs in a process cost system. A process cost system assigns manufacturing costs for raw materials, labor, and overhead to work in process accounts for various departments or manufacturing processes. It transfers the costs of units completed from one department to another as those units move through the manufacturing process. The system transfers the costs of completed work to Finished Goods Inventory. Finally, when inventory is sold, the system transfers costs to Cost of Goods Sold.

4 Make the journal entries to assign manufacturing costs in a process cost system. Entries to assign the costs of raw materials, labor, and overhead consist of a credit to Raw Materials Inventory, Factory Labor, and Manufacturing Overhead, and a debit to Work in Process for each department. Entries to record the cost of goods transferred to another department are a credit to Work in Process for the department whose work is finished and a debit to the department to which the goods are transferred. The entry to record units completed and transferred to the warehouse is a credit to Work in Process for the department whose work is finished and a debit to Finished Goods Inventory. The entry to record the sale of goods is a credit to Finished Goods Inventory and a debit to Cost of Goods Sold.

5 Compute equivalent units. Equivalent units of production measure work done during a period, expressed in fully completed units. Companies use this measure to determine the cost per unit of completed product. Equivalent units are the sum of units completed and transferred out plus equivalent units of ending work in process.

6 Explain the four steps necessary to prepare a production cost report. The four steps to complete a production cost report are: (1) Compute the physical unit flow—that is, the units to be accounted for and the units accounted for. (2) Compute the equivalent units of production. (3) Compute the unit production costs, expressed in terms of equivalent units of production. (4) Prepare a cost reconciliation schedule, which shows that the total costs accounted for equal the total costs to be accounted for.

7 Prepare a production cost report. The production cost report contains both quantity and cost data for a production department. There are four sections in the report: (1) number of physical units, (2) equivalent units determination, (3) unit costs, and (4) cost reconciliation schedule.

8 Explain just-in-time (JIT) processing. JIT is a manufacturing technique dedicated to producing the right products at the right time as needed. One of the principal accounting effects is that a Raw and In-Process Inventory account replaces both the raw materials and work in process inventory accounts.

9 Explain activity-based costing (ABC). ABC is a method of product costing that focuses on the activities performed to produce products. It assigns the cost of the activities to products by using cost drivers that measure the activities performed. The primary objective of ABC is accurate and meaningful product costs.

GLOSSARY

Activity-based costing (ABC) A cost accounting system that focuses on the activities performed in manufacturing a specific product. (p. 1000).

Conversion costs The sum of labor costs and overhead costs. (p. 991).

Cost driver Any factor or activity that has a direct cause–effect relationship with the resources consumed. (p. 1000).

Cost reconciliation schedule A schedule that shows that the total costs accounted for equal the total costs to be accounted for. (p. 996).

Equivalent units of production A measure of the work done during the period, expressed in fully completed units. (p. 990).

Just-in-time (JIT) processing A processing system dedicated to producing the right products (or parts) as they are needed. (p. 998).

Operations costing A combination of a process cost and a job order cost system, in which products are manufactured primarily by standardized methods, with some customization. (p. 998).

Physical units Actual units to be accounted for during a period, irrespective of any work performed. (p. 994).

Process cost systems An accounting system used to apply costs to similar products that are mass-produced in a continuous fashion. (p. 984).

Production cost report An internal report for management that shows both production quantity and cost data for a production department. (p. 993).

Total units (costs) accounted for The sum of the units (costs) transferred out during the period plus the units (costs) in process at the end of the period. (pp. 994, 996).

Total units (costs) to be accounted for The sum of the units (costs) started (or transferred) into production during the period plus the units (costs) in process at the beginning of the period. (pp. 994, 996).

Unit production costs Costs expressed in terms of equivalent units of production. (p. 995).

Weighted-average method Method used to compute equivalent units of production which considers the degree of completion (weighting) of the units completed and transferred out and the ending work in process. (p. 990).

APPENDIX 21A   Example of Traditional Costing versus Activity-Based Costing

LEARNING OBJECTIVE 10

Apply activity-based costing to specific company data.

Production and Cost Data

In this appendix, we present an example that compares activity-based costing to traditional costing. Assume that Atlas Company produces two abdominal-training products, the Ab Bench and the Ab Coaster. The Ab Bench is a high-volume item totaling 25,000 units annually. The Ab Coaster is a low-volume item totaling only 5,000 units per year. Each product requires one hour of direct labor for completion. Therefore, total annual direct labor hours are 30,000 (25,000 + 5,000). Expected annual manufacturing overhead costs are $900,000. The predetermined overhead rate is $30 ($900,000 ÷ 30,000) per direct labor hour.

The direct materials cost per unit is $40 for the Ab Bench and $30 for the Ab Coaster. The direct labor cost is $12 per unit for each product.

Unit Costs Under Traditional Costing

Illustration 21A-1 shows the unit cost for each product under traditional costing.

Illustration 21A-1
Units costs—traditional costing

	Products	
Manufacturing Costs	Ab Bench	Ab Coaster
Direct materials	$40	$30
Direct labor	12	12
Overhead	30*	30*
Total unit cost	$82	$72

*Predetermined overhead rate × Direct labor hours = $30 × 1 hr = $30

Unit Costs Under ABC

Let's now calculate unit costs under ABC, in order to compare activity-based costing with a traditional costing system. The first step is to determine overhead rates under ABC.

DETERMINING OVERHEAD RATES UNDER ABC

Analysis reveals that Atlas Company's expected annual overhead costs of $900,000 relate to three activities—machine setups, machining, and inspections. Illustration 21A-2 shows the cost driver and overhead rate for each activity.

Activity	Cost Driver	Total Expected Overhead Cost	Total Expected Use of Driver	Activity-Based Overhead Rate
Machine setups	Number of setups	$300,000	1,500	**$200** per setup
Machining	Machine hours	500,000	50,000	**$10** per machine hour
Inspections	Number of inspections	100,000	2,000	**$50** per inspection

Illustration 21A-2
Computing overhead rates—ABC

ASSIGNING OVERHEAD COSTS TO PRODUCTS UNDER ABC

In assigning costs, it is necessary to know the expected number of cost drivers for each product. Because of its low volume, the Ab Coaster requires more setups and inspections than the Ab Bench. The expected number of cost drivers for each product is as follows.

	Products		Total
Cost Driver	Ab Bench	Ab Coaster	Usage
Number of machine setups	500	1,000	1,500
Machine hours	30,000	20,000	50,000
Number of inspections	500	1,500	2,000

Illustration 21A-3
Expected number of cost drivers

Using these data, Atlas can assign the expected annual overhead cost to each product as follows.

Activity	Ab Bench Number	Ab Bench Cost	Ab Coaster Number	Ab Coaster Cost	Total Cost
Machine setups ($200)	500	$100,000	1,000	$200,000	$300,000
Machining ($10)	30,000	300,000	20,000	200,000	500,000
Inspections ($50)	500	25,000	1,500	75,000	100,000
Total assigned costs (a)		$425,000		$475,000	$900,000
Units produced (b)		25,000		5,000	
Overhead cost per unit [(a) ÷ (b)]		$17		$95	

Illustration 21A-4
Assignment of overhead costs to products

These data show that under ABC, overhead costs are shifted from the high-volume product (Ab Bench) to the low-volume product (Ab Coaster). This shift results in more accurate costing for two reasons:

1. Low-volume products often require more special handling, such as more machine setups and inspections, than high-volume products. This is true for Atlas Company. Thus, the low-volume product frequently is responsible for more overhead costs per unit than a high-volume product.

2. Assigning overhead using ABC will usually increase the cost per unit for low-volume products as compared to a traditional overhead allocation. Therefore, traditional cost drivers such as direct labor hours are usually not appropriate for assigning overhead costs to low-volume products.

Comparing Unit Costs

A comparison of unit manufacturing costs under traditional costing and ABC shows the following significant differences.

Illustration 21A-5
Comparison of unit product costs

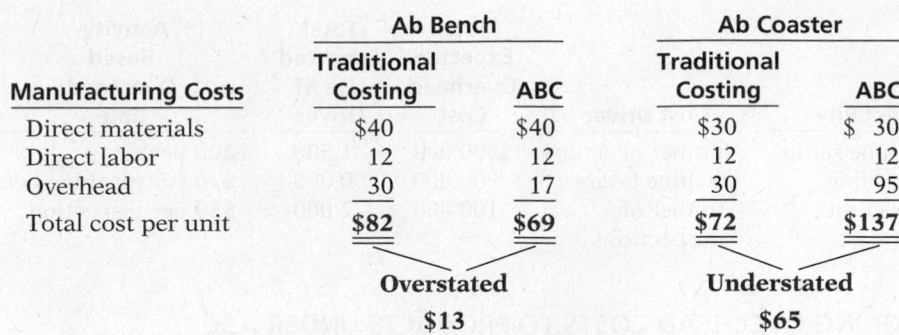

Manufacturing Costs	Ab Bench Traditional Costing	Ab Bench ABC	Ab Coaster Traditional Costing	Ab Coaster ABC
Direct materials	$40	$40	$30	$ 30
Direct labor	12	12	12	12
Overhead	30	17	30	95
Total cost per unit	$82	$69	$72	$137
	Overstated $13		Understated $65	

The comparison shows that unit costs under traditional costing have been significantly distorted. The cost of the Ab Bench has been overstated $13 per unit ($82 − $69). The cost of the Ab Coaster has been understated $65 per unit ($137 − $72). The differences are attributable to how Atlas Company assigns manufacturing overhead. A likely consequence of the differences is that Atlas has been overpricing the Ab Bench and possibly losing market share to competitors. It also has been sacrificing profitability by underpricing the Ab Coaster.

As illustrated in the above case, ABC involves the following steps.

1. Identify the major activities that pertain to the manufacture of specific products.
2. Accumulate manufacturing overhead costs by activities.
3. Identify the cost driver(s) that accurately measure(s) each activity's contribution to the finished product.
4. Assign manufacturing overhead costs for each activity to products, using the cost driver(s).

Benefits of ABC

The primary benefit of ABC is **more accurate product costing**. Here's why:

1. **ABC leads to more cost pools** being used to assign overhead costs to products. Instead of one plantwide pool (or even departmental pools) and a single cost driver, companies use numerous activity cost pools with more relevant cost drivers. Costs are assigned more directly on the basis of the cost drivers used to produce each product.
2. **ABC leads to enhanced control over overhead costs.** Under ABC, companies can trace many overhead costs directly to activities—allowing some indirect costs to be identified as direct costs. Thus, managers have become more aware of their responsibility to control the activities that generate those costs.
3. **ABC leads to better management decisions.** More accurate product costing should contribute to setting selling prices that can help achieve desired product profitability levels. In addition, more accurate cost data could be helpful in deciding whether to make or buy a product part or component, and sometimes even whether to eliminate a product.

Activity-based costing does not change the amount of overhead costs. What it does do is allocate those overhead costs in a more accurate manner. Furthermore, if the scorekeeping is more realistic and more accurate, managers should be able to better understand cost behavior and overall profitability.

Limitations of ABC

Although ABC systems often provide better product cost data than traditional volume-based systems, there are limitations:

1. **ABC can be expensive to use.** The increased cost of identifying multiple activities and applying numerous cost drivers discourages many companies from using ABC. Activity-based costing systems are more complex than traditional costing systems—sometimes significantly more complex. So companies must ask, is the cost of implementation greater than the benefit of greater accuracy? Sometimes it may be. For some companies, there may be no need to consider ABC at all because their existing system is sufficient. If the costs of ABC outweigh the benefits, then the company should not implement ABC.

2. **Some arbitrary allocations continue.** Even though more overhead costs can be assigned directly to products through ABC's multiple activity cost pools, certain overhead costs remain to be allocated by means of some arbitrary volume-based cost driver such as labor or machine hours.

SUMMARY OF LEARNING OBJECTIVE FOR APPENDIX 21A

10 Apply activity-based costing to specific company data. In applying ABC, it is necessary to compute the overhead rate for each activity by dividing total expected overhead by the total expected usage of the cost driver. The overhead cost for each activity is then assigned to products on the basis of each product's use of the cost driver.

Self-Test, Brief Exercises, Exercises, Problem Set A, and many more resources are available for practice in *WileyPLUS*.

Note: All asterisked Questions, Exercises, and Problems relate to material in the appendix to the chapter.

SELF-TEST QUESTIONS

Answers are on page 1028.

(LO 1) 1. Which of the following items is **not** characteristic of a process cost system?
  (a) Once production begins, it continues until the finished product emerges.
  (b) The products produced are heterogeneous in nature.
  (c) The focus is on continually producing homogeneous products.
  (d) When the finished product emerges, all units have precisely the same amount of materials, labor, and overhead.

(LO 2) 2. Indicate which of the following statements is **not** correct.
  (a) Both a job order and a process cost system track the same three manufacturing cost elements—direct materials, direct labor, and manufacturing overhead.
  (b) A job order cost system uses only one work in process account, whereas a process cost system uses multiple work in process accounts.
  (c) Manufacturing costs are accumulated the same way in a job order and in a process cost system.

  (d) Manufacturing costs are assigned the same way in a job order and in a process cost system.

3. In a process cost system, the flow of costs is: (LO 3)
  (a) work in process, cost of goods sold, finished goods.
  (b) finished goods, work in process, cost of goods sold.
  (c) finished goods, cost of goods sold, work in process.
  (d) work in process, finished goods, cost of goods sold.

4. In making journal entries to assign raw materials   (LO 4) costs, a company using process costing:
  (a) debits Finished Goods Inventory.
  (b) often debits two or more work in process accounts.
  (c) generally credits two or more work in process accounts.
  (d) credits Finished Goods Inventory.

5. In a process cost system, manufacturing overhead: (LO 4)
  (a) is assigned to finished goods at the end of each accounting period.
  (b) is assigned to a work in process account for each job as the job is completed.

(c) is assigned to a work in process account for each production department on the basis of a predetermined overhead rate.

(d) is assigned to a work in process account for each production department as overhead costs are incurred.

(LO 5)   **6.** Conversion costs are the sum of:
  (a) fixed and variable overhead costs.
  (b) labor costs and overhead costs.
  (c) direct material costs and overhead costs.
  (d) direct labor and indirect labor costs.

(LO 5)   **7.** The Mixing Department's output during the period consists of 20,000 units completed and transferred out, and 5,000 units in ending work in process 60% complete as to materials and conversion costs. Beginning inventory is 1,000 units, 40% complete as to materials and conversion costs. The equivalent units of production are:
  (a) 22,600.   **(c)** 24,000.
  (b) 23,000.   **(d)** 25,000.

(LO 6)   **8.** In RYZ Company, there are zero units in beginning work in process, 7,000 units started into production, and 500 units in ending work in process 20% completed. The physical units to be accounted for are:
  (a) 7,000.   **(c)** 7,500.
  (b) 7,360.   **(d)** 7,340.

(LO 6)   **9.** Mora Company has 2,000 units in beginning work in process, 20% complete as to conversion costs, 23,000 units transferred out to finished goods, and 3,000 units in ending work in process $33\frac{1}{3}$% complete as to conversion costs. The beginning and ending inventory is fully complete as to materials costs. Equivalent units for materials and conversion costs are, respectively:
  (a) 22,000, 24,000.   **(c)** 26,000, 24,000.
  (b) 24,000, 26,000.   **(d)** 26,000, 26,000.

(LO 6)   **10.** Fortner Company has no beginning work in process; 9,000 units are transferred out and 3,000 units in ending work in process are one-third finished as to conversion costs and fully complete as to materials cost. If total materials cost is $60,000, the unit materials cost is:
  (a) $5.00.
  (b) $5.45 rounded.
  (c) $6.00.
  (d) No correct answer is given.

(LO 6)   **11.** Largo Company has unit costs of $10 for materials and $30 for conversion costs. If there are 2,500 units in ending work in process, 40% complete as to conversion costs, and fully complete as to materials cost, the total cost assignable to the ending work in process inventory is:
  (a) $45,000.
  (b) $55,000.
  (c) $75,000.
  (d) $100,000.

12. A production cost report: (LO 7)
  (a) is an external report.
  (b) shows both the production quantity and cost data related to a department.
  (c) shows equivalent units of production but not physical units.
  (d) contains six sections.

13. In a production cost report, units to be accounted for   (LO 7) are calculated as:
  (a) Units started into production + Units in ending work in process.
  (b) Units started into production − Units in beginning work in process.
  (c) Units transferred out + Units in beginning work in process.
  (d) Units started into production + Units in beginning work in process.

14. Under just-in-time processing: (LO 8)
  (a) raw materials are received just in time for use in production.
  (b) subassembly parts are completed just in time for use in assembling finished goods.
  (c) finished goods are completed just in time to be sold.
  (d) All of the above.

15. The primary objective of just-in-time processing is   (LO 8) to:
  (a) accumulate overhead in activity cost pools.
  (b) eliminate or reduce all manufacturing inventories.
  (c) identify relevant activity cost drivers.
  (d) identify value-added activities.

16. Activity-based costing: (LO 9)
  (a) assumes that the cost of a product is equal to the sum of the costs of all activities performed to manufacture it.
  (b) has become more widespread as overhead costs have been decreasing relative to materials and labor costs.
  (c) is similar to a conventional cost accounting system in accounting for direct labor and manufacturing overhead but differs in regard to direct materials.
  (d) uses a single unit-level basis to allocate overhead costs to products.

17. Activity-based costing (ABC):   (LO 9)
  (a) can be used only in a process cost system.
  (b) focuses on units of production.
  (c) focuses on activities performed to produce a product.
  (d) uses only a single basis of allocation.

*18. The overhead rate for Machine Setups is $100 per setup.   (LO 10) Products A and B have 80 and 60 setups, respectively. The overhead assigned to each product is:
  (a) Product A $8,000, Product B $8,000.
  (b) Product A $8,000, Product B $6,000.
  (c) Product A $6,000, Product B $6,000.
  (d) Product A $6,000, Product B $8,000.

Go to the book's companion website, www.wiley.com/college/weygandt, for additional Self-Test Questions.

✔ The Navigator

QUESTIONS

1. Identify which costing system—job order or process cost—the following companies would primarily use: (a) Quaker Oats, (b) Jif Peanut Butter, (c) Gulf Craft (luxury yachts), and (d) Warner Bros. Motion Pictures.

2. Contrast the primary focus of job order cost accounting and of process cost accounting.

3. What are the similarities between a job order and a process cost system?

4. Your roommate is confused about the features of process cost accounting. Identify and explain the distinctive features for your roommate.

5. Sam Bowyer believes there are no significant differences in the flow of costs between job order cost accounting and process cost accounting. Is Bowyer correct? Explain.

6. (a) What source documents are used in assigning (1) materials and (2) labor to production in a process cost system?
   (b) What criterion and basis are commonly used in allocating overhead to processes?

7. At Ely Company, overhead is assigned to production departments at the rate of $5 per machine hour. In July, machine hours were 3,000 in the Machining Department and 2,400 in the Assembly Department. Prepare the entry to assign overhead to production.

8. Mark Haley is uncertain about the steps used to prepare a production cost report. State the procedures that are required in the sequence in which they are performed.

9. John Harbeck is confused about computing physical units. Explain to John how physical units to be accounted for and physical units accounted for are determined.

10. What is meant by the term "equivalent units of production"?

11. How are equivalent units of production computed?

12. Coats Company had zero units of beginning work in process. During the period, 9,000 units were completed, and there were 600 units of ending work in process. What were the units started into production?

13. Sanchez Co. has zero units of beginning work in process. During the period, 12,000 units were completed, and there were 500 units of ending work in process one-fifth complete as to conversion cost and 100% complete as to materials cost. What were the equivalent units of production for (a) materials and (b) conversion costs?

14. Hindi Co. started 3,000 units during the period. Its beginning inventory is 500 units one-fourth complete as to conversion costs and 100% complete as to materials costs. Its ending inventory is 300 units one-fifth complete as to conversion costs and 100% complete as to materials costs. How many units were transferred out this period?

15. Clauss Company transfers out 14,000 units and has 2,000 units of ending work in process that are 25% complete. Materials are entered at the beginning of the process and there is no beginning work in process. Assuming unit materials costs of $3 and unit conversion costs of $5, what are the costs to be assigned to units (a) transferred out and (b) in ending work in process?

16. (a) Ann Quinn believes the production cost report is an external report for stockholders. Is Ann correct? Explain.
    (b) Identify the sections in a production cost report.

17. What purposes are served by a production cost report?

18. At Trent Company, there are 800 units of ending work in process that are 100% complete as to materials and 40% complete as to conversion costs. If the unit cost of materials is $3 and the total costs assigned to the 800 units is $6,000, what is the per unit conversion cost?

19. What is the difference between operations costing and a process cost system?

20. How does a company decide whether to use a job order or a process cost system?

21. (a) Describe the philosophy and approach of just-in-time processing.
    (b) Identify the major elements of JIT processing.

22. (a) What are the principal differences between activity-based costing (ABC) and traditional product costing?
    (b) What assumptions must be met for ABC costing to be useful?

23. Chopra Co. identifies the following activities that pertain to manufacturing overhead: Materials Handling, Machine Setups, Factory Machine Maintenance, Factory Supervision, and Quality Control. For each activity, identify an appropriate cost driver.

*24. (a) What steps are involved in developing an activity-based costing system?
     (b) What are the benefits of ABC costing?

BRIEF EXERCISES

BE21-1 Weber Company purchases $45,000 of raw materials on account, and it incurs $60,000 of factory labor costs. Journalize the two transactions on March 31 assuming the labor costs are not paid until April.

Journalize entries for accumulating costs.
(LO 4)

BE21-2 Data for Weber Company are given in BE21-1. Supporting records show that (a) the Assembly Department used $24,000 of raw materials and $35,000 of the factory labor, and (b) the Finishing Department used the remainder. Journalize the assignment of the costs to the processing departments on March 31.

Journalize the assignment of materials and labor costs.
(LO 4)

Journalize the assignment of overhead costs.

(LO 4)

BE21-3 Factory labor data for Weber Company are given in BE21-2. Manufacturing overhead is assigned to departments on the basis of 200% of labor costs. Journalize the assignment of overhead to the Assembly and Finishing Departments.

Compute equivalent units of production.

(LO 5)

BE21-4 Goode Company has the following production data for selected months.

Month	Beginning Work in Process	Units Transferred Out	Ending Work in Process Units	% Complete as to Conversion Cost
January	–0–	35,000	10,000	40%
March	–0–	40,000	8,000	75
July	–0–	45,000	16,000	25

Compute equivalent units of production for materials and conversion costs, assuming materials are entered at the beginning of the process.

Compute unit costs of production.

(LO 6)

BE21-5 In Lopez Company, total material costs are $36,000, and total conversion costs are $54,000. Equivalent units of production are materials 10,000 and conversion costs 12,000. Compute the unit costs for materials, conversion costs, and total manufacturing costs.

Assign costs to units transferred out and in process.

(LO 6)

BE21-6 Trek Company has the following production data for April: units transferred out 40,000, and ending work in process 5,000 units that are 100% complete for materials and 40% complete for conversion costs. If unit materials cost is $4 and unit conversion cost is $7, determine the costs to be assigned to the units transferred out and the units in ending work in process.

Compute unit costs.

(LO 6)

BE21-7 Production costs chargeable to the Finishing Department in June in Cascio Company are materials $16,000, labor $29,500, overhead $18,000. Equivalent units of production are materials 20,000 and conversion costs 19,000. Compute the unit costs for materials and conversion costs.

Prepare cost reconciliation schedule.

(LO 6)

BE21-8 Data for Cascio Company are given in BE21-7. Production records indicate that 18,000 units were transferred out, and 2,000 units in ending work in process were 50% complete as to conversion cost and 100% complete as to materials. Prepare a cost reconciliation schedule.

Compute equivalent units of production.

(LO 5)

BE21-9 The Smelting Department of Mathews Company has the following production and cost data for November.

> Production: Beginning work in process 2,000 units that are 100% complete as to materials and 20% complete as to conversion costs; units transferred out 8,000 units; and ending work in process 7,000 units that are 100% complete as to materials and 40% complete as to conversion costs.

Compute the equivalent units of production for (a) materials and (b) conversion costs for the month of November.

Understand contemporary developments.

(LO 8, 9)

BE21-10 Sam Snead has formulated the following list of statements about contemporary developments in managerial accounting.

1. Just-in-time processing results in a push approach; that is, raw materials are pushed through each process.
2. A primary objective of just-in-time processing is to eliminate all manufacturing inventories.
3. A major disadvantage of just-in-time processing is lower product quality.
4. A primary benefit of activity-based costing is more accurate and meaningful product costing.
5. A major advantage of activity-based costing is that it uses a single unit-level basis, such as direct labor or machine hours, to allocate overhead.

Identify each statement as true or false. If false, indicate how to correct the statement to make it true.

Compute activity-based overhead rates.

(LO 10)

*BE21-11 Mordica Company identifies three activities in its manufacturing process: machine setups, machining, and inspections. Estimated annual overhead cost for each activity is $150,000, $325,000, and $87,500, respectively. The cost driver for each activity and the expected annual usage are: number of setups 2,500, machine hours 25,000, and number of inspections 1,750. Compute the overhead rate for each activity.

> DO IT! Review

DO IT! 21-1 Indicate whether each of the following statements is true or false.

1. Many hospitals use job order costing for small, routine medical procedures.
2. A manufacturer of computer flash drives would use a job order cost system.
3. A process cost system uses multiple work in process accounts.
4. A process cost system keeps track of costs on job cost sheets.

Compare job order and process cost systems.
(LO 1, 2)

DO IT! 21-2 Kopa Company manufactures CH-21 through two processes: Mixing and Packaging. In July, the following costs were incurred.

	Mixing	Packaging
Raw materials used	$10,000	$28,000
Factory labor costs	8,000	36,000
Manufacturing overhead costs	12,000	54,000

Units completed at a cost of $21,000 in the Mixing Department are transferred to the Packaging Department. Units completed at a cost of $106,000 in the Packaging Department are transferred to Finished Goods. Journalize the assignment of these costs to the two processes and the transfer of units as appropriate.

Assign and journalize manufacturing costs.
(LO 4)

DO IT! 21-3 The assembly department has the following production data for the current month.

Beginning Work in Process	Units Transferred Out	Ending Work in Process
–0–	20,000	12,000

Materials are entered at the beginning of the process. The ending work in process units are 70% complete as to conversion costs. Compute the equivalent units of production for (a) materials and (b) conversion costs.

Compute equivalent units.
(LO 5)

DO IT! 21-4 In March, Kelly Company had the following unit production costs: materials $10 and conversion costs $8. On March 1, it had zero work in process. During March, Kelly transferred out 22,000 units. As of March 31, 4,000 units that were 40% complete as to conversion costs and 100% complete as to materials were in ending work in process.

(a) Compute the total units to be accounted for.
(b) Compute the equivalent units of production.
(c) Prepare a cost reconciliation schedule, including the costs of materials transferred out and the costs of materials in process.

Prepare cost reconciliation schedule.
(LO 6, 7)

DO IT! 21-5 Indicate whether each of the following statements is true or false.

1. Just-in-time processing is also known as just-in-case processing.
2. Companies that use just-in-time processing complete finished goods just in time to be sold.
3. A major benefit of just-in-time processing is enhanced product quality.
4. An ABC system is similar to conventional costing systems in accounting for period costs but differs in regard to manufacturing costs.
5. The primary benefit of ABC is significant reduction or elimination of manufacturing inventories.
6. In recent years, the amount of direct labor used in many industries has greatly decreased and total overhead costs have significantly increased.

Answer questions about JIT and ABC.
(LO 8, 9)

EXERCISES

E21-1 Robert Mallory has prepared the following list of statements about process cost accounting.

1. Process cost systems are used to apply costs to similar products that are mass-produced in a continuous fashion.
2. A process cost system is used when each finished unit is indistinguishable from another.

Understand process cost accounting.
(LO 1, 2)

3. Companies that produce soft drinks, motion pictures, and computer chips would all use process cost accounting.
4. In a process cost system, costs are tracked by individual jobs.
5. Job order costing and process costing track different manufacturing cost elements.
6. Both job order costing and process costing account for direct materials, direct labor, and manufacturing overhead.
7. Costs flow through the accounts in the same basic way for both job order costing and process costing.
8. In a process cost system, only one work in process account is used.
9. In a process cost system, costs are summarized in a job cost sheet.
10. In a process cost system, the unit cost is total manufacturing costs for the period divided by the equivalent units produced during the period.

Instructions
Identify each statement as true or false. If false, indicate how to correct the statement.

Journalize transactions.
(LO 4)

E21-2 Harrelson Company manufactures pizza sauce through two production departments: Cooking and Canning. In each process, materials and conversion costs are incurred evenly throughout the process. For the month of April, the work in process accounts show the following debits.

	Cooking	Canning
Beginning work in process	$ –0–	$ 4,000
Materials	21,000	9,000
Labor	8,500	7,000
Overhead	31,500	25,800
Costs transferred in		53,000

Instructions
Journalize the April transactions.

Answer questions on costs and production.
(LO 3, 5, 6)

E21-3 The ledger of Custer Company has the following work in process account.

Work in Process—Painting						
5/1	Balance	3,590	5/31	Transferred out	?
5/31	Materials	5,160			
5/31	Labor	2,740			
5/31	Overhead	1,380			
5/31	Balance	?			

Production records show that there were 400 units in the beginning inventory, 30% complete, 1,400 units started, and 1,500 units transferred out. The beginning work in process had materials cost of $2,040 and conversion costs of $1,550. The units in ending inventory were 40% complete. Materials are entered at the beginning of the painting process.

Instructions
(a) How many units are in process at May 31?
(b) What is the unit materials cost for May?
(c) What is the unit conversion cost for May?
(d) What is the total cost of units transferred out in May?
(e) What is the cost of the May 31 inventory?

Journalize transactions for two processes.
(LO 4)

E21-4 Schrager Company has two production departments: Cutting and Assembly. July 1 inventories are Raw Materials $4,200, Work in Process—Cutting $2,900, Work in Process—Assembly $10,600, and Finished Goods $31,000. During July, the following transactions occurred.

1. Purchased $62,500 of raw materials on account.
2. Incurred $60,000 of factory labor. (Credit Factory Wages Payable.)
3. Incurred $70,000 of manufacturing overhead; $40,000 was paid and the remainder is unpaid.
4. Requisitioned materials for Cutting $15,700 and Assembly $8,900.
5. Used factory labor for Cutting $33,000 and Assembly $27,000.
6. Applied overhead at the rate of $18 per machine hour. Machine hours were Cutting 1,680 and Assembly 1,720.

7. Transferred goods costing $67,600 from the Cutting Department to the Assembly Department.

8. Transferred goods costing $134,900 from Assembly to Finished Goods.

9. Sold goods costing $150,000 for $200,000 on account.

Instructions
Journalize the transactions. (Omit explanations.)

E21-5 In Wayne Company, materials are entered at the beginning of each process. Work in process inventories, with the percentage of work done on conversion costs, and production data for its Sterilizing Department in selected months during 2014 are as follows.

Compute physical units and equivalent units of production.
(LO 5, 6)

	Beginning Work in Process		Units	Ending Work in Process	
Month	Units	Conversion Cost%	Transferred Out	Units	Conversion Cost%
January	–0–	—	9,000	2,000	60
March	–0–	—	12,000	3,000	30
May	–0–	—	16,000	7,000	80
July	–0–	—	10,000	1,500	·40

Instructions
(a) Compute the physical units for January and May.
(b) Compute the equivalent units of production for (1) materials and (2) conversion costs for each month.

E21-6 The Cutting Department of Cassel Company has the following production and cost data for July.

Determine equivalent units, unit costs, and assignment of costs.
(LO 5, 6)

Production	Costs	
1. Transferred out 12,000 units.	Beginning work in process	$ –0–
2. Started 3,000 units that are 60%	Materials	45,000
complete as to conversion	Labor	16,200
costs and 100% complete as	Manufacturing overhead	18,300
to materials at July 31.		

Materials are entered at the beginning of the process. Conversion costs are incurred uniformly during the process.

Instructions
(a) Determine the equivalent units of production for (1) materials and (2) conversion costs.
(b) Compute unit costs and prepare a cost reconciliation schedule.

E21-7 The Sanding Department of Richards Furniture Company has the following production and manufacturing cost data for March 2014, the first month of operation.

Prepare a production cost report.
(LO 5, 6, 7)   XLS

Production: 9,000 units finished and transferred out; 3,000 units started that are 100% complete as to materials and 20% complete as to conversion costs.

Manufacturing costs: Materials $33,000; labor $24,000; overhead $36,000.

Instructions
Prepare a production cost report.

E21-8 The Blending Department of Luongo Company has the following cost and production data for the month of April.

Determine equivalent units, unit costs, and assignment of costs.
(LO 5, 6)

Costs:	
Work in process, April 1	
Direct materials: 100% complete	$100,000
Conversion costs: 20% complete	70,000
Cost of work in process, April 1	$170,000
Costs incurred during production in April	
Direct materials	$ 800,000
Conversion costs	365,000
Costs incurred in April	$1,165,000

Units transferred out totaled 17,000. Ending work in process was 1,000 units that are 100% complete as to materials and 40% complete as to conversion costs.

Instructions

(a) Compute the equivalent units of production for (1) materials and (2) conversion costs for the month of April.

(b) Compute the unit costs for the month.

(c) Determine the costs to be assigned to the units transferred out and in ending work in process.

Determine equivalent units, unit costs, and assignment of costs.

(LO 5, 6)

E21-9 Kostrivas Company has gathered the following information.

Units in beginning work in process	–0–
Units started into production	40,000
Units in ending work in process	6,000
Percent complete in ending work in process:	
Conversion costs	40%
Materials	100%
Costs incurred:	
Direct materials	$72,000
Direct labor	$81,000
Overhead	$101,000

Instructions

(a) Compute equivalent units of production for materials and for conversion costs.

(b) Determine the unit costs of production.

(c) Show the assignment of costs to units transferred out and in process.

Determine equivalent units, unit costs, and assignment of costs.

(LO 5, 6)

E21-10 Overton Company has gathered the following information.

Units in beginning work in process	20,000
Units started into production	164,000
Units in ending work in process	24,000
Percent complete in ending work in process:	
Conversion costs	60%
Materials	100%
Costs incurred:	
Direct materials	$101,200
Direct labor	$164,800
Overhead	$184,000

Instructions

(a) Compute equivalent units of production for materials and for conversion costs.

(b) Determine the unit costs of production.

(c) Show the assignment of costs to units transferred out and in process.

Compute equivalent units, unit costs, and costs assigned.

(LO 5, 6)

E21-11 The Polishing Department of Harbin Company has the following production and manufacturing cost data for September. Materials are entered at the beginning of the process.

Production: Beginning inventory 1,600 units that are 100% complete as to materials and 30% complete as to conversion costs; units started during the period are 38,400; ending inventory of 5,000 units 10% complete as to conversion costs.

Manufacturing costs: Beginning inventory costs, comprised of $20,000 of materials and $43,180 of conversion costs; materials costs added in Polishing during the month, $177,200; labor and overhead applied in Polishing during the month, $125,680 and $257,140, respectively.

Instructions

(a) Compute the equivalent units of production for materials and conversion costs for the month of September.

(b) Compute the unit costs for materials and conversion costs for the month.

(c) Determine the costs to be assigned to the units transferred out and in process.

Explain the production cost report.

(LO 7)

E21-12 David Skaros has recently been promoted to production manager, and so he has just started to receive various managerial reports. One of the reports he has received is the production cost report that you prepared. It showed that his department had 2,000 equivalent units in ending inventory. His department has had a history of not keeping enough inventory on hand to meet demand. He has come to you, very angry, and wants to know why you credited him with only 2,000 units when he knows he had at least twice that many on hand.

Instructions

Explain to him why his production cost report showed only 2,000 equivalent units in ending inventory. Write an informal memo. Be kind and explain very clearly why he is mistaken.

E21-13 The Welding Department of Thorpe Company has the following production and manufacturing cost data for February 2014. All materials are added at the beginning of the process.

Prepare a production cost report.

(LO 5, 6, 7)

Manufacturing Costs			Production Data	
Beginning work in process			Beginning work in process	15,000 units
Materials	$18,000			1/10 complete
Conversion costs	14,175	$ 32,175	Units transferred out	49,000
Materials		180,000	Units started	45,000
Labor		52,380	Ending work in process	11,000 units
Overhead		61,445		1/5 complete

Instructions

Prepare a production cost report for the Welding Department for the month of February.

E21-14 Remington Shipping, Inc. is contemplating the use of process costing to track the costs of its operations. The operation consists of three segments (departments): receiving, shipping, and delivery. Containers are received at Remington's docks and sorted according to the ship they will be carried on. The containers are loaded onto a ship, which carries them to the appropriate port of destination. The containers are then off-loaded and delivered to the receiving company.

Remington Shipping wants to begin using process costing in the shipping department. Direct materials represent the fuel costs to run the ship, and "Containers in transit" represents work in process. Listed below is information about the shipping department's first month's activity.

Compute physical units and equivalent units of production.

(LO 5, 6)

Containers in transit, April 1	0°
Containers loaded	1,200
Containers in transit, April 30	350, 40% of direct materials and 20% of conversion costs

Instructions

(a) Determine the physical flow of containers for the month.

(b) Calculate the equivalent units for direct materials and conversion costs.

E21-15 Royale Mortgage Company uses a process cost system to accumulate costs in its loan application department. When an application is completed, it is forwarded to the loan department for final processing. The following processing and cost data pertain to September.

Determine equivalent units, unit costs, and assignment of costs.

(LO 5, 6)

1. Applications in process on September 1, 100
2. Applications started in September, 900
3. Completed applications during September, 800
4. Applications still in process at September 30 were 100% complete as to materials (forms) and 60% complete as to conversion costs.

Beginning WIP:	
Direct materials	$ 1,000
Conversion costs	3,960
September costs:	
Direct materials	$ 4,500
Direct labor	12,000
Overhead	9,340

Materials are the forms used in the application process, and these costs are incurred at the beginning of the process. Conversion costs are incurred uniformly during the process.

Instructions

(a) Determine the equivalent units of service (production) for materials and conversion costs.

(b) Compute the unit costs and prepare a cost reconciliation schedule.

Compute overhead rates and assign overhead using ABC.

(LO 10)

*E21-16 Major Instrument, Inc. manufactures two products: missile range instruments and space pressure gauges. During April, 50 range instruments and 300 pressure gauges were produced, and overhead costs of $94,500 were estimated. An analysis of estimated overhead costs reveals the following activities.

Activities	Cost Drivers	Total Cost
1. Materials handling	Number of requisitions	$40,000
2. Machine setups	Number of setups	27,500
3. Quality inspections	Number of inspections	27,000
		$94,500

The cost driver volume for each product was as follows.

Cost Drivers	Instruments	Gauges	Total
Number of requisitions	400	600	1,000
Number of setups	200	300	500
Number of inspections	200	400	600

Instructions

(a) Determine the overhead rate for each activity.

(b) Assign the manufacturing overhead costs for April to the two products using activity-based costing.

(c) ◄——— Write a memorandum to the president of Major Instrument explaining the benefits of activity-based costing.

Compute product cost using traditional costing and ABC.

(LO 10)

*E21-17 Kowalski Company manufactures a number of specialized machine parts. Part Compo-24 uses $35 of direct materials and $15 of direct labor per unit. Kowalski's estimated manufacturing overhead is as follows.

Materials handling	$150,000
Machining	180,000
Factory supervision	138,000
Total	$468,000

Overhead is applied based on direct labor costs, which were estimated at $200,000.

Kowalski is considering adopting activity-based costing. The cost drivers are estimated at:

Activity	Cost Driver	Expected Use
Materials handling	Weight of materials	50,000 pounds
Machining	Machine hours	20,000 hours
Factory supervision	Direct labor hours	12,000 hours

Instructions

(a) Compute the cost of 1,000 units of Compo-24 using the current traditional costing system.

(b) Compute the cost of 1,000 units of Compo-24 using the proposed activity-based costing system. Assume the 1,000 units use 2,500 pounds of materials, 500 machine hours, and 1,000 direct labor hours.

EXERCISES: SET B AND CHALLENGE EXERCISES

Visit the book's companion website, at **www.wiley.com/college/weygandt**, and choose the Student Companion site to access Exercise Set B and Challenge Exercises.

PROBLEMS: SET A

Journalize transactions.

(LO 3, 4)

P21-1A Conwell Company manufactures its product, Vitadrink, through two manufacturing processes: Mixing and Packaging. All materials are entered at the beginning of each process. On October 1, 2014, inventories consisted of Raw Materials $26,000, Work in Process—Mixing $0, Work in Process—Packaging $250,000, and Finished Goods $289,000.

The beginning inventory for Packaging consisted of 10,000 units that were 50% complete as to conversion costs and fully complete as to materials. During October, 50,000 units were started into production in the Mixing Department and the following transactions were completed.

1. Purchased $300,000 of raw materials on account.
2. Issued raw materials for production: Mixing $210,000 and Packaging $45,000.
3. Incurred labor costs of $258,900.
4. Used factory labor: Mixing $182,500 and Packaging $76,400.
5. Incurred $810,000 of manufacturing overhead on account.
6. Applied manufacturing overhead on the basis of $24 per machine hour. Machine hours were 28,000 in Mixing and 6,000 in Packaging.
7. Transferred 45,000 units from Mixing to Packaging at a cost of $979,000.
8. Transferred 53,000 units from Packaging to Finished Goods at a cost of $1,315,000.
9. Sold goods costing $1,604,000 for $2,500,000 on account.

Instructions
Journalize the October transactions.

P21-2A Rosenthal Company manufactures bowling balls through two processes: Molding and Packaging. In the Molding Department, the urethane, rubber, plastics, and other materials are molded into bowling balls. In the Packaging Department, the balls are placed in cartons and sent to the finished goods warehouse. All materials are entered at the beginning of each process. Labor and manufacturing overhead are incurred uniformly throughout each process. Production and cost data for the Molding Department during June 2014 are presented below.

Complete four steps necessary to prepare a production cost report.
(LO 5, 6, 7)

Production Data	June
Beginning work in process units	–0–
Units started into production	22,000
Ending work in process units	2,000
Percent complete—ending inventory	40%

Cost Data	
Materials	$198,000
Labor	53,600
Overhead	112,800
Total	$364,400

Instructions
(a) Prepare a schedule showing physical units of production.
(b) Determine the equivalent units of production for materials and conversion costs.
(c) Compute the unit costs of production.
(d) Determine the costs to be assigned to the units transferred out and in process for June.
(e) Prepare a production cost report for the Molding Department for the month of June.

P21-3A Seagren Industries Inc. manufactures in separate processes furniture for homes. In each process, materials are entered at the beginning, and conversion costs are incurred uniformly. Production and cost data for the first process in making two products in two different manufacturing plants are as follows.

Complete four steps necessary to prepare a production cost report.
(LO 5, 6, 7)

	Cutting Department	
	Plant 1	Plant 2
Production Data—July	T12-Tables	C10-Chairs
Work in process units, July 1	–0–	–0–
Units started into production	19,000	16,000
Work in process units, July 31	3,000	500
Work in process percent complete	60%	80%

Cost Data—July		
Work in process, July 1	$ –0–	$ –0–
Materials	380,000	288,000
Labor	234,200	110,000
Overhead	104,000	96,700
Total	$718,200	$494,700

Instructions
(a) For each plant:
    (1) Compute the physical units of production.
    (2) Compute equivalent units of production for materials and for conversion costs.
    (3) Determine the unit costs of production.
    (4) Show the assignment of costs to units transferred out and in process.
(b) Prepare the production cost report for Plant 1 for July 2014.

Assign costs and prepare production cost report.

(LO 5, 6, 7)

P21-4A Rivera Company has several processing departments. Costs charged to the Assembly Department for November 2014 totaled $2,280,000 as follows.

Work in process, November 1		
Materials	$79,000	
Conversion costs	48,150	$ 127,150
Materials added		1,589,000
Labor		225,920
Overhead		337,930

Production records show that 35,000 units were in beginning work in process 30% complete as to conversion costs, 660,000 units were started into production, and 25,000 units were in ending work in process 40% complete as to conversion costs. Materials are entered at the beginning of each process.

Instructions
(a) Determine the equivalent units of production and the unit production costs for the Assembly Department.
(b) Determine the assignment of costs to goods transferred out and in process.
(c) Prepare a production cost report for the Assembly Department.

Determine equivalent units and unit costs and assign costs.

(LO 5, 6, 7)

P21-5A Morse Company manufactures basketballs. Materials are added at the beginning of the production process and conversion costs are incurred uniformly. Production and cost data for the month of July 2014 are as follows.

Production Data—Basketballs	Units	Percent Complete
Work in process units, July 1	500	60%
Units started into production	1,250	
Work in process units, July 31	600	40%

Cost Data—Basketballs		
Work in process, July 1		
Materials	$750	
Conversion costs	600	$1,350
Direct materials		2,400
Direct labor		1,580
Manufacturing overhead		1,295

Instructions
(a) Calculate the following.
    (1) The equivalent units of production for materials and conversion costs.
    (2) The unit costs of production for materials and conversion costs.
    (3) The assignment of costs to units transferred out and in process at the end of the accounting period.
(b) Prepare a production cost report for the month of July for the basketballs.

Compute equivalent units and complete production cost report.

(LO 5, 7)

P21-6A Hamilton Processing Company uses a weighted-average process cost system and manufactures a single product—a premium rug shampoo and cleaner. The manufacturing activity for the month of October has just been completed. A partially completed production cost report for the month of October for the Mixing and Cooking Department is shown on the next page.

Instructions
(a) Prepare a schedule that shows how the equivalent units were computed so that you can complete the "Quantities: Units accounted for" equivalent units section shown in the production cost report, and compute October unit costs.
(b) Complete the following "Cost Reconciliation Schedule" part of the production cost report.

HAMILTON PROCESSING COMPANY
Mixing and Cooking Department
Production Cost Report
For the Month Ended October 31

Quantities	Physical Units	Equivalent Units Materials	Equivalent Units Conversion Costs
Units to be accounted for			
Work in process, October 1 (all materials, 70% conversion costs)	20,000		
Started into production	150,000		
Total units	170,000		
Units accounted for			
Transferred out	120,000	?	?
Work in process, October 31 (60% materials, 40% conversion costs)	50,000	?	?
Total units accounted for	170,000	?	?

Costs

Unit costs	Materials	Conversion Costs	Total
Total cost	$240,000	$105,000	$345,000
Equivalent units	?	?	
Unit costs	$? +	$? =	$?

Costs to be accounted for	
Work in process, October 1	$ 30,000
Started into production	315,000
Total costs	$345,000

Cost Reconciliation Schedule

Costs accounted for		
Transferred out		$?
Work in process, October 31		
Materials	$?	
Conversion costs	?	?
Total costs		$?

*P21-7A Schultz Electronics manufactures two large-screen television models: the Royale which sells for $1,600, and a new model, the Majestic, which sells for $1,300. The production cost computed per unit under traditional costing for each model in 2014 was as follows.

Assign overhead to products using ABC and evaluate decision.

(LO 10)

Traditional Costing	Royale	Majestic
Direct materials	$ 700	$420
Direct labor ($20 per hour)	120	100
Manufacturing overhead ($38 per DLH)	228	190
Total per unit cost	$1,048	$710

In 2014, Schultz manufactured 25,000 units of the Royale and 10,000 units of the Majestic. The overhead rate of $38 per direct labor hour was determined by dividing total expected manufacturing overhead of $7,600,000 by the total direct labor hours (200,000) for the two models.

Under traditional costing, the gross profit on the models was Royale $552 or ($1,600 − $1,048), and Majestic $590 or ($1,300 − $710). Because of this difference, management is considering phasing out the Royale model and increasing the production of the Majestic model.

Before finalizing its decision, management asks Schultz's controller to prepare an analysis using activity-based costing (ABC). The controller accumulates the following information about overhead for the year ended December 31, 2014.

Activities	Cost Drivers	Estimated Overhead	Expected Use of Cost Drivers	Activity-Based Overhead Rate
Purchasing	Number of orders	$1,200,000	40,000	$30/order
Machine setups	Number of setups	900,000	18,000	$50/setup
Machining	Machine hours	4,800,000	120,000	$40/hour
Quality control	Number of inspections	700,000	28,000	$25/inspection

The cost drivers used for each product were:

Cost Drivers	Royale	Majestic	Total
Purchase orders	17,000	23,000	40,000
Machine setups	5,000	13,000	18,000
Machine hours	75,000	45,000	120,000
Inspections	11,000	17,000	28,000

Instructions
(a) Assign the total 2014 manufacturing overhead costs to the two products using activity-based costing (ABC) and determine the overhead cost per unit.
(b) What was the cost per unit and gross profit of each model using ABC costing?
(c) ———— Are management's future plans for the two models sound? Explain.

PROBLEMS: SET B

Journalize transactions.
(LO 3, 4)

P21-1B Wilbury Company manufactures a nutrient, Everlife, through two manufacturing processes: Blending and Packaging. All materials are entered at the beginning of each process. On August 1, 2014, inventories consisted of Raw Materials $5,000, Work in Process— Blending $0, Work in Process—Packaging $3,945, and Finished Goods $7,500. The beginning inventory for Packaging consisted of 500 units, two-fifths complete as to conversion costs and fully complete as to materials. During August, 9,000 units were started into production in Blending, and the following transactions were completed.

1. Purchased $25,000 of raw materials on account.
2. Issued raw materials for production: Blending $18,930 and Packaging $9,140.
3. Incurred labor costs of $25,770.
4. Used factory labor: Blending $15,320 and Packaging $10,450.
5. Incurred $36,500 of manufacturing overhead on account.
6. Applied manufacturing overhead at the rate of $28 per machine hour. Machine hours were Blending 900 and Packaging 300.
7. Transferred 8,200 units from Blending to Packaging at a cost of $44,940.
8. Transferred 8,600 units from Packaging to Finished Goods at a cost of $67,490.
9. Sold goods costing $62,000 for $90,000 on account.

Instructions
Journalize the August transactions.

Complete four steps necessary to prepare a production cost report.
(LO 5, 6, 7)

P21-2B Steiner Corporation manufactures water skis through two processes: Molding and Packaging. In the Molding Department, fiberglass is heated and shaped into the form of a ski. In the Packaging Department, the skis are placed in cartons and sent to the finished goods warehouse. Materials are entered at the beginning of both processes. Labor and manufacturing overhead are incurred uniformly throughout each process. Production and cost data for the Molding Department for January 2014 are presented below.

Production Data	January
Beginning work in process units	–0–
Units started into production	50,000
Ending work in process units	2,500
Percent complete—ending inventory	40%

Cost Data	January
Materials	$510,000
Labor	92,500
Overhead	150,000
Total	$752,500

Instructions

(a) Compute the physical units of production.
(b) Determine the equivalent units of production for materials and conversion costs.
(c) Compute the unit costs of production.
(d) Determine the costs to be assigned to the units transferred out and in process.
(e) Prepare a production cost report for the Molding Department for the month of January.

P21-3B Borman Corporation manufactures in separate processes refrigerators and freezers for homes. In each process, materials are entered at the beginning and conversion costs are incurred uniformly. Production and cost data for the first process in making two products in two different manufacturing plants are as follows.

Complete four steps necessary to prepare a production cost report.
(LO 5, 6, 7)

	Stamping Department	
	Plant A	**Plant B**
Production Data—June	**R12 Refrigerators**	**F24 Freezers**
Work in process units, June 1	–0–	–0–
Units started into production	20,000	20,000
Work in process units, June 30	4,000	2,500
Work in process percent complete	75%	60%

Cost Data—June		
Work in process, June 1	$ –0–	$ –0–
Materials	840,000	720,000
Labor	245,000	259,000
Overhead	420,000	292,000
Total	$1,505,000	$1,271,000

Instructions

(a) For each plant:
 (1) Compute the physical units of production.
 (2) Compute equivalent units of production for materials and for conversion costs.
 (3) Determine the unit costs of production.
 (4) Show the assignment of costs to units transferred out and in process.
(b) Prepare the production cost report for Plant A for June 2014.

P21-4B Luxman Company has several processing departments. Costs charged to the Assembly Department for October 2014 totaled $1,298,400 as follows.

Assign costs and prepare production cost report.
(LO 5, 6, 7)

Work in process, October 1		
Materials	$29,000	
Conversion costs	16,500	$ 45,500
Materials added		1,006,000
Labor		138,900
Overhead		108,000

Production records show that 25,000 units were in beginning work in process 40% complete as to conversion cost, 435,000 units were started into production, and 35,000 units were in ending work in process 40% complete as to conversion costs. Materials are entered at the beginning of each process.

Instructions

(a) Determine the equivalent units of production and the unit production costs for the Assembly Department.
(b) Determine the assignment of costs to goods transferred out and in process.
(c) Prepare a production cost report for the Assembly Department.

Determine equivalent units and unit costs and assign costs.
(LO 5, 6, 7)

P21-5B Swinn Company manufactures bicycles. Materials are added at the beginning of the production process, and conversion costs are incurred uniformly. Production and cost data for the month of May are as follows.

Production Data—Bicycles	Units	Percent Complete
Work in process units, May 1	500	80%
Units started in production	2,000	
Work in process units, May 31	800	40%

Cost Data—Bicycles		
Work in process, May 1		
Materials	$15,000	
Conversion costs	18,000	$33,000
Direct materials		50,000
Direct labor		19,020
Manufacturing overhead		33,680

Instructions
(a) Calculate the following.
   (1) The equivalent units of production for materials and conversion costs.
   (2) The unit costs of production for materials and conversion costs.
   (3) The assignment of costs to units transferred out and in process at the end of the accounting period.
(b) Prepare a production cost report for the month of May for the bicycles.

Compute equivalent units and complete production cost report.
(LO 5, 7)

P21-6B Venuchi Cleaner Company uses a weighted-average process cost system and manufactures a single product—an all-purpose liquid cleaner. The manufacturing activity for the month of March has just been completed. A partially completed production cost report for the month of March for the mixing and blending department is shown below.

VENUCHI CLEANER COMPANY
Mixing and Blending Department
Production Cost Report
For the Month Ended March 31

		Equivalent Units	
Quantities	Physical Units	Materials	Conversion Costs
Units to be accounted for			
Work in process, March 1	10,000		
Started into production	76,000		
Total units	86,000		
Units accounted for			
Transferred out	66,000	?	?
Work in process, March 31			
(60% materials, 20% conversion costs)	20,000	?	?
Total units	86,000	?	?

Costs			
Unit costs	Materials	Conversion Costs	Total
Total cost	$156,000	$98,000	$254,000
Equivalent units	?	?	
Unit costs	$? +	$? =	$?
Costs to be accounted for			
Work in process, March 1			$ 8,700
Started into production			245,300
Total costs			$254,000

Cost Reconciliation Schedule	Materials	Conversion Costs	Total
Costs accounted for			
Transferred out			$?
Work in process, March 31			
Materials	$?		
Conversion costs		?	?
Total costs			$?

Instructions

(a) Prepare a schedule that shows how the equivalent units were computed so that you can complete the "Quantities: Units accounted for" equivalent units section shown in the production cost report above, and compute March unit costs.

(b) Complete the "Cost Reconciliation Schedule" part of the production cost report above.

PROBLEMS: SET C

Visit the book's companion website, at **www.wiley.com/college/weygandt**, and choose the Student Companion site to access Problem Set C.

WATERWAYS CONTINUING PROBLEM

(*Note:* This is a continuation of the Waterways Problem from Chapters 19 through 20.)

WCP21 Because most of the parts for its irrigation systems are standard, Waterways handles the majority of its manufacturing as a process cost system. There are multiple process departments. Three of these departments are the Molding, Cutting, and Welding departments. All items eventually end up in the Packaging department which prepares items for sale in kits or individually. This problem asks you to help Waterways calculate equivalent units and prepare a production cost report.

Go to the book's companion website, at **www.wiley.com/college/weygandt**, *to see the completion of this problem.*

Broadening Your Perspective

Management Decision-Making

Decision-Making Problem: Current Designs

BYP21-1 Building a kayak using the composite method is a very labor-intensive process. In the fabrication department, the kayaks go through several steps as employees carefully place layers of Kevlar® in a mold and then use resin to fuse together the layers. The excess resin is removed with a vacuum process, and the upper shell and lower shell are removed from the molds and assembled. The seat, hatch, and other components are added in the finishing department.

    At the beginning of April, Current Designs had 30 kayaks in process in the fabrication department. Rick Thrune, the production manager, estimated that about 80% of the material costs had been added to these boats, which were about 50% complete with respect to the conversion costs. The cost of this inventory had been calculated to be $8,400 in materials and $9,000 in conversion costs.

During April, 72 boats were started. At the end of the month, the 35 kayaks in the ending inventory had 20% of the materials and 40% of the conversion costs already added to them.

A review of the accounting records for April showed that materials with a cost of $17,500 had been requisitioned by this department and that the conversion costs for the month were $39,600.

Instructions
Complete a production cost report for April 2014 for the fabrication department using the weighted-average method.

Decision-Making Across the Organization

BYP21-2 Florida Beach Company manufactures sunscreen lotion, called Surtan, in 11-ounce plastic bottles. Surtan is sold in a competitive market. As a result, management is very cost-conscious. Surtan is manufactured through two processes: mixing and filling. Materials are entered at the beginning of each process, and labor and manufacturing overhead occur uniformly throughout each process. Unit costs are based on the cost per gallon of Surtan using the weighted-average costing approach.

On June 30, 2014, Mary Ritzman, the chief accountant for the past 20 years, opted to take early retirement. Her replacement, Joe Benili, had extensive accounting experience with motels in the area but only limited contact with manufacturing accounting. During July, Joe correctly accumulated the following production quantity and cost data for the Mixing Department.

Production quantities: Work in process, July 1, 8,000 gallons 75% complete; started into production 100,000 gallons; work in process, July 31, 5,000 gallons 20% complete. Materials are added at the beginning of the process.

Production costs: Beginning work in process $88,000, comprised of $21,000 of materials costs and $67,000 of conversion costs; incurred in July: materials $573,000, conversion costs $765,000.

Joe then prepared a production cost report on the basis of physical units started into production. His report showed a production cost of $14.26 per gallon of Surtan. The management of Florida Beach was surprised at the high unit cost. The president comes to you, as Mary's top assistant, to review Joe's report and prepare a correct report if necessary.

Instructions
With the class divided into groups, answer the following questions.

(a) Show how Joe arrived at the unit cost of $14.26 per gallon of Surtan.
(b) What error(s) did Joe make in preparing his production cost report?
(c) Prepare a correct production cost report for July.

Managerial Analysis

BYP21-3 Harris Furniture Company manufactures living room furniture through two departments: Framing and Upholstering. Materials are entered at the beginning of each process. For May, the following cost data are obtained from the two work in process accounts.

	Framing	Upholstering
Work in process, May 1	$ –0–	$?
Materials	450,000	?
Conversion costs	261,000	330,000
Costs transferred in	–0–	600,000
Costs transferred out	600,000	?
Work in process, May 31	111,000	?

Instructions
Answer the following questions.

(a) If 3,000 sofas were started into production on May 1 and 2,500 sofas were transferred to Upholstering, what was the unit cost of materials for May in the Framing Department?
(b) Using the data in (a) above, what was the per unit conversion cost of the sofas transferred to Upholstering?
(c) Continuing the assumptions in (a) above, what is the percentage of completion of the units in process at May 31 in the Framing Department?

Real-World Focus

BYP21-4 Paintball is now played around the world. The process of making paintballs is actually quite similar to the process used to make certain medical pills. In fact, paintballs were previously often made at the same factories that made pharmaceuticals.

Address: **www.youtube.com/watch?v=iQG5m4AK4uY**, or go to **www.wiley.com/college/weygandt**

Instructions
View that video at the site listed above and then answer the following questions.

(a) Describe in sequence the primary steps used to manufacture paintballs.
(b) Explain the costs incurred by the company that would fall into each of the following categories: materials, labor, and overhead. Of these categories, which do you think would be the greatest cost in making paintballs?
(c) Discuss whether a paintball manufacturer would use job order costing or process costing.

Critical Thinking

Communication Activity

BYP21-5 Diane Barone was a good friend of yours in high school and is from your home town. While you chose to major in accounting when you both went away to college, she majored in marketing and management. You have recently been promoted to accounting manager for the Snack Foods Division of Melton Enterprises, and your friend was promoted to regional sales manager for the same division of Melton. Diane recently telephoned you. She explained that she was familiar with job cost sheets, which had been used by the Special Projects division where she had formerly worked. She was, however, very uncomfortable with the production cost reports prepared by your division. She emailed you a list of her particular questions:

1. Since Melton occasionally prepares snack foods for special orders in the Snack Foods Division, why don't we track costs of the orders separately?
2. What is an equivalent unit?
3. Why am I getting four production cost reports? Isn't there one Work in Process account?

Instructions
Prepare a memo to Diane. Answer her questions, and include any additional information you think would be helpful. You may write informally, but do use proper grammar and punctuation.

Ethics Case

BYP21-6 R. B. Dillman Company manufactures a high-tech component that passes through two production processing departments, Molding and Assembly. Department managers are partially compensated on the basis of units of products completed and transferred out relative to units of product put into production. This was intended as encouragement to be efficient and to minimize waste.

Jan Wooten is the department head in the Molding Department, and Tony Ferneti is her quality control inspector. During the month of June, Jan had three new employees who were not yet technically skilled. As a result, many of the units produced in June had minor molding defects. In order to maintain the department's normal high rate of completion, Jan told Tony to pass through inspection and on to the Assembly Department all units that had defects nondetectable to the human eye. "Company and industry tolerances on this product are too high anyway," says Jan. "Less than 2% of the units we produce are subjected in the market to the stress tolerance we've designed into them. The odds of those 2% being any of this month's units are even less. Anyway, we're saving the company money."

Instructions
(a) Who are the potential stakeholders involved in this situation?
(b) What alternatives does Tony have in this situation? What might the company do to prevent this situation from occurring?

Considering People, Planet, and Profit

BYP21-7 In a recent year, an oil refinery in Texas City, Texas, on the Houston Ship Channel exploded. The explosion killed 15 people and sent a plume of smoke hundreds of feet into the air. The blast started as a fire in the section of the plant that increased the octane of the gasoline that was produced at the refinery. The Houston Ship Channel is the main waterway that allows commerce to flow from the Gulf of Mexico into Houston.

The Texas Commission on Environmental Quality expressed concern about the release of nitrogen oxides, benzene, and other known carcinogens as a result of the blast. Neighbors of the plant complained that the plant had been emitting carcinogens for years and that the regulators had ignored their complaints about emissions and unsafe working conditions.

Instructions

(a) Outline the costs that the company now faces as a result of the accident.
(b) How could the company have reduced the costs associated with the accident?

Answers to Chapter Questions

Answers to Insight and Accounting Across the Organization Questions

p. 992 Haven't I Seen That Before?   Q: In what ways might the relative composition (materials, labor, and overhead) of a remanufactured product's cost differ from that of a newly made product? **A:** We would expect that the materials costs would be substantially reduced since the bulk of the physical product is being reused. The labor component might increase, and the level of automation might decrease, since remanufacturing a product requires identification and replacement of malfunctioning components. This process might not be as easily automated as the production of a new product.

p. 1001 Using ABC to Aid in Employee Evaluation   Q: What positive implications does application of ABC have for the employees of this company? **A:** ABC will make these employees more aware of which activities cost the company more money. They will be motivated to reduce their use of these activities in order to improve their individual performance.

Answers to Self-Test Questions

1. b   **2.** d   **3.** d   **4.** b   **5.** c   **6.** b   **7.** b [20,000 + (5,000 × 60%)]   **8.** a   **9.** c (23,000 + 3,000), [23,000 + (3,000 × 33⅓%)]   **10.** a [\$60,000 ÷ (9,000 + 3,000)]   **11.** b [(\$10 × 2,500) + (\$30 × 2,500 × 40%)]   **12.** b   **13.** d   **14.** d   **15.** b   **16.** a   **17.** c   *18. b (\$100 × 80); (\$100 × 60)

✔ The Navigator

22 | Cost-Volume-Profit

Don't Worry—Just Get Big

It wasn't that Jeff Bezos didn't have a good job. He was a vice president at a Wall Street firm. But, he quit his job, moved to Seattle, and started an online retailer, which he named Amazon.com. Like any good entrepreneur, Jeff strove to keep his initial investment small. Operations were run out of his garage. And, to avoid the need for a warehouse, he took orders for books and had them shipped from other distributors' warehouses. One board member recalls how excited the board was whenever an order came in from a customer in a state that Amazon had never serviced before.

By its fourth month, Amazon was selling 100 books a day. In its first full year, it had $15.7 million in sales. The next year, sales increased eightfold. Two years later, sales were $1.6 billion.

Although its sales growth was impressive, Amazon's ability to lose money was equally amazing. One analyst nicknamed it Amazon.bomb, while another, predicting its demise, called it Amazon.toast. Why was it losing money? The company used every available dollar to reinvest in itself. It built massive warehouses and bought increasingly sophisticated (and expensive)

computer systems to improve its distribution system. This desire to grow as fast as possible was captured in a T-shi slogan at its company picnic, which read "Eat another ho dog, get big fast." This buying binge was increasing the company's fixed costs at a rate that exceeded its sales gr Skeptics were predicting that Amazon would soon run o cash. It didn't.

In the fourth quarter of 2010 (only 15 years after its wor headquarters were located in a garage), Amazon reporte quarterly revenues of $12.95 billion and quarterly incom $416 million. But, even as it announced record profits, it share price fell by 9%. Why? Because although the com was predicting that its sales revenue in the next quarter would increase by at least 28%, it predicted that its ope profit would fall by at least 2% and perhaps by as much 34%. The company made no apologies. It explained tha was in the process of expanding from 39 distribution ce to 52. As Amazon's finance chief noted, "You're not as productive on those assets for some time. I'm very pleas with the investments we're making and we've shown ov our history that we've been able to make great returns c capital we invest in." In other words, eat another hot dc

✔ **The Navigator**

Learning Objectives

✔ The Navigator

After studying this chapter, you should be able to:

[1] Distinguish between variable and fixed costs.

[2] Explain the significance of the relevant range.

[3] Explain the concept of mixed costs.

[4] List the five components of cost-volume-profit analysis.

[5] Indicate what contribution margin is and how it can be expressed.

[6] Identify the three ways to determine the break-even point.

[7] Give the formulas for determining sales required to earn target net income.

[8] Define margin of safety, and give the formulas for computing it.

[9] Describe the essential features of a cost-volume-profit income statement.

Watch the Southwest Airlines video in WileyPLUS to learn more about cost-volume-profit analysis in the real world.

Source: Christine Frey and John Cook, "How Amazon.com Survived, Thrived and Turned a Profit," *Seattle Post* (January 28, 2008); and Stu Woo, "Sticker Shock Over Amazon Growth," *Wall Street Journal Online* (January 28, 2011).

Preview of Chapter 22

 The Navigator

As the Feature Story indicates, to manage any size business you must understand how costs respond to changes in sales volume and the effect of costs and revenues on profits. A prerequisite to understanding cost-volume-profit (CVP) relationships is knowledge of how costs behave. In this chapter, we first explain the considerations involved in cost behavior analysis. Then, we discuss and illustrate CVP analysis.

The content and organization of Chapter 22 are as follows.

COST-VOLUME-PROFIT	
Cost Behavior Analysis	**Cost-Volume-Profit Analysis**
• Variable costs • Fixed costs • Relevant range • Mixed costs • Identifying variable and fixed costs	• Basic components • CVP income statement • Break-even analysis • Target net income • Margin of safety • Changes in business environment • CVP income statement revisited

Cost Behavior Analysis

LEARNING OBJECTIVE 1

Distinguish between variable and fixed costs.

Cost behavior analysis is the study of how specific costs respond to changes in the level of business activity. As you might expect, some costs change, and others remain the same. For example, for an airline company such as Southwest or United, the longer the flight, the higher the fuel costs. On the other hand, Massachusetts General Hospital's costs to staff the emergency room on any given night are relatively constant regardless of the number of patients treated. A knowledge of cost behavior helps management plan operations and decide between alternative courses of action. Cost behavior analysis applies to all types of entities.

The starting point in cost behavior analysis is measuring the key business activities. Activity levels may be expressed in terms of sales dollars (in a retail company), miles driven (in a trucking company), room occupancy (in a hotel), or dance classes taught (by a dance studio). Many companies use more than one measurement base. A manufacturer, for example, may use direct labor hours or units of output for manufacturing costs, and sales revenue or units sold for selling expenses.

For an activity level to be useful in cost behavior analysis, changes in the level or volume of activity should be correlated with changes in costs. The activity level selected is referred to as the activity (or volume) index. The **activity index** identifies the activity that causes changes in the behavior of costs. With an appropriate activity index, companies can classify the behavior of costs in response to changes in activity levels into three categories: variable, fixed, or mixed.

Variable Costs

Variable costs are costs that vary **in total** directly and proportionately with changes in the activity level. If the level increases 10%, total variable costs will increase 10%. If the level of activity decreases by 25%, total variable costs will decrease 25%. Examples of variable costs include direct materials and direct labor for a manufacturer; cost of goods sold, sales commissions, and freight-out for a merchandiser; and gasoline in airline and trucking companies. A variable cost may also be defined as a cost that **remains the same per unit at every level of activity**.

To illustrate the behavior of a variable cost, assume that Damon Company manufactures tablet computers that contain a $10 camera. The activity index is the number of tablet computers produced. As Damon manufactures each tablet, the total cost of cameras used increases by $10. As part (a) of Illustration 22-1

Illustration 22-1
Behavior of total and unit variable costs

Helpful Hint True or false: Variable costs per unit change directly and proportionately with changes in activity. Answer: False. Per unit costs remain constant at all levels of activity.

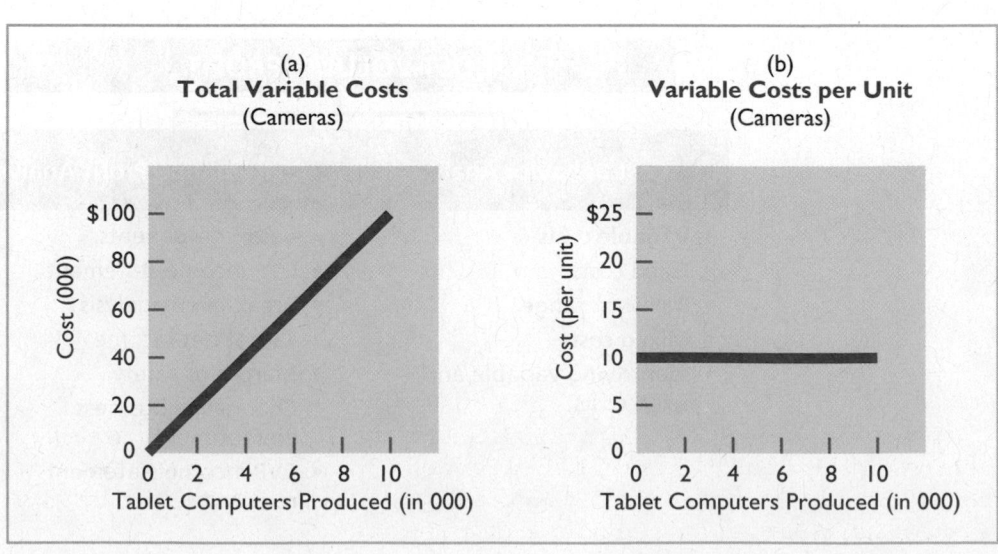

shows, total cost of the cameras will be $20,000 if Damon produces 2,000 tablets, and $100,000 when it produces 10,000 tablets. We also can see that a variable cost remains the same per unit as the level of activity changes. As part (b) of Illustration 22-1 shows, the unit cost of $10 for the cameras is the same whether Damon produces 2,000 or 10,000 tablets.

Companies that rely heavily on labor to manufacture a product, such as Nike or Reebok, or to perform a service, such as Hilton or Marriott, are likely to have many variable costs. In contrast, companies that use a high proportion of machinery and equipment in producing revenue, such as AT&T or Duke Energy Co., may have few variable costs.

Fixed Costs

Fixed costs are costs that **remain the same in total** regardless of changes in the activity level. Examples include property taxes, insurance, rent, supervisory salaries, and depreciation on buildings and equipment. Because total fixed costs remain constant as activity changes, it follows that **fixed costs per unit vary inversely with activity. As volume increases, unit cost declines, and vice versa.**

To illustrate the behavior of fixed costs, assume that Damon Company leases its productive facilities at a cost of $10,000 per month. Total fixed costs of the facilities will remain constant at every level of activity, as part (a) of Illustration 22-2 shows. But, **on a per unit basis, the cost of rent will decline as activity increases**, as part (b) of Illustration 22-2 shows. At 2,000 units, the unit cost per tablet computer is $5 ($10,000 ÷ 2,000). When Damon produces 10,000 tablets, the unit cost of the rent is only $1 per tablet ($10,000 ÷ 10,000).

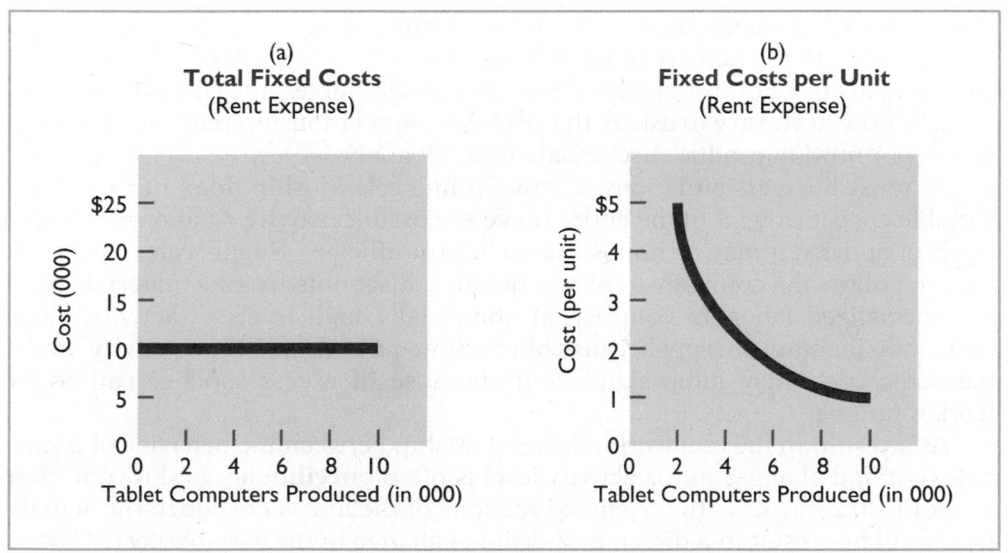

Illustration 22-2
Behavior of total and unit fixed costs

The trend for many manufacturers is to have more fixed costs and fewer variable costs. This trend is the result of increased use of automation and less use of employee labor. As a result, depreciation and lease charges (fixed costs) increase, whereas direct labor costs (variable costs) decrease.

© Jani Bryson/iStockphoto

PEOPLE, PLANET, AND PROFIT INSIGHT

Gardens in the Sky

Because of population increases, the United Nations' Food and Agriculture Organization esti-mates that food production will need to increase by 70% by 2050. Also, by 2050, roughly 70% of people will live in cities, which means more food needs to be hauled further to get it to the consumer. To address the lack of farmable land and reduce the cost of transporting produce, some have suggested building "vertical farming" skyscrapers in cities. This sounds great, but do the numbers work? Some variable costs would be reduced. For example, the use of pesticides, herbicides, fuel costs for shipping, and water would all drop. Soil erosion would be a non-issue since plants would be grown hydroponically (in a solution of water and minerals), and land requirements would be reduced because of vertical structures. But, other costs would be higher. First, there is the cost of the building. Also, any multistory building would require artificial lighting for plants on lower floors.

Until these cost challenges can be overcome, it appears that these skyscrapers will not break even. On the other hand, rooftop greenhouses on existing city structures already appear finan-cially viable. For example, a 15,000 square-foot rooftop greenhouse in Brooklyn already pro-duces roughly 30 tons of vegetables per year for local residents.

Source: "Vertical Farming: Does It Really Stack Up?" *The Economist* (December 9, 2010).

 What are some of the variable and fixed costs that are impacted by hydroponic farming? (See page 1073.)

Relevant Range

LEARNING OBJECTIVE 2

Explain the significance of the relevant range.

In Illustration 22-1 part (a) (page 1033), a straight line is drawn throughout the entire range of the activity index for total variable costs. In essence, the assump-tion is that the costs are **linear**. If a relationship is linear (that is, straight-line), then changes in the activity index will result in a direct, proportional change in the variable cost. For example, if the activity level doubles, the cost doubles.

It is now necessary to ask: Is the straight-line relationship realistic? Does the linear assumption produce useful data for CVP analysis?

In most business situations, a straight-line relationship **does not exist** for variable costs throughout the entire range of possible activity. At abnormally low levels of activity, it may be impossible to be cost-efficient. Small-scale operations may not allow the company to obtain quantity discounts for raw materials or to use specialized labor. In contrast, at abnormally high levels of activity, labor costs may increase sharply because of overtime pay. Also, at high activity levels, materials costs may jump significantly because of excess spoilage caused by worker fatigue.

As a result, in the real world, the relationship between the behavior of a vari-able cost and changes in the activity level is often **curvilinear**, as shown in part (a) of Illustration 22-3. In the curved sections of the line, a change in the activity index will not result in a direct, proportional change in the variable cost. That is, a doubling of the activity index will not result in an exact doubling of the variable cost. The variable cost may more than double, or it may be less than double.

Total fixed costs also do not have a straight-line relationship over the entire range of activity. Some fixed costs will not change. But it is possible for management to change other fixed costs. For example, in some instances, salaried employees (fixed) are replaced with freelance workers (variable). Illustration 22-3, part (b), shows an example of the behavior of total fixed costs through all potential levels of activity.

Helpful Hint Fixed costs that may be changeable include research, such as new product development, and management training programs.

Illustration 22-3
Nonlinear behavior of variable and fixed costs

For most companies, operating at almost zero or at 100% capacity is the exception rather than the rule. Instead, companies often operate over a somewhat narrower range, such as 40–80% of capacity. The range over which a company expects to operate during a year is called the **relevant range** of the activity index. Within the relevant range, as both diagrams in Illustration 22-4 show, a straight-line relationship generally exists for both variable and fixed costs.

Alternative Terminology
The relevant range is also called the *normal* or *practical range.*

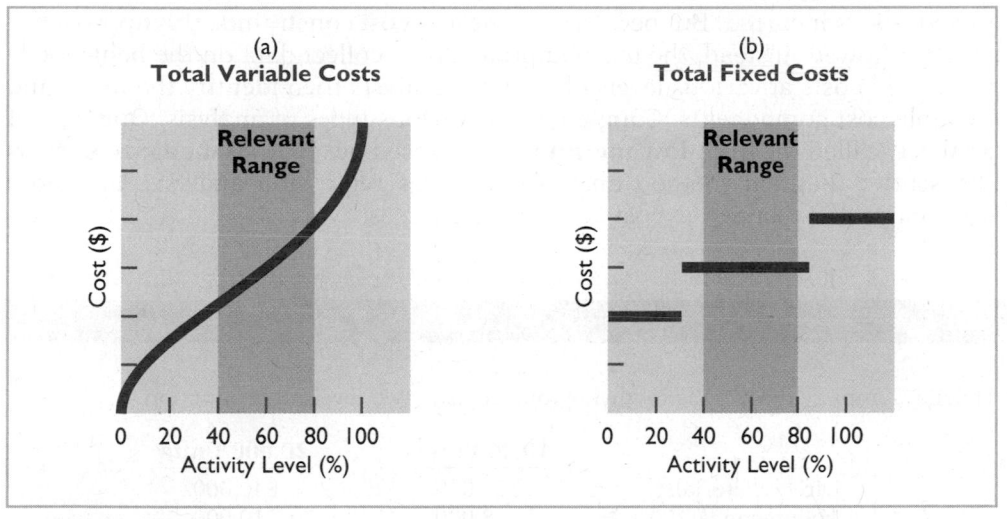

Illustration 22-4
Linear behavior within relevant range

As you can see, although the linear (straight-line) relationship may not be completely realistic, **the linear assumption produces useful data for CVP analysis as long as the level of activity remains within the relevant range.**

Mixed Costs

Mixed costs are costs that contain both a variable element and a fixed element. **Mixed costs, therefore, change in total but not proportionately with changes in the activity level.**

The rental of a U-Haul truck is a good example of a mixed cost. Assume that local rental terms for a 17-foot truck, including insurance, are $50 per day plus 50 cents per mile. When determining the cost of a one-day rental, the per day charge is a fixed cost (with respect to miles driven), whereas the mileage charge is a variable cost. Illustration 22-5 (page 1036) shows the rental cost for a one-day rental.

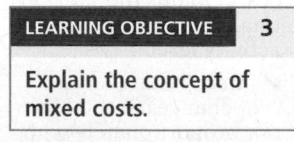

LEARNING OBJECTIVE   **3**

Explain the concept of mixed costs.

Illustration 22-5
Behavior of a mixed cost

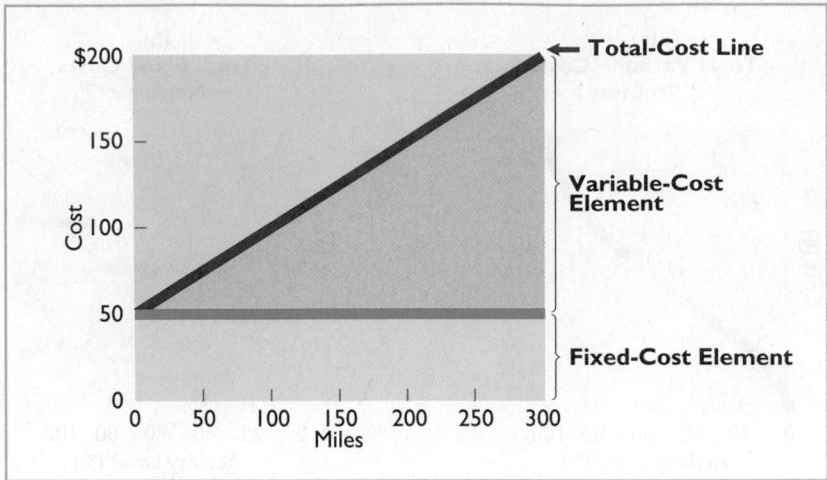

In this case, the fixed-cost element is the cost of having the service available. The variable-cost element is the cost of actually using the service. Another example of a mixed cost is utility costs (electric, telephone, and so on), where there is a flat service fee plus a usage charge.

For purposes of CVP analysis, **mixed costs must be classified into their fixed and variable elements**. How does management make the classification? One possibility is to determine the variable and fixed components each time a mixed cost is incurred. But because of time and cost constraints, this approach is rarely followed. Instead, the usual approach is to collect data on the behavior of the mixed costs at various levels of activity. Analysts then identify the fixed- and variable-cost components. Companies use various types of analysis. One type of analysis, called the **high-low method**, is discussed next. Other methods, such as the scatter diagram method and least squares regression analysis, are more appropriately explained in cost accounting courses.

> **DO IT!**

Types of Costs

Helena Company reports the following total costs at two levels of production.

	10,000 Units	20,000 Units
Direct materials	$20,000	$40,000
Maintenance	8,000	10,000
Direct labor	17,000	34,000
Indirect materials	1,000	2,000
Depreciation	4,000	4,000
Utilities	3,000	5,000
Rent	6,000	6,000

Classify each cost as variable, fixed, or mixed.

Action Plan

✔ Recall that a variable cost varies in total directly and proportionately with each change in activity level.

✔ Recall that a fixed cost remains the same in total with each change in activity level.

✔ Recall that a mixed cost changes in total but not proportionately with each change in activity level.

Solution

Direct materials, direct labor, and indirect materials are variable costs.
Depreciation and rent are fixed costs.
Maintenance and utilities are mixed costs.

Related exercise material: **BE22-1, BE22-2, E22-1, E22-2, E22-4,** and **DO IT!** 22-1.

 The Navigator

HIGH-LOW METHOD

The **high-low method** uses the total costs incurred at the high and low levels of activity to classify mixed costs into fixed and variable components. The difference in costs between the high and low levels represents variable costs, since only the variable-cost element can change as activity levels change.

The steps in computing fixed and variable costs under this method are as follows.

1. Determine variable cost per unit from the following formula.

$$\begin{array}{c} \text{Change in} \\ \text{Total Costs} \end{array} \div \begin{array}{c} \text{High minus Low} \\ \text{Activity Level} \end{array} = \begin{array}{c} \text{Variable Cost} \\ \text{per Unit} \end{array}$$

To illustrate, assume that Metro Transit Company has the following mainte-nance costs and mileage data for its fleet of buses over a 6-month period.

Month	Miles Driven	Total Cost	Month	Miles Driven	Total Cost
January	20,000	$30,000	April	50,000	$63,000
February	40,000	48,000	May	30,000	42,000
March	35,000	49,000	June	43,000	61,000

The high and low levels of activity are 50,000 miles in April and 20,000 miles in January. The maintenance costs at these two levels are $63,000 and $30,000, respectively. The difference in maintenance costs is $33,000 ($63,000 − $30,000), and the difference in miles is 30,000 (50,000 − 20,000). Therefore, for Metro Transit, variable cost per unit is $1.10, computed as follows.

$$\$33,000 \div 30,000 = \$1.10$$

2. Determine the fixed costs by subtracting the total variable costs at either the high or the low activity level from the total cost at that activity level.

For Metro Transit, the computations are shown in Illustration 22-8.

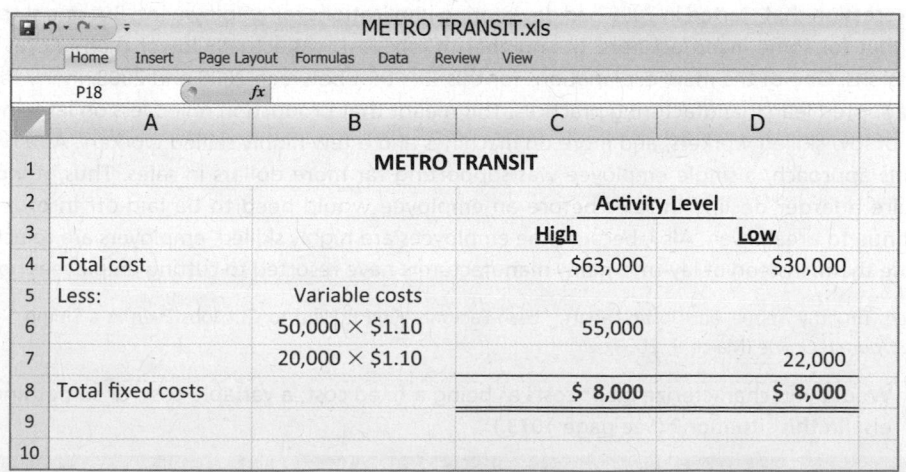

	A	B	C	D
1		**METRO TRANSIT**		
2			Activity Level	
3			High	Low
4	Total cost		$63,000	$30,000
5	Less:	Variable costs		
6		50,000 × $1.10	55,000	
7		20,000 × $1.10		22,000
8	Total fixed costs		$ 8,000	$ 8,000
9				
10				

Maintenance costs are therefore $8,000 per month of fixed costs plus $1.10 per mile of variable costs. This is represented by the following formula:

$$\text{Maintenance costs} = \$8,000 + (\$1.10 \times \text{Miles driven})$$

For example, at 45,000 miles, estimated maintenance costs would be $8,000 fixed and $49,500 variable ($1.10 × 45,000) for a total of $57,500.

The graph in Illustration 22-9 plots the 6-month data for Metro Transit Company. The red line drawn in the graph connects the high and low data points, and therefore represents the equation that we just solved using the high-low method. The red, "high-low" line intersects the y-axis at $8,000 (the fixed-cost level), and it rises by $1.10 per unit (the variable cost per unit). Note that a completely different line would result if we chose any two of the other data points. That is, by choosing any two other data points, we would end up with a different estimate of fixed costs and a different variable cost per unit. Thus, from this scatter plot, we can see that while the high-low method is simple, the result is rather arbitrary. A better approach, which uses information from all the data points to estimate fixed and variable costs, is called **regression analysis**. A discussion of regression analysis is provided in a supplement on the book's companion website.

Illustration 22-9
Scatter plot for Metro Transit Company

pidjoe/iStockphoto

MANAGEMENT INSIGHT

Skilled Labor Is Truly Essential

The recession that started in 2008 had devastating implications for employment. But one surprise was that for some manufacturers, the number of jobs lost was actually lower than in previous recessions. One of the main explanations for this was that between 2000 and 2008, many factories adopted lean manufacturing practices. This meant that production relied less on large numbers of low-skilled workers, and more on machines and a few highly skilled workers. As a result of this approach, a single employee was supporting far more dollars in sales. Thus, it would require a larger decline in sales before an employee would need to be laid-off in order to continue to break even. Also, because the employees are highly skilled, employers are reluctant to lose them. Instead of lay-offs, many manufacturers have resorted to cutting employees hours.

Source: Timothy Aeppel and Justin Lahart, "Lean Factories Find It Hard to Cut Jobs Even in a Slump," *Wall Street Journal Online* (March 9, 2009).

 Would you characterize labor costs as being a fixed cost, a variable cost, or something else in this situation? (See page 1073.)

Importance of Identifying Variable and Fixed Costs

Why is it important to segregate costs into variable and fixed elements? The answer may become apparent if we look at the following four business decisions.

1. If American Airlines is to make a profit when it reduces all domestic fares by 30%, what reduction in costs or increase in passengers will be required?
   Answer: To make a profit when it cuts domestic fares by 30%, American Airlines will have to increase the number of passengers or cut its variable costs for those flights. Its fixed costs will not change.

2. If Ford Motor Company meets workers' demands for higher wages, what increase in sales revenue will be needed to maintain current profit levels?
   Answer: Higher wages at Ford Motor Company will increase the variable costs of manufacturing automobiles. To maintain present profit levels, Ford will have to cut other variable costs or increase the price of its automobiles.

3. If United States Steel Corp.'s program to modernize plant facilities through significant equipment purchases reduces the work force by 50%, what will be the effect on the cost of producing one ton of steel?
   Answer: The modernizing of plant facilities at United States Steel Corp. changes the proportion of fixed and variable costs of producing one ton of steel. Fixed costs increase because of higher depreciation charges, whereas variable costs decrease due to the reduction in the number of steelworkers.

4. What happens if Kellogg increases its advertising expenses but cannot increase prices because of competitive pressure?
   Answer: Sales volume must be increased to cover the increase in fixed advertising costs.

> DO IT!

High-Low Method   Byrnes Company accumulates the following data concerning a mixed cost, using units produced as the activity level.

	Units Produced	Total Cost
March	9,800	$14,740
April	8,500	13,250
May	7,000	11,100
June	7,600	12,000
July	8,100	12,460

Action Plan

✔ Determine the highest and lowest levels of activity.

✔ Compute variable cost per unit as: Change in total costs ÷ (High − low activity level) = Variable cost per unit.

✔ Compute fixed cost as: Total cost − (Variable cost per unit × Units produced) = Fixed cost.

(a) Compute the variable- and fixed-cost elements using the high-low method.
(b) Estimate the total cost if the company produces 6,000 units.

Solution

(a) Variable cost: ($14,740 − $11,100) ÷ (9,800 − 7,000) = $1.30 per unit
    Fixed cost: $14,740 − $12,740 ($1.30 × 9,800 units) = $2,000
        or $11,100 − $9,100 ($1.30 × 7,000) = $2,000
(b) Total cost to produce 6,000 units: $2,000 + $7,800 ($1.30 × 6,000) = $9,800

Related exercise material: **BE22-3, BE22-4, BE22-5, E22-3, E22-5, E22-6, and DO IT! 22-2.**

 ✔ The Navigator

Cost-Volume-Profit Analysis

LEARNING OBJECTIVE   4

List the five components of cost-volume-profit analysis.

Cost-volume-profit (CVP) analysis is the study of the effects of changes in costs and volume on a company's profits. CVP analysis is important in profit planning. It also is a critical factor in such management decisions as setting selling prices, determining product mix, and maximizing use of production facilities.

Basic Components

CVP analysis considers the interrelationships among the components shown in Illustration 22-10.

Volume or level of activity   **Unit selling prices**   **Variable costs per unit**   **Total fixed costs**   **Sales mix**

Illustration 22-10
Components of CVP analysis

The following assumptions underlie each CVP analysis.

1. The behavior of both costs and revenues is linear throughout the relevant range of the activity index.
2. Costs can be classified accurately as either variable or fixed.
3. Changes in activity are the only factors that affect costs.
4. All units produced are sold.
5. When more than one type of product is sold, the sales mix will remain constant. That is, the percentage that each product represents of total sales will stay the same. Sales mix complicates CVP analysis because different products will have different cost relationships. In this chapter, we assume a single product.

When these assumptions are not valid, the CVP analysis may be inaccurate.

CVP Income Statement

LEARNING OBJECTIVE   5

Indicate what contribution margin is and how it can be expressed.

Because CVP is so important for decision-making, management often wants this information reported in a **cost-volume-profit (CVP) income statement** format for internal use. The CVP income statement classifies costs as variable or fixed and computes a contribution margin. **Contribution margin (CM)** is the amount of revenue remaining after deducting variable costs. It is often stated both as a total amount and on a per unit basis.

We will use Vargo Video Company to illustrate a CVP income statement. Vargo Video produces a high-definition digital camcorder with 15× optical zoom and a wide-screen, high-resolution LCD monitor. Relevant data for the camcorders sold by this company in June 2014 are as follows.

Illustration 22-11
Assumed selling and cost data for Vargo Video

Unit selling price of camcorder	$500
Unit variable costs	$300
Total monthly fixed costs	$200,000
Units sold	1,600

The CVP income statement for Vargo Video therefore would be reported as follows.

Illustration 22-12
CVP income statement, with net income

VARGO VIDEO COMPANY
CVP Income Statement
For the Month Ended June 30, 2014

	Total
Sales (1,600 camcorders)	$ 800,000
Variable costs	480,000
Contribution margin	320,000
Fixed costs	200,000
Net income	**$120,000**

A traditional income statement and a CVP income statement both report the same net income of $120,000. However a traditional income statement does not classify costs as variable or fixed, and therefore it does not report a contribution margin. In addition, sometimes per unit amounts and percentage of sales amounts are shown on a CVP income statement to facilitate CVP analysis. *Homework assignments specify which columns to present.*

In the applications of CVP analysis that follow, we assume that the term "cost" includes all costs and expenses related to production and sale of the product. That is, cost includes manufacturing costs plus selling and administrative expenses.

CONTRIBUTION MARGIN PER UNIT

Illustration 22-14 shows Vargo Video's CVP income statement at the point where net income equals zero. It shows a contribution margin of $200,000, and a contribution margin per unit of $200 ($500 − $300). The formula for **contribution margin per unit** and the computation for Vargo Video are:

Illustration 22-13
Formula for contribution margin per unit

Unit Selling Price	−	Unit Variable Costs	=	Contribution Margin per Unit
$500	−	$300	=	$200

Contribution margin per unit indicates that for every camcorder sold, the selling price exceeds the variable costs by $200. Vargo generates $200 per unit sold to cover fixed costs and contribute to net income. Because Vargo Video has fixed costs of $200,000, it must sell 1,000 camcorders ($200,000 ÷ $200) to cover its fixed costs. At the point where total contribution margin exactly equals fixed costs, Vargo will report net income of zero. At this point, referred to as the **break-even point**, total costs (variable plus fixed) exactly equal total revenue.

Illustration 22-14
CVP income statement, with zero net income

VARGO VIDEO COMPANY
CVP Income Statement
For the Month Ended June 30, 2014

	Total	Per Unit
Sales (1,000 camcorders)	$ 500,000	$ 500
Variable costs	300,000	300
Contribution margin	200,000	**$200**
Fixed costs	200,000	
Net income	$ −0−	

It follows that for every camcorder sold above the break-even point of 1,000 units, **net income increases by the amount of the contribution margin per unit, $200**. For example, assume that Vargo sold one more camcorder, for a total of 1,001 camcorders sold. In this case, Vargo reports net income of $200, as shown in Illustration 22-15.

Illustration 22-15
CVP income statement, with net income and per unit data

VARGO VIDEO COMPANY
CVP Income Statement
For the Month Ended June 30, 2014

	Total	Per Unit
Sales (1,001 camcorders)	$500,500	$500
Variable costs	300,300	300
Contribution margin	200,200	**$200**
Fixed costs	200,000	
Net income	$ 200	

CONTRIBUTION MARGIN RATIO

Some managers prefer to use a contribution margin ratio in CVP analysis. The contribution margin ratio is the contribution margin expressed as a percentage of sales, as shown in Illustration 22-16.

Illustration 22-16
CVP income statement, with net income and percent of sales data

VARGO VIDEO COMPANY
CVP Income Statement
For the Month Ended June 30, 2014

	Total	Percent of Sales
Sales (1,001 camcorders)	$500,500	100%
Variable costs	300,300	60
Contribution margin	200,200	**40%**
Fixed costs	200,000	
Net income	$ 200	

Alternatively, the **contribution margin ratio** is the contribution margin per unit divided by the unit selling price. For Vargo Video, the ratio is as follows.

Illustration 22-17
Formula for contribution margin ratio

Contribution Margin per Unit	÷	Unit Selling Price	=	Contribution Margin Ratio
$200	÷	$500	=	40%

The contribution margin ratio of 40% means that Vargo generates 40 cents of contribution margin with each dollar of sales. That is, $0.40 of each sales dollar (40% × $1) is available to apply to fixed costs and to contribute to net income.

This expression of contribution margin is very helpful in determining the effect of changes in sales on net income. For example, if Vargo's sales increase $100,000, net income will increase $40,000 (40% × $100,000). Thus, by using the contribution margin ratio, managers can quickly determine increases in net income from any change in sales.

We can also see this effect through a CVP income statement. Assume that Vargo Video's current sales are $500,000 and it wants to know the effect of a $100,000 (200-unit) increase in sales. Vargo prepares a comparative CVP income statement analysis as follows.

Illustration 22-18
Comparative CVP income statements

VARGO VIDEO COMPANY
CVP Income Statements
For the Month Ended June 30, 2014

	No Change			With Change		
	Total	Per Unit	Percent of Sales	Total	Per Unit	Percent of Sales
Sales	$500,000	$500	100%	$600,000	$500	100%
Variable costs	300,000	300	60	360,000	300	60
Contribution margin	200,000	$200	40%	240,000	$200	40%
Fixed costs	200,000			200,000		
Net income	$ –0–			$ 40,000		

The $40,000 increase in net income can be calculated on either a contribution margin per unit basis (200 units × $200 per unit) or using the contribution margin ratio times the increase in sales dollars (40% × $100,000). Note that the contribution margin per unit and contribution margin as a percentage of sales remain unchanged by the increase in sales.

Study these CVP income statements carefully. The concepts presented in these statements are used extensively in this and later chapters.

Break-Even Analysis

A key relationship in CVP analysis is the level of activity at which total revenues equal total costs (both fixed and variable)—the **break-even point**. At this volume of sales, the company will realize no income but will suffer no loss. The process of finding the break-even point is called **break-even analysis**. Knowledge of the break-even point is useful to management when it decides whether to introduce new product lines, change sales prices on established products, or enter new market areas.

LEARNING OBJECTIVE   6

Identify the three ways to determine the break-even point.

The break-even point can be:

1. Computed from a mathematical equation.
2. Computed by using contribution margin.
3. Derived from a cost-volume-profit (CVP) graph.

The break-even point can be expressed either in **sales units** or **sales dollars**.

MATHEMATICAL EQUATION
The first line of Illustration 22-19 shows a common equation used for CVP analysis. When net income is set to zero, this equation can be used to calculate the break-even point.

Illustration 22-19
Basic CVP equation

Required Sales	−	Variable Costs	−	Fixed Costs	=	Net Income
$500Q	−	$300Q	−	$200,000	=	$0

As shown in Illustration 22-14 (page 1041), net income equals zero when the contribution margin (sales minus variable costs) is equal to fixed costs.

To reflect this, Illustration 22-20 rewrites the equation with contribution margin (sales minus variable costs) on the left side, and fixed costs and net income on the right. We can compute the break-even point **in units** by **using unit selling prices** and **unit variable costs**. The computation for Vargo Video is:

Illustration 22-20
Computation of break-even point in units

Required Sales	−	Variable Costs	−	Fixed Costs	=	Net Income
$500Q	−	$300Q	−	$200,000	=	$0
$500Q	−	$300Q	=	$200,000	+	$0

$$\$200Q = \$200,000$$

$$Q = \frac{\$200,000}{\$200} = \frac{\text{Fixed Costs}}{\text{Contribution Margin per Unit}}$$

$$Q = 1,000 \text{ units}$$

where
$$Q = \text{sales volume in units}$$
$$\$500 = \text{selling price}$$
$$\$300 = \text{variable costs per unit}$$
$$\$200,000 = \text{total fixed costs}$$

Thus, Vargo Video must sell 1,000 units to break even.

To find the amount of **sales dollars** required to break even, we multiply the units sold at the break-even point times the selling price per unit, as shown below.

$$1,000 \times \$500 = \$500,000 \text{ (break-even sales dollars)}$$

CONTRIBUTION MARGIN TECHNIQUE

Many managers employ the contribution margin to compute the break-even point.

CONTRIBUTION MARGIN IN UNITS The final step in Illustration 22-20 divides fixed costs by the contribution margin per unit (highlighted in red). Thus, rather than walk through all of the steps of the equation approach, we can simply employ this formula shown in Illustration 22-21.

Illustration 22-21
Formula for break-even point in units using contribution margin per unit

Fixed Costs	÷	Contribution Margin per Unit	=	Break-Even Point in Units
$200,000	÷	$200	=	1,000 units

Why does this formula work? The contribution margin per unit is the net amount by which each sale exceeds the variable costs per unit. Every sale generates this much money to pay off fixed costs. Consequently, if we divide fixed costs by the contribution margin per unit, we know how many units we need to sell to break even.

CONTRIBUTION MARGIN RATIO As we will see in the next chapter, when a company has numerous products, it is not practical to determine the contribution margin per unit for each product. In this case, using the contribution margin ratio is very useful for determining the break-even point in total dollars (rather than units). Recall that the contribution margin ratio is the amount of contribution margin that is generated from each dollar of sales. Therefore, to determine the sales dollars needed to cover fixed costs, we divide fixed costs by the contribution margin ratio, as shown in Illustration 22-22.

Fixed Costs	÷	Contribution Margin Ratio	=	Break-Even Point in Dollars
$200,000	÷	40%	=	$500,000

Illustration 22-22
Formula for break-even point in dollars using contribution margin ratio

To apply this formula to Vargo, consider that its 40% contribution margin ratio means that for every dollar sold, it generates 40 cents of contribution margin. The question is, how many dollars of sales does Vargo need in order to generate total contribution margin of $200,000 to pay off fixed costs? We divide the fixed costs of $200,000 by the 40 cents of contribution margin generated by each dollar of sales to arrive at $500,000 ($200,000 ÷ 40%). To prove this result, if we generate 40 cents of contribution margin for each dollar of sales, then the total contribution margin generated by $500,000 in sales is $200,000 ($500,000 × 40%).

SERVICE COMPANY INSIGHT

Charter Flights Offer a Good Deal

The Internet is wringing inefficiencies out of nearly every industry. While commercial aircraft spend roughly 4,000 hours a year in the air, chartered aircraft are flown only 500 hours annually. That means that they are sitting on the ground—not making any money—about 90% of the time. One company, FlightServe, saw a business opportunity in that fact. For about the same cost as a first-class ticket, FlightServe decided to match up executives with charter flights in small "private jets." The executive would get a more comfortable ride and could avoid the hassle of big airports. FlightServe noted that the average charter jet has eight seats. When all eight seats were full, the company would have an 80% profit margin. It would break even at an average of 3.3 full seats per flight.

Source: "Jet Set Go," *The Economist* (March 18, 2000), p. 68.

 How did FlightServe determine that it would break even with 3.3 seats full per flight? (See page 1073.)

GRAPHIC PRESENTATION
An effective way to find the break-even point is to prepare a break-even graph. Because this graph also shows costs, volume, and profits, it is referred to as a **cost-volume-profit (CVP) graph**.

As the CVP graph in Illustration 22-23 (page 1046) shows, sales volume is recorded along the horizontal axis. This axis should extend to the maximum level of expected sales. Both total revenues (sales) and total costs (fixed plus variable) are recorded on the vertical axis.

Illustration 22-23
CVP graph

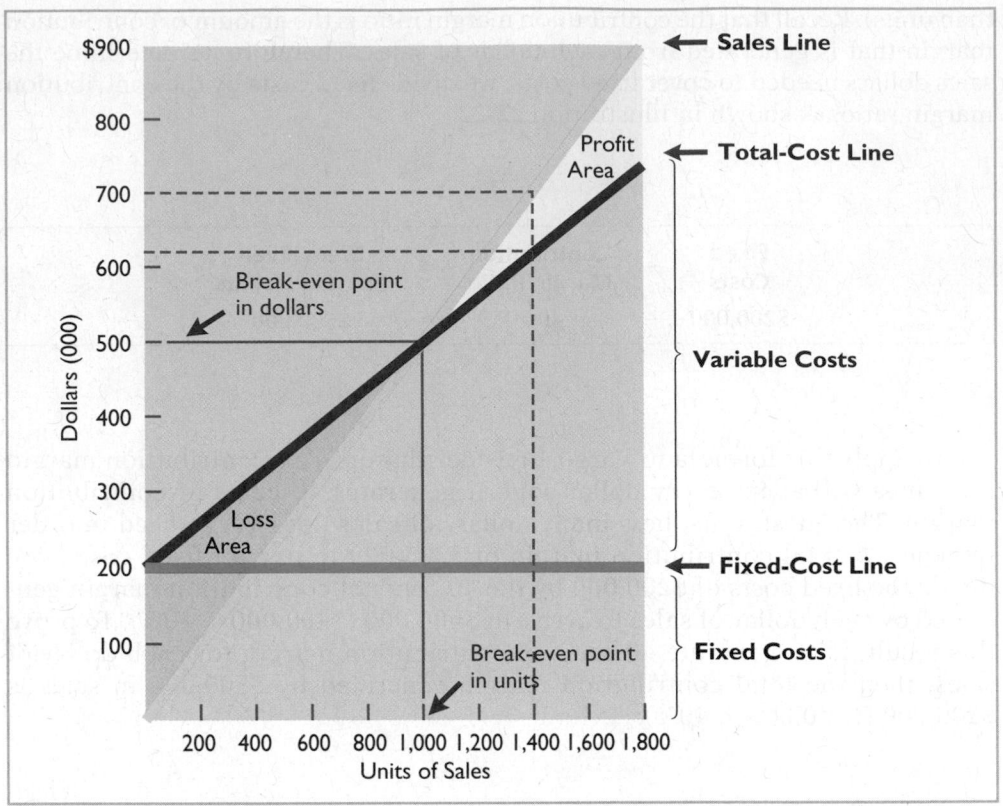

The construction of the graph, using the data for Vargo Video, is as follows.

1. Plot the sales line, starting at the zero activity level. For every camcorder sold, total revenue increases by $500. For example, at 200 units, sales are $100,000. At the upper level of activity (1,800 units), sales are $900,000. The revenue line is assumed to be linear through the full range of activity.

2. Plot the total fixed costs using a horizontal line. For the camcorders, this line is plotted at $200,000. The fixed costs are the same at every level of activity.

3. Plot the total-cost line. This starts at the fixed-cost line at zero activity. It increases by the variable costs at each level of activity. For each camcorder, variable costs are $300. Thus, at 200 units, total variable costs are $60,000, and the total cost is $260,000. At 1,800 units, total variable costs are $540,000, and total cost is $740,000. On the graph, the amount of the variable costs can be derived from the difference between the total-cost and fixed-cost lines at each level of activity.

4. Determine the break-even point from the intersection of the total-cost line and the sales line. The break-even point in dollars is found by drawing a horizontal line from the break-even point to the vertical axis. The break-even point in units is found by drawing a vertical line from the break-even point to the horizontal axis. For the camcorders, the break-even point is $500,000 of sales, or 1,000 units. At this sales level, Vargo Video will cover costs but make no profit.

The CVP graph also shows both the net income and net loss areas. Thus, the amount of income or loss at each level of sales can be derived from the sales and total-cost lines.

A CVP graph is useful because the effects of a change in any element in the CVP analysis can be quickly seen. For example, a 10% increase in selling price will change the location of the sales line. Likewise, the effects on total costs of wage increases can be quickly observed.

> **DO IT!**

Break-Even Analysis

Action Plan

✔ Apply the formula: Sales − Variable costs − Fixed costs = Net income.

✔ Apply the formula: Fixed costs ÷ Contribution margin per unit = Break-even point in units.

Lombardi Company has a unit selling price of $400, variable costs per unit of $240, and fixed costs of $180,000. Compute the break-even point in units using (a) a mathematical equation and (b) contribution margin per unit.

Solution

(a) The equation is $400Q − $240Q − $180,000 = $0; ($400Q − $240Q) = $180,000. The break-even point in units is 1,125. (b) The contribution margin per unit is $160 ($400 − $240). The formula therefore is $180,000 ÷ $160, and the break-even point in units is 1,125.

Related exercise material: **BE22-6, BE22-7, BE22-8, BE22-9, E22-8, E22-9, E22-10, E22-11, E22-12, E22-13, and DO IT! 22-3.**

 The Navigator

Target Net Income

Rather than simply "breaking even," management usually sets an income objective often called **target net income**. It indicates the sales necessary to achieve a specified level of income. Companies determine the sales necessary to achieve target net income by using one of the three approaches discussed earlier.

LEARNING OBJECTIVE   7

Give the formulas for determining sales required to earn target net income.

MATHEMATICAL EQUATION

We know that at the break-even point no profit or loss results for the company. By adding an amount for target net income to the same basic equation, we obtain the following formula for determining required sales.

Required Sales	−	Variable Costs	−	Fixed Costs	=	Target Net Income

Illustration 22-24
Formula for required sales to meet target net income

Recall that once the break-even point has been reached so that fixed costs are covered, each additional unit sold increases net income by the amount of the contribution margin per unit. We can rewrite the equation with contribution margin (sales minus variable costs) on the left-hand side, and fixed costs and net income on the right. Assuming that target net income is $120,000 for Vargo Video, the computation of required sales in units is as follows.

Illustration 22-25
Computation of required sales

Required Sales	−	Variable Costs	−	Fixed Costs	=	Target Net Income
$500Q	−	$300Q	−	$200,000	=	$120,000
$500Q	−	$300Q	=	$200,000	+	$120,000

$$\$200Q = \$200,000 + \$120,000$$

$$Q = \frac{\$200,000 + \$120,000}{\$200} = \frac{\text{Fixed Costs} + \text{Net Target Income}}{\text{Contribution Margin per Unit}}$$

$$Q = 1,600$$

where

$$Q = \text{sales volume}$$
$$\$500 = \text{selling price}$$
$$\$300 = \text{variable costs per unit}$$
$$\$200,000 = \text{total fixed costs}$$
$$\$120,000 = \text{target net income}$$

Vargo must sell 1,600 units to achieve target net income of $120,000. The sales dollars required to achieve the target net income is found by multiplying the units sold by the unit selling price [(1,600 × $500) = $800,000].

CONTRIBUTION MARGIN TECHNIQUE

As in the case of break-even sales, we can compute in either units or dollars the sales required to meet target net income. The formula to compute required sales in units for Vargo Video using the contribution margin per unit can be seen in the final step of the equation approach in Illustration 22-25 (shown in red). We simply divide the sum of fixed costs and target net income by the contribution margin per unit. Illustration 22-26 shows this for Vargo.

Illustration 22-26
Formula for required sales in units using contribution margin per unit

$\left(\begin{array}{c}\text{Fixed Costs +}\\\text{Target Net Income}\end{array}\right)$	÷	Contribution Margin per Unit	=	Required Sales in Units
($200,000 + $120,000)	÷	$200	=	1,600 units

To achieve its desired target net income of $120,000, Vargo must sell 1,600 camcorders.

The formula to compute the required sales in dollars for Vargo Video using the contribution margin ratio is shown below.

Illustration 22-27
Formula for required sales in dollars using contribution margin ratio

$\left(\begin{array}{c}\text{Fixed Costs +}\\\text{Target Net Income}\end{array}\right)$	÷	Contribution Margin Ratio	=	Required Sales in Dollars
($200,000 + $120,000)	÷	40%	=	$800,000

To achieve its desired target net income of $120,000, Vargo must generate sales of $800,000.

GRAPHIC PRESENTATION

We also can use the CVP graph in Illustration 22-23 (on page 1046) to find the sales required to meet target net income. In the profit area of the graph, the distance between the sales line and the total-cost line at any point equals net income. We can find required sales by analyzing the differences between the two lines until the desired net income is found.

For example, suppose Vargo Video sells 1,400 camcorders. Illustration 22-23 shows that a vertical line drawn at 1,400 units intersects the sales line at $700,000 and the total cost line at $620,000. The difference between the two amounts represents the net income (profit) of $80,000.

Margin of Safety

LEARNING OBJECTIVE   8

Define margin of safety, and give the formulas for computing it.

Margin of safety is the difference between actual or expected sales and sales at the break-even point. It measures the "cushion" that a particular level of sales provides. It tells us how far sales could fall before the company begins operating at a loss. The margin of safety is expressed in dollars or as a ratio.

The formula for stating the **margin of safety in dollars** is actual (or expected) sales minus break-even sales. Assuming that actual (expected) sales for Vargo Video are $750,000, the computation is:

Actual (Expected) Sales	−	Break-Even Sales	=	Margin of Safety in Dollars
$750,000	−	$500,000	=	$250,000

Illustration 22-28
Formula for margin of safety in dollars

Vargo's margin of safety is $250,000. Its sales could fall $250,000 before it operates at a loss.

The **margin of safety ratio** is the margin of safety in dollars divided by actual (or expected) sales. The formula and computation for determining the margin of safety ratio are:

Margin of Safety in Dollars	÷	Actual (Expected) Sales	=	Margin of Safety Ratio
$250,000	÷	$750,000	=	33%

Illustration 22-29
Formula for margin of safety ratio

This means that the company's sales could fall by 33% before it would be operating at a loss.

The higher the dollars or the percentage, the greater the margin of safety. Management continuously evaluates the adequacy of the margin of safety in terms of such factors as the vulnerability of the product to competitive pressures and to downturns in the economy.

SERVICE COMPANY INSIGHT

How a Rolling Stones' Tour Makes Money

Computation of break-even and margin of safety is important for service companies. Consider how the promoter for the Rolling Stones' tour used the break-even point and margin of safety. For example, one outdoor show should bring 70,000 individuals for a gross of $2.45 million. The promoter guarantees $1.2 million to the Rolling Stones. In addition, 20% of gross goes to the stadium in which the performance is staged. Add another $400,000 for other expenses such as ticket takers, parking attendants, advertising, and so on. The promoter also shares in sales of T-shirts and memorabilia for which the promoter will net over $7 million during the tour. From a successful Rolling Stones' tour, the promoter could make $35 million!

Yael/Retna

? What amount of sales dollars are required for the promoter to break even? (See page 1073.)

> DO IT!

Margin of Safety; Required Sales

Mabo Company makes calculators that sell for $20 each. For the coming year, management expects fixed costs to total $220,000 and variable costs to be $9 per unit.

(a) Compute break-even point in units using the mathematical equation.
(b) Compute break-even point in dollars using the contribution margin (CM) ratio.
(c) Compute the margin of safety percentage assuming actual sales are $500,000.
(d) Compute the sales required in dollars to earn net income of $165,000.

Solution

(a) Sales − Variable costs − Fixed costs = Net income
$$\$20Q - \$9Q - \$220{,}000 = \$0$$
$$\$11Q = \$220{,}000$$
$$Q = 20{,}000 \text{ units}$$

(b) Contribution margin per unit = Unit selling price − Unit variable costs
$$\$11 = \$20 - \$9$$
Contribution margin ratio = Contribution margin per unit ÷ Unit selling price
$$55\% = \$11 \div \$20$$
Break-even point in dollars = Fixed cost ÷ Contribution margin ratio
$$= \$220{,}000 \div 55\%$$
$$= \$400{,}000$$

(c) Margin of safety $= \dfrac{\text{Actual sales} - \text{Break-even sales}}{\text{Actual sales}}$

$$= \frac{\$500{,}000 - \$400{,}000}{\$500{,}000}$$

$$= 20\%$$

(d) Required sales − Variable costs − Fixed costs = Net income
$$\$20Q - \$9Q - \$220{,}000 = \$165{,}000$$
$$\$11Q = \$385{,}000$$
$$Q = 35{,}000 \text{ units}$$
$$35{,}000 \text{ units} \times \$20 = \$700{,}000 \text{ required sales}$$

Related exercise material: **BE22-6, BE22-7, BE22-8, E22-5, E22-6, E22-7, E22-8, E22-9, E22-10, E22-11, E22-12, E22-13, and DO IT! 22-4.**

✔ **The Navigator**

CVP and Changes in the Business Environment

When the personal computer was introduced, it sold for $2,500. Today, similar computers sell for much less. Recently, when oil prices rose, the break-even point for airline companies such as American and Northwest rose dramatically. Because of lower prices for imported steel, the demand for domestic steel dropped significantly. The point should be clear: Business conditions change rapidly, and management must respond intelligently to these changes. CVP analysis can help.

To better understand how CVP analysis works, let's look at three independent situations that might occur at Vargo Video. Each case uses the original camcorder sales and cost data, which were as follows.

Illustration 22-30
Original camcorder sales and cost data

Unit selling price	$500
Unit variable cost	$300
Total fixed costs	$200,000
Break-even sales	$500,000 or 1,000 units

CASE 1 A competitor is offering a 10% discount on the selling price of its camcorders. Management must decide whether to offer a similar discount.

Question: What effect will a 10% discount on selling price have on the break-even point for camcorders?

Answer: A 10% discount on selling price reduces the selling price per unit to $450 [$500 − ($500 × 10%)]. Variable costs per unit remain unchanged at $300. Thus, the contribution margin per unit is $150. Assuming no change in fixed costs, break-even point is 1,333 units, computed as follows.

Fixed Costs	÷	Contribution Margin per Unit	=	Break-Even Point in Units
$200,000	÷	$150	=	1,333 units (rounded)

Illustration 22-31
Computation of break-even sales in units

For Vargo Video, this change requires monthly sales to increase by 333 units, or 33$\frac{1}{3}$%, in order to break even. In reaching a conclusion about offering a 10% discount to customers, management must determine how likely it is to achieve the increased sales. Also, management should estimate the possible loss of sales if the competitor's discount price is not matched.

CASE II To meet the threat of foreign competition, management invests in new robotic equipment that will lower the amount of direct labor required to make camcorders. The company estimates that total fixed costs will increase 30% and that variable cost per unit will decrease 30%.

Question: What effect will the new equipment have on the sales volume required to break even?

Answer: Total fixed costs become $260,000 [$200,000 + (30% × $200,000)]. The variable cost per unit becomes $210 [$300 − (30% × $300)]. The new break-even point is approximately 897 units, computed as follows.

Fixed Costs	÷	Contribution Margin per Unit	=	Break-Even Point in Units
$260,000	÷	($500 − $210)	=	897 units (rounded)

Illustration 22-32
Computation of break-even sales in units

These changes appear to be advantageous for Vargo Video. The break-even point is reduced by approximately 10%, or 100 units.

CASE III Vargo's principal supplier of raw materials has just announced a price increase. The higher cost is expected to increase the variable cost of camcorders by $25 per unit. Management decides to hold the line on the selling price of the camcorders. It plans a cost-cutting program that will save $17,500 in fixed costs per month. Vargo is currently realizing monthly net income of $80,000 on sales of 1,400 camcorders.

Question: What increase in units sold will be needed to maintain the same level of net income?

Answer: The variable cost per unit increases to $325 ($300 + $25). Fixed costs are reduced to $182,500 ($200,000 − $17,500). Because of the change in variable cost, the contribution margin per unit becomes $175 ($500 − $325). The required number of units sold to achieve the target net income is computed as follows.

Fixed Costs + Target Net Income	÷	Contribution Margin per Unit	=	Required Sales in Units
($182,500 + $80,000)	÷	$175	=	1,500

Illustration 22-33
Computation of required sales

To achieve the required sales, Vargo will have to sell 1,500 camcorders, an increase of 100 units. If this does not seem to be a reasonable expectation, management will either have to make further cost reductions or accept less net income if the selling price remains unchanged.

CVP Income Statement Revisited

Earlier in the chapter we presented a simple CVP income statement. When companies prepare a CVP income statement, they provide more detail about specific variable and fixed-cost items.

To illustrate a more detailed CVP income statement, we will assume that Vargo Video reaches its target net income of $120,000 (see Illustration 22-25 on page 1047). The following information is obtained on the $680,000 of costs that were incurred in June to produce and sell 1,600 units.

Illustration 22-34
Assumed cost and expense data

	Variable	Fixed	Total
Cost of goods sold	$400,000	$120,000	$520,000
Selling expenses	60,000	40,000	100,000
Administrative expenses	20,000	40,000	60,000
	$480,000	$200,000	$680,000

The detailed CVP income statement for Vargo is shown below.

Illustration 22-35
Detailed CVP income statement

VARGO VIDEO COMPANY
CVP Income Statement
For the Month Ended June 30, 2014

		Total	Per Unit
Sales		$ 800,000	$ 500
Variable expenses			
Cost of goods sold	$400,000		
Selling expenses	60,000		
Administrative expenses	20,000		
Total variable expenses		480,000	300
Contribution margin		320,000	$200
Fixed expenses			
Cost of goods sold	120,000		
Selling expenses	40,000		
Administrative expenses	40,000		
Total fixed expenses		200,000	
Net income		$120,000	

> Comprehensive DO IT!

B.T. Hernandez Company, maker of high-quality flashlights, has experienced steady growth over the last 6 years. However, increased competition has led Mr. Hernandez, the president, to believe that an aggressive campaign is needed next year to maintain the company's present growth. The company's accountant has presented Mr. Hernandez with the data on the next page for the current year, 2014, for use in preparing next year's advertising campaign.

Cost Schedules

Variable costs	
Direct labor per flashlight	$ 8.00
Direct materials	4.00
Variable overhead	3.00
Variable cost per flashlight	$15.00
Fixed costs	
Manufacturing	$ 25,000
Selling	40,000
Administrative	70,000
Total fixed costs	$135,000
Selling price per flashlight	$25.00
Expected sales, 2014 (20,000 flashlights)	$500,000

Mr. Hernandez has set the sales target for the year 2015 at a level of $550,000 (22,000 flashlights).

Instructions
(Ignore any income tax considerations.)

(a) What is the projected operating income for 2014 at the 20,000 expected sales level?

(b) What is the contribution margin per unit for 2014?

(c) What is the break-even point in units for 2014?

(d) Mr. Hernandez believes that to attain the sales target in the year 2015, the company must incur an additional selling expense of $10,000 for advertising in 2015, with all other costs remaining constant. What will be the break-even point in dollar sales for 2015 if the company spends the additional $10,000?

(e) If the company spends the additional $10,000 for advertising in 2015, what is the sales level in dollars required to equal 2014 operating income?

Solution to Comprehensive DO IT!

Action Plan
✔ Know the formulas.

✔ Recognize that variable costs change with sales volume; fixed costs do not.

✔ Avoid computational errors.

(a)

Expected sales			$500,000
Less:			
Variable cost (20,000 flashlights × $15)	$300,000		
Fixed costs	135,000		435,000
Projected operating income			$ 65,000

(b)

Selling price per flashlight	$25
Variable cost per flashlight	15
Contribution margin per unit	$10

(c) Fixed costs ÷ Contribution margin per unit = Break-even point in units
$135,000 ÷ $10 = 13,500 units

(d) Fixed costs ÷ Contribution margin ratio = Break-even point in dollars
$145,000 ÷ 40% = $362,500

Fixed costs (from 2014)	$135,000
Additional advertising expense	10,000
Fixed costs (2015)	$145,000

Contribution margin per unit (b) $10
Contribution margin ratio = Contribution margin per unit ÷ Unit selling price
40% = $10 ÷ $25

(e) Required sales = (Fixed costs + Target net income) ÷ Contribution margin ratio
$525,000 = ($145,000 + $65,000) ÷ 40%

 The Navigator

SUMMARY OF LEARNING OBJECTIVES

1 **Distinguish between variable and fixed costs.** Variable costs are costs that vary in total directly and proportionately with changes in the activity index. Fixed costs are costs that remain the same in total regardless of changes in the activity index.

2 **Explain the significance of the relevant range.** The relevant range is the range of activity in which a company expects to operate during a year. It is important in CVP analysis because the behavior of costs is assumed to be linear throughout the relevant range.

3 **Explain the concept of mixed costs.** Mixed costs increase in total but not proportionately with changes in the activity level. For purposes of CVP analysis, mixed costs must be classified into their fixed and variable elements. One method that management may use to classify these costs is the high-low method.

4 **List the five components of cost-volume-profit analysis.** The five components of CVP analysis are (a) volume or level of activity, (b) unit selling prices, (c) variable cost per unit, (d) total fixed costs, and (e) sales mix.

5 **Indicate what contribution margin is and how it can be expressed.** Contribution margin is the amount of revenue remaining after deducting variable costs. It is identified in a CVP income statement, which classifies costs as variable or fixed. It can be expressed as a per unit amount or as a ratio.

6 **Identify the three ways to determine the break-even point.** The break-even point can be (a) computed from a mathematical equation, (b) computed by using a contribution margin technique, and (c) derived from a CVP graph.

7 **Give the formulas for determining sales required to earn target net income.** The general formula for required sales is Required sales − Variable costs − Fixed costs = Target net income. Two other formulas are Required sales in units = (Fixed costs + Target net income) ÷ Contribution margin per unit, and Required sales in dollars = (Fixed costs + Target net income) ÷ Contribution margin ratio.

8 **Define margin of safety, and give the formulas for computing it.** Margin of safety is the difference between actual or expected sales and sales at the break-even point. The formulas for margin of safety are: Actual (expected) sales − Break-even sales = Margin of safety in dollars; Margin of safety in dollars ÷ Actual (expected) sales = Margin of safety ratio.

9 **Describe the essential features of a cost-volume-profit income statement.** The CVP income statement classifies costs and expenses as variable or fixed and reports contribution margin in the body of the statement.

GLOSSARY

Activity index The activity that causes changes in the behavior of costs. (p. 1032).

Break-even point The level of activity at which total revenues equal total costs. (p. 1041).

Contribution margin (CM) The amount of revenue remaining after deducting variable costs. (p. 1040).

Contribution margin per unit The amount of revenue remaining per unit after deducting variable costs; calculated as unit selling price minus unit variable cost. (p. 1041).

Contribution margin ratio The percentage of each dollar of sales that is available to apply to fixed costs and contribute to net income; calculated as contribution margin per unit divided by unit selling price. (p. 1042).

Cost behavior analysis The study of how specific costs respond to changes in the level of business activity. (p. 1032).

Cost-volume-profit (CVP) analysis The study of the effects of changes in costs and volume on a company's profits. (p. 1040).

Cost-volume-profit (CVP) graph A graph showing the relationship between costs, volume, and profits. (p. 1045).

Cost-volume-profit (CVP) income statement A statement for internal use that classifies costs as fixed or variable and reports contribution margin in the body of the statement. (p. 1040).

Fixed costs Costs that remain the same in total regardless of changes in the activity level. (p. 1033).

High-low method A mathematical method that uses the total costs incurred at the high and low levels of activity to classify mixed costs into fixed and variable components. (p. 1037).

Margin of safety The difference between actual or expected sales and sales at the break-even point. (p. 1048).

Mixed costs Costs that contain both a variable and a fixed cost element and change in total but not proportionately with changes in the activity level. (p. 1035).

Relevant range The range of the activity index over which the company expects to operate during the year. (p. 1035).

Target net income The income objective set by management. (p. 1047).

Variable costs Costs that vary in total directly and proportionately with changes in the activity level. (p. 1032).

APPENDIX 22A   Variable Costing

In earlier chapters, we classified both variable and fixed manufacturing costs as product costs. In job order costing, for example, a job is assigned the costs of direct materials, direct labor, and **both** variable and fixed manufacturing overhead. This costing approach is referred to as **full** or **absorption costing**. It is so named because all manufacturing costs are charged to, or absorbed by, the product. Absorption costing is the approach used for external reporting under generally accepted accounting principles.

> **LEARNING OBJECTIVE 10**
>
> Explain the difference between absorption costing and variable costing.

An alternative approach is to use **variable costing**. Under variable costing, only direct materials, direct labor, and variable manufacturing overhead costs are considered product costs. Companies recognize fixed manufacturing overhead costs as period costs (expenses) when incurred. Illustration 22A-1 shows the difference between absorption costing and variable costing.

Absorption Costing		Variable Costing
	Fixed	
Product Cost ←——— Manufacturing ———→ Period Cost		
	Overhead	

Illustration 22A-1
Difference between absorption costing and variable costing

Under both absorption and variable costing selling and administrative expenses are period costs.

Companies may not use variable costing for external financial reports because generally accepted accounting principles require that fixed manufacturing overhead be accounted for as a product cost.

Example Comparing Absorption Costing with Variable Costing

To illustrate absorption and variable costing, assume that Premium Products Corporation manufactures a polyurethane sealant, called Fix-It, for car windshields. Relevant data for Fix-It in January 2014, the first month of production, are as follows.

Selling price	$20 per unit.
Units	Produced 30,000; sold 20,000; beginning inventory zero.
Variable unit costs	Manufacturing $9 (direct materials $5, direct labor $3, and variable overhead $1).
	Selling and administrative expenses $2.
Fixed costs	Manufacturing overhead $120,000.
	Selling and administrative expenses $15,000.

Illustration 22A-2
Sealant sales and cost data for Premium Products Corporation

The per unit manufacturing cost under each costing approach is computed in Illustration 22A-3.

Type of Cost	Absorption Costing	Variable Costing
Direct materials	$ 5	$5
Direct labor	3	3
Variable manufacturing overhead	1	1
Fixed manufacturing overhead		
($120,000 ÷ 30,000 units produced)	4	0
Manufacturing cost per unit	$13	$9

Illustration 22A-3
Computation of per unit manufacturing cost

The manufacturing cost per unit is $4 higher ($13 − $9) for absorption costing. This occurs because fixed manufacturing overhead costs are a product cost under absorption costing. Under variable costing, they are, instead, a period cost, and so they are expensed. Based on these data, each unit sold and each unit remaining in inventory is costed under absorption costing at $13 and under variable costing at $9.

Absorption Costing Example

Illustration 22A-4 shows the income statement for Premium Products using absorption costing. It shows that cost of goods manufactured is $390,000, computed by multiplying the 30,000 units produced times the manufacturing cost per unit of $13 (see Illustration 22A-3). Cost of goods sold is $260,000, after subtracting ending inventory of $130,000. Under absorption costing, $40,000 of the fixed overhead (10,000 units × $4) is deferred to a future period as part of the cost of ending inventory.

Illustration 22A-4
Absorption costing income statement

Helpful Hint The income statement format in Illustration 22A-4 is the same as that used under generally accepted accounting principles.

PREMIUM PRODUCTS CORPORATION
Income Statement
For the Month Ended January 31, 2014
Absorption Costing

Sales (20,000 units × $20)		$400,000
Cost of goods sold		
Inventory, January 1	$ –0–	
Cost of goods manufactured (30,000 units × $13)	390,000	
Cost of goods available for sale	390,000	
Inventory, January 31 (10,000 units × $13)	**130,000**	
Cost of goods sold (20,000 units × $13)		260,000
Gross profit		140,000
Variable selling and administrative expenses		
(20,000 × $2)	40,000	
Fixed selling and administrative expenses	15,000	55,000
Net Income		**$ 85,000**

Variable Costing Example

As Illustration 22A-5 shows, companies use the cost-volume-profit format in preparing a variable costing income statement. The variable manufacturing cost of $270,000 is computed by multiplying the 30,000 units produced times variable manufacturing cost of $9 per unit (see Illustration 22A-3). As in absorption costing, both variable and fixed selling and administrative expenses are treated as period costs.

There is one primary difference between variable and absorption costing. Under variable costing, companies charge the fixed manufacturing overhead as an expense in the current period. Fixed manufacturing overhead costs of the current period, therefore, are not deferred to future periods through the ending inventory. As a result, absorption costing will show a **higher net income number** than variable costing **whenever units produced exceed units sold**. This difference can be seen in the income statements in Illustrations 22A-4 and 22A-5. There is a $40,000 difference in the ending inventories ($130,000 under

PREMIUM PRODUCTS CORPORATION Income Statement For the Month Ended January 31, 2014 Variable Costing		
Sales (20,000 units × $20)		$ 400,000
Variable cost of goods sold		
Inventory, January 1	$ –0–	
Variable cost of goods manufactured		
(30,000 units × $9)	270,000	
Variable cost of goods available for sale	270,000	
Inventory, January 31 (10,000 units × $9)	**90,000**	
Variable cost of goods sold	180,000	
Variable selling and administrative expenses		
(20,000 units × $2)	40,000	220,000
Contribution margin		180,000
Fixed manufacturing overhead	120,000	
Fixed selling and administrative expenses	15,000	135,000
Net income		**$ 45,000**

Illustration 22A-5
Variable costing income statement

Helpful Hint Note the difference in the computation of the ending inventory: $9 per unit here, $13 per unit in Illustration 22A-4.

absorption costing versus $90,000 under variable costing). Under absorption costing, $40,000 of the fixed overhead costs (10,000 units × $4) has been deferred to a future period as part of inventory. In contrast, under variable costing, all fixed manufacturing costs are expensed in the current period.

The following relationships apply:

- When units produced exceed units sold (as shown), income from operations under absorption costing is higher than variable costing.

- When units produced are less than units sold, income from operations under absorption costing is lower than variable costing.

- When units produced and sold are the same, income from operations will be equal under the two costing approaches. In this case, there is no increase in ending inventory. So fixed overhead costs of the current period are not deferred to future periods through the ending inventory.

Illustration 22A-6 summarizes the foregoing effects of the two costing approaches on income from operations.

Illustration 22A-6
Summary of income effects

Rationale for Variable Costing

The purpose of fixed manufacturing costs is **to have productive facilities available for use**. A company incurs these costs whether it operates at zero or at 100% of capacity. Thus, proponents of variable costing argue that these costs are period costs and therefore should be expensed when incurred.

Supporters of absorption costing defend the assignment of fixed manufacturing overhead costs to inventory. They say that these costs are as much a cost of getting a product ready for sale as direct materials or direct labor. Accordingly, they contend, these costs should not be matched with revenues until the product is sold.

The use of variable costing is acceptable **only for internal use by management**. It cannot be used in determining product costs in financial statements prepared in accordance with generally accepted accounting principles because it understates inventory costs. To comply with the matching principle, a company must use absorption costing for its work in process and finished goods inventories. Similarly, companies must use absorption costing for income tax purposes.

SUMMARY OF LEARNING OBJECTIVE FOR APPENDIX 22A

The Navigator

10 Explain the difference between absorption costing and variable costing. Under absorption costing, fixed manufacturing costs are product costs. Under variable costing, fixed manufacturing costs are period costs.

GLOSSARY FOR APPENDIX 22A

Absorption costing A costing approach in which all manufacturing costs are charged to the product. (p. 1055).

Variable costing A costing approach in which only variable manufacturing costs are product costs, and fixed manufacturing costs are period costs (expenses). (p. 1055).

Self-Test, Brief Exercises, Exercises, Problem Set A, and many more components are available for practice in *WileyPLUS*.

*****Note:** All asterisked Questions, Exercises, and Problems relate to material in the appendix to the chapter.

SELF-TEST QUESTIONS

Answers are on page 1073.

(LO 1) **1.** Variable costs are costs that:
   (a) vary in total directly and proportionately with changes in the activity level.
   (b) remain linear outside of the relevant range.
   (c) vary inversely with changes in the activity level.
   (d) remain constant in total with changes in the activity level.

(LO 2) **2.** The relevant range is:
   (a) the range of activity in which variable costs will be curvilinear.
   (b) the range of activity in which fixed costs will be curvilinear.
   (c) the range over which the company expects to operate during a year.
   (d) usually from zero to 100% of operating capacity.

3. Mixed costs consist of a: (LO 3)
   (a) variable-cost element and a fixed-cost element.
   (b) fixed-cost element and a controllable-cost element.
   (c) relevant-cost element and a controllable-cost element.
   (d) variable-cost element and a relevant-cost element.

4. Your phone service provider offers a plan that is clas- (LO 3) sified as a mixed cost. The cost per month for 1,000 minutes is $50. If you use 2,000 minutes this month, your cost will be:
   (a) $50.   (c) more than $100.
   (b) $100.   (d) between $50 and $100.

5. Which of the following is **not** involved in CVP (LO 4) analysis?
   (a) Sales mix.   (c) Fixed costs per unit.
   (b) Unit selling prices. (d) Volume or level of activity.

(LO 5) **6.** Contribution margin:
  (a) is revenue remaining after deducting variable costs.
  (b) may not be expressed as contribution margin per unit.
  (c) is selling price less cost of goods sold.
  (d) is the same as gross margin.

(LO 5) **7.** When comparing a traditional income statement to a CVP income statement:
  (a) net income will always be greater on the traditional statement.
  (b) net income will always be less on the traditional statement.
  (c) net income will always be identical on both.
  (d) net income will be greater or less depending on the sales volume.

(LO 6) **8.** Brownstone Company's contribution margin ratio is 30%. If Brownstone's sales revenue is $100 greater than its break-even sales in dollars, its net income:
  (a) will be $100.
  (b) will be $70.
  (c) will be $30.
  (d) cannot be determined without knowing fixed costs.

(LO 6) **9.** Gossen Company is planning to sell 200,000 pliers for $4 per unit. The contribution margin ratio is 25%. If Gossen will break even at this level of sales, what are the fixed costs?
  (a) $100,000.   **(c)** $200,000.
  (b) $160,000.   **(d)** $300,000.

(LO 7) **10.** The mathematical equation for computing required sales to obtain target net income is Required sales =
  (a) Variable costs + Target net income.
  (b) Variable costs + Fixed costs + Target net income.
  (c) Fixed costs + Target net income.
  (d) No correct answer is given.

11. Marshall Company had actual sales of $600,000 when (LO 8) break-even sales were $420,000. What is the margin of safety ratio?
  (a) 25%.   **(c)** $33^{1}/_{3}$%.
  (b) 30%.   **(d)** 45%.

12. Margin of safety is computed as: (LO 8)
  (a) Actual sales − Break-even sales.
  (b) Contribution margin − Fixed costs.
  (c) Break-even sales − Variable costs.
  (d) Actual sales − Contribution margin.

13. On a CVP income statement: (LO 9)
  (a) Sales − Cost of goods sold = Contribution margin.
  (b) Sales − Variable costs − Fixed costs = Contribution margin.
  (c) Sales − Variable costs = Contribution margin.
  (d) Sales − Fixed costs = Contribution margin.

14. Cournot Company sells 100,000 wrenches for $12 a unit. (LO 9) Fixed costs are $300,000, and net income is $200,000. What should be reported as variable expenses in the CVP income statement?
  (a) $700,000.
  (b) $900,000.
  (c) $500,000.
  (d) $1,000,000.

****15.** Under variable costing, fixed manufacturing costs are (LO 10) classified as:
  (a) period costs.
  (b) product costs.
  (c) both period and product costs.
  (d) neither period nor product costs.

Go to the book's companion website, www.wiley.com/college/weygandt, for additional Self-Test Questions.

 ✔ **The Navigator**

QUESTIONS

1. (a) What is cost behavior analysis?
  (b) Why is cost behavior analysis important to management?

2. (a) Scott Winter asks your help in understanding the term "activity index." Explain the meaning and importance of this term for Scott.
  (b) State the two ways that variable costs may be defined.

3. Contrast the effects of changes in the activity level on total fixed costs and on unit fixed costs.

4. J. P. Alexander claims that the relevant range concept is important only for variable costs.
  (a) Explain the relevant range concept.
  (b) Do you agree with J. P.'s claim? Explain.

5. "The relevant range is indispensable in cost behavior analysis." Is this true? Why or why not?

6. Adam Antal is confused. He does not understand why rent on his apartment is a fixed cost and rent on a Hertz rental truck is a mixed cost. Explain the difference to Adam.

7. How should mixed costs be classified in CVP analysis? What approach is used to effect the appropriate classification?

8. At the high and low levels of activity during the month, direct labor hours are 90,000 and 40,000, respectively. The related costs are $165,000 and $100,000. What are the fixed and variable costs at any level of activity?

9. "Cost-volume-profit (CVP) analysis is based entirely on unit costs." Do you agree? Explain.

10. Faye Dunn defines contribution margin as the amount of profit available to cover operating expenses. Is there any truth in this definition? Discuss.

11. Marshall Company's GWhiz calculator sells for $40. Variable costs per unit are estimated to be $26. What are the contribution margin per unit and the contribution margin ratio?

12. "Break-even analysis is of limited use to management because a company cannot survive by just breaking even." Do you agree? Explain.

13. Total fixed costs are $26,000 for Daz Inc. It has a contribution margin per unit of $15, and a contribution margin ratio of 25%. Compute the break-even sales in dollars.

14. Peggy Turnbull asks your help in constructing a CVP graph. Explain to Peggy (a) how the break-even point is plotted, and (b) how the level of activity and dollar sales at the break-even point are determined.

15. Define the term "margin of safety." If Revere Company expects to sell 1,250 units of its product at $12 per unit, and break-even sales for the product are $13,200, what is the margin of safety ratio?

16. Huang Company's break-even sales are $500,000. Assuming fixed costs are $180,000, what sales volume is needed to achieve a target net income of $90,000?

17. The traditional income statement for Pace Company shows sales $900,000, cost of goods sold $600,000, and operating expenses $200,000. Assuming all costs and expenses are 70% variable and 30% fixed, prepare a CVP income statement through contribution margin.

*18. Distinguish between absorption costing and variable costing.

*19. (a) What is the major rationale for the use of variable costing? (b) Discuss why variable costing may not be used for financial reporting purposes.

BRIEF EXERCISES

Classify costs as variable, fixed, or mixed.
(LO 1, 3)

BE22-1 Monthly production costs in Pesavento Company for two levels of production are as follows.

Cost	2,000 Units	4,000 Units
Indirect labor	$10,000	$20,000
Supervisory salaries	5,000	5,000
Maintenance	4,000	7,000

Indicate which costs are variable, fixed, and mixed, and give the reason for each answer.

Diagram the behavior of costs within the relevant range.
(LO 2)

BE22-2 For Lodes Company, the relevant range of production is 40–80% of capacity. At 40% of capacity, a variable cost is $4,000 and a fixed cost is $6,000. Diagram the behavior of each cost within the relevant range assuming the behavior is linear.

Diagram the behavior of a mixed cost.
(LO 3)

BE22-3 For Hunt Company, a mixed cost is $15,000 plus $18 per direct labor hour. Diagram the behavior of the cost using increments of 500 hours up to 2,500 hours on the horizontal axis and increments of $15,000 up to $60,000 on the vertical axis.

Determine variable- and fixed-cost elements using the high-low method.
(LO 3)

BE22-4 Bruno Company accumulates the following data concerning a mixed cost, using miles as the activity level.

	Miles Driven	Total Cost		Miles Driven	Total Cost
January	8,000	$14,150	March	8,500	$15,000
February	7,500	13,500	April	8,200	14,490

Compute the variable- and fixed-cost elements using the high-low method.

Determine missing amounts for contribution margin.
(LO 5)

BE22-5 Determine the missing amounts.

	Unit Selling Price	Unit Variable Costs	Contribution Margin per Unit	Contribution Margin Ratio
1.	$640	$352	(a)	(b)
2.	$300	(c)	$93	(d)
3.	(e)	(f)	$325	25%

Compute the break-even point.
(LO 6)

BE22-6 Rice Company has a unit selling price of $520, variable costs per unit of $286, and fixed costs of $163,800. Compute the break-even point in units using (a) the mathematical equation and (b) contribution margin per unit.

Compute the break-even point.
(LO 6)

BE22-7 Acorn Corp. had total variable costs of $180,000, total fixed costs of $170,000, and total revenues of $300,000. Compute the required sales in dollars to break even.

Compute sales for target net income.
(LO 7)

BE22-8 For Flynn Company, variable costs are 70% of sales, and fixed costs are $195,000. Management's net income goal is $75,000. Compute the required sales in dollars needed to achieve management's target net income of $75,000. (Use the contribution margin approach.)

BE22-9 Deines Corporation has fixed costs of $480,000. It has a unit selling price of $6, unit variable costs of $4.40, and a target net income of $1,500,000. Compute the required sales in units to achieve its target net income.

Compute the required sales in units for target net income.
(LO 7)

BE22-10 For Stevens Company, actual sales are $1,000,000 and break-even sales are $840,000. Compute (a) the margin of safety in dollars and (b) the margin of safety ratio.

Compute the margin of safety and the margin of safety ratio.
(LO 8)

BE22-11 Radial Inc. had sales of $2,400,000 for the first quarter of 2014. In making the sales, the company incurred the costs and expenses shown below.

Prepare CVP income statement.
(LO 9)

	Variable	Fixed
Cost of goods sold	$920,000	$440,000
Selling expenses	70,000	45,000
Administrative expenses	86,000	98,000

Prepare a CVP income statement for the quarter ended March 31, 2014.

*BE22-12 Howser Company's fixed overhead costs are $4 per unit, and its variable overhead costs are $8 per unit. In the first month of operations, 50,000 units are produced, and 48,000 units are sold. Write a short memo to the chief financial officer explaining which costing approach will produce the higher income and what the difference will be.

Compute net income under absorption and variable costing.
(LO 10)

> DO IT! Review

DO IT! 22-1 Helena Company reports the following total costs at two levels of production.

Classify types of costs.
(LO 1, 3)

	5,000 Units	10,000 Units
Indirect labor	$ 3,000	$ 6,000
Property taxes	7,000	7,000
Direct labor	28,000	56,000
Direct materials	22,000	44,000
Depreciation	4,000	4,000
Utilities	5,000	7,000
Maintenance	9,000	11,000

Classify each cost as variable, fixed, or mixed.

DO IT! 22-2 Westerville Company accumulates the following data concerning a mixed cost, using units produced as the activity level.

Compute costs using high-low method and estimate total cost.
(LO 3)

	Units Produced	Total Cost
March	10,000	$18,000
April	9,000	16,650
May	10,500	18,580
June	8,800	16,200
July	9,500	17,100

(a) Compute the variable- and fixed-cost elements using the high-low method.
(b) Estimate the total cost if the company produces 9,200 units.

DO IT! 22-3 Larissa Company has a unit selling price of $250, variable costs per unit of $170, and fixed costs of $140,000. Compute the break-even point in units using (a) the mathematical equation and (b) contribution margin per unit.

Compute break-even point in units.
(LO 6)

DO IT! 22-4 Presto Company makes radios that sell for $30 each. For the coming year, management expects fixed costs to total $220,000 and variable costs to be $18 per unit.

Compute break-even point, margin of safety ratio, and sales for target net income.
(LO 6, 7, 8)

(a) Compute the break-even point in dollars using the contribution margin (CM) ratio.
(b) Compute the margin of safety ratio assuming actual sales are $800,000.
(c) Compute the sales dollars required to earn net income of $140,000.

Define and classify variable, fixed, and mixed costs.
(LO 1, 3)

E22-1 Turgro Company manufactures a single product. Annual production costs incurred in the manufacturing process are shown below for two levels of production.

	Costs Incurred			
Production in Units	5,000		10,000	
Production Costs	Total Cost	Cost/ Unit	Total Cost	Cost/ Unit
Direct materials	$8,000	$1.60	$16,000	$1.60
Direct labor	9,500	1.90	19,000	1.90
Utilities	2,000	0.40	3,500	0.35
Rent	4,000	0.80	4,000	0.40
Maintenance	800	0.16	1,100	0.11
Supervisory salaries	1,000	0.20	1,000	0.10

Instructions
(a) Define the terms variable costs, fixed costs, and mixed costs.
(b) Classify each cost above as either variable, fixed, or mixed.

Determine fixed and variable costs using the high-low method and prepare graph.
(LO 1, 3)

E22-2 The controller of Furgee Industries has collected the following monthly expense data for use in analyzing the cost behavior of maintenance costs.

Month	Total Maintenance Costs	Total Machine Hours
January	$2,500	300
February	3,000	350
March	3,600	500
April	4,500	690
May	3,200	400
June	4,900	700

Instructions
(a) Determine the fixed- and variable-cost components using the high-low method.
(b) Prepare a graph showing the behavior of maintenance costs, and identify the fixed- and variable-cost elements. Use 100-hour increments and $1,000 cost increments.

Classify variable, fixed, and mixed costs.
(LO 1, 3)

E22-3 Family Furniture Corporation incurred the following costs.
1. Wood used in the production of furniture.
2. Fuel used in delivery trucks.
3. Straight-line depreciation on factory building.
4. Screws used in the production of furniture.
5. Sales staff salaries.
6. Sales commissions.
7. Property taxes.
8. Insurance on buildings.
9. Hourly wages of furniture craftsmen.
10. Salaries of factory supervisors.
11. Utilities expense.
12. Telephone bill.

Instructions
Identify the costs above as variable, fixed, or mixed.

Explain assumptions underlying CVP analysis.
(LO 4)

E22-4 Jim Taylor wants Taylor Company to use CVP analysis to study the effects of changes in costs and volume on the company. Taylor has heard that certain assumptions must be valid in order for CVP analysis to be useful.

Instructions
Prepare a memo to Jim Taylor concerning the assumptions that underlie CVP analysis.

E22-5 In the month of June, Jose Hebert's Beauty Salon gave 4,000 haircuts, shampoos, and permanents at an average price of $30. During the month, fixed costs were $16,800 and variable costs were 75% of sales.

Compute contribution margin, break-even point, and margin of safety.
(LO 5, 6, 8)

Instructions
(a) Determine the contribution margin in dollars, per unit and as a ratio.
(b) Using the contribution margin technique, compute the break-even point in dollars and in units.
(c) Compute the margin of safety in dollars and as a ratio.

E22-6 Glacial Company estimates that variable costs will be 62.5% of sales, and fixed costs will total $600,000. The selling price of the product is $4.

Prepare a CVP graph and compute break-even point and margin of safety.
(LO 6, 8)

Instructions
(a) Prepare a CVP graph, assuming maximum sales of $3,200,000. (*Note:* Use $400,000 increments for sales and costs and 100,000 increments for units.)
(b) Compute the break-even point in (1) units and (2) dollars.
(c) Compute the margin of safety in (1) dollars and (2) as a ratio, assuming actual sales are $2 million.

E22-7 All That Blooms performs environmentally friendly lawn services for homeowners. Its operating costs are as follows.

Compute break-even point in units and dollars.
(LO 5, 6)

Depreciation	$1,400 per month
Advertising	$200 per month
Insurance	$2,000 per month
Weed and feed materials	$12 per lawn
Direct labor	$10 per lawn
Fuel	$2 per lawn

All That Blooms charges $60 per treatment for the average single-family lawn.

Instructions
Determine the company's break-even point in (a) number of lawns serviced per month and (b) dollars.

E22-8 The Green Acres Inn is trying to determine its break-even point. The inn has 50 rooms that it rents at $60 a night. Operating costs are as follows.

Compute break-even point.
(LO 5, 6)

Salaries	$6,200 per month
Utilities	$1,100 per month
Depreciation	$1,000 per month
Maintenance	$100 per month
Maid service	$11 per room
Other costs	$28 per room

Instructions
Determine the inn's break-even point in (a) number of rented rooms per month and (b) dollars.

E22-9 In the month of March, Style Salon services 560 clients at an average price of $120. During the month, fixed costs were $21,024 and variable costs were 60% of sales.

Compute contribution margin and break-even point.
(LO 5, 6)

Instructions
(a) Determine the contribution margin in dollars, per unit, and as a ratio.
(b) Using the contribution margin technique, compute the break-even point in dollars and in units.

E22-10 Kare Kars provides shuttle service between four hotels near a medical center and an international airport. Kare Kars uses two 10-passenger vans to offer 12 round trips per day. A recent month's activity in the form of a cost-volume-profit income statement is shown below.

Compute break-even point.
(LO 5, 6)

Fare revenues (1,440 fares)		$36,000
Variable costs		
Fuel	$ 5,040	
Tolls and parking	3,100	
Maintenance	860	9,000
Contribution margin		27,000
Fixed costs		
Salaries	12,700	
Depreciation	1,300	
Insurance	1,000	15,000
Net income		$12,000

Instructions

(a) Calculate the break-even point in (1) dollars and (2) number of fares.

(b) Without calculations, determine the contribution margin at the break-even point.

Compute variable costs per unit, contribution margin ratio, and increase in fixed costs.

(LO 5, 6)

E22-11 In 2013, Manhoff Company had a break-even point of $350,000 based on a selling price of $5 per unit and fixed costs of $112,000. In 2014, the selling price and the variable costs per unit did not change, but the break-even point increased to $420,000.

Instructions

(a) Compute the variable costs per unit and the contribution margin ratio for 2013.

(b) Compute the increase in fixed costs for 2014.

Prepare CVP income statements.

(LO 5, 6, 9)

E22-12 Cannes Company has the following information available for September 2014.

Unit selling price of video game consoles	$ 400
Unit variable costs	$ 275
Total fixed costs	$52,000
Units sold	600

Instructions

(a) Compute the contribution margin per unit.

(b) Prepare a CVP income statement that shows both total and per unit amounts.

(c) Compute Cannes' break-even point in units.

(d) Prepare a CVP income statement for the break-even point that shows both total and per unit amounts.

Compute various components to derive target net income under different assumptions.

(LO 6, 7)

E22-13 Naylor Company had $210,000 of net income in 2013 when the selling price per unit was $150, the variable costs per unit were $90, and the fixed costs were $570,000. Management expects per unit data and total fixed costs to remain the same in 2014. The president of Naylor Company is under pressure from stockholders to increase net income by $52,000 in 2014.

Instructions

(a) Compute the number of units sold in 2013.

(b) Compute the number of units that would have to be sold in 2014 to reach the stockholders' desired profit level.

(c) Assume that Naylor Company sells the same number of units in 2014 as it did in 2013. What would the selling price have to be in order to reach the stockholders' desired profit level?

Compute net income under different alternatives.

(LO 7)

E22-14 Cottonwood Company reports the following operating results for the month of August: sales $400,000 (units 5,000); variable costs $210,000; and fixed costs $90,000. Management is considering the following independent courses of action to increase net income.

1. Increase selling price by 10% with no change in total variable costs or units sold.

2. Reduce variable costs to 45% of sales.

Instructions

Compute the net income to be earned under each alternative. Which course of action will produce the highest net income?

Prepare a CVP income statement before and after changes in business environment.

(LO 9)

E22-15 Hall Company had sales in 2014 of $1,560,000 on 60,000 units. Variable costs totaled $720,000, and fixed costs totaled $500,000.

A new raw material is available that will decrease the variable costs per unit by 25% (or $3.00). However, to process the new raw material, fixed operating costs will increase by $150,000. Management feels that one-half of the decline in the variable costs per unit should be passed on to customers in the form of a sales price reduction. The marketing department expects that this sales price reduction will result in a 5% increase in the number of units sold.

Instructions

Prepare a projected CVP income statement for 2014 (a) assuming the changes have not been made, and (b) assuming that changes are made as described.

Compute total product cost and prepare an income statement using variable costing.

(LO 10)

*E22-16 Linus Company manufactures and distributes industrial air compressors. The following costs are available for the year ended December 31, 2014. The company has no beginning inventory. In 2014, 1,500 units were produced, but only 1,300 units were sold. The unit selling price was $4,500. Costs and expenses were as follows.

Variable costs per unit		
Direct materials	$	1,000
Direct labor		1,500
Variable manufacturing overhead		500
Variable selling and administrative expenses		60
Annual fixed costs and expenses		
Manufacturing overhead		$1,400,000
Selling and administrative expenses		100,000

Instructions

(a) Compute the manufacturing cost of one unit of product using variable costing.

(b) Prepare a 2014 income statement for Linus Company using variable costing.

*E22-17 Montier Corporation produces one product. Its cost includes direct materials ($10 per unit), direct labor ($8 per unit), variable overhead ($5 per unit), fixed manufacturing ($225,000), and fixed selling and administrative ($30,000). In October 2014, Montier produced 25,000 units and sold 20,000 at $50 each.

Prepare absorption cost and variable cost income statements.

(LO 10)

Instructions

(a) Prepare an absorption costing income statement.

(b) Prepare a variable costing income statement.

(c) Explain the difference in net income in the two income statements.

EXERCISES: SET B AND CHALLENGE EXERCISES

Visit the book's companion website, at **www.wiley.com/college/weygandt**, and choose the Student Companion site to access Exercise Set B and Challenge Exercises.

PROBLEMS: SET A

P22-1A Telly Savalas owns the Bonita Barber Shop. He employs four barbers and pays each a base rate of $1,000 per month. One of the barbers serves as the manager and receives an extra $500 per month. In addition to the base rate, each barber also receives a commission of $4.50 per haircut.

Other costs are as follows.

Advertising	$200 per month
Rent	$1,100 per month
Barber supplies	$0.30 per haircut
Utilities	$175 per month plus $0.20 per haircut
Magazines	$25 per month

Telly currently charges $10 per haircut.

Determine variable and fixed costs, compute break-even point, prepare a CVP graph, and determine net income.

(LO 1, 3, 5, 6)

Instructions

(a) Determine the variable costs per haircut and the total monthly fixed costs.

(b) Compute the break-even point in units and dollars.

(c) Prepare a CVP graph, assuming a maximum of 1,800 haircuts in a month. Use increments of 300 haircuts on the horizontal axis and $3,000 on the vertical axis.

(d) Determine net income, assuming 1,700 haircuts are given in a month.

(a) VC $5

Prepare a CVP income statement, compute break-even point, contribution margin ratio, margin of safety ratio, and sales for target net income.

(LO 5, 6, 7, 8, 9)

P22-2A Jorge Company bottles and distributes B-Lite, a diet soft drink. The beverage is sold for 50 cents per 16-ounce bottle to retailers, who charge customers 75 cents per bottle. For the year 2014, management estimates the following revenues and costs.

Sales	$1,800,000	Selling expenses—variable	$70,000
Direct materials	430,000	Selling expenses—fixed	65,000
Direct labor	360,000	Administrative expenses—	
Manufacturing overhead—		variable	20,000
variable	380,000	Administrative expenses—	
Manufacturing overhead—		fixed	60,000
fixed	280,000		

Instructions

(a) Prepare a CVP income statement for 2014 based on management's estimates. (Show column for total amounts only.)

(b) (1) 2,700,000 units
(c) CM ratio 30%

(b) Compute the break-even point in (1) units and (2) dollars.

(c) Compute the contribution margin ratio and the margin of safety ratio. (Round to nearest full percent.)

(d) Determine the sales dollars required to earn net income of $180,000.

Compute break-even point under alternative courses of action.

(LO 5, 6)

P22-3A Dousmann Corp.'s sales slumped badly in 2014. For the first time in its history, it operated at a loss. The company's income statement showed the following results from selling 500,000 units of product: sales $2,500,000; total costs and expenses $2,600,000; and net loss $100,000. Costs and expenses consisted of the amounts shown below.

	Total	Variable	Fixed
Cost of goods sold	$2,140,000	$1,540,000	$600,000
Selling expenses	250,000	92,000	158,000
Administrative expenses	210,000	68,000	142,000
	$2,600,000	$1,700,000	$900,000

Management is considering the following independent alternatives for 2015.

1. Increase unit selling price 20% with no change in costs, expenses, and sales volume.
2. Change the compensation of salespersons from fixed annual salaries totaling $150,000 to total salaries of $60,000 plus a 5% commission on sales.

Instructions

(a) Compute the break-even point in dollars for 2014.

(b) Alternative 1 $2,093,023

(b) Compute the break-even point in dollars under each of the alternative courses of action. (Round all ratios to nearest full percent.) Which course of action do you recommend?

Compute break-even point and margin of safety ratio, and prepare a CVP income statement before and after changes in business environment.

(LO 5, 6, 8, 9)

P22-4A Mary Willis is the advertising manager for Bargain Shoe Store. She is currently working on a major promotional campaign. Her ideas include the installation of a new lighting system and increased display space that will add $24,000 in fixed costs to the $270,000 currently spent. In addition, Mary is proposing that a 5% price decrease ($40 to $38) will produce a 20% increase in sales volume (20,000 to 24,000). Variable costs will remain at $24 per pair of shoes. Management is impressed with Mary's ideas but concerned about the effects that these changes will have on the break-even point and the margin of safety.

Instructions

(a) Compute the current break-even point in units, and compare it to the break-even point in units if Mary's ideas are used.

(b) Current margin of safety ratio 16%

(b) Compute the margin of safety ratio for current operations and after Mary's changes are introduced. (Round to nearest full percent.)

(c) Prepare a CVP income statement for current operations and after Mary's changes are introduced. (Show column for total amounts only.) Would you make the changes suggested?

Compute contribution margin, fixed costs, break-even point, sales for target net income, and margin of safety ratio.

(LO 5, 6, 7, 8)

P22-5A Mozena Corporation has collected the following information after its first year of sales. Sales were $1,500,000 on 100,000 units; selling expenses $250,000 (40% variable and 60% fixed); direct materials $511,000; direct labor $290,000; administrative expenses $270,000 (20% variable and 80% fixed); manufacturing overhead $350,000 (70% variable and 30% fixed). Top management has asked you to do a CVP analysis so that it can make plans for the coming year. It has projected that unit sales will increase by 10% next year.

Instructions

(a) Compute (1) the contribution margin for the current year and the projected year, and (2) the fixed costs for the current year. (Assume that fixed costs will remain the same in the projected year.)

(b) Compute the break-even point in units and sales dollars for the current year.

(c) The company has a target net income of $200,000. What is the required sales in dollars for the company to meet its target?

(d) If the company meets its target net income number, by what percentage could its sales fall before it is operating at a loss? That is, what is its margin of safety ratio?

(b) 157,000 units

*P22-6A Gardner Company produces plastic that is used for injection-molding applications such as gears for small motors. In 2013, the first year of operations, Gardner produced 4,000 tons of plastic and sold 2,500 tons. In 2014, the production and sales results were exactly reversed. In each year, the selling price per ton was $2,000, variable manufacturing costs were 15% of the sales price of units produced, variable selling expenses were 10% of the selling price of units sold, fixed manufacturing costs were $2,000,000, and fixed administrative expenses were $500,000.

Prepare income statements under absorption costing and variable costing for a company with beginning inventory, and reconcile differences.

(LO 10)

Instructions

(a) Prepare income statements for each year using variable costing. (Use the format from Illustration 22A-5.)

(b) Prepare income statements for each year using absorption costing. (Use the format from Illustration 22A-4.)

(c) Reconcile the differences each year in net income under the two costing approaches.

(d) ——— Comment on the effects of production and sales on net income under the two costing approaches.

(a) 2014 $3,500,000

(b) 2014 $2,750,000

PROBLEMS: SET B

P22-1B The Sasoon Barber Shop employs four barbers. One barber, who also serves as the manager, is paid a salary of $3,000 per month. The other barbers are paid $1,500 per month. In addition, each barber is paid a commission of $3 per haircut. Other monthly costs are store rent $700 plus 60 cents per haircut, depreciation on equipment $400, barber supplies 40 cents per haircut, utilities $300, and advertising $100. The price of a haircut is $10.

Determine variable and fixed costs, compute break-even point, prepare a CVP graph, and determine net income.

(LO 1, 3, 5, 6)

Instructions

(a) Determine the variable costs per haircut and the total monthly fixed costs.

(b) Compute the break-even point in units and dollars.

(c) Prepare a CVP graph, assuming a maximum of 1,800 haircuts in a month. Use increments of 300 haircuts on the horizontal axis and $3,000 increments on the vertical axis.

(d) Determine the net income, assuming 1,800 haircuts are given in a month.

(a) VC $4

P22-2B All Frute Company bottles and distributes Frute Ade, a fruit drink. The beverage is sold for 50 cents per 16-ounce bottle to retailers, who charge customers 70 cents per bottle. For the year 2014, management estimates the following revenues and costs.

Prepare a CVP income statement, compute break-even point, contribution margin ratio, margin of safety ratio, and sales for target net income.

(LO 5, 6, 7, 8, 9)

Sales	$2,500,000	Selling expenses—variable	$ 80,000
Direct materials	360,000	Selling expenses—fixed	250,000
Direct labor	450,000	Administrative expenses—	
Manufacturing overhead—		variable	40,000
variable	270,000	Administrative expenses—	
Manufacturing overhead—		fixed	150,000
fixed	380,000		

Instructions

(a) Prepare a CVP income statement for 2014 based on management's estimates. (Show column for total amounts only.)

(b) Compute the break-even point in (1) units and (2) dollars.

(c) Compute the contribution margin ratio and the margin of safety ratio.

(d) Determine the sales dollars required to earn net income of $624,000.

(b) (1) 3,000,000 units

(c) CM ratio 52%

Compute break-even point under alternative courses of action.

(LO 5, 6)

P22-3B Olgivie Company had a bad year in 2013. For the first time in its history, it operated at a loss. The company's income statement showed the following results from selling 60,000 units of product: sales $1,800,000; total costs and expenses $2,010,000; and net loss $210,000. Costs and expenses consisted of the amounts shown below.

	Total	Variable	Fixed
Cost of goods sold	$1,350,000	$ 930,000	$420,000
Selling expenses	480,000	125,000	355,000
Administrative expenses	180,000	115,000	65,000
	$2,010,000	$1,170,000	$840,000

Management is considering the following independent alternatives for 2014.

1. Increase unit selling price 25% with no change in costs, expenses, and sales volume.
2. Change the compensation of salespersons from fixed annual salaries totaling $200,000 to total salaries of $20,000 plus a 5% commission on net sales.
3. Purchase new high-tech factory machinery that will change the proportion between variable and fixed cost of goods sold to 50:50.

Instructions
(a) Compute the break-even point in dollars for 2013.

(b) Alternative 1, $1,750,000

(b) Compute the break-even point in dollars under each of the alternative courses of action. (Round all ratios to nearest full percent.) Which course of action do you recommend?

Compute break-even point and margin of safety ratio, and prepare a CVP income statement before and after changes in business environment.

(LO 5, 6, 8, 9)

P22-4B Alma Ortiz is the advertising manager for CostLess Shoe Store. She is currently working on a major promotional campaign. Her ideas include the installation of a new lighting system and increased display space that will add $18,000 in fixed costs to the $216,000 currently spent. In addition, Alma is proposing that a 10% price decrease (from $30 to $27) will produce an increase in sales volume from 20,000 to 24,000 units. Variable costs will remain at $12 per pair of shoes. Management is impressed with Alma's ideas but concerned about the effects that these changes will have on the break-even point and the margin of safety.

Instructions
(a) Compute the current break-even point in units, and compare it to the break-even point in units if Alma's ideas are used.

(b) Current margin of safety ratio 40%

(b) Compute the margin of safety ratio for current operations and after Alma's changes are introduced. (Round to nearest full percent.)
(c) Prepare a CVP income statement for current operations and after Alma's changes are introduced. (Show column for total amounts only.) Would you make the changes suggested?

Compute break-even point and margin of safety ratio, and prepare a CVP income statement before and after changes in business environment.

(LO 5, 6, 7, 8)

P22-5B Isaac Corporation has collected the following information after its first year of sales. Sales were $1,800,000 on 100,000 units; selling expenses $400,000 (30% variable and 70% fixed); direct materials $456,000; direct labor $250,000; administrative expenses $484,000 (50% variable and 50% fixed); manufacturing overhead $480,000 (40% variable and 60% fixed). Top management has asked you to do a CVP analysis so that it can make plans for the coming year. It has projected that unit sales will increase by 20% next year.

Instructions
(a) Compute (1) the contribution margin for the current year and the projected year, and (2) the fixed costs for the current year. (Assume that fixed costs will remain the same in the projected year.)

(b) 150,000 units

(b) Compute the break-even point in units and sales dollars.
(c) The company has a target net income of $213,000. What is the required sales in dollars for the company to meet its target?
(d) If the company meets its target net income number, by what percentage could its sales fall before it is operating at a loss? That is, what is its margin of safety ratio?
(e) The company is considering a purchase of equipment that would reduce its direct labor costs by $100,000 and would change its manufacturing overhead costs to 10% variable and 90% fixed (assume total manufacturing overhead cost is $480,000, as above). It is also considering switching to a pure commission basis for its sales staff. This would change selling expenses to 80% variable and 20% fixed (assume total selling expense is $400,000, as above). Compute (1) the contribution margin and (2) the contribution margin ratio, and recompute (3) the break-even point in sales dollars. Comment on the effect each of management's proposed changes has on the break-even point.

*P22-6B FAB produces fabrics that are used for clothing and other applications. In 2013, the first year of operations, FAB produced 500,000 yards of fabric and sold 400,000 yards. In 2014, the production and sales results were exactly reversed. In each year, selling price per yard was $2.50, variable manufacturing costs were 30% of the sales price of units produced, variable selling expenses were 10% of the selling price of units sold, fixed manufacturing costs were $400,000, and fixed administrative expenses were $100,000.

Prepare income statements under absorption costing and variable costing for a company with beginning inventory, and reconcile differences.

(LO 6, 10)

Instructions
(a) Prepare income statements for each year using variable costing. (Use the format from Illustration 22A-5.)

(b) Prepare income statements for each year using absorption costing. (Use the format from Illustration 22A-4.)

(c) Reconcile the differences each year in income from operations under the two costing approaches.

(d) ◆━━━ Comment on the effects of production and sales on net income under the two costing approaches.

(a) 2013 Net income
    $100,000

(b) 2013 Net income
    $180,000

PROBLEMS: SET C

Visit the book's companion website, at **www.wiley.com/college/weygandt**, and choose the Student Companion site to access Problem Set C.

WATERWAYS CONTINUING PROBLEM

(*Note:* This is a continuation of the Waterways Problem from Chapters 19 through 21.)

WCP22 The Vice President for Sales and Marketing at Waterways Corporation is planning for production needs to meet sales demand in the coming year. He is also trying to determine how the company's profits might be increased in the coming year. This problem asks you to use cost-volume-profit concepts to help Waterways understand contribution margins of some of its products and to decide whether to mass-produce certain products.

*Go to the book's companion website, **www.wiley.com/college/weygandt**, to find the remainder of this problem.*

Broadening Your Perspective

Management Decision-Making

Decision-Making Problem: Current Designs

BYP22-1 Bill Johnson, sales manager, and Diane Buswell, controller, at Current Designs are beginning to analyze the cost considerations for one of the composite models of the kayak division. They have provided the following production and operational costs necessary to produce one composite kayak.

Kevlar®	$250 per kayak
Resin and supplies	$100 per kayak
Finishing kit (seat, rudder, ropes, etc.)	$170 per kayak
Labor	$420 per kayak
Selling and administrative expenses—variable	$400 per kayak
Selling and administrative expenses—fixed	$119,700 per year
Manufacturing overhead—fixed	$240,000 per year

Bill and Diane have asked you to provide a cost-volume-profit analysis, to help them finalize the budget projections for the upcoming year. Bill has informed you that the selling price of the composite kayak will be $2,000.

Instructions
(a) Calculate variable costs per unit.
(b) Determine the contribution margin per unit.
(c) Using the contribution margin per unit, determine the break-even point in units for this product line.
(d) Assume that Current Designs plans to earn $270,600 on this product line. Using the contribution margin per unit, calculate the number of units that need to be sold to achieve this goal.
(e) Based on the most recent sales forecast, Current Designs plans to sell 1,000 units of this model. Using your results from part (c), calculate the margin of safety and the margin of safety ratio.

Decision-Making Across the Organization

BYP22-2 Creative Ideas Company has decided to introduce a new product. The new product can be manufactured by either a capital-intensive method or a labor-intensive method. The manufacturing method will not affect the quality of the product. The estimated manufacturing costs by the two methods are as follows.

	Capital-Intensive	Labor-Intensive
Direct materials	$5 per unit	$5.50 per unit
Direct labor	$6 per unit	$8.00 per unit
Variable overhead	$3 per unit	$4.50 per unit
Fixed manufacturing costs	$2,524,000	$1,550,000

Creative Ideas' market research department has recommended an introductory unit sales price of $32. The incremental selling expenses are estimated to be $502,000 annually plus $2 for each unit sold, regardless of manufacturing method.

Instructions
With the class divided into groups, answer the following.

(a) Calculate the estimated break-even point in annual unit sales of the new product if Creative Ideas Company uses the:
  (1) Capital-intensive manufacturing method.
  (2) Labor-intensive manufacturing method.
(b) Determine the annual unit sales volume at which Creative Ideas Company would be indifferent between the two manufacturing methods.
(c) Explain the circumstance under which Creative Ideas should employ each of the two manufacturing methods.

(CMA adapted)

Managerial Analysis

BYP22-3 The condensed income statement for the Peri and Paul partnership for 2014 is as follows.

PERI AND PAUL COMPANY
Income Statement
For the Year Ended December 31, 2014

Sales revenue (240,000 units)		$1,200,000
Cost of goods sold		800,000
Gross profit		400,000
Operating expenses		
Selling	$280,000	
Administrative	150,000	430,000
Net loss		$ (30,000)

A cost behavior analysis indicates that 75% of the cost of goods sold are variable, 42% of the selling expenses are variable, and 40% of the administrative expenses are variable.

Instructions

(Round to nearest unit, dollar, and percentage, where necessary. Use the CVP income statement format in computing profits.)

(a) Compute the break-even point in total sales dollars and in units for 2014.

(b) Peri has proposed a plan to get the partnership "out of the red" and improve its profitability. She feels that the quality of the product could be substantially improved by spending $0.25 more per unit on better raw materials. The selling price per unit could be increased to only $5.25 because of competitive pressures. Peri estimates that sales volume will increase by 25%. What effect would Peri's plan have on the profits and the break-even point in dollars of the partnership? (Round the contribution margin ratio to two decimal places.)

(c) Paul was a marketing major in college. He believes that sales volume can be increased only by intensive advertising and promotional campaigns. He therefore proposed the following plan as an alternative to Peri's: (1) Increase variable selling expenses to $0.59 per unit, (2) lower the selling price per unit by $0.25, and (3) increase fixed selling expenses by $40,000. Paul quoted an old marketing research report that said that sales volume would increase by 60% if these changes were made. What effect would Paul's plan have on the profits and the break-even point in dollars of the partnership?

(d) Which plan should be accepted? Explain your answer.

Real-World Focus

BYP22-4 The Coca-Cola Company hardly needs an introduction. A line taken from the cover of a recent annual report says it all: If you measured time in servings of Coca-Cola, "a billion Coca-Cola's ago was yesterday morning." On average, every U.S. citizen drinks 363 8-ounce servings of Coca-Cola products each year. Coca-Cola's primary line of business is the making and selling of syrup to bottlers. These bottlers then sell the finished bottles and cans of Coca-Cola to the consumer.

In the annual report of Coca-Cola, the information shown below was provided.

THE COCA-COLA COMPANY
Management Discussion

Our gross margin declined to 61 percent this year from 62 percent in the prior year, primarily due to costs for materials such as sweeteners and packaging.

The increases [in selling expenses] in the last two years were primarily due to higher marketing expenditures in support of our Company's volume growth.

We measure our sales volume in two ways: (1) gallon shipments of concentrates and syrups and (2) unit cases of finished product (bottles and cans of Coke sold by bottlers).

Instructions

Answer the following questions.

(a) Are sweeteners and packaging a variable cost or a fixed cost? What is the impact on the contribution margin of an increase in the per unit cost of sweeteners or packaging? What are the implications for profitability?

(b) In your opinion, are marketing expenditures a fixed cost, variable cost, or mixed cost to The Coca-Cola Company? Give justification for your answer.

(c) Which of the two measures cited for measuring volume represents the activity index as defined in this chapter? Why might Coca-Cola use two different measures?

BYP22-5 The May 21, 2010, edition of the *Wall Street Journal* includes an article by Jeffrey Trachtenberg entitled "E-Books Rewrite Bookselling."

Instructions

Read the article and answer the following questions.

(a) What aspect of Barnes and Noble's current structure puts it at risk if electronic books become a significant portion of book sales?

(b) What was Barnes and Noble's primary competitive advantage in a "paper book" world? How has this advantage been eliminated by e-books?

(c) What event do the authors say might eventually be viewed as the big turning point for e-books?

(d) What amount does Barnes and Noble earn on a $25 hardcover book? How much would it likely earn on an e-book version of the same title? What implications does this have for Barnes and Noble versus its competitors?

(e) What two mistakes does the author suggest that Barnes and Noble made that left it ill-prepared for an e-book environment?

Critical Thinking

Communication Activity

BYP22-6 Your roommate asks for your help on the following questions about CVP analysis formulas.

(a) How can the mathematical equation for break-even sales show both sales units and sales dollars?

(b) How do the formulas differ for contribution margin per unit and contribution margin ratio?

(c) How can contribution margin be used to determine break-even sales in units and in dollars?

Instructions

Write a memo to your roommate stating the relevant formulas and answering each question.

Ethics Case

BYP22-7 Scott Bestor is an accountant for Westfield Company. Early this year, Scott made a highly favorable projection of sales and profits over the next 3 years for Westfield's hot-selling computer PLEX. As a result of the projections Scott presented to senior management, the company decided to expand production in this area. This decision led to dislocations of some plant personnel who were reassigned to one of the company's newer plants in another state. However, no one was fired, and in fact the company expanded its work force slightly.

Unfortunately, Scott rechecked his computations on the projections a few months later and found that he had made an error that would have reduced his projections substantially. Luckily, sales of PLEX have exceeded projections so far, and management is satisfied with its decision. Scott, however, is not sure what to do. Should he confess his honest mistake and jeopardize his possible promotion? He suspects that no one will catch the error because sales of PLEX have exceeded his projections, and it appears that profits will materialize close to his projections.

Instructions

(a) Who are the stakeholders in this situation?

(b) Identify the ethical issues involved in this situation.

(c) What are the possible alternative actions for Scott? What would you do in Scott's position?

All About You

BYP22-8 Cost-volume-profit analysis can also be used in making personal financial decisions. For example, the purchase of a new car is one of your biggest personal expenditures. It is important that you carefully analyze your options.

Suppose that you are considering the purchase of a hybrid vehicle. Let's assume the following facts: The hybrid will initially cost an additional $4,500 above the cost of a traditional vehicle. The hybrid will get 40 miles per gallon of gas, and the traditional car will get 30 miles per gallon. Also, assume that the cost of gas is $3.60 per gallon.

Instructions

Using the facts above, answer the following questions.

(a) What is the variable gasoline cost of going one mile in the hybrid car? What is the variable cost of going one mile in the traditional car?

(b) Using the information in part (a), if "miles" is your unit of measure, what is the "contribution margin" of the hybrid vehicle relative to the traditional vehicle? That is, express the variable cost savings on a per-mile basis.

(c) How many miles would you have to drive in order to break even on your investment in the hybrid car?

(d) What other factors might you want to consider?

Considering People, Planet, and Profit

BYP22-9 Many politicians, scientists, economists, and businesspeople have become concerned about the potential implications of global warming. The largest source of the emissions thought to contribute to global warming is from coal-fired power plants. The cost of alternative energy has declined, but it is still higher than coal. In 1980, wind-power electricity cost 80 cents per kilowatt hour. Using today's highly efficient turbines with rotor diameters of up to 125 meters, the cost can be as low as 4 cents (about the same as coal), or as much as 20 cents in places with less wind.

Some people have recently suggested that conventional cost comparisons are not adequate because they do not take environmental costs into account. For example, while coal is a very cheap energy source, it is also a significant contributor of greenhouse gases. Should environmental costs be incorporated into decision formulas when planners evaluate new power plants? The basic arguments for and against are as follows.

YES: As long as environmental costs are ignored, renewable energy will appear to be too expensive relative to coal.

NO: If one country decides to incorporate environmental costs into its decision-making process but other countries do not, the country that does so will be at a competitive disadvantage because its products will cost more to produce.

Instructions
Write a response indicating your position regarding this situation. Provide support for your view.

Answers to Chapter Questions

Answers to Insight and Accounting Across the Organization Questions

p. 1034 Gardens in the Sky   Q: What are some of the variable and fixed costs that are impacted by hydroponic farming? **A:** Compared to traditional methods, hydroponic farming would reduce the use of pesticides, herbicides, fuel, and water. Soil erosion would be eliminated, and land requirements would drop. But, fixed costs related to constructing greenhouses, suitable vertical planters, as well as investments in artificial lighting could be high.

p. 1038 Skilled Labor Is Truly Essential   Q: Would you characterize labor costs as being a fixed cost, a variable cost, or something else in this situation? **A:** Because these labor costs are essentially unchanged for most levels of production, they are primarily fixed. However, it could be described as being a "step function." If production gets too far outside the normal range, workers' hours will change. If production goes too low, hours are cut, and if it goes too high, overtime hours are needed.

p. 1045 Charter Flights Offer a Good Deal   Q: How did FlightServe determine that it would break even with 3.3 seats full per flight? **A:** FlightServe determined its break-even point with the following formula: Fixed costs ÷ Contribution margin per seat occupied = Break-even point in seats.

p. 1049 How a Rolling Stones' Tour Makes Money   Q: What amount of sales dollars are required for the promoter to break even?
A: Fixed costs = $1,200,000 + $400,000 = $1,600,000
   Contribution margin ratio = 80%
   Break-even sales = $1,600,000 ÷ .80 = $2,000,000

Answers to Self-Test Questions

1. a **2.** c **3.** a **4.** d **5.** c **6.** a **7.** c **8.** c ($100 × 30%) **9.** c ($800,000 × 25%) **10.** b **11.** b $600,000 − $420,000 = $180,000; $180,000 ÷ $600,000 = 30% **12.** a **13.** c **14.** a ($100,000 × $12) − ($300,000 + $200,000) ***15.** a

 The Navigator

✔ Remember to go back to The Navigator box on the chapter opening page and check off your completed work.

23 | Budgetary Planning

Feature Story

Was This the Next Amazon.com? Not Quite

So you came up with a great idea for a product. You started a company, and you are selling stuff so fast that you can barely keep up. No problem, right? However, without proper planning and budgeting, your success could be short-lived. In some cases, failure is actually brought on by rapid, uncontrolled growth.

One such example was online discount bookseller, www.Positively-You.com. One of the website's co-founders, Lyle Bowline, had never run a business. However, his experience as an assistant director of an entrepreneurial center had provided him with knowledge about the do's and don'ts of small business. To minimize costs, he started the company small and simple. He invested $5,000 in computer equipment and ran the business out of his basement. In the early months, even though sales were only about $2,000 a month, the company actually made a profit because it kept its costs low (a feat few other dot-coms could boast of).

Things changed dramatically when the company received national publicity in the financial press. Suddenly, the company's sales increased to $50,000 a month—fully 25 times the previous level. The "simple" little business suddenly needed a business plan, a strategic plan, and a budget. It needed to rent office space and to hire employees.

Initially, members of a local book club donated time to he meet the sudden demand. Some put in so much tha eventually the company hired them. Quickly, the number paid employees ballooned. The sudden growth necessitat detailed planning and budgeting. The need for a proper budget was accentuated by the fact that the company's g profit was only 16 cents on each dollar of goods sold. Thi meant that after paying for its inventory, the company ha only 16 cents of every dollar to cover its remaining opera costs.

Unfortunately, the company never got things under contr Within a few months, sales had plummeted to $12,000 month. At this level of sales, the company could not mee mountain of monthly expenses that it had accumulated i trying to grow. Ironically, the company's sudden success, the turmoil it created, appears to have been what eventu caused the company to fail.

Watch the Babycakes video in WileyPLUS to learn more about budgetary planning in the real world.

✔ The Navigator

- Scan Learning Objectives
- Read Feature Story
- Read Preview
- Read text and answer **DO IT!** p. 1080
  - p. 1083 ■ p. 1085 ■ p. 1089
  - p. 1094
- Work Comprehensive **DO IT! 1** p. 1097
  - **2** p. 1099
- Review Summary of Learning Objectives
- Answer Self-Test Questions
- Complete Assignments
- Go to *WileyPLUS* for practice and tutorials

Learning Objectives

✔ The Navigator

After studying this chapter, you should be able to:

[1] Indicate the benefits of budgeting.

[2] State the essentials of effective budgeting.

[3] Identify the budgets that comprise the master budget.

[4] Describe the sources for preparing the budgeted income statement.

[5] Explain the principal sections of a cash budget.

[6] Indicate the applicability of budgeting in nonmanufacturing companies.

Preview of Chapter 23

✔ The Navigator

As the Feature Story about Positively-You.com indicates, budgeting is critical to financial well-being. As a student, you budget your study time and your money. Families budget income and expenses. Governmental agencies budget revenues and expenditures. Businesses use budgets in planning and controlling their operations.

Our primary focus in this chapter is budgeting—specifically, how budgeting is used as a **planning** tool by management. Through budgeting, it should be possible for management to maintain enough cash to pay creditors, to have sufficient raw materials to meet production requirements, and to have adequate finished goods to meet expected sales.

The content and organization of Chapter 23 are as follows.

BUDGETARY PLANNING

Budgeting Basics	Preparing the Operating Budgets	Preparing the Financial Budgets	Budgeting in Non-manufacturing Companies
• Budgeting and accounting • Benefits • Essentials of effective budgeting • Length of budget period • Budgeting process • Budgeting and human behavior • Budgeting and long-range planning • The master budget	• Sales • Production • Direct materials • Direct labor • Manufacturing overhead • Selling and administrative expense • Budgeted income statement	• Cash • Budgeted balance sheet	• Merchandisers • Service • Not-for-profit

Budgeting Basics

One of management's major responsibilities is planning. As explained in Chapter 19, **planning** is the process of establishing company-wide objectives. A successful organization makes both long-term and short-term plans. These plans establish the objectives of the company and the proposed way of accomplishing them.

A **budget** is a formal written statement of management's plans for a specified future time period, expressed in financial terms. It represents the primary method of communicating agreed-upon objectives throughout the organization. Once adopted, a budget becomes an important basis for evaluating performance. It promotes efficiency and serves as a deterrent to waste and inefficiency. We consider the role of budgeting as a **control device** in Chapter 24.

Budgeting and Accounting

Accounting information makes major contributions to the budgeting process. From the accounting records, companies can obtain historical data on revenues, costs, and expenses. These data are helpful in formulating future budget goals.

Normally, accountants have the responsibility for presenting management's budgeting goals in financial terms. In this role, they translate management's plans and communicate the budget to employees throughout the company. They prepare periodic budget reports that provide the basis for measuring performance and comparing actual results with planned objectives. The budget itself, and the administration of the budget, however, are entirely management responsibilities.

The Benefits of Budgeting

The primary benefits of budgeting are:

1. It requires all levels of management to **plan ahead** and to formalize goals on a recurring basis.

2. It provides **definite objectives** for evaluating performance at each level of responsibility.

3. It creates an **early warning system** for potential problems so that management can make changes before things get out of hand.

4. It facilitates the **coordination of activities** within the business. It does this by correlating the goals of each segment with overall company objectives. Thus, the company can integrate production and sales promotion with expected sales.

5. It results in greater **management awareness** of the entity's overall operations and the impact on operations of external factors, such as economic trends.

6. It **motivates personnel** throughout the organization to meet planned objectives.

A budget is an aid to management; it is not a substitute for management. A budget cannot operate or enforce itself. Companies can realize the benefits of budgeting only when managers carefully administer budgets.

Essentials of Effective Budgeting

Effective budgeting depends on a **sound organizational structure**. In such a structure, authority and responsibility for all phases of operations are clearly defined. Budgets based on **research and analysis** are more likely to result in realistic goals that will contribute to the growth and profitability of a company.

And, the effectiveness of a budget program is directly related to its **acceptance by all levels of management**.

Once adopted, the budget is an important tool for evaluating performance. Managers should systematically and periodically review variations between actual and expected results to determine their cause(s). However, individuals should not be held responsible for variations that are beyond their control.

Length of the Budget Period

The budget period is not necessarily one year in length. **A budget may be prepared for any period of time.** Various factors influence the length of the budget period. These factors include the type of budget, the nature of the organization, the need for periodic appraisal, and prevailing business conditions.

The budget period should be long enough to provide an attainable goal under normal business conditions. Ideally, the time period should minimize the impact of seasonal or cyclical fluctuations. On the other hand, the budget period should not be so long that reliable estimates are impossible.

The **most common budget period is one year**. The annual budget, in turn, is often supplemented by monthly and quarterly budgets. Many companies use **continuous 12-month budgets**. These budgets drop the month just ended and add a future month. One advantage of continuous budgeting is that it keeps management planning a full year ahead.

ACCOUNTING ACROSS THE ORGANIZATION

Businesses Often Feel Too Busy to Plan for the Future

A study by Willard & Shullman Group Ltd. found that fewer than 14% of businesses with less than 500 employees do an annual budget or have a written business plan. For many small businesses, the basic assumption is that, "As long as I sell as much as I can, and keep my employees paid, I'm doing OK." A few small business owners even say that they see no need for budgeting and planning. Most small business owners, though, say that they understand that budgeting and planning are critical for survival and growth. But given the long hours that they already work addressing day-to-day challenges, they also say that they are "just too busy to plan for the future."

 Describe a situation in which a business "sells as much as it can" but cannot "keep its employees paid." (See page 1120.)

The Budgeting Process

The development of the budget for the coming year generally starts several months before the end of the current year. The budgeting process usually begins with the collection of data from each organizational unit of the company. Past performance is often the starting point from which future budget goals are formulated.

The budget is developed within the framework of a **sales forecast**. This forecast shows potential sales for the industry and the company's expected share of such sales. Sales forecasting involves a consideration of various factors: (1) general economic conditions, (2) industry trends, (3) market research studies, (4) anticipated advertising and promotion, (5) previous market share, (6) changes in prices, and (7) technological developments. The input of sales personnel and top management is essential to the sales forecast.

In small companies like Positively-You.com, the budgeting process is often informal. In larger companies, a **budget committee** has responsibility for coordinating the preparation of the budget. The committee ordinarily includes the president, treasurer, chief accountant (controller), and management personnel from each of the major areas of the company, such as sales, production, and research. The budget committee serves as a review board where managers can defend their budget goals and requests. Differences are reviewed, modified if necessary, and reconciled. The budget is then put in its final form by the budget committee, approved, and distributed.

Budgeting and Human Behavior

A budget can have a significant impact on human behavior. If done well, it can inspire managers to higher levels of performance. However, if done poorly, budgets can discourage additional effort and pull down the morale of managers. Why do these diverse effects occur? The answer is found in how the budget is developed and administered.

In developing the budget, each level of management should be invited to participate. This "bottom-to-top" approach is referred to as **participative budgeting**. One advantage of participative budgeting is that lower-level managers have more detailed knowledge of their specific area and thus are able to provide more accurate budgetary estimates. Also, when lower-level managers participate in the budgeting process, they are more likely to perceive the resulting budget as fair. The overall goal is to reach agreement on a budget that the managers consider fair and achievable, but which also meets the corporate goals set by top management. When this goal is met, the budget will provide positive motivation for the managers. In contrast, if managers view the budget as unfair and unrealistic, they may feel discouraged and uncommitted to budget goals. The risk of having unrealistic budgets is generally greater when the budget is developed from top management down to lower management than vice versa. Illustration 23-1 graphically displays the flow of budget data from bottom to top under participative budgeting.

Illustration 23-1
Flow of budget data under participative budgeting

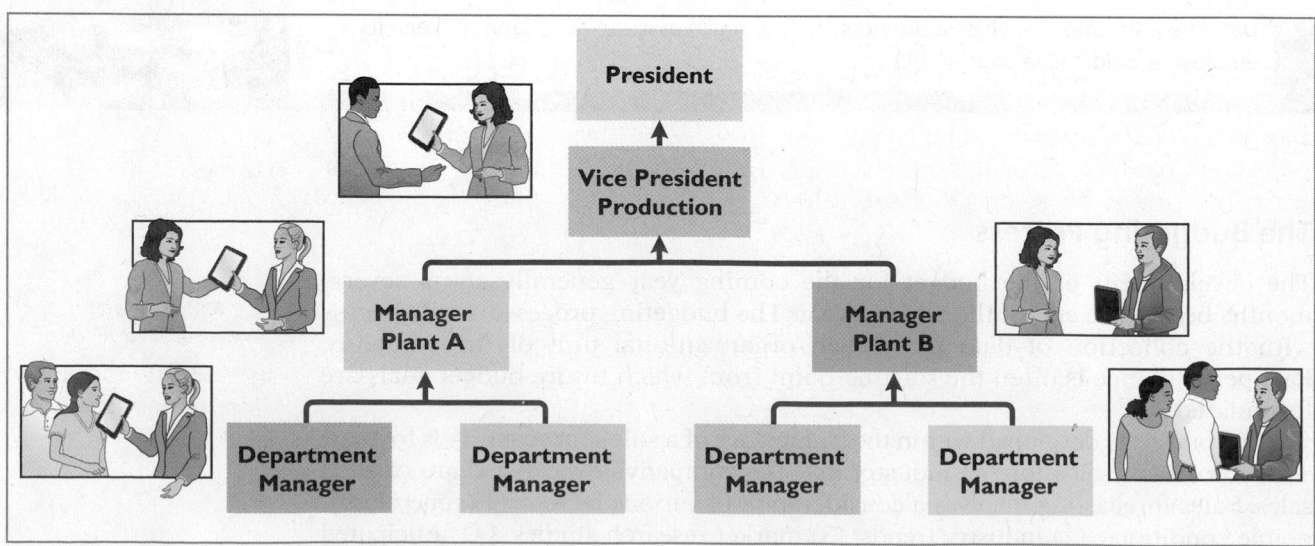

For example, at one time, in an effort to revive its plummeting stock, Time Warner's top management determined and publicly announced bold new financial goals for the coming year. Unfortunately, these goals were not reached. The next year, the company got a new CEO who said the company would now actually set reasonable goals that it could meet. The new budgets were developed with each operating unit setting what it felt were optimistic but attainable goals. In the words of one manager, using this approach created a sense of teamwork.

Participative budgeting does, however, have potential disadvantages. First, the "give and take" of participative budgeting is time-consuming (and thus more costly). Under a "top-down" approach, the budget is simply developed by top management and then dictated to lower-level managers. A second disadvantage is that participative budgeting can foster budgetary "gaming" through budgetary slack. **Budgetary slack** occurs when managers intentionally underestimate budgeted revenues or overestimate budgeted expenses in order to make it easier to achieve budgetary goals. To minimize budgetary slack, higher-level managers must carefully review and thoroughly question the budget projections provided to them by employees whom they supervise.

For the budget to be effective, top management must completely support the budget. The budget is an important basis for evaluating performance. It also can be used as a positive aid in achieving projected goals. The effect of an evaluation is positive when top management tempers criticism with advice and assistance. In contrast, a manager is likely to respond negatively if top management uses the budget exclusively to assess blame. A budget should not be used as a pressure device to force improved performance. In sum, a budget can be a manager's friend or a foe.

> ### Ethics Note
> Unrealistic budgets can lead to unethical employee behavior such as cutting corners on the job or distorting internal financial reports.

Budgeting and Long-Range Planning

Budgeting and long-range planning are not the same. One important difference is the **time period involved**. The maximum length of a budget is usually one year, and budgets are often prepared for shorter periods of time, such as a month or a quarter. In contrast, long-range planning usually encompasses a period of at least five years.

A second significant difference is in **emphasis**. Budgeting focuses on achieving specific short-term goals, such as meeting annual profit objectives. **Long-range planning**, on the other hand, identifies long-term goals, selects strategies to achieve those goals, and develops policies and plans to implement the strategies. In long-range planning, management also considers anticipated trends in the economic and political environment and how the company should cope with them.

The final difference between budgeting and long-range planning relates to the **amount of detail presented**. Budgets, as you will see in this chapter, can be very detailed. Long-range plans contain considerably less detail. The data in long-range plans are intended more for a review of progress toward long-term goals than as a basis of control for achieving specific results. The primary objective of long-range planning is to develop the best strategy to maximize the company's performance over an extended future period.

Helpful Hint In comparing a budget with a long-range plan: (1) Which has more detail? (2) Which is done for a longer period of time? (3) Which is more concerned with short-term goals? Answers: (1) Budget. (2) Long-range plan. (3) Budget.

The Master Budget

The term "budget" is actually a shorthand term to describe a variety of budget documents. All of these documents are combined into a master budget. The **master budget** is a set of interrelated budgets that constitutes a plan of action for a specified time period.

The master budget contains two classes of budgets. **Operating budgets** are the individual budgets that result in the preparation of the budgeted income statement. These budgets establish goals for the company's sales and production personnel. In contrast, **financial budgets** focus primarily on the cash resources

> **LEARNING OBJECTIVE   3**
>
> Identify the budgets that comprise the master budget.

needed to fund expected operations and planned capital expenditures. Financial budgets include the capital expenditure budget, the cash budget, and the budgeted balance sheet.

Illustration 23-2 pictures the individual budgets included in a master budget, and the sequence in which they are prepared. The company first develops the operating budgets, beginning with the sales budget. Then, it prepares the financial budgets. We will explain and illustrate each budget shown in Illustration 23-2 except the capital expenditure budget. That budget is discussed under the topic of capital budgeting in Chapter 26.

Illustration 23-2
Components of the master budget

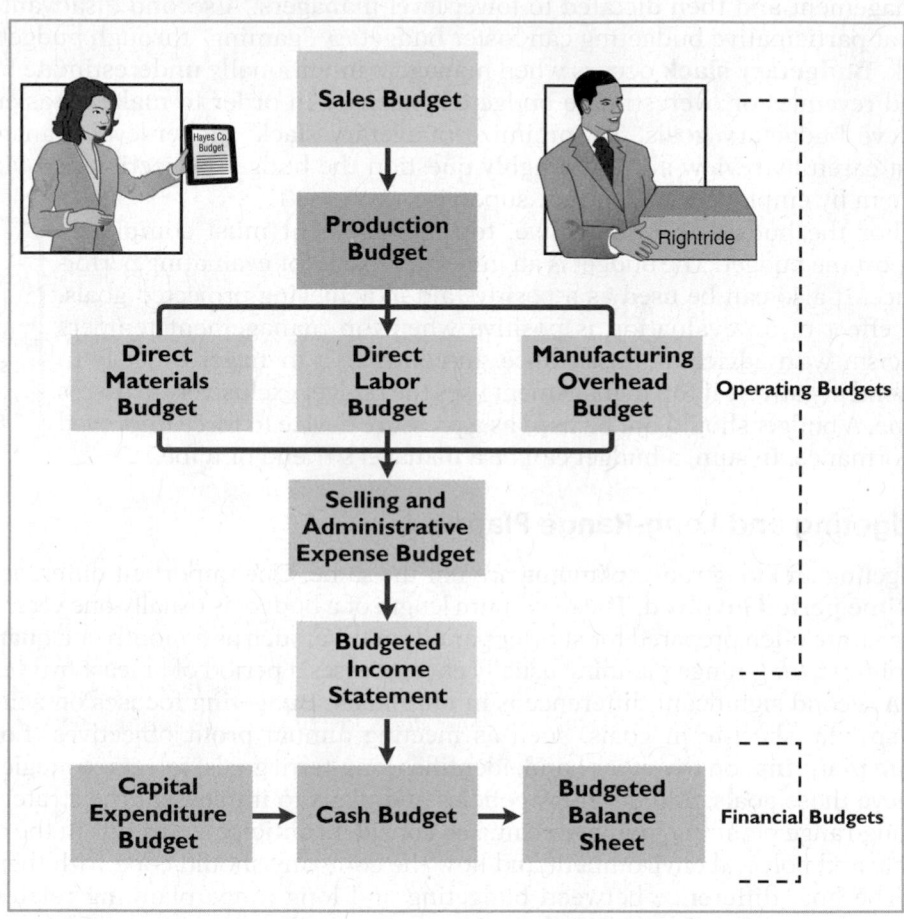

DO IT!

Budget Terminology

Use this list of terms to complete the sentences that follow.

Long-range planning	Participative budgeting
Sales forecast	Operating budgets
Master budget	Financial budgets

1. A _____ shows potential sales for the industry and a company's expected share of such sales.

2. _____ are used as the basis for the preparation of the budgeted income statement.

3. The _____ is a set of interrelated budgets that constitutes a plan of action for a specified time period.

4. _____ identifies long-term goals, selects strategies to achieve these goals, and develops policies and plans to implement the strategies.

5. Lower-level managers are more likely to perceive results as fair and achievable under a _____ approach.

6. _____ focus primarily on the cash resources needed to fund expected operations and planned capital expenditures.

Solution

1. Sales forecast.	4. Long-range planning.
2. Operating budgets.	5. Participative budgeting.
3. Master budget.	6. Financial budgets.

Related exercise material: **BE23-1, E23-1, and DO IT! 23-1.**

✔ The Navigator

Preparing the Operating Budgets

We use a case study of Hayes Company in preparing the operating budgets. Hayes manufactures and sells a single product, an ergonomically designed bike seat with multiple customizable adjustments, called the Rightride. The budgets are prepared by quarters for the year ending December 31, 2014. Hayes Company begins its annual budgeting process on September 1, 2013, and it completes the budget for 2014 by December 1, 2013.

Sales Budget

As shown in the master budget in Illustration 23-2, **the sales budget is prepared first**. Each of the other budgets depends on the sales budget. The **sales budget** is derived from the sales forecast. It represents management's best estimate of sales revenue for the budget period. An inaccurate sales budget may adversely affect net income. For example, an overly optimistic sales budget may result in excessive inventories that may have to be sold at reduced prices. In contrast, an unduly pessimistic sales budget may result in loss of sales revenue due to inventory shortages.

For example, at one time Amazon.com significantly underestimated demand for its e-book reader, the Kindle. As a consequence, it did not produce enough Kindles and was completely sold out of the readers well before the holiday shopping season. Not only did this represent a huge lost opportunity for Amazon.com, but it exposed it to potential competitors, who were eager to provide customers with alternatives to the Kindle.

Forecasting sales is challenging. For example, consider the forecasting challenges faced by major sports arenas, whose revenues depend on the success of the home team. Madison Square Garden's revenues from April to June were $193 million during a year when the Knicks made the NBA playoffs. But revenues were only $133.2 million a couple of years later when the team did not make the playoffs. Or, consider the challenges faced by Hollywood movie producers in predicting the complicated revenue stream produced by a new movie. Movie theater ticket sales represent only 20% of total revenue. The bulk of revenue comes from global sales, DVDs, video-on-demand, merchandising products, and videogames, all of which are difficult to forecast.

The sales budget is prepared by multiplying the expected unit sales volume for each product by its anticipated unit selling price. Hayes Company expects sales volume to be 3,000 units in the first quarter, with 500-unit increases in each succeeding quarter. Illustration 23-3 (page 1082) shows the sales budget for the year, by quarter, based on a sales price of $60 per unit.

Helpful Hint For a retail or manufacturing company, what is the starting point in preparing the master budget, and why? Answer: The sales budget is the starting point for the master budget. It sets the level of activity for other functions such as production and purchasing.

Illustration 23-3
Sales budget

	A	B	C	D	E	F
1		**HAYES COMPANY**				
2		**Sales Budget**				
3		**For the Year Ending December 31, 2014**				
4		Quarter				
5		1	2	3	4	Year
6	Expected unit sales	3,000	3,500	4,000	4,500	15,000
7	Unit selling price	× $60	× $60	× $60	× $60	× $60
8	Total sales	$180,000	$210,000	$240,000	$270,000	$900,000

Some companies classify the anticipated sales revenue as cash or credit sales and by geographical regions, territories, or salespersons.

Marcela Barsse/iStockphoto

SERVICE COMPANY INSIGHT

The Implications of Budgetary Optimism

Companies aren't the only ones that have to estimate revenues. Governments at all levels (e.g., local, state, or federal) prepare annual budgets. Most are required to submit balanced budgets, that is, estimated revenues are supposed to cover anticipated expenditures. Unfortunately, estimating government revenues can be as difficult as, or even more difficult than, estimating company revenues. The accuracy of government estimates is most critical during economic downturns. If governments fail to anticipate lower revenues during the planning stage, they often later have to make much larger, more disruptive cuts than would have been originally necessary.

For example, during 2009, the median state government overestimated revenues by 10.2%, with four state governments missing by more than 25%. What makes estimation so difficult for these governments? Most states rely on income taxes, which fluctuate widely with economic gyrations. Some states rely on sales taxes, which are problematic because the laws regarding sales taxes haven't adjusted for the shift from manufacturing to service companies and from brick-and-mortar stores to online sales.

Source: Conor Dougherty, "States Fumble Revenue Forecasts," *Wall Street Journal Online* (March 2, 2011).

? Why is it important that government budgets accurately estimate future revenues during economic downturns? (See page 1120.)

Production Budget

The **production budget** shows the number of units of a product to produce to meet anticipated sales demand. Production requirements are determined from the following formula.[1]

Illustration 23-4
Production requirements formula

Budgeted Sales Units	+	Desired Ending Finished Goods Units	−	Beginning Finished Goods Units	=	Required Production Units

A realistic estimate of ending inventory is essential in scheduling production requirements. Excessive inventories in one quarter may lead to cutbacks

---

[1]This formula ignores any work in process inventories, which are assumed to be nonexistent in Hayes Company.

in production and employee layoffs in a subsequent quarter. On the other hand, inadequate inventories may result either in added costs for overtime work or in lost sales. Hayes Company believes it can meet future sales requirements by maintaining an ending inventory equal to 20% of the next quarter's budgeted sales volume. For example, the ending finished goods inventory for the first quarter is 700 units (20% × anticipated second-quarter sales of 3,500 units). Illustration 23-5 shows the production budget.

Units of Finished Goods Inventory	
Beg. Inv.	
Required Prod. Units	Sales
End. Inv.	

Hayes Company Production Budget.xls

Home   Insert   Page Layout   Formulas   Data   Review   View

P18   fx

	A	B	C	D	E	F	G	H	I	J
1		**HAYES COMPANY**								
2		**Production Budget**								
3		**For the Year Ending December 31, 2014**								
4					Quarter					
5		1		2		3		4		Year
6	Expected unit sales (Illustration 23-3)	3,000		3,500		4,000		4,500		
7	Add: Desired ending finished goods units[a]	700		800		900		1,000	[b]	
8	Total required units	3,700		4,300		4,900		5,500		
9	Less: Beginning finished goods units	600	[c]	700		800		900		
10	**Required production units**	3,100		3,600		4,100		4,600		15,400
11										
12	[a]20% of next quarter's sales									
13	[b]Expected 2015 first-quarter sales, 5,000 units × 20%									
14	[c]20% of estimated first-quarter 2014 sales units									

Units of Finished Goods Inventory	
600	
3,100	3,000
700	

Illustration 23-5
Production budget

The production budget, in turn, provides the basis for the budgeted costs for each manufacturing cost element, as explained in the following pages.

> DO IT!

Production Budget

Becker Company estimates that 2014 unit sales will be 12,000 in quarter 1, 16,000 in quarter 2, and 20,000 in quarter 3, at a unit selling price of $30. Management desires to have ending finished goods inventory equal to 15% of the next quarter's expected unit sales. Prepare a production budget by quarter for the first six months of 2014.

Action Plan

✔ Begin with budgeted sales in units.

✔ Add desired ending finished goods inventory.

✔ Subtract beginning finished goods inventory.

Solution

BECKER COMPANY Production Budget For the Six Months Ending June 30, 2014			
	Quarter		**Six Months**
	1	**2**	
Expected unit sales	12,000	16,000	
Add: Desired ending finished goods	2,400	3,000	
Total required units	14,400	19,000	
Less: Beginning finished goods inventory	1,800	2,400	
Required production units	12,600	16,600	29,200

Related exercise material: **BE23-3, E23-4, E23-6, and DO IT! 23-2.**

 The Navigator

Direct Materials Budget

The **direct materials budget** shows both the quantity and cost of direct materials to be purchased. The quantities of direct materials are derived from the following formula.

Illustration 23-6
Formula for direct materials quantities

Direct Materials Units Required for Production	+	Desired Ending Direct Materials Units	−	Beginning Direct Materials Units	=	Required Direct Materials Units to Be Purchased

Units of Direct Materials

Beg. Inv.	
Direct Materials Purchases	Direct Materials Required for Prod.
End. Inv.	

After the company determines the number of units to purchase, it can compute the budgeted cost of direct materials to be purchased. It does so by multiplying the required units of direct materials by the anticipated cost per unit.

The desired ending inventory is again a key component in the budgeting process. For example, inadequate inventories could result in temporary shutdowns of production. Because of its close proximity to suppliers, Hayes Company maintains an ending inventory of raw materials equal to 10% of the next quarter's production requirements. The manufacture of each Rightride requires 2 pounds of raw materials, and the expected cost per pound is $4. Illustration 23-7 shows the direct materials budget. Assume that the desired ending direct materials amount is 1,020 pounds for the fourth quarter of 2014.

Illustration 23-7
Direct materials budget

Units of Direct Materials (1st Qtr.)

620	
6,300	6,200
720	

	Hayes Company Direct Materials Budget.xls				
	Home Insert Page Layout Formulas Data Review View				
	P18 fx				

	A	C	E	G	I	K
1	**HAYES COMPANY**					
2	**Direct Materials Budget**					
3	**For the Year Ending December 31, 2014**					
4		Quarter				
5		1	2	3	4	Year
6	Units to be produced (Illustration 23-5)	3,100	3,600	4,100	4,600	
7	Direct materials per unit	× 2	× 2	× 2	× 2	
8	Total pounds needed for production	6,200	7,200	8,200	9,200	
9	Add: Desired ending direct materials (pounds)ᵃ	720	820	920	1,020	
10	Total materials required	6,920	8,020	9,120	10,220	
11	Less: Beginning direct materials (pounds)	620 ᵇ	720	820	920	
12	Direct materials purchases	6,300	7,300	8,300	9,300	
13	Cost per pound	× $4	× $4	× $4	× $4	
14	**Total cost of direct materials purchases**	**$25,200**	**$29,200**	**$33,200**	**$37,200**	**$124,800**
15						
16	ᵃ10% of next quarter's production requirements					
17	ᵇ10% of estimated first-quarter pounds needed for production					
18						

MANAGEMENT INSIGHT

Betting That Prices Won't Fall

Sometimes things happen that cause managers to reevaluate their normal purchasing patterns. Consider, for example, the predicament that businesses faced when the price of many raw materials recently skyrocketed. Rubber, cotton, oil, corn, wheat, steel, copper, and spices—prices for seemingly everything were going straight up. Anticipating that prices might continue to go up, many managers decided to stockpile much larger quantities of raw materials to avoid paying even higher prices in the future. For example, after cotton prices rose 92%, one manager of a printed T-shirt manufacturer decided to stockpile a huge supply of plain T-shirts in anticipation of additional price increases. While he normally has about 30 boxes of T-shirts in inventory, he purchased 2,500 boxes.

Source: Liam Pleven and Matt Wirz, "Companies Stock Up as Commodities Prices Rise," *Wall Street Journal Online* (February 3, 2011).

? What are the potential downsides of stockpiling a huge amount of raw materials? (See page 1120.)

> DO IT!

Master Budget

Action Plan

✔ Know the form and content of the sales budget.

✔ Prepare the sales budget first, as the basis for the other budgets.

✔ Determine the units that must be produced to meet anticipated sales.

✔ Know how to compute the beginning and ending finished goods units.

✔ Determine the materials required to meet production needs.

✔ Know how to compute the beginning and ending direct materials units.

Soriano Company is preparing its master budget for 2014. Relevant data pertaining to its sales, production, and direct materials budgets are as follows.

Sales. Sales for the year are expected to total 1,200,000 units. Quarterly sales, as a percentage of total sales, are 20%, 25%, 30%, and 25%, respectively. The sales price is expected to be $50 per unit for the first three quarters and $55 per unit beginning in the fourth quarter. Sales in the first quarter of 2015 are expected to be 10% higher than the budgeted sales for the first quarter of 2014.

Production. Management desires to maintain the ending finished goods inventories at 25% of the next quarter's budgeted sales volume.

Direct materials. Each unit requires 3 pounds of raw materials at a cost of $5 per pound. Management desires to maintain raw materials inventories at 5% of the next quarter's production requirements. Assume the production requirements for the first quarter of 2015 are 810,000 pounds.

Prepare the sales, production, and direct materials budgets by quarters for 2014.

Solution

Soriano Company Sales Budget.xls

Home | Insert | Page Layout | Formulas | Data | Review | View

P18   *fx*

	A	B	C	D	E	F
1		**SORIANO COMPANY**				
2		**Sales Budget**				
3		**For the Year Ending December 31, 2014**				
4				Quarter		
5		1	2	3	4	Year
6	Expected unit sales	240,000	300,000	360,000	300,000	1,200,000
7	Unit selling price	× $50	× $50	× $50	× $55	—
8	Total sales	$12,000,000	$15,000,000	$18,000,000	$16,500,000	$61,500,000

Soriano Company Production Budget.xls

Home | Insert | Page Layout | Formulas | Data | Review | View

P18 | fx

SORIANO COMPANY
Production Budget
For the Year Ending December 31, 2014

	A	1	2	3	4	Year
		Quarter				
6	Expected unit sales	240,000	300,000	360,000	300,000	
7	Add: Desired ending finished goods units[a]	75,000	90,000	75,000	66,000 [b]	
8	Total required units	315,000	390,000	435,000	366,000	
9	Less: Beginning finished goods units	60,000 [c]	75,000	90,000	75,000	
10	**Required production units**	**255,000**	**315,000**	**345,000**	**291,000**	**1,206,000**

[a]25% of next quarter's unit sales
[b]Estimated first-quarter 2015 sales units: 240,000 + (240,000 × 10%) = 264,000: 264,000 × 25%
[c]25% of estimated first-quarter 2014 sales units (240,000 × 25%)

Soriano Company Direct Materials Budget.xls

Home | Insert | Page Layout | Formulas | Data | Review | View

P18 | fx

SORIANO COMPANY
Direct Materials Budget
For the Year Ending December 31, 2014

	A	B	C	D	E	F	G	H
		Quarter						Year
		1		2	3	4		
6	Units to be produced	255,000		315,000	345,000	291,000		
7	Direct materials per unit	× 3		× 3	× 3	× 3		
8	Total pounds needed for production	765,000		945,000	1,035,000	873,000		
9	Add: Desired ending direct materials (pounds)	47,250		51,750	43,650	40,500 [a]		
10	Total materials required	812,250		996,750	1,078,650	913,500		
11	Less: Beginning direct materials (pounds)	38,250 [b]		47,250	51,750	43,650		
12	Direct materials purchases	774,000		949,500	1,026,900	869,850		
13	Cost per pound	× $5		× $5	× $5	× $5		
14	**Total cost of direct materials purchases**	**$3,870,000**		**$4,747,500**	**$5,134,500**	**$4,349,250**		**$18,101,250**

[a]Estimated first-quarter 2015 production requirements: 810,000 × 5% = 40,500
[b]5% of estimated first-quarter pounds needed for production

---

Related exercise material: **BE23-2, BE23-3, BE23-4, E23-2, E23-3, E23-4, E23-5, E23-6, and DO IT! 23-2.**

 The Navigator

Direct Labor Budget

Like the direct materials budget, the **direct labor budget** contains the quantity (hours) and cost of direct labor necessary to meet production requirements. The total direct labor cost is derived from the following formula.

Illustration 23-8
Formula for direct labor cost

Units to Be Produced	×	Direct Labor Time per Unit	×	Direct Labor Cost per Hour	=	Total Direct Labor Cost

Direct labor hours are determined from the production budget. At Hayes Company, two hours of direct labor are required to produce each unit of finished goods. The anticipated hourly wage rate is $10. Illustration 23-9 shows these data.

Illustration 23-9
Direct labor budget

Hayes Company Direct Labor Budget.xls

Home   Insert   Page Layout   Formulas   Data   Review   View

P18   fx

	A	B	C	D	E	F	G	H	I	J
1			HAYES COMPANY							
2			Direct Labor Budget							
3			For the Year Ending December 31, 2014							
4							Quarter			
5			1		2		3		4	Year
6	Units to be produced (Illustration 23-5)		3,100		3,600		4,100		4,600	
7	Direct labor time (hours) per unit		× 2		× 2		× 2		× 2	
8	Total required direct labor hours		6,200		7,200		8,200		9,200	
9	Direct labor cost per hour		× $10		× $10		× $10		× $10	
10	Total direct labor cost		$62,000		$72,000		$82,000		$92,000	$308,000
11										

The direct labor budget is critical in maintaining a labor force that can meet the expected levels of production.

Helpful Hint An important assumption in Illustration 23-9 is that the company can add to and subtract from its work force as needed so that the $10 per hour labor cost applies to a wide range of possible production activity.

Manufacturing Overhead Budget

The **manufacturing overhead budget** shows the expected manufacturing overhead costs for the budget period. As Illustration 23-10 (page 1088) shows, **this budget distinguishes between variable and fixed overhead costs**. Hayes Company expects variable costs to fluctuate with production volume on the basis of the following rates per direct labor hour: indirect materials $1.00, indirect labor $1.40, utilities $0.40, and maintenance $0.20. Thus, for the 6,200 direct labor hours to produce 3,100 units, budgeted indirect materials are $6,200 (6,200 × $1), and budgeted indirect labor is $8,680 (6,200 × $1.40). Hayes also recognizes that some maintenance is fixed. The amounts reported for fixed costs are assumed for our example. The accuracy of budgeted overhead cost estimates can be greatly improved by employing activity-based costing.

At Hayes Company, overhead is applied to production on the basis of direct labor hours. Thus, as Illustration 23-10 shows, the budgeted annual rate is $8 per hour ($246,400 ÷ 30,800).

Selling and Administrative Expense Budget

Hayes Company combines its operating expenses into one budget, the **selling and administrative expense budget**. This budget projects anticipated selling and administrative expenses for the budget period. This budget (Illustration 23-11, page 1088) also classifies expenses as either variable or fixed. In this case, the variable expense rates per unit of sales are sales commissions $3 and freight-out $1. Variable expenses per quarter are based on the unit sales from the sales budget (Illustration 23-3, page 1082). For example, Hayes expects sales in the first quarter to be 3,000 units. Thus, Sales Commissions Expense is $9,000 (3,000 × $3), and Freight-Out is $3,000 (3,000 × $1). Fixed expenses are based on assumed data.

Illustration 23-10
Manufacturing overhead budget

Hayes Company Manufacturing Overhead Budget.xls

Home   Insert   Page Layout   Formulas   Data   Review   View

P18   *fx*

HAYES COMPANY
Manufacturing Overhead Budget
For the Year Ending December 31, 2014

	Quarter				
A	1	2	3	4	Year
Variable costs					
Indirect materials ($1.00/hour)	$ 6,200	$ 7,200	$ 8,200	$ 9,200	$ 30,800
Indirect labor ($1.40/hour)	8,680	10,080	11,480	12,880	43,120
Utilities ($0.40/hour)	2,480	2,880	3,280	3,680	12,320
Maintenance ($0.20/hour)	1,240	1,440	1,640	1,840	6,160
Total variable costs	18,600	21,600	24,600	27,600	92,400
Fixed costs					
Supervisory salaries	20,000	20,000	20,000	20,000	80,000
Depreciation	3,800	3,800	3,800	3,800	15,200
Property taxes and insurance	9,000	9,000	9,000	9,000	36,000
Maintenance	5,700	5,700	5,700	5,700	22,800
Total fixed costs	38,500	38,500	38,500	38,500	154,000
Total manufacturing overhead	**$57,100**	**$60,100**	**$63,100**	**$66,100**	**$246,400**
Direct labor hours (Illustration 23-9)	6,200	7,200	8,200	9,200	30,800
Manufacturing overhead rate per direct labor hour ($246,400 ÷ 30,800)					$8

Illustration 23-11
Selling and administrative expense budget

Hayes Company Manufacturing Selling and Administrative Expense Budget.xls

Home   Insert   Page Layout   Formulas   Data   Review   View

P18   *fx*

HAYES COMPANY
Selling and Administrative Expense Budget
For the Year Ending December 31, 2014

	Quarter				
A	1	2	3	4	Year
Budgeted sales in units (Illustration 23-3)	3,000	3,500	4,000	4,500	15,000
Variable expenses					
Sales commissions ($3 per unit)	$ 9,000	$10,500	$12,000	$13,500	$ 45,000
Freight-out ($1 per unit)	3,000	3,500	4,000	4,500	15,000
Total variable expenses	12,000	14,000	16,000	18,000	60,000
Fixed expenses					
Advertising	5,000	5,000	5,000	5,000	20,000
Sales salaries	15,000	15,000	15,000	15,000	60,000
Office salaries	7,500	7,500	7,500	7,500	30,000
Depreciation	1,000	1,000	1,000	1,000	4,000
Property taxes and insurance	1,500	1,500	1,500	1,500	6,000
Total fixed expenses	30,000	30,000	30,000	30,000	120,000
Total selling and administrative expenses	**$42,000**	**$44,000**	**$46,000**	**$48,000**	**$180,000**

Budgeted Income Statement

The **budgeted income statement** is the important end-product of the operating budgets. This budget indicates the expected profitability of operations for the budget period. The budgeted income statement provides the basis for evaluating company performance. Budgeted income statements often act as a call to action. For example, a board member at XM Satellite Radio Holdings felt that budgeted costs were too high relative to budgeted revenues. When management refused to cut its marketing and programming costs, the board member resigned. He felt that without the cuts, the company risked financial crisis.

As you would expect, the budgeted income statement is prepared from the various operating budgets. For example, to find the cost of goods sold, Hayes Company must first determine the total unit cost of producing one Rightride, as follows.

> **LEARNING OBJECTIVE   4**
>
> Describe the sources for preparing the budgeted income statement.

Illustration 23-12
Computation of total unit cost

	Cost of One Rightride			
Cost Element	**Illustration**	**Quantity**	**Unit Cost**	**Total**
Direct materials	23-7	2 pounds	$ 4.00	$ 8.00
Direct labor	23-9	2 hours	$10.00	20.00
Manufacturing overhead	23-10	2 hours	$ 8.00	16.00
Total unit cost				**$44.00**

Hayes Company then determines cost of goods sold by multiplying the units sold by the unit cost. Its budgeted cost of goods sold is $660,000 (15,000 × $44). All data for the income statement come from the individual operating budgets except the following: (1) interest expense is expected to be $100, and (2) income taxes are estimated to be $12,000. Illustration 23-13 shows the budgeted income statement.

Illustration 23-13
Budgeted income statement

HAYES COMPANY	
Budgeted Income Statement	
For the Year Ending December 31, 2014	
Sales revenue (Illustration 23-3)	$900,000
Cost of goods sold (15,000 × $44)	660,000
Gross profit	240,000
Selling and administrative expenses (Illustration 23-11)	180,000
Income from operations	60,000
Interest expense	100
Income before income taxes	59,900
Income tax expense	12,000
Net income	$ 47,900

> **DO IT!**

Budgeted Income Statement

Soriano Company is preparing its budgeted income statement for 2014. Relevant data pertaining to its sales, production, and direct materials budgets can be found in the **DO IT!** exercise on page 1085.

In addition, Soriano budgets 0.5 hours of direct labor per unit, labor costs at $15 per hour, and manufacturing overhead at $25 per direct labor hour. Its budgeted selling and administrative expenses for 2014 are $12,000,000.

(a) Calculate the budgeted total unit cost. (b) Prepare the budgeted income statement for 2014.

Solution

(a)

Cost Element	Quantity	Unit Cost	Total
Direct materials	3.0 pounds	$ 5	$ 15.00
Direct labor	0.5 hours	$15	7.50
Manufacturing overhead	0.5 hours	$25	12.50
Total unit cost			**$35.00**

(b)

SORIANO COMPANY
Budgeted Income Statement
For the Year Ending December 31, 2014

Sales revenue (1,200,000 units from sales budget, page 1085)	$61,500,000
Cost of goods sold (1,200,000 × $35.00/unit)	42,000,000
Gross profit	19,500,000
Selling and administrative expenses	12,000,000
Net income	$ 7,500,000

Related exercise material: **BE23-8, E23-9, E23-11, and DO IT! 23-3.**

 ✔ **The Navigator**

Preparing the Financial Budgets

As shown in Illustration 23-2 (page 1080), the financial budgets consist of the capital expenditure budget, the cash budget, and the budgeted balance sheet. We will discuss the capital expenditure budget in Chapter 26. The other budgets are explained in the following sections.

Cash Budget

The **cash budget** shows anticipated cash flows. Because cash is so vital, this budget is often considered to be the most important financial budget.

The cash budget contains three sections (cash receipts, cash disbursements, and financing) and the beginning and ending cash balances, as shown in Illustration 23-14.

Illustration 23-14
Basic form of a cash budget

ANY COMPANY
Cash Budget

Beginning cash balance	$X,XXX
Add: Cash receipts (itemized)	X,XXX
Total available cash	X,XXX
Less: Cash disbursements (itemized)	X,XXX
Excess (deficiency) of available cash over cash disbursements	X,XXX
Financing	X,XXX
Ending cash balance	$X,XXX

The **cash receipts section** includes expected receipts from the company's principal source(s) of revenue. These are usually cash sales and collections from customers on credit sales. This section also shows anticipated receipts of interest and dividends, and proceeds from planned sales of investments, plant assets, and the company's capital stock.

The **cash disbursements section** shows expected cash payments. Such payments include direct materials, direct labor, manufacturing overhead, and selling and administrative expenses. This section also includes projected payments for income taxes, dividends, investments, and plant assets.

The **financing section** shows expected borrowings and the repayment of the borrowed funds plus interest. Companies need this section when there is a cash deficiency or when the cash balance is below management's minimum required balance.

Data in the cash budget are prepared in sequence. The ending cash balance of one period becomes the beginning cash balance for the next period. Companies obtain data for preparing the cash budget from other budgets and from information provided by management. In practice, cash budgets are often prepared for the year on a monthly basis.

To minimize detail, we will assume that Hayes Company prepares an annual cash budget by quarters. Its cash budget is based on the following assumptions.

1. The January 1, 2014, cash balance is expected to be $38,000. Hayes wishes to maintain a balance of at least $15,000.

2. Sales (Illustration 23-3, page 1082): 60% are collected in the quarter sold and 40% are collected in the following quarter. Accounts receivable of $60,000 at December 31, 2013, are expected to be collected in full in the first quarter of 2014.

3. Short-term investments are expected to be sold for $2,000 cash in the first quarter.

4. Direct materials (Illustration 23-7, page 1084): 50% are paid in the quarter purchased and 50% are paid in the following quarter. Accounts payable of $10,600 at December 31, 2013, are expected to be paid in full in the first quarter of 2014.

5. Direct labor (Illustration 23-9, page 1087): 100% is paid in the quarter incurred.

6. Manufacturing overhead (Illustration 23-10, page 1088) and selling and administrative expenses (Illustration 23-11, page 1088): All items except depreciation are paid in the quarter incurred.

7. Management plans to purchase a truck in the second quarter for $10,000 cash.

8. Hayes makes equal quarterly payments of its estimated annual income taxes.

9. Loans are repaid in the earliest quarter in which there is sufficient cash (that is, when the cash on hand exceeds the $15,000 minimum required balance).

In preparing the cash budget, it is useful to prepare schedules for collections from customers (assumption No. 2) and cash payments for direct materials (assumption No. 4). These schedules are shown in Illustrations 23-15 and 23-16 (page 1092).

Illustration 23-15
Collections from customers

HAYES COMPANY
Schedule of Expected Collections from Customers

| | | Collections by Quarter | | | |
	Sales[a]	1	2	3	4
Accounts receivable, 12/31/13		$ 60,000			
First quarter	$180,000	108,000[b]	$ 72,000[c]		
Second quarter	210,000		126,000	$ 84,000	
Third quarter	240,000			144,000	$ 96,000
Fourth quarter	270,000				162,000
Total collections		$168,000	$198,000	$228,000	$258,000

[a]Per Illustration 23-3; [b]$180,000 × .60; [c]$180,000 × .40

Illustration 23-16
Payments for direct materials

		Payments by Quarter			
	Purchases[a]	1	2	3	4
Accounts payable, 12/31/13		$10,600			
First quarter	$25,200	12,600[b]	$12,600[c]		
Second quarter	29,200		14,600	$14,600	
Third quarter	33,200			16,600	$16,600
Fourth quarter	37,200				18,600
Total payments		$23,200	$27,200	$31,200	$35,200

HAYES COMPANY
Schedule of Expected Payments for Direct Materials

[a]Per Illustration 23-7; [b]$25,200 × .50; [c]$25,200 × .50

Illustration 23-17 shows the cash budget for Hayes Company. The budget indicates that Hayes will need $3,000 of financing in the second quarter to maintain a minimum cash balance of $15,000. Since there is an excess of available cash over disbursements of $22,500 at the end of the third quarter, the borrowing, plus $100 interest, is repaid in this quarter.

Illustration 23-17
Cash budget

Hayes Company Cash Budget.xls

	A	B	C	D	E	F	G	H	I	J
1			**HAYES COMPANY**							
2			**Cash Budget**							
3			**For the Year Ending December 31, 2014**							
4					Quarter					
5		Assumption	1		2		3		4	
6	Beginning cash balance	1	$ 38,000		$ 25,500		$ 15,000		$ 19,400	
7	**Add: Receipts**									
8	Collections from customers	2	168,000		198,000		228,000		258,000	
9	Sale of securities	3	2,000		0		0		0	
10	Total receipts		170,000		198,000		228,000		258,000	
11	Total available cash		208,000		223,500		243,000		277,400	
12	**Less: Disbursements**									
13	Direct materials	4	23,200		27,200		31,200		35,200	
14	Direct labor	5	62,000		72,000		82,000		92,000	
15	Manufacturing overhead	6	53,300	a	56,300		59,300		62,300	
16	Selling and administrative expenses	6	41,000	b	43,000		45,000		47,000	
17	Purchase of truck	7	0		10,000		0		0	
18	Income tax expense	8	3,000		3,000		3,000		3,000	
19	Total disbursements		182,500		211,500		220,500		239,500	
20	Excess (deficiency) of available cash over cash disbursements		25,500		12,000		22,500		37,900	
21	**Financing**									
22	Add: Borrowings		0		**3,000**		0		0	
23	Less: Repayments including interest	9	0		0		**3,100**		0	
24	Ending cash balance		$ 25,500		$ 15,000		$ 19,400		$ 37,900	
25										
26	a$57,100 − $3,800 depreciation									
27	b$42,000 − $1,000 depreciation									

A cash budget contributes to more effective cash management. It shows managers when additional financing is necessary well before the actual need arises. And, it indicates when excess cash is available for investments or other purposes.

SERVICE COMPANY INSIGHT

Without a Budget, Can the Games Begin?

Behind the grandeur of the Olympic Games lies a huge financial challenge—how to keep budgeted costs in line with revenues. For example, the 2006 Winter Olympics in Turin, Italy, narrowly avoided going into bankruptcy before the Games even started. In order for the event to remain solvent, organizers cancelled glitzy celebrations and shifted promotional responsibilities to an Italian state-run agency. Despite these efforts, after the Games were over, the Italian government created a lottery game to cover its financial losses.

As another example, organizers of the 2002 Winter Olympics in Salt Lake City cut budgeted costs by $200 million shortly before the events began. According to the chief operating and financial officer, the organizers went through every line item in the budget, sorting each one into "must have" versus "nice to have." As a result, the Salt Lake City Games produced a surplus of $100 million.

Source: Gabriel Kahn and Roger Thurow, "In Turin, Paying for Games Went Down to the Wire," *Wall Street Journal* (February 10, 2006).

? Why does it matter whether the Olympic Games exceed their budget? (See page 1120.)

Marianna Day Massey/Zuma Press/NewsCom

Budgeted Balance Sheet

The **budgeted balance sheet** is a projection of financial position at the end of the budget period. This budget is developed from the budgeted balance sheet for the preceding year and the budgets for the current year. Pertinent data from the budgeted balance sheet at December 31, 2013, are as follows.

Buildings and equipment	$182,000	Common stock	$225,000
Accumulated depreciation	$ 28,800	Retained earnings	$ 46,480

Illustration 23-18 shows Hayes Company's budgeted balance sheet at December 31, 2014.

Illustration 23-18
Budgeted balance sheet

HAYES COMPANY		
Budgeted Balance Sheet		
December 31, 2014		
Assets		
Cash		$ 37,900
Accounts receivable		108,000
Finished goods inventory		44,000
Raw materials inventory		4,080
Buildings and equipment	$192,000	
Less: Accumulated depreciation	48,000	144,000
Total assets		$337,980

Illustration 23-18
(*continued*)

Liabilities and Stockholders' Equity	
Accounts payable	$ 18,600
Common stock	225,000
Retained earnings	94,380
Total liabilities and stockholders' equity	$337,980

The computations and sources of the amounts are explained below.

Cash: Ending cash balance $37,900, shown in the cash budget (Illustration 23-17, page 1092).

Accounts receivable: 40% of fourth-quarter sales $270,000, shown in the schedule of expected collections from customers (Illustration 23-15, page 1091).

Finished goods inventory: Desired ending inventory 1,000 units, shown in the production budget (Illustration 23-5, page 1083) times the total unit cost $44 (shown in Illustration 23-12, page 1089).

Raw materials inventory: Desired ending inventory 1,020 pounds, times the cost per pound $4, shown in the direct materials budget (Illustration 23-7, page 1084).

Buildings and equipment: December 31, 2013, balance $182,000, plus purchase of truck for $10,000 (Illustration 23-17, page 1092).

Accumulated depreciation: December 31, 2013, balance $28,800, plus $15,200 depreciation shown in manufacturing overhead budget (Illustration 23-10, page 1088) and $4,000 depreciation shown in selling and administrative expense budget (Illustration 23-11, page 1088).

Accounts payable: 50% of fourth-quarter purchases $37,200, shown in schedule of expected payments for direct materials (Illustration 23-16, page 1092).

Common stock: Unchanged from the beginning of the year.

Retained earnings: December 31, 2013, balance $46,480, plus net income $47,900, shown in budgeted income statement (Illustration 23-13, page 1089).

After budget data are entered into the computer, Hayes prepares the various budgets (sales, cash, etc.), as well as the budgeted financial statements. Using spreadsheets, management can also perform "what if" (sensitivity) analyses based on different hypothetical assumptions. For example, suppose that sales managers project that sales will be 10% higher in the coming quarter. What impact does this change have on the rest of the budgeting process and the financing needs of the business? The impact of the various assumptions on the budget is quickly determined by the spreadsheet. Armed with these analyses, managers make more informed decisions about the impact of various projects. They also anticipate future problems and business opportunities. As seen in this chapter, budgeting is an excellent use of electronic spreadsheets.

> **DO IT!**

Cash Budget

Martian Company management wants to maintain a minimum monthly cash balance of $15,000. At the beginning of March, the cash balance is $16,500, expected cash receipts for March are $210,000, and cash disbursements are expected to be $220,000. How much cash, if any, must be borrowed to maintain the desired minimum monthly balance?

Solution

Action Plan

✔ Write down the basic form of the cash budget, starting with the beginning cash balance, adding cash receipts for the period, deducting cash disbursements, and identifying the needed financing to achieve the desired minimum ending cash balance.

✔ Insert the data given into the outlined form of the cash budget.

MARTIAN COMPANY
Cash Budget
For the Month Ending March 31, 2014

Beginning cash balance	$ 16,500
Add: Cash receipts for March	210,000
Total available cash	226,500
Less: Cash disbursements for March	220,000
Excess of available cash over cash disbursements	6,500
Financing	8,500
Ending cash balance	$ 15,000

To maintain the desired minimum cash balance of $15,000, Martian Company must borrow $8,500 of cash.

Related exercise material: **BE23-9, E23-11, E23-12, E23-13, and DO IT! 23-4.**

 The Navigator

Budgeting in Nonmanufacturing Companies

Budgeting is not limited to manufacturers. Budgets are also used by merchandisers, service companies, and not-for-profit organizations.

LEARNING OBJECTIVE 6

Indicate the applicability of budgeting in nonmanufacturing companies.

Merchandisers

As in manufacturing operations, the sales budget for a merchandiser is both the starting point and the key factor in the development of the master budget. The major differences between the master budgets of a merchandiser and a manufacturer are these:

1. A merchandiser **uses a merchandise purchases budget instead of a production budget**.

2. A merchandiser **does not use the manufacturing budgets (direct materials, direct labor, and manufacturing overhead)**.

The **merchandise purchases budget** shows the estimated cost of goods to be purchased to meet expected sales. The formula for determining budgeted merchandise purchases is:

Budgeted Cost of Goods Sold	+	Desired Ending Merchandise Inventory	−	Beginning Merchandise Inventory	=	Required Merchandise Purchases

Illustration 23-19
Merchandise purchases formula

To illustrate, assume that the budget committee of Lima Company is preparing the merchandise purchases budget for July 2014. It estimates that budgeted sales will be $300,000 in July and $320,000 in August. Cost of goods sold is expected to be 70% of sales—that is, $210,000 in July (.70 × $300,000) and $224,000 in August (.70 × $320,000). The company's desired ending inventory is 30% of the following month's cost of goods sold. Required merchandise purchases for July are $214,200, computed as follows.

Illustration 23-20
Merchandise purchases budget

LIMA COMPANY Merchandise Purchases Budget For the Month Ending July 31, 2014	
Budgeted cost of goods sold ($300,000 × 70%)	$ 210,000
Add: Desired ending merchandise inventory ($224,000 × 30%)	67,200
Total	277,200
Less: Beginning merchandise inventory ($210,000 × 30%)	63,000
Required merchandise purchases for July	**$214,200**

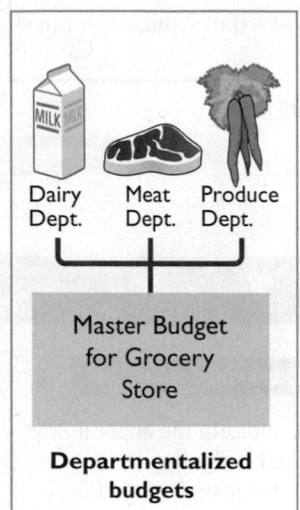

Departmentalized budgets

When a merchandiser is departmentalized, it prepares separate budgets for each department. For example, a grocery store prepares sales budgets and purchases budgets for each of its major departments, such as meats, dairy, and produce. The store then combines these budgets into a master budget for the store. When a retailer has branch stores, it prepares separate master budgets for each store. Then, it incorporates these budgets into master budgets for the company as a whole.

Service Companies

In a service company, such as a public accounting firm, a law office, or a medical practice, the critical factor in budgeting is **coordinating professional staff needs with anticipated services**. If a firm is overstaffed, several problems may result: Labor costs are disproportionately high. Profits are lower because of the additional salaries. Staff turnover sometimes increases because of lack of challenging work. In contrast, if a service company is understaffed, it may lose revenue because existing and prospective client needs for service cannot be met. Also, professional staff may seek other jobs because of excessive workloads.

Service companies can obtain budget data for service revenue from **expected output** or **expected input**. When output is used, it is necessary to determine the expected billings of clients for services performed. In a public accounting firm, for example, output is the sum of its billings in auditing, tax, and consulting services. When input data are used, each professional staff member projects his or her billable time. The firm then applies billing rates to billable time to produce expected service revenue.

Not-for-Profit Organizations

Budgeting is just as important for not-for-profit organizations as for profit-oriented businesses. The budget process, however, is different. In most cases, not-for-profit entities budget **on the basis of cash flows (expenditures and receipts), rather than on a revenue and expense basis**. Further, the starting point in the process is usually expenditures, not receipts. For the not-for-profit entity, management's task generally is to find the receipts needed to support the planned expenditures. The activity index is also likely to be significantly different. For example, in a not-for-profit entity, such as a university, budgeted faculty positions may be based on full-time equivalent students or credit hours expected to be taught in a department.

For some governmental units, voters approve the budget. In other cases, such as state governments and the federal government, legislative approval is required. After the budget is adopted, it must be followed. Overspending is often illegal. In governmental budgets, authorizations tend to be on a line-by-line basis. That is, the budget for a municipality may have a specified authorization for police and fire protection, garbage collection, street paving, and so on. The line-item authorization of governmental budgets significantly limits the amount of discretion management can exercise. The city manager often cannot use savings from one line item, such as street paving, to cover increased spending in another line item, such as snow removal.

SERVICE COMPANY INSIGHT

Budget Shortfalls as Far as the Eye Can See

All organizations need to stick to budgets. The Museum of Contemporary Art in Los Angeles learned this the hard way. Over a 10-year period, its endowment shrunk from $50 million to $6 million as its newly hired director strove to build the museum's reputation through spending. The director consistently ran budget deficits, which eventually threatened the museum's survival.

The most recent recession has created budgeting challenges for nearly all governmental agencies. Tax revenues dropped rapidly as earnings declined and unemployment skyrocketed. At the same time, sources of debt financing dried up. To meet a projected shortfall of nearly $50 billion, California proposed to cut the school year by five days, give state workers two unpaid days off per month, and raise the state's sales tax percentage. Even Princeton University, with the largest endowment per student of any U.S. university ($2 million per student), experienced a 25% drop in the value of its endowment when the financial markets plunged. Because the endowment supports 45% of the university's $1.25 billion budget, when the endowment fell the university had to make cuts. Many raises were capped at $2,000, administrative budgets were cut by 5%, and major construction projects were put on hold.

Source: Edward Wyatt and Jori Finkel, "Soaring in Art, Museum Trips Over Finances," *Wall Street Journal Online* (December 4, 2008); and Stu Woo, "California's Plans to Close Gap Become More Drastic," *Wall Street Journal Online* (January 8, 2009); and John Hechinger, "Princeton Cuts Budget as Endowment Slides," *Wall Street Journal Online* (January 9, 2009).

? Why would a university's budgeted scholarships probably fall when the stock market suffers a serious drop? (See page 1120.)

> Comprehensive DO IT! 1

Barrett Company has completed all operating budgets other than the income statement for 2014. Selected data from these budgets follow.

Sales revenue: $300,000
Purchases of raw materials: $145,000
Ending inventory of raw materials: $15,000
Direct labor: $40,000
Manufacturing overhead: $73,000, including $3,000 of depreciation expense
Selling and administrative expenses: $36,000 including depreciation expense of $1,000
Interest expense: $1,000
Principal payment on note: $2,000
Dividends declared: $2,000
Income tax rate: 30%

Other information:

Assume that the number of units produced equals the number sold.

Year-end accounts receivable: 4% of 2014 sales.

Year-end accounts payable: 50% of ending inventory of raw materials.

Interest, direct labor, manufacturing overhead, and selling and administrative expenses other than depreciation are paid as incurred.

Dividends declared and income taxes for 2014 will not be paid until 2015.

BARRETT COMPANY		
Balance Sheet		
December 31, 2013		

Assets

Cash		$20,000
Raw materials inventory		10,000
Equipment	$40,000	
Less: Accumulated depreciation	4,000	36,000
Total assets		$66,000

Liabilities and Stockholders' Equity

Accounts payable		$ 5,000
Notes payable		22,000
Total liabilities		$27,000
Common stock	25,000	
Retained earnings	14,000	39,000
Total liabilities and stockholders' equity		$66,000

Instructions

(a) Calculate budgeted cost of goods sold.

(b) Prepare a budgeted income statement for the year ending December 31, 2014.

(c) Prepare a budgeted balance sheet as of December 31, 2014.

Solution to Comprehensive DO IT! 1

Action Plan

✔ Recall that beginning raw materials inventory plus purchases less ending raw materials inventory equals direct materials used.

✔ Prepare the budgeted income statement before the budgeted balance sheet.

✔ Use the standard form of a cash budget to determine cash on the budgeted balance sheet.

✔ Add budgeted depreciation expense to accumulated depreciation at the beginning of the year to determine accumulated depreciation on the budgeted balance sheet.

(a) Beginning raw materials + Purchases − Ending raw materials = Cost of direct materials used ($10,000 + $145,000 − $15,000 = $140,000)

Direct materials used + Direct labor + Manufacturing overhead = Cost of goods sold ($140,000 + $40,000 + $73,000 = $253,000)

(b)

BARRETT COMPANY		
Budgeted Income Statement		
For the Year Ending December 31, 2014		

Sales revenue		$300,000
Cost of goods sold		253,000
Gross profit		47,000
Selling and administrative expenses	$36,000	
Interest expense	1,000	37,000
Income before income tax expense		10,000
Income tax expense (30%)		3,000
Net income		$ 7,000

Action Plan (cont'd)

✔ Add budgeted net income to retained earnings from the beginning of the year and subtract dividends declared to determine retained earnings on the budgeted balance sheet.

✔ Verify that total assets equal total liabilities and stockholders' equity on the budgeted balance sheet.

(c)

BARRETT COMPANY
Budgeted Balance Sheet
December 31, 2014

Assets

Cash$^{(1)}$		$17,500
Accounts receivable (4% × $300,000)		12,000
Raw materials inventory		15,000
Equipment	$40,000	
Less: Accumulated depreciation	8,000	32,000
Total assets		$76,500

Liabilities and Stockholders' Equity

Accounts payable (50% × $15,000)	$ 7,500	
Income taxes payable	3,000	
Dividends payable	2,000	
Note payable	20,000	
Total liabilities		$32,500
Common stock	25,000	
Retained earnings$^{(2)}$	19,000	44,000
Total liabilities and stockholders' equity		$76,500

$^{(1)}$Beginning cash balance		$ 20,000
Add: Collections from customers		
(96% × $300,000 sales)		288,000
Total available cash		308,000
Less: Disbursements		
Direct materials ($5,000 + $145,000 − $7,500)	$142,500	
Direct labor	40,000	
Manufacturing overhead	70,000	
Selling and administrative expenses	35,000	
Total disbursements		287,500
Excess of available cash over cash disbursements		20,500
Financing		
Less: Repayment of principal and interest		3,000
Ending cash balance		$ 17,500

$^{(2)}$Beginning retained earnings + Net income − Dividends declared = Ending retained earnings ($14,000 + $7,000 − $2,000 = $19,000)

 The Navigator

> Comprehensive DO IT! 2

Action Plan

✔ Know the form and content of the sales budget.

✔ Prepare the sales budget first as the basis for the other budgets.

✔ Determine the units that must be produced to meet anticipated sales.

✔ Know how to compute the beginning and ending finished goods units.

Asheville Company is preparing its master budget for 2014. Relevant data pertaining to its sales and production budgets are as follows.

Sales. Sales for the year are expected to total 2,100,000 units. Quarterly sales, as a percentage of total sales, are 15%, 25%, 35%, and 25%, respectively. The sales price is expected to be $70 per unit for the first three quarters and $75 per unit beginning in the fourth quarter. Sales in the first quarter of 2015 are expected to be 10% higher than the budgeted sales volume for the first quarter of 2014.

Production. Management desires to maintain ending finished goods inventories at 20% of the next quarter's budgeted sales volume.

Instructions

Prepare the sales budget and production budget by quarters for 2014.

Solution to Comprehensive DO IT! 2

ASHEVILLE COMPANY
Sales Budget
For the Year Ending December 31, 2014

| | Quarter | | | | |
	1	2	3	4	Year
Expected unit sales	315,000	525,000	735,000	525,000	2,100,000
Unit selling price	× $70	× $70	× $70	× $75	—
Total sales	$22,050,000	$36,750,000	$51,450,000	$39,375,000	$149,625,000

ASHEVILLE COMPANY
Production Budget
For the Year Ending December 31, 2014

| | Quarter | | | | |
	1	2	3	4	Year
Expected unit sales	315,000	525,000	735,000	525,000	
Add: Desired ending finished goods units	105,000	147,000	105,000	69,300[a]	
Total required units	420,000	672,000	840,000	594,300	
Less: Beginning finished goods units	63,000[b]	105,000	147,000	105,000	
Required production units	357,000	567,000	693,000	489,300	2,106,300

[a]Estimated first-quarter 2015 sales volume 315,000 + (315,000 × 10%) = 346,500; 346,500 × 20%
[b]20% of estimated first-quarter 2014 sales units (315,000 × 20%)

 The Navigator

SUMMARY OF LEARNING OBJECTIVES

 The Navigator

1 Indicate the benefits of budgeting. The primary advantages of budgeting are that it (a) requires management to plan ahead, (b) provides definite objectives for evaluating performance, (c) creates an early warning system for potential problems, (d) facilitates coordination of activities, (e) results in greater management awareness, and (f) motivates personnel to meet planned objectives.

2 State the essentials of effective budgeting. The essentials of effective budgeting are (a) sound organizational structure, (b) research and analysis, and (c) acceptance by all levels of management.

3 Identify the budgets that comprise the master budget. The master budget consists of the following budgets: (a) sales, (b) production, (c) direct materials, (d) direct labor, (e) manufacturing overhead, (f) selling and administrative expense, (g) budgeted income statement, (h) capital expenditure budget, (i) cash budget, and (j) budgeted balance sheet.

4 Describe the sources for preparing the budgeted income statement. The budgeted income statement is prepared from (a) the sales budget; (b) the budgets for direct materials, direct labor, and manufacturing overhead; and (c) the selling and administrative expense budget.

5 Explain the principal sections of a cash budget. The cash budget has three sections (receipts, disbursements, and financing) and the beginning and ending cash balances.

6 Indicate the applicability of budgeting in nonmanufacturing companies. Budgeting may be used by merchandisers for development of a merchandise purchases budget. In service companies, budgeting is a critical factor in coordinating staff needs with anticipated services. In not-for-profit organizations, the starting point in budgeting is usually expenditures, not receipts.

GLOSSARY

Budget A formal written statement of management's plans for a specified future time period, expressed in financial terms. (p. 1076).

Budget committee A group responsible for coordinating the preparation of the budget. (p. 1078).

Budgetary slack The amount by which a manager intentionally underestimates budgeted revenues or overestimates budgeted expenses in order to make it easier to achieve budgetary goals. (p. 1079).

Budgeted balance sheet A projection of financial position at the end of the budget period. (p. 1093).

Budgeted income statement An estimate of the expected profitability of operations for the budget period. (p. 1089).

Cash budget A projection of anticipated cash flows. (p. 1090).

Direct labor budget A projection of the quantity and cost of direct labor necessary to meet production requirements. (p. 1086).

Direct materials budget An estimate of the quantity and cost of direct materials to be purchased. (p. 1084).

Financial budgets Individual budgets that focus primarily on the cash resources needed to fund expected operations and planned capital expenditures. (p. 1079).

Long-range planning A formalized process of identifying long-term goals, selecting strategies to achieve those goals, and developing policies and plans to implement the strategies. (p. 1079).

Manufacturing overhead budget An estimate of expected manufacturing overhead costs for the budget period. (p. 1087).

Master budget A set of interrelated budgets that constitutes a plan of action for a specific time period. (p. 1079).

Merchandise purchases budget The estimated cost of goods to be purchased by a merchandiser to meet expected sales. (p. 1095).

Operating budgets Individual budgets that result in a budgeted income statement. (p. 1079).

Participative budgeting A budgetary approach that starts with input from lower-level managers and works upward so that managers at all levels participate. (p. 1078).

Production budget A projection of the units that must be produced to meet anticipated sales. (p. 1082).

Sales budget An estimate of expected sales revenue for the budget period. (p. 1081).

Sales forecast The projection of potential sales for the industry and the company's expected share of such sales. (p. 1077).

Selling and administrative expense budget A projection of anticipated selling and administrative expenses for the budget period. (p. 1087).

 Self-Test, Brief Exercises, Exercises, Problem Set A, and many more resources are available for practice in *WileyPLUS*.

SELF-TEST QUESTIONS

Answers are on page 1120.

(LO 1) **1.** Which of the following is **not** a benefit of budgeting?
  (a) Management can plan ahead.
  (b) An early warning system is provided for potential problems.
  (c) It enables disciplinary action to be taken at every level of responsibility.
  (d) The coordination of activities is facilitated.

(LO 1) **2.** A budget:
  (a) is the responsibility of management accountants.
  (b) is the primary method of communicating agreed-upon objectives throughout an organization.
  (c) ignores past performance because it represents management's plans for a future time period.
  (d) may promote efficiency but has no role in evaluating performance.

(LO 2) **3.** The essentials of effective budgeting do **not** include:
  (a) top-down budgeting.
  (b) management acceptance.
  (c) research and analysis.
  (d) sound organizational structure.

(LO 2) **4.** Compared to budgeting, long-range planning generally has the:
  (a) same amount of detail.
  (b) longer time period.
  (c) same emphasis.
  (d) same time period.

5. A sales budget is: (LO 3)
  (a) derived from the production budget.
  (b) management's best estimate of sales revenue for the year.
  (c) not the starting point for the master budget.
  (d) prepared only for credit sales.

6. The formula for the production budget is budgeted (LO 3) sales in units plus:
  (a) desired ending merchandise inventory less beginning merchandise inventory.
  (b) beginning finished goods units less desired ending finished goods units.
  (c) desired ending direct materials units less beginning direct materials units.
  (d) desired ending finished goods units less beginning finished goods units.

7. Direct materials inventories are kept in pounds in Byrd (LO 3) Company, and the total pounds of direct materials needed for production is 9,500. If the beginning inventory is 1,000 pounds and the desired ending inventory is 2,200 pounds, the total pounds to be purchased is:
  (a) 9,400.   (c) 9,700.
  (b) 9,500.   (d) 10,700.

(LO 3) 8. The formula for computing the direct labor budget is to multiply the direct labor cost per hour by the:
   (a) total required direct labor hours.
   (b) physical units to be produced.
   (c) equivalent units to be produced.
   (d) No correct answer is given.

(LO 4) 9. Each of the following budgets is used in preparing the budgeted income statement **except** the:
   (a) sales budget.
   (b) selling and administrative budget.
   (c) capital expenditure budget.
   (d) direct labor budget.

(LO 4) 10. The budgeted income statement is:
   (a) the end-product of the operating budgets.
   (b) the end-product of the financial budgets.
   (c) the starting point of the master budget.
   (d) dependent on cash receipts and cash disbursements.

(LO 5) 11. The budgeted balance sheet is:
   (a) developed from the budgeted balance sheet for the preceding year and the budgets for the current year.
   (b) the last operating budget prepared.
   (c) used to prepare the cash budget.
   (d) All of the above.

(LO 5) 12. The format of a cash budget is:
   (a) Beginning cash balance + Cash receipts + Cash from financing − Cash disbursements = Ending cash balance.
   (b) Beginning cash balance + Cash receipts − Cash disbursements +/− Financing = Ending cash balance.

   (c) Beginning cash balance + Net income − Cash dividends = Ending cash balance.
   (d) Beginning cash balance + Cash revenues − Cash expenses = Ending cash balance.

(LO 5) 13. Expected direct materials purchases in Read Company are $70,000 in the first quarter and $90,000 in the second quarter. Forty percent (40%) of the purchases are paid in cash as incurred, and the balance is paid in the following quarter. The budgeted cash payments for purchases in the second quarter are:
   (a) $96,000.   (c) $78,000.
   (b) $90,000.   (d) $72,000.

(LO 6) 14. The budget for a merchandiser differs from a budget for a manufacturer because:
   (a) a merchandise purchases budget replaces the production budget.
   (b) the manufacturing budgets are not applicable.
   (c) None of the above.
   (d) Both (a) and (b) above.

(LO 6) 15. In most cases, not-for-profit entities:
   (a) prepare budgets using the same steps as those used by profit-oriented businesses.
   (b) know budgeted cash receipts at the beginning of a time period, so they budget only for expenditures.
   (c) begin the budgeting process by budgeting expenditures rather than receipts.
   (d) can ignore budgets because they are not expected to generate net income.

Go to the book's companion website, www.wiley.com/college/weygandt, for additional Self-Test Questions.

The Navigator

QUESTIONS

1. (a) What is a budget?
   (b) How does a budget contribute to good management?

2. Kate Cey and Joe Coulter are discussing the benefits of budgeting. They ask you to identify the primary advantages of budgeting. Comply with their request.

3. Jane Gilligan asks your help in understanding the essentials of effective budgeting. Identify the essentials for Jane.

4. (a) "Accounting plays a relatively unimportant role in budgeting." Do you agree? Explain.
   (b) What responsibilities does management have in budgeting?

5. What criteria are helpful in determining the length of the budget period? What is the most common budget period?

6. Lori Wilkins maintains that the only difference between budgeting and long-range planning is time. Do you agree? Why or why not?

7. What is participative budgeting? What are its potential benefits? What are its potential disadvantages?

8. What is budgetary slack? What incentive do managers have to create budgetary slack?

9. Distinguish between a master budget and a sales forecast.

10. What budget is the starting point in preparing the master budget? What may result if this budget is inaccurate?

11. "The production budget shows both unit production data and unit cost data." Is this true? Explain.

12. Alou Company has 20,000 beginning finished goods units. Budgeted sales units are 160,000. If management desires 15,000 ending finished goods units, what are the required units of production?

13. In preparing the direct materials budget for Quan Company, management concludes that required purchases are 64,000 units. If 52,000 direct materials units are required in production and there are 9,000

units of beginning direct materials, what is the desired units of ending direct materials?

14. The production budget of Justus Company calls for 80,000 units to be produced. If it takes 45 minutes to make one unit and the direct labor rate is $16 per hour, what is the total budgeted direct labor cost?

15. Ortiz Company's manufacturing overhead budget shows total variable costs of $198,000 and total fixed costs of $162,000. Total production in units is expected to be 150,000. It takes 20 minutes to make one unit, and the direct labor rate is $15 per hour. Express the manufacturing overhead rate as (a) a percentage of direct labor cost, and (b) an amount per direct labor hour.

16. Everly Company's variable selling and administrative expenses are 12% of net sales. Fixed expenses are $50,000 per quarter. The sales budget shows expected sales of $200,000 and $240,000 in the first and second quarters, respectively. What are the total budgeted selling and administrative expenses for each quarter?

17. For Goody Company, the budgeted cost for one unit of product is direct materials $10, direct labor $20, and manufacturing overhead 80% of direct labor cost. If 25,000 units are expected to be sold at $65 each, what is the budgeted gross profit?

18. Indicate the supporting schedules used in preparing a budgeted income statement through gross profit for a manufacturer.

19. Identify the three sections of a cash budget. What balances are also shown in this budget?

20. Noterman Company has credit sales of $600,000 in January. Past experience suggests that 40% is collected in the month of sale, 50% in the month following the sale, and 10% in the second month following the sale. Compute the cash collections from January sales in January, February, and March.

21. What is the formula for determining required merchandise purchases for a merchandiser?

22. How may expected revenues in a service company be computed?

BRIEF EXERCISES

BE23-1 Chicksaw Company uses the following budgets: Balance Sheet, Capital Expenditure, Cash, Direct Labor, Direct Materials, Income Statement, Manufacturing Overhead, Production, Sales, and Selling and Administrative. Prepare a diagram of the interrelationships of the budgets in the master budget. Indicate whether each budget is an operating or a financial budget.

Prepare a diagram of a master budget.
(LO 3)

BE23-2 Palermo Company estimates that unit sales will be 10,000 in quarter 1; 12,000 in quarter 2; 15,000 in quarter 3; and 18,000 in quarter 4. Using a sales price of $70 per unit, prepare the sales budget by quarters for the year ending December 31, 2014.

Prepare a sales budget.
(LO 3)

BE23-3 Sales budget data for Palermo Company are given in BE23-2. Management desires to have an ending finished goods inventory equal to 25% of the next quarter's expected unit sales. Prepare a production budget by quarters for the first 6 months of 2014.

Prepare a production budget for 2 quarters.
(LO 3)

BE23-4 Perine Company has 2,000 pounds of raw materials in its December 31, 2013, ending inventory. Required production for January and February of 2014 are 4,000 and 5,000 units, respectively. Two pounds of raw materials are needed for each unit, and the estimated cost per pound is $6. Management desires an ending inventory equal to 25% of next month's materials requirements. Prepare the direct materials budget for January.

Prepare a direct materials budget for 1 month.
(LO 3)

BE23-5 For Mize Company, units to be produced are 5,000 in quarter 1 and 6,000 in quarter 2. It takes 1.6 hours to make a finished unit, and the expected hourly wage rate is $15 per hour. Prepare a direct labor budget by quarters for the 6 months ending June 30, 2014.

Prepare a direct labor budget for 2 quarters.
(LO 3)

BE23-6 For Roche Inc., variable manufacturing overhead costs are expected to be $20,000 in the first quarter of 2014, with $5,000 increments in each of the remaining three quarters. Fixed overhead costs are estimated to be $40,000 in each quarter. Prepare the manufacturing overhead budget by quarters and in total for the year.

Prepare a manufacturing overhead budget.
(LO 3)

BE23-7 Noble Company classifies its selling and administrative expense budget into variable and fixed components. Variable expenses are expected to be $22,000 in the first quarter, and $4,000 increments are expected in the remaining quarters of 2014. Fixed expenses are expected to be $40,000 in each quarter. Prepare the selling and administrative expense budget by quarters and in total for 2014.

Prepare a selling and administrative expense budget.
(LO 3)

BE23-8 North Company has completed all of its operating budgets. The sales budget for the year shows 50,000 units and total sales of $2,250,000. The total unit cost of making one unit of sales is $25. Selling and administrative expenses are expected to be $300,000.

Prepare a budgeted income statement for the year.
(LO 4)

Income taxes are estimated to be $210,000. Prepare a budgeted income statement for the year ending December 31, 2014.

Prepare data for a cash budget.
(LO 5)

BE23-9 Bruno Industries expects credit sales for January, February, and March to be $200,000, $260,000, and $300,000, respectively. It is expected that 75% of the sales will be collected in the month of sale, and 25% will be collected in the following month. Compute cash collections from customers for each month.

Determine required merchandise purchases for 1 month.
(LO 6)

BE23-10 Moore Wholesalers is preparing its merchandise purchases budget. Budgeted sales are $400,000 for April and $480,000 for May. Cost of goods sold is expected to be 65% of sales. The company's desired ending inventory is 20% of the following month's cost of goods sold. Compute the required purchases for April.

> ## DO IT! Review

Identify budget terminology.
(LO 2, 3)

DO IT! 23-1 Use this list of terms to complete the sentences that follow.

Long-range plans	Participative budgeting
Sales forecast	Operating budgets
Master budget	Financial budgets

1. _____ establish goals for the company's sales and production personnel.
2. The _____ is a set of interrelated budgets that constitutes a plan of action for a specified time period.
3. _____ reduces the risk of having unrealistic budgets.
4. _____ include the cash budget and the budgeted balance sheet.
5. The budget is formed within the framework of a _____.
6. _____ contain considerably less detail than budgets.

Prepare sales, production, and direct materials budgets.
(LO 3)

DO IT! 23-2 Ash Creek Company is preparing its master budget for 2014. Relevant data pertaining to its sales, production, and direct materials budgets are as follows.

Sales. Sales for the year are expected to total 1,000,000 units. Quarterly sales are 20%, 20%, 30%, and 30%, respectively. The sales price is expected to be $40 per unit for the first three quarters and $45 per unit beginning in the fourth quarter. Sales in the first quarter of 2015 are expected to be 20% higher than the budgeted sales for the first quarter of 2014.

Production. Management desires to maintain the ending finished goods inventories at 25% of the next quarter's budgeted sales volume.

Direct materials. Each unit requires 2 pounds of raw materials at a cost of $12 per pound. Management desires to maintain raw materials inventories at 10% of the next quarter's production requirements. Assume the production requirements for first quarter of 2015 are 450,000 pounds.

Prepare the sales, production, and direct materials budgets by quarters for 2014.

Calculate budgeted total unit cost and prepare budgeted income statement.
(LO 4)

DO IT! 23-3 Ash Creek Company is preparing its budgeted income statement for 2014. Relevant data pertaining to its sales, production, and direct materials budgets can be found in **DO IT!** 23-2.

In addition, Ash Creek budgets 0.3 hours of direct labor per unit, labor costs at $15 per hour, and manufacturing overhead at $20 per direct labor hour. Its budgeted selling and administrative expenses for 2014 are $6,000,000.

(a) Calculate the budgeted total unit cost.
(b) Prepare the budgeted income statement for 2014.

Determine amount of financing needed.
(LO 5)

DO IT! 23-4 Batista Company management wants to maintain a minimum monthly cash balance of $20,000. At the beginning of April, the cash balance is $25,000, expected cash receipts for April are $245,000, and cash disbursements are expected to be $255,000. How much cash, if any, must be borrowed to maintain the desired minimum monthly balance?

EXERCISES

E23-1 ┄┄┄ Adler Company has always done some planning for the future, but the company has never prepared a formal budget. Now that the company is growing larger, it is considering preparing a budget.

Explain the concept of budgeting.
(LO 1, 2, 3)

Instructions
Write a memo to Jim Dixon, the president of Adler Company, in which you define budgeting, identify the budgets that comprise the master budget, identify the primary benefits of budgeting, and discuss the essentials of effective budgeting.

E23-2 Edington Electronics Inc. produces and sells two models of pocket calculators, XQ-103 and XQ-104. The calculators sell for $15 and $25, respectively. Because of the intense competition Edington faces, management budgets sales semiannually. Its projections for the first 2 quarters of 2014 are as follows.

Prepare a sales budget for 2 quarters.
(LO 3)

Product	Unit Sales	
	Quarter 1	**Quarter 2**
XQ-103	20,000	22,000
XQ-104	12,000	15,000

No changes in selling prices are anticipated.

Instructions
Prepare a sales budget for the 2 quarters ending June 30, 2014. List the products and show for each quarter and for the 6 months, units, selling price, and total sales by product and in total.

E23-3 Garza and Neely, CPAs, are preparing their service revenue (sales) budget for the coming year (2014). The practice is divided into three departments: auditing, tax, and consulting. Billable hours for each department, by quarter, are provided below.

Prepare a sales budget for 4 quarters.
(LO 3, 6)

Department	Quarter 1	Quarter 2	Quarter 3	Quarter 4
Auditing	2,300	1,600	2,000	2,400
Tax	3,000	2,200	2,000	2,500
Consulting	1,500	1,500	1,500	1,500

Average hourly billing rates are auditing $80, tax $90, and consulting $100.

Instructions
Prepare the service revenue (sales) budget for 2014 by listing the departments and showing for each quarter and the year in total, billable hours, billable rate, and total revenue.

E23-4 Turney Company produces and sells automobile batteries, the heavy-duty HD-240. The 2014 sales forecast is as follows.

Prepare quarterly production budgets.
(LO 3)

Quarter	HD-240
1	5,000
2	7,000
3	8,000
4	10,000

The January 1, 2014, inventory of HD-240 is 2,000 units. Management desires an ending inventory each quarter equal to 40% of the next quarter's sales. Sales in the first quarter of 2015 are expected to be 25% higher than sales in the same quarter in 2014.

Instructions
Prepare quarterly production budgets for each quarter and in total for 2014.

E23-5 Dallas Industries has adopted the following production budget for the first 4 months of 2014.

Prepare a direct materials purchases budget.
(LO 3)

Month	Units	Month	Units
January	10,000	March	5,000
February	8,000	April	4,000

Each unit requires 2 pounds of raw materials costing $2 per pound. On December 31, 2013, the ending raw materials inventory was 4,000 pounds. Management wants to have a raw materials inventory at the end of the month equal to 20% of next month's production requirements.

Instructions
Prepare a direct materials purchases budget by month for the first quarter.

Prepare production and direct materials budgets by quarters for 6 months.
(LO 3)

E23-6 On January 1, 2014, the Hardin Company budget committee has reached agreement on the following data for the 6 months ending June 30, 2014.

Sales units: First quarter 5,000; second quarter 6,000; third quarter 7,000.

Ending raw materials inventory: 40% of the next quarter's production requirements.

Ending finished goods inventory: 25% of the next quarter's expected sales units.

Third-quarter production: 7,200 units.

The ending raw materials and finished goods inventories at December 31, 2013, follow the same percentage relationships to production and sales that occur in 2014. Three pounds of raw materials are required to make each unit of finished goods. Raw materials purchased are expected to cost $4 per pound.

Instructions
(a) Prepare a production budget by quarters for the 6-month period ended June 30, 2014.
(b) Prepare a direct materials budget by quarters for the 6-month period ended June 30, 2014.

Prepare a direct labor budget.
(LO 3)

E23-7 Rodriguez, Inc., is preparing its direct labor budget for 2014 from the following production budget based on a calendar year.

Quarter	Units	Quarter	Units
1	20,000	3	35,000
2	25,000	4	30,000

Each unit requires 1.5 hours of direct labor.

Instructions
Prepare a direct labor budget for 2014. Wage rates are expected to be $16 for the first 2 quarters and $18 for quarters 3 and 4.

Prepare a manufacturing overhead budget for the year.
(LO 3)

E23-8 Atlanta Company is preparing its manufacturing overhead budget for 2014. Relevant data consist of the following.

Units to be produced (by quarters): 10,000, 12,000, 14,000, 16,000.

Direct labor: time is 1.5 hours per unit.

Variable overhead costs per direct labor hour: indirect materials $0.80; indirect labor $1.20; and maintenance $0.50.

Fixed overhead costs per quarter: supervisory salaries $35,000; depreciation $15,000; and maintenance $12,000.

Instructions
Prepare the manufacturing overhead budget for the year, showing quarterly data.

Prepare a selling and administrative expense budget for 2 quarters.
(LO 3)

E23-9 Duncan Company combines its operating expenses for budget purposes in a selling and administrative expense budget. For the first 6 months of 2014, the following data are available.

1. Sales: 20,000 units quarter 1; 22,000 units quarter 2.
2. Variable costs per dollar of sales: sales commissions 5%, delivery expense 2%, and advertising 4%.
3. Fixed costs per quarter: sales salaries $10,000, office salaries $8,000, depreciation $4,200, insurance $1,500, utilities $800, and repairs expense $500.
4. Unit selling price: $20.

Instructions
Prepare a selling and administrative expense budget by quarters for the first 6 months of 2014.

E23-10 Fuqua Company's sales budget projects unit sales of part 198Z of 10,000 units in January, 12,000 units in February, and 13,000 units in March. Each unit of part 198Z requires 4 pounds of materials, which cost $2 per pound. Fuqua Company desires its ending raw materials inventory to equal 40% of the next month's production requirements, and its ending finished goods inventory to equal 20% of the next month's expected unit sales. These goals were met at December 31, 2013.

Prepare a production and a direct materials budget.
(LO 3)

Instructions
(a) Prepare a production budget for January and February 2014.
(b) Prepare a direct materials budget for January 2014.

E23-11 Dalby Company has accumulated the following budget data for the year 2014.

1. Sales: 30,000 units, unit selling price $85.
2. Cost of one unit of finished goods: direct materials 2 pounds at $5 per pound, direct labor 3 hours at $15 per hour, and manufacturing overhead $5 per direct labor hour.
3. Inventories (raw materials only): beginning, 10,000 pounds; ending, 15,000 pounds.
4. Selling and administrative expenses: $200,000.
5. Income taxes: 30% of income before income taxes.

Prepare a budgeted income statement for the year.
(LO 4)

Instructions
(a) Prepare a schedule showing the computation of cost of goods sold for 2014.
(b) Prepare a budgeted income statement for 2014.

E23-12 Danner Company expects to have a cash balance of $45,000 on January 1, 2014. Relevant monthly budget data for the first 2 months of 2014 are as follows.

Prepare a cash budget for 2 months.
(LO 5)

Collections from customers: January $85,000, February $150,000.

Payments for direct materials: January $50,000, February $75,000.

Direct labor: January $30,000, February $45,000. Wages are paid in the month they are incurred.

Manufacturing overhead: January $21,000, February $25,000. These costs include depreciation of $1,500 per month. All other overhead costs are paid as incurred.

Selling and administrative expenses: January $15,000, February $20,000. These costs are exclusive of depreciation. They are paid as incurred.

Sales of marketable securities in January are expected to realize $12,000 in cash. Danner Company has a line of credit at a local bank that enables it to borrow up to $25,000. The company wants to maintain a minimum monthly cash balance of $20,000.

Instructions
Prepare a cash budget for January and February.

E23-13 Aaron Corporation is projecting a cash balance of $30,000 in its December 31, 2013, balance sheet. Aaron's schedule of expected collections from customers for the first quarter of 2014 shows total collections of $180,000. The schedule of expected payments for direct materials for the first quarter of 2014 shows total payments of $41,000. Other information gathered for the first quarter of 2014 is sale of equipment $3,000; direct labor $70,000, manufacturing overhead $35,000, selling and administrative expenses $45,000; and purchase of securities $14,000. Aaron wants to maintain a balance of at least $25,000 cash at the end of each quarter.

Prepare a cash budget.
(LO 5)

Instructions
Prepare a cash budget for the first quarter.

E23-14 LRF Company's budgeted sales and direct materials purchases are as follows.

Prepare schedules of expected collections and payments.
(LO 5)

	Budgeted Sales	Budgeted D.M. Purchases
January	$200,000	$30,000
February	220,000	36,000
March	270,000	40,000

LRF's sales are 30% cash and 70% credit. Credit sales are collected 10% in the month of sale, 50% in the month following sale, and 36% in the second month following sale; 4% are uncollectible. LRF's purchases are 50% cash and 50% on account. Purchases on account are paid 40% in the month of purchase, and 60% in the month following purchase.

Instructions
(a) Prepare a schedule of expected collections from customers for March.
(b) Prepare a schedule of expected payments for direct materials for March.

Prepare schedules for cash receipts and cash payments, and determine ending balances for balance sheet.

(LO 5, 6)

E23-15 Green Landscaping Inc. is preparing its budget for the first quarter of 2014. The next step in the budgeting process is to prepare a cash receipts schedule and a cash payments schedule. To that end the following information has been collected.

Clients usually pay 60% of their fee in the month that service is performed, 30% the month after, and 10% the second month after receiving service.

Actual service revenue for 2013 and expected service revenues for 2014 are November 2013, $80,000; December 2013, $90,000; January 2014, $100,000; February 2014, $120,000; March 2014, $140,000.

Purchases of landscaping supplies (direct materials) are paid 60% in the month of purchase and 40% the following month. Actual purchases for 2013 and expected purchases for 2014 are December 2013, $14,000; January 2014, $12,000; February 2014, $15,000; March 2014, $18,000.

Instructions

(a) Prepare the following schedules for each month in the first quarter of 2014 and for the quarter in total:

(1) Expected collections from clients.

(2) Expected payments for landscaping supplies.

(b) Determine the following balances at March 31, 2014:

(1) Accounts receivable.

(2) Accounts payable.

Prepare a cash budget for 2 quarters.

(LO 5, 6)

E23-16 Lager Dental Clinic is a medium-sized dental service specializing in family dental care. The clinic is currently preparing the master budget for the first 2 quarters of 2014. All that remains in this process is the cash budget. The following information has been collected from other portions of the master budget and elsewhere.

Beginning cash balance	$ 30,000
Required minimum cash balance	25,000
Payment of income taxes (2nd quarter)	4,000
Professional salaries:	
1st quarter	140,000
2nd quarter	140,000
Interest from investments (2nd quarter)	7,000
Overhead costs:	
1st quarter	75,000
2nd quarter	100,000
Selling and administrative costs, including	
$2,000 depreciation:	
1st quarter	50,000
2nd quarter	70,000
Purchase of equipment (2nd quarter)	50,000
Sale of equipment (1st quarter)	12,000
Collections from clients:	
1st quarter	230,000
2nd quarter	380,000
Interest payments (2nd quarter)	400

Instructions

Prepare a cash budget for each of the first two quarters of 2014.

Prepare a purchases budget and budgeted income statement for a merchandiser.

(LO 6)

E23-17 In May 2014, the budget committee of Grand Stores assembles the following data in preparation of budgeted merchandise purchases for the month of June.

1. Expected sales: June $500,000, July $600,000.

2. Cost of goods sold is expected to be 75% of sales.

3. Desired ending merchandise inventory is 30% of the following (next) month's cost of goods sold.

4. The beginning inventory at June 1 will be the desired amount.

Instructions

(a) Compute the budgeted merchandise purchases for June.

(b) Prepare the budgeted income statement for June through gross profit.

Visit the book's companion website, at **www.wiley.com/college/weygandt**, and choose the Student Companion site to access Exercise Set B and Challenge Exercises.

PROBLEMS: SET A

P23-1A Glendo Farm Supply Company manufactures and sells a pesticide called Snare. The following data are available for preparing budgets for Snare for the first 2 quarters of 2014.

Prepare budgeted income statement and supporting budgets.

(LO 3, 4)

1. Sales: quarter 1, 30,000 bags; quarter 2, 42,000 bags. Selling price is $60 per bag.
2. Direct materials: each bag of Snare requires 4 pounds of Gumm at a cost of $3.80 per pound and 6 pounds of Tarr at $1.50 per pound.
3. Desired inventory levels:

Type of Inventory	January 1	April 1	July 1
Snare (bags)	8,000	15,000	18,000
Gumm (pounds)	9,000	10,000	13,000
Tarr (pounds)	14,000	20,000	25,000

4. Direct labor: direct labor time is 15 minutes per bag at an hourly rate of $16 per hour.
5. Selling and administrative expenses are expected to be 15% of sales plus $175,000 per quarter.
6. Income taxes are expected to be 30% of income from operations.

Your assistant has prepared two budgets: (1) The manufacturing overhead budget shows expected costs to be 150% of direct labor cost. (2) The direct materials budget for Tarr shows the cost of Tarr purchases to be $297,000 in quarter 1 and $439,500 in quarter 2.

Instructions
Prepare the budgeted income statement for the first 6 months and all required operating budgets by quarters. (*Note:* Use variable and fixed in the selling and administrative expense budget.) Do not prepare the manufacturing overhead budget or the direct materials budget for Tarr.

Net income $601,720
Cost per bag $34.20

P23-2A Deleon Inc. is preparing its annual budgets for the year ending December 31, 2014. Accounting assistants furnish the data shown below.

Prepare sales, production, direct materials, direct labor, and income statement budgets.

(LO 3, 4)

	Product JB 50	Product JB 60
Sales budget:		
Anticipated volume in units	400,000	200,000
Unit selling price	$20	$25
Production budget:		
Desired ending finished goods units	30,000	15,000
Beginning finished goods units	25,000	10,000
Direct materials budget:		
Direct materials per unit (pounds)	2	3
Desired ending direct materials pounds	30,000	10,000
Beginning direct materials pounds	40,000	15,000
Cost per pound	$3	$4
Direct labor budget:		
Direct labor time per unit	0.4	0.6
Direct labor rate per hour	$12	$12
Budgeted income statement:		
Total unit cost	$13	$20

An accounting assistant has prepared the detailed manufacturing overhead budget and the selling and administrative expense budget. The latter shows selling expenses of $560,000 for product JB 50 and $360,000 for product JB 60, and administrative expenses of $540,000 for product JB 50 and $340,000 for product JB 60. Income taxes are expected to be 30%.

Instructions

Prepare the following budgets for the year. Show data for each product. Quarterly budgets should not be prepared.

(a) Sales   **(d)** Direct labor
(b) Production   **(e)** Income statement (*Note:* Income taxes are
(c) Direct materials   not allocated to the products.)

P23-3A Marsh Industries had sales in 2013 of $6,400,000 and gross profit of $1,100,000. Management is considering two alternative budget plans to increase its gross profit in 2014.

Plan A would increase the selling price per unit from $8.00 to $8.40. Sales volume would decrease by 10% from its 2013 level. Plan B would decrease the selling price per unit by $0.50. The marketing department expects that the sales volume would increase by 100,000 units.

At the end of 2013, Marsh has 38,000 units of inventory on hand. If Plan A is accepted, the 2014 ending inventory should be equal to 5% of the 2014 sales. If Plan B is accepted, the ending inventory should be equal to 60,000 units. Each unit produced will cost $1.80 in direct labor, $1.30 in direct materials, and $1.20 in variable overhead. The fixed overhead for 2014 should be $1,895,000.

Instructions

(a) Prepare a sales budget for 2014 under each plan.
(b) Prepare a production budget for 2014 under each plan.
(c) Compute the production cost per unit under each plan. Why is the cost per unit different for each of the two plans? (Round to two decimals.)
(d) Which plan should be accepted? (*Hint:* Compute the gross profit under each plan.)

P23-4A Colter Company prepares monthly cash budgets. Relevant data from operating budgets for 2014 are:

	January	February
Sales revenue	$360,000	$400,000
Direct materials purchases	120,000	125,000
Direct labor	90,000	100,000
Manufacturing overhead	70,000	75,000
Selling and administrative expenses	79,000	85,000

All sales are on account. Collections are expected to be 50% in the month of sale, 30% in the first month following the sale, and 20% in the second month following the sale. Sixty percent (60%) of direct materials purchases are paid in cash in the month of purchase, and the balance due is paid in the month following the purchase. All other items above are paid in the month incurred except for selling and administrative expenses that include $1,000 of depreciation per month.

Other data:

1. Credit sales: November 2013, $250,000; December 2013, $320,000.
2. Purchases of direct materials: December 2013, $100,000.
3. Other receipts: January—collection of December 31, 2013, notes receivable $15,000; February—proceeds from sale of securities $6,000.
4. Other disbursements: February—payment of $6,000 cash dividend.

The company's cash balance on January 1, 2014, is expected to be $60,000. The company wants to maintain a minimum cash balance of $50,000.

Instructions

(a) Prepare schedules for (1) expected collections from customers and (2) expected payments for direct materials purchases for January and February.
(b) Prepare a cash budget for January and February in columnar form.

Left margin notes:

(a) Total sales $13,000,000
(b) Required production units:
    JB 50, 405,000
    JB 60, 205,000
(c) Total cost of direct materials purchases $4,840,000
(d) Total direct labor cost $3,420,000
(e) Net income $1,400,000

Prepare sales and production budgets and compute cost per unit under two plans.

(LO 3, 4)

(c) Unit cost: Plan A $6.94
    Plan B $6.36
(d) Gross profit:
    Plan A $1,051,200
    Plan B $1,026,000

Prepare cash budget for 2 months.

(LO 5)

(a) January: collections $326,000 payments $112,000
(b) Ending cash balance:
    January $51,000
    February $50,000

P23-5A Krause Industries' balance sheet at December 31, 2013, is presented below.

Prepare budgeted income statement and balance sheet.
(LO 4, 5)

KRAUSE INDUSTRIES
Balance Sheet
December 31, 2013

Assets

Current assets		
Cash		$ 7,500
Accounts receivable		82,500
Finished goods inventory (1,000 units)		15,000
Total current assets		105,000
Property, plant, and equipment		
Equipment	$40,000	
Less: Accumulated depreciation	10,000	30,000
Total assets		$135,000

Liabilities and Stockholders' Equity

Liabilities		
Notes payable		$ 25,000
Accounts payable		45,000
Total liabilities		70,000
Stockholders' equity		
Common stock	$40,000	
Retained earnings	25,000	
Total stockholders' equity		65,000
Total liabilities and stockholders' equity		$135,000

Additional information accumulated for the budgeting process is as follows.
   Budgeted data for the year 2014 include the following.

	4th Qtr. of 2014	Year 2014 Total
Sales budget (8,000 units at $32)	$76,800	$256,000
Direct materials used	17,000	62,500
Direct labor	12,500	50,900
Manufacturing overhead applied	10,000	48,600
Selling and administrative expenses	18,000	75,000

   To meet sales requirements and to have 3,000 units of finished goods on hand at December 31, 2014, the production budget shows 9,000 required units of output. The total unit cost of production is expected to be $18. Krause Industries uses the first-in, first-out (FIFO) inventory costing method. Selling and administrative expenses include $4,000 for depreciation on equipment. Interest expense is expected to be $3,500 for the year. Income taxes are expected to be 40% of income before income taxes.
   All sales and purchases are on account. It is expected that 60% of quarterly sales are collected in cash within the quarter and the remainder is collected in the following quarter. Direct materials purchased from suppliers are paid 50% in the quarter incurred and the remainder in the following quarter. Purchases in the fourth quarter were the same as the materials used. In 2014, the company expects to purchase additional equipment costing $9,000. It expects to pay $8,000 on notes payable plus all interest due and payable to December 31 (included in interest expense $3,500, above). Accounts payable at December 31, 2014, include amounts due suppliers (see above) plus other accounts payable of $6,500. In 2014, the company expects to declare and pay an $8,000 cash dividend. Unpaid income taxes at December 31 will be $5,000. The company's cash budget shows an expected cash balance of $6,980 at December 31, 2014.

Instructions
Prepare a budgeted income statement for 2014 and a budgeted balance sheet at December 31, 2014. In preparing the income statement, you will need to compute cost of goods

Net income $32,700
Total assets $126,700

manufactured (direct materials + direct labor + manufacturing overhead) and finished goods inventory (December 31, 2014).

Prepare purchases and income statement budgets for a merchandiser.

(LO 6)

P23-6A The budget committee of Litwin Company collects the following data for its San Miguel Store in preparing budgeted income statements for May and June 2014.

1. Sales for May are expected to be $800,000. Sales in June and July are expected to be 5% higher than the preceding month.
2. Cost of goods sold is expected to be 75% of sales.
3. Company policy is to maintain ending merchandise inventory at 15% of the following month's cost of goods sold.
4. Operating expenses are estimated to be:

Sales salaries	$30,000 per month
Advertising	6% of monthly sales
Delivery expense	3% of monthly sales
Sales commissions	5% of monthly sales
Rent expense	$5,000 per month
Depreciation	$800 per month
Utilities	$600 per month
Insurance	$500 per month

(a) Purchases:
  May $604,500
  June $634,725
(b) Net income:
  May $35,770
  June $38,850

5. Income taxes are estimated to be 30% of income from operations.

Instructions
(a) Prepare the merchandise purchases budget for each month in columnar form.
(b) Prepare budgeted income statements for each month in columnar form. Show in the statements the details of cost of goods sold.

PROBLEMS: SET B

Prepare budgeted income statement and supporting budgets.

(LO 3, 4)

P23-1B Mercer Farm Supply Company manufactures and sells a fertilizer called Basic II. The following data are available for preparing budgets for Basic II for the first 2 quarters of 2014.

1. Sales: quarter 1, 40,000 bags; quarter 2, 50,000 bags. Selling price is $63 per bag.
2. Direct materials: each bag of Basic II requires 5 pounds of Crup at a cost of $3.80 per pound and 10 pounds of Dert at $1.50 per pound.
3. Desired inventory levels:

Type of Inventory	January 1	April 1	July 1
Basic II (bags)	10,000	15,000	20,000
Crup (pounds)	9,000	12,000	15,000
Dert (pounds)	15,000	20,000	25,000

4. Direct labor: direct labor time is 15 minutes per bag at an hourly rate of $12 per hour.
5. Selling and administrative expenses are expected to be 10% of sales plus $150,000 per quarter.
6. Income taxes are expected to be 30% of income from operations.

Your assistant has prepared two budgets: (1) The manufacturing overhead budget shows expected costs to be 100% of direct labor cost. (2) The direct materials budget for Dert which shows the cost of Dert to be $682,500 in quarter 1 and $832,500 in quarter 2.

Net income $842,100
Cost per bag $40.00

Prepare sales, production, direct materials, direct labor, and income statement budgets.

(LO 3, 4)

Instructions
Prepare the budgeted income statement for the first 6 months of 2014 and all required supporting budgets by quarters. (*Note:* Use variable and fixed in the selling and administrative expense budget.) Do not prepare the manufacturing overhead budget or the direct materials budget for Dert.

P23-2B Urbina Inc. is preparing its annual budgets for the year ending December 31, 2014. Accounting assistants furnish the following data.

	Product LN 35	Product LN 40
Sales budget:		
Anticipated volume in units	400,000	240,000
Unit selling price	$25	$35
Production budget:		
Desired ending finished goods units	20,000	25,000
Beginning finished goods units	30,000	15,000
Direct materials budget:		
Direct materials per unit (pounds)	2	3
Desired ending direct materials pounds	50,000	10,000
Beginning direct materials pounds	40,000	20,000
Cost per pound	$2	$3
Direct labor budget:		
Direct labor time per unit	0.5	0.75
Direct labor rate per hour	$12	$12
Budgeted income statement:		
Total unit cost	$12	$22

An accounting assistant has prepared the detailed manufacturing overhead budget and the selling and administrative expense budget. The latter shows selling expenses of $750,000 for product LN 35 and $580,000 for product LN 40, and administrative expenses of $420,000 for product LN 35 and $380,000 for product LN 40. Income taxes are expected to be 30%.

Instructions

Prepare the following budgets for the year. Show data for each product. You do not need to prepare quarterly budgets.

(a) Sales
(b) Production
(c) Direct materials
(d) Direct labor
(e) Income statement (*Note:* Income taxes are not allocated to the products.)

(a) Total sales $18,400,000
(b) Required production units: LN 35, 390,000
(c) Total cost of direct materials purchases $3,800,000
(d) Total direct labor cost $4,590,000
(e) Net income $4,333,000

P23-3B Ogleby Industries has sales in 2013 of $5,600,000 (800,000 units) and gross profit of $1,344,000. Management is considering two alternative budget plans to increase its gross profit in 2014.

Plan A would increase the selling price per unit from $7.00 to $7.60. Sales volume would decrease by 5% from its 2013 level. Plan B would decrease the selling price per unit by 5%. The marketing department expects that the sales volume would increase by 150,000 units.

At the end of 2013, Ogleby has 70,000 units on hand. If Plan A is accepted, the 2014 ending inventory should be equal to 90,000 units. If Plan B is accepted, the ending inventory should be equal to 100,000 units. Each unit produced will cost $2.00 in direct materials, $1.50 in direct labor, and $0.50 in variable overhead. The fixed overhead for 2014 should be $980,000.

Prepare sales and production budgets and compute cost per unit under two plans.

(LO 3, 4)

Instructions

(a) Prepare a sales budget for 2014 under (1) Plan A and (2) Plan B.
(b) Prepare a production budget for 2014 under (1) Plan A and (2) Plan B.
(c) Compute the cost per unit under (1) Plan A and (2) Plan B. Explain why the cost per unit is different for each of the two plans. (Round to two decimals.)
(d) Which plan should be accepted? (*Hint:* Compute the gross profit under each plan.)

(c) Unit cost:
   Plan A $5.26
   Plan B $5.00
(d) Gross profit:
   Plan A $1,778,400
   Plan B $1,567,500

P23-4B Derby Company prepares monthly cash budgets. Relevant data from operating budgets for 2014 are:

Prepare cash budget for 2 months.

(LO 5)

	January	February
Sales revenue	$350,000	$400,000
Direct materials purchases	110,000	120,000
Direct labor	85,000	115,000
Manufacturing overhead	60,000	75,000
Selling and administrative expenses	75,000	80,000

All sales are on account. Collections are expected to be 60% in the month of sale, 25% in the first month following the sale, and 15% in the second month following the sale. Thirty percent (30%) of direct materials purchases are paid in cash in the month of purchase, and the balance due is paid in the month following the purchase. All other items above are paid in the month incurred. Depreciation has been excluded from manufacturing overhead and selling and administrative expenses.

Other data:

1. Credit sales: November 2013, $200,000; December 2013, $290,000.
2. Purchases of direct materials: December 2013, $90,000.
3. Other receipts: January—collection of December 31, 2013, interest receivable $3,000; February—proceeds from sale of securities $5,000.
4. Other disbursements: February—payment of $20,000 for land.

The company's cash balance on January 1, 2014, is expected to be $50,000. The company wants to maintain a minimum cash balance of $40,000.

(a) January:
collections $312,500
payments $96,000
(b) Ending cash balance:
January $49,500
February $40,000

Instructions

(a) Prepare schedules for (1) expected collections from customers and (2) expected payments for direct materials purchases.
(b) Prepare a cash budget for January and February in columnar form.

Prepare purchases and income statement budgets for a merchandiser.

(LO 6)

XLS

P23-5B The budget committee of Widner Company collects the following data for its Westwood Store in preparing budgeted income statements for July and August 2014.

1. Expected sales: July $400,000, August $450,000, September $500,000.
2. Cost of goods sold is expected to be 65% of sales.
3. Company policy is to maintain ending merchandise inventory at 15% of the following month's cost of goods sold.
4. Operating expenses are estimated to be:

Sales salaries	$50,000 per month
Advertising	5% of monthly sales
Delivery expense	2% of monthly sales
Sales commissions	4% of monthly sales
Rent expense	$3,000 per month
Depreciation	$700 per month
Utilities	$500 per month
Insurance	$300 per month

5. Income taxes are estimated to be 30% of income from operations.

(a) Purchases: July $264,875
August $297,375
(b) Net income: July $29,050
August $37,450

Instructions

(a) Prepare the merchandise purchases budget for each month in columnar form.
(b) Prepare budgeted income statements for each month in columnar form. Show the details of cost of goods sold in the statements.

PROBLEMS: SET C

Visit the book's companion website, at **www.wiley.com/college/weygandt**, and choose the Student Companion site to access Problem Set C.

WATERWAYS CONTINUING PROBLEM

(This is a continuation of the Waterways Problem from Chapters 19 through 22.)

WCP23 Waterways Corporation is preparing its budget for the coming year, 2014. The first step is to plan for the first quarter of that coming year. The company has gathered information from its managers in preparation of the budgeting process. This problem asks you to prepare the various budgets that comprise the master budget for 2014.

Go to the book's companion website, at **www.wiley.com/college/weygandt**, *to see the completion of this problem.*

Broadening Your Perspective

Management Decision-Making

Decision-Making Problem: Current Designs

BYP23-1 Diane Buswell is preparing the 2013 budget for one of Current Designs' rotomolded kayaks. Extensive meetings with members of the sales department and executive team have resulted in the following unit sales projections for 2013.

Quarter 1	1,000 kayaks
Quarter 2	1,500 kayaks
Quarter 3	750 kayaks
Quarter 4	750 kayaks

Current Designs' policy is to have finished goods ending inventory in a quarter equal to 20% of the next quarter's anticipated sales. Preliminary sales projections for 2014 are 1,100 units for the first quarter and 1,500 units for the second quarter. Ending inventory of finished goods at December 31, 2012, will be 200 rotomolded kayaks.

Production of each kayak requires 54 pounds of polyethylene powder and a finishing kit (rope, seat, hardware, etc.). Company policy is that the ending inventory of polyethylene powder should be 25% of the amount needed for production in the next quarter. Assume that the ending inventory of polyethylene powder on December 31, 2012, is 19,400 pounds. The finishing kits can be assembled as they are needed. As a result, Current Designs does not maintain a significant inventory of the finishing kits.

The polyethylene powder used in these kayaks costs $1.50 per pound, and the finishing kits cost $170 each. Production of a single kayak requires 2 hours of time by more experienced, type I employees and 3 hours of finishing time by type II employees. The type I employees are paid $15 per hour, and the type II employees are paid $12 per hour.

Selling and administrative expenses for this line are expected to be $45 per unit sold plus $7,500 per quarter. Manufacturing overhead is assigned at 150% of labor costs.

Instructions
Prepare the production budget, direct materials budget, direct labor budget, manufacturing overhead budget, and selling and administrative budget for this product line by quarter and in total for 2013.

Decision-Making Across the Organization

BYP23-2 Palmer Corporation operates on a calendar-year basis. It begins the annual budgeting process in late August when the president establishes targets for the total dollar sales and net income before taxes for the next year.

The sales target is given first to the marketing department. The marketing manager formulates a sales budget by product line in both units and dollars. From this budget, sales quotas by product line in units and dollars are established for each of the corporation's sales districts. The marketing manager also estimates the cost of the marketing activities required to support the target sales volume and prepares a tentative marketing expense budget.

The executive vice president uses the sales and profit targets, the sales budget by product line, and the tentative marketing expense budget to determine the dollar amounts that can be devoted to manufacturing and corporate office expense. The executive vice president prepares the budget for corporate expenses. She then forwards to the production department the product-line sales budget in units and the total dollar amount that can be devoted to manufacturing.

The production manager meets with the factory managers to develop a manufacturing plan that will produce the required units when needed within the cost constraints set by the executive vice president. The budgeting process usually comes to a halt at this point because the production department does not consider the financial resources allocated to be adequate.

When this standstill occurs, the vice president of finance, the executive vice president, the marketing manager, and the production manager meet together to determine the final budgets for each of the areas. This normally results in a modest increase in the total amount available for manufacturing costs and cuts in the marketing expense and corporate office expense budgets. The total sales and net income figures proposed by the president are seldom changed. Although the participants are seldom pleased with the compromise, these budgets are final. Each executive then develops a new detailed budget for the operations in his or her area.

None of the areas has achieved its budget in recent years. Sales often run below the target. When budgeted sales are not achieved, each area is expected to cut costs so that the president's profit target can be met. However, the profit target is seldom met because costs are not cut enough. In fact, costs often run above the original budget in all functional areas (marketing, production, and corporate office).

The president is disturbed that Palmer has not been able to meet the sales and profit targets. He hired a consultant with considerable experience with companies in Palmer's industry. The consultant reviewed the budgets for the past 4 years. He concluded that the product line sales budgets were reasonable and that the cost and expense budgets were adequate for the budgeted sales and production levels.

Instructions

With the class divided into groups, answer the following.

(a) Discuss how the budgeting process employed by Palmer Corporation contributes to the failure to achieve the president's sales and profit targets.

(b) Suggest how Palmer Corporation's budgeting process could be revised to correct the problems.

(c) Should the functional areas be expected to cut their costs when sales volume falls below budget? Explain your answer.

(CMA adapted)

Managerial Analysis

BYP23-3 Elliot & Hesse Inc. manufactures ergonomic devices for computer users. Some of its more popular products include glare screens (for computer monitors), keyboard stands with wrist rests, and carousels that allow easy access to discs. Over the past 5 years, it experienced rapid growth, with sales of all products increasing 20% to 50% each year.

Last year, some of the primary manufacturers of computers began introducing new products with some of the ergonomic designs, such as glare screens and wrist rests, already built in. As a result, sales of Elliot & Hesse's accessory devices have declined somewhat. The company believes that the disc carousels will probably continue to show growth, but that the other products will probably continue to decline. When the next year's budget was prepared, increases were built into research and development so that replacement products could be developed or the company could expand into some other product line. Some product lines being considered are general-purpose ergonomic devices including back supports, foot rests, and sloped writing pads.

The most recent results have shown that sales decreased more than was expected for the glare screens. As a result, the company may have a shortage of funds. Top management has therefore asked that all expenses be reduced 10% to compensate for these reduced sales. Summary budget information is as follows.

Direct materials	$240,000
Direct labor	110,000
Insurance	50,000
Depreciation	90,000
Machine repairs	30,000
Sales salaries	50,000
Office salaries	80,000
Factory salaries (indirect labor)	50,000
Total	$700,000

Instructions

Using the information above, answer the following questions.

(a) What are the implications of reducing each of the costs? For example, if the company reduces direct materials costs, it may have to do so by purchasing lower-quality materials. This may affect sales in the long run.

(b) Based on your analysis in (a), what do you think is the best way to obtain the $70,000 in cost savings requested? Be specific. Are there any costs that cannot or should not be reduced? Why?

Real-World Focus

BYP23-4 Network Computing Devices, Inc. was founded in 1988 in Mountain View, California. The company develops software products such as X-terminals, Z-mail, PC X-ware, and related hardware products. The following is a discussion by management in its annual report.

NETWORK COMPUTING DEVICES, INC.
Management Discussion

The Company's operating results have varied significantly, particularly on a quarterly basis, as a result of a number of factors, including general economic conditions affecting industry demand for computer products, the timing and market acceptance of new product introductions by the Company and its competitors, the timing of significant orders from large customers, periodic changes in product pricing and discounting due to competitive factors, and the availability of key components, such as video monitors and electronic subassemblies, some of which require substantial order lead times. The Company's operating results may fluctuate in the future as a result of these and other factors, including the Company's success in developing and introducing new products, its product and customer mix, and the level of competition which it experiences. The Company operates with a small backlog. Sales and operating results, therefore, generally depend on the volume and timing of orders received, which are difficult to forecast. The Company has experienced slowness in orders from some customers during the first quarter of each calendar year due to budgeting cycles common in the computer industry. In addition, sales in Europe typically are adversely affected in the third calendar quarter as many European customers reduce their business activities during the month of August.

  Due to the Company's rapid growth rate and the effect of new product introductions on quarterly revenues, these seasonal trends have not materially impacted the Company's results of operations to date. However, as the Company's product lines mature and its rate of revenue growth declines, these seasonal factors may become more evident. Additionally, the Company's international sales are denominated in U.S. dollars, and an increase or decrease in the value of the U.S. dollar relative to foreign currencies could make the Company's products less or more competitive in those markets.

Instructions
(a) Identify the factors that affect the budgeting process at Network Computing Devices, Inc.
(b) Explain the additional budgeting concerns created by the international operations of the company.

BYP23-5 Information regarding many approaches to budgeting can be found on the Web. The following activity investigates the merits of "zero-based" budgeting, as discussed by Michael LaFaive, Director of Financial Policy of the Mackinac Center for Public Policy.

Address: **www.mackinac.org/article.aspx?ID5=928**, or go to **www.wiley.com/college/weygandt**

Instructions
Read the article at the website and answer the following questions.

(a) How does zero-based budgeting differ from standard budgeting procedures?
(b) What are some potential advantages of zero-based budgeting?
(c) What are some potential disadvantages of zero-based budgeting?
(d) How often do departments in Oklahoma undergo zero-based budgeting?

Critical Thinking

Communication Activity

BYP23-6 In order to better serve their rural patients, Drs. Joe and Rick Parcells (brothers) began giving safety seminars. Especially popular were their "emergency-preparedness" talks given to farmers. Many people asked whether the "kit" of materials the doctors recommended for common farm emergencies was commercially available.

After checking with several suppliers, the doctors realized that no other company offered the supplies they recommended in their seminars, packaged in the way they described. Their wives, Megan and Sue, agreed to make a test package by ordering supplies from various medical supply companies and assembling them into a "kit" that could be sold at the seminars. When these kits proved a runaway success, the sisters-in-law decided to market them. At the advice of their accountant, they organized this venture as a separate company, called Life Protection Products (LPP), with Megan Parcells as CEO and Sue Parcells as Secretary-Treasurer.

LPP soon started receiving requests for the kits from all over the country, as word spread about their availability. Even without advertising, LPP was able to sell its full inventory every month. However, the company was becoming financially strained. Megan and Sue had about $100,000 in savings, and they invested about half that amount initially. They believed that this venture would allow them to make money. However, at the present time, only about $30,000 of the cash remains, and the company is constantly short of cash.

Megan has come to you for advice. She does not understand why the company is having cash flow problems. She and Sue have not even been withdrawing salaries. However, they have rented a local building and have hired two more full-time workers to help them cope with the increasing demand. They do not think they could handle the demand without this additional help.

Megan is also worried that the cash problems mean that the company may not be able to support itself. She has prepared the cash budget shown below. All seminar customers pay for their products in full at the time of purchase. In addition, several large companies have ordered the kits for use by employees who work in remote sites. They have requested credit terms and have been allowed to pay in the month following the sale. These large purchasers amount to about 25% of the sales at the present time. LPP purchases the materials for the kits about 2 months ahead of time. Megan and Sue are considering slowing the growth of the company by simply purchasing less materials, which will mean selling fewer kits.

The workers are paid weekly. Megan and Sue need about $15,000 cash on hand at the beginning of the month to pay for purchases of raw materials. Right now they have been using cash from their savings, but as noted, only $30,000 is left.

Instructions

Write a response to Megan Parcells. Explain why LPP is short of cash. Will this company be able to support itself? Explain your answer. Make any recommendations you deem appropriate.

LIFE PROTECTION PRODUCTS
Cash Budget
For the Quarter Ending June 30, 2014

	April	May	June
Cash balance, beginning	$15,000	$15,000	$15,000
Cash received			
From prior month sales	5,000	7,500	12,500
From current sales	15,000	22,500	37,500
Total cash on hand	35,000	45,000	65,000
Cash payments			
To employees	3,000	3,000	3,000
For products	25,000	35,000	45,000
Miscellaneous expenses	5,000	6,000	7,000
Postage	1,000	1,000	1,000
Total cash payments	34,000	45,000	56,000
Cash balance	$ 1,000	$ 0	$ 9,000
Borrow from savings	$14,000	$15,000	$ 1,000
Borrow from bank?	$ 0	$ 0	$ 5,000

Ethics Case

BYP23-7 You are an accountant in the budgetary, projections, and special projects department of Fernetti Conductor, Inc., a large manufacturing company. The president, Richard Brown, asks you on very short notice to prepare some sales and income projections covering the next 2 years of the company's much heralded new product lines. He wants these projections for a series of speeches he is making while on a 2-week trip to eight East Coast brokerage firms. The president hopes to bolster Fernetti's stock sales and price.

You work 23 hours in 2 days to compile the projections, hand-deliver them to the president, and are swiftly but graciously thanked as he departs. A week later, you find time to go over some of your computations and discover a miscalculation that makes the projections grossly overstated. You quickly inquire about the president's itinerary and learn that he has made half of his speeches and has half yet to make. You are in a quandary as to what to do.

Instructions
(a) What are the consequences of telling the president of your gross miscalculations?
(b) What are the consequences of not telling the president of your gross miscalculations?
(c) What are the ethical considerations to you and the president in this situation?

All About You

BYP23-8 In order to get your personal finances under control, you need to prepare a personal budget. Assume that you have compiled the following information regarding your expected cash flows for a typical month.

Rent payment	$ 500	Miscellaneous costs	$210
Interest income	50	Savings	50
Income tax withheld	300	Eating out	150
Electricity bill	85	Telephone and Internet costs	125
Groceries	100	Student loan payments	375
Wages earned	2,500	Entertainment costs	250
Insurance	100	Transportation costs	150

Instructions
Using the information above, prepare a personal budget. In preparing this budget, use the format found at **http://financialplan.about.com/cs/budgeting/l/blbudget.htm**. Just skip any unused line items.

Considering Your Costs and Benefits

BYP23-9 You might hear people say that they "need to learn to live within a budget." The funny thing is that most people who say this haven't actually prepared a personal budget, nor do they intend to. Instead, what they are referring to is a vaguely defined, poorly specified collection of rough ideas of how much they should spend on various aspects of their lives. However, you can't live within or even outside of something that doesn't exist. With that in mind, let's take a look at one aspect of personal-budget templates.

Many personal-budget worksheet templates that are provided for college students treat student loans as an income source. See, for example, the template provided at **http://financialplan. about.com/cs/budgeting/l/blmocolbud.htm**. Based on your knowledge of accounting, is this correct?

YES: Student loans provide a source of cash, which can be used to pay costs. As the saying goes, "It all spends the same." Therefore, student loans are income.

NO: Student loans must eventually be repaid; therefore, they are not income. As the name suggests, they are loans.

Instructions
Write a response indicating your position regarding this situation. Provide support for your view.

Answers to Chapter Questions

Answers to Insight and Accounting Across the Organization Questions

p. 1077 Businesses Often Feel Too Busy to Plan for the Future **Q:** Describe a situation in which a business "sells as much as it can" but cannot "keep its employees paid." **A:** If sales are made to customers on credit and collection is slow, the company may find that it does not have enough cash to pay employees or suppliers. Without these resources, the company will fail to survive.

p. 1082 The Implications of Budgetary Optimism **Q:** Why is it important that government budgets accurately estimate future revenues during economic downturns? **A:** Accuracy of government revenue estimates is especially important during economic downturns because most governments must balance their budgets. If anticipated revenues in one period do not match expectations, then the shortfall must be made up in the next period. This can result in much steeper, more disruptive cuts than might have been necessary had the government anticipated the revenue decline more accurately and consequently started cutting expenditures sooner.

p. 1085 Betting That Prices Won't Fall **Q:** What are the potential downsides of stockpiling a huge amount of raw materials? **A:** If prices continue to go up, these managers will avoid paying higher prices until their inventory runs out. However, it is a risky strategy. First of all, prices fluctuate. If a price goes up by 90% in a year, it can also go down by 90%. If this happens, the managers will be stuck with overpriced raw materials. Second, if the economy slows down, it might take a lot longer to sell their inventory than they had planned. There are many costs associated with holding large quantities of inventory. The additional storage, insurance, and handling costs can be very expensive, and obsolescence can occur.

p. 1093 Without a Budget, Can the Games Begin? **Q:** Why does it matter whether the Olympic Games exceed their budget? **A:** If the Olympic Games exceed their budget, taxpayers of the sponsoring community and country will end up footing the bill. Depending on the size of the losses, and the resources of the community, this could produce a substantial burden. As a result, other communities might be reluctant to host the Olympics in the future.

p. 1097 Budget Shortfalls as Far as the Eye Can See **Q:** Why would a university's budgeted scholarships probably fall when the stock market suffers a serious drop? **A:** Scholarships typically cannot be paid out of the "principal" portion of donations made to scholarship endowment funds. Instead, scholarships are usually funded through earnings generated by endowment investments. Any excess earnings above current-year scholarship needs can be used for scholarships in subsequent years. But a serious drop in the value of endowment investments can wipe out previous earnings, in some cases completely eliminating funds available for scholarships.

Answers to Self-Test Questions

1. c **2.** b **3.** a **4.** b **5.** b **6.** d **7.** d $(9,500 + 2,200 − 1,000)$ **8.** a **9.** c **10.** a **11.** a **12.** b **13.** c $[(\$70,000 \times 60\%) + (\$90,000 \times 40\%)]$ **14.** d **15.** c

24 | Budgetary Control and Responsibility Accounting

Turning Trash Into Treasure

Vancouver teenager Brian Scudamore needed to raise money to pay his way through college. With $700 and a strong desire to do it on his own, he established a junk removal company. Fifteen years later, 1-800-GOT-JUNK? had 113 franchise partners across Canada and the United States, and projected revenues of more than $60 million.

"It was a high-school business project that was out of control," says Cameron Herold, vice president of operations.

While the exponential growth of 1-800-GOT-JUNK? may seem unwieldy (at one point it had five consecutive years of 100% compounded growth), it has in fact involved sound financial planning, budgeting, and cash management. The company only spends money it has; it has no outside investors or debt.

Managing this growth involves forecasting everything by creating a "painted picture" of what the company will look

like in three years. The company knows its staffing plans training requirements, and overhead and office space ne well in advance. "That filters back to our budgeting proc Herold says. "We'll sit down and say, 'If this is where we going, what are all the components of that?' . . . Then w bring it back to zero and say, 'What's it going to cost us' Where does it fit into the budget?'"

Key to the company's growth management was the introd of franchising. "We chose franchising because our franchis partners would actually finance our growth," Herold notes addition to the initial franchise fee, franchisees pay the hea office 8% of their sales, plus another 7% to run the centra call center.

While the company has used franchising to manage grow a frugal approach to day-to-day costs has also been inte to its budgeting success. "We're always looking for way cut costs," Herold says. This includes establishing strateg relationships with the local coffee shop, doing regular co

 The Navigator

- ■ Scan Learning Objectives
- ■ Read Feature Story
- ■ Read Preview
- ■ Read text and answer **DO IT!** p. 1132
  - ■ p. 1134 ■ p. 1145 ■ p. 1148
- ■ Work Comprehensive **DO IT! 1** p. 1149
  - ■ **2** p. 1150
- ■ Review Summary of Learning Objectives
- ■ Answer Self-Test Questions
- ■ Complete Assignments
- ■ Go to *WileyPLUS* for practice and tutorials

Learning Objectives The Navigator

After studying this chapter, you should be able to:

[1] Describe the concept of budgetary control.

[2] Evaluate the usefulness of static budget reports.

[3] Explain the development of flexible budgets and the usefulness of flexible budget reports.

[4] Describe the concept of responsibility accounting.

[5] Indicate the features of responsibility reports for cost centers.

[6] Identify the content of responsibility reports for profit centers.

[7] Explain the basis and formula used in evaluating performance in investment centers.

© Clackson/iStockphoto

analyses of office equipment and changing suppliers when needed, and buying office furniture in bulk from liquidators at 10 cents on the dollar. As Herold points out, "All those little things start to really add up."

Watch the Tribeca Grand video in WileyPLUS to learn more about budgeting in the real world.

Preview of Chapter 24

 The Navigator

In contrast to Chapter 23, we now consider how budgets are used by management to control operations. In the Feature Story on 1-800-GOT-JUNK?, we see that management uses the budget to adapt to the business environment. This chapter focuses on two aspects of management control: (1) budgetary control and (2) responsibility accounting.

The content and organization of Chapter 24 are as follows.

BUDGETARY CONTROL AND RESPONSIBILITY ACCOUNTING

Budgetary Control	Static Budget Reports	Flexible Budgets	Responsibility Accounting	Types of Responsibility Centers
• Budget reports • Control activities • Reporting systems	• Examples • Uses and limitations	• Why flexible budgets? • Development • Case study • Reports	• Controllable vs. noncontrollable • Performance evaluation • Reporting system	• Cost centers • Profit centers • Investment centers

Budgetary Control

LEARNING OBJECTIVE 1

Describe the concept of budgetary control.

One of management's functions is to control company operations. Control consists of the steps taken by management to see that planned objectives are met. We now ask: How do budgets contribute to control of operations?

The use of budgets in controlling operations is known as **budgetary control**. Such control takes place by means of **budget reports** that compare actual results with planned objectives. The use of budget reports is based on the belief that planned objectives lose much of their potential value without some monitoring of progress along the way. Just as your professors give midterm exams to evaluate your progress, top management requires periodic reports on the progress of department managers toward their planned objectives.

Budget reports provide management with feedback on operations. The feedback for a crucial objective, such as having enough cash on hand to pay bills, may be made daily. For other objectives, such as meeting budgeted annual sales and operating expenses, monthly budget reports may suffice. Budget reports are prepared as frequently as needed. From these reports, management analyzes any differences between actual and planned results and determines their causes. Management then takes corrective action, or it decides to modify future plans. Budgetary control involves the activities shown in Illustration 24-1.

Illustration 24-1
Budgetary control activities

Budgetary control works best when a company has a formalized reporting system. The system does the following:

1. Identifies the name of the budget report, such as the sales budget or the manufacturing overhead budget.
2. States the frequency of the report, such as weekly or monthly.
3. Specifies the purpose of the report.
4. Indicates the primary recipient(s) of the report.

Illustration 24-2 provides a partial budgetary control system for a manufacturing company. Note the frequency of the reports and their emphasis on control. For example, there is a daily report on scrap and a weekly report on labor.

Name of Report	Frequency	Purpose	Primary Recipient(s)
Sales	Weekly	Determine whether sales goals are met	Top management and sales manager
Labor	Weekly	Control direct and indirect labor costs	Vice president of production and production department managers
Scrap	Daily	Determine efficient use of materials	Production manager
Departmental overhead costs	Monthly	Control overhead costs	Department manager
Selling expenses	Monthly	Control selling expenses	Sales manager
Income statement	Monthly and quarterly	Determine whether income goals are met	Top management

Illustration 24-2
Budgetary control reporting system

Static Budget Reports

You learned in Chapter 23 that the master budget formalizes management's planned objectives for the coming year. When used in budgetary control, each budget included in the master budget is considered to be static. A **static budget** is a projection of budget data **at one level of activity**. These budgets do not consider data for different levels of activity. As a result, companies always compare actual results with budget data at the activity level that was used in developing the master budget.

LEARNING OBJECTIVE	2

Evaluate the usefulness of static budget reports.

Examples

To illustrate the role of a static budget in budgetary control, we will use selected data prepared for Hayes Company in Chapter 23. Budget and actual sales data for the Rightride product in the first and second quarters of 2014 are as follows.

Sales	First Quarter	Second Quarter	Total
Budgeted	$180,000	$210,000	$390,000
Actual	179,000	199,500	378,500
Difference	$ 1,000	$ 10,500	$ 11,500

Illustration 24-3
Budget and actual sales data

The sales budget report for Hayes Company's first quarter is shown below. The right-most column reports the difference between the budgeted and actual amounts.

HAYES COMPANY
Sales Budget Report
For the Quarter Ended March 31, 2014

Illustration 24-4
Sales budget report—first quarter

Product Line	Budget	Actual	Difference Favorable F Unfavorable U
Rightride*	$180,000	$179,000	**$1,000 U**

*In practice, each product line would be included in the report.

The report shows that sales are $1,000 under budget—an unfavorable result. This difference is less than 1% of budgeted sales ($1,000 ÷ $180,000 = .0056). Top management's reaction to unfavorable differences is often influenced by the

Alternative Terminology
The difference between budget and actual is sometimes called a *budget variance.*

materiality (significance) of the difference. Since the difference of $1,000 is immaterial in this case, we assume that Hayes Company management takes no specific corrective action.

Illustration 24-5 shows the budget report for the second quarter. It contains one new feature: cumulative year-to-date information. This report indicates that sales for the second quarter are $10,500 below budget. This is 5% of budgeted sales ($10,500 ÷ $210,000). Top management may now conclude that the difference between budgeted and actual sales requires investigation.

HAYES COMPANY
Sales Budget Report
For the Quarter Ended June 30, 2014

| | Second Quarter | | | Year-to-Date | | |
| | | | Difference | | | Difference |
Product Line	Budget	Actual	Favorable F Unfavorable U	Budget	Actual	Favorable F Unfavorable U
Rightride	$210,000	$199,500	**$10,500 U**	$390,000	$378,500	**$11,500 U**

Illustration 24-5
Sales budget report—second quarter

Management's analysis should start by asking the sales manager the cause(s) of the shortfall. Managers should consider the need for corrective action. For example, management may decide to spur sales by offering sales incentives to customers or by increasing the advertising of Rightrides. Or, if management concludes that a downturn in the economy is responsible for the lower sales, it may modify planned sales and profit goals for the remainder of the year.

Uses and Limitations

From these examples, you can see that a master sales budget is useful in evaluating the performance of a sales manager. It is now necessary to ask: Is the master budget appropriate for evaluating a manager's performance in controlling costs? Recall that in a static budget, data are not modified or adjusted, regardless of changes in activity. It follows, then, that a static budget is appropriate in evaluating a manager's effectiveness in controlling costs when:

1. The actual level of activity closely approximates the master budget activity level, and/or
2. The behavior of the costs in response to changes in activity is fixed.

A static budget report is, therefore, appropriate for **fixed manufacturing costs** and for **fixed selling and administrative expenses**. But, as you will see shortly, static budget reports may not be a proper basis for evaluating a manager's performance in controlling variable costs.

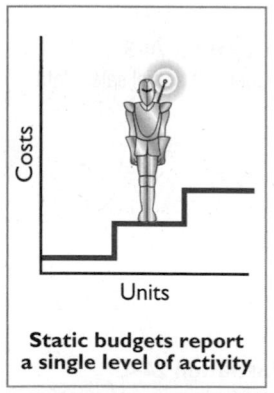
Static budgets report a single level of activity

Flexible Budgets

LEARNING OBJECTIVE **3**

Explain the development of flexible budgets and the usefulness of flexible budget reports.

In contrast to a static budget, which is based on one level of activity, a **flexible budget** projects budget data for various levels of activity. In essence, **the flexible budget is a series of static budgets at different levels of activity**. The flexible budget recognizes that the budgetary process is more useful if it is adaptable to changed operating conditions.

Flexible budgets can be prepared for each of the types of budgets included in the master budget. For example, Marriott Hotels can budget revenue and net income on the basis of 60%, 80%, and 100% of room occupancy. Similarly,

American Van Lines can budget its operating expenses on the basis of various levels of truck-miles driven. Duke Energy can budget revenue and net income on the basis of estimated billions of kwh (kilowatt hours) of residential, commercial, and industrial electricity generated. In the following pages, we will illustrate a flexible budget for manufacturing overhead.

Why Flexible Budgets?

Assume that you are the manager in charge of manufacturing overhead in the Assembly Department of Barton Robotics. In preparing the manufacturing overhead budget for 2014, you prepare the following static budget based on a production volume of 10,000 units of robotic controls.

Flexible budgets are static budgets at different activity levels

BARTON ROBOTICS Manufacturing Overhead Budget (Static) Assembly Department For the Year Ended December 31, 2014	
Budgeted production in units (robotic controls)	10,000
Budgeted costs	
Indirect materials	$ 250,000
Indirect labor	260,000
Utilities	190,000
Depreciation	280,000
Property taxes	70,000
Supervision	50,000
	$1,100,000

Helpful Hint The master budget described in Chapter 23 is based on a static budget.

Illustration 24-6
Static overhead budget

Fortunately for the company, the demand for robotic controls has increased, and Barton produces and sells 12,000 units during the year, rather than 10,000. You are elated: Increased sales means increased profitability, which should mean a bonus or a raise for you and the employees in your department. Unfortunately, a comparison of Assembly Department actual and budgeted costs has put you on the spot. The budget report is shown below.

Illustration 24-7
Overhead static budget report

	A	B	C	D	E
1		BARTON ROBOTICS			
2		Manufacturing Overhead Static Budget Report			
3		For the Year Ended December 31, 2014			
4				Difference	
5		Budget	Actual	Favorable - F Unfavorable - U	
6	Production in units	10,000	12,000		
7					
8	Costs				
9	Indirect materials	$ 250,000	$ 295,000	$ 45,000	U
10	Indirect labor	260,000	312,000	52,000	U
11	Utilities	190,000	225,000	35,000	U
12	Depreciation	280,000	280,000	0	
13	Property taxes	70,000	70,000	0	
14	Supervision	50,000	50,000	0	
15		$1,100,000	$1,232,000	$132,000	U
16					

This comparison uses budget data based on the original activity level (10,000 robotic controls). It indicates that the Assembly Department is significantly **over budget** for three of the six overhead costs. There is a total unfavorable difference of $132,000, which is 12% over budget ($132,000 ÷ $1,100,000). Your supervisor is very unhappy! Instead of sharing in the company's success, you may find yourself looking for another job. What went wrong?

When you calm down and carefully examine the manufacturing overhead budget, you identify the problem: The budget data are not relevant! At the time the budget was developed, the company anticipated that only 10,000 units would be produced, **not** 12,000. Comparing actual with budgeted variable costs is meaningless. As production increases, the budget allowances for variable costs should increase proportionately. The variable costs in this example are indirect materials, indirect labor, and utilities.

Analyzing the budget data for these costs at 10,000 units, you arrive at the following per unit results.

Illustration 24-8
Variable costs per unit

Item	Total Cost	Per Unit
Indirect materials	$250,000	$25
Indirect labor	260,000	26
Utilities	190,000	19
	$700,000	$70

Illustration 24-9 calculates the budgeted variable costs at 12,000 units.

Illustration 24-9
Budgeted variable costs, 12,000 units

Item	Computation	Total
Indirect materials	$25 × 12,000	$300,000
Indirect labor	26 × 12,000	312,000
Utilities	19 × 12,000	228,000
		$840,000

Because fixed costs do not change in total as activity changes, the budgeted amounts for these costs remain the same. Illustration 24-10 shows the budget report based on the flexible budget for **12,000 units** of production. (Compare this with Illustration 24-7.)

This report indicates that the Assembly Department's costs are **under budget**— a favorable difference. Instead of worrying about being fired, you may be in line for a bonus or a raise after all! As this analysis shows, the only appropriate comparison is between actual costs at 12,000 units of production and budgeted costs at 12,000 units. Flexible budget reports provide this comparison.

Developing the Flexible Budget

The flexible budget uses the master budget as its basis. To develop the flexible budget, management uses the following steps.

1. Identify the activity index and the relevant range of activity.
2. Identify the variable costs, and determine the budgeted variable cost per unit of activity for each cost.
3. Identify the fixed costs, and determine the budgeted amount for each cost.
4. Prepare the budget for selected increments of activity within the relevant range.

Illustration 24-10
Overhead flexible budget report

		Barton Robotics.xls			
Home	Insert	Page Layout Formulas Data Review View			
P18		fx			

	A	B	C	D	E
1		**BARTON ROBOTICS**			
2		**Manufacturing Overhead Flexible Budget Report**			
3		**For the Year Ended December 31, 2014**			
4				Difference	
5		Budget	Actual	Favorable - F Unfavorable - U	
6	Production in units	12,000	12,000		
7					
8	Variable costs				
9	Indirect materials ($25)	$ 300,000	$ 295,000	$5,000	F
10	Indirect labor ($26)	312,000	312,000	0	
11	Utilities ($19)	228,000	225,000	3,000	F
12	Total variable costs	840,000	832,000	8,000	F
13					
14	Fixed costs				
15	Depreciation	280,000	280,000	0	
16	Property taxes	70,000	70,000	0	
17	Supervision	50,000	50,000	0	
18	Total fixed costs	400,000	400,000	0	
19	Total costs	$1,240,000	$1,232,000	$8,000	F
20					

The activity index chosen should significantly influence the costs being budgeted. For manufacturing overhead costs, for example, the activity index is usually the same as the index used in developing the predetermined overhead rate—that is, direct labor hours or machine hours. For selling and administrative expenses, the activity index usually is sales or net sales.

The choice of the increment of activity is largely a matter of judgment. For example, if the relevant range is 8,000 to 12,000 direct labor hours, increments of 1,000 hours may be selected. The flexible budget is then prepared for each increment within the relevant range.

SERVICE COMPANY INSIGHT

Just What the Doctor Ordered?

Nobody is immune from the effects of declining revenues—not even movie stars. When the number of viewers of the television show "House," a medical drama, declined by almost 20%, Fox Broadcasting said it wanted to cut the license fee that it paid to NBCUniversal by 20%. What would NBCUniversal do in response? It might cut the size of the show's cast, which would reduce the payroll costs associated with the show. Or, it could reduce the number of episodes that take advantage of the full cast. Alternatively, it might threaten to quit providing the show to Fox altogether and instead present the show on its own NBC-affiliated channels.

Source: Sam Schechner, "Media Business Shorts: NBCU, Fox Taking Scalpel to 'House'," *Wall Street Journal Online* (April 17, 2011).

? Explain how the use of flexible budgets might help to identify the best solution to this problem. (See page 1174.)

Fox Broadcasting Company/Album/Newscom

Flexible Budget—A Case Study

To illustrate the flexible budget, we use Fox Company. Fox's management uses a **flexible budget for monthly comparisons** of actual and budgeted manufacturing overhead costs of the Finishing Department. The master budget for the year ending December 31, 2014, shows expected **annual** operating capacity of 120,000 direct labor hours and the following overhead costs.

Illustration 24-11
Master budget data

Variable Costs		Fixed Costs	
Indirect materials	$180,000	Depreciation	$180,000
Indirect labor	240,000	Supervision	120,000
Utilities	60,000	Property taxes	60,000
Total	$480,000	Total	$360,000

The four steps for developing the flexible budget are applied as follows.

STEP 1. Identify the activity index and the relevant range of activity. The activity index is direct labor hours. The relevant range is 8,000–12,000 direct labor hours per **month**.

STEP 2. Identify the variable costs, and determine the budgeted variable cost per unit of activity for each cost. There are three variable costs. The variable cost per unit is found by dividing each total budgeted cost by the direct labor hours used in preparing the annual master budget (120,000 hours). For Fox Company, the computations are:

Illustration 24-12
Computation of variable cost per direct labor hour

Variable Costs	Computation	Variable Cost per Direct Labor Hour
Indirect materials	$180,000 ÷ 120,000	**$1.50**
Indirect labor	$240,000 ÷ 120,000	**2.00**
Utilities	$ 60,000 ÷ 120,000	**0.50**
Total		**$4.00**

STEP 3. Identify the fixed costs, and determine the budgeted amount for each cost. There are three fixed costs. Since Fox desires **monthly budget data**, it divides each annual budgeted cost by 12 to find the monthly amounts. For Fox Company, the monthly budgeted fixed costs are depreciation $15,000, supervision $10,000, and property taxes $5,000.

STEP 4. Prepare the budget for selected increments of activity within the relevant range. Management prepares the budget in increments of 1,000 direct labor hours.

Illustration 24-13 shows Fox's flexible budget.

Illustration 24-13
Monthly overhead flexible budget

	A	B	C	D	E	F
1	FOX COMPANY					
2	Monthly Manufacturing Overhead Flexible Budget					
3	Finishing Department					
4	For Months During the Year 2014					
5	Activity level					
6	Direct labor hours	8,000	9,000	10,000	11,000	12,000
7	Variable costs					
8	Indirect materials ($1.50)a	$12,000b	$13,500	$15,000	$16,500	$18,000
9	Indirect labor ($2.00)a	16,000c	18,000	20,000	22,000	24,000
10	Utilities ($0.50)a	4,000d	4,500	5,000	5,500	6,000
11	Total variable costs	32,000	36,000	40,000	44,000	48,000
12	Fixed costs					
13	Depreciation	15,000	15,000	15,000	15,000	15,000
14	Supervision	10,000	10,000	10,000	10,000	10,000
15	Property taxes	5,000	5,000	5,000	5,000	5,000
16	Total fixed costs	30,000	30,000	30,000	30,000	30,000
17	Total costs	$62,000	$66,000	$70,000	$74,000	$78,000
19	aCost per direct labor hour; b8,000 x $1.50; c8,000 x $2.00; d8,000 x $0.50					

Fox uses the formula below to determine total budgeted costs at any level of activity.

Illustration 24-14
Formula for total budgeted costs

$$\text{Fixed Costs} + \text{Variable Costs*} = \text{Total Budgeted Costs}$$

*Total variable cost per unit of activity × Activity level.

For Fox, fixed costs are $30,000, and total variable cost per direct labor hour is $4 ($1.50 + $2.00 + $0.50). At 9,000 direct labor hours, total budgeted costs are $66,000 [$30,000 + ($4 × 9,000)]. At 8,622 direct labor hours, total budgeted costs are $64,488 [$30,000 + ($4 × 8,622)].

Total budgeted costs can also be shown graphically, as in Illustration 24-15 (page 1132). In the graph, the horizontal axis represents the activity index, and costs are indicated on the vertical axis. The graph highlights two activity levels (10,000 and 12,000). As shown, total budgeted costs at these activity levels are $70,000 [$30,000 + ($4 × 10,000)] and $78,000 [$30,000 + ($4 × 12,000)], respectively.

Helpful Hint Using the data given for Fox, what amount of total costs would be budgeted for 10,600 direct labor hours? Answer: $30,000 fixed + $42,400 variable (i.e., 10,600 × $4) = $72,400 total.

Illustration 24-15
Graphic flexible budget data highlighting 10,000 and 12,000 activity levels

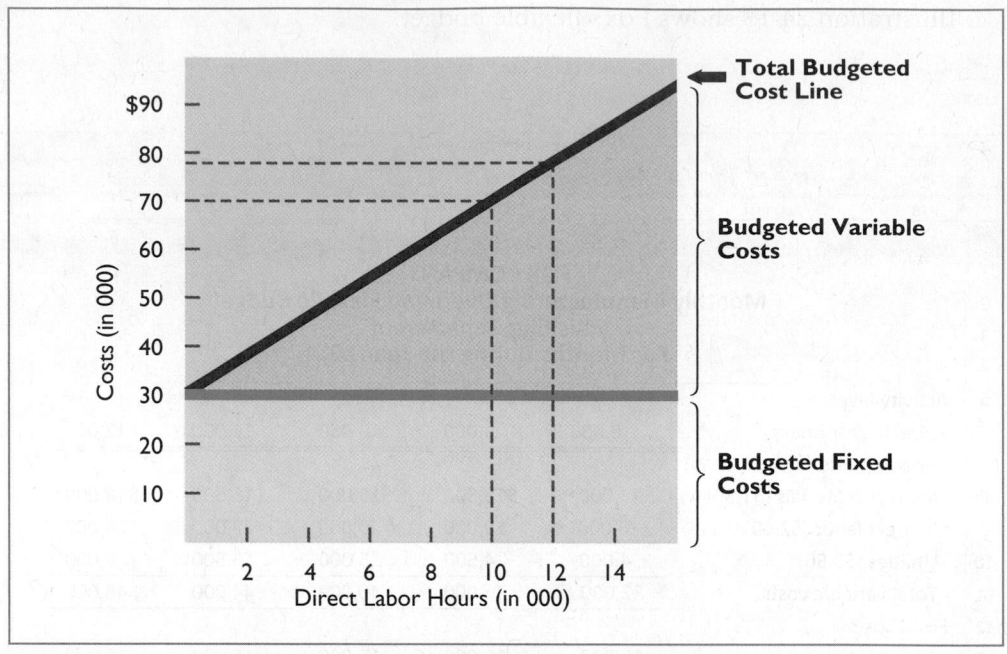

> DO IT!

Flexible Budgets

In Strassel Company's flexible budget graph, the fixed cost line and the total budgeted cost line intersect the vertical axis at $36,000. The total budgeted cost line is $186,000 at an activity level of 50,000 direct labor hours. Compute total budgeted costs at 30,000 direct labor hours.

Action Plan

✔ Apply the formula: Fixed costs + Variable costs (Total variable cost per unit × Activity level) = Total budgeted costs.

Solution

Using the graph, fixed costs are $36,000, and variable costs are $3 per direct labor hour [($186,000 − $36,000) ÷ 50,000]. Thus, at 30,000 direct labor hours, total budgeted costs are $126,000 [$36,000 + ($3 × 30,000)].

Related exercise material: **BE24-4, E24-3, E24-5, and DO IT! 24-1.**

✔ **The Navigator**

Flexible Budget Reports

Flexible budget reports are another type of internal report. The flexible budget report consists of two sections: (1) production data for a selected activity index, such as direct labor hours, and (2) cost data for variable and fixed costs. The report provides a basis for evaluating a manager's performance in two areas: production control and cost control. Flexible budget reports are widely used in production and service departments.

Illustration 24-16 shows a budget report for the Finishing Department of Fox Company for the month of January. In this month, 9,000 hours are worked. The budget data are therefore based on the flexible budget for 9,000 hours in Illustration 24-13 (page 1131). The actual cost data are assumed.

Illustration 24-16
Overhead flexible budget report

		Fox Company.xls			
Home	Insert	Page Layout Formulas Data Review View			
P18		fx			
	A	B	C	D	E
1		**FOX COMPANY**			
2		**Manufacturing Overhead Flexible Budget Report**			
3		**Finishing Department**			
4		**For the Month Ended January 31, 2014**			
5				Difference	
6		Budget at	Actual costs at	Favorable - F	
7	Direct labor hours (DLH)	9,000 DLH	9,000 DLH	Unfavorable - U	
8					
9	Variable costs				
10	Indirect materials ($1.50)*	$13,500	$14,000	$ 500	U
11	Indirect labor ($2.00)*	18,000	17,000	1,000	F
12	Utilities ($0.50)*	4,500	4,600	100	U
13	Total variable costs	36,000	35,600	400	F
14					
15	Fixed costs				
16	Depreciation	15,000	15,000	0	
17	Supervision	10,000	10,000	0	
18	Property taxes	5,000	5,000	0	
19	Total fixed costs	30,000	30,000	0	
20	Total costs	$66,000	$65,600	$ 400	F
21					
22	*Cost per direct labor hour				

How appropriate is this report in evaluating the Finishing Department manager's performance in controlling overhead costs? The report clearly provides a reliable basis. Both actual and budget costs are based on the activity level worked during January. Since variable costs generally are incurred directly by the department, the difference between the budget allowance for those hours and the actual costs is the responsibility of the department manager.

In subsequent months, Fox Company will prepare other flexible budget reports. For each month, the budget data are based on the actual activity level attained. In February that level may be 11,000 direct labor hours, in July 10,000, and so on.

Note that this flexible budget is based on a single cost driver. A more accurate budget often can be developed using the activity-based costing concepts explained in Chapter 21.

© Eric Isselée/iStockphoto

SERVICE COMPANY INSIGHT

Budgets and the Exotic Newcastle Disease

Exotic Newcastle Disease, one of the most infectious bird diseases in the world, kills so swiftly that many victims die before any symptoms appear. When it broke out in Southern California, it could have spelled disaster for the San Diego Zoo. "We have one of the most valuable collections of birds in the world, if not *the* most valuable," says Paula Brock, CFO of the Zoological Society of San Diego, which operates the zoo.

Bird exhibits were closed to the public for several months (the disease, which is harmless to humans, can be carried on clothes and shoes). The tires of arriving delivery trucks were sanitized, as were the shoes of anyone visiting the zoo's nonpublic areas. Zookeeper uniforms had to be changed and cleaned daily. And ultimately, the zoo, with $150 million in revenues, spent almost half a million dollars on quarantine measures.

It worked: No birds got sick. Better yet, the damage to the rest of the zoo's budget was minimized by another protective measure: the monthly budget reforecast. "When we get a hit like this, we still have to find a way to make our bottom line," says Brock. Thanks to a new planning process Brock had introduced a year earlier, the zoo's scientists were able to raise the financial alarm as they redirected resources to ward off the disease. "Because we had timely awareness," she says, "we were able to make adjustments to weather the storm."

Budget reforecasting is nothing new. (The San Diego Zoo's annual static budget was behind the times before Brock took over as CFO.) But the reaction of the zoo's staff shows the benefits of Brock's immediate efforts to link strategy to the process. It's a move long touted by consultants as a key way to improve people's involvement in budgeting.

"To keep your company on a path, it has to have some kind of map," says Brock. "The budgeting-and-planning process is that map. I cannot imagine an organization feeling in control if it didn't have that sort of discipline."

Source: Tim Reason, "Budgeting in the Real World," *CFO Magazine* (July 12, 2005), *www.cfodirect.com/cfopublic.nsf/vContentPrint/649A82C8FF8AB06B85257037004* (accessed July 2005).

 What is the major benefit of tying a budget to the overall goals of the company? (See page 1175.)

> DO IT!

Flexible Budget Reports

Lawler Company expects to produce 40,000 units of product CV93 during the current year. Budgeted variable manufacturing costs per unit are direct materials $6, direct labor $15, and overhead $24. Annual budgeted fixed manufacturing overhead costs are $120,000 for depreciation and $60,000 for supervision.

In the current month, Lawler produced 5,000 units and incurred the following costs: direct materials $33,900, direct labor $74,200, variable overhead $120,500, depreciation $10,000, and supervision $5,000.

Prepare a flexible budget report. (*Note:* You do not have to prepare the heading.) Were costs controlled?

Solution

Action Plan

✔ Use budget for actual units produced.

✔ Classify each cost as variable or fixed.

✔ Determine monthly fixed costs by dividing annual amounts by 12.

✔ Determine the difference as favorable or unfavorable.

✔ Determine the difference in total variable costs, total fixed costs, and total costs.

	A	B	C	D	
		Budget at	Actual costs at	Difference Favorable - F	
1					
2					
3	Units produced	5,000 units	5,000 units	Unfavorable - U	
4					
5	Variable costs				
6	Direct materials ($6)	$ 30,000	$ 33,900	$3,900	U
7	Direct labor ($15)	75,000	74,200	800	F
8	Overhead ($24)	120,000	120,500	500	U
9	Total variable costs	225,000	228,600	3,600	U
10					
11	Fixed costs				
12	Depreciation	10,000	10,000	0	
13	Supervision	5,000	5,000	0	
14	Total fixed costs	15,000	15,000	0	
15	Total costs	$240,000	$243,600	$3,600	U
16					
17					

Spreadsheet: Lawler Company.xls — Home | Insert | Page Layout | Formulas | Data | Review | View — cell P18

The responsibility report indicates that actual direct labor was only about 1% different from the budget, and overhead was less than half a percent different. Both appear to have been well-controlled.

This was not the case for direct materials. Its 13% unfavorable difference should probably be investigated.

Actual fixed costs had no difference from budget and were well-controlled.

Related exercise material: **BE24-5, E24-4, E24-6, E24-8, and DO IT! 24-2.**

✔ The Navigator

Responsibility Accounting

Like budgeting, responsibility accounting is an important part of management accounting. **Responsibility accounting** involves accumulating and reporting costs (and revenues, where relevant) on the basis of the manager who has the authority to make the day-to-day decisions about the items. Under responsibility accounting, a manager's performance is evaluated on matters directly under that manager's control. Responsibility accounting can be used at every level of management in which the following conditions exist.

LEARNING OBJECTIVE   4

Describe the concept of responsibility accounting.

1. Costs and revenues can be directly associated with the specific level of management responsibility.

2. The costs and revenues can be controlled by employees at the level of responsibility with which they are associated.

3. Budget data can be developed for evaluating the manager's effectiveness in controlling the costs and revenues.

Illustration 24-17 depicts levels of responsibility for controlling costs.

Illustration 24-17
Responsibility for controllable costs at varying levels of management

WI Cheese Company

"I'm responsible for controlling costs in my **department**."

"I'm responsible for controlling costs in my **division**."

"The big cheese"

"I'm responsible for controlling **company** costs."

Department Manager   **Division Manager**   **President**

Responsibility accounting gives managers responsibility for controllable costs at each level of authority

Helpful Hint All companies use responsibility accounting. Without some form of responsibility accounting, there would be chaos in discharging management's control function.

Under responsibility accounting, any individual who controls a specified set of activities can be a responsibility center. Thus, responsibility accounting may extend from the lowest level of control to the top strata of management. Once responsibility is established, the company first measures and reports the effectiveness of the individual's performance for the specified activity. It then reports that measure upward throughout the organization.

Responsibility accounting is especially valuable in a decentralized company. **Decentralization** means that the control of operations is delegated to many managers throughout the organization. The term **segment** is sometimes used to identify an area of responsibility in decentralized operations. Under responsibility accounting, companies prepare segment reports periodically, such as monthly, quarterly, and annually, to evaluate managers' performance.

Responsibility accounting is an essential part of any effective system of budgetary control. The reporting of costs and revenues under responsibility accounting differs from budgeting in two respects:

1. A distinction is made between controllable and noncontrollable items.

2. Performance reports either emphasize or include only items controllable by the individual manager.

Responsibility accounting applies to both profit and not-for-profit entities. For-profit entities seek to maximize net income. Not-for-profit entities wish to perform services as efficiently as possible.

MANAGEMENT INSIGHT
Competition versus Collaboration

Many compensation and promotion programs encourage competition among employees for pay raises. To get ahead you have to perform better than your fellow employees. While this may encourage hard work, it does not foster collaboration, and it can lead to distrust and disloyalty. Such results have led some companies to believe that cooperation and collaboration are essential in order to succeed in today's environment. For example, division managers might increase collaboration (and reduce costs) by sharing design and marketing resources or by jointly negotiating with suppliers. In addition, companies can reduce the need to hire and lay off employees by sharing employees across divisions as human resource needs increase and decrease.

As a consequence, many companies now explicitly include measures of collaboration in their performance measures. For example, Procter & Gamble measures collaboration in employees' annual performance reviews. At Cisco Systems the assessment of an employee's teamwork can affect the annual bonus by as much as 20%.

Source: Carol Hymowitz, "Rewarding Competitors Over Collaboration No Longer Makes Sense," *Wall Street Journal* (February 13, 2006).

? How might managers of separate divisions be able to reduce division costs through collaboration? (See page 1175.)

Controllable versus Noncontrollable Revenues and Costs

All costs and revenues are controllable at some level of responsibility within a company. This truth underscores the adage by the CEO of any organization that "the buck stops here." Under responsibility accounting, the critical issue is **whether the cost or revenue is controllable at the level of responsibility with which it is associated**. A cost over which a manager has control is called a **controllable cost**. From this definition, it follows that:

1. All costs are controllable by top management because of the broad range of its authority.
2. Fewer costs are controllable as one moves down to each lower level of managerial responsibility because of the manager's decreasing authority.

In general, **costs incurred directly by a level of responsibility are controllable at that level**. In contrast, costs incurred indirectly and allocated to a responsibility level are **noncontrollable costs** at that level.

Helpful Hint Are there more or fewer controllable costs as you move to higher levels of management? Answer: More.

Helpful Hint The longer the time span, the more likely that the cost becomes controllable.

Principles of Performance Evaluation

Performance evaluation is at the center of responsibility accounting. It is a management function that compares actual results with budget goals. It involves both behavioral and reporting principles.

MANAGEMENT BY EXCEPTION

Management by exception means that top management's review of a budget report is focused either entirely or primarily on differences between actual results and planned objectives. This approach enables top management to focus on problem areas. For example, many companies now use online reporting systems for employees to file their travel and entertainment expense reports. In addition to cutting reporting time in half, the online system enables managers to quickly analyze variances from travel budgets. This cuts down on expense account "padding" such as spending too much on meals or falsifying documents for costs that were never actually incurred.

Management by exception does not mean that top management will investigate every difference. For this approach to be effective, there must be guidelines for identifying an exception. The usual criteria are materiality and controllability.

MATERIALITY Without quantitative guidelines, management would have to investigate every budget difference regardless of the amount. Materiality is usually expressed as a percentage difference from budget. For example, management may set the percentage difference at 5% for important items and 10% for other items. Managers will investigate all differences either over or under budget by the specified percentage. Costs over budget warrant investigation to determine why they were not controlled. Likewise, costs under budget merit investigation to determine whether costs critical to profitability are being curtailed. For example, if maintenance costs are budgeted at $80,000 but only $40,000 is spent, major unexpected breakdowns in productive facilities may occur in the future.

Alternatively, a company may specify a single percentage difference from budget for all items and supplement this guideline with a minimum dollar limit. For example, the exception criteria may be stated at 5% of budget or more than $10,000.

CONTROLLABILITY OF THE ITEM Exception guidelines are more restrictive for controllable items than for items the manager cannot control. In fact, there may be no guidelines for noncontrollable items. For example, a large unfavorable difference between actual and budgeted property tax expense may not be flagged for investigation because the only possible causes are an unexpected increase in the tax rate or in the assessed value of the property. An investigation into the difference would be useless: The manager cannot control either cause.

BEHAVIORAL PRINCIPLES

The human factor is critical in evaluating performance. Behavioral principles include the following.

1. **Managers of responsibility centers should have direct input into the process of establishing budget goals of their area of responsibility.** Without such input, managers may view the goals as unrealistic or arbitrarily set by top management. Such views adversely affect the managers' motivation to meet the targeted objectives.

2. **The evaluation of performance should be based entirely on matters that are controllable by the manager being evaluated.** Criticism of a manager on matters outside his or her control reduces the effectiveness of the evaluation process. It leads to negative reactions by a manager and to doubts about the fairness of the company's evaluation policies.

3. **Top management should support the evaluation process.** As explained earlier, the evaluation process begins at the lowest level of responsibility and extends upward to the highest level of management. Managers quickly lose faith in the process when top management ignores, overrules, or bypasses established procedures for evaluating a manager's performance.

4. **The evaluation process must allow managers to respond to their evaluations.** Evaluation is not a one-way street. Managers should have the opportunity to defend their performance. Evaluation without feedback is both impersonal and ineffective.

5. The evaluation should identify both good and poor performance. Praise for good performance is a powerful motivating factor for a manager. This is especially true when a manager's compensation includes rewards for meeting budget goals.

REPORTING PRINCIPLES

Performance evaluation under responsibility accounting should be based on certain reporting principles. These principles pertain primarily to the internal reports that provide the basis for evaluating performance. Performance reports should:

1. Contain only data that are controllable by the manager of the responsibility center.
2. Provide accurate and reliable budget data to measure performance.
3. Highlight significant differences between actual results and budget goals.
4. Be tailor-made for the intended evaluation.
5. Be prepared at reasonable time intervals.

In recent years, companies have come under increasing pressure from influential shareholder groups to do a better job of linking executive pay to corporate performance. For example, software maker Siebel Systems unveiled a new incentive plan after lengthy discussions with the California Public Employees' Retirement System. One unique feature of the plan is that managers' targets will be publicly disclosed at the beginning of each year for investors to evaluate.

MANAGEMENT INSIGHT

Flexible Manufacturing Requires Flexible Accounting

Flexible budgeting is useful because it enables managers to evaluate performance in light of changing conditions. But the ability to react quickly to changing conditions is even more important. Among automobile manufacturing facilities in the U.S., nobody's plants are more flexible than Honda. The manufacturing facilities of some auto companies can make slight alterations to the features of a vehicle in response to changes in demand for particular features. But for most plants, to switch from production of one type of vehicle to a completely different type of vehicle, when demand for types of vehicles shifts, typically takes months and costs hundreds of millions of dollars. But at the Honda plant, the switch takes minutes. For example, it takes about five minutes to install different hand-like parts on the robots so they can switch from making Civic compacts to the longer, taller CR-V crossover. This ability to adjust quickly to changing demand gave Honda a huge advantage when gas prices surged and demand for more fuel-efficient cars increased quickly.

Source: Kate Linebaugh, "Honda's Flexible Plants Provide Edge," *Wall Street Journal Online* (September 23, 2008).

 What implications do these improvements in production capabilities have for management accounting information and performance evaluation within the organization? (See page 1175.)

Responsibility Reporting System

A **responsibility reporting system** involves the preparation of a report for each level of responsibility in the company's organization chart. To illustrate such a system, we use the partial organization chart and production departments of Francis Chair Company in Illustration 24-18 (page 1140).

Report A
President sees summary data of vice presidents.

Report B
Vice president sees summary of controllable costs in his/her functional area.

Report C
Plant manager sees summary of controllable costs for each department in the plant.

Report D
Department manager sees controllable costs of his/her department.

Illustration 24-18
Partial organization chart

The responsibility reporting system begins with the lowest level of responsibility for controlling costs and moves upward to each higher level. Illustration 24-19 details the connections between levels.

A brief description of the four reports for Francis Chair Company is as follows.

1. **Report D** is typical of reports that go to department managers. Similar reports are prepared for the managers of the Fabricating, Assembly, and Enameling Departments.

2. **Report C** is an example of reports that are sent to plant managers. It shows the costs of the Chicago plant that are controllable at the second level of responsibility. In addition, Report C shows summary data for each department that is controlled by the plant manager. Similar reports are prepared for the Detroit and St. Louis plant managers.

3. **Report B** illustrates the reports at the third level of responsibility. It shows the controllable costs of the vice president of production and summary data on the three assembly plants for which this officer is responsible. Similar reports are prepared for the vice presidents of sales and finance.

4. **Report A** is typical of reports that go to the top level of responsibility—the president. It shows the controllable costs and expenses of this office and summary data on the vice presidents that are accountable to the president.

Illustration 24-19
Responsibility reporting system

Report A
President sees summary data of vice presidents.

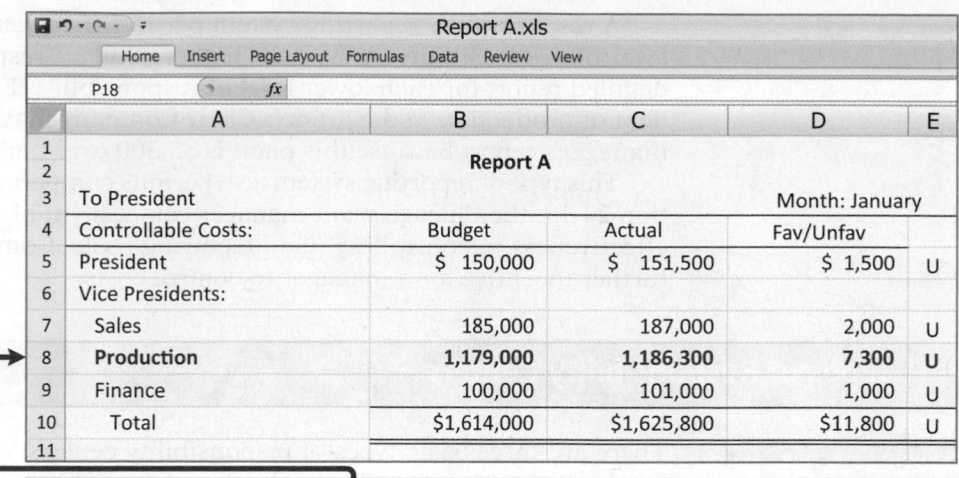

Report A.xls

	A	B	C	D	E
1			**Report A**		
2					
3	To President			Month: January	
4	Controllable Costs:	Budget	Actual	Fav/Unfav	
5	President	$ 150,000	$ 151,500	$ 1,500	U
6	Vice Presidents:				
7	Sales	185,000	187,000	2,000	U
8	**Production**	**1,179,000**	**1,186,300**	**7,300**	U
9	Finance	100,000	101,000	1,000	U
10	Total	$1,614,000	$1,625,800	$11,800	U
11					

Report B
Vice president sees summary of controllable costs in his/her functional area.

Report B.xls

	A	B	C	D	E
1			**Report B**		
2					
3	To Vice President Production			Month: January	
4	Controllable Costs:	Budget	Actual	Fav/Unfav	
5	VP Production	$ 125,000	$ 126,000	$ 1,000	U
6	Assembly Plants:				
7	Detroit	420,000	418,000	2,000	F
8	**Chicago**	**304,000**	**309,300**	**5,300**	U
9	St. Louis	330,000	333,000	3,000	U
10	Total	$1,179,000	$1,186,300	$ 7,300	U
11					

Report C
Plant manager sees summary of controllable costs for each department in the plant.

Report C.xls

	A	B	C	D	E
1			**Report C**		
2					
3	To Plant Manager-Chicago			Month: January	
4	Controllable Costs:	Budget	Actual	Fav/Unfav	
5	Chicago Plant	$110,000	$113,000	$3,000	U
6	Departments:				
7	**Fabricating**	**84,000**	**85,300**	**1,300**	U
8	Enameling	62,000	64,000	2,000	U
9	Assembly	48,000	47,000	1,000	F
10	Total	$304,000	$309,300	$5,300	U
11					

Report D
Department manager sees controllable costs of his/her department.

Report D.xls

	A	B	C	D	E
1			**Report D**		
2					
3	To Fabricating Dept. Manager			Month: January	
4	Controllable Costs:	Budget	Actual	Fav/Unfav	
5	Direct Materials	$20,000	$20,500	$ 500	U
6	Direct Labor	40,000	41,000	1,000	U
7	Overhead	24,000	23,800	200	F
8	Total	$84,000	$85,300	$1,300	U
9					

A responsibility reporting system permits management by exception at each level of responsibility. And, each higher level of responsibility can obtain the detailed report for each lower level of responsibility. For example, the vice president of production in the Francis Chair Company may request the Chicago plant manager's report because this plant is $5,300 over budget.

This type of reporting system also permits comparative evaluations. In Illustration 24-19, the Chicago plant manager can easily rank the department managers' effectiveness in controlling manufacturing costs. Comparative rankings provide further incentive for a manager to control costs.

Types of Responsibility Centers

LEARNING OBJECTIVE **5**

Indicate the features of responsibility reports for cost centers.

Helpful Hint (1) Is the jewelry department of Macy's department store a profit center or a cost center? (2) Is the props department of a movie studio a profit center or a cost center? Answers: (1) Profit center. (2) Cost center.

There are three basic types of responsibility centers: cost centers, profit centers, and investment centers. These classifications indicate the degree of responsibility the manager has for the performance of the center.

A **cost center** incurs costs (and expenses) but does not directly generate revenues. Managers of cost centers have the authority to incur costs. They are evaluated on their ability to control costs. **Cost centers are usually either production departments or service departments.** Production departments participate directly in making the product. Service departments perform only support services. In a Ford Motor Company automobile plant, the welding, painting, and assembling departments are production departments. Ford's maintenance, cafeteria, and human resources departments are service departments. All of them are cost centers.

A **profit center** incurs costs (and expenses) and also generates revenues. Managers of profit centers are judged on the profitability of their centers. Examples of profit centers include the individual departments of a retail store, such as clothing, furniture, and automotive products, and branch offices of banks.

Like a profit center, an **investment center** incurs costs (and expenses) and generates revenues. In addition, an investment center has control over decisions regarding the assets available for use. Investment center managers are evaluated on both the profitability of the center and the rate of return earned on the funds invested. Investment centers are often associated with subsidiary companies. Utility Duke Energy has operating divisions such as electric utility, energy trading, and natural gas. Investment center managers control or significantly influence investment decisions related to such matters as plant expansion and entry into new market areas. Illustration 24-20 depicts the three types of responsibility centers.

Illustration 24-20
Types of responsibility centers

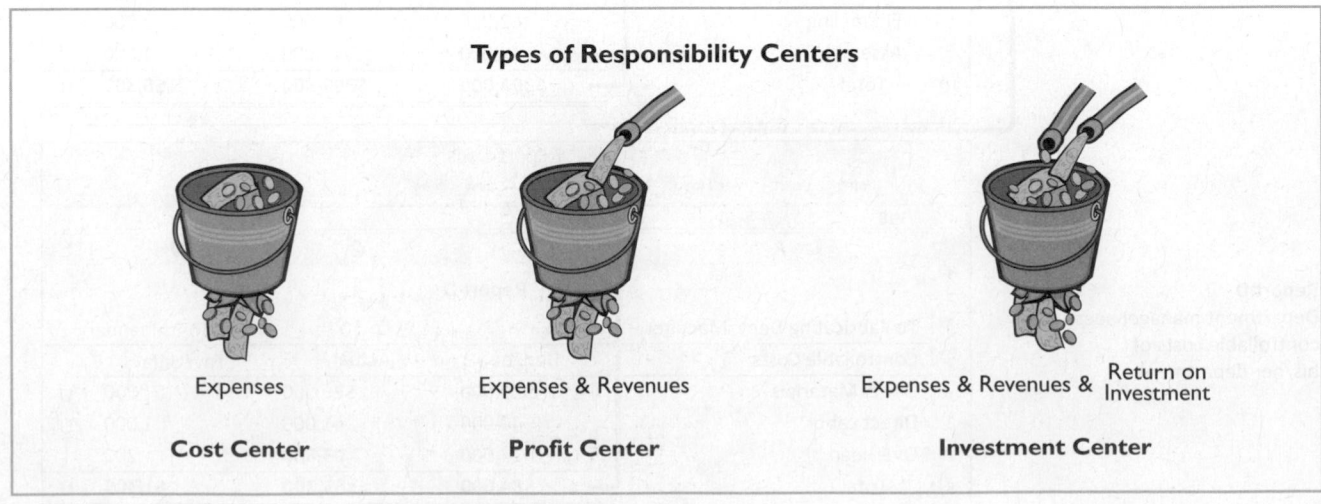

Types of Responsibility Centers

Expenses

Cost Center

Expenses & Revenues

Profit Center

Expenses & Revenues & Return on Investment

Investment Center

Responsibility Accounting for Cost Centers

The evaluation of a manager's performance for cost centers is based on his or her ability to meet budgeted goals for controllable costs. **Responsibility reports for cost centers compare actual controllable costs with flexible budget data.**

Illustration 24-21 shows a responsibility report. The report is adapted from the flexible budget report for Fox Company in Illustration 24-16 (page 1133). It assumes that the Finishing Department manager is able to control all manufacturing overhead costs except depreciation, property taxes, and his own monthly salary of $6,000. The remaining $4,000 ($10,000 − $6,000) of supervision costs are assumed to apply to other supervisory personnel within the Finishing Department, whose salaries are controllable by the manager.

Illustration 24-21
Responsibility report for a cost center

Controllable Costs	Budget	Actual	Difference Favorable - F Unfavorable - U	
Indirect materials	$13,500	$14,000	$ 500	U
Indirect labor	18,000	17,000	$1,000	F
Utilities	4,500	4,600	100	U
Supervision	4,000	4,000	0	
	$40,000	$39,600	$ 400	F

FOX COMPANY / Finishing Department / Responsibility Report / For the Month Ended January 31, 2014

The report in Illustration 24-21 includes **only controllable costs**, and no distinction is made between variable and fixed costs. The responsibility report continues the concept of management by exception. In this case, top management may request an explanation of the $1,000 favorable difference in indirect labor and/or the $500 unfavorable difference in indirect materials.

Responsibility Accounting for Profit Centers

To evaluate the performance of a profit center manager, upper management needs detailed information about both controllable revenues and controllable costs. The operating revenues earned by a profit center, such as sales, are controllable by the manager. All variable costs (and expenses) incurred by the center are also controllable by the manager because they vary with sales. However, to determine the controllability of fixed costs, it is necessary to distinguish between direct and indirect fixed costs.

LEARNING OBJECTIVE 6

Identify the content of responsibility reports for profit centers.

DIRECT AND INDIRECT FIXED COSTS

A profit center may have both direct and indirect fixed costs. **Direct fixed costs** relate specifically to one center and are incurred for the sole benefit of that center. Examples of such costs include the salaries established by the profit center manager for supervisory personnel and the cost of a timekeeping department for the center's employees. Since these fixed costs can be traced directly to a center, they are also called **traceable costs**. **Most direct fixed costs are controllable by the profit center manager.**

In contrast, **indirect fixed costs** pertain to a company's overall operating activities and are incurred for the benefit of more than one profit center. Management allocates indirect fixed costs to profit centers on some type of equitable basis. For example, property taxes on a building occupied by more than one center may be allocated on the basis of square feet of floor space used by each center. Or, the costs of a company's human resources department may be allocated to profit centers on the basis of the number of employees in each center. Because these fixed costs apply to more than one center, they are also called **common costs**. **Most indirect fixed costs are not controllable by the profit center manager.**

RESPONSIBILITY REPORT

The responsibility report for a profit center shows budgeted and actual **controllable revenues and costs**. The report is prepared using the cost-volume-profit income statement explained in Chapter 22. In the report:

1. Controllable fixed costs are deducted from contribution margin.
2. The excess of contribution margin over controllable fixed costs is identified as **controllable margin**.
3. Noncontrollable fixed costs are not reported.

Illustration 24-22 shows the responsibility report for the manager of the Marine Division, a profit center of Mantle Company. For the year, the Marine Division also had $60,000 of indirect fixed costs that were not controllable by the profit center manager.

Illustration 24-22
Responsibility report for profit center

	A	B	C	D	E
		MANTLE COMPANY			
		Marine Division			
		Responsibility Report			
		For the Year Ended December 31, 2014			
				Difference	
				Favorable - F	
		Budget	Actual	Unfavorable - U	
7	Sales revenue	$1,200,000	$1,150,000	$50,000	U
8	Variable costs				
9	Cost of goods sold	500,000	490,000	10,000	F
10	Selling and administrative	160,000	156,000	4,000	F
11	Total	660,000	646,000	14,000	F
12	Contribution margin	540,000	504,000	36,000	U
13	**Controllable fixed costs**				
14	Cost of goods sold	100,000	100,000	0	
15	Selling and administrative	80,000	80,000	0	
16	Total	180,000	180,000	0	
17	**Controllable margin**	$ 360,000	$ 324,000	$36,000	U

Controllable margin is considered to be the best measure of the manager's performance **in controlling revenues and costs**. The report in Illustration 24-22 shows that the manager's performance was below budgeted expectations by 10%

($36,000 ÷ $360,000). Top management would likely investigate the causes of this unfavorable result. Note that the report does not show the Marine Division's noncontrollable fixed costs of $60,000. These costs would be included in a report on the profitability of the profit center.

Management also may choose to see **monthly** responsibility reports for profit centers. In addition, responsibility reports may include cumulative year-to-date results.

> **DO IT!**

Profit Center Responsibility Report

Midwest Division operates as a profit center. It reports the following for the year:

	Budget	Actual
Sales revenue	$1,500,000	$1,700,000
Variable costs	700,000	800,000
Controllable fixed costs	400,000	400,000
Noncontrollable fixed costs	200,000	200,000

Prepare a responsibility report for the Midwest Division for December 31, 2014.

Action Plan

✔ Deduct variable costs from sales revenue to show contribution margin.

✔ Deduct controllable fixed costs from the contribution margin to show controllable margin.

✔ Do not report noncontrollable fixed costs.

Solution

MIDWEST DIVISION			
Responsibility Report			
For the Year Ended December 31, 2014			
			Difference
			Favorable F
	Budget	Actual	Unfavorable U
Sales revenue	$1,500,000	$1,700,000	$200,000 F
Variable costs	700,000	800,000	100,000 U
Contribution margin	800,000	900,000	100,000 F
Controllable fixed costs	400,000	400,000	–0–
Controllable margin	$ 400,000	$ 500,000	$100,000 F

Related exercise material: **BE24-7, E24-13, and DO IT! 24-3.**

✔ **The Navigator**

Responsibility Accounting for Investment Centers

As explained earlier, an investment center manager can control or significantly influence the investment funds available for use. Thus, the primary basis for evaluating the performance of a manager of an investment center is **return on investment (ROI)**. The return on investment is considered to be a useful performance measurement because it shows the **effectiveness of the manager in utilizing the assets at his or her disposal**.

> **LEARNING OBJECTIVE   7**
>
> Explain the basis and formula used in evaluating performance in investment centers.

RETURN ON INVESTMENT (ROI)

The formula for computing ROI for an investment center, together with assumed illustrative data, is shown in Illustration 24-23.

Controllable Margin	÷	Average Operating Assets	=	Return on Investment (ROI)
$1,000,000	÷	$5,000,000	=	20%

Illustration 24-23
ROI formula

Both factors in the formula are controllable by the investment center manager. Operating assets consist of current assets and plant assets used in operations by the center and controlled by the manager. Nonoperating assets such as idle plant assets and land held for future use are excluded. Average operating assets are usually based on the cost or book value of the assets at the beginning and end of the year.

RESPONSIBILITY REPORT

The scope of the investment center manager's responsibility significantly affects the content of the performance report. Since an investment center is an independent entity for operating purposes, **all fixed costs are controllable by its manager**. For example, the manager is responsible for depreciation on investment center assets. Therefore, more fixed costs are identified as controllable in the performance report for an investment center manager than in a performance report for a profit center manager. The report also shows budgeted and actual ROI below controllable margin.

To illustrate this responsibility report, we will now assume that the Marine Division of Mantle Company is an investment center. It has budgeted and actual average operating assets of $2,000,000. The manager can control $60,000 of fixed costs that were not controllable when the division was a profit center. Illustration 24-24 shows the division's responsibility report.

Illustration 24-24
Responsibility report for investment center

	A	B	C	D	E
1		MANTLE COMPANY			
2		Marine Division			
3		Responsibility Report			
4		For the Year Ended December 31, 2014			
5				Difference	
6		Budget	Actual	Favorable - F Unfavorable - U	
7	Sales revenue	$ 1,200,000	$ 1,150,000	$ 50,000	U
8	Variable costs				
9	Cost of goods sold	500,000	490,000	10,000	F
10	Selling and administrative	160,000	156,000	4,000	F
11	Total	660,000	646,000	14,000	F
12	Contribution margin	540,000	504,000	36,000	U
13	**Controllable fixed costs**				
14	Cost of goods sold	100,000	100,000	0	
15	Selling and administrative	80,000	80,000	0	
16	**Other fixed costs**	60,000	60,000	0	
17	Total	$ 240,000	$ 240,000	0	
18	**Controllable margin**	$ 300,000	$ 264,000	$ 36,000	U
19	**Return on investment**	15.0%	13.2%	1.8%	U
20		(a)	(b)	(c)	
21					
22		(a) $ 300,000 / $2,000,000	(b) $ 264,000 / $2,000,000	(c) $ 36,000 / $2,000,000	
23					

The report shows that the manager's performance based on ROI was below budget expectations by 1.8% (15.0% versus 13.2%). Top management would likely want an explanation of the reasons for this unfavorable result.

JUDGMENTAL FACTORS IN ROI

The return on investment approach includes two judgmental factors:

1. **Valuation of operating assets.** Operating assets may be valued at acquisition cost, book value, appraised value, or fair value. The first two bases are readily available from the accounting records.

2. **Margin (income) measure.** This measure may be controllable margin, income from operations, or net income.

Each of the alternative values for operating assets can provide a reliable basis for evaluating a manager's performance as long as it is consistently applied between reporting periods. However, the use of income measures other than controllable margin will not result in a valid basis for evaluating the performance of an investment center manager.

IMPROVING ROI

The manager of an investment center can improve ROI by increasing controllable margin, and/or reducing average operating assets. To illustrate, we will use the following assumed data for the Laser Division of Berra Company.

Sales revenue	$2,000,000
Variable costs	1,100,000
Contribution margin (45%)	900,000
Controllable fixed costs	300,000
Controllable margin (a)	$ 600,000
Average operating assets (b)	$5,000,000
Return on investment (a) ÷ (b)	**12%**

Illustration 24-25
Assumed data for Laser Division

INCREASING CONTROLLABLE MARGIN Controllable margin can be increased by increasing sales or by reducing variable and controllable fixed costs as follows.

1. **Increase sales 10%.** Sales will increase $200,000 ($2,000,000 × .10). Assuming no change in the contribution margin percentage of 45%, contribution margin will increase $90,000 ($200,000 × .45). Controllable margin will increase by the same amount because controllable fixed costs will not change. Thus, controllable margin becomes $690,000 ($600,000 + $90,000). The new ROI is 13.8%, computed as follows.

$$\text{ROI} = \frac{\text{Controllable margin}}{\text{Average operating assets}} = \frac{\$690,000}{\$5,000,000} = 13.8\%$$

Illustration 24-26
ROI computation—increase in sales

An increase in sales benefits both the investment center and the company if it results in new business. It would not benefit the company if the increase was achieved at the expense of other investment centers.

2. **Decrease variable and fixed costs 10%.** Total costs decrease $140,000 [($1,100,000 + $300,000) × .10]. This reduction results in a corresponding increase in controllable margin. Thus, controllable margin becomes $740,000 ($600,000 + $140,000). The new ROI is 14.8%, computed as follows.

$$\text{ROI} = \frac{\text{Controllable margin}}{\text{Average operating assets}} = \frac{\$740,000}{\$5,000,000} = 14.8\%$$

Illustration 24-27
ROI computation—decrease in costs

This course of action is clearly beneficial when the reduction in costs is the result of eliminating waste and inefficiency. But, a reduction in costs that results from cutting expenditures on vital activities, such as required maintenance and inspections, is not likely to be acceptable to top management.

REDUCING AVERAGE OPERATING ASSETS Assume that average operating assets are reduced 10% or $500,000 ($5,000,000 × .10). Average operating assets become $4,500,000 ($5,000,000 − $500,000). Since controllable margin remains unchanged at $600,000, the new ROI is 13.3%, computed as follows.

Illustration 24-28
ROI computation—decrease in operating assets

$$\text{ROI} = \frac{\text{Controllable margin}}{\text{Average operating assets}} = \frac{\$600,000}{\$4,500,000} = \textbf{13.3\%}$$

Reductions in operating assets may or may not be prudent. It is beneficial to eliminate overinvestment in inventories and to dispose of excessive plant assets. However, it is unwise to reduce inventories below expected needs or to dispose of essential plant assets.

© YinYang/iStockphoto

ACCOUNTING ACROSS THE ORGANIZATION

Does Hollywood Look at ROI?

If Hollywood were run like a real business, where things like return on investment mattered, there would be one unchallenged, sacred principle that studio chieftains would never violate: Make lots of G-rated movies.

No matter how you slice the movie business—by star vehicles, by budget levels, or by sequels or franchises—by far the best return on investment comes from the not-so-glamorous world of G-rated films. The problem is, these movies represent only 3% of the total films made in a typical year.

Take 2003: According to Motion Picture Association of America statistics, of the 940 movies released that year, only 29 were G-rated. Yet the highest-grossing movie of the year, *Finding Nemo*, was G-rated. . . . On the flip side are the R-rated films, which dominate the total releases and yet yield the worst return on investment. A whopping 646 R-rated films were released in 2003—69% of the total output—but only four of the top-20 grossing movies of the year were R-rated films.

This trend—G-rated movies are good for business but underproduced; R-rated movies are bad for business, and yet overdone—is something that has been driving economists batty for the past several years.

Source: David Grainger, "The Dysfunctional Family-Film Business," *Fortune* (January 10, 2005), pp. 20–21.

 What might be the reason that movie studios do not produce G-rated movies as much as R-rated ones? (See page 1175.)

> ## DO IT!

Performance Evaluation

The service division of Metro Industries reported the following results for 2014.

Sales revenue	$400,000
Variable costs	320,000
Controllable fixed costs	40,800
Average operating assets	280,000

Management is considering the following independent courses of action in 2015 in order to maximize the return on investment for this division.

1. Reduce average operating assets by $80,000, with no change in controllable margin.
2. Increase sales $80,000, with no change in the contribution margin percentage.
(a) Compute the controllable margin and the return on investment for 2014.
(b) Compute the controllable margin and the expected return on investment for each proposed alternative.

Solution

Action Plan

✔ Recall key formulas: Sales revenue − Variable costs = Contribution margin.

✔ Contribution margin ÷ Sales revenue = Contribution margin percentage.

✔ Contribution margin − Controllable fixed costs = Controllable margin.

✔ Return on investment = Controllable margin ÷ Average operating assets.

(a) Return on investment for 2014

Sales revenue	$400,000
Variable costs	320,000
Contribution margin	80,000
Controllable fixed costs	40,800
Controllable margin	$ 39,200

Return on investment $\dfrac{\$39,200}{\$280,000} = 14\%$

(b) Expected return on investment for alternative 1:

$$\dfrac{\$39,200}{\$280,000 - \$80,000} = 19.6\%$$

Expected return on investment for alternative 2:

Sales revenue ($400,000 + $80,000)	$480,000
Variable costs ($320,000/$400,000 × $480,000)	384,000
Contribution margin	96,000
Controllable fixed costs	40,800
Controllable margin	$ 55,200

Return on investment $\dfrac{\$55,200}{\$280,000} = 19.7\%$

Related exercise material: **BE24-8, BE24-9, BE24-10, E24-14, E24-15, and DO IT! 24-4.**

✔ **The Navigator**

> ## Comprehensive DO IT! 1

Glenda Company uses a flexible budget for manufacturing overhead based on direct labor hours. For 2014, the master overhead budget for the Packaging Department based on 300,000 direct labor hours was as follows.

Variable Costs		Fixed Costs	
Indirect labor	$360,000	Supervision	$ 60,000
Supplies and lubricants	150,000	Depreciation	24,000
Maintenance	210,000	Property taxes	18,000
Utilities	120,000	Insurance	12,000
	$840,000		$114,000

During July, 24,000 direct labor hours were worked. The company incurred the following variable costs in July: indirect labor $30,200, supplies and lubricants $11,600, maintenance $17,500, and utilities $9,200. Actual fixed overhead costs were the same as monthly budgeted fixed costs.

Instructions

Prepare a flexible budget report for the Packaging Department for July.

Solution to Comprehensive DO IT! 1

GLENDA COMPANY
Manufacturing Overhead Budget Report (Flexible)
Packaging Department
For the Month Ended July 31, 2014

Direct labor hours (DLH)	Budget 24,000 DLH	Actual Costs 24,000 DLH	Difference Favorable F Unfavorable U
Variable costs			
Indirect labor ($1.20ᵃ)	$28,800	$30,200	$1,400 U
Supplies and lubricants ($0.50ᵃ)	12,000	11,600	400 F
Maintenance ($0.70ᵃ)	16,800	17,500	700 U
Utilities ($0.40ᵃ)	9,600	9,200	400 F
Total variable	67,200	68,500	1,300 U
Fixed costs			
Supervision	$ 5,000ᵇ	$ 5,000	–0–
Depreciation	2,000ᵇ	2,000	–0–
Property taxes	1,500ᵇ	1,500	–0–
Insurance	1,000ᵇ	1,000	–0–
Total fixed	9,500	9,500	–0–
Total costs	$76,700	$78,000	$1,300 U

ᵃ($360,000 ÷ 300,000; $150,000 ÷ 300,000; $210,000 ÷ 300,000; $120,000 ÷ 300,000).
ᵇAnnual cost divided by 12.

 The Navigator

> **Comprehensive DO IT! 2**

The manufacturing overhead budget for Reebles Company contains the following items.

Variable costs	
Indirect materials	$25,000
Indirect labor	12,000
Maintenance expenses	10,000
Manufacturing supplies	6,000
Total variable	$53,000

Fixed costs	
Supervision	$17,000
Inspection costs	1,000
Insurance expenses	2,000
Depreciation	15,000
Total fixed	$35,000

The budget was based on an estimated 2,000 units being produced. During November, 1,500 units were produced, and the following costs incurred.

Variable costs	
Indirect materials	$25,200
Indirect labor	13,500
Maintenance expenses	8,200
Manufacturing supplies	5,100
Total variable	$52,000
Fixed costs	
Supervision	$19,300
Inspection costs	1,200
Insurance expenses	2,200
Depreciation	14,700
Total fixed	$37,400

Instructions

(a) Determine which items would be controllable by Ed Lopat, the production manager. (Assume "supervision" excludes Lopat's own salary.)

(b) How much should have been spent during the month for the manufacture of the 1,500 units?

(c) Prepare a flexible manufacturing overhead budget report for Mr. Lopat.

(d) Prepare a responsibility report. Include only the costs that would have been controllable by Mr. Lopat. In an attached memo, describe clearly for Mr. Lopat the areas in which his performance needs to be improved.

Solution to Comprehensive DO IT! 2

(a) Ed Lopat should be able to control all the variable costs and the fixed costs of supervision and inspection. Insurance and depreciation ordinarily are not the responsibility of the department manager.

(b) The total variable cost per unit is $26.50 ($53,000 ÷ 2,000). The total budgeted cost during the month to manufacture 1,500 units is variable costs $39,750 (1,500 × $26.50) plus fixed costs ($35,000), for a total of $74,750 ($39,750 + $35,000).

(c)

REEBLES COMPANY
Production Department
Manufacturing Overhead Budget Report (Flexible)
For the Month Ended November 30, 2014

	Budget at 1,500 Units	Actual at 1,500 Units	Difference Favorable F Unfavorable U
Variable costs			
Indirect materials ($12.50)	$18,750	$25,200	$ 6,450 U
Indirect labor ($6)	9,000	13,500	4,500 U
Maintenance ($5)	7,500	8,200	700 U
Manufacturing supplies ($3)	4,500	5,100	600 U
Total variable	39,750	52,000	12,250 U
Fixed costs			
Supervision	17,000	19,300	2,300 U
Inspection	1,000	1,200	200 U
Insurance	2,000	2,200	200 U
Depreciation	15,000	14,700	300 F
Total fixed	35,000	37,400	2,400 U
Total costs	$74,750	$89,400	$14,650 U

(d) Because a production department is a cost center, the responsibility report should include only the costs that are controllable by the production manager. In this type of report, no distinction is made between variable and fixed costs. Budget data in the report should be based on the units actually produced.

REEBLES COMPANY
Production Department
Manufacturing Overhead Responsibility Report
For the Month Ended November 30, 2014

Controllable Costs	Budget	Actual	Difference Favorable F Unfavorable U
Indirect materials	$18,750	$25,200	$ 6,450 U
Indirect labor	9,000	13,500	4,500 U
Maintenance	7,500	8,200	700 U
Manufacturing supplies	4,500	5,100	600 U
Supervision	17,000	19,300	2,300 U
Inspection	1,000	1,200	200 U
Total	$57,750	$72,500	$14,750 U

To: Mr. Ed Lopat, Production Manager

From: _____, Vice President of Production

Subject: Performance Evaluation for the Month of November

Your performance in controlling costs that are your responsibility was very disappointing in the month of November. As indicated in the accompanying responsibility report, total costs were $14,750 over budget. On a percentage basis, costs were 26% over budget. As you can see, actual costs were over budget for every cost item. In three instances, costs were significantly over budget (indirect materials 34%, indirect labor 50%, and supervision 14%).

Ed, it is imperative that you get costs under control in your department as soon as possible.

I think we need to talk about ways to implement more effective cost control measures. I would like to meet with you in my office at 9 a.m. on Wednesday to discuss possible alternatives.

 The Navigator

SUMMARY OF LEARNING OBJECTIVES

 The Navigator

1 Describe the concept of budgetary control. Budgetary control consists of (a) preparing periodic budget reports that compare actual results with planned objectives, (b) analyzing the differences to determine their causes, (c) taking appropriate corrective action, and (d) modifying future plans, if necessary.

2 Evaluate the usefulness of static budget reports. Static budget reports are useful in evaluating the progress toward planned sales and profit goals. They are also appropriate in assessing a manager's effectiveness in controlling costs when (a) actual activity closely approximates the master budget activity level, and/or (b) the behavior of the costs in response to changes in activity is fixed.

3 Explain the development of flexible budgets and the usefulness of flexible budget reports. To develop the flexible budget it is necessary to: (a) Identify the activity index and the relevant range of activity. (b) Identify the variable costs, and determine the budgeted variable cost per unit of activity for each cost. (c) Identify the fixed costs, and determine the budgeted amount for each cost. (d) Prepare the budget for selected increments of activity within the relevant range. Flexible budget reports permit an evaluation of a manager's performance in controlling production and costs.

4 Describe the concept of responsibility accounting. Responsibility accounting involves accumulating and reporting revenues and costs on the basis of the individual manager who has the authority to make the day-to-day decisions about the items. The evaluation of a manager's performance is based on the matters directly under the manager's control. In responsibility accounting, it is necessary to distinguish between controllable and noncontrollable fixed costs and to identify three types of responsibility centers: cost, profit, and investment.

5 Indicate the features of responsibility reports for cost centers. Responsibility reports for cost centers compare actual costs with flexible budget data. The reports show only controllable costs, and no distinction is made between variable and fixed costs.

6 Identify the content of responsibility reports for profit centers. Responsibility reports show contribution margin, controllable fixed costs, and controllable margin for each profit center.

7 Explain the basis and formula used in evaluating performance in investment centers. The primary basis for evaluating performance in investment centers is return on investment (ROI). The formula for computing ROI for investment centers is Controllable margin ÷ Average operating assets.

GLOSSARY

Budgetary control The use of budgets to control operations. (p. 1124).

Controllable cost A cost over which a manager has control. (p. 1137).

Controllable margin Contribution margin less controllable fixed costs. (p. 1144).

Cost center A responsibility center that incurs costs but does not directly generate revenues. (p. 1142).

Decentralization Control of operations is delegated to many managers throughout the organization. (p. 1136).

Direct fixed costs Costs that relate specifically to a responsibility center and are incurred for the sole benefit of the center. (p. 1143).

Flexible budget A projection of budget data for various levels of activity. (p. 1126).

Indirect fixed costs Costs that are incurred for the benefit of more than one profit center. (p. 1144).

Investment center A responsibility center that incurs costs, generates revenues, and has control over decisions regarding the assets available for use. (p. 1142).

Management by exception The review of budget reports by top management focused entirely or primarily

on differences between actual results and planned objectives. (p. 1137).

Noncontrollable costs Costs incurred indirectly and allocated to a responsibility center that are not controllable at that level. (p. 1137).

Profit center A responsibility center that incurs costs and also generates revenues. (p. 1142).

Responsibility accounting A part of management accounting that involves accumulating and reporting revenues and costs on the basis of the manager who has the authority to make the day-to-day decisions about the items. (p. 1135).

Responsibility reporting system The preparation of reports for each level of responsibility in the company's organization chart. (p. 1139).

Return on investment (ROI) A measure of management's effectiveness in utilizing assets at its disposal in an investment center. (p. 1145).

Segment An area of responsibility in decentralized operations. (p. 1136).

Static budget A projection of budget data at one level of activity. (p. 1125).

 **Self-Test, Brief Exercises, Exercises, Problem Set A, and many more resources are available for practice in *WileyPLUS*.**

SELF-TEST QUESTIONS

Answers are on page 1175.

(LO 1) **1.** Budgetary control involves all but one of the following:
  (a) modifying future plans.
  (b) analyzing differences.
  (c) using static budgets.
  (d) determining differences between actual and planned results.

(LO 1) **2.** Budget reports are prepared:
  (a) daily.   (c) monthly.
  (b) weekly.   (d) All of these choices are correct.

(LO 1) **3.** A production manager in a manufacturing company would most likely receive a:
  (a) sales report.
  (b) income statement.

  (c) scrap report.
  (d) shipping department overhead report.

(LO 2) **4.** A static budget is:
  (a) a projection of budget data at several levels of activity within the relevant range of activity.
  (b) a projection of budget data at a single level of activity.
  (c) compared to a flexible budget in a budget report.
  (d) never appropriate in evaluating a manager's effectiveness in controlling costs.

(LO 2) **5.** A static budget is useful in controlling costs when cost behavior is:
  (a) mixed.   (c) variable.
  (b) fixed.   (d) linear.

(LO 3)   6. At zero direct labor hours in a flexible budget graph, the total budgeted cost line intersects the vertical axis at $30,000. At 10,000 direct labor hours, a horizontal line drawn from the total budgeted cost line intersects the vertical axis at $90,000. Fixed and variable costs may be expressed as:
   (a) $30,000 fixed plus $6 per direct labor hour variable.
   (b) $30,000 fixed plus $9 per direct labor hour variable.
   (c) $60,000 fixed plus $3 per direct labor hour variable.
   (d) $60,000 fixed plus $6 per direct labor hour variable.

(LO 3)   7. At 9,000 direct labor hours, the flexible budget for indirect materials is $27,000. If $28,000 of indirect materials costs are incurred at 9,200 direct labor hours, the flexible budget report should show the following difference for indirect materials:
   (a) $1,000 unfavorable.   (c) $400 favorable.
   (b) $1,000 favorable.   (d) $400 unfavorable.

(LO 4)   8. Under responsibility accounting, the evaluation of a manager's performance is based on matters that the manager:
   (a) directly controls.
   (b) directly and indirectly controls.
   (c) indirectly controls.
   (d) has shared responsibility for with another manager.

(LO 4)   9. Responsibility centers include:
   (a) cost centers.
   (b) profit centers.
   (c) investment centers.
   (d) All of these choices are correct.

(LO 5)   10. Responsibility reports for cost centers:
   (a) distinguish between fixed and variable costs.
   (b) use static budget data.
   (c) include both controllable and noncontrollable costs.
   (d) include only controllable costs.

(LO 5)   11. The accounting department of a manufacturing company is an example of:
   (a) a cost center.   (c) an investment center.
   (b) a profit center.   (d) a contribution center.

(LO 6)   12. To evaluate the performance of a profit center manager, upper management needs detailed information about:
   (a) controllable costs.
   (b) controllable revenues.
   (c) controllable costs and revenues.
   (d) controllable costs and revenues and average operating assets.

(LO 6)   13. In a responsibility report for a profit center, controllable fixed costs are deducted from contribution margin to show:
   (a) profit center margin.
   (b) controllable margin.
   (c) net income.
   (d) income from operations.

(LO 7)   14. In the formula for return on investment (ROI), the factors for controllable margin and operating assets are, respectively:
   (a) controllable margin percentage and total operating assets.
   (b) controllable margin dollars and average operating assets.
   (c) controllable margin dollars and total assets.
   (d) controllable margin percentage and average operating assets.

(LO 7)   15. A manager of an investment center can improve ROI by:
   (a) increasing average operating assets.
   (b) reducing sales.
   (c) increasing variable costs.
   (d) reducing variable and/or controllable fixed costs.

Go to the book's companion website, www.wiley.com/college/weygandt, for additional Self-Test Questions.

 The Navigator

QUESTIONS

1. (a) What is budgetary control?
   (b) Fred Barone is describing budgetary control. What steps should be included in Fred's description?
2. The following purposes are part of a budgetary reporting system: (a) Determine efficient use of materials. (b) Control overhead costs. (c) Determine whether income objectives are being met. For each purpose, indicate the name of the report, the frequency of the report, and the primary recipient(s) of the report.
3. How may a budget report for the second quarter differ from a budget report for the first quarter?
4. Ken Bay questions the usefulness of a master sales budget in evaluating sales performance. Is there justification for Ken's concern? Explain.
5. Under what circumstances may a static budget be an appropriate basis for evaluating a manager's effectiveness in controlling costs?

6. "A flexible budget is really a series of static budgets." Is this true? Why?
7. The static manufacturing overhead budget based on 40,000 direct labor hours shows budgeted indirect labor costs of $54,000. During March, the department incurs $64,000 of indirect labor while working 45,000 direct labor hours. Is this a favorable or unfavorable performance? Why?
8. A static overhead budget based on 40,000 direct labor hours shows Factory Insurance $6,500 as a fixed cost. At the 50,000 direct labor hours worked in March, factory insurance costs were $6,300. Is this a favorable or unfavorable performance? Why?
9. Megan Pedigo is confused about how a flexible budget is prepared. Identify the steps for Megan.
10. Cali Company has prepared a graph of flexible budget data. At zero direct labor hours, the total budgeted

cost line intersects the vertical axis at $20,000. At 10,000 direct labor hours, the line drawn from the total budgeted cost line intersects the vertical axis at $85,000. How may the fixed and variable costs be expressed?

11. The flexible budget formula is fixed costs $50,000 plus variable costs of $4 per direct labor hour. What is the total budgeted cost at (a) 9,000 hours and (b) 12,345 hours?

12. What is management by exception? What criteria may be used in identifying exceptions?

13. What is responsibility accounting? Explain the purpose of responsibility accounting.

14. Eve Rooney is studying for an accounting examination. Describe for Eve what conditions are necessary for responsibility accounting to be used effectively.

15. Distinguish between controllable and noncontrollable costs.

16. How do responsibility reports differ from budget reports?

17. What is the relationship, if any, between a responsibility reporting system and a company's organization chart?

18. Distinguish among the three types of responsibility centers.

19. (a) What costs are included in a performance report for a cost center? (b) In the report, are variable and fixed costs identified?

20. How do direct fixed costs differ from indirect fixed costs? Are both types of fixed costs controllable?

21. Jane Nott is confused about controllable margin reported in an income statement for a profit center. How is this margin computed, and what is its primary purpose?

22. What is the primary basis for evaluating the performance of the manager of an investment center? Indicate the formula for this basis.

23. Explain the ways that ROI can be improved.

24. Indicate two behavioral principles that pertain to (a) the manager being evaluated and (b) top management.

BRIEF EXERCISES

BE24-1 For the quarter ended March 31, 2014, Maris Company accumulates the following sales data for its product, Garden-Tools: $310,000 budget; $305,000 actual. Prepare a static budget report for the quarter.

Prepare static budget report.
(LO 2)

BE24-2 Data for Maris Company are given in BE24-1. In the second quarter, budgeted sales were $380,000, and actual sales were $384,000. Prepare a static budget report for the second quarter and for the year to date.

Prepare static budget report for 2 quarters.
(LO 2)

BE24-3 In Paige Company, direct labor is $20 per hour. The company expects to operate at 10,000 direct labor hours each month. In January 2014, direct labor totaling $204,000 is incurred in working 10,400 hours. Prepare (a) a static budget report and (b) a flexible budget report. Evaluate the usefulness of each report.

Show usefulness of flexible budgets in evaluating performance.
(LO 3)

BE24-4 Gundy Company expects to produce 1,200,000 units of Product XX in 2014. Monthly production is expected to range from 80,000 to 120,000 units. Budgeted variable manufacturing costs per unit are direct materials $5, direct labor $6, and overhead $8. Budgeted fixed manufacturing costs per unit for depreciation are $2 and for supervision are $1. Prepare a flexible manufacturing budget for the relevant range value using 20,000 unit increments.

Prepare a flexible budget for variable costs.
(LO 3)

BE24-5 Data for Gundy Company are given in BE24-4. In March 2014, the company incurs the following costs in producing 100,000 units: direct materials $525,000, direct labor $596,000, and variable overhead $805,000. Actual fixed costs were equal to budgeted fixed costs. Prepare a flexible budget report for March. Were costs controlled?

Prepare flexible budget report.
(LO 3)

BE24-6 In the Assembly Department of Hannon Company, budgeted and actual manufacturing overhead costs for the month of April 2014 were as follows.

Prepare a responsibility report for a cost center.
(LO 5)

	Budget	Actual
Indirect materials	$16,000	$14,300
Indirect labor	20,000	20,600
Utilities	10,000	10,850
Supervision	5,000	5,000

All costs are controllable by the department manager. Prepare a responsibility report for April for the cost center.

Prepare a responsibility report for a profit center.
(LO 6)

BE24-7 Elbert Company accumulates the following summary data for the year ending December 31, 2014, for its Water Division, which it operates as a profit center: sales revenue—$2,000,000 budget, $2,080,000 actual; variable costs—$1,000,000 budget, $1,060,000 actual; and controllable fixed costs—$300,000 budget, $305,000 actual. Prepare a responsibility report for the Water Division.

Prepare a responsibility report for an investment center.
(LO 7)

BE24-8 For the year ending December 31, 2014, Cobb Company accumulates the following data for the Plastics Division which it operates as an investment center: contribution margin—$700,000 budget, $710,000 actual; controllable fixed costs—$300,000 budget, $302,000 actual. Average operating assets for the year were $2,000,000. Prepare a responsibility report for the Plastics Division beginning with contribution margin.

Compute return on investment using the ROI formula.
(LO 7)

BE24-9 For its three investment centers, Kaspar Company accumulates the following data:

	I	II	III
Sales revenue	$2,000,000	$4,000,000	$ 4,000,000
Controllable margin	1,300,000	2,000,000	3,600,000
Average operating assets	5,000,000	8,000,000	12,000,000

Compute the return on investment (ROI) for each center.

Compute return on investment under changed conditions.
(LO 7)

BE24-10 Data for the investment centers for Kaspar Company are given in BE24-9. The centers expect the following changes in the next year: (I) increase sales 15%; (II) decrease costs $400,000; (III) decrease average operating assets $500,000. Compute the expected return on investment (ROI) for each center. Assume center I has a contribution margin percentage of 70%.

> DO IT! Review

Compute total budgeted costs in flexible budget.
(LO 3)

DO IT! 24-1 In Pargo Company's flexible budget graph, the fixed cost line and the total budgeted cost line intersect the vertical axis at $90,000. The total budgeted cost line is $330,000 at an activity level of 50,000 direct labor hours. Compute total budgeted costs at 65,000 direct labor hours.

Prepare and evaluate a flexible budget report.
(LO 3)

DO IT! 24-2 Mussatto Company expects to produce 50,000 units of product IOA during the current year. Budgeted variable manufacturing costs per unit are direct materials $7, direct labor $13, and overhead $18. Annual budgeted fixed manufacturing overhead costs are $96,000 for depreciation and $45,600 for supervision.

In the current month, Mussatto produced 6,000 units and incurred the following costs: direct materials $38,850, direct labor $76,440, variable overhead $116,640, depreciation $8,000, and supervision $4,000.

Prepare a flexible budget report. (*Note:* You do not need to prepare the heading.) Were costs controlled?

Prepare a responsibility report.
(LO 6)

DO IT! 24-3 The Wellstone Division operates as a profit center. It reports the following for the year.

	Budget	Actual
Sales revenue	$2,000,000	$1,860,000
Variable costs	800,000	760,000
Controllable fixed costs	550,000	550,000
Noncontrollable fixed costs	250,000	250,000

Prepare a responsibility report for the Wellstone Division at December 31, 2014.

Compute ROI and expected return on investments.
(LO 7)

DO IT! 24-4 The service division of Raney Industries reported the following results for 2013.

Sales revenue	$500,000
Variable costs	300,000
Controllable fixed costs	75,000
Average operating assets	625,000

Management is considering the following independent courses of action in 2014 in order to maximize the return on investment for this division.

1. Reduce average operating assets by $125,000, with no change in controllable margin.
2. Increase sales $100,000, with no change in the contribution margin percentage.

(a) Compute the controllable margin and the return on investment for 2013. (b) Compute the controllable margin and the expected return on investment for each proposed alternative.

✔ **The Navigator**

EXERCISES

E24-1 Mike Trusler has prepared the following list of statements about budgetary control.

1. Budget reports compare actual results with planned objectives.
2. All budget reports are prepared on a weekly basis.
3. Management uses budget reports to analyze differences between actual and planned results and determine their causes.
4. As a result of analyzing budget reports, management may either take corrective action or modify future plans.
5. Budgetary control works best when a company has an informal reporting system.
6. The primary recipients of the sales report are the sales manager and the vice president of production.
7. The primary recipient of the scrap report is the production manager.
8. A static budget is a projection of budget data at one level of activity.
9. Top management's reaction to unfavorable differences is not influenced by the materiality of the difference.
10. A static budget is not appropriate in evaluating a manager's effectiveness in controlling costs unless the actual activity level approximates the static budget activity level or the behavior of the costs is fixed.

Understand the concept of budgetary control.

(LO 1, 2, 3)

Instructions
Identify each statement as true or false. If false, indicate how to correct the statement.

E24-2 Crede Company budgeted selling expenses of $30,000 in January, $35,000 in February, and $40,000 in March. Actual selling expenses were $31,200 in January, $34,525 in February, and $46,000 in March.

Prepare and evaluate static budget report.

(LO 2)

Instructions
(a) Prepare a selling expense report that compares budgeted and actual amounts by month and for the year to date.
(b) What is the purpose of the report prepared in (a), and who would be the primary recipient?
(c) What would be the likely result of management's analysis of the report?

E24-3 Thome Company uses a flexible budget for manufacturing overhead based on direct labor hours. Variable manufacturing overhead costs per direct labor hour are as follows.

Prepare flexible manufacturing overhead budget.

(LO 3)

Indirect labor	$1.00
Indirect materials	0.60
Utilities	0.40

Fixed overhead costs per month are supervision $4,000, depreciation $1,200, and property taxes $800. The company believes it will normally operate in a range of 7,000–10,000 direct labor hours per month.

Instructions
Prepare a monthly manufacturing overhead flexible budget for 2014 for the expected range of activity, using increments of 1,000 direct labor hours.

Prepare flexible budget reports for manufacturing overhead costs, and comment on findings.

(LO 3)

E24-4 Using the information in E24-3, assume that in July 2014, Thome Company incurs the following manufacturing overhead costs.

Variable Costs		Fixed Costs	
Indirect labor	$8,800	Supervision	$4,000
Indirect materials	5,300	Depreciation	1,200
Utilities	3,200	Property taxes	800

Instructions

(a) Prepare a flexible budget performance report, assuming that the company worked 9,000 direct labor hours during the month.

(b) Prepare a flexible budget performance report, assuming that the company worked 8,500 direct labor hours during the month.

(c) ●━━━ Comment on your findings.

Prepare flexible selling expense budget.

(LO 3)

E24-5 DeWitt Company uses flexible budgets to control its selling expenses. Monthly sales are expected to range from $170,000 to $200,000. Variable costs and their percentage relationship to sales are sales commissions 6%, advertising 4%, traveling 3%, and delivery 2%. Fixed selling expenses will consist of sales salaries $35,000, depreciation on delivery equipment $7,000, and insurance on delivery equipment $1,000.

Instructions

Prepare a monthly flexible budget for each $10,000 increment of sales within the relevant range for the year ending December 31, 2014.

Prepare flexible budget reports for selling expenses.

(LO 3)

E24-6 The actual selling expenses incurred in March 2014 by DeWitt Company are as follows.

Variable Expenses		Fixed Expenses	
Sales commissions	$11,000	Sales salaries	$35,000
Advertising	6,900	Depreciation	7,000
Travel	5,100	Insurance	1,000
Delivery	3,450		

Instructions

(a) Prepare a flexible budget performance report for March using the budget data in E24-5, assuming that March sales were $170,000.

(b) Prepare a flexible budget performance report, assuming that March sales were $180,000.

(c) ●━━━ Comment on the importance of using flexible budgets in evaluating the performance of the sales manager.

Prepare flexible budget and responsibility report for manufacturing overhead.

(LO 3, 5)

E24-7 Lowell Company's manufacturing overhead budget for the first quarter of 2014 contained the following data.

Variable Costs		Fixed Costs	
Indirect materials	$12,000	Supervisory salaries	$36,000
Indirect labor	10,000	Depreciation	7,000
Utilities	8,000	Property taxes and insurance	8,000
Maintenance	6,000	Maintenance	5,000

Actual variable costs were indirect materials $13,900, indirect labor $9,500, utilities $8,700, and maintenance $5,000. Actual fixed costs equaled budgeted costs except for property taxes and insurance, which were $8,400. The actual activity level equaled the budgeted level.

All costs are considered controllable by the production department manager except for depreciation, and property taxes and insurance.

Instructions

(a) Prepare a manufacturing overhead flexible budget report for the first quarter.

(b) Prepare a responsibility report for the first quarter.

Prepare flexible budget report, and answer question.

(LO 2, 3)

E24-8 As sales manager, Joe Batista was given the following static budget report for selling expenses in the Clothing Department of Soria Company for the month of October.

SORIA COMPANY
Clothing Department
Budget Report
For the Month Ended October 31, 2014

	Budget	Actual	Difference Favorable F Unfavorable U
Sales in units	8,000	10,000	2,000 F
Variable expenses			
Sales commissions	$ 2,400	$ 2,600	$ 200 U
Advertising expense	720	850	130 U
Travel expense	3,600	4,100	500 U
Free samples given out	1,600	1,400	200 F
Total variable	8,320	8,950	630 U
Fixed expenses			
Rent	1,500	1,500	–0–
Sales salaries	1,200	1,200	–0–
Office salaries	800	800	–0–
Depreciation—autos (sales staff)	500	500	–0–
Total fixed	4,000	4,000	–0–
Total expenses	$12,320	$12,950	$ 630 U

As a result of this budget report, Joe was called into the president's office and congratulated on his fine sales performance. He was reprimanded, however, for allowing his costs to get out of control. Joe knew something was wrong with the performance report that he had been given. However, he was not sure what to do, and comes to you for advice.

Instructions
(a) Prepare a budget report based on flexible budget data to help Joe.
(b) Should Joe have been reprimanded? Explain.

E24-9 Kirkland Plumbing Company is a newly formed company specializing in plumbing services for home and business. The owner, Lenny Kirkland, had divided the company into two segments: Home Plumbing Services and Business Plumbing Services. Each segment is run by its own supervisor, while basic selling and administrative services are shared by both segments.

Prepare and discuss a responsibility report.
(LO 3, 5)

Lenny has asked you to help him create a performance reporting system that will allow him to measure each segment's performance in terms of its profitability. To that end, the following information has been collected on the Home Plumbing Services segment for the first quarter of 2014.

	Budget	Actual
Service revenue	$25,000	$26,000
Allocated portion of:		
Building depreciation	11,000	11,000
Advertising	5,000	4,200
Billing	3,500	3,000
Property taxes	1,200	1,000
Material and supplies	1,600	1,200
Supervisory salaries	9,000	9,500
Insurance	4,000	3,600
Wages	3,000	3,250
Gas and oil	2,800	3,400
Equipment depreciation	1,500	1,300

Instructions
(a) Prepare a responsibility report for the first quarter of 2014 for the Home Plumbing Services segment.
(b) ——— Write a memo to Lenny Kirkland discussing the principles that should be used when preparing performance reports.

E24-10 Venetian Company has two production departments, Fabricating and Assembling. At a department managers' meeting, the controller uses flexible budget graphs to explain total budgeted costs. Separate graphs based on direct labor hours are used for each department. The graphs show the following.

1. At zero direct labor hours, the total budgeted cost line and the fixed cost line intersect the vertical axis at $50,000 in the Fabricating Department and $40,000 in the Assembling Department.
2. At normal capacity of 50,000 direct labor hours, the line drawn from the total budgeted cost line intersects the vertical axis at $150,000 in the Fabricating Department, and $120,000 in the Assembling Department.

Instructions
(a) State the total budgeted cost formula for each department.
(b) Compute the total budgeted cost for each department, assuming actual direct labor hours worked were 53,000 and 47,000, in the Fabricating and Assembling Departments, respectively.
(c) Prepare the flexible budget graph for the Fabricating Department, assuming the maximum direct labor hours in the relevant range is 100,000. Use increments of 10,000 direct labor hours on the horizontal axis and increments of $50,000 on the vertical axis.

E24-11 Fultz Company's organization chart includes the president; the vice president of production; three assembly plants—Dallas, Atlanta, and Tucson; and two departments within each plant—Machining and Finishing. Budget and actual manufacturing cost data for July 2014 are as follows.

Finishing Department—Dallas: direct materials $41,500 actual, $44,000 budget; direct labor $83,400 actual, $82,000 budget; manufacturing overhead $51,000 actual, $49,200 budget.

Machining Department—Dallas: total manufacturing costs $220,000 actual, $219,000 budget.

Atlanta Plant: total manufacturing costs $424,000 actual, $421,000 budget.

Tucson Plant: total manufacturing costs $494,200 actual, $496,500 budget.

The Dallas plant manager's office costs were $95,000 actual and $92,000 budget. The vice president of production's office costs were $132,000 actual and $130,000 budget. Office costs are not allocated to departments and plants.

Instructions
Using the format on page 1141, prepare the reports in a responsibility system for:
(a) The Finishing Department—Dallas.
(b) The plant manager—Dallas.
(c) The vice president of production.

E24-12 The Mixing Department manager of Malone Company is able to control all overhead costs except rent, property taxes, and salaries. Budgeted monthly overhead costs for the Mixing Department, in alphabetical order, are:

Indirect labor	$12,000	Property taxes	$ 1,000
Indirect materials	7,700	Rent	1,800
Lubricants	1,675	Salaries	10,000
Maintenance	3,500	Utilities	5,000

Actual costs incurred for January 2014 are indirect labor $12,250; indirect materials $10,200; lubricants $1,650; maintenance $3,500; property taxes $1,100; rent $1,800; salaries $10,000; and utilities $6,400.

Instructions
(a) Prepare a responsibility report for January 2014.
(b) What would be the likely result of management's analysis of the report?

E24-13 Deitz Inc. has three divisions which are operated as profit centers. Actual operating data for the divisions listed alphabetically are as follows.

Operating Data	Women's Shoes	Men's Shoes	Children's Shoes
Contribution margin	$250,000	(3)	$180,000
Controllable fixed costs	100,000	(4)	(5)
Controllable margin	(1)	$ 90,000	95,000
Sales revenue	600,000	450,000	(6)
Variable costs	(2)	320,000	250,000

Instructions

(a) Compute the missing amounts. Show computations.

(b) Prepare a responsibility report for the Women's Shoes Division assuming (1) the data are for the month ended June 30, 2014, and (2) all data equal budget except variable costs which are $10,000 over budget.

E24-14 The Sports Equipment Division of Harrington Company is operated as a profit center. Sales for the division were budgeted for 2014 at $900,000. The only variable costs budgeted for the division were cost of goods sold ($440,000) and selling and administrative ($60,000). Fixed costs were budgeted at $100,000 for cost of goods sold, $90,000 for selling and administrative, and $70,000 for noncontrollable fixed costs. Actual results for these items were:

Prepare a responsibility report for a profit center, and compute ROI.

(LO 6, 7)

Sales revenue	$880,000
Cost of goods sold	
Variable	408,000
Fixed	105,000
Selling and administrative	
Variable	61,000
Fixed	66,000
Noncontrollable fixed	90,000

Instructions

(a) Prepare a responsibility report for the Sports Equipment Division for 2014.

(b) Assume the division is an investment center, and average operating assets were $1,000,000. The noncontrollable fixed costs are controllable at the investment center level. Compute ROI.

E24-15 The West Division of Nieto Company reported the following data for the current year.

Compute ROI for current year and for possible future changes.

(LO 7)

Sales revenue	$3,000,000
Variable costs	1,980,000
Controllable fixed costs	600,000
Average operating assets	5,000,000

Top management is unhappy with the investment center's return on investment (ROI). It asks the manager of the West Division to submit plans to improve ROI in the next year. The manager believes it is feasible to consider the following independent courses of action.

1. Increase sales by $320,000 with no change in the contribution margin percentage.
2. Reduce variable costs by $150,000.
3. Reduce average operating assets by 4%.

Instructions

(a) Compute the return on investment (ROI) for the current year.

(b) Using the ROI formula, compute the ROI under each of the proposed courses of action. (Round to one decimal.)

E24-16 The Dinkle and Frizell Dental Clinic performs both preventive and orthodontic dental services. The two owners, Reese Dinkle and Anita Frizell, operate the clinic as two separate investment centers: Preventive Services and Orthodontic Services. Each of them is in charge of one of the centers: Reese for Preventive Services and Anita for Orthodontic Services. Each month, they prepare an income statement for the two centers to evaluate performance and make decisions about how to improve the operational efficiency and profitability of the clinic.

Prepare a responsibility report for an investment center.

(LO 7)

Recently, they have been concerned about the profitability of the Preventive Services operations. For several months, it has been reporting a loss. The responsibility report for the month of May 2014 is shown on page 1162.

	Actual	Difference from Budget
Service revenue	$ 40,000	$1,000 F
Variable costs		
Filling materials	5,000	100 U
Novocain	3,900	100 U
Supplies	1,900	350 F
Dental assistant wages	2,500	–0–
Utilities	500	110 U
Total variable costs	13,800	40 F
Fixed costs		
Allocated portion of receptionist's salary	3,000	200 U
Dentist salary	9,800	400 U
Equipment depreciation	6,000	–0–
Allocated portion of building depreciation	15,000	1,000 U
Total fixed costs	33,800	1,600 U
Operating income (loss)	$ (7,600)	$ 560 U

In addition, the owners know that the investment in operating assets at the beginning of the month was $82,400, and it was $77,600 at the end of the month. They have asked for your assistance in evaluating their current performance reporting system.

Instructions

(a) Prepare a responsibility report for an investment center as illustrated in the chapter.

(b) ●———— Write a memo to the owners discussing the deficiencies of their current reporting system.

Prepare missing amounts in responsibility reports for three investment centers.

(LO 7)

E24-17 The Pletcher Transportation Company uses a responsibility reporting system to measure the performance of its three investment centers: Planes, Taxis, and Limos. Segment performance is measured using a system of responsibility reports and return on investment calculations. The allocation of resources within the company and the segment managers' bonuses are based in part on the results shown in these reports.

Recently, the company was the victim of a computer virus that deleted portions of the company's accounting records. This was discovered when the current period's responsibility reports were being prepared. The printout of the actual operating results appeared as follows.

	Planes	Taxis	Limos
Service revenue	$?	$500,000	$?
Variable costs	5,500,000	?	300,000
Contribution margin	?	250,000	480,000
Controllable fixed costs	1,500,000	?	?
Controllable margin	?	80,000	240,000
Average operating assets	25,000,000	?	1,500,000
Return on investment	13%	10%	?

Instructions
Determine the missing pieces of information above.

EXERCISES: SET B AND CHALLENGE EXERCISES

Visit the book's companion website, at **www.wiley.com/college/weygandt**, and choose the Student Companion site to access Exercise Set B and Challenge Exercises.

PROBLEMS: SET A

P24-1A Cook Company estimates that 300,000 direct labor hours will be worked during the coming year, 2014, in the Packaging Department. On this basis, the budgeted manufacturing overhead cost data, shown below, are computed for the year.

Prepare flexible budget and budget report for manufacturing overhead.

(LO 3)

Fixed Overhead Costs		Variable Overhead Costs	
Supervision	$ 96,000	Indirect labor	$126,000
Depreciation	72,000	Indirect materials	90,000
Insurance	30,000	Repairs	54,000
Rent	24,000	Utilities	72,000
Property taxes	18,000	Lubricants	18,000
	$240,000		$360,000

It is estimated that direct labor hours worked each month will range from 27,000 to 36,000 hours.

During October, 27,000 direct labor hours were worked and the following overhead costs were incurred.

Fixed overhead costs: supervision $8,000, depreciation $6,000, insurance $2,460, rent $2,000, and property taxes $1,500.

Variable overhead costs: indirect labor $12,432, indirect materials $7,680, repairs $4,800, utilities $6,840, and lubricants $1,920.

Instructions
(a) Prepare a monthly manufacturing overhead flexible budget for each increment of 3,000 direct labor hours over the relevant range for the year ending December 31, 2014.
(b) Prepare a flexible budget report for October.
(c) ━━━ Comment on management's efficiency in controlling manufacturing overhead costs in October.

(a) Total costs: DLH 27,000, $52,400; DLH 36,000, $63,200

(b) Difference $1,232 U

P24-2A Zelmer Company manufactures tablecloths. Sales have grown rapidly over the past 2 years. As a result, the president has installed a budgetary control system for 2014. The following data were used in developing the master manufacturing overhead budget for the Ironing Department, which is based on an activity index of direct labor hours.

Prepare flexible budget, budget report, and graph for manufacturing overhead.

(LO 3)

Variable Costs	Rate per Direct Labor Hour	Annual Fixed Costs	
Indirect labor	$0.40	Supervision	$48,000
Indirect materials	0.50	Depreciation	18,000
Factory utilities	0.30	Insurance	12,000
Factory repairs	0.20	Rent	30,000

The master overhead budget was prepared on the expectation that 480,000 direct labor hours will be worked during the year. In June, 41,000 direct labor hours were worked. At that level of activity, actual costs were as shown below.

Variable—per direct labor hour: indirect labor $0.44, indirect materials $0.48, factory utilities $0.32, and factory repairs $0.25.

Fixed: same as budgeted.

Instructions
(a) Prepare a monthly manufacturing overhead flexible budget for the year ending December 31, 2014, assuming production levels range from 35,000 to 50,000 direct labor hours. Use increments of 5,000 direct labor hours.
(b) Prepare a budget report for June comparing actual results with budget data based on the flexible budget.
(c) Were costs effectively controlled? Explain.
(d) State the formula for computing the total budgeted costs for the Ironing Department.
(e) Prepare the flexible budget graph, showing total budgeted costs at 35,000 and 45,000 direct labor hours. Use increments of 5,000 direct labor hours on the horizontal axis and increments of $10,000 on the vertical axis.

(a) Total costs: 35,000 DLH, $58,000; 50,000 DLH, $79,000

(b) Budget $66,400
Actual $70,090

State total budgeted cost formula, and prepare flexible budget reports for 2 time periods.

(LO 2, 3)

P24-3A Hill Company uses budgets in controlling costs. The August 2014 budget report for the company's Assembling Department is as follows.

HILL COMPANY
Budget Report
Assembling Department
For the Month Ended August 31, 2014

Manufacturing Costs	Budget	Actual	Difference Favorable F Unfavorable U
Variable costs			
Direct materials	$ 48,000	$ 47,000	$1,000 F
Direct labor	54,000	51,200	2,800 F
Indirect materials	24,000	24,200	200 U
Indirect labor	18,000	17,500	500 F
Utilities	15,000	14,900	100 F
Maintenance	6,000	6,200	200 U
Total variable	165,000	161,000	4,000 F
Fixed costs			
Rent	12,000	12,000	–0–
Supervision	17,000	17,000	–0–
Depreciation	6,000	6,000	–0–
Total fixed	35,000	35,000	–0–
Total costs	$200,000	$196,000	$4,000 F

The monthly budget amounts in the report were based on an expected production of 60,000 units per month or 720,000 units per year. The Assembling Department manager is pleased with the report and expects a raise, or at least praise for a job well done. The company president, however, is unhappy with the results for August because only 58,000 units were produced.

Instructions
(a) State the total monthly budgeted cost formula.

(b) Budget $194,500

(b) Prepare a budget report for August using flexible budget data. Why does this report provide a better basis for evaluating performance than the report based on static budget data?

(c) Budget $211,000
   Actual $212,100

(c) In September, 64,000 units were produced. Prepare the budget report using flexible budget data, assuming (1) each variable cost was 10% higher than its actual cost in August, and (2) fixed costs were the same in September as in August.

Prepare responsibility report for a profit center.

(LO 6)

P24-4A Clarke Inc. operates the Patio Furniture Division as a profit center. Operating data for this division for the year ended December 31, 2014, are as shown below.

	Budget	Difference from Budget
Sales revenue	$2,500,000	$50,000 F
Cost of goods sold		
Variable	1,300,000	41,000 F
Controllable fixed	200,000	3,000 U
Selling and administrative		
Variable	220,000	6,000 U
Controllable fixed	50,000	2,000 U
Noncontrollable fixed costs	70,000	4,000 U

In addition, Clarke incurs $180,000 of indirect fixed costs that were budgeted at $175,000. Twenty percent (20%) of these costs are allocated to the Patio Furniture Division.

Instructions

(a) Prepare a responsibility report for the Patio Furniture Division for the year.

(b) ━━━ Comment on the manager's performance in controlling revenues and costs.

(c) Identify any costs excluded from the responsibility report and explain why they were excluded.

(a) Contribution margin
$85,000 F
Controllable margin
$80,000 F

P24-5A Suppan Company manufactures a variety of tools and industrial equipment. The company operates through three divisions. Each division is an investment center. Operating data for the Home Division for the year ended December 31, 2014, and relevant budget data are as follows.

Prepare responsibility report for an investment center, and compute ROI.

(LO 7)

	Actual	Comparison with Budget
Sales revenue	$1,400,000	$100,000 favorable
Variable cost of goods sold	675,000	55,000 unfavorable
Variable selling and administrative expenses	125,000	25,000 unfavorable
Controllable fixed cost of goods sold	170,000	On target
Controllable fixed selling and administrative expenses	80,000	On target

Average operating assets for the year for the Home Division were $2,000,000 which was also the budgeted amount.

Instructions

(a) Prepare a responsibility report (in thousands of dollars) for the Home Division.

(b) Evaluate the manager's performance. Which items will likely be investigated by top management?

(c) Compute the expected ROI in 2014 for the Home Division, assuming the following independent changes to actual data.

(1) Variable cost of goods sold is decreased by 5%.

(2) Average operating assets are decreased by 10%.

(3) Sales are increased by $200,000, and this increase is expected to increase contribution margin by $85,000.

(a) Controllable margin:
Budget $330;
Actual $350

P24-6A Durham Company uses a responsibility reporting system. It has divisions in Denver, Seattle, and San Diego. Each division has three production departments: Cutting, Shaping, and Finishing. The responsibility for each department rests with a manager who reports to the division production manager. Each division manager reports to the vice president of production. There are also vice presidents for marketing and finance. All vice presidents report to the president.

In January 2014, controllable actual and budget manufacturing overhead cost data for the departments and divisions were as shown below.

Prepare reports for cost centers under responsibility accounting, and comment on performance of managers.

(LO 4)

Manufacturing Overhead	Actual	Budget
Individual costs—Cutting Department—Seattle		
Indirect labor	$ 73,000	$ 70,000
Indirect materials	47,900	46,000
Maintenance	20,500	18,000
Utilities	20,100	17,000
Supervision	22,000	20,000
	$183,500	$171,000
Total costs		
Shaping Department—Seattle	$158,000	$148,000
Finishing Department—Seattle	210,000	205,000
Denver division	678,000	673,000
San Diego division	722,000	715,000

Additional overhead costs were incurred as follows: Seattle division production manager—actual costs $52,500, budget $51,000; vice president of production—actual costs $65,000, budget $64,000; president—actual costs $76,400, budget $74,200. These expenses are not allocated.

The vice presidents who report to the president, other than the vice president of production, had the following expenses.

Vice President	Actual	Budget
Marketing	$133,600	$130,000
Finance	109,000	104,000

Instructions

(a) (1) $12,500 U
  (2) $29,000 U
  (3) $42,000 U
  (4) $52,800 U

(a) Using the format on page 1141, prepare the following responsibility reports.
   (1) Manufacturing overhead—Cutting Department manager—Seattle division.
   (2) Manufacturing overhead—Seattle division manager.
   (3) Manufacturing overhead—vice president of production.
   (4) Manufacturing overhead and expenses—president.
(b) Comment on the comparative performances of:
   (1) Department managers in the Seattle division.
   (2) Division managers.
   (3) Vice presidents.

PROBLEMS: SET B

Prepare flexible budget and budget report for manufacturing overhead.

(LO 3)

P24-1B Speier Company estimates that 240,000 direct labor hours will be worked during 2014 in the Assembly Department. On this basis, the following budgeted manufacturing overhead data are computed.

Variable Overhead Costs		Fixed Overhead Costs	
Indirect labor	$ 72,000	Supervision	$ 75,600
Indirect materials	48,000	Depreciation	30,000
Repairs	36,000	Insurance	12,000
Utilities	24,000	Rent	9,600
Lubricants	12,000	Property taxes	6,000
	$192,000		$133,200

It is estimated that direct labor hours worked each month will range from 18,000 to 24,000 hours.

During January, 20,000 direct labor hours were worked and the following overhead costs were incurred.

Variable Overhead Costs		Fixed Overhead Costs	
Indirect labor	$ 6,200	Supervision	$ 6,300
Indirect materials	3,600	Depreciation	2,500
Repairs	2,300	Insurance	1,000
Utilities	1,700	Rent	850
Lubricants	1,050	Property taxes	500
	$14,850		$11,150

Instructions

(a) Total costs: 18,000 DLH, $25,500; 24,000 DLH, $30,300

(b) Budget $27,100
   Actual $26,000

(a) Prepare a monthly flexible manufacturing overhead budget for each increment of 2,000 direct labor hours over the relevant range for the year ending December 31, 2014.
(b) Prepare a manufacturing overhead budget report for January.
(c) ◄———— Comment on management's efficiency in controlling manufacturing overhead costs in January.

Prepare flexible budget, budget report, and graph for manufacturing overhead.

(LO 3)

P24-2B Gonzalez Company produces one product, Olpe. Because of wide fluctuations in demand for Olpe, the Assembly Department experiences significant variations in monthly production levels.

The annual master manufacturing overhead budget is based on 300,000 direct labor hours. In July, 27,500 labor hours were worked. The master manufacturing overhead budget for the year and the actual overhead costs incurred in July are as follows.

Overhead Costs	Master Budget (annual)	Actual in July
Variable		
Indirect labor	$300,000	$26,000
Indirect materials	150,000	11,350
Utilities	90,000	8,050
Maintenance	60,000	5,400
Fixed		
Supervision	144,000	12,000
Depreciation	96,000	8,000
Insurance and taxes	60,000	5,000
Total	$900,000	$75,800

Instructions
(a) Prepare a monthly flexible overhead budget for the year ending December 31, 2014, assuming monthly production levels range from 22,500 to 30,000 direct labor hours. Use increments of 2,500 direct labor hours.
(b) Prepare a budget report for the month of July 2014, comparing actual results with budget data based on the flexible budget.
(c) ────── Were costs effectively controlled? Explain.
(d) State the formula for computing the total monthly budgeted costs in the Gonzalez Company.
(e) Prepare the flexible budget graph showing total budgeted costs at 25,000 and 27,500 direct labor hours. Use increments of 5,000 on the horizontal axis and increments of $10,000 on the vertical axis.

(a) Total costs: 22,500 DLH, $70,000; 30,000 DLH, $85,000

(b) Budget $80,000 Actual $75,800

P24-3B Hardesty Company uses budgets in controlling costs. The May 2014 budget report for the company's Packaging Department is as follows.

State total budgeted cost formula, and prepare flexible budget reports for 2 time periods.

(LO 2, 3)

HARDESTY COMPANY
Budget Report
Packaging Department
For the Month Ended May 31, 2014

Manufacturing Costs	Budget	Actual	Difference Favorable F Unfavorable U
Variable costs			
Direct materials	$ 40,000	$ 41,000	$1,000 U
Direct labor	45,000	47,300	2,300 U
Indirect materials	15,000	15,200	200 U
Indirect labor	12,500	13,000	500 U
Utilities	10,000	9,600	400 F
Maintenance	7,500	8,000	500 U
Total variable	130,000	134,100	4,100 U
Fixed costs			
Rent	10,000	10,000	–0–
Supervision	7,000	7,000	–0–
Depreciation	4,000	4,000	–0–
Total fixed	21,000	21,000	–0–
Total costs	$151,000	$155,100	$4,100 U

The monthly budget amounts in the report were based on an expected production of 50,000 units per month or 600,000 units per year.

The company president was displeased with the department manager's performance. The department manager, who thought he had done a good job, could not understand the unfavorable results. In May, 55,000 units were produced.

Instructions

(a) State the total budgeted cost formula.

(b) Budget $164,000

(b) Prepare a budget report for May using flexible budget data. Why does this report provide a better basis for evaluating performance than the report based on static budget data?

(c) Budget $125,000
Actual $128,280

(c) In June, 40,000 units were produced. Prepare the budget report using flexible budget data, assuming (1) each variable cost was 20% less in June than its actual cost in May, and (2) fixed costs were the same in the month of June as in May.

Prepare responsibility report for a profit center.
(LO 6)

P24-4B Guzman Inc. operates the Home Appliance Division as a profit center. Operating data for this division for the year ended December 31, 2014, are shown below.

	Budget	Difference from Budget
Sales revenue	$2,400,000	$90,000 U
Cost of goods sold		
Variable	1,200,000	58,000 U
Controllable fixed	200,000	8,000 F
Selling and administrative		
Variable	240,000	8,000 F
Controllable fixed	60,000	3,000 U
Noncontrollable fixed costs	50,000	2,000 U

In addition, Guzman incurs $150,000 of indirect fixed costs that were budgeted at $155,000. Twenty percent (20%) of these costs are allocated to the Home Appliance Division. None of these costs are controllable by the division manager.

Instructions

(a) Contribution margin
$140,000 U
Controllable margin
$135,000 U

(a) Prepare a responsibility report for the Home Appliance Division (a profit center) for the year.

(b) ◄———— Comment on the manager's performance in controlling revenues and costs.

(c) Identify any costs excluded from the responsibility report and explain why they were excluded.

Prepare responsibility report for an investment center, and compute ROI.
(LO 7)

P24-5B Strauss Company manufactures a variety of garden and lawn equipment. The company operates through three divisions. Each division is an investment center. Operating data for the Lawnmower Division for the year ended December 31, 2014, and relevant budget data are as follows.

	Actual	Comparison with Budget
Sales revenue	$2,900,000	$150,000 unfavorable
Variable cost of goods sold	1,400,000	100,000 unfavorable
Variable selling and administrative expenses	300,000	40,000 favorable
Controllable fixed cost of goods sold	270,000	On target
Controllable fixed selling and administrative expenses	140,000	On target

Average operating assets for the year for the Lawnmower Division were $5,000,000, which was also the budgeted amount.

Instructions

(a) Controllable margin:
Budget $1,000
Actual $790

(a) Prepare a responsibility report (in thousands of dollars) for the Lawnmower Division.

(b) Evaluate the manager's performance. Which items will likely be investigated by top management?

(c) Compute the expected ROI in 2014 for the Lawnmower Division, assuming the following independent changes to actual data.

  (1) Variable cost of goods sold is decreased by 20%.

  (2) Average operating assets are decreased by 24%.

  (3) Sales are increased by $700,000, and this increase is expected to increase contribution margin by $260,000.

Prepare reports for cost centers under responsibility accounting, and comment on performance of managers.
(LO 4)

P24-6B Gore Company uses a responsibility reporting system. It has divisions in San Francisco, Phoenix, and Tulsa. Each division has three production departments: Cutting, Shaping, and Finishing. The responsibility for each department rests with a manager who reports to the division production manager. Each division manager reports to the vice president of production. There are also vice presidents for marketing and finance. All vice presidents report to the president.

In January 2014, controllable actual and budget manufacturing overhead cost data for the departments and divisions were as shown below.

Manufacturing Overhead	Actual	Budget
Individual costs—Cutting Department—Phoenix		
Indirect labor	$ 95,000	$ 90,000
Indirect materials	62,700	61,000
Maintenance	27,400	25,000
Utilities	25,200	20,000
Supervision	31,000	28,000
	$241,300	$224,000
Total costs		
Shaping Department—Phoenix	$190,000	$177,000
Finishing Department—Phoenix	250,000	245,000
San Francisco division	724,000	715,000
Tulsa division	760,000	750,000

Additional overhead costs were incurred as follows: Phoenix division production manager—actual costs $73,100, budget $70,000; vice president of production—actual costs $72,000, budget $70,000; president—actual costs $94,200, budget $91,300. These expenses are not allocated.

The vice presidents, who report to the president (other than the vice president of production), had the following expenses.

Vice President	Actual	Budget
Marketing	$167,200	$160,000
Finance	125,000	120,000

Instructions
(a) Using the format on page 1141, prepare the following responsibility reports.
   (1) Manufacturing overhead—Cutting Department manager—Phoenix division.
   (2) Manufacturing overhead—Phoenix division manager.
   (3) Manufacturing overhead—vice president of production.
   (4) Manufacturing overhead and expenses—president.
(b) Comment on the comparative performances of:
   (1) Department managers in the Phoenix division.
   (2) Division managers.
   (3) Vice presidents.

(a) (1) $17,300 U
(2) $38,400 U
(3) $59,400 U
(4) $74,500 U

PROBLEMS: SET C

Visit the book's companion website, at **www.wiley.com/college/weygandt**, and choose the Student Companion site to access Problem Set C.

WATERWAYS CONTINUING PROBLEM

(*Note:* This is a continuation of the Waterways Problem from Chapters 19 through 23.)

WCP24 Waterways Corporation is continuing its budget preparations. This problem gives you static budget information as well as actual overhead costs, and asks you to calculate amounts related to budgetary control and responsibility accounting.

Go to the book's companion website, at **www.wiley.com/college/weygandt**, *to find the completion of this problem.*

Broadening Your Perspective

Management Decision-Making

Decision-Making Problem: Current Designs

BYP24-1 The Current Designs staff has prepared the annual manufacturing budget for the roto-molded line based on an estimated annual production of 4,000 kayaks during 2013. Each kayak will require 54 pounds of polyethylene powder and a finishing kit (rope, seat, hardware, etc.). The polyethylene powder used in these kayaks costs $1.50 per pound, and the finishing kits cost $170 each. Each kayak will use two kinds of labor—2 hours of type I labor from people who run the oven and trim the plastic, and 3 hours of work from type II workers who attach the hatches and seat and other hardware. The type I employees are paid $15 per hour, and the type II are paid $12 per hour.
Manufacturing overhead is budgeted at $396,000 for 2013, broken down as follows.

Variable costs	
Indirect materials	$ 40,000
Manufacturing supplies	53,800
Maintenance and utilities	88,000
	181,800
Fixed costs	
Supervision	90,000
Insurance	14,400
Depreciation	109,800
	214,200
Total	$396,000

During the first quarter, ended March 31, 2013, 1,050 units were actually produced with the following costs.

Polyethylene powder	$ 87,000
Finishing kits	178,840
Type I labor	31,500
Type II labor	39,060
Indirect materials	10,500
Manufacturing supplies	14,150
Maintenance and utilities	26,000
Supervision	20,000
Insurance	3,600
Depreciation	27,450
Total	$438,100

Instructions
(a) Prepare the annual manufacturing budget for 2013, assuming that 4,000 kayaks will be produced.
(b) Prepare the flexible budget for manufacturing for the quarter ended March 31, 2013. Assume activity levels of 900, 1,000, and 1,050 kayaks.
(c) Assuming the rotomolded line is treated as a profit center, prepare a flexible budget report for manufacturing for the quarter ended March 31, 2013, when 1,050 kayaks were produced.

Decision-Making Across the Organization

BYP24-2 Green Pastures is a 400-acre farm on the outskirts of the Kentucky Bluegrass, specializing in the boarding of broodmares and their foals. A recent economic downturn in the thoroughbred industry has led to a decline in breeding activities, and it has made the boarding business extremely competitive. To meet the competition, Green Pastures planned in 2014 to entertain clients, advertise more extensively, and absorb expenses formerly paid by clients such as veterinary and blacksmith fees.

The budget report for 2014 is presented below. As shown, the static income statement budget for the year is based on an expected 21,900 boarding days at $25 per mare. The variable expenses per mare per day were budgeted: feed $5, veterinary fees $3, blacksmith fees $0.25, and supplies $0.55. All other budgeted expenses were either semifixed or fixed.

During the year, management decided not to replace a worker who quit in March, but it did issue a new advertising brochure and did more entertaining of clients.[1]

GREEN PASTURES
Static Budget Income Statement
For the Year Ended December 31, 2014

	Actual	Master Budget	Difference
Number of mares	52	60	8 U
Number of boarding days	19,000	21,900	2,900 U
Sales revenue	$380,000	$547,500	$167,500 U
Less: Variable expenses			
Feed	104,390	109,500	5,110 F
Veterinary fees	58,838	65,700	6,862 F
Blacksmith fees	4,984	5,475	491 F
Supplies	10,178	12,045	1,867 F
Total variable expenses	178,390	192,720	14,330 F
Contribution margin	201,610	354,780	153,170 U
Less: Fixed expenses			
Depreciation	40,000	40,000	–0–
Insurance	11,000	11,000	–0–
Utilities	12,000	14,000	2,000 F
Repairs and maintenance	10,000	11,000	1,000 F
Labor	88,000	95,000	7,000 F
Advertisement	12,000	8,000	4,000 U
Entertainment	7,000	5,000	2,000 U
Total fixed expenses	180,000	184,000	4,000 F
Net income	$ 21,610	$170,780	$149,170 U

Instructions

With the class divided into groups, answer the following.

(a) Based on the static budget report:

(1) What was the primary cause(s) of the loss in net income?

(2) Did management do a good, average, or poor job of controlling expenses?

(3) Were management's decisions to stay competitive sound?

(b) Prepare a flexible budget report for the year.

(c) Based on the flexible budget report, answer the three questions in part (a) above.

(d) What course of action do you recommend for the management of Green Pastures?

Managerial Analysis

BYP24-3 Lanier Company manufactures expensive watch cases sold as souvenirs. Three of its sales departments are Retail Sales, Wholesale Sales, and Outlet Sales. The Retail Sales Department is a profit center. The Wholesale Sales Department is a cost center. Its managers merely take orders from customers who purchase through the company's wholesale catalog. The Outlet Sales Department is an investment center because each manager is given full responsibility for an outlet store location. The manager can hire and discharge employees, purchase, maintain, and sell equipment, and in general is fairly independent of company control.

Mary Gammel is a manager in the Retail Sales Department. Stephen Flott manages the Wholesale Sales Department. Jose Gomez manages the Golden Gate Club outlet store in San Francisco. The following are the budget responsibility reports for each of the three departments.

---

[1]Data for this case are based on Hans Sprohge and John Talbott, "New Applications for Variance Analysis," *Journal of Accountancy* (AICPA, New York), April 1989, pp. 137–141.

Budget

	Retail Sales	Wholesale Sales	Outlet Sales
Sales revenue	$ 750,000	$ 400,000	$200,000
Variable costs			
Cost of goods sold	150,000	100,000	25,000
Advertising	100,000	30,000	5,000
Sales salaries	75,000	15,000	3,000
Printing	10,000	20,000	5,000
Travel	20,000	30,000	2,000
Fixed costs			
Rent	50,000	30,000	10,000
Insurance	5,000	2,000	1,000
Depreciation	75,000	100,000	40,000
Investment in assets	1,000,000	1,200,000	800,000

Actual Results

	Retail Sales	Wholesale Sales	Outlet Sales
Sales revenue	$ 750,000	$ 400,000	$200,000
Variable costs			
Cost of goods sold	192,000	122,000	26,500
Advertising	100,000	30,000	5,000
Sales salaries	75,000	15,000	3,000
Printing	10,000	20,000	5,000
Travel	14,000	21,000	1,500
Fixed costs			
Rent	40,000	50,000	12,300
Insurance	5,000	2,000	1,000
Depreciation	80,000	90,000	56,000
Investment in assets	1,000,000	1,200,000	800,000

Instructions
(a) Determine which of the items should be included in the responsibility report for each of the three managers.
(b) Compare the budgeted measures with the actual results. Decide which results should be called to the attention of each manager.

Real-World Focus

BYP24-4 Computer Associates International, Inc., the world's leading business software company, delivers the end-to-end infrastructure to enable e-business through innovative technology, services, and education. Computer Associates has 19,000 employees worldwide and recently had revenue of over $6 billion.

Presented below is information from the company's annual report.

COMPUTER ASSOCIATES INTERNATIONAL, INC.
Management Discussion

The Company has experienced a pattern of business whereby revenue for its third and fourth fiscal quarters reflects an increase over first- and second-quarter revenue. The Company attributes this increase to clients' increased spending at the end of their calendar year budgetary periods and the culmination of its annual sales plan. Since the Company's costs do not increase proportionately with the third- and fourth-quarters' increase in revenue, the higher revenue in these quarters results in greater profit margins and income. Fourth-quarter profitability is traditionally affected by significant new hirings, training, and education expenditures for the succeeding year.

Instructions
(a) Why don't the company's costs increase proportionately as the revenues increase in the third and fourth quarters?
(b) What type of budgeting seems appropriate for the Computer Associates situation?

BYP24-5 There are many useful resources regarding budgeting available on websites. The following activity investigates the results of a comprehensive budgeting study.

Address: **http://www.accountingweb.com/sites/default/files/centage_ioma.pdf**

Instructions
Go to the address above and then answer the following questions.
(a) What are cited as the two most common "pain points" of budgeting?
(b) What percentage of companies that participated in the survey said that they prepare annual budgets? Of those that prepare budgets, what percentage say that they start the budgeting process by first generating sales projections?
(c) What is the most common amount of time for the annual budgeting process?
(d) When evaluating variances from budgeted amounts, what was the most commonly defined range of acceptable tolerance levels?
(e) The study defines three types of consequences for varying from budgeted amounts. How does it describe "severe" consequences?

Critical Thinking

Communication Activity

BYP24-6 The manufacturing overhead budget for Fleming Company contains the following items.

Variable costs		Fixed costs	
Indirect materials	$22,000	Supervision	$17,000
Indirect labor	12,000	Inspection costs	1,000
Maintenance expense	10,000	Insurance expense	2,000
Manufacturing supplies	6,000	Depreciation	15,000
Total variable	$50,000	Total fixed	$35,000

The budget was based on an estimated 2,000 units being produced. During the past month, 1,500 units were produced, and the following costs incurred.

Variable costs		Fixed costs	
Indirect materials	$22,500	Supervision	$18,400
Indirect labor	13,500	Inspection costs	1,200
Maintenance expense	8,200	Insurance expense	2,200
Manufacturing supplies	5,000	Depreciation	14,700
Total variable	$49,200	Total fixed	$36,500

Instructions
(a) Determine which items would be controllable by Fred Bedner, the production manager.
(b) How much should have been spent during the month for the manufacture of the 1,500 units?
(c) Prepare a flexible manufacturing overhead budget report for Mr. Bedner.
(d) Prepare a responsibility report. Include only the costs that would have been controllable by Mr. Bedner. Assume that the supervision cost above includes Mr. Bedner's salary of $10,000, both at budget and actual. In an attached memo, describe clearly for Mr. Bedner the areas in which his performance needs to be improved.

Ethics Case

BYP24-7 American Products Corporation participates in a highly competitive industry. In order to meet this competition and achieve profit goals, the company has chosen the decentralized form of organization. Each manager of a decentralized investment center is measured on the basis of profit contribution, market penetration, and return on investment. Failure to meet the objectives established by corporate management for these measures has not been acceptable and usually has resulted in demotion or dismissal of an investment center manager.

An anonymous survey of managers in the company revealed that the managers feel the pressure to compromise their personal ethical standards to achieve the corporate objectives. For example, at certain plant locations there was pressure to reduce quality control to a level which could not assure that all unsafe products would be rejected. Also, sales personnel were encouraged to use questionable sales tactics to obtain orders, including gifts and other incentives to purchasing agents.

The chief executive officer is disturbed by the survey findings. In his opinion, such behavior cannot be condoned by the company. He concludes that the company should do something about this problem.

Instructions
(a) Who are the stakeholders (the affected parties) in this situation?
(b) Identify the ethical implications, conflicts, or dilemmas in the above described situation.
(c) What might the company do to reduce the pressures on managers and decrease the ethical conflicts?

(CMA adapted)

All About You

BYP24-8 It is one thing to prepare a personal budget; it is another thing to stick to it. Financial planners have suggested various mechanisms to provide support for enforcing personal budgets. One approach is called "envelope budgeting."

Instructions
Read the article provided at **http://en.wikipedia.org/wiki/Envelope_budgeting**, and answer the following questions.
(a) Summarize the process of envelope budgeting.
(b) Evaluate whether you think you would benefit from envelope budgeting. What do you think are its strengths and weaknesses relative to your situation?

Considering Your Costs and Benefits

BYP24-9 Preparing a personal budget is a great first step toward control over your personal finances. It is especially useful to prepare a budget when you face a big decision. For most people, the biggest decision they will ever make is whether to purchase a house. The percentage of people in the United States who own a home is high compared to many other countries. This is partially the result of U.S. government programs and incentives that encourage home ownership. For example, the interest on a home mortgage is tax-deductible.

Before purchasing a house, you should first consider whether buying it is the best choice for you. Suppose you just graduated from college and are moving to a new community. Should you immediately buy a new home?

YES: If I purchase a home, I am making my housing cost more like a "fixed cost," thus minimizing increases in my future housing costs. Also, I benefit from the appreciation in my home's value. Although recent turbulence in the economy has caused home prices in many communities to decline, I know that over the long term, home prices have increased across the country.

NO: I just moved to a new town, so I don't know the housing market. I am new to my job, so I don't know whether I will like it or my new community. Also, if my job does go well, it is likely that my income will increase in the next few years, so I will able to afford a better house if I wait. Therefore, the flexibility provided by renting is very valuable to me at this point in my life.

Instructions
Write a response indicating your position regarding this situation. Provide support for your view.

Answers to Chapter Questions

Answers to Insight and Accounting Across the Organization Questions

p. 1129 Just What the Doctor Ordered? **Q:** Explain how the use of flexible budgets might help to identify the best solution to this problem. **A:** A fixed budget assumes a particular level of activity. In the case of television shows, the number of viewers can impact revenues and costs. NBCUniversal could prepare alternative budgets at varying levels of activities and assume various cost structures depending on the number of cast members and other factors. Experimenting with different scenarios could help the network identify an approach that maintains an acceptable level of income as revenues decline.

p. 1134 Budgets and the Exotic Newcastle Disease   Q: What is the major benefit of tying a budget to the overall goals of the company? **A:** People working on a budgeting process that is clearly guided and focused by strategic goals spend less time arguing about irrelevant details and more time focusing on the items that matter.

p. 1137 Competition versus Collaboration   Q: How might managers of separate divisions be able to reduce division costs through collaboration? **A:** Division managers might reduce costs by sharing design and marketing resources or by jointly negotiating with suppliers. In addition, they can reduce the need to hire and lay off employees by sharing staff across divisions as human resource needs change.

p. 1139 Flexible Manufacturing Requires Flexible Accounting   Q: What implications do these improvements in production capabilities have for management accounting information and performance evaluation within the organization? **A:** In order to maximize the potential of flexible manufacturing facilities, managers need to be supplied with information on a more frequent basis. In turn, the tools used to evaluate performance need to take into account what information management had at its disposal, and what decisions were made in response to this information.

p. 1148 Does Hollywood Look at ROI?   Q: What might be the reason that movie studios do not produce G-rated movies as much as R-rated ones? **A:** Perhaps Hollywood believes that big-name stars or large budgets, both of which are typical of R-rated movies, sell movies. However, one study recently concluded, "We can't find evidence that stars help movies, and we can't find evidence that bigger budgets increase return on investment." Some film companies are going out of their way to achieve at least a PG rating.

Answers to Self-Test Questions

1. c **2.** d **3.** c **4.** b **5.** b **6.** a ($90,000 − $30,000) ÷ 10,000 **7.** d $28,000 − [9,200 × ($27,000 ÷ 9,000)] **8.** a **9.** d **10.** d **11.** a **12.** c **13.** b **14.** b **15.** d

✔ The Navigator

25 | Standard Costs and Balanced Scorecard

80,000 Different Caffeinated Combinations

When Howard Schultz purchased a small Seattle coffee-roasting business in 1987, he set out to create a new kind of company. He thought the company should sell coffee by the cup in its store, in addition to the bags of roasted beans it already sold. He also felt that the store shouldn't just sell coffee but also a pleasant atmosphere and experience. Schultz saw the store as a place where you could order a beverage, custom-made to your unique tastes, in an environment that would give you the sense that you had escaped, if only momentarily, from the chaos we call life. Finally, Schultz believed that the company would prosper if employees shared in its success.

In a little more than 20 years, Howard Schultz's company, Starbucks, grew from that one store to over 17,000 locations in 54 countries. That is an incredible rate of growth, and it didn't happen by accident. While Starbucks does everything it can to maximize the customer's experience, behind the scenes it needs to control costs. Consider the almost infinite options of beverage combinations and variations

at Starbucks. The company must determine the most efficient way to make each beverage, it must communica these methods in the form of standards to its employees and it must then evaluate whether those standards are being met.

Schultz's book, *Onward: How Starbucks Fought for Its Li Without Losing Its Soul*, describes a painful period in wh Starbucks had to close 600 stores and lay off thousands employees. However, when a prominent shareholder sugg that the company eliminate its employee health-care plan, many other companies had done, Schultz refused. The hea care plan represented one of the company's most tangible commitments to employee well-being as well as to corpor social responsibility. Schultz feels strongly that providing he care to the company's employees is an essential part of the standard cost of a cup of Starbucks' coffee.

Watch the Starbucks video in WileyPLUS to learn more a how the company sets standards. Watch the Southwest Airlines video in WileyPLUS to learn more about the use the balanced scorecard in the real world.

 The Navigator

- Scan Learning Objectives
- Read Feature Story
- Read Preview
- Read text and answer **DO IT!** p. 1183
    - p. 1188 ■ p. 1192 ■ p. 1197
- Work Comprehensive **DO IT!** p. 1198
- Review Summary of Learning Objectives
- Answer Self-Test Questions
- Complete Assignments
- Go to *WileyPLUS* for practice and tutorials

Learning Objectives   **The Navigator**

After studying this chapter, you should be able to:

[1] Distinguish between a standard and a budget.

[2] Identify the advantages of standard costs.

[3] Describe how companies set standards.

[4] State the formulas for determining direct materials and direct labor variances.

[5] State the formula for determining the total manufacturing overhead variance.

[6] Discuss the reporting of variances.

[7] Prepare an income statement for management under a standard costing system.

[8] Describe the balanced scorecard approach to performance evaluation.

Bloomberg/Getty Images

Preview of Chapter 25

 The Navigator

Standards are a fact of life. You met the admission standards for the school you are attending. The vehicle that you drive had to meet certain governmental emissions standards. The hamburgers and salads that you eat in a restaurant have to meet certain health and nutritional standards before they can be sold. As described in our Feature Story, Starbucks has standards for the costs of its materials, labor, and overhead. The reason for standards in these cases is very simple. They help to ensure that overall product quality is high while keeping costs under control.

In this chapter, we continue the study of controlling costs. You will learn how to evaluate performance using standard costs and a balanced scorecard.

The content and organization of Chapter 25 are as follows.

STANDARD COSTS AND BALANCED SCORECARD

The Need for Standards	Setting Standard Costs	Analyzing and Reporting Variances from Standards	Balanced Scorecard
• Standards vs. budgets • Why standard costs?	• Ideal vs. normal • Case study	• Direct materials variances • Direct labor variances • Manufacturing overhead variances • Reporting variances • Statement presentation	• Financial perspective • Customer perspective • Internal process perspective • Learning and growth perspective

The Need for Standards

LEARNING OBJECTIVE **1**

Distinguish between a standard and a budget.

Standards are common in business. Those imposed by government agencies are often called **regulations**. They include the Fair Labor Standards Act, the Equal Employment Opportunity Act, and a multitude of environmental standards. Standards established internally by a company may extend to personnel matters, such as employee absenteeism and ethical codes of conduct, quality control standards for products, and standard costs for goods and services. In managerial accounting, **standard costs** are predetermined unit costs, which companies use as measures of performance.

We will focus on manufacturing operations in this chapter. But you should also recognize that standard costs also apply to many types of service businesses as well. For example, a fast-food restaurant such as McDonald's knows the price it should pay for pickles, beef, buns, and other ingredients. It also knows how much time it should take an employee to flip hamburgers. If the company pays too much for pickles or if employees take too much time to prepare Big Macs, McDonald's notices the deviations and takes corrective action. Not-for-profit entities, such as universities, charitable organizations, and governmental agencies, also may use standard costs as measures of performance.

Distinguishing Between Standards and Budgets

Both **standards** and **budgets** are predetermined costs, and both contribute to management planning and control. There is a difference, however, in the way the terms are expressed. A standard is a **unit** amount. A budget is a **total** amount. Thus, it is customary to state that the **standard cost** of direct labor for a unit of product is, say, $10. If the company produces 5,000 units of the product, the $50,000 of direct labor is the **budgeted** labor cost. A standard is the budgeted **cost per unit** of product. A standard is therefore concerned with each individual cost component that makes up the entire budget.

There are important accounting differences between budgets and standards. Except in the application of manufacturing overhead to jobs and processes, budget data are not journalized in cost accounting systems. In contrast, as we illustrate in Appendix 25A, standard costs may be incorporated into cost accounting systems. Also, a company may report its inventories at standard cost in its financial statements, but it would not report inventories at budgeted costs.

Why Standard Costs?

LEARNING OBJECTIVE **2**

Identify the advantages of standard costs.

Standard costs offer a number of advantages to an organization, as shown in Illustration 25-1.

The organization will realize these advantages only when standard costs are carefully established and prudently used. Using standards solely as a way to place blame can have a negative effect on managers and employees. To minimize this effect, many companies offer wage incentives to those who meet the standards.

Setting Standard Costs

LEARNING OBJECTIVE **3**

Describe how companies set standards.

The setting of standard costs to produce a unit of product is a difficult task. It requires input from all persons who have responsibility for costs and quantities. To determine the standard cost of direct materials, management consults purchasing agents, product managers, quality control engineers, and production supervisors. In setting the standard cost for direct labor, managers obtain pay

Advantages of Standard Costs

Facilitate management planning

Promote greater economy by making employees more "cost-conscious"

Useful in setting selling prices

Contribute to management control by providing basis for evaluation of cost control

Useful in highlighting variances in management by exception

Simplify costing of inventories and reduce clerical costs

Illustration 25-1
Advantages of standard costs

rate data from the payroll department. Industrial engineers generally determine the labor time requirements. The managerial accountant provides important input for the standard-setting process by accumulating historical cost data and by knowing how costs respond to changes in activity levels.

To be effective in controlling costs, standard costs need to be current at all times. Thus, standards are under continuous review. They should change whenever managers determine that the existing standard is not a good measure of performance. Circumstances that warrant revision of a standard include changed wage rates resulting from a new union contract, a change in product specifications, or the implementation of a new manufacturing method.

Ideal versus Normal Standards

Companies set standards at one of two levels: ideal or normal. **Ideal standards** represent optimum levels of performance under perfect operating conditions. **Normal standards** represent efficient levels of performance that are attainable under expected operating conditions.

Some managers believe ideal standards will stimulate workers to ever-increasing improvement. However, most managers believe that ideal standards lower the morale of the entire workforce because they are difficult, if not impossible, to meet. Very few companies use ideal standards.

Most companies that use standards set them at a normal level. Properly set, normal standards should be **rigorous but attainable**. Normal standards allow for rest periods, machine breakdowns, and other "normal" contingencies in the production process. In the remainder of this chapter, we will assume that standard costs are set at a normal level.

Ethics Note

When standards are set too high, employees sometimes feel pressure to consider unethical practices to meet these standards.

ACCOUNTING ACROSS THE ORGANIZATION

How Do Standards Help a Business?

A number of organizations, including corporations, consultants, and governmental agencies, share information regarding performance standards in an effort to create a standard set of measures for thousands of business processes. The group, referred to as the Open Standards Benchmarking Collaborative, includes IBM, Procter and Gamble, the U.S. Navy, and the World Bank. Companies that are interested in participating can go to the group's website and enter their information.

Source: William M. Bulkeley, "Business, Agencies to Standardize Their Benchmarks," *Wall Street Journal* (May 19, 2004).

? How will the creation of such standards help a business or organization? (See page 1225.)

A Case Study

To establish the standard cost of producing a product, it is necessary to establish standards for each manufacturing cost element—direct materials, direct labor, and manufacturing overhead. The standard for each element is derived from the standard price to be paid and the standard quantity to be used.

To illustrate, we use an extended example. Xonic Beverage Company uses standard costs to measure performance at the production facility of its caffeinated energy drink, Xonic Tonic. Xonic produces one-gallon containers of concentrated syrup that it sells to coffee and smoothie shops, and other retail outlets. The syrup is mixed with ice water or ice "slush" before serving. The potency of the beverage varies depending on the amount of concentrated syrup used.

DIRECT MATERIALS

The **direct materials price standard** is the cost per unit of direct materials that should be incurred. This standard is based on the purchasing department's best estimate of the **cost of raw materials**. This cost is frequently based on current purchase prices. The price standard also includes an amount for related costs such as receiving, storing, and handling. The materials price standard per pound of material for Xonic Tonic is:

Illustration 25-2
Setting direct materials price standard

Item	Price
Purchase price, net of discounts	$ 2.70
Freight	0.20
Receiving and handling	0.10
Standard direct materials price per pound	**$3.00**

The **direct materials quantity standard** is the quantity of direct materials that should be used per unit of finished goods. This standard is expressed as a physical measure, such as pounds, barrels, or board feet. In setting the standard, management considers both the quality and quantity of materials required to manufacture the product. The standard includes allowances for unavoidable waste and normal spoilage. The standard quantity per unit for Xonic Tonic is as follows.

Item	Quantity (Pounds)
Required materials	3.5
Allowance for waste	0.4
Allowance for spoilage	0.1
Standard direct materials quantity per unit	**4.0**

Illustration 25-3
Setting direct materials quantity standard

   The standard direct materials cost per unit is the standard direct materials price times the standard direct materials quantity. For Xonic, the standard direct materials cost per gallon of Xonic Tonic is $12.00 ($3 × 4 pounds).

DIRECT LABOR

The **direct labor price standard** is the rate per hour that should be incurred for direct labor. This standard is based on current wage rates, adjusted for anticipated changes such as cost of living adjustments (COLAs). The price standard also generally includes employer payroll taxes and fringe benefits, such as paid holidays and vacations. For Xonic, the direct labor price standard is as follows.

Alternative Terminology
The direct labor price standard is also called the *direct labor rate standard*.

Item	Price
Hourly wage rate	$ 12.50
COLA	0.25
Payroll taxes	0.75
Fringe benefits	1.50
Standard direct labor rate per hour	**$15.00**

Illustration 25-4
Setting direct labor price standard

   The **direct labor quantity standard** is the time that should be required to make one unit of the product. This standard is especially critical in labor-intensive companies. Allowances should be made in this standard for rest periods, cleanup, machine setup, and machine downtime. For Xonic, the direct labor quantity standard is as follows.

Alternative Terminology
The direct labor quantity standard is also called the *direct labor efficiency standard*.

Item	Quantity (Hours)
Actual production time	1.5
Rest periods and cleanup	0.2
Setup and downtime	0.3
Standard direct labor hours per unit	**2.0**

Illustration 25-5
Setting direct labor quantity standard

   The standard direct labor cost per unit is the standard direct labor rate times the standard direct labor hours. For Xonic, the standard direct labor cost per gallon is $30 ($15 × 2 hours).

MANUFACTURING OVERHEAD

For manufacturing overhead, companies use a **standard predetermined overhead rate** in setting the standard. This overhead rate is determined by dividing budgeted overhead costs by an expected standard activity index. For example, the index may be standard direct labor hours or standard machine hours.

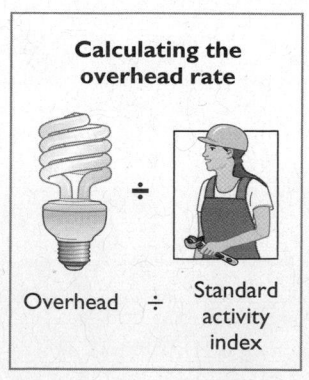

Calculating the overhead rate

Overhead ÷ Standard activity index

As discussed in Chapter 21, many companies employ activity-based costing (ABC) to allocate overhead costs. Because ABC uses multiple activity indices to allocate overhead costs, it results in a better correlation between activities and costs incurred than do other methods. As a result, the use of ABC can significantly improve the usefulness of standard costing for management decision-making.

Xonic uses standard direct labor hours as the activity index. The company expects to produce 13,200 gallons of Xonic Tonic during the year at normal capacity. **Normal capacity** is the average activity output that a company should experience over the long run. Since it takes two direct labor hours for each gallon, total standard direct labor hours are 26,400 (13,200 gallons × 2 hours).

At normal capacity of 26,400 direct labor hours, overhead costs are expected to be $132,000. Of that amount, $79,200 are variable and $52,800 are fixed. Illustration 25-6 shows computation of the standard predetermined overhead rates for Xonic.

Illustration 25-6
Computing predetermined overhead rates

Budgeted Overhead Costs	Amount	÷	Standard Direct Labor Hours	=	Overhead Rate per Direct Labor Hour
Variable	$ 79,200		26,400		$3.00
Fixed	52,800		26,400		2.00
Total	$132,000		26,400		$5.00

The standard manufacturing overhead rate per unit is the predetermined overhead rate times the activity index quantity standard. For Xonic, which uses direct labor hours as its activity index, the standard manufacturing overhead rate per gallon of Xonic Tonic is $10 ($5 × 2 hours).

TOTAL STANDARD COST PER UNIT

After a company has established the standard quantity and price per unit of product, it can determine the total standard cost. The total standard cost per unit is the sum of the standard costs of direct materials, direct labor, and manufacturing overhead. The total standard cost per gallon of Xonic Tonic is $52, as shown on the following standard cost card.

Illustration 25-7
Standard cost per gallon of Xonic Tonic

Product: Xonic Tonic		**Unit Measure: Gallon**		
Manufacturing Cost Elements	Standard Quantity	× Standard Price	=	Standard Cost
Direct materials	4 pounds	$ 3.00		$12.00
Direct labor	2 hours	$15.00		30.00
Manufacturing overhead	2 hours	$ 5.00		10.00
				$52.00

The company prepares a standard cost card for each product. This card provides the basis for determining variances from standards.

MANAGEMENT INSIGHT

How Can We Make Susan's Chili Profitable?

Susan's Chili Factory manufactures and sells chili. The cost of manufacturing Susan's chili consists of the costs of raw materials, labor to convert the basic ingredients to chili, and overhead. Managers need to develop three standards for materials: (1) What should be the formula (mix) of ingredients for one gallon of chili? (2) What should be the normal wastage (or shrinkage) for the individual ingredients? (3) What should be the standard cost for the individual ingredients that go into the chili?

Susan's Chili Factory also illustrates how managers can use standard costs in controlling costs. Suppose that summer droughts have reduced crop yields. As a result, prices have doubled for beans, onions, and peppers. In this case, actual costs will be significantly higher than standard costs, which will cause management to evaluate the situation. Similarly, assume that poor maintenance caused the onion-dicing blades to become dull. As a result, usage of onions to make a gallon of chili tripled. Because this deviation is quickly highlighted through standard costs, managers can take corrective action promptly.

Source: Adapted from David R. Beran, "Cost Reduction Through Control Reporting," *Management Accounting* (April 1982), pp. 29–33.

© Manuel Gutjahr/iStockphoto

? How might management use this raw materials cost information? (See page 1225.)

> DO IT!

Standard Costs

Action Plan

✔ Know that standard costs are predetermined unit costs.

✔ To establish the standard cost of producing a product, establish the standard for each manufacturing cost element—direct materials, direct labor, and manufacturing overhead.

✔ Compute the standard cost for each element from the standard price to be paid and the standard quantity to be used.

Ridette Inc. accumulated the following standard cost data concerning product Cty31.

Direct materials per unit: 1.5 pounds at $4 per pound.
Direct labor per unit: 0.25 hours at $13 per hour.
Manufacturing overhead: predetermined rate is 120% of direct labor cost.

Compute the standard cost of one unit of product Cty31.

Solution

Manufacturing Cost Element	Standard Quantity	×	Standard Price	=	Standard Cost
Direct materials	1.5 pounds		$4.00		$ 6.00
Direct labor	0.25 hours		$13.00		3.25
Manufacturing overhead	120% of direct labor cost		$3.25		3.90
Total					$13.15

Related exercise material: **BE25-2, BE25-3, E25-1, E25-2, E25-3, and DO IT! 25-1.**

 The Navigator

Analyzing and Reporting Variances from Standards

LEARNING OBJECTIVE **4**

State the formulas for determining direct materials and direct labor variances.

One of the major management uses of standard costs is to identify variances from standards. **Variances** are the differences between total actual costs and total standard costs.

To illustrate, assume that in producing 1,000 gallons of Xonic Tonic in the month of June, Xonic incurred the following costs.

Illustration 25-8
Actual production costs

Direct materials	$13,020
Direct labor	31,080
Variable overhead	6,500
Fixed overhead	4,400
Total actual costs	$55,000

Companies determine total standard costs by multiplying the units produced by the standard cost per unit. The total standard cost of Xonic Tonic is $52,000 (1,000 gallons × $52). Thus, the total variance is $3,000, as shown below.

Illustration 25-9
Computation of total variance

Actual costs	$55,000
Less: Standard costs	52,000
Total variance	**$ 3,000**

Alternative Terminology
In business, the term *variance* is also used to indicate differences between total budgeted and total actual costs.

Note that the variance is expressed in total dollars, and not on a per unit basis.

When actual costs exceed standard costs, the variance is **unfavorable**. The $3,000 variance in June for Xonic Tonic is unfavorable. An unfavorable variance has a negative connotation. It suggests that the company paid too much for one or more of the manufacturing cost elements or that it used the elements inefficiently.

If actual costs are less than standard costs, the variance is **favorable**. A favorable variance has a positive connotation. It suggests efficiencies in incurring manufacturing costs and in using direct materials, direct labor, and manufacturing overhead.

However, be careful: A favorable variance could be obtained by using inferior materials. In printing wedding invitations, for example, a favorable variance could result from using an inferior grade of paper. Or, a favorable variance might be achieved in installing tires on an automobile assembly line by tightening only half of the lug bolts. A variance is not favorable if the company has sacrificed quality control standards.

To interpret a variance, you must analyze its components. A variance can result from differences related to the cost of materials, labor, or overhead. Illustration 25-10 shows that the total variance is the sum of the materials, labor, and overhead variances.

Illustration 25-10
Components of total variance

Materials Variance + Labor Variance + Overhead Variance = Total Variance

In the following discussion, you will see that the materials variance and the labor variance are the sum of variances resulting from price differences and quantity differences. Illustration 25-11 shows a format for computing the price and quantity variances.

Illustration 25-11
Breakdown of materials or labor variance into price and quantity variances

Note that the left side of the matrix is actual cost (actual quantity times actual price). The right hand is standard cost (standard quantity times standard price). The only additional element you need in order to compute the price and quantity variances is the middle element, the actual quantity at the standard price.

Direct Materials Variances

Part of Xonic's total variance of $3,000 is due to a materials variance. In completing the order for 1,000 gallons of Xonic Tonic, the company used 4,200 pounds of direct materials. The direct materials were purchased at a price of $3.10 per unit. From Illustration 25-3, we know that Xonic's standards require it to use 4 pounds of materials per gallon produced, so it should have only used 4,000 (4 × 1,000) pounds of direct materials to produce 1,000 gallons. Illustration 25-2 shows that the standard cost of each pound of direct materials is $3 instead of the $3.10 actually paid. Illustration 25-12 shows that the **total materials variance** is computed as the difference between the amount paid (actual quantity times actual price) and the amount that should have been paid based on standards (standard quantity times standard price of materials).

Actual Quantity × Actual Price (AQ) × (AP)	−	Standard Quantity × Standard Price (SQ) × (SP)	=	Total Materials Variance (TMV)
(4,200 × $3.10)	−	(4,000 × $3.00)	=	$1,020 U

Illustration 25-12
Formula for total materials variance

Thus, for Xonic, the total materials variance is $1,020 ($13,020 − $12,000) unfavorable.

The total materials variance could be caused by differences in the price paid for the materials or by differences in the amount of materials used. Illustration 25-13 (page 1186) shows that the total materials variance is the sum of the materials price variance and the materials quantity variance.

Illustration 25-13
Components of total materials variance

Materials Price Variance + Materials Quantity Variance = Total Materials Variance

The materials price variance results from a difference between the actual price and the standard price. Illustration 25-14 shows that the **materials price variance** is computed as the difference between the actual amount paid (actual quantity of materials times actual price) and the standard amount that should have been paid for the materials used (actual quantity of materials times standard price).[1]

Illustration 25-14
Formula for materials price variance

Actual Quantity × Actual Price (AQ) × (AP)	−	Actual Quantity × Standard Price (AQ) × (SP)	=	Materials Price Variance (MPV)
(4,200 × $3.10)	−	(4,200 × $3.00)	=	$420 U

Helpful Hint The alternative formula is:

$$AQ \times (AP - SP) = MPV$$

For Xonic, the materials price variance is $420 ($13,020 − $12,600) unfavorable.

The price variance can also be computed by multiplying the actual quantity purchased by the difference between the actual and standard price per unit. The computation in this case is 4,200 × ($3.10 − $3.00) = $420 U.

As seen in Illustration 25-13, the other component of the materials variance is the quantity variance. The quantity variance results from differences between the amount of material actually used and the amount that should have been used. As shown in Illustration 25-15, the **materials quantity variance** is computed as the difference between the standard cost of the actual quantity (actual quantity times standard price) and the standard cost of the amount that should have been used (standard quantity times standard price for materials).

Illustration 25-15
Formula for materials quantity variance

Actual Quantity × Standard Price (AQ) × (SP)	−	Standard Quantity × Standard Price (SQ) × (SP)	=	Materials Quantity Variance (MQV)
(4,200 × $3.00)	−	(4,000 × $3.00)	=	$600 U

Thus, for Xonic, the materials quantity variance is $600 ($12,600 − $12,000) unfavorable.

Helpful Hint The alternative formula is:

$$SP \times (AQ - SQ) = MQV$$

The quantity variance can also be computed by applying the standard price to the difference between actual and standard quantities used. The computation in this example is $3.00 × (4,200 − 4,000) = $600 U.

The total materials variance of $1,020 U, therefore, consists of the following.

Illustration 25-16
Summary of materials variances

Materials price variance	$ 420 U
Materials quantity variance	600 U
Total materials variance	**$1,020 U**

---

[1]Assume that all materials purchased during the period are used in production and that no units remain in inventory at the end of the period.

Companies sometimes use a matrix to analyze a variance. **When the matrix is used, a company computes the amounts using the formulas for each cost element first and then computes the variances.** Illustration 25-17 shows the completed matrix for the direct materials variance for Xonic. The matrix provides a convenient structure for determining each variance.

Illustration 25-17
Matrix for direct materials variances

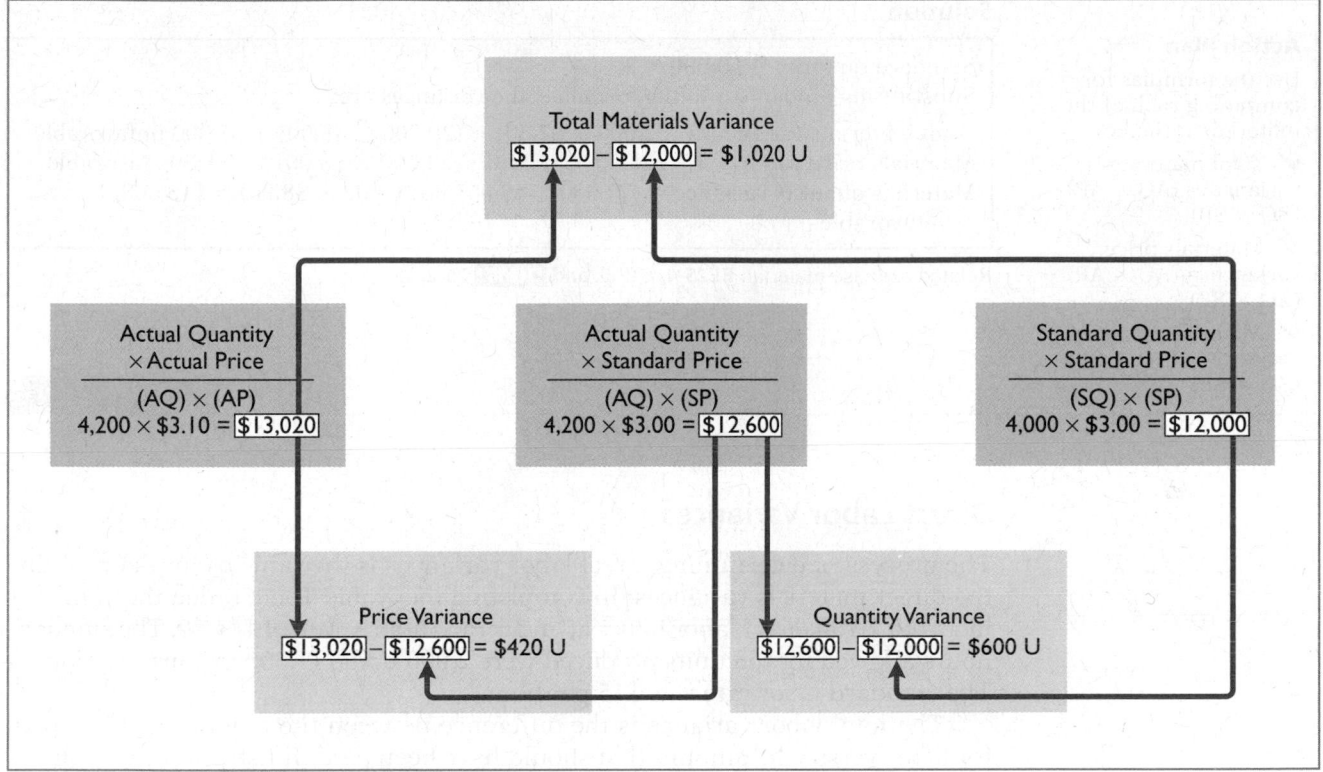

CAUSES OF MATERIALS VARIANCES

What are the causes of a variance? The causes may relate to both internal and external factors. The investigation of a **materials price variance usually begins in the purchasing department**. Many factors affect the price paid for raw materials. These include availability of quantity and cash discounts, the quality of the materials requested, and the delivery method used. To the extent that these factors are considered in setting the price standard, the purchasing department is responsible for any variances.

However, a variance may be beyond the control of the purchasing department. Sometimes, for example, prices may rise faster than expected. Moreover, actions by groups over which the company has no control, such as the OPEC nations' oil price increases, may cause an unfavorable variance. For example, during a recent year, Kraft Foods and Kellogg Company both experienced unfavorable materials price variances when the cost of dairy and wheat products jumped unexpectedly. There are also times when a production department may be responsible for the price variance. This may occur when a rush order forces the company to pay a higher price for the materials.

The starting point for determining the cause(s) of a significant **materials quantity variance is in the production department**. If the variances are due to inexperienced workers, faulty machinery, or carelessness, the production department is responsible. However, if the materials obtained by the purchasing department were of inferior quality, then the purchasing department is responsible.

> **DO IT!**

Direct Materials Variances

The standard cost of Wonder Walkers includes two units of direct materials at $8.00 per unit. During July, the company buys 22,000 units of direct materials at $7.50 and uses those materials to produce 10,000 Wonder Walkers. Compute the total, price, and quantity variances for materials.

Solution

Action Plan

Use the formulas for computing each of the materials variances:

✔ Total materials variance = (AQ × AP) − (SQ × SP)

✔ Materials price variance = (AQ × AP) − (AQ × SP)

✔ Materials quantity variance = (AQ × SP) − (SQ × SP)

Standard quantity = 10,000 × 2.
Substituting amounts into the formulas, the variances are:

Total materials variance = (22,000 × $7.50) − (20,000 × $8.00) = $5,000 unfavorable

Materials price variance = (22,000 × $7.50) − (22,000 × $8.00) = $11,000 favorable

Materials quantity variance = (22,000 × $8.00) − (20,000 × $8.00) = $16,000 unfavorable

Related exercise material: **BE25-4, E25-5, and DO IT! 25-2.**

 ✔ **The Navigator**

Direct Labor Variances

The process of determining direct labor variances is the same as for determining the direct materials variances. In completing the Xonic Tonic order, the company incurred 2,100 direct labor hours at an average hourly rate of $14.80. The standard hours allowed for the units produced were 2,000 hours (1,000 gallons × 2 hours). The standard labor rate was $15 per hour.

The total labor variance is the difference between the amount actually paid for labor versus the amount that should have been paid. Illustration 25-18 shows that the **total labor variance** is computed as the difference between the amount actually paid for labor (actual hours times actual rate) and the amount that should have been paid (standard hours times standard rate for labor).

Illustration 25-18
Formula for total labor variance

Actual Hours × Actual Rate (AH) × (AR)	−	Standard Hours × Standard Rate (SH) × (SR)	=	Total Labor Variance (TLV)
(2,100 × $14.80)	−	(2,000 × $15.00)	=	$1,080 U

The total labor variance is $1,080 ($31,080 − $30,000) unfavorable.

The total labor variance is caused by differences in the labor rate or difference in labor hours. Illustration 25-19 shows that the total labor variance is the sum of the labor price variance and the labor quantity variance.

Illustration 25-19
Components of total labor variance

Labor Price Variance + Labor Quantity Variance = Total Labor Variance

The labor price variance results from the difference between the rate paid to workers versus the rate that was supposed to be paid. Illustration 25-20 shows that the **labor price variance** is computed as the difference between the actual amount paid (actual hours times actual rate) and the amount that should have been paid for the number of hours worked (actual hours times standard rate for labor).

Illustration 25-20
Formula for labor price variance

Actual Hours × Actual Rate (AH) × (AR)	–	Actual Hours × Standard Rate (AH) × (SR)	=	Labor Price Variance (LPV)
(2,100 × $14.80)	–	(2,100 × $15.00)	=	$420 F

For Xonic, the labor price variance is $420 ($31,080 − $31,500) favorable.

The labor price variance can also be computed by multiplying actual hours worked by the difference between the actual pay rate and the standard pay rate. The computation in this example is 2,100 × ($15.00 − $14.80) = $420 F.

The other component of the total labor variance is the labor quantity variance. The labor quantity variance results from the difference between the actual number of labor hours and the number of hours that should have been worked for the quantity produced. Illustration 25-21 shows that the **labor quantity variance** is computed as the difference between the amount that should have been paid for the hours worked (actual hours times standard rate) and the amount that should have been paid for the amount of hours that should have been worked (standard hours times standard rate for labor).

Helpful Hint The alternative formula is:

$$\boxed{AH} \times \boxed{AR - SR} = \boxed{LPV}$$

Illustration 25-21
Formula for labor quantity variance

Actual Hours × Standard Rate (AH) × (SR)	–	Standard Hours × Standard Rate (SH) × (SR)	=	Labor Quantity Variance (LQV)
(2,100 × $15.00)	–	(2,000 × $15.00)	=	$1,500 U

Thus, for Xonic, the labor quantity variance is $1,500 ($31,500 − $30,000) unfavorable.

The same result can be obtained by multiplying the standard rate by the difference between actual hours worked and standard hours allowed. In this case, the computation is $15.00 × (2,100 − 2,000) = $1,500 U.

The total direct labor variance of $1,080 U, therefore, consists of:

Helpful Hint The alternative formula is:

$$\boxed{SR} \times \boxed{AH - SH} = \boxed{LQV}$$

Labor price variance	$ 420 F
Labor quantity variance	1,500 U
Total direct labor variance	**$1,080 U**

Illustration 25-22
Summary of labor variances

These results can also be obtained from the matrix in Illustration 25-23 (page 1190).

CAUSES OF LABOR VARIANCES

Labor price variances usually result from two factors: (1) paying workers **different wages than expected**, and (2) **misallocation of workers**. In companies where pay rates are determined by union contracts, labor price variances should be infrequent. When workers are not unionized, there is a much higher likelihood of such variances. The responsibility for these variances rests with the manager who authorized the wage change.

"What caused labor price variances?"
Personnel decisions

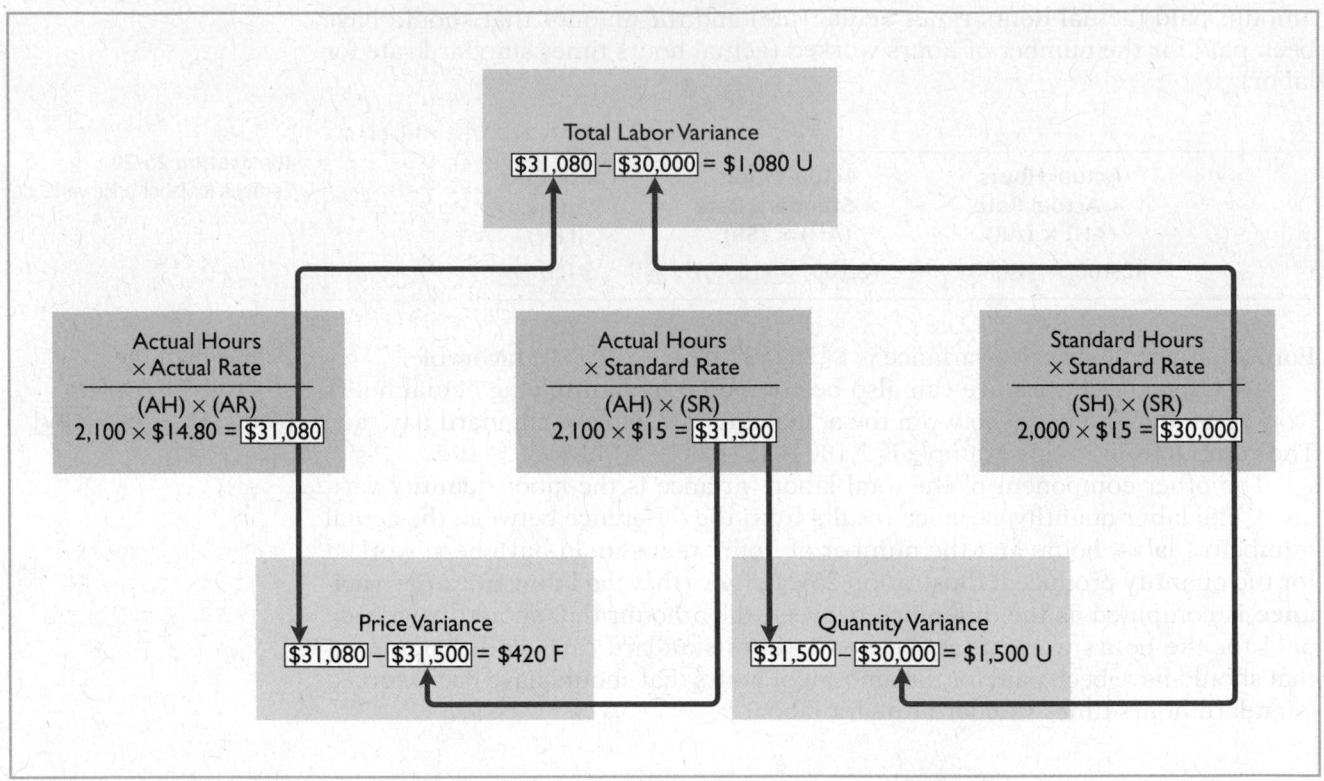

Illustration 25-23
Matrix for direct labor variances

"What caused labor quantity variances?"

Production Dept.

Misallocation of the workforce refers to using skilled workers in place of unskilled workers and vice versa. The use of an inexperienced worker instead of an experienced one will result in a favorable price variance because of the lower pay rate of the unskilled worker. An unfavorable price variance would result if a skilled worker were substituted for an inexperienced one. The production department generally is responsible for labor price variances resulting from misallocation of the workforce.

Labor quantity variances relate to the **efficiency of workers**. The cause of a quantity variance generally can be traced to the production department. The causes of an unfavorable variance may be poor training, worker fatigue, faulty machinery, or carelessness. These causes are the responsibility of the **production department**. However, if the excess time is due to inferior materials, the responsibility falls outside the production department.

Manufacturing Overhead Variances

The **total overhead variance** is the difference between the actual overhead costs and overhead costs applied based on standard hours allowed for the amount of goods produced. As indicated in Illustration 25-8 (page 1184), Xonic incurred overhead costs of $10,900 to produce 1,000 gallons of Xonic Tonic in June. The computation of the actual overhead is comprised of a variable and a fixed component. Illustration 25-24 shows this computation.

Illustration 25-24
Actual overhead costs

Variable overhead	$ 6,500
Fixed overhead	4,400
Total actual overhead	**$10,900**

To find the total overhead variance in a standard costing system, we determine the overhead costs applied based on standard hours allowed. **Standard hours allowed** are the hours that **should** have been worked for the units produced. Overhead costs for Xonic Tonic are applied based on direct labor hours. Because it takes two hours of direct labor to produce one gallon of Xonic Tonic, for the 1,000-gallon Xonic Tonic order, the standard hours allowed are 2,000 hours (1,000 gallons × 2 hours). We then apply the predetermined overhead rate to the 2,000 standard hours allowed.

Recall from Illustration 25-6 (page 1182) that the amount of budgeted overhead costs at normal capacity of $132,000 was divided by normal capacity of 26,400 direct labor hours, to arrive at a predetermined overhead rate of $5 ($132,000 ÷ 26,400). The predetermined rate of $5 is then multiplied by the 2,000 standard hours allowed, to determine the overhead costs applied.

Illustration 25-25 shows the formula for the total overhead variance and the calculation for Xonic for the month of June.

Actual Overhead	−	Overhead Applied*	=	Total Overhead Variance
$10,900 ($6,500 + $4,400)	−	$10,000 ($5 × 2,000 hours)	=	$900 U

*Based on standard hours allowed.

Illustration 25-25
Formula for total overhead variance

Thus, for Xonic, the total overhead variance is $900 unfavorable.

The overhead variance is generally analyzed through a price and a quantity variance. (These computations are discussed in more detail in advanced courses.) The name usually given to the price variance is the **overhead controllable variance**; the quantity variance is referred to as the **overhead volume variance**. Appendix 25B discusses how the total overhead variance can be broken down into these two variances.

CAUSES OF MANUFACTURING OVERHEAD VARIANCES

One reason for an overhead variance relates to over- or underspending on overhead items. For example, overhead may include indirect labor for which a company paid wages higher than the standard labor price allowed. Or, the price of electricity to run the company's machines increased, and the company did not anticipate this additional cost. Companies should investigate any spending variances, to determine whether they will continue in the future. Generally, the responsibility for these variances rests with the production department.

The overhead variance can also result from the inefficient use of overhead. For example, because of poor maintenance, a number of the manufacturing machines are experiencing breakdowns on a consistent basis, leading to reduced production. Or, the flow of materials through the production process is impeded because of a lack of skilled labor to perform the necessary production tasks, due to a lack of planning. In both of these cases, the production department is responsible for the cause of these variances. On the other hand, overhead can also be underutilized because of a lack of sales orders. When the cause is a lack of sales orders, the responsibility rests outside the production department. For example, at one point Chrysler experienced a very significant unfavorable overhead variance because plant capacity was maintained at excessively high levels, due to overly optimistic sales forecasts.

Archer Colin/SIPA/NewsCom

PEOPLE, PLANET, AND PROFIT INSIGHT

What's Brewing at Starbucks?

It is one thing for a company to say it is committed to corporate social responsibility. It is another thing for the company to actually spell out measurable goals. Recently, Starbucks published its 10th annual *Global Responsibility Report* in which it describes its goals, achievements, and even its shortcomings related to corporate social responsibility. For example, the company achieved its goal of getting more than 50% of its electricity from renewable sources. It then set its sights higher by setting a goal of 100% within five years. The company also has numerous goals related to purchasing coffee from sources that are certified as responsibly grown and ethically traded; providing funds for loans to coffee farmers; and partnerships with Conservation International to provide training to farmers on ecologically friendly growing. Further, the company reduced water consumption by more than 20% in a two-year period. Finally, it made a significant investment in programs to increase recycling of paper and plastic at its stores.

The report also candidly explains that the company did not meet its goal to cut energy consumption by 25%. It also fell far short of its goal of getting customers to reuse their cups. In those instances where it didn't achieve its goals, Starbucks set new goals and described steps it would take to achieve them. You can view the company's *Global Responsibility Report* at **www.starbucks.com/2010report**.

Source: "Starbucks Launches 10th Global Responsibility Report," *Business Wire* (April 18, 2011).

? What implications does Starbucks' commitment to corporate social responsibility have for the standard cost of a cup of coffee? (See page 1225.)

> DO IT!

Labor and Manufacturing Overhead Variances

Action Plan
✔ Use the formulas for computing each of the variances:
Total labor variance =
(AH × AR) − (SH × SR)
Labor price variance =
(AH × AR) − (AH × SR)
Labor quantity variance =
(AH × SR) − (SH × SR)
Total overhead variance =
Actual overhead −
Overhead applied*

*Based on standard hours allowed.

The standard cost of Product YY includes 3 hours of direct labor at $12.00 per hour. The predetermined overhead rate is $20.00 per direct labor hour. During July, the company incurred 3,500 hours of direct labor at an average rate of $12.40 per hour and $71,300 of manufacturing overhead costs. It produced 1,200 units.

(a) Compute the total, price, and quantity variances for labor. (b) Compute the total overhead variance.

Solution

Substituting amounts into the formulas, the variances are:

Total labor variance = (3,500 × $12.40) − (3,600 × $12.00) = $200 unfavorable

Labor price variance = (3,500 × $12.40) − (3,500 × $12.00) = $1,400 unfavorable

Labor quantity variance = (3,500 × $12.00) − (3,600 × $12.00) = $1,200 favorable

Total overhead variance = $71,300 − $72,000* = $700 favorable

*3,600 hours × $20.00

Related exercise material: **BE25-5, BE25-6, E25-4, E25-6, E25-7, E25-8, E25-10, and DO IT! 25-3.**

 ✔ **The Navigator**

Reporting Variances

All variances should be reported to appropriate levels of management as soon as possible. The sooner managers are informed, the sooner they can evaluate problems and take corrective action.

LEARNING OBJECTIVE 6

Discuss the reporting of variances.

The form, content, and frequency of variance reports vary considerably among companies. One approach is to prepare a weekly report for each department that has primary responsibility for cost control. Under this approach, materials price variances are reported to the purchasing department, and all other variances are reported to the production department that did the work. The following report for Xonic, with the materials for the Xonic Tonic order listed first, illustrates this approach.

XONIC Variance Report—Purchasing Department For Week Ended June 8, 2014					
Type of Materials	Quantity Purchased	Actual Price	Standard Price	Price Variance	Explanation
X100	4,200 lbs.	$3.10	$3.00	$ 420 U	Rush order
X142	1,200 units	2.75	2.80	60 F	Quantity discount
A85	600 doz.	5.20	5.10	60 U	Regular supplier on strike
Total price variance				$420 U	

Illustration 25-26
Materials price variance report

The explanation column is completed after consultation with the purchasing department manager.

Variance reports facilitate the principle of "management by exception" explained in Chapter 24. For example, the vice president of purchasing can use the report shown above to evaluate the effectiveness of the purchasing department manager. Or, the vice president of production can use production department variance reports to determine how well each production manager is controlling costs. In using variance reports, top management normally looks for **significant variances**. These may be judged on the basis of some quantitative measure, such as more than 10% of the standard or more than $1,000.

Statement Presentation of Variances

In income statements **prepared for management** under a standard cost accounting system, **cost of goods sold is stated at standard cost and the variances are disclosed separately**. Unfavorable variances increase cost of goods sold, while favorable variances decrease cost of goods sold. Illustration 25-27 (page 1194) shows the presentation of variances in an income statement. This income statement is based on the production and sale of 1,000 units of Xonic Tonic at $70 per unit. It also assumes selling and administrative costs of $3,000. Observe that each variance is shown, as well as the total net variance. In this example, variations from standard costs reduced net income by $3,000.

LEARNING OBJECTIVE 7

Prepare an income statement for management under a standard costing system.

Standard costs may be used in financial statements prepared for stockholders and other external users. The costing of inventories at standard costs is in accordance with generally accepted accounting principles when there are no significant differences between actual costs and standard costs. Hewlett-Packard and Jostens, Inc., for example, report their inventories at standard costs. However, if there are significant differences between actual and standard costs, the financial statements must report inventories and cost of goods sold at actual costs.

Illustration 25-27
Variances in income statement for management

XONIC Income Statement For the Month Ended June 30, 2014		
Sales revenue		$70,000
Cost of goods sold (at standard)		52,000
Gross profit (at standard)		18,000
Variances		
Materials price	$ 420 U	
Materials quantity	600 U	
Labor price	420 F	
Labor quantity	1,500 U	
Overhead	900 U	
Total variance unfavorable		**3,000**
Gross profit (actual)		15,000
Selling and administrative expenses		3,000
Net income		$12,000

It is also possible to show the variances in an income statement prepared in the variable costing (CVP) format. To do so, it is necessary to analyze the overhead variances into variable and fixed components. This type of analysis is explained in cost accounting textbooks.

Balanced Scorecard

LEARNING OBJECTIVE 8

Describe the balanced scorecard approach to performance evaluation.

Financial measures (measurement of dollars), such as variance analysis and return on investment (ROI), are useful tools for evaluating performance. However, many companies now supplement these financial measures with nonfinancial measures to better assess performance and anticipate future results. For example, airlines like Delta, American, and United use capacity utilization as an important measure to understand and predict future performance. Newspaper publishers such as the *New York Times* and the *Chicago Tribune* use circulation figures as another measure by which to assess performance. Penske Automotive Group, the owner of 300 dealerships, rewards executives for meeting employee retention targets. Illustration 25-28 lists some key nonfinancial measures used in various industries.

Most companies recognize that both financial and nonfinancial measures can provide useful insights into what is happening in the company. As a result, many companies now use a broad-based measurement approach, called the **balanced scorecard**, to evaluate performance. The **balanced scorecard** incorporates financial and nonfinancial measures in an integrated system that links performance measurement with a company's strategic goals. Nearly 50% of the largest companies in the United States, including Unilever, Chase, and Wal-Mart Stores, Inc., are using the balanced scorecard approach.

The balanced scorecard evaluates company performance from a series of "perspectives." The four most commonly employed perspectives are as follows.

1. The **financial perspective** is the most traditional view of the company. It employs financial measures of performance used by most firms.

Industry		Measure
Automobiles		Capacity utilization of plants.
		Average age of key assets.
		Impact of strikes.
		Brand-loyalty statistics.
Computer Systems		Market profile of customer end-products.
		Number of new products.
		Employee stock ownership percentages.
		Number of scientists and technicians used in R&D.
Chemicals		Customer satisfaction data.
		Factors affecting customer product selection.
		Number of patents and trademarks held.
		Customer brand awareness.
Regional Banks		Number of ATMs by state.
		Number of products used by average customer.
		Percentage of customer service calls handled by interactive voice response units.
		Personnel cost per employee.
		Credit card retention rates.

Source: Financial Accounting Standards Board, *Business Reporting: Insights into Enhancing Voluntary Disclosures* (Norwalk, Conn.: FASB, 2001).

Illustration 25-28
Nonfinancial measures used in various industries

2. The **customer perspective** evaluates the company from the viewpoint of those people who buy its products or services. This view compares the company to competitors in terms of price, quality, product innovation, customer service, and other dimensions.

3. The **internal process perspective** evaluates the internal operating processes critical to success. All critical aspects of the value chain—including product development, production, delivery, and after-sale service—are evaluated to ensure that the company is operating effectively and efficiently.

4. The **learning and growth perspective** evaluates how well the company develops and retains its employees. This would include evaluation of such things as employee skills, employee satisfaction, training programs, and information dissemination.

Within each perspective, the balanced scorecard identifies objectives that contribute to attainment of strategic goals. Illustration 25-29 (page 1196) shows examples of objectives within each perspective.

The objectives are linked across perspectives in order to tie performance measurement to company goals. The financial-perspective objectives are normally set first, and then objectives are set in the other perspectives in order to accomplish the financial goals.

For example, within the financial perspective, a common goal is to increase profit per dollars invested as measured by ROI. In order to increase ROI, a customer-perspective objective might be to increase customer satisfaction as measured by the percentage of customers who would recommend the product to a friend. In order to increase customer satisfaction, an internal-process-perspective objective might be to increase product quality as measured by the percentage

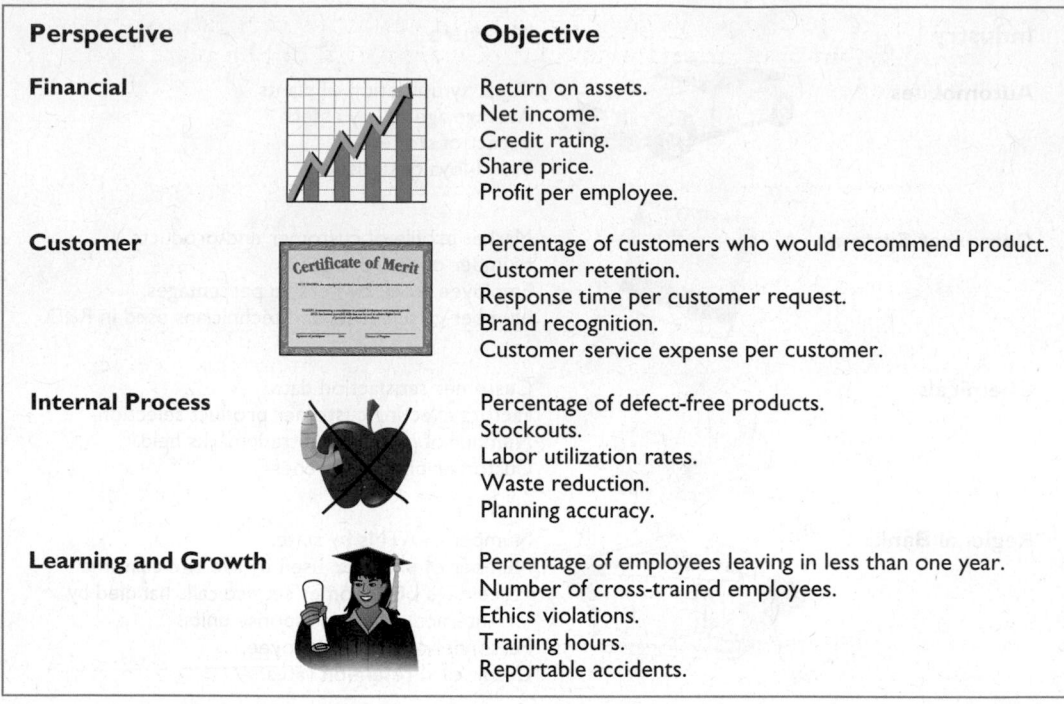

Illustration 25-29
Examples of objectives within the four perspectives of balanced scorecard

of defect-free units. Finally, in order to increase the percentage of defect-free units, the learning-and-growth-perspective objective might be to reduce factory employee turnover as measured by the percentage of employees leaving in under one year.

Illustration 25-30 illustrates this linkage across perspectives.

Illustration 25-30
Linked process across balanced scorecard perspectives

Through this linked process, the company can better understand how to achieve its goals and what measures to use to evaluate performance.

In summary, the balanced scorecard does the following:

1. Employs both **financial and nonfinancial measures**. (For example, ROI is a financial measure; employee turnover is a nonfinancial measure.)

2. **Creates linkages** so that high-level corporate goals can be communicated all the way down to the shop floor.

3. **Provides measurable objectives for nonfinancial measures** such as product quality, rather than vague statements such as "We would like to improve quality."

4. Integrates all of the company's goals into a single performance measurement system, so that **an inappropriate amount of weight will not be placed on any single goal**.

SERVICE COMPANY INSIGHT

It May Be Time to Fly United Again

Many of the benefits of a balanced scorecard approach are evident in the improved operations at United Airlines. At the time it filed for bankruptcy, United had a reputation for some of the worst service in the airline business. But when Glenn Tilton took over as United's chief executive officer, he recognized that things had to change.

He implemented an incentive program that allows all of United's 63,000 employees to earn a bonus of 2.5% or more of their wages if the company "exceeds its goals for on-time flight departures and for customer intent to fly United again." After instituting this program, the company's on-time departures were among the best, its customer complaints were reduced considerably, and the number of customers who said that they would fly United again was at its highest level ever.

Source: Susan Carey, "Friendlier Skies: In Bankruptcy, United Airlines Forges a Path to Better Service," *Wall Street Journal* (June 15, 2004).

? Which of the perspectives of a balanced scorecard were the focus of United's CEO? (See page 1225.)

© Gene Chutka/iStockphoto

> DO IT!

Balanced Scorecard

Action Plan

✔ The financial perspective employs traditional financial measures of performance.

✔ The customer perspective evaluates company performance as seen by the people who buy its products or services.

✔ The internal process perspective evaluates the internal operating processes critical to success.

✔ The learning and growth perspective evaluates how well the company develops and retains its employees.

Indicate which of the four perspectives in the balanced scorecard is most likely associated with the objectives that follow.

1. Percentage of repeat customers.

2. Number of suggestions for improvement from employees.

3. Contribution margin.

4. Brand recognition.

5. Number of cross-trained employees.

6. Amount of setup time.

Solution

> **1.** Customer perspective.
>
> **2.** Learning and growth perspective.
>
> **3.** Financial perspective.
>
> **4.** Customer perspective.
>
> **5.** Learning and growth perspective.
>
> **6.** Internal process perspective.

Related exercise material: **BE25-7, E25-16, and DO IT! 25-4.**

 The Navigator

> Comprehensive DO IT!

Manlow Company makes a cologne called Allure. The standard cost for one bottle of Allure is as follows.

			Standard		
Manufacturing Cost Elements	**Quantity**	×	**Price**	=	**Cost**
Direct materials	6 oz.	×	$ 0.90	=	$ 5.40
Direct labor	0.5 hrs.	×	$12.00	=	6.00
Manufacturing overhead	0.5 hrs.	×	$ 4.80	=	2.40
					$13.80

During the month, the following transactions occurred in manufacturing 10,000 bottles of Allure.

1. 58,000 ounces of materials were purchased at $1.00 per ounce.
2. All the materials purchased were used to produce the 10,000 bottles of Allure.
3. 4,900 direct labor hours were worked at a total labor cost of $56,350.
4. Variable manufacturing overhead incurred was $15,000 and fixed overhead incurred was $10,400.

The manufacturing overhead rate of $4.80 is based on a normal capacity of 5,200 direct labor hours. The total budget at this capacity is $10,400 fixed and $14,560 variable.

Instructions
(a) Compute the total variance and the variances for direct materials and direct labor elements.
(b) Compute the total variance for manufacturing overhead.

Solution to Comprehensive DO IT!

Action Plan

✔ Check to make sure the total variance and the sum of the individual variances are equal.

✔ Find the price variance first, then the quantity variance.

✔ Base budgeted overhead costs on flexible budget data.

✔ Base overhead applied on standard hours allowed.

✔ Ignore actual hours worked in computing overhead variances.

(a)

Total Variance

Actual costs incurred	
Direct materials	$ 58,000
Direct labor	56,350
Manufacturing overhead	25,400
	139,750
Standard cost (10,000 × $13.80)	138,000
Total variance	$ 1,750 U

Direct Materials Variances

Total = $58,000 (58,000 × $1.00) − $54,000 (60,000 × $0.90) = $4,000 U
Price = $58,000 (58,000 × $1.00) − $52,200 (58,000 × $0.90) = $5,800 U
Quantity = $52,200 (58,000 × $0.90) − $54,000 (60,000 × $0.90) = $1,800 F

Direct Labor Variances

Total = $56,350 (4,900 × $11.50) − $60,000 (5,000 × $12.00) = $3,650 F
Price = $56,350 (4,900 × $11.50) − $58,800 (4,900 × $12.00) = $2,450 F
Quantity = $58,800 (4,900 × $12.00) − $60,000 (5,000 × $12.00) = $1,200 F

(b)

Overhead Variance

Total = $25,400 ($15,000 + $10,400) − $24,000 (5,000 × $4.80) = $1,400 U

✔ The Navigator

SUMMARY OF LEARNING OBJECTIVES

1 **Distinguish between a standard and a budget.** Both standards and budgets are predetermined costs. The primary difference is that a standard is a unit amount, whereas a budget is a total amount. A standard may be regarded as the budgeted cost per unit of product.

2 **Identify the advantages of standard costs.** Standard costs offer a number of advantages. They (a) facilitate management planning, (b) promote greater economy, (c) are useful in setting selling prices, (d) contribute to management control, (e) permit "management by exception," and (f) simplify the costing of inventories and reduce clerical costs.

3 **Describe how companies set standards.** The direct materials price standard should be based on the delivered cost of raw materials plus an allowance for receiving and handling. The direct materials quantity standard should establish the required quantity plus an allowance for waste and spoilage.

The direct labor price standard should be based on current wage rates and anticipated adjustments such as COLAs. It also generally includes payroll taxes and fringe benefits. Direct labor quantity standards should be based on required production time plus an allowance for rest periods, cleanup, machine setup, and machine downtime.

For manufacturing overhead, a standard predetermined overhead rate is used. It is based on an expected standard activity index such as standard direct labor hours or standard machine hours.

4 **State the formulas for determining direct materials and direct labor variances.** The formulas for the direct materials variances are:

$$\begin{pmatrix} \text{Actual quantity} \\ \times \text{ Actual price} \end{pmatrix} - \begin{pmatrix} \text{Standard quantity} \\ \times \text{ Standard price} \end{pmatrix} = \begin{matrix} \text{Total} \\ \text{materials} \\ \text{variance} \end{matrix}$$

$$\begin{pmatrix} \text{Actual quantity} \\ \times \text{ Actual price} \end{pmatrix} - \begin{pmatrix} \text{Actual quantity} \\ \times \text{ Standard price} \end{pmatrix} = \begin{matrix} \text{Materials} \\ \text{price} \\ \text{variance} \end{matrix}$$

$$\begin{pmatrix} \text{Actual quantity} \\ \times \text{ Standard price} \end{pmatrix} - \begin{pmatrix} \text{Standard quantity} \\ \times \text{ Standard price} \end{pmatrix} = \begin{matrix} \text{Materials} \\ \text{quantity} \\ \text{variance} \end{matrix}$$

The formulas for the direct labor variances are:

$$\begin{pmatrix} \text{Actual hours} \\ \times \text{ Actual rate} \end{pmatrix} - \begin{pmatrix} \text{Standard hours} \\ \times \text{ Standard rate} \end{pmatrix} = \begin{matrix} \text{Total} \\ \text{labor} \\ \text{variance} \end{matrix}$$

$$\begin{pmatrix} \text{Actual hours} \\ \times \text{ Actual rate} \end{pmatrix} - \begin{pmatrix} \text{Actual hours} \\ \times \text{ Standard rate} \end{pmatrix} = \begin{matrix} \text{Labor} \\ \text{price} \\ \text{variance} \end{matrix}$$

$$\begin{pmatrix} \text{Actual hours} \\ \times \text{ Standard rate} \end{pmatrix} - \begin{pmatrix} \text{Standard hours} \\ \times \text{ Standard rate} \end{pmatrix} = \begin{matrix} \text{Labor} \\ \text{quantity} \\ \text{variance} \end{matrix}$$

5 **State the formula for determining the total manufacturing overhead variance.** The formula for the total manufacturing overhead variance is:

$$\begin{pmatrix} \text{Actual} \\ \text{overhead} \end{pmatrix} - \begin{pmatrix} \text{Overhead} \\ \text{applied at} \\ \text{standard hours} \\ \text{allowed} \end{pmatrix} = \begin{matrix} \text{Total overhead} \\ \text{variance} \end{matrix}$$

6 **Discuss the reporting of variances.** Variances are reported to management in variance reports. The reports facilitate management by exception by highlighting significant differences.

7 **Prepare an income statement for management under a standard costing system.** Under a standard costing system, an income statement prepared for management will report cost of goods sold at standard cost and then disclose each variance separately.

8 **Describe the balanced scorecard approach to performance evaluation.** The balanced scorecard incorporates financial and nonfinancial measures in an integrated system that links performance measurement and a company's strategic goals. It employs four perspectives: financial, customer, internal process, and learning and growth. Objectives are set within each of these perspectives that link to objectives within the other perspectives.

GLOSSARY

Balanced scorecard An approach that incorporates financial and nonfinancial measures in an integrated system that links performance measurement and a company's strategic goals. (p. 1194).

Customer perspective A viewpoint employed in the balanced scorecard to evaluate the company from the perspective of those people who buy and use its products or services. (p. 1195).

Direct labor price standard The rate per hour that should be incurred for direct labor. (p. 1181).

Direct labor quantity standard The time that should be required to make one unit of product. (p. 1181).

Direct materials price standard The cost per unit of direct materials that should be incurred. (p. 1180).

Direct materials quantity standard The quantity of direct materials that should be used per unit of finished goods. (p. 1180).

Financial perspective A viewpoint employed in the balanced scorecard to evaluate a company's performance using financial measures. (p. 1194).

Ideal standards Standards based on the optimum level of performance under perfect operating conditions. (p. 1179).

Internal process perspective A viewpoint employed in the balanced scorecard to evaluate the effectiveness and efficiency of a company's value chain, including product development, production, delivery, and after-sale service. (p. 1195).

Labor price variance The difference between the actual hours times the actual rate and the actual hours times the standard rate for labor. (p. 1188).

Labor quantity variance The difference between actual hours times the standard rate and standard hours times the standard rate for labor. (p. 1189).

Learning and growth perspective A viewpoint employed in the balanced scorecard to evaluate how well a company develops and retains its employees. (p. 1195).

Materials price variance The difference between the actual quantity times the actual price and the actual quantity times the standard price for materials. (p. 1186).

Materials quantity variance The difference between the actual quantity times the standard price and the standard quantity times the standard price for materials. (p. 1186).

Normal capacity The average activity output that a company should experience over the long run. (p. 1182).

Normal standards Standards based on an efficient level of performance that are attainable under expected operating conditions. (p. 1179).

Standard costs Predetermined unit costs which companies use as measures of performance. (p. 1178).

Standard hours allowed The hours that should have been worked for the units produced. (p. 1191).

Standard predetermined overhead rate An overhead rate determined by dividing budgeted overhead costs by an expected standard activity index. (p. 1181).

Total labor variance The difference between actual hours times the actual rate and standard hours times the standard rate for labor. (p. 1188).

Total materials variance The difference between the actual quantity times the actual price and the standard quantity times the standard price of materials. (p. 1185).

Total overhead variance The difference between actual overhead costs and overhead costs applied to work done, based on standard hours allowed. (p. 1190).

Variance The difference between total actual costs and total standard costs. (p. 1184).

APPENDIX 25A   Standard Cost Accounting System

LEARNING OBJECTIVE   9

Identify the features of a standard cost accounting system.

A **standard cost accounting system** is a double-entry system of accounting. In this system, companies use standard costs in making entries, and they formally recognize variances in the accounts. Companies may use a standard cost system with either job order or process costing.

In this appendix, we will explain and illustrate a **standard cost, job order cost accounting system**. The system is based on two important assumptions:

1. Variances from standards are recognized at the earliest opportunity.
2. The Work in Process account is maintained exclusively on the basis of standard costs.

In practice, there are many variations among standard cost systems. The system described here should prepare you for systems you see in the "real world."

Journal Entries

We will use the transactions of Xonic to illustrate the journal entries. Note as you study the entries that the major difference between the entries here and those for the job order cost accounting system in Chapter 20 is the **variance accounts**.

1. Purchase raw materials on account for $13,020 when the standard cost is $12,600.

Raw Materials Inventory	12,600	
Materials Price Variance	420	
Accounts Payable		13,020
(To record purchase of materials)		

Xonic debits the inventory account for actual quantities at standard cost. This enables the perpetual materials records to show actual quantities. Xonic debits the price variance, which is unfavorable, to Materials Price Variance.

2. Incur direct labor costs of $31,080 when the standard labor cost is $31,500.

Factory Labor	31,500	
Labor Price Variance		420
Factory Wages Payable		31,080
(To record direct labor costs)		

Like the Raw Materials Inventory account, Xonic debits Factory Labor for actual hours worked at the standard hourly rate of pay. In this case, the labor variance is favorable. Thus, Xonic credits Labor Price Variance.

3. Incur actual manufacturing overhead costs of $10,900.

Manufacturing Overhead	10,900	
Accounts Payable/Cash/Acc. Depreciation		10,900
(To record overhead incurred)		

The controllable overhead variance (see Appendix 25B) is not recorded at this time. It depends on standard hours applied to work in process. This amount is not known at the time overhead is incurred.

4. Issue raw materials for production at a cost of $12,600 when the standard cost is $12,000.

Work in Process Inventory	12,000	
Materials Quantity Variance	600	
Raw Materials Inventory		12,600
(To record issuance of raw materials)		

Xonic debits Work in Process Inventory for standard materials quantities used at standard prices. It debits the variance account because the variance is unfavorable. The company credits Raw Materials Inventory for actual quantities at standard prices.

5. Assign factory labor to production at a cost of $31,500 when standard cost is $30,000.

Work in Process Inventory	30,000	
Labor Quantity Variance	1,500	
Factory Labor		31,500
(To assign factory labor to jobs)		

Xonic debits Work in Process Inventory for standard labor hours at standard rates. It debits the unfavorable variance to Labor Quantity Variance. The credit to Factory Labor produces a zero balance in this account.

6. Apply manufacturing overhead to production $10,000.

Work in Process Inventory	10,000	
Manufacturing Overhead		10,000
(To assign overhead to jobs)		

Xonic debits Work in Process Inventory for standard hours allowed multiplied by the standard overhead rate.

7. Transfer completed work to finished goods $52,000.

Finished Goods Inventory	52,000	
Work in Process Inventory		52,000
(To record transfer of completed work to finished goods)		

In this example, both inventory accounts are at standard cost.

8. Sell the 1,000 gallons of Xonic Tonic for $70,000.

Accounts Receivable	70,000	
Cost of Goods Sold	52,000	
Sales		70,000
Finished Goods Inventory		52,000
(To record sale of finished goods and the cost of goods sold)		

The company debits Cost of Goods Sold at standard cost. Gross profit, in turn, is the difference between sales and the standard cost of goods sold.

9. Recognize unfavorable total overhead variance:

Overhead Variance	900	
Manufacturing Overhead		900
(To recognize overhead variances)		

Prior to this entry, a debit balance of $900 existed in Manufacturing Overhead. This entry therefore produces a zero balance in the Manufacturing Overhead account. The information needed for this entry is often not available until the end of the accounting period.

Ledger Accounts

Illustration 25A-1 shows the cost accounts for Xonic after posting the entries. Note that five variance accounts are included in the ledger. The remaining accounts are the same as those illustrated for a job order cost system in Chapter 20, in which only actual costs were used.

Illustration 25A-1
Cost accounts with variances

Helpful Hint All debit balances in variance accounts indicate unfavorable variances. All credit balances indicate favorable variances.

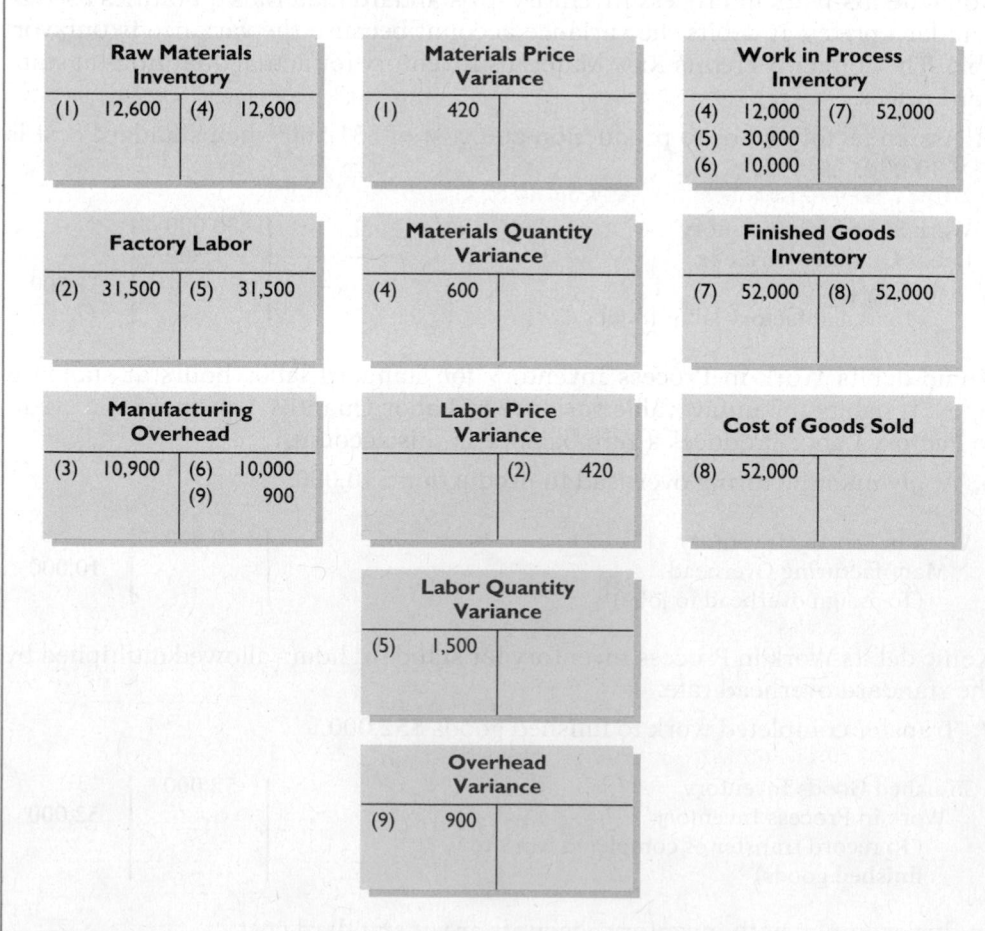

SUMMARY OF LEARNING OBJECTIVE FOR APPENDIX 25A

9 Identify the features of a standard cost accounting system. In a standard cost accounting system, companies journalize and post standard costs, and they maintain separate variance accounts in the ledger.

GLOSSARY FOR APPENDIX 25A

Standard cost accounting system A double-entry system of accounting in which standard costs are used in making entries and variances are recognized in the accounts. (p. 1200).

APPENDIX 25B   A Closer Look at Overhead Variances

As indicated in the chapter, the total overhead variance is generally analyzed through a price variance and a quantity variance. The name usually given to the price variance is the **overhead controllable variance**; the quantity variance is referred to as the **overhead volume variance**.

LEARNING OBJECTIVE   10

Compute overhead controllable and volume variance.

Overhead Controllable Variance

The **overhead controllable variance** shows whether overhead costs are effectively controlled. To compute this variance, the company compares actual overhead costs incurred with budgeted costs for the **standard hours allowed**. The budgeted costs are determined from a flexible manufacturing overhead budget. The concepts related to a flexible budget were discussed in Chapter 24.

For Xonic, the budget formula for manufacturing overhead is variable manufacturing overhead cost of $3 per hour of labor plus fixed manufacturing overhead costs of $4,400 ($52,800 ÷ 12, per Illustration 25-6 on page 1182). Illustration 25B-1 shows the monthly flexible budget for Xonic.

Illustration 25B-1
Flexible budget using standard direct labor hours

XONIC
Flexible Manufacturing Overhead Monthly Budget

	B	C	D	E
Activity Index				
Standard direct labor hours	1,800	2,000	2,200	2,400
Costs				
Variable costs				
Indirect materials	$1,800	$ 2,000	$ 2,200	$ 2,400
Indirect labor	2,700	3,000	3,300	3,600
Utilities	900	1,000	1,100	1,200
Total variable costs	5,400	6,000	6,600	7,200
Fixed costs				
Supervision	3,000	3,000	3,000	3,000
Depreciation	1,400	1,400	1,400	1,400
Total fixed costs	4,400	4,400	4,400	4,400
Total costs	$9,800	$10,400	$11,000	$11,600

As shown, the budgeted costs for 2,000 standard hours are $10,400 ($6,000 variable and $4,400 fixed).

Illustration 25B-2 shows the formula for the overhead controllable variance and the calculation for Xonic at 1,000 units of output (2,000 standard labor hours).

Illustration 25B-2
Formula for overhead
controllable variance

Actual Overhead	−	Overhead Budgeted*	=	Overhead Controllable Variance
$10,900	−	$10,400	=	$500 U
($6,500 + $4,400)		($6,000 + $4,400)		

*Based on standard hours allowed.

The overhead controllable variance for Xonic is $500 unfavorable.

Most controllable variances are associated with variable costs, which are controllable costs. Fixed costs are often known at the time the budget is prepared and are therefore not as likely to deviate from the budgeted amount. In Xonic's case, all of the overhead controllable variance is due to the difference between the actual variable overhead costs ($6,500) and the budgeted variable costs ($6,000).

Management can compare actual and budgeted overhead for each manufacturing overhead cost that contributes to the controllable variance. In addition, management can develop cost and quantity variances for each overhead cost, such as indirect materials and indirect labor.

Overhead Volume Variance

The **overhead volume variance** is the difference between normal capacity hours and standard hours allowed times the fixed overhead rate. The overhead volume variance relates to whether fixed costs were under- or overapplied during the year. For example, the overhead volume variance answers the question of whether Xonic effectively used its fixed costs. If Xonic produces less Xonic Tonic than normal capacity would allow, an unfavorable variance results. Conversely, if Xonic produces more Xonic Tonic than what is considered normal capacity, a favorable variance results.

The formula for computing the overhead volume variance is as follows.

Illustration 25B-3
Formula for overhead volume
variance

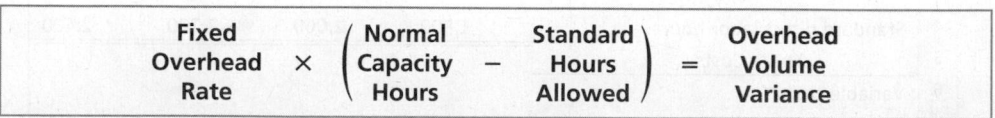

Fixed Overhead Rate	×	(Normal Capacity Hours	−	Standard Hours Allowed)	=	Overhead Volume Variance

To illustrate the fixed overhead rate computation, recall that Xonic budgeted fixed overhead cost for the year of $52,800 (Illustration 25-6 on page 1182). At normal capacity, 26,400 standard direct labor hours are required. The fixed overhead rate is therefore $2 per hour ($52,800 ÷ 26,400 hours).

Xonic produced 1,000 units of Xonic Tonic in June. The standard hours allowed for the 1,000 gallons produced in June is 2,000 (1,000 gallons × 2 hours). For Xonic, normal capacity for June is 1,100, so standard direct labor hours for June at normal capacity is 2,200 (26,400 annual hours ÷ 12 months). The computation of the overhead volume variance in this case is as follows.

Fixed Overhead Rate	×	(Normal Capacity Hours	−	Standard Hours Allowed)	=	Overhead Volume Variance
$2	×	(2,200	−	2,000)	=	$400 U

Illustration 25B-4
Computation of overhead volume variance for Xonic

In Xonic's case, a $400 unfavorable volume variance results. The volume variance is unfavorable because Xonic produced only 1,000 gallons rather than the normal capacity of 1,100 gallons in the month of June. As a result, it underapplied fixed overhead for that period.

In computing the overhead variances, it is important to remember the following.

1. Standard hours allowed are used in each of the variances.
2. Budgeted costs for the controllable variance are derived from the flexible budget.
3. The controllable variance generally pertains to variable costs.
4. The volume variance pertains solely to fixed costs.

SUMMARY OF LEARNING OBJECTIVE FOR APPENDIX 25B

 The Navigator

10 Compute overhead controllable and volume variance. The total overhead variance is generally analyzed through a price variance and a quantity variance.

The name usually given to the price variance is the overhead controllable variance. The quantity variance is referred to as the overhead volume variance.

GLOSSARY FOR APPENDIX 25B

Overhead controllable variance The difference between actual overhead incurred and overhead budgeted for the standard hours allowed. (p. 1203).

Overhead volume variance The difference between normal capacity hours and standard hours allowed times the fixed overhead rate. (p. 1204).

 Self-Test, Brief Exercises, Exercises, Problem Set A, and many more resources are available for practice in *WileyPLUS*.

*Note:** All asterisked Questions, Exercises, and Problems relate to material in the appendices to the chapter.

SELF-TEST QUESTIONS

Answers are on page 1225.

(LO 1) 1. Standards differ from budgets in that:
   (a) budgets but not standards may be used in valuing inventories.
   (b) budgets but not standards may be journalized and posted.
   (c) budgets are a total amount and standards are a unit amount.
   (d) only budgets contribute to management planning and control.

2. Standard costs: (LO 1)
   (a) are imposed by governmental agencies.
   (b) are predetermined unit costs which companies use as measures of performance.
   (c) can be used by manufacturing companies but not by service or not-for-profit companies.
   (d) All of these responses are correct.

(LO 2)　**3.** The advantages of standard costs include all of the following **except**:
- **(a)** management by exception may be used.
- **(b)** management planning is facilitated.
- **(c)** they may simplify the costing of inventories.
- **(d)** management must use a static budget.

(LO 3)　**4.** Normal standards:
- **(a)** allow for rest periods, machine breakdowns, and setup time.
- **(b)** represent levels of performance under perfect operating conditions.
- **(c)** are rarely used because managers believe they lower workforce morale.
- **(d)** are more likely than ideal standards to result in unethical practices.

(LO 3)　**5.** The setting of standards is:
- **(a)** a managerial accounting decision.
- **(b)** a management decision.
- **(c)** a worker decision.
- **(d)** preferably set at the ideal level of performance.

(LO 4)　**6.** Each of the following formulas is correct **except**:
- **(a)** Labor price variance = (Actual hours × Actual rate) − (Actual hours × Standard rate).
- **(b)** Total overhead variance = Actual overhead − Overhead applied.
- **(c)** Materials price variance = (Actual quantity × Actual price) − (Standard quantity × Standard price).
- **(d)** Labor quantity variance = (Actual hours × Standard rate) − (Standard hours × Standard rate).

(LO 4)　**7.** In producing product AA, 6,300 pounds of direct materials were used at a cost of $1.10 per pound. The standard was 6,000 pounds at $1.00 per pound. The direct materials quantity variance is:
- **(a)** $330 unfavorable.　　**(c)** $600 unfavorable.
- **(b)** $300 unfavorable.　　**(d)** $630 unfavorable.

(LO 4)　**8.** In producing product ZZ, 14,800 direct labor hours were used at a rate of $8.20 per hour. The standard was 15,000 hours at $8.00 per hour. Based on these data, the direct labor:
- **(a)** quantity variance is $1,600 favorable.
- **(b)** quantity variance is $1,600 unfavorable.
- **(c)** price variance is $2,960 favorable.
- **(d)** price variance is $2,960 unfavorable.

(LO 5)　**9.** Which of the following is **correct** about the total overhead variance?
- **(a)** Budgeted overhead and budgeted overhead applied are the same.
- **(b)** Total actual overhead is composed of variable overhead, fixed overhead, and period costs.
- **(c)** Standard hours actually worked are used in computing the variance.
- **(d)** Standard hours allowed for the work done is the measure used in computing the variance.

(LO 5)　**10.** The formula for computing the total overhead variance is:

- **(a)** actual overhead less overhead applied.
- **(b)** overhead budgeted less overhead applied.
- **(c)** actual overhead less overhead budgeted.
- **(d)** No correct answer is given.

11. Which of the following is **incorrect** about variance reports? (LO 6)
- **(a)** They facilitate "management by exception."
- **(b)** They should only be sent to the top level of management.
- **(c)** They should be prepared as soon as possible.
- **(d)** They may vary in form, content, and frequency among companies.

12. In using variance reports to evaluate cost control, (LO 6) management normally looks into:
- **(a)** all variances.
- **(b)** favorable variances only.
- **(c)** unfavorable variances only.
- **(d)** both favorable and unfavorable variances that exceed a predetermined quantitative measure such as a percentage or dollar amount.

13. Generally accepted accounting principles allow a (LO 7) company to:
- **(a)** report inventory at standard cost but cost of goods sold must be reported at actual cost.
- **(b)** report cost of goods sold at standard cost but inventory must be reported at actual cost.
- **(c)** report inventory and cost of goods sold at standard cost as long as there are no significant differences between actual and standard cost.
- **(d)** report inventory and cost of goods sold only at actual costs; standard costing is never permitted.

14. Which of the following would **not** be an objective (LO 8) used in the customer perspective of the balanced scorecard approach?
- **(a)** Percentage of customers who would recommend product to a friend.
- **(b)** Customer retention.
- **(c)** Brand recognition.
- **(d)** Earnings per share.

*15. Which of the following is **incorrect** about a standard (LO 9) cost accounting system?
- **(a)** It is applicable to job order costing.
- **(b)** It is applicable to process costing.
- **(c)** It reports only favorable variances.
- **(d)** It keeps separate accounts for each variance.

*16. The formula to compute the overhead volume vari- (LO 10) ance is:
- **(a)** Fixed overhead rate × (Standard hours − Actual hours).
- **(b)** Fixed overhead rate × (Normal capacity hours − Actual hours).
- **(c)** Fixed overhead rate × (Normal capacity hours − Standard hours allowed).
- **(d)** (Variable overhead rate + Fixed overhead rate) × (Normal capacity hours − Standard hours allowed).

Go to the book's companion website, www.wiley.com/college/weygandt, for additional Self-Test Questions.

✔ **The Navigator**

QUESTIONS

1. (a) "Standard costs are the expected total cost of completing a job." Is this correct? Explain.
   (b) "A standard imposed by a governmental agency is known as a regulation." Do you agree? Explain.
2. (a) Explain the similarities and differences between standards and budgets.
   (b) Contrast the accounting for standards and budgets.
3. Standard costs facilitate management planning. What are the other advantages of standard costs?
4. Contrast the roles of the management accountant and management in setting standard costs.
5. Distinguish between an ideal standard and a normal standard.
6. What factors should be considered in setting (a) the direct materials price standard and (b) the direct materials quantity standard?
7. "The objective in setting the direct labor quantity standard is to determine the aggregate time required to make one unit of product." Do you agree? What allowances should be made in setting this standard?
8. How is the predetermined overhead rate determined when standard costs are used?
9. What is the difference between a favorable cost variance and an unfavorable cost variance?
10. In each of the following formulas, supply the words that should be inserted for each number in parentheses.
    (a) (Actual quantity × (1)) − (Standard quantity × (2)) = Total materials variance
    (b) ((3) × Actual price) − (Actual quantity × (4)) = Materials price variance
    (c) (Actual quantity × (5)) − ((6) × Standard price) = Materials quantity variance
11. In the direct labor variance matrix, there are three factors: (1) Actual hours × Actual rate, (2) Actual hours × Standard rate, and (3) Standard hours × Standard rate. Using the numbers, indicate the formulas for each of the direct labor variances.
12. Mikan Company's standard predetermined overhead rate is $9 per direct labor hour. For the month of June, 26,000 actual hours were worked, and 27,000

standard hours were allowed. How much overhead was applied?
13. How often should variances be reported to management? What principle may be used with variance reports?
14. What circumstances may cause the purchasing department to be responsible for both an unfavorable materials price variance and an unfavorable materials quantity variance?
15. What are the four perspectives used in the balanced scorecard? Discuss the nature of each, and how the perspectives are linked.
16. Kerry James says that the balanced scorecard was created to replace financial measures as the primary mechanism for performance evaluation. He says that it uses only nonfinancial measures. Is this true?
17. What are some examples of nonfinancial measures used by companies to evaluate performance?
18. (a) How are variances reported in income statements prepared for management? (b) May standard costs be used in preparing financial statements for stockholders? Explain.
*19. (a) Explain the basic features of a standard cost accounting system. (b) What type of balance will exist in the variance account when (1) the materials price variance is unfavorable and (2) the labor quantity variance is favorable?
*20. If the $9 per hour overhead rate in Question 12 includes $5 variable, and actual overhead costs were $248,000, what is the overhead controllable variance for June? The normal capacity hours were 28,000. Is the variance favorable or unfavorable?
*21. What is the purpose of computing the overhead volume variance? What is the basic formula for this variance?
*22. Alma Ortiz does not understand why the overhead volume variance indicates that fixed overhead costs are under- or overapplied. Clarify this matter for Alma.
*23. John Hsu is attempting to outline the important points about overhead variances on a class examination. List four points that John should include in his outline.

BRIEF EXERCISES

BE25-1 Perez Company uses both standards and budgets. For the year, estimated production of Product X is 500,000 units. Total estimated cost for materials and labor are $1,300,000 and $1,700,000. Compute the estimates for (a) a standard cost and (b) a budgeted cost.

Distinguish between a standard and a budget.
(LO 1)

BE25-2 Tang Company accumulates the following data concerning raw materials in making one gallon of finished product: (1) Price—net purchase price $2.30, freight-in $0.20, and receiving and handling $0.10. (2) Quantity—required materials 3.6 pounds, allowance for waste and spoilage 0.4 pounds. Compute the following.

Set direct materials standard.
(LO 3)

(a) Standard direct materials price per gallon.
(b) Standard direct materials quantity per gallon.
(c) Total standard materials cost per gallon.

Set direct labor standard.
(LO 3)

BE25-3 Labor data for making one gallon of finished product in Tang Company are as follows: (1) Price—hourly wage rate $13.00, payroll taxes $0.80, and fringe benefits $1.20. (2) Quantity—actual production time 1.1 hours, rest periods and cleanup 0.25 hours, and setup and downtime 0.15 hours. Compute the following.

(a) Standard direct labor rate per hour.
(b) Standard direct labor hours per gallon.
(c) Standard labor cost per gallon.

Compute direct materials variances.
(LO 4)

BE25-4 Simba Company's standard materials cost per unit of output is $10 (2 pounds × $5). During July, the company purchases and uses 3,200 pounds of materials costing $16,192 in making 1,500 units of finished product. Compute the total, price, and quantity materials variances.

Compute direct labor variances.
(LO 4)

BE25-5 Hartley Company's standard labor cost per unit of output is $22 (2 hours × $11 per hour). During August, the company incurs 2,100 hours of direct labor at an hourly cost of $10.80 per hour in making 1,000 units of finished product. Compute the total, price, and quantity labor variances.

Compute total overhead variance.
(LO 5)

BE25-6 In October, Roby Company reports 21,000 actual direct labor hours, and it incurs $118,000 of manufacturing overhead costs. Standard hours allowed for the work done is 20,400 hours. The predetermined overhead rate is $6 per direct labor hour. Compute the total overhead variance.

Match balanced scorecard perspectives.
(LO 8)

BE25-7 The four perspectives in the balanced scorecard are (1) financial, (2) customer, (3) internal process, and (4) learning and growth. Match each of the following objectives with the perspective it is most likely associated with: (a) Plant capacity utilization. (b) Employee work days missed due to injury. (c) Return on assets. (d) Brand recognition.

Journalize materials variances.
(LO 9)

*BE25-8 Journalize the following transactions for Combs Company.

(a) Purchased 6,000 units of raw materials on account for $11,500. The standard cost was $12,000.
(b) Issued 5,600 units of raw materials for production. The standard units were 5,800.

Journalize labor variances.
(LO 9)

*BE25-9 Journalize the following transactions for Dewey, Inc.

(a) Incurred direct labor costs of $24,000 for 3,000 hours. The standard labor cost was $25,500.
(b) Assigned 3,000 direct labor hours costing $24,000 to production. Standard hours were 3,150.

Compute the overhead controllable variance.
(LO 10)

*BE25-10 Some overhead data for Roby Company are given in BE25-6. In addition, the flexible manufacturing overhead budget shows that budgeted costs are $4 variable per direct labor hour and $50,000 fixed. Compute the overhead controllable variance.

Compute overhead volume variance.
(LO 10)

*BE25-11 Using the data in BE25-6 and BE25-10, compute the overhead volume variance. Normal capacity was 25,000 direct labor hours.

> DO IT! Review

Compute standard cost.
(LO 3)

DO IT! 25-1 Jacque Company accumulated the following standard cost data concerning product I-Tal.

Direct materials per unit: 2 pounds at $5 per pound
Direct labor per unit: 0.2 hours at $15 per hour
Manufacturing overhead: Predetermined rate is 125% of direct labor cost

Compute the standard cost of one unit of product I-Tal.

Compute materials variance.
(LO 4)

DO IT! 25-2 The standard cost of product 777 includes 2 units of direct materials at $6.00 per unit. During August, the company bought 29,000 units of materials at $6.30 and used those materials to produce 16,000 units. Compute the total, price, and quantity variances for materials.

DO IT! 25-3 The standard cost of product 5252 includes 1.9 hours of direct labor at $14.00 per hour. The predetermined overhead rate is $22.00 per direct labor hour. During July, the company incurred 4,100 hours of direct labor at an average rate of $14.30 per hour and $81,300 of manufacturing overhead costs. It produced 2,000 units.

Compute labor and manufacturing overhead variances.

(LO 4, 5)

(a) Compute the total, price, and quantity variances for labor. (b) Compute the total overhead variance.

DO IT! 25-4 Indicate which of the four perspectives in the balanced scorecard is most likely associated with the objectives that follow.

Match balance scorecard perspectives and their objectives.

(LO 8)

1. Ethics violations.
2. Credit rating.
3. Customer retention.
4. Stockouts.
5. Reportable accidents.
6. Brand recognition.

EXERCISES

E25-1 Shannon Company is planning to produce 2,000 units of product in 2014. Each unit requires 3 pounds of materials at $5 per pound and a half-hour of labor at $15 per hour. The overhead rate is 70% of direct labor.

Compute budget and standard.

(LO 1, 2, 3)

Instructions

(a) Compute the budgeted amounts for 2014 for direct materials to be used, direct labor, and applied overhead.
(b) Compute the standard cost of one unit of product.
(c) What are the potential advantages to a corporation of using standard costs?

E25-2 Hank Itzek manufactures and sells homemade wine, and he wants to develop a standard cost per gallon. The following are required for production of a 50-gallon batch.

Compute standard materials costs.

(LO 3)

3,000 ounces of grape concentrate at $0.06 per ounce
54 pounds of granulated sugar at $0.30 per pound
60 lemons at $0.60 each
50 yeast tablets at $0.25 each
50 nutrient tablets at $0.20 each
2,600 ounces of water at $0.005 per ounce

Hank estimates that 4% of the grape concentrate is wasted, 10% of the sugar is lost, and 25% of the lemons cannot be used.

Instructions

Compute the standard cost of the ingredients for one gallon of wine. (Carry computations to two decimal places.)

E25-3 Kimm Company has gathered the following information about its product.

Compute standard cost per unit.

(LO 3)

Direct materials. Each unit of product contains 4.5 pounds of materials. The average waste and spoilage per unit produced under normal conditions is 0.5 pounds. Materials cost $5 per pound, but Kimm always takes the 2% cash discount all of its suppliers offer. Freight costs average $0.25 per pound.

Direct labor. Each unit requires 2 hours of labor. Setup, cleanup, and downtime average 0.3 hours per unit. The average hourly pay rate of Kimm's employees is $12. Payroll taxes and fringe benefits are an additional $3 per hour.

Manufacturing overhead. Overhead is applied at a rate of $7 per direct labor hour.

Instructions

Compute Kimm's total standard cost per unit.

Compute labor cost and labor quantity variance.

(LO 3, 4)

E25-4 Monte Services, Inc. is trying to establish the standard labor cost of a typical oil change. The following data have been collected from time and motion studies conducted over the past month.

Actual time spent on the oil change	1.0 hour
Hourly wage rate	$12
Payroll taxes	10% of wage rate
Setup and downtime	20% of actual labor time
Cleanup and rest periods	30% of actual labor time
Fringe benefits	25% of wage rate

Instructions

(a) Determine the standard direct labor hours per oil change.
(b) Determine the standard direct labor hourly rate.
(c) Determine the standard direct labor cost per oil change.
(d) If an oil change took 1.6 hours at the standard hourly rate, what was the direct labor quantity variance?

Compute materials price and quantity variances.

(LO 4)

E25-5 The standard cost of Product B manufactured by MIT Company includes three units of direct materials at $5.00 per unit. During June, 29,000 units of direct materials are purchased at a cost of $4.70 per unit, and 29,000 units of direct materials are used to produce 9,500 units of Product B.

Instructions

(a) Compute the total materials variance and the price and quantity variances.
(b) Repeat (a), assuming the purchase price is $5.15 and the quantity purchased and used is 28,000 units.

Compute labor price and quantity variances.

(LO 4)

E25-6 Lewis Company's standard labor cost of producing one unit of Product DD is 4 hours at the rate of $12.00 per hour. During August, 40,600 hours of labor are incurred at a cost of $12.15 per hour to produce 10,000 units of Product DD.

Instructions

(a) Compute the total labor variance.
(b) Compute the labor price and quantity variances.
(c) Repeat (b), assuming the standard is 4.1 hours of direct labor at $12.25 per hour.

Compute materials and labor variances.

(LO 4)

E25-7 Nona Inc., which produces a single product, has prepared the following standard cost sheet for one unit of the product.

Direct materials (8 pounds at $2.50 per pound)	$20
Direct labor (3 hours at $12.00 per hour)	$36

During the month of April, the company manufactures 235 units and incurs the following actual costs.

Direct materials purchased and used (1,900 pounds)	$5,035
Direct labor (700 hours)	$8,260

Instructions

Compute the total, price, and quantity variances for materials and labor.

Compute the materials and labor variances and list reasons for unfavorable variances.

(LO 4)

E25-8 The following direct materials and direct labor data pertain to the operations of Laurel Company for the month of August.

Costs		Quantities	
Actual labor rate	$13 per hour	Actual hours incurred and used	4,150 hours
Actual materials price	$128 per ton	Actual quantity of materials purchased and used	1,220 tons
Standard labor rate	$12.50 per hour	Standard hours used	4,300 hours
Standard materials price	$130 per ton	Standard quantity of materials used	1,200 tons

Instructions

(a) Compute the total, price, and quantity variances for materials and labor.
(b) ———— Provide two possible explanations for each of the unfavorable variances calculated above, and suggest where responsibility for the unfavorable result might be placed.

E25-9 During March 2014, Toby Tool & Die Company worked on four jobs. A review of direct labor costs reveals the following summary data.

Prepare a variance report for direct labor.

(LO 4, 6)

Job Number	Actual Hours	Actual Costs	Standard Hours	Standard Costs	Total Variance
A257	221	$4,420	225	$4,500	$ 80 F
A258	450	9,450	430	8,600	850 U
A259	300	6,180	300	6,000	180 U
A260	116	2,088	110	2,200	112 F
Total variance					$838 U

Analysis reveals that Job A257 was a repeat job. Job A258 was a rush order that required overtime work at premium rates of pay. Job A259 required a more experienced replacement worker on one shift. Work on Job A260 was done for one day by a new trainee when a regular worker was absent.

Instructions
Prepare a report for the plant supervisor on direct labor cost variances for March. The report should have columns for (1) Job No., (2) Actual Hours, (3) Standard Hours, (4) Quantity Variance, (5) Actual Rate, (6) Standard Rate, (7) Price Variance, and (8) Explanation.

E25-10 Manufacturing overhead data for the production of Product H by Smart Company are as follows.

Compute overhead variance.

(LO 5)

Overhead incurred for 52,000 actual direct labor hours worked	$263,000
Overhead rate (variable $3; fixed $2) at normal capacity of 54,000 direct labor hours	$5
Standard hours allowed for work done	51,000

Instructions
Compute the total overhead variance.

E25-11 Byrd Company produces one product, a putter called GO-Putter. Byrd uses a standard cost system and determines that it should take one hour of direct labor to produce one GO-Putter. The normal production capacity for this putter is 100,000 units per year. The total budgeted overhead at normal capacity is $850,000 comprised of $250,000 of variable costs and $600,000 of fixed costs. Byrd applies overhead on the basis of direct labor hours.

Compute overhead variances.

(LO 5)

During the current year, Byrd produced 95,000 putters, worked 94,000 direct labor hours, and incurred variable overhead costs of $256,000 and fixed overhead costs of $600,000.

Instructions
(a) Compute the predetermined variable overhead rate and the predetermined fixed overhead rate.
(b) Compute the applied overhead for Byrd for the year.
(c) Compute the total overhead variance.

E25-12 Wales Company purchased (at a cost of $10,800) and used 2,400 pounds of materials during May. Wales's standard cost of materials per unit produced is based on 2 pounds per unit at a cost $5 per pound. Production in May was 1,070 units.

Compute variances for materials.

(LO 4)

Instructions
(a) Compute the total, price, and quantity variances for materials.
(b) Assume Wales also had an unfavorable labor quantity variance. What is a possible scenario that would provide one cause for the variances computed in (a) and the unfavorable labor quantity variance?

E25-13 Picard Landscaping plants grass seed as the basic landscaping for business campuses. During a recent month, the company worked on three projects (Remington, Chang, and Wyco). The company is interested in controlling the materials costs, namely the grass seed, for these plantings projects.

Prepare a variance report.

(LO 4, 6)

In order to provide management with useful cost control information, the company uses standard costs and prepares monthly variance reports. Analysis reveals that the purchasing agent mistakenly purchased poor-quality seed for the Remington project. The Chang project, however, received higher-than-standard-quality seed that was on sale. The Wyco project received standard-quality seed. However, the price had increased and a new employee was used to spread the seed.

Shown below are quantity and cost data for each project.

Project	Actual Quantity	Actual Costs	Standard Quantity	Standard Costs	Total Variance
Remington	500 lbs.	$1,200	460 lbs.	$1,150	$ 50 U
Chang	400	920	410	1,025	105 F
Wyco	550	1,430	480	1,200	230 U
Total variance					$175 U

Instructions

(a) Prepare a variance report for the purchasing department with the following columns: (1) Project, (2) Actual Pounds Purchased, (3) Actual Price, (4) Standard Price, (5) Price Variance, and (6) Explanation.

(b) Prepare a variance report for the production department with the following columns: (1) Project, (2) Actual Pounds, (3) Standard Pounds, (4) Standard Price, (5) Quantity Variance, and (6) Explanation.

Complete variance report.
(LO 6)

E25-14 Burte Corporation prepared the following variance report.

BURTE CORPORATION
Variance Report—Purchasing Department
For the Week Ended January 9, 2014

Type of Materials	Quantity Purchased	Actual Price	Standard Price	Price Variance	Explanation
Rogue11	? lbs.	$5.20	$5.00	$5,000 ?	Price increase
Storm17	7,000 oz.	?	3.30	1,050 U	Rush order
Beast29	22,000 units	0.40	?	440 F	Bought larger quantity

Instructions
Fill in the appropriate amounts or letters for the question marks in the report.

Prepare income statement for management.
(LO 7)

E25-15 Fisk Company uses a standard cost accounting system. During January, the company reported the following manufacturing variances.

Materials price variance	$1,200 U	Labor quantity variance	$750 U
Materials quantity variance	800 F	Overhead variance	800 U
Labor price variance	550 U		

In addition, 8,000 units of product were sold at $8 per unit. Each unit sold had a standard cost of $5. Selling and administrative expenses were $8,000 for the month.

Instructions
Prepare an income statement for management for the month ended January 31, 2014.

Identify performance evaluation terminology.
(LO 3, 8)

E25-16 The following is a list of terms related to performance evaluation.

1. Balanced scorecard
2. Variance
3. Learning and growth perspective
4. Nonfinancial measures
5. Customer perspective
6. Internal process perspective
7. Ideal standards
8. Normal standards

Instructions
Match each of the following descriptions with one of the terms above.

(a) The difference between total actual costs and total standard costs.

(b) An efficient level of performance that is attainable under expected operating conditions.

(c) An approach that incorporates financial and nonfinancial measures in an integrated system that links performance measurement and a company's strategic goals.

(d) A viewpoint employed in the balanced scorecard to evaluate how well a company develops and retains its employees.

(e) An evaluation tool that is not based on dollars.

(f) A viewpoint employed in the balanced scorecard to evaluate the company from the perspective of those people who buy its products or services.

(g) An optimum level of performance under perfect operating conditions.

(h) A viewpoint employed in the balanced scorecard to evaluate the efficiency and effectiveness of the company's value chain.

***E25-17** Vista Company installed a standard cost system on January 1. Selected transactions for the month of January are as follows.

Journalize entries in a standard cost accounting system.

(LO 9)

1. Purchased 18,000 units of raw materials on account at a cost of $4.50 per unit. Standard cost was $4.40 per unit.

2. Issued 18,000 units of raw materials for jobs that required 17,500 standard units of raw materials.

3. Incurred 7,650 actual hours of direct labor at an actual rate of $10 per hour. The standard rate is $11 per hour. (Credit Factory Wages Payable.)

4. Performed 7,650 hours of direct labor on jobs when standard hours were 7,700.

5. Applied overhead to jobs at the rate of 100% of direct labor cost for standard hours allowed.

Instructions
Journalize the January transactions.

***E25-18** Stiller Company uses a standard cost accounting system. Some of the ledger accounts have been destroyed in a fire. The controller asks your help in reconstructing some missing entries and balances.

Answer questions concerning missing entries and balances.

(LO 4, 5, 9)

Instructions
Answer the following questions.

(a) Materials Price Variance shows a $2,000 unfavorable balance. Accounts Payable shows $128,000 of raw materials purchases. What was the amount debited to Raw Materials Inventory for raw materials purchased?

(b) Materials Quantity Variance shows a $3,000 favorable balance. Raw Materials Inventory shows a zero balance. What was the amount debited to Work in Process Inventory for direct materials used?

(c) Labor Price Variance shows a $1,500 favorable balance. Factory Labor shows a debit of $140,000 for wages incurred. What was the amount credited to Factory Wages Payable?

(d) Factory Labor shows a credit of $140,000 for direct labor used. Labor Quantity Variance shows a $900 favorable balance. What was the amount debited to Work in Process for direct labor used?

(e) Overhead applied to Work in Process totaled $165,000. If the total overhead variance was $1,200 favorable, what was the amount of overhead costs debited to Manufacturing Overhead?

***E25-19** Data for Nona Inc. are given in E25-7.

Journalize entries for materials and labor variances.

(LO 9)

Instructions
Journalize the entries to record the materials and labor variances.

***E25-20** The information shown below was taken from the annual manufacturing overhead cost budget of Samantha Company.

Compute manufacturing overhead variances and interpret findings.

(LO 10)

Variable manufacturing overhead costs	$34,650
Fixed manufacturing overhead costs	$19,800
Normal production level in labor hours	16,500
Normal production level in units	4,125
Standard labor hours per unit	4

During the year, 4,000 units were produced, 16,100 hours were worked, and the actual manufacturing overhead was $55,000. Actual fixed manufacturing overhead costs equaled budgeted fixed manufacturing overhead costs. Overhead is applied on the basis of direct labor hours.

Instructions

(a) Compute the total, fixed, and variable predetermined manufacturing overhead rates.

(b) Compute the total, controllable, and volume overhead variances.

(c) ▬▬▬ Briefly interpret the overhead controllable and volume variances computed in (b).

Compute overhead variances.
(LO 10)

*E25-21 The loan department of Calgary Bank uses standard costs to determine the overhead cost of processing loan applications. During the current month, a fire occurred, and the accounting records for the department were mostly destroyed. The data shown below were salvaged from the ashes.

Standard variable overhead rate per hour	$9
Standard hours per application	2
Standard hours allowed	2,000
Standard fixed overhead rate per hour	$6
Actual fixed overhead cost	$12,600
Variable overhead budget based on standard hours allowed	$18,000
Fixed overhead budget	$12,600
Overhead controllable variance	$ 1,200 U

Instructions

(a) Determine the following.

　(1) Total actual overhead cost.

　(2) Actual variable overhead cost.

　(3) Variable overhead costs applied.

　(4) Fixed overhead costs applied.

　(5) Overhead volume variance.

(b) Determine how many loans were processed.

Compute variances.
(LO 10)

*E25-22 Alona Company's overhead rate was based on estimates of $200,000 for overhead costs and 20,000 direct labor hours. Alona's standards allow 2 hours of direct labor per unit produced. Production in May was 900 units, and actual overhead incurred in May was $19,000. The overhead budgeted for 1,800 standard direct labor hours is $17,600 ($5,000 fixed and $12,600 variable).

Instructions

(a) Compute the total, controllable, and volume variances for overhead.

(b) What are possible causes of the variances computed in part (a)?

EXERCISES: SET B AND CHALLENGE EXERCISES

Visit the book's companion website, at **www.wiley.com/college/weygandt**, and choose the Student Companion site to access Exercise Set B and Challenge Exercises.

PROBLEMS: SET A

Compute variances.
(LO 4, 5)

P25-1A Costello Corporation manufactures a single product. The standard cost per unit of product is shown below.

Direct materials—1 pound plastic at $7.00 per pound	$ 7.00
Direct labor—1.6 hours at $12.00 per hour	19.20
Variable manufacturing overhead	12.00
Fixed manufacturing overhead	4.00
Total standard cost per unit	$42.20

The predetermined manufacturing overhead rate is $10 per direct labor hour ($16.00 ÷ 1.6). It was computed from a master manufacturing overhead budget based on normal production of 8,000 direct labor hours (5,000 units) for the month. The master budget showed total variable costs of $60,000 ($7.50 per hour) and total fixed overhead costs of $20,000 ($2.50 per hour). Actual costs for October in producing 4,900 units were as follows.

Direct materials (5,100 pounds)	$ 36,720
Direct labor (7,500 hours)	93,750
Variable overhead	59,700
Fixed overhead	21,000
Total manufacturing costs	$211,170

The purchasing department buys the quantities of raw materials that are expected to be used in production each month. Raw materials inventories, therefore, can be ignored.

Instructions
(a) Compute all of the materials and labor variances.
(b) Compute the total overhead variance.

(a) MPV $1,020 U

P25-2A Ayala Corporation accumulates the following data relative to jobs started and finished during the month of June 2014.

Compute variances, and prepare income statement.
(LO 4, 5, 7)

Costs and Production Data	Actual	Standard
Raw materials unit cost	$2.25	$2.10
Raw materials units used	10,600	10,000
Direct labor payroll	$120,960	$120,000
Direct labor hours worked	14,400	15,000
Manufacturing overhead incurred	$189,500	
Manufacturing overhead applied		$193,500
Machine hours expected to be used at normal capacity		42,500
Budgeted fixed overhead for June		$55,250
Variable overhead rate per machine hour		$3.00
Fixed overhead rate per machine hour		$1.30

Overhead is applied on the basis of standard machine hours. Three hours of machine time are required for each direct labor hour. The jobs were sold for $400,000. Selling and administrative expenses were $40,000. Assume that the amount of raw materials purchased equaled the amount used.

Instructions
(a) Compute all of the variances for (1) direct materials and (2) direct labor.
(b) Compute the total overhead variance.
(c) Prepare an income statement for management. (Ignore income taxes.)

(a) LQV $4,800 F

P25-3A Hopkins Clothiers is a small company that manufactures tall-men's suits. The company has used a standard cost accounting system. In May 2014, 11,200 suits were produced. The following standard and actual cost data applied to the month of May when normal capacity was 14,000 direct labor hours. All materials purchased were used.

Compute and identify significant variances.
(LO 4, 5, 6)

Cost Element	Standard (per unit)	Actual
Direct materials	8 yards at $4.40 per yard	$375,575 for 90,500 yards ($4.15 per yard)
Direct labor	1.2 hours at $13.40 per hour	$200,220 for 14,200 hours ($14.10 per hour)
Overhead	1.2 hours at $6.10 per hour (fixed $3.50; variable $2.60)	$49,000 fixed overhead $37,000 variable overhead

Overhead is applied on the basis of direct labor hours. At normal capacity, budgeted fixed overhead costs were $49,000, and budgeted variable overhead was $36,400.

Instructions
(a) Compute the total, price, and quantity variances for (1) materials and (2) labor.
(b) Compute the total overhead variance.
(c) ———— Which of the materials and labor variances should be investigated if management considers a variance of more than 4% from standard to be significant?

(a) MPV $22,625 F

P25-4A Kansas Company uses a standard cost accounting system. In 2014, the company produced 28,000 units. Each unit took several pounds of direct materials and 1.6 standard hours of direct labor at a standard hourly rate of $12.00. Normal capacity was 50,000 direct labor hours. During the year, 117,000 pounds of raw materials were purchased at $0.92 per pound. All materials purchased were used during the year.

Instructions
(a) If the materials price variance was $3,510 favorable, what was the standard materials price per pound?
(b) If the materials quantity variance was $4,750 unfavorable, what was the standard materials quantity per unit?
(c) What were the standard hours allowed for the units produced?
(d) If the labor quantity variance was $7,200 unfavorable, what were the actual direct labor hours worked?
(e) If the labor price variance was $9,080 favorable, what was the actual rate per hour?
(f) If total budgeted manufacturing overhead was $360,000 at normal capacity, what was the predetermined overhead rate?
(g) What was the standard cost per unit of product?
(h) How much overhead was applied to production during the year?
(i) Using one or more answers above, what were the total costs assigned to work in process?

P25-5A Pace Labs, Inc. provides mad cow disease testing for both state and federal governmental agricultural agencies. Because the company's customers are governmental agencies, prices are strictly regulated. Therefore, Pace Labs must constantly monitor and control its testing costs. Shown below are the standard costs for a typical test.

Direct materials (2 test tubes @ $1.46 per tube)	$ 2.92
Direct labor (1 hour @ $24 per hour)	24.00
Variable overhead (1 hour @ $6 per hour)	6.00
Fixed overhead (1 hour @ $10 per hour)	10.00
Total standard cost per test	$42.92

The lab does not maintain an inventory of test tubes. Therefore, the tubes purchased each month are used that month. Actual activity for the month of November 2014, when 1,500 tests were conducted, resulted in the following.

Direct materials (3,050 test tubes)	$ 4,209
Direct labor (1,600 hours)	36,800
Variable overhead	7,400
Fixed overhead	15,000

Monthly budgeted fixed overhead is $14,000. Revenues for the month were $75,000, and selling and administrative expenses were $5,000.

Instructions
(a) Compute the price and quantity variances for direct materials and direct labor.
(b) Compute the total overhead variance.
(c) Prepare an income statement for management.
(d) Provide possible explanations for each unfavorable variance.

*P25-6A Jorgensen Corporation uses standard costs with its job order cost accounting system. In January, an order (Job No. 12) for 1,900 units of Product B was received. The standard cost of one unit of Product B is as follows.

Direct materials	3 pounds at $1.00 per pound	$ 3.00
Direct labor	1 hour at $8.00 per hour	8.00
Overhead	2 hours (variable $4.00 per machine hour; fixed $2.25 per machine hour)	12.50
Standard cost per unit		$23.50

Normal capacity for the month was 4,200 machine hours. During January, the following transactions applicable to Job No. 12 occurred.

1. Purchased 6,200 pounds of raw materials on account at $1.05 per pound.
2. Requisitioned 6,200 pounds of raw materials for Job No. 12.

3. Incurred 2,000 hours of direct labor at a rate of $7.80 per hour.
4. Worked 2,000 hours of direct labor on Job No. 12.
5. Incurred manufacturing overhead on account $25,000.
6. Applied overhead to Job No. 12 on basis of standard machine hours allowed.
7. Completed Job No. 12.
8. Billed customer for Job No. 12 at a selling price of $65,000.

Instructions
(a) Journalize the transactions.
(b) Post to the job order cost accounts.
(c) Prepare the entry to recognize the total overhead variance.
(d) Prepare the January 2014 income statement for management. Assume selling and administrative expenses were $2,000.

(d) NI $15,890

*P25-7A Using the information in P25-1A, compute the overhead controllable variance and the overhead volume variance.

Compute overhead control-lable and volume variances.
(LO 10)

*P25-8A Using the information in P25-2A, compute the overhead controllable variance and the overhead volume variance.

Compute overhead control-lable and volume variances.
(LO 10)

*P25-9A Using the information in P25-3A, compute the overhead controllable variance and the overhead volume variance.

Compute overhead control-lable and volume variances.
(LO 10)

*P25-10A Using the information in P25-5A, compute the overhead controllable variance and the overhead volume variance.

Compute overhead control-lable and volume variances.
(LO 10)

PROBLEMS: SET B

P25-1B Buil Corporation manufactures a single product. The standard cost per unit of product is as follows.

Compute variances.
(LO 4, 5)

Direct materials—2 pounds of plastic at $6 per pound	$12
Direct labor—2 hours at $13 per hour	26
Variable manufacturing overhead	7
Fixed manufacturing overhead	5
Total standard cost per unit	$50

The master manufacturing overhead budget for the month based on normal productive capacity of 20,000 direct labor hours (10,000 units) shows total variable costs of $70,000 ($3.50 per labor hour) and total fixed costs of $50,000 ($2.50 per labor hour). Normal productive capacity is 20,000 direct labor hours. Overhead is applied on the basis of direct labor hours. Actual costs for November in producing 9,700 units were as follows.

Direct materials (20,000 pounds)	$119,000
Direct labor (19,600 hours)	256,760
Variable overhead	68,800
Fixed overhead	50,000
Total manufacturing costs	$494,560

The purchasing department normally buys the quantities of raw materials that are expected to be used in production each month. Raw materials inventories, therefore, can be ignored.

Instructions
(a) Compute all of the materials and labor variances.
(b) Compute the total overhead variance.

(a) MPV $1,000 F

Compute variances, and prepare income statement.

(LO 4, 5, 7)

XLS

P25-2B Huang Company uses a standard cost accounting system to account for the manufacture of exhaust fans. In July 2014, it accumulates the following data relative to 1,800 units started and finished.

Cost and Production Data	Actual	Standard
Raw materials		
Units purchased	21,000	
Units used	21,000	22,000
Unit cost	$3.70	$3.50
Direct labor		
Hours worked	3,450	3,600
Hourly rate	$11.50	$12.00
Manufacturing overhead		
Incurred	$94,800	
Applied		$100,800

Manufacturing overhead was applied on the basis of direct labor hours. Normal capacity for the month was 3,400 direct labor hours. At normal capacity, budgeted overhead costs were $16 per labor hour variable and $12 per labor hour fixed. Total budgeted fixed overhead costs were $40,800.

Jobs finished during the month were sold for $270,000. Selling and administrative expenses were $20,000.

Instructions

(a) LQV $1,800 F

(a) Compute all of the variances for (1) direct materials and (2) direct labor.
(b) Compute the total overhead variance.
(c) Prepare an income statement for management. (Ignore income taxes.)

Compute and identify significant variances.

(LO 4, 5, 6)

P25-3B Zimmerman Clothiers manufactures women's business suits. The company uses a standard cost accounting system. In March 2014, 15,700 suits were made. The following standard and actual cost data applied to the month of March when normal capacity was 20,000 direct labor hours. All materials purchased were used in production.

Cost Element	Standard (per unit)	Actual
Direct materials	5 yards at $6.75 per yard	$547,200 for 76,000 yards ($7.20 per yard)
Direct labor	1.0 hours at $11.45 per hour	$165,760 for 14,800 hours ($11.20 per hour)
Overhead	1.0 hours at $9.40 per hour (fixed $6.25; variable $3.15)	$120,000 fixed overhead $49,000 variable overhead

Overhead is applied on the basis of direct labor hours. At normal capacity, budgeted fixed overhead costs were $125,000, and budgeted variable overhead costs were $63,000.

Instructions

(a) MPV $34,200 U

(a) Compute the total, price, and quantity variances for (1) materials and (2) labor.
(b) Compute the total overhead variance.
(c) ———— Which of the materials and labor variances should be investigated if management considers a variance of more than 5% from standard to be significant?

Answer questions about variances.

(LO 4, 5)

P25-4B Beta Company uses a standard cost accounting system. In 2014, 45,000 units were produced. Each unit took several pounds of direct materials and 2 standard hours of direct labor at a standard hourly rate of $12.00. Normal capacity was 86,000 direct labor hours. During the year, 200,000 pounds of raw materials were purchased at $1.00 per pound. All materials purchased were used during the year.

Instructions

(a) If the materials price variance was $10,000 unfavorable, what was the standard materials price per pound?

(b) 5.0 pounds

(b) If the materials quantity variance was $23,750 favorable, what was the standard materials quantity per unit?
(c) What were the standard hours allowed for the units produced?
(d) If the labor quantity variance was $10,080 unfavorable, what were the actual direct labor hours worked?

(e) If the labor price variance was $18,168 favorable, what was the actual rate per hour?
(f) If total budgeted manufacturing overhead was $713,800 at normal capacity, what was the predetermined overhead rate per direct labor hour?

(f) $8.30 per DLH

(g) What was the standard cost per unit of product?
(h) How much overhead was applied to production during the year?
(i) Using selected answers above, what were the total costs assigned to work in process?

P25-5B Bonita Labs performs steroid testing services to high schools, colleges, and universities. Because the company deals solely with educational institutions, the price of each test is strictly regulated. Therefore, the costs incurred must be carefully monitored and controlled. Shown below are the standard costs for a typical test.

Compute variances, prepare an income statement, and explain unfavorable variances.

(LO 4, 5, 7)

Direct materials (1 petri dish @ $1.80 per dish)	$ 1.80
Direct labor (0.5 hours @ $20.50 per hour)	10.25
Variable overhead (0.5 hours @ $8 per hour)	4.00
Fixed overhead (0.5 hours @ $5 per hour)	2.50
Total standard cost per test	$18.55

The lab does not maintain an inventory of petri dishes. Therefore, the dishes purchased each month are used that month. Actual activity for the month of May 2014, when 2,500 tests were conducted, resulted in the following.

Direct materials (2,530 dishes)	$ 5,060
Direct labor (1,240 hours)	26,040
Variable overhead	10,100
Fixed overhead	5,700

Monthly budgeted fixed overhead is $6,000. Revenues for the month were $55,000, and selling and administrative expenses were $2,000.

Instructions
(a) Compute the price and quantity variances for direct materials and direct labor.

(a) LQV $205 F

(b) Compute the total overhead variance.
(c) Prepare an income statement for management.
(d) Provide possible explanations for each unfavorable variance.

*P25-6B Frio Company uses standard costs with its job order cost accounting system. In January, an order (Job No. 84) was received for 5,500 units of Product D. The standard cost of 1 unit of Product D is as follows.

Journalize and post standard cost entries, and prepare income statement.

(LO 4, 5, 7, 9)

Direct materials—1.5 pounds at $4.00 per pound	$ 6.00
Direct labor—1 hour at $9.00 per hour	9.00
Overhead—1 hour (variable $7.40; fixed $8.00)	15.40
Standard cost per unit	$30.40

Overhead is applied on the basis of direct labor hours. Normal capacity for the month of January was 6,000 direct labor hours. During January, the following transactions applicable to Job No. 84 occurred.

1. Purchased 8,100 pounds of raw materials on account at $3.70 per pound.
2. Requisitioned 8,100 pounds of raw materials for production.
3. Incurred 5,200 hours of direct labor at $9.20 per hour.
4. Worked 5,200 hours of direct labor on Job No. 84.
5. Incurred $87,500 of manufacturing overhead on account.
6. Applied overhead to Job No. 84 on the basis of direct labor hours.
7. Transferred Job No. 84 to finished goods.
8. Billed customer for Job No. 84 at a selling price of $270,000.

Instructions
(a) Journalize the transactions.
(b) Post to the job order cost accounts.
(c) Prepare the entry to recognize the total overhead variance.
(d) Prepare the January 2014 income statement for management. Assume selling and administrative expenses were $60,000.

(d) NI $44,690

Compute overhead controllable and volume variances.

(LO 10)

*P25-7B Using the information in P25-1B, compute the overhead controllable variance and the overhead volume variance.

Compute overhead controllable and volume variances.

(LO 10)

*P25-8B Using the information in P25-2B, compute the overhead controllable variance and the overhead volume variance.

Compute overhead controllable and volume variances.

(LO 10)

*P25-9B Using the information in P25-3B, compute the overhead controllable variance and the overhead volume variance.

Compute overhead controllable and volume variances.

(LO 10)

*P25-10B Using the information in P25-5B, compute the overhead controllable variance and the overhead volume variance.

PROBLEMS: SET C

Visit the book's companion website, at **www.wiley.com/college/weygandt**, and choose the Student Companion site to access Problem Set C.

WATERWAYS CONTINUING PROBLEM

(This is a continuation of the Waterways Problem from Chapters 19 through 24.)

WCP25 Waterways Corporation uses very stringent standard costs in evaluating its manufacturing efficiency. These standards are not "ideal" at this point, but management is working toward that as a goal. This problem asks you to calculate and evaluate the company's variances.

Go to the book's companion website, at **www.wiley.com/college/weygandt**, *to find the completion of this problem.*

Broadening Your Perspective

Management Decision-Making

Decision-Making Problem: Current Designs

BYP25-1 The executive team at Current Designs has gathered to evaluate the company's operations for the last month. One of the topics on the agenda is the special order from Huegel Hollow, which was presented in BYP20-1. Recall that Current Designs had a special order to produce a batch of 20 kayaks for a client, and you were asked to determine the cost of the order and the cost per kayak.

Mike Cichanowski asked the others if the special order caused any particular problems in the production process. Dave Thill, the production manager, made the following comments: "Since we wanted to complete this order quickly and make a good first impression on this new customer, we had some of our most experienced type I workers run the rotomold oven and do the trimming. They were very efficient and were able to complete that part of the manufacturing process even more quickly than the regular crew. However, the finishing on these kayaks required a different technique than what we usually use, so our type II workers took a little longer than usual for that part of the process."

Deb Welch, who is in charge of the purchasing function, said, "We had to pay a little more for the polyethylene powder for this order because the customer wanted a color that we don't usually stock. We also ordered a little extra since we wanted to make sure that we had enough to allow us to calibrate the equipment. The calibration was a little tricky, and we used all of the powder that we had purchased. Since the number of kayaks in the order was fairly small, we were able to use some rope and other parts that were left over from last year's production in the finishing kits. We've seen a price increase for these components in the last year, so using the parts that we already had in inventory cut our costs for the finishing kits."

Instructions

(a) Based on the comments above, predict whether each of the following variances will be favorable or unfavorable. If you don't have enough information to make a prediction, use "NEI" to indicate "Not Enough Information."

(1) Quantity variance for polyethylene powder.
(2) Price variance for polyethylene powder.
(3) Quantity variance for finishing kits.
(4) Price variance for finishing kits.
(5) Quantity variance for type I workers.
(6) Price variance for type I workers.
(7) Quantity variance for type II workers.
(8) Price variance for type II workers.

(b) Diane Buswell examined some of the accounting records and reported that Current Designs purchased 1,200 pounds of pellets for this order at a total cost of $2,040. Twenty (20) finishing kits were assembled at a total cost of $3,240. The payroll records showed that the type I employees worked 38 hours on this project at a total cost of $570. The type II finishing employees worked 65 hours at a total cost of $796.25. A total of 20 kayaks were produced for this order.

   The standards that had been developed for this model of kayak were used in BYP20-1 and are reproduced here. For each kayak:

   54 pounds of polyethylene powder at $1.50 per pound

   1 finishing kit (rope, seat, hardware, etc.) at $170

   2 hours of type I labor from people who run the oven and trim the plastic at a standard wage rate of $15 per hour

   3 hours of type II labor from people who attach the hatches and seat and other hardware at a standard wage rate of $12 per hour.

Calculate the eight variances that are listed in part (a) of this problem.

Decision-Making Across the Organization

BYP25-2 Milton Professionals, a management consulting firm, specializes in strategic planning for financial institutions. James Hahn and Sara Norton, partners in the firm, are assembling a new strategic planning model for use by clients. The model is designed for use on most personal computers and replaces a rather lengthy manual model currently marketed by the firm. To market the new model, James and Sara will need to provide clients with an estimate of the number of labor hours and computer time needed to operate the model. The model is currently being test-marketed at five small financial institutions. These financial institutions are listed below, along with the number of combined computer/labor hours used by each institution to run the model one time.

Financial Institutions	Computer/Labor Hours Required
Midland National	25
First State	45
Financial Federal	40
Pacific America	30
Lakeview National	30
Total	170
Average	34

   Any company that purchases the new model will need to purchase user manuals for the system. User manuals will be sold to clients in cases of 20, at a cost of $320 per case. One manual must be used each time the model is run because each manual includes a nonreusable computer-accessed password for operating the system. Also required are specialized computer forms that are sold only by Milton. The specialized forms are sold in packages of 250, at a cost of $60 per package. One application of the model requires the use of 50 forms. This amount includes two forms that are generally wasted in each application due to printer alignment errors. The overall cost of the strategic planning model to clients is $12,000. Most clients will use the model four times annually.

Milton must provide its clients with estimates of ongoing costs incurred in operating the new planning model, and would like to do so in the form of standard costs.

Instructions

With the class divided into groups, answer the following.

(a) What factors should be considered in setting a standard for computer/labor hours?
(b) What alternatives for setting a standard for computer/labor hours might be used?
(c) What standard for computer/labor hours would you select? Justify your answer.
(d) Determine the standard materials cost associated with the user manuals and computer forms for each application of the strategic planning model.

Managerial Analysis

*BYP25-3 Ana Carillo and Associates is a medium-sized company located near a large metropolitan area in the Midwest. The company manufactures cabinets of mahogany, oak, and other fine woods for use in expensive homes, restaurants, and hotels. Although some of the work is custom, many of the cabinets are a standard size.

One such non-custom model is called Luxury Base Frame. Normal production is 1,000 units. Each unit has a direct labor hour standard of 5 hours. Overhead is applied to production based on standard direct labor hours. During the most recent month, only 900 units were produced; 4,500 direct labor hours were allowed for standard production, but only 4,000 hours were used. Standard and actual overhead costs were as follows.

	Standard (1,000 units)	Actual (900 units)
Indirect materials	$ 12,000	$ 12,300
Indirect labor	43,000	51,000
(Fixed) Manufacturing supervisors' salaries	22,500	22,000
(Fixed) Manufacturing office employees' salaries	13,000	12,500
(Fixed) Engineering costs	27,000	25,000
Computer costs	10,000	10,000
Electricity	2,500	2,500
(Fixed) Manufacturing building depreciation	8,000	8,000
(Fixed) Machinery depreciation	3,000	3,000
(Fixed) Trucks and forklift depreciation	1,500	1,500
Small tools	700	1,400
(Fixed) Insurance	500	500
(Fixed) Property taxes	300	300
Total	$144,000	$150,000

Instructions

(a) Determine the overhead application rate.
(b) Determine how much overhead was applied to production.
(c) Calculate the total overhead variance, controllable variance, and volume variance.
(d) Decide which overhead variances should be investigated.
(e) Discuss causes of the overhead variances. What can management do to improve its performance next month?

Real-World Focus

BYP25-4 Glassmaster Company is organized as two divisions and one subsidiary. One division focuses on the manufacture of filaments such as fishing line and sewing thread; the other division manufactures antennas and specialty fiberglass products. Its subsidiary manufactures flexible steel wire controls and molded control panels.

The annual report of Glassmaster provides the following information.

GLASSMASTER COMPANY
Management Discussion

Gross profit margins for the year improved to 20.9% of sales compared to last year's 18.5%. All operations reported improved margins due in large part to improved operating efficiencies as a result of cost reduction measures implemented during the second and third quarters of the fiscal year and increased manufacturing throughout due to higher unit volume sales. Contributing to the improved margins was a favorable materials price variance due to competitive pricing by suppliers as a result of soft demand for petrochemical-based products. This favorable variance is temporary and will begin to reverse itself as stronger worldwide demand for commodity products improves in tandem with the economy. Partially offsetting these positive effects on profit margins were competitive pressures on sales prices of certain product lines. The company responded with pricing strategies designed to maintain and/or increase market share.

Instructions

(a) Is it apparent from the information whether Glassmaster utilizes standard costs?

(b) Do you think the price variance experienced should lead to changes in standard costs for the next fiscal year?

BYP25-5 The Balanced Scorecard Institute (**www.balancedscorecard.org**) is a great resource for information about implementing the balanced scorecard. One item of interest provided at its website is an example of a balanced scorecard for a regional airline.

Address: **http://www.balancedscorecard.org/portals/0/pdf/regional_airline.pdf**, or go to **www.wiley.com/college/weygandt**

Instructions

Go to the address above and answer the following questions.

(a) What are the objectives identified for the airline for each perspective?

(b) What measures are used for the objectives in the customer perspective?

(c) What initiatives are planned to achieve the objective in the learning perspective?

BYP25-6 The December 22, 2009, edition of the *Wall Street Journal* has an article by Kevin Kelliker entitled "In Risky Move, GM to Run Plants Around Clock."

Instructions

Read the article and answer the following questions.

(a) According to the article, what is the normal industry standard for plants to be considered operating at full capacity?

(b) What ideal standard is the company hoping to achieve?

(c) What reasons are given in the article for why most companies do not operate a third shift? How does GM propose to overcome these issues?

(d) What are some potential drawbacks of the midnight shift? What implications does this have for variances from standards?

(e) What potential sales/marketing disadvantage does the third shift create?

Critical Thinking

Communication Activity

BYP25-7 The setting of standards is critical to the effective use of standards in evaluating performance.

Instructions

Explain the following in a memo to your instructor.

(a) The comparative advantages and disadvantages of ideal versus normal standards.

(b) The factors that should be included in setting the price and quantity standards for direct materials, direct labor, and manufacturing overhead.

Ethics Case

BYP25-8 At Symond Company, production workers in the Painting Department are paid on the basis of productivity. The labor time standard for a unit of production is established through periodic time studies conducted by Douglas Management Consultants. In a time study, the actual time required to complete a specific task by a worker is observed. Allowances are then made for preparation time, rest periods, and cleanup time. Bill Carson is one of several veterans in the Painting Department.

Bill is informed by Douglas that he will be used in the time study for the painting of a new product. The findings will be the basis for establishing the labor time standard for the next 6 months. During the test, Bill deliberately slows his normal work pace in an effort to obtain a labor time standard that will be easy to meet. Because it is a new product, the Douglas representative who conducted the test is unaware that Bill did not give the test his best effort.

Instructions

(a) Who was benefited and who was harmed by Bill's actions?

(b) Was Bill ethical in the way he performed the time study test?

(c) What measure(s) might the company take to obtain valid data for setting the labor time standard?

All About You

BYP25-9 From the time you first entered school many years ago, instructors have been measuring and evaluating you by imposing standards. In addition, many of you will pursue professions that administer professional examinations to attain recognized certification. Recently, a federal commission presented proposals suggesting all public colleges and universities should require standardized tests to measure their students' learning.

Instructions

Read the article at **www.signonsandiego.com/uniontrib/20060811/news_1n11colleges.html**, and answer the following questions.

(a) What areas of concern did the panel's recommendations address?

(b) What are possible advantages of standard testing?

(c) What are possible disadvantages of standard testing?

(d) Would you be in favor of standardized tests?

Considering Your Costs and Benefits

BYP25-10 Do you think that standard costs are used only in making products like wheel bearings and hamburgers? Think again. Standards influence virtually every aspect of our lives. For example, the next time you call to schedule an appointment with your doctor, ask the receptionist how many minutes the appointment is scheduled for. Doctors are under increasing pressure to see more patients each day, which means the time spent with each patient is shorter. As insurance companies and employers push for reduced medical costs, every facet of medicine has been standardized and analyzed. Doctors, nurses, and other medical staff are evaluated in every part of their operations to ensure maximum efficiency. While keeping medical treatment affordable seems like a worthy goal, what are the potential implications for the quality of health care? Does a focus on the bottom line result in a reduction in the quality of health care?

A simmering debate has centered on a very basic question: To what extent should accountants, through financial measures, influence the type of medical care that you receive? Suppose that your local medical facility is in danger of closing because it has been losing money. Should the facility put in place incentives that provide bonuses to doctors if they meet certain standard-cost targets for the cost of treating specific ailments?

YES: If the facility is in danger of closing, then someone should take steps to change the medical practices to reduce costs. A closed medical facility is of no use to me, my family, or the community.

NO: I don't want an accountant deciding the right medical treatment for me. My family and I deserve the best medical care.

Instructions

Write a response indicating your position regarding this situation. Provide support for your view.

Answers to Chapter Questions

Answers to Insight and Accounting Across the Organization Questions

p. 1180 How Do Standards Help a Business?   Q: How will the creation of such standards help a business or organization? **A:** A business or organization may use the data to compare its performance relative to others with regard to common practices such as processing a purchase order or filling a sales order. Armed with this information, an organization can determine which areas to focus on with improvement campaigns.

p. 1183 How Can We Make Susan's Chili Profitable?   Q: How might management use this raw materials cost information? **A:** Management might decide to increase the price of its chili. Or, it might revise its recipes to use cheaper ingredients. Or, it might eliminate some products until ingredients are available at costs closer to standard. Regarding the waste due to dull blades, management should reconsider its maintenance policy, to balance the cost of maintenance versus the cost of wasted product.

p. 1192 What's Brewing at Starbucks?   Q: What implications does Starbucks' commitment to corporate social responsibility have for the standard cost of a cup of coffee? **A:** Starbucks' *Global Responsibility Report* explicitly describes its goals related to corporate social responsibility. By including measurable objectives, it signals that it is committed to meeting these goals. As a consequence of setting measurable objectives, when the company determines the standard costs of its products, it needs to factor in the costs of these programs. For example, if renewable energy costs more per kilowatt, then the company must include this added cost in its determination of its products' costs.

p. 1197 It May Be Time to Fly United Again   Q: Which of the perspectives of a balanced scorecard were the focus of United's CEO? **A:** Improving on-time flight departures is an objective within the internal process perspective. Customer intent to fly United again is an objective within the customer perspective.

Answers to Self-Test Questions

1. c **2.** b **3.** d **4.** a **5.** b **6.** c **7.** b $[(6,300 \times \$1.00) - (6,000 \times \$1.00)]$ **8.** a $[(14,800 \times \$8.00) - (15,000 \times \$8.00)]$ **9.** d **10.** a **11.** b **12.** d **13.** c **14.** d ***15.** c ***16.** c

✔ **The Navigator**

Feature Story

Make It or Buy It?

When is a manufacturer not a manufacturer? When it outsources. An extension of the classic "make or buy" decision, outsourcing involves hiring other companies to make all or part of a product or to perform services. Who is outsourcing? Nike, General Motors, Sara Lee, and Hewlett-Packard, to name a few. Even a recent trade journal article for small cabinetmakers outlined the pros and cons of building cabinet doors and drawers internally, or outsourcing them to other shops.

Gibson Greetings, Inc., one of the country's largest sellers of greeting cards, has experienced both the pros and cons of outsourcing. In April one year, it announced it would out-source the manufacturing of all of its cards and gift wrap. Gibson's stock price shot up quickly because investors believed the strategy could save the company $10 million a year, primarily by reducing manufacturing costs. But later in the same year, Gibson got a taste of the negative side of outsourcing: When one of its suppliers was unable to me its production schedule, about $20 million of Christmas cards went to stores a month later than scheduled.

Outsourcing is often a point of dispute in labor negotiati Although many of the jobs lost to outsourcing go overse that is not always the case. In fact, a recent trend is to h out work to vendors located close to the company. This reduces shipping costs and can improve coordination of e

One company that has benefited from local outsourcing Solectron Corporation in Silicon Valley. It makes things li cell phones, printers, and computers for high-tech comp in the region. To the surprise of many, it has kept thousa of people employed in California rather than watching t jobs go overseas. What is its secret? It produces high-qu products efficiently. Solectron has to be efficient because operates on a very thin profit margin—that is, it makes a amount of money on each part—but it makes millions a

✔ The Navigator

- Scan Learning Objectives
- Read Feature Story
- Read Preview
- Read text and answer **DO IT!** p. 1232
  - p. 1234   ▪ p. 1238   ▪ p. 1242
  - p. 1244   ▪ p. 1249
- Work Comprehensive **DO IT!** p. 1250
- Review Summary of Learning Objectives
- Answer Self-Test Questions
- Complete Assignments
- Go to *WileyPLUS* for practice and tutorials

Learning Objectives

After studying this chapter, you should be able to:

[1] Identify the steps in management's decision-making process.

[2] Describe the concept of incremental analysis.

[3] Identify the relevant costs in accepting an order at a special price.

[4] Identify the relevant costs in a make-or-buy decision.

[5] Identify the relevant costs in determining whether to sell or process materials further.

[6] Identify the relevant costs to be considered in repairing, retaining, or replacing equipment.

[7] Identify the relevant costs in deciding whether to eliminate an unprofitable segment or product.

[8] Determine which products to make and sell when resources are limited.

[9] Contrast annual rate of return and cash payback in capital budgeting.

[10] Distinguish between the net present value and internal rate of return methods.

© Izabela Habur/iStockphoto

millions of parts. It has proved the logic of outsourcing as a management decision, both for the companies for which it makes parts and for its owners and employees.

Watch the Method video in WileyPLUS to learn more about incremental analysis in the real world, and the Holland America Line video to learn more about capital budgeting in the real world.

Preview of Chapter 26

✔ The Navigator

An important purpose of management accounting is to provide managers with relevant information for decision-making. Companies of all sorts must make product decisions. Philip Morris decided to cut prices to raise market share. Oral-B Laboratories opted to produce a new, higher-priced ($5) toothbrush. General Motors discontinued making the Buick Riviera and announced the closure of its Oldsmobile Division. Quaker Oats decided to sell off a line of beverages, at a price more than $1 billion less than it paid for that product line only a few years before. Ski manufacturers like Dynastar had to decide whether to use their limited resources to make snowboards instead of downhill skis.

This chapter begins with an explanation of management's decision-making process. It then considers the topics of incremental analysis and capital budgeting. The content and organization of Chapter 26 are as follows.

INCREMENTAL ANALYSIS AND CAPITAL BUDGETING

Incremental Analysis	Capital Budgeting
• Management's decision-making process	• Evaluation process
• Incremental analysis approach	• Annual rate of return
• Accept special-price order	• Cash payback
• Make or buy	• Discounted cash flow: NPV and IRR
• Sell or process further	
• Repair, retain, or replace equipment	
• Eliminate unprofitable segment	
• Allocate limited resources	

Incremental Analysis

LEARNING OBJECTIVE **1**

Identify the steps in management's decision-making process.

Management's Decision-Making Process

Making decisions is an important management function. Management's decision-making process does not always follow a set pattern because decisions vary significantly in their scope, urgency, and importance. It is possible, though, to identify some steps that are frequently involved in the process. These steps are shown in Illustration 26-1.

Accounting's contribution to the decision-making process occurs primarily in Steps 2 and 4—evaluating possible courses of action, and reviewing results. In Step 2, for each possible course of action, relevant revenue and cost data are provided. These show the expected overall effect on net income. In Step 4, internal reports are prepared that review the actual impact of the decision.

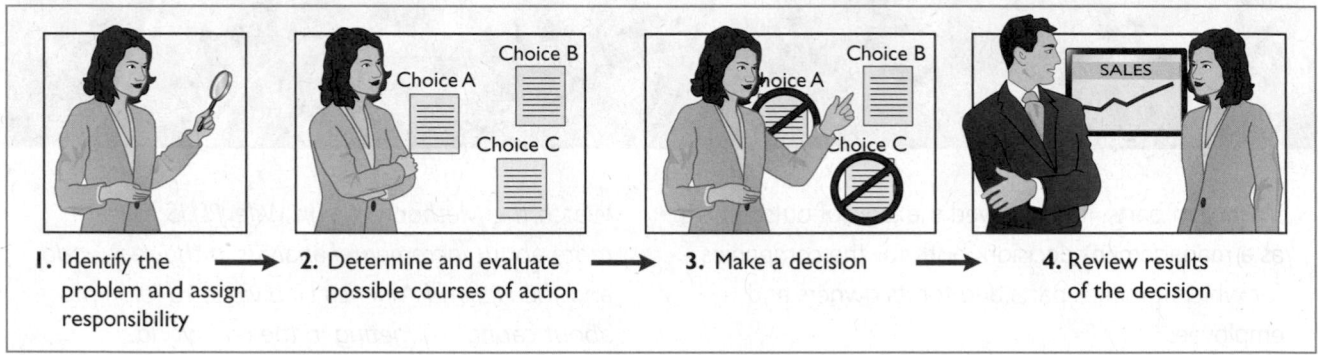

1. Identify the problem and assign responsibility → **2.** Determine and evaluate possible courses of action → **3.** Make a decision → **4.** Review results of the decision

Illustration 26-1
Management's decision-making process

In making business decisions, management ordinarily considers both financial and nonfinancial information. **Financial** information is related to revenues and costs and their effect on the company's overall profitability. **Nonfinancial** information relates to such factors as the effect of the decision on employee turnover, the environment, or the overall image of the company in the community. (These are considerations that we touched on in our Chapter 19 discussion of corporate social responsibility.) Although nonfinancial information can be as important as financial information, we will focus primarily on financial information that is relevant to the decision.

Incremental Analysis Approach

LEARNING OBJECTIVE **2**

Describe the concept of incremental analysis.

Decisions involve a choice among alternative courses of action. Suppose you face the personal financial decision of whether to purchase or lease a car. The financial data relate to the cost of leasing versus the cost of purchasing. For example, leasing would involve periodic lease payments; purchasing would require "up-front" payment of the purchase price. In other words, the financial data relevant to the decision are the data that would vary in the future among the possible alternatives. The process used to identify the financial data that change under alternative courses of action is called **incremental analysis**. In some cases, you will find that when you use incremental analysis, both costs **and** revenues will vary. In other cases, only costs **or** revenues will vary.

Alternative Terminology
Incremental analysis is also called *differential analysis* because the analysis focuses on differences.

Just as your decision to buy or lease a car will affect your future financial situation, similar decisions, on a larger scale, will affect a company's future. Incremental analysis identifies the probable effects of those decisions on future earnings. Such analysis inevitably involves estimates and uncertainty. Gathering data for incremental analyses may involve market analysts, engineers, and accountants. In quantifying the data, the accountant is expected to produce the most reliable information available at the time the decision must be made.

How Incremental Analysis Works

The basic approach in incremental analysis is illustrated in the following example.

Illustration 26-2
Basic approach in incremental analysis

	Incremental Analysis.xls		
Home Insert Page Layout Formulas Data Review View			
P18 fx			
A	B	C	D
1	**Alternative A**	**Alternative B**	**Net Income Increase (Decrease)**
2 Revenues	$125,000	$110,000	$ (15,000)
3 Costs	100,000	80,000	20,000
4 Net income	$ 25,000	$ 30,000	$ 5,000
5			

This example compares alternative B with alternative A. The net income column shows the differences between the alternatives. In this case, incremental revenue will be $15,000 less under alternative B than under alternative A. But a $20,000 incremental cost savings will be realized.[1] Thus, alternative B will produce $5,000 more net income than alternative A.

In the following pages, you will encounter three important cost concepts used in incremental analysis, as defined and discussed in Illustration 26-3.

Illustration 26-3
Key cost concepts in incremental analysis

- **Relevant cost**   In incremental analysis, the only factors to be considered are those costs and revenues that differ across alternatives. Those factors are called **relevant costs**. Costs and revenues that do not differ across alternatives can be ignored when trying to choose between alternatives.

- **Opportunity cost**   Often in choosing one course of action, the company must give up the opportunity to benefit from some other course of action. For example, if a machine is used to make one type of product, the benefit of making another type of product with that machine is lost. This lost benefit is referred to as **opportunity cost**.

- **Sunk cost**   Costs that have already been incurred and will not be changed or avoided by any present or future decisions are referred to as **sunk costs**. For example, the amount you spent in the past to purchase or repair a machine should have no bearing on your decision whether to buy a new machine. **Sunk costs are not relevant costs.**

---

[1]Although income taxes are sometimes important in incremental analysis, they are ignored in the chapter for simplicity's sake.

Incremental analysis sometimes involves changes that at first glance might seem contrary to your intuition. For example, sometimes variable costs **do not change** under the alternative courses of action. Also, sometimes fixed costs **do change**. For example, direct labor, normally a variable cost, is not an incremental cost in deciding between two new factory machines if each asset requires the same amount of direct labor. In contrast, rent expense, normally a fixed cost, is an incremental cost in a decision whether to continue occupancy of a building or to purchase or lease a new building.

It is also important to understand that **the approaches to incremental analysis discussed in this chapter do not take into consideration the time value of money**. That is, amounts to be paid or received in future years are not discounted for the cost of interest. Time value of money is addressed later in this chapter as well as in Appendix G.

A number of different types of decisions involve incremental analysis. The more common types of decisions are whether to:

1. Accept an order at a special price.
2. Make or buy component parts or finished products.
3. Sell products or process them further.
4. Repair, retain, or replace equipment.
5. Eliminate an unprofitable business segment or product.

We will consider each of these types of decisions in the following pages.

©Tina Spruce/iStockphoto

SERVICE COMPANY INSIGHT

That Letter from AmEx Might Not Be a Bill

No doubt every one of you has received an invitation from a credit card company to open a new account—some of you have probably received three in one day. But how many of you have received an offer of $300 to close out your credit card account? American Express decided to offer some of its customers $300 if they would give back their credit card. You could receive the $300 even if you hadn't paid off your balance yet, as long as you agreed to give up your credit card.

Source: Aparajita Saha-Bubna and Lauren Pollock, "AmEx Offers Some Holders $300 to Pay and Leave," *Wall Street Journal Online* (February 23, 2009).

 What are the relevant costs that American Express would need to know in order to determine to whom to make this offer? (See page 1271.)

Accept an Order at a Special Price

LEARNING OBJECTIVE **3**

Identify the relevant costs in accepting an order at a special price.

Sometimes a company may have an opportunity to obtain additional business if it is willing to make a major price concession to a specific customer. To illustrate, assume that Sunbelt Company produces 100,000 Smoothie blenders per month, which is 80% of plant capacity. Variable manufacturing costs are $8 per unit. Fixed manufacturing costs are $400,000, or $4 per unit. The Smoothie blenders are normally sold directly to retailers at $20 each. Sunbelt has an offer from Kensington Co. (a foreign wholesaler) to purchase an additional 2,000 blenders at $11 per unit. Acceptance of the offer would not affect normal sales of the product, and the additional units can be manufactured without increasing plant capacity. What should management do?

If management makes its decision on the basis of the total cost per unit of $12 ($8 variable + $4 fixed), the order would be rejected because costs per unit ($12) would exceed revenues per unit ($11) by $1 per unit. However, since the units can be produced within existing plant capacity, the special order **will not increase fixed costs**. Let's identify the relevant data for the decision. First, the variable manufacturing costs will increase $16,000 ($8 × 2,000). Second, the expected revenue will increase $22,000 ($11 × 2,000). Thus, as shown in Illustration 26-4, Sunbelt will increase its net income by $6,000 by accepting this special order.

	Incremental Analysis - Accepting an order at a special price.xls			
	Home Insert Page Layout Formulas Data Review View			
	P18	fx		
	A	B	C	D
1		**Reject Order**	**Accept Order**	**Net Income Increase (Decrease)**
2	Revenues	$0	$22,000	$ 22,000
3	Costs	0	16,000	(16,000)
4	Net income	$0	$ 6,000	$ 6,000
5				

Illustration 26-4
Incremental analysis—accepting an order at a special price

Two points should be emphasized. First, we assume that sales of the product in other markets **would not be affected by this special order**. If other sales were affected, then Sunbelt would have to consider the lost sales in making the decision. Second, if Sunbelt is operating **at full capacity**, it is likely that the special order would be rejected. Under such circumstances, the company would have to expand plant capacity. In that case, the special order would have to absorb these additional fixed manufacturing costs, as well as the variable manufacturing costs.

SERVICE COMPANY INSIGHT

Giving Away the Store?

In an earlier chapter, we discussed Amazon.com's incredible growth. However, some analysts have questioned whether some of the methods that Amazon uses to increase its sales make good business sense. For example, a few years ago, Amazon initiated a "Prime" free-shipping subscription program. For a $79 fee per year, Amazon's customers get free shipping on as many goods as they want to buy. At the time, CEO Jeff Bezos promised that the program would be costly in the short-term but benefit the company in the long-term. Six years later, it was true that Amazon's sales had grown considerably. It was also estimated that its Prime customers buy two to three times as much as non-Prime customers. But, its shipping costs rose from 2.8% of sales to 4% of sales, which is remarkably similar to the drop in its gross margin from 24% to 22.3%. Perhaps even less easy to justify is a proposal by Mr. Bezos to start providing a free Internet movie-streaming service to Amazon's Prime customers. Perhaps some incremental analysis is in order?

© Klenger/iStockphoto

Source: Martin Peers, "Amazon's Prime Numbers," *Wall Street Journal Online* (February 3, 2011).

? What are the relevant revenues and costs that Amazon should consider relative to the decision whether to offer the Prime free-shipping subscription? (See page 1271.)

> **DO IT!**

Special Orders

Cobb Company incurs costs of $28 per unit ($18 variable and $10 fixed) to make a product that normally sells for $42. A foreign wholesaler offers to buy 5,000 units at $25 each. Cobb will incur additional shipping costs of $1 per unit. Compute the increase or decrease in net income Cobb will realize by accepting the special order, assuming Cobb has excess operating capacity. Should Cobb Company accept the special order?

Solution

Action Plan

✔ Identify all revenues that will change as a result of accepting the order.

✔ Identify all costs that will change as a result of accepting the order, and net this amount against the change in revenues.

	Reject	Accept	Net Income Increase (Decrease)
Revenue	$–0–	$125,000*	$125,000
Costs	–0–	95,000**	(95,000)
Net income	$–0–	$ 30,000	$ 30,000

*5,000 × $25
**(5,000 × $18) + (5,000 × $1)

The analysis indicates net income will increase by $30,000; therefore, Cobb Company should accept the special order.

Related exercise material: **BE26-3, E26-2, E26-3,** and **DO IT!** 26-1.

✔ The Navigator

Make or Buy

When a manufacturer assembles component parts in producing a finished product, management must decide whether to make or buy the components. The decision to buy parts or services is often referred to as outsourcing. For example, as discussed in the Feature Story, a company such as General Motors Corporation may either make or buy the batteries, tires, and radios used in its cars. Similarly, Hewlett-Packard Corporation may make or buy the electronic circuitry, cases, and printer heads for its printers. Boeing recently sold some of its commercial aircraft factories in an effort to cut production costs and focus instead on engineering and final assembly rather than manufacturing. The decision to make or buy components should be made on the basis of incremental analysis.

Baron Company makes motorcycles and scooters. It incurs the following annual costs in producing 25,000 ignition switches for scooters.

Illustration 26-5
Annual product cost data

Direct materials	$ 50,000
Direct labor	75,000
Variable manufacturing overhead	40,000
Fixed manufacturing overhead	60,000
Total manufacturing costs	$225,000
Total cost per unit ($225,000 ÷ 25,000)	**$9.00**

Instead of making its own switches, Baron Company might purchase the ignition switches from Ignition, Inc. at a price of $8 per unit. What should management do?

At first glance, it appears that management should purchase the ignition switches for $8 rather than make them at a cost of $9. However, a review of operations indicates that if the ignition switches are purchased from Ignition, Inc., all of Baron's variable costs but only $10,000 of its fixed manufacturing costs will be eliminated (avoided). Thus, $50,000 of the fixed manufacturing costs will remain if the ignition switches are purchased. The relevant costs for incremental analysis, therefore, are as shown below.

	Incremental Analysis - Make or buy.xls		
	A	B Make	C Buy	D Net Income Increase (Decrease)
2	Direct materials	$ 50,000	$ 0	$ 50,000
3	Direct labor	75,000	0	75,000
4	Variable manufacturing costs	40,000	0	40,000
5	Fixed manufacturing costs	60,000	50,000	10,000
6	Purchase price (25,000 × $8)	0	200,000	(200,000)
7	Total annual cost	$225,000	$250,000	$ (25,000)

Illustration 26-6
Incremental analysis—make or buy

This analysis indicates that Baron Company would incur $25,000 of additional costs by buying the ignition switches rather than making them. Therefore, Baron should continue to make the ignition switches even though the total manufacturing cost is $1 higher per unit than the purchase price. The primary cause of this result is that, even if the company purchases the ignition switches, it will still have fixed costs of $50,000 to absorb.

OPPORTUNITY COST

The foregoing make-or-buy analysis is complete only if it is assumed that the productive capacity used to make the ignition switches cannot be converted to another purpose. If there is an opportunity to use this productive capacity in some other manner, then this opportunity cost must be considered. As indicated earlier, **opportunity cost** is the potential benefit that may be obtained by following an alternative course of action.

To illustrate, assume that through buying the switches, Baron Company can use the released productive capacity to generate additional income of $38,000 from producing a different product. This lost income is an additional cost of continuing to make the switches in the make-or-buy decision. This opportunity cost is therefore added to the "Make" column for comparison. As shown in Illustration 26-7, it is now advantageous to buy the ignition switches. The company's income would increase by $13,000.

Ethics Note

In the make-or-buy decision, it is important for management to take into account the social impact of its choice. For instance, buying may be the most economically feasible solution, but such action could result in the closure of a manufacturing plant that employs many good workers.

	Incremental Analysis - Make or buy with opportunity cost.xls		
	A	B Make	C Buy	D Net Income Increase (Decrease)
2	Total annual cost	$225,000	$250,000	$(25,000)
3	Opportunity cost	38,000	0	38,000
4	Total cost	$263,000	$250,000	$ 13,000

Illustration 26-7
Incremental analysis—make or buy, with opportunity cost

The qualitative factors in this decision include the possible loss of jobs for employees who produce the ignition switches. In addition, management must assess how well the supplier will be able to satisfy the company's quality control standards at the quoted price per unit.

> **DO IT!**

Make or Buy

Action Plan

✔ Look for the costs that change.

✔ Ignore the costs that do not change.

✔ Use the format in the chapter for your answer.

✔ Recognize that opportunity cost can make a difference.

Juanita Company must decide whether to make or buy some of its components for the appliances it produces. The costs of producing 166,000 electrical cords for its appliances are as follows.

Direct materials	$90,000	Variable overhead	$32,000
Direct labor	$20,000	Fixed overhead	$24,000

Instead of making the electrical cords at an average cost per unit of $1.00 ($166,000 ÷ 166,000), the company has an opportunity to buy the cords at $0.90 per unit. If the company purchases the cords, all variable costs and one-fourth of the fixed costs will be eliminated.

(a) Prepare an incremental analysis showing whether the company should make or buy the electrical cords. (b) Will your answer be different if the released productive capacity will generate additional income of $5,000?

Solution

(a)

	Make	Buy	Net Income Increase (Decrease)
Direct materials	$ 90,000	$ –0–	$ 90,000
Direct labor	20,000	–0–	20,000
Variable manufacturing costs	32,000	–0–	32,000
Fixed manufacturing costs	24,000	18,000*	6,000
Purchase price	–0–	149,400**	(149,400)
Total cost	$166,000	$167,400	$ (1,400)

*.75 × $24,000
**$166,000 × .90

This analysis indicates that Juanita Company will incur $1,400 of additional costs if it buys the electrical cords rather than making them.

(b)

	Make	Buy	Net Income Increase (Decrease)
Total cost	$166,000	$167,400	$(1,400)
Opportunity cost	5,000	–0–	5,000
Total cost	$171,000	$167,400	$ 3,600

Yes, the answer is different: The analysis shows that net income will be increased by $3,600 if Juanita Company purchases the electrical cords rather than making them.

Related exercise material: **BE26-4, E26-4, and DO IT! 26-2.**

✔ **The Navigator**

LEARNING OBJECTIVE 5

Identify the relevant costs in determining whether to sell or process materials further.

Sell or Process Further

Many manufacturers have the option of selling products at a given point in the production cycle or continuing to process with the expectation of selling them at a later point at a higher price. For example, a bicycle manufacturer such as Trek could sell its bicycles to retailers either unassembled or assembled. A furniture manufacturer such as Ethan Allen could sell its dining room sets to furniture stores either unfinished or finished. The sell-or-process-further decision should be made on the basis of incremental analysis. The basic decision rule is: **Process further as long as the incremental revenue from such processing exceeds the incremental processing costs.**

Assume, for example, that Woodmasters Inc. makes tables. It sells unfinished tables for $50. The cost to manufacture an unfinished table is $35, computed as follows.

Direct materials	$15
Direct labor	10
Variable manufacturing overhead	6
Fixed manufacturing overhead	4
Manufacturing cost per unit	**$35**

Illustration 26-8
Per unit cost of unfinished table

Woodmasters currently has unused productive capacity that is expected to continue indefinitely. Some of this capacity could be used to finish the tables and sell them at $60 per unit. For a finished table, direct materials will increase $2 and direct labor costs will increase $4. Variable manufacturing overhead costs will increase by $2.40 (60% of direct labor). No increase is anticipated in fixed manufacturing overhead.

Should the company sell the unfinished tables, or should it process them further? The incremental analysis on a per unit basis is as follows.

Helpful Hint Current net income is known. Net income from processing further is an estimate. In making its decision, management could add a "risk" factor for the estimate.

Incremental Analysis - Sell or process further.xls			
Home Insert Page Layout Formulas Data Review View			
P18 fx			
A	B	C	D
1	**Sell Unfinished**	**Process Further**	**Net Income Increase (Decrease)**
2 Sales price per unit	$50.00	$60.00	$10.00
3 Cost per unit			
4 Direct materials	15.00	17.00	(2.00)
5 Direct labor	10.00	14.00	(4.00)
6 Variable manufacturing overhead	6.00	8.40	(2.40)
7 Fixed manufacturing overhead	4.00	4.00	0.00
8 Total	35.00	43.40	(8.40)
9 Net income per unit	$15.00	$16.60	$ 1.60
10			

Illustration 26-9
Incremental analysis—sell or process further

It would be advantageous for Woodmasters to process the tables further. The incremental revenue of $10.00 from the additional processing is $1.60 higher than the incremental processing costs of $8.40.

Repair, Retain, or Replace Equipment

Management often has to decide whether to continue using an asset, repair, or replace it. For example, Delta Airlines must decide whether to replace old jets with new, more fuel-efficient ones. To illustrate, assume that Jeffcoat Company

LEARNING OBJECTIVE   6

Identify the relevant costs to be considered in repairing, retaining, or replacing equipment.

has a factory machine that originally cost $110,000. It has a balance in Accumulated Depreciation of $70,000, so its book value is $40,000. It has a remaining useful life of four years. The company is considering replacing this machine with a new machine. A new machine is available that costs $120,000. It is expected to have zero salvage value at the end of its four-year useful life. If the new machine is acquired, variable manufacturing costs are expected to decrease from $160,000 to $125,000 annually, and the old unit could be sold for $5,000. The incremental analysis for the **four-year period** is as follows.

Incremental Analysis - Retain or replace equipment.xls

	A	B	C	D	E	F
1		Retain Equipment		Replace Equipment		Net Income Increase (Decrease)
2	Variable manufacturing costs	$640,000ᵃ		$500,000ᵇ		$ 140,000
3	New machine cost			120,000		(120,000)
4	Sale of old machine			(5,000)		5,000
5	Total	$640,000		$615,000		$ 25,000
6						
7	ᵃ(4 years × $160,000)					
8	ᵇ(4 years × $125,000)					
9						

Illustration 26-10
Incremental analysis—retain or replace equipment

In this case, it would be to the company's advantage to replace the equipment. The lower variable manufacturing costs due to replacement more than offset the cost of the new equipment. Note that the $5,000 received from the sale of the old machine is relevant to the decision because it will only be received if the company chooses to replace its equipment. In general, any trade-in allowance or cash disposal value of existing assets is relevant to the decision to retain or replace equipment.

One other point should be mentioned regarding Jeffcoat's decision: **The book value of the old machine does not affect the decision.** Book value is a **sunk cost**, which is a cost that cannot be changed by any present or future decision. **Sunk costs are not relevant in incremental analysis.** In this example, if the asset is retained, book value will be depreciated over its remaining useful life. Or, if the new unit is acquired, book value will be recognized as a loss of the current period. Thus, the effect of book value on current and future earnings is the same regardless of the replacement decision.

Eliminate an Unprofitable Segment or Product

Management sometimes must decide whether to eliminate an unprofitable business segment or product. For example, in recent years, many airlines quit servicing certain cities or cut back on the number of flights. Goodyear quit producing several brands in the low-end tire market. Again, the key is to **focus on the relevant costs—the data that change under the alternative courses of action**. To illustrate, assume that Venus Company manufactures tennis racquets in three models: Pro, Master, and Champ. Pro and Master are profitable lines. Champ (highlighted in red in Illustration 26-11) operates at a loss. Condensed income statement data are as follows.

	Pro	Master	Champ	Total
Sales revenue	$800,000	$300,000	$100,000	$1,200,000
Variable costs	520,000	210,000	90,000	820,000
Contribution margin	280,000	90,000	10,000	380,000
Fixed costs	80,000	50,000	30,000	160,000
Net income	$200,000	$ 40,000	$ (20,000)	$ 220,000

Illustration 26-11
Segment income data

Helpful Hint A decision to discontinue a segment based solely on the bottom line—net loss—is inappropriate.

You might think that total net income will increase by $20,000 to $240,000 if the unprofitable Champ line of racquets is eliminated. However, **net income may actually decrease if the Champ line is discontinued**. The reason is that the fixed costs allocated to the Champ racquets will have to be absorbed by the other products. To illustrate, assume that the $30,000 of fixed costs applicable to the unprofitable segment are allocated $2/3$ to the Pro model and $1/3$ to the Master model if the Champ model is eliminated. Fixed costs will increase to $100,000 ($80,000 + $20,000) in the Pro line and to $60,000 ($50,000 + $10,000) in the Master line. The revised income statement is:

	Pro	Master	Total
Sales revenue	$800,000	$300,000	$1,100,000
Variable costs	520,000	210,000	730,000
Contribution margin	280,000	90,000	370,000
Fixed costs	**100,000**	**60,000**	160,000
Net income	$180,000	$ 30,000	$ 210,000

Illustration 26-12
Income data after eliminating unprofitable product line

Total net income has decreased $10,000 ($220,000 − $210,000). This result is also obtained in the following incremental analysis of the Champ racquets.

Illustration 26-13
Incremental analysis— eliminating unprofitable segment with no reduction in fixed costs

Incremental Analysis - Eliminating an unprofitable segment.xls

Home   Insert   Page Layout   Formulas   Data   Review   View

P18   fx

	A	B	C	D
1		Continue	Eliminate	Net Income Increase (Decrease)
2	Sales revenue	$100,000	$ 0	$(100,000)
3	Variable costs	90,000	0	90,000
4	Contribution margin	10,000	0	(10,000)
5	Fixed costs	30,000	30,000	0
6	Net income	$(20,000)	$(30,000)	$ (10,000)
7				

The loss in net income is attributable to the Champ line's contribution margin ($10,000) that will not be realized if the segment is discontinued.

In deciding on the future status of an unprofitable segment, management should consider the effect of elimination on related product lines. It may be possible for continuing product lines to obtain some or all of the sales lost by the discontinued product line. In some businesses, services or products may be linked—for example, free checking accounts at a bank, or coffee at a donut shop.

In addition, management should consider the effect of eliminating the product line on employees who may have to be discharged or retrained.

© Max Blain/iStockphoto

MANAGEMENT INSIGHT

Time to Move to a New Neighborhood?

If you have ever moved, then you know how complicated and costly it can be. Now consider what it would be like for a manufacturing company with 260 employees and a 170,000-square-foot facility to move from southern California to Idaho. That is what Buck Knives did in order to save its company from financial ruin. Electricity rates in Idaho were half those in California, workers' compensation was one-third the cost, and factory wages were 20% lower. Combined, this would reduce manufacturing costs by $600,000 per year. Moving the factory would cost about $8.5 million, plus $4 million to move key employees. Offsetting these costs was the estimated $11 million selling price of the California property. Based on these estimates, the move would pay for itself in three years.

Ultimately, the company received only $7.5 million for its California property, only 58 of 75 key employees were willing to move, construction was delayed by a year which caused the new plant to increase in price by $1.5 million, and wages surged in Idaho due to low unemployment. Despite all of these complications, though, the company considers the move a great success.

Source: Chris Lydgate, "The Buck Stopped," *Inc. Magazine* (May 2006), pp. 87–95.

 What were some of the factors that complicated the company's decision to move? How should the company have incorporated such factors into its incremental analysis? (See page 1271.)

> ## DO IT!

Unprofitable Segments

Lambert, Inc. manufactures several types of accessories. For the year, the knit hats and scarves line had sales revenue of $400,000, variable expenses of $310,000, and fixed expenses of $120,000. Therefore, the knit hats and scarves line had a net loss of $30,000. If Lambert eliminates the knit hats and scarves line, $20,000 of fixed costs will remain. Prepare an analysis showing whether the company should eliminate the knit hats and scarves line.

Solution

	Continue	Eliminate	Net Income Increase (Decrease)
Sales revenue	$400,000	$ 0	$(400,000)
Variable costs	310,000	0	310,000
Contribution margin	90,000	0	(90,000)
Fixed costs	120,000	20,000	100,000
Net income	$ (30,000)	$(20,000)	$ 10,000

The analysis indicates that Lambert should eliminate the knit hats and scarves line because net income will increase $10,000.

Action Plan

✔ Identify the revenues that will change as a result of eliminating a product line.

✔ Identify all costs that will change as a result of eliminating a product line, and net the amount against the revenues.

Related exercise material: **BE26-7, E26-8, E26-9, and DO IT! 26-3.**

 The Navigator

Allocate Limited Resources

Companies, like individuals, face limited resources. For a retail department store, the limited resource may be floor space. For a manufacturing company, the limited resource may be raw materials, direct labor hours, or machine capacity. When a company has limited resources, management must decide which products to make and sell in order to maximize net income.

To illustrate, assume that Collins Company manufactures deluxe and standard pen and pencil sets. The limiting resource is machine capacity, which is 3,600 hours per month. Relevant data consist of the following.

	Deluxe Sets	Standard Sets
Contribution margin per unit	$8	$6
Machine hours required	0.4	0.2

Illustration 26-14
Contribution margin and machine hours

The deluxe sets may appear to be more profitable since they have a higher contribution margin ($8) than the standard sets ($6). However, the standard sets take fewer machine hours to produce than the deluxe sets. Therefore, it is necessary to find the **contribution margin per unit of limited resource**—in this case, contribution margin per machine hour. This is obtained by dividing the contribution margin per unit of each product by the number of units of the limited resource required for each product, as shown in Illustration 26-15.

Helpful Hint CM alone is not enough in this decision. The key factor is CM per unit of limited resource.

	Deluxe Sets	Standard Sets
Contribution margin per unit (a)	$8	$6
Machine hours required (b)	0.4	0.2
Contribution margin per unit of limited resource [(a) ÷ (b)]	$20	$30

Illustration 26-15
Contribution margin per unit of limited resource

The computation shows that the standard sets have a higher contribution margin per unit of limited resource. This would suggest that, given sufficient demand for standard sets, the company should shift the sales mix to produce more standard sets or increase machine capacity. If Collins Company is able to increase machine capacity from 3,600 hours to 4,200 hours, the additional 600 hours could be used to produce either the standard or deluxe pen and pencil sets. The total contribution margin under each alternative is found by multiplying the machine hours by the contribution margin per unit of limited resource, as shown below.

	Produce Deluxe Sets	Produce Standard Sets
Machine hours (a)	600	600
Contribution margin per unit of limited resource (b)	$20	$30
Contribution margin [(a) × (b)]	$12,000	$18,000

Illustration 26-16
Incremental analysis—computation of total contribution margin

From this analysis, we see that to maximize net income, all of the increased capacity should be used to make and sell the standard sets.

Capital Budgeting

Individuals make capital expenditures when they buy a new home, car, or television set. Similarly, businesses make capital expenditures when they modernize plant facilities or expand operations. Companies like Holland America Line must constantly determine how to invest their resources. Other examples: Dell announced plans to spend $1 billion on data centers for cloud computing. Exxon announced that two wells off the Brazilian coast, which it had spent hundreds of millions to drill, would produce no oil. Renault and Nissan spent over $5 billion during a nearly 20-year period to develop electric cars, such as the Leaf.

In business, as for individuals, the amount of possible capital expenditures usually exceeds the funds available for such expenditures. Thus, the resources available must be allocated (budgeted) among the competing alternatives. The process of making capital expenditure decisions in business is known as **capital budgeting**. Capital budgeting involves choosing among various capital projects to find the one(s) that will maximize a company's return on its financial investment.

Evaluation Process

Many companies follow a carefully prescribed process in capital budgeting. At least once a year, top management requests proposals for projects from each department. A capital budgeting committee screens the proposals and submits its findings to the officers of the company. The officers, in turn, select the projects they believe to be most worthy of funding. They submit this list to the board of directors. Ultimately, the directors approve the capital expenditure budget for the year. Illustration 26-17 shows this process.

1. Project proposals are requested from departments, plants, and authorized personnel.

2. Proposals are screened by a capital budget committee.

3. Officers determine which projects are worthy of funding.

4. Board of directors approves capital budget.

Illustration 26-17
Corporate capital budget authorization process

The involvement of top management and the board of directors in the process demonstrates the importance of capital budgeting decisions. These decisions often have a significant impact on a company's future profitability. In fact, poor capital budgeting decisions have led to the bankruptcy of some companies.

Accounting data are indispensable in assessing the probable effects of capital expenditures. To provide management with relevant data for capital budgeting decisions, you should be familiar with the quantitative techniques that may be used. The three most common techniques are: (1) annual rate of return, (2) cash payback, and (3) discounted cash flow. We demonstrate each of these techniques in the following sections. To illustrate the three quantitative techniques, assume that Reno Company is considering an investment of $130,000 in new equipment. The new equipment is expected to last 5 years and have zero salvage value at the end of its useful life. Reno uses the straight-line method of depreciation for accounting purposes. The expected annual revenues and costs of the new product that will be produced from the investment are:

Sales revenue		$200,000
Less: Costs and expenses		
Manufacturing costs (exclusive of depreciation)	$132,000	
Depreciation expenses ($130,000 ÷ 5)	26,000	
Selling and administrative expenses	22,000	180,000
Income before income taxes		20,000
Income tax expense		7,000
Net income		$ 13,000

Illustration 26-18
Estimated annual net income from capital expenditure

MANAGEMENT INSIGHT

Investing for the Future

Monitoring capital expenditure amounts is one way to learn about a company's growth potential. Few companies can grow if they don't make significant capital investments. Here is a list of well-known companies and the amounts and types of their capital expenditures in a recent year.

Company Name	Amount	Types of Expenditures
Campbell Soup Company	$283 million	Acquisitions and plant expansions.
Barrick Gold Corporation	$228 million	Land acquisition and mine expansion.
Dell Computer Corporation	$329 million	Manufacturing and office facilities.
Sears, Roebuck and Co.	$925 million	New stores.
Nike Inc.	$186 million	Warehouse locations, management information systems.

© Mark Evans/iStockphoto

 Why is it important for top management to constantly monitor the nature, amount, and success of a company's capital expenditures? (See page 1271.)

Annual Rate of Return

The **annual rate of return method** is based directly on accrual accounting data rather than on cash flows. It indicates **the profitability of a capital expenditure** by dividing expected annual net income by the average investment. Illustration 26-19 shows the formula for computing annual rate of return.

Expected Annual Net Income	÷	Average Investment	=	Annual Rate of Return

Illustration 26-19
Annual rate of return formula

Expected annual net income is obtained from the projected income statement. Reno Company's expected annual net income is $13,000. Average investment is derived from the following formula.

Illustration 26-20
Formula for computing average investment

$$\frac{\text{Original Investment} + \text{Value at End of Useful Life}}{2} = \text{Average Investment}$$

The value at the end of useful life is the asset's salvage value, if any. For Reno Company, average investment is $65,000 [($130,000 + $0) ÷ 2]. The expected annual rate of return for Reno's investment in new equipment is therefore 20%, computed as follows.

$$\$13,000 \div \$65,000 = 20\%$$

Management then compares this annual rate of return with its **required rate of return** for investments of similar risk. The required rate of return is generally based on the company's **cost of capital**. The **cost of capital** is the rate of return that management expects to pay on all borrowed and equity funds. The cost of capital is a company-wide (or sometimes a division-wide) rate; it does not relate to the cost of funding a specific project.

Helpful Hint A capital budgeting decision based on only one technique may be misleading. It is often wise to analyze the investment from a number of different perspectives.

The annual rate of return decision rule is: **A project is acceptable if its rate of return is greater than management's required rate of return. It is unacceptable when the reverse is true.** When companies use the rate of return technique in deciding among several acceptable projects, **the higher the rate of return for a given risk, the more attractive the investment**.

The principal advantages of this method are the simplicity of its calculation and management's familiarity with the accounting terms used in the computation. A major limitation of the annual rate of return method is that it does not consider the time value of money. For example, no consideration is given as to whether cash inflows will occur early or late in the life of the investment. As explained in Appendix G, recognition of the time value of money can make a significant difference between the future value and the discounted present value of an investment. A second disadvantage is that this method relies on accrual accounting numbers rather than expected cash flows.

> ## DO IT!

Annual Rate of Return

Watertown Paper Corporation is considering adding another machine for the manufacture of corrugated cardboard. The machine would cost $900,000. It would have an estimated life of 6 years and no salvage value. The company estimates that annual revenue would increase by $400,000 and that annual expenses excluding depreciation would increase by $190,000. It uses the straight-line method to compute depreciation expense. Management has a required rate of return of 9%. Compute the annual rate of return.

Solution

Action Plan

✔ Expected annual net income = Annual revenues − Annual expenses (including depreciation expense).

✔ Annual rate of return = Expected annual net income/Average investment.

✔ Average investment = (Original investment + Value at end of useful life)/2.

Revenues		$400,000
Less:		
Expenses (excluding depreciation)	$190,000	
Depreciation ($900,000/6 years)	150,000	340,000
Annual net income		$ 60,000

Average investment = ($900,000 + 0)/2 = $450,000.
Annual rate of return = $60,000/$450,000 = 13.3%.

Since the annual rate of return (13.33%) is greater than Watertown's required rate of return (9%), the proposed project is acceptable.

Related exercise material: **BE26-10, E26-11, and DO IT! 26-4.**

 The Navigator

Cash Payback

The **cash payback technique** identifies the time period required to recover the cost of the capital investment from the net annual cash flow produced by the investment. Illustration 26-21 presents the formula for computing the cash payback period assuming equal annual cash flows.

Illustration 26-21
Cash payback formula

Cost of Capital Investment	÷	Net Annual Cash Flow	=	Cash Payback Period

Net annual cash flow is approximated by taking net income and adding back depreciation expense. Depreciation expense is added back because depreciation on the capital expenditure does not involve an annual outflow of cash. Accordingly, the depreciation deducted in determining net income must be added back to determine net annual cash flows.

In the Reno Company example, net annual cash flow is $39,000, as shown below.

Illustration 26-22
Computation of net annual cash flow

Net income	$ 13,000
Add: Depreciation expense	26,000
Net annual cash flow	**$39,000**

The cash payback period in this example is therefore 3.33 years, computed as follows.

$$\$130,000 \div \$39,000 = 3.33 \text{ years}$$

Evaluation of the payback period is often related to the expected useful life of the asset. For example, assume that at Reno Company a project is unacceptable if the payback period is longer than 60% of the asset's expected useful life. The 3.33-year payback period in this case is 67% of the project's expected useful life. Thus, the project is unacceptable.

It follows that when the payback method is used to decide among acceptable alternative projects, **the shorter the payback period, the more attractive the investment**. This is true for two reasons. First, the earlier the investment is recovered, the sooner the company can use the cash funds for other purposes. Second, the risk of loss from obsolescence and changed economic conditions is less in a shorter payback period.

The preceding computation of the cash payback period assumes **equal** net annual cash flows in each year of the investment's life. In many cases, this assumption is not valid. In the case of **uneven** net annual cash flows, the company determines the cash payback period when the cumulative net cash flows from the investment equal the cost of the investment.

To illustrate, assume that Chen Company proposes an investment in a new website that is estimated to cost $300,000. Illustration 26-23 shows the proposed investment cost, net annual cash flows, cumulative net cash flows, and the cash payback period.

Illustration 26-23
Net annual cash flow schedule

Year	Investment	Net Annual Cash Flow	Cumulative Net Cash Flow
0	$300,000		
1		$ 60,000	$ 60,000
2		90,000	150,000
3		90,000	240,000
4		120,000	360,000
5		100,000	460,000

Cash payback period = 3.5 years

As Illustration 26-23 shows, at the end of year 3, cumulative net cash flow of $240,000 is less than the investment cost of $300,000. However, at the end of year 4, the cumulative net cash flow of $360,000 exceeds the investment cost. The net cash flow needed in year 4 to equal the investment cost is $60,000 ($300,000 − $240,000). Assuming the net cash flow occurs evenly during year 4, we then divide this amount by the net annual cash flow in year 4 ($120,000) to determine the point during the year when the cash payback occurs. Thus, we get 0.50 ($60,000/$120,000), or half of the year, and the cash payback period is 3.5 years.

The cash payback method may be useful as an initial screening tool. It may be the most critical factor in the capital budgeting decision for a company that desires a fast turnaround of its investment because of a weak cash position. Like the annual rate of return, cash payback is relatively easy to compute and understand.

However, cash payback is not ordinarily the only basis for the capital budgeting decision because it **ignores the expected profitability of the project**. To illustrate, assume that Projects A and B have the same payback period, but Project A's useful life is double that of Project B's. Project A's earning power, therefore, is twice as long as Project B's. A further—and major—disadvantage of this technique is that it ignores the time value of money.

© Pictafolio/iStockphoto

MANAGEMENT INSIGHT

Can You Hear Me—Better?

What's better than 3G wireless service? 4G. But the question for wireless service providers is whether customers will be willing to pay extra for that improvement. Verizon has already spent billions on the upgrade, but customer usage might be slow in coming. First, there aren't that many 4G-compatible devices, and coverage will be spotty. Also, most applications don't really need higher speeds. Verizon is hoping that its investment in 4G works out better than its $23 billion investment in its FIOS fiber-wired network for TV and ultrahigh-speed Internet. One analyst estimates that the present value of each FIOS customer is $800 less than the cost of the connection.

Source: Martin Peers, "Investors: Beware Verizon's Generation GAP," *Wall Street Journal Online* (January 26, 2010).

 Based on the potentially slow initial adoption of 4G by customers, how might the conclusions of a cash payback analysis of Verizon's 4G investment differ from a present value analysis? (See page 1271.)

> DO IT!

Cash Payback Period

Watertown Paper Corporation is considering adding another machine for the manufacture of corrugated cardboard. The machine would cost $900,000. It would have an estimated life of 6 years and no salvage value. The company estimates that annual cash inflows would increase by $400,000 and that annual cash outflows would increase by $190,000. Compute the cash payback period.

Solution

Action Plan

✔ Annual cash inflows − Annual cash outflows = Net annual cash flow.

✔ Cash payback period = Cost of capital investment/ Net annual cash flow.

Estimated annual cash inflows	$400,000
Estimated annual cash outflows	190,000
Net annual cash flow	$210,000

Cash payback period = $900,000/$210,000 = 4.3 years.

Related exercise material: **BE26-9, E26-10, E26-11, and DO IT! 26-4.**

 The Navigator

Discounted Cash Flow

The **discounted cash flow technique** is generally recognized as the best conceptual approach to making capital budgeting decisions. This technique considers both the estimated total net cash flows from the investment and the time value of money. The expected total net cash flow consists of the sum of the annual net cash flows plus the estimated liquidation proceeds when the asset is sold for salvage at the end of its useful life. But because liquidation proceeds are generally immaterial, we ignore them in subsequent discussions.

Two methods are used with the discounted cash flow technique: (1) net present value, and (2) internal rate of return. **Before we discuss the methods, we recommend that you examine Appendix G if you need a review of present value concepts.**

NET PRESENT VALUE METHOD

The **net present value (NPV) method** involves discounting net cash flows to their present value and then comparing that present value with the capital outlay required by the investment. The difference between these two amounts is referred to as **net present value (NPV)**. Company management determines what interest rate to use in discounting the future net cash flows. This rate, often referred to as the **discount rate** or **required rate of return**, is discussed in a later section.

The NVP decision rule is this: **A proposal is acceptable when net present value is zero or positive.** At either of those values, the rate of return on the investment equals or exceeds the required rate of return. When net present value is negative, the project is unacceptable. Illustration 26-24 shows the net present value decision criteria.

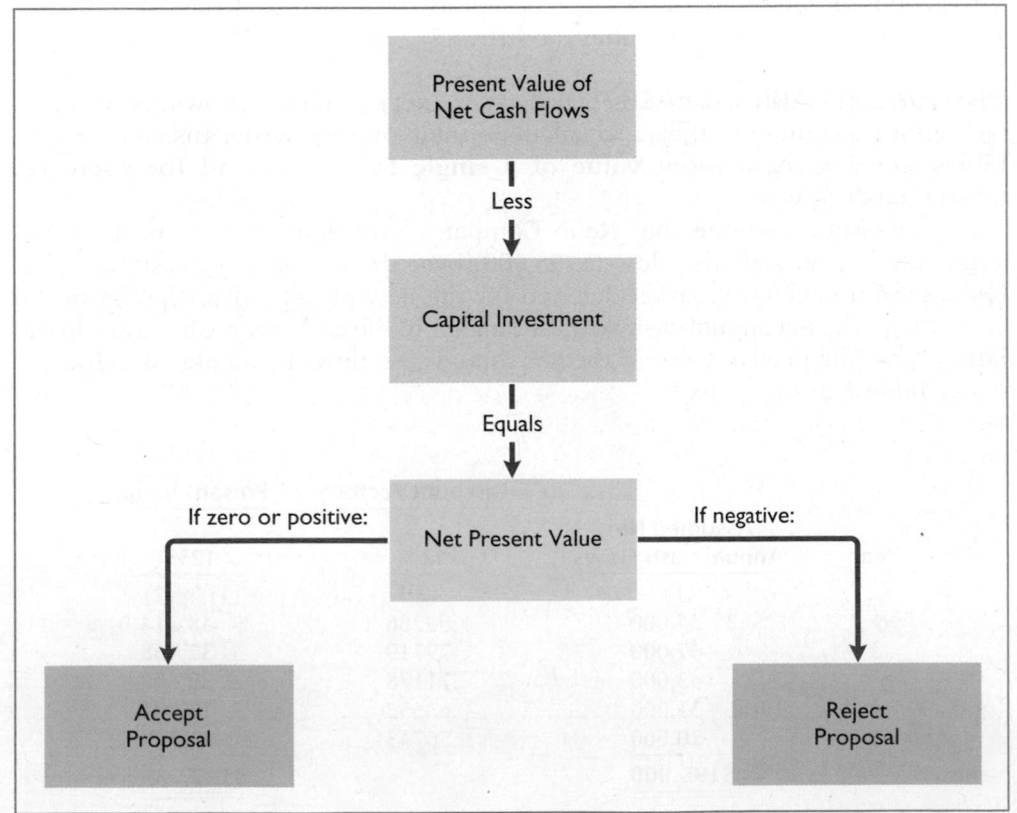

Illustration 26-24
Net present value decision criteria

Ethics Note

Discounted future cash flows may not take into account all of the important considerations needed to make an informed capital budgeting decision. Other issues, for example, could include worker safety, product quality, and environmental impact.

When making a selection among acceptable proposals, **the higher the positive net present value, the more attractive the investment**. The application of this method to two cases is described in the next two sections. In each case, we assume that the investment has no salvage value at the end of its useful life.

EQUAL NET ANNUAL CASH FLOWS Reno Company's net annual cash flows are $39,000. If we assume this amount is **uniform over the asset's useful life**, we can compute the present value of the net annual cash flows by using the present value of an annuity of 1 for 5 payments (in Table 2, Appendix G). The computation at a rate of return of 12% is:

Illustration 26-25
Present value of net annual cash flows

	Present Value at 12%
Discount factor for 5 periods	3.60478
Present value of net annual cash flows:	
$39,000 × 3.60478	**$140,586**

The analysis of the proposal by the net present value method is as follows.

Illustration 26-26
Computation of net present value

	12%
Present value of net annual cash flows	$140,586
Capital investment	130,000
Net present value	**$ 10,586**

Helpful Hint The ABC Co. expects equal net annual cash flows over an asset's 5-year useful life.

What discount factor should it use in determining present values if management wants (1) a 12% return or (2) a 15% return?

Answer: Using Table 2, the factors are (1) 3.60478 and (2) 3.35216.

The proposed capital expenditure is acceptable at a required rate of return of 12% because the net present value is positive.

UNEQUAL NET ANNUAL CASH FLOWS When net annual cash flows are unequal, we cannot use annuity tables to calculate their present value. Instead, we use tables showing the **present value of a single future amount for each net annual cash flow**.

To illustrate, assume that Reno Company management expects the same aggregate net annual cash flow ($195,000) over the life of the investment. But because of a declining market demand for the new product over the life of the equipment, the net annual cash flows are higher in the early years and lower in the later years. The present value of the net annual cash flows is calculated as follows using Table 1 in Appendix G.

Illustration 26-27
Computation of present value of unequal annual cash flows

Year	Assumed Net Annual Cash Flows	Discount Factor 12%	Present Value 12%
	(1)	(2)	(1) × (2)
1	$ 54,000	.89286	$ 48,214
2	47,000	.79719	37,468
3	43,000	.71178	30,607
4	31,000	.63552	19,701
5	20,000	.56743	11,349
	$195,000		$147,339

Therefore, the analysis of the proposal by the net present value method is as follows.

Illustration 26-28
Analysis of proposal using net present value method

	12%
Present value of net annual cash flows	$147,339
Capital investment	130,000
Net present value	**$ 17,339**

In this example, the present value of the net annual cash flows is greater than the $130,000 capital investment. Thus, the project is acceptable at a 12% required rate of return. The difference between the present values using the 12% rate under equal net annual cash flows ($140,586) and unequal net annual cash flows ($147,339) is due to the pattern of the net cash flows.

MANAGEMENT INSIGHT

Seeing the Big Picture

Inaccurate trend forecasting and market positioning are more detrimental to capital investment decisions than using the wrong discount rate. Ampex patented the VCR but failed to see its market potential. Westinghouse made the same mistake with the flat-screen video display. More often, companies adopt projects or businesses only to discontinue them in response to market changes. Texas Instruments announced it would stop manufacturing computer chips, after it had made substantial capital investments that enabled it to become one of the world's leading suppliers. The company dropped out of some 12 business lines in only a few years.

Source: World Research Advisory Inc. (London, August 1998), p. 4.

? How important is the choice of discount rate in making capital budgeting decisions? (See page 1271.)

© Don Bayley/iStockphoto

INTERNAL RATE OF RETURN METHOD

The **internal rate of return method** differs from the net present value method in that it finds the **interest yield of the potential investment**. The **internal rate of return (IRR)** is the interest rate that will cause the present value of the proposed capital expenditure to equal the present value of the expected net annual cash flows. Because it recognizes the time value of money, the internal rate of return method is (like the NPV method) a discounted cash flow technique. The determination of the internal rate of return involves two steps.

Step 1. Compute the internal rate of return factor. The formula for this factor is:

Illustration 26-29
Formula for internal rate of return factor

Capital Investment	÷	Net Annual Cash Flow	=	Internal Rate of Return Factor

The computation for Reno Company, assuming equal net annual cash flows,[2] is:

$$\$130{,}000 \div \$39{,}000 = 3.3333$$

---

[2]When net annual cash flows are equal, the internal rate of return factor is the same as the cash payback period.

Step 2. Use the factor and the present value of an annuity of 1 table to find the internal rate of return. Table 2 of Appendix G is used in this step. The internal rate of return is the discount factor that is closest to the internal rate of return factor for the time period covered by the net annual cash flows.

For Reno Company, the net annual cash flows are expected to continue for 5 years. Thus, it is necessary to read across the period-5 row in Table 2 to find the discount factor. The row for 5 periods is reproduced below for your convenience.

TABLE 2
PRESENT VALUE OF AN ANNUITY OF 1

(n) Periods	5%	6%	7%	8%	9%	10%	11%	12%	15%
5	4.32948	4.21236	4.10020	3.99271	3.88965	3.79079	3.69590	3.60478	3.35216

In this case, the closest discount factor to 3.3333 is 3.35216, which represents an interest rate of approximately 15%. The rate of return can be further determined by interpolation, but since we are using estimated net annual cash flows, such precision is seldom required.

Once managers know the internal rate of return, they compare it to the company's required rate of return (the discount rate). The IRR decision rule is as follows: **Accept the project when the internal rate of return is equal to or greater than the required rate of return. Reject the project when the internal rate of return is less than the required rate of return.** Illustration 26-30 below shows these relationships. Assuming the required rate of return is 10% for Reno Company, the project is acceptable because the 15% internal rate of return is greater than the required rate.

Illustration 26-30
Internal rate of return decision criteria

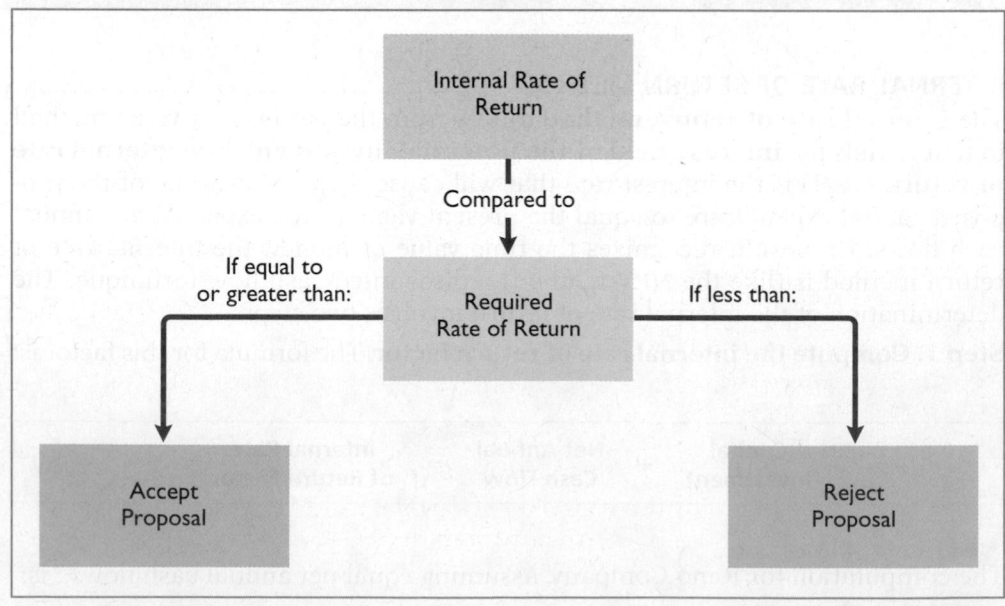

The IRR method is widely used in practice. Most managers find the internal rate of return easy to interpret.

Comparing Discounted Cash Flow Methods

Illustration 26-31 compares the two discounted cash flow methods—net present value and internal rate of return. When properly used, either method provides management with relevant quantitative data for making capital budgeting decisions.

	Net Present Value	Internal Rate of Return
1. Objective	Compute net present value (a dollar amount).	Compute internal rate of return (a percentage).
2. Decision rule	If net present value is zero or positive, accept the proposal. If net present value is negative, reject the proposal	If internal rate of return is equal to or greater than the required rate of return, accept the proposal. If internal rate of return is less than the required rate of return, reject the proposal.

Illustration 26-31
Comparison of discounted cash flow methods

> ## DO IT!

Discounted Cash Flow

Watertown Paper Corporation is considering adding another machine for the manufacture of corrugated cardboard. The machine would cost $900,000. It would have an estimated life of 6 years and no salvage value. The company estimates that annual cash inflows would increase by $400,000 and that annual cash outflows would increase by $190,000. Management has a required rate of return of 9%.

(a) Calculate the net present value on this project, and discuss whether it should be accepted.

(b) Calculate the internal rate of return on this project, and discuss whether it should be accepted.

Solution

Action Plan

✔ Compute net annual cash flow: Estimated annual cash inflows − Estimated annual cash outflows.

✔ Use the NPV technique to calculate the difference between net cash flows and the initial investment.

✔ Accept the project if the net present value is positive.

✔ Compute the IRR factor: Capital investment ÷ Net annual cash flows.

✔ Look up the factor in the present value of an annuity table to find the internal rate of return.

✔ Accept the project if the internal rate of return is equal to or greater than the required rate of return.

(a)

Estimated annual cash inflows		$400,000
Estimated annual cash outflows		190,000
Net annual cash flow		$210,000

	Cash Flow	9% Discount Factor	Present Value
Present value of net annual cash flows	$210,000	4.48592*	$942,043
Capital investment			900,000
Net present value			$ 42,043

*Table 2, Appendix G

Since the net present value is greater than zero, Watertown should accept the project.

(b) $900,000 ÷ 210,000 = 4.285714. Using Table 2 of Appendix G and the factors that correspond with the six-period row, 4.285714 is between the factors for 10% and 11%. Since the project has an internal rate that is greater than 10% and the required rate of return is only 9%, Watertown should accept the project.

Related exercise material: **BE26-11, BE26-12, BE26-13, E26-10, E26-11, E26-12, E26-13, and DO IT! 26-5.**

 The Navigator

> ## Comprehensive DO IT!

Sierra Company is considering a long-term capital investment project called ZIP. The project will require an investment of $120,000, and it will have a useful life of 4 years. Annual net income for ZIP is expected to be: Year 1 $12,000; Year 2 $10,000; Year 3 $8,000; and Year 4 $6,000. Depreciation is computed by the straight-line method with no salvage value. The company's cost of capital is 12%.

Instructions
(a) Compute the annual rate of return for the project.
(b) Compute the cash payback period for the project. (Round to two decimals.)
(c) Compute the net present value for the project. (Round to nearest dollar.)
(d) Should the project be accepted? Why?

Solution to Comprehensive DO IT!

Action Plan

✔ To compute annual rate of return, divide expected annual net income by average investment.

✔ To compute cash payback, divide cost of the investment by net annual cash flows.

✔ Recall that net annual cash flow equals annual net income plus annual depreciation expense.

✔ Be careful to use the correct discount factor in using the net present value method.

(a) $9,000 ($36,000 ÷ 4) ÷ $60,000 ($120,000 ÷ 2) = 15%
(b) Depreciation expense is $120,000 ÷ 4 years = $30,000.
   Net annual cash flows are:
Year 1	$12,000 + $30,000 =	$42,000
Year 2	$10,000 + $30,000 =	$40,000
Year 3	$8,000 + $30,000 =	$38,000
Year 4	$6,000 + $30,000 =	$36,000

   Cumulative net cash flows would be $82,000 ($42,000 + $40,000) at the end of year 2 and $120,000 ($42,000 + $40,000 + $38,000) at the end of year 3. Since the cumulative net cash flows at the end of year 3 exactly equal the initial cash investment of $120,000, the cash payback period is 3 years.

(c)

Year	Discount Factor	Net Annual Cash Flow	Present Value
1	.89286	$42,000	$ 37,500
2	.79719	40,000	31,888
3	.71178	38,000	27,048
4	.63552	36,000	22,879
			119,315
		Capital investment	120,000
		Negative net present value	$ (685)

(d) The annual rate of return of 15% is good. However, the cash payback period is 75% of the project's useful life, and net present value is negative. The recommendation is to reject the project.

✔ The Navigator

SUMMARY OF LEARNING OBJECTIVES

✔ The Navigator

1 **Identify the steps in management's decision-making process.** Management's decision-making process is: (a) identify the problem and assign responsibility, (b) determine and evaluate possible courses of action, (c) make the decision, and (d) review the results of the decision.

2 **Describe the concept of incremental analysis.** Incremental analysis identifies financial data that change under alternative courses of action. These data are relevant to the decision because they will vary in the future among the possible alternatives.

3 **Identify the relevant costs in accepting an order at a special price.** The relevant information in accepting an order at a special price is the difference between the variable costs to produce the special order and expected revenues.

4 **Identify the relevant costs in a make-or-buy decision.** In a make-or-buy decision, the relevant costs are (a) the manufacturing costs that will be saved, (b) the purchase price, and (c) opportunity costs.

5 **Identify the relevant costs in determining whether to sell or process materials further.** The decision rule for

whether to sell or process materials further is: Process further as long as the incremental revenue from processing exceeds the incremental processing costs.

6 Identify the relevant costs to be considered in repairing, retaining, or replacing equipment. The factors to consider in determining whether equipment should be retained or replaced are the effects on variable costs and the cost of the new equipment. Also, any trade-in allowance or cash disposal value of the existing asset must be considered.

7 Identify the relevant costs in deciding whether to eliminate an unprofitable segment or product. In deciding whether to eliminate an unprofitable segment, determine the contribution margin, if any, produced by the segment and the disposition of the segment's fixed expenses.

8 Determine which products to make and sell when resources are limited. When a company has limited resources, find the contribution margin per unit of limited resource. Then multiply this amount by the units of limited resource to determine which product maximizes net income.

9 Contrast annual rate of return and cash payback in capital budgeting. The **annual rate of return** is obtained by dividing expected annual net income by the average investment. The higher the rate of return, the more attractive the investment. The **cash payback** technique identifies the time period to recover the cost of the investment. The formula is: Cost of capital expenditure divided by estimated net annual cash flow equals cash payback period. The shorter the payback period, the more attractive the investment.

10 Distinguish between the net present value and internal rate of return methods. Under the **net present value** method, compare the present value of future net cash flows with the capital investment to determine net present value. The NPV decision rule is: Accept the project if net present value is zero or positive. Reject the investment if net present value is negative.

Under the **internal rate of return** method, find the interest yield of the potential investment. The IRR decision rule is: Accept the project when the internal rate of return is equal to or greater than the required rate of return. Reject the project when the internal rate of return is less than the required rate.

GLOSSARY

Annual rate of return method Determines the profitability of a capital expenditure by dividing expected annual net income by the average investment. (p. 1241).

Capital budgeting The process of making capital expenditure decisions in business. (p. 1240).

Cash payback technique Identifies the time period required to recover the cost of a capital investment from the net annual cash flow produced by the investment. (p. 1243).

Cost of capital The rate of return that management expects to pay on all borrowed and equity funds. (p. 1242).

Discounted cash flow technique Considers both the estimated total net cash flows from the investment and the time value of money. (p. 1245).

Incremental analysis The process of identifying the financial data that change under alternative courses of action. (p. 1228).

Internal rate of return (IRR) The rate that will cause the present value of the proposed capital expenditure

to equal the present value of the expected net annual cash flows. (p. 1247).

Internal rate of return (IRR) method Finds the interest yield of the potential investment. (p. 1247).

Net present value (NPV) The difference that results when the original capital outlay is subtracted from the discounted net cash flows. (p. 1245).

Net present value (NPV) method Discounts net cash flows to their present value and then compares that present value to the capital outlay required by the investment. (p. 1245).

Opportunity cost The potential benefit that may be obtained from following an alternative course of action. (p. 1229).

Required rate of return The rate that is generally based on the company's cost of capital. (p. 1242).

Sunk cost A cost that cannot be changed by any present or future decision. (p. 1229).

 Self-Test, Brief Exercises, Exercises, Problem Set A, and many more components are available for practice in *WileyPLUS*.

SELF-TEST QUESTIONS

Answers are on page 1271.

(LO 1) **1.** Three of the steps in management's decision-making process are as follows. (1) Review results of decision. (2) Identify the problem. (3) Make the decision. The steps are performed in the following order:

(a) (1), (2), (3).　　　(c) (2), (1), (3).
(b) (3), (2), (1).　　　(d) (2), (3), (1).

2. Incremental analysis is the process of identifying the (LO 2) financial data that:

(a) do not change under alternative courses of action.
(b) change under alternative courses of action.
(c) are mixed under alternative courses of action.
(d) No correct answer is given.

(LO 3) 3. It costs a company $14 of variable costs and $6 of fixed costs to produce product A that sells for $30. A foreign buyer offers to purchase 3,000 units at $18 each. If the special offer is accepted and produced with unused capacity, net income will:
(a) decrease $6,000.   (c) increase $12,000.
(b) increase $6,000.   (d) increase $9,000.

(LO 3) 4. Jobart Company is currently operating at full capacity. It is considering buying a part from an outside supplier rather than making it in-house. If Jobart purchases the part, it can use the released productive capacity to generate additional income of $30,000 from producing a different product. When conducting incremental analysis in this make-or-buy decision, the company should:
(a) ignore the $30,000.
(b) add $30,000 to other costs in the "Make" column.
(c) add $30,000 to other costs in the "Buy" column.
(d) subtract $30,000 from the other costs in the "Make" column.

(LO 4) 5. In a make-or-buy decision, relevant costs are:
(a) manufacturing costs that will be saved.
(b) the purchase price of the units.
(c) opportunity costs.
(d) All of these.

(LO 5) 6. The decision rule in a sell-or-process-further decision is: Process further as long as the incremental revenue from processing exceeds:
(a) incremental processing costs.
(b) variable processing costs.
(c) fixed processing costs.
(d) No correct answer is given.

(LO 5) 7. Walton, Inc. makes an unassembled product that it currently sells for $55. Production costs are $20. Walton is considering assembling the product and selling it for $68. The cost to assemble the product is estimated at $12. What decision should Walton make?
(a) Sell before assembly; net income per unit will be $12 greater.
(b) Sell before assembly; net income per unit will be $1 greater.
(c) Process further; net income per unit will be $13 greater.
(d) Process further; net income per unit will be $1 greater.

(LO 6) 8. In a decision to repair, retain, or replace equipment, the book value of the old equipment is a(n):
(a) opportunity cost.
(b) sunk cost.

(c) incremental cost.
(d) marginal cost.

(LO 7) 9. If an unprofitable segment is eliminated:
(a) net income will always increase.
(b) variable expenses of the eliminated segment will have to be absorbed by other segments.
(c) fixed expenses allocated to the eliminated segment will have to be absorbed by other segments.
(d) net income will always decrease.

(LO 7) 10. A segment of Hazard Inc. has the following data.

Sales revenue	$200,000
Variable costs	$140,000
Fixed costs	$100,000

If this segment is eliminated, 50% of the fixed costs will be eliminated, and the rest will be allocated to the remaining segments. What should Hazard do?
(a) Eliminate the segment; net income will be $50,000 greater.
(b) Eliminate the segment; net income will be $10,000 greater.
(c) Keep the segment; net income will be $200,000 greater.
(d) Keep the segment; net income will be $10,000 greater.

(LO 8) 11. If the contribution margin per unit is $15 and it takes 3.0 machine hours to produce the unit, the contribution margin per unit of limited resource is:
(a) $25.   (c) $45.
(b) $5.   (d) No correct answer is given.

(LO 9) 12. Which of the following is **incorrect** about the annual rate of return method?
(a) The calculation is simple.
(b) The accounting terms used are familiar to management.
(c) The timing of the net cash flows is not considered.
(d) The time value of money is considered.

(LO 9) 13. What is a weakness of the cash payback approach?
(a) It uses accrual-based accounting numbers.
(b) It ignores the time value of money.
(c) It is complicated to compute.
(d) It cannot be used if a project has uneven net annual cash flows.

(LO 10) 14. A project should be accepted if its internal rate of return exceeds:
(a) zero.
(b) the rate of return on a government bond.
(c) the company's required rate of return.
(d) the rate the company pays on borrowed funds.

(LO 10) 15. A positive net present value means that the:
(a) project's rate of return is less than the cutoff rate.
(b) project's rate of return exceeds the required rate of return.
(c) project's rate of return equals the required rate of return.
(d) project is unacceptable.

Go to the book's companion website, www.wiley.com/college/weygandt, for additional Self-Test Questions.

✔ **The Navigator**

QUESTIONS

1. What steps are frequently involved in management's decision-making process?
2. Your roommate, Anna Polis, contends that accounting contributes to most of the steps in management's decision-making process. Is your roommate correct? Explain.
3. "Incremental analysis involves the accumulation of information concerning a single course of action." Do you agree? Why?
4. Sydney Greene asks your help concerning the relevance of variable and fixed costs in incremental analysis. Help Sydney with his problem.
5. What data are relevant in deciding whether to accept an order at a special price?
6. Emil Company has an opportunity to buy parts at $9 each that currently cost $12 to make. What manufacturing costs are relevant to this make-or-buy decision?
7. Define the term opportunity cost. How may this cost be relevant in a make-or-buy decision?
8. What is the decision rule in deciding whether to sell a product or process it further?
9. Your roommate, Gale Dunham, is confused about sunk costs. Explain to your roommate the meaning of sunk costs and their relevance to a decision to retain or replace equipment.
10. Huang Inc. has one product line that is unprofitable. What circumstances may cause overall company net income to be lower if the unprofitable product line is eliminated?
11. How is the contribution margin per unit of limited resources computed?
12. Describe the process a company may use in screening and approving the capital expenditure budget.
13. Your classmate, Mike Dawson, is confused about the factors that are included in the annual rate of return method. What is the formula for this method?
14. Sveta Pace is trying to understand the term cost of capital. Define the term, and indicate its relevance to the decision rule under the annual rate of return method.
15. Tom Wells claims the formula for the cash payback technique is the same as the formula for the annual rate of return method. Is Tom correct? What is the formula for the cash payback technique?
16. What are the advantages and disadvantages of the cash payback technique?
17. Two types of present value tables may be used with the discounted cash flow technique. Identify the tables and the circumstance(s) when each table should be used.
18. What is the decision rule under the net present value method?
19. Identify the steps required in using the internal rate of return method.
20. El Cajon Company uses the internal rate of return method. What is the decision rule for this method?

BRIEF EXERCISES

BE26-1 The steps in management's decision-making process are listed in random order below. Indicate the order in which the steps should be executed.

_____ Make a decision.

_____ Identify the problem and assign responsibility.

_____ Review results of the decision.

_____ Determine and evaluate possible courses of action.

Identify the steps in management's decision-making process.
(LO 1)

BE26-2 Bogart Company is considering two alternatives. Alternative A will have revenues of $160,000 and costs of $100,000. Alternative B will have revenues of $180,000 and costs of $125,000. Compare Alternative A to Alternative B showing incremental revenues, costs, and net income.

Determine incremental changes.
(LO 2)

BE26-3 At Jaymes Company, it costs $30 per unit ($20 variable and $10 fixed) to make a product at full capacity that normally sells for $45. A foreign wholesaler offers to buy 3,000 units at $25 each. Jaymes will incur special shipping costs of $2 per unit. Assuming that Jaymes has excess operating capacity, indicate the net income (loss) Jaymes would realize by accepting the special order.

Determine whether to accept a special order.
(LO 3)

BE26-4 Manson Industries incurs unit costs of $8 ($5 variable and $3 fixed) in making a subassembly part for its finished product. A supplier offers to make 10,000 of the assembly part at $6 per unit. If the offer is accepted, Manson will save all variable costs but no fixed costs. Prepare an analysis showing the total cost saving, if any, Manson will realize by buying the part.

Determine whether to make or buy a part.
(LO 4)

BE26-5 Chudrick Inc. makes unfinished bookcases that it sells for $62. Production costs are $36 variable and $10 fixed. Because it has unused capacity, Chudrick is considering finishing the bookcases and selling them for $70. Variable finishing costs are expected to

Determine whether to sell or process further.
(LO 5)

be $7 per unit with no increase in fixed costs. Prepare an analysis on a per unit basis showing whether Chudrick should sell unfinished or finished bookcases.

Determine whether to retain or replace equipment.

(LO 6)

BE26-6 Kobe Company has a factory machine with a book value of $90,000 and a remaining useful life of 5 years. It can be sold for $30,000. A new machine is available at a cost of $300,000. This machine will have a 5-year useful life with no salvage value. The new machine will lower annual variable manufacturing costs from $600,000 to $500,000. Prepare an analysis showing whether the old machine should be retained or replaced.

Determine whether to eliminate an unprofitable segment.

(LO 7)

BE26-7 Lisah, Inc., manufactures golf clubs in three models. For the year, the Big Bart line has a net loss of $10,000 from sales $200,000, variable costs $180,000, and fixed costs $30,000. If the Big Bart line is eliminated, $20,000 of fixed costs will remain. Prepare an analysis showing whether the Big Bart line should be eliminated.

Show allocation of limited resources.

(LO 8)

BE26-8 In Viejo Company, data concerning two products are: Contribution margin per unit—Product A $11, Product B $12; machine hours required for one unit—Product A 2, Product B 2.5. Compute the contribution margin per unit of limited resource for each product.

Compute the cash payback period for a capital investment.

(LO 9)

BE26-9 Bella Company is considering purchasing new equipment for $450,000. It is expected that the equipment will produce net annual cash flows of $50,000 over its 10-year useful life. Annual depreciation will be $45,000. Compute the cash payback period.

Compute annual rate of return.

(LO 9)

BE26-10 Mecha Oil Company is considering investing in a new oil well. It is expected that the oil well will increase annual revenues by $130,000 and will increase annual expenses by $70,000 including depreciation. The oil well will cost $470,000 and will have a $10,000 salvage value at the end of its 10-year useful life. Calculate the annual rate of return.

Compute net present value of an investment.

(LO 10)

BE26-11 Beacon Company is considering two different, mutually exclusive capital expenditure proposals. Project A will cost $400,000, has an expected useful life of 10 years, a salvage value of zero, and is expected to increase net annual cash flows by $70,000. Project B will cost $280,000, has an expected useful life of 10 years, a salvage value of zero, and is expected to increase net annual cash flows by $50,000. A discount rate of 9% is appropriate for both projects. Compute the net present value of each project. Which project should be accepted?

Calculate internal rate of return.

(LO 10)

BE26-12 Horowitz Company is evaluating the purchase of a rebuilt spot-welding machine to be used in the manufacture of a new product. The machine will cost $176,000, has an estimated useful life of 7 years, a salvage value of zero, and will increase net annual cash flows by $33,740. What is its approximate internal rate of return?

Compute net present value of an investment.

(LO 10)

BE26-13 Hsung Company accumulates the following data concerning a proposed capital investment: cash cost $215,000, net annual cash flows $40,000, present value factor of cash inflows for 10 years 5.65 (rounded). Determine the net present value, and indicate whether the investment should be made.

> DO IT! Review

Evaluate special order.

(LO 3)

DO IT! 26-1 Maize Company incurs a cost of $35 per unit, of which $20 is variable, to make a product that normally sells for $58. A foreign wholesaler offers to buy 6,000 units at $30 each. Maize will incur additional costs of $3 per unit to imprint a logo and to pay for shipping. Compute the increase or decrease in net income Maize will realize by accepting the special order, assuming Maize has sufficient excess operating capacity. Should Maize Company accept the special order?

Evaluate make-or-buy opportunity.

(LO 4)

DO IT! 26-2 Rubble Company must decide whether to make or buy some of its components. The costs of producing 60,000 switches for its generators are as follows.

Direct materials	$30,000	Variable overhead	$45,000
Direct labor	$42,000	Fixed overhead	$60,000

Instead of making the switches at an average cost of $2.95 ($177,000 ÷ 60,000), the company has an opportunity to buy the switches at $2.70 per unit. If the company purchases the switches, all the variable costs and one-fourth of the fixed costs will be eliminated.

(a) Prepare an incremental analysis showing whether the company should make or buy the switches. (b) Would your answer be different if the released productive capacity will generate additional income of $34,000?

DO IT! 26-3 Gator Corporation manufactures several types of accessories. For the year, the gloves and mittens line had sales revenue of $500,000, variable expenses of $370,000, and fixed expenses of $150,000. Therefore, the gloves and mittens line had a net loss of $20,000. If Gator eliminates the line, $38,000 of fixed costs will remain.

Analyze whether to eliminate unprofitable segment.
(LO 7)

Prepare an analysis showing whether the company should eliminate the gloves and mittens line.

DO IT! 26-4 Minkle Company is considering purchasing new equipment for $350,000. The equipment has a 5-year useful life, and depreciation would be $70,000 (assuming straight-line depreciation and zero salvage value). The purchase of the equipment should increase net income by $50,000 each year for 5 years. (a) Compute the annual rate of return. (b) Compute the cash payback period.

Compute capital budgeting measures.
(LO 9)

DO IT! 26-5 Bentoli Box Corporation is considering adding another machine for the manufacture of corrugated cardboard. The machine would cost $680,000. It would have an estimated life of 6 years and no salvage value. The company estimates that annual cash inflows would increase by $300,000 and that annual cash outflows would increase by $140,000. Management has a required rate of return of 10%.

Compute discounted cash flow measures.
(LO 10)

(a) Calculate the net present value on this project, and discuss whether it should be accepted. (b) Calculate the internal rate of return on this project, and discuss whether it should be accepted.

EXERCISES

E26-1 Ortega has prepared the following list of statements about decision-making and incremental analysis.

Analyze statements about decision-making and incremental analysis.
(LO 1, 2)

1. The first step in management's decision-making process is, "Determine and evaluate possible courses of action."
2. The final step in management's decision-making process is to actually make the decision.
3. Accounting's contribution to management's decision-making process occurs primarily in evaluating possible courses of action and in reviewing the results.
4. In making business decisions, management ordinarily considers only financial information because it is objectively determined.
5. Decisions involve a choice among alternative courses of action.
6. The process used to identify the financial data that change under alternative courses of action is called incremental analysis.
7. Costs that are the same under all alternative courses of action sometimes affect the decision.
8. When using incremental analysis, some costs will always change under alternative courses of action, but revenues will not.
9. Variable costs will change under alternative courses of action, but fixed costs will not.

Instructions
Identify each statement as true or false. If false, indicate how to correct the statement.

E26-2 Leno Company manufactures toasters. For the first 8 months of 2014, the company reported the following operating results while operating at 75% of plant capacity:

Use incremental analysis for special-order decision.
(LO 3)

Sales revenue (350,000 units)	$4,375,000
Cost of goods sold	2,600,000
Gross profit	1,775,000
Operating expenses	840,000
Net income	$ 935,000

Cost of goods sold was 70% variable and 30% fixed; operating expenses were 75% variable and 25% fixed.

In September, Leno Company receives a special order for 15,000 toasters at $7.60 each from Centro Company of Ciudad Juarez. Acceptance of the order would result in an additional $3,000 of shipping costs but no increase in fixed operating expenses.

Instructions
(a) Prepare an incremental analysis for the special order.
(b) ———— Should Leno Company accept the special order? Why or why not?

Use incremental analysis for special-order decision.
(LO 3)

E26-3 Gruden Company produces golf discs which it normally sells to retailers for $7 each. The cost of manufacturing 20,000 golf discs is:

Materials	$ 10,000
Labor	30,000
Variable overhead	20,000
Fixed overhead	40,000
Total	$100,000

Gruden also incurs 5% sales commission ($0.35) on each disc sold.

McGee Corporation offers Gruden $4.80 per disc for 5,000 discs. McGee would sell the discs under its own brand name in foreign markets not yet served by Gruden. If Gruden accepts the offer, its fixed overhead will increase from $40,000 to $46,000 due to the purchase of a new imprinting machine. No sales commission will result from the special order.

Instructions
(a) Prepare an incremental analysis for the special order.
(b) Should Gruden accept the special order? Why or why not?
(c) What assumptions underlie the decision made in part (b)?

Use incremental analysis for make-or-buy decision.
(LO 4)

E26-4 Schopp Inc. has been manufacturing its own shades for its table lamps. The company is currently operating at 100% of capacity, and variable manufacturing overhead is charged to production at the rate of 70% of direct labor cost. The direct materials and direct labor cost per unit to make the lamp shades are $4 and $5, respectively. Normal production is 30,000 table lamps per year.

A supplier offers to make the lamp shades at a price of $12.75 per unit. If Schopp Inc. accepts the supplier's offer, all variable manufacturing costs will be eliminated, but the $45,000 of fixed manufacturing overhead currently being charged to the lamp shades will have to be absorbed by other products.

Instructions
(a) Prepare the incremental analysis for the decision to make or buy the lamp shades.
(b) ———— Should Schopp Inc. buy the lamp shades?
(c) ———— Would your answer be different in (b) if the productive capacity released by not making the lamp shades could be used to produce income of $25,000?

Use incremental analysis for sell-or-process-further decision.
(LO 5)

E26-5 Rachel Rey recently opened her own basketweaving studio. She sells finished baskets in addition to the raw materials needed by customers to weave baskets of their own. Rachel has put together a variety of raw material kits, each including materials at various stages of completion. Unfortunately, owing to space limitations, Rachel is unable to carry all varieties of kits originally assembled and must choose between two basic packages.

The basic introductory kit includes undyed, uncut reeds (with dye included) for weaving one basket. This basic package costs Rachel $14 and sells for $30. The second kit, called Stage 2, includes cut reeds that have already been dyed. With this kit the customer need only soak the reeds and weave the basket. Rachel is able to produce the second kit by using the basic materials included in the first kit and adding one hour of her own time, which she values at $18 per hour. Because she is more efficient at cutting and dying reeds than her average customer, Rachel is able to make two kits of the dyed reeds, in one hour, from one kit of undyed reeds. The Stage 2 kit sells for $35.

Instructions
Determine whether Rachel's basketweaving shop should carry the basic introductory kit with undyed and uncut reeds or the Stage 2 kit with reeds already dyed and cut. Prepare an incremental analysis to support your answer.

E26-6 Loh Gear Bikes could sell its bicycles to retailers either assembled or unassembled. The cost of an unassembled bike is as follows.

Use incremental analysis for sell-or-process-further decision.

(LO 5)

Direct materials	$150
Direct labor	70
Variable overhead (70% of direct labor)	49
Fixed overhead (30% of direct labor)	21
Manufacturing cost per unit	$290

The unassembled bikes are sold to retailers at $400 each.

Loh Gear currently has unused productive capacity that is expected to continue indefinitely; management has concluded that some of this capacity can be used to assemble the bikes and sell them at $440 each. Assembling the bikes will increase direct materials by $10 per bike, and direct labor by $10 per bike. Additional variable overhead will be incurred at the normal rates, but there will be no additional fixed overhead as a result of assembling the bikes.

Instructions
(a) Prepare an incremental analysis for the sell-or-process-further decision.
(b) Should Loh Gear sell or process further? Why or why not?

E26-7 Johnson Enterprises uses a computer to handle its sales invoices. Lately, business has been so good that it takes an extra 3 hours per night, plus every third Saturday, to keep up with the volume of sales invoices. Management is considering updating its computer with a faster model that would eliminate all of the overtime processing.

Use incremental analysis for retaining or replacing equipment decision.

(LO 6)

	Current Machine	New Machine
Original purchase cost	$15,000	$25,000
Accumulated depreciation	$ 6,000	—
Estimated annual operating costs	$25,000	$20,000
Useful life	5 years	5 years

If sold now, the current machine would have a salvage value of $6,000. If operated for the remainder of its useful life, the current machine would have zero salvage value. The new machine is expected to have zero salvage value after 5 years.

Instructions
Should the current machine be replaced?

E26-8 Judy Jean, a recent graduate of Rolling's accounting program, evaluated the operating performance of Artie Company's six divisions. Judy made the following presentation to Artie's board of directors and suggested the Huron Division be eliminated. "If the Huron Division is eliminated," she said, "our total profits would increase by $26,000."

Use incremental analysis concerning elimination of division.

(LO 7)

	The Other Five Divisions	Huron Division	Total
Sales revenue	$1,664,200	$ 100,000	$1,764,200
Cost of goods sold	978,520	76,000	1,054,520
Gross profit	685,680	24,000	709,680
Operating expenses	527,940	50,000	577,940
Net income	$ 157,740	$ (26,000)	$ 131,740

In the Huron Division, cost of goods sold is $61,000 variable and $15,000 fixed, and operating expenses are $26,000 variable and $24,000 fixed. None of the Huron Division's fixed costs will be eliminated if the division is discontinued.

Instructions
Is Judy right about eliminating the Huron Division? Prepare a schedule to support your answer.

E26-9 Cawley Company makes three models of tasers. Information on the three products is given as follows.

Use incremental analysis for elimination of a product line.

(LO 7)

	Tingler	Shocker	Stunner
Sales revenue	$300,000	$500,000	$200,000
Variable expenses	150,000	200,000	145,000
Contribution margin	150,000	300,000	55,000
Fixed expenses	120,000	230,000	95,000
Net income	$ 30,000	$ 70,000	$ (40,000)

Fixed expenses consist of $300,000 of common costs allocated to the three products based on relative sales, and additional fixed expenses of $30,000 (Tingler), $80,000 (Shocker), and $35,000 (Stunner). The common costs will be incurred regardless of how many models are produced. The other fixed expenses would be eliminated if a model is phased out.

James Watt, an executive with the company, feels the Stunner line should be discontinued to increase the company's net income.

Instructions
(a) Compute current net income for Cawley Company.
(b) Compute net income by product line and in total for Cawley Company if the company discontinues the Stunner product line. (*Hint:* Allocate the $300,000 common costs to the two remaining product lines based on their relative sales.)
(c) Should Cawley eliminate the Stunner product line? Why or why not?

Compute cash payback period and net present value.

(LO 9, 10)

E26-10 Doug's Custom Construction Company is considering three new projects, each requiring an equipment investment of $22,000. Each project will last for 3 years and produce the following net annual cash flows.

Year	AA	BB	CC
1	$ 7,000	$10,000	$13,000
2	9,000	10,000	12,000
3	12,000	10,000	11,000
Total	$28,000	$30,000	$36,000

The equipment's salvage value is zero, and Doug uses straight-line depreciation. Doug will not accept any project with a cash payback period over 2 years. Doug's required rate of return is 12%.

Instructions
(a) Compute each project's payback period, indicating the most desirable project and the least desirable project using this method. (Round to two decimals and assume in your computations that cash flows occur evenly throughout the year.)
(b) Compute the net present value of each project. Does your evaluation change? (Round to nearest dollar.)

Compute annual rate of return, cash payback period, and net present value.

(LO 9, 10)

E26-11 Vilas Company is considering a capital investment of $190,000 in additional productive facilities. The new machinery is expected to have a useful life of 5 years with no salvage value. Depreciation is by the straight-line method. During the life of the investment, annual net income and net annual cash flows are expected to be $12,000 and $50,000, respectively. Vilas has a 12% cost of capital rate, which is the required rate of return on the investment.

Instructions
(Round to two decimals.)

(a) Compute (1) the cash payback period and (2) the annual rate of return on the proposed capital expenditure.
(b) Using the discounted cash flow technique, compute the net present value.

Determine internal rate of return.

(LO 10)

E26-12 Ueker Company is considering three capital expenditure projects. Relevant data for the projects are as follows.

Project	Investment	Annual Income	Life of Project
22A	$240,000	$16,700	6 years
23A	270,000	20,600	9 years
24A	280,000	17,500	7 years

Annual income is constant over the life of the project. Each project is expected to have zero salvage value at the end of the project. Ueker Company uses the straight-line method of depreciation.

Instructions
(a) Determine the internal rate of return for each project. Round the internal rate of return factor to three decimals.
(b) If Ueker Company's required rate of return is 11%, which projects are acceptable?

E26-13 Leung Corporation is considering investing in two different projects. It could invest in both, neither, or just one of the projects. The forecasts for the projects are as follows.

Compute net present value and recommend project.

(LO 10)

	Project A	**Project B**
Capital investment	$200,000	$300,000
Net annual cash flows	$50,000	$65,000
Length of project	5 years	7 years

The required rate of return acceptable to Leung is 9%.

Instructions
(a) Compute the net present value of the two projects.
(b) What capital budgeting decision should Leung make?
(c) Project A could be modified. By spending $25,000 more initially, the net annual cash flows could be increased by $10,000 per year. Would this change Leung's decision?

EXERCISES: SET B AND CHALLENGE EXERCISES

Visit the book's website, at **www.wiley.com/college/weygandt**, and choose the Student Companion site to access Exercise Set B.

PROBLEMS: SET A

P26-1A ShurShot Sports Inc. manufactures basketballs for the National Basketball Association (NBA). For the first 6 months of 2014, the company reported the following operating results while operating at 80% of plant capacity and producing 120,000 units.

Use incremental analysis for special order and identify nonfinancial factors in the decision.

(LO 3)

	Amount
Sales revenue	$4,800,000
Cost of goods sold	3,600,000
Selling and administrative expenses	405,000
Net income	$ 795,000

Fixed costs for the period were cost of goods sold $960,000, and selling and administrative expenses $225,000.

In July, normally a slack manufacturing month, ShurShot Sports receives a special order for 10,000 basketballs at $27 each from the Greek Basketball Association (GBA). Acceptance of the order would increase variable selling and administrative expenses $0.50 per unit because of shipping costs but would not increase fixed costs and expenses.

Instructions
(a) Prepare an incremental analysis for the special order.
(b) Should ShurShot Sports Inc. accept the special order? Explain your answer.
(c) What is the minimum selling price on the special order to produce net income of $4.00 per ball?
(d) ———— What nonfinancial factors should management consider in making its decision?

Use incremental analysis related to make or buy, consider opportunity cost, and identify nonfinancial factors.

(LO 4)

P26-2A The management of Shatner Manufacturing Company is trying to decide whether to continue manufacturing a part or to buy it from an outside supplier. The part, called CISCO, is a component of the company's finished product.

The following information was collected from the accounting records and production data for the year ending December 31, 2014.

1. 8,000 units of CISCO were produced in the Machining Department.
2. Variable manufacturing costs applicable to the production of each CISCO unit were: direct materials $4.80, direct labor $4.30, indirect labor $0.43, utilities $0.40.
3. Fixed manufacturing costs applicable to the production of CISCO were:

Cost Item	Direct	Allocated
Depreciation	$2,100	$ 900
Property taxes	500	200
Insurance	900	600
	$3,500	$1,700

All variable manufacturing and direct fixed costs will be eliminated if CISCO is purchased. Allocated costs will have to be absorbed by other production departments.

4. The lowest quotation for 8,000 CISCO units from a supplier is $80,000.
5. If CISCO units are purchased, freight and inspection costs would be $0.35 per unit, and receiving costs totaling $1,300 per year would be incurred by the Machining Department.

Instructions

(a) Prepare an incremental analysis for CISCO. Your analysis should have columns for (1) Make CISCO, (2) Buy CISCO, and (3) Net Income Increase/(Decrease).

(b) Based on your analysis, what decision should management make?

(c) Would the decision be different if Shatner Company has the opportunity to produce $3,000 of net income with the facilities currently being used to manufacture CISCO? Show computations.

(d) ⸻ What nonfinancial factors should management consider in making its decision?

Compute gain or loss, and determine if equipment should be replaced.

(LO 6)

P26-3A Last year (2013), Richter Condos installed a mechanized elevator for its tenants. The owner of the company, Ron Richter, recently returned from an industry equipment exhibition where he watched a computerized elevator demonstrated. He was impressed with the elevator's speed, comfort of ride, and cost efficiency. Upon returning from the exhibition, he asked his purchasing agent to collect price and operating cost data on the new elevator. In addition, he asked the company's accountant to provide him with cost data on the company's elevator. This information is presented below.

	Old Elevator	New Elevator
Purchase price	$120,000	$160,000
Estimated salvage value	0	0
Estimated useful life	5 years	4 years
Depreciation method	Straight-line	Straight-line
Annual operating costs other than depreciation:		
Variable	$ 35,000	$ 10,000
Fixed	23,000	8,500

Annual revenues are $240,000, and selling and administrative expenses are $29,000, regardless of which elevator is used. If the old elevator is replaced now, at the beginning of 2014, Richter Condos will be able to sell it for $25,000.

Instructions

(a) Determine any gain or loss if the old elevator is replaced.

(b) Prepare a 4-year summarized income statement for each of the following assumptions:
  (1) The old elevator is retained.
  (2) The old elevator is replaced.

(c) Using incremental analysis, determine if the old elevator should be replaced.

(d) ⸻ Write a memo to Ron Richter explaining why any gain or loss should be ignored in the decision to replace the old elevator.

P26-4A Gutierrez Company has four operating divisions. During the first quarter of 2014, the company reported aggregate income from operations of $213,000 and the following divisional results.

Prepare incremental analysis concerning elimination of divisions.

(LO 7)

	Division			
	I	**II**	**III**	**IV**
Sales revenue	$250,000	$200,000	$500,000	$450,000
Cost of goods sold	200,000	192,000	300,000	250,000
Selling and administrative expenses	75,000	60,000	60,000	50,000
Income (loss) from operations	$ (25,000)	$ (52,000)	$140,000	$150,000

Analysis reveals the following percentages of variable costs in each division.

	I	II	III	IV
Cost of goods sold	75%	90%	80%	75%
Selling and administrative expenses	40	70	50	60

Discontinuance of any division would save 50% of the fixed costs and expenses for that division.

Top management is very concerned about the unprofitable divisions (I and II). Consensus is that one or both of the divisions should be discontinued.

Instructions

(a) Compute the contribution margin for Divisions I and II.

(b) Prepare an incremental analysis concerning the possible discontinuance of (1) Division I and (2) Division II. What course of action do you recommend for each division?

(c) Prepare a columnar condensed income statement for Gutierrez Company, assuming Division II is eliminated. (Use the CVP format.) Division II's unavoidable fixed costs are allocated equally to the continuing divisions.

(d) Reconcile the total income from operations ($213,000) with the total income from operations without Division II.

P26-5A Henkel Company is considering three long-term capital investment proposals. Each investment has a useful life of 5 years. Relevant data on each project are as follows.

Compute annual rate of return, cash payback, and net present value.

(LO 9, 10)

	Project Kilo	**Project Lima**	**Project Oscar**
Capital investment	$150,000	$165,000	$200,000
Annual net income:			
Year 1	14,000	18,000	27,000
2	14,000	17,000	23,000
3	14,000	16,000	21,000
4	14,000	12,000	13,000
5	14,000	9,000	12,000
Total	$ 70,000	$ 72,000	$ 96,000

Depreciation is computed by the straight-line method with no salvage value. The company's cost of capital is 15%. (Assume that cash flows occur evenly throughout the year.)

Instructions

(a) Compute the cash payback period for each project. (Round to two decimals.)

(b) Compute the net present value for each project. (Round to nearest dollar.)

(c) Compute the annual rate of return for each project. (Round to two decimals.) (*Hint:* Use average annual net income in your computation.)

(d) Rank the projects on each of the foregoing bases. Which project do you recommend?

P26-6A Lon Timur is an accounting major at a midwestern state university located approximately 60 miles from a major city. Many of the students attending the university are from the metropolitan area and visit their homes regularly on the weekends. Lon, an entrepreneur at heart, realizes that few good commuting alternatives are available for students doing weekend travel. He believes that a weekend commuting service could be organized and run profitably from several suburban and downtown shopping mall locations. Lon has gathered the following investment information.

Compute annual rate of return, cash payback, and net present value.

(LO 9, 10)

1. Five used vans would cost a total of $75,000 to purchase and would have a 3-year useful life with negligible salvage value. Lon plans to use straight-line depreciation.
2. Ten drivers would have to be employed at a total annual payroll expense of $48,000.

3. Other annual out-of-pocket expenses associated with running the commuter service would include Gasoline $16,000, Maintenance $3,300, Repairs $4,000, Insurance $4,200, and Advertising $2,500.
4. Lon has visited several financial institutions to discuss funding. The best interest rate he has been able to negotiate is 15%. Use this rate for cost of capital.
5. Lon expects each van to make ten round trips weekly and carry an average of six students each trip. The service is expected to operate 30 weeks each year, and each student will be charged $12.00 for a round-trip ticket.

Instructions
(a) Determine the annual (1) net income and (2) net annual cash flows for the commuter service.
(b) Compute (1) the cash payback period and (2) the annual rate of return. (Round to two decimals.)
(c) Compute the net present value of the commuter service. (Round to the nearest dollar.)
(d) ⬤▬▬ What should Lon conclude from these computations?

Compute net present value and internal rate of return.

(LO 10)

P26-7A Goltra Clinic is considering investing in new heart-monitoring equipment. It has two options: Option A would have an initial lower cost but would require a significant expenditure for rebuilding after 4 years. Option B would require no rebuilding expenditure, but its maintenance costs would be higher. Since the Option B machine is of initial higher quality, it is expected to have a salvage value at the end of its useful life. The following estimates were made of the cash flows. The company's cost of capital is 8%.

	Option A	Option B
Initial cost	$160,000	$227,000
Annual cash inflows	$70,000	$80,000
Annual cash outflows	$30,000	$26,000
Cost to rebuild (end of year 4)	$50,000	$0
Salvage value	$0	$8,000
Estimated useful life	7 years	7 years

Instructions
(a) Compute the (1) net present value and (2) internal rate of return for each option. (*Hint:* To solve for internal rate of return, experiment with alternative discount rates to arrive at a net present value of zero.)
(b) Which option should be accepted?

PROBLEMS: SET B

Use incremental analysis for special order and identify nonfinancial factors in decision.

(LO 3)

P26-1B Morello Inc. manufactures basketballs for the National Basketball Association (NBA). For the first 6 months of 2014, the company reported the following operating results while operating at 90% of plant capacity and producing 90,000 units.

	Amount	Per Unit
Sales revenue	$4,500,000	$50
Cost of goods sold	3,060,000	34
Selling and administrative expenses	360,000	4
Net income	$1,080,000	$12

Fixed costs for the period were cost of goods sold $900,000, and selling and administrative expenses $180,000.

In July, normally a slack manufacturing month, Morello receives a special order for 10,000 basketballs at $30 each from the Chinese Basketball Association (CBA). Acceptance of the order would increase variable selling and administrative expenses $0.50 per unit because of shipping costs but would not increase fixed costs and expenses.

Instructions
(a) Prepare an incremental analysis for the special order.
(b) Should Morello Inc. accept the special order?
(c) What is the minimum selling price on the special order to produce net income of $5.50 per ball?
(d) ⬤▬▬ What nonfinancial factors should management consider in making its decision?

P26-2B The management of Gill Corporation is trying to decide whether to continue manufacturing a part or to buy it from an outside supplier. The part, called FIZBE, is a component of the company's finished product.

Use incremental analysis related to make or buy; consider opportunity cost and identify nonfinancial factors.
(LO 4)

The following information was collected from the accounting records and production data for the year ending December 31, 2014.

1. 5,000 units of FIZBE were produced in the Machining Department.
2. Variable manufacturing costs applicable to the production of each FIZBE unit were: direct materials $4.75, direct labor $4.60, indirect labor $0.45, utilities $0.35.
3. Fixed manufacturing costs applicable to the production of FIZBE were:

Cost Item	Direct	Allocated
Depreciation	$1,100	$ 900
Property taxes	500	200
Insurance	900	600
	$2,500	$1,700

All variable manufacturing and direct fixed costs will be eliminated if FIZBE is purchased. Allocated costs will have to be absorbed by other production departments.
4. The lowest quotation for 5,000 FIZBE units from a supplier is $56,000.
5. If FIZBE units are purchased, freight and inspection costs would be $0.30 per unit, and receiving costs totaling $500 per year would be incurred by the Machining Department.

Instructions
(a) Prepare an incremental analysis for FIZBE. Your analysis should have columns for (1) Make FIZBE, (2) Buy FIZBE, and (3) Net Income Increase/(Decrease).
(b) Based on your analysis, what decision should management make?
(c) Would the decision be different if Gill Corporation has the opportunity to produce $6,000 of net income with the facilities currently being used to manufacture FIZBE? Show computations.
(d) ━━━━ What nonfinancial factors should management consider in making its decision?

P26-3B Last year (2013), Simmons Company installed new factory equipment. The owner of the company, Gene Simmons, recently returned from an industry equipment exhibition where he watched computerized equipment demonstrated. He was impressed with the equipment's speed and cost efficiency. Upon returning from the exhibition, he asked his purchasing agent to collect price and operating cost data on the new equipment. In addition, he asked the company's accountant to provide him with cost data on the company's equipment. This information is presented below.

Compute gain or loss, and determine if equipment should be replaced.
(LO 6)

	Old Equipment	New Equipment
Purchase price	$210,000	$250,000
Estimated salvage value	0	0
Estimated useful life	5 years	4 years
Depreciation method	Straight-line	Straight-line
Annual operating costs other than depreciation:		
Variable	$50,000	$12,000
Fixed	30,000	5,000

Annual revenues are $360,000, and selling and administrative expenses are $45,000, regardless of which equipment is used. If the old equipment is replaced now, at the beginning of 2014, Simmons Company will be able to sell it for $58,000.

Instructions
(a) Determine any gain or loss if the old equipment is replaced.
(b) Prepare a 4-year summarized income statement for each of the following assumptions:
    (1) The old equipment is retained.
    (2) The old equipment is replaced.
(c) Using incremental analysis, determine if the old equipment should be replaced.
(d) ━━━━ Write a memo to Gene Simmons explaining why any gain or loss should be ignored in the decision to replace the old equipment.

Prepare incremental analysis
concerning elimination of
divisions.

(LO 7)**P26-4B** Panda Corporation has four operating divisions. During the first quarter of 2014, the company reported aggregate income from operations of $129,000 and the divisional results shown below.

	Division			
	I	**II**	**III**	**IV**
Sales revenue	$510,000	$400,000	$310,000	$170,000
Cost of goods sold	300,000	250,000	270,000	156,000
Selling and administrative expenses	60,000	80,000	75,000	70,000
Income (loss) from operations	$150,000	$ 70,000	$ (35,000)	$ (56,000)

Analysis reveals the following percentages of variable costs in each division.

	I	**II**	**III**	**IV**
Cost of goods sold	70%	80%	70%	90%
Selling and administrative expenses	40	50	60	70

Discontinuance of any division would save 50% of the fixed costs and expenses for that division.

Top management is very concerned about the unprofitable divisions (III and IV). Consensus is that one or both of the divisions should be discontinued.

Instructions
(a) Compute the contribution margin for Divisions III and IV.
(b) Prepare an incremental analysis concerning the possible discontinuance of (1) Division III and (2) Division IV. What course of action do you recommend for each division?
(c) Prepare a columnar condensed income statement for Panda Corporation, assuming Division IV is eliminated. (Use the CVP format.) Division IV's unavoidable fixed costs are allocated equally to the continuing divisions.
(d) Reconcile the total income from operations ($129,000) with the total income from operations without Division IV.

Compute annual rate of
return, cash payback, and net
present value.

(LO 9, 10)

P26-5B The Borders and Noble partnership is considering three long-term capital investment proposals. Each investment has a useful life of 5 years. Relevant data on each project are as follows.

	Project Mary	**Project Winnie**	**Project Sarah**
Capital investment	$140,000	$175,000	$190,000
Annual net income:			
Year 1	10,000	12,500	19,000
2	10,000	12,000	16,000
3	10,000	11,000	14,000
4	10,000	8,000	9,000
5	10,000	6,000	8,000
Total	$ 50,000	$ 49,500	$ 66,000

Depreciation is computed by the straight-line method with no salvage value. The company's cost of capital is 12%. (Assume cash flows occur evenly throughout the year.)

Instructions
(a) Compute the cash payback period for each project. (Round to two decimals.)
(b) Compute the net present value for each project. (Round to nearest dollar.)
(c) Compute the annual rate of return for each project. (Round to two decimals.) (*Hint:* Use average annual net income in your computation.)
(d) Rank the projects on each of the foregoing bases. Which project do you recommend?

Compute annual rate of
return, cash payback, and net
present value.

(LO 9, 10)

P26-6B Ben Paul is an accounting major at a western university located approximately 60 miles from a major city. Many of the students attending the university are from the metropolitan area and visit their homes regularly on the weekends. Ben, an entrepreneur at heart, realizes that few good commuting alternatives are available for students doing weekend travel. He believes that a weekend commuting service could be organized and run profitably from several suburban and downtown shopping mall locations. Ben has gathered the following investment information.

1. Five used vans would cost a total of $90,000 to purchase and would have a 3-year useful life with negligible salvage value. Ben plans to use straight-line depreciation.
2. Ten drivers would have to be employed at a total annual payroll expense of $43,000.
3. Other annual out-of-pocket expenses associated with running the commuter service would include Gasoline $26,000, Maintenance $4,000, Repairs $5,300, Insurance $4,500, and Advertising $2,200.
4. Ben desires to earn a return of 15% on his investment.
5. Ben expects each van to make ten round trips weekly and carry an average of six students each trip. The service is expected to operate 32 weeks each year, and each student will be charged $15 for a round-trip ticket.

Instructions
(a) Determine the annual (1) net income and (2) net annual cash flows for the commuter service.
(b) Compute (1) the cash payback period and (2) the annual rate of return. (Round to two decimals.)
(c) Compute the net present value of the commuter service. (Round to the nearest dollar.)
(d) ━━━ What should Ben conclude from these computations?

P26-7B Platteville Eye Clinic is considering investing in new optical-scanning equipment. It has two options: Option A would have an initial lower cost but would require a significant expenditure for rebuilding after 3 years. Option B would require no rebuilding expenditure, but its maintenance costs would be higher. Since the Option B machine is of initial higher quality, it is expected to have a salvage value at the end of its useful life. The following estimates were made of the cash flows. The company's cost of capital is 11%.

Compute net present value and internal rate of return.
(LO 10)

	Option A	Option B
Initial cost	$100,000	$160,000
Annual cash inflows	$56,000	$60,000
Annual cash outflows	$24,000	$24,000
Cost to rebuild (end of year 3)	$53,000	$0
Salvage value	$0	$24,000
Estimated useful life	6 years	6 years

Instructions
(a) Compute the (1) net present value and (2) internal rate of return for each option. (*Hint:* To solve for internal rate of return, experiment with alternative discount rates to arrive at a net present value of zero.)
(b) Which option should be accepted?

PROBLEMS: SET C

Visit the book's companion website, at **www.wiley.com/college/weygandt**, and choose the Student Companion site to access Problem Set C.

COMPREHENSIVE PROBLEM: CHAPTERS 19 TO 26

CP26 You would like to start a business manufacturing a unique model of bicycle helmet. In preparation for an interview with the bank to discuss your financing needs, you need to provide the following information. A number of assumptions are required; clearly note all assumptions that you make.

Instructions
(a) Identify the types of costs that would likely be involved in making this product.
(b) Set up five columns as indicated.

	Product Costs			
Item	Direct Materials	Direct Labor	Manufacturing Overhead	Period Costs

Classify the costs you identified in (a) into the manufacturing cost classifications of product costs (direct materials, direct labor, and manufacturing overhead) and period costs.

(c) Assign hypothetical monthly dollar figures to the costs you identified in (a) and (b).

(d) Assume you have no raw materials or work in process beginning or ending inventories. Prepare a projected cost of goods manufactured schedule for the first month of operations.

(e) Project the number of helmets you expect to produce the first month of operations. Compute the cost to produce one bicycle helmet. Review the result to ensure it is reasonable; if not, return to part (c) and adjust the monthly dollar figures you assigned accordingly.

(f) What type of cost accounting system will you likely use—job order or process costing?

(g) Explain how you would assign costs in either the job order or process costing system you plan to use.

(h) Classify your costs as either variable or fixed costs. For simplicity, assign all costs to either variable or fixed, assuming there are no mixed costs, using the format shown.

Item	Variable Costs	Fixed Costs	Total Costs

(i) Compute the unit variable cost, using the production number you determined in (e).

(j) Project the number of helmets you anticipate selling the first month of operations. Set a unit selling price, and compute both the contribution margin per unit and the contribution margin ratio.

(k) Determine your break-even point in dollars and in units.

(l) Prepare projected operating budgets (sales, production, direct materials, direct labor, manufacturing overhead, selling and administrative expense, and income statement). You will need to make assumptions for each of the following:

Direct materials budget:	Quantity of direct materials required to produce one helmet; cost per unit of quantity; desired ending direct materials (assume none).
Direct labor budget:	Direct labor time required per helmet; direct labor cost per hour.
Budgeted income statement:	Income tax expense is 45% of income from operations.

(m) Prepare a cash budget for the month. Assume the percentage of sales that will be collected from customers is 75%, and the percentage of direct materials that will be paid in the current month is 75%.

(n) Determine a relevant range of activity, using the number of helmets produced as your activity index. Recast your manufacturing overhead budget into a flexible monthly budget for two additional activity levels.

(o) Identify one potential cause of materials, direct labor, and manufacturing overhead variances for your product.

(p) Assume that you wish to purchase production equipment that costs $720,000. Determine the cash payback period, utilizing the monthly cash flow that you computed in part (m) multiplied by 12 months (for simplicity).

(q) Identify any nonfinancial factors that should be considered before commencing your business venture.

WATERWAYS CONTINUING PROBLEM

(This is a continuation of the Waterways Problem from Chapters 19 through 25.)

WCP26 Waterways Corporation puts much emphasis on cash flow when it plans for capital investments. The company chose its discount rate of 8% based on the rate of return it must pay its owners and creditors. Using that rate, Waterways then uses different methods to determine the best decisions for making capital outlays. Waterways is considering buying five new backhoes to replace the backhoes it now has. This problem asks you to evaluate that decision, using various capital budgeting techniques.

Go to the book's companion website, **www.wiley.com/college/weygandt,** *to find the remainder of this problem.*

Broadening Your Perspective

Decision-Making Problems: Current Designs

BYP26-1 Recently, Mike Cichanowski, owner and CEO of Current Designs, received a phone call from the president of a brewing company. He was calling to inquire about the possibility of Current Designs producing "floating coolers" for a promotion his company was planning. These coolers resemble a kayak but are about one-third the size. They are used to float food and beverages while paddling down the river on a weekend leisure trip. The company would be interested in purchasing 100 coolers for the upcoming summer. It is willing to pay $250 per cooler. The brewing company would pick up the coolers upon completion of the order.

Mike met with Diane Buswell, controller, to identify how much it would cost Current Designs to produce the coolers. After careful analysis, the following costs were identified.

Direct materials	$80/unit	Variable overhead	$20/unit
Direct labor	$60/unit	Fixed overhead	$1,000

Current Designs would be able to modify an existing mold to produce the coolers. The cost of these modifications would be approximately $2,000.

Instructions

(a) Prepare an incremental analysis to determine whether Current Designs should accept this special order to produce the coolers.

(b) Discuss additional factors that Mike and Diane should consider if Current Designs is currently operating at full capacity.

BYP26-2 A company that manufactures recreational pedal boats has approached Mike Cichanowski to ask if he would be interested in using Current Designs' rotomold expertise and equipment to produce some of the pedal boat components. Mike is intrigued by the idea and thinks it would be an interesting way of complementing the present product line.

One of Mike's hesitations about the proposal is that the pedal boats are a different shape than the kayaks that Current Designs produces. As a result, the company would need to buy an additional rotomold oven in order to produce the pedal boat components. This project clearly involves risks, and Mike wants to make sure that the returns justify the risks. In this case, since this is a new venture, Mike thinks that a 15% discount rate is appropriate to use to evaluate the project.

As an intern at Current Designs, Mike has asked you to prepare an initial evaluation of this proposal. To aid in your analysis, he has provided the following information and assumptions.

1. The new rotomold oven will have a cost of $256,000, a salvage value of $0, and an 8-year useful life. Straight-line depreciation will be used.

2. The projected revenues, costs, and results for each of the 8 years of this project are as follows.

Sales revenue		$220,000
Less:		
Manufacturing costs	$140,000	
Depreciation	32,000	
Shipping and administrative costs	22,000	194,000
Income before income taxes		26,000
Income tax expense		10,800
Net income		$ 15,200

Instructions

(a) Compute the annual rate of return. (Round to two decimal places.)

(b) Compute the payback period. (Round to two decimal places.)

(c) Compute the NPV using a discount rate of 9%. (Round to nearest dollar.) Should the proposal be accepted using this discount rate?

(d) Compute the NPV using a discount rate of 15%. (Round to nearest dollar.) Should the proposal be accepted using this discount rate?

Decision-Making Across the Organization

BYP26-3 Aurora Company is considering the purchase of a new machine. The invoice price of the machine is $140,000, freight charges are estimated to be $4,000, and installation costs are expected to be $6,000. Salvage value of the new equipment is expected to be zero after a useful life of 5 years. Existing equipment could be retained and used for an additional 5 years if the new machine is not purchased. At that time, the salvage value of the equipment would be zero. If the new machine is purchased now, the existing machine would have to be scrapped. Aurora's accountant, Lisah Huang, has accumulated the following data regarding annual sales and expenses with and without the new machine.

1. Without the new machine, Aurora can sell 12,000 units of product annually at a per unit selling price of $100. If the new machine is purchased, the number of units produced and sold would increase by 10%, and the selling price would remain the same.
2. The new machine is faster than the old machine, and it is more efficient in its usage of materials. With the old machine the gross profit rate will be 25% of sales, whereas the rate will be 30% of sales with the new machine.
3. Annual selling expenses are $180,000 with the current equipment. Because the new equipment would produce a greater number of units to be sold, annual selling expenses are expected to increase by 10% if it is purchased.
4. Annual administrative expenses are expected to be $100,000 with the old machine, and $113,000 with the new machine.
5. The current book value of the existing machine is $36,000. Aurora uses straight-line depreciation.

Instructions
With the class divided into groups, prepare an incremental analysis for the 5 years showing whether Aurora should keep the existing machine or buy the new machine. (Ignore income tax effects.)

Managerial Analysis

BYP26-4 MiniTek manufactures private-label small electronic products, such as alarm clocks, calculators, kitchen timers, stopwatches, and automatic pencil sharpeners. Some of the products are sold as sets, and others are sold individually. Products are studied as to their sales potential, and then cost estimates are made. The Engineering Department develops production plans, and then production begins. The company has generally had very successful product introductions. Only two products introduced by the company have been discontinued.

One of the products currently sold is a multi-alarm clock. The clock has four alarms that can be programmed to sound at various times and for varying lengths of time. The company has experienced a great deal of difficulty in making the circuit boards for the clocks. The production process has never operated smoothly. The product is unprofitable at the present time, primarily because of warranty repairs and product recalls. Two models of the clocks were recalled, for example, because they sometimes caused an electric shock when the alarms were being shut off. The Engineering Department is attempting to revise the manufacturing process, but the revision will take another 6 months at least.

The clocks were very popular when they were introduced, and since they are private-label, the company has not suffered much from the recalls. Presently, the company has a very large order for several items from Kmart Stores. The order includes 5,000 of the multi-alarm clocks. When the company suggested that Kmart purchase the clocks from another manufacturer, Kmart threatened to rescind the entire order unless the clocks were included.

The company has therefore investigated the possibility of having another company make the clocks for them. The clocks were bid for the Kmart order based on an estimated $6.90 cost to manufacture:

Circuit board, 1 each @ $2.00	$2.00
Plastic case, 1 each @ $0.80	0.80
Alarms, 4 @ $0.15 each	0.60
Labor, 15 minutes @ $12/hour	3.00
Overhead, $2.00 per labor hour	0.50

MiniTek could purchase clocks to fill the Kmart order for $10 from Trans-Tech Asia, a Korean manufacturer with a very good quality record. Trans-Tech has offered to reduce the price to $7.50 after MiniTek has been a customer for 6 months, placing an order of at least 1,000 units per month. If MiniTek becomes a "preferred customer" by purchasing 15,000 units per year, the price would be reduced still further to $4.50.

Omega Products, a local manufacturer, has also offered to make clocks for MiniTek. They have offered to sell 5,000 clocks for $5 each. However, Omega Products has been in business for only 6 months. They have experienced significant turnover in their labor force, and the local press has reported that the owners may face tax evasion charges soon. The owner of Omega Products is an electronic engineer, however, and the quality of the clocks is likely to be good.

If MiniTek decides to purchase the clocks from either Trans-Tech or Omega, all the costs to manufacture could be avoided, except a total of $5,000 in overhead costs for machine depreciation. The machinery is fairly new, and has no alternate use.

Instructions

(a) What is the difference in profit under each of the alternatives if the clocks are to be sold for $14.50 each to Kmart?

(b) What are the most important nonfinancial factors that MiniTek should consider when making this decision?

(c) What do you think MiniTek should do in regard to the Kmart order? What should it do in regard to continuing to manufacture the multi-alarm clocks? Be prepared to defend your answer.

Real-World Focus

BYP26-5 Founded in 1983, Beverly Hills Fan Company is located in Woodland Hills, California. With 23 employees and sales of less than $10 million, the company is relatively small. Management feels that there is potential for growth in the upscale market for ceiling fans and lighting. They are particularly optimistic about growth in Mexican and Canadian markets.

Presented below is information from the president's letter in the company's annual report.

BEVERLY HILLS FAN COMPANY
President's Letter

An aggressive product development program was initiated during the past year resulting in new ceiling fan models planned for introduction this year. Award winning industrial designer Ron Rezek created several new fan models for the Beverly Hills Fan and L.A. Fan lines, including a new Showroom Collection, designed specifically for the architectural and designer markets. Each of these models has received critical acclaim, and order commitments for this year have been outstanding. Additionally, our Custom Color and special order fans continued to enjoy increasing popularity and sales gains as more and more customers desire fans that match their specific interior decors. Currently, Beverly Hills Fan Company offers a product line of over 100 models of contemporary, traditional, and transitional ceiling fans.

Instructions

(a) What points did the company management need to consider before deciding to offer the special-order fans to customers?

(b) How would incremental analysis be employed to assist in this decision?

BYP26-6 Campbell Soup Company is an international provider of soup products. Management is very interested in continuing to grow the company in its core business, while "spinning off" those businesses that are not part of its core operation.

Address: **www.campbellsoups.com**, or go to **www.wiley.com/college/weygandt**

Steps

1. Go to the home page of Campbell Soup Company at the address shown above.

2. Choose the annual report dated July 29, 2012.

Instructions

Review the financial statements and management's discussion and analysis, and answer the following questions.

(a) What was the total amount of capital expenditures for the fiscal year ending July 29, 2012, and how does this amount compare with the previous year?

(b) What interest rate did the company pay on new borrowings for the fiscal year ending July 29, 2012?

(c) Assume that this year's capital expenditures are expected to increase cash flows by $42 million. What is the expected internal rate of return (IRR) for these capital expenditures? (Assume a 10-year period for the cash flows.)

Communication Activity

BYP26-7 Refer back to E26-11 to address the following.

Instructions
Prepare a memo to Maria Fierro, your supervisor. Show your calculations from E26-11, (a) and (b). In one or two paragraphs, discuss important nonfinancial considerations. Make any assumptions you believe to be necessary. Make a recommendation based on your analysis.

Ethics Case

BYP26-8 NuComp Company operates in a state where corporate taxes and workers' compensation insurance rates have recently doubled. NuComp's president has just assigned you the task of preparing an economic analysis and making a recommendation relative to moving the entire operation to Missouri. The president is slightly in favor of such a move because Missouri is his boyhood home and he also owns a fishing lodge there.

You have just completed building your dream house, moved in, and sodded the lawn. Your children are all doing well in school and sports and, along with your spouse, want no part of a move to Missouri. If the company does move, so will you because the town is a one-industry community and you and your spouse will have to move to have employment. Moving when everyone else does will cause you to take a big loss on the sale of your house. The same hardships will be suffered by your coworkers, and the town will be devastated.

In compiling the costs of moving versus not moving, you have latitude in the assumptions you make, the estimates you compute, and the discount rates and time periods you project. You are in a position to influence the decision singlehandedly.

Instructions
(a) Who are the stakeholders in this situation?
(b) What are the ethical issues in this situation?
(c) What would you do in this situation?

All About You

BYP26-9 Managerial accounting techniques can be used in a wide variety of settings. As we have frequently pointed out, you can use them in many personal situations. They also can be useful in trying to find solutions for societal issues that appear to be hard to solve.

Instructions
Read the *Fortune* article, "The Toughest Customers: How Hardheaded Business Metrics Can Help the Hard-core Homeless," by Cait Murphy, available at **http://money.cnn.com/magazines/fortune/ fortune_archive/2006/04/03/8373067/index.htm**. Answer the following questions.
(a) How does the article define "chronic" homelessness?
(b) In what ways does homelessness cost a city money? What are the estimated costs of a chronic homeless person to various cities?
(c) What are the steps suggested to address the problem?
(d) What is the estimated cost of implementing this program in New York? What results have been seen?
(e) In terms of incremental analysis, frame the relevant costs in this situation.

Considering Your Costs and Benefits

BYP26-10 School costs money. Is this an expenditure that you should have avoided? A year of tuition at a public four-year college costs about $8,655, and a year of tuition at a public two-year college costs about $1,359. If you did not go to college, you might avoid mountains of school-related debt. In fact, each year, about 600,000 students decide to drop out of school. Many of them never return. Suppose that you are working two jobs and going to college, and that you are not making ends meet. Your grades are suffering due to your lack of available study time. You feel depressed. Should you drop out of school?

YES: You can always go back to school. If your grades are bad and you are depressed, what good is school doing you anyway?

NO: Once you drop out, it is very hard to get enough momentum to go back. Dropping out will dramatically reduce your long-term opportunities. It is better to stay in school, even if you take only one class per semester. While you cannot go back and redo your initial decision, you can look at some facts to evaluate the wisdom of your decision.

Instructions

Write a response indicating your position regarding this situation. Provide support for your view.

Answers to Chapter Questions

Answers to Insight and Accounting Across the Organization Questions

p. 1230 That Letter from AmEx Might Not Be a Bill   Q: What are the relevant costs that American Express would need to know in order to determine to whom to make this offer? **A:** Clearly, American Express would make this offer to those customers that are most likely to default on their bills. The most important relevant cost would be the "expected loss" that an at-risk customer posed. If a customer has a high probability of defaulting, and if the expected loss exceeds the $300 cost, then American Express can probably save money by paying that customer to quit using its card so that the customer doesn't incur an even bigger bill.

p. 1231 Giving Away the Store?   Q: What are the relevant revenues and costs that Amazon should consider relative to the decision whether to offer the Prime free-shipping subscription? **A:** The relevant revenues to consider would be the estimated change in revenue that would result from offering free shipping and the $79 annual fee for a Prime subscription. The relevant costs would be the estimated additional shipping costs that the company would incur.

p. 1238 Time to Move to a New Neighborhood?   Q: What were some of the factors that complicated the company's decision to move? How should the company have incorporated such factors into its incremental analysis? **A:** The company received only $7.5 million for its California property, only 58 of 75 key employees were willing to move, construction was delayed by a year which caused the new plant to increase in price by $1.5 million, and wages surged in Idaho due to low unemployment. In performing incremental analysis of the decision to move, a company should perform sensitivity analysis. This would include evaluating the impact on the decision if all costs were, for example, 10% higher than expected or if cost savings were 10% lower than expected.

p. 1241 Investing for the Future   Q: Why is it important for top management to constantly monitor the nature, amount, and success of a company's capital expenditures? **A:** In order to remain competitive and to grow, companies must continually invest in new opportunities. However, not all projects will be successful, so management must continually monitor projects to ensure that continuation of the investment is in the company's best interest.

p. 1244 Can You Hear Me—Better?   Q: Based on the potentially slow initial adoption of 4G by customers, how might the conclusions of a cash payback analysis of Verizon's 4G investment differ from a present value analysis? **A:** If the initial adoption of 4G by customers is slow, then the amount of cash received in the early years will be low. This would lengthen the cash payback period, making it unlikely that the investment would get high marks with this test. However, the long-run potential of 4G is probably quite high as more people switch to smart phones and consequently increase their use of services that benefit from a high-speed connection. These later cash flows may well be large enough that they provide a positive net present value amount.

p. 1247 Seeing the Big Picture   Q: How important is the choice of discount rate in making capital budgeting decisions? **A:** The point of this discussion is that errors in implementation, as well as the accuracy of the estimated future benefits and costs as measured by cash inflows and outflows, is what matters the most when making capital expenditure decisions. While the choice of discount rates will result in incremental differences in present value calculations, "missing the big picture" has the potential to cause much bigger decision errors. Underestimating potential future cash inflows can result in missed opportunities. Underestimating future costs can result in failed investments.

Answers to Self-Test Questions

1. d   **2.** b   **3.** c [($18 − $14) × 3,000]   **4.** b   **5.** d   **6.** a   **7.** d ($68 − $55) − $12   **8.** b   **9.** c   **10.** d ($200,000 − $140,000 − $50,000)   **11.** b ($15 ÷ 3)   **12.** d   **13.** b   **14.** c   **15.** b

✔ **The Navigator**

✔ Remember to go back to The Navigator box on the chapter opening page and check off your completed work.

Once each year, a corporation communicates to its stockholders and other interested parties by issuing a complete set of audited financial statements. The **annual report**, as this communication is called, summarizes the financial results of the company's operations for the year and its plans for the future. Many annual reports are attractive, multicolored, glossy public relations pieces, containing pictures of corporate officers and directors as well as photos and descriptions of new products and new buildings. Yet the basic function of every annual report is to report financial information, almost all of which is a product of the corporation's accounting system.

The content and organization of corporate annual reports have become fairly standardized. Excluding the public relations part of the report (pictures, products, etc.), the following are the traditional financial portions of the annual report:

- Financial Highlights
- Letter to the Stockholders
- Management's Discussion and Analysis
- Financial Statements
- Notes to the Financial Statements
- Management's Responsibility for Financial Reporting
- Management's Report on Internal Control over Financial Reporting
- Report of Independent Registered Public Accounting Firm
- Selected Financial Data

The official SEC filing of the annual report is called a **Form 10-K**, which often omits the public relations pieces found in most standard annual reports. On the following pages, we present Apple Inc.'s financial statements taken from the company's 2011 Form 10-K. To access Apple's Form 10-K, including notes to the financial statements, follow these steps:

1. Go to **http://investor.apple.com**.
2. Select the Financial History tab.
3. Select 2011 10-K Annual Report filed Oct 26, 2011.
4. Item 8, on page 42, provides an index to the consolidated financial statements and notes. The Notes to Consolidated Financial Statements, for example, begin on page 47.

CONSOLIDATED STATEMENTS OF OPERATIONS
(In millions, except number of shares which are reflected in thousands and per share amounts)

Three years ended September 24, 2011	2011	2010	2009
Net sales	$108,249	$ 65,225	$ 42,905
Cost of sales	64,431	39,541	25,683
Gross margin	43,818	25,684	17,222
Operating expenses:			
Research and development	2,429	1,782	1,333
Selling, general and administrative	7,599	5,517	4,149
Total operating expenses	10,028	7,299	5,482
Operating income	33,790	18,385	11,740
Other income and expense	415	155	326
Income before provision for income taxes	34,205	18,540	12,066
Provision for income taxes	8,283	4,527	3,831
Net income	$ 25,922	$ 14,013	$ 8,235
Earnings per common share:			
Basic	$ 28.05	$ 15.41	$ 9.22
Diluted	$ 27.68	$ 15.15	$ 9.08
Shares used in computing earnings per share:			
Basic	924,258	909,461	893,016
Diluted	936,645	924,712	907,005

See accompanying Notes to Consolidated Financial Statements.

CONSOLIDATED BALANCE SHEETS
(In millions, except number of shares which are reflected in thousands)

	September 24, 2011	September 25, 2010
ASSETS:		
Current assets:		
Cash and cash equivalents	$ 9,815	$ 11,261
Short-term marketable securities	16,137	14,359
Accounts receivable, less allowances of $53 and $55, respectively	5,369	5,510
Inventories	776	1,051
Deferred tax assets	2,014	1,636
Vendor non-trade receivables	6,348	4,414
Other current assets	4,529	3,447
Total current assets	44,988	41,678
Long-term marketable securities	55,618	25,391
Property, plant and equipment, net	7,777	4,768
Goodwill	896	741
Acquired intangible assets, net	3,536	342
Other assets	3,556	2,263
Total assets	$ 116,371	$ 75,183
LIABILITIES AND SHAREHOLDERS' EQUITY:		
Current liabilities:		
Accounts payable	$ 14,632	$ 12,015
Accrued expenses	9,247	5,723
Deferred revenue	4,091	2,984
Total current liabilities	27,970	20,722
Deferred revenue – non-current	1,686	1,139
Other non-current liabilities	10,100	5,531
Total liabilities	39,756	27,392
Commitments and contingencies		
Shareholders' equity:		
Common stock, no par value; 1,800,000 shares authorized; 929,277 and 915,970 shares issued and outstanding, respectively	13,331	10,668
Retained earnings	62,841	37,169
Accumulated other comprehensive income/(loss)	443	(46)
Total shareholders' equity	76,615	47,791
Total liabilities and shareholders' equity	$ 116,371	$ 75,183

See accompanying Notes to Consolidated Financial Statements.

CONSOLIDATED STATEMENTS OF SHAREHOLDERS' EQUITY
(In millions, except number of shares which are reflected in thousands)

	Common Stock		Retained Earnings	Accumulated Other Comprehensive Income/ (Loss)	Total Shareholders' Equity
	Shares	Amount			
Balances as of September 27, 2008	888,326	$ 7,177	$ 15,129	$ (9)	$22,297
Components of comprehensive income:					
Net income	0	0	8,235	0	8,235
Change in foreign currency translation	0	0	0	(14)	(14)
Change in unrealized gains/losses on marketable securities, net of tax	0	0	0	118	118
Change in unrecognized gains/losses on derivative instruments, net of tax	0	0	0	(18)	(18)
Total comprehensive income					8,321
Share-based compensation	0	707	0	0	707
Common stock issued under stock plans, net of shares withheld for employee taxes	11,480	404	(11)	0	393
Tax benefit from equity awards, including transfer pricing adjustments	0	(78)	0	0	(78)
Balances as of September 26, 2009	899,806	8,210	23,353	77	31,640
Components of comprehensive income:					
Net income	0	0	14,013	0	14,013
Change in foreign currency translation	0	0	0	7	7
Change in unrealized gains/losses on marketable securities, net of tax	0	0	0	123	123
Change in unrecognized gains/losses on derivative instruments, net of tax	0	0	0	(253)	(253)
Total comprehensive income					13,890
Share-based compensation	0	876	0	0	876
Common stock issued under stock plans, net of shares withheld for employee taxes	16,164	703	(197)	0	506
Tax benefit from equity awards, including transfer pricing adjustments	0	879	0	0	879
Balances as of September 25, 2010	915,970	10,668	37,169	(46)	47,791
Components of comprehensive income:					
Net income	0	0	25,922	0	25,922
Change in foreign currency translation	0	0	0	(12)	(12)
Change in unrealized gains/losses on marketable securities, net of tax	0	0	0	(41)	(41)
Change in unrecognized gains/losses on derivative instruments, net of tax	0	0	0	542	542
Total comprehensive income					26,411
Share-based compensation	0	1,168	0	0	1,168
Common stock issued under stock plans, net of shares withheld for employee taxes	13,307	561	(250)	0	311
Tax benefit from equity awards, including transfer pricing adjustments	0	934	0	0	934
Balances as of September 24, 2011	929,277	$13,331	$ 62,841	$ 443	$76,615

See accompanying Notes to Consolidated Financial Statements.

CONSOLIDATED STATEMENTS OF CASH FLOWS
(In millions)

Three years ended September 24, 2011	2011	2010	2009
Cash and cash equivalents, beginning of the year	$ 11,261	$ 5,263	$ 11,875
Operating activities:			
Net income	25,922	14,013	8,235
Adjustments to reconcile net income to cash generated by operating activities:			
Depreciation, amortization and accretion	1,814	1,027	734
Share-based compensation expense	1,168	879	710
Deferred income tax expense	2,868	1,440	1,040
Changes in operating assets and liabilities:			
Accounts receivable, net	143	(2,142)	(939)
Inventories	275	(596)	54
Vendor non-trade receivables	(1,934)	(2,718)	586
Other current and non-current assets	(1,391)	(1,610)	(713)
Accounts payable	2,515	6,307	92
Deferred revenue	1,654	1,217	521
Other current and non-current liabilities	4,495	778	(161)
Cash generated by operating activities	37,529	18,595	10,159
Investing activities:			
Purchases of marketable securities	(102,317)	(57,793)	(46,724)
Proceeds from maturities of marketable securities	20,437	24,930	19,790
Proceeds from sales of marketable securities	49,416	21,788	10,888
Payments made in connection with business acquisitions, net of cash acquired	(244)	(638)	0
Payments for acquisition of property, plant and equipment	(4,260)	(2,005)	(1,144)
Payments for acquisition of intangible assets	(3,192)	(116)	(69)
Other	(259)	(20)	(175)
Cash used in investing activities	(40,419)	(13,854)	(17,434)
Financing activities:			
Proceeds from issuance of common stock	831	912	475
Excess tax benefits from equity awards	1,133	751	270
Taxes paid related to net share settlement of equity awards	(520)	(406)	(82)
Cash generated by financing activities	1,444	1,257	663
(Decrease)/increase in cash and cash equivalents	(1,446)	5,998	(6,612)
Cash and cash equivalents, end of the year	$ 9,815	$ 11,261	$ 5,263
Supplemental cash flow disclosure:			
Cash paid for income taxes, net	$ 3,338	$ 2,697	$ 2,997

See accompanying Notes to Consolidated Financial Statements.

Specimen Financial Statements: PepsiCo, Inc.

PepsiCo, Inc. is a world leader in convenient snacks, foods, and beverages. The following are PepsiCo's financial statements as presented in its 2011 annual report. To access PepsiCo's complete annual report, including notes to the financial statements, follow these steps:

1. Go to **www.pepsico.com**.
2. Select Annual Reports under the Investors tab.
3. Select the 2011 Annual Report Download.
4. An index to the company's financials is provided on page 23. The Notes to Consolidated Financial Statements, for example, begin on page 56.

Consolidated Statement of Income

Fiscal years ended December 31, 2011, December 25, 2010 and December 26, 2009
(in millions except per share amounts)

	2011	2010	2009
Net Revenue	$66,504	$57,838	$43,232
Cost of sales	31,593	26,575	20,099
Selling, general and administrative expenses	25,145	22,814	15,026
Amortization of intangible assets	133	117	63
Operating Profit	9,633	8,332	8,044
Bottling equity income	–	735	365
Interest expense	(856)	(903)	(397)
Interest income and other	57	68	67
Income before income taxes	8,834	8,232	8,079
Provision for income taxes	2,372	1,894	2,100
Net income	6,462	6,338	5,979
Less: Net income attributable to noncontrolling interests	19	18	33
Net Income Attributable to PepsiCo	$ 6,443	$ 6,320	$ 5,946
Net Income Attributable to PepsiCo per Common Share			
Basic	$ 4.08	$ 3.97	$ 3.81
Diluted	$ 4.03	$ 3.91	$ 3.77
Weighted-average common shares outstanding			
Basic	1,576	1,590	1,558
Diluted	1,597	1,614	1,577
Cash dividends declared per common share	$ 2.025	$ 1.89	$ 1.775

See accompanying notes to consolidated financial statements

Consolidated Statement of Cash Flows

Fiscal years ended December 31, 2011, December 25, 2010 and December 26, 2009
(in millions)

	2011	2010	2009
Operating Activities			
Net income	$ 6,462	$ 6,338	$ 5,979
Depreciation and amortization	2,737	2,327	1,635
Stock-based compensation expense	326	299	227
Restructuring and impairment charges	383	–	36
Cash payments for restructuring charges	(31)	(31)	(196)
Merger and integration costs	329	808	50
Cash payments for merger and integration costs	(377)	(385)	(49)
Gain on previously held equity interests in PBG and PAS	–	(958)	–
Asset write-off	–	145	–
Non-cash foreign exchange loss related to Venezuela devaluation	–	120	–
Excess tax benefits from share-based payment arrangements	(70)	(107)	(42)
Pension and retiree medical plan contributions	(349)	(1,734)	(1,299)
Pension and retiree medical plan expenses	571	453	423
Bottling equity income, net of dividends	–	42	(235)
Deferred income taxes and other tax charges and credits	495	500	284
Change in accounts and notes receivable	(666)	(268)	188
Change in inventories	(331)	276	17
Change in prepaid expenses and other current assets	(27)	144	(127)
Change in accounts payable and other current liabilities	520	488	(133)
Change in income taxes payable	(340)	123	319
Other, net	(688)	(132)	(281)
Net Cash Provided by Operating Activities	8,944	8,448	6,796
Investing Activities			
Capital spending	(3,339)	(3,253)	(2,128)
Sales of property, plant and equipment	84	81	58
Acquisitions of PBG and PAS, net of cash and cash equivalents acquired	–	(2,833)	–
Acquisition of manufacturing and distribution rights from DPSG	–	(900)	–
Acquisition of WBD, net of cash and cash equivalents acquired	(2,428)	–	–
Investment in WBD	(164)	(463)	–
Other acquisitions and investments in noncontrolled affiliates	(601)	(83)	(500)
Divestitures	780	12	99
Cash restricted for pending acquisitions	–	–	15
Short-term investments, by original maturity			
More than three months—purchases	–	(12)	(29)
More than three months—maturities	21	29	71
Three months or less, net	45	(229)	13
Other investing, net	(16)	(17)	–
Net Cash Used for Investing Activities	(5,618)	(7,668)	(2,401)
Financing Activities			
Proceeds from issuances of long-term debt	$ 3,000	$ 6,451	$ 1,057
Payments of long-term debt	(1,596)	(59)	(226)
Debt repurchase	(771)	(500)	–
Short-term borrowings, by original maturity			
More than three months—proceeds	523	227	26
More than three months—payments	(559)	(96)	(81)
Three months or less, net	339	2,351	(963)
Cash dividends paid	(3,157)	(2,978)	(2,732)
Share repurchases—common	(2,489)	(4,978)	–
Share repurchases—preferred	(7)	(5)	(7)
Proceeds from exercises of stock options	945	1,038	413
Excess tax benefits from share-based payment arrangements	70	107	42
Acquisition of noncontrolling interests	(1,406)	(159)	–
Other financing	(27)	(13)	(26)
Net Cash (Used for)/Provided by Financing Activities	(5,135)	1,386	(2,497)
Effect of exchange rate changes on cash and cash equivalents	(67)	(166)	(19)
Net (Decrease)/Increase in Cash and Cash Equivalents	(1,876)	2,000	1,879
Cash and Cash Equivalents, Beginning of Year	5,943	3,943	2,064
Cash and Cash Equivalents, End of Year	$ 4,067	$ 5,943	$ 3,943
Non-cash activity:			
Issuance of common stock and equity awards in connection with our acquisitions of PBG and PAS, as reflected in investing and financing activities	–	$ 4,451	–

See accompanying notes to consolidated financial statements

Consolidated Balance Sheet

December 31, 2011 and December 25, 2010
(in millions except per share amounts)

	2011	2010
ASSETS		
Current Assets		
Cash and cash equivalents	$ 4,067	$ 5,943
Short-term investments	358	426
Accounts and notes receivable, net	6,912	6,323
Inventories	3,827	3,372
Prepaid expenses and other current assets	2,277	1,505
Total Current Assets	17,441	17,569
Property, Plant and Equipment, net	19,698	19,058
Amortizable Intangible Assets, net	1,888	2,025
Goodwill	16,800	14,661
Other nonamortizable intangible assets	14,557	11,783
Nonamortizable Intangible Assets	31,357	26,444
Investments in Noncontrolled Affiliates	1,477	1,368
Other Assets	1,021	1,689
Total Assets	$ 72,882	$ 68,153
LIABILITIES AND EQUITY		
Current Liabilities		
Short-term obligations	$ 6,205	$ 4,898
Accounts payable and other current liabilities	11,757	10,923
Income taxes payable	192	71
Total Current Liabilities	18,154	15,892
Long-Term Debt Obligations	20,568	19,999
Other Liabilities	8,266	6,729
Deferred Income Taxes	4,995	4,057
Total Liabilities	51,983	46,677
Commitments and Contingencies		
Preferred Stock, no par value	41	41
Repurchased Preferred Stock	(157)	(150)
PepsiCo Common Shareholders' Equity		
Common stock, par value 1²/₃¢ per share (authorized 3,600 shares, issued 1,865 shares)	31	31
Capital in excess of par value	4,461	4,527
Retained earnings	40,316	37,090
Accumulated other comprehensive loss	(6,229)	(3,630)
Repurchased common stock, at cost (301 and 284 shares, respectively)	(17,875)	(16,745)
Total PepsiCo Common Shareholders' Equity	20,704	21,273
Noncontrolling interests	311	312
Total Equity	20,899	21,476
Total Liabilities and Equity	$ 72,882	$ 68,153

See accompanying notes to consolidated financial statements

Consolidated Statement of Equity

Fiscal years ended December 31, 2011, December 25, 2010 and December 26, 2009
(in millions)

	2011		2010		2009	
	Shares	Amount	Shares	Amount	Shares	Amount
Preferred Stock	0.8	$ 41	0.8	$ 41	0.8	$ 41
Repurchased Preferred Stock						
Balance, beginning of year	(0.6)	(150)	(0.6)	(145)	(0.5)	(138)
Redemptions	(–)	(7)	(–)	(5)	(0.1)	(7)
Balance, end of year	(0.6)	(157)	(0.6)	(150)	(0.6)	(145)
Common Stock						
Balance, beginning of year	1,865	31	1,782	30	1,782	30
Shares issued in connection with our acquisitions of PBG and PAS	–	–	83	1	–	–
Balance, end of year	1,865	31	1,865	31	1,782	30
Capital in Excess of Par Value						
Balance, beginning of year		4,527		250		351
Stock-based compensation expense		326		299		227
Stock option exercises/RSUs converted[a]		(361)		(500)		(292)
Withholding tax on RSUs converted		(56)		(68)		(36)
Equity issued in connection with our acquisitions of PBG and PAS		–		4,451		–
Other		25		95		–
Balance, end of year		4,461		4,527		250
Retained Earnings						
Balance, beginning of year		37,090		33,805		30,638
Net income attributable to PepsiCo		6,443		6,320		5,946
Cash dividends declared — common		(3,192)		(3,028)		(2,768)
Cash dividends declared — preferred		(1)		(1)		(2)
Cash dividends declared — RSUs		(24)		(12)		(9)
Other		–		6		–
Balance, end of year		40,316		37,090		33,805
Accumulated Other Comprehensive Loss						
Balance, beginning of year		(3,630)		(3,794)		(4,694)
Currency translation adjustment		(1,529)		312		800
Cash flow hedges, net of tax:						
Net derivative losses		(83)		(111)		(55)
Reclassification of net losses to net income		14		53		28
Pension and retiree medical, net of tax:						
Net pension and retiree medical (losses)/gains		(1,110)		(280)		21
Reclassification of net losses to net income		133		166		86
Unrealized (losses)/gains on securities, net of tax		(8)		23		20
Other		(16)		1		–
Balance, end of year		(6,229)		(3,630)		(3,794)
Repurchased Common Stock						
Balance, beginning of year	(284)	(16,745)	(217)	(13,383)	(229)	(14,122)
Share repurchases	(39)	(2,489)	(76)	(4,978)	–	–
Stock option exercises	20	1,251	24	1,487	11	649
Other	2	108	(15)	129	1	90
Balance, end of year	(301)	(17,875)	(284)	(16,745)	(217)	(13,383)
Total Common Shareholders' Equity		20,704		21,273		16,908
Noncontrolling Interests						
Balance, beginning of year		312		638		476
Net income attributable to noncontrolling interests		19		18		33
Distributions to noncontrolling interests, net		(24)		(6)		–
Currency translation adjustment		65		(13)		(12)
Acquisitions and divestitures		(57)		(326)		150
Other, net		(4)		1		(9)
Balance, end of year		311		312		638
Total Equity		$ 20,899		$ 21,476		$ 17,442

(a) Includes total tax benefits of $43 million in 2011, $75 million in 2010 and $31 million in 2009.

(Continued on following page)

Consolidated Statement of Equity
(continued)

Fiscal years ended December 31, 2011, December 25, 2010 and December 26, 2009 (in millions)	2011	2010	2009
Comprehensive Income			
Net income	$ 6,462	$6,338	$5,979
Other comprehensive (loss)/income			
Currency translation adjustment	(1,464)	299	788
Cash flow hedges, net of tax	(69)	(58)	(27)
Pension and retiree medical, net of tax:			
Net prior service (cost)/credit	(10)	22	(3)
Net (losses)/gains	(967)	(136)	110
Unrealized (losses)/gains on securities, net of tax	(8)	23	20
Other	(16)	1	–
	(2,534)	151	888
Comprehensive income	3,928	6,489	6,867
Comprehensive income attributable to noncontrolling interests	(84)	(5)	(21)
Comprehensive Income Attributable to PepsiCo	$ 3,844	$6,484	$6,846

See accompanying notes to consolidated financial statements

Specimen Financial Statements: The Coca-Cola Company

The Coca-Cola Company is a global leader in the beverage industry. It offers hundreds of brands, including soft drinks, fruit juices, sports drinks and other beverages in more than 200 countries. The following are Coca-Cola's financial statements as presented in its 2011 annual report. To access Coca-Cola's complete annual report, including notes to the financial statements, follow these steps:

1. Go to **www.thecoca-colacompany.com**.
2. Select Reports & Financial Information under the Investors tab.
3. Select Annual & Other Reports and then 2011 Annual Report on Form 10-K.
4. Use the Bookmarks section on the left to find specific information. The Notes to Consolidated Financial Statements, for example, begin on page 82.

THE COCA-COLA COMPANY AND SUBSIDIARIES
CONSOLIDATED STATEMENTS OF INCOME

Year Ended December 31,	2011	2010	2009
(In millions except per share data)			
NET OPERATING REVENUES	$ 46,542	$ 35,119	$ 30,990
Cost of goods sold	18,216	12,693	11,088
GROSS PROFIT	28,326	22,426	19,902
Selling, general and administrative expenses	17,440	13,158	11,358
Other operating charges	732	819	313
OPERATING INCOME	10,154	8,449	8,231
Interest income	483	317	249
Interest expense	417	733	355
Equity income (loss) — net	690	1,025	781
Other income (loss) — net	529	5,185	40
INCOME BEFORE INCOME TAXES	11,439	14,243	8,946
Income taxes	2,805	2,384	2,040
CONSOLIDATED NET INCOME	8,634	11,859	6,906
Less: Net income attributable to noncontrolling interests	62	50	82
NET INCOME ATTRIBUTABLE TO SHAREOWNERS OF THE COCA-COLA COMPANY	$ 8,572	$ 11,809	$ 6,824
BASIC NET INCOME PER SHARE[1]	$ 3.75	$ 5.12	$ 2.95
DILUTED NET INCOME PER SHARE[1]	$ 3.69	$ 5.06	$ 2.93
AVERAGE SHARES OUTSTANDING	2,284	2,308	2,314
Effect of dilutive securities	39	25	15
AVERAGE SHARES OUTSTANDING ASSUMING DILUTION	2,323	2,333	2,329

[1] Basic net income per share and diluted net income per share are calculated based on net income attributable to shareowners of The Coca-Cola Company.

Refer to Notes to Consolidated Financial Statements.

THE COCA-COLA COMPANY AND SUBSIDIARIES

CONSOLIDATED BALANCE SHEETS

December 31,	2011	2010
(In millions except par value)		
ASSETS		
CURRENT ASSETS		
Cash and cash equivalents	$ 12,803	$ 8,517
Short-term investments	1,088	2,682
TOTAL CASH, CASH EQUIVALENTS AND SHORT-TERM INVESTMENTS	13,891	11,199
Marketable securities	144	138
Trade accounts receivable, less allowances of $83 and $48, respectively	4,920	4,430
Inventories	3,092	2,650
Prepaid expenses and other assets	3,450	3,162
TOTAL CURRENT ASSETS	25,497	21,579
EQUITY METHOD INVESTMENTS	7,233	6,954
OTHER INVESTMENTS, PRINCIPALLY BOTTLING COMPANIES	1,141	631
OTHER ASSETS	3,495	2,121
PROPERTY, PLANT AND EQUIPMENT — net	14,939	14,727
TRADEMARKS WITH INDEFINITE LIVES	6,430	6,356
BOTTLERS' FRANCHISE RIGHTS WITH INDEFINITE LIVES	7,770	7,511
GOODWILL	12,219	11,665
OTHER INTANGIBLE ASSETS	1,250	1,377
TOTAL ASSETS	$ 79,974	$ 72,921
LIABILITIES AND EQUITY		
CURRENT LIABILITIES		
Accounts payable and accrued expenses	$ 9,009	$ 8,859
Loans and notes payable	12,871	8,100
Current maturities of long-term debt	2,041	1,276
Accrued income taxes	362	273
TOTAL CURRENT LIABILITIES	24,283	18,508
LONG-TERM DEBT	13,656	14,041
OTHER LIABILITIES	5,420	4,794
DEFERRED INCOME TAXES	4,694	4,261
THE COCA-COLA COMPANY SHAREOWNERS' EQUITY		
Common stock, $0.25 par value; Authorized — 5,600 shares;		
Issued — 3,520 and 3,520 shares, respectively	880	880
Capital surplus	11,212	10,057
Reinvested earnings	53,550	49,278
Accumulated other comprehensive income (loss)	(2,703)	(1,450)
Treasury stock, at cost — 1,257 and 1,228 shares, respectively	(31,304)	(27,762)
EQUITY ATTRIBUTABLE TO SHAREOWNERS OF THE COCA-COLA COMPANY	31,635	31,003
EQUITY ATTRIBUTABLE TO NONCONTROLLING INTERESTS	286	314
TOTAL EQUITY	31,921	31,317
TOTAL LIABILITIES AND EQUITY	$ 79,974	$ 72,921

Refer to Notes to Consolidated Financial Statements.

THE COCA-COLA COMPANY AND SUBSIDIARIES
CONSOLIDATED STATEMENTS OF CASH FLOWS

Year Ended December 31,	2011	2010	2009
(In millions)			
OPERATING ACTIVITIES			
Consolidated net income	$ 8,634	$ 11,859	$ 6,906
Depreciation and amortization	1,954	1,443	1,236
Stock-based compensation expense	354	380	241
Deferred income taxes	1,028	617	353
Equity (income) loss — net of dividends	(269)	(671)	(359)
Foreign currency adjustments	7	151	61
Significant (gains) losses on sales of assets — net	(220)	(645)	(43)
Other significant (gains) losses — net	—	(4,713)	—
Other operating charges	214	264	134
Other items	(335)	477	221
Net change in operating assets and liabilities	(1,893)	370	(564)
Net cash provided by operating activities	9,474	9,532	8,186
INVESTING ACTIVITIES			
Purchases of short-term investments	(4,057)	(4,579)	(2,130)
Proceeds from disposals of short-term investments	5,647	4,032	—
Acquisitions and investments	(977)	(2,511)	(300)
Purchases of other investments	(787)	(132)	(22)
Proceeds from disposals of bottling companies and other investments	562	972	240
Purchases of property, plant and equipment	(2,920)	(2,215)	(1,993)
Proceeds from disposals of property, plant and equipment	101	134	104
Other investing activities	(93)	(106)	(48)
Net cash provided by (used in) investing activities	(2,524)	(4,405)	(4,149)
FINANCING ACTIVITIES			
Issuances of debt	27,495	15,251	14,689
Payments of debt	(22,530)	(13,403)	(12,326)
Issuances of stock	1,569	1,666	664
Purchases of stock for treasury	(4,513)	(2,961)	(1,518)
Dividends	(4,300)	(4,068)	(3,800)
Other financing activities	45	50	(2)
Net cash provided by (used in) financing activities	(2,234)	(3,465)	(2,293)
EFFECT OF EXCHANGE RATE CHANGES ON CASH AND CASH EQUIVALENTS	(430)	(166)	576
CASH AND CASH EQUIVALENTS			
Net increase (decrease) during the year	4,286	1,496	2,320
Balance at beginning of year	8,517	7,021	4,701
Balance at end of year	$ 12,803	$ 8,517	$ 7,021

Refer to Notes to Consolidated Financial Statements.

THE COCA-COLA COMPANY AND SUBSIDIARIES
CONSOLIDATED STATEMENTS OF SHAREOWNERS' EQUITY

Year Ended December 31,	2011	2010	2009
(In millions except per share data)			
EQUITY ATTRIBUTABLE TO SHAREOWNERS OF THE COCA-COLA COMPANY			
NUMBER OF COMMON SHARES OUTSTANDING			
Balance at beginning of year	2,292	2,303	2,312
Purchases of treasury stock	(63)	(49)	(26)
Treasury stock issued to employees related to stock compensation plans	34	38	17
Balance at end of year	2,263	2,292	2,303
COMMON STOCK	$ 880	$ 880	$ 880
CAPITAL SURPLUS			
Balance at beginning of year	10,057	8,537	7,966
Stock issued to employees related to stock compensation plans	724	855	339
Replacement share-based awards issued in connection with an acquisition	—	237	—
Tax benefit (charge) from employees' stock option and restricted stock plans	79	48	(6)
Stock-based compensation	354	380	238
Other activities	(2)	—	—
Balance at end of year	11,212	10,057	8,537
REINVESTED EARNINGS			
Balance at beginning of year	49,278	41,537	38,513
Net income attributable to shareowners of The Coca-Cola Company	8,572	11,809	6,824
Dividends (per share — $1.88, $1.76 and $1.64 in 2011, 2010 and 2009, respectively)	(4,300)	(4,068)	(3,800)
Balance at end of year	53,550	49,278	41,537
ACCUMULATED OTHER COMPREHENSIVE INCOME (LOSS)			
Balance at beginning of year	(1,450)	(757)	(2,674)
Net foreign currency translation adjustment	(640)	(935)	1,824
Net gain (loss) on derivatives	145	(120)	34
Net change in unrealized gain on available-for-sale securities	(7)	102	(52)
Net change in pension and other benefit liabilities	(751)	260	111
Net other comprehensive income (loss)	(1,253)	(693)	1,917
Balance at end of year	(2,703)	(1,450)	(757)
TREASURY STOCK			
Balance at beginning of year	(27,762)	(25,398)	(24,213)
Stock issued to employees related to stock compensation plans	830	824	333
Purchases of treasury stock	(4,372)	(3,188)	(1,518)
Balance at end of year	(31,304)	(27,762)	(25,398)
TOTAL EQUITY ATTRIBUTABLE TO SHAREOWNERS OF THE COCA-COLA COMPANY	$ 31,635	$ 31,003	$ 24,799
EQUITY ATTRIBUTABLE TO NONCONTROLLING INTERESTS			
Balance at beginning of year	$ 314	$ 547	$ 390
Net income attributable to noncontrolling interests	62	50	82
Net foreign currency translation adjustment	(52)	(12)	49
Dividends paid to noncontrolling interests	(38)	(32)	(14)
Contributions by noncontrolling interests	—	1	40
Increase due to business combinations	—	13	—
Deconsolidation of certain variable interest entities	—	(253)	—
TOTAL EQUITY ATTRIBUTABLE TO NONCONTROLLING INTERESTS	$ 286	$ 314	$ 547
COMPREHENSIVE INCOME			
Consolidated net income	$ 8,634	$ 11,859	$ 6,906
Consolidated net other comprehensive income (loss)	(1,305)	(705)	1,966
CONSOLIDATED COMPREHENSIVE INCOME	$ 7,329	$ 11,154	$ 8,872

Refer to Notes to Consolidated Financial Statements.

Specimen Financial Statements: Amazon.com, Inc.

Amazon.com, Inc. is the world's largest online retailer. It also produces consumer electronics—notably the Kindle e-book reader and the Kindle Fire Tablet computer—and is a major provider of cloud computing services. The following are Amazon's financial statements as presented in the company's 2011 annual report. To access Amazon's complete annual report, including notes to the financial statements, follow these steps:

1. Go to **www.amazon.com**.
2. Select the Investor Relations link at the bottom of the page and then select the 2011 Annual Report under Annual Reports and Proxies.
3. Use the Bookmarks section on the left to find specific information. The Notes to Consolidated Financial Statements, for example, begin on page 40.

AMAZON.COM, INC.

CONSOLIDATED STATEMENTS OF CASH FLOWS

(in millions)

	Year Ended December 31,		
	2011	2010	2009
CASH AND CASH EQUIVALENTS, BEGINNING OF PERIOD	$ 3,777	$ 3,444	$ 2,769
OPERATING ACTIVITIES:			
Net income	631	1,152	902
Adjustments to reconcile net income to net cash from operating activities:			
Depreciation of fixed assets, including internal-use software and website development, and other amortization	1,083	568	378
Stock-based compensation	557	424	341
Other operating expense (income), net	154	106	103
Losses (gains) on sales of marketable securities, net	(4)	(2)	(4)
Other expense (income), net	(56)	(79)	(15)
Deferred income taxes	136	4	81
Excess tax benefits from stock-based compensation	(62)	(259)	(105)
Changes in operating assets and liabilities:			
Inventories	(1,777)	(1,019)	(531)
Accounts receivable, net and other	(866)	(295)	(481)
Accounts payable	2,997	2,373	1,859
Accrued expenses and other	1,067	740	300
Additions to unearned revenue	1,064	687	1,054
Amortization of previously unearned revenue	(1,021)	(905)	(589)
Net cash provided by operating activities	3,903	3,495	3,293
INVESTING ACTIVITIES:			
Purchases of fixed assets, including internal-use software and website development	(1,811)	(979)	(373)
Acquisitions, net of cash acquired, and other	(705)	(352)	(40)
Sales and maturities of marketable securities and other investments	6,843	4,250	1,966
Purchases of marketable securities and other investments	(6,257)	(6,279)	(3,890)
Net cash used in investing activities	(1,930)	(3,360)	(2,337)
FINANCING ACTIVITIES:			
Excess tax benefits from stock-based compensation	62	259	105
Common stock repurchased	(277)	—	—
Proceeds from long-term debt and other	177	143	87
Repayments of long-term debt, capital lease, and finance lease obligations	(444)	(221)	(472)
Net cash provided by (used in) financing activities	(482)	181	(280)
Foreign-currency effect on cash and cash equivalents	1	17	(1)
Net increase in cash and cash equivalents	1,492	333	675
CASH AND CASH EQUIVALENTS, END OF PERIOD	$ 5,269	$ 3,777	$ 3,444
SUPPLEMENTAL CASH FLOW INFORMATION:			
Cash paid for interest on long term debt	$ 14	$ 11	$ 32
Cash paid for income taxes (net of refunds)	33	75	48
Fixed assets acquired under capital leases	753	405	147
Fixed assets acquired under build-to-suit leases	259	172	188

See accompanying notes to consolidated financial statements.

AMAZON.COM, INC.

CONSOLIDATED STATEMENTS OF OPERATIONS
(in millions, except per share data)

	Year Ended December 31,		
	2011	2010	2009
Net product sales	$42,000	$30,792	$22,273
Net services sales	6,077	3,412	2,236
Total net sales	48,077	34,204	24,509
Operating expenses (1):			
Cost of sales	37,288	26,561	18,978
Fulfillment	4,576	2,898	2,052
Marketing	1,630	1,029	680
Technology and content	2,909	1,734	1,240
General and administrative	658	470	328
Other operating expense (income), net	154	106	102
Total operating expenses	47,215	32,798	23,380
Income from operations	862	1,406	1,129
Interest income	61	51	37
Interest expense	(65)	(39)	(34)
Other income (expense), net	76	79	29
Total non-operating income (expense)	72	91	32
Income before income taxes	934	1,497	1,161
Provision for income taxes	(291)	(352)	(253)
Equity-method investment activity, net of tax	(12)	7	(6)
Net income	$ 631	$ 1,152	$ 902
Basic earnings per share	$ 1.39	$ 2.58	$ 2.08
Diluted earnings per share	$ 1.37	$ 2.53	$ 2.04
Weighted average shares used in computation of earnings per share:			
Basic	453	447	433
Diluted	461	456	442

(1) Includes stock-based compensation as follows:

Fulfillment	$ 133	$ 90	$ 79
Marketing	39	27	20
Technology and content	292	223	182
General and administrative	93	84	60

See accompanying notes to consolidated financial statements.

AMAZON.COM, INC.

CONSOLIDATED BALANCE SHEETS
(in millions, except per share data)

	December 31,	
	2011	**2010**
ASSETS		
Current assets:		
Cash and cash equivalents	$ 5,269	$ 3,777
Marketable securities	4,307	4,985
Inventories	4,992	3,202
Accounts receivable, net and other	2,571	1,587
Deferred tax assets	351	196
Total current assets	17,490	13,747
Fixed assets, net	4,417	2,414
Deferred tax assets	28	22
Goodwill	1,955	1,349
Other assets	1,388	1,265
Total assets	$25,278	$18,797
LIABILITIES AND STOCKHOLDERS' EQUITY		
Current liabilities:		
Accounts payable	$11,145	$ 8,051
Accrued expenses and other	3,751	2,321
Total current liabilities	14,896	10,372
Long-term liabilities	2,625	1,561
Commitments and contingencies		
Stockholders' equity:		
Preferred stock, $0.01 par value:		
Authorized shares — 500		
Issued and outstanding shares — none	0	0
Common stock, $0.01 par value:		
Authorized shares — 5,000		
Issued shares — 473 and 468		
Outstanding shares — 455 and 451	5	5
Treasury stock, at cost	(877)	(600)
Additional paid-in capital	6,990	6,325
Accumulated other comprehensive loss	(316)	(190)
Retained earnings	1,955	1,324
Total stockholders' equity	7,757	6,864
Total liabilities and stockholders' equity	$25,278	$18,797

See accompanying notes to consolidated financial statements.

AMAZON.COM, INC.

CONSOLIDATED STATEMENTS OF STOCKHOLDERS' EQUITY

(in millions)

	Common Stock Shares	Amount	Treasury Stock	Additional Paid-In Capital	Accumulated Other Comprehensive Income (Loss)	Retained Earnings (Accumulated Deficit)	Total Stockholders' Equity
Balance at December 31, 2008	428	$ 4	$(600)	$4,121	$(123)	$ (730)	$2,672
Net income	—	—	—	—	—	902	902
Foreign currency translation gains, net of tax	—	—	—	—	62	—	62
Change in unrealized gains on available-for-sale securities, net of tax	—	—	—	—	4	—	4
Amortization of unrealized loss on terminated Euro Currency Swap, net of tax	—	—	—	—	1	—	1
Comprehensive income							969
Exercise of common stock options	7	—	—	19	—	—	19
Issuance of common stock for acquisition activity	9	1	—	1,144	—	—	1,145
Excess tax benefits from stock-based compensation	—	—	—	103	—	—	103
Stock-based compensation and issuance of employee benefit plan stock	—	—	—	349	—	—	349
Balance at December 31, 2009	444	5	(600)	5,736	(56)	172	5,257
Net income	—	—	—	—	—	1,152	1,152
Foreign currency translation gains, net of tax	—	—	—	—	(137)	—	(137)
Change in unrealized gains on available-for-sale securities, net of tax	—	—	—	—	3	—	3
Comprehensive income							1,018
Exercise of common stock options	7	—	—	16	—	—	16
Excess tax benefits from stock-based compensation	—	—	—	145	—	—	145
Stock-based compensation and issuance of employee benefit plan stock	—	—	—	428	—	—	428
Balance at December 31, 2010	451	5	(600)	6,325	(190)	1,324	6,864
Net income	—	—	—	—	—	631	631
Foreign currency translation gains, net of tax	—	—	—	—	(123)	—	(123)
Change in unrealized gains on available-for-sale securities, net of tax	—	—	—	—	(3)	—	(3)
Comprehensive income							505
Exercise of common stock options	5	—	—	7	—	—	7
Repurchase of common stock	(1)	—	(277)	—	—	—	(277)
Excess tax benefits from stock-based compensation	—	—	—	62	—	—	62
Stock-based compensation and issuance of employee benefit plan stock	—	—	—	569	—	—	569
Issuance of common stock for acquisition activity	—	—	—	27	—	—	27
Balance at December 31, 2011	455	$ 5	$(877)	$6,990	$(316)	$1,955	$7,757

See accompanying notes to consolidated financial statements.

Appendix E | Specimen Financial Statements: Wal-Mart Stores, Inc.

In 2012, Wal-Mart Stores, Inc. celebrated "50 years of helping customers save money and live better." The following are Wal-Mart's financial statements as presented in the company's 2012 annual report. To access Wal-Mart's complete annual report, including notes to the financial statements, follow these steps:

1. Go to **http://corporate.walmart.com**.
2. Select Annual Reports under the Investors tab.
3. Select the 2012 Annual Report (Wal-Mart's fiscal year ends January 31).
4. The Notes to Consolidated Financial Statements begin on page 38.

Consolidated Statements of Income

	Fiscal Years Ended January 31,		
(Amounts in millions except per share data)	2012	2011	2010
Revenues:			
Net sales	$443,854	$418,952	$405,132
Membership and other income	3,096	2,897	2,953
	446,950	421,849	408,085
Costs and expenses:			
Cost of sales	335,127	314,946	304,106
Operating, selling, general and administrative expenses	85,265	81,361	79,977
Operating income	26,558	25,542	24,002
Interest:			
Debt	2,034	1,928	1,787
Capital leases	288	277	278
Interest income	(162)	(201)	(181)
Interest, net	2,160	2,004	1,884
Income from continuing operations before income taxes	24,398	23,538	22,118
Provision for income taxes:			
Current	6,742	6,703	7,643
Deferred	1,202	876	(487)
	7,944	7,579	7,156
Income from continuing operations	16,454	15,959	14,962
Income (loss) from discontinued operations, net of tax	(67)	1,034	(79)
Consolidated net income	16,387	16,993	14,883
Less consolidated net income attributable to noncontrolling interest	(688)	(604)	(513)
Consolidated net income attributable to Walmart	$ 15,699	$ 16,389	$ 14,370
Basic net income per common share:			
Basic income per common share from continuing operations attributable to Walmart	$ 4.56	$ 4.20	$ 3.74
Basic income (loss) per common share from discontinued operations attributable to Walmart	(0.02)	0.28	(0.02)
Basic net income per common share attributable to Walmart	$ 4.54	$ 4.48	$ 3.72
Diluted net income per common share:			
Diluted income per common share from continuing operations attributable to Walmart	$ 4.54	$ 4.18	$ 3.73
Diluted income (loss) per common share from discontinued operations attributable to Walmart	(0.02)	0.29	(0.02)
Diluted net income per common share attributable to Walmart	$ 4.52	$ 4.47	$ 3.71
Weighted-average common shares outstanding:			
Basic	3,460	3,656	3,866
Diluted	3,474	3,670	3,877
Dividends declared per common share	$ 1.46	$ 1.21	$ 1.09

See accompanying notes.

Consolidated Balance Sheets

	As of January 31,	
(Amounts in millions except per share data)	**2012**	2011
ASSETS		
Current assets:		
Cash and cash equivalents	$ 6,550	$ 7,395
Receivables, net	5,937	5,089
Inventories	40,714	36,437
Prepaid expenses and other	1,685	2,960
Current assets of discontinued operations	89	131
Total current assets	54,975	52,012
Property and equipment:		
Property and equipment	155,002	148,584
Less accumulated depreciation	(45,399)	(43,486)
Property and equipment, net	109,603	105,098
Property under capital lease:		
Property under capital lease	5,936	5,905
Less accumulated amortization	(3,215)	(3,125)
Property under capital lease, net	2,721	2,780
Goodwill	20,651	16,763
Other assets and deferred charges	5,456	4,129
Total assets	**$193,406**	**$180,782**
LIABILITIES AND EQUITY		
Current liabilities:		
Short-term borrowings	$ 4,047	$ 1,031
Accounts payable	36,608	33,676
Accrued liabilities	18,154	18,701
Accrued income taxes	1,164	157
Long-term debt due within one year	1,975	4,655
Obligations under capital leases due within one year	326	336
Current liabilities of discontinued operations	26	47
Total current liabilities	62,300	58,603
Long-term debt	44,070	40,692
Long-term obligations under capital leases	3,009	3,150
Deferred income taxes and other	7,862	6,682
Redeemable noncontrolling interest	404	408
Commitments and contingencies		
Equity:		
Preferred stock ($0.10 par value; 100 shares authorized, none issued)	—	—
Common stock ($0.10 par value; 11,000 shares authorized, 3,418 and 3,516 issued and outstanding at January 31, 2012 and 2011, respectively)	342	352
Capital in excess of par value	3,692	3,577
Retained earnings	68,691	63,967
Accumulated other comprehensive income (loss)	(1,410)	646
Total Walmart shareholders' equity	71,315	68,542
Noncontrolling interest	4,446	2,705
Total equity	75,761	71,247
Total liabilities and equity	**$193,406**	**$180,782**

See accompanying notes.

Consolidated Statements of Shareholders' Equity

(Amounts in millions, except per share data)	Common Stock Shares	Common Stock Amount	Capital in Excess of Par Value	Retained Earnings	Accumulated Other Comprehensive Income (Loss)	Total Walmart Shareholders' Equity	Noncontrolling Interest	Total Equity
Balances — February 1, 2009	3,925	$ 393	$3,920	$ 63,344	$(2,688)	$ 64,969	$1,794	$ 66,763
Consolidated net income (excludes redeemable noncontrolling interest)	—	—	—	14,370	—	14,370	499	14,869
Other comprehensive income	—	—	—	—	2,618	2,618	64	2,682
Cash dividends ($1.09 per share)	—	—	—	(4,217)	—	(4,217)	—	(4,217)
Purchase of Company stock	(145)	(15)	(246)	(7,136)	—	(7,397)	—	(7,397)
Purchase of redeemable noncontrolling interest	—	—	(288)	—	—	(288)	—	(288)
Other	6	—	417	(4)	—	413	(177)	236
Balances — January 31, 2010	3,786	378	3,803	66,357	(70)	70,468	2,180	72,648
Consolidated net income (excludes redeemable noncontrolling interest)	—	—	—	16,389	—	16,389	584	16,973
Other comprehensive income	—	—	—	—	716	716	162	878
Cash dividends ($1.21 per share)	—	—	—	(4,437)	—	(4,437)	—	(4,437)
Purchase of Company stock	(280)	(28)	(487)	(14,319)	—	(14,834)	—	(14,834)
Other	10	2	261	(23)	—	240	(221)	19
Balances — January 31, 2011	3,516	352	3,577	63,967	646	68,542	2,705	71,247
Consolidated net income (excludes redeemable noncontrolling interest)	—	—	—	15,699	—	15,699	627	16,326
Other comprehensive loss	—	—	—	—	(2,056)	(2,056)	(660)	(2,716)
Cash dividends ($1.46 per share)	—	—	—	(5,048)	—	(5,048)	—	(5,048)
Purchase of Company stock	(113)	(11)	(229)	(5,930)	—	(6,170)	—	(6,170)
Noncontrolling interest of acquired entity	—	—	—	—	—	—	1,988	1,988
Other	15	1	344	3	—	348	(214)	134
Balances — January 31, 2012	3,418	$ 342	$3,692	$ 68,691	$(1,410)	$ 71,315	$4,446	$ 75,761

See accompanying notes.

Consolidated Statements of Comprehensive Income

(Amounts in millions)	Fiscal Years Ended January 31, 2012	2011	2010
Consolidated net income:			
Consolidated net income [1]	$16,387	$16,993	$14,883
Other comprehensive income:			
Currency translation [2]	(2,758)	1,137	2,854
Net change in fair values of derivatives	(67)	(17)	94
Change in minimum pension liability	43	(145)	(220)
Total comprehensive income	13,605	17,968	17,611
Less amounts attributable to the noncontrolling interest:			
Consolidated net income [1]	(688)	(604)	(513)
Currency translation [2]	726	(259)	(110)
Amounts attributable to the noncontrolling interest	38	(863)	(623)
Comprehensive income attributable to Walmart	**$13,643**	$17,105	$16,988

(1) Includes $61 million, $20 million and $14 million in fiscal 2012, 2011 and 2010, respectively, related to the redeemable noncontrolling interest.

(2) Includes $(66) million, $97 million and $46 million in fiscal 2012, 2011 and 2010, respectively, related to the redeemable noncontrolling interest.

See accompanying notes.

Consolidated Statements of Cash Flows

(Amounts in millions)	Fiscal Years Ended January 31,		
	2012	2011	2010
Cash flows from operating activities:			
Consolidated net income	$ 16,387	$ 16,993	$ 14,883
Loss (income) from discontinued operations, net of tax	67	(1,034)	79
Income from continuing operations	16,454	15,959	14,962
Adjustments to reconcile income from continuing operations to net cash provided by operating activities:			
Depreciation and amortization	8,130	7,641	7,157
Deferred income taxes	1,050	651	(504)
Other operating activities	398	1,087	318
Changes in certain assets and liabilities, net of effects of acquisitions:			
Accounts receivable	(796)	(733)	(297)
Inventories	(3,727)	(3,205)	2,213
Accounts payable	2,687	2,676	1,052
Accrued liabilities	59	(433)	1,348
Net cash provided by operating activities	24,255	23,643	26,249
Cash flows from investing activities:			
Payments for property and equipment	(13,510)	(12,699)	(12,184)
Proceeds from disposal of property and equipment	580	489	1,002
Investments and business acquisitions, net of cash acquired	(3,548)	(202)	—
Other investing activities	(131)	219	(438)
Net cash used in investing activities	(16,609)	(12,193)	(11,620)
Cash flows from financing activities:			
Net change in short-term borrowings	3,019	503	(1,033)
Proceeds from issuance of long-term debt	5,050	11,396	5,546
Payments of long-term debt	(4,584)	(4,080)	(6,033)
Dividends paid	(5,048)	(4,437)	(4,217)
Purchase of Company stock	(6,298)	(14,776)	(7,276)
Purchase of redeemable noncontrolling interest	—	—	(436)
Payment of capital lease obligations	(355)	(363)	(346)
Other financing activities	(242)	(271)	(396)
Net cash used in financing activities	(8,458)	(12,028)	(14,191)
Effect of exchange rates on cash and cash equivalents	(33)	66	194
Net increase (decrease) in cash and cash equivalents	(845)	(512)	632
Cash and cash equivalents at beginning of year	7,395	7,907	7,275
Cash and cash equivalents at end of year	$ 6,550	$ 7,395	$ 7,907
Supplemental disclosure of cash flow information:			
Income tax paid	$ 5,899	$ 6,984	$ 7,389
Interest paid	2,346	2,163	2,141

See accompanying notes.

Specimen Financial Statements: Zetar plc

Zetar plc is a leading U.K. manufacturer of confectionery and natural snacks with a reputation for quality and product innovation. Note that its financial statements are IFRS-based and are presented in British pounds (£). To access the company's complete 2011 annual report, including notes to the financial statements, follow these steps:

1. Go to **www.zetarplc.com**.
2. Select Reports & Presentations under the Investors tab.
3. Select Report & Accounts for the year ended 30th April 2011.
4. Use the Bookmarks sections on the left to navigate through the annual report. The Notes to the consolidated financial statements, for example, begin on page 28.

Consolidated income statement

FOR THE YEAR ENDED 30 APRIL 2011

	Note	2011 Adjusted[1] results £'000	2011 Adjusting items £'000	2011 Total £'000	2010 Adjusted[1] results £'000	2010 Adjusting items £'000	2010 Total £'000
Revenue	5	134,998	–	134,998	131,922	–	131,922
Cost of sales		(107,677)	–	(107,677)	(105,112)	–	(105,112)
Gross profit		27,321	–	27,321	26,810	–	26,810
Distribution costs		(5,550)	–	(5,550)	(5,495)	–	(5,495)
Administrative expenses:							
– other administrative expenses		(14,271)	(267)	(14,538)	(14,003)	–	(14,003)
– amortisation of intangible assets	15	–	(170)	(170)	–	(299)	(299)
– share-based payments	10	–	(330)	(330)	–	(287)	(287)
Operating profit		7,500	(767)	6,733	7,312	(586)	6,726
Finance income	9	3	–	3	11	–	11
Finance costs	9	(793)	(308)	(1,101)	(968)	201	(767)
Profit from continuing operations before taxation		6,710	(1,075)	5,635	6,355	(385)	5,970
Tax on profit from continuing activities	11	(1,764)	108	(1,656)	(1,722)	20	(1,702)
Net result from continuing operations		4,946	(967)	3,979	4,633	(365)	4,268
Net result from discontinued operations	34	–	503	503	–	–	–
Profit for the year		4,946	(464)	4,482	4,633	(365)	4,268
Basic earnings per share (p)	13			35.1			32.6
Diluted earnings/per share (p)	13			34.9			32.6
Adjusted basic earnings per share (p)[1]	13	38.7			35.4		
Adjusted diluted earnings per share (p)[1]	13	38.5			35.4		

[1] Adjusted operating profit and adjusted earnings per share are stated before one-off items, amortisation of intangible assets, share-based payments and the fair value movement on financial instruments.

Consolidated statement of comprehensive income

FOR THE YEAR ENDED 30 APRIL 2011

	2011 Total £'000	2010 Total £'000
Profit for the year	4,482	4,268
Other comprehensive income:		
– currency translation differences	245	(917)
Other comprehensive income	245	(917)
Total comprehensive income for the year	4,727	3,351
Attributable to:		
– owners of the parent	4,727	3,351

Consolidated balance sheet
AT 30 APRIL 2011

	Note	2011 £'000	2010 £'000
Non-current assets			
Goodwill	14	**30,520**	30,342
Other intangible assets	15	**140**	309
Property, plant and equipment	16	**16,583**	14,886
Deferred tax asset	22	**149**	213
		47,392	45,750
Current assets			
Inventories	17	**16,453**	16,039
Trade and other receivables	18	**24,935**	19,062
Cash at bank	27	**4,282**	4,257
		45,670	39,358
Total assets		**93,062**	85,108
Current liabilities			
Trade and other payables	19	**(25,075)**	(25,176)
Deferred consideration	12	**(38)**	–
Current tax liabilities		**(620)**	(524)
Obligations under finance leases	20	**(75)**	(90)
Derivative financial instruments	30	**(157)**	(406)
Borrowings and overdrafts	21	**(14,509)**	(12,885)
		(40,474)	(39,081)
Net current assets		**5,196**	277
Non-current liabilities			
Deferred consideration		**–**	(300)
Deferred tax liabilities	22	**(1,750)**	(1,605)
Obligations under finance leases	20	**(15)**	(77)
Borrowings and overdrafts	21	**(4,536)**	(2,290)
		(6,301)	(4,272)
Total liabilities		**(46,775)**	(43,353)
Net assets		**46,287**	41,755
Equity			
Share capital	23	**1,324**	1,324
Share premium account	24	**28,266**	28,266
Merger reserve		**3,411**	3,411
Equity reserve	25	**2,664**	2,089
Retained earnings	25	**10,622**	6,665
Total equity attributable to equity holders of the parent		**46,287**	41,755

The financial statements were approved by the Board for issue on 20 July 2011.

Consolidated cash flow statement
FOR THE YEAR ENDED 30 APRIL 2011

	Note	2011 £'000	2010 £'000
Cash flow from operating activities			
Profit from continuing operations before taxation		5,635	5,970
Finance costs		1,101	767
Interest income		(3)	(11)
Share-based payments		330	287
Depreciation	6	2,267	2,337
Loss/(profit) on sale of plant and equipment	6	9	(113)
Amortisation of intangible assets	6	170	299
Net movement in working capital		(6,040)	(179)
Decrease/(increase) in inventories		72	(1,720)
(Increase)/decrease in receivables		(5,295)	128
(Decrease)/increase in payables		(817)	1,413
Total cash flow from operations		3,469	9,357
Net interest paid	9	(1,347)	(957)
Tax paid		(1,369)	(1,415)
Total cash flow from operating activities		753	6,985
Cash flow from investing activities			
Purchase of property, plant and equipment		(3,789)	(2,098)
Proceeds from sale of plant and equipment		45	259
Disposal of subsidiary		500	–
Total cash impact of acquisitions		(848)	(220)
Acquisition of business		(483)	(220)
Net borrowings assumed on acquisition		(365)	–
Net cash flow from investing activities		(4,092)	(2,059)
Cash flow from financing activities			
Net proceeds from issue of ordinary share capital		–	14
Purchase of own shares		(525)	(250)
Proceeds from new borrowings		7,000	–
Repayment of borrowings		(5,174)	(2,545)
Finance lease repayments		(91)	(214)
Net cash flow from financing activities		1,210	(2,995)
Net (decrease)/increase in cash and cash equivalents		(2,129)	1,931
Cash and cash equivalents at beginning of the year		(6,608)	(8,127)
Effect of foreign exchange rate movements		96	(412)
Cash and cash equivalents at the end of the year		(8,641)	(6,608)
Cash and cash equivalents comprise:			
– cash at bank	27	4,282	4,257
– bank overdraft	27	(12,923)	(10,865)
		(8,641)	(6,608)

Consolidated statement of changes in equity
FOR THE YEAR ENDED 30 APRIL 2011

		Attributable to equity holders of the parent				
	Share capital £'000	Share premium account £'000	Merger reserve £'000	Equity reserve £'000	Retained earnings £'000	Total £'000
Balance at 1 May 2009	1,324	28,252	3,411	2,719	2,647	38,353
Comprehensive income						
Profit for the year	–	–	–	–	4,268	4,268
Other comprehensive income						
Exchange (loss) on translation of foreign operations	–	–	–	(917)	–	(917)
Total other comprehensive income	–	–	–	(917)	–	(917)
Total comprehensive income	–	–	–	(917)	4,268	3,351
Transactions with owners:						
– issue of new ordinary shares	–	14	–	–	–	14
– purchase of own shares	–	–	–	–	(250)	(250)
– share-based payment charge	–	–	–	287	–	287
Total transactions with owners	–	14	–	287	(250)	51
Balance at 30 April 2010	1,324	28,266	3,411	2,089	6,665	41,755
Comprehensive income						
Profit for the year	–	–	–	–	4,482	4,482
Other comprehensive income						
Exchange gain on translation of foreign operations	–	–	–	245	–	245
Total other comprehensive income	–	–	–	245	–	245
Total comprehensive income	–	–	–	245	4,482	4,727
Transactions with owners:						
– purchase of own shares	–	–	–	–	(525)	(525)
– share-based payment charge	–	–	–	330	–	330
Total transactions with owners	–	–	–	330	(525)	(195)
Balance at 30 April 2011	1,324	28,266	3,411	2,664	10,622	46,287

Time Value of Money

Learning Objectives

After studying this appendix, you should be able to:

[1] Distinguish between simple and compound interest.

[2] Identify the variables fundamental to solving present value problems.

[3] Solve for present value of a single amount.

[4] Solve for present value of an annuity.

[5] Compute the present value of notes and bonds.

Nature of Interest

Would you rather receive $1,000 today or a year from now? You should prefer to receive the $1,000 today because you can invest the $1,000 and earn interest on it. As a result, you will have more than $1,000 a year from now. What this example illustrates is the concept of the **time value of money**. Everyone prefers to receive money today rather than in the future because of the interest factor.

Interest is payment for the use of another person's money. It is the difference between the amount borrowed or invested (called the **principal**) and the amount repaid or collected. The amount of interest to be paid or collected is usually stated as a rate over a specific period of time. The rate of interest is generally stated as an **annual rate**.

The amount of interest involved in any financing transaction is based on three elements:

1. **Principal (p):** The original amount borrowed or invested.
2. **Interest Rate (i):** An annual percentage of the principal.
3. **Time (n):** The number of years that the principal is borrowed or invested.

Simple Interest

Simple interest is computed on the principal amount only. It is the return on the principal for one period. Simple interest is usually expressed as shown in Illustration G-1.

Interest	=	Principal	×	Rate	×	Time
		p		*i*		*n*

For example, if you borrowed $5,000 for 2 years at a simple interest rate of 6% annually, you would pay $600 in total interest computed as follows.

$$Interest = p \times i \times n$$
$$= \$5,000 \times .06 \times 2$$
$$= \$600$$

Illustration G-1
Interest computation

LEARNING OBJECTIVE   **1**

Distinguish between simple and compound interest.

Compound Interest

Compound interest is computed on principal **and** on any interest earned that has not been paid or withdrawn. It is the return on the principal for two or more time periods. Compounding computes interest not only on the principal but also on the interest earned to date on that principal, assuming the interest is left on deposit.

To illustrate the difference between simple and compound interest, assume that you deposit $1,000 in Bank Two, where it will earn **simple interest** of 9% per year, and you deposit another $1,000 in Citizens Bank, where it will earn compound interest of 9% per year **compounded annually**. Also assume that in both cases you will not withdraw any interest until three years from the date of deposit. Illustration G-2 shows the computation of interest you will receive and the accumulated year-end balances.

Illustration G-2
Simple versus compound interest

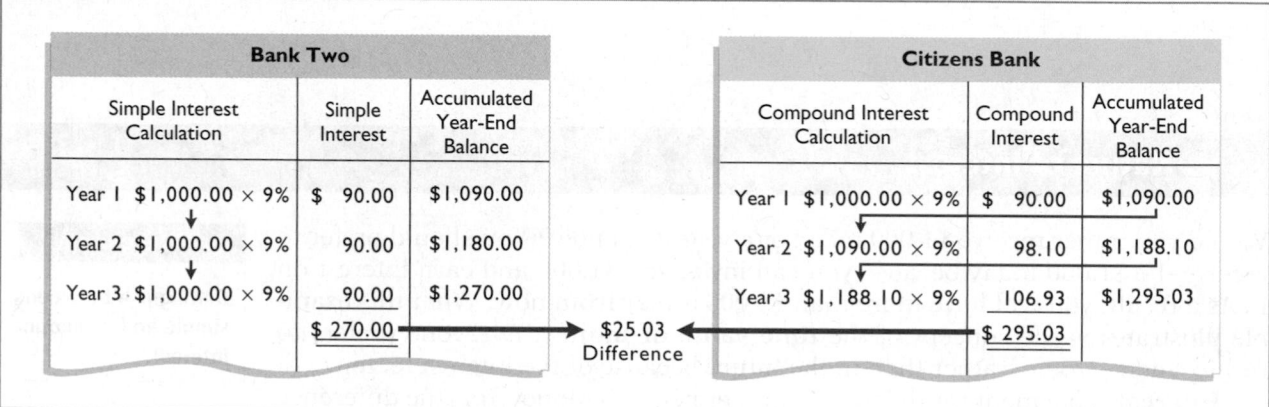

Bank Two				Citizens Bank		
Simple Interest Calculation	Simple Interest	Accumulated Year-End Balance		Compound Interest Calculation	Compound Interest	Accumulated Year-End Balance
Year 1 $1,000.00 × 9%	$ 90.00	$1,090.00		Year 1 $1,000.00 × 9%	$ 90.00	$1,090.00
Year 2 $1,000.00 × 9%	90.00	$1,180.00		Year 2 $1,090.00 × 9%	98.10	$1,188.10
Year 3 $1,000.00 × 9%	90.00	$1,270.00		Year 3 $1,188.10 × 9%	106.93	$1,295.03
	$ 270.00		$25.03 Difference		$ 295.03	

Note in Illustration G-2 that simple interest uses the initial principal of $1,000 to compute the interest in all three years. Compound interest uses the accumulated balance (principal plus interest to date) at each year-end to compute interest in the succeeding year—which explains why your compound interest account is larger.

Obviously, if you had a choice between investing your money at simple interest or at compound interest, you would choose compound interest, all other things—especially risk—being equal. In the example, compounding provides $25.03 of additional interest income. For practical purposes, compounding assumes that unpaid interest earned becomes a part of the principal. The accumulated balance at the end of each year becomes the new principal on which interest is earned during the next year.

Illustration G-2 indicates that you should invest your money at the bank that compounds interest annually. Most business situations use compound interest. Simple interest is generally applicable only to short-term situations of one year or less.

Present Value Concepts

LEARNING OBJECTIVE   2

Identify the variables fundamental to solving present value problems.

The **present value** is the value now of a given amount to be paid or received in the future, assuming compound interest. The present value is based on three variables: (1) the dollar amount to be received (future amount), (2) the length of time until the amount is received (number of periods), and (3) the interest rate (the discount rate). The process of determining the present value is referred to as **discounting the future amount**.

In this textbook, we use present value computations in measuring several items. For example, Chapter 15 computed the present value of the principal and interest payments to determine the market price of a bond. In addition, determining the amount to be reported for notes payable and lease liabilities involves present value computations.

Present Value of a Single Amount

To illustrate present value, assume that you want to invest a sum of money that will yield $1,000 at the end of one year. What amount would you need to invest today to have $1,000 one year from now? Illustration G-3 shows the formula for calculating present value.

> **LEARNING OBJECTIVE   3**
>
> **Solve for present value of a single amount.**

$$\text{Present Value} = \text{Future Value} \div (1 + i)^n$$

Illustration G-3
Formula for present value

Thus, if you want a 10% rate of return, you would compute the present value of $1,000 for one year as follows.

$$
\begin{aligned}
PV &= FV \div (1 + i)^n \\
&= \$1{,}000 \div (1 + .10)^1 \\
&= \$1{,}000 \div 1.10 \\
&= \$909.09
\end{aligned}
$$

We know the future amount ($1,000), the discount rate (10%), and the number of periods (1). These variables are depicted in the time diagram in Illustration G-4.

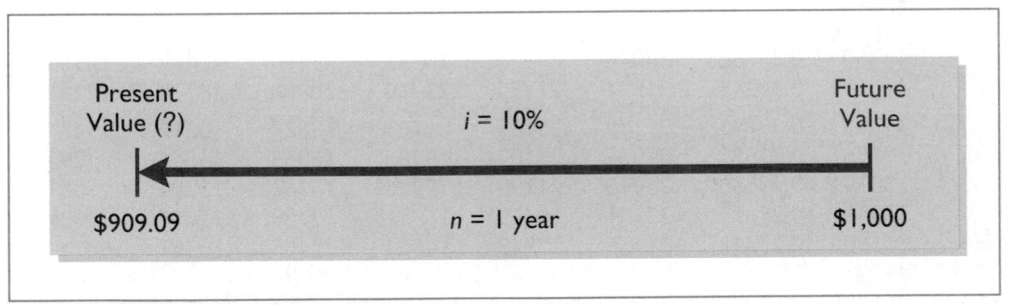

Illustration G-4
Finding present value if discounted for one period

If you receive the single amount of $1,000 **in two years**, discounted at 10% $[PV = \$1{,}000 \div (1 + .10)^2]$, the present value of your $1,000 is $826.45 ($1,000 ÷ 1.21), as shown in Illustration G-5.

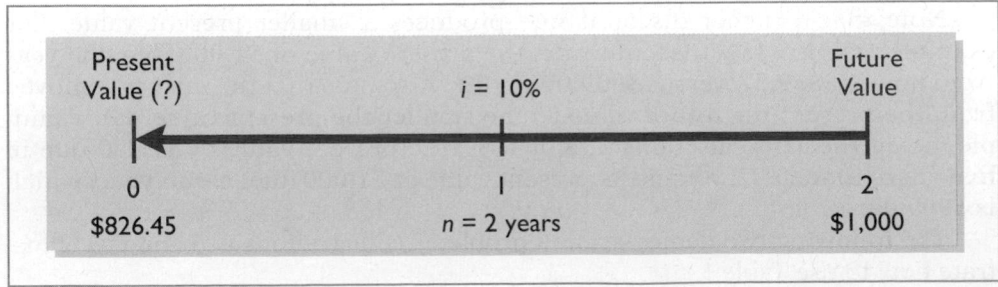

Illustration G-5
Finding present value if discounted for two periods

You also could find the present value of your amount through tables that show the present value of 1 for *n* periods. In Table 1 below, *n* (represented in the table's rows) is the number of discounting periods involved. The percentages (represented in the table's columns) are the periodic interest rates or discount rates. The 5-digit decimal numbers in the intersections of the rows and columns are called the **present value of 1 factors**.

When using Table 1 to determine present value, you multiply the future value by the present value factor specified at the intersection of the number of periods and the discount rate.

TABLE 1
Present Value of 1

(*n*) Periods	4%	5%	6%	7%	8%	9%	10%	11%	12%	15%
1	.96154	.95238	.94340	0.93458	.92593	.91743	.90909	.90090	.89286	.86957
2	.92456	.90703	.89000	0.87344	.85734	.84168	.82645	.81162	.79719	.75614
3	.88900	.86384	.83962	0.81630	.79383	.77218	.75132	.73119	.71178	.65752
4	.85480	.82270	.79209	0.76290	.73503	.70843	.68301	.65873	.63552	.57175
5	.82193	.78353	.74726	0.71299	.68058	.64993	.62092	.59345	.56743	.49718
6	.79031	.74622	.70496	0.66634	.63017	.59627	.56447	.53464	.50663	.43233
7	.75992	.71068	.66506	0.62275	.58349	.54703	.51316	.48166	.45235	.37594
8	.73069	.67684	.62741	0.58201	.54027	.50187	.46651	.43393	.40388	.32690
9	.70259	.64461	.59190	0.54393	.50025	.46043	.42410	.39092	.36061	.28426
10	.67556	.61391	.55839	0.50835	.46319	.42241	.38554	.35218	.32197	.24719
11	.64958	.58468	.52679	0.47509	.42888	.38753	.35049	.31728	.28748	.21494
12	.62460	.55684	.49697	0.44401	.39711	.35554	.31863	.28584	.25668	.18691
13	.60057	.53032	.46884	0.41496	.36770	.32618	.28966	.25751	.22917	.16253
14	.57748	.50507	.44230	0.38782	.34046	.29925	.26333	.23199	.20462	.14133
15	.55526	.48102	.41727	0.36245	.31524	.27454	.23939	.20900	.18270	.12289
16	.53391	.45811	.39365	0.33873	.29189	.25187	.21763	.18829	.16312	.10687
17	.51337	.43630	.37136	0.31657	.27027	.23107	.19785	.16963	.14564	.09293
18	.49363	.41552	.35034	0.29586	.25025	.21199	.17986	.15282	.13004	.08081
19	.47464	.39573	.33051	0.27615	.23171	.19449	.16351	.13768	.11611	.07027
20	.45639	.37689	.31180	0.25842	.21455	.17843	.14864	.12403	.10367	.06110

For example, the present value factor for one period at a discount rate of 10% is .90909, which equals the $909.09 ($1,000 × .90909) computed in Illustration G-4. For two periods at a discount rate of 10%, the present value factor is .82645, which equals the $826.45 ($1,000 × .82645) computed previously.

Note that a higher discount rate produces a smaller present value. For example, using a 15% discount rate, the present value of $1,000 due one year from now is $869.57, versus $909.09 at 10%. Also note that the further removed from the present the future value is, the smaller the present value. For example, using the same discount rate of 10%, the present value of $1,000 due in **five years** is $620.92, versus the present value of $1,000 due in **one year**, which is $909.09.

The following two demonstration problems (Illustrations G-6 and G-7) illustrate how to use Table 1.

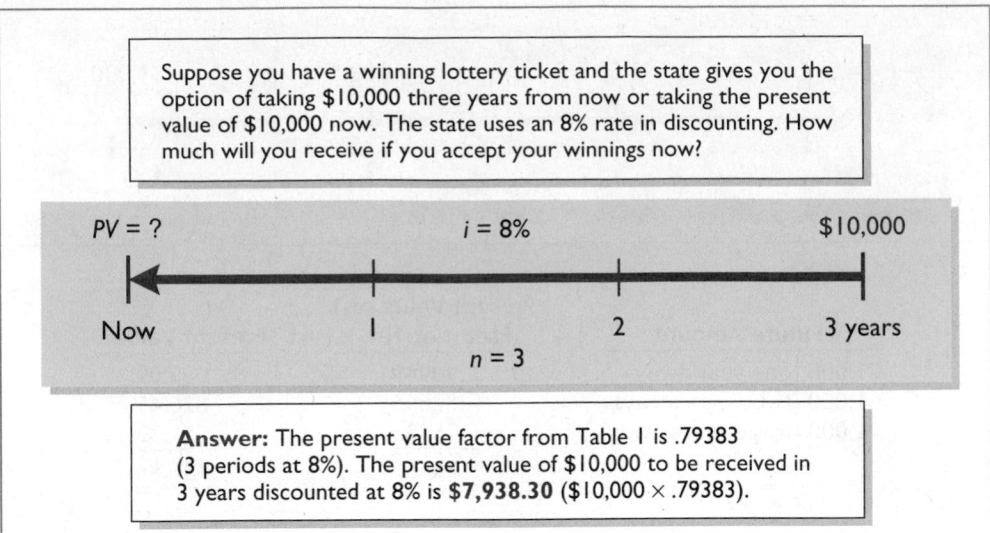

Suppose you have a winning lottery ticket and the state gives you the option of taking $10,000 three years from now or taking the present value of $10,000 now. The state uses an 8% rate in discounting. How much will you receive if you accept your winnings now?

PV = ?   *i* = 8% $10,000

Now   1   2   3 years

n = 3

Answer: The present value factor from Table 1 is .79383 (3 periods at 8%). The present value of $10,000 to be received in 3 years discounted at 8% is **$7,938.30** ($10,000 × .79383).

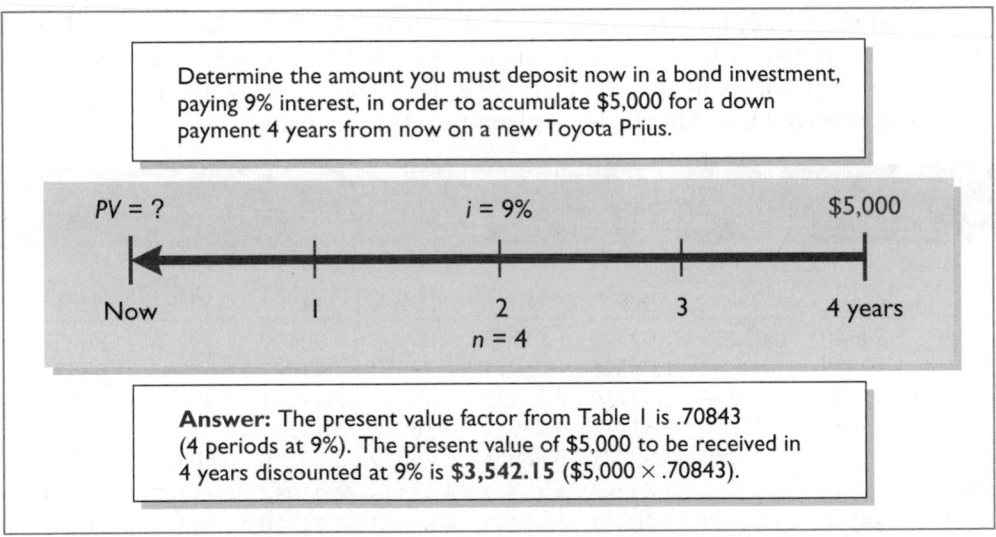

Determine the amount you must deposit now in a bond investment, paying 9% interest, in order to accumulate $5,000 for a down payment 4 years from now on a new Toyota Prius.

PV = ?   *i* = 9% $5,000

Now   1   2   3   4 years

n = 4

Answer: The present value factor from Table 1 is .70843 (4 periods at 9%). The present value of $5,000 to be received in 4 years discounted at 9% is **$3,542.15** ($5,000 × .70843).

Present Value of an Annuity

The preceding discussion involved the discounting of only a single future amount. Businesses and individuals frequently engage in transactions in which a **series** of equal dollar amounts are to be received or paid at evenly spaced time intervals (periodically). Examples of a series of periodic receipts or payments are loan agreements, installment sales, mortgage notes, lease (rental) contracts, and pension obligations. As discussed in Chapter 15, these periodic receipts or payments are **annuities**.

The **present value of an annuity** is the value now of a series of future receipts or payments, discounted assuming compound interest. In computing the present value of an annuity, you need to know (1) the discount rate, (2) the number of discount periods, and (3) the amount of the periodic receipts or payments.

To illustrate how to compute the present value of an annuity, assume that you will receive $1,000 cash annually for three years at a time when the discount rate is 10%. Illustration G-8 (page G6) depicts this situation, and Illustration G-9 (page G6) shows the computation of its present value.

LEARNING OBJECTIVE   4

Solve for present value of an annuity.

Illustration G-8
Time diagram for a three-year annuity

Illustration G-9
Present value of a series of future amounts computation

Present Value of 1

Future Amount	×	Factor at 10%	=	Present Value
$1,000 (one year away)		.90909		$ 909.09
1,000 (two years away)		.82645		826.45
1,000 (three years away)		.75132		751.32
		2.48686		**$2,486.86**

This method of calculation is required when the periodic cash flows are not uniform in each period. However, when the future receipts are the same in each period, there are two other ways to compute present value. First, you can multiply the annual cash flow by the sum of the three present value factors. In the previous example, $1,000 × 2.48686 equals $2,486.86. The second method is to use annuity tables. As illustrated in Table 2, these tables show the present value of 1 to be received periodically for a given number of periods.

TABLE 2
Present Value of an Annuity of 1

(n) Periods	4%	5%	6%	7%	8%	9%	10%	11%	12%	15%
1	.96154	.95238	.94340	0.93458	.92593	.91743	.90909	.90090	.89286	.86957
2	1.88609	1.85941	1.83339	1.80802	1.78326	1.75911	1.73554	1.71252	1.69005	1.62571
3	2.77509	2.72325	2.67301	2.62432	2.57710	2.53130	2.48685	2.44371	2.40183	2.28323
4	3.62990	3.54595	3.46511	3.38721	3.31213	3.23972	3.16986	3.10245	3.03735	2.85498
5	4.45182	4.32948	4.21236	4.10020	3.99271	3.88965	3.79079	3.69590	3.60478	3.35216
6	5.24214	5.07569	4.91732	4.76654	4.62288	4.48592	4.35526	4.23054	4.11141	3.78448
7	6.00205	5.78637	5.58238	5.38929	5.20637	5.03295	4.86842	4.71220	4.56376	4.16042
8	6.73274	6.46321	6.20979	5.97130	5.74664	5.53482	5.33493	5.14612	4.96764	4.48732
9	7.43533	7.10782	6.80169	6.51523	6.24689	5.99525	5.75902	5.53705	5.32825	4.77158
10	8.11090	7.72173	7.36009	7.02358	6.71008	6.41766	6.14457	5.88923	5.65022	5.01877
11	8.76048	8.30641	7.88687	7.49867	7.13896	6.80519	6.49506	6.20652	5.93770	5.23371
12	9.38507	8.86325	8.38384	7.94269	7.53608	7.16073	6.81369	6.49236	6.19437	5.42062
13	9.98565	9.39357	8.85268	8.35765	7.90378	7.48690	7.10336	6.74987	6.42355	5.58315
14	10.56312	9.89864	9.29498	8.74547	8.24424	7.78615	7.36669	6.98187	6.62817	5.72448
15	11.11839	10.37966	9.71225	9.10791	8.55948	8.06069	7.60608	7.19087	6.81086	5.84737
16	11.65230	10.83777	10.10590	9.44665	8.85137	8.31256	7.82371	7.37916	6.97399	5.95424
17	12.16567	11.27407	10.47726	9.76322	9.12164	8.54363	8.02155	7.54879	7.11963	6.04716
18	12.65930	11.68959	10.82760	10.05909	9.37189	8.75563	8.20141	7.70162	7.24967	6.12797
19	13.13394	12.08532	11.15812	10.33560	9.60360	8.95012	8.36492	7.83929	7.36578	6.19823
20	13.59033	12.46221	11.46992	10.59401	9.81815	9.12855	8.51356	7.96333	7.46944	6.25933

Table 2 shows that the present value of an annuity of 1 factor for three periods at 10% is 2.48685.[1] (This present value factor is the total of the three individual present value factors, as shown in Illustration G-9.) Applying this amount to the annual cash flow of $1,000 produces a present value of $2,486.85.

[1]The difference of .00001 between 2.48686 and 2.48685 is due to rounding.

The following demonstration problem (Illustration G-10) illustrates how to use Table 2.

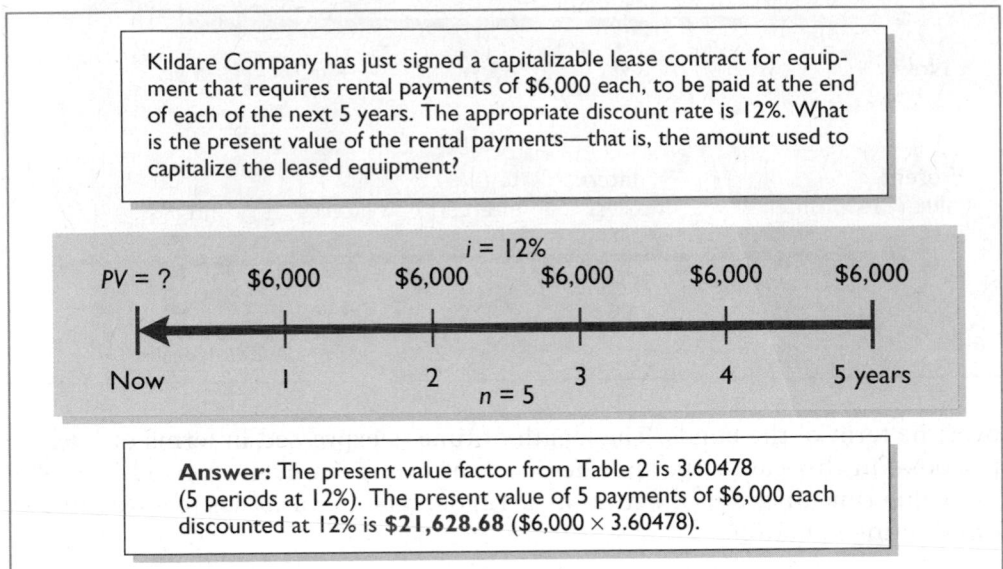

Kildare Company has just signed a capitalizable lease contract for equipment that requires rental payments of $6,000 each, to be paid at the end of each of the next 5 years. The appropriate discount rate is 12%. What is the present value of the rental payments—that is, the amount used to capitalize the leased equipment?

$i = 12\%$

PV = ? $6,000 $6,000 $6,000 $6,000 $6,000

Now   1   2   3   4   5 years
$n = 5$

Answer: The present value factor from Table 2 is 3.60478 (5 periods at 12%). The present value of 5 payments of $6,000 each discounted at 12% is **$21,628.68** ($6,000 × 3.60478).

Illustration G-10
Demonstration problem—Using Table 2 for *PV* of an annuity of 1

Time Periods and Discounting

In the preceding calculations, the discounting was done on an **annual** basis using an **annual** interest rate. Discounting may also be done over shorter periods of time such as monthly, quarterly, or semiannually.

When the time frame is less than one year, you need to convert the annual interest rate to the applicable time frame. Assume, for example, that the investor in Illustration G-8 received $500 **semiannually** for three years instead of $1,000 annually. In this case, the number of periods becomes six (3 × 2), the discount rate is 5% (10% ÷ 2), the present value factor from Table 2 is 5.07569, and the present value of the future cash flows is $2,537.85 (5.07569 × $500). This amount is slightly higher than the $2,486.86 computed in Illustration G-9 because interest is paid twice during the same year. Therefore, interest is earned on the first half-year's interest.

Computing the Present Value of a Long-Term Note or Bond

The present value (or market price) of a long-term note or bond is a function of three variables: (1) the payment amounts, (2) the length of time until the amounts are paid, and (3) the discount rate. Our illustration uses a five-year bond issue.

LEARNING OBJECTIVE   **5**

Compute the present value of notes and bonds.

The first variable—dollars to be paid—is made up of two elements: (1) a series of interest payments (an annuity), and (2) the principal amount (a single sum). To compute the present value of the bond, we must discount both the interest payments and the principal amount—two different computations. The time diagrams for a bond due in five years are shown in Illustration G-11 (page G8).

When the investor's market interest rate is equal to the bond's contractual interest rate, the present value of the bonds will equal the face value of the bonds. To illustrate, assume a bond issue of 10%, five-year bonds with a face value of $100,000 with interest payable **semiannually** on January 1 and July 1. If the discount rate is the same as the contractual rate, the bonds will sell at face value. In this case, the investor will receive the following: (1) $100,000 at maturity, and (2) a series of ten $5,000 interest payments [($100,000 × 10%) ÷ 2]

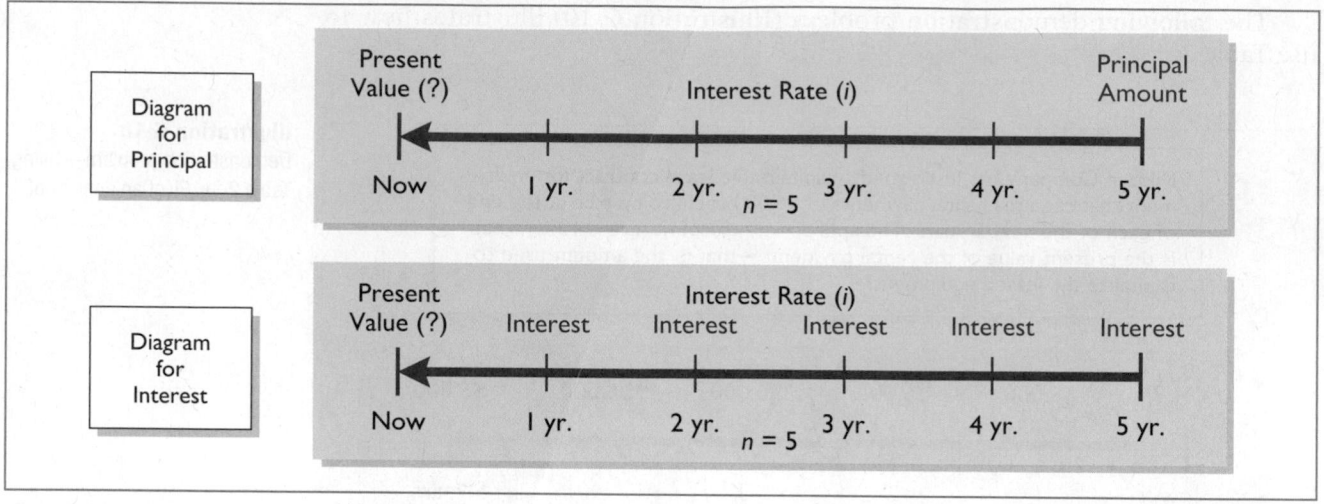

Illustration G-11
Present value of a bond time diagram

over the term of the bonds. The length of time is expressed in terms of interest periods—in this case—10, and the discount rate per interest period, 5%. The following time diagram (Illustration G-12) depicts the variables involved in this discounting situation.

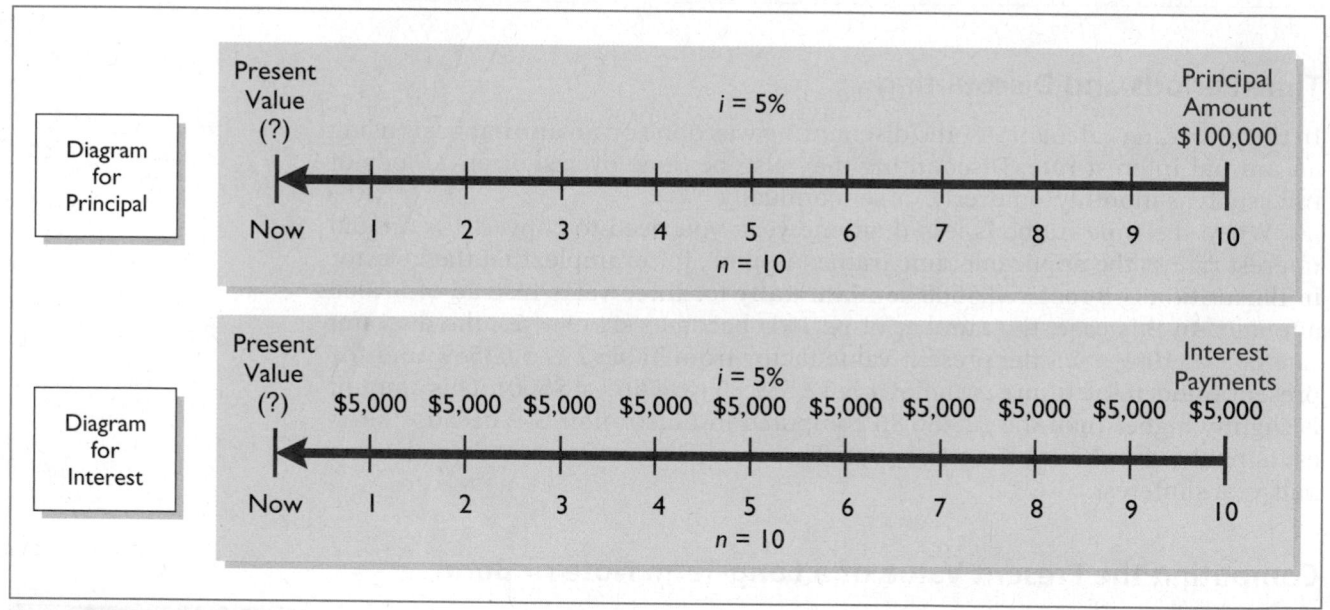

Illustration G-12
Time diagram for present value of a 10%, five-year bond paying interest semiannually

Illustration G-13 shows the computation of the present value of these bonds.

10% Contractual Rate—10% Discount Rate

Present value of principal to be received at maturity	
$100,000 × PV of 1 due in 10 periods at 5%	
$100,000 × .61391 (Table 1)	$ 61,391
Present value of interest to be received periodically	
over the term of the bonds	
$5,000 × PV of 1 due periodically for 10 periods at 5%	
$5,000 × 7.72173 (Table 2)	38,609*
Present value of bonds	**$100,000**

Illustration G-13
Present value of principal and interest—face value

*Rounded

Now assume that the investor's required rate of return is 12%, not 10%. The future amounts are again $100,000 and $5,000, respectively, but now a discount rate of 6% (12% ÷ 2) must be used. The present value of the bonds is $92,639, as computed in Illustration G-14.

Illustration G-14
Present value of principal and interest—discount

10% Contractual Rate—12% Discount Rate

Present value of principal to be received at maturity	
$100,000 × .55839 (Table 1)	$55,839
Present value of interest to be received periodically	
over the term of the bonds	
$5,000 × 7.36009 (Table 2)	36,800
Present value of bonds	**$92,639**

Conversely, if the discount rate is 8% and the contractual rate is 10%, the present value of the bonds is $108,111, computed as shown in Illustration G-15.

Illustration G-15
Present value of principal and interest—premium

10% Contractual Rate—8% Discount Rate

Present value of principal to be received at maturity	
$100,000 × .67556 (Table 1)	$ 67,556
Present value of interest to be received periodically	
over the term of the bonds	
$5,000 × 8.11090 (Table 2)	40,555
Present value of bonds	**$108,111**

The above discussion relies on present value tables in solving present value problems. Many people use spreadsheets such as Excel or financial calculators (some even on websites) to compute present values, without the use of tables. Many calculators, especially financial calculators, have present value (*PV*) functions that allow you to calculate present values by merely inputting the proper amount, discount rate, and periods, and then pressing the PV key. Appendix H illustrates how to use a financial calculator in various business situations.

SUMMARY OF LEARNING OBJECTIVES

1 Distinguish between simple and compound interest. Simple interest is computed on the principal only, while compound interest is computed on the principal and any interest earned that has not been withdrawn.

2 Identify the variables fundamental to solving present value problems. The following three variables are fundamental to solving present value problems: (1) the future amount, (2) the number of periods, and (3) the interest rate (the discount rate).

3 Solve for present value of a single amount. Prepare a time diagram of the problem. Identify the future amount, the number of discounting periods, and the discount (interest) rate. Using the present value of a single amount table, multiply the future amount by the present value factor specified at the intersection of the number of periods and the discount rate.

4 Solve for present value of an annuity. Prepare a time diagram of the problem. Identify the future annuity payments, the number of discounting periods, and the discount (interest) rate. Using the present value of an annuity of 1 table, multiply the amount of the annuity payments by the present value factor specified at the intersection of the number of periods and the interest rate.

5 Compute the present value of notes and bonds. To determine the present value of the principal amount: Multiply the principal amount (a single future amount) by the present value factor (from the present value of 1 table) intersecting at the number of periods (number of interest payments) and the discount rate.

To determine the present value of the series of interest payments: Multiply the amount of the interest payment by the present value factor (from the present value of an annuity of 1 table) intersecting at the number of periods (number of interest payments) and the discount rate. Add the present value of the principal amount to the present value of the interest payments to arrive at the present value of the note or bond.

GLOSSARY

Annuity A series of equal dollar amounts to be paid or received at evenly spaced time intervals (periodically). (p. G5).

Compound interest The interest computed on the principal and any interest earned that has not been paid or withdrawn. (p. G2).

Discounting the future amount(s) The process of determining present value. (p. G2).

Interest Payment for the use of another's money. (p. G1).

Present value The value now of a given amount to be paid or received in the future, assuming compound interest. (p. G2).

Present value of an annuity The value now of a series of future receipts or payments, discounted assuming compound interest. (p. G5).

Principal The amount borrowed or invested. (p. G1).

Simple interest The interest computed on the principal only. (p. G1).

BRIEF EXERCISES

Use present value tables.
(LO 3, 4)

Use tables to solve exercises.

BEG-1 For each of the following cases, indicate (a) to what interest rate columns, and (b) to what number of periods you would refer in looking up the discount rate.

1. In Table 1 (present value of 1):

	Annual Rate	Number of Years Involved	Compounding per Year
Case A	12%	6	Annually
Case B	10%	15	Annually
Case C	8%	12	Semiannually

2. In Table 2 (present value of an annuity of 1):

	Annual Rate	Number of Years Involved	Number of Payments Involved	Frequency of Payments
Case A	8%	20	20	Annually
Case B	10%	5	5	Annually
Case C	12%	4	8	Semiannually

Determine present values.
(LO 3, 4)

BEG-2 (a) What is the present value of $30,000 due 8 periods from now, discounted at 8%? (b) What is the present value of $30,000 to be received at the end of each of 6 periods, discounted at 9%?

Compute the present value of a single-sum investment.
(LO 3)

BEG-3 Chaffee Company is considering an investment that will return a lump sum of $600,000 5 years from now. What amount should Chaffee Company pay for this investment in order to earn a 10% return?

Compute the present value of a single-sum investment.
(LO 3)

BEG-4 Lloyd Company earns 9% on an investment that will return $700,000 8 years from now. What is the amount Lloyd should invest now in order to earn this rate of return?

Compute the present value of a single-sum, zero-interest-bearing note.
(LO 3)

BEG-5 Drake Company sold a 5-year, zero-interest-bearing $36,000 note receivable to Glenn Inc. Glenn wishes to earn 10% over the remaining 4 years of the note. How much cash will Drake receive upon sale of the note?

Compute the present value of a single-sum, zero-interest-bearing note.
(LO 3)

BEG-6 Delgado Company issues a 3-year, zero-interest-bearing $60,000 note. The interest rate used to discount the zero-interest-bearing note is 8%. What are the cash proceeds that Delgado Company should receive?

BEG-7 Shea Company is considering investing in an annuity contract that will return $40,000 annually at the end of each year for 15 years. What amount should Shea Company pay for this investment if it earns a 6% return?

Compute the present value of an annuity investment.
(LO 4)

BEG-8 Littleton Company earns 11% on an investment that pays back $100,000 at the end of each of the next 4 years. What is the amount Littleton Company invested to earn the 11% rate of return?

Compute the present value of an annuity investment.
(LO 4)

BEG-9 Trenton Railroad Co. is about to issue $200,000 of 10-year bonds paying a 10% interest rate, with interest payable semiannually. The discount rate for such securities is 8%. How much can Trenton expect to receive for the sale of these bonds?

Compute the present value of bonds.
(LO 3, 4, 5)

BEG-10 Assume the same information as in BEG-9 except that the discount rate is 10% instead of 8%. In this case, how much can Trenton expect to receive from the sale of these bonds?

Compute the present value of bonds.
(LO 3, 4, 5)

BEG-11 Lewis Company receives a $75,000, 6-year note bearing interest of 8% (paid annually) from a customer at a time when the discount rate is 9%. What is the present value of the note received by Lewis Company?

Compute the present value of a note.
(LO 3, 4, 5)

BEG-12 Jarl Company issued 8%, 8-year, $1,000,000 par value bonds that pay interest semiannually on October 1 and April 1. The bonds are dated April 1, 2014, and are issued on that date. The discount rate of interest for such bonds on April 1, 2014, is 10%. What cash proceeds did Jarl receive from issuance of the bonds?

Compute the present value of bonds.
(LO 3, 4, 5)

BEG-13 Bill Broadman owns a garage and is contemplating purchasing a tire retreading machine for $16,280. After estimating costs and revenues, Bill projects a net cash flow from the retreading machine of $2,800 annually for 8 years. Bill hopes to earn a return of 11% on such investments. What is the present value of the retreading operation? Should Bill Broadman purchase the retreading machine?

Compute the value of a machine for purposes of making a purchase decision.
(LO 4, 5)

BEG-14 Biju Company issues a 10%, 6-year mortgage note on January 1, 2014, to obtain financing for new equipment. Land is used as collateral for the note. The terms provide for semiannual installment payments of $78,978. What were the cash proceeds received from the issuance of the note?

Compute the present value of a note.
(LO 4)

BEG-15 Preet Company is considering purchasing equipment. The equipment will produce the following cash flows: Year 1, $30,000; Year 2, $40,000; Year 3, $60,000. Preet requires a minimum rate of return of 12%. What is the maximum price Preet should pay for this equipment?

Compute the maximum price to pay for a machine.
(LO 4, 5)

BEG-16 If Monica Ramirez invests $2,745 now, she will receive $10,000 at the end of 15 years. What annual rate of interest will Monica earn on her investment? (*Hint:* Use Table 1.)

Compute the interest rate on a single sum.
(LO 3)

BEG-17 Hellen Bos has been offered the opportunity of investing $51,316 now. The investment will earn 10% per year and at the end of that time will return Hellen $100,000. How many years must Hellen wait to receive $100,000? (*Hint:* Use Table 1.)

Compute the number of periods of a single sum.
(LO 3)

BEG-18 Natasha Anapova purchased an investment for $11,469.92. From this investment, she will receive $1,000 annually for the next 20 years, starting one year from now. What rate of interest will Natasha's investment be earning for her? (*Hint:* Use Table 2.)

Compute the interest rate on an annuity.
(LO 4)

BEG-19 Kaley Perry invests $8,559.48 now for a series of $1,000 annual returns, beginning one year from now. Kaley will earn a return of 8% on the initial investment. How many annual payments of $1,000 will Kaley receive? (*Hint:* Use Table 2.)

Compute the number of periods of an annuity.
(LO 4)

BEG-20 Vesuvius Company needs $10,000 on January 1, 2017. It is starting a fund on January 1, 2014.

Compute the amount to be invested.
(LO 3)

Instructions
Compute the amount that must be invested in the fund on January 1, 2014, to produce a $10,000 balance on January 1, 2017, if:

(a) The fund earns 8% per year compounded annually.
(b) The fund earns 8% per year compounded semiannually.
(c) The fund earns 12% per year compounded annually.
(d) The fund earns 12% per year compounded semiannually.

BEG-21 Twan Company needs $10,000 on January 1, 2019. It is starting a fund to produce that amount.

Compute the amount to be invested.
(LO 3)

Instructions

Compute the amount that must be invested in the fund to produce a $10,000 balance on January 1, 2019, if:

(a) The initial investment is made January 1, 2014, and the fund earns 6% per year.
(b) The initial investment is made January 1, 2016, and the fund earns 6% per year.
(c) The initial investment is made January 1, 2014, and the fund earns 10% per year.
(d) The initial investment is made January 1, 2016, and the fund earns 10% per year.

Select the better payment option.

(LO 4)

BEG-22 Cullen Corporation is buying new equipment. It can pay $39,500 today (option 1), or $10,000 today and 5 yearly payments of $8,000 each, starting in one year (option 2).

Instructions

Which option should Cullen select? (Assume a discount rate of 10%.)

Compute the cost of an investment, amount received, and rate of return.

(LO 4)

BEG-23 Phelps Corporation is considering several investments.

Instructions

(a) One investment returns $10,000 per year for 5 years and provides a return of 10%. What is the cost of this investment?
(b) Another investment costs $50,000 and returns a certain amount per year for 10 years, providing an 8% return. What amount is received each year?
(c) A third investment costs $70,000 and returns $11,971 each year for 15 years. What is the rate of return on this investment?

Select the best payment option.

(LO 4)

BEG-24 You are the beneficiary of a trust fund. The fund gives you the option of receiving $5,000 per year for 10 years, $9,000 per year for 5 years, or $30,000 today.

Instructions

If the desired rate of return is 8%, which option should you select?

Compute the semiannual car payment.

(LO 4)

BEG-25 You are purchasing a car for $24,000, and you obtain financing as follows: $2,400 down payment, 12% interest, semiannual payments over 5 years.

Instructions

Compute the payment you will make every 6 months.

Compute the present value of bonds.

(LO 3, 4, 5)

BEG-26 Alamos Corporation is considering purchasing bonds of Garcia Company as an investment. The bonds have a face value of $40,000 with a 10% interest rate. The bonds mature in 4 years and pay interest semiannually.

Instructions

(a) What is the most Alamos should pay for the bonds if it desires a 12% return?
(b) What is the most Alamos should pay for the bonds if it desires an 8% return?

Compute the present value of bonds.

(LO 3, 4, 5)

BEG-27 Arnez Corporation is considering purchasing bonds of Ball Company as an investment. The bonds have a face value of $90,000 with a 9% interest rate. The bonds mature in 6 years and pay interest semiannually.

Instructions

(a) What is the most Arnez should pay for the bonds if it desires a 10% return?
(b) What is the most Arnez should pay for the bonds if it desires an 8% return?

COMPANY INDEX

Notes

Notes

Notes

Notes

Notes

Notes

ACCOUNTING EQUATION (Chapter 2)

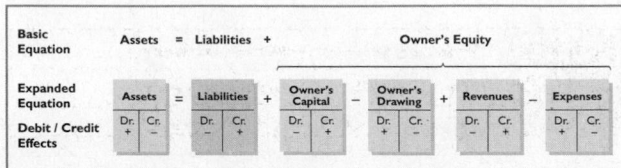

	Assets	=	Liabilities	+				Owner's Equity							
Basic Equation	Assets	=	Liabilities	+				Owner's Equity							
Expanded Equation	Assets	=	Liabilities	+	Owner's Capital	−	Owner's Drawing	+	Revenues	−	Expenses				
Debit / Credit Effects	Dr. +	Cr. −	Dr. −	Cr. +	Dr. −	Cr. +	Dr. +	Cr. −	Dr. −	Cr. +	Dr. +	Cr. −

ADJUSTING ENTRIES (Chapter 3)

	Type	Adjusting Entry	
Deferrals	1. Prepaid expenses	Dr. Expenses	Cr. Assets
	2. Unearned revenues	Dr. Liabilities	Cr. Revenues
Accruals	1. Accrued revenues	Dr. Assets	Cr. Revenues
	2. Accrued expenses	Dr. Expenses	Cr. Liabilities

Note: Each adjusting entry will affect one or more income statement accounts and one or more balance sheet accounts.

Interest Computation

Interest = Face value of note × Annual interest rate × Time in terms of one year

CLOSING ENTRIES (Chapter 4)

Purpose: (1) Update the Owner's Capital account in the ledger by transferring net income (loss) and Owner's Drawings to Owner's Capital. (2) Prepare the temporary accounts (revenue, expense, Owner's Drawings) for the next period's postings by reducing their balances to zero.

Process

1. Debit each revenue account for its balance (assuming normal balances), and credit Income Summary for total revenues.
2. Debit Income Summary for total expenses, and credit each expense account for its balance (assuming normal balances).

    STOP AND CHECK: Does the balance in your Income Summary account equal the net income (loss) reported in the income statement?

3. Debit (credit) Income Summary, and credit (debit) Owner's Capital for the amount of net income (loss).
4. Debit Owner's Capital for the balance in the Owner's Drawings account, and credit Owner's Drawings for the same amount.

    STOP AND CHECK: Does the balance in your Owner's Capital account equal the ending balance reported in the balance sheet and the owner's equity statement? Are all of your temporary account balances zero?

ACCOUNTING CYCLE (Chapter 4)

Optional steps: If a worksheet is prepared, Steps 4, 5, and 6 are incorporated in the worksheet. If reversing entries are prepared, they occur between Steps 9 and 1 as discussed below.

INVENTORY (Chapters 5 and 6)

Ownership

Freight Terms	Ownership of goods on public carrier resides with:	Who pays freight costs:
FOB shipping point	Buyer	Buyer
FOB destination	Seller	Seller

Perpetual vs. Periodic Journal Entries

Event	Perpetual	Periodic*
Purchase of goods	Inventory 　Cash (A/P)	Purchases 　Cash (A/P)
Freight (shipping point)	Inventory 　Cash	Freight-In 　Cash
Return of goods	Cash (or A/P) 　Inventory	Cash (or A/P) 　Purchase Ret. and All.
Sale of goods	Cash (or A/R) 　Sales Revenue Cost of Goods Sold 　Inventory	Cash (or A/R) 　Sales Revenue No entry
Sales returns and allowances	Sales Ret. and All. 　Accounts Receivable Inventory 　Cost of Goods Sold	Sales Ret. and All. 　Accounts Receivable No entry
Sales discounts	Cash Sales Discounts 　Accounts Receivable	Cash Sales Discounts 　Accounts Receivable
End of period	No entry	Closing or adjusting entry required

*Covered in appendix.

Cost Flow Methods

- Specific identification
- First-in, first-out (FIFO)
- Weighted-average
- Last-in, first-out (LIFO)

FRAUD, INTERNAL CONTROL, AND CASH (Chapter 8)

The Fraud Triangle

Opportunity

Financial pressure △ Rationalization

Principles of Internal Control Activities

- Establishment of responsibility
- Segregation of duties
- Documentation procedures
- Physical controls
- Independent internal verification
- Human resource controls

Bank Reconciliation

Bank	Books
Balance per bank statement Add: Deposit in transit	Balance per books Add: Unrecorded credit memoranda from bank statement
Deduct: Outstanding checks	Deduct: Unrecorded debit memoranda from bank statement
Adjusted cash balance	Adjusted cash balance

Note: 1. Errors should be offset (added or deducted) on the side that made the error.
2. Adjusting journal entries should only be made on the books.

STOP AND CHECK: Does the adjusted cash balance in the Cash account equal the reconciled balance?

RAPID REVIEW
Chapter Content

RECEIVABLES (Chapter 9)

Methods to Account for Uncollectible Accounts

Direct write-off method	Record bad debt expense when the company determines a particular account to be uncollectible.
Allowance methods: Percentage-of-sales	At the end of each period, estimate the amount of credit sales uncollectible. Debit Bad Debt Expense and credit Allowance for Doubtful Accounts for this amount. As specific accounts become uncollectible, debit Allowance for Doubtful Accounts and credit Accounts Receivable.
Percentage-of-receivables	At the end of each period, estimate the amount of uncollectible receivables. Debit Bad Debt Expense and credit Allowance for Doubtful Accounts in an amount that results in a balance in the allowance account equal to the estimate of uncollectibles. As specific accounts become uncollectible, debit Allowance for Doubtful Accounts and credit Accounts Receivable.

PLANT ASSETS (Chapter 10)

Presentation

Tangible Assets	Intangible Assets
Property, plant, and equipment	Intangible assets (patents, copyrights, trademarks, franchises, goodwill)
Natural resources	

Computation of Annual Depreciation Expense

Straight-line	$\dfrac{\text{Cost} - \text{Salvage value}}{\text{Useful life (in years)}}$
Units-of-activity	$\dfrac{\text{Cost} - \text{Salvage value}}{\text{Useful life (in units)}} \times$ Units of activity during year
Declining-balance	Book value at beginning of year $\times$ Declining balance rate* *Declining-balance rate = 1 ÷ Useful life (in years)

Note: If depreciation is calculated for partial periods, the straight-line and declining-balance methods must be adjusted for the relevant proportion of the year. Multiply the annual depreciation expense by the number of months expired in the year divided by 12 months.

SHAREHOLDERS' EQUITY (Chapter 13)

Comparison of Equity Accounts

Proprietorship	Partnership	Corporation
Owner's equity Owner's capital	Partner's equity Name, Capital Name, Capital	Stockholders' equity Common stock Retained earnings

No-Par Value vs. Par Value Stock Journal Entries

No-Par Value	Par Value

Cash
   Common Stock
	Cash
	   Common Stock (par value)
	   Paid-in Capital in Excess of Par—Common Stock

DIVIDENDS (Chapter 14)

Comparison of Dividend Effects

	Cash	Common Stock	Retained Earnings
Cash dividend	↓	No effect	↓
Stock dividend	No effect	↑	↓
Stock split	No effect	No effect	No effect

BONDS (Chapter 15)

Premium	Market interest rate < Contractual interest rate
Face Value	Market interest rate = Contractual interest rate
Discount	Market interest rate > Contractual interest rate

INVESTMENTS (Chapter 16)

Comparison of Long-Term Bond Investment and Liability Journal Entries

Event	Investor	Investee

Purchase / issue of bonds	Debt Investments
	   Cash
		Cash
		   Bonds Payable

Interest receipt / payment	Cash
	   Interest Revenue
		Interest Expense
		   Cash

Comparison of Cost and Equity Methods of Accounting for Long-Term Stock Investments

Event	Cost	Equity

Acquisition	Stock Investments
	   Cash
		Stock Investments
		   Cash

Investee reports earnings	No entry	Stock Investments Investment Revenue

Investee pays dividends	Cash
	   Dividend Revenue
		Cash
		   Stock Investments

Trading and Available-for-Sale Securities

Trading	Report at fair value with changes reported in net income.
Available-for-sale	Report at fair value with changes reported in the stockholders' equity section.

STATEMENT OF CASH FLOWS (Chapter 17)

Cash flows from operating activities (**indirect method**)

Net income		
Add:	Losses on disposals of assets	$ X
	Amortization and depreciation	X
	Decreases in current assets	X
	Increases in current liabilities	X
Deduct:	Gains on disposals of assets	(X)
	Increases in current assets	(X)
	Decreases in current liabilities	(X)
Net cash provided (used) by operating activities		$ X

Cash flows from operating activities (**direct method**)

Cash receipts
(Examples: from sales of goods and services to customers, from receipts of interest and dividends on loans and investments) $ X
Cash payments
(Examples: to suppliers, for operating expenses, for interest, for taxes) (X)
Net cash provided (used) by operating activities $ X

PRESENTATION OF NON-TYPICAL ITEMS (Chapter 18)

Prior period adjustments (Chapter 14)	Statement of retained earnings (adjustment of beginning retained earnings)
Discontinued operations	Income statement (presented separately after "Income from continuing operations")
Extraordinary items	Income statement (presented separately after "Income before extraordinary items")
Changes in accounting principle	In most instances, use the new method in current period and restate previous year's results using new method. For changes in depreciation and amortization methods, use the new method in the current period but do not restate previous periods.

RAPID REVIEW
Chapter Content

MANAGERIAL ACCOUNTING (Chapter 19)

Characteristics of Managerial Accounting

Primary Users	Internal users
Reports	Internal reports issued as needed
Purpose	Special purpose for a particular user
Content	Pertains to subunits, may be detailed, use of relevant data
Verification	No independent audits

Types of Manufacturing Costs

Direct materials	Raw materials directly associated with finished product
Direct labor	Work of employees directly associated with turning raw materials into finished product
Manufacturing overhead	Costs indirectly associated with manufacture of finished product

JOB ORDER AND PROCESS COSTING (Chapters 20 and 21)

Types of Accounting Systems

Job order	Costs are assigned to each unit or each batch of goods
Process cost	Costs are applied to similar products that are mass-produced in a continuous fashion

Job Order and Process Cost Flow

COST-VOLUME-PROFIT (Chapter 22)

Types of Costs

Variable costs	Vary in total directly and proportionately with changes in activity level
Fixed costs	Remain the same in total regardless of change in activity level
Mixed costs	Contain both a fixed and a variable element

CVP Income Statement Format

	Total	Per Unit
Sales revenue	$xx	$xx
Variable costs	xx	xx
Contribution margin	xx	$xx
Fixed costs	xx	
Net income	$xx	

Contribution Margin per Unit

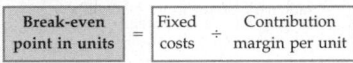

$$\text{Contribution margin per unit} = \text{Unit selling price} - \text{Unit variable costs}$$

Break-Even Point

$$\text{Break-even point in units} = \text{Fixed costs} \div \text{Contribution margin per unit}$$

Target Net Income

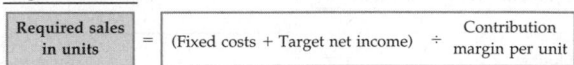

$$\text{Required sales in units} = (\text{Fixed costs} + \text{Target net income}) \div \text{Contribution margin per unit}$$

BUDGETS (Chapter 23)

Components of the Master Budget

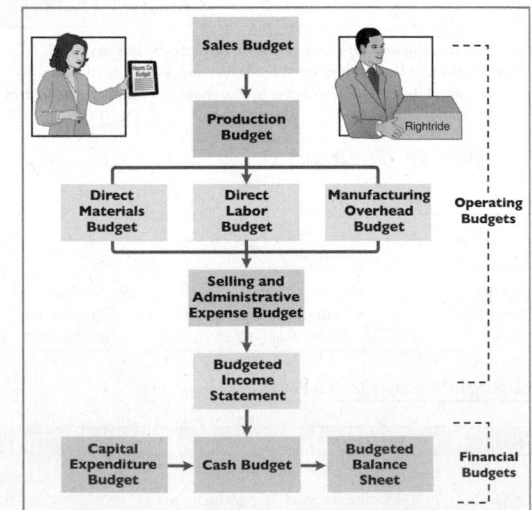

RESPONSIBILITY ACCOUNTING (Chapter 24)

Types of Responsibility Centers

Cost	Profit	Investment
Expenses only	Expenses and Revenues	Expenses and Revenues and ROI

Return on Investment

Return on investment (ROI)	=	Investment center controllable margin	÷	Average investment center operating assets

STANDARD COSTS (Chapter 25)

Standard Cost Variances

Total materials variance	=	Materials price variance	+	Materials quantity variance

Total labor variance	=	Labor price variance	+	Labor quantity variance

Total overhead variance	=	Overhead controllable variance	+	Overhead volume variance

Materials price variance	=	$AQ \times AP$	−	$AQ \times SP$

Materials quantity variance	=	$AQ \times SP$	−	$SQ \times SP$

Labor price variance	=	$AH \times AR$	−	$AH \times SR$

Labor quantity variance	=	$AH \times SR$	−	$SH \times SR$

Overhead variance	=	Actual overhead	−	Overhead applied

INCREMENTAL ANALYSIS AND CAPITAL BUDGETING (Chapter 26)

Incremental Analysis

1. Identify the relevant costs associated with each alternative. Relevant costs are those costs and revenues that differ across alternatives. Choose the alternative that maximizes net income.
2. Opportunity costs are those benefits that are given up when one alternative is chosen instead of another one. Opportunity costs are relevant costs.
3. Sunk costs have already been incurred and will not be changed or avoided by any future decision. Sunk costs are not relevant costs.

Annual Rate of Return

Annual rate of return	=	Expected annual net income	÷	Average investment

Cash Payback

Cash payback period	=	Cost of capital investment	÷	Net annual cash flow

Discounted Cash Flow Approaches

Net Present Value	Internal Rate of Return
Compute net present value (a dollar amount). If net present value is zero or positive, accept the proposal. If net present value is negative, reject the proposal.	Compute internal rate of return (a percentage). If internal rate of return is equal to or greater than the minimum required rate of return, accept the proposal. If internal rate of return is less than the minimum rate, reject the proposal.

RAPID REVIEW
Financial Statements

Order of Preparation

Statement Type	Date
1. Income statement	For the period ended
2. Retained earnings statement	For the period ended
3. Balance sheet	As of the end of the period
4. Statement of cash flows	For the period ended

Income Statement (perpetual inventory system)

COMPANY NAME Income Statement For the Period Ended		
Sales revenues		
Sales revenue	$ X	
Less: Sales returns and allowances	X	
Sales discounts	X	
Net sales		$ X
Cost of goods sold		X
Gross profit		X
Operating expenses		
(Examples: store salaries, advertising, delivery, rent, depreciation, utilities, insurance)		X
Income from operations		X
Other revenues and gains		
(Examples: interest, gains)	X	
Other expenses and losses		
(Examples: interest, losses)	X	X
Income before income taxes		X
Income tax expense		X
Net income		$ X

Income Statement (periodic inventory system)

COMPANY NAME Income Statement For the Period Ended			
Sales revenues			
Sales revenue	$ X		
Less: Sales returns and allowances	X		
Sales discounts	X		
Net sales			$ X
Cost of goods sold			
Beginning inventory		X	
Purchases	$ X		
Less: Purchase returns and allowances	X		
Net purchases	X		
Add: Freight-in	X		
Cost of goods purchased		X	
Cost of goods available for sale		X	
Less: Ending inventory		X	
Cost of goods sold			X
Gross profit			X
Operating expenses			
(Examples: store salaries, advertising, delivery, rent, depreciation, utilities, insurance)			X
Income from operations			X
Other revenues and gains			
(Examples: interest, gains)		X	
Other expenses and losses			
(Examples: interest, losses)		X	X
Income before income taxes			X
Income tax expense			X
Net income			$ X

Retained Earnings Statement

COMPANY NAME Retained Earnings Statement For the Period Ended	
Retained earnings, beginning of period	$ X
Add: Net income (or deduct net loss)	X
	X
Deduct: Dividends	X
Retained earnings, end of period	$ X

STOP AND CHECK: Net income (loss) presented on the retained earnings statement must equal the net income (loss) presented on the income statement.

Balance Sheet

COMPANY NAME Balance Sheet As of the End of the Period			
Assets			
Current assets			
(Examples: cash, short-term debt investments, accounts receivable, inventory, prepaids)			$ X
Long-term investments			
(Examples: investments in bonds, investments in stocks)			X
Property, plant, and equipment			
Land		$ X	
Buildings and equipment	$ X		
Less: Accumulated depreciation	X	X	X
Intangible assets			X
Total assets			$ X
Liabilities and Stockholders' Equity			
Liabilities			
Current liabilities			
(Examples: notes payable, accounts payable, accruals, unearned revenues, current portion of notes payable)			$ X
Long-term liabilities			
(Examples: notes payable, bonds payable)			X
Total liabilities			X
Stockholders' equity			
Common stock			X
Retained earnings			X
Total liabilities and stockholders' equity			$ X

STOP AND CHECK: Total assets on the balance sheet must equal total liabilities and stockholders' equity; and, ending retained earnings on the balance sheet must equal ending retained earnings on the retained earnings statement.

Statement of Cash Flows

COMPANY NAME Statement of Cash Flows For the Period Ended	
Cash flows from operating activities	
(*Note:* May be prepared using the direct or indirect method)	
Net cash provided (used) by operating activities	$ X
Cash flows from investing activities	
(Examples: purchase / sale of long-term assets)	
Net cash provided (used) by investing activities	X
Cash flows from financing activities	
(Examples: issue / repayment of long-term liabilities, issue of stock, payment of dividends)	
Net cash provided (used) by financing activities	X
Net increase (decrease) in cash	X
Cash, beginning of the period	X
Cash, end of the period	$ X

STOP AND CHECK: Cash, end of the period, on the statement of cash flows must equal cash presented on the balance sheet.